AF718360

THE BEST LAWYERS IN AMERICA

THE BEST LAWYERS IN AMERICA

STEVEN NAIFEH

AND

GREGORY WHITE SMITH

Harvard Law School 1977

SENIOR EDITORS

William David Brooks

Stephen Ashley Geddes

EDITORS

James Barr - Kathy Bauer - Erin Brooks

Carl Dawson - Andrew Duke - Phillip Greer

Ted Jones - Daniel Lutz - Cathy Shaw - Jeremy Wilson

2009

WOODWARD / WHITE

Aiken, South Carolina

The Best Lawyers in America® and Best Lawyers® are exclusive trademarks and service marks of Woodward/White, Inc.

Copyright ©2008 by Woodward/White, Inc.
All rights reserved. This book, or parts thereof, must not be reproduced in any form without permission.

Published and distributed by Woodward/White, Inc.
129 First Avenue, SW, Aiken, SC 29801

PLEASE NOTE

Woodward/White has used its best efforts in assembling material for inclusion in The Best Lawyers in America® 2009 but does not warrant that the information contained in the book is complete or accurate, and does not assume, and hereby disclaims, any liability to any person for any loss or damage caused by errors or omissions in The Best Lawyers in America® 2009 whether such errors or omissions result from negligence, accident, or any other cause.

Woodward/White makes every reasonable effort to check all of its lists against publicly-available records on lawyers who have been sanctioned by their state bar associations. Lawyers are removed from the lists if they have had a significant, fully-adjudicated sanction within the past ten to fifteen years depending on their state bar's standards for imposing sanctions and on the manner in which information about sanctions is made available to the public, both of which vary widely from state to state.

No commercial use of the information in this book may be made without permission. No fees may be charged, directly or indirectly, for the use of the information in this book without permission.

Library of Congress Cataloging in Publication Data

Naifeh, Steven W., 1952-
The best lawyers in America.

1. Lawyers--United States--Directories. 2. Lawyers--United States--Rating of. 3.Lawyers--Specialties and specialists--United States--Directories. I. Smith, Gregory White. II. Title.

ISBN 978-0980025330 (v. 1)
ISBN 978-0980025347 (v. 2)
ISBN 978-0980025354 (2 vol. set)

PRINTED IN THE UNITED STATES OF AMERICA

CONTENTS – Volume I

Volume II

INTRODUCTION

We proudly present the fifteenth edition of *The Best Lawyers in America*®. For more than a quarter of a century, *Best Lawyers*® has been regarded – by both the legal profession and the public – as the definitive guide to legal excellence in the United States. *Best Lawyers* has received accolades from presidents of the American Bar Association, officials of state bar groups, corporate counsel, and journalists, all of whom have recognized that our lists provide an important service to the bar and to the public.

Best Lawyers has been featured in numerous national and regional publications and broadcasts, including the *New York Times* and *60 Minutes*. Our lists have appeared in *The Washington Post*, the *Los Angeles Times*, and *New York Magazine*, and are the basis of more than fifty *Best Lawyers* features in regional and city magazines, as well as professional and business publications such as *Corporate Counsel*. The *Best Lawyers* database is also available on every Bloomberg Terminal worldwide.

Of all the attention *Best Lawyers* has received, however, we continue to be most gratified by the support of the thousands of attorneys who participate in our surveys and help make *Best Lawyers* what *The American Lawyer* recognized as "the most respected referral list of attorneys in practice."

In an age when almost everything is for sale, we are proud that the print edition of *The Best Lawyers in America* is still the only advertisement-free, peer-reviewed listing of attorneys available anywhere. Lawyers who are listed in *Best Lawyers* are not required or allowed to make payments to be listed; nor are they required to make any purchase to be listed. We independently verify all of the information included in our listings; lawyers are not required to verify or respond in any way to be listed. Best Lawyers also makes every effort to confirm that each lawyer on our list is in good standing with the ethics committee of his or her state bar association at the time of publication.

COMPILING THE FIFTEENTH EDITION

The method used to compile *Best Lawyers* is fundamentally the same as it was when the first edition was compiled more than twenty-five years ago. Lawyers are chosen for inclusion based solely on a vote of their peers. Because listings cannot be bought, and no purchase is required to be included, *Best Lawyers* remains the gold standard of reliability and integrity in lawyer ratings.

The survey for the 2009 edition began with a nomination pool consisting of (1) all lawyers whose names appeared in the fourteenth edition of *Best Lawyers*; (2) lawyers who had been nominated for but not listed in the previous edition (except in cases where the votes are very low, lawyers nominated but not listed remain in the nomination pool for two editions, at which time, if they have not been voted onto the list, they are removed from the pool); (3) new nominations solicited from the 36,000 attorneys listed in the previous edition; (4) nominations solicited from marketing officers at firms with marketing departments (limited according to the size of the firm); (5) lawyers who had been nominated *sua sponte* during the year since the previous survey.

The voting pool for *Best Lawyers* is far more transparent than that of any other peer-review survey of the legal profession. For the fifteenth edition, the pool consisted of all the lawyers listed in the previous edition. *Best Lawyers* polls only a select group of prominent and respected attorneys. We believe that the quality of a peer-review survey is no better than the quality of its voting pool. A referring lawyer or potential client wants to know whom the top lawyers in the relevant field would recommend. This has been the basis of *Best Lawyers*' polling method since its introduction in 1983.

Some lawyers were asked to vote only on nominees in their own specialty in their own jurisdiction. Lawyers in closely related specialties were asked to vote across specialties, as were lawyers in smaller jurisdictions. In a few instances, where specialties are national or international in nature, lawyers were asked to vote nationally as well as locally. Voting lawyers were also given an opportunity to offer more detailed comments on nominees. In all, more than 2.5 million individual evaluations were processed in compiling this new edition.

As in previous surveys, we provided voting lawyers with only the following general guideline for determining if a nominee should be listed among "the best": "If you had a close friend or relative who needed a real estate lawyer (for example), and you could not handle the case yourself – for reasons of conflict of interest or time – to whom would you refer them?" All votes and comments were solicited with a guarantee of confidentiality – a critical factor in the viability and validity of *Best Lawyers* surveys.

To ensure the continued rigor of the selection process, we urged lawyers to use only their highest standards when voting, and to evaluate each attorney based only on his or her individual merits. The additional comments allowed us to more accurately compare and weigh voting patterns. Over the years, we have developed methodological tools to identify and correct for anomalies in both the nomination and the voting process, including the potentially distorting impact of partner votes.

Ultimately, of course, a lawyer's inclusion in these lists is based on the subjective judgments of his or her fellow attorneys. While it is true that the lists may at times disproportionately reward visibility or popularity, we remain confident that the breadth of our survey, the candor of our respondents, and the sophistication of our polling methodology largely correct for any biases, and that these lists continue to represent the most reliable, accurate, and useful guide to the best lawyers in the United States available anywhere.

BESTLAWYERS.COM

The 2009 edition of *The Best Lawyers in America* is available online at www.bestlawyers.com. Online listings make it possible for lawyers included in the fifteenth edition to provide additional biographical information that cannot be included in the book due to space limitations. Lawyers can link their listings either to a custom-built Best Lawyers bio page or to an existing firm web page. Firm links also are available at www.bestlawyers.com. We have improved our website's search functionality by making it possible to search for lawyers by subspecialty as well as by specialty.

BESTLAWYERS INTERNATIONAL

Best Lawyers has begun expanding its surveys to include legal communities around the globe. We have published three editions of *The Best Lawyers in Canada* and, by January 2009, we will have released *Best Lawyers* lists for Argentina, Australia, Azerbaijan, Bahrain, Belarus, Brazil, Chile, Georgia, Ireland, Israel, Japan, Kazakhstan, Kenya, Kuwait, Mexico, Moldova, New Zealand, Oman, Qatar, Russia, Saudi Arabia, Singapore, South Africa, South Korea, Spain, Ukraine, the United Arab Emirates, and the United Kingdom. By the end of 2009, we expect to complete our listings of the top attorneys in every country worldwide, using the same rigorous peer-review methodology and maintaining the same absolute integrity that have made *Best Lawyers* the premier lawyer referral service in the United States.

CLIENT COMMENTS

To help potential clients better understand the particular skills of lawyers listed in *Best Lawyers*, our website now features client comments. Although client comments, by themselves, cannot be used to generate an accurate list of outstanding lawyers and should not be solely relied upon to choose a lawyer (even minimally qualified lawyers can produce a few testimonials from satisfied clients), we believe that "customer reviews" can help potential clients better assess the particular strengths and skills of lawyers who have won the respect of their peers through *Best Lawyers*' surveys. The client comments on BestLawyers.com are detailed and, in most cases, attributed to specific clients – important criteria for a reliable recommendation.

We invite all the lawyers listed in the fifteenth edition of *Best Lawyers* (except those in the seven states that currently prohibit testimonials and endorsements) to help us identify and contact any of their clients who are willing to provide comments about them on BestLawyers.com.

BEST LAWYERS "SELECT"

Best Lawyers also fulfills special research requests. For clients who have multi-jurisdictional legal matters, who require unique legal skill-sets, or who need lawyers in out-of-the-way places – Best Lawyers provides customized searches.

Based on a client's specific requirements, Best Lawyers will search its vast, annually-updated database of more than 2.5 million evaluations and identify the lawyer or firm that has the right skills, the right experience, the right connections, and the right team for the assignment. Our Select service has also helped law firms identify "correspondent" lawyers or firms in distant legal markets that share special or unusual legal expertise.

TRADEMARKS

Due to our long history and distinguished reputation, Best Lawyers has secured federal trademark and service-mark protection for the marks "The Best Lawyers in America" and "Best Lawyers." Any list of lawyers that uses these marks in commerce without written permission is in violation of federal law. Publications that license our lists are required to place an "®" beside each occurrence of "The Best Lawyers in America" or "Best Lawyers."

THE EDITORS

Steven Naifeh and Gregory White Smith are both Harvard-trained attorneys. Mr. Naifeh worked briefly for the New York firm of Milbank, Tweed, Hadley & McCloy; Mr. Smith, for the San Francisco firm of Morrison & Foerster. They have written twelve nonfiction books including four national bestsellers: most recently, *On a Street Called Easy, In A Cottage Called Joye* (Little Brown, 1996), and *Making Miracles Happen* (Little Brown, 1997). Their book *Jackson Pollock: An American Saga* (Clarkson Potter, 1990) won the Pulitzer Prize for biography and was a nonfiction finalist for the National Book Award in 1991. Naifeh and

Smith are currently working on a biography of Vincent van Gogh to be published by Random House in 2010.

The principal editors for the fifteenth edition of *Best Lawyers* were James Barr, Erin Brooks, William D. Brooks, Kathy Bauer, Carl Dawson, Andrew Duke, Stephen Geddes, Phillip Greer, Jennifer Herring, Ted Jones, Daniel Lutz, Catherine Shaw, and Jeremy Wilson. The editors would once again like to acknowledge the contribution of Stephen Geddes and his team in updating and streamlining a data-heavy process that is increasingly software- and Internet-dependent.

- ⑩ *Lawyers who have been listed in* Best Lawyers *for at least ten years.*
- ⑳ *Lawyers who have been listed in* Best Lawyers *for at least twenty years.*
- ㉕ *Lawyers who have been listed in* Best Lawyers *for at least twenty-five years.*

*We would like to acknowledge our debt
to the thousands of attorneys who gave of their time and expertise
in the process of compiling these lists.*

THE BEST LAWYERS IN AMERICA

I

ALABAMA - NEBRASKA

ALABAMA

ADMINISTRATIVE LAW

Athens

P. Michael Cole · Wilmer & Lee · 315 West Market Street · Athens, AL 35611 · 256-232-2010

Birmingham

Ronald W. Farley · Burr & Forman · http://www.burr.com · 420 North 20th Street, Suite 3400 · Birmingham, AL 35203-3284 · 205-251-3000

Montgomery

George Azar · Azar, Azar & Moore · 2740 Zelda Road, Fourth Floor · P.O. Box 2028 · Montgomery, AL 36102-2028 · 334-265-8551

Wendell Cauley · Bradley Arant Rose & White · http://www.bradleyarant.com · Alabama Center for Commerce, Suite 780 · 401 Adams Avenue · Montgomery, AL 36104 · 334-956-7700

Mark D. Wilkerson · Wilkerson & Bryan · 405 South Hull Street · P.O. Box 830 · Montgomery, AL 36101-0830 · 334-265-1500

ALTERNATIVE DISPUTE RESOLUTION

Birmingham

James Patrick Alexander · (25) · Littler Mendelson · Wachovia Tower, Suite 2730 · 420 Twentieth Street North · Birmingham, AL 35203 · 205-421-4700

Charles L. Denaburg · (10) · Najjar Denaburg · 2125 Morris Avenue · Birmingham, AL 35203 · 205-250-8400

Arthur J. Hanes, Jr. · Dominick, Fletcher, Yeilding, Wood & Lloyd · http://www.dfy.com · 2121 Highland Avenue South · P.O. Box 1387 · Birmingham, AL 35201 · 205-939-0033

Thad G. Long · (10) · Bradley Arant Rose & White · http://www.bradleyarant.com · One Federal Place · 1819 Fifth Avenue North · Birmingham, AL 35203-2119 · 205-521-8000

Rodney A. Max · Upchurch Watson White & Max · 2000-A SouthBridge Parkway, Suite 400 · Birmingham, AL 35209 · 205-933-9033

Edward P. Meyerson · Baker, Donelson, Bearman, Caldwell & Berkowitz · http://www.bakerdonelson.com · Wachovia Tower, Suite 1600 · 420 Twentieth Street North · Birmingham, AL 35203 · 205-328-0480

Sam C. Pointer, Jr. · Lightfoot, Franklin & White · The Clark Building · 400 Twentieth Street North · Birmingham, AL 35203 · 205-581-0700

Kenneth O. Simon · Christian & Small · http://www.csattorneys.com · 505 North 20th Street, Suite 1800 · Birmingham, AL 35203-2696 · 205-795-6588

Fern H. Singer · Baker, Donelson, Bearman, Caldwell & Berkowitz · http://www.bakerdonelson.com · Wachovia Tower, Suite 1600 · 420 Twentieth Street North · Birmingham, AL 35203 · 205-328-0480

Clarence M. Small, Jr. · (20) · Christian & Small · http://www.csattorneys.com · 505 North 20th Street, Suite 1800 · Birmingham, AL 35203-2696 · 205-795-6588

George M. Van Tassel, Jr. · Sirote & Permutt · 2311 Highland Avenue South · P.O. Box 55727 · Birmingham, AL 35255-5727 · 205-930-5100

J. Mark White · ⑩ · White Arnold & Dowd · 2025 Third Avenue North, Suite 500 · Birmingham, AL 35203 · 205-323-1888

Huntsville

H. Harold Stephens · Bradley Arant Rose & White · http://www.bradleyarant.com · 200 Clinton Avenue West, Suite 900 · Huntsville, AL 35801-4900 · 256-517-5100

Montgomery

William D. Coleman · ⑩ · Capell & Howard · http://www.capellhoward.com · 150 South Perry Street · P.O. Box 2069 · Montgomery, AL 36102-2069 · 334-241-8000

Frank H. McFadden · Capell & Howard · http://www.capellhoward.com · 150 South Perry Street · P.O. Box 2069 · Montgomery, AL 36102-2069 · 334-241-8000

Opelika

Phillip Adams, Jr. · Adams, Umbach, Davidson & White · Walker Building · 205 South Ninth Street · P.O. Box 2069 · Opelika, AL 36803 · 334-745-6466

ANTITRUST LAW

Birmingham

Michael S. Denniston · Bradley Arant Rose & White · http://www.bradleyarant.com · One Federal Place · 1819 Fifth Avenue North · Birmingham, AL 35203-2119 · 205-521-8000

Gary M. London · Burr & Forman · http://www.burr.com · 420 North 20th Street, Suite 3400 · Birmingham, AL 35203-3284 · 205-251-3000

Thad G. Long · ⑩ · Bradley Arant Rose & White · http://www.bradleyarant.com · One Federal Place · 1819 Fifth Avenue North · Birmingham, AL 35203-2119 · 205-521-8000

George G. Lynn · Maynard Cooper & Gale · http://www.maynardcooper.com · Regions/Harbert Plaza, Suite 2400 · 1901 Sixth Avenue North · Birmingham, AL 35203-2602 · 205-254-1000

Crawford S. McGivaren, Jr. · ⑳ · Cabaniss, Johnston, Gardner, Dumas & O'Neal · http://www.cabaniss.com · 2001 Park Place North, Suite 700 · P.O. Box 830612 · Birmingham, AL 35283-0612 · 205-716-5200

Fairhope

David A. Bagwell · ⑩ · David A. Bagwell · 400 Fairhope Avenue, Suite 2-E · P.O. Box 2126 · Fairhope, AL 36533 · 251-928-2970

Mobile

Warren C. Herlong, Jr. · Helmsing, Leach, Herlong, Newman & Rouse · http://www.helmsinglaw.com · The LaClede Building, Suite 2000 · 150 Government Street · P.O. Box 2767 · Mobile, AL 36652 · 251-432-5521

APPELLATE LAW

Birmingham

Ed R. Haden · Balch & Bingham · http://www.balch.com · 1710 Sixth Avenue North · Birmingham, AL 35203-2015 · 205-251-8100

Matthew H. Lembke · Bradley Arant Rose & White · http://www.bradleyarant.com · One Federal Place · 1819 Fifth Avenue North · Birmingham, AL 35203-2119 · 205-521-8000

Kevin C. Newsom · Bradley Arant Rose & White · http://www.bradleyarant.com · One Federal Place · 1819 Fifth Avenue North · Birmingham, AL 35203-2119 · 205-521-8000

Deborah Alley Smith · Christian & Small · http://www.csattorneys.com · 505 North 20th Street, Suite 1800 · Birmingham, AL 35203-2696 · 205-795-6588

Susan S. Wagner · Baker, Donelson, Bearman, Caldwell & Berkowitz · http://www.bakerdonelson.com · Wachovia Tower, Suite 1600 · 420 Twentieth Street North · Birmingham, AL 35203 · 205-328-0480

Huntsville

Scott Burnett Smith · Bradley Arant Rose & White · http://www.bradleyarant.com · 200 Clinton Avenue West, Suite 900 · Huntsville, AL 35801-4900 · 256-517-5100

Mobile

Forrest S. Latta · Burr & Forman · http://www.burr.com · Colonial Bank Centre, Suite 400 · 41 West I-65 Service Road North · P.O. Box 16046 · Mobile, AL 36616 · 251-344-5151

Thomas M. O'Hara · McDowell Knight Roedder & Sledge · Riverview Plaza, Suite 900 · 63 South Royal Street · P.O. Box 350 · Mobile, AL 36601 · 251-432-5300

William E. Shreve, Jr. · Lyons, Pipes & Cook · Two North Royal Street · P.O. Box 2727 · Mobile, AL 36652-2727 · 251-432-4481

William W. Watts III · Hudson & Watts · One St. Louis Centre, Suite 2500 · P.O. Box 989 · Mobile, AL 36601 · 251-432-7200

Montgomery

David R. Boyd · ⑩ · Balch & Bingham · http://www.balch.com · 105 Tallapoosa Street, Suite 200 · P.O. Box 78 · Montgomery, AL 36101-0078 · 334-834-6500

Walter R. Byars · Steiner, Crum & Byars · Regions Bank Building, Eighth Floor · Eight Commerce Street P.O. Box 668 · Montgomery, AL 36101-0668 · 334-832-8800

Robert A. Huffaker · ⑳ · Rushton, Stakely, Johnston & Garrett · http://www.rsjg.com · 184 Commerce Street · P.O. Box 270 · Montgomery, AL 36101-0270 · 334-206-3100

W. Joseph McCorkle, Jr. · Balch & Bingham · http://www.balch.com · 105 Tallapoosa Street, Suite 200 · P.O. Box 78 · Montgomery, AL 36101-0078 · 334-834-6500

Oakley W. Melton, Jr. · ⑳ · Melton, Espy & Williams · 255 Dexter Avenue · P.O. Drawer 5130 · Montgomery, AL 36103-5130 · 334-263-6621

Tuscaloosa

R. Bernard Harwood · Rosen Harwood · 2117 Jack Warner Parkway · Tuscaloosa, AL 35401 · 205-344-5000

BANKING LAW

Birmingham

Kay K. Bains · ⑩ · Bradley Arant Rose & White · http://www.bradleyarant.com · One Federal Place · 1819 Fifth Avenue North · Birmingham, AL 35203-2119 · 205-521-8000

H. Hampton Boles · ⑩ · Balch & Bingham · http://www.balch.com · 1901 Sixth Avenue North, Suite 1500 Birmingham, AL 35203-4644 · 205-251-8100

Michael Brandt · Wallace, Jordan, Ratliff & Brandt · http://www.wallacejordan.com · 800 Shades Creek Parkway, Suite 400 · P.O. Box 530910 · Birmingham, AL 35253 · 205-870-0555

Steven A. Brickman · Sirote & Permutt · 2311 Highland Avenue South · P.O. Box 55727 · Birmingham, AL 35255-5727 · 205-930-5100

Larry B. Childs · Waller Lansden Dortch & Davis · http://www.wallerlaw.com · 1901 Sixth Avenue North, Suite 1400 · Birmingham, AL 35203 · 205-214-6380

J. Paul Compton, Jr. · ⑩ · Bradley Arant Rose & White · http://www.bradleyarant.com · One Federal Place · 1819 Fifth Avenue North · Birmingham, AL 35203-2119 · 205-521-8000

L. Susan Doss · Bradley Arant Rose & White · http://www.bradleyarant.com · One Federal Place · 1819 Fifth Avenue North · Birmingham, AL 35203-2119 · 205-521-8000

J. David Dresher · ⑩ · Bradley Arant Rose & White · http://www.bradleyarant.com · One Federal Place · 1819 Fifth Avenue North · Birmingham, AL 35203-2119 · 205-521-8000

Carolyn L. Duncan · Cabaniss, Johnston, Gardner, Dumas & O'Neal · http://www.cabaniss.com · 2001 Park Place North, Suite 700 · P.O. Box 830612 · Birmingham, AL 35283-0612 · 205-716-5200

Haskins W. Jones · Johnston Barton Proctor & Rose · Colonial Brookwood Center, Suite 901 · 569 Brookwood Village · Birmingham, AL 35209 · 205-458-9400

Barry S. Marks · Marks & Weinberg · Park Place Tower, Suite 525 · 2001 Park Place North · Birmingham, AL 35203 · 205-251-8301

Gail L. Mills · Burr & Forman · http://www.burr.com · 420 North 20th Street, Suite 3400 · Birmingham, AL 35203-3284 · 205-251-3000

Dwight L. Mixson, Jr. · ⑩ · Burr & Forman · http://www.burr.com · 420 North 20th Street, Suite 3400 · Birmingham, AL 35203-3284 · 205-251-3000

Randall H. Morrow · Maynard Cooper & Gale · http://www.maynardcooper.com · Regions/Harbert Plaza, Suite 2400 · 1901 Sixth Avenue North · Birmingham, AL 35203-2602 · 205-254-1000

Richard L. Pearson · Balch & Bingham · http://www.balch.com · 1901 Sixth Avenue North, Suite 1500 · Birmingham, AL 35203-4644 · 205-251-8100

Charles C. Pinckney · Adams and Reese · http://www.adamsandreese.com · Concord Center, Suite 1100 · 2100 Third Avenue North · Birmingham, AL 35203 · 205-250-5000

J. Fred Powell · ⑩ · Burr & Forman · http://www.burr.com · 420 North 20th Street, Suite 3400 · Birmingham, AL 35203-3284 · 205-251-3000

Maurice L. Shevin · Sirote & Permutt · 2311 Highland Avenue South · P.O. Box 55727 · Birmingham, AL 35255-5727 · 205-930-5100

Henry E. Simpson · ⑩ · Adams and Reese · http://www.adamsandreese.com · Concord Center, Suite 1100 · 2100 Third Avenue North · Birmingham, AL 35203 · 205-250-5000

Joseph G. Stewart · ⑩ · Burr & Forman · http://www.burr.com · 420 North 20th Street, Suite 3400 · Birmingham, AL 35203-3284 · 205-251-3000

Laurence D. Vinson, Jr. · ⑩ · Bradley Arant Rose & White · http://www.bradleyarant.com · One Federal Place · 1819 Fifth Avenue North · Birmingham, AL 35203-2119 · 205-521-8000

Paul S. Ware · Bradley Arant Rose & White · http://www.bradleyarant.com · One Federal Place · 1819 Fifth Avenue North · Birmingham, AL 35203-2119 · 205-521-8000

Michael D. Waters · ⑩ · Balch & Bingham · http://www.balch.com · 1901 Sixth Avenue North, Suite 1500 Birmingham, AL 35203-4644 · 205-251-8100

Lois S. Woodward · Balch & Bingham · http://www.balch.com · 1901 Sixth Avenue North, Suite 1500 · Birmingham, AL 35203-4644 · 205-251-8100

William S. Wright · Balch & Bingham · http://www.balch.com · 1901 Sixth Avenue North, Suite 1500 · Birmingham, AL 35203-4644 · 205-251-8100

Kenneth T. Wyatt · Bradley Arant Rose & White · http://www.bradleyarant.com · One Federal Place · 1819 Fifth Avenue North · Birmingham, AL 35203-2119 · 205-521-8000

Mobile

Alan C. Christian · Johnstone, Adams, Bailey, Gordon & Harris · http://www.johnstoneadams.com · One St. Louis Centre, Suite 4000 · One Saint Louis Street · P.O. Box 1988 · Mobile, AL 36633-1988 · 251-432-7682

Stephen G. Crawford · ⑩ · Hand Arendall · http://www.handarendall.com · RSA Tower, Suite 30200 · 11 North Water Street · Mobile, AL 36602 · 251-432-5511

Ronald P. Davis · ⑩ · Vickers, Riis, Murray and Curran · Regions Bank Building, 11th Floor · 106 St. Francis Street · P.O. Drawer 2568 · Mobile, AL 36652 · 251-432-9772

J. W. Goodloe, Jr. · ⑩ · Vickers, Riis, Murray and Curran · Regions Bank Building, 11th Floor · 106 St. Francis Street · P.O. Drawer 2568 · Mobile, AL 36652 · 251-432-9772

John C. H. Miller, Jr. · Jones Walker · http://www.joneswalker.com · 254 State Street · P.O. Box 46 · Mobile, AL 36601 · 251-432-1414

J. Manson Murray · ⑩ · Vickers, Riis, Murray and Curran · Regions Bank Building, 11th Floor · 106 St. Francis Street · P.O. Drawer 2568 · Mobile, AL 36652 · 251-432-9772

Thomas P. Oldweiler · Armbrecht Jackson · Riverview Plaza, 13th Floor · 63 South Royal Street · P.O. Box 290 · Mobile, AL 36601-0290 · 251-405-1300

E. B. Peebles III · ⑩ · Armbrecht Jackson · Riverview Plaza, 13th Floor · 63 South Royal Street · P.O. Box 290 · Mobile, AL 36601-0290 · 251-405-1300

Wesley Pipes IV · ⑩ · Wesley Pipes · 107 Saint Francis Street, Suite 2411 · P.O. Box 249 · Mobile, AL 36601 · 251-434-6455

Ronald A. Snider · Jones Walker · http://www.joneswalker.com · 254 State Street · P.O. Box 46 · Mobile, AL 36601 · 251-432-1414

Donald J. Stewart · ⑩ · Cabaniss, Johnston, Gardner, Dumas & O'Neal · http://www.cabaniss.com · 63 South Royal Street, Suite 700 · P.O. Box 2906 · Mobile, AL 36652-2906 · 251-415-7300

George M. Walker · Hand Arendall · http://www.handarendall.com · RSA Tower, Suite 30200 · 11 North Water Street · Mobile, AL 36602 · 251-432-5511

Richard A. Wright · Jones Walker · http://www.joneswalker.com · 254 State Street · P.O. Box 46 · Mobile, AL 36601 · 251-432-1414

BANKRUPTCY AND CREDITOR-DEBTOR RIGHTS LAW

Birmingham

Robert H. Adams · ⑩ · Haskell, Slaughter, Young & Rediker · http://www.hsy.com · Park Place Tower, Suite 1400 · 2001 Park Place North · Birmingham, AL 35203 · 205-251-1000

David B. Anderson · ⑩ · Anderson & Associates · Financial Center, Suite 1450 · 505 Twentieth Street North · Birmingham, AL 35203-4635 · 205-324-1230

Jay R. Bender · Bradley Arant Rose & White · http://www.bradleyarant.com · One Federal Place · 1819 Fifth Avenue North · Birmingham, AL 35203-2119 · 205-521-8000

Richard P. Carmody · ⑩ · Adams and Reese · http://www.adamsandreese.com · Concord Center, Suite 1100 · 2100 Third Avenue North · Birmingham, AL 35203 · 205-250-5000

J. Patrick Darby · Bradley Arant Rose & White · http://www.bradleyarant.com · One Federal Place · 1819 Fifth Avenue North · Birmingham, AL 35203-2119 · 205-521-8000

Charles L. Denaburg · ⑩ · Najjar Denaburg · 2125 Morris Avenue · Birmingham, AL 35203 · 205-250-8400

N. Christian Glenos · Bradley Arant Rose & White · http://www.bradleyarant.com · One Federal Place · 1819 Fifth Avenue North · Birmingham, AL 35203-2119 · 205-521-8000

Michael L. Hall · Burr & Forman · http://www.burr.com · 420 North 20th Street, Suite 3400 · Birmingham, AL 35203-3284 · 205-251-3000

Clark R. Hammond · Johnston Barton Proctor & Rose · Colonial Brookwood Center, Suite 901 · 569 Brookwood Village · Birmingham, AL 35209 · 205-458-9400

Joe A. Joseph · Burr & Forman · http://www.burr.com · 420 North 20th Street, Suite 3400 · Birmingham, AL 35203-3284 · 205-251-3000

Jayna Partain Lamar · Maynard Cooper & Gale · http://www.maynardcooper.com · Regions/Harbert Plaza, Suite 2400 · 1901 Sixth Avenue North · Birmingham, AL 35203-2602 · 205-254-1000

Timothy M. Lupinacci · Baker, Donelson, Bearman, Caldwell & Berkowitz · http://www.bakerdonelson.com · Wachovia Tower, Suite 1600 · 420 Twentieth Street North · Birmingham, AL 35203 · 205-328-0480

Derek F. Meek · Burr & Forman · http://www.burr.com · 420 North 20th Street, Suite 3400 · Birmingham, AL 35203-3284 · 205-251-3000

George M. Neal, Jr. · Sirote & Permutt · 2311 Highland Avenue South · P.O. Box 55727 · Birmingham, AL 35255-5727 · 205-930-5100

Thomas E. Reynolds · Haskell, Slaughter, Young & Rediker · http://www.hsy.com · Park Place Tower, Suite 1400 · 2001 Park Place North · Birmingham, AL 35203 · 205-251-1000

Robert B. Rubin · 20 · Burr & Forman · http://www.burr.com · 420 North 20th Street, Suite 3400 · Birmingham, AL 35203-3284 · 205-251-3000

Ted Stuckenschneider · Ted Stuckenschneider · http://www.birminghambankruptcylawyer.net · 205 North 20th Street, Suite 427 · Birmingham, AL 35203 · 205-324-5631

W. Clark Watson · Balch & Bingham · http://www.balch.com · 1901 Sixth Avenue North, Suite 1500 · Birmingham, AL 35203-4644 · 205-251-8100

Donald M. Wright · Sirote & Permutt · 2311 Highland Avenue South · P.O. Box 55727 · Birmingham, AL 35255-5727 · 205-930-5100

Mobile

Henry A. Callaway III · Hand Arendall · http://www.handarendall.com · RSA Tower, Suite 30200 · 11 North Water Street · Mobile, AL 36602 · 251-432-5511

George W. Finkbohner, Jr. · 20 · The Finkbohner Law Firm · 2866 Dauphin Street, Suite O · P.O. Box 3085 · Mobile, AL 36652 · 251-472-8388

Irvin Grodsky · 10 · Irvin Grodsky · 454 Dauphin Street · P.O. Box 3123 · Mobile, AL 36652 · 251-433-3657

Christopher I. Gruenewald · Armbrecht Jackson · Riverview Plaza, 13th Floor · 63 South Royal Street · P.O. Box 290 · Mobile, AL 36601-0290 · 251-405-1300

Jeffery J. Hartley · Helmsing, Leach, Herlong, Newman & Rouse · http://www.helmsinglaw.com · The LaClede Building, Suite 2000 · 150 Government Street · P.O. Box 2767 · Mobile, AL 36652 · 251-432-5521

Donald J. Stewart · 10 · Cabaniss, Johnston, Gardner, Dumas & O'Neal · http://www.cabaniss.com · 63 South Royal Street, Suite 700 · P.O. Box 2906 · Mobile, AL 36652-2906 · 251-415-7300

Lawrence B. Voit · 10 · Silver, Voit & Thompson · 4317-A Midmost Drive · Mobile, AL 36609 · 251-343-0800

BET-THE-COMPANY LITIGATION

Birmingham

D. Leon Ashford · 10 · Hare, Wynn, Newell & Newton · The Historic Massey Building, Suite 800 · 2025 Third Avenue North · Birmingham, AL 35203 · 205-328-5330

W. Michael Atchison · 10 · Starnes & Atchison · 100 Brookwood Place, Seventh Floor · P.O. Box 598512 · Birmingham, AL 35259-8512 · 205-868-6000

Michael L. Edwards · 20 · Balch & Bingham · http://www.balch.com · 1710 Sixth Avenue North · Birmingham, AL 35203-2015 · 205-251-8100

Samuel H. Franklin · ⑳ · Lightfoot, Franklin & White · The Clark Building · 400 Twentieth Street North · Birmingham, AL 35203 · 205-581-0700

James W. Gewin · ㉕ · Bradley Arant Rose & White · http://www.bradleyarant.com · One Federal Place · 1819 Fifth Avenue North · Birmingham, AL 35203-2119 · 205-521-8000

Hobart A. McWhorter, Jr. · ⑳ · Bradley Arant Rose & White · http://www.bradleyarant.com · One Federal Place · 1819 Fifth Avenue North · Birmingham, AL 35203-2119 · 205-521-8000

John H. Morrow · ㉕ · Bradley Arant Rose & White · http://www.bradleyarant.com · One Federal Place · 1819 Fifth Avenue North · Birmingham, AL 35203-2119 · 205-521-8000

Scott A. Powell · ⑩ · Hare, Wynn, Newell & Newton · The Historic Massey Building, Suite 800 · 2025 Third Avenue North · Birmingham, AL 35203 · 205-328-5330

Mobile

Broox G. Holmes · ⑳ · Armbrecht Jackson · Riverview Plaza, 13th Floor · 63 South Royal Street · P.O. Box 290 · Mobile, AL 36601-0290 · 251-405-1300

John N. Leach, Jr. · ⑳ · Helmsing, Leach, Herlong, Newman & Rouse · http://www.helmsinglaw.com · The LaClede Building, Suite 2000 · 150 Government Street · P.O. Box 2767 · Mobile, AL 36652 · 251-432-5521

Steven L. Nicholas · Cunningham, Bounds, Yance, Crowder & Brown · http://www.cbcbb.com · 1601 Dauphin Street · P.O. Box 66705 · Mobile, AL 36660 · 251-471-6191

Montgomery

David R. Boyd · ⑩ · Balch & Bingham · http://www.balch.com · 105 Tallapoosa Street, Suite 200 · P.O. Box 78 · Montgomery, AL 36101-0078 · 334-834-6500

William D. Coleman · ⑩ · Capell & Howard · http://www.capellhoward.com · 150 South Perry Street · P.O. Box 2069 · Montgomery, AL 36102-2069 · 334-241-8000

Joseph C. Espy III · ⑩ · Melton, Espy & Williams · 255 Dexter Avenue · P.O. Drawer 5130 · Montgomery, AL 36103-5130 · 334-263-6621

Tabor R. Novak, Jr. · ⑩ · Ball, Ball, Matthews & Novak · 2000 Interstate Park Drive, Suite 204 · P.O. Box 2148 · Montgomery, AL 36102-2148 · 334-387-7680

Robert D. Segall · ⑳ · Copeland, Franco, Screws & Gill · 444 South Perry Street · P.O. Box 347 · Montgomery, AL 36101-0347 · 334-834-1180

Charles A. Stewart III · Bradley Arant Rose & White · http://www.bradleyarant.com · Alabama Center for Commerce, Suite 780 · 401 Adams Avenue · Montgomery, AL 36104 · 334-956-7700

BIOTECHNOLOGY LAW

Birmingham

T. Gregory Peterson · Bradley Arant Rose & White · http://www.bradleyarant.com · One Federal Place · 1819 Fifth Avenue North · Birmingham, AL 35203-2119 · 205-521-8000

Huntsville

Scott E. Ludwig · ⑩ · Bradley Arant Rose & White · http://www.bradleyarant.com · 200 Clinton Avenue West, Suite 900 · Huntsville, AL 35801-4900 · 256-517-5100

COMMERCIAL LITIGATION

Alexander City

Larry W. Morris · ⑩ · Morris, Haynes & Hornsby · 131 Main Street · P.O. Box 1660 · Alexander City, AL 35011-1660 · 256-329-2000

Bay Minette

Allan R. Chason · Chason & Chason · 300 D'Olive Street · P.O. Box 100 · Bay Minette, AL 36507 · 251-937-2191

Birmingham

Edward S. Allen · Balch & Bingham · http://www.balch.com · 1710 Sixth Avenue North · Birmingham, AL 35203-2015 · 205-251-8100

D. Leon Ashford · ⑩ · Hare, Wynn, Newell & Newton · The Historic Massey Building, Suite 800 · 2025 Third Avenue North · Birmingham, AL 35203 · 205-328-5330

W. Michael Atchison · ⑩ · Starnes & Atchison · 100 Brookwood Place, Seventh Floor · P.O. Box 598512 · Birmingham, AL 35259-8512 · 205-868-6000

W. Percy Badham III · Badham & Buck · Wachovia Tower, Suite 2585 · 420 North 20th Street · Birmingham, AL 35203 · 205-521-0036

Frank M. Bainbridge · ⑩ · Bainbridge, Mims, Rogers & Smith · Luckie Building, Suite 415 · 600 Luckie Drive · P.O. Box 530886 · Birmingham, AL 35253-2450 · 205-879-1100

Lee E. Bains, Jr. · Maynard Cooper & Gale · http://www.maynardcooper.com · Regions/Harbert Plaza, Suite 2400 · 1901 Sixth Avenue North · Birmingham, AL 35203-2602 · 205-254-1000

S. Allen Baker, Jr. · Balch & Bingham · http://www.balch.com · 1710 Sixth Avenue North · Birmingham, AL 35203-2015 · 205-251-8100

Robert R. Baugh · Sirote & Permutt · 2311 Highland Avenue South · P.O. Box 55727 · Birmingham, AL 35255-5727 · 205-930-5100

John N. Bolus · Maynard Cooper & Gale · http://www.maynardcooper.com · Regions/Harbert Plaza, Suite 2400 · 1901 Sixth Avenue North · Birmingham, AL 35203-2602 · 205-254-1000

Andrew P. Campbell · ⑩ · Campbell, Gidiere, Lee, Sinclair & Williams · 2100-A Southbridge Parkway, Suite 450 · Birmingham, AL 35209 · 205-803-0051

Lawrence B. Clark · Baker, Donelson, Bearman, Caldwell & Berkowitz · http://www.bakerdonelson.com Wachovia Tower, Suite 1600 · 420 Twentieth Street North · Birmingham, AL 35203 · 205-328-0480

Julia Boaz Cooper · Bradley Arant Rose & White · http://www.bradleyarant.com · One Federal Place · 1819 Fifth Avenue North · Birmingham, AL 35203-2119 · 205-521-8000

J. Mason Davis, Jr. · Sirote & Permutt · 2311 Highland Avenue South · P.O. Box 55727 · Birmingham, AL 35255-5727 · 205-930-5100

Luther M. Dorr, Jr. · Maynard Cooper & Gale · http://www.maynardcooper.com · Regions/Harbert Plaza, Suite 2400 · 1901 Sixth Avenue North · Birmingham, AL 35203-2602 · 205-254-1000

Augusta S. Dowd · White Arnold & Dowd · 2025 Third Avenue North, Suite 500 · Birmingham, AL 35203 · 205-323-1888

Tom Dutton · ⑩ · Pittman, Hooks, Dutton, Kirby & Hellums · Park Place Tower, Suite 1100 · 2001 Park Place North · Birmingham, AL 35203 · 205-322-8880

Robert D. Eckinger · Adams and Reese · http://www.adamsandreese.com · Concord Center, Suite 1100 · 2100 Third Avenue North · Birmingham, AL 35203 · 205-250-5000

Michael L. Edwards · ⑳ · Balch & Bingham · http://www.balch.com · 1710 Sixth Avenue North · Birmingham, AL 35203-2015 · 205-251-8100

Samuel H. Franklin · ⑳ · Lightfoot, Franklin & White · The Clark Building · 400 Twentieth Street North · Birmingham, AL 35203 · 205-581-0700

Michael Freeman · Balch & Bingham · http://www.balch.com · 1901 Sixth Avenue North, Suite 1500 · Birmingham, AL 35203-4644 · 205-251-8100

Fournier J. Gale III · ㉕ · Maynard Cooper & Gale · http://www.maynardcooper.com · Regions/Harbert Plaza, Suite 2400 · 1901 Sixth Avenue North · Birmingham, AL 35203-2602 · 205-254-1000

James W. Gewin · ㉕ · Bradley Arant Rose & White · http://www.bradleyarant.com · One Federal Place · 1819 Fifth Avenue North · Birmingham, AL 35203-2119 · 205-521-8000

John E. Goodman · Bradley Arant Rose & White · http://www.bradleyarant.com · One Federal Place · 1819 Fifth Avenue North · Birmingham, AL 35203-2119 · 205-521-8000

James L. Goyer III · Maynard Cooper & Gale · http://www.maynardcooper.com · Regions/Harbert Plaza, Suite 2400 · 1901 Sixth Avenue North · Birmingham, AL 35203-2602 · 205-254-1000

Gregory H. Hawley · White Arnold & Dowd · 2025 Third Avenue North, Suite 500 · Birmingham, AL 35203 · 205-323-1888

James C. Huckaby, Jr. · Christian & Small · http://www.csattorneys.com · 505 North 20th Street, Suite 1800 · Birmingham, AL 35203-2696 · 205-795-6588

David G. Hymer · Bradley Arant Rose & White · http://www.bradleyarant.com · One Federal Place · 1819 Fifth Avenue North · Birmingham, AL 35203-2119 · 205-521-8000

Stephen C. Jackson · Maynard Cooper & Gale · http://www.maynardcooper.com · Regions/Harbert Plaza, Suite 2400 · 1901 Sixth Avenue North · Birmingham, AL 35203-2602 · 205-254-1000

John M. Johnson · Lightfoot, Franklin & White · The Clark Building · 400 Twentieth Street North · Birmingham, AL 35203 · 205-581-0700

G. Douglas Jones · Whatley Drake & Kallas · 2001 Park Place North, Suite 1000 · P.O. Box 10647 · Birmingham, AL 35202-0647 · 205-328-9576

M. Christian King · Lightfoot, Franklin & White · The Clark Building · 400 Twentieth Street North · Birmingham, AL 35203 · 205-581-0700

William C. Knight, Jr. · ㉕ · Burr & Forman · http://www.burr.com · 420 North 20th Street, Suite 3400 · Birmingham, AL 35203-3284 · 205-251-3000

Matthew H. Lembke · Bradley Arant Rose & White · http://www.bradleyarant.com · One Federal Place · 1819 Fifth Avenue North · Birmingham, AL 35203-2119 · 205-521-8000

Warren B. Lightfoot · (25) · Lightfoot, Franklin & White · The Clark Building · 400 Twentieth Street North · Birmingham, AL 35203 · 205-581-0700

Thad G. Long · (10) · Bradley Arant Rose & White · http://www.bradleyarant.com · One Federal Place · 1819 Fifth Avenue North · Birmingham, AL 35203-2119 · 205-521-8000

Joseph B. Mays, Jr. · (10) · Bradley Arant Rose & White · http://www.bradleyarant.com · One Federal Place · 1819 Fifth Avenue North · Birmingham, AL 35203-2119 · 205-521-8000

Crawford S. McGivaren, Jr. · (20) · Cabaniss, Johnston, Gardner, Dumas & O'Neal · http://www.cabaniss.com · 2001 Park Place North, Suite 700 · P.O. Box 830612 · Birmingham, AL 35283-0612 · 205-716-5200

Michael D. McKibben · Bradley Arant Rose & White · http://www.bradleyarant.com · One Federal Place · 1819 Fifth Avenue North · Birmingham, AL 35203-2119 · 205-521-8000

Hobart A. McWhorter, Jr. · (20) · Bradley Arant Rose & White · http://www.bradleyarant.com · One Federal Place · 1819 Fifth Avenue North · Birmingham, AL 35203-2119 · 205-521-8000

Tony G. Miller · Maynard Cooper & Gale · http://www.maynardcooper.com · Regions/Harbert Plaza, Suite 2400 · 1901 Sixth Avenue North · Birmingham, AL 35203-2602 · 205-254-1000

John C. Morrow · Burr & Forman · http://www.burr.com · 420 North 20th Street, Suite 3400 · Birmingham, AL 35203-3284 · 205-251-3000

John H. Morrow · (25) · Bradley Arant Rose & White · http://www.bradleyarant.com · One Federal Place · 1819 Fifth Avenue North · Birmingham, AL 35203-2119 · 205-521-8000

James L. North · (10) · James L. North & Associates · Title Building, Suite 700 · 300 Twenty-First Street North · Birmingham, AL 35203 · 205-251-0252

Richard F. Ogle · (10) · Christian & Small · http://www.csattorneys.com · 505 North 20th Street, Suite 1800 Birmingham, AL 35203-2696 · 205-795-6588

J. Vernon Patrick, Jr. · (20) · Haskell, Slaughter, Young & Rediker · http://www.hsy.com · Park Place Tower, Suite 1400 · 2001 Park Place North · Birmingham, AL 35203 · 205-251-1000

Michael R. Pennington · (10) · Bradley Arant Rose & White · http://www.bradleyarant.com · One Federal Place · 1819 Fifth Avenue North · Birmingham, AL 35203-2119 · 205-521-8000

Scott A. Powell · (10) · Hare, Wynn, Newell & Newton · The Historic Massey Building, Suite 800 · 2025 Third Avenue North · Birmingham, AL 35203 · 205-328-5330

James L. Priester · Maynard Cooper & Gale · http://www.maynardcooper.com · Regions/Harbert Plaza, Suite 2400 · 1901 Sixth Avenue North · Birmingham, AL 35203-2602 · 205-254-1000

J. Michael Rediker · (20) · Haskell, Slaughter, Young & Rediker · http://www.hsy.com · Park Place Tower, Suite 1400 · 2001 Park Place North · Birmingham, AL 35203 · 205-251-1000

Alan T. Rogers · Balch & Bingham · http://www.balch.com · 1710 Sixth Avenue North · Birmingham, AL 35203-2015 · 205-251-8100

Bruce Rogers · Bainbridge, Mims, Rogers & Smith · Luckie Building, Suite 415 · 600 Luckie Drive · P.O. Box 530886 · Birmingham, AL 35253-2450 · 205-879-1100

Stephen A. Rowe · Adams and Reese · http://www.adamsandreese.com · Concord Center, Suite 1100 · 2100 Third Avenue North · Birmingham, AL 35203 · 205-250-5000

Robert H. Rutherford · Burr & Forman · http://www.burr.com · 420 North 20th Street, Suite 3400 · Birmingham, AL 35203-3284 · 205-251-3000

A. Inge Selden III · Maynard Cooper & Gale · http://www.maynardcooper.com · Regions/Harbert Plaza, Suite 2400 · 1901 Sixth Avenue North · Birmingham, AL 35203-2602 · 205-254-1000

Charles E. Sharp, Sr. · ⑳ · Sadler Sullivan · Wachovia Tower, Suite 2500 · 420 North 20th Street · Birmingham, AL 35203-5203 · 205-326-4166

Henry E. Simpson · ⑩ · Adams and Reese · http://www.adamsandreese.com · Concord Center, Suite 1100 · 2100 Third Avenue North · Birmingham, AL 35203 · 205-250-5000

Deborah Alley Smith · Christian & Small · http://www.csattorneys.com · 505 North 20th Street, Suite 1800 · Birmingham, AL 35203-2696 · 205-795-6588

Richard E. Smith · Christian & Small · http://www.csattorneys.com · 505 North 20th Street, Suite 1800 · Birmingham, AL 35203-2696 · 205-795-6588

Daniel D. Sparks · Christian & Small · http://www.csattorneys.com · 505 North 20th Street, Suite 1800 · Birmingham, AL 35203-2696 · 205-795-6588

Sharon D. Stuart · Christian & Small · http://www.csattorneys.com · 505 North 20th Street, Suite 1800 · Birmingham, AL 35203-2696 · 205-795-6588

J. Mark White · ⑩ · White Arnold & Dowd · 2025 Third Avenue North, Suite 500 · Birmingham, AL 35203 · 205-323-1888

J. Gusty Yearout · Yearout & Traylor · 800 Shades Creek Parkway, Suite 500 · Birmingham, AL 35209 · 205-414-8160

Lee H. Zell · ⑩ · Balch & Bingham · http://www.balch.com · 1710 Sixth Avenue North · Birmingham, AL 35203-2015 · 205-251-8100

Brewton

Edward T. Hines · Thompson, Garrett & Hines · 218 Belleville Avenue · P.O. Box 387 · Brewton, AL 36427-0387 · 251-867-6063

Fairhope

David A. Bagwell · ⑩ · David A. Bagwell · 400 Fairhope Avenue, Suite 2-E · P.O. Box 2126 · Fairhope, AL 36533 · 251-928-2970

Huntsville

J. R. Brooks · Lanier Ford Shaver & Payne · http://www.lfsp.com · 200 West Side Square, Suite 5000 · P.O. Box 2087 · Huntsville, AL 35804-2087 · 256-535-1100

Julian D. Butler · Sirote & Permutt · 305 Church Street, Suite 800 · P.O. Box 18248 · Huntsville, AL 35804 · 256-536-1711

W. Stanley Rodgers · ⑳ · Lanier Ford Shaver & Payne · http://www.lfsp.com · 200 West Side Square, Suite 5000 · P.O. Box 2087 · Huntsville, AL 35804-2087 · 256-535-1100

George W. Royer, Jr. · Lanier Ford Shaver & Payne · http://www.lfsp.com · 200 West Side Square, Suite 5000 · P.O. Box 2087 · Huntsville, AL 35804-2087 · 256-535-1100

Jasper

Edward R. Jackson · Jackson, Fikes, Hood & Brakefield · 1816 Third Avenue, Suite 200 · P.O. Box 748 · Jasper, AL 35502-0748 · 205-387-2171

Mobile

Walter M. Cook, Jr. · Lyons, Pipes & Cook · Two North Royal Street · P.O. Box 2727 · Mobile, AL 36652-2727 · 251-432-4481

William M. Cunningham, Jr. · Burns, Cunningham & Mackey · 50 St. Emanuel Street · P.O. Box 1583 · Mobile, AL 36633 · 334-432-0612

Edward A. Dean · 10 · Armbrecht Jackson · Riverview Plaza, 13th Floor · 63 South Royal Street · P.O. Box 290 · Mobile, AL 36601-0290 · 251-405-1300

William H. Hardie, Jr. · 20 · Johnstone, Adams, Bailey, Gordon & Harris · http://www.johnstoneadams.com · One St. Louis Centre, Suite 4000 · One Saint Louis Street · P.O. Box 1988 · Mobile, AL 36633-1988 · 251-432-7682

Ben H. Harris III · Jones Walker · http://www.joneswalker.com · 254 State Street · P.O. Box 46 · Mobile, AL 36601 · 251-432-1414

Broox G. Holmes · 20 · Armbrecht Jackson · Riverview Plaza, 13th Floor · 63 South Royal Street · P.O. Box 290 · Mobile, AL 36601-0290 · 251-405-1300

John N. Leach, Jr. · 20 · Helmsing, Leach, Herlong, Newman & Rouse · http://www.helmsinglaw.com · The LaClede Building, Suite 2000 · 150 Government Street · P.O. Box 2767 · Mobile, AL 36652 · 251-432-5521

Peter S. Mackey · Burns, Cunningham & Mackey · 50 St. Emanuel Street · P.O. Box 1583 · Mobile, AL 36633 · 334-432-0612

Brian P. McCarthy · McDowell Knight Roedder & Sledge · Riverview Plaza, Suite 900 · 63 South Royal Street · P.O. Box 350 · Mobile, AL 36601 · 251-432-5300

M. Kathleen Miller · Armbrecht Jackson · Riverview Plaza, 13th Floor · 63 South Royal Street · P.O. Box 290 · Mobile, AL 36601-0290 · 251-405-1300

James B. Newman · Helmsing, Leach, Herlong, Newman & Rouse · http://www.helmsinglaw.com · The LaClede Building, Suite 2000 · 150 Government Street · P.O. Box 2767 · Mobile, AL 36652 · 251-432-5521

Steven L. Nicholas · Cunningham, Bounds, Yance, Crowder & Brown · http://www.cbcbb.com · 1601 Dauphin Street · P.O. Box 66705 · Mobile, AL 36660 · 251-471-6191

Caine O'Rear III · 10 · Hand Arendall · http://www.handarendall.com · RSA Tower, Suite 30200 · 11 North Water Street · Mobile, AL 36602 · 251-432-5511

Stephen C. Olen · 10 · Cunningham, Bounds, Yance, Crowder & Brown · http://www.cbcbb.com · 1601 Dauphin Street · P.O. Box 66705 · Mobile, AL 36660 · 251-471-6191

Sandy G. Robinson · 10 · Cabaniss, Johnston, Gardner, Dumas & O'Neal · http://www.cabaniss.com · 63 South Royal Street, Suite 700 · P.O. Box 2906 · Mobile, AL 36652-2906 · 251-415-7300

Benjamen T. Rowe · 10 · Cabaniss, Johnston, Gardner, Dumas & O'Neal · http://www.cabaniss.com · 63 South Royal Street, Suite 700 · P.O. Box 2906 · Mobile, AL 36652-2906 · 251-415-7300

Thomas S. Rue · Johnstone, Adams, Bailey, Gordon & Harris · http://www.johnstoneadams.com · One St. Louis Centre, Suite 4000 · One Saint Louis Street · P.O. Box 1988 · Mobile, AL 36633-1988 · 251-432-7682

A. Edwin Stuardi III · Armbrecht Jackson · Riverview Plaza, 13th Floor · 63 South Royal Street · P.O. Box 290 · Mobile, AL 36601-0290 · 251-405-1300

Cooper C. Thurber · Lyons, Pipes & Cook · Two North Royal Street · P.O. Box 2727 · Mobile, AL 36652-2727 · 251-432-4481

George M. Walker · Hand Arendall · http://www.handarendall.com · RSA Tower, Suite 30200 · 11 North Water Street · Mobile, AL 36602 · 251-432-5511

Forrest C. Wilson III · McDowell Knight Roedder & Sledge · Riverview Plaza, Suite 900 · 63 South Royal Street · P.O. Box 350 · Mobile, AL 36601 · 251-432-5300

Montgomery

Dennis R. Bailey · Rushton, Stakely, Johnston & Garrett · http://www.rsjg.com · 184 Commerce Street · P.O. Box 270 · Montgomery, AL 36101-0270 · 334-206-3100

David R. Boyd · ⑩ · Balch & Bingham · http://www.balch.com · 105 Tallapoosa Street, Suite 200 · P.O. Box 78 · Montgomery, AL 36101-0078 · 334-834-6500

Philip H. Butler · Bradley Arant Rose & White · http://www.bradleyarant.com · Alabama Center for Commerce, Suite 780 · 401 Adams Avenue · Montgomery, AL 36104 · 334-956-7700

Walter R. Byars · Steiner, Crum & Byars · Regions Bank Building, Eighth Floor · Eight Commerce Street P.O. Box 668 · Montgomery, AL 36101-0668 · 334-832-8800

James A. Byram, Jr. · Balch & Bingham · http://www.balch.com · 105 Tallapoosa Street, Suite 200 · P.O. Box 78 · Montgomery, AL 36101-0078 · 334-834-6500

William D. Coleman · ⑩ · Capell & Howard · http://www.capellhoward.com · 150 South Perry Street · P.O. Box 2069 · Montgomery, AL 36102-2069 · 334-241-8000

Lee H. Copeland · Copeland, Franco, Screws & Gill · 444 South Perry Street · P.O. Box 347 · Montgomery, AL 36101-0347 · 334-834-1180

Joseph C. Espy III · ⑩ · Melton, Espy & Williams · 255 Dexter Avenue · P.O. Drawer 5130 · Montgomery, AL 36103-5130 · 334-263-6621

Richard H. Gill · ⑩ · Copeland, Franco, Screws & Gill · 444 South Perry Street · P.O. Box 347 · Montgomery, AL 36101-0347 · 334-834-1180

John A. Henig, Jr. · ⑩ · Copeland, Franco, Screws & Gill · 444 South Perry Street · P.O. Box 347 · Montgomery, AL 36101-0347 · 334-834-1180

Robert A. Huffaker · ⑳ · Rushton, Stakely, Johnston & Garrett · http://www.rsjg.com · 184 Commerce Street · P.O. Box 270 · Montgomery, AL 36101-0270 · 334-206-3100

Thomas S. Lawson, Jr. · Capell & Howard · http://www.capellhoward.com · 150 South Perry Street · P.O. Box 2069 · Montgomery, AL 36102-2069 · 334-241-8000

W. Joseph McCorkle, Jr. · Balch & Bingham · http://www.balch.com · 105 Tallapoosa Street, Suite 200 · P.O. Box 78 · Montgomery, AL 36101-0078 · 334-834-6500

Oakley W. Melton, Jr. · ⑳ · Melton, Espy & Williams · 255 Dexter Avenue · P.O. Drawer 5130 · Montgomery, AL 36103-5130 · 334-263-6621

Robert F. Northcutt · Capell & Howard · http://www.capellhoward.com · 150 South Perry Street · P.O. Box 2069 · Montgomery, AL 36102-2069 · 334-241-8000

Tabor R. Novak, Jr. · ⑩ · Ball, Ball, Matthews & Novak · 2000 Interstate Park Drive, Suite 204 · P.O. Box 2148 · Montgomery, AL 36102-2148 · 334-387-7680

Charles B. Paterson · Balch & Bingham · http://www.balch.com · 105 Tallapoosa Street, Suite 200 · P.O. Box 78 · Montgomery, AL 36101-0078 · 334-834-6500

Robert D. Segall · ⑳ · Copeland, Franco, Screws & Gill · 444 South Perry Street · P.O. Box 347 · Montgomery, AL 36101-0347 · 334-834-1180

Charles A. Stewart III · Bradley Arant Rose & White · http://www.bradleyarant.com · Alabama Center for Commerce, Suite 780 · 401 Adams Avenue · Montgomery, AL 36104 · 334-956-7700

Dorman Walker · Balch & Bingham · http://www.balch.com · 105 Tallapoosa Street, Suite 200 · P.O. Box 78 · Montgomery, AL 36101-0078 · 334-834-6500

George Walton Walker III · Copeland, Franco, Screws & Gill · 444 South Perry Street · P.O. Box 347 · Montgomery, AL 36101-0347 · 334-834-1180

James N. Walter, Jr. · Capell & Howard · http://www.capellhoward.com · 150 South Perry Street · P.O. Box 2069 · Montgomery, AL 36102-2069 · 334-241-8000

Opelika

William F. Horsley · ⑩ · Samford & Denson · 709 Avenue A · P.O. Box 2345 · Opelika, AL 36803-2345 · 334-745-3504

Robert T. Meadows III · Capell & Howard · http://www.capellhoward.com · 3120 Frederick Road, Suite B · P.O. Drawer 2268 · Opelika, AL 36803 · 334-501-1540

Tuscaloosa

William J. Donald, Jr. · ⑩ · Donald, Randall & Donald · AmSouth Building, Ninth Floor · 2330 University Boulevard · Tuscaloosa, AL 35403 · 205-758-2585

COMMUNICATIONS LAW

Montgomery

Dennis R. Bailey · Rushton, Stakely, Johnston & Garrett · http://www.rsjg.com · 184 Commerce Street · P.O. Box 270 · Montgomery, AL 36101-0270 · 334-206-3100

CONSTRUCTION LAW

Birmingham

James F. Archibald III · Bradley Arant Rose & White · http://www.bradleyarant.com · One Federal Place 1819 Fifth Avenue North · Birmingham, AL 35203-2119 · 205-521-8000

Axel Bolvig III · Bradley Arant Rose & White · http://www.bradleyarant.com · One Federal Place · 1819 Fifth Avenue North · Birmingham, AL 35203-2119 · 205-521-8000

William S. Fishburne III · Burr & Forman · http://www.burr.com · 420 North 20th Street, Suite 3400 · Birmingham, AL 35203-3284 · 205-251-3000

Edward P. Meyerson · Baker, Donelson, Bearman, Caldwell & Berkowitz · http://www.bakerdonelson.com · Wachovia Tower, Suite 1600 · 420 Twentieth Street North · Birmingham, AL 35203 · 205-328-0480

J. David Pugh · Bradley Arant Rose & White · http://www.bradleyarant.com · One Federal Place · 1819 Fifth Avenue North · Birmingham, AL 35203-2119 · 205-521-8000

E. Mabry Rogers · Bradley Arant Rose & White · http://www.bradleyarant.com · One Federal Place · 1819 Fifth Avenue North · Birmingham, AL 35203-2119 · 205-521-8000

Walter J. Sears III · Bradley Arant Rose & White · http://www.bradleyarant.com · One Federal Place · 1819 Fifth Avenue North · Birmingham, AL 35203-2119 · 205-521-8000

R. Carlton Smyly · Cabaniss, Johnston, Gardner, Dumas & O'Neal · http://www.cabaniss.com · 2001 Park Place North, Suite 700 · P.O. Box 830612 · Birmingham, AL 35283-0612 · 205-716-5200

Luther Graves Stiff III · Starnes & Atchison · 100 Brookwood Place, Seventh Floor · P.O. Box 598512 · Birmingham, AL 35259-8512 · 205-868-6000

E. Glenn Waldrop, Jr. · Lightfoot, Franklin & White · The Clark Building · 400 Twentieth Street North Birmingham, AL 35203 · 205-581-0700

Mobile

Clifford C. Brady · Brady Radcliff & Brown · 1600 Wachovia Bank Building · 61 Saint Joseph Street · P.O. Box 1668 · Mobile, AL 36633 · 251-405-0077

I. David Cherniak · Johnstone, Adams, Bailey, Gordon & Harris · http://www.johnstoneadams.com · One St. Louis Centre, Suite 4000 · One Saint Louis Street · P.O. Box 1988 · Mobile, AL 36633-1988 · 251-432-7682

C. William Daniels, Jr. · Burr & Forman · http://www.burr.com · Colonial Bank Centre, Suite 400 · 41 West I-65 Service Road North · P.O. Box 16046 · Mobile, AL 36616 · 251-344-5151

James P. Green · Wright Green · 1495 University Boulevard · P.O. Box 16818 · Mobile, AL 36616 · 251-344-7744

William Alexander Moseley · Hand Arendall · http://www.handarendall.com · RSA Tower, Suite 30200 · 11 North Water Street · Mobile, AL 36602 · 251-432-5511

Caine O'Rear III · ⑩ · Hand Arendall · http://www.handarendall.com · RSA Tower, Suite 30200 · 11 North Water Street · Mobile, AL 36602 · 251-432-5511

Montgomery

William D. Coleman · ⑩ · Capell & Howard · http://www.capellhoward.com · 150 South Perry Street · P.O. Box 2069 · Montgomery, AL 36102-2069 · 334-241-8000

J. Lister Hubbard · Capell & Howard · http://www.capellhoward.com · 150 South Perry Street · P.O. Box 2069 · Montgomery, AL 36102-2069 · 334-241-8000

R. Brooke Lawson III · Capell & Howard · http://www.capellhoward.com · 150 South Perry Street · P.O. Box 2069 · Montgomery, AL 36102-2069 · 334-241-8000

Frank H. McFadden · Capell & Howard · http://www.capellhoward.com · 150 South Perry Street · P.O. Box 2069 · Montgomery, AL 36102-2069 · 334-241-8000

CORPORATE GOVERNANCE AND COMPLIANCE LAW

Birmingham

Gregory S. Curran · Maynard Cooper & Gale · http://www.maynardcooper.com · Regions/Harbert Plaza, Suite 2400 · 1901 Sixth Avenue North · Birmingham, AL 35203-2602 · 205-254-1000

Mark L. Drew · Maynard Cooper & Gale · http://www.maynardcooper.com · Regions/Harbert Plaza, Suite 2400 · 1901 Sixth Avenue North · Birmingham, AL 35203-2602 · 205-254-1000

Christopher B. Harmon · Maynard Cooper & Gale · http://www.maynardcooper.com · Regions/Harbert Plaza, Suite 2400 · 1901 Sixth Avenue North · Birmingham, AL 35203-2602 · 205-254-1000

William W. Horton · Haskell, Slaughter, Young & Rediker · http://www.hsy.com · Park Place Tower, Suite 1400 · 2001 Park Place North · Birmingham, AL 35203 · 205-251-1000

B. G. Minisman, Jr. · (10) · Baker, Donelson, Bearman, Caldwell & Berkowitz · http://www.bakerdonelson.com · Wachovia Tower, Suite 1600 · 420 Twentieth Street North · Birmingham, AL 35203 · 205-328-0480

John K. Molen · (10) · Bradley Arant Rose & White · http://www.bradleyarant.com · One Federal Place · 1819 Fifth Avenue North · Birmingham, AL 35203-2119 · 205-521-8000

Timothy J. Tracy · Balch & Bingham · http://www.balch.com · 1901 Sixth Avenue North, Suite 1500 · Birmingham, AL 35203-4644 · 205-251-8100

Paul S. Ware · Bradley Arant Rose & White · http://www.bradleyarant.com · One Federal Place · 1819 Fifth Avenue North · Birmingham, AL 35203-2119 · 205-521-8000

Mobile

Eric J. Dyas · Jones Walker · http://www.joneswalker.com · 254 State Street · P.O. Box 46 · Mobile, AL 36601 · 251-432-1414

Gregory R. Jones · (10) · Hand Arendall · http://www.handarendall.com · RSA Tower, Suite 30200 · 11 North Water Street · Mobile, AL 36602 · 251-432-5511

John C. H. Miller, Jr. · Jones Walker · http://www.joneswalker.com · 254 State Street · P.O. Box 46 · Mobile, AL 36601 · 251-432-1414

CORPORATE LAW

Birmingham

Matthew A. Aiken · Balch & Bingham · http://www.balch.com · 1901 Sixth Avenue North, Suite 1500 · Birmingham, AL 35203-4644 · 205-251-8100

Louis H. Anders · (25) · Burr & Forman · http://www.burr.com · 420 North 20th Street, Suite 3400 · Birmingham, AL 35203-3284 · 205-251-3000

Suzanne Ashe · Balch & Bingham · http://www.balch.com · 1901 Sixth Avenue North, Suite 1500 · Birmingham, AL 35203-4644 · 205-251-8100

Walter M. Beale, Jr. · Balch & Bingham · http://www.balch.com · 1901 Sixth Avenue North, Suite 1500 · Birmingham, AL 35203-4644 · 205-251-8100

Birch Bowdre · Wallace, Jordan, Ratliff & Brandt · http://www.wallacejordan.com · 800 Shades Creek Parkway, Suite 400 · P.O. Box 530910 · Birmingham, AL 35253 · 205-870-0555

Thomas H. Brinkley · Maynard Cooper & Gale · http://www.maynardcooper.com · Regions/Harbert Plaza, Suite 2400 · 1901 Sixth Avenue North · Birmingham, AL 35203-2602 · 205-254-1000

F. Gerald Burnett · Cabaniss, Johnston, Gardner, Dumas & O'Neal · http://www.cabaniss.com · 2001 Park Place North, Suite 700 · P.O. Box 830612 · Birmingham, AL 35283-0612 · 205-716-5200

Thomas Neely Carruthers · ㉕ · Bradley Arant Rose & White · http://www.bradleyarant.com · One Federal Place · 1819 Fifth Avenue North · Birmingham, AL 35203-2119 · 205-521-8000

James W. Childs, Jr. · Bradley Arant Rose & White · http://www.bradleyarant.com · One Federal Place · 1819 Fifth Avenue North · Birmingham, AL 35203-2119 · 205-521-8000

Edward R. Christian · Burr & Forman · http://www.burr.com · 420 North 20th Street, Suite 3400 · Birmingham, AL 35203-3284 · 205-251-3000

Richard J. Cohn · ㉕ · Sirote & Permutt · 2311 Highland Avenue South · P.O. Box 55727 · Birmingham, AL 35255-5727 · 205-930-5100

J. Paul Compton, Jr. · ⑩ · Bradley Arant Rose & White · http://www.bradleyarant.com · One Federal Place · 1819 Fifth Avenue North · Birmingham, AL 35203-2119 · 205-521-8000

Roy J. Crawford · ⑳ · Cabaniss, Johnston, Gardner, Dumas & O'Neal · http://www.cabaniss.com · 2001 Park Place North, Suite 700 · P.O. Box 830612 · Birmingham, AL 35283-0612 · 205-716-5200

Gregory S. Curran · Maynard Cooper & Gale · http://www.maynardcooper.com · Regions/Harbert Plaza, Suite 2400 · 1901 Sixth Avenue North · Birmingham, AL 35203-2602 · 205-254-1000

C. Fred Daniels · ⑩ · Cabaniss, Johnston, Gardner, Dumas & O'Neal · http://www.cabaniss.com · 2001 Park Place North, Suite 700 · P.O. Box 830612 · Birmingham, AL 35283-0612 · 205-716-5200

J. Mason Davis, Jr. · Sirote & Permutt · 2311 Highland Avenue South · P.O. Box 55727 · Birmingham, AL 35255-5727 · 205-930-5100

L. Susan Doss · Bradley Arant Rose & White · http://www.bradleyarant.com · One Federal Place · 1819 Fifth Avenue North · Birmingham, AL 35203-2119 · 205-521-8000

Mark L. Drew · Maynard Cooper & Gale · http://www.maynardcooper.com · Regions/Harbert Plaza, Suite 2400 · 1901 Sixth Avenue North · Birmingham, AL 35203-2602 · 205-254-1000

John P. Dulin, Jr. · Maynard Cooper & Gale · http://www.maynardcooper.com · Regions/Harbert Plaza, Suite 2400 · 1901 Sixth Avenue North · Birmingham, AL 35203-2602 · 205-254-1000

Denson Nauls Franklin III · Bradley Arant Rose & White · http://www.bradleyarant.com · One Federal Place · 1819 Fifth Avenue North · Birmingham, AL 35203-2119 · 205-521-8000

Robert E. Lee Garner · Haskell, Slaughter, Young & Rediker · http://www.hsy.com · Park Place Tower, Suite 1400 · 2001 Park Place North · Birmingham, AL 35203 · 205-251-1000

John B. Grenier · ⑩ · Bradley Arant Rose & White · http://www.bradleyarant.com · One Federal Place · 1819 Fifth Avenue North · Birmingham, AL 35203-2119 · 205-521-8000

Christopher B. Harmon · Maynard Cooper & Gale · http://www.maynardcooper.com · Regions/Harbert Plaza, Suite 2400 · 1901 Sixth Avenue North · Birmingham, AL 35203-2602 · 205-254-1000

William Lyle Hinds, Jr. · (25) · Bradley Arant Rose & White · http://www.bradleyarant.com · One Federal Place · 1819 Fifth Avenue North · Birmingham, AL 35203-2119 · 205-521-8000

J. Fred Kingren · Hand Arendall · http://www.handarendall.com · Park Place Tower, Suite 1200 · 2001 Park Place North · Birmingham, AL 35203 · 205-324-4400

Thomas O. Kolb · Baker, Donelson, Bearman, Caldwell & Berkowitz · http://www.bakerdonelson.com · Wachovia Tower, Suite 1600 · 420 Twentieth Street North · Birmingham, AL 35203 · 205-328-0480

Harold B. Kushner · (20) · Bradley Arant Rose & White · http://www.bradleyarant.com · One Federal Place 1819 Fifth Avenue North · Birmingham, AL 35203-2119 · 205-521-8000

Ronald A. Levitt · (10) · Sirote & Permutt · 2311 Highland Avenue South · P.O. Box 55727 · Birmingham, AL 35255-5727 · 205-930-5100

Jack B. Levy · (10) · Balch & Bingham · http://www.balch.com · 1901 Sixth Avenue North, Suite 1500 · Birmingham, AL 35203-4644 · 205-251-8100

J. Kris Lowry · Maynard Cooper & Gale · http://www.maynardcooper.com · Regions/Harbert Plaza, Suite 2400 · 1901 Sixth Avenue North · Birmingham, AL 35203-2602 · 205-254-1000

Barry S. Marks · Marks & Weinberg · Park Place Tower, Suite 525 · 2001 Park Place North · Birmingham, AL 35203 · 205-251-8301

Daniel H. Markstein III · (25) · Maynard Cooper & Gale · http://www.maynardcooper.com · Regions/Harbert Plaza, Suite 2400 · 1901 Sixth Avenue North · Birmingham, AL 35203-2602 · 205-254-1000

C. Henry Marston · Walston, Wells & Birchall · One Federal Place, Suite 1100 · 1819 Fifth Avenue North Birmingham, AL 35203 · 205-244-5200

B. G. Minisman, Jr. · (10) · Baker, Donelson, Bearman, Caldwell & Berkowitz · http://www.bakerdonelson.com · Wachovia Tower, Suite 1600 · 420 Twentieth Street North · Birmingham, AL 35203 · 205-328-0480

John K. Molen · (10) · Bradley Arant Rose & White · http://www.bradleyarant.com · One Federal Place · 1819 Fifth Avenue North · Birmingham, AL 35203-2119 · 205-521-8000

James L. North · (10) · James L. North & Associates · Title Building, Suite 700 · 300 Twenty-First Street North · Birmingham, AL 35203 · 205-251-0252

M. Beth O'Neill · Maynard Cooper & Gale · http://www.maynardcooper.com · Regions/Harbert Plaza, Suite 2400 · 1901 Sixth Avenue North · Birmingham, AL 35203-2602 · 205-254-1000

Virginia C. Patterson · Bradley Arant Rose & White · http://www.bradleyarant.com · One Federal Place · 1819 Fifth Avenue North · Birmingham, AL 35203-2119 · 205-521-8000

Sidney T. Philips · Leitman, Siegal & Payne · The Land Title Building, Suite 400 · 600 North 20th Street · Birmingham, AL 35203 · 205-251-5900

Robert B. Phillips II · Baker, Donelson, Bearman, Caldwell & Berkowitz · http://www.bakerdonelson.com · Wachovia Tower, Suite 1600 · 420 Twentieth Street North · Birmingham, AL 35203 · 205-328-0480

J. Fred Powell · (10) · Burr & Forman · http://www.burr.com · 420 North 20th Street, Suite 3400 · Birmingham, AL 35203-3284 · 205-251-3000

Gene T. Price · Burr & Forman · http://www.burr.com · 420 North 20th Street, Suite 3400 · Birmingham, AL 35203-3284 · 205-251-3000

James E. Rotch · ⑩ · Bradley Arant Rose & White · http://www.bradleyarant.com · One Federal Place · 1819 Fifth Avenue North · Birmingham, AL 35203-2119 · 205-521-8000

Maurice L. Shevin · Sirote & Permutt · 2311 Highland Avenue South · P.O. Box 55727 · Birmingham, AL 35255-5727 · 205-930-5100

D. J. Simonetti · ⑩ · Baker, Donelson, Bearman, Caldwell & Berkowitz · http://www.bakerdonelson.com Wachovia Tower, Suite 1600 · 420 Twentieth Street North · Birmingham, AL 35203 · 205-328-0480

Jack P. Stephenson, Jr. · ⑩ · Burr & Forman · http://www.burr.com · 420 North 20th Street, Suite 3400 · Birmingham, AL 35203-3284 · 205-251-3000

Joseph G. Stewart · ⑩ · Burr & Forman · http://www.burr.com · 420 North 20th Street, Suite 3400 · Birmingham, AL 35203-3284 · 205-251-3000

George M. Taylor III · Burr & Forman · http://www.burr.com · 420 North 20th Street, Suite 3400 · Birmingham, AL 35203-3284 · 205-251-3000

W. Lee Thuston · ⑩ · Burr & Forman · http://www.burr.com · 420 North 20th Street, Suite 3400 · Birmingham, AL 35203-3284 · 205-251-3000

Timothy J. Tracy · Balch & Bingham · http://www.balch.com · 1901 Sixth Avenue North, Suite 1500 · Birmingham, AL 35203-4644 · 205-251-8100

Laurence D. Vinson, Jr. · ⑩ · Bradley Arant Rose & White · http://www.bradleyarant.com · One Federal Place · 1819 Fifth Avenue North · Birmingham, AL 35203-2119 · 205-521-8000

Robert C. Walthall · ㉕ · Bradley Arant Rose & White · http://www.bradleyarant.com · One Federal Place 1819 Fifth Avenue North · Birmingham, AL 35203-2119 · 205-521-8000

Paul S. Ware · Bradley Arant Rose & White · http://www.bradleyarant.com · One Federal Place · 1819 Fifth Avenue North · Birmingham, AL 35203-2119 · 205-521-8000

James C. Wilson, Jr. · Baker, Donelson, Bearman, Caldwell & Berkowitz · http://www.bakerdonelson.com · Wachovia Tower, Suite 1600 · 420 Twentieth Street North · Birmingham, AL 35203 · 205-328-0480

Huntsville

Hall B. Bryant III · Bradley Arant Rose & White · http://www.bradleyarant.com · 200 Clinton Avenue West, Suite 900 · Huntsville, AL 35801-4900 · 256-517-5100

Scott E. Ludwig · ⑩ · Bradley Arant Rose & White · http://www.bradleyarant.com · 200 Clinton Avenue West, Suite 900 · Huntsville, AL 35801-4900 · 256-517-5100

John Wynn · ⑩ · Lanier Ford Shaver & Payne · http://www.lfsp.com · 200 West Side Square, Suite 5000 · P.O. Box 2087 · Huntsville, AL 35804-2087 · 256-535-1100

Mobile

Stephen G. Crawford · ⑩ · Hand Arendall · http://www.handarendall.com · RSA Tower, Suite 30200 · 11 North Water Street · Mobile, AL 36602 · 251-432-5511

Zebulon Montgomery Pike Inge, Jr. · ⑩ · Vickers, Riis, Murray and Curran · Regions Bank Building, 11th Floor · 106 St. Francis Street · P.O. Drawer 2568 · Mobile, AL 36652 · 251-432-9772

W. David Johnson · Adams and Reese · http://www.adamsandreese.com · RSA Battle House Tower, Suite 23200 · 11 North Water Street · Mobile, AL 36602 · 251-433-3234

George A. LeMaistre · Jones Walker · http://www.joneswalker.com · 254 State Street · P.O. Box 46 · Mobile, AL 36601 · 251-432-1414

Victor H. Lott, Jr. · Adams and Reese · http://www.adamsandreese.com · RSA Battle House Tower, Suite 23200 · 11 North Water Street · Mobile, AL 36602 · 251-433-3234

T. Bruce McGowin · Hand Arendall · http://www.handarendall.com · RSA Tower, Suite 30200 · 11 North Water Street · Mobile, AL 36602 · 251-432-5511

John C. H. Miller, Jr. · Jones Walker · http://www.joneswalker.com · 254 State Street · P.O. Box 46 · Mobile, AL 36601 · 251-432-1414

Brooks P. Milling · Hand Arendall · http://www.handarendall.com · RSA Tower, Suite 30200 · 11 North Water Street · Mobile, AL 36602 · 251-432-5511

J. Manson Murray · ⑩ · Vickers, Riis, Murray and Curran · Regions Bank Building, 11th Floor · 106 St. Francis Street · P.O. Drawer 2568 · Mobile, AL 36652 · 251-432-9772

E. B. Peebles III · ⑩ · Armbrecht Jackson · Riverview Plaza, 13th Floor · 63 South Royal Street · P.O. Box 290 · Mobile, AL 36601-0290 · 251-405-1300

James Dale Smith · Armbrecht Jackson · Riverview Plaza, 13th Floor · 63 South Royal Street · P.O. Box 290 · Mobile, AL 36601-0290 · 251-405-1300

Ronald A. Snider · Jones Walker · http://www.joneswalker.com · 254 State Street · P.O. Box 46 · Mobile, AL 36601 · 251-432-1414

Montgomery

John F. Andrews · ⑩ · Capell & Howard · http://www.capellhoward.com · 150 South Perry Street · P.O. Box 2069 · Montgomery, AL 36102-2069 · 334-241-8000

Richard H. Gill · ⑩ · Copeland, Franco, Screws & Gill · 444 South Perry Street · P.O. Box 347 · Montgomery, AL 36101-0347 · 334-834-1180

Henry H. Hutchinson · ⑳ · Capell & Howard · http://www.capellhoward.com · 150 South Perry Street · P.O. Box 2069 · Montgomery, AL 36102-2069 · 334-241-8000

D. Kyle Johnson · ⑩ · Capell & Howard · http://www.capellhoward.com · 150 South Perry Street · P.O. Box 2069 · Montgomery, AL 36102-2069 · 334-241-8000

Thomas G. Mancuso · ⑩ · Haskell, Slaughter, Young & Rediker · http://www.hsy.com · 305 South Lawrence Street · Montgomery, AL 36104 · 334-265-8573

Robert D. Thorington · Bradley Arant Rose & White · http://www.bradleyarant.com · Alabama Center for Commerce, Suite 780 · 401 Adams Avenue · Montgomery, AL 36104 · 334-956-7700

DUI/DWI DEFENSE

Birmingham

William N. Clark · ⑩ · Redden, Mills & Clark · Financial Center, Suite 940 · 505 Twentieth Street North Birmingham, AL 35203 · 205-322-0457

Maxwell H. Pulliam · Christian & Small · http://www.csattorneys.com · 505 North 20th Street, Suite 1800 Birmingham, AL 35203-2696 · 205-795-6588

Stephen W. Shaw · Redden, Mills & Clark · Financial Center, Suite 940 · 505 Twentieth Street North · Birmingham, AL 35203 · 205-322-0457

Thomas J. Spina · Fawal & Spina · 1330 Twenty-First Way South, Suite 200 · Birmingham, AL 35205 · 205-939-1330

Huntsville

Phillip B. Price, Sr. · Price and Flowers Law Firm · 217 Randolph Avenue, SE · Huntsville, AL 35801-4825 · 256-536-6000

Mobile

Kenneth A. Nixon · Lyons, Pipes & Cook · Two North Royal Street · P.O. Box 2727 · Mobile, AL 36652-2727 · 251-432-4481

Montgomery

John T. Kirk · John T. Kirk · 445 South Decatur Street · P.O. Box 1412 · Montgomery, AL 36102 · 334-264-1498

EDUCATION LAW

Birmingham

Carl E. Johnson, Jr. · Bishop, Colvin, Johnson & Kent · 1910 First Avenue North · Birmingham, AL 35203-4006 · 205-251-2881

Donald B. Sweeney, Jr. · Bradley Arant Rose & White · http://www.bradleyarant.com · One Federal Place · 1819 Fifth Avenue North · Birmingham, AL 35203-2119 · 205-521-8000

Huntsville

J. R. Brooks · Lanier Ford Shaver & Payne · http://www.lfsp.com · 200 West Side Square, Suite 5000 · P.O. Box 2087 · Huntsville, AL 35804-2087 · 256-535-1100

William W. Sanderson, Jr. · Lanier Ford Shaver & Payne · http://www.lfsp.com · 200 West Side Square, Suite 5000 · P.O. Box 2087 · Huntsville, AL 35804-2087 · 256-535-1100

Mobile

Robert C. Campbell III · Campbell, Duke & Prine · Regions Tower, Suite 700 · 851 East I-65 Service Road South · Mobile, AL 36606 · 251-476-2400

Montgomery

David R. Boyd · ⑩ · Balch & Bingham · http://www.balch.com · 105 Tallapoosa Street, Suite 200 · P.O. Box 78 · Montgomery, AL 36101-0078 · 334-834-6500

ELDER LAW

Birmingham

Joel A. Mendler · (25) · Sirote & Permutt · 2311 Highland Avenue South · P.O. Box 55727 · Birmingham, AL 35255-5727 · 205-930-5100

EMINENT DOMAIN AND CONDEMNATION LAW

Birmingham

Charles A. J. Beavers, Jr. · (25) · Bradley Arant Rose & White · http://www.bradleyarant.com · One Federal Place · 1819 Fifth Avenue North · Birmingham, AL 35203-2119 · 205-521-8000

Jesse P. Evans III · (10) · Haskell, Slaughter, Young & Rediker · http://www.hsy.com · Park Place Tower, Suite 1400 · 2001 Park Place North · Birmingham, AL 35203 · 205-251-1000

Mobile

Warren C. Herlong, Jr. · Helmsing, Leach, Herlong, Newman & Rouse · http://www.helmsinglaw.com · The LaClede Building, Suite 2000 · 150 Government Street · P.O. Box 2767 · Mobile, AL 36652 · 251-432-5521

EMPLOYEE BENEFITS LAW

Birmingham

Elizabeth G. Beaube · Maynard Cooper & Gale · http://www.maynardcooper.com · Regions/Harbert Plaza, Suite 2400 · 1901 Sixth Avenue North · Birmingham, AL 35203-2602 · 205-254-1000

Joseph S. Bluestein · (10) · Sirote & Permutt · 2311 Highland Avenue South · P.O. Box 55727 · Birmingham, AL 35255-5727 · 205-930-5100

James S. Christie, Jr. · Bradley Arant Rose & White · http://www.bradleyarant.com · One Federal Place · 1819 Fifth Avenue North · Birmingham, AL 35203-2119 · 205-521-8000

C. Fred Daniels · (10) · Cabaniss, Johnston, Gardner, Dumas & O'Neal · http://www.cabaniss.com · 2001 Park Place North, Suite 700 · P.O. Box 830612 · Birmingham, AL 35283-0612 · 205-716-5200

David S. Dunkle · (20) · Cabaniss, Johnston, Gardner, Dumas & O'Neal · http://www.cabaniss.com · 2001 Park Place North, Suite 700 · P.O. Box 830612 · Birmingham, AL 35283-0612 · 205-716-5200

Kevin J. Henderson · (10) · Bradley Arant Rose & White · http://www.bradleyarant.com · One Federal Place · 1819 Fifth Avenue North · Birmingham, AL 35203-2119 · 205-521-8000

Jack B. Levy · (10) · Balch & Bingham · http://www.balch.com · 1901 Sixth Avenue North, Suite 1500 · Birmingham, AL 35203-4644 · 205-251-8100

Jackson M. Payne · Leitman, Siegal & Payne · The Land Title Building, Suite 400 · 600 North 20th Street · Birmingham, AL 35203 · 205-251-5900

Terry Price · Ford & Harrison · http://www.fordharrison.com · 2100 Third Avenue North, Suite 400 · Birmingham, AL 35203 · 205-244-5900

James L. Priester · Maynard Cooper & Gale · http://www.maynardcooper.com · Regions/Harbert Plaza, Suite 2400 · 1901 Sixth Avenue North · Birmingham, AL 35203-2602 · 205-254-1000

Frances King Quick · Adams and Reese · http://www.adamsandreese.com · Concord Center, Suite 1100 · 2100 Third Avenue North · Birmingham, AL 35203 · 205-250-5000

Laura Schiele Robinson · Balch & Bingham · http://www.balch.com · 1901 Sixth Avenue North, Suite 1500 · Birmingham, AL 35203-4644 · 205-251-8100

William E. Shanks, Jr. · ⑩ · Balch & Bingham · http://www.balch.com · 1901 Sixth Avenue North, Suite 1500 · Birmingham, AL 35203-4644 · 205-251-8100

D. J. Simonetti · ⑩ · Baker, Donelson, Bearman, Caldwell & Berkowitz · http://www.bakerdonelson.com Wachovia Tower, Suite 1600 · 420 Twentieth Street North · Birmingham, AL 35203 · 205-328-0480

Dana L. Thrasher · ⑩ · Constangy, Brooks & Smith · http://www.constangy.com · One Federal Place, Suite 900 · 1819 Fifth Avenue North · Birmingham, AL 35203-2618 · 205-252-9321

A. Brand Walton, Jr. · ⑳ · Burr & Forman · http://www.burr.com · 420 North 20th Street, Suite 3400 · Birmingham, AL 35203-3284 · 205-251-3000

Mobile

Thomas F. Garth · ⑩ · Lyons, Pipes & Cook · Two North Royal Street · P.O. Box 2727 · Mobile, AL 36652-2727 · 251-432-4481

Montgomery

D. Kyle Johnson · ⑩ · Capell & Howard · http://www.capellhoward.com · 150 South Perry Street · P.O. Box 2069 · Montgomery, AL 36102-2069 · 334-241-8000

ENERGY LAW

Birmingham

M. Stanford Blanton · Balch & Bingham · http://www.balch.com · 1710 Sixth Avenue North · Birmingham, AL 35203-2015 · 205-251-8100

Fournier J. Gale III · ㉕ · Maynard Cooper & Gale · http://www.maynardcooper.com · Regions/Harbert Plaza, Suite 2400 · 1901 Sixth Avenue North · Birmingham, AL 35203-2602 · 205-254-1000

Lyle D. Larson · Balch & Bingham · http://www.balch.com · 1710 Sixth Avenue North · Birmingham, AL 35203-2015 · 205-251-8100

S. Chris Still · Balch & Bingham · http://www.balch.com · 1710 Sixth Avenue North · Birmingham, AL 35203-2015 · 205-251-8100

Andrew Tunnell · Balch & Bingham · http://www.balch.com · 1710 Sixth Avenue North · Birmingham, AL 35203-2015 · 205-251-8100

H. Thomas Wells, Jr. · Maynard Cooper & Gale · http://www.maynardcooper.com · Regions/Harbert Plaza, Suite 2400 · 1901 Sixth Avenue North · Birmingham, AL 35203-2602 · 205-254-1000

Mobile

Conrad P. Armbrecht · ⑳ · Armbrecht Jackson · Riverview Plaza, 13th Floor · 63 South Royal Street · P.O. Box 290 · Mobile, AL 36601-0290 · 251-405-1300

Neil C. Johnston · ⑩ · Hand Arendall · http://www.handarendall.com · RSA Tower, Suite 30200 · 11 North Water Street · Mobile, AL 36602 · 251-432-5511

Montgomery

Walter R. Byars · Steiner, Crum & Byars · Regions Bank Building, Eighth Floor · Eight Commerce Street P.O. Box 668 · Montgomery, AL 36101-0668 · 334-832-8800

Tuscaloosa

William T. Watson · ⑩ · Watson, deGraffenried, Hardin & Tyra · 1651 McFarland Boulevard North · Tuscaloosa, AL 35406 · 205-345-1577

ENVIRONMENTAL LAW

Birmingham

William S. Cox III · Lightfoot, Franklin & White · The Clark Building · 400 Twentieth Street North · Birmingham, AL 35203 · 205-581-0700

Ronald W. Farley · Burr & Forman · http://www.burr.com · 420 North 20th Street, Suite 3400 · Birmingham, AL 35203-3284 · 205-251-3000

J. Ross Forman III · Burr & Forman · http://www.burr.com · 420 North 20th Street, Suite 3400 · Birmingham, AL 35203-3284 · 205-251-3000

Fournier J. Gale III · ㉕ · Maynard Cooper & Gale · http://www.maynardcooper.com · Regions/Harbert Plaza, Suite 2400 · 1901 Sixth Avenue North · Birmingham, AL 35203-2602 · 205-254-1000

Andrew Robert Greene · ⑩ · Bradley Arant Rose & White · http://www.bradleyarant.com · One Federal Place · 1819 Fifth Avenue North · Birmingham, AL 35203-2119 · 205-521-8000

John M. Johnson · Lightfoot, Franklin & White · The Clark Building · 400 Twentieth Street North · Birmingham, AL 35203 · 205-581-0700

Steven G. McKinney · Balch & Bingham · http://www.balch.com · 1901 Sixth Avenue North, Suite 1500 · Birmingham, AL 35203-4644 · 205-251-8100

Adam K. Peck · Lightfoot, Franklin & White · The Clark Building · 400 Twentieth Street North · Birmingham, AL 35203 · 205-581-0700

Harlan I. Prater IV · Lightfoot, Franklin & White · The Clark Building · 400 Twentieth Street North · Birmingham, AL 35203 · 205-581-0700

Rebecca W. Pritchett · Pritchett Law Firm · 2001 Park Place North, Suite 810 · Birmingham, AL 35203 · 205-583-9090

William H. Satterfield · ⑳ · Balch & Bingham · http://www.balch.com · 1901 Sixth Avenue North, Suite 1500 · Birmingham, AL 35203-4644 · 205-251-8100

Alfred F. Smith, Jr. · Bainbridge, Mims, Rogers & Smith · Luckie Building, Suite 415 · 600 Luckie Drive P.O. Box 530886 · Birmingham, AL 35253-2450 · 205-879-1100

Jarred O. Taylor II · Maynard Cooper & Gale · http://www.maynardcooper.com · Regions/Harbert Plaza, Suite 2400 · 1901 Sixth Avenue North · Birmingham, AL 35203-2602 · 205-254-1000

Sid J. Trant · Bradley Arant Rose & White · http://www.bradleyarant.com · One Federal Place · 1819 Fifth Avenue North · Birmingham, AL 35203-2119 · 205-521-8000

J. Alan Truitt · Maynard Cooper & Gale · http://www.maynardcooper.com · Regions/Harbert Plaza, Suite 2400 · 1901 Sixth Avenue North · Birmingham, AL 35203-2602 · 205-254-1000

H. Thomas Wells, Jr. · Maynard Cooper & Gale · http://www.maynardcooper.com · Regions/Harbert Plaza, Suite 2400 · 1901 Sixth Avenue North · Birmingham, AL 35203-2602 · 205-254-1000

Mobile

Conrad P. Armbrecht · ⑳ · Armbrecht Jackson · Riverview Plaza, 13th Floor · 63 South Royal Street · P.O. Box 290 · Mobile, AL 36601-0290 · 251-405-1300

Neil C. Johnston · ⑩ · Hand Arendall · http://www.handarendall.com · RSA Tower, Suite 30200 · 11 North Water Street · Mobile, AL 36602 · 251-432-5511

T. Bruce McGowin · Hand Arendall · http://www.handarendall.com · RSA Tower, Suite 30200 · 11 North Water Street · Mobile, AL 36602 · 251-432-5511

Montgomery

Thomas J. Methvin · Beasley, Allen, Crow, Methvin, Portis & Miles · 218 Commerce Street · P.O. Box 4160 · Montgomery, AL 36103-4160 · 334-269-2343

EQUIPMENT FINANCE LAW

Birmingham

Barry S. Marks · Marks & Weinberg · Park Place Tower, Suite 525 · 2001 Park Place North · Birmingham, AL 35203 · 205-251-8301

Laurence D. Vinson, Jr. · ⑩ · Bradley Arant Rose & White · http://www.bradleyarant.com · One Federal Place · 1819 Fifth Avenue North · Birmingham, AL 35203-2119 · 205-521-8000

FAMILY LAW

Birmingham

Stephen R. Arnold · ㉕ · White Arnold & Dowd · 2025 Third Avenue North, Suite 500 · Birmingham, AL 35203 · 205-323-1888

Robert C. Barnett · ㉕ · Robert C. Barnett · Age Herald Building, Suite 100 · 2107 Fifth Avenue North · Birmingham, AL 35203 · 205-252-9751

J. Ronald Boyd · ⑩ · Boyd, Fernambucq, Vincent & Dunn · 2801 University Boulevard, Suite 302 · Birmingham, AL 35233 · 205-930-9000

Robin L. Burrell · Najjar Denaburg · 2125 Morris Avenue · Birmingham, AL 35203 · 205-250-8400

William N. Clark · ⑩ · Redden, Mills & Clark · Financial Center, Suite 940 · 505 Twentieth Street North Birmingham, AL 35203 · 205-322-0457

Terry M. Cromer · Durward & Cromer · 2015 Second Avenue North, Suite 100 · Birmingham, AL 35203 205-324-6654

Gerard J. Durward · ㉕ · Durward & Cromer · 2015 Second Avenue North, Suite 100 · Birmingham, AL 35203 · 205-324-6654

George Richard Fernambucq · Boyd, Fernambucq, Vincent & Dunn · 2801 University Boulevard, Suite 302 · Birmingham, AL 35233 · 205-930-9000

L. Stephen Wright, Jr. · ⑩ · Najjar Denaburg · 2125 Morris Avenue · Birmingham, AL 35203 · 205-250-8400

Mobile

Donald M. Briskman · Briskman & Binion · 205 Church Street · P.O. Box 43 · Mobile, AL 36602 · 251-433-7600

J. Jerry Pilgrim · ⑩ · J. Jerry Pilgrim & Associates · 63 South Royal Street, Suite 503 · Mobile, AL 36602 251-432-7645

Michael D. Sherman · Micheal D. Sherman · 205 Saint Emanuel Street, First Floor · Mobile, AL 36602 · 251-694-6000

Joseph C. Sullivan, Jr. · Hamilton, Butler, Riddick, Tarlton & Sullivan · 107 St. Francis Street, Suite 1407 · P.O. Box 1743 · Mobile, AL 36633 · 251-432-7517

Montgomery

Joseph C. Espy III · ⑩ · Melton, Espy & Williams · 255 Dexter Avenue · P.O. Drawer 5130 · Montgomery, AL 36103-5130 · 334-263-6621

John A. Henig, Jr. · ⑩ · Copeland, Franco, Screws & Gill · 444 South Perry Street · P.O. Box 347 · Montgomery, AL 36101-0347 · 334-834-1180

Oakley W. Melton, Jr. · ⑳ · Melton, Espy & Williams · 255 Dexter Avenue · P.O. Drawer 5130 · Montgomery, AL 36103-5130 · 334-263-6621

J. Floyd Minor · ⑩ · Minor & Olszewski · 458 South Lawrence Street · P.O. Box 164 · Montgomery, AL 36101 · 334-265-6200

Pelham

Douglas L. Key · Key, Greer, Frawley, Key, Harrison & Simpson · 2163 Pelham Parkway · Pelham, AL 35124-1161 · 205-987-2211

FIRST AMENDMENT LAW

Birmingham

Gilbert E. Johnston, Jr. · ⑩ · Johnston Barton Proctor & Rose · Colonial Brookwood Center, Suite 901 · 569 Brookwood Village · Birmingham, AL 35209 · 205-458-9400

Warren B. Lightfoot · ㉕ · Lightfoot, Franklin & White · The Clark Building · 400 Twentieth Street North · Birmingham, AL 35203 · 205-581-0700

John H. Morrow · ㉕ · Bradley Arant Rose & White · http://www.bradleyarant.com · One Federal Place · 1819 Fifth Avenue North · Birmingham, AL 35203-2119 · 205-521-8000

Huntsville

E. Cutter Hughes · ⑩ · Bradley Arant Rose & White · http://www.bradleyarant.com · 200 Clinton Avenue West, Suite 900 · Huntsville, AL 35801-4900 · 256-517-5100

Mobile

Edward S. Sledge III · ⑩ · McDowell Knight Roedder & Sledge · Riverview Plaza, Suite 900 · 63 South Royal Street · P.O. Box 350 · Mobile, AL 36601 · 251-432-5300

FRANCHISE LAW

Birmingham

Linda A. Friedman · ⑩ · Bradley Arant Rose & White · http://www.bradleyarant.com · One Federal Place 1819 Fifth Avenue North · Birmingham, AL 35203-2119 · 205-521-8000

GOVERNMENT RELATIONS LAW

Birmingham

M. Stanford Blanton · Balch & Bingham · http://www.balch.com · 1710 Sixth Avenue North · Birmingham, AL 35203-2015 · 205-251-8100

Edward A. Hosp · Maynard Cooper & Gale · http://www.maynardcooper.com · Regions/Harbert Plaza, Suite 2400 · 1901 Sixth Avenue North · Birmingham, AL 35203-2602 · 205-254-1000

Stephen W. Still · Maynard Cooper & Gale · http://www.maynardcooper.com · Regions/Harbert Plaza, Suite 2400 · 1901 Sixth Avenue North · Birmingham, AL 35203-2602 · 205-254-1000

Luther J. Strange III · Bradley Arant Rose & White · http://www.bradleyarant.com · One Federal Place · 1819 Fifth Avenue North · Birmingham, AL 35203-2119 · 205-521-8000

Montgomery

Alvin L. Fox, Jr. · Maynard Cooper & Gale · http://www.maynardcooper.com · RSA Union Building, Suite 650 · 100 North Union Street · Montgomery, AL 36104 · 334-262-2001

HEALTH CARE LAW

Birmingham

Howard E. Bogard · Burr & Forman · http://www.burr.com · 420 North 20th Street, Suite 3400 · Birmingham, AL 35203-3284 · 205-251-3000

Richard J. Brockman · Johnston Barton Proctor & Rose · Colonial Brookwood Center, Suite 901 · 569 Brookwood Village · Birmingham, AL 35209 · 205-458-9400

Clark A. Cooper · Christian & Small · http://www.csattorneys.com · 505 North 20th Street, Suite 1800 · Birmingham, AL 35203-2696 · 205-795-6588

Deane K. Corliss · ⑩ · Bradley Arant Rose & White · http://www.bradleyarant.com · One Federal Place · 1819 Fifth Avenue North · Birmingham, AL 35203-2119 · 205-521-8000

Roy J. Crawford · ⑳ · Cabaniss, Johnston, Gardner, Dumas & O'Neal · http://www.cabaniss.com · 2001 Park Place North, Suite 700 · P.O. Box 830612 · Birmingham, AL 35283-0612 · 205-716-5200

Susan Dominick Doughton · ⑩ · Dominick, Fletcher, Yeilding, Wood & Lloyd · http://www.dfy.com · 2121 Highland Avenue South · P.O. Box 1387 · Birmingham, AL 35201 · 205-939-0033

William W. Horton · Haskell, Slaughter, Young & Rediker · http://www.hsy.com · Park Place Tower, Suite 1400 · 2001 Park Place North · Birmingham, AL 35203 · 205-251-1000

M. Ann Huckstep · Adams and Reese · http://www.adamsandreese.com · Concord Center, Suite 1100 · 2100 Third Avenue North · Birmingham, AL 35203 · 205-250-5000

David M. Hunt · Johnston Barton Proctor & Rose · Colonial Brookwood Center, Suite 901 · 569 Brookwood Village · Birmingham, AL 35209 · 205-458-9400

Cavender C. Kimble · Balch & Bingham · http://www.balch.com · 1710 Sixth Avenue North · Birmingham, AL 35203-2015 · 205-251-8100

Andrew Lemons · Baker, Donelson, Bearman, Caldwell & Berkowitz · http://www.bakerdonelson.com · Wachovia Tower, Suite 1600 · 420 Twentieth Street North · Birmingham, AL 35203 · 205-328-0480

Ronald A. Levitt · ⑩ · Sirote & Permutt · 2311 Highland Avenue South · P.O. Box 55727 · Birmingham, AL 35255-5727 · 205-930-5100

Jack B. Levy · ⑩ · Balch & Bingham · http://www.balch.com · 1901 Sixth Avenue North, Suite 1500 · Birmingham, AL 35203-4644 · 205-251-8100

Colin H. Luke · Balch & Bingham · http://www.balch.com · 1901 Sixth Avenue North, Suite 1500 · Birmingham, AL 35203-4644 · 205-251-8100

Laurence J. McDuff · Adams and Reese · http://www.adamsandreese.com · Concord Center, Suite 1100 · 2100 Third Avenue North · Birmingham, AL 35203 · 205-250-5000

B. G. Minisman, Jr. · ⑩ · Baker, Donelson, Bearman, Caldwell & Berkowitz · http://www.bakerdonelson.com · Wachovia Tower, Suite 1600 · 420 Twentieth Street North · Birmingham, AL 35203 · 205-328-0480

Lenora W. Pate · Sirote & Permutt · 2311 Highland Avenue South · P.O. Box 55727 · Birmingham, AL 35255-5727 · 205-930-5100

James M. Pool · Maynard Cooper & Gale · http://www.maynardcooper.com · Regions/Harbert Plaza, Suite 2400 · 1901 Sixth Avenue North · Birmingham, AL 35203-2602 · 205-254-1000

James L. Priester · Maynard Cooper & Gale · http://www.maynardcooper.com · Regions/Harbert Plaza, Suite 2400 · 1901 Sixth Avenue North · Birmingham, AL 35203-2602 · 205-254-1000

Joseph T. Ritchey · Sirote & Permutt · 2311 Highland Avenue South · P.O. Box 55727 · Birmingham, AL 35255-5727 · 205-930-5100

William B. Stewart · Wallace, Jordan, Ratliff & Brandt · http://www.wallacejordan.com · 800 Shades Creek Parkway, Suite 400 · P.O. Box 530910 · Birmingham, AL 35253 · 205-870-0555

Mobile

R. Alan Alexander · Helmsing, Leach, Herlong, Newman & Rouse · http://www.helmsinglaw.com · The LaClede Building, Suite 2000 · 150 Government Street · P.O. Box 2767 · Mobile, AL 36652 · 251-432-5521

Scott A. Browning · Johnstone, Adams, Bailey, Gordon & Harris · http://www.johnstoneadams.com · One St. Louis Centre, Suite 4000 · One Saint Louis Street · P.O. Box 1988 · Mobile, AL 36633-1988 · 251-432-7682

Wade B. Perry, Jr. · ⑩ · Johnstone, Adams, Bailey, Gordon & Harris · http://www.johnstoneadams.com · One St. Louis Centre, Suite 4000 · One Saint Louis Street · P.O. Box 1988 · Mobile, AL 36633-1988 · 251-432-7682

Montgomery

Thomas J. Methvin · Beasley, Allen, Crow, Methvin, Portis & Miles · 218 Commerce Street · P.O. Box 4160 · Montgomery, AL 36103-4160 · 334-269-2343

John T. Mooresmith · ⑩ · Burr & Forman · http://www.burr.com · RSA Tower, Suite 1950 · 201 Monroe Street · Montgomery, AL 36104 · 334-241-7000

INFORMATION TECHNOLOGY LAW

Birmingham

Paul M. Sykes · Bradley Arant Rose & White · http://www.bradleyarant.com · One Federal Place · 1819 Fifth Avenue North · Birmingham, AL 35203-2119 · 205-521-8000

INSURANCE LAW

Birmingham

Lee E. Bains, Jr. · Maynard Cooper & Gale · http://www.maynardcooper.com · Regions/Harbert Plaza, Suite 2400 · 1901 Sixth Avenue North · Birmingham, AL 35203-2602 · 205-254-1000

Paul P. Bolus · Bradley Arant Rose & White · http://www.bradleyarant.com · One Federal Place · 1819 Fifth Avenue North · Birmingham, AL 35203-2119 · 205-521-8000

J. Paul Compton, Jr. · ⑩ · Bradley Arant Rose & White · http://www.bradleyarant.com · One Federal Place · 1819 Fifth Avenue North · Birmingham, AL 35203-2119 · 205-521-8000

Edgar M. Elliott IV · Christian & Small · http://www.csattorneys.com · 505 North 20th Street, Suite 1800 · Birmingham, AL 35203-2696 · 205-795-6588

Roger C. Foster · Laney & Foster · Two Perimeter Park South, Suite 426 · P.O. Box 43798 · Birmingham, AL 35243 · 205-298-8440

John M. Fraley · Haskell, Slaughter, Young & Rediker · http://www.hsy.com · Park Place Tower, Suite 1400 · 2001 Park Place North · Birmingham, AL 35203 · 205-251-1000

Robert S. Given · Burr & Forman · http://www.burr.com · 420 North 20th Street, Suite 3400 · Birmingham, AL 35203-3284 · 205-251-3000

C. William Gladden · Hand Arendall · http://www.handarendall.com · Park Place Tower, Suite 1200 · 2001 Park Place North · Birmingham, AL 35203 · 205-324-4400

Jeffrey M. Grantham · Maynard Cooper & Gale · http://www.maynardcooper.com · Regions/Harbert Plaza, Suite 2400 · 1901 Sixth Avenue North · Birmingham, AL 35203-2602 · 205-254-1000

J. Mark Hart · Haskell, Slaughter, Young & Rediker · http://www.hsy.com · Park Place Tower, Suite 1400 2001 Park Place North · Birmingham, AL 35203 · 205-251-1000

Stephen C. Jackson · Maynard Cooper & Gale · http://www.maynardcooper.com · Regions/Harbert Plaza, Suite 2400 · 1901 Sixth Avenue North · Birmingham, AL 35203-2602 · 205-254-1000

James A. Kee, Jr. · Kee & Selby · http://www.keeselby.com · 1900 International Park Drive, Suite 220 · Birmingham, AL 35243 · 205-968-9900

Cavender C. Kimble · Balch & Bingham · http://www.balch.com · 1710 Sixth Avenue North · Birmingham, AL 35203-2015 · 205-251-8100

Michael D. Mulvaney · Maynard Cooper & Gale · http://www.maynardcooper.com · Regions/Harbert Plaza, Suite 2400 · 1901 Sixth Avenue North · Birmingham, AL 35203-2602 · 205-254-1000

Bert S. Nettles · Haskell, Slaughter, Young & Rediker · http://www.hsy.com · Park Place Tower, Suite 1400 · 2001 Park Place North · Birmingham, AL 35203 · 205-251-1000

Alan T. Rogers · Balch & Bingham · http://www.balch.com · 1710 Sixth Avenue North · Birmingham, AL 35203-2015 · 205-251-8100

Carol Ann Smith · Carol Ann Smith · 2000-A SouthBridge Parkway, Suite 405 · Birmingham, AL 35209 · 205-802-2214

John B. Tally, Jr. · Rumberger, Kirk & Caldwell · Lakeshore Park Plaza, Suite 125 · 2204 Lakeshore Drive · Birmingham, AL 35209-6739 · 205-327-5550

William B. Wahlheim, Jr. · Maynard Cooper & Gale · http://www.maynardcooper.com · Regions/Harbert Plaza, Suite 2400 · 1901 Sixth Avenue North · Birmingham, AL 35203-2602 · 205-254-1000

Katharine Anne Weber · Maynard Cooper & Gale · http://www.maynardcooper.com · Regions/Harbert Plaza, Suite 2400 · 1901 Sixth Avenue North · Birmingham, AL 35203-2602 · 205-254-1000

Mobile

Orrin K. Ames III · Hand Arendall · http://www.handarendall.com · RSA Tower, Suite 30200 · 11 North Water Street · Mobile, AL 36602 · 251-432-5511

M. Warren Butler · Starnes & Atchison · Battle House Tower, 34th Floor · 11 North Water Street · Mobile, AL 36602 · 251-433-6049

Walter T. Gilmer, Jr. · McDowell Knight Roedder & Sledge · Riverview Plaza, Suite 900 · 63 South Royal Street · P.O. Box 350 · Mobile, AL 36601 · 251-432-5300

Forrest S. Latta · Burr & Forman · http://www.burr.com · Colonial Bank Centre, Suite 400 · 41 West I-65 Service Road North · P.O. Box 16046 · Mobile, AL 36616 · 251-344-5151

Caroline C. McCarthy · Lyons, Pipes & Cook · Two North Royal Street · P.O. Box 2727 · Mobile, AL 36652-2727 · 251-432-4481

M. Kathleen Miller · Armbrecht Jackson · Riverview Plaza, 13th Floor · 63 South Royal Street · P.O. Box 290 · Mobile, AL 36601-0290 · 251-405-1300

Henry T. Morrissette · Hand Arendall · http://www.handarendall.com · RSA Tower, Suite 30200 · 11 North Water Street · Mobile, AL 36602 · 251-432-5511

Benjamen T. Rowe · ⑩ · Cabaniss, Johnston, Gardner, Dumas & O'Neal · http://www.cabaniss.com · 63 South Royal Street, Suite 700 · P.O. Box 2906 · Mobile, AL 36652-2906 · 251-415-7300

William E. Shreve, Jr. · Lyons, Pipes & Cook · Two North Royal Street · P.O. Box 2727 · Mobile, AL 36652-2727 · 251-432-4481

Charles C. Simpson III · Johnstone, Adams, Bailey, Gordon & Harris · http://www.johnstoneadams.com · One St. Louis Centre, Suite 4000 · One Saint Louis Street · P.O. Box 1988 · Mobile, AL 36633-1988 · 251-432-7682

Cooper C. Thurber · Lyons, Pipes & Cook · Two North Royal Street · P.O. Box 2727 · Mobile, AL 36652-2727 · 251-432-4481

Montgomery

James A. Byram, Jr. · Balch & Bingham · http://www.balch.com · 105 Tallapoosa Street, Suite 200 · P.O. Box 78 · Montgomery, AL 36101-0078 · 334-834-6500

James W. Garrett, Jr. · Rushton, Stakely, Johnston & Garrett · http://www.rsjg.com · 184 Commerce Street · P.O. Box 270 · Montgomery, AL 36101-0270 · 334-206-3100

Tabor R. Novak, Jr. · ⑩ · Ball, Ball, Matthews & Novak · 2000 Interstate Park Drive, Suite 204 · P.O. Box 2148 · Montgomery, AL 36102-2148 · 334-387-7680

Robert C. Ward, Jr. · Rushton, Stakely, Johnston & Garrett · http://www.rsjg.com · 184 Commerce Street P.O. Box 270 · Montgomery, AL 36101-0270 · 334-206-3100

INTELLECTUAL PROPERTY LAW

Birmingham

Linda A. Friedman · ⑩ · Bradley Arant Rose & White · http://www.bradleyarant.com · One Federal Place 1819 Fifth Avenue North · Birmingham, AL 35203-2119 · 205-521-8000

Thad G. Long · ⑩ · Bradley Arant Rose & White · http://www.bradleyarant.com · One Federal Place · 1819 Fifth Avenue North · Birmingham, AL 35203-2119 · 205-521-8000

Paul M. Sykes · Bradley Arant Rose & White · http://www.bradleyarant.com · One Federal Place · 1819 Fifth Avenue North · Birmingham, AL 35203-2119 · 205-521-8000

Huntsville

Frank M. Caprio · Bradley Arant Rose & White · http://www.bradleyarant.com · 200 Clinton Avenue West, Suite 900 · Huntsville, AL 35801-4900 · 256-517-5100

Mobile

David R. Quittmeyer · ⑩ · Hand Arendall · http://www.handarendall.com · RSA Tower, Suite 30200 · 11 North Water Street · Mobile, AL 36602 · 251-432-5511

INTERNATIONAL TRADE AND FINANCE LAW

Birmingham

James C. Wilson, Jr. · Baker, Donelson, Bearman, Caldwell & Berkowitz · http://www.bakerdonelson.com · Wachovia Tower, Suite 1600 · 420 Twentieth Street North · Birmingham, AL 35203 · 205-328-0480

Frank M. Young III · Haskell, Slaughter, Young & Rediker · http://www.hsy.com · Park Place Tower, Suite 1400 · 2001 Park Place North · Birmingham, AL 35203 · 205-251-1000

LABOR AND EMPLOYMENT LAW

Birmingham

James Patrick Alexander · ㉕ · Littler Mendelson · Wachovia Tower, Suite 2730 · 420 Twentieth Street North · Birmingham, AL 35203 · 205-421-4700

Mitchell G. Allen · Maynard Cooper & Gale · http://www.maynardcooper.com · Regions/Harbert Plaza, Suite 2400 · 1901 Sixth Avenue North · Birmingham, AL 35203-2602 · 205-254-1000

David R. Arendall · Arendall & Associates · 2018 Morris Avenue · Birmingham, AL 35203 · 205-252-1550

Beverly P. Baker · Ogletree Deakins · http://www.ogletreedeakins.com · One Federal Place, Suite 1000 · 1819 Fifth Avenue North · Birmingham, AL 35203-2118 · 205-328-1900

Stephen E. Brown · ⑩ · Maynard Cooper & Gale · http://www.maynardcooper.com · Regions/Harbert Plaza, Suite 2400 · 1901 Sixth Avenue North · Birmingham, AL 35203-2602 · 205-254-1000

Richard Carrigan · Ogletree Deakins · http://www.ogletreedeakins.com · One Federal Place, Suite 1000 · 1819 Fifth Avenue North · Birmingham, AL 35203-2118 · 205-328-1900

Robert F. Childs, Jr. · ⑩ · Wiggins, Childs, Quinn & Pantazis · The Kress Building · 301 Nineteenth Street North · Birmingham, AL 35203-3213 · 205-314-0500

John J. Coleman III · ⑩ · Burr & Forman · http://www.burr.com · 420 North 20th Street, Suite 3400 · Birmingham, AL 35203-3284 · 205-251-3000

John James Coleman, Jr. · ㉕ · Bradley Arant Rose & White · http://www.bradleyarant.com · One Federal Place · 1819 Fifth Avenue North · Birmingham, AL 35203-2119 · 205-521-8000

Thomas Andrew Davis · Jackson Lewis · http://www.jacksonlewis.com · First Commercial Bank Building, Suite 870 · 800 Shades Creek Parkway · Birmingham, AL 35209 · 205-332-3100

Marcel L. Debruge · Burr & Forman · http://www.burr.com · 420 North 20th Street, Suite 3400 · Birmingham, AL 35203-3284 · 205-251-3000

Sydney F. Frazier, Jr. · ⑩ · Cabaniss, Johnston, Gardner, Dumas & O'Neal · http://www.cabaniss.com · 2001 Park Place North, Suite 700 · P.O. Box 830612 · Birmingham, AL 35283-0612 · 205-716-5200

Barry V. Frederick · ⑩ · The Frederick Firm · 5409 Trace Ridge Lane · Birmingham, AL 35244-3940 · 205-739-0043

Mac B. Greaves · Burr & Forman · http://www.burr.com · 420 North 20th Street, Suite 3400 · Birmingham, AL 35203-3284 · 205-251-3000

William K. Hancock · Adams and Reese · http://www.adamsandreese.com · Concord Center, Suite 1100 · 2100 Third Avenue North · Birmingham, AL 35203 · 205-250-5000

John W. Hargrove · Bradley Arant Rose & White · http://www.bradleyarant.com · One Federal Place · 1819 Fifth Avenue North · Birmingham, AL 35203-2119 · 205-521-8000

Alicia Kay Haynes · Haynes & Haynes · 1600 Woodmere Drive · Birmingham, AL 35226 · 205-879-0377

Harry L. Hopkins · Ogletree Deakins · http://www.ogletreedeakins.com · One Federal Place, Suite 1000 · 1819 Fifth Avenue North · Birmingham, AL 35203-2118 · 205-328-1900

J. Fredric Ingram · ㉕ · Burr & Forman · http://www.burr.com · 420 North 20th Street, Suite 3400 · Birmingham, AL 35203-3284 · 205-251-3000

Frank S. James III · Baker, Donelson, Bearman, Caldwell & Berkowitz · http://www.bakerdonelson.com · Wachovia Tower, Suite 1600 · 420 Twentieth Street North · Birmingham, AL 35203 · 205-328-0480

Abdul K. Kallon · Bradley Arant Rose & White · http://www.bradleyarant.com · One Federal Place · 1819 Fifth Avenue North · Birmingham, AL 35203-2119 · 205-521-8000

Peyton Lacy, Jr. · ⑳ · Ogletree Deakins · http://www.ogletreedeakins.com · One Federal Place, Suite 1000 · 1819 Fifth Avenue North · Birmingham, AL 35203-2118 · 205-328-1900

Jeffrey A. Lee · Maynard Cooper & Gale · http://www.maynardcooper.com · Regions/Harbert Plaza, Suite 2400 · 1901 Sixth Avenue North · Birmingham, AL 35203-2602 · 205-254-1000

Heather Leonard · Heather Leonard · 2108 Rocky Ridge Road, Suite One · Birmingham, AL 35216 · 205-978-7899

J. Patrick Logan · ⑩ · Johnston Barton Proctor & Rose · Colonial Brookwood Center, Suite 901 · 569 Brookwood Village · Birmingham, AL 35209 · 205-458-9400

Michael L. Lucas · Burr & Forman · http://www.burr.com · 420 North 20th Street, Suite 3400 · Birmingham, AL 35203-3284 · 205-251-3000

James Walker May · ⑩ · Littler Mendelson · Wachovia Tower, Suite 2730 · 420 Twentieth Street North · Birmingham, AL 35203 · 205-421-4700

David J. Middlebrooks · ⑩ · Lehr, Middlebrooks & Vreeland · 2021 Third Avenue North · P.O. Box 11945 · Birmingham, AL 35202-1945 · 205-326-3002

T. Matthew Miller · Bradley Arant Rose & White · http://www.bradleyarant.com · One Federal Place · 1819 Fifth Avenue North · Birmingham, AL 35203-2119 · 205-521-8000

Chris Mitchell · Maynard Cooper & Gale · http://www.maynardcooper.com · Regions/Harbert Plaza, Suite 2400 · 1901 Sixth Avenue North · Birmingham, AL 35203-2602 · 205-254-1000

Patrick K. Nakamura · ⑩ · Nakamura, Quinn, Walls, Weaver & Davies · Lakeshore Park Plaza, Suite 130 2204 Lakeshore Drive · Birmingham, AL 35209 · 205-870-9989

Carol Sue Nelson · Maynard Cooper & Gale · http://www.maynardcooper.com · Regions/Harbert Plaza, Suite 2400 · 1901 Sixth Avenue North · Birmingham, AL 35203-2602 · 205-254-1000

Timothy A. Palmer · Ogletree Deakins · http://www.ogletreedeakins.com · One Federal Place, Suite 1000 1819 Fifth Avenue North · Birmingham, AL 35203-2118 · 205-328-1900

James C. Pennington · Ogletree Deakins · http://www.ogletreedeakins.com · One Federal Place, Suite 1000 · 1819 Fifth Avenue North · Birmingham, AL 35203-2118 · 205-328-1900

Charles Michael Quinn · ⑩ · Wiggins, Childs, Quinn & Pantazis · The Kress Building · 301 Nineteenth Street North · Birmingham, AL 35203-3213 · 205-314-0500

John D. Saxon · John D. Saxon · http://www.saxonattorney.com · 2119 Third Avenue North · Birmingham, AL 35203-3314 · 205-324-0223

Fern H. Singer · Baker, Donelson, Bearman, Caldwell & Berkowitz · http://www.bakerdonelson.com · Wachovia Tower, Suite 1600 · 420 Twentieth Street North · Birmingham, AL 35203 · 205-328-0480

David M. Smith · ⑩ · Maynard Cooper & Gale · http://www.maynardcooper.com · Regions/Harbert Plaza, Suite 2400 · 1901 Sixth Avenue North · Birmingham, AL 35203-2602 · 205-254-1000

Jay D. St. Clair · ⑩ · Littler Mendelson · Wachovia Tower, Suite 2730 · 420 Twentieth Street North · Birmingham, AL 35203 · 205-421-4700

Marion Jefferson Starling III · Balch & Bingham · http://www.balch.com · 1710 Sixth Avenue North · Birmingham, AL 35203-2015 · 205-251-8100

Steven M. Stastny · Ford & Harrison · http://www.fordharrison.com · 2100 Third Avenue North, Suite 400 · Birmingham, AL 35203 · 205-244-5900

Arnold W. Umbach III · Starnes & Atchison · 100 Brookwood Place, Seventh Floor · P.O. Box 598512 · Birmingham, AL 35259-8512 · 205-868-6000

Albert L. Vreeland · Lehr, Middlebrooks & Vreeland · 2021 Third Avenue North · P.O. Box 11945 · Birmingham, AL 35202-1945 · 205-326-3002

Joe R. Whatley, Jr. · (20) · Whatley Drake & Kallas · 2001 Park Place North, Suite 1000 · P.O. Box 10647 · Birmingham, AL 35202-0647 · 205-328-9576

Anne R. Yuengert · Bradley Arant Rose & White · http://www.bradleyarant.com · One Federal Place · 1819 Fifth Avenue North · Birmingham, AL 35203-2119 · 205-521-8000

Huntsville

T. Dwight Sloan · Wilmer & Lee · 100 Washington Street, Suite 200 · P.O. Box 2168 · Huntsville, AL 35804 · 256-533-0202

John A. Wilmer · Wilmer & Lee · 100 Washington Street, Suite 200 · P.O. Box 2168 · Huntsville, AL 35804 · 256-533-0202

Mobile

Henry H. Brewster, Jr. · Stein, Brewster & Pilcher · 205 North Conception Street · P.O. Box 1051 · Mobile, AL 36633-1051 · 251-433-2002

Celia Josephine Collins · Johnstone, Adams, Bailey, Gordon & Harris · http://www.johnstoneadams.com · One St. Louis Centre, Suite 4000 · One Saint Louis Street · P.O. Box 1988 · Mobile, AL 36633-1988 · 251-432-7682

Willis C. Darby, Jr. · Willis C. Darby · 200 St. Anthony Street · P.O. Box 2565 · Mobile, AL 36652-0000 · 251-432-2635

J. Cecil Gardner · (25) · Gardner, Middlebrooks, Gibbons, Kittrell, Olsen, Walker & Hill · 1119 Government Street · P.O. Drawer 3103 · Mobile, AL 36652 · 251-433-8100

Frank McRight · (25) · Burr & Forman · http://www.burr.com · Colonial Bank Centre, Suite 400 · 41 West I-65 Service Road North · P.O. Box 16046 · Mobile, AL 36616 · 251-344-5151

Paul D. Myrick · (10) · Jackson Myrick · Riverview Plaza, Suite 1100 · 63 South Royal Street · Mobile, AL 36602 · 251-432-1811

Mary E. Olsen · Gardner, Middlebrooks, Gibbons, Kittrell, Olsen, Walker & Hill · 1119 Government Street · P.O. Drawer 3103 · Mobile, AL 36652 · 251-433-8100

Patricia J. Ponder · Hand Arendall · http://www.handarendall.com · RSA Tower, Suite 30200 · 11 North Water Street · Mobile, AL 36602 · 251-432-5511

Sandy G. Robinson · (10) · Cabaniss, Johnston, Gardner, Dumas & O'Neal · http://www.cabaniss.com · 63 South Royal Street, Suite 700 · P.O. Box 2906 · Mobile, AL 36652-2906 · 251-415-7300

Kirk C. Shaw · (10) · Armbrecht Jackson · Riverview Plaza, 13th Floor · 63 South Royal Street · P.O. Box 290 · Mobile, AL 36601-0290 · 251-405-1300

Patrick H. Sims · Cabaniss, Johnston, Gardner, Dumas & O'Neal · http://www.cabaniss.com · 63 South Royal Street, Suite 700 · P.O. Box 2906 · Mobile, AL 36652-2906 · 251-415-7300

Edward L.D. Smith · Edward L.D. Smith · Seven North Lawrence Street · P.O. Box 927 · Mobile, AL 36601-0927 · 251-431-9000

Gregory B. Stein · ⑳ · Stein, Brewster & Pilcher · 205 North Conception Street · P.O. Box 1051 · Mobile, AL 36633-1051 · 251-433-2002

William K. Thomas · Cabaniss, Johnston, Gardner, Dumas & O'Neal · http://www.cabaniss.com · 63 South Royal Street, Suite 700 · P.O. Box 2906 · Mobile, AL 36652-2906 · 251-415-7300

William C. Tidwell III · ㉕ · Hand Arendall · http://www.handarendall.com · RSA Tower, Suite 30200 · 11 North Water Street · Mobile, AL 36602 · 251-432-5511

Kimberly C. Walker · Gardner, Middlebrooks, Gibbons, Kittrell, Olsen, Walker & Hill · 1119 Government Street · P.O. Drawer 3103 · Mobile, AL 36652 · 251-433-8100

Montgomery

Henry C. Barnett, Jr. · Capell & Howard · http://www.capellhoward.com · 150 South Perry Street · P.O. Box 2069 · Montgomery, AL 36102-2069 · 334-241-8000

Bruce J. Downey III · ⑳ · Capell & Howard · http://www.capellhoward.com · 150 South Perry Street · P.O. Box 2069 · Montgomery, AL 36102-2069 · 334-241-8000

LAND USE & ZONING LAW

Birmingham

Charles A. J. Beavers, Jr. · ㉕ · Bradley Arant Rose & White · http://www.bradleyarant.com · One Federal Place · 1819 Fifth Avenue North · Birmingham, AL 35203-2119 · 205-521-8000

Douglas P. Corretti · ㉕ · Corretti, Newsome & Hawkins · 1804 Seventh Avenue North · Birmingham, AL 35203 · 205-251-1164

John F. DeBuys, Jr. · Burr & Forman · http://www.burr.com · 420 North 20th Street, Suite 3400 · Birmingham, AL 35203-3284 · 205-251-3000

Jesse P. Evans III · ⑩ · Haskell, Slaughter, Young & Rediker · http://www.hsy.com · Park Place Tower, Suite 1400 · 2001 Park Place North · Birmingham, AL 35203 · 205-251-1000

Thad G. Long · ⑩ · Bradley Arant Rose & White · http://www.bradleyarant.com · One Federal Place · 1819 Fifth Avenue North · Birmingham, AL 35203-2119 · 205-521-8000

LEVERAGED BUYOUTS AND PRIVATE EQUITY LAW

Birmingham

Denson Nauls Franklin III · Bradley Arant Rose & White · http://www.bradleyarant.com · One Federal Place · 1819 Fifth Avenue North · Birmingham, AL 35203-2119 · 205-521-8000

B. G. Minisman, Jr. · ⑩ · Baker, Donelson, Bearman, Caldwell & Berkowitz · http://www.bakerdonelson.com · Wachovia Tower, Suite 1600 · 420 Twentieth Street North · Birmingham, AL 35203 · 205-328-0480

John K. Molen · (10) · Bradley Arant Rose & White · http://www.bradleyarant.com · One Federal Place · 1819 Fifth Avenue North · Birmingham, AL 35203-2119 · 205-521-8000

MARITIME LAW

Mobile

J. Hodge Alves III · (10) · Hand Arendall · http://www.handarendall.com · RSA Tower, Suite 30200 · 11 North Water Street · Mobile, AL 36602 · 251-432-5511

Joe E. Basenberg · Hand Arendall · http://www.handarendall.com · RSA Tower, Suite 30200 · 11 North Water Street · Mobile, AL 36602 · 251-432-5511

Douglas L. Brown · (10) · Brady Radcliff & Brown · 1600 Wachovia Bank Building · 61 Saint Joseph Street · P.O. Box 1668 · Mobile, AL 36633 · 251-405-0077

Blane H. Crutchfield · Hand Arendall · http://www.handarendall.com · RSA Tower, Suite 30200 · 11 North Water Street · Mobile, AL 36602 · 251-432-5511

John P. Kavanagh, Jr. · Burr & Forman · http://www.burr.com · Colonial Bank Centre, Suite 400 · 41 West I-65 Service Road North · P.O. Box 16046 · Mobile, AL 36616 · 251-344-5151

Alexander F. Lankford III · (20) · Hand Arendall · http://www.handarendall.com · RSA Tower, Suite 30200 11 North Water Street · Mobile, AL 36602 · 251-432-5511

M. Kathleen Miller · Armbrecht Jackson · Riverview Plaza, 13th Floor · 63 South Royal Street · P.O. Box 290 · Mobile, AL 36601-0290 · 251-405-1300

Abram L. Philips, Jr. · (20) · Burr & Forman · http://www.burr.com · Colonial Bank Centre, Suite 400 · 41 West I-65 Service Road North · P.O. Box 16046 · Mobile, AL 36616 · 251-344-5151

Marion A. Quina, Jr. · Lyons, Pipes & Cook · Two North Royal Street · P.O. Box 2727 · Mobile, AL 36652-2727 · 251-432-4481

Donald C. Radcliff · (10) · Brady Radcliff & Brown · 1600 Wachovia Bank Building · 61 Saint Joseph Street P.O. Box 1668 · Mobile, AL 36633 · 251-405-0077

A. Clay Rankin III · (10) · Hand Arendall · http://www.handarendall.com · RSA Tower, Suite 30200 · 11 North Water Street · Mobile, AL 36602 · 251-432-5511

Thomas S. Rue · Johnstone, Adams, Bailey, Gordon & Harris · http://www.johnstoneadams.com · One St. Louis Centre, Suite 4000 · One Saint Louis Street · P.O. Box 1988 · Mobile, AL 36633-1988 · 251-432-7682

G. Hamp Uzzelle III · (20) · Hand Arendall · http://www.handarendall.com · RSA Tower, Suite 30200 · 11 North Water Street · Mobile, AL 36602 · 251-432-5511

MASS TORT LITIGATION

Birmingham

John R. Chiles · Burr & Forman · http://www.burr.com · 420 North 20th Street, Suite 3400 · Birmingham, AL 35203-3284 · 205-251-3000

Augusta S. Dowd · White Arnold & Dowd · 2025 Third Avenue North, Suite 500 · Birmingham, AL 35203 · 205-323-1888

Russell Jackson Drake · Whatley Drake & Kallas · 2001 Park Place North, Suite 1000 · P.O. Box 10647 · Birmingham, AL 35202-0647 · 205-328-9576

James W. Gewin · ㉕ · Bradley Arant Rose & White · http://www.bradleyarant.com · One Federal Place · 1819 Fifth Avenue North · Birmingham, AL 35203-2119 · 205-521-8000

F. M. Haston III · Bradley Arant Rose & White · http://www.bradleyarant.com · One Federal Place · 1819 Fifth Avenue North · Birmingham, AL 35203-2119 · 205-521-8000

James C. Huckaby, Jr. · Christian & Small · http://www.csattorneys.com · 505 North 20th Street, Suite 1800 · Birmingham, AL 35203-2696 · 205-795-6588

Michael R. Pennington · ⑩ · Bradley Arant Rose & White · http://www.bradleyarant.com · One Federal Place · 1819 Fifth Avenue North · Birmingham, AL 35203-2119 · 205-521-8000

Maibeth J. Porter · Maynard Cooper & Gale · http://www.maynardcooper.com · Regions/Harbert Plaza, Suite 2400 · 1901 Sixth Avenue North · Birmingham, AL 35203-2602 · 205-254-1000

Leila H. Watson · Cory, Watson, Crowder & DeGaris · 2131 Magnolia Avenue · Birmingham, AL 35205-2836 · 205-328-2200

H. Thomas Wells, Jr. · Maynard Cooper & Gale · http://www.maynardcooper.com · Regions/Harbert Plaza, Suite 2400 · 1901 Sixth Avenue North · Birmingham, AL 35203-2602 · 205-254-1000

J. Mark White · ⑩ · White Arnold & Dowd · 2025 Third Avenue North, Suite 500 · Birmingham, AL 35203 · 205-323-1888

Mobile

Joseph P. H. Babington · Helmsing, Leach, Herlong, Newman & Rouse · http://www.helmsinglaw.com · The LaClede Building, Suite 2000 · 150 Government Street · P.O. Box 2767 · Mobile, AL 36652 · 251-432-5521

Joe E. Basenberg · Hand Arendall · http://www.handarendall.com · RSA Tower, Suite 30200 · 11 North Water Street · Mobile, AL 36602 · 251-432-5511

George M. Walker · Hand Arendall · http://www.handarendall.com · RSA Tower, Suite 30200 · 11 North Water Street · Mobile, AL 36602 · 251-432-5511

Montgomery

Andy D. Birchfield, Jr. · Beasley, Allen, Crow, Methvin, Portis & Miles · 218 Commerce Street · P.O. Box 4160 · Montgomery, AL 36103-4160 · 334-269-2343

Thomas J. Methvin · Beasley, Allen, Crow, Methvin, Portis & Miles · 218 Commerce Street · P.O. Box 4160 · Montgomery, AL 36103-4160 · 334-269-2343

MEDICAL MALPRACTICE LAW

Birmingham

D. Leon Ashford · ⑩ · Hare, Wynn, Newell & Newton · The Historic Massey Building, Suite 800 · 2025 Third Avenue North · Birmingham, AL 35203 · 205-328-5330

Walter W. Bates · Starnes & Atchison · 100 Brookwood Place, Seventh Floor · P.O. Box 598512 · Birmingham, AL 35259-8512 · 205-868-6000

Thomas W. Christian · 20 · Christian & Small · http://www.csattorneys.com · 505 North 20th Street, Suite 1800 · Birmingham, AL 35203-2696 · 205-795-6588

Robert E. Cooper · Christian & Small · http://www.csattorneys.com · 505 North 20th Street, Suite 1800 · Birmingham, AL 35203-2696 · 205-795-6588

Michael A. Florie · 10 · Starnes & Atchison · 100 Brookwood Place, Seventh Floor · P.O. Box 598512 · Birmingham, AL 35259-8512 · 205-868-6000

Samuel H. Franklin · 20 · Lightfoot, Franklin & White · The Clark Building · 400 Twentieth Street North · Birmingham, AL 35203 · 205-581-0700

Stephen D. Heninger · 20 · Heninger, Garrison & Davis · 2224 First Avenue North · Birmingham, AL 35203 · 205-326-3336

Robert P. Mackenzie III · Starnes & Atchison · 100 Brookwood Place, Seventh Floor · P.O. Box 598512 · Birmingham, AL 35259-8512 · 205-868-6000

Michael D. McKibben · Bradley Arant Rose & White · http://www.bradleyarant.com · One Federal Place · 1819 Fifth Avenue North · Birmingham, AL 35203-2119 · 205-521-8000

Joseph S. Miller · Starnes & Atchison · 100 Brookwood Place, Seventh Floor · P.O. Box 598512 · Birmingham, AL 35259-8512 · 205-868-6000

David W. Proctor · Johnston Barton Proctor & Rose · Colonial Brookwood Center, Suite 901 · 569 Brookwood Village · Birmingham, AL 35209 · 205-458-9400

Randal H. Sellers · Starnes & Atchison · 100 Brookwood Place, Seventh Floor · P.O. Box 598512 · Birmingham, AL 35259-8512 · 205-868-6000

Michael K. Wright · Starnes & Atchison · 100 Brookwood Place, Seventh Floor · P.O. Box 598512 · Birmingham, AL 35259-8512 · 205-868-6000

Decatur

John S. Key · Eyster, Key, Tubb, Weaver & Roth · Eyster Building · 402 Moulton Street East · P.O. Box 1607 · Decatur, AL 35602-1607 · 256-353-6761

Huntsville

Daniel F. Beasley · Lanier Ford Shaver & Payne · http://www.lfsp.com · 200 West Side Square, Suite 5000 · P.O. Box 2087 · Huntsville, AL 35804-2087 · 256-535-1100

George E. Knox, Jr. · Lanier Ford Shaver & Payne · http://www.lfsp.com · 200 West Side Square, Suite 5000 · P.O. Box 2087 · Huntsville, AL 35804-2087 · 256-535-1100

Mobile

R. Alan Alexander · Helmsing, Leach, Herlong, Newman & Rouse · http://www.helmsinglaw.com · The LaClede Building, Suite 2000 · 150 Government Street · P.O. Box 2767 · Mobile, AL 36652 · 251-432-5521

M. Kathleen Miller · Armbrecht Jackson · Riverview Plaza, 13th Floor · 63 South Royal Street · P.O. Box 290 · Mobile, AL 36601-0290 · 251-405-1300

W. Boyd Reeves · 20 · Armbrecht Jackson · Riverview Plaza, 13th Floor · 63 South Royal Street · P.O. Box 290 · Mobile, AL 36601-0290 · 251-405-1300

A. Edwin Stuardi III · Armbrecht Jackson · Riverview Plaza, 13th Floor · 63 South Royal Street · P.O. Box 290 · Mobile, AL 36601-0290 · 251-405-1300

Norman E. Waldrop, Jr. · Armbrecht Jackson · Riverview Plaza, 13th Floor · 63 South Royal Street · P.O. Box 290 · Mobile, AL 36601-0290 · 251-405-1300

Michael A. Worel · Cunningham, Bounds, Yance, Crowder & Brown · http://www.cbcbb.com · 1601 Dauphin Street · P.O. Box 66705 · Mobile, AL 36660 · 251-471-6191

Montgomery

Richard B. Garrett · ⑩ · Rushton, Stakely, Johnston & Garrett · http://www.rsjg.com · 184 Commerce Street · P.O. Box 270 · Montgomery, AL 36101-0270 · 334-206-3100

Thomas H. Keene · ⑩ · Rushton, Stakely, Johnston & Garrett · http://www.rsjg.com · 184 Commerce Street · P.O. Box 270 · Montgomery, AL 36101-0270 · 334-206-3100

MERGERS & ACQUISITIONS LAW

Birmingham

Thomas Neely Carruthers · ㉕ · Bradley Arant Rose & White · http://www.bradleyarant.com · One Federal Place · 1819 Fifth Avenue North · Birmingham, AL 35203-2119 · 205-521-8000

James W. Childs, Jr. · Bradley Arant Rose & White · http://www.bradleyarant.com · One Federal Place · 1819 Fifth Avenue North · Birmingham, AL 35203-2119 · 205-521-8000

Gregory S. Curran · Maynard Cooper & Gale · http://www.maynardcooper.com · Regions/Harbert Plaza, Suite 2400 · 1901 Sixth Avenue North · Birmingham, AL 35203-2602 · 205-254-1000

Mark L. Drew · Maynard Cooper & Gale · http://www.maynardcooper.com · Regions/Harbert Plaza, Suite 2400 · 1901 Sixth Avenue North · Birmingham, AL 35203-2602 · 205-254-1000

Denson Nauls Franklin III · Bradley Arant Rose & White · http://www.bradleyarant.com · One Federal Place · 1819 Fifth Avenue North · Birmingham, AL 35203-2119 · 205-521-8000

John B. Grenier · ⑩ · Bradley Arant Rose & White · http://www.bradleyarant.com · One Federal Place · 1819 Fifth Avenue North · Birmingham, AL 35203-2119 · 205-521-8000

Colin H. Luke · Balch & Bingham · http://www.balch.com · 1901 Sixth Avenue North, Suite 1500 · Birmingham, AL 35203-4644 · 205-251-8100

B. G. Minisman, Jr. · ⑩ · Baker, Donelson, Bearman, Caldwell & Berkowitz · http://www.bakerdonelson.com · Wachovia Tower, Suite 1600 · 420 Twentieth Street North · Birmingham, AL 35203 · 205-328-0480

John K. Molen · ⑩ · Bradley Arant Rose & White · http://www.bradleyarant.com · One Federal Place · 1819 Fifth Avenue North · Birmingham, AL 35203-2119 · 205-521-8000

Virginia C. Patterson · Bradley Arant Rose & White · http://www.bradleyarant.com · One Federal Place · 1819 Fifth Avenue North · Birmingham, AL 35203-2119 · 205-521-8000

Timothy J. Tracy · Balch & Bingham · http://www.balch.com · 1901 Sixth Avenue North, Suite 1500 · Birmingham, AL 35203-4644 · 205-251-8100

Paul S. Ware · Bradley Arant Rose & White · http://www.bradleyarant.com · One Federal Place · 1819 Fifth Avenue North · Birmingham, AL 35203-2119 · 205-521-8000

MUNICIPAL LAW

Birmingham

Wyatt Rushton Haskell · Haskell, Slaughter, Young & Rediker · http://www.hsy.com · Park Place Tower, Suite 1400 · 2001 Park Place North · Birmingham, AL 35203 · 205-251-1000

Donald B. Sweeney, Jr. · Bradley Arant Rose & White · http://www.bradleyarant.com · One Federal Place · 1819 Fifth Avenue North · Birmingham, AL 35203-2119 · 205-521-8000

Mobile

Donald J. Stewart · ⑩ · Cabaniss, Johnston, Gardner, Dumas & O'Neal · http://www.cabaniss.com · 63 South Royal Street, Suite 700 · P.O. Box 2906 · Mobile, AL 36652-2906 · 251-415-7300

NATURAL RESOURCES LAW

Birmingham

Fournier J. Gale III · ㉕ · Maynard Cooper & Gale · http://www.maynardcooper.com · Regions/Harbert Plaza, Suite 2400 · 1901 Sixth Avenue North · Birmingham, AL 35203-2602 · 205-254-1000

H. Thomas Wells, Jr. · Maynard Cooper & Gale · http://www.maynardcooper.com · Regions/Harbert Plaza, Suite 2400 · 1901 Sixth Avenue North · Birmingham, AL 35203-2602 · 205-254-1000

Mobile

Conrad P. Armbrecht · ⑳ · Armbrecht Jackson · Riverview Plaza, 13th Floor · 63 South Royal Street · P.O. Box 290 · Mobile, AL 36601-0290 · 251-405-1300

Duane A. Graham · Armbrecht Jackson · Riverview Plaza, 13th Floor · 63 South Royal Street · P.O. Box 290 · Mobile, AL 36601-0290 · 251-405-1300

Neil C. Johnston · ⑩ · Hand Arendall · http://www.handarendall.com · RSA Tower, Suite 30200 · 11 North Water Street · Mobile, AL 36602 · 251-432-5511

Tuscaloosa

William T. Watson · ⑩ · Watson, deGraffenried, Hardin & Tyra · 1651 McFarland Boulevard North · Tuscaloosa, AL 35406 · 205-345-1577

NON-PROFIT/CHARITIES LAW

Birmingham

Timothy A. Bush · Sirote & Permutt · 2311 Highland Avenue South · P.O. Box 55727 · Birmingham, AL 35255-5727 · 205-930-5100

K. Wood Herren · Bradley Arant Rose & White · http://www.bradleyarant.com · One Federal Place · 1819 Fifth Avenue North · Birmingham, AL 35203-2119 · 205-521-8000

William D. Lineberry · Balch & Bingham · http://www.balch.com · 1710 Sixth Avenue North · Birmingham, AL 35203-2015 · 205-251-8100

James M. Pool · Maynard Cooper & Gale · http://www.maynardcooper.com · Regions/Harbert Plaza, Suite 2400 · 1901 Sixth Avenue North · Birmingham, AL 35203-2602 · 205-254-1000

Hardwick C. Walthall · Maynard Cooper & Gale · http://www.maynardcooper.com · Regions/Harbert Plaza, Suite 2400 · 1901 Sixth Avenue North · Birmingham, AL 35203-2602 · 205-254-1000

Huntsville

Scott E. Ludwig · ⑩ · Bradley Arant Rose & White · http://www.bradleyarant.com · 200 Clinton Avenue West, Suite 900 · Huntsville, AL 35801-4900 · 256-517-5100

Mobile

Thomas F. Garth · ⑩ · Lyons, Pipes & Cook · Two North Royal Street · P.O. Box 2727 · Mobile, AL 36652-2727 · 251-432-4481

Montgomery

Warren C. Matthews · Burr & Forman · http://www.burr.com · RSA Tower, Suite 1950 · 201 Monroe Street · Montgomery, AL 36104 · 334-241-7000

NON-WHITE-COLLAR CRIMINAL DEFENSE

Birmingham

Emory Anthony, Jr. · Emory Anthony, Jr. · 2015 First Avenue North · Birmingham, AL 35203-4101 · 205-458-1100

William N. Clark · ⑩ · Redden, Mills & Clark · Financial Center, Suite 940 · 505 Twentieth Street North Birmingham, AL 35203 · 205-322-0457

Richard S. Jaffe · Jaffe, Strickland, Drennan & Dodd · http://www.rjaffelaw.com · The Alexander House · 2320 Arlington Avenue · Birmingham, AL 35205-4112 · 205-930-9800

Anthony A. Joseph · Maynard Cooper & Gale · http://www.maynardcooper.com · Regions/Harbert Plaza, Suite 2400 · 1901 Sixth Avenue North · Birmingham, AL 35203-2602 · 205-254-1000

John Lentine · Sheffield, Sheffield & Lentine, P.C. · 205 Twentieth Street North, Suite 323 · Birmingham, AL 35203-4705 · 205-328-1365

Maxwell H. Pulliam · Christian & Small · http://www.csattorneys.com · 505 North 20th Street, Suite 1800 Birmingham, AL 35203-2696 · 205-795-6588

John C. Robbins · Polson & Robbins · Park Place Tower, Suite 925 · 2001 Park Place North · Birmingham, AL 35203 · 205-252-7000

Thomas J. Spina · Fawal & Spina · 1330 Twenty-First Way South, Suite 200 · Birmingham, AL 35205 · 205-939-1330

Glennon F. Threatt, Jr. · Threatt & Blocton · Two 20th Street North, Suite 920 · Birmingham, AL 35203-4007 · 205-251-8747

Huntsville

Bruce Alan Gardner · Bruce A. Gardner · 125 Holmes Avenue · P.O. Box 18636 · Huntsville, AL 35804-8636 · 256-533-5756

Mobile

Donald M. Briskman · Briskman & Binion · 205 Church Street · P.O. Box 43 · Mobile, AL 36602 · 251-433-7600

Robert F. Clark · ⑩ · Clark & Deen · 207 Church Street · P.O. Box 2705 · Mobile, AL 36652 · 251-433-5860

T. Jefferson Deen III · ⑩ · Deen Law · 207 Church Street · P.O. Box 2705 · Mobile, AL 36652 · 251-433-5860

Dennis Knizley · Dennis J. Knizley · Seven North Lawrence Street · Mobile, AL 36602-2111 · 251-432-3799

Kenneth A. Nixon · Lyons, Pipes & Cook · Two North Royal Street · P.O. Box 2727 · Mobile, AL 36652-2727 · 251-432-4481

Montgomery

George L. Beck, Jr. · ⑳ · Capell & Howard · http://www.capellhoward.com · 150 South Perry Street · P.O. Box 2069 · Montgomery, AL 36102-2069 · 334-241-8000

Ronald W. Wise · ⑩ · Ronald W. Wise · 2000 Interstate Park Drive, Suite 105 · Montgomery, AL 36109 · 334-260-0003

Opelika

Joseph L. Dean, Jr. · ⑩ · Dean & Barrett · 457 South 10th Street · P.O. Box 231 · Opelika, AL 36803-0231 · 334-749-2222

OIL & GAS LAW

Mobile

Conrad P. Armbrecht · ⑳ · Armbrecht Jackson · Riverview Plaza, 13th Floor · 63 South Royal Street · P.O. Box 290 · Mobile, AL 36601-0290 · 251-405-1300

Alan C. Christian · Johnstone, Adams, Bailey, Gordon & Harris · http://www.johnstoneadams.com · One St. Louis Centre, Suite 4000 · One Saint Louis Street · P.O. Box 1988 · Mobile, AL 36633-1988 · 251-432-7682

Tuscaloosa

William T. Watson · ⑩ · Watson, deGraffenried, Hardin & Tyra · 1651 McFarland Boulevard North · Tuscaloosa, AL 35406 · 205-345-1577

PERSONAL INJURY LITIGATION

Alexander City

Larry W. Morris · ⑩ · Morris, Haynes & Hornsby · 131 Main Street · P.O. Box 1660 · Alexander City, AL 35011-1660 · 256-329-2000

M. Clay Alspaugh · ⑳ · Smith & Alspaugh · Financial Center, Suite 1100 · 505 Twentieth Street North · Birmingham, AL 35203 · 205-324-8910

D. Leon Ashford · ⑩ · Hare, Wynn, Newell & Newton · The Historic Massey Building, Suite 800 · 2025 Third Avenue North · Birmingham, AL 35203 · 205-328-5330

W. Michael Atchison · ⑩ · Starnes & Atchison · 100 Brookwood Place, Seventh Floor · P.O. Box 598512 · Birmingham, AL 35259-8512 · 205-868-6000

S. Allen Baker, Jr. · Balch & Bingham · http://www.balch.com · 1710 Sixth Avenue North · Birmingham, AL 35203-2015 · 205-251-8100

James C. Barton, Jr. · Johnston Barton Proctor & Rose · Colonial Brookwood Center, Suite 901 · 569 Brookwood Village · Birmingham, AL 35209 · 205-458-9400

Walter W. Bates · Starnes & Atchison · 100 Brookwood Place, Seventh Floor · P.O. Box 598512 · Birmingham, AL 35259-8512 · 205-868-6000

Robert R. Baugh · Sirote & Permutt · 2311 Highland Avenue South · P.O. Box 55727 · Birmingham, AL 35255-5727 · 205-930-5100

Michael K. Beard · Marsh, Rickard & Bryan · 800 Shades Creek Parkway, Suite 600-D · Birmingham, AL 35209-4532 · 205-879-1981

Michael L. Bell · Lightfoot, Franklin & White · The Clark Building · 400 Twentieth Street North · Birmingham, AL 35203 · 205-581-0700

H. Lanier Brown II · Huie, Fernambucq & Stewart · Building Three, Suite 200 · 2801 Highway 280 South · Birmingham, AL 35223-2484 · 205-251-1193

Frank O. Burge, Jr. · ⑳ · Burge & Burge · 2001 Park Place North, Suite 850 · Birmingham, AL 35203-3284 · 205-251-9000

Philip J. Carroll III · Bradley Arant Rose & White · http://www.bradleyarant.com · One Federal Place · 1819 Fifth Avenue North · Birmingham, AL 35203-2119 · 205-521-8000

Steven F. Casey · Balch & Bingham · http://www.balch.com · 1710 Sixth Avenue North · Birmingham, AL 35203-2015 · 205-251-8100

Stanley A. Cash · ⑩ · Huie, Fernambucq & Stewart · Building Three, Suite 200 · 2801 Highway 280 South · Birmingham, AL 35223-2484 · 205-251-1193

Thomas W. Christian · ⑳ · Christian & Small · http://www.csattorneys.com · 505 North 20th Street, Suite 1800 · Birmingham, AL 35203-2696 · 205-795-6588

Lawrence B. Clark · Baker, Donelson, Bearman, Caldwell & Berkowitz · http://www.bakerdonelson.com Wachovia Tower, Suite 1600 · 420 Twentieth Street North · Birmingham, AL 35203 · 205-328-0480

Brittin T. Coleman · Bradley Arant Rose & White · http://www.bradleyarant.com · One Federal Place · 1819 Fifth Avenue North · Birmingham, AL 35203-2119 · 205-521-8000

Edward O. Conerly · ⑳ · Hall, Conerly & Bolvig · Financial Center, Suite 1400 · 505 North 20th Street · Birmingham, AL 35203 · 205-251-8143

Robert E. Cooper · Christian & Small · http://www.csattorneys.com · 505 North 20th Street, Suite 1800 · Birmingham, AL 35203-2696 · 205-795-6588

Michael A. Florie · 10 · Starnes & Atchison · 100 Brookwood Place, Seventh Floor · P.O. Box 598512 · Birmingham, AL 35259-8512 · 205-868-6000

Samuel H. Franklin · 20 · Lightfoot, Franklin & White · The Clark Building · 400 Twentieth Street North · Birmingham, AL 35203 · 205-581-0700

Ralph D. Gaines III · Gaines, Wolter & Kinney · 3500 Blue Lake Drive, Suite 425 · Birmingham, AL 35243 · 205-980-5888

James W. Gewin · 25 · Bradley Arant Rose & White · http://www.bradleyarant.com · One Federal Place · 1819 Fifth Avenue North · Birmingham, AL 35203-2119 · 205-521-8000

C. William Gladden · Hand Arendall · http://www.handarendall.com · Park Place Tower, Suite 1200 · 2001 Park Place North · Birmingham, AL 35203 · 205-324-4400

Stephen D. Heninger · 20 · Heninger, Garrison & Davis · 2224 First Avenue North · Birmingham, AL 35203 · 205-326-3336

L. Andrew Hollis · 10 · Hollis & Wright · Financial Center, Suite 1500 · 505 North 20th Street · Birmingham, AL 35203 · 205-324-3600

Gilbert E. Johnston, Jr. · 10 · Johnston Barton Proctor & Rose · Colonial Brookwood Center, Suite 901 · 569 Brookwood Village · Birmingham, AL 35209 · 205-458-9400

Warren B. Lightfoot · 25 · Lightfoot, Franklin & White · The Clark Building · 400 Twentieth Street North · Birmingham, AL 35203 · 205-581-0700

David H. Marsh · 10 · Marsh, Rickard & Bryan · 800 Shades Creek Parkway, Suite 600-D · Birmingham, AL 35209-4532 · 205-879-1981

Eugene D. Martenson · 20 · Huie, Fernambucq & Stewart · Building Three, Suite 200 · 2801 Highway 280 South · Birmingham, AL 35223-2484 · 205-251-1193

Crawford S. McGivaren, Jr. · 20 · Cabaniss, Johnston, Gardner, Dumas & O'Neal · http://www.cabaniss.com · 2001 Park Place North, Suite 700 · P.O. Box 830612 · Birmingham, AL 35283-0612 · 205-716-5200

Hobart A. McWhorter, Jr. · 20 · Bradley Arant Rose & White · http://www.bradleyarant.com · One Federal Place · 1819 Fifth Avenue North · Birmingham, AL 35203-2119 · 205-521-8000

John C. Morrow · Burr & Forman · http://www.burr.com · 420 North 20th Street, Suite 3400 · Birmingham, AL 35203-3284 · 205-251-3000

John H. Morrow · 25 · Bradley Arant Rose & White · http://www.bradleyarant.com · One Federal Place · 1819 Fifth Avenue North · Birmingham, AL 35203-2119 · 205-521-8000

Alex W. Newton · 25 · Hare, Wynn, Newell & Newton · The Historic Massey Building, Suite 800 · 2025 Third Avenue North · Birmingham, AL 35203 · 205-328-5330

Adam K. Peck · Lightfoot, Franklin & White · The Clark Building · 400 Twentieth Street North · Birmingham, AL 35203 · 205-581-0700

W. Lee Pittman · 10 · Pittman, Hooks, Dutton, Kirby & Hellums · Park Place Tower, Suite 1100 · 2001 Park Place North · Birmingham, AL 35203 · 205-322-8880

Scott A. Powell · 10 · Hare, Wynn, Newell & Newton · The Historic Massey Building, Suite 800 · 2025 Third Avenue North · Birmingham, AL 35203 · 205-328-5330

Harlan I. Prater IV · Lightfoot, Franklin & White · The Clark Building · 400 Twentieth Street North · Birmingham, AL 35203 · 205-581-0700

James R. Pratt III · ⑩ · Hare, Wynn, Newell & Newton · The Historic Massey Building, Suite 800 · 2025 Third Avenue North · Birmingham, AL 35203 · 205-328-5330

David W. Proctor · Johnston Barton Proctor & Rose · Colonial Brookwood Center, Suite 901 · 569 Brookwood Village · Birmingham, AL 35209 · 205-458-9400

S. Shay Samples · ⑩ · Hare, Wynn, Newell & Newton · The Historic Massey Building, Suite 800 · 2025 Third Avenue North · Birmingham, AL 35203 · 205-328-5330

John P. Scott, Jr. · Starnes & Atchison · 100 Brookwood Place, Seventh Floor · P.O. Box 598512 · Birmingham, AL 35259-8512 · 205-868-6000

John W. Scott · Scott Dukes & Geisler · Concord Center, Suite 700 · 2100 Third Avenue North · Birmingham, AL 35203 · 205-251-2300

Randal H. Sellers · Starnes & Atchison · 100 Brookwood Place, Seventh Floor · P.O. Box 598512 · Birmingham, AL 35259-8512 · 205-868-6000

Charles E. Sharp, Sr. · ⑳ · Sadler Sullivan · Wachovia Tower, Suite 2500 · 420 North 20th Street · Birmingham, AL 35203-5203 · 205-326-4166

Henry E. Simpson · ⑩ · Adams and Reese · http://www.adamsandreese.com · Concord Center, Suite 1100 · 2100 Third Avenue North · Birmingham, AL 35203 · 205-250-5000

James E. Simpson · ⑩ · Adams and Reese · http://www.adamsandreese.com · Concord Center, Suite 1100 2100 Third Avenue North · Birmingham, AL 35203 · 205-250-5000

Clarence M. Small, Jr. · ⑳ · Christian & Small · http://www.csattorneys.com · 505 North 20th Street, Suite 1800 · Birmingham, AL 35203-2696 · 205-795-6588

William W. Smith · ⑩ · Smith & Alspaugh · Financial Center, Suite 1100 · 505 Twentieth Street North · Birmingham, AL 35203 · 205-324-8910

D. Alan Thomas · ⑩ · Huie, Fernambucq & Stewart · Building Three, Suite 200 · 2801 Highway 280 South · Birmingham, AL 35223-2484 · 205-251-1193

James J. Thompson, Jr. · ⑩ · Hare, Wynn, Newell & Newton · The Historic Massey Building, Suite 800 2025 Third Avenue North · Birmingham, AL 35203 · 205-328-5330

Steve A. Tucker · Cabaniss, Johnston, Gardner, Dumas & O'Neal · http://www.cabaniss.com · 2001 Park Place North, Suite 700 · P.O. Box 830612 · Birmingham, AL 35283-0612 · 205-716-5200

Jere F. White, Jr. · ⑩ · Lightfoot, Franklin & White · The Clark Building · 400 Twentieth Street North · Birmingham, AL 35203 · 205-581-0700

Terrel Wynn · Hare, Wynn, Newell & Newton · The Historic Massey Building, Suite 800 · 2025 Third Avenue North · Birmingham, AL 35203 · 205-328-5330

J. Gusty Yearout · Yearout & Traylor · 800 Shades Creek Parkway, Suite 500 · Birmingham, AL 35209 · 205-414-8160

Butler

William L. Utsey · Utsey & Utsey · 112 South Mulberry Avenue · P.O. Box 615 · Butler, AL 36904-2524 · 205-459-3791

Dothan

Rufus R. Smith, Jr. · ⑩ · Rufus R. Smith, Jr. & Associates · 129 South Saint Andrews Street · P.O. Box 6629 · Dothan, AL 36302 · 334-671-7959

Gadsden

Gregory S. Cusimano · ⑩ · Cusimano, Keener, Roberts & Raley · http://www.alabamatortlaw.com · 153 South Ninth Street · Gadsden, AL 35901 · 256-543-0400

Guntersville

Randy H. Beard · Beard & Beard · 416 Gunter Avenue · Guntersville, AL 35976 · 256-582-3189

Huntsville

Joseph M. Cloud · ⑩ · Joseph M. Cloud · 521 Madison Street, Suite 102 · P.O. Box 428 · Huntsville, AL 35804 · 256-534-0545

Gary V. Conchin · Morris, Conchin & King · 129 Washington Street · P.O. Box 248 · Huntsville, AL 35804 · 256-536-0588

Harvey B. Morris · Morris, Conchin & King · 129 Washington Street · P.O. Box 248 · Huntsville, AL 35804 · 256-536-0588

Donna S. Pate · Lanier Ford Shaver & Payne · http://www.lfsp.com · 200 West Side Square, Suite 5000 · P.O. Box 2087 · Huntsville, AL 35804-2087 · 256-535-1100

W. Stanley Rodgers · ⑳ · Lanier Ford Shaver & Payne · http://www.lfsp.com · 200 West Side Square, Suite 5000 · P.O. Box 2087 · Huntsville, AL 35804-2087 · 256-535-1100

Thomas H. Siniard · ⑩ · Siniard, Timberlake & League · 125 Holmes Avenue · Huntsville, AL 35801 · 256-536-0770

H. Harold Stephens · Bradley Arant Rose & White · http://www.bradleyarant.com · 200 Clinton Avenue West, Suite 900 · Huntsville, AL 35801-4900 · 256-517-5100

Jackson

Gaines C. McCorquodale · McCorquodale and McCorquodale · 226 Commerce Street · P.O. Drawer 1137 · Jackson, AL 36545-1137 · 251-246-9015

Jasper

Edward R. Jackson · Jackson, Fikes, Hood & Brakefield · 1816 Third Avenue, Suite 200 · P.O. Box 748 · Jasper, AL 35502-0748 · 205-387-2171

Morris Savage · ⑩ · Bankhead & Savage · 311 Eighteenth Street West · P.O. Box 462 · Jasper, AL 35501 205-384-4574

Mobile

Joseph P. H. Babington · Helmsing, Leach, Herlong, Newman & Rouse · http://www.helmsinglaw.com · The LaClede Building, Suite 2000 · 150 Government Street · P.O. Box 2767 · Mobile, AL 36652 · 251-432-5521

Gregory B. Breedlove · Cunningham, Bounds, Yance, Crowder & Brown · http://www.cbcbb.com · 1601 Dauphin Street · P.O. Box 66705 · Mobile, AL 36660 · 251-471-6191

Joseph M. Brown, Jr. · ⑩ · Cunningham, Bounds, Yance, Crowder & Brown · http://www.cbcbb.com · 1601 Dauphin Street · P.O. Box 66705 · Mobile, AL 36660 · 251-471-6191

Peter F. Burns · Burns, Cunningham & Mackey · 50 St. Emanuel Street · P.O. Box 1583 · Mobile, AL 36633 · 334-432-0612

John T. Crowder, Jr. · ⑩ · Cunningham, Bounds, Yance, Crowder & Brown · http://www.cbcbb.com · 1601 Dauphin Street · P.O. Box 66705 · Mobile, AL 36660 · 251-471-6191

Robert T. Cunningham, Jr. · ⑳ · Cunningham, Bounds, Yance, Crowder & Brown · http://www.cbcbb.com · 1601 Dauphin Street · P.O. Box 66705 · Mobile, AL 36660 · 251-471-6191

William M. Cunningham, Jr. · Burns, Cunningham & Mackey · 50 St. Emanuel Street · P.O. Box 1583 · Mobile, AL 36633 · 334-432-0612

George W. Finkbohner III · Cunningham, Bounds, Yance, Crowder & Brown · http://www.cbcbb.com · 1601 Dauphin Street · P.O. Box 66705 · Mobile, AL 36660 · 251-471-6191

A. Danner Frazer, Jr. · ⑩ · Frazer, Greene, Upchurch & Baker · AmSouth Bank Building, Suite 2206 · 107 Saint Francis Street · P.O. Box 1686 · Mobile, AL 36602 · 251-431-6020

Broox G. Holmes · ⑳ · Armbrecht Jackson · Riverview Plaza, 13th Floor · 63 South Royal Street · P.O. Box 290 · Mobile, AL 36601-0290 · 251-405-1300

Fred W. Killion, Jr. · ⑩ · Killion Law Firm · 2513 Dauphin Street · P.O. Box 7807 · Mobile, AL 36670 · 251-476-5900

Michael D. Knight · ⑩ · McDowell Knight Roedder & Sledge · Riverview Plaza, Suite 900 · 63 South Royal Street · P.O. Box 350 · Mobile, AL 36601 · 251-432-5300

John N. Leach, Jr. · ⑳ · Helmsing, Leach, Herlong, Newman & Rouse · http://www.helmsinglaw.com · The LaClede Building, Suite 2000 · 150 Government Street · P.O. Box 2767 · Mobile, AL 36652 · 251-432-5521

Jerry A. McDowell · ⑩ · McDowell Knight Roedder & Sledge · Riverview Plaza, Suite 900 · 63 South Royal Street · P.O. Box 350 · Mobile, AL 36601 · 251-432-5300

R. Boyd Miller · ⑩ · Cabaniss, Johnston, Gardner, Dumas & O'Neal · http://www.cabaniss.com · 63 South Royal Street, Suite 700 · P.O. Box 2906 · Mobile, AL 36652-2906 · 251-415-7300

W. Boyd Reeves · ⑳ · Armbrecht Jackson · Riverview Plaza, 13th Floor · 63 South Royal Street · P.O. Box 290 · Mobile, AL 36601-0290 · 251-405-1300

William C. Roedder, Jr. · ⑩ · McDowell Knight Roedder & Sledge · Riverview Plaza, Suite 900 · 63 South Royal Street · P.O. Box 350 · Mobile, AL 36601 · 251-432-5300

Benjamen T. Rowe · ⑩ · Cabaniss, Johnston, Gardner, Dumas & O'Neal · http://www.cabaniss.com · 63 South Royal Street, Suite 700 · P.O. Box 2906 · Mobile, AL 36652-2906 · 251-415-7300

Edward S. Sledge III · ⑩ · McDowell Knight Roedder & Sledge · Riverview Plaza, Suite 900 · 63 South Royal Street · P.O. Box 350 · Mobile, AL 36601 · 251-432-5300

Michael E. Upchurch · Frazer, Greene, Upchurch & Baker · AmSouth Bank Building, Suite 2206 · 107 Saint Francis Street · P.O. Box 1686 · Mobile, AL 36602 · 251-431-6020

Norman E. Waldrop, Jr. · Armbrecht Jackson · Riverview Plaza, 13th Floor · 63 South Royal Street · P.O. Box 290 · Mobile, AL 36601-0290 · 251-405-1300

Michael A. Worel · Cunningham, Bounds, Yance, Crowder & Brown · http://www.cbcbb.com · 1601 Dauphin Street · P.O. Box 66705 · Mobile, AL 36660 · 251-471-6191

Montgomery

Jere L. Beasley · ⑩ · Beasley, Allen, Crow, Methvin, Portis & Miles · 218 Commerce Street · P.O. Box 4160 · Montgomery, AL 36103-4160 · 334-269-2343

William H. Brittain II · Ball, Ball, Matthews & Novak · 2000 Interstate Park Drive, Suite 204 · P.O. Box 2148 · Montgomery, AL 36102-2148 · 334-387-7680

Walter R. Byars · Steiner, Crum & Byars · Regions Bank Building, Eighth Floor · Eight Commerce Street P.O. Box 668 · Montgomery, AL 36101-0668 · 334-832-8800

Ronald G. Davenport · Rushton, Stakely, Johnston & Garrett · http://www.rsjg.com · 184 Commerce Street · P.O. Box 270 · Montgomery, AL 36101-0270 · 334-206-3100

Joseph C. Espy III · ⑩ · Melton, Espy & Williams · 255 Dexter Avenue · P.O. Drawer 5130 · Montgomery, AL 36103-5130 · 334-263-6621

Richard B. Garrett · ⑩ · Rushton, Stakely, Johnston & Garrett · http://www.rsjg.com · 184 Commerce Street · P.O. Box 270 · Montgomery, AL 36101-0270 · 334-206-3100

Richard H. Gill · ⑩ · Copeland, Franco, Screws & Gill · 444 South Perry Street · P.O. Box 347 · Montgomery, AL 36101-0347 · 334-834-1180

Fred D. Gray, Sr. · ⑩ · Gray, Langford, Sapp, McGowan, Gray & Nathanson · 400 South Union Street, Suite 205 · P.O. Box 830239 · Montgomery, AL 36104 · 334-727-4830

Thomas H. Keene · ⑩ · Rushton, Stakely, Johnston & Garrett · http://www.rsjg.com · 184 Commerce Street · P.O. Box 270 · Montgomery, AL 36101-0270 · 334-206-3100

James Douglas McElvy · Azar, Azar & Moore · 2740 Zelda Road, Fourth Floor · P.O. Box 2028 · Montgomery, AL 36102-2028 · 334-265-8551

William C. McGowin · Bradley Arant Rose & White · http://www.bradleyarant.com · Alabama Center for Commerce, Suite 780 · 401 Adams Avenue · Montgomery, AL 36104 · 334-956-7700

Oakley W. Melton, Jr. · ⑳ · Melton, Espy & Williams · 255 Dexter Avenue · P.O. Drawer 5130 · Montgomery, AL 36103-5130 · 334-263-6621

Thomas J. Methvin · Beasley, Allen, Crow, Methvin, Portis & Miles · 218 Commerce Street · P.O. Box 4160 · Montgomery, AL 36103-4160 · 334-269-2343

F. Chadwick Morriss · Rushton, Stakely, Johnston & Garrett · http://www.rsjg.com · 184 Commerce Street · P.O. Box 270 · Montgomery, AL 36101-0270 · 334-206-3100

Tabor R. Novak, Jr. · ⑩ · Ball, Ball, Matthews & Novak · 2000 Interstate Park Drive, Suite 204 · P.O. Box 2148 · Montgomery, AL 36102-2148 · 334-387-7680

Robert D. Segall · ⑳ · Copeland, Franco, Screws & Gill · 444 South Perry Street · P.O. Box 347 · Montgomery, AL 36101-0347 · 334-834-1180

Frank J. Stakely · Rushton, Stakely, Johnston & Garrett · http://www.rsjg.com · 184 Commerce Street · P.O. Box 270 · Montgomery, AL 36101-0270 · 334-206-3100

Fred W. Tyson · Rushton, Stakely, Johnston & Garrett · http://www.rsjg.com · 184 Commerce Street · P.O. Box 270 · Montgomery, AL 36101-0270 · 334-206-3100

George Walton Walker III · Copeland, Franco, Screws & Gill · 444 South Perry Street · P.O. Box 347 · Montgomery, AL 36101-0347 · 334-834-1180

Frank M. Wilson · Frank M. Wilson · 504 South Perry Street · Montgomery, AL 36102 · 334-263-2560

Opelika

J. Tutt Barrett · Dean & Barrett · 457 South 10th Street · P.O. Box 231 · Opelika, AL 36803-0231 · 334-749-2222

Phenix City

James R. McKoon, Jr. · McKoon & Thomas · 925 Broad Street · P.O. Box 3220 · Phenix City, AL 36868 334-297-2300

Talladega

Charles P. Gaines · ⑩ · Gaines, Gaines & Rasco · 127 North Street · P.O. Box 275 · Talladega, AL 35160 256-362-2386

Tuscaloosa

William J. Donald, Jr. · ⑩ · Donald, Randall & Donald · AmSouth Building, Ninth Floor · 2330 University Boulevard · Tuscaloosa, AL 35403 · 205-758-2585

PRODUCT LIABILITY LITIGATION

Birmingham

D. Leon Ashford · ⑩ · Hare, Wynn, Newell & Newton · The Historic Massey Building, Suite 800 · 2025 Third Avenue North · Birmingham, AL 35203 · 205-328-5330

H. Lanier Brown II · Huie, Fernambucq & Stewart · Building Three, Suite 200 · 2801 Highway 280 South · Birmingham, AL 35223-2484 · 205-251-1193

Thomas W. Christian · ⑳ · Christian & Small · http://www.csattorneys.com · 505 North 20th Street, Suite 1800 · Birmingham, AL 35203-2696 · 205-795-6588

Lawrence B. Clark · Baker, Donelson, Bearman, Caldwell & Berkowitz · http://www.bakerdonelson.com Wachovia Tower, Suite 1600 · 420 Twentieth Street North · Birmingham, AL 35203 · 205-328-0480

Brittin T. Coleman · Bradley Arant Rose & White · http://www.bradleyarant.com · One Federal Place · 1819 Fifth Avenue North · Birmingham, AL 35203-2119 · 205-521-8000

Samuel H. Franklin · ⑳ · Lightfoot, Franklin & White · The Clark Building · 400 Twentieth Street North · Birmingham, AL 35203 · 205-581-0700

F. M. Haston III · Bradley Arant Rose & White · http://www.bradleyarant.com · One Federal Place · 1819 Fifth Avenue North · Birmingham, AL 35203-2119 · 205-521-8000

Stephen D. Heninger · ⑳ · Heninger, Garrison & Davis · 2224 First Avenue North · Birmingham, AL 35203 · 205-326-3336

Eugene D. Martenson · ⑳ · Huie, Fernambucq & Stewart · Building Three, Suite 200 · 2801 Highway 280 South · Birmingham, AL 35223-2484 · 205-251-1193

John C. Morrow · Burr & Forman · http://www.burr.com · 420 North 20th Street, Suite 3400 · Birmingham, AL 35203-3284 · 205-251-3000

Adam K. Peck · Lightfoot, Franklin & White · The Clark Building · 400 Twentieth Street North · Birmingham, AL 35203 · 205-581-0700

Kenneth M. Perry · Bradley Arant Rose & White · http://www.bradleyarant.com · One Federal Place · 1819 Fifth Avenue North · Birmingham, AL 35203-2119 · 205-521-8000

Sam C. Pointer, Jr. · Lightfoot, Franklin & White · The Clark Building · 400 Twentieth Street North · Birmingham, AL 35203 · 205-581-0700

Maibeth J. Porter · Maynard Cooper & Gale · http://www.maynardcooper.com · Regions/Harbert Plaza, Suite 2400 · 1901 Sixth Avenue North · Birmingham, AL 35203-2602 · 205-254-1000

J. Banks Sewell III · Lightfoot, Franklin & White · The Clark Building · 400 Twentieth Street North · Birmingham, AL 35203 · 205-581-0700

James E. Simpson · ⑩ · Adams and Reese · http://www.adamsandreese.com · Concord Center, Suite 1100 2100 Third Avenue North · Birmingham, AL 35203 · 205-250-5000

D. Alan Thomas · ⑩ · Huie, Fernambucq & Stewart · Building Three, Suite 200 · 2801 Highway 280 South · Birmingham, AL 35223-2484 · 205-251-1193

H. Thomas Wells, Jr. · Maynard Cooper & Gale · http://www.maynardcooper.com · Regions/Harbert Plaza, Suite 2400 · 1901 Sixth Avenue North · Birmingham, AL 35203-2602 · 205-254-1000

Jere F. White, Jr. · ⑩ · Lightfoot, Franklin & White · The Clark Building · 400 Twentieth Street North · Birmingham, AL 35203 · 205-581-0700

Mobile

Joseph P. H. Babington · Helmsing, Leach, Herlong, Newman & Rouse · http://www.helmsinglaw.com · The LaClede Building, Suite 2000 · 150 Government Street · P.O. Box 2767 · Mobile, AL 36652 · 251-432-5521

Michael D. Knight · ⑩ · McDowell Knight Roedder & Sledge · Riverview Plaza, Suite 900 · 63 South Royal Street · P.O. Box 350 · Mobile, AL 36601 · 251-432-5300

Jerry A. McDowell · ⑩ · McDowell Knight Roedder & Sledge · Riverview Plaza, Suite 900 · 63 South Royal Street · P.O. Box 350 · Mobile, AL 36601 · 251-432-5300

Benjamen T. Rowe · ⑩ · Cabaniss, Johnston, Gardner, Dumas & O'Neal · http://www.cabaniss.com · 63 South Royal Street, Suite 700 · P.O. Box 2906 · Mobile, AL 36652-2906 · 251-415-7300

Cooper C. Thurber · Lyons, Pipes & Cook · Two North Royal Street · P.O. Box 2727 · Mobile, AL 36652-2727 · 251-432-4481

PROFESSIONAL MALPRACTICE LAW

Birmingham

Eugene D. Martenson · ⑳ · Huie, Fernambucq & Stewart · Building Three, Suite 200 · 2801 Highway 280 South · Birmingham, AL 35223-2484 · 205-251-1193

Crawford S. McGivaren, Jr. · ⑳ · Cabaniss, Johnston, Gardner, Dumas & O'Neal · http://www.cabaniss.com · 2001 Park Place North, Suite 700 · P.O. Box 830612 · Birmingham, AL 35283-0612 · 205-716-5200

PROJECT FINANCE LAW

Birmingham

Ray D. Gibbons · Bradley Arant Rose & White · http://www.bradleyarant.com · One Federal Place · 1819 Fifth Avenue North · Birmingham, AL 35203-2119 · 205-521-8000

J. Kris Lowry · Maynard Cooper & Gale · http://www.maynardcooper.com · Regions/Harbert Plaza, Suite 2400 · 1901 Sixth Avenue North · Birmingham, AL 35203-2602 · 205-254-1000

PUBLIC FINANCE LAW

Birmingham

James L. Birchall · Walston, Wells & Birchall · One Federal Place, Suite 1100 · 1819 Fifth Avenue North Birmingham, AL 35203 · 205-244-5200

John H. Burton, Jr. · Presley, Burton & Collier · Protective Center, Suite 700 · 2801 Highway 280 South Birmingham, AL 35223-2483 · 205-423-3600

J. Foster Clark · Balch & Bingham · http://www.balch.com · 1901 Sixth Avenue North, Suite 1500 · Birmingham, AL 35203-4644 · 205-251-8100

Mark E. Ezell · Haskell, Slaughter, Young & Rediker · http://www.hsy.com · Park Place Tower, Suite 1400 · 2001 Park Place North · Birmingham, AL 35203 · 205-251-1000

J. Thomas Francis · Balch & Bingham · http://www.balch.com · 1901 Sixth Avenue North, Suite 1500 · Birmingham, AL 35203-4644 · 205-251-8100

P. Nicholas Greenwood · Hand Arendall · http://www.handarendall.com · Park Place Tower, Suite 1200 · 2001 Park Place North · Birmingham, AL 35203 · 205-324-4400

A. Lee Martin · Haskell, Slaughter, Young & Rediker · http://www.hsy.com · Park Place Tower, Suite 1400 · 2001 Park Place North · Birmingham, AL 35203 · 205-251-1000

Kathryn J. Ottensmeyer · Balch & Bingham · http://www.balch.com · 1710 Sixth Avenue North · Birmingham, AL 35203-2015 · 205-251-8100

J. Hobson Presley, Jr. · Presley, Burton & Collier · Protective Center, Suite 700 · 2801 Highway 280 South · Birmingham, AL 35223-2483 · 205-423-3600

William M. Slaughter · Haskell, Slaughter, Young & Rediker · http://www.hsy.com · Park Place Tower, Suite 1400 · 2001 Park Place North · Birmingham, AL 35203 · 205-251-1000

S. Douglas Williams, Jr. · Maynard Cooper & Gale · http://www.maynardcooper.com · Regions/Harbert Plaza, Suite 2400 · 1901 Sixth Avenue North · Birmingham, AL 35203-2602 · 205-254-1000

Alan K. Zeigler · Bradley Arant Rose & White · http://www.bradleyarant.com · One Federal Place · 1819 Fifth Avenue North · Birmingham, AL 35203-2119 · 205-521-8000

Mobile

R. Preston Bolt, Jr. · Hand Arendall · http://www.handarendall.com · RSA Tower, Suite 30200 · 11 North Water Street · Mobile, AL 36602 · 251-432-5511

William B. Givhan · Hand Arendall · http://www.handarendall.com · RSA Tower, Suite 30200 · 11 North Water Street · Mobile, AL 36602 · 251-432-5511

Montgomery

John F. Andrews · (10) · Capell & Howard · http://www.capellhoward.com · 150 South Perry Street · P.O. Box 2069 · Montgomery, AL 36102-2069 · 334-241-8000

W. Stanley Gregory · (10) · Bradley Arant Rose & White · http://www.bradleyarant.com · Alabama Center for Commerce, Suite 780 · 401 Adams Avenue · Montgomery, AL 36104 · 334-956-7700

Christopher S. Simmons · (10) · Rushton, Stakely, Johnston & Garrett · http://www.rsjg.com · 184 Commerce Street · P.O. Box 270 · Montgomery, AL 36101-0270 · 334-206-3100

Robert D. Thorington · Bradley Arant Rose & White · http://www.bradleyarant.com · Alabama Center for Commerce, Suite 780 · 401 Adams Avenue · Montgomery, AL 36104 · 334-956-7700

RAILROAD LAW

Birmingham

Crawford S. McGivaren, Jr. · (20) · Cabaniss, Johnston, Gardner, Dumas & O'Neal · http://www.cabaniss.com · 2001 Park Place North, Suite 700 · P.O. Box 830612 · Birmingham, AL 35283-0612 · 205-716-5200

Michael Ray · Sadler Sullivan · Wachovia Tower, Suite 2500 · 420 North 20th Street · Birmingham, AL 35203-5203 · 205-326-4166

Charles E. Sharp, Sr. · (20) · Sadler Sullivan · Wachovia Tower, Suite 2500 · 420 North 20th Street · Birmingham, AL 35203-5203 · 205-326-4166

Steve A. Tucker · Cabaniss, Johnston, Gardner, Dumas & O'Neal · http://www.cabaniss.com · 2001 Park Place North, Suite 700 · P.O. Box 830612 · Birmingham, AL 35283-0612 · 205-716-5200

Turner B. Williams · Burr & Forman · http://www.burr.com · 420 North 20th Street, Suite 3400 · Birmingham, AL 35203-3284 · 205-251-3000

REAL ESTATE LAW

Anniston

Jay F. Pumroy · Wilson, Dillion, Pumroy & James · 1431 Leighton Avenue · P.O. Box 2333 · Anniston, AL 36202-2333 · 256-236-4222

Birmingham

Scott A. Abney · Maynard Cooper & Gale · http://www.maynardcooper.com · Regions/Harbert Plaza, Suite 2400 · 1901 Sixth Avenue North · Birmingham, AL 35203-2602 · 205-254-1000

Kay K. Bains · ⑩ · Bradley Arant Rose & White · http://www.bradleyarant.com · One Federal Place · 1819 Fifth Avenue North · Birmingham, AL 35203-2119 · 205-521-8000

Charles A. J. Beavers, Jr. · ㉕ · Bradley Arant Rose & White · http://www.bradleyarant.com · One Federal Place · 1819 Fifth Avenue North · Birmingham, AL 35203-2119 · 205-521-8000

H. Hampton Boles · ⑩ · Balch & Bingham · http://www.balch.com · 1901 Sixth Avenue North, Suite 1500 Birmingham, AL 35203-4644 · 205-251-8100

Michael Brandt · Wallace, Jordan, Ratliff & Brandt · http://www.wallacejordan.com · 800 Shades Creek Parkway, Suite 400 · P.O. Box 530910 · Birmingham, AL 35253 · 205-870-0555

Steven A. Brickman · Sirote & Permutt · 2311 Highland Avenue South · P.O. Box 55727 · Birmingham, AL 35255-5727 · 205-930-5100

Thomas C. Clark III · Maynard Cooper & Gale · http://www.maynardcooper.com · Regions/Harbert Plaza, Suite 2400 · 1901 Sixth Avenue North · Birmingham, AL 35203-2602 · 205-254-1000

Douglas P. Corretti · ㉕ · Corretti, Newsome & Hawkins · 1804 Seventh Avenue North · Birmingham, AL 35203 · 205-251-1164

John F. DeBuys, Jr. · Burr & Forman · http://www.burr.com · 420 North 20th Street, Suite 3400 · Birmingham, AL 35203-3284 · 205-251-3000

Jesse P. Evans III · ⑩ · Haskell, Slaughter, Young & Rediker · http://www.hsy.com · Park Place Tower, Suite 1400 · 2001 Park Place North · Birmingham, AL 35203 · 205-251-1000

Frank C. Galloway, Jr. · ㉕ · Hand Arendall · http://www.handarendall.com · Park Place Tower, Suite 1200 · 2001 Park Place North · Birmingham, AL 35203 · 205-324-4400

H. Chervis Isom · ⑳ · Baker, Donelson, Bearman, Caldwell & Berkowitz · http://www.bakerdonelson.com · Wachovia Tower, Suite 1600 · 420 Twentieth Street North · Birmingham, AL 35203 · 205-328-0480

W. Benjamin Johnson · Burr & Forman · http://www.burr.com · 420 North 20th Street, Suite 3400 · Birmingham, AL 35203-3284 · 205-251-3000

Haskins W. Jones · Johnston Barton Proctor & Rose · Colonial Brookwood Center, Suite 901 · 569 Brookwood Village · Birmingham, AL 35209 · 205-458-9400

Denise W. Killebrew · ⑩ · Baker, Donelson, Bearman, Caldwell & Berkowitz · http://www.bakerdonelson.com · Wachovia Tower, Suite 1600 · 420 Twentieth Street North · Birmingham, AL 35203 · 205-328-0480

Randolph H. Lanier · ㉕ · Balch & Bingham · http://www.balch.com · 1901 Sixth Avenue North, Suite 1500 · Birmingham, AL 35203-4644 · 205-251-8100

Jerome K. Lanning · ㉕ · Johnston Barton Proctor & Rose · Colonial Brookwood Center, Suite 901 · 569 Brookwood Village · Birmingham, AL 35209 · 205-458-9400

Dwight L. Mixson, Jr. · ⑩ · Burr & Forman · http://www.burr.com · 420 North 20th Street, Suite 3400 · Birmingham, AL 35203-3284 · 205-251-3000

Stephen R. Monk · ⑩ · Bradley Arant Rose & White · http://www.bradleyarant.com · One Federal Place · 1819 Fifth Avenue North · Birmingham, AL 35203-2119 · 205-521-8000

Randall H. Morrow · Maynard Cooper & Gale · http://www.maynardcooper.com · Regions/Harbert Plaza, Suite 2400 · 1901 Sixth Avenue North · Birmingham, AL 35203-2602 · 205-254-1000

James J. Odom, Jr. · James J. Odom · 211 Yeager Parkway, Suite B · P.O. Box 11244 · Birmingham, AL 35202 · 205-664-8691

J. Fred Powell · ⑩ · Burr & Forman · http://www.burr.com · 420 North 20th Street, Suite 3400 · Birmingham, AL 35203-3284 · 205-251-3000

Robert R. Sexton · ⑩ · Maynard Cooper & Gale · http://www.maynardcooper.com · Regions/Harbert Plaza, Suite 2400 · 1901 Sixth Avenue North · Birmingham, AL 35203-2602 · 205-254-1000

Dawn Helms Sharff · Bradley Arant Rose & White · http://www.bradleyarant.com · One Federal Place · 1819 Fifth Avenue North · Birmingham, AL 35203-2119 · 205-521-8000

Bradley G. Siegal · Leitman, Siegal & Payne · The Land Title Building, Suite 400 · 600 North 20th Street · Birmingham, AL 35203 · 205-251-5900

F. Don Siegal · Leitman, Siegal & Payne · The Land Title Building, Suite 400 · 600 North 20th Street · Birmingham, AL 35203 · 205-251-5900

Adam J. Sigman · Maynard Cooper & Gale · http://www.maynardcooper.com · Regions/Harbert Plaza, Suite 2400 · 1901 Sixth Avenue North · Birmingham, AL 35203-2602 · 205-254-1000

David C. Skinner · David C. Skinner · 2700 Rogers Drive, Suite 208 · Birmingham, AL 35209 · 205-871-9566

Felton W. Smith · Balch & Bingham · http://www.balch.com · 1901 Sixth Avenue North, Suite 1500 · Birmingham, AL 35203-4644 · 205-251-8100

Carol H. Stewart · Burr & Forman · http://www.burr.com · 420 North 20th Street, Suite 3400 · Birmingham, AL 35203-3284 · 205-251-3000

Phillip G. Stutts · Leitman, Siegal & Payne · The Land Title Building, Suite 400 · 600 North 20th Street Birmingham, AL 35203 · 205-251-5900

William R. Sylvester · ⑩ · Walston, Wells & Birchall · One Federal Place, Suite 1100 · 1819 Fifth Avenue North · Birmingham, AL 35203 · 205-244-5200

Bobby C. Underwood · ⑩ · Bradley Arant Rose & White · http://www.bradleyarant.com · One Federal Place · 1819 Fifth Avenue North · Birmingham, AL 35203-2119 · 205-521-8000

Meade Whitaker, Jr. · Bradley Arant Rose & White · http://www.bradleyarant.com · One Federal Place · 1819 Fifth Avenue North · Birmingham, AL 35203-2119 · 205-521-8000

Gwen L. Windle · Haskell, Slaughter, Young & Rediker · http://www.hsy.com · Park Place Tower, Suite 1400 · 2001 Park Place North · Birmingham, AL 35203 · 205-251-1000

William S. Wright · Balch & Bingham · http://www.balch.com · 1901 Sixth Avenue North, Suite 1500 · Birmingham, AL 35203-4644 · 205-251-8100

Huntsville

Daniel M. Wilson · Maynard Cooper & Gale · http://www.maynardcooper.com · 655 Gallatin Street · Huntsville, AL 35801 · 256-551-0171

Mobile

I. David Cherniak · Johnstone, Adams, Bailey, Gordon & Harris · http://www.johnstoneadams.com · One St. Louis Centre, Suite 4000 · One Saint Louis Street · P.O. Box 1988 · Mobile, AL 36633-1988 · 251-432-7682

Warren C. Herlong, Jr. · Helmsing, Leach, Herlong, Newman & Rouse · http://www.helmsinglaw.com · The LaClede Building, Suite 2000 · 150 Government Street · P.O. Box 2767 · Mobile, AL 36652 · 251-432-5521

Neil C. Johnston · ⑩ · Hand Arendall · http://www.handarendall.com · RSA Tower, Suite 30200 · 11 North Water Street · Mobile, AL 36602 · 251-432-5511

Vivian G. Johnston, Jr. · ㉕ · Hand Arendall · http://www.handarendall.com · RSA Tower, Suite 30200 · 11 North Water Street · Mobile, AL 36602 · 251-432-5511

Stova F. McFadden · ⑳ · McFadden, Lyon & Rouse · 718 Downtowner Boulevard · Mobile, AL 36609-5499 · 251-342-9172

T. Bruce McGowin · Hand Arendall · http://www.handarendall.com · RSA Tower, Suite 30200 · 11 North Water Street · Mobile, AL 36602 · 251-432-5511

Harold D. Parkman · ⑳ · Hand Arendall · http://www.handarendall.com · RSA Tower, Suite 30200 · 11 North Water Street · Mobile, AL 36602 · 251-432-5511

Beth M. Rouse · McFadden, Lyon & Rouse · 718 Downtowner Boulevard · Mobile, AL 36609-5499 · 251-342-9172

Montgomery

Shapard D. Ashley · Capell & Howard · http://www.capellhoward.com · 150 South Perry Street · P.O. Box 2069 · Montgomery, AL 36102-2069 · 334-241-8000

Jeffrey W. Blitz · ⑩ · Rushton, Stakely, Johnston & Garrett · http://www.rsjg.com · 184 Commerce Street P.O. Box 270 · Montgomery, AL 36101-0270 · 334-206-3100

James M. Edwards · Balch & Bingham · http://www.balch.com · 105 Tallapoosa Street, Suite 200 · P.O. Box 78 · Montgomery, AL 36101-0078 · 334-834-6500

William I. Eskridge · Rushton, Stakely, Johnston & Garrett · http://www.rsjg.com · 184 Commerce Street P.O. Box 270 · Montgomery, AL 36101-0270 · 334-206-3100

William Inge Hill, Jr. · ⑳ · Hill, Hill, Carter, Franco, Cole & Black · 425 South Perry Street · P.O. Box 116 · Montgomery, AL 36101-0116 · 334-834-7600

William K. Martin · ⑩ · Capell & Howard · http://www.capellhoward.com · 150 South Perry Street · P.O. Box 2069 · Montgomery, AL 36102-2069 · 334-241-8000

Katherine Palmer Smith · Capell & Howard · http://www.capellhoward.com · 150 South Perry Street · P.O. Box 2069 · Montgomery, AL 36102-2069 · 334-241-8000

SECURITIES LAW

Birmingham

Suzanne Ashe · Balch & Bingham · http://www.balch.com · 1901 Sixth Avenue North, Suite 1500 · Birmingham, AL 35203-4644 · 205-251-8100

James W. Childs, Jr. · Bradley Arant Rose & White · http://www.bradleyarant.com · One Federal Place · 1819 Fifth Avenue North · Birmingham, AL 35203-2119 · 205-521-8000

J. Paul Compton, Jr. · ⑩ · Bradley Arant Rose & White · http://www.bradleyarant.com · One Federal Place · 1819 Fifth Avenue North · Birmingham, AL 35203-2119 · 205-521-8000

John H. Cooper · ⑩ · Sirote & Permutt · 2311 Highland Avenue South · P.O. Box 55727 · Birmingham, AL 35255-5727 · 205-930-5100

Gregory S. Curran · Maynard Cooper & Gale · http://www.maynardcooper.com · Regions/Harbert Plaza, Suite 2400 · 1901 Sixth Avenue North · Birmingham, AL 35203-2602 · 205-254-1000

L. Susan Doss · Bradley Arant Rose & White · http://www.bradleyarant.com · One Federal Place · 1819 Fifth Avenue North · Birmingham, AL 35203-2119 · 205-521-8000

Carolyn L. Duncan · Cabaniss, Johnston, Gardner, Dumas & O'Neal · http://www.cabaniss.com · 2001 Park Place North, Suite 700 · P.O. Box 830612 · Birmingham, AL 35283-0612 · 205-716-5200

Robert E. Lee Garner · Haskell, Slaughter, Young & Rediker · http://www.hsy.com · Park Place Tower, Suite 1400 · 2001 Park Place North · Birmingham, AL 35203 · 205-251-1000

John B. Grenier · ⑩ · Bradley Arant Rose & White · http://www.bradleyarant.com · One Federal Place · 1819 Fifth Avenue North · Birmingham, AL 35203-2119 · 205-521-8000

Christopher B. Harmon · Maynard Cooper & Gale · http://www.maynardcooper.com · Regions/Harbert Plaza, Suite 2400 · 1901 Sixth Avenue North · Birmingham, AL 35203-2602 · 205-254-1000

William K. Holbrook · Haskell, Slaughter, Young & Rediker · http://www.hsy.com · Park Place Tower, Suite 1400 · 2001 Park Place North · Birmingham, AL 35203 · 205-251-1000

Thomas L. Krebs · Haskell, Slaughter, Young & Rediker · http://www.hsy.com · Park Place Tower, Suite 1400 · 2001 Park Place North · Birmingham, AL 35203 · 205-251-1000

Daniel H. Markstein III · ㉕ · Maynard Cooper & Gale · http://www.maynardcooper.com · Regions/Harbert Plaza, Suite 2400 · 1901 Sixth Avenue North · Birmingham, AL 35203-2602 · 205-254-1000

C. Henry Marston · Walston, Wells & Birchall · One Federal Place, Suite 1100 · 1819 Fifth Avenue North Birmingham, AL 35203 · 205-244-5200

B. G. Minisman, Jr. · ⑩ · Baker, Donelson, Bearman, Caldwell & Berkowitz · http://www.bakerdonelson.com · Wachovia Tower, Suite 1600 · 420 Twentieth Street North · Birmingham, AL 35203 · 205-328-0480

John K. Molen · ⑩ · Bradley Arant Rose & White · http://www.bradleyarant.com · One Federal Place · 1819 Fifth Avenue North · Birmingham, AL 35203-2119 · 205-521-8000

J. Vernon Patrick, Jr. · ⑳ · Haskell, Slaughter, Young & Rediker · http://www.hsy.com · Park Place Tower, Suite 1400 · 2001 Park Place North · Birmingham, AL 35203 · 205-251-1000

Richard L. Pearson · Balch & Bingham · http://www.balch.com · 1901 Sixth Avenue North, Suite 1500 · Birmingham, AL 35203-4644 · 205-251-8100

J. Michael Rediker · ⑳ · Haskell, Slaughter, Young & Rediker · http://www.hsy.com · Park Place Tower, Suite 1400 · 2001 Park Place North · Birmingham, AL 35203 · 205-251-1000

J. Michael Savage · Maynard Cooper & Gale · http://www.maynardcooper.com · Regions/Harbert Plaza, Suite 2400 · 1901 Sixth Avenue North · Birmingham, AL 35203-2602 · 205-254-1000

Jack P. Stephenson, Jr. · ⑩ · Burr & Forman · http://www.burr.com · 420 North 20th Street, Suite 3400 · Birmingham, AL 35203-3284 · 205-251-3000

Paul S. Ware · Bradley Arant Rose & White · http://www.bradleyarant.com · One Federal Place · 1819 Fifth Avenue North · Birmingham, AL 35203-2119 · 205-521-8000

Montgomery

Richard H. Gill · ⑩ · Copeland, Franco, Screws & Gill · 444 South Perry Street · P.O. Box 347 · Montgomery, AL 36101-0347 · 334-834-1180

Thomas G. Mancuso · ⑩ · Haskell, Slaughter, Young & Rediker · http://www.hsy.com · 305 South Lawrence Street · Montgomery, AL 36104 · 334-265-8573

TAX LAW

Birmingham

Louis H. Anders · ㉕ · Burr & Forman · http://www.burr.com · 420 North 20th Street, Suite 3400 · Birmingham, AL 35203-3284 · 205-251-3000

Harold I. Apolinsky · ㉕ · Sirote & Permutt · 2311 Highland Avenue South · P.O. Box 55727 · Birmingham, AL 35255-5727 · 205-930-5100

Steven A. Benefield · Christian & Small · http://www.csattorneys.com · 505 North 20th Street, Suite 1800 Birmingham, AL 35203-2696 · 205-795-6588

Thomas H. Brinkley · Maynard Cooper & Gale · http://www.maynardcooper.com · Regions/Harbert Plaza, Suite 2400 · 1901 Sixth Avenue North · Birmingham, AL 35203-2602 · 205-254-1000

William J. Bryant · Feld, Hyde, Wertheimer, Bryant & Stone · http://www.feldhyde.com · 2000 SouthBridge Parkway, Suite 500 · Birmingham, AL 35209 · 205-802-7575

F. Gerald Burnett · Cabaniss, Johnston, Gardner, Dumas & O'Neal · http://www.cabaniss.com · 2001 Park Place North, Suite 700 · P.O. Box 830612 · Birmingham, AL 35283-0612 · 205-716-5200

Thomas Neely Carruthers · ㉕ · Bradley Arant Rose & White · http://www.bradleyarant.com · One Federal Place · 1819 Fifth Avenue North · Birmingham, AL 35203-2119 · 205-521-8000

Ross N. Cohen · Haskell, Slaughter, Young & Rediker · http://www.hsy.com · Park Place Tower, Suite 1400 · 2001 Park Place North · Birmingham, AL 35203 · 205-251-1000

John H. Cooper · ⑩ · Sirote & Permutt · 2311 Highland Avenue South · P.O. Box 55727 · Birmingham, AL 35255-5727 · 205-930-5100

Roy J. Crawford · ⑳ · Cabaniss, Johnston, Gardner, Dumas & O'Neal · http://www.cabaniss.com · 2001 Park Place North, Suite 700 · P.O. Box 830612 · Birmingham, AL 35283-0612 · 205-716-5200

C. Fred Daniels · ⑩ · Cabaniss, Johnston, Gardner, Dumas & O'Neal · http://www.cabaniss.com · 2001 Park Place North, Suite 700 · P.O. Box 830612 · Birmingham, AL 35283-0612 · 205-716-5200

Bingham D. Edwards, Jr. · Balch & Bingham · http://www.balch.com · 1901 Sixth Avenue North, Suite 1500 · Birmingham, AL 35203-4644 · 205-251-8100

Bruce P. Ely · ⑩ · Bradley Arant Rose & White · http://www.bradleyarant.com · One Federal Place · 1819 Fifth Avenue North · Birmingham, AL 35203-2119 · 205-521-8000

Glenn E. Estess · Wallace, Jordan, Ratliff & Brandt · http://www.wallacejordan.com · 800 Shades Creek Parkway, Suite 400 · P.O. Box 530910 · Birmingham, AL 35253 · 205-870-0555

Stuart J. Frentz · ⑩ · Bradley Arant Rose & White · http://www.bradleyarant.com · One Federal Place · 1819 Fifth Avenue North · Birmingham, AL 35203-2119 · 205-521-8000

Christopher R. Grissom · Bradley Arant Rose & White · http://www.bradleyarant.com · One Federal Place · 1819 Fifth Avenue North · Birmingham, AL 35203-2119 · 205-521-8000

K. Wood Herren · Bradley Arant Rose & White · http://www.bradleyarant.com · One Federal Place · 1819 Fifth Avenue North · Birmingham, AL 35203-2119 · 205-521-8000

William Lyle Hinds, Jr. · ㉕ · Bradley Arant Rose & White · http://www.bradleyarant.com · One Federal Place · 1819 Fifth Avenue North · Birmingham, AL 35203-2119 · 205-521-8000

Russell L. Irby III · Johnston Barton Proctor & Rose · Colonial Brookwood Center, Suite 901 · 569 Brookwood Village · Birmingham, AL 35209 · 205-458-9400

Harold B. Kushner · ⑳ · Bradley Arant Rose & White · http://www.bradleyarant.com · One Federal Place 1819 Fifth Avenue North · Birmingham, AL 35203-2119 · 205-521-8000

Bradley W. Lard · Bradley Arant Rose & White · http://www.bradleyarant.com · One Federal Place · 1819 Fifth Avenue North · Birmingham, AL 35203-2119 · 205-521-8000

Alex B. Leath · Balch & Bingham · http://www.balch.com · 1901 Sixth Avenue North, Suite 1500 · Birmingham, AL 35203-4644 · 205-251-8100

Ronald A. Levitt · ⑩ · Sirote & Permutt · 2311 Highland Avenue South · P.O. Box 55727 · Birmingham, AL 35255-5727 · 205-930-5100

Curtis O. Liles III · Liles & Rushin · 505 Twentieth Street North, Suite 625 · Birmingham, AL 35203-2605 · 205-263-4900

John F. Lyle III · Adams and Reese · http://www.adamsandreese.com · Concord Center, Suite 1100 · 2100 Third Avenue North · Birmingham, AL 35203 · 205-250-5000

Thomas J. Mahoney, Jr. · Baker, Donelson, Bearman, Caldwell & Berkowitz · http://www.bakerdonelson.com · Wachovia Tower, Suite 1600 · 420 Twentieth Street North · Birmingham, AL 35203 · 205-328-0480

Daniel H. Markstein III · ㉕ · Maynard Cooper & Gale · http://www.maynardcooper.com · Regions/Harbert Plaza, Suite 2400 · 1901 Sixth Avenue North · Birmingham, AL 35203-2602 · 205-254-1000

Jim G. Mclaughlin · Maynard Cooper & Gale · http://www.maynardcooper.com · Regions/Harbert Plaza, Suite 2400 · 1901 Sixth Avenue North · Birmingham, AL 35203-2602 · 205-254-1000

Sidney T. Philips · Leitman, Siegal & Payne · The Land Title Building, Suite 400 · 600 North 20th Street · Birmingham, AL 35203 · 205-251-5900

J. William Rose, Jr. · Johnston Barton Proctor & Rose · Colonial Brookwood Center, Suite 901 · 569 Brookwood Village · Birmingham, AL 35209 · 205-458-9400

Bradley J. Sklar · Sirote & Permutt · 2311 Highland Avenue South · P.O. Box 55727 · Birmingham, AL 35255-5727 · 205-930-5100

William R. Sylvester · ⑩ · Walston, Wells & Birchall · One Federal Place, Suite 1100 · 1819 Fifth Avenue North · Birmingham, AL 35203 · 205-244-5200

Robert C. Walthall · ㉕ · Bradley Arant Rose & White · http://www.bradleyarant.com · One Federal Place 1819 Fifth Avenue North · Birmingham, AL 35203-2119 · 205-521-8000

Brian T. Williams · Dominick, Fletcher, Yeilding, Wood & Lloyd · http://www.dfy.com · 2121 Highland Avenue South · P.O. Box 1387 · Birmingham, AL 35201 · 205-939-0033

David M. Wooldridge · ⑩ · Sirote & Permutt · 2311 Highland Avenue South · P.O. Box 55727 · Birmingham, AL 35255-5727 · 205-930-5100

Decatur

Dow M. Perry · ⑩ · Harris, Caddell & Shanks · 214 Johnston Street, SE · P.O. Box 2688 · Decatur, AL 35602-2688 · 256-340-8000

Dothan

G. David Johnston · ⑩ · Johnston, Hinesley, Flowers, Clenney & Turner · 291 North Oates Street · Dothan, AL 36303 · 334-793-1115

Foley

Gregory L. Leatherbury, Jr. · ㉕ · Hand Arendall · http://www.handarendall.com · 112 West Laurel Avenue · Foley, AL 36535 · 251-970-5511

Huntsville

Scott E. Ludwig · ⑩ · Bradley Arant Rose & White · http://www.bradleyarant.com · 200 Clinton Avenue West, Suite 900 · Huntsville, AL 35801-4900 · 256-517-5100

John Wynn · ⑩ · Lanier Ford Shaver & Payne · http://www.lfsp.com · 200 West Side Square, Suite 5000 · P.O. Box 2087 · Huntsville, AL 35804-2087 · 256-535-1100

Mobile

G. Porter Brock, Jr. · ⑳ · Hand Arendall · http://www.handarendall.com · RSA Tower, Suite 30200 · 11 North Water Street · Mobile, AL 36602 · 251-432-5511

Robert M. Galloway · Galloway, Wettermark, Everest, Rutens & Gaillard · 3263 Cottage Hill Road · P.O. Box 16629 · Mobile, AL 36616-0629 · 251-476-4493

Thomas F. Garth · ⑩ · Lyons, Pipes & Cook · Two North Royal Street · P.O. Box 2727 · Mobile, AL 36652-2727 · 251-432-4481

Frederick G. Helmsing · ⑩ · Helmsing, Leach, Herlong, Newman & Rouse · http://www.helmsinglaw.com · The LaClede Building, Suite 2000 · 150 Government Street · P.O. Box 2767 · Mobile, AL 36652 · 251-432-5521

Zebulon Montgomery Pike Inge, Jr. · ⑩ · Vickers, Riis, Murray and Curran · Regions Bank Building, 11th Floor · 106 St. Francis Street · P.O. Drawer 2568 · Mobile, AL 36652 · 251-432-9772

Vivian G. Johnston, Jr. · ㉕ · Hand Arendall · http://www.handarendall.com · RSA Tower, Suite 30200 · 11 North Water Street · Mobile, AL 36602 · 251-432-5511

Robert H. Rouse · Helmsing, Leach, Herlong, Newman & Rouse · http://www.helmsinglaw.com · The LaClede Building, Suite 2000 · 150 Government Street · P.O. Box 2767 · Mobile, AL 36652 · 251-432-5521

R. Gregory Watts · ⑩ · Johnstone, Adams, Bailey, Gordon & Harris · http://www.johnstoneadams.com · One St. Louis Centre, Suite 4000 · One Saint Louis Street · P.O. Box 1988 · Mobile, AL 36633-1988 · 251-432-7682

Montgomery

Robert E. L. Gilpin · ⑩ · Kaufman, Gilpin, McKenzie, Thomas & Weiss · Lakeview Center, Suite 300 · 2660 East Chase Lane · Montgomery, AL 36117 · 334-244-1111

W. Stanley Gregory · ⑩ · Bradley Arant Rose & White · http://www.bradleyarant.com · Alabama Center for Commerce, Suite 780 · 401 Adams Avenue · Montgomery, AL 36104 · 334-956-7700

Gerald W. Hartley · ⑳ · Hartley & Hartley · 8650 Minnie Brown Road, Suite 124 · Montgomery, AL 36117-7433 · 334-481-6904

Henry H. Hutchinson · ⑳ · Capell & Howard · http://www.capellhoward.com · 150 South Perry Street · P.O. Box 2069 · Montgomery, AL 36102-2069 · 334-241-8000

James Theodore Jackson · ⑩ · Rushton, Stakely, Johnston & Garrett · http://www.rsjg.com · 184 Commerce Street · P.O. Box 270 · Montgomery, AL 36101-0270 · 334-206-3100

D. Kyle Johnson · ⑩ · Capell & Howard · http://www.capellhoward.com · 150 South Perry Street · P.O. Box 2069 · Montgomery, AL 36102-2069 · 334-241-8000

Jeff Kohn · ⑩ · Sasser, Bolton, Stidham & Sefton · 100 Colonial Bank Boulevard, Suite B201 · P.O. Drawer 242127 · Montgomery, AL 36117 · 334-532-3400

Daniel L. Lindsey · Rushton, Stakely, Johnston & Garrett · http://www.rsjg.com · 184 Commerce Street · P.O. Box 270 · Montgomery, AL 36101-0270 · 334-206-3100

Thomas G. Mancuso · ⑩ · Haskell, Slaughter, Young & Rediker · http://www.hsy.com · 305 South Lawrence Street · Montgomery, AL 36104 · 334-265-8573

Alan E. Rothfeder · Copeland, Franco, Screws & Gill · 444 South Perry Street · P.O. Box 347 · Montgomery, AL 36101-0347 · 334-834-1180

James M. Scott · ㉕ · Capell & Howard · http://www.capellhoward.com · 150 South Perry Street · P.O. Box 2069 · Montgomery, AL 36102-2069 · 334-241-8000

Christopher S. Simmons · ⑩ · Rushton, Stakely, Johnston & Garrett · http://www.rsjg.com · 184 Commerce Street · P.O. Box 270 · Montgomery, AL 36101-0270 · 334-206-3100

Debra D. Spain · ⑩ · Capell & Howard · http://www.capellhoward.com · 150 South Perry Street · P.O. Box 2069 · Montgomery, AL 36102-2069 · 334-241-8000

W. Holt Speir III · ⑩ · Capell & Howard · http://www.capellhoward.com · 150 South Perry Street · P.O. Box 2069 · Montgomery, AL 36102-2069 · 334-241-8000

Helen Crump Wells · ⑩ · Rushton, Stakely, Johnston & Garrett · http://www.rsjg.com · 184 Commerce Street · P.O. Box 270 · Montgomery, AL 36101-0270 · 334-206-3100

M. Courtney Williams · Capell & Howard · http://www.capellhoward.com · 150 South Perry Street · P.O. Box 2069 · Montgomery, AL 36102-2069 · 334-241-8000

TIMBER LAW

Birmingham

Kay K. Bains · ⑩ · Bradley Arant Rose & White · http://www.bradleyarant.com · One Federal Place · 1819 Fifth Avenue North · Birmingham, AL 35203-2119 · 205-521-8000

Mobile

Candace D. Johnson · Adams and Reese · http://www.adamsandreese.com · RSA Battle House Tower, Suite 23200 · 11 North Water Street · Mobile, AL 36602 · 251-433-3234

Neil C. Johnston · ⑩ · Hand Arendall · http://www.handarendall.com · RSA Tower, Suite 30200 · 11 North Water Street · Mobile, AL 36602 · 251-432-5511

TRANSPORTATION LAW

Birmingham

D. Leon Ashford · ⑩ · Hare, Wynn, Newell & Newton · The Historic Massey Building, Suite 800 · 2025 Third Avenue North · Birmingham, AL 35203 · 205-328-5330

Michael K. Beard · Marsh, Rickard & Bryan · 800 Shades Creek Parkway, Suite 600-D · Birmingham, AL 35209-4532 · 205-879-1981

John W. Clark, Jr. · Clark, Oncale, Hair & Smith · 800 Shades Creek Parkway, Suite 850 · Birmingham, AL 35209 · 205-397-2900

Turner B. Williams · Burr & Forman · http://www.burr.com · 420 North 20th Street, Suite 3400 · Birmingham, AL 35203-3284 · 205-251-3000

TRUSTS AND ESTATES

Birmingham

Harold I. Apolinsky · ㉕ · Sirote & Permutt · 2311 Highland Avenue South · P.O. Box 55727 · Birmingham, AL 35255-5727 · 205-930-5100

Ross N. Cohen · Haskell, Slaughter, Young & Rediker · http://www.hsy.com · Park Place Tower, Suite 1400 · 2001 Park Place North · Birmingham, AL 35203 · 205-251-1000

C. Fred Daniels · ⑩ · Cabaniss, Johnston, Gardner, Dumas & O'Neal · http://www.cabaniss.com · 2001 Park Place North, Suite 700 · P.O. Box 830612 · Birmingham, AL 35283-0612 · 205-716-5200

Louis B. Feld · ⑩ · Feld, Hyde, Wertheimer, Bryant & Stone · http://www.feldhyde.com · 2000 SouthBridge Parkway, Suite 500 · Birmingham, AL 35209 · 205-802-7575

William Lyle Hinds, Jr. · ㉕ · Bradley Arant Rose & White · http://www.bradleyarant.com · One Federal Place · 1819 Fifth Avenue North · Birmingham, AL 35203-2119 · 205-521-8000

Nancy C. Hughes · ⑩ · Hughes & Scalise · 600 Luckie Drive, Suite 405 · Birmingham, AL 35223 · 205-871-0300

Elizabeth H. Hutchins · Sirote & Permutt · 2311 Highland Avenue South · P.O. Box 55727 · Birmingham, AL 35255-5727 · 205-930-5100

Gregory D. Hyde · ⑩ · Feld, Hyde, Wertheimer, Bryant & Stone · http://www.feldhyde.com · 2000 SouthBridge Parkway, Suite 500 · Birmingham, AL 35209 · 205-802-7575

Cynthia Lamar-Hart · Maynard Cooper & Gale · http://www.maynardcooper.com · Regions/Harbert Plaza, Suite 2400 · 1901 Sixth Avenue North · Birmingham, AL 35203-2602 · 205-254-1000

Daniel H. Markstein III · ㉕ · Maynard Cooper & Gale · http://www.maynardcooper.com · Regions/Harbert Plaza, Suite 2400 · 1901 Sixth Avenue North · Birmingham, AL 35203-2602 · 205-254-1000

Melinda M. Mathews · ⑩ · Sirote & Permutt · 2311 Highland Avenue South · P.O. Box 55727 · Birmingham, AL 35255-5727 · 205-930-5100

Douglas L. McWhorter · Dominick, Fletcher, Yeilding, Wood & Lloyd · http://www.dfy.com · 2121 Highland Avenue South · P.O. Box 1387 · Birmingham, AL 35201 · 205-939-0033

Joel A. Mendler · ㉕ · Sirote & Permutt · 2311 Highland Avenue South · P.O. Box 55727 · Birmingham, AL 35255-5727 · 205-930-5100

Anne W. Mitchell · ⑩ · Baker, Donelson, Bearman, Caldwell & Berkowitz · http://www.bakerdonelson.com · Wachovia Tower, Suite 1600 · 420 Twentieth Street North · Birmingham, AL 35203 · 205-328-0480

J. Sanford Mullins III · Sirote & Permutt · 2311 Highland Avenue South · P.O. Box 55727 · Birmingham, AL 35255-5727 · 205-930-5100

Howard W. Neiswender · Balch & Bingham · http://www.balch.com · 1901 Sixth Avenue North, Suite 1500 · Birmingham, AL 35203-4644 · 205-251-8100

Jackson M. Payne · Leitman, Siegal & Payne · The Land Title Building, Suite 400 · 600 North 20th Street · Birmingham, AL 35203 · 205-251-5900

Bruce A. Rawls · Burr & Forman · http://www.burr.com · 420 North 20th Street, Suite 3400 · Birmingham, AL 35203-3284 · 205-251-3000

J. William Rose, Jr. · Johnston Barton Proctor & Rose · Colonial Brookwood Center, Suite 901 · 569 Brookwood Village · Birmingham, AL 35209 · 205-458-9400

Kirby Sevier · ⑳ · Maynard Cooper & Gale · http://www.maynardcooper.com · Regions/Harbert Plaza, Suite 2400 · 1901 Sixth Avenue North · Birmingham, AL 35203-2602 · 205-254-1000

Dale B. Stone · ⑩ · Feld, Hyde, Wertheimer, Bryant & Stone · http://www.feldhyde.com · 2000 SouthBridge Parkway, Suite 500 · Birmingham, AL 35209 · 205-802-7575

M. Allison Taylor · Maynard Cooper & Gale · http://www.maynardcooper.com · Regions/Harbert Plaza, Suite 2400 · 1901 Sixth Avenue North · Birmingham, AL 35203-2602 · 205-254-1000

Judith F. Todd · ⑩ · Sirote & Permutt · 2311 Highland Avenue South · P.O. Box 55727 · Birmingham, AL 35255-5727 · 205-930-5100

Leonard Wertheimer III · ⑳ · Feld, Hyde, Wertheimer, Bryant & Stone · http://www.feldhyde.com · 2000 SouthBridge Parkway, Suite 500 · Birmingham, AL 35209 · 205-802-7575

Brian T. Williams · Dominick, Fletcher, Yeilding, Wood & Lloyd · http://www.dfy.com · 2121 Highland Avenue South · P.O. Box 1387 · Birmingham, AL 35201 · 205-939-0033

Ralph H. Yeilding · ⑩ · Bradley Arant Rose & White · http://www.bradleyarant.com · One Federal Place · 1819 Fifth Avenue North · Birmingham, AL 35203-2119 · 205-521-8000

Foley

Gregory L. Leatherbury, Jr. · ㉕ · Hand Arendall · http://www.handarendall.com · 112 West Laurel Avenue · Foley, AL 36535 · 251-970-5511

Huntsville

Scott E. Ludwig · ⑩ · Bradley Arant Rose & White · http://www.bradleyarant.com · 200 Clinton Avenue West, Suite 900 · Huntsville, AL 35801-4900 · 256-517-5100

S. Dagnal Rowe · Wilmer & Lee · 100 Washington Street, Suite 200 · P.O. Box 2168 · Huntsville, AL 35804 · 256-533-0202

Mobile

G. Porter Brock, Jr. · ⑳ · Hand Arendall · http://www.handarendall.com · RSA Tower, Suite 30200 · 11 North Water Street · Mobile, AL 36602 · 251-432-5511

Harwell E. Coale, Jr. · Coale, Dukes, Kirkpatrick & Crowley · 2610-B Dauphin Street, Suite 101 · Mobile, AL 36606 · 251-471-2625

John J. Crowley, Jr. · Coale, Dukes, Kirkpatrick & Crowley · 2610-B Dauphin Street, Suite 101 · Mobile, AL 36606 · 251-471-2625

J. Michael Druhan, Jr. · Johnston Druhan · Bayport Building, Suite 201 · Five Dauphin Street · P.O. Box 154 · Mobile, AL 36601 · 251-432-0738

Thomas F. Garth · ⑩ · Lyons, Pipes & Cook · Two North Royal Street · P.O. Box 2727 · Mobile, AL 36652-2727 · 251-432-4481

Duane A. Graham · Armbrecht Jackson · Riverview Plaza, 13th Floor · 63 South Royal Street · P.O. Box 290 · Mobile, AL 36601-0290 · 251-405-1300

Lyman F. Holland, Jr. · ⑳ · Hand Arendall · http://www.handarendall.com · RSA Tower, Suite 30200 · 11 North Water Street · Mobile, AL 36602 · 251-432-5511

Zebulon Montgomery Pike Inge, Jr. · ⑩ · Vickers, Riis, Murray and Curran · Regions Bank Building, 11th Floor · 106 St. Francis Street · P.O. Drawer 2568 · Mobile, AL 36652 · 251-432-9772

Vivian G. Johnston, Jr. · ㉕ · Hand Arendall · http://www.handarendall.com · RSA Tower, Suite 30200 · 11 North Water Street · Mobile, AL 36602 · 251-432-5511

Shirley M. Justice · ⑩ · Sirote & Permutt · One St. Louis Centre, Suite 1000 · P.O. Drawer 2025 · Mobile, AL 36602 · 251-432-1671

Robert H. Rouse · Helmsing, Leach, Herlong, Newman & Rouse · http://www.helmsinglaw.com · The LaClede Building, Suite 2000 · 150 Government Street · P.O. Box 2767 · Mobile, AL 36652 · 251-432-5521

R. Gregory Watts · ⑩ · Johnstone, Adams, Bailey, Gordon & Harris · http://www.johnstoneadams.com · One St. Louis Centre, Suite 4000 · One Saint Louis Street · P.O. Box 1988 · Mobile, AL 36633-1988 · 251-432-7682

Montgomery

Gerald W. Hartley · ⑳ · Hartley & Hartley · 8650 Minnie Brown Road, Suite 124 · Montgomery, AL 36117-7433 · 334-481-6904

D. Kyle Johnson · ⑩ · Capell & Howard · http://www.capellhoward.com · 150 South Perry Street · P.O. Box 2069 · Montgomery, AL 36102-2069 · 334-241-8000

Christopher S. Simmons · ⑩ · Rushton, Stakely, Johnston & Garrett · http://www.rsjg.com · 184 Commerce Street · P.O. Box 270 · Montgomery, AL 36101-0270 · 334-206-3100

Debra D. Spain · ⑩ · Capell & Howard · http://www.capellhoward.com · 150 South Perry Street · P.O. Box 2069 · Montgomery, AL 36102-2069 · 334-241-8000

W. Holt Speir III · ⑩ · Capell & Howard · http://www.capellhoward.com · 150 South Perry Street · P.O. Box 2069 · Montgomery, AL 36102-2069 · 334-241-8000

Helen Crump Wells · ⑩ · Rushton, Stakely, Johnston & Garrett · http://www.rsjg.com · 184 Commerce Street · P.O. Box 270 · Montgomery, AL 36101-0270 · 334-206-3100

VENTURE CAPITAL LAW

Birmingham

James W. Childs, Jr. · Bradley Arant Rose & White · http://www.bradleyarant.com · One Federal Place · 1819 Fifth Avenue North · Birmingham, AL 35203-2119 · 205-521-8000

Gregory S. Curran · Maynard Cooper & Gale · http://www.maynardcooper.com · Regions/Harbert Plaza, Suite 2400 · 1901 Sixth Avenue North · Birmingham, AL 35203-2602 · 205-254-1000

Thomas O. Kolb · Baker, Donelson, Bearman, Caldwell & Berkowitz · http://www.bakerdonelson.com · Wachovia Tower, Suite 1600 · 420 Twentieth Street North · Birmingham, AL 35203 · 205-328-0480

B. G. Minisman, Jr. · ⑩ · Baker, Donelson, Bearman, Caldwell & Berkowitz · http://www.bakerdonelson.com · Wachovia Tower, Suite 1600 · 420 Twentieth Street North · Birmingham, AL 35203 · 205-328-0480

WATER LAW

Birmingham

William S. Cox III · Lightfoot, Franklin & White · The Clark Building · 400 Twentieth Street North · Birmingham, AL 35203 · 205-581-0700

Mobile

Neil C. Johnston · ⑩ · Hand Arendall · http://www.handarendall.com · RSA Tower, Suite 30200 · 11 North Water Street · Mobile, AL 36602 · 251-432-5511

WHITE-COLLAR CRIMINAL DEFENSE

Birmingham

William N. Clark · ⑩ · Redden, Mills & Clark · Financial Center, Suite 940 · 505 Twentieth Street North Birmingham, AL 35203 · 205-322-0457

Richard S. Jaffe · Jaffe, Strickland, Drennan & Dodd · http://www.rjaffelaw.com · The Alexander House · 2320 Arlington Avenue · Birmingham, AL 35205-4112 · 205-930-9800

Anthony A. Joseph · Maynard Cooper & Gale · http://www.maynardcooper.com · Regions/Harbert Plaza, Suite 2400 · 1901 Sixth Avenue North · Birmingham, AL 35203-2602 · 205-254-1000

John Lentine · Sheffield, Sheffield & Lentine, P.C. · 205 Twentieth Street North, Suite 323 · Birmingham, AL 35203-4705 · 205-328-1365

Joseph B. Mays, Jr. · (10) · Bradley Arant Rose & White · http://www.bradleyarant.com · One Federal Place · 1819 Fifth Avenue North · Birmingham, AL 35203-2119 · 205-521-8000

Robert J. McLean · Robert J. McLean · 1330 Twenty-First Way South · P.O. Box 430024 · Birmingham, AL 35243-1024 · 205-933-1250

Maxwell H. Pulliam · Christian & Small · http://www.csattorneys.com · 505 North 20th Street, Suite 1800 Birmingham, AL 35203-2696 · 205-795-6588

Jack W. Selden · Bradley Arant Rose & White · http://www.bradleyarant.com · One Federal Place · 1819 Fifth Avenue North · Birmingham, AL 35203-2119 · 205-521-8000

Thomas J. Spina · Fawal & Spina · 1330 Twenty-First Way South, Suite 200 · Birmingham, AL 35205 · 205-939-1330

James R. Sturdivant · Sirote & Permutt · 2311 Highland Avenue South · P.O. Box 55727 · Birmingham, AL 35255-5727 · 205-930-5100

Glennon F. Threatt, Jr. · Threatt & Blocton · Two 20th Street North, Suite 920 · Birmingham, AL 35203-4007 · 205-251-8747

J. Mark White · (10) · White Arnold & Dowd · 2025 Third Avenue North, Suite 500 · Birmingham, AL 35203 · 205-323-1888

Huntsville

Bruce Alan Gardner · Bruce A. Gardner · 125 Holmes Avenue · P.O. Box 18636 · Huntsville, AL 35804-8636 · 256-533-5756

Mobile

T. Jefferson Deen III · (10) · Deen Law · 207 Church Street · P.O. Box 2705 · Mobile, AL 36652 · 251-433-5860

Frederick G. Helmsing · (10) · Helmsing, Leach, Herlong, Newman & Rouse · http://www.helmsinglaw.com · The LaClede Building, Suite 2000 · 150 Government Street · P.O. Box 2767 · Mobile, AL 36652 · 251-432-5521

Kenneth A. Nixon · Lyons, Pipes & Cook · Two North Royal Street · P.O. Box 2727 · Mobile, AL 36652-2727 · 251-432-4481

Montgomery

George L. Beck, Jr. · (20) · Capell & Howard · http://www.capellhoward.com · 150 South Perry Street · P.O. Box 2069 · Montgomery, AL 36102-2069 · 334-241-8000

Ronald W. Wise · (10) · Ronald W. Wise · 2000 Interstate Park Drive, Suite 105 · Montgomery, AL 36109 · 334-260-0003

Vestavia Hills

Ronald Ray Brunson · Ronald Ray Brunson · 4379 Boulder Lake Circle · Vestavia Hills, AL 35242-7499 · 205-967-6242

WORKERS' COMPENSATION LAW

Birmingham

Stephen E. Brown · ⑩ · Maynard Cooper & Gale · http://www.maynardcooper.com · Regions/Harbert Plaza, Suite 2400 · 1901 Sixth Avenue North · Birmingham, AL 35203-2602 · 205-254-1000

Charles F. Carr · ⑩ · Carr, Allison, Pugh, Howard, Oliver & Sisson · 100 Vestavia Parkway · Birmingham, AL 35216 · 205-822-2006

John S. Civils · ⑩ · Huie, Fernambucq & Stewart · Building Three, Suite 200 · 2801 Highway 280 South · Birmingham, AL 35223-2484 · 205-251-1193

Charles H. Clark, Jr. · ⑩ · Huie, Fernambucq & Stewart · Building Three, Suite 200 · 2801 Highway 280 South · Birmingham, AL 35223-2484 · 205-251-1193

John J. Coleman III · ⑩ · Burr & Forman · http://www.burr.com · 420 North 20th Street, Suite 3400 · Birmingham, AL 35203-3284 · 205-251-3000

William Anthony Davis III · ⑩ · Starnes & Atchison · 100 Brookwood Place, Seventh Floor · P.O. Box 598512 · Birmingham, AL 35259-8512 · 205-868-6000

Anthony N. Fox · Scott, Sullivan, Streetman & Fox · 2450 Valleydale Road · P.O. Box 380548 · Birmingham, AL 35244 · 205-967-9675

Patricia G. Fraley · ⑩ · Patricia Guthrie Fraley · P.O. Box 530124 · Birmingham, AL 35253-0124 · 205-871-3496

Sydney F. Frazier, Jr. · ⑩ · Cabaniss, Johnston, Gardner, Dumas & O'Neal · http://www.cabaniss.com · 2001 Park Place North, Suite 700 · P.O. Box 830612 · Birmingham, AL 35283-0612 · 205-716-5200

Robert W. Lee, Jr. · ⑩ · Robert W. Lee & Associates · Two North 20th Street, Suite 1350 · Birmingham, AL 35203 · 205-323-1061

James N. Nolan · ⑩ · Constangy, Brooks & Smith · http://www.constangy.com · One Federal Place, Suite 900 · 1819 Fifth Avenue North · Birmingham, AL 35203-2618 · 205-252-9321

Thomas L. Oliver II · Carr, Allison, Pugh, Howard, Oliver & Sisson · 100 Vestavia Parkway · Birmingham, AL 35216 · 205-822-2006

Linda W. Pope · Wainwright, Pope & McMeekin · Two Metroplex Drive, Suite 305 · Birmingham, AL 35209 · 205-802-7455

Bennett L. Pugh · Carr, Allison, Pugh, Howard, Oliver & Sisson · 100 Vestavia Parkway · Birmingham, AL 35216 · 205-822-2006

Thomas S. Spires · ⑩ · Smith, Spires & Peddy · 2015 Second Avenue North, Suite 200 · Birmingham, AL 35203 · 205-251-5885

Jay D. St. Clair · ⑩ · Littler Mendelson · Wachovia Tower, Suite 2730 · 420 Twentieth Street North · Birmingham, AL 35203 · 205-421-4700

John F. Whitaker · ⑩ · Whitaker, Mudd, Simms, Luke & Wells · http://www.wmslawfirm.com · 2001 Park Place, Suite 400 · Birmingham, AL 35203-2798 · 205-639-5300

Gadsden

Gina D. Coggin · Rhea Boyd Rhea & Coggin · 930 Forrest Avenue · P.O. Box 8486 · Gadsden, AL 35901-3623 · 256-547-6801

Donald R. Rhea · ⑩ · Rhea Boyd Rhea & Coggin · 930 Forrest Avenue · P.O. Box 8486 · Gadsden, AL 35901-3623 · 256-547-6801

Huntsville

Frederick L. Fohrell · Wilmer & Lee · 100 Washington Street, Suite 200 · P.O. Box 2168 · Huntsville, AL 35804 · 256-533-0202

Ralph W. Hornsby, Sr. · Hornsby, Watson, Hornsby, Blackwell & McKown · 1110 Gleneagles Drive · Huntsville, AL 35801 · 256-650-5500

Thomas H. Siniard · ⑩ · Siniard, Timberlake & League · 125 Holmes Avenue · Huntsville, AL 35801 · 256-536-0770

R. Wayne Wolfe · ⑩ · Wolfe, Jones & Boswell · 905 Bob Wallace Avenue, Suite 100 · Huntsville, AL 35801 · 256-534-2205

Mobile

Grover E. Asmus · ⑩ · Asmus & Gaddy · 107 St. Francis Street, Suite 1500 · P.O. Box 553 · Mobile, AL 36601 · 251-439-7600

Douglas L. Brown · ⑩ · Brady Radcliff & Brown · 1600 Wachovia Bank Building · 61 Saint Joseph Street · P.O. Box 1668 · Mobile, AL 36633 · 251-405-0077

Scott G. Brown · Armbrecht Jackson · Riverview Plaza, 13th Floor · 63 South Royal Street · P.O. Box 290 Mobile, AL 36601-0290 · 251-405-1300

Richard E. Browning · ⑩ · Richard E. Browning · 3800 Airport Boulevard, Suite 202 · P.O. Box 160284 · Mobile, AL 36616 · 251-304-0909

Celia Josephine Collins · Johnstone, Adams, Bailey, Gordon & Harris · http://www.johnstoneadams.com · One St. Louis Centre, Suite 4000 · One Saint Louis Street · P.O. Box 1988 · Mobile, AL 36633-1988 · 251-432-7682

Richard W. Franklin · Armbrecht Jackson · Riverview Plaza, 13th Floor · 63 South Royal Street · P.O. Box 290 · Mobile, AL 36601-0290 · 251-405-1300

P. Vincent Gaddy · Asmus & Gaddy · 107 St. Francis Street, Suite 1500 · P.O. Box 553 · Mobile, AL 36601 · 251-439-7600

Ben H. Harris, Jr. · Johnstone, Adams, Bailey, Gordon & Harris · http://www.johnstoneadams.com · One St. Louis Centre, Suite 4000 · One Saint Louis Street · P.O. Box 1988 · Mobile, AL 36633-1988 · 251-432-7682

Michael G. Huey · ⑩ · Huey Law Firm · 1059 Dauphin Street · P.O. Drawer 1806 · Mobile, AL 36633-1806 · 251-433-6622

John F. Janecky · Johnstone, Adams, Bailey, Gordon & Harris · http://www.johnstoneadams.com · One St. Louis Centre, Suite 4000 · One Saint Louis Street · P.O. Box 1988 · Mobile, AL 36633-1988 · 251-432-7682

Frank E. Leon · ⑩ · Frank Leon · 2500 Dauphin Street · Mobile, AL 36606 · 251-445-4400

James P. Meador · Legg & Meador · 202 South Royal Street · Mobile, AL 36602-3008 · 251-706-1001

R. Boyd Miller · ⑩ · Cabaniss, Johnston, Gardner, Dumas & O'Neal · http://www.cabaniss.com · 63 South Royal Street, Suite 700 · P.O. Box 2906 · Mobile, AL 36652-2906 · 251-415-7300

William E. Pipkin, Jr. · Austill Lewis Simms Pipkin & Moore · Commerce Building, Suite 508 · 118 North Royal Street · P.O. Box 2885 · Mobile, AL 36652-2885 · 251-431-9006

Sandy G. Robinson · ⑩ · Cabaniss, Johnston, Gardner, Dumas & O'Neal · http://www.cabaniss.com · 63 South Royal Street, Suite 700 · P.O. Box 2906 · Mobile, AL 36652-2906 · 251-415-7300

Ian D. Rosenthal · Cabaniss, Johnston, Gardner, Dumas & O'Neal · http://www.cabaniss.com · 63 South Royal Street, Suite 700 · P.O. Box 2906 · Mobile, AL 36652-2906 · 251-415-7300

Tracy P. Turner · Johnstone, Adams, Bailey, Gordon & Harris · http://www.johnstoneadams.com · One St. Louis Centre, Suite 4000 · One Saint Louis Street · P.O. Box 1988 · Mobile, AL 36633-1988 · 251-432-7682

Jay A. York · ⑩ · York & Legg · 3290 Dauphin Street, Suite 200 · P.O. Box 16207 · Mobile, AL 36616 · 251-471-3377

Montgomery

William P. Cobb II · ⑩ · Balch & Bingham · http://www.balch.com · 105 Tallapoosa Street, Suite 200 · P.O. Box 78 · Montgomery, AL 36101-0078 · 334-834-6500

Michael M. Eley · ⑩ · Webb & Eley · 7475 Halcion Pointe Drive · P.O. Box 240909 · Montgomery, AL 36124 · 334-262-1850

Talladega

Charles P. Gaines · ⑩ · Gaines, Gaines & Rasco · 127 North Street · P.O. Box 275 · Talladega, AL 35160 256-362-2386

Tuscaloosa

Steven W. Ford · ⑩ · Ford & Abernathy · 621 Greensboro Avenue · P.O. Box 20263 · Tuscaloosa, AL 35402 · 205-349-2000

ALASKA

ADMINISTRATIVE LAW

Anchorage

Julian L. Mason III · ⑳ · Ashburn & Mason · 1227 West Ninth Avenue, Suite 200 · Anchorage, AK 99501-5914 · 907-276-4331

ALTERNATIVE DISPUTE RESOLUTION

Anchorage

Elaine M. Andrews · Andrews Resolution Services · 2131 Belair Drive · Anchorage, AK 99517-1345 · 907-222-7648

William M. Bankston · ⑩ · Bankston, Gronning, O'Hara, Sedor, Givens & Heaphey · 601 West Fifth Avenue, Suite 900 · Anchorage, AK 99501 · 907-276-1711

Glenn E. Cravez · Law Office of Glenn E. Cravez · 421 W First Avenue, Suite 250 · Anchorage, AK 99501 · 907-276-3370

Paul L. Davis · K&L Gates · 420 L Street, Suite 400 · Anchorage, AK 99501-1971 · 907-276-1969

Jeffrey M. Feldman · ⑩ · Feldman, Orlansky & Sanders · 500 L Street, Suite 400 · Anchorage, AK 99501 907-272-3538

Bruce E. Gagnon · ㉕ · Atkinson, Conway & Gagnon · 420 L Street, Suite 500 · Anchorage, AK 99501-1989 · 907-276-1700

Parry E. Grover · ⑳ · Davis Wright Tremaine · 701 West Eighth Avenue, Suite 800 · Anchorage, AK 99501-3468 · 907-257-5300

Roger F. Holmes · ⑳ · Biss & Holmes · 3948 Clay Products Drive · Anchorage, AK 99517-1014 · 907-248-8013

Thomas P. Owens, Jr. · ㉕ · Thomas P. Owens, Jr. · 3705 Arctic Boulevard, Suite 2717 · Anchorage, AK 99503-5774 · 907-274-6883

Nelson G. Page · Burr, Pease & Kurtz · 810 N Street, Suite 300 · Anchorage, AK 99501-3293 · 907-276-6100

David B. Ruskin · David B. Ruskin · 601 West Fifth Avenue, Suite 700 · Anchorage, AK 99501-5901 · 907-277-1711

Eric T. Sanders · Feldman, Orlansky & Sanders · 500 L Street, Suite 400 · Anchorage, AK 99501 · 907-272-3538

Douglas J. Serdahely · Patton Boggs · 601 West Fifth Avenue, Suite 700 · Anchorage, AK 99501 · 907-263-6300

John A. Treptow · ⑩ · Dorsey & Whitney · 1031 West Fourth Avenue, Suite 600 · Anchorage, AK 99501-5907 · 907-276-4557

APPELLATE LAW

Anchorage

Valerie L. Brown · Law Office of Valerie L. Brown · P.O. Box 91659 · Anchorage, AK 99509 · 907-272-4544

Jeffrey M. Feldman · ⑩ · Feldman, Orlansky & Sanders · 500 L Street, Suite 400 · Anchorage, AK 99501 907-272-3538

Patrick B. Gilmore · Atkinson, Conway & Gagnon · 420 L Street, Suite 500 · Anchorage, AK 99501-1989 907-276-1700

Susan Orlansky · Feldman, Orlansky & Sanders · 500 L Street, Suite 400 · Anchorage, AK 99501 · 907-272-3538

BANKRUPTCY AND CREDITOR-DEBTOR RIGHTS LAW

Anchorage

Michelle L. Boutin · Jermain, Dunnagan & Owens · 3000 A Street, Suite 300 · Anchorage, AK 99503 · 907-563-8844

David H. Bundy · ⑩ · David H. Bundy · 3201 C Street, Suite 301 · Anchorage, AK 99503 · 907-248-8431

Cabot Christianson · 10 · Christianson & Spraker · 911 West Eighth Avenue, Suite 302 · Anchorage, AK 99501 · 907-258-6016

Patrick B. Gilmore · Atkinson, Conway & Gagnon · 420 L Street, Suite 500 · Anchorage, AK 99501-1989 907-276-1700

Michael R. Mills · Dorsey & Whitney · 1031 West Fourth Avenue, Suite 600 · Anchorage, AK 99501-5907 907-276-4557

Frederick J. Odsen · 10 · Hughes Pfiffner Gorski Seedorf & Odsen · http://www.hpglaw.net · 3900 C Street, Suite 1001 · Anchorage, AK 99503-5931 · 907-274-7522

David W. Oesting · 25 · Davis Wright Tremaine · 701 West Eighth Avenue, Suite 800 · Anchorage, AK 99501-3468 · 907-257-5300

John C. Siemers · 10 · Burr, Pease & Kurtz · 810 N Street, Suite 300 · Anchorage, AK 99501-3293 · 907-276-6100

Spencer C. Sneed · 10 · Dorsey & Whitney · 1031 West Fourth Avenue, Suite 600 · Anchorage, AK 99501-5907 · 907-276-4557

Gary A. Spraker · Christianson & Spraker · 911 West Eighth Avenue, Suite 302 · Anchorage, AK 99501 · 907-258-6016

Diane F. Vallentine · Jermain, Dunnagan & Owens · 3000 A Street, Suite 300 · Anchorage, AK 99503 · 907-563-8844

Fairbanks

James D. DeWitt · 20 · Guess & Rudd · Key Bank Building, Suite 500 · 100 Cushman Street · Fairbanks, AK 99701 · 907-452-8986

COMMERCIAL LITIGATION

Anchorage

Mark E. Ashburn · 10 · Ashburn & Mason · 1227 West Ninth Avenue, Suite 200 · Anchorage, AK 99501-5914 · 907-276-4331

William M. Bankston · 10 · Bankston, Gronning, O'Hara, Sedor, Givens & Heaphey · 601 West Fifth Avenue, Suite 900 · Anchorage, AK 99501 · 907-276-1711

Ronald L. Bliss · 10 · Bliss, Wilkens & Clayton · 500 L Street, Suite 200 · Anchorage, AK 99501-5909 · 907-276-2999

Robert C. Bundy · Dorsey & Whitney · 1031 West Fourth Avenue, Suite 600 · Anchorage, AK 99501-5907 · 907-276-4557

Jon S. Dawson · Davis Wright Tremaine · 701 West Eighth Avenue, Suite 800 · Anchorage, AK 99501-3468 · 907-257-5300

Kenneth P. Eggers · Groh Eggers · 2600 Cordova Street, Suite 110 · Anchorage, AK 99503-3934 · 907-562-6474

Jeffrey M. Feldman · 10 · Feldman, Orlansky & Sanders · 500 L Street, Suite 400 · Anchorage, AK 99501 907-272-3538

Charles P. Flynn · ⑳ · Burr, Pease & Kurtz · 810 N Street, Suite 300 · Anchorage, AK 99501-3293 · 907-276-6100

Bruce E. Gagnon · ㉕ · Atkinson, Conway & Gagnon · 420 L Street, Suite 500 · Anchorage, AK 99501-1989 · 907-276-1700

Michael C. Geraghty · DeLisio, Moran, Geraghty & Zobel · 943 West Sixth Avenue · Anchorage, AK 99501-2033 · 907-279-9574

Patrick B. Gilmore · Atkinson, Conway & Gagnon · 420 L Street, Suite 500 · Anchorage, AK 99501-1989 907-276-1700

Andrew Guidi · Delaney Wiles · 1007 West Third Avenue, Suite 400 · Anchorage, AK 99501-1990 · 907-279-3581

James N. Leik · Perkins Coie · http://www.perkinscoie.com · 1029 West Third Avenue, Suite 300 · Anchorage, AK 99501-1981 · 907-279-8561

Peter Maassen · Ingaldson, Maassen & Fitzgerald · 813 West Third Avenue · Anchorage, AK 99501 · 907-258-8750

Julian L. Mason III · ⑳ · Ashburn & Mason · 1227 West Ninth Avenue, Suite 200 · Anchorage, AK 99501-5914 · 907-276-4331

David W. Oesting · ㉕ · Davis Wright Tremaine · 701 West Eighth Avenue, Suite 800 · Anchorage, AK 99501-3468 · 907-257-5300

Susan Orlansky · Feldman, Orlansky & Sanders · 500 L Street, Suite 400 · Anchorage, AK 99501 · 907-272-3538

Nelson G. Page · Burr, Pease & Kurtz · 810 N Street, Suite 300 · Anchorage, AK 99501-3293 · 907-276-6100

Timothy J. Petumenos · Birch, Horton, Bittner & Cherot · 1127 West Seventh Avenue · Anchorage, AK 99501 · 907-276-1550

Frank A. Pfiffner · Hughes Pfiffner Gorski Seedorf & Odsen · http://www.hpglaw.net · 3900 C Street, Suite 1001 · Anchorage, AK 99503-5931 · 907-274-7522

Eric T. Sanders · Feldman, Orlansky & Sanders · 500 L Street, Suite 400 · Anchorage, AK 99501 · 907-272-3538

Douglas J. Serdahely · Patton Boggs · 601 West Fifth Avenue, Suite 700 · Anchorage, AK 99501 · 907-263-6300

John A. Treptow · ⑩ · Dorsey & Whitney · 1031 West Fourth Avenue, Suite 600 · Anchorage, AK 99501-5907 · 907-276-4557

Howard S. Trickey · Jermain, Dunnagan & Owens · 3000 A Street, Suite 300 · Anchorage, AK 99503 · 907-563-8844

Terrance A. Turner · ⑩ · Turner & Mede · 1500 West 33rd Avenue, Suite 200 · Anchorage, AK 99503-3502 · 907-276-3963

Diane F. Vallentine · Jermain, Dunnagan & Owens · 3000 A Street, Suite 300 · Anchorage, AK 99503 · 907-563-8844

William B. Rozell · ⑳ · William B. Rozell · 2575-1 Douglas Highway · P.O. Box 20730 · Juneau, AK 99802 · 907-586-0142

CONSTRUCTION LAW

Anchorage

William M. Bankston · ⑩ · Bankston, Gronning, O'Hara, Sedor, Givens & Heaphey · 601 West Fifth Avenue, Suite 900 · Anchorage, AK 99501 · 907-276-1711

David M. Freeman · Holmes Weddle & Barcott · 701 West Eighth Avenue, Suite 700 · Anchorage, AK 99501-3408 · 907-274-0666

Michael C. Geraghty · DeLisio, Moran, Geraghty & Zobel · 943 West Sixth Avenue · Anchorage, AK 99501-2033 · 907-279-9574

Traeger Machetanz · Oles Morrison Rinker & Baker · 745 West Fourth Avenue, Suite 502 · Anchorage, AK 99501 · 907-258-0106

Frank A. Pfiffner · Hughes Pfiffner Gorski Seedorf & Odsen · http://www.hpglaw.net · 3900 C Street, Suite 1001 · Anchorage, AK 99503-5931 · 907-274-7522

Raymond H. Royce III · Law Offices of Royce & Brain · 1407 West 31st Avenue, Seventh Floor · Anchorage, AK 99503-3678 · 907-258-6792

W. Michael Stephenson · Jermain, Dunnagan & Owens · 3000 A Street, Suite 300 · Anchorage, AK 99503 · 907-563-8844

CORPORATE LAW

Anchorage

William M. Bankston · ⑩ · Bankston, Gronning, O'Hara, Sedor, Givens & Heaphey · 601 West Fifth Avenue, Suite 900 · Anchorage, AK 99501 · 907-276-1711

Kathryn A. Black · Birch, Horton, Bittner & Cherot · 1127 West Seventh Avenue · Anchorage, AK 99501 907-276-1550

Philip Blumstein · Landye Bennett Blumstein · 701 West Eighth Avenue, Suite 1200 · Anchorage, AK 99501 · 907-276-5152

Jon S. Dawson · Davis Wright Tremaine · 701 West Eighth Avenue, Suite 800 · Anchorage, AK 99501-3468 · 907-257-5300

Brian W. Durrell · Durrell Law Group · 1400 West Benson Boulevard, Suite 370 · Anchorage, AK 99503 · 907-258-3224

Bruce E. Gagnon · ㉕ · Atkinson, Conway & Gagnon · 420 L Street, Suite 500 · Anchorage, AK 99501-1989 · 907-276-1700

Andrew E. Hoge · ⑳ · Hartig Rhodes Hoge & Lekisch · 717 K Street · Anchorage, AK 99501 · 907-276-1592

Chris Foote Hyatt · Hartig Rhodes Hoge & Lekisch · 717 K Street · Anchorage, AK 99501 · 907-276-1592

Jerome H. Juday · Atkinson, Conway & Gagnon · 420 L Street, Suite 500 · Anchorage, AK 99501-1989 · 907-276-1700

Barbara Simpson Kraft · Davis Wright Tremaine · 701 West Eighth Avenue, Suite 800 · Anchorage, AK 99501-3468 · 907-257-5300

Julian L. Mason III · ⑳ · Ashburn & Mason · 1227 West Ninth Avenue, Suite 200 · Anchorage, AK 99501-5914 · 907-276-4331

Joseph M. Moran · DeLisio, Moran, Geraghty & Zobel · 943 West Sixth Avenue · Anchorage, AK 99501-2033 · 907-279-9574

Steven T. O'Hara · ⑩ · Bankston, Gronning, O'Hara, Sedor, Givens & Heaphey · 601 West Fifth Avenue, Suite 900 · Anchorage, AK 99501 · 907-276-1711

Joseph Reece · Davis Wright Tremaine · 701 West Eighth Avenue, Suite 800 · Anchorage, AK 99501-3468 · 907-257-5300

Richard M. Rosston · Dorsey & Whitney · 1031 West Fourth Avenue, Suite 600 · Anchorage, AK 99501-5907 · 907-276-4557

Jane Sauer · Manley & Brautigam · 845 K Street · Anchorage, AK 99501 · 907-334-5600

Terrance A. Turner · ⑩ · Turner & Mede · 1500 West 33rd Avenue, Suite 200 · Anchorage, AK 99503-3502 · 907-276-3963

EMINENT DOMAIN AND CONDEMNATION LAW

Anchorage

Donald W. McClintock III · Ashburn & Mason · 1227 West Ninth Avenue, Suite 200 · Anchorage, AK 99501-5914 · 907-276-4331

Steven S. Tervooren · Hughes Pfiffner Gorski Seedorf & Odsen · http://www.hpglaw.net · 3900 C Street, Suite 1001 · Anchorage, AK 99503-5931 · 907-274-7522

EMPLOYEE BENEFITS LAW

Anchorage

Randall G. Simpson · Jermain, Dunnagan & Owens · 3000 A Street, Suite 300 · Anchorage, AK 99503 · 907-563-8844

ENERGY LAW

Anchorage

Andrew E. Hoge · ⑳ · Hartig Rhodes Hoge & Lekisch · 717 K Street · Anchorage, AK 99501 · 907-276-1592

Julian L. Mason III · ⑳ · Ashburn & Mason · 1227 West Ninth Avenue, Suite 200 · Anchorage, AK 99501-5914 · 907-276-4331

Joseph M. Moran · DeLisio, Moran, Geraghty & Zobel · 943 West Sixth Avenue · Anchorage, AK 99501-2033 · 907-279-9574

A. William Saupe · ⑩ · Ashburn & Mason · 1227 West Ninth Avenue, Suite 200 · Anchorage, AK 99501-5914 · 907-276-4331

Robert E. Stoller · Robert E. Stoller · 800 East Dimond Boulevard, Suite 3-537 · Anchorage, AK 99515-2046 · 907-522-2299

Louis R. Veerman · Guess & Rudd · 510 L Street, Suite 700 · Anchorage, AK 99501 · 907-793-2200

ENVIRONMENTAL LAW

Anchorage

Rebecca Bernard · Trustees for Alaska · 1026 West Fourth Avenue, Suite 201 · Anchorage, AK 99501 · 907-276-4244

Eric B. Fjelstad · Perkins Coie · http://www.perkinscoie.com · 1029 West Third Avenue, Suite 300 · Anchorage, AK 99501-1981 · 907-279-8561

Thomas E. Meacham · ⑳ · Thomas E. Meacham · 9500 Prospect Drive · Anchorage, AK 99516-1062 · 907-346-1077

David W. Oesting · ㉕ · Davis Wright Tremaine · 701 West Eighth Avenue, Suite 800 · Anchorage, AK 99501-3468 · 907-257-5300

Susan E. Reeves · Reeves Amodio · 500 L Street, Suite 300 · Anchorage, AK 99501 · 907-222-7100

Peter Van Tuyn · Bessenyey & Van Tuyn · 310 K Street, Suite 200 · Anchorage, AK 99501 · 907-278-2000

Douglas

Robert K. Reges, Jr. · The Reges Law Firm · 226 St. Ann's Avenue, Suite A · Douglas, AK 99824 · 907-790-2777

Juneau

William B. Rozell · ⑳ · William B. Rozell · 2575-1 Douglas Highway · P.O. Box 20730 · Juneau, AK 99802 · 907-586-0142

FAMILY LAW

Anchorage

Bruce A. Bookman · Bookman & Helm · 471 West 36th Avenue, Suite 204 · Anchorage, AK 99503 · 907-865-0800

Jennifer A. Coughlin · K&L Gates · 420 L Street, Suite 400 · Anchorage, AK 99501-1971 · 907-276-1969

Roberta C. Erwin · Law Office of Joseph P. Palmier · 121 West Fireweed Lane, Suite 208 · Anchorage, AK 99503 · 907-279-8522

Jennifer L. Holland · Law Offices of Jennifer L. Holland · 880 H Street, Suite 201 · Anchorage, AK 99501 · 907-279-9940

Lynda A. Limon · Lynda A. Limon · 606 E Street, Suite 203 · Anchorage, AK 99501 · 907-279-2889

Janet D. Platt · Janet D. Platt · 711 M Street, Suite 101 · Anchorage, AK 99501-3307 · 907-276-1515

R. Scott Taylor · Feldman, Orlansky & Sanders · 500 L Street, Suite 400 · Anchorage, AK 99501 · 907-272-3538

FIRST AMENDMENT LAW

Anchorage

D. John McKay · ⑩ · D. John McKay · 117 East Cook Avenue · Anchorage, AK 99501 · 907-274-3154

GAMING LAW

Anchorage

Dan K. Coffey · Dan K. Coffey · 207 East Northern Lights Boulevard, Suite 200 · Anchorage, AK 99503-2731 · 907-274-3385

Charles A. Dunnagan · ㉕ · Jermain, Dunnagan & Owens · 3000 A Street, Suite 300 · Anchorage, AK 99503 · 907-563-8844

Laurel J. Peterson · Laurel J. Peterson · 805 West Third Avenue, Suite 200 · Anchorage, AK 99501-2001 907-278-1568

HEALTH CARE LAW

Anchorage

Robert J. Dickson · ⑩ · Atkinson, Conway & Gagnon · 420 L Street, Suite 500 · Anchorage, AK 99501-1989 · 907-276-1700

Roger F. Holmes · ⑳ · Biss & Holmes · 3948 Clay Products Drive · Anchorage, AK 99517-1014 · 907-248-8013

John A. Treptow · ⑩ · Dorsey & Whitney · 1031 West Fourth Avenue, Suite 600 · Anchorage, AK 99501-5907 · 907-276-4557

INSURANCE LAW

Anchorage

Kimberlee A. Colbo · Hughes Pfiffner Gorski Seedorf & Odsen · http://www.hpglaw.net · 3900 C Street, Suite 1001 · Anchorage, AK 99503-5931 · 907-274-7522

John A. Treptow · ⑩ · Dorsey & Whitney · 1031 West Fourth Avenue, Suite 600 · Anchorage, AK 99501-5907 · 907-276-4557

Jimmy E. White · Hughes Pfiffner Gorski Seedorf & Odsen · http://www.hpglaw.net · 3900 C Street, Suite 1001 · Anchorage, AK 99503-5931 · 907-274-7522

Gary A. Zipkin · Guess & Rudd · 510 L Street, Suite 700 · Anchorage, AK 99501 · 907-793-2200

INTELLECTUAL PROPERTY LAW

Anchorage

D. John McKay · ⑩ · D. John McKay · 117 East Cook Avenue · Anchorage, AK 99501 · 907-274-3154

LABOR AND EMPLOYMENT LAW

Anchorage

Thomas M. Daniel · ⑩ · Perkins Coie · http://www.perkinscoie.com · 1029 West Third Avenue, Suite 300 Anchorage, AK 99501-1981 · 907-279-8561

Paul L. Davis · K&L Gates · 420 L Street, Suite 400 · Anchorage, AK 99501-1971 · 907-276-1969

Charles A. Dunnagan · ㉕ · Jermain, Dunnagan & Owens · 3000 A Street, Suite 300 · Anchorage, AK 99503 · 907-563-8844

William J. Evans · Dorsey & Whitney · 1031 West Fourth Avenue, Suite 600 · Anchorage, AK 99501-5907 · 907-276-4557

Saul R. Friedman · Jermain, Dunnagan & Owens · 3000 A Street, Suite 300 · Anchorage, AK 99503 · 907-563-8844

Parry E. Grover · ⑳ · Davis Wright Tremaine · 701 West Eighth Avenue, Suite 800 · Anchorage, AK 99501-3468 · 907-257-5300

Lee Holen · ⑩ · Lee Holen · 608 West Fourth Avenue, Suite 21 · Anchorage, AK 99501-2340 · 907-278-0298

William F. Mede · Turner & Mede · 1500 West 33rd Avenue, Suite 200 · Anchorage, AK 99503-3502 · 907-276-3963

Bradley D. Owens · Jermain, Dunnagan & Owens · 3000 A Street, Suite 300 · Anchorage, AK 99503 · 907-563-8844

Thomas P. Owens III · Burr, Pease & Kurtz · 810 N Street, Suite 300 · Anchorage, AK 99501-3293 · 907-276-6100

Thomas P. Owens, Jr. · ㉕ · Thomas P. Owens, Jr. · 3705 Arctic Boulevard, Suite 2717 · Anchorage, AK 99503-5774 · 907-274-6883

Joseph Reece · Davis Wright Tremaine · 701 West Eighth Avenue, Suite 800 · Anchorage, AK 99501-3468 · 907-257-5300

Randall G. Simpson · Jermain, Dunnagan & Owens · 3000 A Street, Suite 300 · Anchorage, AK 99503 · 907-563-8844

John A. Treptow · ⑩ · Dorsey & Whitney · 1031 West Fourth Avenue, Suite 600 · Anchorage, AK 99501-5907 · 907-276-4557

Howard S. Trickey · Jermain, Dunnagan & Owens · 3000 A Street, Suite 300 · Anchorage, AK 99503 · 907-563-8844

Fairbanks

William B. Schendel · ⑳ · Winfree Law Office · 250 Cushman Street, Suite 500 · Fairbanks, AK 99701-4629 · 907-451-6500

LAND USE & ZONING LAW

Anchorage

Louisiana W. Cutler · K&L Gates · 420 L Street, Suite 400 · Anchorage, AK 99501-1971 · 907-276-1969

Gordon J. Tans · Perkins Coie · http://www.perkinscoie.com · 1029 West Third Avenue, Suite 300 · Anchorage, AK 99501-1981 · 907-279-8561

Joan M. Travostino · K&L Gates · 420 L Street, Suite 400 · Anchorage, AK 99501-1971 · 907-276-1969

LEGAL MALPRACTICE LAW

Anchorage

Howard A. Lazar · Delaney, Wiles, Hayes, Gerety, Ellis & Young · 1007 West Third Avenue, Suite 400 · Anchorage, AK 99501 · 907-279-3581

Frank A. Pfiffner · Hughes Pfiffner Gorski Seedorf & Odsen · http://www.hpglaw.net · 3900 C Street, Suite 1001 · Anchorage, AK 99503-5931 · 907-274-7522

MARITIME LAW

Anchorage

Ronald L. Bliss · ⑩ · Bliss, Wilkens & Clayton · 500 L Street, Suite 200 · Anchorage, AK 99501-5909 · 907-276-2999

Douglas R. Davis · Keesal, Young & Logan · 1029 West Third Avenue, Sixth Floor · Anchorage, AK 99501-1954 · 907-279-9696

Herbert H. Ray, Jr. · Keesal, Young & Logan · 1029 West Third Avenue, Sixth Floor · Anchorage, AK 99501-1954 · 907-279-9696

MEDICAL MALPRACTICE LAW

Anchorage

Keith E. Brown · Brown, Waller & Gibbs · 821 North Street, Suite 202 · Anchorage, AK 99501-3285 · 907-276-2050

Timothy Lamb · Delaney, Wiles, Hayes, Gerety, Ellis & Young · 1007 West Third Avenue, Suite 400 · Anchorage, AK 99501 · 907-279-3581

Howard A. Lazar · Delaney, Wiles, Hayes, Gerety, Ellis & Young · 1007 West Third Avenue, Suite 400 · Anchorage, AK 99501 · 907-279-3581

Matthew K. Peterson · Clapp, Peterson , Van Flein, Tiemessen & Thorsness · 711 H Street, Suite 620 · Anchorage, AK 99501-3454 · 907-272-9272

MERGERS & ACQUISITIONS LAW

Anchorage

Kathryn A. Black · Birch, Horton, Bittner & Cherot · 1127 West Seventh Avenue · Anchorage, AK 99501 907-276-1550

Philip Blumstein · Landye Bennett Blumstein · 701 West Eighth Avenue, Suite 1200 · Anchorage, AK 99501 · 907-276-5152

Jon S. Dawson · Davis Wright Tremaine · 701 West Eighth Avenue, Suite 800 · Anchorage, AK 99501-3468 · 907-257-5300

Brian W. Durrell · Durrell Law Group · 1400 West Benson Boulevard, Suite 370 · Anchorage, AK 99503 · 907-258-3224

Chris Foote Hyatt · Hartig Rhodes Hoge & Lekisch · 717 K Street · Anchorage, AK 99501 · 907-276-1592

Barbara Simpson Kraft · Davis Wright Tremaine · 701 West Eighth Avenue, Suite 800 · Anchorage, AK 99501-3468 · 907-257-5300

Richard M. Rosston · Dorsey & Whitney · 1031 West Fourth Avenue, Suite 600 · Anchorage, AK 99501-5907 · 907-276-4557

MINING LAW

Anchorage

Thomas E. Meacham · (20) · Thomas E. Meacham · 9500 Prospect Drive · Anchorage, AK 99516-1062 · 907-346-1077

Joseph J. Perkins, Jr. · (10) · Guess & Rudd · 510 L Street, Suite 700 · Anchorage, AK 99501 · 907-793-2200

MUNICIPAL LAW

Anchorage

Brian Carter Boyd · Boyd, Chandler & Falconer · 911 West Eighth Avenue, Suite 302 · Anchorage, AK 99501 · 907-272-8401

Louisiana W. Cutler · K&L Gates · 420 L Street, Suite 400 · Anchorage, AK 99501-1971 · 907-276-1969

Michael Gatti · Wohlforth, Johnson, Brecht, Cartledge & Brooking · 900 West Fifth Avenue, Suite 600 · Anchorage, AK 99501 · 907-276-6401

Gordon J. Tans · Perkins Coie · http://www.perkinscoie.com · 1029 West Third Avenue, Suite 300 · Anchorage, AK 99501-1981 · 907-279-8561

Joan M. Travostino · K&L Gates · 420 L Street, Suite 400 · Anchorage, AK 99501-1971 · 907-276-1969

William M. Walker · Walker & Levesque · 731 N Street · Anchorage, AK 99501 · 907-278-7000

NATIVE AMERICAN LAW

Anchorage

David S. Case · Landye Bennett Blumstein · 701 West Eighth Avenue, Suite 1200 · Anchorage, AK 99501 · 907-276-5152

Lloyd B. Miller · Sonosky, Chambers, Sachse, Endreson & Perry · 900 West Fifth Avenue, Suite 700 · Anchorage, AK 99501-2029 · 907-258-6377

R. Scott Taylor · Feldman, Orlansky & Sanders · 500 L Street, Suite 400 · Anchorage, AK 99501 · 907-272-3538

Juneau

Myra M. Munson · Sonosky, Chambers, Sachse, Endreson & Perry · 318 Fourth Street · Juneau, AK 99801 · 907-586-5880

NATURAL RESOURCES LAW

Anchorage

Douglas R. Davis · Keesal, Young & Logan · 1029 West Third Avenue, Sixth Floor · Anchorage, AK 99501-1954 · 907-279-9696

Heather H. Grahame · ⑩ · Dorsey & Whitney · 1031 West Fourth Avenue, Suite 600 · Anchorage, AK 99501-5907 · 907-276-4557

F. Stephen Mahoney · Manley & Brautigam · 845 K Street · Anchorage, AK 99501 · 907-334-5600

Thomas E. Meacham · ⑳ · Thomas E. Meacham · 9500 Prospect Drive · Anchorage, AK 99516-1062 · 907-346-1077

Joseph J. Perkins, Jr. · ⑩ · Guess & Rudd · 510 L Street, Suite 700 · Anchorage, AK 99501 · 907-793-2200

Robert E. Stoller · Robert E. Stoller · 800 East Dimond Boulevard, Suite 3-537 · Anchorage, AK 99515-2046 · 907-522-2299

Peter Van Tuyn · Bessenyey & Van Tuyn · 310 K Street, Suite 200 · Anchorage, AK 99501 · 907-278-2000

Juneau

William B. Rozell · ⑳ · William B. Rozell · 2575-1 Douglas Highway · P.O. Box 20730 · Juneau, AK 99802 · 907-586-0142

NON-PROFIT/CHARITIES LAW

Anchorage

F. Stephen Mahoney · Manley & Brautigam · 845 K Street · Anchorage, AK 99501 · 907-334-5600

Steven T. O'Hara · ⑩ · Bankston, Gronning, O'Hara, Sedor, Givens & Heaphey · 601 West Fifth Avenue, Suite 900 · Anchorage, AK 99501 · 907-276-1711

NON-WHITE-COLLAR CRIMINAL DEFENSE

Anchorage

Sidney K. Billingslea · Sidney K. Billingslea · 134 West 15th Avenue · Anchorage, AK 99501 · 907-277-9119

Robert C. Bundy · Dorsey & Whitney · 1031 West Fourth Avenue, Suite 600 · Anchorage, AK 99501-5907 · 907-276-4557

Rex Lamont Butler · Rex Lamont Butler & Associates · 745 West Fourth Avenue · Anchorage, AK 99501-2136 · 907-272-1497

Brian Doherty · Doherty & Menard · Resolution Plaza, Suite 500 · 1029 West Third Avenue · Anchorage, AK 99501-1982 · 907-279-4506

Jeffrey M. Feldman · ⑩ · Feldman, Orlansky & Sanders · 500 L Street, Suite 400 · Anchorage, AK 99501 907-272-3538

Carmen L. Gutierrez · Carmen L. Gutierrez · 510 L Street, Suite 306 · Anchorage, AK 99501-1952 · 907-274-2800

James H. McComas · ⑩ · Friedman, Rubin & White · 1227 West Ninth Avenue, Suite 201 · Anchorage, AK 99501 · 907-258-0704

Amy R. Menard · Doherty & Menard · Resolution Plaza, Suite 500 · 1029 West Third Avenue · Anchorage, AK 99501-1982 · 907-279-4506

John M. Murtagh · John M. Murtagh · 1101 West Seventh Avenue · Anchorage, AK 99501-3301 · 907-274-8664

Christine S. Schleuss · ⑩ · Suddock & Schleuss · 500 L Street, Suite 300 · Anchorage, AK 99501 · 907-258-7807

Cynthia L. Strout · ⑩ · Cynthia L. Strout · 733 West Fourth Avenue, Suite 401 · Anchorage, AK 99501 · 907-276-0377

Phillip Paul Weidner · ⑳ · Phillip Paul Weidner & Associates · 330 L Street, Suite 200 · Anchorage, AK 99501 · 907-277-7000

OIL & GAS LAW

Anchorage

F. Stephen Mahoney · Manley & Brautigam · 845 K Street · Anchorage, AK 99501 · 907-334-5600

Thomas E. Meacham · ⑳ · Thomas E. Meacham · 9500 Prospect Drive · Anchorage, AK 99516-1062 · 907-346-1077

PERSONAL INJURY LITIGATION

Anchorage

Keith E. Brown · Brown, Waller & Gibbs · 821 North Street, Suite 202 · Anchorage, AK 99501-3285 · 907-276-2050

Ray R. Brown · Dillon & Findley · 1049 West Fifth Avenue, Suite 100 · Anchorage, AK 99501 · 907-277-5400

William T. Council · ⑩ · William T. Council · 2295 Arcadia Drive · Anchorage, AK 99517-1341 · 907-222-7929

Jeffrey M. Feldman · ⑩ · Feldman, Orlansky & Sanders · 500 L Street, Suite 400 · Anchorage, AK 99501 907-272-3538

Michael C. Geraghty · DeLisio, Moran, Geraghty & Zobel · 943 West Sixth Avenue · Anchorage, AK 99501-2033 · 907-279-9574

Roger F. Holmes · ⑳ · Biss & Holmes · 3948 Clay Products Drive · Anchorage, AK 99517-1014 · 907-248-8013

Jonathon A. Katcher · Pope & Katcher · 401 West First Avenue, Suite 220 · Anchorage, AK 99501 · 907-272-8577

Timothy Lamb · Delaney, Wiles, Hayes, Gerety, Ellis & Young · 1007 West Third Avenue, Suite 400 · Anchorage, AK 99501 · 907-279-3581

Howard A. Lazar · Delaney, Wiles, Hayes, Gerety, Ellis & Young · 1007 West Third Avenue, Suite 400 · Anchorage, AK 99501 · 907-279-3581

Mauri Long · ⑩ · Dillon & Findley · 1049 West Fifth Avenue, Suite 100 · Anchorage, AK 99501 · 907-277-5400

W. Michael Moody · ⑩ · Atkinson, Conway & Gagnon · 420 L Street, Suite 500 · Anchorage, AK 99501-1989 · 907-276-1700

Matthew K. Peterson · Clapp, Peterson , Van Flein, Tiemessen & Thorsness · 711 H Street, Suite 620 · Anchorage, AK 99501-3454 · 907-272-9272

Douglas Pope · Pope & Katcher · 401 West First Avenue, Suite 220 · Anchorage, AK 99501 · 907-272-8577

Robert L. Richmond · Richmond & Quinn · 360 K Street, Suite 200 · Anchorage, AK 99501-2038 · 907-276-5727

Kenneth S. Roosa · Cooke Roosa · 3700 Jewel Lake Road · Anchorage, AK 99502 · 907-276-2744

Eric T. Sanders · Feldman, Orlansky & Sanders · 500 L Street, Suite 400 · Anchorage, AK 99501 · 907-272-3538

Christine S. Schleuss · ⑩ · Suddock & Schleuss · 500 L Street, Suite 300 · Anchorage, AK 99501 · 907-258-7807

Michael J. Schneider · ⑩ · Law Offices of Michael J. Schneider · 880 N Street, Suite 202 · Anchorage, AK 99501 · 907-277-9306

Randall G. Simpson · Jermain, Dunnagan & Owens · 3000 A Street, Suite 300 · Anchorage, AK 99503 · 907-563-8844

Steven S. Tervooren · Hughes Pfiffner Gorski Seedorf & Odsen · http://www.hpglaw.net · 3900 C Street, Suite 1001 · Anchorage, AK 99503-5931 · 907-274-7522

Howard S. Trickey · Jermain, Dunnagan & Owens · 3000 A Street, Suite 300 · Anchorage, AK 99503 · 907-563-8844

Diane F. Vallentine · Jermain, Dunnagan & Owens · 3000 A Street, Suite 300 · Anchorage, AK 99503 · 907-563-8844

Richard E. Vollertsen · 10 · Atkinson, Conway & Gagnon · 420 L Street, Suite 500 · Anchorage, AK 99501-1989 · 907-276-1700

Juneau

Paul L. Dillon · Dillon & Findley · 350 North Franklin Street · Juneau, AK 99801 · 907-586-4000

Michael L. Lessmeier · Lessmeier & Winters · Vintage Business Park, Suite 100 · 3000 Vintage Boulevard · Juneau, AK 99801 · 907-796-4999

William B. Rozell · 20 · William B. Rozell · 2575-1 Douglas Highway · P.O. Box 20730 · Juneau, AK 99802 · 907-586-0142

PRODUCT LIABILITY LITIGATION

Anchorage

James N. Leik · Perkins Coie · http://www.perkinscoie.com · 1029 West Third Avenue, Suite 300 · Anchorage, AK 99501-1981 · 907-279-8561

W. Michael Moody · 10 · Atkinson, Conway & Gagnon · 420 L Street, Suite 500 · Anchorage, AK 99501-1989 · 907-276-1700

Neil T. O'Donnell · Atkinson, Conway & Gagnon · 420 L Street, Suite 500 · Anchorage, AK 99501-1989 · 907-276-1700

Matthew K. Peterson · Clapp, Peterson , Van Flein, Tiemessen & Thorsness · 711 H Street, Suite 620 · Anchorage, AK 99501-3454 · 907-272-9272

Daniel T. Quinn · Richmond & Quinn · 360 K Street, Suite 200 · Anchorage, AK 99501-2038 · 907-276-5727

Steven S. Tervooren · Hughes Pfiffner Gorski Seedorf & Odsen · http://www.hpglaw.net · 3900 C Street, Suite 1001 · Anchorage, AK 99503-5931 · 907-274-7522

PROFESSIONAL MALPRACTICE LAW

Anchorage

Bruce E. Gagnon · 25 · Atkinson, Conway & Gagnon · 420 L Street, Suite 500 · Anchorage, AK 99501-1989 · 907-276-1700

John A. Treptow · 10 · Dorsey & Whitney · 1031 West Fourth Avenue, Suite 600 · Anchorage, AK 99501-5907 · 907-276-4557

REAL ESTATE LAW

Anchorage

William M. Bankston · 10 · Bankston, Gronning, O'Hara, Sedor, Givens & Heaphey · 601 West Fifth Avenue, Suite 900 · Anchorage, AK 99501 · 907-276-1711

Brian W. Durrell · Durrell Law Group · 1400 West Benson Boulevard, Suite 370 · Anchorage, AK 99503 · 907-258-3224

Bruce E. Gagnon · 25 · Atkinson, Conway & Gagnon · 420 L Street, Suite 500 · Anchorage, AK 99501-1989 · 907-276-1700

Peter C. Ginder · 20 · The Law Offices of Peter C. Ginder · 810 N Street, Suite 201 · Anchorage, AK 99501 · 907-258-6001

Andrew E. Hoge · 20 · Hartig Rhodes Hoge & Lekisch · 717 K Street · Anchorage, AK 99501 · 907-276-1592

Chris Foote Hyatt · Hartig Rhodes Hoge & Lekisch · 717 K Street · Anchorage, AK 99501 · 907-276-1592

Ann C. Liburd · Burr, Pease & Kurtz · 810 N Street, Suite 300 · Anchorage, AK 99501-3293 · 907-276-6100

Donald W. McClintock III · Ashburn & Mason · 1227 West Ninth Avenue, Suite 200 · Anchorage, AK 99501-5914 · 907-276-4331

James H. McCollum · James H. McCollum · 510 L Street, Suite 540 · Anchorage, AK 99501-1959 · 907-770-7773

Frederick J. Odsen · 10 · Hughes Pfiffner Gorski Seedorf & Odsen · http://www.hpglaw.net · 3900 C Street, Suite 1001 · Anchorage, AK 99503-5931 · 907-274-7522

Joseph Reece · Davis Wright Tremaine · 701 West Eighth Avenue, Suite 800 · Anchorage, AK 99501-3468 · 907-257-5300

Richard M. Rosston · Dorsey & Whitney · 1031 West Fourth Avenue, Suite 600 · Anchorage, AK 99501-5907 · 907-276-4557

Gordon F. Schadt · Schadt Law Office · 2909 Arctic Boulevard, Suite 103 · Anchorage, AK 99503-3810 · 907-562-0990

Joan M. Travostino · K&L Gates · 420 L Street, Suite 400 · Anchorage, AK 99501-1971 · 907-276-1969

Terrance A. Turner · 10 · Turner & Mede · 1500 West 33rd Avenue, Suite 200 · Anchorage, AK 99503-3502 · 907-276-3963

SECURITIES LAW

Anchorage

Bruce E. Gagnon · 25 · Atkinson, Conway & Gagnon · 420 L Street, Suite 500 · Anchorage, AK 99501-1989 · 907-276-1700

TAX LAW

Anchorage

Peter B. Brautigam · Manley & Brautigam · 845 K Street · Anchorage, AK 99501 · 907-334-5600

Robert C. Brink · Hartig Rhodes Hoge & Lekisch · 717 K Street · Anchorage, AK 99501 · 907-276-1592

Brian W. Durrell · Durrell Law Group · 1400 West Benson Boulevard, Suite 370 · Anchorage, AK 99503 · 907-258-3224

F. Stephen Mahoney · Manley & Brautigam · 845 K Street · Anchorage, AK 99501 · 907-334-5600

Robert L. Manley · ⑳ · Manley & Brautigam · 845 K Street · Anchorage, AK 99501 · 907-334-5600

Steven T. O'Hara · ⑩ · Bankston, Gronning, O'Hara, Sedor, Givens & Heaphey · 601 West Fifth Avenue, Suite 900 · Anchorage, AK 99501 · 907-276-1711

David G. Shaftel · ⑳ · Law Offices of David G. Shaftel · 1029 West Third Avenue, Suite 600 · Anchorage, AK 99501 · 907-276-6015

TIMBER LAW

Anchorage

James D. Linxwiler · Guess & Rudd · 510 L Street, Suite 700 · Anchorage, AK 99501 · 907-793-2200

TRANSPORTATION LAW

Anchorage

Michael K. Nave · Guess & Rudd · 510 L Street, Suite 700 · Anchorage, AK 99501 · 907-793-2200

TRUSTS AND ESTATES

Anchorage

Peter B. Brautigam · Manley & Brautigam · 845 K Street · Anchorage, AK 99501 · 907-334-5600

Robert C. Brink · Hartig Rhodes Hoge & Lekisch · 717 K Street · Anchorage, AK 99501 · 907-276-1592

Trigg T. Davis · ⑳ · Davis, Randall, Anderson & Mathis · 405 West 36th Avenue, Suite 200 · Anchorage, AK 99503-5872 · 907-561-4420

Brian W. Durrell · Durrell Law Group · 1400 West Benson Boulevard, Suite 370 · Anchorage, AK 99503 · 907-258-3224

Peter C. Ginder · ⑳ · The Law Offices of Peter C. Ginder · 810 N Street, Suite 201 · Anchorage, AK 99501 · 907-258-6001

Robert L. Manley · ⑳ · Manley & Brautigam · 845 K Street · Anchorage, AK 99501 · 907-334-5600

Steven T. O'Hara · ⑩ · Bankston, Gronning, O'Hara, Sedor, Givens & Heaphey · 601 West Fifth Avenue, Suite 900 · Anchorage, AK 99501 · 907-276-1711

David G. Shaftel · ⑳ · Law Offices of David G. Shaftel · 1029 West Third Avenue, Suite 600 · Anchorage, AK 99501 · 907-276-6015

WATER LAW

Anchorage

Thomas E. Meacham · (20) · Thomas E. Meacham · 9500 Prospect Drive · Anchorage, AK 99516-1062 · 907-346-1077

WHITE-COLLAR CRIMINAL DEFENSE

Anchorage

Mark E. Ashburn · (10) · Ashburn & Mason · 1227 West Ninth Avenue, Suite 200 · Anchorage, AK 99501-5914 · 907-276-4331

Sidney K. Billingslea · Sidney K. Billingslea · 134 West 15th Avenue · Anchorage, AK 99501 · 907-277-9119

Robert C. Bundy · Dorsey & Whitney · 1031 West Fourth Avenue, Suite 600 · Anchorage, AK 99501-5907 · 907-276-4557

Rex Lamont Butler · Rex Lamont Butler & Associates · 745 West Fourth Avenue · Anchorage, AK 99501-2136 · 907-272-1497

Brent R. Cole · Marston & Cole · 745 West Fourth Avenue, Suite 502 · Anchorage, AK 99501-2136 · 907-277-8001

Brian Doherty · Doherty & Menard · Resolution Plaza, Suite 500 · 1029 West Third Avenue · Anchorage, AK 99501-1982 · 907-279-4506

Jeffrey M. Feldman · (10) · Feldman, Orlansky & Sanders · 500 L Street, Suite 400 · Anchorage, AK 99501 907-272-3538

Carmen L. Gutierrez · Carmen L. Gutierrez · 510 L Street, Suite 306 · Anchorage, AK 99501-1952 · 907-274-2800

James H. McComas · (10) · Friedman, Rubin & White · 1227 West Ninth Avenue, Suite 201 · Anchorage, AK 99501 · 907-258-0704

Amy R. Menard · Doherty & Menard · Resolution Plaza, Suite 500 · 1029 West Third Avenue · Anchorage, AK 99501-1982 · 907-279-4506

John M. Murtagh · John M. Murtagh · 1101 West Seventh Avenue · Anchorage, AK 99501-3301 · 907-274-8664

Christine S. Schleuss · (10) · Suddock & Schleuss · 500 L Street, Suite 300 · Anchorage, AK 99501 · 907-258-7807

Douglas J. Serdahely · Patton Boggs · 601 West Fifth Avenue, Suite 700 · Anchorage, AK 99501 · 907-263-6300

Cynthia L. Strout · (10) · Cynthia L. Strout · 733 West Fourth Avenue, Suite 401 · Anchorage, AK 99501 · 907-276-0377

Phillip Paul Weidner · (20) · Phillip Paul Weidner & Associates · 330 L Street, Suite 200 · Anchorage, AK 99501 · 907-277-7000

WORKERS' COMPENSATION LAW

Anchorage

Chancy Croft · ⑩ · Chancy Croft Law Office · 738 H Street · Anchorage, AK 99501 · 907-272-3508

Michael J. Jensen · Law Offices of Michael J. Jensen · 12350 Industry Way, Suite 208 · Anchorage, AK 99515 · 907-277-8000

Joseph A. Kalamarides · ⑩ · Kalamarides & Lambert · 711 H Street, Suite 450 · Anchorage, AK 99501 · 907-276-2135

Randall J. Weddle · ⑩ · Holmes Weddle & Barcott · 701 West Eighth Avenue, Suite 700 · Anchorage, AK 99501-3408 · 907-274-0666

Patricia Zobel · ⑩ · DeLisio, Moran, Geraghty & Zobel · 943 West Sixth Avenue · Anchorage, AK 99501-2033 · 907-279-9574

ARIZONA

ADMINISTRATIVE LAW

Phoenix

Joan S. Burke · Osborn Maledon · http://www.omlaw.com · The Phoenix Plaza, Twenty-First Floor · 2929 North Central Avenue · Phoenix, AZ 85012-2793 · 602-640-9000

Thomas H. Campbell · Lewis and Roca · http://www.lrlaw.com · 40 North Central Avenue, Suite 1900 · Phoenix, AZ 85004 · 602-262-5311

Michael M. Grant · Gallagher & Kennedy · http://www.gknet.com · 2575 East Camelback Road · Phoenix, AZ 85016-9225 · 602-530-8000

J. Scott Rhodes · Jennings, Strouss & Salmon · http://www.jsslaw.com · The Collier Center, 11th Floor · 201 East Washington Street · Phoenix, AZ 85004-2385 · 602-262-5911

Tucson

Michael F. McNulty · ❿ · Lewis and Roca · http://www.lrlaw.com · One South Church Avenue, Suite 700 Tucson, AZ 85701-1627 · 520-622-2090

ALTERNATIVE DISPUTE RESOLUTION

Phoenix

Shawn K. Aiken · Hebert Schenk · http://www.hs-law.com · 4742 North 24th Street, Suite 100 · Phoenix, AZ 85014 · 602-248-8203

Gerald W. Alston · Jennings, Strouss & Salmon · http://www.jsslaw.com · The Collier Center, 11th Floor 201 East Washington Street · Phoenix, AZ 85004-2385 · 602-262-5911

Gary L. Birnbaum · ❿ · Mariscal, Weeks, McIntyre & Friedlander · http://www.mwmf.com · 2901 North Central Avenue, Suite 200 · Phoenix, AZ 85012-2705 · 602-285-5000

Paul F. Eckstein · ㉕ · Perkins Coie Brown & Bain · http://www.perkinscoie.com · 2901 North Central Avenue, Suite 2000 · Phoenix, AZ 85012-2788 · 602-351-8000

Sherman D. Fogel · Fogel & Bronnenkant · 2850 East Camelback Road, Suite 200 · Phoenix, AZ 85016 · 602-264-3330

Richard A. Friedlander · Mariscal, Weeks, McIntyre & Friedlander · http://www.mwmf.com · 2901 North Central Avenue, Suite 200 · Phoenix, AZ 85012-2705 · 602-285-5000

Richard N. Goldsmith · Lewis and Roca · http://www.lrlaw.com · 40 North Central Avenue, Suite 1900 · Phoenix, AZ 85004 · 602-262-5311

Bruce E. Meyerson · Miller LaSota & Peters · 722 East Osborn, Suite 100 · Phoenix, AZ 85014-5245 · 602-248-2900

Michael S. Rubin · Mariscal, Weeks, McIntyre & Friedlander · http://www.mwmf.com · 2901 North Central Avenue, Suite 200 · Phoenix, AZ 85012-2705 · 602-285-5000

Stephen H. Scott · Scott & Skelly · 1313 East Osborn Road, Suite 120 · Phoenix, AZ 85014-0001 · 602-277-8228

Christopher M. Skelly · Scott & Skelly · 1313 East Osborn Road, Suite 120 · Phoenix, AZ 85014-0001 · 602-277-8228

Scottsdale

Marvin S. Cohen · Sacks Tierney · http://www.sackstierney.com · 4250 North Drinkwater Boulevard, Fourth Floor · Scottsdale, AZ 85251-3693 · 480-425-2600

Amy L. Lieberman · Insight Employment Mediation · http://www.insightemployment.com · 21090 North Pima Road · Scottsdale, AZ 85255 · 480-246-3366

David C. Tierney · Sacks Tierney · http://www.sackstierney.com · 4250 North Drinkwater Boulevard, Fourth Floor · Scottsdale, AZ 85251-3693 · 480-425-2600

Tucson

Lawrence H. Fleischman · The Fleischman Law Firm · 2850 North Swan Road, Suite 120 · Tucson, AZ 85712 · 520-326-6400

S. Jeffrey Minker · S. Jeffrey Minker · 860 West Ina Road · Tucson, AZ 85704-4405 · 520-797-7800

Thomas A. Zlaket · Thomas A. Zlaket · 310 South Williams Boulevard, Suite 170 · Tucson, AZ 85711-4446 · 520-750-0250

ANTITRUST LAW

Phoenix

Charles A. Blanchard · Perkins Coie Brown & Bain · http://www.perkinscoie.com · 2901 North Central Avenue, Suite 2000 · Phoenix, AZ 85012-2788 · 602-351-8000

John J. Bouma · ⑩ · Snell & Wilmer · One Arizona Center · 400 East Van Buren Street · Phoenix, AZ 85004-2202 · 602-382-6000

Timothy J. Burke · Fennemore Craig · http://www.fclaw.com · 3003 North Central Avenue, Suite 2600 · Phoenix, AZ 85012-2913 · 602-916-5000

H. Michael Clyde · Perkins Coie Brown & Bain · http://www.perkinscoie.com · 2901 North Central Avenue, Suite 2000 · Phoenix, AZ 85012-2788 · 602-351-8000

Brett L. Dunkelman · Osborn Maledon · http://www.omlaw.com · The Phoenix Plaza, Twenty-First Floor · 2929 North Central Avenue · Phoenix, AZ 85012-2793 · 602-640-9000

Paul F. Eckstein · ㉕ · Perkins Coie Brown & Bain · http://www.perkinscoie.com · 2901 North Central Avenue, Suite 2000 · Phoenix, AZ 85012-2788 · 602-351-8000

Douglas Gerlach · Jennings, Strouss & Salmon · http://www.jsslaw.com · The Collier Center, 11th Floor · 201 East Washington Street · Phoenix, AZ 85004-2385 · 602-262-5911

Andrew S. Gordon · Coppersmith Gordon Schermer & Brockelman · 2800 North Central Avenue, Suite 1000 · Phoenix, AZ 85004-1007 · 602-224-0999

William J. Maledon · ⑩ · Osborn Maledon · http://www.omlaw.com · The Phoenix Plaza, Twenty-First Floor · 2929 North Central Avenue · Phoenix, AZ 85012-2793 · 602-640-9000

Daniel McAuliffe · ⑩ · Snell & Wilmer · One Arizona Center · 400 East Van Buren Street · Phoenix, AZ 85004-2202 · 602-382-6000

Karen C. Owens · ⑩ · Coppersmith Gordon Schermer & Brockelman · 2800 North Central Avenue, Suite 1000 · Phoenix, AZ 85004-1007 · 602-224-0999

Randall S. Papetti · Lewis and Roca · http://www.lrlaw.com · 40 North Central Avenue, Suite 1900 · Phoenix, AZ 85004 · 602-262-5311

Deana S. Peck · Quarles & Brady · http://www.quarles.com · One Renaissance Square · Two North Central Avenue · Phoenix, AZ 85004-2391 · 602-229-5200

Charles S. Price · Mariscal, Weeks, McIntyre & Friedlander · http://www.mwmf.com · 2901 North Central Avenue, Suite 200 · Phoenix, AZ 85012-2705 · 602-285-5000

Lawrence G. Scarborough · Bryan Cave · One Renaissance Square, Suite 2200 · Two North Central Avenue · Phoenix, AZ 85004-4406 · 602-364-7000

Richard A. Segal · ㉕ · Gust Rosenfeld · http://www.gustlaw.com · 201 East Washington Street, Suite 800 Phoenix, AZ 85004-2327 · 602-257-7422

Tucson

David J. Leonard · ㉕ · Leonard & Felker · 7440 North Oracle Road, Building Two · Tucson, AZ 85704 · 520-622-7737

APPELLATE LAW

Phoenix

Timothy J. Berg · Fennemore Craig · http://www.fclaw.com · 3003 North Central Avenue, Suite 2600 · Phoenix, AZ 85012-2913 · 602-916-5000

David B. Earl · Jennings, Strouss & Salmon · http://www.jsslaw.com · The Collier Center, 11th Floor · 201 East Washington Street · Phoenix, AZ 85004-2385 · 602-262-5911

Paul F. Eckstein · ㉕ · Perkins Coie Brown & Bain · http://www.perkinscoie.com · 2901 North Central Avenue, Suite 2000 · Phoenix, AZ 85012-2788 · 602-351-8000

Susan M. Freeman · ⑩ · Lewis and Roca · http://www.lrlaw.com · 40 North Central Avenue, Suite 1900 · Phoenix, AZ 85004 · 602-262-5311

Eileen Dennis GilBride · Jones, Skelton & Hochuli · 2901 North Central Avenue, Suite 800 · Phoenix, AZ 85012 · 602-263-1700

Larry A. Hammond · ⑩ · Osborn Maledon · http://www.omlaw.com · The Phoenix Plaza, Twenty-First Floor · 2929 North Central Avenue · Phoenix, AZ 85012-2793 · 602-640-9000

Mark I. Harrison · ⑩ · Osborn Maledon · http://www.omlaw.com · The Phoenix Plaza, Twenty-First Floor · 2929 North Central Avenue · Phoenix, AZ 85012-2793 · 602-640-9000

Thomas L. Hudson · Osborn Maledon · http://www.omlaw.com · The Phoenix Plaza, Twenty-First Floor 2929 North Central Avenue · Phoenix, AZ 85012-2793 · 602-640-9000

Lawrence A. Kasten · Lewis and Roca · http://www.lrlaw.com · 40 North Central Avenue, Suite 1900 · Phoenix, AZ 85004 · 602-262-5311

Daniel McAuliffe · ⑩ · Snell & Wilmer · One Arizona Center · 400 East Van Buren Street · Phoenix, AZ 85004-2202 · 602-382-6000

Joel W. Nomkin · Perkins Coie Brown & Bain · http://www.perkinscoie.com · 2901 North Central Avenue, Suite 2000 · Phoenix, AZ 85012-2788 · 602-351-8000

Kenneth J. Sherk · ⑩ · Fennemore Craig · http://www.fclaw.com · 3003 North Central Avenue, Suite 2600 · Phoenix, AZ 85012-2913 · 602-916-5000

Paul G. Ulrich · Paul G. Ulrich · 131 East El Caminito Drive · Phoenix, AZ 85020-3503 · 602-248-9465

Charles W. Wirken · Gust Rosenfeld · http://www.gustlaw.com · 201 East Washington Street, Suite 800 · Phoenix, AZ 85004-2327 · 602-257-7422

Tucson

Scott H. Gan · Mesch, Clark & Rothschild · 259 North Meyer Avenue · Tucson, AZ 85701-1090 · 520-624-8886

Michael J. Meehan · ⑳ · Munger Chadwick · National Bank Plaza, Suite 300 · 333 North Wilmot · Tucson, AZ 85711-2634 · 520-721-1900

BANKING LAW

Phoenix

Joel P. Hoxie · Snell & Wilmer · One Arizona Center · 400 East Van Buren Street · Phoenix, AZ 85004-2202 · 602-382-6000

Robert L. Matia · Squire Sanders · http://www.ssd.com · Two Renaissance Square, Suite 2700 · 40 North Central Avenue · Phoenix, AZ 85004-4498 · 602-528-4000

Matthew Mehr · Quarles & Brady · http://www.quarles.com · One Renaissance Square · Two North Central Avenue · Phoenix, AZ 85004-2391 · 602-229-5200

Brent F. Moody · ⑩ · Brent F. Moody · 4806 North Thirty-Fifth Place · Phoenix, AZ 85018-3468 · 602-957-7042

Henry A. Perras · Quarles & Brady · http://www.quarles.com · One Renaissance Square · Two North Central Avenue · Phoenix, AZ 85004-2391 · 602-229-5200

Lawrence C. Petrowski · Stinson Morrison Hecker · http://www.stinson.com · 1850 North Central Avenue, Suite 2100 · Phoenix, AZ 85004-4584 · 602-279-1600

Gil Rudolph · Greenberg Traurig · http://www.gtlaw.com · 2375 East Camelback Road, Suite 700 · Phoenix, AZ 85016 · 602-445-8000

David Sprentall · Snell & Wilmer · One Arizona Center · 400 East Van Buren Street · Phoenix, AZ 85004-2202 · 602-382-6000

Kent W. Stevens · ⑩ · Quarles & Brady · http://www.quarles.com · One Renaissance Square · Two North Central Avenue · Phoenix, AZ 85004-2391 · 602-229-5200

Peter A. Terry · Quarles & Brady · http://www.quarles.com · One Renaissance Square · Two North Central Avenue · Phoenix, AZ 85004-2391 · 602-229-5200

Jeffrey H. Verbin · ⑩ · Greenberg Traurig · http://www.gtlaw.com · 2375 East Camelback Road, Suite 700 · Phoenix, AZ 85016 · 602-445-8000

Craig K. Williams · Snell & Wilmer · One Arizona Center · 400 East Van Buren Street · Phoenix, AZ 85004-2202 · 602-382-6000

Tucson

Roy W. Kyle · ⑩ · Lewis and Roca · http://www.lrlaw.com · One South Church Avenue, Suite 700 · Tucson, AZ 85701-1627 · 520-622-2090

James F. Morrow · ⑩ · Quarles & Brady · http://www.quarles.com · One South Church Street, Suite 1700 Tucson, AZ 85701-1621 · 520-770-8700

Nicholas W. O'Keeffe · Quarles & Brady · http://www.quarles.com · One South Church Street, Suite 1700 Tucson, AZ 85701-1621 · 520-770-8700

Curt D. Reimann · Snell & Wilmer · One South Church Avenue, Suite 1500 · Tucson, AZ 85701-1630 · 520-882-1200

BANKRUPTCY AND CREDITOR-DEBTOR RIGHTS LAW

Phoenix

C. Taylor Ashworth · ⑩ · Stinson Morrison Hecker · http://www.stinson.com · 1850 North Central Avenue, Suite 2100 · Phoenix, AZ 85004-4584 · 602-279-1600

Steven N. Berger · Engelman Berger · Security Title Plaza, Suite 700 · 3636 North Central Avenue · Phoenix, AZ 85012 · 602-271-9090

Michael W. Carmel · Michael W. Carmel · 80 East Columbus · Phoenix, AZ 85012-2334 · 602-264-4965

John R. Clemency · Greenberg Traurig · http://www.gtlaw.com · 2375 East Camelback Road, Suite 700 · Phoenix, AZ 85016 · 602-445-8000

Daniel P. Collins · Collins, May, Potenza, Baran & Gillespie · 201 North Central Avenue, Suite 2210 · Phoenix, AZ 85004-4424 · 602-252-1900

Joseph E. Cotterman · Gallagher & Kennedy · http://www.gknet.com · 2575 East Camelback Road · Phoenix, AZ 85016-9225 · 602-530-8000

James E. Cross · Osborn Maledon · http://www.omlaw.com · The Phoenix Plaza, Twenty-First Floor · 2929 North Central Avenue · Phoenix, AZ 85012-2793 · 602-640-9000

John J. Dawson · 25 · Quarles & Brady · http://www.quarles.com · One Renaissance Square · Two North Central Avenue · Phoenix, AZ 85004-2391 · 602-229-5200

S. Cary Forrester · Forrester & Worth · 3636 North Central Avenue, Suite 700 · Phoenix, AZ 85012-1985 602-271-4250

Susan M. Freeman · 10 · Lewis and Roca · http://www.lrlaw.com · 40 North Central Avenue, Suite 1900 · Phoenix, AZ 85004 · 602-262-5311

Donald L. Gaffney · 10 · Snell & Wilmer · One Arizona Center · 400 East Van Buren Street · Phoenix, AZ 85004-2202 · 602-382-6000

Gary A. Gotto · Keller Rohrback · 3101 North Central Avenue, Suite 1400 · Phoenix, AZ 85012-2600 · 602-248-0088

Craig D. Hansen · Squire Sanders · http://www.ssd.com · Two Renaissance Square, Suite 2700 · 40 North Central Avenue · Phoenix, AZ 85004-4498 · 602-528-4000

John A. Harris · Quarles & Brady · http://www.quarles.com · One Renaissance Square · Two North Central Avenue · Phoenix, AZ 85004-2391 · 602-229-5200

Robert P. Harris · Quarles & Brady · http://www.quarles.com · One Renaissance Square · Two North Central Avenue · Phoenix, AZ 85004-2391 · 602-229-5200

Carolyn J. Johnsen · Jennings, Strouss & Salmon · http://www.jsslaw.com · The Collier Center, 11th Floor · 201 East Washington Street · Phoenix, AZ 85004-2385 · 602-262-5911

Jordan A. Kroop · Squire Sanders · http://www.ssd.com · Two Renaissance Square, Suite 2700 · 40 North Central Avenue · Phoenix, AZ 85004-4498 · 602-528-4000

Richard M. Lorenzen · Perkins Coie Brown & Bain · http://www.perkinscoie.com · 2901 North Central Avenue, Suite 2000 · Phoenix, AZ 85012-2788 · 602-351-8000

William Novotny · Mariscal, Weeks, McIntyre & Friedlander · http://www.mwmf.com · 2901 North Central Avenue, Suite 200 · Phoenix, AZ 85012-2705 · 602-285-5000

Peter J. Rathwell · 20 · Snell & Wilmer · One Arizona Center · 400 East Van Buren Street · Phoenix, AZ 85004-2202 · 602-382-6000

Cathy L. Reece · Fennemore Craig · http://www.fclaw.com · 3003 North Central Avenue, Suite 2600 · Phoenix, AZ 85012-2913 · 602-916-5000

Paul Sala · Allen, Sala & Bayne · Viad Corporate Center, Suite 1150 · 1850 North Central Avenue · Phoenix, AZ 85004 · 602-256-6000

Thomas J. Salerno · 10 · Squire Sanders · http://www.ssd.com · Two Renaissance Square, Suite 2700 · 40 North Central Avenue · Phoenix, AZ 85004-4498 · 602-528-4000

Dale C. Schian · Schian Walker · 3550 North Central Avenue, Suite 1700 · Phoenix, AZ 85012-2115 · 602-277-1501

Brian Sirower · Quarles & Brady · http://www.quarles.com · One Renaissance Square · Two North Central Avenue · Phoenix, AZ 85004-2391 · 602-229-5200

Gerald K. Smith · 20 · Lewis and Roca · http://www.lrlaw.com · 40 North Central Avenue, Suite 1900 · Phoenix, AZ 85004 · 602-262-5311

Brian N. Spector · Jennings, Strouss & Salmon · http://www.jsslaw.com · The Collier Center, 11th Floor · 201 East Washington Street · Phoenix, AZ 85004-2385 · 602-262-5911

Warren J. Stapleton · Osborn Maledon · http://www.omlaw.com · The Phoenix Plaza, Twenty-First Floor · 2929 North Central Avenue · Phoenix, AZ 85012-2793 · 602-640-9000

Bradley J. Stevens · Jennings, Strouss & Salmon · http://www.jsslaw.com · The Collier Center, 11th Floor 201 East Washington Street · Phoenix, AZ 85004-2385 · 602-262-5911

Tucson

Susan G. Boswell · ⑳ · Quarles & Brady · http://www.quarles.com · One South Church Street, Suite 1700 Tucson, AZ 85701-1621 · 520-770-8700

Rob M. Charles, Jr. · Lewis and Roca · http://www.lrlaw.com · One South Church Avenue, Suite 700 · Tucson, AZ 85701-1627 · 520-622-2090

Scott D. Gibson · ⑩ · Gibson, Nakamura & Green · 2941 North Swan Road, Suite 101 · Tucson, AZ 85712 · 520-722-2600

Michael McGrath · ⑩ · Mesch, Clark & Rothschild · 259 North Meyer Avenue · Tucson, AZ 85701-1090 520-624-8886

Lowell E. Rothschild · ㉕ · Mesch, Clark & Rothschild · 259 North Meyer Avenue · Tucson, AZ 85701-1090 · 520-624-8886

Brenda Moody Whinery · Mesch, Clark & Rothschild · 259 North Meyer Avenue · Tucson, AZ 85701-1090 · 520-624-8886

BET-THE-COMPANY LITIGATION

Phoenix

Peter D. Baird · ㉕ · Lewis and Roca · http://www.lrlaw.com · 40 North Central Avenue, Suite 1900 · Phoenix, AZ 85004 · 602-262-5311

Gary L. Birnbaum · ⑩ · Mariscal, Weeks, McIntyre & Friedlander · http://www.mwmf.com · 2901 North Central Avenue, Suite 200 · Phoenix, AZ 85012-2705 · 602-285-5000

James R. Condo · Snell & Wilmer · One Arizona Center · 400 East Van Buren Street · Phoenix, AZ 85004-2202 · 602-382-6000

Paul F. Eckstein · ㉕ · Perkins Coie Brown & Bain · http://www.perkinscoie.com · 2901 North Central Avenue, Suite 2000 · Phoenix, AZ 85012-2788 · 602-351-8000

Larry A. Hammond · ⑩ · Osborn Maledon · http://www.omlaw.com · The Phoenix Plaza, Twenty-First Floor · 2929 North Central Avenue · Phoenix, AZ 85012-2793 · 602-640-9000

Ed Hendricks, Sr. · ㉕ · Meyer Hendricks · 3131 East CamelbackRoad, Suite 310 · Phoenix, AZ 85016 · 602-604-2100

Joseph E. Mais · Perkins Coie Brown & Bain · http://www.perkinscoie.com · 2901 North Central Avenue, Suite 2000 · Phoenix, AZ 85012-2788 · 602-351-8000

William J. Maledon · ⑩ · Osborn Maledon · http://www.omlaw.com · The Phoenix Plaza, Twenty-First Floor · 2929 North Central Avenue · Phoenix, AZ 85012-2793 · 602-640-9000

David B. Rosenbaum · Osborn Maledon · http://www.omlaw.com · The Phoenix Plaza, Twenty-First Floor · 2929 North Central Avenue · Phoenix, AZ 85012-2793 · 602-640-9000

Tucson

Gerald Maltz · ㉕ · Haralson, Miller, Pitt, Feldman & McAnally · One South Church Avenue, Suite 900 · Tucson, AZ 85701 · 520-792-3836

Jeffrey Willis · Snell & Wilmer · One South Church Avenue, Suite 1500 · Tucson, AZ 85701-1630 · 520-882-1200

BIOTECHNOLOGY LAW

Phoenix

Frank X. Curci · Jennings, Strouss & Salmon · http://www.jsslaw.com · The Collier Center, 11th Floor · 201 East Washington Street · Phoenix, AZ 85004-2385 · 602-262-5911

Scottsdale

Robert F. Copple · Copple & Associates · 9274 East Desert Trail · Scottsdale, AZ 85260 · 480-614-5771

COMMERCIAL LITIGATION

Phoenix

Shawn K. Aiken · Hebert Schenk · http://www.hs-law.com · 4742 North 24th Street, Suite 100 · Phoenix, AZ 85014 · 602-248-8203

Gerald W. Alston · Jennings, Strouss & Salmon · http://www.jsslaw.com · The Collier Center, 11th Floor 201 East Washington Street · Phoenix, AZ 85004-2385 · 602-262-5911

Peter D. Baird · ㉕ · Lewis and Roca · http://www.lrlaw.com · 40 North Central Avenue, Suite 1900 · Phoenix, AZ 85004 · 602-262-5311

Keith Beauchamp · Lewis and Roca · http://www.lrlaw.com · 40 North Central Avenue, Suite 1900 · Phoenix, AZ 85004 · 602-262-5311

James J. Belanger · Cheifetz Iannitelli Marcolini · http://www.cimlaw.com · Viad Tower, 19th Floor · 1850 North Central Avenue · Phoenix, AZ 85004 · 602-952-6000

Timothy J. Berg · Fennemore Craig · http://www.fclaw.com · 3003 North Central Avenue, Suite 2600 · Phoenix, AZ 85012-2913 · 602-916-5000

Gary L. Birnbaum · ⑩ · Mariscal, Weeks, McIntyre & Friedlander · http://www.mwmf.com · 2901 North Central Avenue, Suite 200 · Phoenix, AZ 85012-2705 · 602-285-5000

Donald W. Bivens · Snell & Wilmer · One Arizona Center · 400 East Van Buren Street · Phoenix, AZ 85004-2202 · 602-382-6000

Charles A. Blanchard · Perkins Coie Brown & Bain · http://www.perkinscoie.com · 2901 North Central Avenue, Suite 2000 · Phoenix, AZ 85012-2788 · 602-351-8000

John J. Bouma · ⑩ · Snell & Wilmer · One Arizona Center · 400 East Van Buren Street · Phoenix, AZ 85004-2202 · 602-382-6000

Francis J. Burke, Jr. · Steptoe & Johnson · http://www.steptoe.com · Collier Center, 16th Floor · 201 East Washington Street · Phoenix, AZ 85004-2382 · 602-257-5200

Howard Ross Cabot · Perkins Coie Brown & Bain · http://www.perkinscoie.com · 2901 North Central Avenue, Suite 2000 · Phoenix, AZ 85012-2788 · 602-351-8000

José A. Cárdenas · Lewis and Roca · http://www.lrlaw.com · 40 North Central Avenue, Suite 1900 · Phoenix, AZ 85004 · 602-262-5311

H. Michael Clyde · Perkins Coie Brown & Bain · http://www.perkinscoie.com · 2901 North Central Avenue, Suite 2000 · Phoenix, AZ 85012-2788 · 602-351-8000

Richard S. Cohen · ⑩ · Ford & Harrison · http://www.fordharrison.com · 2525 East Camelback Road, Suite 450 · Phoenix, AZ 85016 · 602-627-3500

James R. Condo · Snell & Wilmer · One Arizona Center · 400 East Van Buren Street · Phoenix, AZ 85004-2202 · 602-382-6000

R. Douglas Dalton · Dalton · http://www.daltonplc.com · 1850 North Central Avenue, Suite 1100 · Phoenix, AZ 85004 · 602-224-2444

Dale A. Danneman · Lewis and Roca · http://www.lrlaw.com · 40 North Central Avenue, Suite 1900 · Phoenix, AZ 85004 · 602-262-5311

Barbara J. Dawson · Snell & Wilmer · One Arizona Center · 400 East Van Buren Street · Phoenix, AZ 85004-2202 · 602-382-6000

John E. DeWulf · Roshka DeWulf & Patten · http://www.rdp-law.com · One Arizona Center, Suite 800 · 400 East Van Buren Street · Phoenix, AZ 85004 · 602-256-6100

William W. Drury, Jr. · Renaud Cook Drury Mesaros · Phelps Dodge Tower, Suite 900 · One North Central Avenue · Phoenix, AZ 85004 · 602-307-9900

Jay S. Dushoff · ㉕ · Gallagher & Kennedy · http://www.gknet.com · 2575 East Camelback Road · Phoenix, AZ 85016-9225 · 602-530-8000

Paul F. Eckstein · ㉕ · Perkins Coie Brown & Bain · http://www.perkinscoie.com · 2901 North Central Avenue, Suite 2000 · Phoenix, AZ 85012-2788 · 602-351-8000

Andrew M. Federhar · Fennemore Craig · http://www.fclaw.com · 3003 North Central Avenue, Suite 2600 · Phoenix, AZ 85012-2913 · 602-916-5000

Susan M. Freeman · ⑩ · Lewis and Roca · http://www.lrlaw.com · 40 North Central Avenue, Suite 1900 · Phoenix, AZ 85004 · 602-262-5311

Mark A. Fuller · Gallagher & Kennedy · http://www.gknet.com · 2575 East Camelback Road · Phoenix, AZ 85016-9225 · 602-530-8000

Douglas Gerlach · Jennings, Strouss & Salmon · http://www.jsslaw.com · The Collier Center, 11th Floor · 201 East Washington Street · Phoenix, AZ 85004-2385 · 602-262-5911

Andrew S. Gordon · Coppersmith Gordon Schermer & Brockelman · 2800 North Central Avenue, Suite 1000 · Phoenix, AZ 85004-1007 · 602-224-0999

Andrew F. Halaby · Snell & Wilmer · One Arizona Center · 400 East Van Buren Street · Phoenix, AZ 85004-2202 · 602-382-6000

Richard A. Halloran · Lewis and Roca · http://www.lrlaw.com · 40 North Central Avenue, Suite 1900 · Phoenix, AZ 85004 · 602-262-5311

Barry D. Halpern · ⑩ · Snell & Wilmer · One Arizona Center · 400 East Van Buren Street · Phoenix, AZ 85004-2202 · 602-382-6000

Larry A. Hammond · ⑩ · Osborn Maledon · http://www.omlaw.com · The Phoenix Plaza, Twenty-First Floor · 2929 North Central Avenue · Phoenix, AZ 85012-2793 · 602-640-9000

Roger T. Hargrove · Fennemore Craig · http://www.fclaw.com · 3003 North Central Avenue, Suite 2600 · Phoenix, AZ 85012-2913 · 602-916-5000

Marty Harper · Shughart Thomson & Kilroy · http://www.stklaw.com · Security Title Plaza, Suite 1200 · 3636 North Central Avenue · Phoenix, AZ 85012-0001 · 602-650-2000

Mark I. Harrison · ⑩ · Osborn Maledon · http://www.omlaw.com · The Phoenix Plaza, Twenty-First Floor · 2929 North Central Avenue · Phoenix, AZ 85012-2793 · 602-640-9000

Ed Hendricks, Sr. · ㉕ · Meyer Hendricks · 3131 East CamelbackRoad, Suite 310 · Phoenix, AZ 85016 · 602-604-2100

Charles W. Herf · Quarles & Brady · http://www.quarles.com · One Renaissance Square · Two North Central Avenue · Phoenix, AZ 85004-2391 · 602-229-5200

Richard G. Himelrick · Tiffany & Bosco · Camelback Esplanade II, Third Floor · 2525 East Camelback Road · Phoenix, AZ 85016-4237 · 602-255-6000

Joel P. Hoxie · Snell & Wilmer · One Arizona Center · 400 East Van Buren Street · Phoenix, AZ 85004-2202 · 602-382-6000

Thomas L. Hudson · Osborn Maledon · http://www.omlaw.com · The Phoenix Plaza, Twenty-First Floor 2929 North Central Avenue · Phoenix, AZ 85012-2793 · 602-640-9000

Michael K. Kennedy · Gallagher & Kennedy · http://www.gknet.com · 2575 East Camelback Road · Phoenix, AZ 85016-9225 · 602-530-8000

Robert V. Kerrick · Tiffany & Bosco · Camelback Esplanade II, Third Floor · 2525 East Camelback Road · Phoenix, AZ 85016-4237 · 602-255-6000

Michael R. King · Gammage & Burnham · http://www.gblaw.com · One Renaissance Square, 18th Floor · Two North Central Avenue · Phoenix, AZ 85004 · 602-256-0566

Emil J. Kotalik, Jr. · Peshkin & Kotalik · 3030 North Central Avenue, Suite 1106 · Phoenix, AZ 85012-2718 · 602-248-7770

N. Warner Lee · Ryley Carlock & Applewhite · http://www.rcalaw.com · Phelps Dodge Tower, Suite 1200 One North Central Avenue · Phoenix, AZ 85004-4417 · 602-258-7701

John Lemaster · Ryley Carlock & Applewhite · http://www.rcalaw.com · Phelps Dodge Tower, Suite 1200 · One North Central Avenue · Phoenix, AZ 85004-4417 · 602-258-7701

Joseph E. Mais · Perkins Coie Brown & Bain · http://www.perkinscoie.com · 2901 North Central Avenue, Suite 2000 · Phoenix, AZ 85012-2788 · 602-351-8000

William J. Maledon · ⑩ · Osborn Maledon · http://www.omlaw.com · The Phoenix Plaza, Twenty-First Floor · 2929 North Central Avenue · Phoenix, AZ 85012-2793 · 602-640-9000

Michael C. Manning · Stinson Morrison Hecker · http://www.stinson.com · 1850 North Central Avenue, Suite 2100 · Phoenix, AZ 85004-4584 · 602-279-1600

Don P. Martin · Quarles & Brady · http://www.quarles.com · One Renaissance Square · Two North Central Avenue · Phoenix, AZ 85004-2391 · 602-229-5200

Daniel McAuliffe · ⑩ · Snell & Wilmer · One Arizona Center · 400 East Van Buren Street · Phoenix, AZ 85004-2202 · 602-382-6000

Robert H. McKirgan · Lewis and Roca · http://www.lrlaw.com · 40 North Central Avenue, Suite 1900 · Phoenix, AZ 85004 · 602-262-5311

Joel W. Nomkin · Perkins Coie Brown & Bain · http://www.perkinscoie.com · 2901 North Central Avenue, Suite 2000 · Phoenix, AZ 85012-2788 · 602-351-8000

Jennifer P. Nore · Snell & Wilmer · One Arizona Center · 400 East Van Buren Street · Phoenix, AZ 85004-2202 · 602-382-6000

Michael J. O'Connor · Jennings, Strouss & Salmon · http://www.jsslaw.com · The Collier Center, 11th Floor · 201 East Washington Street · Phoenix, AZ 85004-2385 · 602-262-5911

Kevin E. O'Malley · Gallagher & Kennedy · http://www.gknet.com · 2575 East Camelback Road · Phoenix, AZ 85016-9225 · 602-530-8000

Pamela M. Overton · Greenberg Traurig · http://www.gtlaw.com · 2375 East Camelback Road, Suite 700 · Phoenix, AZ 85016 · 602-445-8000

David A. Paige · Quarles & Brady · http://www.quarles.com · One Renaissance Square · Two North Central Avenue · Phoenix, AZ 85004-2391 · 602-229-5200

Randall S. Papetti · Lewis and Roca · http://www.lrlaw.com · 40 North Central Avenue, Suite 1900 · Phoenix, AZ 85004 · 602-262-5311

Rodolfo Parga, Jr. · Ryley Carlock & Applewhite · http://www.rcalaw.com · Phelps Dodge Tower, Suite 1200 · One North Central Avenue · Phoenix, AZ 85004-4417 · 602-258-7701

Deana S. Peck · Quarles & Brady · http://www.quarles.com · One Renaissance Square · Two North Central Avenue · Phoenix, AZ 85004-2391 · 602-229-5200

Craig W. Phillips · Lewis and Roca · http://www.lrlaw.com · 40 North Central Avenue, Suite 1900 · Phoenix, AZ 85004 · 602-262-5311

Charles S. Price · Mariscal, Weeks, McIntyre & Friedlander · http://www.mwmf.com · 2901 North Central Avenue, Suite 200 · Phoenix, AZ 85012-2705 · 602-285-5000

David E. Rauch · Snell & Wilmer · One Arizona Center · 400 East Van Buren Street · Phoenix, AZ 85004-2202 · 602-382-6000

Patricia Lee Refo · Snell & Wilmer · One Arizona Center · 400 East Van Buren Street · Phoenix, AZ 85004-2202 · 602-382-6000

Scott W. Rodgers · Osborn Maledon · http://www.omlaw.com · The Phoenix Plaza, Twenty-First Floor · 2929 North Central Avenue · Phoenix, AZ 85012-2793 · 602-640-9000

David B. Rosenbaum · Osborn Maledon · http://www.omlaw.com · The Phoenix Plaza, Twenty-First Floor · 2929 North Central Avenue · Phoenix, AZ 85012-2793 · 602-640-9000

Paul J. Roshka, Jr. · Roshka DeWulf & Patten · http://www.rdp-law.com · One Arizona Center, Suite 800 400 East Van Buren Street · Phoenix, AZ 85004 · 602-256-6100

Michael S. Rubin · Mariscal, Weeks, McIntyre & Friedlander · http://www.mwmf.com · 2901 North Central Avenue, Suite 200 · Phoenix, AZ 85012-2705 · 602-285-5000

James A. Ryan · Quarles & Brady · http://www.quarles.com · One Renaissance Square · Two North Central Avenue · Phoenix, AZ 85004-2391 · 602-229-5200

Barry R. Sanders · Mariscal, Weeks, McIntyre & Friedlander · http://www.mwmf.com · 2901 North Central Avenue, Suite 200 · Phoenix, AZ 85012-2705 · 602-285-5000

Richard A. Segal · (25) · Gust Rosenfeld · http://www.gustlaw.com · 201 East Washington Street, Suite 800 Phoenix, AZ 85004-2327 · 602-257-7422

John G. Sestak, Jr. · Jennings, Strouss & Salmon · http://www.jsslaw.com · The Collier Center, 11th Floor · 201 East Washington Street · Phoenix, AZ 85004-2385 · 602-262-5911

Kenneth J. Sherk · (10) · Fennemore Craig · http://www.fclaw.com · 3003 North Central Avenue, Suite 2600 · Phoenix, AZ 85012-2913 · 602-916-5000

Andrew R. Sherwood · Quarles & Brady · http://www.quarles.com · One Renaissance Square · Two North Central Avenue · Phoenix, AZ 85004-2391 · 602-229-5200

Robert A. Shull · Mariscal, Weeks, McIntyre & Friedlander · http://www.mwmf.com · 2901 North Central Avenue, Suite 200 · Phoenix, AZ 85012-2705 · 602-285-5000

Jesse B. Simpson · Lewis and Roca · http://www.lrlaw.com · 40 North Central Avenue, Suite 1900 · Phoenix, AZ 85004 · 602-262-5311

Louis A. Stahl · Quarles & Brady · http://www.quarles.com · One Renaissance Square · Two North Central Avenue · Phoenix, AZ 85004-2391 · 602-229-5200

Geoffrey M.T. Sturr · Osborn Maledon · http://www.omlaw.com · The Phoenix Plaza, Twenty-First Floor 2929 North Central Avenue · Phoenix, AZ 85012-2793 · 602-640-9000

Shane R. Swindle · Perkins Coie Brown & Bain · http://www.perkinscoie.com · 2901 North Central Avenue, Suite 2000 · Phoenix, AZ 85012-2788 · 602-351-8000

Timothy J. Thomason · Mariscal, Weeks, McIntyre & Friedlander · http://www.mwmf.com · 2901 North Central Avenue, Suite 200 · Phoenix, AZ 85012-2705 · 602-285-5000

John C. West · Jennings, Strouss & Salmon · http://www.jsslaw.com · The Collier Center, 11th Floor · 201 East Washington Street · Phoenix, AZ 85004-2385 · 602-262-5911

Lonnie J. Williams, Jr. · (10) · Quarles & Brady · http://www.quarles.com · One Renaissance Square · Two North Central Avenue · Phoenix, AZ 85004-2391 · 602-229-5200

Scottsdale

Jeffrey S. Leonard · Sacks Tierney · http://www.sackstierney.com · 4250 North Drinkwater Boulevard, Fourth Floor · Scottsdale, AZ 85251-3693 · 480-425-2600

David C. Tierney · Sacks Tierney · http://www.sackstierney.com · 4250 North Drinkwater Boulevard, Fourth Floor · Scottsdale, AZ 85251-3693 · 480-425-2600

Tucson

A. Bates Butler III · Fennemore Craig · http://www.fclaw.com · One South Church Avenue, Suite 1000 · Tucson, AZ 85701-1627 · 520-879-6800

Thomas Chandler · (25) · The Law Office of Thomas Chandler · 126 West River Road · Tucson, AZ 85701-0001 · 520-623-4353

George J. Feulner · Feulner Dorris · 310 South Williams Boulevard, Suite 240 · Tucson, AZ 85711-7704 · 520-622-4866

John Gabroy · ⑩ · Gabroy, Rollman & Bossé · 3507 North Campbell Avenue, Suite 111 · Tucson, AZ 85719 · 520-320-1300

Bruce R. Heurlin · Heurlin Sherlock Panahi · 1636 North Swan Road, Suite 200 · Tucson, AZ 85712-4096 · 520-319-1200

John N. Iurino · Lewis and Roca · http://www.lrlaw.com · One South Church Avenue, Suite 700 · Tucson, AZ 85701-1627 · 520-622-2090

Craig H. Kaufman · Quarles & Brady · http://www.quarles.com · One South Church Street, Suite 1700 · Tucson, AZ 85701-1621 · 520-770-8700

George Krauja · Fennemore Craig · http://www.fclaw.com · One South Church Avenue, Suite 1000 · Tucson, AZ 85701-1627 · 520-879-6800

Gerald Maltz · ㉕ · Haralson, Miller, Pitt, Feldman & McAnally · One South Church Avenue, Suite 900 · Tucson, AZ 85701 · 520-792-3836

Michael J. Meehan · ⑳ · Munger Chadwick · National Bank Plaza, Suite 300 · 333 North Wilmot · Tucson, AZ 85711-2634 · 520-721-1900

William N. Poorten III · Snell & Wilmer · One South Church Avenue, Suite 1500 · Tucson, AZ 85701-1630 · 520-882-1200

Richard M. Rollman · Gabroy, Rollman & Bossé · 3507 North Campbell Avenue, Suite 111 · Tucson, AZ 85719 · 520-320-1300

Dennis Rosen · Dennis Rosen · 1670 East River Road, Suite 124 · Tucson, AZ 85718-8900 · 520-319-9191

Michael J.S. Rusing · Rusing & Lopez · 6262 North Swan Road, Suite 200 · Tucson, AZ 85718 · 520-792-4800

Cary S. Sandman · Waterfall, Economidis, Caldwell, Hanshaw & Villamana · http://www.wechv.com · Williams Centre, Eighth Floor · 5210 East Williams Circle · Tucson, AZ 85711 · 520-790-5828

Tom Slutes · ⑩ · Slutes Sakrison & Rogers · 4801 East Broadway Boulevard, Suite 301 · Tucson, AZ 85711-0001 · 520-624-6691

Jeffrey Willis · Snell & Wilmer · One South Church Avenue, Suite 1500 · Tucson, AZ 85701-1630 · 520-882-1200

COMMUNICATIONS LAW

Phoenix

Joan S. Burke · Osborn Maledon · http://www.omlaw.com · The Phoenix Plaza, Twenty-First Floor · 2929 North Central Avenue · Phoenix, AZ 85012-2793 · 602-640-9000

Jeffrey W. Crockett · Snell & Wilmer · One Arizona Center · 400 East Van Buren Street · Phoenix, AZ 85004-2202 · 602-382-6000

Randall C. Nelson · Osborn Maledon · http://www.omlaw.com · The Phoenix Plaza, Twenty-First Floor · 2929 North Central Avenue · Phoenix, AZ 85012-2793 · 602-640-9000

Michael W. Patten · Roshka DeWulf & Patten · http://www.rdp-law.com · One Arizona Center, Suite 800 400 East Van Buren Street · Phoenix, AZ 85004 · 602-256-6100

Phoenix

Mark E. Barker · Jennings Haug & Cunningham · 2800 North Central Avenue, Suite 1800 · Phoenix, AZ 85004-1049 · 602-234-7800

David J. Cantelme · Cantelme & Brown · 3030 North Central Avenue, Suite 1109 · Phoenix, AZ 85012 · 602-200-0104

James R. Condo · Snell & Wilmer · One Arizona Center · 400 East Van Buren Street · Phoenix, AZ 85004-2202 · 602-382-6000

Jason Ebe · Snell & Wilmer · One Arizona Center · 400 East Van Buren Street · Phoenix, AZ 85004-2202 602-382-6000

Richard A. Friedlander · Mariscal, Weeks, McIntyre & Friedlander · http://www.mwmf.com · 2901 North Central Avenue, Suite 200 · Phoenix, AZ 85012-2705 · 602-285-5000

Jeffrey J. Goulder · Stinson Morrison Hecker · http://www.stinson.com · 1850 North Central Avenue, Suite 2100 · Phoenix, AZ 85004-4584 · 602-279-1600

Marty Harper · Shughart Thomson & Kilroy · http://www.stklaw.com · Security Title Plaza, Suite 1200 · 3636 North Central Avenue · Phoenix, AZ 85012-0001 · 602-650-2000

William F. Haug · Jennings Haug & Cunningham · 2800 North Central Avenue, Suite 1800 · Phoenix, AZ 85004-1049 · 602-234-7800

Frances J. Haynes · Lewis and Roca · http://www.lrlaw.com · 40 North Central Avenue, Suite 1900 · Phoenix, AZ 85004 · 602-262-5311

Michael J. Holden · Holden Willits Murphy · Two North Central Avenue, Suite 1700 · Phoenix, AZ 85016 · 602-508-6210

Stephen Jackson · Warner, Angle, Hallam, Jackson & Formanek · 3550 North Central Avenue, Suite 1500 · Phoenix, AZ 85012-2188 · 602-264-7101

John Randall Jefferies · Fennemore Craig · http://www.fclaw.com · 3003 North Central Avenue, Suite 2600 · Phoenix, AZ 85012-2913 · 602-916-5000

Curtis A. Jennings · Jennings Haug & Cunningham · 2800 North Central Avenue, Suite 1800 · Phoenix, AZ 85004-1049 · 602-234-7800

Charles Keller · Snell & Wilmer · One Arizona Center · 400 East Van Buren Street · Phoenix, AZ 85004-2202 · 602-382-6000

Michael R. King · Gammage & Burnham · http://www.gblaw.com · One Renaissance Square, 18th Floor · Two North Central Avenue · Phoenix, AZ 85004 · 602-256-0566

D. Kim Lough · Jennings Haug & Cunningham · 2800 North Central Avenue, Suite 1800 · Phoenix, AZ 85004-1049 · 602-234-7800

Jay M. Mann · Mann, Berens & Wisner · 3300 North Central Avenue, Suite 2400 · Phoenix, AZ 85012-2513 · 602-258-6200

Joseph E. McGarry · Lewis and Roca · http://www.lrlaw.com · 40 North Central Avenue, Suite 1900 · Phoenix, AZ 85004 · 602-262-5311

Stephen E. Richman · Mariscal, Weeks, McIntyre & Friedlander · http://www.mwmf.com · 2901 North Central Avenue, Suite 200 · Phoenix, AZ 85012-2705 · 602-285-5000

Robert F. Roos · Lewis and Roca · http://www.lrlaw.com · 40 North Central Avenue, Suite 1900 · Phoenix, AZ 85004 · 602-262-5311

James J. Sienicki · Snell & Wilmer · One Arizona Center · 400 East Van Buren Street · Phoenix, AZ 85004-2202 · 602-382-6000

E. Jeffrey Walsh · Greenberg Traurig · http://www.gtlaw.com · 2375 East Camelback Road, Suite 700 · Phoenix, AZ 85016 · 602-445-8000

Scottsdale

Sharon B. Shively · Sacks Tierney · http://www.sackstierney.com · 4250 North Drinkwater Boulevard, Fourth Floor · Scottsdale, AZ 85251-3693 · 480-425-2600

David C. Tierney · Sacks Tierney · http://www.sackstierney.com · 4250 North Drinkwater Boulevard, Fourth Floor · Scottsdale, AZ 85251-3693 · 480-425-2600

Tucson

Melvin C. Cohen · Mesch, Clark & Rothschild · 259 North Meyer Avenue · Tucson, AZ 85701-1090 · 520-624-8886

CORPORATE GOVERNANCE AND COMPLIANCE LAW

Phoenix

Jon Cohen · 25 · Snell & Wilmer · One Arizona Center · 400 East Van Buren Street · Phoenix, AZ 85004-2202 · 602-382-6000

Michael Donahey · Snell & Wilmer · One Arizona Center · 400 East Van Buren Street · Phoenix, AZ 85004-2202 · 602-382-6000

Matthew P. Feeney · 10 · Snell & Wilmer · One Arizona Center · 400 East Van Buren Street · Phoenix, AZ 85004-2202 · 602-382-6000

Robert S. Kant · Greenberg Traurig · http://www.gtlaw.com · 2375 East Camelback Road, Suite 700 · Phoenix, AZ 85016 · 602-445-8000

Richard Lieberman · Jennings, Strouss & Salmon · http://www.jsslaw.com · The Collier Center, 11th Floor · 201 East Washington Street · Phoenix, AZ 85004-2385 · 602-262-5911

Steven D. Pidgeon · 10 · DLA Piper · 2415 East Camelback Road, Suite 700 · Phoenix, AZ 85016-4245 · 480-606-5100

Frank M. Placenti · Squire Sanders · http://www.ssd.com · Two Renaissance Square, Suite 2700 · 40 North Central Avenue · Phoenix, AZ 85004-4498 · 602-528-4000

Joseph P. Richardson · Squire Sanders · http://www.ssd.com · Two Renaissance Square, Suite 2700 · 40 North Central Avenue · Phoenix, AZ 85004-4498 · 602-528-4000

CORPORATE LAW

Phoenix

James E. Brophy · Ryley Carlock & Applewhite · http://www.rcalaw.com · Phelps Dodge Tower, Suite 1200 · One North Central Avenue · Phoenix, AZ 85004-4417 · 602-258-7701

Tom Chauncey II · Gust Rosenfeld · http://www.gustlaw.com · 201 East Washington Street, Suite 800 · Phoenix, AZ 85004-2327 · 602-257-7422

Jon Cohen · ㉕ · Snell & Wilmer · One Arizona Center · 400 East Van Buren Street · Phoenix, AZ 85004-2202 · 602-382-6000

Joseph M. Crabb · Squire Sanders · http://www.ssd.com · Two Renaissance Square, Suite 2700 · 40 North Central Avenue · Phoenix, AZ 85004-4498 · 602-528-4000

Thomas H. Curzon · ⑩ · Osborn Maledon · http://www.omlaw.com · The Phoenix Plaza, Twenty-First Floor · 2929 North Central Avenue · Phoenix, AZ 85012-2793 · 602-640-9000

Scott D. DeWald · Lewis and Roca · http://www.lrlaw.com · 40 North Central Avenue, Suite 1900 · Phoenix, AZ 85004 · 602-262-5311

Michael Donahey · Snell & Wilmer · One Arizona Center · 400 East Van Buren Street · Phoenix, AZ 85004-2202 · 602-382-6000

Steven P. Emerick · Quarles & Brady · http://www.quarles.com · One Renaissance Square · Two North Central Avenue · Phoenix, AZ 85004-2391 · 602-229-5200

Matthew P. Feeney · ⑩ · Snell & Wilmer · One Arizona Center · 400 East Van Buren Street · Phoenix, AZ 85004-2202 · 602-382-6000

Jere M. Friedman · Friedman Law · 2398 East Camelback Road, Suite 925 · Phoenix, AZ 85016-0001 · 602-955-3800

Gary A. Gotto · Keller Rohrback · 3101 North Central Avenue, Suite 1400 · Phoenix, AZ 85012-2600 · 602-248-0088

William M. Hardin · ⑩ · Osborn Maledon · http://www.omlaw.com · The Phoenix Plaza, Twenty-First Floor · 2929 North Central Avenue · Phoenix, AZ 85012-2793 · 602-640-9000

William A. Hicks III · Ballard Spahr Andrews & Ingersoll · 3300 Tower, Suite 1800 · 3300 North Central Avenue · Phoenix, AZ 85012-2518 · 602-798-5400

Christopher D. Johnson · ⑩ · Squire Sanders · http://www.ssd.com · Two Renaissance Square, Suite 2700 · 40 North Central Avenue · Phoenix, AZ 85004-4498 · 602-528-4000

Robert S. Kant · Greenberg Traurig · http://www.gtlaw.com · 2375 East Camelback Road, Suite 700 · Phoenix, AZ 85016 · 602-445-8000

Andrew P. Kelly · Osborn Maledon · http://www.omlaw.com · The Phoenix Plaza, Twenty-First Floor · 2929 North Central Avenue · Phoenix, AZ 85012-2793 · 602-640-9000

Anne L. Kleindienst · ⑩ · Fennemore Craig · http://www.fclaw.com · 3003 North Central Avenue, Suite 2600 · Phoenix, AZ 85012-2913 · 602-916-5000

Steven T. Lawrence · Gallagher & Kennedy · http://www.gknet.com · 2575 East Camelback Road · Phoenix, AZ 85016-9225 · 602-530-8000

Karen C. McConnell · Ballard Spahr Andrews & Ingersoll · 3300 Tower, Suite 1800 · 3300 North Central Avenue · Phoenix, AZ 85012-2518 · 602-798-5400

P. Robert Moya · ⑳ · Quarles & Brady · http://www.quarles.com · One Renaissance Square · Two North Central Avenue · Phoenix, AZ 85004-2391 · 602-229-5200

Randall C. Nelson · Osborn Maledon · http://www.omlaw.com · The Phoenix Plaza, Twenty-First Floor · 2929 North Central Avenue · Phoenix, AZ 85012-2793 · 602-640-9000

Timothy E. Pickrell · Squire Sanders · http://www.ssd.com · Two Renaissance Square, Suite 2700 · 40 North Central Avenue · Phoenix, AZ 85004-4498 · 602-528-4000

Steven D. Pidgeon · ⑩ · DLA Piper · 2415 East Camelback Road, Suite 700 · Phoenix, AZ 85016-4245 · 480-606-5100

Joseph P. Richardson · Squire Sanders · http://www.ssd.com · Two Renaissance Square, Suite 2700 · 40 North Central Avenue · Phoenix, AZ 85004-4498 · 602-528-4000

Frederick H. Rosenfeld · ㉕ · Gust Rosenfeld · http://www.gustlaw.com · 201 East Washington Street, Suite 800 · Phoenix, AZ 85004-2327 · 602-257-7422

Scott W. Ruby · Gust Rosenfeld · http://www.gustlaw.com · 201 East Washington Street, Suite 800 · Phoenix, AZ 85004-2327 · 602-257-7422

Jack N. Rudel · Jennings, Strouss & Salmon · http://www.jsslaw.com · The Collier Center, 11th Floor · 201 East Washington Street · Phoenix, AZ 85004-2385 · 602-262-5911

Stephen M. Savage · ⑩ · Ballard Spahr Andrews & Ingersoll · 3300 Tower, Suite 1800 · 3300 North Central Avenue · Phoenix, AZ 85012-2518 · 602-798-5400

Dean C. Short II · Gallagher & Kennedy · http://www.gknet.com · 2575 East Camelback Road · Phoenix, AZ 85016-9225 · 602-530-8000

Norman C. Storey · Squire Sanders · http://www.ssd.com · Two Renaissance Square, Suite 2700 · 40 North Central Avenue · Phoenix, AZ 85004-4498 · 602-528-4000

Sarah A. Strunk · Fennemore Craig · http://www.fclaw.com · 3003 North Central Avenue, Suite 2600 · Phoenix, AZ 85012-2913 · 602-916-5000

Scott K. Weiss · Greenberg Traurig · http://www.gtlaw.com · 2375 East Camelback Road, Suite 700 · Phoenix, AZ 85016 · 602-445-8000

Nancy L. White · Steptoe & Johnson · http://www.steptoe.com · Collier Center, 16th Floor · 201 East Washington Street · Phoenix, AZ 85004-2382 · 602-257-5200

Scottsdale

Gregory L. Mast · ⑩ · Mast Law Firm · 2415 East Camelback Road, Suite 1050 · Scottsdale, AZ 85016 · 480-990-2114

Seymour Sacks · ㉕ · Sacks Tierney · http://www.sackstierney.com · 4250 North Drinkwater Boulevard, Fourth Floor · Scottsdale, AZ 85251-3693 · 480-425-2600

Tucson

Larry R. Adamson · ㉕ · Duffield, Young, Adamson · 3430 East Sunrise Drive, Suite 200 · Tucson, AZ 85718-3236 · 520-792-1181

Gabriel Beckmann · Lewis and Roca · http://www.lrlaw.com · One South Church Avenue, Suite 700 · Tucson, AZ 85701-1627 · 520-622-2090

Richard Duffield · ㉕ · Duffield, Young, Adamson · 3430 East Sunrise Drive, Suite 200 · Tucson, AZ 85718-3236 · 520-792-1181

Eugene C. Gieseler · ㉕ · Duffield, Young, Adamson · 3430 East Sunrise Drive, Suite 200 · Tucson, AZ 85718-3236 · 520-792-1181

Lawrence M. Hecker, Jr. · ⑩ · Hecker & Muehlebach · 405 West Franklin Street · Tucson, AZ 85701-8209 · 520-798-3803

Russell E. Jones · ⑳ · Waterfall, Economidis, Caldwell, Hanshaw & Villamana · http://www.wechv.com · Williams Centre, Eighth Floor · 5210 East Williams Circle · Tucson, AZ 85711 · 520-790-5828

Oscar S. Lizardi · Rusing & Lopez · 6262 North Swan Road, Suite 200 · Tucson, AZ 85718 · 520-792-4800

Gordon G. Waterfall · ㉕ · Waterfall, Economidis, Caldwell, Hanshaw & Villamana · http://www.wechv.com · Williams Centre, Eighth Floor · 5210 East Williams Circle · Tucson, AZ 85711 · 520-790-5828

DUI/DWI DEFENSE

Phoenix

Larry I. Kazan · ⑩ · Debus, Kazan & Westerhausen · 335 East Palm Lane · Phoenix, AZ 85004 · 602-257-8900

Tucson

Stephen Paul Barnard · Stephen Paul Barnard · 945 North Stone Avenue · Tucson, AZ 85705-7746 · 520-624-2494

Michael J. Bloom · ⑩ · Michael J. Bloom · 100 North Stone Avenue, Suite 701 · Tucson, AZ 85701-1516 520-882-9904

EDUCATION LAW

Flagstaff

C. Benson Hufford · Hufford, Horstman, Mongini, Parnell & Tucker · 120 North Beaver Street · P.O. Box B · Flagstaff, AZ 86001 · 928-226-0000

Mesa

Denise Lowell-Britt · Udall Shumway & Lyons · 30 West First Street · Mesa, AZ 85201 · 480-461-5300

Phoenix

Charles W. Herf · Quarles & Brady · http://www.quarles.com · One Renaissance Square · Two North Central Avenue · Phoenix, AZ 85004-2391 · 602-229-5200

Gary L. Lassen · Gary L. Lassen · 2020 North Central Avenue, Suite 1100 · Phoenix, AZ 85004 · 602-252-1205

Gordon Lewis · Jones, Skelton & Hochuli · 2901 North Central Avenue, Suite 800 · Phoenix, AZ 85012 · 602-263-1700

Tucson

Denise M. Bainton · DeConcini McDonald Yetwin & Lacy · 2525 East Broadway Boulevard, Suite 200 · Tucson, AZ 85716-5300 · 520-322-5000

John C. Richardson · DeConcini McDonald Yetwin & Lacy · 2525 East Broadway Boulevard, Suite 200 · Tucson, AZ 85716-5300 · 520-322-5000

ELDER LAW

Phoenix

Charles L. Arnold · Frazer Ryan Goldberg & Arnold · http://www.frgaglaw.com · 3101 North Central Avenue, Suite 1600 · Phoenix, AZ 85012-2615 · 602-277-2010

Bridget O'Brien Swartz · Law Office of Bridget O'Brien Swartz · 2999 North 44th Street, Suite 325 · Phoenix, AZ 85018 · 602-955-7886

Prescott

Chester B. McLaughlin IV · Law Office of Chester B. McLaughlin · 1577 Plaza West Drive, Suite B · Prescott, AZ 86303 · 928-443-9934

Sun City

Warner B. Bair II · Warner B. Bair II · 13211 North 103rd Avenue, Suite Three · Sun City, AZ 85351-3031 · 623-974-2421

Catherine J. Leas · Catherine J. Leas · 10451 Palmeras Drive, Suite 208 · Sun City, AZ 85373-2081 · 623-875-9501

Tucson

Allan D. Bogutz · Bogutz & Gordon · 3503 North Campbell Avenue, Suite 101 · Tucson, AZ 85719 · 520-321-9700

Robert B. Fleming · Fleming & Curti · 330 North Granada Avenue · Tucson, AZ 85701 · 520-622-0400

Craig Gordon · Bogutz & Gordon · 3503 North Campbell Avenue, Suite 101 · Tucson, AZ 85719 · 520-321-9700

EMINENT DOMAIN AND CONDEMNATION LAW

Phoenix

Martin A. Aronson · Morrill & Aronson · One East Camelback Road, Suite 340 · Phoenix, AZ 85012-1648 · 602-263-8993

Gary L. Birnbaum · ⑩ · Mariscal, Weeks, McIntyre & Friedlander · http://www.mwmf.com · 2901 North Central Avenue, Suite 200 · Phoenix, AZ 85012-2705 · 602-285-5000

James T. Braselton · Mariscal, Weeks, McIntyre & Friedlander · http://www.mwmf.com · 2901 North Central Avenue, Suite 200 · Phoenix, AZ 85012-2705 · 602-285-5000

Jay S. Dushoff · ㉕ · Gallagher & Kennedy · http://www.gknet.com · 2575 East Camelback Road · Phoenix, AZ 85016-9225 · 602-530-8000

Steven A. Hirsch · Bryan Cave · One Renaissance Square, Suite 2200 · Two North Central Avenue · Phoenix, AZ 85004-4406 · 602-364-7000

Robert V. Kerrick · Tiffany & Bosco · Camelback Esplanade II, Third Floor · 2525 East Camelback Road · Phoenix, AZ 85016-4237 · 602-255-6000

Dale S. Zeitlin · Zeitlin & Zeitlin · 5050 North 40th Street, Suite 330 · Phoenix, AZ 85018-2194 · 602-648-5222

Douglas G. Zimmerman · Jennings, Strouss & Salmon · http://www.jsslaw.com · The Collier Center, 11th Floor · 201 East Washington Street · Phoenix, AZ 85004-2385 · 602-262-5911

Tucson

G. Lawrence Schubart · Stubbs & Schubart · 340 North Main Avenue · Tucson, AZ 85701 · 520-623-5466

EMPLOYEE BENEFITS LAW

Phoenix

Nancy Kay Campbell · Snell & Wilmer · One Arizona Center · 400 East Van Buren Street · Phoenix, AZ 85004-2202 · 602-382-6000

David N. Heap · ⑩ · Fennemore Craig · http://www.fclaw.com · 3003 North Central Avenue, Suite 2600 · Phoenix, AZ 85012-2913 · 602-916-5000

Neil H. Hiller · ⑩ · Fennemore Craig · http://www.fclaw.com · 3003 North Central Avenue, Suite 2600 · Phoenix, AZ 85012-2913 · 602-916-5000

Thomas R. Hoecker · ⑩ · Snell & Wilmer · One Arizona Center · 400 East Van Buren Street · Phoenix, AZ 85004-2202 · 602-382-6000

Anne L. Leary · Gallagher & Kennedy · http://www.gknet.com · 2575 East Camelback Road · Phoenix, AZ 85016-9225 · 602-530-8000

David E. Manch · ⑳ · Lewis and Roca · http://www.lrlaw.com · 40 North Central Avenue, Suite 1900 · Phoenix, AZ 85004 · 602-262-5311

Michael E. Pietzsch · ⑳ · Pietzsch, Bonnett & Womack · http://www.usbenefitslaw.com · 2702 North Third Street, Suite 3000 · Phoenix, AZ 85004 · 602-604-6200

Cynthia L. Shupe · ⑩ · Fennemore Craig · http://www.fclaw.com · 3003 North Central Avenue, Suite 2600 · Phoenix, AZ 85012-2913 · 602-916-5000

Marvin S. Swift, Jr. · Snell & Wilmer · One Arizona Center · 400 East Van Buren Street · Phoenix, AZ 85004-2202 · 602-382-6000

Robert J. Werner · Onsager, Werner & Oberg · 3200 North Central Avenue, Suite 1800 · Phoenix, AZ 85012-2443 · 602-631-6790

Charles W. Whetstine · ⑩ · Frazer Ryan Goldberg & Arnold · http://www.frgaglaw.com · 3101 North Central Avenue, Suite 1600 · Phoenix, AZ 85012-2615 · 602-277-2010

Tucson

Steven L. Bossé · ⑳ · Gabroy, Rollman & Bossé · 3507 North Campbell Avenue, Suite 111 · Tucson, AZ 85719 · 520-320-1300

Bryan E. Daum · ⑳ · Bryan E. Daum · 6262 North Swan Road, Suite 130 · Tucson, AZ 85718-0001 · 520-577-5155

Eugene C. Gieseler · ㉕ · Duffield, Young, Adamson · 3430 East Sunrise Drive, Suite 200 · Tucson, AZ 85718-3236 · 520-792-1181

Douglas J. Newman · ⑳ · Douglas J. Newman · 2650 North Country Club Road · Tucson, AZ 85716-1651 · 520-325-2053

ENERGY LAW

Phoenix

Timothy J. Berg · Fennemore Craig · http://www.fclaw.com · 3003 North Central Avenue, Suite 2600 · Phoenix, AZ 85012-2913 · 602-916-5000

Thomas H. Campbell · Lewis and Roca · http://www.lrlaw.com · 40 North Central Avenue, Suite 1900 · Phoenix, AZ 85004 · 602-262-5311

C. Webb Crockett · ⑩ · Fennemore Craig · http://www.fclaw.com · 3003 North Central Avenue, Suite 2600 · Phoenix, AZ 85012-2913 · 602-916-5000

Jeffrey W. Crockett · Snell & Wilmer · One Arizona Center · 400 East Van Buren Street · Phoenix, AZ 85004-2202 · 602-382-6000

Michael M. Grant · Gallagher & Kennedy · http://www.gknet.com · 2575 East Camelback Road · Phoenix, AZ 85016-9225 · 602-530-8000

Jerry L. Haggard · ⑳ · Jerry L. Haggard · 1248 East Victor Hugo Avenue · Phoenix, AZ 85022-4950 · 602-863-1119

Norman D. James · Fennemore Craig · http://www.fclaw.com · 3003 North Central Avenue, Suite 2600 · Phoenix, AZ 85012-2913 · 602-916-5000

Jay I. Moyes · Moyes Sellers & Sims · 1850 North Central Avenue, Suite 1100 · Phoenix, AZ 85009-0001 602-604-2141

Michael W. Patten · Roshka DeWulf & Patten · http://www.rdp-law.com · One Arizona Center, Suite 800 400 East Van Buren Street · Phoenix, AZ 85004 · 602-256-6100

Carlos Ronstadt · ⑩ · Snell & Wilmer · One Arizona Center · 400 East Van Buren Street · Phoenix, AZ 85004-2202 · 602-382-6000

Kenneth C. Sundlof, Jr. · Jennings, Strouss & Salmon · http://www.jsslaw.com · The Collier Center, 11th Floor · 201 East Washington Street · Phoenix, AZ 85004-2385 · 602-262-5911

Tucson

John C. Lacy · ⑳ · DeConcini McDonald Yetwin & Lacy · 2525 East Broadway Boulevard, Suite 200 · Tucson, AZ 85716-5300 · 520-322-5000

Lawrence V. Robertson, Jr. · Munger Chadwick · National Bank Plaza, Suite 300 · 333 North Wilmot · Tucson, AZ 85711-2634 · 520-721-1900

ENTERTAINMENT LAW

Phoenix

Michael L. Gallagher · ⑩ · Gallagher & Kennedy · http://www.gknet.com · 2575 East Camelback Road · Phoenix, AZ 85016-9225 · 602-530-8000

William J. Maledon · ⑩ · Osborn Maledon · http://www.omlaw.com · The Phoenix Plaza, Twenty-First Floor · 2929 North Central Avenue · Phoenix, AZ 85012-2793 · 602-640-9000

ENVIRONMENTAL LAW

Phoenix

Robert D. Anderson · Fennemore Craig · http://www.fclaw.com · 3003 North Central Avenue, Suite 2600 Phoenix, AZ 85012-2913 · 602-916-5000

Lauren J. Caster · ⑩ · Fennemore Craig · http://www.fclaw.com · 3003 North Central Avenue, Suite 2600 Phoenix, AZ 85012-2913 · 602-916-5000

Carla A. Consoli · Lewis and Roca · http://www.lrlaw.com · 40 North Central Avenue, Suite 1900 · Phoenix, AZ 85004 · 602-262-5311

J. Stanton Curry · ⑩ · Gallagher & Kennedy · http://www.gknet.com · 2575 East Camelback Road · Phoenix, AZ 85016-9225 · 602-530-8000

James G. Derouin · ⑳ · Steptoe & Johnson · http://www.steptoe.com · Collier Center, 16th Floor · 201 East Washington Street · Phoenix, AZ 85004-2382 · 602-257-5200

Joseph A. Drazek · Quarles & Brady · http://www.quarles.com · One Renaissance Square · Two North Central Avenue · Phoenix, AZ 85004-2391 · 602-229-5200

Phillip F. Fargotstein · Fennemore Craig · http://www.fclaw.com · 3003 North Central Avenue, Suite 2600 · Phoenix, AZ 85012-2913 · 602-916-5000

Roger K. Ferland · ⑩ · Quarles & Brady · http://www.quarles.com · One Renaissance Square · Two North Central Avenue · Phoenix, AZ 85004-2391 · 602-229-5200

Kathleen Ferris · ⑩ · Kathleen Ferris · 2415 East Camelback Road, Suite 700 · Phoenix, AZ 85016 · 602-381-2561

Karen S. Gaylord · Salmon, Lewis & Weldon · 2850 East Camelback Road, Suite 200 · Phoenix, AZ 85016 · 602-801-9060

Norman D. James · Fennemore Craig · http://www.fclaw.com · 3003 North Central Avenue, Suite 2600 · Phoenix, AZ 85012-2913 · 602-916-5000

James W. Johnson · ⑳ · Fennemore Craig · http://www.fclaw.com · 3003 North Central Avenue, Suite 2600 · Phoenix, AZ 85012-2913 · 602-916-5000

David P. Kimball III · ⑳ · Gallagher & Kennedy · http://www.gknet.com · 2575 East Camelback Road · Phoenix, AZ 85016-9225 · 602-530-8000

M. Byron Lewis · ⑩ · Salmon, Lewis & Weldon · 2850 East Camelback Road, Suite 200 · Phoenix, AZ 85016 · 602-801-9060

Mark A. McGinnis · Salmon, Lewis & Weldon · 2850 East Camelback Road, Suite 200 · Phoenix, AZ 85016 · 602-801-9060

Lisa M. McKnight · Salmon, Lewis & Weldon · 2850 East Camelback Road, Suite 200 · Phoenix, AZ 85016 · 602-801-9060

Dalva L. Moellenberg · ⑩ · Gallagher & Kennedy · http://www.gknet.com · 2575 East Camelback Road · Phoenix, AZ 85016-9225 · 602-530-8000

Daniel L. Muchow · Quarles & Brady · http://www.quarles.com · One Renaissance Square · Two North Central Avenue · Phoenix, AZ 85004-2391 · 602-229-5200

Lucas J. Narducci · Bryan Cave · One Renaissance Square, Suite 2200 · Two North Central Avenue · Phoenix, AZ 85004-4406 · 602-364-7000

Patrick Paul · Snell & Wilmer · One Arizona Center · 400 East Van Buren Street · Phoenix, AZ 85004-2202 · 602-382-6000

Michael J. Pearce · Maguire & Pearce · 2999 North 44th Street, Suite 630 · Phoenix, AZ 85018-0001 · 602-277-2195

Sheryl A. Sweeney · Ryley Carlock & Applewhite · http://www.rcalaw.com · Phelps Dodge Tower, Suite 1200 · One North Central Avenue · Phoenix, AZ 85004-4417 · 602-258-7701

Shane R. Swindle · Perkins Coie Brown & Bain · http://www.perkinscoie.com · 2901 North Central Avenue, Suite 2000 · Phoenix, AZ 85012-2788 · 602-351-8000

Christopher D. Thomas · Squire Sanders · http://www.ssd.com · Two Renaissance Square, Suite 2700 · 40 North Central Avenue · Phoenix, AZ 85004-4498 · 602-528-4000

Richard W. Tobin II · Lewis and Roca · http://www.lrlaw.com · 40 North Central Avenue, Suite 1900 · Phoenix, AZ 85004 · 602-262-5311

David L. Wallis · Gallagher & Kennedy · http://www.gknet.com · 2575 East Camelback Road · Phoenix, AZ 85016-9225 · 602-530-8000

Nicholas J. Wallwork · Steptoe & Johnson · http://www.steptoe.com · Collier Center, 16th Floor · 201 East Washington Street · Phoenix, AZ 85004-2382 · 602-257-5200

John B. Weldon, Jr. · ⑩ · Salmon, Lewis & Weldon · 2850 East Camelback Road, Suite 200 · Phoenix, AZ 85016 · 602-801-9060

G. Van Velsor Wolf, Jr. · Snell & Wilmer · One Arizona Center · 400 East Van Buren Street · Phoenix, AZ 85004-2202 · 602-382-6000

Scottsdale

Charles A. Bischoff · Jorden Bischoff & Hiser · 7272 East Indian School Road, Suite 360 · Scottsdale, AZ 85251 · 480-505-3900

Eric L. Hiser · Jorden Bischoff & Hiser · 7272 East Indian School Road, Suite 360 · Scottsdale, AZ 85251 480-505-3900

Tucson

Michael F. McNulty · ⑩ · Lewis and Roca · http://www.lrlaw.com · One South Church Avenue, Suite 700 Tucson, AZ 85701-1627 · 520-622-2090

EQUIPMENT FINANCE LAW

Phoenix

Steven P. Emerick · Quarles & Brady · http://www.quarles.com · One Renaissance Square · Two North Central Avenue · Phoenix, AZ 85004-2391 · 602-229-5200

Jeffrey H. Verbin · ⑩ · Greenberg Traurig · http://www.gtlaw.com · 2375 East Camelback Road, Suite 700 · Phoenix, AZ 85016 · 602-445-8000

ETHICS AND PROFESSIONAL RESPONSIBILITY LAW

Phoenix

J. Scott Rhodes · Jennings, Strouss & Salmon · http://www.jsslaw.com · The Collier Center, 11th Floor · 201 East Washington Street · Phoenix, AZ 85004-2385 · 602-262-5911

FAMILY LAW

Phoenix

Barry L. Brody · Barry L. Brody · 5050 East Thomas Road · Phoenix, AZ 85018 · 602-381-0111

Todd H. Franks · Franks & Sheldon · 2111 East Highland Avenue, Suite 145 · Phoenix, AZ 85016 · 602-230-1265

Philip C. Gerard · ⑳ · The Cavanagh Law Firm · 1850 North Central Avenue, Suite 2400 · Phoenix, AZ 85004 · 602-322-4000

Charles R. Hallam · ⑩ · Warner, Angle, Hallam, Jackson & Formanek · 3550 North Central Avenue, Suite 1500 · Phoenix, AZ 85012-2188 · 602-264-7101

John E. Herrick · John E. Herrick · 2600 North Central Avenue, Suite 900 · Phoenix, AZ 85004 · 602-264-1001

Robert A. Jensen · ㉕ · Law Office of Robert Jensen · 2025 North Third Street, Suite 150 · Phoenix, AZ 85004-0001 · 602-230-1118

Robert L. Schwartz · ⑩ · Mariscal, Weeks, McIntyre & Friedlander · http://www.mwmf.com · 2901 North Central Avenue, Suite 200 · Phoenix, AZ 85012-2705 · 602-285-5000

Tucson

John R. Bolt · ⑩ · Donau & Bolt · 3505 North Campbell Avenue, Suite 501 · Tucson, AZ 85719-2033 · 520-795-8710

Peter Economidis · ㉕ · Waterfall, Economidis, Caldwell, Hanshaw & Villamana · http://www.wechv.com Williams Centre, Eighth Floor · 5210 East Williams Circle · Tucson, AZ 85711 · 520-790-5828

Leonard Karp · ⑳ · Karp & Weiss · 3060 North Swan Road · Tucson, AZ 85712-1225 · 520-325-4200

David H. Lieberthal · ⑩ · David H. Lieberthal · 3900 East Broadway Boulevard, Suite 210 · Tucson, AZ 85711-0001 · 520-547-7740

Kathleen A. McCarthy · ⑩ · Kathleen A. McCarthy & Associates · 300 North Main Avenue, Suite 203 · Tucson, AZ 85701-8230 · 520-623-0341

Alyce L. Pennington · DeConcini McDonald Yetwin & Lacy · 2525 East Broadway Boulevard, Suite 200 Tucson, AZ 85716-5300 · 520-322-5000

James L. Stroud · ⑳ · Stompoly & Stroud · http://www.stompoly.com · 3567 East Sunrise Drive, Suite 133 · Tucson, AZ 85718 · 520-628-8300

W. Patrick Traynor · ⑩ · Waterfall, Economidis, Caldwell, Hanshaw & Villamana · http://www.wechv.com · Williams Centre, Eighth Floor · 5210 East Williams Circle · Tucson, AZ 85711 · 520-790-5828

FAMILY LAW MEDIATION

Phoenix

Barry L. Brody · Barry L. Brody · 5050 East Thomas Road · Phoenix, AZ 85018 · 602-381-0111

Robert L. Schwartz · ⑩ · Mariscal, Weeks, McIntyre & Friedlander · http://www.mwmf.com · 2901 North Central Avenue, Suite 200 · Phoenix, AZ 85012-2705 · 602-285-5000

Tucson

Peter Economidis · ㉕ · Waterfall, Economidis, Caldwell, Hanshaw & Villamana · http://www.wechv.com Williams Centre, Eighth Floor · 5210 East Williams Circle · Tucson, AZ 85711 · 520-790-5828

Pamela A. Liberty · Liberty, O'Neill and Bibbens · 1590 East Grant Road · Tucson, AZ 85719-3314 · 520-322-9003

FIRST AMENDMENT LAW

Phoenix

David J. Bodney · ⑩ · Steptoe & Johnson · http://www.steptoe.com · Collier Center, 16th Floor · 201 East Washington Street · Phoenix, AZ 85004-2382 · 602-257-5200

Paul F. Eckstein · ㉕ · Perkins Coie Brown & Bain · http://www.perkinscoie.com · 2901 North Central Avenue, Suite 2000 · Phoenix, AZ 85012-2788 · 602-351-8000

Tucson

Michael J. Meehan · ⑳ · Munger Chadwick · National Bank Plaza, Suite 300 · 333 North Wilmot · Tucson, AZ 85711-2634 · 520-721-1900

FRANCHISE LAW

Phoenix

John L. Hay · ⑩ · Gust Rosenfeld · http://www.gustlaw.com · 201 East Washington Street, Suite 800 · Phoenix, AZ 85004-2327 · 602-257-7422

Anne L. Kleindienst · ⑩ · Fennemore Craig · http://www.fclaw.com · 3003 North Central Avenue, Suite 2600 · Phoenix, AZ 85012-2913 · 602-916-5000

Christina M. Noyes · Gust Rosenfeld · http://www.gustlaw.com · 201 East Washington Street, Suite 800 · Phoenix, AZ 85004-2327 · 602-257-7422

James A. Ullman · ⑩ · Greenberg Traurig · http://www.gtlaw.com · 2375 East Camelback Road, Suite 700 Phoenix, AZ 85016 · 602-445-8000

Susan E. Wells · ⑩ · Susan E. Wells · 10810 North Tatum Boulevard, Suite 102-201 · Phoenix, AZ 85028 480-368-9300

Quinn P. Williams · ⑩ · Greenberg Traurig · http://www.gtlaw.com · 2375 East Camelback Road, Suite 700 · Phoenix, AZ 85016 · 602-445-8000

Charles W. Wirken · Gust Rosenfeld · http://www.gustlaw.com · 201 East Washington Street, Suite 800 · Phoenix, AZ 85004-2327 · 602-257-7422

Jeffrey H. Wolf · Greenberg Traurig · http://www.gtlaw.com · 2375 East Camelback Road, Suite 700 · Phoenix, AZ 85016 · 602-445-8000

Scottsdale

Robin C. Carter · ⑩ · Robin C. Carter · 5520 East Charter Oak · Scottsdale, AZ 85254-0001 · 520-795-5445

GAMING LAW

Phoenix

Bradley Bledsoe Downes · Bledsoe Downes & Rosier · 4805 East Thistle Landing Drive, Suite 110 · Phoenix, AZ 85044 · 480-346-4214

Paul F. Eckstein · ㉕ · Perkins Coie Brown & Bain · http://www.perkinscoie.com · 2901 North Central Avenue, Suite 2000 · Phoenix, AZ 85012-2788 · 602-351-8000

Glenn M. Feldman · Mariscal, Weeks, McIntyre & Friedlander · http://www.mwmf.com · 2901 North Central Avenue, Suite 200 · Phoenix, AZ 85012-2705 · 602-285-5000

Stephen M. Hart · Lewis and Roca · http://www.lrlaw.com · 40 North Central Avenue, Suite 1900 · Phoenix, AZ 85004 · 602-262-5311

Heidi McNeil Staudenmaier · Snell & Wilmer · One Arizona Center · 400 East Van Buren Street · Phoenix, AZ 85004-2202 · 602-382-6000

Tempe

Eric N. Dahlstrom · Rothstein, Donatelli, Hughes, Dahlstrom, Schoenburg & Bienvenu · 80 East Rio Salado Parkway, Suite 305 · Tempe, AZ 85281-9103 · 480-921-9296

Michael C. Shiel · Rothstein, Donatelli, Hughes, Dahlstrom, Schoenburg & Bienvenu · 80 East Rio Salado Parkway, Suite 305 · Tempe, AZ 85281-9103 · 480-921-9296

Tucson

Luis A. Ochoa · Quarles & Brady · http://www.quarles.com · One South Church Street, Suite 1700 · Tucson, AZ 85701-1621 · 520-770-8700

Daniel J. Quigley · Quigley & Whitehill · http://www.qw-law.com · 2730 East Broadway, Suite 160 · Tucson, AZ 85716-5384 · 520-326-4600

GOVERNMENT RELATIONS LAW

Phoenix

Charles A. Blanchard · Perkins Coie Brown & Bain · http://www.perkinscoie.com · 2901 North Central Avenue, Suite 2000 · Phoenix, AZ 85012-2788 · 602-351-8000

Wendy G. Briggs · Veridus · 343 West Roosevelt Street · Phoenix, AZ 85003-0001 · 602-229-1129

Michael Preston Green · Fennemore Craig · http://www.fclaw.com · 3003 North Central Avenue, Suite 2600 · Phoenix, AZ 85012-2913 · 602-916-5000

Donald G. Isaacson · Isaacson & Duffy · 3101 North Central Avenue, Suite 740 · Phoenix, AZ 85012 · 602-274-2200

John K. Mangum · Law Office of John K. Mangum · 318 West Roosevelt Street · Phoenix, AZ 85003-0001 · 602-252-5222

Patrick Paul · Snell & Wilmer · One Arizona Center · 400 East Van Buren Street · Phoenix, AZ 85004-2202 · 602-382-6000

Jeffrey A. Sandquist · Veridus · 343 West Roosevelt Street · Phoenix, AZ 85003-0001 · 602-229-1129

Lee Stein · Perkins Coie Brown & Bain · http://www.perkinscoie.com · 2901 North Central Avenue, Suite 2000 · Phoenix, AZ 85012-2788 · 602-351-8000

HEALTH CARE LAW

Phoenix

Richard B. Burnham · ⑩ · Gammage & Burnham · http://www.gblaw.com · One Renaissance Square, 18th Floor · Two North Central Avenue · Phoenix, AZ 85004 · 602-256-0566

Gerald K. Gaffaney · Mariscal, Weeks, McIntyre & Friedlander · http://www.mwmf.com · 2901 North Central Avenue, Suite 200 · Phoenix, AZ 85012-2705 · 602-285-5000

Paul J. Giancola · Snell & Wilmer · One Arizona Center · 400 East Van Buren Street · Phoenix, AZ 85004-2202 · 602-382-6000

Andrew S. Gordon · Coppersmith Gordon Schermer & Brockelman · 2800 North Central Avenue, Suite 1000 · Phoenix, AZ 85004-1007 · 602-224-0999

Barry D. Halpern · ⑩ · Snell & Wilmer · One Arizona Center · 400 East Van Buren Street · Phoenix, AZ 85004-2202 · 602-382-6000

Kraig J. Marton · ⑩ · Jaburg & Wilk · http://www.jaburgwilk.com · 3200 North Central Avenue, Suite 2000 · Phoenix, AZ 85012 · 602-248-1000

Robert J. Milligan · Milligan, Lawless, Taylor, Murphy & Bailey · 4647 North 32nd Street, Suite B185 · Phoenix, AZ 85018-0001 · 602-792-3501

Roger N. Morris · Quarles & Brady · http://www.quarles.com · One Renaissance Square · Two North Central Avenue · Phoenix, AZ 85004-2391 · 602-229-5200

Stephen W. Myers · Myers & Jenkins · One East Camelback Road, Suite 500 · Phoenix, AZ 85012-2910 · 602-200-7900

Julie M. Nelson · Coppersmith Gordon Schermer & Brockelman · 2800 North Central Avenue, Suite 1000 · Phoenix, AZ 85004-1007 · 602-224-0999

Karen C. Owens · ⑩ · Coppersmith Gordon Schermer & Brockelman · 2800 North Central Avenue, Suite 1000 · Phoenix, AZ 85004-1007 · 602-224-0999

Calvin L. Raup · Raup & Hergenroether · Two North Central Avenue · Phoenix, AZ 85004-0001 · 602-229-8961

Terry M. Roman · ⑩ · Snell & Wilmer · One Arizona Center · 400 East Van Buren Street · Phoenix, AZ 85004-2202 · 602-382-6000

Kristen B. Rosati · Coppersmith Gordon Schermer & Brockelman · 2800 North Central Avenue, Suite 1000 · Phoenix, AZ 85004-1007 · 602-224-0999

Lawrence Rosenfeld · Greenberg Traurig · http://www.gtlaw.com · 2375 East Camelback Road, Suite 700 Phoenix, AZ 85016 · 602-445-8000

Beth J. Schermer · ⑩ · Coppersmith Gordon Schermer & Brockelman · 2800 North Central Avenue, Suite 1000 · Phoenix, AZ 85004-1007 · 602-224-0999

Susan L. Watchman · Gammage & Burnham · http://www.gblaw.com · One Renaissance Square, 18th Floor · Two North Central Avenue · Phoenix, AZ 85004 · 602-256-0566

John C. West · Jennings, Strouss & Salmon · http://www.jsslaw.com · The Collier Center, 11th Floor · 201 East Washington Street · Phoenix, AZ 85004-2385 · 602-262-5911

Scottsdale

Steven M. Goldstein · Sacks Tierney · http://www.sackstierney.com · 4250 North Drinkwater Boulevard, Fourth Floor · Scottsdale, AZ 85251-3693 · 480-425-2600

IMMIGRATION LAW

Goodyear

Christopher J. Brelje · ⑩ · Brelje and Associates · 3080 North Litchfield Road, Suite 220 · Goodyear, AZ 85338 · 623-536-5750

Phoenix

Lisa D. Duran · Quarles & Brady · http://www.quarles.com · One Renaissance Square · Two North Central Avenue · Phoenix, AZ 85004-2391 · 602-229-5200

Nancy-Jo Merritt · ⑩ · Fennemore Craig · http://www.fclaw.com · 3003 North Central Avenue, Suite 2600 · Phoenix, AZ 85012-2913 · 602-916-5000

Rebecca A. Winterscheidt · Snell & Wilmer · One Arizona Center · 400 East Van Buren Street · Phoenix, AZ 85004-2202 · 602-382-6000

Tucson

Zada A. Edgar-Soto · ⑩ · The Law Office of Zada Edgar-Soto · 1661 North Swan Road, Suite 150 · Tucson, AZ 85712-1571 · 520-327-3545

Gloria A. Goldman · ⑩ · Goldman & Goldman · 1575 West Ina Road · Tucson, AZ 85704 · 520-797-9229

Tarik H. Sultan · ⑩ · Wolf & Sultan · http://www.azimm.com · 5151 East Broadway Boulevard, Suite 1750 · Tucson, AZ 85701-3705 · 520-882-9633

INFORMATION TECHNOLOGY LAW

Phoenix

Fredric D. Bellamy · Steptoe & Johnson · http://www.steptoe.com · Collier Center, 16th Floor · 201 East Washington Street · Phoenix, AZ 85004-2382 · 602-257-5200

George L. Paul · Lewis and Roca · http://www.lrlaw.com · 40 North Central Avenue, Suite 1900 · Phoenix, AZ 85004 · 602-262-5311

INSURANCE LAW

Phoenix

Floyd P. Bienstock · Steptoe & Johnson · http://www.steptoe.com · Collier Center, 16th Floor · 201 East Washington Street · Phoenix, AZ 85004-2382 · 602-257-5200

Douglas L. Christian · Harper, Christian, Dichter & Graif · http://www.hcdglaw.com · 2700 North Central Avenue, Suite 1200 · Phoenix, AZ 85004 · 602-792-1700

Steven Guy · Snell & Wilmer · One Arizona Center · 400 East Van Buren Street · Phoenix, AZ 85004-2202 · 602-382-6000

Emil J. Kotalik, Jr. · Peshkin & Kotalik · 3030 North Central Avenue, Suite 1106 · Phoenix, AZ 85012-2718 · 602-248-7770

Steven Plitt · Kunz Plitt Hyland Demlong & Klefield · http://www.kunzlegal.com · 3838 North Central Avenue, Suite 1500 · Phoenix, AZ 85012 · 602-331-4600

Tempe

Wayne C. Arnett · Arnett & Arnett · 4600 South Mill Avenue, Suite 100 · Tempe, AZ 85282 · 480-839-4600

Tucson

Peter Collins, Jr. · Gust Rosenfeld · http://www.gustlaw.com · One South Church Avenue, Suite 1900 · Tucson, AZ 85701-1627 · 520-628-7070

INTELLECTUAL PROPERTY LAW

Phoenix

Paul E. Burns · Gallagher & Kennedy · http://www.gknet.com · 2575 East Camelback Road · Phoenix, AZ 85016-9225 · 602-530-8000

Chad S. Campbell · Perkins Coie Brown & Bain · http://www.perkinscoie.com · 2901 North Central Avenue, Suite 2000 · Phoenix, AZ 85012-2788 · 602-351-8000

John E. Cummerford · Greenberg Traurig · http://www.gtlaw.com · 2375 East Camelback Road, Suite 700 · Phoenix, AZ 85016 · 602-445-8000

Brett L. Dunkelman · Osborn Maledon · http://www.omlaw.com · The Phoenix Plaza, Twenty-First Floor · 2929 North Central Avenue · Phoenix, AZ 85012-2793 · 602-640-9000

Paul F. Eckstein · ㉕ · Perkins Coie Brown & Bain · http://www.perkinscoie.com · 2901 North Central Avenue, Suite 2000 · Phoenix, AZ 85012-2788 · 602-351-8000

Gerald L. Fellows · Greenberg Traurig · http://www.gtlaw.com · 2375 East Camelback Road, Suite 700 · Phoenix, AZ 85016 · 602-445-8000

Sean D. Garrison · Lewis and Roca · http://www.lrlaw.com · 40 North Central Avenue, Suite 1900 · Phoenix, AZ 85004 · 602-262-5311

Richard A. Halloran · Lewis and Roca · http://www.lrlaw.com · 40 North Central Avenue, Suite 1900 · Phoenix, AZ 85004 · 602-262-5311

Ray K. Harris · Fennemore Craig · http://www.fclaw.com · 3003 North Central Avenue, Suite 2600 · Phoenix, AZ 85012-2913 · 602-916-5000

Charles Hauff · Snell & Wilmer · One Arizona Center · 400 East Van Buren Street · Phoenix, AZ 85004-2202 · 602-382-6000

Jonathan M. James · Perkins Coie Brown & Bain · http://www.perkinscoie.com · 2901 North Central Avenue, Suite 2000 · Phoenix, AZ 85012-2788 · 602-351-8000

Charles W. Jirauch · Quarles & Brady · http://www.quarles.com · One Renaissance Square · Two North Central Avenue · Phoenix, AZ 85004-2391 · 602-229-5200

Brian W. LaCorte · Gallagher & Kennedy · http://www.gknet.com · 2575 East Camelback Road · Phoenix, AZ 85016-9225 · 602-530-8000

Sid Leach · Snell & Wilmer · One Arizona Center · 400 East Van Buren Street · Phoenix, AZ 85004-2202 602-382-6000

David E. Rauch · Snell & Wilmer · One Arizona Center · 400 East Van Buren Street · Phoenix, AZ 85004-2202 · 602-382-6000

Bruce E. Samuels · Lewis and Roca · http://www.lrlaw.com · 40 North Central Avenue, Suite 1900 · Phoenix, AZ 85004 · 602-262-5311

Howard Sobelman · Snell & Wilmer · One Arizona Center · 400 East Van Buren Street · Phoenix, AZ 85004-2202 · 602-382-6000

Scottsdale

Glenn S. Bacal · ⑩ · Holme Roberts & Owen · http://www.hro.com · Promenade Corporate Center, Suite 300 · 16427 North Scottsdale Road · Scottsdale, AZ 85254-1597 · 480-624-4500

INTERNATIONAL ARBITRATION

Phoenix

Gerald W. Alston · Jennings, Strouss & Salmon · http://www.jsslaw.com · The Collier Center, 11th Floor 201 East Washington Street · Phoenix, AZ 85004-2385 · 602-262-5911

Philip A. Robbins · ㉕ · Jennings, Strouss & Salmon · http://www.jsslaw.com · The Collier Center, 11th Floor · 201 East Washington Street · Phoenix, AZ 85004-2385 · 602-262-5911

INTERNATIONAL TRADE AND FINANCE LAW

Nogales

Hector G. Arana · Fennemore Craig · http://www.fclaw.com · 420 West Mariposa Road, Suite 200 · Nogales, AZ 85621-1074 · 520-281-3480

Phoenix

Gerald W. Alston · Jennings, Strouss & Salmon · http://www.jsslaw.com · The Collier Center, 11th Floor 201 East Washington Street · Phoenix, AZ 85004-2385 · 602-262-5911

Tucson

D. Michael Mandig · Waterfall, Economidis, Caldwell, Hanshaw & Villamana · http://www.wechv.com · Williams Centre, Eighth Floor · 5210 East Williams Circle · Tucson, AZ 85711 · 520-790-5828

LABOR AND EMPLOYMENT LAW

Phoenix

Daniel C. Barr · Perkins Coie Brown & Bain · http://www.perkinscoie.com · 2901 North Central Avenue, Suite 2000 · Phoenix, AZ 85012-2788 · 602-351-8000

Gerald Barrett · ⑳ · Ward, Keenan & Barrett · 3838 North Central Avenue, Suite 1720 · Phoenix, AZ 85012-0001 · 602-279-1717

Stephanie M. Cerasano · Ford & Harrison · http://www.fordharrison.com · 2525 East Camelback Road, Suite 450 · Phoenix, AZ 85016 · 602-627-3500

Charles L. Chester · Ryley Carlock & Applewhite · http://www.rcalaw.com · Phelps Dodge Tower, Suite 1200 · One North Central Avenue · Phoenix, AZ 85004-4417 · 602-258-7701

Joseph T. Clees · Ogletree Deakins · http://www.ogletreedeakins.com · 2415 Camelback Road, Suite 800 Phoenix, AZ 85016 · 602-778-3700

Richard S. Cohen · ⑩ · Ford & Harrison · http://www.fordharrison.com · 2525 East Camelback Road, Suite 450 · Phoenix, AZ 85016 · 602-627-3500

Robert J. Deeny · ㉕ · Sherman & Howard · 1850 North Central Avenue, Suite 500 · Phoenix, AZ 85004-4546 · 602-636-2000

John Alan Doran · Greenberg Traurig · http://www.gtlaw.com · 2375 East Camelback Road, Suite 700 · Phoenix, AZ 85016 · 602-445-8000

John J. Egbert · Jennings, Strouss & Salmon · http://www.jsslaw.com · The Collier Center, 11th Floor · 201 East Washington Street · Phoenix, AZ 85004-2385 · 602-262-5911

Troy P. Foster · Ford & Harrison · http://www.fordharrison.com · 2525 East Camelback Road, Suite 450 · Phoenix, AZ 85016 · 602-627-3500

Donald R. Gilbert · Fennemore Craig · http://www.fclaw.com · 3003 North Central Avenue, Suite 2600 · Phoenix, AZ 85012-2913 · 602-916-5000

David F. Gomez · ⑩ · Gomez & Petitti · 2525 East Camelback Road, Suite 860 · Phoenix, AZ 85016 · 602-957-8686

N. Douglas Grimwood · ⑩ · The Grimwood Law Firm · 301 East Bethany Home Road, Suite A-205 · Phoenix, AZ 85012-1269 · 602-265-4995

Robert D. Haws · Gust Rosenfeld · http://www.gustlaw.com · 201 East Washington Street, Suite 800 · Phoenix, AZ 85004-2327 · 602-257-7422

William R. Hayden · ⑳ · Snell & Wilmer · One Arizona Center · 400 East Van Buren Street · Phoenix, AZ 85004-2202 · 602-382-6000

Charles W. Herf · Quarles & Brady · http://www.quarles.com · One Renaissance Square · Two North Central Avenue · Phoenix, AZ 85004-2391 · 602-229-5200

Donald Peder Johnsen · Gallagher & Kennedy · http://www.gknet.com · 2575 East Camelback Road · Phoenix, AZ 85016-9225 · 602-530-8000

Robert K. Jones · Jackson Lewis · http://www.jacksonlewis.com · 2390 East Camelback Road, Suite 305 · Phoenix, AZ 85016 · 602-714-7044

Lawrence A. Katz · ⑳ · Steptoe & Johnson · http://www.steptoe.com · Collier Center, 16th Floor · 201 East Washington Street · Phoenix, AZ 85004-2382 · 602-257-5200

Michael J. Keenan · ⑳ · Ward, Keenan & Barrett · 3838 North Central Avenue, Suite 1720 · Phoenix, AZ 85012-0001 · 602-279-1717

Thomas J. Kennedy · Sherman & Howard · 1850 North Central Avenue, Suite 500 · Phoenix, AZ 85004-4546 · 602-636-2000

Gordon Lewis · Jones, Skelton & Hochuli · 2901 North Central Avenue, Suite 800 · Phoenix, AZ 85012 · 602-263-1700

John F. Lomax, Jr. · Greenberg Traurig · http://www.gtlaw.com · 2375 East Camelback Road, Suite 700 · Phoenix, AZ 85016 · 602-445-8000

Stanley Lubin · ㉕ · Lubin & Enoch · 349 North Fourth Avenue · Phoenix, AZ 85003 · 602-234-0008

Kraig J. Marton · ⑩ · Jaburg & Wilk · http://www.jaburgwilk.com · 3200 North Central Avenue, Suite 2000 · Phoenix, AZ 85012 · 602-248-1000

Michael D. Moberly · Ryley Carlock & Applewhite · http://www.rcalaw.com · Phelps Dodge Tower, Suite 1200 · One North Central Avenue · Phoenix, AZ 85004-4417 · 602-258-7701

Nathan R. Niemuth · Ryley Carlock & Applewhite · http://www.rcalaw.com · Phelps Dodge Tower, Suite 1200 · One North Central Avenue · Phoenix, AZ 85004-4417 · 602-258-7701

J. Mark Ogden · Littler Mendelson · Camelback Esplanade, Suite 900 · 2425 East Camelback Road · Phoenix, AZ 85016-4242 · 602-474-3600

Michael J. Petitti, Jr. · Gomez & Petitti · 2525 East Camelback Road, Suite 860 · Phoenix, AZ 85016 · 602-957-8686

Jon E. Pettibone · ⑳ · Quarles & Brady · http://www.quarles.com · One Renaissance Square · Two North Central Avenue · Phoenix, AZ 85004-2391 · 602-229-5200

Janice Procter-Murphy · Fennemore Craig · http://www.fclaw.com · 3003 North Central Avenue, Suite 2600 · Phoenix, AZ 85012-2913 · 602-916-5000

Stephanie J. Quincy · Steptoe & Johnson · http://www.steptoe.com · Collier Center, 16th Floor · 201 East Washington Street · Phoenix, AZ 85004-2382 · 602-257-5200

Scott W. Rodgers · Osborn Maledon · http://www.omlaw.com · The Phoenix Plaza, Twenty-First Floor · 2929 North Central Avenue · Phoenix, AZ 85012-2793 · 602-640-9000

Lawrence Rosenfeld · Greenberg Traurig · http://www.gtlaw.com · 2375 East Camelback Road, Suite 700 Phoenix, AZ 85016 · 602-445-8000

Bradley H. Schleier · Schleier Law Offices · 3101 North Central Avenue, Suite 1090 · Phoenix, AZ 85012-2640 · 602-277-0157

Tod F. Schleier · ⑳ · Schleier Law Offices · 3101 North Central Avenue, Suite 1090 · Phoenix, AZ 85012-2640 · 602-277-0157

David A. Selden · ⑩ · Ballard Spahr Andrews & Ingersoll · 3300 Tower, Suite 1800 · 3300 North Central Avenue · Phoenix, AZ 85012-2518 · 602-798-5400

James Burr Shields II · James Burr Shields · 382 East Palm Lane · Phoenix, AZ 85004-1531 · 602-307-0780

Ralph B. Sievwright · ⑳ · Twitty, Sievwright & Mills · 2702 North Third Street, Suite 4007 · Phoenix, AZ 85004-4608 · 602-248-9424

Ronald J. Stolkin · ⑳ · Fennemore Craig · http://www.fclaw.com · 3003 North Central Avenue, Suite 2600 · Phoenix, AZ 85012-2913 · 602-916-5000

Richard K. Walker · Quarles & Brady · http://www.quarles.com · One Renaissance Square · Two North Central Avenue · Phoenix, AZ 85004-2391 · 602-229-5200

Lonnie J. Williams, Jr. · ⑩ · Quarles & Brady · http://www.quarles.com · One Renaissance Square · Two North Central Avenue · Phoenix, AZ 85004-2391 · 602-229-5200

Rebecca A. Winterscheidt · Snell & Wilmer · One Arizona Center · 400 East Van Buren Street · Phoenix, AZ 85004-2202 · 602-382-6000

Tempe

Kent Brockelman · Coppersmith Gordon Schermer & Brockelman · 2800 North Central Avenue, Suite 1000 · Tempe, AZ 85004 · 602-224-0999

Kimberly A. Fatica · Coppersmith Gordon Schermer & Brockelman · 2800 North Central Avenue, Suite 1000 · Tempe, AZ 85004 · 602-224-0999

Tucson

Donald T. Awerkamp · Awerkamp & Bonilla · 313 South Convent Avenue · Tucson, AZ 85701 · 520-798-5282

Sandra S. Froman · ⑩ · Sandra S. Froman · 200 West Magee Road, Suite 140 · Tucson, AZ 85704-6492 · 520-498-1860

John Gabroy · ⑩ · Gabroy, Rollman & Bossé · 3507 North Campbell Avenue, Suite 111 · Tucson, AZ 85719 · 520-320-1300

James K. Mackie · Ogletree Deakins · http://www.ogletreedeakins.com · 6760 North Oracle Road, Suite 200 · Tucson, AZ 85704-5608 · 520-544-0300

Gerald Maltz · ㉕ · Haralson, Miller, Pitt, Feldman & McAnally · One South Church Avenue, Suite 900 · Tucson, AZ 85701 · 520-792-3836

Tibor Nagy, Jr. · ⑩ · Ogletree Deakins · http://www.ogletreedeakins.com · 6760 North Oracle Road, Suite 200 · Tucson, AZ 85704-5608 · 520-544-0300

John A. Robertson · ⑳ · Snell & Wilmer · One South Church Avenue, Suite 1500 · Tucson, AZ 85701-1630 · 520-882-1200

Armand Salese · ⑳ · Law Offices of Armand Salese · 145 South Sixth Avenue · Tucson, AZ 85701 · 520-903-0825

LAND USE & ZONING LAW

Phoenix

Stephen W. Anderson · Gammage & Burnham · http://www.gblaw.com · One Renaissance Square, 18th Floor · Two North Central Avenue · Phoenix, AZ 85004 · 602-256-0566

Dana S. Belknap · Gallagher & Kennedy · http://www.gknet.com · 2575 East Camelback Road · Phoenix, AZ 85016-9225 · 602-530-8000

Edwin C. Bull · Burch & Cracchiolo · http://www.bcattorneys.com · 702 East Osborn Road, Suite 200 · P.O. Box 16882 · Phoenix, AZ 85011 · 602-274-7611

Rebecca Lynne Burnham · ⑩ · Greenberg Traurig · http://www.gtlaw.com · 2375 East Camelback Road, Suite 700 · Phoenix, AZ 85016 · 602-445-8000

Michael J. Curley · ⑩ · Earl Curley & Lagarde · 3101 North Central Avenue, Suite 1000 · Phoenix, AZ 85012 · 602-265-0094

Jay S. Dushoff · ㉕ · Gallagher & Kennedy · http://www.gknet.com · 2575 East Camelback Road · Phoenix, AZ 85016-9225 · 602-530-8000

Stephen C. Earl · ⑩ · Earl Curley & Lagarde · 3101 North Central Avenue, Suite 1000 · Phoenix, AZ 85012 · 602-265-0094

Grady Gammage, Jr. · ⑩ · Gammage & Burnham · http://www.gblaw.com · One Renaissance Square, 18th Floor · Two North Central Avenue · Phoenix, AZ 85004 · 602-256-0566

Jeffrey D. Gross · Gallagher & Kennedy · http://www.gknet.com · 2575 East Camelback Road · Phoenix, AZ 85016-9225 · 602-530-8000

Robert V. Kerrick · Tiffany & Bosco · Camelback Esplanade II, Third Floor · 2525 East Camelback Road · Phoenix, AZ 85016-4237 · 602-255-6000

Lynne A. Lagarde · ⑩ · Earl Curley & Lagarde · 3101 North Central Avenue, Suite 1000 · Phoenix, AZ 85012 · 602-265-0094

Larry S. Lazarus · Lazarus & Associates · The Lazarus Professional Building · 420 West Roosevelt · Phoenix, AZ 85003-1325 · 602-340-0900

Michael J. Phalen · Fennemore Craig · http://www.fclaw.com · 3003 North Central Avenue, Suite 2600 · Phoenix, AZ 85012-2913 · 602-916-5000

Scott A. Rose · The Cavanagh Law Firm · 1850 North Central Avenue, Suite 2400 · Phoenix, AZ 85004 · 602-322-4000

Michael B. Withey · Withey Morris · 2525 East Arizona Biltmore Circle, Suite A-212 · Phoenix, AZ 85016-0001 · 602-230-0600

Scottsdale

John V. Berry · Berry & Damore · 6750 East Camelback Road, Suite 100 · Scottsdale, AZ 85251 · 480-385-2727

Paul E. Gilbert · ⑩ · Beus Gilbert · 4800 North Scottsdale Road, Suite 6000 · Scottsdale, AZ 85251-7630 · 480-429-3000

Douglas A. Jorden · Jorden Bischoff & Hiser · 7272 East Indian School Road, Suite 360 · Scottsdale, AZ 85251 · 480-505-3900

Tucson

Frank S. Bangs, Jr. · Lewis and Roca · http://www.lrlaw.com · One South Church Avenue, Suite 700 · Tucson, AZ 85701-1627 · 520-622-2090

Mary Beth Savel · Lewis and Roca · http://www.lrlaw.com · One South Church Avenue, Suite 700 · Tucson, AZ 85701-1627 · 520-622-2090

S. L. Schorr · ⑳ · Lewis and Roca · http://www.lrlaw.com · One South Church Avenue, Suite 700 · Tucson, AZ 85701-1627 · 520-622-2090

G. Lawrence Schubart · Stubbs & Schubart · 340 North Main Avenue · Tucson, AZ 85701 · 520-623-5466

Keri L. Silvyn · Lewis and Roca · http://www.lrlaw.com · One South Church Avenue, Suite 700 · Tucson, AZ 85701-1627 · 520-622-2090

LEGAL MALPRACTICE LAW

Phoenix

Peter D. Baird · ㉕ · Lewis and Roca · http://www.lrlaw.com · 40 North Central Avenue, Suite 1900 · Phoenix, AZ 85004 · 602-262-5311

Gary L. Birnbaum · ⑩ · Mariscal, Weeks, McIntyre & Friedlander · http://www.mwmf.com · 2901 North Central Avenue, Suite 200 · Phoenix, AZ 85012-2705 · 602-285-5000

John J. Bouma · ⑩ · Snell & Wilmer · One Arizona Center · 400 East Van Buren Street · Phoenix, AZ 85004-2202 · 602-382-6000

Timothy J. Burke · Fennemore Craig · http://www.fclaw.com · 3003 North Central Avenue, Suite 2600 · Phoenix, AZ 85012-2913 · 602-916-5000

James R. Condo · Snell & Wilmer · One Arizona Center · 400 East Van Buren Street · Phoenix, AZ 85004-2202 · 602-382-6000

Brian M. Goodwin · Shughart Thomson & Kilroy · http://www.stklaw.com · Security Title Plaza, Suite 1200 · 3636 North Central Avenue · Phoenix, AZ 85012-0001 · 602-650-2000

Mark I. Harrison · ⑩ · Osborn Maledon · http://www.omlaw.com · The Phoenix Plaza, Twenty-First Floor · 2929 North Central Avenue · Phoenix, AZ 85012-2793 · 602-640-9000

Ed Hendricks, Sr. · ㉕ · Meyer Hendricks · 3131 East CamelbackRoad, Suite 310 · Phoenix, AZ 85016 · 602-604-2100

Don P. Martin · Quarles & Brady · http://www.quarles.com · One Renaissance Square · Two North Central Avenue · Phoenix, AZ 85004-2391 · 602-229-5200

David E. Rauch · Snell & Wilmer · One Arizona Center · 400 East Van Buren Street · Phoenix, AZ 85004-2202 · 602-382-6000

Patricia Lee Refo · Snell & Wilmer · One Arizona Center · 400 East Van Buren Street · Phoenix, AZ 85004-2202 · 602-382-6000

J. Scott Rhodes · Jennings, Strouss & Salmon · http://www.jsslaw.com · The Collier Center, 11th Floor · 201 East Washington Street · Phoenix, AZ 85004-2385 · 602-262-5911

Kenneth J. Sherk · ⑩ · Fennemore Craig · http://www.fclaw.com · 3003 North Central Avenue, Suite 2600 · Phoenix, AZ 85012-2913 · 602-916-5000

Andrew R. Sherwood · Quarles & Brady · http://www.quarles.com · One Renaissance Square · Two North Central Avenue · Phoenix, AZ 85004-2391 · 602-229-5200

Tucson

Dan Cavett · ⑩ · Cavett & Fulton · 6035 East Grant Road · Tucson, AZ 85712 · 520-733-0100

Douglas H. Clark, Jr. · ⑩ · Mesch, Clark & Rothschild · 259 North Meyer Avenue · Tucson, AZ 85701-1090 · 520-624-8886

Richard Davis · Mesch, Clark & Rothschild · 259 North Meyer Avenue · Tucson, AZ 85701-1090 · 520-624-8886

LEVERAGED BUYOUTS AND PRIVATE EQUITY LAW

Phoenix

P. Robert Moya · ⑳ · Quarles & Brady · http://www.quarles.com · One Renaissance Square · Two North Central Avenue · Phoenix, AZ 85004-2391 · 602-229-5200

MASS TORT LITIGATION

Phoenix

Stephen M. Bressler · Lewis and Roca · http://www.lrlaw.com · 40 North Central Avenue, Suite 1900 · Phoenix, AZ 85004 · 602-262-5311

Sheila Carmody · Snell & Wilmer · One Arizona Center · 400 East Van Buren Street · Phoenix, AZ 85004-2202 · 602-382-6000

Craig W. Phillips · Lewis and Roca · http://www.lrlaw.com · 40 North Central Avenue, Suite 1900 · Phoenix, AZ 85004 · 602-262-5311

Robert J. Pohlman · Ryley Carlock & Applewhite · http://www.rcalaw.com · Phelps Dodge Tower, Suite 1200 · One North Central Avenue · Phoenix, AZ 85004-4417 · 602-258-7701

Nicholas J. Wallwork · Steptoe & Johnson · http://www.steptoe.com · Collier Center, 16th Floor · 201 East Washington Street · Phoenix, AZ 85004-2382 · 602-257-5200

Tucson

Cynthia T. Kuhn · Rusing & Lopez · 6262 North Swan Road, Suite 200 · Tucson, AZ 85718 · 520-792-4800

Phoenix

Neil C. Alden · Jardine, Baker, Hickman & Houston · 3300 North Central Avenue, Suite 2600 · Phoenix, AZ 85012 · 602-200-9777

James R. Broening · ⑩ · Broening, Oberg, Woods & Wilson · http://www.bowwlaw.com · 1122 East Jefferson Street · Phoenix, AZ 85034 · 602-271-7700

Stephen A. Bullington · Jones, Skelton & Hochuli · 2901 North Central Avenue, Suite 800 · Phoenix, AZ 85012 · 602-263-1700

Jeffrey J. Campbell · Campbell, Yost, Clare & Norell · 101 North First Avenue, Suite 2500 · Phoenix, AZ 85003 · 602-322-1600

Steve D. Copple · Copple, Boehm & Murphy · 3550 North Central Avenue, Suite 1800 · Phoenix, AZ 85012 · 602-528-4700

Frederick M. Cummings · Jennings, Strouss & Salmon · http://www.jsslaw.com · The Collier Center, 11th Floor · 201 East Washington Street · Phoenix, AZ 85004-2385 · 602-262-5911

Shawn M. Cunningham · Harris, Powers & Cunningham · 361 East Coronado, Suite 101 · P.O. Box 13568 Phoenix, AZ 85004-1525 · 602-271-9344

Harding B. Cure · The Cavanagh Law Firm · 1850 North Central Avenue, Suite 2400 · Phoenix, AZ 85004 · 602-322-4000

Jay A. Fradkin · Jennings, Strouss & Salmon · http://www.jsslaw.com · The Collier Center, 11th Floor · 201 East Washington Street · Phoenix, AZ 85004-2385 · 602-262-5911

Peter A. Guerrero · Roush, McCracken, Guerrero, Miller & Ortega · 650 North Third Avenue · Phoenix, AZ 85003 · 602-253-3554

Barry D. Halpern · ⑩ · Snell & Wilmer · One Arizona Center · 400 East Van Buren Street · Phoenix, AZ 85004-2202 · 602-382-6000

William R. Jones, Jr. · ㉕ · Jones, Skelton & Hochuli · 2901 North Central Avenue, Suite 800 · Phoenix, AZ 85012 · 602-263-1700

John A. Micheaels · Beale Micheaels & Slack · 1440 East Missouri Avenue, Suite 150 · Phoenix, AZ 85014 · 602-285-1444

Anthony J. Palumbo · Palumbo, Wolfe, Sahlman & Palumbo · 2800 North Central Avenue, Suite 1400 · Phoenix, AZ 85004 · 602-265-5777

Frank I. Powers · Harris, Powers & Cunningham · 361 East Coronado, Suite 101 · P.O. Box 13568 · Phoenix, AZ 85004-1525 · 602-271-9344

Calvin L. Raup · Raup & Hergenroether · Two North Central Avenue · Phoenix, AZ 85004-0001 · 602-229-8961

William H. Sandweg III · Sandweg & Ager · http://www.phoenixmedicalmalpracticeattorneys.com · 1221 East Osborn Road, Suite 100 · Phoenix, AZ 85014 · 602-648-3201

J. Russell Skelton · ⑩ · Jones, Skelton & Hochuli · 2901 North Central Avenue, Suite 800 · Phoenix, AZ 85012 · 602-263-1700

Howard M. Snyder · Snyder & Wenner · 2200 East Camelback Road, Suite 213 · Phoenix, AZ 85016-9096 · 602-224-0005

David A. Wenner · ⑩ · Snyder & Wenner · 2200 East Camelback Road, Suite 213 · Phoenix, AZ 85016-9096 · 602-224-0005

Elliot G. Wolfe · ⑳ · Palumbo, Wolfe, Sahlman & Palumbo · 2800 North Central Avenue, Suite 1400 · Phoenix, AZ 85004 · 602-265-5777

Tempe

Bruce D. Crawford · Crawford & Kline · 1920 East Southern Avenue, Suite 101 · Tempe, AZ 85282 · 480-491-5100

Tucson

Dan Cavett · ⑩ · Cavett & Fulton · 6035 East Grant Road · Tucson, AZ 85712 · 520-733-0100

Barry M. Davis · ⑩ · Piccarreta & Davis · http://www.pd-law.com · 145 South Sixth Avenue · Tucson, AZ 85701-2007 · 520-622-6900

Ronald D. Mercaldo · Law Offices of Ronald D. Mercaldo · 6713 East Camino Principal · Tucson, AZ 85715 · 520-624-1400

Catherine M. Woods · Rusing & Lopez · 6262 North Swan Road, Suite 200 · Tucson, AZ 85718 · 520-792-4800

MERGERS & ACQUISITIONS LAW

Phoenix

Jon Cohen · ㉕ · Snell & Wilmer · One Arizona Center · 400 East Van Buren Street · Phoenix, AZ 85004-2202 · 602-382-6000

Joseph M. Crabb · Squire Sanders · http://www.ssd.com · Two Renaissance Square, Suite 2700 · 40 North Central Avenue · Phoenix, AZ 85004-4498 · 602-528-4000

Thomas H. Curzon · ⑩ · Osborn Maledon · http://www.omlaw.com · The Phoenix Plaza, Twenty-First Floor · 2929 North Central Avenue · Phoenix, AZ 85012-2793 · 602-640-9000

Michael Donahey · Snell & Wilmer · One Arizona Center · 400 East Van Buren Street · Phoenix, AZ 85004-2202 · 602-382-6000

Matthew P. Feeney · ⑩ · Snell & Wilmer · One Arizona Center · 400 East Van Buren Street · Phoenix, AZ 85004-2202 · 602-382-6000

Greg R. Hall · DLA Piper · 2415 East Camelback Road, Suite 700 · Phoenix, AZ 85016-4245 · 480-606-5100

Robert S. Kant · Greenberg Traurig · http://www.gtlaw.com · 2375 East Camelback Road, Suite 700 · Phoenix, AZ 85016 · 602-445-8000

Michael L. Kaplan · Greenberg Traurig · http://www.gtlaw.com · 2375 East Camelback Road, Suite 700 · Phoenix, AZ 85016 · 602-445-8000

Richard Lieberman · Jennings, Strouss & Salmon · http://www.jsslaw.com · The Collier Center, 11th Floor · 201 East Washington Street · Phoenix, AZ 85004-2385 · 602-262-5911

Bruce E. Macdonough · Greenberg Traurig · http://www.gtlaw.com · 2375 East Camelback Road, Suite 700 · Phoenix, AZ 85016 · 602-445-8000

Karen C. McConnell · Ballard Spahr Andrews & Ingersoll · 3300 Tower, Suite 1800 · 3300 North Central Avenue · Phoenix, AZ 85012-2518 · 602-798-5400

P. Robert Moya · ⑳ · Quarles & Brady · http://www.quarles.com · One Renaissance Square · Two North Central Avenue · Phoenix, AZ 85004-2391 · 602-229-5200

Steven D. Pidgeon · ⑩ · DLA Piper · 2415 East Camelback Road, Suite 700 · Phoenix, AZ 85016-4245 · 480-606-5100

Frank M. Placenti · Squire Sanders · http://www.ssd.com · Two Renaissance Square, Suite 2700 · 40 North Central Avenue · Phoenix, AZ 85004-4498 · 602-528-4000

Joseph P. Richardson · Squire Sanders · http://www.ssd.com · Two Renaissance Square, Suite 2700 · 40 North Central Avenue · Phoenix, AZ 85004-4498 · 602-528-4000

Tucson

Roy W. Kyle · ⑩ · Lewis and Roca · http://www.lrlaw.com · One South Church Avenue, Suite 700 · Tucson, AZ 85701-1627 · 520-622-2090

MINING LAW

Phoenix

Jerry L. Haggard · ⑳ · Jerry L. Haggard · 1248 East Victor Hugo Avenue · Phoenix, AZ 85022-4950 · 602-863-1119

Carlos Ronstadt · ⑩ · Snell & Wilmer · One Arizona Center · 400 East Van Buren Street · Phoenix, AZ 85004-2202 · 602-382-6000

Tucson

John C. Lacy · ⑳ · DeConcini McDonald Yetwin & Lacy · 2525 East Broadway Boulevard, Suite 200 · Tucson, AZ 85716-5300 · 520-322-5000

MUNICIPAL LAW

Phoenix

Bryant D. Barber · Lewis and Roca · http://www.lrlaw.com · 40 North Central Avenue, Suite 1900 · Phoenix, AZ 85004 · 602-262-5311

Lori V. Berke · Berke Law Firm · 1601 North Seventh Street, Suite 360 · Phoenix, AZ 85006 · 602-254-8800

Brian M. Goodwin · Shughart Thomson & Kilroy · http://www.stklaw.com · Security Title Plaza, Suite 1200 · 3636 North Central Avenue · Phoenix, AZ 85012-0001 · 602-650-2000

Thomas K. Irvine · Shughart Thomson & Kilroy · http://www.stklaw.com · Security Title Plaza, Suite 1200 · 3636 North Central Avenue · Phoenix, AZ 85012-0001 · 602-650-2000

MUTUAL FUNDS LAW

Phoenix

Matthew P. Feeney · ⑩ · Snell & Wilmer · One Arizona Center · 400 East Van Buren Street · Phoenix, AZ 85004-2202 · 602-382-6000

NATIVE AMERICAN LAW

Phoenix

Paul F. Eckstein · ㉕ · Perkins Coie Brown & Bain · http://www.perkinscoie.com · 2901 North Central Avenue, Suite 2000 · Phoenix, AZ 85012-2788 · 602-351-8000

Glenn M. Feldman · Mariscal, Weeks, McIntyre & Friedlander · http://www.mwmf.com · 2901 North Central Avenue, Suite 200 · Phoenix, AZ 85012-2705 · 602-285-5000

Stephen M. Hart · Lewis and Roca · http://www.lrlaw.com · 40 North Central Avenue, Suite 1900 · Phoenix, AZ 85004 · 602-262-5311

Mark Ohre · Snell & Wilmer · One Arizona Center · 400 East Van Buren Street · Phoenix, AZ 85004-2202 · 602-382-6000

Heidi McNeil Staudenmaier · Snell & Wilmer · One Arizona Center · 400 East Van Buren Street · Phoenix, AZ 85004-2202 · 602-382-6000

Scottsdale

Judith M. Dworkin · Sacks Tierney · http://www.sackstierney.com · 4250 North Drinkwater Boulevard, Fourth Floor · Scottsdale, AZ 85251-3693 · 480-425-2600

Tempe

Eric N. Dahlstrom · Rothstein, Donatelli, Hughes, Dahlstrom, Schoenburg & Bienvenu · 80 East Rio Salado Parkway, Suite 305 · Tempe, AZ 85281-9103 · 480-921-9296

Michael C. Shiel · Rothstein, Donatelli, Hughes, Dahlstrom, Schoenburg & Bienvenu · 80 East Rio Salado Parkway, Suite 305 · Tempe, AZ 85281-9103 · 480-921-9296

Tucson

Robert C. Brauchli · Brauchli & Brauchli · 6650 North Oracle Road, Suite 110 · Tucson, AZ 85704-5604 · 520-742-2191

Luis A. Ochoa · Quarles & Brady · http://www.quarles.com · One South Church Street, Suite 1700 · Tucson, AZ 85701-1621 · 520-770-8700

Daniel J. Quigley · Quigley & Whitehill · http://www.qw-law.com · 2730 East Broadway, Suite 160 · Tucson, AZ 85716-5384 · 520-326-4600

NATURAL RESOURCES LAW

Phoenix

Robert D. Anderson · Fennemore Craig · http://www.fclaw.com · 3003 North Central Avenue, Suite 2600 Phoenix, AZ 85012-2913 · 602-916-5000

Lauren J. Caster · ⑩ · Fennemore Craig · http://www.fclaw.com · 3003 North Central Avenue, Suite 2600 Phoenix, AZ 85012-2913 · 602-916-5000

Jeffrey W. Crockett · Snell & Wilmer · One Arizona Center · 400 East Van Buren Street · Phoenix, AZ 85004-2202 · 602-382-6000

Margaret R. Gallogly · Fennemore Craig · http://www.fclaw.com · 3003 North Central Avenue, Suite 2600 · Phoenix, AZ 85012-2913 · 602-916-5000

Jerry L. Haggard · ⑳ · Jerry L. Haggard · 1248 East Victor Hugo Avenue · Phoenix, AZ 85022-4950 · 602-863-1119

Norman D. James · Fennemore Craig · http://www.fclaw.com · 3003 North Central Avenue, Suite 2600 · Phoenix, AZ 85012-2913 · 602-916-5000

James W. Johnson · ⑳ · Fennemore Craig · http://www.fclaw.com · 3003 North Central Avenue, Suite 2600 · Phoenix, AZ 85012-2913 · 602-916-5000

M. Byron Lewis · ⑩ · Salmon, Lewis & Weldon · 2850 East Camelback Road, Suite 200 · Phoenix, AZ 85016 · 602-801-9060

Mark A. McGinnis · Salmon, Lewis & Weldon · 2850 East Camelback Road, Suite 200 · Phoenix, AZ 85016 · 602-801-9060

Michael J. Pearce · Maguire & Pearce · 2999 North 44th Street, Suite 630 · Phoenix, AZ 85018-0001 · 602-277-2195

Sheryl A. Sweeney · Ryley Carlock & Applewhite · http://www.rcalaw.com · Phelps Dodge Tower, Suite 1200 · One North Central Avenue · Phoenix, AZ 85004-4417 · 602-258-7701

John B. Weldon, Jr. · ⑩ · Salmon, Lewis & Weldon · 2850 East Camelback Road, Suite 200 · Phoenix, AZ 85016 · 602-801-9060

Tucson

John C. Lacy · ⑳ · DeConcini McDonald Yetwin & Lacy · 2525 East Broadway Boulevard, Suite 200 · Tucson, AZ 85716-5300 · 520-322-5000

Michael F. McNulty · ⑩ · Lewis and Roca · http://www.lrlaw.com · One South Church Avenue, Suite 700 Tucson, AZ 85701-1627 · 520-622-2090

NON-PROFIT/CHARITIES LAW

Phoenix

Ellis M. Carter · Fennemore Craig · http://www.fclaw.com · 3003 North Central Avenue, Suite 2600 · Phoenix, AZ 85012-2913 · 602-916-5000

Kendis K. Muscheid · Fennemore Craig · http://www.fclaw.com · 3003 North Central Avenue, Suite 2600 Phoenix, AZ 85012-2913 · 602-916-5000

Alfred J. Olsen · ㉕ · Olsen-Smith · http://www.olsensmith.com · Virginia Financial Plaza, Suite 3300 · 301 East Virginia Avenue · Phoenix, AZ 85004-1267 · 602-254-1040

Tucson

Paul D. Slosser · ⑳ · Slosser, Hudgins, Struse & Freund · 6750 North Oracle Road · Tucson, AZ 85704-5618 · 520-575-5555

NON-WHITE-COLLAR CRIMINAL DEFENSE

Phoenix

James J. Belanger · Cheifetz Iannitelli Marcolini · http://www.cimlaw.com · Viad Tower, 19th Floor · 1850 North Central Avenue · Phoenix, AZ 85004 · 602-952-6000

Michael E. Benchoff · ㉕ · Michael E. Benchoff · 6121 North Third Avenue · Phoenix, AZ 85013 · 602-253-1687

Larry L. Debus · ㉕ · Debus, Kazan & Westerhausen · 335 East Palm Lane · Phoenix, AZ 85004 · 602-257-8900

Clark L. Derrick · Kimerer & Derrick · 221 East Indianola Avenue · Phoenix, AZ 85012-2002 · 602-279-5900

Tom E. Henze · ⑩ · Gallagher & Kennedy · http://www.gknet.com · 2575 East Camelback Road · Phoenix, AZ 85016-9225 · 602-530-8000

Larry I. Kazan · ⑩ · Debus, Kazan & Westerhausen · 335 East Palm Lane · Phoenix, AZ 85004 · 602-257-8900

Michael D. Kimerer · ㉕ · Kimerer & Derrick · 221 East Indianola Avenue · Phoenix, AZ 85012-2002 · 602-279-5900

Craig Mehrens · Mehrens and Wilemon · 99 East Virginia Avenue, Suite 220 · Phoenix, AZ 85004 · 602-258-5151

Tucson

Michael J. Bloom · ⑩ · Michael J. Bloom · 100 North Stone Avenue, Suite 701 · Tucson, AZ 85701-1516 520-882-9904

Stanton Bloom · Stanton Bloom · 145 South Sixth Avenue · Tucson, AZ 85701-0001 · 520-623-5821

Alfred S. Donau III · Donau & Bolt · 3505 North Campbell Avenue, Suite 501 · Tucson, AZ 85719-2033 520-795-8710

Walter B. Nash III · Law Offices of Nash & Kirchner · P.O. Box 2310 · Tucson, AZ 85702-2310 · 520-792-1613

Michael L. Piccarreta · ⑩ · Piccarreta & Davis · http://www.pd-law.com · 145 South Sixth Avenue · Tucson, AZ 85701-2007 · 520-622-6900

Stephen M. Weiss · Karp & Weiss · 3060 North Swan Road · Tucson, AZ 85712-1225 · 520-325-4200

Lake Havasu City

Denis R. Malm · ⑩ · Wachtel, Biehn & Malm · 2240 McCulloch Boulevard · Lake Havasu City, AZ 86403 · 928-855-5115

Phoenix

Thomas G. Bakker · Olson, Jantsch & Bakker · 7243 North Sixteenth Street · Phoenix, AZ 85020-5203 · 602-861-2705

Michael A. Beale · ⑳ · Beale Micheaels & Slack · 1440 East Missouri Avenue, Suite 150 · Phoenix, AZ 85014 · 602-285-1444

Robert W. Boatman · Gallagher & Kennedy · http://www.gknet.com · 2575 East Camelback Road · Phoenix, AZ 85016-9225 · 602-530-8000

James R. Broening · ⑩ · Broening, Oberg, Woods & Wilson · http://www.bowwlaw.com · 1122 East Jefferson Street · Phoenix, AZ 85034 · 602-271-7700

Douglas L. Christian · Harper, Christian, Dichter & Graif · http://www.hcdglaw.com · 2700 North Central Avenue, Suite 1200 · Phoenix, AZ 85004 · 602-792-1700

Vaughn Crawford · Snell & Wilmer · One Arizona Center · 400 East Van Buren Street · Phoenix, AZ 85004-2202 · 602-382-6000

Frederick M. Cummings · Jennings, Strouss & Salmon · http://www.jsslaw.com · The Collier Center, 11th Floor · 201 East Washington Street · Phoenix, AZ 85004-2385 · 602-262-5911

Shawn M. Cunningham · Harris, Powers & Cunningham · 361 East Coronado, Suite 101 · P.O. Box 13568 Phoenix, AZ 85004-1525 · 602-271-9344

John M. Curtin · Robbins & Curtin · 301 East Bethany Home Road, Suite B-100 · Phoenix, AZ 85012 · 602-285-0100

John D. Everroad · Fennemore Craig · http://www.fclaw.com · 3003 North Central Avenue, Suite 2600 · Phoenix, AZ 85012-2913 · 602-916-5000

Scott M. Finical · Fennemore Craig · http://www.fclaw.com · 3003 North Central Avenue, Suite 2600 · Phoenix, AZ 85012-2913 · 602-916-5000

Jay A. Fradkin · Jennings, Strouss & Salmon · http://www.jsslaw.com · The Collier Center, 11th Floor · 201 East Washington Street · Phoenix, AZ 85004-2385 · 602-262-5911

Gerald K. Gaffaney · Mariscal, Weeks, McIntyre & Friedlander · http://www.mwmf.com · 2901 North Central Avenue, Suite 200 · Phoenix, AZ 85012-2705 · 602-285-5000

Brian M. Goodwin · Shughart Thomson & Kilroy · http://www.stklaw.com · Security Title Plaza, Suite 1200 · 3636 North Central Avenue · Phoenix, AZ 85012-0001 · 602-650-2000

Andrew S. Gordon · Coppersmith Gordon Schermer & Brockelman · 2800 North Central Avenue, Suite 1000 · Phoenix, AZ 85004-1007 · 602-224-0999

Edward G. Hochuli · Jones, Skelton & Hochuli · 2901 North Central Avenue, Suite 800 · Phoenix, AZ 85012 · 602-263-1700

Steven J. Hulsman · Lewis and Roca · http://www.lrlaw.com · 40 North Central Avenue, Suite 1900 · Phoenix, AZ 85004 · 602-262-5311

William R. Jones, Jr. · ㉕ · Jones, Skelton & Hochuli · 2901 North Central Avenue, Suite 800 · Phoenix, AZ 85012 · 602-263-1700

Michael K. Kennedy · Gallagher & Kennedy · http://www.gknet.com · 2575 East Camelback Road · Phoenix, AZ 85016-9225 · 602-530-8000

James J. Leonard, Jr. · ⑳ · Palumbo, Wolfe, Sahlman & Palumbo · 2800 North Central Avenue, Suite 1400 · Phoenix, AZ 85004 · 602-265-5777

John T. Masterson · Jones, Skelton & Hochuli · 2901 North Central Avenue, Suite 800 · Phoenix, AZ 85012 · 602-263-1700

Patrick J. McGroder III · ⑩ · Gallagher & Kennedy · http://www.gknet.com · 2575 East Camelback Road · Phoenix, AZ 85016-9225 · 602-530-8000

John A. Micheaels · Beale Micheaels & Slack · 1440 East Missouri Avenue, Suite 150 · Phoenix, AZ 85014 · 602-285-1444

Arthur G. Newman, Jr. · Treon, Aguirre & Newman · 2700 North Central Avenue, Suite 1400 · Phoenix, AZ 85004-1133 · 602-285-4400

Raymond M. Norris · Treon, Aguirre & Newman · 2700 North Central Avenue, Suite 1400 · Phoenix, AZ 85004-1133 · 602-285-4400

Douglas C. Northup · Fennemore Craig · http://www.fclaw.com · 3003 North Central Avenue, Suite 2600 Phoenix, AZ 85012-2913 · 602-916-5000

Michael J. O'Connor · Jennings, Strouss & Salmon · http://www.jsslaw.com · The Collier Center, 11th Floor · 201 East Washington Street · Phoenix, AZ 85004-2385 · 602-262-5911

Duane A. Olson · Olson, Jantsch & Bakker · 7243 North Sixteenth Street · Phoenix, AZ 85020-5203 · 602-861-2705

Frank A. Parks · ㉕ · Sanders & Parks · 3030 North Third Street, Suite 1300 · Phoenix, AZ 85012 · 602-532-5600

Warren E. Platt · ㉕ · Snell & Wilmer · One Arizona Center · 400 East Van Buren Street · Phoenix, AZ 85004-2202 · 602-382-6000

Richard S. Plattner · ⑩ · Plattner Verderame · 316 East Flower Street · P.O. Box 36570 · Phoenix, AZ 85067-6570 · 602-266-2002

Frank I. Powers · Harris, Powers & Cunningham · 361 East Coronado, Suite 101 · P.O. Box 13568 · Phoenix, AZ 85004-1525 · 602-271-9344

Calvin L. Raup · Raup & Hergenroether · Two North Central Avenue · Phoenix, AZ 85004-0001 · 602-229-8961

Philip A. Robbins · ㉕ · Jennings, Strouss & Salmon · http://www.jsslaw.com · The Collier Center, 11th Floor · 201 East Washington Street · Phoenix, AZ 85004-2385 · 602-262-5911

Thomas M. Ryan · Treon, Aguirre & Newman · 2700 North Central Avenue, Suite 1400 · Phoenix, AZ 85004-1133 · 602-285-4400

William H. Sandweg III · Sandweg & Ager · http://www.phoenixmedicalmalpracticeattorneys.com · 1221 East Osborn Road, Suite 100 · Phoenix, AZ 85014 · 602-648-3201

Howard M. Snyder · Snyder & Wenner · 2200 East Camelback Road, Suite 213 · Phoenix, AZ 85016-9096 · 602-224-0005

Timothy J. Thomason · Mariscal, Weeks, McIntyre & Friedlander · http://www.mwmf.com · 2901 North Central Avenue, Suite 200 · Phoenix, AZ 85012-2705 · 602-285-5000

William L. Thorpe · Fennemore Craig · http://www.fclaw.com · 3003 North Central Avenue, Suite 2600 · Phoenix, AZ 85012-2913 · 602-916-5000

Thomas L. Toone · Beer & Toone · 76 East Mitchell Drive · Phoenix, AZ 85012 · 602-263-0900

Richard T. Treon · ㉕ · Treon, Aguirre & Newman · 2700 North Central Avenue, Suite 1400 · Phoenix, AZ 85004-1133 · 602-285-4400

Kenneth L. Tucker · ⑩ · Tucker & Miller · 1440 East Missouri Avenue, Suite C-115 · Phoenix, AZ 85014-0001 · 602-870-5511

Frank Verderame · Plattner Verderame · 316 East Flower Street · P.O. Box 36570 · Phoenix, AZ 85067-6570 · 602-266-2002

David A. Wenner · ⑩ · Snyder & Wenner · 2200 East Camelback Road, Suite 213 · Phoenix, AZ 85016-9096 · 602-224-0005

Elliot G. Wolfe · ⑳ · Palumbo, Wolfe, Sahlman & Palumbo · 2800 North Central Avenue, Suite 1400 · Phoenix, AZ 85004 · 602-265-5777

Richard J. Woods · ⑩ · The Cavanagh Law Firm · 1850 North Central Avenue, Suite 2400 · Phoenix, AZ 85004 · 602-322-4000

Terrence P. Woods · Broening, Oberg, Woods & Wilson · http://www.bowwlaw.com · 1122 East Jefferson Street · Phoenix, AZ 85034 · 602-271-7700

Prescott

Michael R. Murphy · ⑩ · Murphy, Schmitt, Hathaway & Wilson · http://www.mshwlaw.com/attorneys.htm · Elks Building, Third Floor · 117 East Gurley Street · Prescott, AZ 86301-3813 · 928-445-6860

Robert E. Schmitt · Murphy, Schmitt, Hathaway & Wilson · http://www.mshwlaw.com/attorneys.htm · Elks Building, Third Floor · 117 East Gurley Street · Prescott, AZ 86301-3813 · 928-445-6860

Scottsdale

H. Christian Bode · Bode & Collins · 7377 East Doubletree Ranch Road, Suite A210 · Scottsdale, AZ 85258-2053 · 480-355-5020

Mark O'Connor · Herzog and O'Connor · 7333 East Doubletree Ranch Road, Suite 280 · Scottsdale, AZ 85258-2023 · 480-998-3855

Tempe

Bruce D. Crawford · Crawford & Kline · 1920 East Southern Avenue, Suite 101 · Tempe, AZ 85282 · 480-491-5100

Peter G. Kline · Crawford & Kline · 1920 East Southern Avenue, Suite 101 · Tempe, AZ 85282 · 480-491-5100

Reed C. Tolman · Tolman Osborne & Keenan · 1920 East Southern Avenue, Suite 104 · Tempe, AZ 85282-7518 · 480-897-1020

Dan Cavett · ⑩ · Cavett & Fulton · 6035 East Grant Road · Tucson, AZ 85712 · 520-733-0100

Douglas H. Clark, Jr. · ⑩ · Mesch, Clark & Rothschild · 259 North Meyer Avenue · Tucson, AZ 85701-1090 · 520-624-8886

Peter Collins, Jr. · Gust Rosenfeld · http://www.gustlaw.com · One South Church Avenue, Suite 1900 · Tucson, AZ 85701-1627 · 520-628-7070

Thomas G. Cotter · Haralson, Miller, Pitt, Feldman & McAnally · One South Church Avenue, Suite 900 · Tucson, AZ 85701 · 520-792-3836

Barry M. Davis · ⑩ · Piccarreta & Davis · http://www.pd-law.com · 145 South Sixth Avenue · Tucson, AZ 85701-2007 · 520-622-6900

Richard Davis · Mesch, Clark & Rothschild · 259 North Meyer Avenue · Tucson, AZ 85701-1090 · 520-624-8886

Elliot A. Glicksman · Elliot A. Glicksman · http://www.glicksmanlaw.com · 145 South Sixth Avenue · Tucson, AZ 85701 · 520-628-8878

Richard D. Grand · ㉕ · Richard D. Grand · 6870 North Andrea Doria Drive · Tucson, AZ 85704 · 520-622-8855

Dale Haralson · ㉕ · Haralson, Miller, Pitt, Feldman & McAnally · One South Church Avenue, Suite 900 · Tucson, AZ 85701 · 520-792-3836

Marshall Humphrey III · Humphrey & Peterson · 3861 East Third Street · Tucson, AZ 85716-4646 · 520-795-1900

Barry A. MacBan · MacBan Law Offices · 1795 East Skyline Drive, Suite 155 · Tucson, AZ 85718 · 520-624-6446

Bruce G. Macdonald · McNamara, Goldsmith, Jackson & Macdonald · 1670 East River Road, Suite 200 · Tucson, AZ 85718 · 520-624-0126

Ronald D. Mercaldo · Law Offices of Ronald D. Mercaldo · 6713 East Camino Principal · Tucson, AZ 85715 · 520-624-1400

JoJene E. Mills · ⑩ · Law Office of JoJene E. Mills · 1670 East River Road, Suite 270 · Tucson, AZ 85718-0001 · 520-529-3200

Michael J.S. Rusing · Rusing & Lopez · 6262 North Swan Road, Suite 200 · Tucson, AZ 85718 · 520-792-4800

Ted A. Schmidt · Kinerk, Beal, Schmidt, Dyer & Sethi · 1790 East River Road, Suite 300 · Tucson, AZ 85718 · 520-790-5600

Tom Slutes · ⑩ · Slutes Sakrison & Rogers · 4801 East Broadway Boulevard, Suite 301 · Tucson, AZ 85711-0001 · 520-624-6691

D. B. Udall · ⑳ · Udall Law Firm · 4801 East Broadway, Suite 400 · Tucson, AZ 85711 · 520-623-4353

Eugene Zlaket · Eugene Zlaket · P.O. Box 40246 · Tucson, AZ 85717-0246 · 520-327-8777

Thomas A. Zlaket · Thomas A. Zlaket · 310 South Williams Boulevard, Suite 170 · Tucson, AZ 85711-4446 · 520-750-0250

Wickenburg

Richard W. Abbuhl · Richard W. Abbuhl · 2075 West Silverlode Drive · Wickenburg, AZ 85390-0001 · 602-689-2702

PRODUCT LIABILITY LITIGATION

Phoenix

Stephen M. Bressler · Lewis and Roca · http://www.lrlaw.com · 40 North Central Avenue, Suite 1900 · Phoenix, AZ 85004 · 602-262-5311

Vaughn Crawford · Snell & Wilmer · One Arizona Center · 400 East Van Buren Street · Phoenix, AZ 85004-2202 · 602-382-6000

Brian M. Goodwin · Shughart Thomson & Kilroy · http://www.stklaw.com · Security Title Plaza, Suite 1200 · 3636 North Central Avenue · Phoenix, AZ 85012-0001 · 602-650-2000

Warren E. Platt · 25 · Snell & Wilmer · One Arizona Center · 400 East Van Buren Street · Phoenix, AZ 85004-2202 · 602-382-6000

Elliot G. Wolfe · 20 · Palumbo, Wolfe, Sahlman & Palumbo · 2800 North Central Avenue, Suite 1400 · Phoenix, AZ 85004 · 602-265-5777

Tucson

Stephen T. Portell · Quarles & Brady · http://www.quarles.com · One South Church Street, Suite 1700 · Tucson, AZ 85701-1621 · 520-770-8700

Amy M. Samberg · Snell & Wilmer · One South Church Avenue, Suite 1500 · Tucson, AZ 85701-1630 · 520-882-1200

PROFESSIONAL MALPRACTICE LAW

Phoenix

Barry D. Halpern · 10 · Snell & Wilmer · One Arizona Center · 400 East Van Buren Street · Phoenix, AZ 85004-2202 · 602-382-6000

John A. Micheaels · Beale Micheaels & Slack · 1440 East Missouri Avenue, Suite 150 · Phoenix, AZ 85014 · 602-285-1444

Tucson

Peter Akmajian · Udall Law Firm · 4801 East Broadway, Suite 400 · Tucson, AZ 85711 · 520-623-4353

Catherine M. Woods · Rusing & Lopez · 6262 North Swan Road, Suite 200 · Tucson, AZ 85718 · 520-792-4800

PUBLIC FINANCE LAW

Phoenix

Michael Cafiso · Greenberg Traurig · http://www.gtlaw.com · 2375 East Camelback Road, Suite 700 · Phoenix, AZ 85016 · 602-445-8000

William R. DeHaan · Greenberg Traurig · http://www.gtlaw.com · 2375 East Camelback Road, Suite 700 · Phoenix, AZ 85016 · 602-445-8000

Brigitte F. Green · Greenberg Traurig · http://www.gtlaw.com · 2375 East Camelback Road, Suite 700 · Phoenix, AZ 85016 · 602-445-8000

William A. Hicks III · Ballard Spahr Andrews & Ingersoll · 3300 Tower, Suite 1800 · 3300 North Central Avenue · Phoenix, AZ 85012-2518 · 602-798-5400

Keith C. Hoskins · Gust Rosenfeld · http://www.gustlaw.com · 201 East Washington Street, Suite 800 · Phoenix, AZ 85004-2327 · 602-257-7422

Charles E. James, Jr. · Squire Sanders · http://www.ssd.com · Two Renaissance Square, Suite 2700 · 40 North Central Avenue · Phoenix, AZ 85004-4498 · 602-528-4000

Robert L. Matia · Squire Sanders · http://www.ssd.com · Two Renaissance Square, Suite 2700 · 40 North Central Avenue · Phoenix, AZ 85004-4498 · 602-528-4000

Timothy E. Pickrell · Squire Sanders · http://www.ssd.com · Two Renaissance Square, Suite 2700 · 40 North Central Avenue · Phoenix, AZ 85004-4498 · 602-528-4000

Frederick H. Rosenfeld · ㉕ · Gust Rosenfeld · http://www.gustlaw.com · 201 East Washington Street, Suite 800 · Phoenix, AZ 85004-2327 · 602-257-7422

Scott W. Ruby · Gust Rosenfeld · http://www.gustlaw.com · 201 East Washington Street, Suite 800 · Phoenix, AZ 85004-2327 · 602-257-7422

George C. Spilsbury · Jennings, Strouss & Salmon · http://www.jsslaw.com · The Collier Center, 11th Floor · 201 East Washington Street · Phoenix, AZ 85004-2385 · 602-262-5911

William F. Wilder · Ryley Carlock & Applewhite · http://www.rcalaw.com · Phelps Dodge Tower, Suite 1200 · One North Central Avenue · Phoenix, AZ 85004-4417 · 602-258-7701

Scottsdale

Timothy C. Nash · Kutak Rock · 8601 North Scottsdale Road, Suite 300 · Scottsdale, AZ 85253-2742 · 480-429-5000

Tucson

James W. Zeeb · Law Offices of James W. Zeeb · 405 West Franklin Street · Tucson, AZ 85701-8209 · 520-798-3803

RAILROAD LAW

Phoenix

William L. Thorpe · Fennemore Craig · http://www.fclaw.com · 3003 North Central Avenue, Suite 2600 · Phoenix, AZ 85012-2913 · 602-916-5000

Tucson

Lloyd L. Rabb III · Rabb Penny Law Firm · 3320 North Campbell Avenue, Suite 150 · Tucson, AZ 85719 · 520-888-6740

Phoenix

Andrew Abraham · Burch & Cracchiolo · http://www.bcattorneys.com · 702 East Osborn Road, Suite 200 P.O. Box 16882 · Phoenix, AZ 85011 · 602-274-7611

Stephen W. Anderson · Gammage & Burnham · http://www.gblaw.com · One Renaissance Square, 18th Floor · Two North Central Avenue · Phoenix, AZ 85004 · 602-256-0566

Thomas Arendt · Arendt Law Group · 5009 East Washington, Suite 125 · Phoenix, AZ 85034-0001 · 602-244-1400

Timothy W. Barton · ⑩ · Gust Rosenfeld · http://www.gustlaw.com · 201 East Washington Street, Suite 800 · Phoenix, AZ 85004-2327 · 602-257-7422

Robert C. Bates · ⑩ · Snell & Wilmer · One Arizona Center · 400 East Van Buren Street · Phoenix, AZ 85004-2202 · 602-382-6000

Gary L. Birnbaum · ⑩ · Mariscal, Weeks, McIntyre & Friedlander · http://www.mwmf.com · 2901 North Central Avenue, Suite 200 · Phoenix, AZ 85012-2705 · 602-285-5000

Neil David Biskind · Biskind Hunt · 11201 North Tatum Boulevard, Suite 330 · Phoenix, AZ 85028 · 602-955-4433

James T. Braselton · Mariscal, Weeks, McIntyre & Friedlander · http://www.mwmf.com · 2901 North Central Avenue, Suite 200 · Phoenix, AZ 85012-2705 · 602-285-5000

Alexander L. Broadfoot · Gallagher & Kennedy · http://www.gknet.com · 2575 East Camelback Road · Phoenix, AZ 85016-9225 · 602-530-8000

Edwin C. Bull · Burch & Cracchiolo · http://www.bcattorneys.com · 702 East Osborn Road, Suite 200 · P.O. Box 16882 · Phoenix, AZ 85011 · 602-274-7611

Rebecca Lynne Burnham · ⑩ · Greenberg Traurig · http://www.gtlaw.com · 2375 East Camelback Road, Suite 700 · Phoenix, AZ 85016 · 602-445-8000

George T. Cole · Fennemore Craig · http://www.fclaw.com · 3003 North Central Avenue, Suite 2600 · Phoenix, AZ 85012-2913 · 602-916-5000

James B. Connor · Gallagher & Kennedy · http://www.gknet.com · 2575 East Camelback Road · Phoenix, AZ 85016-9225 · 602-530-8000

Michael J. Curley · ⑩ · Earl Curley & Lagarde · 3101 North Central Avenue, Suite 1000 · Phoenix, AZ 85012 · 602-265-0094

David A. Durfee · Gallagher & Kennedy · http://www.gknet.com · 2575 East Camelback Road · Phoenix, AZ 85016-9225 · 602-530-8000

Jay S. Dushoff · ㉕ · Gallagher & Kennedy · http://www.gknet.com · 2575 East Camelback Road · Phoenix, AZ 85016-9225 · 602-530-8000

Donald E. Dyekman · Mariscal, Weeks, McIntyre & Friedlander · http://www.mwmf.com · 2901 North Central Avenue, Suite 200 · Phoenix, AZ 85012-2705 · 602-285-5000

Stephen C. Earl · ⑩ · Earl Curley & Lagarde · 3101 North Central Avenue, Suite 1000 · Phoenix, AZ 85012 · 602-265-0094

George M. Esahak-Gage · Jennings, Strouss & Salmon · http://www.jsslaw.com · The Collier Center, 11th Floor · 201 East Washington Street · Phoenix, AZ 85004-2385 · 602-262-5911

Lee E. Esch · Jennings, Strouss & Salmon · http://www.jsslaw.com · The Collier Center, 11th Floor · 201 East Washington Street · Phoenix, AZ 85004-2385 · 602-262-5911

Fred C. Fathe · ⑩ · Mariscal, Weeks, McIntyre & Friedlander · http://www.mwmf.com · 2901 North Central Avenue, Suite 200 · Phoenix, AZ 85012-2705 · 602-285-5000

Dean J. Formanek · Warner, Angle, Hallam, Jackson & Formanek · 3550 North Central Avenue, Suite 1500 · Phoenix, AZ 85012-2188 · 602-264-7101

Grady Gammage, Jr. · ⑩ · Gammage & Burnham · http://www.gblaw.com · One Renaissance Square, 18th Floor · Two North Central Avenue · Phoenix, AZ 85004 · 602-256-0566

Diane M. Haller · Quarles & Brady · http://www.quarles.com · One Renaissance Square · Two North Central Avenue · Phoenix, AZ 85004-2391 · 602-229-5200

Kyle B. Hettinger · Perkins Coie Brown & Bain · http://www.perkinscoie.com · 2901 North Central Avenue, Suite 2000 · Phoenix, AZ 85012-2788 · 602-351-8000

Gordon E. Hunt · Biskind Hunt · 11201 North Tatum Boulevard, Suite 330 · Phoenix, AZ 85028 · 602-955-4433

James R. Huntwork · ⑳ · Salmon, Lewis & Weldon · 2850 East Camelback Road, Suite 200 · Phoenix, AZ 85016 · 602-801-9060

R. Neil Irwin · Bryan Cave · One Renaissance Square, Suite 2200 · Two North Central Avenue · Phoenix, AZ 85004-4406 · 602-364-7000

Gerald L. Jacobs · ⑩ · Greenberg Traurig · http://www.gtlaw.com · 2375 East Camelback Road, Suite 700 · Phoenix, AZ 85016 · 602-445-8000

Gary G. Keltner · Jennings, Strouss & Salmon · http://www.jsslaw.com · The Collier Center, 11th Floor · 201 East Washington Street · Phoenix, AZ 85004-2385 · 602-262-5911

Robert V. Kerrick · Tiffany & Bosco · Camelback Esplanade II, Third Floor · 2525 East Camelback Road · Phoenix, AZ 85016-4237 · 602-255-6000

Charles M. King · ⑩ · Fennemore Craig · http://www.fclaw.com · 3003 North Central Avenue, Suite 2600 Phoenix, AZ 85012-2913 · 602-916-5000

Jay S. Kramer · Fennemore Craig · http://www.fclaw.com · 3003 North Central Avenue, Suite 2600 · Phoenix, AZ 85012-2913 · 602-916-5000

David W. Kreutzberg · Squire Sanders · http://www.ssd.com · Two Renaissance Square, Suite 2700 · 40 North Central Avenue · Phoenix, AZ 85004-4498 · 602-528-4000

William L. Kurtz · Fennemore Craig · http://www.fclaw.com · 3003 North Central Avenue, Suite 2600 · Phoenix, AZ 85012-2913 · 602-916-5000

Lynne A. Lagarde · ⑩ · Earl Curley & Lagarde · 3101 North Central Avenue, Suite 1000 · Phoenix, AZ 85012 · 602-265-0094

David L. Lansky · ⑩ · Mariscal, Weeks, McIntyre & Friedlander · http://www.mwmf.com · 2901 North Central Avenue, Suite 200 · Phoenix, AZ 85012-2705 · 602-285-5000

K. David Lindner · Squire Sanders · http://www.ssd.com · Two Renaissance Square, Suite 2700 · 40 North Central Avenue · Phoenix, AZ 85004-4498 · 602-528-4000

Steven L. Lisker · Lisker, Page & Gibson · http://www.liskerlaw.com · 2355 East Camelback Road, Suite 615 · Phoenix, AZ 85016 · 602-778-4300

Ronald E. Lowe · ⑩ · Perkins Coie Brown & Bain · http://www.perkinscoie.com · 2901 North Central Avenue, Suite 2000 · Phoenix, AZ 85012-2788 · 602-351-8000

Thayne Lowe · Osborn Maledon · http://www.omlaw.com · The Phoenix Plaza, Twenty-First Floor · 2929 North Central Avenue · Phoenix, AZ 85012-2793 · 602-640-9000

Richard Mallery · Snell & Wilmer · One Arizona Center · 400 East Van Buren Street · Phoenix, AZ 85004-2202 · 602-382-6000

Bruce B. May · ㉕ · Jennings, Strouss & Salmon · http://www.jsslaw.com · The Collier Center, 11th Floor · 201 East Washington Street · Phoenix, AZ 85004-2385 · 602-262-5911

Thomas J. McDonald · Gammage & Burnham · http://www.gblaw.com · One Renaissance Square, 18th Floor · Two North Central Avenue · Phoenix, AZ 85004 · 602-256-0566

Jeffrey Miller · Gammage & Burnham · http://www.gblaw.com · One Renaissance Square, 18th Floor · Two North Central Avenue · Phoenix, AZ 85004 · 602-256-0566

Don J. Miner · Fennemore Craig · http://www.fclaw.com · 3003 North Central Avenue, Suite 2600 · Phoenix, AZ 85012-2913 · 602-916-5000

Linda M. Mitchell · Lewis and Roca · http://www.lrlaw.com · 40 North Central Avenue, Suite 1900 · Phoenix, AZ 85004 · 602-262-5311

Gordon A. Mohr · ⑩ · Mohr, Hackett, Pederson, Blakley & Randolph · 2800 North Central Avenue, Suite 1100 · Phoenix, AZ 85004-1043 · 602-240-3000

Michael V. Mulchay · Michael V. Mulchay · 4545 East Shea Boulevard, Suite 208 · Phoenix, AZ 85028-0001 · 602-264-4232

Robert H. Nagle · Nagle Law Group · 4530 East Shea Boulevard, Suite 140 · Phoenix, AZ 85028-1621 · 602-595-6951

Mark A. Nesvig · Fennemore Craig · http://www.fclaw.com · 3003 North Central Avenue, Suite 2600 · Phoenix, AZ 85012-2913 · 602-916-5000

Jones Osborn II · Osborn Maledon · http://www.omlaw.com · The Phoenix Plaza, Twenty-First Floor · 2929 North Central Avenue · Phoenix, AZ 85012-2793 · 602-640-9000

David M. Paltzik · Greenberg Traurig · http://www.gtlaw.com · 2375 East Camelback Road, Suite 700 · Phoenix, AZ 85016 · 602-445-8000

M. Virginia Perry · Ballard Spahr Andrews & Ingersoll · 3300 Tower, Suite 1800 · 3300 North Central Avenue · Phoenix, AZ 85012-2518 · 602-798-5400

Jody K. Pokorski · Snell & Wilmer · One Arizona Center · 400 East Van Buren Street · Phoenix, AZ 85004-2202 · 602-382-6000

Terry L. Rakow · The Cavanagh Law Firm · 1850 North Central Avenue, Suite 2400 · Phoenix, AZ 85004 · 602-322-4000

Robert P. Robinson · Fennemore Craig · http://www.fclaw.com · 3003 North Central Avenue, Suite 2600 Phoenix, AZ 85012-2913 · 602-916-5000

Scott A. Rose · The Cavanagh Law Firm · 1850 North Central Avenue, Suite 2400 · Phoenix, AZ 85004 · 602-322-4000

Derek L. Sorenson · Quarles & Brady · http://www.quarles.com · One Renaissance Square · Two North Central Avenue · Phoenix, AZ 85004-2391 · 602-229-5200

D. Randall Stokes · Lewis and Roca · http://www.lrlaw.com · 40 North Central Avenue, Suite 1900 · Phoenix, AZ 85004 · 602-262-5311

Lesa J. Storey · Greenberg Traurig · http://www.gtlaw.com · 2375 East Camelback Road, Suite 700 · Phoenix, AZ 85016 · 602-445-8000

Norman C. Storey · Squire Sanders · http://www.ssd.com · Two Renaissance Square, Suite 2700 · 40 North Central Avenue · Phoenix, AZ 85004-4498 · 602-528-4000

Michael E. Tiffany · Tiffany & Bosco · Camelback Esplanade II, Third Floor · 2525 East Camelback Road · Phoenix, AZ 85016-4237 · 602-255-6000

Kenneth Van Winkle, Jr. · Lewis and Roca · http://www.lrlaw.com · 40 North Central Avenue, Suite 1900 · Phoenix, AZ 85004 · 602-262-5311

Jay D. Wiley · ⑳ · Snell & Wilmer · One Arizona Center · 400 East Van Buren Street · Phoenix, AZ 85004-2202 · 602-382-6000

Craig K. Williams · Snell & Wilmer · One Arizona Center · 400 East Van Buren Street · Phoenix, AZ 85004-2202 · 602-382-6000

Peter A. Winkler · Mariscal, Weeks, McIntyre & Friedlander · http://www.mwmf.com · 2901 North Central Avenue, Suite 200 · Phoenix, AZ 85012-2705 · 602-285-5000

Michael B. Withey · Withey Morris · 2525 East Arizona Biltmore Circle, Suite A-212 · Phoenix, AZ 85016-0001 · 602-230-0600

Joyce Kline Wright · Snell & Wilmer · One Arizona Center · 400 East Van Buren Street · Phoenix, AZ 85004-2202 · 602-382-6000

Gary R. Zwillinger · Zwillinger, Georgelos & Greek · 2425 East Camelback Road, Suite 600 · Phoenix, AZ 85016-0001 · 602-224-7888

Scottsdale

Stephen Aron Benson · Sacks Tierney · http://www.sackstierney.com · 4250 North Drinkwater Boulevard, Fourth Floor · Scottsdale, AZ 85251-3693 · 480-425-2600

John V. Berry · Berry & Damore · 6750 East Camelback Road, Suite 100 · Scottsdale, AZ 85251 · 480-385-2727

William P. Connealy · Tobin, Hoff & Connealy · 4250 North Drinkwater Boulevard, Suite 170 · Scottsdale, AZ 85251-3981 · 480-385-1234

Paul E. Gilbert · ⑩ · Beus Gilbert · 4800 North Scottsdale Road, Suite 6000 · Scottsdale, AZ 85251-7630 · 480-429-3000

Gregory L. Mast · ⑩ · Mast Law Firm · 2415 East Camelback Road, Suite 1050 · Scottsdale, AZ 85016 · 480-990-2114

Seymour Sacks · ㉕ · Sacks Tierney · http://www.sackstierney.com · 4250 North Drinkwater Boulevard, Fourth Floor · Scottsdale, AZ 85251-3693 · 480-425-2600

Shawn E. Tobin · Tobin, Hoff & Connealy · 4250 North Drinkwater Boulevard, Suite 170 · Scottsdale, AZ 85251-3981 · 480-385-1234

Frank S. Bangs, Jr. · Lewis and Roca · http://www.lrlaw.com · One South Church Avenue, Suite 700 · Tucson, AZ 85701-1627 · 520-622-2090

Benjamin W. Bauer · Fennemore Craig · http://www.fclaw.com · One South Church Avenue, Suite 1000 · Tucson, AZ 85701-1627 · 520-879-6800

Michael D. Botwin · Michael D. Botwin · 3507 North Campbell Avenue, Suite 111 · Tucson, AZ 85719 · 520-577-1337

Robert A. Fortuno · Robert A. Fortuno · 350 South Williams Boulevard, Suite 150 · Tucson, AZ 85711-7461 · 520-299-4610

T. Patrick Griffin · Haralson, Miller, Pitt, Feldman & McAnally · One South Church Avenue, Suite 900 · Tucson, AZ 85701 · 520-792-3836

John N. Iurino · Lewis and Roca · http://www.lrlaw.com · One South Church Avenue, Suite 700 · Tucson, AZ 85701-1627 · 520-622-2090

Patricio P. Lopez III · Rusing & Lopez · 6262 North Swan Road, Suite 200 · Tucson, AZ 85718 · 520-792-4800

Linda C. McNulty · Lewis and Roca · http://www.lrlaw.com · One South Church Avenue, Suite 700 · Tucson, AZ 85701-1627 · 520-622-2090

James F. Morrow · (10) · Quarles & Brady · http://www.quarles.com · One South Church Street, Suite 1700 Tucson, AZ 85701-1621 · 520-770-8700

Deborah Oseran · Mendelsohn & Oseran · 3915 East Broadway Boulevard, Suite 301 · Tucson, AZ 85711-0001 · 520-325-7500

Curt D. Reimann · Snell & Wilmer · One South Church Avenue, Suite 1500 · Tucson, AZ 85701-1630 · 520-882-1200

Andrew D. Schorr · Lewis and Roca · http://www.lrlaw.com · One South Church Avenue, Suite 700 · Tucson, AZ 85701-1627 · 520-622-2090

Lewis D. Schorr · Lewis and Roca · http://www.lrlaw.com · One South Church Avenue, Suite 700 · Tucson, AZ 85701-1627 · 520-622-2090

S. L. Schorr · (20) · Lewis and Roca · http://www.lrlaw.com · One South Church Avenue, Suite 700 · Tucson, AZ 85701-1627 · 520-622-2090

G. Lawrence Schubart · Stubbs & Schubart · 340 North Main Avenue · Tucson, AZ 85701 · 520-623-5466

Marc Geoffrey Simon · (10) · Snell & Wilmer · One South Church Avenue, Suite 1500 · Tucson, AZ 85701-1630 · 520-882-1200

Celeste M. Steen · Lewis and Roca · http://www.lrlaw.com · One South Church Avenue, Suite 700 · Tucson, AZ 85701-1627 · 520-622-2090

Joe F. Tarver, Jr. · (10) · Joe F. Tarver · 4710 North Caida Place · Tucson, AZ 85718-6728 · 520-318-0800

M. Roxanne Veliz · Snell & Wilmer · One South Church Avenue, Suite 1500 · Tucson, AZ 85701-1630 · 520-882-1200

Richard M. Yetwin · DeConcini McDonald Yetwin & Lacy · 2525 East Broadway Boulevard, Suite 200 · Tucson, AZ 85716-5300 · 520-322-5000

SECURITIES LAW

Phoenix

John J. Bouma · ⑩ · Snell & Wilmer · One Arizona Center · 400 East Van Buren Street · Phoenix, AZ 85004-2202 · 602-382-6000

Jon Cohen · ㉕ · Snell & Wilmer · One Arizona Center · 400 East Van Buren Street · Phoenix, AZ 85004-2202 · 602-382-6000

Scott D. DeWald · Lewis and Roca · http://www.lrlaw.com · 40 North Central Avenue, Suite 1900 · Phoenix, AZ 85004 · 602-262-5311

Michael Donahey · Snell & Wilmer · One Arizona Center · 400 East Van Buren Street · Phoenix, AZ 85004-2202 · 602-382-6000

W. T. Eggleston, Jr. · Fennemore Craig · http://www.fclaw.com · 3003 North Central Avenue, Suite 2600 Phoenix, AZ 85012-2913 · 602-916-5000

Steven P. Emerick · Quarles & Brady · http://www.quarles.com · One Renaissance Square · Two North Central Avenue · Phoenix, AZ 85004-2391 · 602-229-5200

Matthew P. Feeney · ⑩ · Snell & Wilmer · One Arizona Center · 400 East Van Buren Street · Phoenix, AZ 85004-2202 · 602-382-6000

Jere M. Friedman · Friedman Law · 2398 East Camelback Road, Suite 925 · Phoenix, AZ 85016-0001 · 602-955-3800

Martin R. Galbut · Galbut & Galbut · http://www.galbutlaw.com · Camelback Esplanade, Suite 1020 · 2425 East Camelback Road · Phoenix, AZ 85016 · 602-955-1455

William M. Hardin · ⑩ · Osborn Maledon · http://www.omlaw.com · The Phoenix Plaza, Twenty-First Floor · 2929 North Central Avenue · Phoenix, AZ 85012-2793 · 602-640-9000

Christopher D. Johnson · ⑩ · Squire Sanders · http://www.ssd.com · Two Renaissance Square, Suite 2700 · 40 North Central Avenue · Phoenix, AZ 85004-4498 · 602-528-4000

Robert S. Kant · Greenberg Traurig · http://www.gtlaw.com · 2375 East Camelback Road, Suite 700 · Phoenix, AZ 85016 · 602-445-8000

Richard Lieberman · Jennings, Strouss & Salmon · http://www.jsslaw.com · The Collier Center, 11th Floor · 201 East Washington Street · Phoenix, AZ 85004-2385 · 602-262-5911

Bruce E. Macdonough · Greenberg Traurig · http://www.gtlaw.com · 2375 East Camelback Road, Suite 700 · Phoenix, AZ 85016 · 602-445-8000

Karen C. McConnell · Ballard Spahr Andrews & Ingersoll · 3300 Tower, Suite 1800 · 3300 North Central Avenue · Phoenix, AZ 85012-2518 · 602-798-5400

P. Robert Moya · ⑳ · Quarles & Brady · http://www.quarles.com · One Renaissance Square · Two North Central Avenue · Phoenix, AZ 85004-2391 · 602-229-5200

Steven D. Pidgeon · ⑩ · DLA Piper · 2415 East Camelback Road, Suite 700 · Phoenix, AZ 85016-4245 · 480-606-5100

Frank M. Placenti · Squire Sanders · http://www.ssd.com · Two Renaissance Square, Suite 2700 · 40 North Central Avenue · Phoenix, AZ 85004-4498 · 602-528-4000

Joseph P. Richardson · Squire Sanders · http://www.ssd.com · Two Renaissance Square, Suite 2700 · 40 North Central Avenue · Phoenix, AZ 85004-4498 · 602-528-4000

Paul J. Roshka, Jr. · Roshka DeWulf & Patten · http://www.rdp-law.com · One Arizona Center, Suite 800 400 East Van Buren Street · Phoenix, AZ 85004 · 602-256-6100

Christopher S. Stachowiak · Osborn Maledon · http://www.omlaw.com · The Phoenix Plaza, Twenty-First Floor · 2929 North Central Avenue · Phoenix, AZ 85012-2793 · 602-640-9000

SPORTS LAW

Phoenix

Michael L. Gallagher · ⑩ · Gallagher & Kennedy · http://www.gknet.com · 2575 East Camelback Road · Phoenix, AZ 85016-9225 · 602-530-8000

William J. Maledon · ⑩ · Osborn Maledon · http://www.omlaw.com · The Phoenix Plaza, Twenty-First Floor · 2929 North Central Avenue · Phoenix, AZ 85012-2793 · 602-640-9000

Patrick J. McGroder III · ⑩ · Gallagher & Kennedy · http://www.gknet.com · 2575 East Camelback Road · Phoenix, AZ 85016-9225 · 602-530-8000

Dean C. Short II · Gallagher & Kennedy · http://www.gknet.com · 2575 East Camelback Road · Phoenix, AZ 85016-9225 · 602-530-8000

Tucson

Burton J. Kinerk · ⑩ · Kinerk, Beal, Schmidt, Dyer & Sethi · 1790 East River Road, Suite 300 · Tucson, AZ 85718 · 520-790-5600

TAX LAW

Mesa

Paul J. Mooney · Mooney, Wright & Moore · Mesa Financial Plaza, Suite 16000 · 1201 South Alma School Road · Mesa, AZ 85210-0001 · 480-615-7500

Jim L. Wright · Mooney, Wright & Moore · Mesa Financial Plaza, Suite 16000 · 1201 South Alma School Road · Mesa, AZ 85210-0001 · 480-615-7500

Phoenix

Timothy D. Brown · Gallagher & Kennedy · http://www.gknet.com · 2575 East Camelback Road · Phoenix, AZ 85016-9225 · 602-530-8000

John R. Christian · ㉕ · Jennings, Strouss & Salmon · http://www.jsslaw.com · The Collier Center, 11th Floor · 201 East Washington Street · Phoenix, AZ 85004-2385 · 602-262-5911

Patrick Derdenger · ⑩ · Steptoe & Johnson · http://www.steptoe.com · Collier Center, 16th Floor · 201 East Washington Street · Phoenix, AZ 85004-2382 · 602-257-5200

Anthony V. Ehmann · ㉕ · Fennemore Craig · http://www.fclaw.com · 3003 North Central Avenue, Suite 2600 · Phoenix, AZ 85012-2913 · 602-916-5000

Jeffrey B. Fugal · Quarles & Brady · http://www.quarles.com · One Renaissance Square · Two North Central Avenue · Phoenix, AZ 85004-2391 · 602-229-5200

Yale F. Goldberg · 10 · Frazer Ryan Goldberg & Arnold · http://www.frgaglaw.com · 3101 North Central Avenue, Suite 1600 · Phoenix, AZ 85012-2615 · 602-277-2010

David L. Haga, Jr. · 20 · Fennemore Craig · http://www.fclaw.com · 3003 North Central Avenue, Suite 2600 · Phoenix, AZ 85012-2913 · 602-916-5000

Gregg Hanks · Fennemore Craig · http://www.fclaw.com · 3003 North Central Avenue, Suite 2600 · Phoenix, AZ 85012-2913 · 602-916-5000

Susan Ward Harris · Frazer Ryan Goldberg & Arnold · http://www.frgaglaw.com · 3101 North Central Avenue, Suite 1600 · Phoenix, AZ 85012-2615 · 602-277-2010

Neil H. Hiller · 10 · Fennemore Craig · http://www.fclaw.com · 3003 North Central Avenue, Suite 2600 · Phoenix, AZ 85012-2913 · 602-916-5000

Neal Kurn · 20 · Fennemore Craig · http://www.fclaw.com · 3003 North Central Avenue, Suite 2600 · Phoenix, AZ 85012-2913 · 602-916-5000

Stephen E. Lee · 20 · Jennings, Strouss & Salmon · http://www.jsslaw.com · The Collier Center, 11th Floor · 201 East Washington Street · Phoenix, AZ 85004-2385 · 602-262-5911

Kendis K. Muscheid · Fennemore Craig · http://www.fclaw.com · 3003 North Central Avenue, Suite 2600 Phoenix, AZ 85012-2913 · 602-916-5000

Alfred J. Olsen · 25 · Olsen-Smith · http://www.olsensmith.com · Virginia Financial Plaza, Suite 3300 · 301 East Virginia Avenue · Phoenix, AZ 85004-1267 · 602-254-1040

Richard C. Onsager · Onsager, Werner & Oberg · 3200 North Central Avenue, Suite 1800 · Phoenix, AZ 85012-2443 · 602-631-6790

Brad S. Ostroff · 10 · Frazer Ryan Goldberg & Arnold · http://www.frgaglaw.com · 3101 North Central Avenue, Suite 1600 · Phoenix, AZ 85012-2615 · 602-277-2010

Martha Patrick · Burch & Cracchiolo · http://www.bcattorneys.com · 702 East Osborn Road, Suite 200 · P.O. Box 16882 · Phoenix, AZ 85011 · 602-274-7611

Michael E. Pietzsch · 20 · Pietzsch, Bonnett & Womack · http://www.usbenefitslaw.com · 2702 North Third Street, Suite 3000 · Phoenix, AZ 85004 · 602-604-6200

Leslie A. Plattner · 20 · Plattner, Schneidman & Schneider · 4201 North Twenty-Fourth Street, Suite 100 Phoenix, AZ 85016-4663 · 602-274-7955

Charles A. Pulaski, Jr. · 10 · Snell & Wilmer · One Arizona Center · 400 East Van Buren Street · Phoenix, AZ 85004-2202 · 602-382-6000

Les Raatz · Mariscal, Weeks, McIntyre & Friedlander · http://www.mwmf.com · 2901 North Central Avenue, Suite 200 · Phoenix, AZ 85012-2705 · 602-285-5000

Thomas J. Shumard · 10 · Thomas J. Shumard · 4715 North 32nd Street, Suite 105 · Phoenix, AZ 85018-3300 · 602-224-9706

Susan K. Smith · 10 · Olsen-Smith · http://www.olsensmith.com · Virginia Financial Plaza, Suite 3300 · 301 East Virginia Avenue · Phoenix, AZ 85004-1267 · 602-254-1040

David E. Weiss, Jr. · (20) · Snell & Wilmer · One Arizona Center · 400 East Van Buren Street · Phoenix, AZ 85004-2202 · 602-382-6000

Scottsdale

Max K. Boyer · Boyer, Dolasinski, Miller & Martin · 4250 North Drinkwater Boulevard, Suite 120 · Scottsdale, AZ 85251 · 480-505-3480

Stephen S. Case · (25) · Stephen S. Case · 6220 North Fifty-First Place · Scottsdale, AZ 85253-5478 · 602-840-8562

Stephen E. Silver · (20) · Silver Lockwood · Finova Corporate Center, Sixth Floor · 4800 North Scottsdale Road · Scottsdale, AZ 85251-0001 · 480-429-3360

Tucson

Susan M. Freund · (10) · Slosser, Hudgins, Struse & Freund · 6750 North Oracle Road · Tucson, AZ 85704-5618 · 520-575-5555

Gregory V. Gadarian · (10) · Gregory V. Gadarian · 2200 East River Road, Suite 123 · Tucson, AZ 85718-6579 · 520-529-2242

Steven W. Phillips · (10) · Phillips, Moeller & Conway · Rockwell House · 405 West Franklin Street · Tucson, AZ 85701-8209 · 520-798-3803

Gordon G. Waterfall · (25) · Waterfall, Economidis, Caldwell, Hanshaw & Villamana · http://www.wechv.com · Williams Centre, Eighth Floor · 5210 East Williams Circle · Tucson, AZ 85711 · 520-790-5828

TECHNOLOGY LAW

Phoenix

Frank X. Curci · Jennings, Strouss & Salmon · http://www.jsslaw.com · The Collier Center, 11th Floor · 201 East Washington Street · Phoenix, AZ 85004-2385 · 602-262-5911

TRUSTS AND ESTATES

Phoenix

David Case · Ryley Carlock & Applewhite · http://www.rcalaw.com · Phelps Dodge Tower, Suite 1200 · One North Central Avenue · Phoenix, AZ 85004-4417 · 602-258-7701

John R. Christian · (25) · Jennings, Strouss & Salmon · http://www.jsslaw.com · The Collier Center, 11th Floor · 201 East Washington Street · Phoenix, AZ 85004-2385 · 602-262-5911

Brenda K. Church · Frazer Ryan Goldberg & Arnold · http://www.frgaglaw.com · 3101 North Central Avenue, Suite 1600 · Phoenix, AZ 85012-2615 · 602-277-2010

Louis F. Comus, Jr. · (20) · Fennemore Craig · http://www.fclaw.com · 3003 North Central Avenue, Suite 2600 · Phoenix, AZ 85012-2913 · 602-916-5000

Michael A. Cronin · (10) · Maynard, Cronin, Erickson, Curran & Sparks · 3200 North Central Avenue, Suite 1800 · Phoenix, AZ 85012 · 602-279-8500

Rita A. Eisenfeld · (10) · Fennemore Craig · http://www.fclaw.com · 3003 North Central Avenue, Suite 2600 Phoenix, AZ 85012-2913 · 602-916-5000

Neal Kurn · (20) · Fennemore Craig · http://www.fclaw.com · 3003 North Central Avenue, Suite 2600 · Phoenix, AZ 85012-2913 · 602-916-5000

Richard L. Lassen · Jennings, Strouss & Salmon · http://www.jsslaw.com · The Collier Center, 11th Floor 201 East Washington Street · Phoenix, AZ 85004-2385 · 602-262-5911

Hope E. Leibsohn · (10) · Lewis and Roca · http://www.lrlaw.com · 40 North Central Avenue, Suite 1900 · Phoenix, AZ 85004 · 602-262-5311

Alfred J. Olsen · (25) · Olsen-Smith · http://www.olsensmith.com · Virginia Financial Plaza, Suite 3300 · 301 East Virginia Avenue · Phoenix, AZ 85004-1267 · 602-254-1040

Les Raatz · Mariscal, Weeks, McIntyre & Friedlander · http://www.mwmf.com · 2901 North Central Avenue, Suite 200 · Phoenix, AZ 85012-2705 · 602-285-5000

James W. Ryan · Frazer Ryan Goldberg & Arnold · http://www.frgaglaw.com · 3101 North Central Avenue, Suite 1600 · Phoenix, AZ 85012-2615 · 602-277-2010

Thomas J. Shumard · (10) · Thomas J. Shumard · 4715 North 32nd Street, Suite 105 · Phoenix, AZ 85018-3300 · 602-224-9706

Susan K. Smith · (10) · Olsen-Smith · http://www.olsensmith.com · Virginia Financial Plaza, Suite 3300 · 301 East Virginia Avenue · Phoenix, AZ 85004-1267 · 602-254-1040

Bridget O'Brien Swartz · Law Office of Bridget O'Brien Swartz · 2999 North 44th Street, Suite 325 · Phoenix, AZ 85018 · 602-955-7886

Michael J. Tucker · Michael J. Tucker · 2702 North Third Street, Suite 3000 · Phoenix, AZ 85004 · 602-280-1500

John C. Vryhof · Snell & Wilmer · One Arizona Center · 400 East Van Buren Street · Phoenix, AZ 85004-2202 · 602-382-6000

David E. Weiss, Jr. · (20) · Snell & Wilmer · One Arizona Center · 400 East Van Buren Street · Phoenix, AZ 85004-2202 · 602-382-6000

Richard H. Whitney · (25) · Gust Rosenfeld · http://www.gustlaw.com · 201 East Washington Street, Suite 800 · Phoenix, AZ 85004-2327 · 602-257-7422

Scottsdale

John R. Becker · Becker & House · Kierland Corporate Center, Suite 370 · 7047 East Greenway Parkway Scottsdale, AZ 85254 · 480-240-4020

Stephen S. Case · (25) · Stephen S. Case · 6220 North Fifty-First Place · Scottsdale, AZ 85253-5478 · 602-840-8562

Gregory M. Kruzel · Braun Siler Kruzel · 14811 North Kierland Boulevard, Suite 500 · Scottsdale, AZ 85254 · 480-951-8044

W John Lischer · (10) · Lischer Batts & Lyons · 8767 East Via De Ventura, Suite 270 · Scottsdale, AZ 85258-3383 · 480-922-4684

E. Dennis Siler · (10) · Braun Siler Kruzel · 14811 North Kierland Boulevard, Suite 500 · Scottsdale, AZ 85254 · 480-951-8044

Robert B. Fleming · Fleming & Curti · 330 North Granada Avenue · Tucson, AZ 85701 · 520-622-0400

Gregory V. Gadarian · ⑩ · Gregory V. Gadarian · 2200 East River Road, Suite 123 · Tucson, AZ 85718-6579 · 520-529-2242

Charles Giddings · Snell & Wilmer · One South Church Avenue, Suite 1500 · Tucson, AZ 85701-1630 · 520-882-1200

Eugene C. Gieseler · ㉕ · Duffield, Young, Adamson · 3430 East Sunrise Drive, Suite 200 · Tucson, AZ 85718-3236 · 520-792-1181

K. Alexander Hobson · Duffield, Young, Adamson · 3430 East Sunrise Drive, Suite 200 · Tucson, AZ 85718-3236 · 520-792-1181

G. Eugene Isaak · ⑳ · Haralson, Miller, Pitt, Feldman & McAnally · One South Church Avenue, Suite 900 · Tucson, AZ 85701 · 520-792-3836

John D. Kendall · Waterfall, Economidis, Caldwell, Hanshaw & Villamana · http://www.wechv.com · Williams Centre, Eighth Floor · 5210 East Williams Circle · Tucson, AZ 85711 · 520-790-5828

Steven W. Phillips · ⑩ · Phillips, Moeller & Conway · Rockwell House · 405 West Franklin Street · Tucson, AZ 85701-8209 · 520-798-3803

Paul D. Slosser · ⑳ · Slosser, Hudgins, Struse & Freund · 6750 North Oracle Road · Tucson, AZ 85704-5618 · 520-575-5555

Robert M. Struse · ⑩ · Slosser, Hudgins, Struse & Freund · 6750 North Oracle Road · Tucson, AZ 85704-5618 · 520-575-5555

Gordon G. Waterfall · ㉕ · Waterfall, Economidis, Caldwell, Hanshaw & Villamana · http://www.wechv.com · Williams Centre, Eighth Floor · 5210 East Williams Circle · Tucson, AZ 85711 · 520-790-5828

Craig H. Wisnom · Bogutz & Gordon · 3503 North Campbell Avenue, Suite 101 · Tucson, AZ 85719 · 520-321-9700

VENTURE CAPITAL LAW

Phoenix

Daniel McEvers Mahoney · Snell & Wilmer · One Arizona Center · 400 East Van Buren Street · Phoenix, AZ 85004-2202 · 602-382-6000

Quinn P. Williams · ⑩ · Greenberg Traurig · http://www.gtlaw.com · 2375 East Camelback Road, Suite 700 · Phoenix, AZ 85016 · 602-445-8000

WATER LAW

Phoenix

Robert D. Anderson · Fennemore Craig · http://www.fclaw.com · 3003 North Central Avenue, Suite 2600 Phoenix, AZ 85012-2913 · 602-916-5000

Lauren J. Caster · ⑩ · Fennemore Craig · http://www.fclaw.com · 3003 North Central Avenue, Suite 2600 Phoenix, AZ 85012-2913 · 602-916-5000

Cynthia M. Chandley · Ryley Carlock & Applewhite · http://www.rcalaw.com · Phelps Dodge Tower, Suite 1200 · One North Central Avenue · Phoenix, AZ 85004-4417 · 602-258-7701

Jeffrey W. Crockett · Snell & Wilmer · One Arizona Center · 400 East Van Buren Street · Phoenix, AZ 85004-2202 · 602-382-6000

Margaret R. Gallogly · Fennemore Craig · http://www.fclaw.com · 3003 North Central Avenue, Suite 2600 · Phoenix, AZ 85012-2913 · 602-916-5000

Norman D. James · Fennemore Craig · http://www.fclaw.com · 3003 North Central Avenue, Suite 2600 · Phoenix, AZ 85012-2913 · 602-916-5000

James W. Johnson · ⑳ · Fennemore Craig · http://www.fclaw.com · 3003 North Central Avenue, Suite 2600 · Phoenix, AZ 85012-2913 · 602-916-5000

M. Byron Lewis · ⑩ · Salmon, Lewis & Weldon · 2850 East Camelback Road, Suite 200 · Phoenix, AZ 85016 · 602-801-9060

Mark A. McGinnis · Salmon, Lewis & Weldon · 2850 East Camelback Road, Suite 200 · Phoenix, AZ 85016 · 602-801-9060

Michael J. Pearce · Maguire & Pearce · 2999 North 44th Street, Suite 630 · Phoenix, AZ 85018-0001 · 602-277-2195

L. William Staudenmaier · Ryley Carlock & Applewhite · http://www.rcalaw.com · Phelps Dodge Tower, Suite 1200 · One North Central Avenue · Phoenix, AZ 85004-4417 · 602-258-7701

Sheryl A. Sweeney · Ryley Carlock & Applewhite · http://www.rcalaw.com · Phelps Dodge Tower, Suite 1200 · One North Central Avenue · Phoenix, AZ 85004-4417 · 602-258-7701

John B. Weldon, Jr. · ⑩ · Salmon, Lewis & Weldon · 2850 East Camelback Road, Suite 200 · Phoenix, AZ 85016 · 602-801-9060

Pinetop-Lakeside

David A. Brown · Brown & Brown · P.O. Box 3128 · Pinetop-Lakeside, AZ 85935 · 928-367-3235

Tucson

L. Anthony Fines · Law Office of L. Anthony Fines · 33 North Stone Avenue, Suite 1850 · Tucson, AZ 85701-0001 · 520-547-2890

Michael F. McNulty · ⑩ · Lewis and Roca · http://www.lrlaw.com · One South Church Avenue, Suite 700 Tucson, AZ 85701-1627 · 520-622-2090

WHITE-COLLAR CRIMINAL DEFENSE

Phoenix

James J. Belanger · Cheifetz Iannitelli Marcolini · http://www.cimlaw.com · Viad Tower, 19th Floor · 1850 North Central Avenue · Phoenix, AZ 85004 · 602-952-6000

Michael E. Benchoff · ㉕ · Michael E. Benchoff · 6121 North Third Avenue · Phoenix, AZ 85013 · 602-253-1687

Francis J. Burke, Jr. · Steptoe & Johnson · http://www.steptoe.com · Collier Center, 16th Floor · 201 East Washington Street · Phoenix, AZ 85004-2382 · 602-257-5200

Larry L. Debus · ㉕ · Debus, Kazan & Westerhausen · 335 East Palm Lane · Phoenix, AZ 85004 · 602-257-8900

Clark L. Derrick · Kimerer & Derrick · 221 East Indianola Avenue · Phoenix, AZ 85012-2002 · 602-279-5900

Stephen M. Dichter · ⑩ · Harper, Christian, Dichter & Graif · http://www.hcdglaw.com · 2700 North Central Avenue, Suite 1200 · Phoenix, AZ 85004 · 602-792-1700

Jordan L. Green · ㉕ · Perkins Coie Brown & Bain · http://www.perkinscoie.com · 2901 North Central Avenue, Suite 2000 · Phoenix, AZ 85012-2788 · 602-351-8000

Larry A. Hammond · ⑩ · Osborn Maledon · http://www.omlaw.com · The Phoenix Plaza, Twenty-First Floor · 2929 North Central Avenue · Phoenix, AZ 85012-2793 · 602-640-9000

Tom E. Henze · ⑩ · Gallagher & Kennedy · http://www.gknet.com · 2575 East Camelback Road · Phoenix, AZ 85016-9225 · 602-530-8000

Michael D. Kimerer · ㉕ · Kimerer & Derrick · 221 East Indianola Avenue · Phoenix, AZ 85012-2002 · 602-279-5900

Craig Mehrens · Mehrens and Wilemon · 99 East Virginia Avenue, Suite 220 · Phoenix, AZ 85004 · 602-258-5151

Edward F. Novak · ⑩ · Mariscal, Weeks, McIntyre & Friedlander · http://www.mwmf.com · 2901 North Central Avenue, Suite 200 · Phoenix, AZ 85012-2705 · 602-285-5000

Lee Stein · Perkins Coie Brown & Bain · http://www.perkinscoie.com · 2901 North Central Avenue, Suite 2000 · Phoenix, AZ 85012-2788 · 602-351-8000

Tucson

Stanton Bloom · Stanton Bloom · 145 South Sixth Avenue · Tucson, AZ 85701-0001 · 520-623-5821

A. Bates Butler III · Fennemore Craig · http://www.fclaw.com · One South Church Avenue, Suite 1000 · Tucson, AZ 85701-1627 · 520-879-6800

Alfred S. Donau III · Donau & Bolt · 3505 North Campbell Avenue, Suite 501 · Tucson, AZ 85719-2033 520-795-8710

Bruce R. Heurlin · Heurlin Sherlock Panahi · 1636 North Swan Road, Suite 200 · Tucson, AZ 85712-4096 · 520-319-1200

Michael L. Piccarreta · ⑩ · Piccarreta & Davis · http://www.pd-law.com · 145 South Sixth Avenue · Tucson, AZ 85701-2007 · 520-622-6900

Stephen M. Weiss · Karp & Weiss · 3060 North Swan Road · Tucson, AZ 85712-1225 · 520-325-4200

WORKERS' COMPENSATION LAW

Flagstaff

Thomas C. Whitley · ⑩ · Taylor & Associates · 2323 North Walgreens Street, Suite 104 · P.O. Box 22516 · Flagstaff, AZ 86002-2516 · 928-526-4160

Donald L. Cross · ⑩ · Cross & Lieberman · 2001 West Camelback Road, Suite 270 · Phoenix, AZ 85015 · 602-650-2856

Julie A. Doherty · ⑩ · Doherty & Venezia · 4000 North Central Avenue, Suite 1720 · Phoenix, AZ 85012-3510 · 602-277-0980

David W. Earl · Cross & Lieberman · 2001 West Camelback Road, Suite 270 · Phoenix, AZ 85015 · 602-650-2856

Gregory L. Folger · ⑩ · Jones, Skelton & Hochuli · 2901 North Central Avenue, Suite 800 · Phoenix, AZ 85012 · 602-263-1700

J. Terence Fox · ⑩ · J. Terence Fox · 934 West McDowell Road · Phoenix, AZ 85007-1730 · 602-274-6828

R. Kent Klein · ⑩ · Klein, Lundmark, Barberich & LaMont · 5333 North Seventh Street, Suite B-112 · P.O. Box 33997 · Phoenix, AZ 85067-3997 · 602-279-9777

Dennis R. Kurth · ⑩ · Taylor & Associates · 320 East Virginia Avenue, Suite 100 · Phoenix, AZ 85004 · 602-254-1977

K. Casey Kurth · ⑩ · Jardine, Baker, Hickman & Houston · 3300 North Central Avenue, Suite 2600 · Phoenix, AZ 85012 · 602-200-9777

Terrence Kurth · ⑩ · Jones, Skelton & Hochuli · 2901 North Central Avenue, Suite 800 · Phoenix, AZ 85012 · 602-263-1700

Steven C. Lester · ⑩ · Steven C. Lester · 1100 East Washington Street, Suite 100 · Phoenix, AZ 85034-1045 · 602-253-1956

Lawrence H. Lieberman · ⑩ · Cross & Lieberman · 2001 West Camelback Road, Suite 270 · Phoenix, AZ 85015 · 602-650-2856

R. Todd Lundmark · ⑩ · Klein, Lundmark, Barberich & LaMont · 5333 North Seventh Street, Suite B-112 · P.O. Box 33997 · Phoenix, AZ 85067-3997 · 602-279-9777

Mark R. Mignella · Mark R. Mignella · 7007 North 18th Street · P.O. Box 32325 · Phoenix, AZ 85064-2325 · 602-385-3785

Charles G. Rehling II · ⑩ · Jones, Skelton & Hochuli · 2901 North Central Avenue, Suite 800 · Phoenix, AZ 85012 · 602-263-1700

Alan M. Schiffman · Schiffman Law Office · http://www.schiffmanlaw.com · 4506 North Twelfth Street · Phoenix, AZ 85014-4201 · 602-266-2667

Roger A. Schwartz · Taylor & Associates · 320 East Virginia Avenue, Suite 100 · Phoenix, AZ 85004 · 602-254-1977

J. Russell Skelton · ⑩ · Jones, Skelton & Hochuli · 2901 North Central Avenue, Suite 800 · Phoenix, AZ 85012 · 602-263-1700

Richard E. Taylor · ⑩ · Taylor & Associates · 320 East Virginia Avenue, Suite 100 · Phoenix, AZ 85004 · 602-254-1977

Stephen L. Weiss · ⑩ · Taylor & Associates · 320 East Virginia Avenue, Suite 100 · Phoenix, AZ 85004 · 602-254-1977

Charles M. Wilmer · Charles M. Wilmer, Sole Practitioner · 2504 North Third Street · Phoenix, AZ 85004-1125 · 602-241-9424

Charles M. Wilmer, Jr. · ⑩ · Wilmer, Messer & Testini · 202 East Earl, Suite 400 · P.O. Box 25051 · Phoenix, AZ 85002-5051 · 602-532-0301

Thomas C. Wilmer · Thomas C. Wilmer · 2504 North Third Street · Phoenix, AZ 85004-1308 · 602-230-1188

Robert E. Wisniewski · Robert E. Wisniewski · 519 East Thomas Road · P.O. Box 33217 · Phoenix, AZ 85067-3217 · 602-234-3700

Tucson

Brian Clymer · ⑩ · Brian Clymer · 2601 North Campbell Avenue, Suite 203 · Tucson, AZ 85719 · 520-323-1234

J. Stephen Dix · ⑩ · Dix, Forman & Kern · 2606 East 10th Street · P.O. Box 43517 · Tucson, AZ 85733 · 520-748-0800

Robert J. Forman · ⑩ · Dix, Forman & Kern · 2606 East 10th Street · P.O. Box 43517 · Tucson, AZ 85733 · 520-748-0800

Arthur V. Gage · Arthur V. Gage · 2573 North First Avenue · Tucson, AZ 85719 · 520-881-8300

Carol L. Lohmann · ⑩ · Law Office of Carol L. Lohmann · 627 North Seventh Avenue · Tucson, AZ 85701-0001 · 520-628-7700

Patrick R. McNamara · ⑩ · Tretschok McNamara & Miller · 2606 East One Tenth Street · Tucson, AZ 85733-2887 · 520-622-2833

M. Ted Moeller · Moeller Law Office · 2929 East Broadway Boulevard · Tucson, AZ 85716-4748 · 520-795-8852

Dee-Dee Samet · ⑩ · Dee-Dee Samet · 717 North Sixth Avenue · Tucson, AZ 85705 · 520-624-8595

Pamela A. Treadwell-Rubin · Goering, Roberts, Rubin, Brogna, Enos & Treadwell-Rubin · http://www.azdefenselaw.com · 3320 North Campbell Avenue, Suite 200 · Tucson, AZ 85719-2371 · 520-577-9300

ARKANSAS

ADMINISTRATIVE LAW

Little Rock

Frederick K. Campbell · Mitchell, Williams, Selig, Gates & Woodyard · http://www.mitchellwilliamslaw.com · 425 West Capitol Avenue, Suite 1800 · Little Rock, AR 72201-3525 501-688-8800

Doak Foster · Mitchell, Williams, Selig, Gates & Woodyard · http://www.mitchellwilliamslaw.com · 425 West Capitol Avenue, Suite 1800 · Little Rock, AR 72201-3525 · 501-688-8800

Allan W. Horne · Dover Dixon Horne · http://www.doverdixonhorne.com · Metropolitan Tower, 37th Floor · 425 West Capitol Avenue · Little Rock, AR 72201 · 501-375-9151

T. Ark Monroe III · Mitchell, Williams, Selig, Gates & Woodyard · http://www.mitchellwilliamslaw.com · 425 West Capitol Avenue, Suite 1800 · Little Rock, AR 72201-3525 · 501-688-8800

Nicholas Thompson · Mitchell, Williams, Selig, Gates & Woodyard · http://www.mitchellwilliamslaw.com · 425 West Capitol Avenue, Suite 1800 · Little Rock, AR 72201-3525 501-688-8800

William H. L. Woodyard III · Mitchell, Williams, Selig, Gates & Woodyard · http://www.mitchellwilliamslaw.com · 425 West Capitol Avenue, Suite 1800 · Little Rock, AR 72201-3525 501-688-8800

ALTERNATIVE DISPUTE RESOLUTION

Fort Smith

Robert E. Hornberger · ADR, Inc. · 404 North Seventh Street · P.O. Box 8064 · Fort Smith, AR 72902-8064 · 479-783-1776

Little Rock

John A. Davis III · ADR, Inc. · 1501 North University Avenue, Suite 420 · Little Rock, AR 72207 · 501-376-2121

John D. Davis · ⑩ · Wright, Lindsey & Jennings · http://www.wlj.com · 200 West Capitol Avenue, Suite 2300 · Little Rock, AR 72201-3699 · 501-371-0808

Frank S. Hamlin · ADR, Inc. · 1501 North University Avenue, Suite 420 · Little Rock, AR 72207 · 501-376-2121

Sidney H. McCollum · ADR, Inc. · 1501 North University Avenue, Suite 420 · Little Rock, AR 72207 · 501-376-2121

ANTITRUST LAW

Little Rock

Philip S. Anderson · ⑩ · Williams & Anderson · http://www.williamsanderson.com · Stephens Building, 22nd Floor · 111 Center Street · Little Rock, AR 72201 · 501-372-0800

Peter G. Kumpe · ⑩ · Williams & Anderson · http://www.williamsanderson.com · Stephens Building, 22nd Floor · 111 Center Street · Little Rock, AR 72201 · 501-372-0800

Robert Shults · ㉕ · Shults Law Firm · 200 West Capitol Avenue, Suite 1600 · Little Rock, AR 72201-3637 · 501-375-2301

James M. Simpson · ⑩ · Friday, Eldredge & Clark · http://www.fridayfirm.com · 400 West Capitol Avenue, Suite 2000 · Little Rock, AR 72201-3522 · 501-376-2011

APPELLATE LAW

Fayetteville

R. Christopher Lawson · Friday, Eldredge & Clark · http://www.fridayfirm.com · 3425 North Futrall Drive, Suite 103 · Fayetteville, AR 72703-6252 · 479-695-2011

Little Rock

Philip S. Anderson · ⑩ · Williams & Anderson · http://www.williamsanderson.com · Stephens Building, 22nd Floor · 111 Center Street · Little Rock, AR 72201 · 501-372-0800

Jess L. Askew III · Williams & Anderson · http://www.williamsanderson.com · Stephens Building, 22nd Floor · 111 Center Street · Little Rock, AR 72201 · 501-372-0800

E. B. Chiles IV · Quattlebaum, Grooms, Tull & Burrow · http://www.qgtb.com · 111 Center Street, Suite 1900 · Little Rock, AR 72201-4420 · 501-379-1700

Patrick J. Goss · ⑩ · Rose Law Firm · 120 East Fourth Street · Little Rock, AR 72201-2893 · 501-375-9131

Philip E. Kaplan · ㉕ · Williams & Anderson · http://www.williamsanderson.com · Stephens Building, 22nd Floor · 111 Center Street · Little Rock, AR 72201 · 501-372-0800

Troy A. Price · Wright, Lindsey & Jennings · http://www.wlj.com · 200 West Capitol Avenue, Suite 2300 · Little Rock, AR 72201-3699 · 501-371-0808

Roger D. Rowe · Lax, Vaughan, Fortson, McKenzie & Rowe · Cantrell West Building, Suite 201 · 11300 Cantrell Road · Little Rock, AR 72212 · 501-376-6565

Robert S. Shafer · Friday, Eldredge & Clark · http://www.fridayfirm.com · 400 West Capitol Avenue, Suite 2000 · Little Rock, AR 72201-3522 · 501-376-2011

BANKING LAW

Jonesboro

Ralph W. Waddell · Barrett & Deacon · Mercantile Center, Third Floor · 300 South Church Street · P.O. Box 1700 · Jonesboro, AR 72403 · 870-931-1700

Little Rock

Garland W. Binns, Jr. · Dover Dixon Horne · http://www.doverdixonhorne.com · Metropolitan Tower, 37th Floor · 425 West Capitol Avenue · Little Rock, AR 72201 · 501-375-9151

Patrick A. Burrow · Quattlebaum, Grooms, Tull & Burrow · http://www.qgtb.com · 111 Center Street, Suite 1900 · Little Rock, AR 72201-4420 · 501-379-1700

Randal B. Frazier · Kutak Rock · 124 West Capitol Avenue, Suite 2000 · Little Rock, AR 72201-3706 · 501-975-3000

Donald H. Henry · ⑩ · Mitchell, Williams, Selig, Gates & Woodyard · http://www.mitchellwilliamslaw.com · 425 West Capitol Avenue, Suite 1800 · Little Rock, AR 72201-3525 501-688-8800

John Kooistra III · Williams & Anderson · http://www.williamsanderson.com · Stephens Building, 22nd Floor · 111 Center Street · Little Rock, AR 72201 · 501-372-0800

David B. Vandergriff · Quattlebaum, Grooms, Tull & Burrow · http://www.qgtb.com · 111 Center Street, Suite 1900 · Little Rock, AR 72201-4420 · 501-379-1700

William A. Waddell · ⑩ · Friday, Eldredge & Clark · http://www.fridayfirm.com · 400 West Capitol Avenue, Suite 2000 · Little Rock, AR 72201-3522 · 501-376-2011

BANKRUPTCY AND CREDITOR-DEBTOR RIGHTS LAW

Crossett

Thomas S. Streetman · Streetman & Meeks · 302 Main Street · P.O. Drawer A · Crossett, AR 71635 · 870-364-2213

Fayetteville

Jill R. Jacoway · Jacoway Law Firm · 26 West Center, Suite 203 · P.O. Box 3456 · Fayetteville, AR 72701 479-521-2621

Little Rock

Charles W. Baker · ⑩ · Rose Law Firm · 120 East Fourth Street · Little Rock, AR 72201-2893 · 501-375-9131

Charles T. Coleman · ⑩ · Wright, Lindsey & Jennings · http://www.wlj.com · 200 West Capitol Avenue, Suite 2300 · Little Rock, AR 72201-3699 · 501-371-0808

James F. Dowden · ⑩ · James F. Dowden · 212 Center Street, 10th Floor · Little Rock, AR 72201 · 501-324-4700

Judy Simmons Henry · Wright, Lindsey & Jennings · http://www.wlj.com · 200 West Capitol Avenue, Suite 2300 · Little Rock, AR 72201-3699 · 501-371-0808

Lance R. Miller · Mitchell, Williams, Selig, Gates & Woodyard · http://www.mitchellwilliamslaw.com · 425 West Capitol Avenue, Suite 1800 · Little Rock, AR 72201-3525 · 501-688-8800

Richard L. Ramsay · Eichenbaum, Liles & Heister · Union National Bank Building, Suite 1400 · 124 West Capitol Avenue · Little Rock, AR 72201-3717 · 501-376-4531

Isaac A. Scott, Jr. · ⑩ · Wright, Lindsey & Jennings · http://www.wlj.com · 200 West Capitol Avenue, Suite 2300 · Little Rock, AR 72201-3699 · 501-371-0808

Stan D. Smith · Mitchell, Williams, Selig, Gates & Woodyard · http://www.mitchellwilliamslaw.com · 425 West Capitol Avenue, Suite 1800 · Little Rock, AR 72201-3525 · 501-688-8800

Geoffrey B. Treece · Quattlebaum, Grooms, Tull & Burrow · http://www.qgtb.com · 111 Center Street, Suite 1900 · Little Rock, AR 72201-4420 · 501-379-1700

North Little Rock

David A. Grace · ⑩ · Hardin & Grace · 500 Main Street, Suite A · P.O. Box 5851 · North Little Rock, AR 72119 · 501-378-7900

Siloam Springs

John Terry Lee · John Terry Lee · 106 South Broadway Street · P.O. Box 1348 · Siloam Springs, AR 72761-1348 · 479-524-2337

Springdale

William M. Clark, Jr. · Cypert, Crouch, Clark & Harwell · 111 Holcomb Street · P.O. Box 1400 · Springdale, AR 72765-1400 · 479-751-5222

BET-THE-COMPANY LITIGATION

Batesville

H. David Blair · ⑩ · Blair & Stroud · http://www.blastlaw.com · Municipal Building, Suite 201 · 500 East Main Street · P.O. Box 2135 · Batesville, AR 72501 · 870-793-8350

Fayetteville

John C. Everett · ⑩ · Everett & Wales · 1944 East Joyce Boulevard · P.O. Box 8370 · Fayetteville, AR 72703-8370 · 479-443-0292

Little Rock

William M. Griffin III · ⑩ · Friday, Eldredge & Clark · http://www.fridayfirm.com · 400 West Capitol Avenue, Suite 2000 · Little Rock, AR 72201-3522 · 501-376-2011

Philip E. Kaplan · ㉕ · Williams & Anderson · http://www.williamsanderson.com · Stephens Building, 22nd Floor · 111 Center Street · Little Rock, AR 72201 · 501-372-0800

COMMERCIAL LITIGATION

Batesville

H. David Blair · ⑩ · Blair & Stroud · http://www.blastlaw.com · Municipal Building, Suite 201 · 500 East Main Street · P.O. Box 2135 · Batesville, AR 72501 · 870-793-8350

El Dorado

Brian H. Ratcliff · Shackleford, Phillips, Wineland & Ratcliff · 100 East Church Street · P.O. Box 1718 · El Dorado, AR 71731-1718 · 870-862-5523

Dennis L. Shackleford · ㉕ · Shackleford, Phillips, Wineland & Ratcliff · 100 East Church Street · P.O. Box 1718 · El Dorado, AR 71731-1718 · 870-862-5523

Floyd M. Thomas, Jr. · Compton, Prewett, Thomas & Hickey · 423 North Washington Avenue · El Dorado, AR 71730-5615 · 870-862-3478

Fayetteville

Constance G. Clark · Davis, Wright, Clark, Butt & Carithers · http://www.daviswrightlaw.com · 19 East Mountain Street · P.O. Box 1688 · Fayetteville, AR 72702-1688 · 479-521-7600

Sidney P. Davis, Jr. · ⑩ · Davis, Wright, Clark, Butt & Carithers · http://www.daviswrightlaw.com · 19 East Mountain Street · P.O. Box 1688 · Fayetteville, AR 72702-1688 · 479-521-7600

John C. Everett · ⑩ · Everett & Wales · 1944 East Joyce Boulevard · P.O. Box 8370 · Fayetteville, AR 72703-8370 · 479-443-0292

Robert Jones III · Connor & Winters · 211 East Dickson Street · Fayetteville, AR 72701 · 479-582-5711

Fort Smith

C. Wayne Harris · Warner, Smith & Harris · 400 Rogers Avenue · P.O. Box 1626 · Fort Smith, AR 72901 · 479-782-6041

Charles R. Ledbetter · ⑩ · Ledbetter, Cogbill, Arnold & Harrison · 622 Parker Avenue · P.O. Box 185 · Fort Smith, AR 72902-0185 · 479-782-7294

Helena

David Solomon · ⑩ · David Solomon · 427 Cherry Street · P.O. Box 490 · Helena, AR 72342-3301 · 870-338-7427

Jonesboro

Barry Deacon · Barrett & Deacon · Mercantile Center, Third Floor · 300 South Church Street · P.O. Box 1700 · Jonesboro, AR 72403 · 870-931-1700

Little Rock

H. William Allen · ⑩ · Allen Law Firm · http://www.arbusinesslitigation.com · Centre Place, Ninth Floor 212 Center Street · Little Rock, AR 72201-2416 · 501-374-7100

Philip S. Anderson · ⑩ · Williams & Anderson · http://www.williamsanderson.com · Stephens Building, 22nd Floor · 111 Center Street · Little Rock, AR 72201 · 501-372-0800

Jess L. Askew III · Williams & Anderson · http://www.williamsanderson.com · Stephens Building, 22nd Floor · 111 Center Street · Little Rock, AR 72201 · 501-372-0800

John K. Baker · Mitchell, Williams, Selig, Gates & Woodyard · http://www.mitchellwilliamslaw.com · 425 West Capitol Avenue, Suite 1800 · Little Rock, AR 72201-3525 · 501-688-8800

R. T. Beard III · ⑩ · Mitchell, Williams, Selig, Gates & Woodyard · http://www.mitchellwilliamslaw.com · 425 West Capitol Avenue, Suite 1800 · Little Rock, AR 72201-3525 · 501-688-8800

Cathleen V. Compton · ⑩ · Cathleen V. Compton · 114 South Pulaski Street · Little Rock, AR 72201 · 501-372-0080

Gary D. Corum · Wilson, Engstrom, Corum & Coulter · 200 South Commerce, Suite 600 · P.O. Box 71 · Little Rock, AR 72203 · 501-375-6453

Nate Coulter · Wilson, Engstrom, Corum & Coulter · 200 South Commerce, Suite 600 · P.O. Box 71 · Little Rock, AR 72203 · 501-375-6453

Kevin A. Crass · Friday, Eldredge & Clark · http://www.fridayfirm.com · 400 West Capitol Avenue, Suite 2000 · Little Rock, AR 72201-3522 · 501-376-2011

Richard T. Donovan · Rose Law Firm · 120 East Fourth Street · Little Rock, AR 72201-2893 · 501-375-9131

Timothy O. Dudley · ⑩ · Timothy O. Dudley · 114 South Pulaski Street · Little Rock, AR 72201-1924 · 501-372-0080

Patrick J. Goss · ⑩ · Rose Law Firm · 120 East Fourth Street · Little Rock, AR 72201-2893 · 501-375-9131

William M. Griffin III · ⑩ · Friday, Eldredge & Clark · http://www.fridayfirm.com · 400 West Capitol Avenue, Suite 2000 · Little Rock, AR 72201-3522 · 501-376-2011

Christopher J. Heller · Friday, Eldredge & Clark · http://www.fridayfirm.com · 400 West Capitol Avenue, Suite 2000 · Little Rock, AR 72201-3522 · 501-376-2011

D. Michael Huckabay, Sr. · ⑩ · Huckabay, Munson, Rowlett & Moore · http://www.hmrmlaw.com · Regions Center, Suite 1900 · 400 West Capitol Avenue · Little Rock, AR 72201 · 501-374-6535

M. Samuel Jones III · Mitchell, Williams, Selig, Gates & Woodyard · http://www.mitchellwilliamslaw.com · 425 West Capitol Avenue, Suite 1800 · Little Rock, AR 72201-3525 501-688-8800

Philip E. Kaplan · ㉕ · Williams & Anderson · http://www.williamsanderson.com · Stephens Building, 22nd Floor · 111 Center Street · Little Rock, AR 72201 · 501-372-0800

Peter G. Kumpe · ⑩ · Williams & Anderson · http://www.williamsanderson.com · Stephens Building, 22nd Floor · 111 Center Street · Little Rock, AR 72201 · 501-372-0800

John G. Lile · ⑩ · Wright, Lindsey & Jennings · http://www.wlj.com · 200 West Capitol Avenue, Suite 2300 · Little Rock, AR 72201-3699 · 501-371-0808

Bruce E. Munson · Huckabay, Munson, Rowlett & Moore · http://www.hmrmlaw.com · Regions Center, Suite 1900 · 400 West Capitol Avenue · Little Rock, AR 72201 · 501-374-6535

Elizabeth R. Murray · Friday, Eldredge & Clark · http://www.fridayfirm.com · 400 West Capitol Avenue, Suite 2000 · Little Rock, AR 72201-3522 · 501-376-2011

David M. Powell · Williams & Anderson · http://www.williamsanderson.com · Stephens Building, 22nd Floor · 111 Center Street · Little Rock, AR 72201 · 501-372-0800

Steven W. Quattlebaum · Quattlebaum, Grooms, Tull & Burrow · http://www.qgtb.com · 111 Center Street, Suite 1900 · Little Rock, AR 72201-4420 · 501-379-1700

Gordon S. Rather, Jr. · ⑩ · Wright, Lindsey & Jennings · http://www.wlj.com · 200 West Capitol Avenue, Suite 2300 · Little Rock, AR 72201-3699 · 501-371-0808

Roger D. Rowe · Lax, Vaughan, Fortson, McKenzie & Rowe · Cantrell West Building, Suite 201 · 11300 Cantrell Road · Little Rock, AR 72212 · 501-376-6565

Beverly A. Rowlett · ⑩ · Huckabay, Munson, Rowlett & Moore · http://www.hmrmlaw.com · Regions Center, Suite 1900 · 400 West Capitol Avenue · Little Rock, AR 72201 · 501-374-6535

Charles L. Schlumberger · Quattlebaum, Grooms, Tull & Burrow · http://www.qgtb.com · 111 Center Street, Suite 1900 · Little Rock, AR 72201-4420 · 501-379-1700

Michael N. Shannon · Quattlebaum, Grooms, Tull & Burrow · http://www.qgtb.com · 111 Center Street, Suite 1900 · Little Rock, AR 72201-4420 · 501-379-1700

Steven T. Shults · ⑩ · Shults Law Firm · 200 West Capitol Avenue, Suite 1600 · Little Rock, AR 72201-3637 · 501-375-2301

John E. Tull III · Quattlebaum, Grooms, Tull & Burrow · http://www.qgtb.com · 111 Center Street, Suite 1900 · Little Rock, AR 72201-4420 · 501-379-1700

William A. Waddell · ⑩ · Friday, Eldredge & Clark · http://www.fridayfirm.com · 400 West Capitol Avenue, Suite 2000 · Little Rock, AR 72201-3522 · 501-376-2011

Teresa M. Wineland · Williams & Anderson · http://www.williamsanderson.com · Stephens Building, 22nd Floor · 111 Center Street · Little Rock, AR 72201 · 501-372-0800

Pine Bluff

Stephen A. Matthews · ㉕ · Bridges, Young, Matthews & Drake · 315 East Eighth Avenue · P.O. Box 7808 · Pine Bluff, AR 71611 · 870-534-5532

Rogers

James G. Lingle · Lingle Law Firm · 110 South Dixieland Road · Rogers, AR 72758 · 479-636-7899

Marshall S. Ney · Mitchell, Williams, Selig, Gates & Woodyard · http://www.mitchellwilliamslaw.com · 5414 Pinnacle Point Drive, Suite 500 · Rogers, AR 72758-8131 · 479-464-5650

COMMUNICATIONS LAW

Little Rock

Jess L. Askew III · Williams & Anderson · http://www.williamsanderson.com · Stephens Building, 22nd Floor · 111 Center Street · Little Rock, AR 72201 · 501-372-0800

Lawrence Chisenhall · Chisenhall, Nestrud & Julian · Regions Bank Building, Suite 2840 · 400 West Capitol Avenue · Little Rock, AR 72201 · 501-372-5800

CONSTRUCTION LAW

Little Rock

Allen C. Dobson · Cross Gunter Witherspoon & Galchus · http://www.cgwg.com · 500 President Clinton Avenue, Suite 200 · Little Rock, AR 72201 · 501-371-9999

Jack East III · Jack East III · 2725 Cantrell Road, Suite 202 · Little Rock, AR 72202 · 501-372-3278

Cyril Hollingsworth · Dover Dixon Horne · http://www.doverdixonhorne.com · Metropolitan Tower, 37th Floor · 425 West Capitol Avenue · Little Rock, AR 72201 · 501-375-9151

Jeffrey H. Moore · Friday, Eldredge & Clark · http://www.fridayfirm.com · 400 West Capitol Avenue, Suite 2000 · Little Rock, AR 72201-3522 · 501-376-2011

David M. Powell · Williams & Anderson · http://www.williamsanderson.com · Stephens Building, 22nd Floor · 111 Center Street · Little Rock, AR 72201 · 501-372-0800

John Dewey Watson · Friday, Eldredge & Clark · http://www.fridayfirm.com · 400 West Capitol Avenue, Suite 2000 · Little Rock, AR 72201-3522 · 501-376-2011

North Little Rock

David A. Grace · ⑩ · Hardin & Grace · 500 Main Street, Suite A · P.O. Box 5851 · North Little Rock, AR 72119 · 501-378-7900

CORPORATE LAW

Jonesboro

Ralph W. Waddell · Barrett & Deacon · Mercantile Center, Third Floor · 300 South Church Street · P.O. Box 1700 · Jonesboro, AR 72403 · 870-931-1700

Philip S. Anderson · ⑩ · Williams & Anderson · http://www.williamsanderson.com · Stephens Building, 22nd Floor · 111 Center Street · Little Rock, AR 72201 · 501-372-0800

Paul B. Benham III · ⑳ · Friday, Eldredge & Clark · http://www.fridayfirm.com · 400 West Capitol Avenue, Suite 2000 · Little Rock, AR 72201-3522 · 501-376-2011

C. Douglas Buford, Jr. · Mitchell, Williams, Selig, Gates & Woodyard · http://www.mitchellwilliamslaw.com · 425 West Capitol Avenue, Suite 1800 · Little Rock, AR 72201-3525 501-688-8800

Walter M. Ebel III · Friday, Eldredge & Clark · http://www.fridayfirm.com · 400 West Capitol Avenue, Suite 2000 · Little Rock, AR 72201-3522 · 501-376-2011

Price C. Gardner · Friday, Eldredge & Clark · http://www.fridayfirm.com · 400 West Capitol Avenue, Suite 2000 · Little Rock, AR 72201-3522 · 501-376-2011

H. Watt Gregory III · Kutak Rock · 124 West Capitol Avenue, Suite 2000 · Little Rock, AR 72201-3706 · 501-975-3000

Paul W. Hoover, Jr. · Williams & Anderson · http://www.williamsanderson.com · Stephens Building, 22nd Floor · 111 Center Street · Little Rock, AR 72201 · 501-372-0800

Donald T. Jack, Jr. · ⑩ · Jack, Nelson & Jones · The Metropolitan Tower, Suite 3400 · 425 West Capitol Avenue · Little Rock, AR 72201 · 501-375-1122

Walter E. May · Mitchell, Williams, Selig, Gates & Woodyard · http://www.mitchellwilliamslaw.com · 425 West Capitol Avenue, Suite 1800 · Little Rock, AR 72201-3525 · 501-688-8800

T. Ark Monroe III · Mitchell, Williams, Selig, Gates & Woodyard · http://www.mitchellwilliamslaw.com · 425 West Capitol Avenue, Suite 1800 · Little Rock, AR 72201-3525 · 501-688-8800

John S. Selig · ⑩ · Mitchell, Williams, Selig, Gates & Woodyard · http://www.mitchellwilliamslaw.com · 425 West Capitol Avenue, Suite 1800 · Little Rock, AR 72201-3525 · 501-688-8800

Robert Shults · ㉕ · Shults Law Firm · 200 West Capitol Avenue, Suite 1600 · Little Rock, AR 72201-3637 · 501-375-2301

Nicholas Thompson · Mitchell, Williams, Selig, Gates & Woodyard · http://www.mitchellwilliamslaw.com · 425 West Capitol Avenue, Suite 1800 · Little Rock, AR 72201-3525 501-688-8800

Paragould

Ray A. Goodwin · Goodwin Moore · 511 South Fourth Street · P.O. Box 726 · Paragould, AR 72450 · 870-239-2225

DUI/DWI DEFENSE

Fayetteville

Christina D. Comstock · Everett & Wales · 1944 East Joyce Boulevard · P.O. Box 8370 · Fayetteville, AR 72703-8370 · 479-443-0292

Little Rock

David H. Williams · The Law Office of David H. Williams · 212 Center Street, Second Floor · Little Rock, AR 72201 · 501-372-0038

EDUCATION LAW

Little Rock

Christopher J. Heller · Friday, Eldredge & Clark · http://www.fridayfirm.com · 400 West Capitol Avenue, Suite 2000 · Little Rock, AR 72201-3522 · 501-376-2011

EMPLOYEE BENEFITS LAW

Little Rock

Bryant Cranford · Rose Law Firm · 120 East Fourth Street · Little Rock, AR 72201-2893 · 501-375-9131

Gregory B. Graham · 20 · Overbey, Graham, Strigel & Wesbrook · Pavilion Centre, Suite 240 · 8315 Cantrell Road · Little Rock, AR 72227-2355 · 501-664-8105

Joseph B. Hurst, Jr. · 20 · Friday, Eldredge & Clark · http://www.fridayfirm.com · 400 West Capitol Avenue, Suite 2000 · Little Rock, AR 72201-3522 · 501-376-2011

Alexandra A. Ifrah · Friday, Eldredge & Clark · http://www.fridayfirm.com · 400 West Capitol Avenue, Suite 2000 · Little Rock, AR 72201-3522 · 501-376-2011

A. Wyckliff Nisbet, Jr. · 20 · Friday, Eldredge & Clark · http://www.fridayfirm.com · 400 West Capitol Avenue, Suite 2000 · Little Rock, AR 72201-3522 · 501-376-2011

Thomas L. Overbey · 25 · Overbey, Graham, Strigel & Wesbrook · Pavilion Centre, Suite 240 · 8315 Cantrell Road · Little Rock, AR 72227-2355 · 501-664-8105

Craig H. Westbrook · 20 · Overbey, Graham, Strigel & Wesbrook · Pavilion Centre, Suite 240 · 8315 Cantrell Road · Little Rock, AR 72227-2355 · 501-664-8105

ENERGY LAW

Little Rock

Lawrence Chisenhall · Chisenhall, Nestrud & Julian · Regions Bank Building, Suite 2840 · 400 West Capitol Avenue · Little Rock, AR 72201 · 501-372-5800

Stephen N. Joiner · Rose Law Firm · 120 East Fourth Street · Little Rock, AR 72201-2893 · 501-375-9131

Nathan M. Norton · Wright, Lindsey & Jennings · http://www.wlj.com · 200 West Capitol Avenue, Suite 2300 · Little Rock, AR 72201-3699 · 501-371-0808

Scott C. Trotter · Perkins & Trotter · One Information Way, Suite 200 · P.O. Box 251618 · Little Rock, AR 72225-1618 · 501-603-9000

ENVIRONMENTAL LAW

Fayetteville

Colene Gaston · Gaston Law Office · 2949 North Point Circle, Suite Three · Fayetteville, AR 72704 · 479-521-3148

Little Rock

Sherry P. Bartley · ⑩ · Mitchell, Williams, Selig, Gates & Woodyard · http://www.mitchellwilliamslaw.com · 425 West Capitol Avenue, Suite 1800 · Little Rock, AR 72201-3525 501-688-8800

Joseph Henry Bates III · Cauley Bowman Carney & Williams · 11311 Arcade Drive, Suite 200 · P.O. Box 25438 · Little Rock, AR 72212 · 501-312-8500

Ann P. Faitz · Chisenhall, Nestrud & Julian · Regions Bank Building, Suite 2840 · 400 West Capitol Avenue · Little Rock, AR 72201 · 501-372-5800

Allan Gates · ⑩ · Mitchell, Williams, Selig, Gates & Woodyard · http://www.mitchellwilliamslaw.com · 425 West Capitol Avenue, Suite 1800 · Little Rock, AR 72201-3525 · 501-688-8800

Samuel E. Ledbetter · McMath Woods · http://www.mcmathlaw.com · 711 West Third Street · Little Rock, AR 72201 · 501-396-5400

Kelly M. McQueen · Perkins & Trotter · One Information Way, Suite 200 · P.O. Box 251618 · Little Rock, AR 72225-1618 · 501-603-9000

Charles R. Nestrud · ⑩ · Chisenhall, Nestrud & Julian · Regions Bank Building, Suite 2840 · 400 West Capitol Avenue · Little Rock, AR 72201 · 501-372-5800

G. Alan Perkins · ⑩ · Perkins & Trotter · One Information Way, Suite 200 · P.O. Box 251618 · Little Rock, AR 72225-1618 · 501-603-9000

Brian Rosenthal · Rose Law Firm · 120 East Fourth Street · Little Rock, AR 72201-2893 · 501-375-9131

Marcella J. Taylor · Mitchell, Williams, Selig, Gates & Woodyard · http://www.mitchellwilliamslaw.com · 425 West Capitol Avenue, Suite 1800 · Little Rock, AR 72201-3525 · 501-688-8800

Walter G. Wright, Jr. · Mitchell, Williams, Selig, Gates & Woodyard · http://www.mitchellwilliamslaw.com · 425 West Capitol Avenue, Suite 1800 · Little Rock, AR 72201-3525 501-688-8800

FAMILY LAW

Hot Springs National Park

Bryan J. Reis · The Farrar Firm · First National Bank Building, Third Floor, Suite Five · 135 Section Line Road · Hot Springs National Park, AR 71913 · 501-525-3130

Little Rock

Marcia Barnes · Mitchell, Blackstock, Barnes, Wagoner, Ivers & Sneddon · 1010 West Third Street · P.O. Box 1510 · Little Rock, AR 72203-1510 · 501-378-7870

Barry E. Coplin · ⑩ · Coplin & Heuer · 124 West Capitol Avenue, Suite 1650 · Little Rock, AR 72201 · 501-707-0300

Stephen C. Engstrom · ⑩ · Wilson, Engstrom, Corum & Coulter · 200 South Commerce, Suite 600 · P.O. Box 71 · Little Rock, AR 72203 · 501-375-6453

Sam Hilburn · Hilburn, Calhoon, Harper, Pruniski & Calhoun · U.S. Bank Building North, Suite 800 · One Riverfront Place · Little Rock, AR 72114 · 501-372-0110

Henry Hodges · Hodges Law Firm · 400 West Capitol Avenue, Suite 1722 · Little Rock, AR 72201-3402 · 501-375-0400

Judson C. Kidd · Dodds, Kidd & Ryan · 313 West Second Street · Little Rock, AR 72201 · 501-375-9901

W. Michael Reif · Dover Dixon Horne · http://www.doverdixonhorne.com · Metropolitan Tower, 37th Floor · 425 West Capitol Avenue · Little Rock, AR 72201 · 501-375-9151

Gary B. Rogers · Dover Dixon Horne · http://www.doverdixonhorne.com · Metropolitan Tower, 37th Floor · 425 West Capitol Avenue · Little Rock, AR 72201 · 501-375-9151

Jack Wagoner III · Mitchell, Blackstock, Barnes, Wagoner, Ivers & Sneddon · 1010 West Third Street · P.O. Box 1510 · Little Rock, AR 72203-1510 · 501-378-7870

Paragould

Harry Truman Moore · ⑩ · Goodwin Moore · 511 South Fourth Street · P.O. Box 726 · Paragould, AR 72450 · 870-239-2225

Rogers

David R. Matthews · Matthews, Campbell, Rhoads, McClure, Thompson & Fryauf · 119 South Second Street · Rogers, AR 72756 · 479-636-0875

FIRST AMENDMENT LAW

Little Rock

Philip S. Anderson · ⑩ · Williams & Anderson · http://www.williamsanderson.com · Stephens Building, 22nd Floor · 111 Center Street · Little Rock, AR 72201 · 501-372-0800

Jess L. Askew III · Williams & Anderson · http://www.williamsanderson.com · Stephens Building, 22nd Floor · 111 Center Street · Little Rock, AR 72201 · 501-372-0800

Kristine G. Baker · Quattlebaum, Grooms, Tull & Burrow · http://www.qgtb.com · 111 Center Street, Suite 1900 · Little Rock, AR 72201-4420 · 501-379-1700

Philip E. Kaplan · ㉕ · Williams & Anderson · http://www.williamsanderson.com · Stephens Building, 22nd Floor · 111 Center Street · Little Rock, AR 72201 · 501-372-0800

John T. Lavey · ㉕ · Lavey & Burnett · 904 West Second Street · P.O. Box 2657 · Little Rock, AR 72201 · 501-376-2269

Troy A. Price · Wright, Lindsey & Jennings · http://www.wlj.com · 200 West Capitol Avenue, Suite 2300 · Little Rock, AR 72201-3699 · 501-371-0808

John E. Tull III · Quattlebaum, Grooms, Tull & Burrow · http://www.qgtb.com · 111 Center Street, Suite 1900 · Little Rock, AR 72201-4420 · 501-379-1700

North Little Rock

Morgan E. Welch · Welch & Kitchens · One Riverfront Place, Suite 413 · North Little Rock, AR 72114 · 501-978-3030

FRANCHISE LAW

Little Rock

David M. Powell · Williams & Anderson · http://www.williamsanderson.com · Stephens Building, 22nd Floor · 111 Center Street · Little Rock, AR 72201 · 501-372-0800

Roger D. Rowe · Lax, Vaughan, Fortson, McKenzie & Rowe · Cantrell West Building, Suite 201 · 11300 Cantrell Road · Little Rock, AR 72212 · 501-376-6565

William A. Waddell · ⑩ · Friday, Eldredge & Clark · http://www.fridayfirm.com · 400 West Capitol Avenue, Suite 2000 · Little Rock, AR 72201-3522 · 501-376-2011

GOVERNMENT RELATIONS LAW

Little Rock

T. Ark Monroe III · Mitchell, Williams, Selig, Gates & Woodyard · http://www.mitchellwilliamslaw.com · 425 West Capitol Avenue, Suite 1800 · Little Rock, AR 72201-3525 · 501-688-8800

Nicholas Thompson · Mitchell, Williams, Selig, Gates & Woodyard · http://www.mitchellwilliamslaw.com · 425 West Capitol Avenue, Suite 1800 · Little Rock, AR 72201-3525 501-688-8800

HEALTH CARE LAW

Fort Smith

Elizabeth Andreoli · Hardin, Jesson & Terry · Arvest Bank Building, Suite 500 · 5000 Rogers Avenue · P.O. Box 10127 · Fort Smith, AR 72917-0127 · 479-452-2200

Little Rock

Charles B. Cliett, Jr. · Mitchell, Williams, Selig, Gates & Woodyard · http://www.mitchellwilliamslaw.com · 425 West Capitol Avenue, Suite 1800 · Little Rock, AR 72201-3525 501-688-8800

David L. Ivers · Mitchell, Blackstock, Barnes, Wagoner, Ivers & Sneddon · 1010 West Third Street · P.O. Box 1510 · Little Rock, AR 72203-1510 · 501-378-7870

Donald T. Jack, Jr. · ⑩ · Jack, Nelson & Jones · The Metropolitan Tower, Suite 3400 · 425 West Capitol Avenue · Little Rock, AR 72201 · 501-375-1122

Michael W. Mitchell · ⑩ · Mitchell, Blackstock, Barnes, Wagoner, Ivers & Sneddon · 1010 West Third Street · P.O. Box 1510 · Little Rock, AR 72203-1510 · 501-378-7870

Lee J. Muldrow · ⑩ · Wright, Lindsey & Jennings · http://www.wlj.com · 200 West Capitol Avenue, Suite 2300 · Little Rock, AR 72201-3699 · 501-371-0808

IMMIGRATION LAW

Little Rock

Melissa McJunkins Duke · Cross Gunter Witherspoon & Galchus · http://www.cgwg.com · 500 President Clinton Avenue, Suite 200 · Little Rock, AR 72201 · 501-371-9999

Donna Smith Galchus · Cross Gunter Witherspoon & Galchus · http://www.cgwg.com · 500 President Clinton Avenue, Suite 200 · Little Rock, AR 72201 · 501-371-9999

Lonoke

Kathy W. Goss · Kathy Woodward Goss · 604 South Center Street · P.O. Box 448 · Lonoke, AR 72086-0448 · 501-676-6522

INSURANCE LAW

Little Rock

Frederick K. Campbell · Mitchell, Williams, Selig, Gates & Woodyard · http://www.mitchellwilliamslaw.com · 425 West Capitol Avenue, Suite 1800 · Little Rock, AR 72201-3525 501-688-8800

Charles B. Cliett, Jr. · Mitchell, Williams, Selig, Gates & Woodyard · http://www.mitchellwilliamslaw.com · 425 West Capitol Avenue, Suite 1800 · Little Rock, AR 72201-3525 501-688-8800

Doak Foster · Mitchell, Williams, Selig, Gates & Woodyard · http://www.mitchellwilliamslaw.com · 425 West Capitol Avenue, Suite 1800 · Little Rock, AR 72201-3525 · 501-688-8800

Allan W. Horne · Dover Dixon Horne · http://www.doverdixonhorne.com · Metropolitan Tower, 37th Floor · 425 West Capitol Avenue · Little Rock, AR 72201 · 501-375-9151

T. Ark Monroe III · Mitchell, Williams, Selig, Gates & Woodyard · http://www.mitchellwilliamslaw.com · 425 West Capitol Avenue, Suite 1800 · Little Rock, AR 72201-3525 · 501-688-8800

Jeffrey Thomas · Mitchell, Williams, Selig, Gates & Woodyard · http://www.mitchellwilliamslaw.com · 425 West Capitol Avenue, Suite 1800 · Little Rock, AR 72201-3525 · 501-688-8800

Nicholas Thompson · Mitchell, Williams, Selig, Gates & Woodyard · http://www.mitchellwilliamslaw.com · 425 West Capitol Avenue, Suite 1800 · Little Rock, AR 72201-3525 501-688-8800

INTELLECTUAL PROPERTY LAW

Little Rock

Ray F. Cox, Jr. · Wright, Lindsey & Jennings · http://www.wlj.com · 200 West Capitol Avenue, Suite 2300 · Little Rock, AR 72201-3699 · 501-371-0808

J. Charles Dougherty · Wright, Lindsey & Jennings · http://www.wlj.com · 200 West Capitol Avenue, Suite 2300 · Little Rock, AR 72201-3699 · 501-371-0808

Harold J. Evans · Williams & Anderson · http://www.williamsanderson.com · Stephens Building, 22nd Floor · 111 Center Street · Little Rock, AR 72201 · 501-372-0800

Hermann Ivester · Mitchell, Williams, Selig, Gates & Woodyard · http://www.mitchellwilliamslaw.com · 425 West Capitol Avenue, Suite 1800 · Little Rock, AR 72201-3525 · 501-688-8800

Kathryn Bennet Perkins · Rose Law Firm · 120 East Fourth Street · Little Rock, AR 72201-2893 · 501-375-9131

INTERNATIONAL ARBITRATION

Little Rock

David M. Powell · Williams & Anderson · http://www.williamsanderson.com · Stephens Building, 22nd Floor · 111 Center Street · Little Rock, AR 72201 · 501-372-0800

LABOR AND EMPLOYMENT LAW

Fort Smith

Benjamin H. Shipley III · ⑩ · Cross Gunter Witherspoon & Galchus · http://www.cgwg.com · 5401 Rogers Avenue, Suite 200 · Fort Smith, AR 72903 · 479-783-8200

Jonesboro

Paul D. Waddell · Barrett & Deacon · Mercantile Center, Third Floor · 300 South Church Street · P.O. Box 1700 · Jonesboro, AR 72403 · 870-931-1700

Little Rock

Tim Boe · ㉕ · Rose Law Firm · 120 East Fourth Street · Little Rock, AR 72201-2893 · 501-375-9131

John L. Burnett · ⑳ · Lavey & Burnett · 904 West Second Street · P.O. Box 2657 · Little Rock, AR 72201 · 501-376-2269

J. Bruce Cross · ⑩ · Cross Gunter Witherspoon & Galchus · http://www.cgwg.com · 500 President Clinton Avenue, Suite 200 · Little Rock, AR 72201 · 501-371-9999

John D. Davis · ⑩ · Wright, Lindsey & Jennings · http://www.wlj.com · 200 West Capitol Avenue, Suite 2300 · Little Rock, AR 72201-3699 · 501-371-0808

Oscar E. Davis, Jr. · ⑩ · Friday, Eldredge & Clark · http://www.fridayfirm.com · 400 West Capitol Avenue, Suite 2000 · Little Rock, AR 72201-3522 · 501-376-2011

Allen C. Dobson · Cross Gunter Witherspoon & Galchus · http://www.cgwg.com · 500 President Clinton Avenue, Suite 200 · Little Rock, AR 72201 · 501-371-9999

Byron L. Freeland · Mitchell, Williams, Selig, Gates & Woodyard · http://www.mitchellwilliamslaw.com · 425 West Capitol Avenue, Suite 1800 · Little Rock, AR 72201-3525 · 501-688-8800

Kathlyn Graves · ⑩ · Mitchell, Williams, Selig, Gates & Woodyard · http://www.mitchellwilliamslaw.com 425 West Capitol Avenue, Suite 1800 · Little Rock, AR 72201-3525 · 501-688-8800

Russell A. Gunter · ㉕ · Cross Gunter Witherspoon & Galchus · http://www.cgwg.com · 500 President Clinton Avenue, Suite 200 · Little Rock, AR 72201 · 501-371-9999

Regina Haralson · Kaplan, Brewer, Maxey & Haralson · 111 Center Street, Suite 2200 · Little Rock, AR 72201-4424 · 501-372-0400

Melva Harmon · ⑩ · Melva Harmon · Stephens Building, Suite 1200 · 111 Center Street · Little Rock, AR 72201 · 501-372-1133

Christopher J. Heller · Friday, Eldredge & Clark · http://www.fridayfirm.com · 400 West Capitol Avenue, Suite 2000 · Little Rock, AR 72201-3522 · 501-376-2011

Dan L. Herrington · Friday, Eldredge & Clark · http://www.fridayfirm.com · 400 West Capitol Avenue, Suite 2000 · Little Rock, AR 72201-3522 · 501-376-2011

Denise Hoggard · Chisenhall, Nestrud & Julian · Regions Bank Building, Suite 2840 · 400 West Capitol Avenue · Little Rock, AR 72201 · 501-372-5800

Philip E. Kaplan · ㉕ · Williams & Anderson · http://www.williamsanderson.com · Stephens Building, 22nd Floor · 111 Center Street · Little Rock, AR 72201 · 501-372-0800

John T. Lavey · ㉕ · Lavey & Burnett · 904 West Second Street · P.O. Box 2657 · Little Rock, AR 72201 · 501-376-2269

David P. Martin · Rose Law Firm · 120 East Fourth Street · Little Rock, AR 72201-2893 · 501-375-9131

JoAnn C. Maxey · ⑩ · Williams & Anderson · http://www.williamsanderson.com · Stephens Building, 22nd Floor · 111 Center Street · Little Rock, AR 72201 · 501-372-0800

Michael S. Moore · Friday, Eldredge & Clark · http://www.fridayfirm.com · 400 West Capitol Avenue, Suite 2000 · Little Rock, AR 72201-3522 · 501-376-2011

Elizabeth R. Murray · Friday, Eldredge & Clark · http://www.fridayfirm.com · 400 West Capitol Avenue, Suite 2000 · Little Rock, AR 72201-3522 · 501-376-2011

Janet Pulliam · Williams & Anderson · http://www.williamsanderson.com · Stephens Building, 22nd Floor 111 Center Street · Little Rock, AR 72201 · 501-372-0800

Richard A. Roderick · Cross Gunter Witherspoon & Galchus · http://www.cgwg.com · 500 President Clinton Avenue, Suite 200 · Little Rock, AR 72201 · 501-371-9999

Scotty M. Shively · ⑩ · Cross Gunter Witherspoon & Galchus · http://www.cgwg.com · 500 President Clinton Avenue, Suite 200 · Little Rock, AR 72201 · 501-371-9999

Frederick S. Ursery · Friday, Eldredge & Clark · http://www.fridayfirm.com · 400 West Capitol Avenue, Suite 2000 · Little Rock, AR 72201-3522 · 501-376-2011

Brian A. Vandiver · Cross Gunter Witherspoon & Galchus · http://www.cgwg.com · 500 President Clinton Avenue, Suite 200 · Little Rock, AR 72201 · 501-371-9999

Carolyn B. Witherspoon · ⑩ · Cross Gunter Witherspoon & Galchus · http://www.cgwg.com · 500 President Clinton Avenue, Suite 200 · Little Rock, AR 72201 · 501-371-9999

Leigh Anne Yeargan · Mitchell, Williams, Selig, Gates & Woodyard · http://www.mitchellwilliamslaw.com · 425 West Capitol Avenue, Suite 1800 · Little Rock, AR 72201-3525 501-688-8800

Mountainburg

Michael R. Jones · ⑩ · Gilker and Jones · 9222 North Highway 71 · Mountainburg, AR 72946 · 479-783-3109

Pine Bluff

Spencer F. Robinson · ⑩ · Ramsay, Bridgforth, Harrelson and Starling · Simmons First National Building, 11th Floor · 501 Main Street · P.O. Box 8509 · Pine Bluff, AR 71611-8509 · 870-535-9000

LAND USE & ZONING LAW

Little Rock

W. Christopher Barrier · ⑩ · Mitchell, Williams, Selig, Gates & Woodyard · http://www.mitchellwilliamslaw.com · 425 West Capitol Avenue, Suite 1800 · Little Rock, AR 72201-3525 501-688-8800

LEGAL MALPRACTICE LAW

Little Rock

Donald H. Bacon · Friday, Eldredge & Clark · http://www.fridayfirm.com · 400 West Capitol Avenue, Suite 2000 · Little Rock, AR 72201-3522 · 501-376-2011

Edwin L. Lowther, Jr. · ⑩ · Wright, Lindsey & Jennings · http://www.wlj.com · 200 West Capitol Avenue, Suite 2300 · Little Rock, AR 72201-3699 · 501-371-0808

MASS TORT LITIGATION

Little Rock

Sherry P. Bartley · ⑩ · Mitchell, Williams, Selig, Gates & Woodyard · http://www.mitchellwilliamslaw.com · 425 West Capitol Avenue, Suite 1800 · Little Rock, AR 72201-3525 501-688-8800

Steven W. Quattlebaum · Quattlebaum, Grooms, Tull & Burrow · http://www.qgtb.com · 111 Center Street, Suite 1900 · Little Rock, AR 72201-4420 · 501-379-1700

Gordon S. Rather, Jr. · ⑩ · Wright, Lindsey & Jennings · http://www.wlj.com · 200 West Capitol Avenue, Suite 2300 · Little Rock, AR 72201-3699 · 501-371-0808

MEDIA LAW

Little Rock

Jess L. Askew III · Williams & Anderson · http://www.williamsanderson.com · Stephens Building, 22nd Floor · 111 Center Street · Little Rock, AR 72201 · 501-372-0800

John E. Tull III · Quattlebaum, Grooms, Tull & Burrow · http://www.qgtb.com · 111 Center Street, Suite 1900 · Little Rock, AR 72201-4420 · 501-379-1700

MEDICAL MALPRACTICE LAW

Batesville

H. David Blair · (10) · Blair & Stroud · http://www.blastlaw.com · Municipal Building, Suite 201 · 500 East Main Street · P.O. Box 2135 · Batesville, AR 72501 · 870-793-8350

Fayetteville

Kelly Carithers · Davis, Wright, Clark, Butt & Carithers · http://www.daviswrightlaw.com · 19 East Mountain Street · P.O. Box 1688 · Fayetteville, AR 72702-1688 · 479-521-7600

Walter B. Cox · (10) · Cox, Cox & Estes · Arvest Square, Suite 302 · 75 Northeast Avenue · P.O. Box 878 · Fayetteville, AR 72702 · 479-251-7900

Sidney P. Davis, Jr. · (10) · Davis, Wright, Clark, Butt & Carithers · http://www.daviswrightlaw.com · 19 East Mountain Street · P.O. Box 1688 · Fayetteville, AR 72702-1688 · 479-521-7600

James R. Estes · Cox, Cox & Estes · Arvest Square, Suite 302 · 75 Northeast Avenue · P.O. Box 878 · Fayetteville, AR 72702 · 479-251-7900

Walker Dale Garrett · Bassett Law Firm · 221 North College Avenue · P.O. Box 3618 · Fayetteville, AR 72702-3618 · 479-521-9996

Fort Smith

Charles R. Ledbetter · (10) · Ledbetter, Cogbill, Arnold & Harrison · 622 Parker Avenue · P.O. Box 185 · Fort Smith, AR 72902-0185 · 479-782-7294

Jonesboro

Bobby R. McDaniel · (25) · McDaniel & Wells · 400 South Main Street · Jonesboro, AR 72401 · 870-932-5950

Paul D. McNeill · Womack, Landis, Phelps, McNeill & McDaniel · 301 West Washington · P.O. Box 3077 Jonesboro, AR 72401 · 870-932-0900

Paul D. Waddell · Barrett & Deacon · Mercantile Center, Third Floor · 300 South Church Street · P.O. Box 1700 · Jonesboro, AR 72403 · 870-931-1700

Little Rock

Overton S. Anderson · Anderson, Murphy & Hopkins · 400 West Capital Avenue, Suite 2470 · Little Rock, AR 72201 · 501-372-1887

T. Michelle Ator · Friday, Eldredge & Clark · http://www.fridayfirm.com · 400 West Capitol Avenue, Suite 2000 · Little Rock, AR 72201-3522 · 501-376-2011

Donald H. Bacon · Friday, Eldredge & Clark · http://www.fridayfirm.com · 400 West Capitol Avenue, Suite 2000 · Little Rock, AR 72201-3522 · 501-376-2011

Timothy L. Boone · Huckabay, Munson, Rowlett & Moore · http://www.hmrmlaw.com · Regions Center, Suite 1900 · 400 West Capitol Avenue · Little Rock, AR 72201 · 501-374-6535

Ken Cook · Mitchell, Williams, Selig, Gates & Woodyard · http://www.mitchellwilliamslaw.com · 425 West Capitol Avenue, Suite 1800 · Little Rock, AR 72201-3525 · 501-688-8800

Mariam T. Hopkins · Anderson, Murphy & Hopkins · 400 West Capital Avenue, Suite 2470 · Little Rock, AR 72201 · 501-372-1887

D. Michael Huckabay, Sr. · ⑩ · Huckabay, Munson, Rowlett & Moore · http://www.hmrmlaw.com · Regions Center, Suite 1900 · 400 West Capitol Avenue · Little Rock, AR 72201 · 501-374-6535

Bruce E. Munson · Huckabay, Munson, Rowlett & Moore · http://www.hmrmlaw.com · Regions Center, Suite 1900 · 400 West Capitol Avenue · Little Rock, AR 72201 · 501-374-6535

Laura Hensley Smith · ⑩ · Friday, Eldredge & Clark · http://www.fridayfirm.com · 400 West Capitol Avenue, Suite 2000 · Little Rock, AR 72201-3522 · 501-376-2011

Springdale

Robert J. Lambert · Roy, Lambert & Lovelace · 2706 South Dividend Drive · P.O. Drawer 7030 · Springdale, AR 72766-7030 · 479-756-8510

MERGERS & ACQUISITIONS LAW

Fayetteville

James W. Smith · Friday, Eldredge & Clark · http://www.fridayfirm.com · 3425 North Futrall Drive, Suite 103 · Fayetteville, AR 72703-6252 · 479-695-2011

Little Rock

Paul B. Benham III · ⑳ · Friday, Eldredge & Clark · http://www.fridayfirm.com · 400 West Capitol Avenue, Suite 2000 · Little Rock, AR 72201-3522 · 501-376-2011

C. Douglas Buford, Jr. · Mitchell, Williams, Selig, Gates & Woodyard · http://www.mitchellwilliamslaw.com · 425 West Capitol Avenue, Suite 1800 · Little Rock, AR 72201-3525 501-688-8800

Kevin R. Burns · Rose Law Firm · 120 East Fourth Street · Little Rock, AR 72201-2893 · 501-375-9131

Walter M. Ebel III · Friday, Eldredge & Clark · http://www.fridayfirm.com · 400 West Capitol Avenue, Suite 2000 · Little Rock, AR 72201-3522 · 501-376-2011

Gregory B. Graham · ⑳ · Overbey, Graham, Strigel & Wesbrook · Pavilion Centre, Suite 240 · 8315 Cantrell Road · Little Rock, AR 72227-2355 · 501-664-8105

H. Watt Gregory III · Kutak Rock · 124 West Capitol Avenue, Suite 2000 · Little Rock, AR 72201-3706 · 501-975-3000

MUNICIPAL LAW

Little Rock

M. Jane Dickey · Rose Law Firm · 120 East Fourth Street · Little Rock, AR 72201-2893 · 501-375-9131

Hal Joseph Kemp · Kemp Duckett Spradley & Curry · 111 Center Street, Suite 1300 · Little Rock, AR 72201 · 501-372-7243

David F. Menz · Williams & Anderson · http://www.williamsanderson.com · Stephens Building, 22nd Floor · 111 Center Street · Little Rock, AR 72201 · 501-372-0800

J. Shepherd Russell III · Friday, Eldredge & Clark · http://www.fridayfirm.com · 400 West Capitol Avenue, Suite 2000 · Little Rock, AR 72201-3522 · 501-376-2011

John William Spivey III · ⑩ · Wright, Lindsey & Jennings · http://www.wlj.com · 200 West Capitol Avenue, Suite 2300 · Little Rock, AR 72201-3699 · 501-371-0808

Gordon M. Wilbourn · Kutak Rock · 124 West Capitol Avenue, Suite 2000 · Little Rock, AR 72201-3706 501-975-3000

NON-PROFIT/CHARITIES LAW

Little Rock

Sarah Cotton · Friday, Eldredge & Clark · http://www.fridayfirm.com · 400 West Capitol Avenue, Suite 2000 · Little Rock, AR 72201-3522 · 501-376-2011

Byron M. Eiseman, Jr. · ㉕ · Friday, Eldredge & Clark · http://www.fridayfirm.com · 400 West Capitol Avenue, Suite 2000 · Little Rock, AR 72201-3522 · 501-376-2011

James E. Harris · ⑳ · Friday, Eldredge & Clark · http://www.fridayfirm.com · 400 West Capitol Avenue, Suite 2000 · Little Rock, AR 72201-3522 · 501-376-2011

W. Wilson Jones · ⑩ · Rose Law Firm · 120 East Fourth Street · Little Rock, AR 72201-2893 · 501-375-9131

K. Coleman Westbrook, Jr. · Friday, Eldredge & Clark · http://www.fridayfirm.com · 400 West Capitol Avenue, Suite 2000 · Little Rock, AR 72201-3522 · 501-376-2011

NON-WHITE-COLLAR CRIMINAL DEFENSE

Fayetteville

John C. Everett · ⑩ · Everett & Wales · 1944 East Joyce Boulevard · P.O. Box 8370 · Fayetteville, AR 72703-8370 · 479-443-0292

Warner H. Taylor · Taylor Law Firm · 303 East Millsap Road · P.O. Box 8310 · Fayetteville, AR 72703 · 479-443-5222

Fort Smith

Eddie N. Christian, Sr. · ⑩ · Christian & Byars · 502 Garrison Avenue · Fort Smith, AR 72901 · 479-782-9147

Jonesboro

Bill W. Bristow · Bristow & Richardson · 216 East Washington Street · Jonesboro, AR 72401-3102 · 870-935-9000

Bobby R. McDaniel · ㉕ · McDaniel & Wells · 400 South Main Street · Jonesboro, AR 72401 · 870-932-5950

Little Rock

Cathleen V. Compton · ⑩ · Cathleen V. Compton · 114 South Pulaski Street · Little Rock, AR 72201 · 501-372-0080

Timothy O. Dudley · ⑩ · Timothy O. Dudley · 114 South Pulaski Street · Little Rock, AR 72201-1924 · 501-372-0080

John Wesley Hall · John Wesley Hall · 1311 Broadway · Little Rock, AR 72202-4843 · 501-371-9131

J. Blake Hendrix · Blake Hendrix · 308 South Louisiana Street · Little Rock, AR 72201 · 501-376-0679

Richard E. Holiman · Holiman Law Firm · 400 West Capitol Avenue, Suite 1700 · Little Rock, AR 72201 · 501-375-1170

Jack T. Lassiter · ⑩ · Hatfield & Lassiter · 401 West Capitol Avenue, Suite 502 · Little Rock, AR 72201-3437 · 501-374-9010

Jeff Rosenzweig · Jeff Rosenzweig · 300 Spring Building, Suite 310 · Third and Spring Streets · Little Rock, AR 72201 · 501-372-5247

West Memphis

Kent J. Rubens · Rieves, Rubens & Mayton · http://www.rrmlawyers.com · 304 East Broadway · P.O. Box 1359 · West Memphis, AR 72301-3174 · 870-735-3420

OIL & GAS LAW

Fort Smith

Thomas A. Daily · Daily & Woods · 58 South Sixth Avenue · P.O. Box 1446 · Fort Smith, AR 72902 · 479-782-0361

Robert M. Honea · Hardin, Jesson & Terry · Arvest Bank Building, Suite 500 · 5000 Rogers Avenue · P.O. Box 10127 · Fort Smith, AR 72917-0127 · 479-452-2200

Little Rock

G. Alan Perkins · ⑩ · Perkins & Trotter · One Information Way, Suite 200 · P.O. Box 251618 · Little Rock, AR 72225-1618 · 501-603-9000

Magnolia

Carolyn J. Clegg · Keith, Clegg & Epley · McAlester Building, Suite 205 · 124 South Jackson · P.O. Drawer 1029 · Magnolia, AR 71754-1029 · 870-234-3550

PERSONAL INJURY LITIGATION

Arkadelphia

Rodney P. Moore · Wright, Berry, Hughes & Moore · http://www.arklaw.com · 303 Professional Park Drive · P.O. Drawer 947 · Arkadelphia, AR 71923 · 870-246-6796

Batesville

H. David Blair · ⑩ · Blair & Stroud · http://www.blastlaw.com · Municipal Building, Suite 201 · 500 East Main Street · P.O. Box 2135 · Batesville, AR 72501 · 870-793-8350

Bryant

Ted Boswell · ㉕ · The Boswell Law Firm · http://www.boswellaw.com · 45 North Third Street · P.O. Box 798 · Bryant, AR 72089-0798 · 501-847-3031

El Dorado

Brian H. Ratcliff · Shackleford, Phillips, Wineland & Ratcliff · 100 East Church Street · P.O. Box 1718 · El Dorado, AR 71731-1718 · 870-862-5523

Dennis L. Shackleford · ㉕ · Shackleford, Phillips, Wineland & Ratcliff · 100 East Church Street · P.O. Box 1718 · El Dorado, AR 71731-1718 · 870-862-5523

Floyd M. Thomas, Jr. · Compton, Prewett, Thomas & Hickey · 423 North Washington Avenue · El Dorado, AR 71730-5615 · 870-862-3478

Fayetteville

Kelly Carithers · Davis, Wright, Clark, Butt & Carithers · http://www.daviswrightlaw.com · 19 East Mountain Street · P.O. Box 1688 · Fayetteville, AR 72702-1688 · 479-521-7600

Walter B. Cox · ⑩ · Cox, Cox & Estes · Arvest Square, Suite 302 · 75 Northeast Avenue · P.O. Box 878 · Fayetteville, AR 72702 · 479-251-7900

Sidney P. Davis, Jr. · ⑩ · Davis, Wright, Clark, Butt & Carithers · http://www.daviswrightlaw.com · 19 East Mountain Street · P.O. Box 1688 · Fayetteville, AR 72702-1688 · 479-521-7600

James R. Estes · Cox, Cox & Estes · Arvest Square, Suite 302 · 75 Northeast Avenue · P.O. Box 878 · Fayetteville, AR 72702 · 479-251-7900

Walker Dale Garrett · Bassett Law Firm · 221 North College Avenue · P.O. Box 3618 · Fayetteville, AR 72702-3618 · 479-521-9996

Robert L. Jones III · Conner & Winters · http://www.cwlaw.com · 211 East Dickson Street · Fayetteville, AR 72701 · 479-582-5711

Don A. Taylor · Davis, Wright, Clark, Butt & Carithers · http://www.daviswrightlaw.com · 19 East Mountain Street · P.O. Box 1688 · Fayetteville, AR 72702-1688 · 479-521-7600

Forrest City

B. Michael Easley · ⑩ · Easley & Houseal · 510 East Cross Street · P.O. Box 1115 · Forrest City, AR 72335 · 870-633-1447

Fort Smith

Charles R. Ledbetter · ⑩ · Ledbetter, Cogbill, Arnold & Harrison · 622 Parker Avenue · P.O. Box 185 · Fort Smith, AR 72902-0185 · 479-782-7294

Douglas O. Smith, Jr. · ⑩ · Warner, Smith & Harris · 400 Rogers Avenue · P.O. Box 1626 · Fort Smith, AR 72901 · 479-782-6041

G. Alan Wooten · Warner, Smith & Harris · 400 Rogers Avenue · P.O. Box 1626 · Fort Smith, AR 72901 · 479-782-6041

Jonesboro

Alfred F. Angulo · Barrett & Deacon · Mercantile Center, Third Floor · 300 South Church Street · P.O. Box 1700 · Jonesboro, AR 72403 · 870-931-1700

Bill W. Bristow · Bristow & Richardson · 216 East Washington Street · Jonesboro, AR 72401-3102 · 870-935-9000

John C. Deacon · ⑩ · Barrett & Deacon · Mercantile Center, Third Floor · 300 South Church Street · P.O. Box 1700 · Jonesboro, AR 72403 · 870-931-1700

Bobby R. McDaniel · ㉕ · McDaniel & Wells · 400 South Main Street · Jonesboro, AR 72401 · 870-932-5950

Paul D. McNeill · Womack, Landis, Phelps, McNeill & McDaniel · 301 West Washington · P.O. Box 3077 Jonesboro, AR 72401 · 870-932-0900

John V. Phelps · ⑩ · Womack, Landis, Phelps, McNeill & McDaniel · 301 West Washington · P.O. Box 3077 · Jonesboro, AR 72401 · 870-932-0900

Phillip J. Wells · McDaniel & Wells · 400 South Main Street · Jonesboro, AR 72401 · 870-932-5950

Little Rock

Overton S. Anderson · Anderson, Murphy & Hopkins · 400 West Capital Avenue, Suite 2470 · Little Rock, AR 72201 · 501-372-1887

Donald H. Bacon · Friday, Eldredge & Clark · http://www.fridayfirm.com · 400 West Capitol Avenue, Suite 2000 · Little Rock, AR 72201-3522 · 501-376-2011

Michael D. Barnes · Wright, Lindsey & Jennings · http://www.wlj.com · 200 West Capitol Avenue, Suite 2300 · Little Rock, AR 72201-3699 · 501-371-0808

Sherry P. Bartley · ⑩ · Mitchell, Williams, Selig, Gates & Woodyard · http://www.mitchellwilliamslaw.com · 425 West Capitol Avenue, Suite 1800 · Little Rock, AR 72201-3525 501-688-8800

R. T. Beard III · ⑩ · Mitchell, Williams, Selig, Gates & Woodyard · http://www.mitchellwilliamslaw.com · 425 West Capitol Avenue, Suite 1800 · Little Rock, AR 72201-3525 · 501-688-8800

Timothy L. Boone · Huckabay, Munson, Rowlett & Moore · http://www.hmrmlaw.com · Regions Center, Suite 1900 · 400 West Capitol Avenue · Little Rock, AR 72201 · 501-374-6535

Dan F. Bufford · Laser Law Firm · 101 South Spring Street, Suite 300 · Little Rock, AR 72201-2488 · 501-376-2981

Michelle H. Cauley · Mitchell, Williams, Selig, Gates & Woodyard · http://www.mitchellwilliamslaw.com 425 West Capitol Avenue, Suite 1800 · Little Rock, AR 72201-3525 · 501-688-8800

Robert M. Cearley, Jr. · ⑩ · Cearley Law Firm · Centre Place, Second Floor · 212 Center Street · Little Rock, AR 72201 · 501-372-5600

Cathleen V. Compton · ⑩ · Cathleen V. Compton · 114 South Pulaski Street · Little Rock, AR 72201 · 501-372-0080

Kevin A. Crass · Friday, Eldredge & Clark · http://www.fridayfirm.com · 400 West Capitol Avenue, Suite 2000 · Little Rock, AR 72201-3522 · 501-376-2011

David M. Donovan · Watts, Donovan & Tilley · Arkansas Capital Commerce Center, Suite 200 · 200 South Commerce Street · Little Rock, AR 72201-1769 · 501-372-1406

Timothy O. Dudley · ⑩ · Timothy O. Dudley · 114 South Pulaski Street · Little Rock, AR 72201-1924 · 501-372-0080

Roger A. Glasgow · Wright, Lindsey & Jennings · http://www.wlj.com · 200 West Capitol Avenue, Suite 2300 · Little Rock, AR 72201-3699 · 501-371-0808

William M. Griffin III · ⑩ · Friday, Eldredge & Clark · http://www.fridayfirm.com · 400 West Capitol Avenue, Suite 2000 · Little Rock, AR 72201-3522 · 501-376-2011

Robert L. Henry III · ⑩ · Barber, McCaskill, Jones & Hale · Regions Center, Suite 2700 · 400 West Capitol Avenue · Little Rock, AR 72201-3414 · 501-372-6175

Mariam T. Hopkins · Anderson, Murphy & Hopkins · 400 West Capital Avenue, Suite 2470 · Little Rock, AR 72201 · 501-372-1887

D. Michael Huckabay, Sr. · ⑩ · Huckabay, Munson, Rowlett & Moore · http://www.hmrmlaw.com · Regions Center, Suite 1900 · 400 West Capitol Avenue · Little Rock, AR 72201 · 501-374-6535

Don Michael Huckabay, Jr. · Huckabay, Munson, Rowlett & Moore · http://www.hmrmlaw.com · Regions Center, Suite 1900 · 400 West Capitol Avenue · Little Rock, AR 72201 · 501-374-6535

Jim L. Julian · ⑩ · Chisenhall, Nestrud & Julian · Regions Bank Building, Suite 2840 · 400 West Capitol Avenue · Little Rock, AR 72201 · 501-372-5800

Edwin L. Lowther, Jr. · ⑩ · Wright, Lindsey & Jennings · http://www.wlj.com · 200 West Capitol Avenue, Suite 2300 · Little Rock, AR 72201-3699 · 501-371-0808

Robert M. McHenry · McHenry, McHenry & Taylor · 8210 Henderson Road · Little Rock, AR 72210 · 501-372-3425

James Bruce McMath · ⑩ · McMath Woods · http://www.mcmathlaw.com · 711 West Third Street · Little Rock, AR 72201 · 501-396-5400

Stuart P. Miller · Mitchell, Williams, Selig, Gates & Woodyard · http://www.mitchellwilliamslaw.com · 425 West Capitol Avenue, Suite 1800 · Little Rock, AR 72201-3525 · 501-688-8800

John E. Moore · Huckabay, Munson, Rowlett & Moore · http://www.hmrmlaw.com · Regions Center, Suite 1900 · 400 West Capitol Avenue · Little Rock, AR 72201 · 501-374-6535

Bruce E. Munson · Huckabay, Munson, Rowlett & Moore · http://www.hmrmlaw.com · Regions Center, Suite 1900 · 400 West Capitol Avenue · Little Rock, AR 72201 · 501-374-6535

Lyn P. Pruitt · Mitchell, Williams, Selig, Gates & Woodyard · http://www.mitchellwilliamslaw.com · 425 West Capitol Avenue, Suite 1800 · Little Rock, AR 72201-3525 · 501-688-8800

Gordon S. Rather, Jr. · ⑩ · Wright, Lindsey & Jennings · http://www.wlj.com · 200 West Capitol Avenue, Suite 2300 · Little Rock, AR 72201-3699 · 501-371-0808

Beverly A. Rowlett · ⑩ · Huckabay, Munson, Rowlett & Moore · http://www.hmrmlaw.com · Regions Center, Suite 1900 · 400 West Capitol Avenue · Little Rock, AR 72201 · 501-374-6535

Donald S. Ryan · ⑩ · Dodds, Kidd & Ryan · 313 West Second Street · Little Rock, AR 72201 · 501-375-9901

Michael N. Shannon · Quattlebaum, Grooms, Tull & Burrow · http://www.qgtb.com · 111 Center Street, Suite 1900 · Little Rock, AR 72201-4420 · 501-379-1700

James M. Simpson · ⑩ · Friday, Eldredge & Clark · http://www.fridayfirm.com · 400 West Capitol Avenue, Suite 2000 · Little Rock, AR 72201-3522 · 501-376-2011

Jeff Singleton · Mitchell, Williams, Selig, Gates & Woodyard · http://www.mitchellwilliamslaw.com · 425 West Capitol Avenue, Suite 1800 · Little Rock, AR 72201-3525 · 501-688-8800

Laura Hensley Smith · ⑩ · Friday, Eldredge & Clark · http://www.fridayfirm.com · 400 West Capitol Avenue, Suite 2000 · Little Rock, AR 72201-3522 · 501-376-2011

James F. Swindoll · Law Offices of James Swindoll · 212 Center Street, Suite 300 · Little Rock, AR 72201 · 501-374-1290

James W. Tilley · Watts, Donovan & Tilley · Arkansas Capital Commerce Center, Suite 200 · 200 South Commerce Street · Little Rock, AR 72201-1769 · 501-372-1406

Frederick S. Ursery · Friday, Eldredge & Clark · http://www.fridayfirm.com · 400 West Capitol Avenue, Suite 2000 · Little Rock, AR 72201-3522 · 501-376-2011

Richard N. Watts · Watts, Donovan & Tilley · Arkansas Capital Commerce Center, Suite 200 · 200 South Commerce Street · Little Rock, AR 72201-1769 · 501-372-1406

Teresa M. Wineland · Williams & Anderson · http://www.williamsanderson.com · Stephens Building, 22nd Floor · 111 Center Street · Little Rock, AR 72201 · 501-372-0800

Mountain Home

Frank Bailey · Bailey & Oliver · http://www.imaginejustice.com · 506 Hospital Drive · Mountain Home, AR 72653 · 870-425-6041

North Little Rock

Clyde Tab Turner · Turner & Associates · 4705 Somers Avenue, Suite 100 · North Little Rock, AR 72116 · 501-791-2277

Pine Bluff

Stephen A. Matthews · ㉕ · Bridges, Young, Matthews & Drake · 315 East Eighth Avenue · P.O. Box 7808 · Pine Bluff, AR 71611 · 870-534-5532

West Memphis

Elton A. Rieves III · ⑩ · Rieves, Rubens & Mayton · http://www.rrmlawyers.com · 304 East Broadway · P.O. Box 1359 · West Memphis, AR 72301-3174 · 870-735-3420

PRODUCT LIABILITY LITIGATION

Batesville

H. David Blair · ⑩ · Blair & Stroud · http://www.blastlaw.com · Municipal Building, Suite 201 · 500 East Main Street · P.O. Box 2135 · Batesville, AR 72501 · 870-793-8350

Jonesboro

Barry Deacon · Barrett & Deacon · Mercantile Center, Third Floor · 300 South Church Street · P.O. Box 1700 · Jonesboro, AR 72403 · 870-931-1700

Little Rock

Michael D. Barnes · Wright, Lindsey & Jennings · http://www.wlj.com · 200 West Capitol Avenue, Suite 2300 · Little Rock, AR 72201-3699 · 501-371-0808

Robert M. Cearley, Jr. · ⑩ · Cearley Law Firm · Centre Place, Second Floor · 212 Center Street · Little Rock, AR 72201 · 501-372-5600

Edwin L. Lowther, Jr. · ⑩ · Wright, Lindsey & Jennings · http://www.wlj.com · 200 West Capitol Avenue, Suite 2300 · Little Rock, AR 72201-3699 · 501-371-0808

Bruce E. Munson · Huckabay, Munson, Rowlett & Moore · http://www.hmrmlaw.com · Regions Center, Suite 1900 · 400 West Capitol Avenue · Little Rock, AR 72201 · 501-374-6535

Lyn P. Pruitt · Mitchell, Williams, Selig, Gates & Woodyard · http://www.mitchellwilliamslaw.com · 425 West Capitol Avenue, Suite 1800 · Little Rock, AR 72201-3525 · 501-688-8800

Gordon S. Rather, Jr. · ⑩ · Wright, Lindsey & Jennings · http://www.wlj.com · 200 West Capitol Avenue, Suite 2300 · Little Rock, AR 72201-3699 · 501-371-0808

Richard N. Watts · Watts, Donovan & Tilley · Arkansas Capital Commerce Center, Suite 200 · 200 South Commerce Street · Little Rock, AR 72201-1769 · 501-372-1406

North Little Rock

Clyde Tab Turner · Turner & Associates · 4705 Somers Avenue, Suite 100 · North Little Rock, AR 72116 · 501-791-2277

PROFESSIONAL MALPRACTICE LAW

Batesville

H. David Blair · ⑩ · Blair & Stroud · http://www.blastlaw.com · Municipal Building, Suite 201 · 500 East Main Street · P.O. Box 2135 · Batesville, AR 72501 · 870-793-8350

Little Rock

Timothy O. Dudley · ⑩ · Timothy O. Dudley · 114 South Pulaski Street · Little Rock, AR 72201-1924 · 501-372-0080

David A. Littleton · Anderson, Murphy & Hopkins · 400 West Capital Avenue, Suite 2470 · Little Rock, AR 72201 · 501-372-1887

David M. Powell · Williams & Anderson · http://www.williamsanderson.com · Stephens Building, 22nd Floor · 111 Center Street · Little Rock, AR 72201 · 501-372-0800

West Memphis

Kent J. Rubens · Rieves, Rubens & Mayton · http://www.rrmlawyers.com · 304 East Broadway · P.O. Box 1359 · West Memphis, AR 72301-3174 · 870-735-3420

PROJECT FINANCE LAW

Little Rock

Harold W. Hamlin · Mitchell, Williams, Selig, Gates & Woodyard · http://www.mitchellwilliamslaw.com · 425 West Capitol Avenue, Suite 1800 · Little Rock, AR 72201-3525 · 501-688-8800

David F. Menz · Williams & Anderson · http://www.williamsanderson.com · Stephens Building, 22nd Floor · 111 Center Street · Little Rock, AR 72201 · 501-372-0800

J. Shepherd Russell III · Friday, Eldredge & Clark · http://www.fridayfirm.com · 400 West Capitol Avenue, Suite 2000 · Little Rock, AR 72201-3522 · 501-376-2011

W. Jackson Williams · Williams & Anderson · http://www.williamsanderson.com · Stephens Building, 22nd Floor · 111 Center Street · Little Rock, AR 72201 · 501-372-0800

PUBLIC FINANCE LAW

Little Rock

Robert B. Beach, Jr. · Friday, Eldredge & Clark · http://www.fridayfirm.com · 400 West Capitol Avenue, Suite 2000 · Little Rock, AR 72201-3522 · 501-376-2011

James A. Buttry · Friday, Eldredge & Clark · http://www.fridayfirm.com · 400 West Capitol Avenue, Suite 2000 · Little Rock, AR 72201-3522 · 501-376-2011

M. Jane Dickey · Rose Law Firm · 120 East Fourth Street · Little Rock, AR 72201-2893 · 501-375-9131

James E. Hathaway III · Kutak Rock · 124 West Capitol Avenue, Suite 2000 · Little Rock, AR 72201-3706 · 501-975-3000

Thomas P. Leggett · Friday, Eldredge & Clark · http://www.fridayfirm.com · 400 West Capitol Avenue, Suite 2000 · Little Rock, AR 72201-3522 · 501-376-2011

David F. Menz · Williams & Anderson · http://www.williamsanderson.com · Stephens Building, 22nd Floor · 111 Center Street · Little Rock, AR 72201 · 501-372-0800

J. Shepherd Russell III · Friday, Eldredge & Clark · http://www.fridayfirm.com · 400 West Capitol Avenue, Suite 2000 · Little Rock, AR 72201-3522 · 501-376-2011

John William Spivey III · ⑩ · Wright, Lindsey & Jennings · http://www.wlj.com · 200 West Capitol Avenue, Suite 2300 · Little Rock, AR 72201-3699 · 501-371-0808

Gordon M. Wilbourn · Kutak Rock · 124 West Capitol Avenue, Suite 2000 · Little Rock, AR 72201-3706 501-975-3000

W. Jackson Williams · Williams & Anderson · http://www.williamsanderson.com · Stephens Building, 22nd Floor · 111 Center Street · Little Rock, AR 72201 · 501-372-0800

RAILROAD LAW

Jonesboro

Barry Deacon · Barrett & Deacon · Mercantile Center, Third Floor · 300 South Church Street · P.O. Box 1700 · Jonesboro, AR 72403 · 870-931-1700

John C. Deacon · ⑩ · Barrett & Deacon · Mercantile Center, Third Floor · 300 South Church Street · P.O. Box 1700 · Jonesboro, AR 72403 · 870-931-1700

Little Rock

Scott H. Tucker · Friday, Eldredge & Clark · http://www.fridayfirm.com · 400 West Capitol Avenue, Suite 2000 · Little Rock, AR 72201-3522 · 501-376-2011

Frederick S. Ursery · Friday, Eldredge & Clark · http://www.fridayfirm.com · 400 West Capitol Avenue, Suite 2000 · Little Rock, AR 72201-3522 · 501-376-2011

REAL ESTATE LAW

Fort Smith

Thomas A. Daily · Daily & Woods · 58 South Sixth Avenue · P.O. Box 1446 · Fort Smith, AR 72902 · 479-782-0361

L. Cody Hayes · Pryor, Robertson & Barry · 315 North Seventh Street · P.O. Drawer 848 · Fort Smith, AR 72902-0848 · 479-782-8813

Little Rock

W. Christopher Barrier · ⑩ · Mitchell, Williams, Selig, Gates & Woodyard · http://www.mitchellwilliamslaw.com · 425 West Capitol Avenue, Suite 1800 · Little Rock, AR 72201-3525 501-688-8800

C. Tad Bohannon · Wright, Lindsey & Jennings · http://www.wlj.com · 200 West Capitol Avenue, Suite 2300 · Little Rock, AR 72201-3699 · 501-371-0808

Darrell D. Dover · ㉕ · Dover Dixon Horne · http://www.doverdixonhorne.com · Metropolitan Tower, 37th Floor · 425 West Capitol Avenue · Little Rock, AR 72201 · 501-375-9151

Timothy W. Grooms · ⑩ · Quattlebaum, Grooms, Tull & Burrow · http://www.qgtb.com · 111 Center Street, Suite 1900 · Little Rock, AR 72201-4420 · 501-379-1700

Harold W. Hamlin · Mitchell, Williams, Selig, Gates & Woodyard · http://www.mitchellwilliamslaw.com · 425 West Capitol Avenue, Suite 1800 · Little Rock, AR 72201-3525 · 501-688-8800

Paul W. Hoover, Jr. · Williams & Anderson · http://www.williamsanderson.com · Stephens Building, 22nd Floor · 111 Center Street · Little Rock, AR 72201 · 501-372-0800

Hal Joseph Kemp · Kemp Duckett Spradley & Curry · 111 Center Street, Suite 1300 · Little Rock, AR 72201 · 501-372-7243

David F. Menz · Williams & Anderson · http://www.williamsanderson.com · Stephens Building, 22nd Floor · 111 Center Street · Little Rock, AR 72201 · 501-372-0800

James M. Saxton · ⑩ · Friday, Eldredge & Clark · http://www.fridayfirm.com · 400 West Capitol Avenue, Suite 2000 · Little Rock, AR 72201-3522 · 501-376-2011

John William Spivey III · ⑩ · Wright, Lindsey & Jennings · http://www.wlj.com · 200 West Capitol Avenue, Suite 2300 · Little Rock, AR 72201-3699 · 501-371-0808

Jay T. Taylor · Friday, Eldredge & Clark · http://www.fridayfirm.com · 400 West Capitol Avenue, Suite 2000 · Little Rock, AR 72201-3522 · 501-376-2011

North Little Rock

Stuart W. Hankins · Hankins Law Firm · 800 West Fourth Street · P.O. Box 5151 · North Little Rock, AR 72119 · 501-371-9226

SECURITIES LAW

Little Rock

Paul B. Benham III · ⑳ · Friday, Eldredge & Clark · http://www.fridayfirm.com · 400 West Capitol Avenue, Suite 2000 · Little Rock, AR 72201-3522 · 501-376-2011

Garland W. Binns, Jr. · Dover Dixon Horne · http://www.doverdixonhorne.com · Metropolitan Tower, 37th Floor · 425 West Capitol Avenue · Little Rock, AR 72201 · 501-375-9151

C. Douglas Buford, Jr. · Mitchell, Williams, Selig, Gates & Woodyard · http://www.mitchellwilliamslaw.com · 425 West Capitol Avenue, Suite 1800 · Little Rock, AR 72201-3525 501-688-8800

Walter M. Ebel III · Friday, Eldredge & Clark · http://www.fridayfirm.com · 400 West Capitol Avenue, Suite 2000 · Little Rock, AR 72201-3522 · 501-376-2011

M. Sean Hatch · Wright, Lindsey & Jennings · http://www.wlj.com · 200 West Capitol Avenue, Suite 2300 · Little Rock, AR 72201-3699 · 501-371-0808

Charles C. Price · Wright, Lindsey & Jennings · http://www.wlj.com · 200 West Capitol Avenue, Suite 2300 · Little Rock, AR 72201-3699 · 501-371-0808

John S. Selig · ⑩ · Mitchell, Williams, Selig, Gates & Woodyard · http://www.mitchellwilliamslaw.com · 425 West Capitol Avenue, Suite 1800 · Little Rock, AR 72201-3525 · 501-688-8800

STRUCTURED FINANCE LAW

Little Rock

J. Shepherd Russell III · Friday, Eldredge & Clark · http://www.fridayfirm.com · 400 West Capitol Avenue, Suite 2000 · Little Rock, AR 72201-3522 · 501-376-2011

W. Jackson Williams · Williams & Anderson · http://www.williamsanderson.com · Stephens Building, 22nd Floor · 111 Center Street · Little Rock, AR 72201 · 501-372-0800

TAX LAW

El Dorado

Joseph Hickey · ⑩ · Compton, Prewett, Thomas & Hickey · 423 North Washington Avenue · El Dorado, AR 71730-5615 · 870-862-3478

Fayetteville

James Lee Moore III · ⑩ · Reece, Moore, Pendergraft · 75 North East Avenue, Suite 500 · P.O. Box 1788 Fayetteville, AR 72702 · 479-443-2705

James W. Smith · Friday, Eldredge & Clark · http://www.fridayfirm.com · 3425 North Futrall Drive, Suite 103 · Fayetteville, AR 72703-6252 · 479-695-2011

Jonesboro

Robert S. Jones · Barrett & Deacon · Mercantile Center, Third Floor · 300 South Church Street · P.O. Box 1700 · Jonesboro, AR 72403 · 870-931-1700

Tom D. Womack · Womack, Landis, Phelps, McNeill & McDaniel · 301 West Washington · P.O. Box 3077 · Jonesboro, AR 72401 · 870-932-0900

Little Rock

Samuel R. Baxter · Baxter & Jewell · One Information Way, Suite 210 · Little Rock, AR 72202-2289 · 501-664-9555

J. Lee Brown · Friday, Eldredge & Clark · http://www.fridayfirm.com · 400 West Capitol Avenue, Suite 2000 · Little Rock, AR 72201-3522 · 501-376-2011

C. Brantly Buck · Rose Law Firm · 120 East Fourth Street · Little Rock, AR 72201-2893 · 501-375-9131

Bryant Cranford · Rose Law Firm · 120 East Fourth Street · Little Rock, AR 72201-2893 · 501-375-9131

Walter M. Ebel III · Friday, Eldredge & Clark · http://www.fridayfirm.com · 400 West Capitol Avenue, Suite 2000 · Little Rock, AR 72201-3522 · 501-376-2011

Byron M. Eiseman, Jr. · ㉕ · Friday, Eldredge & Clark · http://www.fridayfirm.com · 400 West Capitol Avenue, Suite 2000 · Little Rock, AR 72201-3522 · 501-376-2011

Price C. Gardner · Friday, Eldredge & Clark · http://www.fridayfirm.com · 400 West Capitol Avenue, Suite 2000 · Little Rock, AR 72201-3522 · 501-376-2011

Gregory B. Graham · ⑳ · Overbey, Graham, Strigel & Wesbrook · Pavilion Centre, Suite 240 · 8315 Cantrell Road · Little Rock, AR 72227-2355 · 501-664-8105

W. Wilson Jones · ⑩ · Rose Law Firm · 120 East Fourth Street · Little Rock, AR 72201-2893 · 501-375-9131

John C. Lessel · ⑩ · John C. Lessel · 11601 Pleasant Ridge Road, Suite 301 · Little Rock, AR 72212 · 501-954-9000

Thomas L. Overbey · ㉕ · Overbey, Graham, Strigel & Wesbrook · Pavilion Centre, Suite 240 · 8315 Cantrell Road · Little Rock, AR 72227-2355 · 501-664-8105

Michael O. Parker · Dover Dixon Horne · http://www.doverdixonhorne.com · Metropolitan Tower, 37th Floor · 425 West Capitol Avenue · Little Rock, AR 72201 · 501-375-9151

John B. Peace · Dover Dixon Horne · http://www.doverdixonhorne.com · Metropolitan Tower, 37th Floor · 425 West Capitol Avenue · Little Rock, AR 72201 · 501-375-9151

John R. Tisdale · Wright, Lindsey & Jennings · http://www.wlj.com · 200 West Capitol Avenue, Suite 2300 · Little Rock, AR 72201-3699 · 501-371-0808

Thomas C. Vaughan, Jr. · Lax, Vaughan, Fortson, McKenzie & Rowe · Cantrell West Building, Suite 201 · 11300 Cantrell Road · Little Rock, AR 72212 · 501-376-6565

Craig H. Westbrook · ⑳ · Overbey, Graham, Strigel & Wesbrook · Pavilion Centre, Suite 240 · 8315 Cantrell Road · Little Rock, AR 72227-2355 · 501-664-8105

Pine Bluff

Ted N. Drake · ㉕ · Bridges, Young, Matthews & Drake · 315 East Eighth Avenue · P.O. Box 7808 · Pine Bluff, AR 71611 · 870-534-5532

Anthony A. Hilliard · Ramsay, Bridgforth, Harrelson and Starling · Simmons First National Building, 11th Floor · 501 Main Street · P.O. Box 8509 · Pine Bluff, AR 71611-8509 · 870-535-9000

TECHNOLOGY LAW

Little Rock

Ray F. Cox, Jr. · Wright, Lindsey & Jennings · http://www.wlj.com · 200 West Capitol Avenue, Suite 2300 · Little Rock, AR 72201-3699 · 501-371-0808

J. Charles Dougherty · Wright, Lindsey & Jennings · http://www.wlj.com · 200 West Capitol Avenue, Suite 2300 · Little Rock, AR 72201-3699 · 501-371-0808

Harold J. Evans · Williams & Anderson · http://www.williamsanderson.com · Stephens Building, 22nd Floor · 111 Center Street · Little Rock, AR 72201 · 501-372-0800

TRUSTS AND ESTATES

El Dorado

Joseph Hickey · ⑩ · Compton, Prewett, Thomas & Hickey · 423 North Washington Avenue · El Dorado, AR 71730-5615 · 870-862-3478

Fayetteville

William Jackson Butt II · Davis, Wright, Clark, Butt & Carithers · http://www.daviswrightlaw.com · 19 East Mountain Street · P.O. Box 1688 · Fayetteville, AR 72702-1688 · 479-521-7600

James Lee Moore III · ⑩ · Reece, Moore, Pendergraft · 75 North East Avenue, Suite 500 · P.O. Box 1788 Fayetteville, AR 72702 · 479-443-2705

James W. Smith · Friday, Eldredge & Clark · http://www.fridayfirm.com · 3425 North Futrall Drive, Suite 103 · Fayetteville, AR 72703-6252 · 479-695-2011

Fort Smith

Patrick Neill Moore · Warner, Smith & Harris · 400 Rogers Avenue · P.O. Box 1626 · Fort Smith, AR 72901 · 479-782-6041

Jonesboro

Robert S. Jones · Barrett & Deacon · Mercantile Center, Third Floor · 300 South Church Street · P.O. Box 1700 · Jonesboro, AR 72403 · 870-931-1700

Tom D. Womack · Womack, Landis, Phelps, McNeill & McDaniel · 301 West Washington · P.O. Box 3077 · Jonesboro, AR 72401 · 870-932-0900

Little Rock

Steve Bauman · ⑩ · Mitchell, Williams, Selig, Gates & Woodyard · http://www.mitchellwilliamslaw.com · 425 West Capitol Avenue, Suite 1800 · Little Rock, AR 72201-3525 · 501-688-8800

William Thomas Baxter · ⑩ · Friday, Eldredge & Clark · http://www.fridayfirm.com · 400 West Capitol Avenue, Suite 2000 · Little Rock, AR 72201-3522 · 501-376-2011

J. Lee Brown · Friday, Eldredge & Clark · http://www.fridayfirm.com · 400 West Capitol Avenue, Suite 2000 · Little Rock, AR 72201-3522 · 501-376-2011

C. Brantly Buck · Rose Law Firm · 120 East Fourth Street · Little Rock, AR 72201-2893 · 501-375-9131

Jeffrey H. Dixon · Mitchell, Williams, Selig, Gates & Woodyard · http://www.mitchellwilliamslaw.com · 425 West Capitol Avenue, Suite 1800 · Little Rock, AR 72201-3525 · 501-688-8800

Byron M. Eiseman, Jr. · ㉕ · Friday, Eldredge & Clark · http://www.fridayfirm.com · 400 West Capitol Avenue, Suite 2000 · Little Rock, AR 72201-3522 · 501-376-2011

James E. Harris · ⑳ · Friday, Eldredge & Clark · http://www.fridayfirm.com · 400 West Capitol Avenue, Suite 2000 · Little Rock, AR 72201-3522 · 501-376-2011

Richard F. Hatfield · ㉕ · Hatfield & Lassiter · 401 West Capitol Avenue, Suite 502 · Little Rock, AR 72201-3437 · 501-374-9010

William Dixon Haught · ㉕ · Haught & Wade · 111 Center Street, Suite 1320 · Little Rock, AR 72201 · 501-375-5257

W. Wilson Jones · ⑩ · Rose Law Firm · 120 East Fourth Street · Little Rock, AR 72201-2893 · 501-375-9131

John C. Lessel · ⑩ · John C. Lessel · 11601 Pleasant Ridge Road, Suite 301 · Little Rock, AR 72212 · 501-954-9000

Thomas L. Overbey · ㉕ · Overbey, Graham, Strigel & Wesbrook · Pavilion Centre, Suite 240 · 8315 Cantrell Road · Little Rock, AR 72227-2355 · 501-664-8105

George N. Plastiras · Plastiras Law Firm · Gans House · 1010 West Third Street · P.O. Box 1510 · Little Rock, AR 72203-1510 · 501-376-7410

Christopher T. Rogers · Mitchell, Williams, Selig, Gates & Woodyard · http://www.mitchellwilliamslaw.com · 425 West Capitol Avenue, Suite 1800 · Little Rock, AR 72201-3525 501-688-8800

Jean D. Stockburger · ⑩ · Mitchell, Williams, Selig, Gates & Woodyard · http://www.mitchellwilliamslaw.com · 425 West Capitol Avenue, Suite 1800 · Little Rock, AR 72201-3525 501-688-8800

John Cogan Wade · ⑩ · Haught & Wade · 111 Center Street, Suite 1320 · Little Rock, AR 72201 · 501-375-5257

K. Coleman Westbrook, Jr. · Friday, Eldredge & Clark · http://www.fridayfirm.com · 400 West Capitol Avenue, Suite 2000 · Little Rock, AR 72201-3522 · 501-376-2011

Pine Bluff

Ted N. Drake · ㉕ · Bridges, Young, Matthews & Drake · 315 East Eighth Avenue · P.O. Box 7808 · Pine Bluff, AR 71611 · 870-534-5532

Anthony A. Hilliard · Ramsay, Bridgforth, Harrelson and Starling · Simmons First National Building, 11th Floor · 501 Main Street · P.O. Box 8509 · Pine Bluff, AR 71611-8509 · 870-535-9000

WHITE-COLLAR CRIMINAL DEFENSE

Fayetteville

John C. Everett · ⑩ · Everett & Wales · 1944 East Joyce Boulevard · P.O. Box 8370 · Fayetteville, AR 72703-8370 · 479-443-0292

Warner H. Taylor · Taylor Law Firm · 303 East Millsap Road · P.O. Box 8310 · Fayetteville, AR 72703 · 479-443-5222

Fort Smith

Eddie N. Christian, Sr. · ⑩ · Christian & Byars · 502 Garrison Avenue · Fort Smith, AR 72901 · 479-782-9147

Jonesboro

Bill W. Bristow · Bristow & Richardson · 216 East Washington Street · Jonesboro, AR 72401-3102 · 870-935-9000

Bobby R. McDaniel · ㉕ · McDaniel & Wells · 400 South Main Street · Jonesboro, AR 72401 · 870-932-5950

Little Rock

Cathleen V. Compton · ⑩ · Cathleen V. Compton · 114 South Pulaski Street · Little Rock, AR 72201 · 501-372-0080

Timothy O. Dudley · ⑩ · Timothy O. Dudley · 114 South Pulaski Street · Little Rock, AR 72201-1924 · 501-372-0080

John Wesley Hall · John Wesley Hall · 1311 Broadway · Little Rock, AR 72202-4843 · 501-371-9131

J. Blake Hendrix · Blake Hendrix · 308 South Louisiana Street · Little Rock, AR 72201 · 501-376-0679

Richard E. Holiman · Holiman Law Firm · 400 West Capitol Avenue, Suite 1700 · Little Rock, AR 72201 · 501-375-1170

Jack T. Lassiter · ⑩ · Hatfield & Lassiter · 401 West Capitol Avenue, Suite 502 · Little Rock, AR 72201-3437 · 501-374-9010

William C. McArthur · ㉕ · William C. McArthur · 300 Spring Building, Suite 620 · Little Rock, AR 72201-2444 · 501-376-6173

Jeff Rosenzweig · Jeff Rosenzweig · 300 Spring Building, Suite 310 · Third and Spring Streets · Little Rock, AR 72201 · 501-372-5247

West Memphis

Kent J. Rubens · Rieves, Rubens & Mayton · http://www.rrmlawyers.com · 304 East Broadway · P.O. Box 1359 · West Memphis, AR 72301-3174 · 870-735-3420

El Dorado

Brian H. Ratcliff · Shackleford, Phillips, Wineland & Ratcliff · 100 East Church Street · P.O. Box 1718 · El Dorado, AR 71731-1718 · 870-862-5523

Fayetteville

Constance G. Clark · Davis, Wright, Clark, Butt & Carithers · http://www.daviswrightlaw.com · 19 East Mountain Street · P.O. Box 1688 · Fayetteville, AR 72702-1688 · 479-521-7600

Fort Smith

Eddie H. Walker, Jr. · ⑩ · Walker, Shock, Cox & Harp · 400 North Sixth Street · P.O. Box 998 · Fort Smith, AR 72902-0998 · 479-783-7600

Jonesboro

Phillip J. Wells · McDaniel & Wells · 400 South Main Street · Jonesboro, AR 72401 · 870-932-5950

Little Rock

Silas H. Brewer, Jr. · ⑩ · Kaplan, Brewer, Maxey & Haralson · 111 Center Street, Suite 2200 · Little Rock, AR 72201-4424 · 501-372-0400

John D. Davis · ⑩ · Wright, Lindsey & Jennings · http://www.wlj.com · 200 West Capitol Avenue, Suite 2300 · Little Rock, AR 72201-3699 · 501-371-0808

William M. Griffin III · ⑩ · Friday, Eldredge & Clark · http://www.fridayfirm.com · 400 West Capitol Avenue, Suite 2000 · Little Rock, AR 72201-3522 · 501-376-2011

Betty J. Hardy · Friday, Eldredge & Clark · http://www.fridayfirm.com · 400 West Capitol Avenue, Suite 2000 · Little Rock, AR 72201-3522 · 501-376-2011

Michael R. Mayton · Rieves, Rubens & Mayton · http://www.rrmlawyers.com · The Lyon Building, Suite 345 · 401 West Capitol Avenue · Little Rock, AR 72201-4823 · 501-376-0504

Lee J. Muldrow · ⑩ · Wright, Lindsey & Jennings · http://www.wlj.com · 200 West Capitol Avenue, Suite 2300 · Little Rock, AR 72201-3699 · 501-371-0808

Randy P. Murphy · Anderson, Murphy & Hopkins · 400 West Capital Avenue, Suite 2470 · Little Rock, AR 72201 · 501-372-1887

Frank B. Newell · Laser Law Firm · 101 South Spring Street, Suite 300 · Little Rock, AR 72201-2488 · 501-376-2981

Eric Newkirk · Rieves, Rubens & Mayton · http://www.rrmlawyers.com · The Lyon Building, Suite 345 · 401 West Capitol Avenue · Little Rock, AR 72201-4823 · 501-376-0504

Guy Alton Wade · Friday, Eldredge & Clark · http://www.fridayfirm.com · 400 West Capitol Avenue, Suite 2000 · Little Rock, AR 72201-3522 · 501-376-2011

Carol Worley · Worley Wood & Parrish · One Financial Centre Parkway, Suite 411 · 650 South Shackleford Road · Little Rock, AR 72211 · 501-225-3535

Pine Bluff

Michael Dennis · Bridges, Young, Matthews & Drake · 315 East Eighth Avenue · P.O. Box 7808 · Pine Bluff, AR 71611 · 870-534-5532

Texarkana

Gregory Giles · Harrelson, Moore & Giles · 1206 State Line Avenue · P.O. Box 2631 · Texarkana, AR 71854 · 870-774-5191

CALIFORNIA

ADMINISTRATIVE LAW

Emeryville

Amitai Schwartz · Amitai Schwartz · Watergate Towers, Suite 1286 · 2000 Powell Street · Emeryville, CA 94608 · 510-597-1775

Los Angeles

Terese A. Mosher Beluris · McDermott Will & Emery · 2049 Century Park East, 38th Floor · Los Angeles, CA 90067-3218 · 310-277-4110

Arthur Robert Chenen · Theodora Oringher Miller & Richman · 2029 Century Park East, Six Floor · Los Angeles, CA 90067-2907 · 310-557-2009

Henry R. Fenton · Fenton & Nelson · 11835 West Olympic Boulevard, Suite 925 · Los Angeles, CA 90064 · 310-444-5244

Donald A. Goldman · McDermott Will & Emery · 2049 Century Park East, 38th Floor · Los Angeles, CA 90067-3218 · 310-277-4110

James Robert Lahana · Fenigstein & Kaufman · 1900 Avenue of the Stars, Suite 2300 · Los Angeles, CA 90067-4314 · 310-201-0777

Manhattan Beach

John D. Harwell · Law Office of John D. Harwell · 225 Twenty-Seventh Street · Manhattan Beach, CA 90266 · 310-546-7078

Oakland

Lyle C. Cavin, Jr. · Lyle C. Cavin, Jr. · 201 Fourth Street, Suite 102 · Oakland, CA 94607 · 510-444-2501

Rolling Hills Estates

Russell Iungerich · Iungerich & Spackman · 28441 Highridge Road, Suite 201 · Rolling Hills Estates, CA 90274-4871 · 310-697-0288

Sacramento

James P. Corn · Stoel Rives · http://www.stoel.com · 980 Ninth Street, Suite 1900 · Sacramento, CA 95814 · 916-447-0700

San Diego

Nancy O. Dix · DLA Piper · 401 B Street, Suite 1700 · San Diego, CA 92101-4297 · 619-699-2700

San Francisco

Fred H. Altshuler · Altshuler Berzon · 177 Post Street, Suite 300 · San Francisco, CA 94108 · 415-421-7151

Allan J. Joseph · Rogers Joseph O'Donnell · 311 California Street, 10th Floor · San Francisco, CA 94104-2695 · 415-956-2828

Martin A. Mattes · ⑩ · Nossaman · http://www.nossaman.com · 50 California Street, 34th Floor · San Francisco, CA 94111-4707 · 415-398-3600

Neil H. O'Donnell · Rogers Joseph O'Donnell · 311 California Street, 10th Floor · San Francisco, CA 94104-2695 · 415-956-2828

Edward W. O'Neill · Davis Wright Tremaine · 505 Montgomery Street, Suite 800 · San Francisco, CA 94111-6533 · 415-276-6500

ADVERTISING LAW

Los Angeles

Robert A. Darwell · Sheppard, Mullin, Richter & Hampton · http://www.sheppardmullin.com · 1901 Avenue of the Stars, Suite 1600 · Los Angeles, CA 90067 · 310-228-3700

ALTERNATIVE DISPUTE RESOLUTION

Clovis

Douglas E. Noll · Noll Associates · 20124 Tollhouse Road · P.O. Box 2336 · Clovis, CA 93613 · 800-785-4487

Encino

Jeffrey Krivis · First Mediation Corporation · 16501 Ventura Boulevard, Suite 606 · Encino, CA 91436 · 818-784-4544

Fresno

John J. Mccauley · McCauley and Associates · 8365 North Fresno Street, Suite 110 · Fresno, CA 93720-1548 · 800-848-5591

Irvine

Don W. Martens · (10) · Knobbe, Martens, Olson & Bear · 2040 Main Street, 14th Floor · Irvine, CA 92614 949-760-0404

Long Beach

Michael D. Moorhead · Judicate West · One World Trade Center, Suite 1650 · Long Beach, CA 90831-0002 · 562-432-8340

Los Angeles

James N. Adler · (25) · James N. Adler Mediation & Arbitration · 1034 Selby Avenue · Los Angeles, CA 90024-3106 · 310-209-8548

Eleanor Oths Barr · ADR Services · 1900 Avenue of the Stars, Suite 250 · Los Angeles, CA 90067 · 310-201-0010

Russell A. Bostrom · Judicate West · 12100 Wilshire Boulevard, Suite 650 · Los Angeles, CA 90025 · 310-442-2100

Christine W.S. Byrd · Irell & Manella · 1800 Avenue of the Stars, Suite 900 · Los Angeles, CA 90067-4276 · 310-277-1010

George D. Calkins II · Cox, Castle & Nicholson · 2049 Century Park East, 28th Floor · Los Angeles, CA 90067 · 310-277-4222

Richard Chernick · JAMS · 707 Wilshire Boulevard, 46th Floor · Los Angeles, CA 90017 · 213-620-1133

Kenneth C. Gibbs · Gibbs, Giden, Locher & Turner · 1880 Century Park East, 12th Floor · Los Angeles, CA 90067-1621 · 310-552-3400

Jay Cordell Horton · Judicate West · 12100 Wilshire Boulevard, Suite 650 · Los Angeles, CA 90025 · 310-442-2100

Patrick M. Kelly · Wilson Elser Moskowitz Edelman & Dicker · 555 South Flower Street, Suite 2900 · Los Angeles, CA 90071-2407 · 213-443-5100

Jeff Kichaven · JAMS · 707 Wilshire Boulevard, 46th Floor · Los Angeles, CA 90017 · 213-620-1133

Ralph R. Mabey · ⑳ · Stutman, Treister & Glatt · 1901 Avenue of the Stars, 12th Floor · Los Angeles, CA 90067 · 310-228-5600

Denise R. Madigan · ADR Services · 1900 Avenue of the Stars, Suite 250 · Los Angeles, CA 90067 · 310-201-0010

Richard R. Mainland · Fulbright & Jaworski · http://www.fulbright.com · 555 South Flower Street, 41st Floor · Los Angeles, CA 90071 · 213-892-9200

Eugene Charles Moscovitch · ADR Services · 1900 Avenue of the Stars, Suite 250 · Los Angeles, CA 90067 · 310-201-0010

Alexander S. Polsky · JAMS · 707 Wilshire Boulevard, 46th Floor · Los Angeles, CA 90017 · 213-620-1133

Janet Rubin Fields · Judicate West · 12100 Wilshire Boulevard, Suite 650 · Los Angeles, CA 90025 · 310-442-2100

Steven J. Stone · JAMS · 707 Wilshire Boulevard, 46th Floor · Los Angeles, CA 90017 · 213-620-1133

Dickran M. Tevrizian · JAMS · 707 Wilshire Boulevard, 46th Floor · Los Angeles, CA 90017 · 213-620-1133

Ralph O. Williams III · ADR Services · 1900 Avenue of the Stars, Suite 250 · Los Angeles, CA 90067 · 310-201-0010

Malibu

Max Factor III · Factor Mediation Services · 21355 Pacific Coast Highway, Suite 200 · Malibu, CA 90265 310-456-3500

Monterey

Charles R. Keller · Fenton & Keller · 2801 Monterey Salinas Highway · P.O. Box 791 · Monterey, CA 93942-0791 · 831-373-1241

Newport Beach

Layn R. Phillips · Irell & Manella · 840 Newport Center Drive, Suite 400 · Newport Beach, CA 92660-6324 · 949-760-0991

Oakland

Bette B. Epstein · Reed Smith · 1999 Harrison Street, Suite 2400 · P.O. Box 2084 · Oakland, CA 94604-3572 · 510-763-2000

William A. Quinby · Wulff, Quinby & Sochynsky · 1901 Harrison Street, Suite 1420 · Oakland, CA 94612 510-663-5222

Yaroslav Sochynsky · Wulff, Quinby & Sochynsky · 1901 Harrison Street, Suite 1420 · Oakland, CA 94612 · 510-663-5222

Vivien B. Williamson · Vivien B. Williamson · 1939 Harrison Street, Suite 520 · Oakland, CA 94612 · 510-452-1300

Randall W. Wulff · Wulff, Quinby & Sochynsky · 1901 Harrison Street, Suite 1420 · Oakland, CA 94612 · 510-663-5222

Orange

John K. Trotter · JAMS · 500 North State College Boulevard, Suite 600 · Orange, CA 92868 · 714-939-1300

Pasadena

Les J. Weinstein · Sheldon Mak Rose & Anderson · 100 Corson Street, Third Floor · Pasadena, CA 91103-3842 · 626-796-4000

San Diego

Douglas A. Glass · Glass Mediations · http://www.glassmediations.com · 2550 Fifth Avenue, Suite 605 · San Diego, CA 92103 · 619-234-7790

Craig Higgs · Higgs, Fletcher & Mack · 401 West A Street, Suite 2600 · San Diego, CA 92101-7910 · 619-236-1551

Scott S. Markus · Markus Kruis Mediation · 402 West Broadway, Suite 700 · San Diego, CA 92101 · 619-239-2020

Thomas E. Sharkey · (10) · Sharkey, Roberts & Chodzko · 402 West Broadway, Suite 2000 · P.O. Box 3089 San Diego, CA 92101 · 619-239-8499

Maureen A. Summers · Summers & Shives · 8755 Aero Drive, Suite 230 · San Diego, CA 92123-1750 · 858-874-1800

San Francisco

Zela G. Claiborne · JAMS · Two Embarcadero Center, Suite 1500 · San Francisco, CA 94111 · 415-982-5267

Bruce A. Edwards · JAMS · Two Embarcadero Center, Suite 1500 · San Francisco, CA 94111 · 415-982-5267

Robert B. Kaplan · Jeffer, Mangels, Butler & Marmaro · Two Embarcadero Center, Fifth Floor · San Francisco, CA 94111 · 415-398-8080

Daniel J. Kelly · (20) · Walkup, Melodia, Kelly & Schoenberger · http://www.walkuplawoffice.com · 650 California Street, 26th Floor · San Francisco, CA 94108 · 415-981-7210

Edward A. Panelli · JAMS · Two Embarcadero Center, Suite 1500 · San Francisco, CA 94111 · 415-982-5267

David A. Rotman · Gregorio Haldeman · 201 Mission Street, Suite 1900 · San Francisco, CA 94105 · 415-543-3366

Mark S. Rudy · (10) · Rudy, Exelrod & Zieff · http://www.reztlaw.com · 351 California Street, Suite 700 · San Francisco, CA 94104 · 415-434-9800

Daniel Weinstein · JAMS · Two Embarcadero Center, Suite 1500 · San Francisco, CA 94111 · 415-982-5267

Rebecca Westerfield · JAMS · Two Embarcadero Center, Suite 1500 · San Francisco, CA 94111 · 415-982-5267

Ray L. Wong · Duane Morris · Spear Tower, Suite 2000 · One Market · San Francisco, CA 94105-1104 · 415-957-3000

San Jose

Thomas H. R. Denver · Mediation Masters · 96 North Third Street, Suite 300 · San Jose, CA 95112 · 408-280-7883

Charles F. Hawkins · Mediation Masters · 96 North Third Street, Suite 300 · San Jose, CA 95112 · 408-280-7883

Leonard Sprinkles · Mediation Masters · 96 North Third Street, Suite 300 · San Jose, CA 95112 · 408-280-7883

San Juan Capistrano

John Leo Wagner · The Wagner Law Firm · http://www.wagneradr.com · 31331 Via Del Verde · San Juan Capistrano, CA 92675-6320 · 949-248-3137

Santa Ana

Troy D. Roe · Judicate West · 1851 East First Street, Suite 1450 · Santa Ana, CA 92705 · 714-834-1340

William Sheffield · Judicate West · 1851 East First Street, Suite 1450 · Santa Ana, CA 92705 · 714-834-1340

Santa Barbara

Kevin T. McIvers · McIvers & Slater · 211 East Anapamu Street · Santa Barbara, CA 93101 · 805-897-3843

Santa Monica

Viggo Boserup · JAMS · 1601 Cloverfield Boulevard, Suite 370 South · Santa Monica, CA 90404 · 310-392-3044

Deborah J. Rothman · Deborah J. Rothman · http://www.deborahrothman.com · 13101 Washington Boulevard, Suite 456 · Santa Monica, CA 90066 · 310-452-9891

Santa Rosa

William L. Bettinelli · JAMS · 50 Old Courthouse Square, Suite 600 · Santa Rosa, CA 95404 · 707-527-5267

John F. DeMeo · ⑩ · DeMeo DeMeo & West · 565 West College Avenue · Santa Rosa, CA 95401 · 707-545-3232

Robert A. Murray · Arbitration & Mediation Center · 111 Santa Rosa Avenue, Suite 202 · Santa Rosa, CA 95404 · 707-525-9409

Toluca Lake

Gig Kyriacou · The Mediation Offices of Gig Kyriacou · 4110 Cahuenga Boulevard · Toluca Lake, CA 91602 · 818-769-9347

Valencia

Steven G. Mehta · Mehta & Mann · 27200 Tourney Road, Suite 475 · Valencia, CA 91355 · 661-284-1818

Walnut Creek

Michael J. Ney · McNamara, Dodge, Ney, Beatty, Slattery, Pfalzer, Borges & Brothers · 1211 Newell Avenue · Walnut Creek, CA 94596-5331 · 925-939-5330

ANTITRUST LAW

Irvine

Juan C. Basombrio · Dorsey & Whitney · 38 Technology Drive, Suite 100 · Irvine, CA 92618-5310 · 949-932-3600

Los Angeles

Aton Arbisser · Kaye Scholer · 1999 Avenue of the Stars, Suite 1700 · Los Angeles, CA 90067-6048 · 310-788-1000

William T. Bisset · Hughes Hubbard & Reed · http://www.hugheshubbard.com · 350 South Grand Avenue, Suite 3600 · Los Angeles, CA 90071-3442 · 213-613-2800

Maxwell M. Blecher · ⑩ · Blecher & Collins · 515 South Figueroa Street, 17th Floor · Los Angeles, CA 90071 · 213-622-4222

Robert E. Cooper · ⑩ · Gibson, Dunn & Crutcher · 333 South Grand Avenue · Los Angeles, CA 90071-3197 · 213-229-7000

Carole E. Handler · Wildman, Harrold, Allen & Dixon · 5900 Wilshire Boulevard, Suite 2600 · Los Angeles, CA 90036-5013 · 323-951-9681

Chad S. Hummel · Manatt, Phelps & Phillips · 11355 West Olympic Boulevard · Los Angeles, CA 90064 310-312-4000

Bradley S. Phillips · Munger, Tolles & Olson · 355 South Grand Avenue, 35th Floor · Los Angeles, CA 90071-1560 · 213-683-9100

Ronald C. Redcay · Arnold & Porter · 777 South Figueroa Street, 44th Floor · Los Angeles, CA 90017-5844 · 213-243-4000

Charles H. Samel · Latham & Watkins · 355 South Grand Avenue · Los Angeles, CA 90071-1560 · 213-485-1234

Darryl L. Snider · Sheppard, Mullin, Richter & Hampton · 333 South Hope Street, 48th Floor · Los Angeles, CA 90071-1448 · 213-620-1780

Michael H. Steinberg · Sullivan & Cromwell · 1888 Century Park East, 21st Floor · Los Angeles, CA 90067-1725 · 310-712-6600

Daniel G. Swanson · Gibson, Dunn & Crutcher · 333 South Grand Avenue · Los Angeles, CA 90071-3197 · 213-229-7000

Menlo Park

Christopher B. Hockett · Davis Polk & Wardwell · 1600 El Camino Real · Menlo Park, CA 94025 · 650-752-2000

Mountain View

Tyler A. Baker · Fenwick & West · Silicon Valley Center · 801 California Street · Mountain View, CA 94041-2008 · 650-988-8500

Mark S. Ostrau · Fenwick & West · Silicon Valley Center · 801 California Street · Mountain View, CA 94041-2008 · 650-988-8500

Palo Alto

Charles T. Compton · Wilson Sonsini Goodrich & Rosati · 650 Page Mill Road · Palo Alto, CA 94304-1050 · 650-493-9300

Robert P. Taylor · ⑩ · Mintz, Levin, Cohn, Ferris, Glovsky and Popeo · 1400 Page Mill Road · Palo Alto, CA 94304-1124 · 650-251-7700

San Diego

Jeffery M. Shohet · DLA Piper · 401 B Street, Suite 1700 · San Diego, CA 92101-4297 · 619-699-2700

San Francisco

Geraldine M. Alexis · Perkins Coie · http://www.perkinscoie.com · Four Embarcadero Center, Suite 2400 San Francisco, CA 94111-4131 · 415-344-7000

James R. Atwood · Covington & Burling · One Front Street · San Francisco, CA 94111-5356 · 415-591-6000

David M. Balabanian · ⑩ · Bingham McCutchen · http://www.bingham.com · Three Embarcadero Center · San Francisco, CA 94111-4067 · 415-393-2000

Stephen V. Bomse · ⑩ · Orrick, Herrington & Sutcliffe · The Orrick Building · 405 Howard Street · San Francisco, CA 94105-2669 · 415-773-5700

George A. Cumming, Jr. · Morgan Lewis & Bockius · Spear Street Tower · One Market · San Francisco, CA 94105-1596 · 415-442-1000

Marie L. Fiala · Heller Ehrman · 333 Bush Street · San Francisco, CA 94104-2878 · 415-772-6000

Paul R. Griffin · Thelen Reid Brown Raysman & Steiner · 101 Second Street, Suite 1800 · San Francisco, CA 94105-3601 · 415-371-1200

Forrest A. Hainline III · Goodwin Procter · Three Embarcadero Center, 24th Floor · San Francisco, CA 94111 · 415-733-6000

Gary L. Halling · Sheppard, Mullin, Richter & Hampton · http://www.sheppardmullin.com · Four Embarcadero Center, 17th Floor · San Francisco, CA 94111 · 415-434-9100

Terry J. Houlihan · Bingham McCutchen · http://www.bingham.com · Three Embarcadero Center · San Francisco, CA 94111-4067 · 415-393-2000

Holly A. House · Bingham McCutchen · http://www.bingham.com · Three Embarcadero Center · San Francisco, CA 94111-4067 · 415-393-2000

James L. Hunt · ⑩ · Bingham McCutchen · http://www.bingham.com · Three Embarcadero Center · San Francisco, CA 94111-4067 · 415-393-2000

Mark A. Lemley · Keker & Van Nest · http://www.kvn.com · 710 Sansome Street · San Francisco, CA 94111 · 415-391-5400

Jesse W. Markham, Jr. · Holme Roberts & Owen · http://www.hro.com · 560 Mission Street, 25th Floor · San Francisco, CA 94105-2994 · 415-268-2000

James McGinnis · Sheppard, Mullin, Richter & Hampton · http://www.sheppardmullin.com · Four Embarcadero Center, 17th Floor · San Francisco, CA 94111 · 415-434-9100

Alfred C. Pfeiffer, Jr. · Latham & Watkins · 505 Montgomery Street, Suite 2000 · San Francisco, CA 94111-6538 · 415-391-0600

Donn P. Pickett · Bingham McCutchen · http://www.bingham.com · Three Embarcadero Center · San Francisco, CA 94111-4067 · 415-393-2000

M. Laurence Popofsky · 20 · Orrick, Herrington & Sutcliffe · The Orrick Building · 405 Howard Street · San Francisco, CA 94105-2669 · 415-773-5700

Penelope A. Preovolos · Morrison & Foerster · http://www.mofo.com · 425 Market Street · San Francisco, CA 94105-2482 · 415-268-7000

Robert B. Pringle · Thelen Reid Brown Raysman & Steiner · 101 Second Street, Suite 1800 · San Francisco, CA 94105-3601 · 415-371-1200

Robert A. Rosenfeld · Orrick, Herrington & Sutcliffe · The Orrick Building · 405 Howard Street · San Francisco, CA 94105-2669 · 415-773-5700

Joel S. Sanders · Gibson, Dunn & Crutcher · Post Montgomery Center, Suite 3100 · One Montgomery Street · San Francisco, CA 94104-4505 · 415-393-8200

Guido Saveri · Saveri & Saveri · 111 Pine Street, Suite 1700 · San Francisco, CA 94111 · 415-217-6810

Bruce L. Simon · Pearson, Simon, Soter, Warshaw & Penny · 44 Montgomery Street, Suite 1430 · San Francisco, CA 94104-4610 · 415-433-9000

Gary R. Spratling · Gibson, Dunn & Crutcher · Post Montgomery Center, Suite 3100 · One Montgomery Street · San Francisco, CA 94104-4505 · 415-393-8200

Daniel M. Wall · Latham & Watkins · 505 Montgomery Street, Suite 2000 · San Francisco, CA 94111-6538 · 415-391-0600

APPELLATE LAW

Berkeley

Victoria J. De Goff · De Goff and Sherman · 1916 Los Angeles Avenue · Berkeley, CA 94707 · 510-524-1840

Joseph A. Hearst · Joseph A. Hearst · PMB 525 · 1563 Solano Avenue · Berkeley, CA 94707 · 510-528-6863

Richard I. Sherman · 10 · De Goff and Sherman · 1916 Los Angeles Avenue · Berkeley, CA 94707 · 510-524-1840

Burbank

Charlotte E. Costan · Charlotte E. Costan · P.O. Box 3083 · Burbank, CA 91508 · 818-842-8932

Costa Mesa

Richard A. Derevan · Snell & Wilmer · 600 Anton Boulevard, Suite 1400 · Costa Mesa, CA 92626-7689 · 714-427-7000

East Palo Alto

Michael J. Reagan · DLA Piper · 2000 University Avenue · East Palo Alto, CA 94303-2214 · 650-833-2000

Emeryville

Amitai Schwartz · Amitai Schwartz · Watergate Towers, Suite 1286 · 2000 Powell Street · Emeryville, CA 94608 · 510-597-1775

Encino

Peter Abrahams · Horvitz & Levy · 15760 Ventura Boulevard, 18th Floor · Encino, CA 91436-3000 · 818-995-0800

David M. Axelrad · Horvitz & Levy · 15760 Ventura Boulevard, 18th Floor · Encino, CA 91436-3000 · 818-995-0800

Frederic D. Cohen · Horvitz & Levy · 15760 Ventura Boulevard, 18th Floor · Encino, CA 91436-3000 · 818-995-0800

David S. Ettinger · Horvitz & Levy · 15760 Ventura Boulevard, 18th Floor · Encino, CA 91436-3000 · 818-995-0800

Ellis J. Horvitz · ⑩ · Horvitz & Levy · 15760 Ventura Boulevard, 18th Floor · Encino, CA 91436-3000 · 818-995-0800

Barry R. Levy · Horvitz & Levy · 15760 Ventura Boulevard, 18th Floor · Encino, CA 91436-3000 · 818-995-0800

Lisa Perrochet · Horvitz & Levy · 15760 Ventura Boulevard, 18th Floor · Encino, CA 91436-3000 · 818-995-0800

John A. Taylor, Jr. · Horvitz & Levy · 15760 Ventura Boulevard, 18th Floor · Encino, CA 91436-3000 · 818-995-0800

Mitchell C. Tilner · Horvitz & Levy · 15760 Ventura Boulevard, 18th Floor · Encino, CA 91436-3000 · 818-995-0800

Irvine

William J. Kopeny · ⑩ · William Kopeny & Associates · http://www.writsnappeals.com · 16485 Laguna Canyon Road, Suite 230 · Irvine, CA 92618 · 949-453-2243

Los Angeles

Mitchell E. Abbott · Richards, Watson & Gershon · 355 South Grand Avenue, 40th Floor · Los Angeles, CA 90071-3101 · 213-626-8484

Michael M. Berger · Manatt, Phelps & Phillips · 11355 West Olympic Boulevard · Los Angeles, CA 90064 · 310-312-4000

Laura W. Brill · Irell & Manella · 1800 Avenue of the Stars, Suite 900 · Los Angeles, CA 90067-4276 · 310-277-1010

Barry Fischer · Law Office of Barry Fischer · 1925 Century Park East, Suite 1150 · Los Angeles, CA 90067 · 310-788-0900

Robert S. Gerstein · Law Office of Robert S. Gerstein · 12400 Wilshiere Boulevard, Suite 1300 · Los Angeles, CA 90025-1019 · 310-820-1939

Irving H. Greines · ⑩ · Greines, Martin, Stein & Richland · 5900 Wilshire Boulevard, 12th Floor · Los Angeles, CA 90036 · 310-859-7811

Harvey M. Grossman · Law Office of Harvey M. Grossman · 500 North Highland Avenue · P.O. Box 360919 · Los Angeles, CA 90036-1419 · 323-957-1236

Rita Gunasekaran · Haight, Brown & Bonesteel · 6080 Center Drive, Suite 800 · Los Angeles, CA 90045 310-215-7100

James M. Harris · Sidley Austin · 555 West Fifth Street, 40th Floor · Los Angeles, CA 90013 · 213-896-6000

Rex S. Heinke · ⑩ · Akin Gump Strauss Hauer & Feld · 2029 Century Park East, Suite 2400 · Los Angeles, CA 90067-3012 · 310-229-1000

Edward J. Horowitz · Edward J. Horowitz · 1151 Bienveneda Avenue · P.O. Box 967 · Los Angeles, CA 90272 · 310-826-6619

Shirley M. Hufstedler · ⑩ · Morrison & Foerster · http://www.mofo.com · 555 West Fifth Street, Suite 3500 · Los Angeles, CA 90013-1024 · 213-892-5200

Edward P. Lazarus · Akin Gump Strauss Hauer & Feld · 2029 Century Park East, Suite 2400 · Los Angeles, CA 90067-3012 · 310-229-1000

Michael J. Lightfoot · ⑳ · Lightfoot Vandevelde Sadowsky Crouchley Rutherford & Levine · 800 Wilshire Boulevard, Suite 500 · Los Angeles, CA 90017 · 213-622-4750

Elwood Lui · Jones Day · 555 South Flower Street, 50th Floor · Los Angeles, CA 90071 · 213-489-3939

Robin Meadow · Greines, Martin, Stein & Richland · 5900 Wilshire Boulevard, 12th Floor · Los Angeles, CA 90036 · 310-859-7811

William A. Norris · Akin Gump Strauss Hauer & Feld · 2029 Century Park East, Suite 2400 · Los Angeles, CA 90067-3012 · 310-229-1000

Marc J. Poster · Greines, Martin, Stein & Richland · 5900 Wilshire Boulevard, 12th Floor · Los Angeles, CA 90036 · 310-859-7811

Barbara W. Ravitz · Greines, Martin, Stein & Richland · 5900 Wilshire Boulevard, 12th Floor · Los Angeles, CA 90036 · 310-859-7811

Kent L. Richland · Greines, Martin, Stein & Richland · 5900 Wilshire Boulevard, 12th Floor · Los Angeles, CA 90036 · 310-859-7811

Gregory R. Smith · Irell & Manella · 1800 Avenue of the Stars, Suite 900 · Los Angeles, CA 90067-4276 · 310-277-1010

Kenneth W. Starr · Kirkland & Ellis · 777 South Figueroa Street, Suite 3400 · Los Angeles, CA 90017-5800 · 213-680-8400

Martin Stein · Greines, Martin, Stein & Richland · 5900 Wilshire Boulevard, 12th Floor · Los Angeles, CA 90036 · 310-859-7811

Barry Tarlow · ㉕ · Tarlow & Berk · 9119 West Sunset Boulevard · Los Angeles, CA 90069 · 310-278-2111

Thomas D. Warren · Baker Hostetler · http://www.bakerlaw.com · 12100 Wilshire Boulevard, 15th Floor · Los Angeles, CA 90025 · 310-820-8800

Roy G. Weatherup · Lewis, Brisbois, Bisgaard & Smith · 221 North Figueroa Street, Suite 1200 · Los Angeles, CA 90012-2601 · 213-250-1800

Marina Del Rey

Stephen A. Kroft · ⑩ · Stephen A. Kroft · 4807 Roma Court · Marina Del Rey, CA 90292 · 310-822-4024

Mill Valley

Eric S. Multhaup · Eric S. Multhaup · 20 Sunnyside Avenue, Suite A · Mill Valley, CA 94941 · 415-821-6000

Northridge

Mark A. Hart · Mark A. Hart · 9420 Reseda Boulevard · P.O. Box 520 · Northridge, CA 91324-6000 · 818-363-0419

Novato

Elliot L. Bien · Bien & Summers · 23 Palomino Road · Novato, CA 94947 · 415-898-2900

Oakland

Jon B. Eisenberg · Eisenberg & Hancock · 1970 Broadway, Suite 1200 · Oakland, CA 94612 · 510-452-2581

Ellen Lake · Ellen Lake · 4230 Lakeshore Avenue · Oakland, CA 94610-1136 · 510-272-9393

E. Elizabeth Summers · Bien & Summers · 3932 Reinhardt Drive · Oakland, CA 94619 · 510-531-3106

Rolling Hills Estates

Russell Iungerich · Iungerich & Spackman · 28441 Highridge Road, Suite 201 · Rolling Hills Estates, CA 90274-4871 · 310-697-0288

Sacramento

Jay-Allen Eisen · Jay-Allen Eisen Law Corporation · 2431 Capitol Avenue · Sacramento, CA 95816 · 916-444-6171

Michael T. Fogarty · McDonough Holland & Allen · http://www.mhalaw.com · 555 Capitol Mall, Ninth Floor · Sacramento, CA 95814-4692 · 916-444-3900

Charity Kenyon · Kenyon-Yeates · 3400 Cottage Way, Suite K · Sacramento, CA 95825 · 916-609-5000

San Diego

Charles A. Bird · Luce, Forward, Hamilton & Scripps · http://www.luce.com · 600 West Broadway, Suite 2600 · San Diego, CA 92101 · 619-236-1414

Martin N. Buchanan · Niddrie Fish and Buchanan · Symphony Towers Building, Suite 2640 · 750 B Street · San Diego, CA 92101 · 619-238-6065

Kathryn E. Karcher · Ravin Glovinsky · 401 B Street, Suite 2450 · San Diego, CA 92101 · 206-335-1631

Lynda A. Romero · Law Office of Lynda Romero · 5173 Waring Road, Suite 220 · San Diego, CA 92120 · 619-286-6992

Laura G. Schaefer · Boyce & Schaefer · 934 Twenty-Third Street · San Diego, CA 92102-1911 · 619-232-3320

Charles M. Sevilla · 20 · The Law Office of Charles Sevilla · 1010 Second Avenue, Suite 1825 · San Diego, CA 92101-4902 · 619-232-2222

Karin D. Vogel · Sheppard, Mullin, Richter & Hampton · http://www.sheppardmullin.com · 501 West Broadway, 19th Floor · San Diego, CA 92101 · 619-338-6500

Lewis A. Wenzell · 10 · Lewis A. Wenzell · 5070 Narragansett Avenue, Suite 303 · San Diego, CA 92107-3028 · 619-224-9422

San Francisco

Jeffrey L. Bleich · Munger, Tolles & Olson · 560 Mission Street, 27th Floor · San Francisco, CA 94105-9781 · 415-512-4000

Jerome I. Braun · Farella Braun & Martel · Russ Building, 17th Floor · 235 Montgomery Street · San Francisco, CA 94104 · 415-954-4400

Raymond A. Cardozo · Reed Smith · Two Embarcadero Center, Suite 2000 · San Francisco, CA 94111 · 415-543-8700

Peter W. Davis · 10 · Reed Smith · Two Embarcadero Center, Suite 2000 · San Francisco, CA 94111 · 415-543-8700

Jerome B. Falk, Jr. · 25 · Howard, Rice, Nemerovski, Canady, Falk & Rabkin · Three Embarcadero Center, Seventh Floor · San Francisco, CA 94111-4024 · 415-434-1600

Paul D. Fogel · Reed Smith · Two Embarcadero Center, Suite 2000 · San Francisco, CA 94111 · 415-543-8700

Kevin M. Fong · Pillsbury Winthrop Shaw Pittman · http://www.pillsburylaw.com · 50 Fremont Street · P.O. Box 7880 · San Francisco, CA 94120-7880 · 415-983-1000

David M. Heilbron · 10 · David M. Heilbron · Three Embarcadero Center · C/O Bingham McCutchen · San Francisco, CA 94111-4067 · 415-393-2177

Steven A. Hirsch · Keker & Van Nest · http://www.kvn.com · 710 Sansome Street · San Francisco, CA 94111 · 415-391-5400

Raoul D. Kennedy · 20 · Skadden, Arps, Slate, Meagher & Flom · Four Embarcadero Center, Suite 3800 · San Francisco, CA 94111 · 415-984-6400

Daniel M. Kolkey · Gibson, Dunn & Crutcher · Post Montgomery Center, Suite 3100 · One Montgomery Street · San Francisco, CA 94104-4505 · 415-393-8200

Ephraim Margolin · 25 · Law Office of Ephraim Margolin · Union Square, Suite 400 · 240 Stockton Street San Francisco, CA 94108-5318 · 415-421-4347

Steven L. Mayer · Howard, Rice, Nemerovski, Canady, Falk & Rabkin · Three Embarcadero Center, Seventh Floor · San Francisco, CA 94111-4024 · 415-434-1600

John R. Reese · Bingham McCutchen · http://www.bingham.com · Three Embarcadero Center · San Francisco, CA 94111-4067 · 415-393-2000

Dennis P. Riordan · ⑩ · Riordan & Horgan · 523 Octavia Street · San Francisco, CA 94102 · 415-431-3472

Michael Rubin · Altshuler Berzon · 177 Post Street, Suite 300 · San Francisco, CA 94108 · 415-421-7151

Robert J. Stumpf, Jr. · Sheppard, Mullin, Richter & Hampton · http://www.sheppardmullin.com · Four Embarcadero Center, 17th Floor · San Francisco, CA 94111 · 415-434-9100

Sanford Svetcov · Lerach Coughlin Stoia Geller Rudman & Robbins · 100 Pine Street, Suite 2600 · San Francisco, CA 94111 · 415-288-4545

Douglas R. Young · ⑩ · Farella Braun & Martel · Russ Building, 17th Floor · 235 Montgomery Street · San Francisco, CA 94104 · 415-954-4400

Santa Monica

Dennis A. Fischer · Dennis A. Fischer · 1448 Fifteenth Street, Suite 206 · Santa Monica, CA 90404 · 310-451-4815

Robert E. Hinerfeld · Robert E. Hinerfeld · 371 Twenty-Fourth Street · Santa Monica, CA 90402-2517 · 310-394-4902

Ventura

Wendy C. Lascher · Lascher & Lascher · http://www.lascher.com · 605 Poli Street · P.O. Box 25540 · Ventura, CA 93002 · 805-648-3228

Walnut Creek

Stephen L. Kostka · Bingham McCutchen · http://www.bingham.com · 1333 North California Boulevard, Suite 210 · Walnut Creek, CA 94596-1270 · 925-937-8000

Woodland Hills

Roland Wrinkle · Grassini & Wrinkle · 20750 Ventura Boulevard, Suite 221 · Woodland Hills, CA 91364 · 818-348-1717

BANKING LAW

Costa Mesa

Joseph L. Coleman · Snell & Wilmer · 600 Anton Boulevard, Suite 1400 · Costa Mesa, CA 92626-7689 · 714-427-7000

Dean A. Demetre · Sheppard, Mullin, Richter & Hampton · http://www.sheppardmullin.com · 650 Town Center Drive, Fourth Floor · Costa Mesa, CA 92626 · 714-513-5100

Ellen R. Marshall · Manatt, Phelps & Phillips · Park Tower, 14th Floor · 695 Town Center Drive · Costa Mesa, CA 92626 · 714-371-2500

East Palo Alto

Craig M. Tighe · DLA Piper · 2000 University Avenue · East Palo Alto, CA 94303-2214 · 650-833-2000

Dennis B. Arnold · ⑩ · Gibson, Dunn & Crutcher · 333 South Grand Avenue · Los Angeles, CA 90071-3197 · 213-229-7000

Gordon M. Bava · ⑩ · Manatt, Phelps & Phillips · 11355 West Olympic Boulevard · Los Angeles, CA 90064 · 310-312-4000

Alan G. Benjamin · Orrick, Herrington & Sutcliffe · 777 South Figueroa Street, Suite 3200 · Los Angeles, CA 90017-5855 · 213-629-2020

John D. Berchild, Jr. · Sheppard, Mullin, Richter & Hampton · http://www.sheppardmullin.com · 333 South Hope Street, 48th Floor · Los Angeles, CA 90071-1448 · 213-620-1780

T. Hale Boggs · ⑩ · Manatt, Phelps & Phillips · 11355 West Olympic Boulevard · Los Angeles, CA 90064 310-312-4000

Anthony R. Callobre · Bingham McCutchen · http://www.bingham.com · 355 South Grand Avenue, Suite 4400 · Los Angeles, CA 90071-3106 · 213-680-6400

Robert C. Colton · Buchalter Nemer · 1000 Wilshire Boulevard, Suite 1500 · Los Angeles, CA 90017-2457 · 213-891-0700

Gene R. Elerding · ⑩ · Manatt, Phelps & Phillips · 11355 West Olympic Boulevard · Los Angeles, CA 90064 · 310-312-4000

Stanley F. Farrar · ⑩ · Sullivan & Cromwell · 1888 Century Park East, 21st Floor · Los Angeles, CA 90067-1725 · 310-712-6600

Hydee R. Feldstein · Sullivan & Cromwell · 1888 Century Park East, 21st Floor · Los Angeles, CA 90067-1725 · 310-712-6600

Edwin F. Feo · ⑩ · Milbank, Tweed, Hadley & McCloy · http://www.milbank.com · 601 South Figueroa Street, 30th Floor · Los Angeles, CA 90017-5735 · 213-892-4000

Henry M. Fields · ⑩ · Morrison & Foerster · http://www.mofo.com · 555 West Fifth Street, Suite 3500 · Los Angeles, CA 90013-1024 · 213-892-5200

Barry V. Freeman · Jeffer, Mangels, Butler & Marmaro · 1900 Avenue of the Stars, Seventh Floor · Los Angeles, CA 90067-4308 · 310-203-8080

Joseph Gabai · Morrison & Foerster · http://www.mofo.com · 555 West Fifth Street, Suite 3500 · Los Angeles, CA 90013-1024 · 213-892-5200

T. J. Grasmick · Manatt, Phelps & Phillips · 11355 West Olympic Boulevard · Los Angeles, CA 90064 · 310-312-4000

John Francis Hilson · ⑩ · Paul Hastings · 515 South Flower Street, 25th Floor · Los Angeles, CA 90071 · 213-683-6000

Paul H. Irving · ⑩ · Manatt, Phelps & Phillips · 11355 West Olympic Boulevard · Los Angeles, CA 90064 310-312-4000

John M. Jameson · Latham & Watkins · 355 South Grand Avenue · Los Angeles, CA 90071-1560 · 213-485-1234

Kathryn I. Johnstone · Morrison & Foerster · http://www.mofo.com · 555 West Fifth Street, Suite 3500 · Los Angeles, CA 90013-1024 · 213-892-5200

Brian D. Kilb · Gibson, Dunn & Crutcher · 2029 Century Park East, 40th Floor · Los Angeles, CA 90067-3026 · 310-552-8500

Matthew T. Kirby · ⑩ · O'Melveny & Myers · 400 South Hope Street, 10th Floor · Los Angeles, CA 90071-2899 · 213-430-6000

Warren R. Loui · Mayer Brown · 350 South Grand Avenue, 25th Floor · Los Angeles, CA 90071-1503 · 213-229-9500

David J. McCarty · Sheppard, Mullin, Richter & Hampton · http://www.sheppardmullin.com · 333 South Hope Street, 48th Floor · Los Angeles, CA 90071-1448 · 213-620-1780

Frederick B. McLane · ⑩ · O'Melveny & Myers · 1999 Avenue of the Stars, Seventh Floor · Los Angeles, CA 90067-6035 · 310-553-6700

John E. Mendez · Latham & Watkins · 355 South Grand Avenue · Los Angeles, CA 90071-1560 · 213-485-1234

Brian E. Newhouse · Mayer Brown · 350 South Grand Avenue, 25th Floor · Los Angeles, CA 90071-1503 213-229-9500

Christine M. Olsen · ⑩ · O'Melveny & Myers · 400 South Hope Street, 10th Floor · Los Angeles, CA 90071-2899 · 213-430-6000

Thomas D. Phelps · ⑩ · Manatt, Phelps & Phillips · 11355 West Olympic Boulevard · Los Angeles, CA 90064 · 310-312-4000

William T. Quicksilver · ⑩ · Manatt, Phelps & Phillips · 11355 West Olympic Boulevard · Los Angeles, CA 90064 · 310-312-4000

Harold P. Reichwald · Manatt, Phelps & Phillips · 11355 West Olympic Boulevard · Los Angeles, CA 90064 · 310-312-4000

Gary B. Rosenbaum · McDermott Will & Emery · 2049 Century Park East, 38th Floor · Los Angeles, CA 90067-3218 · 310-277-4110

Mary B. Ruhl · Latham & Watkins · 355 South Grand Avenue · Los Angeles, CA 90071-1560 · 213-485-1234

Neil W. Rust · White & Case · http://www.whitecase.com · 633 West Fifth Street, Suite 1900 · Los Angeles, CA 90071-2007 · 213-620-7700

Gary D. Samson · McGuireWoods · http://www.mcguirewoods.com · 1800 Century Park East, Eighth Floor · Los Angeles, CA 90067 · 310-315-8200

Harry C. Sigman · ⑩ · Harry C. Sigman · P.O. Box 67608 · Los Angeles, CA 90067-0608 · 310-277-2247

Pauline M. Stevens · Morrison & Foerster · http://www.mofo.com · 555 West Fifth Street, Suite 3500 · Los Angeles, CA 90013-1024 · 213-892-5200

William P. Wade · ⑩ · K&L Gates · 10100 Santa Monica Boulevard, Seventh Floor · Los Angeles, CA 90067 · 310-552-5000

Charles E. Washburn, Jr. · ⑩ · Manatt, Phelps & Phillips · 11355 West Olympic Boulevard · Los Angeles, CA 90064 · 310-312-4000

Steven O. Weise · ⑩ · Heller Ehrman · 333 South Hope Street, 39th Floor · Los Angeles, CA 90071-1406 213-689-0200

Donna J. Zenor · Morrison & Foerster · http://www.mofo.com · 555 West Fifth Street, Suite 3500 · Los Angeles, CA 90013-1024 · 213-892-5200

San Diego

Kurt L. Kicklighter · Luce, Forward, Hamilton & Scripps · http://www.luce.com · 600 West Broadway, Suite 2600 · San Diego, CA 92101 · 619-236-1414

San Francisco

Barry A. Abbott · Howard, Rice, Nemerovski, Canady, Falk & Rabkin · Three Embarcadero Center, Seventh Floor · San Francisco, CA 94111-4024 · 415-434-1600

Roland E. Brandel · ⑩ · Morrison & Foerster · http://www.mofo.com · 425 Market Street · San Francisco, CA 94105-2482 · 415-268-7000

Peter H. Carson · Bingham McCutchen · http://www.bingham.com · Three Embarcadero Center · San Francisco, CA 94111-4067 · 415-393-2000

Thomas Y. Coleman · Orrick, Herrington & Sutcliffe · The Orrick Building · 405 Howard Street · San Francisco, CA 94105-2669 · 415-773-5700

G. Larry Engel · Morrison & Foerster · http://www.mofo.com · 425 Market Street · San Francisco, CA 94105-2482 · 415-268-7000

Kevin B. Fisher · Paul Hastings · 55 Second Street, 24th Floor · San Francisco, CA 94105 · 415-856-7000

George P. Haley · Pillsbury Winthrop Shaw Pittman · http://www.pillsburylaw.com · 50 Fremont Street · P.O. Box 7880 · San Francisco, CA 94120-7880 · 415-983-1000

William L. Harvey · Winston & Strawn · 101 California Street, 39th Floor · San Francisco, CA 94111-5802 · 415-591-1000

George A. Hisert · ⑩ · Bingham McCutchen · http://www.bingham.com · Three Embarcadero Center · San Francisco, CA 94111-4067 · 415-393-2000

F. Daniel Leventhal · Morrison & Foerster · http://www.mofo.com · 425 Market Street · San Francisco, CA 94105-2482 · 415-268-7000

Pamela J. Martinson · Bingham McCutchen · http://www.bingham.com · Three Embarcadero Center · San Francisco, CA 94111-4067 · 415-393-2000

Jill Matichak · O'Melveny & Myers · Embarcadero Center West · 275 Battery Street · San Francisco, CA 94111-3305 · 415-984-8700

Rodney R. Peck · ⑩ · Pillsbury Winthrop Shaw Pittman · http://www.pillsburylaw.com · 50 Fremont Street · P.O. Box 7880 · San Francisco, CA 94120-7880 · 415-983-1000

Denis T. Rice · ⑳ · Howard, Rice, Nemerovski, Canady, Falk & Rabkin · Three Embarcadero Center, Seventh Floor · San Francisco, CA 94111-4024 · 415-434-1600

James M. Rockett · Bingham McCutchen · http://www.bingham.com · Three Embarcadero Center · San Francisco, CA 94111-4067 · 415-393-2000

Joseph A. Scherer · Cooley Godward Kronish · 101 California Street, Fifth Floor · San Francisco, CA 94111-5800 · 415-693-2000

Dennis M. Talbott · ⑩ · Severson & Werson · One Embarcadero Center, Suite 2600 · San Francisco, CA 94111 · 415-398-3344

Maureen A. Young · Bingham McCutchen · http://www.bingham.com · Three Embarcadero Center · San Francisco, CA 94111-4067 · 415-393-2000

Robert Alan Zadek · Buchalter Nemer · 333 Market Street, 25th Floor · San Francisco, CA 94105-2102 · 415-227-0900

Walnut Creek

Karl Geier · Miller, Starr & Regalia · 1331 North California Boulevard, Fifth Floor · P.O. Box 8177 · Walnut Creek, CA 94596 · 925-935-9400

BANKRUPTCY AND CREDITOR-DEBTOR RIGHTS LAW

Aptos

Alan D. Pedlar · ⑩ · The Law Office of Alan Pedlar · 1112 Via Malibu · Aptos, CA 95003 · 831-688-2667

Calabasas

David Gould · David Gould · 23801 Calabasas Road, Suite 2032 · Calabasas, CA 91302 · 818-222-8092

Costa Mesa

Alan H. Martin · Sheppard, Mullin, Richter & Hampton · http://www.sheppardmullin.com · 650 Town Center Drive, Fourth Floor · Costa Mesa, CA 92626 · 714-513-5100

Cupertino

Janice M. Murray · Murray & Murray · 19400 Stevens Creek Boulevard, Suite 200 · Cupertino, CA 95014-2548 · 650-852-9000

John Walshe Murray · ⑩ · Murray & Murray · 19400 Stevens Creek Boulevard, Suite 200 · Cupertino, CA 95014-2548 · 650-852-9000

Irvine

Oscar Garza · Gibson, Dunn & Crutcher · 3161 Michelson Drive · Irvine, CA 92612-4412 · 949-451-3800

Ronald Rus · Rus, Miliband & Smith · Citicorp Plaza, Seventh Floor · 2600 Michelson Drive · Irvine, CA 92612 · 949-752-7100

Nanette D. Sanders · Ringstad & Sanders · 2030 Main Street, Suite 1200 · Irvine, CA 92614 · 949-851-7450

Lafayette

Andrea A. Wirum · ⑩ · Andrea Wirum · P.O. Box 1108 · Lafayette, CA 94549 · 415-294-7710

Los Angeles

Dennis B. Arnold · ⑩ · Gibson, Dunn & Crutcher · 333 South Grand Avenue · Los Angeles, CA 90071-3197 · 213-229-7000

Edward T. Attanasio · Klee, Tuchin, Bogdanoff & Stern · 1919 Avenue of the Stars, 39th Floor · Los Angeles, CA 90067-6049 · 310-407-4000

Bruce Bennett · ⑩ · Hennigan, Bennett & Dorman · 865 South Figueroa Street, Suite 2900 · Los Angeles, CA 90017 · 213-694-1200

Lee R. Bogdanoff · Klee, Tuchin, Bogdanoff & Stern · 1919 Avenue of the Stars, 39th Floor · Los Angeles, CA 90067-6049 · 310-407-4000

Gregory A. Bray · Milbank, Tweed, Hadley & McCloy · http://www.milbank.com · 601 South Figueroa Street, 30th Floor · Los Angeles, CA 90017-5735 · 213-892-4000

Richard W. Brunette, Jr. · Sheppard, Mullin, Richter & Hampton · http://www.sheppardmullin.com · 333 South Hope Street, 48th Floor · Los Angeles, CA 90071-1448 · 213-620-1780

Daniel J. Bussel · Klee, Tuchin, Bogdanoff & Stern · 1919 Avenue of the Stars, 39th Floor · Los Angeles, CA 90067-6049 · 310-407-4000

Marc S. Cohen · ⑩ · Kaye Scholer · 1999 Avenue of the Stars, Suite 1700 · Los Angeles, CA 90067-6048 · 310-788-1000

Jeffrey H. Davidson · Stutman, Treister & Glatt · 1901 Avenue of the Stars, 12th Floor · Los Angeles, CA 90067 · 310-228-5600

Peter A. Davidson · Moldo Davidson Fraioli Seror & Sestanovich · 2029 Century Park East, 21st Floor · Los Angeles, CA 90067 · 310-551-3100

Van C. Durrer II · Skadden, Arps, Slate, Meagher & Flom · 300 South Grand Avenue, Suite 3400 · Los Angeles, CA 90071 · 213-687-5000

Richard W. Esterkin · Morgan Lewis & Bockius · 300 South Grand Avenue, 22nd Floor · Los Angeles, CA 90071-3132 · 213-612-2500

Ronald L. Fein · ㉕ · RL Fein · 1901 Avenue of The Stars, 12th Floor · Los Angeles, CA 90067 · 310-228-5780

Alan M. Feld · Manatt, Phelps & Phillips · 11355 West Olympic Boulevard · Los Angeles, CA 90064 · 310-312-4000

Hydee R. Feldstein · Sullivan & Cromwell · 1888 Century Park East, 21st Floor · Los Angeles, CA 90067-1725 · 310-712-6600

Peter Gilhuly · Latham & Watkins · 355 South Grand Avenue · Los Angeles, CA 90071-1560 · 213-485-1234

Herman L. Glatt · ㉕ · Stutman, Treister & Glatt · 1901 Avenue of the Stars, 12th Floor · Los Angeles, CA 90067 · 310-228-5600

Brad R. Godshall · Pachulski, Stang, Ziehl, Young, Jones & Weintraub · 10100 Santa Monica Boulevard, Suite 1100 · Los Angeles, CA 90067-4100 · 310-277-6910

Eric D. Goldberg · Stutman, Treister & Glatt · 1901 Avenue of the Stars, 12th Floor · Los Angeles, CA 90067 · 310-228-5600

Robert A. Greenfield · ⑩ · Stutman, Treister & Glatt · 1901 Avenue of the Stars, 12th Floor · Los Angeles, CA 90067 · 310-228-5600

Richard W. Havel · ⑩ · Sidley Austin · 555 West Fifth Street, 40th Floor · Los Angeles, CA 90013 · 213-896-6000

Milton B. Hyman · ⑩ · Irell & Manella · 1800 Avenue of the Stars, Suite 900 · Los Angeles, CA 90067-4276 · 310-277-1010

Robbin L. Itkin · Steptoe & Johnson · http://www.steptoe.com · 2121 Avenue of the Stars, Suite 2800 · Los Angeles, CA 90067 · 310-734-3200

Evan M. Jones · O'Melveny & Myers · 400 South Hope Street, 10th Floor · Los Angeles, CA 90071-2899 213-430-6000

Ivan L. Kallick · Manatt, Phelps & Phillips · 11355 West Olympic Boulevard · Los Angeles, CA 90064 · 310-312-4000

Eve H. Karasik · Stutman, Treister & Glatt · 1901 Avenue of the Stars, 12th Floor · Los Angeles, CA 90067 · 310-228-5600

Matthew T. Kirby · ⑩ · O'Melveny & Myers · 400 South Hope Street, 10th Floor · Los Angeles, CA 90071-2899 · 213-430-6000

Gary E. Klausner · Stutman, Treister & Glatt · 1901 Avenue of the Stars, 12th Floor · Los Angeles, CA 90067 · 310-228-5600

Kenneth N. Klee · ⑳ · Klee, Tuchin, Bogdanoff & Stern · 1919 Avenue of the Stars, 39th Floor · Los Angeles, CA 90067-6049 · 310-407-4000

Robert A. Klyman · Latham & Watkins · 355 South Grand Avenue · Los Angeles, CA 90071-1560 · 213-485-1234

Jeffrey C. Krause · Stutman, Treister & Glatt · 1901 Avenue of the Stars, 12th Floor · Los Angeles, CA 90067 · 310-228-5600

Thomas R. Kreller · Milbank, Tweed, Hadley & McCloy · http://www.milbank.com · 601 South Figueroa Street, 30th Floor · Los Angeles, CA 90017-5735 · 213-892-4000

Mette H. Kurth · Sheppard, Mullin, Richter & Hampton · http://www.sheppardmullin.com · 1901 Avenue of the Stars, Suite 1600 · Los Angeles, CA 90067 · 310-228-3700

Ben H. Logan III · ⑩ · O'Melveny & Myers · 400 South Hope Street, 10th Floor · Los Angeles, CA 90071-2899 · 213-430-6000

Michael S. Lurey · ⑳ · Latham & Watkins · 355 South Grand Avenue · Los Angeles, CA 90071-1560 · 213-485-1234

Ralph R. Mabey · ⑳ · Stutman, Treister & Glatt · 1901 Avenue of the Stars, 12th Floor · Los Angeles, CA 90067 · 310-228-5600

David J. McCarty · Sheppard, Mullin, Richter & Hampton · http://www.sheppardmullin.com · 333 South Hope Street, 48th Floor · Los Angeles, CA 90071-1448 · 213-620-1780

Frank A. Merola · Stutman, Treister & Glatt · 1901 Avenue of the Stars, 12th Floor · Los Angeles, CA 90067 · 310-228-5600

Byron Z. Moldo · Moldo Davidson Fraioli Seror & Sestanovich · 2029 Century Park East, 21st Floor · Los Angeles, CA 90067 · 310-551-3100

Robert J. Moore · ⑩ · Milbank, Tweed, Hadley & McCloy · http://www.milbank.com · 601 South Figueroa Street, 30th Floor · Los Angeles, CA 90017-5735 · 213-892-4000

Sally S. Neely · ⑩ · Sidley Austin · 555 West Fifth Street, 40th Floor · Los Angeles, CA 90013 · 213-896-6000

Isaac M. Pachulski · ⑩ · Stutman, Treister & Glatt · 1901 Avenue of the Stars, 12th Floor · Los Angeles, CA 90067 · 310-228-5600

Richard M. Pachulski · ⑩ · Pachulski, Stang, Ziehl, Young, Jones & Weintraub · 10100 Santa Monica Boulevard, Suite 1100 · Los Angeles, CA 90067-4100 · 310-277-6910

Thomas E. Patterson · Klee, Tuchin, Bogdanoff & Stern · 1919 Avenue of the Stars, 39th Floor · Los Angeles, CA 90067-6049 · 310-407-4000

Lawrence Peitzman · ㉕ · Peitzman, Weg & Kempinsky · 10100 Santa Monica Boulevard, Suite 1450 · Los Angeles, CA 90067 · 310-552-3100

Richard T. Peters · ⑳ · Sidley Austin · 555 West Fifth Street, 40th Floor · Los Angeles, CA 90013 · 213-896-6000

Stephan M. Ray · Stutman, Treister & Glatt · 1901 Avenue of the Stars, 12th Floor · Los Angeles, CA 90067 · 310-228-5600

Eric E. Sagerman · Winston & Strawn · 333 South Grand Avenue, 38th Floor · Los Angeles, CA 90071-1543 · 213-615-1700

David Seror · Moldo Davidson Fraioli Seror & Sestanovich · 2029 Century Park East, 21st Floor · Los Angeles, CA 90067 · 310-551-3100

K. John Shaffer · Stutman, Treister & Glatt · 1901 Avenue of the Stars, 12th Floor · Los Angeles, CA 90067 · 310-228-5600

Mark Shinderman · Munger, Tolles & Olson · 355 South Grand Avenue, 35th Floor · Los Angeles, CA 90071-1560 · 213-683-9100

David P. Simonds · Akin Gump Strauss Hauer & Feld · 2029 Century Park East, Suite 2400 · Los Angeles, CA 90067-3012 · 310-229-1000

David M. Stern · ⑩ · Klee, Tuchin, Bogdanoff & Stern · 1919 Avenue of the Stars, 39th Floor · Los Angeles, CA 90067-6049 · 310-407-4000

Michael L. Tuchin · Klee, Tuchin, Bogdanoff & Stern · 1919 Avenue of the Stars, 39th Floor · Los Angeles, CA 90067-6049 · 310-407-4000

Mark S. Wallace · Stutman, Treister & Glatt · 1901 Avenue of the Stars, 12th Floor · Los Angeles, CA 90067 · 310-228-5600

Stephen H. Warren · O'Melveny & Myers · 400 South Hope Street, 10th Floor · Los Angeles, CA 90071-2899 · 213-430-6000

George C. Webster II · Stutman, Treister & Glatt · 1901 Avenue of the Stars, 12th Floor · Los Angeles, CA 90067 · 310-228-5600

Howard J. Weg · ⑩ · Peitzman, Weg & Kempinsky · 10100 Santa Monica Boulevard, Suite 1450 · Los Angeles, CA 90067 · 310-552-3100

Richard L. Wynne · Kirkland & Ellis · 777 South Figueroa Street, Suite 3400 · Los Angeles, CA 90017-5800 · 213-680-8400

Martin S. Zohn · Proskauer Rose · http://www.proskauer.com · 2049 Century Park East, 32nd Floor · Los Angeles, CA 90067-3206 · 310-557-2900

Newport Beach

Paul J. Couchot · Winthrop Couchot · http://www.winthropcouchot.com · 660 Newport Center Drive, Fourth Floor · Newport Beach, CA 92660 · 949-720-4100

William N. Lobel · Irell & Manella · 840 Newport Center Drive, Suite 400 · Newport Beach, CA 92660-6324 · 949-760-0991

Marc J. Winthrop · ⑩ · Winthrop Couchot · http://www.winthropcouchot.com · 660 Newport Center Drive, Fourth Floor · Newport Beach, CA 92660 · 949-720-4100

Oakland

Michael D. Cooper · Wendel, Rosen, Black & Dean · 1111 Broadway, 24th Floor · P.O. Box 2047 · Oakland, CA 94604-2047 · 510-834-6600

Sacramento

Steven H. Felderstein · ⑳ · Felderstein Fitzgerald Willoughby & Pascuzzi · http://www.ffwplaw.com · The Wells Fargo Center, Suite 1450 · 400 Capitol Mall · Sacramento, CA 95814-4434 · 916-329-7400

Donald W. Fitzgerald · Felderstein Fitzgerald Willoughby & Pascuzzi · http://www.ffwplaw.com · The Wells Fargo Center, Suite 1450 · 400 Capitol Mall · Sacramento, CA 95814-4434 · 916-329-7400

R. Dale Ginter · Downey Brand · 555 Capitol Mall, 10th Floor · Sacramento, CA 95814 · 916-444-1000

Marc A. Levinson · ⑩ · Orrick, Herrington & Sutcliffe · 400 Capitol Mall, Suite 3000 · Sacramento, CA 95814-4497 · 916-447-9200

Paul J. Pascuzzi · Felderstein Fitzgerald Willoughby & Pascuzzi · http://www.ffwplaw.com · The Wells Fargo Center, Suite 1450 · 400 Capitol Mall · Sacramento, CA 95814-4434 · 916-329-7400

Thomas A. Willoughby · Felderstein Fitzgerald Willoughby & Pascuzzi · http://www.ffwplaw.com · The Wells Fargo Center, Suite 1450 · 400 Capitol Mall · Sacramento, CA 95814-4434 · 916-329-7400

San Diego

Michael T. Andrew · ⑩ · Luce, Forward, Hamilton & Scripps · http://www.luce.com · 600 West Broadway, Suite 2600 · San Diego, CA 92101 · 619-236-1414

Mikel R. Bistrow · ⑩ · Duane Morris · 101 West Broadway, Suite 900 · San Diego, CA 92101-8285 · 619-744-2200

Jeffry A. Davis · ⑩ · Mintz, Levin, Cohn, Ferris, Glovsky and Popeo · 3580 Carmel Mountain Road, Suite 300 · San Diego, CA 92130 · 858-314-1500

Margaret M. Mann · Sheppard, Mullin, Richter & Hampton · http://www.sheppardmullin.com · 501 West Broadway, 19th Floor · San Diego, CA 92101 · 619-338-6500

David L. Osias · ⑩ · Allen Matkins Leck Gamble Mallory & Natsis · 501 West Broadway, 15th Floor · San Diego, CA 92101-3541 · 619-233-1155

Victor A. Vilaplana · ⑩ · Foley & Lardner · 402 West Broadway, Suite 2100 · San Diego, CA 92101 · 619-234-6655

Dennis J. Wickham · Seltzer Caplan McMahon Vitek · Symphony Towers, Suite 2100 · 750 B Street · San Diego, CA 92101 · 619-685-3003

San Francisco

Michael H. Ahrens · ⑩ · Sheppard, Mullin, Richter & Hampton · http://www.sheppardmullin.com · Four Embarcadero Center, 17th Floor · San Francisco, CA 94111 · 415-434-9100

Peter J. Benvenutti · ⑳ · Heller Ehrman · 333 Bush Street · San Francisco, CA 94104-2878 · 415-772-6000

Peter G. Bertrand · Buchalter Nemer · 333 Market Street, 25th Floor · San Francisco, CA 94105-2102 · 415-227-0900

Robert L. Eisenbach III · Cooley Godward Kronish · 101 California Street, Fifth Floor · San Francisco, CA 94111-5800 · 415-693-2000

G. Larry Engel · ⑩ · Morrison & Foerster · http://www.mofo.com · 425 Market Street · San Francisco, CA 94105-2482 · 415-268-7000

Ellen A. Friedman · Friedman Dumas & Springwater · 150 Spear Street, Suite 1600 · San Francisco, CA 94105 · 415-834-3800

Debra J. Grassgreen · Pachulski, Stang, Ziehl, Young, Jones & Weintraub · 150 California Street, 15th Floor · San Francisco, CA 94111-4500 · 415-263-7000

Frederick D. Holden, Jr. · ⑳ · Orrick, Herrington & Sutcliffe · The Orrick Building · 405 Howard Street San Francisco, CA 94105-2669 · 415-773-5700

Michael A. Isaacs · Luce, Forward, Hamilton & Scripps · http://www.luce.com · 121 Spear Street, Suite 200 · San Francisco, CA 94105-1582 · 415-356-4600

Robert E. Izmirian · ㉕ · Buchalter Nemer · 333 Market Street, 25th Floor · San Francisco, CA 94105-2102 · 415-227-0900

J. Michael Kelly · Cooley Godward Kronish · 101 California Street, Fifth Floor · San Francisco, CA 94111-5800 · 415-693-2000

Henry C. Kevane · Pachulski, Stang, Ziehl, Young, Jones & Weintraub · 150 California Street, 15th Floor San Francisco, CA 94111-4500 · 415-263-7000

William J. Lafferty · Howard, Rice, Nemerovski, Canady, Falk & Rabkin · Three Embarcadero Center, Seventh Floor · San Francisco, CA 94111-4024 · 415-434-1600

Adam A. Lewis · Morrison & Foerster · http://www.mofo.com · 425 Market Street · San Francisco, CA 94105-2482 · 415-268-7000

James L. Lopes · ⑳ · Howard, Rice, Nemerovski, Canady, Falk & Rabkin · Three Embarcadero Center, Seventh Floor · San Francisco, CA 94111-4024 · 415-434-1600

Charles P. Maher · Luce, Forward, Hamilton & Scripps · http://www.luce.com · 121 Spear Street, Suite 200 · San Francisco, CA 94105-1582 · 415-356-4600

Merle C. Meyers · Meyers Law Group · 44 Montgomery Street, Suite 1010 · San Francisco, CA 94104 · 415-362-7500

Randy E. Michelson · Randy E. Michelson · 746 Fourth Avenue · San Francisco, CA 94118 · 415-407-8100

Patrick A. Murphy · ㉕ · Winston & Strawn · 101 California Street, 39th Floor · San Francisco, CA 94111-5802 · 415-591-1000

Ron M. Oliner · Duane Morris · Spear Tower, Suite 2000 · One Market · San Francisco, CA 94105-1104 · 415-957-3000

Andrea T. Porter · ⑩ · Friedman Dumas & Springwater · 150 Spear Street, Suite 1600 · San Francisco, CA 94105 · 415-834-3800

Randy Rogers · Winston & Strawn · 101 California Street, 39th Floor · San Francisco, CA 94111-5802 · 415-591-1000

Harvey S. Schochet · Davis Wright Tremaine · 505 Montgomery Street, Suite 800 · San Francisco, CA 94111-6533 · 415-276-6500

Michael St. James · St. James Law · http://www.stjames-law.com · 155 Montgomery Street, Suite 1004 · San Francisco, CA 94104 · 415-391-7566

Suzzanne S. Uhland · O'Melveny & Myers · Embarcadero Center West · 275 Battery Street · San Francisco, CA 94111-3305 · 415-984-8700

Philip S. Warden · ⑳ · Pillsbury Winthrop Shaw Pittman · http://www.pillsburylaw.com · 50 Fremont Street · P.O. Box 7880 · San Francisco, CA 94120-7880 · 415-983-1000

San Jose

Bernard S. Greenfield · ⑩ · McGrane Greenfield · 40 South Market Street, Seventh Floor · San Jose, CA 95113 · 408-995-5600

Santa Barbara

Joel R. Ohlgren · ⑩ · Sheppard, Mullin, Richter & Hampton · http://www.sheppardmullin.com · 1111 Chapala Street, Third Floor · Santa Barbara, CA 93101 · 805-879-1800

Santa Monica

Michael H. Goldstein · Greenberg Traurig · http://www.gtlaw.com · 2450 Colorado Avenue, Suite 400-E · Santa Monica, CA 90404 · 310-586-7700

BET-THE-COMPANY LITIGATION

Burlingame

Joseph W. Cotchett · ⑩ · Cotchett, Pitre & McCarthy · San Francisco Airport Office Center, Suite 200 · 840 Malcolm Road · Burlingame, CA 94010 · 650-697-6000

Los Angeles

Maxwell M. Blecher · ⑩ · Blecher & Collins · 515 South Figueroa Street, 17th Floor · Los Angeles, CA 90071 · 213-622-4222

Brad D. Brian · ⑩ · Munger, Tolles & Olson · 355 South Grand Avenue, 35th Floor · Los Angeles, CA 90071-1560 · 213-683-9100

Hillel Chodos · ⑩ · Hillel Chodos · 1559 South Sepulveda Boulevard · Los Angeles, CA 90025 · 310-473-8666

Morgan Chu · ⑩ · Irell & Manella · 1800 Avenue of the Stars, Suite 900 · Los Angeles, CA 90067-4276 · 310-277-1010

Robert E. Cooper · ⑩ · Gibson, Dunn & Crutcher · 333 South Grand Avenue · Los Angeles, CA 90071-3197 · 213-229-7000

Larry R. Feldman · ⑩ · Kaye Scholer · 1999 Avenue of the Stars, Suite 1700 · Los Angeles, CA 90067-6048 · 310-788-1000

Irving H. Greines · ⑩ · Greines, Martin, Stein & Richland · 5900 Wilshire Boulevard, 12th Floor · Los Angeles, CA 90036 · 310-859-7811

J. Michael Hennigan · Hennigan, Bennett & Dorman · 865 South Figueroa Street, Suite 2900 · Los Angeles, CA 90017 · 213-694-1200

Seth M. Hufstedler · ⑳ · Morrison & Foerster · http://www.mofo.com · 555 West Fifth Street, Suite 3500 Los Angeles, CA 90013-1024 · 213-892-5200

Shirley M. Hufstedler · ⑩ · Morrison & Foerster · http://www.mofo.com · 555 West Fifth Street, Suite 3500 · Los Angeles, CA 90013-1024 · 213-892-5200

Thomas J. Nolan · Skadden, Arps, Slate, Meagher & Flom · 300 South Grand Avenue, Suite 3400 · Los Angeles, CA 90071 · 213-687-5000

Ronald L. Olson · ⑳ · Munger, Tolles & Olson · 355 South Grand Avenue, 35th Floor · Los Angeles, CA 90071-1560 · 213-683-9100

John J. Quinn · ⑩ · JAMS · 707 Wilshire Boulevard, 46th Floor · Los Angeles, CA 90017 · 213-620-1133

Palo Alto

Boris Feldman · ⑩ · Wilson Sonsini Goodrich & Rosati · 650 Page Mill Road · Palo Alto, CA 94304-1050 · 650-493-9300

Redwood Shores

Robert P. Feldman · Quinn Emanuel Urquhart Oliver & Hedges · 555 Twin Dolphin Drive, Suite 560 · Redwood Shores, CA 94065 · 650-801-5000

San Diego

Robert S. Brewer, Jr. · ⑩ · McKenna Long & Aldridge · Symphony Towers, Suite 3300 · 750 B Street · San Diego, CA 92101-8105 · 619-595-5400

Gerald L. McMahon · ⑩ · Seltzer Caplan McMahon Vitek · Symphony Towers, Suite 2100 · 750 B Street San Diego, CA 92101 · 619-685-3003

David J. Noonan · ⑩ · Kirby, Noonan, Lance & Hoge · 350 Tenth Avenue, Suite 1300 · San Diego, CA 92101-8700 · 619-231-8666

Don G. Rushing · Morrison & Foerster · http://www.mofo.com · 12531 High Bluff Drive, Suite 100 · San Diego, CA 92130-2040 · 858-720-5100

Reginald A. Vitek · ⑩ · Seltzer Caplan McMahon Vitek · Symphony Towers, Suite 2100 · 750 B Street · San Diego, CA 92101 · 619-685-3003

Michael J. Weaver · ⑩ · Latham & Watkins · 600 West Broadway, Suite 1800 · San Diego, CA 92101-3375 · 619-236-1234

San Francisco

Jeffrey L. Bleich · Munger, Tolles & Olson · 560 Mission Street, 27th Floor · San Francisco, CA 94105-9781 · 415-512-4000

Daniel Bookin · ⑩ · O'Melveny & Myers · Embarcadero Center West · 275 Battery Street · San Francisco, CA 94111-3305 · 415-984-8700

James J. Brosnahan · ㉕ · Morrison & Foerster · http://www.mofo.com · 425 Market Street · San Francisco, CA 94105-2482 · 415-268-7000

Kevin J. Dunne · ⑩ · Sedgwick, Detert, Moran & Arnold · Steuart Tower, Eighth Floor · One Market Plaza · San Francisco, CA 94105 · 415-781-7900

Jerome B. Falk, Jr. · ㉕ · Howard, Rice, Nemerovski, Canady, Falk & Rabkin · Three Embarcadero Center, Seventh Floor · San Francisco, CA 94111-4024 · 415-434-1600

Melvin R. Goldman · ⑳ · Morrison & Foerster · http://www.mofo.com · 425 Market Street · San Francisco, CA 94105-2482 · 415-268-7000

John W. Keker · ㉕ · Keker & Van Nest · http://www.kvn.com · 710 Sansome Street · San Francisco, CA 94111 · 415-391-5400

Raoul D. Kennedy · ⑳ · Skadden, Arps, Slate, Meagher & Flom · Four Embarcadero Center, Suite 3800 · San Francisco, CA 94111 · 415-984-6400

Jack W. Londen · Morrison & Foerster · http://www.mofo.com · 425 Market Street · San Francisco, CA 94105-2482 · 415-268-7000

M. Laurence Popofsky · ⑳ · Orrick, Herrington & Sutcliffe · The Orrick Building · 405 Howard Street · San Francisco, CA 94105-2669 · 415-773-5700

Douglas M. Schwab · ⑩ · Hogan & Hartson · Four Embarcadero Center, 22nd Floor · San Francisco, CA 94111 · 415-519-5312

Robert A. Van Nest · Keker & Van Nest · http://www.kvn.com · 710 Sansome Street · San Francisco, CA 94111 · 415-391-5400

Santa Monica

Marshall B. Grossman · ⑩ · Bingham McCutchen · http://www.bingham.com · The Water Garden, Fourth Floor · 1620 Twenty-Sixth Street · Santa Monica, CA 90404-4060 · 310-907-1000

BIOTECHNOLOGY LAW

East Palo Alto

Bruce W. Jenett · DLA Piper · 2000 University Avenue · East Palo Alto, CA 94303-2214 · 650-833-2000

Alan Kalin · Bingham McCutchen · http://www.bingham.com · 1900 University Avenue · East Palo Alto, CA 94303-2223 · 650-849-4400

Menlo Park

Michael W. Hall · Latham & Watkins · 140 Scott Drive · Menlo Park, CA 94025 · 650-328-4600

Alan C. Mendelson · ⑩ · Latham & Watkins · 140 Scott Drive · Menlo Park, CA 94025 · 650-328-4600

Mountain View

Ann M. Caviani Pease · Dechert · 2440 West El Camino Real, Suite 700 · Mountain View, CA 94040-1499 · 650-813-4800

Palo Alto

Laura A. Berezin · Cooley Godward Kronish · 3175 Hanover Street · Palo Alto, CA 94304-1130 · 650-843-5000

Thomas E. Ciotti · ⑩ · Morrison & Foerster · http://www.mofo.com · 755 Page Mill Road · Palo Alto, CA 94304-1018 · 650-813-5600

Kenneth A. Clark · Wilson Sonsini Goodrich & Rosati · 650 Page Mill Road · Palo Alto, CA 94304-1050 · 650-493-9300

William Gaede · McDermott Will & Emery · 3150 Porter Drive · Palo Alto, CA 94304-1212 · 650-813-5000

Suzanne S. Hooper · Cooley Godward Kronish · 3175 Hanover Street · Palo Alto, CA 94304-1130 · 650-843-5000

Robert L. Jones · Cooley Godward Kronish · 3175 Hanover Street · Palo Alto, CA 94304-1130 · 650-843-5000

Barbara Kosacz · Cooley Godward Kronish · 3175 Hanover Street · Palo Alto, CA 94304-1130 · 650-843-5000

J. Casey McGlynn · Wilson Sonsini Goodrich & Rosati · 650 Page Mill Road · Palo Alto, CA 94304-1050 · 650-493-9300

Glen Y. Sato · Cooley Godward Kronish · 3175 Hanover Street · Palo Alto, CA 94304-1130 · 650-843-5000

San Diego

Gregg I. Anderson · ⑩ · Knobbe, Martens, Olson & Bear · 550 West C Street, Suite 1200 · San Diego, CA 92101 · 619-235-8550

L. Kay Chandler · Cooley Godward Kronish · 4401 Eastgate Mall · San Diego, CA 92121-1909 · 858-550-6000

Peng Chen · Morrison & Foerster · http://www.mofo.com · 12531 High Bluff Drive, Suite 100 · San Diego, CA 92130-2040 · 858-720-5100

Thomas A. Coll · Cooley Godward Kronish · 4401 Eastgate Mall · San Diego, CA 92121-1909 · 858-550-6000

Lisa A. Haile · DLA Piper · 4365 Executive Drive, Suite 1100 · San Diego, CA 92121-2133 · 858-677-1400

Anthony M. Insogna · Jones Day · 12265 El Camino Real, Suite 200 · San Diego, CA 92130-4096 · 858-314-1200

Richard A. Kaufman · Heller Ehrman · 4350 La Jolla Village Drive, Seventh Floor · San Diego, CA 92122-1246 · 858-450-8400

Kate H. Murashige · ⑩ · Morrison & Foerster · http://www.mofo.com · 12531 High Bluff Drive, Suite 100 San Diego, CA 92130-2040 · 858-720-5100

Frederick T. Muto · ⑩ · Cooley Godward Kronish · 4401 Eastgate Mall · San Diego, CA 92121-1909 · 858-550-6000

Faye H. Russell · Latham & Watkins · 12636 High Bluff Drive, Suite 400 · San Diego, CA 92130 · 858-523-5400

Mark R. Wicker · Morrison & Foerster · http://www.mofo.com · 12531 High Bluff Drive, Suite 100 · San Diego, CA 92130-2040 · 858-720-5100

San Francisco

Jonathan S. Dickstein · Morrison & Foerster · http://www.mofo.com · 425 Market Street · San Francisco, CA 94105-2482 · 415-268-7000

James C. Snipes · Covington & Burling · One Front Street · San Francisco, CA 94111-5356 · 415-591-6000

Thomas E. Sparks, Jr. · ⑩ · Pillsbury Winthrop Shaw Pittman · http://www.pillsburylaw.com · 50 Fremont Street · P.O. Box 7880 · San Francisco, CA 94120-7880 · 415-983-1000

San Marcos

Cathryn Campbell · Needle & Rosenberg · 950 Boardwalk, Suite 201 · San Marcos, CA 92078-2600 · 760-916-1150

CIVIL RIGHTS LAW

Oakland

Barry Goldstein · Goldstein, Demchak, Baller, Borgen & Dardarian · 300 Lakeside Drive, Suite 1000 · Oakland, CA 94612-3534 · 510-763-9800

San Diego

Michael R. Marrinan · Law Office of Michael R. Marrinan · 614 Fifth Avenue, Suite D · San Diego, CA 92101 · 619-238-6900

COLLABORATIVE LAW: FAMILY LAW

Los Angeles

Frederick J. Glassman · Mayer & Glassman · 12400 Wilshire Boulevard, Suite 400 · Los Angeles, CA 90025 · 310-207-0007

COMMERCIAL LITIGATION

Berkeley

Victoria J. De Goff · De Goff and Sherman · 1916 Los Angeles Avenue · Berkeley, CA 94707 · 510-524-1840

Beverly Hills

Allan Browne · ⑩ · Dreier Stein Kahan Browne Woods George · 450 North Roxbury Drive, Seventh Floor · Beverly Hills, CA 90210-4231 · 310-274-7100

Anthony M. Glassman · Glassman, Browning & Saltsman · 360 North Bedford Drive, Suite 204 · Beverly Hills, CA 90210-5157 · 310-278-5100

Edward A. Woods · Dreier Stein Kahan Browne Woods George · 450 North Roxbury Drive, Seventh Floor · Beverly Hills, CA 90210-4231 · 310-274-7100

Burlingame

Joseph W. Cotchett · ⑩ · Cotchett, Pitre & McCarthy · San Francisco Airport Office Center, Suite 200 · 840 Malcolm Road · Burlingame, CA 94010 · 650-697-6000

Claremont

Herbert Hafif · ⑩ · Herbert Hafif · 269 West Bonita Avenue · Claremont, CA 91711-4784 · 909-624-1671

Costa Mesa

Glenn Dassoff · Paul Hastings · 695 Town Center Drive, 17th Floor · Costa Mesa, CA 92626 · 714-668-6200

Robert J. Gibson · Snell & Wilmer · 600 Anton Boulevard, Suite 1400 · Costa Mesa, CA 92626-7689 · 714-427-7000

Steven Graham · Snell & Wilmer · 600 Anton Boulevard, Suite 1400 · Costa Mesa, CA 92626-7689 · 714-427-7000

Michael T. Hornak · Rutan & Tucker · http://www.rutan.com · 611 Anton Boulevard, Suite 1400 · P.O. Box 1950 · Costa Mesa, CA 92628-1950 · 714-641-5100

John B. Hurlbut, Jr. · Rutan & Tucker · http://www.rutan.com · 611 Anton Boulevard, Suite 1400 · P.O. Box 1950 · Costa Mesa, CA 92628-1950 · 714-641-5100

Donald L. Morrow · ⑩ · Paul Hastings · 695 Town Center Drive, 17th Floor · Costa Mesa, CA 92626 · 714-668-6200

William S. O'Hare · Snell & Wilmer · 600 Anton Boulevard, Suite 1400 · Costa Mesa, CA 92626-7689 · 714-427-7000

Thomas J. Umberg · Manatt, Phelps & Phillips · Park Tower, 14th Floor · 695 Town Center Drive · Costa Mesa, CA 92626 · 714-371-2500

Dean J. Zipser · Manatt, Phelps & Phillips · Park Tower, 14th Floor · 695 Town Center Drive · Costa Mesa, CA 92626 · 714-371-2500

East Palo Alto

Paul Alexander · Howrey · 1950 University Avenue, Fourth Floor · East Palo Alto, CA 94303 · 650-798-3555

William J. Goines · Greenberg Traurig · http://www.gtlaw.com · 1900 University Avenue, Fifth Floor · East Palo Alto, CA 94303 · 650-328-8500

Elk Grove

John E. Cassinat · Cassinat Law Corporation · 4815 Laguna Park Drive, Suite C · Elk Grove, CA 95758 · 916-393-3030

Encino

Ellis J. Horvitz · ⑩ · Horvitz & Levy · 15760 Ventura Boulevard, 18th Floor · Encino, CA 91436-3000 · 818-995-0800

Barry R. Levy · Horvitz & Levy · 15760 Ventura Boulevard, 18th Floor · Encino, CA 91436-3000 · 818-995-0800

Irvine

Martha K. Gooding · Howrey · Four Park Plaza, Suite 1700 · Irvine, CA 92614 · 949-721-6900

William B. Grenner · K&L Gates · 1900 Main Street, Suite 600 · Irvine, CA 92614-7319 · 949-253-0900

Stuart P. Jasper · Jasper & Jasper · 19800 MacArthur Boulevard, Suite 860 · Irvine, CA 92612-2493 · 949-756-1560

Thomas R. Malcolm · ⑩ · Jones Day · Three Park Plaza, Suite 1100 · Irvine, CA 92614-2592 · 949-851-3939

Robert Palmer · Gibson, Dunn & Crutcher · 3161 Michelson Drive · Irvine, CA 92612-4412 · 949-451-3800

Kathleen O. Peterson · K&L Gates · 1900 Main Street, Suite 600 · Irvine, CA 92614-7319 · 949-253-0900

Daniel L. Rasmussen · Payne & Fears · Jamboree Center, Suite 1100 · Four Park Plaza · Irvine, CA 92614 · 949-851-1100

Steven P. Rice · Crowell & Moring · Three Park Plaza, 20th Floor · Irvine, CA 92614-8505 · 949-263-8400

Richard S. Ruben · Jones Day · Three Park Plaza, Suite 1100 · Irvine, CA 92614-2592 · 949-851-3939

Wayne W. Smith · Gibson, Dunn & Crutcher · 3161 Michelson Drive · Irvine, CA 92612-4412 · 949-451-3800

Jeffrey T. Thomas · Gibson, Dunn & Crutcher · 3161 Michelson Drive · Irvine, CA 92612-4412 · 949-451-3800

Meryl L. Young · Gibson, Dunn & Crutcher · 3161 Michelson Drive · Irvine, CA 92612-4412 · 949-451-3800

Long Beach

Samuel A. Keesal, Jr. · ⑩ · Keesal, Young & Logan · 400 Oceangate · P.O. Box 1730 · Long Beach, CA 90801-1730 · 562-436-2000

Scott T. Pratt · Keesal, Young & Logan · 400 Oceangate · P.O. Box 1730 · Long Beach, CA 90801-1730 · 562-436-2000

Terry Ross · Keesal, Young & Logan · 400 Oceangate · P.O. Box 1730 · Long Beach, CA 90801-1730 · 562-436-2000

Thomas G. Stolpman · ⑳ · Stolpman, Krissman, Elber & Silver · 111 West Ocean Boulevard, 19th Floor · Long Beach, CA 90802 · 562-435-8300

J. Stephen Young · Keesal, Young & Logan · 400 Oceangate · P.O. Box 1730 · Long Beach, CA 90801-1730 · 562-436-2000

Los Angeles

Seth Aronson · O'Melveny & Myers · 400 South Hope Street, 10th Floor · Los Angeles, CA 90071-2899 · 213-430-6000

James Asperger · O'Melveny & Myers · 400 South Hope Street, 10th Floor · Los Angeles, CA 90071-2899 · 213-430-6000

Jane H. Barrett · Morrison & Foerster · http://www.mofo.com · 555 West Fifth Street, Suite 3500 · Los Angeles, CA 90013-1024 · 213-892-5200

Maxwell M. Blecher · ⑩ · Blecher & Collins · 515 South Figueroa Street, 17th Floor · Los Angeles, CA 90071 · 213-622-4222

Brad D. Brian · ⑩ · Munger, Tolles & Olson · 355 South Grand Avenue, 35th Floor · Los Angeles, CA 90071-1560 · 213-683-9100

James H. Broderick, Jr. · Squire Sanders · http://www.ssd.com · 555 South Flower Street, 31st Floor · Los Angeles, CA 90071-2300 · 213-624-2500

Anthony S. Castanares · Stutman, Treister & Glatt · 1901 Avenue of the Stars, 12th Floor · Los Angeles, CA 90067 · 310-228-5600

Patrick A. Cathcart · Adorno & Yoss · 633 West Fifth Street, Suite 1150 · Los Angeles, CA 90071 · 213-229-2400

Hillel Chodos · ⑩ · Hillel Chodos · 1559 South Sepulveda Boulevard · Los Angeles, CA 90025 · 310-473-8666

Morgan Chu · ⑩ · Irell & Manella · 1800 Avenue of the Stars, Suite 900 · Los Angeles, CA 90067-4276 · 310-277-1010

Andrew S. Clare · Loeb & Loeb · 10100 Santa Monica Boulevard, Suite 2200 · Los Angeles, CA 90067-4164 · 310-282-2000

Robert E. Cooper · ⑩ · Gibson, Dunn & Crutcher · 333 South Grand Avenue · Los Angeles, CA 90071-3197 · 213-229-7000

James E. Curry · Sheppard, Mullin, Richter & Hampton · http://www.sheppardmullin.com · 1901 Avenue of the Stars, Suite 1600 · Los Angeles, CA 90067 · 310-228-3700

Jeffrey S. Davidson · Kirkland & Ellis · 777 South Figueroa Street, Suite 3400 · Los Angeles, CA 90017-5800 · 213-680-8400

Craig J. de Recat · Manatt, Phelps & Phillips · 11355 West Olympic Boulevard · Los Angeles, CA 90064 310-312-4000

Jack P. Dicanio · Skadden, Arps, Slate, Meagher & Flom · 300 South Grand Avenue, Suite 3400 · Los Angeles, CA 90071 · 213-687-5000

Peter Brown Dolan · ⑳ · The Dolan Law Firm · Citigroup Center, Suite 1750 · 444 South Flower Street · Los Angeles, CA 90071-2924 · 213-689-0333

John A. Donovan · Skadden, Arps, Slate, Meagher & Flom · 300 South Grand Avenue, Suite 3400 · Los Angeles, CA 90071 · 213-687-5000

Helen L. Duncan · Fulbright & Jaworski · http://www.fulbright.com · 555 South Flower Street, 41st Floor Los Angeles, CA 90071 · 213-892-9200

Bonnie E. Eskenazi · Greenberg Glusker · 1900 Avenue of the Stars, 21st Floor · Los Angeles, CA 90067 310-553-3610

Larry R. Feldman · ⑩ · Kaye Scholer · 1999 Avenue of the Stars, Suite 1700 · Los Angeles, CA 90067-6048 · 310-788-1000

Robert W. Fischer, Jr. · Fulbright & Jaworski · http://www.fulbright.com · 555 South Flower Street, 41st Floor · Los Angeles, CA 90071 · 213-892-9200

Alan E. Friedman · Jones Day · 555 South Flower Street, 50th Floor · Los Angeles, CA 90071 · 213-489-3939

Harvey R. Friedman · Greenberg Glusker · 1900 Avenue of the Stars, 21st Floor · Los Angeles, CA 90067 · 310-553-3610

Arthur N. Greenberg · Greenberg Glusker · 1900 Avenue of the Stars, 21st Floor · Los Angeles, CA 90067 · 310-553-3610

Michael A. Greene · Greenberg Glusker · 1900 Avenue of the Stars, 21st Floor · Los Angeles, CA 90067 · 310-553-3610

Raymond E. Hane III · Waller Lansden Dortch & Davis · http://www.wallerlaw.com · 333 South Grand Avenue, Suite 1800 · Los Angeles, CA 90071 · 213-362-3680

Kenneth R. Heitz · Irell & Manella · 1800 Avenue of the Stars, Suite 900 · Los Angeles, CA 90067-4276 · 310-277-1010

J. Michael Hennigan · Hennigan, Bennett & Dorman · 865 South Figueroa Street, Suite 2900 · Los Angeles, CA 90017 · 213-694-1200

Mark C. Holscher · Kirkland & Ellis · 777 South Figueroa Street, Suite 3400 · Los Angeles, CA 90017-5800 · 213-680-8400

Seth M. Hufstedler · ⑳ · Morrison & Foerster · http://www.mofo.com · 555 West Fifth Street, Suite 3500 Los Angeles, CA 90013-1024 · 213-892-5200

Shirley M. Hufstedler · ⑩ · Morrison & Foerster · http://www.mofo.com · 555 West Fifth Street, Suite 3500 · Los Angeles, CA 90013-1024 · 213-892-5200

Chad S. Hummel · Manatt, Phelps & Phillips · 11355 West Olympic Boulevard · Los Angeles, CA 90064 310-312-4000

Laurence J. Hutt · Arnold & Porter · 777 South Figueroa Street, 44th Floor · Los Angeles, CA 90017-5844 · 213-243-4000

Andrei Iancu · Irell & Manella · 1800 Avenue of the Stars, Suite 900 · Los Angeles, CA 90067-4276 · 310-277-1010

Michael C. Kelley · Sidley Austin · 555 West Fifth Street, 40th Floor · Los Angeles, CA 90013 · 213-896-6000

Patrick M. Kelly · Wilson Elser Moskowitz Edelman & Dicker · 555 South Flower Street, Suite 2900 · Los Angeles, CA 90071-2407 · 213-443-5100

Richard B. Kendall · Irell & Manella · 1800 Avenue of the Stars, Suite 900 · Los Angeles, CA 90067-4276 310-277-1010

Dennis E. Kinnaird · ㉕ · Foley & Lardner · 555 South Flower Street, Suite 3500 · Los Angeles, CA 90071-2300 · 213-972-4500

Gail E. Lees · Gibson, Dunn & Crutcher · 333 South Grand Avenue · Los Angeles, CA 90071-3197 · 213-229-7000

Norman Levine · Greenberg Glusker · 1900 Avenue of the Stars, 21st Floor · Los Angeles, CA 90067 · 310-553-3610

Gregory A. Long · Sheppard, Mullin, Richter & Hampton · http://www.sheppardmullin.com · 333 South Hope Street, 48th Floor · Los Angeles, CA 90071-1448 · 213-620-1780

Brian C. Lysaght · ⑩ · Christensen, Glaser, Fink, Jacobs, Weil & Shapiro · 10250 Constellation Boulevard, 19th Floor · Los Angeles, CA 90067 · 310-553-3000

Richard R. Mainland · Fulbright & Jaworski · http://www.fulbright.com · 555 South Flower Street, 41st Floor · Los Angeles, CA 90071 · 213-892-9200

Robert P. Mallory · McDermott Will & Emery · 2049 Century Park East, 38th Floor · Los Angeles, CA 90067-3218 · 310-277-4110

Robert E. Mangels · Jeffer, Mangels, Butler & Marmaro · 1900 Avenue of the Stars, Seventh Floor · Los Angeles, CA 90067-4308 · 310-203-8080

Steven A. Marenberg · Irell & Manella · 1800 Avenue of the Stars, Suite 900 · Los Angeles, CA 90067-4276 · 310-277-1010

Marc Marmaro · Jeffer, Mangels, Butler & Marmaro · 1900 Avenue of the Stars, Seventh Floor · Los Angeles, CA 90067-4308 · 310-203-8080

Richard Marmaro · Skadden, Arps, Slate, Meagher & Flom · 300 South Grand Avenue, Suite 3400 · Los Angeles, CA 90071 · 213-687-5000

Peter H. Mason · Fulbright & Jaworski · http://www.fulbright.com · 555 South Flower Street, 41st Floor · Los Angeles, CA 90071 · 213-892-9200

Alejandro Mayorkas · O'Melveny & Myers · 1999 Avenue of the Stars, Seventh Floor · Los Angeles, CA 90067-6035 · 310-553-6700

Anthony Murray · ⑩ · Loeb & Loeb · 10100 Santa Monica Boulevard, Suite 2200 · Los Angeles, CA 90067-4164 · 310-282-2000

Mark A. Neubauer · Steptoe & Johnson · http://www.steptoe.com · 2121 Avenue of the Stars, Suite 2800 · Los Angeles, CA 90067 · 310-734-3200

Thomas J. Nolan · Skadden, Arps, Slate, Meagher & Flom · 300 South Grand Avenue, Suite 3400 · Los Angeles, CA 90071 · 213-687-5000

Kevin O'Connell · ⑩ · Manatt, Phelps & Phillips · 11355 West Olympic Boulevard · Los Angeles, CA 90064 · 310-312-4000

Michael J. O'Connor · White O'Connor Fink & Brenner · 10100 Santa Monica Boulevard, Suite 2300 · Los Angeles, CA 90067 · 310-712-6100

Pierce O'Donnell · ⑩ · O'Donnell & Shaeffer · 550 South Hope Street, Suite 1000 · Los Angeles, CA 90071-2627 · 213-347-0290

Ronald L. Olson · ⑳ · Munger, Tolles & Olson · 355 South Grand Avenue, 35th Floor · Los Angeles, CA 90071-1560 · 213-683-9100

Ronald M. Oster · Paul Hastings · 515 South Flower Street, 25th Floor · Los Angeles, CA 90071 · 213-683-6000

Peter I. Ostroff · Sidley Austin · 555 West Fifth Street, 40th Floor · Los Angeles, CA 90013 · 213-896-6000

Charles E. Patterson · Morrison & Foerster · http://www.mofo.com · 555 West Fifth Street, Suite 3500 · Los Angeles, CA 90013-1024 · 213-892-5200

Daniel Petrocelli · O'Melveny & Myers · 1999 Avenue of the Stars, Seventh Floor · Los Angeles, CA 90067-6035 · 310-553-6700

Debra E. Pole · Sidley Austin · 555 West Fifth Street, 40th Floor · Los Angeles, CA 90013 · 213-896-6000

Glenn Pomerantz · Munger, Tolles & Olson · 355 South Grand Avenue, 35th Floor · Los Angeles, CA 90071-1560 · 213-683-9100

John B. Quinn · Quinn Emanuel Urquhart Oliver & Hedges · 865 South Figueroa Street, 10th Floor · Los Angeles, CA 90017 · 213-443-3000

John J. Quinn · ⑩ · JAMS · 707 Wilshire Boulevard, 46th Floor · Los Angeles, CA 90017 · 213-620-1133

Miles N. Ruthberg · Latham & Watkins · 355 South Grand Avenue · Los Angeles, CA 90071-1560 · 213-485-1234

Robert A. Sacks · Sullivan & Cromwell · 1888 Century Park East, 21st Floor · Los Angeles, CA 90067-1725 · 310-712-6600

Charles H. Samel · Latham & Watkins · 355 South Grand Avenue · Los Angeles, CA 90071-1560 · 213-485-1234

Robert S. Schulman · Fulbright & Jaworski · http://www.fulbright.com · 555 South Flower Street, 41st Floor · Los Angeles, CA 90071 · 213-892-9200

Peter S. Selvin · Loeb & Loeb · 10100 Santa Monica Boulevard, Suite 2200 · Los Angeles, CA 90067-4164 · 310-282-2000

Michael A. Sherman · Bingham McCutchen · http://www.bingham.com · 355 South Grand Avenue, Suite 4400 · Los Angeles, CA 90071-3106 · 213-680-6400

Henry Shields, Jr. · Irell & Manella · 1800 Avenue of the Stars, Suite 900 · Los Angeles, CA 90067-4276 · 310-277-1010

David Siegel · Irell & Manella · 1800 Avenue of the Stars, Suite 900 · Los Angeles, CA 90067-4276 · 310-277-1010

Lawrence Silver · ⑩ · Silver & Field · 11150 West Olympic Boulevard, Suite 980 · Los Angeles, CA 90025 · 310-477-7640

John W. Spiegel · Munger, Tolles & Olson · 355 South Grand Avenue, 35th Floor · Los Angeles, CA 90071-1560 · 213-683-9100

Kenneth W. Starr · Kirkland & Ellis · 777 South Figueroa Street, Suite 3400 · Los Angeles, CA 90017-5800 · 213-680-8400

David M. Stern · ⑩ · Klee, Tuchin, Bogdanoff & Stern · 1919 Avenue of the Stars, 39th Floor · Los Angeles, CA 90067-6049 · 310-407-4000

Gregory P. Stone · ⑩ · Munger, Tolles & Olson · 355 South Grand Avenue, 35th Floor · Los Angeles, CA 90071-1560 · 213-683-9100

William F. Sullivan · Paul Hastings · 515 South Flower Street, 25th Floor · Los Angeles, CA 90071 · 213-683-6000

Peter R. Taft · ⑳ · Munger, Tolles & Olson · 355 South Grand Avenue, 35th Floor · Los Angeles, CA 90071-1560 · 213-683-9100

Douglas L. Thorpe · Douglas L. Thorpe · 1508 Old Oak Road · Los Angeles, CA 90049-2504 · 310-230-9556

A. William Urquhart · Quinn Emanuel Urquhart Oliver & Hedges · 865 South Figueroa Street, 10th Floor · Los Angeles, CA 90017 · 213-443-3000

Bruce G. Vanyo · ⑳ · Katten Muchin Rosenman · 2029 Century Park East, Suite 2600 · Los Angeles, CA 90067-3012 · 310-788-4400

Eric S. Waxman · Skadden, Arps, Slate, Meagher & Flom · 300 South Grand Avenue, Suite 3400 · Los Angeles, CA 90071 · 213-687-5000

Jeffrey I. Weinberger · Munger, Tolles & Olson · 355 South Grand Avenue, 35th Floor · Los Angeles, CA 90071-1560 · 213-683-9100

Alexander F. Wiles · Irell & Manella · 1800 Avenue of the Stars, Suite 900 · Los Angeles, CA 90067-4276 310-277-1010

Richard T. Williams · Holland & Knight · http://www.hklaw.com · 633 West Fifth Street, 21st Floor · Los Angeles, CA 90071 · 213-896-2400

Marina Del Rey

Stephen A. Kroft · ⑩ · Stephen A. Kroft · 4807 Roma Court · Marina Del Rey, CA 90292 · 310-822-4024

Menlo Park

Paul H. Dawes · ⑩ · Latham & Watkins · 140 Scott Drive · Menlo Park, CA 94025 · 650-328-4600

Mission Viejo

Maureen E. Callahan · Borchard & Callahan · 25909 Pala, Suite 300 · Mission Viejo, CA 92691 · 949-457-9505

Mountain View

Susan S. Muck · Fenwick & West · Silicon Valley Center · 801 California Street · Mountain View, CA 94041-2008 · 650-988-8500

Newport Beach

Alan J. Droste · King Parret & Droste · 450 Newport Center Drive, Suite 500 · Newport Beach, CA 92660 · 949-644-3400

Andra Barmash Greene · Irell & Manella · 840 Newport Center Drive, Suite 400 · Newport Beach, CA 92660-6324 · 949-760-0991

Marc S. Maister · Irell & Manella · 840 Newport Center Drive, Suite 400 · Newport Beach, CA 92660-6324 · 949-760-0991

Richard M. Sherman, Jr. · Irell & Manella · 840 Newport Center Drive, Suite 400 · Newport Beach, CA 92660-6324 · 949-760-0991

Michael G. Yoder · O'Melveny & Myers · 610 Newport Center Drive, 17th Floor · Newport Beach, CA 92660 · 949-760-9600

Oakland

Stephen G. Blitch · Reed Smith · 1999 Harrison Street, Suite 2400 · P.O. Box 2084 · Oakland, CA 94604-3572 · 510-763-2000

Palo Alto

Norman J. Blears · Hogan & Hartson · 525 University Avenue, Second Floor · Palo Alto, CA 94301 · 415-244-8684

John W. Clark · ⑩ · John W. Clark · 2600 El Camino Real, Suite 410 · Palo Alto, CA 94306 · 650-354-3605

Donald M. Falk · Mayer Brown · Two Palo Alto Square, Suite 300 · 3000 El Camino Real · Palo Alto, CA 94306-2112 · 650-331-2000

Boris Feldman · ⑩ · Wilson Sonsini Goodrich & Rosati · 650 Page Mill Road · Palo Alto, CA 94304-1050 · 650-493-9300

Nicki F. Locker · Wilson Sonsini Goodrich & Rosati · 650 Page Mill Road · Palo Alto, CA 94304-1050 · 650-493-9300

Stephen C. Neal · ⑩ · Cooley Godward Kronish · Five Palo Alto Square · 3000 El Camino Real · Palo Alto, CA 94306-2155 · 650-843-5000

Darryl P. Rains · Morrison & Foerster · http://www.mofo.com · 755 Page Mill Road · Palo Alto, CA 94304-1018 · 650-813-5600

Steven M. Schatz · ⑩ · Wilson Sonsini Goodrich & Rosati · 650 Page Mill Road · Palo Alto, CA 94304-1050 · 650-493-9300

David S. Steuer · Wilson Sonsini Goodrich & Rosati · 650 Page Mill Road · Palo Alto, CA 94304-1050 · 650-493-9300

Rancho Palos Verdes

Donald C. Smaltz · ⑳ · Spiegel Liao & Kagay · 3323 Crownview Drive · Rancho Palos Verdes, CA 90275 310-514-3444

Redwood Shores

Robert P. Feldman · Quinn Emanuel Urquhart Oliver & Hedges · 555 Twin Dolphin Drive, Suite 560 · Redwood Shores, CA 94065 · 650-801-5000

Robert T. Haslam · Covington & Burling · 333 Twin Dolphin Drive, Suite 700 · Redwood Shores, CA 94065-1418 · 650-632-4700

Riverside

Terry D. Bridges · ⑩ · Reid & Hellyer · 3880 Lemon Street, Fifth Floor · P.O. Box 1300 · Riverside, CA 92502-1300 · 951-682-1771

David G. Moore · ⑩ · Reid & Hellyer · 3880 Lemon Street, Fifth Floor · P.O. Box 1300 · Riverside, CA 92502-1300 · 951-682-1771

Sacramento

Dale C. Campbell · Weintraub Genshlea Chediak · 400 Capitol Mall, 11th Floor · Sacramento, CA 95814-4407 · 916-558-6000

Kathleen Finnerty · Greenberg Traurig · http://www.gtlaw.com · 1201 K Street, Suite 1100 · Sacramento, CA 95814 · 916-442-1111

Edward P. Freidberg · ⑩ · Freidberg & Parker · 650 University Avenue, Suite 205 · Sacramento, CA 95825 · 916-929-9060

Joseph S. Genshlea · ⑩ · Weintraub Genshlea Chediak · 400 Capitol Mall, 11th Floor · Sacramento, CA 95814-4407 · 916-558-6000

Stephen L. Goff · McDonough Holland & Allen · http://www.mhalaw.com · 555 Capitol Mall, Ninth Floor · Sacramento, CA 95814-4692 · 916-444-3900

Stephen J. Meyer · Downey Brand · 555 Capitol Mall, 10th Floor · Sacramento, CA 95814 · 916-444-1000

David A. Riegels · David A. Riegels, Attorney at Law · 4208 H Street · P.O. Box 19579 · Sacramento, CA 95819-0579 · 916-739-0988

Charles J. Stevens · ⑩ · Stevens & O'Connell · 400 Capitol Mall, Suite 1400 · Sacramento, CA 95814-4498 · 916-329-9111

San Diego

Eric M. Acker · Morrison & Foerster · http://www.mofo.com · 12531 High Bluff Drive, Suite 100 · San Diego, CA 92130-2040 · 858-720-5100

John Allcock · ⑩ · DLA Piper · 401 B Street, Suite 1700 · San Diego, CA 92101-4297 · 619-699-2700

Michael Attanasio · Cooley Godward Kronish · 4401 Eastgate Mall · San Diego, CA 92121-1909 · 858-550-6000

Charles A. Bird · Luce, Forward, Hamilton & Scripps · http://www.luce.com · 600 West Broadway, Suite 2600 · San Diego, CA 92101 · 619-236-1414

William S. Boggs · DLA Piper · 401 B Street, Suite 1700 · San Diego, CA 92101-4297 · 619-699-2700

Robert S. Brewer, Jr. · ⑩ · McKenna Long & Aldridge · Symphony Towers, Suite 3300 · 750 B Street · San Diego, CA 92101-8105 · 619-595-5400

Juanita R. Brooks · ⑳ · Fish & Richardson · 12390 El Camino Real · San Diego, CA 92130 · 858-678-5070

Robert W. Brownlie · DLA Piper · 401 B Street, Suite 1700 · San Diego, CA 92101-4297 · 619-699-2700

Douglas M. Butz · ⑩ · Butz, Dunn, DeSantis & Bingham · 101 West Broadway, Suite 1700 · San Diego, CA 92101-8289 · 619-233-4777

Edward D. Chapin · ⑳ · Chapin Wheeler · http://www.chapinwheeler.com · 550 West C Street, Suite 2000 · San Diego, CA 92101 · 619-241-4810

Luke R. Corbett · ⑩ · Butz, Dunn, DeSantis & Bingham · 101 West Broadway, Suite 1700 · San Diego, CA 92101-8289 · 619-233-4777

Charles H. Dick, Jr. · ⑩ · Baker & McKenzie · 12544 High Bluff Drive, Third Floor · San Diego, CA 92130-3051 · 858-523-6200

Donald A. English · English & Gloven · 550 West C Street, Suite 1800 · San Diego, CA 92101 · 619-338-6610

Koji Fukumura · Cooley Godward Kronish · 4401 Eastgate Mall · San Diego, CA 92121-1909 · 858-550-6000

William E. Grauer · Cooley Godward Kronish · 4401 Eastgate Mall · San Diego, CA 92121-1909 · 858-550-6000

Michael L. Kirby · Kirby, Noonan, Lance & Hoge · 350 Tenth Avenue, Suite 1300 · San Diego, CA 92101-8700 · 619-231-8666

David E. Kleinfeld · Foley & Lardner · 11250 El Camino Real, Suite 200 · San Diego, CA 92130 · 858-847-6700

John H. L'Estrange · Wright & L'Estrange · 401 West A Street, Suite 2250 · San Diego, CA 92101-8103 · 619-231-4844

Daniel G. Lamb, Jr. · Pillsbury Winthrop Shaw Pittman · http://www.pillsburylaw.com · 501 West Broadway, Suite 1100 · San Diego, CA 92101-3575 · 619-234-5000

Harvey R. Levine · ⑳ · Levine, Steinberg, Miller & Huver · 550 West C Street, Suite 1810 · San Diego, CA 92101-8596 · 619-231-9449

John F. McGuire, Jr. · ⑳ · Thorsnes Bartolotta McGuire · http://www.tbmlawyers.com · 2550 Fifth Avenue, 11th Floor · San Diego, CA 92103 · 619-236-9363

Gerald L. McMahon · ⑩ · Seltzer Caplan McMahon Vitek · Symphony Towers, Suite 2100 · 750 B Street San Diego, CA 92101 · 619-685-3003

Cary W. Miller · ⑩ · Hooper, Lundy & Bookman · 101 West Broadway, Suite 1330 · San Diego, CA 92101 · 619-744-7300

David J. Noonan · ⑩ · Kirby, Noonan, Lance & Hoge · 350 Tenth Avenue, Suite 1300 · San Diego, CA 92101-8700 · 619-231-8666

Don G. Rushing · Morrison & Foerster · http://www.mofo.com · 12531 High Bluff Drive, Suite 100 · San Diego, CA 92130-2040 · 858-720-5100

Jeffery M. Shohet · DLA Piper · 401 B Street, Suite 1700 · San Diego, CA 92101-4297 · 619-699-2700

Nancy Stagg · Fish & Richardson · 12390 El Camino Real · San Diego, CA 92130 · 858-678-5070

Robert G. Steiner · ⑳ · Luce, Forward, Hamilton & Scripps · http://www.luce.com · 600 West Broadway, Suite 2600 · San Diego, CA 92101 · 619-236-1414

Anthony M. Stiegler · Cooley Godward Kronish · 4401 Eastgate Mall · San Diego, CA 92121-1909 · 858-550-6000

Steven M. Strauss · Cooley Godward Kronish · 4401 Eastgate Mall · San Diego, CA 92121-1909 · 858-550-6000

Edward Patrick Swan, Jr. · Luce, Forward, Hamilton & Scripps · http://www.luce.com · 600 West Broadway, Suite 2600 · San Diego, CA 92101 · 619-236-1414

Stephen P. Swinton · ⑩ · Latham & Watkins · 600 West Broadway, Suite 1800 · San Diego, CA 92101-3375 · 619-236-1234

Reginald A. Vitek · ⑩ · Seltzer Caplan McMahon Vitek · Symphony Towers, Suite 2100 · 750 B Street · San Diego, CA 92101 · 619-685-3003

Michael J. Weaver · ⑩ · Latham & Watkins · 600 West Broadway, Suite 1800 · San Diego, CA 92101-3375 · 619-236-1234

Shirli Fabbri Weiss · DLA Piper · 401 B Street, Suite 1700 · San Diego, CA 92101-4297 · 619-699-2700

Daniel M. White · 10 · White, Oliver & Amundson · http://www.whiteoliver.com · 550 West C Street, Suite 950 · San Diego, CA 92101-3353 · 619-239-0300

Robert C. Wright · Wright & L'Estrange · 401 West A Street, Suite 2250 · San Diego, CA 92101-8103 · 619-231-4844

San Francisco

Gordon C. Atkinson · 10 · Cooley Godward Kronish · 101 California Street, Fifth Floor · San Francisco, CA 94111-5800 · 415-693-2000

David M. Balabanian · 10 · Bingham McCutchen · http://www.bingham.com · Three Embarcadero Center · San Francisco, CA 94111-4067 · 415-393-2000

Jonathan R. Bass · 10 · Coblentz, Patch, Duffy & Bass · http://www.coblentzlaw.com · One Ferry Building, Suite 200 · San Francisco, CA 94111-4213 · 415-391-4800

James P. Bennett · Morrison & Foerster · http://www.mofo.com · 425 Market Street · San Francisco, CA 94105-2482 · 415-268-7000

Jeffrey L. Bleich · Munger, Tolles & Olson · 560 Mission Street, 27th Floor · San Francisco, CA 94105-9781 · 415-512-4000

Stephen V. Bomse · 10 · Orrick, Herrington & Sutcliffe · The Orrick Building · 405 Howard Street · San Francisco, CA 94105-2669 · 415-773-5700

Daniel Bookin · 10 · O'Melveny & Myers · Embarcadero Center West · 275 Battery Street · San Francisco, CA 94111-3305 · 415-984-8700

James J. Brosnahan · 25 · Morrison & Foerster · http://www.mofo.com · 425 Market Street · San Francisco, CA 94105-2482 · 415-268-7000

Donald W. Brown · Covington & Burling · One Front Street · San Francisco, CA 94111-5356 · 415-591-6000

John L. Cooper · 10 · Farella Braun & Martel · Russ Building, 17th Floor · 235 Montgomery Street · San Francisco, CA 94104 · 415-954-4400

Josef D. Cooper · 20 · Cooper & Kirkham · 655 Montgomery Street, Suite 1700 · San Francisco, CA 94111 · 415-788-3030

Patrick J. Coughlin · Lerach Coughlin Stoia Geller Rudman & Robbins · 100 Pine Street, Suite 2600 · San Francisco, CA 94111 · 415-288-4545

Kevin J. Dunne · 10 · Sedgwick, Detert, Moran & Arnold · Steuart Tower, Eighth Floor · One Market Plaza · San Francisco, CA 94105 · 415-781-7900

Daralyn J. Durie · Keker & Van Nest · http://www.kvn.com · 710 Sansome Street · San Francisco, CA 94111 · 415-391-5400

Jordan Eth · Morrison & Foerster · http://www.mofo.com · 425 Market Street · San Francisco, CA 94105-2482 · 415-268-7000

Jerome B. Falk, Jr. · 25 · Howard, Rice, Nemerovski, Canady, Falk & Rabkin · Three Embarcadero Center, Seventh Floor · San Francisco, CA 94111-4024 · 415-434-1600

Marie L. Fiala · Heller Ehrman · 333 Bush Street · San Francisco, CA 94104-2878 · 415-772-6000

Frederick S. Fields · Coblentz, Patch, Duffy & Bass · http://www.coblentzlaw.com · One Ferry Building, Suite 200 · San Francisco, CA 94111-4213 · 415-391-4800

Paul T. Friedman · Morrison & Foerster · http://www.mofo.com · 425 Market Street · San Francisco, CA 94105-2482 · 415-268-7000

Robert C. Friese · Shartsis Friese · http://www.sflaw.com · One Maritime Plaza, 18th Floor · San Francisco, CA 94111 · 415-421-6500

Melvin R. Goldman · 20 · Morrison & Foerster · http://www.mofo.com · 425 Market Street · San Francisco, CA 94105-2482 · 415-268-7000

Arturo J. González · Morrison & Foerster · http://www.mofo.com · 425 Market Street · San Francisco, CA 94105-2482 · 415-268-7000

Robert A. Goodin · Goodin, MacBride, Squeri, Ritchie & Day · 505 Sansome Street, Suite 900 · San Francisco, CA 94111 · 415-392-7900

Susan J. Harriman · Keker & Van Nest · http://www.kvn.com · 710 Sansome Street · San Francisco, CA 94111 · 415-391-5400

David M. Heilbron · 10 · David M. Heilbron · Three Embarcadero Center · C/O Bingham McCutchen · San Francisco, CA 94111-4067 · 415-393-2177

Richard M. Heimann · Lieff Cabraser Heimann & Bernstein · Embarcadero Center West, Suite 3000 · 275 Battery Street · San Francisco, CA 94111-3339 · 415-956-1000

James L. Hunt · 10 · Bingham McCutchen · http://www.bingham.com · Three Embarcadero Center · San Francisco, CA 94111-4067 · 415-393-2000

Eliot S. Jubelirer · Schiff Hardin · Spear Street Tower, 32nd Floor · One Market · San Francisco, CA 94105 · 415-901-8700

Robert A. Julian · Winston & Strawn · 101 California Street, 39th Floor · San Francisco, CA 94111-5802 · 415-591-1000

John W. Keker · 25 · Keker & Van Nest · http://www.kvn.com · 710 Sansome Street · San Francisco, CA 94111 · 415-391-5400

Raoul D. Kennedy · 20 · Skadden, Arps, Slate, Meagher & Flom · Four Embarcadero Center, Suite 3800 · San Francisco, CA 94111 · 415-984-6400

Rachel Krevans · Morrison & Foerster · http://www.mofo.com · 425 Market Street · San Francisco, CA 94105-2482 · 415-268-7000

Matthew L. Larrabee · Heller Ehrman · 333 Bush Street · San Francisco, CA 94104-2878 · 415-772-6000

Mark A. Lemley · Keker & Van Nest · http://www.kvn.com · 710 Sansome Street · San Francisco, CA 94111 · 415-391-5400

Gregory P. Lindstrom · 10 · Latham & Watkins · 505 Montgomery Street, Suite 2000 · San Francisco, CA 94111-6538 · 415-391-0600

Jan Nielsen Little · Keker & Van Nest · http://www.kvn.com · 710 Sansome Street · San Francisco, CA 94111 · 415-391-5400

Jack W. Londen · Morrison & Foerster · http://www.mofo.com · 425 Market Street · San Francisco, CA 94105-2482 · 415-268-7000

Michael R. Marron · McQuaid Bedford & Van Zandt · 221 Main Street, 16th Floor · San Francisco, CA 94105-1936 · 415-905-0200

Robert A. Mittelstaedt · Jones Day · 555 California Street, 26th Floor · San Francisco, CA 94104 · 415-626-3939

Charles O. Morgan, Jr. · 25 · Law Office of Charles O. Morgan, Jr. · Cathedral Hill Office Building, Suite 333 · 1255 Post Street · San Francisco, CA 94109 · 415-292-8030

James N. Penrod · 10 · Morgan Lewis & Bockius · Spear Street Tower · One Market · San Francisco, CA 94105-1596 · 415-442-1000

Donn P. Pickett · Bingham McCutchen · http://www.bingham.com · Three Embarcadero Center · San Francisco, CA 94111-4067 · 415-393-2000

M. Laurence Popofsky · 20 · Orrick, Herrington & Sutcliffe · The Orrick Building · 405 Howard Street · San Francisco, CA 94105-2669 · 415-773-5700

Robert B. Pringle · Thelen Reid Brown Raysman & Steiner · 101 Second Street, Suite 1800 · San Francisco, CA 94105-3601 · 415-371-1200

Laurence F. Pulgram · Fenwick & West · 555 California Street, 12th Floor · San Francisco, CA 94104 · 415-875-2300

Donald J. Putterman · Kasowitz, Benson, Torres & Friedman · 101 California Street, Suite 2050 · San Francisco, CA 94111 · 415-421-6140

Paul A. Renne · 20 · Cooley Godward Kronish · 101 California Street, Fifth Floor · San Francisco, CA 94111-5800 · 415-693-2000

Denis T. Rice · 20 · Howard, Rice, Nemerovski, Canady, Falk & Rabkin · Three Embarcadero Center, Seventh Floor · San Francisco, CA 94111-4024 · 415-434-1600

John H. Riddle · Nixon Peabody · One Embarcadero Center, 18th Floor · San Francisco, CA 94111-3996 415-984-8200

George A. Riley · O'Melveny & Myers · Embarcadero Center West · 275 Battery Street · San Francisco, CA 94111-3305 · 415-984-8700

Robert A. Rosenfeld · Orrick, Herrington & Sutcliffe · The Orrick Building · 405 Howard Street · San Francisco, CA 94105-2669 · 415-773-5700

Jerome C. Roth · Munger, Tolles & Olson · 560 Mission Street, 27th Floor · San Francisco, CA 94105-9781 · 415-512-4000

Douglas M. Schwab · 10 · Hogan & Hartson · Four Embarcadero Center, 22nd Floor · San Francisco, CA 94111 · 415-519-5312

Richard L. Seabolt · Duane Morris · Spear Tower, Suite 2000 · One Market · San Francisco, CA 94105-1104 · 415-957-3000

Arthur J. Shartsis · 10 · Shartsis Friese · http://www.sflaw.com · One Maritime Plaza, 18th Floor · San Francisco, CA 94111 · 415-421-6500

Bruce L. Simon · Pearson, Simon, Soter, Warshaw & Penny · 44 Montgomery Street, Suite 1430 · San Francisco, CA 94104-4610 · 415-433-9000

Stephen M. Snyder · Snyder Miller & Orton · 111 Sutter Street, Suite 1950 · San Francisco, CA 94104 · 415-962-4400

Jon B. Streeter · Keker & Van Nest · http://www.kvn.com · 710 Sansome Street · San Francisco, CA 94111 · 415-391-5400

Ragesh K. Tangri · Keker & Van Nest · http://www.kvn.com · 710 Sansome Street · San Francisco, CA 94111 · 415-391-5400

Robert W. Tarun · Baker & McKenzie · Two Embarcadero Center, 11th Floor · San Francisco, CA 94111-3802 · 415-576-3000

Robert A. Van Nest · Keker & Van Nest · http://www.kvn.com · 710 Sansome Street · San Francisco, CA 94111 · 415-391-5400

Stephen S. Walters · 10 · Allen Matkins Leck Gamble Mallory & Natsis · Three Embarcadero Center, 12th Floor · San Francisco, CA 94111-4074 · 415-837-1515

Douglas R. Young · 10 · Farella Braun & Martel · Russ Building, 17th Floor · 235 Montgomery Street · San Francisco, CA 94104 · 415-954-4400

Joel Zeldin · Shartsis Friese · http://www.sflaw.com · One Maritime Plaza, 18th Floor · San Francisco, CA 94111 · 415-421-6500

San Jose

Daniel J. Bergeson · Bergeson · http://www.be-law.com · 303 Almaden Boulevard, Suite 500 · San Jose, CA 95110-2712 · 408-291-6200

William Faulkner · McManis Faulkner · http://www.mcmanisfaulkner.com · Fairmont Plaza, 10th Floor · 50 West San Fernando Street · San Jose, CA 95113-2415 · 408-279-8700

Carl L. McConnell · Hoge, Fenton, Jones & Appel · http://www.hogefenton.com · 60 South Market Street, Suite 1400 · San Jose, CA 95113-2396 · 408-287-9501

James McManis · 10 · McManis Faulkner · http://www.mcmanisfaulkner.com · Fairmont Plaza, 10th Floor 50 West San Fernando Street · San Jose, CA 95113-2415 · 408-279-8700

Allen J. Ruby · 20 · Ruby & Schofield · 125 South Market Street, Suite 1001 · San Jose, CA 95113-2285 · 408-998-8500

Jesse F. Ruiz · Robinson & Wood · 227 North First Street · San Jose, CA 95113 · 408-298-7120

Santa Ana

Daniel J. Callahan · Callahan & Blaine · http://www.callahan-law.com · Three Hutton Centre Drive, Ninth Floor · Santa Ana, CA 92707 · 714-241-4444

Santa Barbara

A. Barry Cappello · Cappello & Noël · 831 State Street · Santa Barbara, CA 93101-3227 · 805-564-2444

Thomas G. Foley, Jr. · Foley Bezek Behle & Curtis · 15 West Carrillo Street · Santa Barbara, CA 93101 · 805-962-9495

J. Terry Schwartz · Price, Postel & Parma · 200 East Carrillo Street, Suite 400 · P.O. Box 99 · Santa Barbara, CA 93102-0099 · 805-962-0011

Santa Monica

Bruce A. Friedman · Bingham McCutchen · http://www.bingham.com · The Water Garden, Fourth Floor 1620 Twenty-Sixth Street · Santa Monica, CA 90404-4060 · 310-907-1000

Marshall B. Grossman · ⑩ · Bingham McCutchen · http://www.bingham.com · The Water Garden, Fourth Floor · 1620 Twenty-Sixth Street · Santa Monica, CA 90404-4060 · 310-907-1000

Frank Kaplan · Bingham McCutchen · http://www.bingham.com · The Water Garden, Fourth Floor · 1620 Twenty-Sixth Street · Santa Monica, CA 90404-4060 · 310-907-1000

Dale F. Kinsella · ⑩ · Kinsella Weitzman Iser Kump & Aldisert · http://www.kwikalaw.com · 808 Wilshire Boulevard, Third Floor · Santa Monica, CA 90401 · 310-566-9800

Frank E. Merideth, Jr. · Greenberg Traurig · http://www.gtlaw.com · 2450 Colorado Avenue, Suite 400-E Santa Monica, CA 90404 · 310-586-7700

Gwyn D. Quillen · Bingham McCutchen · http://www.bingham.com · The Water Garden, Fourth Floor · 1620 Twenty-Sixth Street · Santa Monica, CA 90404-4060 · 310-907-1000

Howard L. Weitzman · Kinsella Weitzman Iser Kump & Aldisert · http://www.kwikalaw.com · 808 Wilshire Boulevard, Third Floor · Santa Monica, CA 90401 · 310-566-9800

Santa Rosa

John F. DeMeo · ⑩ · DeMeo DeMeo & West · 565 West College Avenue · Santa Rosa, CA 95401 · 707-545-3232

Patrick W. Emery · Abbey, Weitzenberg, Warren & Emery · 100 Stony Point Road, Suite 200 · P.O. Box 1566 · Santa Rosa, CA 95402-1566 · 707-542-5050

C. Kenneth James, Jr. · C. Kenneth James, Jr. · 476 Hillsdale Drive · Santa Rosa, CA 95409 · 707-539-1794

Michael D. Senneff · Senneff, Freeman & Bluestone · 50 Old Courthouse Square, Suite 401 · P.O. Box 3729 · Santa Rosa, CA 95402 · 707-526-4250

W. Barton Weitzenberg · Abbey, Weitzenberg, Warren & Emery · 100 Stony Point Road, Suite 200 · P.O. Box 1566 · Santa Rosa, CA 95402-1566 · 707-542-5050

Walnut Creek

Richard G. Carlston · Miller, Starr & Regalia · 1331 North California Boulevard, Fifth Floor · P.O. Box 8177 · Walnut Creek, CA 94596 · 925-935-9400

Clement L. Glynn · Glynn & Finley · 100 Pringle Avenue, Suite 500 · Walnut Creek, CA 94596 · 925-210-2800

Eugene H. Miller · Miller, Starr & Regalia · 1331 North California Boulevard, Fifth Floor · P.O. Box 8177 Walnut Creek, CA 94596 · 925-935-9400

Michael P. Verna · Bowles & Verna · 2121 North California Boulevard, Suite 875 · P.O. Box 8180 · Walnut Creek, CA 94596 · 925-935-3300

Westlake Village

Edward M. Medvene · ⑩ · Law Office of Edward M. Medvene · 1014 South Westlake Boulevard, Suite 14-185 · Westlake Village, CA 91361 · 805-497-2788

COMMUNICATIONS LAW

Los Angeles

Henry Weissmann · Munger, Tolles & Olson · 355 South Grand Avenue, 35th Floor · Los Angeles, CA 90071-1560 · 213-683-9100

Oakland

Leon M. Bloomfield · Wilson & Bloomfield · 1901 Harrison Street, Suite 1630 · Oakland, CA 94612 · 510-625-8250

Palo Alto

Earl Nicholas Selby · ⑩ · Law Offices of Earl Nicholas Selby · 418 Florence Street · Palo Alto, CA 94301 650-323-0990

San Francisco

Peter A. Casciato · Peter A. Casciato · 355 Bryant Street, Suite 410 · San Francisco, CA 94107 · 415-291-8661

Michael B. Day · ⑩ · Goodin, MacBride, Squeri, Ritchie & Day · 505 Sansome Street, Suite 900 · San Francisco, CA 94111 · 415-392-7900

Mark Fogelman · Reed Smith · Two Embarcadero Center, Suite 2000 · San Francisco, CA 94111 · 415-543-8700

Thomas J. MacBride, Jr. · ⑩ · Goodin, MacBride, Squeri, Ritchie & Day · 505 Sansome Street, Suite 900 San Francisco, CA 94111 · 415-392-7900

Martin A. Mattes · ⑩ · Nossaman · http://www.nossaman.com · 50 California Street, 34th Floor · San Francisco, CA 94111-4707 · 415-398-3600

James D. Squeri · ⑩ · Goodin, MacBride, Squeri, Ritchie & Day · 505 Sansome Street, Suite 900 · San Francisco, CA 94111 · 415-392-7900

Suzanne K. Toller · Davis Wright Tremaine · 505 Montgomery Street, Suite 800 · San Francisco, CA 94111-6533 · 415-276-6500

Walnut Creek

William H. Booth · ⑩ · William H. Booth · 1500 Newell Avenue, Fifth Floor · Walnut Creek, CA 94596 · 925-296-2460

CONSTRUCTION LAW

El Segundo

Timothy M. Truax · Law Offices of Timothy M. Truax · 222 North Sepulveda Boulevard, Suite 2000 · El Segundo, CA 90245 · 310-662-4755

Irvine

W. Jeffrey Burch · Watt, Tieder, Hoffar & Fitzgerald · http://www.wthf.com · 2040 Main Street, Suite 300 · Irvine, CA 92614 · 949-852-6700

Michael G. Long · Watt, Tieder, Hoffar & Fitzgerald · http://www.wthf.com · 2040 Main Street, Suite 300 Irvine, CA 92614 · 949-852-6700

Los Angeles

Fred G. Bennett · Quinn Emanuel Urquhart Oliver & Hedges · 865 South Figueroa Street, 10th Floor · Los Angeles, CA 90017 · 213-443-3000

Robert J. Cathcart · Allen Matkins Leck Gamble Mallory & Natsis · 515 South Figueroa Street, Ninth Floor · Los Angeles, CA 90071-3398 · 213-622-5555

John B. Clark · Thelen Reid Brown Raysman & Steiner · 333 South Hope Street, Suite 2900 · Los Angeles, CA 90071-3048 · 213-576-8000

David P. Dapper · Akerman Senterfitt · http://www.akerman.com · 725 South Figueroa Street, 38th Floor Los Angeles, CA 90017-5438 · 213-688-9500

Patrick J. Duffy III · Monteleone & McCrory · 725 South Figueroa Street, Suite 3200 · Los Angeles, CA 90017-5446 · 213-612-9900

Harold E. Hamersmith · Sheppard, Mullin, Richter & Hampton · http://www.sheppardmullin.com · 333 South Hope Street, 48th Floor · Los Angeles, CA 90071-1448 · 213-620-1780

Robert L. Ivey · Holland & Knight · http://www.hklaw.com · 633 West Fifth Street, 21st Floor · Los Angeles, CA 90071 · 213-896-2400

Bernard S. Kamine · Kamine Ungerer · http://www.ku-law.com · 523 West Sixth Street, Suite 546 · Los Angeles, CA 90014 · 213-972-0119

Michael F. Minchella · Monteleone & McCrory · 725 South Figueroa Street, Suite 3200 · Los Angeles, CA 90017-5446 · 213-612-9900

Timothy L. Pierce · K&L Gates · 10100 Santa Monica Boulevard, Seventh Floor · Los Angeles, CA 90067 · 310-552-5000

Lawrence Teplin · Cox, Castle & Nicholson · 2049 Century Park East, 28th Floor · Los Angeles, CA 90067 · 310-277-4222

Robert B. Thum · Thelen Reid Brown Raysman & Steiner · 333 South Hope Street, Suite 2900 · Los Angeles, CA 90071-3048 · 213-576-8000

Glenn E. Turner III · Gibbs, Giden, Locher & Turner · 1880 Century Park East, 12th Floor · Los Angeles, CA 90067-1621 · 310-552-3400

Oakland

Roger M. Hughes · Bell, Rosenberg & Hughes · 1300 Clay Street, Suite 1000 · Oakland, CA 94612 · 510-832-8585

Pasadena

Gordon Hunt · Hunt, Ortmann, Blasco, Palffy & Rossell · 301 North Lake Avenue, Seventh Floor · Pasadena, CA 91101 · 626-440-5200

Dale A. Ortmann · Hunt, Ortmann, Blasco, Palffy & Rossell · 301 North Lake Avenue, Seventh Floor · Pasadena, CA 91101 · 626-440-5200

Sacramento

William A. Lichtig · McDonough Holland & Allen · http://www.mhalaw.com · 555 Capitol Mall, Ninth Floor · Sacramento, CA 95814-4692 · 916-444-3900

D. Michael Schoenfeld · Murphy Austin Adams Schoenfeld · http://www.murphyaustin.com · 304 S Street · P.O. Box 1319 · Sacramento, CA 95812-1319 · 916-446-2300

San Diego

Peter J. Ippolito · McKenna Long & Aldridge · Symphony Towers, Suite 3300 · 750 B Street · San Diego, CA 92101-8105 · 619-595-5400

Craig A. Ramseyer · Procopio, Cory, Hargreaves & Savitch · 530 B Street, 21st Floor · San Diego, CA 92101 · 619-238-1900

Steven M. Strauss · Cooley Godward Kronish · 4401 Eastgate Mall · San Diego, CA 92121-1909 · 858-550-6000

San Francisco

Howard William Ashcraft, Jr. · Hanson Bridgett · http://www.hansonbridgett.com · 425 Market Street, 26th Floor · San Francisco, CA 94105 · 415-777-3200

Deborah S. Ballati · Farella Braun & Martel · Russ Building, 17th Floor · 235 Montgomery Street · San Francisco, CA 94104 · 415-954-4400

David Buoncristiani · Thelen Reid Brown Raysman & Steiner · 101 Second Street, Suite 1800 · San Francisco, CA 94105-3601 · 415-371-1200

Alan E. Harris · Farella Braun & Martel · Russ Building, 17th Floor · 235 Montgomery Street · San Francisco, CA 94104 · 415-954-4400

John R. Heisse II · Thelen Reid Brown Raysman & Steiner · 101 Second Street, Suite 1800 · San Francisco, CA 94105-3601 · 415-371-1200

Stephen V. O'Neal · Thelen Reid Brown Raysman & Steiner · 101 Second Street, Suite 1800 · San Francisco, CA 94105-3601 · 415-371-1200

Michael J. Plishner · Bingham McCutchen · http://www.bingham.com · Three Embarcadero Center · San Francisco, CA 94111-4067 · 415-393-2000

Charles M. Sink · Farella Braun & Martel · Russ Building, 17th Floor · 235 Montgomery Street · San Francisco, CA 94104 · 415-954-4400

Jeffrey A. Sykes · Farella Braun & Martel · Russ Building, 17th Floor · 235 Montgomery Street · San Francisco, CA 94104 · 415-954-4400

Stephen Zovickian · Bingham McCutchen · http://www.bingham.com · Three Embarcadero Center · San Francisco, CA 94111-4067 · 415-393-2000

San Jose

Stevan C. Adelman · Miller, Morton, Caillat & Nevis · 25 Metro Drive, Seventh Floor · San Jose, CA 95110 · 408-292-1765

David S. Henningsen · Robinson & Wood · 227 North First Street · San Jose, CA 95113 · 408-298-7120

Frank J. Hughes · Miller, Morton, Caillat & Nevis · 25 Metro Drive, Seventh Floor · San Jose, CA 95110 408-292-1765

Michael D. McSweeney · Hoge, Fenton, Jones & Appel · http://www.hogefenton.com · 60 South Market Street, Suite 1400 · San Jose, CA 95113-2396 · 408-287-9501

Lester G. Sachs · Law Offices of Lester G. Sachs · 1905 The Alameda · San Jose, CA 95126-1428 · 408-296-1988

CORPORATE GOVERNANCE AND COMPLIANCE LAW

Costa Mesa

James J. Scheinkman · Snell & Wilmer · 600 Anton Boulevard, Suite 1400 · Costa Mesa, CA 92626-7689 714-427-7000

East Palo Alto

Diane Holt Frankle · DLA Piper · 2000 University Avenue · East Palo Alto, CA 94303-2214 · 650-833-2000

Irvine

Keith P. Bishop · Allen Matkins Leck Gamble Mallory & Natsis · 1900 Main Street, Fifth Floor · Irvine, CA 92614-7321 · 949-553-1313

Los Angeles

Brad D. Brian · ⑩ · Munger, Tolles & Olson · 355 South Grand Avenue, 35th Floor · Los Angeles, CA 90071-1560 · 213-683-9100

Neal H. Brockmeyer · ㉕ · Heller Ehrman · 333 South Hope Street, 39th Floor · Los Angeles, CA 90071-1406 · 213-689-0200

Jerome L. Coben · Skadden, Arps, Slate, Meagher & Flom · 300 South Grand Avenue, Suite 3400 · Los Angeles, CA 90071 · 213-687-5000

Stanley F. Farrar · ⑩ · Sullivan & Cromwell · 1888 Century Park East, 21st Floor · Los Angeles, CA 90067-1725 · 310-712-6600

Frank H. Golay, Jr. · ⑩ · Sullivan & Cromwell · 1888 Century Park East, 21st Floor · Los Angeles, CA 90067-1725 · 310-712-6600

Steven K. Hazen · Steven K. Hazen · 149 South Barrington Avenue, Suite 245 · Los Angeles, CA 90049-3310 · 310-377-4356

Brian J. McCarthy · Skadden, Arps, Slate, Meagher & Flom · 300 South Grand Avenue, Suite 3400 · Los Angeles, CA 90071 · 213-687-5000

Alison S. Ressler · Sullivan & Cromwell · 1888 Century Park East, 21st Floor · Los Angeles, CA 90067-1725 · 310-712-6600

Paul D. Tosetti · ⑩ · Latham & Watkins · 355 South Grand Avenue · Los Angeles, CA 90071-1560 · 213-485-1234

Diana L. Walker · ⑩ · O'Melveny & Myers · 400 South Hope Street, 10th Floor · Los Angeles, CA 90071-2899 · 213-430-6000

Newport Beach

William T. Gay · Gordon & Rees · 4675 MacArthur Court, Suite 800 · Newport Beach, CA 92660 · 949-255-6950

Palo Alto

Eric C. Jensen · Cooley Godward Kronish · 3175 Hanover Street · Palo Alto, CA 94304-1130 · 650-843-5000

Page Mailliard · Wilson Sonsini Goodrich & Rosati · 650 Page Mill Road · Palo Alto, CA 94304-1050 · 650-493-9300

Scott D. Miller · Sullivan & Cromwell · 1870 Embarcadero Road · Palo Alto, CA 94303-3308 · 650-461-5600

Erik J. Olson · Morrison & Foerster · http://www.mofo.com · 755 Page Mill Road · Palo Alto, CA 94304-1018 · 650-813-5600

John L. Savva · Sullivan & Cromwell · 1870 Embarcadero Road · Palo Alto, CA 94303-3308 · 650-461-5600

Richard Scudellari · Reed Smith · 1510 Page Mill Road, Suite 110 · Palo Alto, CA 94304 · 650-352-0500

John Sheridan · Wilson Sonsini Goodrich & Rosati · 650 Page Mill Road · Palo Alto, CA 94304-1050 · 650-493-9300

William D. Sherman · ㉕ · Morrison & Foerster · http://www.mofo.com · 755 Page Mill Road · Palo Alto, CA 94304-1018 · 650-813-5600

Larry W. Sonsini · ㉕ · Wilson Sonsini Goodrich & Rosati · 650 Page Mill Road · Palo Alto, CA 94304-1050 · 650-493-9300

Nancy H. Wojtas · Cooley Godward Kronish · 3175 Hanover Street · Palo Alto, CA 94304-1130 · 650-843-5000

Sacramento

David C. Adams · Weintraub Genshlea Chediak · 400 Capitol Mall, 11th Floor · Sacramento, CA 95814-4407 · 916-558-6000

Scott E. Bartel · Bullivant Houser Bailey · 1415 L Street, Suite 1000 · Sacramento, CA 95814 · 916-930-2500

San Francisco

David B. Bayless · Covington & Burling · One Front Street · San Francisco, CA 94111-5356 · 415-591-6000

Nathaniel M. Cartmell III · Pillsbury Winthrop Shaw Pittman · http://www.pillsburylaw.com · 50 Fremont Street · P.O. Box 7880 · San Francisco, CA 94120-7880 · 415-983-1000

Richard H. Koppes · Jones Day · 555 California Street, 26th Floor · San Francisco, CA 94104 · 415-626-3939

Robert M. Mattson, Jr. · Morrison & Foerster · http://www.mofo.com · 425 Market Street · San Francisco, CA 94105-2482 · 415-268-7000

Costa Mesa

David M. Bosko · ⑳ · Sheppard, Mullin, Richter & Hampton · http://www.sheppardmullin.com · 650 Town Center Drive, Fourth Floor · Costa Mesa, CA 92626 · 714-513-5100

Thomas J. Crane · Rutan & Tucker · http://www.rutan.com · 611 Anton Boulevard, Suite 1400 · P.O. Box 1950 · Costa Mesa, CA 92628-1950 · 714-641-5100

James W. Loss · Bingham McCutchen · http://www.bingham.com · 600 Anton Boulevard, 18th Floor · Costa Mesa, CA 92626 · 714-830-0600

East Palo Alto

Peter M. Astiz · DLA Piper · 2000 University Avenue · East Palo Alto, CA 94303-2214 · 650-833-2000

Bartley C. Deamer · ⑳ · Bingham McCutchen · http://www.bingham.com · 1900 University Avenue · East Palo Alto, CA 94303-2223 · 650-849-4400

Gregory M. Gallo · ⑩ · DLA Piper · 2000 University Avenue · East Palo Alto, CA 94303-2214 · 650-833-2000

Henry Lesser · ⑳ · DLA Piper · 2000 University Avenue · East Palo Alto, CA 94303-2214 · 650-833-2000

Dennis C. Sullivan · DLA Piper · 2000 University Avenue · East Palo Alto, CA 94303-2214 · 650-833-2000

Glendora

Joel Franklin McIntyre · Joel Franklyn McIntyre · 180 North Pennsylvania Avenue · P.O. Box 426 · Glendora, CA 91740 · 626-914-6771

Irvine

R. Patrick Arrington · ⑩ · Dorsey & Whitney · 38 Technology Drive, Suite 100 · Irvine, CA 92618-5310 949-932-3600

Ellen S. Bancroft · Dorsey & Whitney · 38 Technology Drive, Suite 100 · Irvine, CA 92618-5310 · 949-932-3600

Los Angeles

Robert L. Adler · ⑳ · Munger, Tolles & Olson · 355 South Grand Avenue, 35th Floor · Los Angeles, CA 90071-1560 · 213-683-9100

Gary Apfel · Dewey & LeBoeuf · 333 South Grand Avenue, Suite 2600 · Los Angeles, CA 90071-1530 · 213-621-6000

Willie R. Barnes · ⑩ · Musick, Peeler & Garrett · One Wilshire Boulevard, Suite 2000 · Los Angeles, CA 90017 · 213-629-7600

Kenneth R. Bender · ⑩ · Paul Hastings · 515 South Flower Street, 25th Floor · Los Angeles, CA 90071 · 213-683-6000

Richard L. Bernacchi · ⑩ · Irell & Manella · 1800 Avenue of the Stars, Suite 900 · Los Angeles, CA 90067-4276 · 310-277-1010

Joel M. Bernstein · McDermott Will & Emery · 2049 Century Park East, 38th Floor · Los Angeles, CA 90067-3218 · 310-277-4110

Andrew E. Bogen · 20 · Gibson, Dunn & Crutcher · 333 South Grand Avenue · Los Angeles, CA 90071-3197 · 213-229-7000

T. Hale Boggs · 10 · Manatt, Phelps & Phillips · 11355 West Olympic Boulevard · Los Angeles, CA 90064 310-312-4000

Lawrence M. Braun · Sheppard, Mullin, Richter & Hampton · http://www.sheppardmullin.com · 333 South Hope Street, 48th Floor · Los Angeles, CA 90071-1448 · 213-620-1780

Neal H. Brockmeyer · 25 · Heller Ehrman · 333 South Hope Street, 39th Floor · Los Angeles, CA 90071-1406 · 213-689-0200

Tim C. Bruinsma · Fulbright & Jaworski · http://www.fulbright.com · 555 South Flower Street, 41st Floor Los Angeles, CA 90071 · 213-892-9200

Robert R. Carlson · 25 · Paul Hastings · 515 South Flower Street, 25th Floor · Los Angeles, CA 90071 · 213-683-6000

Louis M. Castruccio · 20 · Irell & Manella · 1800 Avenue of the Stars, Suite 900 · Los Angeles, CA 90067-4276 · 310-277-1010

Jerome L. Coben · Skadden, Arps, Slate, Meagher & Flom · 300 South Grand Avenue, Suite 3400 · Los Angeles, CA 90071 · 213-687-5000

Jeffrey H. Cohen · Skadden, Arps, Slate, Meagher & Flom · 300 South Grand Avenue, Suite 3400 · Los Angeles, CA 90071 · 213-687-5000

Michael C. Cohen · Morrison & Foerster · http://www.mofo.com · 555 West Fifth Street, Suite 3500 · Los Angeles, CA 90013-1024 · 213-892-5200

Robert C. Colton · Buchalter Nemer · 1000 Wilshire Boulevard, Suite 1500 · Los Angeles, CA 90017-2457 · 213-891-0700

Michael J. Connell · 25 · Quateman · 1801 Century Park East, Suite 1801 · Los Angeles, CA 90067 · 310-556-7755

Andrew J. Demetriou · Fulbright & Jaworski · http://www.fulbright.com · 555 South Flower Street, 41st Floor · Los Angeles, CA 90071 · 213-892-9200

David A. Ebershoff · Fulbright & Jaworski · http://www.fulbright.com · 555 South Flower Street, 41st Floor · Los Angeles, CA 90071 · 213-892-9200

Gregory C. Fant · Arnold & Porter · 777 South Figueroa Street, 44th Floor · Los Angeles, CA 90017-5844 213-243-4000

Stanley F. Farrar · 10 · Sullivan & Cromwell · 1888 Century Park East, 21st Floor · Los Angeles, CA 90067-1725 · 310-712-6600

Ronald L. Fein · 25 · RL Fein · 1901 Avenue of The Stars, 12th Floor · Los Angeles, CA 90067 · 310-228-5780

Ronald K. Fujikawa · Greenberg Glusker · 1900 Avenue of the Stars, 21st Floor · Los Angeles, CA 90067 310-553-3610

Joseph J. Giunta · Skadden, Arps, Slate, Meagher & Flom · 300 South Grand Avenue, Suite 3400 · Los Angeles, CA 90071 · 213-687-5000

Frank H. Golay, Jr. · ⑩ · Sullivan & Cromwell · 1888 Century Park East, 21st Floor · Los Angeles, CA 90067-1725 · 310-712-6600

William D. Gould · ⑳ · TroyGould · http://www.troygould.com · 1801 Century Park East, Suite 1600 · Los Angeles, CA 90067 · 310-553-4441

Rodrigo A. Guerra, Jr. · Skadden, Arps, Slate, Meagher & Flom · 300 South Grand Avenue, Suite 3400 · Los Angeles, CA 90071 · 213-687-5000

Theodore E. Guth · ⑩ · Manatt, Phelps & Phillips · 11355 West Olympic Boulevard · Los Angeles, CA 90064 · 310-312-4000

John F. Hartigan · ⑩ · Morgan Lewis & Bockius · 300 South Grand Avenue, 22nd Floor · Los Angeles, CA 90071-3132 · 213-612-2500

Harry L. Hathaway · ⑩ · Fulbright & Jaworski · http://www.fulbright.com · 555 South Flower Street, 41st Floor · Los Angeles, CA 90071 · 213-892-9200

Steven K. Hazen · Steven K. Hazen · 149 South Barrington Avenue, Suite 245 · Los Angeles, CA 90049-3310 · 310-377-4356

Kenneth R. Heitz · Irell & Manella · 1800 Avenue of the Stars, Suite 900 · Los Angeles, CA 90067-4276 · 310-277-1010

Mary Ellen Kanoff · Latham & Watkins · 355 South Grand Avenue · Los Angeles, CA 90071-1560 · 213-485-1234

Andrew E. Katz · Mitchell Silberberg & Knupp · 11377 West Olympic Boulevard · Los Angeles, CA 90064 · 310-312-2000

George D. Kieffer · Manatt, Phelps & Phillips · 11355 West Olympic Boulevard · Los Angeles, CA 90064 310-312-4000

Robert B. Knauss · ⑩ · Munger, Tolles & Olson · 355 South Grand Avenue, 35th Floor · Los Angeles, CA 90071-1560 · 213-683-9100

Moshe J. Kupietzky · Sidley Austin · 555 West Fifth Street, 40th Floor · Los Angeles, CA 90013 · 213-896-6000

Brian J. McCarthy · Skadden, Arps, Slate, Meagher & Flom · 300 South Grand Avenue, Suite 3400 · Los Angeles, CA 90071 · 213-687-5000

Frederick B. McLane · ⑩ · O'Melveny & Myers · 1999 Avenue of the Stars, Seventh Floor · Los Angeles, CA 90067-6035 · 310-553-6700

Peter M. Menard · Sheppard, Mullin, Richter & Hampton · http://www.sheppardmullin.com · 333 South Hope Street, 48th Floor · Los Angeles, CA 90071-1448 · 213-620-1780

Bruce D. Meyer · ⑩ · Gibson, Dunn & Crutcher · 333 South Grand Avenue · Los Angeles, CA 90071-3197 · 213-229-7000

Robert K. Montgomery · ⑳ · Gibson, Dunn & Crutcher · 2029 Century Park East, 40th Floor · Los Angeles, CA 90067-3026 · 310-552-8500

Ashok W. Mukhey · Irell & Manella · 1800 Avenue of the Stars, Suite 900 · Los Angeles, CA 90067-4276 310-277-1010

Gregg A. Noel · Skadden, Arps, Slate, Meagher & Flom · 300 South Grand Avenue, Suite 3400 · Los Angeles, CA 90071 · 213-687-5000

Alison S. Ressler · Sullivan & Cromwell · 1888 Century Park East, 21st Floor · Los Angeles, CA 90067-1725 · 310-712-6600

David K. Robbins · Bingham McCutchen · http://www.bingham.com · 355 South Grand Avenue, Suite 4400 · Los Angeles, CA 90071-3106 · 213-680-6400

Thomas C. Sadler · Latham & Watkins · 355 South Grand Avenue · Los Angeles, CA 90071-1560 · 213-485-1234

Nicholas P. Saggese · Skadden, Arps, Slate, Meagher & Flom · 300 South Grand Avenue, Suite 3400 · Los Angeles, CA 90071 · 213-687-5000

Richard A. Shortz · Morgan Lewis & Bockius · 300 South Grand Avenue, 22nd Floor · Los Angeles, CA 90071-3132 · 213-612-2500

Lisa Specht · Manatt, Phelps & Phillips · 11355 West Olympic Boulevard · Los Angeles, CA 90064 · 310-312-4000

Allen Z. Sussman · Reed Smith · 355 South Grand Avenue, Suite 2900 · Los Angeles, CA 90071 · 213-457-8000

Paul D. Tosetti · ⑩ · Latham & Watkins · 355 South Grand Avenue · Los Angeles, CA 90071-1560 · 213-485-1234

Diana L. Walker · ⑩ · O'Melveny & Myers · 400 South Hope Street, 10th Floor · Los Angeles, CA 90071-2899 · 213-430-6000

James R. Walther · Mayer Brown · 350 South Grand Avenue, 25th Floor · Los Angeles, CA 90071-1503 · 213-229-9500

John B. Watkins · WilmerHale · http://www.wilmerhale.com · 350 South Grand Avenue, Suite 2100 · Los Angeles, CA 90071 · 213-443-5300

Menlo Park

Francis S. Currie · Davis Polk & Wardwell · 1600 El Camino Real · Menlo Park, CA 94025 · 650-752-2000

Paul H. Dawes · ⑩ · Latham & Watkins · 140 Scott Drive · Menlo Park, CA 94025 · 650-328-4600

Robert V. Gunderson, Jr. · ⑩ · Gunderson Dettmer Stough Villeneuve Franklin & Hachigian · 155 Constitution Drive · Menlo Park, CA 94025 · 650-321-2400

Michael W. Hall · Latham & Watkins · 140 Scott Drive · Menlo Park, CA 94025 · 650-328-4600

Christopher L. Kaufman · ㉕ · Latham & Watkins · 140 Scott Drive · Menlo Park, CA 94025 · 650-328-4600

Peter F. Kerman · Latham & Watkins · 140 Scott Drive · Menlo Park, CA 94025 · 650-328-4600

Alan C. Mendelson · ⑩ · Latham & Watkins · 140 Scott Drive · Menlo Park, CA 94025 · 650-328-4600

Patrick A. Pohlen · Latham & Watkins · 140 Scott Drive · Menlo Park, CA 94025 · 650-328-4600

Brooks Stough · Gunderson Dettmer Stough Villeneuve Franklin & Hachigian · 155 Constitution Drive · Menlo Park, CA 94025 · 650-321-2400

Mountain View

Gordon K. Davidson · ⑩ · Fenwick & West · Silicon Valley Center · 801 California Street · Mountain View, CA 94041-2008 · 650-988-8500

Mark C. Stevens · Fenwick & West · Silicon Valley Center · 801 California Street · Mountain View, CA 94041-2008 · 650-988-8500

Newport Beach

William T. Gay · Gordon & Rees · 4675 MacArthur Court, Suite 800 · Newport Beach, CA 92660 · 949-255-6950

Gary J. Singer · O'Melveny & Myers · 610 Newport Center Drive, 17th Floor · Newport Beach, CA 92660 · 949-760-9600

Palo Alto

Lee F. Benton · ⑩ · Cooley Godward Kronish · 3175 Hanover Street · Palo Alto, CA 94304-1130 · 650-843-5000

Richard E. Climan · ⑩ · Cooley Godward Kronish · 3175 Hanover Street · Palo Alto, CA 94304-1130 · 650-843-5000

Craig E. Dauchy · ⑩ · Cooley Godward Kronish · 3175 Hanover Street · Palo Alto, CA 94304-1130 · 650-843-5000

Jorge A. del Calvo · Pillsbury Winthrop Shaw Pittman · http://www.pillsburylaw.com · 2475 Hanover Street · Palo Alto, CA 94304-1114 · 650-233-4500

John A. Fore · Wilson Sonsini Goodrich & Rosati · 650 Page Mill Road · Palo Alto, CA 94304-1050 · 650-493-9300

James F. Fulton, Jr. · Cooley Godward Kronish · 3175 Hanover Street · Palo Alto, CA 94304-1130 · 650-843-5000

John M. Geschke · Cooley Godward Kronish · 3175 Hanover Street · Palo Alto, CA 94304-1130 · 650-843-5000

William H. Hinman, Jr. · ⑩ · Simpson Thacher · 2550 Hanover Street · Palo Alto, CA 94304 · 650-251-5000

Suzanne S. Hooper · Cooley Godward Kronish · 3175 Hanover Street · Palo Alto, CA 94304-1130 · 650-843-5000

Eric C. Jensen · Cooley Godward Kronish · 3175 Hanover Street · Palo Alto, CA 94304-1130 · 650-843-5000

Robert L. Jones · Cooley Godward Kronish · 3175 Hanover Street · Palo Alto, CA 94304-1130 · 650-843-5000

Thomas W. Kellerman · Morgan Lewis & Bockius · Two Palo Alto Square, Suite 700 · 3000 El Camino Real · Palo Alto, CA 94306-2121 · 650-843-4000

Martin W. Korman · Wilson Sonsini Goodrich & Rosati · 650 Page Mill Road · Palo Alto, CA 94304-1050 650-493-9300

Barbara Kosacz · Cooley Godward Kronish · 3175 Hanover Street · Palo Alto, CA 94304-1130 · 650-843-5000

Katharine A. Martin · Wilson Sonsini Goodrich & Rosati · 650 Page Mill Road · Palo Alto, CA 94304-1050 · 650-493-9300

Henry P. Massey, Jr. · ㉕ · Wilson Sonsini Goodrich & Rosati · 650 Page Mill Road · Palo Alto, CA 94304-1050 · 650-493-9300

Timothy J. Moore · Cooley Godward Kronish · 3175 Hanover Street · Palo Alto, CA 94304-1130 · 650-843-5000

Michael C. Phillips · Morrison & Foerster · http://www.mofo.com · 755 Page Mill Road · Palo Alto, CA 94304-1018 · 650-813-5600

John V. Roos · Wilson Sonsini Goodrich & Rosati · 650 Page Mill Road · Palo Alto, CA 94304-1050 · 650-493-9300

Jeffrey D. Saper · Wilson Sonsini Goodrich & Rosati · 650 Page Mill Road · Palo Alto, CA 94304-1050 · 650-493-9300

David J. Segre · Wilson Sonsini Goodrich & Rosati · 650 Page Mill Road · Palo Alto, CA 94304-1050 · 650-493-9300

John Sheridan · Wilson Sonsini Goodrich & Rosati · 650 Page Mill Road · Palo Alto, CA 94304-1050 · 650-493-9300

William D. Sherman · ㉕ · Morrison & Foerster · http://www.mofo.com · 755 Page Mill Road · Palo Alto, CA 94304-1018 · 650-813-5600

Larry W. Sonsini · ㉕ · Wilson Sonsini Goodrich & Rosati · 650 Page Mill Road · Palo Alto, CA 94304-1050 · 650-493-9300

Mark P. Tanoury · Cooley Godward Kronish · 3175 Hanover Street · Palo Alto, CA 94304-1130 · 650-843-5000

Nicholas Unkovic · Squire Sanders · http://www.ssd.com · 600 Hansen Way · Palo Alto, CA 94304-1043 · 650-856-6500

Ann Yvonne Walker · Wilson Sonsini Goodrich & Rosati · 650 Page Mill Road · Palo Alto, CA 94304-1050 · 650-493-9300

Mark B. Weeks · Cooley Godward Kronish · 3175 Hanover Street · Palo Alto, CA 94304 · 650-843-5000

Riverside

Jane W. Carney · Roth Carney Knudsen · 3850 Vine Street, Suite 240 · Riverside, CA 92507 · 951-682-6500

George M. Reyes · Best Best & Krieger · 3750 University Avenue, Suite 400 · P.O. Box 1028 · Riverside, CA 92502 · 951-686-1450

Bruce D. Varner · Varner & Brandt · 3750 University Avenue, Suite 610 · Riverside, CA 92501 · 951-274-7777

Sacramento

Christopher Chediak · Weintraub Genshlea Chediak · 400 Capitol Mall, 11th Floor · Sacramento, CA 95814-4407 · 916-558-6000

John E. Di Gusto · Boutin Dentino Gibson Di Giusto Hodell · 555 Capitol Mall, Suite 1500 · Sacramento, CA 95814 · 916-321-4444

Jeffrey M. Koewler · Downey Brand · 555 Capitol Mall, 10th Floor · Sacramento, CA 95814 · 916-444-1000

San Diego

Craig S. Andrews · ⑩ · DLA Piper · 4365 Executive Drive, Suite 1100 · San Diego, CA 92121-2133 · 858-677-1400

Knox Bell · DLA Piper · 4365 Executive Drive, Suite 1100 · San Diego, CA 92121-2133 · 858-677-1400

Barry M. Clarkson · Latham & Watkins · 12636 High Bluff Drive, Suite 400 · San Diego, CA 92130 · 858-523-5400

Thomas A. Coll · Cooley Godward Kronish · 4401 Eastgate Mall · San Diego, CA 92121-1909 · 858-550-6000

Robert G. Copeland · ⑳ · Sheppard, Mullin, Richter & Hampton · http://www.sheppardmullin.com · 501 West Broadway, 19th Floor · San Diego, CA 92101 · 619-338-6500

Michael S. Kagnoff · DLA Piper · 4365 Executive Drive, Suite 1100 · San Diego, CA 92121-2133 · 858-677-1400

John B. McNeece III · Luce, Forward, Hamilton & Scripps · http://www.luce.com · 600 West Broadway, Suite 2600 · San Diego, CA 92101 · 619-236-1414

Frederick T. Muto · ⑩ · Cooley Godward Kronish · 4401 Eastgate Mall · San Diego, CA 92121-1909 · 858-550-6000

Cameron Jay Rains · DLA Piper · 4365 Executive Drive, Suite 1100 · San Diego, CA 92121-2133 · 858-677-1400

Faye H. Russell · Latham & Watkins · 12636 High Bluff Drive, Suite 400 · San Diego, CA 92130 · 858-523-5400

David R. Snyder · ⑩ · Pillsbury Winthrop Shaw Pittman · http://www.pillsburylaw.com · 501 West Broadway, Suite 1100 · San Diego, CA 92101-3575 · 619-234-5000

Scott N. Wolfe · ⑩ · Latham & Watkins · 12636 High Bluff Drive, Suite 400 · San Diego, CA 92130 · 858-523-5400

San Francisco

Barry A. Abbott · Howard, Rice, Nemerovski, Canady, Falk & Rabkin · Three Embarcadero Center, Seventh Floor · San Francisco, CA 94111-4024 · 415-434-1600

Shane M. Byrne · Baker & McKenzie · Two Embarcadero Center, 11th Floor · San Francisco, CA 94111-3802 · 415-576-3000

John W. Campbell · Morrison & Foerster · http://www.mofo.com · 425 Market Street · San Francisco, CA 94105-2482 · 415-268-7000

Richard W. Canady · ⑩ · Howard, Rice, Nemerovski, Canady, Falk & Rabkin · Three Embarcadero Center, Seventh Floor · San Francisco, CA 94111-4024 · 415-434-1600

Nathaniel M. Cartmell III · Pillsbury Winthrop Shaw Pittman · http://www.pillsburylaw.com · 50 Fremont Street · P.O. Box 7880 · San Francisco, CA 94120-7880 · 415-983-1000

Frank E. Farella · ㉕ · Farella Braun & Martel · Russ Building, 17th Floor · 235 Montgomery Street · San Francisco, CA 94104 · 415-954-4400

Kenneth Guernsey · Cooley Godward Kronish · 101 California Street, Fifth Floor · San Francisco, CA 94111-5800 · 415-693-2000

Leslie P. Jay · ⑳ · Orrick, Herrington & Sutcliffe · The Orrick Building · 405 Howard Street · San Francisco, CA 94105-2669 · 415-773-5700

John W. Larson · ⑳ · Morgan Lewis & Bockius · Spear Street Tower · One Market · San Francisco, CA 94105-1596 · 415-442-1000

Samuel M. Livermore · Cooley Godward Kronish · 101 California Street, Fifth Floor · San Francisco, CA 94111-5800 · 415-693-2000

Bruce Alan Mann · ㉕ · Morrison & Foerster · http://www.mofo.com · 425 Market Street · San Francisco, CA 94105-2482 · 415-268-7000

Deborah A. Marshall · Howard, Rice, Nemerovski, Canady, Falk & Rabkin · Three Embarcadero Center, Seventh Floor · San Francisco, CA 94111-4024 · 415-434-1600

Ronald B. Moskovitz · Morgan Lewis & Bockius · Spear Street Tower · One Market · San Francisco, CA 94105-1596 · 415-442-1000

Robert G. O'Connor · Wilson Sonsini Goodrich & Rosati · Spear Tower, Suite 3300 · One Market Street · San Francisco, CA 94105-1126 · 415-947-2000

Richard M. Phillips · ⑳ · K&L Gates · 55 Second Street, Suite 1700 · San Francisco, CA 94105-3493 · 415-882-8200

Lawrence B. Rabkin · Howard, Rice, Nemerovski, Canady, Falk & Rabkin · Three Embarcadero Center, Seventh Floor · San Francisco, CA 94111-4024 · 415-434-1600

Sean M. Rhatigan · Crosby, Heafey, Roach & May · Two Embarcadero Center, Suite 2000 · San Francisco, CA 94111 · 415-543-8700

Denis T. Rice · ⑳ · Howard, Rice, Nemerovski, Canady, Falk & Rabkin · Three Embarcadero Center, Seventh Floor · San Francisco, CA 94111-4024 · 415-434-1600

Thomas E. Sparks, Jr. · ⑩ · Pillsbury Winthrop Shaw Pittman · http://www.pillsburylaw.com · 50 Fremont Street · P.O. Box 7880 · San Francisco, CA 94120-7880 · 415-983-1000

Blair W. White · Pillsbury Winthrop Shaw Pittman · http://www.pillsburylaw.com · 50 Fremont Street · P.O. Box 7880 · San Francisco, CA 94120-7880 · 415-983-1000

Stanton D. Wong · Pillsbury Winthrop Shaw Pittman · http://www.pillsburylaw.com · 50 Fremont Street · P.O. Box 7880 · San Francisco, CA 94120-7880 · 415-983-1000

Douglas M. Young · Baker & McKenzie · Two Embarcadero Center, 11th Floor · San Francisco, CA 94111-3802 · 415-576-3000

Thomas A. Zimmer · Holland & Knight · http://www.hklaw.com · 50 California Street, Suite 2800 · San Francisco, CA 94111-4624 · 415-743-6900

San Jose

Daniel J. Bergeson · Bergeson · http://www.be-law.com · 303 Almaden Boulevard, Suite 500 · San Jose, CA 95110-2712 · 408-291-6200

Thomas R. Hogan · Hogan, Holmes & Usoz · 333 West Santa Clara Street, Suite 800 · San Jose, CA 95113-1713 · 408-292-7600

Stephen S. McCray · Hoge, Fenton, Jones & Appel · http://www.hogefenton.com · 60 South Market Street, Suite 1400 · San Jose, CA 95113-2396 · 408-287-9501

Anthony J. Trepel · Trepel Law Offices · 40 South Market Street, Seventh Floor · San Jose, CA 95113-2367 · 408-275-0501

Santa Barbara

C. Thomas Hopkins · Sheppard, Mullin, Richter & Hampton · http://www.sheppardmullin.com · 1111 Chapala Street, Third Floor · Santa Barbara, CA 93101 · 805-879-1800

David E. Lafitte · Stradling Yocca Carlson & Rauth · 800 Anacapa Street, Suite A · Santa Barbara, CA 93101 · 805-564-0065

Santa Monica

Robert L. Kahan · Dreier Stein Kahan Browne Woods George · The Water Garden · North Tower, Sixth Floor · 1620 Twenty-Sixth Street · Santa Monica, CA 90404 · 310-828-9050

Thomas S. Loo · Greenberg Traurig · http://www.gtlaw.com · 2450 Colorado Avenue, Suite 400-E · Santa Monica, CA 90404 · 310-586-7700

Santa Rosa

Richard W. Abbey · Abbey, Weitzenberg, Warren & Emery · 100 Stony Point Road, Suite 200 · P.O. Box 1566 · Santa Rosa, CA 95402-1566 · 707-542-5050

Clayton E. Clement · Clement, Fitzpatrick & Kenworthy · 3333 Mendocino Avenue · Santa Rosa, CA 95403 · 707-523-1181

Robert S. Rutherfurd · Anderson, Zeigler, Disharoon, Gallagher & Gray · 50 Old Courthouse Square, Fifth Floor · P.O. Box 1498 · Santa Rosa, CA 95404 · 707-545-4910

Kirt F. Zeigler · Anderson, Zeigler, Disharoon, Gallagher & Gray · 50 Old Courthouse Square, Fifth Floor P.O. Box 1498 · Santa Rosa, CA 95404 · 707-545-4910

DERIVATIVES LAW

Los Angeles

William F. Sullivan · Paul Hastings · 515 South Flower Street, 25th Floor · Los Angeles, CA 90071 · 213-683-6000

Palo Alto

John C. Dwyer · Cooley Godward Kronish · Five Palo Alto Square · 3000 El Camino Real · Palo Alto, CA 94306-2155 · 650-843-5000

William S. Freeman · Cooley Godward Kronish · Five Palo Alto Square · 3000 El Camino Real · Palo Alto, CA 94306-2155 · 650-843-5000

San Diego

Robert W. Brownlie · DLA Piper · 401 B Street, Suite 1700 · San Diego, CA 92101-4297 · 619-699-2700

William E. Grauer · Cooley Godward Kronish · 4401 Eastgate Mall · San Diego, CA 92121-1909 · 858-550-6000

Michael G. Rhodes · Cooley Godward Kronish · 4401 Eastgate Mall · San Diego, CA 92121-1909 · 858-550-6000

Shirli Fabbri Weiss · DLA Piper · 401 B Street, Suite 1700 · San Diego, CA 92101-4297 · 619-699-2700

DUI/DWI DEFENSE

Century City

Richard A. Hutton · Hutton and Wilson · 1880 Century Park East, Suite 710 · Century City, CA 90067 · 310-550-7720

Riverside

Christopher B. Harmon · Harmon & Harmon · The Loring Building, Suite 250 · 3685 Main Street · Riverside, CA 92501 · 951-329-9324

San Diego

John G. Phillips · John G. Phillips · 1010 Second Avenue, Suite 1840 · San Diego, CA 92101 · 619-234-0163

Thomas J. Warwick, Jr. · Grimes & Warwick · 2664 Fourth Avenue · San Diego, CA 92103-6515 · 619-232-9700

Santa Rosa

Richard J. Ingram · Harrington & Ingram · 438 First Street, Fourth Floor · Santa Rosa, CA 95401 · 707-573-8123

ELDER LAW

Laguna Hills

Fay Blix · Fay Blix · 23601 Moulton Parkway, Suite 220 · Laguna Hills, CA 92653 · 949-454-2205

San Diego

Sheila S. Trexler · Neil, Dymott, Frank, McFall & Trexler · http://www.neildymott.com · 1010 Second Avenue, Suite 2500 · San Diego, CA 92101-4959 · 619-238-1712

EMINENT DOMAIN AND CONDEMNATION LAW

Irvine

John C. Murphy · Luce, Forward, Hamilton & Scripps · http://www.luce.com · 2040 Main Street, Suite 600 · Irvine, CA 92614 · 949-732-3700

Los Angeles

Michael M. Berger · Manatt, Phelps & Phillips · 11355 West Olympic Boulevard · Los Angeles, CA 90064 · 310-312-4000

Kevin H. Brogan · Hill, Farrer & Burrill · One California Plaza, 37th Floor · 300 South Grand Avenue · Los Angeles, CA 90071-3147 · 213-620-0460

Edward C. Burg · Manatt, Phelps & Phillips · 11355 West Olympic Boulevard · Los Angeles, CA 90064 · 310-312-4000

Gideon Kanner · Manatt, Phelps & Phillips · 11355 West Olympic Boulevard · Los Angeles, CA 90064 · 310-312-4000

Gary A. Kovacic · Sullivan, Workman and Dee · 800 South Figueroa Street, Suite 1200 · Los Angeles, CA 90017-2521 · 213-624-5544

George M. Soneff · Manatt, Phelps & Phillips · 11355 West Olympic Boulevard · Los Angeles, CA 90064 310-312-4000

Oakland

Alice M. Beasley · Erickson, Beasley, Hewitt & Wilson · 483 Ninth Street, Suite 200 · Oakland, CA 94607 · 510-839-3448

Sacramento

James S. Burling · Pacific Legal Foundation · 3900 Lennane Drive, Suite 200 · Sacramento, CA 95834 · 916-419-7111

John V. Diepenbrock · ⑳ · Diepenbrock Harrison · 400 Capitol Mall, Suite 1800 · Sacramento, CA 95814 · 916-446-4469

Gary Alan Livaich · Desmond, Nolan, Livaich & Cunningham · 15th & S Building · 1830 Fifteenth Street · Sacramento, CA 95811 · 916-443-2051

Ronald A. Zumbrun · The Zumbrun Law Firm · 3800 Watt Avenue, Suite 101 · Sacramento, CA 95821 · 916-486-5900

San Jose

Norman E. Matteoni · Matteoni, O'Laughlin & Hechtman · 848 The Alameda · San Jose, CA 95126 · 408-293-4300

Walnut Creek

Clement L. Glynn · Glynn & Finley · 100 Pringle Avenue, Suite 500 · Walnut Creek, CA 94596 · 925-210-2800

EMPLOYEE BENEFITS LAW

East Palo Alto

P. Garth Gartrell · ⑩ · Greenberg Traurig · http://www.gtlaw.com · 1900 University Avenue, Fifth Floor · East Palo Alto, CA 94303 · 650-328-8500

Folsom

Jeffrey C. Chang · ⑩ · Chang, Ruthenberg & Long · 620 Coolidge Drive, Suite 350 · Folsom, CA 95630-3155 · 916-357-5660

Kevin G. Long · Chang, Ruthenberg & Long · 620 Coolidge Drive, Suite 350 · Folsom, CA 95630-3155 · 916-357-5660

Kenneth W. Ruthenberg, Jr. · Chang, Ruthenberg & Long · 620 Coolidge Drive, Suite 350 · Folsom, CA 95630-3155 · 916-357-5660

Irvine

Joseph P. Busch III · Gibson, Dunn & Crutcher · 3161 Michelson Drive · Irvine, CA 92612-4412 · 949-451-3800

Los Angeles

Bruce L. Ashton · Reish Luftman Reicher & Cohen · http://www.reish.com · 11755 Wilshire Boulevard, 10th Floor · Los Angeles, CA 90025-1539 · 310-478-5656

James D. C. Barrall · ⑩ · Latham & Watkins · 355 South Grand Avenue · Los Angeles, CA 90071-1560 · 213-485-1234

David E. Gordon · ⑳ · O'Melveny & Myers · 400 South Hope Street, 10th Floor · Los Angeles, CA 90071-2899 · 213-430-6000

Linda Griffey · O'Melveny & Myers · 400 South Hope Street, 10th Floor · Los Angeles, CA 90071-2899 · 213-430-6000

Mark H. Hess · ⑩ · Manatt, Phelps & Phillips · 11355 West Olympic Boulevard · Los Angeles, CA 90064 310-312-4000

Robert K. Johnson · ⑳ · Munger, Tolles & Olson · 355 South Grand Avenue, 35th Floor · Los Angeles, CA 90071-1560 · 213-683-9100

Thomas A. Kirschbaum · ⑩ · Irell & Manella · 1800 Avenue of the Stars, Suite 900 · Los Angeles, CA 90067-4276 · 310-277-1010

Jay Adams Knight · Musick, Peeler & Garrett · One Wilshire Boulevard, Suite 2000 · Los Angeles, CA 90017 · 213-629-7600

Michael A. Lawson · Skadden, Arps, Slate, Meagher & Flom · 300 South Grand Avenue, Suite 3400 · Los Angeles, CA 90071 · 213-687-5000

Ethan Lipsig · ⑩ · Paul Hastings · 515 South Flower Street, 25th Floor · Los Angeles, CA 90071 · 213-683-6000

Robert J. Lowe · Mitchell Silberberg & Knupp · 11377 West Olympic Boulevard · Los Angeles, CA 90064 · 310-312-2000

C. Frederick Reish · ⑩ · Reish Luftman Reicher & Cohen · http://www.reish.com · 11755 Wilshire Boulevard, 10th Floor · Los Angeles, CA 90025-1539 · 310-478-5656

Robert W. Ridley · Farmer & Ridley · 333 South Hope Street, Suite 3750 · Los Angeles, CA 90071 · 213-626-0291

Robin M. Schachter · Akin Gump Strauss Hauer & Feld · 2029 Century Park East, Suite 2400 · Los Angeles, CA 90067-3012 · 310-229-1000

David West · ⑩ · Gibson, Dunn & Crutcher · 333 South Grand Avenue · Los Angeles, CA 90071-3197 · 213-229-7000

Menlo Park

Renee R. Deming · Cooley Godward Kronish · Building Three, Suite 230 · 3000 Sand Hill Road · Menlo Park, CA 94025 · 650-843-5033

Richard A. Grimm · Heller Ehrman · 275 Middlefield Road · Menlo Park, CA 94025-3506 · 650-324-7000

Sharon J. Hendricks · Heller Ehrman · 275 Middlefield Road · Menlo Park, CA 94025-3506 · 650-324-7000

Daniel Niehans · Gunderson Dettmer Stough Villeneuve Franklin & Hachigian · 155 Constitution Drive · Menlo Park, CA 94025 · 650-321-2400

Mountain View

Scott P. Spector · Fenwick & West · Silicon Valley Center · 801 California Street · Mountain View, CA 94041-2008 · 650-988-8500

Newport Beach

Wayne S. Jacobsen · O'Melveny & Myers · 610 Newport Center Drive, 17th Floor · Newport Beach, CA 92660 · 949-760-9600

R. Craig Scott · ⑩ · Scott & Whitehead · 1301 Dove Street, Suite 1000 · Newport Beach, CA 92660 · 949-222-0166

Palo Alto

John E. Aguirre · Wilson Sonsini Goodrich & Rosati · 650 Page Mill Road · Palo Alto, CA 94304-1050 · 650-493-9300

S. James DiBernardo · Morgan Lewis & Bockius · Two Palo Alto Square, Suite 700 · 3000 El Camino Real · Palo Alto, CA 94306-2121 · 650-843-4000

Maureen J. Gorman · ⑩ · Mayer Brown · Two Palo Alto Square, Suite 300 · 3000 El Camino Real · Palo Alto, CA 94306-2112 · 650-331-2000

Zaitun Poonja · Morgan Lewis & Bockius · Two Palo Alto Square, Suite 700 · 3000 El Camino Real · Palo Alto, CA 94306-2121 · 650-843-4000

Pasadena

Thomas E. Shardlow · ⑩ · Shardlow & Vick · 790 East Colorado Boulevard, Ninth Floor · Pasadena, CA 91101 · 626-584-1600

Steven E. Trytten · Anglin, Flewelling, Rasmussen, Campbell & Trytten · 199 South Los Robles Avenue, Suite 600 · Pasadena, CA 91101-2459 · 626-535-1900

Rancho Santa Fe

Louis A. Mezzullo · ⑳ · Luce, Forward, Hamilton & Scripps · http://www.luce.com · 6050 El Tordo · P.O. Box 2329 · Rancho Santa Fe, CA 92067-2329 · 858-756-4410

Riverside

Richard D. Roth · Roth Carney Knudsen · 3850 Vine Street, Suite 240 · Riverside, CA 92507 · 951-682-6500

San Diego

Lawrence S. Branton · ⑳ · Branton & Wilson · 701 B Street, Suite 1255 · San Diego, CA 92101-8187 · 619-236-1891

Robert K. Butterfield · Butterfield Schechter · 10616 Scripps Summit Court, Suite 200 · San Diego, CA 92131-3961 · 858-444-2300

Daniel N. Riesenberg · ⑳ · Pillsbury Winthrop Shaw Pittman · http://www.pillsburylaw.com · 12255 El Camino Real, Suite 300 · San Diego, CA 92130-4088 · 619-234-5000

Jan H. Webster · Pillsbury Winthrop Shaw Pittman · http://www.pillsburylaw.com · 12255 El Camino Real, Suite 300 · San Diego, CA 92130-4088 · 619-234-5000

San Francisco

James P. Baker · Jones Day · 555 California Street, 26th Floor · San Francisco, CA 94104 · 415-626-3939

William D. Berry · Orrick, Herrington & Sutcliffe · The Orrick Building · 405 Howard Street · San Francisco, CA 94105-2669 · 415-773-5700

Mark H. Boxer · DLA Piper · 153 Townsend Street, Suite 800 · San Francisco, CA 94107-1957 · 415-836-2500

David F. Boyle · DLA Piper · 153 Townsend Street, Suite 800 · San Francisco, CA 94107-1957 · 415-836-2500

Julie Burbank · Trucker Huss · http://www.truckerhuss.com · 120 Montgomery Street, 23rd Floor · San Francisco, CA 94104-4398 · 415-788-3111

Edward D. Burmeister, Jr. · Baker & McKenzie · Two Embarcadero Center, 11th Floor · San Francisco, CA 94111-3802 · 415-576-3000

David S. Foster · ⑩ · Thelen Reid Brown Raysman & Steiner · 101 Second Street, Suite 1800 · San Francisco, CA 94105-3601 · 415-371-1200

Richard A. Gilbert · Orrick, Herrington & Sutcliffe · The Orrick Building · 405 Howard Street · San Francisco, CA 94105-2669 · 415-773-5700

R. Bradford Huss · ⑩ · Trucker Huss · http://www.truckerhuss.com · 120 Montgomery Street, 23rd Floor San Francisco, CA 94104-4398 · 415-788-3111

Thomas Z. Reicher · Cooley Godward Kronish · 101 California Street, Fifth Floor · San Francisco, CA 94111-5800 · 415-693-2000

Barry H. Sacks · The Law Offices of Barry H. Sacks · 2557 Clay Street · San Francisco, CA 94115 · 415-346-6095

Benjamin F. Spater · Trucker Huss · http://www.truckerhuss.com · 120 Montgomery Street, 23rd Floor · San Francisco, CA 94104-4398 · 415-788-3111

Charles A. Storke · Trucker Huss · http://www.truckerhuss.com · 120 Montgomery Street, 23rd Floor · San Francisco, CA 94104-4398 · 415-788-3111

Lee A. Trucker · ⑩ · Trucker Huss · http://www.truckerhuss.com · 120 Montgomery Street, 23rd Floor · San Francisco, CA 94104-4398 · 415-788-3111

ENERGY LAW

Los Angeles

Gregory R. McClintock · Akerman Senterfitt · http://www.akerman.com · 725 South Figueroa Street, 38th Floor · Los Angeles, CA 90017-5438 · 213-688-9500

Charles Read · O'Melveny & Myers · 400 South Hope Street, 10th Floor · Los Angeles, CA 90071-2899 · 213-430-6000

John W. Spiegel · Munger, Tolles & Olson · 355 South Grand Avenue, 35th Floor · Los Angeles, CA 90071-1560 · 213-683-9100

Henry Weissmann · Munger, Tolles & Olson · 355 South Grand Avenue, 35th Floor · Los Angeles, CA 90071-1560 · 213-683-9100

Riverside

Arthur L. Littleworth · ⑩ · Best Best & Krieger · 3750 University Avenue, Suite 400 · P.O. Box 1028 · Riverside, CA 92502 · 951-686-1450

Michelle Ouellette · Best Best & Krieger · 3750 University Avenue, Suite 400 · P.O. Box 1028 · Riverside, CA 92502 · 951-686-1450

Gregory K. Wilkinson · Best Best & Krieger · 3750 University Avenue, Suite 400 · P.O. Box 1028 · Riverside, CA 92502 · 951-686-1450

Roseville

Dennis W. DeCuir · Dennis W. De Cuir · 2999 Douglas Boulevard, Suite 325 · Roseville, CA 95661-3839 916-788-1022

Sacramento

Dan L. Carroll · Downey Brand · 555 Capitol Mall, 10th Floor · Sacramento, CA 95814 · 916-444-1000

Christopher T. Ellison · Ellison, Schneider & Harris · 2015 H Street · Sacramento, CA 95814-3109 · 916-447-2166

Stuart L. Somach · ⑩ · Somach, Simmons & Dunn · http://www.somachlaw.com · Hall of Justice Building, Third Floor · 813 Sixth Street · Sacramento, CA 95814-2403 · 916-446-7979

San Francisco

Michael B. Day · ⑩ · Goodin, MacBride, Squeri, Ritchie & Day · 505 Sansome Street, Suite 900 · San Francisco, CA 94111 · 415-392-7900

Marie L. Fiala · Heller Ehrman · 333 Bush Street · San Francisco, CA 94104-2878 · 415-772-6000

Steven F. Greenwald · Davis Wright Tremaine · 505 Montgomery Street, Suite 800 · San Francisco, CA 94111-6533 · 415-276-6500

Joseph M. Karp · Winston & Strawn · 101 California Street, 39th Floor · San Francisco, CA 94111-5802 · 415-591-1000

William D. Kissinger · Bingham McCutchen · http://www.bingham.com · Three Embarcadero Center · San Francisco, CA 94111-4067 · 415-393-2000

Thomas J. MacBride, Jr. · ⑩ · Goodin, MacBride, Squeri, Ritchie & Day · 505 Sansome Street, Suite 900 San Francisco, CA 94111 · 415-392-7900

Joseph M. Malkin · Orrick, Herrington & Sutcliffe · The Orrick Building · 405 Howard Street · San Francisco, CA 94105-2669 · 415-773-5700

Martin A. Mattes · ⑩ · Nossaman · http://www.nossaman.com · 50 California Street, 34th Floor · San Francisco, CA 94111-4707 · 415-398-3600

Edward W. O'Neill · Davis Wright Tremaine · 505 Montgomery Street, Suite 800 · San Francisco, CA 94111-6533 · 415-276-6500

Martin S. Schenker · Cooley Godward Kronish · 101 California Street, Fifth Floor · San Francisco, CA 94111-5800 · 415-693-2000

James D. Squeri · ⑩ · Goodin, MacBride, Squeri, Ritchie & Day · 505 Sansome Street, Suite 900 · San Francisco, CA 94111 · 415-392-7900

Walnut Creek

William H. Booth · ⑩ · William H. Booth · 1500 Newell Avenue, Fifth Floor · Walnut Creek, CA 94596 · 925-296-2460

Gordon P. Erspamer · Morrison & Foerster · http://www.mofo.com · 101 Ygnacio Valley Road, Suite 450 Walnut Creek, CA 94596-4095 · 925-295-3300

Peter W. Hanschen · ⑩ · Morrison & Foerster · http://www.mofo.com · 101 Ygnacio Valley Road, Suite 450 · Walnut Creek, CA 94596-4095 · 925-295-3300

ENTERTAINMENT LAW

Atherton

Donald S. Engel · ⑳ · Engel & Engel · 71 Atherton Avenue · Atherton, CA 94027 · 650-386-3312

Beverly Hills

Michael Bergman · Weissmann, Wolff, Bergman, Coleman, Grodin & Evall · 9665 Wilshire Boulevard, Ninth Floor · Beverly Hills, CA 90212-2345 · 310-858-7888

Jacob A. Bloom · Bloom Hergott Diemer Rosenthal & LaViolette · 150 South Rodeo Drive, Third Floor · Beverly Hills, CA 90212 · 310-859-6880

Thomas M. Hansen · ⑩ · Hansen, Jacobson, Teller, Hoberman, Newman & Warren · 450 North Roxbury Drive, Eighth Floor · Beverly Hills, CA 90210-4222 · 310-271-8777

Alan S. Hergott · Bloom Hergott Diemer Rosenthal & LaViolette · 150 South Rodeo Drive, Third Floor · Beverly Hills, CA 90212 · 310-859-6880

Craig Jacobson · Hansen, Jacobson, Teller, Hoberman, Newman & Warren · 450 North Roxbury Drive, Eighth Floor · Beverly Hills, CA 90210-4222 · 310-271-8777

Seth I. Lichtenstein · Goldring, Hertz & Lichtenstein · 450 North Roxbury Drive, Eighth Floor · Beverly Hills, CA 90210-4222 · 310-271-8777

Jeffrey L. Nagin · ⑩ · Rosenfeld, Meyer & Susman · 9601 Wilshire Boulevard, Suite 710 · Beverly Hills, CA 90210-5288 · 310-858-7700

Jeanne Newman · Hansen, Jacobson, Teller, Hoberman, Newman & Warren · 450 North Roxbury Drive, Eighth Floor · Beverly Hills, CA 90210-4222 · 310-271-8777

Donald S. Passman · ⑳ · Gang, Tyre, Ramer & Brown · 132 South Rodeo Drive · Beverly Hills, CA 90212-2425 · 310-777-4800

Bruce M. Ramer · ⑳ · Gang, Tyre, Ramer & Brown · 132 South Rodeo Drive · Beverly Hills, CA 90212-2425 · 310-777-4800

Eric Weissmann · ⑳ · Weissmann, Wolff, Bergman, Coleman, Grodin & Evall · 9665 Wilshire Boulevard, Ninth Floor · Beverly Hills, CA 90212-2345 · 310-858-7888

Capitola

Judy Alexander · Law Office of Judy Alexander · 1500 Forty-First Avenue, Suite 290 · Capitola, CA 95010 · 831-479-3488

Claremont

Frank N. Darras · Shernoff Bidart & Darras · 600 South Indian Hill Boulevard · Claremont, CA 91711 · 909-621-4935

Los Angeles

Leslie B. Abell · Myman, Abell, Fineman, Greenspan & Light · 11601 Wilshire Boulevard, Suite 2200 · Los Angeles, CA 90025 · 310-231-0800

Fredric I. Bernstein · Proskauer Rose · http://www.proskauer.com · 2049 Century Park East, 32nd Floor · Los Angeles, CA 90067-3206 · 310-557-2900

Charles J. Biederman · Manatt, Phelps & Phillips · 11355 West Olympic Boulevard · Los Angeles, CA 90064 · 310-312-4000

John G. Branca · ⑳ · Ziffren, Brittenham, Branca, Fischer, Gilbert-Lurie, Stiffelman, Cook, Johnson, Lande & Wolf · 1801 Century Park West · Los Angeles, CA 90067-6406 · 310-552-3388

Harry M. Brittenham · ⑳ · Ziffren, Brittenham, Branca, Fischer, Gilbert-Lurie, Stiffelman, Cook, Johnson, Lande & Wolf · 1801 Century Park West · Los Angeles, CA 90067-6406 · 310-552-3388

Alan M. Brunswick · Manatt, Phelps & Phillips · 11355 West Olympic Boulevard · Los Angeles, CA 90064 · 310-312-4000

P. John Burke · Akin Gump Strauss Hauer & Feld · 2029 Century Park East, Suite 2400 · Los Angeles, CA 90067-3012 · 310-229-1000

Joseph Calabrese · O'Melveny & Myers · 1999 Avenue of the Stars, Seventh Floor · Los Angeles, CA 90067-6035 · 310-553-6700

William L. Cole · Mitchell Silberberg & Knupp · 11377 West Olympic Boulevard · Los Angeles, CA 90064 · 310-312-2000

Melanie K. Cook · Ziffren, Brittenham, Branca, Fischer, Gilbert-Lurie, Stiffelman, Cook, Johnson, Lande & Wolf · 1801 Century Park West · Los Angeles, CA 90067-6406 · 310-552-3388

Robert A. Darwell · Sheppard, Mullin, Richter & Hampton · http://www.sheppardmullin.com · 1901 Avenue of the Stars, Suite 1600 · Los Angeles, CA 90067 · 310-228-3700

Bert H. Deixler · Proskauer Rose · http://www.proskauer.com · 2049 Century Park East, 32nd Floor · Los Angeles, CA 90067-3206 · 310-557-2900

John A. Donovan · Skadden, Arps, Slate, Meagher & Flom · 300 South Grand Avenue, Suite 3400 · Los Angeles, CA 90071 · 213-687-5000

Scott A. Edelman · Gibson, Dunn & Crutcher · 2029 Century Park East, 40th Floor · Los Angeles, CA 90067-3026 · 310-552-8500

Craig A. Emanuel · Loeb & Loeb · 10100 Santa Monica Boulevard, Suite 2200 · Los Angeles, CA 90067-4164 · 310-282-2000

Howard D. Fabrick · Akin Gump Strauss Hauer & Feld · 2029 Century Park East, Suite 2400 · Los Angeles, CA 90067-3012 · 310-229-1000

Steven E. Fayne · Akin Gump Strauss Hauer & Feld · 2029 Century Park East, Suite 2400 · Los Angeles, CA 90067-3012 · 310-229-1000

Bertram Fields · ⑳ · Greenberg Glusker · 1900 Avenue of the Stars, 21st Floor · Los Angeles, CA 90067 · 310-553-3610

Samuel N. Fischer · Ziffren, Brittenham, Branca, Fischer, Gilbert-Lurie, Stiffelman, Cook, Johnson, Lande & Wolf · 1801 Century Park West · Los Angeles, CA 90067-6406 · 310-552-3388

Russell J. Frackman · Mitchell Silberberg & Knupp · 11377 West Olympic Boulevard · Los Angeles, CA 90064 · 310-312-2000

John T. Frankenheimer · ⑳ · Loeb & Loeb · 10100 Santa Monica Boulevard, Suite 2200 · Los Angeles, CA 90067-4164 · 310-282-2000

Clifford Ward Gilbert · Ziffren, Brittenham, Branca, Fischer, Gilbert-Lurie, Stiffelman, Cook, Johnson, Lande & Wolf · 1801 Century Park West · Los Angeles, CA 90067-6406 · 310-552-3388

Patricia Glaser · Christensen, Glaser, Fink, Jacobs, Weil & Shapiro · 10250 Constellation Boulevard, 19th Floor · Los Angeles, CA 90067 · 310-553-3000

Susan A. Grode · Katten Muchin Rosenman · 2029 Century Park East, Suite 2600 · Los Angeles, CA 90067-3012 · 310-788-4400

Barry L. Hirsch · ⑳ · Hirsch Wallerstein Matlof & Fishman · 10100 Santa Monica Boulevard, Suite 1700 · Los Angeles, CA 90067 · 310-703-1700

James R. Jackoway · Jackoway Tyerman Wertheimer Austen Mandelbaum Morris & Klein · 1925 Century Park East, 22nd Floor · Los Angeles, CA 90067 · 310-553-0305

Richard B. Kendall · Irell & Manella · 1800 Avenue of the Stars, Suite 900 · Los Angeles, CA 90067-4276 310-277-1010

Barry B. Langberg · Stroock & Stroock & Lavan · 2029 Century Park East · Los Angeles, CA 90067-3086 310-556-5800

John H. Lavely, Jr. · Lavely & Singer · 2049 Century Park East, Suite 2400 · Los Angeles, CA 90067-2906 · 310-556-3501

Thomas Glen Leo · Sheppard, Mullin, Richter & Hampton · http://www.sheppardmullin.com · 1901 Avenue of the Stars, Suite 1600 · Los Angeles, CA 90067 · 310-228-3700

Gerald A. Margolis · Manatt, Phelps & Phillips · 11355 West Olympic Boulevard · Los Angeles, CA 90064 · 310-312-4000

Michael A. Mayerson · ⑩ · Loeb & Loeb · 10100 Santa Monica Boulevard, Suite 2200 · Los Angeles, CA 90067-4164 · 310-282-2000

Schuyler M. Moore · Stroock & Stroock & Lavan · 2029 Century Park East · Los Angeles, CA 90067-3086 · 310-556-5800

Christopher C. Murray · ⑩ · O'Melveny & Myers · 1999 Avenue of the Stars, Seventh Floor · Los Angeles, CA 90067-6035 · 310-553-6700

David Nochimson · ⑩ · Ziffren, Brittenham, Branca, Fischer, Gilbert-Lurie, Stiffelman, Cook, Johnson, Lande & Wolf · 1801 Century Park West · Los Angeles, CA 90067-6406 · 310-552-3388

Michael J. O'Connor · White O'Connor Fink & Brenner · 10100 Santa Monica Boulevard, Suite 2300 · Los Angeles, CA 90067 · 310-712-6100

L. Lee Phillips · ⑳ · Manatt, Phelps & Phillips · 11355 West Olympic Boulevard · Los Angeles, CA 90064 · 310-312-4000

Marissa J. Román · Akin Gump Strauss Hauer & Feld · 2029 Century Park East, Suite 2400 · Los Angeles, CA 90067-3012 · 310-229-1000

Ronald S. Rosen · TroyGould · http://www.troygould.com · 1801 Century Park East, Suite 1600 · Los Angeles, CA 90067 · 310-553-4441

Henry Shields, Jr. · Irell & Manella · 1800 Avenue of the Stars, Suite 900 · Los Angeles, CA 90067-4276 · 310-277-1010

Martin D. Singer · Lavely & Singer · 2049 Century Park East, Suite 2400 · Los Angeles, CA 90067-2906 · 310-556-3501

Gary S. Stiffelman · Ziffren, Brittenham, Branca, Fischer, Gilbert-Lurie, Stiffelman, Cook, Johnson, Lande & Wolf · 1801 Century Park West · Los Angeles, CA 90067-6406 · 310-552-3388

Henry J. Tashman · Davis Wright Tremaine · 865 South Figueroa Street, Suite 2400 · Los Angeles, CA 90017-2566 · 213-633-6800

Barry W. Tyerman · ⑩ · Jackoway Tyerman Wertheimer Austen Mandelbaum Morris & Klein · 1925 Century Park East, 22nd Floor · Los Angeles, CA 90067 · 310-553-0305

Lawrence J. Ulman · Gibson, Dunn & Crutcher · 2029 Century Park East, 40th Floor · Los Angeles, CA 90067-3026 · 310-552-8500

Andrew M. White · White O'Connor Fink & Brenner · 10100 Santa Monica Boulevard, Suite 2300 · Los Angeles, CA 90067 · 310-712-6100

Bryan L. Wolf · Ziffren, Brittenham, Branca, Fischer, Gilbert-Lurie, Stiffelman, Cook, Johnson, Lande & Wolf · 1801 Century Park West · Los Angeles, CA 90067-6406 · 310-552-3388

Juliette C. Youngblood · Irell & Manella · 1800 Avenue of the Stars, Suite 900 · Los Angeles, CA 90067-4276 · 310-277-1010

Kenneth Ziffren · ⑳ · Ziffren, Brittenham, Branca, Fischer, Gilbert-Lurie, Stiffelman, Cook, Johnson, Lande & Wolf · 1801 Century Park West · Los Angeles, CA 90067-6406 · 310-552-3388

Palo Alto

James M. Chadwick · Sheppard, Mullin, Richter & Hampton · http://www.sheppardmullin.com · 2225 East Bayshore Road, Suite 205 · Palo Alto, CA 94303 · 650-320-1777

Daniel H. Black · Greenberg Traurig · http://www.gtlaw.com · 2450 Colorado Avenue, Suite 400-E · Santa Monica, CA 90404 · 310-586-7700

Jay L. Cooper · (20) · Greenberg Traurig · http://www.gtlaw.com · 2450 Colorado Avenue, Suite 400-E · Santa Monica, CA 90404 · 310-586-7700

Ernest Del · Del, Shaw, Moonves, Tanaka, Finkelstein & Lezcano · 2120 Colorado Avenue, Suite 200 · Santa Monica, CA 90404 · 310-979-7900

Marcia J. Harris · Dreier Stein Kahan Browne Woods George · The Water Garden · North Tower, Sixth Floor · 1620 Twenty-Sixth Street · Santa Monica, CA 90404 · 310-828-9050

Lawrence Y. Iser · Kinsella Weitzman Iser Kump & Aldisert · http://www.kwikalaw.com · 808 Wilshire Boulevard, Third Floor · Santa Monica, CA 90401 · 310-566-9800

Steven Katleman · Greenberg Traurig · http://www.gtlaw.com · 2450 Colorado Avenue, Suite 400-E · Santa Monica, CA 90404 · 310-586-7700

Dale F. Kinsella · (10) · Kinsella Weitzman Iser Kump & Aldisert · http://www.kwikalaw.com · 808 Wilshire Boulevard, Third Floor · Santa Monica, CA 90401 · 310-566-9800

Richard I. Leher · Greenberg Traurig · http://www.gtlaw.com · 2450 Colorado Avenue, Suite 400-E · Santa Monica, CA 90404 · 310-586-7700

Michael J. Plonsker · Dreier Stein Kahan Browne Woods George · The Water Garden · North Tower, Sixth Floor · 1620 Twenty-Sixth Street · Santa Monica, CA 90404 · 310-828-9050

Samuel R. Pryor · Dreier Stein Kahan Browne Woods George · The Water Garden · North Tower, Sixth Floor · 1620 Twenty-Sixth Street · Santa Monica, CA 90404 · 310-828-9050

Alan U. Schwartz · Greenberg Traurig · http://www.gtlaw.com · 2450 Colorado Avenue, Suite 400-E · Santa Monica, CA 90404 · 310-586-7700

Nina L. Shaw · Del, Shaw, Moonves, Tanaka, Finkelstein & Lezcano · 2120 Colorado Avenue, Suite 200 · Santa Monica, CA 90404 · 310-979-7900

Stanton L. Stein · Dreier Stein Kahan Browne Woods George · The Water Garden · North Tower, Sixth Floor · 1620 Twenty-Sixth Street · Santa Monica, CA 90404 · 310-828-9050

Howard L. Weitzman · Kinsella Weitzman Iser Kump & Aldisert · http://www.kwikalaw.com · 808 Wilshire Boulevard, Third Floor · Santa Monica, CA 90401 · 310-566-9800

ENVIRONMENTAL LAW

East Palo Alto

Christopher P. Berka · Bingham McCutchen · http://www.bingham.com · 1900 University Avenue · East Palo Alto, CA 94303-2223 · 650-849-4400

Irvine

Robert D. Thornton · Nossaman · http://www.nossaman.com · 18101 Von Karman Avenue, Suite 1800 · Irvine, CA 92612-0177 · 949-833-7800

Long Beach

Elizabeth P. Beazley · Keesal, Young & Logan · 400 Oceangate · P.O. Box 1730 · Long Beach, CA 90801-1730 · 562-436-2000

Los Angeles

Patrick W. Dennis · ⑩ · Gibson, Dunn & Crutcher · 333 South Grand Avenue · Los Angeles, CA 90071-3197 · 213-229-7000

Bruce P. Howard · ⑩ · Latham & Watkins · 355 South Grand Avenue · Los Angeles, CA 90071-1560 · 213-485-1234

Colin Lennard · Fulbright & Jaworski · http://www.fulbright.com · 555 South Flower Street, 41st Floor · Los Angeles, CA 90071 · 213-892-9200

Gene A. Lucero · Latham & Watkins · 355 South Grand Avenue · Los Angeles, CA 90071-1560 · 213-485-1234

Gregory R. McClintock · Akerman Senterfitt · http://www.akerman.com · 725 South Figueroa Street, 38th Floor · Los Angeles, CA 90017-5438 · 213-688-9500

Martin J. McTigue · O'Melveny & Myers · 400 South Hope Street, 10th Floor · Los Angeles, CA 90071-2899 · 213-430-6000

Sharon F. Rubalcava · Weston Benshoof Rochefort Rubalcava MacCuish · 333 South Hope Street, 16th Floor · Los Angeles, CA 90071 · 213-576-1000

Jocelyn N. Thompson · Weston Benshoof Rochefort Rubalcava MacCuish · 333 South Hope Street, 16th Floor · Los Angeles, CA 90071 · 213-576-1000

Robert A. Wyman, Jr. · ⑩ · Latham & Watkins · 355 South Grand Avenue · Los Angeles, CA 90071-1560 · 213-485-1234

Oakland

Donnell Van Noppen III · ⑩ · Earth Justice · 426 Seventeenth Street, Sixth Floor · Oakland, CA 94612 · 510-550-6700

Riverside

Arthur L. Littleworth · ⑩ · Best Best & Krieger · 3750 University Avenue, Suite 400 · P.O. Box 1028 · Riverside, CA 92502 · 951-686-1450

Michelle Ouellette · Best Best & Krieger · 3750 University Avenue, Suite 400 · P.O. Box 1028 · Riverside, CA 92502 · 951-686-1450

Gregory K. Wilkinson · Best Best & Krieger · 3750 University Avenue, Suite 400 · P.O. Box 1028 · Riverside, CA 92502 · 951-686-1450

Sacramento

Mark D. Harrison · Diepenbrock Harrison · 400 Capitol Mall, Suite 1800 · Sacramento, CA 95814 · 916-446-4469

Timothy M. Taylor · Stoel Rives · http://www.stoel.com · 980 Ninth Street, Suite 1900 · Sacramento, CA 95814 · 916-447-0700

Tina A. Thomas · Remy, Thomas, Moose and Manley · 455 Capitol Mall, Suite 210 · Sacramento, CA 95814 · 916-443-2745

San Francisco

John F. Barg · Barg Coffin Lewis & Trapp · http://www.bcltlaw.com · 350 California Street, 22nd Floor · San Francisco, CA 94104-1435 · 415-228-5400

Michael R. Barr · ⑳ · Pillsbury Winthrop Shaw Pittman · http://www.pillsburylaw.com · 50 Fremont Street · P.O. Box 7880 · San Francisco, CA 94120-7880 · 415-983-1000

James A. Bruen · ⑳ · Farella Braun & Martel · Russ Building, 17th Floor · 235 Montgomery Street · San Francisco, CA 94104 · 415-954-4400

Christopher J. Carr · Morrison & Foerster · http://www.mofo.com · 425 Market Street · San Francisco, CA 94105-2482 · 415-268-7000

Richard C. Coffin · Barg Coffin Lewis & Trapp · http://www.bcltlaw.com · 350 California Street, 22nd Floor · San Francisco, CA 94104-1435 · 415-228-5400

Michèle B. Corash · ⑩ · Morrison & Foerster · http://www.mofo.com · 425 Market Street · San Francisco, CA 94105-2482 · 415-268-7000

Pamela S. Duffy · ⑩ · Coblentz, Patch, Duffy & Bass · http://www.coblentzlaw.com · One Ferry Building, Suite 200 · San Francisco, CA 94111-4213 · 415-391-4800

John D. Edgcomb · Edgcomb Law Group · 115 Sansome Street, Suite 700 · San Francisco, CA 94104-3603 · 415-399-1555

Robert L. Falk · Morrison & Foerster · http://www.mofo.com · 425 Market Street · San Francisco, CA 94105-2482 · 415-268-7000

Ronald C. Hausmann · ⑳ · Munger, Tolles & Olson · 560 Mission Street, 27th Floor · San Francisco, CA 94105-9781 · 415-512-4000

Jennifer L. Hernandez · Holland & Knight · http://www.hklaw.com · 50 California Street, Suite 2800 · San Francisco, CA 94111-4624 · 415-743-6900

Karen J. Nardi · Bingham McCutchen · http://www.bingham.com · Three Embarcadero Center · San Francisco, CA 94111-4067 · 415-393-2000

Sandi L. Nichols · Allen Matkins Leck Gamble Mallory & Natsis · Three Embarcadero Center, 12th Floor · San Francisco, CA 94111-4074 · 415-837-1515

Trenton H. Norris · Arnold & Porter · 90 New Montgomery Street, Suite 600 · San Francisco, CA 94105 · 415-356-3000

Margaret N. Rosegay · Pillsbury Winthrop Shaw Pittman · http://www.pillsburylaw.com · 50 Fremont Street · P.O. Box 7880 · San Francisco, CA 94120-7880 · 415-983-1000

Deborah J. Schmall · Paul Hastings · 55 Second Street, 24th Floor · San Francisco, CA 94105 · 415-856-7000

Michael J. Steel · Morrison & Foerster · http://www.mofo.com · 425 Market Street · San Francisco, CA 94105-2482 · 415-268-7000

Robert D. Wyatt · ⑩ · Allen Matkins Leck Gamble Mallory & Natsis · Three Embarcadero Center, 12th Floor · San Francisco, CA 94111-4074 · 415-837-1515

Michael H. Zischke · Cox, Castle & Nicholson · 555 California Street, 10th Floor · San Francisco, CA 94104 · 415-392-4200

San Rafael

Gary T. Ragghianti · Ragghianti Freitas · 874 Fourth Street, Suite D · San Rafael, CA 94901-3246 · 415-453-9433

Walnut Creek

Patricia E. Curtin · Morgan Miller Blair · 1331 North California Boulevard, Suite 200 · Walnut Creek, CA 94596-4544 · 925-937-3600

Bruce Reed Goodmiller · Morrison & Foerster · http://www.mofo.com · 101 Ygnacio Valley Road, Suite 450 · Walnut Creek, CA 94596-4095 · 925-295-3300

Stephen L. Kostka · Bingham McCutchen · http://www.bingham.com · 1333 North California Boulevard, Suite 210 · Walnut Creek, CA 94596-1270 · 925-937-8000

EQUIPMENT FINANCE LAW

Los Angeles

John D. Berchild, Jr. · Sheppard, Mullin, Richter & Hampton · http://www.sheppardmullin.com · 333 South Hope Street, 48th Floor · Los Angeles, CA 90071-1448 · 213-620-1780

Robert C. Colton · Buchalter Nemer · 1000 Wilshire Boulevard, Suite 1500 · Los Angeles, CA 90017-2457 · 213-891-0700

Joseph M. Malinowski · Kaye Scholer · 1999 Avenue of the Stars, Suite 1700 · Los Angeles, CA 90067-6048 · 310-788-1000

Gary D. Samson · McGuireWoods · http://www.mcguirewoods.com · 1800 Century Park East, Eighth Floor · Los Angeles, CA 90067 · 310-315-8200

Richard K. Smith, Jr. · White & Case · http://www.whitecase.com · 633 West Fifth Street, Suite 1900 · Los Angeles, CA 90071-2007 · 213-620-7700

Steven O. Weise · ⑩ · Heller Ehrman · 333 South Hope Street, 39th Floor · Los Angeles, CA 90071-1406 213-689-0200

San Diego

Eli W. Mansour · Luce, Forward, Hamilton & Scripps · http://www.luce.com · 11988 El Camino Real, Suite 200 · San Diego, CA 92130-2594 · 858-720-6300

San Francisco

Barry A. Dubin · Cooper, White & Cooper · 201 California Street, 17th Floor · San Francisco, CA 94111-3013 · 415-433-1900

Barry Graynor · Cooley Godward Kronish · 101 California Street, Fifth Floor · San Francisco, CA 94111-5800 · 415-693-2000

George A. Hisert · ⑩ · Bingham McCutchen · http://www.bingham.com · Three Embarcadero Center · San Francisco, CA 94111-4067 · 415-393-2000

William B. Piels · Holland & Knight · http://www.hklaw.com · 50 California Street, Suite 2800 · San Francisco, CA 94111-4624 · 415-743-6900

Dennis M. Talbott · ⑩ · Severson & Werson · One Embarcadero Center, Suite 2600 · San Francisco, CA 94111 · 415-398-3344

Robert Alan Zadek · Buchalter Nemer · 333 Market Street, 25th Floor · San Francisco, CA 94105-2102 · 415-227-0900

Thomas A. Zimmer · Holland & Knight · http://www.hklaw.com · 50 California Street, Suite 2800 · San Francisco, CA 94111-4624 · 415-743-6900

ETHICS AND PROFESSIONAL RESPONSIBILITY LAW

South Pasadena

Ellen Anne Pansky · Pansky & Markle · 1010 Sycamore Avenue, Suite 101 · South Pasadena, CA 91030 · 213-626-7300

Walnut Creek

Carol Langford · Carol Langford · 100 Pringle Avenue, Suite 570 · Walnut Creek, CA 94596 · 925-938-3870

FAMILY LAW

Bakersfield

Edward J. Thomas · Law Office of Edward J. Thomas · 5201 California Avenue, Suite 400 · Bakersfield, CA 93309-1673 · 661-322-1777

Berkeley

Richard I. Sherman · ⑩ · De Goff and Sherman · 1916 Los Angeles Avenue · Berkeley, CA 94707 · 510-524-1840

Beverly Hills

Ronald W. Anteau · ⑩ · Kolodny & Anteau · West Tower, Ninth Floor · 9100 Wilshire Boulevard · Beverly Hills, CA 90212-3425 · 310-271-5533

Bruce A. Clemens · ⑩ · Jaffe & Clemens · 433 North Camden Drive, Suite 1000 · Beverly Hills, CA 90210 · 310-550-7477

William J. Glucksman · Kolodny & Anteau · West Tower, Ninth Floor · 9100 Wilshire Boulevard · Beverly Hills, CA 90212-3425 · 310-271-5533

Neal Raymond Hersh · Hersh, Mannis & Bogen · 9150 Wilshire Boulevard, Suite 209 · Beverly Hills, CA 90212 · 310-786-1910

Daniel J. Jaffe · ⑳ · Jaffe & Clemens · 433 North Camden Drive, Suite 1000 · Beverly Hills, CA 90210 · 310-550-7477

Robert S. Kaufman · Kaufman, Young, Spiegel, Robinson & Kenerson · 301 North Cannon Drive, Suite 300 · Beverly Hills, CA 90210-4724 · 310-887-5100

Stephen A. Kolodny · ⑩ · Kolodny & Anteau · West Tower, Ninth Floor · 9100 Wilshire Boulevard · Beverly Hills, CA 90212-3425 · 310-271-5533

Craig B. Leeds · Leeds, Wender & Rosenfeld · http://www.beverlyhillslaw.com · 9107 Wilshire Boulevard, Suite 300 · Beverly Hills, CA 90210 · 310-278-7560

David M. Luboff · Jaffe & Clemens · 433 North Camden Drive, Suite 1000 · Beverly Hills, CA 90210 · 310-550-7477

Ronald A. Rosenfeld · ⑩ · Leeds, Wender & Rosenfeld · http://www.beverlyhillslaw.com · 9107 Wilshire Boulevard, Suite 300 · Beverly Hills, CA 90210 · 310-278-7560

Melvyn J. Ross · Law Offices of Melvyn J. Ross · 9401 Wilshire Boulevard, Suite 1250 · Beverly Hills, CA 90212-2926 · 310-278-4000

William S. Ryden · Jaffe & Clemens · 433 North Camden Drive, Suite 1000 · Beverly Hills, CA 90210 · 310-550-7477

Lance S. Spiegel · Kaufman, Young, Spiegel, Robinson & Kenerson · 301 North Cannon Drive, Suite 300 Beverly Hills, CA 90210-4724 · 310-887-5100

Peter M. Walzer · Walzer & Melcher · 499 North Canon Drive, Fourth Floor · Beverly Hills, CA 90210 · 310-557-0915

Claremont

Thomas C. Brayton · ⑩ · Jones & Brayton · 250 West First Street, Suite 320 · Claremont, CA 91711 · 909-447-8500

Corte Madera

Madeleine Simborg · ⑩ · Simborg & Killingsworth · 770 Tamalpais Drive, Suite 401-A · Corte Madera, CA 94925 · 415-924-7171

Costa Mesa

Saul M. Gelbart · Stegmeier & Gelbart · 3090 Bristol Street, Suite 220 · Costa Mesa, CA 92626 · 714-957-6116

Eleanor A. Stegmeier · ⑩ · Stegmeier & Gelbart · 3090 Bristol Street, Suite 220 · Costa Mesa, CA 92626 714-957-6116

El Cajon

S. Michael Love · ⑳ · McDougal, Love, Eckis, Smith, Boehmer & Foley · 460 North Magnolia Avenue · P.O. Drawer 1466 · El Cajon, CA 92022-1466 · 619-440-4444

Fresno

Stephen A. Kalemkarian · ⑳ · Stephen A. Kalemkarian · 371 East Bullard, Suite 115 · Fresno, CA 93710-5217 · 559-435-2525

Half Moon Bay

Marc H. Gradstein · Gradstein & Gorman · 80 Stone Pine Road, Suite 101 · Half Moon Bay, CA 94019 · 650-560-0123

Lafayette

Diane G. Michelsen · Law Offices of Diane Michelsen · 3190 Old Tunnel Road · Lafayette, CA 94549-4133 · 925-945-1880

Los Angeles

Glenn S. Buzard · Buter, Buzard, Dunaetz & Fishbein · 11611 San Vicente Boulevard, Suite 820 · Los Angeles, CA 90049 · 310-820-6700

Bruce E. Cooperman · Wasser, Cooperman & Carter · One Century Plaza, Suite 1200 · 2029 Century Park East · Los Angeles, CA 90067 · 310-277-7117

Patrick DeCarolis, Jr. · Trope & DeCarolis · 11620 Wilshire Boulevard, Suite 710 · Los Angeles, CA 90025 · 310-405-7373

Thomas Paine Dunlap · Trope & Trope · 12121 Wilshire Boulevard, Suite 801 · Los Angeles, CA 90025 · 310-207-8228

John A. Foley · Wasser, Cooperman & Carter · One Century Plaza, Suite 1200 · 2029 Century Park East · Los Angeles, CA 90067 · 310-277-7117

Judith R. Forman · Law Offices of Judith R. Forman · 11355 West Olympic Boulevard · Los Angeles, CA 90064 · 310-444-8840

Manley Freid · ⑩ · Freid and Goldsman · 2029 Century Park East, Suite 860 · Los Angeles, CA 90067 · 310-552-2700

Larry A. Ginsberg · Harris-Ginsberg · http://www.harris-ginsberg.com · 6500 Wilshire Boulevard, Suite 1870 · Los Angeles, CA 90048 · 310-444-6333

Melvin S. Goldsman · Freid and Goldsman · 2029 Century Park East, Suite 860 · Los Angeles, CA 90067 310-552-2700

Suzanne Harris · Harris-Ginsberg · http://www.harris-ginsberg.com · 6500 Wilshire Boulevard, Suite 1870 Los Angeles, CA 90048 · 310-444-6333

Anne C. Kiley · Trope & Trope · 12121 Wilshire Boulevard, Suite 801 · Los Angeles, CA 90025 · 310-207-8228

Steven Knowles · ⑩ · Trope & Trope · 12121 Wilshire Boulevard, Suite 801 · Los Angeles, CA 90025 · 310-207-8228

Stacy D. Phillips · Phillips, Lerner, Lauzon & Jamra · One Century Plaza, Suite 1200 · 2029 Century Park East · Los Angeles, CA 90067 · 310-277-7117

David J. Radis · Law Office of David J. Radis · 1901 Avenue Of The Stars, Suite 1900 · Los Angeles, CA 90067 · 310-552-0536

Richard A. Stilz · Law Offices of Richard A. Stilz · 11845 West Olympic Boulevard, Suite 1000 · Los Angeles, CA 90064 · 310-312-8100

Sorrell Trope · ⑳ · Trope & Trope · 12121 Wilshire Boulevard, Suite 801 · Los Angeles, CA 90025 · 310-207-8228

Dennis M. Wasser · ㉕ · Wasser, Cooperman & Carter · One Century Plaza, Suite 1200 · 2029 Century Park East · Los Angeles, CA 90067 · 310-277-7117

Laura Wasser · Wasser, Cooperman & Carter · One Century Plaza, Suite 1200 · 2029 Century Park East · Los Angeles, CA 90067 · 310-277-7117

Menlo Park

Clifford R. Chernick · Law Offices of Clifford Ross Chernick · http://www.chernicklaw.com · 770 Menlo Avenue, Suite 101 · Menlo Park, CA 94025-4736 · 650-327-5570

Napa

Robert E. Blevans · Lewis & Blevans · 1005 Coombs Street · Napa, CA 94559 · 707-226-9928

Roger J. Lewis · Lewis & Blevans · 1005 Coombs Street · Napa, CA 94559 · 707-226-9928

Newport Beach

Steven E. Briggs · ⑩ · Law Offices of Steven E. Briggs · 2700 Newport Boulevard, Suite 172 · Newport Beach, CA 92663 · 949-673-7410

Mark E. Minyard · ⑩ · Minyard and Morris · 1811 Quail Street · Newport Beach, CA 92660 · 949-724-1111

Michael A. Morris · Minyard and Morris · 1811 Quail Street · Newport Beach, CA 92660 · 949-724-1111

Gerald J. Phillips · Phillips, Whisnant, Gazin & Gorczyca · 230 Newport Center Drive, Third Floor · Newport Beach, CA 92660 · 949-644-4007

John R. Schilling · ⑩ · John R. Schilling · Tower One, Suite 590 · 4675 MacArthur Court · Newport Beach, CA 92660 · 949-833-8833

Philip G. Seastrom · Philip G. Seastrom & Associates · 4695 MacArthur Court, Suite 1450 · Newport Beach, CA 92660 · 949-474-0800

Jaqueline A. Whisnant · Phillips, Whisnant, Gazin & Gorczyca · 230 Newport Center Drive, Third Floor Newport Beach, CA 92660 · 949-644-4007

Oakland

Lorin B. Blum · ⑩ · Blum, Braz & Gibbs · http://www.bbgfamilylaw.com · 1939 Harrison Street, Suite 818 Oakland, CA 94612-3533 · 510-465-3927

Garrett C. Dailey · ⑩ · Law Offices of Garrett C. Dailey · 2915 McClure Street · Oakland, CA 94609 · 510-465-3920

Donna T. Gibbs · Blum, Braz & Gibbs · http://www.bbgfamilylaw.com · 1939 Harrison Street, Suite 818 · Oakland, CA 94612-3533 · 510-465-3927

Marjory A. Kaplan · Law Office of Marjory A. Kaplan · 1300 Clay Street, Suite 820 · Oakland, CA 94612 510-763-5611

Sarah H. Leverett · ⑩ · Sarah H. Leverett · 1939 Harrison Street, Suite 710 · Oakland, CA 94612 · 510-832-6600

Deborah J. Marx · Deborah J. Marx · 1300 Clay Street, Suite 820 · Oakland, CA 94612 · 510-763-5611

Miriam Steinbock · Miriam Steinbock · 1300 Clay Street, Suite 820 · Oakland, CA 94612 · 510-763-5611

Ronald A. Wagner · ⑳ · Wagner & Wagner · 1939 Harrison Street, Suite 600 · Oakland, CA 94612 · 510-763-3395

Sandra F. Wagner · ⑩ · Wagner & Wagner · 1939 Harrison Street, Suite 600 · Oakland, CA 94612 · 510-763-3395

Oceanside

Karen M. Heffron · Greenman, Lacy, Klein, O'Harra & Heffron · 900 Pier View Way · P.O. Box 299 · Oceanside, CA 92049-0299 · 760-722-1234

Orange

Robert P. Des Jardins · Robert P. Des Jardins · 333 City Boulevard West, Suite 1210 · Orange, CA 92868 714-634-2779

David L. Price · ⑳ · David L. Price · One City Boulevard West, Suite 1400 · Orange, CA 92868 · 714-634-0200

Thomas P. Stabile · ⑩ · Schwamb & Stabile · 333 City Boulevard West, Suite 710 · Orange, CA 92868 · 714-937-3911

Palo Alto

Jessica F. Arner · ⑩ · Lakin Spears · Embarcadero Place, Suite 110 · 2400 Geng Road · Palo Alto, CA 94303 · 650-328-7000

Pasadena

Don Mike Anthony · Hahn & Hahn · 301 East Colorado Boulevard, Ninth Floor · Pasadena, CA 91101-1977 · 626-796-9123

Lee W. Salisbury · Lee W. Salisbury · 225 South Lake Avenue, Suite 550 · Pasadena, CA 91101-3004 · 626-449-4812

Redwood City

Lana L. Norris · ⑩ · Norris Family Law · http://www.norrisfamilylaw.com · 555 Twin Dolphin Drive, Suite 165 · Redwood City, CA 94065 · 650-622-3500

Philip S. Silvestri · Silvestri Silvestri & Mialocq · 550 Price Avenue, Suite A · Redwood City, CA 94063 · 650-367-0442

Richmond

Francis A. Watson, Jr. · ⑳ · Watson, Hoffe & Hass · 3700 Barrett Avenue · P.O. Box 5001 · Richmond, CA 94805-2297 · 510-237-3700

Roseville

Gary Ralph O'Dell · Law Office of Gary R. O'Dell · 2220 Douglas Boulevard, Suite 200 · Roseville, CA 95661 · 916-786-7078

Sacramento

Anthony S. Dick · ㉕ · Dick & Wagner · 797 University Avenue · Sacramento, CA 95825-6732 · 916-920-9504

Camille H. Hemmer · ⑩ · Law Office of Camille H. Hemmer · 555 University Avenue, Suite 125 · Sacramento, CA 95825 · 916-922-8500

Robert J. O'Hair · ⑩ · Woodruff O'Hair, Posner & Salinger · 2251 Fair Oaks Boulevard, Suite 100 · Sacramento, CA 95825 · 916-920-0211

Nancy Perkovich · ⑩ · Perkovich and Perkovich · 3425 American River Drive · Sacramento, CA 95864 · 916-973-1122

Stephen James Wagner · ⑳ · Dick & Wagner · 797 University Avenue · Sacramento, CA 95825-6732 · 916-920-9504

D. Thomas Woodruff · Woodruff O'Hair, Posner & Salinger · 2251 Fair Oaks Boulevard, Suite 100 · Sacramento, CA 95825 · 916-920-0211

San Bernardino

Charles W. Richardson · ⑩ · Charles W. Richardson · 330 North D Street, Suite 405 · San Bernardino, CA 92401 · 909-889-4495

San Diego

James D. Allen · ⑩ · Allen-Magidson · 401 West A Street, Suite 2050 · San Diego, CA 92101 · 619-232-2050

Bruce M. Beals · Bruce M. Beals · 550 West B Street, Suite 200 · San Diego, CA 92101-3537 · 619-231-6811

Sharon Ann Blanchet · Ashworth, Blanchet, Christensen & Kalemkiarian · 2250 Third Avenue · San Diego, CA 92101 · 619-234-8585

Meredith L. Brown · Brown & Brown · The Plaza at La Jolla Village, Suite 230 · 4370 La Jolla Village Drive · San Diego, CA 92122 · 858-450-5035

Kim W. Cheatum · Law Office of Kim W. Cheatum · 101 West Broadway, Suite 1700 · San Diego, CA 92101-8289 · 619-233-9977

Gordon D. Cruse · Gordon D. Cruse · 110 West C Street, Suite 2300 · San Diego, CA 92101-3910 · 619-696-9922

Hildy L. Fentin · Stocks & Fentin · 600 B Street, Suite 2050 · San Diego, CA 92101 · 619-231-2025

Warren E. Haviland · Huntington & Haviland · 402 West Broadway, Suite 400 · San Diego, CA 92101 · 619-233-9500

Rex L. Jones III · ⑩ · Jones Barnes · 401 B Street, Suite 2200 · San Diego, CA 92101 · 619-544-7090

Nicholas A. Leto, Jr. · ⑩ · Veltmann & Leto · 1620 Fifth Avenue, Suite 700 · San Diego, CA 92101-2743 619-232-7384

Gerald L. McMahon · ⑩ · Seltzer Caplan McMahon Vitek · Symphony Towers, Suite 2100 · 750 B Street San Diego, CA 92101 · 619-685-3003

Sandra J. Morris · ⑩ · Sandra J. Morris · 3200 Fourth Avenue, Suite 101 · San Diego, CA 92103-5716 · 619-296-6060

Janis K. Stocks · ⑩ · Stocks & Fentin · 600 B Street, Suite 2050 · San Diego, CA 92101 · 619-231-2025

Nancy Taylor · Hargreaves & Taylor · 750 B Street, Suite 2300 · San Diego, CA 92101 · 619-238-5501

James S. Veltmann · ⑩ · Veltmann & Leto · 1620 Fifth Avenue, Suite 700 · San Diego, CA 92101-2743 · 619-232-7384

Robert C. Wood · ⑩ · Hervey & Wood · 1620 Fifth Avenue, Suite 800 · San Diego, CA 92101 · 619-238-1223

San Francisco

Nordin F. Blacker · ⑳ · Law Office of Nordin Blacker · 505 Sansome Street, Suite 400 · San Francisco, CA 94111 · 415-397-3222

Christopher F. Emley · ⑩ · Christopher F. Emley · 240 Stockton Street, Suite 400 · San Francisco, CA 94108-5306 · 415-392-1991

Max Gutierrez, Jr. · ㉕ · Morgan Lewis & Bockius · Spear Street Tower · One Market · San Francisco, CA 94105-1596 · 415-442-1000

Pamela E. Pierson · ⑳ · Pierson, Coats & Palash · 685 Market Street, Suite 370 · San Francisco, CA 94105 · 415-495-4499

Diana E. Richmond · ㉕ · Sideman & Bancroft · One Embarcadero Center, Eighth Floor · San Francisco, CA 94111 · 415-392-1960

William R. Russell · Russell Law Firm · 1340 Clay Street, Suite 25-P · San Francisco, CA 94109 · 415-421-8888

Lowell H. Sucherman · ⑳ · Sucherman Insalaco · 100 Spear Street, Suite 1640 · San Francisco, CA 94105 415-357-5050

Bernard Wolf · ⑩ · Law Offices of Bernard N. Wolf · 225 Bush Street, Suite 1439 · San Francisco, CA 94104 · 415-788-7030

San Jose

William L. Dok · ⑳ · Dok, Levy & Perrin · 1550 The Alameda, Suite 300 · San Jose, CA 95126 · 408-287-7790

Philip L. Hammer · ⑳ · Hoge, Fenton, Jones & Appel · http://www.hogefenton.com · 60 South Market Street, Suite 1400 · San Jose, CA 95113-2396 · 408-287-9501

Donelle C. Morgan · Morgan Duffy-Smith & Tidalgo · 1960 The Alameda, Suite 220 · San Jose, CA 95126 · 408-244-4570

Robert C. Redding · Madden & Redding · 1625 The Alameda, Suite 801 · San Jose, CA 95126 · 408-275-8100

Neville K. Spadafore · ⑩ · Lundell & Spadafore · 1065 Asbury Street · San Jose, CA 95126-1855 · 408-292-1717

Hugh T. Thomson · ㉕ · Law Offices of Hugh Thomson · 95 South Market Street, Suite 410 · San Jose, CA 95113-2312 · 408-298-4000

San Mateo

Richard C. Berra · ⑳ · Berra Stross & Wallacker · 155 Bovet Road, Suite 202 · San Mateo, CA 94402 · 650-349-9920

Joseph P. Crawford · Hanson Family Law Group · 411 Borel Avenue, Suite 440 · San Mateo, CA 94402 · 650-524-2144

Belinda Hanson · Hanson Family Law Group · 411 Borel Avenue, Suite 440 · San Mateo, CA 94402 · 650-524-2144

Harry A. Hanson, Jr. · ㉕ · Hanson Family Law Group · 411 Borel Avenue, Suite 440 · San Mateo, CA 94402 · 650-524-2144

Kristi Cotton Spence · ⑩ · Law Office of Kristi Cotton Spence · 1777 Borel Place, Suite 204 · San Mateo, CA 94402 · 650-350-1110

San Rafael

Richard F. Barry · ㉕ · Law Office of Richard F. Barry · 1000 Fourth Street, Suite 650 · P.O. Box 151257 · San Rafael, CA 94915-1257 · 415-453-0360

Sharon F. Mah · Sharon F. Mah · 999 Fifth Avenue, Suite 200 · San Rafael, CA 94901 · 415-454-9680

John P. McCall · ⑳ · Riede McCall Mason & Mussallem · 999 Fifth Avenue, Suite 200 · San Rafael, CA 94901-2986 · 415-454-9880

Santa Ana

Judith Anne Curtin · Judith Anne Curtin · Three Imperial Promenade, Suite 510 · Santa Ana, CA 92707 714-957-5834

Santa Monica

Connolly Oyler · ⑩ · Oyler & Woldman · 233 Wilshire Boulevard, Suite 400 · Santa Monica, CA 90401 · 310-917-1040

Santa Rosa

Margaret L. Anderson · Margaret L. Anderson · http://www.margaretlanderson.com · 829 Sonoma Avenue · Santa Rosa, CA 95404 · 707-546-4677

Catherine A. Conner · Conner, Lawrence & Rodney · 829 Sonoma Avenue · Santa Rosa, CA 95404 · 707-523-0480

David A. Gonzalez · David A. Gonzalez · 3510 Unocal Place, Suite 325 · Santa Rosa, CA 95403-0900 · 707-528-4106

Gregory F. Jilka · Gregory A. Jilka · 829 Sonoma Avenue, Suite Four · Santa Rosa, CA 95404 · 707-546-4677

Lawrence A. Moskowitz · Perry, Johnson, Anderson, Miller & Moskowitz · http://www.perrylaw.net · 438 First Street, Fourth Floor · Santa Rosa, CA 95401 · 707-525-8800

Amy Rodney · Conner, Lawrence & Rodney · 829 Sonoma Avenue · Santa Rosa, CA 95404 · 707-523-0480

Torrance

Christopher M. Moore · Moore Bryan & Schroff · http://www.moorebryanschroff.com · California Bank and Trust Tower, Suite 490 · 21515 Hawthorne Boulevard · Torrance, CA 90503-6511 · 310-540-8855

Ventura

Gregory W. Herring · Ferguson, Case, Orr, Paterson & Cunningham · 1050 South Kimball Road · Ventura, CA 93004 · 805-659-6800

Vista

James A. Hennenhoefer · ⑳ · James A. Hennenhoefer · 316 South Melrose Drive, Suite 200 · Vista, CA 92081 · 760-941-2260

Walnut Creek

Brigeda D. Bank · Fox and Bank · http://www.foxandbank.com · 1333 California Boulevard, Suite 555 · Walnut Creek, CA 94596 · 925-933-9000

A. Kathryn Fox · Fox and Bank · http://www.foxandbank.com · 1333 California Boulevard, Suite 555 · Walnut Creek, CA 94596 · 925-933-9000

Steven D. Hallert · ⑳ · Hallert & Hallert · 710 South Broadway, Suite 312 · Walnut Creek, CA 94596 · 925-933-4033

Peter G. Loewenstein · Law Offices of Peter G. Loewenstein · http://www.petergloewenstein.com · Two Ygnacio Center, Suite 430 · 2033 North Main Street · Walnut Creek, CA 94596-3748 · 925-256-3300

John E. Manoogian · ⑩ · John E. Manoogian · 2175 North California Boulevard, Suite 715 · Walnut Creek, CA 94596-3503 · 925-930-6585

John S. May · Law Offices of John S. May · 2700 Ygnacio Valley Road, Suite 265 · Walnut Creek, CA 94598 · 925-935-6302

Lee C. Pearce · ⑩ · Law Offices of Lee C. Pearce · 1333 North California Boulevard, Suite 540 · Walnut Creek, CA 94596-4533 · 925-946-0450

Andrew Ross · Whiting, Fallon & Ross · 101 Ygnacio Valley Road, Suite 250 · Walnut Creek, CA 94596 · 925-296-6000

William F. Whiting · Whiting, Fallon, Ross & Abel · 101 Ygnacio Valley Road, Suite 250 · Walnut Creek, CA 94596 · 925-296-6000

FAMILY LAW MEDIATION

Berkeley

Martina Reaves · Martina Reaves · 1708 Beverly Place · Berkeley, CA 94707 · 510-559-2685

Beverly Hills

Ronald A. Rosenfeld · ⑩ · Leeds, Wender & Rosenfeld · http://www.beverlyhillslaw.com · 9107 Wilshire Boulevard, Suite 300 · Beverly Hills, CA 90210 · 310-278-7560

Corte Madera

Madeleine Simborg · ⑩ · Simborg & Killingsworth · 770 Tamalpais Drive, Suite 401-A · Corte Madera, CA 94925 · 415-924-7171

Los Angeles

Franklin R. Garfield · Garfield & Tepper & Raskin · 1801 Century Park East, Suite 2300 · Los Angeles, CA 90067-2325 · 310-277-1981

Frederick J. Glassman · Mayer & Glassman · 12400 Wilshire Boulevard, Suite 400 · Los Angeles, CA 90025 · 310-207-0007

Joan Patsy Ostroy · Law Office of Joan Patsy Ostroy · 12100 Wilshire Boulevard, Suite 1940 · Los Angeles, CA 90025-7126 · 310-820-7971

Oakland

Miriam Steinbock · Miriam Steinbock · 1300 Clay Street, Suite 820 · Oakland, CA 94612 · 510-763-5611

San Diego

Gordon D. Cruse · Gordon D. Cruse · 110 West C Street, Suite 2300 · San Diego, CA 92101-3910 · 619-696-9922

Hildy L. Fentin · Stocks & Fentin · 600 B Street, Suite 2050 · San Diego, CA 92101 · 619-231-2025

San Francisco

Diana E. Richmond · (25) · Sideman & Bancroft · One Embarcadero Center, Eighth Floor · San Francisco, CA 94111 · 415-392-1960

San Mateo

Richard C. Berra · (20) · Berra Stross & Wallacker · 155 Bovet Road, Suite 202 · San Mateo, CA 94402 · 650-349-9920

Harry A. Hanson, Jr. · (25) · Hanson Family Law Group · 411 Borel Avenue, Suite 440 · San Mateo, CA 94402 · 650-524-2144

Kristi Cotton Spence · (10) · Law Office of Kristi Cotton Spence · 1777 Borel Place, Suite 204 · San Mateo, CA 94402 · 650-350-1110

Santa Rosa

William B. Doty · William B. Doty · 823 Sonoma Avenue · Santa Rosa, CA 95404 · 707-542-1150

Walnut Creek

A. Kathryn Fox · Fox and Bank · http://www.foxandbank.com · 1333 California Boulevard, Suite 555 · Walnut Creek, CA 94596 · 925-933-9000

FIRST AMENDMENT LAW

Beverly Hills

Anthony M. Glassman · Glassman, Browning & Saltsman · 360 North Bedford Drive, Suite 204 · Beverly Hills, CA 90210-5157 · 310-278-5100

Alan L. Isaacman · (10) · Isaacman, Kaufman & Painter · 8484 Wilshire Boulevard, Suite 850 · Beverly Hills, CA 90211 · 323-782-7700

Los Angeles

Gary L. Bostwick · Bostwick & Jassy · 12400 Wilshire Boulevard, Suite 400 · Los Angeles, CA 90025 · 310-979-6059

Theodore J. Boutrous, Jr. · Gibson, Dunn & Crutcher · 333 South Grand Avenue · Los Angeles, CA 90071-3197 · 213-229-7000

Stephen G. Contopulos · Sidley Austin · 555 West Fifth Street, 40th Floor · Los Angeles, CA 90013 · 213-896-6000

Rex S. Heinke · ⑩ · Akin Gump Strauss Hauer & Feld · 2029 Century Park East, Suite 2400 · Los Angeles, CA 90067-3012 · 310-229-1000

Kelli L. Sager · ⑩ · Davis Wright Tremaine · 865 South Figueroa Street, Suite 2400 · Los Angeles, CA 90017-2566 · 213-633-6800

John H. Weston · ⑩ · Weston, Garrou, Walters & Mooney · 12121 Wilshire Boulevard, Suite 900 · Los Angeles, CA 90025-1176 · 310-442-0072

Monterey

Neil L. Shapiro · ⑩ · Law Offices of Neil L. Shapiro · http://www.nshapiro.com · 2100 Garden Road, Suite C · Monterey, CA 93940 · 831-372-3700

Palo Alto

James M. Chadwick · Sheppard, Mullin, Richter & Hampton · http://www.sheppardmullin.com · 2225 East Bayshore Road, Suite 205 · Palo Alto, CA 94303 · 650-320-1777

Sacramento

Charity Kenyon · Kenyon-Yeates · 3400 Cottage Way, Suite K · Sacramento, CA 95825 · 916-609-5000

San Diego

John Allcock · ⑩ · DLA Piper · 401 B Street, Suite 1700 · San Diego, CA 92101-4297 · 619-699-2700

Guylyn Remmenga Cummins · ⑩ · Sheppard, Mullin, Richter & Hampton · http://www.sheppardmullin.com · 501 West Broadway, 19th Floor · San Diego, CA 92101 · 619-338-6500

Gregory D. Roper · ⑩ · Luce, Forward, Hamilton & Scripps · http://www.luce.com · 600 West Broadway, Suite 2600 · San Diego, CA 92101 · 619-236-1414

San Francisco

Thomas R. Burke · Davis Wright Tremaine · 505 Montgomery Street, Suite 800 · San Francisco, CA 94111-6533 · 415-276-6500

Duffy Carolan · Davis Wright Tremaine · 505 Montgomery Street, Suite 800 · San Francisco, CA 94111-6533 · 415-276-6500

Edward P. Davis, Jr. · ⑩ · Orrick, Herrington & Sutcliffe · The Orrick Building · 405 Howard Street · San Francisco, CA 94105-2669 · 415-773-5700

Roger R. Myers · Holme Roberts & Owen · http://www.hro.com · 560 Mission Street, 25th Floor · San Francisco, CA 94105-2994 · 415-268-2000

Karl Olson · Levy, Ram & Olson · 639 Front Street, Fourth Floor · San Francisco, CA 94111 · 415-433-4949

James M. Wagstaffe · ⑩ · Kerr & Wagstaffe · 100 Spear Street, Suite 1800 · San Francisco, CA 94105-1528 · 415-371-8500

Santa Monica

Terence J. Clark · ⑩ · Greenberg Traurig · http://www.gtlaw.com · 2450 Colorado Avenue, Suite 400-E · Santa Monica, CA 90404 · 310-586-7700

FRANCHISE LAW

Encino

David C. Gurnick · Lewitt Hackman Shapiro Marshall and Harlin · 16633 Ventura Boulevard, 11th Floor Encino, CA 91436-1865 · 818-990-2120

Los Angeles

Michael K. Lindsey · Paul Hastings · 515 South Flower Street, 25th Floor · Los Angeles, CA 90071 · 213-683-6000

Rochelle B. Spandorf · Sonnenschein Nath & Rosenthal · 601 South Figueroa Street, Suite 2500 · Los Angeles, CA 90017-5704 · 213-623-9300

Phyllis Alden Truby · Phyllis Alden Truby · 12121 Wilshire Boulevard, Suite 600 · Los Angeles, CA 90025-1188 · 310-481-6772

San Francisco

Patrick J. Carter · Law Offices of Patrick J. Carter · 2523 Twenty-Eighth Avenue · San Francisco, CA 94116 · 415-665-7494

Robert L. Ebe · Nixon Peabody · One Embarcadero Center, 18th Floor · San Francisco, CA 94111-3996 · 415-984-8200

Santa Monica

Kenneth R. Costello · Bryan Cave · 120 Broadway, Suite 300 · Santa Monica, CA 90401-2386 · 310-576-2100

Susan A. Grueneberg · Dreier Stein Kahan Browne Woods George · The Water Garden · North Tower, Sixth Floor · 1620 Twenty-Sixth Street · Santa Monica, CA 90404 · 310-828-9050

Robert L. Kahan · Dreier Stein Kahan Browne Woods George · The Water Garden · North Tower, Sixth Floor · 1620 Twenty-Sixth Street · Santa Monica, CA 90404 · 310-828-9050

Jonathan C. Solish · Bryan Cave · 120 Broadway, Suite 300 · Santa Monica, CA 90401-2386 · 310-576-2100

GAMING LAW

Los Angeles

Jerome L. Levine · Holland & Knight · http://www.hklaw.com · 633 West Fifth Street, 21st Floor · Los Angeles, CA 90071 · 213-896-2400

Teresa E. Poust · Holland & Knight · http://www.hklaw.com · 633 West Fifth Street, 21st Floor · Los Angeles, CA 90071 · 213-896-2400

Newport Beach

Stephen B. Otto · Good, Wildman, Hegness & Walley · 5000 Campus Drive · Newport Beach, CA 92660 949-720-1300

Oakland

Patricia A. Prochaska · Patricia A. Prochaska · 375 Cavour Street · Oakland, CA 94618 · 510-601-9760

Sacramento

Howard L. Dickstein · Dickstein & Zerbi · 1530 J Street, Suite 250 · Sacramento, CA 95814 · 916-244-8550

Harlan Wayne Goodson · Harlan W. Goodson · 1126 Second Street, Suite 108 · Sacramento, CA 95814 · 916-422-3476

John K. Maloney · Maloney & Tabor · 2386 Fair Oaks Boulevard · Sacramento, CA 95825-4741 · 916-485-5690

Robert S. Tabor · Maloney & Tabor · 2386 Fair Oaks Boulevard · Sacramento, CA 95825-4741 · 916-485-5690

Jane G. Zerbi · Dickstein & Zerbi · 1530 J Street, Suite 250 · Sacramento, CA 95814 · 916-244-8550

San Rafael

George Forman · Forman & Associates · 4340 Redwood Highway, Suite F-228 · San Rafael, CA 94903 · 415-491-2310

Santa Monica

Mark R. Moskowitz · Greenberg Traurig · http://www.gtlaw.com · 2450 Colorado Avenue, Suite 400-E · Santa Monica, CA 90404 · 310-586-7700

Santa Rosa

Anthony Cohen · Clement, Fitzpatrick & Kenworthy · 3333 Mendocino Avenue · Santa Rosa, CA 95403 707-523-1181

GOVERNMENT RELATIONS LAW

Los Angeles

Robert M. Hertzberg · Mayer Brown · 350 South Grand Avenue, 25th Floor · Los Angeles, CA 90071-1503 · 213-229-9500

Philip R. Recht · Mayer Brown · 350 South Grand Avenue, 25th Floor · Los Angeles, CA 90071-1503 · 213-229-9500

Lisa Specht · Manatt, Phelps & Phillips · 11355 West Olympic Boulevard · Los Angeles, CA 90064 · 310-312-4000

Sacramento

Gene Livingston · Greenberg Traurig · http://www.gtlaw.com · 1201 K Street, Suite 1100 · Sacramento, CA 95814 · 916-442-1111

Steven A. Merksamer · Nielsen, Merksamer, Parrinello, Mueller & Naylor · 1415 L Street, Suite 1200 · Sacramento, CA 95814 · 916-446-6752

San Diego

Nancy O. Dix · DLA Piper · 401 B Street, Suite 1700 · San Diego, CA 92101-4297 · 619-699-2700

HEALTH CARE LAW

Burlingame

Keith P. Bartel · Carr, McClellan, Ingersoll, Thompson & Horn · 216 Park Road · P.O. Box 513 · Burlingame, CA 94010 · 650-342-9600

Claremont

Frank N. Darras · Shernoff Bidart & Darras · 600 South Indian Hill Boulevard · Claremont, CA 91711 · 909-621-4935

Costa Mesa

Martin J. Thompson · Manatt, Phelps & Phillips · Park Tower, 14th Floor · 695 Town Center Drive · Costa Mesa, CA 92626 · 714-371-2500

East Palo Alto

Ross E. Campbell · ⑩ · Bingham McCutchen · http://www.bingham.com · 1900 University Avenue · East Palo Alto, CA 94303-2223 · 650-849-4400

Encino

Ellis J. Horvitz · ⑩ · Horvitz & Levy · 15760 Ventura Boulevard, 18th Floor · Encino, CA 91436-3000 · 818-995-0800

Lafayette

A. Robert Singer · ⑩ · Law Office of A. Robert Singer · One West Wind Road · Lafayette, CA 94549-2115 · 925-926-0439

Los Angeles

Timothy P. Blanchard · McDermott Will & Emery · 2049 Century Park East, 38th Floor · Los Angeles, CA 90067-3218 · 310-277-4110

Lloyd A. Bookman · Hooper, Lundy & Bookman · 1875 Century Park East, Suite 1600 · Los Angeles, CA 90067-2799 · 310-551-8111

Lowell C. Brown · Arent Fox · Gas Company Tower, 48th Floor · 555 West Fifth Street · Los Angeles, CA 90013 · 213-629-7400

Arthur Robert Chenen · Theodora Oringher Miller & Richman · 2029 Century Park East, Six Floor · Los Angeles, CA 90067-2907 · 310-557-2009

Andrew J. Demetriou · Fulbright & Jaworski · http://www.fulbright.com · 555 South Flower Street, 41st Floor · Los Angeles, CA 90071 · 213-892-9200

George C. Demos · O'Melveny & Myers · 400 South Hope Street, 10th Floor · Los Angeles, CA 90071-2899 · 213-430-6000

Kathleen H. Drummy · Davis Wright Tremaine · 865 South Figueroa Street, Suite 2400 · Los Angeles, CA 90017-2566 · 213-633-6800

Henry R. Fenton · Fenton & Nelson · 11835 West Olympic Boulevard, Suite 925 · Los Angeles, CA 90064 · 310-444-5244

Donald A. Goldman · McDermott Will & Emery · 2049 Century Park East, 38th Floor · Los Angeles, CA 90067-3218 · 310-277-4110

Russell Hayman · McDermott Will & Emery · 2049 Century Park East, 38th Floor · Los Angeles, CA 90067-3218 · 310-277-4110

Patric Hooper · ⑩ · Hooper, Lundy & Bookman · 1875 Century Park East, Suite 1600 · Los Angeles, CA 90067-2799 · 310-551-8111

Mark A. Kadzielski · Fulbright & Jaworski · http://www.fulbright.com · 555 South Flower Street, 41st Floor · Los Angeles, CA 90071 · 213-892-9200

Terri D. Keville · Manatt, Phelps & Phillips · 11355 West Olympic Boulevard · Los Angeles, CA 90064 · 310-312-4000

James Robert Lahana · Fenigstein & Kaufman · 1900 Avenue of the Stars, Suite 2300 · Los Angeles, CA 90067-4314 · 310-201-0777

Barry S. Landsberg · ⑩ · Manatt, Phelps & Phillips · 11355 West Olympic Boulevard · Los Angeles, CA 90064 · 310-312-4000

J. Robert Liset · Musick, Peeler & Garrett · One Wilshire Boulevard, Suite 2000 · Los Angeles, CA 90017 · 213-629-7600

Robert W. Lundy, Jr. · Hooper, Lundy & Bookman · 1875 Century Park East, Suite 1600 · Los Angeles, CA 90067-2799 · 310-551-8111

Douglas M. Mancino · ⑩ · McDermott Will & Emery · 2049 Century Park East, 38th Floor · Los Angeles, CA 90067-3218 · 310-277-4110

Jeremy N. Miller · Miller Health Law Group · 2049 Century Park East, Suite 2250 · Los Angeles, CA 90067 · 310-277-9003

Ira J. Rappeport · McDermott Will & Emery · 2049 Century Park East, 38th Floor · Los Angeles, CA 90067-3218 · 310-277-4110

J. Peter Rich · McDermott Will & Emery · 2049 Century Park East, 38th Floor · Los Angeles, CA 90067-3218 · 310-277-4110

James R. Schwartz · Manatt, Phelps & Phillips · 11355 West Olympic Boulevard · Los Angeles, CA 90064 · 310-312-4000

Richard F. Seiden · Foley & Lardner · 2029 Century Park East, Suite 3500 · Los Angeles, CA 90067-3021 · 310-277-2223

W. Bradley Tully · Hooper, Lundy & Bookman · 1875 Century Park East, Suite 1600 · Los Angeles, CA 90067-2799 · 310-551-8111

Carl I. Weissburg · ⑩ · Foley & Lardner · 2029 Century Park East, Suite 3500 · Los Angeles, CA 90067-3021 · 310-277-2223

Manhattan Beach

John D. Harwell · Law Office of John D. Harwell · 225 Twenty-Seventh Street · Manhattan Beach, CA 90266 · 310-546-7078

Redlands

Jeffrey S. Raynes · Law Office of Jeffrey Raynes · 1780 Orange Tree Lane · Redlands, CA 92374 · 909-793-6800

Sacramento

Stephen L. Goff · McDonough Holland & Allen · http://www.mhalaw.com · 555 Capitol Mall, Ninth Floor · Sacramento, CA 95814-4692 · 916-444-3900

San Diego

James G. Harrigan · Higgs, Fletcher & Mack · 401 West A Street, Suite 2600 · San Diego, CA 92101-7910 · 619-236-1551

Cary W. Miller · ⑩ · Hooper, Lundy & Bookman · 101 West Broadway, Suite 1330 · San Diego, CA 92101 · 619-744-7300

Michael R. Moore · Sheppard, Mullin, Richter & Hampton · http://www.sheppardmullin.com · 501 West Broadway, 19th Floor · San Diego, CA 92101 · 619-338-6500

George L. Root, Jr. · Procopio, Cory, Hargreaves & Savitch · 530 B Street, 21st Floor · San Diego, CA 92101 · 619-238-1900

R. Michael Scarano, Jr. · Foley & Lardner · 11250 El Camino Real, Suite 200 · San Diego, CA 92130 · 858-847-6700

San Francisco

John O. Chesley · Ropes & Gray · http://www.ropesgray.com · One Embarcadero Center, Suite 2200 · San Francisco, CA 94111-3711 · 415-315-6300

Paul R. DeMuro · ⑩ · Latham & Watkins · 505 Montgomery Street, Suite 2000 · San Francisco, CA 94111-6538 · 415-391-0600

James R. Dutro · Latham & Watkins · 505 Montgomery Street, Suite 2000 · San Francisco, CA 94111-6538 · 415-391-0600

Daniel B. Higgins · ⑩ · Paul Hastings · 55 Second Street, 24th Floor · San Francisco, CA 94105 · 415-856-7000

Gerald M. Hinkley · Davis Wright Tremaine · 505 Montgomery Street, Suite 800 · San Francisco, CA 94111-6533 · 415-276-6500

Laurence W. Kessenick · Kessenick Phillips & Gamma · 44 Montgomery Street, Suite 3380 · San Francisco, CA 94104 · 415-362-9400

Glenn L. Krinsky · Ropes & Gray · http://www.ropesgray.com · One Embarcadero Center, Suite 2200 · San Francisco, CA 94111-3711 · 415-315-6300

M. Steven Lipton · Davis Wright Tremaine · 505 Montgomery Street, Suite 800 · San Francisco, CA 94111-6533 · 415-276-6500

Mitchell J. Olejko · Ropes & Gray · http://www.ropesgray.com · One Embarcadero Center, Suite 2200 · San Francisco, CA 94111-3711 · 415-315-6300

Gerald R. Peters · ⑩ · Latham & Watkins · 505 Montgomery Street, Suite 2000 · San Francisco, CA 94111-6538 · 415-391-0600

Steven V. Schnier · ⑩ · Hanson Bridgett · http://www.hansonbridgett.com · 425 Market Street, 26th Floor · San Francisco, CA 94105 · 415-777-3200

Harry Shulman · Davis Wright Tremaine · 505 Montgomery Street, Suite 800 · San Francisco, CA 94111-6533 · 415-276-6500

Paul T. Smith · Davis Wright Tremaine · 505 Montgomery Street, Suite 800 · San Francisco, CA 94111-6533 · 415-276-6500

Ross E. Stromberg · ⑩ · Jones Day · 555 California Street, 26th Floor · San Francisco, CA 94104 · 415-626-3939

Gayl A. Westendorf · Paul Hastings · 55 Second Street, 24th Floor · San Francisco, CA 94105 · 415-856-7000

IMMIGRATION LAW

Irvine

Debi Gloria · Paparelli & Partners · Four Park Plaza, Suite 200 · Irvine, CA 92614-8560 · 949-955-5555

David Hirson · Fragomen, Del Rey, Bernsen & Loewy · http://www.fragomen.com · 18401 Von Karman Avenue, Suite 255 · Irvine, CA 92612-1596 · 949-261-0209

Angelo A. Paparelli · ⑩ · Paparelli & Partners · Four Park Plaza, Suite 200 · Irvine, CA 92614-8560 · 949-955-5555

Yoshiko I. Robertson · Paparelli & Partners · Four Park Plaza, Suite 200 · Irvine, CA 92614-8560 · 949-955-5555

Susan K. Wehrer · Paparelli & Partners · Four Park Plaza, Suite 200 · Irvine, CA 92614-8560 · 949-955-5555

La Jolla

Grace A. Zimmerman · The Law Office of Grace Zimmerman · 817 Silverado Street · La Jolla, CA 92037 858-454-1965

Los Angeles

Timothy S. Barker · Fragomen, Del Rey, Bernsen & Loewy · http://www.fragomen.com · 11150 West Olympic Boulevard, Suite 1000 · Los Angeles, CA 90064 · 310-820-3322

Frida P. Glucoft · Mitchell Silberberg & Knupp · 11377 West Olympic Boulevard · Los Angeles, CA 90064 · 310-312-2000

Howard Hom · Law Office of Howard Hom · 600 Wilshire Boulevard, Suite 1550 · Los Angeles, CA 90017 · 213-387-0954

Mark A. Ivener · ⑩ · Ivener & Fullmer · 11601 Wilshire Boulevard, Suite 2280 · Los Angeles, CA 90025 · 310-477-3000

Peter A. Schey · ⑩ · Center for Human Rights and Constitutional Law · 256 South Occidental Boulevard Los Angeles, CA 90057 · 213-388-8693

Carl Shusterman · ⑩ · Law Offices of Carl Shusterman · 600 Wilshire Boulevard, Suite 1550 · Los Angeles, CA 90017 · 213-623-4592

Oakland

E. Norton Tooby · Law Offices of Norton Tooby · 6333 Telegraph Avenue, Suite 200 · Oakland, CA 94609 · 510-601-1300

Pasadena

Josie Gonzalez · ⑩ · Gonzalez & Harris · 35 Northlake Avenue, Suite 710 · Pasadena, CA 91101 · 626-229-9806

San Diego

Fausta M. Albi · Larrabee Mehlman Albi Coker · 10145 Pacific Heights Boulevard, Suite 910 · P.O. Box 919016 · San Diego, CA 92121-9016 · 858-642-0420

Robert A. Mautino · ⑩ · Mautino & Mautino · 1059 Tenth Avenue · San Diego, CA 92101 · 619-235-9177

Sharon R. Mehlman · Larrabee Mehlman Albi Coker · 10145 Pacific Heights Boulevard, Suite 910 · P.O. Box 919016 · San Diego, CA 92121-9016 · 858-642-0420

Diana Vellos Coker · Larrabee Mehlman Albi Coker · 10145 Pacific Heights Boulevard, Suite 910 · P.O. Box 919016 · San Diego, CA 92121-9016 · 858-642-0420

San Francisco

Jeff T. Appleman · Berry, Appleman & Leiden · 353 Sacramento Street, Suite 1300 · San Francisco, CA 94111-3633 · 415-398-1800

David P. Berry · Berry, Appleman & Leiden · 353 Sacramento Street, Suite 1300 · San Francisco, CA 94111-3633 · 415-398-1800

Christine Brigagliano · Van Der Hout, Brigagliano & Nightingale · 180 Sutter Street, Fifth Floor · San Francisco, CA 94104-4001 · 415-981-3000

Atessa Chehrazi · Jackson & Hertogs · 170 Columbus Avenue, Fourth Floor · San Francisco, CA 94133-5160 · 415-986-4559

Nancy Ann Fellom · Fellom & Solorio · 231 Sansome Street, Sixth Floor · San Francisco, CA 94104-2304 415-362-1212

Hope M. Frye · Lawler & Lawler · http://www.aboutvisas.com · 201 Filbert Street, Suite 400 · San Francisco, CA 94133 · 415-391-2010

Martin J. Lawler · ⑩ · Lawler & Lawler · http://www.aboutvisas.com · 201 Filbert Street, Suite 400 · San Francisco, CA 94133 · 415-391-2010

Warren R. Leiden · Berry, Appleman & Leiden · 353 Sacramento Street, Suite 1300 · San Francisco, CA 94111-3633 · 415-398-1800

Lance D. Nagel · Morgan Lewis & Bockius · Spear Street Tower · One Market · San Francisco, CA 94105-1596 · 415-442-1000

Norman C. Plotkin · Jackson & Hertogs · 170 Columbus Avenue, Fourth Floor · San Francisco, CA 94133-5160 · 415-986-4559

Donald L. Ungar · ⑩ · Simmons & Ungar · 50 California Street, Suite 470 · San Francisco, CA 94111 · 415-421-0860

Marc Van Der Hout · ⑩ · Van Der Hout, Brigagliano & Nightingale · 180 Sutter Street, Fifth Floor · San Francisco, CA 94104-4001 · 415-981-3000

Ronald Wada · Tafapolsky & Smith · 90 New Montgomery Street · San Francisco, CA 94105 · 415-975-9800

San Jose

Donald Freiberg · Law Offices of Donald Freiburg · 1550 The Alameda, Suite 209 · San Jose, CA 95126-2304 · 408-995-0621

Marcine Anne Seid · Law Offices of Marcine A. Seid · 1530 The Alameda, Suite 310 · San Jose, CA 95126-2303 · 408-271-9888

Millie-Ann Marquez-Li Sumcad · Schwerin and Sumcad · 84 West Santa Clara Street, Suite 550 · San Jose, CA 95113 · 408-295-4232

Santa Clara

Cynthia Juarez Lange · ⑩ · Fragomen, Del Rey, Bernsen & Loewy · http://www.fragomen.com · 2804 Mission College Boulevard, Second Floor · Santa Clara, CA 95054-1803 · 408-919-0600

Santa Monica

Tien-Li Loke Walsh · Wolfsdorf Immigration Law Group · http://www.wolfsdorf.com · 1416 Second Street · Santa Monica, CA 90401 · 310-570-4088

Bernard P. Wolfsdorf · Wolfsdorf Immigration Law Group · http://www.wolfsdorf.com · 1416 Second Street · Santa Monica, CA 90401 · 310-570-4088

South San Francisco

Edward R. Litwin · ⑩ · Litwin & Associates · 1435 Huntington Avenue, Suite 336 · South San Francisco, CA 94080-5966 · 650-588-7100

Studio City

John B. Bartos · The Miller Law Offices · 12441 Ventura Boulevard · Studio City, CA 91604 · 818-508-9005

Charles M. Miller · ⑩ · The Miller Law Offices · 12441 Ventura Boulevard · Studio City, CA 91604 · 818-508-9005

Terri Senesac Miller · The Miller Law Offices · 12441 Ventura Boulevard · Studio City, CA 91604 · 818-508-9005

INFORMATION TECHNOLOGY LAW

Berkeley

Katherine C. Spelman · Cobalt · 821 Bancroft Way · Berkeley, CA 94710 · 510-841-9800

East Palo Alto

Maureen S. Dorney · DLA Piper · 2000 University Avenue · East Palo Alto, CA 94303-2214 · 650-833-2000

Heather J. Meeker · Greenberg Traurig · http://www.gtlaw.com · 1900 University Avenue, Fifth Floor · East Palo Alto, CA 94303 · 650-328-8500

Mark F. Radcliffe · DLA Piper · 2000 University Avenue · East Palo Alto, CA 94303-2214 · 650-833-2000

Los Angeles

Richard L. Bernacchi · ⑩ · Irell & Manella · 1800 Avenue of the Stars, Suite 900 · Los Angeles, CA 90067-4276 · 310-277-1010

Morgan Chu · ⑩ · Irell & Manella · 1800 Avenue of the Stars, Suite 900 · Los Angeles, CA 90067-4276 · 310-277-1010

Ronald L. Johnston · Arnold & Porter · 777 South Figueroa Street, 44th Floor · Los Angeles, CA 90017-5844 · 213-243-4000

David Nimmer · ⑩ · Irell & Manella · 1800 Avenue of the Stars, Suite 900 · Los Angeles, CA 90067-4276 310-277-1010

Clark B. Siegel · Irell & Manella · 1800 Avenue of the Stars, Suite 900 · Los Angeles, CA 90067-4276 · 310-277-1010

Menlo Park

Anthony R. Klein · Latham & Watkins · 140 Scott Drive · Menlo Park, CA 94025 · 650-328-4600

Daniel R. Mummery · Latham & Watkins · 140 Scott Drive · Menlo Park, CA 94025 · 650-328-4600

Glenn G. Nash · Latham & Watkins · 140 Scott Drive · Menlo Park, CA 94025 · 650-328-4600

Mountain View

Stuart P. Meyer · Fenwick & West · Silicon Valley Center · 801 California Street · Mountain View, CA 94041-2008 · 650-988-8500

Palo Alto

Suzanne Y. Bell · Wilson Sonsini Goodrich & Rosati · 650 Page Mill Road · Palo Alto, CA 94304-1050 · 650-493-9300

Ian N. Feinberg · Mayer Brown · Two Palo Alto Square, Suite 300 · 3000 El Camino Real · Palo Alto, CA 94306-2112 · 650-331-2000

Françoise Gilbert · IT Law Group · http://www.itlawgroup.com · 555 Bryant Street, Suite 603 · Palo Alto, CA 94301 · 650-328-1800

Michael D. Stern · Cooley Godward Kronish · 3175 Hanover Street · Palo Alto, CA 94304-1130 · 650-843-5000

Portola Valley

Susan H. Nycum · Susan H. Nycum · 35 Granada Court · Portola Valley, CA 94028 · 650-851-3304

Sacramento

Scott W. Pink · DLA Piper · 400 Capitol Mall, Suite 2400 · Sacramento, CA 95814-4428 · 916-930-3200

San Francisco

Laurie S. Hane · Morrison & Foerster · http://www.mofo.com · 425 Market Street · San Francisco, CA 94105-2482 · 415-268-7000

David L. Hayes · Fenwick & West · 555 California Street, 12th Floor · San Francisco, CA 94104 · 415-875-2300

J. Thomas McCarthy · ⑩ · Morrison & Foerster · http://www.mofo.com · 425 Market Street · San Francisco, CA 94105-2482 · 415-268-7000

Denis T. Rice · ⑳ · Howard, Rice, Nemerovski, Canady, Falk & Rabkin · Three Embarcadero Center, Seventh Floor · San Francisco, CA 94111-4024 · 415-434-1600

William I. Schwartz · Morrison & Foerster · http://www.mofo.com · 425 Market Street · San Francisco, CA 94105-2482 · 415-268-7000

Stacy Snowman · DLA Piper · 153 Townsend Street, Suite 800 · San Francisco, CA 94107-1957 · 415-836-2500

San Jose

Stephen N. Hollman · Business & Technology Law Group · 160 West Santa Clara Street, Suite 1050 · San Jose, CA 95113 · 408-282-1949

Santa Monica

Ian C. Ballon · Greenberg Traurig · http://www.gtlaw.com · 2450 Colorado Avenue, Suite 400-E · Santa Monica, CA 90404 · 310-586-7700

INSURANCE LAW

Campbell

Randy M. Hess · Adleson, Hess & Kelly · 577 Salmar Avenue, Second Floor · Campbell, CA 95008 · 408-341-0234

Claremont

Michael J. Bidart · Shernoff Bidart & Darras · 600 South Indian Hill Boulevard · Claremont, CA 91711 · 909-621-4935

Frank N. Darras · Shernoff Bidart & Darras · 600 South Indian Hill Boulevard · Claremont, CA 91711 · 909-621-4935

William M. Shernoff · ⑳ · Shernoff Bidart & Darras · 600 South Indian Hill Boulevard · Claremont, CA 91711 · 909-621-4935

Los Angeles

David B. Babbe · Morrison & Foerster · http://www.mofo.com · 555 West Fifth Street, Suite 3500 · Los Angeles, CA 90013-1024 · 213-892-5200

Jonathan Bank · Locke Lord Bissell & Liddell · 300 South Grand Avenue, Suite 800 · Los Angeles, CA 90071 · 213-485-1500

Robert H. Berkes · Berkes Crane Robinson & Seal · http://www.bcrslaw.com · 515 South Figueroa Street, Suite 1500 · Los Angeles, CA 90071 · 213-955-1150

R. Jeff Carlisle · Lynberg & Watkins · International Tower Plaza, 16th Floor · 888 South Figueroa Street · Los Angeles, CA 90017-5449 · 213-624-8700

Patrick A. Cathcart · Adorno & Yoss · 633 West Fifth Street, Suite 1150 · Los Angeles, CA 90071 · 213-229-2400

Nancy Sher Cohen · Proskauer Rose · 2049 Century Park East, 32nd Floor · Los Angeles, CA 90067-3206 310-557-2900

Steven M. Crane · Berkes Crane Robinson & Seal · http://www.bcrslaw.com · 515 South Figueroa Street, Suite 1500 · Los Angeles, CA 90071 · 213-955-1150

Linda Dakin-Grimm · Milbank, Tweed, Hadley & McCloy · http://www.milbank.com · 601 South Figueroa Street, 30th Floor · Los Angeles, CA 90017-5735 · 213-892-4000

Stephen N. Goldberg · Dickstein Shapiro · http://www.dicksteinshapiro.com · 2049 Century Park East, Suite 700 · Los Angeles, CA 90067-3109 · 310-772-8300

David M. Halbreich · Reed Smith · 355 South Grand Avenue, Suite 2900 · Los Angeles, CA 90071 · 213-457-8000

Michel Yves Horton · Morgan Lewis & Bockius · 300 South Grand Avenue, 22nd Floor · Los Angeles, CA 90071-3132 · 213-612-2500

Kent R. Keller · Barger & Wolen · 633 West Fifth Street, 47th Floor · Los Angeles, CA 90071-2043 · 213-680-2800

Ronald D. Kent · Sonnenschein Nath & Rosenthal · 601 South Figueroa Street, Suite 2500 · Los Angeles, CA 90017-5704 · 213-623-9300

R. DeWitt Kirwan · Akin Gump Strauss Hauer & Feld · 2029 Century Park East, Suite 2400 · Los Angeles, CA 90067-3012 · 310-229-1000

Dean J. Kitchens · Gibson, Dunn & Crutcher · 333 South Grand Avenue · Los Angeles, CA 90071-3197 · 213-229-7000

Cary B. Lerman · Munger, Tolles & Olson · 355 South Grand Avenue, 35th Floor · Los Angeles, CA 90071-1560 · 213-683-9100

Margaret Levy · Manatt, Phelps & Phillips · 11355 West Olympic Boulevard · Los Angeles, CA 90064 · 310-312-4000

G. Andrew Lundberg · Latham & Watkins · 355 South Grand Avenue · Los Angeles, CA 90071-1560 · 213-485-1234

Royal F. Oakes · Barger & Wolen · 633 West Fifth Street, 47th Floor · Los Angeles, CA 90071-2043 · 213-680-2800

Ronald M. Oster · Paul Hastings · 515 South Flower Street, 25th Floor · Los Angeles, CA 90071 · 213-683-6000

Kirk A. Pasich · Dickstein Shapiro · http://www.dicksteinshapiro.com · 2049 Century Park East, Suite 700 Los Angeles, CA 90067-3109 · 310-772-8300

Randall J. Peters · Lynberg & Watkins · International Tower Plaza, 16th Floor · 888 South Figueroa Street · Los Angeles, CA 90017-5449 · 213-624-8700

Deborah A. Pitts · Duane Morris · 633 West Fifth Street, Suite 4600 · Los Angeles, CA 90071-2065 · 213-689-7400

Ronald R. Robinson · Berkes Crane Robinson & Seal · http://www.bcrslaw.com · 515 South Figueroa Street, Suite 1500 · Los Angeles, CA 90071 · 213-955-1150

Peter K. Rosen · Latham & Watkins · 355 South Grand Avenue · Los Angeles, CA 90071-1560 · 213-485-1234

Peter S. Selvin · Loeb & Loeb · 10100 Santa Monica Boulevard, Suite 2200 · Los Angeles, CA 90067-4164 · 310-282-2000

Randolph P. Sinnott · Sinnott, Dito, Moura & Puebla · 707 Wilshire Boulevard, Suite 3200 · Los Angeles, CA 90017 · 213-996-4200

David W. Steuber · Howrey · 550 South Hope Street, Suite 1100 · Los Angeles, CA 90071 · 213-892-1800

Mark Wood · O'Melveny & Myers · 400 South Hope Street, 10th Floor · Los Angeles, CA 90071-2899 · 213-430-6000

Newport Beach

Gregory L. Dillion · Newmeyer & Dillion · 895 Dove Street, Fifth Floor · Newport Beach, CA 92660 · 949-854-7000

Marc S. Maister · Irell & Manella · 840 Newport Center Drive, Suite 400 · Newport Beach, CA 92660-6324 · 949-760-0991

Oakland

Ralph A. Lombardi · Lombardi, Loper & Conant · 1999 Harrison Street, 26th Floor · Oakland, CA 94612 510-433-2600

Redwood Shores

Mark G. Bonino · Hayes, Davis, Bonino, Ellingson, McLay & Scott · 203 Redwood Shores Parkway, Suite 480 · Redwood Shores, CA 94065 · 650-637-9100

San Diego

R. Randal Crispen · Luce, Forward, Hamilton & Scripps · http://www.luce.com · 600 West Broadway, Suite 2600 · San Diego, CA 92101 · 619-236-1414

Charles A. Danaher · Luce, Forward, Hamilton & Scripps · http://www.luce.com · 600 West Broadway, Suite 2600 · San Diego, CA 92101 · 619-236-1414

Peter Klee · Luce, Forward, Hamilton & Scripps · http://www.luce.com · 600 West Broadway, Suite 2600 · San Diego, CA 92101 · 619-236-1414

Mitchell L. Lathrop · Duane Morris · 101 West Broadway, Suite 900 · San Diego, CA 92101-8285 · 619-744-2200

Harvey R. Levine · ⑳ · Levine, Steinberg, Miller & Huver · 550 West C Street, Suite 1810 · San Diego, CA 92101-8596 · 619-231-9449

Scott W. Sonne · Luce, Forward, Hamilton & Scripps · http://www.luce.com · 600 West Broadway, Suite 2600 · San Diego, CA 92101 · 619-236-1414

Kristine L. Wilkes · Latham & Watkins · 600 West Broadway, Suite 1800 · San Diego, CA 92101-3375 · 619-236-1234

San Francisco

Barry A. Abbott · Howard, Rice, Nemerovski, Canady, Falk & Rabkin · Three Embarcadero Center, Seventh Floor · San Francisco, CA 94111-4024 · 415-434-1600

Donald W. Brown · Covington & Burling · One Front Street · San Francisco, CA 94111-5356 · 415-591-6000

Barry L. Bunshoft · Duane Morris · Spear Tower, Suite 2000 · One Market · San Francisco, CA 94105-1104 · 415-957-3000

Grace A. Carter · Paul Hastings · 55 Second Street, 24th Floor · San Francisco, CA 94105 · 415-856-7000

Martin Checov · O'Melveny & Myers · Embarcadero Center West · 275 Battery Street · San Francisco, CA 94111-3305 · 415-984-8700

Scott P. DeVries · Winston & Strawn · 101 California Street, 39th Floor · San Francisco, CA 94111-5802 · 415-591-1000

Donald E. Dorfman · Nixon Peabody · One Embarcadero Center, 18th Floor · San Francisco, CA 94111-3996 · 415-984-8200

William R. Friedrich · Farella Braun & Martel · Russ Building, 17th Floor · 235 Montgomery Street · San Francisco, CA 94104 · 415-954-4400

Paul E. B. Glad · Sonnenschein Nath & Rosenthal · 525 Market Street, 26th Floor · San Francisco, CA 94105-2708 · 415-882-5000

David B. Goodwin · Covington & Burling · One Front Street · San Francisco, CA 94111-5356 · 415-591-6000

Lawrence A. Hobel · Covington & Burling · One Front Street · San Francisco, CA 94111-5356 · 415-591-6000

Raoul D. Kennedy · ⑳ · Skadden, Arps, Slate, Meagher & Flom · Four Embarcadero Center, Suite 3800 · San Francisco, CA 94111 · 415-984-6400

Barry S. Levin · Heller Ehrman · 333 Bush Street · San Francisco, CA 94104-2878 · 415-772-6000

Philip R. Matthews · Duane Morris · Spear Tower, Suite 2000 · One Market · San Francisco, CA 94105-1104 · 415-957-3000

Kurt W. Melchior · Nossaman · http://www.nossaman.com · 50 California Street, 34th Floor · San Francisco, CA 94111-4707 · 415-398-3600

Ann M. Mooney · Cooley Godward Kronish · 101 California Street, Fifth Floor · San Francisco, CA 94111-5800 · 415-693-2000

Richard L. Seabolt · Duane Morris · Spear Tower, Suite 2000 · One Market · San Francisco, CA 94105-1104 · 415-957-3000

Paul W. Sugarman · Heller Ehrman · 333 Bush Street · San Francisco, CA 94104-2878 · 415-772-6000

Ray L. Wong · Duane Morris · Spear Tower, Suite 2000 · One Market · San Francisco, CA 94105-1104 · 415-957-3000

San Jose

Bradley A. Bening · Willoughby, Stuart and Bening · Fairmont Plaza, Suite 400 · 50 West San Fernando Street · San Jose, CA 95113 · 408-289-1972

Ronald J. Cook · Willoughby, Stuart and Bening · Fairmont Plaza, Suite 400 · 50 West San Fernando Street · San Jose, CA 95113 · 408-289-1972

Alexander F. Stuart · Willoughby, Stuart and Bening · Fairmont Plaza, Suite 400 · 50 West San Fernando Street · San Jose, CA 95113 · 408-289-1972

Randall E. Willoughby · (10) · Willoughby, Stuart and Bening · Fairmont Plaza, Suite 400 · 50 West San Fernando Street · San Jose, CA 95113 · 408-289-1972

Santa Monica

Bruce A. Friedman · Bingham McCutchen · http://www.bingham.com · The Water Garden, Fourth Floor 1620 Twenty-Sixth Street · Santa Monica, CA 90404-4060 · 310-907-1000

Walnut Creek

Michael J. Ney · McNamara, Dodge, Ney, Beatty, Slattery, Pfalzer, Borges & Brothers · 1211 Newell Avenue · Walnut Creek, CA 94596-5331 · 925-939-5330

INTELLECTUAL PROPERTY LAW

Aliso Viejo

Bruce B. Brunda · Stetina, Brunda, Garred & Brucker · 75 Enterprise, Suite 250 · Aliso Viejo, CA 92656 · 949-855-1246

Costa Mesa

Albin H. Gess · Snell & Wilmer · 600 Anton Boulevard, Suite 1400 · Costa Mesa, CA 92626-7689 · 714-427-7000

Joseph W. Price, Jr. · Snell & Wilmer · 600 Anton Boulevard, Suite 1400 · Costa Mesa, CA 92626-7689 · 714-427-7000

Dean J. Zipser · Manatt, Phelps & Phillips · Park Tower, 14th Floor · 695 Town Center Drive · Costa Mesa, CA 92626 · 714-371-2500

Cupertino

Lloyd R. Day, Jr. · Day Casebeer Madrid & Batchelder · 20300 Stevens Creek Boulevard, Suite 400 · Cupertino, CA 95014 · 408-873-0110

East Palo Alto

William F. Abrams · Bingham McCutchen · http://www.bingham.com · 1900 University Avenue · East Palo Alto, CA 94303-2223 · 650-849-4400

Byde W. Clawson · Bingham McCutchen · http://www.bingham.com · 1900 University Avenue · East Palo Alto, CA 94303-2223 · 650-849-4400

Hollywood

Jeffrey C. Briggs · Briggs Law · http://www.jbriggslaw.com · 6381 Hollywood Boulevard, Suite 530 · Hollywood, CA 90028 · 323-461-5400

Irvine

Joseph S. Cianfrani · Knobbe, Martens, Olson & Bear · 2040 Main Street, 14th Floor · Irvine, CA 92614 · 949-760-0404

R. Scott Feldmann · Crowell & Moring · Three Park Plaza, 20th Floor · Irvine, CA 92614-8505 · 949-263-8400

James W. Geriak · ⑩ · Orrick, Herrington & Sutcliffe · Four Park Plaza, Suite 1600 · Irvine, CA 92614-2558 · 949-567-6700

Russell B. Hill · Howrey · Four Park Plaza, Suite 1700 · Irvine, CA 92614 · 949-721-6900

Howard J. Klein · Klein, O'Neill & Singh · 43 Corporate Park, Suite 204 · Irvine, CA 92606 · 949-955-1920

Don W. Martens · ⑩ · Knobbe, Martens, Olson & Bear · 2040 Main Street, 14th Floor · Irvine, CA 92614 949-760-0404

Kimberley Chen Nobles · Crowell & Moring · Three Park Plaza, 20th Floor · Irvine, CA 92614-8505 · 949-263-8400

Joseph R. Re · Knobbe, Martens, Olson & Bear · 2040 Main Street, 14th Floor · Irvine, CA 92614 · 949-760-0404

William C. Rooklidge · Howrey · Four Park Plaza, Suite 1700 · Irvine, CA 92614 · 949-721-6900

David A. Segal · Gibson, Dunn & Crutcher · 3161 Michelson Drive · Irvine, CA 92612-4412 · 949-451-3800

John B. Sganga, Jr. · Knobbe, Martens, Olson & Bear · 2040 Main Street, 14th Floor · Irvine, CA 92614 · 949-760-0404

Los Angeles

Charles S. Barquist · Morrison & Foerster · http://www.mofo.com · 555 West Fifth Street, Suite 3500 · Los Angeles, CA 90013-1024 · 213-892-5200

Wayne Barsky · Gibson, Dunn & Crutcher · 2029 Century Park East, 40th Floor · Los Angeles, CA 90067-3026 · 310-552-8500

Laura W. Brill · Irell & Manella · 1800 Avenue of the Stars, Suite 900 · Los Angeles, CA 90067-4276 · 310-277-1010

Elliot N. Brown · Irell & Manella · 1800 Avenue of the Stars, Suite 900 · Los Angeles, CA 90067-4276 · 310-277-1010

Merl John Carson · Foley & Lardner · 555 South Flower Street, Suite 3500 · Los Angeles, CA 90071-2300 · 213-972-4500

Morgan Chu · ⑩ · Irell & Manella · 1800 Avenue of the Stars, Suite 900 · Los Angeles, CA 90067-4276 · 310-277-1010

Gary A. Clark · Sheppard, Mullin, Richter & Hampton · http://www.sheppardmullin.com · 333 South Hope Street, 48th Floor · Los Angeles, CA 90071-1448 · 213-620-1780

Richard de Bodo · Hogan & Hartson · 1999 Avenue of the Stars, Suite 1400 · Los Angeles, CA 90067 · 310-785-4600

Mark A. Flagel · Latham & Watkins · 355 South Grand Avenue · Los Angeles, CA 90071-1560 · 213-485-1234

Gary N. Frischling · Irell & Manella · 1800 Avenue of the Stars, Suite 900 · Los Angeles, CA 90067-4276 310-277-1010

Ronald L. Johnston · Arnold & Porter · 777 South Figueroa Street, 44th Floor · Los Angeles, CA 90017-5844 · 213-243-4000

Robert G. Krupka · ⑩ · Kirkland & Ellis · 777 South Figueroa Street, Suite 3400 · Los Angeles, CA 90017-5800 · 213-680-8400

Frederick A. Lorig · Quinn Emanuel Urquhart Oliver & Hedges · 865 South Figueroa Street, 10th Floor · Los Angeles, CA 90017 · 213-443-3000

Michael L. Lovitz · Connolly Bove Lodge & Hutz · http://www.cblh.com · 333 South Grand Avenue, Suite 2300 · Los Angeles, CA 90071 · 213-787-2500

John D. McConaghy · Connolly Bove Lodge & Hutz · http://www.cblh.com · 333 South Grand Avenue, Suite 2300 · Los Angeles, CA 90071 · 213-787-2500

David Nimmer · ⑩ · Irell & Manella · 1800 Avenue of the Stars, Suite 900 · Los Angeles, CA 90067-4276 310-277-1010

Jeffrey M. Olson · Sidley Austin · 555 West Fifth Street, 40th Floor · Los Angeles, CA 90013 · 213-896-6000

Louis P. Petrich · Leopold, Petrich & Smith · 2049 Century Park East, Suite 3110 · Los Angeles, CA 90067-3274 · 310-277-3333

Edward G. Poplawski · Sidley Austin · 555 West Fifth Street, 40th Floor · Los Angeles, CA 90013 · 213-896-6000

Laurence H. Pretty · ⑩ · The Law Office of Laurence H. Pretty · http://www.laurencepretty.com · 633 West Fifth Street, 28th Floor · Los Angeles, CA 90071 · 213-223-2050

Ronald S. Rosen · TroyGould · http://www.troygould.com · 1801 Century Park East, Suite 1600 · Los Angeles, CA 90067 · 310-553-4441

Robert A. Sacks · Sullivan & Cromwell · 1888 Century Park East, 21st Floor · Los Angeles, CA 90067-1725 · 310-712-6600

Mark A. Samuels · O'Melveny & Myers · 400 South Hope Street, 10th Floor · Los Angeles, CA 90071-2899 · 213-430-6000

Victor G. Savikas · Jones Day · 555 South Flower Street, 50th Floor · Los Angeles, CA 90071 · 213-489-3939

Robert Schwartz · O'Melveny & Myers · 1999 Avenue of the Stars, Seventh Floor · Los Angeles, CA 90067-6035 · 310-553-6700

Lionel S. Sobel · Southwestern Law School · 3050 Wilshire Boulevard · Los Angeles, CA 90010 · 310-738-6756

Jonathan H. Steinberg · Irell & Manella · 1800 Avenue of the Stars, Suite 900 · Los Angeles, CA 90067-4276 · 310-277-1010

Robert Steinberg · Latham & Watkins · 355 South Grand Avenue · Los Angeles, CA 90071-1560 · 213-485-1234

Jane Shay Wald · Irell & Manella · 1800 Avenue of the Stars, Suite 900 · Los Angeles, CA 90067-4276 · 310-277-1010

Robert C. Weiss · Jones Day · 555 South Flower Street, 50th Floor · Los Angeles, CA 90071 · 213-489-3939

Gregory B. Wood · Fulbright & Jaworski · http://www.fulbright.com · 555 South Flower Street, 41st Floor · Los Angeles, CA 90071 · 213-892-9200

Donald L. Zachary · Spillane Shaeffer Aronoff Bandlow · 1880 Century Park East, Suite 1004 · Los Angeles, CA 90067-1623 · 310-229-9300

Malibu

Steven M. Weinberg · Cowan, DeBaets, Abrahams & Sheppard · 30765 Pacific Coast Highway, Suite 411 Malibu, CA 90265 · 310-457-6100

Menlo Park

William L. Anthony, Jr. · Orrick, Herrington & Sutcliffe · 1000 Marsh Road · Menlo Park, CA 94025-1015 · 650-614-7400

Neel Chatterjee · Orrick, Herrington & Sutcliffe · 1000 Marsh Road · Menlo Park, CA 94025-1015 · 650-614-7400

Gerald P. Dodson · Goodwin Procter · 135 Commonwealth Drive · Menlo Park, CA 94025-1105 · 650-752-3100

G. Hopkins Guy III · Orrick, Herrington & Sutcliffe · 1000 Marsh Road · Menlo Park, CA 94025-1015 · 650-614-7400

Mountain View

James J. Elacqua · Dechert · 2440 West El Camino Real, Suite 700 · Mountain View, CA 94040-1499 · 650-813-4800

Lynn H. Pasahow · ⑩ · Fenwick & West · Silicon Valley Center · 801 California Street · Mountain View, CA 94041-2008 · 650-988-8500

Darryl M. Woo · Fenwick & West · Silicon Valley Center · 801 California Street · Mountain View, CA 94041-2008 · 650-988-8500

Mitchell Zimmerman · Fenwick & West · Silicon Valley Center · 801 California Street · Mountain View, CA 94041-2008 · 650-988-8500

Newport Beach

Andra Barmash Greene · Irell & Manella · 840 Newport Center Drive, Suite 400 · Newport Beach, CA 92660-6324 · 949-760-0991

Palo Alto

Thomas E. Ciotti · ⑩ · Morrison & Foerster · http://www.mofo.com · 755 Page Mill Road · Palo Alto, CA 94304-1018 · 650-813-5600

Kenneth A. Clark · Wilson Sonsini Goodrich & Rosati · 650 Page Mill Road · Palo Alto, CA 94304-1050 · 650-493-9300

William Gaede · McDermott Will & Emery · 3150 Porter Drive · Palo Alto, CA 94304-1212 · 650-813-5000

Robert J. Goldman · Ropes & Gray · http://www.ropesgray.com · 525 University Avenue, Suite 300 · Palo Alto, CA 94301-1917 · 650-617-4000

Terrence P. McMahon · McDermott Will & Emery · 3150 Porter Drive · Palo Alto, CA 94304-1212 · 650-813-5000

Gladys H. Monroy · Morrison & Foerster · http://www.mofo.com · 755 Page Mill Road · Palo Alto, CA 94304-1018 · 650-813-5600

C. Larry O'Rourke · Finnegan, Henderson, Farabow, Garrett & Dunner · http://www.finnegan.com · Stanford Research Park · 3300 Hillview Avenue · Palo Alto, CA 94304-1203 · 650-849-6600

James Pooley · Morrison & Foerster · http://www.mofo.com · 755 Page Mill Road · Palo Alto, CA 94304-1018 · 650-813-5600

Mark D. Rowland · Ropes & Gray · http://www.ropesgray.com · 525 University Avenue, Suite 300 · Palo Alto, CA 94301-1917 · 650-617-4000

Ron E. Shulman · Wilson Sonsini Goodrich & Rosati · 650 Page Mill Road · Palo Alto, CA 94304-1050 · 650-493-9300

Robert P. Taylor · ⑩ · Mintz, Levin, Cohn, Ferris, Glovsky and Popeo · 1400 Page Mill Road · Palo Alto, CA 94304-1124 · 650-251-7700

Jerry D. Voight · Finnegan, Henderson, Farabow, Garrett & Dunner · http://www.finnegan.com · Stanford Research Park · 3300 Hillview Avenue · Palo Alto, CA 94304-1203 · 650-849-6600

Pasedena

Robert A. Schroeder · Sheldon Mak Rose & Anderson · 100 East Corson Street, Third Floor · Pasedena, CA 91103-3842 · 626-796-4000

Jeffrey G. Sheldon · Sheldon Mak Rose & Anderson · 100 East Corson Street, Third Floor · Pasedena, CA 91103-3842 · 626-796-4000

Redwood Shores

Robert T. Haslam · Covington & Burling · 333 Twin Dolphin Drive, Suite 700 · Redwood Shores, CA 94065-1418 · 650-632-4700

Matthew D. Powers · Weil Gotshal & Manges · 201 Redwood Shores Parkway, Fifth Floor · Redwood Shores, CA 94065 · 650-802-3000

Edward R. Reines · Weil Gotshal & Manges · 201 Redwood Shores Parkway, Fifth Floor · Redwood Shores, CA 94065 · 650-802-3000

Claude M. Stern · Quinn Emanuel Urquhart Oliver & Hedges · 555 Twin Dolphin Drive, Suite 560 · Redwood Shores, CA 94065 · 650-801-5000

Sacramento

Christopher Chediak · Weintraub Genshlea Chediak · 400 Capitol Mall, 11th Floor · Sacramento, CA 95814-4407 · 916-558-6000

Scott W. Pink · DLA Piper · 400 Capitol Mall, Suite 2400 · Sacramento, CA 95814-4428 · 916-930-3200

San Diego

John Allcock · ⑩ · DLA Piper · 401 B Street, Suite 1700 · San Diego, CA 92101-4297 · 619-699-2700

Gregg I. Anderson · ⑩ · Knobbe, Martens, Olson & Bear · 550 West C Street, Suite 1200 · San Diego, CA 92101 · 619-235-8550

Juanita R. Brooks · ⑳ · Fish & Richardson · 12390 El Camino Real · San Diego, CA 92130 · 858-678-5070

Peng Chen · Morrison & Foerster · http://www.mofo.com · 12531 High Bluff Drive, Suite 100 · San Diego, CA 92130-2040 · 858-720-5100

David C. Doyle · Morrison & Foerster · http://www.mofo.com · 12531 High Bluff Drive, Suite 100 · San Diego, CA 92130-2040 · 858-720-5100

John E. Gartman · Fish & Richardson · 12390 El Camino Real · San Diego, CA 92130 · 858-678-5070

Lisa A. Haile · DLA Piper · 4365 Executive Drive, Suite 1100 · San Diego, CA 92121-2133 · 858-677-1400

Anthony M. Insogna · Jones Day · 12265 El Camino Real, Suite 200 · San Diego, CA 92130-4096 · 858-314-1200

Ned Israelsen · Knobbe, Martens, Olson & Bear · 550 West C Street, Suite 1200 · San Diego, CA 92101 · 619-235-8550

Randall E. Kay · DLA Piper · 401 B Street, Suite 1700 · San Diego, CA 92101-4297 · 619-699-2700

David E. Kleinfeld · Foley & Lardner · 11250 El Camino Real, Suite 200 · San Diego, CA 92130 · 858-847-6700

Stephen S. Korniczky · Paul Hastings · 3579 Valley Centre Drive · San Diego, CA 92130 · 858-720-2500

Kate H. Murashige · ⑩ · Morrison & Foerster · http://www.mofo.com · 12531 High Bluff Drive, Suite 100 San Diego, CA 92130-2040 · 858-720-5100

Douglas E. Olson · Duane Morris · 101 West Broadway, Suite 900 · San Diego, CA 92101-8285 · 619-744-2200

Stephen P. Swinton · ⑩ · Latham & Watkins · 600 West Broadway, Suite 1800 · San Diego, CA 92101-3375 · 619-236-1234

Mark R. Wicker · Morrison & Foerster · http://www.mofo.com · 12531 High Bluff Drive, Suite 100 · San Diego, CA 92130-2040 · 858-720-5100

San Francisco

Andrew P. Bridges · Winston & Strawn · 101 California Street, 39th Floor · San Francisco, CA 94111-5802 · 415-591-1000

Henry C. Bunsow · Howrey · 525 Market Street, Suite 3600 · San Francisco, CA 94105-2708 · 415-848-4900

Jeffrey R. Chanin · Keker & Van Nest · http://www.kvn.com · 710 Sansome Street · San Francisco, CA 94111 · 415-391-5400

Daralyn J. Durie · Keker & Van Nest · http://www.kvn.com · 710 Sansome Street · San Francisco, CA 94111 · 415-391-5400

Robert D. Fram · Covington & Burling · One Front Street · San Francisco, CA 94111-5356 · 415-591-6000

Thomas J. Friel, Jr. · Cooley Godward Kronish · 101 California Street, Fifth Floor · San Francisco, CA 94111-5800 · 415-693-2000

Martin R. Glick · Howard, Rice, Nemerovski, Canady, Falk & Rabkin · Three Embarcadero Center, Seventh Floor · San Francisco, CA 94111-4024 · 415-434-1600

Paul Goldstein · ⑩ · Morrison & Foerster · http://www.mofo.com · 425 Market Street · San Francisco, CA 94105-2482 · 415-268-7000

David L. Hayes · Fenwick & West · 555 California Street, 12th Floor · San Francisco, CA 94104 · 415-875-2300

Michael A. Jacobs · Morrison & Foerster · http://www.mofo.com · 425 Market Street · San Francisco, CA 94105-2482 · 415-268-7000

Leo L. Lam · Keker & Van Nest · http://www.kvn.com · 710 Sansome Street · San Francisco, CA 94111 · 415-391-5400

Mark A. Lemley · Keker & Van Nest · http://www.kvn.com · 710 Sansome Street · San Francisco, CA 94111 · 415-391-5400

Jack W. Londen · Morrison & Foerster · http://www.mofo.com · 425 Market Street · San Francisco, CA 94105-2482 · 415-268-7000

J. Thomas McCarthy · ⑩ · Morrison & Foerster · http://www.mofo.com · 425 Market Street · San Francisco, CA 94105-2482 · 415-268-7000

Harold J. McElhinny · Morrison & Foerster · http://www.mofo.com · 425 Market Street · San Francisco, CA 94105-2482 · 415-268-7000

Michael H. Page · Keker & Van Nest · http://www.kvn.com · 710 Sansome Street · San Francisco, CA 94111 · 415-391-5400

George A. Riley · O'Melveny & Myers · Embarcadero Center West · 275 Battery Street · San Francisco, CA 94111-3305 · 415-984-8700

Thomas F. Smegal, Jr. · ⑩ · Law Offices of Thomas F. Smegal, Jr. · One Sansome Street, 35th Floor · San Francisco, CA 94104 · 415-217-8383

Neil A. Smith · ⑩ · Sheppard, Mullin, Richter & Hampton · http://www.sheppardmullin.com · Four Embarcadero Center, 17th Floor · San Francisco, CA 94111 · 415-434-9100

Jon B. Streeter · Keker & Van Nest · http://www.kvn.com · 710 Sansome Street · San Francisco, CA 94111 · 415-391-5400

Stephen E. Taylor · Taylor & Company Law Offices · One Ferry Building, Suite 355 · San Francisco, CA 94111 · 415-788-8200

San Jose

Daniel J. Bergeson · Bergeson · http://www.be-law.com · 303 Almaden Boulevard, Suite 500 · San Jose, CA 95110-2712 · 408-291-6200

Santa Monica

Ian C. Ballon · Greenberg Traurig · http://www.gtlaw.com · 2450 Colorado Avenue, Suite 400-E · Santa Monica, CA 90404 · 310-586-7700

Terence J. Clark · ⑩ · Greenberg Traurig · http://www.gtlaw.com · 2450 Colorado Avenue, Suite 400-E · Santa Monica, CA 90404 · 310-586-7700

INTERNATIONAL ARBITRATION

Monterey

Charles R. Keller · Fenton & Keller · 2801 Monterey Salinas Highway · P.O. Box 791 · Monterey, CA 93942-0791 · 831-373-1241

INTERNATIONAL TRADE AND FINANCE LAW

Los Angeles

Warren Christopher · O'Melveny & Myers · 1999 Avenue of the Stars, Seventh Floor · Los Angeles, CA 90067-6035 · 310-553-6700

Francis W. Costello · Holland & Knight · http://www.hklaw.com · 633 West Fifth Street, 21st Floor · Los Angeles, CA 90071 · 213-896-2400

Stanley F. Farrar · ⑩ · Sullivan & Cromwell · 1888 Century Park East, 21st Floor · Los Angeles, CA 90067-1725 · 310-712-6600

Peter A. Gelles · Peter Gelles · 1801 Century Park East, Suite 1520 · Los Angeles, CA 90067 · 310-201-7900

Albert S. Golbert · Golbert & Associates · One Bunker Hill, Eighth Floor · 601 West Fifth Street · Los Angeles, CA 90071-2094 · 213-891-9641

John R. Liebman · McKenna Long & Aldridge · 444 South Flower Street, Eighth Floor · Los Angeles, CA 90071-2901 · 213-688-1000

Robert E. Lutz II · Southwestern University School of Law · 3050 Wilshire Boulevard · Los Angeles, CA 90010 · 213-738-6700

Neal S. Millard · White & Case · http://www.whitecase.com · 633 West Fifth Street, Suite 1900 · Los Angeles, CA 90071-2007 · 213-620-7700

LABOR AND EMPLOYMENT LAW

Alameda

W. Daniel Boone · Weinberg, Roger & Rosenfeld · 1001 Marina Village Parkway, Suite 200 · Alameda, CA 94501-1091 · 510-337-1001

David A. Rosenfeld · Weinberg, Roger & Rosenfeld · 1001 Marina Village Parkway, Suite 200 · Alameda, CA 94501-1091 · 510-337-1001

Stewart Weinberg · ㉕ · Weinberg, Roger & Rosenfeld · 1001 Marina Village Parkway, Suite 200 · Alameda, CA 94501-1091 · 510-337-1001

Berkeley

Della Hinn Bahan · Bahan and Associates · 125 University Avenue, Suite 102 · Berkeley, CA 94710 · 510-845-0740

Brad S. Seligman · The Impact Fund · 125 University Avenue, Suite 102 · Berkeley, CA 94710 · 510-845-3473

Beverly Hills

Scott R. Ames · Serratore - Ames · 9595 Wilshire Boulevard, Suite 201 · Beverly Hills, CA 90212 · 310-205-2460

Steven J. Rottman · Rottman-Kaplan · 9350 Wilshire Boulevard, Suite 300 · Beverly Hills, CA 90212 · 310-288-3700

David A. Wimmer · Swerdlow Florence Sanchez Swerdlow & Wimmer · http://www.swerdlowlaw.com · 9401 Wilshire Boulevard, Suite 828 · Beverly Hills, CA 90212 · 310-288-3980

Burbank

Leo Geffner · ㉕ · Bush, Quinonez, Gottlieb, Singer, Lopez, Kohanski, Adelstein & Dickinson · 3500 West Olive Avenue, Suite 1100 · Burbank, CA 91505 · 818-973-3200

Burlingame

Charles E. Voltz · ⑳ · Law Office of Charles E. Voltz · 433 Airport Boulevard, Suite 231 · P.O. Box 323 · Burlingame, CA 94011 · 650-685-8010

Costa Mesa

Stephen L. Berry · Paul Hastings · 695 Town Center Drive, 17th Floor · Costa Mesa, CA 92626 · 714-668-6200

James P. Carter · Paul Hastings · 695 Town Center Drive, 17th Floor · Costa Mesa, CA 92626 · 714-668-6200

Frank Cronin · Snell & Wilmer · 600 Anton Boulevard, Suite 1400 · Costa Mesa, CA 92626-7689 · 714-427-7000

Howard C. Hay · ㉕ · Paul Hastings · 695 Town Center Drive, 17th Floor · Costa Mesa, CA 92626 · 714-668-6200

Michael A. Hood · ⑩ · Paul Hastings · 695 Town Center Drive, 17th Floor · Costa Mesa, CA 92626 · 714-668-6200

Christy D. Joseph · Snell & Wilmer · 600 Anton Boulevard, Suite 1400 · Costa Mesa, CA 92626-7689 · 714-427-7000

David C. Larsen · ⑳ · Rutan & Tucker · http://www.rutan.com · 611 Anton Boulevard, Suite 1400 · P.O. Box 1950 · Costa Mesa, CA 92628-1950 · 714-641-5100

James L. Morris · Rutan & Tucker · http://www.rutan.com · 611 Anton Boulevard, Suite 1400 · P.O. Box 1950 · Costa Mesa, CA 92628-1950 · 714-641-5100

Gold River

Christopher H. Whelan · ⑩ · Christopher H. Whelan · 11246 Gold Express Drive, Suite 100 · Gold River, CA 95670-4425 · 916-635-5577

Irvine

William D. Claster · ⑩ · Gibson, Dunn & Crutcher · 3161 Michelson Drive · Irvine, CA 92612-4412 · 949-451-3800

William M. Crosby · Barnes, Crosby, Fitzgerald & Zeman · 18101 Von Karman Avenue, Suite 120 · Irvine, CA 92614 · 949-852-1100

Daniel F. Fears · Payne & Fears · Jamboree Center, Suite 1100 · Four Park Plaza · Irvine, CA 92614 · 949-851-1100

James J. McDonald, Jr. · Fisher & Phillips · http://www.laborlawyers.com · 18400 Von Karman Avenue, Suite 400 · Irvine, CA 92612 · 949-851-2424

Robert A. Naeve · Jones Day · Three Park Plaza, Suite 1100 · Irvine, CA 92614-2592 · 949-851-3939

James L. Payne · Payne & Fears · Jamboree Center, Suite 1100 · Four Park Plaza · Irvine, CA 92614 · 949-851-1100

John M. Polson · Fisher & Phillips · http://www.laborlawyers.com · 18400 Von Karman Avenue, Suite 400 · Irvine, CA 92612 · 949-851-2424

Daniel L. Rasmussen · Payne & Fears · Jamboree Center, Suite 1100 · Four Park Plaza · Irvine, CA 92614 · 949-851-1100

Gabrielle Wirth · Dorsey & Whitney · 38 Technology Drive, Suite 100 · Irvine, CA 92618-5310 · 949-932-3600

Laguna Hills

Michelle A. Reinglass · Law Office of Michelle A. Reinglass · 23161 Millcreek Drive, Suite 170 · Laguna Hills, CA 92653 · 949-587-0460

Long Beach

Paul E. Crost · ⑳ · Law Office of Paul E. Crost · 5318 East Second Street, Suite 381 · Long Beach, CA 90803 · 562-608-8433

Los Angeles

Leslie L. Abbott · Paul Hastings · 515 South Flower Street, 25th Floor · Los Angeles, CA 90071 · 213-683-6000

George W. Abele · Paul Hastings · 515 South Flower Street, 25th Floor · Los Angeles, CA 90071 · 213-683-6000

Nancy L. Abell · ⑳ · Paul Hastings · 515 South Flower Street, 25th Floor · Los Angeles, CA 90071 · 213-683-6000

Hirsch Adell · Reich, Adell, Crost & Cvitan · 3550 Wilshire Boulevard, Suite 2000 · Los Angeles, CA 90010-2314 · 213-386-3860

James N. Adler · ㉕ · James N. Adler Mediation & Arbitration · 1034 Selby Avenue · Los Angeles, CA 90024-3106 · 310-209-8548

Elena R. Baca · Paul Hastings · 515 South Flower Street, 25th Floor · Los Angeles, CA 90071 · 213-683-6000

Jeffrey A. Berman · ⑩ · Sidley Austin · 555 West Fifth Street, 40th Floor · Los Angeles, CA 90013 · 213-896-6000

Jonathan W. Biddle · ⑩ · Law Offices of Jonathan W. Biddle · One Wilshire Boulevard, Suite 2200 · Los Angeles, CA 90017-3321 · 213-629-8720

William L. Cole · Mitchell Silberberg & Knupp · 11377 West Olympic Boulevard · Los Angeles, CA 90064 · 310-312-2000

Alexander Cvitan · Reich, Adell, Crost & Cvitan · 3550 Wilshire Boulevard, Suite 2000 · Los Angeles, CA 90010-2314 · 213-386-3860

Robert M. Dohrmann · ㉕ · Schwartz, Steinsapir, Dohrmann & Sommers · 6300 Wilshire Boulevard, Suite 2000 · Los Angeles, CA 90048-5268 · 323-655-4700

Steven G. Drapkin · Steven Drapkin · 11377 West Olympic Boulevard, Suite 900 · Los Angeles, CA 90064-1683 · 310-914-7909

William J. Emanuel · Littler Mendelson · 2049 Century Park East, Fifth Floor · Los Angeles, CA 90067-3107 · 310-553-0308

Howard D. Fabrick · Akin Gump Strauss Hauer & Feld · 2029 Century Park East, Suite 2400 · Los Angeles, CA 90067-3012 · 310-229-1000

Alan V. Friedman · ㉕ · Munger, Tolles & Olson · 355 South Grand Avenue, 35th Floor · Los Angeles, CA 90071-1560 · 213-683-9100

Bernard D. Gold · ⑩ · Proskauer Rose · http://www.proskauer.com · 2049 Century Park East, 32nd Floor Los Angeles, CA 90067-3206 · 310-557-2900

Nathan Goldberg · ⑩ · Allred, Maroko & Goldberg · 6300 Wilshire Boulevard, Suite 1500 · Los Angeles, CA 90048 · 323-302-4773

Paul Grossman · ㉕ · Paul Hastings · 515 South Flower Street, 25th Floor · Los Angeles, CA 90071 · 213-683-6000

Pamela L. Hemminger · ⑩ · Gibson, Dunn & Crutcher · 333 South Grand Avenue · Los Angeles, CA 90071-3197 · 213-229-7000

Toni J. Jaramilla · Law Office of Toni Jaramilla · 10100 Santa Monica Boulevard, Suite 300 · Los Angeles, CA 90067 · 310-551-3020

Eric H. Joss · Paul Hastings · 515 South Flower Street, 25th Floor · Los Angeles, CA 90071 · 213-683-6000

David D. Kadue · Seyfarth Shaw · One Century Plaza, Suite 3300 · 2029 Century Park East · Los Angeles, CA 90067-3063 · 310-277-7200

Diane L. Kimberlin · Littler Mendelson · 2049 Century Park East, Fifth Floor · Los Angeles, CA 90067-3107 · 310-553-0308

Gordon E. Krischer · ⑩ · O'Melveny & Myers · 400 South Hope Street, 10th Floor · Los Angeles, CA 90071-2899 · 213-430-6000

J. Al Latham, Jr. · Paul Hastings · 515 South Flower Street, 25th Floor · Los Angeles, CA 90071 · 213-683-6000

Dolores Y. Leal · Allred, Maroko & Goldberg · 6300 Wilshire Boulevard, Suite 1500 · Los Angeles, CA 90048 · 323-302-4773

Stuart Libicki · Schwartz, Steinsapir, Dohrmann & Sommers · 6300 Wilshire Boulevard, Suite 2000 · Los Angeles, CA 90048-5268 · 323-655-4700

Ethan Lipsig · ⑩ · Paul Hastings · 515 South Flower Street, 25th Floor · Los Angeles, CA 90071 · 213-683-6000

Michael Maroko · ⑩ · Allred, Maroko & Goldberg · 6300 Wilshire Boulevard, Suite 1500 · Los Angeles, CA 90048 · 323-302-4773

Everett F. Meiners · Parker, Milliken, Clark, O'Hara & Samuelian · 555 South Flower Street, 13th Floor · Los Angeles, CA 90071 · 213-683-6500

Lawrence A. Michaels · Mitchell Silberberg & Knupp · 11377 West Olympic Boulevard · Los Angeles, CA 90064 · 310-312-2000

Dennis F. Moss · Spiro Moss Barness Harrison & Barge · 11377 West Olympic Boulevard, Fifth Floor · Los Angeles, CA 90064 · 310-235-2468

Anthony T. Oliver, Jr. · ⑳ · Parker, Milliken, Clark, O'Hara & Samuelian · 555 South Flower Street, 13th Floor · Los Angeles, CA 90071 · 213-683-6500

Robert T. Olmos · Allred, Maroko & Goldberg · 6300 Wilshire Boulevard, Suite 1500 · Los Angeles, CA 90048 · 323-302-4773

Anthony J. Oncidi · Proskauer Rose · http://www.proskauer.com · 2049 Century Park East, 32nd Floor · Los Angeles, CA 90067-3206 · 310-557-2900

Lester G. Ostrov · Lester G. Ostrov · 11845 West Olympic Boulevard, Suite 1245 · Los Angeles, CA 90064 · 310-477-0424

Joseph L. Paller, Jr. · Gilbert & Sackman · 3699 Wilshire Boulevard, Suite 1200 · Los Angeles, CA 90010-2732 · 323-938-3000

George A. Pappy · ㉕ · Reich, Adell, Crost & Cvitan · 3550 Wilshire Boulevard, Suite 2000 · Los Angeles, CA 90010-2314 · 213-386-3860

Lee T. Paterson · Winston & Strawn · 333 South Grand Avenue, 38th Floor · Los Angeles, CA 90071-1543 · 213-615-1700

Michael P. Posner · Posner & Rosen · 3600 Wilshire Boulevard, Suite 1800 · Los Angeles, CA 90010 · 213-389-6050

Lyne A. Richardson · Ford & Harrison · http://www.fordharrison.com · 350 South Grand Avenue, Suite 2300 · Los Angeles, CA 90071 · 213-237-2400

Howard Z. Rosen · Posner & Rosen · 3600 Wilshire Boulevard, Suite 1800 · Los Angeles, CA 90010 · 213-389-6050

Terry E. Sanchez · ⑩ · Munger, Tolles & Olson · 355 South Grand Avenue, 35th Floor · Los Angeles, CA 90071-1560 · 213-683-9100

Deborah Crandall Saxe · Jones Day · 555 South Flower Street, 50th Floor · Los Angeles, CA 90071 · 213-489-3939

Karl A. Schmidt · Parker, Milliken, Clark, O'Hara & Samuelian · 555 South Flower Street, 13th Floor · Los Angeles, CA 90071 · 213-683-6500

Steven M. Schneider · Mitchell Silberberg & Knupp · 11377 West Olympic Boulevard · Los Angeles, CA 90064 · 310-312-2000

Richard J. Simmons · Sheppard, Mullin, Richter & Hampton · http://www.sheppardmullin.com · 333 South Hope Street, 48th Floor · Los Angeles, CA 90071-1448 · 213-620-1780

Ann Kane Smith · Thelen Reid Brown Raysman & Steiner · 333 South Hope Street, Suite 2900 · Los Angeles, CA 90071-3048 · 213-576-8000

Laurence D. Steinsapir · ㉕ · Schwartz, Steinsapir, Dohrmann & Sommers · 6300 Wilshire Boulevard, Suite 2000 · Los Angeles, CA 90048-5268 · 323-655-4700

George A. Stohner · Morgan Lewis & Bockius · 300 South Grand Avenue, 22nd Floor · Los Angeles, CA 90071-3132 · 213-612-2500

Framroze M. Virjee · O'Melveny & Myers · 400 South Hope Street, 10th Floor · Los Angeles, CA 90071-2899 · 213-430-6000

William Stewart Waldo · ⑳ · Paul Hastings · 515 South Flower Street, 25th Floor · Los Angeles, CA 90071 · 213-683-6000

Jeffrey K. Winikow · Jeffrey K. Winikow · 1801 Century Park East, Suite 1520 · Los Angeles, CA 90067 · 310-552-3450

Stuart H. Young, Jr. · ⑩ · Hill, Farrer & Burrill · One California Plaza, 37th Floor · 300 South Grand Avenue · Los Angeles, CA 90071-3147 · 213-620-0460

James A. Zapp · ⑩ · Paul Hastings · 515 South Flower Street, 25th Floor · Los Angeles, CA 90071 · 213-683-6000

Manhattan Beach

Nancy Bornn · Bornn & Surls · 1500 Rosecrans Avenue, Suite 500 · Manhattan Beach, CA 90266 · 310-706-4055

Curtis L. Surls · Bornn & Surls · 1500 Rosecrans Avenue, Suite 500 · Manhattan Beach, CA 90266 · 310-706-4055

Menlo Park

Lynne C. Hermle · Orrick, Herrington & Sutcliffe · 1000 Marsh Road · Menlo Park, CA 94025-1015 · 650-614-7400

Mission Viejo

Don D. Sessions · Sessions & Kimball · 23456 Madero, Suite 170 · Mission Viejo, CA 92691-7913 · 949-380-0900

Mountain View

Victor Schachter · ⑩ · Fenwick & West · Silicon Valley Center · 801 California Street · Mountain View, CA 94041-2008 · 650-988-8500

Newport Beach

R. Craig Scott · ⑩ · Scott & Whitehead · 1301 Dove Street, Suite 1000 · Newport Beach, CA 92660 · 949-222-0166

Oakland

Morris J. Baller · Goldstein, Demchak, Baller, Borgen & Dardarian · 300 Lakeside Drive, Suite 1000 · Oakland, CA 94612-3534 · 510-763-9800

Duane B. Beeson · ㉕ · Beeson, Tayer & Bodine · 1404 Franklin Street, Fifth Floor · Oakland, CA 94612 510-625-9700

David Borgen · Goldstein, Demchak, Baller, Borgen & Dardarian · 300 Lakeside Drive, Suite 1000 · Oakland, CA 94612-3534 · 510-763-9800

Kathryn B. Dickson · Dickson- Ross · 1970 Broadway, Suite 1045 · Oakland, CA 94612 · 510-268-1999

Henry S. Hewitt · ⑩ · Erickson, Beasley, Hewitt & Wilson · 483 Ninth Street, Suite 200 · Oakland, CA 94607 · 510-839-3448

Jean K. Hyams · Boxer & Gerson · 300 Frank H. Ogawa Plaza, Suite 500 · Oakland, CA 94612 · 510-835-8870

Bill Lann Lee · Lewis, Feinberg, Lee, Renaker & Jackson · 1330 Broadway, Suite 1800 · Oakland, CA 94612 · 510-839-6824

Leslie F. Levy · Boxer & Gerson · 300 Frank H. Ogawa Plaza, Suite 500 · Oakland, CA 94612 · 510-835-8870

Jody I. LeWitter · Siegel & LeWitter · 1939 Harrison Street, Suite 307 · Oakland, CA 94612 · 510-452-5000

Jeff Ross · Dickson Ross · 1970 Broadway, Suite 1045 · Oakland, CA 94612 · 510-268-1999

Ronald E. Yank · ⑩ · Ronald Yank · 5598 Lawton Avenue · Oakland, CA 94618 · 510-547-2907

Palo Alto

Fred W. Alvarez · Wilson Sonsini Goodrich & Rosati · 650 Page Mill Road · Palo Alto, CA 94304-1050 · 650-493-9300

Frederick D. Baron · Cooley Godward Kronish · 3175 Hanover Street · Palo Alto, CA 94304-1130 · 650-843-5000

Cynthia L. Jackson · Baker & McKenzie · 660 Hansen Way · P.O. Box 60309 · Palo Alto, CA 94304-0309 650-856-2400

Melinda S. Riechert · Morgan Lewis & Bockius · Two Palo Alto Square, Suite 700 · 3000 El Camino Real Palo Alto, CA 94306-2121 · 650-843-4000

Gregory Tenhoff · Cooley Godward Kronish · 3175 Hanover Street · Palo Alto, CA 94304-1130 · 650-843-5000

Raymond L. Wheeler · ⑳ · Morrison & Foerster · http://www.mofo.com · 755 Page Mill Road · Palo Alto, CA 94304-1018 · 650-813-5600

Thomas E. Wilson · Morrison & Foerster · http://www.mofo.com · 755 Page Mill Road · Palo Alto, CA 94304-1018 · 650-813-5600

Pasadena

Ellen Greenstone · ⑩ · Rothner, Segall & Greenstone · 510 South Marengo Avenue · Pasadena, CA 91101 · 626-796-7555

Barbara E. Hadsell · ⑩ · Hadsell & Stormer · 128 North Fair Oaks Avenue, Suite 204 · Pasadena, CA 91103 · 626-585-9600

Virginia Keeny · Hadsell & Stormer · 128 North Fair Oaks Avenue, Suite 204 · Pasadena, CA 91103 · 626-585-9600

Randall R. Renick · Hadsell, Stormer, Keeny, Richardson & Renick · 128 North Fair Oaks Avenue, Suite 204 · Pasadena, CA 91103 · 626-585-9600

Anne K. Richardson · Hadsell & Stormer · 128 North Fair Oaks Avenue, Suite 204 · Pasadena, CA 91103 626-585-9600

Glenn E. Rothner · ⑳ · Rothner, Segall & Greenstone · 510 South Marengo Avenue · Pasadena, CA 91101 · 626-796-7555

Anthony R. Segall · Rothner, Segall & Greenstone · 510 South Marengo Avenue · Pasadena, CA 91101 · 626-796-7555

Dan Stormer · ⑩ · Hadsell & Stormer · 128 North Fair Oaks Avenue, Suite 204 · Pasadena, CA 91103 · 626-585-9600

Riverside

Terry D. Bridges · ⑩ · Reid & Hellyer · 3880 Lemon Street, Fifth Floor · P.O. Box 1300 · Riverside, CA 92502-1300 · 951-682-1771

Vincent P. Nolan · Law Office of Vincent P. Nolan · 3877 Twelfth Street · Riverside, CA 92501-3527 · 909-788-1747

Sacramento

Daniel J. Coyle · Downey Brand · 555 Capitol Mall, 10th Floor · Sacramento, CA 95814 · 916-444-1000

Richard R. Gray · Littler Mendelson · 2520 Venture Oaks Way, Suite 390 · Sacramento, CA 95833-4227 · 916-830-7200

Daniel J. McVeigh · Downey Brand · 555 Capitol Mall, 10th Floor · Sacramento, CA 95814 · 916-444-1000

Gary M. Messing · Carroll, Burdick & McDonough · 1007 Seventh Street, Suite 200 · Sacramento, CA 95814 · 916-446-5297

David L. Perrault · Hardy Erich Brown & Wilson · 1000 G Street, Second Floor · Sacramento, CA 95814 · 916-449-3800

Charles L. Post · Weintraub Genshlea Chediak · 400 Capitol Mall, 11th Floor · Sacramento, CA 95814-4407 · 916-558-6000

San Diego

Robert W. Bell, Jr. · ⑳ · Paul, Plevin, Sullivan & Connaughton · 401 B Street, 10th Floor · San Diego, CA 92101 · 619-237-5200

Harvey C. Berger · Pope, Berger & Williams · 550 West C Street, Suite 1400 · San Diego, CA 92101 · 619-234-1222

Kathryn A. Bernert · Luce, Forward, Hamilton & Scripps · http://www.luce.com · 11988 El Camino Real, Suite 200 · San Diego, CA 92130-2594 · 858-720-6300

J. Rod Betts · Paul, Plevin, Sullivan & Connaughton · 401 B Street, 10th Floor · San Diego, CA 92101 · 619-237-5200

John D. Collins · ⑳ · Sheppard, Mullin, Richter & Hampton · http://www.sheppardmullin.com · 12275 El Camino Real, Suite 200 · San Diego, CA 92130 · 858-720-8900

L. B. Edleson · Edleson & Rezzo · Emerald Plaza, 27th Floor · 402 West Broadway · San Diego, CA 92101-8567 · 619-230-8402

George S. Howard, Jr. · ⑩ · Jones Day · 12265 El Camino Real, Suite 200 · San Diego, CA 92130-4096 · 858-314-1200

Robert A. Levy · Luce, Forward, Hamilton & Scripps · http://www.luce.com · 600 West Broadway, Suite 2600 · San Diego, CA 92101 · 619-236-1414

Anthony F. Pantoni · Anthony F. Pantoni · 401 West A Street, Suite 2300 · San Diego, CA 92101 · 619-235-4400

Richard A. Paul · ⑳ · Paul, Plevin, Sullivan & Connaughton · 401 B Street, 10th Floor · San Diego, CA 92101 · 619-237-5200

Fred M. Plevin · Paul, Plevin, Sullivan & Connaughton · 401 B Street, 10th Floor · San Diego, CA 92101 619-237-5200

Richard D. Prochazka · ⑳ · Richard D. Prochazka · 2525 Camino Del Rio South, Suite 209 · San Diego, CA 92108 · 619-296-7677

Mark S. Pulliam · Latham & Watkins · 600 West Broadway, Suite 1800 · San Diego, CA 92101-3375 · 619-236-1234

Jeremy A. Roth · Littler Mendelson · 501 West Broadway, Suite 900 · San Diego, CA 92101-3577 · 619-232-0441

Renee S. Schor · Schor & Freeland · 600 B Street, Suite 2200 · San Diego, CA 92101 · 619-906-2400

Theodore R. Scott · Littler Mendelson · 501 West Broadway, Suite 900 · San Diego, CA 92101-3577 · 619-232-0441

Abby B. Silverman · Baker & McKenzie · 12544 High Bluff Drive, Third Floor · San Diego, CA 92130-3051 · 858-523-6200

Fern M. Steiner · ⑳ · Tosdal, Smith, Steiner & Wax · 401 West A Street, Suite 320 · San Diego, CA 92101-7911 · 619-239-7200

David P. Strauss · Strauss and Asher · 1111 Sixth Avenue, Suite 404 · San Diego, CA 92101 · 619-618-2407

Michael C. Sullivan · Paul, Plevin, Sullivan & Connaughton · 401 B Street, 10th Floor · San Diego, CA 92101 · 619-237-5200

Thomas L. Tosdal · ⑳ · Tosdal, Smith, Steiner & Wax · 401 West A Street, Suite 320 · San Diego, CA 92101-7911 · 619-239-7200

Claudette G. Wilson · Wilson Petty Kosmo & Turner · 550 West C Street, Suite 1050 · San Diego, CA 92101-3532 · 619-236-9600

John L. Anderson · ⑳ · Neyhart, Anderson, Freitas, Flynn & Grosball · 44 Montgomery Street, Suite 2080 · San Francisco, CA 94104-6702 · 415-677-9440

Douglas H. Barton · ⑩ · Hanson Bridgett · http://www.hansonbridgett.com · 425 Market Street, 26th Floor · San Francisco, CA 94105 · 415-777-3200

Alan Berkowitz · Bingham McCutchen · http://www.bingham.com · Three Embarcadero Center · San Francisco, CA 94111-4067 · 415-393-2000

Stephen P. Berzon · Altshuler Berzon · 177 Post Street, Suite 300 · San Francisco, CA 94108 · 415-421-7151

Charles S. Birenbaum · Winston & Strawn · 101 California Street, 39th Floor · San Francisco, CA 94111-5802 · 415-591-1000

Paul W. Cane, Jr. · ⑩ · Paul Hastings · 55 Second Street, 24th Floor · San Francisco, CA 94105 · 415-856-7000

Jeffrey B. Demain · Altshuler Berzon · 177 Post Street, Suite 300 · San Francisco, CA 94108 · 415-421-7151

Gilmore F. Diekmann, Jr. · ⑳ · Seyfarth Shaw · 560 Mission Street, Suite 3100 · San Francisco, CA 94105-2930 · 415-397-2823

Rebecca D. Eisen · Morgan Lewis & Bockius · Spear Street Tower · One Market · San Francisco, CA 94105-1596 · 415-442-1000

Alan B. Exelrod · ⑳ · Rudy, Exelrod & Zieff · http://www.reztlaw.com · 351 California Street, Suite 700 · San Francisco, CA 94104 · 415-434-9800

James M. Finberg · Altshuler Berzon · 177 Post Street, Suite 300 · San Francisco, CA 94108 · 415-421-7151

Patricia K. Gillette · ⑩ · Orrick, Herrington & Sutcliffe · The Orrick Building · 405 Howard Street · San Francisco, CA 94105-2669 · 415-773-5700

Patrick M. Glenn · Hanson Bridgett · http://www.hansonbridgett.com · 425 Market Street, 26th Floor · San Francisco, CA 94105 · 415-777-3200

E. Jeffrey Grube · Paul Hastings · 55 Second Street, 24th Floor · San Francisco, CA 94105 · 415-856-7000

Dov M. Grunschlag · Carter, Carter, Fries and Grunschlag · 44 Montgomery Street, 25th Floor · San Francisco, CA 94104 · 415-989-4800

Michael C. Hallerud · Thelen Reid Brown Raysman & Steiner · 101 Second Street, Suite 1800 · San Francisco, CA 94105-3601 · 415-371-1200

Philip E. Kay · The Law Office of Philip Kay · 736 Forty-Third Avenue · San Francisco, CA 94121 · 415-387-6622

Judith Droz Keyes · ⑩ · Davis Wright Tremaine · 505 Montgomery Street, Suite 800 · San Francisco, CA 94111-6533 · 415-276-6500

Robert P. Kristoff · Paul Hastings · 55 Second Street, 24th Floor · San Francisco, CA 94105 · 415-856-7000

Barbara A. Lawless · Lawless & Lawless · 180 Montgomery Street, Suite 2000 · San Francisco, CA 94104 415-391-7555

Robert M. Lieber · ㉕ · Margolis & Tisman · 111 Pine Street, Suite 1620 · San Francisco, CA 94111 · 415-986-2144

Garry G. Mathiason · Littler Mendelson · 650 California Street, 20th Floor · San Francisco, CA 94108-2693 · 415-433-1940

Fraser A. McAlpine · ⑩ · Hunton & Williams · 575 Market Street, Suite 3700 · San Francisco, CA 94105 415-975-3700

Richard G. McCracken · Davis, Cowell & Bowe · 595 Market Street, Suite 1400 · San Francisco, CA 94105 · 415-597-7200

John A. McGuinn · ⑩ · McGuinn, Hillsman & Palefsky · 535 Pacific Avenue · San Francisco, CA 94133 · 415-421-9292

Stephen M. Murphy · Law Office of Stephen M. Murphy · 180 Montgomery Street, Suite 940 · San Francisco, CA 94104 · 415-986-1338

Timothy J. Murphy · ⑳ · Fisher & Phillips · http://www.laborlawyers.com · One Embarcadero Center, Suite 2340 · 501 Fourteenth Street · San Francisco, CA 94111-3712 · 415-490-9000

Peter D. Nussbaum · ㉕ · Altshuler Berzon · 177 Post Street, Suite 300 · San Francisco, CA 94108 · 415-421-7151

Cliff Palefsky · ⑳ · McGuinn, Hillsman & Palefsky · 535 Pacific Avenue · San Francisco, CA 94133 · 415-421-9292

Michael Rubin · Altshuler Berzon · 177 Post Street, Suite 300 · San Francisco, CA 94108 · 415-421-7151

Mark S. Rudy · ⑩ · Rudy, Exelrod & Zieff · http://www.reztlaw.com · 351 California Street, Suite 700 · San Francisco, CA 94104 · 415-434-9800

Jerrold C. Schaefer · ⑩ · Hanson Bridgett · http://www.hansonbridgett.com · 425 Market Street, 26th Floor · San Francisco, CA 94105 · 415-777-3200

James Severson · Bingham McCutchen · http://www.bingham.com · Three Embarcadero Center · San Francisco, CA 94111-4067 · 415-393-2000

Linda E. Shostak · Morrison & Foerster · http://www.mofo.com · 425 Market Street · San Francisco, CA 94105-2482 · 415-268-7000

Gary R. Siniscalco · Orrick, Herrington & Sutcliffe · The Orrick Building · 405 Howard Street · San Francisco, CA 94105-2669 · 415-773-5700

Cecily A. Waterman · Morgan Lewis & Bockius · Spear Street Tower · One Market · San Francisco, CA 94105-1596 · 415-442-1000

M. Kirby C. Wilcox · ⑳ · Paul Hastings · 55 Second Street, 24th Floor · San Francisco, CA 94105 · 415-856-7000

Jeffrey D. Wohl · ⑩ · Paul Hastings · 55 Second Street, 24th Floor · San Francisco, CA 94105 · 415-856-7000

Steven G. Zieff · Rudy, Exelrod & Zieff · http://www.reztlaw.com · 351 California Street, Suite 700 · San Francisco, CA 94104 · 415-434-9800

San Jose

Robert C. Coelho · Hoge, Fenton, Jones & Appel · http://www.hogefenton.com · 60 South Market Street, Suite 1400 · San Jose, CA 95113-2396 · 408-287-9501

Kathryn K. Meier · Hoge, Fenton, Jones & Appel · http://www.hogefenton.com · 60 South Market Street, Suite 1400 · San Jose, CA 95113-2396 · 408-287-9501

San Mateo

William C. Quackenbush · ⑩ · Quackenbush & Quackenbush · 1700 South El Camino Real, Suite 408 · San Mateo, CA 94402 · 650-578-8300

Santa Monica

Diana P. Scott · Greenberg Traurig · http://www.gtlaw.com · 2450 Colorado Avenue, Suite 400-E · Santa Monica, CA 90404 · 310-586-7700

Stephen H. Silver · ⑩ · Silver Hadden, Silver, Wexler & Levine · 1428 Second Street · P.O. Box 2161 · Santa Monica, CA 90407-2161 · 310-393-1486

Santa Rosa

Amy Rodney · Conner, Lawrence & Rodney · 829 Sonoma Avenue · Santa Rosa, CA 95404 · 707-523-0480

Sherman Oaks

Mary Lee Wegner · Law Offices of Mary Lee Wegner · 4708 Cedros Avenue · Sherman Oaks, CA 91403 · 818-990-2298

Tustin

Harris E. Kershnar · Harris E. Kershnar · 17592 Irvine Boulevard · Tustin, CA 92780-3105 · 714-730-5300

Universal City

Kenneth R. Ballard · Ballard, Rosenberg, Golper & Savitt · 10 Universal City Plaza, 16th Floor · Universal City, CA 91608-1097 · 818-508-3700

John B. Golper · Ballard, Rosenberg, Golper & Savitt · 10 Universal City Plaza, 16th Floor · Universal City, CA 91608-1097 · 818-508-3700

Richard S. Rosenberg · Ballard, Rosenberg, Golper & Savitt · 10 Universal City Plaza, 16th Floor · Universal City, CA 91608-1097 · 818-508-3700

Linda Miller Savitt · Ballard, Rosenberg, Golper & Savitt · 10 Universal City Plaza, 16th Floor · Universal City, CA 91608-1097 · 818-508-3700

LAND USE & ZONING LAW

Carmichael

George E. Phillips · George E. Phillips · 2306 Garfield Avenue · Carmichael, CA 95608 · 916-979-4800

Costa Mesa

Susan K. Hori · Manatt, Phelps & Phillips · Park Tower, 14th Floor · 695 Town Center Drive · Costa Mesa, CA 92626 · 714-371-2500

Timothy Paone · Manatt, Phelps & Phillips · Park Tower, 14th Floor · 695 Town Center Drive · Costa Mesa, CA 92626 · 714-371-2500

Los Angeles

Kenneth B. Bley · ⑩ · Cox, Castle & Nicholson · 2049 Century Park East, 28th Floor · Los Angeles, CA 90067 · 310-277-4222

Linda J. Bozung · DLA Piper · 1999 Avenue of the Stars, Suite 400 · Los Angeles, CA 90067-6023 · 310-595-3000

Stanley W. Lamport · Cox, Castle & Nicholson · 2049 Century Park East, 28th Floor · Los Angeles, CA 90067 · 310-277-4222

George J. Mihlsten · ⑩ · Latham & Watkins · 355 South Grand Avenue · Los Angeles, CA 90071-1560 · 213-485-1234

Margaret Moore Sohagi · The Sohagi Law Group · 10880 Wilshire Boulevard, Suite 900-A · Los Angeles, CA 90024-4110 · 310-475-5700

Lucinda Starrett · Latham & Watkins · 355 South Grand Avenue · Los Angeles, CA 90071-1560 · 213-485-1234

John W. Whitaker · ⑳ · DLA Piper · 550 South Hope Street, Suite 2300 · Los Angeles, CA 90071-2678 · 213-330-7700

Sacramento

William W. Abbott · Abbott & Kinderman · 2100 Twenty-First Street · Sacramento, CA 95818 · 916-456-9595

Joseph E. Coomes, Jr. · McDonough Holland & Allen · http://www.mhalaw.com · 555 Capitol Mall, Ninth Floor · Sacramento, CA 95814-4692 · 916-444-3900

John V. Diepenbrock · ⑳ · Diepenbrock Harrison · 400 Capitol Mall, Suite 1800 · Sacramento, CA 95814 · 916-446-4469

Edward J. Quinn, Jr. · McDonough Holland & Allen · http://www.mhalaw.com · 555 Capitol Mall, Ninth Floor · Sacramento, CA 95814-4692 · 916-444-3900

Tina A. Thomas · Remy, Thomas, Moose and Manley · 455 Capitol Mall, Suite 210 · Sacramento, CA 95814 · 916-443-2745

Ronald A. Zumbrun · The Zumbrun Law Firm · 3800 Watt Avenue, Suite 101 · Sacramento, CA 95821 · 916-486-5900

San Diego

James R. Dawe · ⑩ · Seltzer Caplan McMahon Vitek · Symphony Towers, Suite 2100 · 750 B Street · San Diego, CA 92101 · 619-685-3003

Christopher W. Garrett · Latham & Watkins · 600 West Broadway, Suite 1800 · San Diego, CA 92101-3375 · 619-236-1234

Paul E. Robinson · Hecht Solberg Robinson Goldberg & Bagley · One America Plaza, Eighth Floor · 600 West Broadway · San Diego, CA 92101 · 619-239-3444

Karen M. ZoBell · DLA Piper · 401 B Street, Suite 1700 · San Diego, CA 92101-4297 · 619-699-2700

San Francisco

John Briscoe · Briscoe, Ivester & Bazel · 155 Sansome Street, Seventh Floor · San Francisco, CA 94104 · 415-402-2700

William K. Coblentz · 25 · Coblentz, Patch, Duffy & Bass · http://www.coblentzlaw.com · One Ferry Building, Suite 200 · San Francisco, CA 94111-4213 · 415-391-4800

Susan R. Diamond · Morgan Lewis & Bockius · Spear Street Tower · One Market · San Francisco, CA 94105-1596 · 415-442-1000

Pamela S. Duffy · 10 · Coblentz, Patch, Duffy & Bass · http://www.coblentzlaw.com · One Ferry Building, Suite 200 · San Francisco, CA 94111-4213 · 415-391-4800

Robert C. Herr · 20 · Pillsbury Winthrop Shaw Pittman · http://www.pillsburylaw.com · 50 Fremont Street · P.O. Box 7880 · San Francisco, CA 94120-7880 · 415-983-1000

David M. Madway · Sheppard, Mullin, Richter & Hampton · http://www.sheppardmullin.com · Four Embarcadero Center, 17th Floor · San Francisco, CA 94111 · 415-434-9100

R. Clark Morrison · Cox, Castle & Nicholson · 555 California Street, 10th Floor · San Francisco, CA 94104 · 415-392-4200

Harry O'Brien · Coblentz, Patch, Duffy & Bass · http://www.coblentzlaw.com · One Ferry Building, Suite 200 · San Francisco, CA 94111-4213 · 415-391-4800

E. Clement Shute, Jr. · 10 · Shute, Mihaly & Weinberger · 396 Hayes Street · San Francisco, CA 94102 · 415-552-7272

Robert A. Thompson · 25 · Sheppard, Mullin, Richter & Hampton · http://www.sheppardmullin.com · Four Embarcadero Center, 17th Floor · San Francisco, CA 94111 · 415-434-9100

Robert J. Uram · Sheppard, Mullin, Richter & Hampton · http://www.sheppardmullin.com · Four Embarcadero Center, 17th Floor · San Francisco, CA 94111 · 415-434-9100

Tay C. Via · Coblentz, Patch, Duffy & Bass · http://www.coblentzlaw.com · One Ferry Building, Suite 200 San Francisco, CA 94111-4213 · 415-391-4800

Michael B. Wilmar · Sheppard, Mullin, Richter & Hampton · http://www.sheppardmullin.com · Four Embarcadero Center, 17th Floor · San Francisco, CA 94111 · 415-434-9100

Michael H. Zischke · Cox, Castle & Nicholson · 555 California Street, 10th Floor · San Francisco, CA 94104 · 415-392-4200

San Rafael

Gary T. Ragghianti · Ragghianti Freitas · 874 Fourth Street, Suite D · San Rafael, CA 94901-3246 · 415-453-9433

Tahoe City

Michael B. Brown · Stoel Rives · http://www.stoel.com · 3000 North Lake Boulevard, Suite One · P.O. Box 7336 · Tahoe City, CA 96145 · 530-583-2116

Walnut Creek

Patricia E. Curtin · Morgan Miller Blair · 1331 North California Boulevard, Suite 200 · Walnut Creek, CA 94596-4544 · 925-937-3600

David A. Gold · Morrison & Foerster · http://www.mofo.com · 101 Ygnacio Valley Road, Suite 450 · Walnut Creek, CA 94596-4095 · 925-295-3300

Bruce Reed Goodmiller · Morrison & Foerster · http://www.mofo.com · 101 Ygnacio Valley Road, Suite 450 · Walnut Creek, CA 94596-4095 · 925-295-3300

Stephen L. Kostka · Bingham McCutchen · http://www.bingham.com · 1333 North California Boulevard, Suite 210 · Walnut Creek, CA 94596-1270 · 925-937-8000

Geoffrey L. Robinson · Bingham McCutchen · http://www.bingham.com · 1333 North California Boulevard, Suite 210 · Walnut Creek, CA 94596-1270 · 925-937-8000

Cecily T. Talbert · Bingham McCutchen · http://www.bingham.com · 1333 North California Boulevard, Suite 210 · Walnut Creek, CA 94596-1270 · 925-937-8000

Wilson F. Wendt · Miller, Starr & Regalia · 1331 North California Boulevard, Fifth Floor · P.O. Box 8177 Walnut Creek, CA 94596 · 925-935-9400

LEGAL MALPRACTICE LAW

Burlingame

Joseph W. Cotchett · ⑩ · Cotchett, Pitre & McCarthy · San Francisco Airport Office Center, Suite 200 · 840 Malcolm Road · Burlingame, CA 94010 · 650-697-6000

Costa Mesa

H. Gilbert Jones · ⑳ · Lewis, Brisbois, Bisgaard & Smith · 650 Town Center Drive, Suite 1400 · Costa Mesa, CA 92626-1925 · 714-545-9200

William S. O'Hare · Snell & Wilmer · 600 Anton Boulevard, Suite 1400 · Costa Mesa, CA 92626-7689 · 714-427-7000

Long Beach

Samuel A. Keesal, Jr. · ⑩ · Keesal, Young & Logan · 400 Oceangate · P.O. Box 1730 · Long Beach, CA 90801-1730 · 562-436-2000

Los Angeles

Robert C. Baker · ⑩ · Baker, Keener & Nahra · 633 West Fifth Street, 54th Floor · Los Angeles, CA 90071 · 213-241-0900

Brad D. Brian · ⑩ · Munger, Tolles & Olson · 355 South Grand Avenue, 35th Floor · Los Angeles, CA 90071-1560 · 213-683-9100

Peter Q. Ezzell · Haight, Brown & Bonesteel · 6080 Center Drive, Suite 800 · Los Angeles, CA 90045 · 310-215-7100

Larry R. Feldman · ⑩ · Kaye Scholer · 1999 Avenue of the Stars, Suite 1700 · Los Angeles, CA 90067-6048 · 310-788-1000

Kurt C. Peterson · Reed Smith · 1901 Avenue of the Stars, Suite 700 · Los Angeles, CA 90067-6078 · 310-734-5200

John J. Quinn · ⑩ · JAMS · 707 Wilshire Boulevard, 46th Floor · Los Angeles, CA 90017 · 213-620-1133

Redwood City

John M. Bentley · ⑳ · Ropers, Majeski, Kohn & Bentley · 1001 Marshall Street, Suite 300 · Redwood City, CA 94063-2052 · 650-364-8200

Sacramento

Edward P. Freidberg · ⑩ · Freidberg & Parker · 650 University Avenue, Suite 205 · Sacramento, CA 95825 · 916-929-9060

James R. Kirby II · Segal & Kirby · 770 L Street, Suite 1440 · Sacramento, CA 95814 · 916-441-0828

San Diego

Douglas M. Butz · ⑩ · Butz, Dunn, DeSantis & Bingham · 101 West Broadway, Suite 1700 · San Diego, CA 92101-8289 · 619-233-4777

Douglas R. Reynolds · ⑩ · Law Office of Douglas R. Reynolds · 4525 Idaho Street, Suite Eight · San Diego, CA 92116 · 619-573-7800

San Francisco

Daralyn J. Durie · Keker & Van Nest · http://www.kvn.com · 710 Sansome Street · San Francisco, CA 94111 · 415-391-5400

Susan J. Harriman · Keker & Van Nest · http://www.kvn.com · 710 Sansome Street · San Francisco, CA 94111 · 415-391-5400

Ronald E. Mallen · ⑩ · Hinshaw & Culbertson · http://www.hinshawlaw.com · One California Street, 18th Floor · San Francisco, CA 94111 · 415-362-6000

Joseph P. McMonigle · ⑩ · Long & Levit · 465 California Street, Fifth Floor · San Francisco, CA 91404 · 415-397-2222

James N. Penrod · ⑩ · Morgan Lewis & Bockius · Spear Street Tower · One Market · San Francisco, CA 94105-1596 · 415-442-1000

Elliot R. Peters · Keker & Van Nest · http://www.kvn.com · 710 Sansome Street · San Francisco, CA 94111 · 415-391-5400

Robert A. Van Nest · Keker & Van Nest · http://www.kvn.com · 710 Sansome Street · San Francisco, CA 94111 · 415-391-5400

San Jose

Jesse F. Ruiz · Robinson & Wood · 227 North First Street · San Jose, CA 95113 · 408-298-7120

St. Helena

Peter R. Thompson · Thompson & Thompson · 836 Chiles Avenue · St. Helena, CA 94574 · 707-968-9770

Costa Mesa

David M. Bosko · ⑳ · Sheppard, Mullin, Richter & Hampton · http://www.sheppardmullin.com · 650 Town Center Drive, Fourth Floor · Costa Mesa, CA 92626 · 714-513-5100

James W. Loss · Bingham McCutchen · http://www.bingham.com · 600 Anton Boulevard, 18th Floor · Costa Mesa, CA 92626 · 714-830-0600

Peter J. Tennyson · Paul Hastings · 695 Town Center Drive, 17th Floor · Costa Mesa, CA 92626 · 714-668-6200

East Palo Alto

John Howard Clowes · DLA Piper · 2000 University Avenue · East Palo Alto, CA 94303-2214 · 650-833-2000

Bartley C. Deamer · ⑳ · Bingham McCutchen · http://www.bingham.com · 1900 University Avenue · East Palo Alto, CA 94303-2223 · 650-849-4400

Gregory M. Gallo · ⑩ · DLA Piper · 2000 University Avenue · East Palo Alto, CA 94303-2214 · 650-833-2000

James M. Koshland · DLA Piper · 2000 University Avenue · East Palo Alto, CA 94303-2214 · 650-833-2000

Henry Lesser · ⑳ · DLA Piper · 2000 University Avenue · East Palo Alto, CA 94303-2214 · 650-833-2000

Irvine

Keith P. Bishop · Allen Matkins Leck Gamble Mallory & Natsis · 1900 Main Street, Fifth Floor · Irvine, CA 92614-7321 · 949-553-1313

Los Angeles

Lawrence M. Braun · Sheppard, Mullin, Richter & Hampton · http://www.sheppardmullin.com · 333 South Hope Street, 48th Floor · Los Angeles, CA 90071-1448 · 213-620-1780

Gary J. Cohen · Sidley Austin · 555 West Fifth Street, 40th Floor · Los Angeles, CA 90013 · 213-896-6000

Ray LaSoya · Hughes Hubbard & Reed · http://www.hugheshubbard.com · 350 South Grand Avenue, Suite 3600 · Los Angeles, CA 90071-3442 · 213-613-2800

Bruce D. Meyer · ⑩ · Gibson, Dunn & Crutcher · 333 South Grand Avenue · Los Angeles, CA 90071-3197 · 213-229-7000

Robert K. Montgomery · ⑳ · Gibson, Dunn & Crutcher · 2029 Century Park East, 40th Floor · Los Angeles, CA 90067-3026 · 310-552-8500

Bradford P. Weirick · Gibson, Dunn & Crutcher · 333 South Grand Avenue · Los Angeles, CA 90071-3197 · 213-229-7000

John A. Weissenbach · Kirkland & Ellis · 777 South Figueroa Street, Suite 3400 · Los Angeles, CA 90017-5800 · 213-680-8400

Menlo Park

Scott C. Dettmer · Gunderson Dettmer Stough Villeneuve Franklin & Hachigian · 155 Constitution Drive · Menlo Park, CA 94025 · 650-321-2400

Robert V. Gunderson, Jr. · ⑩ · Gunderson Dettmer Stough Villeneuve Franklin & Hachigian · 155 Constitution Drive · Menlo Park, CA 94025 · 650-321-2400

Michael W. Hall · Latham & Watkins · 140 Scott Drive · Menlo Park, CA 94025 · 650-328-4600

Christopher L. Kaufman · ㉕ · Latham & Watkins · 140 Scott Drive · Menlo Park, CA 94025 · 650-328-4600

Donald M. Keller, Jr. · Orrick, Herrington & Sutcliffe · 1000 Marsh Road · Menlo Park, CA 94025-1015 · 650-614-7400

Peter F. Kerman · Latham & Watkins · 140 Scott Drive · Menlo Park, CA 94025 · 650-328-4600

Alan C. Mendelson · ⑩ · Latham & Watkins · 140 Scott Drive · Menlo Park, CA 94025 · 650-328-4600

Brooks Stough · Gunderson Dettmer Stough Villeneuve Franklin & Hachigian · 155 Constitution Drive · Menlo Park, CA 94025 · 650-321-2400

Thomas F. Villeneuve · Gunderson Dettmer Stough Villeneuve Franklin & Hachigian · 155 Constitution Drive · Menlo Park, CA 94025 · 650-321-2400

Mountain View

Gordon K. Davidson · ⑩ · Fenwick & West · Silicon Valley Center · 801 California Street · Mountain View, CA 94041-2008 · 650-988-8500

Mark C. Stevens · Fenwick & West · Silicon Valley Center · 801 California Street · Mountain View, CA 94041-2008 · 650-988-8500

Palo Alto

Aaron J. Alter · Wilson Sonsini Goodrich & Rosati · 650 Page Mill Road · Palo Alto, CA 94304-1050 · 650-493-9300

Lee F. Benton · ⑩ · Cooley Godward Kronish · 3175 Hanover Street · Palo Alto, CA 94304-1130 · 650-843-5000

Steven E. Bochner · Wilson Sonsini Goodrich & Rosati · 650 Page Mill Road · Palo Alto, CA 94304-1050 650-493-9300

Kenneth A. Clark · Wilson Sonsini Goodrich & Rosati · 650 Page Mill Road · Palo Alto, CA 94304-1050 · 650-493-9300

Craig E. Dauchy · ⑩ · Cooley Godward Kronish · 3175 Hanover Street · Palo Alto, CA 94304-1130 · 650-843-5000

Jorge A. del Calvo · Pillsbury Winthrop Shaw Pittman · http://www.pillsburylaw.com · 2475 Hanover Street · Palo Alto, CA 94304-1114 · 650-233-4500

Robert P. Latta · Wilson Sonsini Goodrich & Rosati · 650 Page Mill Road · Palo Alto, CA 94304-1050 · 650-493-9300

J. Casey McGlynn · Wilson Sonsini Goodrich & Rosati · 650 Page Mill Road · Palo Alto, CA 94304-1050 · 650-493-9300

Timothy J. Moore · Cooley Godward Kronish · 3175 Hanover Street · Palo Alto, CA 94304-1130 · 650-843-5000

Mario M. Rosati · Wilson Sonsini Goodrich & Rosati · 650 Page Mill Road · Palo Alto, CA 94304-1050 · 650-493-9300

David J. Segre · Wilson Sonsini Goodrich & Rosati · 650 Page Mill Road · Palo Alto, CA 94304-1050 · 650-493-9300

William D. Sherman · ㉕ · Morrison & Foerster · http://www.mofo.com · 755 Page Mill Road · Palo Alto, CA 94304-1018 · 650-813-5600

Larry W. Sonsini · ㉕ · Wilson Sonsini Goodrich & Rosati · 650 Page Mill Road · Palo Alto, CA 94304-1050 · 650-493-9300

Mark P. Tanoury · Cooley Godward Kronish · 3175 Hanover Street · Palo Alto, CA 94304-1130 · 650-843-5000

Pasadena

Dana M. Warren · Dana M. Warren · 790 East Colorado Boulevard, Ninth Floor · Pasadena, CA 91101 · 626-240-0687

Sacramento

David C. Adams · Weintraub Genshlea Chediak · 400 Capitol Mall, 11th Floor · Sacramento, CA 95814-4407 · 916-558-6000

San Diego

Craig S. Andrews · ⑩ · DLA Piper · 4365 Executive Drive, Suite 1100 · San Diego, CA 92121-2133 · 858-677-1400

Ross L. Burningham · DLA Piper · 4365 Executive Drive, Suite 1100 · San Diego, CA 92121-2133 · 858-677-1400

Thomas A. Coll · Cooley Godward Kronish · 4401 Eastgate Mall · San Diego, CA 92121-1909 · 858-550-6000

Robert G. Copeland · ⑳ · Sheppard, Mullin, Richter & Hampton · http://www.sheppardmullin.com · 501 West Broadway, 19th Floor · San Diego, CA 92101 · 619-338-6500

Michael S. Kagnoff · DLA Piper · 4365 Executive Drive, Suite 1100 · San Diego, CA 92121-2133 · 858-677-1400

Frederick T. Muto · ⑩ · Cooley Godward Kronish · 4401 Eastgate Mall · San Diego, CA 92121-1909 · 858-550-6000

Cameron Jay Rains · DLA Piper · 4365 Executive Drive, Suite 1100 · San Diego, CA 92121-2133 · 858-677-1400

Faye H. Russell · Latham & Watkins · 12636 High Bluff Drive, Suite 400 · San Diego, CA 92130 · 858-523-5400

David R. Snyder · ⑩ · Pillsbury Winthrop Shaw Pittman · http://www.pillsburylaw.com · 501 West Broadway, Suite 1100 · San Diego, CA 92101-3575 · 619-234-5000

Scott N. Wolfe · ⑩ · Latham & Watkins · 12636 High Bluff Drive, Suite 400 · San Diego, CA 92130 · 858-523-5400

San Francisco

Kenneth Guernsey · Cooley Godward Kronish · 101 California Street, Fifth Floor · San Francisco, CA 94111-5800 · 415-693-2000

Jeffrey C. Hammes · Kirkland & Ellis · 555 California Street · San Francisco, CA 94104 · 415-439-1400

MARITIME LAW

Long Beach

William H. Collier, Jr. · ⑩ · Keesal, Young & Logan · 400 Oceangate · P.O. Box 1730 · Long Beach, CA 90801-1730 · 562-436-2000

Samuel A. Keesal, Jr. · ⑩ · Keesal, Young & Logan · 400 Oceangate · P.O. Box 1730 · Long Beach, CA 90801-1730 · 562-436-2000

Albert E. Peacock III · Keesal, Young & Logan · 400 Oceangate · P.O. Box 1730 · Long Beach, CA 90801-1730 · 562-436-2000

Scott T. Pratt · Keesal, Young & Logan · 400 Oceangate · P.O. Box 1730 · Long Beach, CA 90801-1730 · 562-436-2000

Michael L. Swain · Swain & Dipolito · 555 East Ocean Boulevard, Suite 400 · Long Beach, CA 90802-5051 · 562-983-7833

Joseph A. Walsh II · Keesal, Young & Logan · 400 Oceangate · P.O. Box 1730 · Long Beach, CA 90801-1730 · 562-436-2000

Los Angeles

Robert J. Zapf · Duane Morris · 633 West Fifth Street, Suite 4600 · Los Angeles, CA 90071-2065 · 213-689-7400

Oakland

Lyle C. Cavin, Jr. · Lyle C. Cavin, Jr. · 201 Fourth Street, Suite 102 · Oakland, CA 94607 · 510-444-2501

San Francisco

Forrest Booth · Severson & Werson · One Embarcadero Center, Suite 2600 · San Francisco, CA 94111 · 415-398-3344

Eric M. Danoff · ⑩ · Emard, Danoff, Port, Tamulski & Paetzold · 49 Stevenson Street, Suite 400 · San Francisco, CA 94105 · 415-227-9455

Charles S. Donovan · Sheppard, Mullin, Richter & Hampton · http://www.sheppardmullin.com · Four Embarcadero Center, 17th Floor · San Francisco, CA 94111 · 415-434-9100

Stanley L. Gibson · Gibson, Robb & Lindh · 100 First Street, 27th Floor · San Francisco, CA 94105 · 415-348-6000

John D. Giffin · Keesal, Young & Logan · Four Embarcadero Center, Suite 1500 · San Francisco, CA 94111 · 415-398-6000

Rupert Hansen · Cox, Wootton, Griffin, Hansen & Poulos · 190 The Embarcadero · San Francisco, CA 94105-1201 · 415-438-4600

John R. Hillsman · McGuinn, Hillsman & Palefsky · 535 Pacific Avenue · San Francisco, CA 94133 · 415-421-9292

James B. Nebel · Flynn, Delich & Wise · One California Street, Suite 350 · San Francisco, CA 94111 · 415-693-5566

George W. Nowell · George W. Nowell · 120 Montgomery Street, Suite 1900 · San Francisco, CA 94104-4322 · 415-362-1333

Raymond M. Paetzold · Emard, Danoff, Port, Tamulski & Paetzold · 49 Stevenson Street, Suite 400 · San Francisco, CA 94105 · 415-227-9455

Marilyn Raia · Bullivant Houser Bailey · 601 California Street, Suite 1800 · San Francisco, CA 94108-2823 415-352-2700

James J. Tamulski · Emard, Danoff, Port, Tamulski & Paetzold · 49 Stevenson Street, Suite 400 · San Francisco, CA 94105 · 415-227-9455

Matthew Vafidis · Holland & Knight · http://www.hklaw.com · 50 California Street, Suite 2800 · San Francisco, CA 94111-4624 · 415-743-6900

Richard C. Wootton · Cox, Wootton, Griffin, Hansen & Poulos · 190 The Embarcadero · San Francisco, CA 94105-1201 · 415-438-4600

Walnut Creek

Kent J. Clancy · ⑩ · Kent J. Clancy · 10 Winfield Lane · Walnut Creek, CA 94595 · 925-943-1145

MASS TORT LITIGATION

Burlingame

Joseph W. Cotchett · ⑩ · Cotchett, Pitre & McCarthy · San Francisco Airport Office Center, Suite 200 · 840 Malcolm Road · Burlingame, CA 94010 · 650-697-6000

El Segundo

Michael L. Armitage · Waters & Kraus · 222 North Sepulveda Boulevard, Suite 1900 · El Segundo, CA 90245 · 310-414-8146

Irvine

Gregory F. Hurley · Greenberg Traurig · http://www.gtlaw.com · 3161 Michelson Drive, Suite 1000 · Irvine, CA 92612-4410 · 949-732-6500

Robert W. Loewen · Gibson, Dunn & Crutcher · 3161 Michelson Drive · Irvine, CA 92612-4412 · 949-451-3800

Los Angeles

Sharon J. Arkin · The Arkin Law Firm · 333 South Grand Avenue, 25th Floor · Los Angeles, CA 90071 · 213-943-1344

Gennaro A. Filice III · Filice Brown Eassa & McLeod · http://www.filicebrown.com · 300 South Grand Avenue, 14th Floor · Los Angeles, CA 90071-3124 · 213-687-2666

Thomas V. Girardi · ㉕ · Girardi and Keese · http://www.girardikeese.com · 1126 Wilshire Boulevard · Los Angeles, CA 90017-1904 · 213-977-0211

E. Lee Horton · Waller Lansden Dortch & Davis · http://www.wallerlaw.com · 333 South Grand Avenue, Suite 1800 · Los Angeles, CA 90071 · 213-362-3680

Walter J. Lack · Engstrom, Lipscomb & Lack · 10100 Santa Monica Boulevard, 16th Floor · Los Angeles, CA 90067 · 310-552-3800

Neal R. Marder · Winston & Strawn · 333 South Grand Avenue, 38th Floor · Los Angeles, CA 90071-1543 · 213-615-1700

Jeffrey Brian Margulies · Fulbright & Jaworski · http://www.fulbright.com · 555 South Flower Street, 41st Floor · Los Angeles, CA 90071 · 213-892-9200

Kevin C. Mayer · Liner Yankelevitz Sunshine & Regenstreif · 1100 Glendon Avenue, 14th Floor · Los Angeles, CA 90024-3503 · 310-500-3500

V. Thomas Meador III · Morgan Lewis & Bockius · 300 South Grand Avenue, 22nd Floor · Los Angeles, CA 90071-3132 · 213-612-2500

J. Richard Morrissey · Pillsbury Winthrop Shaw Pittman · http://www.pillsburylaw.com · 725 South Figueroa Street, Suite 2800 · Los Angeles, CA 90017-5406 · 213-488-7100

Elliott D. Olson · Sedgwick, Detert, Moran & Arnold · 801 South Figueroa Street, 19th Floor · Los Angeles, CA 90017-5556 · 213-426-6900

Debra E. Pole · Sidley Austin · 555 West Fifth Street, 40th Floor · Los Angeles, CA 90013 · 213-896-6000

Ellen K. Reisman · Arnold & Porter · 777 South Figueroa Street, 44th Floor · Los Angeles, CA 90017-5844 · 213-243-4000

Lawrence P. Riff · Steptoe & Johnson · http://www.steptoe.com · 633 West Fifth Street, Suite 700 · Los Angeles, CA 90071 · 213-439-9400

David A. Rosen · Rose, Klein & Marias · 801 South Grand Avenue, 11th Floor · Los Angeles, CA 90017-4645 · 213-784-2801

Peter R. Taft · ⑳ · Munger, Tolles & Olson · 355 South Grand Avenue, 35th Floor · Los Angeles, CA 90071-1560 · 213-683-9100

Newport Beach

Ramon Rossi Lopez · Lopez McHugh · 100 Bayview Circle, Suite 5600 · Newport Beach, CA 92660 · 949-737-1501

Mark P. Robinson, Jr. · Robinson, Calcagnie & Robinson · 620 Newport Center Drive, Seventh Floor · Newport Beach, CA 92660 · 949-720-1288

Oakland

Denise Abrams · Kazan, McClain, Abrams, Lyons, Farrise & Greenwood · 171 Twelfth Street, Third Floor · Oakland, CA 94607 · 510-465-7728

Steven Kazan · Kazan, McClain, Abrams, Lyons, Farrise & Greenwood · 171 Twelfth Street, Third Floor Oakland, CA 94607 · 510-465-7728

Dianna Lyons · Kazan, McClain, Abrams, Lyons, Farrise & Greenwood · 171 Twelfth Street, Third Floor Oakland, CA 94607 · 510-465-7728

David M. McClain · Kazan, McClain, Abrams, Lyons, Farrise & Greenwood · 171 Twelfth Street, Third Floor · Oakland, CA 94607 · 510-465-7728

Orinda

Luke Ellis · Gillin, Jacobson, Ellis & Larsen · http://www.gjel.com · Two Theater Square, Suite 230 · Orinda, CA 94563 · 925-253-5800

San Diego

Harvey C. Berger · Pope, Berger & Williams · 550 West C Street, Suite 1400 · San Diego, CA 92101 · 619-234-1222

William S. Boggs · DLA Piper · 401 B Street, Suite 1700 · San Diego, CA 92101-4297 · 619-699-2700

Donald A. English · English & Gloven · 550 West C Street, Suite 1800 · San Diego, CA 92101 · 619-338-6610

Frederick Schenk · Casey, Gerry, Schenk, Francavilla, Blatt & Penfield · http://www.cglaw.com · 110 Laurel Street · San Diego, CA 92101-1486 · 619-238-1811

San Francisco

Thomas J. Brandi · ⑩ · The Brandi Law Firm · 354 Pine Street, Third Floor · San Francisco, CA 94104 · 415-989-1800

James A. Bruen · ⑳ · Farella Braun & Martel · Russ Building, 17th Floor · 235 Montgomery Street · San Francisco, CA 94104 · 415-954-4400

Ernest J. Getto · Latham & Watkins · 505 Montgomery Street, Suite 2000 · San Francisco, CA 94111-6538 · 415-391-0600

Nicholas W. Heldt · Sedgwick, Detert, Moran & Arnold · Steuart Tower, Eighth Floor · One Market Plaza · San Francisco, CA 94105 · 415-781-7900

Steven J. Skikos · Lopez, Hodes, Restaino, Milman & Skikos · 625 Market Street, 11th Floor · San Francisco, CA 94105 · 415-956-5257

Thomas L. Van Wyngarden · Chapman and Cutler · 595 Market Street, 26th Floor · San Francisco, CA 94105-2839 · 415-541-0500

MEDIA LAW

Los Angeles

Theodore J. Boutrous, Jr. · Gibson, Dunn & Crutcher · 333 South Grand Avenue · Los Angeles, CA 90071-3197 · 213-229-7000

Ruth Fisher · Gibson, Dunn & Crutcher · 2029 Century Park East, 40th Floor · Los Angeles, CA 90067-3026 · 310-552-8500

Rex S. Heinke · ⑩ · Akin Gump Strauss Hauer & Feld · 2029 Century Park East, Suite 2400 · Los Angeles, CA 90067-3012 · 310-229-1000

Mark B. Helm · Munger, Tolles & Olson · 355 South Grand Avenue, 35th Floor · Los Angeles, CA 90071-1560 · 213-683-9100

Steven M. Perry · Munger, Tolles & Olson · 355 South Grand Avenue, 35th Floor · Los Angeles, CA 90071-1560 · 213-683-9100

Kelli L. Sager · ⑩ · Davis Wright Tremaine · 865 South Figueroa Street, Suite 2400 · Los Angeles, CA 90017-2566 · 213-633-6800

Lawrence J. Ulman · Gibson, Dunn & Crutcher · 2029 Century Park East, 40th Floor · Los Angeles, CA 90067-3026 · 310-552-8500

Bruce A. Wessel · Irell & Manella · 1800 Avenue of the Stars, Suite 900 · Los Angeles, CA 90067-4276 · 310-277-1010

Alonzo Wickers IV · Davis Wright Tremaine · 865 South Figueroa Street, Suite 2400 · Los Angeles, CA 90017-2566 · 213-633-6800

San Diego

Guylyn Remmenga Cummins · ⑩ · Sheppard, Mullin, Richter & Hampton · http://www.sheppardmullin.com · 501 West Broadway, 19th Floor · San Diego, CA 92101 · 619-338-6500

Gregory D. Roper · ⑩ · Luce, Forward, Hamilton & Scripps · http://www.luce.com · 600 West Broadway, Suite 2600 · San Diego, CA 92101 · 619-236-1414

San Francisco

Thomas R. Burke · Davis Wright Tremaine · 505 Montgomery Street, Suite 800 · San Francisco, CA 94111-6533 · 415-276-6500

Craig Cardon · Sheppard, Mullin, Richter & Hampton · http://www.sheppardmullin.com · Four Embarcadero Center, 17th Floor · San Francisco, CA 94111 · 415-434-9100

Duffy Carolan · Davis Wright Tremaine · 505 Montgomery Street, Suite 800 · San Francisco, CA 94111-6533 · 415-276-6500

MEDICAL MALPRACTICE LAW

El Segundo

Robert N. Stone · ⑩ · Stone, Dolginer & Wenzel · 2321 Rosecrans Avenue, Suite 2220 · El Segundo, CA 90245 · 310-643-0070

Long Beach

Richard D. Carroll · Carroll, Kelly, Trotter, Franzen & McKenna · 111 West Ocean Boulevard, 14th Floor · P.O. Box 22636 · Long Beach, CA 90801-5636 · 562-432-5855

Samuel A. Keesal, Jr. · ⑩ · Keesal, Young & Logan · 400 Oceangate · P.O. Box 1730 · Long Beach, CA 90801-1730 · 562-436-2000

Michael J. Trotter · Carroll, Kelly, Trotter, Franzen & McKenna · 111 West Ocean Boulevard, 14th Floor P.O. Box 22636 · Long Beach, CA 90801-5636 · 562-432-5855

Los Angeles

Steven A. Heimberg · Heimberg Law Group · http://www.heimberglaw.com · 1801 Century Park East, Suite 1920 · Los Angeles, CA 90067-2313 · 310-553-1799

Russell Kussman · ⑩ · Kussman & Whitehill · http://www.kussmanwhitehill.com · 10866 Wilshire Boulevard, Suite 1470 · Los Angeles, CA 90024 · 310-474-4411

Philip Michels · Law Offices of Michels & Watkins · 11755 Wilshire Boulevard, Suite 1300 · Los Angeles, CA 90025-1540 · 310-444-1200

James D. Nichols · ⑩ · Bonne, Bridges, Mueller, O'Keefe & Nichols · http://www.bonnebridges.com · 3699 Wilshire Boulevard, 10th Floor · Los Angeles, CA 90010-2719 · 213-480-1900

David J. O'Keefe · ⑳ · Bonne, Bridges, Mueller, O'Keefe & Nichols · http://www.bonnebridges.com · 3699 Wilshire Boulevard, 10th Floor · Los Angeles, CA 90010-2719 · 213-480-1900

Newport Beach

Kenneth Marshall Silberberg · ⑳ · The Law Offices of Marshall Silberberg · 660 Newport Center Drive, Suite 340 · Newport Beach, CA 92660 · 949-718-0960

Redlands

Jeffrey S. Raynes · Law Office of Jeffrey Raynes · 1780 Orange Tree Lane · Redlands, CA 92374 · 909-793-6800

Sacramento

Noel M. Ferris · The Law Office of Noel M. Ferris · 1001 G Street, Suite 301 · Sacramento, CA 95814 · 916-492-9911

Leo H. Schuering, Jr. · ⑳ · Schuering, Zimmerman, Scully, Tweedy & Doyle · 400 University Avenue · Sacramento, CA 95825 · 916-567-0400

San Bernardino

Robert K. Warford · Reback, McAndrews & Kjar · 215 North D Street, Suite 303 · San Bernardino, CA 92401 · 909-889-4665

San Diego

Richard D. Barton · Higgs, Fletcher & Mack · 401 West A Street, Suite 2600 · San Diego, CA 92101-7910 · 619-236-1551

Cynthia Chihak · Cynthia Chihak · 12555 High Bluff Drive, Suite 150 · San Diego, CA 92130 · 858-481-7252

Robert W. Frank · Neil, Dymott, Frank, McFall & Trexler · http://www.neildymott.com · 1010 Second Avenue, Suite 2500 · San Diego, CA 92101-4959 · 619-238-1712

William M. Low · Higgs, Fletcher & Mack · 401 West A Street, Suite 2600 · San Diego, CA 92101-7910 · 619-236-1551

Virginia C. Nelson · ⑩ · Law Offices of Virginia Nelson · http://www.vcnlaw.com · 550 West C Street, Suite 2050 · San Diego, CA 92101 · 619-232-5503

Gregory W. Pollack · Higgs, Fletcher & Mack · 401 West A Street, Suite 2600 · San Diego, CA 92101-7910 · 619-236-1551

Dennis A. Schoville · ⑩ · Schoville & Arnell · Carriage House · 2404 Broadway · San Diego, CA 92102 · 619-232-9901

Kenneth M. Sigelman · Kenneth M. Sigelman and Associates · 1901 First Avenue, Second Floor · San Diego, CA 92101 · 619-238-3813

Sheila S. Trexler · Neil, Dymott, Frank, McFall & Trexler · http://www.neildymott.com · 1010 Second Avenue, Suite 2500 · San Diego, CA 92101-4959 · 619-238-1712

San Francisco

James S. Bostwick · ㉕ · Bostwick & Associates · Four Embarcadero Center, Suite 750 · San Francisco, CA 94111 · 415-421-8300

James M. Goodman · Hassard Bonnington · http://www.hassard.com · Two Embarcadero Center, Suite 1800 · San Francisco, CA 94111 · 415-288-9800

Daniel J. Kelly · ⑳ · Walkup, Melodia, Kelly & Schoenberger · http://www.walkuplawoffice.com · 650 California Street, 26th Floor · San Francisco, CA 94108 · 415-981-7210

Paul V. Melodia · ⑩ · Walkup, Melodia, Kelly & Schoenberger · http://www.walkuplawoffice.com · 650 California Street, 26th Floor · San Francisco, CA 94108 · 415-981-7210

Scott D. Righthand · Law Office of Scott Righthand · 465 California Street, Suite 300 · San Francisco, CA 94104 · 415-544-0115

San Jose

Bradley M. Corsiglia · Corsiglia McMahon & Allard · 96 North Thrird Street, Suite 620 · San Jose, CA 95112 · 408-289-1417

David Sheuerman · Sheuerman, Martini & Tabari · 1033 Willow Street · San Jose, CA 95125 · 408-918-3707

Cyrus Ali Tabari · Sheuerman, Martini & Tabari · 1033 Willow Street · San Jose, CA 95125 · 408-918-3707

Santa Ana

Margaret M. Holm · Bonne, Bridges, Mueller, O'Keefe & Nichols · http://www.bonnebridges.com · 1851 East First Street, Suite 810 · Santa Ana, CA 92705-3930 · 714-835-1157

Tustin

Christopher J. Day · Day, Day & Brown · 301 West First Street · Tustin, CA 92780 · 714-832-4811

Walnut Creek

Thomas J. Donnelly · Donnelly Nelson Depolo & Murray · 2401 Shadelands Drive, Suite 120 · Walnut Creek, CA 94598-2428 · 925-287-8181

G. Patrick Galloway · ⑩ · Galloway, Lucchese, Everson & Picchi · 1676 North California Boulevard, Fifth Floor · Walnut Creek, CA 94596 · 925-930-9090

David R. Lucchese · ⑩ · Galloway, Lucchese, Everson & Picchi · 1676 North California Boulevard, Fifth Floor · Walnut Creek, CA 94596 · 925-930-9090

James M. Nelson · Donnelly Nelson Depolo & Murray · 2401 Shadelands Drive, Suite 120 · Walnut Creek, CA 94598-2428 · 925-287-8181

MERGERS & ACQUISITIONS LAW

Costa Mesa

Charles K. Ruck · Latham & Watkins · 650 Town Center Drive, 20th Floor · Costa Mesa, CA 92626-1925 · 714-540-1235

East Palo Alto

Peter M. Astiz · DLA Piper · 2000 University Avenue · East Palo Alto, CA 94303-2214 · 650-833-2000

Bartley C. Deamer · ⑳ · Bingham McCutchen · http://www.bingham.com · 1900 University Avenue · East Palo Alto, CA 94303-2223 · 650-849-4400

Diane Holt Frankle · DLA Piper · 2000 University Avenue · East Palo Alto, CA 94303-2214 · 650-833-2000

Gregory M. Gallo · ⑩ · DLA Piper · 2000 University Avenue · East Palo Alto, CA 94303-2214 · 650-833-2000

Henry Lesser · ⑳ · DLA Piper · 2000 University Avenue · East Palo Alto, CA 94303-2214 · 650-833-2000

Glendora

Joel Franklin McIntyre · Joel Franklyn McIntyre · 180 North Pennsylvania Avenue · P.O. Box 426 · Glendora, CA 91740 · 626-914-6771

Irvine

John J. Giovannone · Greenberg Traurig · http://www.gtlaw.com · 3161 Michelson Drive, Suite 1000 · Irvine, CA 92612-4410 · 949-732-6500

John M. Williams III · Gibson, Dunn & Crutcher · 3161 Michelson Drive · Irvine, CA 92612-4412 · 949-451-3800

Los Angeles

Gary Apfel · Dewey & LeBoeuf · 333 South Grand Avenue, Suite 2600 · Los Angeles, CA 90071-1530 · 213-621-6000

Andrew E. Bogen · ⑳ · Gibson, Dunn & Crutcher · 333 South Grand Avenue · Los Angeles, CA 90071-3197 · 213-229-7000

Lawrence M. Braun · Sheppard, Mullin, Richter & Hampton · http://www.sheppardmullin.com · 333 South Hope Street, 48th Floor · Los Angeles, CA 90071-1448 · 213-620-1780

Neal H. Brockmeyer · ㉕ · Heller Ehrman · 333 South Hope Street, 39th Floor · Los Angeles, CA 90071-1406 · 213-689-0200

Tim C. Bruinsma · Fulbright & Jaworski · http://www.fulbright.com · 555 South Flower Street, 41st Floor Los Angeles, CA 90071 · 213-892-9200

Jerome L. Coben · Skadden, Arps, Slate, Meagher & Flom · 300 South Grand Avenue, Suite 3400 · Los Angeles, CA 90071 · 213-687-5000

Andrew J. Demetriou · Fulbright & Jaworski · http://www.fulbright.com · 555 South Flower Street, 41st Floor · Los Angeles, CA 90071 · 213-892-9200

Robert E. Denham · Munger, Tolles & Olson · 355 South Grand Avenue, 35th Floor · Los Angeles, CA 90071-1560 · 213-683-9100

David A. Ebershoff · Fulbright & Jaworski · http://www.fulbright.com · 555 South Flower Street, 41st Floor · Los Angeles, CA 90071 · 213-892-9200

Stanley F. Farrar · ⑩ · Sullivan & Cromwell · 1888 Century Park East, 21st Floor · Los Angeles, CA 90067-1725 · 310-712-6600

Ronald L. Fein · ㉕ · RL Fein · 1901 Avenue of The Stars, 12th Floor · Los Angeles, CA 90067 · 310-228-5780

Ronald K. Fujikawa · Greenberg Glusker · 1900 Avenue of the Stars, 21st Floor · Los Angeles, CA 90067 310-553-3610

Joseph J. Giunta · Skadden, Arps, Slate, Meagher & Flom · 300 South Grand Avenue, Suite 3400 · Los Angeles, CA 90071 · 213-687-5000

Frank H. Golay, Jr. · ⑩ · Sullivan & Cromwell · 1888 Century Park East, 21st Floor · Los Angeles, CA 90067-1725 · 310-712-6600

William D. Gould · ⑳ · TroyGould · http://www.troygould.com · 1801 Century Park East, Suite 1600 · Los Angeles, CA 90067 · 310-553-4441

Steven L. Grossman · O'Melveny & Myers · 1999 Avenue of the Stars, Seventh Floor · Los Angeles, CA 90067-6035 · 310-553-6700

John F. Hartigan · ⑩ · Morgan Lewis & Bockius · 300 South Grand Avenue, 22nd Floor · Los Angeles, CA 90071-3132 · 213-612-2500

Harry L. Hathaway · ⑩ · Fulbright & Jaworski · http://www.fulbright.com · 555 South Flower Street, 41st Floor · Los Angeles, CA 90071 · 213-892-9200

Joan L. Lesser · Irell & Manella · 1800 Avenue of the Stars, Suite 900 · Los Angeles, CA 90067-4276 · 310-277-1010

Brian J. McCarthy · Skadden, Arps, Slate, Meagher & Flom · 300 South Grand Avenue, Suite 3400 · Los Angeles, CA 90071 · 213-687-5000

Bruce D. Meyer · ⑩ · Gibson, Dunn & Crutcher · 333 South Grand Avenue · Los Angeles, CA 90071-3197 · 213-229-7000

Robert K. Montgomery · ⑳ · Gibson, Dunn & Crutcher · 2029 Century Park East, 40th Floor · Los Angeles, CA 90067-3026 · 310-552-8500

Alison S. Ressler · Sullivan & Cromwell · 1888 Century Park East, 21st Floor · Los Angeles, CA 90067-1725 · 310-712-6600

David K. Robbins · Bingham McCutchen · http://www.bingham.com · 355 South Grand Avenue, Suite 4400 · Los Angeles, CA 90071-3106 · 213-680-6400

Nicholas P. Saggese · Skadden, Arps, Slate, Meagher & Flom · 300 South Grand Avenue, Suite 3400 · Los Angeles, CA 90071 · 213-687-5000

Alvin G. Segel · Irell & Manella · 1800 Avenue of the Stars, Suite 900 · Los Angeles, CA 90067-4276 · 310-277-1010

Paul D. Tosetti · ⑩ · Latham & Watkins · 355 South Grand Avenue · Los Angeles, CA 90071-1560 · 213-485-1234

James R. Walther · Mayer Brown · 350 South Grand Avenue, 25th Floor · Los Angeles, CA 90071-1503 · 213-229-9500

John B. Watkins · WilmerHale · http://www.wilmerhale.com · 350 South Grand Avenue, Suite 2100 · Los Angeles, CA 90071 · 213-443-5300

Bradford P. Weirick · Gibson, Dunn & Crutcher · 333 South Grand Avenue · Los Angeles, CA 90071-3197 · 213-229-7000

Menlo Park

Francis S. Currie · Davis Polk & Wardwell · 1600 El Camino Real · Menlo Park, CA 94025 · 650-752-2000

Christopher L. Kaufman · ㉕ · Latham & Watkins · 140 Scott Drive · Menlo Park, CA 94025 · 650-328-4600

Donald M. Keller, Jr. · Orrick, Herrington & Sutcliffe · 1000 Marsh Road · Menlo Park, CA 94025-1015 · 650-614-7400

William Kelly · Davis Polk & Wardwell · 1600 El Camino Real · Menlo Park, CA 94025 · 650-752-2000

Peter F. Kerman · Latham & Watkins · 140 Scott Drive · Menlo Park, CA 94025 · 650-328-4600

Alan C. Mendelson · ⑩ · Latham & Watkins · 140 Scott Drive · Menlo Park, CA 94025 · 650-328-4600

Steven J. Tonsfeldt · Heller Ehrman · 275 Middlefield Road · Menlo Park, CA 94025-3506 · 650-324-7000

Mission Viejo

Robert R. Beauchamp · Beauchamp & Associates · 23120 Alicia Parkway, Suite 200 · Mission Viejo, CA 92692 · 949-598-9624

Mountain View

Douglas N. Cogen · Fenwick & West · Silicon Valley Center · 801 California Street · Mountain View, CA 94041-2008 · 650-988-8500

Mark C. Stevens · Fenwick & West · Silicon Valley Center · 801 California Street · Mountain View, CA 94041-2008 · 650-988-8500

Newport Beach

William T. Gay · Gordon & Rees · 4675 MacArthur Court, Suite 800 · Newport Beach, CA 92660 · 949-255-6950

David Krinsky · O'Melveny & Myers · 610 Newport Center Drive, 17th Floor · Newport Beach, CA 92660 · 949-760-9600

Gary J. Singer · O'Melveny & Myers · 610 Newport Center Drive, 17th Floor · Newport Beach, CA 92660 · 949-760-9600

Palo Alto

Mark A. Bertelsen · Wilson Sonsini Goodrich & Rosati · 650 Page Mill Road · Palo Alto, CA 94304-1050 · 650-493-9300

Richard Capelouto · Simpson Thacher · 2550 Hanover Street · Palo Alto, CA 94304 · 650-251-5000

Richard E. Climan · ⑩ · Cooley Godward Kronish · 3175 Hanover Street · Palo Alto, CA 94304-1130 · 650-843-5000

Jorge A. del Calvo · Pillsbury Winthrop Shaw Pittman · http://www.pillsburylaw.com · 2475 Hanover Street · Palo Alto, CA 94304-1114 · 650-233-4500

Keith A. Flaum · Cooley Godward Kronish · 3175 Hanover Street · Palo Alto, CA 94304-1130 · 650-843-5000

Suzanne S. Hooper · Cooley Godward Kronish · 3175 Hanover Street · Palo Alto, CA 94304-1130 · 650-843-5000

Thomas W. Kellerman · Morgan Lewis & Bockius · Two Palo Alto Square, Suite 700 · 3000 El Camino Real · Palo Alto, CA 94306-2121 · 650-843-4000

Kenton J. King · Skadden, Arps, Slate, Meagher & Flom · 525 University Avenue, Suite 1100 · Palo Alto, CA 94301 · 650-470-4500

Martin W. Korman · Wilson Sonsini Goodrich & Rosati · 650 Page Mill Road · Palo Alto, CA 94304-1050 650-493-9300

Henry P. Massey, Jr. · ㉕ · Wilson Sonsini Goodrich & Rosati · 650 Page Mill Road · Palo Alto, CA 94304-1050 · 650-493-9300

Scott D. Miller · Sullivan & Cromwell · 1870 Embarcadero Road · Palo Alto, CA 94303-3308 · 650-461-5600

Michael C. Phillips · Morrison & Foerster · http://www.mofo.com · 755 Page Mill Road · Palo Alto, CA 94304-1018 · 650-813-5600

Jeffrey D. Saper · Wilson Sonsini Goodrich & Rosati · 650 Page Mill Road · Palo Alto, CA 94304-1050 · 650-493-9300

David J. Segre · Wilson Sonsini Goodrich & Rosati · 650 Page Mill Road · Palo Alto, CA 94304-1050 · 650-493-9300

William D. Sherman · ㉕ · Morrison & Foerster · http://www.mofo.com · 755 Page Mill Road · Palo Alto, CA 94304-1018 · 650-813-5600

Larry W. Sonsini · ㉕ · Wilson Sonsini Goodrich & Rosati · 650 Page Mill Road · Palo Alto, CA 94304-1050 · 650-493-9300

San Diego

Frederick T. Muto · ⑩ · Cooley Godward Kronish · 4401 Eastgate Mall · San Diego, CA 92121-1909 · 858-550-6000

Carl R. Sanchez · Paul Hastings · 3579 Valley Centre Drive · San Diego, CA 92130 · 858-720-2500

Jeffery M. Shohet · DLA Piper · 401 B Street, Suite 1700 · San Diego, CA 92101-4297 · 619-699-2700

Deyan P. Spiridonov · Paul Hastings · 3579 Valley Centre Drive · San Diego, CA 92130 · 858-720-2500

Scott M. Stanton · Morrison & Foerster · http://www.mofo.com · 12531 High Bluff Drive, Suite 100 · San Diego, CA 92130-2040 · 858-720-5100

San Francisco

Steve L. Camahort · O'Melveny & Myers · Embarcadero Center West · 275 Battery Street · San Francisco, CA 94111-3305 · 415-984-8700

Richard W. Canady · ⑩ · Howard, Rice, Nemerovski, Canady, Falk & Rabkin · Three Embarcadero Center, Seventh Floor · San Francisco, CA 94111-4024 · 415-434-1600

Nathaniel M. Cartmell III · Pillsbury Winthrop Shaw Pittman · http://www.pillsburylaw.com · 50 Fremont Street · P.O. Box 7880 · San Francisco, CA 94120-7880 · 415-983-1000

Jeffrey C. Hammes · Kirkland & Ellis · 555 California Street · San Francisco, CA 94104 · 415-439-1400

Michael J. Kennedy · O'Melveny & Myers · Embarcadero Center West · 275 Battery Street · San Francisco, CA 94111-3305 · 415-984-8700

John W. Larson · ⑳ · Morgan Lewis & Bockius · Spear Street Tower · One Market · San Francisco, CA 94105-1596 · 415-442-1000

Deborah A. Marshall · Howard, Rice, Nemerovski, Canady, Falk & Rabkin · Three Embarcadero Center, Seventh Floor · San Francisco, CA 94111-4024 · 415-434-1600

Ronald B. Moskovitz · Morgan Lewis & Bockius · Spear Street Tower · One Market · San Francisco, CA 94105-1596 · 415-442-1000

Michael G. O'Bryan · Morrison & Foerster · http://www.mofo.com · 425 Market Street · San Francisco, CA 94105-2482 · 415-268-7000

Robert G. O'Connor · Wilson Sonsini Goodrich & Rosati · Spear Tower, Suite 3300 · One Market Street · San Francisco, CA 94105-1126 · 415-947-2000

Daniel E. Titelbaum · Luce, Forward, Hamilton & Scripps · 121 Spear Street, Suite 200 · San Francisco, CA 94105-1582 · 415-356-4600

Robert S. Townsend · Morrison & Foerster · http://www.mofo.com · 425 Market Street · San Francisco, CA 94105-2482 · 415-268-7000

MINING LAW

Sacramento

Patrick G. Mitchell · Downey Brand · 555 Capitol Mall, 10th Floor · Sacramento, CA 95814 · 916-444-1000

MUNICIPAL LAW

Los Angeles

Gerald M. Fisher · Freeman, Freeman & Smiley · 3415 South Sepulveda Boulevard, Suite 1200 · Los Angeles, CA 90034 · 310-255-6100

Sacramento

Joseph E. Coomes, Jr. · McDonough Holland & Allen · http://www.mhalaw.com · 555 Capitol Mall, Ninth Floor · Sacramento, CA 95814-4692 · 916-444-3900

Edward J. Quinn, Jr. · McDonough Holland & Allen · http://www.mhalaw.com · 555 Capitol Mall, Ninth Floor · Sacramento, CA 95814-4692 · 916-444-3900

Harriet A. Steiner · McDonough Holland & Allen · http://www.mhalaw.com · 555 Capitol Mall, Ninth Floor · Sacramento, CA 95814-4692 · 916-444-3900

MUTUAL FUNDS LAW

Los Angeles

Robert R. Carlson · ㉕ · Paul Hastings · 515 South Flower Street, 25th Floor · Los Angeles, CA 90071 · 213-683-6000

NATIVE AMERICAN LAW

Los Angeles

Jerome L. Levine · Holland & Knight · http://www.hklaw.com · 633 West Fifth Street, 21st Floor · Los Angeles, CA 90071 · 213-896-2400

Teresa E. Poust · Holland & Knight · http://www.hklaw.com · 633 West Fifth Street, 21st Floor · Los Angeles, CA 90071 · 213-896-2400

Oakland

Patricia A. Prochaska · Patricia A. Prochaska · 375 Cavour Street · Oakland, CA 94618 · 510-601-9760

Sacramento

Howard L. Dickstein · Dickstein & Zerbi · 1530 J Street, Suite 250 · Sacramento, CA 95814 · 916-244-8550

Jane G. Zerbi · Dickstein & Zerbi · 1530 J Street, Suite 250 · Sacramento, CA 95814 · 916-244-8550

San Rafael

George Forman · Forman & Associates · 4340 Redwood Highway, Suite F-228 · San Rafael, CA 94903 · 415-491-2310

NATURAL RESOURCES LAW

Los Angeles

Gregory R. McClintock · Akerman Senterfitt · http://www.akerman.com · 725 South Figueroa Street, 38th Floor · Los Angeles, CA 90017-5438 · 213-688-9500

Riverside

Arthur L. Littleworth · ⑩ · Best Best & Krieger · 3750 University Avenue, Suite 400 · P.O. Box 1028 · Riverside, CA 92502 · 951-686-1450

Michelle Ouellette · Best Best & Krieger · 3750 University Avenue, Suite 400 · P.O. Box 1028 · Riverside, CA 92502 · 951-686-1450

Gregory K. Wilkinson · Best Best & Krieger · 3750 University Avenue, Suite 400 · P.O. Box 1028 · Riverside, CA 92502 · 951-686-1450

Sacramento

James M. Day, Jr. · Day Carter & Murphy · 3620 American River Drive, Suite 205 · Sacramento, CA 95864 · 916-570-2500

Christopher T. Ellison · Ellison, Schneider & Harris · 2015 H Street · Sacramento, CA 95814-3109 · 916-447-2166

Stuart L. Somach · ⑩ · Somach, Simmons & Dunn · http://www.somachlaw.com · Hall of Justice Building, Third Floor · 813 Sixth Street · Sacramento, CA 95814-2403 · 916-446-7979

Ann L. Trowbridge · Day Carter & Murphy · 3620 American River Drive, Suite 205 · Sacramento, CA 95864 · 916-570-2500

San Francisco

Christopher J. Carr · Morrison & Foerster · http://www.mofo.com · 425 Market Street · San Francisco, CA 94105-2482 · 415-268-7000

R. Clark Morrison · Cox, Castle & Nicholson · 555 California Street, 10th Floor · San Francisco, CA 94104 · 415-392-4200

Edward W. O'Neill · Davis Wright Tremaine · 505 Montgomery Street, Suite 800 · San Francisco, CA 94111-6533 · 415-276-6500

Robert J. Uram · Sheppard, Mullin, Richter & Hampton · http://www.sheppardmullin.com · Four Embarcadero Center, 17th Floor · San Francisco, CA 94111 · 415-434-9100

Edgar B. Washburn · Morrison & Foerster · http://www.mofo.com · 425 Market Street · San Francisco, CA 94105-2482 · 415-268-7000

Gary D. Weatherford · Weatherford & Taaffe · 255 California Street, 10th Floor · San Francisco, CA 94111-4916 · 415-989-7300

Walnut Creek

William H. Booth · ⑩ · William H. Booth · 1500 Newell Avenue, Fifth Floor · Walnut Creek, CA 94596 · 925-296-2460

NON-PROFIT/CHARITIES LAW

Los Angeles

Leah M. Bishop · ⑩ · Loeb & Loeb · 10100 Santa Monica Boulevard, Suite 2200 · Los Angeles, CA 90067-4164 · 310-282-2000

Reynolds T. Cafferata · Rodriguez, Horii, Choi & Cafferata · 777 South Figueroa Street, Suite 2150 · Los Angeles, CA 90017 · 213-892-7700

William C. Choi · Rodriguez, Horii, Choi & Cafferata · 777 South Figueroa Street, Suite 2150 · Los Angeles, CA 90017 · 213-892-7700

Paul N. Frimmer · ㉕ · Irell & Manella · 1800 Avenue of the Stars, Suite 900 · Los Angeles, CA 90067-4276 · 310-277-1010

Jon J. Gallo · ㉕ · Greenberg Glusker · 1900 Avenue of the Stars, 21st Floor · Los Angeles, CA 90067 · 310-553-3610

Douglas M. Mancino · ⑩ · McDermott Will & Emery · 2049 Century Park East, 38th Floor · Los Angeles, CA 90067-3218 · 310-277-4110

David Wheeler Newman · Mitchell Silberberg & Knupp · 11377 West Olympic Boulevard · Los Angeles, CA 90064 · 310-312-2000

James R. Schwartz · Manatt, Phelps & Phillips · 11355 West Olympic Boulevard · Los Angeles, CA 90064 · 310-312-4000

Stuart P. Tobisman · ⑳ · Loeb & Loeb · 10100 Santa Monica Boulevard, Suite 2200 · Los Angeles, CA 90067-4164 · 310-282-2000

J. Patrick Whaley · ⑩ · Musick, Peeler & Garrett · One Wilshire Boulevard, Suite 2000 · Los Angeles, CA 90017 · 213-629-7600

North Hollywood

Edmond R. Davis · ㉕ · Davis & Whalen · 5200 Lankershim Boulevard, Suite 380 · North Hollywood, CA 91601 · 818-752-2880

Rancho Santa Fe

Frederick R. Vandeveer · Luce, Forward, Hamilton & Scripps · http://www.luce.com · 6050 El Tordo · P.O. Box 2329 · Rancho Santa Fe, CA 92067-2329 · 858-756-4410

San Diego

Ellen Whelan · DLA Piper · 4365 Executive Drive, Suite 1100 · San Diego, CA 92121-2133 · 858-677-1400

San Francisco

Betsy Buchalter Adler · Adler & Colvin · Russ Building, Suite 1220 · 235 Montgomery Street · San Francisco, CA 94104 · 415-421-7555

Gregory L. Colvin · Adler & Colvin · Russ Building, Suite 1220 · 235 Montgomery Street · San Francisco, CA 94104 · 415-421-7555

Jill S. Dodd · Manatt, Phelps & Phillips · One Embarcadero Center, 30th Floor · San Francisco, CA 94111 · 415-291-7400

Erik D. Dryburgh · Adler & Colvin · Russ Building, Suite 1220 · 235 Montgomery Street · San Francisco, CA 94104 · 415-421-7555

Rosemary E. Fei · Adler & Colvin · Russ Building, Suite 1220 · 235 Montgomery Street · San Francisco, CA 94104 · 415-421-7555

Pamela S. Kaufmann · Hanson Bridgett · http://www.hansonbridgett.com · 425 Market Street, 26th Floor · San Francisco, CA 94105 · 415-777-3200

Ingrid H. Mittermaier · Adler & Colvin · Russ Building, Suite 1220 · 235 Montgomery Street · San Francisco, CA 94104 · 415-421-7555

Cynthia R. Rowland · Coblentz, Patch, Duffy & Bass · http://www.coblentzlaw.com · One Ferry Building, Suite 200 · San Francisco, CA 94111-4213 · 415-391-4800

Thomas Silk, Jr. · The Law Offices of Thomas Silk · 1408 Kearny Street · San Francisco, CA 94133 · 415-986-6000

Charles G. Stephenson · ⑳ · Tufts Stephenson & Kasper · 235 Montgomery Street, Suite 1035 · San Francisco, CA 94104-5300 · 415-705-5300

Myron G. Sugarman · ⑳ · Cooley Godward Kronish · 101 California Street, Fifth Floor · San Francisco, CA 94111-5800 · 415-693-2000

Robert A. Wexler · Adler & Colvin · Russ Building, Suite 1220 · 235 Montgomery Street · San Francisco, CA 94104 · 415-421-7555

NON-WHITE-COLLAR CRIMINAL DEFENSE

Auburn

Thomas Leupp · Leupp, Wachob & Woodall · 149 Court Street · Auburn, CA 95603 · 530-888-1100

Berkeley

Cristina C. Arguedas · ⑳ · Arguedas, Cassman & Headley · http://www.achlaw.com · 803 Hearst Avenue Berkeley, CA 94710 · 510-845-3000

Ted W. Cassman · Arguedas, Cassman & Headley · http://www.achlaw.com · 803 Hearst Avenue · Berkeley, CA 94710 · 510-845-3000

Harold J. Rosenthal · Harold J. Rosenthal · 803 Hearst Avenue · Berkeley, CA 94710 · 510-981-1800

James S. Thomson · James S. Thomson · 819 Delaware Street · Berkeley, CA 94710 · 510-525-9123

Costa Mesa

Joel Levine · ㉕ · Law Office of Joel Levine · 695 Town Center Drive, Suite 875 · Costa Mesa, CA 92626 714-662-4462

Paul S. Meyer · ⑩ · Law Office of Paul S. Meyer · 695 Town Center Drive, Suite 875 · Costa Mesa, CA 92626 · 714-754-6500

Danville

William E. Gagen, Jr. · Gagen, McCoy, McMahon & Armstrong · 279 Front Street · P.O. Box 218 · Danville, CA 94526 · 925-837-0585

Hayward

Philip A. Schnayerson · ⑳ · Garcia, Schnayerson & Mockus · 225 West Winton Avenue, Suite 208 · Hayward, CA 94544 · 510-887-7445

Irvine

Jack M. Earley · ⑩ · The Law Office of Jack M. Earley · 19900 MacArthur Boulevard, Suite 850 · Irvine, CA 92612-8422 · 949-476-8900

Jennifer L. Keller · Law Offices of Jennifer L. Keller · 18500 Von Karman Avenue, Suite 560 · Irvine, CA 92612 · 949-476-8700

William J. Kopeny · ⑩ · William Kopeny & Associates · http://www.writsnappeals.com · 16485 Laguna Canyon Road, Suite 230 · Irvine, CA 92618 · 949-453-2243

Los Angeles

Blair B. Berk · Tarlow & Berk · 9119 West Sunset Boulevard · Los Angeles, CA 90069 · 310-278-2111

Harland W. Braun · ⑳ · Harland W. Braun · 1880 Century Park East, Suite 710 · Los Angeles, CA 90067-1608 · 310-277-4777

Bradley W. Brunon · ⑳ · Bradley W. Brunon · 12100 Wilshire Boulevard, 15th Floor · Los Angeles, CA 90025-7120 · 310-820-4484

Bryan D. Daly · Mayer Brown · 350 South Grand Avenue, 25th Floor · Los Angeles, CA 90071-1503 · 213-229-9500

Stanley I. Greenberg · ㉕ · Stanley I. Greenberg · 6080 Center Drive, Suite 800 · Los Angeles, CA 90045-1574 · 310-215-7509

Janet I. Levine · ⑩ · Lightfoot Vandevelde Sadowsky Crouchley Rutherford & Levine · 800 Wilshire Boulevard, Suite 500 · Los Angeles, CA 90017 · 213-622-4750

Leonard B. Levine · ⑩ · Leonard B. Levine · 1901 Avenue of the Stars, Suite 615 · Los Angeles, CA 90067-6008 · 310-553-6510

Thomas A. Mesereau, Jr. · Mesereau & Yu · 10390 Santa Monica Boulevard · Los Angeles, CA 90025 · 310-789-1177

Alvin S. Michaelson · ⑳ · Law Offices of Alvin S. Michaelson · 1901 Avenue of the Stars, Suite 615 · Los Angeles, CA 90067-6018 · 310-278-4984

Donald M. Re · ⑩ · Donald M. Re · 624 South Grand Avenue, 22nd Floor · Los Angeles, CA 90017 · 213-623-4234

Barry Tarlow · ㉕ · Tarlow & Berk · 9119 West Sunset Boulevard · Los Angeles, CA 90069 · 310-278-2111

John Yzurdiaga · John Yzurdiaga · 800 Wilshire Boulevard, Suite 1510 · Los Angeles, CA 90017 · 213-622-9262

Manhattan Beach

Mark O. Heaney · ㉕ · Mark O. Heaney · 2808 Alma Avenue · Manhattan Beach, CA 90266 · 310-545-6774

Mill Valley

M. Gerald Schwartzbach · ⑳ · M. Gerald Schwartzbach · 655 Redwood Highway, Suite 277 · Mill Valley, CA 94941-3057 · 415-388-2343

Orange

John D. Barnett · ⑩ · Law Office of John D. Barnett · One City Boulevard West, Fifth Floor · Orange, CA 92868 · 714-634-3397

Palo Alto

Michael W. Armstrong · Nolan, Armstrong & Barton · 600 University Avenue · Palo Alto, CA 94301-2076 · 650-326-2980

Thomas J. Nolan · ⑳ · Nolan, Armstrong & Barton · 600 University Avenue · Palo Alto, CA 94301-2076 · 650-326-2980

Riverside

Virginia M. Blumenthal · ⑳ · Blumenthal Law Offices · The Riverside Barrister Building · 3993 Market Street · Riverside, CA 92501 · 951-682-5110

Steven L. Harmon · ⑳ · Harmon & Harmon · The Loring Building, Suite 250 · 3685 Main Street · Riverside, CA 92501 · 951-329-9324

Sacramento

Clyde M. Blackmon · ⑳ · Blackmon & Associates · 813 Sixth Street, Suite 450 · Sacramento, CA 95814-2403 · 916-441-0824

Quin Denvir · Rothschild Wishek & Sands · http://www.rwslaw.com · 901 F Street, Suite 200 · Sacramento, CA 95814 · 916-444-9845

Donald H. Heller · Donald H. Heller · http://www.donaldhellerlaw.com · 655 University Avenue, Suite 215 · Sacramento, CA 95825 · 916-974-3500

Michael Rothschild · ⑩ · Rothschild Wishek & Sands · http://www.rwslaw.com · 901 F Street, Suite 200 · Sacramento, CA 95814 · 916-444-9845

Christopher H. Wing · ⑩ · Christopher H. Wing · 1101 East Street · Sacramento, CA 95814 · 916-441-4888

M. Bradley Wishek · Rothschild Wishek & Sands · http://www.rwslaw.com · 901 F Street, Suite 200 · Sacramento, CA 95814 · 916-444-9845

Salinas

Thomas S. Worthington · ⑳ · The Worthington Law Centre · http://www.worthingtonlawcentre.com · 215 West Alisal Street · Salinas, CA 93901 · 831-758-1688

San Bernardino

C. Patrick Milligan · ⑩ · Milligan & Beswick · 323 West Court Street, Suite 402 · San Bernardino, CA 92401-1697 · 909-889-1178

Grover L. Porter · Grover Porter · 355 North Sierra Way · San Bernardino, CA 92410 · 909-884-0586

San Diego

Robert E. Boyce · Boyce & Schaefer · 934 Twenty-Third Street · San Diego, CA 92102-1911 · 619-232-3320

Nelson P. Brav · Brav & Schwartz · 4026 Dove Street · San Diego, CA 92103-1998 · 619-293-7350

Ezekiel E. Cortez · ⑩ · Ezekiel E. Cortez · http://www.ezekielecortez.com · 1010 Second Avenue, Suite 1850 · San Diego, CA 92101 · 619-237-0309

John G. Cotsirilos · ⑩ · John G. Cotsirilos · 2442 Fourth Avenue · San Diego, CA 92101 · 619-232-6022

Steven E. Feldman · Law Offices of Steven E. Feldman · 934 Twenty-Third Street · San Diego, CA 92102 · 619-232-8649

Howard B. Frank · Frank & Milchen · 136 Redwood Street · San Diego, CA 92103-5690 · 619-574-1888

Charles L. Goldberg · ㉕ · Seltzer Caplan McMahon Vitek · Symphony Towers, Suite 2100 · 750 B Street San Diego, CA 92101 · 619-685-3003

Robert L. Grimes · ⑩ · Grimes & Warwick · 2664 Fourth Avenue · San Diego, CA 92103-6515 · 619-232-9700

Peter J. Hughes · ㉕ · Peter J. Hughes · 1010 Second Avenue, Suite 1840 · San Diego, CA 92101 · 619-234-6696

Eugene G. Iredale · ⑳ · Eugene G. Iredale · 105 West F Street, Fourth Floor · San Diego, CA 92101-6036 · 619-233-1525

Knut S. Johnson · Knut S. Johnson · 1010 Second Avenue, Suite 1850 · San Diego, CA 92101 · 619-232-7080

Michael R. Marrinan · Law Office of Michael R. Marrinan · 614 Fifth Avenue, Suite D · San Diego, CA 92101 · 619-238-6900

Michael N. Pancer · ⑳ · Michael N. Pancer · 105 West F Street, Fourth Floor · San Diego, CA 92101 · 619-236-1826

John G. Phillips · John G. Phillips · 1010 Second Avenue, Suite 1840 · San Diego, CA 92101 · 619-234-0163

Christopher J. Plourd · Christopher J. Plourd · 1168 Union Street, Suite 303 · San Diego, CA 92101 · 619-615-6200

Frank J. Ragen II · ⑩ · Frank J. Ragen · 105 West F Street, Suite 215 · San Diego, CA 92101 · 619-231-4330

Charles M. Sevilla · ⑳ · The Law Office of Charles Sevilla · 1010 Second Avenue, Suite 1825 · San Diego, CA 92101-4902 · 619-232-2222

Milton J. Silverman, Jr. · ㉕ · Milton J. Silverman · The Quartermass-Wilde House · 2404 Broadway · San Diego, CA 92102 · 619-231-6611

Thomas J. Warwick, Jr. · Grimes & Warwick · 2664 Fourth Avenue · San Diego, CA 92103-6515 · 619-232-9700

Lewis A. Wenzell · ⑩ · Lewis A. Wenzell · 5070 Narragansett Avenue, Suite 303 · San Diego, CA 92107-3028 · 619-224-9422

San Francisco

Nanci Lynne Clarence · ⑩ · Clarence & Dyer · 899 Ellis Street · San Francisco, CA 94109 · 415-749-1800

George J. Cotsirilos, Jr. · Cotsirilos & Campisano · 250 Montgomery Street, Suite 1100 · San Francisco, CA 94104-3420 · 415-397-2373

Gilbert Eisenberg · ㉕ · Law Office of Gilbert Eisenberg · 400 Montgomery Street, Suite 200 · San Francisco, CA 94104 · 415-433-3476

William M. Goodman · ⑩ · Kasowitz, Benson, Torres & Friedman · 101 California Street, Suite 2050 · San Francisco, CA 94111 · 415-421-6140

John W. Keker · ㉕ · Keker & Van Nest · http://www.kvn.com · 710 Sansome Street · San Francisco, CA 94111 · 415-391-5400

Richard B. Mazer · Law Office of Richard B. Mazer · 99 Divisadero Street · San Francisco, CA 94117 · 415-621-4100

William L. Osterhoudt · ⑳ · William L. Osterhoudt · 135 Belvedere Street · San Francisco, CA 94117 · 415-664-4600

Dennis P. Riordan · ⑩ · Riordan & Horgan · 523 Octavia Street · San Francisco, CA 94102 · 415-431-3472

Marshall M. Schulman · ⑳ · Law Offices of Marshall M. Schulman · 120 Montgomery Street, Suite 1600 San Francisco, CA 94104 · 415-837-0702

Karen L. Snell · ⑩ · Karen L. Snell · 102 Buena Vista Terrace · San Francisco, CA 94117 · 415-225-7592

Edward W. Swanson · Swanson, McNamara & Haller · 300 Montgomery Street, Suite 1100 · San Francisco, CA 94104 · 415-477-3800

Marcus S. Topel · ⑳ · Kasowitz, Benson, Torres & Friedman · 101 California Street, Suite 2050 · San Francisco, CA 94111 · 415-421-6140

Doron Weinberg · ㉕ · Weinberg & Wilder · 523 Octavia Street · San Francisco, CA 94102 · 415-431-3472

San Jose

Guyton N. Jinkerson · ⑳ · Guyton N. Jinkerson · http://www.guytonjinkerson.com · 510 North Third Street · San Jose, CA 95112 · 408-297-8555

Alan M. Lagod · ⑩ · Lagod & Christensen · 360 West Hedding Street · San Jose, CA 95110 · 408-288-5025

Steven R. Manchester · ⑩ · Manchester, Williams & Seibert · 125 South Market Street, Suite 1100 · San Jose, CA 95113 · 408-287-6193

Kenneth W. Robinson · ⑩ · Law Offices of Kenneth W. Robinson · 1065 Asbury Street · San Jose, CA 95126 · 408-294-4477

Allen J. Ruby · ⑳ · Ruby & Schofield · 125 South Market Street, Suite 1001 · San Jose, CA 95113-2285 · 408-998-8500

Frank R. Ubhaus · ㉕ · Berliner Cohen · 10 Almaden Boulevard, 11th Floor · San Jose, CA 95113-2233 · 408-286-5800

John L. Williams, Jr. · ⑳ · Manchester, Williams & Seibert · 125 South Market Street, Suite 1100 · San Jose, CA 95113 · 408-287-6193

Santa Ana

Allan H. Stokke · ⑳ · Stokke & Riddet · Three Imperial Promenade, Suite 750 · Santa Ana, CA 92707-5903 · 714-662-2400

Santa Cruz

Paul B. Meltzer · ⑩ · Law Offices of Paul B. Meltzer · 511 Water Street · Santa Cruz, CA 95060 · 831-426-6000

Santa Monica

William J. Genego · Nasatir, Hirsch, Podberesky & Genego · Main Street Law Building · 2115 Main Street · Santa Monica, CA 90405 · 310-399-3259

Richard G. Hirsch · ⑳ · Nasatir, Hirsch, Podberesky & Genego · Main Street Law Building · 2115 Main Street · Santa Monica, CA 90405 · 310-399-3259

Marcia A. Morrissey · ⑩ · Marcia A. Morrissey · 2115 Main Street · Santa Monica, CA 90405 · 310-399-3259

Michael D. Nasatir · ⑳ · Nasatir, Hirsch, Podberesky & Genego · Main Street Law Building · 2115 Main Street · Santa Monica, CA 90405 · 310-399-3259

Vicki I. Podberesky · Nasatir, Hirsch, Podberesky & Genego · Main Street Law Building · 2115 Main Street · Santa Monica, CA 90405 · 310-399-3259

Edward A. Rucker · ⑩ · Edward A. Rucker · 1717 Fourth Street, Third Floor · Santa Monica, CA 90401 · 310-928-6620

Victor Sherman · Sherman & Sherman · 2115 Main Street · Santa Monica, CA 90405 · 310-399-3259

Santa Rosa

Chris P. Andrian · Andrian & Gallenson · 1100 Mendocino Avenue · Santa Rosa, CA 95401-4311 · 707-527-9381

Richard J. Ingram · Harrington & Ingram · 438 First Street, Fourth Floor · Santa Rosa, CA 95401 · 707-573-8123

Jamie O. Thistlethwaite · Jamie Olsen Thistlethwaite · 444 Tenth Street, Fourth Floor · Santa Rosa, CA 95401-5267 · 707-578-9254

L. Stephen Turer · L. Stephen Turer · 610 Davis Street · Santa Rosa, CA 95401 · 707-546-1551

Ukiah

Susan B. Jordan · ㉕ · Susan B. Jordan · 515 South School Street · Ukiah, CA 95482 · 707-462-2151

Ann C. Moorman · Law Offices of Ann Moorman · 308 South School Street · Ukiah, CA 95482 · 707-462-1844

Vista

Richard D. Muir · ㉕ · Richard D. Muir · 122 Escondido Avenue, Suite 102 · Vista, CA 92084-6055 · 760-726-6131

OIL & GAS LAW

Walnut Creek

Peter W. Hanschen · ⑩ · Morrison & Foerster · http://www.mofo.com · 101 Ygnacio Valley Road, Suite 450 · Walnut Creek, CA 94596-4095 · 925-295-3300

PERSONAL INJURY LITIGATION

Berkeley

Victoria J. De Goff · De Goff and Sherman · 1916 Los Angeles Avenue · Berkeley, CA 94707 · 510-524-1840

Beverly Hills

Gary A. Dordick · Law Offices of Gary Dordick · 509 South Beverly Drive · Beverly Hills, CA 90212 · 310-551-0949

Burbank

George E. Peterson · ⑩ · Peterson & Bradford · 100 North First Street, Suite 300 · Burbank, CA 91502-1845 · 818-562-5800

Burlingame

Niall P. McCarthy · Cotchett, Pitre & McCarthy · San Francisco Airport Office Center, Suite 200 · 840 Malcolm Road · Burlingame, CA 94010 · 650-697-6000

Frank M. Pitre · Cotchett, Pitre & McCarthy · San Francisco Airport Office Center, Suite 200 · 840 Malcolm Road · Burlingame, CA 94010 · 650-697-6000

Cardiff

Michael Goldstein · The Law Offices of Michael Goldstein · 120 Birmingham Drive, Suite 200 · Cardiff, CA 92007-1753 · 760-436-1801

Claremont

Michael J. Bidart · Shernoff Bidart & Darras · 600 South Indian Hill Boulevard · Claremont, CA 91711 · 909-621-4935

Herbert Hafif · ⑩ · Herbert Hafif · 269 West Bonita Avenue · Claremont, CA 91711-4784 · 909-624-1671

William M. Shernoff · ⑳ · Shernoff Bidart & Darras · 600 South Indian Hill Boulevard · Claremont, CA 91711 · 909-621-4935

Coronado

Amy G. Langerman · ⑩ · Amy G. Langerman · 951 Coronado Avenue · Coronado, CA 92118-0000 · 619-437-4579

Costa Mesa

W. Douglas Easton · Law Offices of W. Douglas Easton · 650 Town Center Drive, Suite 800 · Costa Mesa, CA 92626 · 714-850-4590

H. Gilbert Jones · ⑳ · Lewis, Brisbois, Bisgaard & Smith · 650 Town Center Drive, Suite 1400 · Costa Mesa, CA 92626-1925 · 714-545-9200

Todd C. Theodora · Theodora, Oringher, Miller & Richman · 535 Anton Boulevard, Ninth Floor · Costa Mesa, CA 92626-7109 · 714-549-6200

El Segundo

Robert N. Stone · ⑩ · Stone, Dolginer & Wenzel · 2321 Rosecrans Avenue, Suite 2220 · El Segundo, CA 90245 · 310-643-0070

Mark D. Wenzel · Stone, Dolginer & Wenzel · 2321 Rosecrans Avenue, Suite 2220 · El Segundo, CA 90245 · 310-643-0070

Emeryville

Nelson C. Barry, Sr. · ⑳ · Bishop, Barry, Howe, Haney & Ryder · Watergate Tower III, 14th Floor · 2000 Powell Street · Emeryville, CA 94608 · 510-596-0888

Glendale

George R. Hillsinger · ⑳ · Gonzalez & Hulbert · 101 North Brand Boulevard, Suite 1880 · Glendale, CA 91203 · 818-844-0188

Hayward

Rick Simons · Furtado, Jaspovice & Simons · 22274 Main Street · Hayward, CA 94541 · 510-582-1080

Indio

Thomas T. Anderson · ⑳ · Thomas T. Anderson · http://www.ttalawfirm.com · 45926 Oasis Street · Indio, CA 92201 · 760-347-3364

Irvine

Daniel M. Hodes · Lopez, Hodes, Restaino, Milman & Skikos · 9210 Irvine Center Drive · Irvine, CA 92618 · 949-640-8222

Long Beach

Jeffrey S. Behar · ⑩ · Ford, Walker, Haggerty & Behar · One World Trade Center, 27th Floor · Long Beach, CA 90831-2700 · 562-983-2500

Richard D. Carroll · Carroll, Kelly, Trotter, Franzen & McKenna · 111 West Ocean Boulevard, 14th Floor · P.O. Box 22636 · Long Beach, CA 90801-5636 · 562-432-5855

Dennis M. Elber · ⑩ · Stolpman, Krissman, Elber & Silver · 111 West Ocean Boulevard, 19th Floor · Long Beach, CA 90802 · 562-435-8300

Joel Krissman · Stolpman, Krissman, Elber & Silver · 111 West Ocean Boulevard, 19th Floor · Long Beach, CA 90802 · 562-435-8300

Dennis J. Sinclitico · ⑩ · Sinclitico & Burns · 330 Golden Shore, Suite 410 · Long Beach, CA 90802-4246 562-628-1919

Thomas G. Stolpman · ⑳ · Stolpman, Krissman, Elber & Silver · 111 West Ocean Boulevard, 19th Floor · Long Beach, CA 90802 · 562-435-8300

Timothy L. Walker · ⑳ · Ford, Walker, Haggerty & Behar · One World Trade Center, 27th Floor · Long Beach, CA 90831-2700 · 562-983-2500

Los Angeles

Robert C. Baker · ⑩ · Baker, Keener & Nahra · 633 West Fifth Street, 54th Floor · Los Angeles, CA 90071 · 213-241-0900

William G. Baumgaertner · Haight, Brown & Bonesteel · 6080 Center Drive, Suite 800 · Los Angeles, CA 90045 · 310-215-7100

Michael J. Bonesteel · Haight, Brown & Bonesteel · 6080 Center Drive, Suite 800 · Los Angeles, CA 90045 · 310-215-7100

Kevin R. Boyle · Panish Shea & Boyle · 11111 Santa Monica Boulevard, Suite 700 · Los Angeles, CA 90025 · 310-477-1700

Roy M. Brisbois · Lewis, Brisbois, Bisgaard & Smith · 221 North Figueroa Street, Suite 1200 · Los Angeles, CA 90012-2601 · 213-250-1800

Peter Q. Ezzell · Haight, Brown & Bonesteel · 6080 Center Drive, Suite 800 · Los Angeles, CA 90045 · 310-215-7100

Larry R. Feldman · ⑩ · Kaye Scholer · 1999 Avenue of the Stars, Suite 1700 · Los Angeles, CA 90067-6048 · 310-788-1000

Thomas V. Girardi · ㉕ · Girardi and Keese · http://www.girardikeese.com · 1126 Wilshire Boulevard · Los Angeles, CA 90017-1904 · 213-977-0211

Roger L. Gordon · ⑩ · Gordon, Edelstein, Krepack, Grant, Felton & Goldstein · 3580 Wilshire Boulevard, Suite 1800 · Los Angeles, CA 90010 · 213-739-7000

Steven A. Heimberg · Heimberg Law Group · http://www.heimberglaw.com · 1801 Century Park East, Suite 1920 · Los Angeles, CA 90067-2313 · 310-553-1799

E. Lee Horton · Waller Lansden Dortch & Davis · http://www.wallerlaw.com · 333 South Grand Avenue, Suite 1800 · Los Angeles, CA 90071 · 213-362-3680

Don Howarth · Howarth & Smith · 523 West Sixth Street, Suite 728 · Los Angeles, CA 90014 · 213-955-9400

Howard D. Krepack · Gordon, Edelstein, Krepack, Grant, Felton & Goldstein · 3580 Wilshire Boulevard, Suite 1800 · Los Angeles, CA 90010 · 213-739-7000

Russell Kussman · ⑩ · Kussman & Whitehill · http://www.kussmanwhitehill.com · 10866 Wilshire Boulevard, Suite 1470 · Los Angeles, CA 90024 · 310-474-4411

Walter J. Lack · Engstrom, Lipscomb & Lack · 10100 Santa Monica Boulevard, 16th Floor · Los Angeles, CA 90067 · 310-552-3800

David R. Lira · Girardi and Keese · http://www.girardikeese.com · 1126 Wilshire Boulevard · Los Angeles, CA 90017-1904 · 213-977-0211

Garo Mardirossian · Mardirossian & Associates · 6311 Wilshire Boulevard · Los Angeles, CA 90048 · 323-653-6311

Philip Michels · Law Offices of Michels & Watkins · 11755 Wilshire Boulevard, Suite 1300 · Los Angeles, CA 90025-1540 · 310-444-1200

Milton A. Miller · Latham & Watkins · 355 South Grand Avenue · Los Angeles, CA 90071-1560 · 213-485-1234

James D. Nichols · ⑩ · Bonne, Bridges, Mueller, O'Keefe & Nichols · http://www.bonnebridges.com · 3699 Wilshire Boulevard, 10th Floor · Los Angeles, CA 90010-2719 · 213-480-1900

David J. O'Keefe · ⑳ · Bonne, Bridges, Mueller, O'Keefe & Nichols · http://www.bonnebridges.com · 3699 Wilshire Boulevard, 10th Floor · Los Angeles, CA 90010-2719 · 213-480-1900

Brian Panish · Panish Shea & Boyle · 11111 Santa Monica Boulevard, Suite 700 · Los Angeles, CA 90025 310-477-1700

Michael J. Piuze · ⑩ · Michael J. Piuze · 11755 Wilshire Boulevard, Suite 1170 · Los Angeles, CA 90025 · 310-312-1102

Debra E. Pole · Sidley Austin · 555 West Fifth Street, 40th Floor · Los Angeles, CA 90013 · 213-896-6000

David M. Ring · Taylor & Ring · 10900 Wilshire Boulevard, Suite 920 · Los Angeles, CA 90024 · 310-209-4100

Jerome L. Ringler · ⑩ · Ringler Kearney Alvarez · 633 West Fifth Street, 28th Floor · Los Angeles, CA 90071 · 213-473-1900

Adam K. Shea · Panish Shea & Boyle · 11111 Santa Monica Boulevard, Suite 700 · Los Angeles, CA 90025 · 310-477-1700

Suzelle M. Smith · Howarth & Smith · 523 West Sixth Street, Suite 728 · Los Angeles, CA 90014 · 213-955-9400

John C. Taylor · ⑩ · Taylor & Ring · 10900 Wilshire Boulevard, Suite 920 · Los Angeles, CA 90024 · 310-209-4100

N. Denise Taylor · ⑩ · Taylor Blessey · 350 South Grand Avenue, Suite 3850 · Los Angeles, CA 90071-3125 · 213-687-1600

David E. Wood · David E. Wood · 1881 Century Park East, Suite 612 · Los Angeles, CA 90067 · 310-286-0900

Walter M. Yoka · Yoka & Smith · 777 South Figueroa Street, Suite 4200 · Los Angeles, CA 90017 · 213-427-2300

Newport Beach

Mark P. Robinson, Jr. · Robinson, Calcagnie & Robinson · 620 Newport Center Drive, Seventh Floor · Newport Beach, CA 92660 · 949-720-1288

Ronald B. Schwartz · Ronald B. Schwartz · 202 Newport Center Drive, Second Floor · Newport Beach, CA 92660 · 949-644-7283

Kenneth Marshall Silberberg · ⑳ · The Law Offices of Marshall Silberberg · 660 Newport Center Drive, Suite 340 · Newport Beach, CA 92660 · 949-718-0960

Michael Paul Thomas · ⑩ · Law Office of Michael Paul Thomas · 2901 West Pacific Coast Highway, Suite 200 · Newport Beach, CA 92663 · 949-258-4349

Oakland

Stephen G. Blitch · Reed Smith · 1999 Harrison Street, Suite 2400 · P.O. Box 2084 · Oakland, CA 94604-3572 · 510-763-2000

Richard H. Carlson · Anthony & Carlson · 1999 Harrison Street, Suite 2000 · Oakland, CA 94612-3582 · 510-835-8400

J. Gary Gwilliam · ⑩ · Gwilliam, Ivary, Chiosso, Cavalli & Brewer · 1999 Harrison Street, Suite 1600 · Oakland, CA 94612 · 510-832-5411

Gerald C. Sterns · ㉕ · Sterns & Walker · Clocktower Building · 901 Clay Street · Oakland, CA 94607 · 510-267-0500

Orinda

Luke Ellis · Gillin, Jacobson, Ellis & Larsen · http://www.gjel.com · Two Theater Square, Suite 230 · Orinda, CA 94563 · 925-253-5800

Andrew R. Gillin · Gillin, Jacobson, Ellis & Larsen · http://www.gjel.com · Two Theater Square, Suite 230 · Orinda, CA 94563 · 925-253-5800

Jim Larsen · Gillin, Jacobson, Ellis & Larsen · http://www.gjel.com · Two Theater Square, Suite 230 · Orinda, CA 94563 · 925-253-5800

Pasadena

Kevin Meenan · The Meenan Lariviere Law Firm · Penthouse, Ninth Floor · 790 East Colorado Boulevard · Pasadena, CA 91101-2193 · 626-398-0000

Rancho Mirage

G. Dana Hobart · ⑩ · G. Dana Hobart · http://www.legalethicsexpert.com · 36989 Palmdale Road · Rancho Mirage, CA 92270 · 760-324-1013

Rancho Palos Verdes

Robert J. Chávez · Wilkes & McHugh · 500 Silver Spur Road, Suite 200 · Rancho Palos Verdes, CA 90275 · 877-406-3003

Redding

Dugan Barr · Barr & Mudford · 1824 Court Street · Redding, CA 96001 · 530-243-8008

Redlands

Florentino R. Garza · ㉕ · Garza & Garza · 1980 Orange Tree Lane, Suite 280 · Redlands, CA 92374 · 909-798-0663

Jeffrey S. Raynes · Law Office of Jeffrey Raynes · 1780 Orange Tree Lane · Redlands, CA 92374 · 909-793-6800

Douglas F. Welebir · Welebir Tierney & Weck · http://www.wtw-law.com · 2068 Orange Tree Lane, Suite 215 · Redlands, CA 92374-4555 · 909-335-0444

Redwood City

John M. Bentley · ⑳ · Ropers, Majeski, Kohn & Bentley · 1001 Marshall Street, Suite 300 · Redwood City, CA 94063-2052 · 650-364-8200

Riverside

Don G. Grant · Thompson & Colegate · 3610 Fourteenth Street · P.O. Box 1299 · Riverside, CA 92502 · 951-682-5550

David G. Moore · ⑩ · Reid & Hellyer · 3880 Lemon Street, Fifth Floor · P.O. Box 1300 · Riverside, CA 92502-1300 · 951-682-1771

Roseville

Steven H. Gurnee · Gurnee & Daniels · 2240 Douglas Boulevard, Suite 150 · Roseville, CA 95661-3875 · 916-797-3100

Sacramento

James T. Anwyl · Anwyl, Scoffield & Stepp · 2180 Harvard Street, Suite 200 · Sacramento, CA 95815-3318 · 916-565-1800

Joseph J. Babich · Dreyer, Babich, Buccola & Callaham · 20 Bicentennial Circle · Sacramento, CA 95826 916-379-3500

Theodore D. Bolling, Jr. · ⑳ · Bolling, Walter & Gawthrop · 8880 Cal Center Drive, Suite 400 · P.O. Box 255200 · Sacramento, CA 95865 · 916-369-0777

Robert A. Buccola · Dreyer, Babich, Buccola & Callaham · 20 Bicentennial Circle · Sacramento, CA 95826 · 916-379-3500

William C. Callaham · Dreyer, Babich, Buccola & Callaham · 20 Bicentennial Circle · Sacramento, CA 95826 · 916-379-3500

Gary B. Callahan · Wilcoxen, Callahan, Montgomery and Deacon · 2114 K Street · Sacramento, CA 95816 · 916-442-2777

Douglas DeVries · Devries Law Firm · 1792 Tribute Road, Suite 480 · Sacramento, CA 95815 · 916-473-4343

Roger A. Dreyer · ⑩ · Dreyer, Babich, Buccola & Callaham · 20 Bicentennial Circle · Sacramento, CA 95826 · 916-379-3500

Edward P. Freidberg · ⑩ · Freidberg & Parker · 650 University Avenue, Suite 205 · Sacramento, CA 95825 · 916-929-9060

Mark E. Merin · Law Office of Mark Merin · 2001 P Street, Suite 100 · Sacramento, CA 95814-5213 · 916-443-6911

Curtis R. Namba · Namba Law Offices · 735 University Drive · Sacramento, CA 95825 · 916-922-6300

Russell G. Porter · ⑩ · Porter Scott · 350 University Avenue, Suite 200 · Sacramento, CA 95825 · 916-929-1481

John M. Poswall · ⑳ · Poswall White & Cutler · 1001 G Street, Suite 301 · Sacramento, CA 95814 · 916-449-1300

Leo H. Schuering, Jr. · ⑳ · Schuering, Zimmerman, Scully, Tweedy & Doyle · 400 University Avenue · Sacramento, CA 95825 · 916-567-0400

R. Parker White · Poswall White & Cutler · 1001 G Street, Suite 301 · Sacramento, CA 95814 · 916-449-1300

Daniel E. Wilcoxen · Wilcoxen, Callahan, Montgomery and Deacon · 2114 K Street · Sacramento, CA 95816 · 916-442-2777

San Bernardino

Robert K. Warford · Reback, McAndrews & Kjar · 215 North D Street, Suite 303 · San Bernardino, CA 92401 · 909-889-4665

San Diego

Vincent J. Bartolotta, Jr. · ⑳ · Thorsnes Bartolotta McGuire · http://www.tbmlawyers.com · 2550 Fifth Avenue, 11th Floor · San Diego, CA 92103 · 619-236-9363

Richard D. Barton · Higgs, Fletcher & Mack · 401 West A Street, Suite 2600 · San Diego, CA 92101-7910 · 619-236-1551

Nelson P. Brav · Brav & Schwartz · 4026 Dove Street · San Diego, CA 92103-1998 · 619-293-7350

Alan K. Brubaker · ⑩ · Wingert, Grebing, Brubaker & Goodwin · http://www.wingertlaw.com · One America Plaza, Seventh Floor · 600 West Broadway · San Diego, CA 92101-3370 · 619-232-8151

Douglas M. Butz · ⑩ · Butz, Dunn, DeSantis & Bingham · 101 West Broadway, Suite 1700 · San Diego, CA 92101-8289 · 619-233-4777

David S. Casey, Jr. · Casey, Gerry, Schenk, Francavilla, Blatt & Penfield · http://www.cglaw.com · 110 Laurel Street · San Diego, CA 92101-1486 · 619-238-1811

Edward D. Chapin · ⑳ · Chapin Wheeler · http://www.chapinwheeler.com · 550 West C Street, Suite 2000 · San Diego, CA 92101 · 619-241-4810

Cynthia Chihak · Cynthia Chihak · 12555 High Bluff Drive, Suite 150 · San Diego, CA 92130 · 858-481-7252

Steven J. Cologne · Higgs, Fletcher & Mack · 401 West A Street, Suite 2600 · San Diego, CA 92101-7910 619-236-1551

George E. Fleming · ⑩ · Baker & McKenzie · 12544 High Bluff Drive, Third Floor · San Diego, CA 92130-3051 · 858-523-6200

John H. Gomez · The Gomez Law Firm · http://thegomezfirm.com · 625 Broadway, Suite 600 · San Diego, CA 92101 · 619-237-3490

Charles R. Grebing · ⑩ · Wingert, Grebing, Brubaker & Goodwin · http://www.wingertlaw.com · One America Plaza, Seventh Floor · 600 West Broadway · San Diego, CA 92101-3370 · 619-232-8151

Robert M. Juskie · Wingert, Grebing, Brubaker & Goodwin · http://www.wingertlaw.com · One America Plaza, Seventh Floor · 600 West Broadway · San Diego, CA 92101-3370 · 619-232-8151

Lawrence J. Kouns · Luce, Forward, Hamilton & Scripps · http://www.luce.com · 600 West Broadway, Suite 2600 · San Diego, CA 92101 · 619-236-1414

Harvey R. Levine · ⑳ · Levine, Steinberg, Miller & Huver · 550 West C Street, Suite 1810 · San Diego, CA 92101-8596 · 619-231-9449

William M. Low · Higgs, Fletcher & Mack · 401 West A Street, Suite 2600 · San Diego, CA 92101-7910 · 619-236-1551

James A. Mangione · Wingert, Grebing, Brubaker & Goodwin · http://www.wingertlaw.com · One America Plaza, Seventh Floor · 600 West Broadway · San Diego, CA 92101-3370 · 619-232-8151

Craig R. McClellan · ⑩ · The McClellan Law Firm · http://www.mcclellanlaw.com · 1144 State Street · San Diego, CA 92101 · 619-231-0505

John F. McGuire, Jr. · ⑳ · Thorsnes Bartolotta McGuire · http://www.tbmlawyers.com · 2550 Fifth Avenue, 11th Floor · San Diego, CA 92103 · 619-236-9363

Michael I. Neil · ⑳ · Neil, Dymott, Frank, McFall & Trexler · http://www.neildymott.com · 1010 Second Avenue, Suite 2500 · San Diego, CA 92101-4959 · 619-238-1712

Virginia C. Nelson · ⑩ · Law Offices of Virginia Nelson · http://www.vcnlaw.com · 550 West C Street, Suite 2050 · San Diego, CA 92101 · 619-232-5503

Gregory W. Pollack · Higgs, Fletcher & Mack · 401 West A Street, Suite 2600 · San Diego, CA 92101-7910 · 619-236-1551

Kevin F. Quinn · Thorsnes Bartolotta McGuire · http://www.tbmlawyers.com · 2550 Fifth Avenue, 11th Floor · San Diego, CA 92103 · 619-236-9363

Dennis A. Schoville · ⑩ · Schoville & Arnell · Carriage House · 2404 Broadway · San Diego, CA 92102 · 619-232-9901

Milton J. Silverman, Jr. · ㉕ · Milton J. Silverman · The Quartermass-Wilde House · 2404 Broadway · San Diego, CA 92102 · 619-231-6611

Robert F. Vaage · Robert F. Vaage · 110 West C Street, Suite 2105 · San Diego, CA 92101-3905 · 619-338-0505

Daniel M. White · ⑩ · White, Oliver & Amundson · http://www.whiteoliver.com · 550 West C Street, Suite 950 · San Diego, CA 92101-3353 · 619-239-0300

San Francisco

Albert R. Abramson · ㉕ · Abramson Smith Waldsmith · http://www.aswllp.com · 44 Montgomery Street, Suite 3340 · San Francisco, CA 94104 · 415-421-7995

Robert S. Arns · The Arns Law Firm · 515 Folsom Street, Third Floor · San Francisco, CA 94105 · 415-495-7800

David B. Baum · ㉕ · Baum & Blake · http://www.baumblake.com · One Sansome Street, Suite 3500 · San Francisco, CA 94104 · 415-956-5544

Martin Blake · Baum & Blake · http://www.baumblake.com · One Sansome Street, Suite 3500 · San Francisco, CA 94104 · 415-956-5544

James S. Bostwick · ㉕ · Bostwick & Associates · Four Embarcadero Center, Suite 750 · San Francisco, CA 94111 · 415-421-8300

Thomas J. Brandi · ⑩ · The Brandi Law Firm · 354 Pine Street, Third Floor · San Francisco, CA 94104 · 415-989-1800

James J. Brosnahan · ㉕ · Morrison & Foerster · http://www.mofo.com · 425 Market Street · San Francisco, CA 94105-2482 · 415-268-7000

Donald W. Brown · Covington & Burling · One Front Street · San Francisco, CA 94111-5356 · 415-591-6000

Elizabeth J. Cabraser · Lieff Cabraser Heimann & Bernstein · Embarcadero Center West, Suite 3000 · 275 Battery Street · San Francisco, CA 94111-3339 · 415-956-1000

John W. Crowley · ⑩ · Crowley, Stringer & Fenske · 456 Montgomery Street, 17th Floor · San Francisco, CA 94104-1233 · 415-989-1100

Matthew D. Davis · Walkup, Melodia, Kelly & Schoenberger · http://www.walkuplawoffice.com · 650 California Street, 26th Floor · San Francisco, CA 94108 · 415-981-7210

Robert C. Gebhardt · Jeffer, Mangels, Butler & Marmaro · Two Embarcadero Center, Fifth Floor · San Francisco, CA 94111 · 415-398-8080

James M. Goodman · Hassard Bonnington · http://www.hassard.com · Two Embarcadero Center, Suite 1800 · San Francisco, CA 94111 · 415-288-9800

John R. Hillsman · McGuinn, Hillsman & Palefsky · 535 Pacific Avenue · San Francisco, CA 94133 · 415-421-9292

John W. Keker · ㉕ · Keker & Van Nest · http://www.kvn.com · 710 Sansome Street · San Francisco, CA 94111 · 415-391-5400

Daniel J. Kelly · ⑳ · Walkup, Melodia, Kelly & Schoenberger · http://www.walkuplawoffice.com · 650 California Street, 26th Floor · San Francisco, CA 94108 · 415-981-7210

Michael A. Kelly · ⑩ · Walkup, Melodia, Kelly & Schoenberger · http://www.walkuplawoffice.com · 650 California Street, 26th Floor · San Francisco, CA 94108 · 415-981-7210

Lawrence E. Kern · Kern, Noda, Devine & Segal · Sutter Plaza, Suite 600 · 1388 Sutter Street · San Francisco, CA 94109 · 415-474-1900

David B. Lynch · Low, Ball & Lynch · 505 Montgomery Street, Seventh Floor · San Francisco, CA 94111-2584 · 415-981-6630

Robert T. Lynch · ⑩ · Lynch, Gilardi & Grummer · 475 Sansome Street, Suite 1800 · San Francisco, CA 94111 · 415-397-2800

Michael R. Marron · McQuaid Bedford & Van Zandt · 221 Main Street, 16th Floor · San Francisco, CA 94105-1936 · 415-905-0200

Cynthia McGuinn · Veen Law Firm · 711 Van Ness Avenue, Suite 220 · P.O. Box 7296 · San Francisco, CA 94120-7296 · 415-673-4800

John A. McGuinn · ⑩ · McGuinn, Hillsman & Palefsky · 535 Pacific Avenue · San Francisco, CA 94133 · 415-421-9292

Paul V. Melodia · ⑩ · Walkup, Melodia, Kelly & Schoenberger · http://www.walkuplawoffice.com · 650 California Street, 26th Floor · San Francisco, CA 94108 · 415-981-7210

Charles O. Morgan, Jr. · ㉕ · Law Office of Charles O. Morgan, Jr. · Cathedral Hill Office Building, Suite 333 · 1255 Post Street · San Francisco, CA 94109 · 415-292-8030

Dennis F. Moriarty · Cesari, Werner and Moriarty · 360 Post Street, Sutie 500 · San Francisco, CA 94108 415-391-1113

Edward J. Nevin · ⑩ · Nevin & Absalom · http://www.sfpiandlaborlawyers.com · 22 Battery Street, Suite 333 · San Francisco, CA 94111-5514 · 415-392-5040

James N. Penrod · ⑩ · Morgan Lewis & Bockius · Spear Street Tower · One Market · San Francisco, CA 94105-1596 · 415-442-1000

Gregory C. Read · Sedgwick, Detert, Moran & Arnold · Steuart Tower, Eighth Floor · One Market Plaza San Francisco, CA 94105 · 415-781-7900

Ronald H. Rouda · ⑩ · Rouda, Feder, Tietjen & Zanobini · 44 Montgomery Street, Suite 4000 · San Francisco, CA 94104 · 415-398-5398

Douglas S. Saeltzer · Walkup, Melodia, Kelly & Schoenberger · http://www.walkuplawoffice.com · 650 California Street, 26th Floor · San Francisco, CA 94108 · 415-981-7210

Randall H. Scarlett · Scarlett Law Group · Barbary Coast Building · 536 Pacific Avenue · San Francisco, CA 94133 · 415-352-6264

Richard H. Schoenberger · Walkup, Melodia, Kelly & Schoenberger · http://www.walkuplawoffice.com · 650 California Street, 26th Floor · San Francisco, CA 94108 · 415-981-7210

William B. Smith · ⑩ · Abramson Smith Waldsmith · http://www.aswllp.com · 44 Montgomery Street, Suite 3340 · San Francisco, CA 94104 · 415-421-7995

N. Kathleen Strickland · Ropers, Majeski, Kohn & Bentley · 201 Spear Street, Suite 1000 · San Francisco, CA 94105 · 415-543-4800

William L. Veen · Veen Law Firm · 711 Van Ness Avenue, Suite 220 · P.O. Box 7296 · San Francisco, CA 94120-7296 · 415-673-4800

San Jose

Robert H. Bohn, Sr. · Bohn and Bohn · http://www.bohnlaw.com · 152 North Third Street, Suite 200 · San Jose, CA 95112 · 408-279-4222

Archie S. Robinson · ⑳ · Robinson & Wood · 227 North First Street · San Jose, CA 95113 · 408-298-7120

John C. Stein · ⑩ · The Boccardo Law Firm · 111 West St. John Street, Suite 400 · P.O. Box 15001 · San Jose, CA 95115-0001 · 408-298-5678

Randall E. Willoughby · ⑩ · Willoughby, Stuart and Bening · Fairmont Plaza, Suite 400 · 50 West San Fernando Street · San Jose, CA 95113 · 408-289-1972

San Mateo

Terry O'Reilly · O'Reilly & Danko · http://www.oreillylaw.com · 1900 O'Farrell Street, Suite 360 · San Mateo, CA 94403 · 650-358-5901

San Rafael

J. Francis George III · Law Offices of J. Frank George · 912 Lootens Place, Second Floor · San Rafael, CA 94901-3110 · 415-721-2040

Santa Ana

Wylie A. Aitken · ⑳ · Aitken, Aitken & Cohn · Three MacArthur Place, Suite 800 · P.O. Box 2555 · Santa Ana, CA 92707-0555 · 714-434-1424

Daniel J. Callahan · Callahan & Blaine · http://www.callahan-law.com · Three Hutton Centre Drive, Ninth Floor · Santa Ana, CA 92707 · 714-241-4444

Santa Monica

Bruce A. Broillet · ⑳ · Greene Broillet & Wheeler · http://www.greene-broillet.com · 100 Wilshire Boulevard, 21st Floor · P.O. Box 2131 · Santa Monica, CA 90407 · 310-576-1200

John F. Denove · Cheong, Denove, Rowell & Bennett · 10100 Santa Monica Boulevard, Suite 2460 · Santa Monica, CA 90067-4007 · 310-277-4857

Browne Greene · ⑳ · Greene Broillet & Wheeler · http://www.greene-broillet.com · 100 Wilshire Boulevard, 21st Floor · P.O. Box 2131 · Santa Monica, CA 90407 · 310-576-1200

Ian Buddy Herzog · ⑩ · The Law Offices of Ian Herzog · 233 Wilshire Boulevard, Suite 550 · Santa Monica, CA 90401 · 310-458-6660

Mark T. Quigley · Greene Broillet & Wheeler · http://www.greene-broillet.com · 100 Wilshire Boulevard, 21st Floor · P.O. Box 2131 · Santa Monica, CA 90407 · 310-576-1200

Christine D. Spagnoli · Greene Broillet & Wheeler · http://www.greene-broillet.com · 100 Wilshire Boulevard, 21st Floor · P.O. Box 2131 · Santa Monica, CA 90407 · 310-576-1200

Geoffrey S. Wells · Greene Broillet & Wheeler · http://www.greene-broillet.com · 100 Wilshire Boulevard, 21st Floor · P.O. Box 2131 · Santa Monica, CA 90407 · 310-576-1200

Timothy J. Wheeler · ⑩ · Greene Broillet & Wheeler · http://www.greene-broillet.com · 100 Wilshire Boulevard, 21st Floor · P.O. Box 2131 · Santa Monica, CA 90407 · 310-576-1200

Santa Rosa

John F. DeMeo · ⑩ · DeMeo DeMeo & West · 565 West College Avenue · Santa Rosa, CA 95401 · 707-545-3232

C. Kenneth James, Jr. · C. Kenneth James, Jr. · 476 Hillsdale Drive · Santa Rosa, CA 95409 · 707-539-1794

Thomas R. Kenney, Jr. · Law Offices of Thomas R. Kenney · 608 College Avenue · P.O. Box 1516 · Santa Rosa, CA 95402-1516 · 707-575-7715

Michael D. Senneff · Senneff, Freeman & Bluestone · 50 Old Courthouse Square, Suite 401 · P.O. Box 3729 · Santa Rosa, CA 95402 · 707-526-4250

Saratoga

Salvador A. Liccardo · The Liccardo Law Firm · http://www.liccardo.com · 14510 Big Basin Way, Suite 242 · Saratoga, CA 95070 · 408-872-3764

Torrance

Gerald E. Agnew, Jr. · ⑩ · AgnewBrusavich · http://www.agnewbrusavich.com · 20355 Hawthorne Boulevard · Torrance, CA 90503 · 310-793-1400

Bruce M. Brusavich · AgnewBrusavich · http://www.agnewbrusavich.com · 20355 Hawthorne Boulevard · Torrance, CA 90503 · 310-793-1400

Tustin

Christopher J. Day · Day, Day & Brown · 301 West First Street · Tustin, CA 92780 · 714-832-4811

Walnut Creek

Thomas J. Donnelly · Donnelly Nelson Depolo & Murray · 2401 Shadelands Drive, Suite 120 · Walnut Creek, CA 94598-2428 · 925-287-8181

Martin J. Everson · Galloway, Lucchese, Everson & Picchi · 1676 North California Boulevard, Fifth Floor · Walnut Creek, CA 94596 · 925-930-9090

G. Patrick Galloway · ⑩ · Galloway, Lucchese, Everson & Picchi · 1676 North California Boulevard, Fifth Floor · Walnut Creek, CA 94596 · 925-930-9090

Peter J. Hinton · ⑩ · Hinton, Alfert & Sumner · 1646 North California Boulevard, Suite 600 · Walnut Creek, CA 94596-4113 · 925-932-6006

David R. Lucchese · ⑩ · Galloway, Lucchese, Everson & Picchi · 1676 North California Boulevard, Fifth Floor · Walnut Creek, CA 94596 · 925-930-9090

Michael J. Ney · McNamara, Dodge, Ney, Beatty, Slattery, Pfalzer, Borges & Brothers · 1211 Newell Avenue · Walnut Creek, CA 94596-5331 · 925-939-5330

Michael P. Verna · Bowles & Verna · 2121 North California Boulevard, Suite 875 · P.O. Box 8180 · Walnut Creek, CA 94596 · 925-935-3300

West Los Angeles

Charles B. O'Reilly · ⑳ · Law Offices of Charles B. O'Reilly · 12304 Santa Monica Boulevard, Suite 300 · West Los Angeles, CA 90025 · 310-820-3404

Woodland Hills

Lawrence P. Grassini · ⑳ · Grassini & Wrinkle · 20750 Ventura Boulevard, Suite 221 · Woodland Hills, CA 91364 · 818-348-1717

Roland Wrinkle · Grassini & Wrinkle · 20750 Ventura Boulevard, Suite 221 · Woodland Hills, CA 91364 · 818-348-1717

PRIVATE FUNDS LAW

Los Angeles

T. Hale Boggs · ⑩ · Manatt, Phelps & Phillips · 11355 West Olympic Boulevard · Los Angeles, CA 90064 310-312-4000

Gary J. Cohen · Sidley Austin · 555 West Fifth Street, 40th Floor · Los Angeles, CA 90013 · 213-896-6000

Stanley F. Farrar · ⑩ · Sullivan & Cromwell · 1888 Century Park East, 21st Floor · Los Angeles, CA 90067-1725 · 310-712-6600

Frank H. Golay, Jr. · ⑩ · Sullivan & Cromwell · 1888 Century Park East, 21st Floor · Los Angeles, CA 90067-1725 · 310-712-6600

Alison S. Ressler · Sullivan & Cromwell · 1888 Century Park East, 21st Floor · Los Angeles, CA 90067-1725 · 310-712-6600

William P. Wade · ⑩ · K&L Gates · 10100 Santa Monica Boulevard, Seventh Floor · Los Angeles, CA 90067 · 310-552-5000

Bradford P. Weirick · Gibson, Dunn & Crutcher · 333 South Grand Avenue · Los Angeles, CA 90071-3197 · 213-229-7000

Menlo Park

Francis S. Currie · Davis Polk & Wardwell · 1600 El Camino Real · Menlo Park, CA 94025 · 650-752-2000

Palo Alto

John A. Dado · Cooley Godward Kronish · 3175 Hanover Street · Palo Alto, CA 94304-1130 · 650-843-5000

Craig E. Dauchy · ⑩ · Cooley Godward Kronish · 3175 Hanover Street · Palo Alto, CA 94304-1130 · 650-843-5000

Scott D. Miller · Sullivan & Cromwell · 1870 Embarcadero Road · Palo Alto, CA 94303-3308 · 650-461-5600

Michael J. Nooney · Simpson Thacher · 2550 Hanover Street · Palo Alto, CA 94304 · 650-251-5000

John L. Savva · Sullivan & Cromwell · 1870 Embarcadero Road · Palo Alto, CA 94303-3308 · 650-461-5600

Mark P. Tanoury · Cooley Godward Kronish · 3175 Hanover Street · Palo Alto, CA 94304-1130 · 650-843-5000

Sacramento

Charles S. Farman · Morrison & Foerster · http://www.mofo.com · 400 Capitol Mall, Suite 2600 · Sacramento, CA 95814 · 916-448-3200

San Francisco

John P. Broadhurst · Shartsis Friese · http://www.sflaw.com · One Maritime Plaza, 18th Floor · San Francisco, CA 94111 · 415-421-6500

Robert S. Fore · Goodwin Procter · Three Embarcadero Center, 24th Floor · San Francisco, CA 94111 · 415-733-6000

Daniel W. Frank · Cooley Godward Kronish · 101 California Street, Fifth Floor · San Francisco, CA 94111-5800 · 415-693-2000

Ronald B. Moskovitz · Morgan Lewis & Bockius · Spear Street Tower · One Market · San Francisco, CA 94105-1596 · 415-442-1000

Peter M. Phleger · Morgan Lewis & Bockius · Spear Street Tower · One Market · San Francisco, CA 94105-1596 · 415-442-1000

Mark D. Whatley · Howard, Rice, Nemerovski, Canady, Falk & Rabkin · Three Embarcadero Center, Seventh Floor · San Francisco, CA 94111-4024 · 415-434-1600

PRODUCT LIABILITY LITIGATION

Costa Mesa

Robert J. Gibson · Snell & Wilmer · 600 Anton Boulevard, Suite 1400 · Costa Mesa, CA 92626-7689 · 714-427-7000

Gary Wolensky · Snell & Wilmer · 600 Anton Boulevard, Suite 1400 · Costa Mesa, CA 92626-7689 · 714-427-7000

Emeryville

Lori A. Schweitzer · Becherer, Kannett & Schweitzer · 2200 Powell Street, Suite 805 · Emeryville, CA 94608 · 510-658-3600

Long Beach

Dennis M. Elber · ⑩ · Stolpman, Krissman, Elber & Silver · 111 West Ocean Boulevard, 19th Floor · Long Beach, CA 90802 · 562-435-8300

Samuel A. Keesal, Jr. · ⑩ · Keesal, Young & Logan · 400 Oceangate · P.O. Box 1730 · Long Beach, CA 90801-1730 · 562-436-2000

Joel Krissman · Stolpman, Krissman, Elber & Silver · 111 West Ocean Boulevard, 19th Floor · Long Beach, CA 90802 · 562-435-8300

Thomas G. Stolpman · ⑳ · Stolpman, Krissman, Elber & Silver · 111 West Ocean Boulevard, 19th Floor · Long Beach, CA 90802 · 562-435-8300

Los Angeles

Ralph A. Campillo · Sedgwick, Detert, Moran & Arnold · 801 South Figueroa Street, 19th Floor · Los Angeles, CA 90017-5556 · 213-426-6900

Jan E. Dodd · Kaye Scholer · 1999 Avenue of the Stars, Suite 1700 · Los Angeles, CA 90067-6048 · 310-788-1000

Peter Q. Ezzell · Haight, Brown & Bonesteel · 6080 Center Drive, Suite 800 · Los Angeles, CA 90045 · 310-215-7100

Larry R. Feldman · ⑩ · Kaye Scholer · 1999 Avenue of the Stars, Suite 1700 · Los Angeles, CA 90067-6048 · 310-788-1000

Pierce O'Donnell · ⑩ · O'Donnell & Shaeffer · 550 South Hope Street, Suite 1000 · Los Angeles, CA 90071-2627 · 213-347-0290

David J. O'Keefe · ⑳ · Bonne, Bridges, Mueller, O'Keefe & Nichols · http://www.bonnebridges.com · 3699 Wilshire Boulevard, 10th Floor · Los Angeles, CA 90010-2719 · 213-480-1900

Elliott D. Olson · Sedgwick, Detert, Moran & Arnold · 801 South Figueroa Street, 19th Floor · Los Angeles, CA 90017-5556 · 213-426-6900

Brian Panish · Panish Shea & Boyle · 11111 Santa Monica Boulevard, Suite 700 · Los Angeles, CA 90025 · 310-477-1700

Debra E. Pole · Sidley Austin · 555 West Fifth Street, 40th Floor · Los Angeles, CA 90013 · 213-896-6000

Adam K. Shea · Panish Shea & Boyle · 11111 Santa Monica Boulevard, Suite 700 · Los Angeles, CA 90025 · 310-477-1700

Walter M. Yoka · Yoka & Smith · 777 South Figueroa Street, Suite 4200 · Los Angeles, CA 90017 · 213-427-2300

James J. Yukevich · Yukevich Calfo & Cavanaugh · 601 South Figeroua Street, 38th Floor · Los Angeles, CA 90017 · 213-362-7777

Oakland

Gerald C. Sterns · ㉕ · Sterns & Walker · Clocktower Building · 901 Clay Street · Oakland, CA 94607 · 510-267-0500

Sacramento

John M. Poswall · ⑳ · Poswall White & Cutler · 1001 G Street, Suite 301 · Sacramento, CA 95814 · 916-449-1300

San Diego

William S. Boggs · DLA Piper · 401 B Street, Suite 1700 · San Diego, CA 92101-4297 · 619-699-2700

Robert J. Francavilla · Casey, Gerry, Schenk, Francavilla, Blatt & Penfield · http://www.cglaw.com · 110 Laurel Street · San Diego, CA 92101-1486 · 619-238-1811

John H. Gomez · The Gomez Law Firm · http://thegomezfirm.com · 625 Broadway, Suite 600 · San Diego, CA 92101 · 619-237-3490

Lawrence J. Kouns · Luce, Forward, Hamilton & Scripps · http://www.luce.com · 600 West Broadway, Suite 2600 · San Diego, CA 92101 · 619-236-1414

Harvey R. Levine · ⑳ · Levine, Steinberg, Miller & Huver · 550 West C Street, Suite 1810 · San Diego, CA 92101-8596 · 619-231-9449

Don G. Rushing · Morrison & Foerster · http://www.mofo.com · 12531 High Bluff Drive, Suite 100 · San Diego, CA 92130-2040 · 858-720-5100

Dennis A. Schoville · ⑩ · Schoville & Arnell · Carriage House · 2404 Broadway · San Diego, CA 92102 · 619-232-9901

San Francisco

Albert R. Abramson · ㉕ · Abramson Smith Waldsmith · http://www.aswllp.com · 44 Montgomery Street, Suite 3340 · San Francisco, CA 94104 · 415-421-7995

James S. Bostwick · ㉕ · Bostwick & Associates · Four Embarcadero Center, Suite 750 · San Francisco, CA 94111 · 415-421-8300

Kevin J. Dunne · ⑩ · Sedgwick, Detert, Moran & Arnold · Steuart Tower, Eighth Floor · One Market Plaza · San Francisco, CA 94105 · 415-781-7900

Michael F. Healy · Sedgwick, Detert, Moran & Arnold · Steuart Tower, Eighth Floor · One Market Plaza San Francisco, CA 94105 · 415-781-7900

Michael A. Kelly · ⑩ · Walkup, Melodia, Kelly & Schoenberger · http://www.walkuplawoffice.com · 650 California Street, 26th Floor · San Francisco, CA 94108 · 415-981-7210

Charles F. Preuss · Drinker Biddle & Reath · 50 Fremont Street · San Francisco, CA 94105-2235 · 415-591-7500

Gregory C. Read · Sedgwick, Detert, Moran & Arnold · Steuart Tower, Eighth Floor · One Market Plaza San Francisco, CA 94105 · 415-781-7900

Luanne Sacks · DLA Piper · 153 Townsend Street, Suite 800 · San Francisco, CA 94107-1957 · 415-836-2500

N. Kathleen Strickland · Ropers, Majeski, Kohn & Bentley · 201 Spear Street, Suite 1000 · San Francisco, CA 94105 · 415-543-4800

Donald F. Zimmer, Jr. · King & Spalding · Four Embarcadero Center, Suite 3500 · San Francisco, CA 94111 · 415-318-1220

San Mateo

Terry O'Reilly · O'Reilly & Danko · http://www.oreillylaw.com · 1900 O'Farrell Street, Suite 360 · San Mateo, CA 94403 · 650-358-5901

Santa Monica

Bruce A. Broillet · ⑳ · Greene Broillet & Wheeler · http://www.greene-broillet.com · 100 Wilshire Boulevard, 21st Floor · P.O. Box 2131 · Santa Monica, CA 90407 · 310-576-1200

Christine D. Spagnoli · Greene Broillet & Wheeler · http://www.greene-broillet.com · 100 Wilshire Boulevard, 21st Floor · P.O. Box 2131 · Santa Monica, CA 90407 · 310-576-1200

Geoffrey S. Wells · Greene Broillet & Wheeler · http://www.greene-broillet.com · 100 Wilshire Boulevard, 21st Floor · P.O. Box 2131 · Santa Monica, CA 90407 · 310-576-1200

Torrance

Gerald E. Agnew, Jr. · ⑩ · AgnewBrusavich · http://www.agnewbrusavich.com · 20355 Hawthorne Boulevard · Torrance, CA 90503 · 310-793-1400

Bruce M. Brusavich · AgnewBrusavich · http://www.agnewbrusavich.com · 20355 Hawthorne Boulevard · Torrance, CA 90503 · 310-793-1400

Woodland Hills

Lawrence P. Grassini · ⑳ · Grassini & Wrinkle · 20750 Ventura Boulevard, Suite 221 · Woodland Hills, CA 91364 · 818-348-1717

PROFESSIONAL MALPRACTICE LAW

Beverly Hills

James R. Rosen · Law Offices of James R. Rosen · 468 North Camden Drive, Suite 300 · Beverly Hills, CA 90210 · 310-285-1727

Burbank

George E. Peterson · ⑩ · Peterson & Bradford · 100 North First Street, Suite 300 · Burbank, CA 91502-1845 · 818-562-5800

Long Beach

Samuel A. Keesal, Jr. · ⑩ · Keesal, Young & Logan · 400 Oceangate · P.O. Box 1730 · Long Beach, CA 90801-1730 · 562-436-2000

Los Angeles

Larry R. Feldman · ⑩ · Kaye Scholer · 1999 Avenue of the Stars, Suite 1700 · Los Angeles, CA 90067-6048 · 310-788-1000

Steven A. Heimberg · Heimberg Law Group · http://www.heimberglaw.com · 1801 Century Park East, Suite 1920 · Los Angeles, CA 90067-2313 · 310-553-1799

Russell Kussman · ⑩ · Kussman & Whitehill · http://www.kussmanwhitehill.com · 10866 Wilshire Boulevard, Suite 1470 · Los Angeles, CA 90024 · 310-474-4411

Philip Michels · Law Offices of Michels & Watkins · 11755 Wilshire Boulevard, Suite 1300 · Los Angeles, CA 90025-1540 · 310-444-1200

David J. O'Keefe · ⑳ · Bonne, Bridges, Mueller, O'Keefe & Nichols · http://www.bonnebridges.com · 3699 Wilshire Boulevard, 10th Floor · Los Angeles, CA 90010-2719 · 213-480-1900

Sacramento

John M. Poswall · ⑳ · Poswall White & Cutler · 1001 G Street, Suite 301 · Sacramento, CA 95814 · 916-449-1300

Santa Monica

Bruce A. Broillet · ⑳ · Greene Broillet & Wheeler · http://www.greene-broillet.com · 100 Wilshire Boulevard, 21st Floor · P.O. Box 2131 · Santa Monica, CA 90407 · 310-576-1200

Woodland Hills

Lawrence P. Grassini · ⑳ · Grassini & Wrinkle · 20750 Ventura Boulevard, Suite 221 · Woodland Hills, CA 91364 · 818-348-1717

PROJECT FINANCE LAW

Los Angeles

Edwin F. Feo · ⑩ · Milbank, Tweed, Hadley & McCloy · http://www.milbank.com · 601 South Figueroa Street, 30th Floor · Los Angeles, CA 90017-5735 · 213-892-4000

Richard A. Shortz · Morgan Lewis & Bockius · 300 South Grand Avenue, 22nd Floor · Los Angeles, CA 90071-3132 · 213-612-2500

Edward W. Zaelke · Chadbourne & Parke · http://www.chadbourne.com · 350 South Grand Avenue, Suite 3300 · Los Angeles, CA 90071 · 213-892-1000

San Francisco

Thomas B. Glascock · Orrick, Herrington & Sutcliffe · The Orrick Building · 405 Howard Street · San Francisco, CA 94105-2669 · 415-773-5700

George P. Haley · Pillsbury Winthrop Shaw Pittman · http://www.pillsburylaw.com · 50 Fremont Street · P.O. Box 7880 · San Francisco, CA 94120-7880 · 415-983-1000

David C. Spielberg · Orrick, Herrington & Sutcliffe · The Orrick Building · 405 Howard Street · San Francisco, CA 94105-2669 · 415-773-5700

Mark P. Weitzel · Orrick, Herrington & Sutcliffe · The Orrick Building · 405 Howard Street · San Francisco, CA 94105-2669 · 415-773-5700

PUBLIC FINANCE LAW

Davis

Ronald E. Lee · Ronald E. Lee · 803 Second Street, Suite G · Davis, CA 95616 · 530-756-1180

Los Angeles

Eugene J. Carron · Orrick, Herrington & Sutcliffe · 777 South Figueroa Street, Suite 3200 · Los Angeles, CA 90017-5855 · 213-629-2020

Stephen T. Cole · Fulbright & Jaworski · http://www.fulbright.com · 555 South Flower Street, 41st Floor · Los Angeles, CA 90071 · 213-892-9200

Lewis G. Feldman · ⑩ · Goodwin Procter · 10250 Constellation Boulevard, 21st Floor · Los Angeles, CA 90067 · 310-788-5100

Donald L. Hunt · Fulbright & Jaworski · http://www.fulbright.com · 555 South Flower Street, 41st Floor · Los Angeles, CA 90071 · 213-892-9200

Lisalee Anne Wells · Fulbright & Jaworski · http://www.fulbright.com · 555 South Flower Street, 41st Floor · Los Angeles, CA 90071 · 213-892-9200

Sacramento

Perry E. Israel · Law Office of Perry Israel · 3436 American River Drive, Suite Nine · Sacramento, CA 95864 · 916-485-6645

Jenna C. Magan · Orrick, Herrington & Sutcliffe · 400 Capitol Mall, Suite 3000 · Sacramento, CA 95814-4497 · 916-447-9200

John R. Myers · Orrick, Herrington & Sutcliffe · 400 Capitol Mall, Suite 3000 · Sacramento, CA 95814-4497 · 916-447-9200

Diane S. Potter · Orrick, Herrington & Sutcliffe · 400 Capitol Mall, Suite 3000 · Sacramento, CA 95814-4497 · 916-447-9200

San Francisco

Roger L. Davis · Orrick, Herrington & Sutcliffe · The Orrick Building · 405 Howard Street · San Francisco, CA 94105-2669 · 415-773-5700

John H. Knox · Orrick, Herrington & Sutcliffe · The Orrick Building · 405 Howard Street · San Francisco, CA 94105-2669 · 415-773-5700

Gerald J. McGovern · Sidley Austin · 555 California Street, Suite 2000 · San Francisco, CA 94104 · 415-772-1200

Eric D. Tashman · Sidley Austin · 555 California Street, Suite 2000 · San Francisco, CA 94104 · 415-772-1200

REAL ESTATE LAW

Beverly Hills

Lee Silver · Ervin, Cohen & Jessup · 9401 Wilshire Boulevard, Ninth Floor · Beverly Hills, CA 90212-2974 · 310-273-6333

Costa Mesa

Randall M. Babbush · Rutan & Tucker · http://www.rutan.com · 611 Anton Boulevard, Suite 1400 · P.O. Box 1950 · Costa Mesa, CA 92628-1950 · 714-641-5100

Joseph L. Coleman · Snell & Wilmer · 600 Anton Boulevard, Suite 1400 · Costa Mesa, CA 92626-7689 · 714-427-7000

Marcello F. DeFrenza · Garrett DeFrenza Stiepel · Park Tower, Suite 500 · 695 Town Center Drive · Costa Mesa, CA 92626-1924 · 714-384-4300

John C. Garrett · ⑩ · Garrett DeFrenza Stiepel · Park Tower, Suite 500 · 695 Town Center Drive · Costa Mesa, CA 92626-1924 · 714-384-4300

Susan K. Hori · Manatt, Phelps & Phillips · Park Tower, 14th Floor · 695 Town Center Drive · Costa Mesa, CA 92626 · 714-371-2500

Steven A. McHolm · Snell & Wilmer · 600 Anton Boulevard, Suite 1400 · Costa Mesa, CA 92626-7689 · 714-427-7000

John F. Simonis · Paul Hastings · 695 Town Center Drive, 17th Floor · Costa Mesa, CA 92626 · 714-668-6200

Henry R. Stiepel · Garrett DeFrenza Stiepel · Park Tower, Suite 500 · 695 Town Center Drive · Costa Mesa, CA 92626-1924 · 714-384-4300

East Palo Alto

Carol K. Dillon · Bingham McCutchen · http://www.bingham.com · 1900 University Avenue · East Palo Alto, CA 94303-2223 · 650-849-4400

Patrick J. McGaraghan · DLA Piper · 2000 University Avenue · East Palo Alto, CA 94303-2214 · 650-833-2000

Toni P. Wise · Greenberg Traurig · http://www.gtlaw.com · 1900 University Avenue, Fifth Floor · East Palo Alto, CA 94303 · 650-328-8500

Encino

Herbert J. Strickstein · ㉕ · Herbert J. Strickstein · 16633 Ventura Boulevard, Suite 1400 · Encino, CA 91436 · 310-553-4888

Irvine

Gary S. McKitterick · Allen Matkins Leck Gamble Mallory & Natsis · 1900 Main Street, Fifth Floor · Irvine, CA 92614-7321 · 949-553-1313

John C. Murphy · Luce, Forward, Hamilton & Scripps · http://www.luce.com · 2040 Main Street, Suite 600 · Irvine, CA 92614 · 949-732-3700

Richard S. Ruben · Jones Day · Three Park Plaza, Suite 1100 · Irvine, CA 92614-2592 · 949-851-3939

Arthur O. Spaulding, Jr. · Cox, Castle & Nicholson · 19800 MacArthur Boulevard, Suite 500 · Irvine, CA 92612 · 949-476-2111

Los Angeles

Frederick L. Allen · ⑳ · Allen Matkins Leck Gamble Mallory & Natsis · 515 South Figueroa Street, Ninth Floor · Los Angeles, CA 90071-3398 · 213-622-5555

Keith A. Allen-Niesen · Manatt, Phelps & Phillips · 11355 West Olympic Boulevard · Los Angeles, CA 90064 · 310-312-4000

Rand S. April · Skadden, Arps, Slate, Meagher & Flom · 300 South Grand Avenue, Suite 3400 · Los Angeles, CA 90071 · 213-687-5000

Dennis B. Arnold · ⑩ · Gibson, Dunn & Crutcher · 333 South Grand Avenue · Los Angeles, CA 90071-3197 · 213-229-7000

Don Berger · Latham & Watkins · 355 South Grand Avenue · Los Angeles, CA 90071-1560 · 213-485-1234

Margaret Frick Bertisch · Kennerly Lamishaw & Rossi · 707 Wilshire Boulevard, Suite 1400 · Los Angeles, CA 90071 · 213-312-1250

Kenneth B. Bley · ⑩ · Cox, Castle & Nicholson · 2049 Century Park East, 28th Floor · Los Angeles, CA 90067 · 310-277-4222

Linda J. Bozung · DLA Piper · 1999 Avenue of the Stars, Suite 400 · Los Angeles, CA 90067-6023 · 310-595-3000

Stevens A. Carey · Pircher, Nichols & Meeks · 1925 Century Park East, 17th Floor · Los Angeles, CA 90067 · 310-201-8900

Anthony Ciasulli · Morgan Lewis & Bockius · 300 South Grand Avenue, 22nd Floor · Los Angeles, CA 90071-3132 · 213-612-2500

Stephen Claman · ⑳ · Greenberg Glusker · 1900 Avenue of the Stars, 21st Floor · Los Angeles, CA 90067 · 310-553-3610

William F. Delvac · Latham & Watkins · 355 South Grand Avenue · Los Angeles, CA 90071-1560 · 213-485-1234

Louis P. Eatman · ⑩ · Proskauer Rose · http://www.proskauer.com · 2049 Century Park East, 32nd Floor · Los Angeles, CA 90067-3206 · 310-557-2900

Robert M. Eller · ⑳ · Manatt, Phelps & Phillips · 11355 West Olympic Boulevard · Los Angeles, CA 90064 · 310-312-4000

Aaftab Esmail · Bocarsly, Emden, Cowan, Esmail, Parker & Arndt · 633 West Fifth Street, 70th Floor · Los Angeles, CA 90071 · 213-239-8000

Philip N. Feder · Paul Hastings · 515 South Flower Street, 25th Floor · Los Angeles, CA 90071 · 213-683-6000

Steven A. Fein · DLA Piper · 550 South Hope Street, Suite 2300 · Los Angeles, CA 90071-2678 · 213-330-7700

Lewis G. Feldman · ⑩ · Goodwin Procter · 10250 Constellation Boulevard, 21st Floor · Los Angeles, CA 90067 · 310-788-5100

Thomas R. Fileti · Morrison & Foerster · http://www.mofo.com · 555 West Fifth Street, Suite 3500 · Los Angeles, CA 90013-1024 · 213-892-5200

Amy R. Forbes · Gibson, Dunn & Crutcher · 2029 Century Park East, 40th Floor · Los Angeles, CA 90067-3026 · 310-552-8500

Douglas B. Frank · Proskauer Rose · http://www.proskauer.com · 2049 Century Park East, 32nd Floor · Los Angeles, CA 90067-3206 · 310-557-2900

Bruce W. Fraser · Sidley Austin · 555 West Fifth Street, 40th Floor · Los Angeles, CA 90013 · 213-896-6000

Gary A. Glick · Cox, Castle & Nicholson · 2049 Century Park East, 28th Floor · Los Angeles, CA 90067 · 310-277-4222

Timi A. Hallem · Manatt, Phelps & Phillips · 11355 West Olympic Boulevard · Los Angeles, CA 90064 · 310-312-4000

Louis A. Huskins · ⑳ · Irell & Manella · 1800 Avenue of the Stars, Suite 900 · Los Angeles, CA 90067-4276 · 310-277-1010

Ursula H. Hyman · Latham & Watkins · 355 South Grand Avenue · Los Angeles, CA 90071-1560 · 213-485-1234

Sandra Gerson Kanengiser · Irell & Manella · 1800 Avenue of the Stars, Suite 900 · Los Angeles, CA 90067-4276 · 310-277-1010

Nancy N. Kennerly · Kennerly Lamishaw & Rossi · 707 Wilshire Boulevard, Suite 1400 · Los Angeles, CA 90071 · 213-312-1250

Michael S. Klein · Klein & Weisz · 12401 Wilshire Boulevard, Second Floor · Los Angeles, CA 90025 · 310-447-7000

John H. Kuhl · Cox, Castle & Nicholson · 2049 Century Park East, 28th Floor · Los Angeles, CA 90067 · 310-277-4222

Matt Lamishaw · Kennerly Lamishaw & Rossi · 707 Wilshire Boulevard, Suite 1400 · Los Angeles, CA 90071 · 213-312-1250

Gary M. Laughlin · Pircher, Nichols & Meeks · 1925 Century Park East, 17th Floor · Los Angeles, CA 90067 · 310-201-8900

Thomas J. Leanse · Katten Muchin Rosenman · 2029 Century Park East, Suite 2600 · Los Angeles, CA 90067-3012 · 310-788-4400

Marvin Leon · ㉕ · Mitchell Silberberg & Knupp · 11377 West Olympic Boulevard · Los Angeles, CA 90064 · 310-312-2000

Michael L. Matkins · ⑳ · Allen Matkins Leck Gamble Mallory & Natsis · 515 South Figueroa Street, Ninth Floor · Los Angeles, CA 90071-3398 · 213-622-5555

Richard C. Mendelson · DLA Piper · 550 South Hope Street, Suite 2300 · Los Angeles, CA 90071-2678 · 213-330-7700

Michael E. Meyer · ⑳ · DLA Piper · 550 South Hope Street, Suite 2300 · Los Angeles, CA 90071-2678 · 213-330-7700

George J. Mihlsten · ⑩ · Latham & Watkins · 355 South Grand Avenue · Los Angeles, CA 90071-1560 · 213-485-1234

O'Malley M. Miller · ⑳ · Munger, Tolles & Olson · 355 South Grand Avenue, 35th Floor · Los Angeles, CA 90071-1560 · 213-683-9100

Allan G. Mutchnik · Skadden, Arps, Slate, Meagher & Flom · 300 South Grand Avenue, Suite 3400 · Los Angeles, CA 90071 · 213-687-5000

Anton N. Natsis · ⑩ · Allen Matkins Leck Gamble Mallory & Natsis · 1901 Avenue of the Stars, Suite 1800 · Los Angeles, CA 90067-6019 · 310-788-2400

Phillip G. Nichols · Pircher, Nichols & Meeks · 1925 Century Park East, 17th Floor · Los Angeles, CA 90067 · 310-201-8900

Dean C. Pappas · Goodwin Procter · 10250 Constellation Boulevard, 21st Floor · Los Angeles, CA 90067 310-788-5100

Leo J. Pircher · ㉕ · Pircher, Nichols & Meeks · 1925 Century Park East, 17th Floor · Los Angeles, CA 90067 · 310-201-8900

Patrick A. Ramsey · ⑩ · Paul Hastings · 515 South Flower Street, 25th Floor · Los Angeles, CA 90071 · 213-683-6000

James D. Richman · Arnold & Porter · 777 South Figueroa Street, 44th Floor · Los Angeles, CA 90017-5844 · 213-243-4000

James M. Rishwain, Jr. · Pillsbury Winthrop Shaw Pittman · http://www.pillsburylaw.com · 725 South Figueroa Street, Suite 2800 · Los Angeles, CA 90017-5406 · 213-488-7100

Michael E. Scheinberg · Pircher, Nichols & Meeks · 1925 Century Park East, 17th Floor · Los Angeles, CA 90067 · 310-201-8900

Thomas R. Sestanovich · Moldo Davidson Fraioli Seror & Sestanovich · 2029 Century Park East, 21st Floor · Los Angeles, CA 90067 · 310-551-3100

Michael F. Sfregola · Gibson, Dunn & Crutcher · 333 South Grand Avenue · Los Angeles, CA 90071-3197 · 213-229-7000

Jesse Sharf · ⑩ · Gibson, Dunn & Crutcher · 2029 Century Park East, 40th Floor · Los Angeles, CA 90067-3026 · 310-552-8500

Betty M. Shumener · DLA Piper · 550 South Hope Street, Suite 2300 · Los Angeles, CA 90071-2678 · 213-330-7700

Ronald I. Silverman · ⑩ · Cox, Castle & Nicholson · 2049 Century Park East, 28th Floor · Los Angeles, CA 90067 · 310-277-4222

Stephanie C. Silvers · Pircher, Nichols & Meeks · 1925 Century Park East, 17th Floor · Los Angeles, CA 90067 · 310-201-8900

Michael G. Smooke · ⑩ · Fulbright & Jaworski · http://www.fulbright.com · 555 South Flower Street, 41st Floor · Los Angeles, CA 90071 · 213-892-9200

John M. Tipton · Allen Matkins Leck Gamble Mallory & Natsis · 1901 Avenue of the Stars, Suite 1800 · Los Angeles, CA 90067-6019 · 310-788-2400

Richard S. Volpert · ㉕ · Munger, Tolles & Olson · 355 South Grand Avenue, 35th Floor · Los Angeles, CA 90071-1560 · 213-683-9100

Ira J. Waldman · Cox, Castle & Nicholson · 2049 Century Park East, 28th Floor · Los Angeles, CA 90067 310-277-4222

Paul R. Walker · ⑳ · Sidley Austin · 555 West Fifth Street, 40th Floor · Los Angeles, CA 90013 · 213-896-6000

William S. Waller · Pillsbury Winthrop Shaw Pittman · http://www.pillsburylaw.com · 725 South Figueroa Street, Suite 2800 · Los Angeles, CA 90017-5406 · 213-488-7100

Alan Wayte · ㉕ · DLA Piper · 550 South Hope Street, Suite 2300 · Los Angeles, CA 90071-2678 · 213-330-7700

Peter M. Weil · Christensen, Glaser, Fink, Jacobs, Weil & Shapiro · 10250 Constellation Boulevard, 19th Floor · Los Angeles, CA 90067 · 310-553-3000

Pamela Lynne Westhoff · DLA Piper · 550 South Hope Street, Suite 2300 · Los Angeles, CA 90071-2678 213-330-7700

Benzion J. Westreich · Katten Muchin Rosenman · 2029 Century Park East, Suite 2600 · Los Angeles, CA 90067-3012 · 310-788-4400

John W. Whitaker · ⑳ · DLA Piper · 550 South Hope Street, Suite 2300 · Los Angeles, CA 90071-2678 · 213-330-7700

Robert E. Williams · ⑩ · Sheppard, Mullin, Richter & Hampton · http://www.sheppardmullin.com · 333 South Hope Street, 48th Floor · Los Angeles, CA 90071-1448 · 213-620-1780

Mathew A. Wyman · Cox, Castle & Nicholson · 2049 Century Park East, 28th Floor · Los Angeles, CA 90067 · 310-277-4222

Newport Beach

Alan J. Droste · King Parret & Droste · 450 Newport Center Drive, Suite 500 · Newport Beach, CA 92660 · 949-644-3400

Roy S. Geiger · Irell & Manella · 840 Newport Center Drive, Suite 400 · Newport Beach, CA 92660-6324 949-760-0991

Anthony W. Pierotti · Irell & Manella · 840 Newport Center Drive, Suite 400 · Newport Beach, CA 92660-6324 · 949-760-0991

Richard M. Sherman, Jr. · Irell & Manella · 840 Newport Center Drive, Suite 400 · Newport Beach, CA 92660-6324 · 949-760-0991

Oakland

Michael A. Dean · ㉕ · Wendel, Rosen, Black & Dean · 1111 Broadway, 24th Floor · P.O. Box 2047 · Oakland, CA 94604-2047 · 510-834-6600

Charles A. Hansen · Wendel, Rosen, Black & Dean · 1111 Broadway, 24th Floor · P.O. Box 2047 · Oakland, CA 94604-2047 · 510-834-6600

Orinda

John R. Hetland · ⑩ · Hetland & Kneeland · 20 Redcoach Lane · Orinda, CA 94563 · 510-548-5900

Palo Alto

Philip J. Levine · Morrison & Foerster · http://www.mofo.com · 755 Page Mill Road · Palo Alto, CA 94304-1018 · 650-813-5600

Bradford C. O'Brien · Wilson Sonsini Goodrich & Rosati · 650 Page Mill Road · Palo Alto, CA 94304-1050 · 650-493-9300

David M. Van Atta · Hanna & Van Atta · 525 University Avenue, Suite 705 · Palo Alto, CA 94301-1921 · 650-321-5700

Pope Valley

Reverdy Johnson · ⑳ · Reverdy Johnson · 6027 Pope Valley Road · P.O. Box 145 · Pope Valley, CA 94567-0145 · 707-965-3430

Rancho Santa Fe

Eric O. Freeberg · ⑩ · Eric O. Freeberg · 14639 Calle Carla · P.O. Box 9440 · Rancho Santa Fe, CA 92067-4440 · 858-756-6632

Riverside

Frank J. Delany · The Law Offices of Frank J. Delany · 3801 University Avenue, Suite 260 · Riverside, CA 92501 · 951-682-9260

Roseville

Curtis C. Sproul · Sproul Trost · 3721 Douglas Boulevard, Suite 300 · Roseville, CA 95661 · 916-783-6262

Sacramento

Russell J. Austin · ⑩ · Murphy Austin Adams Schoenfeld · http://www.murphyaustin.com · 304 S Street · P.O. Box 1319 · Sacramento, CA 95812-1319 · 916-446-2300

John V. Diepenbrock · ⑳ · Diepenbrock Harrison · 400 Capitol Mall, Suite 1800 · Sacramento, CA 95814 · 916-446-4469

Karen L. Diepenbrock · Diepenbrock Harrison · 400 Capitol Mall, Suite 1800 · Sacramento, CA 95814 · 916-446-4469

Patricia D. Elliott · McDonough Holland & Allen · http://www.mhalaw.com · 555 Capitol Mall, Ninth Floor · Sacramento, CA 95814-4692 · 916-444-3900

Jeffry R. Jones · McDonough Holland & Allen · http://www.mhalaw.com · 555 Capitol Mall, Ninth Floor Sacramento, CA 95814-4692 · 916-444-3900

Larry L. Rader · ⑩ · Rader, Rader, Goulart & Gray · 2617 K Street, Suite 200 · Sacramento, CA 95816-5185 · 916-446-7577

David J. Spottiswood · ⑩ · McDonough Holland & Allen · http://www.mhalaw.com · 555 Capitol Mall, Ninth Floor · Sacramento, CA 95814-4692 · 916-444-3900

Charles W. Trainor · Trainor Fairbrook · 980 Fulton Avenue · P.O. Box 255824 · Sacramento, CA 95865 · 916-929-7000

San Diego

David W. Bagley II · Hecht Solberg Robinson Goldberg & Bagley · One America Plaza, Eighth Floor · 600 West Broadway · San Diego, CA 92101 · 619-239-3444

Robert J. Bell · Luce, Forward, Hamilton & Scripps · http://www.luce.com · 600 West Broadway, Suite 2600 · San Diego, CA 92101 · 619-236-1414

Robert D. Buell · Luce, Forward, Hamilton & Scripps · http://www.luce.com · 600 West Broadway, Suite 2600 · San Diego, CA 92101 · 619-236-1414

Robert Caplan · ㉕ · Seltzer Caplan McMahon Vitek · Symphony Towers, Suite 2100 · 750 B Street · San Diego, CA 92101 · 619-685-3003

Jeffrey A. Chine · Luce, Forward, Hamilton & Scripps · http://www.luce.com · 600 West Broadway, Suite 2600 · San Diego, CA 92101 · 619-236-1414

Susan L. Daly · Hecht Solberg Robinson Goldberg & Bagley · One America Plaza, Eighth Floor · 600 West Broadway · San Diego, CA 92101 · 619-239-3444

James R. Dawe · ⑩ · Seltzer Caplan McMahon Vitek · Symphony Towers, Suite 2100 · 750 B Street · San Diego, CA 92101 · 619-685-3003

Brian C. Fish · Luce, Forward, Hamilton & Scripps · http://www.luce.com · 600 West Broadway, Suite 2600 · San Diego, CA 92101 · 619-236-1414

Gordon L. Gerson · Gerson Law Firm · http://www.gersonlaw.com · 9255 Towne Centre Drive, Suite 300 · San Diego, CA 92121 · 858-452-5400

Louis E. Goebel · ㉕ · Law Offices of Louis E. Goebel · 110 West A Street, Suite 600 · San Diego, CA 92101 · 619-239-2611

Mark Hagarty · Luce, Forward, Hamilton & Scripps · http://www.luce.com · 600 West Broadway, Suite 2600 · San Diego, CA 92101 · 619-236-1414

A. John Hecht · Hecht Solberg Robinson Goldberg & Bagley · One America Plaza, Eighth Floor · 600 West Broadway · San Diego, CA 92101 · 619-239-3444

Valentine S. Hoy · Luce, Forward, Hamilton & Scripps · http://www.luce.com · 600 West Broadway, Suite 2600 · San Diego, CA 92101 · 619-236-1414

Gregory Dean Judkins · Judkins Glatt & Hulme · 530 B Street, Suite 1800 · San Diego, CA 92101 · 619-232-4604

Richard L. Kintz · ⑳ · Sheppard, Mullin, Richter & Hampton · http://www.sheppardmullin.com · 12275 El Camino Real, Suite 200 · San Diego, CA 92130 · 858-720-8900

Paul E. Robinson · Hecht Solberg Robinson Goldberg & Bagley · One America Plaza, Eighth Floor · 600 West Broadway · San Diego, CA 92101 · 619-239-3444

Nancy T. Scull · ⑩ · Luce, Forward, Hamilton & Scripps · http://www.luce.com · 600 West Broadway, Suite 2600 · San Diego, CA 92101 · 619-236-1414

Brian T. Seltzer · Seltzer Caplan McMahon Vitek · Symphony Towers, Suite 2100 · 750 B Street · San Diego, CA 92101 · 619-685-3003

Bruce P. Shepherd · Latham & Watkins · 600 West Broadway, Suite 1800 · San Diego, CA 92101-3375 · 619-236-1234

Steven M. Strauss · Cooley Godward Kronish · 4401 Eastgate Mall · San Diego, CA 92121-1909 · 858-550-6000

Steven S. Wall · Luce, Forward, Hamilton & Scripps · http://www.luce.com · 600 West Broadway, Suite 2600 · San Diego, CA 92101 · 619-236-1414

Karen M. ZoBell · DLA Piper · 401 B Street, Suite 1700 · San Diego, CA 92101-4297 · 619-699-2700

San Francisco

Peter Aitelli · Morrison & Foerster · http://www.mofo.com · 425 Market Street · San Francisco, CA 94105-2482 · 415-268-7000

Timothy N. Brown · ⑩ · Timothy N. Brown · 70 Clifford Terrace · San Francisco, CA 94117 · 415-753-2629

Leslie M. Browne · ⑩ · Ellman Burke Hoffman & Johnson · 601 California Street, 19th Floor · San Francisco, CA 94108 · 415-777-2727

Michael J. Burke · Ellman Burke Hoffman & Johnson · 601 California Street, 19th Floor · San Francisco, CA 94108 · 415-777-2727

Stephen K. Cassidy · ㉕ · Cassidy, Shimko, Dawson & Kawakami · 20 California Street, Suite 500 · San Francisco, CA 94111 · 415-788-2040

Paul Churchill · Goodwin Procter · Three Embarcadero Center, 24th Floor · San Francisco, CA 94111 · 415-733-6000

William K. Coblentz · ㉕ · Coblentz, Patch, Duffy & Bass · http://www.coblentzlaw.com · One Ferry Building, Suite 200 · San Francisco, CA 94111-4213 · 415-391-4800

Stephen A. Cowan · ㉕ · DLA Piper · 153 Townsend Street, Suite 800 · San Francisco, CA 94107-1957 · 415-836-2500

Pamela S. Duffy · ⑩ · Coblentz, Patch, Duffy & Bass · http://www.coblentzlaw.com · One Ferry Building, Suite 200 · San Francisco, CA 94111-4213 · 415-391-4800

Howard N. Ellman · ㉕ · Ellman Burke Hoffman & Johnson · 601 California Street, 19th Floor · San Francisco, CA 94108 · 415-777-2727

Craig B. Etlin · Morrison & Foerster · http://www.mofo.com · 425 Market Street · San Francisco, CA 94105-2482 · 415-268-7000

Stephen R. Finn · ㉕ · Morgan Lewis & Bockius · Spear Street Tower · One Market · San Francisco, CA 94105-1596 · 415-442-1000

M. Manuel Fishman · Cooley Godward Kronish · 101 California Street, Fifth Floor · San Francisco, CA 94111-5800 · 415-693-2000

John C. Gamble · ⑩ · Allen Matkins Leck Gamble Mallory & Natsis · Three Embarcadero Center, 12th Floor · San Francisco, CA 94111-4074 · 415-837-1515

Robert C. Herr · ⑳ · Pillsbury Winthrop Shaw Pittman · http://www.pillsburylaw.com · 50 Fremont Street · P.O. Box 7880 · San Francisco, CA 94120-7880 · 415-983-1000

Bruce W. Hyman · ㉕ · Allen Matkins Leck Gamble Mallory & Natsis · Three Embarcadero Center, 12th Floor · San Francisco, CA 94111-4074 · 415-837-1515

David H. Kremer · ⑩ · Shartsis Friese · http://www.sflaw.com · One Maritime Plaza, 18th Floor · San Francisco, CA 94111 · 415-421-6500

Michael H. Liever · Orrick, Herrington & Sutcliffe · The Orrick Building · 405 Howard Street · San Francisco, CA 94105-2669 · 415-773-5700

Richard C. Mallory · ⑳ · Allen Matkins Leck Gamble Mallory & Natsis · Three Embarcadero Center, 12th Floor · San Francisco, CA 94111-4074 · 415-837-1515

R. Clark Morrison · Cox, Castle & Nicholson · 555 California Street, 10th Floor · San Francisco, CA 94104 · 415-392-4200

Mary G. Murphy · Gibson, Dunn & Crutcher · Post Montgomery Center, Suite 3100 · One Montgomery Street · San Francisco, CA 94104-4505 · 415-393-8200

William G. Murray, Jr. · ⑩ · Orrick, Herrington & Sutcliffe · The Orrick Building · 405 Howard Street · San Francisco, CA 94105-2669 · 415-773-5700

Noel W. Nellis · ㉕ · Orrick, Herrington & Sutcliffe · The Orrick Building · 405 Howard Street · San Francisco, CA 94105-2669 · 415-773-5700

Harry O'Brien · Coblentz, Patch, Duffy & Bass · http://www.coblentzlaw.com · One Ferry Building, Suite 200 · San Francisco, CA 94111-4213 · 415-391-4800

Jay L. Paxton · Ellman Burke Hoffman & Johnson · 601 California Street, 19th Floor · San Francisco, CA 94108 · 415-777-2727

Alan J. Robin · Shartsis Friese · http://www.sflaw.com · One Maritime Plaza, 18th Floor · San Francisco, CA 94111 · 415-421-6500

Richard H. Rosenthal · Cox, Castle & Nicholson · 555 California Street, 10th Floor · San Francisco, CA 94104 · 415-392-4200

Charles H. Seaman · ⑩ · Reed Smith · Two Embarcadero Center, Suite 2000 · San Francisco, CA 94111 · 415-543-8700

Brian D. Smith · Heller Ehrman · 333 Bush Street · San Francisco, CA 94104-2878 · 415-772-6000

James R. Stillman · Ellman Burke Hoffman & Johnson · 601 California Street, 19th Floor · San Francisco, CA 94108 · 415-777-2727

Robert A. Thompson · ㉕ · Sheppard, Mullin, Richter & Hampton · http://www.sheppardmullin.com · Four Embarcadero Center, 17th Floor · San Francisco, CA 94111 · 415-434-9100

Charles V. Thornton · ㉕ · Paul Hastings · 55 Second Street, 24th Floor · San Francisco, CA 94105 · 415-856-7000

Scott C. Verges · ⑩ · MBV Law · 855 Front Street · San Francisco, CA 94111 · 415-781-4400

Caryl B. Welborn · ⑩ · DLA Piper · 153 Townsend Street, Suite 800 · San Francisco, CA 94107-1957 · 415-836-2500

Michael H. Zischke · Cox, Castle & Nicholson · 555 California Street, 10th Floor · San Francisco, CA 94104 · 415-392-4200

San Jose

Sanford A. Berliner · ⑩ · Berliner Cohen · 10 Almaden Boulevard, 11th Floor · San Jose, CA 95113-2233 408-286-5800

Geoffrey C. Etnire · Hoge, Fenton, Jones & Appel · http://www.hogefenton.com · 60 South Market Street, Suite 1400 · San Jose, CA 95113-2396 · 408-287-9501

Samuel L. Farb · Berliner Cohen · 10 Almaden Boulevard, 11th Floor · San Jose, CA 95113-2233 · 408-286-5800

Michael D. McSweeney · Hoge, Fenton, Jones & Appel · http://www.hogefenton.com · 60 South Market Street, Suite 1400 · San Jose, CA 95113-2396 · 408-287-9501

San Rafael

Gary T. Ragghianti · Ragghianti Freitas · 874 Fourth Street, Suite D · San Rafael, CA 94901-3246 · 415-453-9433

Santa Monica

Jonathan S. Gross · Gilchrist & Rutter · 1299 Ocean Avenue, Suite 900 · Santa Monica, CA 90401 · 310-393-4000

Paul S. Rutter · ⑩ · Gilchrist & Rutter · 1299 Ocean Avenue, Suite 900 · Santa Monica, CA 90401 · 310-393-4000

William S. Small · Bingham McCutchen · http://www.bingham.com · The Water Garden, Fourth Floor · 1620 Twenty-Sixth Street · Santa Monica, CA 90404-4060 · 310-907-1000

Santa Rosa

James L. Beyers · Beyers Costin · 200 Fourth Street, Suite 400 · Santa Rosa, CA 95402 · 707-547-2000

Clayton E. Clement · Clement, Fitzpatrick & Kenworthy · 3333 Mendocino Avenue · Santa Rosa, CA 95403 · 707-523-1181

Christopher G. Costin · Beyers Costin · 200 Fourth Street, Suite 400 · Santa Rosa, CA 95402 · 707-547-2000

Randall Kenworthy · Clement, Fitzpatrick & Kenworthy · 3333 Mendocino Avenue · Santa Rosa, CA 95403 · 707-523-1181

Solana Beach

Michael E. Gleason · ⑩ · Gleason & Gleason · 777 South Highway 101, Suite 123 · Solana Beach, CA 92075 · 858-350-0572

Walnut Creek

James M. Frassetto · Miller, Starr & Regalia · 1331 North California Boulevard, Fifth Floor · P.O. Box 8177 · Walnut Creek, CA 94596 · 925-935-9400

Edward S. Merrill · Bingham McCutchen · http://www.bingham.com · 1333 North California Boulevard, Suite 210 · Walnut Creek, CA 94596-1270 · 925-937-8000

Eugene H. Miller · Miller, Starr & Regalia · 1331 North California Boulevard, Fifth Floor · P.O. Box 8177 Walnut Creek, CA 94596 · 925-935-9400

Edmund L. Regalia · ⑩ · Miller, Starr & Regalia · 1331 North California Boulevard, Fifth Floor · P.O. Box 8177 · Walnut Creek, CA 94596 · 925-935-9400

Gary E. Rosenberg · Miller, Starr & Regalia · 1331 North California Boulevard, Fifth Floor · P.O. Box 8177 · Walnut Creek, CA 94596 · 925-935-9400

George Speir · Miller, Starr & Regalia · 1331 North California Boulevard, Fifth Floor · P.O. Box 8177 · Walnut Creek, CA 94596 · 925-935-9400

Marvin B. Starr · ㉕ · Miller, Starr & Regalia · 1331 North California Boulevard, Fifth Floor · P.O. Box 8177 · Walnut Creek, CA 94596 · 925-935-9400

Wilson F. Wendt · Miller, Starr & Regalia · 1331 North California Boulevard, Fifth Floor · P.O. Box 8177 Walnut Creek, CA 94596 · 925-935-9400

SECURITIES LAW

East Palo Alto

John Howard Clowes · DLA Piper · 2000 University Avenue · East Palo Alto, CA 94303-2214 · 650-833-2000

Gregory M. Gallo · ⑩ · DLA Piper · 2000 University Avenue · East Palo Alto, CA 94303-2214 · 650-833-2000

Dennis C. Sullivan · DLA Piper · 2000 University Avenue · East Palo Alto, CA 94303-2214 · 650-833-2000

Long Beach

Michael M. Gless · ⑩ · Keesal, Young & Logan · 400 Oceangate · P.O. Box 1730 · Long Beach, CA 90801-1730 · 562-436-2000

Los Angeles

Kenneth J. Baronsky · Milbank, Tweed, Hadley & McCloy · http://www.milbank.com · 601 South Figueroa Street, 30th Floor · Los Angeles, CA 90017-5735 · 213-892-4000

Jennifer Bellah Maguire · Gibson, Dunn & Crutcher · 333 South Grand Avenue · Los Angeles, CA 90071-3197 · 213-229-7000

Joel M. Bernstein · McDermott Will & Emery · 2049 Century Park East, 38th Floor · Los Angeles, CA 90067-3218 · 310-277-4110

Karen E. Bertero · Gibson, Dunn & Crutcher · 333 South Grand Avenue · Los Angeles, CA 90071-3197 · 213-229-7000

Neal H. Brockmeyer · ㉕ · Heller Ehrman · 333 South Hope Street, 39th Floor · Los Angeles, CA 90071-1406 · 213-689-0200

Robert R. Carlson · ㉕ · Paul Hastings · 515 South Flower Street, 25th Floor · Los Angeles, CA 90071 · 213-683-6000

Hillel T. Cohn · Morrison & Foerster · http://www.mofo.com · 555 West Fifth Street, Suite 3500 · Los Angeles, CA 90013-1024 · 213-892-5200

Michael J. Connell · ㉕ · Quateman · 1801 Century Park East, Suite 1801 · Los Angeles, CA 90067 · 310-556-7755

Stanley F. Farrar · ⑩ · Sullivan & Cromwell · 1888 Century Park East, 21st Floor · Los Angeles, CA 90067-1725 · 310-712-6600

Ronald L. Fein · ㉕ · RL Fein · 1901 Avenue of The Stars, 12th Floor · Los Angeles, CA 90067 · 310-228-5780

Ronald K. Fujikawa · Greenberg Glusker · 1900 Avenue of the Stars, 21st Floor · Los Angeles, CA 90067 310-553-3610

Frank H. Golay, Jr. · ⑩ · Sullivan & Cromwell · 1888 Century Park East, 21st Floor · Los Angeles, CA 90067-1725 · 310-712-6600

Steven L. Grossman · O'Melveny & Myers · 1999 Avenue of the Stars, Seventh Floor · Los Angeles, CA 90067-6035 · 310-553-6700

Theodore E. Guth · ⑩ · Manatt, Phelps & Phillips · 11355 West Olympic Boulevard · Los Angeles, CA 90064 · 310-312-4000

John F. Hartigan · ⑩ · Morgan Lewis & Bockius · 300 South Grand Avenue, 22nd Floor · Los Angeles, CA 90071-3132 · 213-612-2500

J. Scott Hodgkins · Latham & Watkins · 355 South Grand Avenue · Los Angeles, CA 90071-1560 · 213-485-1234

Pamela B. Kelly · Latham & Watkins · 355 South Grand Avenue · Los Angeles, CA 90071-1560 · 213-485-1234

Theodore H. Latty · Hughes Hubbard & Reed · http://www.hugheshubbard.com · 350 South Grand Avenue, Suite 3600 · Los Angeles, CA 90071-3442 · 213-613-2800

Jonathan K. Layne · Gibson, Dunn & Crutcher · 2029 Century Park East, 40th Floor · Los Angeles, CA 90067-3026 · 310-552-8500

Brian J. McCarthy · Skadden, Arps, Slate, Meagher & Flom · 300 South Grand Avenue, Suite 3400 · Los Angeles, CA 90071 · 213-687-5000

Frederick B. McLane · ⑩ · O'Melveny & Myers · 1999 Avenue of the Stars, Seventh Floor · Los Angeles, CA 90067-6035 · 310-553-6700

Gregg A. Noel · Skadden, Arps, Slate, Meagher & Flom · 300 South Grand Avenue, Suite 3400 · Los Angeles, CA 90071 · 213-687-5000

Alison S. Ressler · Sullivan & Cromwell · 1888 Century Park East, 21st Floor · Los Angeles, CA 90067-1725 · 310-712-6600

Cynthia A. Rotell · Latham & Watkins · 355 South Grand Avenue · Los Angeles, CA 90071-1560 · 213-485-1234

Nicholas P. Saggese · Skadden, Arps, Slate, Meagher & Flom · 300 South Grand Avenue, Suite 3400 · Los Angeles, CA 90071 · 213-687-5000

Dale E. Short · TroyGould · http://www.troygould.com · 1801 Century Park East, Suite 1600 · Los Angeles, CA 90067 · 310-553-4441

Edward Sonnenschein, Jr. · Latham & Watkins · 355 South Grand Avenue · Los Angeles, CA 90071-1560 · 213-485-1234

Mark A. Stegemoeller · Latham & Watkins · 355 South Grand Avenue · Los Angeles, CA 90071-1560 · 213-485-1234

John B. Watkins · WilmerHale · http://www.wilmerhale.com · 350 South Grand Avenue, Suite 2100 · Los Angeles, CA 90071 · 213-443-5300

Menlo Park

Francis S. Currie · Davis Polk & Wardwell · 1600 El Camino Real · Menlo Park, CA 94025 · 650-752-2000

Bruce K. Dallas · Davis Polk & Wardwell · 1600 El Camino Real · Menlo Park, CA 94025 · 650-752-2000

Paul H. Dawes · ⑩ · Latham & Watkins · 140 Scott Drive · Menlo Park, CA 94025 · 650-328-4600

Alan F. Denenberg · Davis Polk & Wardwell · 1600 El Camino Real · Menlo Park, CA 94025 · 650-752-2000

Christopher L. Kaufman · ㉕ · Latham & Watkins · 140 Scott Drive · Menlo Park, CA 94025 · 650-328-4600

Donald M. Keller, Jr. · Orrick, Herrington & Sutcliffe · 1000 Marsh Road · Menlo Park, CA 94025-1015 · 650-614-7400

Alan C. Mendelson · ⑩ · Latham & Watkins · 140 Scott Drive · Menlo Park, CA 94025 · 650-328-4600

Brooks Stough · Gunderson Dettmer Stough Villeneuve Franklin & Hachigian · 155 Constitution Drive · Menlo Park, CA 94025 · 650-321-2400

Edward J. Wes, Jr. · Perkins Coie · http://www.perkinscoie.com · 101 Jefferson Drive · Menlo Park, CA 94025-1114 · 650-838-4300

Mountain View

Gordon K. Davidson · ⑩ · Fenwick & West · Silicon Valley Center · 801 California Street · Mountain View, CA 94041-2008 · 650-988-8500

Laird H. Simons III · Fenwick & West · Silicon Valley Center · 801 California Street · Mountain View, CA 94041-2008 · 650-988-8500

Jeffrey R. Vetter · Fenwick & West · Silicon Valley Center · 801 California Street · Mountain View, CA 94041-2008 · 650-988-8500

Newport Beach

Gary J. Singer · O'Melveny & Myers · 610 Newport Center Drive, 17th Floor · Newport Beach, CA 92660 · 949-760-9600

Palo Alto

Aaron J. Alter · Wilson Sonsini Goodrich & Rosati · 650 Page Mill Road · Palo Alto, CA 94304-1050 · 650-493-9300

Laura A. Berezin · Cooley Godward Kronish · 3175 Hanover Street · Palo Alto, CA 94304-1130 · 650-843-5000

Mark A. Bertelsen · Wilson Sonsini Goodrich & Rosati · 650 Page Mill Road · Palo Alto, CA 94304-1050 · 650-493-9300

Steven E. Bochner · Wilson Sonsini Goodrich & Rosati · 650 Page Mill Road · Palo Alto, CA 94304-1050 650-493-9300

Jorge A. del Calvo · Pillsbury Winthrop Shaw Pittman · http://www.pillsburylaw.com · 2475 Hanover Street · Palo Alto, CA 94304-1114 · 650-233-4500

Boris Feldman · ⑩ · Wilson Sonsini Goodrich & Rosati · 650 Page Mill Road · Palo Alto, CA 94304-1050 · 650-493-9300

John A. Fore · Wilson Sonsini Goodrich & Rosati · 650 Page Mill Road · Palo Alto, CA 94304-1050 · 650-493-9300

John M. Geschke · Cooley Godward Kronish · 3175 Hanover Street · Palo Alto, CA 94304-1130 · 650-843-5000

William H. Hinman, Jr. · ⑩ · Simpson Thacher · 2550 Hanover Street · Palo Alto, CA 94304 · 650-251-5000

Suzanne S. Hooper · Cooley Godward Kronish · 3175 Hanover Street · Palo Alto, CA 94304-1130 · 650-843-5000

Eric C. Jensen · Cooley Godward Kronish · 3175 Hanover Street · Palo Alto, CA 94304-1130 · 650-843-5000

Kevin P. Kennedy · Simpson Thacher · 2550 Hanover Street · Palo Alto, CA 94304 · 650-251-5000

Kenton J. King · Skadden, Arps, Slate, Meagher & Flom · 525 University Avenue, Suite 1100 · Palo Alto, CA 94301 · 650-470-4500

Henry P. Massey, Jr. · ㉕ · Wilson Sonsini Goodrich & Rosati · 650 Page Mill Road · Palo Alto, CA 94304-1050 · 650-493-9300

Timothy J. Moore · Cooley Godward Kronish · 3175 Hanover Street · Palo Alto, CA 94304-1130 · 650-843-5000

Jeffrey D. Saper · Wilson Sonsini Goodrich & Rosati · 650 Page Mill Road · Palo Alto, CA 94304-1050 · 650-493-9300

David J. Segre · Wilson Sonsini Goodrich & Rosati · 650 Page Mill Road · Palo Alto, CA 94304-1050 · 650-493-9300

William D. Sherman · ㉕ · Morrison & Foerster · http://www.mofo.com · 755 Page Mill Road · Palo Alto, CA 94304-1018 · 650-813-5600

Gregory C. Smith · Skadden, Arps, Slate, Meagher & Flom · 525 University Avenue, Suite 1100 · Palo Alto, CA 94301 · 650-470-4500

Larry W. Sonsini · ㉕ · Wilson Sonsini Goodrich & Rosati · 650 Page Mill Road · Palo Alto, CA 94304-1050 · 650-493-9300

Sacramento

Scott E. Bartel · Bullivant Houser Bailey · 1415 L Street, Suite 1000 · Sacramento, CA 95814 · 916-930-2500

Daniel B. Eng · Bullivant Houser Bailey · 1415 L Street, Suite 1000 · Sacramento, CA 95814 · 916-930-2500

San Diego

Koji Fukumura · Cooley Godward Kronish · 4401 Eastgate Mall · San Diego, CA 92121-1909 · 858-550-6000

William E. Grauer · Cooley Godward Kronish · 4401 Eastgate Mall · San Diego, CA 92121-1909 · 858-550-6000

Cheston J. Larson · Latham & Watkins · 12636 High Bluff Drive, Suite 400 · San Diego, CA 92130 · 858-523-5400

Frederick T. Muto · ⑩ · Cooley Godward Kronish · 4401 Eastgate Mall · San Diego, CA 92121-1909 · 858-550-6000

Michael G. Rhodes · Cooley Godward Kronish · 4401 Eastgate Mall · San Diego, CA 92121-1909 · 858-550-6000

Shirli Fabbri Weiss · DLA Piper · 401 B Street, Suite 1700 · San Diego, CA 92101-4297 · 619-699-2700

San Francisco

W. Hardy Callcott · Bingham McCutchen · http://www.bingham.com · Three Embarcadero Center · San Francisco, CA 94111-4067 · 415-393-2000

Richard W. Canady · ⑩ · Howard, Rice, Nemerovski, Canady, Falk & Rabkin · Three Embarcadero Center, Seventh Floor · San Francisco, CA 94111-4024 · 415-434-1600

Nathaniel M. Cartmell III · Pillsbury Winthrop Shaw Pittman · http://www.pillsburylaw.com · 50 Fremont Street · P.O. Box 7880 · San Francisco, CA 94120-7880 · 415-983-1000

Tracy K. Edmonson · Latham & Watkins · 505 Montgomery Street, Suite 2000 · San Francisco, CA 94111-6538 · 415-391-0600

Robert C. Friese · Shartsis Friese · http://www.sflaw.com · One Maritime Plaza, 18th Floor · San Francisco, CA 94111 · 415-421-6500

Kenneth Guernsey · Cooley Godward Kronish · 101 California Street, Fifth Floor · San Francisco, CA 94111-5800 · 415-693-2000

John W. Larson · ⑳ · Morgan Lewis & Bockius · Spear Street Tower · One Market · San Francisco, CA 94105-1596 · 415-442-1000

Bruce Alan Mann · ㉕ · Morrison & Foerster · http://www.mofo.com · 425 Market Street · San Francisco, CA 94105-2482 · 415-268-7000

Deborah A. Marshall · Howard, Rice, Nemerovski, Canady, Falk & Rabkin · Three Embarcadero Center, Seventh Floor · San Francisco, CA 94111-4024 · 415-434-1600

Richard M. Phillips · ⑳ · K&L Gates · 55 Second Street, Suite 1700 · San Francisco, CA 94105-3493 · 415-882-8200

Paul C. Pringle · Sidley Austin · 555 California Street, Suite 2000 · San Francisco, CA 94104 · 415-772-1200

Denis T. Rice · ⑳ · Howard, Rice, Nemerovski, Canady, Falk & Rabkin · Three Embarcadero Center, Seventh Floor · San Francisco, CA 94111-4024 · 415-434-1600

Gilbert R. Serota · Howard, Rice, Nemerovski, Canady, Falk & Rabkin · Three Embarcadero Center, Seventh Floor · San Francisco, CA 94111-4024 · 415-434-1600

Santa Monica

Robert L. Kahan · Dreier Stein Kahan Browne Woods George · The Water Garden · North Tower, Sixth Floor · 1620 Twenty-Sixth Street · Santa Monica, CA 90404 · 310-828-9050

SPORTS LAW

Claremont

Frank N. Darras · Shernoff Bidart & Darras · 600 South Indian Hill Boulevard · Claremont, CA 91711 · 909-621-4935

Los Angeles

Douglas B. Adler · Skadden, Arps, Slate, Meagher & Flom · 300 South Grand Avenue, Suite 3400 · Los Angeles, CA 90071 · 213-687-5000

Mark M. Rosenthal · Jeffer, Mangels, Butler & Marmaro · 1900 Avenue of the Stars, Seventh Floor · Los Angeles, CA 90067-4308 · 310-203-8080

STRUCTURED FINANCE LAW

Los Angeles

Sandra Lee Montgomery · Bingham McCutchen · http://www.bingham.com · 355 South Grand Avenue, Suite 4400 · Los Angeles, CA 90071-3106 · 213-680-6400

Richard K. Smith, Jr. · White & Case · http://www.whitecase.com · 633 West Fifth Street, Suite 1900 · Los Angeles, CA 90071-2007 · 213-620-7700

Palo Alto

Andrew J. Hirsch · Wilson Sonsini Goodrich & Rosati · 650 Page Mill Road · Palo Alto, CA 94304-1050 · 650-493-9300

San Francisco

Teveia R. Barnes · Foley & Lardner · One Maritime Plaza, Suite 600 · San Francisco, CA 94111 · 415-434-4484

David V. Biesemeyer · Thelen Reid Brown Raysman & Steiner · 101 Second Street, Suite 1800 · San Francisco, CA 94105-3601 · 415-371-1200

Peter H. Carson · Bingham McCutchen · http://www.bingham.com · Three Embarcadero Center · San Francisco, CA 94111-4067 · 415-393-2000

Pamela J. Martinson · Bingham McCutchen · http://www.bingham.com · Three Embarcadero Center · San Francisco, CA 94111-4067 · 415-393-2000

David B. McMullen · Chapman and Cutler · 595 Market Street, 26th Floor · San Francisco, CA 94105-2839 · 415-541-0500

William B. Piels · Holland & Knight · http://www.hklaw.com · 50 California Street, Suite 2800 · San Francisco, CA 94111-4624 · 415-743-6900

Joseph A. Scherer · Cooley Godward Kronish · 101 California Street, Fifth Floor · San Francisco, CA 94111-5800 · 415-693-2000

Peter S. Szurley · Chapman and Cutler · 595 Market Street, 26th Floor · San Francisco, CA 94105-2839 · 415-541-0500

William S. Veatch · Morrison & Foerster · http://www.mofo.com · 425 Market Street · San Francisco, CA 94105-2482 · 415-268-7000

Maureen A. Young · Bingham McCutchen · http://www.bingham.com · Three Embarcadero Center · San Francisco, CA 94111-4067 · 415-393-2000

Thomas A. Zimmer · Holland & Knight · http://www.hklaw.com · 50 California Street, Suite 2800 · San Francisco, CA 94111-4624 · 415-743-6900

Santa Monica

Mark Birnbaum · Perkins Coie · http://www.perkinscoie.com · South Tower, Sixth Floor · 1620 Twenty-Sixth Street · Santa Monica, CA 90404-4013 · 310-788-9900

TAX LAW

Beverly Hills

Kenneth M. Barish · Kajan Mather and Barish · 9777 Wilshire Boulevard, Suite 805 · Beverly Hills, CA 90212 · 310-278-6080

Elliott H. Kajan · Kajan Mather and Barish · 9777 Wilshire Boulevard, Suite 805 · Beverly Hills, CA 90212 · 310-278-6080

Steven R. Mather · Kajan Mather and Barish · 9777 Wilshire Boulevard, Suite 805 · Beverly Hills, CA 90212 · 310-278-6080

Dennis L. Perez · Hochman, Salkin, Rettig, Toscher & Perez · 9150 Wilshire Boulevard, Suite 300 · Beverly Hills, CA 90212 · 310-281-3200

Charles P. Rettig · Hochman, Salkin, Rettig, Toscher & Perez · 9150 Wilshire Boulevard, Suite 300 · Beverly Hills, CA 90212 · 310-281-3200

Edward M. Robbins, Jr. · Hochman, Salkin, Rettig, Toscher & Perez · 9150 Wilshire Boulevard, Suite 300 · Beverly Hills, CA 90212 · 310-281-3200

Avram Salkin · Hochman, Salkin, Rettig, Toscher & Perez · 9150 Wilshire Boulevard, Suite 300 · Beverly Hills, CA 90212 · 310-281-3200

Steven R. Toscher · Hochman, Salkin, Rettig, Toscher & Perez · 9150 Wilshire Boulevard, Suite 300 · Beverly Hills, CA 90212 · 310-281-3200

Cerritos

John E. James · Atkinson, Andelson, Loya, Ruud & Romo · 17871 Park Plaza Drive · Cerritos, CA 90703-8597 · 562-653-3200

Claremont

Marshall W. Taylor · Taylor, Simonson & Winter · 144 North Indian Hill Boulevard · Claremont, CA 91711 · 909-625-4785

Costa Mesa

Roger A. Grad · Snell & Wilmer · 600 Anton Boulevard, Suite 1400 · Costa Mesa, CA 92626-7689 · 714-427-7000

Paul F. Marx · ⑩ · Rutan & Tucker · http://www.rutan.com · 611 Anton Boulevard, Suite 1400 · P.O. Box 1950 · Costa Mesa, CA 92628-1950 · 714-641-5100

Folsom

Kevin G. Long · Chang, Ruthenberg & Long · 620 Coolidge Drive, Suite 350 · Folsom, CA 95630-3155 · 916-357-5660

Kenneth W. Ruthenberg, Jr. · Chang, Ruthenberg & Long · 620 Coolidge Drive, Suite 350 · Folsom, CA 95630-3155 · 916-357-5660

Gold River

Richard Todd Luoma · Richard Todd Luoma · 11290 Stanford Court Lane, Suite 210 · Gold River, CA 95670 · 916-853-2090

Irvine

Jeffrey C. Joy · Greenberg Traurig · http://www.gtlaw.com · 3161 Michelson Drive, Suite 1000 · Irvine, CA 92612-4410 · 949-732-6500

Los Angeles

C. David Anderson · ⑳ · Loeb & Loeb · 10100 Santa Monica Boulevard, Suite 2200 · Los Angeles, CA 90067-4164 · 310-282-2000

Hatef Behnia · Gibson, Dunn & Crutcher · 333 South Grand Avenue · Los Angeles, CA 90071-3197 · 213-229-7000

Robert Blashek · O'Melveny & Myers · 1999 Avenue of the Stars, Seventh Floor · Los Angeles, CA 90067-6035 · 310-553-6700

Michael I. Blaylock · Carlsmith Ball · 444 South Flower Street, Ninth Floor · Los Angeles, CA 90071-2901 · 213-955-1200

David S. Boyce · Jones Day · 555 South Flower Street, 50th Floor · Los Angeles, CA 90071 · 213-489-3939

Karen S. Bryan · Latham & Watkins · 355 South Grand Avenue · Los Angeles, CA 90071-1560 · 213-485-1234

James F. Childs, Jr. · ⑳ · Jones Day · 555 South Flower Street, 50th Floor · Los Angeles, CA 90071 · 213-489-3939

William R. Christian · Rodi, Pollock, Pettker, Galbraith & Cahill · http://www.rodipollock.com · 444 South Flower Street, Suite 1700 · Los Angeles, CA 90071-2901 · 213-895-4900

John J. Clair, Jr. · Latham & Watkins · 355 South Grand Avenue · Los Angeles, CA 90071-1560 · 213-485-1234

Terence Floyd Cuff · ⑩ · Loeb & Loeb · 10100 Santa Monica Boulevard, Suite 2200 · Los Angeles, CA 90067-4164 · 310-282-2000

Michael D. Fernhoff · Kaye Scholer · 1999 Avenue of the Stars, Suite 1700 · Los Angeles, CA 90067-6048 310-788-1000

Elliot G. Freier · Irell & Manella · 1800 Avenue of the Stars, Suite 900 · Los Angeles, CA 90067-4276 · 310-277-1010

Paul N. Frimmer · ㉕ · Irell & Manella · 1800 Avenue of the Stars, Suite 900 · Los Angeles, CA 90067-4276 · 310-277-1010

Mitchell M. Gaswirth · Proskauer Rose · http://www.proskauer.com · 2049 Century Park East, 32nd Floor Los Angeles, CA 90067-3206 · 310-557-2900

Thomas W. Henning · ⑩ · Allen Matkins Leck Gamble Mallory & Natsis · 515 South Figueroa Street, Ninth Floor · Los Angeles, CA 90071-3398 · 213-622-5555

Paul Gordon Hoffman · ⑩ · Hoffman, Sabban & Watenmaker · 10880 Wilshire Boulevard, Suite 2200 · Los Angeles, CA 90024 · 310-470-6010

Milton B. Hyman · ⑩ · Irell & Manella · 1800 Avenue of the Stars, Suite 900 · Los Angeles, CA 90067-4276 · 310-277-1010

Nancy L. Iredale · ⑩ · Paul Hastings · 515 South Flower Street, 25th Floor · Los Angeles, CA 90071 · 213-683-6000

Paul Issler · Gibson, Dunn & Crutcher · 333 South Grand Avenue · Los Angeles, CA 90071-3197 · 213-229-7000

Robert K. Johnson · ⑳ · Munger, Tolles & Olson · 355 South Grand Avenue, 35th Floor · Los Angeles, CA 90071-1560 · 213-683-9100

Moshe J. Kushman · Skadden, Arps, Slate, Meagher & Flom · 300 South Grand Avenue, Suite 3400 · Los Angeles, CA 90071 · 213-687-5000

Dudley M. Lang · McKenna Long & Aldridge · 444 South Flower Street, Eighth Floor · Los Angeles, CA 90071-2901 · 213-688-1000

Thomas N. Lawson · Loeb & Loeb · 10100 Santa Monica Boulevard, Suite 2200 · Los Angeles, CA 90067-4164 · 310-282-2000

C. Bruce Levine · Greenberg Glusker · 1900 Avenue of the Stars, 21st Floor · Los Angeles, CA 90067 · 310-553-3610

Schuyler M. Moore · Stroock & Stroock & Lavan · 2029 Century Park East · Los Angeles, CA 90067-3086 · 310-556-5800

David Wheeler Newman · Mitchell Silberberg & Knupp · 11377 West Olympic Boulevard · Los Angeles, CA 90064 · 310-312-2000

Sanford Presant · DLA Piper · 1999 Avenue of the Stars, Suite 400 · Los Angeles, CA 90067-6023 · 310-595-3000

Joel Rabinovitz · Irell & Manella · 1800 Avenue of the Stars, Suite 900 · Los Angeles, CA 90067-4276 · 310-277-1010

Scott H. Racine · Akin Gump Strauss Hauer & Feld · 2029 Century Park East, Suite 2400 · Los Angeles, CA 90067-3012 · 310-229-1000

Stephen D. Rose · Munger, Tolles & Olson · 355 South Grand Avenue, 35th Floor · Los Angeles, CA 90071-1560 · 213-683-9100

Edwin G. Schuck, Jr. · Holme Roberts & Owen · http://www.hro.com · 777 South Figueroa Street, Suite 2800 · Los Angeles, CA 90017-5826 · 213-572-4300

Paul A. Sczudlo · Loeb & Loeb · 10100 Santa Monica Boulevard, Suite 2200 · Los Angeles, CA 90067-4164 · 310-282-2000

Raj Tanden · Proskauer Rose · http://www.proskauer.com · 2049 Century Park East, 32nd Floor · Los Angeles, CA 90067-3206 · 310-557-2900

Mark S. Wallace · Stutman, Treister & Glatt · 1901 Avenue of the Stars, 12th Floor · Los Angeles, CA 90067 · 310-228-5600

William P. Wasserman · ㉕ · Ernst & Young · 725 South Figueroa Street, Suite 200 · Los Angeles, CA 90017-5418 · 213-977-3200

J. Patrick Whaley · ⑩ · Musick, Peeler & Garrett · One Wilshire Boulevard, Suite 2000 · Los Angeles, CA 90017 · 213-629-7600

William S. Woods II · Ernst & Young · 725 South Figueroa Street, Suite 200 · Los Angeles, CA 90017-5418 · 213-977-3200

Mountain View

James P. Fuller · ⑳ · Fenwick & West · Silicon Valley Center · 801 California Street · Mountain View, CA 94041-2008 · 650-988-8500

Oakland

Karen L. Hawkins · ⑩ · Taggart & Hawkins · 1901 Harrison Street, Suite 1600 · Oakland, CA 94612 · 510-893-9999

Palo Alto

Frederick R. Chilton · McDermott Will & Emery · 3150 Porter Drive · Palo Alto, CA 94304-1212 · 650-813-5000

Roy E. Crawford · ⑳ · McDermott Will & Emery · 3150 Porter Drive · Palo Alto, CA 94304-1212 · 650-813-5000

Ivan H. Humphreys · Wilson Sonsini Goodrich & Rosati · 650 Page Mill Road · Palo Alto, CA 94304-1050 · 650-493-9300

Larry R. Langdon · Mayer Brown · Two Palo Alto Square, Suite 300 · 3000 El Camino Real · Palo Alto, CA 94306-2112 · 650-331-2000

Robert H. Miller · Cooley Godward Kronish · 3175 Hanover Street · Palo Alto, CA 94304-1130 · 650-843-5000

John M. Peterson, Jr. · Baker & McKenzie · 660 Hansen Way · P.O. Box 60309 · Palo Alto, CA 94304-0309 · 650-856-2400

Thomas S. Wisialowski · Paul Hastings · 1117 South California Avenue · Palo Alto, CA 94304-1106 · 650-320-1800

Rancho Santa Fe

Louis A. Mezzullo · ⑳ · Luce, Forward, Hamilton & Scripps · http://www.luce.com · 6050 El Tordo · P.O. Box 2329 · Rancho Santa Fe, CA 92067-2329 · 858-756-4410

Redlands

John K. Mirau · Mirau, Edwards, Cannon, Harter & Lewin · 1806 Orange Tree Lane, Suite C · Redlands, CA 92374 · 909-793-0200

Paul M. Shimoff · McPeters McAlearney Shimoff & Hatt · Washington Mutual Bank Building, Second Floor · Four West Redlands Boulevard · P.O. Box 2084 · Redlands, CA 92373-0661 · 909-792-8919

Sacramento

James Clarke · McDonough Holland & Allen · http://www.mhalaw.com · 555 Capitol Mall, Ninth Floor · Sacramento, CA 95814-4692 · 916-444-3900

Perry E. Israel · Law Office of Perry Israel · 3436 American River Drive, Suite Nine · Sacramento, CA 95864 · 916-485-6645

James L. Leet · McDonough Holland & Allen · http://www.mhalaw.com · 555 Capitol Mall, Ninth Floor · Sacramento, CA 95814-4692 · 916-444-3900

Regina J. Schroder · Bullivant Houser Bailey · 1415 L Street, Suite 1000 · Sacramento, CA 95814 · 916-930-2500

San Diego

David C. Boatwright · Procopio, Cory, Hargreaves & Savitch · 530 B Street, 21st Floor · San Diego, CA 92101 · 619-238-1900

George L. Damoose · ⑳ · Procopio, Cory, Hargreaves & Savitch · 530 B Street, 21st Floor · San Diego, CA 92101 · 619-238-1900

David J. Dorne · Seltzer Caplan McMahon Vitek · Symphony Towers, Suite 2100 · 750 B Street · San Diego, CA 92101 · 619-685-3003

Richard L. Kintz · ⑳ · Sheppard, Mullin, Richter & Hampton · http://www.sheppardmullin.com · 12275 El Camino Real, Suite 200 · San Diego, CA 92130 · 858-720-8900

Mark L. Mann · Luce, Forward, Hamilton & Scripps · http://www.luce.com · 600 West Broadway, Suite 2600 · San Diego, CA 92101 · 619-236-1414

Richard L. Parker · Heller Ehrman · 4350 La Jolla Village Drive, Seventh Floor · San Diego, CA 92122-1246 · 858-450-8400

Richard A. Shaw · ㉕ · Higgs, Fletcher & Mack · 401 West A Street, Suite 2600 · San Diego, CA 92101-7910 · 619-236-1551

Darryl Steinhause · Luce, Forward, Hamilton & Scripps · http://www.luce.com · 600 West Broadway, Suite 2600 · San Diego, CA 92101 · 619-236-1414

Lawrence I. Tannenbaum · DLA Piper · 401 B Street, Suite 1700 · San Diego, CA 92101-4297 · 619-699-2700

J. Clancy Wilson · ⑩ · Branton & Wilson · 701 B Street, Suite 1255 · San Diego, CA 92101-8187 · 619-236-1891

San Francisco

Jeffry A. Bernstein · ⑳ · Coblentz, Patch, Duffy & Bass · http://www.coblentzlaw.com · One Ferry Building, Suite 200 · San Francisco, CA 94111-4213 · 415-391-4800

Grady M. Bolding · ⑩ · Orrick, Herrington & Sutcliffe · The Orrick Building · 405 Howard Street · San Francisco, CA 94105-2669 · 415-773-5700

William E. Bonano · Pillsbury Winthrop Shaw Pittman · http://www.pillsburylaw.com · 50 Fremont Street · P.O. Box 7880 · San Francisco, CA 94120-7880 · 415-983-1000

Julie A. Divola · Pillsbury Winthrop Shaw Pittman · http://www.pillsburylaw.com · 50 Fremont Street · P.O. Box 7880 · San Francisco, CA 94120-7880 · 415-983-1000

Jill S. Dodd · Manatt, Phelps & Phillips · One Embarcadero Center, 30th Floor · San Francisco, CA 94111 · 415-291-7400

David S. Foster · ⑩ · Thelen Reid Brown Raysman & Steiner · 101 Second Street, Suite 1800 · San Francisco, CA 94105-3601 · 415-371-1200

Joanne M. Garvey · ㉕ · Sheppard, Mullin, Richter & Hampton · Four Embarcadero Center, 17th Floor · San Francisco, CA 94111 · 415-434-9100

David R. Gerson · Wilson Sonsini Goodrich & Rosati · Spear Tower, Suite 3300 · One Market Street · San Francisco, CA 94105-1126 · 415-947-2000

Richard L. Greene · ㉕ · Greene, Radovsky, Maloney & Share · Four Embarcadero Center, Suite 4000 · San Francisco, CA 94111 · 415-981-1400

William T. Hutton · ⑳ · Coblentz, Patch, Duffy & Bass · http://www.coblentzlaw.com · One Ferry Building, Suite 200 · San Francisco, CA 94111-4213 · 415-391-4800

Gary P. Kaplan · Howard, Rice, Nemerovski, Canady, Falk & Rabkin · Three Embarcadero Center, Seventh Floor · San Francisco, CA 94111-4024 · 415-434-1600

Thomas F. Kostic · ㉕ · Morrison & Foerster · http://www.mofo.com · 425 Market Street · San Francisco, CA 94105-2482 · 415-268-7000

Alvin T. Levitt · ㉕ · Manatt, Phelps & Phillips · One Embarcadero Center, 30th Floor · San Francisco, CA 94111 · 415-291-7400

Stuart S. Lipton · Howard, Rice, Nemerovski, Canady, Falk & Rabkin · Three Embarcadero Center, Seventh Floor · San Francisco, CA 94111-4024 · 415-434-1600

Susan C. Philpot · ⑩ · Cooley Godward Kronish · 101 California Street, Fifth Floor · San Francisco, CA 94111-5800 · 415-693-2000

Jordan P. Rose · Manatt, Phelps & Phillips · One Embarcadero Center, 30th Floor · San Francisco, CA 94111 · 415-291-7400

C. Jean Ryan · Sideman & Bancroft · One Embarcadero Center, Eighth Floor · San Francisco, CA 94111 415-392-1960

Richard J. Sideman · ⑩ · Sideman & Bancroft · One Embarcadero Center, Eighth Floor · San Francisco, CA 94111 · 415-392-1960

Lawrence B. Silver · ㉕ · Greene, Radovsky, Maloney & Share · Four Embarcadero Center, Suite 4000 · San Francisco, CA 94111 · 415-981-1400

Myron G. Sugarman · ⑳ · Cooley Godward Kronish · 101 California Street, Fifth Floor · San Francisco, CA 94111-5800 · 415-693-2000

Jeffrey M. Vesely · Pillsbury Winthrop Shaw Pittman · http://www.pillsburylaw.com · 50 Fremont Street · P.O. Box 7880 · San Francisco, CA 94120-7880 · 415-983-1000

Louis Stevan Weller · ⑩ · Deloitte & Touche · 50 Fremont Street, Suite 3100 · San Francisco, CA 94105-2230 · 415-783-4000

George G. Wolf · Orrick, Herrington & Sutcliffe · The Orrick Building · 405 Howard Street · San Francisco, CA 94105-2669 · 415-773-5700

Cameron W. Wolfe, Jr. · ⑳ · Orrick, Herrington & Sutcliffe · The Orrick Building · 405 Howard Street · San Francisco, CA 94105-2669 · 415-773-5700

Robert W. Wood · Wood & Porter · 333 Sacramento Street · San Francisco, CA 94111 · 415-834-1800

San Jose

Clarence J. Ferrari, Jr. · ⑩ · Ferrari Ottoboni · 333 West Santa Clara Street, Suite 700 · San Jose, CA 95113-1716 · 408-280-0535

John F. Hopkins · ⑩ · Hopkins & Carley · The Letitia Building · 70 South First Street · P.O. Box 1469 · San Jose, CA 95109-1469 · 408-286-9800

Alan J. Pinner · Berliner Cohen · 10 Almaden Boulevard, 11th Floor · San Jose, CA 95113-2233 · 408-286-5800

John F. Ramsbacher · Ramsbacher Prokey · 125 South Market Street, Suite 1150 · San Jose, CA 95113 · 408-293-3616

Filmore E. Rose · ⑩ · Beck, Ross, Bismonte & Finley · Fairmont Plaza, Suite 1300 · 50 West San Fernando Street · San Jose, CA 95113 · 408-938-7900

Scott A. Ross · Beck, Ross, Bismonte & Finley · Fairmont Plaza, Suite 1300 · 50 West San Fernando Street · San Jose, CA 95113 · 408-938-7900

Robert E. Temmerman, Jr. · ⑩ · Temmerman & Cilley · 2502 Stevens Creek Boulevard · San Jose, CA 95128-1654 · 408-998-9500

Santa Ana

Terrence J. Moore · Moore & Associates · 1010 North Ross Street South, Suite 200 · Santa Ana, CA 92701 · 714-541-2500

A. Lavar Taylor · Law Offices of A. Lavar Taylor · Six Hutton Centre Drive, Suite 880 · Santa Ana, CA 92707-0516 · 714-546-0445

Santa Barbara

John W. Ambrecht · Ambrecht & Associates · 1224 Coast Village Circle, Suite 32 · Santa Barbara, CA 93108 · 805-965-1329

Santa Monica

M. Katharine Davidson · Dreier Stein Kahan Browne Woods George · The Water Garden · North Tower, Sixth Floor · 1620 Twenty-Sixth Street · Santa Monica, CA 90404 · 310-828-9050

Carol Perrin · Greenberg Traurig · http://www.gtlaw.com · 2450 Colorado Avenue, Suite 400-E · Santa Monica, CA 90404 · 310-586-7700

Santa Rosa

Edwin C. Anderson · ⑩ · Anderson, Zeigler, Disharoon, Gallagher & Gray · 50 Old Courthouse Square, Fifth Floor · P.O. Box 1498 · Santa Rosa, CA 95404 · 707-545-4910

Kirt F. Zeigler · Anderson, Zeigler, Disharoon, Gallagher & Gray · 50 Old Courthouse Square, Fifth Floor P.O. Box 1498 · Santa Rosa, CA 95404 · 707-545-4910

TECHNOLOGY LAW

East Palo Alto

William F. Abrams · Bingham McCutchen · http://www.bingham.com · 1900 University Avenue · East Palo Alto, CA 94303-2223 · 650-849-4400

Los Angeles

Morgan Chu · ⑩ · Irell & Manella · 1800 Avenue of the Stars, Suite 900 · Los Angeles, CA 90067-4276 · 310-277-1010

Menlo Park

Glenn G. Nash · Latham & Watkins · 140 Scott Drive · Menlo Park, CA 94025 · 650-328-4600

Thomas F. Villeneuve · Gunderson Dettmer Stough Villeneuve Franklin & Hachigian · 155 Constitution Drive · Menlo Park, CA 94025 · 650-321-2400

Mountain View

Christopher Scott Graham · Dechert · 2440 West El Camino Real, Suite 700 · Mountain View, CA 94040-1499 · 650-813-4800

Ann M. Caviani Pease · Dechert · 2440 West El Camino Real, Suite 700 · Mountain View, CA 94040-1499 · 650-813-4800

Palo Alto

Kenneth A. Clark · Wilson Sonsini Goodrich & Rosati · 650 Page Mill Road · Palo Alto, CA 94304-1050 · 650-493-9300

William S. Coats · White & Case · http://www.whitecase.com · Five Palo Alto Square, Ninth Floor · 3000 El Camino Real · Palo Alto, CA 94306 · 650-213-0300

Eric Reifschneider · Cooley Godward Kronish · 3175 Hanover Street · Palo Alto, CA 94304-1130 · 650-843-5000

Michael D. Stern · Cooley Godward Kronish · 3175 Hanover Street · Palo Alto, CA 94304-1130 · 650-843-5000

Redwood Shores

Matthew D. Powers · Weil Gotshal & Manges · 201 Redwood Shores Parkway, Fifth Floor · Redwood Shores, CA 94065 · 650-802-3000

San Diego

Michael G. Rhodes · Cooley Godward Kronish · 4401 Eastgate Mall · San Diego, CA 92121-1909 · 858-550-6000

Kent M. Walker · Cooley Godward Kronish · 4401 Eastgate Mall · San Diego, CA 92121-1909 · 858-550-6000

San Francisco

John Crittenden · Cooley Godward Kronish · 101 California Street, Fifth Floor · San Francisco, CA 94111-5800 · 415-693-2000

James G. Gilliland, Jr. · Townsend and Townsend and Crew · http://www.townsend.com · Two Embarcadero Center, Eighth Floor · San Francisco, CA 94111-3834 · 415-576-0200

George A. Riley · O'Melveny & Myers · Embarcadero Center West · 275 Battery Street · San Francisco, CA 94111-3305 · 415-984-8700

Santa Monica

Ian C. Ballon · Greenberg Traurig · http://www.gtlaw.com · 2450 Colorado Avenue, Suite 400-E · Santa Monica, CA 90404 · 310-586-7700

TIMBER LAW

San Francisco

Edgar B. Washburn · Morrison & Foerster · http://www.mofo.com · 425 Market Street · San Francisco, CA 94105-2482 · 415-268-7000

TRANSPORTATION LAW

San Francisco

Thomas J. MacBride, Jr. · ⑩ · Goodin, MacBride, Squeri, Ritchie & Day · 505 Sansome Street, Suite 900 San Francisco, CA 94111 · 415-392-7900

TRUSTS AND ESTATES

Beverly Hills

Jane Peebles · Karlin & Peebles · 8383 Wilshire Boulevard, Suite 649 · Beverly Hills, CA 90211 · 323-852-0030

Corona del Mar

Russell G. Allen · Russell G. Allen · 2101 East Coast Highway, Suite 215 · Corona del Mar, CA 92625-1900 · 949-760-4090

Costa Mesa

David W. Evans · Snell & Wilmer · 600 Anton Boulevard, Suite 1400 · Costa Mesa, CA 92626-7689 · 714-427-7000

Randolph B. Godshall · Sheppard, Mullin, Richter & Hampton · http://www.sheppardmullin.com · 650 Town Center Drive, Fourth Floor · Costa Mesa, CA 92626 · 714-513-5100

Timothy J. Kay · Snell & Wilmer · 600 Anton Boulevard, Suite 1400 · Costa Mesa, CA 92626-7689 · 714-427-7000

Paul F. Marx · ⑩ · Rutan & Tucker · http://www.rutan.com · 611 Anton Boulevard, Suite 1400 · P.O. Box 1950 · Costa Mesa, CA 92628-1950 · 714-641-5100

H. Neal Wells III · Slovak Baron & Empey · 650 Town Center Drive, Suite 1400 · Costa Mesa, CA 92626 714-435-9592

Encino

James R. Birnberg · ⑩ · Oldman, Cooley, Leighton, Sallus, Gold & Birnberg · Penthouse, Suite A · 16133 Ventura Boulevard · Encino, CA 91436-2447 · 818-986-8080

Marshal A. Oldman · Oldman, Cooley, Leighton, Sallus, Gold & Birnberg · Penthouse, Suite A · 16133 Ventura Boulevard · Encino, CA 91436-2447 · 818-986-8080

Marc L. Sallus · Oldman, Cooley, Leighton, Sallus, Gold & Birnberg · Penthouse, Suite A · 16133 Ventura Boulevard · Encino, CA 91436-2447 · 818-986-8080

Garden Grove

Michelle West · Michelle West · 12431 Lewis Street, Suite 102 · Garden Grove, CA 92840 · 714-703-1500

Glendale

Eric Andrew Ashton, Jr. · Edwards, Ashton & Gin · 100 West Broadway, Suite 860 · Glendale, CA 91210 · 818-247-7380

Greenbrae

Alan D. Bonapart · ⑳ · Bancroft & McAlister · 300 Drake's Landing Road, Suite 200 · Greenbrae, CA 94904 · 415-464-8855

George R. Dirkes · Bancroft & McAlister · 300 Drake's Landing Road, Suite 200 · Greenbrae, CA 94904 · 415-464-8855

Robert A. Mills · ㉕ · Bancroft & McAlister · 300 Drake's Landing Road, Suite 200 · Greenbrae, CA 94904 · 415-464-8855

Irvine

Douglas K. Freeman · Freeman, Freeman & Smiley · 1920 Main Street, Suite 1050 · Irvine, CA 92614 · 949-252-2777

Joseph C. Obegi · ⑩ · Freeman, Freeman & Smiley · 1920 Main Street, Suite 1050 · Irvine, CA 92614 · 949-252-2777

La Jolla

Edward V. Brennan · ⑳ · Newnham, Fitzpatrick, Weston & Brennan · 7777 Fay Avenue, Suite 202 · La Jolla, CA 92037 · 858-459-3821

Stephen L. Newnham III · ㉕ · Newnham, Fitzpatrick, Weston & Brennan · 7777 Fay Avenue, Suite 202 · La Jolla, CA 92037 · 858-459-3821

David Weston · ⑩ · Newnham, Fitzpatrick, Weston & Brennan · 7777 Fay Avenue, Suite 202 · La Jolla, CA 92037 · 858-459-3821

Lafayette

William L. Hoisington · ⑳ · William L. Hoisington · 3620 Happy Valley, Suite 201 · P.O. Box 1288 · Lafayette, CA 94549-1288 · 925-962-1022

Laguna Beach

Kim R. Hubbard · Law Office of Kim R. Hubbard · 668 North Coast Highway, Suite 239 · Laguna Beach, CA 92651 · 949-376-4505

Laguna Hills

Fay Blix · Fay Blix · 23601 Moulton Parkway, Suite 220 · Laguna Hills, CA 92653 · 949-454-2205

Los Angeles

Robert Bennett · ⑩ · Greenberg Glusker · 1900 Avenue of the Stars, 21st Floor · Los Angeles, CA 90067 310-553-3610

Leah M. Bishop · ⑩ · Loeb & Loeb · 10100 Santa Monica Boulevard, Suite 2200 · Los Angeles, CA 90067-4164 · 310-282-2000

Reynolds T. Cafferata · Rodriguez, Horii, Choi & Cafferata · 777 South Figueroa Street, Suite 2150 · Los Angeles, CA 90017 · 213-892-7700

William R. Christian · Rodi, Pollock, Pettker, Galbraith & Cahill · http://www.rodipollock.com · 444 South Flower Street, Suite 1700 · Los Angeles, CA 90071-2901 · 213-895-4900

Allan B. Cutrow · ⑩ · Mitchell Silberberg & Knupp · 11377 West Olympic Boulevard · Los Angeles, CA 90064 · 310-312-2000

William Finestone · Finestone & Richter · 11601 Wilshire Boulevard, Suite 1900 · Los Angeles, CA 90025-1755 · 310-575-0800

Paul N. Frimmer · ㉕ · Irell & Manella · 1800 Avenue of the Stars, Suite 900 · Los Angeles, CA 90067-4276 · 310-277-1010

Jon J. Gallo · ㉕ · Greenberg Glusker · 1900 Avenue of the Stars, 21st Floor · Los Angeles, CA 90067 · 310-553-3610

Andrew S. Garb · ⑳ · Loeb & Loeb · 10100 Santa Monica Boulevard, Suite 2200 · Los Angeles, CA 90067-4164 · 310-282-2000

Mitchell M. Gaswirth · Proskauer Rose · http://www.proskauer.com · 2049 Century Park East, 32nd Floor Los Angeles, CA 90067-3206 · 310-557-2900

Joseph G. Gorman, Jr. · ⑳ · Sheppard, Mullin, Richter & Hampton · http://www.sheppardmullin.com · 333 South Hope Street, 48th Floor · Los Angeles, CA 90071-1448 · 213-620-1780

Steven L. Guise · Munger, Tolles & Olson · 355 South Grand Avenue, 35th Floor · Los Angeles, CA 90071-1560 · 213-683-9100

James M. Hassan · Musick, Peeler & Garrett · One Wilshire Boulevard, Suite 2000 · Los Angeles, CA 90017 · 213-629-7600

Harry L. Hathaway · ⑩ · Fulbright & Jaworski · http://www.fulbright.com · 555 South Flower Street, 41st Floor · Los Angeles, CA 90071 · 213-892-9200

Susan J. Hazard · ⑩ · Musick, Peeler & Garrett · One Wilshire Boulevard, Suite 2000 · Los Angeles, CA 90017 · 213-629-7600

Geraldine S. Hemmerling · ㉕ · Hirsch Wallerstein Matlof & Fishman · 10100 Santa Monica Boulevard, Suite 1700 · Los Angeles, CA 90067 · 310-703-1700

Lynard C. Hinojosa · ⑩ · Hinojosa & Wallet · 2215 Colby Avenue · Los Angeles, CA 90064-1504 · 310-473-7000

Paul Gordon Hoffman · ⑩ · Hoffman, Sabban & Watenmaker · 10880 Wilshire Boulevard, Suite 2200 · Los Angeles, CA 90024 · 310-470-6010

Nancy Howard · ⑩ · Sheppard, Mullin, Richter & Hampton · http://www.sheppardmullin.com · 333 South Hope Street, 48th Floor · Los Angeles, CA 90071-1448 · 213-620-1780

Carol A. Johnston · Katten Muchin Rosenman · 2029 Century Park East, Suite 2600 · Los Angeles, CA 90067-3012 · 310-788-4400

Arnold D. Kahn · ⑩ · Greenberg Glusker · 1900 Avenue of the Stars, 21st Floor · Los Angeles, CA 90067 310-553-3610

Andrew M. Katzenstein · Proskauer Rose · 2049 Century Park East, 32nd Floor · Los Angeles, CA 90067-3206 · 310-557-2900

Edward A. Landry · ㉕ · Musick, Peeler & Garrett · One Wilshire Boulevard, Suite 2000 · Los Angeles, CA 90017 · 213-629-7600

Jeffrey M. Loeb · Loeb & Loeb · 10100 Santa Monica Boulevard, Suite 2200 · Los Angeles, CA 90067-4164 · 310-282-2000

Jonathan C. Lurie · ⑩ · McDermott Will & Emery · 2049 Century Park East, 38th Floor · Los Angeles, CA 90067-3218 · 310-277-4110

Burton A. Mitchell · Jeffer, Mangels, Butler & Marmaro · 1900 Avenue of the Stars, Seventh Floor · Los Angeles, CA 90067-4308 · 310-203-8080

David C. Nelson · Loeb & Loeb · 10100 Santa Monica Boulevard, Suite 2200 · Los Angeles, CA 90067-4164 · 310-282-2000

David Wheeler Newman · Mitchell Silberberg & Knupp · 11377 West Olympic Boulevard · Los Angeles, CA 90064 · 310-312-2000

John D. Pettker · ⑩ · Rodi, Pollock, Pettker, Galbraith & Cahill · http://www.rodipollock.com · 444 South Flower Street, Suite 1700 · Los Angeles, CA 90071-2901 · 213-895-4900

John T. Rogers, Jr. · Luce, Forward, Hamilton & Scripps · http://www.luce.com · 601 South Figueroa, Suite 3900 · Los Angeles, CA 90017 · 213-892-4992

Bruce S. Ross · ⑩ · Holland & Knight · http://www.hklaw.com · 633 West Fifth Street, 21st Floor · Los Angeles, CA 90071 · 213-896-2400

Nina M. Sabban · Hoffman, Sabban & Watenmaker · 10880 Wilshire Boulevard, Suite 2200 · Los Angeles, CA 90024 · 310-470-6010

Sussan H. Shore · ⑩ · Weinstock, Manion, Reisman, Shore & Neumann · 1875 Century Park East, Suite 2000 · Los Angeles, CA 90067 · 310-553-8844

Richard L. Stack · ⑩ · Overton, Lyman & Prince · 520 South Grand Avenue, Seventh Floor · Los Angeles, CA 90071 · 213-683-5281

Adam F. Streisand · Loeb & Loeb · 10100 Santa Monica Boulevard, Suite 2200 · Los Angeles, CA 90067-4164 · 310-282-2000

Stuart P. Tobisman · ⑳ · Loeb & Loeb · 10100 Santa Monica Boulevard, Suite 2200 · Los Angeles, CA 90067-4164 · 310-282-2000

Andrew M. Wallet · Hinojosa & Wallet · 2215 Colby Avenue · Los Angeles, CA 90064-1504 · 310-473-7000

Alan S. Watenmaker · ⑩ · Hoffman, Sabban & Watenmaker · 10880 Wilshire Boulevard, Suite 2200 · Los Angeles, CA 90024 · 310-470-6010

Kenneth S. Wolf · ⑩ · Hoffman, Sabban & Watenmaker · 10880 Wilshire Boulevard, Suite 2200 · Los Angeles, CA 90024 · 310-470-6010

Los Gatos

Michael G. Desmarais · Law Office of Michael G. Desmarais · 16450 Los Gatos Boulevard, Suite 208 · Los Gatos, CA 95032 · 408-356-6886

Manhattan Beach

Matthew S. Rae, Jr. · ⑩ · Darling Hall & Rae · 600 John Street · Manhattan Beach, CA 90266 · 310-372-9193

Mill Valley

Sterling L. Ross, Jr. · Robb & Ross · 591 Redwood Highway, Suite 2250 · Mill Valley, CA 94910 · 415-332-3831

Monterey

William H. Soskin · Law Offices of William H. Soskin · 2100 Garden Road, Suite F · Monterey, CA 93940 · 831-649-8006

Napa

Francis J. Collin, Jr. · ⑳ · Dickenson, Peatman & Fogarty · 809 Coombs Street · Napa, CA 94559-2799 · 707-252-7122

W. Scott Thomas · Dickenson, Peatman & Fogarty · 809 Coombs Street · Napa, CA 94559-2799 · 707-252-7122

Newport Beach

James B. MacDonald · Casey & Richards · 610 Newport Center Drive, Suite 650 · Newport Beach, CA 92660-6474 · 949-640-5200

Michael V. Vollmer · ⑩ · Law Office of Michael V. Vollmer · 4770 Von Karman Avenue · Newport Beach, CA 92660-2123 · 949-474-9088

North Hollywood

Edmond R. Davis · ㉕ · Davis & Whalen · 5200 Lankershim Boulevard, Suite 380 · North Hollywood, CA 91601 · 818-752-2880

Michael R. Whalen · ⑩ · Davis & Whalen · 5200 Lankershim Boulevard, Suite 380 · North Hollywood, CA 91601 · 818-752-2880

Oakland

Monica Dell'Osso · Burnham Brown · 1901 Harrison Street, 11th Floor · P.O. Box 119 · Oakland, CA 94604-0119 · 510-444-6800

Margaret M. Hand · Law Office of Margaret M. Hand · 1939 Harrison Street, Suite 200 · Oakland, CA 94612 · 510-444-6044

John L. McDonnell, Jr. · ㉕ · Reed Smith · 1999 Harrison Street, Suite 2400 · P.O. Box 2084 · Oakland, CA 94604-3572 · 510-763-2000

Orinda

John A. Hartog · John A. Hartog · Four Orinda Way, Suite 250-B · Orinda, CA 94563 · 925-253-1717

Palm Springs

Robert A. Schlesinger · ⑩ · Robert A. Schlesinger · 559 South Palm Canyon Drive, Suite B-208 · P.O. Box 2268 · Palm Springs, CA 92263 · 760-325-2076

Palo Alto

Peter LaBoskey · Wilson Sonsini Goodrich & Rosati · 650 Page Mill Road · Palo Alto, CA 94304-1050 · 650-493-9300

Pasadena

Clark R. Byam · ⑩ · Hahn & Hahn · 301 East Colorado Boulevard, Ninth Floor · Pasadena, CA 91101-1977 · 626-796-9123

Theodore E. Calleton · ⑳ · Calleton Merritt De Francisco & Real-Salas · 131 North El Molino Avenue, Suite 300 · Pasadena, CA 91101 · 626-395-0860

Susan T. House · ⑩ · Hahn & Hahn · 301 East Colorado Boulevard, Ninth Floor · Pasadena, CA 91101-1977 · 626-796-9123

Marc R. Isaacson · Hahn & Hahn · 301 East Colorado Boulevard, Ninth Floor · Pasadena, CA 91101-1977 · 626-796-9123

William S. Johnstone, Jr. · ⑩ · Hahn & Hahn · 301 East Colorado Boulevard, Ninth Floor · Pasadena, CA 91101-1977 · 626-796-9123

Valerie J. Merritt · ⑩ · Calleton Merritt De Francisco & Real-Salas · 131 North El Molino Avenue, Suite 300 · Pasadena, CA 91101 · 626-395-0860

Karl I. Swaidan · Hahn & Hahn · 301 East Colorado Boulevard, Ninth Floor · Pasadena, CA 91101-1977 · 626-796-9123

Steven E. Trytten · Anglin, Flewelling, Rasmussen, Campbell & Trytten · 199 South Los Robles Avenue, Suite 600 · Pasadena, CA 91101-2459 · 626-535-1900

Petaluma

Robert Disharoon · Anderson, Zeigler, Disharoon, Gallagher & Gray · The Grace Building · 17 Keller Street · Petaluma, CA 94952 · 707-763-0937

Rancho Santa Fe

Jack G. Charney · Luce, Forward, Hamilton & Scripps · http://www.luce.com · 6050 El Tordo · P.O. Box 2329 · Rancho Santa Fe, CA 92067-2329 · 858-756-4410

James M. Cowley · Luce, Forward, Hamilton & Scripps · http://www.luce.com · 6050 El Tordo · P.O. Box 2329 · Rancho Santa Fe, CA 92067-2329 · 858-756-4410

Barry C. Fitzpatrick · ⑩ · Luce, Forward, Hamilton & Scripps · http://www.luce.com · 6050 El Tordo · P.O. Box 2329 · Rancho Santa Fe, CA 92067-2329 · 858-756-4410

Louis A. Mezzullo · ⑳ · Luce, Forward, Hamilton & Scripps · http://www.luce.com · 6050 El Tordo · P.O. Box 2329 · Rancho Santa Fe, CA 92067-2329 · 858-756-4410

Frederick R. Vandeveer · Luce, Forward, Hamilton & Scripps · http://www.luce.com · 6050 El Tordo · P.O. Box 2329 · Rancho Santa Fe, CA 92067-2329 · 858-756-4410

Sacramento

Frayda L. Bruton · California Trust & Estate Counselors · 400 Capitol Mall, 11th Floor · Sacramento, CA 95814-3324 · 916-444-8826

Thomas A. Craven · ⑩ · Thomas A. Craven · 400 Capitol Mall, 17th Floor · Sacramento, CA 95814-4419 · 916-442-8325

James L. Deeringer · Downey Brand · 555 Capitol Mall, 10th Floor · Sacramento, CA 95814 · 916-444-1000

Malcolm S. Weintraub · ⑩ · Weintraub Genshlea Chediak · 400 Capitol Mall, 11th Floor · Sacramento, CA 95814-4407 · 916-558-6000

San Diego

Meredith G. Alcock · Abbene, Alcock & Liska · 1010 Second Avenue, Suite 1350 · San Diego, CA 92101 619-236-1323

William E. Beamer · ⑳ · Beamer, Lauth, Steinley & Bond · 401 B Street, Suite 1530 · San Diego, CA 92101 · 619-235-6800

Stephen A. Bond · Beamer, Lauth, Steinley & Bond · 401 B Street, Suite 1530 · San Diego, CA 92101 · 619-235-6800

Theodore J. Cranston · ⑳ · DLA Piper · 4365 Executive Drive, Suite 1100 · San Diego, CA 92121-2133 · 858-677-1400

James H. Garrett · James H. Garrett · 550 West C Street, Suite 2050 · San Diego, CA 92101-8584 · 619-230-0052

Mary Gillick · Luce, Forward, Hamilton & Scripps · http://www.luce.com · 600 West Broadway, Suite 2600 · San Diego, CA 92101 · 619-236-1414

James Goodwin · Wingert, Grebing, Brubaker & Goodwin · http://www.wingertlaw.com · One America Plaza, Seventh Floor · 600 West Broadway · San Diego, CA 92101-3370 · 619-232-8151

Ralph E. Hughes · Glenn, Wright, Jacobs & Schell · Wells Fargo Building, Suite 2400 · 401 B Street · San Diego, CA 92101-4200 · 619-239-1211

Carol K. Kao · Luce, Forward, Hamilton & Scripps · http://www.luce.com · 600 West Broadway, Suite 2600 · San Diego, CA 92101 · 619-236-1414

James E. Lauth · Beamer, Lauth, Steinley & Bond · 401 B Street, Suite 1530 · San Diego, CA 92101 · 619-235-6800

James D. Miller · ⑩ · James D. Miller · 1010 Second Avenue, Suite 1350 · San Diego, CA 92101-4913 · 619-236-1323

Margaret Anne Payne · ⑳ · Higgs, Fletcher & Mack · 401 West A Street, Suite 2600 · San Diego, CA 92101-7910 · 619-236-1551

Martin H. Steinley · Beamer, Lauth, Steinley & Bond · 401 B Street, Suite 1530 · San Diego, CA 92101 · 619-235-6800

Ellen L. van Hoften · DLA Piper · 4365 Executive Drive, Suite 1100 · San Diego, CA 92121-2133 · 858-677-1400

Ellen Whelan · DLA Piper · 4365 Executive Drive, Suite 1100 · San Diego, CA 92121-2133 · 858-677-1400

San Francisco

George T. Argyris · Thelen Reid Brown Raysman & Steiner · 101 Second Street, Suite 1800 · San Francisco, CA 94105-3601 · 415-371-1200

D. Keith Bilter · ㉕ · Friedman, McCubbin, Spalding, Bilter, Roosevelt, Montgomery & Hastings · 425 California Street, 25th Floor · San Francisco, CA 94104 · 415-434-1363

Jill S. Dodd · Manatt, Phelps & Phillips · One Embarcadero Center, 30th Floor · San Francisco, CA 94111 · 415-291-7400

Raymond G. Ellis · ⑳ · Orrick, Herrington & Sutcliffe · The Orrick Building · 405 Howard Street · San Francisco, CA 94105-2669 · 415-773-5700

Philip B. Feldman · Coblentz, Patch, Duffy & Bass · http://www.coblentzlaw.com · One Ferry Building, Suite 200 · San Francisco, CA 94111-4213 · 415-391-4800

K. Bruce Friedman · ㉕ · Friedman, McCubbin, Spalding, Bilter, Roosevelt, Montgomery & Hastings · 425 California Street, 25th Floor · San Francisco, CA 94104 · 415-434-1363

Max Gutierrez, Jr. · ㉕ · Morgan Lewis & Bockius · Spear Street Tower · One Market · San Francisco, CA 94105-1596 · 415-442-1000

Diana M. Hastings · Friedman, McCubbin, Spalding, Bilter, Roosevelt, Montgomery & Hastings · 425 California Street, 25th Floor · San Francisco, CA 94104 · 415-434-1363

Theodore A. Hellman · Hanson Bridgett · http://www.hansonbridgett.com · 425 Market Street, 26th Floor · San Francisco, CA 94105 · 415-777-3200

Debra L. Kasper · Tufts Stephenson & Kasper · 235 Montgomery Street, Suite 1035 · San Francisco, CA 94104-5300 · 415-705-5300

Richard S. Kinyon · ⑳ · Morrison & Foerster · http://www.mofo.com · 425 Market Street · San Francisco, CA 94105-2482 · 415-268-7000

Ronald H. Malone · Shartsis Friese · http://www.sflaw.com · One Maritime Plaza, 18th Floor · San Francisco, CA 94111 · 415-421-6500

Donald J. McCubbin · ⑩ · Friedman, McCubbin, Spalding, Bilter, Roosevelt, Montgomery & Hastings · 425 California Street, 25th Floor · San Francisco, CA 94104 · 415-434-1363

James P. Mitchell · Coblentz, Patch, Duffy & Bass · http://www.coblentzlaw.com · One Ferry Building, Suite 200 · San Francisco, CA 94111-4213 · 415-391-4800

George F. Montgomery II · ⑩ · Friedman, McCubbin, Spalding, Bilter, Roosevelt, Montgomery & Hastings · 425 California Street, 25th Floor · San Francisco, CA 94104 · 415-434-1363

Genevieve M. Moore · Morrison & Foerster · http://www.mofo.com · 425 Market Street · San Francisco, CA 94105-2482 · 415-268-7000

Michael A. Roosevelt · ⑩ · Friedman, McCubbin, Spalding, Bilter, Roosevelt, Montgomery & Hastings · 425 California Street, 25th Floor · San Francisco, CA 94104 · 415-434-1363

Seth M. Skootsky · Skootsky & Der · http://www.skootskyder.com · 90 New Montgomery Street, Suite 905 · San Francisco, CA 94105 · 415-979-9800

Philip F. Spalding · ⑳ · Friedman, McCubbin, Spalding, Bilter, Roosevelt, Montgomery & Hastings · 425 California Street, 25th Floor · San Francisco, CA 94104 · 415-434-1363

Charles G. Stephenson · ⑳ · Tufts Stephenson & Kasper · 235 Montgomery Street, Suite 1035 · San Francisco, CA 94104-5300 · 415-705-5300

Myron G. Sugarman · ⑳ · Cooley Godward Kronish · 101 California Street, Fifth Floor · San Francisco, CA 94111-5800 · 415-693-2000

Nelson H. Wild · Law Office of Nelson H. Wild · 332 Pine Street, Suite 710 · San Francisco, CA 94104-3230 · 415-399-1600

Charles P. Wolff · Evans, Latham and Campisi · One Post Street, Suite 600 · San Francisco, CA 94104 · 415-421-0288

Thomas B. Worth · Law Offices of Thomas B. Worth · 425 California Street, Suite 2500 · San Francisco, CA 94104 · 415-434-2226

San Jose

James P. Cilley · Temmerman & Cilley · 2502 Stevens Creek Boulevard · San Jose, CA 95128-1654 · 408-998-9500

Clarence J. Ferrari, Jr. · ⑩ · Ferrari Ottoboni · 333 West Santa Clara Street, Suite 700 · San Jose, CA 95113-1716 · 408-280-0535

Janice Fox · Hoge, Fenton, Jones & Appel · http://www.hogefenton.com · 60 South Market Street, Suite 1400 · San Jose, CA 95113-2396 · 408-287-9501

John F. Hopkins · ⑩ · Hopkins & Carley · The Letitia Building · 70 South First Street · P.O. Box 1469 · San Jose, CA 95109-1469 · 408-286-9800

Alan J. Pinner · Berliner Cohen · 10 Almaden Boulevard, 11th Floor · San Jose, CA 95113-2233 · 408-286-5800

James V. Quillinan V · Hopkins & Carley · The Letitia Building · 70 South First Street · P.O. Box 1469 · San Jose, CA 95109-1469 · 408-286-9800

John F. Ramsbacher · Ramsbacher Prokey · 125 South Market Street, Suite 1150 · San Jose, CA 95113 · 408-293-3616

Filmore E. Rose · ⑩ · Beck, Ross, Bismonte & Finley · Fairmont Plaza, Suite 1300 · 50 West San Fernando Street · San Jose, CA 95113 · 408-938-7900

Scott A. Ross · Beck, Ross, Bismonte & Finley · Fairmont Plaza, Suite 1300 · 50 West San Fernando Street · San Jose, CA 95113 · 408-938-7900

Robert E. Temmerman, Jr. · ⑩ · Temmerman & Cilley · 2502 Stevens Creek Boulevard · San Jose, CA 95128-1654 · 408-998-9500

San Luis Obispo

J. Keith George · George-Cyr · 694 Santa Rosa · P.O. Box 12710 · San Luis Obispo, CA 93406 · 805-528-3394

Warren A. Sinsheimer III · ⑩ · Sinsheimer Juhnke Lebens & McIvor · 1010 Peach Street · P.O. Box 31 · San Luis Obispo, CA 93406 · 805-541-2800

Santa Barbara

John W. Ambrecht · Ambrecht & Associates · 1224 Coast Village Circle, Suite 32 · Santa Barbara, CA 93108 · 805-965-1329

Sandra J. Chan · Sandra J. Chan · Eight East Figueroa, Suite 210 · P.O. Box 5145 · Santa Barbara, CA 93150-5145 · 805-969-4286

Santa Monica

Lawrence H. Heller · Bryan Cave · 120 Broadway, Suite 300 · Santa Monica, CA 90401-2386 · 310-576-2100

Santa Rosa

Edwin C. Anderson · ⑩ · Anderson, Zeigler, Disharoon, Gallagher & Gray · 50 Old Courthouse Square, Fifth Floor · P.O. Box 1498 · Santa Rosa, CA 95404 · 707-545-4910

William M. Andrews · William M. Andrews · 420 Aviation Boulevard, Suite 204 · Santa Rosa, CA 95403 · 707-546-3183

Bradford J. DeMeo · DeMeo DeMeo & West · 565 West College Avenue · Santa Rosa, CA 95401 · 707-545-3232

Steven M. Goldberg · Friedemann Goldberg · 420 Aviation Boulevard, Suite 201 · Santa Rosa, CA 95403 707-543-4900

Kirt F. Zeigler · Anderson, Zeigler, Disharoon, Gallagher & Gray · 50 Old Courthouse Square, Fifth Floor P.O. Box 1498 · Santa Rosa, CA 95404 · 707-545-4910

Sherman Oaks

Irwin D. Goldring · ⑩ · Irwin D. Goldring · P.O. Box 56205 · Sherman Oaks, CA 91413 · 818-986-0304

Woodland Hills

Jack A. Rameson III · Law Offices of Jack A. Rameson, III · 5855 Topanga Canyon Boulevard, Suite 400 Woodland Hills, CA 91367-4621 · 818-703-7500

Danville

Daniel J. O'Connor · Daniel J. O'Connor · P.O. Box 847 · Danville, CA 94526-0847 · 925-838-4102

East Palo Alto

John Howard Clowes · DLA Piper · 2000 University Avenue · East Palo Alto, CA 94303-2214 · 650-833-2000

Gregory M. Gallo · ⑩ · DLA Piper · 2000 University Avenue · East Palo Alto, CA 94303-2214 · 650-833-2000

James M. Koshland · DLA Piper · 2000 University Avenue · East Palo Alto, CA 94303-2214 · 650-833-2000

Los Angeles

Lawrence C. Weeks · Lawrence C. Weeks · 333 South Grand Avenue, 25th Floor · Los Angeles, CA 90071 · 213-596-7851

Bradford P. Weirick · Gibson, Dunn & Crutcher · 333 South Grand Avenue · Los Angeles, CA 90071-3197 · 213-229-7000

Menlo Park

Scott C. Dettmer · Gunderson Dettmer Stough Villeneuve Franklin & Hachigian · 155 Constitution Drive · Menlo Park, CA 94025 · 650-321-2400

Robert V. Gunderson, Jr. · ⑩ · Gunderson Dettmer Stough Villeneuve Franklin & Hachigian · 155 Constitution Drive · Menlo Park, CA 94025 · 650-321-2400

Michael W. Hall · Latham & Watkins · 140 Scott Drive · Menlo Park, CA 94025 · 650-328-4600

Christopher L. Kaufman · ㉕ · Latham & Watkins · 140 Scott Drive · Menlo Park, CA 94025 · 650-328-4600

Donald M. Keller, Jr. · Orrick, Herrington & Sutcliffe · 1000 Marsh Road · Menlo Park, CA 94025-1015 · 650-614-7400

Alan C. Mendelson · ⑩ · Latham & Watkins · 140 Scott Drive · Menlo Park, CA 94025 · 650-328-4600

Daniel E. O'Connor · Gunderson Dettmer Stough Villeneuve Franklin & Hachigian · 155 Constitution Drive · Menlo Park, CA 94025 · 650-321-2400

Brooks Stough · Gunderson Dettmer Stough Villeneuve Franklin & Hachigian · 155 Constitution Drive · Menlo Park, CA 94025 · 650-321-2400

Thomas F. Villeneuve · Gunderson Dettmer Stough Villeneuve Franklin & Hachigian · 155 Constitution Drive · Menlo Park, CA 94025 · 650-321-2400

Mitchell S. Zuklie · Orrick, Herrington & Sutcliffe · 1000 Marsh Road · Menlo Park, CA 94025-1015 · 650-614-7400

Mountain View

Gordon K. Davidson · ⑩ · Fenwick & West · Silicon Valley Center · 801 California Street · Mountain View, CA 94041-2008 · 650-988-8500

Palo Alto

Aaron J. Alter · Wilson Sonsini Goodrich & Rosati · 650 Page Mill Road · Palo Alto, CA 94304-1050 · 650-493-9300

Steven E. Bochner · Wilson Sonsini Goodrich & Rosati · 650 Page Mill Road · Palo Alto, CA 94304-1050 650-493-9300

Craig E. Dauchy · ⑩ · Cooley Godward Kronish · 3175 Hanover Street · Palo Alto, CA 94304-1130 · 650-843-5000

Jorge A. del Calvo · Pillsbury Winthrop Shaw Pittman · http://www.pillsburylaw.com · 2475 Hanover Street · Palo Alto, CA 94304-1114 · 650-233-4500

James F. Fulton, Jr. · Cooley Godward Kronish · 3175 Hanover Street · Palo Alto, CA 94304-1130 · 650-843-5000

Eric C. Jensen · Cooley Godward Kronish · 3175 Hanover Street · Palo Alto, CA 94304-1130 · 650-843-5000

Robert P. Latta · Wilson Sonsini Goodrich & Rosati · 650 Page Mill Road · Palo Alto, CA 94304-1050 · 650-493-9300

Mark A. Medearis · Cooley Godward Kronish · 3175 Hanover Street · Palo Alto, CA 94304-1130 · 650-843-5000

J. Casey McGlynn · Wilson Sonsini Goodrich & Rosati · 650 Page Mill Road · Palo Alto, CA 94304-1050 · 650-493-9300

Timothy J. Moore · Cooley Godward Kronish · 3175 Hanover Street · Palo Alto, CA 94304-1130 · 650-843-5000

Arthur F. Schneiderman · Wilson Sonsini Goodrich & Rosati · 650 Page Mill Road · Palo Alto, CA 94304-1050 · 650-493-9300

Larry W. Sonsini · ㉕ · Wilson Sonsini Goodrich & Rosati · 650 Page Mill Road · Palo Alto, CA 94304-1050 · 650-493-9300

Mark P. Tanoury · Cooley Godward Kronish · 3175 Hanover Street · Palo Alto, CA 94304-1130 · 650-843-5000

Mark B. Weeks · Cooley Godward Kronish · 3175 Hanover Street · Palo Alto, CA 94304 · 650-843-5000

Pasadena

Dana M. Warren · Dana M. Warren · 790 East Colorado Boulevard, Ninth Floor · Pasadena, CA 91101 · 626-240-0687

San Diego

Craig S. Andrews · ⑩ · DLA Piper · 4365 Executive Drive, Suite 1100 · San Diego, CA 92121-2133 · 858-677-1400

Ross L. Burningham · DLA Piper · 4365 Executive Drive, Suite 1100 · San Diego, CA 92121-2133 · 858-677-1400

Thomas A. Coll · Cooley Godward Kronish · 4401 Eastgate Mall · San Diego, CA 92121-1909 · 858-550-6000

Robert G. Copeland · ⑳ · Sheppard, Mullin, Richter & Hampton · http://www.sheppardmullin.com · 501 West Broadway, 19th Floor · San Diego, CA 92101 · 619-338-6500

John A. de Groot · Morrison & Foerster · http://www.mofo.com · 12531 High Bluff Drive, Suite 100 · San Diego, CA 92130-2040 · 858-720-5100

Michael S. Kagnoff · DLA Piper · 4365 Executive Drive, Suite 1100 · San Diego, CA 92121-2133 · 858-677-1400

Frederick T. Muto · ⑩ · Cooley Godward Kronish · 4401 Eastgate Mall · San Diego, CA 92121-1909 · 858-550-6000

David R. Snyder · ⑩ · Pillsbury Winthrop Shaw Pittman · http://www.pillsburylaw.com · 501 West Broadway, Suite 1100 · San Diego, CA 92101-3575 · 619-234-5000

Scott N. Wolfe · ⑩ · Latham & Watkins · 12636 High Bluff Drive, Suite 400 · San Diego, CA 92130 · 858-523-5400

San Francisco

Kenneth Guernsey · Cooley Godward Kronish · 101 California Street, Fifth Floor · San Francisco, CA 94111-5800 · 415-693-2000

J. Randall Lewis · Wilson Sonsini Goodrich & Rosati · Spear Tower, Suite 3300 · One Market Street · San Francisco, CA 94105-1126 · 415-947-2000

WATER LAW

Costa Mesa

Richard G. Montevideo · Rutan & Tucker · http://www.rutan.com · 611 Anton Boulevard, Suite 1400 · P.O. Box 1950 · Costa Mesa, CA 92628-1950 · 714-641-5100

Paul N. Singarella · Latham & Watkins · 650 Town Center Drive, 20th Floor · Costa Mesa, CA 92626-1925 · 714-540-1235

Fresno

Gary W. Sawyers · Law Office of Gary W. Sawyers · 6715 North Palm Avenue, Suite 116 · Fresno, CA 93704 · 559-438-5656

Riverside

Arthur L. Littleworth · ⑩ · Best Best & Krieger · 3750 University Avenue, Suite 400 · P.O. Box 1028 · Riverside, CA 92502 · 951-686-1450

Gregory K. Wilkinson · Best Best & Krieger · 3750 University Avenue, Suite 400 · P.O. Box 1028 · Riverside, CA 92502 · 951-686-1450

Sacramento

Michael A. Campos · Stoel Rives · http://www.stoel.com · 980 Ninth Street, Suite 1900 · Sacramento, CA 95814 · 916-447-0700

Kristen Troy Castaños · Stoel Rives · http://www.stoel.com · 980 Ninth Street, Suite 1900 · Sacramento, CA 95814 · 916-447-0700

Roberta L. Larson · Somach, Simmons & Dunn · http://www.somachlaw.com · Hall of Justice Building, Third Floor · 813 Sixth Street · Sacramento, CA 95814-2403 · 916-446-7979

David E. Lindgren · Downey Brand · 555 Capitol Mall, 10th Floor · Sacramento, CA 95814 · 916-444-1000

Anne J. Schneider · Ellison, Schneider & Harris · 2015 H Street · Sacramento, CA 95814-3109 · 916-447-2166

Stuart L. Somach · ⑩ · Somach, Simmons & Dunn · http://www.somachlaw.com · Hall of Justice Building, Third Floor · 813 Sixth Street · Sacramento, CA 95814-2403 · 916-446-7979

Melissa A. Thorme · Downey Brand · 555 Capitol Mall, 10th Floor · Sacramento, CA 95814 · 916-444-1000

Craig M. Wilson · Stoel Rives · http://www.stoel.com · 980 Ninth Street, Suite 1900 · Sacramento, CA 95814 · 916-447-0700

San Francisco

Thomas M. Berliner · Duane Morris · Spear Tower, Suite 2000 · One Market · San Francisco, CA 94105-1104 · 415-957-3000

John Briscoe · Briscoe, Ivester & Bazel · 155 Sansome Street, Seventh Floor · San Francisco, CA 94104 · 415-402-2700

Robert J. Uram · Sheppard, Mullin, Richter & Hampton · http://www.sheppardmullin.com · Four Embarcadero Center, 17th Floor · San Francisco, CA 94111 · 415-434-9100

Visalia

Daniel M. Dooley · Dooley, Herr & Peltzer · 100 Willow Plaza, Suite 300 · Visalia, CA 93291-6206 · 559-636-0200

Walnut Creek

Roderick E. Walston · Best Best & Krieger · 2001 North Main Street, Suite 390 · Walnut Creek, CA 94596 · 925-977-3300

WHITE-COLLAR CRIMINAL DEFENSE

Auburn

Thomas Leupp · Leupp, Wachob & Woodall · 149 Court Street · Auburn, CA 95603 · 530-888-1100

Berkeley

Cristina C. Arguedas · ⑳ · Arguedas, Cassman & Headley · http://www.achlaw.com · 803 Hearst Avenue Berkeley, CA 94710 · 510-845-3000

Ted W. Cassman · Arguedas, Cassman & Headley · http://www.achlaw.com · 803 Hearst Avenue · Berkeley, CA 94710 · 510-845-3000

James S. Thomson · James S. Thomson · 819 Delaware Street · Berkeley, CA 94710 · 510-525-9123

Beverly Hills

Stephen D. Miller · ㉕ · Law Offices of Stephen D. Miller · 360 North Bedford Drive, Suite 204 · Beverly Hills, CA 90210 · 310-247-0080

Costa Mesa

Joel Levine · ㉕ · Law Office of Joel Levine · 695 Town Center Drive, Suite 875 · Costa Mesa, CA 92626 714-662-4462

Paul S. Meyer · ⑩ · Law Office of Paul S. Meyer · 695 Town Center Drive, Suite 875 · Costa Mesa, CA 92626 · 714-754-6500

Hayward

Philip A. Schnayerson · ⑳ · Garcia, Schnayerson & Mockus · 225 West Winton Avenue, Suite 208 · Hayward, CA 94544 · 510-887-7445

Irvine

Jack M. Earley · ⑩ · The Law Office of Jack M. Earley · 19900 MacArthur Boulevard, Suite 850 · Irvine, CA 92612-8422 · 949-476-8900

Jennifer L. Keller · Law Offices of Jennifer L. Keller · 18500 Von Karman Avenue, Suite 560 · Irvine, CA 92612 · 949-476-8700

William J. Kopeny · ⑩ · William Kopeny & Associates · http://www.writsnappeals.com · 16485 Laguna Canyon Road, Suite 230 · Irvine, CA 92618 · 949-453-2243

Thomas R. Malcolm · ⑩ · Jones Day · Three Park Plaza, Suite 1100 · Irvine, CA 92614-2592 · 949-851-3939

Los Angeles

Manuel A. Abascal · Latham & Watkins · 355 South Grand Avenue · Los Angeles, CA 90071-1560 · 213-485-1234

Mark E. Beck · ⑩ · Orrick, Herrington & Sutcliffe · 777 South Figueroa Street, Suite 3200 · Los Angeles, CA 90017-5855 · 213-629-2020

Terry W. Bird · ⑩ · Bird, Marella, Boxer, Wolpert, Nessim, Drooks & Lincenberg · 1875 Century Park East, 23rd Floor · Los Angeles, CA 90067-2561 · 310-201-2100

Robert C. Bonner · Gibson, Dunn & Crutcher · 333 South Grand Avenue · Los Angeles, CA 90071-3197 213-229-7000

Harland W. Braun · ⑳ · Harland W. Braun · 1880 Century Park East, Suite 710 · Los Angeles, CA 90067-1608 · 310-277-4777

Brad D. Brian · ⑩ · Munger, Tolles & Olson · 355 South Grand Avenue, 35th Floor · Los Angeles, CA 90071-1560 · 213-683-9100

Bradley W. Brunon · ⑳ · Bradley W. Brunon · 12100 Wilshire Boulevard, 15th Floor · Los Angeles, CA 90025-7120 · 310-820-4484

Steve Cochran · Katten Muchin Rosenman · 2029 Century Park East, Suite 2600 · Los Angeles, CA 90067-3012 · 310-788-4400

Robert L. Corbin · ⑩ · Law Offices of Corbin & Fitzgerald · 601 West Fifth Street, Suite 1150 · Los Angeles, CA 90071-2024 · 213-612-0001

Bryan D. Daly · Mayer Brown · 350 South Grand Avenue, 25th Floor · Los Angeles, CA 90071-1503 · 213-229-9500

Jack P. Dicanio · Skadden, Arps, Slate, Meagher & Flom · 300 South Grand Avenue, Suite 3400 · Los Angeles, CA 90071 · 213-687-5000

Kimberly A. Dunne · Sidley Austin · 555 West Fifth Street, 40th Floor · Los Angeles, CA 90013 · 213-896-6000

Frederick D. Friedman · Jones Day · 555 South Flower Street, 50th Floor · Los Angeles, CA 90071 · 213-489-3939

Gordon A. Greenberg · McDermott Will & Emery · 2049 Century Park East, 38th Floor · Los Angeles, CA 90067-3218 · 310-277-4110

Stanley I. Greenberg · ㉕ · Stanley I. Greenberg · 6080 Center Drive, Suite 800 · Los Angeles, CA 90045-1574 · 310-215-7509

Jan Lawrence Handzlik · ㉕ · Howrey · 550 South Hope Street, Suite 1100 · Los Angeles, CA 90071 · 213-892-1800

Russell Hayman · McDermott Will & Emery · 2049 Century Park East, 38th Floor · Los Angeles, CA 90067-3218 · 310-277-4110

Brian J. Hennigan · ⑩ · Irell & Manella · 1800 Avenue of the Stars, Suite 900 · Los Angeles, CA 90067-4276 · 310-277-1010

Thomas E. Holliday · ⑳ · Gibson, Dunn & Crutcher · 333 South Grand Avenue · Los Angeles, CA 90071-3197 · 213-229-7000

Mark C. Holscher · Kirkland & Ellis · 777 South Figueroa Street, Suite 3400 · Los Angeles, CA 90017-5800 · 213-680-8400

John C. Hueston · Irell & Manella · 1800 Avenue of the Stars, Suite 900 · Los Angeles, CA 90067-4276 · 310-277-1010

Pamela L. Johnston · Foley & Lardner · 555 South Flower Street, Suite 3500 · Los Angeles, CA 90071-2300 · 213-972-4500

Dennis E. Kinnaird · ㉕ · Foley & Lardner · 555 South Flower Street, Suite 3500 · Los Angeles, CA 90071-2300 · 213-972-4500

Carolyn June Kubota · O'Melveny & Myers · 400 South Hope Street, 10th Floor · Los Angeles, CA 90071-2899 · 213-430-6000

Janet I. Levine · ⑩ · Lightfoot Vandevelde Sadowsky Crouchley Rutherford & Levine · 800 Wilshire Boulevard, Suite 500 · Los Angeles, CA 90017 · 213-622-4750

Michael J. Lightfoot · ⑳ · Lightfoot Vandevelde Sadowsky Crouchley Rutherford & Levine · 800 Wilshire Boulevard, Suite 500 · Los Angeles, CA 90017 · 213-622-4750

Gary S. Lincenberg · Bird, Marella, Boxer, Wolpert, Nessim, Drooks & Lincenberg · 1875 Century Park East, 23rd Floor · Los Angeles, CA 90067-2561 · 310-201-2100

Vincent J. Marella · ㉕ · Bird, Marella, Boxer, Wolpert, Nessim, Drooks & Lincenberg · 1875 Century Park East, 23rd Floor · Los Angeles, CA 90067-2561 · 310-201-2100

Richard Marmaro · Skadden, Arps, Slate, Meagher & Flom · 300 South Grand Avenue, Suite 3400 · Los Angeles, CA 90071 · 213-687-5000

Alejandro Mayorkas · O'Melveny & Myers · 1999 Avenue of the Stars, Seventh Floor · Los Angeles, CA 90067-6035 · 310-553-6700

Alvin S. Michaelson · ⑳ · Law Offices of Alvin S. Michaelson · 1901 Avenue of the Stars, Suite 615 · Los Angeles, CA 90067-6018 · 310-278-4984

Ronald J. Nessim · Bird, Marella, Boxer, Wolpert, Nessim, Drooks & Lincenberg · 1875 Century Park East, 23rd Floor · Los Angeles, CA 90067-2561 · 310-201-2100

Thomas J. Nolan · Skadden, Arps, Slate, Meagher & Flom · 300 South Grand Avenue, Suite 3400 · Los Angeles, CA 90071 · 213-687-5000

Brian O'Neill · ⑳ · Jones Day · 555 South Flower Street, 50th Floor · Los Angeles, CA 90071 · 213-489-3939

Ronald L. Olson · ⑳ · Munger, Tolles & Olson · 355 South Grand Avenue, 35th Floor · Los Angeles, CA 90071-1560 · 213-683-9100

Anthony Pacheco · Proskauer Rose · http://www.proskauer.com · 2049 Century Park East, 32nd Floor · Los Angeles, CA 90067-3206 · 310-557-2900

S. Thomas Pollack · ⑩ · Irell & Manella · 1800 Avenue of the Stars, Suite 900 · Los Angeles, CA 90067-4276 · 310-277-1010

Michael J. Proctor · Caldwell, Leslie, Newcombe & Pettit · 1000 Wilshire Boulevard, Suite 600 · Los Angeles, CA 90017-2463 · 213-629-9040

John J. Quinn · ⑩ · JAMS · 707 Wilshire Boulevard, 46th Floor · Los Angeles, CA 90017 · 213-620-1133

Jeffrey M. Rawitz · Jones Day · 555 South Flower Street, 50th Floor · Los Angeles, CA 90071 · 213-489-3939

Donald M. Re · ⑩ · Donald M. Re · 624 South Grand Avenue, 22nd Floor · Los Angeles, CA 90017 · 213-623-4234

James L. Sanders · McDermott Will & Emery · 2049 Century Park East, 38th Floor · Los Angeles, CA 90067-3218 · 310-277-4110

David J. Schindler · Latham & Watkins · 355 South Grand Avenue · Los Angeles, CA 90071-1560 · 213-485-1234

David M. Stern · ⑩ · Klee, Tuchin, Bogdanoff & Stern · 1919 Avenue of the Stars, 39th Floor · Los Angeles, CA 90067-6049 · 310-407-4000

Brian A. Sun · ⑩ · Jones Day · 555 South Flower Street, 50th Floor · Los Angeles, CA 90071 · 213-489-3939

Barry Tarlow · ㉕ · Tarlow & Berk · 9119 West Sunset Boulevard · Los Angeles, CA 90069 · 310-278-2111

John D. Vandevelde · ㉕ · Lightfoot Vandevelde Sadowsky Crouchley Rutherford & Levine · 800 Wilshire Boulevard, Suite 500 · Los Angeles, CA 90017 · 213-622-4750

David K. Willingham · Caldwell, Leslie, Newcombe & Pettit · 1000 Wilshire Boulevard, Suite 600 · Los Angeles, CA 90017-2463 · 213-629-9040

Debra Wong Yang · Gibson, Dunn & Crutcher · 333 South Grand Avenue · Los Angeles, CA 90071-3197 213-229-7000

John Yzurdiaga · John Yzurdiaga · 800 Wilshire Boulevard, Suite 1510 · Los Angeles, CA 90017 · 213-622-9262

Manhattan Beach

Mark O. Heaney · ㉕ · Mark O. Heaney · 2808 Alma Avenue · Manhattan Beach, CA 90266 · 310-545-6774

Mill Valley

M. Gerald Schwartzbach · ⑳ · M. Gerald Schwartzbach · 655 Redwood Highway, Suite 277 · Mill Valley, CA 94941-3057 · 415-388-2343

Orange

John D. Barnett · ⑩ · Law Office of John D. Barnett · One City Boulevard West, Fifth Floor · Orange, CA 92868 · 714-634-3397

Ronald G. Brower · Brower & Associates · 1043 Civic Center Drive, W, Suite 200 · Orange, CA 92703 · 714-997-4400

Palo Alto

Michael W. Armstrong · Nolan, Armstrong & Barton · 600 University Avenue · Palo Alto, CA 94301-2076 · 650-326-2980

Stephen C. Neal · ⑩ · Cooley Godward Kronish · Five Palo Alto Square · 3000 El Camino Real · Palo Alto, CA 94306-2155 · 650-843-5000

Thomas J. Nolan · ⑳ · Nolan, Armstrong & Barton · 600 University Avenue · Palo Alto, CA 94301-2076 · 650-326-2980

Redwood Shores

Robert P. Feldman · Quinn Emanuel Urquhart Oliver & Hedges · 555 Twin Dolphin Drive, Suite 560 · Redwood Shores, CA 94065 · 650-801-5000

Riverside

Virginia M. Blumenthal · ⑳ · Blumenthal Law Offices · The Riverside Barrister Building · 3993 Market Street · Riverside, CA 92501 · 951-682-5110

Steven L. Harmon · ⑳ · Harmon & Harmon · The Loring Building, Suite 250 · 3685 Main Street · Riverside, CA 92501 · 951-329-9324

Sacramento

Clyde M. Blackmon · ⑳ · Blackmon & Associates · 813 Sixth Street, Suite 450 · Sacramento, CA 95814-2403 · 916-441-0824

Quin Denvir · Rothschild Wishek & Sands · http://www.rwslaw.com · 901 F Street, Suite 200 · Sacramento, CA 95814 · 916-444-9845

Donald H. Heller · Donald H. Heller · http://www.donaldhellerlaw.com · 655 University Avenue, Suite 215 · Sacramento, CA 95825 · 916-974-3500

Nancy Luque · DLA Piper · 400 Capitol Mall, Suite 2400 · Sacramento, CA 95814-4428 · 916-930-3200

George L. O'Connell · ⑩ · Stevens & O'Connell · 400 Capitol Mall, Suite 1400 · Sacramento, CA 95814-4498 · 916-329-9111

Michael Rothschild · ⑩ · Rothschild Wishek & Sands · http://www.rwslaw.com · 901 F Street, Suite 200 · Sacramento, CA 95814 · 916-444-9845

Malcolm S. Segal · ⑩ · Segal & Kirby · 770 L Street, Suite 1440 · Sacramento, CA 95814 · 916-441-0828

Charles J. Stevens · ⑩ · Stevens & O'Connell · 400 Capitol Mall, Suite 1400 · Sacramento, CA 95814-4498 · 916-329-9111

Christopher H. Wing · ⑩ · Christopher H. Wing · 1101 East Street · Sacramento, CA 95814 · 916-441-4888

M. Bradley Wishek · Rothschild Wishek & Sands · http://www.rwslaw.com · 901 F Street, Suite 200 · Sacramento, CA 95814 · 916-444-9845

Salinas

Thomas S. Worthington · ⑳ · The Worthington Law Centre · http://www.worthingtonlawcentre.com · 215 West Alisal Street · Salinas, CA 93901 · 831-758-1688

San Bernardino

C. Patrick Milligan · ⑩ · Milligan & Beswick · 323 West Court Street, Suite 402 · San Bernardino, CA 92401-1697 · 909-889-1178

Grover L. Porter · Grover Porter · 355 North Sierra Way · San Bernardino, CA 92410 · 909-884-0586

San Clemente

Thomas H. Bienert, Jr. · Bienert, Miller, Weitzel & Katzman · 115 Avenida Miramar · San Clemente, CA 92672 · 949-369-3700

H. Dean Steward · H. Dean Steward · 107 Avenida Miramar, Suite C · San Clemente, CA 92672 · 949-481-4900

San Diego

Michael Attanasio · Cooley Godward Kronish · 4401 Eastgate Mall · San Diego, CA 92121-1909 · 858-550-6000

Nelson P. Brav · Brav & Schwartz · 4026 Dove Street · San Diego, CA 92103-1998 · 619-293-7350

Robert S. Brewer, Jr. · ⑩ · McKenna Long & Aldridge · Symphony Towers, Suite 3300 · 750 B Street · San Diego, CA 92101-8105 · 619-595-5400

Juanita R. Brooks · ⑳ · Fish & Richardson · 12390 El Camino Real · San Diego, CA 92130 · 858-678-5070

Ezekiel E. Cortez · ⑩ · Ezekiel E. Cortez · http://www.ezekielecortez.com · 1010 Second Avenue, Suite 1850 · San Diego, CA 92101 · 619-237-0309

John G. Cotsirilos · ⑩ · John G. Cotsirilos · 2442 Fourth Avenue · San Diego, CA 92101 · 619-232-6022

Raymond J. Coughlan, Jr. · ⑩ · Coughlan, Semmer & Lipman · Koll Center, Suite 400 · 501 West Broadway · San Diego, CA 92101-3505 · 619-232-0800

Steven E. Feldman · Law Offices of Steven E. Feldman · 934 Twenty-Third Street · San Diego, CA 92102 · 619-232-8649

Charles L. Goldberg · ㉕ · Seltzer Caplan McMahon Vitek · Symphony Towers, Suite 2100 · 750 B Street San Diego, CA 92101 · 619-685-3003

Robert L. Grimes · ⑩ · Grimes & Warwick · 2664 Fourth Avenue · San Diego, CA 92103-6515 · 619-232-9700

Patrick Q. Hall · Seltzer Caplan McMahon Vitek · Symphony Towers, Suite 2100 · 750 B Street · San Diego, CA 92101 · 619-685-3003

Peter J. Hughes · ㉕ · Peter J. Hughes · 1010 Second Avenue, Suite 1840 · San Diego, CA 92101 · 619-234-6696

Eugene G. Iredale · ⑳ · Eugene G. Iredale · 105 West F Street, Fourth Floor · San Diego, CA 92101-6036 · 619-233-1525

Knut S. Johnson · Knut S. Johnson · 1010 Second Avenue, Suite 1850 · San Diego, CA 92101 · 619-232-7080

Charles G. LaBella · LaBella & McNamara · 401 West A Street, Suite 1150 · San Diego, CA 92101 · 619-696-9200

Michael L. Lipman · ⑩ · Coughlan, Semmer & Lipman · Koll Center, Suite 400 · 501 West Broadway · San Diego, CA 92101-3505 · 619-232-0800

Michael R. Marrinan · Law Office of Michael R. Marrinan · 614 Fifth Avenue, Suite D · San Diego, CA 92101 · 619-238-6900

Michael N. Pancer · ⑳ · Michael N. Pancer · 105 West F Street, Fourth Floor · San Diego, CA 92101 · 619-236-1826

John G. Phillips · John G. Phillips · 1010 Second Avenue, Suite 1840 · San Diego, CA 92101 · 619-234-0163

Christopher J. Plourd · Christopher J. Plourd · 1168 Union Street, Suite 303 · San Diego, CA 92101 · 619-615-6200

Frank J. Ragen II · ⑩ · Frank J. Ragen · 105 West F Street, Suite 215 · San Diego, CA 92101 · 619-231-4330

Lynda A. Romero · Law Office of Lynda Romero · 5173 Waring Road, Suite 220 · San Diego, CA 92120 · 619-286-6992

Robert D. Rose · Sheppard, Mullin, Richter & Hampton · http://www.sheppardmullin.com · 501 West Broadway, 19th Floor · San Diego, CA 92101 · 619-338-6500

Charles M. Sevilla · ⑳ · The Law Office of Charles Sevilla · 1010 Second Avenue, Suite 1825 · San Diego, CA 92101-4902 · 619-232-2222

Milton J. Silverman, Jr. · ㉕ · Milton J. Silverman · The Quartermass-Wilde House · 2404 Broadway · San Diego, CA 92102 · 619-231-6611

Edward Patrick Swan, Jr. · Luce, Forward, Hamilton & Scripps · http://www.luce.com · 600 West Broadway, Suite 2600 · San Diego, CA 92101 · 619-236-1414

Frank T. Vecchione · Frank Vecchione · 105 West F Street, Suite 215 · San Diego, CA 92101 · 619-231-3653

Thomas J. Warwick, Jr. · Grimes & Warwick · 2664 Fourth Avenue · San Diego, CA 92103-6515 · 619-232-9700

Lewis A. Wenzell · ⑩ · Lewis A. Wenzell · 5070 Narragansett Avenue, Suite 303 · San Diego, CA 92107-3028 · 619-224-9422

San Francisco

Daniel Bookin · ⑩ · O'Melveny & Myers · Embarcadero Center West · 275 Battery Street · San Francisco, CA 94111-3305 · 415-984-8700

James J. Brosnahan · ㉕ · Morrison & Foerster · http://www.mofo.com · 425 Market Street · San Francisco, CA 94105-2482 · 415-268-7000

Walter F. Brown, Jr. · Orrick, Herrington & Sutcliffe · The Orrick Building · 405 Howard Street · San Francisco, CA 94105-2669 · 415-773-5700

Nanci Lynne Clarence · ⑩ · Clarence & Dyer · 899 Ellis Street · San Francisco, CA 94109 · 415-749-1800

John D. Cline · ⑩ · Jones Day · 555 California Street, 26th Floor · San Francisco, CA 94104 · 415-626-3939

George J. Cotsirilos, Jr. · Cotsirilos & Campisano · 250 Montgomery Street, Suite 1100 · San Francisco, CA 94104-3420 · 415-397-2373

Gilbert Eisenberg · ㉕ · Law Office of Gilbert Eisenberg · 400 Montgomery Street, Suite 200 · San Francisco, CA 94104 · 415-433-3476

William M. Goodman · ⑩ · Kasowitz, Benson, Torres & Friedman · 101 California Street, Suite 2050 · San Francisco, CA 94111 · 415-421-6140

Melinda Haag · Orrick, Herrington & Sutcliffe · The Orrick Building · 405 Howard Street · San Francisco, CA 94105-2669 · 415-773-5700

John W. Keker · ㉕ · Keker & Van Nest · http://www.kvn.com · 710 Sansome Street · San Francisco, CA 94111 · 415-391-5400

Jan Nielsen Little · Keker & Van Nest · http://www.kvn.com · 710 Sansome Street · San Francisco, CA 94111 · 415-391-5400

Mary McNamara · Swanson, McNamara & Haller · 300 Montgomery Street, Suite 1100 · San Francisco, CA 94104 · 415-477-3800

George D. Niespolo · Duane Morris · Spear Tower, Suite 2000 · One Market · San Francisco, CA 94105-1104 · 415-957-3000

William L. Osterhoudt · ⑳ · William L. Osterhoudt · 135 Belvedere Street · San Francisco, CA 94117 · 415-664-4600

Elliot R. Peters · Keker & Van Nest · http://www.kvn.com · 710 Sansome Street · San Francisco, CA 94111 · 415-391-5400

John Potter · Quinn Emanuel Urquhart Oliver & Hedges · 50 California Street, 22nd Floor · San Francisco, CA 94111 · 415-875-6600

Dennis P. Riordan · ⑩ · Riordan & Horgan · 523 Octavia Street · San Francisco, CA 94102 · 415-431-3472

Jerome C. Roth · Munger, Tolles & Olson · 560 Mission Street, 27th Floor · San Francisco, CA 94105-9781 · 415-512-4000

Michael J. Shepard · Hogan & Hartson · Four Embarcadero Center, 22nd Floor · San Francisco, CA 94111 · 415-519-5312

Karen L. Snell · ⑩ · Karen L. Snell · 102 Buena Vista Terrace · San Francisco, CA 94117 · 415-225-7592

Edward W. Swanson · Swanson, McNamara & Haller · 300 Montgomery Street, Suite 1100 · San Francisco, CA 94104 · 415-477-3800

Robert W. Tarun · Baker & McKenzie · Two Embarcadero Center, 11th Floor · San Francisco, CA 94111-3802 · 415-576-3000

Marcus S. Topel · ⑳ · Kasowitz, Benson, Torres & Friedman · 101 California Street, Suite 2050 · San Francisco, CA 94111 · 415-421-6140

Robert A. Van Nest · Keker & Van Nest · http://www.kvn.com · 710 Sansome Street · San Francisco, CA 94111 · 415-391-5400

Doron Weinberg · ㉕ · Weinberg & Wilder · 523 Octavia Street · San Francisco, CA 94102 · 415-431-3472

Douglas R. Young · ⑩ · Farella Braun & Martel · Russ Building, 17th Floor · 235 Montgomery Street · San Francisco, CA 94104 · 415-954-4400

San Jose

Craig M. Brown · Craig M. Brown · 333 West Santa Clara Street, Suite 260 · San Jose, CA 95113-1714 · 408-286-8844

Guyton N. Jinkerson · ⑳ · Guyton N. Jinkerson · http://www.guytonjinkerson.com · 510 North Third Street · San Jose, CA 95112 · 408-297-8555

Alan M. Lagod · ⑩ · Lagod & Christensen · 360 West Hedding Street · San Jose, CA 95110 · 408-288-5025

Steven R. Manchester · ⑩ · Manchester, Williams & Seibert · 125 South Market Street, Suite 1100 · San Jose, CA 95113 · 408-287-6193

James McManis · ⑩ · McManis Faulkner · http://www.mcmanisfaulkner.com · Fairmont Plaza, 10th Floor 50 West San Fernando Street · San Jose, CA 95113-2415 · 408-279-8700

Kenneth W. Robinson · ⑩ · Law Offices of Kenneth W. Robinson · 1065 Asbury Street · San Jose, CA 95126 · 408-294-4477

Allen J. Ruby · ⑳ · Ruby & Schofield · 125 South Market Street, Suite 1001 · San Jose, CA 95113-2285 · 408-998-8500

Frank R. Ubhaus · ㉕ · Berliner Cohen · 10 Almaden Boulevard, 11th Floor · San Jose, CA 95113-2233 · 408-286-5800

John L. Williams, Jr. · ⑳ · Manchester, Williams & Seibert · 125 South Market Street, Suite 1100 · San Jose, CA 95113 · 408-287-6193

Santa Ana

James D. Riddet · ⑳ · Stokke & Riddet · Three Imperial Promenade, Suite 750 · Santa Ana, CA 92707-5903 · 714-662-2400

Allan H. Stokke · ⑳ · Stokke & Riddet · Three Imperial Promenade, Suite 750 · Santa Ana, CA 92707-5903 · 714-662-2400

Santa Barbara

Robert M. Sanger · ⑩ · Sanger & Swysen · 233 East Carrillo Street, Suite C · Santa Barbara, CA 93101 · 805-962-4887

Santa Cruz

Paul B. Meltzer · ⑩ · Law Offices of Paul B. Meltzer · 511 Water Street · Santa Cruz, CA 95060 · 831-426-6000

Santa Monica

William J. Genego · Nasatir, Hirsch, Podberesky & Genego · Main Street Law Building · 2115 Main Street · Santa Monica, CA 90405 · 310-399-3259

Richard G. Hirsch · ⑳ · Nasatir, Hirsch, Podberesky & Genego · Main Street Law Building · 2115 Main Street · Santa Monica, CA 90405 · 310-399-3259

Evan A. Jenness · Law Offices of Evan Jenness · Main Street Law Building · 2115 Main Street · Santa Monica, CA 90405 · 310-399-3259

Michael D. Nasatir · ⑳ · Nasatir, Hirsch, Podberesky & Genego · Main Street Law Building · 2115 Main Street · Santa Monica, CA 90405 · 310-399-3259

Vicki I. Podberesky · Nasatir, Hirsch, Podberesky & Genego · Main Street Law Building · 2115 Main Street · Santa Monica, CA 90405 · 310-399-3259

Victor Sherman · Sherman & Sherman · 2115 Main Street · Santa Monica, CA 90405 · 310-399-3259

Santa Rosa

Chris P. Andrian · Andrian & Gallenson · 1100 Mendocino Avenue · Santa Rosa, CA 95401-4311 · 707-527-9381

Jamie O. Thistlethwaite · Jamie Olsen Thistlethwaite · 444 Tenth Street, Fourth Floor · Santa Rosa, CA 95401-5267 · 707-578-9254

L. Stephen Turer · L. Stephen Turer · 610 Davis Street · Santa Rosa, CA 95401 · 707-546-1551

Ukiah

Susan B. Jordan · ㉕ · Susan B. Jordan · 515 South School Street · Ukiah, CA 95482 · 707-462-2151

Ann C. Moorman · Law Offices of Ann Moorman · 308 South School Street · Ukiah, CA 95482 · 707-462-1844

Vista

Richard D. Muir · ㉕ · Richard D. Muir · 122 Escondido Avenue, Suite 102 · Vista, CA 92084-6055 · 760-726-6131

Westlake Village

Edward M. Medvene · ⑩ · Law Office of Edward M. Medvene · 1014 South Westlake Boulevard, Suite 14-185 · Westlake Village, CA 91361 · 805-497-2788

WORKERS' COMPENSATION LAW

Antioch

Thomas M. Pegnim · Pegnim & Herrera · 3105 Lone Tree Way, Suite A · Antioch, CA 94509-4974 · 925-776-4500

Beverly Hills

Lester J. Friedman · The Law Offices of Lester J. Friedman · 9777 Wilshire Boulevard, Suite 1015 · Beverly Hills, CA 90212-1901 · 310-275-1433

Cupertino

Brett A. Borah · ⑩ · Borah & Shaffer · 20111 Stevens Creek Boulevard, Suite 230 · Cupertino, CA 95014 408-996-8650

Encino

Donald S. Lucien · ⑩ · The Law Office of Donald S. Lucien · 16133 Ventura Boulevard, Suite 680 · Encino, CA 91436 · 818-906-2500

Fremont

Raymond E. Frost · Raymond E. Frost & Associates · 39510 Paseo Padre Parkway, Suite 300 · Fremont, CA 94538 · 510-792-5310

Grover Beach

William A. Herreras · ⑩ · Law Office of William A. Herreras · 200 South 13th Street, Suite 212 · P.O. Box 387 · Grover Beach, CA 93433-2263 · 805-473-8550

Irvine

Lloyd B. Rowe · ⑩ · Lloyd B. Rowe · P.O. Box 52888 · Irvine, CA 92619-9998 · 310-532-2072

Long Beach

W. Joseph Truce · ⑩ · Kegel, Tobin & Truce · 3580 Wilshire Boulevard, Suite 1000 · P.O. Box 76907 · Long Beach, CA 90076-0907 · 213-380-3880

Los Angeles

Elliot S. Berkowitz · ⑩ · The Law Offices of Berkowitz & Cohen · 6500 Wilshire Boulevard, Suite 1860 · Los Angeles, CA 90048 · 323-651-5151

Sheldon S. Cohen · The Law Offices of Berkowitz & Cohen · 6500 Wilshire Boulevard, Suite 1860 · Los Angeles, CA 90048 · 323-651-5151

Mark Edelstein · ⑩ · Gordon, Edelstein, Krepack, Grant, Felton & Goldstein · 3580 Wilshire Boulevard, Suite 1800 · Los Angeles, CA 90010 · 213-739-7000

G. Ronald Feenberg · ⑩ · Rose, Klein & Marias · 801 South Grand Avenue, 11th Floor · Los Angeles, CA 90017-4645 · 213-784-2801

Richard I. Felton · ⑩ · Gordon, Edelstein, Krepack, Grant, Felton & Goldstein · 3580 Wilshire Boulevard, Suite 1800 · Los Angeles, CA 90010 · 213-739-7000

Irwin L. Goldstein · ⑩ · Gordon, Edelstein, Krepack, Grant, Felton & Goldstein · 3580 Wilshire Boulevard, Suite 1800 · Los Angeles, CA 90010 · 213-739-7000

Sherry E. Grant · ⑩ · Gordon, Edelstein, Krepack, Grant, Felton & Goldstein · 3580 Wilshire Boulevard, Suite 1800 · Los Angeles, CA 90010 · 213-739-7000

Marvin N. Shapiro · ⑩ · Rose, Klein & Marias · 801 South Grand Avenue, 11th Floor · Los Angeles, CA 90017-4645 · 213-784-2801

Modesto

John B. Frailing · ⑩ · Frailing, Rockwell & Kelly · 1600 G Street, Suite 203 · P.O. Box 0142 · Modesto, CA 95353 · 209-521-2552

Oakland

Stewart N. Boxer · Boxer & Gerson · 300 Frank H. Ogawa Plaza, Suite 500 · Oakland, CA 94612 · 510-835-8870

Robert J. Cavallero · Mullen & Filippi · 555 Twelfth Street, Suite 2050 · Oakland, CA 94607 · 510-444-1532

Michael G. Gerson · ⑩ · Boxer & Gerson · 300 Frank H. Ogawa Plaza, Suite 500 · Oakland, CA 94612 · 510-835-8870

John M. Harrigan · Boxer & Gerson · 300 Frank H. Ogawa Plaza, Suite 500 · Oakland, CA 94612 · 510-835-8870

Ontario

Robert I. Vines · ⑩ · Rose, Klein & Marias · 3633 East Inland Empire Boulevard, Suite 400 · P.O. Box 51464 · Ontario, CA 91761-1064 · 909-581-9476

Palm Desert

Jeffrey M. Wilson · ⑩ · Wilson, Pesota & Fox · 73-710 Fred Waring Drive, Suite 210 · Palm Desert, CA 92260 · 760-776-6830

Pleasant Hill

Mark E. Gearheart · ⑩ · Gearheart & Otis · 367 Civic Drive, Suite 17 · P.O. Box 23588 · Pleasant Hill, CA 94523 · 925-671-9777

Sacramento

Arthur V. Azevedo · ⑩ · Green & Azevedo · 1722 H Street, Suite 100 · Sacramento, CA 95814 · 209-526-3560

Melissa C. Brown · ⑩ · Farrell, Fraulob & Brown · 2315 Capitol Avenue · Sacramento, CA 95816 · 916-442-5835

Marc G. Marcus · Marcus & Regalado · 3031 F Streeet, Suite 100 · Sacramento, CA 95816 · 916-441-1611

Dudley R. Phenix · Jones, Clifford, McDevitt, Naekel & Johnson · 117 J Street, Suite 301 · Sacramento, CA 95814-2212 · 916-443-2284

Salinas

N. Michael Rucka · ⑩ · Rucka, O'Boyle, Lombardo & McKenna · 245 West Laurel Drive · Salinas, CA 93906 · 831-443-1051

Stephen D. Sprenkle · ⑩ · The Law Office of Stephen D. Sprenkle · 1184 Monroe Street, Suite Five · P.O. Box 3500 · Salinas, CA 93912 · 831-449-8011

San Bernardino

Laurence R. Lerner · ⑩ · Lerner, Moore, Strasser, Silva & Cunningham · 141 North Arrowhead Avenue, Suite One · San Bernardino, CA 92408 · 909-889-1131

San Francisco

Francis V. Clifford · ⑩ · Jones, Clifford, Johnson and Johnson · 100 Van Ness Avenue, 19th Floor · San Francisco, CA 94102 · 415-431-5310

Joseph C. Waxman · ⑩ · Law Offices of Waxman & Brodie · 114 Sansome Street, Suite 1205 · San Francisco, CA 94104 · 415-956-5505

San Jose

William J. Armstrong · Armstrong Law Firm · Two North Second Street, Suite 1200 · San Jose, CA 95113 · 408-279-6400

Thomas J. Boyle · ⑩ · Stanek & Boyle · 425 East Santa Clara Street, Suite 220 · San Jose, CA 95113 · 408-279-2584

Thomas J. Butts · ⑩ · Butts & Johnson · 481 North First Street, Suite Five · San Jose, CA 95112 · 408-293-4818

Joseph V. Capurro · ⑩ · Capurro, Rocha & Schmidt · 99 Almaden Boulevard, Suite 1075 · San Jose, CA 95113 · 408-292-8131

Michael P. Holmes · Laughlin, Falbo, Levy & Moresi · 1520 The Alameda, Suite 200 · San Jose, CA 95126-2377 · 408-286-8801

Arthur L. Johnson, Jr. · ⑩ · Butts & Johnson · 481 North First Street, Suite Five · San Jose, CA 95112 · 408-293-4818

Herbert S. Stanek · ⑩ · Stanek & Boyle · 425 East Santa Clara Street, Suite 220 · San Jose, CA 95113 · 408-279-2584

San Rafael

Linda Joanne Brown · ⑩ · Linda Joanne Brown · 999 Fifth Avenue, Suite 350 · San Rafael, CA 94901 · 415-925-9212

Santa Ana

David J. Baziak · Baziak & Steevens · 1327 North Broadway · Santa Ana, CA 92706-3998 · 714-547-5184

Thomas F. Martin · ⑩ · Thomas F. Martin · 2107 North Broadway, Suite 206 · Santa Ana, CA 92706 · 714-547-5025

Torrance

Michael A. Ozurovich · ⑩ · Ozurovich & Schwartz · 3655 Torrance Boulevard, Suite 405 · Torrance, CA 90503 · 310-540-2283

Woodland Hills

Donald P. Tobin · ⑩ · Tobin Lucks · 21300 Victory Boulevard, Third Floor · P.O. Box 4502 · Woodland Hills, CA 91365-4502 · 818-226-3400

COLORADO

ADMINISTRATIVE LAW

Boulder

Jean E. Dubofsky · Jean E. Dubofsky · 1000 Rosehill Drive · Boulder, CO 80302-7148 · 303-447-3510

Denver

Mark G. Grueskin · Isaacson Rosenbaum · 633 Seventeenth Street, Suite 2200 · Denver, CO 80202 · 303-292-5656

Laura Lindley · ⑩ · Bjork Lindley Little · 1600 Stout Street, Suite 1400 · Denver, CO 80202 · 303-892-1400

John F. Shepherd · ⑩ · Holland & Hart · 555 Seventeenth Street, Suite 3200 · Denver, CO 80202-3739 · 303-295-8000

Linda L. Siderius · McConnell Siderius Fleischner Houghtaling & Craigmile · Denver Corporate Center, Tower I, Suite 200 · 4700 South Syracuse · Denver, CO 80237 · 303-480-0400

Ezekiel J. Williams · Faegre & Benson · Wells Fargo Center, Suite 3200 · 1700 Lincoln Street · Denver, CO 80203-4532 · 303-607-3500

Frederick Y. Yu · ⑩ · Sherman & Howard · 633 Seventeenth Street, Suite 3000 · Denver, CO 80202-3624 · 303-297-2900

ADVERTISING LAW

Denver

Claude Wild III · Greenberg Traurig · http://www.gtlaw.com · The Tabor Center, Suite 2400 · 1200 Seventeenth Street · Denver, CO 80202 · 303-572-6500

ALTERNATIVE DISPUTE RESOLUTION

Boulder

Steven Meyrich · Steven Meyrich · 4845 Pearl East Circle, Suite 101 · Boulder, CO 80301 · 303-440-8238

Denver

Bennett S. Aisenberg · Bennett S. Aisenberg · 1600 Broadway, Suite 2350 · Denver, CO 80202 · 303-861-2500

Gary Blum · Silver & DeBoskey · The Smith Mansion · 1801 York Street · Denver, CO 80206 · 303-399-3000

Daniel C. Himelspach · Dispute Management · 1801 Williams Steet, Suite 300 · Denver, CO 80218 · 303-321-1115

Leslie M. Lawson · Dispute Management · 1801 Williams Steet, Suite 300 · Denver, CO 80218 · 303-321-1115

James M. Lyons · ⑩ · Rothgerber Johnson & Lyons · One Tabor Center, Suite 3000 · 1200 Seventeenth Street · Denver, CO 80202-5855 · 303-623-9000

Joan Harcourt McWilliams · McWilliams Mediation Group · http://www.mcwilliamsmediation.com · P.O. Box 6216 · Denver, CO 80206 · 303-830-0171

William E. Murane · ⑳ · Holland & Hart · 555 Seventeenth Street, Suite 3200 · Denver, CO 80202-3739 303-295-8000

Gordon W. Netzorg · ⑩ · Netzorg McKeever Koclanes & Bernhardt · http://www.nmkb.com · 1670 Broadway, Suite 500 · Denver, CO 80202 · 303-864-1000

Helen C. Shreves · Helen C. Shreves · 3200 Cherry Creek South Drive, Suite 600 · Denver, CO 80209-3244 · 303-777-7833

Michael A. Williams · ⑳ · Michael A. Williams · 950 Seventeenth Street, Suite 1700 · Denver, CO 80202 303-785-7999

Golden

Steve A. Mains · Steve Mains · 2103 Montane Drive East · Golden, CO 80401 · 303-526-7677

Greenwood Village

Joe Epstein · Conflict Resolution Services · 5445 DTC Parkway, Suite 770 · Greenwood Village, CO 80111 · 303-355-2314

ANTITRUST LAW

Denver

Dale R. Harris · ⑩ · Davis Graham & Stubbs · http://www.dgslaw.com · 1550 Seventeenth Street, Suite 500 · Denver, CO 80202 · 303-892-9400

James E. Hartley · Holland & Hart · 555 Seventeenth Street, Suite 3200 · Denver, CO 80202-3739 · 303-295-8000

Robert F. Hill · ⑩ · Hill & Robbins · 1441 Eighteenth Street, Suite 100 · Denver, CO 80202 · 303-296-8100

Steven M. Kaufmann · Morrison & Foerster · http://www.mofo.com · Republic Plaza, Suite 5200 · 370 Seventeenth Street · Denver, CO 80202-5638 · 303-592-1500

Gale T. Miller · Davis Graham & Stubbs · http://www.dgslaw.com · 1550 Seventeenth Street, Suite 500 · Denver, CO 80202 · 303-892-9400

David G. Palmer · ㉕ · Greenberg Traurig · http://www.gtlaw.com · The Tabor Center, Suite 2400 · 1200 Seventeenth Street · Denver, CO 80202 · 303-572-6500

John Shively · Faegre & Benson · Wells Fargo Center, Suite 3200 · 1700 Lincoln Street · Denver, CO 80203-4532 · 303-607-3500

B. Lawrence Theis · ⑩ · Holme Roberts & Owen · http://www.hro.com · 1700 Lincoln Street, Suite 4100 · Denver, CO 80203-4541 · 303-861-7000

Lawrence W. Treece · Sherman & Howard · 633 Seventeenth Street, Suite 3000 · Denver, CO 80202-3624 · 303-297-2900

Robert E. Youle · ⑩ · Sherman & Howard · 633 Seventeenth Street, Suite 3000 · Denver, CO 80202-3624 · 303-297-2900

APPELLATE LAW

Boulder

Jean E. Dubofsky · Jean E. Dubofsky · 1000 Rosehill Drive · Boulder, CO 80302-7148 · 303-447-3510

Elizabeth A. Phelan · Holland & Hart · One Boulder Plaza, Suite 300 · 1800 Broadway · Boulder, CO 80302-5144 · 303-473-2700

Colorado Springs

Walter H. Sargent · Walter H. Sargent · 1632 North Cascade Avenue · Colorado Springs, CO 80907 · 719-577-4510

Denver

Susan Foreman · Susan Foreman · 303 Sixteenth Street, Suite 200 · Denver, CO 80202 · 303-825-3050

Walter W. Garnsey, Jr. · ㉕ · Kelly Garnsey Hubbell & Lass · http://www.kghllaw.com · 1441 Eighteenth Street, Suite 300 · Denver, CO 80202-1255 · 303-296-9412

Marcy G. Glenn · Holland & Hart · 555 Seventeenth Street, Suite 3200 · Denver, CO 80202-3739 · 303-295-8000

Richard P. Holme · ⑩ · Davis Graham & Stubbs · http://www.dgslaw.com · 1550 Seventeenth Street, Suite 500 · Denver, CO 80202 · 303-892-9400

Bradley A. Levin · Roberts Levin & Rosenberg · http://www.robertslevin.com · 1660 Wynkoop Street, Suite 800 · Denver, CO 80202 · 303-575-9390

Andrew M. Low · ⑩ · Davis Graham & Stubbs · http://www.dgslaw.com · 1550 Seventeenth Street, Suite 500 · Denver, CO 80202 · 303-892-9400

J. Nicholas McKeever, Jr. · Netzorg McKeever Koclanes & Bernhardt · http://www.nmkb.com · 1670 Broadway, Suite 500 · Denver, CO 80202 · 303-864-1000

Norman R. Mueller · Haddon Morgan Mueller Jordan Mackey & Foreman · 150 East 10th Avenue · Denver, CO 80203-2740 · 303-831-7364

Ronald H. Nemirow · Kennedy Childs & Fogg · Independence Plaza, Suite 2500 · 1050 Seventeenth Street · Denver, CO 80265 · 303-825-2700

Dean S. Neuwirth · Dean Neuwirth · http://www.deanneuwirth.com · 303 Sixteenth Street, Suite 200 · Denver, CO 80202 · 303-629-9700

Thomas L. Roberts · ⑩ · Roberts Levin & Rosenberg · http://www.robertslevin.com · 1660 Wynkoop Street, Suite 800 · Denver, CO 80202 · 303-575-9390

Richard A. Westfall · Hale Friesen · 1430 Wynkoop, Suite 300 · Denver, CO 80202 · 720-904-6000

BANKING LAW

Colorado Springs

Bruce T. Buell · ⑩ · Buell & Ezell · 24 South Weber Street, Suite 375 · Colorado Springs, CO 80903-1506 719-471-4511

James T. Flynn · ⑩ · Flynn, Wright & Fredman · Plaza Of The Rockies, Suite 202 · 111 South Tejon Street · Colorado Springs, CO 80903-3300 · 719-578-8444

Denver

I. Thomas Bieging · Bieging Shapiro & Burrus · 4582 South Ulster Street Parkway, Suite 1650 · Denver, CO 80237 · 720-488-0220

Richard L. Eason · ⑩ · Berenbaum, Weinshienk & Eason · http://www.bwelaw.com · Republic Plaza, 48th Floor · 370 Seventeenth Street · Denver, CO 80202 · 303-825-0800

Tennyson W. Grebenar · ⑩ · Rothgerber Johnson & Lyons · One Tabor Center, Suite 3000 · 1200 Seventeenth Street · Denver, CO 80202-5855 · 303-623-9000

William P. Johnson · ⑩ · Rothgerber Johnson & Lyons · One Tabor Center, Suite 3000 · 1200 Seventeenth Street · Denver, CO 80202-5855 · 303-623-9000

Richard M. Koon · ⑩ · Holland & Hart · 555 Seventeenth Street, Suite 3200 · Denver, CO 80202-3739 · 303-295-8000

John W. Low · ⑩ · Sherman & Howard · 633 Seventeenth Street, Suite 3000 · Denver, CO 80202-3624 · 303-297-2900

John E. Moye · ⑩ · Moye White · 16 Market Square, Sixth Floor · 1400 Sixteenth Street · Denver, CO 80202-1486 · 303-292-2900

William E. Murane · ⑳ · Holland & Hart · 555 Seventeenth Street, Suite 3200 · Denver, CO 80202-3739 303-295-8000

Gordon W. Netzorg · ⑩ · Netzorg McKeever Koclanes & Bernhardt · http://www.nmkb.com · 1670 Broadway, Suite 500 · Denver, CO 80202 · 303-864-1000

Arthur E. Otten, Jr. · ⑩ · Otten, Johnson, Robinson, Neff & Ragonetti · 950 Seventeenth Street, Suite 1600 · Denver, CO 80202 · 303-825-8400

David G. Palmer · ㉕ · Greenberg Traurig · http://www.gtlaw.com · The Tabor Center, Suite 2400 · 1200 Seventeenth Street · Denver, CO 80202 · 303-572-6500

BANKRUPTCY AND CREDITOR-DEBTOR RIGHTS LAW

Boulder

Darrell M. Daley · Faegre & Benson · 1900 Fifteenth Street · Boulder, CO 80302-5414 · 303-447-7700

Denver

Steven Abelman · Brownstein Hyatt Farber Schreck · http://www.bhfs.com · 410 Seventeenth Street, Suite 2200 · Denver, CO 80202-4432 · 303-223-1100

Bart B. Burnett · Pearson, Horowitz & Burnett · 1775 Sherman, 31st Floor · Denver, CO 80203 · 303-298-1999

Craig A. Christensen · ⑳ · Lindquist & Vennum · http://www.lindquist.com · 600 Seventeenth Street, Suite 1800 South · Denver, CO 80202-5441 · 303-573-5900

Carl A. Eklund · ⑳ · Ballard Spahr Andrews & Ingersoll · 1225 Seventeenth Street, Suite 2300 · Denver, CO 80202-5596 · 303-292-2400

Douglas W. Jessop · Jessop & Company · 303 East 17th Avenue, Suite 930 · Denver, CO 80203-1264 · 303-860-7700

Glen E. Keller, Jr. · ⑳ · Davis Graham & Stubbs · http://www.dgslaw.com · 1550 Seventeenth Street, Suite 500 · Denver, CO 80202 · 303-892-9400

Lee M. Kutner · Kutner Miller Brinen · 303 East 17th Avenue, Suite 500 · Denver, CO 80203 · 303-832-2400

Harrie F. Lewis · Lindquist & Vennum · http://www.lindquist.com · 600 Seventeenth Street, Suite 1800 South · Denver, CO 80202-5441 · 303-573-5900

James T. Markus · Block Markus & Williams · 1700 Lincoln Street, Suite 4000 · Denver, CO 80203 · 303-830-0800

Paul D. Rubner · ⑩ · Paul D. Rubner, Attorney at Law · 1600 Broadway, Suite 2600 · Denver, CO 80202 303-832-2616

Gregory Williams · Block Markus & Williams · 1700 Lincoln Street, Suite 4000 · Denver, CO 80203 · 303-830-0800

John F. Young · Block Markus & Williams · 1700 Lincoln Street, Suite 4000 · Denver, CO 80203 · 303-830-0800

BET-THE-COMPANY LITIGATION

Denver

Frederick J. Baumann · Rothgerber Johnson & Lyons · One Tabor Center, Suite 3000 · 1200 Seventeenth Street · Denver, CO 80202-5855 · 303-623-9000

Jeffrey A. Chase · 20 · Jacobs, Chase, Frick, Kleinkopf & Kelley · Independence Plaza, Suite 1500 · 1050 Seventeenth Street · Denver, CO 80265 · 303-685-4800

Harold A. Haddon · 25 · Haddon Morgan Mueller Jordan Mackey & Foreman · 150 East 10th Avenue · Denver, CO 80203-2740 · 303-831-7364

Robert F. Hill · 10 · Hill & Robbins · 1441 Eighteenth Street, Suite 100 · Denver, CO 80202 · 303-296-8100

James M. Lyons · 10 · Rothgerber Johnson & Lyons · One Tabor Center, Suite 3000 · 1200 Seventeenth Street · Denver, CO 80202-5855 · 303-623-9000

Daniel M. Reilly · 10 · Reilly Pozner · http://www.litigationcolorado.com · The Kittredge Building, Suite 700 · 511 Sixteenth Street · Denver, CO 80202 · 303-893-6100

James E. Scarboro · Arnold & Porter · 370 Seventeenth Street, Suite 4500 · Denver, CO 80202-1370 · 303-863-1000

Roger P. Thomasch · 20 · Ballard Spahr Andrews & Ingersoll · 1225 Seventeenth Street, Suite 2300 · Denver, CO 80202-5596 · 303-292-2400

BIOTECHNOLOGY LAW

Littleton

Barry J. Swanson · Swanson Bratschun · 8210 SouthPark Terrace · Littleton, CO 80120 · 303-268-0066

COMMERCIAL LITIGATION

Boulder

Jean E. Dubofsky · Jean E. Dubofsky · 1000 Rosehill Drive · Boulder, CO 80302-7148 · 303-447-3510

William D. Meyer · Hutchinson Black and Cook · 921 Walnut Street, Suite 200 · Boulder, CO 80302 · 303-442-6514

Broomfield

James E. Nesland · Cooley Godward Kronish · 380 Interlocken Crescent, Suite 900 · Broomfield, CO 80021-8023 · 720-566-4000

Denver

Scott S. Barker · Holland & Hart · 555 Seventeenth Street, Suite 3200 · Denver, CO 80202-3739 · 303-295-8000

Frederick J. Baumann · Rothgerber Johnson & Lyons · One Tabor Center, Suite 3000 · 1200 Seventeenth Street · Denver, CO 80202-5855 · 303-623-9000

Michael H. Berger · Jacobs, Chase, Frick, Kleinkopf & Kelley · Independence Plaza, Suite 1500 · 1050 Seventeenth Street · Denver, CO 80265 · 303-685-4800

I. Thomas Bieging · Bieging Shapiro & Burrus · 4582 South Ulster Street Parkway, Suite 1650 · Denver, CO 80237 · 720-488-0220

Richard Caschette · Starrs Mihm & Caschette · 707 Seventeenth Street, Suite 2600 · Denver, CO 80202 · 303-592-5900

Charles L. Casteel · ⑩ · Davis Graham & Stubbs · http://www.dgslaw.com · 1550 Seventeenth Street, Suite 500 · Denver, CO 80202 · 303-892-9400

Gary Ceriani · Davis & Ceriani · 1350 Seventeenth Street, Suite 400 · Denver, CO 80202 · 303-534-9000

Jeffrey A. Chase · ⑳ · Jacobs, Chase, Frick, Kleinkopf & Kelley · Independence Plaza, Suite 1500 · 1050 Seventeenth Street · Denver, CO 80265 · 303-685-4800

F. Stephen Collins · Ducker, Montgomery, Aronstein & Bess · One Civic Center Plaza, Suite 1400 · 1560 Broadway · Denver, CO 80202-1548 · 303-861-2828

Osborne J. Dykes III · Fulbright & Jaworski · http://www.fulbright.com · Republic Plaza, Suite 2150 · 370 Seventeenth Street · Denver, CO 80202-5638 · 303-801-2700

Ann Frick · ⑩ · Jacobs, Chase, Frick, Kleinkopf & Kelley · Independence Plaza, Suite 1500 · 1050 Seventeenth Street · Denver, CO 80265 · 303-685-4800

Michael J. Gallagher · Davis Graham & Stubbs · http://www.dgslaw.com · 1550 Seventeenth Street, Suite 500 · Denver, CO 80202 · 303-892-9400

Walter W. Garnsey, Jr. · ㉕ · Kelly Garnsey Hubbell & Lass · http://www.kghllaw.com · 1441 Eighteenth Street, Suite 300 · Denver, CO 80202-1255 · 303-296-9412

Charles Goldberg · Rothgerber Johnson & Lyons · One Tabor Center, Suite 3000 · 1200 Seventeenth Street · Denver, CO 80202-5855 · 303-623-9000

Hugh Q. Gottschalk · Wheeler Trigg Kennedy · http://www.wtklaw.com · 1801 California Street, Suite 3600 · Denver, CO 80202-2617 · 303-244-1800

Harold A. Haddon · ㉕ · Haddon Morgan Mueller Jordan Mackey & Foreman · 150 East 10th Avenue · Denver, CO 80203-2740 · 303-831-7364

John Lawrence Hamil · Hamil/Hecht · 140 East 19th Avenue, Suite 600 · Denver, CO 80203-1035 · 303-830-1383

Dale R. Harris · ⑩ · Davis Graham & Stubbs · http://www.dgslaw.com · 1550 Seventeenth Street, Suite 500 · Denver, CO 80202 · 303-892-9400

Robert F. Hill · ⑩ · Hill & Robbins · 1441 Eighteenth Street, Suite 100 · Denver, CO 80202 · 303-296-8100

Daniel S. Hoffman · ⑩ · Hogan & Hartson · One Tabor Center, Suite 1500 · 1200 Seventeenth Street · Denver, CO 80202 · 303-899-7300

Peter C. Houtsma · Holland & Hart · 555 Seventeenth Street, Suite 3200 · Denver, CO 80202-3739 · 303-295-8000

Gary M. Jackson · DiManna & Jackson · http://www.dimanna-jackson.com · 1741 High Street · Denver, CO 80218 · 303-320-4848

Thomas P. Johnson · ⑩ · Davis Graham & Stubbs · http://www.dgslaw.com · 1550 Seventeenth Street, Suite 500 · Denver, CO 80202 · 303-892-9400

Edwin S. Kahn · ⑳ · Kelly Garnsey Hubbell & Lass · http://www.kghllaw.com · 1441 Eighteenth Street, Suite 300 · Denver, CO 80202-1255 · 303-296-9412

Gregory B. Kanan · Rothgerber Johnson & Lyons · One Tabor Center, Suite 3000 · 1200 Seventeenth Street · Denver, CO 80202-5855 · 303-623-9000

Steven M. Kaufmann · Morrison & Foerster · http://www.mofo.com · Republic Plaza, Suite 5200 · 370 Seventeenth Street · Denver, CO 80202-5638 · 303-592-1500

Christopher J. Koenigs · Sherman & Howard · 633 Seventeenth Street, Suite 3000 · Denver, CO 80202-3624 · 303-297-2900

G. Stephen Long · Shughart Thomson & Kilroy · http://www.stklaw.com · Independence Plaza, Suite 2300 · 1050 Seventeenth Street · Denver, CO 80265 · 303-572-9300

Andrew M. Low · ⑩ · Davis Graham & Stubbs · http://www.dgslaw.com · 1550 Seventeenth Street, Suite 500 · Denver, CO 80202 · 303-892-9400

James M. Lyons · ⑩ · Rothgerber Johnson & Lyons · One Tabor Center, Suite 3000 · 1200 Seventeenth Street · Denver, CO 80202-5855 · 303-623-9000

Pamela Robillard Mackey · Haddon Morgan Mueller Jordan Mackey & Foreman · 150 East 10th Avenue Denver, CO 80203-2740 · 303-831-7364

Michael S. McCarthy · Faegre & Benson · Wells Fargo Center, Suite 3200 · 1700 Lincoln Street · Denver, CO 80203-4532 · 303-607-3500

Jane Michaels · ⑩ · Holland & Hart · 555 Seventeenth Street, Suite 3200 · Denver, CO 80202-3739 · 303-295-8000

Gale T. Miller · Davis Graham & Stubbs · http://www.dgslaw.com · 1550 Seventeenth Street, Suite 500 · Denver, CO 80202 · 303-892-9400

Norman R. Mueller · Haddon Morgan Mueller Jordan Mackey & Foreman · 150 East 10th Avenue · Denver, CO 80203-2740 · 303-831-7364

William E. Murane · ⑳ · Holland & Hart · 555 Seventeenth Street, Suite 3200 · Denver, CO 80202-3739 303-295-8000

Gordon W. Netzorg · ⑩ · Netzorg McKeever Koclanes & Bernhardt · http://www.nmkb.com · 1670 Broadway, Suite 500 · Denver, CO 80202 · 303-864-1000

Reid Neureiter · Jacobs, Chase, Frick, Kleinkopf & Kelley · Independence Plaza, Suite 1500 · 1050 Seventeenth Street · Denver, CO 80265 · 303-685-4800

Michael L. O'Donnell · Wheeler Trigg Kennedy · http://www.wtklaw.com · 1801 California Street, Suite 3600 · Denver, CO 80202-2617 · 303-244-1800

David G. Palmer · ㉕ · Greenberg Traurig · http://www.gtlaw.com · The Tabor Center, Suite 2400 · 1200 Seventeenth Street · Denver, CO 80202 · 303-572-6500

Daniel M. Reilly · ⑩ · Reilly Pozner · http://www.litigationcolorado.com · The Kittredge Building, Suite 700 · 511 Sixteenth Street · Denver, CO 80202 · 303-893-6100

John M. Richilano · Richilano & Gilligan · 633 Seventeenth Street, Suite 1700 · Denver, CO 80202-1185 303-893-8000

James E. Scarboro · Arnold & Porter · 370 Seventeenth Street, Suite 4500 · Denver, CO 80202-1370 · 303-863-1000

Daniel F. Shea · Hogan & Hartson · One Tabor Center, Suite 1500 · 1200 Seventeenth Street · Denver, CO 80202 · 303-899-7300

Kevin M. Shea · Ballard Spahr Andrews & Ingersoll · 1225 Seventeenth Street, Suite 2300 · Denver, CO 80202-5596 · 303-292-2400

B. Lawrence Theis · ⑩ · Holme Roberts & Owen · http://www.hro.com · 1700 Lincoln Street, Suite 4100 · Denver, CO 80203-4541 · 303-861-7000

Roger P. Thomasch · ⑳ · Ballard Spahr Andrews & Ingersoll · 1225 Seventeenth Street, Suite 2300 · Denver, CO 80202-5596 · 303-292-2400

Tucker K. Trautman · ⑳ · Dorsey & Whitney · Republic Plaza Building, Suite 4700 · 370 Seventeenth Street · Denver, CO 80202-5647 · 303-629-3400

Lawrence W. Treece · Sherman & Howard · 633 Seventeenth Street, Suite 3000 · Denver, CO 80202-3624 · 303-297-2900

John R. Trigg · Wheeler Trigg Kennedy · http://www.wtklaw.com · 1801 California Street, Suite 3600 · Denver, CO 80202-2617 · 303-244-1800

John F. Walsh · Hill & Robbins · 1441 Eighteenth Street, Suite 100 · Denver, CO 80202 · 303-296-8100

Michael A. Williams · ⑳ · Michael A. Williams · 950 Seventeenth Street, Suite 1700 · Denver, CO 80202 303-785-7999

Julie M. Williamson · Bieging Shapiro & Burrus · 4582 South Ulster Street Parkway, Suite 1650 · Denver, CO 80237 · 720-488-0220

Robert E. Youle · ⑩ · Sherman & Howard · 633 Seventeenth Street, Suite 3000 · Denver, CO 80202-3624 · 303-297-2900

Steamboat Springs

James J. Moylan · ⑩ · James J. Moylan · 31685 Inca Way · P.O. Box 775965 · Steamboat Springs, CO 80477-5965 · 970-870-0730

COMMUNICATIONS LAW

Denver

Rebecca B. DeCook · Moye White · 16 Market Square, Sixth Floor · 1400 Sixteenth Street · Denver, CO 80202-1486 · 303-292-2900

Mark W. Williams · Sherman & Howard · 633 Seventeenth Street, Suite 3000 · Denver, CO 80202-3624 · 303-297-2900

Greenwood Village

Thorvald A. Nelson · Holland & Hart · 8390 East Crescent Parkway, Suite 400 · Greenwood Village, CO 80111-2800 · 303-290-1600

CONSTRUCTION LAW

Boulder

C. Brad Peterson · Hutchinson Black and Cook · 921 Walnut Street, Suite 200 · Boulder, CO 80302 · 303-442-6514

Denver

J. David Arkell · Faegre & Benson · Wells Fargo Center, Suite 3200 · 1700 Lincoln Street · Denver, CO 80203-4532 · 303-607-3500

William A. Bianco · Davis Graham & Stubbs · http://www.dgslaw.com · 1550 Seventeenth Street, Suite 500 · Denver, CO 80202 · 303-892-9400

Eugene R. Commander · Shughart Thomson & Kilroy · http://www.stklaw.com · Independence Plaza, Suite 2300 · 1050 Seventeenth Street · Denver, CO 80265 · 303-572-9300

Michael J. Cook · Sherman & Howard · 633 Seventeenth Street, Suite 3000 · Denver, CO 80202-3624 · 303-297-2900

Bret Gunnell · Sherman & Howard · 633 Seventeenth Street, Suite 3000 · Denver, CO 80202-3624 · 303-297-2900

Byrum C. Lee, Jr. · Lee & Associates · 1444 Blake Street · Denver, CO 80202 · 303-291-0733

CORPORATE GOVERNANCE AND COMPLIANCE LAW

Broomfield

Michael L. Platt · Cooley Godward Kronish · 380 Interlocken Crescent, Suite 900 · Broomfield, CO 80021-8023 · 720-566-4000

Denver

H. Gregory Austin · ⑳ · Holland & Hart · 555 Seventeenth Street, Suite 3200 · Denver, CO 80202-3739 · 303-295-8000

Robert R. Keatinge · ⑩ · Holland & Hart · 555 Seventeenth Street, Suite 3200 · Denver, CO 80202-3739 303-295-8000

Cathy S. Krendl · ⑩ · Krendl Krendl Sachnoff & Way · http://www.krendl.com · 370 Seventeenth Street, Suite 5350 · Denver, CO 80202 · 303-629-2600

Ronald Levine II · Davis Graham & Stubbs · http://www.dgslaw.com · 1550 Seventeenth Street, Suite 500 · Denver, CO 80202 · 303-892-9400

Mark R. Levy · ⑳ · Holland & Hart · 555 Seventeenth Street, Suite 3200 · Denver, CO 80202-3739 · 303-295-8000

John L. McCabe · ⑩ · Davis Graham & Stubbs · http://www.dgslaw.com · 1550 Seventeenth Street, Suite 500 · Denver, CO 80202 · 303-892-9400

John E. Moye · ⑩ · Moye White · 16 Market Square, Sixth Floor · 1400 Sixteenth Street · Denver, CO 80202-1486 · 303-292-2900

Jennings J. Newcom · Davis Graham & Stubbs · http://www.dgslaw.com · 1550 Seventeenth Street, Suite 500 · Denver, CO 80202 · 303-892-9400

W. Dean Salter · ⑩ · Holme Roberts & Owen · http://www.hro.com · 1700 Lincoln Street, Suite 4100 · Denver, CO 80203-4541 · 303-861-7000

Peter H. Schwartz · Davis Graham & Stubbs · http://www.dgslaw.com · 1550 Seventeenth Street, Suite 500 · Denver, CO 80202 · 303-892-9400

Anthony van Westrum · ⑩ · Anthony van Westrum · 621 Seventeenth Street, Suite 1515 · Denver, CO 80293-1501 · 303-295-1515

James F. Wood · ⑩ · Sherman & Howard · 633 Seventeenth Street, Suite 3000 · Denver, CO 80202-3624 303-297-2900

Lester R. Woodward · ㉕ · Davis Graham & Stubbs · http://www.dgslaw.com · 1550 Seventeenth Street, Suite 500 · Denver, CO 80202 · 303-892-9400

CORPORATE LAW

Boulder

David M. Packard · Packard and Dierking · WaterStreet, Suite 200 · 2595 Canyon Boulevard · Boulder, CO 80302-5620 · 303-447-0450

Allen Sparkman · Sparkman Shaffer Perlick · 2338 Broadway · Boulder, CO 80304 · 303-449-6543

Broomfield

James C.T. Linfield · Cooley Godward Kronish · 380 Interlocken Crescent, Suite 900 · Broomfield, CO 80021-8023 · 720-566-4000

Francis Wheeler · Cooley Godward Kronish · 380 Interlocken Crescent, Suite 900 · Broomfield, CO 80021-8023 · 720-566-4000

Denver

Betty C. Arkell · Holland & Hart · 555 Seventeenth Street, Suite 3200 · Denver, CO 80202-3739 · 303-295-8000

H. Gregory Austin · ⑳ · Holland & Hart · 555 Seventeenth Street, Suite 3200 · Denver, CO 80202-3739 · 303-295-8000

Harold S. Bloomenthal · ㉕ · Holme Roberts & Owen · http://www.hro.com · 1700 Lincoln Street, Suite 4100 · Denver, CO 80203-4541 · 303-861-7000

Stephen M. Brett · Sherman & Howard · 633 Seventeenth Street, Suite 3000 · Denver, CO 80202-3624 · 303-297-2900

J. William Callison · Faegre & Benson · Wells Fargo Center, Suite 3200 · 1700 Lincoln Street · Denver, CO 80203-4532 · 303-607-3500

Bruce Ducker · ⑩ · Ducker, Montgomery, Aronstein & Bess · One Civic Center Plaza, Suite 1400 · 1560 Broadway · Denver, CO 80202-1548 · 303-861-2828

Josiah O. Hatch III · Ducker, Montgomery, Aronstein & Bess · One Civic Center Plaza, Suite 1400 · 1560 Broadway · Denver, CO 80202-1548 · 303-861-2828

Paul Hilton · ⑩ · Hogan & Hartson · One Tabor Center, Suite 1500 · 1200 Seventeenth Street · Denver, CO 80202 · 303-899-7300

Robert R. Keatinge · ⑩ · Holland & Hart · 555 Seventeenth Street, Suite 3200 · Denver, CO 80202-3739 303-295-8000

Francis P. King · ㉕ · Robinson, Diss & Clowdus · Lincoln Center Building, Suite 2500 · 1660 Lincoln Street · Denver, CO 80264 · 303-861-4154

Cathy S. Krendl · ⑩ · Krendl Krendl Sachnoff & Way · http://www.krendl.com · 370 Seventeenth Street, Suite 5350 · Denver, CO 80202 · 303-629-2600

Ronald Levine II · Davis Graham & Stubbs · http://www.dgslaw.com · 1550 Seventeenth Street, Suite 500 · Denver, CO 80202 · 303-892-9400

Mark R. Levy · ⑳ · Holland & Hart · 555 Seventeenth Street, Suite 3200 · Denver, CO 80202-3739 · 303-295-8000

John G. Lewis · ⑳ · Ireland, Stapleton, Pryor & Pascoe · 1675 Broadway, Suite 2600 · Denver, CO 80202 303-623-2700

Blair L. Lockwood · Faegre & Benson · Wells Fargo Center, Suite 3200 · 1700 Lincoln Street · Denver, CO 80203-4532 · 303-607-3500

John W. Low · ⑩ · Sherman & Howard · 633 Seventeenth Street, Suite 3000 · Denver, CO 80202-3624 · 303-297-2900

John L. McCabe · ⑩ · Davis Graham & Stubbs · http://www.dgslaw.com · 1550 Seventeenth Street, Suite 500 · Denver, CO 80202 · 303-892-9400

Steven D. Miller · Sherman & Howard · 633 Seventeenth Street, Suite 3000 · Denver, CO 80202-3624 · 303-297-2900

Robert C. Montgomery · Ducker, Montgomery, Aronstein & Bess · One Civic Center Plaza, Suite 1400 · 1560 Broadway · Denver, CO 80202-1548 · 303-861-2828

John E. Moye · ⑩ · Moye White · 16 Market Square, Sixth Floor · 1400 Sixteenth Street · Denver, CO 80202-1486 · 303-292-2900

Patricia A. Peterson · Davis Graham & Stubbs · http://www.dgslaw.com · 1550 Seventeenth Street, Suite 500 · Denver, CO 80202 · 303-892-9400

Richard M. Russo · Gibson, Dunn & Crutcher · 1801 California Street, Suite 4200 · Denver, CO 80202-2642 · 303-298-5700

Michael A. Sabian · ⑩ · Shughart Thomson & Kilroy · http://www.stklaw.com · Independence Plaza, Suite 2300 · 1050 Seventeenth Street · Denver, CO 80265 · 303-572-9300

W. Dean Salter · ⑩ · Holme Roberts & Owen · http://www.hro.com · 1700 Lincoln Street, Suite 4100 · Denver, CO 80203-4541 · 303-861-7000

Bruce D. Stocks · Perkins Coie · http://www.perkinscoie.com · 1899 Wynkoop Street, Suite 700 · Denver, CO 80202-1043 · 303-291-2300

Anthony van Westrum · ⑩ · Anthony van Westrum · 621 Seventeenth Street, Suite 1515 · Denver, CO 80293-1501 · 303-295-1515

Edward White III · Moye White · 16 Market Square, Sixth Floor · 1400 Sixteenth Street · Denver, CO 80202-1486 · 303-292-2900

James F. Wood · ⑩ · Sherman & Howard · 633 Seventeenth Street, Suite 3000 · Denver, CO 80202-3624 303-297-2900

Lester R. Woodward · ㉕ · Davis Graham & Stubbs · http://www.dgslaw.com · 1550 Seventeenth Street, Suite 500 · Denver, CO 80202 · 303-892-9400

Douglas R. Wright · Faegre & Benson · Wells Fargo Center, Suite 3200 · 1700 Lincoln Street · Denver, CO 80203-4532 · 303-607-3500

EDUCATION LAW

Boulder

Richard E. Bump · Caplan and Earnest · One Boulder Plaza, Suite 200 · 1800 Broadway · Boulder, CO 80302-5289 · 303-443-8010

EMINENT DOMAIN AND CONDEMNATION LAW

Centennial

Mark E. May · May and Associates · 8008 East Arapahoe Court, Suite 100 · Centennial, CO 80112 · 720-529-1300

Denver

Jody Harper Alderman · Grimshaw & Harring · http://www.grimshawharring.com · 1700 Lincoln Street, Suite 3800 · Denver, CO 80203 · 303-839-3800

Karen L. Brody · Lowe, Fell & Skogg · Republic Plaza, Suite 4900 · 370 Seventeenth Street · Denver, CO 80202 · 720-359-8200

Robert R. Duncan · Duncan Ostrander & Dingess · 3600 South Yosemite Street, Suite 500 · Denver, CO 80237-1829 · 303-779-0200

Leslie A. Fields · Faegre & Benson · Wells Fargo Center, Suite 3200 · 1700 Lincoln Street · Denver, CO 80203-4532 · 303-607-3500

Malcom M. Murray · Murray Dahl Kuechenmeister & Renaud · 2401 Fifthteenth Street, Suite 200 · Denver, CO 80202 · 303-493-6670

Donald M. Ostrander · Duncan Ostrander & Dingess · 3600 South Yosemite Street, Suite 500 · Denver, CO 80237-1829 · 303-779-0200

Wayne B. Schroeder · Grimshaw & Harring · http://www.grimshawharring.com · 1700 Lincoln Street, Suite 3800 · Denver, CO 80203 · 303-839-3800

Kenneth K. Skogg · Lowe, Fell & Skogg · Republic Plaza, Suite 4900 · 370 Seventeenth Street · Denver, CO 80202 · 720-359-8200

John R. Sperber · Faegre & Benson · Wells Fargo Center, Suite 3200 · 1700 Lincoln Street · Denver, CO 80203-4532 · 303-607-3500

Greenwood Village

Douglas S. Widlund · Butcher & Widlund · 7400 East Orchard Road, Suite 150-S · Greenwood Village, CO 80111 · 303-839-1550

Lakewood

William M. Schell · Opperman & Schell · 3609 South Wadsworth Boulevard, Suite 140 · Lakewood, CO 80235 · 303-623-1970

EMPLOYEE BENEFITS LAW

Denver

Cindy S. Birley · Davis Graham & Stubbs · http://www.dgslaw.com · 1550 Seventeenth Street, Suite 500 · Denver, CO 80202 · 303-892-9400

Carolyn E. Daniels · Holme Roberts & Owen · http://www.hro.com · 1700 Lincoln Street, Suite 4100 · Denver, CO 80203-4541 · 303-861-7000

Fred J. Diss · ⑩ · Robinson, Diss & Clowdus · Lincoln Center Building, Suite 2500 · 1660 Lincoln Street Denver, CO 80264 · 303-861-4154

Jane O. Francis · Holland & Hart · 555 Seventeenth Street, Suite 3200 · Denver, CO 80202-3739 · 303-295-8000

Irene F. Gallagher · Holme Roberts & Owen · http://www.hro.com · 1700 Lincoln Street, Suite 4100 · Denver, CO 80203-4541 · 303-861-7000

Marcia Chadwick Holt · ⑳ · Davis Graham & Stubbs · http://www.dgslaw.com · 1550 Seventeenth Street, Suite 500 · Denver, CO 80202 · 303-892-9400

Ellen M. Kelman · Buescher, Goldhammer, Kelman & Dodge · 1563 Gaylord Street · Denver, CO 80206 303-333-7751

Curtis L. Kennedy · Curtis L. Kennedy · 8405 East Princeton Avenue · Denver, CO 80237-1741 · 303-770-0440

Kirk F. Maldonado · ⑩ · Sherman & Howard · 633 Seventeenth Street, Suite 3000 · Denver, CO 80202-3624 · 303-297-2900

David T. Mitzner · ⑩ · Holme Roberts & Owen · http://www.hro.com · 1700 Lincoln Street, Suite 4100 · Denver, CO 80203-4541 · 303-861-7000

Bruce R. Muir · ⑳ · Sherman & Howard · 633 Seventeenth Street, Suite 3000 · Denver, CO 80202-3624 · 303-297-2900

Kathleen Odle · Sherman & Howard · 633 Seventeenth Street, Suite 3000 · Denver, CO 80202-3624 · 303-297-2900

Stephen P. Rickles · Berenbaum, Weinshienk & Eason · http://www.bwelaw.com · Republic Plaza, 48th Floor · 370 Seventeenth Street · Denver, CO 80202 · 303-825-0800

R. Michael Sanchez · ⑳ · Sherman & Howard · 633 Seventeenth Street, Suite 3000 · Denver, CO 80202-3624 · 303-297-2900

Sheldon H. Smith · ⑩ · Holme Roberts & Owen · http://www.hro.com · 1700 Lincoln Street, Suite 4100 · Denver, CO 80203-4541 · 303-861-7000

Kirsten Stewart · Sherman & Howard · 633 Seventeenth Street, Suite 3000 · Denver, CO 80202-3624 · 303-297-2900

Greenwood Village

Ralph W. Shaw · The Shaw Law Firm · 6400 South Fiddler's Green Circle, Suite 500 · Greenwood Village, CO 80111 · 303-327-5544

Denver

Scot Anderson · Davis Graham & Stubbs · http://www.dgslaw.com · 1550 Seventeenth Street, Suite 500 · Denver, CO 80202 · 303-892-9400

James K. Aronstein · ⑩ · Ducker, Montgomery, Aronstein & Bess · One Civic Center Plaza, Suite 1400 · 1560 Broadway · Denver, CO 80202-1548 · 303-861-2828

Michael Beatty · Beatty & Wozniak · Columbine Place, Suite 1100 · 216 Sixteenth Street · Denver, CO 80202-5115 · 303-407-4499

Laura E. Beverage · Jackson Kelly · 1099 Eighteenth Street, Suite 2150 · Denver, CO 80202 · 303-390-0003

Craig Carver · ⑩ · Carver Schwarz McNab & Bailey · Hudson's Bay Centre, Suite 1700 · 1600 Stout Street · Denver, CO 80202 · 303-893-1815

Randall M. Case · Poulson, Odell & Peterson · 1775 Sherman Street, Suite 1400 · Denver, CO 80203 · 303-861-4400

Phillip R. Clark · ⑩ · Holme Roberts & Owen · http://www.hro.com · 1700 Lincoln Street, Suite 4100 · Denver, CO 80203-4541 · 303-861-7000

Franklin Erisman · ⑩ · Holme Roberts & Owen · http://www.hro.com · 1700 Lincoln Street, Suite 4100 · Denver, CO 80203-4541 · 303-861-7000

Richard L. Fanyo · ⑩ · Dufford & Brown · 1700 Broadway, Suite 2100 · Denver, CO 80290-2101 · 303-861-8013

John D. Fognani · ⑩ · Fognani & Faught · 1700 Lincoln Center, Suite 2222 · Denver, CO 80203 · 303-382-6200

Lynn P. Hendrix · ⑩ · Holme Roberts & Owen · http://www.hro.com · 1700 Lincoln Street, Suite 4100 · Denver, CO 80203-4541 · 303-861-7000

Charles L. Kaiser · ⑩ · Davis Graham & Stubbs · http://www.dgslaw.com · 1550 Seventeenth Street, Suite 500 · Denver, CO 80202 · 303-892-9400

James M. King · ⑩ · Baker Hostetler · http://www.bakerlaw.com · 303 East 17th Avenue, Suite 1100 · Denver, CO 80203-1264 · 303-861-0600

Robert G. Lewis · Ducker, Montgomery, Aronstein & Bess · One Civic Center Plaza, Suite 1400 · 1560 Broadway · Denver, CO 80202-1548 · 303-861-2828

Laura Lindley · ⑩ · Bjork Lindley Little · 1600 Stout Street, Suite 1400 · Denver, CO 80202 · 303-892-1400

David R. Little · Bjork Lindley Little · 1600 Stout Street, Suite 1400 · Denver, CO 80202 · 303-892-1400

Judith M. Matlock · ⑩ · Davis Graham & Stubbs · http://www.dgslaw.com · 1550 Seventeenth Street, Suite 500 · Denver, CO 80202 · 303-892-9400

Davis O. O'Connor · ⑳ · Holland & Hart · 555 Seventeenth Street, Suite 3200 · Denver, CO 80202-3739 303-295-8000

William G. Odell · ⑳ · Poulson, Odell & Peterson · 1775 Sherman Street, Suite 1400 · Denver, CO 80203 303-861-4400

Anthony J. Shaheen · ⑩ · Holland & Hart · 555 Seventeenth Street, Suite 3200 · Denver, CO 80202-3739 · 303-295-8000

John F. Shepherd · ⑩ · Holland & Hart · 555 Seventeenth Street, Suite 3200 · Denver, CO 80202-3739 · 303-295-8000

Michael Wozniak · Beatty & Wozniak · Columbine Place, Suite 1100 · 216 Sixteenth Street · Denver, CO 80202-5115 · 303-407-4499

Durango

Thomas P. Dugan · Dugan & Associates · 900 Main Avenue, Suite A · Durango, CO 81301-5179 · 970-259-1770

Greenwood Village

Robert M. Pomeroy, Jr. · ⑩ · Holland & Hart · 8390 East Crescent Parkway, Suite 400 · Greenwood Village, CO 80111-2800 · 303-290-1600

Sedalia

William R. Marsh · ⑳ · William R. Marsh · 6257 Pine Cliff Road · Sedalia, CO 80135-8559 · 303-814-0162

ENTERTAINMENT LAW

Denver

Leigh L. Augustine · Sherman & Howard · 633 Seventeenth Street, Suite 3000 · Denver, CO 80202-3624 303-297-2900

James D. Leonard · Faegre & Benson · Wells Fargo Center, Suite 3200 · 1700 Lincoln Street · Denver, CO 80203-4532 · 303-607-3500

ENVIRONMENTAL LAW

Boulder

S. Macon Cowles III · S. Macon Cowles III · 1680 Wilson Court · Boulder, CO 80304 · 303-447-3062

Jerry W. Raisch · ⑩ · Vranesh & Raisch · 1720 Fourteenth Street, Suite 200 · P.O. Box 871 · Boulder, CO 80306-0871 · 303-443-6151

Eugene J. Riordan · Vranesh & Raisch · 1720 Fourteenth Street, Suite 200 · P.O. Box 871 · Boulder, CO 80306-0871 · 303-443-6151

Denver

William J. Duffy · Davis Graham & Stubbs · http://www.dgslaw.com · 1550 Seventeenth Street, Suite 500 Denver, CO 80202 · 303-892-9400

Ronald M. Eddy · ⑩ · Sherman & Howard · 633 Seventeenth Street, Suite 3000 · Denver, CO 80202-3624 · 303-297-2900

John D. Fognani · ⑩ · Fognani & Faught · 1700 Lincoln Center, Suite 2222 · Denver, CO 80203 · 303-382-6200

Roger L. Freeman · Davis Graham & Stubbs · http://www.dgslaw.com · 1550 Seventeenth Street, Suite 500 · Denver, CO 80202 · 303-892-9400

Kevin S. Hannon · The Law Firm of Kevin Hannon · 1641 Downing Street · Denver, CO 80218 · 303-861-8800

Scott W. Hardt · ⑩ · Temkin Wielga Hardt & Longenecker · 1900 Wazee Street, Suite 303 · Denver, CO 80202 · 303-292-4922

Henry W. Ipsen · ⑳ · Holme Roberts & Owen · http://www.hro.com · 1700 Lincoln Street, Suite 4100 · Denver, CO 80203-4541 · 303-861-7000

John R. Jacus · Davis Graham & Stubbs · http://www.dgslaw.com · 1550 Seventeenth Street, Suite 500 · Denver, CO 80202 · 303-892-9400

Charles L. Kaiser · ⑩ · Davis Graham & Stubbs · http://www.dgslaw.com · 1550 Seventeenth Street, Suite 500 · Denver, CO 80202 · 303-892-9400

Denise W. Kennedy · Holland & Hart · 555 Seventeenth Street, Suite 3200 · Denver, CO 80202-3739 · 303-295-8000

Robert W. Lawrence · ⑩ · Davis Graham & Stubbs · http://www.dgslaw.com · 1550 Seventeenth Street, Suite 500 · Denver, CO 80202 · 303-892-9400

Eugene Megyesy · Dufford & Brown · 1700 Broadway, Suite 2100 · Denver, CO 80290-2101 · 303-861-8013

Zach C. Miller · Davis Graham & Stubbs · http://www.dgslaw.com · 1550 Seventeenth Street, Suite 500 · Denver, CO 80202 · 303-892-9400

Elizabeth A. Mitchell · Holland & Hart · 555 Seventeenth Street, Suite 3200 · Denver, CO 80202-3739 · 303-295-8000

Paul D. Phillips · ⑳ · Holland & Hart · 555 Seventeenth Street, Suite 3200 · Denver, CO 80202-3739 · 303-295-8000

Lori Potter · ⑩ · Kaplan Kirsch Rockwell · 1675 Broadway, Suite 2300 · Denver, CO 80202 · 303-825-7000

Bennett W. Raley · Trout, Raley, Montaño, Witwer & Freeman · 1120 Lincoln Street, Suite 1600 · Denver, CO 80203-2141 · 303-861-1963

David W. Robbins · ⑩ · Hill & Robbins · 1441 Eighteenth Street, Suite 100 · Denver, CO 80202 · 303-296-8100

Linda L. Rockwood · Faegre & Benson · Wells Fargo Center, Suite 3200 · 1700 Lincoln Street · Denver, CO 80203-4532 · 303-607-3500

Ronda Sandquist · Jackson Kelly · 1099 Eighteenth Street, Suite 2150 · Denver, CO 80202 · 303-390-0003

James R. Spaanstra · Faegre & Benson · Wells Fargo Center, Suite 3200 · 1700 Lincoln Street · Denver, CO 80203-4532 · 303-607-3500

Jonathan H. Steeler · Isaacson Rosenbaum · 633 Seventeenth Street, Suite 2200 · Denver, CO 80202 · 303-292-5656

Elizabeth H. Temkin · ⓴ · Temkin Wielga Hardt & Longenecker · 1900 Wazee Street, Suite 303 · Denver, CO 80202 · 303-292-4922

Golden

Richard O. Curley, Jr. · Curley & Associates · 31982 Paradise Circle · Golden, CO 80401 · 720-746-0901

Greenwood Village

J. Kemper Will · Burns, Figa & Will · 6400 South Fiddlers Green Circle, Suite 1000 · Greenwood Village, CO 80111 · 303-796-2626

EQUIPMENT FINANCE LAW

Denver

Keith Block · Block Markus & Williams · 1700 Lincoln Street, Suite 4000 · Denver, CO 80203 · 303-830-0800

John L. McCabe · ⓾ · Davis Graham & Stubbs · http://www.dgslaw.com · 1550 Seventeenth Street, Suite 500 · Denver, CO 80202 · 303-892-9400

FAMILY LAW

Aspen

Ted D. Gardenswartz · Oates Knezevich & Gardenswartz · Aspen Plaza Building, Third Floor · 533 East Hopkins Avenue · Aspen, CO 81611 · 970-920-1700

Castle Rock

Mary Jane Cox Truesdell · Cox & Baker · 858 Happy Canyon Road, Suite 215 · Castle Rock, CO 80108 · 303-688-8588

Centennial

Timothy B. Walker · ⓾ · Mustain-Wood, Walker and Schumacher · 6601 South University Boulevard, Suite 200 · Centennial, CO 80121 · 303-730-0067

Colorado Springs

Thomas R. Cross · ⓾ · The Law Offices of Thomas R. Cross · 118 South Wahsatch Avenue, Suite 250 · Colorado Springs, CO 80903 · 719-471-8299

Lisa M. Dailey · Lisa M. Dailey · 526 South Nevada Avenue · Colorado Springs, CO 80903 · 719-473-0884

Thomas C. Henley · ⓾ · Henley & Henley Gatz · 802 Cheyenne Boulevard · Colorado Springs, CO 80906 · 719-471-4782

David M. Johnson · Johnson & Cord · 24 South Weber Street, Suite 300 · Colorado Springs, CO 80903 · 719-471-4034

John G. Otto · ⓾ · John G. Otto · 305 Main Street · Colorado Springs, CO 80911 · 719-390-7811

E. Michael Canges · ㉕ · Canges, Iwashko, Bethke & Bailey · http://www.cibblaw.com · 950 Seventeenth Street, Suite 1800 · Denver, CO 80202 · 303-860-1900

Diane Carlton · Litvak, Litvak, Mehrtens and Epstein · http://www.familyatty.com · 1900 Grant Street, Suite 500 · Denver, CO 80203-4305 · 303-837-0757

Michael F. DiManna · ⑩ · DiManna & Jackson · http://www.dimanna-jackson.com · 1741 High Street · Denver, CO 80218 · 303-320-4848

Stephen J. Harhai · ⑩ · Stephen J. Harhai · 1928 East 18th Avenue · Denver, CO 80206 · 303-329-8300

Kathleen A. Hogan · McGuane and Hogan · 3773 Cherry Creek North Drive, Suite 950 · Denver, CO 80209 · 303-691-9600

William L. Hunnicutt · ⑳ · Hunnicutt & Appelman · 1600 Stout Street, Suite 1300 · Denver, CO 80202-3132 · 303-572-1900

Robert C. Kaufman · Greenberg Traurig · http://www.gtlaw.com · The Tabor Center, Suite 2400 · 1200 Seventeenth Street · Denver, CO 80202 · 303-572-6500

Mary J. Kelly · ⑩ · Mary J. Kelly · 511 Sixteenth Street, Suite 700 · Denver, CO 80202 · 303-832-5440

Terrance R. Kelly · ㉕ · Kelly Garnsey Hubbell & Lass · http://www.kghllaw.com · 1441 Eighteenth Street, Suite 300 · Denver, CO 80202-1255 · 303-296-9412

Steven C. Lass · Kelly Garnsey Hubbell & Lass · http://www.kghllaw.com · 1441 Eighteenth Street, Suite 300 · Denver, CO 80202-1255 · 303-296-9412

Mark F. Leonard · ⑩ · Brownstein Hyatt Farber Schreck · http://www.bhfs.com · 410 Seventeenth Street, Suite 2200 · Denver, CO 80202-4432 · 303-223-1100

Stanley G. Lipkin · Stephen J. Harhai · 1928 East 18th Avenue · Denver, CO 80206 · 303-329-8300

Lawrence Litvak · ㉕ · Litvak, Litvak, Mehrtens and Epstein · http://www.familyatty.com · 1900 Grant Street, Suite 500 · Denver, CO 80203-4305 · 303-837-0757

Ronald D. Litvak · ⑩ · Litvak, Litvak, Mehrtens and Epstein · http://www.familyatty.com · 1900 Grant Street, Suite 500 · Denver, CO 80203-4305 · 303-837-0757

Steven E. McBride · McBride & Drinkwine · 4601 DTC Boulevard, Suite 1000 · Denver, CO 80237-2570 · 303-740-7422

Frank L. McGuane, Jr. · McGuane and Hogan · 3773 Cherry Creek North Drive, Suite 950 · Denver, CO 80209 · 303-691-9600

Timothy R. J. Mehrtens · ⑩ · Litvak, Litvak, Mehrtens and Epstein · http://www.familyatty.com · 1900 Grant Street, Suite 500 · Denver, CO 80203-4305 · 303-837-0757

Denise Mills · ⑩ · Mills & Weitzenkorn · 1441 Eighteenth Street, Suite 150 · Denver, CO 80202-1250 · 303-292-1441

Neeti Pawar · Neeti Pawar · 1741 High Street · Denver, CO 80218 · 303-333-5686

Jerry N. Snyder · ㉕ · Litvak, Litvak, Mehrtens and Epstein · http://www.familyatty.com · 1900 Grant Street, Suite 500 · Denver, CO 80203-4305 · 303-837-0757

Gina B. Weitzenkorn · Mills & Weitzenkorn · 1441 Eighteenth Street, Suite 150 · Denver, CO 80202-1250 · 303-292-1441

Kimberly R. Willoughby · Willoughby & Eckelberry · 303 East 17th Avenue, Suite 810 · Denver, CO 80203 · 303-839-1770

Durango

Deborah Anderson · ⑩ · Anderson & Baker · 484 Turner Drive North, Suite D · P.O. Box 2507 · Durango, CO 81303-3432 · 970-247-2810

Greenwood Village

Robert T. Hinds, Jr. · ⑳ · Robert T. Hinds, Jr. and Associates · 8490 East Crescent Parkway, Suite 395 · Greenwood Village, CO 80111 · 303-224-9000

Marie Avery Moses · Cook, Cooper & Moses · 5340 South Quebec Street, Suite 345 · Greenwood Village, CO 80111 · 303-623-1130

Highlands Ranch

Barbara C. Quade · ⑩ · Barbara Quade · 9090 South Ridgeline Boulevard, Suite 105 · Highlands Ranch, CO 80129 · 303-987-1127

Lakewood

Peter L. Franklin · Polidori, Franklin & Monahan · 550 South Wadsworth Boulevard, Suite 300 · Lakewood, CO 80226 · 303-936-3300

Lesleigh W. Monahan · Polidori, Franklin & Monahan · 550 South Wadsworth Boulevard, Suite 300 · Lakewood, CO 80226 · 303-936-3300

Gary L. Polidori · ⑩ · Polidori, Franklin & Monahan · 550 South Wadsworth Boulevard, Suite 300 · Lakewood, CO 80226 · 303-936-3300

Littleton

Frances C. Fontana · Fontana & Associates · 5941 South Middlefield Road, Suite 201 · Littleton, CO 80123 · 303-468-2668

Megan M. Sherr · Gutterman Griffiths & Powell · http://www.ggfamilylaw.com · 10375 Park Meadows Drive, Suite 520 · Littleton, CO 80124 · 303-858-8090

FAMILY LAW MEDIATION

Boulder

Steven Meyrich · Steven Meyrich · 4845 Pearl East Circle, Suite 101 · Boulder, CO 80301 · 303-440-8238

Denver

Michael F. DiManna · ⑩ · DiManna & Jackson · http://www.dimanna-jackson.com · 1741 High Street · Denver, CO 80218 · 303-320-4848

Daniel C. Himelspach · Dispute Management · 1801 Williams Steet, Suite 300 · Denver, CO 80218 · 303-321-1115

William L. Hunnicutt · ⑳ · Hunnicutt & Appelman · 1600 Stout Street, Suite 1300 · Denver, CO 80202-3132 · 303-572-1900

Mary J. Kelly · ⑩ · Mary J. Kelly · 511 Sixteenth Street, Suite 700 · Denver, CO 80202 · 303-832-5440

Leslie M. Lawson · Dispute Management · 1801 Williams Steet, Suite 300 · Denver, CO 80218 · 303-321-1115

Joan Harcourt McWilliams · McWilliams Mediation Group · http://www.mcwilliamsmediation.com · P.O. Box 6216 · Denver, CO 80206 · 303-830-0171

Barbara Salomon · ⑩ · Salomon Solutions · P.O. Box 101746 · Denver, CO 80250-1746 · 303-947-1117

Bonnie M. Schriner · Bonnie Marie Schriner · 2635 Seventeenth Street · Denver, CO 80211 · 303-458-5100

Helen C. Shreves · Helen C. Shreves · 3200 Cherry Creek South Drive, Suite 600 · Denver, CO 80209-3244 · 303-777-7833

Highlands Ranch

Elizabeth Henson · Elizabeth Henson · 9090 South Ridgeline Boulevard, Suite 105 · Highlands Ranch, CO 80129 · 303-346-3700

Barbara C. Quade · ⑩ · Barbara Quade · 9090 South Ridgeline Boulevard, Suite 105 · Highlands Ranch, CO 80129 · 303-987-1127

FIRST AMENDMENT LAW

Denver

Christopher P. Beall · Levine Sullivan Koch and Schulz · 1888 Sherman Street, Suite 370 · Denver, CO 80203 · 303-376-2400

Jeffrey A. Chase · ⑳ · Jacobs, Chase, Frick, Kleinkopf & Kelley · Independence Plaza, Suite 1500 · 1050 Seventeenth Street · Denver, CO 80265 · 303-685-4800

Marc D. Flink · Baker Hostetler · http://www.bakerlaw.com · 303 East 17th Avenue, Suite 1100 · Denver, CO 80203-1264 · 303-861-0600

Richard P. Holme · ⑩ · Davis Graham & Stubbs · http://www.dgslaw.com · 1550 Seventeenth Street, Suite 500 · Denver, CO 80202 · 303-892-9400

James W. Hubbell · ⑩ · Kelly Garnsey Hubbell & Lass · http://www.kghllaw.com · 1441 Eighteenth Street, Suite 300 · Denver, CO 80202-1255 · 303-296-9412

A. Bruce Jones · ⑩ · Holland & Hart · 555 Seventeenth Street, Suite 3200 · Denver, CO 80202-3739 · 303-295-8000

Edwin S. Kahn · ⑳ · Kelly Garnsey Hubbell & Lass · http://www.kghllaw.com · 1441 Eighteenth Street, Suite 300 · Denver, CO 80202-1255 · 303-296-9412

Thomas B. Kelley · ⑩ · Levine Sullivan Koch and Schulz · 1888 Sherman Street, Suite 370 · Denver, CO 80203 · 303-376-2400

David A. Lane · Killmer, Lane & Newman · The Odd Fellows Hall, Suite 400 · 1543 Champa Street · Denver, CO 80202 · 303-571-1000

Andrew M. Low · ⑩ · Davis Graham & Stubbs · http://www.dgslaw.com · 1550 Seventeenth Street, Suite 500 · Denver, CO 80202 · 303-892-9400

Daniel Recht · Recht & Kornfeld · http://www.rechtkornfeld.com · 1600 Stout Street, Suite 1000 · Denver, CO 80202 · 303-573-1900

Arthur M. Schwartz · ⑩ · Schwartz & Goldberg · The Tabor Center, Suite 2190 · 1200 Seventeenth Street · Denver, CO 80202 · 303-893-2500

Steven D. Zansberg · Levine Sullivan Koch and Schulz · 1888 Sherman Street, Suite 370 · Denver, CO 80203 · 303-376-2400

FRANCHISE LAW

Denver

Jeffrey Brimer · Snell & Wilmer · Tabor Center, Suite 1900 · 1200 Seventeenth Street · Denver, CO 80202-5854 · 303-634-2000

Kevin P. Hein · Snell & Wilmer · Tabor Center, Suite 1900 · 1200 Seventeenth Street · Denver, CO 80202-5854 · 303-634-2000

Kimberlee I. McCullough · Perkins Coie · http://www.perkinscoie.com · 1899 Wynkoop Street, Suite 700 Denver, CO 80202-1043 · 303-291-2300

GAMING LAW

Colorado Springs

Christopher D. Whitney · Mulliken Weiner Karsh Berg & Jolivet · Alamo Corporate Center, Suite 900 · 102 South Tejon Street · Colorado Springs, CO 80903 · 719-635-8750

Denver

H. Alan Dill · Dill, Dill, Car, Stonbraker & Hutchings · 455 Sherman Street, Suite 300 · Denver, CO 80203 · 303-777-3737

Robert A. Dill · Dill, Dill, Car, Stonbraker & Hutchings · 455 Sherman Street, Suite 300 · Denver, CO 80203 · 303-777-3737

Mark G. Grueskin · Isaacson Rosenbaum · 633 Seventeenth Street, Suite 2200 · Denver, CO 80202 · 303-292-5656

Roger M. Morris · Roger M. Morris · 1775 Sherman Street, Suite 1445 · Denver, CO 80203 · 303-329-0141

Richard L. Nathan · Robinson Waters & O'Dorisio · 1099 Eighteenth Street, 26th Floor · Denver, CO 80202 · 303-297-2600

GOVERNMENT RELATIONS LAW

Denver

Michael F. Feeley · Brownstein Hyatt Farber Schreck · 410 Seventeenth Street, Suite 2200 · Denver, CO 80202-4432 · 303-223-1100

Robert Ferm · Hall & Evans · http://www.hallevans.com · 1125 Seventeenth Street, Suite 600 · Denver, CO 80202 · 303-628-3300

Mark G. Grueskin · Isaacson Rosenbaum · 633 Seventeenth Street, Suite 2200 · Denver, CO 80202 · 303-292-5656

William G. Imig · William G. Imig · 1011 South Valentia Street, Suite 40 · Denver, CO 80247 · 303-337-4822

Martha M. Tierney · Kelly Garnsey Hubbell & Lass · http://www.kghllaw.com · 1441 Eighteenth Street, Suite 300 · Denver, CO 80202-1255 · 303-296-9412

Ted J. Trimpa · Brownstein Hyatt Farber Schreck · http://www.bhfs.com · 410 Seventeenth Street, Suite 2200 · Denver, CO 80202-4432 · 303-223-1100

HEALTH CARE LAW

Boulder

Sharon E. Caulfield · Caplan and Earnest · One Boulder Plaza, Suite 200 · 1800 Broadway · Boulder, CO 80302-5289 · 303-443-8010

Sarah E. Meshak · Caplan and Earnest · One Boulder Plaza, Suite 200 · 1800 Broadway · Boulder, CO 80302-5289 · 303-443-8010

Denver

Gary Blum · Silver & DeBoskey · The Smith Mansion · 1801 York Street · Denver, CO 80206 · 303-399-3000

Fred J. Diss · ⑩ · Robinson, Diss & Clowdus · Lincoln Center Building, Suite 2500 · 1660 Lincoln Street Denver, CO 80264 · 303-861-4154

Bruce A. Johnson · Faegre & Benson · Wells Fargo Center, Suite 3200 · 1700 Lincoln Street · Denver, CO 80203-4532 · 303-607-3500

Ann C. McCullough · Faegre & Benson · Wells Fargo Center, Suite 3200 · 1700 Lincoln Street · Denver, CO 80203-4532 · 303-607-3500

Frederick Miles · ⑩ · Miles & Peters · Sussex Building, Suite 400 · 1430 Larimer Square · Denver, CO 80202 · 303-892-9900

Bruce R. Muir · ⑳ · Sherman & Howard · 633 Seventeenth Street, Suite 3000 · Denver, CO 80202-3624 · 303-297-2900

Gerald A. Niederman · Faegre & Benson · Wells Fargo Center, Suite 3200 · 1700 Lincoln Street · Denver, CO 80203-4532 · 303-607-3500

Frederick Y. Yu · ⑩ · Sherman & Howard · 633 Seventeenth Street, Suite 3000 · Denver, CO 80202-3624 · 303-297-2900

Englewood

Henry C. Cleveland III · ⑩ · Crawford & Cleveland · 7887 East Belleview Avenue, Suite 1100 · Englewood, CO 80111 · 303-228-1622

IMMIGRATION LAW

Centennial

Ann Allott · ⑩ · Allott Immigration Law Firm · 2305 East Arapahoe Road, Suite 100 · Centennial, CO 80122 · 303-797-8055

Denver

Philip M. Alterman · ⑩ · Stern Elkind Curray & Alterman · http://www.secalaw.com · 650 South Cherry Street, Suite 900 · Denver, CO 80246 · 303-692-0111

John S. Castellano · ⑩ · Holland & Hart · 555 Seventeenth Street, Suite 3200 · Denver, CO 80202-3739 303-295-8000

Margaret S. Choi · ⑩ · Lau & Choi · 1930 Sherman Street · Denver, CO 80203 · 303-830-8880

Emily Curray · Stern Elkind Curray & Alterman · http://www.secalaw.com · 650 South Cherry Street, Suite 900 · Denver, CO 80246 · 303-692-0111

Nancy B. Elkind · ⑩ · Stern Elkind Curray & Alterman · http://www.secalaw.com · 650 South Cherry Street, Suite 900 · Denver, CO 80246 · 303-692-0111

Kenneth H. Stern · ⑩ · Stern Elkind Curray & Alterman · http://www.secalaw.com · 650 South Cherry Street, Suite 900 · Denver, CO 80246 · 303-692-0111

INFORMATION TECHNOLOGY LAW

Boulder

Celia F. Rankin · Faegre & Benson · 1900 Fifteenth Street · Boulder, CO 80302-5414 · 303-447-7700

Denver

Peter J. Kinsella · Faegre & Benson · Wells Fargo Center, Suite 3200 · 1700 Lincoln Street · Denver, CO 80203-4532 · 303-607-3500

Timothy B. Scull · Merchant & Gould · 1050 Seventeenth Street, Suite 1950 · Denver, CO 80265-0100 · 303-357-1670

INSURANCE LAW

Boulder

James A. Cederberg · Cederberg Law Firm · 75 Manhattan Drive, Suite 203 · Boulder, CO 80303 · 303-731-3976

Denver

Kevin F. Amatuzio · Montgomery Kolodny Amatuzio & Dusbabek · 1775 Sherman Street, Suite 2100 · Denver, CO 80203 · 303-592-6600

Robert Baldwin · Baldwin & Carpenter · 1512 Larimer Street, Suite 450 · Denver, CO 80202 · 303-623-1832

Christopher Clemenson · Cozen O'Connor · 707 Seventeeth Street, Suite 3100 · Denver, CO 80202 · 720-479-3900

John W. Grund · Grund, Dagner and Nelson · 303 East 17th Avenue, Suite 303 · Denver, CO 80203-1256 · 303-830-7770

Thomas P. Johnson · ⑩ · Davis Graham & Stubbs · http://www.dgslaw.com · 1550 Seventeenth Street, Suite 500 · Denver, CO 80202 · 303-892-9400

Bradley A. Levin · Roberts Levin & Rosenberg · http://www.robertslevin.com · 1660 Wynkoop Street, Suite 800 · Denver, CO 80202 · 303-575-9390

Michael S. McCarthy · Faegre & Benson · Wells Fargo Center, Suite 3200 · 1700 Lincoln Street · Denver, CO 80203-4532 · 303-607-3500

C. Michael Montgomery · Montgomery Kolodny Amatuzio & Dusbabek · 1775 Sherman Street, Suite 2100 · Denver, CO 80203 · 303-592-6600

Christopher R. Mosley · Sherman & Howard · 633 Seventeenth Street, Suite 3000 · Denver, CO 80202-3624 · 303-297-2900

Franklin O'Loughlin · Rothgerber Johnson & Lyons · One Tabor Center, Suite 3000 · 1200 Seventeenth Street · Denver, CO 80202-5855 · 303-623-9000

Thomas L. Roberts · ⑩ · Roberts Levin & Rosenberg · http://www.robertslevin.com · 1660 Wynkoop Street, Suite 800 · Denver, CO 80202 · 303-575-9390

Jon F. Sands · Fisher, Sweetbaum Levin & Sands · http://www.fslpc.com · 1125 Seventeenth Street, Suite 2100 · Denver, CO 80202 · 303-296-3377

John M. Vaught · Wheeler Trigg Kennedy · http://www.wtklaw.com · 1801 California Street, Suite 3600 · Denver, CO 80202-2617 · 303-244-1800

Golden

Dennis B. Polk · Holley, Albertson & Polk · Building Nineteen, Suite 100 · 1667 Cole Boulevard · Golden, CO 80401-3313 · 303-233-7838

Greenwood Village

Michael S. Beaver · Holland & Hart · 8390 East Crescent Parkway, Suite 400 · Greenwood Village, CO 80111-2800 · 303-290-1600

INTELLECTUAL PROPERTY LAW

Boulder

Kent A. Fischmann · Marsh Fischmann & Breyfogle · Canyon Center, Suite 335 · 1881 Ninth Street · Boulder, CO 80302 · 720-562-5500

Scott Havlick · Holland & Hart · One Boulder Plaza, Suite 300 · 1800 Broadway · Boulder, CO 80302-5144 · 303-473-2700

Denver

Glenn K. Beaton · ⑩ · Gibson, Dunn & Crutcher · 1801 California Street, Suite 4200 · Denver, CO 80202-2642 · 303-298-5700

Robert C. Dorr · ⑩ · Dorr, Carson & Birney · One Cherry Center, Suite 800 · 501 South Cherry Street · Denver, CO 80246 · 303-333-3010

Leslie P. Kramer · Faegre & Benson · Wells Fargo Center, Suite 3200 · 1700 Lincoln Street · Denver, CO 80203-4532 · 303-607-3500

George G. Matava · Merchant & Gould · 1050 Seventeenth Street, Suite 1950 · Denver, CO 80265-0100 303-357-1670

Gary M. Polumbus · Dorsey & Whitney · Republic Plaza Building, Suite 4700 · 370 Seventeenth Street · Denver, CO 80202-5647 · 303-629-3400

David N. Schachter · Sherman & Howard · 633 Seventeenth Street, Suite 3000 · Denver, CO 80202-3624 303-297-2900

Timothy B. Scull · Merchant & Gould · 1050 Seventeenth Street, Suite 1950 · Denver, CO 80265-0100 · 303-357-1670

David A. Weinstein · ⑩ · David A. Weinstein · 695 South Colorado Boulevard · Denver, CO 80246 · 303-863-8818

J. Greg Whitehair · Gibson, Dunn & Crutcher · 1801 California Street, Suite 4200 · Denver, CO 80202-2642 · 303-298-5700

Fort Collins

William W. Cochran · Cochran Freund & Young · 2026 Caribou Drive, Suite 201 · Fort Collins, CO 80525 · 970-492-1100

James R. Young · Cochran Freund & Young · 2026 Caribou Drive, Suite 201 · Fort Collins, CO 80525 · 970-492-1100

INTERNATIONAL TRADE AND FINANCE LAW

Denver

Paul Hilton · ⑩ · Hogan & Hartson · One Tabor Center, Suite 1500 · 1200 Seventeenth Street · Denver, CO 80202 · 303-899-7300

LABOR AND EMPLOYMENT LAW

Centennial

Robert J. Truhlar · ⑳ · Truhlar and Truhlar · 7340 East Caley Avenue, Suite 310 · Centennial, CO 80111 · 303-794-2404

Colorado Springs

Craig M. Cornish · ⑳ · Cornish & Dell'Olio · 431 North Cascade Avenue, Suite One · Colorado Springs, CO 80903 · 719-475-1204

Denver

Edwin P. Aro · Hogan & Hartson · One Tabor Center, Suite 1500 · 1200 Seventeenth Street · Denver, CO 80202 · 303-899-7300

William C. Berger · Stettner Miller · Independence Plaza, Suite 700 · 1050 Seventeenth Street · Denver, CO 80265-2008 · 303-534-0273

Thomas B. Buescher · ㉕ · Buescher, Goldhammer, Kelman & Dodge · 1563 Gaylord Street · Denver, CO 80206 · 303-333-7751

Gregory A. Eurich · ㉕ · Holland & Hart · 555 Seventeenth Street, Suite 3200 · Denver, CO 80202-3739 · 303-295-8000

Lynn D. Feiger · ⑳ · Lohf Shaiman Jacobs Hyman & Feiger · Cherry Tower, Suite 900 · 950 South Cherry Street · Denver, CO 80246-2666 · 303-753-9000

Joseph M. Goldhammer · ⑳ · Buescher, Goldhammer, Kelman & Dodge · 1563 Gaylord Street · Denver, CO 80206 · 303-333-7751

Paula D. Greisen · King & Greisen · 1670 York Street · Denver, CO 80206 · 303-298-9878

John M. Husband · ⑳ · Holland & Hart · 555 Seventeenth Street, Suite 3200 · Denver, CO 80202-3739 · 303-295-8000

Curtis L. Kennedy · Curtis L. Kennedy · 8405 East Princeton Avenue · Denver, CO 80237-1741 · 303-770-0440

Darold W. Killmer · ⑩ · Killmer, Lane & Newman · The Odd Fellows Hall, Suite 400 · 1543 Champa Street · Denver, CO 80202 · 303-571-1000

Diane S. King · King & Greisen · 1670 York Street · Denver, CO 80206 · 303-298-9878

Raymond W. Martin · Wheeler Trigg Kennedy · http://www.wtklaw.com · 1801 California Street, Suite 3600 · Denver, CO 80202-2617 · 303-244-1800

William J. Martínez · McNamara, Roseman, Martinez & Kazmierski · 1640 East 18th Avenue · Denver, CO 80218 · 303-333-8700

Todd J. McNamara · McNamara, Roseman, Martinez & Kazmierski · 1640 East 18th Avenue · Denver, CO 80218 · 303-333-8700

Charles W. Newcom · ⑳ · Sherman & Howard · 633 Seventeenth Street, Suite 3000 · Denver, CO 80202-3624 · 303-297-2900

Michael Nosler · Rothgerber Johnson & Lyons · One Tabor Center, Suite 3000 · 1200 Seventeenth Street Denver, CO 80202-5855 · 303-623-9000

K. Preston Oade · ⑩ · Holme Roberts & Owen · http://www.hro.com · 1700 Lincoln Street, Suite 4100 · Denver, CO 80203-4541 · 303-861-7000

Theodore A. Olsen · ⑩ · Sherman & Howard · 633 Seventeenth Street, Suite 3000 · Denver, CO 80202-3624 · 303-297-2900

David D. Powell, Jr. · Brownstein Hyatt Farber Schreck · http://www.bhfs.com · 410 Seventeenth Street, Suite 2200 · Denver, CO 80202-4432 · 303-223-1100

Barry D. Roseman · ⑩ · McNamara, Roseman, Martinez & Kazmierski · 1640 East 18th Avenue · Denver, CO 80218 · 303-333-8700

W. V. Bernie Siebert · Sherman & Howard · 633 Seventeenth Street, Suite 3000 · Denver, CO 80202-3624 · 303-297-2900

Rodney L. Smith · Sherman & Howard · 633 Seventeenth Street, Suite 3000 · Denver, CO 80202-3624 · 303-297-2900

David H. Stacy · Ducker, Montgomery, Aronstein & Bess · One Civic Center Plaza, Suite 1400 · 1560 Broadway · Denver, CO 80202-1548 · 303-861-2828

Charles W. Weese · Jackson Lewis · http://www.jacksonlewis.com · 1050 Seventeeth Street, Suite 2450 · Denver, CO 80265 · 303-892-0404

Glenwood Springs

Sander N. Karp · ⑳ · Leavenworth & Karp · 201 Fourteenth Street, Suite 200 · P.O. Drawer 2030 · Glenwood Springs, CO 81602 · 970-945-2261

Littleton

Kathryn E. Miller · ⑩ · Miller & Steiert · 1901 West Littleton Boulevard, Suite 100 · Littleton, CO 80120-2087 · 303-798-2525

LAND USE & ZONING LAW

Denver

Stephen H. Kaplan · Kaplan Kirsch Rockwell · 1675 Broadway, Suite 2300 · Denver, CO 80202 · 303-825-7000

J. Thomas Macdonald · Otten, Johnson, Robinson, Neff & Ragonetti · 950 Seventeenth Street, Suite 1600 · Denver, CO 80202 · 303-825-8400

Thomas J. Ragonetti · Otten, Johnson, Robinson, Neff & Ragonetti · 950 Seventeenth Street, Suite 1600 Denver, CO 80202 · 303-825-8400

Sarah M. Rockwell · Kaplan Kirsch Rockwell · 1675 Broadway, Suite 2300 · Denver, CO 80202 · 303-825-7000

LEGAL MALPRACTICE LAW

Denver

Shelley B. Don · ⑩ · Don, Hiller & Galleher · 1737 Gaylord Street · Denver, CO 80206 · 303-572-1668

Cecelia A. Fleischner · McConnell Siderius Fleischner Houghtaling & Craigmile · Denver Corporate Center, Tower I, Suite 200 · 4700 South Syracuse · Denver, CO 80237 · 303-480-0400

Daniel S. Hoffman · ⑩ · Hogan & Hartson · One Tabor Center, Suite 1500 · 1200 Seventeenth Street · Denver, CO 80202 · 303-899-7300

Michael L. Hutchinson · Treece, Alfrey, Musat & Bosworth · http://www.tamblaw.com · 999 Eighteenth Street, Suite 1600 · Denver, CO 80202 · 303-292-2700

Joseph C. Jaudon, Jr. · ㉕ · Jaudon & Avery · 600 Grant Street, Suite 505 · Denver, CO 80203 · 303-832-1122

Richard W. Laugesen · ⑩ · Richard W. Laugesen · 1830 South Monroe Street · Denver, CO 80210-3731 303-300-1006

Michael T. McConnell · ⑩ · McConnell Siderius Fleischner Houghtaling & Craigmile · Denver Corporate Center, Tower I, Suite 200 · 4700 South Syracuse · Denver, CO 80237 · 303-480-0400

Daniel Ray McCune · Kennedy Childs & Fogg · Independence Plaza, Suite 2500 · 1050 Seventeenth Street · Denver, CO 80265 · 303-825-2700

Gerald P. McDermott · ⑳ · McDermott Hansen and McLaughlin · 1890 Gaylord Street · Denver, CO 80206-1211 · 303-399-6037

Michael L. O'Donnell · Wheeler Trigg Kennedy · http://www.wtklaw.com · 1801 California Street, Suite 3600 · Denver, CO 80202-2617 · 303-244-1800

John M. Palmeri · Gordon & Rees · 370 Seventeenth Street, Suite 4450 · Denver, CO 80202 · 303-534-5160

Thomas B. Quinn · Gordon & Rees · 370 Seventeenth Street, Suite 4450 · Denver, CO 80202 · 303-534-5160

Elizabeth A. Starrs · Starrs Mihm & Caschette · 707 Seventeenth Street, Suite 2600 · Denver, CO 80202 303-592-5900

Traci L. Van Pelt · McConnell Siderius Fleischner Houghtaling & Craigmile · Denver Corporate Center, Tower I, Suite 200 · 4700 South Syracuse · Denver, CO 80237 · 303-480-0400

LEVERAGED BUYOUTS AND PRIVATE EQUITY LAW

Broomfield

James C.T. Linfield · Cooley Godward Kronish · 380 Interlocken Crescent, Suite 900 · Broomfield, CO 80021-8023 · 720-566-4000

Michael L. Platt · Cooley Godward Kronish · 380 Interlocken Crescent, Suite 900 · Broomfield, CO 80021-8023 · 720-566-4000

Denver

Betty C. Arkell · Holland & Hart · 555 Seventeenth Street, Suite 3200 · Denver, CO 80202-3739 · 303-295-8000

Ronald Levine II · Davis Graham & Stubbs · http://www.dgslaw.com · 1550 Seventeenth Street, Suite 500 · Denver, CO 80202 · 303-892-9400

John G. Lewis · ⑳ · Ireland, Stapleton, Pryor & Pascoe · 1675 Broadway, Suite 2600 · Denver, CO 80202 303-623-2700

B. Scott Pullara · Sherman & Howard · 633 Seventeenth Street, Suite 3000 · Denver, CO 80202-3624 · 303-297-2900

MASS TORT LITIGATION

Boulder

John A. Purvis · ⑳ · Purvis Gray & Murphy · The Exeter Building, Suite 501 · 1050 Walnut Street · Boulder, CO 80302 · 303-442-3366

Denver

Scott S. Barker · Holland & Hart · 555 Seventeenth Street, Suite 3200 · Denver, CO 80202-3739 · 303-295-8000

Linnea Brown · Holme Roberts & Owen · http://www.hro.com · 1700 Lincoln Street, Suite 4100 · Denver, CO 80203-4541 · 303-861-7000

Michael S. Burg · Burg Simpson Eldredge Hersh & Jardine · 40 Inverness Drive, East · Denver, CO 80112 · 303-792-5595

Peter W. Burg · Burg Simpson Eldredge Hersh & Jardine · 40 Inverness Drive, East · Denver, CO 80112 303-792-5595

Osborne J. Dykes III · Fulbright & Jaworski · http://www.fulbright.com · Republic Plaza, Suite 2150 · 370 Seventeenth Street · Denver, CO 80202-5638 · 303-801-2700

John M. Fitzpatrick · Wheeler Trigg Kennedy · http://www.wtklaw.com · 1801 California Street, Suite 3600 · Denver, CO 80202-2617 · 303-244-1800

Kerry N. Jardine · Burg Simpson Eldredge Hersh & Jardine · 40 Inverness Drive, East · Denver, CO 80112 · 303-792-5595

Robert W. Lawrence · ⑩ · Davis Graham & Stubbs · http://www.dgslaw.com · 1550 Seventeenth Street, Suite 500 · Denver, CO 80202 · 303-892-9400

John M. Restaino, Jr. · Burg Simpson Eldredge Hersh & Jardine · 40 Inverness Drive, East · Denver, CO 80112 · 303-792-5595

MEDICAL MALPRACTICE LAW

Boulder

Baine P. Kerr · Hutchinson Black and Cook · 921 Walnut Street, Suite 200 · Boulder, CO 80302 · 303-442-6514

Denver

Edward Bronfin · Kennedy Childs & Fogg · Independence Plaza, Suite 2500 · 1050 Seventeenth Street · Denver, CO 80265 · 303-825-2700

Natalie Brown · Leventhal, Brown & Puga · 950 South Cherry Street, Suite 600 · Denver, CO 80246 · 303-759-9945

John M. Fitzpatrick · Wheeler Trigg Kennedy · http://www.wtklaw.com · 1801 California Street, Suite 3600 · Denver, CO 80202-2617 · 303-244-1800

Mark A. Fogg · Kennedy Childs & Fogg · Independence Plaza, Suite 2500 · 1050 Seventeenth Street · Denver, CO 80265 · 303-825-2700

Neil Hillyard · ⑳ · Hillyard, Wahlberg, Kudla & Sloane · http://www.hwkslaw.com · 4601 DTC Boulevard, Suite 300 · Denver, CO 80237 · 303-571-5302

John Robert Holland · John Robert Holland · 1437 High Street · Denver, CO 80218 · 303-860-1331

Joseph C. Jaudon, Jr. · ㉕ · Jaudon & Avery · 600 Grant Street, Suite 505 · Denver, CO 80203 · 303-832-1122

William L. Keating · (10) · Fogel Keating Wagner Polidori Shafner · http://www.fkwlaw.com · 1290 Broadway, Suite 600 · Denver, CO 80203 · 303-534-0401

Kevin J. Kuhn · Wheeler Trigg Kennedy · http://www.wtklaw.com · 1801 California Street, Suite 3600 · Denver, CO 80202-2617 · 303-244-1800

Jim Leventhal · (10) · Leventhal, Brown & Puga · 950 South Cherry Street, Suite 600 · Denver, CO 80246 · 303-759-9945

Michael T. McConnell · (10) · McConnell Siderius Fleischner Houghtaling & Craigmile · Denver Corporate Center, Tower I, Suite 200 · 4700 South Syracuse · Denver, CO 80237 · 303-480-0400

Gerald P. McDermott · (20) · McDermott Hansen and McLaughlin · 1890 Gaylord Street · Denver, CO 80206-1211 · 303-399-6037

Bruce A. Montoya · Messner & Reeves · 1430 Wynkoop, Suite 400 · Denver, CO 80202 · 303-623-1800

Lorraine Parker · Leventhal, Brown & Puga · 950 South Cherry Street, Suite 600 · Denver, CO 80246 · 303-759-9945

James E. Puga · Leventhal, Brown & Puga · 950 South Cherry Street, Suite 600 · Denver, CO 80246 · 303-759-9945

Fort Collins

T. Thomas Metier · Metier Law Firm · 4828 South College Avenue · Fort Collins, CO 80525 · 970-377-3800

Greenwood Village

Irving G. Johnson · Pryor Johnson Carney Karr Nixon · 5619 DTC Parkway, Suite 1200 · Greenwood Village, CO 80111 · 303-773-3500

Peter W. Pryor · (25) · Pryor Johnson Carney Karr Nixon · 5619 DTC Parkway, Suite 1200 · Greenwood Village, CO 80111 · 303-773-3500

MERGERS & ACQUISITIONS LAW

Boulder

James H. Carroll · Faegre & Benson · 1900 Fifteenth Street · Boulder, CO 80302-5414 · 303-447-7700

Broomfield

James C.T. Linfield · Cooley Godward Kronish · 380 Interlocken Crescent, Suite 900 · Broomfield, CO 80021-8023 · 720-566-4000

Denver

Betty C. Arkell · Holland & Hart · 555 Seventeenth Street, Suite 3200 · Denver, CO 80202-3739 · 303-295-8000

Paul Hilton · (10) · Hogan & Hartson · One Tabor Center, Suite 1500 · 1200 Seventeenth Street · Denver, CO 80202 · 303-899-7300

Cathy S. Krendl · (10) · Krendl Krendl Sachnoff & Way · http://www.krendl.com · 370 Seventeenth Street, Suite 5350 · Denver, CO 80202 · 303-629-2600

Ronald Levine II · Davis Graham & Stubbs · http://www.dgslaw.com · 1550 Seventeenth Street, Suite 500 · Denver, CO 80202 · 303-892-9400

Mark R. Levy · ⑳ · Holland & Hart · 555 Seventeenth Street, Suite 3200 · Denver, CO 80202-3739 · 303-295-8000

John G. Lewis · ⑳ · Ireland, Stapleton, Pryor & Pascoe · 1675 Broadway, Suite 2600 · Denver, CO 80202 303-623-2700

Blair L. Lockwood · Faegre & Benson · Wells Fargo Center, Suite 3200 · 1700 Lincoln Street · Denver, CO 80203-4532 · 303-607-3500

John E. Moye · ⑩ · Moye White · 16 Market Square, Sixth Floor · 1400 Sixteenth Street · Denver, CO 80202-1486 · 303-292-2900

James L. Palenchar · Bartlit, Beck, Herman, Palenchar & Scott · 1899 Wynkoop Street, Eighth Floor · Denver, CO 80202 · 303-592-3100

B. Scott Pullara · Sherman & Howard · 633 Seventeenth Street, Suite 3000 · Denver, CO 80202-3624 · 303-297-2900

Michael A. Sabian · ⑩ · Shughart Thomson & Kilroy · http://www.stklaw.com · Independence Plaza, Suite 2300 · 1050 Seventeenth Street · Denver, CO 80265 · 303-572-9300

W. Dean Salter · ⑩ · Holme Roberts & Owen · http://www.hro.com · 1700 Lincoln Street, Suite 4100 · Denver, CO 80203-4541 · 303-861-7000

Thomas R. Stephens · Bartlit, Beck, Herman, Palenchar & Scott · 1899 Wynkoop Street, Eighth Floor · Denver, CO 80202 · 303-592-3100

James F. Wood · ⑩ · Sherman & Howard · 633 Seventeenth Street, Suite 3000 · Denver, CO 80202-3624 303-297-2900

Douglas R. Wright · Faegre & Benson · Wells Fargo Center, Suite 3200 · 1700 Lincoln Street · Denver, CO 80203-4532 · 303-607-3500

MINING LAW

Denver

James K. Aronstein · ⑩ · Ducker, Montgomery, Aronstein & Bess · One Civic Center Plaza, Suite 1400 · 1560 Broadway · Denver, CO 80202-1548 · 303-861-2828

Laura E. Beverage · Jackson Kelly · 1099 Eighteenth Street, Suite 2150 · Denver, CO 80202 · 303-390-0003

James F. Cress · Holme Roberts & Owen · http://www.hro.com · 1700 Lincoln Street, Suite 4100 · Denver, CO 80203-4541 · 303-861-7000

Franklin Erisman · ⑩ · Holme Roberts & Owen · http://www.hro.com · 1700 Lincoln Street, Suite 4100 · Denver, CO 80203-4541 · 303-861-7000

John D. Fognani · ⑩ · Fognani & Faught · 1700 Lincoln Center, Suite 2222 · Denver, CO 80203 · 303-382-6200

Randall E. Hubbard · Davis Graham & Stubbs · http://www.dgslaw.com · 1550 Seventeenth Street, Suite 500 · Denver, CO 80202 · 303-892-9400

Charles L. Kaiser · ⑩ · Davis Graham & Stubbs · http://www.dgslaw.com · 1550 Seventeenth Street, Suite 500 · Denver, CO 80202 · 303-892-9400

James M. King · ⑩ · Baker Hostetler · http://www.bakerlaw.com · 303 East 17th Avenue, Suite 1100 · Denver, CO 80203-1264 · 303-861-0600

Greenwood Village

Paul J. Schlauch · ⑩ · Holland & Hart · 8390 East Crescent Parkway, Suite 400 · Greenwood Village, CO 80111-2800 · 303-290-1600

Sedalia

William R. Marsh · ⑳ · William R. Marsh · 6257 Pine Cliff Road · Sedalia, CO 80135-8559 · 303-814-0162

MUNICIPAL LAW

Denver

Thomas S. Rice · Senter Goldfarb & Rice · http://www.sgrllc.com · 1700 Broadway, Suite 1700 · Denver, CO 80290 · 303-320-0509

MUTUAL FUNDS LAW

Denver

Reid A. Godbolt · Jones & Keller · 1625 Broadway, 16th Floor · Denver, CO 80202 · 303-573-1600

Glen A. Payne · Jones & Keller · 1625 Broadway, 16th Floor · Denver, CO 80202 · 303-573-1600

Peter H. Schwartz · Davis Graham & Stubbs · http://www.dgslaw.com · 1550 Seventeenth Street, Suite 500 · Denver, CO 80202 · 303-892-9400

Lester R. Woodward · ㉕ · Davis Graham & Stubbs · http://www.dgslaw.com · 1550 Seventeenth Street, Suite 500 · Denver, CO 80202 · 303-892-9400

NATIVE AMERICAN LAW

Boulder

Scott B. McElroy · Greene Meyer & McElroy · 1007 Pearl Street, Suite 220 · Boulder, CO 80302 · 303-442-2021

Denver

Lynn P. Hendrix · ⑩ · Holme Roberts & Owen · http://www.hro.com · 1700 Lincoln Street, Suite 4100 · Denver, CO 80203-4541 · 303-861-7000

Charles L. Kaiser · ⑩ · Davis Graham & Stubbs · http://www.dgslaw.com · 1550 Seventeenth Street, Suite 500 · Denver, CO 80202 · 303-892-9400

Durango

Thomas H. Shipps · Maynes Bradford Shipps & Sheftel · 835 East Second Avenue, Suite 123 · P.O. Box 2717 · Durango, CO 81302-2717 · 970-247-1755

NATURAL RESOURCES LAW

Denver

James K. Aronstein · ⑩ · Ducker, Montgomery, Aronstein & Bess · One Civic Center Plaza, Suite 1400 · 1560 Broadway · Denver, CO 80202-1548 · 303-861-2828

Laura E. Beverage · Jackson Kelly · 1099 Eighteenth Street, Suite 2150 · Denver, CO 80202 · 303-390-0003

Craig Carver · ⑩ · Carver Schwarz McNab & Bailey · Hudson's Bay Centre, Suite 1700 · 1600 Stout Street · Denver, CO 80202 · 303-893-1815

Phillip R. Clark · ⑩ · Holme Roberts & Owen · http://www.hro.com · 1700 Lincoln Street, Suite 4100 · Denver, CO 80203-4541 · 303-861-7000

Gregory R. Danielson · Davis Graham & Stubbs · http://www.dgslaw.com · 1550 Seventeenth Street, Suite 500 · Denver, CO 80202 · 303-892-9400

Franklin Erisman · ⑩ · Holme Roberts & Owen · http://www.hro.com · 1700 Lincoln Street, Suite 4100 · Denver, CO 80203-4541 · 303-861-7000

John D. Fognani · ⑩ · Fognani & Faught · 1700 Lincoln Center, Suite 2222 · Denver, CO 80203 · 303-382-6200

Lynn P. Hendrix · ⑩ · Holme Roberts & Owen · http://www.hro.com · 1700 Lincoln Street, Suite 4100 · Denver, CO 80203-4541 · 303-861-7000

William A. Hillhouse II · White & Jankowski · 511 Sixteenth Street, Suite 500 · Denver, CO 80202-4224 303-595-9441

Randall E. Hubbard · Davis Graham & Stubbs · http://www.dgslaw.com · 1550 Seventeenth Street, Suite 500 · Denver, CO 80202 · 303-892-9400

Charles L. Kaiser · ⑩ · Davis Graham & Stubbs · http://www.dgslaw.com · 1550 Seventeenth Street, Suite 500 · Denver, CO 80202 · 303-892-9400

James M. King · ⑩ · Baker Hostetler · http://www.bakerlaw.com · 303 East 17th Avenue, Suite 1100 · Denver, CO 80203-1264 · 303-861-0600

Robert W. Lawrence · ⑩ · Davis Graham & Stubbs · http://www.dgslaw.com · 1550 Seventeenth Street, Suite 500 · Denver, CO 80202 · 303-892-9400

Robert G. Lewis · Ducker, Montgomery, Aronstein & Bess · One Civic Center Plaza, Suite 1400 · 1560 Broadway · Denver, CO 80202-1548 · 303-861-2828

Laura Lindley · ⑩ · Bjork Lindley Little · 1600 Stout Street, Suite 1400 · Denver, CO 80202 · 303-892-1400

Judith M. Matlock · ⑩ · Davis Graham & Stubbs · http://www.dgslaw.com · 1550 Seventeenth Street, Suite 500 · Denver, CO 80202 · 303-892-9400

Harold G. Morris, Jr. · ⑳ · Lindquist & Vennum · http://www.lindquist.com · 600 Seventeenth Street, Suite 1800 South · Denver, CO 80202-5441 · 303-573-5900

Davis O. O'Connor · ⑳ · Holland & Hart · 555 Seventeenth Street, Suite 3200 · Denver, CO 80202-3739 303-295-8000

William G. Odell · ⑳ · Poulson, Odell & Peterson · 1775 Sherman Street, Suite 1400 · Denver, CO 80203 303-861-4400

David W. Robbins · ⑩ · Hill & Robbins · 1441 Eighteenth Street, Suite 100 · Denver, CO 80202 · 303-296-8100

Anthony J. Shaheen · ⑩ · Holland & Hart · 555 Seventeenth Street, Suite 3200 · Denver, CO 80202-3739 · 303-295-8000

John F. Shepherd · ⑩ · Holland & Hart · 555 Seventeenth Street, Suite 3200 · Denver, CO 80202-3739 · 303-295-8000

Keith Tooley · Welborn, Sullivan, Meck & Tooley · 821 Seventeenth Street, Suite 500 · Denver, CO 80202 · 303-830-2500

Ezekiel J. Williams · Faegre & Benson · Wells Fargo Center, Suite 3200 · 1700 Lincoln Street · Denver, CO 80203-4532 · 303-607-3500

Michael Wozniak · Beatty & Wozniak · Columbine Place, Suite 1100 · 216 Sixteenth Street · Denver, CO 80202-5115 · 303-407-4499

Durango

Thomas P. Dugan · Dugan & Associates · 900 Main Avenue, Suite A · Durango, CO 81301-5179 · 970-259-1770

Thomas H. Shipps · Maynes Bradford Shipps & Sheftel · 835 East Second Avenue, Suite 123 · P.O. Box 2717 · Durango, CO 81302-2717 · 970-247-1755

Glenwood Springs

Scott Balcomb · Balcomb & Green · 818 Colorado Avenue · P.O. Drawer 790 · Glenwood Springs, CO 81602 · 970-945-6546

Loyal E. Leavenworth · Leavenworth & Karp · 201 Fourteenth Street, Suite 200 · P.O. Drawer 2030 · Glenwood Springs, CO 81602 · 970-945-2261

James S. Lochhead · Brownstein Hyatt Farber Schreck · http://www.bhfs.com · 818 Colorado Avenue, Suite 306 · P.O. Box 357 · Glenwood Springs, CO 81602-0357 · 970-945-5302

Greenwood Village

Paul J. Schlauch · ⑩ · Holland & Hart · 8390 East Crescent Parkway, Suite 400 · Greenwood Village, CO 80111-2800 · 303-290-1600

Sedalia

William R. Marsh · ⑳ · William R. Marsh · 6257 Pine Cliff Road · Sedalia, CO 80135-8559 · 303-814-0162

NON-PROFIT/CHARITIES LAW

Boulder

Lynn Kuykendall · Caplan and Earnest · One Boulder Plaza, Suite 200 · 1800 Broadway · Boulder, CO 80302-5289 · 303-443-8010

Colorado Springs

William K. Brown · ⑳ · Holland & Hart · 90 South Cascade Avenue, Suite 1000 · P.O. Box 2340 · Colorado Springs, CO 80903-1645 · 719-475-7730

L. Martin Nussbaum · Rothgerber Johnson & Lyons · Wells Fargo Tower, Suite 1100 · 90 South Cascade Avenue · Colorado Springs, CO 80903-1662 · 719-386-3000

Denver

J. William Callison · Faegre & Benson · Wells Fargo Center, Suite 3200 · 1700 Lincoln Street · Denver, CO 80203-4532 · 303-607-3500

Michael Dubetz · Sherman & Howard · 633 Seventeenth Street, Suite 3000 · Denver, CO 80202-3624 · 303-297-2900

Peter C. Guthery · ⑳ · Berenbaum, Weinshienk & Eason · http://www.bwelaw.com · Republic Plaza, 48th Floor · 370 Seventeenth Street · Denver, CO 80202 · 303-825-0800

Karen Leaffer · Faegre & Benson · Wells Fargo Center, Suite 3200 · 1700 Lincoln Street · Denver, CO 80203-4532 · 303-607-3500

Peter B. Nagel · Peter B. Nagel · 999 Eighteenth Street, Suite 1745 · Denver, CO 80202 · 303-296-4840

James R. Walker · Rothgerber Johnson & Lyons · One Tabor Center, Suite 3000 · 1200 Seventeenth Street · Denver, CO 80202-5855 · 303-623-9000

William E. Walters III · Kelly Garnsey Hubbell & Lass · http://www.kghllaw.com · 1441 Eighteenth Street, Suite 300 · Denver, CO 80202-1255 · 303-296-9412

NON-WHITE-COLLAR CRIMINAL DEFENSE

Boulder

G. Paul McCormick · ⑩ · McCormick & Christoph · 1406 Pearl Street, Suite 200 · Boulder, CO 80302-5307 · 303-443-2281

Colorado Springs

Dennis W. Hartley · ⑩ · Dennis W. Hartley · 1749 South Eighth Street, Suite Five · Colorado Springs, CO 80906-1968 · 719-635-5521

Richard Lewis Tegtmeier · ⑩ · Tegtmeier Law Firm · 104 South Cascade Street, Suite 200 · Colorado Springs, CO 80903-5102 · 719-473-5757

J. Gregory Walta · J. Gregory Walta · 105 East Moreno Avenue · Colorado Springs, CO 80903 · 719-578-8888

Patrick J. Burke · ⑩ · Patrick J. Burke · 303 Sixteenth Street, Suite 200 · Denver, CO 80202 · 303-825-3050

James A. Castle · Castle & Castle · http://www.castleandcastlelaw.com · 1860 Race Street · Denver, CO 80206 · 303-675-0500

Lee D. Foreman · ⑳ · Haddon Morgan Mueller Jordan Mackey & Foreman · 150 East 10th Avenue · Denver, CO 80203-2740 · 303-831-7364

Walter L. Gerash · ⑳ · Walter L. Gerash Law Firm · 1439 Court Place · Denver, CO 80202-5091 · 303-825-5400

Harold A. Haddon · ㉕ · Haddon Morgan Mueller Jordan Mackey & Foreman · 150 East 10th Avenue · Denver, CO 80203-2740 · 303-831-7364

Brian K. Holland · Recht & Kornfeld · http://www.rechtkornfeld.com · 1600 Stout Street, Suite 1000 · Denver, CO 80202 · 303-573-1900

Forrest Wayne Lewis · ⑩ · Forrest W. Lewis · 1600 Broadway, Suite 1525 · Denver, CO 80202 · 303-830-2190

Gary Lozow · ⑩ · Isaacson Rosenbaum · 633 Seventeenth Street, Suite 2200 · Denver, CO 80202 · 303-292-5656

Pamela Robillard Mackey · Haddon Morgan Mueller Jordan Mackey & Foreman · 150 East 10th Avenue Denver, CO 80203-2740 · 303-831-7364

Norman R. Mueller · Haddon Morgan Mueller Jordan Mackey & Foreman · 150 East 10th Avenue · Denver, CO 80203-2740 · 303-831-7364

Jeffrey S. Pagliuca · Haddon Morgan Mueller Jordan Mackey & Foreman · 150 East 10th Avenue · Denver, CO 80203-2740 · 303-831-7364

Larry S. Pozner · ⑳ · Reilly Pozner · http://www.litigationcolorado.com · The Kittredge Building, Suite 700 · 511 Sixteenth Street · Denver, CO 80202 · 303-893-6100

Joseph Saint-Veltri · ㉕ · Joseph Saint-Veltri · 900 Logan Street · Denver, CO 80203 · 303-832-6777

Daniel J. Sears · ⑳ · Daniel J. Sears · 1801 Broadway Street, Suite 1100 · Denver, CO 80202-3839 · 303-292-0110

Harvey A. Steinberg · Springer & Steinberg · http://www.springer-and-steinberg.com · 1600 Broadway, Suite 1200 · Denver, CO 80202 · 303-861-2800

Craig L. Truman · ⑩ · Craig L. Truman · http://www.cltrumanlaw.com · 1444 Wazee Street, Suite 205 · Denver, CO 80202-1326 · 303-595-8008

OIL & GAS LAW

Denver

Craig Carver · ⑩ · Carver Schwarz McNab & Bailey · Hudson's Bay Centre, Suite 1700 · 1600 Stout Street · Denver, CO 80202 · 303-893-1815

Phillip R. Clark · ⑩ · Holme Roberts & Owen · http://www.hro.com · 1700 Lincoln Street, Suite 4100 · Denver, CO 80203-4541 · 303-861-7000

Gregory R. Danielson · Davis Graham & Stubbs · http://www.dgslaw.com · 1550 Seventeenth Street, Suite 500 · Denver, CO 80202 · 303-892-9400

John D. Fognani · ⑩ · Fognani & Faught · 1700 Lincoln Center, Suite 2222 · Denver, CO 80203 · 303-382-6200

Jan Harris · Holland & Hart · 555 Seventeenth Street, Suite 3200 · Denver, CO 80202-3739 · 303-295-8000

Lynn P. Hendrix · ⑩ · Holme Roberts & Owen · http://www.hro.com · 1700 Lincoln Street, Suite 4100 · Denver, CO 80203-4541 · 303-861-7000

Kendor P. Jones · Welborn, Sullivan, Meck & Tooley · 821 Seventeenth Street, Suite 500 · Denver, CO 80202 · 303-830-2500

Robert G. Lewis · Ducker, Montgomery, Aronstein & Bess · One Civic Center Plaza, Suite 1400 · 1560 Broadway · Denver, CO 80202-1548 · 303-861-2828

Laura Lindley · ⑩ · Bjork Lindley Little · 1600 Stout Street, Suite 1400 · Denver, CO 80202 · 303-892-1400

Judith M. Matlock · ⑩ · Davis Graham & Stubbs · http://www.dgslaw.com · 1550 Seventeenth Street, Suite 500 · Denver, CO 80202 · 303-892-9400

Davis O. O'Connor · ⑳ · Holland & Hart · 555 Seventeenth Street, Suite 3200 · Denver, CO 80202-3739 303-295-8000

William G. Odell · ⑳ · Poulson, Odell & Peterson · 1775 Sherman Street, Suite 1400 · Denver, CO 80203 303-861-4400

Michael Wozniak · Beatty & Wozniak · Columbine Place, Suite 1100 · 216 Sixteenth Street · Denver, CO 80202-5115 · 303-407-4499

Durango

Thomas H. Shipps · Maynes Bradford Shipps & Sheftel · 835 East Second Avenue, Suite 123 · P.O. Box 2717 · Durango, CO 81302-2717 · 970-247-1755

PERSONAL INJURY LITIGATION

Arvada

James L. Gilbert · ⑩ · Gilbert, Ollanik & Komyatte · Aspen Business Park, Building IV, Suite 200 · 5400 Ward Road · Arvada, CO 80002 · 303-431-1111

Boulder

S. Macon Cowles III · S. Macon Cowles III · 1680 Wilson Court · Boulder, CO 80304 · 303-447-3062

Jean E. Dubofsky · Jean E. Dubofsky · 1000 Rosehill Drive · Boulder, CO 80302-7148 · 303-447-3510

William R. Gray · ⑩ · Purvis Gray & Murphy · The Exeter Building, Suite 501 · 1050 Walnut Street · Boulder, CO 80302 · 303-442-3366

J. Conard Metcalf · ⑩ · Trine & Metcalf · 2919 Valmont Road, Suite 204 · Boulder, CO 80301 · 303-442-0173

John A. Purvis · ⑳ · Purvis Gray & Murphy · The Exeter Building, Suite 501 · 1050 Walnut Street · Boulder, CO 80302 · 303-442-3366

Robert A. Schuetze · ⑩ · Schuetze & Gordon · 1426 Pearl Street, Suite 202 · Boulder, CO 80302 · 303-444-5944

William A. Trine · ㉕ · Trine & Metcalf · 2919 Valmont Road, Suite 204 · Boulder, CO 80301 · 303-442-0173

Broomfield

Richard F. Schaden · ⑩ · Schaden, Katzman, Lampert & McClune · 9596 Jeffco Airport Avenue · Broomfield, CO 80021 · 303-465-3663

Colorado Springs

Thomas J. Herd · Gaddis, Kin & Herd · 118 South Wahsatch, Suite 100 · Colorado Springs, CO 80903 · 719-471-3848

J. Gregory Walta · J. Gregory Walta · 105 East Moreno Avenue · Colorado Springs, CO 80903 · 719-578-8888

Denver

Alan D. Avery · Jaudon & Avery · 600 Grant Street, Suite 505 · Denver, CO 80203 · 303-832-1122

Robert Baldwin · Baldwin & Carpenter · 1512 Larimer Street, Suite 450 · Denver, CO 80202 · 303-623-1832

Douglas E. Bragg · ㉕ · Douglas E. Bragg · 650 South Cherry Street, Suite 610 · Denver, CO 80246 · 303-571-4030

Charles F. Brega · ㉕ · Lindquist & Vennum · http://www.lindquist.com · 600 Seventeenth Street, Suite 1800 South · Denver, CO 80202-5441 · 303-573-5900

Bradley W. Breslau · Cozen O'Connor · 707 Seventeeth Street, Suite 3100 · Denver, CO 80202 · 720-479-3900

Edward Bronfin · Kennedy Childs & Fogg · Independence Plaza, Suite 2500 · 1050 Seventeenth Street · Denver, CO 80265 · 303-825-2700

Natalie Brown · Leventhal, Brown & Puga · 950 South Cherry Street, Suite 600 · Denver, CO 80246 · 303-759-9945

Ross B. H. Buchanan · Buchanan & Jurdem · 1621 Eighteenth Street, Suite 260 · Denver, CO 80202-1267 · 303-297-2277

Charles L. Casteel · ⑩ · Davis Graham & Stubbs · http://www.dgslaw.com · 1550 Seventeenth Street, Suite 500 · Denver, CO 80202 · 303-892-9400

Shelley B. Don · ⑩ · Don, Hiller & Galleher · 1737 Gaylord Street · Denver, CO 80206 · 303-572-1668

John M. Fitzpatrick · Wheeler Trigg Kennedy · http://www.wtklaw.com · 1801 California Street, Suite 3600 · Denver, CO 80202-2617 · 303-244-1800

Cecelia A. Fleischner · McConnell Siderius Fleischner Houghtaling & Craigmile · Denver Corporate Center, Tower I, Suite 200 · 4700 South Syracuse · Denver, CO 80237 · 303-480-0400

Mark A. Fogg · Kennedy Childs & Fogg · Independence Plaza, Suite 2500 · 1050 Seventeenth Street · Denver, CO 80265 · 303-825-2700

Watson W. Galleher · Don, Hiller & Galleher · 1737 Gaylord Street · Denver, CO 80206 · 303-572-1668

Daniel Gerash · Gerash, Toray & Gerash · http://www.gerashtoray.com · 1775 Sherman Street, Suite 1500 Denver, CO 80203 · 720-496-4744

Walter L. Gerash · ⑳ · Walter L. Gerash Law Firm · 1439 Court Place · Denver, CO 80202-5091 · 303-825-5400

Neil Hillyard · ⑳ · Hillyard, Wahlberg, Kudla & Sloane · http://www.hwkslaw.com · 4601 DTC Boulevard, Suite 300 · Denver, CO 80237 · 303-571-5302

Daniel S. Hoffman · ⑩ · Hogan & Hartson · One Tabor Center, Suite 1500 · 1200 Seventeenth Street · Denver, CO 80202 · 303-899-7300

John Robert Holland · John Robert Holland · 1437 High Street · Denver, CO 80218 · 303-860-1331

Joseph C. Jaudon, Jr. · ㉕ · Jaudon & Avery · 600 Grant Street, Suite 505 · Denver, CO 80203 · 303-832-1122

Bruce J. Kaye · Kaye and Bush · 1200 Fifteenth Street, Suite 200 · Denver, CO 80202 · 303-477-8787

William L. Keating · ⑩ · Fogel Keating Wagner Polidori Shafner · http://www.fkwlaw.com · 1290 Broadway, Suite 600 · Denver, CO 80203 · 303-534-0401

Richard W. Laugesen · ⑩ · Richard W. Laugesen · 1830 South Monroe Street · Denver, CO 80210-3731 303-300-1006

Jim Leventhal · ⑩ · Leventhal, Brown & Puga · 950 South Cherry Street, Suite 600 · Denver, CO 80246 · 303-759-9945

Bradley A. Levin · Roberts Levin & Rosenberg · http://www.robertslevin.com · 1660 Wynkoop Street, Suite 800 · Denver, CO 80202 · 303-575-9390

Michael T. McConnell · ⑩ · McConnell Siderius Fleischner Houghtaling & Craigmile · Denver Corporate Center, Tower I, Suite 200 · 4700 South Syracuse · Denver, CO 80237 · 303-480-0400

Gerald P. McDermott · ⑳ · McDermott Hansen and McLaughlin · 1890 Gaylord Street · Denver, CO 80206-1211 · 303-399-6037

Lee Mickus · Snell & Wilmer · Tabor Center, Suite 1900 · 1200 Seventeenth Street · Denver, CO 80202-5854 · 303-634-2000

Bruce A. Montoya · Messner & Reeves · 1430 Wynkoop, Suite 400 · Denver, CO 80202 · 303-623-1800

Michael L. O'Donnell · Wheeler Trigg Kennedy · http://www.wtklaw.com · 1801 California Street, Suite 3600 · Denver, CO 80202-2617 · 303-244-1800

Lorraine Parker · Leventhal, Brown & Puga · 950 South Cherry Street, Suite 600 · Denver, CO 80246 · 303-759-9945

Steven R. Polidori · Fogel Keating Wagner Polidori Shafner · http://www.fkwlaw.com · 1290 Broadway, Suite 600 · Denver, CO 80203 · 303-534-0401

Daniel M. Reilly · ⑩ · Reilly Pozner · http://www.litigationcolorado.com · The Kittredge Building, Suite 700 · 511 Sixteenth Street · Denver, CO 80202 · 303-893-6100

Thomas L. Roberts · ⑩ · Roberts Levin & Rosenberg · http://www.robertslevin.com · 1660 Wynkoop Street, Suite 800 · Denver, CO 80202 · 303-575-9390

John J. Rossi · ⑩ · Rossi, Cox & Vucinovich · 3801 East Florida Avenue, Suite 905 · Denver, CO 80210-2500 · 303-759-3500

Jeffrey A. Springer · Springer & Steinberg · http://www.springer-and-steinberg.com · 1600 Broadway, Suite 1200 · Denver, CO 80202 · 303-861-2800

Stephen W. Wahlberg · Hillyard, Wahlberg, Kudla & Sloane · http://www.hwkslaw.com · 4601 DTC Boulevard, Suite 300 · Denver, CO 80237 · 303-571-5302

Mary A. Wells · Wells, Anderson & Race · 1700 Broadway, Suite 1020 · Denver, CO 80290 · 303-830-1212

Malcolm E. Wheeler · Wheeler Trigg Kennedy · http://www.wtklaw.com · 1801 California Street, Suite 3600 · Denver, CO 80202-2617 · 303-244-1800

Durango

Michael E. McLachlan · McLachlan & Underell · http://www.mcwhitlaw.com · 813 Main Avenue, Suite 308 · P.O. Box 2867 · Durango, CO 81302 · 970-247-8236

Englewood

W. Randolph Barnhart · Barnhart, Ekker & McNally · http://www.bemllp.com · 7887 East Bellview Avenue, Suite 1200 · Englewood, CO 80111 · 303-793-0700

Robert Craig Ewing · Ewing & Ewing · 3601 South Pennsylvania Street · Englewood, CO 80113-3753 · 303-761-1400

Fort Collins

T. Thomas Metier · Metier Law Firm · 4828 South College Avenue · Fort Collins, CO 80525 · 970-377-3800

Steven B. Ray · The Steve Ray Law Office · 2038 Caribou Drive, Suite 100 · Fort Collins, CO 80525-4326 · 970-266-1210

Greenwood Village

Irving G. Johnson · Pryor Johnson Carney Karr Nixon · 5619 DTC Parkway, Suite 1200 · Greenwood Village, CO 80111 · 303-773-3500

Peter W. Pryor · ㉕ · Pryor Johnson Carney Karr Nixon · 5619 DTC Parkway, Suite 1200 · Greenwood Village, CO 80111 · 303-773-3500

PRIVATE FUNDS LAW

Denver

Reid A. Godbolt · Jones & Keller · 1625 Broadway, 16th Floor · Denver, CO 80202 · 303-573-1600

PRODUCT LIABILITY LITIGATION

Arvada

James L. Gilbert · 10 · Gilbert, Ollanik & Komyatte · Aspen Business Park, Building IV, Suite 200 · 5400 Ward Road · Arvada, CO 80002 · 303-431-1111

Boulder

J. Conard Metcalf · 10 · Trine & Metcalf · 2919 Valmont Road, Suite 204 · Boulder, CO 80301 · 303-442-0173

John A. Purvis · 20 · Purvis Gray & Murphy · The Exeter Building, Suite 501 · 1050 Walnut Street · Boulder, CO 80302 · 303-442-3366

Denver

Charles L. Casteel · 10 · Davis Graham & Stubbs · http://www.dgslaw.com · 1550 Seventeenth Street, Suite 500 · Denver, CO 80202 · 303-892-9400

John M. Fitzpatrick · Wheeler Trigg Kennedy · http://www.wtklaw.com · 1801 California Street, Suite 3600 · Denver, CO 80202-2617 · 303-244-1800

Neil Hillyard · 20 · Hillyard, Wahlberg, Kudla & Sloane · http://www.hwkslaw.com · 4601 DTC Boulevard, Suite 300 · Denver, CO 80237 · 303-571-5302

William L. Keating · 10 · Fogel Keating Wagner Polidori Shafner · http://www.fkwlaw.com · 1290 Broadway, Suite 600 · Denver, CO 80203 · 303-534-0401

Michael L. O'Donnell · Wheeler Trigg Kennedy · http://www.wtklaw.com · 1801 California Street, Suite 3600 · Denver, CO 80202-2617 · 303-244-1800

John R. Trigg · Wheeler Trigg Kennedy · http://www.wtklaw.com · 1801 California Street, Suite 3600 · Denver, CO 80202-2617 · 303-244-1800

Malcolm E. Wheeler · Wheeler Trigg Kennedy · http://www.wtklaw.com · 1801 California Street, Suite 3600 · Denver, CO 80202-2617 · 303-244-1800

Englewood

W. Randolph Barnhart · Barnhart, Ekker & McNally · http://www.bemllp.com · 7887 East Bellview Avenue, Suite 1200 · Englewood, CO 80111 · 303-793-0700

PROFESSIONAL MALPRACTICE LAW

Boulder

John A. Purvis · 20 · Purvis Gray & Murphy · The Exeter Building, Suite 501 · 1050 Walnut Street · Boulder, CO 80302 · 303-442-3366

William A. Trine · 25 · Trine & Metcalf · 2919 Valmont Road, Suite 204 · Boulder, CO 80301 · 303-442-0173

John M. Fitzpatrick · Wheeler Trigg Kennedy · http://www.wtklaw.com · 1801 California Street, Suite 3600 · Denver, CO 80202-2617 · 303-244-1800

Daniel S. Hoffman · ⑩ · Hogan & Hartson · One Tabor Center, Suite 1500 · 1200 Seventeenth Street · Denver, CO 80202 · 303-899-7300

Walter N. Houghtaling · McConnell Siderius Fleischner Houghtaling & Craigmile · Denver Corporate Center, Tower I, Suite 200 · 4700 South Syracuse · Denver, CO 80237 · 303-480-0400

Michael L. Hutchinson · Treece, Alfrey, Musat & Bosworth · http://www.tamblaw.com · 999 Eighteenth Street, Suite 1600 · Denver, CO 80202 · 303-292-2700

Joseph C. Jaudon, Jr. · ㉕ · Jaudon & Avery · 600 Grant Street, Suite 505 · Denver, CO 80203 · 303-832-1122

Michael T. McConnell · ⑩ · McConnell Siderius Fleischner Houghtaling & Craigmile · Denver Corporate Center, Tower I, Suite 200 · 4700 South Syracuse · Denver, CO 80237 · 303-480-0400

Gerald P. McDermott · ⑳ · McDermott Hansen and McLaughlin · 1890 Gaylord Street · Denver, CO 80206-1211 · 303-399-6037

PROJECT FINANCE LAW

Denver

John L. McCabe · ⑩ · Davis Graham & Stubbs · http://www.dgslaw.com · 1550 Seventeenth Street, Suite 500 · Denver, CO 80202 · 303-892-9400

Mark D. Safty · Holland & Hart · 555 Seventeenth Street, Suite 3200 · Denver, CO 80202-3739 · 303-295-8000

David J. Scott · Hogan & Hartson · One Tabor Center, Suite 1500 · 1200 Seventeenth Street · Denver, CO 80202 · 303-899-7300

PUBLIC FINANCE LAW

Denver

James D. Arundel · Kutak Rock · 1801 California Street, Suite 3100 · Denver, CO 80202-2626 · 303-297-2400

Helen C. Atkeson · Hogan & Hartson · One Tabor Center, Suite 1500 · 1200 Seventeenth Street · Denver, CO 80202 · 303-899-7300

Matt Hogan · Sherman & Howard · 633 Seventeenth Street, Suite 3000 · Denver, CO 80202-3624 · 303-297-2900

Kurt A. Kaufmann · Sherman & Howard · 633 Seventeenth Street, Suite 3000 · Denver, CO 80202-3624 303-297-2900

Robert P. Mitchell · Sherman & Howard · 633 Seventeenth Street, Suite 3000 · Denver, CO 80202-3624 303-297-2900

Stanley M. Raine · Sherman & Howard · 633 Seventeenth Street, Suite 3000 · Denver, CO 80202-3624 · 303-297-2900

Dee P. Wisor · Sherman & Howard · 633 Seventeenth Street, Suite 3000 · Denver, CO 80202-3624 · 303-297-2900

RAILROAD LAW

Denver

John J. Rossi · ⑩ · Rossi, Cox & Vucinovich · 3801 East Florida Avenue, Suite 905 · Denver, CO 80210-2500 · 303-759-3500

REAL ESTATE LAW

Aspen

Arthur C. Daily · ⑩ · Holland & Hart · 600 East Main Street, Suite 104 · Aspen, CO 81611 · 970-925-3476

Boulder

Joel C. Davis · ㉕ · Dietze & Davis · Siena Square Building, Suite 400 · 2060 Broadway · Boulder, CO 80302 · 303-447-1375

J. Marcus Painter · Holland & Hart · One Boulder Plaza, Suite 300 · 1800 Broadway · Boulder, CO 80302-5144 · 303-473-2700

Beat U. Steiner · Holland & Hart · One Boulder Plaza, Suite 300 · 1800 Broadway · Boulder, CO 80302-5144 · 303-473-2700

Denver

Robert H. Bach · Holme Roberts & Owen · http://www.hro.com · 1700 Lincoln Street, Suite 4100 · Denver, CO 80203-4541 · 303-861-7000

Edward N. Barad · Brownstein Hyatt Farber Schreck · http://www.bhfs.com · 410 Seventeenth Street, Suite 2200 · Denver, CO 80202-4432 · 303-223-1100

Robert L. Brown · ⑩ · Sherman & Howard · 633 Seventeenth Street, Suite 3000 · Denver, CO 80202-3624 · 303-297-2900

Charles D. Calvin · ⑩ · Faegre & Benson · Wells Fargo Center, Suite 3200 · 1700 Lincoln Street · Denver, CO 80203-4532 · 303-607-3500

Charlton Henry Carpenter · ㉕ · Fairfield & Woods · Wells Fargo Center, Suite 2400 · 1700 Lincoln Street · Denver, CO 80203-4524 · 303-830-2400

Willis Vincent Carpenter · ㉕ · Carpenter & Klatskin · 1500 Denver Club Building · 518 Seventeenth Street · Denver, CO 80202 · 303-534-6315

W. Michael Clowdus · Ballard Spahr Andrews & Ingersoll · 1225 Seventeenth Street, Suite 2300 · Denver, CO 80202-5596 · 303-292-2400

Donald L. Cook · ⑩ · Wood, Ris & Hames · 1775 Sherman Street, Suite 1600 · Denver, CO 80203-4313 · 303-863-7700

James E. Culhane · 25 · Davis Graham & Stubbs · http://www.dgslaw.com · 1550 Seventeenth Street, Suite 500 · Denver, CO 80202 · 303-892-9400

Diane B. Davies · Faegre & Benson · Wells Fargo Center, Suite 3200 · 1700 Lincoln Street · Denver, CO 80203-4532 · 303-607-3500

Lawrence J. Donovan, Jr. · Isaacson Rosenbaum · 633 Seventeenth Street, Suite 2200 · Denver, CO 80202 · 303-292-5656

Rebecca W. Dow · Holland & Hart · 555 Seventeenth Street, Suite 3200 · Denver, CO 80202-3739 · 303-295-8000

Leslie A. Fields · Faegre & Benson · Wells Fargo Center, Suite 3200 · 1700 Lincoln Street · Denver, CO 80203-4532 · 303-607-3500

Rebecca A. Fischer · Sherman & Howard · 633 Seventeenth Street, Suite 3000 · Denver, CO 80202-3624 303-297-2900

Andrew A. Folkerth · Ryley Carlock & Applewhite · http://www.rcalaw.com · 1999 Broadway, Suite 1800 Denver, CO 80202 · 303-863-7500

Teryl Gorrell · Gorrell Giles · 1331 Seventeenth Street, Suite 1000 · Denver, CO 80202 · 303-996-7200

Catherine Hance · Davis Graham & Stubbs · http://www.dgslaw.com · 1550 Seventeenth Street, Suite 500 · Denver, CO 80202 · 303-892-9400

Robert A. Holmes · Holme Roberts & Owen · http://www.hro.com · 1700 Lincoln Street, Suite 4100 · Denver, CO 80203-4541 · 303-861-7000

Paul A. Jacobs · Jacobs, Chase, Frick, Kleinkopf & Kelley · Independence Plaza, Suite 1500 · 1050 Seventeenth Street · Denver, CO 80265 · 303-685-4800

Robert Kaufmann · Brownstein Hyatt Farber Schreck · http://www.bhfs.com · 410 Seventeenth Street, Suite 2200 · Denver, CO 80202-4432 · 303-223-1100

Thomas Patrick Kearns · Fairfield & Woods · Wells Fargo Center, Suite 2400 · 1700 Lincoln Street · Denver, CO 80203-4524 · 303-830-2400

David Kleinkopf · Jacobs, Chase, Frick, Kleinkopf & Kelley · Independence Plaza, Suite 1500 · 1050 Seventeenth Street · Denver, CO 80265 · 303-685-4800

Bruce Lawrence Likoff · 10 · Holme Roberts & Owen · http://www.hro.com · 1700 Lincoln Street, Suite 4100 · Denver, CO 80203-4541 · 303-861-7000

Alan B. Lottner · Lottner Rubin Fishman Brown & Saul · 633 Seventeenth Street, Suite 2700 · Denver, CO 80202-3635 · 303-292-1200

Michael D. Martin · 10 · Holland & Hart · 555 Seventeenth Street, Suite 3200 · Denver, CO 80202-3739 · 303-295-8000

Barry Permut · Isaacson Rosenbaum · 633 Seventeenth Street, Suite 2200 · Denver, CO 80202 · 303-292-5656

Beverly J. Quail · 10 · Ballard Spahr Andrews & Ingersoll · 1225 Seventeenth Street, Suite 2300 · Denver, CO 80202-5596 · 303-292-2400

Thomas J. Ragonetti · Otten, Johnson, Robinson, Neff & Ragonetti · 950 Seventeenth Street, Suite 1600 Denver, CO 80202 · 303-825-8400

Franklin Lee Robinson · ㉕ · Otten, Johnson, Robinson, Neff & Ragonetti · 950 Seventeenth Street, Suite 1600 · Denver, CO 80202 · 303-825-8400

Mark A. Senn · ⑩ · Senn Visciano Kirschenbaum & Merrick · 1801 California Street, Suite 4300 · Denver, CO 80202 · 303-298-1122

Elizabeth Sharrer · Holland & Hart · 555 Seventeenth Street, Suite 3200 · Denver, CO 80202-3739 · 303-295-8000

John D. Sternberg · Otten, Johnson, Robinson, Neff & Ragonetti · 950 Seventeenth Street, Suite 1600 · Denver, CO 80202 · 303-825-8400

Lakewood

Barbara S. Banks · ⑩ · Banks & Imatani · 225 Union Boulevard, Suite 310 · Lakewood, CO 80228 · 303-984-5605

SECURITIES LAW

Broomfield

James C.T. Linfield · Cooley Godward Kronish · 380 Interlocken Crescent, Suite 900 · Broomfield, CO 80021-8023 · 720-566-4000

Denver

Robert J. Ahrenholz · ⑳ · Kutak Rock · 1801 California Street, Suite 3100 · Denver, CO 80202-2626 · 303-297-2400

Harold S. Bloomenthal · ㉕ · Holme Roberts & Owen · http://www.hro.com · 1700 Lincoln Street, Suite 4100 · Denver, CO 80203-4541 · 303-861-7000

Randall J. Fons · Morrison & Foerster · http://www.mofo.com · Republic Plaza, Suite 5200 · 370 Seventeenth Street · Denver, CO 80202-5638 · 303-592-1500

Reid A. Godbolt · Jones & Keller · 1625 Broadway, 16th Floor · Denver, CO 80202 · 303-573-1600

Paul Hilton · ⑩ · Hogan & Hartson · One Tabor Center, Suite 1500 · 1200 Seventeenth Street · Denver, CO 80202 · 303-899-7300

Garth B. Jensen · Holme Roberts & Owen · http://www.hro.com · 1700 Lincoln Street, Suite 4100 · Denver, CO 80203-4541 · 303-861-7000

Ronald Levine II · Davis Graham & Stubbs · http://www.dgslaw.com · 1550 Seventeenth Street, Suite 500 · Denver, CO 80202 · 303-892-9400

Mark R. Levy · ⑳ · Holland & Hart · 555 Seventeenth Street, Suite 3200 · Denver, CO 80202-3739 · 303-295-8000

Patricia A. Peterson · Davis Graham & Stubbs · http://www.dgslaw.com · 1550 Seventeenth Street, Suite 500 · Denver, CO 80202 · 303-892-9400

W. Dean Salter · ⑩ · Holme Roberts & Owen · http://www.hro.com · 1700 Lincoln Street, Suite 4100 · Denver, CO 80203-4541 · 303-861-7000

Peter H. Schwartz · Davis Graham & Stubbs · http://www.dgslaw.com · 1550 Seventeenth Street, Suite 500 · Denver, CO 80202 · 303-892-9400

James F. Wood · ⑩ · Sherman & Howard · 633 Seventeenth Street, Suite 3000 · Denver, CO 80202-3624 303-297-2900

Lester R. Woodward · ㉕ · Davis Graham & Stubbs · http://www.dgslaw.com · 1550 Seventeenth Street, Suite 500 · Denver, CO 80202 · 303-892-9400

Douglas R. Wright · Faegre & Benson · Wells Fargo Center, Suite 3200 · 1700 Lincoln Street · Denver, CO 80203-4532 · 303-607-3500

SPORTS LAW

Denver

Leigh L. Augustine · Sherman & Howard · 633 Seventeenth Street, Suite 3000 · Denver, CO 80202-3624 303-297-2900

James D. Leonard · Faegre & Benson · Wells Fargo Center, Suite 3200 · 1700 Lincoln Street · Denver, CO 80203-4532 · 303-607-3500

STRUCTURED FINANCE LAW

Denver

Keith Block · Block Markus & Williams · 1700 Lincoln Street, Suite 4000 · Denver, CO 80203 · 303-830-0800

Karen L. Chapman · Sherman & Howard · 633 Seventeenth Street, Suite 3000 · Denver, CO 80202-3624 303-297-2900

TAX LAW

Denver

Michael J. Abramovitz · ㉕ · Michael Abramovitz · 1600 Broadway, Suite 2600 · Denver, CO 80202 · 303-592-5454

Theodore B. Atlass · ⑩ · Atlass Professional Corporation · 3665 Cherry Creek North Drive, Suite 100 · Denver, CO 80209-3712 · 303-329-5900

John H. Birkeland · Sherman & Howard · 633 Seventeenth Street, Suite 3000 · Denver, CO 80202-3624 303-297-2900

Charles B. Bruce, Jr. · Holme Roberts & Owen · http://www.hro.com · 1700 Lincoln Street, Suite 4100 · Denver, CO 80203-4541 · 303-861-7000

Douglas M. Cain · ㉕ · Sherman & Howard · 633 Seventeenth Street, Suite 3000 · Denver, CO 80202-3624 · 303-297-2900

J. William Callison · Faegre & Benson · Wells Fargo Center, Suite 3200 · 1700 Lincoln Street · Denver, CO 80203-4532 · 303-607-3500

Adam M. Cohen · Holland & Hart · 555 Seventeenth Street, Suite 3200 · Denver, CO 80202-3739 · 303-295-8000

Barbara Ann Dalvano · Engel & Reiman · The Equitable Building, Suite 500 · 730 Seventeenth Street · Denver, CO 80202 · 303-741-1111

John DeBruyn · ⑩ · DeBruyn Law Offices · 2100 East 14th Avenue · Denver, CO 80206 · 303-377-0707

Fred J. Diss · ⑩ · Robinson, Diss & Clowdus · Lincoln Center Building, Suite 2500 · 1660 Lincoln Street Denver, CO 80264 · 303-861-4154

Michael Dubetz · Sherman & Howard · 633 Seventeenth Street, Suite 3000 · Denver, CO 80202-3624 · 303-297-2900

Theodore Z. Gelt · ⑳ · Gelt & Grassgreen · 303 East 17th Avenue, Suite 910 · Denver, CO 80203 · 303-830-1200

Neil M. Goff · ⑩ · Brownstein Hyatt Farber Schreck · http://www.bhfs.com · 410 Seventeenth Street, Suite 2200 · Denver, CO 80202-4432 · 303-223-1100

Peter C. Guthery · ⑳ · Berenbaum, Weinshienk & Eason · http://www.bwelaw.com · Republic Plaza, 48th Floor · 370 Seventeenth Street · Denver, CO 80202 · 303-825-0800

Robert R. Keatinge · ⑩ · Holland & Hart · 555 Seventeenth Street, Suite 3200 · Denver, CO 80202-3739 303-295-8000

Francis P. King · ㉕ · Robinson, Diss & Clowdus · Lincoln Center Building, Suite 2500 · 1660 Lincoln Street · Denver, CO 80264 · 303-861-4154

Samuel L. Levy · Greenberg Traurig · http://www.gtlaw.com · The Tabor Center, Suite 2400 · 1200 Seventeenth Street · Denver, CO 80202 · 303-572-6500

John R. Maxfield · Holland & Hart · 555 Seventeenth Street, Suite 3200 · Denver, CO 80202-3739 · 303-295-8000

Laurence E. Nemirow · Davis Graham & Stubbs · http://www.dgslaw.com · 1550 Seventeenth Street, Suite 500 · Denver, CO 80202 · 303-892-9400

Richard M. Petkun · Greenberg Traurig · http://www.gtlaw.com · The Tabor Center, Suite 2400 · 1200 Seventeenth Street · Denver, CO 80202 · 303-572-6500

Stephen P. Rickles · Berenbaum, Weinshienk & Eason · http://www.bwelaw.com · Republic Plaza, 48th Floor · 370 Seventeenth Street · Denver, CO 80202 · 303-825-0800

Richard B. Robinson · ⑩ · Robinson, Diss & Clowdus · Lincoln Center Building, Suite 2500 · 1660 Lincoln Street · Denver, CO 80264 · 303-861-4154

John L. Ruppert · Perkins Coie · http://www.perkinscoie.com · 1899 Wynkoop Street, Suite 700 · Denver, CO 80202-1043 · 303-291-2300

Paul T. Ruttum · Ducker, Montgomery, Aronstein & Bess · One Civic Center Plaza, Suite 1400 · 1560 Broadway · Denver, CO 80202-1548 · 303-861-2828

L. William Schmidt, Jr. · Schmidt, Horen & Lockwood · 1050 Seventeenth Street, Suite 1700 · Denver, CO 80265 · 303-436-9121

Paul E. Smith · Holme Roberts & Owen · http://www.hro.com · 1700 Lincoln Street, Suite 4100 · Denver, CO 80203-4541 · 303-861-7000

Raymond L. Sutton, Jr. · ⑩ · Baker Hostetler · http://www.bakerlaw.com · 303 East 17th Avenue, Suite 1100 · Denver, CO 80203-1264 · 303-861-0600

Joseph H. Thibodeau · ⑳ · Law Offices of Joseph H. Thibodeau · 155 South Madison Street, Suite 209 · Denver, CO 80205 · 303-320-1250

James R. Walker · Rothgerber Johnson & Lyons · One Tabor Center, Suite 3000 · 1200 Seventeenth Street · Denver, CO 80202-5855 · 303-623-9000

Robert J. Welter · ㉕ · Holme Roberts & Owen · http://www.hro.com · 1700 Lincoln Street, Suite 4100 · Denver, CO 80203-4541 · 303-861-7000

John R. Wilson · ⑩ · Holland & Hart · 555 Seventeenth Street, Suite 3200 · Denver, CO 80202-3739 · 303-295-8000

Duane Wurzer · ⑩ · Sherman & Howard · 633 Seventeenth Street, Suite 3000 · Denver, CO 80202-3624 303-297-2900

Thomas E. Yearout · Holme Roberts & Owen · http://www.hro.com · 1700 Lincoln Street, Suite 4100 · Denver, CO 80203-4541 · 303-861-7000

Greenwood Village

Robert Alan Poe · ⑩ · Holland & Hart · 8390 East Crescent Parkway, Suite 400 · Greenwood Village, CO 80111-2800 · 303-290-1600

Lakewood

James W. Buchanan III · Buchanan & Stouffer · 141 Union Boulevard, Suite 300 · Lakewood, CO 80228 303-987-3800

TECHNOLOGY LAW

Boulder

Celia F. Rankin · Faegre & Benson · 1900 Fifteenth Street · Boulder, CO 80302-5414 · 303-447-7700

Broomfield

Jim Brogan · Cooley Godward Kronish · 380 Interlocken Crescent, Suite 900 · Broomfield, CO 80021-8023 · 720-566-4000

Denver

Glenn K. Beaton · ⑩ · Gibson, Dunn & Crutcher · 1801 California Street, Suite 4200 · Denver, CO 80202-2642 · 303-298-5700

Kevin S. Crandell · Holland & Hart · 555 Seventeenth Street, Suite 3200 · Denver, CO 80202-3739 · 303-295-8000

Peter J. Kinsella · Faegre & Benson · Wells Fargo Center, Suite 3200 · 1700 Lincoln Street · Denver, CO 80203-4532 · 303-607-3500

Lee R. Osman · Dorsey & Whitney · Republic Plaza Building, Suite 4700 · 370 Seventeenth Street · Denver, CO 80202-5647 · 303-629-3400

Gary M. Polumbus · Dorsey & Whitney · Republic Plaza Building, Suite 4700 · 370 Seventeenth Street · Denver, CO 80202-5647 · 303-629-3400

TRUSTS AND ESTATES

Boulder

Christopher R. Brauchli · ⑳ · Hutchinson Black and Cook · 921 Walnut Street, Suite 200 · Boulder, CO 80302 · 303-442-6514

Constance Tromble Eyster · Hutchinson Black and Cook · 921 Walnut Street, Suite 200 · Boulder, CO 80302 · 303-442-6514

Laura S. Hundley · Holland & Hart · One Boulder Plaza, Suite 300 · 1800 Broadway · Boulder, CO 80302-5144 · 303-473-2700

Lynn Kuykendall · Caplan and Earnest · One Boulder Plaza, Suite 200 · 1800 Broadway · Boulder, CO 80302-5289 · 303-443-8010

Shelly D. Merritt · Shelly D. Merritt · http://www.sdmerrittlaw.com · 1942 Broadway, Suite 314 · Boulder, CO 80302 · 303-413-3477

Colorado Springs

William K. Brown · ⑳ · Holland & Hart · 90 South Cascade Avenue, Suite 1000 · P.O. Box 2340 · Colorado Springs, CO 80903-1645 · 719-475-7730

Bruce T. Buell · ⑩ · Buell & Ezell · 24 South Weber Street, Suite 375 · Colorado Springs, CO 80903-1506 719-471-4511

Stanley C. Kent · ⑩ · Stanley C. Kent · 90 South Cascade Avenue, Suite 1210 · Colorado Springs, CO 80903 · 719-577-4414

Franklin E. Lynch · Kruse & Lynch · Two North Cascade Avenue, Suite 1050 · Colorado Springs, CO 80903 · 719-473-9911

Denver

Theodore B. Atlass · ⑩ · Atlass Professional Corporation · 3665 Cherry Creek North Drive, Suite 100 · Denver, CO 80209-3712 · 303-329-5900

Merry H. Balson · Berenbaum, Weinshienk & Eason · http://www.bwelaw.com · Republic Plaza, 48th Floor · 370 Seventeenth Street · Denver, CO 80202 · 303-825-0800

Carol Berger · Sherman & Howard · 633 Seventeenth Street, Suite 3000 · Denver, CO 80202-3624 · 303-297-2900

Stephen M. Brainerd · Davis Graham & Stubbs · http://www.dgslaw.com · 1550 Seventeenth Street, Suite 500 · Denver, CO 80202 · 303-892-9400

Elizabeth A. Bryant · Elizabeth A. Bryant · 1866 Vine Street · Denver, CO 80206-1122 · 303-398-4000

Douglas M. Cain · ㉕ · Sherman & Howard · 633 Seventeenth Street, Suite 3000 · Denver, CO 80202-3624 · 303-297-2900

Jay H. Chapman · ⑩ · Chapman & Roth · 1355 South Colorado Boulevard, Suite 600 · Denver, CO 80222-3370 · 303-759-4004

Patricia Lester Clowdus · Robinson, Diss & Clowdus · Lincoln Center Building, Suite 2500 · 1660 Lincoln Street · Denver, CO 80264 · 303-861-4154

Kelly Dickson Cooper · Holland & Hart · 555 Seventeenth Street, Suite 3200 · Denver, CO 80202-3739 · 303-295-8000

Nancy R. Crow · Pendleton, Friedberg, Wilson & Hennessey · 1875 Lawrence Street, Tenth Floor · Denver, CO 80202-1898 · 303-839-1204

Barbara Ann Dalvano · Engel & Reiman · The Equitable Building, Suite 500 · 730 Seventeenth Street · Denver, CO 80202 · 303-741-1111

Marc C. Darling · Wade Ash Woods Hill & Farley · 360 South Monroe Street, Suite 400 · Denver, CO 80209 · 303-322-8943

John DeBruyn · ⑩ · DeBruyn Law Offices · 2100 East 14th Avenue · Denver, CO 80206 · 303-377-0707

M. Carl Glatstein · Glatstein & O' Brien · 2696 South Colorado Boulevard, Suite 350 · Denver, CO 80222-5944 · 303-731-3986

Joseph G. Hodges, Jr. · ⑳ · Joseph G. Hodges, Jr. · 3955 East Exposition Avenue, Suite 500 · Denver, CO 80209-5033 · 303-377-0070

Marcia Chadwick Holt · ⑳ · Davis Graham & Stubbs · http://www.dgslaw.com · 1550 Seventeenth Street, Suite 500 · Denver, CO 80202 · 303-892-9400

Laurie A. Hunter · Wade Ash Woods Hill & Farley · 360 South Monroe Street, Suite 400 · Denver, CO 80209 · 303-322-8943

James F. Ingraham · ⑩ · Zisman, Ingraham and Daniel · Ptarmigan Place, Suite 650 · 3773 Cherry Creek North Drive · Denver, CO 80209 · 303-320-0023

Bernard A. Poskus · Poskus, Caton & Klein · 303 East 17th Avenue, Suite 900 · Denver, CO 80203 · 303-832-1600

Victor Quinn · ⑳ · Waggener & Foster · 400 South Colorado Boulevard, Suite 900 · Denver, CO 80246 · 303-860-7344

Stephen P. Rickles · Berenbaum, Weinshienk & Eason · http://www.bwelaw.com · Republic Plaza, 48th Floor · 370 Seventeenth Street · Denver, CO 80202 · 303-825-0800

Richard B. Robinson · ⑩ · Robinson, Diss & Clowdus · Lincoln Center Building, Suite 2500 · 1660 Lincoln Street · Denver, CO 80264 · 303-861-4154

Michelle M. Rose-Hughes · Tuthill & Hughes · 300 South Jackson Street · Denver, CO 80209 · 303-831-7364

Sharon R. Roth · Chapman & Roth · 1355 South Colorado Boulevard, Suite 600 · Denver, CO 80222-3370 · 303-759-4004

L. William Schmidt, Jr. · Schmidt, Horen & Lockwood · 1050 Seventeenth Street, Suite 1700 · Denver, CO 80265 · 303-436-9121

Constance D. Smith · Rothgerber Johnson & Lyons · One Tabor Center, Suite 3000 · 1200 Seventeenth Street · Denver, CO 80202-5855 · 303-623-9000

Robert L. Steenrod, Jr. · R. L. Steenrod, Jr. & Associates · Mattie Silks House · 2009 Market Street · Denver, CO 80205-2022 · 303-534-5100

Bridget Sullivan · Sherman & Howard · 633 Seventeenth Street, Suite 3000 · Denver, CO 80202-3624 · 303-297-2900

Raymond L. Sutton, Jr. · ⑩ · Baker Hostetler · http://www.bakerlaw.com · 303 East 17th Avenue, Suite 1100 · Denver, CO 80203-1264 · 303-861-0600

David Thomas III · ⑩ · Sherman & Howard · 633 Seventeenth Street, Suite 3000 · Denver, CO 80202-3624 · 303-297-2900

Herbert E. Tucker IV · Wade Ash Woods Hill & Farley · 360 South Monroe Street, Suite 400 · Denver, CO 80209 · 303-322-8943

Stephanie M. Tuthill · Tuthill & Hughes · 300 South Jackson Street · Denver, CO 80209 · 303-831-7364

James R. Wade · ⑳ · Wade Ash Woods Hill & Farley · 360 South Monroe Street, Suite 400 · Denver, CO 80209 · 303-322-8943

James R. Walker · Rothgerber Johnson & Lyons · One Tabor Center, Suite 3000 · 1200 Seventeenth Street · Denver, CO 80202-5855 · 303-623-9000

Carol Warnick · Holland & Hart · 555 Seventeenth Street, Suite 3200 · Denver, CO 80202-3739 · 303-295-8000

John A. Warnick · ⑩ · Holme Roberts & Owen · http://www.hro.com · 1700 Lincoln Street, Suite 4100 · Denver, CO 80203-4541 · 303-861-7000

Constance B. Wood · Constance Beck Wood · 1866 Vine Street · Denver, CO 80206 · 303-329-9343

Eugene P. Zuspann II · Zuspann & Zuspann · 1776 South Jackson Street, Suite 520 · Denver, CO 80210-3851 · 303-759-4871

Englewood

Marc A. Chorney · Chorney & Millard · 2000 South Colorado Boulevard Tower Two, Suite 715 · Englewood, CO 80222 · 303-792-5048

Kevin D. Millard · Chorney & Millard · 2000 South Colorado Boulevard Tower Two, Suite 715 · Englewood, CO 80222 · 303-792-5048

Greenwood Village

Susan R. Harris · Susan R. Harris & Associates · 5600 Greenwood Plaza Boulevard, Suite 255 · Greenwood Village, CO 80111 · 303-741-4776

Lakewood

James W. Buchanan III · Buchanan & Stouffer · 141 Union Boulevard, Suite 300 · Lakewood, CO 80228 303-987-3800

Joseph E. Doussard · ⑩ · Doussard, Hodel & Markman · http://www.dhmwlaw.com · 143 Union Boulevard, Suite 770 · Lakewood, CO 80228 · 303-986-1523

Francis Thomas Hill · Frank T. Hill · 143 Union Boulevard, Suite 900 · Lakewood, CO 80228 · 303-980-7911

Littleton

Walter M. Kelly II · Miller & Steiert · 1901 West Littleton Boulevard, Suite 100 · Littleton, CO 80120-2087 · 303-798-2525

Longmont

Jennifer M. Spitz · Stover & Associates · 636 Coffman Street, Suite 301 · Longmont, CO 80501 · 303-682-0433

Thomas L. Stover · ⑩ · Stover & Associates · 636 Coffman Street, Suite 301 · Longmont, CO 80501 · 303-682-0433

Pueblo

David B. Shaw · ⑩ · Shaw & Quigg · 503 North Main Street, Suite 222 · Pueblo, CO 81003-3124 · 719-543-8596

VENTURE CAPITAL LAW

Boulder

James H. Carroll · Faegre & Benson · 1900 Fifteenth Street · Boulder, CO 80302-5414 · 303-447-7700

William R. Roberts · Hogan & Hartson · 1470 Walnut Street, Suite 200 · Boulder, CO 80302 · 720-406-5300

Broomfield

James C.T. Linfield · Cooley Godward Kronish · 380 Interlocken Crescent, Suite 900 · Broomfield, CO 80021-8023 · 720-566-4000

Michael L. Platt · Cooley Godward Kronish · 380 Interlocken Crescent, Suite 900 · Broomfield, CO 80021-8023 · 720-566-4000

WATER LAW

Boulder

David L. Harrison · Moses, Wittemyer, Harrison & Woodruff · 1002 Walnut, Suite 300 · P.O. Box 1440 · Boulder, CO 80302 · 303-443-8782

James R. Montgomery · Moses, Wittemyer, Harrison & Woodruff · 1002 Walnut, Suite 300 · P.O. Box 1440 · Boulder, CO 80302 · 303-443-8782

Jerry W. Raisch · ⑩ · Vranesh & Raisch · 1720 Fourteenth Street, Suite 200 · P.O. Box 871 · Boulder, CO 80306-0871 · 303-443-6151

Denver

Anne J. Castle · Holland & Hart · 555 Seventeenth Street, Suite 3200 · Denver, CO 80202-3739 · 303-295-8000

William A. Hillhouse II · White & Jankowski · 511 Sixteenth Street, Suite 500 · Denver, CO 80202-4224 303-595-9441

David F. Jankowski · White & Jankowski · 511 Sixteenth Street, Suite 500 · Denver, CO 80202-4224 · 303-595-9441

Sarah A. Klahn · White & Jankowski · 511 Sixteenth Street, Suite 500 · Denver, CO 80202-4224 · 303-595-9441

Zach C. Miller · Davis Graham & Stubbs · http://www.dgslaw.com · 1550 Seventeenth Street, Suite 500 · Denver, CO 80202 · 303-892-9400

Dennis M. Montgomery · Hill & Robbins · 1441 Eighteenth Street, Suite 100 · Denver, CO 80202 · 303-296-8100

William A. Paddock · Carlson, Hammond & Paddock · 1700 Lincoln Street, Suite 3900 · Denver, CO 80203-4539 · 303-861-9000

Bennett W. Raley · Trout, Raley, Montaño, Witwer & Freeman · 1120 Lincoln Street, Suite 1600 · Denver, CO 80203-2141 · 303-861-1963

David W. Robbins · ⑩ · Hill & Robbins · 1441 Eighteenth Street, Suite 100 · Denver, CO 80202 · 303-296-8100

Lori J. Satterfield · Holland & Hart · 555 Seventeenth Street, Suite 3200 · Denver, CO 80202-3739 · 303-295-8000

Robert V. Trout · Trout, Raley, Montaño, Witwer & Freeman · 1120 Lincoln Street, Suite 1600 · Denver, CO 80203-2141 · 303-861-1963

Michael D. White · White & Jankowski · 511 Sixteenth Street, Suite 500 · Denver, CO 80202-4224 · 303-595-9441

Glenwood Springs

Scott Balcomb · Balcomb & Green · 818 Colorado Avenue · P.O. Drawer 790 · Glenwood Springs, CO 81602 · 970-945-6546

David C. Hallford · Balcomb & Green · 818 Colorado Avenue · P.O. Drawer 790 · Glenwood Springs, CO 81602 · 970-945-6546

James S. Lochhead · Brownstein Hyatt Farber Schreck · http://www.bhfs.com · 818 Colorado Avenue, Suite 306 · P.O. Box 357 · Glenwood Springs, CO 81602-0357 · 970-945-5302

WHITE-COLLAR CRIMINAL DEFENSE

Boulder

Jean E. Dubofsky · Jean E. Dubofsky · 1000 Rosehill Drive · Boulder, CO 80302-7148 · 303-447-3510

G. Paul McCormick · ⑩ · McCormick & Christoph · 1406 Pearl Street, Suite 200 · Boulder, CO 80302-5307 · 303-443-2281

Patrick T. Murphy · Purvis Gray & Murphy · The Exeter Building, Suite 501 · 1050 Walnut Street · Boulder, CO 80302 · 303-442-3366

Colorado Springs

Dennis W. Hartley · ⑩ · Dennis W. Hartley · 1749 South Eighth Street, Suite Five · Colorado Springs, CO 80906-1968 · 719-635-5521

Richard Lewis Tegtmeier · ⑩ · Tegtmeier Law Firm · 104 South Cascade Street, Suite 200 · Colorado Springs, CO 80903-5102 · 719-473-5757

J. Gregory Walta · J. Gregory Walta · 105 East Moreno Avenue · Colorado Springs, CO 80903 · 719-578-8888

Patrick J. Burke · ⑩ · Patrick J. Burke · 303 Sixteenth Street, Suite 200 · Denver, CO 80202 · 303-825-3050

Lee D. Foreman · ⑳ · Haddon Morgan Mueller Jordan Mackey & Foreman · 150 East 10th Avenue · Denver, CO 80203-2740 · 303-831-7364

Gregory E. Goldberg · Holland & Hart · 555 Seventeenth Street, Suite 3200 · Denver, CO 80202-3739 · 303-295-8000

Harold A. Haddon · ㉕ · Haddon Morgan Mueller Jordan Mackey & Foreman · 150 East 10th Avenue · Denver, CO 80203-2740 · 303-831-7364

Brian K. Holland · Recht & Kornfeld · http://www.rechtkornfeld.com · 1600 Stout Street, Suite 1000 · Denver, CO 80202 · 303-573-1900

Richard K. Kornfeld · Recht & Kornfeld · http://www.rechtkornfeld.com · 1600 Stout Street, Suite 1000 · Denver, CO 80202 · 303-573-1900

Forrest Wayne Lewis · ⑩ · Forrest W. Lewis · 1600 Broadway, Suite 1525 · Denver, CO 80202 · 303-830-2190

Gary Lozow · ⑩ · Isaacson Rosenbaum · 633 Seventeenth Street, Suite 2200 · Denver, CO 80202 · 303-292-5656

James M. Lyons · ⑩ · Rothgerber Johnson & Lyons · One Tabor Center, Suite 3000 · 1200 Seventeenth Street · Denver, CO 80202-5855 · 303-623-9000

Pamela Robillard Mackey · Haddon Morgan Mueller Jordan Mackey & Foreman · 150 East 10th Avenue Denver, CO 80203-2740 · 303-831-7364

Robert N. Miller · Perkins Coie · http://www.perkinscoie.com · 1899 Wynkoop Street, Suite 700 · Denver, CO 80202-1043 · 303-291-2300

Norman R. Mueller · Haddon Morgan Mueller Jordan Mackey & Foreman · 150 East 10th Avenue · Denver, CO 80203-2740 · 303-831-7364

Jeffrey S. Pagliuca · Haddon Morgan Mueller Jordan Mackey & Foreman · 150 East 10th Avenue · Denver, CO 80203-2740 · 303-831-7364

Larry S. Pozner · ⑳ · Reilly Pozner · http://www.litigationcolorado.com · The Kittredge Building, Suite 700 · 511 Sixteenth Street · Denver, CO 80202 · 303-893-6100

John M. Richilano · Richilano & Gilligan · 633 Seventeenth Street, Suite 1700 · Denver, CO 80202-1185 303-893-8000

Daniel J. Sears · ⑳ · Daniel J. Sears · 1801 Broadway Street, Suite 1100 · Denver, CO 80202-3839 · 303-292-0110

Kevin M. Shea · Ballard Spahr Andrews & Ingersoll · 1225 Seventeenth Street, Suite 2300 · Denver, CO 80202-5596 · 303-292-2400

Jeffrey A. Springer · Springer & Steinberg · http://www.springer-and-steinberg.com · 1600 Broadway, Suite 1200 · Denver, CO 80202 · 303-861-2800

Harvey A. Steinberg · Springer & Steinberg · http://www.springer-and-steinberg.com · 1600 Broadway, Suite 1200 · Denver, CO 80202 · 303-861-2800

Craig L. Truman · ⑩ · Craig L. Truman · http://www.cltrumanlaw.com · 1444 Wazee Street, Suite 205 · Denver, CO 80202-1326 · 303-595-8008

WORKERS' COMPENSATION LAW

Colorado Springs

James A. May · ⑩ · Steven U. Mullens · 105 East Moreno, Suite 101 · Colorado Springs, CO 80903 · 719-632-5001

Steven U. Mullens · ⑩ · Steven U. Mullens · 105 East Moreno, Suite 101 · Colorado Springs, CO 80903 · 719-632-5001

Denver

Lawrence D. Blackman · ⑩ · Blackman & Levine · 999 Eighteenth Street, Suite 1755 · Denver, CO 80202-3150 · 303-573-0868

Shelley Phelps Dodge · ⑩ · Buescher, Goldhammer, Kelman & Dodge · 1563 Gaylord Street · Denver, CO 80206 · 303-333-7751

Joseph M. Goldhammer · ⑳ · Buescher, Goldhammer, Kelman & Dodge · 1563 Gaylord Street · Denver, CO 80206 · 303-333-7751

Tama L. Levine · ⑩ · Blackman & Levine · 999 Eighteenth Street, Suite 1755 · Denver, CO 80202-3150 · 303-573-0868

Pepe J. Mendez · ⑩ · Pepe J. Mendez & Associates · 700 Broadway, Suite 1101 · Denver, CO 80203 · 303-831-7670

Fred Ritsema · ⑩ · Ritsema & Lyon · 999 Eighteenth Street, Suite 3100 · Denver, CO 80202 · 303-293-3100

Robert William Turner · ⑩ · Robert William Turner · 1120 Lincoln Street, Suite 1001 · Denver, CO 80203 · 303-830-1803

Durango

Bethiah Beale Crane · ⑩ · Crane & Tejada · 575 East College Drive · Durango, CO 81301 · 970-247-1400

Robert C. Dawes · ⑩ · Dawes, Harriss & Bloodsworth · 572 East Third Avenue · Durango, CO 81301 · 970-247-4411

Grand Junction

David B. Mueller · Withers, Seidman, Rice & Mueller · 101 South Third Street, Suite 265 · P.O. Box 3207 · Grand Junction, CO 81502 · 970-245-9075

Gudrun J. Rice · ⑩ · Withers, Seidman, Rice & Mueller · 101 South Third Street, Suite 265 · P.O. Box 3207 · Grand Junction, CO 81502 · 970-245-9075

Christopher Seidman · ⑩ · Withers, Seidman, Rice & Mueller · 101 South Third Street, Suite 265 · P.O. Box 3207 · Grand Junction, CO 81502 · 970-245-9075

Janet Lynne Frickey · ⑩ · The Frickey Law Firm · 940 Wadsworth Boulevard, Fourth Floor · Lakewood, CO 80214 · 303-237-7373

CONNECTICUT

ALTERNATIVE DISPUTE RESOLUTION

Hartford

William H. Champlin III · Hinckley, Allen & Snyder · http://www.haslaw.com · CityPlace I, 35th Floor · 185 Asylum Street · Hartford, CT 06103-3488 · 860-725-6200

Timothy S. Fisher · McCarter & English · CityPlace I · 185 Asylum Street · Hartford, CT 06103 · 860-275-6700

Joseph G. Lynch · ㉕ · Halloran & Sage · One Goodwin Square · 225 Asylum Street · Hartford, CT 06103 860-522-6103

Louis R. Pepe · ⑩ · Pepe & Hazard · Goodwin Square · 225 Asylum Street · Hartford, CT 06103-4302 · 860-522-5175

Mystic

John Crosskey · John Crosskey · 503 Fishtown Road · Mystic, CT 06355-2041 · 860-536-2813

New Haven

Anthony M. Fitzgerald · ⑳ · Carmody & Torrance · 195 Church Street · P.O. Box 1950 · New Haven, CT 06509-1950 · 203-777-5501

Joseph D. Garrison · ⑳ · Garrison, Levin-Epstein, Chimes & Richardson · 405 Orange Street · New Haven, CT 06511 · 203-777-4425

Beverly J. Hodgson · Beverly J. Hodgson · 130 Huntington Street · New Haven, CT 06511 · 203-497-8571

James F. Stapleton · ⑩ · Day Pitney · One Audubon Street, Sixth Floor · New Haven, CT 06511 · 203-752-5000

West Hartford

Robert P. Wax · Charter Resolution · 14 Stratford Road · West Hartford, CT 06117-2338 · 860-543-0588

ANTITRUST LAW

Hartford

Robert M. Langer · Wiggin and Dana · http://www.wiggin.com · One CityPlace · 185 Asylum Street · Hartford, CT 06103-3402 · 860-297-3700

William M. Rubenstein · Axinn, Veltrop & Harkrider · 90 State House Square, 11th Floor · Hartford, CT 06103-3704 · 860-275-8100

James Sicilian · Day Pitney · The Standard Building · 242 Trumbull Street · Hartford, CT 06103 · 860-275-0100

New Haven

David L. Belt · Jacobs, Grudberg, Belt, Dow & Katz · http://www.jacobslaw.com · 350 Orange Street · P.O. Box 606 · New Haven, CT 06503 · 203-772-3100

APPELLATE LAW

Avon

Thomas C. Clark · Litchfield Cavo · 40 Tower Lane, Suite 200 · Avon, CT 06001 · 860-255-5577

Branford

Richard Emanuel · Richard Emanuel · 601 Plymouth Colony · Branford, CT 06405-4757 · 203-483-6201

Bridgeport

Shelley R. Sadin · Zeldes, Needle & Cooper · http://www.znclaw.com · 1000 Lafayette Boulevard, Fifth Floor · P.O. Box 1740 · Bridgeport, CT 06601-1740 · 203-333-9441

Hartford

Aaron S. Bayer · Wiggin and Dana · http://www.wiggin.com · One CityPlace · 185 Asylum Street · Hartford, CT 06103-3402 · 860-297-3700

G. Eric Brunstad, Jr. · Bingham McCutchen · http://www.bingham.com · One State Street · Hartford, CT 06103-3178 · 860-240-2700

Steven D. Ecker · Cowdery, Ecker & Murphy · 280 Trumbull Street, 22nd Floor · Hartford, CT 06103-2703 · 860-278-5555

John B. Farley · Halloran & Sage · One Goodwin Square · 225 Asylum Street · Hartford, CT 06103 · 860-522-6103

Wesley W. Horton · ⑩ · Horton, Shields & Knox · 90 Gillett Street · Hartford, CT 06105 · 860-522-8338

Sheila A. Huddleston · Shipman & Goodwin · http://www.shipmangoodwin.com · One Constitution Plaza · Hartford, CT 06103-1919 · 860-251-5000

John W. Lemega · Halloran & Sage · One Goodwin Square · 225 Asylum Street · Hartford, CT 06103 · 860-522-6103

Linda L. Morkan · Robinson & Cole · http://www.rc.com · 280 Trumbull Street · Hartford, CT 06103-3597 · 860-275-8200

Michael P. Shea · Day Pitney · The Standard Building · 242 Trumbull Street · Hartford, CT 06103 · 860-275-0100

Jack G. Steigelfest · Howard, Kohn, Sprague & FitzGerald · 237 Buckingham Street · P.O. Box 261798 · Hartford, CT 06126-1798 · 860-525-3101

New Haven

Jeffrey R. Babbin · Wiggin and Dana · http://www.wiggin.com · One Century Tower · 265 Church Street P.O. Box 1832 · New Haven, CT 06508-1832 · 203-498-4400

William H. Clendenen, Jr. · Clendenen & Shea · 400 Orange Street · New Haven, CT 06511 · 203-787-1183

Jonathan M. Freiman · Wiggin and Dana · http://www.wiggin.com · One Century Tower · 265 Church Street · P.O. Box 1832 · New Haven, CT 06508-1832 · 203-498-4400

William F. Gallagher · ⑩ · The Gallagher Law Firm · http://www.gallagher-lawfirm.com · 1377 Ella Grassa Boulevard · P.O. Box 1925 · New Haven, CT 06509 · 203-624-4165

David N. Rosen · 20 · David Rosen & Associates · 400 Orange Street · New Haven, CT 06511 · 203-787-3513

BANKING LAW

Hartford

William W. Bouton III · 10 · Hinckley, Allen & Snyder · http://www.haslaw.com · CityPlace I, 35th Floor 185 Asylum Street · Hartford, CT 06103-3488 · 860-725-6200

J. J. Cranmore · Cranmore, Fitzgerald & Meaney · 49 Wethersfield Avenue · Hartford, CT 06114-1102 · 860-522-9100

James C. Schulwolf · Shipman & Goodwin · http://www.shipmangoodwin.com · One Constitution Plaza · Hartford, CT 06103-1919 · 860-251-5000

R. Jeffrey Smith · Bingham McCutchen · http://www.bingham.com · One State Street · Hartford, CT 06103-3178 · 860-240-2700

David J. Wiese · Tyler Cooper & Alcorn · http://www.tylercooper.com · CityPlace I, 35th Floor · 185 Asylum Street · Hartford, CT 06103-3488 · 860-725-6200

Milford

John W. Hogan, Jr. · Berchem, Moses & Devlin · 75 Broad Street · Milford, CT 06460 · 203-783-1200

Stamford

Michael L. Widland · 10 · Shipman & Goodwin · http://www.shipmangoodwin.com · 300 Atlantic Street, Third Floor · Stamford, CT 06901-3522 · 203-324-8100

BANKRUPTCY AND CREDITOR-DEBTOR RIGHTS LAW

Bridgeport

James Berman · Zeisler & Zeisler · http://www.zeislaw.com · 558 Clinton Avenue · Bridgeport, CT 06605 203-368-4234

Jed Horwitt · Zeisler & Zeisler · http://www.zeislaw.com · 558 Clinton Avenue · Bridgeport, CT 06605 · 203-368-4234

Craig I. Lifland · Zeisler & Zeisler · http://www.zeislaw.com · 558 Clinton Avenue · Bridgeport, CT 06605 · 203-368-4234

James G. Verrillo · Zeisler & Zeisler · http://www.zeislaw.com · 558 Clinton Avenue · Bridgeport, CT 06605 · 203-368-4234

Richard D. Zeisler · 20 · Zeisler & Zeisler · http://www.zeislaw.com · 558 Clinton Avenue · Bridgeport, CT 06605 · 203-368-4234

Hartford

Michael R. Enright · Robinson & Cole · http://www.rc.com · 280 Trumbull Street · Hartford, CT 06103-3597 · 860-275-8200

Evan D. Flaschen · ⑩ · Bracewell & Giuliani · http://www.bgllp.com · 225 Asylum Street, Suite 2600 · Hartford, CT 06103 · 860-947-9000

Ira H. Goldman · ⑩ · Shipman & Goodwin · http://www.shipmangoodwin.com · One Constitution Plaza · Hartford, CT 06103-1919 · 860-251-5000

Jon P. Newton · Reid and Riege · http://www.reidandriege.com · One Financial Plaza, 21st Floor · 755 Main Street · Hartford, CT 06103 · 860-278-1150

John B. Nolan · ⑩ · Day Pitney · The Standard Building · 242 Trumbull Street · Hartford, CT 06103 · 860-275-0100

Michael J. Reilly · Bingham McCutchen · http://www.bingham.com · One State Street · Hartford, CT 06103-3178 · 860-240-2700

Howard L. Siegel · ⑳ · Brown Rudnick · http://www.brbilaw.com · CityPlace I · 185 Asylum Street · Hartford, CT 06103 · 860-509-6500

James J. Tancredi · Day Pitney · The Standard Building · 242 Trumbull Street · Hartford, CT 06103 · 860-275-0100

Robert A. White · ⑩ · Murtha Cullina · CityPlace I, 29th Floor · 185 Asylum Street · Hartford, CT 06103-3469 · 860-240-6000

New Haven

Eric A. Henzy · Reid and Riege · http://www.reidandriege.com · 195 Church Street, 15th Floor · New Haven, CT 06510-1819 · 203-777-8008

Douglas S. Skalka · Neubert, Pepe & Monteith · http://www.npmlaw.com · 195 Church Street, 13th Floor · New Haven, CT 06510 · 203-821-2000

BET-THE-COMPANY LITIGATION

Bridgeport

Jacob D. Zeldes · ㉕ · Zeldes, Needle & Cooper · http://www.znclaw.com · 1000 Lafayette Boulevard, Fifth Floor · P.O. Box 1740 · Bridgeport, CT 06601-1740 · 203-333-9441

Hartford

Francis J. Brady · Murtha Cullina · CityPlace I, 29th Floor · 185 Asylum Street · Hartford, CT 06103-3469 · 860-240-6000

Thomas J. Groark, Jr. · ⑩ · Day Pitney · The Standard Building · 242 Trumbull Street · Hartford, CT 06103 · 860-275-0100

Louis R. Pepe · ⑩ · Pepe & Hazard · Goodwin Square · 225 Asylum Street · Hartford, CT 06103-4302 · 860-522-5175

James A. Wade · ㉕ · Robinson & Cole · http://www.rc.com · 280 Trumbull Street · Hartford, CT 06103-3597 · 860-275-8200

New Haven

Anthony M. Fitzgerald · ⑳ · Carmody & Torrance · 195 Church Street · P.O. Box 1950 · New Haven, CT 06509-1950 · 203-777-5501

BIOTECHNOLOGY LAW

Stamford

James F. Farrington, Jr. · Wiggin and Dana · http://www.wiggin.com · 400 Atlantic Street · P.O. Box 110325 · Stamford, CT 06911-0325 · 203-363-7600

CIVIL RIGHTS LAW

New Haven

Karen Lee Torre · Law Offices of Karen Lee Torre · 51 Elm Street, Suite 307 · New Haven, CT 06510-2049 · 203-865-5541

COMMERCIAL LITIGATION

Bridgeport

David P. Atkins · Pullman & Comley · 850 Main Street · P.O. Box 7006 · Bridgeport, CT 06601-7006 · 203-330-2000

James T. Shearin · Pullman & Comley · 850 Main Street · P.O. Box 7006 · Bridgeport, CT 06601-7006 · 203-330-2000

Jacob D. Zeldes · ㉕ · Zeldes, Needle & Cooper · http://www.znclaw.com · 1000 Lafayette Boulevard, Fifth Floor · P.O. Box 1740 · Bridgeport, CT 06601-1740 · 203-333-9441

Greenwich

James R. Fogarty · ⑳ · Fogarty, Cohen, Selby & Nemiroff · 88 Field Point Road · P.O. Box 2508 · Greenwich, CT 06836-2508 · 203-661-1000

Hartford

Francis J. Brady · Murtha Cullina · CityPlace I, 29th Floor · 185 Asylum Street · Hartford, CT 06103-3469 · 860-240-6000

John B. Farley · Halloran & Sage · One Goodwin Square · 225 Asylum Street · Hartford, CT 06103 · 860-522-6103

William S. Fish, Jr. · Hinckley, Allen & Snyder · http://www.haslaw.com · CityPlace I, 35th Floor · 185 Asylum Street · Hartford, CT 06103-3488 · 860-725-6200

Steven M. Greenspan · Day Pitney · The Standard Building · 242 Trumbull Street · Hartford, CT 06103 860-275-0100

Thomas J. Groark, Jr. · ⑩ · Day Pitney · The Standard Building · 242 Trumbull Street · Hartford, CT 06103 · 860-275-0100

Wesley W. Horton · ⑩ · Horton, Shields & Knox · 90 Gillett Street · Hartford, CT 06105 · 860-522-8338

Charles L. Howard · Shipman & Goodwin · http://www.shipmangoodwin.com · One Constitution Plaza · Hartford, CT 06103-1919 · 860-251-5000

Joseph V. Meaney, Jr. · Cranmore, Fitzgerald & Meaney · 49 Wethersfield Avenue · Hartford, CT 06114-1102 · 860-522-9100

William H. Narwold · Motley Rice · One Corporate Center, 17th Floor · 20 Church Street · Hartford, CT 06103 · 860-882-1681

John B. Nolan · ⑩ · Day Pitney · The Standard Building · 242 Trumbull Street · Hartford, CT 06103 · 860-275-0100

Louis R. Pepe · ⑩ · Pepe & Hazard · Goodwin Square · 225 Asylum Street · Hartford, CT 06103-4302 · 860-522-5175

Craig A. Raabe · Robinson & Cole · http://www.rc.com · 280 Trumbull Street · Hartford, CT 06103-3597 860-275-8200

Paul D. Sanson · Shipman & Goodwin · http://www.shipmangoodwin.com · One Constitution Plaza · Hartford, CT 06103-1919 · 860-251-5000

James A. Wade · ㉕ · Robinson & Cole · http://www.rc.com · 280 Trumbull Street · Hartford, CT 06103-3597 · 860-275-8200

Robert L. Wyld · Shipman & Goodwin · http://www.shipmangoodwin.com · One Constitution Plaza · Hartford, CT 06103-1919 · 860-251-5000

Albert Zakarian · ⑩ · Day Pitney · The Standard Building · 242 Trumbull Street · Hartford, CT 06103 · 860-275-0100

Milford

J. Daniel Sagarin · ⑳ · Hurwitz, Sagarin & Slossberg · 147 North Broad Street · P.O. Box 112 · Milford, CT 06460-0112 · 203-877-8000

New Haven

David L. Belt · Jacobs, Grudberg, Belt, Dow & Katz · http://www.jacobslaw.com · 350 Orange Street · P.O. Box 606 · New Haven, CT 06503 · 203-772-3100

William H. Clendenen, Jr. · Clendenen & Shea · 400 Orange Street · New Haven, CT 06511 · 203-787-1183

Edward Wood Dunham · Wiggin and Dana · http://www.wiggin.com · One Century Tower · 265 Church Street · P.O. Box 1832 · New Haven, CT 06508-1832 · 203-498-4400

Anthony M. Fitzgerald · ⑳ · Carmody & Torrance · 195 Church Street · P.O. Box 1950 · New Haven, CT 06509-1950 · 203-777-5501

David T. Grudberg · Jacobs, Grudberg, Belt, Dow & Katz · http://www.jacobslaw.com · 350 Orange Street · P.O. Box 606 · New Haven, CT 06503 · 203-772-3100

Ira B. Grudberg · ㉕ · Jacobs, Grudberg, Belt, Dow & Katz · http://www.jacobslaw.com · 350 Orange Street · P.O. Box 606 · New Haven, CT 06503 · 203-772-3100

Jonathan Katz · Jacobs, Grudberg, Belt, Dow & Katz · http://www.jacobslaw.com · 350 Orange Street · P.O. Box 606 · New Haven, CT 06503 · 203-772-3100

William H. Prout, Jr. · Wiggin and Dana · http://www.wiggin.com · One Century Tower · 265 Church Street · P.O. Box 1832 · New Haven, CT 06508-1832 · 203-498-4400

David N. Rosen · ⑳ · David Rosen & Associates · 400 Orange Street · New Haven, CT 06511 · 203-787-3513

James F. Stapleton · ⑩ · Day Pitney · One Audubon Street, Sixth Floor · New Haven, CT 06511 · 203-752-5000

Shaun S. Sullivan · ⑳ · Wiggin and Dana · http://www.wiggin.com · One Century Tower · 265 Church Street · P.O. Box 1832 · New Haven, CT 06508-1832 · 203-498-4400

Stamford

Robert P. Dolian · Cummings & Lockwood · http://www.cl-law.com · Six Landmark Square · Stamford, CT 06901 · 203-327-1700

Jay H. Sandak · Sandak Hennessey & Greco · 707 Summer Street, Third Floor · Stamford, CT 06901 · 203-425-4200

Waterbury

James K. Robertson · ⑩ · Carmody & Torrance · 50 Leavenworth Street · P.O. Box 1110 · Waterbury, CT 06721-1110 · 203-573-1200

West Hartford

Richard P. Weinstein · Weinstein & Wisser · 29 South Main Street · West Hartford, CT 06107-2103 · 860-881-2732

Westport

Frank J. Silvestri, Jr. · Levett Rockwood · http://www.levettrockwood.com · 33 Riverside Avenue · P.O. Box 5116 · Westport, CT 06880 · 203-222-0885

COMMUNICATIONS LAW

Hartford

Robert J. Metzler II · ⑩ · Hinckley, Allen & Snyder · http://www.haslaw.com · CityPlace I, 35th Floor · 185 Asylum Street · Hartford, CT 06103-3488 · 860-725-6200

CONSTRUCTION LAW

Hartford

Christopher J. Hug · Robinson & Cole · http://www.rc.com · 280 Trumbull Street · Hartford, CT 06103-3597 · 860-275-8200

Louis R. Pepe · ⑩ · Pepe & Hazard · Goodwin Square · 225 Asylum Street · Hartford, CT 06103-4302 · 860-522-5175

CORPORATE GOVERNANCE AND COMPLIANCE LAW

Hartford

Henry M. Beck, Jr. · Halloran & Sage · One Goodwin Square · 225 Asylum Street · Hartford, CT 06103 · 860-522-6103

Paula Lacey Herman · Day Pitney · The Standard Building · 242 Trumbull Street · Hartford, CT 06103 · 860-275-0100

Jack S. Kennedy · Robinson & Cole · http://www.rc.com · 280 Trumbull Street · Hartford, CT 06103-3597 · 860-275-8200

Hugh P. McGee, Jr. · Murtha Cullina · CityPlace I, 29th Floor · 185 Asylum Street · Hartford, CT 06103-3469 · 860-240-6000

Robert G. Siegel · Day Pitney · The Standard Building · 242 Trumbull Street · Hartford, CT 06103 · 860-275-0100

Stamford

Paul G. Hughes · Murtha Cullina · 177 Broad Street · Stamford, CT 06901 · 203-653-5400

David A. Swerdloff · Day Pitney · One Canterbury Green · Stamford, CT 06901-2047 · 203-977-7300

CORPORATE LAW

Greenwich

R. Scott Beach · Day Pitney · One East Putnam Avenue · Greenwich, CT 06830 · 203-862-7800

Guilford

Irving S. Schloss · (20) · Murtha Cullina · 2488 Boston Post Road · Guilford, CT 06437 · 203-772-7700

Hartford

Henry M. Beck, Jr. · Halloran & Sage · One Goodwin Square · 225 Asylum Street · Hartford, CT 06103 · 860-522-6103

William W. Bouton III · (10) · Hinckley, Allen & Snyder · http://www.haslaw.com · CityPlace I, 35th Floor 185 Asylum Street · Hartford, CT 06103-3488 · 860-725-6200

John M. Horak · Reid and Riege · http://www.reidandriege.com · One Financial Plaza, 21st Floor · 755 Main Street · Hartford, CT 06103 · 860-278-1150

Andrew J. Howat · Reid and Riege · http://www.reidandriege.com · One Financial Plaza, 21st Floor · 755 Main Street · Hartford, CT 06103 · 860-278-1150

Jack S. Kennedy · Robinson & Cole · http://www.rc.com · 280 Trumbull Street · Hartford, CT 06103-3597 · 860-275-8200

Timothy L. Largay · (20) · Murtha Cullina · CityPlace I, 29th Floor · 185 Asylum Street · Hartford, CT 06103-3469 · 860-240-6000

John H. Lawrence, Jr. · Shipman & Goodwin · http://www.shipmangoodwin.com · One Constitution Plaza · Hartford, CT 06103-1919 · 860-251-5000

James I. Lotstein · ⑳ · Edwards Angell Palmer & Dodge · 90 State House Square, Ninth Floor · Hartford, CT 06103 · 860-525-5065

John B. Lynch, Jr. · Robinson & Cole · http://www.rc.com · 280 Trumbull Street · Hartford, CT 06103-3597 · 860-275-8200

Hugh P. McGee, Jr. · Murtha Cullina · CityPlace I, 29th Floor · 185 Asylum Street · Hartford, CT 06103-3469 · 860-240-6000

Willard F. Pinney, Jr. · ⑳ · Murtha Cullina · CityPlace I, 29th Floor · 185 Asylum Street · Hartford, CT 06103-3469 · 860-240-6000

Edward J. Samorajczyk, Jr. · Robinson & Cole · http://www.rc.com · 280 Trumbull Street · Hartford, CT 06103-3597 · 860-275-8200

William T. Sellay · Robinson & Cole · http://www.rc.com · 280 Trumbull Street · Hartford, CT 06103-3597 · 860-275-8200

Robert G. Siegel · Day Pitney · The Standard Building · 242 Trumbull Street · Hartford, CT 06103 · 860-275-0100

Richard S. Smith, Jr. · ⑩ · Murtha Cullina · CityPlace I, 29th Floor · 185 Asylum Street · Hartford, CT 06103-3469 · 860-240-6000

Craig L. Sylvester · Reid and Riege · http://www.reidandriege.com · One Financial Plaza, 21st Floor · 755 Main Street · Hartford, CT 06103 · 860-278-1150

New Haven

Frank J. Marco · Wiggin and Dana · http://www.wiggin.com · One Century Tower · 265 Church Street · P.O. Box 1832 · New Haven, CT 06508-1832 · 203-498-4400

Norwalk

Jennifer N. Boyd · ⑳ · Boyd & Associates · 220 West Norwalk Road · Norwalk, CT 06850 · 203-838-2288

Stamford

David I. Albin · Finn, Dixon & Herling · 177 Broad Street, 15th Floor · Stamford, CT 06901-2048 · 203-325-5000

John T. Capetta · Kelley Drye & Warren · 400 Atlantic Street, 13th Floor · Stamford, CT 06901 · 203-351-8039

Martin A. Clarke · Edwards Angell Palmer & Dodge · Three Stamford Plaza, Seventh Floor · 301 Tresser Boulevard · Stamford, CT 06901 · 203-975-7505

Lawrence P. Coassin · Robinson & Cole · http://www.rc.com · 695 East Main Street · Stamford, CT 06904-2305 · 203-462-7500

Brett W. Dixon · Finn, Dixon & Herling · 177 Broad Street, 15th Floor · Stamford, CT 06901-2048 · 203-325-5000

Harold B. Finn III · ⑳ · Finn, Dixon & Herling · 177 Broad Street, 15th Floor · Stamford, CT 06901-2048 · 203-325-5000

John A. Flaherty · Edwards Angell Palmer & Dodge · Three Stamford Plaza, Seventh Floor · 301 Tresser Boulevard · Stamford, CT 06901 · 203-975-7505

Forrest Lee Griffith III · ⑳ · Day Pitney · One Canterbury Green · Stamford, CT 06901-2047 · 203-977-7300

Michael J. Herling · Finn, Dixon & Herling · 177 Broad Street, 15th Floor · Stamford, CT 06901-2048 · 203-325-5000

Jon T. Hirschoff · ⑩ · Finn, Dixon & Herling · 177 Broad Street, 15th Floor · Stamford, CT 06901-2048 · 203-325-5000

Paul G. Hughes · Murtha Cullina · 177 Broad Street · Stamford, CT 06901 · 203-653-5400

Ernest M. Lorimer · ⑩ · Finn, Dixon & Herling · 177 Broad Street, 15th Floor · Stamford, CT 06901-2048 · 203-325-5000

Richard McGrath · ⑳ · Murtha Cullina · 177 Broad Street · Stamford, CT 06901 · 203-653-5400

David A. Swerdloff · Day Pitney · One Canterbury Green · Stamford, CT 06901-2047 · 203-977-7300

Westport

Paul Berg · Berkowitz, Trager & Trager · http://www.bertralaw.com · Eight Wright Street · P.O. Box 808 · Westport, CT 06880 · 203-226-1001

DUI/DWI DEFENSE

Middletown

Russell S. Palmer · Law Office of Averum J. Sprecher · 90 Court Street · Middletown, CT 06457 · 860-344-9000

New Haven

William F. Dow III · ⑩ · Jacobs, Grudberg, Belt, Dow & Katz · http://www.jacobslaw.com · 350 Orange Street · P.O. Box 606 · New Haven, CT 06503 · 203-772-3100

David T. Grudberg · Jacobs, Grudberg, Belt, Dow & Katz · http://www.jacobslaw.com · 350 Orange Street · P.O. Box 606 · New Haven, CT 06503 · 203-772-3100

Ira B. Grudberg · ㉕ · Jacobs, Grudberg, Belt, Dow & Katz · http://www.jacobslaw.com · 350 Orange Street · P.O. Box 606 · New Haven, CT 06503 · 203-772-3100

John J. Keefe, Jr. · Lynch, Traub, Keefe and Errante · 52 Trumbull Street · P.O. Box 1612 · New Haven, CT 06506-1002 · 203-787-0275

Tara L. Knight · Knight, Conway & Ceritelli · Seven Elm Street, Third Floor · New Haven, CT 06510 · 203-624-6115

Richard William Lynch · Lynch, Traub, Keefe and Errante · 52 Trumbull Street · P.O. Box 1612 · New Haven, CT 06506-1002 · 203-787-0275

Charles Edward Tiernan III · Lynch, Traub, Keefe and Errante · 52 Trumbull Street · P.O. Box 1612 · New Haven, CT 06506-1002 · 203-787-0275

Shelton

James J. Ruane · Ruane Attorneys · One Enterprise Drive · Shelton, CT 06484 · 203-382-0394

EDUCATION LAW

Hartford

Frederick L. Dorsey · Siegel, O'Connor, O'Donnell & Beck · http://www.siegeloconnor.com · 150 Trumbull Street, Fifth Floor · Hartford, CT 06103 · 860-727-8900

Thomas B. Mooney · Shipman & Goodwin · http://www.shipmangoodwin.com · One Constitution Plaza · Hartford, CT 06103-1919 · 860-251-5000

West Hartford

Howard M. Klebanoff · Klebanoff & Alfano · Corporate Center West, Suite 102 · 433 South Main Street · West Hartford, CT 06110 · 860-313-5005

ELDER LAW

Mystic

Deborah J. Tedford · Tedford & Ceddia · 12 Roosevelt Avenue · Mystic, CT 06355 · 860-572-4707

New Haven

Keith Bradoc Gallant · Day Pitney · One Audubon Street, Sixth Floor · New Haven, CT 06511 · 203-752-5000

Stamford

Richard S. Fisher · Cacace, Tusch & Santagata · 777 Summer Street · Stamford, CT 06901-1022 · 203-327-2000

Waterbury

Mark W. Dost · Tinley, Nastri, Renehan & Dost · http://www.tnrdlaw.com · 60 North Main Street, Second Floor · Waterbury, CT 06702 · 203-596-9030

EMINENT DOMAIN AND CONDEMNATION LAW

New Haven

Benson A. Snaider · The Law Office of Benson A. Snaider · 55 Church Street, Suite 403 · New Haven, CT 06510 · 203-777-6426

Michael Susman · ㉕ · Susman, Duffy & Segaloff · 55 Whitney Avenue, Sixth Floor · P.O. Box 1684 · New Haven, CT 06510 · 203-624-9830

Norwalk

Frank W. Murphy · Tierney, Zullo, Flaherty & Murphy · 134 East Avenue · P.O. Box 2028 · Norwalk, CT 06852 · 203-853-7000

EMPLOYEE BENEFITS LAW

Bridgeport

Nancy D. Lapera · ⑩ · Pullman & Comley · 850 Main Street · P.O. Box 7006 · Bridgeport, CT 06601-7006 · 203-330-2000

Hartford

Bruce B. Barth · ⑩ · Robinson & Cole · http://www.rc.com · 280 Trumbull Street · Hartford, CT 06103-3597 · 860-275-8200

John V. Galiette · Reid and Riege · http://www.reidandriege.com · One Financial Plaza, 21st Floor · 755 Main Street · Hartford, CT 06103 · 860-278-1150

Ira H. Goldman · ⑩ · Shipman & Goodwin · http://www.shipmangoodwin.com · One Constitution Plaza · Hartford, CT 06103-1919 · 860-251-5000

John J. Jacobson · ⑳ · Reid and Riege · http://www.reidandriege.com · One Financial Plaza, 21st Floor · 755 Main Street · Hartford, CT 06103 · 860-278-1150

William J. Keenan, Jr. · ⑩ · Murtha Cullina · CityPlace I, 29th Floor · 185 Asylum Street · Hartford, CT 06103-3469 · 860-240-6000

Barrie K. Wetstone · ⑩ · Pullman & Comley · 90 State House Square · Hartford, CT 06103-3702 · 860-424-4300

New Haven

Paul L. Behling · ㉕ · Withers Bergman · 157 Church Street, 19th Floor · P.O. Box 426 · New Haven, CT 06502-0426 · 203-789-1320

Sherry L. Dominick · Wiggin and Dana · http://www.wiggin.com · One Century Tower · 265 Church Street · P.O. Box 1832 · New Haven, CT 06508-1832 · 203-498-4400

West Hartford

Diane M. Fitzgerald · Verrill Dana · http://www.verrilldana.com · 1028 Boulevard, Suite 201 · West Hartford, CT 06119 · 860-228-1023

ENERGY LAW

Hartford

Kenneth C. Baldwin · Robinson & Cole · http://www.rc.com · 280 Trumbull Street · Hartford, CT 06103-3597 · 860-275-8200

Franca L. DeRosa · ⑩ · Brown Rudnick · http://www.brbilaw.com · CityPlace I · 185 Asylum Street · Hartford, CT 06103 · 860-509-6500

David T. Doot · Day Pitney · The Standard Building · 242 Trumbull Street · Hartford, CT 06103 · 860-275-0100

Gerald Garfield · ⑩ · Day Pitney · The Standard Building · 242 Trumbull Street · Hartford, CT 06103 · 860-275-0100

Dwight A. Johnson · ⑩ · Murtha Cullina · CityPlace I, 29th Floor · 185 Asylum Street · Hartford, CT 06103-3469 · 860-240-6000

Paul R. McCary · Murtha Cullina · CityPlace I, 29th Floor · 185 Asylum Street · Hartford, CT 06103-3469 · 860-240-6000

Robert J. Metzler II · ⑩ · Hinckley, Allen & Snyder · http://www.haslaw.com · CityPlace I, 35th Floor · 185 Asylum Street · Hartford, CT 06103-3488 · 860-725-6200

Philip M. Small · Brown Rudnick · http://www.brbilaw.com · CityPlace I · 185 Asylum Street · Hartford, CT 06103 · 860-509-6500

Southport

James E. Rice · Brody, Wilkinson & Ober · 2507 Post Road · Southport, CT 06890 · 203-319-7100

ENVIRONMENTAL LAW

Bridgeport

Christopher P. McCormack · Pullman & Comley · 850 Main Street · P.O. Box 7006 · Bridgeport, CT 06601-7006 · 203-330-2000

Hartford

Thomas M. Armstrong · ⑩ · Reid and Riege · http://www.reidandriege.com · One Financial Plaza, 21st Floor · 755 Main Street · Hartford, CT 06103 · 860-278-1150

Elizabeth Collins Barton · ⑩ · Day Pitney · The Standard Building · 242 Trumbull Street · Hartford, CT 06103 · 860-275-0100

Douglas A. Cohen · ⑩ · Brown Rudnick · http://www.brbilaw.com · CityPlace I · 185 Asylum Street · Hartford, CT 06103 · 860-509-6500

Franca L. DeRosa · ⑩ · Brown Rudnick · http://www.brbilaw.com · CityPlace I · 185 Asylum Street · Hartford, CT 06103 · 860-509-6500

Brian C. Freeman · Robinson & Cole · http://www.rc.com · 280 Trumbull Street · Hartford, CT 06103-3597 · 860-275-8200

Earl W. Phillips, Jr. · ⑩ · Robinson & Cole · http://www.rc.com · 280 Trumbull Street · Hartford, CT 06103-3597 · 860-275-8200

David Platt · Murtha Cullina · CityPlace I, 29th Floor · 185 Asylum Street · Hartford, CT 06103-3469 · 860-240-6000

James P. Ray · Robinson & Cole · http://www.rc.com · 280 Trumbull Street · Hartford, CT 06103-3597 · 860-275-8200

Gregory A. Sharp · ⑩ · Murtha Cullina · CityPlace I, 29th Floor · 185 Asylum Street · Hartford, CT 06103-3469 · 860-240-6000

Philip M. Small · Brown Rudnick · http://www.brbilaw.com · CityPlace I · 185 Asylum Street · Hartford, CT 06103 · 860-509-6500

W. Richard Smith, Jr. · Robinson & Cole · http://www.rc.com · 280 Trumbull Street · Hartford, CT 06103-3597 · 860-275-8200

Mark R. Sussman · ⑩ · Murtha Cullina · CityPlace I, 29th Floor · 185 Asylum Street · Hartford, CT 06103-3469 · 860-240-6000

James A. Thompson, Jr. · ⑩ · Dewey & LeBoeuf · Goodwin Square, 13th Floor · 225 Asylum Street · Hartford, CT 06103 · 860-293-3500

Jane Kimball Warren · ⑩ · McCarter & English · CityPlace I · 185 Asylum Street · Hartford, CT 06103 · 860-275-6700

John E. Wertam · ⑩ · Shipman & Goodwin · http://www.shipmangoodwin.com · One Constitution Plaza · Hartford, CT 06103-1919 · 860-251-5000

Joseph P. Williams · Shipman & Goodwin · http://www.shipmangoodwin.com · One Constitution Plaza · Hartford, CT 06103-1919 · 860-251-5000

Milford

Paul Jacobi · ⑩ · Jacobi & Case · 300 Bic Drive · Milford, CT 06460 · 203-874-7110

New Haven

John R. Bashaw · Day Pitney · One Audubon Street, Sixth Floor · New Haven, CT 06511 · 203-752-5000

Alfred E. Smith, Jr. · ⑩ · Murtha Cullina · Whitney Grove Square, Fourth Floor · Two Whitney Avenue · New Haven, CT 06510 · 203-772-7700

Stamford

Pamela K. Elkow · Robinson & Cole · http://www.rc.com · 695 East Main Street · Stamford, CT 06904-2305 · 203-462-7500

EQUIPMENT FINANCE LAW

Hartford

Michael F. Maglio · Robinson & Cole · http://www.rc.com · 280 Trumbull Street · Hartford, CT 06103-3597 · 860-275-8200

R. Jeffrey Smith · Bingham McCutchen · http://www.bingham.com · One State Street · Hartford, CT 06103-3178 · 860-240-2700

FAMILY LAW

Fairfield

Elaine S. Amendola · ⑩ · Amendola & Amendola · 1248 Post Road, Second Floor · P.O. Box 237 · Fairfield, CT 06430-0237 · 203-319-1143

Richard G. Kent · Meyers Breiner & Kent · 55 Walls Drive, Suite 204 · Fairfield, CT 06824 · 203-255-9410

Michael A. Meyers · ㉕ · Meyers Breiner & Kent · 55 Walls Drive, Suite 204 · Fairfield, CT 06824 · 203-255-9410

Louise T. Truax · Lax & Truax · The Brick Walk, Suite 200-C · 1275 Post Road · P.O. Box 336 · Fairfield, CT 06824 · 203-254-9877

Greenwich

Gary I. Cohen · ⑳ · Law Offices of Gary I. Cohen · 500 West Putnam Avenue, Suite 370 · Greenwich, CT 06830-6096 · 203-622-8787

Thomas D. Colin · Schoonmaker, George & Colin · http://www.sgcfamlaw.com · 81 Holly Hill Lane · P.O. Box 5059 · Greenwich, CT 06831-5059 · 203-862-5000

Wayne D. Effron · ⑩ · Wayne D. Effron · http://www.effronlaw.com · 67 Holly Hill Lane, Suite 301 · Greenwich, CT 06830 · 203-622-1160

Cynthia C. George · ⑩ · Schoonmaker, George & Colin · http://www.sgcfamlaw.com · 81 Holly Hill Lane P.O. Box 5059 · Greenwich, CT 06831-5059 · 203-862-5000

Andrew P. Nemiroff · ⑩ · Fogarty, Cohen, Selby & Nemiroff · 88 Field Point Road · P.O. Box 2508 · Greenwich, CT 06836-2508 · 203-661-1000

Samuel V. Schoonmaker III · ㉕ · Schoonmaker, George & Colin · http://www.sgcfamlaw.com · 81 Holly Hill Lane · P.O. Box 5059 · Greenwich, CT 06831-5059 · 203-862-5000

Hartford

Carlo Forzani · ⑩ · Carlo Forzani · 43 Woodland Street, Suite 500 · Hartford, CT 06105 · 860-251-6790

Wm. Bruce Louden · ㉕ · Louden Legal Group · http://www.loudenlegal.com · 638 Prospect Avenue · Hartford, CT 06105 · 860-231-7150

Christine M. Whitehead · Law Offices of Christine M. Whitehead · 241 Main Street · Hartford, CT 06106 · 860-241-7797

New Canaan

Gaetano Ferro · ⑳ · Marvin, Ferro, Barndollar and Roberts · 220 Elm Street, Suite 100 · New Canaan, CT 06840 · 203-966-9655

Morton E. Marvin · ⑳ · Marvin, Ferro, Barndollar and Roberts · 220 Elm Street, Suite 100 · New Canaan, CT 06840 · 203-966-9655

New Haven

James R. Greenfield · ㉕ · Murphy, Murphy & Nugent · 234 Church Street, Fifth Floor · New Haven, CT 06510-1881 · 203-787-6711

Howard A. Jacobs · ⑩ · Jacobs, Grudberg, Belt, Dow & Katz · http://www.jacobslaw.com · 350 Orange Street · P.O. Box 606 · New Haven, CT 06503 · 203-772-3100

Helen D. Murphy · Murphy, Murphy & Nugent · 234 Church Street, Fifth Floor · New Haven, CT 06510-1881 · 203-787-6711

Jean L. Welty · ⑩ · Welty, Esposito & Wieler · 385 Orange Street · New Haven, CT 06511 · 203-781-0877

New London

Linda L. Mariani · Mariani & Reck · http://www.marianireck.com · 83 Broad Street · New London, CT 06320-1630 · 860-443-5023

Stamford

William T. Fitzmaurice · ⑩ · Fitzmaurice & Siegel · Holly Pond Plaza, Second Floor · 1281 East Main Street · Stamford, CT 06902 · 203-326-5145

Anthony A. Piazza · ⑩ · The Law Firm of Piazza & Simmons · 112 Prospect Street, Third Floor · Stamford, CT 06901 · 203-883-9751

West Hartford

Eliot Nerenberg · Law Offices of Eliot J. Nerenberg · 10 North Main Street, Suite 214 · West Hartford, CT 06107 · 860-232-4881

Gerald A. Roisman · ㉕ · Roisman & McClure · 433 South Main Street, Suite 201 · West Hartford, CT 06110-2815 · 860-521-6701

Westport

Edward Nusbaum · ⑩ · Nusbaum & Parrino · 212 Post Road West · P.O. Box 3239 · Westport, CT 06880-3239 · 203-226-8181

Sarah S. Oldham · Rutkin, Oldham & Needle · Five Imperial Avenue · P.O. Box 295 · Westport, CT 06881 · 203-227-7301

Thomas P. Parrino · Nusbaum & Parrino · 212 Post Road West · P.O. Box 3239 · Westport, CT 06880-3239 · 203-226-8181

Arnold H. Rutkin · ⑩ · Rutkin, Oldham & Needle · Five Imperial Avenue · P.O. Box 295 · Westport, CT 06881 · 203-227-7301

FIRST AMENDMENT LAW

Sandy Hook

Martin B. Margulies · Martin B. Margulies · 79 High Rock Road · Sandy Hook, CT 06482 · 203-426-9846

Stamford

Emanuel Margolis · ⑩ · Wofsey, Rosen, Kweskin & Kuriansky · 600 Summer Street, Suite Seven · Stamford, CT 06901-1490 · 203-327-2300

Westport

Alan Neigher · ⑩ · Alan Neigher · 1804 Post Road East · Westport, CT 06880 · 203-259-0599

FRANCHISE LAW

Bloomfield

Martin A. Clayman · Clayman, Tapper & Baram · Three Regency Drive · Bloomfield, CT 06002-2331 · 860-242-2221

New Haven

Bethany L. Appleby · Wiggin and Dana · http://www.wiggin.com · One Century Tower · 265 Church Street · P.O. Box 1832 · New Haven, CT 06508-1832 · 203-498-4400

Edward Wood Dunham · Wiggin and Dana · http://www.wiggin.com · One Century Tower · 265 Church Street · P.O. Box 1832 · New Haven, CT 06508-1832 · 203-498-4400

Kevin M. Kennedy · Wiggin and Dana · http://www.wiggin.com · One Century Tower · 265 Church Street · P.O. Box 1832 · New Haven, CT 06508-1832 · 203-498-4400

GAMING LAW

New London

Robert D. Tobin · Tobin, Carberry, O'Malley, Riley, Selinger · http://www.tcors.com · 43 Broad Street · P.O. Box 58 · New London, CT 06320-0058 · 860-447-0335

GOVERNMENT RELATIONS LAW

Hartford

David J. McQuade · Murtha Cullina · CityPlace I, 29th Floor · 185 Asylum Street · Hartford, CT 06103-3469 · 860-240-6000

Janemarie W. Murphy · Murtha Cullina · CityPlace I, 29th Floor · 185 Asylum Street · Hartford, CT 06103-3469 · 860-240-6000

Thomas D. Ritter · Brown Rudnick · http://www.brbilaw.com · CityPlace I · 185 Asylum Street · Hartford, CT 06103 · 860-509-6500

HEALTH CARE LAW

Hartford

Michelle Wilcox DeBarge · Wiggin and Dana · http://www.wiggin.com · One CityPlace · 185 Asylum Street · Hartford, CT 06103-3402 · 860-297-3700

H. Kennedy Hudner · Murtha Cullina · CityPlace I, 29th Floor · 185 Asylum Street · Hartford, CT 06103-3469 · 860-240-6000

John H. Lawrence, Jr. · Shipman & Goodwin · http://www.shipmangoodwin.com · One Constitution Plaza · Hartford, CT 06103-1919 · 860-251-5000

Alex Lloyd · ⑩ · Shipman & Goodwin · http://www.shipmangoodwin.com · One Constitution Plaza · Hartford, CT 06103-1919 · 860-251-5000

Thomas S. Marrion · Hinckley, Allen & Snyder · http://www.haslaw.com · CityPlace I, 35th Floor · 185 Asylum Street · Hartford, CT 06103-3488 · 860-725-6200

Maynard R. Miller, Jr. · ⑩ · Reid and Riege · http://www.reidandriege.com · One Financial Plaza, 21st Floor · 755 Main Street · Hartford, CT 06103 · 860-278-1150

Elliott B. Pollack · Pullman & Comley · 90 State House Square · Hartford, CT 06103-3702 · 860-424-4300

Theodore M. Space · ⑩ · Shipman & Goodwin · http://www.shipmangoodwin.com · One Constitution Plaza · Hartford, CT 06103-1919 · 860-251-5000

Theodore J. Tucci · Robinson & Cole · http://www.rc.com · 280 Trumbull Street · Hartford, CT 06103-3597 · 860-275-8200

New Haven

Melinda A. Agsten · ⑩ · Wiggin and Dana · http://www.wiggin.com · One Century Tower · 265 Church Street · P.O. Box 1832 · New Haven, CT 06508-1832 · 203-498-4400

J. Michael Eisner · ⑩ · Eisner & Lugli · 261 Bradley Street · New Haven, CT 06511 · 203-772-0065

Merton G. Gollaher · Wiggin and Dana · http://www.wiggin.com · One Century Tower · 265 Church Street · P.O. Box 1832 · New Haven, CT 06508-1832 · 203-498-4400

Martha Everett Meng · Murtha Cullina · Whitney Grove Square, Fourth Floor · Two Whitney Avenue · New Haven, CT 06510 · 203-772-7700

Stephen E. Ronai · ⑩ · Murtha Cullina · Whitney Grove Square, Fourth Floor · Two Whitney Avenue · New Haven, CT 06510 · 203-772-7700

Maureen Weaver · ⑩ · Wiggin and Dana · http://www.wiggin.com · One Century Tower · 265 Church Street · P.O. Box 1832 · New Haven, CT 06508-1832 · 203-498-4400

Stamford

Paul E. Knag · ⑩ · Murtha Cullina · 177 Broad Street · Stamford, CT 06901 · 203-653-5400

IMMIGRATION LAW

Bloomfield

Jason Y. Gans · ⑩ · Clayman, Tapper & Baram · Three Regency Drive · Bloomfield, CT 06002-2331 · 860-242-2221

Joseph M. Tapper · ⑩ · Clayman, Tapper & Baram · Three Regency Drive · Bloomfield, CT 06002-2331 860-242-2221

Bridgeport

Maria G. Labaredas · Maria G. Labaredas · 961 Huntington Turnpike, Suite 202 · Bridgeport, CT 06610-1247 · 203-374-8881

Hartford

Wayne E. Chapple · ⑩ · The Law Office of Wayne E. Chapple · 241 Main Street, Fifth Floor · Hartford, CT 06106 · 860-525-3000

Eric Fleischmann · Leete, Kosto & Wizner · http://www.lkwvisa.com · 999 Asylum Avenue, Suite 202 · Hartford, CT 06105 · 860-249-8100

Kristin S. Hoffman · Kristin S. Hoffman · 221 Main Street, Suite 501 · Hartford, CT 06106 · 860-241-0078

Elizabeth B. Leete · Leete, Kosto & Wizner · http://www.lkwvisa.com · 999 Asylum Avenue, Suite 202 · Hartford, CT 06105 · 860-249-8100

Daniel E. Marcus · ⑩ · Globman & Marcus · 44 Capitol Avenue, Suite 101 · Hartford, CT 06106 · 860-525-5500

Andrew L. Wizner · Leete, Kosto & Wizner · http://www.lkwvisa.com · 999 Asylum Avenue, Suite 202 · Hartford, CT 06105 · 860-249-8100

Madison

Jennifer Strait Rodriguez · Jennifer Strait Rodriguez · 82 Bradley Road · P.O. Box 166 · Madison, CT 06443 · 203-318-0508

New Haven

Jacqueline DeAndrus Bucar · ⑩ · Murtha Cullina · Whitney Grove Square, Fourth Floor · Two Whitney Avenue · New Haven, CT 06510 · 203-772-7700

North Haven

Michael J. Boyle · Law Offices of Michael J. Boyle · 250 State Street, Unit C-2 · North Haven, CT 06473 203-239-2299

Justin Conlon · Law Offices of Michael J. Boyle · 250 State Street, Unit C-2 · North Haven, CT 06473 · 203-239-2299

Stamford

John J. LaCava · ⑩ · Barr and LaCava · 22 Fifth Street · Stamford, CT 06905 · 203-356-1505

Douglas R. Penn · Barr and LaCava · 22 Fifth Street · Stamford, CT 06905 · 203-356-1505

Westport

Judith Sporn · ⑩ · Judith B. Sporn · 120 Post Road West, Suite 301 · Westport, CT 06880 · 203-226-6171

Wethersfield

Anthony D. Collins · Collins & Martin · 55 Town Line Road, Third Floor · Wethersfield, CT 06109 · 860-761-3400

INSURANCE LAW

Avon

Thomas C. Clark · Litchfield Cavo · 40 Tower Lane, Suite 200 · Avon, CT 06001 · 860-255-5577

Hamden

Jeffrey J. Vita · Saxe Doernberger & Vita · 1952 Whitney Avenue · Hamden, CT 06517 · 203-287-8890

Hartford

Francis J. Brady · Murtha Cullina · CityPlace I, 29th Floor · 185 Asylum Street · Hartford, CT 06103-3469 · 860-240-6000

John B. Farley · Halloran & Sage · One Goodwin Square · 225 Asylum Street · Hartford, CT 06103 · 860-522-6103

Stephen E. Goldman · Robinson & Cole · http://www.rc.com · 280 Trumbull Street · Hartford, CT 06103-3597 · 860-275-8200

Thomas J. Groark, Jr. · ⑩ · Day Pitney · The Standard Building · 242 Trumbull Street · Hartford, CT 06103 · 860-275-0100

John T. Harris · Shipman & Goodwin · http://www.shipmangoodwin.com · One Constitution Plaza · Hartford, CT 06103-1919 · 860-251-5000

Dennis F. Kerrigan, Jr. · Dewey & LeBoeuf · Goodwin Square, 13th Floor · 225 Asylum Street · Hartford, CT 06103 · 860-293-3500

John W. Lemega · Halloran & Sage · One Goodwin Square · 225 Asylum Street · Hartford, CT 06103 · 860-522-6103

Ernest J. Mattei · ⑩ · Day Pitney · The Standard Building · 242 Trumbull Street · Hartford, CT 06103 · 860-275-0100

Kathleen D. Monnes · Day Pitney · The Standard Building · 242 Trumbull Street · Hartford, CT 06103 · 860-275-0100

Philip T. Newbury, Jr. · Howd & Ludorf · 65 Wethersfield Avenue · Hartford, CT 06114-1121 · 860-249-1361

Daniel F. Sullivan · Robinson & Cole · http://www.rc.com · 280 Trumbull Street · Hartford, CT 06103-3597 · 860-275-8200

New Haven

Elizabeth J. Stewart · Murtha Cullina · Whitney Grove Square, Fourth Floor · Two Whitney Avenue · New Haven, CT 06510 · 203-772-7700

Stamford

John H. Kane · Robinson & Cole · http://www.rc.com · 695 East Main Street · Stamford, CT 06904-2305 203-462-7500

INTELLECTUAL PROPERTY LAW

Hartford

Peter L. Costas · ⑩ · Pepe & Hazard · Goodwin Square · 225 Asylum Street · Hartford, CT 06103-4302 · 860-522-5175

New Haven

Francis J. Duffin · Wiggin and Dana · http://www.wiggin.com · One Century Tower · 265 Church Street · P.O. Box 1832 · New Haven, CT 06508-1832 · 203-498-4400

Stamford

Barry Kramer · ⑩ · Edwards Angell Palmer & Dodge · Three Stamford Plaza, Seventh Floor · 301 Tresser Boulevard · Stamford, CT 06901 · 203-975-7505

LABOR AND EMPLOYMENT LAW

Bridgeport

E. Terry Durant · ⑳ · Durant, Nichols, Houston, Hodgson & Cortese-Costa · 1057 Broad Street · Bridgeport, CT 06604-4219 · 203-366-3438

Donald F. Houston · ⑩ · Durant, Nichols, Houston, Hodgson & Cortese-Costa · 1057 Broad Street · Bridgeport, CT 06604-4219 · 203-366-3438

Hartford

Gregg D. Adler · ⑩ · Livingston, Adler, Pulda, Meiklejohn & Kelly · 557 Prospect Avenue · Hartford, CT 06105-2922 · 860-233-9821

Victoria Woodin Chavey · Day Pitney · The Standard Building · 242 Trumbull Street · Hartford, CT 06103 · 860-275-0100

Brian Clemow · ㉕ · Shipman & Goodwin · http://www.shipmangoodwin.com · One Constitution Plaza · Hartford, CT 06103-1919 · 860-251-5000

Thomas M. Cloherty · ⑳ · Murtha Cullina · CityPlace I, 29th Floor · 185 Asylum Street · Hartford, CT 06103-3469 · 860-240-6000

Alice E. DeTora · Robinson & Cole · http://www.rc.com · 280 Trumbull Street · Hartford, CT 06103-3597 · 860-275-8200

Miguel A. Escalera, Jr. · Kainen, Escalera & McHale · 21 Oak Street, Suite 601 · Hartford, CT 06106 · 860-493-0870

Beverly W. Garofalo · Jackson Lewis · http://www.jacksonlewis.com · 90 State House Square, Eighth Floor · Hartford, CT 06103 · 860-522-0404

Burton Kainen · ⑳ · Kainen, Escalera & McHale · 21 Oak Street, Suite 601 · Hartford, CT 06106 · 860-493-0870

Daniel Livingston · ⑩ · Livingston, Adler, Pulda, Meiklejohn & Kelly · 557 Prospect Avenue · Hartford, CT 06105-2922 · 860-233-9821

William G. Madsen · Madsen, Prestley & Parenteau · 44 Capitol Avenue, Suite 201 · Hartford, CT 06106 860-246-2466

Patrick J. McHale · Kainen, Escalera & McHale · 21 Oak Street, Suite 601 · Hartford, CT 06106 · 860-493-0870

Thomas Meiklejohn · Livingston, Adler, Pulda, Meiklejohn & Kelly · 557 Prospect Avenue · Hartford, CT 06105-2922 · 860-233-9821

Thomas B. Mooney · Shipman & Goodwin · http://www.shipmangoodwin.com · One Constitution Plaza · Hartford, CT 06103-1919 · 860-251-5000

Hugh F. Murray III · Murtha Cullina · CityPlace I, 29th Floor · 185 Asylum Street · Hartford, CT 06103-3469 · 860-240-6000

Saranne P. Murray · Shipman & Goodwin · http://www.shipmangoodwin.com · One Constitution Plaza · Hartford, CT 06103-1919 · 860-251-5000

Richard D. O'Connor · ⑳ · Siegel, O'Connor, O'Donnell & Beck · http://www.siegeloconnor.com · 150 Trumbull Street, Fifth Floor · Hartford, CT 06103 · 860-727-8900

Jacques J. Parenteau · Madsen, Prestley & Parenteau · 44 Capitol Avenue, Suite 201 · Hartford, CT 06106 · 860-246-2466

Daniel A. Schwartz · Pullman & Comley · 90 State House Square · Hartford, CT 06103-3702 · 860-424-4300

Felix J. Springer · ⑳ · Day Pitney · The Standard Building · 242 Trumbull Street · Hartford, CT 06103 · 860-275-0100

Richard F. Vitarelli · Robinson & Cole · http://www.rc.com · 280 Trumbull Street · Hartford, CT 06103-3597 · 860-275-8200

Richard Voigt · ⑩ · McCarter & English · CityPlace I · 185 Asylum Street · Hartford, CT 06103 · 860-275-6700

Albert Zakarian · ⑩ · Day Pitney · The Standard Building · 242 Trumbull Street · Hartford, CT 06103 · 860-275-0100

Manchester

Kathleen Eldergill · ⑩ · Beck & Eldergill · http://www.beckeldergilllaw.com · 447 Center Street · Manchester, CT 06040 · 860-646-5606

New Haven

Joseph D. Garrison · ⑳ · Garrison, Levin-Epstein, Chimes & Richardson · 405 Orange Street · New Haven, CT 06511 · 203-777-4425

Peter J. Lefeber · Wiggin and Dana · http://www.wiggin.com · One Century Tower · 265 Church Street · P.O. Box 1832 · New Haven, CT 06508-1832 · 203-498-4400

Ethan A. Levin-Epstein · ⑩ · Garrison, Levin-Epstein, Chimes & Richardson · 405 Orange Street · New Haven, CT 06511 · 203-777-4425

Robert A. Richardson · Garrison, Levin-Epstein, Chimes & Richardson · 405 Orange Street · New Haven, CT 06511 · 203-777-4425

David N. Rosen · ⑳ · David Rosen & Associates · 400 Orange Street · New Haven, CT 06511 · 203-787-3513

Karen Lee Torre · Law Offices of Karen Lee Torre · 51 Elm Street, Suite 307 · New Haven, CT 06510-2049 · 203-865-5541

Barry J. Waters · Murtha Cullina · Whitney Grove Square, Fourth Floor · Two Whitney Avenue · New Haven, CT 06510 · 203-772-7700

John G. Zandy · Wiggin and Dana · http://www.wiggin.com · One Century Tower · 265 Church Street · P.O. Box 1832 · New Haven, CT 06508-1832 · 203-498-4400

New London

Thomas J. Riley · ⑩ · Tobin, Carberry, O'Malley, Riley, Selinger · http://www.tcors.com · 43 Broad Street P.O. Box 58 · New London, CT 06320-0058 · 860-447-0335

North Haven

George E. O'Brien, Jr. · Littler Mendelson · 110 Washington Avenue, Third Floor · North Haven, CT 06473 · 203-234-6344

Stamford

David M. Cohen · ⑩ · Wofsey, Rosen, Kweskin & Kuriansky · 600 Summer Street, Suite Seven · Stamford, CT 06901-1490 · 203-327-2300

Victoria Small de Toledo · ⑩ · Casper & de Toledo · 1458 Bedford Street · Stamford, CT 06905-4727 · 203-325-8600

Kathryn Emmett · Emmett & Glander · 45 Franklin Street · Stamford, CT 06901 · 203-324-7744

A. Robert Fischer · Jackson Lewis · http://www.jacksonlewis.com · 177 Broad Street · P.O. Box 251 · Stamford, CT 06904 · 203-961-0404

David S. Golub · ㉕ · Silver, Golub & Teitell · http://www.sgtlaw.com · 184 Atlantic Street · Stamford, CT 06901 · 203-428-4171

Gary E. Phelan · ⑩ · Outten & Golden · Four Landmark Square, Suite 201 · Stamford, CT 06901 · 203-363-7888

Daniel L. Schwartz · Day Pitney · One Canterbury Green · Stamford, CT 06901-2047 · 203-977-7300

West Hartford

Leon M. Rosenblatt · ⑩ · Leon M. Rosenblatt · 10 North Main Street · West Hartford, CT 06107-1988 · 860-523-8066

LAND USE & ZONING LAW

Bridgeport

Austin K. Wolf · ⑳ · Cohen and Wolf · 1115 Broad Street · P.O. Box 1821 · Bridgeport, CT 06601-1821 · 203-368-0211

Farmington

Robin Messier Pearson · Shipman, Sosensky, Randich & Marks · 135 South Road · Farmington, CT 06032 · 860-606-1700

Greenwich

Bruce F. Cohen · ⑩ · Fogarty, Cohen, Selby & Nemiroff · 88 Field Point Road · P.O. Box 2508 · Greenwich, CT 06836-2508 · 203-661-1000

Hartford

Timothy S. Hollister · Shipman & Goodwin · http://www.shipmangoodwin.com · One Constitution Plaza Hartford, CT 06103-1919 · 860-251-5000

Dwight H. Merriam · ⑩ · Robinson & Cole · http://www.rc.com · 280 Trumbull Street · Hartford, CT 06103-3597 · 860-275-8200

New Haven

Michael Susman · 25 · Susman, Duffy & Segaloff · 55 Whitney Avenue, Sixth Floor · P.O. Box 1684 · New Haven, CT 06510 · 203-624-9830

New London

Glenn T. Carberry · Tobin, Carberry, O'Malley, Riley, Selinger · http://www.tcors.com · 43 Broad Street · P.O. Box 58 · New London, CT 06320-0058 · 860-447-0335

Stamford

Michael J. Cacace · 10 · Cacace, Tusch & Santagata · 777 Summer Street · Stamford, CT 06901-1022 · 203-327-2000

Wilton

Robert A. Fuller · Robert A. Fuller · 75 East Meadow Road · Wilton, CT 06897-4705 · 203-762-5888

LEGAL MALPRACTICE LAW

Bridgeport

David P. Atkins · Pullman & Comley · 850 Main Street · P.O. Box 7006 · Bridgeport, CT 06601-7006 · 203-330-2000

Shelton

Paul E. Pollock · 10 · Bai, Pollock, Blueweiss & Mulcahey · One Corporate Drive · Shelton, CT 06484 · 203-925-8100

LEVERAGED BUYOUTS AND PRIVATE EQUITY LAW

Hartford

Jack S. Kennedy · Robinson & Cole · http://www.rc.com · 280 Trumbull Street · Hartford, CT 06103-3597 · 860-275-8200

New Haven

Frank J. Marco · Wiggin and Dana · http://www.wiggin.com · One Century Tower · 265 Church Street · P.O. Box 1832 · New Haven, CT 06508-1832 · 203-498-4400

Stamford

David I. Albin · Finn, Dixon & Herling · 177 Broad Street, 15th Floor · Stamford, CT 06901-2048 · 203-325-5000

Harold B. Finn III · 20 · Finn, Dixon & Herling · 177 Broad Street, 15th Floor · Stamford, CT 06901-2048 · 203-325-5000

David A. Swerdloff · Day Pitney · One Canterbury Green · Stamford, CT 06901-2047 · 203-977-7300

MASS TORT LITIGATION

New Haven

James F. Early · Early, Ludwick & Sweeney · One Century Tower, 11th Floor · 265 Church Street · P.O. Box 1866 · New Haven, CT 06508-1866 · 203-777-7799

MEDICAL MALPRACTICE LAW

Bridgeport

Robert B. Adelman · ⑩ · Adelman Hirsch & Newman · 1000 Lafayette Boulevard · Bridgeport, CT 06604 · 203-331-8888

Christopher D. Bernard · ⑩ · Koskoff, Koskoff & Bieder · 350 Fairfield Avenue · Bridgeport, CT 06604 203-336-4421

James D. Horwitz · Koskoff, Koskoff & Bieder · 350 Fairfield Avenue · Bridgeport, CT 06604 · 203-336-4421

Michael P. Koskoff · ⑳ · Koskoff, Koskoff & Bieder · 350 Fairfield Avenue · Bridgeport, CT 06604 · 203-336-4421

Joel H. Lichtenstein · Koskoff, Koskoff & Bieder · 350 Fairfield Avenue · Bridgeport, CT 06604 · 203-336-4421

Cindy L. Robinson · ⑩ · Tremont & Sheldon · http://www.tremont-sheldon.com · 64 Lyon Terrace · Bridgeport, CT 06604 · 203-335-5145

Middlebury

Richard A. O'Connor · Sachner & O'Connor · The Crossroads West, Building Two, Suite 2000 · 765 Straits Turnpike · P.O. Box 1323 · Middlebury, CT 06762-1323 · 203-598-7585

Stephen P. Sachner · Sachner & O'Connor · The Crossroads West, Building Two, Suite 2000 · 765 Straits Turnpike · P.O. Box 1323 · Middlebury, CT 06762-1323 · 203-598-7585

New Haven

William F. Gallagher · ⑩ · The Gallagher Law Firm · http://www.gallagher-lawfirm.com · 1377 Ella Grassa Boulevard · P.O. Box 1925 · New Haven, CT 06509 · 203-624-4165

Penny Q. Seaman · Wiggin and Dana · http://www.wiggin.com · One Century Tower · 265 Church Street P.O. Box 1832 · New Haven, CT 06508-1832 · 203-498-4400

Shelton

Gaileen A. Kaufman · Bai, Pollock, Blueweiss & Mulcahey · One Corporate Drive · Shelton, CT 06484 · 203-925-8100

Garie J. Mulcahey · ⑩ · Bai, Pollock, Blueweiss & Mulcahey · One Corporate Drive · Shelton, CT 06484 203-925-8100

Stamford

Daniel E. Ryan III · Ryan, Ryan, Johnson & Deluca · 707 Summer Street · Stamford, CT 06901 · 203-357-9200

Richard A. Silver · ⑳ · Silver, Golub & Teitell · http://www.sgtlaw.com · 184 Atlantic Street · Stamford, CT 06901 · 203-428-4171

Ernest F. Teitell · Silver, Golub & Teitell · http://www.sgtlaw.com · 184 Atlantic Street · Stamford, CT 06901 · 203-428-4171

Angelo A. Ziotas · Silver, Golub & Teitell · http://www.sgtlaw.com · 184 Atlantic Street · Stamford, CT 06901 · 203-428-4171

Waterbury

Augustus R. Southworth III · ⑩ · Carmody & Torrance · 50 Leavenworth Street · P.O. Box 1110 · Waterbury, CT 06721-1110 · 203-573-1200

Westport

Paul J. Pacifico · ⑩ · Law Offices of Paul J. Pacifico · 327 Riverside Avenue · Westport, CT 06880 · 203-761-0644

MERGERS & ACQUISITIONS LAW

Guilford

Irving S. Schloss · ⑳ · Murtha Cullina · 2488 Boston Post Road · Guilford, CT 06437 · 203-772-7700

Hartford

Henry M. Beck, Jr. · Halloran & Sage · One Goodwin Square · 225 Asylum Street · Hartford, CT 06103 · 860-522-6103

Jack S. Kennedy · Robinson & Cole · http://www.rc.com · 280 Trumbull Street · Hartford, CT 06103-3597 · 860-275-8200

Timothy L. Largay · ⑳ · Murtha Cullina · CityPlace I, 29th Floor · 185 Asylum Street · Hartford, CT 06103-3469 · 860-240-6000

James I. Lotstein · ⑳ · Edwards Angell Palmer & Dodge · 90 State House Square, Ninth Floor · Hartford, CT 06103 · 860-525-5065

Hugh P. McGee, Jr. · Murtha Cullina · CityPlace I, 29th Floor · 185 Asylum Street · Hartford, CT 06103-3469 · 860-240-6000

Willard F. Pinney, Jr. · ⑳ · Murtha Cullina · CityPlace I, 29th Floor · 185 Asylum Street · Hartford, CT 06103-3469 · 860-240-6000

William T. Sellay · Robinson & Cole · http://www.rc.com · 280 Trumbull Street · Hartford, CT 06103-3597 · 860-275-8200

Robert G. Siegel · Day Pitney · The Standard Building · 242 Trumbull Street · Hartford, CT 06103 · 860-275-0100

Richard S. Smith, Jr. · ⑩ · Murtha Cullina · CityPlace I, 29th Floor · 185 Asylum Street · Hartford, CT 06103-3469 · 860-240-6000

New Haven

Frank J. Marco · Wiggin and Dana · http://www.wiggin.com · One Century Tower · 265 Church Street · P.O. Box 1832 · New Haven, CT 06508-1832 · 203-498-4400

Stamford

David I. Albin · Finn, Dixon & Herling · 177 Broad Street, 15th Floor · Stamford, CT 06901-2048 · 203-325-5000

Martin A. Clarke · Edwards Angell Palmer & Dodge · Three Stamford Plaza, Seventh Floor · 301 Tresser Boulevard · Stamford, CT 06901 · 203-975-7505

Brett W. Dixon · Finn, Dixon & Herling · 177 Broad Street, 15th Floor · Stamford, CT 06901-2048 · 203-325-5000

Harold B. Finn III · ⑳ · Finn, Dixon & Herling · 177 Broad Street, 15th Floor · Stamford, CT 06901-2048 · 203-325-5000

Michael J. Herling · Finn, Dixon & Herling · 177 Broad Street, 15th Floor · Stamford, CT 06901-2048 · 203-325-5000

Jon T. Hirschoff · ⑩ · Finn, Dixon & Herling · 177 Broad Street, 15th Floor · Stamford, CT 06901-2048 · 203-325-5000

Paul G. Hughes · Murtha Cullina · 177 Broad Street · Stamford, CT 06901 · 203-653-5400

Ernest M. Lorimer · ⑩ · Finn, Dixon & Herling · 177 Broad Street, 15th Floor · Stamford, CT 06901-2048 · 203-325-5000

Richard McGrath · ⑳ · Murtha Cullina · 177 Broad Street · Stamford, CT 06901 · 203-653-5400

David A. Swerdloff · Day Pitney · One Canterbury Green · Stamford, CT 06901-2047 · 203-977-7300

NON-PROFIT/CHARITIES LAW

Hartford

Frank S. Berall · ㉕ · Copp & Berall · 864 Wethersfield Avenue · Hartford, CT 06114-3184 · 860-249-5261

Stamford

David T. Leibell · Wiggin and Dana · http://www.wiggin.com · 400 Atlantic Street · P.O. Box 110325 · Stamford, CT 06911-0325 · 203-363-7600

Nancy P. Marx · Cummings & Lockwood · http://www.cl-law.com · Six Landmark Square · Stamford, CT 06901 · 203-327-1700

Conrad Teitell · ⑩ · Cummings & Lockwood · http://www.cl-law.com · Six Landmark Square · Stamford, CT 06901 · 203-327-1700

NON-WHITE-COLLAR CRIMINAL DEFENSE

Bridgeport

John Robert Gulash, Jr. · ⑩ · Gulash & Riccio · 350 Fairfield Avenue, Suite 703 · P.O. Box 9118 · Bridgeport, CT 06601 · 203-367-7440

Shelley R. Sadin · Zeldes, Needle & Cooper · http://www.znclaw.com · 1000 Lafayette Boulevard, Fifth Floor · P.O. Box 1740 · Bridgeport, CT 06601-1740 · 203-333-9441

Jacob D. Zeldes · ㉕ · Zeldes, Needle & Cooper · http://www.znclaw.com · 1000 Lafayette Boulevard, Fifth Floor · P.O. Box 1740 · Bridgeport, CT 06601-1740 · 203-333-9441

Hartford

Richard R. Brown · ⑩ · Brown, Paindiris & Scott · 100 Pearl Street · Hartford, CT 06103-4506 · 860-522-3343

Craig A. Raabe · Robinson & Cole · http://www.rc.com · 280 Trumbull Street · Hartford, CT 06103-3597 860-275-8200

Hubert J. Santos · ㉕ · Santos & Seeley · 51 Russ Street · Hartford, CT 06106 · 860-249-6548

Hope C. Seeley · Santos & Seeley · 51 Russ Street · Hartford, CT 06106 · 860-249-6548

Milford

J. Daniel Sagarin · ⑳ · Hurwitz, Sagarin & Slossberg · 147 North Broad Street · P.O. Box 112 · Milford, CT 06460-0112 · 203-877-8000

New Haven

William F. Dow III · ⑩ · Jacobs, Grudberg, Belt, Dow & Katz · http://www.jacobslaw.com · 350 Orange Street · P.O. Box 606 · New Haven, CT 06503 · 203-772-3100

David T. Grudberg · Jacobs, Grudberg, Belt, Dow & Katz · http://www.jacobslaw.com · 350 Orange Street · P.O. Box 606 · New Haven, CT 06503 · 203-772-3100

Ira B. Grudberg · ㉕ · Jacobs, Grudberg, Belt, Dow & Katz · http://www.jacobslaw.com · 350 Orange Street · P.O. Box 606 · New Haven, CT 06503 · 203-772-3100

Hugh F. Keefe · ㉕ · Lynch, Traub, Keefe and Errante · 52 Trumbull Street · P.O. Box 1612 · New Haven, CT 06506-1002 · 203-787-0275

John J. Keefe, Jr. · Lynch, Traub, Keefe and Errante · 52 Trumbull Street · P.O. Box 1612 · New Haven, CT 06506-1002 · 203-787-0275

Tara L. Knight · Knight, Conway & Ceritelli · Seven Elm Street, Third Floor · New Haven, CT 06510 · 203-624-6115

Ethan A. Levin-Epstein · ⑩ · Garrison, Levin-Epstein, Chimes & Richardson · 405 Orange Street · New Haven, CT 06511 · 203-777-4425

Richard William Lynch · Lynch, Traub, Keefe and Errante · 52 Trumbull Street · P.O. Box 1612 · New Haven, CT 06506-1002 · 203-787-0275

Richard A. Reeve · Sheehan & Reeve · 139 Orange Street, Suite 301 · New Haven, CT 06510 · 203-787-9026

Michael O. Sheehan · Sheehan & Reeve · 139 Orange Street, Suite 301 · New Haven, CT 06510 · 203-787-9026

Charles Edward Tiernan III · Lynch, Traub, Keefe and Errante · 52 Trumbull Street · P.O. Box 1612 · New Haven, CT 06506-1002 · 203-787-0275

Old Saybrook

Jeremiah Donovan · Jeremiah Donovan and Terry Donovan · 123 Elm Street, Suite 400 · P.O. Box 554 · Old Saybrook, CT 06475-0554 · 860-388-3750

Stamford

Emanuel Margolis · ⑩ · Wofsey, Rosen, Kweskin & Kuriansky · 600 Summer Street, Suite Seven · Stamford, CT 06901-1490 · 203-327-2300

Westport

Andrew B. Bowman · ⑩ · Andrew B. Bowman · 1804 Post Road East · Westport, CT 06880 · 203-259-0599

PERSONAL INJURY LITIGATION

Bridgeport

Robert B. Adelman · ⑩ · Adelman Hirsch & Newman · 1000 Lafayette Boulevard · Bridgeport, CT 06604 · 203-331-8888

Christopher D. Bernard · ⑩ · Koskoff, Koskoff & Bieder · 350 Fairfield Avenue · Bridgeport, CT 06604 203-336-4421

Richard A. Bieder · ⑳ · Koskoff, Koskoff & Bieder · 350 Fairfield Avenue · Bridgeport, CT 06604 · 203-336-4421

William M. Bloss · Koskoff, Koskoff & Bieder · 350 Fairfield Avenue · Bridgeport, CT 06604 · 203-336-4421

James D. Horwitz · Koskoff, Koskoff & Bieder · 350 Fairfield Avenue · Bridgeport, CT 06604 · 203-336-4421

Joshua D. Koskoff · Koskoff, Koskoff & Bieder · 350 Fairfield Avenue · Bridgeport, CT 06604 · 203-336-4421

Michael P. Koskoff · ⑳ · Koskoff, Koskoff & Bieder · 350 Fairfield Avenue · Bridgeport, CT 06604 · 203-336-4421

Joel H. Lichtenstein · Koskoff, Koskoff & Bieder · 350 Fairfield Avenue · Bridgeport, CT 06604 · 203-336-4421

Kathleen Nastri · Koskoff, Koskoff & Bieder · 350 Fairfield Avenue · Bridgeport, CT 06604 · 203-336-4421

Richard L. Newman · Adelman Hirsch & Newman · 1000 Lafayette Boulevard · Bridgeport, CT 06604 · 203-331-8888

Cindy L. Robinson · ⑩ · Tremont & Sheldon · http://www.tremont-sheldon.com · 64 Lyon Terrace · Bridgeport, CT 06604 · 203-335-5145

Robert R. Sheldon · ⑩ · Tremont & Sheldon · http://www.tremont-sheldon.com · 64 Lyon Terrace · Bridgeport, CT 06604 · 203-335-5145

Jason Tremont · Tremont & Sheldon · http://www.tremont-sheldon.com · 64 Lyon Terrace · Bridgeport, CT 06604 · 203-335-5145

Cheshire

Garrett M. Moore, Sr. · ⑩ · Moore, O'Brien, Jacques & Yelenak · 700 West Johnson Avenue, Suite 207 · Cheshire, CT 06410 · 203-272-5881

Guilford

Timothy W. Donahue · Donahue, Durham & Noonan · Concept Park, Suite 306 · 741 Boston Post Road · Guilford, CT 06437 · 203-458-9168

Michael G. Durham · Donahue, Durham & Noonan · Concept Park, Suite 306 · 741 Boston Post Road · Guilford, CT 06437 · 203-458-9168

Patrick Noonan · ⑩ · Donahue, Durham & Noonan · Concept Park, Suite 306 · 741 Boston Post Road · Guilford, CT 06437 · 203-458-9168

Hartford

James D. Bartolini · ⑳ · RisCassi and Davis · 131 Oak Street · P.O. Box 261557 · Hartford, CT 06126-1557 · 860-522-1196

William R. Davis · ⑳ · RisCassi and Davis · 131 Oak Street · P.O. Box 261557 · Hartford, CT 06126-1557 860-522-1196

John C. FitzGerald, Jr. · Cranmore, Fitzgerald & Meaney · 49 Wethersfield Avenue · Hartford, CT 06114-1102 · 860-522-9100

Thomas J. Groark, Jr. · ⑩ · Day Pitney · The Standard Building · 242 Trumbull Street · Hartford, CT 06103 · 860-275-0100

John J. Houlihan, Jr. · RisCassi and Davis · 131 Oak Street · P.O. Box 261557 · Hartford, CT 06126-1557 · 860-522-1196

Michael C. Jainchill · RisCassi and Davis · 131 Oak Street · P.O. Box 261557 · Hartford, CT 06126-1557 · 860-522-1196

John W. Lemega · Halloran & Sage · One Goodwin Square · 225 Asylum Street · Hartford, CT 06103 · 860-522-6103

Joseph G. Lynch · ㉕ · Halloran & Sage · One Goodwin Square · 225 Asylum Street · Hartford, CT 06103 860-522-6103

Ernest J. Mattei · ⑩ · Day Pitney · The Standard Building · 242 Trumbull Street · Hartford, CT 06103 · 860-275-0100

F. Timothy McNamara · ⑳ · F. Timothy McNamara · 102 Oak Street · Hartford, CT 06106 · 860-249-8458

Francis H. Morrison III · ⑩ · Axinn, Veltrop & Harkrider · 90 State House Square, 11th Floor · Hartford, CT 06103-3704 · 860-275-8100

Hubert J. Santos · ㉕ · Santos & Seeley · 51 Russ Street · Hartford, CT 06106 · 860-249-6548

James A. Wade · 25 · Robinson & Cole · http://www.rc.com · 280 Trumbull Street · Hartford, CT 06103-3597 · 860-275-8200

Middlebury

Richard A. O'Connor · Sachner & O'Connor · The Crossroads West, Building Two, Suite 2000 · 765 Straits Turnpike · P.O. Box 1323 · Middlebury, CT 06762-1323 · 203-598-7585

New Haven

Lewis Chimes · Garrison, Levin-Epstein, Chimes & Richardson · 405 Orange Street · New Haven, CT 06511 · 203-777-4425

William H. Clendenen, Jr. · Clendenen & Shea · 400 Orange Street · New Haven, CT 06511 · 203-787-1183

Joel T. Faxon · Stratton Faxon · http://www.strattonfaxon.com · 59 Elm Street · New Haven, CT 06510 · 203-624-9500

Anthony M. Fitzgerald · 20 · Carmody & Torrance · 195 Church Street · P.O. Box 1950 · New Haven, CT 06509-1950 · 203-777-5501

William F. Gallagher · 10 · The Gallagher Law Firm · http://www.gallagher-lawfirm.com · 1377 Ella Grassa Boulevard · P.O. Box 1925 · New Haven, CT 06509 · 203-624-4165

Ira B. Grudberg · 25 · Jacobs, Grudberg, Belt, Dow & Katz · http://www.jacobslaw.com · 350 Orange Street · P.O. Box 606 · New Haven, CT 06503 · 203-772-3100

Howard A. Jacobs · 10 · Jacobs, Grudberg, Belt, Dow & Katz · http://www.jacobslaw.com · 350 Orange Street · P.O. Box 606 · New Haven, CT 06503 · 203-772-3100

Stanley A. Jacobs · 20 · Jacobs & Jacobs · Granite Square, Third Floor · 700 State Street · New Haven, CT 06511 · 203-777-2300

Jonathan Katz · Jacobs, Grudberg, Belt, Dow & Katz · http://www.jacobslaw.com · 350 Orange Street · P.O. Box 606 · New Haven, CT 06503 · 203-772-3100

Margaret P. Mason · LeClair Ryan · 555 Long Wharf Drive, Eighth Floor · New Haven, CT 06511 · 203-331-7138

David N. Rosen · 20 · David Rosen & Associates · 400 Orange Street · New Haven, CT 06511 · 203-787-3513

Penny Q. Seaman · Wiggin and Dana · http://www.wiggin.com · One Century Tower · 265 Church Street P.O. Box 1832 · New Haven, CT 06508-1832 · 203-498-4400

Michael A. Stratton · Stratton Faxon · http://www.strattonfaxon.com · 59 Elm Street · New Haven, CT 06510 · 203-624-9500

Shaun S. Sullivan · 20 · Wiggin and Dana · http://www.wiggin.com · One Century Tower · 265 Church Street · P.O. Box 1832 · New Haven, CT 06508-1832 · 203-498-4400

New London

Thomas W. Boyce, Jr. · 10 · Faulkner & Boyce · 216 Broad Street · P.O. Box 391 · New London, CT 06320 · 860-442-9900

Dale Patrick Faulkner · ㉕ · Faulkner & Boyce · 216 Broad Street · P.O. Box 391 · New London, CT 06320 · 860-442-9900

Robert I. Reardon, Jr. · The Reardon Law Firm · 160 Hempstead Street · P.O. Drawer 1430 · New London, CT 06320 · 860-442-0444

Norwich

Wayne G. Tillinghast · ⑳ · Brown, Jacobson, Tillinghast, Lahan & King · Uncas-Merchants National Bank Building · 22 Courthouse Square · Norwich, CT 06360 · 860-889-3321

Shelton

Jeffrey A. Blueweiss · Bai, Pollock, Blueweiss & Mulcahey · One Corporate Drive · Shelton, CT 06484 · 203-925-8100

Garie J. Mulcahey · ⑩ · Bai, Pollock, Blueweiss & Mulcahey · One Corporate Drive · Shelton, CT 06484 203-925-8100

Paul E. Pollock · ⑩ · Bai, Pollock, Blueweiss & Mulcahey · One Corporate Drive · Shelton, CT 06484 · 203-925-8100

Stamford

Stewart M. Casper · ⑩ · Casper & de Toledo · 1458 Bedford Street · Stamford, CT 06905-4727 · 203-325-8600

Charles A. Deluca · Ryan, Ryan, Johnson & Deluca · 707 Summer Street · Stamford, CT 06901 · 203-357-9200

David S. Golub · ㉕ · Silver, Golub & Teitell · http://www.sgtlaw.com · 184 Atlantic Street · Stamford, CT 06901 · 203-428-4171

Richard A. Silver · ⑳ · Silver, Golub & Teitell · http://www.sgtlaw.com · 184 Atlantic Street · Stamford, CT 06901 · 203-428-4171

Ernest F. Teitell · Silver, Golub & Teitell · http://www.sgtlaw.com · 184 Atlantic Street · Stamford, CT 06901 · 203-428-4171

Angelo A. Ziotas · Silver, Golub & Teitell · http://www.sgtlaw.com · 184 Atlantic Street · Stamford, CT 06901 · 203-428-4171

Wallingford

Terence Zemetis · ⑩ · Delaney, Zemetis & Triplett · 111 South Main Street · P.O. Box 747 · Wallingford, CT 06492 · 203-269-1441

Waterbury

Trudie R. Hamilton · ⑩ · Carmody & Torrance · 50 Leavenworth Street · P.O. Box 1110 · Waterbury, CT 06721-1110 · 203-573-1200

Augustus R. Southworth III · ⑩ · Carmody & Torrance · 50 Leavenworth Street · P.O. Box 1110 · Waterbury, CT 06721-1110 · 203-573-1200

Waterford

Humbert J. Polito, Jr. · Polito and Quinn · 567 Vauxhall Street Extension, Suite 230 · Waterford, CT 06385 · 860-447-3300

Westport

Paul J. Pacifico · ⑩ · Law Offices of Paul J. Pacifico · 327 Riverside Avenue · Westport, CT 06880 · 203-761-0644

PRIVATE FUNDS LAW

New Haven

Paul A. Hughes · Wiggin and Dana · http://www.wiggin.com · One Century Tower · 265 Church Street · P.O. Box 1832 · New Haven, CT 06508-1832 · 203-498-4400

Stamford

Harold B. Finn III · ⑳ · Finn, Dixon & Herling · 177 Broad Street, 15th Floor · Stamford, CT 06901-2048 · 203-325-5000

Michael J. Herling · Finn, Dixon & Herling · 177 Broad Street, 15th Floor · Stamford, CT 06901-2048 · 203-325-5000

PRODUCT LIABILITY LITIGATION

Bridgeport

Robert B. Adelman · ⑩ · Adelman Hirsch & Newman · 1000 Lafayette Boulevard · Bridgeport, CT 06604 · 203-331-8888

New Haven

William F. Gallagher · ⑩ · The Gallagher Law Firm · http://www.gallagher-lawfirm.com · 1377 Ella Grassa Boulevard · P.O. Box 1925 · New Haven, CT 06509 · 203-624-4165

Stamford

Richard A. Silver · ⑳ · Silver, Golub & Teitell · http://www.sgtlaw.com · 184 Atlantic Street · Stamford, CT 06901 · 203-428-4171

Ernest F. Teitell · Silver, Golub & Teitell · http://www.sgtlaw.com · 184 Atlantic Street · Stamford, CT 06901 · 203-428-4171

PROFESSIONAL MALPRACTICE LAW

New Haven

Jonathan Katz · Jacobs, Grudberg, Belt, Dow & Katz · http://www.jacobslaw.com · 350 Orange Street · P.O. Box 606 · New Haven, CT 06503 · 203-772-3100

PROJECT FINANCE LAW

Hartford

Lisa P. Soeder · Soeder & Associates · 241 Asylum Street, Suite 700 · Hartford, CT 06103 · 860-246-1600

Stamford

Ernest M. Lorimer · ⑩ · Finn, Dixon & Herling · 177 Broad Street, 15th Floor · Stamford, CT 06901-2048 · 203-325-5000

PUBLIC FINANCE LAW

Bridgeport

Frank B. Cleary · Pullman & Comley · 850 Main Street · P.O. Box 7006 · Bridgeport, CT 06601-7006 · 203-330-2000

Hartford

S. Frank D'Ercole · Robinson & Cole · http://www.rc.com · 280 Trumbull Street · Hartford, CT 06103-3597 · 860-275-8200

Edmund M. See · Day Pitney · The Standard Building · 242 Trumbull Street · Hartford, CT 06103 · 860-275-0100

Lisa P. Soeder · Soeder & Associates · 241 Asylum Street, Suite 700 · Hartford, CT 06103 · 860-246-1600

Stamford

Frank Giordanella · Murtha Cullina · 177 Broad Street · Stamford, CT 06901 · 203-653-5400

Ernest M. Lorimer · ⑩ · Finn, Dixon & Herling · 177 Broad Street, 15th Floor · Stamford, CT 06901-2048 · 203-325-5000

REAL ESTATE LAW

Avon

Michael R. Levin · ⑳ · Law Offices of Michael Levin · 152 Simsbury Road · Avon, CT 06001 · 860-606-0240

Bridgeport

Austin K. Wolf · ⑳ · Cohen and Wolf · 1115 Broad Street · P.O. Box 1821 · Bridgeport, CT 06601-1821 · 203-368-0211

Farmington

Robin Messier Pearson · Shipman, Sosensky, Randich & Marks · 135 South Road · Farmington, CT 06032 · 860-606-1700

Matthew N. Perlstein · Perlstein & Sandler · 10 Waterside Drive, Suite 303 · Farmington, CT 06032 · 860-677-2177

Mark J. Svonkin · The Law Offices of Mark J. Svonkin · 195 Farmington Avenue, Suite 204 · Farmington, CT 06032 · 860-677-9700

Greenwich

Bruce F. Cohen · ⑩ · Fogarty, Cohen, Selby & Nemiroff · 88 Field Point Road · P.O. Box 2508 · Greenwich, CT 06836-2508 · 203-661-1000

Donat C. Marchand · Ivey, Barnum & O'Mara · 170 Mason Street · Greenwich, CT 06836 · 203-661-6000

Hartford

Frank A. Appicelli · Bingham McCutchen · http://www.bingham.com · One State Street · Hartford, CT 06103-3178 · 860-240-2700

Mark A. Asmar · ⑩ · Brown Rudnick · http://www.brbilaw.com · CityPlace I · 185 Asylum Street · Hartford, CT 06103 · 860-509-6500

Rosemary G. Ayers · Day Pitney · The Standard Building · 242 Trumbull Street · Hartford, CT 06103 · 860-275-0100

Laura G. Ciabarra · Dechert · 90 State House Square, 12th Floor · Hartford, CT 06103-3702 · 860-524-3999

Thomas P. Cody · Robinson & Cole · http://www.rc.com · 280 Trumbull Street · Hartford, CT 06103-3597 · 860-275-8200

Scott P. Consoli · Brown Rudnick · http://www.brbilaw.com · CityPlace I · 185 Asylum Street · Hartford, CT 06103 · 860-509-6500

Paul W. Ford · Ford & Paulekas · 280 Trumbull Street, Suite 2200 · Hartford, CT 06103 · 860-527-0400

John J. Gillies, Jr. · ⑩ · Dechert · 90 State House Square, 12th Floor · Hartford, CT 06103-3702 · 860-524-3999

Herbert A. Krasow · ⑩ · Krasow, Garlick & Hadley · One State Street · Hartford, CT 06103 · 860-549-7100

Diana MacPherson · Robinson & Cole · http://www.rc.com · 280 Trumbull Street · Hartford, CT 06103-3597 · 860-275-8200

James A. McGraw · Day Pitney · The Standard Building · 242 Trumbull Street · Hartford, CT 06103 · 860-275-0100

Dwight H. Merriam · ⑩ · Robinson & Cole · http://www.rc.com · 280 Trumbull Street · Hartford, CT 06103-3597 · 860-275-8200

Mark Oland · ㉕ · Bingham McCutchen · http://www.bingham.com · One State Street · Hartford, CT 06103-3178 · 860-240-2700

R. Jeffrey Smith · Bingham McCutchen · http://www.bingham.com · One State Street · Hartford, CT 06103-3178 · 860-240-2700

New Haven

Susan J. Bryson · Wiggin and Dana · http://www.wiggin.com · One Century Tower · 265 Church Street · P.O. Box 1832 · New Haven, CT 06508-1832 · 203-498-4400

Andrew Lubin · Neubert, Pepe & Monteith · http://www.npmlaw.com · 195 Church Street, 13th Floor · New Haven, CT 06510 · 203-821-2000

James J. Perito · Susman, Duffy & Segaloff · 55 Whitney Avenue, Sixth Floor · P.O. Box 1684 · New Haven, CT 06510 · 203-624-9830

Marjorie F. Shansky · Marjorie F. Shansky · 61 East Grand Avenue · New Haven, CT 06513-4026 · 203-469-3004

Laura M. Sklaver · Susman, Duffy & Segaloff · 55 Whitney Avenue, Sixth Floor · P.O. Box 1684 · New Haven, CT 06510 · 203-624-9830

Michael Susman · ㉕ · Susman, Duffy & Segaloff · 55 Whitney Avenue, Sixth Floor · P.O. Box 1684 · New Haven, CT 06510 · 203-624-9830

Marc A. Wallman · Brenner, Saltzman & Wallman · 271 Whitney Avenue · P.O. Box 1746 · New Haven, CT 06511 · 203-772-2600

New Milford

Gregory J. Cava · Gregory J. Cava · 24 Bank Street, Suite B · New Milford, CT 06776 · 860-350-3650

Southport

Suzanne E. Baldasare · Pepe & Hazard · 30 Jelliff Lane · Southport, CT 06890 · 203-319-4000

Stamford

Frank Lewis Baker III · Robinson & Cole · http://www.rc.com · 695 East Main Street · Stamford, CT 06904-2305 · 203-462-7500

Jerome Berkman · ⑩ · Day Pitney · One Canterbury Green · Stamford, CT 06901-2047 · 203-977-7300

Michael P. Byrne · Day Pitney · One Canterbury Green · Stamford, CT 06901-2047 · 203-977-7300

Michael J. Cacace · ⑩ · Cacace, Tusch & Santagata · 777 Summer Street · Stamford, CT 06901-1022 · 203-327-2000

Steven L. Elbaum · Robinson & Cole · http://www.rc.com · 695 East Main Street · Stamford, CT 06904-2305 · 203-462-7500

Barry C. Hawkins · ⑩ · Shipman & Goodwin · http://www.shipmangoodwin.com · 300 Atlantic Street, Third Floor · Stamford, CT 06901-3522 · 203-324-8100

Michael J. Hinton · Cummings & Lockwood · http://www.cl-law.com · Six Landmark Square · Stamford, CT 06901 · 203-327-1700

Jonathan B. Mills · ⑩ · Cummings & Lockwood · http://www.cl-law.com · Six Landmark Square · Stamford, CT 06901 · 203-327-1700

Thomas P. Skidd, Jr. · ⑩ · Cummings & Lockwood · http://www.cl-law.com · Six Landmark Square · Stamford, CT 06901 · 203-327-1700

Westport

Richard Berkowitz · ⑩ · Berkowitz, Trager & Trager · http://www.bertralaw.com · Eight Wright Street · P.O. Box 808 · Westport, CT 06880 · 203-226-1001

David A. Greenberg · Berkowitz, Trager & Trager · http://www.bertralaw.com · Eight Wright Street · P.O. Box 808 · Westport, CT 06880 · 203-226-1001

Howard D. Komisar · Berkowitz, Trager & Trager · http://www.bertralaw.com · Eight Wright Street · P.O. Box 808 · Westport, CT 06880 · 203-226-1001

Morton R. Ruden · ⑩ · Morton R. Ruden · 19 Ludlow Road · Westport, CT 06881-5071 · 203-454-0909

Steven M. Siegelaub · Berkowitz, Trager & Trager · http://www.bertralaw.com · Eight Wright Street · P.O. Box 808 · Westport, CT 06880 · 203-226-1001

SECURITIES LAW

Bridgeport

Richard Slavin · Cohen and Wolf · 1115 Broad Street · P.O. Box 1821 · Bridgeport, CT 06601-1821 · 203-368-0211

Guilford

Irving S. Schloss · ⑳ · Murtha Cullina · 2488 Boston Post Road · Guilford, CT 06437 · 203-772-7700

Hartford

Timothy L. Largay · ⑳ · Murtha Cullina · CityPlace I, 29th Floor · 185 Asylum Street · Hartford, CT 06103-3469 · 860-240-6000

James I. Lotstein · ⑳ · Edwards Angell Palmer & Dodge · 90 State House Square, Ninth Floor · Hartford, CT 06103 · 860-525-5065

Willard F. Pinney, Jr. · ⑳ · Murtha Cullina · CityPlace I, 29th Floor · 185 Asylum Street · Hartford, CT 06103-3469 · 860-240-6000

Edward J. Samorajczyk, Jr. · Robinson & Cole · http://www.rc.com · 280 Trumbull Street · Hartford, CT 06103-3597 · 860-275-8200

Richard S. Smith, Jr. · ⑩ · Murtha Cullina · CityPlace I, 29th Floor · 185 Asylum Street · Hartford, CT 06103-3469 · 860-240-6000

Stamford

David I. Albin · Finn, Dixon & Herling · 177 Broad Street, 15th Floor · Stamford, CT 06901-2048 · 203-325-5000

Harold B. Finn III · ⑳ · Finn, Dixon & Herling · 177 Broad Street, 15th Floor · Stamford, CT 06901-2048 · 203-325-5000

Michael J. Herling · Finn, Dixon & Herling · 177 Broad Street, 15th Floor · Stamford, CT 06901-2048 · 203-325-5000

Jon T. Hirschoff · ⑩ · Finn, Dixon & Herling · 177 Broad Street, 15th Floor · Stamford, CT 06901-2048 · 203-325-5000

Paul G. Hughes · Murtha Cullina · 177 Broad Street · Stamford, CT 06901 · 203-653-5400

Ernest M. Lorimer · ⑩ · Finn, Dixon & Herling · 177 Broad Street, 15th Floor · Stamford, CT 06901-2048 · 203-325-5000

Richard McGrath · ⑳ · Murtha Cullina · 177 Broad Street · Stamford, CT 06901 · 203-653-5400

David A. Swerdloff · Day Pitney · One Canterbury Green · Stamford, CT 06901-2047 · 203-977-7300

STRUCTURED FINANCE LAW

Hartford

Michael F. Maglio · Robinson & Cole · http://www.rc.com · 280 Trumbull Street · Hartford, CT 06103-3597 · 860-275-8200

R. Jeffrey Smith · Bingham McCutchen · http://www.bingham.com · One State Street · Hartford, CT 06103-3178 · 860-240-2700

TAX LAW

Bantam

Mary M. Ackerly · Ackerly Brown · 782 Bantam Road · P.O. Box 815 · Bantam, CT 06750-0815 · 860-567-0828

Glastonbury

Richard G. Convicer · Convicer & Percy · 41 Hebron Avenue · Glastonbury, CT 06033 · 860-657-9040

Robert J. Percy · Convicer & Percy · 41 Hebron Avenue · Glastonbury, CT 06033 · 860-657-9040

Hartford

Frank S. Berall · ㉕ · Copp & Berall · 864 Wethersfield Avenue · Hartford, CT 06114-3184 · 860-249-5261

Michael L. Coyle · ⑳ · Reid and Riege · http://www.reidandriege.com · One Financial Plaza, 21st Floor · 755 Main Street · Hartford, CT 06103 · 860-278-1150

John E. D'Amico · ⑩ · Updike, Kelly & Spellacy · One State Street, Suite 2400 · P.O. Box 231277 · Hartford, CT 06123-1277 · 860-548-2600

Leslie E. Grodd · ⑩ · Halloran & Sage · One Goodwin Square · 225 Asylum Street · Hartford, CT 06103 · 860-522-6103

Charles H. Lenore · ⑩ · Day Pitney · The Standard Building · 242 Trumbull Street · Hartford, CT 06103 860-275-0100

James B. Lyon · ㉕ · Murtha Cullina · CityPlace I, 29th Floor · 185 Asylum Street · Hartford, CT 06103-3469 · 860-240-6000

John O. Tannenbaum · ⑩ · John O. Tannenbaum · 650 Farmington Avenue · Hartford, CT 06105 · 860-236-6566

Richard W. Tomeo · ㉕ · Robinson & Cole · http://www.rc.com · 280 Trumbull Street · Hartford, CT 06103-3597 · 860-275-8200

New Haven

Paul L. Behling · 25 · Withers Bergman · 157 Church Street, 19th Floor · P.O. Box 426 · New Haven, CT 06502-0426 · 203-789-1320

Stanley N. Bergman · 20 · Withers Bergman · 157 Church Street, 19th Floor · P.O. Box 426 · New Haven, CT 06502-0426 · 203-789-1320

Samuel M. Hurwitz · Brenner, Saltzman & Wallman · 271 Whitney Avenue · P.O. Box 1746 · New Haven, CT 06511 · 203-772-2600

Ronald C. Osach · Silverstein & Osach · 234 Church Street, Suite 903 · P.O. Box 1727 · New Haven, CT 06507 · 203-865-0121

Nathan M. Silverstein · 20 · Silverstein & Osach · 234 Church Street, Suite 903 · P.O. Box 1727 · New Haven, CT 06507 · 203-865-0121

Stamford

Brett W. Dixon · Finn, Dixon & Herling · 177 Broad Street, 15th Floor · Stamford, CT 06901-2048 · 203-325-5000

Michael J. Herling · Finn, Dixon & Herling · 177 Broad Street, 15th Floor · Stamford, CT 06901-2048 · 203-325-5000

TECHNOLOGY LAW

Hartford

Richard L. Green · Thelen Reid Brown Raysman & Steiner · CityPlace II, 10th Floor · 185 Asylum Street · Hartford, CT 06103 · 860-275-6400

New Haven

Mark W. Heaphy · Wiggin and Dana · http://www.wiggin.com · One Century Tower · 265 Church Street · P.O. Box 1832 · New Haven, CT 06508-1832 · 203-498-4400

Simsbury

Diane Duhaime · Jorden Burt · 175 Powder Forest Drive, Suite 201 · Simsbury, CT 06089-9658 · 860-392-5000

TRUSTS AND ESTATES

Avon

Paul E. Mersereau · Drew & Mersereau · 47 West Main Street · Avon, CT 06001 · 860-677-1974

Bantam

Mary M. Ackerly · Ackerly Brown · 782 Bantam Road · P.O. Box 815 · Bantam, CT 06750-0815 · 860-567-0828

Greenwich

Robert T. Gilhuly · ㉕ · Cummings & Lockwood · http://www.cl-law.com · Two Greenwich Plaza · Greenwich, CT 06830-6390 · 203-869-1200

Elizabeth M. Grant · Smith & Grant · Nine Greenwich Office Park · P.O. Box 4459 · Greenwich, CT 06831 · 203-661-1110

Donat C. Marchand · Ivey, Barnum & O'Mara · 170 Mason Street · Greenwich, CT 06836 · 203-661-6000

Edward F. Rodenbach · Cummings & Lockwood · http://www.cl-law.com · Two Greenwich Plaza · Greenwich, CT 06830-6390 · 203-869-1200

Leland C. Selby · ⑩ · Fogarty, Cohen, Selby & Nemiroff · 88 Field Point Road · P.O. Box 2508 · Greenwich, CT 06836-2508 · 203-661-1000

George L. Smith · Smith & Grant · Nine Greenwich Office Park · P.O. Box 4459 · Greenwich, CT 06831 203-661-1110

Guilford

Irving S. Schloss · ⑳ · Murtha Cullina · 2488 Boston Post Road · Guilford, CT 06437 · 203-772-7700

Hartford

Frank S. Berall · ㉕ · Copp & Berall · 864 Wethersfield Avenue · Hartford, CT 06114-3184 · 860-249-5261

James T. Betts · ⑳ · Shipman & Goodwin · http://www.shipmangoodwin.com · One Constitution Plaza · Hartford, CT 06103-1919 · 860-251-5000

Suzanne S. Bocchini · ⑩ · Reid and Riege · http://www.reidandriege.com · One Financial Plaza, 21st Floor · 755 Main Street · Hartford, CT 06103 · 860-278-1150

Steven M. Fast · ⑩ · Day Pitney · The Standard Building · 242 Trumbull Street · Hartford, CT 06103 · 860-275-0100

J. C. David Hadden · Robinson & Cole · http://www.rc.com · 280 Trumbull Street · Hartford, CT 06103-3597 · 860-275-8200

Judith M. Keppelman · ⑩ · Robinson & Cole · http://www.rc.com · 280 Trumbull Street · Hartford, CT 06103-3597 · 860-275-8200

Linda J. McDowell · Robinson & Cole · http://www.rc.com · 280 Trumbull Street · Hartford, CT 06103-3597 · 860-275-8200

Frederick J. Mullen, Jr. · ⑩ · Reid and Riege · http://www.reidandriege.com · One Financial Plaza, 21st Floor · 755 Main Street · Hartford, CT 06103 · 860-278-1150

Robert H. Smith, Jr. · ⑩ · Robinson & Cole · http://www.rc.com · 280 Trumbull Street · Hartford, CT 06103-3597 · 860-275-8200

Lyn G. Walker · ⑩ · Shipman & Goodwin · http://www.shipmangoodwin.com · One Constitution Plaza · Hartford, CT 06103-1919 · 860-251-5000

Martin Wolman · ㉕ · Day Pitney · The Standard Building · 242 Trumbull Street · Hartford, CT 06103 · 860-275-0100

Lakeville

Stuyvesant K. Bearns · ㉕ · Shipman & Goodwin · http://www.shipmangoodwin.com · 12 Porter Street · P.O. Box 1809 · Lakeville, CT 06039 · 860-435-2539

Mystic

Deborah J. Tedford · Tedford & Ceddia · 12 Roosevelt Avenue · Mystic, CT 06355 · 860-572-4707

New Haven

Greg R. Barringer · Reid and Riege · http://www.reidandriege.com · 195 Church Street, 15th Floor · New Haven, CT 06510-1819 · 203-777-8008

Keith Bradoc Gallant · Day Pitney · One Audubon Street, Sixth Floor · New Haven, CT 06511 · 203-752-5000

Carolyn P. Gould · Mulvey, Oliver, Gould & Crotta · 83 Trumbull Street · New Haven, CT 06511 · 203-624-5111

Charles C. Kingsley · ㉕ · Wiggin and Dana · http://www.wiggin.com · One Century Tower · 265 Church Street · P.O. Box 1832 · New Haven, CT 06508-1832 · 203-498-4400

Leonard Leader · Wiggin and Dana · http://www.wiggin.com · One Century Tower · 265 Church Street · P.O. Box 1832 · New Haven, CT 06508-1832 · 203-498-4400

Sara R. Stadler · ⑩ · Murtha Cullina · Whitney Grove Square, Fourth Floor · Two Whitney Avenue · New Haven, CT 06510 · 203-772-7700

Rocky Hill

Jeffrey L. Crown · ㉕ · Jeffrey L. Crown · 21 New Britain Avenue, Suite 208 · Rocky Hill, CT 06067 · 860-257-4330

Southport

Peter T. Mott · Brody, Wilkinson & Ober · 2507 Post Road · Southport, CT 06890 · 203-319-7100

Stamford

Jean Mills Aranha · Connecticut Legal Services · 20 Summer Street · Stamford, CT 06901 · 203-348-9216

Nancy E. Blair · ⑩ · Blair & Potts · Two Stamford Plaza, 10th Floor · 281 Tresser Boulevard · P.O. Box 1214 · Stamford, CT 06901 · 203-327-2333

Daniel L. Daniels · Wiggin and Dana · http://www.wiggin.com · 400 Atlantic Street · P.O. Box 110325 · Stamford, CT 06911-0325 · 203-363-7600

Gregory A. Hayes · Day Pitney · One Canterbury Green · Stamford, CT 06901-2047 · 203-977-7300

Robert J. Miller · ⑩ · Day Pitney · One Canterbury Green · Stamford, CT 06901-2047 · 203-977-7300

John R. Musicaro, Jr. · ⑩ · Cummings & Lockwood · http://www.cl-law.com · Six Landmark Square · Stamford, CT 06901 · 203-327-1700

Arthur G. Potts, Jr. · Blair & Potts · Two Stamford Plaza, 10th Floor · 281 Tresser Boulevard · P.O. Box 1214 · Stamford, CT 06901 · 203-327-2333

Conrad Teitell · ⑩ · Cummings & Lockwood · http://www.cl-law.com · Six Landmark Square · Stamford, CT 06901 · 203-327-1700

Howard S. Tuthill III · ⑩ · Cummings & Lockwood · http://www.cl-law.com · Six Landmark Square · Stamford, CT 06901 · 203-327-1700

Gayle Brian Wilhelm · ㉕ · Cummings & Lockwood · http://www.cl-law.com · Six Landmark Square · Stamford, CT 06901 · 203-327-1700

Waterbury

Mark W. Dost · Tinley, Nastri, Renehan & Dost · http://www.tnrdlaw.com · 60 North Main Street, Second Floor · Waterbury, CT 06702 · 203-596-9030

West Hartford

Paul L. Bourdeau · ⑩ · Cummings & Lockwood · http://www.cl-law.com · Blue Back Square, Suite 400 · 75 Isham Road · West Hartford, CT 06107 · 860-313-4900

B. Dane Dudley · Day Pitney · Blue Black Square, Suite 300 · 75 Isham Road · West Hartford, CT 06107 860-313-5700

Paul A. Hudon · Atlas & Hudon · 95 South Main Street · P.O. Box 270670 · West Hartford, CT 06107 · 860-521-7800

Gina D. Silvestri · Cummings & Lockwood · http://www.cl-law.com · Blue Back Square, Suite 400 · 75 Isham Road · West Hartford, CT 06107 · 860-313-4900

Westport

Amy L.Y. Day · Day & Levy · 27 Imperial Avenue · Westport, CT 06880 · 203-571-1244

WHITE-COLLAR CRIMINAL DEFENSE

Branford

Robert M. Casale · ⑩ · Robert M. Casale · 250 West Main Street, Suite 16 · Branford, CT 06405 · 203-488-6363

Bridgeport

William M. Bloss · Koskoff, Koskoff & Bieder · 350 Fairfield Avenue · Bridgeport, CT 06604 · 203-336-4421

John Robert Gulash, Jr. · ⑩ · Gulash & Riccio · 350 Fairfield Avenue, Suite 703 · P.O. Box 9118 · Bridgeport, CT 06601 · 203-367-7440

Eugene J. Riccio · Gulash & Riccio · 350 Fairfield Avenue, Suite 703 · P.O. Box 9118 · Bridgeport, CT 06601 · 203-367-7440

Shelley R. Sadin · Zeldes, Needle & Cooper · http://www.znclaw.com · 1000 Lafayette Boulevard, Fifth Floor · P.O. Box 1740 · Bridgeport, CT 06601-1740 · 203-333-9441

Jacob D. Zeldes · ㉕ · Zeldes, Needle & Cooper · http://www.znclaw.com · 1000 Lafayette Boulevard, Fifth Floor · P.O. Box 1740 · Bridgeport, CT 06601-1740 · 203-333-9441

Hartford

James W. Bergenn · Shipman & Goodwin · http://www.shipmangoodwin.com · One Constitution Plaza · Hartford, CT 06103-1919 · 860-251-5000

Richard R. Brown · ⑩ · Brown, Paindiris & Scott · 100 Pearl Street · Hartford, CT 06103-4506 · 860-522-3343

James T. Cowdery · Cowdery, Ecker & Murphy · 280 Trumbull Street, 22nd Floor · Hartford, CT 06103-2703 · 860-278-5555

Thomas J. Murphy · Cowdery, Ecker & Murphy · 280 Trumbull Street, 22nd Floor · Hartford, CT 06103-2703 · 860-278-5555

Craig A. Raabe · Robinson & Cole · http://www.rc.com · 280 Trumbull Street · Hartford, CT 06103-3597 860-275-8200

Hubert J. Santos · ㉕ · Santos & Seeley · 51 Russ Street · Hartford, CT 06106 · 860-249-6548

Hope C. Seeley · Santos & Seeley · 51 Russ Street · Hartford, CT 06106 · 860-249-6548

James A. Wade · ㉕ · Robinson & Cole · http://www.rc.com · 280 Trumbull Street · Hartford, CT 06103-3597 · 860-275-8200

Milford

J. Daniel Sagarin · ⑳ · Hurwitz, Sagarin & Slossberg · 147 North Broad Street · P.O. Box 112 · Milford, CT 06460-0112 · 203-877-8000

New Haven

William F. Dow III · ⑩ · Jacobs, Grudberg, Belt, Dow & Katz · http://www.jacobslaw.com · 350 Orange Street · P.O. Box 606 · New Haven, CT 06503 · 203-772-3100

David T. Grudberg · Jacobs, Grudberg, Belt, Dow & Katz · http://www.jacobslaw.com · 350 Orange Street · P.O. Box 606 · New Haven, CT 06503 · 203-772-3100

Ira B. Grudberg · ㉕ · Jacobs, Grudberg, Belt, Dow & Katz · http://www.jacobslaw.com · 350 Orange Street · P.O. Box 606 · New Haven, CT 06503 · 203-772-3100

Hugh F. Keefe · ㉕ · Lynch, Traub, Keefe and Errante · 52 Trumbull Street · P.O. Box 1612 · New Haven, CT 06506-1002 · 203-787-0275

John J. Keefe, Jr. · Lynch, Traub, Keefe and Errante · 52 Trumbull Street · P.O. Box 1612 · New Haven, CT 06506-1002 · 203-787-0275

Tara L. Knight · Knight, Conway & Ceritelli · Seven Elm Street, Third Floor · New Haven, CT 06510 · 203-624-6115

Ethan A. Levin-Epstein · ⑩ · Garrison, Levin-Epstein, Chimes & Richardson · 405 Orange Street · New Haven, CT 06511 · 203-777-4425

Richard William Lynch · Lynch, Traub, Keefe and Errante · 52 Trumbull Street · P.O. Box 1612 · New Haven, CT 06506-1002 · 203-787-0275

Joseph W. Martini · Wiggin and Dana · http://www.wiggin.com · One Century Tower · 265 Church Street · P.O. Box 1832 · New Haven, CT 06508-1832 · 203-498-4400

Charles Edward Tiernan III · Lynch, Traub, Keefe and Errante · 52 Trumbull Street · P.O. Box 1612 · New Haven, CT 06506-1002 · 203-787-0275

Old Saybrook

Jeremiah Donovan · Jeremiah Donovan and Terry Donovan · 123 Elm Street, Suite 400 · P.O. Box 554 · Old Saybrook, CT 06475-0554 · 860-388-3750

Southport

Alfred U. Pavlis · Daly & Pavlis · 107 John Street · Southport, CT 06890 · 203-255-6700

H. James Pickerstein · ⑩ · Pepe & Hazard · 30 Jelliff Lane · Southport, CT 06890 · 203-319-4000

Stamford

David B. Fein · Wiggin and Dana · http://www.wiggin.com · 400 Atlantic Street · P.O. Box 110325 · Stamford, CT 06911-0325 · 203-363-7600

David S. Golub · ㉕ · Silver, Golub & Teitell · http://www.sgtlaw.com · 184 Atlantic Street · Stamford, CT 06901 · 203-428-4171

Emanuel Margolis · ⑩ · Wofsey, Rosen, Kweskin & Kuriansky · 600 Summer Street, Suite Seven · Stamford, CT 06901-1490 · 203-327-2300

Stanley A. Twardy, Jr. · Day Pitney · One Canterbury Green · Stamford, CT 06901-2047 · 203-977-7300

Westport

Andrew B. Bowman · ⑩ · Andrew B. Bowman · 1804 Post Road East · Westport, CT 06880 · 203-259-0599

WORKERS' COMPENSATION LAW

Bridgeport

Robert R. Sheldon · ⑩ · Tremont & Sheldon · http://www.tremont-sheldon.com · 64 Lyon Terrace · Bridgeport, CT 06604 · 203-335-5145

Cheshire

Edward T. Dodd, Jr. · ⑩ · Dodd, Lessack, Ranando & Dalton · 700 West Johnson Avenue, Suite 305 · Cheshire, CT 06410 · 203-272-1883

East Hartford

Richard S. Bartlett · McGann, Bartlett & Brown · 111 Founders Plaza, Suite 1201 · East Hartford, CT 06108 · 860-282-4670

William C. Brown · ⑩ · McGann, Bartlett & Brown · 111 Founders Plaza, Suite 1201 · East Hartford, CT 06108 · 860-282-4670

Jonathan F. Reik · McGann, Bartlett & Brown · 111 Founders Plaza, Suite 1201 · East Hartford, CT 06108 · 860-282-4670

Fairfield

Kevin J. Maher · ⑩ · Maher & Williams · 268 Post Road · P.O. Box 550 · Fairfield, CT 06824 · 203-255-7777

Scott Wilson Williams · Maher & Williams · 268 Post Road · P.O. Box 550 · Fairfield, CT 06824 · 203-255-7777

Glastonbury

Douglas L. Drayton · ⑩ · Pomeranz, Drayton & Stabnick · 95 Glastonbury Boulevard · Glastonbury, CT 06033-4412 · 860-657-8000

Joseph J. Passaretti · Montstream & May · 655 Winding Brooke Drive · P.O. Box 1087 · Glastonbury, CT 06033 · 860-659-1341

James L. Pomeranz · ⑩ · Pomeranz, Drayton & Stabnick · 95 Glastonbury Boulevard · Glastonbury, CT 06033-4412 · 860-657-8000

Nancy S. Rosenbaum · Law Offices of Rosenbaum & Velano · 655 Winding Brook Drive · Glastonbury, CT 06033 · 860-633-9471

Richard T. Stabnick · ⑩ · Pomeranz, Drayton & Stabnick · 95 Glastonbury Boulevard · Glastonbury, CT 06033-4412 · 860-657-8000

Lucas D. Strunk · Pomeranz, Drayton & Stabnick · 95 Glastonbury Boulevard · Glastonbury, CT 06033-4412 · 860-657-8000

Groton

Stephen C. Embry · ⑩ · Embry & Neusner · 118 Poquonnock Road · P.O. Box 1409 · Groton, CT 06340 860-449-0341

David Neusner · Embry & Neusner · 118 Poquonnock Road · P.O. Box 1409 · Groton, CT 06340 · 860-449-0341

Matthew Shafner · ⑩ · O'Brien, Shafner, Stuart, Kelly & Morris · 475 Bridge Street · P.O. Box 929 · Groton, CT 06340 · 860-445-2463

Nathan J. Shafner · Embry & Neusner · 118 Poquonnock Road · P.O. Box 1409 · Groton, CT 06340 · 860-449-0341

Stamford

Stewart M. Casper · ⑩ · Casper & de Toledo · 1458 Bedford Street · Stamford, CT 06905-4727 · 203-325-8600

Woodbridge

Robert F. Carter · ⑩ · Carter, Civitello & Douthat · Woodbridge Office Park, Suite 301 · One Bradley Road · Woodbridge, CT 06525 · 203-389-7000

Donna Civitello · ⑩ · Carter, Civitello & Douthat · Woodbridge Office Park, Suite 301 · One Bradley Road · Woodbridge, CT 06525 · 203-389-7000

DELAWARE

ADMINISTRATIVE LAW

Wilmington

Michael Houghton · Morris, Nichols, Arsht & Tunnell · Chase Manhattan Centre, 18th Floor · 1201 North Market Street · P.O. Box 1347 · Wilmington, DE 19899-1347 · 302-658-9200

Richard D. Kirk · ⑩ · Bayard · 222 Delaware Avenue, Suite 900 · P.O. Box 25130 · Wilmington, DE 19899 · 302-655-5000

ALTERNATIVE DISPUTE RESOLUTION

Wilmington

Victor F. Battaglia · ⑳ · Biggs and Battaglia · 921 Orange Street · P.O. Box 1489 · Wilmington, DE 19899-1489 · 302-655-9677

Vincent A. Bifferato, Sr. · Bifferato Gentilotti · 800 North King Street · P.O. Box 2165 · Wilmington, DE 19801-2165 · 302-429-1900

Grover C. Brown · ⑩ · Gordon, Fournaris & Mammarella · 1925 Lovering Avenue · Wilmington, DE 19806 · 302-652-2900

Joshua W. Martin III · Potter Anderson & Corroon · http://www.potteranderson.com · Hercules Plaza, Sixth Floor · 1313 North Market Street · P.O. Box 951 · Wilmington, DE 19899-0951 · 302-984-6000

Vincent J. Poppiti · Blank Rome · Chase Manhattan Centre, Suite 800 · 1201 Market Street · Wilmington, DE 19801 · 302-425-6400

B. Wilson Redfearn · Tybout, Redfearn & Pell · 750 South Madison Street, Suite 400 · P.O. Box 2092 · Wilmington, DE 19801 · 302-658-6901

Carl Schnee · Bifferato Gentilotti · 800 North King Street · P.O. Box 2165 · Wilmington, DE 19801-2165 302-429-1900

BANKING LAW

Wilmington

Michael Houghton · Morris, Nichols, Arsht & Tunnell · Chase Manhattan Centre, 18th Floor · 1201 North Market Street · P.O. Box 1347 · Wilmington, DE 19899-1347 · 302-658-9200

BANKRUPTCY AND CREDITOR-DEBTOR RIGHTS LAW

Wilmington

Derek C. Abbott · Morris, Nichols, Arsht & Tunnell · Chase Manhattan Centre, 18th Floor · 1201 North Market Street · P.O. Box 1347 · Wilmington, DE 19899-1347 · 302-658-9200

William P. Bowden · Ashby & Geddes · 500 Delaware Avenue, Eighth Floor · P.O. Box 1150 · Wilmington, DE 19899 · 302-654-1888

Robert S. Brady · Young Conaway Stargatt & Taylor · The Brandywine Building, 17th Floor · 1000 West Street · P.O. Box 391 · Wilmington, DE 19899-0391 · 302-571-6600

Mark S. Chehi · Skadden, Arps, Slate, Meagher & Flom · One Rodney Square, Seventh Floor · P.O. Box 636 · Wilmington, DE 19899-0636 · 302-651-3000

Anthony W. Clark · Skadden, Arps, Slate, Meagher & Flom · One Rodney Square, Seventh Floor · P.O. Box 636 · Wilmington, DE 19899-0636 · 302-651-3000

Mark D. Collins · ⑩ · Richards Layton & Finger · One Rodney Square · 920 North King Street · P.O. Box 551 · Wilmington, DE 19899-0551 · 302-651-7700

Daniel J. Defranceschi · Richards Layton & Finger · One Rodney Square · 920 North King Street · P.O. Box 551 · Wilmington, DE 19899-0551 · 302-651-7700

Gregg M. Galardi · Skadden, Arps, Slate, Meagher & Flom · One Rodney Square, Seventh Floor · P.O. Box 636 · Wilmington, DE 19899-0636 · 302-651-3000

Neil B. Glassman · Bayard · 222 Delaware Avenue, Suite 900 · P.O. Box 25130 · Wilmington, DE 19899 · 302-655-5000

Bruce Grohsgal · Pachulski, Stang, Ziehl, Young, Jones & Weintraub · 919 North Market Street, Suite 1700 · P.O. Box 8705 · Wilmington, DE 19899-8705 · 302-652-4100

Laura Davis Jones · ⑩ · Pachulski, Stang, Ziehl, Young, Jones & Weintraub · 919 North Market Street, Suite 1700 · P.O. Box 8705 · Wilmington, DE 19899-8705 · 302-652-4100

John H. Knight · Richards Layton & Finger · One Rodney Square · 920 North King Street · P.O. Box 551 Wilmington, DE 19899-0551 · 302-651-7700

Mark Minuti · Saul Ewing · 222 Delaware Avenue, Suite 1200 · P.O. Box 1266 · Wilmington, DE 19899 · 302-421-6800

Pauline K. Morgan · Young Conaway Stargatt & Taylor · The Brandywine Building, 17th Floor · 1000 West Street · P.O. Box 391 · Wilmington, DE 19899-0391 · 302-571-6600

Michael R. Nestor · Young Conaway Stargatt & Taylor · The Brandywine Building, 17th Floor · 1000 West Street · P.O. Box 391 · Wilmington, DE 19899-0391 · 302-571-6600

James L. Patton, Jr. · ⑩ · Young Conaway Stargatt & Taylor · The Brandywine Building, 17th Floor · 1000 West Street · P.O. Box 391 · Wilmington, DE 19899-0391 · 302-571-6600

Norman L. Pernick · Cole, Schotz, Meisel, Forman & Leonard · http://www.coleschotz.com · 1000 North West Street, Suite 1200 · Wilmington, DE 19801 · 302-652-3131

Laurie Selber Silverstein · Potter Anderson & Corroon · http://www.potteranderson.com · Hercules Plaza, Sixth Floor · 1313 North Market Street · P.O. Box 951 · Wilmington, DE 19899-0951 · 302-984-6000

Stephen W. Spence · ⑩ · Phillips, Goldman & Spence · 1200 North Broom Street · Wilmington, DE 19806-4204 · 302-655-4200

David B. Stratton · Pepper Hamilton · http://www.pepperlaw.com · Hercules Plaza, Suite 5100 · 1313 North Market Street · P.O. Box 1709 · Wilmington, DE 19899-1709 · 302-777-6500

William H. Sudell, Jr. · Morris, Nichols, Arsht & Tunnell · Chase Manhattan Centre, 18th Floor · 1201 North Market Street · P.O. Box 1347 · Wilmington, DE 19899-1347 · 302-658-9200

BET-THE-COMPANY LITIGATION

Wilmington

Lawrence C. Ashby · Ashby & Geddes · 500 Delaware Avenue, Eighth Floor · P.O. Box 1150 · Wilmington, DE 19899 · 302-654-1888

William M. Lafferty · Morris, Nichols, Arsht & Tunnell · Chase Manhattan Centre, 18th Floor · 1201 North Market Street · P.O. Box 1347 · Wilmington, DE 19899-1347 · 302-658-9200

David C. McBride · ⑩ · Young Conaway Stargatt & Taylor · The Brandywine Building, 17th Floor · 1000 West Street · P.O. Box 391 · Wilmington, DE 19899-0391 · 302-571-6600

Robert K. Payson · ㉕ · Potter Anderson & Corroon · http://www.potteranderson.com · Hercules Plaza, Sixth Floor · 1313 North Market Street · P.O. Box 951 · Wilmington, DE 19899-0951 · 302-984-6000

A. Gilchrist Sparks III · ㉕ · Morris, Nichols, Arsht & Tunnell · Chase Manhattan Centre, 18th Floor · 1201 North Market Street · P.O. Box 1347 · Wilmington, DE 19899-1347 · 302-658-9200

Gregory P. Williams · Richards Layton & Finger · One Rodney Square · 920 North King Street · P.O. Box 551 · Wilmington, DE 19899-0551 · 302-651-7700

Donald J. Wolfe, Jr. · ⑩ · Potter Anderson & Corroon · http://www.potteranderson.com · Hercules Plaza, Sixth Floor · 1313 North Market Street · P.O. Box 951 · Wilmington, DE 19899-0951 · 302-984-6000

COMMERCIAL LITIGATION

Wilmington

Jon E. Abramczyk · Morris, Nichols, Arsht & Tunnell · Chase Manhattan Centre, 18th Floor · 1201 North Market Street · P.O. Box 1347 · Wilmington, DE 19899-1347 · 302-658-9200

Frederick H. Alexander · Morris, Nichols, Arsht & Tunnell · Chase Manhattan Centre, 18th Floor · 1201 North Market Street · P.O. Box 1347 · Wilmington, DE 19899-1347 · 302-658-9200

Thomas J. Allingham II · Skadden, Arps, Slate, Meagher & Flom · One Rodney Square, Seventh Floor · P.O. Box 636 · Wilmington, DE 19899-0636 · 302-651-3000

Lawrence C. Ashby · Ashby & Geddes · 500 Delaware Avenue, Eighth Floor · P.O. Box 1150 · Wilmington, DE 19899 · 302-654-1888

R. Franklin Balotti · ㉕ · Richards Layton & Finger · One Rodney Square · 920 North King Street · P.O. Box 551 · Wilmington, DE 19899-0551 · 302-651-7700

Victor F. Battaglia · ⑳ · Biggs and Battaglia · 921 Orange Street · P.O. Box 1489 · Wilmington, DE 19899-1489 · 302-655-9677

Andre G. Bouchard · Bouchard Margules & Friedlander · 222 Delaware Avenue, Suite 1400 · Wilmington, DE 19801 · 302-573-3500

P. Clarkson Collins, Jr. · Morris James · 500 Delaware Avenue, Suite 1500 · P.O. Box 2306 · Wilmington, DE 19899-2306 · 302-888-6800

Arthur L. Dent · Potter Anderson & Corroon · http://www.potteranderson.com · Hercules Plaza, Sixth Floor · 1313 North Market Street · P.O. Box 951 · Wilmington, DE 19899-0951 · 302-984-6000

Jay W. Eisenhofer · Grant & Eisenhofer · Chase Manhattan Centre, Suite 2100 · 1201 North Market Street · Wilmington, DE 19801 · 302-622-7000

C. Barr Flinn · Young Conaway Stargatt & Taylor · The Brandywine Building, 17th Floor · 1000 West Street · P.O. Box 391 · Wilmington, DE 19899-0391 · 302-571-6600

Anne C. Foster · Richards Layton & Finger · One Rodney Square · 920 North King Street · P.O. Box 551 Wilmington, DE 19899-0551 · 302-651-7700

Joel Friedlander · Bouchard Margules & Friedlander · 222 Delaware Avenue, Suite 1400 · Wilmington, DE 19801 · 302-573-3500

Henry E. Gallagher, Jr. · Connolly Bove Lodge & Hutz · http://www.cblh.com · 1007 North Orange Street · P.O. Box 2207 · Wilmington, DE 19899-2207 · 302-658-9141

Stuart M. Grant · Grant & Eisenhofer · Chase Manhattan Centre, Suite 2100 · 1201 North Market Street Wilmington, DE 19801 · 302-622-7000

James S. Green VI · Seitz, Van Ogtrop & Green · 222 Delaware Avenue, Suite 1500 · P.O. Box 68 · Wilmington, DE 19899 · 302-888-0600

Michael Hanrahan · Prickett, Jones & Elliott · 1310 King Street · P.O. Box 1328 · Wilmington, DE 19899 302-888-6500

Richard L. Horwitz · Potter Anderson & Corroon · http://www.potteranderson.com · Hercules Plaza, Sixth Floor · 1313 North Market Street · P.O. Box 951 · Wilmington, DE 19899-0951 · 302-984-6000

Stephen E. Jenkins · Ashby & Geddes · 500 Delaware Avenue, Eighth Floor · P.O. Box 1150 · Wilmington, DE 19899 · 302-654-1888

William M. Lafferty · Morris, Nichols, Arsht & Tunnell · Chase Manhattan Centre, 18th Floor · 1201 North Market Street · P.O. Box 1347 · Wilmington, DE 19899-1347 · 302-658-9200

Lewis H. Lazarus · Morris James · 500 Delaware Avenue, Suite 1500 · P.O. Box 2306 · Wilmington, DE 19899-2306 · 302-888-6800

Martin S. Lessner · Young Conaway Stargatt & Taylor · The Brandywine Building, 17th Floor · 1000 West Street · P.O. Box 391 · Wilmington, DE 19899-0391 · 302-571-6600

David C. McBride · ⑩ · Young Conaway Stargatt & Taylor · The Brandywine Building, 17th Floor · 1000 West Street · P.O. Box 391 · Wilmington, DE 19899-0391 · 302-571-6600

Edward M. McNally · Morris James · 500 Delaware Avenue, Suite 1500 · P.O. Box 2306 · Wilmington, DE 19899-2306 · 302-888-6800

Kenneth J. Nachbar · Morris, Nichols, Arsht & Tunnell · Chase Manhattan Centre, 18th Floor · 1201 North Market Street · P.O. Box 1347 · Wilmington, DE 19899-1347 · 302-658-9200

Stephen C. Norman · Potter Anderson & Corroon · http://www.potteranderson.com · Hercules Plaza, Sixth Floor · 1313 North Market Street · P.O. Box 951 · Wilmington, DE 19899-0951 · 302-984-6000

Robert K. Payson · ㉕ · Potter Anderson & Corroon · http://www.potteranderson.com · Hercules Plaza, Sixth Floor · 1313 North Market Street · P.O. Box 951 · Wilmington, DE 19899-0951 · 302-984-6000

Donald E. Reid · Morris, Nichols, Arsht & Tunnell · Chase Manhattan Centre, 18th Floor · 1201 North Market Street · P.O. Box 1347 · Wilmington, DE 19899-1347 · 302-658-9200

Joseph A. Rosenthal · ⑩ · Rosenthal, Monhait & Goddess · 919 Market Street, Suite 1401 · P.O. Box 1070 · Wilmington, DE 19899-1070 · 302-656-4433

R. Judson Scaggs, Jr. · Morris, Nichols, Arsht & Tunnell · Chase Manhattan Centre, 18th Floor · 1201 North Market Street · P.O. Box 1347 · Wilmington, DE 19899-1347 · 302-658-9200

Collins J. Seitz, Jr. · Connolly Bove Lodge & Hutz · http://www.cblh.com · 1007 North Orange Street · P.O. Box 2207 · Wilmington, DE 19899-2207 · 302-658-9141

James Semple · Morris James · 500 Delaware Avenue, Suite 1500 · P.O. Box 2306 · Wilmington, DE 19899-2306 · 302-888-6800

Kevin R. Shannon · Potter Anderson & Corroon · http://www.potteranderson.com · Hercules Plaza, Sixth Floor · 1313 North Market Street · P.O. Box 951 · Wilmington, DE 19899-0951 · 302-984-6000

Bruce L. Silverstein · Young Conaway Stargatt & Taylor · The Brandywine Building, 17th Floor · 1000 West Street · P.O. Box 391 · Wilmington, DE 19899-0391 · 302-571-6600

A. Gilchrist Sparks III · ㉕ · Morris, Nichols, Arsht & Tunnell · Chase Manhattan Centre, 18th Floor · 1201 North Market Street · P.O. Box 1347 · Wilmington, DE 19899-1347 · 302-658-9200

Pamela S. Tikellis · Chimicles & Tikellis · One Rodney Square · P.O. Box 1035 · Wilmington, DE 19899 302-656-2500

Peter J. Walsh, Jr. · Potter Anderson & Corroon · http://www.potteranderson.com · Hercules Plaza, Sixth Floor · 1313 North Market Street · P.O. Box 951 · Wilmington, DE 19899-0951 · 302-984-6000

Gregory P. Williams · Richards Layton & Finger · One Rodney Square · 920 North King Street · P.O. Box 551 · Wilmington, DE 19899-0551 · 302-651-7700

Donald J. Wolfe, Jr. · ⑩ · Potter Anderson & Corroon · http://www.potteranderson.com · Hercules Plaza, Sixth Floor · 1313 North Market Street · P.O. Box 951 · Wilmington, DE 19899-0951 · 302-984-6000

CORPORATE GOVERNANCE AND COMPLIANCE LAW

Wilmington

E. Norman Veasey · Weil Gotshal & Manges · 1201 North Market Street, Suite 1402 · Wilmington, DE 19801 · 302-656-1410

Wilmington

Jon E. Abramczyk · Morris, Nichols, Arsht & Tunnell · Chase Manhattan Centre, 18th Floor · 1201 North Market Street · P.O. Box 1347 · Wilmington, DE 19899-1347 · 302-658-9200

Frederick H. Alexander · Morris, Nichols, Arsht & Tunnell · Chase Manhattan Centre, 18th Floor · 1201 North Market Street · P.O. Box 1347 · Wilmington, DE 19899-1347 · 302-658-9200

Paul M. Altman · Richards Layton & Finger · One Rodney Square · 920 North King Street · P.O. Box 551 Wilmington, DE 19899-0551 · 302-651-7700

Lawrence C. Ashby · Ashby & Geddes · 500 Delaware Avenue, Eighth Floor · P.O. Box 1150 · Wilmington, DE 19899 · 302-654-1888

R. Franklin Balotti · ㉕ · Richards Layton & Finger · One Rodney Square · 920 North King Street · P.O. Box 551 · Wilmington, DE 19899-0551 · 302-651-7700

Andre G. Bouchard · Bouchard Margules & Friedlander · 222 Delaware Avenue, Suite 1400 · Wilmington, DE 19801 · 302-573-3500

David B. Brown · Potter Anderson & Corroon · http://www.potteranderson.com · Hercules Plaza, Sixth Floor · 1313 North Market Street · P.O. Box 951 · Wilmington, DE 19899-0951 · 302-984-6000

Grover C. Brown · ⑩ · Gordon, Fournaris & Mammarella · 1925 Lovering Avenue · Wilmington, DE 19806 · 302-652-2900

Donald A. Bussard · ⑩ · Richards Layton & Finger · One Rodney Square · 920 North King Street · P.O. Box 551 · Wilmington, DE 19899-0551 · 302-651-7700

P. Clarkson Collins, Jr. · Morris James · 500 Delaware Avenue, Suite 1500 · P.O. Box 2306 · Wilmington, DE 19899-2306 · 302-888-6800

Wendell Fenton · ⑩ · Richards Layton & Finger · One Rodney Square · 920 North King Street · P.O. Box 551 · Wilmington, DE 19899-0551 · 302-651-7700

Jesse A. Finkelstein · ⑩ · Richards Layton & Finger · One Rodney Square · 920 North King Street · P.O. Box 551 · Wilmington, DE 19899-0551 · 302-651-7700

Anne C. Foster · Richards Layton & Finger · One Rodney Square · 920 North King Street · P.O. Box 551 Wilmington, DE 19899-0551 · 302-651-7700

Joel Friedlander · Bouchard Margules & Friedlander · 222 Delaware Avenue, Suite 1400 · Wilmington, DE 19801 · 302-573-3500

Henry E. Gallagher, Jr. · Connolly Bove Lodge & Hutz · http://www.cblh.com · 1007 North Orange Street · P.O. Box 2207 · Wilmington, DE 19899-2207 · 302-658-9141

Mark J. Gentile · Richards Layton & Finger · One Rodney Square · 920 North King Street · P.O. Box 551 Wilmington, DE 19899-0551 · 302-651-7700

Michael D. Goldman · ⑩ · Potter Anderson & Corroon · http://www.potteranderson.com · Hercules Plaza, Sixth Floor · 1313 North Market Street · P.O. Box 951 · Wilmington, DE 19899-0951 · 302-984-6000

Stuart M. Grant · Grant & Eisenhofer · Chase Manhattan Centre, Suite 2100 · 1201 North Market Street Wilmington, DE 19801 · 302-622-7000

John F. Grossbauer · Potter Anderson & Corroon · http://www.potteranderson.com · Hercules Plaza, Sixth Floor · 1313 North Market Street · P.O. Box 951 · Wilmington, DE 19899-0951 · 302-984-6000

David Ley Hamilton · Morris, Nichols, Arsht & Tunnell · Chase Manhattan Centre, 18th Floor · 1201 North Market Street · P.O. Box 1347 · Wilmington, DE 19899-1347 · 302-658-9200

William J. Haubert · Richards Layton & Finger · One Rodney Square · 920 North King Street · P.O. Box 551 · Wilmington, DE 19899-0551 · 302-651-7700

Louis G. Hering · Morris, Nichols, Arsht & Tunnell · Chase Manhattan Centre, 18th Floor · 1201 North Market Street · P.O. Box 1347 · Wilmington, DE 19899-1347 · 302-658-9200

Kurt M. Heyman · Proctor Heyman · 1116 West Street · Wilmington, DE 19801 · 302-472-7300

James L. Holzman · Prickett, Jones & Elliott · 1310 King Street · P.O. Box 1328 · Wilmington, DE 19899 302-888-6500

Stephen E. Jenkins · Ashby & Geddes · 500 Delaware Avenue, Eighth Floor · P.O. Box 1150 · Wilmington, DE 19899 · 302-654-1888

Andrew M. Johnston · Morris, Nichols, Arsht & Tunnell · Chase Manhattan Centre, 18th Floor · 1201 North Market Street · P.O. Box 1347 · Wilmington, DE 19899-1347 · 302-658-9200

John F. Johnston · Morris, Nichols, Arsht & Tunnell · Chase Manhattan Centre, 18th Floor · 1201 North Market Street · P.O. Box 1347 · Wilmington, DE 19899-1347 · 302-658-9200

William D. Johnston · Young Conaway Stargatt & Taylor · The Brandywine Building, 17th Floor · 1000 West Street · P.O. Box 391 · Wilmington, DE 19899-0391 · 302-571-6600

William M. Lafferty · Morris, Nichols, Arsht & Tunnell · Chase Manhattan Centre, 18th Floor · 1201 North Market Street · P.O. Box 1347 · Wilmington, DE 19899-1347 · 302-658-9200

J. Travis Laster · Abrams & Laster · 20 Montchanin Road, Suite 200 · Wilmington, DE 19807 · 302-778-1000

David C. McBride · ⑩ · Young Conaway Stargatt & Taylor · The Brandywine Building, 17th Floor · 1000 West Street · P.O. Box 391 · Wilmington, DE 19899-0391 · 302-571-6600

Elizabeth M. McGeever · Prickett, Jones & Elliott · 1310 King Street · P.O. Box 1328 · Wilmington, DE 19899 · 302-888-6500

Edward M. McNally · Morris James · 500 Delaware Avenue, Suite 1500 · P.O. Box 2306 · Wilmington, DE 19899-2306 · 302-888-6800

Kenneth J. Nachbar · Morris, Nichols, Arsht & Tunnell · Chase Manhattan Centre, 18th Floor · 1201 North Market Street · P.O. Box 1347 · Wilmington, DE 19899-1347 · 302-658-9200

Matthew J. O'Toole · Stevens & Lee · 1105 North Market Street, Seventh Floor · Wilmington, DE 19801 · 302-654-5180

Robert K. Payson · ㉕ · Potter Anderson & Corroon · http://www.potteranderson.com · Hercules Plaza, Sixth Floor · 1313 North Market Street · P.O. Box 951 · Wilmington, DE 19899-0951 · 302-984-6000

Robert B. Pincus · Skadden, Arps, Slate, Meagher & Flom · One Rodney Square, Seventh Floor · P.O. Box 636 · Wilmington, DE 19899-0636 · 302-651-3000

Michael A. Pittenger · Potter Anderson & Corroon · http://www.potteranderson.com · Hercules Plaza, Sixth Floor · 1313 North Market Street · P.O. Box 951 · Wilmington, DE 19899-0951 · 302-984-6000

Vernon R. Proctor · Proctor Heyman · 1116 West Street · Wilmington, DE 19801 · 302-472-7300

Collins J. Seitz, Jr. · Connolly Bove Lodge & Hutz · http://www.cblh.com · 1007 North Orange Street · P.O. Box 2207 · Wilmington, DE 19899-2207 · 302-658-9141

Kevin R. Shannon · Potter Anderson & Corroon · http://www.potteranderson.com · Hercules Plaza, Sixth Floor · 1313 North Market Street · P.O. Box 951 · Wilmington, DE 19899-0951 · 302-984-6000

Bruce L. Silverstein · Young Conaway Stargatt & Taylor · The Brandywine Building, 17th Floor · 1000 West Street · P.O. Box 391 · Wilmington, DE 19899-0391 · 302-571-6600

John H. Small · ⑩ · Prickett, Jones & Elliott · 1310 King Street · P.O. Box 1328 · Wilmington, DE 19899 302-888-6500

A. Gilchrist Sparks III · ㉕ · Morris, Nichols, Arsht & Tunnell · Chase Manhattan Centre, 18th Floor · 1201 North Market Street · P.O. Box 1347 · Wilmington, DE 19899-1347 · 302-658-9200

Robert L. Symonds, Jr. · Stevens & Lee · 1105 North Market Street, Seventh Floor · Wilmington, DE 19801 · 302-654-5180

David J. Teklits · Morris, Nichols, Arsht & Tunnell · Chase Manhattan Centre, 18th Floor · 1201 North Market Street · P.O. Box 1347 · Wilmington, DE 19899-1347 · 302-658-9200

Michael B. Tumas · ⑩ · Potter Anderson & Corroon · http://www.potteranderson.com · Hercules Plaza, Sixth Floor · 1313 North Market Street · P.O. Box 951 · Wilmington, DE 19899-0951 · 302-984-6000

Walter C. Tuthill · Morris, Nichols, Arsht & Tunnell · Chase Manhattan Centre, 18th Floor · 1201 North Market Street · P.O. Box 1347 · Wilmington, DE 19899-1347 · 302-658-9200

Gregory V. Varallo · Richards Layton & Finger · One Rodney Square · 920 North King Street · P.O. Box 551 · Wilmington, DE 19899-0551 · 302-651-7700

Peter J. Walsh, Jr. · Potter Anderson & Corroon · http://www.potteranderson.com · Hercules Plaza, Sixth Floor · 1313 North Market Street · P.O. Box 951 · Wilmington, DE 19899-0951 · 302-984-6000

Scott E. Waxman · Potter Anderson & Corroon · http://www.potteranderson.com · Hercules Plaza, Sixth Floor · 1313 North Market Street · P.O. Box 951 · Wilmington, DE 19899-0951 · 302-984-6000

Edward P. Welch · Skadden, Arps, Slate, Meagher & Flom · One Rodney Square, Seventh Floor · P.O. Box 636 · Wilmington, DE 19899-0636 · 302-651-3000

Gregory P. Williams · Richards Layton & Finger · One Rodney Square · 920 North King Street · P.O. Box 551 · Wilmington, DE 19899-0551 · 302-651-7700

Donald J. Wolfe, Jr. · ⑩ · Potter Anderson & Corroon · http://www.potteranderson.com · Hercules Plaza, Sixth Floor · 1313 North Market Street · P.O. Box 951 · Wilmington, DE 19899-0951 · 302-984-6000

DUI/DWI DEFENSE

Georgetown

Eric G. Mooney · Eric G. Mooney · 11 South Race Street · Georgetown, DE 19947 · 302-856-3070

Wilmington

Louis B. Ferrara · Ferrara Haley Bevis & Collins · 1716 Wawaset Street · Wilmington, DE 19806 · 302-656-7247

E. Dan Lyons · ⑩ · The Lyons Law Firm · 1526 Gilpin Avenue · P.O. Box 579 · Wilmington, DE 19899 · 302-777-5698

ELDER LAW

Wilmington

Mary M. Culley · Morris James · 500 Delaware Avenue, Suite 1500 · P.O. Box 2306 · Wilmington, DE 19899-2306 · 302-888-6800

EMPLOYEE BENEFITS LAW

Wilmington

Timothy J. Snyder · Young Conaway Stargatt & Taylor · The Brandywine Building, 17th Floor · 1000 West Street · P.O. Box 391 · Wilmington, DE 19899-0391 · 302-571-6600

ENVIRONMENTAL LAW

Dover

F. Michael Parkowski · ⑳ · Parkowski, Guerke & Swayze · 116 West Water Street · P.O. Box 598 · Dover, DE 19903-0598 · 302-678-3262

Wilmington

W. Harding Drane, Jr. · Potter Anderson & Corroon · http://www.potteranderson.com · Hercules Plaza, Sixth Floor · 1313 North Market Street · P.O. Box 951 · Wilmington, DE 19899-0951 · 302-984-6000

Anthony G. Flynn · ⑩ · Young Conaway Stargatt & Taylor · The Brandywine Building, 17th Floor · 1000 West Street · P.O. Box 391 · Wilmington, DE 19899-0391 · 302-571-6600

Stephen E. Herrmann · ⑳ · Richards Layton & Finger · One Rodney Square · 920 North King Street · P.O. Box 551 · Wilmington, DE 19899-0551 · 302-651-7700

Timothy Jay Houseal · Young Conaway Stargatt & Taylor · The Brandywine Building, 17th Floor · 1000 West Street · P.O. Box 391 · Wilmington, DE 19899-0391 · 302-571-6600

R. Judson Scaggs, Jr. · Morris, Nichols, Arsht & Tunnell · Chase Manhattan Centre, 18th Floor · 1201 North Market Street · P.O. Box 1347 · Wilmington, DE 19899-1347 · 302-658-9200

Robert W. Whetzel · ⑩ · Richards Layton & Finger · One Rodney Square · 920 North King Street · P.O. Box 551 · Wilmington, DE 19899-0551 · 302-651-7700

FAMILY LAW

Dover

Clay T. Jester · Parkowski, Guerke & Swayze · 116 West Water Street · P.O. Box 598 · Dover, DE 19903-0598 · 302-678-3262

Gerald I.H. Street · Street & Ellis · 426 South State Street · Dover, DE 19901 · 302-735-8400

Hockessin

Jennifer A. Hartnett · Hartnett, Levine & Hartnett · 7301 Lancaster Pike · P.O. Box 220 · Hockessin, DE 19707 · 302-239-4220

Norman E. Levine · Hartnett, Levine & Hartnett · 7301 Lancaster Pike · P.O. Box 220 · Hockessin, DE 19707 · 302-239-4220

Wilmington

Gerald Z. Berkowitz · ⑳ · Berkowitz, Schagrin, Cooper & Dryden · 1218 North Market Street · P.O. Box 1632 · Wilmington, DE 19801 · 302-652-3155

Curtis P. Bounds · Bayard · 222 Delaware Avenue, Suite 900 · P.O. Box 25130 · Wilmington, DE 19899 · 302-655-5000

Christine K. Demsey · Christine K. Demsey · 1328 King Street · Wilmington, DE 19801-3234 · 302-428-3190

Shawn Dougherty · Weik, Nitsche, Dougherty & Componovo · 1300 North Grant Avenue, Suite 101 · Wilmington, DE 19806 · 302-655-4040

Daniel F. Kelleher · ⑩ · Kelleher & Laffey · 1509 Gilpin Avenue · Wilmington, DE 19806 · 302-651-7999

Gretchen S. Knight · Morris James · 500 Delaware Avenue, Suite 1500 · P.O. Box 2306 · Wilmington, DE 19899-2306 · 302-888-6800

H. Alfred Tarrant, Jr. · ㉕ · Cooch and Taylor · 1000 West Street, 10th Floor · Wilmington, DE 19801 · 302-652-3641

FIRST AMENDMENT LAW

Wilmington

Richard G. Elliott, Jr. · ⑩ · Richards Layton & Finger · One Rodney Square · 920 North King Street · P.O. Box 551 · Wilmington, DE 19899-0551 · 302-651-7700

GAMING LAW

Wilmington

Robert L. Thomas · ⑩ · Young Conaway Stargatt & Taylor · The Brandywine Building, 17th Floor · 1000 West Street · P.O. Box 391 · Wilmington, DE 19899-0391 · 302-571-6600

GOVERNMENT RELATIONS LAW

Wilmington

Michael Houghton · Morris, Nichols, Arsht & Tunnell · Chase Manhattan Centre, 18th Floor · 1201 North Market Street · P.O. Box 1347 · Wilmington, DE 19899-1347 · 302-658-9200

HEALTH CARE LAW

Wilmington

Jennifer Gimler Brady · Potter Anderson & Corroon · http://www.potteranderson.com · Hercules Plaza, Sixth Floor · 1313 North Market Street · P.O. Box 951 · Wilmington, DE 19899-0951 · 302-984-6000

Walter P. McEvilly, Jr. · ⑩ · Stevens & Lee · 1105 North Market Street, Seventh Floor · Wilmington, DE 19801 · 302-654-5180

Peter J. Shanley · ⑩ · Shanley & Associates · 800 Delaware Avenue, Tenth Floor · P.O. Box 2283 · Wilmington, DE 19899-2283 · 302-691-6838

William J. Wade · Richards Layton & Finger · One Rodney Square · 920 North King Street · P.O. Box 551 · Wilmington, DE 19899-0551 · 302-651-7700

INFORMATION TECHNOLOGY LAW

Wilmington

Kevin F. Brady · Connolly Bove Lodge & Hutz · http://www.cblh.com · 1007 North Orange Street · P.O. Box 2207 · Wilmington, DE 19899-2207 · 302-658-9141

William R. Denny · Potter Anderson & Corroon · http://www.potteranderson.com · Hercules Plaza, Sixth Floor · 1313 North Market Street · P.O. Box 951 · Wilmington, DE 19899-0951 · 302-984-6000

Richard K. Herrmann · Morris James · 500 Delaware Avenue, Suite 1500 · P.O. Box 2306 · Wilmington, DE 19899-2306 · 302-888-6800

INSURANCE LAW

Hockessin

John S. Spadaro · John Sheehan Spadaro · 724 Yorklyn Road, Suite 375 · Hockessin, DE 19707 · 302-235-7745

Wilmington

Kevin F. Brady · Connolly Bove Lodge & Hutz · http://www.cblh.com · 1007 North Orange Street · P.O. Box 2207 · Wilmington, DE 19899-2207 · 302-658-9141

W. Harding Drane, Jr. · Potter Anderson & Corroon · http://www.potteranderson.com · Hercules Plaza, Sixth Floor · 1313 North Market Street · P.O. Box 951 · Wilmington, DE 19899-0951 · 302-984-6000

Anthony G. Flynn · ⑩ · Young Conaway Stargatt & Taylor · The Brandywine Building, 17th Floor · 1000 West Street · P.O. Box 391 · Wilmington, DE 19899-0391 · 302-571-6600

Richard L. Horwitz · Potter Anderson & Corroon · http://www.potteranderson.com · Hercules Plaza, Sixth Floor · 1313 North Market Street · P.O. Box 951 · Wilmington, DE 19899-0951 · 302-984-6000

Timothy Jay Houseal · Young Conaway Stargatt & Taylor · The Brandywine Building, 17th Floor · 1000 West Street · P.O. Box 391 · Wilmington, DE 19899-0391 · 302-571-6600

John E. James · Potter Anderson & Corroon · http://www.potteranderson.com · Hercules Plaza, Sixth Floor · 1313 North Market Street · P.O. Box 951 · Wilmington, DE 19899-0951 · 302-984-6000

Robert J. Katzenstein · Smith Katzenstein & Furlow · The Corporate Plaza, Suite 1000 · 800 Delaware Avenue · P.O. Box 410 · Wilmington, DE 19899-0410 · 302-652-8400

Mary B. Matterer · Morris James · 500 Delaware Avenue, Suite 1500 · P.O. Box 2306 · Wilmington, DE 19899-2306 · 302-888-6800

INTELLECTUAL PROPERTY LAW

Wilmington

Steven J. Balick · Ashby & Geddes · 500 Delaware Avenue, Eighth Floor · P.O. Box 1150 · Wilmington, DE 19899 · 302-654-1888

Jack B. Blumenfeld · ⑩ · Morris, Nichols, Arsht & Tunnell · Chase Manhattan Centre, 18th Floor · 1201 North Market Street · P.O. Box 1347 · Wilmington, DE 19899-1347 · 302-658-9200

Arthur G. Connolly, Jr. · ⑩ · Connolly Bove Lodge & Hutz · http://www.cblh.com · 1007 North Orange Street · P.O. Box 2207 · Wilmington, DE 19899-2207 · 302-658-9141

Frederick L. Cottrell III · Richards Layton & Finger · One Rodney Square · 920 North King Street · P.O. Box 551 · Wilmington, DE 19899-0551 · 302-651-7700

Paul E. Crawford · ⑩ · Connolly Bove Lodge & Hutz · http://www.cblh.com · 1007 North Orange Street · P.O. Box 2207 · Wilmington, DE 19899-2207 · 302-658-9141

Francis DiGiovanni · Connolly Bove Lodge & Hutz · http://www.cblh.com · 1007 North Orange Street · P.O. Box 2207 · Wilmington, DE 19899-2207 · 302-658-9141

Mary B. Graham · Morris, Nichols, Arsht & Tunnell · Chase Manhattan Centre, 18th Floor · 1201 North Market Street · P.O. Box 1347 · Wilmington, DE 19899-1347 · 302-658-9200

Rudolf E. Hutz · ⑩ · Connolly Bove Lodge & Hutz · http://www.cblh.com · 1007 North Orange Street · P.O. Box 2207 · Wilmington, DE 19899-2207 · 302-658-9141

William J. Marsden · Fish & Richardson · 919 North Market Street, Suite 1100 · P.O. Box 1114 · Wilmington, DE 19899-1114 · 302-652-5070

Maryellen Noreika · Morris, Nichols, Arsht & Tunnell · Chase Manhattan Centre, 18th Floor · 1201 North Market Street · P.O. Box 1347 · Wilmington, DE 19899-1347 · 302-658-9200

Gerard M. O'Rourke · Womble Carlyle Sandridge & Rice · 222 Delaware Avenue, 15th Floor · Wilmington, DE 19801 · 302-252-4320

Patricia Smink Rogowski · Connolly Bove Lodge & Hutz · http://www.cblh.com · 1007 North Orange Street · P.O. Box 2207 · Wilmington, DE 19899-2207 · 302-658-9141

Collins J. Seitz, Jr. · Connolly Bove Lodge & Hutz · http://www.cblh.com · 1007 North Orange Street · P.O. Box 2207 · Wilmington, DE 19899-2207 · 302-658-9141

Rodger D. Smith II · Morris, Nichols, Arsht & Tunnell · Chase Manhattan Centre, 18th Floor · 1201 North Market Street · P.O. Box 1347 · Wilmington, DE 19899-1347 · 302-658-9200

LABOR AND EMPLOYMENT LAW

Wilmington

Gary W. Aber · Aber, Baker & Over · First Federal Plaza, Suite 600 · 702 King Street · P.O. Box 1675 · Wilmington, DE 19899 · 302-472-4900

Victor F. Battaglia · ⑳ · Biggs and Battaglia · 921 Orange Street · P.O. Box 1489 · Wilmington, DE 19899-1489 · 302-655-9677

William W. Bowser · Young Conaway Stargatt & Taylor · The Brandywine Building, 17th Floor · 1000 West Street · P.O. Box 391 · Wilmington, DE 19899-0391 · 302-571-6600

Matthew F. Boyer · Connolly Bove Lodge & Hutz · http://www.cblh.com · 1007 North Orange Street · P.O. Box 2207 · Wilmington, DE 19899-2207 · 302-658-9141

Perry F. Goldlust · Law Offices of Perry Goldlust · 1426 North Clayton Street · Wilmington, DE 19806 · 302-483-2000

Scott A. Holt · Young Conaway Stargatt & Taylor · The Brandywine Building, 17th Floor · 1000 West Street · P.O. Box 391 · Wilmington, DE 19899-0391 · 302-571-6600

Jennifer C. Jauffret · Richards Layton & Finger · One Rodney Square · 920 North King Street · P.O. Box 551 · Wilmington, DE 19899-0551 · 302-651-7700

Kathleen Furey McDonough · Potter Anderson & Corroon · http://www.potteranderson.com · Hercules Plaza, Sixth Floor · 1313 North Market Street · P.O. Box 951 · Wilmington, DE 19899-0951 · 302-984-6000

Thomas S. Neuberger · The Neuberger Firm · Two East Seventh Street, Suite 302 · Wilmington, DE 19801-3707 · 302-655-0582

Sheldon N. Sandler · 25 · Young Conaway Stargatt & Taylor · The Brandywine Building, 17th Floor · 1000 West Street · P.O. Box 391 · Wilmington, DE 19899-0391 · 302-571-6600

Wendy K. Voss · Potter Anderson & Corroon · http://www.potteranderson.com · Hercules Plaza, Sixth Floor · 1313 North Market Street · P.O. Box 951 · Wilmington, DE 19899-0951 · 302-984-6000

Richard R. Wier, Jr. · Richard R. Wier, Jr. · Two Mill Road, Suite 200 · Wilmington, DE 19806 · 302-888-3222

David H. Williams · Morris James · 500 Delaware Avenue, Suite 1500 · P.O. Box 2306 · Wilmington, DE 19899-2306 · 302-888-6800

Barry M. Willoughby · 10 · Young Conaway Stargatt & Taylor · The Brandywine Building, 17th Floor · 1000 West Street · P.O. Box 391 · Wilmington, DE 19899-0391 · 302-571-6600

LAND USE & ZONING LAW

Dover

John W. Paradee · Prickett, Jones & Elliott · 11 North State Street · Dover, DE 19901 · 302-674-3841

Georgetown

James A. Fuqua, Jr. · Fuqua and Yori · 28 The Circle · Georgetown, DE 19947 · 302-856-7777

Wilmington

Richard A. Forsten · Buchanan Ingersoll & Rooney · http://www.bipc.com · The Brandywine Building, Suite 1410 · 1000 West Street · Wilmington, DE 19801-1054 · 302-552-4200

Lisa B. Goodman · Young Conaway Stargatt & Taylor · The Brandywine Building, 17th Floor · 1000 West Street · P.O. Box 391 · Wilmington, DE 19899-0391 · 302-571-6600

Donald Nelson Isken · 10 · Morris, Nichols, Arsht & Tunnell · Chase Manhattan Centre, 18th Floor · 1201 North Market Street · P.O. Box 1347 · Wilmington, DE 19899-1347 · 302-658-9200

William E. Manning · Buchanan Ingersoll & Rooney · http://www.bipc.com · The Brandywine Building, Suite 1410 · 1000 West Street · Wilmington, DE 19801-1054 · 302-552-4200

Pamela J. Scott · Saul Ewing · 222 Delaware Avenue, Suite 1200 · P.O. Box 1266 · Wilmington, DE 19899 · 302-421-6800

Wendie C. Stabler · Saul Ewing · 222 Delaware Avenue, Suite 1200 · P.O. Box 1266 · Wilmington, DE 19899 · 302-421-6800

MASS TORT LITIGATION

Wilmington

Somers S. Price · Potter Anderson & Corroon · http://www.potteranderson.com · Hercules Plaza, Sixth Floor · 1313 North Market Street · P.O. Box 951 · Wilmington, DE 19899-0951 · 302-984-6000

MEDICAL MALPRACTICE LAW

Wilmington

Ben T. Castle · ⑳ · Young Conaway Stargatt & Taylor · The Brandywine Building, 17th Floor · 1000 West Street · P.O. Box 391 · Wilmington, DE 19899-0391 · 302-571-6600

Bartholomew J. Dalton · ⑩ · Dalton & Associates · 1106 West 10th Street · Wilmington, DE 19806 · 302-652-2050

Mason E. Turner, Jr. · ⑳ · Prickett, Jones & Elliott · 1310 King Street · P.O. Box 1328 · Wilmington, DE 19899 · 302-888-6500

Richard A. Zappa · Young Conaway Stargatt & Taylor · The Brandywine Building, 17th Floor · 1000 West Street · P.O. Box 391 · Wilmington, DE 19899-0391 · 302-571-6600

MERGERS & ACQUISITIONS LAW

Wilmington

Frederick H. Alexander · Morris, Nichols, Arsht & Tunnell · Chase Manhattan Centre, 18th Floor · 1201 North Market Street · P.O. Box 1347 · Wilmington, DE 19899-1347 · 302-658-9200

R. Franklin Balotti · ㉕ · Richards Layton & Finger · One Rodney Square · 920 North King Street · P.O. Box 551 · Wilmington, DE 19899-0551 · 302-651-7700

John F. Johnston · Morris, Nichols, Arsht & Tunnell · Chase Manhattan Centre, 18th Floor · 1201 North Market Street · P.O. Box 1347 · Wilmington, DE 19899-1347 · 302-658-9200

Robert B. Pincus · Skadden, Arps, Slate, Meagher & Flom · One Rodney Square, Seventh Floor · P.O. Box 636 · Wilmington, DE 19899-0636 · 302-651-3000

A. Gilchrist Sparks III · ㉕ · Morris, Nichols, Arsht & Tunnell · Chase Manhattan Centre, 18th Floor · 1201 North Market Street · P.O. Box 1347 · Wilmington, DE 19899-1347 · 302-658-9200

Gregory P. Williams · Richards Layton & Finger · One Rodney Square · 920 North King Street · P.O. Box 551 · Wilmington, DE 19899-0551 · 302-651-7700

NON-WHITE-COLLAR CRIMINAL DEFENSE

Wilmington

Joseph A. Hurley · ⑩ · Joseph A. Hurley · http://www.joehurley.com · 1215 King Street · Wilmington, DE 19801 · 302-658-8980

Kathleen M. Jennings · WolfBlock · http://wolfblock.com · Wilmington Trust Center, Suite 1001 · 1100 North Market Street · Wilmington, DE 19801 · 302-777-5860

E. Dan Lyons · ⑩ · The Lyons Law Firm · 1526 Gilpin Avenue · P.O. Box 579 · Wilmington, DE 19899 · 302-777-5698

Eugene J. Maurer, Jr. · ⑩ · Eugene J. Maurer, Jr. · 1201-A King Street · Wilmington, DE 19801 · 302-652-7900

Charles M. Oberly III · WolfBlock · http://wolfblock.com · Wilmington Trust Center, Suite 1001 · 1100 North Market Street · Wilmington, DE 19801 · 302-777-5860

PERSONAL INJURY LITIGATION

Dover

Keith E. Donovan · Morris James · 29 North State Street, Suite 100 · Dover, DE 19901-3832 · 302-678-8815

Wayne N. Elliott · Prickett, Jones & Elliott · 11 North State Street · Dover, DE 19901 · 302-674-3841

Georgetown

Anne L. Naczi · ⑩ · Griffin & Hackett · 116 West Market Street · P.O. Box 612 · Georgetown, DE 19947 302-856-9066

Hockessin

John S. Spadaro · John Sheehan Spadaro · 724 Yorklyn Road, Suite 375 · Hockessin, DE 19707 · 302-235-7745

Newark

Edward B. Carter, Jr. · ⑩ · Kimmel, Carter, Roman & Peltz · Plaza 273 Building, Fourth Floor · 56 West Main Street · Newark, DE 19702 · 302-565-6100

Morton Richard Kimmel · Kimmel, Carter, Roman & Peltz · Plaza 273 Building, Fourth Floor · 56 West Main Street · Newark, DE 19702 · 302-565-6100

Wilmington

Sidney Balick · ⑳ · Balick & Balick · 711 King Street · Wilmington, DE 19801 · 302-658-4265

Victor F. Battaglia · ⑳ · Biggs and Battaglia · 921 Orange Street · P.O. Box 1489 · Wilmington, DE 19899-1489 · 302-655-9677

Stephen P. Casarino · Casarino, Christman & Shalk · Conectiv Building, Suite 200 · 800 North King Street · P.O. Box 1276 · Wilmington, DE 19899 · 302-594-4500

Ben T. Castle · ⑳ · Young Conaway Stargatt & Taylor · The Brandywine Building, 17th Floor · 1000 West Street · P.O. Box 391 · Wilmington, DE 19899-0391 · 302-571-6600

Bartholomew J. Dalton · ⑩ · Dalton & Associates · 1106 West 10th Street · Wilmington, DE 19806 · 302-652-2050

Richard A. DiLiberto, Jr. · Young Conaway Stargatt & Taylor · The Brandywine Building, 17th Floor · 1000 West Street · P.O. Box 391 · Wilmington, DE 19899-0391 · 302-571-6600

Dennis D. Ferri · Morris James · 500 Delaware Avenue, Suite 1500 · P.O. Box 2306 · Wilmington, DE 19899-2306 · 302-888-6800

Richard Galperin · Morris James · 500 Delaware Avenue, Suite 1500 · P.O. Box 2306 · Wilmington, DE 19899-2306 · 302-888-6800

Bruce L. Hudson · Law Office of Bruce L. Hudson · 800 North King Street, Suite 302 · Wilmington, DE 19801-3549 · 302-656-9850

Frederick W. Iobst · Young Conaway Stargatt & Taylor · The Brandywine Building, 17th Floor · 1000 West Street · P.O. Box 391 · Wilmington, DE 19899-0391 · 302-571-6600

Francis J. Jones, Jr. · Morris James · 803 North Broom Street · P.O. Box 2328 · Wilmington, DE 19899-2328 · 302-655-2599

Colin M. Shalk · Casarino, Christman & Shalk · Conectiv Building, Suite 200 · 800 North King Street · P.O. Box 1276 · Wilmington, DE 19899 · 302-594-4500

Melanie K. Sharp · Young Conaway Stargatt & Taylor · The Brandywine Building, 17th Floor · 1000 West Street · P.O. Box 391 · Wilmington, DE 19899-0391 · 302-571-6600

Mason E. Turner, Jr. · ⑳ · Prickett, Jones & Elliott · 1310 King Street · P.O. Box 1328 · Wilmington, DE 19899 · 302-888-6500

Bernard A. Van Ogtrop · ⑳ · Seitz, Van Ogtrop & Green · 222 Delaware Avenue, Suite 1500 · P.O. Box 68 · Wilmington, DE 19899 · 302-888-0600

Neilli Mullen Walsh · ⑩ · Young Conaway Stargatt & Taylor · The Brandywine Building, 17th Floor · 1000 West Street · P.O. Box 391 · Wilmington, DE 19899-0391 · 302-571-6600

Richard A. Zappa · Young Conaway Stargatt & Taylor · The Brandywine Building, 17th Floor · 1000 West Street · P.O. Box 391 · Wilmington, DE 19899-0391 · 302-571-6600

PRODUCT LIABILITY LITIGATION

Wilmington

Somers S. Price · Potter Anderson & Corroon · http://www.potteranderson.com · Hercules Plaza, Sixth Floor · 1313 North Market Street · P.O. Box 951 · Wilmington, DE 19899-0951 · 302-984-6000

REAL ESTATE LAW

Wilmington

Richard P. Beck · ㉕ · Morris James · 500 Delaware Avenue, Suite 1500 · P.O. Box 2306 · Wilmington, DE 19899-2306 · 302-888-6800

Eugene A. DiPrinzio · ⑩ · Young Conaway Stargatt & Taylor · The Brandywine Building, 17th Floor · 1000 West Street · P.O. Box 391 · Wilmington, DE 19899-0391 · 302-571-6600

William S. Gee · Saul Ewing · 222 Delaware Avenue, Suite 1200 · P.O. Box 1266 · Wilmington, DE 19899 · 302-421-6800

Lisa B. Goodman · Young Conaway Stargatt & Taylor · The Brandywine Building, 17th Floor · 1000 West Street · P.O. Box 391 · Wilmington, DE 19899-0391 · 302-571-6600

Donald Nelson Isken · ⑩ · Morris, Nichols, Arsht & Tunnell · Chase Manhattan Centre, 18th Floor · 1201 North Market Street · P.O. Box 1347 · Wilmington, DE 19899-1347 · 302-658-9200

Daniel L. Klein · ⑳ · Richards Layton & Finger · One Rodney Square · 920 North King Street · P.O. Box 551 · Wilmington, DE 19899-0551 · 302-651-7700

Robert J. Krapf · ⑩ · Richards Layton & Finger · One Rodney Square · 920 North King Street · P.O. Box 551 · Wilmington, DE 19899-0551 · 302-651-7700

Christopher J. Lamb · Pepper Hamilton · http://www.pepperlaw.com · Hercules Plaza, Suite 5100 · 1313 North Market Street · P.O. Box 1709 · Wilmington, DE 19899-1709 · 302-777-6500

Richard A. Levine · Young Conaway Stargatt & Taylor · The Brandywine Building, 17th Floor · 1000 West Street · P.O. Box 391 · Wilmington, DE 19899-0391 · 302-571-6600

Thomas Mammarella · Gordon, Fournaris & Mammarella · 1925 Lovering Avenue · Wilmington, DE 19806 · 302-652-2900

William E. Manning · Buchanan Ingersoll & Rooney · http://www.bipc.com · The Brandywine Building, Suite 1410 · 1000 West Street · Wilmington, DE 19801-1054 · 302-552-4200

Wendie C. Stabler · Saul Ewing · 222 Delaware Avenue, Suite 1200 · P.O. Box 1266 · Wilmington, DE 19899 · 302-421-6800

Larry J. Tarabicos · ⑩ · Young Conaway Stargatt & Taylor · The Brandywine Building, 17th Floor · 1000 West Street · P.O. Box 391 · Wilmington, DE 19899-0391 · 302-571-6600

Andrew P. Taylor · ⑳ · Cooch and Taylor · 1000 West Street, 10th Floor · Wilmington, DE 19801 · 302-652-3641

Robert L. Thomas · ⑩ · Young Conaway Stargatt & Taylor · The Brandywine Building, 17th Floor · 1000 West Street · P.O. Box 391 · Wilmington, DE 19899-0391 · 302-571-6600

SECURITIES LAW

Wilmington

R. Franklin Balotti · ㉕ · Richards Layton & Finger · One Rodney Square · 920 North King Street · P.O. Box 551 · Wilmington, DE 19899-0551 · 302-651-7700

Michael A. Pittenger · Potter Anderson & Corroon · http://www.potteranderson.com · Hercules Plaza, Sixth Floor · 1313 North Market Street · P.O. Box 951 · Wilmington, DE 19899-0951 · 302-984-6000

A. Gilchrist Sparks III · ㉕ · Morris, Nichols, Arsht & Tunnell · Chase Manhattan Centre, 18th Floor · 1201 North Market Street · P.O. Box 1347 · Wilmington, DE 19899-1347 · 302-658-9200

Gregory P. Williams · Richards Layton & Finger · One Rodney Square · 920 North King Street · P.O. Box 551 · Wilmington, DE 19899-0551 · 302-651-7700

STRUCTURED FINANCE LAW

Wilmington

Matthew J. O'Toole · Stevens & Lee · 1105 North Market Street, Seventh Floor · Wilmington, DE 19801 · 302-654-5180

Robert L. Symonds, Jr. · Stevens & Lee · 1105 North Market Street, Seventh Floor · Wilmington, DE 19801 · 302-654-5180

Scott E. Waxman · Potter Anderson & Corroon · http://www.potteranderson.com · Hercules Plaza, Sixth Floor · 1313 North Market Street · P.O. Box 951 · Wilmington, DE 19899-0951 · 302-984-6000

TAX LAW

Wilmington

Julian H. Baumann, Jr. · ⑩ · Richards Layton & Finger · One Rodney Square · 920 North King Street · P.O. Box 551 · Wilmington, DE 19899-0551 · 302-651-7700

F. Peter Conaty, Jr. · Richards Layton & Finger · One Rodney Square · 920 North King Street · P.O. Box 551 · Wilmington, DE 19899-0551 · 302-651-7700

Peter S. Gordon · ⑩ · Gordon, Fournaris & Mammarella · 1925 Lovering Avenue · Wilmington, DE 19806 · 302-652-2900

Jerome K. Grossman · ⑩ · Young Conaway Stargatt & Taylor · The Brandywine Building, 17th Floor · 1000 West Street · P.O. Box 391 · Wilmington, DE 19899-0391 · 302-571-6600

William J. Martin III · Martin Conaty & Lunger · 1020 North Bancroft Parkway, Suite 100 · Wilmington, DE 19805 · 302-888-2501

Daniel P. McCollom · Morris James · 500 Delaware Avenue, Suite 1500 · P.O. Box 2306 · Wilmington, DE 19899-2306 · 302-888-6800

W. Donald Sparks II · ⑩ · Richards Layton & Finger · One Rodney Square · 920 North King Street · P.O. Box 551 · Wilmington, DE 19899-0551 · 302-651-7700

Stanford L. Stevenson III · Richards Layton & Finger · One Rodney Square · 920 North King Street · P.O. Box 551 · Wilmington, DE 19899-0551 · 302-651-7700

Leonard S. Togman · ㉕ · Potter Anderson & Corroon · http://www.potteranderson.com · Hercules Plaza, Sixth Floor · 1313 North Market Street · P.O. Box 951 · Wilmington, DE 19899-0951 · 302-984-6000

TECHNOLOGY LAW

Wilmington

William R. Denny · Potter Anderson & Corroon · http://www.potteranderson.com · Hercules Plaza, Sixth Floor · 1313 North Market Street · P.O. Box 951 · Wilmington, DE 19899-0951 · 302-984-6000

Richard K. Herrmann · Morris James · 500 Delaware Avenue, Suite 1500 · P.O. Box 2306 · Wilmington, DE 19899-2306 · 302-888-6800

TRUSTS AND ESTATES

Centreville

Michael A. Friedberg · MacElree Harvey · 5721 Kennett Pike · Centreville, DE 19807-1311 · 302-654-4454

New Castle

Beverly J. Wik · Old Capital Law Firm · The Green, 222 Delaware Street · P.O. Box 470 · New Castle, DE 19720 · 302-221-3000

Wilmington

Richard G. Bacon · 25 · Richards Layton & Finger · One Rodney Square · 920 North King Street · P.O. Box 551 · Wilmington, DE 19899-0551 · 302-651-7700

Robert W. Crowe · 25 · Cooch and Taylor · 1000 West Street, 10th Floor · Wilmington, DE 19801 · 302-652-3641

Mary M. Culley · Morris James · 500 Delaware Avenue, Suite 1500 · P.O. Box 2306 · Wilmington, DE 19899-2306 · 302-888-6800

Peter S. Gordon · 10 · Gordon, Fournaris & Mammarella · 1925 Lovering Avenue · Wilmington, DE 19806 · 302-652-2900

F. Edmund Lynch · 25 · Woloshin, Lynch, Natalie & Gagne · 3200 Concord Pike, Route 202 · P.O. Box 7329 · Wilmington, DE 19803-7329 · 302-477-3200

Richard J. A. Popper · 10 · Young Conaway Stargatt & Taylor · The Brandywine Building, 17th Floor · 1000 West Street · P.O. Box 391 · Wilmington, DE 19899-0391 · 302-571-6600

Thomas R. Pulsifer · 10 · Morris, Nichols, Arsht & Tunnell · Chase Manhattan Centre, 18th Floor · 1201 North Market Street · P.O. Box 1347 · Wilmington, DE 19899-1347 · 302-658-9200

Joanna Reiver · 20 · Gordon, Finaris & Mammarella · 1925 Lovering Avenue · Wilmington, DE 19806 · 302-652-2900

W. Donald Sparks II · 10 · Richards Layton & Finger · One Rodney Square · 920 North King Street · P.O. Box 551 · Wilmington, DE 19899-0551 · 302-651-7700

WHITE-COLLAR CRIMINAL DEFENSE

Wilmington

Joseph A. Hurley · 10 · Joseph A. Hurley · http://www.joehurley.com · 1215 King Street · Wilmington, DE 19801 · 302-658-8980

Kathleen M. Jennings · WolfBlock · http://wolfblock.com · Wilmington Trust Center, Suite 1001 · 1100 North Market Street · Wilmington, DE 19801 · 302-777-5860

E. Dan Lyons · 10 · The Lyons Law Firm · 1526 Gilpin Avenue · P.O. Box 579 · Wilmington, DE 19899 · 302-777-5698

Eugene J. Maurer, Jr. · 10 · Eugene J. Maurer, Jr. · 1201-A King Street · Wilmington, DE 19801 · 302-652-7900

Charles M. Oberly III · WolfBlock · http://wolfblock.com · Wilmington Trust Center, Suite 1001 · 1100 North Market Street · Wilmington, DE 19801 · 302-777-5860

WORKERS' COMPENSATION LAW

Dover

John J. Schmittinger · ⑩ · Schmittinger & Rodriguez · 414 South State Street · P.O. Box 497 · Dover, DE 19903-0497 · 302-674-0140

Newark

Edward B. Carter, Jr. · ⑩ · Kimmel, Carter, Roman & Peltz · Plaza 273 Building, Fourth Floor · 56 West Main Street · Newark, DE 19702 · 302-565-6100

Wilmington

Timothy A. Casey · ⑩ · Marshall, Dennehey, Warner, Coleman & Goggin · 1220 North Market Street, Suite Five · P.O. Box 130 · Wilmington, DE 19801 · 302-552-4300

George B. Heckler, Jr. · Heckler & Frabizzo · The Corporate Plaza, Suite 200 · 800 Delaware Avenue · P.O. Box 128 · Wilmington, DE 19899-0128 · 302-573-4800

Robert W. Ralston · Robert W. Ralston · 1220 North Market Street, Suite 602 · Wilmington, DE 19801 · 302-428-0758

Cassandra F. Roberts · Young Conaway Stargatt & Taylor · The Brandywine Building, 17th Floor · 1000 West Street · P.O. Box 391 · Wilmington, DE 19899-0391 · 302-571-6600

Joseph Weik · Weik, Nitsche, Dougherty & Componovo · 1300 North Grant Avenue, Suite 101 · Wilmington, DE 19806 · 302-655-4040

Michael Weiss · ⑩ · Weiss & Saville · 1220 Market Street, Suite 604 · P.O. Box 370 · Wilmington, DE 19899-0370 · 302-656-0400

Natalie Wolf · Young Conaway Stargatt & Taylor · The Brandywine Building, 17th Floor · 1000 West Street · P.O. Box 391 · Wilmington, DE 19899-0391 · 302-571-6600

DISTRICT OF COLUMBIA

ADMINISTRATIVE LAW

Washington

Terry L. Albertson · Crowell & Moring · 1001 Pennsylvania Avenue, NW · Washington, DC 20004-2595 202-624-2500

Bruce M. Bettigole · Mayer Brown · 1909 K Street, NW · Washington, DC 20006-1101 · 202-263-3000

E. Edward Bruce · Covington & Burling · 1201 Pennsylvania Avenue, NW · Washington, DC 20004-2401 · 202-662-6000

John W. Chierichella · Sheppard, Mullin, Richter & Hampton · http://www.sheppardmullin.com · 1300 I Street, NW, 11th Floor East · Washington, DC 20005 · 202-218-0000

Paul A. Cunningham · Harkins Cunningham · http://www.harkinscunningham.com · 1700 K Street, NW, Suite 400 · Washington, DC 20006-3817 · 202-973-7600

David F. Dowd · Mayer Brown · 1909 K Street, NW · Washington, DC 20006-1101 · 202-263-3000

Michele C. Farquhar · Hogan & Hartson · 555 Thirteenth Street, NW · Washington, DC 20004-1109 · 202-637-5600

Dixie Lynn Johnson · Fried, Frank, Harris, Shriver & Jacobson · 1001 Pennsylvania Avenue, NW · Washington, DC 20004-2505 · 202-639-7000

W. Stanfield Johnson · Crowell & Moring · 1001 Pennsylvania Avenue, NW · Washington, DC 20004-2595 · 202-624-2500

Robert A. Long · Covington & Burling · 1201 Pennsylvania Avenue, NW · Washington, DC 20004-2401 · 202-662-6000

Richard J. Morvillo · Mayer Brown · 1909 K Street, NW · Washington, DC 20006-1101 · 202-263-3000

Mark E. Nagle · Troutman Sanders · 401 Ninth Street, NW, Suite 1000 · Washington, DC 20004-2134 · 202-274-2950

Bernard Nash · Dickstein Shapiro · http://www.dicksteinshapiro.com · 1825 Eye Street, NW · Washington, DC 20006-5403 · 202-420-2200

Steven P. Quarles · ⑩ · Crowell & Moring · 1001 Pennsylvania Avenue, NW · Washington, DC 20004-2595 · 202-624-2500

Bert W. Rein · ⑩ · Wiley Rein · 1776 K Street, NW · Washington, DC 20006-2359 · 202-719-7000

George D. Ruttinger · Crowell & Moring · 1001 Pennsylvania Avenue, NW · Washington, DC 20004-2595 · 202-624-2500

Michael N. Sohn · ⑩ · Arnold & Porter · 555 Twelfth Street, NW · Washington, DC 20004-1206 · 202-942-5000

Thomas M. Susman · Ropes & Gray · http://www.ropesgray.com · One Metro Center, Suite 900 · 700 Twelfth Street, NW · Washington, DC 20005-3948 · 202-508-4600

Daniel E. Troy · Sidley Austin · 1501 K Street, NW · Washington, DC 20005 · 202-736-8000

Carl Lee Vacketta · DLA Piper · 500 Eighth Street, NW · Washington, DC 20004 · 202-799-4000

Edward W. Warren · Kirkland & Ellis · 655 Fifteenth Street, NW · Washington, DC 20005 · 202-879-5000

Richard E. Wiley · ㉕ · Wiley Rein · 1776 K Street, NW · Washington, DC 20006-2359 · 202-719-7000

Louis S. Zimmerman · Fulbright & Jaworski · http://www.fulbright.com · Market Square · 801 Pennsylvania Avenue, NW · Washington, DC 20004-2623 · 202-662-0200

ADVERTISING LAW

Washington

Peter C. Cassat · Dow Lohnes · http://www.dowlohnes.com · 1200 New Hampshire Avenue, NW, Suite 800 · Washington, DC 20036-6802 · 202-776-2000

Michael F. Clayton · Morgan Lewis & Bockius · 1111 Pennsylvania Avenue, NW · Washington, DC 20004 · 202-739-3000

Scott D. Dailard · Dow Lohnes · http://www.dowlohnes.com · 1200 New Hampshire Avenue, NW, Suite 800 · Washington, DC 20036-6802 · 202-776-2000

John P. Feldman · Reed Smith · East Tower, Suite 1100 · 1301 K Street, NW · Washington, DC 20005 · 202-414-9200

D. Reed Freeman, Jr. · Kelley Drye & Warren · Washington Harbour, Suite 400 · 3050 K Street, NW · Washington, DC 20007-5108 · 202-342-8400

Gary D. Hailey · Venable · http://www.venable.com · 575 Seventh Street, NW · Washington, DC 20004-1601 · 202-344-4000

Lewis Rose · Kelley Drye & Warren · Washington Harbour, Suite 400 · 3050 K Street, NW · Washington, DC 20007-5108 · 202-342-8400

John E. Villafranco · Kelley Drye & Warren · Washington Harbour, Suite 400 · 3050 K Street, NW · Washington, DC 20007-5108 · 202-342-8400

Ivan J. Wasserman · Manatt, Phelps & Phillips · One Metro Center, Suite 1100 · 700 Twelfth Street, NW Washington, DC 20005 · 202-585-6500

ALTERNATIVE DISPUTE RESOLUTION

Washington

Adrian L. Bastianelli III · Peckar, Abramson, Bastianelli & Kelley · Two Lafayette Centre, Suite 500 · 1133 Twenty-First Street, NW · Washington, DC 20036 · 202-293-8815

John Bickerman · Bickerman Dispute Resolution · 1201 New York Avenue, NW, Suite 625 · Washington, DC 20005 · 202-289-0400

William J. Bowman · Hogan & Hartson · 555 Thirteenth Street, NW · Washington, DC 20004-1109 · 202-637-5600

Mitchell F. Dolin · Covington & Burling · 1201 Pennsylvania Avenue, NW · Washington, DC 20004-2401 · 202-662-6000

Kenneth R. Feinberg · ⑳ · The Feinberg Group · The Willard Office Building, Suite 390 · 1455 Pennsylvania Avenue, NW · Washington, DC 20004-1008 · 202-371-1110

Eugene D. Gulland · Covington & Burling · 1201 Pennsylvania Avenue, NW · Washington, DC 20004-2401 · 202-662-6000

Larry D. Harris · Greenberg Traurig · http://www.gtlaw.com · 2101 L Street, NW, Suite 1000 · Washington, DC 20037 · 202-331-3100

Judith B. Ittig · Ittig & Ittig · 1420 Ninth Street, NW · Washington, DC 20001-3344 · 202-387-5508

Joshua M. Javits · ⑩ · Dispute Resolution Services · 2023 R Street, NW · Washington, DC 20009 · 202-237-2044

John E. Nolan · ㉕ · Steptoe & Johnson · http://www.steptoe.com · 1330 Connecticut Avenue, NW · Washington, DC 20036 · 202-429-3000

Robert N. Sayler · ㉕ · Covington & Burling · 1201 Pennsylvania Avenue, NW · Washington, DC 20004-2401 · 202-662-6000

William S. Sessions · Holland & Knight · http://www.hklaw.com · 2099 Pennsylvania Avenue, NW, Suite 100 · Washington, DC 20006-6801 · 202-955-3000

Linda R. Singer · JAMS · 555 Thirteenth Street, NW, Suite 400 West · Washington, DC 20004 · 202-942-9180

Stanley Sporkin · Weil Gotshal & Manges · 1300 Eye Street, NW, Suite 900 · Washington, DC 20005 · 202-682-7000

Andrew W. Stephenson · Holland & Knight · http://www.hklaw.com · 2099 Pennsylvania Avenue, NW, Suite 100 · Washington, DC 20006-6801 · 202-955-3000

Roger E. Warin · Steptoe & Johnson · http://www.steptoe.com · 1330 Connecticut Avenue, NW · Washington, DC 20036 · 202-429-3000

ANTITRUST LAW

Washington

Kenneth L. Adams · Dickstein Shapiro · http://www.dicksteinshapiro.com · 1825 Eye Street, NW · Washington, DC 20006-5403 · 202-420-2200

Harvey M. Applebaum · ⑩ · Covington & Burling · 1201 Pennsylvania Avenue, NW · Washington, DC 20004-2401 · 202-662-6000

Mary L. Azcuenaga · Heller Ehrman · 1717 Rhode Island Avenue, NW · Washington, DC 20036-3023 · 202-912-2000

William J. Baer · Arnold & Porter · 555 Twelfth Street, NW · Washington, DC 20004-1206 · 202-942-5000

Donald I. Baker · ㉕ · Baker & Miller · 2401 Pennsylvania Avenue, NW, Suite 300 · Washington, DC 20037 · 202-663-7820

Robert E. Bloch · Mayer Brown · 1909 K Street, NW · Washington, DC 20006-1101 · 202-263-3000

Jeffrey Blumenfeld · Crowell & Moring · 1001 Pennsylvania Avenue, NW · Washington, DC 20004-2595 202-624-2500

Jeffrey W. Brennan · Dechert · 1775 I Street, NW · Washington, DC 20006-2401 · 202-261-3300

John DeQ. Briggs · Howrey · 1299 Pennsylvania Avenue, NW · Washington, DC 20004 · 202-783-0800

Michael F. Brockmeyer · Frommer, Lawrence & Haug · 1667 K Street, NW · Washington, DC 20006 · 202-292-1530

W. Stephen Cannon · Constantine Cannon · 1627 Eye Street, NW, Tenth Floor · Washington, DC 20006 · 202-204-3500

George S. Cary · Cleary Gottlieb Steen & Hamilton · 2000 Pennsylvania Avenue, NW · Washington, DC 20006 · 202-974-1500

C. Benjamin Crisman, Jr. · Skadden, Arps, Slate, Meagher & Flom · 1440 New York Avenue, NW · Washington, DC 20005 · 202-371-7000

Michael Denger · Gibson, Dunn & Crutcher · 1050 Connecticut Avenue, NW · Washington, DC 20036-5306 · 202-955-8500

Paul T. Denis · Dechert · 1775 I Street, NW · Washington, DC 20006-2401 · 202-261-3300

James C. Egan, Jr. · Weil Gotshal & Manges · 1300 Eye Street, NW, Suite 900 · Washington, DC 20005 202-682-7000

Richard J. Favretto · ㉕ · Mayer Brown · 1909 K Street, NW · Washington, DC 20006-1101 · 202-263-3000

Deborah L. Feinstein · Arnold & Porter · 555 Twelfth Street, NW · Washington, DC 20004-1206 · 202-942-5000

Richard A. Feinstein · Boies, Schiller & Flexner · 5301 Wisconsin Avenue, NW · Washington, DC 20015 202-237-2727

Kathryn M. Fenton · Jones Day · 51 Louisiana Avenue, NW · Washington, DC 20001-2113 · 202-879-3939

Roger W. Fones · Morrison & Foerster · http://www.mofo.com · 2000 Pennsylvania Avenue, NW, Suite 5500 · Washington, DC 20006-1888 · 202-887-1500

Kenneth A. Gallo · Paul, Weiss, Rifkind, Wharton & Garrison · 1615 L Street, NW, Suite 1300 · Washington, DC 20036-5694 · 202-223-7300

David I. Gelfand · Cleary Gottlieb Steen & Hamilton · 2000 Pennsylvania Avenue, NW · Washington, DC 20006 · 202-974-1500

James M. Griffin · King & Spalding · 1700 Pennsylvania Avenue, NW, Suite 200 · Washington, DC 20006-4706 · 202-737-0500

Ray V. Hartwell III · Hunton & Williams · 1900 K Street, NW · Washington, DC 20006-1109 · 202-955-1500

Edward P. Henneberry · Orrick, Herrington & Sutcliffe · Columbia Center · 1152 Fifteenth Street, NW · Washington, DC 20005-1706 · 202-339-8400

Peter W. Huber · Kellogg, Huber, Hansen, Todd, Evans & Figel · Sumner Square, Suite 400 · 1615 M Street, NW · Washington, DC 20036 · 202-326-7900

Raymond A. Jacobsen, Jr. · McDermott Will & Emery · 600 Thirteenth Street, NW · Washington, DC 20005-3096 · 202-756-8000

Joseph Kattan · Gibson, Dunn & Crutcher · 1050 Connecticut Avenue, NW · Washington, DC 20036-5306 · 202-955-8500

Michael K. Kellogg · Kellogg, Huber, Hansen, Todd, Evans & Figel · Sumner Square, Suite 400 · 1615 M Street, NW · Washington, DC 20036 · 202-326-7900

Christopher J. Kelly · Mayer Brown · 1909 K Street, NW · Washington, DC 20006-1101 · 202-263-3000

Donald C. Klawiter · Mayer Brown · 1909 K Street, NW · Washington, DC 20006-1101 · 202-263-3000

William J. Kolasky · WilmerHale · http://www.wilmerhale.com · 1875 Pennsylvania Avenue, NW · Washington, DC 20006 · 202-663-6000

Steven R. Kuney · Williams & Connolly · 725 Twelfth Street, NW · Washington, DC 20005-5901 · 202-434-5000

Mark Leddy · Cleary Gottlieb Steen & Hamilton · 2000 Pennsylvania Avenue, NW · Washington, DC 20006 · 202-974-1500

Robert F. Leibenluft · Hogan & Hartson · 555 Thirteenth Street, NW · Washington, DC 20004-1109 · 202-637-5600

Arthur N. Lerner · Crowell & Moring · 1001 Pennsylvania Avenue, NW · Washington, DC 20004-2595 · 202-624-2500

Gregg H. Levy · Covington & Burling · 1201 Pennsylvania Avenue, NW · Washington, DC 20004-2401 · 202-662-6000

Abbott B. Lipsky, Jr. · Latham & Watkins · 555 Eleventh Street, NW, Suite 1000 · Washington, DC 20004-1304 · 202-637-2200

James R. Loftis III · Gibson, Dunn & Crutcher · 1050 Connecticut Avenue, NW · Washington, DC 20036-5306 · 202-955-8500

James W. Lowe · WilmerHale · http://www.wilmerhale.com · 1875 Pennsylvania Avenue, NW · Washington, DC 20006 · 202-663-6000

William C. MacLeod · Kelley Drye & Warren · Washington Harbour, Suite 400 · 3050 K Street, NW · Washington, DC 20007-5108 · 202-342-8400

John M. Majoras · Jones Day · 51 Louisiana Avenue, NW · Washington, DC 20001-2113 · 202-879-3939

Ann Malester · Weil Gotshal & Manges · 1300 Eye Street, NW, Suite 900 · Washington, DC 20005 · 202-682-7000

Janet L. McDavid · Hogan & Hartson · 555 Thirteenth Street, NW · Washington, DC 20004-1109 · 202-637-5600

A. Douglas Melamed · WilmerHale · http://www.wilmerhale.com · 1875 Pennsylvania Avenue, NW · Washington, DC 20006 · 202-663-6000

John J. Miles · Ober, Kaler, Grimes & Shriver · http://www.ober.com · 1401 H Street, NW, Suite 500 · Washington, DC 20005-3324 · 202-408-8400

Thomas Mueller · WilmerHale · http://www.wilmerhale.com · 1875 Pennsylvania Avenue, NW · Washington, DC 20006 · 202-663-6000

John M. Nannes · Skadden, Arps, Slate, Meagher & Flom · 1440 New York Avenue, NW · Washington, DC 20005 · 202-371-7000

Steven A. Newborn · Weil Gotshal & Manges · 1300 Eye Street, NW, Suite 900 · Washington, DC 20005 202-682-7000

Richard G. Parker · O'Melveny & Myers · 1625 Eye Street, NW · Washington, DC 20006-4001 · 202-383-5300

R. Hewitt Pate · Hunton & Williams · 1900 K Street, NW · Washington, DC 20006-1109 · 202-955-1500

Robert Pitofsky · Arnold & Porter · 555 Twelfth Street, NW · Washington, DC 20004-1206 · 202-942-5000

Stephen J. Pollak · ㉕ · Goodwin Procter · 901 New York Avenue, NW · Washington, DC 20001 · 202-346-4000

Mark N. Poovey · Womble Carlyle Sandridge & Rice · 1401 Eye Street, NW, Seventh Floor · Washington, DC 20005 · 202-467-6900

Mark S. Popofsky · Kaye Scholer · The McPherson Building, Suite 1100 · 901 Fifteenth Street, NW · Washington, DC 20005-2327 · 202-682-3500

Phillip A. Proger · Jones Day · 51 Louisiana Avenue, NW · Washington, DC 20001-2113 · 202-879-3939

James F. Rill · Howrey · 1299 Pennsylvania Avenue, NW · Washington, DC 20004 · 202-783-0800

Richard L. Rosen · Arnold & Porter · 555 Twelfth Street, NW · Washington, DC 20004-1206 · 202-942-5000

Douglas E. Rosenthal · ⑩ · Constantine Cannon · 1627 Eye Street, NW, Tenth Floor · Washington, DC 20006 · 202-204-3500

Charles F. Rule · Cadwalader, Wickersham & Taft · http://www.cadwalader.com · 1201 F Street, NW, Suite 1100 · Washington, DC 20004 · 202-862-2200

Robert N. Sayler · ㉕ · Covington & Burling · 1201 Pennsylvania Avenue, NW · Washington, DC 20004-2401 · 202-662-6000

Mark Clifford Schechter · Howrey · 1299 Pennsylvania Avenue, NW · Washington, DC 20004 · 202-783-0800

Marc G. Schildkraut · Howrey · 1299 Pennsylvania Avenue, NW · Washington, DC 20004 · 202-783-0800

Daniel C. Schwartz · Bryan Cave · 700 Thirteenth Street, NW · Washington, DC 20005-3960 · 202-508-6000

Benjamin S. Sharp · Perkins Coie · http://www.perkinscoie.com · 607 Fourteenth Street, NW, Suite 800 · Washington, DC 20005-2003 · 202-628-6600

John H. Shenefield · ㉕ · Morgan Lewis & Bockius · 1111 Pennsylvania Avenue, NW · Washington, DC 20004 · 202-739-3000

Joe Sims · ㉕ · Jones Day · 51 Louisiana Avenue, NW · Washington, DC 20001-2113 · 202-879-3939

Toby G. Singer · Jones Day · 51 Louisiana Avenue, NW · Washington, DC 20001-2113 · 202-879-3939

Robert A. Skitol · Drinker Biddle & Reath · 1500 K Street, NW · Washington, DC 20005-1209 · 202-842-8800

Wm. Randolph Smith · Crowell & Moring · 1001 Pennsylvania Avenue, NW · Washington, DC 20004-2595 · 202-624-2500

Michael N. Sohn · ⑩ · Arnold & Porter · 555 Twelfth Street, NW · Washington, DC 20004-1206 · 202-942-5000

Kevin R. Sullivan · King & Spalding · 1700 Pennsylvania Avenue, NW, Suite 200 · Washington, DC 20006-4706 · 202-737-0500

Steven C. Sunshine · Skadden, Arps, Slate, Meagher & Flom · 1440 New York Avenue, NW · Washington, DC 20005 · 202-371-7000

Willard K. Tom · Morgan Lewis & Bockius · 1111 Pennsylvania Avenue, NW · Washington, DC 20004 · 202-739-3000

Philip L. Verveer · Willkie Farr & Gallagher · 1875 K Street, NW · Washington, DC 20006-1238 · 202-303-1000

Theodore Voorhees, Jr. · Covington & Burling · 1201 Pennsylvania Avenue, NW · Washington, DC 20004-2401 · 202-662-6000

Douglas L. Wald · ⑩ · Arnold & Porter · 555 Twelfth Street, NW · Washington, DC 20004-1206 · 202-942-5000

James R. Weiss · K&L Gates · 1601 K Street, NW · Washington, DC 20006-1600 · 202-778-9000

Joseph F. Winterscheid · McDermott Will & Emery · 600 Thirteenth Street, NW · Washington, DC 20005-3096 · 202-756-8000

Paul Yde · Freshfields Bruckhaus Deringer · 701 Pennsylvania Avenue, NW, Suite 600 · Washington, DC 20004-2692 · 202-777-4500

APPELLATE LAW

Washington

Donald B. Ayer · Jones Day · 51 Louisiana Avenue, NW · Washington, DC 20001-2113 · 202-879-3939

Alfred F. Belcuore · Montedonico, Belcuore & Tazzara · 1020 Nineteenth Street, NW, Suite 420 · Washington, DC 20036 · 202-296-1322

Richard P. Bress · Latham & Watkins · 555 Eleventh Street, NW, Suite 1000 · Washington, DC 20004-1304 · 202-637-2200

Beth S. Brinkmann · Morrison & Foerster · http://www.mofo.com · 2000 Pennsylvania Avenue, NW, Suite 5500 · Washington, DC 20006-1888 · 202-887-1500

E. Edward Bruce · Covington & Burling · 1201 Pennsylvania Avenue, NW · Washington, DC 20004-2401 · 202-662-6000

Peter Buscemi · Morgan Lewis & Bockius · 1111 Pennsylvania Avenue, NW · Washington, DC 20004 · 202-739-3000

Louis R. Cohen · 20 · WilmerHale · http://www.wilmerhale.com · 1875 Pennsylvania Avenue, NW · Washington, DC 20006 · 202-663-6000

Charles J. Cooper · Cooper & Kirk · 1523 New Hampshire Avenue, NW · Washington, DC 20004 · 202-220-9600

Walter Dellinger · O'Melveny & Myers · 1625 Eye Street, NW · Washington, DC 20006-4001 · 202-383-5300

Edward C. DuMont · WilmerHale · http://www.wilmerhale.com · 1875 Pennsylvania Avenue, NW · Washington, DC 20006 · 202-663-6000

Donald R. Dunner · 10 · Finnegan, Henderson, Farabow, Garrett & Dunner · http://www.finnegan.com · 901 New York Avenue, NW · Washington, DC 20001-4413 · 202-408-4000

Roy Englert, Jr. · Robbins, Russell, Englert, Orseck, Untereiner & Sauber · 1801 K Street, NW, Suite 411 · Washington, DC 20006 · 202-775-4500

Miguel A. Estrada · Gibson, Dunn & Crutcher · 1050 Connecticut Avenue, NW · Washington, DC 20036-5306 · 202-955-8500

H. Bartow Farr III · Farr & Taranto · 1220 Nineteenth Street, NW, Suite 800 · Washington, DC 20036-2435 · 202-775-0184

Marc Fiedler · Koonz, McKenney, Johnson, DePaolis & Lightfoot · James Monroe Building, Suite 450 · 2001 Pennsylvania Avenue, NW · Washington, DC 20006 · 202-659-5500

Jonathan S. Franklin · Fulbright & Jaworski · http://www.fulbright.com · Market Square · 801 Pennsylvania Avenue, NW · Washington, DC 20004-2623 · 202-662-0200

David C. Frederick · Kellogg, Huber, Hansen, Todd, Evans & Figel · Sumner Square, Suite 400 · 1615 M Street, NW · Washington, DC 20036 · 202-326-7900

Kenneth S. Geller · Mayer Brown · 1909 K Street, NW · Washington, DC 20006-1101 · 202-263-3000

Laurence Gold · Bredhoff & Kaiser · 805 Fifteenth Street, NW, Suite 1000 · Washington, DC 20005 · 202-842-2600

Thomas C. Goldstein · Akin Gump Strauss Hauer & Feld · Robert S. Strauss Building · 1333 New Hampshire Avenue, NW · Washington, DC 20036-1564 · 202-887-4000

David M. Gossett · Mayer Brown · 1909 K Street, NW · Washington, DC 20006-1101 · 202-263-3000

Kent L. Jones · Sutherland · http://www.sutherland.com · 1275 Pennsylvania Avenue, NW · Washington, DC 20004-2415 · 202-383-0100

Michael K. Kellogg · Kellogg, Huber, Hansen, Todd, Evans & Figel · Sumner Square, Suite 400 · 1615 M Street, NW · Washington, DC 20036 · 202-326-7900

Jeffrey A. Lamken · Baker Botts · http://www.bakerbotts.com · The Warner Building, Suite 1300 · 1299 Pennsylvania Avenue, NW · Washington, DC 20004-2400 · 202-639-7700

Christopher Landau · Kirkland & Ellis · 655 Fifteenth Street, NW · Washington, DC 20005 · 202-879-5000

Gregg H. Levy · Covington & Burling · 1201 Pennsylvania Avenue, NW · Washington, DC 20004-2401 · 202-662-6000

Mark I. Levy · Kilpatrick Stockton · 607 Fourteenth Street, NW, Suite 900 · Washington, DC 20005-2018 202-508-5800

Nathan Lewin · ㉕ · Lewin & Lewin · 1828 L Street, NW, Suite 901 · Washington, DC 20036 · 202-828-1000

Robert A. Long · Covington & Burling · 1201 Pennsylvania Avenue, NW · Washington, DC 20004-2401 · 202-662-6000

Maureen E. Mahoney · Latham & Watkins · 555 Eleventh Street, NW, Suite 1000 · Washington, DC 20004-1304 · 202-637-2200

Alan B. Morrison · Alan B. Morrison · 1600 20th Street, NW · Washington, DC 20009

Glen D. Nager · ⑩ · Jones Day · 51 Louisiana Avenue, NW · Washington, DC 20001-2113 · 202-879-3939

Miriam R. Nemetz · Mayer Brown · 1909 K Street, NW · Washington, DC 20006-1101 · 202-263-3000

John W. Nields, Jr. · Howrey · 1299 Pennsylvania Avenue, NW · Washington, DC 20004 · 202-783-0800

Theodore B. Olson · Gibson, Dunn & Crutcher · 1050 Connecticut Avenue, NW · Washington, DC 20036-5306 · 202-955-8500

Mark Perry · Gibson, Dunn & Crutcher · 1050 Connecticut Avenue, NW · Washington, DC 20036-5306 · 202-955-8500

Carter G. Phillips · Sidley Austin · 1501 K Street, NW · Washington, DC 20005 · 202-736-8000

Andrew J. Pincus · Mayer Brown · 1909 K Street, NW · Washington, DC 20006-1101 · 202-263-3000

Lawrence S. Robbins · Robbins, Russell, Englert, Orseck, Untereiner & Sauber · 1801 K Street, NW, Suite 411 · Washington, DC 20006 · 202-775-4500

Charles A. Rothfeld · Mayer Brown · 1909 K Street, NW · Washington, DC 20006-1101 · 202-263-3000

Gene C. Schaerr · Winston & Strawn · 1700 K Street, NW · Washington, DC 20006-3817 · 202-282-5000

Virginia A. Seitz · Sidley Austin · 1501 K Street, NW · Washington, DC 20005 · 202-736-8000

Paul M. Smith · Jenner & Block · http://www.jenner.com · 1099 New York Avenue, NW, Suite 900 · Washington, DC 20001-4412 · 202-639-6000

Catherine E. Stetson · Hogan & Hartson · 555 Thirteenth Street, NW · Washington, DC 20004-1109 · 202-637-5600

Evan M. Tager · Mayer Brown · 1909 K Street, NW · Washington, DC 20006-1101 · 202-263-3000

Richard G. Taranto · Farr & Taranto · 1220 Nineteenth Street, NW, Suite 800 · Washington, DC 20036-2435 · 202-775-0184

Alan E. Untereiner · Robbins, Russell, Englert, Orseck, Untereiner & Sauber · 1801 K Street, NW, Suite 411 · Washington, DC 20006 · 202-775-4500

Donald B. Verrilli, Jr. · Jenner & Block · http://www.jenner.com · 1099 New York Avenue, NW, Suite 900 · Washington, DC 20001-4412 · 202-639-6000

Edward W. Warren · Kirkland & Ellis · 655 Fifteenth Street, NW · Washington, DC 20005 · 202-879-5000

Seth P. Waxman · WilmerHale · http://www.wilmerhale.com · 1875 Pennsylvania Avenue, NW · Washington, DC 20006 · 202-663-6000

Paul R. Q. Wolfson · WilmerHale · http://www.wilmerhale.com · 1875 Pennsylvania Avenue, NW · Washington, DC 20006 · 202-663-6000

BANKING LAW

Washington

Richard M. Alexander · Arnold & Porter · 555 Twelfth Street, NW · Washington, DC 20004-1206 · 202-942-5000

Christopher Bellini · Gibson, Dunn & Crutcher · 1050 Connecticut Avenue, NW · Washington, DC 20036-5306 · 202-955-8500

Russell J. Bruemmer · WilmerHale · http://www.wilmerhale.com · 1875 Pennsylvania Avenue, NW · Washington, DC 20006 · 202-663-6000

Barkley Clark · ⑩ · Stinson Morrison Hecker · http://www.stinson.com · 1150 Eighteenth Street, NW, Suite 800 · Washington, DC 20036 · 202-785-9100

Frank M. Conner III · DLA Piper · 500 Eighth Street, NW · Washington, DC 20004 · 202-799-4000

A. Patrick Doyle · Arnold & Porter · 555 Twelfth Street, NW · Washington, DC 20004-1206 · 202-942-5000

William S. Eckland · Sidley Austin · 1501 K Street, NW · Washington, DC 20005 · 202-736-8000

L. Richard Fischer · Morrison & Foerster · http://www.mofo.com · 2000 Pennsylvania Avenue, NW, Suite 5500 · Washington, DC 20006-1888 · 202-887-1500

Ronald R. Glancz · Venable · http://www.venable.com · 575 Seventh Street, NW · Washington, DC 20004-1601 · 202-344-4000

John D. Hawke, Jr. · Arnold & Porter · 555 Twelfth Street, NW · Washington, DC 20004-1206 · 202-942-5000

Thomas M. Hefferon · Goodwin Procter · 901 New York Avenue, NW · Washington, DC 20001 · 202-346-4000

Peter E. Heyward · Venable · http://www.venable.com · 575 Seventh Street, NW · Washington, DC 20004-1601 · 202-344-4000

Oliver I. Ireland · Morrison & Foerster · http://www.mofo.com · 2000 Pennsylvania Avenue, NW, Suite 5500 · Washington, DC 20006-1888 · 202-887-1500

Howard S. Jatlow · Dickstein Shapiro · http://www.dicksteinshapiro.com · 1825 Eye Street, NW · Washington, DC 20006-5403 · 202-420-2200

William F. Kroener III · Sullivan & Cromwell · 1701 Pennsylvania Avenue, NW · Washington, DC 20006-5805 · 202-956-7500

Robert M. Kurucza · Morrison & Foerster · http://www.mofo.com · 2000 Pennsylvania Avenue, NW, Suite 5500 · Washington, DC 20006-1888 · 202-887-1500

Dennis J. Lehr · ⑩ · Hogan & Hartson · 555 Thirteenth Street, NW · Washington, DC 20004-1109 · 202-637-5600

Martin E. Lybecker · WilmerHale · http://www.wilmerhale.com · 1875 Pennsylvania Avenue, NW · Washington, DC 20006 · 202-663-6000

Robert E. Mannion · Arnold & Porter · 555 Twelfth Street, NW · Washington, DC 20004-1206 · 202-942-5000

David Medine · WilmerHale · http://www.wilmerhale.com · 1875 Pennsylvania Avenue, NW · Washington, DC 20006 · 202-663-6000

Cantwell F. Muckenfuss III · ⑩ · Gibson, Dunn & Crutcher · 1050 Connecticut Avenue, NW · Washington, DC 20036-5306 · 202-955-8500

John C. Murphy, Jr. · ⑩ · Cleary Gottlieb Steen & Hamilton · 2000 Pennsylvania Avenue, NW · Washington, DC 20006 · 202-974-1500

Mark E. Plotkin · Covington & Burling · 1201 Pennsylvania Avenue, NW · Washington, DC 20004-2401 202-662-6000

Pauline A. Schneider · Orrick, Herrington & Sutcliffe · Columbia Center · 1152 Fifteenth Street, NW · Washington, DC 20005-1706 · 202-339-8400

Gilbert T. Schwartz · Schwartz & Ballen · 1990 M Street, NW, Suite 500 · Washington, DC 20036 · 202-776-0700

Mark R. Spivak · Vinson & Elkins · http://www.velaw.com · The Willard Office Building, Suite 600 · 1455 Pennsylvania Avenue, NW · Washington, DC 20004-1008 · 202-639-6500

Stuart C. Stock · ⑩ · Covington & Burling · 1201 Pennsylvania Avenue, NW · Washington, DC 20004-2401 · 202-662-6000

William J. Sweet, Jr. · Skadden, Arps, Slate, Meagher & Flom · 1440 New York Avenue, NW · Washington, DC 20005 · 202-371-7000

Thomas P. Vartanian · ⑩ · Fried, Frank, Harris, Shriver & Jacobson · 1001 Pennsylvania Avenue, NW · Washington, DC 20004-2505 · 202-639-7000

D. Jean Veta · Covington & Burling · 1201 Pennsylvania Avenue, NW · Washington, DC 20004-2401 · 202-662-6000

John K. Villa · Williams & Connolly · 725 Twelfth Street, NW · Washington, DC 20005-5901 · 202-434-5000

BANKRUPTCY AND CREDITOR-DEBTOR RIGHTS LAW

Washington

Marc E. Albert · Stinson Morrison Hecker · http://www.stinson.com · 1150 Eighteenth Street, NW, Suite 800 · Washington, DC 20036 · 202-785-9100

Michael St. Patrick Baxter · Covington & Burling · 1201 Pennsylvania Avenue, NW · Washington, DC 20004-2401 · 202-662-6000

Michael L. Bernstein · Arnold & Porter · 555 Twelfth Street, NW · Washington, DC 20004-1206 · 202-942-5000

Stephen A. Bogorad · Holland & Knight · http://www.hklaw.com · 2099 Pennsylvania Avenue, NW, Suite 100 · Washington, DC 20006-6801 · 202-955-3000

Paul Bennett Bran · Dickstein Shapiro · http://www.dicksteinshapiro.com · 1825 Eye Street, NW · Washington, DC 20006-5403 · 202-420-2200

Darrell W. Clark · Stinson Morrison Hecker · http://www.stinson.com · 1150 Eighteenth Street, NW, Suite 800 · Washington, DC 20036 · 202-785-9100

Nelson C. Cohen · ⑩ · Zuckerman Spaeder · http://www.zuckerman.com · 1800 M Street, NW, Suite 1000 · Washington, DC 20036-5807 · 202-778-1800

Francis P. Dicello · ⑳ · Reed Smith · East Tower, Suite 1100 · 1301 K Street, NW · Washington, DC 20005 · 202-414-9200

Mary Joanne Dowd · Arent Fox · 1050 Connecticut Avenue, NW · Washington, DC 20036-5339 · 202-857-6000

Mark C. Ellenberg · Cadwalader, Wickersham & Taft · http://www.cadwalader.com · 1201 F Street, NW, Suite 1100 · Washington, DC 20004 · 202-862-2200

Roger Frankel · ㉕ · Orrick, Herrington & Sutcliffe · Columbia Center · 1152 Fifteenth Street, NW · Washington, DC 20005-1706 · 202-339-8400

Bruce Goldstein · ㉕ · Zuckerman Spaeder · http://www.zuckerman.com · 1800 M Street, NW, Suite 1000 Washington, DC 20036-5807 · 202-778-1800

David R. Kuney · ⑩ · Sidley Austin · 1501 K Street, NW · Washington, DC 20005 · 202-736-8000

Richard E. Lear · Holland & Knight · http://www.hklaw.com · 2099 Pennsylvania Avenue, NW, Suite 100 Washington, DC 20006-6801 · 202-955-3000

Daniel M. Litt · ⑩ · Dickstein Shapiro · http://www.dicksteinshapiro.com · 1825 Eye Street, NW · Washington, DC 20006-5403 · 202-420-2200

Janet M. Nesse · Stinson Morrison Hecker · http://www.stinson.com · 1150 Eighteenth Street, NW, Suite 800 · Washington, DC 20036 · 202-785-9100

William J. Perlstein · ⑳ · WilmerHale · http://www.wilmerhale.com · 1875 Pennsylvania Avenue, NW · Washington, DC 20006 · 202-663-6000

Kermit A. Rosenberg · ⑩ · Tighe Patton Armstrong Teasdale · 1747 Pennsylvania Avenue, NW, Suite 300 · Washington, DC 20006 · 202-454-2800

William Daniel Sullivan · ⑩ · Tighe Patton Armstrong Teasdale · 1747 Pennsylvania Avenue, NW, Suite 300 · Washington, DC 20006 · 202-454-2800

Jeffrey L. Tarkenton · Womble Carlyle Sandridge & Rice · 1401 Eye Street, NW, Seventh Floor · Washington, DC 20005 · 202-467-6900

Mark D. Taylor · Kilpatrick Stockton · 607 Fourteenth Street, NW, Suite 900 · Washington, DC 20005-2018 · 202-508-5800

BET-THE-COMPANY LITIGATION

Washington

John D. Aldock · ⑩ · Goodwin Procter · 901 New York Avenue, NW · Washington, DC 20001 · 202-346-4000

Kevin T. Baine · ⑩ · Williams & Connolly · 725 Twelfth Street, NW · Washington, DC 20005-5901 · 202-434-5000

Richard Ben-Veniste · Mayer Brown · 1909 K Street, NW · Washington, DC 20006-1101 · 202-263-3000

Robert S. Bennett · ㉕ · Skadden, Arps, Slate, Meagher & Flom · 1440 New York Avenue, NW · Washington, DC 20005 · 202-371-7000

John M. Bray · ⑩ · King & Spalding · 1700 Pennsylvania Avenue, NW, Suite 200 · Washington, DC 20006-4706 · 202-737-0500

Plato Cacheris · ㉕ · Trout Cacheris · 1350 Connecticut Avenue, NW, Suite 300 · Washington, DC 20036 202-464-3300

Walter Dellinger · O'Melveny & Myers · 1625 Eye Street, NW · Washington, DC 20006-4001 · 202-383-5300

Hamilton P. Fox III · ⑩ · Sutherland · http://www.sutherland.com · 1275 Pennsylvania Avenue, NW · Washington, DC 20004-2415 · 202-383-0100

Jamie Gorelick · WilmerHale · http://www.wilmerhale.com · 1875 Pennsylvania Avenue, NW · Washington, DC 20006 · 202-663-6000

Thomas C. Green · ㉕ · Sidley Austin · 1501 K Street, NW · Washington, DC 20005 · 202-736-8000

Joseph M. Hassett · ⑳ · Hogan & Hartson · 555 Thirteenth Street, NW · Washington, DC 20004-1109 · 202-637-5600

Richard A. Hibey · ⑳ · Miller & Chevalier · http://www.milchev.com · 655 Fifteenth Street, NW, Suite 900 · Washington, DC 20005-5701 · 202-626-5800

Eric H. Holder, Jr. · Covington & Burling · 1201 Pennsylvania Avenue, NW · Washington, DC 20004-2401 · 202-662-6000

William H. Jeffress, Jr. · ⑩ · Baker Botts · http://www.bakerbotts.com · The Warner Building, Suite 1300 1299 Pennsylvania Avenue, NW · Washington, DC 20004-2400 · 202-639-7700

David E. Kendall · ⑩ · Williams & Connolly · 725 Twelfth Street, NW · Washington, DC 20005-5901 · 202-434-5000

William E. McDaniels · ⑳ · Williams & Connolly · 725 Twelfth Street, NW · Washington, DC 20005-5901 · 202-434-5000

William R. McLucas · WilmerHale · http://www.wilmerhale.com · 1875 Pennsylvania Avenue, NW · Washington, DC 20006 · 202-663-6000

R. Stan Mortenson · ㉕ · Baker Botts · http://www.bakerbotts.com · The Warner Building, Suite 1300 · 1299 Pennsylvania Avenue, NW · Washington, DC 20004-2400 · 202-639-7700

Carter G. Phillips · Sidley Austin · 1501 K Street, NW · Washington, DC 20005 · 202-736-8000

Stephen J. Pollak · ㉕ · Goodwin Procter · 901 New York Avenue, NW · Washington, DC 20001 · 202-346-4000

Robert N. Sayler · ㉕ · Covington & Burling · 1201 Pennsylvania Avenue, NW · Washington, DC 20004-2401 · 202-662-6000

Howard M. Shapiro · WilmerHale · http://www.wilmerhale.com · 1875 Pennsylvania Avenue, NW · Washington, DC 20006 · 202-663-6000

Jacob A. Stein · ㉕ · Stein, Mitchell & Mezines · 1100 Connecticut Avenue, NW · Washington, DC 20036 · 202-737-7777

Brendan V. Sullivan, Jr. · ⑩ · Williams & Connolly · 725 Twelfth Street, NW · Washington, DC 20005-5901 · 202-434-5000

William W. Taylor III · ㉕ · Zuckerman Spaeder · http://www.zuckerman.com · 1800 M Street, NW, Suite 1000 · Washington, DC 20036-5807 · 202-778-1800

Mark H. Tuohey · Vinson & Elkins · http://www.velaw.com · The Willard Office Building, Suite 600 · 1455 Pennsylvania Avenue, NW · Washington, DC 20004-1008 · 202-639-6500

John W. Vardaman · ㉕ · Williams & Connolly · 725 Twelfth Street, NW · Washington, DC 20005-5901 · 202-434-5000

John K. Villa · Williams & Connolly · 725 Twelfth Street, NW · Washington, DC 20005-5901 · 202-434-5000

Seth P. Waxman · WilmerHale · http://www.wilmerhale.com · 1875 Pennsylvania Avenue, NW · Washington, DC 20006 · 202-663-6000

BIOTECHNOLOGY LAW

Washington

Stephen A. Bent · Foley & Lardner · Washington Harbour, Suite 500 · 3000 K Street, NW · Washington, DC 20007-5109 · 202-672-5300

Jorge A. Goldstein · Sterne, Kessler, Goldstein & Fox · 1100 New York Avenue, NW · Washington, DC 20005 · 202-371-2600

R. Danny Huntington · Bingham McCutchen · http://www.bingham.com · 2020 K Street, NW · Washington, DC 20006-1806 · 202-373-6000

Paul N. Kokulis · Morgan Lewis & Bockius · 1111 Pennsylvania Avenue, NW · Washington, DC 20004 · 202-739-3000

Areta Kupchyk · Reed Smith · East Tower, Suite 1100 · 1301 K Street, NW · Washington, DC 20005 · 202-414-9200

Jeffrey P. Kushan · Sidley Austin · 1501 K Street, NW · Washington, DC 20005 · 202-736-8000

Erika King Lietzan · Covington & Burling · 1201 Pennsylvania Avenue, NW · Washington, DC 20004-2401 · 202-662-6000

Stephen B. Maebius · Foley & Lardner · Washington Harbour, Suite 500 · 3000 K Street, NW · Washington, DC 20007-5109 · 202-672-5300

Robert B. Nicholas · McDermott Will & Emery · 600 Thirteenth Street, NW · Washington, DC 20005-3096 · 202-756-8000

Teresa Stanek Rea · Crowell & Moring · 1001 Pennsylvania Avenue, NW · Washington, DC 20004-2595 202-624-2500

Colin G. Sandercock · Proskauer Rose · http://www.proskauer.com · 1001 Pennsylvania Avenue NW, Suite 400 South · Washington, DC 20004-2533 · 202-416-6800

Michele M. Simkin · Foley & Lardner · Washington Harbour, Suite 500 · 3000 K Street, NW · Washington, DC 20007-5109 · 202-672-5300

CIVIL RIGHTS LAW

Washington

Linda M. Correia · Webster, Fredrickson Henrichson Correia & Puth · 1775 K Street, NW, Suite 600 · Washington, DC 20006 · 202-659-8510

Bruce A. Fredrickson · Webster, Fredrickson Henrichson Correia & Puth · 1775 K Street, NW, Suite 600 Washington, DC 20006 · 202-659-8510

Douglas B. Huron · Heller, Huron, Chertkof, Lerner, Simon & Salzman · 1730 M Street, NW, Suite 412 · Washington, DC 20036 · 202-293-8090

Debra S. Katz · Katz, Marshall & Banks · http://www.kmblegal.com · 1718 Connecticut Avenue, NW, Sixth Floor · Washington, DC 20009 · 202-299-1140

Carolyn N. Lerner · Heller, Huron, Chertkof, Lerner, Simon & Salzman · 1730 M Street, NW, Suite 412 · Washington, DC 20036 · 202-293-8090

John P. Relman · Relman & Associates · 1225 Nineteenth Street, NW · Washington, DC 20036-2456 · 202-728-1888

Richard A. Salzman · Heller, Huron, Chertkof, Lerner, Simon & Salzman · 1730 M Street, NW, Suite 412 · Washington, DC 20036 · 202-293-8090

Joseph M. Sellers · Cohen, Milstein, Hausfeld & Toll · 1100 New York Avenue, NW, Suite 500 · Washington, DC 20005-3964 · 202-408-4600

David Wachtel · The Bernabei Law Firm · 1775 T Street, NW · Washington, DC 20009-7139 · 202-745-1942

COMMERCIAL LITIGATION

Washington

John D. Aldock · ⑩ · Goodwin Procter · 901 New York Avenue, NW · Washington, DC 20001 · 202-346-4000

Harvey M. Applebaum · ⑩ · Covington & Burling · 1201 Pennsylvania Avenue, NW · Washington, DC 20004-2401 · 202-662-6000

James K. Archibald · Venable · http://www.venable.com · 575 Seventh Street, NW · Washington, DC 20004-1601 · 202-344-4000

Henry W. Asbill · Dewey & LeBoeuf · 1101 New York Avenue, NW, Suite 1100 · Washington, DC 20005-4213 · 202-986-8000

Daniel F. Attridge · Kirkland & Ellis · 655 Fifteenth Street, NW · Washington, DC 20005 · 202-879-5000

Kevin T. Baine · ⑩ · Williams & Connolly · 725 Twelfth Street, NW · Washington, DC 20005-5901 · 202-434-5000

Bruce A. Baird · Covington & Burling · 1201 Pennsylvania Avenue, NW · Washington, DC 20004-2401 · 202-662-6000

Robert B. Barnett · Williams & Connolly · 725 Twelfth Street, NW · Washington, DC 20005-5901 · 202-434-5000

Alan I. Baron · Holland & Knight · http://www.hklaw.com · 2099 Pennsylvania Avenue, NW, Suite 100 · Washington, DC 20006-6801 · 202-955-3000

Michael J. Barta · Baker Botts · http://www.bakerbotts.com · The Warner Building, Suite 1300 · 1299 Pennsylvania Avenue, NW · Washington, DC 20004-2400 · 202-639-7700

Richard W. Beckler · ㉕ · Howrey · 1299 Pennsylvania Avenue, NW · Washington, DC 20004 · 202-783-0800

David Booth Beers · ⑳ · Goodwin Procter · 901 New York Avenue, NW · Washington, DC 20001 · 202-346-4000

Richard Ben-Veniste · Mayer Brown · 1909 K Street, NW · Washington, DC 20006-1101 · 202-263-3000

Robert S. Bennett · ㉕ · Skadden, Arps, Slate, Meagher & Flom · 1440 New York Avenue, NW · Washington, DC 20005 · 202-371-7000

Peter K. Bleakley · ㉕ · Arnold & Porter · 555 Twelfth Street, NW · Washington, DC 20004-1206 · 202-942-5000

William J. Bowman · Hogan & Hartson · 555 Thirteenth Street, NW · Washington, DC 20004-1109 · 202-637-5600

Stephen L. Braga · Baker Botts · http://www.bakerbotts.com · The Warner Building, Suite 1300 · 1299 Pennsylvania Avenue, NW · Washington, DC 20004-2400 · 202-639-7700

John M. Bray · ⑩ · King & Spalding · 1700 Pennsylvania Avenue, NW, Suite 200 · Washington, DC 20006-4706 · 202-737-0500

Pamela A. Bresnahan · Vorys, Sater, Seymour and Pease · 1828 L Street, NW, Suite 1111 · Washington, DC 20036-5109 · 202-467-8800

Lanny A. Breuer · Covington & Burling · 1201 Pennsylvania Avenue, NW · Washington, DC 20004-2401 202-662-6000

Stephen J. Brogan · Jones Day · 51 Louisiana Avenue, NW · Washington, DC 20001-2113 · 202-879-3939

Carol Elder Bruce · Bracewell & Giuliani · http://www.bgllp.com · 2000 K Street, NW, Suite 500 · Washington, DC 20006-1872 · 202-828-5800

Thomas W. Brunner · ⑩ · Wiley Rein · 1776 K Street, NW · Washington, DC 20006-2359 · 202-719-7000

Donald T. Bucklin · ⑳ · Squire Sanders · http://www.ssd.com · 1201 Pennsylvania Avenue, NW, Suite 500 · P.O. Box 407 · Washington, DC 20004-2401 · 202-626-6600

Bobby R. Burchfield · McDermott Will & Emery · 600 Thirteenth Street, NW · Washington, DC 20005-3096 · 202-756-8000

Peter Buscemi · Morgan Lewis & Bockius · 1111 Pennsylvania Avenue, NW · Washington, DC 20004 · 202-739-3000

Graeme W. Bush · Zuckerman Spaeder · http://www.zuckerman.com · 1800 M Street, NW, Suite 1000 · Washington, DC 20036-5807 · 202-778-1800

Dane H. Butswinkas · Williams & Connolly · 725 Twelfth Street, NW · Washington, DC 20005-5901 · 202-434-5000

C. Michael Buxton · Vinson & Elkins · http://www.velaw.com · The Willard Office Building, Suite 600 · 1455 Pennsylvania Avenue, NW · Washington, DC 20004-1008 · 202-639-6500

Plato Cacheris · ㉕ · Trout Cacheris · 1350 Connecticut Avenue, NW, Suite 300 · Washington, DC 20036 202-464-3300

Joe R. Caldwell, Jr. · Baker Botts · http://www.bakerbotts.com · The Warner Building, Suite 1300 · 1299 Pennsylvania Avenue, NW · Washington, DC 20004-2400 · 202-639-7700

Francis D. Carter · Zuckerman Spaeder · http://www.zuckerman.com · 1800 M Street, NW, Suite 1000 · Washington, DC 20036-5807 · 202-778-1800

Louis R. Cohen · ⑳ · WilmerHale · http://www.wilmerhale.com · 1875 Pennsylvania Avenue, NW · Washington, DC 20006 · 202-663-6000

Walter Dellinger · O'Melveny & Myers · 1625 Eye Street, NW · Washington, DC 20006-4001 · 202-383-5300

Sidney Dickstein · ㉕ · Dickstein Shapiro · http://www.dicksteinshapiro.com · 1825 Eye Street, NW · Washington, DC 20006-5403 · 202-420-2200

Mitchell F. Dolin · Covington & Burling · 1201 Pennsylvania Avenue, NW · Washington, DC 20004-2401 · 202-662-6000

Miguel A. Estrada · Gibson, Dunn & Crutcher · 1050 Connecticut Avenue, NW · Washington, DC 20036-5306 · 202-955-8500

Richard J. Favretto · 25 · Mayer Brown · 1909 K Street, NW · Washington, DC 20006-1101 · 202-263-3000

Ralph C. Ferrara · 10 · Dewey & LeBoeuf · 1101 New York Avenue, NW, Suite 1100 · Washington, DC 20005-4213 · 202-986-8000

Mark W. Foster · Zuckerman Spaeder · http://www.zuckerman.com · 1800 M Street, NW, Suite 1000 · Washington, DC 20036-5807 · 202-778-1800

Hamilton P. Fox III · 10 · Sutherland · http://www.sutherland.com · 1275 Pennsylvania Avenue, NW · Washington, DC 20004-2415 · 202-383-0100

Kenneth A. Gallo · Paul, Weiss, Rifkind, Wharton & Garrison · 1615 L Street, NW, Suite 1300 · Washington, DC 20036-5694 · 202-223-7300

Kenneth S. Geller · Mayer Brown · 1909 K Street, NW · Washington, DC 20006-1101 · 202-263-3000

John Gerstein · Ross, Dixon & Bell · 2001 K Street, NW · Washington, DC 20006-1040 · 202-662-2000

Seymour Glanzer · 10 · Dickstein Shapiro · http://www.dicksteinshapiro.com · 1825 Eye Street, NW · Washington, DC 20006-5403 · 202-420-2200

Jamie Gorelick · WilmerHale · http://www.wilmerhale.com · 1875 Pennsylvania Avenue, NW · Washington, DC 20006 · 202-663-6000

Michael J. Grace · Buchanan Ingersoll & Rooney · http://www.bipc.com · 1700 K Street, NW, Suite 300 · Washington, DC 20006-3807 · 202-452-7900

Thomas C. Green · 25 · Sidley Austin · 1501 K Street, NW · Washington, DC 20005 · 202-736-8000

Eugene D. Gulland · Covington & Burling · 1201 Pennsylvania Avenue, NW · Washington, DC 20004-2401 · 202-662-6000

Mark C. Hansen · Kellogg, Huber, Hansen, Todd, Evans & Figel · Sumner Square, Suite 400 · 1615 M Street, NW · Washington, DC 20036 · 202-326-7900

Joseph M. Hassett · 20 · Hogan & Hartson · 555 Thirteenth Street, NW · Washington, DC 20004-1109 · 202-637-5600

David J. Hensler · 10 · Hogan & Hartson · 555 Thirteenth Street, NW · Washington, DC 20004-1109 · 202-637-5600

Richard A. Hibey · 20 · Miller & Chevalier · http://www.milchev.com · 655 Fifteenth Street, NW, Suite 900 · Washington, DC 20005-5701 · 202-626-5800

Robert J. Higgins · 10 · Dickstein Shapiro · http://www.dicksteinshapiro.com · 1825 Eye Street, NW · Washington, DC 20006-5403 · 202-420-2200

Eric H. Holder, Jr. · Covington & Burling · 1201 Pennsylvania Avenue, NW · Washington, DC 20004-2401 · 202-662-6000

Mark D. Hopson · Sidley Austin · 1501 K Street, NW · Washington, DC 20005 · 202-736-8000

A. Stephen Hut, Jr. · WilmerHale · http://www.wilmerhale.com · 1875 Pennsylvania Avenue, NW · Washington, DC 20006 · 202-663-6000

David B. Isbell · 20 · Covington & Burling · 1201 Pennsylvania Avenue, NW · Washington, DC 20004-2401 · 202-662-6000

William D. Iverson · Covington & Burling · 1201 Pennsylvania Avenue, NW · Washington, DC 20004-2401 · 202-662-6000

N. Richard Janis · ⑩ · Janis, Schuelke & Wechsler · 1728 Massachusetts Avenue, NW · Washington, DC 20036 · 202-861-0600

William H. Jeffress, Jr. · ⑩ · Baker Botts · http://www.bakerbotts.com · The Warner Building, Suite 1300 1299 Pennsylvania Avenue, NW · Washington, DC 20004-2400 · 202-639-7700

Robert E. Jordan III · ㉕ · Steptoe & Johnson · http://www.steptoe.com · 1330 Connecticut Avenue, NW Washington, DC 20036 · 202-429-3000

David E. Kendall · ⑩ · Williams & Connolly · 725 Twelfth Street, NW · Washington, DC 20005-5901 · 202-434-5000

David S. Krakoff · Mayer Brown · 1909 K Street, NW · Washington, DC 20006-1101 · 202-263-3000

Steven R. Kuney · Williams & Connolly · 725 Twelfth Street, NW · Washington, DC 20005-5901 · 202-434-5000

Barry William Levine · ⑩ · Dickstein Shapiro · http://www.dicksteinshapiro.com · 1825 Eye Street, NW · Washington, DC 20006-5403 · 202-420-2200

Gregg H. Levy · Covington & Burling · 1201 Pennsylvania Avenue, NW · Washington, DC 20004-2401 · 202-662-6000

Nathan Lewin · ㉕ · Lewin & Lewin · 1828 L Street, NW, Suite 901 · Washington, DC 20036 · 202-828-1000

Robert S. Litt · Arnold & Porter · 555 Twelfth Street, NW · Washington, DC 20004-1206 · 202-942-5000

Mark H. Lynch · ⑩ · Covington & Burling · 1201 Pennsylvania Avenue, NW · Washington, DC 20004-2401 · 202-662-6000

Michael J. Madigan · ⑩ · Akin Gump Strauss Hauer & Feld · Robert S. Strauss Building · 1333 New Hampshire Avenue, NW · Washington, DC 20036-1564 · 202-887-4000

Maureen E. Mahoney · Latham & Watkins · 555 Eleventh Street, NW, Suite 1000 · Washington, DC 20004-1304 · 202-637-2200

Andrew Marks · Crowell & Moring · 1001 Pennsylvania Avenue, NW · Washington, DC 20004-2595 · 202-624-2500

James W. McBride · Baker, Donelson, Bearman, Caldwell & Berkowitz · http://www.bakerdonelson.com Lincoln Square, Sixth Floor · 555 Eleventh Street, NW · Washington, DC 20004 · 202-508-3400

William E. McDaniels · ⑳ · Williams & Connolly · 725 Twelfth Street, NW · Washington, DC 20005-5901 · 202-434-5000

Janet L. McDavid · Hogan & Hartson · 555 Thirteenth Street, NW · Washington, DC 20004-1109 · 202-637-5600

Bruce L. McDonald · ⑳ · Wiley Rein · 1776 K Street, NW · Washington, DC 20006-2359 · 202-719-7000

R. Bruce McLean · ㉕ · Akin Gump Strauss Hauer & Feld · Robert S. Strauss Building · 1333 New Hampshire Avenue, NW · Washington, DC 20036-1564 · 202-887-4000

William R. McLucas · WilmerHale · http://www.wilmerhale.com · 1875 Pennsylvania Avenue, NW · Washington, DC 20006 · 202-663-6000

Christopher B. Mead · London & Mead · 1225 Nineteenth Street, NW, Suite 320 · Washington, DC 20036 · 202-331-3334

Laura Ariane Miller · Nixon Peabody · 401 Ninth Street, NW, Suite 900 · Washington, DC 20004-2128 · 202-585-8000

R. Stan Mortenson · ㉕ · Baker Botts · http://www.bakerbotts.com · The Warner Building, Suite 1300 · 1299 Pennsylvania Avenue, NW · Washington, DC 20004-2400 · 202-639-7700

John E. Nolan · ㉕ · Steptoe & Johnson · http://www.steptoe.com · 1330 Connecticut Avenue, NW · Washington, DC 20036 · 202-429-3000

Lewis Noonberg · DLA Piper · 500 Eighth Street, NW · Washington, DC 20004 · 202-799-4000

Michael Nussbaum · ⑩ · Bonner Kiernan Trebach & Crociata · 1233 Twentieth Street, NW, Eighth Floor · Washington, DC 20036 · 202-712-7000

William D. Nussbaum · ⑩ · Hogan & Hartson · 555 Thirteenth Street, NW · Washington, DC 20004-1109 · 202-637-5600

David W. Ogden · WilmerHale · http://www.wilmerhale.com · 1875 Pennsylvania Avenue, NW · Washington, DC 20006 · 202-663-6000

Thomas E. Patton · ㉕ · Tighe Patton Armstrong Teasdale · 1747 Pennsylvania Avenue, NW, Suite 300 · Washington, DC 20006 · 202-454-2800

Carter G. Phillips · Sidley Austin · 1501 K Street, NW · Washington, DC 20005 · 202-736-8000

Rudolph F. Pierce · ⑩ · Goulston & Storrs · 2001 K Street, NW, Suite 1100 · Washington, DC 20006-1042 · 202-721-0011

Robert Plotkin · McGuireWoods · http://www.mcguirewoods.com · Washington Square, Suite 1200 · 1050 Connecticut Avenue, NW · Washington, DC 20036-5317 · 202-857-1700

Stephen J. Pollak · ㉕ · Goodwin Procter · 901 New York Avenue, NW · Washington, DC 20001 · 202-346-4000

Ethan M. Posner · Covington & Burling · 1201 Pennsylvania Avenue, NW · Washington, DC 20004-2401 202-662-6000

Bert W. Rein · ⑩ · Wiley Rein · 1776 K Street, NW · Washington, DC 20006-2359 · 202-719-7000

Wm. Bradford Reynolds · Howrey · 1299 Pennsylvania Avenue, NW · Washington, DC 20004 · 202-783-0800

Stephen M. Sacks · ⑳ · Arnold & Porter · 555 Twelfth Street, NW · Washington, DC 20004-1206 · 202-942-5000

Robert N. Sayler · ㉕ · Covington & Burling · 1201 Pennsylvania Avenue, NW · Washington, DC 20004-2401 · 202-662-6000

James P. Schaller · Jackson & Campbell · One Lafayette Centre, South Tower · 1120 Twentieth Street, NW · Washington, DC 20036-3437 · 202-457-1600

Howard M. Shapiro · WilmerHale · http://www.wilmerhale.com · 1875 Pennsylvania Avenue, NW · Washington, DC 20006 · 202-663-6000

James E. Sharp · (25) · Sharp & Associates · 1215 Nineteenth Street, NW · Washington, DC 20036 · 202-467-4114

John H. Shenefield · (25) · Morgan Lewis & Bockius · 1111 Pennsylvania Avenue, NW · Washington, DC 20004 · 202-739-3000

Stephen N. Shulman · (25) · Ivins, Phillips & Barker · 1700 Pennsylvania Avenue, NW, Suite 600 · Washington, DC 20006 · 202-393-7600

Theodore Sonde · (10) · Patton Boggs · 2550 M Street, NW · Washington, DC 20037 · 202-457-6000

Stanley Sporkin · Weil Gotshal & Manges · 1300 Eye Street, NW, Suite 900 · Washington, DC 20005 · 202-682-7000

Jacob A. Stein · (25) · Stein, Mitchell & Mezines · 1100 Connecticut Avenue, NW · Washington, DC 20036 · 202-737-7777

Brendan V. Sullivan, Jr. · (10) · Williams & Connolly · 725 Twelfth Street, NW · Washington, DC 20005-5901 · 202-434-5000

Michael S. Sundermeyer · (10) · Williams & Connolly · 725 Twelfth Street, NW · Washington, DC 20005-5901 · 202-434-5000

William W. Taylor III · (25) · Zuckerman Spaeder · http://www.zuckerman.com · 1800 M Street, NW, Suite 1000 · Washington, DC 20036-5807 · 202-778-1800

Henry C. Thumann · (20) · O'Melveny & Myers · 1625 Eye Street, NW · Washington, DC 20006-4001 · 202-383-5300

Robert P. Trout · (10) · Trout Cacheris · 1350 Connecticut Avenue, NW, Suite 300 · Washington, DC 20036 · 202-464-3300

Mark H. Tuohey · Vinson & Elkins · http://www.velaw.com · The Willard Office Building, Suite 600 · 1455 Pennsylvania Avenue, NW · Washington, DC 20004-1008 · 202-639-6500

Steven M. Umin · (20) · Epstein, Becker & Green · 1227 Twenty-Fifth Street, NW, Suite 700 · Washington, DC 20037-1156 · 202-861-0900

John W. Vardaman · (25) · Williams & Connolly · 725 Twelfth Street, NW · Washington, DC 20005-5901 · 202-434-5000

John K. Villa · Williams & Connolly · 725 Twelfth Street, NW · Washington, DC 20005-5901 · 202-434-5000

Roger E. Warin · Steptoe & Johnson · http://www.steptoe.com · 1330 Connecticut Avenue, NW · Washington, DC 20036 · 202-429-3000

Seth P. Waxman · WilmerHale · http://www.wilmerhale.com · 1875 Pennsylvania Avenue, NW · Washington, DC 20006 · 202-663-6000

David N. Webster · (10) · Caplin & Drysdale · http://www.capdale.com · One Thomas Circle, NW, Suite 1100 · Washington, DC 20005 · 202-862-5000

Robert N. Weiner · Arnold & Porter · 555 Twelfth Street, NW · Washington, DC 20004-1206 · 202-942-5000

Laura S. Wertheimer · ⑩ · WilmerHale · http://www.wilmerhale.com · 1875 Pennsylvania Avenue, NW · Washington, DC 20006 · 202-663-6000

Carolyn H. Williams · Williams & Connolly · 725 Twelfth Street, NW · Washington, DC 20005-5901 · 202-434-5000

Paul Martin Wolff · ⑩ · Williams & Connolly · 725 Twelfth Street, NW · Washington, DC 20005-5901 · 202-434-5000

Charles R. Work · ⑩ · McDermott Will & Emery · 600 Thirteenth Street, NW · Washington, DC 20005-3096 · 202-756-8000

Thomas D. Yannucci · Kirkland & Ellis · 655 Fifteenth Street, NW · Washington, DC 20005 · 202-879-5000

COMMUNICATIONS LAW

Washington

James H. Barker · Latham & Watkins · 555 Eleventh Street, NW, Suite 1000 · Washington, DC 20004-1304 · 202-637-2200

Raymond G. Bender · Dow Lohnes · http://www.dowlohnes.com · 1200 New Hampshire Avenue, NW, Suite 800 · Washington, DC 20036-6802 · 202-776-2000

Jonathan D. Blake · Covington & Burling · 1201 Pennsylvania Avenue, NW · Washington, DC 20004-2401 · 202-662-6000

James S. Blaszak · Levine, Blaszak, Block & Boothby · 2001 L Street, NW, Suite 900 · Washington, DC 20036 · 202-857-2550

Colleen L. Boothby · Levine, Blaszak, Block & Boothby · 2001 L Street, NW, Suite 900 · Washington, DC 20036 · 202-857-2550

Henk Brands · Paul, Weiss, Rifkind, Wharton & Garrison · 1615 L Street, NW, Suite 1300 · Washington, DC 20036-5694 · 202-223-7300

Antoinette C. Bush · Skadden, Arps, Slate, Meagher & Flom · 1440 New York Avenue, NW · Washington, DC 20005 · 202-371-7000

Gary M. Epstein · Latham & Watkins · 555 Eleventh Street, NW, Suite 1000 · Washington, DC 20004-1304 · 202-637-2200

Mark L. Evans · Kellogg, Huber, Hansen, Todd, Evans & Figel · Sumner Square, Suite 400 · 1615 M Street, NW · Washington, DC 20036 · 202-326-7900

John R. Feore · Dow Lohnes · http://www.dowlohnes.com · 1200 New Hampshire Avenue, NW, Suite 800 · Washington, DC 20036-6802 · 202-776-2000

Charles D. Ferris · Mintz, Levin, Cohn, Ferris, Glovsky and Popeo · 701 Pennsylvania Avenue, NW · Washington, DC 20004-2608 · 202-434-7300

Kenneth S. Geller · Mayer Brown · 1909 K Street, NW · Washington, DC 20006-1101 · 202-263-3000

Jack Goodman · WilmerHale · http://www.wilmerhale.com · 1875 Pennsylvania Avenue, NW · Washington, DC 20006 · 202-663-6000

Scott B. Harris · Harris, Wiltshire & Grannis · 1200 Eighteenth Street, NW, 12th Floor · Washington, DC 20036-2506 · 202-730-1300

John H. Harwood II · WilmerHale · http://www.wilmerhale.com · 1875 Pennsylvania Avenue, NW · Washington, DC 20006 · 202-663-6000

Peter W. Huber · Kellogg, Huber, Hansen, Todd, Evans & Figel · Sumner Square, Suite 400 · 1615 M Street, NW · Washington, DC 20036 · 202-326-7900

Regina M. Keeney · Lawler, Metzger, Milkman & Keeney · 2001 K Street, NW, Suite 802 · Washington, DC 20006 · 202-777-7700

Michael K. Kellogg · Kellogg, Huber, Hansen, Todd, Evans & Figel · Sumner Square, Suite 400 · 1615 M Street, NW · Washington, DC 20036 · 202-326-7900

Jean L. Kiddoo · Bingham McCutchen · http://www.bingham.com · 3000 K Street, NW · Washington, DC 20007 · 202-424-7500

William T. Lake · WilmerHale · http://www.wilmerhale.com · 1875 Pennsylvania Avenue, NW · Washington, DC 20006 · 202-663-6000

David Lee Lawson · Sidley Austin · 1501 K Street, NW · Washington, DC 20005 · 202-736-8000

Steven Lerman · Leventhal, Senter & Lerman · 2000 North West K Street, Suite 600 · Washington, DC 20006 · 202-429-8970

Henry D. Levine · Levine, Blaszak, Block & Boothby · 2001 L Street, NW, Suite 900 · Washington, DC 20036 · 202-857-2550

Andrew D. Lipman · Bingham McCutchen · http://www.bingham.com · 3000 K Street, NW · Washington, DC 20007 · 202-424-7500

John S. Logan · Dow Lohnes · http://www.dowlohnes.com · 1200 New Hampshire Avenue, NW, Suite 800 · Washington, DC 20036-6802 · 202-776-2000

William F. Maher, Jr. · Morrison & Foerster · http://www.mofo.com · 2000 Pennsylvania Avenue, NW, Suite 5500 · Washington, DC 20006-1888 · 202-887-1500

A. Richard Metzger, Jr. · Lawler, Metzger, Milkman & Keeney · 2001 K Street, NW, Suite 802 · Washington, DC 20006 · 202-777-7700

Ruth Milkman · Lawler, Metzger, Milkman & Keeney · 2001 K Street, NW, Suite 802 · Washington, DC 20006 · 202-777-7700

John T. Nakahata · Harris, Wiltshire & Grannis · 1200 Eighteenth Street, NW, 12th Floor · Washington, DC 20036-2506 · 202-730-1300

Carl W. Northrop · Paul Hastings · 875 Fifteenth Street, NW · Washington, DC 20005 · 202-551-1700

Jonathan E. Nuechterlein · WilmerHale · http://www.wilmerhale.com · 1875 Pennsylvania Avenue, NW · Washington, DC 20006 · 202-663-6000

Andrew Ray · Bingham McCutchen · http://www.bingham.com · 2020 K Street, NW · Washington, DC 20006-1806 · 202-373-6000

Kevin F. Reed · Dow Lohnes · http://www.dowlohnes.com · 1200 New Hampshire Avenue, NW, Suite 800 · Washington, DC 20036-6802 · 202-776-2000

Bert W. Rein · Wiley Rein · 1776 K Street, NW · Washington, DC 20006-2359 · 202-719-7000

Henry M. Rivera · Wiley Rein · 1776 K Street, NW · Washington, DC 20006-2359 · 202-719-7000

John Rogovin · WilmerHale · http://www.wilmerhale.com · 1875 Pennsylvania Avenue, NW · Washington, DC 20006 · 202-663-6000

Peter A. Rohrbach · Hogan & Hartson · 555 Thirteenth Street, NW · Washington, DC 20004-1109 · 202-637-5600

Mace J. Rosenstein · Covington & Burling · 1201 Pennsylvania Avenue, NW · Washington, DC 20004-2401 · 202-662-6000

R. Michael Senkowski · Wiley Rein · 1776 K Street, NW · Washington, DC 20006-2359 · 202-719-7000

Howard J. Symons · Mintz, Levin, Cohn, Ferris, Glovsky and Popeo · 701 Pennsylvania Avenue, NW · Washington, DC 20004-2608 · 202-434-7300

L. Andrew Tollin · Wilkinson Barker Knauer · 2300 North Street, NW, Suite 700 · Washington, DC 20037 · 202-783-4141

Cheryl A. Tritt · Morrison & Foerster · http://www.mofo.com · 2000 Pennsylvania Avenue, NW, Suite 5500 · Washington, DC 20006-1888 · 202-887-1500

Philip L. Verveer · Willkie Farr & Gallagher · 1875 K Street, NW · Washington, DC 20006-1238 · 202-303-1000

R. Clark Wadlow · Sidley Austin · 1501 K Street, NW · Washington, DC 20005 · 202-736-8000

Stephen A. Weiswasser · Covington & Burling · 1201 Pennsylvania Avenue, NW · Washington, DC 20004-2401 · 202-662-6000

Richard E. Wiley · ㉕ · Wiley Rein · 1776 K Street, NW · Washington, DC 20006-2359 · 202-719-7000

William M. Wiltshire · Harris, Wiltshire & Grannis · 1200 Eighteenth Street, NW, 12th Floor · Washington, DC 20036-2506 · 202-730-1300

Christopher J. Wright · Harris, Wiltshire & Grannis · 1200 Eighteenth Street, NW, 12th Floor · Washington, DC 20036-2506 · 202-730-1300

CONSTRUCTION LAW

Washington

Adrian L. Bastianelli III · Peckar, Abramson, Bastianelli & Kelley · Two Lafayette Centre, Suite 500 · 1133 Twenty-First Street, NW · Washington, DC 20036 · 202-293-8815

Herman M. Braude · Braude & Margulies · 1200 Potomac Street, NW · Washington, DC 20007 · 202-471-5400

Bennett D. Greenberg · Seyfarth Shaw · 815 Connecticut Avenue, NW, Suite 500 · Washington, DC 20006-4004 · 202-463-2400

Larry D. Harris · Greenberg Traurig · http://www.gtlaw.com · 2101 L Street, NW, Suite 1000 · Washington, DC 20037 · 202-331-3100

Judith B. Ittig · Ittig & Ittig · 1420 Ninth Street, NW · Washington, DC 20001-3344 · 202-387-5508

Michael Evan Jaffe · Thelen Reid Brown Raysman & Steiner · 701 Eighth Street, NW, Suite 800 · Washington, DC 20001 · 202-508-4000

Joseph A. McManus, Jr. · McManus, Schor, Asmar & Darden · 1155 Fifteenth Street, NW, Suite 900 · Washington, DC 20005 · 202-296-9260

Andrew David Ness · Thelen Reid Brown Raysman & Steiner · 701 Eighth Street, NW, Suite 800 · Washington, DC 20001 · 202-508-4000

Douglas L. Patin · Bradley Arant Rose & White · http://www.bradleyarant.com · 1133 Connecticut Avenue, NW, Twelfth Floor · Washington, DC 20036 · 202-393-7150

Richard McKim Preston · Seyfarth Shaw · 815 Connecticut Avenue, NW, Suite 500 · Washington, DC 20006-4004 · 202-463-2400

Andrew W. Stephenson · Holland & Knight · http://www.hklaw.com · 2099 Pennsylvania Avenue, NW, Suite 100 · Washington, DC 20006-6801 · 202-955-3000

Steven Weber · Holland & Knight · http://www.hklaw.com · 2099 Pennsylvania Avenue, NW, Suite 100 · Washington, DC 20006-6801 · 202-955-3000

Barbara G. Werther · Thelen Reid Brown Raysman & Steiner · 701 Eighth Street, NW, Suite 800 · Washington, DC 20001 · 202-508-4000

CORPORATE GOVERNANCE AND COMPLIANCE LAW

Washington

Bruce A. Baird · Covington & Burling · 1201 Pennsylvania Avenue, NW · Washington, DC 20004-2401 · 202-662-6000

James A. Baker III · Baker Botts · http://www.bakerbotts.com · The Warner Building, Suite 1300 · 1299 Pennsylvania Avenue, NW · Washington, DC 20004-2400 · 202-639-7700

David M. Becker · Cleary Gottlieb Steen & Hamilton · 2000 Pennsylvania Avenue, NW · Washington, DC 20006 · 202-974-1500

Richard Ben-Veniste · Mayer Brown · 1909 K Street, NW · Washington, DC 20006-1101 · 202-263-3000

Lanny A. Breuer · Covington & Burling · 1201 Pennsylvania Avenue, NW · Washington, DC 20004-2401 202-662-6000

David E. Brown, Jr. · Alston + Bird · http://www.alston.com · The Atlantic Building · 950 F Street, NW · Washington, DC 20004-1404 · 202-756-3300

Wallace E. Christner · Venable · http://www.venable.com · 575 Seventh Street, NW · Washington, DC 20004-1601 · 202-344-4000

Bruce E. Coolidge · WilmerHale · http://www.wilmerhale.com · 1875 Pennsylvania Avenue, NW · Washington, DC 20006 · 202-663-6000

Catherine T. Dixon · Weil Gotshal & Manges · 1300 Eye Street, NW, Suite 900 · Washington, DC 20005 202-682-7000

James R. Doty · Baker Botts · http://www.bakerbotts.com · The Warner Building, Suite 1300 · 1299 Pennsylvania Avenue, NW · Washington, DC 20004-2400 · 202-639-7700

Ralph C. Ferrara · ⑩ · Dewey & LeBoeuf · 1101 New York Avenue, NW, Suite 1100 · Washington, DC 20005-4213 · 202-986-8000

Thomas A. Ferrigno · Fulbright & Jaworski · http://www.fulbright.com · Market Square · 801 Pennsylvania Avenue, NW · Washington, DC 20004-2623 · 202-662-0200

Dennis O. Garris · Alston + Bird · http://www.alston.com · The Atlantic Building · 950 F Street, NW · Washington, DC 20004-1404 · 202-756-3300

Joseph I. Goldstein · Mayer Brown · 1909 K Street, NW · Washington, DC 20006-1101 · 202-263-3000

Amy L. Goodman · Gibson, Dunn & Crutcher · 1050 Connecticut Avenue, NW · Washington, DC 20036-5306 · 202-955-8500

Linda L. Griggs · ⑩ · Morgan Lewis & Bockius · 1111 Pennsylvania Avenue, NW · Washington, DC 20004 · 202-739-3000

Bruce A. Hiler · Cadwalader, Wickersham & Taft · http://www.cadwalader.com · 1201 F Street, NW, Suite 1100 · Washington, DC 20004 · 202-862-2200

John J. Huber · ⑩ · Latham & Watkins · 555 Eleventh Street, NW, Suite 1000 · Washington, DC 20004-1304 · 202-637-2200

Michael Hyatte · Sidley Austin · 1501 K Street, NW · Washington, DC 20005 · 202-736-8000

Jerry A. Isenberg · LeClair Ryan · 1101 Connecticut Avenue, NW, Suite 600 · Washington, DC 20036 · 202-659-4140

Dixie Lynn Johnson · Fried, Frank, Harris, Shriver & Jacobson · 1001 Pennsylvania Avenue, NW · Washington, DC 20004-2505 · 202-639-7000

Richard S. Kraut · Dilworth Paxson · 1133 Connecticut Avenue, NW, Suite 620 · Washington, DC 20036 202-452-0900

Brian J. Lane · Gibson, Dunn & Crutcher · 1050 Connecticut Avenue, NW · Washington, DC 20036-5306 · 202-955-8500

Paul S. Maco · Vinson & Elkins · http://www.velaw.com · The Willard Office Building, Suite 600 · 1455 Pennsylvania Avenue, NW · Washington, DC 20004-1008 · 202-639-6500

Colleen P. Mahoney · Skadden, Arps, Slate, Meagher & Flom · 1440 New York Avenue, NW · Washington, DC 20005 · 202-371-7000

David B. H. Martin · Covington & Burling · 1201 Pennsylvania Avenue, NW · Washington, DC 20004-2401 · 202-662-6000

William R. McLucas · WilmerHale · http://www.wilmerhale.com · 1875 Pennsylvania Avenue, NW · Washington, DC 20006 · 202-663-6000

Richard J. Morvillo · Mayer Brown · 1909 K Street, NW · Washington, DC 20006-1101 · 202-263-3000

Ronald O. Mueller · Gibson, Dunn & Crutcher · 1050 Connecticut Avenue, NW · Washington, DC 20036-5306 · 202-955-8500

John F. Olson · ㉕ · Gibson, Dunn & Crutcher · 1050 Connecticut Avenue, NW · Washington, DC 20036-5306 · 202-955-8500

Irving M. Pollack · Fulbright & Jaworski · http://www.fulbright.com · Market Square · 801 Pennsylvania Avenue, NW · Washington, DC 20004-2623 · 202-662-0200

Therese D. Pritchard · Bryan Cave · 700 Thirteenth Street, NW · Washington, DC 20005-3960 · 202-508-6000

William S. Sessions · Holland & Knight · http://www.hklaw.com · 2099 Pennsylvania Avenue, NW, Suite 100 · Washington, DC 20006-6801 · 202-955-3000

Stanley Sporkin · Weil Gotshal & Manges · 1300 Eye Street, NW, Suite 900 · Washington, DC 20005 · 202-682-7000

Dick Thornburgh · K&L Gates · 1601 K Street, NW · Washington, DC 20006-1600 · 202-778-9000

Wallace L. Timmeny · Dechert · 1775 I Street, NW · Washington, DC 20006-2401 · 202-261-3300

John K. Villa · Williams & Connolly · 725 Twelfth Street, NW · Washington, DC 20005-5901 · 202-434-5000

Harry J. Weiss · WilmerHale · http://www.wilmerhale.com · 1875 Pennsylvania Avenue, NW · Washington, DC 20006 · 202-663-6000

CORPORATE LAW

Washington

Robert B. Barnett · Williams & Connolly · 725 Twelfth Street, NW · Washington, DC 20005-5901 · 202-434-5000

Robert F. Bauer · Perkins Coie · http://www.perkinscoie.com · 607 Fourteenth Street, NW, Suite 800 · Washington, DC 20005-2003 · 202-628-6600

Alan J. Berkeley · ⑳ · K&L Gates · 1601 K Street, NW · Washington, DC 20006-1600 · 202-778-9000

Steven B. Boehm · Sutherland · http://www.sutherland.com · 1275 Pennsylvania Avenue, NW · Washington, DC 20004-2415 · 202-383-0100

David E. Brown, Jr. · Alston + Bird · http://www.alston.com · The Atlantic Building · 950 F Street, NW · Washington, DC 20004-1404 · 202-756-3300

Frank M. Conner III · DLA Piper · 500 Eighth Street, NW · Washington, DC 20004 · 202-799-4000

Alan L. Dye · Hogan & Hartson · 555 Thirteenth Street, NW · Washington, DC 20004-1109 · 202-637-5600

Peter D. Ehrenhaft · ⑩ · Harkins Cunningham · http://www.harkinscunningham.com · 1700 K Street, NW, Suite 400 · Washington, DC 20006-3817 · 202-973-7600

Catherine S. Gallagher · Vinson & Elkins · http://www.velaw.com · The Willard Office Building, Suite 600 · 1455 Pennsylvania Avenue, NW · Washington, DC 20004-1008 · 202-639-6500

Dennis O. Garris · Alston + Bird · http://www.alston.com · The Atlantic Building · 950 F Street, NW · Washington, DC 20004-1404 · 202-756-3300

Stephen I. Glover · Gibson, Dunn & Crutcher · 1050 Connecticut Avenue, NW · Washington, DC 20036-5306 · 202-955-8500

Frank R. Goldstein · ⑩ · Sidley Austin · 1501 K Street, NW · Washington, DC 20005 · 202-736-8000

J. Warren Gorrell, Jr. · Hogan & Hartson · 555 Thirteenth Street, NW · Washington, DC 20004-1109 · 202-637-5600

Sandra W. Hallmark · Akin Gump Strauss Hauer & Feld · Robert S. Strauss Building · 1333 New Hampshire Avenue, NW · Washington, DC 20036-1564 · 202-887-4000

Robert E. Jordan III · ㉕ · Steptoe & Johnson · http://www.steptoe.com · 1330 Connecticut Avenue, NW Washington, DC 20036 · 202-429-3000

Steven Kaplan · Arnold & Porter · 555 Twelfth Street, NW · Washington, DC 20004-1206 · 202-942-5000

John Paul Ketels · ⑩ · Clifford Chance · 2001 K Street, NW · Washington, DC 20006-1001 · 202-912-5000

Kenneth A. Letzler · Arnold & Porter · 555 Twelfth Street, NW · Washington, DC 20004-1206 · 202-942-5000

Charles T. Manatt · Manatt, Phelps & Phillips · One Metro Center, Suite 1100 · 700 Twelfth Street, NW Washington, DC 20005 · 202-585-6500

Stanley J. Marcuss · ㉕ · Bryan Cave · 700 Thirteenth Street, NW · Washington, DC 20005-3960 · 202-508-6000

David B. H. Martin · Covington & Burling · 1201 Pennsylvania Avenue, NW · Washington, DC 20004-2401 · 202-662-6000

Stephanie M. Monaco · Mayer Brown · 1909 K Street, NW · Washington, DC 20006-1101 · 202-263-3000

Marilyn Mooney · Fulbright & Jaworski · http://www.fulbright.com · Market Square · 801 Pennsylvania Avenue, NW · Washington, DC 20004-2623 · 202-662-0200

John F. Olson · ㉕ · Gibson, Dunn & Crutcher · 1050 Connecticut Avenue, NW · Washington, DC 20036-5306 · 202-955-8500

John L. Ray · Manatt, Phelps & Phillips · One Metro Center, Suite 1100 · 700 Twelfth Street, NW · Washington, DC 20005 · 202-585-6500

Stephen A. Riddick · Greenberg Traurig · http://www.gtlaw.com · 2101 L Street, NW, Suite 1000 · Washington, DC 20037 · 202-331-3100

Robert S. Risoleo · Sullivan & Cromwell · 1701 Pennsylvania Avenue, NW · Washington, DC 20006-5805 · 202-956-7500

Michael P. Rogan · Skadden, Arps, Slate, Meagher & Flom · 1440 New York Avenue, NW · Washington, DC 20005 · 202-371-7000

Richard H. Rowe · ⑩ · Proskauer Rose · http://www.proskauer.com · 1001 Pennsylvania Avenue NW, Suite 400 South · Washington, DC 20004-2533 · 202-416-6800

George P. Stamas · Kirkland & Ellis · 655 Fifteenth Street, NW · Washington, DC 20005 · 202-879-5000

Richard A. Steinwurtzel · ⑳ · Fried, Frank, Harris, Shriver & Jacobson · 1001 Pennsylvania Avenue, NW Washington, DC 20004-2505 · 202-639-7000

Michael D. Trager · Arnold & Porter · 555 Twelfth Street, NW · Washington, DC 20004-1206 · 202-942-5000

Stephanie Tsacoumis · Gibson, Dunn & Crutcher · 1050 Connecticut Avenue, NW · Washington, DC 20036-5306 · 202-955-8500

Charles R. Wenner · Arnold & Porter · 555 Twelfth Street, NW · Washington, DC 20004-1206 · 202-942-5000

DERIVATIVES LAW

Washington

Geoffrey F. Aronow · Bingham McCutchen · 2020 K Street, NW · Washington, DC 20006-1806 · 202-373-6000

James M. Cain · Sutherland · http://www.sutherland.com · 1275 Pennsylvania Avenue, NW · Washington, DC 20004-2415 · 202-383-0100

Warren N. Davis · Sutherland · http://www.sutherland.com · 1275 Pennsylvania Avenue, NW · Washington, DC 20004-2415 · 202-383-0100

Susan C. Ervin · Dechert · 1775 I Street, NW · Washington, DC 20006-2401 · 202-261-3300

Marshall E. Hanbury · Mayer Brown · 1909 K Street, NW · Washington, DC 20006-1101 · 202-263-3000

Philip McBride Johnson · Skadden, Arps, Slate, Meagher & Flom · 1440 New York Avenue, NW · Washington, DC 20005 · 202-371-7000

M. David Krohn · DLA Piper · 500 Eighth Street, NW · Washington, DC 20004 · 202-799-4000

Charles R. Mills · K&L Gates · 1601 K Street, NW · Washington, DC 20006-1600 · 202-778-9000

Richard J. Morvillo · Mayer Brown · 1909 K Street, NW · Washington, DC 20006-1101 · 202-263-3000

Paul J. Pantano · McDermott Will & Emery · 600 Thirteenth Street, NW · Washington, DC 20005-3096 202-756-8000

Michael L. Spafford · McKee Nelson · 1919 M Street, NW, Suite 200 · Washington, DC 20036 · 202-775-1880

Dennis C. Sullivan · Sullivan & Cromwell · 1701 Pennsylvania Avenue, NW · Washington, DC 20006-5805 · 202-956-7500

Mark D. Young · Kirkland & Ellis · 655 Fifteenth Street, NW · Washington, DC 20005 · 202-879-5000

EDUCATION LAW

Washington

Dennis H. Blumer · Arent Fox · 1050 Connecticut Avenue, NW · Washington, DC 20036-5339 · 202-857-6000

Stanley A. Freeman · Powers, Pyles, Sutter and Verville · http://www.ppsv.com · 1501 M Street, NW, Seventh Floor · Washington, DC 20006 · 202-466-6550

Michael Goldstein · Dow Lohnes · http://www.dowlohnes.com · 1200 New Hampshire Avenue, NW, Suite 800 · Washington, DC 20036-6802 · 202-776-2000

Lee E. Goodman · LeClair Ryan · 1101 Connecticut Avenue, NW, Suite 600 · Washington, DC 20036 · 202-659-4140

Kenneth J. Ingram · Whiteford, Taylor & Preston · http://www.wtplaw.com · 1025 Connecticut Avenue, NW, Suite 400 · Washington, DC 20036-5405 · 202-659-6800

Martin Michaelson · Hogan & Hartson · 555 Thirteenth Street, NW · Washington, DC 20004-1109 · 202-637-5600

Scott R. Palmer · Nelson Mullins Riley & Scarborough · 101 Constitution Avenue, NW, Suite 900 · Washington, DC 20001 · 202-712-2800

Sheldon E. Steinbach · Dow Lohnes · http://www.dowlohnes.com · 1200 New Hampshire Avenue, NW, Suite 800 · Washington, DC 20036-6802 · 202-776-2000

ELDER LAW

Washington

Ralph J. Moore, Jr. · ⑳ · Morgan Lewis & Bockius · 1111 Pennsylvania Avenue, NW · Washington, DC 20004 · 202-739-3000

EMPLOYEE BENEFITS LAW

Washington

Rosina B. Barker · ⑩ · Ivins, Phillips & Barker · 1700 Pennsylvania Avenue, NW, Suite 600 · Washington, DC 20006 · 202-393-7600

Michael R. Bergmann · Skadden, Arps, Slate, Meagher & Flom · 1440 New York Avenue, NW · Washington, DC 20005 · 202-371-7000

Paul Blankenstein · Gibson, Dunn & Crutcher · 1050 Connecticut Avenue, NW · Washington, DC 20036-5306 · 202-955-8500

George H. Bostick · ⑩ · Sutherland · http://www.sutherland.com · 1275 Pennsylvania Avenue, NW · Washington, DC 20004-2415 · 202-383-0100

Gregory C. Braden · Morgan Lewis & Bockius · 1111 Pennsylvania Avenue, NW · Washington, DC 20004 · 202-739-3000

Dan S. Brandenburg · Sanders, Schnabel & Brandenburg · 900 Seventeenth Street, NW, Suite 900 · Washington, DC 20006-2501 · 202-638-2241

Jon W. Breyfogle · Groom Law Group · http://www.groom.com · 1701 Pennsylvania Avenue, NW · Washington, DC 20006-5811 · 202-857-0620

William R. Charyk · Arent Fox · 1050 Connecticut Avenue, NW · Washington, DC 20036-5339 · 202-857-6000

Catherine L. Creech · Ernst & Young · 1101 New York Avenue, NW · Washington, DC 20005-4270 · 202-327-6000

James M. Delaplane, Jr. · Davis & Harman · The Willard, Suite 1200 · 1455 Pennsylvania Avenue, NW · Washington, DC 20004 · 202-347-2230

Robert N. Eccles · ⑩ · O'Melveny & Myers · 1625 Eye Street, NW · Washington, DC 20006-4001 · 202-383-5300

Julie M. Edmond · Covington & Burling · 1201 Pennsylvania Avenue, NW · Washington, DC 20004-2401 · 202-662-6000

Douglas W. Ell · ⑩ · Groom Law Group · http://www.groom.com · 1701 Pennsylvania Avenue, NW · Washington, DC 20006-5811 · 202-857-0620

Carol Connor Flowe · Arent Fox · 1050 Connecticut Avenue, NW · Washington, DC 20036-5339 · 202-857-6000

Gary M. Ford · ⑩ · Groom Law Group · http://www.groom.com · 1701 Pennsylvania Avenue, NW · Washington, DC 20006-5811 · 202-857-0620

Diane J. Fuchs · Womble Carlyle Sandridge & Rice · 1401 Eye Street, NW, Seventh Floor · Washington, DC 20005 · 202-467-6900

Randolf H. Hardock · Davis & Harman · The Willard, Suite 1200 · 1455 Pennsylvania Avenue, NW · Washington, DC 20004 · 202-347-2230

J. Mark Iwry · Sullivan & Cromwell · 1701 Pennsylvania Avenue, NW · Washington, DC 20006-5805 · 202-956-7500

William J. Kilberg · ㉕ · Gibson, Dunn & Crutcher · 1050 Connecticut Avenue, NW · Washington, DC 20036-5306 · 202-955-8500

Steven D. Kittrell · McGuireWoods · http://www.mcguirewoods.com · Washington Square, Suite 1200 · 1050 Connecticut Avenue, NW · Washington, DC 20036-5317 · 202-857-1700

Kurt L.P. Lawson · Hogan & Hartson · 555 Thirteenth Street, NW · Washington, DC 20004-1109 · 202-637-5600

David Levin · Drinker Biddle & Reath · 1500 K Street, NW · Washington, DC 20005-1209 · 202-842-8800

Stuart M. Lewis · ⑳ · Buchanan Ingersoll & Rooney · http://www.bipc.com · 1700 K Street, NW, Suite 300 · Washington, DC 20006-3807 · 202-452-7900

Joyce A. Mader · O'Donoghue & O'Donoghue · 4748 Wisconsin Avenue, NW · Washington, DC 20016 · 202-362-0041

Kent A. Mason · ⑩ · Davis & Harman · The Willard, Suite 1200 · 1455 Pennsylvania Avenue, NW · Washington, DC 20004 · 202-347-2230

Louis T. Mazawey · ⑳ · Groom Law Group · http://www.groom.com · 1701 Pennsylvania Avenue, NW · Washington, DC 20006-5811 · 202-857-0620

Evan Miller · ⑩ · Jones Day · 51 Louisiana Avenue, NW · Washington, DC 20001-2113 · 202-879-3939

Amy N. Moore · ⑩ · Covington & Burling · 1201 Pennsylvania Avenue, NW · Washington, DC 20004-2401 · 202-662-6000

Anne E. Moran · Steptoe & Johnson · http://www.steptoe.com · 1330 Connecticut Avenue, NW · Washington, DC 20036 · 202-429-3000

Daniel L. Morgan · Dickstein Shapiro · http://www.dicksteinshapiro.com · 1825 Eye Street, NW · Washington, DC 20006-5403 · 202-420-2200

Donald J. Myers · Reed Smith · East Tower, Suite 1100 · 1301 K Street, NW · Washington, DC 20005 · 202-414-9200

Melanie F. Nussdorf · ⑩ · Steptoe & Johnson · http://www.steptoe.com · 1330 Connecticut Avenue, NW Washington, DC 20036 · 202-429-3000

Kevin P. O'Brien · ⑩ · Ivins, Phillips & Barker · 1700 Pennsylvania Avenue, NW, Suite 600 · Washington, DC 20006 · 202-393-7600

C. Frederick Oliphant III · ⑳ · Miller & Chevalier · http://www.milchev.com · 655 Fifteenth Street, NW, Suite 900 · Washington, DC 20005-5701 · 202-626-5800

Paul J. Ondrasik, Jr. · Steptoe & Johnson · http://www.steptoe.com · 1330 Connecticut Avenue, NW · Washington, DC 20036 · 202-429-3000

David W. Powell · Groom Law Group · http://www.groom.com · 1701 Pennsylvania Avenue, NW · Washington, DC 20006-5811 · 202-857-0620

Gary G. Quintiere · ⑳ · Miller & Chevalier · http://www.milchev.com · 655 Fifteenth Street, NW, Suite 900 · Washington, DC 20005-5701 · 202-626-5800

Steven J. Sacher · ⑳ · Jones Day · 51 Louisiana Avenue, NW · Washington, DC 20001-2113 · 202-879-3939

Stephen M. Saxon · ⑩ · Groom Law Group · http://www.groom.com · 1701 Pennsylvania Avenue, NW · Washington, DC 20006-5811 · 202-857-0620

Edward A. Scallet · Groom Law Group · http://www.groom.com · 1701 Pennsylvania Avenue, NW · Washington, DC 20006-5811 · 202-857-0620

Thomas G. Schendt · Alston + Bird · http://www.alston.com · The Atlantic Building · 950 F Street, NW · Washington, DC 20004-1404 · 202-756-3300

William A. Schmidt · ⑩ · K&L Gates · 1601 K Street, NW · Washington, DC 20006-1600 · 202-778-9000

Richard C. Shea · Covington & Burling · 1201 Pennsylvania Avenue, NW · Washington, DC 20004-2401 202-662-6000

Serena G. Simons · Venable · http://www.venable.com · 575 Seventh Street, NW · Washington, DC 20004-1601 · 202-344-4000

Richard W. Skillman · Caplin & Drysdale · http://www.capdale.com · One Thomas Circle, NW, Suite 1100 · Washington, DC 20005 · 202-862-5000

W. Mark Smith · Sutherland · http://www.sutherland.com · 1275 Pennsylvania Avenue, NW · Washington, DC 20004-2415 · 202-383-0100

William L. Sollee, Jr. · Ivins, Phillips & Barker · 1700 Pennsylvania Avenue, NW, Suite 600 · Washington, DC 20006 · 202-393-7600

Andree M. St. Martin · Groom Law Group · http://www.groom.com · 1701 Pennsylvania Avenue, NW · Washington, DC 20006-5811 · 202-857-0620

Gary S. Tell · O'Melveny & Myers · 1625 Eye Street, NW · Washington, DC 20006-4001 · 202-383-5300

Peter H. Turza · ⑩ · Gibson, Dunn & Crutcher · 1050 Connecticut Avenue, NW · Washington, DC 20036-5306 · 202-955-8500

John M. Vine · ⑳ · Covington & Burling · 1201 Pennsylvania Avenue, NW · Washington, DC 20004-2401 · 202-662-6000

Martha Jo Wagner · Venable · http://www.venable.com · 575 Seventh Street, NW · Washington, DC 20004-1601 · 202-344-4000

Karen Wahle · O'Melveny & Myers · 1625 Eye Street, NW · Washington, DC 20006-4001 · 202-383-5300

David Weingarten · Slevin & Hart · 1625 Massachusetts Avenue, NW, Suite 450 · Washington, DC 20036 · 202-797-8700

Carol A. Weiser · Sutherland · http://www.sutherland.com · 1275 Pennsylvania Avenue, NW · Washington, DC 20004-2415 · 202-383-0100

Mark D. Wincek · Kilpatrick Stockton · 607 Fourteenth Street, NW, Suite 900 · Washington, DC 20005-2018 · 202-508-5800

ENERGY LAW

Washington

Lawrence G. Acker · Dewey & LeBoeuf · 1101 New York Avenue, NW, Suite 1100 · Washington, DC 20005-4213 · 202-986-8000

David T. Andril · Vinson & Elkins · http://www.velaw.com · The Willard Office Building, Suite 600 · 1455 Pennsylvania Avenue, NW · Washington, DC 20004-1008 · 202-639-6500

Stephen Angle · Vinson & Elkins · http://www.velaw.com · The Willard Office Building, Suite 600 · 1455 Pennsylvania Avenue, NW · Washington, DC 20004-1008 · 202-639-6500

Donna M. Attanasio · White & Case · http://www.whitecase.com · 701 Thirteenth Street, NW · Washington, DC 20005 · 202-626-3600

Stanley W. Balis · Miller, Balis & O'Neil · 1140 Nineteenth Street, NW · Washington, DC 20036 · 202-296-2960

Joseph C. Bell · Hogan & Hartson · 555 Thirteenth Street, NW · Washington, DC 20004-1109 · 202-637-5600

Frederic G. Berner, Jr. · Sidley Austin · 1501 K Street, NW · Washington, DC 20005 · 202-736-8000

David I. Bloom · Mayer Brown · 1909 K Street, NW · Washington, DC 20006-1101 · 202-263-3000

Stephen H. Brose · Steptoe & Johnson · http://www.steptoe.com · 1330 Connecticut Avenue, NW · Washington, DC 20036 · 202-429-3000

James H. Byrd · Miller, Balis & O'Neil · 1140 Nineteenth Street, NW · Washington, DC 20036 · 202-296-2960

Stuart A. Caplan · White & Case · http://www.whitecase.com · 701 Thirteenth Street, NW · Washington, DC 20005 · 202-626-3600

Donald H. Clarke · GKRSE · 1500 K Street, NW, Suite 330 · Washington, DC 20005 · 202-408-5400

Dana Contratto · Crowell & Moring · 1001 Pennsylvania Avenue, NW · Washington, DC 20004-2595 · 202-624-2500

M. Lisanne Crowley · Troutman Sanders · 401 Ninth Street, NW, Suite 1000 · Washington, DC 20004-2134 · 202-274-2950

David D'Alessandro · Stinson Morrison Hecker · http://www.stinson.com · 1150 Eighteenth Street, NW, Suite 800 · Washington, DC 20036 · 202-785-9100

Kelly A. Daly · Stinson Morrison Hecker · http://www.stinson.com · 1150 Eighteenth Street, NW, Suite 800 · Washington, DC 20036 · 202-785-9100

Donald K. Dankner · Winston & Strawn · 1700 K Street, NW · Washington, DC 20006-3817 · 202-282-5000

Clark Evans Downs · ⑩ · Jones Day · 51 Louisiana Avenue, NW · Washington, DC 20001-2113 · 202-879-3939

Thomas Eastment · Baker Botts · http://www.bakerbotts.com · The Warner Building, Suite 1300 · 1299 Pennsylvania Avenue, NW · Washington, DC 20004-2400 · 202-639-7700

George L. Edgar · Morgan Lewis & Bockius · 1111 Pennsylvania Avenue, NW · Washington, DC 20004 · 202-739-3000

Larry F. Eisenstat · Dickstein Shapiro · http://www.dicksteinshapiro.com · 1825 Eye Street, NW · Washington, DC 20006-5403 · 202-420-2200

Eugene R. Elrod · Sidley Austin · 1501 K Street, NW · Washington, DC 20005 · 202-736-8000

John N. Estes III · Skadden, Arps, Slate, Meagher & Flom · 1440 New York Avenue, NW · Washington, DC 20005 · 202-371-7000

Robert S. Fleishman · Covington & Burling · 1201 Pennsylvania Avenue, NW · Washington, DC 20004-2401 · 202-662-6000

Michael J. Fremuth · Andrews Kurth · http://www.andrewskurth.com · 1350 I Street, NW, Suite 1100 · Washington, DC 20005 · 202-662-2700

Carmen L. Gentile · Bruder, Gentile & Marcoux · 1701 Pennsylvania Avenue, NW, Suite 900 · Washington, DC 20006-5807 · 202-296-1500

Michael J. Gergen · Latham & Watkins · 555 Eleventh Street, NW, Suite 1000 · Washington, DC 20004-1304 · 202-637-2200

Douglas G. Green · Steptoe & Johnson · http://www.steptoe.com · 1330 Connecticut Avenue, NW · Washington, DC 20036 · 202-429-3000

Jay Matthew Gutierrez · Morgan Lewis & Bockius · 1111 Pennsylvania Avenue, NW · Washington, DC 20004 · 202-739-3000

Mark R. Haskell · Morgan Lewis & Bockius · 1111 Pennsylvania Avenue, NW · Washington, DC 20004 · 202-739-3000

Barbara K. Heffernan · Schiff Hardin · 1666 K Street NW, Suite 300 · Washington, DC 20006 · 202-778-6400

Kenneth G. Jaffe · Alston + Bird · http://www.alston.com · The Atlantic Building · 950 F Street, NW · Washington, DC 20004-1404 · 202-756-3300

Donald A. Kaplan · K&L Gates · 1601 K Street, NW · Washington, DC 20006-1600 · 202-778-9000

Bruce F. Kiely · Baker Botts · http://www.bakerbotts.com · The Warner Building, Suite 1300 · 1299 Pennsylvania Avenue, NW · Washington, DC 20004-2400 · 202-639-7700

Dennis Lane · Stinson Morrison Hecker · http://www.stinson.com · 1150 Eighteenth Street, NW, Suite 800 · Washington, DC 20036 · 202-785-9100

L. Poe Leggette · Fulbright & Jaworski · http://www.fulbright.com · Market Square · 801 Pennsylvania Avenue, NW · Washington, DC 20004-2623 · 202-662-0200

Kevin J. Lipson · Hogan & Hartson · 555 Thirteenth Street, NW · Washington, DC 20004-1109 · 202-637-5600

Robert Loeffler · Morrison & Foerster · http://www.mofo.com · 2000 Pennsylvania Avenue, NW, Suite 5500 · Washington, DC 20006-1888 · 202-887-1500

Frederick M. Lowther · Dickstein Shapiro · http://www.dicksteinshapiro.com · 1825 Eye Street, NW · Washington, DC 20006-5403 · 202-420-2200

Kenneth T. Maloney · Cullen and Dykman · 1101 Fourteenth Street, NW, Suite 550 · Washington, DC 20005-5633 · 202-223-8890

Michael Manning · Fulbright & Jaworski · http://www.fulbright.com · Market Square · 801 Pennsylvania Avenue, NW · Washington, DC 20004-2623 · 202-662-0200

William L. Massey · Covington & Burling · 1201 Pennsylvania Avenue, NW · Washington, DC 20004-2401 · 202-662-6000

John E. McCaffrey · Stinson Morrison Hecker · http://www.stinson.com · 1150 Eighteenth Street, NW, Suite 800 · Washington, DC 20036 · 202-785-9100

Keith R. McCrea · Sutherland · http://www.sutherland.com · 1275 Pennsylvania Avenue, NW · Washington, DC 20004-2415 · 202-383-0100

John D. McGrane · Morgan Lewis & Bockius · 1111 Pennsylvania Avenue, NW · Washington, DC 20004 202-739-3000

Randolph Q. McManus · Baker Botts · http://www.bakerbotts.com · The Warner Building, Suite 1300 · 1299 Pennsylvania Avenue, NW · Washington, DC 20004-2400 · 202-639-7700

Mark W. Menezes · Hunton & Williams · 1900 K Street, NW · Washington, DC 20006-1109 · 202-955-1500

Richard A. Meserve · Covington & Burling · 1201 Pennsylvania Avenue, NW · Washington, DC 20004-2401 · 202-662-6000

Margaret A. Moore · Van Ness Feldman · 1050 Thomas Jefferson Street, NW, Seventh Floor · Washington, DC 20007-3877 · 202-298-1800

Clifford M. Naeve · Skadden, Arps, Slate, Meagher & Flom · 1440 New York Avenue, NW · Washington, DC 20005 · 202-371-7000

Karol Lyn Newman · Morgan Lewis & Bockius · 1111 Pennsylvania Avenue, NW · Washington, DC 20004 · 202-739-3000

Robert R. Nordhaus · Van Ness Feldman · 1050 Thomas Jefferson Street, NW, Seventh Floor · Washington, DC 20007-3877 · 202-298-1800

Floyd L. Norton IV · Morgan Lewis & Bockius · 1111 Pennsylvania Avenue, NW · Washington, DC 20004 · 202-739-3000

Earle H. O'Donnell · White & Case · http://www.whitecase.com · 701 Thirteenth Street, NW · Washington, DC 20005 · 202-626-3600

Robert A. O'Neil · Miller, Balis & O'Neil · 1140 Nineteenth Street, NW · Washington, DC 20036 · 202-296-2960

Brian D. O'Neill · Dewey & LeBoeuf · 1101 New York Avenue, NW, Suite 1100 · Washington, DC 20005-4213 · 202-986-8000

John B. O'Sullivan · Chadbourne & Parke · http://www.chadbourne.com · 1200 New Hampshire Avenue, NW, Suite 300 · Washington, DC 20036 · 202-974-5600

Glen L. Ortman · Stinson Morrison Hecker · http://www.stinson.com · 1150 Eighteenth Street, NW, Suite 800 · Washington, DC 20036 · 202-785-9100

Mark L. Perlis · Dickstein Shapiro · http://www.dicksteinshapiro.com · 1825 Eye Street, NW · Washington, DC 20006-5403 · 202-420-2200

David B. Raskin · Steptoe & Johnson · http://www.steptoe.com · 1330 Connecticut Avenue, NW · Washington, DC 20036 · 202-429-3000

Harvey L. Reiter · Stinson Morrison Hecker · http://www.stinson.com · 1150 Eighteenth Street, NW, Suite 800 · Washington, DC 20036 · 202-785-9100

Alan I. Robbins · Jennings, Strouss & Salmon · http://www.jsslaw.com · 1700 Pennsylvania Avenue, NW, Suite 500 · Washington, DC 20006-4725 · 202-292-4738

Richard L. Roberts · Steptoe & Johnson · http://www.steptoe.com · 1330 Connecticut Avenue, NW · Washington, DC 20036 · 202-429-3000

William S. Scherman · Skadden, Arps, Slate, Meagher & Flom · 1440 New York Avenue, NW · Washington, DC 20005 · 202-371-7000

David L. Schwartz · Latham & Watkins · 555 Eleventh Street, NW, Suite 1000 · Washington, DC 20004-1304 · 202-637-2200

Charles H. Shoneman · Bracewell & Giuliani · http://www.bgllp.com · 2000 K Street, NW, Suite 500 · Washington, DC 20006-1872 · 202-828-5800

Clifford S. Sikora · Troutman Sanders · 401 Ninth Street, NW, Suite 1000 · Washington, DC 20004-2134 202-274-2950

Kenneth M. Simon · Dickstein Shapiro · http://www.dicksteinshapiro.com · 1825 Eye Street, NW · Washington, DC 20006-5403 · 202-420-2200

Roger E. Smith · Troutman Sanders · 401 Ninth Street, NW, Suite 1000 · Washington, DC 20004-2134 · 202-274-2950

Barry S. Spector · Wright & Talisman · 1200 G Street, NW, Suite 600 · Washington, DC 20005-3802 · 202-393-1200

Michael J. Thompson · Wright & Talisman · 1200 G Street, NW, Suite 600 · Washington, DC 20005-3802 · 202-393-1200

James B. Vasile · Davis Wright Tremaine · 1919 Pennsylvania Avenue, NW, Suite 200 · Washington, DC 20006-3402 · 202-973-4200

Clinton A. Vince · Sonnenschein Nath & Rosenthal · East Tower, Suite 600 · 1301 K Street, NW · Washington, DC 20005-3364 · 202-408-6400

Linda L. Walsh · Hunton & Williams · 1900 K Street, NW · Washington, DC 20006-1109 · 202-955-1500

Jennifer N. Waters · Crowell & Moring · 1001 Pennsylvania Avenue, NW · Washington, DC 20004-2595 202-624-2500

Adam Wenner · Chadbourne & Parke · http://www.chadbourne.com · 1200 New Hampshire Avenue, NW, Suite 300 · Washington, DC 20036 · 202-974-5600

Dena E. Wiggins · Sutherland · http://www.sutherland.com · 1275 Pennsylvania Avenue, NW · Washington, DC 20004-2415 · 202-383-0100

William A. Williams · Sidley Austin · 1501 K Street, NW · Washington, DC 20005 · 202-736-8000

ENTERTAINMENT LAW

Washington

Robert C. Bernius · Nixon Peabody · 401 Ninth Street, NW, Suite 900 · Washington, DC 20004-2128 · 202-585-8000

George H. Cohen · ㉕ · Bredhoff & Kaiser · 805 Fifteenth Street, NW, Suite 1000 · Washington, DC 20005 · 202-842-2600

Robert Corn-Revere · Davis Wright Tremaine · 1919 Pennsylvania Avenue, NW, Suite 200 · Washington, DC 20006-3402 · 202-973-4200

Kenneth M. Kaufman · Manatt, Phelps & Phillips · One Metro Center, Suite 1100 · 700 Twelfth Street, NW · Washington, DC 20005 · 202-585-6500

Gail E. Ross · Lichtman, Trister & Ross · 1666 Connecticut Avenue, NW, Suite 500 · Washington, DC 20009 · 202-328-1666

ENVIRONMENTAL LAW

Washington

Stanley Abramson · Arent Fox · 1050 Connecticut Avenue, NW · Washington, DC 20036-5339 · 202-857-6000

Virginia S. Albrecht · Hunton & Williams · 1900 K Street, NW · Washington, DC 20006-1109 · 202-955-1500

William A. Anderson II · ⑩ · Williams Mullen · http://www.williamsmullen.com · 1666 K Street, NW, Suite 1200 · Washington, DC 20006 · 202-833-9200

James T. Banks · Hogan & Hartson · 555 Thirteenth Street, NW · Washington, DC 20004-1109 · 202-637-5600

Lynn L. Bergeson · ⑩ · Bergeson & Campbell · 1203 Nineteenth Street, NW, Suite 300 · Washington, DC 20036-2401 · 202-557-3800

Kenneth Berlin · Skadden, Arps, Slate, Meagher & Flom · 1440 New York Avenue, NW · Washington, DC 20005 · 202-371-7000

Mitchell H. Bernstein · Van Ness Feldman · 1050 Thomas Jefferson Street, NW, Seventh Floor · Washington, DC 20007-3877 · 202-298-1800

David R. Berz · Weil Gotshal & Manges · 1300 Eye Street, NW, Suite 900 · Washington, DC 20005 · 202-682-7000

James R. Bieke · ⑩ · Goodwin Procter · 901 New York Avenue, NW · Washington, DC 20001 · 202-346-4000

Blake A. Biles · ⑩ · Arnold & Porter · 555 Twelfth Street, NW · Washington, DC 20004-1206 · 202-942-5000

Karl S. Bourdeau · Beveridge & Diamond · 1350 I Street, NW, Suite 700 · Washington, DC 20005-3311 · 202-789-6000

F. William Brownell · Hunton & Williams · 1900 K Street, NW · Washington, DC 20006-1109 · 202-955-1500

Christopher Buckley, Jr. · Gibson, Dunn & Crutcher · 1050 Connecticut Avenue, NW · Washington, DC 20036-5306 · 202-955-8500

David T. Buente, Jr. · ⑩ · Sidley Austin · 1501 K Street, NW · Washington, DC 20005 · 202-736-8000

William M. Bumpers · Baker Botts · http://www.bakerbotts.com · The Warner Building, Suite 1300 · 1299 Pennsylvania Avenue, NW · Washington, DC 20004-2400 · 202-639-7700

Colburn T. Cherney · Ropes & Gray · http://www.ropesgray.com · One Metro Center, Suite 900 · 700 Twelfth Street, NW · Washington, DC 20005-3948 · 202-508-4600

Kipp A. Coddington · Alston + Bird · http://www.alston.com · The Atlantic Building · 950 F Street, NW · Washington, DC 20004-1404 · 202-756-3300

John D. Conner, Jr. · McKenna Long & Aldridge · 1900 K Street, NW · Washington, DC 20006 · 202-496-7500

Henry L. Diamond · Beveridge & Diamond · 1350 I Street, NW, Suite 700 · Washington, DC 20005-3311 · 202-789-6000

Julie R. Domike · Wallace King Domike & Reiskin · Harborside, Suite 500 · 2900 K Street, NW · Washington, DC 20007 · 202-204-1000

Amy L. Edwards · Holland & Knight · http://www.hklaw.com · 2099 Pennsylvania Avenue, NW, Suite 100 · Washington, DC 20006-6801 · 202-955-3000

E. Donald Elliott · Willkie Farr & Gallagher · 1875 K Street, NW · Washington, DC 20006-1238 · 202-303-1000

Norman W. Fichthorn · Hunton & Williams · 1900 K Street, NW · Washington, DC 20006-1109 · 202-955-1500

Andrea Bear Field · ⑳ · Hunton & Williams · 1900 K Street, NW · Washington, DC 20006-1109 · 202-955-1500

G. William Frick · Van Ness Feldman · 1050 Thomas Jefferson Street, NW, Seventh Floor · Washington, DC 20007-3877 · 202-298-1800

Theodore L. Garrett · ⑳ · Covington & Burling · 1201 Pennsylvania Avenue, NW · Washington, DC 20004-2401 · 202-662-6000

Kevin A. Gaynor · Vinson & Elkins · http://www.velaw.com · The Willard Office Building, Suite 600 · 1455 Pennsylvania Avenue, NW · Washington, DC 20004-1008 · 202-639-6500

Mark A. Greenwood · Ropes & Gray · http://www.ropesgray.com · One Metro Center, Suite 900 · 700 Twelfth Street, NW · Washington, DC 20005-3948 · 202-508-4600

Paul Gutermann · Akin Gump Strauss Hauer & Feld · Robert S. Strauss Building · 1333 New Hampshire Avenue, NW · Washington, DC 20036-1564 · 202-887-4000

Samuel I. Gutter · Sidley Austin · 1501 K Street, NW · Washington, DC 20005 · 202-736-8000

Paul E. Hagen · Beveridge & Diamond · 1350 I Street, NW, Suite 700 · Washington, DC 20005-3311 · 202-789-6000

Ridgway M. Hall, Jr. · Crowell & Moring · 1001 Pennsylvania Avenue, NW · Washington, DC 20004-2595 · 202-624-2500

David J. Hayes · Latham & Watkins · 555 Eleventh Street, NW, Suite 1000 · Washington, DC 20004-1304 · 202-637-2200

Jeffrey R. Holmstead · Bracewell & Giuliani · http://www.bgllp.com · 2000 K Street, NW, Suite 500 · Washington, DC 20006-1872 · 202-828-5800

Lisa M. Jaeger · Bracewell & Giuliani · http://www.bgllp.com · 2000 K Street, NW, Suite 500 · Washington, DC 20006-1872 · 202-828-5800

Kenneth M. Kastner · Hogan & Hartson · 555 Thirteenth Street, NW · Washington, DC 20004-1109 · 202-637-5600

Thomas J. Kelly, Jr. · Venable · http://www.venable.com · 575 Seventh Street, NW · Washington, DC 20004-1601 · 202-344-4000

Charles H. Knauss · Bingham McCutchen · http://www.bingham.com · 3000 K Street, NW · Washington, DC 20007 · 202-424-7500

William H. Lewis, Jr. · Morgan Lewis & Bockius · 1111 Pennsylvania Avenue, NW · Washington, DC 20004 · 202-739-3000

Raymond B. Ludwiszewski · Gibson, Dunn & Crutcher · 1050 Connecticut Avenue, NW · Washington, DC 20036-5306 · 202-955-8500

Jonathan Martel · Arnold & Porter · 555 Twelfth Street, NW · Washington, DC 20004-1206 · 202-942-5000

Guy R. Martin · Perkins Coie · http://www.perkinscoie.com · 607 Fourteenth Street, NW, Suite 800 · Washington, DC 20005-2003 · 202-628-6600

Roger J. Marzulla · Marzulla & Marzulla · 1350 Connecticut Avenue, NW, Suite 410 · Washington, DC 20036-1722 · 202-822-6760

David E. Menotti · ⑳ · Pillsbury Winthrop Shaw Pittman · http://www.pillsburylaw.com · 2300 N Street, NW · Washington, DC 20037-1122 · 202-663-8000

Richard A. Meserve · Covington & Burling · 1201 Pennsylvania Avenue, NW · Washington, DC 20004-2401 · 202-662-6000

Thomas H. Milch · Arnold & Porter · 555 Twelfth Street, NW · Washington, DC 20004-1206 · 202-942-5000

Leonard A. Miller · Carter Ledyard & Milburn · 701 Eighth Street, NW, Suite 410 · Washington, DC 20001 · 202-898-1515

Jerome C. Muys · ⑳ · Muys & Associates · 1666 K Street, NW, Suite 700 · Washington, DC 20006 · 202-370-3924

Barry S. Neuman · Carter Ledyard & Milburn · 701 Eighth Street, NW, Suite 410 · Washington, DC 20001 · 202-898-1515

Henry V. Nickel · ⑩ · Hunton & Williams · 1900 K Street, NW · Washington, DC 20006-1109 · 202-955-1500

Charles A. O'Connor III · McKenna Long & Aldridge · 1900 K Street, NW · Washington, DC 20006 · 202-496-7500

William F. Pedersen · ⑳ · William F. Pedersen · http://www.billpedersen.com · 1615 L Street, NW, Suite 1350 · Washington, DC 20036 · 202-296-8884

Richard A. Penna · Van Ness Feldman · 1050 Thomas Jefferson Street, NW, Seventh Floor · Washington, DC 20007-3877 · 202-298-1800

Steven P. Quarles · ⑩ · Crowell & Moring · 1001 Pennsylvania Avenue, NW · Washington, DC 20004-2595 · 202-624-2500

Patrick M. Raher · Hogan & Hartson · 555 Thirteenth Street, NW · Washington, DC 20004-1109 · 202-637-5600

Katherine L. Rhyne · King & Spalding · 1700 Pennsylvania Avenue, NW, Suite 200 · Washington, DC 20006-4706 · 202-737-0500

Steven Schatzow · ⑳ · Steven Schatzow · 2022 Columbia Road, Suite 601 · Washington, DC 20009 · 202-332-3729

Richard E. Schwartz · Crowell & Moring · 1001 Pennsylvania Avenue, NW · Washington, DC 20004-2595 · 202-624-2500

Turner T. Smith, Jr. · ⑩ · Hunton & Williams · 1900 K Street, NW · Washington, DC 20006-1109 · 202-955-1500

Steven P. Solow · Hunton & Williams · 1900 K Street, NW · Washington, DC 20006-1109 · 202-955-1500

Judson W. Starr · Venable · http://www.venable.com · 575 Seventh Street, NW · Washington, DC 20004-1601 · 202-344-4000

Michael W. Steinberg · ⑩ · Morgan Lewis & Bockius · 1111 Pennsylvania Avenue, NW · Washington, DC 20004 · 202-739-3000

Richard G. Stoll · ⑳ · Foley & Lardner · Washington Harbour, Suite 500 · 3000 K Street, NW · Washington, DC 20007-5109 · 202-672-5300

Margaret N. Strand · Venable · http://www.venable.com · 575 Seventh Street, NW · Washington, DC 20004-1601 · 202-344-4000

William L. Thomas · Skadden, Arps, Slate, Meagher & Flom · 1440 New York Avenue, NW · Washington, DC 20005 · 202-371-7000

Allan J. Topol · ⑩ · Covington & Burling · 1201 Pennsylvania Avenue, NW · Washington, DC 20004-2401 · 202-662-6000

Timothy K. Webster · Sidley Austin · 1501 K Street, NW · Washington, DC 20005 · 202-736-8000

David B. Weinberg · ⑩ · Wiley Rein · 1776 K Street, NW · Washington, DC 20006-2359 · 202-719-7000

Kenneth W. Weinstein · Latham & Watkins · 555 Eleventh Street, NW, Suite 1000 · Washington, DC 20004-1304 · 202-637-2200

John L. Wittenborn · Kelley Drye & Warren · Washington Harbour, Suite 400 · 3050 K Street, NW · Washington, DC 20007-5108 · 202-342-8400

Louis S. Zimmerman · Fulbright & Jaworski · http://www.fulbright.com · Market Square · 801 Pennsylvania Avenue, NW · Washington, DC 20004-2623 · 202-662-0200

EQUIPMENT FINANCE LAW

Washington

Barkley Clark · ⑩ · Stinson Morrison Hecker · http://www.stinson.com · 1150 Eighteenth Street, NW, Suite 800 · Washington, DC 20036 · 202-785-9100

Eileen M. Gleimer · Crowell & Moring · 1001 Pennsylvania Avenue, NW · Washington, DC 20004-2595 · 202-624-2500

Edward K. Gross · Vedder Price · 875 Fifteenth Street, NW, Suite 275 · Washington, DC 20005 · 202-312-3320

Lynn A. Soukup · Pillsbury Winthrop Shaw Pittman · http://www.pillsburylaw.com · 2300 N Street, NW · Washington, DC 20037-1122 · 202-663-8000

FAMILY LAW

Washington

Sanford K. Ain · ㉕ · Ain & Bank · http://www.ainbanklaw.com · 1900 M Street, NW, Suite 600 · Washington, DC 20036 · 202-530-3300

Rita M. Bank · ⑳ · Ain & Bank · http://www.ainbanklaw.com · 1900 M Street, NW, Suite 600 · Washington, DC 20036 · 202-530-3300

Mark S. Carlin · Ain & Bank · http://www.ainbanklaw.com · 1900 M Street, NW, Suite 600 · Washington, DC 20036 · 202-530-3300

Jonathan M. Dana · Feldesman Tucker Leifer Fidell · 2001 L Street, NW, Second Floor · Washington, DC 20036 · 202-466-8960

Susan Friedman · Kuder, Smollar & Friedman · 1350 Connecticut Avenue, NW, Suite 600 · Washington, DC 20036 · 202-331-7522

Anne Marie Jackson · Ain & Bank · http://www.ainbanklaw.com · 1900 M Street, NW, Suite 600 · Washington, DC 20036 · 202-530-3300

Armin U. Kuder · ㉕ · Kuder, Smollar & Friedman · 1350 Connecticut Avenue, NW, Suite 600 · Washington, DC 20036 · 202-331-7522

Robert C. Liotta · Liotta, Dranitzke & Engel · 1666 Connecticut Avenue, NW, Suite 250 · Washington, DC 20009-1039 · 202-797-7700

Deborah Luxenberg · Luxenberg, Johnson & Dickens · http://www.luxlaw.com · 1025 Connecticut Avenue, NW, Suite 1000 · Washington, DC 20036 · 202-265-3340

Lauren Shea · Ain & Bank · http://www.ainbanklaw.com · 1900 M Street, NW, Suite 600 · Washington, DC 20036 · 202-530-3300

Paul R. Smollar · Kuder, Smollar & Friedman · 1350 Connecticut Avenue, NW, Suite 600 · Washington, DC 20036 · 202-331-7522

Marna Susan Tucker · ⑳ · Feldesman Tucker Leifer Fidell · 2001 L Street, NW, Second Floor · Washington, DC 20036 · 202-466-8960

FAMILY LAW MEDIATION

Washington

Rita M. Bank · 20 · Ain & Bank · http://www.ainbanklaw.com · 1900 M Street, NW, Suite 600 · Washington, DC 20036 · 202-530-3300

Armin U. Kuder · 25 · Kuder, Smollar & Friedman · 1350 Connecticut Avenue, NW, Suite 600 · Washington, DC 20036 · 202-331-7522

FDA LAW

Washington

David G. Adams · Venable · http://www.venable.com · 575 Seventh Street, NW · Washington, DC 20004-1601 · 202-344-4000

Edward M. Basile · King & Spalding · 1700 Pennsylvania Avenue, NW, Suite 200 · Washington, DC 20006-4706 · 202-737-0500

I. Scott Bass · Sidley Austin · 1501 K Street, NW · Washington, DC 20005 · 202-736-8000

Donald O. Beers · Arnold & Porter · 555 Twelfth Street, NW · Washington, DC 20004-1206 · 202-942-5000

Robert P. Brady · Hogan & Hartson · 555 Thirteenth Street, NW · Washington, DC 20004-1109 · 202-637-5600

Richard M. Cooper · Williams & Connolly · 725 Twelfth Street, NW · Washington, DC 20005-5901 · 202-434-5000

Ellen J. Flannery · Covington & Burling · 1201 Pennsylvania Avenue, NW · Washington, DC 20004-2401 · 202-662-6000

Richard L. Frank · Olsson, Frank and Weeda · 1400 Sixteenth Street, NW, Suite 400 · Washington, DC 20036-2220 · 202-789-1212

Jeffrey N. Gibbs · Hyman, Phelps & McNamara · 700 Thirteenth Street, NW, Suite 1200 · Washington, DC 20005 · 202-737-5600

Mark A. Heller · Goodwin Procter · 901 New York Avenue, NW · Washington, DC 20001 · 202-346-4000

Thomas O. Henteleff · Kleinfeld, Kaplan & Becker · http://www.kkblaw.com · 1140 Nineteenth Street, NW, Suite 900 · Washington, DC 20036 · 202-223-5120

Peter Barton Hutt · 10 · Covington & Burling · 1201 Pennsylvania Avenue, NW · Washington, DC 20004-2401 · 202-662-6000

Richard F. Kingham · Covington & Burling · 1201 Pennsylvania Avenue, NW · Washington, DC 20004-2401 · 202-662-6000

Daniel A. Kracov · Arnold & Porter · 555 Twelfth Street, NW · Washington, DC 20004-1206 · 202-942-5000

Arthur N. Levine · Arnold & Porter · 555 Twelfth Street, NW · Washington, DC 20004-1206 · 202-942-5000

James R. Phelps · Hyman, Phelps & McNamara · 700 Thirteenth Street, NW, Suite 1200 · Washington, DC 20005 · 202-737-5600

Peter O. Safir · Covington & Burling · 1201 Pennsylvania Avenue, NW · Washington, DC 20004-2401 · 202-662-6000

William B. Schultz · Zuckerman Spaeder · http://www.zuckerman.com · 1800 M Street, NW, Suite 1000 · Washington, DC 20036-5807 · 202-778-1800

Daniel E. Troy · Sidley Austin · 1501 K Street, NW · Washington, DC 20005 · 202-736-8000

William W. Vodra · Arnold & Porter · 555 Twelfth Street, NW · Washington, DC 20004-1206 · 202-942-5000

FIRST AMENDMENT LAW

Washington

Kevin T. Baine · ⑩ · Williams & Connolly · 725 Twelfth Street, NW · Washington, DC 20005-5901 · 202-434-5000

Robert C. Bernius · Nixon Peabody · 401 Ninth Street, NW, Suite 900 · Washington, DC 20004-2128 · 202-585-8000

Bruce D. Brown · Baker Hostetler · http://www.bakerlaw.com · Washington Square, Suite 1100 · 1050 Connecticut Avenue, NW · Washington, DC 20036-5304 · 202-861-1500

Robert Corn-Revere · Davis Wright Tremaine · 1919 Pennsylvania Avenue, NW, Suite 200 · Washington, DC 20006-3402 · 202-973-4200

Jonathan D. Hart · Dow Lohnes · http://www.dowlohnes.com · 1200 New Hampshire Avenue, NW, Suite 800 · Washington, DC 20036-6802 · 202-776-2000

Thomas G. Hentoff · Williams & Connolly · 725 Twelfth Street, NW · Washington, DC 20005-5901 · 202-434-5000

David E. Kendall · ⑩ · Williams & Connolly · 725 Twelfth Street, NW · Washington, DC 20005-5901 · 202-434-5000

Lee Levine · ⑩ · Levine Sullivan Koch & Schulz · 1050 Seventeenth Street, NW, Suite 800 · Washington, DC 20036-5514 · 202-508-1100

Andrew Marks · Crowell & Moring · 1001 Pennsylvania Avenue, NW · Washington, DC 20004-2595 · 202-624-2500

Paul M. Smith · Jenner & Block · http://www.jenner.com · 1099 New York Avenue, NW, Suite 900 · Washington, DC 20001-4412 · 202-639-6000

Michael D. Sullivan · Levine Sullivan Koch & Schulz · 1050 Seventeenth Street, NW, Suite 800 · Washington, DC 20036-5514 · 202-508-1100

Charles D. Tobin · Holland & Knight · http://www.hklaw.com · 2099 Pennsylvania Avenue, NW, Suite 100 · Washington, DC 20006-6801 · 202-955-3000

Seth P. Waxman · WilmerHale · http://www.wilmerhale.com · 1875 Pennsylvania Avenue, NW · Washington, DC 20006 · 202-663-6000

Gerson A. Zweifach · ⑩ · Williams & Connolly · 725 Twelfth Street, NW · Washington, DC 20005-5901 202-434-5000

FRANCHISE LAW

Washington

Arthur I. Cantor · Wiley Rein · 1776 K Street, NW · Washington, DC 20006-2359 · 202-719-7000

John F. Dienelt · ⑩ · DLA Piper · 500 Eighth Street, NW · Washington, DC 20004 · 202-799-4000

Steven B. Feirman · Nixon Peabody · 401 Ninth Street, NW, Suite 900 · Washington, DC 20004-2128 · 202-585-8000

Peter J. Klarfeld · Wiley Rein · 1776 K Street, NW · Washington, DC 20006-2359 · 202-719-7000

Andrew P. Loewinger · Nixon Peabody · 401 Ninth Street, NW, Suite 900 · Washington, DC 20004-2128 202-585-8000

Scott McIntosh · DLA Piper · 500 Eighth Street, NW · Washington, DC 20004 · 202-799-4000

Thomas W. Queen · Wiley Rein · 1776 K Street, NW · Washington, DC 20006-2359 · 202-719-7000

Erik B. Wulff · DLA Piper · 500 Eighth Street, NW · Washington, DC 20004 · 202-799-4000

Philip F. Zeidman · ⑩ · DLA Piper · 500 Eighth Street, NW · Washington, DC 20004 · 202-799-4000

GAMING LAW

Washington

Todd Araujo · Akin Gump Strauss Hauer & Feld · Robert S. Strauss Building · 1333 New Hampshire Avenue, NW · Washington, DC 20036-1564 · 202-887-4000

Douglas B. L. Endreson · Sonosky, Chambers, Sachse, Endreson & Perry · 1425 K Street, NW, Suite 600 Washington, DC 20005 · 202-682-0240

Aurene Michele Martin · Ietan Consulting · Robert S. Strauss Building · 1333 New Hampshire Avenue, NW · Washington, DC 20036 · 202-419-3527

Jeffrey T. Smith · Patton Boggs · 2550 M Street, NW · Washington, DC 20037 · 202-457-6000

David O. Stewart · Ropes & Gray · http://www.ropesgray.com · One Metro Center, Suite 900 · 700 Twelfth Street, NW · Washington, DC 20005-3948 · 202-508-4600

Jerry C. Straus · Hobbs, Straus, Dean & Walker · 2120 L Street, NW, Suite 700 · Washington, DC 20037 202-822-8282

Dennis J. Whittlesey · Dickinson Wright · http://www.dickinsonwright.com · 1901 L Street, NW, Suite 800 · Washington, DC 20036-3506 · 202-457-0160

Washington

Howard H. Baker · Baker, Donelson, Bearman, Caldwell & Berkowitz · http://www.bakerdonelson.com · Lincoln Square, Sixth Floor · 555 Eleventh Street, NW · Washington, DC 20004 · 202-508-3400

James Addison Baker IV · Baker Botts · http://www.bakerbotts.com · The Warner Building, Suite 1300 · 1299 Pennsylvania Avenue, NW · Washington, DC 20004-2400 · 202-639-7700

Charlene Barshefsky · WilmerHale · http://www.wilmerhale.com · 1875 Pennsylvania Avenue, NW · Washington, DC 20006 · 202-663-6000

Robert F. Bauer · Perkins Coie · http://www.perkinscoie.com · 607 Fourteenth Street, NW, Suite 800 · Washington, DC 20005-2003 · 202-628-6600

Berl Bernhard · DLA Piper · 500 Eighth Street, NW · Washington, DC 20004 · 202-799-4000

Thomas Hale Boggs, Jr. · Patton Boggs · 2550 M Street, NW · Washington, DC 20037 · 202-457-6000

Antoinette C. Bush · Skadden, Arps, Slate, Meagher & Flom · 1440 New York Avenue, NW · Washington, DC 20005 · 202-371-7000

Martha L. Cochran · Arnold & Porter · 555 Twelfth Street, NW · Washington, DC 20004-1206 · 202-942-5000

James H. Davidson · Polsinelli Shalton Flanigan Suelthaus · http://www.polsinelli.com · 1152 Fifteenth Street, Northwest, Suite 800 · Washington, DC 20005 · 202-783-3300

Roderick DeArment · Covington & Burling · 1201 Pennsylvania Avenue, NW · Washington, DC 20004-2401 · 202-662-6000

Frank J. Donatelli · McGuireWoods · http://www.mcguirewoods.com · Washington Square, Suite 1200 · 1050 Connecticut Avenue, NW · Washington, DC 20036-5317 · 202-857-1700

Stuart E. Eizenstat · Covington & Burling · 1201 Pennsylvania Avenue, NW · Washington, DC 20004-2401 · 202-662-6000

Martin Frost · Polsinelli Shalton Flanigan Suelthaus · http://www.polsinelli.com · 1152 Fifteenth Street, Northwest, Suite 800 · Washington, DC 20005 · 202-783-3300

Mark H. Gitenstein · Mayer Brown · 1909 K Street, NW · Washington, DC 20006-1101 · 202-263-3000

Martin B. Gold · Covington & Burling · 1201 Pennsylvania Avenue, NW · Washington, DC 20004-2401 · 202-662-6000

Richard M. Gold · Holland & Knight · http://www.hklaw.com · 2099 Pennsylvania Avenue, NW, Suite 100 · Washington, DC 20006-6801 · 202-955-3000

Lee E. Goodman · LeClair Ryan · 1101 Connecticut Avenue, NW, Suite 600 · Washington, DC 20036 · 202-659-4140

Theodore R. Groom · ⑩ · Groom Law Group · http://www.groom.com · 1701 Pennsylvania Avenue, NW Washington, DC 20006-5811 · 202-857-0620

Kenneth A. Gross · Skadden, Arps, Slate, Meagher & Flom · 1440 New York Avenue, NW · Washington, DC 20005 · 202-371-7000

Harry L. Gutman · ⑩ · KPMG · 2001 M Street, NW · Washington, DC 20036-3310 · 202-533-3000

Lloyd N. Hand · King & Spalding · 1700 Pennsylvania Avenue, NW, Suite 200 · Washington, DC 20006-4706 · 202-737-0500

Randolf H. Hardock · Davis & Harman · The Willard, Suite 1200 · 1455 Pennsylvania Avenue, NW · Washington, DC 20004 · 202-347-2230

Theodore M. Hester · King & Spalding · 1700 Pennsylvania Avenue, NW, Suite 200 · Washington, DC 20006-4706 · 202-737-0500

Lindsay D. Hooper · Capitol Tax Partners · 101 Constitution Avenue, NW, Suite 675 East · Washington, DC 20001 · 202-289-8700

W. Michael House · Hogan & Hartson · 555 Thirteenth Street, NW · Washington, DC 20004-1109 · 202-637-5600

Elliott H. Levitas · Kilpatrick Stockton · 607 Fourteenth Street, NW, Suite 900 · Washington, DC 20005-2018 · 202-508-5800

Charles S. Levy · WilmerHale · http://www.wilmerhale.com · 1875 Pennsylvania Avenue, NW · Washington, DC 20006 · 202-663-6000

Charles T. Manatt · Manatt, Phelps & Phillips · One Metro Center, Suite 1100 · 700 Twelfth Street, NW Washington, DC 20005 · 202-585-6500

Thurgood Marshall, Jr. · Bingham McCutchen · http://www.bingham.com · 2020 K Street, NW · Washington, DC 20006-1806 · 202-373-6000

David M. McIntosh · Mayer Brown · 1909 K Street, NW · Washington, DC 20006-1101 · 202-263-3000

John A. Merrigan · DLA Piper · 500 Eighth Street, NW · Washington, DC 20004 · 202-799-4000

Michael A. Nemeroff · Sidley Austin · 1501 K Street, NW · Washington, DC 20005 · 202-736-8000

Michael L. Pate · Bracewell & Giuliani · http://www.bgllp.com · 2000 K Street, NW, Suite 500 · Washington, DC 20006-1872 · 202-828-5800

James D. Range · Baker, Donelson, Bearman, Caldwell & Berkowitz · http://www.bakerdonelson.com · Lincoln Square, Sixth Floor · 555 Eleventh Street, NW · Washington, DC 20004 · 202-508-3400

J. Curtis Rich · Van Ness Feldman · 1050 Thomas Jefferson Street, NW, Seventh Floor · Washington, DC 20007-3877 · 202-298-1800

Stephen M. Ryan · McDermott Will & Emery · 600 Thirteenth Street, NW · Washington, DC 20005-3096 · 202-756-8000

Jack L. Schenendorf · Covington & Burling · 1201 Pennsylvania Avenue, NW · Washington, DC 20004-2401 · 202-662-6000

Gerry Sikorski · Holland & Knight · http://www.hklaw.com · 2099 Pennsylvania Avenue, NW, Suite 100 · Washington, DC 20006-6801 · 202-955-3000

Robert S. Strauss · Akin Gump Strauss Hauer & Feld · Robert S. Strauss Building · 1333 New Hampshire Avenue, NW · Washington, DC 20036-1564 · 202-887-4000

Janet R. Studley · Holland & Knight · http://www.hklaw.com · 2099 Pennsylvania Avenue, NW, Suite 100 · Washington, DC 20006-6801 · 202-955-3000

Robert G. Szabo · Van Ness Feldman · 1050 Thomas Jefferson Street, NW, Seventh Floor · Washington, DC 20007-3877 · 202-298-1800

Jonathan Talisman · Capitol Tax Partners · 101 Constitution Avenue, NW, Suite 675 East · Washington, DC 20001 · 202-289-8700

Kirk K. Van Tine · Baker Botts · http://www.bakerbotts.com · The Warner Building, Suite 1300 · 1299 Pennsylvania Avenue, NW · Washington, DC 20004-2400 · 202-639-7700

HEALTH CARE LAW

Washington

Dennis M. Barry · ⑩ · King & Spalding · 1700 Pennsylvania Avenue, NW, Suite 200 · Washington, DC 20006-4706 · 202-737-0500

John T. Brennan, Jr. · Crowell & Moring · 1001 Pennsylvania Avenue, NW · Washington, DC 20004-2595 · 202-624-2500

Lanny A. Breuer · Covington & Burling · 1201 Pennsylvania Avenue, NW · Washington, DC 20004-2401 202-662-6000

Thomas N. Bulleit, Jr. · Hogan & Hartson · 555 Thirteenth Street, NW · Washington, DC 20004-1109 · 202-637-5600

Irwin Cohen · Fulbright & Jaworski · http://www.fulbright.com · Market Square · 801 Pennsylvania Avenue, NW · Washington, DC 20004-2623 · 202-662-0200

H. Guy Collier · McDermott Will & Emery · 600 Thirteenth Street, NW · Washington, DC 20005-3096 · 202-756-8000

Christopher L. Crosswhite · Duane Morris · 505 Ninth Street, NW, Suite 1000 · Washington, DC 20004-2166 · 202-776-7800

Steven B. Epstein · Epstein, Becker & Green · 1227 Twenty-Fifth Street, NW, Suite 700 · Washington, DC 20037-1156 · 202-861-0900

E. Michael Flanagan · Polsinelli Shalton Flanigan Suelthaus · http://www.polsinelli.com · 1152 Fifteenth Street, Northwest, Suite 800 · Washington, DC 20005 · 202-783-3300

Thomas C. Fox · ⑩ · Reed Smith · East Tower, Suite 1100 · 1301 K Street, NW · Washington, DC 20005 202-414-9200

Joel M. Hamme · Powers, Pyles, Sutter and Verville · http://www.ppsv.com · 1501 M Street, NW, Seventh Floor · Washington, DC 20006 · 202-466-6550

Malcolm J. Harkins III · Proskauer Rose · http://www.proskauer.com · 1001 Pennsylvania Avenue NW, Suite 400 South · Washington, DC 20004-2533 · 202-416-6800

Douglas A. Hastings · ⑩ · Epstein, Becker & Green · 1227 Twenty-Fifth Street, NW, Suite 700 · Washington, DC 20037-1156 · 202-861-0900

Peter Barton Hutt · ⑩ · Covington & Burling · 1201 Pennsylvania Avenue, NW · Washington, DC 20004-2401 · 202-662-6000

Thomas Hyatt · Ober, Kaler, Grimes & Shriver · http://www.ober.com · 1401 H Street, NW, Suite 500 · Washington, DC 20005-3324 · 202-408-8400

Paul E. Kalb · Sidley Austin · 1501 K Street, NW · Washington, DC 20005 · 202-736-8000

Christopher L. Keough · King & Spalding · 1700 Pennsylvania Avenue, NW, Suite 200 · Washington, DC 20006-4706 · 202-737-0500

John Daniel Kiser · FoxKiser · 750 Seventeenth Street, NW, Suite 1100 · Washington, DC 20006 · 202-778-2300

Keith M. Korenchuk · Covington & Burling · 1201 Pennsylvania Avenue, NW · Washington, DC 20004-2401 · 202-662-6000

Arthur N. Lerner · Crowell & Moring · 1001 Pennsylvania Avenue, NW · Washington, DC 20004-2595 · 202-624-2500

Gregory M. Luce · Skadden, Arps, Slate, Meagher & Flom · 1440 New York Avenue, NW · Washington, DC 20005 · 202-371-7000

Joel L. Michaels · ⑩ · McDermott Will & Emery · 600 Thirteenth Street, NW · Washington, DC 20005-3096 · 202-756-8000

Diane S. Millman · Powers, Pyles, Sutter and Verville · http://www.ppsv.com · 1501 M Street, NW, Seventh Floor · Washington, DC 20006 · 202-466-6550

Thomas L. Mills · Winston & Strawn · 1700 K Street, NW · Washington, DC 20006-3817 · 202-282-5000

Kirk J. Nahra · Wiley Rein · 1776 K Street, NW · Washington, DC 20006-2359 · 202-719-7000

Patrick K. O'Hare · Ober, Kaler, Grimes & Shriver · http://www.ober.com · 1401 H Street, NW, Suite 500 Washington, DC 20005-3324 · 202-408-8400

Larry A. Oday · Vinson & Elkins · http://www.velaw.com · The Willard Office Building, Suite 600 · 1455 Pennsylvania Avenue, NW · Washington, DC 20004-1008 · 202-639-6500

Ethan M. Posner · Covington & Burling · 1201 Pennsylvania Avenue, NW · Washington, DC 20004-2401 202-662-6000

Galen D. Powers · ⑩ · Powers, Pyles, Sutter and Verville · http://www.ppsv.com · 1501 M Street, NW, Seventh Floor · Washington, DC 20006 · 202-466-6550

Frederick Robinson · Fulbright & Jaworski · http://www.fulbright.com · Market Square · 801 Pennsylvania Avenue, NW · Washington, DC 20004-2623 · 202-662-0200

Martha P. Rogers · Ober, Kaler, Grimes & Shriver · http://www.ober.com · 1401 H Street, NW, Suite 500 Washington, DC 20005-3324 · 202-408-8400

William A. Sarraille · Sidley Austin · 1501 K Street, NW · Washington, DC 20005 · 202-736-8000

Albert W. Shay · Sonnenschein Nath & Rosenthal · East Tower, Suite 600 · 1301 K Street, NW · Washington, DC 20005-3364 · 202-408-6400

Lynn Shapiro Snyder · Epstein, Becker & Green · 1227 Twenty-Fifth Street, NW, Suite 700 · Washington, DC 20037-1156 · 202-861-0900

T. J. Sullivan · Drinker Biddle & Reath · 1500 K Street, NW · Washington, DC 20005-1209 · 202-842-8800

Ronald N. Sutter · ⑩ · Powers, Pyles, Sutter and Verville · http://www.ppsv.com · 1501 M Street, NW, Seventh Floor · Washington, DC 20006 · 202-466-6550

Eugene Tillman · Reed Smith · East Tower, Suite 1100 · 1301 K Street, NW · Washington, DC 20005 · 202-414-9200

Carrie Valiant · Epstein, Becker & Green · 1227 Twenty-Fifth Street, NW, Suite 700 · Washington, DC 20037-1156 · 202-861-0900

Michelle A. Williams · DLA Piper · 500 Eighth Street, NW · Washington, DC 20004 · 202-799-4000

IMMIGRATION LAW

Washington

Andres Benach · Maggio Kattar · 11 Dupont Circle, NW, Suite 775 · Washington, DC 20036 · 202-483-0053

Richard S. Bromberg · Richard S. Bromberg · 2011 Pennsylvania Avenue, NW, Fifth Floor · Washington, DC 20006 · 202-835-0660

Thomas A. Elliot · ⑩ · Elliot & Mayock · 1629 K Street, NW, Twelfth Floor · Washington, DC 20006-1641 · 202-429-1725

Roberta Freedman · Duane Morris · 505 Ninth Street, NW, Suite 1000 · Washington, DC 20004-2166 · 202-776-7800

Karen T. Grisez · Fried, Frank, Harris, Shriver & Jacobson · 1001 Pennsylvania Avenue, NW · Washington, DC 20004-2505 · 202-639-7000

Elliott C. Lichtman · Lichtman, Trister & Ross · 1666 Connecticut Avenue, NW, Suite 500 · Washington, DC 20009 · 202-328-1666

Mark A. Mancini · ⑩ · Wasserman, Mancini & Chang · 1915 I Street, NW, Suite 400 · Washington, DC 20006-2117 · 202-783-8905

Amy M. Nice · Dickstein Shapiro · http://www.dicksteinshapiro.com · 1825 Eye Street, NW · Washington, DC 20006-5403 · 202-420-2200

Jan M. Pederson · ⑩ · The Pederson Immigration Law Group · 2001 L Street, NW, Suite 601 · Washington, DC 20036-4910 · 202-785-1960

Eleanor Pelta · Morgan Lewis & Bockius · 1111 Pennsylvania Avenue, NW · Washington, DC 20004 · 202-739-3000

José I. Pertierra · Law Office of José Pertierra · 1010 Vermont Avenue, NW, Suite 620 · Washington, DC 20005-4902 · 202-783-6666

Mary E. Pivec · ⑩ · Keller and Heckman · Washington Center · 1001 G Street, NW · Washington, DC 20001 · 202-434-4100

Elizabeth A. Quinn · Maggio Kattar · 11 Dupont Circle, NW, Suite 775 · Washington, DC 20036 · 202-483-0053

Linda A. Rahal · Trow & Rahal · http://www.trowlaw.com · 5335 Wisconsin Avenue, NW, Suite 920 · Washington, DC 20015-2003 · 202-537-4830

Robert A. Remes · Carliner & Remes · 1150 Connecticut Avenue, NW, Suite 610 · Washington, DC 20036 · 202-223-0050

Denyse M. Sabagh · ⑩ · Duane Morris · 505 Ninth Street, NW, Suite 1000 · Washington, DC 20004-2166 202-776-7800

Elizabeth E. Stern · Baker & McKenzie · 815 Connecticut Avenue, NW · Washington, DC 20006-4078 · 202-452-7000

Stephen C. Trow · Trow & Rahal · http://www.trowlaw.com · 5335 Wisconsin Avenue, NW, Suite 920 · Washington, DC 20015-2003 · 202-537-4830

Paul W. Virtue · Hogan & Hartson · 555 Thirteenth Street, NW · Washington, DC 20004-1109 · 202-637-5600

Palma R. Yanni · Palma Yanni · 2612 P Street, NW · Washington, DC 20007 · 202-338-1995

INFORMATION TECHNOLOGY LAW

Washington

Jon A. Baumgarten · ⑩ · Proskauer Rose · http://www.proskauer.com · 1001 Pennsylvania Avenue NW, Suite 400 South · Washington, DC 20004-2533 · 202-416-6800

J. Beckwith Burr · WilmerHale · http://www.wilmerhale.com · 1875 Pennsylvania Avenue, NW · Washington, DC 20006 · 202-663-6000

Christopher D. Ford · Alston + Bird · http://www.alston.com · The Atlantic Building · 950 F Street, NW · Washington, DC 20004-1404 · 202-756-3300

Jonathan D. Hart · Dow Lohnes · http://www.dowlohnes.com · 1200 New Hampshire Avenue, NW, Suite 800 · Washington, DC 20036-6802 · 202-776-2000

Daniel A. Masur · Mayer Brown · 1909 K Street, NW · Washington, DC 20006-1101 · 202-263-3000

Randall S. Parks · Hunton & Williams · 1900 K Street, NW · Washington, DC 20006-1109 · 202-955-1500

Carlyle C. Ring, Jr. · Ober, Kaler, Grimes & Shriver · http://www.ober.com · 1401 H Street, NW, Suite 500 · Washington, DC 20005-3324 · 202-408-8400

Lewis Rose · Kelley Drye & Warren · Washington Harbour, Suite 400 · 3050 K Street, NW · Washington, DC 20007-5108 · 202-342-8400

Thomas P. Vartanian · ⑩ · Fried, Frank, Harris, Shriver & Jacobson · 1001 Pennsylvania Avenue, NW · Washington, DC 20004-2505 · 202-639-7000

Robert E. Zahler · Pillsbury Winthrop Shaw Pittman · http://www.pillsburylaw.com · 2300 N Street, NW · Washington, DC 20037-1122 · 202-663-8000

INSURANCE LAW

Washington

William J. Bowman · Hogan & Hartson · 555 Thirteenth Street, NW · Washington, DC 20004-1109 · 202-637-5600

Thomas W. Brunner · ⑩ · Wiley Rein · 1776 K Street, NW · Washington, DC 20006-2359 · 202-719-7000

John G. Buchanan III · Covington & Burling · 1201 Pennsylvania Avenue, NW · Washington, DC 20004-2401 · 202-662-6000

Gary Dixon · Ross, Dixon & Bell · 2001 K Street, NW · Washington, DC 20006-1040 · 202-662-2000

Mitchell F. Dolin · Covington & Burling · 1201 Pennsylvania Avenue, NW · Washington, DC 20004-2401 · 202-662-6000

Laura A. Foggan · Wiley Rein · 1776 K Street, NW · Washington, DC 20006-2359 · 202-719-7000

Scott D. Gilbert · Gilbert Randolph · http://www.gilbertrandolph.com · 1100 New York Avenue, NW, Suite 700 · Washington, DC 20005-3987 · 202-772-2200

William F. Greaney · Covington & Burling · 1201 Pennsylvania Avenue, NW · Washington, DC 20004-2401 · 202-662-6000

John E. Heintz · Kelley Drye & Warren · Washington Harbour, Suite 400 · 3050 K Street, NW · Washington, DC 20007-5108 · 202-342-8400

Clifford B. Hendler · Crowell & Moring · 1001 Pennsylvania Avenue, NW · Washington, DC 20004-2595 202-624-2500

Matthew L. Jacobs · Jenner & Block · http://www.jenner.com · 1099 New York Avenue, NW, Suite 900 · Washington, DC 20001-4412 · 202-639-6000

Paul W. Kalish · Crowell & Moring · 1001 Pennsylvania Avenue, NW · Washington, DC 20004-2595 · 202-624-2500

Leon B. Kellner · Dickstein Shapiro · http://www.dicksteinshapiro.com · 1825 Eye Street, NW · Washington, DC 20006-5403 · 202-420-2200

William J. Kelty III · Locke Lord Bissell & Liddell · 401 Ninth Street, NW, Suite 400 South · Washington, DC 20004 · 202-220-6900

Lorelie S. Masters · Jenner & Block · http://www.jenner.com · 1099 New York Avenue, NW, Suite 900 · Washington, DC 20001-4412 · 202-639-6000

Jerold Oshinsky · Dickstein Shapiro · http://www.dicksteinshapiro.com · 1825 Eye Street, NW · Washington, DC 20006-5403 · 202-420-2200

Mark D. Plevin · Crowell & Moring · 1001 Pennsylvania Avenue, NW · Washington, DC 20004-2595 · 202-624-2500

David M. Raim · Chadbourne & Parke · http://www.chadbourne.com · 1200 New Hampshire Avenue, NW, Suite 300 · Washington, DC 20036 · 202-974-5600

James E. Rocap III · Steptoe & Johnson · http://www.steptoe.com · 1330 Connecticut Avenue, NW · Washington, DC 20036 · 202-429-3000

Robert N. Sayler · ㉕ · Covington & Burling · 1201 Pennsylvania Avenue, NW · Washington, DC 20004-2401 · 202-662-6000

Robert H. Shulman · Howrey · 1299 Pennsylvania Avenue, NW · Washington, DC 20004 · 202-783-0800

William P. Skinner · Covington & Burling · 1201 Pennsylvania Avenue, NW · Washington, DC 20004-2401 · 202-662-6000

Roger E. Warin · Steptoe & Johnson · http://www.steptoe.com · 1330 Connecticut Avenue, NW · Washington, DC 20036 · 202-429-3000

Margaret H. Warner · McDermott Will & Emery · 600 Thirteenth Street, NW · Washington, DC 20005-3096 · 202-756-8000

INTELLECTUAL PROPERTY LAW

Washington

Robert D. Bajefsky · Finnegan, Henderson, Farabow, Garrett & Dunner · http://www.finnegan.com · 901 New York Avenue, NW · Washington, DC 20001-4413 · 202-408-4000

Jon A. Baumgarten · ⑩ · Proskauer Rose · http://www.proskauer.com · 1001 Pennsylvania Avenue NW, Suite 400 South · Washington, DC 20004-2533 · 202-416-6800

Cono A. Carrano · Howrey · 1299 Pennsylvania Avenue, NW · Washington, DC 20004 · 202-783-0800

Michael F. Clayton · Morgan Lewis & Bockius · 1111 Pennsylvania Avenue, NW · Washington, DC 20004 · 202-739-3000

Ruffin B. Cordell · Fish & Richardson · 1425 K Street, NW, Suite 1100 · Washington, DC 20005 · 202-783-5070

William D. Coston · Venable · http://www.venable.com · 575 Seventh Street, NW · Washington, DC 20004-1601 · 202-344-4000

Mark G. Davis · Weil Gotshal & Manges · 1300 Eye Street, NW, Suite 900 · Washington, DC 20005 · 202-682-7000

Donald R. Dunner · ⑩ · Finnegan, Henderson, Farabow, Garrett & Dunner · http://www.finnegan.com · 901 New York Avenue, NW · Washington, DC 20001-4413 · 202-408-4000

Ford F. Farabow, Jr. · ⑩ · Finnegan, Henderson, Farabow, Garrett & Dunner · http://www.finnegan.com · 901 New York Avenue, NW · Washington, DC 20001-4413 · 202-408-4000

Brian E. Ferguson · Weil Gotshal & Manges · 1300 Eye Street, NW, Suite 900 · Washington, DC 20005 · 202-682-7000

E. Anthony Figg · Rothwell, Fidd, Ernst & Manbeck · http://www.rothwellfigg.com · 1425 K Street, NW, Suite 800 · Washington, DC 20005 · 202-783-6040

Christopher Foley · Finnegan, Henderson, Farabow, Garrett & Dunner · http://www.finnegan.com · 901 New York Avenue, NW · Washington, DC 20001-4413 · 202-408-4000

Ann K. Ford · DLA Piper · 500 Eighth Street, NW · Washington, DC 20004 · 202-799-4000

Joel M. Freed · ⑩ · McDermott Will & Emery · 600 Thirteenth Street, NW · Washington, DC 20005-3096 · 202-756-8000

Kenneth A. Gallo · Paul, Weiss, Rifkind, Wharton & Garrison · 1615 L Street, NW, Suite 1300 · Washington, DC 20036-5694 · 202-223-7300

Jorge A. Goldstein · Sterne, Kessler, Goldstein & Fox · 1100 New York Avenue, NW · Washington, DC 20005 · 202-371-2600

Cecilia H. Gonzalez · Howrey · 1299 Pennsylvania Avenue, NW · Washington, DC 20004 · 202-783-0800

Jon D. Grossman · Dickstein Shapiro · http://www.dicksteinshapiro.com · 1825 Eye Street, NW · Washington, DC 20006-5403 · 202-420-2200

Laurence R. Hefter · ⑩ · Finnegan, Henderson, Farabow, Garrett & Dunner · http://www.finnegan.com · 901 New York Avenue, NW · Washington, DC 20001-4413 · 202-408-4000

Douglas B. Henderson · ⑩ · Finnegan, Henderson, Farabow, Garrett & Dunner · http://www.finnegan.com · 901 New York Avenue, NW · Washington, DC 20001-4413 · 202-408-4000

Gary M. Hoffman · Dickstein Shapiro · http://www.dicksteinshapiro.com · 1825 Eye Street, NW · Washington, DC 20006-5403 · 202-420-2200

R. Danny Huntington · Bingham McCutchen · http://www.bingham.com · 2020 K Street, NW · Washington, DC 20006-1806 · 202-373-6000

Thomas Irving · Finnegan, Henderson, Farabow, Garrett & Dunner · http://www.finnegan.com · 901 New York Avenue, NW · Washington, DC 20001-4413 · 202-408-4000

Gerald Ivey · Finnegan, Henderson, Farabow, Garrett & Dunner · http://www.finnegan.com · 901 New York Avenue, NW · Washington, DC 20001-4413 · 202-408-4000

J. Michael Jakes · Finnegan, Henderson, Farabow, Garrett & Dunner · http://www.finnegan.com · 901 New York Avenue, NW · Washington, DC 20001-4413 · 202-408-4000

Kenneth M. Kaufman · Manatt, Phelps & Phillips · One Metro Center, Suite 1100 · 700 Twelfth Street, NW · Washington, DC 20005 · 202-585-6500

Paul N. Kokulis · Morgan Lewis & Bockius · 1111 Pennsylvania Avenue, NW · Washington, DC 20004 · 202-739-3000

Joseph P. Lavelle · Howrey · 1299 Pennsylvania Avenue, NW · Washington, DC 20004 · 202-783-0800

Jack Q. Lever, Jr. · McDermott Will & Emery · 600 Thirteenth Street, NW · Washington, DC 20005-3096 · 202-756-8000

Basil J. Lewris · Finnegan, Henderson, Farabow, Garrett & Dunner · http://www.finnegan.com · 901 New York Avenue, NW · Washington, DC 20001-4413 · 202-408-4000

Anthony V. Lupo · Arent Fox · 1050 Connecticut Avenue, NW · Washington, DC 20036-5339 · 202-857-6000

Raphael V. Lupo · ⑩ · McDermott Will & Emery · 600 Thirteenth Street, NW · Washington, DC 20005-3096 · 202-756-8000

Stephen B. Maebius · Foley & Lardner · Washington Harbour, Suite 500 · 3000 K Street, NW · Washington, DC 20007-5109 · 202-672-5300

Roderick R. McKelvie · Covington & Burling · 1201 Pennsylvania Avenue, NW · Washington, DC 20004-2401 · 202-662-6000

Michael J. Mckeon · Fish & Richardson · 1425 K Street, NW, Suite 1100 · Washington, DC 20005 · 202-783-5070

Kevin M. O'Brien · Baker & McKenzie · 815 Connecticut Avenue, NW · Washington, DC 20006-4078 · 202-452-7000

Thomas P. Olson · WilmerHale · http://www.wilmerhale.com · 1875 Pennsylvania Avenue, NW · Washington, DC 20006 · 202-663-6000

Ralph Oman · Dechert · 1775 I Street, NW · Washington, DC 20006-2401 · 202-261-3300

Charles D. Ossola · Dickstein Shapiro · http://www.dicksteinshapiro.com · 1825 Eye Street, NW · Washington, DC 20006-5403 · 202-420-2200

George F. Pappas · Covington & Burling · 1201 Pennsylvania Avenue, NW · Washington, DC 20004-2401 · 202-662-6000

Margaret K. Pfeiffer · Sullivan & Cromwell · 1701 Pennsylvania Avenue, NW · Washington, DC 20006-5805 · 202-956-7500

Joseph M. Potenza · ⑩ · Banner & Witcoff · 1100 Thirteenth Street, NW, Suite 1200 · Washington, DC 20005-4051 · 202-824-3000

Richard Racine · Finnegan, Henderson, Farabow, Garrett & Dunner · http://www.finnegan.com · 901 New York Avenue, NW · Washington, DC 20001-4413 · 202-408-4000

Richard Rainey · Covington & Burling · 1201 Pennsylvania Avenue, NW · Washington, DC 20004-2401 · 202-662-6000

Thomas J. Scott, Jr. · Goodwin Procter · 901 New York Avenue, NW · Washington, DC 20001 · 202-346-4000

Anthony W. Shaw · Dewey & LeBoeuf · 1101 New York Avenue, NW, Suite 1100 · Washington, DC 20005-4213 · 202-986-8000

Christopher N. Sipes · Covington & Burling · 1201 Pennsylvania Avenue, NW · Washington, DC 20004-2401 · 202-662-6000

Allen M. Sokal · Finnegan, Henderson, Farabow, Garrett & Dunner · http://www.finnegan.com · 901 New York Avenue, NW · Washington, DC 20001-4413 · 202-408-4000

Robert G. Sterne · Sterne, Kessler, Goldstein & Fox · 1100 New York Avenue, NW · Washington, DC 20005 · 202-371-2600

James H. Wallace, Jr. · Wiley Rein · 1776 K Street, NW · Washington, DC 20006-2359 · 202-719-7000

Harold C. Wegner · Foley & Lardner · Washington Harbour, Suite 500 · 3000 K Street, NW · Washington, DC 20007-5109 · 202-672-5300

William K. West, Jr. · ⑩ · Howrey · 1299 Pennsylvania Avenue, NW · Washington, DC 20004 · 202-783-0800

Arthur Wineburg · Akin Gump Strauss Hauer & Feld · Robert S. Strauss Building · 1333 New Hampshire Avenue, NW · Washington, DC 20036-1564 · 202-887-4000

Thomas W. Winland · Finnegan, Henderson, Farabow, Garrett & Dunner · http://www.finnegan.com · 901 New York Avenue, NW · Washington, DC 20001-4413 · 202-408-4000

E. Robert Yoches · Finnegan, Henderson, Farabow, Garrett & Dunner · http://www.finnegan.com · 901 New York Avenue, NW · Washington, DC 20001-4413 · 202-408-4000

INTERNATIONAL ARBITRATION

Washington

Stanimir A. Alexandrov · Sidley Austin · 1501 K Street, NW · Washington, DC 20005 · 202-736-8000

Mitchell F. Dolin · Covington & Burling · 1201 Pennsylvania Avenue, NW · Washington, DC 20004-2401 · 202-662-6000

Oscar M. Garibaldi · Covington & Burling · 1201 Pennsylvania Avenue, NW · Washington, DC 20004-2401 · 202-662-6000

Eugene D. Gulland · Covington & Burling · 1201 Pennsylvania Avenue, NW · Washington, DC 20004-2401 · 202-662-6000

O. Thomas Johnson, Jr. · Covington & Burling · 1201 Pennsylvania Avenue, NW · Washington, DC 20004-2401 · 202-662-6000

Mark A. Kantor · Mark Kantor · 110 Maryland Avenue, NE, Suite 311-B · Washington, DC 20002 · 202-544-4953

Carolyn B. Lamm · White & Case · http://www.whitecase.com · 701 Thirteenth Street, NW · Washington, DC 20005 · 202-626-3600

Darryl S. Lew · White & Case · http://www.whitecase.com · 701 Thirteenth Street, NW · Washington, DC 20005 · 202-626-3600

Lucinda A. Low · Steptoe & Johnson · http://www.steptoe.com · 1330 Connecticut Avenue, NW · Washington, DC 20036 · 202-429-3000

Stuart H. Newberger · Crowell & Moring · 1001 Pennsylvania Avenue, NW · Washington, DC 20004-2595 · 202-624-2500

David Palmeter · Sidley Austin · 1501 K Street, NW · Washington, DC 20005 · 202-736-8000

Jonathan D. Schiller · Boies, Schiller & Flexner · 5301 Wisconsin Avenue, NW · Washington, DC 20015 202-237-2727

Stephen Myron Schwebel · Stephen M. Schwebel · 1501 K Street, NW, Suite 410 · Washington, DC 20005 · 202-736-8328

Abby Cohen Smutny · White & Case · http://www.whitecase.com · 701 Thirteenth Street, NW · Washington, DC 20005 · 202-626-3600

John M. Townsend · Hughes Hubbard & Reed · http://www.hugheshubbard.com · 1775 I Street, NW · Washington, DC 20006-2401 · 202-721-4600

INTERNATIONAL TRADE AND FINANCE LAW

Washington

Irwin P. Altschuler · Greenberg Traurig · http://www.gtlaw.com · 2101 L Street, NW, Suite 1000 · Washington, DC 20037 · 202-331-3100

M. Jean Anderson · Weil Gotshal & Manges · 1300 Eye Street, NW, Suite 900 · Washington, DC 20005 · 202-682-7000

Harvey M. Applebaum · ⑩ · Covington & Burling · 1201 Pennsylvania Avenue, NW · Washington, DC 20004-2401 · 202-662-6000

James L. Bacchus · Greenberg Traurig · http://www.gtlaw.com · 2101 L Street, NW, Suite 1000 · Washington, DC 20037 · 202-331-3100

Howard H. Baker · Baker, Donelson, Bearman, Caldwell & Berkowitz · http://www.bakerdonelson.com · Lincoln Square, Sixth Floor · 555 Eleventh Street, NW · Washington, DC 20004 · 202-508-3400

James Addison Baker IV · Baker Botts · http://www.bakerbotts.com · The Warner Building, Suite 1300 · 1299 Pennsylvania Avenue, NW · Washington, DC 20004-2400 · 202-639-7700

William H. Barringer · Heller Ehrman · 1717 Rhode Island Avenue, NW · Washington, DC 20036-3023 · 202-912-2000

Charlene Barshefsky · WilmerHale · http://www.wilmerhale.com · 1875 Pennsylvania Avenue, NW · Washington, DC 20006 · 202-663-6000

Richard M. Belanger · Sidley Austin · 1501 K Street, NW · Washington, DC 20005 · 202-736-8000

Evan R. Berlack · Baker Botts · http://www.bakerbotts.com · The Warner Building, Suite 1300 · 1299 Pennsylvania Avenue, NW · Washington, DC 20004-2400 · 202-639-7700

Paul F. Brinkman · Alston + Bird · http://www.alston.com · The Atlantic Building · 950 F Street, NW · Washington, DC 20004-1404 · 202-756-3300

Mark Brzezinski · McGuireWoods · http://www.mcguirewoods.com · Washington Square, Suite 1200 · 1050 Connecticut Avenue, NW · Washington, DC 20036-5317 · 202-857-1700

James R. Cannon, Jr. · Williams Mullen · http://www.williamsmullen.com · 1666 K Street, NW, Suite 1200 · Washington, DC 20006 · 202-833-9200

Kathleen W. Cannon · Kelley Drye & Warren · Washington Harbour, Suite 400 · 3050 K Street, NW · Washington, DC 20007-5108 · 202-342-8400

Robert C. Cassidy, Jr. · Robert C. Cassidy · 500 Eighth Street, NW, Suite 3014 · Washington, DC 20004 202-863-7282

Larry Christensen · Miller & Chevalier · http://www.milchev.com · 655 Fifteenth Street, NW, Suite 900 · Washington, DC 20005-5701 · 202-626-5800

Peggy A. Clarke · Blank Rome · Watergate · 600 New Hampshire Avenue, NW · Washington, DC 20037 202-772-5800

Warren E. Connelly · Akin Gump Strauss Hauer & Feld · Robert S. Strauss Building · 1333 New Hampshire Avenue, NW · Washington, DC 20036-1564 · 202-887-4000

Michael J. Coursey · Kelley Drye & Warren · Washington Harbour, Suite 400 · 3050 K Street, NW · Washington, DC 20007-5108 · 202-342-8400

Thomas E. Crocker · Alston + Bird · http://www.alston.com · The Atlantic Building · 950 F Street, NW · Washington, DC 20004-1404 · 202-756-3300

Richard O. Cunningham · Steptoe & Johnson · http://www.steptoe.com · 1330 Connecticut Avenue, NW Washington, DC 20036 · 202-429-3000

Richard N. Dean · Baker & McKenzie · 815 Connecticut Avenue, NW · Washington, DC 20006-4078 · 202-452-7000

Joseph W. Dorn · King & Spalding · 1700 Pennsylvania Avenue, NW, Suite 200 · Washington, DC 20006-4706 · 202-737-0500

Peter D. Ehrenhaft · ⑩ · Harkins Cunningham · http://www.harkinscunningham.com · 1700 K Street, NW, Suite 400 · Washington, DC 20006-3817 · 202-973-7600

Stuart E. Eizenstat · Covington & Burling · 1201 Pennsylvania Avenue, NW · Washington, DC 20004-2401 · 202-662-6000

Christopher P. B. Erckert · Vinson & Elkins · http://www.velaw.com · The Willard Office Building, Suite 600 · 1455 Pennsylvania Avenue, NW · Washington, DC 20004-1008 · 202-639-6500

Jonathan M. Fee · Alston + Bird · http://www.alston.com · The Atlantic Building · 950 F Street, NW · Washington, DC 20004-1404 · 202-756-3300

Benjamin H. Flowe, Jr. · Berliner, Corcoran & Rowe · 1101 Seventeenth Street, NW, Suite 1100 · Washington, DC 20036 · 202-293-5555

F. David Foster · Miller & Chevalier · http://www.milchev.com · 655 Fifteenth Street, NW, Suite 900 · Washington, DC 20005-5701 · 202-626-5800

John D. Greenwald · WilmerHale · http://www.wilmerhale.com · 1875 Pennsylvania Avenue, NW · Washington, DC 20006 · 202-663-6000

Spencer S. Griffith · Akin Gump Strauss Hauer & Feld · Robert S. Strauss Building · 1333 New Hampshire Avenue, NW · Washington, DC 20036-1564 · 202-887-4000

David A. Hartquist · Kelley Drye & Warren · Washington Harbour, Suite 400 · 3050 K Street, NW · Washington, DC 20007-5108 · 202-342-8400

Robert E. Herzstein · 25 · Miller & Chevalier · http://www.milchev.com · 655 Fifteenth Street, NW, Suite 900 · Washington, DC 20005-5701 · 202-626-5800

Lars-Erik Hjelm · Akin Gump Strauss Hauer & Feld · Robert S. Strauss Building · 1333 New Hampshire Avenue, NW · Washington, DC 20036-1564 · 202-887-4000

Gary N. Horlick · WilmerHale · http://www.wilmerhale.com · 1875 Pennsylvania Avenue, NW · Washington, DC 20006 · 202-663-6000

Brenda A. Jacobs · Sidley Austin · 1501 K Street, NW · Washington, DC 20005 · 202-736-8000

James R. Jones · Manatt, Phelps & Phillips · One Metro Center, Suite 1100 · 700 Twelfth Street, NW · Washington, DC 20005 · 202-585-6500

Stephen A. Jones · King & Spalding · 1700 Pennsylvania Avenue, NW, Suite 200 · Washington, DC 20006-4706 · 202-737-0500

Michael Kantor · Mayer Brown · 1909 K Street, NW · Washington, DC 20006-1101 · 202-263-3000

Gilbert B. Kaplan · King & Spalding · 1700 Pennsylvania Avenue, NW, Suite 200 · Washington, DC 20006-4706 · 202-737-0500

Mark Leddy · Cleary Gottlieb Steen & Hamilton · 2000 Pennsylvania Avenue, NW · Washington, DC 20006 · 202-974-1500

Judith Lee · Gibson, Dunn & Crutcher · 1050 Connecticut Avenue, NW · Washington, DC 20036-5306 · 202-955-8500

Charles S. Levy · WilmerHale · http://www.wilmerhale.com · 1875 Pennsylvania Avenue, NW · Washington, DC 20006 · 202-663-6000

Robert A. Lipstein · 10 · Crowell & Moring · 1001 Pennsylvania Avenue, NW · Washington, DC 20004-2595 · 202-624-2500

G. Hamilton Loeb · Paul Hastings · 875 Fifteenth Street, NW · Washington, DC 20005 · 202-551-1700

Lucinda A. Low · Steptoe & Johnson · http://www.steptoe.com · 1330 Connecticut Avenue, NW · Washington, DC 20036 · 202-429-3000

Charles T. Manatt · Manatt, Phelps & Phillips · One Metro Center, Suite 1100 · 700 Twelfth Street, NW Washington, DC 20005 · 202-585-6500

Stanley J. Marcuss · 25 · Bryan Cave · 700 Thirteenth Street, NW · Washington, DC 20005-3960 · 202-508-6000

Mark S. McConnell · Hogan & Hartson · 555 Thirteenth Street, NW · Washington, DC 20004-1109 · 202-637-5600

Ronald I. Meltzer · WilmerHale · http://www.wilmerhale.com · 1875 Pennsylvania Avenue, NW · Washington, DC 20006 · 202-663-6000

Mark A. Moran · Steptoe & Johnson · http://www.steptoe.com · 1330 Connecticut Avenue, NW · Washington, DC 20036 · 202-429-3000

Homer E. Moyer, Jr. · Miller & Chevalier · http://www.milchev.com · 655 Fifteenth Street, NW, Suite 900 · Washington, DC 20005-5701 · 202-626-5800

R. Richard Newcomb · DLA Piper · 500 Eighth Street, NW · Washington, DC 20004 · 202-799-4000

Matthew M. Nolan · Arent Fox · 1050 Connecticut Avenue, NW · Washington, DC 20036-5339 · 202-857-6000

Robert T. Novick · WilmerHale · http://www.wilmerhale.com · 1875 Pennsylvania Avenue, NW · Washington, DC 20006 · 202-663-6000

David Palmeter · Sidley Austin · 1501 K Street, NW · Washington, DC 20005 · 202-736-8000

C. Christopher Parlin · Miller & Chevalier · http://www.milchev.com · 655 Fifteenth Street, NW, Suite 900 · Washington, DC 20005-5701 · 202-626-5800

Steven B. Pfeiffer · Fulbright & Jaworski · http://www.fulbright.com · Market Square · 801 Pennsylvania Avenue, NW · Washington, DC 20004-2623 · 202-662-0200

Amelia Porges · Sidley Austin · 1501 K Street, NW · Washington, DC 20005 · 202-736-8000

Douglas E. Rosenthal · ⑩ · Constantine Cannon · 1627 Eye Street, NW, Tenth Floor · Washington, DC 20006 · 202-204-3500

Paul C. Rosenthal · Kelley Drye & Warren · Washington Harbour, Suite 400 · 3050 K Street, NW · Washington, DC 20007-5108 · 202-342-8400

Richard H. Rowe · ⑩ · Proskauer Rose · http://www.proskauer.com · 1001 Pennsylvania Avenue NW, Suite 400 South · Washington, DC 20004-2533 · 202-416-6800

Lawrence A. Schneider · Arnold & Porter · 555 Twelfth Street, NW · Washington, DC 20004-1206 · 202-942-5000

Stuart P. Seidel · Baker & McKenzie · 815 Connecticut Avenue, NW · Washington, DC 20006-4078 · 202-452-7000

Michael T. Shor · Arnold & Porter · 555 Twelfth Street, NW · Washington, DC 20004-1206 · 202-942-5000

Andrew W. Shoyer · Sidley Austin · 1501 K Street, NW · Washington, DC 20005 · 202-736-8000

Shanker A. Singham · Squire Sanders · http://www.ssd.com · 1201 Pennsylvania Avenue, NW, Suite 500 · P.O. Box 407 · Washington, DC 20004-2401 · 202-626-6600

Valerie A. Slater · Akin Gump Strauss Hauer & Feld · Robert S. Strauss Building · 1333 New Hampshire Avenue, NW · Washington, DC 20036-1564 · 202-887-4000

Jeffrey L. Snyder · Crowell & Moring · 1001 Pennsylvania Avenue, NW · Washington, DC 20004-2595 · 202-624-2500

Robert S. Strauss · Akin Gump Strauss Hauer & Feld · Robert S. Strauss Building · 1333 New Hampshire Avenue, NW · Washington, DC 20036-1564 · 202-887-4000

Mark H. Stumpf · Arnold & Porter · 555 Twelfth Street, NW · Washington, DC 20004-1206 · 202-942-5000

Evelyn M. Suarez · Williams Mullen · http://www.williamsmullen.com · 1666 K Street, NW, Suite 1200 · Washington, DC 20006 · 202-833-9200

Jay Middleton Tannon · ⑩ · DLA Piper · 500 Eighth Street, NW · Washington, DC 20004 · 202-799-4000

Peter D. Trooboff · Covington & Burling · 1201 Pennsylvania Avenue, NW · Washington, DC 20004-2401 · 202-662-6000

Kenneth G. Weigel · Alston + Bird · http://www.alston.com · The Atlantic Building · 950 F Street, NW · Washington, DC 20004-1404 · 202-756-3300

Edwin D. Williamson · Sullivan & Cromwell · 1701 Pennsylvania Avenue, NW · Washington, DC 20006-5805 · 202-956-7500

Thomas B. Wilner · Shearman & Sterling · 801 Pennsylvania Avenue, NW, Suite 900 · Washington, DC 20004-2634 · 202-508-8000

Jeffrey M. Winton · McKenna Long & Aldridge · 1900 K Street, NW · Washington, DC 20006 · 202-496-7500

Alan William Wolff · Dewey & LeBoeuf · 1101 New York Avenue, NW, Suite 1100 · Washington, DC 20005-4213 · 202-986-8000

Clayton Yeutter · Hogan & Hartson · 555 Thirteenth Street, NW · Washington, DC 20004-1109 · 202-637-5600

LABOR AND EMPLOYMENT LAW

Washington

Herve H. Aitken · Ford & Harrison · http://www.fordharrison.com · 1300 Nineteenth Street, NW, Suite 700 · Washington, DC 20036 · 202-719-2000

Robert G. Ames · Venable · http://www.venable.com · 575 Seventh Street, NW · Washington, DC 20004-1601 · 202-344-4000

Jonathan G. Axelrod · ⑩ · Beins, Axelrod, Gleason & Gibson · 1625 Massachusetts Avenue, NW, Suite 500 · Washington, DC 20036 · 202-328-7222

James L. Banks, Jr. · Seyfarth Shaw · 815 Connecticut Avenue, NW, Suite 500 · Washington, DC 20006-4004 · 202-463-2400

Lisa J. Banks · Katz, Marshall & Banks · http://www.kmblegal.com · 1718 Connecticut Avenue, NW, Sixth Floor · Washington, DC 20009 · 202-299-1140

Robert M. Baptiste · ⑳ · Baptiste & Wilder · 1150 Connecticut Avenue, NW, Suite 500 · Washington, DC 20036 · 202-223-0723

Maurice N. Baskin · Venable · http://www.venable.com · 575 Seventh Street, NW · Washington, DC 20004-1601 · 202-344-4000

Hugh J. Beins · ㉕ · Beins, Axelrod, Gleason & Gibson · 1625 Massachusetts Avenue, NW, Suite 500 · Washington, DC 20036 · 202-328-7222

Lynne Bernabei · The Bernabei Law Firm · 1775 T Street, NW · Washington, DC 20009-7139 · 202-745-1942

Charles R. Both · Charles R. Both · 1666 Connecticut Avenue NW, Suite 500 · Washington, DC 20009 · 202-833-9060

Gregory C. Braden · Morgan Lewis & Bockius · 1111 Pennsylvania Avenue, NW · Washington, DC 20004 · 202-739-3000

Barbara B. Brown · ⑩ · Paul Hastings · 875 Fifteenth Street, NW · Washington, DC 20005 · 202-551-1700

Harry W. Burton · Morgan Lewis & Bockius · 1111 Pennsylvania Avenue, NW · Washington, DC 20004 202-739-3000

Barbara Camens · Barr & Camens · 1025 Connecticut Avenue, NW, Suite 712 · Washington, DC 20036-5405 · 202-293-9222

Donald J. Capuano · ⑩ · O'Donoghue & O'Donoghue · 4748 Wisconsin Avenue, NW · Washington, DC 20016 · 202-362-0041

Stephen Z. Chertkof · Heller, Huron, Chertkof, Lerner, Simon & Salzman · 1730 M Street, NW, Suite 412 · Washington, DC 20036 · 202-293-8090

John O'Brien Clarke, Jr. · Highsaw, Mahoney & Clarke · 1050 Seventeenth Street, NW, Suite 590 · Washington, DC 20036 · 202-296-8500

Charles I. Cohen · ⑩ · Morgan Lewis & Bockius · 1111 Pennsylvania Avenue, NW · Washington, DC 20004 · 202-739-3000

George H. Cohen · ㉕ · Bredhoff & Kaiser · 805 Fifteenth Street, NW, Suite 1000 · Washington, DC 20005 · 202-842-2600

Laurence J. Cohen · ㉕ · Sherman, Dunn, Cohen, Leifer & Yellig · 900 Seventh Street, NW, Suite 1000 · Washington, DC 20001 · 202-785-9300

Harold P. Coxson, Jr. · Ogletree Deakins · http://www.ogletreedeakins.com · 2400 N Street, NW, Fifth Floor · Washington, DC 20037 · 202-887-0855

Alison N. Davis · Ford & Harrison · http://www.fordharrison.com · 1300 Nineteenth Street, NW, Suite 700 · Washington, DC 20036 · 202-719-2000

Robert P. Davis · Mayer Brown · 1909 K Street, NW · Washington, DC 20006-1101 · 202-263-3000

David P. Dean · James & Hoffman · 1101 Seventeenth Street, NW, Suite 510 · Washington, DC 20036 · 202-496-0500

Baruch A. Fellner · Gibson, Dunn & Crutcher · 1050 Connecticut Avenue, NW · Washington, DC 20036-5306 · 202-955-8500

Robert B. Fitzpatrick · ⑳ · Fitzpatrick & Associates · Universal Building, Suite 660 · 1825 Connecticut Avenue, NW · Washington, DC 20009-5728 · 202-588-5300

David S. Fortney · Fortney & Scott · 1750 K Street, NW, Suite 325 · Washington, DC 20006 · 202-689-1200

Bruce A. Fredrickson · Webster, Fredrickson Henrichson Correia & Puth · 1775 K Street, NW, Suite 600 Washington, DC 20006 · 202-659-8510

John Gallagher · Paul Hastings · 875 Fifteenth Street, NW · Washington, DC 20005 · 202-551-1700

Robert C. Gombar · ⑳ · McDermott Will & Emery · 600 Thirteenth Street, NW · Washington, DC 20005-3096 · 202-756-8000

Douglas W. Hall · Ford & Harrison · http://www.fordharrison.com · 1300 Nineteenth Street, NW, Suite 700 · Washington, DC 20036 · 202-719-2000

Robert J. Higgins · ⑩ · Dickstein Shapiro · http://www.dicksteinshapiro.com · 1825 Eye Street, NW · Washington, DC 20006-5403 · 202-420-2200

Douglas B. Huron · Heller, Huron, Chertkof, Lerner, Simon & Salzman · 1730 M Street, NW, Suite 412 · Washington, DC 20036 · 202-293-8090

Jeffrey G. Huvelle · Covington & Burling · 1201 Pennsylvania Avenue, NW · Washington, DC 20004-2401 · 202-662-6000

John S. Irving, Jr. · ㉕ · Kirkland & Ellis · 655 Fifteenth Street, NW · Washington, DC 20005 · 202-879-5000

Edgar N. James · James & Hoffman · 1101 Seventeenth Street, NW, Suite 510 · Washington, DC 20036 · 202-496-0500

Joshua M. Javits · ⑩ · Dispute Resolution Services · 2023 R Street, NW · Washington, DC 20009 · 202-237-2044

Ronald M. Johnson · Akin Gump Strauss Hauer & Feld · Robert S. Strauss Building · 1333 New Hampshire Avenue, NW · Washington, DC 20036-1564 · 202-887-4000

Wendy L. Kahn · Zwerdling, Paul, Kahn & Wolly · 1025 Connecticut Avenue, NW, Suite 712 · Washington, DC 20036 · 202-857-5000

Debra S. Katz · Katz, Marshall & Banks · http://www.kmblegal.com · 1718 Connecticut Avenue, NW, Sixth Floor · Washington, DC 20009 · 202-299-1140

Deborah P. Kelly · Dickstein Shapiro · http://www.dicksteinshapiro.com · 1825 Eye Street, NW · Washington, DC 20006-5403 · 202-420-2200

William J. Kilberg · ㉕ · Gibson, Dunn & Crutcher · 1050 Connecticut Avenue, NW · Washington, DC 20036-5306 · 202-955-8500

Barbara J. Kraft · Kraft Eisenmann & Alden · 1001 Pennsylvania Avenue, NW, Suite 600 · Washington, DC 20004 · 202-783-1391

Andrew M. Kramer · ㉕ · Jones Day · 51 Louisiana Avenue, NW · Washington, DC 20001-2113 · 202-879-3939

Kathy L. Krieger · James & Hoffman · 1101 Seventeenth Street, NW, Suite 510 · Washington, DC 20036 202-496-0500

Ian D. Lanoff · ⑳ · Groom Law Group · http://www.groom.com · 1701 Pennsylvania Avenue, NW · Washington, DC 20006-5811 · 202-857-0620

Bruce R. Lerner · Bredhoff & Kaiser · 805 Fifteenth Street, NW, Suite 1000 · Washington, DC 20005 · 202-842-2600

Edward R. Levin · Saul Ewing · The Watergate, Suite 1000 · 2600 Virginia Avenue, NW · Washington, DC 20037-1922 · 202-333-8800

William G. Mahoney · ⑩ · Highsaw, Mahoney & Clarke · 1050 Seventeenth Street, NW, Suite 590 · Washington, DC 20036 · 202-296-8500

Robert Matisoff · ⑩ · O'Donoghue & O'Donoghue · 4748 Wisconsin Avenue, NW · Washington, DC 20016 · 202-362-0041

Neal D. Mollen · Paul Hastings · 875 Fifteenth Street, NW · Washington, DC 20005 · 202-551-1700

Ralph J. Moore, Jr. · ⑳ · Morgan Lewis & Bockius · 1111 Pennsylvania Avenue, NW · Washington, DC 20004 · 202-739-3000

Glen D. Nager · ⑩ · Jones Day · 51 Louisiana Avenue, NW · Washington, DC 20001-2113 · 202-879-3939

Mary K. O'Melveny · Mary K. O'Melveny · 501 Third Street, NW, Suite 800 · Washington, DC 20001-2797 · 202-434-1213

William W. Osborne, Jr. · ⑳ · Osborne Law Offices · 4301 Connecticut Avenue, NW, Suite 108 · Washington, DC 20008 · 202-243-3200

Eleanor Pelta · Morgan Lewis & Bockius · 1111 Pennsylvania Avenue, NW · Washington, DC 20004 · 202-739-3000

Peter J. Petesch · Littler Mendelson · http://www.littler.com/ · 1150 17th Street, Suite 900 · Washington, DC 20036 · 202-842-3400

Harry A. Rissetto · ⑩ · Morgan Lewis & Bockius · 1111 Pennsylvania Avenue, NW · Washington, DC 20004 · 202-739-3000

Steven J. Sacher · ⑳ · Jones Day · 51 Louisiana Avenue, NW · Washington, DC 20001-2113 · 202-879-3939

Richard A. Salzman · Heller, Huron, Chertkof, Lerner, Simon & Salzman · 1730 M Street, NW, Suite 412 · Washington, DC 20036 · 202-293-8090

Joseph E. Santucci, Jr. · Morgan Lewis & Bockius · 1111 Pennsylvania Avenue, NW · Washington, DC 20004 · 202-739-3000

Eugene Scalia · Gibson, Dunn & Crutcher · 1050 Connecticut Avenue, NW · Washington, DC 20036-5306 · 202-955-8500

Judith A. Scott · James & Hoffman · 1101 Seventeenth Street, NW, Suite 510 · Washington, DC 20036 · 202-496-0500

Virginia A. Seitz · Sidley Austin · 1501 K Street, NW · Washington, DC 20005 · 202-736-8000

Paul C. Skelly · Hogan & Hartson · 555 Thirteenth Street, NW · Washington, DC 20004-1109 · 202-637-5600

Robert J. Smith · Morgan Lewis & Bockius · 1111 Pennsylvania Avenue, NW · Washington, DC 20004 · 202-739-3000

Grace E. Speights · Morgan Lewis & Bockius · 1111 Pennsylvania Avenue, NW · Washington, DC 20004 · 202-739-3000

Paul C. Sprenger · ⑩ · Sprenger & Lang · 1400 Eye Street, NW, Suite 500 · Washington, DC 20005 · 202-265-8010

Stanley R. Strauss · ㉕ · Ogletree Deakins · http://www.ogletreedeakins.com · 2400 N Street, NW, Fifth Floor · Washington, DC 20037 · 202-887-0855

Robert H. Stropp, Jr. · Mooney, Green, Baker & Saindon · 1920 L Street, NW, Suite 400 · Washington, DC 20036 · 202-783-0010

Sally M. Tedrow · O'Donoghue & O'Donoghue · 4748 Wisconsin Avenue, NW · Washington, DC 20016 · 202-362-0041

E. Carl Uehlein, Jr. · ⑩ · Morgan Lewis & Bockius · 1111 Pennsylvania Avenue, NW · Washington, DC 20004 · 202-739-3000

Robert M. Weinberg · Bredhoff & Kaiser · 805 Fifteenth Street, NW, Suite 1000 · Washington, DC 20005 · 202-842-2600

Joseph A. Yablonski · Joseph A. Yablonski · 1776 K Street NW, Suite 840 · Washington, DC 20006 · 202-833-9062

Lawrence T. Zimmerman · ㉕ · Lawrence T. Zimmerman · 2101 Connecticut Avenue, NW, Apt 72 · Washington, DC 20008 · 202-232-6967

LAND USE & ZONING LAW

Washington

Christopher H. Collins · Holland & Knight · http://www.hklaw.com · 2099 Pennsylvania Avenue, NW, Suite 100 · Washington, DC 20006-6801 · 202-955-3000

Jacques B. DePuy · Greenstein DeLorme & Luchs · 1620 L Street, NW, Suite 900 · Washington, DC 20036-5605 · 202-452-1400

Maureen E. Dwyer · Pillsbury Winthrop Shaw Pittman · http://www.pillsburylaw.com · 2300 N Street, NW · Washington, DC 20037-1122 · 202-663-8000

John T. Epting · Pillsbury Winthrop Shaw Pittman · http://www.pillsburylaw.com · 2300 N Street, NW · Washington, DC 20037-1122 · 202-663-8000

Phil T. Feola · Pillsbury Winthrop Shaw Pittman · http://www.pillsburylaw.com · 2300 N Street, NW · Washington, DC 20037-1122 · 202-663-8000

Norman Glasgow, Jr. · Holland & Knight · http://www.hklaw.com · 2099 Pennsylvania Avenue, NW, Suite 100 · Washington, DC 20006-6801 · 202-955-3000

Allison C. Prince · Pillsbury Winthrop Shaw Pittman · http://www.pillsburylaw.com · 2300 N Street, NW Washington, DC 20037-1122 · 202-663-8000

Whayne S. Quin · ㉕ · Holland & Knight · http://www.hklaw.com · 2099 Pennsylvania Avenue, NW, Suite 100 · Washington, DC 20006-6801 · 202-955-3000

LEGAL MALPRACTICE LAW

Washington

Stephen L. Braga · Baker Botts · http://www.bakerbotts.com · The Warner Building, Suite 1300 · 1299 Pennsylvania Avenue, NW · Washington, DC 20004-2400 · 202-639-7700

Pamela A. Bresnahan · Vorys, Sater, Seymour and Pease · 1828 L Street, NW, Suite 1111 · Washington, DC 20036-5109 · 202-467-8800

David P. Durbin · Jordan Coyne & Savits · 1100 Connecticut Avenue, NW, Suite 600 · Washington, DC 20036 · 202-296-4747

Aaron L. Handleman · Eccleston & Wolf · 2001 S Street, Suite 310 · Washington, DC 20009 · 202-857-1696

Antonia B. Ianniello · Steptoe & Johnson · http://www.steptoe.com · 1330 Connecticut Avenue, NW · Washington, DC 20036 · 202-429-3000

John Tremain May · Jordan Coyne & Savits · 1100 Connecticut Avenue, NW, Suite 600 · Washington, DC 20036 · 202-296-4747

R. Stan Mortenson · ㉕ · Baker Botts · http://www.bakerbotts.com · The Warner Building, Suite 1300 · 1299 Pennsylvania Avenue, NW · Washington, DC 20004-2400 · 202-639-7700

Roger E. Warin · Steptoe & Johnson · http://www.steptoe.com · 1330 Connecticut Avenue, NW · Washington, DC 20036 · 202-429-3000

David N. Webster · ⑩ · Caplin & Drysdale · http://www.capdale.com · One Thomas Circle, NW, Suite 1100 · Washington, DC 20005 · 202-862-5000

LEVERAGED BUYOUTS AND PRIVATE EQUITY LAW

Washington

Tami Howie · Sonnenschein Nath & Rosenthal · East Tower, Suite 600 · 1301 K Street, NW · Washington, DC 20005-3364 · 202-408-6400

Anthony H. Rickert · DLA Piper · 500 Eighth Street, NW · Washington, DC 20004 · 202-799-4000

Stephen A. Riddick · Greenberg Traurig · http://www.gtlaw.com · 2101 L Street, NW, Suite 1000 · Washington, DC 20037 · 202-331-3100

Paul V. Rogers · Covington & Burling · 1201 Pennsylvania Avenue, NW · Washington, DC 20004-2401 · 202-662-6000

Jay Middleton Tannon · ⑩ · DLA Piper · 500 Eighth Street, NW · Washington, DC 20004 · 202-799-4000

Andrew M. Tucker · Andrews Kurth · http://www.andrewskurth.com · 1350 I Street, NW, Suite 1100 · Washington, DC 20005 · 202-662-2700

MARITIME LAW

Washington

Robert T. Basseches · ㉕ · Goodwin Procter · 901 New York Avenue, NW · Washington, DC 20001 · 202-346-4000

C. Jonathan Benner · Troutman Sanders · 401 Ninth Street, NW, Suite 1000 · Washington, DC 20004-2134 · 202-274-2950

Paul D. Coleman · Hoppel, Mayer & Coleman · 1050 Connecticut Avenue, NW, Tenth Floor · Washington, DC 20036 · 202-296-5460

David B. Cook · Goodwin Procter · 901 New York Avenue, NW · Washington, DC 20001 · 202-346-4000

Marc J. Fink · Sher & Blackwell · 1850 M Street, NW, Suite 900 · Washington, DC 20036 · 202-463-2500

Neal M. Mayer · Hoppel, Mayer & Coleman · 1050 Connecticut Avenue, NW, Tenth Floor · Washington, DC 20036 · 202-296-5460

Charles Papavizas · Winston & Strawn · 1700 K Street, NW · Washington, DC 20006-3817 · 202-282-5000

Stanley O. Sher · Sher & Blackwell · 1850 M Street, NW, Suite 900 · Washington, DC 20036 · 202-463-2500

Jonathan K. Waldron · Blank Rome · Watergate · 600 New Hampshire Avenue, NW · Washington, DC 20037 · 202-772-5800

MASS TORT LITIGATION

Washington

John Beisner · O'Melveny & Myers · 1625 Eye Street, NW · Washington, DC 20006-4001 · 202-383-5300

Lanny A. Breuer · Covington & Burling · 1201 Pennsylvania Avenue, NW · Washington, DC 20004-2401 202-662-6000

Kent A. Gardiner · Crowell & Moring · 1001 Pennsylvania Avenue, NW · Washington, DC 20004-2595 · 202-624-2500

James F. Green · Ashcraft & Gerel · 2000 L Street, NW, Suite 400 · Washington, DC 20036 · 202-783-6400

Carl W. Hampe · Baker & McKenzie · 815 Connecticut Avenue, NW · Washington, DC 20006-4078 · 202-452-7000

Michael W. Heaviside · ⑩ · Ashcraft & Gerel · 2000 L Street, NW, Suite 400 · Washington, DC 20036 · 202-783-6400

Aaron M. Levine · ⑩ · Aaron M. Levine & Associates · 1320 Nineteenth Street, NW, Suite 500 · Washington, DC 20006 · 202-833-8040

Michael L. Martinez · Crowell & Moring · 1001 Pennsylvania Avenue, NW · Washington, DC 20004-2595 · 202-624-2500

David W. Ogden · WilmerHale · http://www.wilmerhale.com · 1875 Pennsylvania Avenue, NW · Washington, DC 20006 · 202-663-6000

Rodney F. Page · Bryan Cave · 700 Thirteenth Street, NW · Washington, DC 20005-3960 · 202-508-6000

Michelle A. Parfitt · Ashcraft & Gerel · 2000 L Street, NW, Suite 400 · Washington, DC 20036 · 202-783-6400

Sara D. Schotland · Cleary Gottlieb Steen & Hamilton · 2000 Pennsylvania Avenue, NW · Washington, DC 20006 · 202-974-1500

Christopher V. Tisi · Ashcraft & Gerel · 2000 L Street, NW, Suite 400 · Washington, DC 20036 · 202-783-6400

Clifford Zatz · Crowell & Moring · 1001 Pennsylvania Avenue, NW · Washington, DC 20004-2595 · 202-624-2500

MEDIA LAW

Washington

Kevin T. Baine · ⑩ · Williams & Connolly · 725 Twelfth Street, NW · Washington, DC 20005-5901 · 202-434-5000

Robert C. Bernius · Nixon Peabody · 401 Ninth Street, NW, Suite 900 · Washington, DC 20004-2128 · 202-585-8000

Robert Corn-Revere · Davis Wright Tremaine · 1919 Pennsylvania Avenue, NW, Suite 200 · Washington, DC 20006-3402 · 202-973-4200

Jonathan D. Hart · Dow Lohnes · http://www.dowlohnes.com · 1200 New Hampshire Avenue, NW, Suite 800 · Washington, DC 20036-6802 · 202-776-2000

Lee Levine · ⑩ · Levine Sullivan Koch & Schulz · 1050 Seventeenth Street, NW, Suite 800 · Washington, DC 20036-5514 · 202-508-1100

Charles D. Tobin · Holland & Knight · http://www.hklaw.com · 2099 Pennsylvania Avenue, NW, Suite 100 · Washington, DC 20006-6801 · 202-955-3000

MEDICAL MALPRACTICE LAW

Washington

Laurie A. Amell · Stein, Mitchell & Mezines · 1100 Connecticut Avenue, NW · Washington, DC 20036 · 202-737-7777

Alfred F. Belcuore · Montedonico, Belcuore & Tazzara · 1020 Nineteenth Street, NW, Suite 420 · Washington, DC 20036 · 202-296-1322

Harlow R. Case · Jack H. Olender & Associates · Farragut Square, Fourth Floor · 888 Seventeenth Street, NW · Washington, DC 20006 · 202-879-7777

Keith W. Donahoe · Donahoe Kearney · http://www.donahoekearney.com · One Farragut Square South, Suite 805 · 1634 Eye Street, NW · Washington, DC 20006 · 202-393-3320

Karen E. Evans · Jack H. Olender & Associates · Farragut Square, Fourth Floor · 888 Seventeenth Street, NW · Washington, DC 20006 · 202-879-7777

L. Palmer Foret · The Law Firm of L. Palmer Foret · 1735 Twentieth Street, NW · Washington, DC 20009 · 202-332-2404

Robert W. Goodson · Wilson Elser Moskowitz Edelman & Dicker · The Colorado Building, Fifth Floor · 1341 G Street, NW · Washington, DC 20005-3105 · 202-626-7660

Bruce J. Klores · ⑩ · Bruce J. Klores & Associates · http://www.klores.com · 1735 Twentieth Street, NW · Washington, DC 20009 · 202-628-8100

Patrick A. Malone · Patrick Malone & Associates · http://www.patrickmalonelaw.com · 1331 H Street, NW, Suite 902 · Washington, DC 20005 · 202-742-1500

Nicholas S. McConnell · ⑩ · Jackson & Campbell · One Lafayette Centre, South Tower · 1120 Twentieth Street, NW · Washington, DC 20036-3437 · 202-457-1600

William E. McDaniels · ⑳ · Williams & Connolly · 725 Twelfth Street, NW · Washington, DC 20005-5901 · 202-434-5000

H. Vincent McKnight, Jr. · Ashcraft & Gerel · 2000 L Street, NW, Suite 400 · Washington, DC 20036 · 202-783-6400

Gerard E. Mitchell · ⑳ · Stein, Mitchell & Mezines · 1100 Connecticut Avenue, NW · Washington, DC 20036 · 202-737-7777

Joseph D. Montedonico · ⑳ · Montedonico, Belcuore & Tazzara · 1020 Nineteenth Street, NW, Suite 420 · Washington, DC 20036 · 202-296-1322

Barry J. Nace · ⑩ · Paulson & Nace · 1615 New Hampshire Avenue, NW, Third Floor · Washington, DC 20009-2520 · 202-463-1999

Jack H. Olender · ⑳ · Jack H. Olender & Associates · Farragut Square, Fourth Floor · 888 Seventeenth Street, NW · Washington, DC 20006 · 202-879-7777

Patrick M. Regan · Regan Zambri & Long · 1919 M Street, NW, Suite 350 · Washington, DC 20036 · 202-463-3030

Melissa Rhea · Jack H. Olender & Associates · Farragut Square, Fourth Floor · 888 Seventeenth Street, NW · Washington, DC 20006 · 202-879-7777

Sandra H. Robinson · Jack H. Olender & Associates · Farragut Square, Fourth Floor · 888 Seventeenth Street, NW · Washington, DC 20006 · 202-879-7777

Daniel Schultz · Schultz & Trombly · 1050 Seventeenth Street, NW, Suite 1250 · Washington, DC 20036-5510 · 202-887-5000

MERGERS & ACQUISITIONS LAW

Washington

Howard B. Adler · Gibson, Dunn & Crutcher · 1050 Connecticut Avenue, NW · Washington, DC 20036-5306 · 202-955-8500

Alan J. Berkeley · ⑳ · K&L Gates · 1601 K Street, NW · Washington, DC 20006-1600 · 202-778-9000

David E. Brown, Jr. · Alston + Bird · http://www.alston.com · The Atlantic Building · 950 F Street, NW · Washington, DC 20004-1404 · 202-756-3300

David N. Brown · ⑳ · Covington & Burling · 1201 Pennsylvania Avenue, NW · Washington, DC 20004-2401 · 202-662-6000

Louis R. Cohen · ⑳ · WilmerHale · http://www.wilmerhale.com · 1875 Pennsylvania Avenue, NW · Washington, DC 20006 · 202-663-6000

Frank M. Conner III · DLA Piper · 500 Eighth Street, NW · Washington, DC 20004 · 202-799-4000

Dennis O. Garris · Alston + Bird · http://www.alston.com · The Atlantic Building · 950 F Street, NW · Washington, DC 20004-1404 · 202-756-3300

Stephen I. Glover · Gibson, Dunn & Crutcher · 1050 Connecticut Avenue, NW · Washington, DC 20036-5306 · 202-955-8500

Frank R. Goldstein · (10) · Sidley Austin · 1501 K Street, NW · Washington, DC 20005 · 202-736-8000

John J. Huber · (10) · Latham & Watkins · 555 Eleventh Street, NW, Suite 1000 · Washington, DC 20004-1304 · 202-637-2200

Alan Jacobs · Heller Ehrman · 1717 Rhode Island Avenue, NW · Washington, DC 20036-3023 · 202-912-2000

John Paul Ketels · (10) · Clifford Chance · 2001 K Street, NW · Washington, DC 20006-1001 · 202-912-5000

Stephen A. Riddick · Greenberg Traurig · http://www.gtlaw.com · 2101 L Street, NW, Suite 1000 · Washington, DC 20037 · 202-331-3100

Richard H. Rowe · (10) · Proskauer Rose · http://www.proskauer.com · 1001 Pennsylvania Avenue NW, Suite 400 South · Washington, DC 20004-2533 · 202-416-6800

Mark J. Silverman · (10) · Steptoe & Johnson · http://www.steptoe.com · 1330 Connecticut Avenue, NW · Washington, DC 20036 · 202-429-3000

Michael N. Sohn · (10) · Arnold & Porter · 555 Twelfth Street, NW · Washington, DC 20004-1206 · 202-942-5000

Richard A. Steinwurtzel · (20) · Fried, Frank, Harris, Shriver & Jacobson · 1001 Pennsylvania Avenue, NW Washington, DC 20004-2505 · 202-639-7000

Andrew P. Varney · Fried, Frank, Harris, Shriver & Jacobson · 1001 Pennsylvania Avenue, NW · Washington, DC 20004-2505 · 202-639-7000

Thomas W. White · WilmerHale · http://www.wilmerhale.com · 1875 Pennsylvania Avenue, NW · Washington, DC 20006 · 202-663-6000

Richard E. Wiley · (25) · Wiley Rein · 1776 K Street, NW · Washington, DC 20006-2359 · 202-719-7000

MINING LAW

Washington

Timothy M. Biddle · Crowell & Moring · 1001 Pennsylvania Avenue, NW · Washington, DC 20004-2595 202-624-2500

Michael S. Giannotto · Goodwin Procter · 901 New York Avenue, NW · Washington, DC 20001 · 202-346-4000

R. Timothy McCrum · Crowell & Moring · 1001 Pennsylvania Avenue, NW · Washington, DC 20004-2595 · 202-624-2500

Steven P. Quarles · (10) · Crowell & Moring · 1001 Pennsylvania Avenue, NW · Washington, DC 20004-2595 · 202-624-2500

MUNICIPAL LAW

Washington

Douglas Patton · Oldaker, Biden and Belair · 818 Connecticut Avenue, NW, Suite 1100 · Washington, DC 20006 · 202-728-1010

Roderic Woodson · Holland & Knight · http://www.hklaw.com · 2099 Pennsylvania Avenue, NW, Suite 100 · Washington, DC 20006-6801 · 202-955-3000

MUTUAL FUNDS LAW

Washington

Marco E. Adelfio · Morrison & Foerster · http://www.mofo.com · 2000 Pennsylvania Avenue, NW, Suite 5500 · Washington, DC 20006-1888 · 202-887-1500

Clifford J. Alexander · ⑳ · K&L Gates · 1601 K Street, NW · Washington, DC 20006-1600 · 202-778-9000

Diane E. Ambler · K&L Gates · 1601 K Street, NW · Washington, DC 20006-1600 · 202-778-9000

James E. Anderson · WilmerHale · http://www.wilmerhale.com · 1875 Pennsylvania Avenue, NW · Washington, DC 20006 · 202-663-6000

Robert G. Bagnall · WilmerHale · http://www.wilmerhale.com · 1875 Pennsylvania Avenue, NW · Washington, DC 20006 · 202-663-6000

Barry P. Barbash · Willkie Farr & Gallagher · 1875 K Street, NW · Washington, DC 20006-1238 · 202-303-1000

Kenneth J. Berman · Debevoise & Plimpton · 555 Thirteenth Street, NW · Washington, DC 20004 · 202-383-8000

Sander M. Bieber · Dechert · 1775 I Street, NW · Washington, DC 20006-2401 · 202-261-3300

Steven B. Boehm · Sutherland · http://www.sutherland.com · 1275 Pennsylvania Avenue, NW · Washington, DC 20004-2415 · 202-383-0100

Ruth S. Epstein · Dechert · 1775 I Street, NW · Washington, DC 20006-2401 · 202-261-3300

Thomas S. Harman · Morgan Lewis & Bockius · 1111 Pennsylvania Avenue, NW · Washington, DC 20004 · 202-739-3000

Robert W. Helm · Dechert · 1775 I Street, NW · Washington, DC 20006-2401 · 202-261-3300

Robert N. Hickey · Sullivan & Worcester · 1666 K Street, NW · Washington, DC 20006 · 202-775-1200

Jane A. Kanter · Dechert · 1775 I Street, NW · Washington, DC 20006-2401 · 202-261-3300

Robert M. Kurucza · Morrison & Foerster · http://www.mofo.com · 2000 Pennsylvania Avenue, NW, Suite 5500 · Washington, DC 20006-1888 · 202-887-1500

Martin E. Lybecker · WilmerHale · http://www.wilmerhale.com · 1875 Pennsylvania Avenue, NW · Washington, DC 20006 · 202-663-6000

David C. Mahaffey · Sullivan & Worcester · 1666 K Street, NW · Washington, DC 20006 · 202-775-1200

R. Charles Miller · K&L Gates · 1601 K Street, NW · Washington, DC 20006-1600 · 202-778-9000

Michael J. Missal · K&L Gates · 1601 K Street, NW · Washington, DC 20006-1600 · 202-778-9000

Stephanie M. Monaco · Mayer Brown · 1909 K Street, NW · Washington, DC 20006-1101 · 202-263-3000

Jack W. Murphy · Dechert · 1775 I Street, NW · Washington, DC 20006-2401 · 202-261-3300

Christopher E. Palmer · Goodwin Procter · 901 New York Avenue, NW · Washington, DC 20001 · 202-346-4000

Jeffrey S. Puretz · Dechert · 1775 I Street, NW · Washington, DC 20006-2401 · 202-261-3300

Stephen E. Roth · Sutherland · http://www.sutherland.com · 1275 Pennsylvania Avenue, NW · Washington, DC 20004-2415 · 202-383-0100

Marianne K. Smythe · WilmerHale · http://www.wilmerhale.com · 1875 Pennsylvania Avenue, NW · Washington, DC 20006 · 202-663-6000

Robert J. Zutz · K&L Gates · 1601 K Street, NW · Washington, DC 20006-1600 · 202-778-9000

NATIVE AMERICAN LAW

Washington

Todd Araujo · Akin Gump Strauss Hauer & Feld · Robert S. Strauss Building · 1333 New Hampshire Avenue, NW · Washington, DC 20036-1564 · 202-887-4000

Virginia W. Boylan · Drinker Biddle & Reath · 1500 K Street, NW · Washington, DC 20005-1209 · 202-842-8800

Reid Peyton Chambers · Sonosky, Chambers, Sachse, Endreson & Perry · 1425 K Street, NW, Suite 600 · Washington, DC 20005 · 202-682-0240

Douglas B. L. Endreson · Sonosky, Chambers, Sachse, Endreson & Perry · 1425 K Street, NW, Suite 600 Washington, DC 20005 · 202-682-0240

Keith M. Harper · Kilpatrick Stockton · 607 Fourteenth Street, NW, Suite 900 · Washington, DC 20005-2018 · 202-508-5800

Danna R. Jackson · Akin Gump Strauss Hauer & Feld · Robert S. Strauss Building · 1333 New Hampshire Avenue, NW · Washington, DC 20036-1564 · 202-887-4000

Aurene Michele Martin · Ietan Consulting · Robert S. Strauss Building · 1333 New Hampshire Avenue, NW · Washington, DC 20036 · 202-419-3527

James T. Meggesto · Akin Gump Strauss Hauer & Feld · Robert S. Strauss Building · 1333 New Hampshire Avenue, NW · Washington, DC 20036-1564 · 202-887-4000

Michael G. Rossetti · Akin Gump Strauss Hauer & Feld · Robert S. Strauss Building · 1333 New Hampshire Avenue, NW · Washington, DC 20036-1564 · 202-887-4000

Lee Shannon · Hobbs, Straus, Dean & Walker · 2120 L Street, NW, Suite 700 · Washington, DC 20037 · 202-822-8282

Jeffrey T. Smith · Patton Boggs · 2550 M Street, NW · Washington, DC 20037 · 202-457-6000

Michael R. Smith · Zuckerman Spaeder · http://www.zuckerman.com · 1800 M Street, NW, Suite 1000 · Washington, DC 20036-5807 · 202-778-1800

Jerry C. Straus · Hobbs, Straus, Dean & Walker · 2120 L Street, NW, Suite 700 · Washington, DC 20037 202-822-8282

Dennis J. Whittlesey · Dickinson Wright · http://www.dickinsonwright.com · 1901 L Street, NW, Suite 800 · Washington, DC 20036-3506 · 202-457-0160

NATURAL RESOURCES LAW

Washington

Lawrence G. Acker · Dewey & LeBoeuf · 1101 New York Avenue, NW, Suite 1100 · Washington, DC 20005-4213 · 202-986-8000

David T. Andril · Vinson & Elkins · http://www.velaw.com · The Willard Office Building, Suite 600 · 1455 Pennsylvania Avenue, NW · Washington, DC 20004-1008 · 202-639-6500

Stanley W. Balis · Miller, Balis & O'Neil · 1140 Nineteenth Street, NW · Washington, DC 20036 · 202-296-2960

Donald C. Baur · Perkins Coie · http://www.perkinscoie.com · 607 Fourteenth Street, NW, Suite 800 · Washington, DC 20005-2003 · 202-628-6600

Timothy M. Biddle · Crowell & Moring · 1001 Pennsylvania Avenue, NW · Washington, DC 20004-2595 202-624-2500

Stephen H. Brose · Steptoe & Johnson · http://www.steptoe.com · 1330 Connecticut Avenue, NW · Washington, DC 20036 · 202-429-3000

Thomas Eastment · Baker Botts · http://www.bakerbotts.com · The Warner Building, Suite 1300 · 1299 Pennsylvania Avenue, NW · Washington, DC 20004-2400 · 202-639-7700

Douglas G. Green · Steptoe & Johnson · http://www.steptoe.com · 1330 Connecticut Avenue, NW · Washington, DC 20036 · 202-429-3000

Mark R. Haskell · Morgan Lewis & Bockius · 1111 Pennsylvania Avenue, NW · Washington, DC 20004 · 202-739-3000

Bruce F. Kiely · Baker Botts · http://www.bakerbotts.com · The Warner Building, Suite 1300 · 1299 Pennsylvania Avenue, NW · Washington, DC 20004-2400 · 202-639-7700

L. Poe Leggette · Fulbright & Jaworski · http://www.fulbright.com · Market Square · 801 Pennsylvania Avenue, NW · Washington, DC 20004-2623 · 202-662-0200

Robert Loeffler · Morrison & Foerster · http://www.mofo.com · 2000 Pennsylvania Avenue, NW, Suite 5500 · Washington, DC 20006-1888 · 202-887-1500

Guy R. Martin · Perkins Coie · http://www.perkinscoie.com · 607 Fourteenth Street, NW, Suite 800 · Washington, DC 20005-2003 · 202-628-6600

Keith R. McCrea · Sutherland · http://www.sutherland.com · 1275 Pennsylvania Avenue, NW · Washington, DC 20004-2415 · 202-383-0100

R. Timothy McCrum · Crowell & Moring · 1001 Pennsylvania Avenue, NW · Washington, DC 20004-2595 · 202-624-2500

Randolph Q. McManus · Baker Botts · http://www.bakerbotts.com · The Warner Building, Suite 1300 · 1299 Pennsylvania Avenue, NW · Washington, DC 20004-2400 · 202-639-7700

Thomas C. Means · Crowell & Moring · 1001 Pennsylvania Avenue, NW · Washington, DC 20004-2595 · 202-624-2500

Margaret A. Moore · Van Ness Feldman · 1050 Thomas Jefferson Street, NW, Seventh Floor · Washington, DC 20007-3877 · 202-298-1800

Jerome C. Muys · ⓴ · Muys & Associates · 1666 K Street, NW, Suite 700 · Washington, DC 20006 · 202-370-3924

Robert R. Nordhaus · Van Ness Feldman · 1050 Thomas Jefferson Street, NW, Seventh Floor · Washington, DC 20007-3877 · 202-298-1800

Steven P. Quarles · ⑩ · Crowell & Moring · 1001 Pennsylvania Avenue, NW · Washington, DC 20004-2595 · 202-624-2500

David B. Raskin · Steptoe & Johnson · http://www.steptoe.com · 1330 Connecticut Avenue, NW · Washington, DC 20036 · 202-429-3000

Steven G. T. Reed · Steptoe & Johnson · http://www.steptoe.com · 1330 Connecticut Avenue, NW · Washington, DC 20036 · 202-429-3000

Richard E. Schwartz · Crowell & Moring · 1001 Pennsylvania Avenue, NW · Washington, DC 20004-2595 · 202-624-2500

Dena E. Wiggins · Sutherland · http://www.sutherland.com · 1275 Pennsylvania Avenue, NW · Washington, DC 20004-2415 · 202-383-0100

William A. Williams · Sidley Austin · 1501 K Street, NW · Washington, DC 20005 · 202-736-8000

NON-PROFIT/CHARITIES LAW

Washington

Edward Jay Beckwith · ⑩ · Baker Hostetler · http://www.bakerlaw.com · Washington Square, Suite 1100 1050 Connecticut Avenue, NW · Washington, DC 20036-5304 · 202-861-1500

Thomas Hyatt · Ober, Kaler, Grimes & Shriver · http://www.ober.com · 1401 H Street, NW, Suite 500 · Washington, DC 20005-3324 · 202-408-8400

Jerald Jacobs · Pillsbury Winthrop Shaw Pittman · http://www.pillsburylaw.com · 2300 N Street, NW · Washington, DC 20037-1122 · 202-663-8000

David I. Kempler · Buchanan Ingersoll & Rooney · http://www.bipc.com · 1700 K Street, NW, Suite 300 · Washington, DC 20006-3807 · 202-452-7900

Jerry J. McCoy · ⑩ · Jerry J. McCoy · 1050 Connecticut Avenue, NW, Suite 1200 · P.O. Box 66491 · Washington, DC 20035-6491 · 202-466-6941

Patrick K. O'Hare · Ober, Kaler, Grimes & Shriver · http://www.ober.com · 1401 H Street, NW, Suite 500 Washington, DC 20005-3324 · 202-408-8400

NON-WHITE-COLLAR CRIMINAL DEFENSE

Washington

Preston Burton · Orrick, Herrington & Sutcliffe · Columbia Center · 1152 Fifteenth Street, NW · Washington, DC 20005-1706 · 202-339-8400

Francis D. Carter · Zuckerman Spaeder · http://www.zuckerman.com · 1800 M Street, NW, Suite 1000 · Washington, DC 20036-5807 · 202-778-1800

John J. Cassidy · ⑩ · Baker Botts · http://www.bakerbotts.com · The Warner Building, Suite 1300 · 1299 Pennsylvania Avenue, NW · Washington, DC 20004-2400 · 202-639-7700

G. Allen Dale · G. Allen Dale · North Building, Suite 900 · 601 Pennsylvania Avenue, NW · Washington, DC 20004-2601 · 202-638-2900

Bernard Grimm · Cozen O'Connor · The Army and Navy Building, Suite 1100 · 1627 I Street, NW · Washington, DC 20006 · 202-912-4800

Mark D. Hopson · Sidley Austin · 1501 K Street, NW · Washington, DC 20005 · 202-736-8000

William H. Jeffress, Jr. · ⑩ · Baker Botts · http://www.bakerbotts.com · The Warner Building, Suite 1300 1299 Pennsylvania Avenue, NW · Washington, DC 20004-2400 · 202-639-7700

William R. Martin · Sutherland · http://www.sutherland.com · 1275 Pennsylvania Avenue, NW · Washington, DC 20004-2415 · 202-383-0100

R. Stan Mortenson · ㉕ · Baker Botts · http://www.bakerbotts.com · The Warner Building, Suite 1300 · 1299 Pennsylvania Avenue, NW · Washington, DC 20004-2400 · 202-639-7700

David Povich · ⑳ · Williams & Connolly · 725 Twelfth Street, NW · Washington, DC 20005-5901 · 202-434-5000

Michele A. Roberts · Akin Gump Strauss Hauer & Feld · Robert S. Strauss Building · 1333 New Hampshire Avenue, NW · Washington, DC 20036-1564 · 202-887-4000

Kenneth M. Robinson · ㉕ · The Robinson Firm · 717 D Street, NW, Suite 400 · Washington, DC 20004-2807 · 202-347-6100

David Schertler · Schertler & Onorato · http://www.schertlerlaw.com · North Building, Ninth Floor · 601 Pennsylvania Avenue, NW · Washington, DC 20036 · 202-628-4199

Randall J. Turk · ⑩ · Baker Botts · http://www.bakerbotts.com · The Warner Building, Suite 1300 · 1299 Pennsylvania Avenue, NW · Washington, DC 20004-2400 · 202-639-7700

OIL & GAS LAW

Washington

G. Mark Cook · Baker Botts · http://www.bakerbotts.com · The Warner Building, Suite 1300 · 1299 Pennsylvania Avenue, NW · Washington, DC 20004-2400 · 202-639-7700

David D'Alessandro · Stinson Morrison Hecker · http://www.stinson.com · 1150 Eighteenth Street, NW, Suite 800 · Washington, DC 20036 · 202-785-9100

Thomas Eastment · Baker Botts · http://www.bakerbotts.com · The Warner Building, Suite 1300 · 1299 Pennsylvania Avenue, NW · Washington, DC 20004-2400 · 202-639-7700

Eugene R. Elrod · Sidley Austin · 1501 K Street, NW · Washington, DC 20005 · 202-736-8000

Bruce F. Kiely · Baker Botts · http://www.bakerbotts.com · The Warner Building, Suite 1300 · 1299 Pennsylvania Avenue, NW · Washington, DC 20004-2400 · 202-639-7700

Mark K. Lewis · Paul Hastings · 875 Fifteenth Street, NW · Washington, DC 20005 · 202-551-1700

Steven R. Miles · Baker Botts · http://www.bakerbotts.com · The Warner Building, Suite 1300 · 1299 Pennsylvania Avenue, NW · Washington, DC 20004-2400 · 202-639-7700

Clifford M. Naeve · Skadden, Arps, Slate, Meagher & Flom · 1440 New York Avenue, NW · Washington, DC 20005 · 202-371-7000

Brian D. O'Neill · Dewey & LeBoeuf · 1101 New York Avenue, NW, Suite 1100 · Washington, DC 20005-4213 · 202-986-8000

PERSONAL INJURY LITIGATION

Washington

Laurie A. Amell · Stein, Mitchell & Mezines · 1100 Connecticut Avenue, NW · Washington, DC 20036 · 202-737-7777

Alfred F. Belcuore · Montedonico, Belcuore & Tazzara · 1020 Nineteenth Street, NW, Suite 420 · Washington, DC 20036 · 202-296-1322

Harlow R. Case · Jack H. Olender & Associates · Farragut Square, Fourth Floor · 888 Seventeenth Street, NW · Washington, DC 20006 · 202-879-7777

Keith W. Donahoe · Donahoe Kearney · http://www.donahoekearney.com · One Farragut Square South, Suite 805 · 1634 Eye Street, NW · Washington, DC 20006 · 202-393-3320

Karen E. Evans · Jack H. Olender & Associates · Farragut Square, Fourth Floor · 888 Seventeenth Street, NW · Washington, DC 20006 · 202-879-7777

Marc Fiedler · Koonz, McKenney, Johnson, DePaolis & Lightfoot · James Monroe Building, Suite 450 · 2001 Pennsylvania Avenue, NW · Washington, DC 20006 · 202-659-5500

L. Palmer Foret · The Law Firm of L. Palmer Foret · 1735 Twentieth Street, NW · Washington, DC 20009 · 202-332-2404

Michael J. Grace · Buchanan Ingersoll & Rooney · http://www.bipc.com · 1700 K Street, NW, Suite 300 · Washington, DC 20006-3807 · 202-452-7900

James F. Green · Ashcraft & Gerel · 2000 L Street, NW, Suite 400 · Washington, DC 20036 · 202-783-6400

Peter C. Grenier · Bode & Grenier · 1150 Connecticut Avenue, NW, Ninth Floor · Washington, DC 20036 · 202-828-4100

David F. Grimaldi · Martell, Donnelly, Grimaldi & Gallagher · 1900 L Street, NW, Suite 401 · Washington, DC 20036 · 202-293-0830

Roger C. Johnson · Koonz, McKenney, Johnson, DePaolis & Lightfoot · James Monroe Building, Suite 450 · 2001 Pennsylvania Avenue, NW · Washington, DC 20006 · 202-659-5500

Bruce J. Klores · ⑩ · Bruce J. Klores & Associates · http://www.klores.com · 1735 Twentieth Street, NW · Washington, DC 20009 · 202-628-8100

Joseph H. Koonz · Koonz, McKenney, Johnson, DePaolis & Lightfoot · James Monroe Building, Suite 450 · 2001 Pennsylvania Avenue, NW · Washington, DC 20006 · 202-659-5500

Lawrence S. Lapidus · Karp, Frosh, Lapidus, Wigodsky & Norwind · 1133 Connecticut Avenue, NW, 11th Floor · Washington, DC 20036 · 202-822-3777

Aaron M. Levine · 10 · Aaron M. Levine & Associates · 1320 Nineteenth Street, NW, Suite 500 · Washington, DC 20006 · 202-833-8040

William P. Lightfoot · Koonz, McKenney, Johnson, DePaolis & Lightfoot · James Monroe Building, Suite 450 · 2001 Pennsylvania Avenue, NW · Washington, DC 20006 · 202-659-5500

John C. Lynch · Macleay, Lynch, Gregg & Lynch · 1629 K Street, NW, Suite 802 · Washington, DC 20006 · 202-785-0123

Patrick A. Malone · Patrick Malone & Associates · http://www.patrickmalonelaw.com · 1331 H Street, NW, Suite 902 · Washington, DC 20005 · 202-742-1500

Nicholas S. McConnell · 10 · Jackson & Campbell · One Lafayette Centre, South Tower · 1120 Twentieth Street, NW · Washington, DC 20036-3437 · 202-457-1600

Gerard E. Mitchell · 20 · Stein, Mitchell & Mezines · 1100 Connecticut Avenue, NW · Washington, DC 20036 · 202-737-7777

Joseph D. Montedonico · 20 · Montedonico, Belcuore & Tazzara · 1020 Nineteenth Street, NW, Suite 420 · Washington, DC 20036 · 202-296-1322

Robert F. Muse · 20 · Stein, Mitchell & Mezines · 1100 Connecticut Avenue, NW · Washington, DC 20036 · 202-737-7777

Barry J. Nace · 10 · Paulson & Nace · 1615 New Hampshire Avenue, NW, Third Floor · Washington, DC 20009-2520 · 202-463-1999

Jack H. Olender · 20 · Jack H. Olender & Associates · Farragut Square, Fourth Floor · 888 Seventeenth Street, NW · Washington, DC 20006 · 202-879-7777

Michelle A. Parfitt · Ashcraft & Gerel · 2000 L Street, NW, Suite 400 · Washington, DC 20036 · 202-783-6400

Patrick M. Regan · Regan Zambri & Long · 1919 M Street, NW, Suite 350 · Washington, DC 20036 · 202-463-3030

Melissa Rhea · Jack H. Olender & Associates · Farragut Square, Fourth Floor · 888 Seventeenth Street, NW · Washington, DC 20006 · 202-879-7777

Sandra H. Robinson · Jack H. Olender & Associates · Farragut Square, Fourth Floor · 888 Seventeenth Street, NW · Washington, DC 20006 · 202-879-7777

Jacob A. Stein · 25 · Stein, Mitchell & Mezines · 1100 Connecticut Avenue, NW · Washington, DC 20036 · 202-737-7777

James W. Taglieri · Cadeaux, Taglieri & Notarius · 1100 Connecticut Avenue, NW, Suite 800 · Washington, DC 20036 · 202-785-3373

Patricia M. Tazzara · Montedonico, Belcuore & Tazzara · 1020 Nineteenth Street, NW, Suite 420 · Washington, DC 20036 · 202-296-1322

Kenneth M. Trombly · Schultz & Trombly · 1050 Seventeenth Street, NW, Suite 1250 · Washington, DC 20036-5510 · 202-887-5000

Stephen L. Urbanczyk · Williams & Connolly · 725 Twelfth Street, NW · Washington, DC 20005-5901 · 202-434-5000

David N. Webster · ⑩ · Caplin & Drysdale · http://www.capdale.com · One Thomas Circle, NW, Suite 1100 · Washington, DC 20005 · 202-862-5000

PRIVATE FUNDS LAW

Washington

Marco E. Adelfio · Morrison & Foerster · http://www.mofo.com · 2000 Pennsylvania Avenue, NW, Suite 5500 · Washington, DC 20006-1888 · 202-887-1500

Diane E. Ambler · K&L Gates · 1601 K Street, NW · Washington, DC 20006-1600 · 202-778-9000

Barry P. Barbash · Willkie Farr & Gallagher · 1875 K Street, NW · Washington, DC 20006-1238 · 202-303-1000

Steven B. Boehm · Sutherland · http://www.sutherland.com · 1275 Pennsylvania Avenue, NW · Washington, DC 20004-2415 · 202-383-0100

Robert H. Rosenblum · K&L Gates · 1601 K Street, NW · Washington, DC 20006-1600 · 202-778-9000

PRODUCT LIABILITY LITIGATION

Washington

John Beisner · O'Melveny & Myers · 1625 Eye Street, NW · Washington, DC 20006-4001 · 202-383-5300

Peter J. Biersteker · Jones Day · 51 Louisiana Avenue, NW · Washington, DC 20001-2113 · 202-879-3939

Lanny A. Breuer · Covington & Burling · 1201 Pennsylvania Avenue, NW · Washington, DC 20004-2401 202-662-6000

Patrick S. Davies · Covington & Burling · 1201 Pennsylvania Avenue, NW · Washington, DC 20004-2401 · 202-662-6000

Kenneth S. Geller · Mayer Brown · 1909 K Street, NW · Washington, DC 20006-1101 · 202-263-3000

Peter T. Grossi, Jr. · Arnold & Porter · 555 Twelfth Street, NW · Washington, DC 20004-1206 · 202-942-5000

Joe G. Hollingsworth · Spriggs & Hollingsworth · 1350 I Street, NW · Washington, DC 20005 · 202-898-5800

Erika Z. Jones · Mayer Brown · 1909 K Street, NW · Washington, DC 20006-1101 · 202-263-3000

Mark H. Lynch · ⑩ · Covington & Burling · 1201 Pennsylvania Avenue, NW · Washington, DC 20004-2401 · 202-662-6000

Michael L. Martinez · Crowell & Moring · 1001 Pennsylvania Avenue, NW · Washington, DC 20004-2595 · 202-624-2500

William E. McDaniels · ⑳ · Williams & Connolly · 725 Twelfth Street, NW · Washington, DC 20005-5901 · 202-434-5000

Robert F. McDermott, Jr. · Jones Day · 51 Louisiana Avenue, NW · Washington, DC 20001-2113 · 202-879-3939

Jack H. Olender · ⑳ · Jack H. Olender & Associates · Farragut Square, Fourth Floor · 888 Seventeenth Street, NW · Washington, DC 20006 · 202-879-7777

Keith A. Teel · Covington & Burling · 1201 Pennsylvania Avenue, NW · Washington, DC 20004-2401 · 202-662-6000

John W. Vardaman · ㉕ · Williams & Connolly · 725 Twelfth Street, NW · Washington, DC 20005-5901 · 202-434-5000

Theodore Voorhees, Jr. · Covington & Burling · 1201 Pennsylvania Avenue, NW · Washington, DC 20004-2401 · 202-662-6000

David N. Webster · ⑩ · Caplin & Drysdale · http://www.capdale.com · One Thomas Circle, NW, Suite 1100 · Washington, DC 20005 · 202-862-5000

Scott L. Winkelman · Crowell & Moring · 1001 Pennsylvania Avenue, NW · Washington, DC 20004-2595 · 202-624-2500

PROFESSIONAL MALPRACTICE LAW

Washington

Stephen L. Braga · Baker Botts · http://www.bakerbotts.com · The Warner Building, Suite 1300 · 1299 Pennsylvania Avenue, NW · Washington, DC 20004-2400 · 202-639-7700

Mark W. Foster · Zuckerman Spaeder · http://www.zuckerman.com · 1800 M Street, NW, Suite 1000 · Washington, DC 20036-5807 · 202-778-1800

R. Stan Mortenson · ㉕ · Baker Botts · http://www.bakerbotts.com · The Warner Building, Suite 1300 · 1299 Pennsylvania Avenue, NW · Washington, DC 20004-2400 · 202-639-7700

Andrew J. Pincus · Mayer Brown · 1909 K Street, NW · Washington, DC 20006-1101 · 202-263-3000

PROJECT FINANCE LAW

Washington

R. Thomas Amis · Alston + Bird · http://www.alston.com · The Atlantic Building · 950 F Street, NW · Washington, DC 20004-1404 · 202-756-3300

Noam Ayali · Chadbourne & Parke · http://www.chadbourne.com · 1200 New Hampshire Avenue, NW, Suite 300 · Washington, DC 20036 · 202-974-5600

Lance T. Brasher · Skadden, Arps, Slate, Meagher & Flom · 1440 New York Avenue, NW · Washington, DC 20005 · 202-371-7000

Jeffrey S. Christie · Skadden, Arps, Slate, Meagher & Flom · 1440 New York Avenue, NW · Washington, DC 20005 · 202-371-7000

Victor J. DeSantis · White & Case · http://www.whitecase.com · 701 Thirteenth Street, NW · Washington, DC 20005 · 202-626-3600

David Evans · Clifford Chance · 2001 K Street, NW · Washington, DC 20006-1001 · 202-912-5000

Roger D. Feldman · Andrews Kurth · http://www.andrewskurth.com · 1350 I Street, NW, Suite 1100 · Washington, DC 20005 · 202-662-2700

Harold I. Freilich · Steptoe & Johnson · http://www.steptoe.com · 1330 Connecticut Avenue, NW · Washington, DC 20036 · 202-429-3000

Maura Goldstein · Baker Botts · http://www.bakerbotts.com · The Warner Building, Suite 1300 · 1299 Pennsylvania Avenue, NW · Washington, DC 20004-2400 · 202-639-7700

Kenneth W. Hansen · Chadbourne & Parke · http://www.chadbourne.com · 1200 New Hampshire Avenue, NW, Suite 300 · Washington, DC 20036 · 202-974-5600

Gregg W. Harris · Fulbright & Jaworski · http://www.fulbright.com · Market Square · 801 Pennsylvania Avenue, NW · Washington, DC 20004-2623 · 202-662-0200

Frederick E. Jenney · Morrison & Foerster · http://www.mofo.com · 2000 Pennsylvania Avenue, NW, Suite 5500 · Washington, DC 20006-1888 · 202-887-1500

Ronald Jonkers · Hills Stern & Morley · North Building, Second Floor · 1120 Twentieth Street, NW · Washington, DC 20036 · 202-822-1600

Martin Klepper · Skadden, Arps, Slate, Meagher & Flom · 1440 New York Avenue, NW · Washington, DC 20005 · 202-371-7000

Keith W. Kriebel · Orrick, Herrington & Sutcliffe · Columbia Center · 1152 Fifteenth Street, NW · Washington, DC 20005-1706 · 202-339-8400

Jonathan A. Maizel · Milbank, Tweed, Hadley & McCloy · http://www.milbank.com · International Square Building, Suite 1100 · 1850 K Street, NW · Washington, DC 20006 · 202-835-7500

Keith Martin · Chadbourne & Parke · http://www.chadbourne.com · 1200 New Hampshire Avenue, NW, Suite 300 · Washington, DC 20036 · 202-974-5600

Catherine McCarthy · Clifford Chance · 2001 K Street, NW · Washington, DC 20006-1001 · 202-912-5000

Christopher C. McIsaac · Clifford Chance · 2001 K Street, NW · Washington, DC 20006-1001 · 202-912-5000

Edward R. Neaher, Jr. · White & Case · http://www.whitecase.com · 701 Thirteenth Street, NW · Washington, DC 20005 · 202-626-3600

Nancy M. Persechino · Bingham McCutchen · http://www.bingham.com · 2020 K Street, NW · Washington, DC 20006-1806 · 202-373-6000

John L. Sachs · Latham & Watkins · 555 Eleventh Street, NW, Suite 1000 · Washington, DC 20004-1304 202-637-2200

Robert F. Shapiro · Chadbourne & Parke · http://www.chadbourne.com · 1200 New Hampshire Avenue, NW, Suite 300 · Washington, DC 20036 · 202-974-5600

Gregory K. Smith · Dewey & LeBoeuf · 1101 New York Avenue, NW, Suite 1100 · Washington, DC 20005-4213 · 202-986-8000

Nicholas J. Spiliotes · Morrison & Foerster · http://www.mofo.com · 2000 Pennsylvania Avenue, NW, Suite 5500 · Washington, DC 20006-1888 · 202-887-1500

Mark R. Spivak · Vinson & Elkins · http://www.velaw.com · The Willard Office Building, Suite 600 · 1455 Pennsylvania Avenue, NW · Washington, DC 20004-1008 · 202-639-6500

Erica A. Ward · Skadden, Arps, Slate, Meagher & Flom · 1440 New York Avenue, NW · Washington, DC 20005 · 202-371-7000

Mark C. Williams · Bingham McCutchen · http://www.bingham.com · 2020 K Street, NW · Washington, DC 20006-1806 · 202-373-6000

Nancy A. Wodka · Bracewell & Giuliani · http://www.bgllp.com · 2000 K Street, NW, Suite 500 · Washington, DC 20006-1872 · 202-828-5800

PUBLIC FINANCE LAW

Washington

Frederic L. Ballard, Jr. · Ballard Spahr Andrews & Ingersoll · 601 Thirteenth Street, NW, Suite 1000 South · Washington, DC 20005-3807 · 202-661-2200

Joseph A. Fanone · Ballard Spahr Andrews & Ingersoll · 601 Thirteenth Street, NW, Suite 1000 South · Washington, DC 20005-3807 · 202-661-2200

William L. Gehrig · Greenberg Traurig · http://www.gtlaw.com · 2101 L Street, NW, Suite 1000 · Washington, DC 20037 · 202-331-3100

Charles S. Henck · Ballard Spahr Andrews & Ingersoll · 601 Thirteenth Street, NW, Suite 1000 South · Washington, DC 20005-3807 · 202-661-2200

John C. Henry · Squire Sanders · http://www.ssd.com · 1201 Pennsylvania Avenue, NW, Suite 500 · P.O. Box 407 · Washington, DC 20004-2401 · 202-626-6600

Andrew R. Kintzinger · Hunton & Williams · 1900 K Street, NW · Washington, DC 20006-1109 · 202-955-1500

Paul S. Maco · Vinson & Elkins · http://www.velaw.com · The Willard Office Building, Suite 600 · 1455 Pennsylvania Avenue, NW · Washington, DC 20004-1008 · 202-639-6500

John M. McNally · Hawkins Delafield & Wood · http://www.hawkins.com · 601 Thirteenth Street, NW, Suite 800 South · Washington, DC 20005 · 202-682-1480

Richard A. Newman · Arent Fox · 1050 Connecticut Avenue, NW · Washington, DC 20036-5339 · 202-857-6000

Mitchell Rapaport · Nixon Peabody · 401 Ninth Street, NW, Suite 900 · Washington, DC 20004-2128 · 202-585-8000

Linda B. Schakel · Ballard Spahr Andrews & Ingersoll · 601 Thirteenth Street, NW, Suite 1000 South · Washington, DC 20005-3807 · 202-661-2200

Pauline A. Schneider · Orrick, Herrington & Sutcliffe · Columbia Center · 1152 Fifteenth Street, NW · Washington, DC 20005-1706 · 202-339-8400

Jeffrey H. Smith · Arnold & Porter · 555 Twelfth Street, NW · Washington, DC 20004-1206 · 202-942-5000

RAILROAD LAW

Washington

Joseph S. Crociata · Bonner Kiernan Trebach & Crociata · 1233 Twentieth Street, NW, Eighth Floor · Washington, DC 20036 · 202-712-7000

Paul A. Cunningham · Harkins Cunningham · http://www.harkinscunningham.com · 1700 K Street, NW, Suite 400 · Washington, DC 20006-3817 · 202-973-7600

Ronald M. Johnson · Akin Gump Strauss Hauer & Feld · Robert S. Strauss Building · 1333 New Hampshire Avenue, NW · Washington, DC 20036-1564 · 202-887-4000

G. Paul Moates · Sidley Austin · 1501 K Street, NW · Washington, DC 20005 · 202-736-8000

Linda J. Morgan · Covington & Burling · 1201 Pennsylvania Avenue, NW · Washington, DC 20004-2401 202-662-6000

Samuel M. Sipe, Jr. · Steptoe & Johnson · http://www.steptoe.com · 1330 Connecticut Avenue, NW · Washington, DC 20036 · 202-429-3000

Stephen A. Trimble · ⑩ · Hamilton & Hamilton · 1900 M Street, NW, Suite 700 · Washington, DC 20036-3518 · 202-463-8282

REAL ESTATE LAW

Washington

Sanford K. Ain · ㉕ · Ain & Bank · http://www.ainbanklaw.com · 1900 M Street, NW, Suite 600 · Washington, DC 20036 · 202-530-3300

C. Richard Beyda · ㉕ · Grossberg, Yochelson, Fox & Beyda · 2000 L Street, NW, Suite 675 · Washington, DC 20036-4907 · 202-296-9696

Earl M. Colson · ⑳ · Arent Fox · 1050 Connecticut Avenue, NW · Washington, DC 20036-5339 · 202-857-6000

Richard G. David · Womble Carlyle Sandridge & Rice · 1401 Eye Street, NW, Seventh Floor · Washington, DC 20005 · 202-467-6900

Jeffry R. Dwyer · ㉕ · Greenberg Traurig · http://www.gtlaw.com · 2101 L Street, NW, Suite 1000 · Washington, DC 20037 · 202-331-3100

Maureen E. Dwyer · Pillsbury Winthrop Shaw Pittman · http://www.pillsburylaw.com · 2300 N Street, NW · Washington, DC 20037-1122 · 202-663-8000

John Engel · Pillsbury Winthrop Shaw Pittman · http://www.pillsburylaw.com · 2300 N Street, NW · Washington, DC 20037-1122 · 202-663-8000

Jay A. Epstien · ⑩ · DLA Piper · 500 Eighth Street, NW · Washington, DC 20004 · 202-799-4000

John T. Epting · Pillsbury Winthrop Shaw Pittman · http://www.pillsburylaw.com · 2300 N Street, NW · Washington, DC 20037-1122 · 202-663-8000

Phil T. Feola · Pillsbury Winthrop Shaw Pittman · http://www.pillsburylaw.com · 2300 N Street, NW · Washington, DC 20037-1122 · 202-663-8000

Wendy L. Fields · Katten Muchin Rosenman · 2900 K Street, NW, Suite 200 · Washington, DC 20007-5201 · 202-625-3500

Stanley J. Fineman · ⑩ · Wilkes Artis · 1150 Eighteenth Street, NW, Suite 400 · Washington, DC 20036-3841 · 202-457-7800

Jeremy B. Fox · Arent Fox · 1050 Connecticut Avenue, NW · Washington, DC 20036-5339 · 202-857-6000

Joseph M. Fries · ㉕ · Arent Fox · 1050 Connecticut Avenue, NW · Washington, DC 20036-5339 · 202-857-6000

Robert J. Gage · Covington & Burling · 1201 Pennsylvania Avenue, NW · Washington, DC 20004-2401 · 202-662-6000

Ronald S. Gart · Seyfarth Shaw · 815 Connecticut Avenue, NW, Suite 500 · Washington, DC 20006-4004 202-463-2400

Lawrence H. Gesner · Venable · http://www.venable.com · 575 Seventh Street, NW · Washington, DC 20004-1601 · 202-344-4000

Norman Glasgow, Jr. · Holland & Knight · http://www.hklaw.com · 2099 Pennsylvania Avenue, NW, Suite 100 · Washington, DC 20006-6801 · 202-955-3000

Michael D. Goodwin · Arnold & Porter · 555 Twelfth Street, NW · Washington, DC 20004-1206 · 202-942-5000

Robert L. Gorham · ⑩ · Holland & Knight · http://www.hklaw.com · 2099 Pennsylvania Avenue, NW, Suite 100 · Washington, DC 20006-6801 · 202-955-3000

Robert G. Gottlieb · Venable · http://www.venable.com · 575 Seventh Street, NW · Washington, DC 20004-1601 · 202-344-4000

Abraham J. Greenstein · Greenstein DeLorme & Luchs · 1620 L Street, NW, Suite 900 · Washington, DC 20036-5605 · 202-452-1400

John D. Hagner · Womble Carlyle Sandridge & Rice · 1401 Eye Street, NW, Seventh Floor · Washington, DC 20005 · 202-467-6900

Frank H. Henneburg · Mayer Brown · 1909 K Street, NW · Washington, DC 20006-1101 · 202-263-3000

Philip M. Horowitz · ⑩ · Venable · http://www.venable.com · 575 Seventh Street, NW · Washington, DC 20004-1601 · 202-344-4000

Gary E. Humes · Arnold & Porter · 555 Twelfth Street, NW · Washington, DC 20004-1206 · 202-942-5000

Howard S. Jatlow · Dickstein Shapiro · http://www.dicksteinshapiro.com · 1825 Eye Street, NW · Washington, DC 20006-5403 · 202-420-2200

David S. Kahn · Holland & Knight · http://www.hklaw.com · 2099 Pennsylvania Avenue, NW, Suite 100 · Washington, DC 20006-6801 · 202-955-3000

Jeffrey R. Keitelman · DLA Piper · 500 Eighth Street, NW · Washington, DC 20004 · 202-799-4000

Frederick L. Klein · DLA Piper · 500 Eighth Street, NW · Washington, DC 20004 · 202-799-4000

Peter R. Kolker · ⑩ · Zuckerman Spaeder · http://www.zuckerman.com · 1800 M Street, NW, Suite 1000 Washington, DC 20036-5807 · 202-778-1800

Kenneth Lore · Bingham McCutchen · http://www.bingham.com · 3000 K Street, NW · Washington, DC 20007 · 202-424-7500

Richard W. Luchs · Greenstein DeLorme & Luchs · 1620 L Street, NW, Suite 900 · Washington, DC 20036-5605 · 202-452-1400

Robert C. MacKichan, Jr. · Holland & Knight · http://www.hklaw.com · 2099 Pennsylvania Avenue, NW, Suite 100 · Washington, DC 20006-6801 · 202-955-3000

Philip N. Margolius · The Margolius Firm · 3000 Connecticut Avenue, NW, Suite 100 · Washington, DC 20008 · 202-332-1800

Keith W. McGlamery · ⑩ · Ballard Spahr Andrews & Ingersoll · 601 Thirteenth Street, NW, Suite 1000 South · Washington, DC 20005-3807 · 202-661-2200

Nelson F. Migdal · Greenberg Traurig · http://www.gtlaw.com · 2101 L Street, NW, Suite 1000 · Washington, DC 20037 · 202-331-3100

Thomas E. D. Millspaugh · WilmerHale · http://www.wilmerhale.com · 1875 Pennsylvania Avenue, NW · Washington, DC 20006 · 202-663-6000

S. Scott Morrison · Katten Muchin Rosenman · 2900 K Street, NW, Suite 200 · Washington, DC 20007-5201 · 202-625-3500

Dennis K. Moyer · Goulston & Storrs · 2001 K Street, NW, Suite 1100 · Washington, DC 20006-1042 · 202-721-0011

Richard A. Newman · Arent Fox · 1050 Connecticut Avenue, NW · Washington, DC 20036-5339 · 202-857-6000

David M. Osnos · ⑳ · Arent Fox · 1050 Connecticut Avenue, NW · Washington, DC 20036-5339 · 202-857-6000

Bruce Parmley · Hogan & Hartson · 555 Thirteenth Street, NW · Washington, DC 20004-1109 · 202-637-5600

Stephen W. Porter · ⑳ · Arnold & Porter · 555 Twelfth Street, NW · Washington, DC 20004-1206 · 202-942-5000

Morton Press · Press & Press · 2150 Wisconsin Avenue, NW, Suite 10 · Washington, DC 20007 · 202-333-6600

Allison C. Prince · Pillsbury Winthrop Shaw Pittman · http://www.pillsburylaw.com · 2300 N Street, NW Washington, DC 20037-1122 · 202-663-8000

Whayne S. Quin · ㉕ · Holland & Knight · http://www.hklaw.com · 2099 Pennsylvania Avenue, NW, Suite 100 · Washington, DC 20006-6801 · 202-955-3000

Franz R. Rassman · Fried, Frank, Harris, Shriver & Jacobson · 1001 Pennsylvania Avenue, NW · Washington, DC 20004-2505 · 202-639-7000

Edward M. Rogers · Nixon Peabody · 401 Ninth Street, NW, Suite 900 · Washington, DC 20004-2128 · 202-585-8000

Barry P. Rosenthal · Bingham McCutchen · http://www.bingham.com · 2020 K Street, NW · Washington, DC 20006-1806 · 202-373-6000

Michael Ruane · Holland & Knight · http://www.hklaw.com · 2099 Pennsylvania Avenue, NW, Suite 100 · Washington, DC 20006-6801 · 202-955-3000

Blake D. Rubin · McDermott Will & Emery · 600 Thirteenth Street, NW · Washington, DC 20005-3096 202-756-8000

Janis B. Schiff · Holland & Knight · http://www.hklaw.com · 2099 Pennsylvania Avenue, NW, Suite 100 · Washington, DC 20006-6801 · 202-955-3000

David C. Silver · Holland & Knight · http://www.hklaw.com · 2099 Pennsylvania Avenue, NW, Suite 100 Washington, DC 20006-6801 · 202-955-3000

Gary S. Smuckler · Morgan Lewis & Bockius · 1111 Pennsylvania Avenue, NW · Washington, DC 20004 202-739-3000

Jeffrey B. Stern · Holland & Knight · http://www.hklaw.com · 2099 Pennsylvania Avenue, NW, Suite 100 Washington, DC 20006-6801 · 202-955-3000

Charles W. Tiedemann · Holland & Knight · http://www.hklaw.com · 2099 Pennsylvania Avenue, NW, Suite 100 · Washington, DC 20006-6801 · 202-955-3000

Stefan F. Tucker · ⑳ · Venable · http://www.venable.com · 575 Seventh Street, NW · Washington, DC 20004-1601 · 202-344-4000

Alan P. Vollmann · Holland & Knight · http://www.hklaw.com · 2099 Pennsylvania Avenue, NW, Suite 100 · Washington, DC 20006-6801 · 202-955-3000

Sheldon J. Weisel · ⑩ · Goulston & Storrs · 2001 K Street, NW, Suite 1100 · Washington, DC 20006-1042 · 202-721-0011

Erica Weiss · Bingham McCutchen · http://www.bingham.com · 2020 K Street, NW · Washington, DC 20006-1806 · 202-373-6000

Edward S. West · Beveridge & Diamond · 1350 I Street, NW, Suite 700 · Washington, DC 20005-3311 · 202-789-6000

Wendelin A. White · Pillsbury Winthrop Shaw Pittman · http://www.pillsburylaw.com · 2300 N Street, NW · Washington, DC 20037-1122 · 202-663-8000

Keith J. Willner · Mayer Brown · 1909 K Street, NW · Washington, DC 20006-1101 · 202-263-3000

Allan R. Winn · Ballard Spahr Andrews & Ingersoll · 601 Thirteenth Street, NW, Suite 1000 South · Washington, DC 20005-3807 · 202-661-2200

Debra D. Yogodzinski · Nixon Peabody · 401 Ninth Street, NW, Suite 900 · Washington, DC 20004-2128 · 202-585-8000

SECURITIES LAW

Washington

Howard B. Adler · Gibson, Dunn & Crutcher · 1050 Connecticut Avenue, NW · Washington, DC 20036-5306 · 202-955-8500

Abigail Arms · Shearman & Sterling · 801 Pennsylvania Avenue, NW, Suite 900 · Washington, DC 20004-2634 · 202-508-8000

James A. Baker III · Baker Botts · http://www.bakerbotts.com · The Warner Building, Suite 1300 · 1299 Pennsylvania Avenue, NW · Washington, DC 20004-2400 · 202-639-7700

William R. Baker III · Latham & Watkins · 555 Eleventh Street, NW, Suite 1000 · Washington, DC 20004-1304 · 202-637-2200

Brandon Becker · WilmerHale · http://www.wilmerhale.com · 1875 Pennsylvania Avenue, NW · Washington, DC 20006 · 202-663-6000

David M. Becker · Cleary Gottlieb Steen & Hamilton · 2000 Pennsylvania Avenue, NW · Washington, DC 20006 · 202-974-1500

Alan J. Berkeley · 20 · K&L Gates · 1601 K Street, NW · Washington, DC 20006-1600 · 202-778-9000

Bruce M. Bettigole · Mayer Brown · 1909 K Street, NW · Washington, DC 20006-1101 · 202-263-3000

Steven B. Boehm · Sutherland · http://www.sutherland.com · 1275 Pennsylvania Avenue, NW · Washington, DC 20004-2415 · 202-383-0100

Catherine Botticelli · Dechert · 1775 I Street, NW · Washington, DC 20006-2401 · 202-261-3300

David Robert Boyd · Boies, Schiller & Flexner · 5301 Wisconsin Avenue, NW · Washington, DC 20015 · 202-237-2727

Gregory S. Bruch · Willkie Farr & Gallagher · 1875 K Street, NW · Washington, DC 20006-1238 · 202-303-1000

Matthew A. Chambers · WilmerHale · http://www.wilmerhale.com · 1875 Pennsylvania Avenue, NW · Washington, DC 20006 · 202-663-6000

Martha L. Cochran · Arnold & Porter · 555 Twelfth Street, NW · Washington, DC 20004-1206 · 202-942-5000

Louis R. Cohen · 20 · WilmerHale · http://www.wilmerhale.com · 1875 Pennsylvania Avenue, NW · Washington, DC 20006 · 202-663-6000

Pat S. Conti · Mayer Brown · 1909 K Street, NW · Washington, DC 20006-1101 · 202-263-3000

Stephen J. Crimmins · Mayer Brown · 1909 K Street, NW · Washington, DC 20006-1101 · 202-263-3000

Meredith B. Cross · WilmerHale · http://www.wilmerhale.com · 1875 Pennsylvania Avenue, NW · Washington, DC 20006 · 202-663-6000

Catherine T. Dixon · Weil Gotshal & Manges · 1300 Eye Street, NW, Suite 900 · Washington, DC 20005 202-682-7000

James R. Doty · Baker Botts · http://www.bakerbotts.com · The Warner Building, Suite 1300 · 1299 Pennsylvania Avenue, NW · Washington, DC 20004-2400 · 202-639-7700

Alan L. Dye · Hogan & Hartson · 555 Thirteenth Street, NW · Washington, DC 20004-1109 · 202-637-5600

Ralph C. Ferrara · 10 · Dewey & LeBoeuf · 1101 New York Avenue, NW, Suite 1100 · Washington, DC 20005-4213 · 202-986-8000

Dennis O. Garris · Alston + Bird · http://www.alston.com · The Atlantic Building · 950 F Street, NW · Washington, DC 20004-1404 · 202-756-3300

Barry R. Goldsmith · Gibson, Dunn & Crutcher · 1050 Connecticut Avenue, NW · Washington, DC 20036-5306 · 202-955-8500

Frank R. Goldstein · 10 · Sidley Austin · 1501 K Street, NW · Washington, DC 20005 · 202-736-8000

Joseph I. Goldstein · Mayer Brown · 1909 K Street, NW · Washington, DC 20006-1101 · 202-263-3000

Amy L. Goodman · Gibson, Dunn & Crutcher · 1050 Connecticut Avenue, NW · Washington, DC 20036-5306 · 202-955-8500

J. Warren Gorrell, Jr. · Hogan & Hartson · 555 Thirteenth Street, NW · Washington, DC 20004-1109 · 202-637-5600

Linda L. Griggs · ⑩ · Morgan Lewis & Bockius · 1111 Pennsylvania Avenue, NW · Washington, DC 20004 · 202-739-3000

Karl A. Groskaufmanis · Fried, Frank, Harris, Shriver & Jacobson · 1001 Pennsylvania Avenue, NW · Washington, DC 20004-2505 · 202-639-7000

Thomas S. Harman · Morgan Lewis & Bockius · 1111 Pennsylvania Avenue, NW · Washington, DC 20004 · 202-739-3000

Bruce A. Hiler · Cadwalader, Wickersham & Taft · http://www.cadwalader.com · 1201 F Street, NW, Suite 1100 · Washington, DC 20004 · 202-862-2200

John J. Huber · ⑩ · Latham & Watkins · 555 Eleventh Street, NW, Suite 1000 · Washington, DC 20004-1304 · 202-637-2200

Paul Huey-Burns · Dechert · 1775 I Street, NW · Washington, DC 20006-2401 · 202-261-3300

Michael Hyatte · Sidley Austin · 1501 K Street, NW · Washington, DC 20005 · 202-736-8000

Jerry A. Isenberg · LeClair Ryan · 1101 Connecticut Avenue, NW, Suite 600 · Washington, DC 20036 · 202-659-4140

Dixie Lynn Johnson · Fried, Frank, Harris, Shriver & Jacobson · 1001 Pennsylvania Avenue, NW · Washington, DC 20004-2505 · 202-639-7000

John Paul Ketels · ⑩ · Clifford Chance · 2001 K Street, NW · Washington, DC 20006-1001 · 202-912-5000

Richard S. Kraut · Dilworth Paxson · 1133 Connecticut Avenue, NW, Suite 620 · Washington, DC 20036 202-452-0900

Brian J. Lane · Gibson, Dunn & Crutcher · 1050 Connecticut Avenue, NW · Washington, DC 20036-5306 · 202-955-8500

Neil S. Lang · Sutherland · http://www.sutherland.com · 1275 Pennsylvania Avenue, NW · Washington, DC 20004-2415 · 202-383-0100

Dennis J. Lehr · ⑩ · Hogan & Hartson · 555 Thirteenth Street, NW · Washington, DC 20004-1109 · 202-637-5600

David C. Mahaffey · Sullivan & Worcester · 1666 K Street, NW · Washington, DC 20006 · 202-775-1200

Colleen P. Mahoney · Skadden, Arps, Slate, Meagher & Flom · 1440 New York Avenue, NW · Washington, DC 20005 · 202-371-7000

David B. H. Martin · Covington & Burling · 1201 Pennsylvania Avenue, NW · Washington, DC 20004-2401 · 202-662-6000

Thomas J. McGonigle · LeClair Ryan · 1101 Connecticut Avenue, NW, Suite 600 · Washington, DC 20036 · 202-659-4140

William R. McLucas · WilmerHale · http://www.wilmerhale.com · 1875 Pennsylvania Avenue, NW · Washington, DC 20006 · 202-663-6000

R. Charles Miller · K&L Gates · 1601 K Street, NW · Washington, DC 20006-1600 · 202-778-9000

Michael J. Missal · K&L Gates · 1601 K Street, NW · Washington, DC 20006-1600 · 202-778-9000

Christian J. Mixter · Morgan Lewis & Bockius · 1111 Pennsylvania Avenue, NW · Washington, DC 20004 · 202-739-3000

R. Stan Mortenson · ㉕ · Baker Botts · http://www.bakerbotts.com · The Warner Building, Suite 1300 · 1299 Pennsylvania Avenue, NW · Washington, DC 20004-2400 · 202-639-7700

Richard J. Morvillo · Mayer Brown · 1909 K Street, NW · Washington, DC 20006-1101 · 202-263-3000

Ronald O. Mueller · Gibson, Dunn & Crutcher · 1050 Connecticut Avenue, NW · Washington, DC 20036-5306 · 202-955-8500

John F. Olson · ㉕ · Gibson, Dunn & Crutcher · 1050 Connecticut Avenue, NW · Washington, DC 20036-5306 · 202-955-8500

Lionel E. Pashkoff · Proskauer Rose · http://www.proskauer.com · 1001 Pennsylvania Avenue NW, Suite 400 South · Washington, DC 20004-2533 · 202-416-6800

Therese D. Pritchard · Bryan Cave · 700 Thirteenth Street, NW · Washington, DC 20005-3960 · 202-508-6000

Frank C. Razzano · Pepper Hamilton · http://www.pepperlaw.com · Hamilton Square · 600 Fourteenth Street, N.W. · Washington, DC 20005-2004 · 202-220-1200

Robert S. Risoleo · Sullivan & Cromwell · 1701 Pennsylvania Avenue, NW · Washington, DC 20006-5805 · 202-956-7500

Michael P. Rogan · Skadden, Arps, Slate, Meagher & Flom · 1440 New York Avenue, NW · Washington, DC 20005 · 202-371-7000

Peter J. Romatowski · ⑩ · Jones Day · 51 Louisiana Avenue, NW · Washington, DC 20001-2113 · 202-879-3939

Peter J. Romeo · ⑳ · Hogan & Hartson · 555 Thirteenth Street, NW · Washington, DC 20004-1109 · 202-637-5600

Richard H. Rowe · ⑩ · Proskauer Rose · http://www.proskauer.com · 1001 Pennsylvania Avenue NW, Suite 400 South · Washington, DC 20004-2533 · 202-416-6800

Brian L. Rubin · Sutherland · http://www.sutherland.com · 1275 Pennsylvania Avenue, NW · Washington, DC 20004-2415 · 202-383-0100

Scott B. Schreiber · Arnold & Porter · 555 Twelfth Street, NW · Washington, DC 20004-1206 · 202-942-5000

Erich T. Schwartz · Skadden, Arps, Slate, Meagher & Flom · 1440 New York Avenue, NW · Washington, DC 20005 · 202-371-7000

David A. Sirignano · Morgan Lewis & Bockius · 1111 Pennsylvania Avenue, NW · Washington, DC 20004 · 202-739-3000

Marianne K. Smythe · WilmerHale · http://www.wilmerhale.com · 1875 Pennsylvania Avenue, NW · Washington, DC 20006 · 202-663-6000

Theodore Sonde · ⑩ · Patton Boggs · 2550 M Street, NW · Washington, DC 20037 · 202-457-6000

Stanley Sporkin · Weil Gotshal & Manges · 1300 Eye Street, NW, Suite 900 · Washington, DC 20005 · 202-682-7000

George P. Stamas · Kirkland & Ellis · 655 Fifteenth Street, NW · Washington, DC 20005 · 202-879-5000

Richard A. Steinwurtzel · ⑳ · Fried, Frank, Harris, Shriver & Jacobson · 1001 Pennsylvania Avenue, NW Washington, DC 20004-2505 · 202-639-7000

John Sture · Gibson, Dunn & Crutcher · 1050 Connecticut Avenue, NW · Washington, DC 20036-5306 · 202-955-8500

Neal Sullivan · Bingham McCutchen · http://www.bingham.com · 2020 K Street, NW · Washington, DC 20006-1806 · 202-373-6000

Wallace L. Timmeny · Dechert · 1775 I Street, NW · Washington, DC 20006-2401 · 202-261-3300

Michael D. Trager · Arnold & Porter · 555 Twelfth Street, NW · Washington, DC 20004-1206 · 202-942-5000

John K. Villa · Williams & Connolly · 725 Twelfth Street, NW · Washington, DC 20005-5901 · 202-434-5000

Harry J. Weiss · WilmerHale · http://www.wilmerhale.com · 1875 Pennsylvania Avenue, NW · Washington, DC 20006 · 202-663-6000

Samuel J. Winer · Foley & Lardner · Washington Harbour, Suite 500 · 3000 K Street, NW · Washington, DC 20007-5109 · 202-672-5300

George G. Yearsich · Morgan Lewis & Bockius · 1111 Pennsylvania Avenue, NW · Washington, DC 20004 · 202-739-3000

Soo J. Yim · WilmerHale · http://www.wilmerhale.com · 1875 Pennsylvania Avenue, NW · Washington, DC 20006 · 202-663-6000

SPORTS LAW

Washington

Lon S. Babby · Williams & Connolly · 725 Twelfth Street, NW · Washington, DC 20005-5901 · 202-434-5000

Andrew H. Friedman · Covington & Burling · 1201 Pennsylvania Avenue, NW · Washington, DC 20004-2401 · 202-662-6000

Douglas G. Gibson · Covington & Burling · 1201 Pennsylvania Avenue, NW · Washington, DC 20004-2401 · 202-662-6000

Mark S. Levinstein · Williams & Connolly · 725 Twelfth Street, NW · Washington, DC 20005-5901 · 202-434-5000

Gregg H. Levy · Covington & Burling · 1201 Pennsylvania Avenue, NW · Washington, DC 20004-2401 · 202-662-6000

Bruce S. Wilson · Covington & Burling · 1201 Pennsylvania Avenue, NW · Washington, DC 20004-2401 202-662-6000

STRUCTURED FINANCE LAW

Washington

John C. Arnholz · McKee Nelson · 1919 M Street, NW, Suite 200 · Washington, DC 20036 · 202-775-1880

Cameron L. Cowan · Orrick, Herrington & Sutcliffe · Columbia Center · 1152 Fifteenth Street, NW · Washington, DC 20005-1706 · 202-339-8400

M. David Krohn · DLA Piper · 500 Eighth Street, NW · Washington, DC 20004 · 202-799-4000

Michael H. Mitchell · Orrick, Herrington & Sutcliffe · Columbia Center · 1152 Fifteenth Street, NW · Washington, DC 20005-1706 · 202-339-8400

Lynn A. Soukup · Pillsbury Winthrop Shaw Pittman · http://www.pillsburylaw.com · 2300 N Street, NW · Washington, DC 20037-1122 · 202-663-8000

TAX LAW

Washington

Donald C. Alexander · 25 · Akin Gump Strauss Hauer & Feld · Robert S. Strauss Building · 1333 New Hampshire Avenue, NW · Washington, DC 20036-1564 · 202-887-4000

Arthur L. Bailey · Steptoe & Johnson · http://www.steptoe.com · 1330 Connecticut Avenue, NW · Washington, DC 20036 · 202-429-3000

John P. Barrie · 10 · Bryan Cave · 700 Thirteenth Street, NW · Washington, DC 20005-3960 · 202-508-6000

Edward Jay Beckwith · 10 · Baker Hostetler · http://www.bakerlaw.com · Washington Square, Suite 1100 1050 Connecticut Avenue, NW · Washington, DC 20036-5304 · 202-861-1500

Dennis P. Bedell · 20 · Miller & Chevalier · http://www.milchev.com · 655 Fifteenth Street, NW, Suite 900 · Washington, DC 20005-5701 · 202-626-5800

Herbert N. Beller · 10 · Sutherland · http://www.sutherland.com · 1275 Pennsylvania Avenue, NW · Washington, DC 20004-2415 · 202-383-0100

Henry J. Birnkrant · Alston + Bird · http://www.alston.com · The Atlantic Building · 950 F Street, NW · Washington, DC 20004-1404 · 202-756-3300

Jody J. Brewster · Skadden, Arps, Slate, Meagher & Flom · 1440 New York Avenue, NW · Washington, DC 20005 · 202-371-7000

James A. Bruton III · Williams & Connolly · 725 Twelfth Street, NW · Washington, DC 20005-5901 · 202-434-5000

Michael J. Caballero · King & Spalding · 1700 Pennsylvania Avenue, NW, Suite 200 · Washington, DC 20006-4706 · 202-737-0500

Linda E. Carlisle · White & Case · http://www.whitecase.com · 701 Thirteenth Street, NW · Washington, DC 20005 · 202-626-3600

Rita A. Cavanagh · Latham & Watkins · 555 Eleventh Street, NW, Suite 1000 · Washington, DC 20004-1304 · 202-637-2200

William R. Charyk · Arent Fox · 1050 Connecticut Avenue, NW · Washington, DC 20036-5339 · 202-857-6000

Robert T. Cole · ⑩ · Alston + Bird · http://www.alston.com · The Atlantic Building · 950 F Street, NW · Washington, DC 20004-1404 · 202-756-3300

Earl M. Colson · ⑳ · Arent Fox · 1050 Connecticut Avenue, NW · Washington, DC 20036-5339 · 202-857-6000

David Cubeta · Miller & Chevalier · http://www.milchev.com · 655 Fifteenth Street, NW, Suite 900 · Washington, DC 20005-5701 · 202-626-5800

Robert E. Culbertson · King & Spalding · 1700 Pennsylvania Avenue, NW, Suite 200 · Washington, DC 20006-4706 · 202-737-0500

Peter M. Daub · Baker & McKenzie · 815 Connecticut Avenue, NW · Washington, DC 20006-4078 · 202-452-7000

Roderick DeArment · Covington & Burling · 1201 Pennsylvania Avenue, NW · Washington, DC 20004-2401 · 202-662-6000

Henry D. DeBerry · ⑩ · Baker Botts · http://www.bakerbotts.com · The Warner Building, Suite 1300 · 1299 Pennsylvania Avenue, NW · Washington, DC 20004-2400 · 202-639-7700

Nicholas J. DeNovio · Latham & Watkins · 555 Eleventh Street, NW, Suite 1000 · Washington, DC 20004-1304 · 202-637-2200

Andrew J. Dubroff · Ernst & Young · 1101 New York Avenue, NW · Washington, DC 20005-4270 · 202-327-6000

Carol A. Dunahoo · Baker & McKenzie · 815 Connecticut Avenue, NW · Washington, DC 20006-4078 · 202-452-7000

H. Stewart Dunn, Jr. · ⑳ · Ivins, Phillips & Barker · 1700 Pennsylvania Avenue, NW, Suite 600 · Washington, DC 20006 · 202-393-7600

Michael C. Durney · Moore & Bruce · 1072 Thomas Jefferson Street, NW · Washington, DC 20007 · 202-965-5300

Michael C. Durst · Steptoe & Johnson · http://www.steptoe.com · 1330 Connecticut Avenue, NW · Washington, DC 20036 · 202-429-3000

F. Scott Farmer · McKee Nelson · 1919 M Street, NW, Suite 200 · Washington, DC 20036 · 202-775-1880

Rocco Femia · Miller & Chevalier · http://www.milchev.com · 655 Fifteenth Street, NW, Suite 900 · Washington, DC 20005-5701 · 202-626-5800

Miriam L. Fisher · Morgan Lewis & Bockius · 1111 Pennsylvania Avenue, NW · Washington, DC 20004 202-739-3000

Eric R. Fox · ⑩ · Ivins, Phillips & Barker · 1700 Pennsylvania Avenue, NW, Suite 600 · Washington, DC 20006 · 202-393-7600

James T. Fuller III · Williams & Connolly · 725 Twelfth Street, NW · Washington, DC 20005-5901 · 202-434-5000

David Garlock · Ernst & Young · 1101 New York Avenue, NW · Washington, DC 20005-4270 · 202-327-6000

Stephen F. Gertzman · ⑳ · Ernst & Young · 1101 New York Avenue, NW · Washington, DC 20005-4270 202-327-6000

Lawrence B. Gibbs · ⑩ · Miller & Chevalier · http://www.milchev.com · 655 Fifteenth Street, NW, Suite 900 · Washington, DC 20005-5701 · 202-626-5800

Kenneth W. Gideon · ⑩ · Skadden, Arps, Slate, Meagher & Flom · 1440 New York Avenue, NW · Washington, DC 20005 · 202-371-7000

Martin D. Ginsburg · ㉕ · Fried, Frank, Harris, Shriver & Jacobson · 1001 Pennsylvania Avenue, NW · Washington, DC 20004-2505 · 202-639-7000

Fred T. Goldberg, Jr. · ⑩ · Skadden, Arps, Slate, Meagher & Flom · 1440 New York Avenue, NW · Washington, DC 20005 · 202-371-7000

Armando Gomez · Skadden, Arps, Slate, Meagher & Flom · 1440 New York Avenue, NW · Washington, DC 20005 · 202-371-7000

Alan W. Granwell · DLA Piper · 500 Eighth Street, NW · Washington, DC 20004 · 202-799-4000

G. Michael Green · Dickstein Shapiro · http://www.dicksteinshapiro.com · 1825 Eye Street, NW · Washington, DC 20006-5403 · 202-420-2200

McGee Grigsby · Latham & Watkins · 555 Eleventh Street, NW, Suite 1000 · Washington, DC 20004-1304 · 202-637-2200

Theodore R. Groom · ⑩ · Groom Law Group · http://www.groom.com · 1701 Pennsylvania Avenue, NW Washington, DC 20006-5811 · 202-857-0620

Harry L. Gutman · ⑩ · KPMG · 2001 M Street, NW · Washington, DC 20036-3310 · 202-533-3000

Sandra W. Hallmark · Akin Gump Strauss Hauer & Feld · Robert S. Strauss Building · 1333 New Hampshire Avenue, NW · Washington, DC 20036-1564 · 202-887-4000

Steven P. Hannes · McDermott Will & Emery · 600 Thirteenth Street, NW · Washington, DC 20005-3096 · 202-756-8000

Walter J. Hellerstein · Sutherland · http://www.sutherland.com · 1275 Pennsylvania Avenue, NW · Washington, DC 20004-2415 · 202-383-0100

Harold J. Heltzer · Crowell & Moring · 1001 Pennsylvania Avenue, NW · Washington, DC 20004-2595 · 202-624-2500

Mary B. Hevener · Baker & McKenzie · 815 Connecticut Avenue, NW · Washington, DC 20006-4078 · 202-452-7000

Lindsay D. Hooper · Capitol Tax Partners · 101 Constitution Avenue, NW, Suite 675 East · Washington, DC 20001 · 202-289-8700

Jasper A. Howard · McKee Nelson · 1919 M Street, NW, Suite 200 · Washington, DC 20036 · 202-775-1880

Joseph G. Howe III · Arnold & Porter · 555 Twelfth Street, NW · Washington, DC 20004-1206 · 202-942-5000

Kent L. Jones · Sutherland · http://www.sutherland.com · 1275 Pennsylvania Avenue, NW · Washington, DC 20004-2415 · 202-383-0100

Alan S. Kaden · ⑩ · Fried, Frank, Harris, Shriver & Jacobson · 1001 Pennsylvania Avenue, NW · Washington, DC 20004-2505 · 202-639-7000

Gerald A. Kafka · Latham & Watkins · 555 Eleventh Street, NW, Suite 1000 · Washington, DC 20004-1304 · 202-637-2200

Robert H. Kapp · Hogan & Hartson · 555 Thirteenth Street, NW · Washington, DC 20004-1109 · 202-637-5600

Kevin M. Keyes · Fried, Frank, Harris, Shriver & Jacobson · 1001 Pennsylvania Avenue, NW · Washington, DC 20004-2505 · 202-639-7000

Kenneth Klein · Mayer Brown · 1909 K Street, NW · Washington, DC 20006-1101 · 202-263-3000

Steven R. Lainoff · ⑩ · KPMG · 2001 M Street, NW · Washington, DC 20036-3310 · 202-533-3000

F. David Lake, Jr. · ㉕ · WilmerHale · http://www.wilmerhale.com · 1875 Pennsylvania Avenue, NW · Washington, DC 20006 · 202-663-6000

Felix B. Laughlin · ⑩ · Dewey & LeBoeuf · 1101 New York Avenue, NW, Suite 1100 · Washington, DC 20005-4213 · 202-986-8000

Matthew D. Lerner · Steptoe & Johnson · http://www.steptoe.com · 1330 Connecticut Avenue, NW · Washington, DC 20036 · 202-429-3000

Patricia G. Lewis · Caplin & Drysdale · http://www.capdale.com · One Thomas Circle, NW, Suite 1100 · Washington, DC 20005 · 202-862-5000

Stuart M. Lewis · ⑳ · Buchanan Ingersoll & Rooney · http://www.bipc.com · 1700 K Street, NW, Suite 300 · Washington, DC 20006-3807 · 202-452-7900

Jerome B. Libin · ⑳ · Sutherland · http://www.sutherland.com · 1275 Pennsylvania Avenue, NW · Washington, DC 20004-2415 · 202-383-0100

John B. Magee · ⑩ · McKee Nelson · 1919 M Street, NW, Suite 200 · Washington, DC 20036 · 202-775-1880

Phillip L. Mann · ⑳ · Miller & Chevalier · http://www.milchev.com · 655 Fifteenth Street, NW, Suite 900 Washington, DC 20005-5701 · 202-626-5800

Keith Martin · Chadbourne & Parke · http://www.chadbourne.com · 1200 New Hampshire Avenue, NW, Suite 300 · Washington, DC 20036 · 202-974-5600

Gregory May · Freshfields Bruckhaus Deringer · 701 Pennsylvania Avenue, NW, Suite 600 · Washington, DC 20004-2692 · 202-777-4500

Suzanne Ross McDowell · Steptoe & Johnson · http://www.steptoe.com · 1330 Connecticut Avenue, NW Washington, DC 20036 · 202-429-3000

William S. McKee · ⑳ · McKee Nelson · 1919 M Street, NW, Suite 200 · Washington, DC 20036 · 202-775-1880

James E. Merritt · ⑩ · Morrison & Foerster · http://www.mofo.com · 2000 Pennsylvania Avenue, NW, Suite 5500 · Washington, DC 20006-1888 · 202-887-1500

Scott D. Michel · Caplin & Drysdale · http://www.capdale.com · One Thomas Circle, NW, Suite 1100 · Washington, DC 20005 · 202-862-5000

Michael R. Miles · Sutherland · http://www.sutherland.com · 1275 Pennsylvania Avenue, NW · Washington, DC 20004-2415 · 202-383-0100

Robert L. Moore II · Miller & Chevalier · http://www.milchev.com · 655 Fifteenth Street, NW, Suite 900 Washington, DC 20005-5701 · 202-626-5800

Clifford E. Muller · Sutherland · http://www.sutherland.com · 1275 Pennsylvania Avenue, NW · Washington, DC 20004-2415 · 202-383-0100

Lon E. Musslewhite · Williams & Connolly · 725 Twelfth Street, NW · Washington, DC 20005-5901 · 202-434-5000

Cono R. Namorato · ⑩ · Caplin & Drysdale · http://www.capdale.com · One Thomas Circle, NW, Suite 1100 · Washington, DC 20005 · 202-862-5000

William F. Nelson · ⑩ · McKee Nelson · 1919 M Street, NW, Suite 200 · Washington, DC 20036 · 202-775-1880

Pamela F. Olson · Skadden, Arps, Slate, Meagher & Flom · 1440 New York Avenue, NW · Washington, DC 20005 · 202-371-7000

Paul W. Oosterhuis · ⑩ · Skadden, Arps, Slate, Meagher & Flom · 1440 New York Avenue, NW · Washington, DC 20005 · 202-371-7000

Marcus S. Owens · Caplin & Drysdale · http://www.capdale.com · One Thomas Circle, NW, Suite 1100 · Washington, DC 20005 · 202-862-5000

Joseph M. Pari · ⑩ · Dewey & LeBoeuf · 1101 New York Avenue, NW, Suite 1100 · Washington, DC 20005-4213 · 202-986-8000

William M. Paul · ⑩ · Covington & Burling · 1201 Pennsylvania Avenue, NW · Washington, DC 20004-2401 · 202-662-6000

James A. Riedy · McDermott Will & Emery · 600 Thirteenth Street, NW · Washington, DC 20005-3096 · 202-756-8000

Christopher S. Rizek · Caplin & Drysdale · http://www.capdale.com · One Thomas Circle, NW, Suite 1100 · Washington, DC 20005 · 202-862-5000

Celia Roady · Morgan Lewis & Bockius · 1111 Pennsylvania Avenue, NW · Washington, DC 20004 · 202-739-3000

H. David Rosenbloom · ⑳ · Caplin & Drysdale · http://www.capdale.com · One Thomas Circle, NW, Suite 1100 · Washington, DC 20005 · 202-862-5000

Blake D. Rubin · McDermott Will & Emery · 600 Thirteenth Street, NW · Washington, DC 20005-3096 202-756-8000

Michael I. Sanders · Blank Rome · Watergate · 600 New Hampshire Avenue, NW · Washington, DC 20037 · 202-772-5800

Paul M. Schmidt · Baker Hostetler · http://www.bakerlaw.com · Washington Square, Suite 1100 · 1050 Connecticut Avenue, NW · Washington, DC 20036-5304 · 202-861-1500

Leslie J. Schneider · Ivins, Phillips & Barker · 1700 Pennsylvania Avenue, NW, Suite 600 · Washington, DC 20006 · 202-393-7600

Abraham Shashy · Dewey & LeBoeuf · 1101 New York Avenue, NW, Suite 1100 · Washington, DC 20005-4213 · 202-986-8000

Mark J. Silverman · ⑩ · Steptoe & Johnson · http://www.steptoe.com · 1330 Connecticut Avenue, NW · Washington, DC 20036 · 202-429-3000

Richard W. Skillman · Caplin & Drysdale · http://www.capdale.com · One Thomas Circle, NW, Suite 1100 · Washington, DC 20005 · 202-862-5000

Giovanna T. Sparagna · Sutherland · http://www.sutherland.com · 1275 Pennsylvania Avenue, NW · Washington, DC 20004-2415 · 202-383-0100

Robert B. Stack · Ivins, Phillips & Barker · 1700 Pennsylvania Avenue, NW, Suite 600 · Washington, DC 20006 · 202-393-7600

Jonathan Talisman · Capitol Tax Partners · 101 Constitution Avenue, NW, Suite 675 East · Washington, DC 20001 · 202-289-8700

Leonard B. Terr · Baker & McKenzie · 815 Connecticut Avenue, NW · Washington, DC 20006-4078 · 202-452-7000

Richard E. Timbie · Caplin & Drysdale · http://www.capdale.com · One Thomas Circle, NW, Suite 1100 · Washington, DC 20005 · 202-862-5000

Charles S. Triplett · Mayer Brown · 1909 K Street, NW · Washington, DC 20006-1101 · 202-263-3000

Thomas A. Troyer · ⑳ · Caplin & Drysdale · http://www.capdale.com · One Thomas Circle, NW, Suite 1100 · Washington, DC 20005 · 202-862-5000

Stefan F. Tucker · ⑳ · Venable · http://www.venable.com · 575 Seventh Street, NW · Washington, DC 20004-1601 · 202-344-4000

Albert H. Turkus · Skadden, Arps, Slate, Meagher & Flom · 1440 New York Avenue, NW · Washington, DC 20005 · 202-371-7000

Robert H. Wellen · ⑩ · Ivins, Phillips & Barker · 1700 Pennsylvania Avenue, NW, Suite 600 · Washington, DC 20006 · 202-393-7600

Thomas F. Wessel · ⑩ · KPMG · 2001 M Street, NW · Washington, DC 20036-3310 · 202-533-3000

Philip R. West · Steptoe & Johnson · http://www.steptoe.com · 1330 Connecticut Avenue, NW · Washington, DC 20036 · 202-429-3000

Reeves C. Westbrook · Covington & Burling · 1201 Pennsylvania Avenue, NW · Washington, DC 20004-2401 · 202-662-6000

Charles W. Wheeler · Alston + Bird · http://www.alston.com · The Atlantic Building · 950 F Street, NW · Washington, DC 20004-1404 · 202-756-3300

Andrea Macintosh Whiteway · McDermott Will & Emery · 600 Thirteenth Street, NW · Washington, DC 20005-3096 · 202-756-8000

Raymond J. Wiacek · Jones Day · 51 Louisiana Avenue, NW · Washington, DC 20001-2113 · 202-879-3939

Gary B. Wilcox · Morgan Lewis & Bockius · 1111 Pennsylvania Avenue, NW · Washington, DC 20004 · 202-739-3000

William J. Wilkins · ⑩ · WilmerHale · http://www.wilmerhale.com · 1875 Pennsylvania Avenue, NW · Washington, DC 20006 · 202-663-6000

B. John Williams, Jr. · Skadden, Arps, Slate, Meagher & Flom · 1440 New York Avenue, NW · Washington, DC 20005 · 202-371-7000

Matthew J. Zinn · ⑩ · Steptoe & Johnson · http://www.steptoe.com · 1330 Connecticut Avenue, NW · Washington, DC 20036 · 202-429-3000

TECHNOLOGY LAW

Washington

Jon A. Baumgarten · ⑩ · Proskauer Rose · http://www.proskauer.com · 1001 Pennsylvania Avenue NW, Suite 400 South · Washington, DC 20004-2533 · 202-416-6800

James M. Burger · Dow Lohnes · http://www.dowlohnes.com · 1200 New Hampshire Avenue, NW, Suite 800 · Washington, DC 20036-6802 · 202-776-2000

Peter C. Cassat · Dow Lohnes · http://www.dowlohnes.com · 1200 New Hampshire Avenue, NW, Suite 800 · Washington, DC 20036-6802 · 202-776-2000

Ralph Oman · Dechert · 1775 I Street, NW · Washington, DC 20006-2401 · 202-261-3300

Richard C. Peet · Foley & Lardner · Washington Harbour, Suite 500 · 3000 K Street, NW · Washington, DC 20007-5109 · 202-672-5300

Julie A. Petruzzelli · Venable · http://www.venable.com · 575 Seventh Street, NW · Washington, DC 20004-1601 · 202-344-4000

Mark E. Plotkin · Covington & Burling · 1201 Pennsylvania Avenue, NW · Washington, DC 20004-2401 202-662-6000

Michael A. Sartori · Venable · http://www.venable.com · 575 Seventh Street, NW · Washington, DC 20004-1601 · 202-344-4000

John I. Stewart, Jr. · Crowell & Moring · 1001 Pennsylvania Avenue, NW · Washington, DC 20004-2595 202-624-2500

Michael S. Tuscan · Cooley Godward Kronish · 777 Sixth Street, NW, Suite 1100 · Washington, DC 20001 · 202-842-7800

Erich E. Veitenheimer III · Cooley Godward Kronish · 777 Sixth Street, NW, Suite 1100 · Washington, DC 20001 · 202-842-7800

David J. Wittenstein · Dow Lohnes · http://www.dowlohnes.com · 1200 New Hampshire Avenue, NW, Suite 800 · Washington, DC 20036-6802 · 202-776-2000

TRANSPORTATION LAW

Washington

Betty Jo Christian · Steptoe & Johnson · http://www.steptoe.com · 1330 Connecticut Avenue, NW · Washington, DC 20036 · 202-429-3000

Nicholas J. Dimichael · Thompson Hine · 1920 N Street, NW, Suite 800 · Washington, DC 20036-1600 · 202-331-8800

Robert M. Jenkins III · Mayer Brown · 1909 K Street, NW · Washington, DC 20006-1101 · 202-263-3000

Anthony J. LaRocca · Steptoe & Johnson · http://www.steptoe.com · 1330 Connecticut Avenue, NW · Washington, DC 20036 · 202-429-3000

C. Michael Loftus · Slover & Loftus · 1224 Seventeenth Street, NW · Washington, DC 20036 · 202-347-7170

G. Paul Moates · Sidley Austin · 1501 K Street, NW · Washington, DC 20005 · 202-736-8000

Linda J. Morgan · Covington & Burling · 1201 Pennsylvania Avenue, NW · Washington, DC 20004-2401 202-662-6000

Michael L. Rosenthal · Covington & Burling · 1201 Pennsylvania Avenue, NW · Washington, DC 20004-2401 · 202-662-6000

Jack L. Schenendorf · Covington & Burling · 1201 Pennsylvania Avenue, NW · Washington, DC 20004-2401 · 202-662-6000

Samuel M. Sipe, Jr. · Steptoe & Johnson · http://www.steptoe.com · 1330 Connecticut Avenue, NW · Washington, DC 20036 · 202-429-3000

TRUSTS AND ESTATES

Washington

Holly M. Bastian · Arent Fox · 1050 Connecticut Avenue, NW · Washington, DC 20036-5339 · 202-857-6000

Edward Jay Beckwith · ⑩ · Baker Hostetler · http://www.bakerlaw.com · Washington Square, Suite 1100 1050 Connecticut Avenue, NW · Washington, DC 20036-5304 · 202-861-1500

Jane C. Bergner · Law Offices of Jane C. Bergner · http://www.dctaxlawfirm.com · 1776 K Street, NW, Suite 800 · Washington, DC 20006 · 202-470-5220

John M. Bixler · Ross, Marsh & Foster · 2001 L Street, NW, Suite 400 · Washington, DC 20036-4910 · 202-822-8888

Doris Blazek-White · ㉕ · Covington & Burling · 1201 Pennsylvania Avenue, NW · Washington, DC 20004-2401 · 202-662-6000

Calvin H. Cobb III · Craighill, Mayfield, Fenwick, Cromelin & Cobb · 4910 Massachusetts Avenue, NW, Suite 215 · Washington, DC 20016-4368 · 202-364-4242

Earl M. Colson · ⑳ · Arent Fox · 1050 Connecticut Avenue, NW · Washington, DC 20036-5339 · 202-857-6000

Paul B. Cromelin III · Craighill, Mayfield, Fenwick, Cromelin & Cobb · 4910 Massachusetts Avenue, NW, Suite 215 · Washington, DC 20016-4368 · 202-364-4242

Michael F. Curtin · ⑳ · Curtin Law Roberson Dunigan & Salans · 1900 M Street, NW, Suite 600 · Washington, DC 20036-3565 · 202-530-3300

William E. Davis · Ross, Marsh & Foster · 2001 L Street, NW, Suite 400 · Washington, DC 20036-4910 · 202-822-8888

Francis E. Fenwick · Craighill, Mayfield, Fenwick, Cromelin & Cobb · 4910 Massachusetts Avenue, NW, Suite 215 · Washington, DC 20016-4368 · 202-364-4242

Ellen K. Harrison · ⑩ · Pillsbury Winthrop Shaw Pittman · http://www.pillsburylaw.com · 2300 N Street, NW · Washington, DC 20037-1122 · 202-663-8000

Beth S. Kaufman · Caplin & Drysdale · http://www.capdale.com · One Thomas Circle, NW, Suite 1100 · Washington, DC 20005 · 202-862-5000

Donald D. Kozusko · Kozusko Harris Vetter Wareh · 1666 K Street, NW, Suite 400 · Washington, DC 20006 · 202-457-7200

George P. Levendis · ⑩ · Levendis Law Group · http://www.levendislaw.com · 1776 K Street, NW, Suite 700 · Washington, DC 20006 · 202-223-8340

John M. Lynham, Jr. · Foley & Lardner · Washington Harbour, Suite 500 · 3000 K Street, NW · Washington, DC 20007-5109 · 202-672-5300

Robert E. Madden · Blank Rome · Watergate · 600 New Hampshire Avenue, NW · Washington, DC 20037 · 202-772-5800

Mary Ann Mancini · Bryan Cave · 700 Thirteenth Street, NW · Washington, DC 20005-3960 · 202-508-6000

Julian E. Markham, Jr. · Thompson, O'Donnell, Markham, Norton & Hannon · 1212 New York Avenue, NW, Suite 1000 · Washington, DC 20005 · 202-289-1133

Richard S. T. Marsh · Ross, Marsh & Foster · 2001 L Street, NW, Suite 400 · Washington, DC 20036-4910 · 202-822-8888

Richard H. Mayfield · Craighill, Mayfield, Fenwick, Cromelin & Cobb · 4910 Massachusetts Avenue, NW, Suite 215 · Washington, DC 20016-4368 · 202-364-4242

Virginia A. McArthur · Law Office of Virginia A. McArthur · 1101 Seventeenth Street, NW, Suite 820 · Washington, DC 20036 · 202-857-3434

Jerry J. McCoy · ⑩ · Jerry J. McCoy · 1050 Connecticut Avenue, NW, Suite 1200 · P.O. Box 66491 · Washington, DC 20035-6491 · 202-466-6941

Ralph J. Moore, Jr. · ⑳ · Morgan Lewis & Bockius · 1111 Pennsylvania Avenue, NW · Washington, DC 20004 · 202-739-3000

Stephen W. Nealon · Hamilton & Hamilton · 1900 M Street, NW, Suite 700 · Washington, DC 20036-3518 · 202-463-8282

Jeanne L. Newlon · Venable · http://www.venable.com · 575 Seventh Street, NW · Washington, DC 20004-1601 · 202-344-4000

Anne J. O'Brien · Arnold & Porter · 555 Twelfth Street, NW · Washington, DC 20004-1206 · 202-942-5000

Lynn K. Pearle · ⑩ · Arent Fox · 1050 Connecticut Avenue, NW · Washington, DC 20036-5339 · 202-857-6000

Lloyd Leva Plaine · ⑩ · Sutherland · http://www.sutherland.com · 1275 Pennsylvania Avenue, NW · Washington, DC 20004-2415 · 202-383-0100

Thomas W. Richardson · Arnold & Porter · 555 Twelfth Street, NW · Washington, DC 20004-1206 · 202-942-5000

Alban Salaman · Holland & Knight · http://www.hklaw.com · 2099 Pennsylvania Avenue, NW, Suite 100 Washington, DC 20006-6801 · 202-955-3000

Laurence E. Salans · Curtin Law Roberson Dunigan & Salans · 1900 M Street, NW, Suite 600 · Washington, DC 20036-3565 · 202-530-3300

Lewis J. Saret · Moore & Bruce · 1072 Thomas Jefferson Street, NW · Washington, DC 20007 · 202-965-5300

A. Christopher Sega · Venable · http://www.venable.com · 575 Seventh Street, NW · Washington, DC 20004-1601 · 202-344-4000

Douglas L. Siegler · Sutherland · http://www.sutherland.com · 1275 Pennsylvania Avenue, NW · Washington, DC 20004-2415 · 202-383-0100

Ira S. Siegler · Ira S. Siegler · 1616 H Street, NW, Suite 900 · Washington, DC 20006-4903 · 202-737-0220

Stefan F. Tucker · 20 · Venable · http://www.venable.com · 575 Seventh Street, NW · Washington, DC 20004-1601 · 202-344-4000

Nicholas D. Ward · 10 · Law Office of Nicholas D. Ward · 1212 New York Avenue, NW, Suite 1000 · Washington, DC 20005 · 202-289-6440

Aen Walker Webster · Buchanan Ingersoll & Rooney · http://www.bipc.com · 1700 K Street, NW, Suite 300 · Washington, DC 20006-3807 · 202-452-7900

VENTURE CAPITAL LAW

Washington

Trevor J. Chaplick · Proskauer Rose · http://www.proskauer.com · 1001 Pennsylvania Avenue NW, Suite 400 South · Washington, DC 20004-2533 · 202-416-6800

Ryan Naftulin · Cooley Godward Kronish · 777 Sixth Street, NW, Suite 1100 · Washington, DC 20001 · 202-842-7800

WATER LAW

Washington

Kristy A. Niehaus Bulleit · Hunton & Williams · 1900 K Street, NW · Washington, DC 20006-1109 · 202-955-1500

Theodore L. Garrett · 20 · Covington & Burling · 1201 Pennsylvania Avenue, NW · Washington, DC 20004-2401 · 202-662-6000

Jerome C. Muys · 20 · Muys & Associates · 1666 K Street, NW, Suite 700 · Washington, DC 20006 · 202-370-3924

WHITE-COLLAR CRIMINAL DEFENSE

Washington

Stephen P. Anthony · Covington & Burling · 1201 Pennsylvania Avenue, NW · Washington, DC 20004-2401 · 202-662-6000

Bruce A. Baird · Covington & Burling · 1201 Pennsylvania Avenue, NW · Washington, DC 20004-2401 · 202-662-6000

Raymond Banoun · ⑳ · Cadwalader, Wickersham & Taft · http://www.cadwalader.com · 1201 F Street, NW, Suite 1100 · Washington, DC 20004 · 202-862-2200

E. Lawrence Barcella, Jr. · ⑩ · Paul Hastings · 875 Fifteenth Street, NW · Washington, DC 20005 · 202-551-1700

Alan I. Baron · Holland & Knight · http://www.hklaw.com · 2099 Pennsylvania Avenue, NW, Suite 100 · Washington, DC 20006-6801 · 202-955-3000

Michael J. Barta · Baker Botts · http://www.bakerbotts.com · The Warner Building, Suite 1300 · 1299 Pennsylvania Avenue, NW · Washington, DC 20004-2400 · 202-639-7700

Robert F. Bauer · Perkins Coie · http://www.perkinscoie.com · 607 Fourteenth Street, NW, Suite 800 · Washington, DC 20005-2003 · 202-628-6600

Richard W. Beckler · ㉕ · Howrey · 1299 Pennsylvania Avenue, NW · Washington, DC 20004 · 202-783-0800

Richard L. Beizer · ⑩ · Crowell & Moring · 1001 Pennsylvania Avenue, NW · Washington, DC 20004-2595 · 202-624-2500

Richard Ben-Veniste · Mayer Brown · 1909 K Street, NW · Washington, DC 20006-1101 · 202-263-3000

Robert S. Bennett · ㉕ · Skadden, Arps, Slate, Meagher & Flom · 1440 New York Avenue, NW · Washington, DC 20005 · 202-371-7000

James A. Bensfield · ⑩ · Miller & Chevalier · http://www.milchev.com · 655 Fifteenth Street, NW, Suite 900 · Washington, DC 20005-5701 · 202-626-5800

Judah Best · ⑳ · Dewey & LeBoeuf · 1101 New York Avenue, NW, Suite 1100 · Washington, DC 20005-4213 · 202-986-8000

Mark J. Biros · Proskauer Rose · http://www.proskauer.com · 1001 Pennsylvania Avenue NW, Suite 400 South · Washington, DC 20004-2533 · 202-416-6800

Stephen L. Braga · Baker Botts · http://www.bakerbotts.com · The Warner Building, Suite 1300 · 1299 Pennsylvania Avenue, NW · Washington, DC 20004-2400 · 202-639-7700

John M. Bray · ⑩ · King & Spalding · 1700 Pennsylvania Avenue, NW, Suite 200 · Washington, DC 20006-4706 · 202-737-0500

Lanny A. Breuer · Covington & Burling · 1201 Pennsylvania Avenue, NW · Washington, DC 20004-2401 202-662-6000

Michael R. Bromwich · Fried, Frank, Harris, Shriver & Jacobson · 1001 Pennsylvania Avenue, NW · Washington, DC 20004-2505 · 202-639-7000

Blair G. Brown · Zuckerman Spaeder · http://www.zuckerman.com · 1800 M Street, NW, Suite 1000 · Washington, DC 20036-5807 · 202-778-1800

Carol Elder Bruce · Bracewell & Giuliani · http://www.bgllp.com · 2000 K Street, NW, Suite 500 · Washington, DC 20006-1872 · 202-828-5800

Gregory S. Bruch · Willkie Farr & Gallagher · 1875 K Street, NW · Washington, DC 20006-1238 · 202-303-1000

Donald T. Bucklin · 20 · Squire Sanders · http://www.ssd.com · 1201 Pennsylvania Avenue, NW, Suite 500 · P.O. Box 407 · Washington, DC 20004-2401 · 202-626-6600

Preston Burton · Orrick, Herrington & Sutcliffe · Columbia Center · 1152 Fifteenth Street, NW · Washington, DC 20005-1706 · 202-339-8400

Dane H. Butswinkas · Williams & Connolly · 725 Twelfth Street, NW · Washington, DC 20005-5901 · 202-434-5000

C. Michael Buxton · Vinson & Elkins · http://www.velaw.com · The Willard Office Building, Suite 600 · 1455 Pennsylvania Avenue, NW · Washington, DC 20004-1008 · 202-639-6500

Ralph J. Caccia · Powell Goldstein · http://www.pogolaw.com · 901 New York Avenue, NW, Third Floor · Washington, DC 20001-4413 · 202-347-0066

Plato Cacheris · 25 · Trout Cacheris · 1350 Connecticut Avenue, NW, Suite 300 · Washington, DC 20036 202-464-3300

Joe R. Caldwell, Jr. · Baker Botts · http://www.bakerbotts.com · The Warner Building, Suite 1300 · 1299 Pennsylvania Avenue, NW · Washington, DC 20004-2400 · 202-639-7700

Francis D. Carter · Zuckerman Spaeder · http://www.zuckerman.com · 1800 M Street, NW, Suite 1000 · Washington, DC 20036-5807 · 202-778-1800

John J. Cassidy · 10 · Baker Botts · http://www.bakerbotts.com · The Warner Building, Suite 1300 · 1299 Pennsylvania Avenue, NW · Washington, DC 20004-2400 · 202-639-7700

Ty Cobb · 10 · Hogan & Hartson · 555 Thirteenth Street, NW · Washington, DC 20004-1109 · 202-637-5600

James M. Cole · Bryan Cave · 700 Thirteenth Street, NW · Washington, DC 20005-3960 · 202-508-6000

Thomas G. Connolly · Harris, Wiltshire & Grannis · 1200 Eighteenth Street, NW, 12th Floor · Washington, DC 20036-2506 · 202-730-1300

Gregory B. Craig · 10 · Williams & Connolly · 725 Twelfth Street, NW · Washington, DC 20005-5901 · 202-434-5000

G. Allen Dale · G. Allen Dale · North Building, Suite 900 · 601 Pennsylvania Avenue, NW · Washington, DC 20004-2601 · 202-638-2900

John M. Dowd · 20 · Akin Gump Strauss Hauer & Feld · Robert S. Strauss Building · 1333 New Hampshire Avenue, NW · Washington, DC 20036-1564 · 202-887-4000

W. Neil Eggleston · Debevoise & Plimpton · 555 Thirteenth Street, NW · Washington, DC 20004 · 202-383-8000

Marc Erik Elias · Perkins Coie · http://www.perkinscoie.com · 607 Fourteenth Street, NW, Suite 800 · Washington, DC 20005-2003 · 202-628-6600

Miguel A. Estrada · Gibson, Dunn & Crutcher · 1050 Connecticut Avenue, NW · Washington, DC 20036-5306 · 202-955-8500

Mitchell S. Ettinger · Skadden, Arps, Slate, Meagher & Flom · 1440 New York Avenue, NW · Washington, DC 20005 · 202-371-7000

Gerald A. Feffer · 20 · Williams & Connolly · 725 Twelfth Street, NW · Washington, DC 20005-5901 · 202-434-5000

Cary M. Feldman · Feldesman Tucker Leifer Fidell · 2001 L Street, NW, Second Floor · Washington, DC 20036 · 202-466-8960

Hamilton P. Fox III · ⑩ · Sutherland · http://www.sutherland.com · 1275 Pennsylvania Avenue, NW · Washington, DC 20004-2415 · 202-383-0100

Scott L. Fredericksen · Foley & Lardner · Washington Harbour, Suite 500 · 3000 K Street, NW · Washington, DC 20007-5109 · 202-672-5300

Steven D. Gordon · Holland & Knight · http://www.hklaw.com · 2099 Pennsylvania Avenue, NW, Suite 100 · Washington, DC 20006-6801 · 202-955-3000

Jamie Gorelick · WilmerHale · http://www.wilmerhale.com · 1875 Pennsylvania Avenue, NW · Washington, DC 20006 · 202-663-6000

Thomas C. Green · ㉕ · Sidley Austin · 1501 K Street, NW · Washington, DC 20005 · 202-736-8000

Bernard Grimm · Cozen O'Connor · The Army and Navy Building, Suite 1100 · 1627 I Street, NW · Washington, DC 20006 · 202-912-4800

Gary G. Grindler · King & Spalding · 1700 Pennsylvania Avenue, NW, Suite 200 · Washington, DC 20006-4706 · 202-737-0500

James Hamilton · Bingham McCutchen · http://www.bingham.com · 2020 K Street, NW · Washington, DC 20006-1806 · 202-373-6000

Mark C. Hansen · Kellogg, Huber, Hansen, Todd, Evans & Figel · Sumner Square, Suite 400 · 1615 M Street, NW · Washington, DC 20036 · 202-326-7900

Thomas A. Hanusik · Crowell & Moring · 1001 Pennsylvania Avenue, NW · Washington, DC 20004-2595 · 202-624-2500

Richard A. Hibey · ⑳ · Miller & Chevalier · http://www.milchev.com · 655 Fifteenth Street, NW, Suite 900 · Washington, DC 20005-5701 · 202-626-5800

Robert J. Higgins · ⑩ · Dickstein Shapiro · http://www.dicksteinshapiro.com · 1825 Eye Street, NW · Washington, DC 20006-5403 · 202-420-2200

Adam S. Hoffinger · Morrison & Foerster · http://www.mofo.com · 2000 Pennsylvania Avenue, NW, Suite 5500 · Washington, DC 20006-1888 · 202-887-1500

Eric H. Holder, Jr. · Covington & Burling · 1201 Pennsylvania Avenue, NW · Washington, DC 20004-2401 · 202-662-6000

Mark D. Hopson · Sidley Austin · 1501 K Street, NW · Washington, DC 20005 · 202-736-8000

Michael E. Horowitz · Cadwalader, Wickersham & Taft · http://www.cadwalader.com · 1201 F Street, NW, Suite 1100 · Washington, DC 20004 · 202-862-2200

Mark J. Hulkower · Steptoe & Johnson · http://www.steptoe.com · 1330 Connecticut Avenue, NW · Washington, DC 20036 · 202-429-3000

Philip T. Inglima · Crowell & Moring · 1001 Pennsylvania Avenue, NW · Washington, DC 20004-2595 · 202-624-2500

N. Richard Janis · ⑩ · Janis, Schuelke & Wechsler · 1728 Massachusetts Avenue, NW · Washington, DC 20036 · 202-861-0600

William H. Jeffress, Jr. · 10 · Baker Botts · http://www.bakerbotts.com · The Warner Building, Suite 1300 1299 Pennsylvania Avenue, NW · Washington, DC 20004-2400 · 202-639-7700

Paula M. Junghans · Zuckerman Spaeder · http://www.zuckerman.com · 1800 M Street, NW, Suite 1000 · Washington, DC 20036-5807 · 202-778-1800

David E. Kendall · 10 · Williams & Connolly · 725 Twelfth Street, NW · Washington, DC 20005-5901 · 202-434-5000

John T. Kotelly · Dickstein Shapiro · http://www.dicksteinshapiro.com · 1825 Eye Street, NW · Washington, DC 20006-5403 · 202-420-2200

David S. Krakoff · Mayer Brown · 1909 K Street, NW · Washington, DC 20006-1101 · 202-263-3000

Alan Kriegel · Skadden, Arps, Slate, Meagher & Flom · 1440 New York Avenue, NW · Washington, DC 20005 · 202-371-7000

William E. Lawler III · Vinson & Elkins · http://www.velaw.com · The Willard Office Building, Suite 600 1455 Pennsylvania Avenue, NW · Washington, DC 20004-1008 · 202-639-6500

Charles S. Leeper · Drinker Biddle & Reath · 1500 K Street, NW · Washington, DC 20005-1209 · 202-842-8800

Barry William Levine · 10 · Dickstein Shapiro · http://www.dicksteinshapiro.com · 1825 Eye Street, NW · Washington, DC 20006-5403 · 202-420-2200

Nathan Lewin · 25 · Lewin & Lewin · 1828 L Street, NW, Suite 901 · Washington, DC 20036 · 202-828-1000

Abbe David Lowell · McDermott Will & Emery · 600 Thirteenth Street, NW · Washington, DC 20005-3096 · 202-756-8000

Robert D. Luskin · Patton Boggs · 2550 M Street, NW · Washington, DC 20037 · 202-457-6000

Michael J. Madigan · 10 · Akin Gump Strauss Hauer & Feld · Robert S. Strauss Building · 1333 New Hampshire Avenue, NW · Washington, DC 20036-1564 · 202-887-4000

William E. McDaniels · 20 · Williams & Connolly · 725 Twelfth Street, NW · Washington, DC 20005-5901 · 202-434-5000

Christopher B. Mead · London & Mead · 1225 Nineteenth Street, NW, Suite 320 · Washington, DC 20036 · 202-331-3334

R. Stan Mortenson · 25 · Baker Botts · http://www.bakerbotts.com · The Warner Building, Suite 1300 · 1299 Pennsylvania Avenue, NW · Washington, DC 20004-2400 · 202-639-7700

Richard J. Morvillo · Mayer Brown · 1909 K Street, NW · Washington, DC 20006-1101 · 202-263-3000

Robert F. Muse · 20 · Stein, Mitchell & Mezines · 1100 Connecticut Avenue, NW · Washington, DC 20036 · 202-737-7777

John W. Nields, Jr. · Howrey · 1299 Pennsylvania Avenue, NW · Washington, DC 20004 · 202-783-0800

Saul M. Pilchen · Skadden, Arps, Slate, Meagher & Flom · 1440 New York Avenue, NW · Washington, DC 20005 · 202-371-7000

Greg Poe · Robbins, Russell, Englert, Orseck, Untereiner & Sauber · 1801 K Street, NW, Suite 411 · Washington, DC 20006 · 202-775-4500

Barry J. Pollack · Kelley Drye & Warren · Washington Harbour, Suite 400 · 3050 K Street, NW · Washington, DC 20007-5108 · 202-342-8400

David Povich · ⑳ · Williams & Connolly · 725 Twelfth Street, NW · Washington, DC 20005-5901 · 202-434-5000

Carl S. Rauh · ⑳ · Skadden, Arps, Slate, Meagher & Flom · 1440 New York Avenue, NW · Washington, DC 20005 · 202-371-7000

Lawrence S. Robbins · Robbins, Russell, Englert, Orseck, Untereiner & Sauber · 1801 K Street, NW, Suite 411 · Washington, DC 20006 · 202-775-4500

Michele A. Roberts · Akin Gump Strauss Hauer & Feld · Robert S. Strauss Building · 1333 New Hampshire Avenue, NW · Washington, DC 20036-1564 · 202-887-4000

James K. Robinson · Cadwalader, Wickersham & Taft · http://www.cadwalader.com · 1201 F Street, NW, Suite 1100 · Washington, DC 20004 · 202-862-2200

Kenneth M. Robinson · ㉕ · The Robinson Firm · 717 D Street, NW, Suite 400 · Washington, DC 20004-2807 · 202-347-6100

Martha P. Rogers · Ober, Kaler, Grimes & Shriver · http://www.ober.com · 1401 H Street, NW, Suite 500 Washington, DC 20005-3324 · 202-408-8400

Peter J. Romatowski · ⑩ · Jones Day · 51 Louisiana Avenue, NW · Washington, DC 20001-2113 · 202-879-3939

Steven M. Salky · Zuckerman Spaeder · http://www.zuckerman.com · 1800 M Street, NW, Suite 1000 · Washington, DC 20036-5807 · 202-778-1800

Richard Sauber · Robbins, Russell, Englert, Orseck, Untereiner & Sauber · 1801 K Street, NW, Suite 411 Washington, DC 20006 · 202-775-4500

David Schertler · Schertler & Onorato · http://www.schertlerlaw.com · North Building, Ninth Floor · 601 Pennsylvania Avenue, NW · Washington, DC 20036 · 202-628-4199

Henry F. Schuelke III · ⑩ · Janis, Schuelke & Wechsler · 1728 Massachusetts Avenue, NW · Washington, DC 20036 · 202-861-0600

Howard M. Shapiro · WilmerHale · http://www.wilmerhale.com · 1875 Pennsylvania Avenue, NW · Washington, DC 20006 · 202-663-6000

James E. Sharp · ㉕ · Sharp & Associates · 1215 Nineteenth Street, NW · Washington, DC 20036 · 202-467-4114

Earl J. Silbert · ㉕ · DLA Piper · 500 Eighth Street, NW · Washington, DC 20004 · 202-799-4000

Barry S. Simon · ⑩ · Williams & Connolly · 725 Twelfth Street, NW · Washington, DC 20005-5901 · 202-434-5000

Joseph T. Small, Jr. · Fulbright & Jaworski · http://www.fulbright.com · Market Square · 801 Pennsylvania Avenue, NW · Washington, DC 20004-2623 · 202-662-0200

DeMaurice F. Smith · Patton Boggs · 2550 M Street, NW · Washington, DC 20037 · 202-457-6000

J. Sedwick Sollers III · King & Spalding · 1700 Pennsylvania Avenue, NW, Suite 200 · Washington, DC 20006-4706 · 202-737-0500

Roger C. Spaeder · ⑩ · Zuckerman Spaeder · http://www.zuckerman.com · 1800 M Street, NW, Suite 1000 · Washington, DC 20036-5807 · 202-778-1800

Mary Spearing · Baker Botts · http://www.bakerbotts.com · The Warner Building, Suite 1300 · 1299 Pennsylvania Avenue, NW · Washington, DC 20004-2400 · 202-639-7700

Stephen R. Spivack · Bradley Arant Rose & White · http://www.bradleyarant.com · 1133 Connecticut Avenue, NW, Twelfth Floor · Washington, DC 20036 · 202-393-7150

Judson W. Starr · Venable · http://www.venable.com · 575 Seventh Street, NW · Washington, DC 20004-1601 · 202-344-4000

Jacob A. Stein · ㉕ · Stein, Mitchell & Mezines · 1100 Connecticut Avenue, NW · Washington, DC 20036 · 202-737-7777

Brendan V. Sullivan, Jr. · ⑩ · Williams & Connolly · 725 Twelfth Street, NW · Washington, DC 20005-5901 · 202-434-5000

Steven C. Tabackman · Tighe Patton Armstrong Teasdale · 1747 Pennsylvania Avenue, NW, Suite 300 · Washington, DC 20006 · 202-454-2800

William W. Taylor III · ㉕ · Zuckerman Spaeder · http://www.zuckerman.com · 1800 M Street, NW, Suite 1000 · Washington, DC 20036-5807 · 202-778-1800

George J. Terwilliger III · White & Case · http://www.whitecase.com · 701 Thirteenth Street, NW · Washington, DC 20005 · 202-626-3600

W. Randolph Teslik · Akin Gump Strauss Hauer & Feld · Robert S. Strauss Building · 1333 New Hampshire Avenue, NW · Washington, DC 20036-1564 · 202-887-4000

Dick Thornburgh · K&L Gates · 1601 K Street, NW · Washington, DC 20006-1600 · 202-778-9000

Robert P. Trout · ⑩ · Trout Cacheris · 1350 Connecticut Avenue, NW, Suite 300 · Washington, DC 20036 · 202-464-3300

Mark H. Tuohey · Vinson & Elkins · http://www.velaw.com · The Willard Office Building, Suite 600 · 1455 Pennsylvania Avenue, NW · Washington, DC 20004-1008 · 202-639-6500

Randall J. Turk · ⑩ · Baker Botts · http://www.bakerbotts.com · The Warner Building, Suite 1300 · 1299 Pennsylvania Avenue, NW · Washington, DC 20004-2400 · 202-639-7700

Laurence A. Urgenson · Kirkland & Ellis · 655 Fifteenth Street, NW · Washington, DC 20005 · 202-879-5000

Barbara Van Gelder · Morgan Lewis & Bockius · 1111 Pennsylvania Avenue, NW · Washington, DC 20004 · 202-739-3000

John W. Vardaman · ㉕ · Williams & Connolly · 725 Twelfth Street, NW · Washington, DC 20005-5901 · 202-434-5000

John K. Villa · Williams & Connolly · 725 Twelfth Street, NW · Washington, DC 20005-5901 · 202-434-5000

F. Joseph Warin · Gibson, Dunn & Crutcher · 1050 Connecticut Avenue, NW · Washington, DC 20036-5306 · 202-955-8500

Seth P. Waxman · WilmerHale · http://www.wilmerhale.com · 1875 Pennsylvania Avenue, NW · Washington, DC 20006 · 202-663-6000

David N. Webster · ⑩ · Caplin & Drysdale · http://www.capdale.com · One Thomas Circle, NW, Suite 1100 · Washington, DC 20005 · 202-862-5000

Lawrence H. Wechsler · ⑩ · Janis, Schuelke & Wechsler · 1728 Massachusetts Avenue, NW · Washington, DC 20036 · 202-861-0600

Reid H. Weingarten · ⑩ · Steptoe & Johnson · http://www.steptoe.com · 1330 Connecticut Avenue, NW · Washington, DC 20036 · 202-429-3000

Peter H. White · Mayer Brown · 1909 K Street, NW · Washington, DC 20006-1101 · 202-263-3000

Paul Martin Wolff · ⑩ · Williams & Connolly · 725 Twelfth Street, NW · Washington, DC 20005-5901 · 202-434-5000

Roger E. Zuckerman · ㉕ · Zuckerman Spaeder · http://www.zuckerman.com · 1800 M Street, NW, Suite 1000 · Washington, DC 20036-5807 · 202-778-1800

WORKERS' COMPENSATION LAW

Washington

Mark L. Schaffer · Ashcraft & Gerel · 2000 L Street, NW, Suite 400 · Washington, DC 20036 · 202-783-6400

FLORIDA

ADMINISTRATIVE LAW

Coral Gables

Mirta P. Canton · Mikki Canton · 5414 Riviera Drive · Coral Gables, FL 33146 · 305-794-9356

Jorge L. López · Jorge Luis Lopez · 131 Madeira Avenue · Coral Gables, FL 33134-4515 · 305-444-6102

Jacksonville

Sidney F. Ansbacher · GrayRobinson · 50 North Laura Street, Suite 1100 · Jacksonville, FL 32202 · 904-598-9929

Miami

Alberto R. Cardenas · Tew Cardenas · http://www.tewlaw.com · Four Seasons Tower, 15th Floor · 1441 Brickell Avenue · Miami, FL 33131-3407 · 305-536-1112

Ira J. Kurzban · a · Kurzban, Kurzban, Weinger & Tetzeli · 2650 Southwest 27th Avenue, Second Floor Miami, FL 33133 · 305-444-0060

Helena Tetzeli · a · Kurzban, Kurzban, Weinger & Tetzeli · 2650 Southwest 27th Avenue, Second Floor · Miami, FL 33133 · 305-444-0060

Orlando

Miranda F. Fitzgerald · a · Lowndes, Drosdick, Doster, Kantor & Reed · 215 North Eola Drive · Orlando, FL 32801 · 407-843-4600

Hal H. Kantor · a · Lowndes, Drosdick, Doster, Kantor & Reed · 215 North Eola Drive · Orlando, FL 32801 · 407-843-4600

R. Duke Woodson · Foley & Lardner · 111 North Orange Avenue, Suite 1800 · P.O. Box 2193 · Orlando, FL 32802-2193 · 407-423-7656

Tallahassee

Martha W. Barnett · a · Holland & Knight · http://www.hklaw.com · Bank of America Building, Suite 600 · 315 South Calhoun Street · Tallahassee, FL 32301 · 850-224-7000

Donna Blanton · Radey, Thomas, Yon & Clark · http://www.radeylaw.com · 301 South Bronough Street, Suite 200 · Tallahassee, FL 32301 · 850-425-6654

Segundo J. Fernandez · Oertel, Fernandez, Cole & Bryant · 301 South Bronough Street, Fifth Floor · P.O. Box 1110 · Tallahassee, FL 32301 · 850-521-0700

Michael J. Glazer · Ausley & McMullen · Washington Square Building · 227 South Calhoun Street · P.O. Box 391 · Tallahassee, FL 32302 · 850-224-9115

Melanie Ann Hines · Berger Singerman · http://www.bergersingerman.com · 125 South Gadsden Street, Suite 300 · Tallahassee, FL 32301 · 850-561-3010

Kenneth G. Oertel · Oertel, Fernandez, Cole & Bryant · 301 South Bronough Street, Fifth Floor · P.O. Box 1110 · Tallahassee, FL 32301 · 850-521-0700

Cathy M. Sellers · Broad and Cassel · Sun Trust Bank Building, Suite 400 · 215 South Monroe Street · Tallahassee, FL 32301 · 850-681-6810

Lawrence E. Sellers · Holland & Knight · http://www.hklaw.com · Bank of America Building, Suite 600 · 315 South Calhoun Street · Tallahassee, FL 32301 · 850-224-7000

Linda Loomis Shelley · Fowler White Boggs Banker · 101 North Monroe Street, Suite 1090 · Tallahassee, FL 32301 · 850-681-0411

John McKager Stipanovich · Fowler White Boggs Banker · 101 North Monroe Street, Suite 1090 · Tallahassee, FL 32301 · 850-681-0411

Daniel H. Thompson · Berger Singerman · http://www.bergersingerman.com · 125 South Gadsden Street, Suite 300 · Tallahassee, FL 32301 · 850-561-3010

Diane D. Tremor · Rose, Sundstrom & Bentley · 2548 Blairstone Pines Drive · P.O. Box 1567 · Tallahassee, FL 32301-1567 · 850-877-6555

Karen D. Walker · Holland & Knight · http://www.hklaw.com · Bank of America Building, Suite 600 · 315 South Calhoun Street · Tallahassee, FL 32301 · 850-224-7000

William E. Williams · GrayRobinson · 301 South Bronough Street, Suite 300 · Tallahassee, FL 32301 · 850-577-9090

Tampa

Rhea F. Law · Fowler White Boggs Banker · 501 East Kennedy Boulevard, Suite 1700 · P.O. Box 1438 · Tampa, FL 33602-5239 · 813-228-7411

Robert A. Shimberg · Hill, Ward & Henderson · http://www.hwhlaw.com · Bank of America Plaza, Suite 3700 · 101 East Kennedy Boulevard · Tampa, FL 33602 · 813-221-3900

David C. Shobe · Fowler White Boggs Banker · 501 East Kennedy Boulevard, Suite 1700 · P.O. Box 1438 Tampa, FL 33602-5239 · 813-228-7411

ALTERNATIVE DISPUTE RESOLUTION

Aventura

David H. Lichter · Higer Lichter & Givner · http://www.hlglawfirm.com · 18305 Biscayne Boulevard, Suite 402 · Aventura, FL 33160 · 305-933-9970

Coral Gables

Phillip A. Hubbart · Phillip Arthur Hubbart · 2655 South Le Jeune Road, Penthouse 1-G · Coral Gables, FL 33134 · 305-374-0650

Leslie J. Lott · a · Lott & Friedland · 355 Alhambra Circle, Suite 1100 · Coral Gables, FL 33134 · 305-448-7089

Gerald T. Wetherington · a · Gerald T Wetherington · 2655 South Le Jeune Road, Penthouse I-G · Coral Gables, FL 33134 · 305-374-0650

Daytona Beach

John J. Upchurch · Upchurch Watson White & Max · 125 South Palmetto Avenue · Daytona Beach, FL 32114 · 386-253-1560

Fort Myers

James L. Nulman · James L. Nulman · 5100 South Cleveland Avenue · Fort Myers, FL 33907-2189 · 239-433-3539

Jacksonville

W. O. Birchfield · a · Birchfield & Humphrey · 1031 LaSalle Street · Jacksonville, FL 32207 · 904-396-6625

Terrance E. Schmidt · a · Bledsoe, Jacobson, Schmidt & Wright · 1301 Riverplace Boulevard, Suite 1818 Jacksonville, FL 32207 · 904-398-1818

Lakeland

Robert G. Stokes · GrayRobinson · One Lake Morton Drive · P.O. Box Three · Lakeland, FL 33802 · 863-284-2200

Maitland

J. Joaquin Fraxedas · Fraxedas Mediation Firm · 1051 Winderley Place, Suite 201 · Maitland, FL 32751 407-661-5757

Lawrence M. Watson, Jr. · Upchurch Watson White & Max · 1060 Maitland Center Commons, Suite 440 Maitland, FL 32751 · 407-661-1123

Miami

José I. Astigarraga · Astigarraga Davis · 701 Brickell Avenue, 16th Floor · Miami, FL 33131 · 305-372-8282

John M. Barkett · Shook, Hardy & Bacon · 201 South Biscayne Boulevard, Suite 2400 · Miami, FL 33131-4332 · 305-358-5171

Stanley A. Beiley · Sacher, Zelman, Hartman, Paul, Beiley & Rolnick · 1401 Brickell Avenue, Seventh Floor · Miami, FL 33131 · 305-371-8797

Edward B. Davis · Akerman Senterfitt · http://www.akerman.com · One Southeast Third Avenue, 25th Floor · Miami, FL 33131-1714 · 305-374-5600

Bruce W. Greer · 2) · Hogan, Greer & Shapiro · 2400 South Dixie Highway, Suite 200 · Miami, FL 33133-3153 · 305-854-8989

James J. Kenny · a · Kenny Nachwalter · Miami Center, Suite 1100 · 201 South Biscayne Boulevard · Miami, FL 33131-2305 · 305-373-1000

Thomas J. Meeks · Carlton Fields · 4000 International Place · 100 Southeast Second Street · P.O. Box 019101 · Miami, FL 33131-9101 · 305-530-0050

Michael Nachwalter · a · Kenny Nachwalter · Miami Center, Suite 1100 · 201 South Biscayne Boulevard Miami, FL 33131-2305 · 305-373-1000

Eduardo Palmer · Rivero Palmer & Mestre · 2525 Ponce De Leon Boulevard, Suite 1000 · Miami, FL 33134-6046 · 305-445-2500

John H. Rooney, Jr. · Shutts & Bowen · http://www.shutts.com · Miami Center, Suite 1500 · 201 South Biscayne Boulevard · Miami, FL 33131 · 305-358-6300

Harry R. Schafer · Kenny Nachwalter · Miami Center, Suite 1100 · 201 South Biscayne Boulevard · Miami, FL 33131-2305 · 305-373-1000

Brian F. Spector · a · Brian F. Spector · http://www.bspector.com · P.O. Box 566206 · Miami, FL 33256-6206 · 305-666-1664

Monticello

Thomas L. Clarke, Jr. · Sunshine Mediation · 4874 Ashville Highway · Monticello, FL 32344-4882 · 863-686-7789

Orlando

Charles W. Abbott · Holland & Knight · http://www.hklaw.com · 200 South Orange Avenue, Suite 2600 · P.O. Box 1526 · Orlando, FL 32802 · 407-425-8500

Christi L. Underwood · Christi L. Underwood · 1615 Edgewater Drive, Suite 180 · P.O. Box 547946 · Orlando, FL 32854-7946 · 407-872-3488

Sarasota

Thomas F. Icard, Jr. · Icard, Merrill, Cullis, Timm, Furen & Ginsburg · http://www.icardmerrill.com · 2033 Main Street, Suite 500 & 600 · P.O. Drawer 4195 · Sarasota, FL 34230 · 941-366-8100

Tampa

William S. Dufoe · Holland & Knight · http://www.hklaw.com · 100 North Tampa Street, Suite 4100 · P.O. Box 1288 · Tampa, FL 33601-1288 · 813-227-8500

Peter J. Grilli · Peter J. Grilli · 3001 West Azeele Street · Tampa, FL 33609 · 813-874-1002

William E. Hahn · William E. Hahn · http://www.whahn-law.com · 310 South Fielding Avenue · Tampa, FL 33606 · 813-250-0660

Mark A. Hanley · Glenn, Rasmussen, Fogarty & Hooker · http://www.glennrasmussen.com · 100 South Ashley Drive, Suite 1300 · Tampa, FL 33602 · 813-229-3333

Mary A. Lau · Lau, Lane, Pieper, Conley & McCreadie · 100 South Ashley Drive, Suite 1700 · P.O. Box 838 · Tampa, FL 33601-0838 · 813-229-2121

Michael F. Nuechterlein · Carlton Fields · Corporate Center Three at International Plaza, Suite 1000 · 4221 West Boy Scout Boulevard · Tampa, FL 33607 · 813-223-7000

Cary R. Singletary · a · Cary R. Singletary · 509 East Jackson Street · Tampa, FL 33602 · 813-301-9339

Winter Park

Jay M. Cohen · Jay M. Cohen · 981 Mayfield Avenue · P.O. Box 2210 · Winter Park, FL 32790-2210 · 407-644-1181

ANTITRUST LAW

Fort Lauderdale

Stuart H. Singer · Boies, Schiller & Flexner · 401 East Las Olas Boulevard, Suite 1200 · Fort Lauderdale, FL 33301 · 954-356-0011

Leesburg

Robert E. Austin, Jr. · Law Offices of Robert E. Austin, Jr. · 1330 Citizens Boulevard, Suite 401 · P.O. Drawer 490200 · Leesburg, FL 34749 · 352-728-1020

Miami

Richard Alan Arnold · a · Kenny Nachwalter · Miami Center, Suite 1100 · 201 South Biscayne Boulevard · Miami, FL 33131-2305 · 305-373-1000

William J. Blechman · Kenny Nachwalter · Miami Center, Suite 1100 · 201 South Biscayne Boulevard · Miami, FL 33131-2305 · 305-373-1000

Barry R. Davidson · 2% · Hunton & Williams · Mellon Financial Center, Suite 2500 · 1111 Brickell Avenue · Miami, FL 33131 · 305-810-2500

James J. Kenny · a · Kenny Nachwalter · Miami Center, Suite 1100 · 201 South Biscayne Boulevard · Miami, FL 33131-2305 · 305-373-1000

Michael Nachwalter · a · Kenny Nachwalter · Miami Center, Suite 1100 · 201 South Biscayne Boulevard Miami, FL 33131-2305 · 305-373-1000

Stephen E. Nagin · Nagin, Gallop & Figueredo · http://www.ngf-law.com · 18001 Old Cutler Road, Suite 556 · Miami, FL 33157-6416 · 305-854-5353

Scott E. Perwin · Kenny Nachwalter · Miami Center, Suite 1100 · 201 South Biscayne Boulevard · Miami, FL 33131-2305 · 305-373-1000

Ronald B. Ravikoff · Akerman Senterfitt · http://www.akerman.com · One Southeast Third Avenue, 25th Floor · Miami, FL 33131-1714 · 305-374-5600

David L. Ross · 2) · Greenberg Traurig · http://www.gtlaw.com · 1221 Brickell Avenue, 22nd Floor · Miami, FL 33131 · 305-579-0500

Lawrence D. Silverman · Silverman Cosgrove & Sammataro · One Biscayne Tower, Suite 2650 · Two South Biscayne Boulevard · Miami, FL 33131 · 305-377-1666

Orlando

Daniel C. Johnson · Carlton Fields · CNL Center at City Commons, Suite 500 · 450 South Orange Avenue · Orlando, FL 32801-3336 · 407-849-0300

Hal K. Litchford · Litchford & Christopher · Bank of America Center, Suite 2200 · 390 North Orange Avenue · P.O. Box 1549 · Orlando, FL 32802 · 407-422-6600

Keith E. Rounsaville · Litchford & Christopher · Bank of America Center, Suite 2200 · 390 North Orange Avenue · P.O. Box 1549 · Orlando, FL 32802 · 407-422-6600

Tallahassee

Jerome Hoffman · Holland & Knight · http://www.hklaw.com · Bank of America Building, Suite 600 · 315 South Calhoun Street · Tallahassee, FL 32301 · 850-224-7000

Robert Scott Palmer · Department of Legal Affairs · 400 South Monroe Street, Suite PL-01 · Tallahassee, FL 32399 · 850-414-3300

Tampa

Stacy D. Blank · Holland & Knight · http://www.hklaw.com · 100 North Tampa Street, Suite 4100 · P.O. Box 1288 · Tampa, FL 33601-1288 · 813-227-8500

Chris S. Coutroulis · Carlton Fields · Corporate Center Three at International Plaza, Suite 1000 · 4221 West Boy Scout Boulevard · Tampa, FL 33607 · 813-223-7000

Jonathan Koch · Bush Ross · http://www.bushross.com · 1801 North Highland Avenue · P.O. Box 3913 · Tampa, FL 33601 · 813-224-9255

APPELLATE LAW

Coral Gables

Phillip A. Hubbart · Phillip Arthur Hubbart · 2655 South Le Jeune Road, Penthouse 1-G · Coral Gables, FL 33134 · 305-374-0650

Fort Lauderdale

Nancy W. Gregoire · Bunnell, Woulfe, Kirschbaum, Keller, McIntyre & Gregoire · One Financial Plaza, Suite 900 · 100 Southeast Third Avenue · Fort Lauderdale, FL 33394 · 954-761-8600

John R. Hargrove · Gordon Hargrove & James · http://www.ghj.com · 2400 East Commercial Boulevard, Suite 1100 · Fort Lauderdale, FL 33308 · 954-958-2500

John H. Pelzer · Ruden, McClosky, Smith, Schuster & Russell · 200 East Broward Boulevard · P.O. Box 1900 · Fort Lauderdale, FL 33302 · 954-764-6660

Beverly A. Pohl · Broad and Cassel · One Financial Plaza, Suite 2700 · 100 Southeast Third Avenue · Fort Lauderdale, FL 33394 · 954-764-7060

Paul R. Regensdorf · Stearns Weaver Miller Weissler Alhadeff & Sitterson · 200 East Las Olas Boulevard, 21st Floor, Penthouse A · Fort Lauderdale, FL 33301 · 954-462-9500

Bruce S. Rogow · 2) · Bruce S. Rogow · Broward Financial Centre, Suite 1930 · 500 East Broward Boulevard · Fort Lauderdale, FL 33394 · 954-767-8909

Jacksonville

James T. Miller · James T. Miller · 233 East Bay Street, Suite 920 · Jacksonville, FL 32202-3456 · 904-791-8824

James C. Rinaman, Jr. · 2) · Marks & Gray · 1200 Riverplace Boulevard, Suite 800 · P.O. Box 447 · Jacksonville, FL 32201 · 904-398-0900

William J. Sheppard · a · Sheppard, White,Thomas & Kachergus · 215 North Washington Street · Jacksonville, FL 32202-2808 · 904-356-9661

Michael G. Tanner · Tanner Bishop · One Independent Drive, Suite 1700 · Jacksonville, FL 32202-5015 904-598-0034

Elizabeth L. White · a · Sheppard, White,Thomas & Kachergus · 215 North Washington Street · Jacksonville, FL 32202-2808 · 904-356-9661

Miami

Joseph D. W. Beeler · Joseph Beeler, P.A. · 800 Brickell Avenue, Penthouse Two · Miami, FL 33131 · 305-372-5110

Laura Besvinick · Hogan & Hartson · Mellon Financial Center, Suite 1900 · 1111 Brickell Avenue · Miami, FL 33131 · 305-459-6500

Joel D. Eaton · 2) · Podhurst Orseck · http://www.podhurst.com · City National Bank Building, Suite 800 25 West Flagler Street · Miami, FL 33130 · 305-358-2800

Arthur J. England, Jr. · a · Greenberg Traurig · http://www.gtlaw.com · 1221 Brickell Avenue, 22nd Floor · Miami, FL 33131 · 305-579-0500

Robert S. Glazier · Law Office of Robert S. Glazier · 540 Brickell Key Drive, Suite C-1 · Miami, FL 33131 · 305-372-5900

Cynthia L. Greene · a · Greene, Smith & Associates · 7340 Southwest 61st Court · Miami, FL 33143 · 786-268-2553

Alan G. Greer · a · Richman Greer · http://www.richmangreer.com · Miami Center, 10th Floor · 201 South Biscayne Boulevard · Miami, FL 33131 · 305-373-4000

Edward G. Guedes · Greenberg Traurig · http://www.gtlaw.com · 1221 Brickell Avenue, 22nd Floor · Miami, FL 33131 · 305-579-0500

Mark Hicks · 2) · Hicks & Kneale · 799 Brickell Plaza, Suite 900 · Miami, FL 33131 · 305-374-8171

Elliot B. Kula · Greenberg Traurig · http://www.gtlaw.com · 1221 Brickell Avenue, 22nd Floor · Miami, FL 33131 · 305-579-0500

Wendy F. Lumish · Carlton Fields · 4000 International Place · 100 Southeast Second Street · P.O. Box 019101 · Miami, FL 33131-9101 · 305-530-0050

Thomas J. Meeks · Carlton Fields · 4000 International Place · 100 Southeast Second Street · P.O. Box 019101 · Miami, FL 33131-9101 · 305-530-0050

Joel S. Perwin · a · Joel S. Perwin · Alfred I. duPont Building, Suite 1422 · 169 East Flagler Street · Miami, FL 33131 · 305-779-6090

Lauri Waldman Ross · Ross & Girten, P.A. · Two Datran Center, Suite 1612 · 9130 South Dadeland Boulevard · Miami, FL 33156 · 305-670-8010

Elizabeth K. Russo · Russo Appellate Firm · 6101 Southwest 76th Street · Miami, FL 33143-5021 · 305-666-4660

Elliot H. Scherker · Greenberg Traurig · http://www.gtlaw.com · 1221 Brickell Avenue, 22nd Floor · Miami, FL 33131 · 305-579-0500

Janice Burton Sharpstein · Jorden Burt · 777 Brickell Avenue, Suite 500 · Miami, FL 33131-2803 · 305-371-2600

Rodolfo Sorondo, Jr. · Holland & Knight · http://www.hklaw.com · 701 Brickell Avenue, Suite 3000 · Miami, FL 33131 · 305-374-8500

G. Richard Strafer · a · G. Richard Strafer · 201 South Biscayne Boulevard, Suite 1380 · Miami, FL 33131 · 305-374-9091

Patrice A. Talisman · Hersch & Talisman · 2937 Southwest 27th Avenue, Suite 206 · Miami, FL 33133 · 305-358-0570

Parker Davidson Thomson · 2) · Hogan & Hartson · Mellon Financial Center, Suite 1900 · 1111 Brickell Avenue · Miami, FL 33131 · 305-459-6500

Miami Beach

Marc Cooper · Marc Cooper Esq · 625 East Dilido Drive · Miami Beach, FL 33139 · 305-525-9185

North Miami Beach

Andrew S. Berman · Young, Berman, Karpf & Gonzalez · http://www.ybkglaw.com · 17071 West Dixie Highway · North Miami Beach, FL 33160 · 305-945-1851

Orlando

Kimberly A. Ashby · Akerman Senterfitt · http://www.akerman.com · CNL Center II at City Commons, Suite 1200 · 420 South Orange Avenue · Orlando, FL 32801-3336 · 407-423-4000

Hal K. Litchford · Litchford & Christopher · Bank of America Center, Suite 2200 · 390 North Orange Avenue · P.O. Box 1549 · Orlando, FL 32802 · 407-422-6600

Shawn G. Rader · Lowndes, Drosdick, Doster, Kantor & Reed · 215 North Eola Drive · Orlando, FL 32801 · 407-843-4600

Palm Beach Gardens

Marjorie Gadarian Graham · Marjorie Gadarian Graham · 11211 Prosperity Farms Road, Suite D-129 · Palm Beach Gardens, FL 33410 · 561-775-1204

Plantation

Joseph S. Kashi · 2) · Sperry, Shapiro & Kashi · 1776 North Pine Island Road, Suite 324 · Plantation, FL 33322 · 954-423-6553

St. Petersburg

Robert Biasotti · Carlton Fields · 200 Central Avenue, Suite 2300 · St. Petersburg, FL 33701 · 727-821-7000

Tallahassee

John R. Beranek · 2) · Ausley & McMullen · Washington Square Building · 227 South Calhoun Street · P.O. Box 391 · Tallahassee, FL 32302 · 850-224-9115

Katherine Eastmoore Giddings · Akerman Senterfitt · http://www.akerman.com · Highpoint Center, Suite 1200 · 106 East College Avenue · Tallahassee, FL 32301 · 850-224-9634

Stephen H. Grimes · Holland & Knight · http://www.hklaw.com · Bank of America Building, Suite 600 · 315 South Calhoun Street · Tallahassee, FL 32301 · 850-224-7000

Major B. Harding · Ausley & McMullen · Washington Square Building · 227 South Calhoun Street · P.O. Box 391 · Tallahassee, FL 32302 · 850-224-9115

Robert Augustus Harper · a · Harper & Harper · 325 West Park Avenue · P.O. Box 10132 · Tallahassee, FL 32302-2132 · 850-224-5900

Joseph W. Hatchett · Akerman Senterfitt · http://www.akerman.com · Highpoint Center, Suite 1200 · 106 East College Avenue · Tallahassee, FL 32301 · 850-224-9634

Barry Richard · Greenberg Traurig · http://www.gtlaw.com · 101 East College Avenue · Tallahassee, FL 32301 · 850-222-6891

Michael R. Ufferman · The Michael Ufferman Law Firm · 2022-1 Raymond Diehl Road · Tallahassee, FL 32308 · 850-386-2345

Tampa

Steven L. Brannock · Holland & Knight · http://www.hklaw.com · 100 North Tampa Street, Suite 4100 · P.O. Box 1288 · Tampa, FL 33601-1288 · 813-227-8500

Raymond T. Elligett, Jr. · Buell & Elligett · 3003 West Azeele Street, Suite 100 · Tampa, FL 33609 · 813-874-2600

Amy Farrior · Buell & Elligett · 3003 West Azeele Street, Suite 100 · Tampa, FL 33609 · 813-874-2600

James E. Felman · Kynes, Markman & Felman · 100 South Ashley Drive, Suite 1300 · P.O. Box 3396 · Tampa, FL 33601-3396 · 813-229-1118

Betsy Gallagher · Kubicki Draper · 201 North Franklin Street, Suite 2550 · Tampa, FL 33602 · 813-204-9776

Tracy Raffles Gunn · Gunn Appellate Practice P.A. · 777 South Harbour Island Boulevard, Suite 770 · Tampa, FL 33602 · 813-695-6833

Stuart C. Markman · Kynes, Markman & Felman · 100 South Ashley Drive, Suite 1300 · P.O. Box 3396 · Tampa, FL 33601-3396 · 813-229-1118

Hala A. Sandridge · Fowler White Boggs Banker · 501 East Kennedy Boulevard, Suite 1700 · P.O. Box 1438 · Tampa, FL 33602-5239 · 813-228-7411

Gary L. Sasso · Carlton Fields · Corporate Center Three at International Plaza, Suite 1000 · 4221 West Boy Scout Boulevard · Tampa, FL 33607 · 813-223-7000

Charles P. Schropp · Schropp Law Firm · 2309 South Macdill Avenue, Suite 101 · Tampa, FL 33629-5918 · 813-418-3320

Wayne Lee Thomas · Wayne Lee Thomas · 707 North Franklin Street, 10th Floor · P.O. Box 1834 · Tampa, FL 33601 · 813-229-3638

George A. Vaka · Vaka, Larson & Johnson · 100 North Tampa Street, Suite 1800 · Tampa, FL 33602 · 813-228-6688

Sylvia H. Walbolt · 2) · Carlton Fields · Corporate Center Three at International Plaza, Suite 1000 · 4221 West Boy Scout Boulevard · Tampa, FL 33607 · 813-223-7000

West Palm Beach

Philip M. Burlington · Burlington & Rockenbach · 2001 Palm Beach Lakes Boulevard, Suite 410 · West Palm Beach, FL 33409 · 561-721-0400

Edna L. Caruso · 2% · Edna L. Caruso · Barristers Building, Suite 3-A · 1615 Forum Place · West Palm Beach, FL 33401 · 561-686-8010

James K. Green · James Kellogg Green · 222 Lakeview Avenue, Suite 1650 · West Palm Beach, FL 33401-6145 · 561-659-2029

Jane Kreusler-Walsh · a · Kreusler-Walsh, Compiani & Vargas · The Flagler Center, Suite 503 · 501 South Flagler Drive · West Palm Beach, FL 33401 · 561-659-5455

Thomas E. Warner · Carlton Fields · Esperante, Suite 1400 · 222 Lakeview Avenue · West Palm Beach, FL 33401 · 561-659-7070

BANKING LAW

Coral Gables

Alcides I. Avila · Avila Rodriguez Hernandez Mena & Ferri · 2525 Ponce De Leon Boulevard, Suite 1225 Coral Gables, FL 33134-6049 · 305-779-3560

Rene V. Murai · Murai, Wald, Biondo & Moreno · Two Alhambra Plaza, Penthouse 1-B · Coral Gables, FL 33134 · 305-444-0101

Fort Lauderdale

Mark K. Somerstein · Ruden, McClosky, Smith, Schuster & Russell · 200 East Broward Boulevard · P.O. Box 1900 · Fort Lauderdale, FL 33302 · 954-764-6660

Jacksonville

J. Kirby Chritton · Rogers Towers · 1301 Riverplace Boulevard, Suite 1500 · Jacksonville, FL 32207 · 904-398-3911

Ivan A. Colao · Holland & Knight · http://www.hklaw.com · 50 North Laura Street, Suite 3900 · P.O. Box 52687 · Jacksonville, FL 32202-2687 · 904-353-2000

Edward L. Kelly · Rogers Towers · 1301 Riverplace Boulevard, Suite 1500 · Jacksonville, FL 32207 · 904-398-3911

Miami

Victor M. Alvarez · White & Case · http://www.whitecase.com · Wachovia Financial Center, Suite 4900 · 200 South Biscayne Boulevard · Miami, FL 33131-2352 · 305-371-2700

Stuart D. Ames · Stearns Weaver Miller Weissler Alhadeff & Sitterson · Museum Tower, Suite 2200 · 150 West Flagler Street · Miami, FL 33130 · 305-789-3200

Scott L. Baena · 2) · Bilzin Sumberg Baena Price & Axelrod · Wachovia Financial Center, Suite 2500 · 200 South Biscayne Boulevard · Miami, FL 33131 · 305-374-7580

Michael Basile · Stroock & Stroock & Lavan · 200 South Biscayne Boulevard · Miami, FL 33131-5323 · 305-358-9900

Bowman Brown · 2% · Shutts & Bowen · http://www.shutts.com · Miami Center, Suite 1500 · 201 South Biscayne Boulevard · Miami, FL 33131 · 305-358-6300

Allison R. Day · Genovese Joblove & Battista · Bank of America Tower at International Place, 44th Floor 100 Southeast Second Street · Miami, FL 33131 · 305-349-2300

Arthur J. Furia · Gunster, Yoakley & Stewart · One Biscayne Tower, Suite 3400 · Two South Biscayne Boulevard · Miami, FL 33131-1897 · 305-376-6000

Peter W. Homer · HomerBonner · Four Seasons Tower, Suite 1200 · 1441 Brickell Avenue · Miami, FL 33131 · 305-350-5100

Carlos E. Loumiet · Hunton & Williams · Mellon Financial Center, Suite 2500 · 1111 Brickell Avenue · Miami, FL 33131 · 305-810-2500

William G. McCullough · Shutts & Bowen · http://www.shutts.com · Miami Center, Suite 1500 · 201 South Biscayne Boulevard · Miami, FL 33131 · 305-358-6300

James E. Morgan III · Squire Sanders · http://www.ssd.com · 200 South Biscayne Boulevard, Suite 4000 · Miami, FL 33131-2398 · 305-577-7000

José E. Sirven · Holland & Knight · http://www.hklaw.com · 701 Brickell Avenue, Suite 3000 · Miami, FL 33131 · 305-374-8500

José F. Valdivia III · Hogan & Hartson · Mellon Financial Center, Suite 1900 · 1111 Brickell Avenue · Miami, FL 33131 · 305-459-6500

Clemente L. Vázquez-Bello · Gunster, Yoakley & Stewart · One Biscayne Tower, Suite 3400 · Two South Biscayne Boulevard · Miami, FL 33131-1897 · 305-376-6000

Diane Noller Wells · Devine Goodman Pallot & Wells · 777 Brickell Avenue, Suite 850 · Miami, FL 33131 · 305-374-8200

Naples

G. Helen Athan · Grant, Fridkin, Pearson, Athan & Crown · Pelican Bay Corporate Centre, Suite 501 · 5551 Ridgewood Drive · Naples, FL 34108-2719 · 239-514-1000

Orlando

Tucker H. Byrd · Greenberg Traurig · http://www.gtlaw.com · 450 South Orange Avenue, Suite 650 · Orlando, FL 32801 · 407-420-1000

J. Thomas Cardwell · a · Akerman Senterfitt · http://www.akerman.com · CNL Center II at City Commons, Suite 1200 · 420 South Orange Avenue · Orlando, FL 32801-3336 · 407-423-4000

Patrick T. Christiansen · a · Akerman Senterfitt · http://www.akerman.com · CNL Center II at City Commons, Suite 1200 · 420 South Orange Avenue · Orlando, FL 32801-3336 · 407-423-4000

J. Jeffrey Deery · Winderweedle, Haines, Ward & Woodman · Bank of America Center, Suite 1500 · 390 North Orange Avenue · P.O. Box 1391 · Orlando, FL 32801 · 407-423-4246

Joseph E. Foster · Akerman Senterfitt · http://www.akerman.com · CNL Center II at City Commons, Suite 1200 · 420 South Orange Avenue · Orlando, FL 32801-3336 · 407-423-4000

John P. Greeley · Smith Mackinnon · Citrus Center, Suite 800 · 255 South Orange Avenue · P.O. Box 2254 · Orlando, FL 32801 · 407-843-7300

Rod Jones · a · Shutts & Bowen · http://www.shutts.com · 300 South Orange Avenue, Suite 1000 · Orlando, FL 32801 · 407-423-3200

Michael A. Ryan · Lowndes, Drosdick, Doster, Kantor & Reed · 215 North Eola Drive · Orlando, FL 32801 · 407-843-4600

Virginia B. Townes · Akerman Senterfitt · http://www.akerman.com · CNL Center II at City Commons, Suite 1200 · 420 South Orange Avenue · Orlando, FL 32801-3336 · 407-423-4000

Tampa

Marvin E. Barkin · 2) · Trenam, Kemker, Scharf, Barkin, Frye, O'Neill & Mullis · http://www.trenam.com · 101 East Kennedy Boulevard, Suite 2700 · P.O. Box 1102 · Tampa, FL 33601-1102 · 813-223-7474

David S. Felman · a · Hill, Ward & Henderson · http://www.hwhlaw.com · Bank of America Plaza, Suite 3700 · 101 East Kennedy Boulevard · Tampa, FL 33602 · 813-221-3900

Robert B. Glenn, Jr. · a · Glenn, Rasmussen, Fogarty & Hooker · http://www.glennrasmussen.com · 100 South Ashley Drive, Suite 1300 · Tampa, FL 33602 · 813-229-3333

Charles L. Stutts · a · Holland & Knight · http://www.hklaw.com · 100 North Tampa Street, Suite 4100 · P.O. Box 1288 · Tampa, FL 33601-1288 · 813-227-8500

BANKRUPTCY AND CREDITOR-DEBTOR RIGHTS LAW

Boca Raton

Robert C. Furr · Furr and Cohen · One Boca Place, Suite 337-W · 2255 Glades Road · Boca Raton, FL 33431 · 561-395-0500

Clearwater

Michael C. Markham · Johnson, Pope, Bokor, Ruppel & Burns · http://www.jpfirm.com · 911 Chestnut Street · P.O. Box 1368 · Clearwater, FL 33756 · 727-461-1818

Fort Lauderdale

John D. Eaton · Berger Singerman · http://www.bergersingerman.com · 350 East Las Olas Boulevard, Suite 1000 · Fort Lauderdale, FL 33301 · 954-525-9900

Brian K. Gart · Berger Singerman · http://www.bergersingerman.com · 350 East Las Olas Boulevard, Suite 1000 · Fort Lauderdale, FL 33301 · 954-525-9900

Michael I. Goldberg · Akerman Senterfitt · http://www.akerman.com · Las Olas Centre II, Suite 1600 · 350 East Los Olas Boulevard · Fort Lauderdale, FL 33301-2229 · 954-463-2700

Joan M. Levit · Akerman Senterfitt · http://www.akerman.com · Las Olas Centre II, Suite 1600 · 350 East Los Olas Boulevard · Fort Lauderdale, FL 33301-2229 · 954-463-2700

Thomas M. Messana · Messana Weinstein & Stern, P.A. · 401 East Las Olas Boulevard · Fort Lauderdale, FL 33301 · 954-712-7400

Chad P. Pugatch · a · Rice Pugatch Robinson & Schiller · 101 Northeast Third Avenue, Suite 1800 · Fort Lauderdale, FL 33301 · 954-462-8000

Arthur Halsey Rice · Rice Pugatch Robinson & Schiller · 101 Northeast Third Avenue, Suite 1800 · Fort Lauderdale, FL 33301 · 954-462-8000

Reggie David Sanger · 2% · Reggie David Sanger · 208 Southeast Ninth Street · Fort Lauderdale, FL 33316-1020 · 954-463-8547

Patrick S. Scott · Law Offices of Patrick S. Scott · 111 Southeast 12th Street, Suite B · Fort Lauderdale, FL 33316 · 954-523-1615

Arthur J. Spector · Berger Singerman · http://www.bergersingerman.com · 350 East Las Olas Boulevard, Suite 1000 · Fort Lauderdale, FL 33301 · 954-525-9900

Jacksonville

Stephen D. Busey · a · Smith Hulsey & Busey · http://www.smithhulsey.com · 225 Water Street, Suite 1800 · Jacksonville, FL 32202 · 904-359-7700

John B. Macdonald · Akerman Senterfitt · http://www.akerman.com · 50 North Laura Street, Suite 2500 · Jacksonville, FL 32202-3646 · 904-798-3700

David E. Otero · Akerman Senterfitt · http://www.akerman.com · 50 North Laura Street, Suite 2500 · Jacksonville, FL 32202-3646 · 904-798-3700

James H. Post · Smith Hulsey & Busey · http://www.smithhulsey.com · 225 Water Street, Suite 1800 · Jacksonville, FL 32202 · 904-359-7700

Miami

Scott L. Baena · 2) · Bilzin Sumberg Baena Price & Axelrod · Wachovia Financial Center, Suite 2500 · 200 South Biscayne Boulevard · Miami, FL 33131 · 305-374-7580

Paul J. Battista · Genovese Joblove & Battista · Bank of America Tower at International Place, 44th Floor 100 Southeast Second Street · Miami, FL 33131 · 305-349-2300

Howard J. Berlin · a · Kluger, Peretz, Kaplan & Berlin · http://www.kpkb.com · Miami Center, Suite 1700 · 201 South Biscayne Boulevard · Miami, FL 33131 · 305-379-9000

Mark D. Bloom · a · Greenberg Traurig · http://www.gtlaw.com · 1221 Brickell Avenue, 22nd Floor · Miami, FL 33131 · 305-579-0500

Oscar R. Cantu · a · Weil Gotshal & Manges · 1395 Brickell Avenue, Suite 1200 · Miami, FL 33131 · 305-577-3100

Francis L. Carter · a · Akerman Senterfitt · http://www.akerman.com · One Southeast Third Avenue, 25th Floor · Miami, FL 33131-1714 · 305-374-5600

David C. Cimo · Genovese Joblove & Battista · Bank of America Tower at International Place, 44th Floor 100 Southeast Second Street · Miami, FL 33131 · 305-349-2300

Allison R. Day · Genovese Joblove & Battista · Bank of America Tower at International Place, 44th Floor 100 Southeast Second Street · Miami, FL 33131 · 305-349-2300

Drew M. Dillworth · Stearns Weaver Miller Weissler Alhadeff & Sitterson · Museum Tower, Suite 2200 · 150 West Flagler Street · Miami, FL 33130 · 305-789-3200

John H. Genovese · 2) · Genovese Joblove & Battista · Bank of America Tower at International Place, 44th Floor · 100 Southeast Second Street · Miami, FL 33131 · 305-349-2300

Gregory S. Grossman · Astigarraga Davis · 701 Brickell Avenue, 16th Floor · Miami, FL 33131 · 305-372-8282

Jordi Guso · Berger Singerman · http://www.bergersingerman.com · 200 South Biscayne Boulevard, Suite 1000 · Miami, FL 33131 · 305-755-9500

Ross R. Hartog · Markowitz, Davis, Ringel & Trusty · http://www.mdrtlaw.com · Two Datran Center, Suite 1225 · 9130 South Dadeland Boulevard · Miami, FL 33156-7849 · 305-670-5000

John B. Hutton III · Greenberg Traurig · http://www.gtlaw.com · 1221 Brickell Avenue, 22nd Floor · Miami, FL 33131 · 305-579-0500

John W. Kozyak · 2) · Kozyak Tropin & Throckmorton · http://www.kttlaw.com · 2525 Ponce de Leon Boulevard, Ninth Floor · Miami, FL 33134 · 305-372-1800

Thomas E. Lauria · White & Case · http://www.whitecase.com · Wachovia Financial Center, Suite 4900 · 200 South Biscayne Boulevard · Miami, FL 33131-2352 · 305-371-2700

Thomas R. Lehman · Tew Cardenas · http://www.tewlaw.com · Four Seasons Tower, 15th Floor · 1441 Brickell Avenue · Miami, FL 33131-3407 · 305-536-1112

James P. S. Leshaw · Greenberg Traurig · http://www.gtlaw.com · 1221 Brickell Avenue, 22nd Floor · Miami, FL 33131 · 305-579-0500

David M. Levine · a · Tew Cardenas · http://www.tewlaw.com · Four Seasons Tower, 15th Floor · 1441 Brickell Avenue · Miami, FL 33131-3407 · 305-536-1112

Corali Lopez-Castro · Kozyak Tropin & Throckmorton · http://www.kttlaw.com · 2525 Ponce de Leon Boulevard, Ninth Floor · Miami, FL 33134 · 305-372-1800

Jerry M. Markowitz · a · Markowitz, Davis, Ringel & Trusty · http://www.mdrtlaw.com · Two Datran Center, Suite 1225 · 9130 South Dadeland Boulevard · Miami, FL 33156-7849 · 305-670-5000

Harold D. Moorefield, Jr. · a · Stearns Weaver Miller Weissler Alhadeff & Sitterson · Museum Tower, Suite 2200 · 150 West Flagler Street · Miami, FL 33130 · 305-789-3200

Mindy A. Mora · Bilzin Sumberg Baena Price & Axelrod · Wachovia Financial Center, Suite 2500 · 200 South Biscayne Boulevard · Miami, FL 33131 · 305-374-7580

Timothy J. Norris · 2) · Duane Morris · 200 South Biscayne Boulevard, Suite 3400 · Miami, FL 33131-2397 · 305-960-2200

Paul L. Orshan · Duane Morris · 200 South Biscayne Boulevard, Suite 3400 · Miami, FL 33131-2397 · 305-960-2200

Craig V. Rasile · Hunton & Williams · Mellon Financial Center, Suite 2500 · 1111 Brickell Avenue · Miami, FL 33131 · 305-810-2500

Patricia Ann Redmond · a · Stearns Weaver Miller Weissler Alhadeff & Sitterson · Museum Tower, Suite 2200 · 150 West Flagler Street · Miami, FL 33130 · 305-789-3200

David L. Rosendorf · Kozyak Tropin & Throckmorton · http://www.kttlaw.com · 2525 Ponce de Leon Boulevard, Ninth Floor · Miami, FL 33134 · 305-372-1800

Peter D. Russin · Meland Russin & Budwick · 3000 Wachovia Financial Center · 200 South Biscayne Boulevard · Miami, FL 33131 · 305-358-6363

Luis Salazar · Greenberg Traurig · http://www.gtlaw.com · 1221 Brickell Avenue, 22nd Floor · Miami, FL 33131 · 305-579-0500

Robert A. Schatzman · 2) · Adorno & Yoss · 2525 Ponce de Leon Boulevard, Suite 400 · Miami, FL 33134 · 305-460-1000

John C. Shawde · Berger Singerman · http://www.bergersingerman.com · 200 South Biscayne Boulevard, Suite 1000 · Miami, FL 33131 · 305-755-9500

Paul Steven Singerman · a · Berger Singerman · http://www.bergersingerman.com · 200 South Biscayne Boulevard, Suite 1000 · Miami, FL 33131 · 305-755-9500

Frank Terzo · GrayRobinson · 1221 Brickell Avenue, Suite 1650 · Miami, FL 33131 · 305-416-6880

Charles W. Throckmorton · Kozyak Tropin & Throckmorton · http://www.kttlaw.com · 2525 Ponce de Leon Boulevard, Ninth Floor · Miami, FL 33134 · 305-372-1800

Diane Noller Wells · Devine Goodman Pallot & Wells · 777 Brickell Avenue, Suite 850 · Miami, FL 33131 · 305-374-8200

Orlando

Andrew M. Brumby · Shutts & Bowen · http://www.shutts.com · 300 South Orange Avenue, Suite 1000 · Orlando, FL 32801 · 407-423-3200

Jules S. Cohen · 2% · Akerman Senterfitt · http://www.akerman.com · CNL Center II at City Commons, Suite 1200 · 420 South Orange Avenue · Orlando, FL 32801-3336 · 407-423-4000

Denise D. Dell-Powell · Akerman Senterfitt · http://www.akerman.com · CNL Center II at City Commons, Suite 1200 · 420 South Orange Avenue · Orlando, FL 32801-3336 · 407-423-4000

James E. Foster · Akerman Senterfitt · http://www.akerman.com · CNL Center II at City Commons, Suite 1200 · 420 South Orange Avenue · Orlando, FL 32801-3336 · 407-423-4000

Joseph E. Foster · Akerman Senterfitt · http://www.akerman.com · CNL Center II at City Commons, Suite 1200 · 420 South Orange Avenue · Orlando, FL 32801-3336 · 407-423-4000

Elizabeth A. Green · Latham, Shuker, Barker, Eden & Beaudine · 390 North Orange Avenue, Suite 600 · P.O. Box 3353 · Orlando, FL 32801 · 407-481-5800

Kenneth D. Herron, Jr. · Wolff, Hill, McFarlin & Herron · 1851 West Colonial Drive · Orlando, FL 32804 · 407-648-0058

Robert F. Higgins · Lowndes, Drosdick, Doster, Kantor & Reed · 215 North Eola Drive · Orlando, FL 32801 · 407-843-4600

Peter N. Hill · Wolff, Hill, McFarlin & Herron · 1851 West Colonial Drive · Orlando, FL 32804 · 407-648-0058

Lynn James Hinson · Dean, Mead, Egerton, Bloodworth, Capouano & Bozarth · http://www.deanmead.com · 800 North Magnolia Avenue, Suite 1500 · P.O. Box 2346 · Orlando, FL 32802-2346 · 407-841-1200

Roy S. Kobert · Broad and Cassel · 390 North Orange Avenue, Suite 1400 · Orlando, FL 32801-4961 · 407-839-4200

Bradley M. Saxton · Winderweedle, Haines, Ward & Woodman · Bank of America Center, Suite 1500 · 390 North Orange Avenue · P.O. Box 1391 · Orlando, FL 32801 · 407-423-4246

R. Scott Shuker · Latham, Shuker, Barker, Eden & Beaudine · 390 North Orange Avenue, Suite 600 · P.O. Box 3353 · Orlando, FL 32801 · 407-481-5800

Robert L. Young · Carlton Fields · CNL Center at City Commons, Suite 500 · 450 South Orange Avenue Orlando, FL 32801-3336 · 407-849-0300

Samuel J. Zusmann, Jr. · a · Holland & Knight · http://www.hklaw.com · 200 South Orange Avenue, Suite 2600 · P.O. Box 1526 · Orlando, FL 32802 · 407-425-8500

Pensacola

Philip Alan Bates · a · Philip A. Bates · 25 West Cedar Street, Suite 550 · Pensacola, FL 32502 · 850-470-0091

John E. Venn, Jr. · John E. Venn, Jr. · 220 West Garden Street, Suite 603 · Pensacola, FL 32502-5732 · 850-438-0005

St. Petersburg

Michael P. Horan · Trenam, Kemker, Scharf, Barkin, Frye, O'Neill & Mullis · http://www.trenam.com · 200 Central Avenue, Suite 1600 · P.O. Box 3542 · St. Petersburg, FL 33731-3542 · 727-896-7171

Tampa

Rod Anderson · Holland & Knight · http://www.hklaw.com · 100 North Tampa Street, Suite 4100 · P.O. Box 1288 · Tampa, FL 33601-1288 · 813-227-8500

Russell M. Blain · Stichter, Riedel, Blain & Prosser · 110 East Madison Street, Suite 200 · Tampa, FL 33602-4700 · 813-229-0144

Noel R. Boeke · Holland & Knight · http://www.hklaw.com · 100 North Tampa Street, Suite 4100 · P.O. Box 1288 · Tampa, FL 33601-1288 · 813-227-8500

Michael P. Brundage · Hill, Ward & Henderson · http://www.hwhlaw.com · Bank of America Plaza, Suite 3700 · 101 East Kennedy Boulevard · Tampa, FL 33602 · 813-221-3900

Roberta A. Colton · a · Trenam, Kemker, Scharf, Barkin, Frye, O'Neill & Mullis · http://www.trenam.com · 101 East Kennedy Boulevard, Suite 2700 · P.O. Box 1102 · Tampa, FL 33601-1102 · 813-223-7474

John D. Emmanuel · Fowler White Boggs Banker · 501 East Kennedy Boulevard, Suite 1700 · P.O. Box 1438 · Tampa, FL 33602-5239 · 813-228-7411

William Keith Fendrick · a · Foley & Lardner · 100 North Tampa Street, Suite 2700 · P.O. Box 3391 · Tampa, FL 33602 · 813-229-2300

Leonard H. Gilbert · a · Holland & Knight · http://www.hklaw.com · 100 North Tampa Street, Suite 4100 · P.O. Box 1288 · Tampa, FL 33601-1288 · 813-227-8500

Robert B. Glenn, Jr. · a · Glenn, Rasmussen, Fogarty & Hooker · http://www.glennrasmussen.com · 100 South Ashley Drive, Suite 1300 · Tampa, FL 33602 · 813-229-3333

John J. Lamoureux · Carlton Fields · Corporate Center Three at International Plaza, Suite 1000 · 4221 West Boy Scout Boulevard · Tampa, FL 33607 · 813-223-7000

Hywel Leonard · Carlton Fields · Corporate Center Three at International Plaza, Suite 1000 · 4221 West Boy Scout Boulevard · Tampa, FL 33607 · 813-223-7000

Gregory M. McCoskey · Glenn, Rasmussen, Fogarty & Hooker · http://www.glennrasmussen.com · 100 South Ashley Drive, Suite 1300 · Tampa, FL 33602 · 813-229-3333

Richard C. Prosser · a · Stichter, Riedel, Blain & Prosser · 110 East Madison Street, Suite 200 · Tampa, FL 33602-4700 · 813-229-0144

Edwin G. Rice · Glenn, Rasmussen, Fogarty & Hooker · http://www.glennrasmussen.com · 100 South Ashley Drive, Suite 1300 · Tampa, FL 33602 · 813-229-3333

Harley E. Riedel II · 2) · Stichter, Riedel, Blain & Prosser · 110 East Madison Street, Suite 200 · Tampa, FL 33602-4700 · 813-229-0144

Lynn W. Sherman · Hill, Ward & Henderson · http://www.hwhlaw.com · Bank of America Plaza, Suite 3700 · 101 East Kennedy Boulevard · Tampa, FL 33602 · 813-221-3900

Robert A. Soriano · a · Greenberg Traurig · http://www.gtlaw.com · Courthouse Plaza, Suite 100 · 625 East Twiggs Street · Tampa, FL 33602 · 813-318-5700

H. Bradley Staggs · Bush Ross · http://www.bushross.com · 1801 North Highland Avenue · P.O. Box 3913 Tampa, FL 33601 · 813-224-9255

Don M. Stichter · 2) · Stichter, Riedel, Blain & Prosser · 110 East Madison Street, Suite 200 · Tampa, FL 33602-4700 · 813-229-0144

Edward M. Waller, Jr. · a · Fowler White Boggs Banker · 501 East Kennedy Boulevard, Suite 1700 · P.O. Box 1438 · Tampa, FL 33602-5239 · 813-228-7411

Jeffrey W. Warren · a · Bush Ross · http://www.bushross.com · 1801 North Highland Avenue · P.O. Box 3913 · Tampa, FL 33601 · 813-224-9255

Mark J. Wolfson · Foley & Lardner · 100 North Tampa Street, Suite 2700 · P.O. Box 3391 · Tampa, FL 33602 · 813-229-2300

William Knight Zewadski · 2) · Trenam, Kemker, Scharf, Barkin, Frye, O'Neill & Mullis · http://www.trenam.com · 101 East Kennedy Boulevard, Suite 2700 · P.O. Box 1102 · Tampa, FL 33601-1102 · 813-223-7474

West Palm Beach

Robert Gilbert · Carlton Fields · Esperante, Suite 1400 · 222 Lakeview Avenue · West Palm Beach, FL 33401 · 561-659-7070

L. Louis Mrachek · a · Page, Mrachek, Fitzgerald & Rose · Flagler Center, Suite 600 · 505 South Flagler Drive · West Palm Beach, FL 33401 · 561-655-2250

Clearwater

F. Wallace Pope, Jr. · a · Johnson, Pope, Bokor, Ruppel & Burns · http://www.jpfirm.com · 911 Chestnut Street · P.O. Box 1368 · Clearwater, FL 33756 · 727-461-1818

Coral Gables

Dean C. Colson · Colson, Hicks & Eidson · http://www.colsonhickseidson.com · 255 Aragon Avenue, Second Floor · Coral Gables, FL 33134 · 305-476-7400

Joseph M. Matthews · a · Colson, Hicks & Eidson · http://www.colsonhickseidson.com · 255 Aragon Avenue, Second Floor · Coral Gables, FL 33134 · 305-476-7400

Gerald B. Wald · Murai, Wald, Biondo & Moreno · Two Alhambra Plaza, Penthouse 1-B · Coral Gables, FL 33134 · 305-444-0101

Jacksonville

Stephen D. Busey · a · Smith Hulsey & Busey · http://www.smithhulsey.com · 225 Water Street, Suite 1800 · Jacksonville, FL 32202 · 904-359-7700

John A. DeVault III · 2) · Bedell, Dittmar, DeVault, Pillans & Coxe · http://www.bedellfirm.com · The Bedell Building · 101 East Adams Street · Jacksonville, FL 32202 · 904-353-0211

Rutledge R. Liles · a · Liles, Gavin, Costantino & George · http://www.lgcglaw.com · One Enterprise Center, Suite 1500 · 225 Water Street · Jacksonville, FL 32202 · 904-634-1100

Charles P. Pillans III · a · Bedell, Dittmar, DeVault, Pillans & Coxe · http://www.bedellfirm.com · The Bedell Building · 101 East Adams Street · Jacksonville, FL 32202 · 904-353-0211

George E. Schulz, Jr. · a · Holland & Knight · http://www.hklaw.com · 50 North Laura Street, Suite 3900 · P.O. Box 52687 · Jacksonville, FL 32202-2687 · 904-353-2000

David M. Wells · a · Gunster, Yoakley & Stewart · One Enterprise Center, Suite 1750 · 225 Water Street Jacksonville, FL 32202-5185 · 904-354-1980

Miami

John M. Brumbaugh · Richman Greer · http://www.richmangreer.com · Miami Center, 10th Floor · 201 South Biscayne Boulevard · Miami, FL 33131 · 305-373-4000

Richard H. Critchlow · a · Kenny Nachwalter · Miami Center, Suite 1100 · 201 South Biscayne Boulevard · Miami, FL 33131-2305 · 305-373-1000

Joel D. Eaton · 2) · Podhurst Orseck · http://www.podhurst.com · City National Bank Building, Suite 800 25 West Flagler Street · Miami, FL 33130 · 305-358-2800

Arthur J. England, Jr. · a · Greenberg Traurig · http://www.gtlaw.com · 1221 Brickell Avenue, 22nd Floor · Miami, FL 33131 · 305-579-0500

Alan G. Greer · a · Richman Greer · http://www.richmangreer.com · Miami Center, 10th Floor · 201 South Biscayne Boulevard · Miami, FL 33131 · 305-373-4000

Robert C. Josefsberg · 2% · Podhurst Orseck · http://www.podhurst.com · City National Bank Building, Suite 800 · 25 West Flagler Street · Miami, FL 33130 · 305-358-2800

John W. Kozyak · 2) · Kozyak Tropin & Throckmorton · http://www.kttlaw.com · 2525 Ponce de Leon Boulevard, Ninth Floor · Miami, FL 33134 · 305-372-1800

Thomas J. Meeks · Carlton Fields · 4000 International Place · 100 Southeast Second Street · P.O. Box 019101 · Miami, FL 33131-9101 · 305-530-0050

Lewis F. Murphy · Squire Sanders · http://www.ssd.com · 200 South Biscayne Boulevard, Suite 4000 · Miami, FL 33131-2398 · 305-577-7000

Michael Nachwalter · a · Kenny Nachwalter · Miami Center, Suite 1100 · 201 South Biscayne Boulevard Miami, FL 33131-2305 · 305-373-1000

Joel S. Perwin · a · Joel S. Perwin · Alfred I. duPont Building, Suite 1422 · 169 East Flagler Street · Miami, FL 33131 · 305-779-6090

Aaron S. Podhurst · 2% · Podhurst Orseck · http://www.podhurst.com · City National Bank Building, Suite 800 · 25 West Flagler Street · Miami, FL 33130 · 305-358-2800

Benjamine Reid · Carlton Fields · 4000 International Place · 100 Southeast Second Street · P.O. Box 019101 · Miami, FL 33131-9101 · 305-530-0050

Herman J. Russomanno · Russomanno & Borrello · 150 West Flagler Street, Suite 2101 · Miami, FL 33130 · 305-373-2101

Marty L. Steinberg · a · Hunton & Williams · Mellon Financial Center, Suite 2500 · 1111 Brickell Avenue · Miami, FL 33131 · 305-810-2500

Harley S. Tropin · a · Kozyak Tropin & Throckmorton · http://www.kttlaw.com · 2525 Ponce de Leon Boulevard, Ninth Floor · Miami, FL 33134 · 305-372-1800

Miami Beach

Marc Cooper · Marc Cooper Esq · 625 East Dilido Drive · Miami Beach, FL 33139 · 305-525-9185

Orlando

Bruce B. Blackwell · King, Blackwell, Downs & Zehnder · 25 East Pine Street · P.O. Box 1631 · Orlando, FL 32802-1631 · 407-422-2472

Darryl M. Bloodworth · 2) · Dean, Mead, Egerton, Bloodworth, Capouano & Bozarth · http://www.deanmead.com · 800 North Magnolia Avenue, Suite 1500 · P.O. Box 2346 · Orlando, FL 32802-2346 · 407-841-1200

J. Thomas Cardwell · a · Akerman Senterfitt · http://www.akerman.com · CNL Center II at City Commons, Suite 1200 · 420 South Orange Avenue · Orlando, FL 32801-3336 · 407-423-4000

Roy B. Dalton · a · Dalton & Carpenter · 720 Rugby Street, Suite 200 · P.O. Box 540116 · Orlando, FL 32804 · 407-843-8470

David B. King · a · King, Blackwell, Downs & Zehnder · 25 East Pine Street · P.O. Box 1631 · Orlando, FL 32802-1631 · 407-422-2472

Eli H. Subin · a · Holland & Knight · http://www.hklaw.com · 200 South Orange Avenue, Suite 2600 · P.O. Box 1526 · Orlando, FL 32802 · 407-425-8500

William B. Wilson · a · Holland & Knight · http://www.hklaw.com · 200 South Orange Avenue, Suite 2600 · P.O. Box 1526 · Orlando, FL 32802 · 407-425-8500

Sarasota

A. Lamar Matthews, Jr. · a · Matthews, Eastmoore, Hardy, Crauwels & Garcia · 1777 Main Street, Suite 500 · P.O. Box 49377 · Sarasota, FL 34230-6377 · 941-366-8888

Tallahassee

Martha W. Barnett · a · Holland & Knight · http://www.hklaw.com · Bank of America Building, Suite 600 · 315 South Calhoun Street · Tallahassee, FL 32301 · 850-224-7000

W. Dexter Douglass · a · Douglass Law Firm · 211 East Call Street · P.O. Box 1674 · Tallahassee, FL 32302 · 850-224-6191

Stephen H. Grimes · Holland & Knight · http://www.hklaw.com · Bank of America Building, Suite 600 · 315 South Calhoun Street · Tallahassee, FL 32301 · 850-224-7000

Kenneth R. Hart · Ausley & McMullen · Washington Square Building · 227 South Calhoun Street · P.O. Box 391 · Tallahassee, FL 32302 · 850-224-9115

Barry Richard · Greenberg Traurig · http://www.gtlaw.com · 101 East College Avenue · Tallahassee, FL 32301 · 850-222-6891

Tampa

Marvin E. Barkin · 2) · Trenam, Kemker, Scharf, Barkin, Frye, O'Neill & Mullis · http://www.trenam.com · 101 East Kennedy Boulevard, Suite 2700 · P.O. Box 1102 · Tampa, FL 33601-1102 · 813-223-7474

Guy M. Burns · a · Johnson, Pope, Bokor, Ruppel & Burns · http://www.jpfirm.com · 403 East Madison Street, Suite 400 · Tampa, FL 33602 · 813-225-2500

William C. Frye · 2) · Trenam, Kemker, Scharf, Barkin, Frye, O'Neill & Mullis · http://www.trenam.com · 101 East Kennedy Boulevard, Suite 2700 · P.O. Box 1102 · Tampa, FL 33601-1102 · 813-223-7474

Benjamin H. Hill III · a · Hill, Ward & Henderson · http://www.hwhlaw.com · Bank of America Plaza, Suite 3700 · 101 East Kennedy Boulevard · Tampa, FL 33602 · 813-221-3900

Stuart C. Markman · Kynes, Markman & Felman · 100 South Ashley Drive, Suite 1300 · P.O. Box 3396 · Tampa, FL 33601-3396 · 813-229-1118

Gary L. Sasso · Carlton Fields · Corporate Center Three at International Plaza, Suite 1000 · 4221 West Boy Scout Boulevard · Tampa, FL 33607 · 813-223-7000

Joseph H. Varner III · a · KnopikVarnerMoore · One Harbour Place, Suite 800 · 777 South Harbour Island Boulevard · Tampa, FL 33602 · 813-221-3131

West Palm Beach

J. Michael Burman · a · Burman, Critton, Luttier & Coleman · 515 North Flagler Drive, Suite 400 · West Palm Beach, FL 33401 · 561-842-2820

Patricia E. Lowry · Squire Sanders · http://www.ssd.com · Phillips Point West, Suite 1900 · 777 South Flagler Drive · West Palm Beach, FL 33401-6198 · 561-650-7200

Sidney A. Stubbs, Jr. · 2) · Jones, Foster, Johnston & Stubbs · 505 South Flagler Drive, Suite 1100 · P.O. Box 3475 · West Palm Beach, FL 33402-3475 · 561-659-3000

BIOTECHNOLOGY LAW

Miami

Paul W. Radensky · McDermott Will & Emery · Miami Center, 22nd Floor · 201 South Biscayne Boulevard · Miami, FL 33131-4336 · 305-358-3500

Tampa

Christopher Paradies · Fowler White Boggs Banker · 501 East Kennedy Boulevard, Suite 1700 · P.O. Box 1438 · Tampa, FL 33602-5239 · 813-228-7411

COMMERCIAL LITIGATION

Aventura

Michael J. Higer · Higer Lichter & Givner · http://www.hlglawfirm.com · 18305 Biscayne Boulevard, Suite 402 · Aventura, FL 33160 · 305-933-9970

Bartow

John W. Frost II · Frost Van den Boom & Smith, P.A. · 395 South Central Avenue · P.O. Box 2188 · Bartow, FL 33830 · 863-533-0314

Clearwater

Joshua Magidson · Macfarlane Ferguson & McMullen · 625 Court Street · P.O. Box 1669 · Clearwater, FL 33757 · 727-441-8966

F. Wallace Pope, Jr. · a · Johnson, Pope, Bokor, Ruppel & Burns · http://www.jpfirm.com · 911 Chestnut Street · P.O. Box 1368 · Clearwater, FL 33756 · 727-461-1818

Coral Gables

Hugo L. Black, Jr. · 2% · Hugo L. Black, Jr., P.A. · 2655 South Le Jeune Road, Penthouse 1-G · Coral Gables, FL 33134 · 305-358-5700

Dean C. Colson · Colson, Hicks & Eidson · http://www.colsonhickseidson.com · 255 Aragon Avenue, Second Floor · Coral Gables, FL 33134 · 305-476-7400

Roberto Martinez · Colson, Hicks & Eidson · http://www.colsonhickseidson.com · 255 Aragon Avenue, Second Floor · Coral Gables, FL 33134 · 305-476-7400

Joseph M. Matthews · a · Colson, Hicks & Eidson · http://www.colsonhickseidson.com · 255 Aragon Avenue, Second Floor · Coral Gables, FL 33134 · 305-476-7400

Wilfredo A. Rodriguez · Avila Rodriguez Hernandez Mena & Ferri · 2525 Ponce De Leon Boulevard, Suite 1225 · Coral Gables, FL 33134-6049 · 305-779-3560

Susan Johnson Tarbe · Colson, Hicks & Eidson · http://www.colsonhickseidson.com · 255 Aragon Avenue, Second Floor · Coral Gables, FL 33134 · 305-476-7400

Gerald B. Wald · Murai, Wald, Biondo & Moreno · Two Alhambra Plaza, Penthouse 1-B · Coral Gables, FL 33134 · 305-444-0101

Gerald T. Wetherington · a · Gerald T Wetherington · 2655 South Le Jeune Road, Penthouse I-G · Coral Gables, FL 33134 · 305-374-0650

Fort Lauderdale

Mitchell W. Berger · Berger Singerman · http://www.bergersingerman.com · 350 East Las Olas Boulevard, Suite 1000 · Fort Lauderdale, FL 33301 · 954-525-9900

Linda A. Conahan · Gunster, Yoakley & Stewart · Las Olas Centre, Suite 1400 · 450 East Las Olas Boulevard · Fort Lauderdale, FL 33301 · 954-462-2000

Steven E. Eisenberg · Steven E. Eisenberg, P.A. · 3109 Stirling Road, Suite 101 · Fort Lauderdale, FL 33312 · 954-981-6533

Maurice M. Garcia · Greenspoon Marder · Trade Centre South, Suite 700 · 100 West Cypress Creek Road · Fort Lauderdale, FL 33309-2140 · 954-491-1120

Ruben M. Garcia · 2) · Ruben M. Garcia · 1209 Southeast Third Avenue · Fort Lauderdale, FL 33316-1905 · 954-462-4600

Robert S. Hackleman · Gunster, Yoakley & Stewart · Las Olas Centre, Suite 1400 · 450 East Las Olas Boulevard · Fort Lauderdale, FL 33301 · 954-462-2000

John R. Hargrove · Gordon Hargrove & James · http://www.ghj.com · 2400 East Commercial Boulevard, Suite 1100 · Fort Lauderdale, FL 33308 · 954-958-2500

Charles H. Lichtman · Berger Singerman · http://www.bergersingerman.com · 350 East Las Olas Boulevard, Suite 1000 · Fort Lauderdale, FL 33301 · 954-525-9900

Paul R. Regensdorf · Stearns Weaver Miller Weissler Alhadeff & Sitterson · 200 East Las Olas Boulevard, 21st Floor, Penthouse A · Fort Lauderdale, FL 33301 · 954-462-9500

Bruce S. Rogow · 2) · Bruce S. Rogow · Broward Financial Centre, Suite 1930 · 500 East Broward Boulevard · Fort Lauderdale, FL 33394 · 954-767-8909

Stuart H. Singer · Boies, Schiller & Flexner · 401 East Las Olas Boulevard, Suite 1200 · Fort Lauderdale, FL 33301 · 954-356-0011

Fort Myers

Carl Joseph Coleman · Fowler White Boggs Banker · 2235 First Street · Fort Myers, FL 33901 · 239-334-7892

John A. Noland · Henderson, Franklin, Starnes & Holt · http://www.henlaw.com · 1715 Monroe Street · P.O. Box 280 · Fort Myers, FL 33902-0280 · 239-344-1100

J. Jeffrey Rice · Goldstein, Buckley, Cechman, Rice and Purtz · 1515 Broadway Street · Fort Myers, FL 33901 · 239-334-1146

Jacksonville

James A. Bledsoe · Bledsoe, Jacobson, Schmidt & Wright · 1301 Riverplace Boulevard, Suite 1818 · Jacksonville, FL 32207 · 904-398-1818

Stephen D. Busey · a · Smith Hulsey & Busey · http://www.smithhulsey.com · 225 Water Street, Suite 1800 · Jacksonville, FL 32202 · 904-359-7700

John A. DeVault III · 2) · Bedell, Dittmar, DeVault, Pillans & Coxe · http://www.bedellfirm.com · The Bedell Building · 101 East Adams Street · Jacksonville, FL 32202 · 904-353-0211

Lawrence J. Hamilton II · Holland & Knight · http://www.hklaw.com · 50 North Laura Street, Suite 3900 P.O. Box 52687 · Jacksonville, FL 32202-2687 · 904-353-2000

Rutledge R. Liles · a · Liles, Gavin, Costantino & George · http://www.lgcglaw.com · One Enterprise Center, Suite 1500 · 225 Water Street · Jacksonville, FL 32202 · 904-634-1100

John B. Macdonald · Akerman Senterfitt · http://www.akerman.com · 50 North Laura Street, Suite 2500 · Jacksonville, FL 32202-3646 · 904-798-3700

Charles P. Pillans III · a · Bedell, Dittmar, DeVault, Pillans & Coxe · http://www.bedellfirm.com · The Bedell Building · 101 East Adams Street · Jacksonville, FL 32202 · 904-353-0211

James H. Post · Smith Hulsey & Busey · http://www.smithhulsey.com · 225 Water Street, Suite 1800 · Jacksonville, FL 32202 · 904-359-7700

James C. Rinaman, Jr. · 2) · Marks & Gray · 1200 Riverplace Boulevard, Suite 800 · P.O. Box 447 · Jacksonville, FL 32201 · 904-398-0900

E. Lanny Russell · Smith Hulsey & Busey · http://www.smithhulsey.com · 225 Water Street, Suite 1800 · Jacksonville, FL 32202 · 904-359-7700

Terrance E. Schmidt · a · Bledsoe, Jacobson, Schmidt & Wright · 1301 Riverplace Boulevard, Suite 1818 Jacksonville, FL 32207 · 904-398-1818

George E. Schulz, Jr. · a · Holland & Knight · http://www.hklaw.com · 50 North Laura Street, Suite 3900 · P.O. Box 52687 · Jacksonville, FL 32202-2687 · 904-353-2000

Michael G. Tanner · Tanner Bishop · One Independent Drive, Suite 1700 · Jacksonville, FL 32202-5015 904-598-0034

David M. Wells · a · Gunster, Yoakley & Stewart · One Enterprise Center, Suite 1750 · 225 Water Street Jacksonville, FL 32202-5185 · 904-354-1980

Steven A. Werber · 2% · Liles, Gavin, Costantino & George · http://www.lgcglaw.com · One Enterprise Center, Suite 1500 · 225 Water Street · Jacksonville, FL 32202 · 904-634-1100

Lakeland

Robert E. Puterbaugh · Peterson & Myers · http://www.petersonmyers.com · 225 East Lemon Street, Suite 300 · P.O. Box 24628 · Lakeland, FL 33802-4628 · 863-683-6511

Robert L. Trohn · GrayRobinson · One Lake Morton Drive · P.O. Box Three · Lakeland, FL 33802 · 863-284-2200

Leesburg

Robert E. Austin, Jr. · Law Offices of Robert E. Austin, Jr. · 1330 Citizens Boulevard, Suite 401 · P.O. Drawer 490200 · Leesburg, FL 34749 · 352-728-1020

Miami

Rudolph F. Aragon · White & Case · http://www.whitecase.com · Wachovia Financial Center, Suite 4900 200 South Biscayne Boulevard · Miami, FL 33131-2352 · 305-371-2700

Richard Alan Arnold · a · Kenny Nachwalter · Miami Center, Suite 1100 · 201 South Biscayne Boulevard · Miami, FL 33131-2305 · 305-373-1000

Tod Aronovitz · Aronovitz Trial Lawyers · Museum Tower, Suite 2700 · 150 West Flagler Street · Miami, FL 33130-1536 · 305-372-2772

José I. Astigarraga · Astigarraga Davis · 701 Brickell Avenue, 16th Floor · Miami, FL 33131 · 305-372-8282

A. J. Barranco · Barranco & Kircher · 150 West Flagler Street, Suite 1400 · Miami, FL 33130 · 305-371-8575

Hilarie Bass · Greenberg Traurig · http://www.gtlaw.com · 1221 Brickell Avenue, 22nd Floor · Miami, FL 33131 · 305-579-0500

Stanley A. Beiley · Sacher, Zelman, Hartman, Paul, Beiley & Rolnick · 1401 Brickell Avenue, Seventh Floor · Miami, FL 33131 · 305-371-8797

Laura Besvinick · Hogan & Hartson · Mellon Financial Center, Suite 1900 · 1111 Brickell Avenue · Miami, FL 33131 · 305-459-6500

Sanford L. Bohrer · a · Holland & Knight · http://www.hklaw.com · 701 Brickell Avenue, Suite 3000 · Miami, FL 33131 · 305-374-8500

John M. Brumbaugh · Richman Greer · http://www.richmangreer.com · Miami Center, 10th Floor · 201 South Biscayne Boulevard · Miami, FL 33131 · 305-373-4000

Dennis M. Campbell · Clarke Silverglate & Campbell · http://csclawfirm.com · 799 Brickell Plaza, Suite 900 · Miami, FL 33131 · 305-377-0700

Michael B. Chavies · Akerman Senterfitt · http://www.akerman.com · One Southeast Third Avenue, 25th Floor · Miami, FL 33131-1714 · 305-374-5600

Mercer K. Clarke · Clarke Silverglate & Campbell · http://csclawfirm.com · 799 Brickell Plaza, Suite 900 · Miami, FL 33131 · 305-377-0700

Jeffrey Michael Cohen · Carlton Fields · 4000 International Place · 100 Southeast Second Street · P.O. Box 019101 · Miami, FL 33131-9101 · 305-530-0050

Stephen M. Corse · White & Case · http://www.whitecase.com · Wachovia Financial Center, Suite 4900 · 200 South Biscayne Boulevard · Miami, FL 33131-2352 · 305-371-2700

Richard H. Critchlow · a · Kenny Nachwalter · Miami Center, Suite 1100 · 201 South Biscayne Boulevard · Miami, FL 33131-2305 · 305-373-1000

Barry R. Davidson · 2% · Hunton & Williams · Mellon Financial Center, Suite 2500 · 1111 Brickell Avenue · Miami, FL 33131 · 305-810-2500

Alvin B. Davis · a · Squire Sanders · http://www.ssd.com · 200 South Biscayne Boulevard, Suite 4000 · Miami, FL 33131-2398 · 305-577-7000

Edward H. Davis, Jr. · Astigarraga Davis · 701 Brickell Avenue, 16th Floor · Miami, FL 33131 · 305-372-8282

Joseph A. DeMaria · Tew Cardenas · http://www.tewlaw.com · Four Seasons Tower, 15th Floor · 1441 Brickell Avenue · Miami, FL 33131-3407 · 305-536-1112

Victor M. Diaz, Jr. · Podhurst Orseck · http://www.podhurst.com · City National Bank Building, Suite 800 · 25 West Flagler Street · Miami, FL 33130 · 305-358-2800

Alan T. Dimond · Greenberg Traurig · http://www.gtlaw.com · 1221 Brickell Avenue, 22nd Floor · Miami, FL 33131 · 305-579-0500

Richard M. Dunn · a · Cozen O'Connor · Wachovia Financial Center, Suite 4410 · 200 South Biscayne Boulevard · Miami, FL 33131-2303 · 305-704-5940

Joel D. Eaton · 2) · Podhurst Orseck · http://www.podhurst.com · City National Bank Building, Suite 800 25 West Flagler Street · Miami, FL 33130 · 305-358-2800

Arthur J. England, Jr. · a · Greenberg Traurig · http://www.gtlaw.com · 1221 Brickell Avenue, 22nd Floor · Miami, FL 33131 · 305-579-0500

Alan H. Fein · Stearns Weaver Miller Weissler Alhadeff & Sitterson · Museum Tower, Suite 2200 · 150 West Flagler Street · Miami, FL 33130 · 305-789-3200

Jeffrey D. Feldman · Feldman Gale · http://www.feldmangale.com · One Biscayne Tower, 30th Floor · Two South Biscayne Boulevard · Miami, FL 33131 · 305-358-5001

Milton M. Ferrell, Jr. · Ferrell Law · 201 South Biscayne Boulevard, 34th Floor · Miami, FL 33131 · 305-371-8585

Jonathan Goodman · Akerman Senterfitt · http://www.akerman.com · One Southeast Third Avenue, 25th Floor · Miami, FL 33131-1714 · 305-374-5600

David C. Goodwin · 2% · Shook, Hardy & Bacon · 201 South Biscayne Boulevard, Suite 2400 · Miami, FL 33131-4332 · 305-358-5171

Alan G. Greer · a · Richman Greer · http://www.richmangreer.com · Miami Center, 10th Floor · 201 South Biscayne Boulevard · Miami, FL 33131 · 305-373-4000

Alice G. Hector · Akerman Senterfitt · http://www.akerman.com · One Southeast Third Avenue, 25th Floor · Miami, FL 33131-1714 · 305-374-5600

Lawrence R. Heller · Gilbride Heller & Brown · One Biscayne Tower, 15th Floor · Two South Biscayne Boulevard · Miami, FL 33131 · 305-358-3580

John M. Hogan · Holland & Knight · http://www.hklaw.com · 701 Brickell Avenue, Suite 3000 · Miami, FL 33131 · 305-374-8500

Peter W. Homer · HomerBonner · Four Seasons Tower, Suite 1200 · 1441 Brickell Avenue · Miami, FL 33131 · 305-350-5100

Eric D. Isicoff · Isicoff, Ragatz & Koenigsberg · 1200 Brickell Avenue, Suite 1900 · Miami, FL 33131 · 305-373-3232

Michael D. Joblove · Genovese Joblove & Battista · Bank of America Tower at International Place, 44th Floor · 100 Southeast Second Street · Miami, FL 33131 · 305-349-2300

Robert C. Josefsberg · 2% · Podhurst Orseck · http://www.podhurst.com · City National Bank Building, Suite 800 · 25 West Flagler Street · Miami, FL 33130 · 305-358-2800

Lawrence A. Kellogg · Tew Cardenas · http://www.tewlaw.com · Four Seasons Tower, 15th Floor · 1441 Brickell Avenue · Miami, FL 33131-3407 · 305-536-1112

James J. Kenny · a · Kenny Nachwalter · Miami Center, Suite 1100 · 201 South Biscayne Boulevard · Miami, FL 33131-2305 · 305-373-1000

Charles C. Kline · White & Case · http://www.whitecase.com · Wachovia Financial Center, Suite 4900 · 200 South Biscayne Boulevard · Miami, FL 33131-2352 · 305-371-2700

Alan J. Kluger · Kluger, Peretz, Kaplan & Berlin · http://www.kpkb.com · Miami Center, Suite 1700 · 201 South Biscayne Boulevard · Miami, FL 33131 · 305-379-9000

Judith M. Korchin · Holland & Knight · http://www.hklaw.com · 701 Brickell Avenue, Suite 3000 · Miami, FL 33131 · 305-374-8500

John W. Kozyak · 2) · Kozyak Tropin & Throckmorton · http://www.kttlaw.com · 2525 Ponce de Leon Boulevard, Ninth Floor · Miami, FL 33134 · 305-372-1800

Peter M. Kramer · Squire Sanders · http://www.ssd.com · 200 South Biscayne Boulevard, Suite 4000 · Miami, FL 33131-2398 · 305-577-7000

Alan D. Lash · Lash & Goldberg · http://www.lashgoldberg.com · Bank of America Tower, Suite 1200 · 100 Southeast Second Street · Miami, FL 33131-2158 · 305-347-4040

Carol A. Licko · Hogan & Hartson · Mellon Financial Center, Suite 1900 · 1111 Brickell Avenue · Miami, FL 33131 · 305-459-6500

Paul R. Lipton · Greenberg Traurig · http://www.gtlaw.com · 1221 Brickell Avenue, 22nd Floor · Miami, FL 33131 · 305-579-0500

Corali Lopez-Castro · Kozyak Tropin & Throckmorton · http://www.kttlaw.com · 2525 Ponce de Leon Boulevard, Ninth Floor · Miami, FL 33134 · 305-372-1800

Wendy F. Lumish · Carlton Fields · 4000 International Place · 100 Southeast Second Street · P.O. Box 019101 · Miami, FL 33131-9101 · 305-530-0050

Pedro J. Martinez-Fraga · Squire Sanders · http://www.ssd.com · 200 South Biscayne Boulevard, Suite 4000 · Miami, FL 33131-2398 · 305-577-7000

Barry L. Meadow · Law Offices of Barry L. Meadow · 169 East Flagler Street, Suite 1542 · Miami, FL 33131-1213 · 305-358-9880

Thomas J. Meeks · Carlton Fields · 4000 International Place · 100 Southeast Second Street · P.O. Box 019101 · Miami, FL 33131-9101 · 305-530-0050

David Milian · Kozyak Tropin & Throckmortón · http://www.kttlaw.com · 2525 Ponce de Leon Boulevard, Ninth Floor · Miami, FL 33134 · 305-372-1800

Edward Mullins · Astigarraga Davis · 701 Brickell Avenue, 16th Floor · Miami, FL 33131 · 305-372-8282

Lewis F. Murphy · Squire Sanders · http://www.ssd.com · 200 South Biscayne Boulevard, Suite 4000 · Miami, FL 33131-2398 · 305-577-7000

Michael Nachwalter · a · Kenny Nachwalter · Miami Center, Suite 1100 · 201 South Biscayne Boulevard Miami, FL 33131-2305 · 305-373-1000

Paul L. Nettleton · Carlton Fields · 4000 International Place · 100 Southeast Second Street · P.O. Box 019101 · Miami, FL 33131-9101 · 305-530-0050

Tracy A. Nichols · Holland & Knight · http://www.hklaw.com · 701 Brickell Avenue, Suite 3000 · Miami, FL 33131 · 305-374-8500

Michael S. Olin · Michael S Olin P.A. · 169 East Flagler Street, Suite 1224 · Miami, FL 33131 · 305-677-5088

Dennis J. Olle · Carlton Fields · 4000 International Place · 100 Southeast Second Street · P.O. Box 019101 Miami, FL 33131-9101 · 305-530-0050

Eduardo Palmer · Rivero Palmer & Mestre · 2525 Ponce De Leon Boulevard, Suite 1000 · Miami, FL 33134-6046 · 305-445-2500

Joel S. Perwin · a · Joel S. Perwin · Alfred I. duPont Building, Suite 1422 · 169 East Flagler Street · Miami, FL 33131 · 305-779-6090

Scott E. Perwin · Kenny Nachwalter · Miami Center, Suite 1100 · 201 South Biscayne Boulevard · Miami, FL 33131-2305 · 305-373-1000

Aaron S. Podhurst · 2% · Podhurst Orseck · http://www.podhurst.com · City National Bank Building, Suite 800 · 25 West Flagler Street · Miami, FL 33130 · 305-358-2800

David C. Pollack · Stearns Weaver Miller Weissler Alhadeff & Sitterson · Museum Tower, Suite 2200 · 150 West Flagler Street · Miami, FL 33130 · 305-789-3200

Peter Prieto · Holland & Knight · http://www.hklaw.com · 701 Brickell Avenue, Suite 3000 · Miami, FL 33131 · 305-374-8500

Craig V. Rasile · Hunton & Williams · Mellon Financial Center, Suite 2500 · 1111 Brickell Avenue · Miami, FL 33131 · 305-810-2500

Ronald B. Ravikoff · Akerman Senterfitt · http://www.akerman.com · One Southeast Third Avenue, 25th Floor · Miami, FL 33131-1714 · 305-374-5600

Mark F. Raymond · Broad and Cassel · One Biscayne Tower, Suite 2100 · Two South Biscayne Boulevard · Miami, FL 33131 · 305-373-9400

Joseph L. Rebak · Tew Cardenas · http://www.tewlaw.com · Four Seasons Tower, 15th Floor · 1441 Brickell Avenue · Miami, FL 33131-3407 · 305-536-1112

C. Ryan Reetz · Squire Sanders · http://www.ssd.com · 200 South Biscayne Boulevard, Suite 4000 · Miami, FL 33131-2398 · 305-577-7000

Benjamine Reid · Carlton Fields · 4000 International Place · 100 Southeast Second Street · P.O. Box 019101 · Miami, FL 33131-9101 · 305-530-0050

William L. Richey · a · William L. Richey · Miami Center, 34th Floor · 201 South Biscayne Boulevard · Miami, FL 33131-4325 · 305-372-8808

David L. Ross · 2) · Greenberg Traurig · http://www.gtlaw.com · 1221 Brickell Avenue, 22nd Floor · Miami, FL 33131 · 305-579-0500

Lauri Waldman Ross · Ross & Girten, P.A. · Two Datran Center, Suite 1612 · 9130 South Dadeland Boulevard · Miami, FL 33156 · 305-670-8010

Herman J. Russomanno · Russomanno & Borrello · 150 West Flagler Street, Suite 2101 · Miami, FL 33130 · 305-373-2101

Thomas G. Schultz · a · Tew Cardenas · http://www.tewlaw.com · Four Seasons Tower, 15th Floor · 1441 Brickell Avenue · Miami, FL 33131-3407 · 305-536-1112

Spencer H. Silverglate · Clarke Silverglate & Campbell · http://csclawfirm.com · 799 Brickell Plaza, Suite 900 · Miami, FL 33131 · 305-377-0700

Lawrence D. Silverman · Silverman Cosgrove & Sammataro · One Biscayne Tower, Suite 2650 · Two South Biscayne Boulevard · Miami, FL 33131 · 305-377-1666

Marlene K. Silverman · Greenberg Traurig · http://www.gtlaw.com · 1221 Brickell Avenue, 22nd Floor · Miami, FL 33131 · 305-579-0500

Holly R. Skolnick · Greenberg Traurig · http://www.gtlaw.com · 1221 Brickell Avenue, 22nd Floor · Miami, FL 33131 · 305-579-0500

Richard Caldwell Smith · 2) · Shook, Hardy & Bacon · 201 South Biscayne Boulevard, Suite 2400 · Miami, FL 33131-4332 · 305-358-5171

Rodolfo Sorondo, Jr. · Holland & Knight · http://www.hklaw.com · 701 Brickell Avenue, Suite 3000 · Miami, FL 33131 · 305-374-8500

Edward Soto · Weil Gotshal & Manges · 1395 Brickell Avenue, Suite 1200 · Miami, FL 33131 · 305-577-3100

Eugene E. Stearns · Stearns Weaver Miller Weissler Alhadeff & Sitterson · Museum Tower, Suite 2200 · 150 West Flagler Street · Miami, FL 33130 · 305-789-3200

Marty L. Steinberg · a · Hunton & Williams · Mellon Financial Center, Suite 2500 · 1111 Brickell Avenue · Miami, FL 33131 · 305-810-2500

C. Thomas Tew · a · Tew Cardenas · http://www.tewlaw.com · Four Seasons Tower, 15th Floor · 1441 Brickell Avenue · Miami, FL 33131-3407 · 305-536-1112

James D. Thomas · Squire Sanders · http://www.ssd.com · 200 South Biscayne Boulevard, Suite 4000 · Miami, FL 33131-2398 · 305-577-7000

Parker Davidson Thomson · 2) · Hogan & Hartson · Mellon Financial Center, Suite 1900 · 1111 Brickell Avenue · Miami, FL 33131 · 305-459-6500

Harley S. Tropin · a · Kozyak Tropin & Throckmorton · http://www.kttlaw.com · 2525 Ponce de Leon Boulevard, Ninth Floor · Miami, FL 33134 · 305-372-1800

Stanley H. Wakshlag · a · Kenny Nachwalter · Miami Center, Suite 1100 · 201 South Biscayne Boulevard · Miami, FL 33131-2305 · 305-373-1000

Mitchell Widom · Bilzin Sumberg Baena Price & Axelrod · Wachovia Financial Center, Suite 2500 · 200 South Biscayne Boulevard · Miami, FL 33131 · 305-374-7580

James D. Wing · Holland & Knight · http://www.hklaw.com · 701 Brickell Avenue, Suite 3000 · Miami, FL 33131 · 305-374-8500

Jon W. Zeder · Ferrell Law · 201 South Biscayne Boulevard, 34th Floor · Miami, FL 33131 · 305-371-8585

Miami Beach

Marc Cooper · Marc Cooper Esq · 625 East Dilido Drive · Miami Beach, FL 33139 · 305-525-9185

Naples

John T. Blakely · Roetzel & Andress · http://www.ralaw.com · Trianon Centre, Third Floor · 850 Park Shore Drive · Naples, FL 34103 · 239-649-6200

Edward K. Cheffy · Cheffy Passidomo Wilson & Johnson · 821 Fifth Avenue South, Suite 201 · Naples, FL 34102 · 239-261-9300

J. Michael Coleman · Coleman, Hazzard & Taylor · Poinciana Professional Park, Suite 304 · 2640 Golden Gate Parkway · Naples, FL 34105 · 239-298-5200

Lawrence A. Farese · Robins, Kaplan, Miller & Ciresi · 711 Fifth Avenue South, Suite 201 · Naples, FL 34102 · 239-430-7070

Jeffrey D. Fridkin · Grant, Fridkin, Pearson, Athan & Crown · Pelican Bay Corporate Centre, Suite 501 · 5551 Ridgewood Drive · Naples, FL 34108-2719 · 239-514-1000

Robert G. Menzies · Roetzel & Andress · http://www.ralaw.com · Trianon Centre, Third Floor · 850 Park Shore Drive · Naples, FL 34103 · 239-649-6200

Cathy S. Reiman · Roetzel & Andress · http://www.ralaw.com · Trianon Centre, Third Floor · 850 Park Shore Drive · Naples, FL 34103 · 239-649-6200

Christopher T. Vernon · Vernon Healy · 3080 Tamiami Trail East · Naples, FL 34112 · 239-649-5390

North Miami Beach

Andrew S. Berman · Young, Berman, Karpf & Gonzalez · http://www.ybkglaw.com · 17071 West Dixie Highway · North Miami Beach, FL 33160 · 305-945-1851

Orange

Christopher C. Skambis · The Skambis Law Firm · 715 Vassar Street · Orange, FL 32804 · 407-649-0090

Orlando

Michael J. Beaudine · Latham, Shuker, Barker, Eden & Beaudine · 390 North Orange Avenue, Suite 600 P.O. Box 3353 · Orlando, FL 32801 · 407-481-5800

Bruce B. Blackwell · King, Blackwell, Downs & Zehnder · 25 East Pine Street · P.O. Box 1631 · Orlando, FL 32802-1631 · 407-422-2472

Darryl M. Bloodworth · 2) · Dean, Mead, Egerton, Bloodworth, Capouano & Bozarth · http://www.deanmead.com · 800 North Magnolia Avenue, Suite 1500 · P.O. Box 2346 · Orlando, FL 32802-2346 · 407-841-1200

John M. Brennan · GrayRobinson · 301 East Pine Street, Suite 1400 · P.O. Box 3068 · Orlando, FL 32802-3068 · 407-843-8880

Andrew M. Brumby · Shutts & Bowen · http://www.shutts.com · 300 South Orange Avenue, Suite 1000 · Orlando, FL 32801 · 407-423-3200

Tucker H. Byrd · Greenberg Traurig · http://www.gtlaw.com · 450 South Orange Avenue, Suite 650 · Orlando, FL 32801 · 407-420-1000

J. Thomas Cardwell · a · Akerman Senterfitt · http://www.akerman.com · CNL Center II at City Commons, Suite 1200 · 420 South Orange Avenue · Orlando, FL 32801-3336 · 407-423-4000

Roy B. Dalton · a · Dalton & Carpenter · 720 Rugby Street, Suite 200 · P.O. Box 540116 · Orlando, FL 32804 · 407-843-8470

Mayanne Downs · King, Blackwell, Downs & Zehnder · 25 East Pine Street · P.O. Box 1631 · Orlando, FL 32802-1631 · 407-422-2472

Michael Elsberry · Lowndes, Drosdick, Doster, Kantor & Reed · 215 North Eola Drive · Orlando, FL 32801 · 407-843-4600

Joseph E. Foster · Akerman Senterfitt · http://www.akerman.com · CNL Center II at City Commons, Suite 1200 · 420 South Orange Avenue · Orlando, FL 32801-3336 · 407-423-4000

James Grodin · Foley & Lardner · 111 North Orange Avenue, Suite 1800 · P.O. Box 2193 · Orlando, FL 32802-2193 · 407-423-7656

Lynn James Hinson · Dean, Mead, Egerton, Bloodworth, Capouano & Bozarth · http://www.deanmead.com · 800 North Magnolia Avenue, Suite 1500 · P.O. Box 2346 · Orlando, FL 32802-2346 · 407-841-1200

John P. Horan · Foley & Lardner · 111 North Orange Avenue, Suite 1800 · P.O. Box 2193 · Orlando, FL 32802-2193 · 407-423-7656

Michael A. Hornreich · Greenberg Traurig · http://www.gtlaw.com · 450 South Orange Avenue, Suite 650 · Orlando, FL 32801 · 407-420-1000

Scott J. Johnson · Holland & Knight · http://www.hklaw.com · 200 South Orange Avenue, Suite 2600 · P.O. Box 1526 · Orlando, FL 32802 · 407-425-8500

David B. King · a · King, Blackwell, Downs & Zehnder · 25 East Pine Street · P.O. Box 1631 · Orlando, FL 32802-1631 · 407-422-2472

Joseph A. Lane · Lowndes, Drosdick, Doster, Kantor & Reed · 215 North Eola Drive · Orlando, FL 32801 · 407-843-4600

Hal K. Litchford · Litchford & Christopher · Bank of America Center, Suite 2200 · 390 North Orange Avenue · P.O. Box 1549 · Orlando, FL 32802 · 407-422-6600

Timothy J. Manor · Lowndes, Drosdick, Doster, Kantor & Reed · 215 North Eola Drive · Orlando, FL 32801 · 407-843-4600

Michael E. Marder · Greenspoon Marder · Capital Plaza I, Suite 500 · 201 East Pine Street · Orlando, FL 32801 · 407-425-6559

Francis M. McDonald, Jr. · Carlton Fields · CNL Center at City Commons, Suite 500 · 450 South Orange Avenue · Orlando, FL 32801-3336 · 407-849-0300

Brian A. McDowell · Holland & Knight · http://www.hklaw.com · 200 South Orange Avenue, Suite 2600 · P.O. Box 1526 · Orlando, FL 32802 · 407-425-8500

Michael P. McMahon · Akerman Senterfitt · http://www.akerman.com · CNL Center II at City Commons, Suite 1200 · 420 South Orange Avenue · Orlando, FL 32801-3336 · 407-423-4000

Howell W. Melton, Jr. · Holland & Knight · http://www.hklaw.com · 200 South Orange Avenue, Suite 2600 · P.O. Box 1526 · Orlando, FL 32802 · 407-425-8500

David S. Oliver · Baker Hostetler · http://www.bakerlaw.com · Sun Trust Center, Suite 2300 · 200 South Orange Avenue · Orlando, FL 32801-3432 · 407-649-4000

William G. Osborne · William G. Osborne · 538 East Washington Street · Orlando, FL 32801 · 407-422-5385

Lawrence J. Phalin · a · Mateer & Harbert · Two Landmark Center, Suite 600 · 225 East Robinson Street · P.O. Box 2854 · Orlando, FL 32801 · 407-425-9044

T. Todd Pittenger · Lowndes, Drosdick, Doster, Kantor & Reed · 450 South Orange Street, Suite 250 · Orlando, FL 32801-3383 · 407-843-4600

Shawn G. Rader · Lowndes, Drosdick, Doster, Kantor & Reed · 215 North Eola Drive · Orlando, FL 32801 · 407-843-4600

Larry M. Roth · Larry M. Roth · 1615 Edgewater Drive, Suite 180 · P.O. Box 547637 · Orlando, FL 32854 · 407-872-2239

Bradley M. Saxton · Winderweedle, Haines, Ward & Woodman · Bank of America Center, Suite 1500 · 390 North Orange Avenue · P.O. Box 1391 · Orlando, FL 32801 · 407-423-4246

Gary R. Soles · Lowndes, Drosdick, Doster, Kantor & Reed · 450 South Orange Street, Suite 250 · Orlando, FL 32801-3383 · 407-843-4600

I. William Spivey II · Greenberg Traurig · http://www.gtlaw.com · 450 South Orange Avenue, Suite 650 · Orlando, FL 32801 · 407-420-1000

Eli H. Subin · a · Holland & Knight · http://www.hklaw.com · 200 South Orange Avenue, Suite 2600 · P.O. Box 1526 · Orlando, FL 32802 · 407-425-8500

James Michael Talley · Fisher, Rushmer, Werrenrath, Dickson, Talley & Dunlap · 20 North Orange Avenue, Suite 1500 · P.O. Box 712 · Orlando, FL 32802-0712 · 407-843-2111

Albert F. Tellechea · Holland & Knight · http://www.hklaw.com · 200 South Orange Avenue, Suite 2600 · P.O. Box 1526 · Orlando, FL 32802 · 407-425-8500

Virginia B. Townes · Akerman Senterfitt · http://www.akerman.com · CNL Center II at City Commons, Suite 1200 · 420 South Orange Avenue · Orlando, FL 32801-3336 · 407-423-4000

Christopher J. Weiss · Holland & Knight · http://www.hklaw.com · 200 South Orange Avenue, Suite 2600 · P.O. Box 1526 · Orlando, FL 32802 · 407-425-8500

Michael Wilson · Broad and Cassel · 390 North Orange Avenue, Suite 1400 · Orlando, FL 32801-4961 · 407-839-4200

William B. Wilson · a · Holland & Knight · http://www.hklaw.com · 200 South Orange Avenue, Suite 2600 · P.O. Box 1526 · Orlando, FL 32802 · 407-425-8500

Terry C. Young · Lowndes, Drosdick, Doster, Kantor & Reed · 215 North Eola Drive · Orlando, FL 32801 · 407-843-4600

Pensacola

H. Edward Moore, Jr. · a · Moore, Hill & Westmoreland · Sun Trust Tower, Ninth Floor · 220 West Garden Street · Pensacola, FL 32502 · 850-434-3541

Sarasota

Charles Bartlett · Icard, Merrill, Cullis, Timm, Furen & Ginsburg · http://www.icardmerrill.com · 2033 Main Street, Suite 500 & 600 · P.O. Drawer 4195 · Sarasota, FL 34230 · 941-366-8100

A. Lamar Matthews, Jr. · a · Matthews, Eastmoore, Hardy, Crauwels & Garcia · 1777 Main Street, Suite 500 · P.O. Box 49377 · Sarasota, FL 34230-6377 · 941-366-8888

St. Petersburg

Steven C. Dupre · Carlton Fields · 200 Central Avenue, Suite 2300 · St. Petersburg, FL 33701 · 727-821-7000

Michael J. Keane · Keane Reese Vesely & Gerdes · Veritas Courtyard · 770 Second Avenue South · St. Petersburg, FL 33701 · 727-823-5000

Lee H. Rightmyer · Carlton Fields · 200 Central Avenue, Suite 2300 · St. Petersburg, FL 33701 · 727-821-7000

Stephen J. Wein · Battaglia, Ross, Dicus & Wein · 980 Tyrone Boulevard · P.O. Box 41100 · St. Petersburg, FL 33743 · 727-381-2300

Stuart

Roy E. Fitzgerald III · Page, Mrachek, Fitzgerald & Rose · 1000 South Monterey Commons Boulevard, Suite 306 · Stuart, FL 34996 · 772-221-7757

Stephen C. Page · Page, Mrachek, Fitzgerald & Rose · 1000 South East Monterey Commons Boulevard, Suite 306 · Stuart, FL 34996 · 772-221-7757

Martha W. Barnett · a · Holland & Knight · http://www.hklaw.com · Bank of America Building, Suite 600 · 315 South Calhoun Street · Tallahassee, FL 32301 · 850-224-7000

Elizabeth L. Bevington · Holland & Knight · http://www.hklaw.com · Bank of America Building, Suite 600 · 315 South Calhoun Street · Tallahassee, FL 32301 · 850-224-7000

Lorence J. Bielby · Greenberg Traurig · http://www.gtlaw.com · 101 East College Avenue · Tallahassee, FL 32301 · 850-222-6891

Daniel C. Brown · Carlton Fields · Suntrust Building, Suite 500 · 215 South Monroe Street · Tallahassee, FL 32301 · 850-224-1585

Robert N. Clarke, Jr. · Ausley & McMullen · Washington Square Building · 227 South Calhoun Street · P.O. Box 391 · Tallahassee, FL 32302 · 850-224-9115

W. Dexter Douglass · a · Douglass Law Firm · 211 East Call Street · P.O. Box 1674 · Tallahassee, FL 32302 · 850-224-6191

Stephen H. Grimes · Holland & Knight · http://www.hklaw.com · Bank of America Building, Suite 600 · 315 South Calhoun Street · Tallahassee, FL 32301 · 850-224-7000

W. Douglas Hall · Carlton Fields · Suntrust Building, Suite 500 · 215 South Monroe Street · Tallahassee, FL 32301 · 850-224-1585

Kenneth R. Hart · Ausley & McMullen · Washington Square Building · 227 South Calhoun Street · P.O. Box 391 · Tallahassee, FL 32302 · 850-224-9115

Jerome Hoffman · Holland & Knight · http://www.hklaw.com · Bank of America Building, Suite 600 · 315 South Calhoun Street · Tallahassee, FL 32301 · 850-224-7000

Kelly Overstreet Johnson · Broad and Cassel · Sun Trust Bank Building, Suite 400 · 215 South Monroe Street · Tallahassee, FL 32301 · 850-681-6810

James P. Judkins · a · Judkins, Simpson & High · 1102 North Gadsden Street · P.O. Box 10368 · Tallahassee, FL 32302 · 850-222-6040

Carl R. Pennington, Jr. · a · Pennington, Moore, Wilkinson, Bell & Dunbar · http://www.penningtonlaw.com · 215 South Monroe Street, Second Floor · P.O. Box 10095 · Tallahassee, FL 32302-2095 · 850-222-3533

Barry Richard · Greenberg Traurig · http://www.gtlaw.com · 101 East College Avenue · Tallahassee, FL 32301 · 850-222-6891

M. Stephen Turner · Broad and Cassel · Sun Trust Bank Building, Suite 400 · 215 South Monroe Street · Tallahassee, FL 32301 · 850-681-6810

Karen D. Walker · Holland & Knight · http://www.hklaw.com · Bank of America Building, Suite 600 · 315 South Calhoun Street · Tallahassee, FL 32301 · 850-224-7000

Tampa

Timothy A. Andreu · Glenn, Rasmussen, Fogarty & Hooker · http://www.glennrasmussen.com · 100 South Ashley Drive, Suite 1300 · Tampa, FL 33602 · 813-229-3333

David C. Banker · Bush Ross · http://www.bushross.com · 1801 North Highland Avenue · P.O. Box 3913 · Tampa, FL 33601 · 813-224-9255

Marvin E. Barkin · 2) · Trenam, Kemker, Scharf, Barkin, Frye, O'Neill & Mullis · http://www.trenam.com · 101 East Kennedy Boulevard, Suite 2700 · P.O. Box 1102 · Tampa, FL 33601-1102 · 813-223-7474

Stacy D. Blank · Holland & Knight · http://www.hklaw.com · 100 North Tampa Street, Suite 4100 · P.O. Box 1288 · Tampa, FL 33601-1288 · 813-227-8500

Karl J. Brandes · Phelps Dunbar · http://www.phelpsdunbar.com · 100 South Ashley Drive, Suite 1900 · Tampa, FL 33602-5311 · 813-472-7550

Mark A. Brown · Carlton Fields · Corporate Center Three at International Plaza, Suite 1000 · 4221 West Boy Scout Boulevard · Tampa, FL 33607 · 813-223-7000

Robert H. Buesing · Trenam, Kemker, Scharf, Barkin, Frye, O'Neill & Mullis · http://www.trenam.com · 101 East Kennedy Boulevard, Suite 2700 · P.O. Box 1102 · Tampa, FL 33601-1102 · 813-223-7474

Guy M. Burns · a · Johnson, Pope, Bokor, Ruppel & Burns · http://www.jpfirm.com · 403 East Madison Street, Suite 400 · Tampa, FL 33602 · 813-225-2500

C. Philip Campbell, Jr. · Shumaker, Loop & Kendrick · Bank of America Plaza, Suite 2800 · 101 East Kennedy Boulevard · Tampa, FL 33602-5150 · 813-229-7600

Michael R. Carey · Carey, O'Malley, Whitaker & Manson · 712 South Oregon Avenue · Tampa, FL 33606 · 813-250-0577

Michael L. Chapman · Holland & Knight · http://www.hklaw.com · 100 North Tampa Street, Suite 4100 · P.O. Box 1288 · Tampa, FL 33601-1288 · 813-227-8500

Michael B. Colgan · Glenn, Rasmussen, Fogarty & Hooker · http://www.glennrasmussen.com · 100 South Ashley Drive, Suite 1300 · Tampa, FL 33602 · 813-229-3333

G. Donovan Conwell, Jr. · Conwell, Sukhia & Kirkpatrick · 2701 North Rocky Point Drive, Suite 1200 · Tampa, FL 33607 · 813-282-8000

Chris S. Coutroulis · Carlton Fields · Corporate Center Three at International Plaza, Suite 1000 · 4221 West Boy Scout Boulevard · Tampa, FL 33607 · 813-223-7000

W. Donald Cox · Fowler White Boggs Banker · 501 East Kennedy Boulevard, Suite 1700 · P.O. Box 1438 Tampa, FL 33602-5239 · 813-228-7411

Katherine C. Donlon · Fowler White Boggs Banker · 501 East Kennedy Boulevard, Suite 1700 · P.O. Box 1438 · Tampa, FL 33602-5239 · 813-228-7411

William S. Dufoe · Holland & Knight · http://www.hklaw.com · 100 North Tampa Street, Suite 4100 · P.O. Box 1288 · Tampa, FL 33601-1288 · 813-227-8500

Stanley H. Eleff · Trenam, Kemker, Scharf, Barkin, Frye, O'Neill & Mullis · http://www.trenam.com · 101 East Kennedy Boulevard, Suite 2700 · P.O. Box 1102 · Tampa, FL 33601-1102 · 813-223-7474

William C. Frye · 2) · Trenam, Kemker, Scharf, Barkin, Frye, O'Neill & Mullis · http://www.trenam.com · 101 East Kennedy Boulevard, Suite 2700 · P.O. Box 1102 · Tampa, FL 33601-1102 · 813-223-7474

D. Lee Fugate · Zuckerman Spaeder · http://www.zuckerman.com · 101 East Kennedy Boulevard, Suite 1200 · Tampa, FL 33602-5838 · 813-221-1010

Edward W. Gerecke · Carlton Fields · Corporate Center Three at International Plaza, Suite 1000 · 4221 West Boy Scout Boulevard · Tampa, FL 33607 · 813-223-7000

Leonard H. Gilbert · a · Holland & Knight · http://www.hklaw.com · 100 North Tampa Street, Suite 4100 · P.O. Box 1288 · Tampa, FL 33601-1288 · 813-227-8500

Richard A. Gilbert · de la Parte & Gilbert · Bank of America Plaza, Suite 3400 · 101 East Kennedy Boulevard · Tampa, FL 33602-5195 · 813-229-2775

Robert B. Glenn, Jr. · a · Glenn, Rasmussen, Fogarty & Hooker · http://www.glennrasmussen.com · 100 South Ashley Drive, Suite 1300 · Tampa, FL 33602 · 813-229-3333

George L. Guerra · Fowler White Boggs Banker · 501 East Kennedy Boulevard, Suite 1700 · P.O. Box 1438 · Tampa, FL 33602-5239 · 813-228-7411

William C. Guerrant, Jr. · Hill, Ward & Henderson · http://www.hwhlaw.com · Bank of America Plaza, Suite 3700 · 101 East Kennedy Boulevard · Tampa, FL 33602 · 813-221-3900

William F. Hamilton · Holland & Knight · http://www.hklaw.com · 100 North Tampa Street, Suite 4100 · P.O. Box 1288 · Tampa, FL 33601-1288 · 813-227-8500

G. Calvin Hayes · Holland & Knight · http://www.hklaw.com · 100 North Tampa Street, Suite 4100 · P.O. Box 1288 · Tampa, FL 33601-1288 · 813-227-8500

Benjamin H. Hill III · a · Hill, Ward & Henderson · http://www.hwhlaw.com · Bank of America Plaza, Suite 3700 · 101 East Kennedy Boulevard · Tampa, FL 33602 · 813-221-3900

Michael S. Hooker · Glenn, Rasmussen, Fogarty & Hooker · http://www.glennrasmussen.com · 100 South Ashley Drive, Suite 1300 · Tampa, FL 33602 · 813-229-3333

Lawrence P. Ingram · Phelps Dunbar · http://www.phelpsdunbar.com · 100 South Ashley Drive, Suite 1900 · Tampa, FL 33602-5311 · 813-472-7550

Frank R. Jakes · Johnson, Pope, Bokor, Ruppel & Burns · http://www.jpfirm.com · 403 East Madison Street, Suite 400 · Tampa, FL 33602 · 813-225-2500

Leslie E. Joughin III · Akerman Senterfitt · http://www.akerman.com · SunTrust Financial Centre, Suite 1700 · 401 East Jackson Street · Tampa, FL 33602-5803 · 813-223-7333

Gregory W. Kehoe · Greenberg Traurig · http://www.gtlaw.com · Courthouse Plaza, Suite 100 · 625 East Twiggs Street · Tampa, FL 33602 · 813-318-5700

Robert E. V. Kelley, Jr. · Hill, Ward & Henderson · http://www.hwhlaw.com · Bank of America Plaza, Suite 3700 · 101 East Kennedy Boulevard · Tampa, FL 33602 · 813-221-3900

Charles F. Ketchey · Trenam, Kemker, Scharf, Barkin, Frye, O'Neill & Mullis · http://www.trenam.com · 101 East Kennedy Boulevard, Suite 2700 · P.O. Box 1102 · Tampa, FL 33601-1102 · 813-223-7474

Bradford D. Kimbro · Holland & Knight · http://www.hklaw.com · 100 North Tampa Street, Suite 4100 · P.O. Box 1288 · Tampa, FL 33601-1288 · 813-227-8500

Peter B. King · Fowler White Boggs Banker · 501 East Kennedy Boulevard, Suite 1700 · P.O. Box 1438 · Tampa, FL 33602-5239 · 813-228-7411

David T. Knight · Hill, Ward & Henderson · http://www.hwhlaw.com · Bank of America Plaza, Suite 3700 101 East Kennedy Boulevard · Tampa, FL 33602 · 813-221-3900

Christopher S. Knopik · KnopikVarnerMoore · One Harbour Place, Suite 800 · 777 South Harbour Island Boulevard · Tampa, FL 33602 · 813-221-3131

Jonathan Koch · Bush Ross · http://www.bushross.com · 1801 North Highland Avenue · P.O. Box 3913 · Tampa, FL 33601 · 813-224-9255

Thomas G. Long · Barnett, Bolt, Kirkwood, Long & McBride · http://www.barnettbolt.com · 601 Bayshore Boulevard, Suite 700 · P.O. Box 3287 · Tampa, FL 33606 · 813-253-2020

Stuart C. Markman · Kynes, Markman & Felman · 100 South Ashley Drive, Suite 1300 · P.O. Box 3396 · Tampa, FL 33601-3396 · 813-229-1118

Margaret D. Mathews · Akerman Senterfitt · http://www.akerman.com · SunTrust Financial Centre, Suite 1700 · 401 East Jackson Street · Tampa, FL 33602-5803 · 813-223-7333

James B. Murphy, Jr. · Shook, Hardy & Bacon · 100 North Tampa Street, Suite 2900 · Tampa, FL 33602-5810 · 813-202-7100

Kevin J. Napper · Carlton Fields · Corporate Center Three at International Plaza, Suite 1000 · 4221 West Boy Scout Boulevard · Tampa, FL 33607 · 813-223-7000

John E. Phillips · Phelps Dunbar · http://www.phelpsdunbar.com · 100 South Ashley Drive, Suite 1900 · Tampa, FL 33602-5311 · 813-472-7550

Darryl R. Richards · Johnson, Pope, Bokor, Ruppel & Burns · http://www.jpfirm.com · 403 East Madison Street, Suite 400 · Tampa, FL 33602 · 813-225-2500

Thomas J. Roehn · Carlton Fields · Corporate Center Three at International Plaza, Suite 1000 · 4221 West Boy Scout Boulevard · Tampa, FL 33607 · 813-223-7000

Richard G. Salazar · Fowler White Boggs Banker · 501 East Kennedy Boulevard, Suite 1700 · P.O. Box 1438 · Tampa, FL 33602-5239 · 813-228-7411

Gary L. Sasso · Carlton Fields · Corporate Center Three at International Plaza, Suite 1000 · 4221 West Boy Scout Boulevard · Tampa, FL 33607 · 813-223-7000

Edward O. Savitz · Bush Ross · http://www.bushross.com · 1801 North Highland Avenue · P.O. Box 3913 Tampa, FL 33601 · 813-224-9255

William J. Schifino, Jr. · Williams Schifino Mangione & Steady · One Tampa City Center, Suite 3200 · 201 North Franklin Street · Tampa, FL 33602 · 813-221-2626

L. Joseph Shaheen, Jr. · Akerman Senterfitt · http://www.akerman.com · SunTrust Financial Centre, Suite 1700 · 401 East Jackson Street · Tampa, FL 33602-5803 · 813-223-7333

Gregg D. Thomas · a · Thomas & LoCicero · 400 North Ashley Drive, Suite 1100 · Tampa, FL 33602 · 813-984-3060

Wayne Lee Thomas · Wayne Lee Thomas · 707 North Franklin Street, 10th Floor · P.O. Box 1834 · Tampa, FL 33601 · 813-229-3638

Kenneth G. Turkel · Williams Schifino Mangione & Steady · One Tampa City Center, Suite 3200 · 201 North Franklin Street · Tampa, FL 33602 · 813-221-2626

Joseph H. Varner III · a · KnopikVarnerMoore · One Harbour Place, Suite 800 · 777 South Harbour Island Boulevard · Tampa, FL 33602 · 813-221-3131

Charles Wachter · Fowler White Boggs Banker · 501 East Kennedy Boulevard, Suite 1700 · P.O. Box 1438 · Tampa, FL 33602-5239 · 813-228-7411

Dennis P. Waggoner · Hill, Ward & Henderson · http://www.hwhlaw.com · Bank of America Plaza, Suite 3700 · 101 East Kennedy Boulevard · Tampa, FL 33602 · 813-221-3900

Sylvia H. Walbolt · 2) · Carlton Fields · Corporate Center Three at International Plaza, Suite 1000 · 4221 West Boy Scout Boulevard · Tampa, FL 33607 · 813-223-7000

Edward M. Waller, Jr. · a · Fowler White Boggs Banker · 501 East Kennedy Boulevard, Suite 1700 · P.O. Box 1438 · Tampa, FL 33602-5239 · 813-228-7411

Morris Weinberg, Jr. · Zuckerman Spaeder · http://www.zuckerman.com · 101 East Kennedy Boulevard, Suite 1200 · Tampa, FL 33602-5838 · 813-221-1010

David B. Weinstein · Greenberg Traurig · http://www.gtlaw.com · Courthouse Plaza, Suite 100 · 625 East Twiggs Street · Tampa, FL 33602 · 813-318-5700

Burton W. Wiand · Fowler White Boggs Banker · 501 East Kennedy Boulevard, Suite 1700 · P.O. Box 1438 · Tampa, FL 33602-5239 · 813-228-7411

Gwynne A. Young · Carlton Fields · Corporate Center Three at International Plaza, Suite 1000 · 4221 West Boy Scout Boulevard · Tampa, FL 33607 · 813-223-7000

Richard M. Zabak · GrayRobinson · 201 North Franklin Street, Suite 2200 · P.O. Box 3324 · Tampa, FL 33601 · 813-273-5000

West Palm Beach

David P. Ackerman · Ackerman, Link and Sartory · 222 Lakeview Avenue, Suite 1250 · West Palm Beach, FL 33401 · 561-838-4100

James W. Beasley, Jr. · 2% · Beasley, Hauser, Kramer & Leonard · The Flagler Center, Suite 1500 · 505 South Flagler Drive · West Palm Beach, FL 33401 · 561-835-0900

Mark F. Bideau · Greenberg Traurig · http://www.gtlaw.com · 777 South Flagler Drive, Suite 300-E · West Palm Beach, FL 33401 · 561-650-7900

J. Michael Burman · a · Burman, Critton, Luttier & Coleman · 515 North Flagler Drive, Suite 400 · West Palm Beach, FL 33401 · 561-842-2820

Margaret L. Cooper · Jones, Foster, Johnston & Stubbs · 505 South Flagler Drive, Suite 1100 · P.O. Box 3475 · West Palm Beach, FL 33402-3475 · 561-659-3000

Robert D. Critton · Burman, Critton, Luttier & Coleman · 515 North Flagler Drive, Suite 400 · West Palm Beach, FL 33401 · 561-842-2820

G. Joseph Curley · Gunster, Yoakley & Stewart · Phillips Point, Suite 500 East · 777 South Flagler Drive West Palm Beach, FL 33401-6194 · 561-655-1980

H. Michael Easley · Jones, Foster, Johnston & Stubbs · 505 South Flagler Drive, Suite 1100 · P.O. Box 3475 · West Palm Beach, FL 33402-3475 · 561-659-3000

Scott Gardner Hawkins · Jones, Foster, Johnston & Stubbs · 505 South Flagler Drive, Suite 1100 · P.O. Box 3475 · West Palm Beach, FL 33402-3475 · 561-659-3000

Richard C. Hutchison · Holland & Knight · http://www.hklaw.com · 222 Lakeview Avenue, Suite 1000 · West Palm Beach, FL 33401 · 561-833-2000

Joseph Ianno, Jr. · Carlton Fields · Esperante, Suite 1400 · 222 Lakeview Avenue · West Palm Beach, FL 33401 · 561-659-7070

Bradford D. Kaufman · Greenberg Traurig · http://www.gtlaw.com · 777 South Flagler Drive, Suite 300-E · West Palm Beach, FL 33401 · 561-650-7900

Alfred LaSorte, Jr. · Shutts & Bowen · http://www.shutts.com · One Clearlake Centre, Suite 500 · 250 Australian Avenue South · West Palm Beach, FL 33401 · 561-650-8500

Patricia Lebow · Broad and Cassel · One North Clematis Street, Suite 500 · West Palm Beach, FL 33401 561-832-3300

Scott J. Link · Ackerman, Link and Sartory · 222 Lakeview Avenue, Suite 1250 · West Palm Beach, FL 33401 · 561-838-4100

John W. Little III · Brigham Moore · http://www.eminentdomain.com · One Clearlake Centre, Suite 1601 250 South Australian Avenue · West Palm Beach, FL 33401-5016 · 561-832-7862

Patricia E. Lowry · Squire Sanders · http://www.ssd.com · Phillips Point West, Suite 1900 · 777 South Flagler Drive · West Palm Beach, FL 33401-6198 · 561-650-7200

L. Louis Mrachek · a · Page, Mrachek, Fitzgerald & Rose · Flagler Center, Suite 600 · 505 South Flagler Drive · West Palm Beach, FL 33401 · 561-655-2250

Gerald F. Richman · a · Richman Greer · http://www.richmangreer.com · One Clearlake Centre, Suite 1504 · 250 Australian Avenue South · West Palm Beach, FL 33401-5016 · 561-803-3500

Peter A. Sachs · Jones, Foster, Johnston & Stubbs · 505 South Flagler Drive, Suite 1100 · P.O. Box 3475 · West Palm Beach, FL 33402-3475 · 561-659-3000

John Scarola · Searcy Denney Scarola Barnhart & Shipley · http://www.searcylaw.com · 2139 Palm Beach Lakes Boulevard · P.O. Drawer 3626 · West Palm Beach, FL 33402-3626 · 561-686-6300

Robert T. Scott · a · Gunster, Yoakley & Stewart · Phillips Point, Suite 500 East · 777 South Flagler Drive · West Palm Beach, FL 33401-6194 · 561-655-1980

Sidney A. Stubbs, Jr. · 2) · Jones, Foster, Johnston & Stubbs · 505 South Flagler Drive, Suite 1100 · P.O. Box 3475 · West Palm Beach, FL 33402-3475 · 561-659-3000

John G. White III · Richman Greer · http://www.richmangreer.com · One Clearlake Centre, Suite 1504 · 250 Australian Avenue South · West Palm Beach, FL 33401-5016 · 561-803-3500

CONSTRUCTION LAW

Bradenton

Donald D. Clark · Donald D. Clark · 8433 Enterprise Circle, Suite 120 · Bradenton, FL 34202-4200 · 941-487-1980

Coral Gables

Richard G. Daniels · Daniels, Kashtan, Downs, Robertson & Magathan · 3300 Ponce De Leon Boulevard Coral Gables, FL 33134 · 305-448-7988

Joseph W. Downs III · Daniels, Kashtan, Downs, Robertson & Magathan · 3300 Ponce De Leon Boulevard · Coral Gables, FL 33134 · 305-448-7988

Michael F. Kashtan · Daniels, Kashtan, Downs, Robertson & Magathan · 3300 Ponce De Leon Boulevard Coral Gables, FL 33134 · 305-448-7988

Steven M. Siegfried · Siegfried, Rivera, Lerner, De La Torre & Sobel · Suntrust Plaza, Suite 1102 · 201 Alhambra Circle · Coral Gables, FL 33134 · 305-442-3334

Stuart H. Sobel · Siegfried, Rivera, Lerner, De La Torre & Sobel · Suntrust Plaza, Suite 1102 · 201 Alhambra Circle · Coral Gables, FL 33134 · 305-442-3334

Fort Lauderdale

Alan C. Brandt, Jr. · Ferencik Libanoff Brandt Bustamante & Williams · 150 South Pine Island Road, Suite 400 · Fort Lauderdale, FL 33324 · 954-474-8080

Alejandro Espino · Vezina, Lawrence & Piscitelli · 300 Southwest First Avenue, Suite 150 · Fort Lauderdale, FL 33301 · 954-728-1270

Robert E. Ferencik, Jr. · Ferencik Libanoff Brandt Bustamante & Williams · 150 South Pine Island Road, Suite 400 · Fort Lauderdale, FL 33324 · 954-474-8080

Melinda S. Gentile · Peckar & Abramson · http://www.pecklaw.com · 401 East Las Olas Boulevard, Suite 1600 · Fort Lauderdale, FL 33301 · 954-764-5222

Joseph W. Lawrence II · Vezina, Lawrence & Piscitelli · 300 Southwest First Avenue, Suite 150 · Fort Lauderdale, FL 33301 · 954-728-1270

Larry R. Leiby · Leiby Stearns and Roberts · 1000 Sawgrass Corporate Parkway, Suite 552 · Fort Lauderdale, FL 33323 · 954-382-9199

Steven B. Lesser · Becker & Poliakoff · 3111 Stirling Road · Fort Lauderdale, FL 33312 · 954-987-7550

Ira L. Libanoff · Ferencik Libanoff Brandt Bustamante & Williams · 150 South Pine Island Road, Suite 400 · Fort Lauderdale, FL 33324 · 954-474-8080

Michael A. Piscitelli · Vezina, Lawrence & Piscitelli · 300 Southwest First Avenue, Suite 150 · Fort Lauderdale, FL 33301 · 954-728-1270

Stephen B. Rakusin · The Rakusin Law Firm · Wachovia Tower, Suite 444 · One East Broward Boulevard · Fort Lauderdale, FL 33301 · 954-356-0496

Michael E. Stearns · Leiby Stearns and Roberts · 1000 Sawgrass Corporate Parkway, Suite 552 · Fort Lauderdale, FL 33323 · 954-382-9199

Lee A. Weintraub · Becker & Poliakoff · 3111 Stirling Road · Fort Lauderdale, FL 33312 · 954-987-7550

Jacksonville

Adam G. Adams III · Rogers Towers · 1301 Riverplace Boulevard, Suite 1500 · Jacksonville, FL 32207 · 904-398-3911

Henry G. (Chip) Bachara · Bachara Construction Law Group · One Independent Drive, Suite 1800 · Jacksonville, FL 32202 · 904-562-1060

Harold S. Lippes · Lippes & Bryan · 800 West Monroe Street · Jacksonville, FL 32202 · 904-633-8781

Jeffrey C. Regan · Regan, Zebouni & Walker · http://www.rzwlaw.com · 9905 Old St. Augustine Road, Suite 400 · Jacksonville, FL 32257 · 904-356-1300

C. Warren Tripp, Jr. · Bedell, Dittmar, DeVault, Pillans & Coxe · http://www.bedellfirm.com · The Bedell Building · 101 East Adams Street · Jacksonville, FL 32202 · 904-353-0211

David M. Wells · a · Gunster, Yoakley & Stewart · One Enterprise Center, Suite 1750 · 225 Water Street Jacksonville, FL 32202-5185 · 904-354-1980

Edward M. Whelan · Gunster, Yoakley & Stewart · One Enterprise Center, Suite 1750 · 225 Water Street Jacksonville, FL 32202-5185 · 904-354-1980

Lake Mary

James M. McCrae · Law Office of Jim McCrae · 1349 South International Parkway, Suite 2421 · Lake Mary, FL 32746 · 407-936-1570

Maitland

Gregory S. Martin · Moye, O'Brien, O'Rourke, Pickert & Martin · 800 South Orlando Avenue · Maitland, FL 32751 · 407-622-5250

James E. Moye · Moye, O'Brien, O'Rourke, Pickert & Martin · 800 South Orlando Avenue · Maitland, FL 32751 · 407-622-5250

Stephen W. Pickert · Moye, O'Brien, O'Rourke, Pickert & Martin · 800 South Orlando Avenue · Maitland, FL 32751 · 407-622-5250

Miami

Stephen M. Corse · White & Case · http://www.whitecase.com · Wachovia Financial Center, Suite 4900 · 200 South Biscayne Boulevard · Miami, FL 33131-2352 · 305-371-2700

Joseph A. DeMaria · Tew Cardenas · http://www.tewlaw.com · Four Seasons Tower, 15th Floor · 1441 Brickell Avenue · Miami, FL 33131-3407 · 305-536-1112

Bruce C. King · Carlton Fields · 4000 International Place · 100 Southeast Second Street · P.O. Box 019101 Miami, FL 33131-9101 · 305-530-0050

Stephen H. Reisman · Peckar & Abramson · http://www.pecklaw.com · One Southeast Third Avenue, Suite 3100 · Miami, FL 33131 · 305-358-2600

Donald S. Rosenberg · 2% · Peckar & Abramson · http://www.pecklaw.com · One Southeast Third Avenue, Suite 3100 · Miami, FL 33131 · 305-358-2600

Neal Sklar · Peckar & Abramson · http://www.pecklaw.com · One Southeast Third Avenue, Suite 3100 · Miami, FL 33131 · 305-358-2600

Gary M. Stein · Peckar & Abramson · http://www.pecklaw.com · One Southeast Third Avenue, Suite 3100 · Miami, FL 33131 · 305-358-2600

R. Earl Welbaum · Welbaum, Guernsey, Hingston, Greenleaf, Gregory, Black & Rune · 901 Ponce de Leon Boulevard, Penthouse Suite · Miami, FL 33134-3009 · 305-441-8900

Naples

Richard C. Grant · Grant, Fridkin, Pearson, Athan & Crown · Pelican Bay Corporate Centre, Suite 501 · 5551 Ridgewood Drive · Naples, FL 34108-2719 · 239-514-1000

Orlando

Kimberly A. Ashby · Akerman Senterfitt · http://www.akerman.com · CNL Center II at City Commons, Suite 1200 · 420 South Orange Avenue · Orlando, FL 32801-3336 · 407-423-4000

Edmund T. Baxa, Jr. · Foley & Lardner · 111 North Orange Avenue, Suite 1800 · P.O. Box 2193 · Orlando, FL 32802-2193 · 407-423-7656

Brian Bennett · Page, Eichenblatt, Bernbaum & Bennett · 214 East Lucerne Circle · Orlando, FL 32801 407-386-1900

Stephen M. Bull · Bull & Associates · 111 North Orange Avenue, Suite 950 · Orlando, FL 32801 · 407-843-5291

Charles J. Cacciabeve · Carlton Fields · CNL Center at City Commons, Suite 500 · 450 South Orange Avenue · Orlando, FL 32801-3336 · 407-849-0300

Daniel H. Coultoff · Latham, Shuker, Barker, Eden & Beaudine · 390 North Orange Avenue, Suite 600 · P.O. Box 3353 · Orlando, FL 32801 · 407-481-5800

John H. Dannecker · Shutts & Bowen · http://www.shutts.com · 300 South Orange Avenue, Suite 1000 · Orlando, FL 32801 · 407-423-3200

Michael R. Gibbons · Lowndes, Drosdick, Doster, Kantor & Reed · 215 North Eola Drive · Orlando, FL 32801 · 407-843-4600

Michael A. Hornreich · Greenberg Traurig · http://www.gtlaw.com · 450 South Orange Avenue, Suite 650 · Orlando, FL 32801 · 407-420-1000

Gregory J. Johansen · Peckar & Abramson · http://www.pecklaw.com · 301 East Pine Street, Suite 730 · Orlando, FL 32801 · 407-999-2440

Jeffrey D. Keiner · GrayRobinson · 301 East Pine Street, Suite 1400 · P.O. Box 3068 · Orlando, FL 32802-3068 · 407-843-8880

Joseph A. Lane · Lowndes, Drosdick, Doster, Kantor & Reed · 215 North Eola Drive · Orlando, FL 32801 · 407-843-4600

Lawrence J. Phalin · a · Mateer & Harbert · Two Landmark Center, Suite 600 · 225 East Robinson Street · P.O. Box 2854 · Orlando, FL 32801 · 407-425-9044

Lilburn R. Railey III · Railey & Harding · 20 North Eola Drive · Orlando, FL 32801-1937 · 407-648-9119

Paul L. SanGiovanni · Shutts & Bowen · http://www.shutts.com · 300 South Orange Avenue, Suite 1000 · Orlando, FL 32801 · 407-423-3200

Ben W. Subin · Holland & Knight · http://www.hklaw.com · 200 South Orange Avenue, Suite 2600 · P.O. Box 1526 · Orlando, FL 32802 · 407-425-8500

Christopher J. Weiss · Holland & Knight · http://www.hklaw.com · 200 South Orange Avenue, Suite 2600 · P.O. Box 1526 · Orlando, FL 32802 · 407-425-8500

Michael Wilson · Broad and Cassel · 390 North Orange Avenue, Suite 1400 · Orlando, FL 32801-4961 · 407-839-4200

Sarasota

David E. Gurley · Gurley Dramis Lazo · 601 South Osprey Avenue · Sarasota, FL 34236-7526 · 941-365-4501

Thomas F. Icard, Jr. · Icard, Merrill, Cullis, Timm, Furen & Ginsburg · http://www.icardmerrill.com · 2033 Main Street, Suite 500 & 600 · P.O. Drawer 4195 · Sarasota, FL 34230 · 941-366-8100

Conrad J. Lazo · Gurley Dramis Lazo · 601 South Osprey Avenue · Sarasota, FL 34236-7526 · 941-365-4501

St. Petersburg

David Bresler · Fowler White Boggs Banker · 501 First Avenue North, Suite 900 · St. Petersburg, FL 33701 · 727-896-0601

Brian P. Deeb · Deeb & Brainerd · 5999 Central Avenue, Suite 202 · St. Petersburg, FL 33710 · 727-384-5999

V. James Dickson · Ruden, McClosky, Smith, Schuster & Russell · 150 Second Avenue North, Suite 1700 · St. Petersburg, FL 33733 · 727-502-8200

Tallahassee

Robert N. Clarke, Jr. · Ausley & McMullen · Washington Square Building · 227 South Calhoun Street · P.O. Box 391 · Tallahassee, FL 32302 · 850-224-9115

Bradley S. Copenhaver · Vezina, Lawrence & Piscitelli · 413 East Park Avenue · Tallahassee, FL 32301 850-224-6205

Frederick J. Springer · Bryant Miller & Olive · 101 North Monroe Street, Suite 900 · Tallahassee, FL 32301 · 850-222-8611

W. Robert Vezina III · Vezina, Lawrence & Piscitelli · 413 East Park Avenue · Tallahassee, FL 32301 · 850-224-6205

Tampa

Robert H. Buesing · Trenam, Kemker, Scharf, Barkin, Frye, O'Neill & Mullis · http://www.trenam.com · 101 East Kennedy Boulevard, Suite 2700 · P.O. Box 1102 · Tampa, FL 33601-1102 · 813-223-7474

Michael R. Carey · Carey, O'Malley, Whitaker & Manson · 712 South Oregon Avenue · Tampa, FL 33606 · 813-250-0577

Anthony Anderson Benton Dogali · Forizs & Dogali · 4301 Anchor Plaza Parkway, Suite 300 · Tampa, FL 33634 · 813-289-0700

Stanley H. Eleff · Trenam, Kemker, Scharf, Barkin, Frye, O'Neill & Mullis · http://www.trenam.com · 101 East Kennedy Boulevard, Suite 2700 · P.O. Box 1102 · Tampa, FL 33601-1102 · 813-223-7474

Timothy A. Hunt · Hill, Ward & Henderson · http://www.hwhlaw.com · Bank of America Plaza, Suite 3700 · 101 East Kennedy Boulevard · Tampa, FL 33602 · 813-221-3900

Leo Meirose · Meirose & Friscia · 5550 West Executive Drive, Suite 250 · Tampa, FL 33609 · 813-289-8800

George J. Meyer · Carlton Fields · Corporate Center Three at International Plaza, Suite 1000 · 4221 West Boy Scout Boulevard · Tampa, FL 33607 · 813-223-7000

Michael F. Nuechterlein · Carlton Fields · Corporate Center Three at International Plaza, Suite 1000 · 4221 West Boy Scout Boulevard · Tampa, FL 33607 · 813-223-7000

Luis Prats · Carlton Fields · Corporate Center Three at International Plaza, Suite 1000 · 4221 West Boy Scout Boulevard · Tampa, FL 33607 · 813-223-7000

Edward O. Savitz · Bush Ross · http://www.bushross.com · 1801 North Highland Avenue · P.O. Box 3913 Tampa, FL 33601 · 813-224-9255

Dale W. Vash · Fowler White Boggs Banker · 501 East Kennedy Boulevard, Suite 1700 · P.O. Box 1438 · Tampa, FL 33602-5239 · 813-228-7411

John S. Vento · Trenam, Kemker, Scharf, Barkin, Frye, O'Neill & Mullis · http://www.trenam.com · 101 East Kennedy Boulevard, Suite 2700 · P.O. Box 1102 · Tampa, FL 33601-1102 · 813-223-7474

Wm. Cary Wright · Carlton Fields · Corporate Center Three at International Plaza, Suite 1000 · 4221 West Boy Scout Boulevard · Tampa, FL 33607 · 813-223-7000

West Palm Beach

Bruce G. Alexander · Casey Ciklin Lubitz Martens & O'Connell · 515 North Flagler Drive, Suite 1900 · West Palm Beach, FL 33401 · 561-832-5900

Winter Park

Brian P. Kirwin · Kirwin Norris · 338 West Morse Boulevard, Suite 150 · Winter Park, FL 32789 · 407-740-6600

V. Frederic Lyon · Lyon Firm · http://www.lyonfirm.com · 1031 West Morse Boulevard, Suite 170 · Winter Park, FL 32789 · 407-647-8900

Bruce Alan Norris · Kirwin Norris · 338 West Morse Boulevard, Suite 150 · Winter Park, FL 32789 · 407-740-6600

CORPORATE GOVERNANCE AND COMPLIANCE LAW

Miami

Jonathan L. Awner · Akerman Senterfitt · http://www.akerman.com · One Southeast Third Avenue, 25th Floor · Miami, FL 33131-1714 · 305-374-5600

Gregory A. Baldwin · Holland & Knight · http://www.hklaw.com · 701 Brickell Avenue, Suite 3000 · Miami, FL 33131 · 305-374-8500

Rodney H. Bell · Holland & Knight · http://www.hklaw.com · 701 Brickell Avenue, Suite 3000 · Miami, FL 33131 · 305-374-8500

Mitchell Eliot Herr · Holland & Knight · http://www.hklaw.com · 701 Brickell Avenue, Suite 3000 · Miami, FL 33131 · 305-374-8500

John M. Hogan · Holland & Knight · http://www.hklaw.com · 701 Brickell Avenue, Suite 3000 · Miami, FL 33131 · 305-374-8500

Teddy D. Klinghoffer · Akerman Senterfitt · http://www.akerman.com · One Southeast Third Avenue, 25th Floor · Miami, FL 33131-1714 · 305-374-5600

Thomas J. Meeks · Carlton Fields · 4000 International Place · 100 Southeast Second Street · P.O. Box 019101 · Miami, FL 33131-9101 · 305-530-0050

Peter Prieto · Holland & Knight · http://www.hklaw.com · 701 Brickell Avenue, Suite 3000 · Miami, FL 33131 · 305-374-8500

Stephen K. Roddenberry · Akerman Senterfitt · http://www.akerman.com · One Southeast Third Avenue, 25th Floor · Miami, FL 33131-1714 · 305-374-5600

Steven Sonberg · Holland & Knight · http://www.hklaw.com · 701 Brickell Avenue, Suite 3000 · Miami, FL 33131 · 305-374-8500

Tampa

Chester E. Bacheller · a · Holland & Knight · http://www.hklaw.com · 100 North Tampa Street, Suite 4100 · P.O. Box 1288 · Tampa, FL 33601-1288 · 813-227-8500

Nathaniel L. Doliner · Carlton Fields · Corporate Center Three at International Plaza, Suite 1000 · 4221 West Boy Scout Boulevard · Tampa, FL 33607 · 813-223-7000

Robert J. Grammig · a · Holland & Knight · http://www.hklaw.com · 100 North Tampa Street, Suite 4100 · P.O. Box 1288 · Tampa, FL 33601-1288 · 813-227-8500

Richard B. Hadlow · a · Holland & Knight · http://www.hklaw.com · 100 North Tampa Street, Suite 4100 · P.O. Box 1288 · Tampa, FL 33601-1288 · 813-227-8500

R. Alan Higbee · Shutts & Bowen · http://www.shutts.com · 100 South Ashley Drive, Suite 1500 · Tampa, FL 33602 · 813-229-8900

Richard M. Leisner · 2% · Trenam, Kemker, Scharf, Barkin, Frye, O'Neill & Mullis · http://www.trenam.com · 101 East Kennedy Boulevard, Suite 2700 · P.O. Box 1102 · Tampa, FL 33601-1102 · 813-223-7474

Robert C. Rasmussen · 2) · Glenn, Rasmussen, Fogarty & Hooker · http://www.glennrasmussen.com · 100 South Ashley Drive, Suite 1300 · Tampa, FL 33602 · 813-229-3333

Gary I. Teblum · a · Trenam, Kemker, Scharf, Barkin, Frye, O'Neill & Mullis · http://www.trenam.com · 101 East Kennedy Boulevard, Suite 2700 · P.O. Box 1102 · Tampa, FL 33601-1102 · 813-223-7474

Martin A. Traber · Foley & Lardner · 100 North Tampa Street, Suite 2700 · P.O. Box 3391 · Tampa, FL 33602 · 813-229-2300

CORPORATE LAW

Boca Raton

Richard E. Heath · 2% · Hodgson Russ · 1801 North Military Trail, Suite 200 · Boca Raton, FL 33431 · 561-394-0500

Stewart H. Lapayowker · Goldstein Lapayowker · 2700 North Military Trail, Suite 130 · Boca Raton, FL 33431 · 561-989-9955

Bonita Springs

Hugh W. Nevin, Jr. · a · Cohen & Grigsby · 27200 Riverview Center Boulevard, Suite 309 · Bonita Springs, FL 34134-4317 · 239-390-1900

Fort Lauderdale

Donn A. Beloff · Greenberg Traurig · http://www.gtlaw.com · 401 East Las Olas Boulevard, Suite 2000 · Fort Lauderdale, FL 33301 · 954-765-0500

Jacksonville

L. Kinder Cannon III · a · Holland & Knight · http://www.hklaw.com · 50 North Laura Street, Suite 3900 · P.O. Box 52687 · Jacksonville, FL 32202-2687 · 904-353-2000

Gardner F. Davis · Foley & Lardner · One Independent Drive, Suite 1300 · P.O. Box 240 · Jacksonville, FL 32201 · 904-359-2000

Linda Y. Kelso · Foley & Lardner · One Independent Drive, Suite 1300 · P.O. Box 240 · Jacksonville, FL 32201 · 904-359-2000

Kenneth M. Kirschner · 2% · Kirschner & Legler · 300A Wharfside Way · Jacksonville, FL 32207 · 904-346-3200

Mitchell W. Legler · 2% · Kirschner & Legler · 300A Wharfside Way · Jacksonville, FL 32207 · 904-346-3200

James L. Main · Holland & Knight · http://www.hklaw.com · 50 North Laura Street, Suite 3900 · P.O. Box 52687 · Jacksonville, FL 32202-2687 · 904-353-2000

Halcyon E. Skinner · McGuireWoods · http://www.mcguirewoods.com · Bank of America Tower, Suite 3300 · 50 North Laura Street · Jacksonville, FL 32202-3661 · 904-798-3200

Miami

Cesar L. Alvarez · a · Greenberg Traurig · http://www.gtlaw.com · 1221 Brickell Avenue, 22nd Floor · Miami, FL 33131 · 305-579-0500

Emilio J. Alvarez-Farré · White & Case · http://www.whitecase.com · Wachovia Financial Center, Suite 4900 · 200 South Biscayne Boulevard · Miami, FL 33131-2352 · 305-371-2700

Stuart D. Ames · Stearns Weaver Miller Weissler Alhadeff & Sitterson · Museum Tower, Suite 2200 · 150 West Flagler Street · Miami, FL 33130 · 305-789-3200

William C. Arnhols · Akerman Senterfitt · http://www.akerman.com · One Southeast Third Avenue, 25th Floor · Miami, FL 33131-1714 · 305-374-5600

Daniel H. Aronson · Bilzin Sumberg Baena Price & Axelrod · Wachovia Financial Center, Suite 2500 · 200 South Biscayne Boulevard · Miami, FL 33131 · 305-374-7580

Jonathan L. Awner · Akerman Senterfitt · http://www.akerman.com · One Southeast Third Avenue, 25th Floor · Miami, FL 33131-1714 · 305-374-5600

Alan D. Axelrod · Bilzin Sumberg Baena Price & Axelrod · Wachovia Financial Center, Suite 2500 · 200 South Biscayne Boulevard · Miami, FL 33131 · 305-374-7580

Rodney H. Bell · Holland & Knight · http://www.hklaw.com · 701 Brickell Avenue, Suite 3000 · Miami, FL 33131 · 305-374-8500

Richard N. Bernstein · Greenberg Traurig · http://www.gtlaw.com · 1221 Brickell Avenue, 22nd Floor · Miami, FL 33131 · 305-579-0500

Bowman Brown · 2% · Shutts & Bowen · http://www.shutts.com · Miami Center, Suite 1500 · 201 South Biscayne Boulevard · Miami, FL 33131 · 305-358-6300

Barry G. Craig · Squire Sanders · http://www.ssd.com · 200 South Biscayne Boulevard, Suite 4000 · Miami, FL 33131-2398 · 305-577-7000

Luis A. de Armas · Shutts & Bowen · http://www.shutts.com · Miami Center, Suite 1500 · 201 South Biscayne Boulevard · Miami, FL 33131 · 305-358-6300

Gary M. Epstein · a · Greenberg Traurig · http://www.gtlaw.com · 1221 Brickell Avenue, 22nd Floor · Miami, FL 33131 · 305-579-0500

Carl A. Fornaris · Greenberg Traurig · http://www.gtlaw.com · 1221 Brickell Avenue, 22nd Floor · Miami, FL 33131 · 305-579-0500

Jorge L. Hernandez-Toraño · Holland & Knight · http://www.hklaw.com · 701 Brickell Avenue, Suite 3000 · Miami, FL 33131 · 305-374-8500

Larry J. Hoffman · 2) · Greenberg Traurig · http://www.gtlaw.com · 1221 Brickell Avenue, 22nd Floor · Miami, FL 33131 · 305-579-0500

Alison W. Miller · Stearns Weaver Miller Weissler Alhadeff & Sitterson · Museum Tower, Suite 2200 · 150 West Flagler Street · Miami, FL 33130 · 305-789-3200

James E. Morgan III · Squire Sanders · http://www.ssd.com · 200 South Biscayne Boulevard, Suite 4000 · Miami, FL 33131-2398 · 305-577-7000

Marshall Pasternack · Bilzin Sumberg Baena Price & Axelrod · Wachovia Financial Center, Suite 2500 · 200 South Biscayne Boulevard · Miami, FL 33131 · 305-374-7580

Stephen K. Roddenberry · Akerman Senterfitt · http://www.akerman.com · One Southeast Third Avenue, 25th Floor · Miami, FL 33131-1714 · 305-374-5600

Ira N. Rosner · Greenberg Traurig · http://www.gtlaw.com · 1221 Brickell Avenue, 22nd Floor · Miami, FL 33131 · 305-579-0500

Philip B. Schwartz · Akerman Senterfitt · http://www.akerman.com · One Southeast Third Avenue, 25th Floor · Miami, FL 33131-1714 · 305-374-5600

José E. Sirven · Holland & Knight · http://www.hklaw.com · 701 Brickell Avenue, Suite 3000 · Miami, FL 33131 · 305-374-8500

Steven Sonberg · Holland & Knight · http://www.hklaw.com · 701 Brickell Avenue, Suite 3000 · Miami, FL 33131 · 305-374-8500

Naples

Mary Beth M. Clary · Porter, Wright, Morris & Arthur · http://www.porterwright.com · 5801 Pelican Bay Boulevard, Suite 300 · Naples, FL 34108-2709 · 239-593-2900

F. Joseph McMackin III · Bond, Schoeneck & King · Northern Trust Building, Suite 250 · 4001 Tamiami Trail North · Naples, FL 34103-3555 · 239-659-3800

John M. Passidomo · Cheffy Passidomo Wilson & Johnson · 821 Fifth Avenue South, Suite 201 · Naples, FL 34102 · 239-261-9300

Orlando

J. Gordon Arkin · Foley & Lardner · 111 North Orange Avenue, Suite 1800 · P.O. Box 2193 · Orlando, FL 32802-2193 · 407-423-7656

Louis T. M. Conti · a · Holland & Knight · http://www.hklaw.com · 200 South Orange Avenue, Suite 2600 · P.O. Box 1526 · Orlando, FL 32802 · 407-425-8500

Richard D. Davidson · Lowndes, Drosdick, Doster, Kantor & Reed · 450 South Orange Street, Suite 250 Orlando, FL 32801-3383 · 407-843-4600

Michael Elsberry · Lowndes, Drosdick, Doster, Kantor & Reed · 215 North Eola Drive · Orlando, FL 32801 · 407-843-4600

Randolph H. Fields · Greenberg Traurig · http://www.gtlaw.com · 450 South Orange Avenue, Suite 650 · Orlando, FL 32801 · 407-420-1000

John P. Greeley · Smith Mackinnon · Citrus Center, Suite 800 · 255 South Orange Avenue · P.O. Box 2254 · Orlando, FL 32801 · 407-843-7300

Robert F. Higgins · Lowndes, Drosdick, Doster, Kantor & Reed · 215 North Eola Drive · Orlando, FL 32801 · 407-843-4600

James J. Hoctor · Lowndes, Drosdick, Doster, Kantor & Reed · 215 North Eola Drive · Orlando, FL 32801 · 407-843-4600

Scott R. MacLeod · Holland & Knight · http://www.hklaw.com · 200 South Orange Avenue, Suite 2600 · P.O. Box 1526 · Orlando, FL 32802 · 407-425-8500

Timothy J. Manor · Lowndes, Drosdick, Doster, Kantor & Reed · 215 North Eola Drive · Orlando, FL 32801 · 407-843-4600

Byrd F. Marshall, Jr. · GrayRobinson · 301 East Pine Street, Suite 1400 · P.O. Box 3068 · Orlando, FL 32802-3068 · 407-843-8880

Thomas M. McAleavey · Holland & Knight · http://www.hklaw.com · 200 South Orange Avenue, Suite 2600 · P.O. Box 1526 · Orlando, FL 32802 · 407-425-8500

Robert W. Mead, Jr. · a · Dean, Mead, Egerton, Bloodworth, Capouano & Bozarth · http://www.deanmead.com · 800 North Magnolia Avenue, Suite 1500 · P.O. Box 2346 · Orlando, FL 32802-2346 · 407-841-1200

Peter E. Reinert · Lowndes, Drosdick, Doster, Kantor & Reed · 215 North Eola Drive · Orlando, FL 32801 · 407-843-4600

Richard M. Robinson · a · GrayRobinson · 301 East Pine Street, Suite 1400 · P.O. Box 3068 · Orlando, FL 32802-3068 · 407-843-8880

John A. Sanders · Foley & Lardner · 111 North Orange Avenue, Suite 1800 · P.O. Box 2193 · Orlando, FL 32802-2193 · 407-423-7656

David L. Schick · GrayRobinson · 301 East Pine Street, Suite 1400 · P.O. Box 3068 · Orlando, FL 32802-3068 · 407-843-8880

Leighton D. Yates, Jr. · a · Holland & Knight · http://www.hklaw.com · 200 South Orange Avenue, Suite 2600 · P.O. Box 1526 · Orlando, FL 32802 · 407-425-8500

St. Petersburg

Joel D. Bronstein · a · Bronstein, Carlson, Gleim & Smith · 150 Second Avenue North, Suite 1100 · St. Petersburg, FL 33701 · 727-898-6688

Tallahassee

James M. Ervin, Jr. · a · Holland & Knight · http://www.hklaw.com · Bank of America Building, Suite 600 · 315 South Calhoun Street · Tallahassee, FL 32301 · 850-224-7000

Mark E. Holcomb · a · Madsen, Goldman & Holcomb · 1705 Metropolitan Boulevard, Suite 101 · Tallahassee, FL 32308-3765 · 850-523-0400

Tampa

Robert E. Aylward · Robert E. Aylward · 600 South Magnolia Avenue, Suite 125 · Tampa, FL 33606-2751 · 813-259-9984

Chester E. Bacheller · a · Holland & Knight · http://www.hklaw.com · 100 North Tampa Street, Suite 4100 · P.O. Box 1288 · Tampa, FL 33601-1288 · 813-227-8500

Anderson L. Baldy III · Holland & Knight · http://www.hklaw.com · 100 North Tampa Street, Suite 4100 P.O. Box 1288 · Tampa, FL 33601-1288 · 813-227-8500

Nelson T. Castellano · Trenam, Kemker, Scharf, Barkin, Frye, O'Neill & Mullis · http://www.trenam.com 101 East Kennedy Boulevard, Suite 2700 · P.O. Box 1102 · Tampa, FL 33601-1102 · 813-223-7474

Mark A. Danzi · Hill, Ward & Henderson · http://www.hwhlaw.com · Bank of America Plaza, Suite 3700 · 101 East Kennedy Boulevard · Tampa, FL 33602 · 813-221-3900

Nathaniel L. Doliner · Carlton Fields · Corporate Center Three at International Plaza, Suite 1000 · 4221 West Boy Scout Boulevard · Tampa, FL 33607 · 813-223-7000

David M. Doney · Fowler White Boggs Banker · 501 East Kennedy Boulevard, Suite 1700 · P.O. Box 1438 Tampa, FL 33602-5239 · 813-228-7411

David S. Felman · a · Hill, Ward & Henderson · http://www.hwhlaw.com · Bank of America Plaza, Suite 3700 · 101 East Kennedy Boulevard · Tampa, FL 33602 · 813-221-3900

John N. Giordano · Bush Ross · http://www.bushross.com · 1801 North Highland Avenue · P.O. Box 3913 Tampa, FL 33601 · 813-224-9255

Robert J. Grammig · a · Holland & Knight · http://www.hklaw.com · 100 North Tampa Street, Suite 4100 · P.O. Box 1288 · Tampa, FL 33601-1288 · 813-227-8500

Richard B. Hadlow · a · Holland & Knight · http://www.hklaw.com · 100 North Tampa Street, Suite 4100 · P.O. Box 1288 · Tampa, FL 33601-1288 · 813-227-8500

Richard M. Leisner · 2% · Trenam, Kemker, Scharf, Barkin, Frye, O'Neill & Mullis · http://www.trenam.com · 101 East Kennedy Boulevard, Suite 2700 · P.O. Box 1102 · Tampa, FL 33601-1102 · 813-223-7474

Harold W. Mullis, Jr. · a · Trenam, Kemker, Scharf, Barkin, Frye, O'Neill & Mullis · http://www.trenam.com · 101 East Kennedy Boulevard, Suite 2700 · P.O. Box 1102 · Tampa, FL 33601-1102 · 813-223-7474

Olga Pina · Fowler White Boggs Banker · 501 East Kennedy Boulevard, Suite 1700 · P.O. Box 1438 · Tampa, FL 33602-5239 · 813-228-7411

Robert C. Rasmussen · 2) · Glenn, Rasmussen, Fogarty & Hooker · http://www.glennrasmussen.com · 100 South Ashley Drive, Suite 1300 · Tampa, FL 33602 · 813-229-3333

R. James Robbins, Jr. · Hill, Ward & Henderson · http://www.hwhlaw.com · Bank of America Plaza, Suite 3700 · 101 East Kennedy Boulevard · Tampa, FL 33602 · 813-221-3900

David C. Shobe · Fowler White Boggs Banker · 501 East Kennedy Boulevard, Suite 1700 · P.O. Box 1438 Tampa, FL 33602-5239 · 813-228-7411

Darrell C. Smith · Shumaker, Loop & Kendrick · Bank of America Plaza, Suite 2800 · 101 East Kennedy Boulevard · Tampa, FL 33602-5150 · 813-229-7600

Gary I. Teblum · a · Trenam, Kemker, Scharf, Barkin, Frye, O'Neill & Mullis · http://www.trenam.com · 101 East Kennedy Boulevard, Suite 2700 · P.O. Box 1102 · Tampa, FL 33601-1102 · 813-223-7474

John I. Van Voris · a · GrayRobinson · 201 North Franklin Street, Suite 2200 · P.O. Box 3324 · Tampa, FL 33601 · 813-273-5000

Gregory C. Yadley · Shumaker, Loop & Kendrick · Bank of America Plaza, Suite 2800 · 101 East Kennedy Boulevard · Tampa, FL 33602-5150 · 813-229-7600

West Palm Beach

Thomas R. McGuigan · 2) · Squire Sanders · http://www.ssd.com · Phillips Point West, Suite 1900 · 777 South Flagler Drive · West Palm Beach, FL 33401-6198 · 561-650-7200

Michael V. Mitrione · a · Gunster, Yoakley & Stewart · Phillips Point, Suite 500 East · 777 South Flagler Drive · West Palm Beach, FL 33401-6194 · 561-655-1980

David L. Perry · Holland & Knight · http://www.hklaw.com · 222 Lakeview Avenue, Suite 1000 · West Palm Beach, FL 33401 · 561-833-2000

DERIVATIVES LAW

Miami

Juan Pablo Cappello · Greenberg Traurig · http://www.gtlaw.com · 1221 Brickell Avenue, 22nd Floor · Miami, FL 33131 · 305-579-0500

Amy G. Dulin · Hughes Hubbard & Reed · http://www.hugheshubbard.com · 201 South Biscayne Boulevard, Suite 2500 · Miami, FL 33131-4332 · 305-358-1666

Timothy J. McCarthy · Hughes Hubbard & Reed · http://www.hugheshubbard.com · 201 South Biscayne Boulevard, Suite 2500 · Miami, FL 33131-4332 · 305-358-1666

Jeffrey S. Tenen · Greenberg Traurig · http://www.gtlaw.com · 1221 Brickell Avenue, 22nd Floor · Miami, FL 33131 · 305-579-0500

DUI/DWI DEFENSE

Miami

Robert Scott Reiff · Law Offices of Robert S. Reiff · 2400 South Dixie Highway, Suite 200 · Miami, FL 33133 · 305-854-5511

EDUCATION LAW

Daytona Beach

Theodore R. Doran · Doran, Wolfe, Ansay & Kundid · 444 Seabreeze Boulevard, Suite 800 · Daytona Beach, FL 32118 · 386-253-1111

Naples

M. Jean Rawson · M. Jean Rawson · 400 Fifth Avenue South · Naples, FL 34102 · 239-263-8206

Orlando

Usher L. Brown · Brown, Garganese, Weiss & D' Agresta · http://www.orlandolaw.net · 111 NorthOrange Avenue, Suite 2000 · P.O. Box 2873 · Orlando, FL 32802-2873 · 407-425-9566

Port Charlotte

Michael R. McKinley · McKinley, Ittersagen, Gunderson & Berntsson · 18401 Murdock Circle, Suite C · Port Charlotte, FL 33948 · 941-627-1000

Tallahassee

Jennifer S. Blohm · Meyer and Brooks · 2544 Blairstone Pines Drive · P.O. Box 1547 · Tallahassee, FL 32302 · 850-878-5212

Thomas W. Brooks · Meyer and Brooks · 2544 Blairstone Pines Drive · P.O. Box 1547 · Tallahassee, FL 32302 · 850-878-5212

Ronald G. Meyer · Meyer and Brooks · 2544 Blairstone Pines Drive · P.O. Box 1547 · Tallahassee, FL 32302 · 850-878-5212

ELDER LAW

Fort Lauderdale

Terry Abrams Berger · Abrams Berger · 2699 Stirling Road, Suite A-301 · Fort Lauderdale, FL 33312 · 305-949-2424

Miami

Candis Trusty · Markowitz, Davis, Ringel & Trusty · http://www.mdrtlaw.com · Two Datran Center, Suite 1225 · 9130 South Dadeland Boulevard · Miami, FL 33156-7849 · 305-670-5000

Orlando

Norma Stanley · Lowndes, Drosdick, Doster, Kantor & Reed · 215 North Eola Drive · Orlando, FL 32801 · 407-843-4600

EMINENT DOMAIN AND CONDEMNATION LAW

Clearwater

James A. Helinger, Jr. · James A. Helinger · 814 Chestnut Street · Clearwater, FL 33756-5642 · 727-443-5373

Fort Lauderdale

Charles R. Forman · Forman Hanratty & Montgomery · 1323 Southeast Third Avenue · Fort Lauderdale, FL 33316 · 954-522-9441

Jacksonville

Andrew Prince Brigham · Brigham Moore · http://www.eminentdomain.com · 2963 Dupont Avenue, Suite Three · Jacksonville, FL 32217-2740 · 904-730-9001

Miami

Ron A. Adams · Brigham Moore · http://www.eminentdomain.com · 2525 Ponce de Leon Boulevard, Suite 625 · Miami, FL 33134-6051 · 305-858-2400

Amy Brigham Boulris · Brigham Moore · http://www.eminentdomain.com · 2525 Ponce de Leon Boulevard, Suite 625 · Miami, FL 33134-6051 · 305-858-2400

Toby Prince Brigham · Brigham Moore · http://www.eminentdomain.com · 2525 Ponce de Leon Boulevard, Suite 625 · Miami, FL 33134-6051 · 305-858-2400

Robert C. Byrne · Brigham Moore · http://www.eminentdomain.com · 2525 Ponce de Leon Boulevard, Suite 625 · Miami, FL 33134-6051 · 305-858-2400

Laura N. Camp · Brigham Moore · http://www.eminentdomain.com · 2525 Ponce de Leon Boulevard, Suite 625 · Miami, FL 33134-6051 · 305-858-2400

Bradley S. Gould · Akerman Senterfitt · http://www.akerman.com · One Southeast Third Avenue, 25th Floor · Miami, FL 33131-1714 · 305-374-5600

Juan M. Muñiz · Brigham Moore · http://www.eminentdomain.com · 2525 Ponce de Leon Boulevard, Suite 625 · Miami, FL 33134-6051 · 305-858-2400

Brian P. Patchen · The Law Offices of Brian P. Patchen · http://www.brianpatchen.com · 1000 Brickell Avenue, Suite 1112 · Miami, FL 33131-3014 · 305-372-1112

Andrew H. Schuster · Brigham Moore · http://www.eminentdomain.com · 2525 Ponce de Leon Boulevard, Suite 625 · Miami, FL 33134-6051 · 305-858-2400

Orlando

Robert Alfert, Jr. · Broad and Cassel · 390 North Orange Avenue, Suite 1400 · Orlando, FL 32801-4961 · 407-839-4200

C. Ken Bishop · Broad and Cassel · 390 North Orange Avenue, Suite 1400 · Orlando, FL 32801-4961 · 407-839-4200

Kurt H. Garber · Wilson, Garber & Small · 437 North Magnolia Avenue · Orlando, FL 32801-1524 · 407-843-4321

Kent Lee Hipp · GrayRobinson · 301 East Pine Street, Suite 1400 · P.O. Box 3068 · Orlando, FL 32802-3068 · 407-843-8880

Tracy A. Marshall · GrayRobinson · 301 East Pine Street, Suite 1400 · P.O. Box 3068 · Orlando, FL 32802-3068 · 407-843-8880

Jay W. Small · Wilson, Garber & Small · 437 North Magnolia Avenue · Orlando, FL 32801-1524 · 407-843-4321

Mary D. Solik · Foley & Lardner · 111 North Orange Avenue, Suite 1800 · P.O. Box 2193 · Orlando, FL 32802-2193 · 407-423-7656

James M. Spoonhour · Lowndes, Drosdick, Doster, Kantor & Reed · 215 North Eola Drive · Orlando, FL 32801 · 407-843-4600

J. Christy Wilson III · Wilson, Garber & Small · 437 North Magnolia Avenue · Orlando, FL 32801-1524 · 407-843-4321

Sarasota

S. William Moore · Brigham Moore · http://www.eminentdomain.com · 3277 East Fruitville Road · Sarasota, FL 34237-6410 · 941-365-3800

St. Petersburg

Jackson H. Bowman IV · Brigham Moore · http://www.eminentdomain.com · 1780 One-Hundred-Second Avenue North, Suite 100 · St. Petersburg, FL 33716-3600 · 727-579-9000

Gregory S. Rix · Brigham Moore · http://www.eminentdomain.com · 1780 One-Hundred-Second Avenue North, Suite 100 · St. Petersburg, FL 33716-3600 · 727-579-9000

Tallahassee

A. J. James Spalla · Akerman Senterfitt · http://www.akerman.com · Highpoint Center, Suite 1200 · 106 East College Avenue · Tallahassee, FL 32301 · 850-224-9634

Charles Stratton · Broad and Cassel · Sun Trust Bank Building, Suite 400 · 215 South Monroe Street · Tallahassee, FL 32301 · 850-681-6810

Tampa

Paul D. Bain · Gaylord Merlin Ludovici Diaz & Bain · http://www.gaylordmerlin.com · 5001 West Cypress Street · Tampa, FL 33607-3803 · 813-221-9000

Mark P. Buell · Buell & Elligett · 3003 West Azeele Street, Suite 100 · Tampa, FL 33609 · 813-874-2600

D. Tobyn DeYoung · D Tobyn Deyoung · 601 Bayshore Boulevard, Suite 840 · Tampa, FL 33606-2761 · 813-253-3755

Andrew G. Diaz · Gaylord Merlin Ludovici Diaz & Bain · http://www.gaylordmerlin.com · 5001 West Cypress Street · Tampa, FL 33607-3803 · 813-221-9000

S. Cary Gaylord · Gaylord Merlin Ludovici Diaz & Bain · http://www.gaylordmerlin.com · 5001 West Cypress Street · Tampa, FL 33607-3803 · 813-221-9000

Robert E. V. Kelley, Jr. · Hill, Ward & Henderson · http://www.hwhlaw.com · Bank of America Plaza, Suite 3700 · 101 East Kennedy Boulevard · Tampa, FL 33602 · 813-221-3900

Lorena Hart Ludovici · Gaylord Merlin Ludovici Diaz & Bain · http://www.gaylordmerlin.com · 5001 West Cypress Street · Tampa, FL 33607-3803 · 813-221-9000

Kimbel L. Merlin · Gaylord Merlin Ludovici Diaz & Bain · http://www.gaylordmerlin.com · 5001 West Cypress Street · Tampa, FL 33607-3803 · 813-221-9000

Marc Ira Sachs · D Tobyn Deyoung · 601 Bayshore Boulevard, Suite 840 · Tampa, FL 33606-2761 · 813-253-3755

William B. Smith · William B. Smith · P.O. Box 18223 · Tampa, FL 33679-8223 · 813-251-0530

West Palm Beach

John W. Little III · Brigham Moore · http://www.eminentdomain.com · One Clearlake Centre, Suite 1601 250 South Australian Avenue · West Palm Beach, FL 33401-5016 · 561-832-7862

H. Adams Weaver, Jr. · Jones, Foster, Johnston & Stubbs · 505 South Flagler Drive, Suite 1100 · P.O. Box 3475 · West Palm Beach, FL 33402-3475 · 561-659-3000

EMPLOYEE BENEFITS LAW

Coral Gables

Charles P. Sacher · a · Sacher, Martini & Sacher · Gables International Plaza, Suite 1101 · 2655 LeJeune Road · Coral Gables, FL 33134-5802 · 305-448-3900

Fort Lauderdale

James B. Davis · 2) · Gunster, Yoakley & Stewart · Las Olas Centre, Suite 1400 · 450 East Las Olas Boulevard · Fort Lauderdale, FL 33301 · 954-462-2000

Lawrence M. Ploucha · a · Atkinson, Diner, Stone, Mankuta & Ploucha · One Financial Plaza, Suite 1400 · 100 Southeast Third Avenue · Fort Lauderdale, FL 33394 · 954-925-5501

Michael L. Trop · a · Adorno & Yoss · 350 East Las Olas Boulevard, Suite 1700 · Fort Lauderdale, FL 33301 · 954-763-1200

Jacksonville

Andrew J. Fawbush · Dewey & LeBoeuf · 50 North Laura Street, Suite 2800 · Jacksonville, FL 32202-3650 · 904-354-8000

Miami

Victoria Chemerys · Ford & Harrison · http://www.fordharrison.com · 100 Southeast Second Street, Suite 4500 · Miami, FL 33131 · 305-808-2100

Sharon Quinn Dixon · a · Stearns Weaver Miller Weissler Alhadeff & Sitterson · Museum Tower, Suite 2200 · 150 West Flagler Street · Miami, FL 33130 · 305-789-3200

Robert J. Friedman · a · Holland & Knight · http://www.hklaw.com · 701 Brickell Avenue, Suite 3000 · Miami, FL 33131 · 305-374-8500

Jonathan H. Green · Jonathan H. Green & Associates · 799 Brickell Plaza, Suite 700 · Miami, FL 33131 · 305-372-5100

Steven B. Lapidus · a · Greenberg Traurig · http://www.gtlaw.com · 1221 Brickell Avenue, 22nd Floor · Miami, FL 33131 · 305-579-0500

Peter E. Salomon · Akerman Senterfitt · http://www.akerman.com · One Southeast Third Avenue, 25th Floor · Miami, FL 33131-1714 · 305-374-5600

Naples

Jeffrey M. Folkman · Hahn Loeser & Parks · 800 Laurel Oak Drive, Suite 600 · Naples, FL 34108 · 239-254-2900

Orlando

Michael J. Canan · a · GrayRobinson · 301 East Pine Street, Suite 1400 · P.O. Box 3068 · Orlando, FL 32802-3068 · 407-843-8880

Richard T. Hurt · Akerman Senterfitt · http://www.akerman.com · CNL Center II at City Commons, Suite 1200 · 420 South Orange Avenue · Orlando, FL 32801-3336 · 407-423-4000

Robert W. Mead, Jr. · a · Dean, Mead, Egerton, Bloodworth, Capouano & Bozarth · http://www.deanmead.com · 800 North Magnolia Avenue, Suite 1500 · P.O. Box 2346 · Orlando, FL 32802-2346 · 407-841-1200

David L. Schick · GrayRobinson · 301 East Pine Street, Suite 1400 · P.O. Box 3068 · Orlando, FL 32802-3068 · 407-843-8880

Joseph Jay Van Heyde II · Dean, Mead, Egerton, Bloodworth, Capouano & Bozarth · http://www.deanmead.com · 800 North Magnolia Avenue, Suite 1500 · P.O. Box 2346 · Orlando, FL 32802-2346 · 407-841-1200

Sarasota

Carol L. Myers · Myers & Shaw · 373 Braden Avenue, Suite 202 · Sarasota, FL 34243-2053 · 941-360-1990

Tampa

Steven K. Barber · Fowler White Boggs Banker · 501 East Kennedy Boulevard, Suite 1700 · P.O. Box 1438 · Tampa, FL 33602-5239 · 813-228-7411

Kelley A. Bosecker · GrayRobinson · 201 North Franklin Street, Suite 2200 · P.O. Box 3324 · Tampa, FL 33601 · 813-273-5000

Joseph D. Edwards · 2) · Squire Sanders · http://www.ssd.com · One Tampa City Center, Suite 2100 · 201 North Franklin Street · Tampa, FL 33602-5164 · 813-202-1300

Bret Hamlin · Hill, Ward & Henderson · http://www.hwhlaw.com · Bank of America Plaza, Suite 3700 · 101 East Kennedy Boulevard · Tampa, FL 33602 · 813-221-3900

Frederick M. Rothenberg · 2% · Holland & Knight · http://www.hklaw.com · 100 North Tampa Street, Suite 4100 · P.O. Box 1288 · Tampa, FL 33601-1288 · 813-227-8500

R. Dennis Tweed · Hill, Ward & Henderson · http://www.hwhlaw.com · Bank of America Plaza, Suite 3700 · 101 East Kennedy Boulevard · Tampa, FL 33602 · 813-221-3900

Alton C. Ward · a · Hill, Ward & Henderson · http://www.hwhlaw.com · Bank of America Plaza, Suite 3700 · 101 East Kennedy Boulevard · Tampa, FL 33602 · 813-221-3900

Roberta Casper Watson · a · Trenam, Kemker, Scharf, Barkin, Frye, O'Neill & Mullis · http://www.trenam.com · 101 East Kennedy Boulevard, Suite 2700 · P.O. Box 1102 · Tampa, FL 33601-1102 · 813-223-7474

West Palm Beach

David E. Bowers · a · Jones, Foster, Johnston & Stubbs · 505 South Flagler Drive, Suite 1100 · P.O. Box 3475 · West Palm Beach, FL 33402-3475 · 561-659-3000

ENERGY LAW

Jacksonville

Sidney F. Ansbacher · GrayRobinson · 50 North Laura Street, Suite 1100 · Jacksonville, FL 32202 · 904-598-9929

Miami

Ira N. Rosner · Greenberg Traurig · http://www.gtlaw.com · 1221 Brickell Avenue, 22nd Floor · Miami, FL 33131 · 305-579-0500

Pensacola

Jeffrey A. Stone · Beggs & Lane · 501 Commendencia Street · P.O. Box 12950 · Pensacola, FL 32591 · 850-432-2451

Tallahassee

James D. Beasley · Ausley & McMullen · Washington Square Building · 227 South Calhoun Street · P.O. Box 391 · Tallahassee, FL 32302 · 850-224-9115

Charles A. Guyton · Squire Sanders · http://www.ssd.com · 215 South Monroe Street, Suite 601 · Tallahassee, FL 32301-1804 · 850-222-2300

D. Bruce May, Jr. · Holland & Knight · http://www.hklaw.com · Bank of America Building, Suite 600 · 315 South Calhoun Street · Tallahassee, FL 32301 · 850-224-7000

Robert W. Pass · Carlton Fields · Suntrust Building, Suite 500 · 215 South Monroe Street · Tallahassee, FL 32301 · 850-224-1585

Gary V. Perko · Hopping Green & Sams · http://www.hgslaw.com · 123 South Calhoun Street · P.O. Box 6526 · Tallahassee, FL 32314 · 850-222-7598

Lee L. Willis · a · Ausley & McMullen · Washington Square Building · 227 South Calhoun Street · P.O. Box 391 · Tallahassee, FL 32302 · 850-224-9115

Tampa

Laurel E. Lockett · Carlton Fields · Corporate Center Three at International Plaza, Suite 1000 · 4221 West Boy Scout Boulevard · Tampa, FL 33607 · 813-223-7000

James Michael Walls · Carlton Fields · Corporate Center Three at International Plaza, Suite 1000 · 4221 West Boy Scout Boulevard · Tampa, FL 33607 · 813-223-7000

ENTERTAINMENT LAW

Brandon

Michael J. McDermott · McDermott & Thacker · 791 West Lumsden Road · Brandon, FL 33511 · 813-684-3131

Fort Lauderdale

Steven E. Eisenberg · Steven E. Eisenberg, P.A. · 3109 Stirling Road, Suite 101 · Fort Lauderdale, FL 33312 · 954-981-6533

Jacksonville

Robert S. Bernstein · Foley & Lardner · One Independent Drive, Suite 1300 · P.O. Box 240 · Jacksonville, FL 32201 · 904-359-2000

Howard G. Butler · Ossi, Najem & Rosario · 1506 Prudential Drive · Jacksonville, FL 32207 · 904-399-0606

Lawrence J. Najem · Ossi, Najem & Rosario · 1506 Prudential Drive · Jacksonville, FL 32207 · 904-399-0606

Michael A. Ossi · Ossi, Najem & Rosario · 1506 Prudential Drive · Jacksonville, FL 32207 · 904-399-0606

Miami

Joseph Z. Fleming · 2% · Greenberg Traurig · http://www.gtlaw.com · 1221 Brickell Avenue, 22nd Floor · Miami, FL 33131 · 305-579-0500

Jorge L. Hernandez-Toraño · Holland & Knight · http://www.hklaw.com · 701 Brickell Avenue, Suite 3000 · Miami, FL 33131 · 305-374-8500

Stanley H. Wakshlag · a · Kenny Nachwalter · Miami Center, Suite 1100 · 201 South Biscayne Boulevard · Miami, FL 33131-2305 · 305-373-1000

Leslie José Zigel · Ziglaw · 4500 Biscayne Boulevard, Suite 201 · Miami, FL 33137 · 305-604-9944

ENVIRONMENTAL LAW

Fort Lauderdale

Rick J. Burgess · Gunster, Yoakley & Stewart · Las Olas Centre, Suite 1400 · 450 East Las Olas Boulevard · Fort Lauderdale, FL 33301 · 954-462-2000

Barbara A. Hall · Greenberg Traurig · http://www.gtlaw.com · 401 East Las Olas Boulevard, Suite 2000 · Fort Lauderdale, FL 33301 · 954-765-0500

Donald R. Hall · Gunster, Yoakley & Stewart · Las Olas Centre, Suite 1400 · 450 East Las Olas Boulevard Fort Lauderdale, FL 33301 · 954-462-2000

Donald C. McClosky · 2% · Ruden, McClosky, Smith, Schuster & Russell · 200 East Broward Boulevard · P.O. Box 1900 · Fort Lauderdale, FL 33302 · 954-764-6660

Dennis D. Mele · a · Ruden, McClosky, Smith, Schuster & Russell · 200 East Broward Boulevard · P.O. Box 1900 · Fort Lauderdale, FL 33302 · 954-764-6660

Debbie M. Orshefsky · Greenberg Traurig · http://www.gtlaw.com · 401 East Las Olas Boulevard, Suite 2000 · Fort Lauderdale, FL 33301 · 954-765-0500

Jacksonville

Donald D. Anderson · McGuireWoods · http://www.mcguirewoods.com · Bank of America Tower, Suite 3300 · 50 North Laura Street · Jacksonville, FL 32202-3661 · 904-798-3200

Henry Dean · GrayRobinson · 50 North Laura Street, Suite 1100 · Jacksonville, FL 32202 · 904-598-9929

Wayne E. Flowers · Lewis, Longman & Walker · http://www.llw-law.com · 245 Riverside Avenue, Suite 150 · Jacksonville, FL 32202 · 904-353-6410

Richard L. Maguire · Rogers Towers · 1301 Riverplace Boulevard, Suite 1500 · Jacksonville, FL 32207 · 904-398-3911

John G. Metcalf · Pappas Metcalf Jenks & Miller · 245 Riverside Avenue, Suite 400 · Jacksonville, FL 32202-4907 · 904-353-1980

M. Lynn Pappas · a · Pappas Metcalf Jenks & Miller · 245 Riverside Avenue, Suite 400 · Jacksonville, FL 32202-4907 · 904-353-1980

Tim E. Sleeth · Smith Hulsey & Busey · http://www.smithhulsey.com · 225 Water Street, Suite 1800 · Jacksonville, FL 32202 · 904-359-7700

Miami

John M. Barkett · Shook, Hardy & Bacon · 201 South Biscayne Boulevard, Suite 2400 · Miami, FL 33131-4332 · 305-358-5171

Kerri L. Barsh · Greenberg Traurig · http://www.gtlaw.com · 1221 Brickell Avenue, 22nd Floor · Miami, FL 33131 · 305-579-0500

Jeffrey S. Bercow · Bercow & Radell · 200 South Biscayne Boulevard, Suite 850 · Miami, FL 33131 · 305-374-5300

Matthew P. Coglianese · Peckar & Abramson · http://www.pecklaw.com · One Southeast Third Avenue, Suite 3100 · Miami, FL 33131 · 305-358-2600

Lucia A. Dougherty · Greenberg Traurig · http://www.gtlaw.com · 1221 Brickell Avenue, 22nd Floor · Miami, FL 33131 · 305-579-0500

Joseph Z. Fleming · 2% · Greenberg Traurig · http://www.gtlaw.com · 1221 Brickell Avenue, 22nd Floor · Miami, FL 33131 · 305-579-0500

Joseph G. Goldstein · Holland & Knight · http://www.hklaw.com · 701 Brickell Avenue, Suite 3000 · Miami, FL 33131 · 305-374-8500

Douglas M. Halsey · White & Case · http://www.whitecase.com · Wachovia Financial Center, Suite 4900 · 200 South Biscayne Boulevard · Miami, FL 33131-2352 · 305-371-2700

T. Neal McAliley · White & Case · http://www.whitecase.com · Wachovia Financial Center, Suite 4900 · 200 South Biscayne Boulevard · Miami, FL 33131-2352 · 305-371-2700

Eileen Ball Mehta · a · Bilzin Sumberg Baena Price & Axelrod · Wachovia Financial Center, Suite 2500 · 200 South Biscayne Boulevard · Miami, FL 33131 · 305-374-7580

Stanley B. Price · 2) · Bilzin Sumberg Baena Price & Axelrod · Wachovia Financial Center, Suite 2500 · 200 South Biscayne Boulevard · Miami, FL 33131 · 305-374-7580

Clifford A. Schulman · 2) · Greenberg Traurig · http://www.gtlaw.com · 1221 Brickell Avenue, 22nd Floor · Miami, FL 33131 · 305-579-0500

Robert H. Traurig · 2% · Greenberg Traurig · http://www.gtlaw.com · 1221 Brickell Avenue, 22nd Floor · Miami, FL 33131 · 305-579-0500

Orlando

Cecelia Bonifay · Akerman Senterfitt · http://www.akerman.com · CNL Center II at City Commons, Suite 1200 · 420 South Orange Avenue · Orlando, FL 32801-3336 · 407-423-4000

Ted R. Brown · Baker Hostetler · http://www.bakerlaw.com · Sun Trust Center, Suite 2300 · 200 South Orange Avenue · Orlando, FL 32801-3432 · 407-649-4000

Miranda F. Fitzgerald · a · Lowndes, Drosdick, Doster, Kantor & Reed · 215 North Eola Drive · Orlando, FL 32801 · 407-843-4600

Hal H. Kantor · a · Lowndes, Drosdick, Doster, Kantor & Reed · 215 North Eola Drive · Orlando, FL 32801 · 407-843-4600

Julie P. Kendig-Schrader · Greenberg Traurig · http://www.gtlaw.com · 450 South Orange Avenue, Suite 650 · Orlando, FL 32801 · 407-420-1000

Thomas K. Maurer · Foley & Lardner · 111 North Orange Avenue, Suite 1800 · P.O. Box 2193 · Orlando, FL 32802-2193 · 407-423-7656

William L. Pence · Akerman Senterfitt · http://www.akerman.com · CNL Center II at City Commons, Suite 1200 · 420 South Orange Avenue · Orlando, FL 32801-3336 · 407-423-4000

Nicholas A. Pope · Lowndes, Drosdick, Doster, Kantor & Reed · 215 North Eola Drive · Orlando, FL 32801 · 407-843-4600

Rory C. Ryan · Holland & Knight · http://www.hklaw.com · 200 South Orange Avenue, Suite 2600 · P.O. Box 1526 · Orlando, FL 32802 · 407-425-8500

Roger W. Sims · ⑩ · Holland & Knight · http://www.hklaw.com · 200 South Orange Avenue, Suite 2600 · P.O. Box 1526 · Orlando, FL 32802 · 407-425-8500

R. Duke Woodson · Foley & Lardner · 111 North Orange Avenue, Suite 1800 · P.O. Box 2193 · Orlando, FL 32802-2193 · 407-423-7656

Tallahassee

Silvia M. Alderman · Akerman Senterfitt · http://www.akerman.com · Highpoint Center, Suite 1200 · 106 East College Avenue · Tallahassee, FL 32301 · 850-224-9634

James S. Alves · ⑩ · Hopping Green & Sams · http://www.hgslaw.com · 123 South Calhoun Street · P.O. Box 6526 · Tallahassee, FL 32314 · 850-222-7598

Robert C. Apgar · Greenberg Traurig · http://www.gtlaw.com · 101 East College Avenue · Tallahassee, FL 32301 · 850-222-6891

Reginald L. Bouthillier · Greenberg Traurig · http://www.gtlaw.com · 101 East College Avenue · Tallahassee, FL 32301 · 850-222-6891

Martha Harrell Chumbler · Carlton Fields · Suntrust Building, Suite 500 · 215 South Monroe Street · Tallahassee, FL 32301 · 850-224-1585

Terry Cole · Oertel, Fernandez, Cole & Bryant · 301 South Bronough Street, Fifth Floor · P.O. Box 1110 · Tallahassee, FL 32301 · 850-521-0700

Peter C. Cunningham · ⑩ · Hopping Green & Sams · http://www.hgslaw.com · 123 South Calhoun Street P.O. Box 6526 · Tallahassee, FL 32314 · 850-222-7598

Lawrence N. Curtin · ⑩ · Holland & Knight · http://www.hklaw.com · Bank of America Building, Suite 600 · 315 South Calhoun Street · Tallahassee, FL 32301 · 850-224-7000

David S. Dee · Young Van Assenderp · Gallie's Hall, Second Floor · 225 South Adams Street · P.O. Box 1833 · Tallahassee, FL 32302 · 850-222-7206

Ralph A. DeMeo · Hopping Green & Sams · http://www.hgslaw.com · 123 South Calhoun Street · P.O. Box 6526 · Tallahassee, FL 32314 · 850-222-7598

Segundo J. Fernandez · Oertel, Fernandez, Cole & Bryant · 301 South Bronough Street, Fifth Floor · P.O. Box 1110 · Tallahassee, FL 32301 · 850-521-0700

William H. Green · ⑩ · Hopping Green & Sams · http://www.hgslaw.com · 123 South Calhoun Street · P.O. Box 6526 · Tallahassee, FL 32314 · 850-222-7598

W. Douglas Hall · Carlton Fields · Suntrust Building, Suite 500 · 215 South Monroe Street · Tallahassee, FL 32301 · 850-224-1585

Wade L. Hopping · ⑳ · Hopping Green & Sams · http://www.hgslaw.com · 123 South Calhoun Street · P.O. Box 6526 · Tallahassee, FL 32314 · 850-222-7598

R. Steven Lewis · Lewis, Longman & Walker · http://www.llw-law.com · 2600 Centennial Place, Suite 100 · Tallahassee, FL 32308 · 850-222-5702

Nancy G. Linnan · Carlton Fields · Suntrust Building, Suite 500 · 215 South Monroe Street · Tallahassee, FL 32301 · 850-224-1585

Anne Longman · Lewis, Longman & Walker · http://www.llw-law.com · 2600 Centennial Place, Suite 100 Tallahassee, FL 32308 · 850-222-5702

Frank E. Matthews · a · Hopping Green & Sams · http://www.hgslaw.com · 123 South Calhoun Street · P.O. Box 6526 · Tallahassee, FL 32314 · 850-222-7598

Kenneth G. Oertel · Oertel, Fernandez, Cole & Bryant · 301 South Bronough Street, Fifth Floor · P.O. Box 1110 · Tallahassee, FL 32301 · 850-521-0700

Eric T. Olsen · Hopping Green & Sams · http://www.hgslaw.com · 123 South Calhoun Street · P.O. Box 6526 · Tallahassee, FL 32314 · 850-222-7598

Philip S. Parsons · a · Young Van Assenderp · Gallie's Hall, Second Floor · 225 South Adams Street · P.O. Box 1833 · Tallahassee, FL 32302 · 850-222-7206

Michael P. Petrovich · Hopping Green & Sams · http://www.hgslaw.com · 123 South Calhoun Street · P.O. Box 6526 · Tallahassee, FL 32314 · 850-222-7598

William D. Preston · a · William D. Preston · http://www.wprestonpa.com · 4832 Kerry Forest Parkway, Suite A · Tallahassee, FL 32309 · 850-668-4986

Douglas Rillstone · Broad and Cassel · Sun Trust Bank Building, Suite 400 · 215 South Monroe Street · Tallahassee, FL 32301 · 850-681-6810

Gary P. Sams · 2) · Hopping Green & Sams · http://www.hgslaw.com · 123 South Calhoun Street · P.O. Box 6526 · Tallahassee, FL 32314 · 850-222-7598

Cathy M. Sellers · Broad and Cassel · Sun Trust Bank Building, Suite 400 · 215 South Monroe Street · Tallahassee, FL 32301 · 850-681-6810

Lawrence E. Sellers · Holland & Knight · http://www.hklaw.com · Bank of America Building, Suite 600 · 315 South Calhoun Street · Tallahassee, FL 32301 · 850-224-7000

Linda Loomis Shelley · Fowler White Boggs Banker · 101 North Monroe Street, Suite 1090 · Tallahassee, FL 32301 · 850-681-0411

Mary F. Smallwood · a · Ruden, McClosky, Smith, Schuster & Russell · 215 South Monroe Street, Suite 815 · Tallahassee, FL 32301 · 850-412-2000

Daniel H. Thompson · Berger Singerman · http://www.bergersingerman.com · 125 South Gadsden Street, Suite 300 · Tallahassee, FL 32301 · 850-561-3010

Jacob D. Varn · Fowler White Boggs Banker · 101 North Monroe Street, Suite 1090 · Tallahassee, FL 32301 · 850-681-0411

Tampa

Gayle Buttram Carlson · Gayle B. Carlson · 3111 West Martin Luther King Boulevard, Suite 100 · P.O. Box 273771 · Tampa, FL 33607 · 813-229-2900

Frank L. Hearne · Mechanik Nuccio Hearne & Wester · 305 South Boulevard · Tampa, FL 33606 · 813-276-1920

Rhea F. Law · Fowler White Boggs Banker · 501 East Kennedy Boulevard, Suite 1700 · P.O. Box 1438 · Tampa, FL 33602-5239 · 813-228-7411

Laurel E. Lockett · Carlton Fields · Corporate Center Three at International Plaza, Suite 1000 · 4221 West Boy Scout Boulevard · Tampa, FL 33607 · 813-223-7000

Ronald H. Noble · Fowler White Boggs Banker · 501 East Kennedy Boulevard, Suite 1700 · P.O. Box 1438 · Tampa, FL 33602-5239 · 813-228-7411

Roger D. Schwenke · 2) · Carlton Fields · Corporate Center Three at International Plaza, Suite 1000 · 4221 West Boy Scout Boulevard · Tampa, FL 33607 · 813-223-7000

Scott I. Steady · Williams Schifino Mangione & Steady · One Tampa City Center, Suite 3200 · 201 North Franklin Street · Tampa, FL 33602 · 813-221-2626

Theodore C. Taub · a · Shumaker, Loop & Kendrick · Bank of America Plaza, Suite 2800 · 101 East Kennedy Boulevard · Tampa, FL 33602-5150 · 813-229-7600

William B. Taylor IV · Macfarlane Ferguson & McMullen · One Tampa City Center, Suite 2000 · 201 North Franklin Street · P.O. Box 1531 · Tampa, FL 33601 · 813-273-4200

David B. Weinstein · Greenberg Traurig · http://www.gtlaw.com · Courthouse Plaza, Suite 100 · 625 East Twiggs Street · Tampa, FL 33602 · 813-318-5700

West Palm Beach

James R. Brindell · a · Gunster, Yoakley & Stewart · Phillips Point, Suite 500 East · 777 South Flagler Drive · West Palm Beach, FL 33401-6194 · 561-655-1980

Terry E. Lewis · Lewis, Longman & Walker · http://www.llw-law.com · 1700 Palm Beach Lakes Boulevard, Suite 1000 · West Palm Beach, FL 33401 · 561-640-0820

Alfred J. Malefatto · Greenberg Traurig · http://www.gtlaw.com · 777 South Flagler Drive, Suite 300-E · West Palm Beach, FL 33401 · 561-650-7900

Stephen A. Walker · Lewis, Longman & Walker · http://www.llw-law.com · 1700 Palm Beach Lakes Boulevard, Suite 1000 · West Palm Beach, FL 33401 · 561-640-0820

E. Lee Worsham · Ruden, McClosky, Smith, Schuster & Russell · 222 Lakeview Avenue, Suite 800 · West Palm Beach, FL 33401-6112 · 561-838-4500

EQUIPMENT FINANCE LAW

Fort Lauderdale

Steven N. Lippman · Rothstein Rosenfeldt Adler · Bank of America Building, Suite 1650 · 401 East Las Olas Boulevard · Fort Lauderdale, FL 33301 · 954-522-3456

Miami

Christian W. Hansen · White & Case · http://www.whitecase.com · Wachovia Financial Center, Suite 4900 · 200 South Biscayne Boulevard · Miami, FL 33131-2352 · 305-371-2700

Barry L. Meadow · Law Offices of Barry L. Meadow · 169 East Flagler Street, Suite 1542 · Miami, FL 33131-1213 · 305-358-9880

Timothy J. Norris · 2) · Duane Morris · 200 South Biscayne Boulevard, Suite 3400 · Miami, FL 33131-2397 · 305-960-2200

Tampa

Leonard H. Gilbert · a · Holland & Knight · http://www.hklaw.com · 100 North Tampa Street, Suite 4100 · P.O. Box 1288 · Tampa, FL 33601-1288 · 813-227-8500

ETHICS AND PROFESSIONAL RESPONSIBILITY LAW

Tallahassee

Barry Richard · Greenberg Traurig · http://www.gtlaw.com · 101 East College Avenue · Tallahassee, FL 32301 · 850-222-6891

FAMILY LAW

Boca Raton

Brenda M. Abrams · Shapiro Blasi Wasserman & Gora · 7777 Glades Road, Suite 400 · Boca Raton, FL 33434 · 561-477-7800

Christopher A. Tiso · Schuttler & Greenberg · 2151 Northwest Boca Raton Boulevard, Suite 100 · Boca Raton, FL 33431 · 561-393-0565

Bradenton

Larry K. Coleman · a · Law Office of Larry K. Coleman · The Riverview Center, Suite 100 · 1111 Third Avenue West · Bradenton, FL 34205 · 941-747-1234

Clearwater

Ky M. Koch · Koch, Smith & Hoffman · 200 North Garden Avenue, Suite A · Clearwater, FL 33755 · 727-446-6248

Kinnear King Smith · Koch, Smith & Hoffman · 200 North Garden Avenue, Suite A · Clearwater, FL 33755 · 727-446-6248

Dunedin

Wayne J. Boyer · a · Boyer and Schiltz · 1968 Bayshore Boulevard · Dunedin, FL 34698 · 727-734-0662

Fort Lauderdale

Marc H. Brawer · Brawer, Hirsch and Associates · http://www.brawerlaw.com · 650 South East Third Avenue, Suite C · Fort Lauderdale, FL 33301 · 954-522-1922

Gordon C. Brydger · Brydger & Porras · http://www.brydgerporras.com · 100 Northeast Third Avenue, Suite 480 · Fort Lauderdale, FL 33301 · 954-527-2855

Michele Kane Cummings · Ruden, McClosky, Smith, Schuster & Russell · 200 East Broward Boulevard · P.O. Box 1900 · Fort Lauderdale, FL 33302 · 954-764-6660

Peter L. Gladstone · Gladstone & Weissman · http://www.gwpa.net · One Financial Plaza, Suite 2208 · Fort Lauderdale, FL 33394 · 954-761-9994

Dale R. Sanders · a · Lyons and Sanders · 600 Northeast Third Avenue · Fort Lauderdale, FL 33304-2689 · 954-467-8700

Roberta G. Stanley · Brinkley, McNerney, Morgan, Solomon & Tatum · 200 East Las Olas Boulevard, Suite 1900 · Fort Lauderdale, FL 33301 · 954-522-2200

Jeffrey A. Weissman · Gladstone & Weissman · http://www.gwpa.net · One Financial Plaza, Suite 2208 · Fort Lauderdale, FL 33394 · 954-761-9994

Fort Myers

Alan J. Rubinstein · 2) · Rubinstein & Holz · 1375 Jackson Street, Suite 304 · P.O. Box 368 · Fort Myers, FL 33902-0368 · 239-332-3400

Hollywood

A. Matthew Miller · 2) · Boies, Schiller & Flexner · 2435 Hollywood Boulevard · Hollywood, FL 33020 · 954-924-0300

Charles Fox Miller · Boies, Schiller & Flexner · 2435 Hollywood Boulevard · Hollywood, FL 33020 · 954-924-0300

James Fox Miller · 2% · Boies, Schiller & Flexner · 2435 Hollywood Boulevard · Hollywood, FL 33020 · 954-924-0300

Jacksonville

Albert J. Datz · 2% · Datz & Datz · 4348 Southpoint Boulevard, Suite 330 · Jacksonville, FL 32216 · 904-296-7440

Samuel S. Jacobson · Bledsoe, Jacobson, Schmidt & Wright · 1301 Riverplace Boulevard, Suite 1818 · Jacksonville, FL 32207 · 904-398-1818

James G. Roberts · Roberts & Reiter · 233 East Bay Street, Suite 725 · Jacksonville, FL 32202-3448 · 904-353-7305

Barry S. Sinoff · Law Office of Barry S. Sinoff · 6960 Bonneval Road, Suite 202 · Jacksonville, FL 32216-6076 · 904-296-2299

Elliot Zisser · 2) · Zisser, Robison, Brown, Nowlis & Maciejewski · One Independent Drive, Suite 3306 · Jacksonville, FL 32202 · 904-353-3222

Lake Park

Martin L. Haines III · a · Martin L Haines III Chartered · 501 North Federal Highway · Lake Park, FL 33403 · 561-863-5400

Miami

A. J. Barranco · Barranco & Kircher · 150 West Flagler Street, Suite 1400 · Miami, FL 33130 · 305-371-8575

Harold Bluestein · Bluestein & Wayne · 2665 South Bayshore Drive, Suite 1204 · Miami, FL 33133 · 305-859-9200

Albert G. Caruana · a · Caruana & Jacobs · http://www.caruanalaw.com · Courthouse Tower, Suite 1000 44 West Flagler Street · Miami, FL 33130 · 305-371-7972

Bruce A. Christensen · a · Richman Greer · http://www.richmangreer.com · Miami Center, 10th Floor · 201 South Biscayne Boulevard · Miami, FL 33131 · 305-373-4000

Marsha B. Elser · 2) · Elser, Foster-Morales & Kopco · Courthouse Tower, Suite 2100 · 44 West Flagler Street · Miami, FL 33130 · 305-577-0090

Melvyn B. Frumkes · 2% · Melvyn B. Frumkes & Associates · Three Grove Isle Drive, Suite 1106 · Miami, FL 33133 · 305-371-5600

Cynthia L. Greene · a · Greene, Smith & Associates · 7340 Southwest 61st Court · Miami, FL 33143 · 786-268-2553

Maurice Jay Kutner · 2) · Kutner and Associates · Courthouse Tower, 11th Floor · 44 West Flagler Street Miami, FL 33130-1806 · 305-377-9411

Barry L. Meadow · Law Offices of Barry L. Meadow · 169 East Flagler Street, Suite 1542 · Miami, FL 33131-1213 · 305-358-9880

Richard C. Milstein · Akerman Senterfitt · http://www.akerman.com · One Southeast Third Avenue, 25th Floor · Miami, FL 33131-1714 · 305-374-5600

Deanna S. Shifrin · Buckner, Shifrin, Rice & Etter · 46 South West First Street, Second Floor · Miami, FL 33130 · 305-679-9744

Jacqueline M. Valdespino · Valdespino & Associates · 2641 Abaco Avenue · Miami, FL 33133-3803 · 305-442-1200

Milton

T. Sol Johnson · a · Johnson, Green & Miller · 6850 Caroline Street · P.O. Box 605 · Milton, FL 32572 · 850-623-3841

Naples

John R. Asbell · a · Asbell, Ho, Klaus & Goetz · 365 Fifth Avenue South, Suite 202 · Naples, FL 34102 · 239-403-9800

Victoria M. Ho · a · Asbell, Ho, Klaus & Goetz · 365 Fifth Avenue South, Suite 202 · Naples, FL 34102 · 239-403-9800

North Miami Beach

Barry S. Franklin · a · Franklin & Criscuolo · 801 Northeast 167th Street, Second Floor · North Miami Beach, FL 33162-3729 · 305-940-4000

Mitchell K. Karpf · Young, Berman, Karpf & Gonzalez · http://www.ybkglaw.com · 17071 West Dixie Highway · North Miami Beach, FL 33160 · 305-945-1851

Orlando

Mayanne Downs · King, Blackwell, Downs & Zehnder · 25 East Pine Street · P.O. Box 1631 · Orlando, FL 32802-1631 · 407-422-2472

Norman Lee Sasser, Jr. · Sasser & Weber · 1217 Mount Vernon Street · Orlando, FL 32803-5417 · 407-896-0491

Michael R. Walsh · 2% · Michael R. Walsh · 326 North Fern Creek Avenue · Orlando, FL 32803 · 407-896-9431

Nancy S. Weber · Sasser & Weber · 1217 Mount Vernon Street · Orlando, FL 32803-5417 · 407-896-0491

Richard D. West · West Green & Associates · http://www.rdwestlaw.com · 711 North Magnolia Avenue · Orlando, FL 32803 · 407-425-8878

Sarasota

Arthur D. Ginsburg · 2% · Icard, Merrill, Cullis, Timm, Furen & Ginsburg · http://www.icardmerrill.com · 2033 Main Street, Suite 500 & 600 · P.O. Drawer 4195 · Sarasota, FL 34230 · 941-366-8100

South Miami

Andrew M. Leinoff · a · Leinoff & Lemos · 7301 Southwest 57th Court, Suite 545 · South Miami, FL 33143 · 305-661-1556

Natalie S. Lemos · Leinoff & Lemos · 7301 Southwest 57th Court, Suite 545 · South Miami, FL 33143 · 305-661-1556

St. Petersburg

Raleigh W. Greene III · R. W. Greene III · 401 Fourth Street North · St. Petersburg, FL 33701 · 727-821-2900

Michael L. Hastings · Hastings and Estreicher · 600 First Avenue North, Suite 306 · St. Petersburg, FL 33701 · 727-895-3600

Tallahassee

Kristin Adamson-Landau · Novey, Mendelson & Adamson · 851 East Park Avenue · Tallahassee, FL 32301-2620 · 850-224-2000

Elaine N. Duggar · a · Gardner, Wadsworth, Duggar, Bist & Wiener · 1300 Thomaswood Drive · Tallahassee, FL 32308-7914 · 850-385-0070

James P. Judkins · a · Judkins, Simpson & High · 1102 North Gadsden Street · P.O. Box 10368 · Tallahassee, FL 32302 · 850-222-6040

Jerome M. Novey · a · Novey, Mendelson & Adamson · 851 East Park Avenue · Tallahassee, FL 32301-2620 · 850-224-2000

Thomas L. Powell · Powell & Mack · 803 North Calhoun Street · Tallahassee, FL 32303 · 850-224-1452

Tampa

Raymond A. Alley, Jr. · a · Raymond A. Alley, Jr. · 708 East Jackson Street · Tampa, FL 33602-5008 · 813-251-8778

Caroline Kapusta Black · Mason Black & Caballero · http://www.mbc-lawoffice.com · 307 South Magnolia Avenue · Tampa, FL 33606-2237 · 813-251-9200

Edna Y. Elliott · a · Law Office of Edna Elliott · 111 South Boulevard · Tampa, FL 33606 · 813-254-5051

Robert W. Fields · 2) · Robert W. Fields · 44 Aegean Avenue · Tampa, FL 33606 · 813-251-1202

Stann W. Givens · a · Knox & Givens · 607 West Horatio Street · Tampa, FL 33606 · 813-254-0034

John Fraser Himes · Himes & Boire · http://www.hbfamilylaw.com · Bank Of America Plaza, Suite 2430 · 101 East Kennedy Boulevard · Tampa, FL 33602 · 813-261-4700

James P. Knox · a · Knox & Givens · 607 West Horatio Street · Tampa, FL 33606 · 813-254-0034

David A. Maney · Maney, Damsker, Jones & Kuhlman · 606 East Madison Street · P.O. Box 172009 · Tampa, FL 33672-2009 · 813-228-7371

Miriam E. Mason · a · Mason Black & Caballero · http://www.mbc-lawoffice.com · 307 South Magnolia Avenue · Tampa, FL 33606-2237 · 813-251-9200

Marian P. McCulloch · Allen Dell · 202 South Rome Avenue, Suite 100 · Tampa, FL 33606 · 813-223-5351

Ronald J. Russo · Ronald J. Russo · Five O One Building, Suite 700 · 501 East Kennedy Boulevard · Tampa, FL 33602-5200 · 813-221-9400

Jeanne T. Tate · Jeanne T. Tate · 418 West Platt Street · Tampa, FL 33606 · 813-258-3355

West Palm Beach

Victoria A. Calebrese · Law Office of Lewis Kapner · http://www.lewiskapner.com · One Clearlake Centre, Suite 1402 · 250 Australian Avenue South · West Palm Beach, FL 33402-5083 · 561-655-3000

Jorge M. Cestero · Sasser, Cestero & Sasser · 1800 Australian Avenue South, Suite 203 · P.O. Box 2907 · West Palm Beach, FL 33402 · 561-689-4378

John T. Christiansen · a · Christiansen & Jacknin · 1555 Palm Beach Lakes Boulevard, Suite 1010 · P.O. Box 3346 · West Palm Beach, FL 33402 · 561-689-1888

Jeffrey D. Fisher · Fisher & Bendeck · 501 South Flagler Drive, Suite 450 · West Palm Beach, FL 33401 561-832-1005

Lewis Kapner · a · Law Office of Lewis Kapner · http://www.lewiskapner.com · One Clearlake Centre, Suite 1402 · 250 Australian Avenue South · West Palm Beach, FL 33402-5083 · 561-655-3000

Mark T. Luttier · Burman, Critton, Luttier & Coleman · 515 North Flagler Drive, Suite 400 · West Palm Beach, FL 33401 · 561-842-2820

Donald J. Sasser · 2) · Sasser, Cestero & Sasser · 1800 Australian Avenue South, Suite 203 · P.O. Box 2907 · West Palm Beach, FL 33402 · 561-689-4378

Thomas J. Sasser · Sasser, Cestero & Sasser · 1800 Australian Avenue South, Suite 203 · P.O. Box 2907 · West Palm Beach, FL 33402 · 561-689-4378

FAMILY LAW MEDIATION

Orlando

Rebecca L. Palmer · Lowndes, Drosdick, Doster, Kantor & Reed · 215 North Eola Drive · Orlando, FL 32801 · 407-843-4600

St. Petersburg

Raleigh W. Greene III · R. W. Greene III · 401 Fourth Street North · St. Petersburg, FL 33701 · 727-821-2900

Tampa

Raymond A. Alley, Jr. · a · Raymond A. Alley, Jr. · 708 East Jackson Street · Tampa, FL 33602-5008 · 813-251-8778

FDA LAW

Boca Raton

Joel B. Rothman · Seiden, Alder, Matthewman & Bloch · http://www.seidenlaw.com · West Tower, Suite 340 · Glades Twin Plaza · 2300 Glades Road · Boca Raton, FL 33431 · 561-416-0170

Fort Lauderdale

Peter A. Quinter · Becker & Poliakoff · 3111 Stirling Road · Fort Lauderdale, FL 33312 · 954-987-7550

FIRST AMENDMENT LAW

Fort Lauderdale

John R. Hargrove · Gordon Hargrove & James · http://www.ghj.com · 2400 East Commercial Boulevard, Suite 1100 · Fort Lauderdale, FL 33308 · 954-958-2500

Bruce S. Rogow · 2) · Bruce S. Rogow · Broward Financial Centre, Suite 1930 · 500 East Broward Boulevard · Fort Lauderdale, FL 33394 · 954-767-8909

Gainesville

Larry G. Turner · Turner & Jones · 204 West University Avenue, Suite Seven · Gainesville, FL 32601-5205 · 352-372-4263

Jacksonville

George D. Gabel, Jr. · a · Holland & Knight · http://www.hklaw.com · 50 North Laura Street, Suite 3900 P.O. Box 52687 · Jacksonville, FL 32202-2687 · 904-353-2000

William J. Sheppard · a · Sheppard, White,Thomas & Kachergus · 215 North Washington Street · Jacksonville, FL 32202-2808 · 904-356-9661

Miami

Laura Besvinick · Hogan & Hartson · Mellon Financial Center, Suite 1900 · 1111 Brickell Avenue · Miami, FL 33131 · 305-459-6500

Sanford L. Bohrer · a · Holland & Knight · http://www.hklaw.com · 701 Brickell Avenue, Suite 3000 · Miami, FL 33131 · 305-374-8500

Thomas R. Julin · a · Hunton & Williams · Mellon Financial Center, Suite 2500 · 1111 Brickell Avenue · Miami, FL 33131 · 305-810-2500

Richard J. Ovelmen · a · Jorden Burt · 777 Brickell Avenue, Suite 500 · Miami, FL 33131-2803 · 305-371-2600

Samuel A. Terilli, Jr. · Ford & Harrison · http://www.fordharrison.com · 100 Southeast Second Street, Suite 4500 · Miami, FL 33131 · 305-808-2100

St. Petersburg

George Karl Rahdert · a · Rahdert, Steele, Bole & Reynolds · 535 Central Avenue · St. Petersburg, FL 33701-3703 · 727-823-4191

Tallahassee

C. Gary Williams · a · Ausley & McMullen · Washington Square Building · 227 South Calhoun Street · P.O. Box 391 · Tallahassee, FL 32302 · 850-224-9115

Tampa

Carol J. LoCicero · Thomas & LoCicero · 400 North Ashley Drive, Suite 1100 · Tampa, FL 33602 · 813-984-3060

Gregg D. Thomas · a · Thomas & LoCicero · 400 North Ashley Drive, Suite 1100 · Tampa, FL 33602 · 813-984-3060

FRANCHISE LAW

Miami

Alejandro Brito · Zarco, Einhorn, Salkowski & Brito · Bank of America Tower, Suite 2700 · 100 Southeast Second Street · Miami, FL 33131 · 305-374-5418

Robert M. Einhorn · Zarco, Einhorn, Salkowski & Brito · Bank of America Tower, Suite 2700 · 100 Southeast Second Street · Miami, FL 33131 · 305-374-5418

Michael D. Joblove · Genovese Joblove & Battista · Bank of America Tower at International Place, 44th Floor · 100 Southeast Second Street · Miami, FL 33131 · 305-349-2300

Jason M. Murray · Carlton Fields · 4000 International Place · 100 Southeast Second Street · P.O. Box 019101 · Miami, FL 33131-9101 · 305-530-0050

Robert F. Salkowski · Zarco, Einhorn, Salkowski & Brito · Bank of America Tower, Suite 2700 · 100 Southeast Second Street · Miami, FL 33131 · 305-374-5418

Robert Zarco · Zarco, Einhorn, Salkowski & Brito · Bank of America Tower, Suite 2700 · 100 Southeast Second Street · Miami, FL 33131 · 305-374-5418

Tallahassee

Dean Bunch · Sutherland · http://www.sutherland.com · 3600 Maclay Boulevard South, Suite 202 · Tallahassee, FL 32312-1267 · 850-907-2500

John W. Forehand · Lewis, Longman & Walker · http://www.llw-law.com · 2600 Centennial Place, Suite 100 · Tallahassee, FL 32308 · 850-222-5702

Tampa

David A. Beyer · DLA Piper · 100 North Tampa, Suite 2200 · Tampa, FL 33602-5809 · 813-229-2111

GOVERNMENT RELATIONS LAW

Fort Lauderdale

Keith M. Poliakoff · Becker & Poliakoff · 3111 Stirling Road · Fort Lauderdale, FL 33312 · 954-987-7550

Edward J. Pozzuoli · Tripp Scott · 110 Southeast Sixth Street, 15th Floor · Fort Lauderdale, FL 33301 · 954-525-7500

Jacksonville

W. O. Birchfield · a · Birchfield & Humphrey · 1031 LaSalle Street · Jacksonville, FL 32207 · 904-396-6625

Paul M. Harden · Paul M. Harden · 1301 Riverplace Boulevard, Suite 2601 · Jacksonville, FL 32207-9032 904-396-5731

Orange Park

John E. Thrasher · Southern Strategy Group · 1303 Oaklanding Lane · Orange Park, FL 32003 · 904-607-2226

Orlando

C. David Brown II · Broad and Cassel · 390 North Orange Avenue, Suite 1400 · Orlando, FL 32801-4961 407-839-4200

Hal H. Kantor · a · Lowndes, Drosdick, Doster, Kantor & Reed · 215 North Eola Drive · Orlando, FL 32801 · 407-843-4600

R. Duke Woodson · Foley & Lardner · 111 North Orange Avenue, Suite 1800 · P.O. Box 2193 · Orlando, FL 32802-2193 · 407-423-7656

Tallahassee

Fred W. Baggett · Greenberg Traurig · http://www.gtlaw.com · 101 East College Avenue · Tallahassee, FL 32301 · 850-222-6891

Martha W. Barnett · a · Holland & Knight · http://www.hklaw.com · Bank of America Building, Suite 600 · 315 South Calhoun Street · Tallahassee, FL 32301 · 850-224-7000

Douglas S. Bell · Pennington, Moore, Wilkinson, Bell & Dunbar · http://www.penningtonlaw.com · 215 South Monroe Street, Second Floor · P.O. Box 10095 · Tallahassee, FL 32302-2095 · 850-222-3533

Samuel P. Bell III · Pennington, Moore, Wilkinson, Bell & Dunbar · http://www.penningtonlaw.com · 215 South Monroe Street, Second Floor · P.O. Box 10095 · Tallahassee, FL 32302-2095 · 850-222-3533

Diane W. Carr · Hopping Green & Sams · http://www.hgslaw.com · 123 South Calhoun Street · P.O. Box 6526 · Tallahassee, FL 32314 · 850-222-7598

Michael J. Cherniga · Greenberg Traurig · http://www.gtlaw.com · 101 East College Avenue · Tallahassee, FL 32301 · 850-222-6891

Martha Harrell Chumbler · Carlton Fields · Suntrust Building, Suite 500 · 215 South Monroe Street · Tallahassee, FL 32301 · 850-224-1585

Hayden R. Dempsey · Greenberg Traurig · http://www.gtlaw.com · 101 East College Avenue · Tallahassee, FL 32301 · 850-222-6891

J. Michael Huey · GrayRobinson · 301 South Bronough Street, Suite 300 · Tallahassee, FL 32301 · 850-577-9090

Nancy G. Linnan · Carlton Fields · Suntrust Building, Suite 500 · 215 South Monroe Street · Tallahassee, FL 32301 · 850-224-1585

Linda Loomis Shelley · Fowler White Boggs Banker · 101 North Monroe Street, Suite 1090 · Tallahassee, FL 32301 · 850-681-0411

John McKager Stipanovich · Fowler White Boggs Banker · 101 North Monroe Street, Suite 1090 · Tallahassee, FL 32301 · 850-681-0411

J. Larry Williams · Akerman Senterfitt · http://www.akerman.com · Highpoint Center, Suite 1200 · 106 East College Avenue · Tallahassee, FL 32301 · 850-224-9634

Tampa

Steven A. Anderson · Ruden, McClosky, Smith, Schuster & Russell · SunTrust Financial Centre, Suite 2700 · 401 East Jackson Street · Tampa, FL 33602 · 813-222-6600

Rhea F. Law · Fowler White Boggs Banker · 501 East Kennedy Boulevard, Suite 1700 · P.O. Box 1438 · Tampa, FL 33602-5239 · 813-228-7411

HEALTH CARE LAW

Altamonte Springs

Gregory Chaires · Chaires, Brooderson & Guerrero · http://www.chlawyers.com · 283 Cranes Roost Boulevard, Suite 165 · Altamonte Springs, FL 32701-3437 · 407-834-2777

Fort Lauderdale

Gabriel L. Imperato · a · Broad and Cassel · One Financial Plaza, Suite 2700 · 100 Southeast Third Avenue · Fort Lauderdale, FL 33394 · 954-764-7060

David C. Peck · Greenberg Traurig · http://www.gtlaw.com · 401 East Las Olas Boulevard, Suite 2000 · Fort Lauderdale, FL 33301 · 954-765-0500

Lester Perling · Broad and Cassel · One Financial Plaza, Suite 2700 · 100 Southeast Third Avenue · Fort Lauderdale, FL 33394 · 954-764-7060

Kathy J. Tayon · Fowler White Boggs Banker · 1200 East Las Olas Boulevard, Suite 400 · Fort Lauderdale, FL 33301 · 954-703-3900

Fort Myers

Thomas P. Clark · Henderson, Franklin, Starnes & Holt · http://www.henlaw.com · 1715 Monroe Street · P.O. Box 280 · Fort Myers, FL 33902-0280 · 239-344-1100

Donna J. Tisch · Fowler White Boggs Banker · 2235 First Street · Fort Myers, FL 33901 · 239-334-7892

Jacksonville

Michael J. Dewberry · Fowler White Boggs Banker · 50 North Laura Street, Suite 2200 · Jacksonville, FL 32202 · 904-598-3100

M. Richard Lewis, Jr. · Smith Hulsey & Busey · http://www.smithhulsey.com · 225 Water Street, Suite 1800 · Jacksonville, FL 32202 · 904-359-7700

Stephen G. Prom · Akerman Senterfitt · http://www.akerman.com · 50 North Laura Street, Suite 2500 · Jacksonville, FL 32202-3646 · 904-798-3700

Miami

Stephen J. Bronis · a · Carlton Fields · 4000 International Place · 100 Southeast Second Street · P.O. Box 019101 · Miami, FL 33131-9101 · 305-530-0050

Ira J. Coleman · McDermott Will & Emery · Miami Center, 22nd Floor · 201 South Biscayne Boulevard · Miami, FL 33131-4336 · 305-358-3500

Maria T. Currier · Holland & Knight · http://www.hklaw.com · 701 Brickell Avenue, Suite 3000 · Miami, FL 33131 · 305-374-8500

Gary Scott Davis · a · McDermott Will & Emery · Miami Center, 22nd Floor · 201 South Biscayne Boulevard · Miami, FL 33131-4336 · 305-358-3500

Joanne B. Erde · a · Duane Morris · 200 South Biscayne Boulevard, Suite 3400 · Miami, FL 33131-2397 305-960-2200

Lewis W. Fishman · a · Law Offices of Lewis W. Fishman · Two Datran Center, Suite 1121 · 9130 South Dadeland Boulevard · Miami, FL 33156-7848 · 305-670-2100

Alan D. Lash · Lash & Goldberg · http://www.lashgoldberg.com · Bank of America Tower, Suite 1200 · 100 Southeast Second Street · Miami, FL 33131-2158 · 305-347-4040

Nanette O'Donnell · Duane Morris · 200 South Biscayne Boulevard, Suite 3400 · Miami, FL 33131-2397 · 305-960-2200

John S. Schwartz · Law Offices of Schwartz and Associates · 200 South East First Street · Miami, FL 33131 · 305-573-9573

Mike Segal · Broad and Cassel · One Biscayne Tower, Suite 2100 · Two South Biscayne Boulevard · Miami, FL 33131 · 305-373-9400

Stephen H. Siegel · Ruden, McClosky, Smith, Schuster & Russell · Bank of America Building, Suite 1900 701 Brickell Avenue · Miami, FL 33131 · 305-789-2700

Jerry J. Sokol · McDermott Will & Emery · Miami Center, 22nd Floor · 201 South Biscayne Boulevard · Miami, FL 33131-4336 · 305-358-3500

William J. Spratt, Jr. · K&L Gates · Wachovia Financial Center, Suite 3900 · 200 South Biscayne Boulevard · Miami, FL 33131-2399 · 305-539-3300

Mark A. Sterling · Hogan & Hartson · Mellon Financial Center, Suite 1900 · 1111 Brickell Avenue · Miami, FL 33131 · 305-459-6500

Jennifer A. Vecchio · McDermott Will & Emery · Miami Center, 22nd Floor · 201 South Biscayne Boulevard · Miami, FL 33131-4336 · 305-358-3500

Orlando

Michael J. Bittman · GrayRobinson · 301 East Pine Street, Suite 1400 · P.O. Box 3068 · Orlando, FL 32802-3068 · 407-843-8880

David L. Evans · Mateer & Harbert · Two Landmark Center, Suite 600 · 225 East Robinson Street · P.O. Box 2854 · Orlando, FL 32801 · 407-425-9044

James F. Heekin, Jr. · Lowndes, Drosdick, Doster, Kantor & Reed · 215 North Eola Drive · Orlando, FL 32801 · 407-843-4600

Richard W. Johns · Foley & Lardner · 111 North Orange Avenue, Suite 1800 · P.O. Box 2193 · Orlando, FL 32802-2193 · 407-423-7656

Laurie J. Levin · Baker Hostetler · http://www.bakerlaw.com · Sun Trust Center, Suite 2300 · 200 South Orange Avenue · Orlando, FL 32801-3432 · 407-649-4000

William G. Mateer · a · Mateer & Harbert · Two Landmark Center, Suite 600 · 225 East Robinson Street · P.O. Box 2854 · Orlando, FL 32801 · 407-425-9044

William F. Sutton, Jr. · Ruden, McClosky, Smith, Schuster & Russell · 111 North Orange Avenue, Suite 1750 · Orlando, FL 32801 · 407-244-8000

Ponte Vedra Beach

Rick Monte Reznicsek · Reznicsek Fraser Hastings · 240 Ponte Vedra Park Drive, Suite 150 · Ponte Vedra Beach, FL 32082 · 904-567-1060

Sarasota

Carol Ann Kalish · Williams Parker Harrison Dietz & Getzen · 200 South Orange Avenue · Sarasota, FL 34236 · 941-366-4800

St. Petersburg

Richard O. Jacobs · Trenam, Kemker, Scharf, Barkin, Frye, O'Neill & Mullis · http://www.trenam.com · 200 Central Avenue, Suite 1600 · P.O. Box 3542 · St. Petersburg, FL 33731-3542 · 727-896-7171

Thomas B. Smith · Bronstein, Carlson, Gleim & Smith · 150 Second Avenue North, Suite 1100 · St. Petersburg, FL 33701 · 727-898-6688

Tallahassee

David C. Ashburn · Greenberg Traurig · http://www.gtlaw.com · 101 East College Avenue · Tallahassee, FL 32301 · 850-222-6891

Michael J. Cherniga · Greenberg Traurig · http://www.gtlaw.com · 101 East College Avenue · Tallahassee, FL 32301 · 850-222-6891

Michael J. Glazer · Ausley & McMullen · Washington Square Building · 227 South Calhoun Street · P.O. Box 391 · Tallahassee, FL 32302 · 850-224-9115

Allen R. Grossman · Metzger, Grossman, Furlow & Bayo · 1408 North Piedmont Way · Tallahassee, FL 32308 · 850-385-1314

Shannon B. Hartsfield · Holland & Knight · http://www.hklaw.com · Bank of America Building, Suite 600 · 315 South Calhoun Street · Tallahassee, FL 32301 · 850-224-7000

Jerome Hoffman · Holland & Knight · http://www.hklaw.com · Bank of America Building, Suite 600 · 315 South Calhoun Street · Tallahassee, FL 32301 · 850-224-7000

Morris H. Miller · a · Holland & Knight · http://www.hklaw.com · Bank of America Building, Suite 600 · 315 South Calhoun Street · Tallahassee, FL 32301 · 850-224-7000

Steven T. Mindlin · a · Rose, Sundstrom & Bentley · 2548 Blairstone Pines Drive · P.O. Box 1567 · Tallahassee, FL 32301-1567 · 850-877-6555

R. Terry Rigsby · Carlton Fields · Suntrust Building, Suite 500 · 215 South Monroe Street · Tallahassee, FL 32301 · 850-224-1585

Tampa

Ronald A. Christaldi · Shumaker, Loop & Kendrick · Bank of America Plaza, Suite 2800 · 101 East Kennedy Boulevard · Tampa, FL 33602-5150 · 813-229-7600

Kirk S. Davis · a · Akerman Senterfitt · http://www.akerman.com · SunTrust Financial Centre, Suite 1700 · 401 East Jackson Street · Tampa, FL 33602-5803 · 813-223-7333

C. Howard Hunter · Hill, Ward & Henderson · http://www.hwhlaw.com · Bank of America Plaza, Suite 3700 · 101 East Kennedy Boulevard · Tampa, FL 33602 · 813-221-3900

James J. Kennedy · Buchanan Ingersoll & Rooney · http://www.bipc.com · SunTrust Financial Centre, Suite 2500 · 401 East Jackson Street · Tampa, FL 33602-5236 · 813-222-8180

Bruce D. Lamb · Ruden, McClosky, Smith, Schuster & Russell · SunTrust Financial Centre, Suite 2700 · 401 East Jackson Street · Tampa, FL 33602 · 813-222-6600

Cynthia A. Mikos · Law Office of Cynthia A. Mikos · http://www.camlaw.net · 202 South Rome Avenue, Suite 100 · Tampa, FL 33606 · 813-223-5351

Barbara R. Pankau · a · Pankau Law Firm · 5920 River Terrace · Tampa, FL 33604 · 813-223-1757

R. Andrew Rock · Buchanan Ingersoll & Rooney · http://www.bipc.com · SunTrust Financial Centre, Suite 2500 · 401 East Jackson Street · Tampa, FL 33602-5236 · 813-222-8180

Joseph W. Rugg · Akerman Senterfitt · http://www.akerman.com · SunTrust Financial Centre, Suite 1700 401 East Jackson Street · Tampa, FL 33602-5803 · 813-223-7333

Richard M. Sebek · Fowler White Boggs Banker · 501 East Kennedy Boulevard, Suite 1700 · P.O. Box 1438 · Tampa, FL 33602-5239 · 813-228-7411

Edward M. Waller, Jr. · a · Fowler White Boggs Banker · 501 East Kennedy Boulevard, Suite 1700 · P.O. Box 1438 · Tampa, FL 33602-5239 · 813-228-7411

Don B. Weinbren · Trenam, Kemker, Scharf, Barkin, Frye, O'Neill & Mullis · http://www.trenam.com · 101 East Kennedy Boulevard, Suite 2700 · P.O. Box 1102 · Tampa, FL 33601-1102 · 813-223-7474

Vero Beach

Valerie Goodwin Larcombe · Indian River Medical Center · Indian River Medical Center · 1000 36th Street · Vero Beach, FL 32960 · 772-567-4311

West Palm Beach

James A. Farrell · Shutts & Bowen · http://www.shutts.com · One Clearlake Centre, Suite 500 · 250 Australian Avenue South · West Palm Beach, FL 33401 · 561-650-8500

IMMIGRATION LAW

Coral Gables

Jeffrey N. Brauwerman · a · Brauwerman, June & Morgado · http://www.brauwermanlaw.com · 137 Madeira Avenue · Coral Gables, FL 33134 · 305-758-1234

Eugenio Hernandez · Avila Rodriguez Hernandez Mena & Ferri · 2525 Ponce De Leon Boulevard, Suite 1225 · Coral Gables, FL 33134-6049 · 305-779-3560

Miami

Michael A. Bander · Bander & Scarlatelli · 444 Brickell Avenue, Suite 300 · Miami, FL 33131 · 305-358-5800

David S. Berger · a · Bernstein & Berger · 100 North Biscayne Boulevard, Suite 1602 · Miami, FL 33132 305-371-4555

Magda Montiel Davis · a · Montiel Davis & Fonte · 111 Northeast First Street, Fifth Floor · Miami, FL 33132 · 305-446-1151

Kari Ann Fonte · Montiel Davis & Fonte · 111 Northeast First Street, Fifth Floor · Miami, FL 33132 · 305-446-1151

Tammy Fox-Isicoff · Rifkin and Fox-Isicoff · 1110 Brickell Avenue, Suite 210 · Miami, FL 33131 · 305-371-2777

Mary E. Kramer · Mary E. Kramer · 168 Southeast First Street · Miami, FL 33131 · 305-374-2300

Ira J. Kurzban · a · Kurzban, Kurzban, Weinger & Tetzeli · 2650 Southwest 27th Avenue, Second Floor Miami, FL 33133 · 305-444-0060

John P. Pratt · Kurzban, Kurzban, Weinger & Tetzeli · 2650 Southwest 27th Avenue, Second Floor · Miami, FL 33133 · 305-444-0060

Anis N. Saleh · Law Offices of Saleh & Associates · SunTrust International Center, Suite 1870 · One Southeast Third Avenue · Miami, FL 33131 · 305-379-2661

Michael Shane · Law Offices of Michael Shane · One Datran Center, Penthouse Two, Suite 1810 · 9100 South Dadeland Boulevard · Miami, FL 33156 · 305-671-8777

Helena Tetzeli · a · Kurzban, Kurzban, Weinger & Tetzeli · 2650 Southwest 27th Avenue, Second Floor · Miami, FL 33133 · 305-444-0060

Sarah Lea Tobocman · Gunster, Yoakley & Stewart · One Biscayne Tower, Suite 3400 · Two South Biscayne Boulevard · Miami, FL 33131-1897 · 305-376-6000

Oldsmar

Dilip Patel · Dilip Patel · http://www.dplawfirm.com · Cypress Lakes Professional Center · 140 Pine Avenue North · Oldsmar, FL 34677 · 813-855-0066

Gerald P. Seipp · a · Dilip Patel · http://www.dplawfirm.com · Cypress Lakes Professional Center · 140 Pine Avenue North · Oldsmar, FL 34677 · 813-855-0066

Orlando

Daniel R. Aidif · Daniel R. Aidif · 501 East South Street, Suite A · Orlando, FL 32801 · 407-841-4855

Teresa B. Finer · Lowndes, Drosdick, Doster, Kantor & Reed · 215 North Eola Drive · Orlando, FL 32801 · 407-843-4600

Philip M. Zyne · a · Philip M. Zyne · 1978 Bridgewater Drive · Orlando, FL 32746 · 407-833-8951

Tampa

William J. Flynn III · Fowler White Boggs Banker · 501 East Kennedy Boulevard, Suite 1700 · P.O. Box 1438 · Tampa, FL 33602-5239 · 813-228-7411

John E. Lund · Lund & O'Flaherty · Tampa Theater Building, Suite 800 · 707 North Franklin Street · Tampa, FL 33602-4419 · 813-224-9988

Winter Park

Edward Charles Beshara · Law Offices of Edward Beshara · 1850 Lee Road, Suite 300 · Winter Park, FL 32789 · 407-629-6455

INFORMATION TECHNOLOGY LAW

Boca Raton

Joel B. Rothman · Seiden, Alder, Matthewman & Bloch · http://www.seidenlaw.com · West Tower, Suite 340 · Glades Twin Plaza · 2300 Glades Road · Boca Raton, FL 33431 · 561-416-0170

Celebration

Thomas A. Sadaka · Seiden, Alder, Matthewman & Bloch · http://www.seidenlaw.com · Celebration Corporate Center, Suite 201 · 1420 Celebration Boulevard · Celebration, FL 34747 · 407-566-2110

Coral Gables

Ury Fischer · Lott & Friedland · 355 Alhambra Circle, Suite 1100 · Coral Gables, FL 33134 · 305-448-7089

Miami

Mark D. Grossman · Grossman Law Group · http://www.ecomputerlaw.com · 999 Ponce de Leon Boulevard, Suite 705 · Miami, FL 33134 · 305-443-8180

Samuel A. Lewis · Feldman Gale · http://www.feldmangale.com · One Biscayne Tower, 30th Floor · Two South Biscayne Boulevard · Miami, FL 33131 · 305-358-5001

José I. Rojas · Rojas Law Firm · Two Datran Center, Suite 1209 · 9130 South Dadeland Boulevard · Miami, FL 33156 · 305-446-4000

Tampa

G. Donovan Conwell, Jr. · Conwell, Sukhia & Kirkpatrick · 2701 North Rocky Point Drive, Suite 1200 · Tampa, FL 33607 · 813-282-8000

Andrew C. Greenberg · Carlton Fields · Corporate Center Three at International Plaza, Suite 1000 · 4221 West Boy Scout Boulevard · Tampa, FL 33607 · 813-223-7000

Harvey S. Kauget · Phelps Dunbar · http://www.phelpsdunbar.com · 100 South Ashley Drive, Suite 1900 · Tampa, FL 33602-5311 · 813-472-7550

INSURANCE LAW

Jacksonville

Thomas C. Dearing · Fowler White Boggs Banker · 50 North Laura Street, Suite 2200 · Jacksonville, FL 32202 · 904-598-3100

Rutledge R. Liles · a · Liles, Gavin, Costantino & George · http://www.lgcglaw.com · One Enterprise Center, Suite 1500 · 225 Water Street · Jacksonville, FL 32202 · 904-634-1100

Frederick D. Page · Holland & Knight · http://www.hklaw.com · 50 North Laura Street, Suite 3900 · P.O. Box 52687 · Jacksonville, FL 32202-2687 · 904-353-2000

James C. Rinaman, Jr. · Marks & Gray · 1200 Riverplace Boulevard, Suite 800 · P.O. Box 447 · Jacksonville, FL 32201 · 904-398-0900

Miami

Marcy Levine Aldrich · Akerman Senterfitt · http://www.akerman.com · One Southeast Third Avenue, 25th Floor · Miami, FL 33131-1714 · 305-374-5600

Steven J. Brodie · Carlton Fields · 4000 International Place · 100 Southeast Second Street · P.O. Box 019101 · Miami, FL 33131-9101 · 305-530-0050

Bowman Brown · Shutts & Bowen · http://www.shutts.com · Miami Center, Suite 1500 · 201 South Biscayne Boulevard · Miami, FL 33131 · 305-358-6300

Jeffrey Michael Cohen · Carlton Fields · 4000 International Place · 100 Southeast Second Street · P.O. Box 019101 · Miami, FL 33131-9101 · 305-530-0050

Bernard Jacobson · Akerman Senterfitt · http://www.akerman.com · One Southeast Third Avenue, 25th Floor · Miami, FL 33131-1714 · 305-374-5600

John E. Meagher · Shutts & Bowen · http://www.shutts.com · Miami Center, Suite 1500 · 201 South Biscayne Boulevard · Miami, FL 33131 · 305-358-6300

Lewis F. Murphy · Squire Sanders · http://www.ssd.com · 200 South Biscayne Boulevard, Suite 4000 · Miami, FL 33131-2398 · 305-577-7000

Nina Whiston · Akerman Senterfitt · http://www.akerman.com · One Southeast Third Avenue, 25th Floor Miami, FL 33131-1714 · 305-374-5600

Jon W. Zeder · Ferrell Law · 201 South Biscayne Boulevard, 34th Floor · Miami, FL 33131 · 305-371-8585

Orlando

Janet L. Brown · Boehm, Brown, Fischer, Harwood, Kelly & Scheihing · 101 Southhall Lane, Suite 375 · P.O. Box 2593 · Orlando, FL 32751 · 407-660-0990

Susan B. Harwood · Boehm, Brown, Fischer, Harwood, Kelly & Scheihing · 101 Southhall Lane, Suite 375 · P.O. Box 2593 · Orlando, FL 32751 · 407-660-0990

David C. Schwartz · Fowler White Boggs Banker · SunTrust Center, Suite 1950 · 200 South Orange Avenue · Orlando, FL 32801 · 407-406-5500

Richard S. Womble · Rissman, Weisberg, Barrett, Hurt, Donahue & McLain · Capital Plaza, 15th Floor · 201 East Pine Street · P.O. Box 4940 · Orlando, FL 32801 · 407-839-0120

Palm Beach Gardens

Fred A. Cunningham · Slawson Cunningham Whalen & Gaspari · 2401 PGA Boulevard, Suite 140 · Palm Beach Gardens, FL 33410-3590 · 561-625-6260

Tallahassee

Daniel C. Brown · Carlton Fields · Suntrust Building, Suite 500 · 215 South Monroe Street · Tallahassee, FL 32301 · 850-224-1585

P. Bruce Culpepper · Akerman Senterfitt · http://www.akerman.com · Highpoint Center, Suite 1200 · 106 East College Avenue · Tallahassee, FL 32301 · 850-224-9634

Mark K. Delegal · Pennington, Moore, Wilkinson, Bell & Dunbar · http://www.penningtonlaw.com · 215 South Monroe Street, Second Floor · P.O. Box 10095 · Tallahassee, FL 32302-2095 · 850-222-3533

Thomas J. Jones · Holland & Knight · http://www.hklaw.com · Bank of America Building, Suite 600 · 315 South Calhoun Street · Tallahassee, FL 32301 · 850-224-7000

Allan J. Katz · Akerman Senterfitt · http://www.akerman.com · Highpoint Center, Suite 1200 · 106 East College Avenue · Tallahassee, FL 32301 · 850-224-9634

Edward L. Kutter · Akerman Senterfitt · http://www.akerman.com · Highpoint Center, Suite 1200 · 106 East College Avenue · Tallahassee, FL 32301 · 850-224-9634

Thomas J. Maida · Foley & Lardner · 106 East College Avenue, Suite 900 · Tallahassee, FL 32301 · 850-222-6100

Harry O. Thomas · Radey, Thomas, Yon & Clark · http://www.radeylaw.com · 301 South Bronough Street, Suite 200 · Tallahassee, FL 32301 · 850-425-6654

Gary P. Timin · Squire Sanders · http://www.ssd.com · 215 South Monroe Street, Suite 601 · Tallahassee, FL 32301-1804 · 850-222-2300

David A. Yon · Radey, Thomas, Yon & Clark · http://www.radeylaw.com · 301 South Bronough Street, Suite 200 · Tallahassee, FL 32301 · 850-425-6654

Tampa

Bruce A. Aebel · Fowler White Boggs Banker · 501 East Kennedy Boulevard, Suite 1700 · P.O. Box 1438 · Tampa, FL 33602-5239 · 813-228-7411

W. Donald Cox · Fowler White Boggs Banker · 501 East Kennedy Boulevard, Suite 1700 · P.O. Box 1438 Tampa, FL 33602-5239 · 813-228-7411

Matthew L. Litsky · Phelps Dunbar · http://www.phelpsdunbar.com · 100 South Ashley Drive, Suite 1900 Tampa, FL 33602-5311 · 813-472-7550

William F. Merlin, Jr. · Merlin Law Group · 777 South Harbour Island Boulevard, Suite 950 · Tampa, FL 33602 · 813-229-1000

Daniel P. Mitchell · Barr Murman Tonelli Slother & Sleet · 201 East Kennedy Boulevard, Suite 1700 · P.O. Box 172669 · Tampa, FL 33602 · 813-223-3951

Charles P. Schropp · Schropp Law Firm · 2309 South Macdill Avenue, Suite 101 · Tampa, FL 33629-5918 · 813-418-3320

George A. Vaka · Vaka, Larson & Johnson · 100 North Tampa Street, Suite 1800 · Tampa, FL 33602 · 813-228-6688

West Palm Beach

Michael S. Smith · Lesser, Lesser, Landy & Smith · 101 Northpoint Parkway · West Palm Beach, FL 33407 · 561-655-2028

INTELLECTUAL PROPERTY LAW

Boca Raton

Frank J. Benasutti · Benasutti Mediation Center · One Boca Commerce Center, Suite 211 · 551 Northwest 77th Street · Boca Raton, FL 33487 · 561-994-5959

Steven M. Greenberg · Carey Rodriguez Greenberg & Paul · 950 Peninsula Corporate Circle, Suite 3200 · Boca Raton, FL 33487 · 561-922-3845

Terri Meyers · Kluger, Peretz, Kaplan & Berlin · http://www.kpkb.com · Penninsula Executive Center, Suite 300 · 2385 Northwest Executive Center Drive · Boca Raton, FL 33431 · 561-443-0800

Coral Gables

David K. Friedland · Lott & Friedland · 355 Alhambra Circle, Suite 1100 · Coral Gables, FL 33134 · 305-448-7089

Leslie J. Lott · a · Lott & Friedland · 355 Alhambra Circle, Suite 1100 · Coral Gables, FL 33134 · 305-448-7089

Mark E. Stein · Lott & Friedland · 355 Alhambra Circle, Suite 1100 · Coral Gables, FL 33134 · 305-448-7089

Fort Lauderdale

John Christopher · Christopher & Weisberg · http://www.cwiplaw.com · 200 East Las Olas Boulevard, Suite 2040 · Fort Lauderdale, FL 33301 · 954-828-1488

Steven E. Eisenberg · Steven E. Eisenberg, P.A. · 3109 Stirling Road, Suite 101 · Fort Lauderdale, FL 33312 · 954-981-6533

Barry L. Haley · Malin, Haley & DiMaggio · 1936 South Andrews Avenue · Fort Lauderdale, FL 33316 · 954-763-3303

Robert C. Kain · Robert C. Kain · 750 Southeast Third Avenue, Suite 100 · Fort Lauderdale, FL 33316-1153 · 954-768-9002

Jeffrey H. Kamenetsky · Christopher & Weisberg · http://www.cwiplaw.com · 200 East Las Olas Boulevard, Suite 2040 · Fort Lauderdale, FL 33301 · 954-828-1488

Daniel Polley · Daniel Polley · 1215 East Broward Boulevard · Fort Lauderdale, FL 33301 · 954-234-2417

Donald S. Showalter · GrayRobinson · 401 East Las Olas Boulevard, Suite 1850 · Fort Lauderdale, FL 33301 · 954-761-8111

Gainesville

David R. Saliwanchik · Saliwanchik, Lloyd & Saliwanchik · 3107 South West Williston Road · Gainesville, FL 32614-2950 · 352-375-8100

Jacksonville

Rutledge R. Liles · a · Liles, Gavin, Costantino & George · http://www.lgcglaw.com · One Enterprise Center, Suite 1500 · 225 Water Street · Jacksonville, FL 32202 · 904-634-1100

Frederick D. Page · Holland & Knight · http://www.hklaw.com · 50 North Laura Street, Suite 3900 · P.O. Box 52687 · Jacksonville, FL 32202-2687 · 904-353-2000

Miami

Stephanie C. Alvarez · Feldman Gale · http://www.feldmangale.com · One Biscayne Tower, 30th Floor · Two South Biscayne Boulevard · Miami, FL 33131 · 305-358-5001

John C. Carey · Carey Rodriguez Greenberg & Paul · 1395 Brickell Avenue, Suite 700 · Miami, FL 33131 · 305-372-7474

Michael C. Cesarano · Feldman Gale · http://www.feldmangale.com · One Biscayne Tower, 30th Floor · Two South Biscayne Boulevard · Miami, FL 33131 · 305-358-5001

Michael B. Chesal · Kluger, Peretz, Kaplan & Berlin · http://www.kpkb.com · Miami Center, Suite 1700 · 201 South Biscayne Boulevard · Miami, FL 33131 · 305-379-9000

Jorge T. Espinosa · Espinosa Trueba PL · 3001 South West Third Avenue · Miami, FL 33129 · 305-854-0900

Jeffrey D. Feldman · Feldman Gale · http://www.feldmangale.com · One Biscayne Tower, 30th Floor · Two South Biscayne Boulevard · Miami, FL 33131 · 305-358-5001

James A. Gale · Feldman Gale · http://www.feldmangale.com · One Biscayne Tower, 30th Floor · Two South Biscayne Boulevard · Miami, FL 33131 · 305-358-5001

Kenneth R. Hartmann · Kozyak Tropin & Throckmorton · http://www.kttlaw.com · 2525 Ponce de Leon Boulevard, Ninth Floor · Miami, FL 33134 · 305-372-1800

Jennie S. Malloy · Malloy & Malloy · 2800 Southwest Third Avenue · Miami, FL 33129 · 305-858-8000

John C. Malloy III · Malloy & Malloy · 2800 Southwest Third Avenue · Miami, FL 33129 · 305-858-8000

Gail A. McQuilkin · Kozyak Tropin & Throckmorton · http://www.kttlaw.com · 2525 Ponce de Leon Boulevard, Ninth Floor · Miami, FL 33134 · 305-372-1800

Janet T. Munn · Feldman Gale · http://www.feldmangale.com · One Biscayne Tower, 30th Floor · Two South Biscayne Boulevard · Miami, FL 33131 · 305-358-5001

Stephen E. Nagin · Nagin, Gallop & Figueredo · http://www.ngf-law.com · 18001 Old Cutler Road, Suite 556 · Miami, FL 33157-6416 · 305-854-5353

Steven I. Peretz · Kluger, Peretz, Kaplan & Berlin · http://www.kpkb.com · Miami Center, Suite 1700 · 201 South Biscayne Boulevard · Miami, FL 33131 · 305-379-9000

Harry R. Schafer · Kenny Nachwalter · Miami Center, Suite 1100 · 201 South Biscayne Boulevard · Miami, FL 33131-2305 · 305-373-1000

Naples

Jeanne L. Seewald · Hahn Loeser & Parks · 800 Laurel Oak Drive, Suite 600 · Naples, FL 34108 · 239-254-2900

Orlando

Herbert L. Allen · Allen, Dyer, Doppelt, Milbrath & Gilchrist · http://www.addmg.com · 255 South Orange Avenue, Suite 1401 · Orlando, FL 32801 · 407-841-2330

James H. Beusse · Beusse, Brownlee, Wolter, Mora & Maire · 390 North Orange Avenue, Suite 2500 · Orlando, FL 32801 · 407-926-7700

Ava K. Doppelt · Allen, Dyer, Doppelt, Milbrath & Gilchrist · http://www.addmg.com · 255 South Orange Avenue, Suite 1401 · Orlando, FL 32801 · 407-841-2330

Brian R. Gilchrist · Allen, Dyer, Doppelt, Milbrath & Gilchrist · http://www.addmg.com · 255 South Orange Avenue, Suite 1401 · Orlando, FL 32801 · 407-841-2330

Christine Q. McLeod · Beusse, Brownlee, Wolter, Mora & Maire · 390 North Orange Avenue, Suite 2500 Orlando, FL 32801 · 407-926-7700

Stephen D. Milbrath · Allen, Dyer, Doppelt, Milbrath & Gilchrist · http://www.addmg.com · 255 South Orange Avenue, Suite 1401 · Orlando, FL 32801 · 407-841-2330

Lori T. Milvain · Latham, Shuker, Barker, Eden & Beaudine · 390 North Orange Avenue, Suite 600 · P.O. Box 3353 · Orlando, FL 32801 · 407-481-5800

T. Todd Pittenger · Lowndes, Drosdick, Doster, Kantor & Reed · 450 South Orange Street, Suite 250 · Orlando, FL 32801-3383 · 407-843-4600

Stuart

Stephen C. Page · Page, Mrachek, Fitzgerald & Rose · 1000 South East Monterey Commons Boulevard, Suite 306 · Stuart, FL 34996 · 772-221-7757

Tampa

G. Donovan Conwell, Jr. · Conwell, Sukhia & Kirkpatrick · 2701 North Rocky Point Drive, Suite 1200 · Tampa, FL 33607 · 813-282-8000

Andrew C. Greenberg · Carlton Fields · Corporate Center Three at International Plaza, Suite 1000 · 4221 West Boy Scout Boulevard · Tampa, FL 33607 · 813-223-7000

William F. Hamilton · Holland & Knight · http://www.hklaw.com · 100 North Tampa Street, Suite 4100 · P.O. Box 1288 · Tampa, FL 33601-1288 · 813-227-8500

Frank R. Jakes · Johnson, Pope, Bokor, Ruppel & Burns · http://www.jpfirm.com · 403 East Madison Street, Suite 400 · Tampa, FL 33602 · 813-225-2500

Harvey S. Kauget · Phelps Dunbar · http://www.phelpsdunbar.com · 100 South Ashley Drive, Suite 1900 · Tampa, FL 33602-5311 · 813-472-7550

Monica B. Mason · Fowler White Boggs Banker · 501 East Kennedy Boulevard, Suite 1700 · P.O. Box 1438 · Tampa, FL 33602-5239 · 813-228-7411

C. Douglas McDonald, Jr. · Carlton Fields · Corporate Center Three at International Plaza, Suite 1000 · 4221 West Boy Scout Boulevard · Tampa, FL 33607 · 813-223-7000

Stefan V. Stein · a · Holland & Knight · http://www.hklaw.com · 100 North Tampa Street, Suite 4100 · P.O. Box 1288 · Tampa, FL 33601-1288 · 813-227-8500

J. Todd Timmerman · Shumaker, Loop & Kendrick · Bank of America Plaza, Suite 2800 · 101 East Kennedy Boulevard · Tampa, FL 33602-5150 · 813-229-7600

West Palm Beach

Gregory A. Nelson · Akerman Senterfitt · http://www.akerman.com · Esperante Building, Suite 400 · 222 Lakeview Avenue · West Palm Beach, FL 33401-6183 · 561-653-5000

J. Rodman Steele, Jr. · Akerman Senterfitt · http://www.akerman.com · Esperante Building, Suite 400 · 222 Lakeview Avenue · West Palm Beach, FL 33401-6183 · 561-653-5000

INTERNATIONAL ARBITRATION

Coral Gables

Wilfredo A. Rodriguez · Avila Rodriguez Hernandez Mena & Ferri · 2525 Ponce De Leon Boulevard, Suite 1225 · Coral Gables, FL 33134-6049 · 305-779-3560

José I. Astigarraga · Astigarraga Davis · 701 Brickell Avenue, 16th Floor · Miami, FL 33131 · 305-372-8282

Burton A. Landy · Akerman Senterfitt · http://www.akerman.com · One Southeast Third Avenue, 25th Floor · Miami, FL 33131-1714 · 305-374-5600

Pedro J. Martinez-Fraga · Squire Sanders · http://www.ssd.com · 200 South Biscayne Boulevard, Suite 4000 · Miami, FL 33131-2398 · 305-577-7000

Edward Mullins · Astigarraga Davis · 701 Brickell Avenue, 16th Floor · Miami, FL 33131 · 305-372-8282

Eduardo Palmer · Rivero Palmer & Mestre · 2525 Ponce De Leon Boulevard, Suite 1000 · Miami, FL 33134-6046 · 305-445-2500

C. Ryan Reetz · Squire Sanders · http://www.ssd.com · 200 South Biscayne Boulevard, Suite 4000 · Miami, FL 33131-2398 · 305-577-7000

William L. Richey · a · William L. Richey · Miami Center, 34th Floor · 201 South Biscayne Boulevard · Miami, FL 33131-4325 · 305-372-8808

John H. Rooney, Jr. · Shutts & Bowen · http://www.shutts.com · Miami Center, Suite 1500 · 201 South Biscayne Boulevard · Miami, FL 33131 · 305-358-6300

INTERNATIONAL TRADE AND FINANCE LAW

Miami

Cesar L. Alvarez · a · Greenberg Traurig · http://www.gtlaw.com · 1221 Brickell Avenue, 22nd Floor · Miami, FL 33131 · 305-579-0500

Victor M. Alvarez · White & Case · http://www.whitecase.com · Wachovia Financial Center, Suite 4900 · 200 South Biscayne Boulevard · Miami, FL 33131-2352 · 305-371-2700

Bowman Brown · 2% · Shutts & Bowen · http://www.shutts.com · Miami Center, Suite 1500 · 201 South Biscayne Boulevard · Miami, FL 33131 · 305-358-6300

Jose A. Casal · Holland & Knight · http://www.hklaw.com · 701 Brickell Avenue, Suite 3000 · Miami, FL 33131 · 305-374-8500

Luis A. de Armas · Shutts & Bowen · http://www.shutts.com · Miami Center, Suite 1500 · 201 South Biscayne Boulevard · Miami, FL 33131 · 305-358-6300

D. Bruce Hoffman · Hunton & Williams · Mellon Financial Center, Suite 2500 · 1111 Brickell Avenue · Miami, FL 33131 · 305-810-2500

Adolfo E. Jimenez · Holland & Knight · http://www.hklaw.com · 701 Brickell Avenue, Suite 3000 · Miami, FL 33131 · 305-374-8500

Carlos E. Loumiet · Hunton & Williams · Mellon Financial Center, Suite 2500 · 1111 Brickell Avenue · Miami, FL 33131 · 305-810-2500

George Mencio, Jr. · Holland & Knight · http://www.hklaw.com · 701 Brickell Avenue, Suite 3000 · Miami, FL 33131 · 305-374-8500

Patricia Menendez Cambo · Greenberg Traurig · http://www.gtlaw.com · 1221 Brickell Avenue, 22nd Floor · Miami, FL 33131 · 305-579-0500

Luis J. Perez · Hogan & Hartson · Mellon Financial Center, Suite 1900 · 1111 Brickell Avenue · Miami, FL 33131 · 305-459-6500

Stephen K. Roddenberry · Akerman Senterfitt · http://www.akerman.com · One Southeast Third Avenue, 25th Floor · Miami, FL 33131-1714 · 305-374-5600

Miguel A. Zaldivar, Jr. · Hogan & Hartson · Mellon Financial Center, Suite 1900 · 1111 Brickell Avenue Miami, FL 33131 · 305-459-6500

Orlando

Louis Frey, Jr. · Lowndes, Drosdick, Doster, Kantor & Reed · 215 North Eola Drive · Orlando, FL 32801 · 407-843-4600

Thomas M. McAleavey · Holland & Knight · http://www.hklaw.com · 200 South Orange Avenue, Suite 2600 · P.O. Box 1526 · Orlando, FL 32802 · 407-425-8500

Tampa

Chester E. Bacheller · a · Holland & Knight · http://www.hklaw.com · 100 North Tampa Street, Suite 4100 · P.O. Box 1288 · Tampa, FL 33601-1288 · 813-227-8500

Robert J. Grammig · a · Holland & Knight · http://www.hklaw.com · 100 North Tampa Street, Suite 4100 · P.O. Box 1288 · Tampa, FL 33601-1288 · 813-227-8500

Richard A. Jacobson · Fowler White Boggs Banker · 501 East Kennedy Boulevard, Suite 1700 · P.O. Box 1438 · Tampa, FL 33602-5239 · 813-228-7411

William M. Sharp · Sharp & Associates · 4890 West Kennedy Boulevard, Suite 900 · Tampa, FL 33609-1850 · 813-286-4199

LABOR AND EMPLOYMENT LAW

Altamonte Springs

Patricia R. Sigman · Sigman & Sigman · 211 Maitland Avenue · Altamonte Springs, FL 32701 · 407-332-1200

Boca Raton

Allan H. Weitzman · Proskauer Rose · http://www.proskauer.com · 2255 Glades Road, Suite 340 West · Boca Raton, FL 33431-7383 · 561-241-7400

Bonita Springs

John E. Lyncheski · a · Cohen & Grigsby · 27200 Riverview Center Boulevard, Suite 309 · Bonita Springs, FL 34134-4317 · 239-390-1900

Clearwater

J. Robert McCormack · Persante & McCormack · Building 15 · 2555 Enterprise Road · Clearwater, FL 33763-1118 · 727-796-7666

Joan M. Vecchioli · Johnson, Pope, Bokor, Ruppel & Burns · http://www.jpfirm.com · 911 Chestnut Street · P.O. Box 1368 · Clearwater, FL 33756 · 727-461-1818

Coral Gables

Robert L. Norton · a · Allen, Norton & Blue · http://www.anblaw.com · 121 Majorca Avenue, Suite 300 · Coral Gables, FL 33134 · 305-445-7801

Susan Potter Norton · a · Allen, Norton & Blue · http://www.anblaw.com · 121 Majorca Avenue, Suite 300 · Coral Gables, FL 33134 · 305-445-7801

Peter L. Sampo · Allen, Norton & Blue · http://www.anblaw.com · 121 Majorca Avenue, Suite 300 · Coral Gables, FL 33134 · 305-445-7801

Donald Slesnick · Slesnick & Casey · 2701 Ponce de Leon Boulevard, Suite 200 · Coral Gables, FL 33134-6020 · 305-448-5672

Robert A. Sugarman · 2) · Sugarman & Susskind · 100 Miracle Mile, Suite 300 · Coral Gables, FL 33134-5429 · 305-529-2801

Howard S. Susskind · 2) · Sugarman & Susskind · 100 Miracle Mile, Suite 300 · Coral Gables, FL 33134-5429 · 305-529-2801

Robert E. Weisberg · 2) · Robert E. Weisberg · 1450 Madruga Avenue, Suite 302 · Coral Gables, FL 33146-3164 · 305-666-6095

Fort Lauderdale

Charles S. Caulkins · Fisher & Phillips · http://www.laborlawyers.com · 450 East Las Olas Boulevard, Suite 800 · Fort Lauderdale, FL 33301 · 954-525-4800

James Polkinghorn · Fisher & Phillips · http://www.laborlawyers.com · 450 East Las Olas Boulevard, Suite 800 · Fort Lauderdale, FL 33301 · 954-525-4800

Christopher D. Robinson · Fisher & Phillips · http://www.laborlawyers.com · 450 East Las Olas Boulevard, Suite 800 · Fort Lauderdale, FL 33301 · 954-525-4800

Stuart A. Rosenfeldt · Rothstein Rosenfeldt Adler · Bank of America Building, Suite 1650 · 401 East Las Olas Boulevard · Fort Lauderdale, FL 33301 · 954-522-3456

Scott W. Rothstein · Rothstein Rosenfeldt Adler · Bank of America Building, Suite 1650 · 401 East Las Olas Boulevard · Fort Lauderdale, FL 33301 · 954-522-3456

Leonard K. Samuels · Berger Singerman · http://www.bergersingerman.com · 350 East Las Olas Boulevard, Suite 1000 · Fort Lauderdale, FL 33301 · 954-525-9900

Jon K. Stage · Stearns Weaver Miller Weissler Alhadeff & Sitterson · 200 East Las Olas Boulevard, 21st Floor, Penthouse A · Fort Lauderdale, FL 33301 · 954-462-9500

Cathy M. Stutin · Fisher & Phillips · http://www.laborlawyers.com · 450 East Las Olas Boulevard, Suite 800 · Fort Lauderdale, FL 33301 · 954-525-4800

Gainesville

Neil Chonin · a · Southern Legal Council Inc · 1229 North West 12th Avenue · Gainesville, FL 32601 · 352-271-8890

Paul A. Donnelly · Donnelly & Gross · 204 West University Avenue, Suite Five · Gainesville, FL 32601 · 352-374-4001

Laura A. Gross · Donnelly & Gross · 204 West University Avenue, Suite Five · Gainesville, FL 32601 · 352-374-4001

Larry G. Turner · Turner & Jones · 204 West University Avenue, Suite Seven · Gainesville, FL 32601-5205 · 352-372-4263

Jacksonville

William H. Andrews · 2) · GrayRobinson · 50 North Laura Street, Suite 1100 · Jacksonville, FL 32202 · 904-598-9929

Scott S. Cairns · McGuireWoods · http://www.mcguirewoods.com · Bank of America Tower, Suite 3300 · 50 North Laura Street · Jacksonville, FL 32202-3661 · 904-798-3200

Patrick D. Coleman · 2) · GrayRobinson · 50 North Laura Street, Suite 1100 · Jacksonville, FL 32202 · 904-598-9929

Peter Reed Corbin · a · Ford & Harrison · http://www.fordharrison.com · 225 Water Street, Suite 710 · Jacksonville, FL 32202 · 904-357-2000

Thomas A. Delegal III · Delegal Law Offices · 424 East Monroe Street · Jacksonville, FL 32202 · 904-633-5000

Michael J. Dewberry · Fowler White Boggs Banker · 50 North Laura Street, Suite 2200 · Jacksonville, FL 32202 · 904-598-3100

John F. Dickinson · a · Constangy, Brooks & Smith · http://www.constangy.com · 200 West Forsyth Street, Suite 1700 · P.O. Box 41099 · Jacksonville, FL 32203-1099 · 904-356-8900

John E. Duvall · Ford & Harrison · http://www.fordharrison.com · 225 Water Street, Suite 710 · Jacksonville, FL 32202 · 904-357-2000

Guy O. Farmer II · 2% · Holland & Knight · http://www.hklaw.com · 50 North Laura Street, Suite 3900 · P.O. Box 52687 · Jacksonville, FL 32202-2687 · 904-353-2000

Michael K. Grogan · 2) · Allen, Norton & Blue · http://www.anblaw.com · 800 West Monroe Street · Jacksonville, FL 32202 · 904-562-4480

G. Thomas Harper · a · Harper & Gerlach · 4110 Southpoint Boulevard, Suite 228 · Jacksonville, FL 32216 · 904-296-7000

Eric J. Holshouser · a · Fowler White Boggs Banker · 50 North Laura Street, Suite 2200 · Jacksonville, FL 32202 · 904-598-3100

Kevin E. Hyde · a · Foley & Lardner · One Independent Drive, Suite 1300 · P.O. Box 240 · Jacksonville, FL 32201 · 904-359-2000

F. Damon Kitchen · Constangy, Brooks & Smith · http://www.constangy.com · 200 West Forsyth Street, Suite 1700 · P.O. Box 41099 · Jacksonville, FL 32203-1099 · 904-356-8900

Richard N. Margulies · Jackson Lewis · http://www.jacksonlewis.com · Aetna Building, 12th Floor · 841 Prudential Drive · Jacksonville, FL 32207 · 904-638-2655

Michael G. Prendergast · GrayRobinson · 50 North Laura Street, Suite 1100 · Jacksonville, FL 32202 · 904-598-9929

Robert G. Riegel, Jr. · Fowler White Boggs Banker · 50 North Laura Street, Suite 2200 · Jacksonville, FL 32202 · 904-598-3100

David B. Sacks · Law Office of David B. Sacks · 1017 LaSalle Street · Jacksonville, FL 32207 · 904-634-1122

William J. Sheppard · a · Sheppard, White,Thomas & Kachergus · 215 North Washington Street · Jacksonville, FL 32202-2808 · 904-356-9661

Archibald J. Thomas III · Archibald J. Thomas, III · Riverplace Tower, Suite 1640 · 1301 Riverplace Boulevard · Jacksonville, FL 32207 · 904-396-2322

Kenneth B. Wright · Bledsoe, Jacobson, Schmidt & Wright · 1301 Riverplace Boulevard, Suite 1818 · Jacksonville, FL 32207 · 904-398-1818

Maitland

John M. Finnigan · Finnigan Law Firm · 1700 Maitland Avenue · Maitland, FL 32751-3321 · 407-478-3700

Melbourne

Andrew S. Hament · Ford & Harrison · http://www.fordharrison.com · One Harbor Place, Suite 501 · 1901 South Harbor City Boulevard · Melbourne, FL 32901 · 321-724-5970

Miami

David E. Block · Jackson Lewis · http://www.jacksonlewis.com · One Biscayne Tower, Suite 3500 · Two South Biscayne Boulevard · Miami, FL 33131 · 305-577-7600

James S. Bramnick · Akerman Senterfitt · http://www.akerman.com · One Southeast Third Avenue, 25th Floor · Miami, FL 33131-1714 · 305-374-5600

Joan M. Canny · Morgan Lewis & Bockius · 5300 Wachovia Financial Center · 200 South Biscayne Boulevard · Miami, FL 33131-2339 · 305-415-3000

Kelly-Ann G. Cartwright · Holland & Knight · http://www.hklaw.com · 701 Brickell Avenue, Suite 3000 · Miami, FL 33131 · 305-374-8500

Michael W. Casey III · 2) · Epstein, Becker & Green · Wachovia Financial Center, Suite 4300 · 200 South Biscayne Boulevard · Miami, FL 33131 · 305-579-3200

Mark R. Cheskin · Hogan & Hartson · Mellon Financial Center, Suite 1900 · 1111 Brickell Avenue · Miami, FL 33131 · 305-459-6500

Terence G. Connor · Hunton & Williams · Mellon Financial Center, Suite 2500 · 1111 Brickell Avenue · Miami, FL 33131 · 305-810-2500

James C. Crosland · Bryant Miller & Olive · One Biscayne Tower, Suite 1480 · Two South Biscayne Boulevard · Miami, FL 33131 · 305-374-7349

Patrick G. DeBlasio III · Jackson Lewis · http://www.jacksonlewis.com · One Biscayne Tower, Suite 3500 · Two South Biscayne Boulevard · Miami, FL 33131 · 305-577-7600

David M. DeMaio · Ogletree Deakins · http://www.ogletreedeakins.com · 701 Brickell Avenue, Suite 2020 · Miami, FL 33131 · 305-374-0506

Susan N. Eisenberg · Akerman Senterfitt · http://www.akerman.com · One Southeast Third Avenue, 25th Floor · Miami, FL 33131-1714 · 305-374-5600

Joseph Z. Fleming · 2% · Greenberg Traurig · http://www.gtlaw.com · 1221 Brickell Avenue, 22nd Floor · Miami, FL 33131 · 305-579-0500

Pedro P. Forment · Ford & Harrison · http://www.fordharrison.com · 100 Southeast Second Street, Suite 4500 · Miami, FL 33131 · 305-808-2100

W. Russell Hamilton III · Stearns Weaver Miller Weissler Alhadeff & Sitterson · Museum Tower, Suite 2200 · 150 West Flagler Street · Miami, FL 33130 · 305-789-3200

Christopher P. Hammon · Ogletree Deakins · http://www.ogletreedeakins.com · 701 Brickell Avenue, Suite 2020 · Miami, FL 33131 · 305-374-0506

Marilyn J. Holifield · Holland & Knight · http://www.hklaw.com · 701 Brickell Avenue, Suite 3000 · Miami, FL 33131 · 305-374-8500

Robert T. Kofman · Stearns Weaver Miller Weissler Alhadeff & Sitterson · Museum Tower, Suite 2200 · 150 West Flagler Street · Miami, FL 33130 · 305-789-3200

Kathleen M. Phillips · Phillips Richard & Rind · 9360 Southwest 72nd Street, Suite 283 · Miami, FL 33173-3283 · 305-412-8322

William R. Radford · Ford & Harrison · http://www.fordharrison.com · 100 Southeast Second Street, Suite 4500 · Miami, FL 33131 · 305-808-2100

Ronald M. Rosengarten · Greenberg Traurig · http://www.gtlaw.com · 1221 Brickell Avenue, 22nd Floor Miami, FL 33131 · 305-579-0500

Rene F. Ruiz · Ford & Harrison · http://www.fordharrison.com · 100 Southeast Second Street, Suite 4500 · Miami, FL 33131 · 305-808-2100

Samuel A. Terilli, Jr. · Ford & Harrison · http://www.fordharrison.com · 100 Southeast Second Street, Suite 4500 · Miami, FL 33131 · 305-808-2100

Patricia H. Thompson · Carlton Fields · 4000 International Place · 100 Southeast Second Street · P.O. Box 019101 · Miami, FL 33131-9101 · 305-530-0050

Robert S. Turk · Stearns Weaver Miller Weissler Alhadeff & Sitterson · Museum Tower, Suite 2200 · 150 West Flagler Street · Miami, FL 33130 · 305-789-3200

Richard D. Tuschman · Epstein, Becker & Green · Wachovia Financial Center, Suite 4300 · 200 South Biscayne Boulevard · Miami, FL 33131 · 305-579-3200

Courtney B. Wilson · a · Littler Mendelson · One Biscayne Tower, Suite 1500 · Two South Biscayne Boulevard · Miami, FL 33131 · 305-400-7500

Mark E. Zelek · Morgan Lewis & Bockius · 5300 Wachovia Financial Center · 200 South Biscayne Boulevard · Miami, FL 33131-2339 · 305-415-3000

Naples

Jon D. Fishbane · Roetzel & Andress · http://www.ralaw.com · Trianon Centre, Third Floor · 850 Park Shore Drive · Naples, FL 34103 · 239-649-6200

Orlando

Lori R. Benton · Ford & Harrison · http://www.fordharrison.com · 300 South Orange Avenue, Suite 1300 · P.O. Box 60 · Orlando, FL 32801 · 407-418-2300

James G. Brown · 2) · Ford & Harrison · http://www.fordharrison.com · 300 South Orange Avenue, Suite 1300 · P.O. Box 60 · Orlando, FL 32801 · 407-418-2300

Carlos J. Burruezo · Littler Mendelson · 4767 New Broad Street · Orlando, FL 32814 · 407-514-2637

Joyce Ackerbaum Cox · Baker Hostetler · http://www.bakerlaw.com · Sun Trust Center, Suite 2300 · 200 South Orange Avenue · Orlando, FL 32801-3432 · 407-649-4000

Joseph Egan, Jr. · 2) · Egan, Lev & Siwica · 231 East Colonial Drive · P.O. Box 2231 · Orlando, FL 32802 · 407-422-1400

Charles Robinson Fawsett · Shutts & Bowen · http://www.shutts.com · 300 South Orange Avenue, Suite 1000 · Orlando, FL 32801 · 407-423-3200

Thomas C. Garwood, Jr. · 2) · Ford & Harrison · http://www.fordharrison.com · 300 South Orange Avenue, Suite 1300 · P.O. Box 60 · Orlando, FL 32801 · 407-418-2300

Dorothy F. Green · Latham, Shuker, Barker, Eden & Beaudine · 390 North Orange Avenue, Suite 600 · P.O. Box 3353 · Orlando, FL 32801 · 407-481-5800

Mary Ruth Houston · Shutts & Bowen · http://www.shutts.com · 300 South Orange Avenue, Suite 1000 · Orlando, FL 32801 · 407-423-3200

David V. Kornreich · 2) · Fisher & Phillips · http://www.laborlawyers.com · 1250 Lincoln Plaza · 300 South Orange Avenue · Orlando, FL 32801 · 407-541-0888

Randall W. Lord · Jackson Lewis · http://www.jacksonlewis.com · 390 North Orange Avenue, Suite 1285 · Orlando, FL 32801-1641 · 407-246-8440

Jeffrey E. Mandel · Fisher & Phillips · http://www.laborlawyers.com · 1250 Lincoln Plaza · 300 South Orange Avenue · Orlando, FL 32801 · 407-541-0888

Allen J. McKenna · Ford & Harrison · http://www.fordharrison.com · 300 South Orange Avenue, Suite 1300 · P.O. Box 60 · Orlando, FL 32801 · 407-418-2300

Susan K. McKenna · a · Jackson Lewis · http://www.jacksonlewis.com · 390 North Orange Avenue, Suite 1285 · Orlando, FL 32801-1641 · 407-246-8440

Patrick M. Muldowney · Baker Hostetler · http://www.bakerlaw.com · Sun Trust Center, Suite 2300 · 200 South Orange Avenue · Orlando, FL 32801-3432 · 407-649-4000

Daniel P. O'Gorman · Ford & Harrison · http://www.fordharrison.com · 300 South Orange Avenue, Suite 1300 · P.O. Box 60 · Orlando, FL 32801 · 407-418-2300

Morey Raiskin · Lowndes, Drosdick, Doster, Kantor & Reed · 215 North Eola Drive · Orlando, FL 32801 · 407-843-4600

M. Susan Sacco · Ford & Harrison · http://www.fordharrison.com · 300 South Orange Avenue, Suite 1300 P.O. Box 60 · Orlando, FL 32801 · 407-418-2300

Kevin W. Shaughnessy · Baker Hostetler · http://www.bakerlaw.com · Sun Trust Center, Suite 2300 · 200 South Orange Avenue · Orlando, FL 32801-3432 · 407-649-4000

Susan T. Spradley · GrayRobinson · 301 East Pine Street, Suite 1400 · P.O. Box 3068 · Orlando, FL 32802-3068 · 407-843-8880

Charles E. Williams, Jr. · Littler Mendelson · 4767 New Broad Street · Orlando, FL 32814 · 407-514-2637

Kay L. Wolf · Ford & Harrison · http://www.fordharrison.com · 300 South Orange Avenue, Suite 1300 · P.O. Box 60 · Orlando, FL 32801 · 407-418-2300

Benton N. Wood · Fisher & Phillips · http://www.laborlawyers.com · 1250 Lincoln Plaza · 300 South Orange Avenue · Orlando, FL 32801 · 407-541-0888

Donald C. Works III · Jackson Lewis · http://www.jacksonlewis.com · 390 North Orange Avenue, Suite 1285 · Orlando, FL 32801-1641 · 407-246-8440

Aaron L. Zandy · Ford & Harrison · http://www.fordharrison.com · 300 South Orange Avenue, Suite 1300 P.O. Box 60 · Orlando, FL 32801 · 407-418-2300

Palm Harbor

Wolfgang M. Florin · Florin Roebig · 777 Alderman Road · Palm Harbor, FL 34683 · 727-786-5000

Christopher D. Gray · Florin Roebig · 777 Alderman Road · Palm Harbor, FL 34683 · 727-786-5000

David J. Linesch · a · The Linesch Firm · 700 Bee Pond Road · Palm Harbor, FL 34683 · 727-786-0000

Angela E. Outten · Reeser, Rodnite, Outten & Zdravko · 3411 Palm Harbor Boulevard, Suite A · Palm Harbor, FL 34683 · 727-787-5919

Pensacola

Ralph A. Peterson · Beggs & Lane · 501 Commendencia Street · P.O. Box 12950 · Pensacola, FL 32591 · 850-432-2451

Plantation

Robert D. Klausner · a · Klausner & Kaufman · 10059 Northwest First Court · Plantation, FL 33324 · 954-916-1202

St. Petersburg

Phyllis J. Towzey · Phyllis J. Towzey · http://www.towzey.com · The Kress Building, Suite 401 · 475 Central Avenue · St. Petersburg, FL 33701-3846 · 727-895-1200

Tallahassee

Leonard A. Carson · Carson & Adkins · 2958 Wellington Circle North, Suite 200 · Tallahassee, FL 32309 · 850-894-1009

Kelly Overstreet Johnson · Broad and Cassel · Sun Trust Bank Building, Suite 400 · 215 South Monroe Street · Tallahassee, FL 32301 · 850-681-6810

Robert E. Larkin III · Allen, Norton & Blue · http://www.anblaw.com · 906 North Monroe Street · Tallahassee, FL 32303 · 850-561-3503

James W. Linn · Lewis, Longman & Walker · http://www.llw-law.com · 2600 Centennial Place, Suite 100 Tallahassee, FL 32308 · 850-222-5702

Michael Mattimore · Allen, Norton & Blue · http://www.anblaw.com · 906 North Monroe Street · Tallahassee, FL 32303 · 850-561-3503

William E. Powers, Jr. · Allen, Norton & Blue · http://www.anblaw.com · 906 North Monroe Street · Tallahassee, FL 32303 · 850-561-3503

Robert J. Sniffen · Sniffen Law Firm · 211 East Call Street · Tallahassee, FL 32301 · 850-205-1996

Tampa

W. Reynolds Allen · a · Allen, Norton & Blue · http://www.anblaw.com · Hyde Park Plaza, Suite 225 · 324 South Hyde Park Avenue · Tampa, FL 33606 · 813-251-1210

John-Edward Alley · 2% · Ford & Harrison · http://www.fordharrison.com · 101 East Kennedy Boulevard, Suite 900 · Tampa, FL 33602-5133 · 813-261-7800

George Barford · Carlton Fields · Corporate Center Three at International Plaza, Suite 1000 · 4221 West Boy Scout Boulevard · Tampa, FL 33607 · 813-223-7000

Cathy Jo Beveridge · Fowler White Boggs Banker · 501 East Kennedy Boulevard, Suite 1700 · P.O. Box 1438 · Tampa, FL 33602-5239 · 813-228-7411

Heather B. Brock · Fowler White Boggs Banker · 501 East Kennedy Boulevard, Suite 1700 · P.O. Box 1438 · Tampa, FL 33602-5239 · 813-228-7411

Frank E. Brown · Macfarlane Ferguson & McMullen · One Tampa City Center, Suite 2000 · 201 North Franklin Street · P.O. Box 1531 · Tampa, FL 33601 · 813-273-4200

Karen Meyer Buesing · Akerman Senterfitt · http://www.akerman.com · SunTrust Financial Centre, Suite 1700 · 401 East Jackson Street · Tampa, FL 33602-5803 · 813-223-7333

William B. deMeza, Jr. · Holland & Knight · http://www.hklaw.com · 100 North Tampa Street, Suite 4100 · P.O. Box 1288 · Tampa, FL 33601-1288 · 813-227-8500

Matthew K. Fenton · Wenzel & Fenton · 633 North Franklin Street, Suite 500 · Tampa, FL 33602 · 813-224-0431

Theresa M. Gallion · Fisher & Phillips · http://www.laborlawyers.com · SunTrust Financial Centre, Suite 2525 · 401 East Jackson Street · Tampa, FL 33602 · 813-769-7500

Thomas M. Gonzalez · 2) · Thompson, Sizemore, Gonzalez & Hearing · http://www.tsg-law.com · One Tampa City Center, Suite 1600 · 201 North Franklin Street · P.O. Box 639 · Tampa, FL 33601 · 813-273-0050

Tony B. Griffin · a · Ruden, McClosky, Smith, Schuster & Russell · SunTrust Financial Centre, Suite 2700 · 401 East Jackson Street · Tampa, FL 33602 · 813-222-6600

Robert D. Hall, Jr. · a · Ford & Harrison · http://www.fordharrison.com · 101 East Kennedy Boulevard, Suite 900 · Tampa, FL 33602-5133 · 813-261-7800

Mark A. Hanley · Glenn, Rasmussen, Fogarty & Hooker · http://www.glennrasmussen.com · 100 South Ashley Drive, Suite 1300 · Tampa, FL 33602 · 813-229-3333

Gregory A. Hearing · Thompson, Sizemore, Gonzalez & Hearing · http://www.tsg-law.com · One Tampa City Center, Suite 1600 · 201 North Franklin Street · P.O. Box 639 · Tampa, FL 33601 · 813-273-0050

Tracey K. Jaensch · Ford & Harrison · http://www.fordharrison.com · 101 East Kennedy Boulevard, Suite 900 · Tampa, FL 33602-5133 · 813-261-7800

Kevin D. Johnson · Thompson, Sizemore, Gonzalez & Hearing · http://www.tsg-law.com · One Tampa City Center, Suite 1600 · 201 North Franklin Street · P.O. Box 639 · Tampa, FL 33601 · 813-273-0050

Mark F. Kelly · a · Kelly & McKee · 1718 East Seventh Avenue, Suite 301 · Tampa, FL 33605 · 813-248-6400

Mary A. Lau · Lau, Lane, Pieper, Conley & McCreadie · 100 South Ashley Drive, Suite 1700 · P.O. Box 838 · Tampa, FL 33601-0838 · 813-229-2121

Michael D. Malfitano · a · Constangy, Brooks & Smith · http://www.constangy.com · 100 North Tampa Street, Suite 3350 · Tampa, FL 33602 · 813-223-7166

John P. McAdams · Carlton Fields · Corporate Center Three at International Plaza, Suite 1000 · 4221 West Boy Scout Boulevard · Tampa, FL 33607 · 813-223-7000

Dennis M. McClelland · Phelps Dunbar · http://www.phelpsdunbar.com · 100 South Ashley Drive, Suite 1900 · Tampa, FL 33602-5311 · 813-472-7550

Richard C. McCrea, Jr. · a · Greenberg Traurig · http://www.gtlaw.com · Courthouse Plaza, Suite 100 · 625 East Twiggs Street · Tampa, FL 33602 · 813-318-5700

Janet Goldberg McEnery · Macfarlane Ferguson & McMullen · One Tampa City Center, Suite 2000 · 201 North Franklin Street · P.O. Box 1531 · Tampa, FL 33601 · 813-273-4200

Robert F. McKee · Kelly & McKee · 1718 East Seventh Avenue, Suite 301 · Tampa, FL 33605 · 813-248-6400

Edmund J. McKenna · Ford & Harrison · http://www.fordharrison.com · 101 East Kennedy Boulevard, Suite 900 · Tampa, FL 33602-5133 · 813-261-7800

Grant D. Petersen · Ogletree Deakins · http://www.ogletreedeakins.com · 100 North Tampa Street, Suite 3600 · Tampa, FL 33602 · 813-289-1247

John E. Phillips · Phelps Dunbar · http://www.phelpsdunbar.com · 100 South Ashley Drive, Suite 1900 · Tampa, FL 33602-5311 · 813-472-7550

Tammie L. Rattray · Ford & Harrison · http://www.fordharrison.com · 101 East Kennedy Boulevard, Suite 900 · Tampa, FL 33602-5133 · 813-261-7800

John W. Robinson IV · a · Fowler White Boggs Banker · 501 East Kennedy Boulevard, Suite 1700 · P.O. Box 1438 · Tampa, FL 33602-5239 · 813-228-7411

Cynthia N. Sass · Cynthia N. Sass · 601 West Drive Martin Luther King, Jr. Boulevard · Tampa, FL 33603 · 813-251-5599

Scott T. Silverman · Akerman Senterfitt · http://www.akerman.com · SunTrust Financial Centre, Suite 1700 · 401 East Jackson Street · Tampa, FL 33602-5803 · 813-223-7333

Sam Smith · Burr & Smith · 442 West Kennedy Boulevard, Suite 300 · Tampa, FL 33606 · 813-253-2010

Thomas T. Steele · Steele, Watson & Benner · 201 East Kennedy Boulevard, Suite 425 · Tampa, FL 33602 · 813-223-2060

David J. Stefany · Allen, Norton & Blue · http://www.anblaw.com · Hyde Park Plaza, Suite 225 · 324 South Hyde Park Avenue · Tampa, FL 33606 · 813-251-1210

James R. Wiley · Carlton Fields · Corporate Center Three at International Plaza, Suite 1000 · 4221 West Boy Scout Boulevard · Tampa, FL 33607 · 813-223-7000

Peter W. Zinober · 2) · Greenberg Traurig · http://www.gtlaw.com · Courthouse Plaza, Suite 100 · 625 East Twiggs Street · Tampa, FL 33602 · 813-318-5700

Kevin D. Zwetsch · Fowler White Boggs Banker · 501 East Kennedy Boulevard, Suite 1700 · P.O. Box 1438 · Tampa, FL 33602-5239 · 813-228-7411

West Palm Beach

G. Joseph Curley · Gunster, Yoakley & Stewart · Phillips Point, Suite 500 East · 777 South Flagler Drive West Palm Beach, FL 33401-6194 · 561-655-1980

Christine D. Hanley · Christine D. Hanley & Associates · http://www.cdhanley.com · 1000 Southern Boulevard, Second Floor · West Palm Beach, FL 33405 · 561-659-5646

Patricia E. Lowry · Squire Sanders · http://www.ssd.com · Phillips Point West, Suite 1900 · 777 South Flagler Drive · West Palm Beach, FL 33401-6198 · 561-650-7200

I. Jeffrey Pheterson · Buckingham, Doolittle & Burroughs · http://www.bdblaw.com · Northbridge Centre · 515 North Flagler Drive · West Palm Beach, FL 33401 · 561-653-3318

John S. Trimper · Jones, Foster, Johnston & Stubbs · 505 South Flagler Drive, Suite 1100 · P.O. Box 3475 · West Palm Beach, FL 33402-3475 · 561-659-3000

Winter Park

Wayne L. Helsby · Allen, Norton & Blue · http://www.anblaw.com · 1477 West Fairbanks Avenue, Suite 100 · Winter Park, FL 32789-7113 · 407-571-2152

Travis R. Hollifield · Hollifield Legal Centre for Women · 147 East Lyman Avenue, Suite C · Winter Park, FL 32789 · 407-599-9590

Mark E. Levitt · Allen, Norton & Blue · http://www.anblaw.com · 1477 West Fairbanks Avenue, Suite 100 Winter Park, FL 32789-7113 · 407-571-2152

Jill S. Schwartz · Jill S. Schwartz & Associates · 180 North Park Avenue, Suite 200 · Winter Park, FL 32789-7401 · 407-647-8911

Gary D. Wilson · Jill S. Schwartz & Associates · 180 North Park Avenue, Suite 200 · Winter Park, FL 32789-7401 · 407-647-8911

Winter Springs

Thomas J. Pilacek · 2) · Pilacek & Associates · Red Willow Plaza · 5844 Red Bug Lake Road · Winter Springs, FL 32708-5011 · 407-660-9595

LAND USE & ZONING LAW

Fort Lauderdale

Susan F. Delegal · Billing Cochran Heath Lyles Mauro & Anderson · 888 Southeast Third Avenue, Suite 301 · Fort Lauderdale, FL 33316-1159 · 954-764-7150

Scott J. Fuerst · Ruden, McClosky, Smith, Schuster & Russell · 200 East Broward Boulevard · P.O. Box 1900 · Fort Lauderdale, FL 33302 · 954-764-6660

Samuel S. Goren · Goren, Cherof, Doody & Ezrol · 3099 East Commercial Boulevard, Suite 200 · Fort Lauderdale, FL 33308-4500 · 954-771-4500

Donald R. Hall · Gunster, Yoakley & Stewart · Las Olas Centre, Suite 1400 · 450 East Las Olas Boulevard Fort Lauderdale, FL 33301 · 954-462-2000

Robert B. Lochrie III · Lochrie & Chakas · 1401 East Broward Boulevard, Suite 200 · Fort Lauderdale, FL 33301 · 954-779-1119

Donald C. McClosky · 2% · Ruden, McClosky, Smith, Schuster & Russell · 200 East Broward Boulevard · P.O. Box 1900 · Fort Lauderdale, FL 33302 · 954-764-6660

Dennis D. Mele · a · Ruden, McClosky, Smith, Schuster & Russell · 200 East Broward Boulevard · P.O. Box 1900 · Fort Lauderdale, FL 33302 · 954-764-6660

Debbie M. Orshefsky · Greenberg Traurig · http://www.gtlaw.com · 401 East Las Olas Boulevard, Suite 2000 · Fort Lauderdale, FL 33301 · 954-765-0500

Fort Myers

Beverly Grady · Roetzel & Andress · http://www.ralaw.com · 2320 First Street, Suite 1000 · Fort Myers, FL 33901 · 239-337-3850

James T. Humphrey · Fowler White Boggs Banker · 2235 First Street · Fort Myers, FL 33901 · 239-334-7892

Jacksonville

Brenna M. Durden · Lewis, Longman & Walker · http://www.llw-law.com · 245 Riverside Avenue, Suite 150 · Jacksonville, FL 32202 · 904-353-6410

Theodore R. Hainline, Jr. · Rogers Towers · 1301 Riverplace Boulevard, Suite 1500 · Jacksonville, FL 32207 · 904-398-3911

Susan C. McDonald · Rogers Towers · 1301 Riverplace Boulevard, Suite 1500 · Jacksonville, FL 32207 · 904-398-3911

John G. Metcalf · Pappas Metcalf Jenks & Miller · 245 Riverside Avenue, Suite 400 · Jacksonville, FL 32202-4907 · 904-353-1980

M. Lynn Pappas · a · Pappas Metcalf Jenks & Miller · 245 Riverside Avenue, Suite 400 · Jacksonville, FL 32202-4907 · 904-353-1980

Lake Wales

Jack P. Brandon · Peterson & Myers · http://www.petersonmyers.com · 130 East Central Avenue · Lake Wales, FL 33853 · 863-676-7611

Miami

Kerri L. Barsh · Greenberg Traurig · http://www.gtlaw.com · 1221 Brickell Avenue, 22nd Floor · Miami, FL 33131 · 305-579-0500

Jeffrey S. Bass · Shubin & Bass · http://www.shubinbass.com · 46 Southwest First Street, Third Floor · Miami, FL 33130 · 305-381-6060

Jeffrey S. Bercow · Bercow & Radell · 200 South Biscayne Boulevard, Suite 850 · Miami, FL 33131 · 305-374-5300

Lucia A. Dougherty · Greenberg Traurig · http://www.gtlaw.com · 1221 Brickell Avenue, 22nd Floor · Miami, FL 33131 · 305-579-0500

Joseph Z. Fleming · 2% · Greenberg Traurig · http://www.gtlaw.com · 1221 Brickell Avenue, 22nd Floor · Miami, FL 33131 · 305-579-0500

Joseph G. Goldstein · Holland & Knight · http://www.hklaw.com · 701 Brickell Avenue, Suite 3000 · Miami, FL 33131 · 305-374-8500

Juan J. Mayol Lopez, Jr. · Holland & Knight · http://www.hklaw.com · 701 Brickell Avenue, Suite 3000 · Miami, FL 33131 · 305-374-8500

Carter N. McDowell · Bilzin Sumberg Baena Price & Axelrod · Wachovia Financial Center, Suite 2500 · 200 South Biscayne Boulevard · Miami, FL 33131 · 305-374-7580

Eileen Ball Mehta · a · Bilzin Sumberg Baena Price & Axelrod · Wachovia Financial Center, Suite 2500 · 200 South Biscayne Boulevard · Miami, FL 33131 · 305-374-7580

Stanley B. Price · 2) · Bilzin Sumberg Baena Price & Axelrod · Wachovia Financial Center, Suite 2500 · 200 South Biscayne Boulevard · Miami, FL 33131 · 305-374-7580

Clifford A. Schulman · 2) · Greenberg Traurig · http://www.gtlaw.com · 1221 Brickell Avenue, 22nd Floor · Miami, FL 33131 · 305-579-0500

John K. Shubin · Shubin & Bass · http://www.shubinbass.com · 46 Southwest First Street, Third Floor · Miami, FL 33130 · 305-381-6060

Robert H. Traurig · 2% · Greenberg Traurig · http://www.gtlaw.com · 1221 Brickell Avenue, 22nd Floor · Miami, FL 33131 · 305-579-0500

Naples

R. Bruce Anderson · Roetzel & Andress · http://www.ralaw.com · Trianon Centre, Third Floor · 850 Park Shore Drive · Naples, FL 34103 · 239-649-6200

John M. Passidomo · Cheffy Passidomo Wilson & Johnson · 821 Fifth Avenue South, Suite 201 · Naples, FL 34102 · 239-261-9300

George L. Varnadoe · Cheffy Passidomo Wilson & Johnson · 821 Fifth Avenue South, Suite 201 · Naples, FL 34102 · 239-261-9300

Orlando

Cecelia Bonifay · Akerman Senterfitt · http://www.akerman.com · CNL Center II at City Commons, Suite 1200 · 420 South Orange Avenue · Orlando, FL 32801-3336 · 407-423-4000

C. David Brown II · Broad and Cassel · 390 North Orange Avenue, Suite 1400 · Orlando, FL 32801-4961 407-839-4200

Miranda F. Fitzgerald · a · Lowndes, Drosdick, Doster, Kantor & Reed · 215 North Eola Drive · Orlando, FL 32801 · 407-843-4600

Hal H. Kantor · a · Lowndes, Drosdick, Doster, Kantor & Reed · 215 North Eola Drive · Orlando, FL 32801 · 407-843-4600

Nicholas A. Pope · Lowndes, Drosdick, Doster, Kantor & Reed · 215 North Eola Drive · Orlando, FL 32801 · 407-843-4600

Thomas T. Ross · a · Akerman Senterfitt · http://www.akerman.com · CNL Center II at City Commons, Suite 1200 · 420 South Orange Avenue · Orlando, FL 32801-3336 · 407-423-4000

Roger W. Sims · a · Holland & Knight · http://www.hklaw.com · 200 South Orange Avenue, Suite 2600 · P.O. Box 1526 · Orlando, FL 32802 · 407-425-8500

R. Duke Woodson · Foley & Lardner · 111 North Orange Avenue, Suite 1800 · P.O. Box 2193 · Orlando, FL 32802-2193 · 407-423-7656

Sarasota

Charles D. Bailey, Jr. · Williams Parker Harrison Dietz & Getzen · 200 South Orange Avenue · Sarasota, FL 34236 · 941-366-4800

Michael J. Furen · Icard, Merrill, Cullis, Timm, Furen & Ginsburg · http://www.icardmerrill.com · 2033 Main Street, Suite 500 & 600 · P.O. Drawer 4195 · Sarasota, FL 34230 · 941-366-8100

William W. Merrill III · Icard, Merrill, Cullis, Timm, Furen & Ginsburg · http://www.icardmerrill.com · 2033 Main Street, Suite 500 & 600 · P.O. Drawer 4195 · Sarasota, FL 34230 · 941-366-8100

Tallahassee

Robert C. Apgar · Greenberg Traurig · http://www.gtlaw.com · 101 East College Avenue · Tallahassee, FL 32301 · 850-222-6891

Martha Harrell Chumbler · Carlton Fields · Suntrust Building, Suite 500 · 215 South Monroe Street · Tallahassee, FL 32301 · 850-224-1585

W. Douglas Hall · Carlton Fields · Suntrust Building, Suite 500 · 215 South Monroe Street · Tallahassee, FL 32301 · 850-224-1585

Wade L. Hopping · 2) · Hopping Green & Sams · http://www.hgslaw.com · 123 South Calhoun Street · P.O. Box 6526 · Tallahassee, FL 32314 · 850-222-7598

Margaret-Ray Kemper · Ruden, McClosky, Smith, Schuster & Russell · 215 South Monroe Street, Suite 815 · Tallahassee, FL 32301 · 850-412-2000

Nancy G. Linnan · Carlton Fields · Suntrust Building, Suite 500 · 215 South Monroe Street · Tallahassee, FL 32301 · 850-224-1585

Frank E. Matthews · a · Hopping Green & Sams · http://www.hgslaw.com · 123 South Calhoun Street · P.O. Box 6526 · Tallahassee, FL 32314 · 850-222-7598

David L. Powell · Hopping Green & Sams · http://www.hgslaw.com · 123 South Calhoun Street · P.O. Box 6526 · Tallahassee, FL 32314 · 850-222-7598

Cari L. Roth · Bryant Miller & Olive · 101 North Monroe Street, Suite 900 · Tallahassee, FL 32301 · 850-222-8611

Gary P. Sams · 2) · Hopping Green & Sams · http://www.hgslaw.com · 123 South Calhoun Street · P.O. Box 6526 · Tallahassee, FL 32314 · 850-222-7598

Cathy M. Sellers · Broad and Cassel · Sun Trust Bank Building, Suite 400 · 215 South Monroe Street · Tallahassee, FL 32301 · 850-681-6810

Linda Loomis Shelley · Fowler White Boggs Banker · 101 North Monroe Street, Suite 1090 · Tallahassee, FL 32301 · 850-681-0411

Mary F. Smallwood · a · Ruden, McClosky, Smith, Schuster & Russell · 215 South Monroe Street, Suite 815 · Tallahassee, FL 32301 · 850-412-2000

Dan R. Stengle · Hopping Green & Sams · http://www.hgslaw.com · 123 South Calhoun Street · P.O. Box 6526 · Tallahassee, FL 32314 · 850-222-7598

Tampa

Keith W. Bricklemyer · Bricklemyer Smolker & Bolves · http://www.bsbfirm.com · 500 East Kennedy Boulevard, Suite 200 · Tampa, FL 33602-4708 · 813-223-3888

Gina K. Grimes · Hill, Ward & Henderson · http://www.hwhlaw.com · Bank of America Plaza, Suite 3700 101 East Kennedy Boulevard · Tampa, FL 33602 · 813-221-3900

Rhea F. Law · Fowler White Boggs Banker · 501 East Kennedy Boulevard, Suite 1700 · P.O. Box 1438 · Tampa, FL 33602-5239 · 813-228-7411

David M. Mechanik · Mechanik Nuccio Hearne & Wester · 305 South Boulevard · Tampa, FL 33606 · 813-276-1920

James Shimberg, Jr. · Holland & Knight · http://www.hklaw.com · 100 North Tampa Street, Suite 4100 · P.O. Box 1288 · Tampa, FL 33601-1288 · 813-227-8500

Theodore C. Taub · a · Shumaker, Loop & Kendrick · Bank of America Plaza, Suite 2800 · 101 East Kennedy Boulevard · Tampa, FL 33602-5150 · 813-229-7600

Ronald L. Weaver · Stearns Weaver Miller Weissler Alhadeff & Sitterson · SunTrust Financial Centre, Suite 2200 · 401 East Jackson Street · P.O. Box 3299 · Tampa, FL 33601 · 813-223-4800

Andrea E. Zelman · Fowler White Boggs Banker · 501 East Kennedy Boulevard, Suite 1700 · P.O. Box 1438 · Tampa, FL 33602-5239 · 813-228-7411

West Palm Beach

James R. Brindell · a · Gunster, Yoakley & Stewart · Phillips Point, Suite 500 East · 777 South Flagler Drive · West Palm Beach, FL 33401-6194 · 561-655-1980

Ronald K. Kolins · Greenberg Traurig · http://www.gtlaw.com · 777 South Flagler Drive, Suite 300-E · West Palm Beach, FL 33401 · 561-650-7900

LEGAL MALPRACTICE LAW

Fort Lauderdale

Maurice M. Garcia · Greenspoon Marder · Trade Centre South, Suite 700 · 100 West Cypress Creek Road · Fort Lauderdale, FL 33309-2140 · 954-491-1120

D. David Keller · Bunnell, Woulfe, Kirschbaum, Keller, McIntyre & Gregoire · One Financial Plaza, Suite 900 · 100 Southeast Third Avenue · Fort Lauderdale, FL 33394 · 954-761-8600

Jacksonville

John A. DeVault III · 2) · Bedell, Dittmar, DeVault, Pillans & Coxe · http://www.bedellfirm.com · The Bedell Building · 101 East Adams Street · Jacksonville, FL 32202 · 904-353-0211

Robert H. Farnell II · Bedell, Dittmar, DeVault, Pillans & Coxe · http://www.bedellfirm.com · The Bedell Building · 101 East Adams Street · Jacksonville, FL 32202 · 904-353-0211

Rutledge R. Liles · a · Liles, Gavin, Costantino & George · http://www.lgcglaw.com · One Enterprise Center, Suite 1500 · 225 Water Street · Jacksonville, FL 32202 · 904-634-1100

Miami

Richard H. Critchlow · a · Kenny Nachwalter · Miami Center, Suite 1100 · 201 South Biscayne Boulevard · Miami, FL 33131-2305 · 305-373-1000

Alan G. Greer · a · Richman Greer · http://www.richmangreer.com · Miami Center, 10th Floor · 201 South Biscayne Boulevard · Miami, FL 33131 · 305-373-4000

Andrew C. Hall · Hall, Lamb and Hall · http://www.hlhlawfirm.com · Grand Bay Plaza, Penthouse One · 2665 South Bayshore Drive · Miami, FL 33133 · 305-374-5030

Ronald L. Kammer · Hinshaw & Culbertson · http://www.hinshawlaw.com · 9155 South Dadeland Boulevard, Suite 1600 · Miami, FL 33156 · 305-358-7747

Robert Michael Klein · Stephens, Lynn, Klein, LaCava, Hoffman & Puya · Two Datran Center, Penthouse II · 9130 South Dadeland Boulevard · Miami, FL 33156 · 305-670-3700

Edward A. Moss · a · Shook, Hardy & Bacon · 201 South Biscayne Boulevard, Suite 2400 · Miami, FL 33131-4332 · 305-358-5171

Michael Nachwalter · a · Kenny Nachwalter · Miami Center, Suite 1100 · 201 South Biscayne Boulevard Miami, FL 33131-2305 · 305-373-1000

Warren R. Trazenfeld · Warren R. Trazenfeld · 3225 Aviation Avenue, Suite 600 · Miami, FL 33133-4741 · 305-860-1100

Orlando

Jerry R. Linscott · a · Baker Hostetler · http://www.bakerlaw.com · Sun Trust Center, Suite 2300 · 200 South Orange Avenue · Orlando, FL 32801-3432 · 407-649-4000

St. Petersburg

Thomas D. Masterson · Masterson Law Group · 699 First Avenue North · St. Petersburg, FL 33701 · 727-896-3641

Tallahassee

Thomas J. Guilday · Guilday, Tucker, Schwartz & Simpson · 1983 Centre Pointe Boulevard, Suite 200 · P.O. Box 12500 · Tallahassee, FL 32317-2500 · 850-224-7091

Mary K. Simpson · Guilday, Tucker, Schwartz & Simpson · 1983 Centre Pointe Boulevard, Suite 200 · P.O. Box 12500 · Tallahassee, FL 32317-2500 · 850-224-7091

Tampa

Anthony W. Cunningham · 2% · Cunningham Law Group · 100 South Ashley Drive, Suite 280 · Tampa, FL 33602-5300 · 813-223-1700

Frank H. Gassler · Fowler White Boggs Banker · 501 East Kennedy Boulevard, Suite 1700 · P.O. Box 1438 · Tampa, FL 33602-5239 · 813-228-7411

Benjamin H. Hill III · a · Hill, Ward & Henderson · http://www.hwhlaw.com · Bank of America Plaza, Suite 3700 · 101 East Kennedy Boulevard · Tampa, FL 33602 · 813-221-3900

Brett J. Preston · Hill, Ward & Henderson · http://www.hwhlaw.com · Bank of America Plaza, Suite 3700 101 East Kennedy Boulevard · Tampa, FL 33602 · 813-221-3900

Gary L. Sasso · Carlton Fields · Corporate Center Three at International Plaza, Suite 1000 · 4221 West Boy Scout Boulevard · Tampa, FL 33607 · 813-223-7000

Stephen H. Sears · Macfarlane Ferguson & McMullen · One Tampa City Center, Suite 2000 · 201 North Franklin Street · P.O. Box 1531 · Tampa, FL 33601 · 813-273-4200

West Palm Beach

David J. Sales · Searcy Denney Scarola Barnhart & Shipley · http://www.searcylaw.com · 2139 Palm Beach Lakes Boulevard · P.O. Drawer 3626 · West Palm Beach, FL 33402-3626 · 561-686-6300

John G. White III · Richman Greer · http://www.richmangreer.com · One Clearlake Centre, Suite 1504 · 250 Australian Avenue South · West Palm Beach, FL 33401-5016 · 561-803-3500

LEVERAGED BUYOUTS AND PRIVATE EQUITY LAW

Fort Lauderdale

Donn A. Beloff · Greenberg Traurig · http://www.gtlaw.com · 401 East Las Olas Boulevard, Suite 2000 · Fort Lauderdale, FL 33301 · 954-765-0500

Miami

Daniel H. Aronson · Bilzin Sumberg Baena Price & Axelrod · Wachovia Financial Center, Suite 2500 · 200 South Biscayne Boulevard · Miami, FL 33131 · 305-374-7580

Jonathan L. Awner · Akerman Senterfitt · http://www.akerman.com · One Southeast Third Avenue, 25th Floor · Miami, FL 33131-1714 · 305-374-5600

Jorge L. Freeland · White & Case · http://www.whitecase.com · Wachovia Financial Center, Suite 4900 · 200 South Biscayne Boulevard · Miami, FL 33131-2352 · 305-371-2700

Teddy D. Klinghoffer · Akerman Senterfitt · http://www.akerman.com · One Southeast Third Avenue, 25th Floor · Miami, FL 33131-1714 · 305-374-5600

Stephen K. Roddenberry · Akerman Senterfitt · http://www.akerman.com · One Southeast Third Avenue, 25th Floor · Miami, FL 33131-1714 · 305-374-5600

Tampa

David S. Felman · a · Hill, Ward & Henderson · http://www.hwhlaw.com · Bank of America Plaza, Suite 3700 · 101 East Kennedy Boulevard · Tampa, FL 33602 · 813-221-3900

Robert J. Grammig · a · Holland & Knight · http://www.hklaw.com · 100 North Tampa Street, Suite 4100 · P.O. Box 1288 · Tampa, FL 33601-1288 · 813-227-8500

Gary I. Teblum · a · Trenam, Kemker, Scharf, Barkin, Frye, O'Neill & Mullis · http://www.trenam.com · 101 East Kennedy Boulevard, Suite 2700 · P.O. Box 1102 · Tampa, FL 33601-1102 · 813-223-7474

Gregory C. Yadley · Shumaker, Loop & Kendrick · Bank of America Plaza, Suite 2800 · 101 East Kennedy Boulevard · Tampa, FL 33602-5150 · 813-229-7600

MARITIME LAW

Coral Gables

John W. Keller III · a · Keller & Bolz · 121 Majorca Avenue, Suite 200 · Coral Gables, FL 33134 · 305-529-8500

Michael T. Moore · Moore & Company · http://www.moore-and-co.net · 355 Alhambra Circle, Suite 1100 Coral Gables, FL 33134 · 786-221-0600

Fort Lauderdale

Ronald A. FitzGerald · a · Conrad & Scherer · 633 South Federal Highway, Eighth Floor · P.O. Box 14723 · Fort Lauderdale, FL 33302 · 954-462-5500

Jacksonville

George D. Gabel, Jr. · a · Holland & Knight · http://www.hklaw.com · 50 North Laura Street, Suite 3900 P.O. Box 52687 · Jacksonville, FL 32202-2687 · 904-353-2000

James F. Moseley, Jr. · Moseley, Prichard, Parrish, Knight & Jones · 501 West Bay Street · Jacksonville, FL 32202 · 904-356-1306

James F. Moseley, Sr. · 2) · Moseley, Prichard, Parrish, Knight & Jones · 501 West Bay Street · Jacksonville, FL 32202 · 904-356-1306

Robert B. Parrish · a · Moseley, Prichard, Parrish, Knight & Jones · 501 West Bay Street · Jacksonville, FL 32202 · 904-356-1306

Edward Alfred White · Law Office of Edward A. White · Blackstone Building, Suite 901 · 233 East Bay Street · Jacksonville, FL 32202-3456 · 904-356-6500

Melbourne

Theodore L. Shinkle · GrayRobinson · 1800 West Hibiscus Boulevard, Suite 138 · P.O. Box 1870 · Melbourne, FL 32901 · 321-727-8100

Miami

Andrew W. Anderson · Houck Anderson · 200 South Biscayne Boulevard, Suite 300 · Miami, FL 33131 · 305-372-9044

Mark R. Houck · Houck Anderson · 200 South Biscayne Boulevard, Suite 300 · Miami, FL 33131 · 305-372-9044

James N. Hurley · Fowler White Burnett · Espirito Santo Plaza, 14th Floor · 1395 Brickell Avenue · Miami, FL 33131-3302 · 305-789-9200

Allan R. Kelley · Fowler White Burnett · Espirito Santo Plaza, 14th Floor · 1395 Brickell Avenue · Miami, FL 33131-3302 · 305-789-9200

Curtis J. Mase · Mase & Lara · 80 Southwest Eighth Street, Suite 2700 · Miami, FL 33130 · 305-377-3770

Tampa

Timothy C. Conley · Lau, Lane, Pieper, Conley & McCreadie · 100 South Ashley Drive, Suite 1700 · P.O. Box 838 · Tampa, FL 33601-0838 · 813-229-2121

Anthony J. Cuva · Akerman Senterfitt · http://www.akerman.com · SunTrust Financial Centre, Suite 1700 · 401 East Jackson Street · Tampa, FL 33602-5803 · 813-223-7333

David W. McCreadie · a · Lau, Lane, Pieper, Conley & McCreadie · 100 South Ashley Drive, Suite 1700 P.O. Box 838 · Tampa, FL 33601-0838 · 813-229-2121

John J. McLaughlin · a · Wagner, Vaughan, McLaughlin & Brennan · 601 Bayshore Boulevard, Suite 910 · Tampa, FL 33606 · 813-225-4000

Jacob J. Munch · Munch & Munch · 600 South Magnolia Avenue, Suite 325 · Tampa, FL 33606 · 813-254-1557

Carl R. Nelson · Fowler White Boggs Banker · 501 East Kennedy Boulevard, Suite 1700 · P.O. Box 1438 · Tampa, FL 33602-5239 · 813-228-7411

Nathaniel G. W. Pieper · a · Lau, Lane, Pieper, Conley & McCreadie · 100 South Ashley Drive, Suite 1700 · P.O. Box 838 · Tampa, FL 33601-0838 · 813-229-2121

Roger A. Vaughan, Jr. · 2) · Wagner, Vaughan, McLaughlin & Brennan · 708 East Jackson Street · Tampa, FL 33602 · 813-223-7421

Allen K. Von Spiegelfeld · Fowler White Boggs Banker · 501 East Kennedy Boulevard, Suite 1700 · P.O. Box 1438 · Tampa, FL 33602-5239 · 813-228-7411

MASS TORT LITIGATION

Coral Gables

Lewis S. Eidson · Colson, Hicks & Eidson · http://www.colsonhickseidson.com · 255 Aragon Avenue, Second Floor · Coral Gables, FL 33134 · 305-476-7400

David M. Lipman · The Law Office of David M. Lipman · 5901 South West 74th Street, Suite 304 · Coral Gables, FL 33146-2435 · 305-662-2600

Jacksonville

Wayne Hogan · a · Terrell Hogan Ellis Yegelwel · Blackstone Building, Eighth Floor · 233 East Bay Street · Jacksonville, FL 32202 · 904-722-2228

Evan J. Yegelwel · Terrell Hogan Ellis Yegelwel · Blackstone Building, Eighth Floor · 233 East Bay Street · Jacksonville, FL 32202 · 904-722-2228

Miami

Wendy F. Lumish · Carlton Fields · 4000 International Place · 100 Southeast Second Street · P.O. Box 019101 · Miami, FL 33131-9101 · 305-530-0050

Benjamine Reid · Carlton Fields · 4000 International Place · 100 Southeast Second Street · P.O. Box 019101 · Miami, FL 33131-9101 · 305-530-0050

Pensacola

J. Michael Papantonio · a · Levin, Papantonio, Thomas, Mitchell, Echsner & Proctor · 316 South Baylen Street, Suite 600 · P.O. Box 12308 · Pensacola, FL 32591 · 850-435-7000

Troy Rafferty · Levin, Papantonio, Thomas, Mitchell, Echsner & Proctor · 316 South Baylen Street, Suite 600 · P.O. Box 12308 · Pensacola, FL 32591 · 850-435-7000

Tampa

John-Edward Alley · 2% · Ford & Harrison · http://www.fordharrison.com · 101 East Kennedy Boulevard, Suite 900 · Tampa, FL 33602-5133 · 813-261-7800

Kevin J. Napper · Carlton Fields · Corporate Center Three at International Plaza, Suite 1000 · 4221 West Boy Scout Boulevard · Tampa, FL 33607 · 813-223-7000

Gary L. Sasso · Carlton Fields · Corporate Center Three at International Plaza, Suite 1000 · 4221 West Boy Scout Boulevard · Tampa, FL 33607 · 813-223-7000

West Palm Beach

Mark F. Bideau · Greenberg Traurig · http://www.gtlaw.com · 777 South Flagler Drive, Suite 300-E · West Palm Beach, FL 33401 · 561-650-7900

Patricia E. Lowry · Squire Sanders · http://www.ssd.com · Phillips Point West, Suite 1900 · 777 South Flagler Drive · West Palm Beach, FL 33401-6198 · 561-650-7200

John Scarola · Searcy Denney Scarola Barnhart & Shipley · http://www.searcylaw.com · 2139 Palm Beach Lakes Boulevard · P.O. Drawer 3626 · West Palm Beach, FL 33402-3626 · 561-686-6300

MEDIA LAW

Jacksonville

George D. Gabel, Jr. · a · Holland & Knight · http://www.hklaw.com · 50 North Laura Street, Suite 3900 P.O. Box 52687 · Jacksonville, FL 32202-2687 · 904-353-2000

Lake Mary

Frank S. Ioppolo, Jr. · Precision Play Media, Inc. · 3300 W Lake Mary Boulevard, Suite 300 · Lake Mary, FL 32746 · 407-320-7229

Miami

Sanford L. Bohrer · a · Holland & Knight · http://www.hklaw.com · 701 Brickell Avenue, Suite 3000 · Miami, FL 33131 · 305-374-8500

Adolfo E. Jimenez · Holland & Knight · http://www.hklaw.com · 701 Brickell Avenue, Suite 3000 · Miami, FL 33131 · 305-374-8500

Thomas R. Julin · a · Hunton & Williams · Mellon Financial Center, Suite 2500 · 1111 Brickell Avenue · Miami, FL 33131 · 305-810-2500

Richard J. Ovelmen · a · Jorden Burt · 777 Brickell Avenue, Suite 500 · Miami, FL 33131-2803 · 305-371-2600

Orlando

Judith M. Mercier · Holland & Knight · http://www.hklaw.com · 200 South Orange Avenue, Suite 2600 · P.O. Box 1526 · Orlando, FL 32802 · 407-425-8500

Tampa

Gregg D. Thomas · a · Thomas & LoCicero · 400 North Ashley Drive, Suite 1100 · Tampa, FL 33602 · 813-984-3060

MEDICAL MALPRACTICE LAW

Clearwater

James A. Martin, Jr. · Macfarlane Ferguson & McMullen · 625 Court Street · P.O. Box 1669 · Clearwater, FL 33757 · 727-441-8966

Coral Gables

Stuart Z. Grossman · a · Grossman Roth · http://www.grossmanroth.com · 2525 Ponce De Leon Boulevard, Suite 1150 · Coral Gables, FL 33134 · 305-442-8666

Neal A. Roth · Grossman Roth · http://www.grossmanroth.com · 2525 Ponce De Leon Boulevard, Suite 1150 · Coral Gables, FL 33134 · 305-442-8666

Jacksonville

Jeptha F. Barbour · Marks & Gray · 1200 Riverplace Boulevard, Suite 800 · P.O. Box 447 · Jacksonville, FL 32201 · 904-398-0900

Earl E. Googe, Jr. · Smith Hulsey & Busey · http://www.smithhulsey.com · 225 Water Street, Suite 1800 Jacksonville, FL 32202 · 904-359-7700

Corinne C. Hodak · a · The Hodak Law Firm · 1920 San Marco Boulevard · Jacksonville, FL 32207 · 904-399-2008

William E. Kuntz · Smith Hulsey & Busey · http://www.smithhulsey.com · 225 Water Street, Suite 1800 · Jacksonville, FL 32202 · 904-359-7700

Rodney S. Margol · Margol & Pennington · 320 North First Street, Suite 609 · Jacksonville, FL 32250 · 904-355-7508

C. Rufus Pennington III · Margol & Pennington · 320 North First Street, Suite 609 · Jacksonville, FL 32250 · 904-355-7508

Robert F. Spohrer · Spohrer & Dodd · 701 West Adams Street · Jacksonville, FL 32204 · 904-309-6500

Miami

Walter S. Holland · Ferraro & Associates · 4000 Ponce De Leon Boulevard, Suite 700 · Miami, FL 33146 305-375-0111

Andrew Needle · Needle & Ellenberg · http://www.needleellenberg.com · 1401 Brickell Avenue, Suite 900 · Miami, FL 33131 · 305-530-0000

Benjamine Reid · Carlton Fields · 4000 International Place · 100 Southeast Second Street · P.O. Box 019101 · Miami, FL 33131-9101 · 305-530-0050

Orange

Rafael E. Martinez · McEwan, Martinez & Dukes · 108 East Central Boulevard · P.O. Box 753 · Orange, FL 32801 · 407-423-8571

Orlando

Dan H. Honeywell · a · Wooten, Honeywell, Kimbrough, Gibson, Doherty & Normand · 236 South Lucerne Circle · P.O. Box 568188 · Orlando, FL 32856-8188 · 407-843-7060

Jennings L. Hurt III · Rissman, Weisberg, Barrett, Hurt, Donahue & McLain · Capital Plaza, 15th Floor · 201 East Pine Street · P.O. Box 4940 · Orlando, FL 32801 · 407-839-0120

Henry W. Jewett II · Rissman, Weisberg, Barrett, Hurt, Donahue & McLain · Capital Plaza, 15th Floor · 201 East Pine Street · P.O. Box 4940 · Orlando, FL 32801 · 407-839-0120

Palm Beach Gardens

Sean C. Domnick · Domnick & Shevin · 5100 PGA Boulevard, Suite 317 · Palm Beach Gardens, FL 33418-3956 · 561-630-5363

St. Petersburg

Jeffrey M. Goodis · Thompson Goodis Thompson Groseclose & Richardson · 700 Central Avenue, Suite 500 · P.O. Box 90 · St. Petersburg, FL 33731 · 727-823-0540

Thomas D. Masterson · Masterson Law Group · 699 First Avenue North · St. Petersburg, FL 33701 · 727-896-3641

Tallahassee

Craig Ashley Dennis · Dennis, Jackson, Martin & Fontela · 2367 Centreville Road · Tallahassee, FL 32308 · 850-422-3345

S. William Fuller, Jr. · Fuller Mitchell Hood & Stephens · 2565 Barrington Circle · Tallahassee, FL 32308 · 850-222-0770

Tampa

David C. Banker · Bush Ross · http://www.bushross.com · 1801 North Highland Avenue · P.O. Box 3913 · Tampa, FL 33601 · 813-224-9255

Robert E. Banker · 2) · Fowler White Boggs Banker · 501 East Kennedy Boulevard, Suite 1700 · P.O. Box 1438 · Tampa, FL 33602-5239 · 813-228-7411

Kenneth A. Beytin · Burton, Schulte, Weekley, Hoeler, McLaughlin & Beytin · 100 South Ashley Drive, Suite 600 · Tampa, FL 33602 · 813-221-0955

Richard K. Bowers · Fowler White Boggs Banker · 501 East Kennedy Boulevard, Suite 1700 · P.O. Box 1438 · Tampa, FL 33602-5239 · 813-228-7411

James D. Clark · Alley, Clark, Greiwe & Fulmer · 701 East Washington Street · Tampa, FL 33602 · 813-222-0977

Troy J. Crotts · Bush Ross · http://www.bushross.com · 1801 North Highland Avenue · P.O. Box 3913 · Tampa, FL 33601 · 813-224-9255

Kirk S. Davis · a · Akerman Senterfitt · http://www.akerman.com · SunTrust Financial Centre, Suite 1700 · 401 East Jackson Street · Tampa, FL 33602-5803 · 813-223-7333

James J. Evangelista · Bush Ross · http://www.bushross.com · 1801 North Highland Avenue · P.O. Box 3913 · Tampa, FL 33601 · 813-224-9255

Carl A. Goldman · Morgan Lamb Goldman & Valles · 2701 North Rocky Point Drive, Suite 410 · Tampa, FL 33607 · 813-281-9700

Donald Greiwe · Alley, Clark, Greiwe & Fulmer · 701 East Washington Street · Tampa, FL 33602 · 813-222-0977

William E. Hahn · William E. Hahn · http://www.whahn-law.com · 310 South Fielding Avenue · Tampa, FL 33606 · 813-250-0660

Benjamin H. Hill III · a · Hill, Ward & Henderson · http://www.hwhlaw.com · Bank of America Plaza, Suite 3700 · 101 East Kennedy Boulevard · Tampa, FL 33602 · 813-221-3900

John L. Holcomb · Hill, Ward & Henderson · http://www.hwhlaw.com · Bank of America Plaza, Suite 3700 · 101 East Kennedy Boulevard · Tampa, FL 33602 · 813-221-3900

C. Howard Hunter · Hill, Ward & Henderson · http://www.hwhlaw.com · Bank of America Plaza, Suite 3700 · 101 East Kennedy Boulevard · Tampa, FL 33602 · 813-221-3900

Christopher S. Knopik · KnopikVarnerMoore · One Harbour Place, Suite 800 · 777 South Harbour Island Boulevard · Tampa, FL 33602 · 813-221-3131

Louis J. LaCava · Stephens, Lynn, Klein, LaCava, Hoffman & Puya · Bank of America Plaza, Suite 2500 · 101 East Kennedy Boulevard · Tampa, FL 33602 · 813-209-9611

Roland J. Lamb · Morgan Lamb Goldman & Valles · 2701 North Rocky Point Drive, Suite 410 · Tampa, FL 33607 · 813-281-9700

Rodney W. Morgan · Morgan Lamb Goldman & Valles · 2701 North Rocky Point Drive, Suite 410 · Tampa, FL 33607 · 813-281-9700

Clifford L. Somers · Barr Murman Tonelli Slother & Sleet · 201 East Kennedy Boulevard, Suite 1700 · P.O. Box 172669 · Tampa, FL 33602 · 813-223-3951

Henry E. Valenzuela · Valenzuela & Stern · 100 North Tampa Street, Suite 1825 · Tampa, FL 33602 · 813-272-1000

C. Steven Yerrid · 2) · The Yerrid Law Firm · Bank of America Plaza, Suite 3910 · 101 East Kennedy Boulevard · Tampa, FL 33602 · 813-222-8222

West Palm Beach

Theodore Babbitt · 2) · Babbitt Johnson Osborne & LeClainche · 1450 Centrepark Boulevard, Suite 100 · West Palm Beach, FL 33401 · 561-684-2500

F. Gregory Barnhart · a · Searcy Denney Scarola Barnhart & Shipley · http://www.searcylaw.com · 2139 Palm Beach Lakes Boulevard · P.O. Drawer 3626 · West Palm Beach, FL 33402-3626 · 561-686-6300

Mark W. Clark · Lytal, Reiter, Clark, Fountain & Williams · 515 North Flagler Drive, 10th Floor · West Palm Beach, FL 33401 · 561-655-1990

Christopher M. Larmoyeux · a · Larmoyeux & Bone · 550 South Quadrille Boulevard, Suite 200 · West Palm Beach, FL 33401 · 561-832-9400

Darryl L. Lewis · Searcy Denney Scarola Barnhart & Shipley · http://www.searcylaw.com · 2139 Palm Beach Lakes Boulevard · P.O. Drawer 3626 · West Palm Beach, FL 33402-3626 · 561-686-6300

Lake Lytal, Jr. · a · Lytal, Reiter, Clark, Fountain & Williams · 515 North Flagler Drive, 10th Floor · West Palm Beach, FL 33401 · 561-655-1990

Joseph J. Reiter · 2) · Lytal, Reiter, Clark, Fountain & Williams · 515 North Flagler Drive, 10th Floor · West Palm Beach, FL 33401 · 561-655-1990

John Scarola · Searcy Denney Scarola Barnhart & Shipley · http://www.searcylaw.com · 2139 Palm Beach Lakes Boulevard · P.O. Drawer 3626 · West Palm Beach, FL 33402-3626 · 561-686-6300

Christian D. Searcy, Sr. · 2% · Searcy Denney Scarola Barnhart & Shipley · http://www.searcylaw.com · 2139 Palm Beach Lakes Boulevard · P.O. Drawer 3626 · West Palm Beach, FL 33402-3626 · 561-686-6300

John A. Shipley · Searcy Denney Scarola Barnhart & Shipley · http://www.searcylaw.com · 2139 Palm Beach Lakes Boulevard · P.O. Drawer 3626 · West Palm Beach, FL 33402-3626 · 561-686-6300

Karen E. Terry · Searcy Denney Scarola Barnhart & Shipley · http://www.searcylaw.com · 2139 Palm Beach Lakes Boulevard · P.O. Drawer 3626 · West Palm Beach, FL 33402-3626 · 561-686-6300

MERGERS & ACQUISITIONS LAW

Jacksonville

L. Kinder Cannon III · a · Holland & Knight · http://www.hklaw.com · 50 North Laura Street, Suite 3900 · P.O. Box 52687 · Jacksonville, FL 32202-2687 · 904-353-2000

J. Kirby Chritton · Rogers Towers · 1301 Riverplace Boulevard, Suite 1500 · Jacksonville, FL 32207 · 904-398-3911

Gardner F. Davis · Foley & Lardner · One Independent Drive, Suite 1300 · P.O. Box 240 · Jacksonville, FL 32201 · 904-359-2000

Linda Y. Kelso · Foley & Lardner · One Independent Drive, Suite 1300 · P.O. Box 240 · Jacksonville, FL 32201 · 904-359-2000

Miami

Emilio J. Alvarez-Farré · White & Case · http://www.whitecase.com · Wachovia Financial Center, Suite 4900 · 200 South Biscayne Boulevard · Miami, FL 33131-2352 · 305-371-2700

Daniel H. Aronson · Bilzin Sumberg Baena Price & Axelrod · Wachovia Financial Center, Suite 2500 · 200 South Biscayne Boulevard · Miami, FL 33131 · 305-374-7580

Jonathan L. Awner · Akerman Senterfitt · http://www.akerman.com · One Southeast Third Avenue, 25th Floor · Miami, FL 33131-1714 · 305-374-5600

Alan D. Axelrod · Bilzin Sumberg Baena Price & Axelrod · Wachovia Financial Center, Suite 2500 · 200 South Biscayne Boulevard · Miami, FL 33131 · 305-374-7580

Rodney H. Bell · Holland & Knight · http://www.hklaw.com · 701 Brickell Avenue, Suite 3000 · Miami, FL 33131 · 305-374-8500

Bowman Brown · 2% · Shutts & Bowen · http://www.shutts.com · Miami Center, Suite 1500 · 201 South Biscayne Boulevard · Miami, FL 33131 · 305-358-6300

Luis A. de Armas · Shutts & Bowen · http://www.shutts.com · Miami Center, Suite 1500 · 201 South Biscayne Boulevard · Miami, FL 33131 · 305-358-6300

Bernard Jacobson · Akerman Senterfitt · http://www.akerman.com · One Southeast Third Avenue, 25th Floor · Miami, FL 33131-1714 · 305-374-5600

Teddy D. Klinghoffer · Akerman Senterfitt · http://www.akerman.com · One Southeast Third Avenue, 25th Floor · Miami, FL 33131-1714 · 305-374-5600

Alison W. Miller · Stearns Weaver Miller Weissler Alhadeff & Sitterson · Museum Tower, Suite 2200 · 150 West Flagler Street · Miami, FL 33130 · 305-789-3200

Stephen K. Roddenberry · Akerman Senterfitt · http://www.akerman.com · One Southeast Third Avenue, 25th Floor · Miami, FL 33131-1714 · 305-374-5600

Abigail C. Watts-Fitzgerald · Hunton & Williams · Mellon Financial Center, Suite 2500 · 1111 Brickell Avenue · Miami, FL 33131 · 305-810-2500

Orlando

Richard D. Davidson · Lowndes, Drosdick, Doster, Kantor & Reed · 450 South Orange Street, Suite 250 Orlando, FL 32801-3383 · 407-843-4600

Randolph H. Fields · Greenberg Traurig · http://www.gtlaw.com · 450 South Orange Avenue, Suite 650 · Orlando, FL 32801 · 407-420-1000

Russell P. Hintze · Greenberg Traurig · http://www.gtlaw.com · 450 South Orange Avenue, Suite 650 · Orlando, FL 32801 · 407-420-1000

Byrd F. Marshall, Jr. · GrayRobinson · 301 East Pine Street, Suite 1400 · P.O. Box 3068 · Orlando, FL 32802-3068 · 407-843-8880

Thomas M. McAleavey · Holland & Knight · http://www.hklaw.com · 200 South Orange Avenue, Suite 2600 · P.O. Box 1526 · Orlando, FL 32802 · 407-425-8500

Peter E. Reinert · Lowndes, Drosdick, Doster, Kantor & Reed · 215 North Eola Drive · Orlando, FL 32801 · 407-843-4600

Leighton D. Yates, Jr. · a · Holland & Knight · http://www.hklaw.com · 200 South Orange Avenue, Suite 2600 · P.O. Box 1526 · Orlando, FL 32802 · 407-425-8500

Tampa

Chester E. Bacheller · a · Holland & Knight · http://www.hklaw.com · 100 North Tampa Street, Suite 4100 · P.O. Box 1288 · Tampa, FL 33601-1288 · 813-227-8500

Curt P. Creely · Foley & Lardner · 100 North Tampa Street, Suite 2700 · P.O. Box 3391 · Tampa, FL 33602 · 813-229-2300

Nathaniel L. Doliner · Carlton Fields · Corporate Center Three at International Plaza, Suite 1000 · 4221 West Boy Scout Boulevard · Tampa, FL 33607 · 813-223-7000

R. Alan Higbee · Shutts & Bowen · http://www.shutts.com · 100 South Ashley Drive, Suite 1500 · Tampa, FL 33602 · 813-229-8900

Carolyn T. Long · Foley & Lardner · 100 North Tampa Street, Suite 2700 · P.O. Box 3391 · Tampa, FL 33602 · 813-229-2300

Robert C. Rasmussen · 2) · Glenn, Rasmussen, Fogarty & Hooker · http://www.glennrasmussen.com · 100 South Ashley Drive, Suite 1300 · Tampa, FL 33602 · 813-229-3333

David C. Shobe · Fowler White Boggs Banker · 501 East Kennedy Boulevard, Suite 1700 · P.O. Box 1438 Tampa, FL 33602-5239 · 813-228-7411

Darrell C. Smith · Shumaker, Loop & Kendrick · Bank of America Plaza, Suite 2800 · 101 East Kennedy Boulevard · Tampa, FL 33602-5150 · 813-229-7600

Martin A. Traber · Foley & Lardner · 100 North Tampa Street, Suite 2700 · P.O. Box 3391 · Tampa, FL 33602 · 813-229-2300

Steven W. Vazquez · Foley & Lardner · 100 North Tampa Street, Suite 2700 · P.O. Box 3391 · Tampa, FL 33602 · 813-229-2300

Gregory C. Yadley · Shumaker, Loop & Kendrick · Bank of America Plaza, Suite 2800 · 101 East Kennedy Boulevard · Tampa, FL 33602-5150 · 813-229-7600

MUNICIPAL LAW

Fort Lauderdale

Samuel S. Goren · Goren, Cherof, Doody & Ezrol · 3099 East Commercial Boulevard, Suite 200 · Fort Lauderdale, FL 33308-4500 · 954-771-4500

Gary A. Poliakoff · Becker & Poliakoff · 3111 Stirling Road · Fort Lauderdale, FL 33312 · 954-987-7550

Fort Myers

James T. Humphrey · Fowler White Boggs Banker · 2235 First Street · Fort Myers, FL 33901 · 239-334-7892

Orlando

Usher L. Brown · Brown, Garganese, Weiss & D' Agresta · http://www.orlandolaw.net · 111 NorthOrange Avenue, Suite 2000 · P.O. Box 2873 · Orlando, FL 32802-2873 · 407-425-9566

Anthony A. Garganese · Brown, Garganese, Weiss & D' Agresta · http://www.orlandolaw.net · 111 NorthOrange Avenue, Suite 2000 · P.O. Box 2873 · Orlando, FL 32802-2873 · 407-425-9566

Tallahassee

Robert L. Nabors · Nabors, Giblin & Nickerson · 1500 Mahan Drive, Suite 200 · Tallahassee, FL 32308 · 850-224-4070

Gregory T. Stewart · Nabors, Giblin & Nickerson · 1500 Mahan Drive, Suite 200 · Tallahassee, FL 32308 · 850-224-4070

Tampa

Rhea F. Law · Fowler White Boggs Banker · 501 East Kennedy Boulevard, Suite 1700 · P.O. Box 1438 · Tampa, FL 33602-5239 · 813-228-7411

NATURAL RESOURCES LAW

Tallahassee

Lawrence N. Curtin · a · Holland & Knight · http://www.hklaw.com · Bank of America Building, Suite 600 · 315 South Calhoun Street · Tallahassee, FL 32301 · 850-224-7000

NON-PROFIT/CHARITIES LAW

Miami

Henry H. Raattama, Jr. · 2) · Akerman Senterfitt · http://www.akerman.com · One Southeast Third Avenue, 25th Floor · Miami, FL 33131-1714 · 305-374-5600

Tampa

Leslie J. Barnett · 2% · Barnett, Bolt, Kirkwood, Long & McBride · http://www.barnettbolt.com · 601 Bayshore Boulevard, Suite 700 · P.O. Box 3287 · Tampa, FL 33606 · 813-253-2020

Peter T. Kirkwood · Barnett, Bolt, Kirkwood, Long & McBride · http://www.barnettbolt.com · 601 Bayshore Boulevard, Suite 700 · P.O. Box 3287 · Tampa, FL 33606 · 813-253-2020

Frank J. Rief · Akerman Senterfitt · http://www.akerman.com · SunTrust Financial Centre, Suite 1700 · 401 East Jackson Street · Tampa, FL 33602-5803 · 813-223-7333

NON-WHITE-COLLAR CRIMINAL DEFENSE

Boca Raton

H. Dohn Williams, Jr. · a · H. Dohn Williams, Jr. · 990 Northwest Fifth Street · Boca Raton, FL 33486 · 561-929-5432

Clearwater

Denis M. de Vlaming · a · Denis M. de Vlaming · 1101 Turner Street · Clearwater, FL 33756 · 727-461-0525

George E. Tragos · Tragos & Sartres · Suntrust Bank Building, Suite 800 · 600 Cleveland Street · Clearwater, FL 33755 · 727-441-9030

Coral Gables

Joel Hirschhorn · 2% · Hirschhorn & Bieber · http://www.aquitall.com · 550 Biltmore Way, Penthouse 3-A Coral Gables, FL 33134 · 305-445-5320

Fort Lauderdale

J. David Bogenschutz · 2) · Bogenschutz, Dutko & Kroll · Third Fifth Bank Building, Suite 500 · 600 South Andrews Avenue · Fort Lauderdale, FL 33301 · 954-764-2500

Michael E. Dutko · Bogenschutz, Dutko & Kroll · Third Fifth Bank Building, Suite 500 · 600 South Andrews Avenue · Fort Lauderdale, FL 33301 · 954-764-2500

Fred Haddad · a · Fred Haddad · One Financial Plaza, Suite 2612 · Fort Lauderdale, FL 33394 · 954-467-6767

Bruce M. Lyons · 2) · Lyons and Sanders · 600 Northeast Third Avenue · Fort Lauderdale, FL 33304-2689 · 954-467-8700

Bruce L. Udolf · Berger Singerman · http://www.bergersingerman.com · 350 East Las Olas Boulevard, Suite 1000 · Fort Lauderdale, FL 33301 · 954-525-9900

Bruce A. Zimet · 2) · Bruce A. Zimet · One Financial Plaza, Suite 2612 · Fort Lauderdale, FL 33394 · 954-764-7081

Fort Myers

Peter D. Aiken · Peter D. Aiken · 2575 Cleveland Avenue · Fort Myers, FL 33901 · 239-334-8890

Gainesville

Robert S. Griscti · a · Law Firm of Robert S. Griscti · 204 West University Avenue, Suite Six · P.O. Box 508 · Gainesville, FL 32602 · 352-375-4460

Larry G. Turner · Turner & Jones · 204 West University Avenue, Suite Seven · Gainesville, FL 32601-5205 · 352-372-4263

Jacksonville

O. David Barksdale · Bedell, Dittmar, DeVault, Pillans & Coxe · http://www.bedellfirm.com · The Bedell Building · 101 East Adams Street · Jacksonville, FL 32202 · 904-353-0211

Henry M. Coxe III · 2) · Bedell, Dittmar, DeVault, Pillans & Coxe · http://www.bedellfirm.com · The Bedell Building · 101 East Adams Street · Jacksonville, FL 32202 · 904-353-0211

Albert J. Datz · 2% · Datz & Datz · 4348 Southpoint Boulevard, Suite 330 · Jacksonville, FL 32216 · 904-296-7440

Curtis S. Fallgatter · Fallgatter, Farmand & Catlin · 200 East Forsyth Street · Jacksonville, FL 32202 · 904-353-5800

Charles B. Lembcke · Charles B. Lembcke · 1300 Riverplace Boulevard, Suite 605 · Jacksonville, FL 32207 · 904-355-5467

William J. Sheppard · a · Sheppard, White,Thomas & Kachergus · 215 North Washington Street · Jacksonville, FL 32202-2808 · 904-356-9661

D. Gray Thomas · Sheppard, White,Thomas & Kachergus · 215 North Washington Street · Jacksonville, FL 32202-2808 · 904-356-9661

Elizabeth L. White · a · Sheppard, White,Thomas & Kachergus · 215 North Washington Street · Jacksonville, FL 32202-2808 · 904-356-9661

Robert S. Willis · Willis and Weinbaum · 503 East Monroe Street · Jacksonville, FL 32202 · 904-356-0990

Miami

William Aaron · Law Offices of William Aaron · Wachovia Financial Center, Suite 2770 · 200 South Biscayne Boulevard · Miami, FL 33131 · 305-371-5800

Joseph D. W. Beeler · Joseph Beeler, P.A. · 800 Brickell Avenue, Penthouse Two · Miami, FL 33131 · 305-372-5110

Donald I. Bierman · 2% · Bierman, Shohat, Loewy & Pizzi · 800 Brickell Avenue, Penthouse Two · Miami, FL 33131-2911 · 305-358-7000

Melvin S. Black · a · Melvin S. Black · Grove Forest Plaza, Suite 202 · 2937 Southwest 27th Avenue · Miami, FL 33133 · 305-443-1600

Roy Black · 2) · Black, Srebnick Kornspan & Stumpf · http://www.royblack.com · Miami Center, Suite 1300 · 201 South Biscayne Boulevard · Miami, FL 33131 · 305-371-6421

Stephen J. Bronis · a · Carlton Fields · 4000 International Place · 100 Southeast Second Street · P.O. Box 019101 · Miami, FL 33131-9101 · 305-530-0050

Edward A. Carhart · 2% · Edward A. Carhart · 5300 Southwest 76th Street · Miami, FL 33143-5852 · 305-567-1066

Jack M. Denaro · 2% · Jack M. Denaro · 7700 North Kendall Drive, Suite 504 · Miami, FL 33156 · 305-274-9550

Joel M. Denaro · Law Offices of Joel Denaro · 777 Brickell Avenue, Suite 400 · Miami, FL 33131-2812 · 305-371-1883

H. Scott Fingerhut · H. Scott Fingerhut · 2400 South Dixie Highway, Second Floor · Miami, FL 33133-3156 · 305-285-0500

Richard L. Hersch · Hersch & Talisman · 2937 Southwest 27th Avenue, Suite 206 · Miami, FL 33133 · 305-358-0570

Milton Hirsch · a · Milton Hirsch · Two Datran Center, Suite 1200 · 9130 South Dadeland Boulevard · Miami, FL 33156 · 305-670-0077

James J. Hogan · a · Hogan, Greer & Shapiro · 2400 South Dixie Highway, Suite 200 · Miami, FL 33133-3153 · 305-854-8989

John M. Hogan · Holland & Knight · http://www.hklaw.com · 701 Brickell Avenue, Suite 3000 · Miami, FL 33131 · 305-374-8500

Robert C. Josefsberg · 2% · Podhurst Orseck · http://www.podhurst.com · City National Bank Building, Suite 800 · 25 West Flagler Street · Miami, FL 33130 · 305-358-2800

Albert J. Krieger · 2) · Albert J. Krieger, P.A. · 2701 South Bayshore Drive, Suite 315 · Miami, FL 33133-3307 · 786-573-4912

Ira N. Loewy · Bierman, Shohat, Loewy & Pizzi · 800 Brickell Avenue, Penthouse Two · Miami, FL 33131-2911 · 305-358-7000

David Oscar Markus · David Oscar Markus · Alfred I. duPont Building, Suite 1200 · 169 East Flagler Street · Miami, FL 33131-1205 · 305-379-6667

Jane Wollner Moscowitz · a · Moscowitz & Moscowitz · Mellon Financial Center, Suite 2050 · 1111 Brickell Avenue · Miami, FL 33131 · 305-379-8300

Norman A. Moscowitz · a · Moscowitz & Moscowitz · Mellon Financial Center, Suite 2050 · 1111 Brickell Avenue · Miami, FL 33131 · 305-379-8300

Rebekah J. Poston · Squire Sanders · http://www.ssd.com · 200 South Biscayne Boulevard, Suite 4000 · Miami, FL 33131-2398 · 305-577-7000

Peter Prieto · Holland & Knight · http://www.hklaw.com · 701 Brickell Avenue, Suite 3000 · Miami, FL 33131 · 305-374-8500

Jose M. Quiñon · a · Jose M. Quiñon · 2333 Brickell Avenue, Suite A-1 · Miami, FL 33129 · 305-858-5700

Robert Scott Reiff · Law Offices of Robert S. Reiff · 2400 South Dixie Highway, Suite 200 · Miami, FL 33133 · 305-854-5511

William L. Richey · a · William L. Richey · Miami Center, 34th Floor · 201 South Biscayne Boulevard · Miami, FL 33131-4325 · 305-372-8808

Michael J. Rosen · Michael J. Rosen · Grove Forest Plaza, Suite 101 · 2937 Southwest 27th Avenue · Miami, FL 33133 · 305-446-6116

Jon A. Sale · a · Sale & Weintraub · 200 Southeast Second Street, Suite 4300 · Miami, FL 33131-2112 · 305-374-1818

Mark Seiden · Mark Seiden · 777 Brickell Avenue, Suite 400 · Miami, FL 33131-2803 · 305-577-4981

Hy Shapiro · Hogan, Greer & Shapiro · 2400 South Dixie Highway, Suite 200 · Miami, FL 33133-3153 · 305-854-8989

Richard A. Sharpstein · a · Jorden Burt · 777 Brickell Avenue, Suite 500 · Miami, FL 33131-2803 · 305-371-2600

Edward R. Shohat · 2) · Bierman, Shohat, Loewy & Pizzi · 800 Brickell Avenue, Penthouse Two · Miami, FL 33131-2911 · 305-358-7000

H. T. Smith, Jr. · a · H. T. Smith · 1017 Northwest Ninth Court · Miami, FL 33136-3012 · 305-324-1845

Neal R. Sonnett · 2% · Neal R. Sonnett · http://www.sonnettlaw.com · One Biscayne Tower, Twenty Sixth Floor · Two South Biscayne Boulevard · Miami, FL 33131-1802 · 305-358-2000

Howard M. Srebnick · Black, Srebnick Kornspan & Stumpf · http://www.royblack.com · Miami Center, Suite 1300 · 201 South Biscayne Boulevard · Miami, FL 33131 · 305-371-6421

Marty L. Steinberg · a · Hunton & Williams · Mellon Financial Center, Suite 2500 · 1111 Brickell Avenue · Miami, FL 33131 · 305-810-2500

G. Richard Strafer · a · G. Richard Strafer · 201 South Biscayne Boulevard, Suite 1380 · Miami, FL 33131 · 305-374-9091

Orlando

Mark L. Horwitz · Law Offices of Mark L. Horwitz · http://www.mlhorwitzlaw.com · 17 East Pine Street · Orlando, FL 32801 · 407-401-7224

Robert A. Leventhal · Leventhal & Slaughter · 111 North Orange Avenue, Suite 700 · Orlando, FL 32801 · 407-849-6161

James M. Russ · 2% · Law Offices of James M. Russ · Tinker Building · 18 West Pine Street · Orlando, FL 32801-2697 · 407-849-6050

William J. Sheaffer · William J. Sheaffer · http://www.defenselaw.net · 609 East Central Boulevard · Orlando, FL 32801 · 407-423-1066

Harrison T. Slaughter, Jr. · Leventhal & Slaughter · 111 North Orange Avenue, Suite 700 · Orlando, FL 32801 · 407-849-6161

Pensacola

Barry W. Beroset · Beroset & Keene · 1622 North Ninth Avenue · Pensacola, FL 32503 · 850-438-3111

Leo A. Thomas · a · Levin, Papantonio, Thomas, Mitchell, Echsner & Proctor · 316 South Baylen Street, Suite 600 · P.O. Box 12308 · Pensacola, FL 32591 · 850-435-7000

Sarasota

Derek Byrd · The Byrd Law Firm · 2151 Main Street, Suite 201 · Sarasota, FL 34237 · 941-954-3400

Tallahassee

Stephen S. Dobson III · Dobson, Davis & Smith · 610 North Duval Street · Tallahassee, FL 32301 · 850-224-2683

Richard A. Greenberg · Rumberger, Kirk & Caldwell · 215 South Monroe Street, Suite 130 · P.O. Box 10507 · Tallahassee, FL 32302-2507 · 850-222-6550

Robert Augustus Harper · a · Harper & Harper · 325 West Park Avenue · P.O. Box 10132 · Tallahassee, FL 32302-2132 · 850-224-5900

Robert Augustus Harper III · Harper & Harper · 325 West Park Avenue · P.O. Box 10132 · Tallahassee, FL 32302-2132 · 850-224-5900

James P. Judkins · a · Judkins, Simpson & High · 1102 North Gadsden Street · P.O. Box 10368 · Tallahassee, FL 32302 · 850-222-6040

Larry D. Simpson · a · Judkins, Simpson & High · 1102 North Gadsden Street · P.O. Box 10368 · Tallahassee, FL 32302 · 850-222-6040

Tampa

Ronald K. Cacciatore · 2% · Ronald K. Cacciatore · 100 North Tampa Street, Suite 2835 · Tampa, FL 33602 · 813-223-4831

Barry A. Cohen · 2% · Cohen, Jayson & Foster · 201 East Kennedy Boulevard, Suite 1000 · Tampa, FL 33602-5829 · 813-225-1655

James E. Felman · Kynes, Markman & Felman · 100 South Ashley Drive, Suite 1300 · P.O. Box 3396 · Tampa, FL 33601-3396 · 813-229-1118

John M. Fitzgibbons · a · John M. Fitzgibbons · 707 North Franklin Street, Suite 700 · Tampa, FL 33602 · 813-221-8800

Marcelino J. Huerta III · Marcelino J. Huerta III · http://www.tampacase.com · 109 North Brush Street, Suite 200 · Tampa, FL 33602-4163 · 813-229-7623

William F. Jung · Jung & Sisco · http://www.jungandsisco.com · Wachovia Center, Suite 1240 · 100 South Ashley Drive · Tampa, FL 33602 · 813-225-1988

Edward J. Page · Carlton Fields · Corporate Center Three at International Plaza, Suite 1000 · 4221 West Boy Scout Boulevard · Tampa, FL 33607 · 813-223-7000

Gary R. Trombley · 2) · Trombley & Hanes · Tampa Theatre Building, 10th Floor · 707 North Franklin Street · Tampa, FL 33602 · 813-229-7918

West Palm Beach

Joseph R. Atterbury · Atterbury, Goldberger, Richardson & Weiss · 250 Australian Avenue South, Suite 1400 · West Palm Beach, FL 33401-5012 · 561-659-8300

Jack A. Goldberger · Atterbury, Goldberger, Richardson & Weiss · 250 Australian Avenue South, Suite 1400 · West Palm Beach, FL 33401-5012 · 561-659-8300

Richard G. Lubin · a · Richard G. Lubin · 1217 South Flagler Drive, Second Floor · West Palm Beach, FL 33401-6706 · 561-655-2040

David Louis Roth · a · Roth & Duncan · 515 North Flagler Drive, Suite 325 · P.O. Box 770 · West Palm Beach, FL 33402 · 561-655-5529

Winter Park

Kirk N. Kirkconnell · Kirkconnell, Lindsey, Snure & Yates · 1150 Louisiana Avenue, Suite One · P.O. Box 2728 · Winter Park, FL 32790-2728 · 407-644-7600

Warren W. Lindsey · Kirkconnell, Lindsey, Snure & Yates · 1150 Louisiana Avenue, Suite One · P.O. Box 2728 · Winter Park, FL 32790-2728 · 407-644-7600

Michael J. Snure · Kirkconnell, Lindsey, Snure & Yates · 1150 Louisiana Avenue, Suite One · P.O. Box 2728 · Winter Park, FL 32790-2728 · 407-644-7600

PERSONAL INJURY LITIGATION

Boca Raton

Richard J. Roselli · Roselli & McNelis · http://rosellimcnelis.com · Sanctuary Centre, Suite 202-E · 4800 North Federal Highway · Boca Raton, FL 33431-3415 · 561-826-0826

Clearwater

Thomas W. Carey · Carey & Leisure · 622 Bypass Drive, Suite 100 · Clearwater, FL 33764 · 727-799-3900

Coral Gables

Dean C. Colson · Colson, Hicks & Eidson · http://www.colsonhickseidson.com · 255 Aragon Avenue, Second Floor · Coral Gables, FL 33134 · 305-476-7400

David H. Gold · David H. Gold, P.A. · 328 Minorca Avenue, First Floor · Coral Gables, FL 33134 · 303-567-2525

Ervin A. Gonzalez · Colson, Hicks & Eidson · http://www.colsonhickseidson.com · 255 Aragon Avenue, Second Floor · Coral Gables, FL 33134 · 305-476-7400

Stuart Z. Grossman · a · Grossman Roth · http://www.grossmanroth.com · 2525 Ponce De Leon Boulevard, Suite 1150 · Coral Gables, FL 33134 · 305-442-8666

Michael A. Haggard · The Haggard Law Firm · 330 Alhambra Circle, First Floor · Coral Gables, FL 33134 · 305-446-5700

William Andrew Haggard · a · The Haggard Law Firm · 330 Alhambra Circle, First Floor · Coral Gables, FL 33134 · 305-446-5700

Phillip A. Hubbart · Phillip Arthur Hubbart · 2655 South Le Jeune Road, Penthouse 1-G · Coral Gables, FL 33134 · 305-374-0650

Robert K. Tucker · George, Hartz & Lundeen · 4800 LeJeune Road · Coral Gables, FL 33146-1819 · 305-662-4800

Andrew B. Yaffa · Grossman Roth · http://www.grossmanroth.com · 2525 Ponce De Leon Boulevard, Suite 1150 · Coral Gables, FL 33134 · 305-442-8666

Fort Lauderdale

Walter G. Campbell, Jr. · a · Krupnick Campbell Malone Buser Slama Hancock Liberman & McKee · 700 Southeast Third Avenue, Suite 100 · Fort Lauderdale, FL 33316-1186 · 954-763-8181

Jay Cohen · Law Office of Jay Cohen · 200 Southwest First Avenue, 12th Floor · Fort Lauderdale, FL 33301 · 954-763-6939

Kelly D. Hancock · Krupnick Campbell Malone Buser Slama Hancock Liberman & McKee · 700 Southeast Third Avenue, Suite 100 · Fort Lauderdale, FL 33316-1186 · 954-763-8181

Neal W. Hirschfeld · Greenspoon Marder · Trade Centre South, Suite 700 · 100 West Cypress Creek Road · Fort Lauderdale, FL 33309-2140 · 954-491-1120

Gordon James III · Gordon Hargrove & James · http://www.ghj.com · 2400 East Commercial Boulevard, Suite 1100 · Fort Lauderdale, FL 33308 · 954-958-2500

Robert W. Kelley · Kelley Uustal · Courthouse Law Plaza, Third Floor · 700 Southeast Third Avenue · Fort Lauderdale, FL 33316-1153 · 954-522-6601

Jon E. Krupnick · ⑳ · Krupnick Campbell Malone Buser Slama Hancock Liberman & McKee · 700 Southeast Third Avenue, Suite 100 · Fort Lauderdale, FL 33316-1186 · 954-763-8181

Scott S. Liberman · Krupnick Campbell Malone Buser Slama Hancock Liberman & McKee · 700 Southeast Third Avenue, Suite 100 · Fort Lauderdale, FL 33316-1186 · 954-763-8181

Kevin A. Malone · ⑩ · Krupnick Campbell Malone Buser Slama Hancock Liberman & McKee · 700 Southeast Third Avenue, Suite 100 · Fort Lauderdale, FL 33316-1186 · 954-763-8181

Douglas M. McIntosh · McIntosh, Sawran, Peltz & Cartaya · 1776 East Sunrise Boulevard · Fort Lauderdale, FL 33304-3067 · 954-765-1001

Robert J. McKee · Krupnick Campbell Malone Buser Slama Hancock Liberman & McKee · 700 Southeast Third Avenue, Suite 100 · Fort Lauderdale, FL 33316-1186 · 954-763-8181

Dennis M. O'Hara · Wicker, Smith, O'Hara, McCoy, Graham & Ford · SunTrust Center, Suite 1400 · 515 East Las Olas Boulevard · Fort Lauderdale, FL 33301 · 954-847-4800

Diana Santa Maria · Law Offices of Diana Santa Maria · 5220 South University Drive, Suite 205C · Fort Lauderdale, FL 33328 · 954-434-1077

Sheldon J. Schlesinger · ㉕ · Sheldon J. Schlesinger · 1212 Southeast Third Avenue · Fort Lauderdale, FL 33316-1906 · 954-467-8800

Joseph J. Slama · Krupnick Campbell Malone Buser Slama Hancock Liberman & McKee · 700 Southeast Third Avenue, Suite 100 · Fort Lauderdale, FL 33316-1186 · 954-763-8181

John J. Uustal · Kelley Uustal · Courthouse Law Plaza, Third Floor · 700 Southeast Third Avenue · Fort Lauderdale, FL 33316-1153 · 954-522-6601

Fort Myers

Jeffrey R. Garvin · Garvin Law Firm · http://www.garvinlegal.com · 7800 University Pointe Drive, Suite 100 · Fort Myers, FL 33907 · 239-277-0005

Patrick E. Geraghty · Geraghty Dougherty & Edwards · 2225 First Street · P.O. Box 1605 · Fort Myers, FL 33902-1605 · 239-334-9500

Kim Patrick Hart · Law Office of Kim Patrick Hart · http://www.kimhartlaw.com · 2205 McGregor Boulevard · P.O. Box 2485 · Fort Myers, FL 33902 · 239-337-4800

Allan M. Parvey · Parvey & Frankel · SunTrust Plaza, Suite 100 · 2069 First Street · Fort Myers, FL 33901 · 239-334-0300

Bruce M. Stanley, Sr. · Henderson, Franklin, Starnes & Holt · http://www.henlaw.com · 1715 Monroe Street · P.O. Box 280 · Fort Myers, FL 33902-0280 · 239-344-1100

Wallace Von Arx · Fowler White Boggs Banker · 2235 First Street · Fort Myers, FL 33901 · 239-334-7892

Jeptha F. Barbour · Marks & Gray · 1200 Riverplace Boulevard, Suite 800 · P.O. Box 447 · Jacksonville, FL 32201 · 904-398-0900

Robert J. Beckham · 2) · Holland & Knight · http://www.hklaw.com · 50 North Laura Street, Suite 3900 · P.O. Box 52687 · Jacksonville, FL 32202-2687 · 904-353-2000

Thomas E. Bishop · Tanner Bishop · One Independent Drive, Suite 1700 · Jacksonville, FL 32202-5015 904-598-0034

James E. Cobb · 2) · Peek, Cobb & Edwards · 1301 Riverplace Boulevard, Suite 1609 · Jacksonville, FL 32207 · 904-399-1609

Howard C. Coker · a · Coker, Schickel, Sorenson & Daniel · 136 East Bay Street · P.O. Box 1860 · Jacksonville, FL 32201 · 904-356-6071

William M. Corley · Marks & Gray · 1200 Riverplace Boulevard, Suite 800 · P.O. Box 447 · Jacksonville, FL 32201 · 904-398-0900

Robert H. Farnell II · Bedell, Dittmar, DeVault, Pillans & Coxe · http://www.bedellfirm.com · The Bedell Building · 101 East Adams Street · Jacksonville, FL 32202 · 904-353-0211

William C. Gentry · 2) · William C. Gentry · 136 East Bay Street, Suite 300 · Jacksonville, FL 32202-3415 · 904-356-4100

Victor M. Halbach, Jr. · Marks & Gray · 1200 Riverplace Boulevard, Suite 800 · P.O. Box 447 · Jacksonville, FL 32201 · 904-398-0900

Corinne C. Hodak · a · The Hodak Law Firm · 1920 San Marco Boulevard · Jacksonville, FL 32207 · 904-399-2008

Wayne Hogan · a · Terrell Hogan Ellis Yegelwel · Blackstone Building, Eighth Floor · 233 East Bay Street · Jacksonville, FL 32202 · 904-722-2228

Samuel S. Jacobson · Bledsoe, Jacobson, Schmidt & Wright · 1301 Riverplace Boulevard, Suite 1818 · Jacksonville, FL 32207 · 904-398-1818

William E. Kuntz · Smith Hulsey & Busey · http://www.smithhulsey.com · 225 Water Street, Suite 1800 · Jacksonville, FL 32202 · 904-359-7700

Rutledge R. Liles · a · Liles, Gavin, Costantino & George · http://www.lgcglaw.com · One Enterprise Center, Suite 1500 · 225 Water Street · Jacksonville, FL 32202 · 904-634-1100

Dominic C. MacKenzie · Holland & Knight · http://www.hklaw.com · 50 North Laura Street, Suite 3900 · P.O. Box 52687 · Jacksonville, FL 32202-2687 · 904-353-2000

James F. Moseley, Sr. · 2) · Moseley, Prichard, Parrish, Knight & Jones · 501 West Bay Street · Jacksonville, FL 32202 · 904-356-1306

Michael J. Obringer · Marshall, Dennehey, Warner, Coleman & Goggin · 200 West Forsyth Street, Suite 1400 · Jacksonville, FL 32202-3427 · 904-358-4200

James C. Rinaman, Jr. · 2) · Marks & Gray · 1200 Riverplace Boulevard, Suite 800 · P.O. Box 447 · Jacksonville, FL 32201 · 904-398-0900

Robert F. Spohrer · Spohrer & Dodd · 701 West Adams Street · Jacksonville, FL 32204 · 904-309-6500

Kristen M. Van der Linde · Boyd & Jenerette · http://www.boyd-jenerette.com · The Levy Building, Suite 400 · 201 North Hogan Street · Jacksonville, FL 32202 · 904-353-6241

Edward Alfred White · Law Office of Edward A. White · Blackstone Building, Suite 901 · 233 East Bay Street · Jacksonville, FL 32202-3456 · 904-356-6500

Lakeland

Jonathan B. Trohn · Valenti Campbell Trohn Tamayo & Aranda, P.A. · 1701 South Florida Avenue · Lakeland, FL 33803-2262 · 863-686-0043

Robert L. Trohn · GrayRobinson · One Lake Morton Drive · P.O. Box Three · Lakeland, FL 33802 · 863-284-2200

Melbourne

S. Sammy Cacciatore, Jr. · 2% · Nance, Cacciatore, Hamilton, Barger, Nance & Cacciatore · 525 North Harbor City Boulevard · P.O. Drawer 361817 · Melbourne, FL 32936 · 321-777-7777

James H. Nance · Nance, Cacciatore, Hamilton, Barger, Nance & Cacciatore · 525 North Harbor City Boulevard · P.O. Drawer 361817 · Melbourne, FL 32936 · 321-777-7777

Miami

Tod Aronovitz · Aronovitz Trial Lawyers · Museum Tower, Suite 2700 · 150 West Flagler Street · Miami, FL 33130-1536 · 305-372-2772

Edward R. Blumberg · Deutsch & Blumberg · New World Tower, Suite 2802 · 100 North Biscayne Boulevard · Miami, FL 33132 · 305-358-6329

Henry Burnett · 2) · Fowler White Burnett · Espirito Santo Plaza, 14th Floor · 1395 Brickell Avenue · Miami, FL 33131-3302 · 305-789-9200

Mercer K. Clarke · Clarke Silverglate & Campbell · http://csclawfirm.com · 799 Brickell Plaza, Suite 900 · Miami, FL 33131 · 305-377-0700

Richard P. Cole · Cole, Scott & Kissane · http://www.csklegal.com · Pacific National Bank Building, Third Floor · 1390 Brickell Avenue · Miami, FL 33131 · 305-350-5300

Andrew S. Connell, Jr. · Marlow, Connell, Valerius, Abrams, Adler, Newman, Lewis & Blevins · 4000 Ponce de Leon Boulevard, Suite 570 · Miami, FL 33146 · 305-446-0500

Steven K. Deutsch · Deutsch & Blumberg · New World Tower, Suite 2802 · 100 North Biscayne Boulevard · Miami, FL 33132 · 305-358-6329

Victor M. Diaz, Jr. · Podhurst Orseck · http://www.podhurst.com · City National Bank Building, Suite 800 · 25 West Flagler Street · Miami, FL 33130 · 305-358-2800

Manuel L. Dobrinsky · Freidin & Dobrinsky · One Biscayne Tower, Suite 3100 · Two South Biscayne Boulevard · Miami, FL 33131 · 305-371-3666

Richard M. Dunn · a · Cozen O'Connor · Wachovia Financial Center, Suite 4410 · 200 South Biscayne Boulevard · Miami, FL 33131-2303 · 305-704-5940

Joel D. Eaton · 2) · Podhurst Orseck · http://www.podhurst.com · City National Bank Building, Suite 800 25 West Flagler Street · Miami, FL 33130 · 305-358-2800

Andrew L. Ellenberg · Needle & Ellenberg · http://www.needleellenberg.com · 1401 Brickell Avenue, Suite 900 · Miami, FL 33131 · 305-530-0000

Gary D. Fox · a · Stewart Tilghman Fox & Bianchi · One Southeast Third Avenue, Suite 3000 · Miami, FL 33131-1764 · 305-358-6644

Philip Freidin · Freidin & Dobrinsky · One Biscayne Tower, Suite 3100 · Two South Biscayne Boulevard Miami, FL 33131 · 305-371-3666

Alan Goldfarb · Alan Goldfarb, P.A. · 100 South East Second Street, Suite 3900 · Miami, FL 33131 · 305-371-3111

David C. Goodwin · 2% · Shook, Hardy & Bacon · 201 South Biscayne Boulevard, Suite 2400 · Miami, FL 33131-4332 · 305-358-5171

Walter S. Holland · Ferraro & Associates · 4000 Ponce De Leon Boulevard, Suite 700 · Miami, FL 33146 305-375-0111

Christopher E. Knight · Fowler White Burnett · Espirito Santo Plaza, 14th Floor · 1395 Brickell Avenue · Miami, FL 33131-3302 · 305-789-9200

Arno Kutner · a · Kutner, Rubinoff & Moss · 501 Northeast First Avenue, Suite 300 · P.O. Box 9700 · Miami, FL 33101-9700 · 305-358-6200

Ira H. Leesfield · Leesfield Leighton & Partners · 2350 South Dixie Highway · Miami, FL 33133 · 305-854-4900

John E. Leighton · Leesfield Leighton & Partners · 2350 South Dixie Highway · Miami, FL 33133 · 305-854-4900

Jonathon P. Lynn · Stephens, Lynn, Klein, LaCava, Hoffman & Puya · Two Datran Center, Penthouse II · 9130 South Dadeland Boulevard · Miami, FL 33156 · 305-670-3700

Steven C. Marks · Podhurst Orseck · http://www.podhurst.com · City National Bank Building, Suite 800 · 25 West Flagler Street · Miami, FL 33130 · 305-358-2800

Jackson F. McCoy · Wicker, Smith, O'Hara, McCoy, Graham & Ford · Grove Plaza Building, Fifth Floor 2900 Middle Street · Miami, FL 33133 · 305-448-3939

Barry L. Meadow · Law Offices of Barry L. Meadow · 169 East Flagler Street, Suite 1542 · Miami, FL 33131-1213 · 305-358-9880

Edward A. Moss · a · Shook, Hardy & Bacon · 201 South Biscayne Boulevard, Suite 2400 · Miami, FL 33131-4332 · 305-358-5171

Andrew Needle · Needle & Ellenberg · http://www.needleellenberg.com · 1401 Brickell Avenue, Suite 900 · Miami, FL 33131 · 305-530-0000

Robert L. Parks · 2% · Law Offices of Robert L. Parks · 2121 Ponce de Leon, Suite 505 · Miami, FL 33134 · 305-445-4430

Aaron S. Podhurst · 2% · Podhurst Orseck · http://www.podhurst.com · City National Bank Building, Suite 800 · 25 West Flagler Street · Miami, FL 33130 · 305-358-2800

Benjamine Reid · Carlton Fields · 4000 International Place · 100 Southeast Second Street · P.O. Box 019101 · Miami, FL 33131-9101 · 305-530-0050

Stanley M. Rosenblatt · 2% · Stanley M. Rosenblatt · Concord Building, 12th Floor · 66 West Flagler Street · Miami, FL 33130-1807 · 305-374-6131

Herman J. Russomanno · Russomanno & Borrello · 150 West Flagler Street, Suite 2101 · Miami, FL 33130 · 305-373-2101

Elliot H. Scherker · Greenberg Traurig · http://www.gtlaw.com · 1221 Brickell Avenue, 22nd Floor · Miami, FL 33131 · 305-579-0500

Larry S. Stewart · 2) · Stewart Tilghman Fox & Bianchi · One Southeast Third Avenue, Suite 3000 · Miami, FL 33131-1764 · 305-358-6644

Lee Philip Teichner · Holland & Knight · http://www.hklaw.com · 701 Brickell Avenue, Suite 3000 · Miami, FL 33131 · 305-374-8500

Orlando

Alexander Murphree Clem · Morgan & Morgan · 20 North Orange Avenue, Suite 1600 · Orlando, FL 32801 · 407-420-1414

Roy B. Dalton · a · Dalton & Carpenter · 720 Rugby Street, Suite 200 · P.O. Box 540116 · Orlando, FL 32804 · 407-843-8470

Leon H. Handley · a · Rumberger, Kirk & Caldwell · Lincoln Plaza, Suite 1400 · 300 South Orange Avenue · P.O. Box 1873 · Orlando, FL 32802-1873 · 407-872-7300

Dan H. Honeywell · a · Wooten, Honeywell, Kimbrough, Gibson, Doherty & Normand · 236 South Lucerne Circle · P.O. Box 568188 · Orlando, FL 32856-8188 · 407-843-7060

Jennings L. Hurt III · Rissman, Weisberg, Barrett, Hurt, Donahue & McLain · Capital Plaza, 15th Floor · 201 East Pine Street · P.O. Box 4940 · Orlando, FL 32801 · 407-839-0120

J. Scott Kirk · a · Rumberger, Kirk & Caldwell · Lincoln Plaza, Suite 1400 · 300 South Orange Avenue · P.O. Box 1873 · Orlando, FL 32802-1873 · 407-872-7300

Francis M. McDonald, Jr. · Carlton Fields · CNL Center at City Commons, Suite 500 · 450 South Orange Avenue · Orlando, FL 32801-3336 · 407-849-0300

Keith R. Mitnik · Morgan & Morgan · 20 North Orange Avenue, Suite 1600 · Orlando, FL 32801 · 407-420-1414

C. Richard Newsome · Newsome Law Firm · http://www.newsomelaw.com · 20 North Orange Avenue, Suite 800 · Orlando, FL 32801 · 407-648-5977

E. Clay Parker · a · Law Offices of E. Clay Parker · 108 East Hillcrest Street · Orlando, FL 32801 · 407-425-4910

Council Wooten, Jr. · Wooten, Honeywell, Kimbrough, Gibson, Doherty & Normand · 236 South Lucerne Circle · P.O. Box 568188 · Orlando, FL 32856-8188 · 407-843-7060

Palm Beach Gardens

Fred A. Cunningham · Slawson Cunningham Whalen & Gaspari · 2401 PGA Boulevard, Suite 140 · Palm Beach Gardens, FL 33410-3590 · 561-625-6260

Sean C. Domnick · Domnick & Shevin · 5100 PGA Boulevard, Suite 317 · Palm Beach Gardens, FL 33418-3956 · 561-630-5363

Theodore J. Leopold · Ricci Leopold · 2925 PGA Boulevard, Suite 200 · Palm Beach Gardens, FL 33410 561-684-6500

Edward M. Ricci · a · Ricci Leopold · 2925 PGA Boulevard, Suite 200 · Palm Beach Gardens, FL 33410 561-684-6500

Richard W. Slawson · a · Slawson Cunningham Whalen & Gaspari · 2401 PGA Boulevard, Suite 140 · Palm Beach Gardens, FL 33410-3590 · 561-625-6260

Pensacola

Robert G. Kerrigan · Kerrigan, Estess, Rankin, McLeod & Thompson · 400 East Government Street · P.O. Box 12009 · Pensacola, FL 32501 · 850-444-4444

Fredric G. Levin · 2% · Levin, Papantonio, Thomas, Mitchell, Echsner & Proctor · 316 South Baylen Street, Suite 600 · P.O. Box 12308 · Pensacola, FL 32591 · 850-435-7000

J. Michael Papantonio · a · Levin, Papantonio, Thomas, Mitchell, Echsner & Proctor · 316 South Baylen Street, Suite 600 · P.O. Box 12308 · Pensacola, FL 32591 · 850-435-7000

Plantation

Joseph S. Kashi · 2) · Sperry, Shapiro & Kashi · 1776 North Pine Island Road, Suite 324 · Plantation, FL 33322 · 954-423-6553

Sarasota

William E. Partridge · Grossman, Roth and Partridge · SouthTrust Bank Plaza, Suite 777 · 1800 Second Street · Sarasota, FL 34236 · 941-365-8666

St. Petersburg

William F. Blews · a · William F. Blews · 111 Second Avenue, NE, Suite 904 · P.O. Box 417 · St. Petersburg, FL 33731-0417 · 727-822-8322

David Bresler · Fowler White Boggs Banker · 501 First Avenue North, Suite 900 · St. Petersburg, FL 33701 · 727-896-0601

Thomas D. Masterson · Masterson Law Group · 699 First Avenue North · St. Petersburg, FL 33701 · 727-896-3641

Jeffrey P. Winkler · Fowler White Boggs Banker · 501 First Avenue North, Suite 900 · St. Petersburg, FL 33701 · 727-896-0601

Tallahassee

John R. Beranek · 2) · Ausley & McMullen · Washington Square Building · 227 South Calhoun Street · P.O. Box 391 · Tallahassee, FL 32302 · 850-224-9115

Cecil L. Davis, Jr. · Fowler White Boggs Banker · 101 North Monroe Street, Suite 1090 · Tallahassee, FL 32301 · 850-681-0411

W. Dexter Douglass · a · Douglass Law Firm · 211 East Call Street · P.O. Box 1674 · Tallahassee, FL 32302 · 850-224-6191

C. David Fonvielle · Fonvielle Lewis Foote & Messer · 3375-A Capital Circle, NE · Tallahassee, FL 32308 · 850-422-7773

S. William Fuller, Jr. · Fuller Mitchell Hood & Stephens · 2565 Barrington Circle · Tallahassee, FL 32308 · 850-222-0770

Karen Gievers · Karen A. Gievers · 524 East College Avenue, Suite Two · Tallahassee, FL 32301 · 850-222-1961

Donald M. Hinkle · Hinkle & Foran · 1545 Raymond Diehl Road, Suite 150 · Tallahassee, FL 32308 · 850-205-2055

Halley B. Lewis III · Fonvielle Lewis Foote & Messer · 3375-A Capital Circle, NE · Tallahassee, FL 32308 · 850-422-7773

Tampa

David C. Banker · Bush Ross · http://www.bushross.com · 1801 North Highland Avenue · P.O. Box 3913 · Tampa, FL 33601 · 813-224-9255

Robert E. Banker · 2) · Fowler White Boggs Banker · 501 East Kennedy Boulevard, Suite 1700 · P.O. Box 1438 · Tampa, FL 33602-5239 · 813-228-7411

L. Robert Bourgeois · Fowler White Boggs Banker · 501 East Kennedy Boulevard, Suite 1700 · P.O. Box 1438 · Tampa, FL 33602-5239 · 813-228-7411

Richard K. Bowers · Fowler White Boggs Banker · 501 East Kennedy Boulevard, Suite 1700 · P.O. Box 1438 · Tampa, FL 33602-5239 · 813-228-7411

Weldon "Web" Earl Brennan · Brennan, Holden, Kavouklis · 115 South Newport Avenue · Tampa, FL 33606 · 813-254-7770

Mark P. Buell · Buell & Elligett · 3003 West Azeele Street, Suite 100 · Tampa, FL 33609 · 813-874-2600

James D. Clark · Alley, Clark, Greiwe & Fulmer · 701 East Washington Street · Tampa, FL 33602 · 813-222-0977

Barry A. Cohen · 2% · Cohen, Jayson & Foster · 201 East Kennedy Boulevard, Suite 1000 · Tampa, FL 33602-5829 · 813-225-1655

Troy J. Crotts · Bush Ross · http://www.bushross.com · 1801 North Highland Avenue · P.O. Box 3913 · Tampa, FL 33601 · 813-224-9255

Anthony W. Cunningham · 2% · Cunningham Law Group · 100 South Ashley Drive, Suite 280 · Tampa, FL 33602-5300 · 813-223-1700

James J. Evangelista · Bush Ross · http://www.bushross.com · 1801 North Highland Avenue · P.O. Box 3913 · Tampa, FL 33601 · 813-224-9255

Frank H. Gassler · Fowler White Boggs Banker · 501 East Kennedy Boulevard, Suite 1700 · P.O. Box 1438 · Tampa, FL 33602-5239 · 813-228-7411

Richard A. Gilbert · de la Parte & Gilbert · Bank of America Plaza, Suite 3400 · 101 East Kennedy Boulevard · Tampa, FL 33602-5195 · 813-229-2775

Lee D. Gunn IV · Gunn Law Group · 777 South Harbour Island Boulevard, Suite 765 · Tampa, FL 33602 813-228-7070

William E. Hahn · William E. Hahn · http://www.whahn-law.com · 310 South Fielding Avenue · Tampa, FL 33606 · 813-250-0660

John L. Holcomb · Hill, Ward & Henderson · http://www.hwhlaw.com · Bank of America Plaza, Suite 3700 · 101 East Kennedy Boulevard · Tampa, FL 33602 · 813-221-3900

C. Howard Hunter · Hill, Ward & Henderson · http://www.hwhlaw.com · Bank of America Plaza, Suite 3700 · 101 East Kennedy Boulevard · Tampa, FL 33602 · 813-221-3900

Christopher S. Knopik · KnopikVarnerMoore · One Harbour Place, Suite 800 · 777 South Harbour Island Boulevard · Tampa, FL 33602 · 813-221-3131

John Krentzman · Fowler White Boggs Banker · 501 East Kennedy Boulevard, Suite 1700 · P.O. Box 1438 · Tampa, FL 33602-5239 · 813-228-7411

Bennie Lazzara, Jr. · a · Wilkes & McHugh · One North Dale Mabry Highway, Suite 800 · Tampa, FL 33609-2755 · 813-873-0026

Joseph K. Lopez · Fowler White Boggs Banker · 501 East Kennedy Boulevard, Suite 1700 · P.O. Box 1438 · Tampa, FL 33602-5239 · 813-228-7411

Gary W. Martin · Fowler White Boggs Banker · 501 East Kennedy Boulevard, Suite 1700 · P.O. Box 1438 Tampa, FL 33602-5239 · 813-228-7411

Timothy L. McHugh · Wilkes & McHugh · One North Dale Mabry Highway, Suite 800 · Tampa, FL 33609-2755 · 813-873-0026

Kevin J. Napper · Carlton Fields · Corporate Center Three at International Plaza, Suite 1000 · 4221 West Boy Scout Boulevard · Tampa, FL 33607 · 813-223-7000

Martin W. Palmer · Fowler White Boggs Banker · 501 East Kennedy Boulevard, Suite 1700 · P.O. Box 1438 · Tampa, FL 33602-5239 · 813-228-7411

Bradley E. Powers · Fowler White Boggs Banker · 501 East Kennedy Boulevard, Suite 1700 · P.O. Box 1438 · Tampa, FL 33602-5239 · 813-228-7411

Michael S. Rywant · Rywant, Alvarez, Jones, Russo & Guyton · Perry Paint & Glass Building, Suite 500 · 109 North Brush Street · Tampa, FL 33601 · 813-229-7007

Stephen H. Sears · Macfarlane Ferguson & McMullen · One Tampa City Center, Suite 2000 · 201 North Franklin Street · P.O. Box 1531 · Tampa, FL 33601 · 813-273-4200

Robert M. Stoler · Williams Schifino Mangione & Steady · One Tampa City Center, Suite 3200 · 201 North Franklin Street · Tampa, FL 33602 · 813-221-2626

Dale M. Swope · Swope Rodante · 1234 Fifth Avenue East · Tampa, FL 33605 · 813-273-0017

Douglas J. Titus, Jr. · George & Titus · 100 South Ashley Drive, Suite 1290 · Tampa, FL 33602-5309 · 813-273-0355

David R. Tyrrell · Hill, Ward & Henderson · http://www.hwhlaw.com · Bank of America Plaza, Suite 3700 101 East Kennedy Boulevard · Tampa, FL 33602 · 813-221-3900

Henry E. Valenzuela · Valenzuela & Stern · 100 North Tampa Street, Suite 1825 · Tampa, FL 33602 · 813-272-1000

Roger A. Vaughan, Jr. · 2) · Wagner, Vaughan, McLaughlin & Brennan · 708 East Jackson Street · Tampa, FL 33602 · 813-223-7421

Alan F. Wagner · Wagner, Vaughan, McLaughlin & Brennan · 601 Bayshore Boulevard, Suite 910 · Tampa, FL 33606 · 813-225-4000

Bill Wagner · 2% · Wagner, Vaughan, McLaughlin & Brennan · 601 Bayshore Boulevard, Suite 910 · Tampa, FL 33606 · 813-225-4000

James L. Wilkes II · Wilkes & McHugh · One North Dale Mabry Highway, Suite 800 · Tampa, FL 33609-2755 · 813-873-0026

C. Steven Yerrid · 2) · The Yerrid Law Firm · Bank of America Plaza, Suite 3910 · 101 East Kennedy Boulevard · Tampa, FL 33602 · 813-222-8222

West Palm Beach

Theodore Babbitt · 2) · Babbitt Johnson Osborne & LeClainche · 1450 Centrepark Boulevard, Suite 100 · West Palm Beach, FL 33401 · 561-684-2500

F. Gregory Barnhart · a · Searcy Denney Scarola Barnhart & Shipley · http://www.searcylaw.com · 2139 Palm Beach Lakes Boulevard · P.O. Drawer 3626 · West Palm Beach, FL 33402-3626 · 561-686-6300

Edna L. Caruso · 2% · Edna L. Caruso · Barristers Building, Suite 3-A · 1615 Forum Place · West Palm Beach, FL 33401 · 561-686-8010

Mark W. Clark · Lytal, Reiter, Clark, Fountain & Williams · 515 North Flagler Drive, 10th Floor · West Palm Beach, FL 33401 · 561-655-1990

Donald R. Fountain, Jr. · Lytal, Reiter, Clark, Fountain & Williams · 515 North Flagler Drive, 10th Floor · West Palm Beach, FL 33401 · 561-655-1990

Christopher M. Larmoyeux · a · Larmoyeux & Bone · 550 South Quadrille Boulevard, Suite 200 · West Palm Beach, FL 33401 · 561-832-9400

Lake Lytal, Jr. · a · Lytal, Reiter, Clark, Fountain & Williams · 515 North Flagler Drive, 10th Floor · West Palm Beach, FL 33401 · 561-655-1990

Robert M. Montgomery, Jr. · 2% · Montgomery & Associates · 1016 Clearwater Place · P.O. Drawer 3086 West Palm Beach, FL 33402 · 561-832-2880

David C. Prather · Lytal, Reiter, Clark, Fountain & Williams · 515 North Flagler Drive, 10th Floor · West Palm Beach, FL 33401 · 561-655-1990

Justus W. Reid · a · Reid and Zobel · 222 Lakeview Avenue, Suite 1160 · West Palm Beach, FL 33401-6145 · 561-659-7700

Joseph J. Reiter · 2) · Lytal, Reiter, Clark, Fountain & Williams · 515 North Flagler Drive, 10th Floor · West Palm Beach, FL 33401 · 561-655-1990

John Scarola · Searcy Denney Scarola Barnhart & Shipley · http://www.searcylaw.com · 2139 Palm Beach Lakes Boulevard · P.O. Drawer 3626 · West Palm Beach, FL 33402-3626 · 561-686-6300

Christian D. Searcy, Sr. · 2% · Searcy Denney Scarola Barnhart & Shipley · http://www.searcylaw.com · 2139 Palm Beach Lakes Boulevard · P.O. Drawer 3626 · West Palm Beach, FL 33402-3626 · 561-686-6300

Michael S. Smith · Lesser, Lesser, Landy & Smith · 101 Northpoint Parkway · West Palm Beach, FL 33407 · 561-655-2028

Christopher K. Speed · 2) · Searcy Denney Scarola Barnhart & Shipley · http://www.searcylaw.com · 2139 Palm Beach Lakes Boulevard · P.O. Drawer 3626 · West Palm Beach, FL 33402-3626 · 561-686-6300

Roy R. Watson · a · Adams, Coogler, Watson & Merkel · 1555 Palm Beach Lakes Boulevard, Suite 1600 · P.O. Box 2069 · West Palm Beach, FL 33402 · 561-478-4500

David J. White · Searcy Denney Scarola Barnhart & Shipley · http://www.searcylaw.com · 2139 Palm Beach Lakes Boulevard · P.O. Drawer 3626 · West Palm Beach, FL 33402-3626 · 561-686-6300

Winter Park

Michael Maher · 2% · The Maher Law Firm · http://www.maherlawfirm.com · 631 West Morse Boulevard, Suite 200 · Winter Park, FL 32789 · 407-839-0866

PRIVATE FUNDS LAW

Miami

Jorge L. Freeland · White & Case · http://www.whitecase.com · Wachovia Financial Center, Suite 4900 · 200 South Biscayne Boulevard · Miami, FL 33131-2352 · 305-371-2700

Ethan W. Johnson · Morgan Lewis & Bockius · 5300 Wachovia Financial Center · 200 South Biscayne Boulevard · Miami, FL 33131-2339 · 305-415-3000

Teddy D. Klinghoffer · Akerman Senterfitt · http://www.akerman.com · One Southeast Third Avenue, 25th Floor · Miami, FL 33131-1714 · 305-374-5600

Jason S. Oletsky · Kluger, Peretz, Kaplan & Berlin · http://www.kpkb.com · Miami Center, Suite 1700 · 201 South Biscayne Boulevard · Miami, FL 33131 · 305-379-9000

Jeffrey M. Oshinsky · Stearns Weaver Miller Weissler Alhadeff & Sitterson · Museum Tower, Suite 2200 150 West Flagler Street · Miami, FL 33130 · 305-789-3200

Tampa

David S. Felman · a · Hill, Ward & Henderson · http://www.hwhlaw.com · Bank of America Plaza, Suite 3700 · 101 East Kennedy Boulevard · Tampa, FL 33602 · 813-221-3900

PRODUCT LIABILITY LITIGATION

Coral Gables

Dean C. Colson · Colson, Hicks & Eidson · http://www.colsonhickseidson.com · 255 Aragon Avenue, Second Floor · Coral Gables, FL 33134 · 305-476-7400

Lewis S. Eidson · Colson, Hicks & Eidson · http://www.colsonhickseidson.com · 255 Aragon Avenue, Second Floor · Coral Gables, FL 33134 · 305-476-7400

Jacksonville

Jeptha F. Barbour · Marks & Gray · 1200 Riverplace Boulevard, Suite 800 · P.O. Box 447 · Jacksonville, FL 32201 · 904-398-0900

Victor M. Halbach, Jr. · Marks & Gray · 1200 Riverplace Boulevard, Suite 800 · P.O. Box 447 · Jacksonville, FL 32201 · 904-398-0900

Rutledge R. Liles · a · Liles, Gavin, Costantino & George · http://www.lgcglaw.com · One Enterprise Center, Suite 1500 · 225 Water Street · Jacksonville, FL 32202 · 904-634-1100

Dominic C. MacKenzie · Holland & Knight · http://www.hklaw.com · 50 North Laura Street, Suite 3900 · P.O. Box 52687 · Jacksonville, FL 32202-2687 · 904-353-2000

Raymond P. Reid, Jr. · Pajcic & Pajcic · One Independent Drive, Suite 1900 · Jacksonville, FL 32202 · 904-358-8881

James C. Rinaman, Jr. · 2) · Marks & Gray · 1200 Riverplace Boulevard, Suite 800 · P.O. Box 447 · Jacksonville, FL 32201 · 904-398-0900

Miami

Mercer K. Clarke · Clarke Silverglate & Campbell · http://csclawfirm.com · 799 Brickell Plaza, Suite 900 · Miami, FL 33131 · 305-377-0700

Richard M. Dunn · a · Cozen O'Connor · Wachovia Financial Center, Suite 4410 · 200 South Biscayne Boulevard · Miami, FL 33131-2303 · 305-704-5940

Robert L. Parks · 2% · Law Offices of Robert L. Parks · 2121 Ponce de Leon, Suite 505 · Miami, FL 33134 · 305-445-4430

Benjamine Reid · Carlton Fields · 4000 International Place · 100 Southeast Second Street · P.O. Box 019101 · Miami, FL 33131-9101 · 305-530-0050

Orlando

Francis M. McDonald, Jr. · Carlton Fields · CNL Center at City Commons, Suite 500 · 450 South Orange Avenue · Orlando, FL 32801-3336 · 407-849-0300

Larry M. Roth · Larry M. Roth · 1615 Edgewater Drive, Suite 180 · P.O. Box 547637 · Orlando, FL 32854 · 407-872-2239

David C. Schwartz · Fowler White Boggs Banker · SunTrust Center, Suite 1950 · 200 South Orange Avenue · Orlando, FL 32801 · 407-406-5500

Palm Beach Gardens

Edward M. Ricci · a · Ricci Leopold · 2925 PGA Boulevard, Suite 200 · Palm Beach Gardens, FL 33410 561-684-6500

Pensacola

J. Michael Papantonio · a · Levin, Papantonio, Thomas, Mitchell, Echsner & Proctor · 316 South Baylen Street, Suite 600 · P.O. Box 12308 · Pensacola, FL 32591 · 850-435-7000

Tallahassee

Lance J. Block · The Law Offices of Lance Block · P.O. Box 840 · Tallahassee, FL 32302 · 850-599-1980

Tampa

Anthony W. Cunningham · 2% · Cunningham Law Group · 100 South Ashley Drive, Suite 280 · Tampa, FL 33602-5300 · 813-223-1700

Frank H. Gassler · Fowler White Boggs Banker · 501 East Kennedy Boulevard, Suite 1700 · P.O. Box 1438 · Tampa, FL 33602-5239 · 813-228-7411

Edward W. Gerecke · Carlton Fields · Corporate Center Three at International Plaza, Suite 1000 · 4221 West Boy Scout Boulevard · Tampa, FL 33607 · 813-223-7000

Kevin J. Napper · Carlton Fields · Corporate Center Three at International Plaza, Suite 1000 · 4221 West Boy Scout Boulevard · Tampa, FL 33607 · 813-223-7000

David R. Tyrrell · Hill, Ward & Henderson · http://www.hwhlaw.com · Bank of America Plaza, Suite 3700 101 East Kennedy Boulevard · Tampa, FL 33602 · 813-221-3900

West Palm Beach

Theodore Babbitt · 2) · Babbitt Johnson Osborne & LeClainche · 1450 Centrepark Boulevard, Suite 100 · West Palm Beach, FL 33401 · 561-684-2500

Patricia E. Lowry · Squire Sanders · http://www.ssd.com · Phillips Point West, Suite 1900 · 777 South Flagler Drive · West Palm Beach, FL 33401-6198 · 561-650-7200

Joseph J. Reiter · 2) · Lytal, Reiter, Clark, Fountain & Williams · 515 North Flagler Drive, 10th Floor · West Palm Beach, FL 33401 · 561-655-1990

David J. Sales · Searcy Denney Scarola Barnhart & Shipley · http://www.searcylaw.com · 2139 Palm Beach Lakes Boulevard · P.O. Drawer 3626 · West Palm Beach, FL 33402-3626 · 561-686-6300

Christian D. Searcy, Sr. · 2% · Searcy Denney Scarola Barnhart & Shipley · http://www.searcylaw.com · 2139 Palm Beach Lakes Boulevard · P.O. Drawer 3626 · West Palm Beach, FL 33402-3626 · 561-686-6300

PROFESSIONAL MALPRACTICE LAW

Coral Gables

Dean C. Colson · Colson, Hicks & Eidson · http://www.colsonhickseidson.com · 255 Aragon Avenue, Second Floor · Coral Gables, FL 33134 · 305-476-7400

Jacksonville

Robert J. Beckham · 2) · Holland & Knight · http://www.hklaw.com · 50 North Laura Street, Suite 3900 · P.O. Box 52687 · Jacksonville, FL 32202-2687 · 904-353-2000

James C. Rinaman, Jr. · 2) · Marks & Gray · 1200 Riverplace Boulevard, Suite 800 · P.O. Box 447 · Jacksonville, FL 32201 · 904-398-0900

Miami

Laura Besvinick · Hogan & Hartson · Mellon Financial Center, Suite 1900 · 1111 Brickell Avenue · Miami, FL 33131 · 305-459-6500

Stanley M. Rosenblatt · 2% · Stanley M. Rosenblatt · Concord Building, 12th Floor · 66 West Flagler Street · Miami, FL 33130-1807 · 305-374-6131

Tampa

Robert E. Banker · 2) · Fowler White Boggs Banker · 501 East Kennedy Boulevard, Suite 1700 · P.O. Box 1438 · Tampa, FL 33602-5239 · 813-228-7411

Anthony W. Cunningham · 2% · Cunningham Law Group · 100 South Ashley Drive, Suite 280 · Tampa, FL 33602-5300 · 813-223-1700

James J. Evangelista · Bush Ross · http://www.bushross.com · 1801 North Highland Avenue · P.O. Box 3913 · Tampa, FL 33601 · 813-224-9255

Benjamin H. Hill III · a · Hill, Ward & Henderson · http://www.hwhlaw.com · Bank of America Plaza, Suite 3700 · 101 East Kennedy Boulevard · Tampa, FL 33602 · 813-221-3900

Edward O. Savitz · Bush Ross · http://www.bushross.com · 1801 North Highland Avenue · P.O. Box 3913 Tampa, FL 33601 · 813-224-9255

PROJECT FINANCE LAW

Miami

Joseph W. Pallot · Devine Goodman Pallot & Wells · 777 Brickell Avenue, Suite 850 · Miami, FL 33131 305-374-8200

Thomas R. Woolsey · Hogan & Hartson · Mellon Financial Center, Suite 1900 · 1111 Brickell Avenue · Miami, FL 33131 · 305-459-6500

Miguel A. Zaldivar, Jr. · Hogan & Hartson · Mellon Financial Center, Suite 1900 · 1111 Brickell Avenue Miami, FL 33131 · 305-459-6500

PUBLIC FINANCE LAW

Jacksonville

Chauncey W. Lever, Jr. · Foley & Lardner · One Independent Drive, Suite 1300 · P.O. Box 240 · Jacksonville, FL 32201 · 904-359-2000

Lakeland

Henry M. Morgan, Jr. · GrayRobinson · One Lake Morton Drive · P.O. Box Three · Lakeland, FL 33802 · 863-284-2200

Richard B. Stephens · Holland & Knight · http://www.hklaw.com · 2115 Harden Boulevard · Lakeland, FL 33803 · 863-682-1161

Edward W. Vogel III · Holland & Knight · http://www.hklaw.com · 2115 Harden Boulevard · Lakeland, FL 33803 · 863-682-1161

Miami

Albert A. Del Castillo · Squire Sanders · http://www.ssd.com · 200 South Biscayne Boulevard, Suite 4000 Miami, FL 33131-2398 · 305-577-7000

Robert C. Gang · Greenberg Traurig · http://www.gtlaw.com · 1221 Brickell Avenue, 22nd Floor · Miami, FL 33131 · 305-579-0500

Bruce H. Giles-Klein · Greenberg Traurig · http://www.gtlaw.com · 1221 Brickell Avenue, 22nd Floor · Miami, FL 33131 · 305-579-0500

Luis Reiter · Squire Sanders · http://www.ssd.com · 200 South Biscayne Boulevard, Suite 4000 · Miami, FL 33131-2398 · 305-577-7000

Orlando

Kenneth R. Artin · Bryant Miller & Olive · 135 West Central Boulevard, Suite 700 · Orlando, FL 32801 · 407-426-7001

Warren S. Bloom · Greenberg Traurig · http://www.gtlaw.com · 450 South Orange Avenue, Suite 650 · Orlando, FL 32801 · 407-420-1000

Randall C. Clement · Bryant Miller & Olive · 135 West Central Boulevard, Suite 700 · Orlando, FL 32801 · 407-426-7001

Michael A. Ryan · Lowndes, Drosdick, Doster, Kantor & Reed · 215 North Eola Drive · Orlando, FL 32801 · 407-843-4600

Jéan E. Wilson · Greenberg Traurig · http://www.gtlaw.com · 450 South Orange Avenue, Suite 650 · Orlando, FL 32801 · 407-420-1000

Tallahassee

Randall W. Hanna · Bryant Miller & Olive · 101 North Monroe Street, Suite 900 · Tallahassee, FL 32301 850-222-8611

Tampa

Duane D. Draper · Bryant Miller & Olive · One Tampa City Center, Suite 2700 · Tampa, FL 33602 · 813-273-6677

Frank N. Fleischer · GrayRobinson · 201 North Franklin Street, Suite 2200 · P.O. Box 3324 · Tampa, FL 33601 · 813-273-5000

L. Thomas Giblin · Nabors, Giblin & Nickerson · 2502 North Rocky Point Drive, Suite 1060 · Tampa, FL 33607 · 813-281-2222

Alexandra M. MacLennan · Squire Sanders · http://www.ssd.com · One Tampa City Center, Suite 2100 · 201 North Franklin Street · Tampa, FL 33602-5164 · 813-202-1300

Steven E. Miller · Nabors, Giblin & Nickerson · 2502 North Rocky Point Drive, Suite 1060 · Tampa, FL 33607 · 813-281-2222

John R. Stokes · Nabors, Giblin & Nickerson · 2502 North Rocky Point Drive, Suite 1060 · Tampa, FL 33607 · 813-281-2222

West Palm Beach

Mark E. Raymond · Holland & Knight · http://www.hklaw.com · 222 Lakeview Avenue, Suite 1000 · West Palm Beach, FL 33401 · 561-833-2000

RAILROAD LAW

Jacksonville

William Higginbotham · Moody, Strople, Kloeppel, Basilone & Higginbotham · 7400 Baymeadows Way, Suite 105 · Jacksonville, FL 32256 · 904-256-0018

Ronald R. Oberdier · Oberdier & Oberdier · 6620 Southpoint Drive South, Suite 200 · Jacksonville, FL 32216-0940 · 904-721-4161

REAL ESTATE LAW

Boca Raton

Jeffrey Deutch · Broad and Cassel · Corporate Centre of Boca Raton, Suite 300 · 7777 Glades Road · Boca Raton, FL 33434 · 561-483-7000

Dennis W. Hillier · Greenberg Traurig · http://www.gtlaw.com · 5100 Town Center Circle, Suite 400 · Boca Raton, FL 33486 · 561-955-7600

Richard Macfarland · Broad and Cassel · Corporate Centre of Boca Raton, Suite 300 · 7777 Glades Road · Boca Raton, FL 33434 · 561-483-7000

Andrew S. Robins · Proskauer Rose · http://www.proskauer.com · 2255 Glades Road, Suite 340 West · Boca Raton, FL 33431-7383 · 561-241-7400

Bonita Springs

Thad D. Kirkpatrick · Cohen & Grigsby · 27200 Riverview Center Boulevard, Suite 309 · Bonita Springs, FL 34134-4317 · 239-390-1900

Clearwater

Roger A. Larson · Johnson, Pope, Bokor, Ruppel & Burns · http://www.jpfirm.com · 911 Chestnut Street P.O. Box 1368 · Clearwater, FL 33756 · 727-461-1818

Coral Gables

Rene V. Murai · Murai, Wald, Biondo & Moreno · Two Alhambra Plaza, Penthouse 1-B · Coral Gables, FL 33134 · 305-444-0101

Coral Springs

John Hume · John Hume · 1401 North University Drive, Suite 402 · Coral Springs, FL 33071-6088 · 954-755-5154

Destin

W. Christopher Hart · a · Clark, Partington, Hart, Larry, Bond & Stackhouse · 34990 Emerald Coast Parkway, Suite 301 · Destin, FL 32541 · 850-650-3304

Fort Lauderdale

Drake M. Batchelder · Akerman Senterfitt · http://www.akerman.com · Las Olas Centre II, Suite 1600 · 350 East Los Olas Boulevard · Fort Lauderdale, FL 33301-2229 · 954-463-2700

James L. Berger · Berger Singerman · http://www.bergersingerman.com · 350 East Las Olas Boulevard, Suite 1000 · Fort Lauderdale, FL 33301 · 954-525-9900

Conrad J. Boyle · Mombach, Boyle and Hardin · Broward Financial Centre, Suite 1950 · 500 East Broward Boulevard · Fort Lauderdale, FL 33394-3079 · 954-467-2200

Susan F. Delegal · Billing Cochran Heath Lyles Mauro & Anderson · 888 Southeast Third Avenue, Suite 301 · Fort Lauderdale, FL 33316-1159 · 954-764-7150

Marshall J. Emas · Shutts & Bowen · http://www.shutts.com · 200 East Broward Boulevard, Suite 2100 · Fort Lauderdale, FL 33301 · 954-524-5505

Scott J. Fuerst · Ruden, McClosky, Smith, Schuster & Russell · 200 East Broward Boulevard · P.O. Box 1900 · Fort Lauderdale, FL 33302 · 954-764-6660

Jonathan S. Gelman · Greenberg Traurig · http://www.gtlaw.com · 401 East Las Olas Boulevard, Suite 2000 · Fort Lauderdale, FL 33301 · 954-765-0500

Bruce D. Goorland · Ruden, McClosky, Smith, Schuster & Russell · 200 East Broward Boulevard · P.O. Box 1900 · Fort Lauderdale, FL 33302 · 954-764-6660

Samuel S. Goren · Goren, Cherof, Doody & Ezrol · 3099 East Commercial Boulevard, Suite 200 · Fort Lauderdale, FL 33308-4500 · 954-771-4500

Mark F. Grant · Ruden, McClosky, Smith, Schuster & Russell · 200 East Broward Boulevard · P.O. Box 1900 · Fort Lauderdale, FL 33302 · 954-764-6660

Gerald Greenspoon · Greenspoon Marder · Trade Centre South, Suite 700 · 100 West Cypress Creek Road · Fort Lauderdale, FL 33309-2140 · 954-491-1120

Donald R. Hall · Gunster, Yoakley & Stewart · Las Olas Centre, Suite 1400 · 450 East Las Olas Boulevard Fort Lauderdale, FL 33301 · 954-462-2000

Stephen F. Katz · Greenberg Traurig · http://www.gtlaw.com · 401 East Las Olas Boulevard, Suite 2000 · Fort Lauderdale, FL 33301 · 954-765-0500

Donald C. McClosky · 2% · Ruden, McClosky, Smith, Schuster & Russell · 200 East Broward Boulevard · P.O. Box 1900 · Fort Lauderdale, FL 33302 · 954-764-6660

Geoffrey S. Mombach · Mombach, Boyle and Hardin · Broward Financial Centre, Suite 1950 · 500 East Broward Boulevard · Fort Lauderdale, FL 33394-3079 · 954-467-2200

Stephen B. Moss · Holland & Knight · http://www.hklaw.com · One East Broward Boulevard, Suite 1300 · P.O. Box 14070 · Fort Lauderdale, FL 33302-4070 · 954-525-1000

Debbie M. Orshefsky · Greenberg Traurig · http://www.gtlaw.com · 401 East Las Olas Boulevard, Suite 2000 · Fort Lauderdale, FL 33301 · 954-765-0500

Eric D. Rapkin · Akerman Senterfitt · http://www.akerman.com · Las Olas Centre II, Suite 1600 · 350 East Los Olas Boulevard · Fort Lauderdale, FL 33301-2229 · 954-463-2700

Brian J. Sherr · Greenberg Traurig · http://www.gtlaw.com · 401 East Las Olas Boulevard, Suite 2000 · Fort Lauderdale, FL 33301 · 954-765-0500

John L. Shiekman · Ruden, McClosky, Smith, Schuster & Russell · 200 East Broward Boulevard · P.O. Box 1900 · Fort Lauderdale, FL 33302 · 954-764-6660

Peter D. Slavis · Ruden, McClosky, Smith, Schuster & Russell · 200 East Broward Boulevard · P.O. Box 1900 · Fort Lauderdale, FL 33302 · 954-764-6660

Barry E. Somerstein · a · Ruden, McClosky, Smith, Schuster & Russell · 200 East Broward Boulevard · P.O. Box 1900 · Fort Lauderdale, FL 33302 · 954-764-6660

Mark K. Somerstein · Ruden, McClosky, Smith, Schuster & Russell · 200 East Broward Boulevard · P.O. Box 1900 · Fort Lauderdale, FL 33302 · 954-764-6660

Roger H. Staley · a · Saunders Curtis Et Al · 6550 North Federal Highway, Suite 510 · Fort Lauderdale, FL 33308-1423 · 954-229-1956

Adele I. Stone · Atkinson, Diner, Stone, Mankuta & Ploucha · One Financial Plaza, Suite 1400 · 100 Southeast Third Avenue · Fort Lauderdale, FL 33394 · 954-925-5501

Peter L. Tunis · Greenberg Traurig · http://www.gtlaw.com · 401 East Las Olas Boulevard, Suite 2000 · Fort Lauderdale, FL 33301 · 954-765-0500

Fort Myers

Garey F. Butler · Fowler White Boggs Banker · 2235 First Street · Fort Myers, FL 33901 · 239-334-7892

W. O. Birchfield · a · Birchfield & Humphrey · 1031 LaSalle Street · Jacksonville, FL 32207 · 904-396-6625

Charles E. Commander III · 2% · Foley & Lardner · One Independent Drive, Suite 1300 · P.O. Box 240 · Jacksonville, FL 32201 · 904-359-2000

David C. Cook · Foley & Lardner · One Independent Drive, Suite 1300 · P.O. Box 240 · Jacksonville, FL 32201 · 904-359-2000

William J. Deas · William J. Deas · 2215 River Boulevard · Jacksonville, FL 32203 · 904-387-9292

Brenna M. Durden · Lewis, Longman & Walker · http://www.llw-law.com · 245 Riverside Avenue, Suite 150 · Jacksonville, FL 32202 · 904-353-6410

Allan T. Geiger · a · Rogers Towers · 1301 Riverplace Boulevard, Suite 1500 · Jacksonville, FL 32207 · 904-398-3911

Doris Sussman Goldstein · New Town Law · 2656 Beauclerc Road · P.O. Box 23646 · Jacksonville, FL 32241 · 904-730-2960

Theodore R. Hainline, Jr. · Rogers Towers · 1301 Riverplace Boulevard, Suite 1500 · Jacksonville, FL 32207 · 904-398-3911

Karl B. Hanson, Jr. · Fowler White Boggs Banker · 50 North Laura Street, Suite 2200 · Jacksonville, FL 32202 · 904-598-3100

Thomas M. Jenks · Pappas Metcalf Jenks & Miller · 245 Riverside Avenue, Suite 400 · Jacksonville, FL 32202-4907 · 904-353-1980

Kenneth M. Keefe, Jr. · McGuireWoods · http://www.mcguirewoods.com · Bank of America Tower, Suite 3300 · 50 North Laura Street · Jacksonville, FL 32202-3661 · 904-798-3200

G. Preston Keyes · Smith Hulsey & Busey · http://www.smithhulsey.com · 225 Water Street, Suite 1800 · Jacksonville, FL 32202 · 904-359-7700

Emerson M. Lotzia · Foley & Lardner · One Independent Drive, Suite 1300 · P.O. Box 240 · Jacksonville, FL 32201 · 904-359-2000

John G. Metcalf · Pappas Metcalf Jenks & Miller · 245 Riverside Avenue, Suite 400 · Jacksonville, FL 32202-4907 · 904-353-1980

Terry A. Moore · GrayRobinson · 50 North Laura Street, Suite 1100 · Jacksonville, FL 32202 · 904-598-9929

M. Lynn Pappas · a · Pappas Metcalf Jenks & Miller · 245 Riverside Avenue, Suite 400 · Jacksonville, FL 32202-4907 · 904-353-1980

Bryan L. Putnal · Smith Hulsey & Busey · http://www.smithhulsey.com · 225 Water Street, Suite 1800 · Jacksonville, FL 32202 · 904-359-7700

William E. Scheu · a · Rogers Towers · 1301 Riverplace Boulevard, Suite 1500 · Jacksonville, FL 32207 904-398-3911

Bert C. Simon · Gartner, Brock and Simon · 1660 Prudential Drive, Suite 203 · P.O. Box 10697 · Jacksonville, FL 32247-0697 · 904-399-0870

Douglas G. Stanford · Smith, Gambrell & Russell · http://www.sgrlaw.com · Bank of America Tower, Suite 2600 · 50 North Laura Street · Jacksonville, FL 32202 · 904-598-6100

Carl M. Stewart · Taylor, Stewart, Houston & Duss · 1050 Riverside Avenue · Jacksonville, FL 32204-4123 · 904-354-9000

James S. Taylor · 2% · Taylor, Stewart, Houston & Duss · 1050 Riverside Avenue · Jacksonville, FL 32204-4123 · 904-354-9000

Melissa S. Turra · Holland & Knight · http://www.hklaw.com · 50 North Laura Street, Suite 3900 · P.O. Box 52687 · Jacksonville, FL 32202-2687 · 904-353-2000

Harry M. Wilson III · a · Smith Hulsey & Busey · http://www.smithhulsey.com · 225 Water Street, Suite 1800 · Jacksonville, FL 32202 · 904-359-7700

Miami

E. Richard Alhadeff · Stearns Weaver Miller Weissler Alhadeff & Sitterson · Museum Tower, Suite 2200 150 West Flagler Street · Miami, FL 33130 · 305-789-3200

Suzanne M. Amaducci-Adams · Bilzin Sumberg Baena Price & Axelrod · Wachovia Financial Center, Suite 2500 · 200 South Biscayne Boulevard · Miami, FL 33131 · 305-374-7580

Ralph B. Bekkevold · Greenberg Traurig · http://www.gtlaw.com · 1221 Brickell Avenue, 22nd Floor · Miami, FL 33131 · 305-579-0500

Miami

Jonathan D. Beloff · Beloff & Schwartz · 1111 Lincoln Road, Suite 400 · Miami, FL 33139 · 305-673-1101

Miami

Jeffrey S. Bercow · Bercow & Radell · 200 South Biscayne Boulevard, Suite 850 · Miami, FL 33131 · 305-374-5300

Michael A. Berke · Akerman Senterfitt · http://www.akerman.com · One Southeast Third Avenue, 25th Floor · Miami, FL 33131-1714 · 305-374-5600

Brian L. Bilzin · a · Bilzin Sumberg Baena Price & Axelrod · Wachovia Financial Center, Suite 2500 · 200 South Biscayne Boulevard · Miami, FL 33131 · 305-374-7580

William R. Bloom · Holland & Knight · http://www.hklaw.com · 701 Brickell Avenue, Suite 3000 · Miami, FL 33131 · 305-374-8500

Burt Bruton · Greenberg Traurig · http://www.gtlaw.com · 1221 Brickell Avenue, 22nd Floor · Miami, FL 33131 · 305-579-0500

Kevin D. Cowan · Shutts & Bowen · http://www.shutts.com · Miami Center, Suite 1500 · 201 South Biscayne Boulevard · Miami, FL 33131 · 305-358-6300

Lucia A. Dougherty · Greenberg Traurig · http://www.gtlaw.com · 1221 Brickell Avenue, 22nd Floor · Miami, FL 33131 · 305-579-0500

Marc L. Faust · Katz Barron Squitero Faust · http://www.katzbarron.com · 2699 South Bayshore Drive, Seventh Floor · Miami, FL 33133-5408 · 305-856-2444

Barry Frank · Weil Gotshal & Manges · 1395 Brickell Avenue, Suite 1200 · Miami, FL 33131 · 305-577-3100

Robert E. Gallagher, Jr. · Stearns Weaver Miller Weissler Alhadeff & Sitterson · Museum Tower, Suite 2200 · 150 West Flagler Street · Miami, FL 33130 · 305-789-3200

Laura R. Gangemi Vignola · Greenberg Traurig · http://www.gtlaw.com · 1221 Brickell Avenue, 22nd Floor · Miami, FL 33131 · 305-579-0500

Chava Eve Genet · Stearns Weaver Miller Weissler Alhadeff & Sitterson · Museum Tower, Suite 2200 · 150 West Flagler Street · Miami, FL 33130 · 305-789-3200

Richard J. Giusto · Greenberg Traurig · http://www.gtlaw.com · 1221 Brickell Avenue, 22nd Floor · Miami, FL 33131 · 305-579-0500

Steven E. Goldman · Greenberg Traurig · http://www.gtlaw.com · 1221 Brickell Avenue, 22nd Floor · Miami, FL 33131 · 305-579-0500

Joseph G. Goldstein · Holland & Knight · http://www.hklaw.com · 701 Brickell Avenue, Suite 3000 · Miami, FL 33131 · 305-374-8500

Matthew B. Gorson · 2) · Greenberg Traurig · http://www.gtlaw.com · 1221 Brickell Avenue, 22nd Floor · Miami, FL 33131 · 305-579-0500

K. Lawrence Gragg · a · White & Case · http://www.whitecase.com · Wachovia Financial Center, Suite 4900 · 200 South Biscayne Boulevard · Miami, FL 33131-2352 · 305-371-2700

John F. Halula · Holland & Knight · http://www.hklaw.com · 701 Brickell Avenue, Suite 3000 · Miami, FL 33131 · 305-374-8500

Osmond C. Howe, Jr. · a · Howe, Robinson & Watkins · Courvoisier Centre One, Suite 504 · 501 Brickell Key Drive · Miami, FL 33131 · 305-377-1274

Michael D. Katz · Katz Barron Squitero Faust · http://www.katzbarron.com · 2699 South Bayshore Drive, Seventh Floor · Miami, FL 33133-5408 · 305-856-2444

David S. Kenin · 2) · Greenberg Traurig · http://www.gtlaw.com · 1221 Brickell Avenue, 22nd Floor · Miami, FL 33131 · 305-579-0500

Nancy B. Lash · Greenberg Traurig · http://www.gtlaw.com · 1221 Brickell Avenue, 22nd Floor · Miami, FL 33131 · 305-579-0500

Juan P. Loumiet · Greenberg Traurig · http://www.gtlaw.com · 1221 Brickell Avenue, 22nd Floor · Miami, FL 33131 · 305-579-0500

Juan J. Mayol Lopez, Jr. · Holland & Knight · http://www.hklaw.com · 701 Brickell Avenue, Suite 3000 · Miami, FL 33131 · 305-374-8500

Brian J. McDonough · Stearns Weaver Miller Weissler Alhadeff & Sitterson · Museum Tower, Suite 2200 · 150 West Flagler Street · Miami, FL 33130 · 305-789-3200

Francisco J. Menendez · Stearns Weaver Miller Weissler Alhadeff & Sitterson · Museum Tower, Suite 2200 · 150 West Flagler Street · Miami, FL 33130 · 305-789-3200

Stanley B. Price · 2) · Bilzin Sumberg Baena Price & Axelrod · Wachovia Financial Center, Suite 2500 · 200 South Biscayne Boulevard · Miami, FL 33131 · 305-374-7580

Albert D. Quentel · 2) · Greenberg Traurig · http://www.gtlaw.com · 1221 Brickell Avenue, 22nd Floor · Miami, FL 33131 · 305-579-0500

Neil S. Rollnick · Adorno & Yoss · 2525 Ponce de Leon Boulevard, Suite 400 · Miami, FL 33134 · 305-460-1000

Donald S. Rosenberg · 2% · Peckar & Abramson · http://www.pecklaw.com · One Southeast Third Avenue, Suite 3100 · Miami, FL 33131 · 305-358-2600

Janice L. Russell · Akerman Senterfitt · http://www.akerman.com · One Southeast Third Avenue, 25th Floor · Miami, FL 33131-1714 · 305-374-5600

Gary Saul · Greenberg Traurig · http://www.gtlaw.com · 1221 Brickell Avenue, 22nd Floor · Miami, FL 33131 · 305-579-0500

Barry N. Semet · Fowler White Burnett · Espirito Santo Plaza, 14th Floor · 1395 Brickell Avenue · Miami, FL 33131-3302 · 305-789-9200

James W. Shindell · Bilzin Sumberg Baena Price & Axelrod · Wachovia Financial Center, Suite 2500 · 200 South Biscayne Boulevard · Miami, FL 33131 · 305-374-7580

Harry B. Smith · 2) · Ruden, McClosky, Smith, Schuster & Russell · Bank of America Building, Suite 1900 · 701 Brickell Avenue · Miami, FL 33131 · 305-789-2700

Andrew M. Smulian · Akerman Senterfitt · http://www.akerman.com · One Southeast Third Avenue, 25th Floor · Miami, FL 33131-1714 · 305-374-5600

Carey A. Stiss · Bilzin Sumberg Baena Price & Axelrod · Wachovia Financial Center, Suite 2500 · 200 South Biscayne Boulevard · Miami, FL 33131 · 305-374-7580

John C. Sumberg · Bilzin Sumberg Baena Price & Axelrod · Wachovia Financial Center, Suite 2500 · 200 South Biscayne Boulevard · Miami, FL 33131 · 305-374-7580

Brian Tague · Tew Cardenas · http://www.tewlaw.com · Four Seasons Tower, 15th Floor · 1441 Brickell Avenue · Miami, FL 33131-3407 · 305-536-1112

Robert H. Traurig · 2% · Greenberg Traurig · http://www.gtlaw.com · 1221 Brickell Avenue, 22nd Floor · Miami, FL 33131 · 305-579-0500

Steven J. Vainder · White & Case · http://www.whitecase.com · Wachovia Financial Center, Suite 4900 · 200 South Biscayne Boulevard · Miami, FL 33131-2352 · 305-371-2700

H. William Walker, Jr. · White & Case · http://www.whitecase.com · Wachovia Financial Center, Suite 4900 · 200 South Biscayne Boulevard · Miami, FL 33131-2352 · 305-371-2700

J. Donald Wasil · Shutts & Bowen · http://www.shutts.com · Miami Center, Suite 1500 · 201 South Biscayne Boulevard · Miami, FL 33131 · 305-358-6300

William A. Weber · Hughes Hubbard & Reed · http://www.hugheshubbard.com · 201 South Biscayne Boulevard, Suite 2500 · Miami, FL 33131-4332 · 305-358-1666

Robert I. Weissler · Stearns Weaver Miller Weissler Alhadeff & Sitterson · Museum Tower, Suite 2200 · 150 West Flagler Street · Miami, FL 33130 · 305-789-3200

Julie A. S. Williamson · Akerman Senterfitt · http://www.akerman.com · One Southeast Third Avenue, 25th Floor · Miami, FL 33131-1714 · 305-374-5600

Naples

G. Helen Athan · Grant, Fridkin, Pearson, Athan & Crown · Pelican Bay Corporate Centre, Suite 501 · 5551 Ridgewood Drive · Naples, FL 34108-2719 · 239-514-1000

W. Jeffrey Cecil · Porter, Wright, Morris & Arthur · http://www.porterwright.com · 5801 Pelican Bay Boulevard, Suite 300 · Naples, FL 34108-2709 · 239-593-2900

Jay F. Cook · Law Offices of Jay F. Cook · 1415 Panther Lane, Suite 313 · Naples, FL 34109 · 239-591-6648

Richard C. Grant · Grant, Fridkin, Pearson, Athan & Crown · Pelican Bay Corporate Centre, Suite 501 · 5551 Ridgewood Drive · Naples, FL 34108-2719 · 239-514-1000

C. Neil Gregory · Roetzel & Andress · http://www.ralaw.com · Trianon Centre, Third Floor · 850 Park Shore Drive · Naples, FL 34103 · 239-649-6200

Paul K. Heuerman · Roetzel & Andress · http://www.ralaw.com · Trianon Centre, Third Floor · 850 Park Shore Drive · Naples, FL 34103 · 239-649-6200

Kevin R. Lottes · Quarles & Brady · http://www.quarles.com · 1395 Panther Lane, Suite 300 · Naples, FL 34109-7874 · 941-262-5959

Mark J. Price · Roetzel & Andress · http://www.ralaw.com · Trianon Centre, Third Floor · 850 Park Shore Drive · Naples, FL 34103 · 239-649-6200

David N. Sexton · Bond, Schoeneck & King · Northern Trust Building, Suite 250 · 4001 Tamiami Trail North · Naples, FL 34103-3555 · 239-659-3800

Stephen E. Thompson · Roetzel & Andress · http://www.ralaw.com · Trianon Centre, Third Floor · 850 Park Shore Drive · Naples, FL 34103 · 239-649-6200

Orlando

James Balletta · GrayRobinson · 301 East Pine Street, Suite 1400 · P.O. Box 3068 · Orlando, FL 32802-3068 · 407-843-8880

William A. Beckett · Lowndes, Drosdick, Doster, Kantor & Reed · 215 North Eola Drive · Orlando, FL 32801 · 407-843-4600

William R. Bird, Jr. · Lowndes, Drosdick, Doster, Kantor & Reed · 215 North Eola Drive · Orlando, FL 32801 · 407-843-4600

Cecelia Bonifay · Akerman Senterfitt · http://www.akerman.com · CNL Center II at City Commons, Suite 1200 · 420 South Orange Avenue · Orlando, FL 32801-3336 · 407-423-4000

Stephen J. Bozarth · a · Dean, Mead, Egerton, Bloodworth, Capouano & Bozarth · http://www.deanmead.com · 800 North Magnolia Avenue, Suite 1500 · P.O. Box 2346 · Orlando, FL 32802-2346 · 407-841-1200

Jacqueline Bozzuto · Lowndes, Drosdick, Doster, Kantor & Reed · 215 North Eola Drive · Orlando, FL 32801 · 407-843-4600

C. David Brown II · Broad and Cassel · 390 North Orange Avenue, Suite 1400 · Orlando, FL 32801-4961 407-839-4200

Ted R. Brown · Baker Hostetler · http://www.bakerlaw.com · Sun Trust Center, Suite 2300 · 200 South Orange Avenue · Orlando, FL 32801-3432 · 407-649-4000

William E. Doster · a · Lowndes, Drosdick, Doster, Kantor & Reed · 215 North Eola Drive · Orlando, FL 32801 · 407-843-4600

William T. Dymond, Jr. · Lowndes, Drosdick, Doster, Kantor & Reed · 215 North Eola Drive · Orlando, FL 32801 · 407-843-4600

Ted B. Edwards · Foley & Lardner · 111 North Orange Avenue, Suite 1800 · P.O. Box 2193 · Orlando, FL 32802-2193 · 407-423-7656

Orlando L. Evora · Greenberg Traurig · http://www.gtlaw.com · 450 South Orange Avenue, Suite 650 · Orlando, FL 32801 · 407-420-1000

Peter J. Fides II · Greenberg Traurig · http://www.gtlaw.com · 450 South Orange Avenue, Suite 650 · Orlando, FL 32801 · 407-420-1000

Richard J. Fildes · a · Lowndes, Drosdick, Doster, Kantor & Reed · 215 North Eola Drive · Orlando, FL 32801 · 407-843-4600

Phillip R. Finch · GrayRobinson · 301 East Pine Street, Suite 1400 · P.O. Box 3068 · Orlando, FL 32802-3068 · 407-843-8880

Miranda F. Fitzgerald · a · Lowndes, Drosdick, Doster, Kantor & Reed · 215 North Eola Drive · Orlando, FL 32801 · 407-843-4600

Thomas E. Francis · Lowndes, Drosdick, Doster, Kantor & Reed · 215 North Eola Drive · Orlando, FL 32801 · 407-843-4600

Richard T. Fulton · Baker Hostetler · http://www.bakerlaw.com · Sun Trust Center, Suite 2300 · 200 South Orange Avenue · Orlando, FL 32801-3432 · 407-649-4000

Aaron J. Gorovitz · Lowndes, Drosdick, Doster, Kantor & Reed · 215 North Eola Drive · Orlando, FL 32801 · 407-843-4600

Michael J. Grindstaff · Shutts & Bowen · http://www.shutts.com · 300 South Orange Avenue, Suite 1000 · Orlando, FL 32801 · 407-423-3200

Martha Anderson Hartley · Greenberg Traurig · http://www.gtlaw.com · 450 South Orange Avenue, Suite 650 · Orlando, FL 32801 · 407-420-1000

Hal H. Kantor · a · Lowndes, Drosdick, Doster, Kantor & Reed · 215 North Eola Drive · Orlando, FL 32801 · 407-843-4600

Frederick W. Leonhardt · GrayRobinson · 301 East Pine Street, Suite 1400 · P.O. Box 3068 · Orlando, FL 32802-3068 · 407-843-8880

Peter L. Lopez · Lowndes, Drosdick, Doster, Kantor & Reed · 215 North Eola Drive · Orlando, FL 32801 · 407-843-4600

John F. Lowndes · 2% · Lowndes, Drosdick, Doster, Kantor & Reed · 215 North Eola Drive · Orlando, FL 32801 · 407-843-4600

Timothy J. Manor · Lowndes, Drosdick, Doster, Kantor & Reed · 215 North Eola Drive · Orlando, FL 32801 · 407-843-4600

A. Guy Neff · Holland & Knight · http://www.hklaw.com · 200 South Orange Avenue, Suite 2600 · P.O. Box 1526 · Orlando, FL 32802 · 407-425-8500

Daniel T. O'Keefe · Shutts & Bowen · http://www.shutts.com · 300 South Orange Avenue, Suite 1000 · Orlando, FL 32801 · 407-423-3200

Rosemary O'Shea · Baker Hostetler · http://www.bakerlaw.com · Sun Trust Center, Suite 2300 · 200 South Orange Avenue · Orlando, FL 32801-3432 · 407-649-4000

Nicholas A. Pope · Lowndes, Drosdick, Doster, Kantor & Reed · 215 North Eola Drive · Orlando, FL 32801 · 407-843-4600

Shawn G. Rader · Lowndes, Drosdick, Doster, Kantor & Reed · 215 North Eola Drive · Orlando, FL 32801 · 407-843-4600

Paul E. Rosenthal · Foley & Lardner · 111 North Orange Avenue, Suite 1800 · P.O. Box 2193 · Orlando, FL 32802-2193 · 407-423-7656

Thomas T. Ross · a · Akerman Senterfitt · http://www.akerman.com · CNL Center II at City Commons, Suite 1200 · 420 South Orange Avenue · Orlando, FL 32801-3336 · 407-423-4000

Michael A. Ryan · Lowndes, Drosdick, Doster, Kantor & Reed · 215 North Eola Drive · Orlando, FL 32801 · 407-843-4600

James E. L. Seay · a · Holland & Knight · http://www.hklaw.com · 200 South Orange Avenue, Suite 2600 P.O. Box 1526 · Orlando, FL 32802 · 407-425-8500

James Slater · Broad and Cassel · 390 North Orange Avenue, Suite 1400 · Orlando, FL 32801-4961 · 407-839-4200

James M. Spoonhour · Lowndes, Drosdick, Doster, Kantor & Reed · 215 North Eola Drive · Orlando, FL 32801 · 407-843-4600

Michael J. Sullivan · Greenberg Traurig · http://www.gtlaw.com · 450 South Orange Avenue, Suite 650 · Orlando, FL 32801 · 407-420-1000

Scott C. Thompson · Lowndes, Drosdick, Doster, Kantor & Reed · 215 North Eola Drive · Orlando, FL 32801 · 407-843-4600

Jeffrey P. Wieland · Akerman Senterfitt · http://www.akerman.com · CNL Center II at City Commons, Suite 1200 · 420 South Orange Avenue · Orlando, FL 32801-3336 · 407-423-4000

Jim Willard · Shutts & Bowen · http://www.shutts.com · 300 South Orange Avenue, Suite 1000 · Orlando, FL 32801 · 407-423-3200

R. Duke Woodson · Foley & Lardner · 111 North Orange Avenue, Suite 1800 · P.O. Box 2193 · Orlando, FL 32802-2193 · 407-423-7656

Jon C. Yergler · a · Lowndes, Drosdick, Doster, Kantor & Reed · 215 North Eola Drive · Orlando, FL 32801 · 407-843-4600

Pensacola

Patrick G. Emmanuel · 2% · Emmanuel, Sheppard & Condon · 30 South Spring Street · P.O. Drawer 1271 Pensacola, FL 32591 · 850-433-6581

John W. Monroe, Jr. · a · Emmanuel, Sheppard & Condon · 30 South Spring Street · P.O. Drawer 1271 Pensacola, FL 32591 · 850-433-6581

Sarasota

Michael J. Furen · Icard, Merrill, Cullis, Timm, Furen & Ginsburg · http://www.icardmerrill.com · 2033 Main Street, Suite 500 & 600 · P.O. Drawer 4195 · Sarasota, FL 34230 · 941-366-8100

J. Michael Hartenstine · Williams Parker Harrison Dietz & Getzen · 200 South Orange Avenue · Sarasota, FL 34236 · 941-366-4800

St. Petersburg

Louie N. Adcock, Jr. · Fisher & Sauls · 100 Second Avenue South, Suite 701 · St. Petersburg, FL 33701 · 727-822-2033

Anthony S. Battaglia · 2) · Battaglia, Ross, Dicus & Wein · 980 Tyrone Boulevard · P.O. Box 41100 · St. Petersburg, FL 33743 · 727-381-2300

Mary Jo Carney · Powell, Carney, Gross, Maller & Ramsay · Bank of America Tower, Suite 1210 · One Progress Plaza · St. Petersburg, FL 33701 · 727-898-9011

Robert Decker · Decker Beeler · South Tower, 100 Second Avenue South, Suite 303 · St. Petersburg, FL 33701 · 727-821-6677

Joel B. Giles · Carlton Fields · 200 Central Avenue, Suite 2300 · St. Petersburg, FL 33701 · 727-821-7000

R. Donald Mastry · Trenam, Kemker, Scharf, Barkin, Frye, O'Neill & Mullis · http://www.trenam.com · 200 Central Avenue, Suite 1600 · P.O. Box 3542 · St. Petersburg, FL 33731-3542 · 727-896-7171

James N. Powell · Powell, Carney, Gross, Maller & Ramsay · Bank of America Tower, Suite 1210 · One Progress Plaza · St. Petersburg, FL 33701 · 727-898-9011

David R. Punzak · Carlton Fields · 200 Central Avenue, Suite 2300 · St. Petersburg, FL 33701 · 727-821-7000

Tallahassee

Nancy G. Linnan · Carlton Fields · Suntrust Building, Suite 500 · 215 South Monroe Street · Tallahassee, FL 32301 · 850-224-1585

Robert R. McDonald · Greenberg Traurig · http://www.gtlaw.com · 101 East College Avenue · Tallahassee, FL 32301 · 850-222-6891

David L. Powell · Hopping Green & Sams · http://www.hgslaw.com · 123 South Calhoun Street · P.O. Box 6526 · Tallahassee, FL 32314 · 850-222-7598

Dan R. Stengle · Hopping Green & Sams · http://www.hgslaw.com · 123 South Calhoun Street · P.O. Box 6526 · Tallahassee, FL 32314 · 850-222-7598

Tampa

J. Alan Asendorf · Trenam, Kemker, Scharf, Barkin, Frye, O'Neill & Mullis · http://www.trenam.com · 101 East Kennedy Boulevard, Suite 2700 · P.O. Box 1102 · Tampa, FL 33601-1102 · 813-223-7474

Michael A. Bedke · DLA Piper · 100 North Tampa, Suite 2200 · Tampa, FL 33602-5809 · 813-229-2111

Keith W. Bricklemyer · Bricklemyer Smolker & Bolves · http://www.bsbfirm.com · 500 East Kennedy Boulevard, Suite 200 · Tampa, FL 33602-4708 · 813-223-3888

David R. Brittain · Trenam, Kemker, Scharf, Barkin, Frye, O'Neill & Mullis · http://www.trenam.com · 101 East Kennedy Boulevard, Suite 2700 · P.O. Box 1102 · Tampa, FL 33601-1102 · 813-223-7474

Jeffrey Drew Butt · Squire Sanders · http://www.ssd.com · One Tampa City Center, Suite 2100 · 201 North Franklin Street · Tampa, FL 33602-5164 · 813-202-1300

C. Graham Carothers, Jr. · Shumaker, Loop & Kendrick · Bank of America Plaza, Suite 2800 · 101 East Kennedy Boulevard · Tampa, FL 33602-5150 · 813-229-7600

Charles H. Carver · McNamara & Carver · 2907 West Bay To Bay Boulevard, Suite 201 · Tampa, FL 33629-8161 · 813-837-0727

Preston O. Cockey, Jr. · a · Preston O. Cockey, Jr. · 110 East Madison Street, Suite 204 · Tampa, FL 33602-4718 · 813-275-5015

Aileen S. Davis · Akerman Senterfitt · http://www.akerman.com · SunTrust Financial Centre, Suite 1700 · 401 East Jackson Street · Tampa, FL 33602-5803 · 813-223-7333

Richard D. Eckhard · Holland & Knight · http://www.hklaw.com · 100 North Tampa Street, Suite 4100 · P.O. Box 1288 · Tampa, FL 33601-1288 · 813-227-8500

Jeanette M. Flores · GrayRobinson · 201 North Franklin Street, Suite 2200 · P.O. Box 3324 · Tampa, FL 33601 · 813-273-5000

Robert S. Freedman · Carlton Fields · Corporate Center Three at International Plaza, Suite 1000 · 4221 West Boy Scout Boulevard · Tampa, FL 33607 · 813-223-7000

Gina K. Grimes · Hill, Ward & Henderson · http://www.hwhlaw.com · Bank of America Plaza, Suite 3700 101 East Kennedy Boulevard · Tampa, FL 33602 · 813-221-3900

Thomas N. Henderson III · 2) · Hill, Ward & Henderson · http://www.hwhlaw.com · Bank of America Plaza, Suite 3700 · 101 East Kennedy Boulevard · Tampa, FL 33602 · 813-221-3900

Stephen M. Hudoba · Hill, Ward & Henderson · http://www.hwhlaw.com · Bank of America Plaza, Suite 3700 · 101 East Kennedy Boulevard · Tampa, FL 33602 · 813-221-3900

W. Kent Ihrig · Shumaker, Loop & Kendrick · Bank of America Plaza, Suite 2800 · 101 East Kennedy Boulevard · Tampa, FL 33602-5150 · 813-229-7600

John S. Inglis · Shumaker, Loop & Kendrick · Bank of America Plaza, Suite 2800 · 101 East Kennedy Boulevard · Tampa, FL 33602-5150 · 813-229-7600

Jonathan P. Jennewein · Hill, Ward & Henderson · http://www.hwhlaw.com · Bank of America Plaza, Suite 3700 · 101 East Kennedy Boulevard · Tampa, FL 33602 · 813-221-3900

Robert E. V. Kelley, Jr. · Hill, Ward & Henderson · http://www.hwhlaw.com · Bank of America Plaza, Suite 3700 · 101 East Kennedy Boulevard · Tampa, FL 33602 · 813-221-3900

Ruth Barnes Kinsolving · Carlton Fields · Corporate Center Three at International Plaza, Suite 1000 · 4221 West Boy Scout Boulevard · Tampa, FL 33607 · 813-223-7000

Stephen L. Kussner · GrayRobinson · 201 North Franklin Street, Suite 2200 · P.O. Box 3324 · Tampa, FL 33601 · 813-273-5000

Rhea F. Law · Fowler White Boggs Banker · 501 East Kennedy Boulevard, Suite 1700 · P.O. Box 1438 · Tampa, FL 33602-5239 · 813-228-7411

Edgel C. Lester · Carlton Fields · Corporate Center Three at International Plaza, Suite 1000 · 4221 West Boy Scout Boulevard · Tampa, FL 33607 · 813-223-7000

Richard C. Linquanti · a · Carlton Fields · Corporate Center Three at International Plaza, Suite 1000 · 4221 West Boy Scout Boulevard · Tampa, FL 33607 · 813-223-7000

Thomas M. Little · Foley & Lardner · 100 North Tampa Street, Suite 2700 · P.O. Box 3391 · Tampa, FL 33602 · 813-229-2300

Barbara H. Luikart · Phelps Dunbar · http://www.phelpsdunbar.com · 100 South Ashley Drive, Suite 1900 · Tampa, FL 33602-5311 · 813-472-7550

Steven H. Mezer · Bush Ross · http://www.bushross.com · 1801 North Highland Avenue · P.O. Box 3913 · Tampa, FL 33601 · 813-224-9255

Stephen J. Mitchell · 2) · Squire Sanders · http://www.ssd.com · One Tampa City Center, Suite 2100 · 201 North Franklin Street · Tampa, FL 33602-5164 · 813-202-1300

Samuel P. Queirolo · Bryant Miller & Olive · One Tampa City Center, Suite 2700 · Tampa, FL 33602 · 813-273-6677

Mary H. Quinlan · Trenam, Kemker, Scharf, Barkin, Frye, O'Neill & Mullis · http://www.trenam.com · 101 East Kennedy Boulevard, Suite 2700 · P.O. Box 1102 · Tampa, FL 33601-1102 · 813-223-7474

Fred S. Ridley · Foley & Lardner · 100 North Tampa Street, Suite 2700 · P.O. Box 3391 · Tampa, FL 33602 · 813-229-2300

R. James Robbins, Jr. · Hill, Ward & Henderson · http://www.hwhlaw.com · Bank of America Plaza, Suite 3700 · 101 East Kennedy Boulevard · Tampa, FL 33602 · 813-221-3900

Roger D. Schwenke · 2) · Carlton Fields · Corporate Center Three at International Plaza, Suite 1000 · 4221 West Boy Scout Boulevard · Tampa, FL 33607 · 813-223-7000

James Shimberg, Jr. · Holland & Knight · http://www.hklaw.com · 100 North Tampa Street, Suite 4100 · P.O. Box 1288 · Tampa, FL 33601-1288 · 813-227-8500

W. Lawrence Smith · Hill, Ward & Henderson · http://www.hwhlaw.com · Bank of America Plaza, Suite 3700 · 101 East Kennedy Boulevard · Tampa, FL 33602 · 813-221-3900

Richard H. Sollner · Trenam, Kemker, Scharf, Barkin, Frye, O'Neill & Mullis · http://www.trenam.com · 101 East Kennedy Boulevard, Suite 2700 · P.O. Box 1102 · Tampa, FL 33601-1102 · 813-223-7474

Stephen J. Szabo · Foley & Lardner · 100 North Tampa Street, Suite 2700 · P.O. Box 3391 · Tampa, FL 33602 · 813-229-2300

Theodore C. Taub · a · Shumaker, Loop & Kendrick · Bank of America Plaza, Suite 2800 · 101 East Kennedy Boulevard · Tampa, FL 33602-5150 · 813-229-7600

Michael J. Virgadamo · Carlton Fields · Corporate Center Three at International Plaza, Suite 1000 · 4221 West Boy Scout Boulevard · Tampa, FL 33607 · 813-223-7000

Ronald L. Weaver · Stearns Weaver Miller Weissler Alhadeff & Sitterson · SunTrust Financial Centre, Suite 2200 · 401 East Jackson Street · P.O. Box 3299 · Tampa, FL 33601 · 813-223-4800

Donald H. Whittemore · Phelps Dunbar · http://www.phelpsdunbar.com · 100 South Ashley Drive, Suite 1900 · Tampa, FL 33602-5311 · 813-472-7550

Viera

R. Mason Blake · Dean, Mead, Egerton, Bloodworth, Capouano & Bozarth · http://www.deanmead.com · 8240 Devereux Drive, Suite 100 · Viera, FL 32940 · 321-259-8900

West Palm Beach

Larry B. Alexander · a · Jones, Foster, Johnston & Stubbs · 505 South Flagler Drive, Suite 1100 · P.O. Box 3475 · West Palm Beach, FL 33402-3475 · 561-659-3000

Jerry E. Aron · a · Jerry E. Aron · 2505 MetroCentre Boulevard, Suite 301 · West Palm Beach, FL 33407 561-478-0511

Howard Bregman · Greenberg Traurig · http://www.gtlaw.com · 777 South Flagler Drive, Suite 300-E · West Palm Beach, FL 33401 · 561-650-7900

Alan J. Ciklin · a · Casey Ciklin Lubitz Martens & O'Connell · 515 North Flagler Drive, Suite 1900 · West Palm Beach, FL 33401 · 561-832-5900

Laurie L. Gildan · Greenberg Traurig · http://www.gtlaw.com · 777 South Flagler Drive, Suite 300-E · West Palm Beach, FL 33401 · 561-650-7900

Thomas A. Hanson · Carlton Fields · Esperante, Suite 1400 · 222 Lakeview Avenue · West Palm Beach, FL 33401 · 561-659-7070

Alfred LaSorte, Jr. · Shutts & Bowen · http://www.shutts.com · One Clearlake Centre, Suite 500 · 250 Australian Avenue South · West Palm Beach, FL 33401 · 561-650-8500

Wendy Sartory Link · Ackerman, Link and Sartory · 222 Lakeview Avenue, Suite 1250 · West Palm Beach, FL 33401 · 561-838-4100

Arthur J. Menor · Shutts & Bowen · http://www.shutts.com · One Clearlake Centre, Suite 500 · 250 Australian Avenue South · West Palm Beach, FL 33401 · 561-650-8500

John T. Metzger · McDonald Hopkins · 505 South Flagler Drive, Suite 300 · West Palm Beach, FL 33401 · 561-472-2121

Hugh William Perry · Gunster, Yoakley & Stewart · Phillips Point, Suite 500 East · 777 South Flagler Drive · West Palm Beach, FL 33401-6194 · 561-655-1980

Marvin S. Rosen · ⑳ · Ruden, McClosky, Smith, Schuster & Russell · 222 Lakeview Avenue, Suite 800 · West Palm Beach, FL 33401-6112 · 561-838-4500

Winter Park

Randolph J. Rush · Winderweedle, Haines, Ward & Woodman · 329 Park Avenue North, Second Floor · P.O. Box 880 · Winter Park, FL 32790-0880 · 407-423-4246

SECURITIES LAW

Fort Lauderdale

Donn A. Beloff · Greenberg Traurig · http://www.gtlaw.com · 401 East Las Olas Boulevard, Suite 2000 · Fort Lauderdale, FL 33301 · 954-765-0500

Jacksonville

L. Kinder Cannon III · ⑩ · Holland & Knight · http://www.hklaw.com · 50 North Laura Street, Suite 3900 · P.O. Box 52687 · Jacksonville, FL 32202-2687 · 904-353-2000

Linda Y. Kelso · Foley & Lardner · One Independent Drive, Suite 1300 · P.O. Box 240 · Jacksonville, FL 32201 · 904-359-2000

Miami

Daniel H. Aronson · Bilzin Sumberg Baena Price & Axelrod · Wachovia Financial Center, Suite 2500 · 200 South Biscayne Boulevard · Miami, FL 33131 · 305-374-7580

Rodney H. Bell · Holland & Knight · http://www.hklaw.com · 701 Brickell Avenue, Suite 3000 · Miami, FL 33131 · 305-374-8500

Richard E. Brodsky · Tabas, Freedman, Soloff & Miller · http://www.tfsmlaw.com · Ingraham Building, Suite 919 · 25 Southeast Second Avenue · Miami, FL 33131 · 305-375-8171

J. Thomas Cookson · Akerman Senterfitt · http://www.akerman.com · One Southeast Third Avenue, 25th Floor · Miami, FL 33131-1714 · 305-374-5600

Luis A. de Armas · Shutts & Bowen · http://www.shutts.com · Miami Center, Suite 1500 · 201 South Biscayne Boulevard · Miami, FL 33131 · 305-358-6300

Gary M. Epstein · a · Greenberg Traurig · http://www.gtlaw.com · 1221 Brickell Avenue, 22nd Floor · Miami, FL 33131 · 305-579-0500

Carl A. Fornaris · Greenberg Traurig · http://www.gtlaw.com · 1221 Brickell Avenue, 22nd Floor · Miami, FL 33131 · 305-579-0500

Alan G. Greer · a · Richman Greer · http://www.richmangreer.com · Miami Center, 10th Floor · 201 South Biscayne Boulevard · Miami, FL 33131 · 305-373-4000

Mitchell Eliot Herr · Holland & Knight · http://www.hklaw.com · 701 Brickell Avenue, Suite 3000 · Miami, FL 33131 · 305-374-8500

Lawrence A. Kellogg · Tew Cardenas · http://www.tewlaw.com · Four Seasons Tower, 15th Floor · 1441 Brickell Avenue · Miami, FL 33131-3407 · 305-536-1112

Enrique J. Martin · Greenberg Traurig · http://www.gtlaw.com · 1221 Brickell Avenue, 22nd Floor · Miami, FL 33131 · 305-579-0500

Thomas J. Meeks · Carlton Fields · 4000 International Place · 100 Southeast Second Street · P.O. Box 019101 · Miami, FL 33131-9101 · 305-530-0050

Alison W. Miller · Stearns Weaver Miller Weissler Alhadeff & Sitterson · Museum Tower, Suite 2200 · 150 West Flagler Street · Miami, FL 33130 · 305-789-3200

Lewis F. Murphy · Squire Sanders · http://www.ssd.com · 200 South Biscayne Boulevard, Suite 4000 · Miami, FL 33131-2398 · 305-577-7000

Barbara J. Oikle · Greenberg Traurig · http://www.gtlaw.com · 1221 Brickell Avenue, 22nd Floor · Miami, FL 33131 · 305-579-0500

Stephen K. Roddenberry · Akerman Senterfitt · http://www.akerman.com · One Southeast Third Avenue, 25th Floor · Miami, FL 33131-1714 · 305-374-5600

Ira N. Rosner · Greenberg Traurig · http://www.gtlaw.com · 1221 Brickell Avenue, 22nd Floor · Miami, FL 33131 · 305-579-0500

Steven Sonberg · Holland & Knight · http://www.hklaw.com · 701 Brickell Avenue, Suite 3000 · Miami, FL 33131 · 305-374-8500

C. Thomas Tew · a · Tew Cardenas · http://www.tewlaw.com · Four Seasons Tower, 15th Floor · 1441 Brickell Avenue · Miami, FL 33131-3407 · 305-536-1112

Stanley H. Wakshlag · a · Kenny Nachwalter · Miami Center, Suite 1100 · 201 South Biscayne Boulevard · Miami, FL 33131-2305 · 305-373-1000

David E. Wells · Hunton & Williams · Mellon Financial Center, Suite 2500 · 1111 Brickell Avenue · Miami, FL 33131 · 305-810-2500

Naples

Mary Beth M. Clary · Porter, Wright, Morris & Arthur · http://www.porterwright.com · 5801 Pelican Bay Boulevard, Suite 300 · Naples, FL 34108-2709 · 239-593-2900

Christopher T. Vernon · Vernon Healy · 3080 Tamiami Trail East · Naples, FL 34112 · 239-649-5390

Orlando

Thomas M. McAleavey · Holland & Knight · http://www.hklaw.com · 200 South Orange Avenue, Suite 2600 · P.O. Box 1526 · Orlando, FL 32802 · 407-425-8500

Tampa

Chester E. Bacheller · a · Holland & Knight · http://www.hklaw.com · 100 North Tampa Street, Suite 4100 · P.O. Box 1288 · Tampa, FL 33601-1288 · 813-227-8500

Guy M. Burns · a · Johnson, Pope, Bokor, Ruppel & Burns · http://www.jpfirm.com · 403 East Madison Street, Suite 400 · Tampa, FL 33602 · 813-225-2500

Nelson T. Castellano · Trenam, Kemker, Scharf, Barkin, Frye, O'Neill & Mullis · http://www.trenam.com 101 East Kennedy Boulevard, Suite 2700 · P.O. Box 1102 · Tampa, FL 33601-1102 · 813-223-7474

Curt P. Creely · Foley & Lardner · 100 North Tampa Street, Suite 2700 · P.O. Box 3391 · Tampa, FL 33602 · 813-229-2300

Nathaniel L. Doliner · Carlton Fields · Corporate Center Three at International Plaza, Suite 1000 · 4221 West Boy Scout Boulevard · Tampa, FL 33607 · 813-223-7000

Robert J. Grammig · a · Holland & Knight · http://www.hklaw.com · 100 North Tampa Street, Suite 4100 · P.O. Box 1288 · Tampa, FL 33601-1288 · 813-227-8500

Richard M. Leisner · 2% · Trenam, Kemker, Scharf, Barkin, Frye, O'Neill & Mullis · http://www.trenam.com · 101 East Kennedy Boulevard, Suite 2700 · P.O. Box 1102 · Tampa, FL 33601-1102 · 813-223-7474

Robert C. Rasmussen · 2) · Glenn, Rasmussen, Fogarty & Hooker · http://www.glennrasmussen.com · 100 South Ashley Drive, Suite 1300 · Tampa, FL 33602 · 813-229-3333

David C. Shobe · Fowler White Boggs Banker · 501 East Kennedy Boulevard, Suite 1700 · P.O. Box 1438 Tampa, FL 33602-5239 · 813-228-7411

Darrell C. Smith · Shumaker, Loop & Kendrick · Bank of America Plaza, Suite 2800 · 101 East Kennedy Boulevard · Tampa, FL 33602-5150 · 813-229-7600

Gary I. Teblum · a · Trenam, Kemker, Scharf, Barkin, Frye, O'Neill & Mullis · http://www.trenam.com · 101 East Kennedy Boulevard, Suite 2700 · P.O. Box 1102 · Tampa, FL 33601-1102 · 813-223-7474

Martin A. Traber · Foley & Lardner · 100 North Tampa Street, Suite 2700 · P.O. Box 3391 · Tampa, FL 33602 · 813-229-2300

Steven W. Vazquez · Foley & Lardner · 100 North Tampa Street, Suite 2700 · P.O. Box 3391 · Tampa, FL 33602 · 813-229-2300

Gregory C. Yadley · Shumaker, Loop & Kendrick · Bank of America Plaza, Suite 2800 · 101 East Kennedy Boulevard · Tampa, FL 33602-5150 · 813-229-7600

SPORTS LAW

St. Petersburg

Ben J. Hayes · Carlton Fields · 200 Central Avenue, Suite 2300 · St. Petersburg, FL 33701 · 727-821-7000

STRUCTURED FINANCE LAW

Miami

Victor M. Alvarez · White & Case · http://www.whitecase.com · Wachovia Financial Center, Suite 4900 · 200 South Biscayne Boulevard · Miami, FL 33131-2352 · 305-371-2700

Juan Pablo Cappello · Greenberg Traurig · http://www.gtlaw.com · 1221 Brickell Avenue, 22nd Floor · Miami, FL 33131 · 305-579-0500

Amy G. Dulin · Hughes Hubbard & Reed · http://www.hugheshubbard.com · 201 South Biscayne Boulevard, Suite 2500 · Miami, FL 33131-4332 · 305-358-1666

George Mencio, Jr. · Holland & Knight · http://www.hklaw.com · 701 Brickell Avenue, Suite 3000 · Miami, FL 33131 · 305-374-8500

Jeffrey S. Tenen · Greenberg Traurig · http://www.gtlaw.com · 1221 Brickell Avenue, 22nd Floor · Miami, FL 33131 · 305-579-0500

TAX LAW

Boca Raton

Robert A. Chaves · Gutter Chaves Josepher · Boca Corporate Center, Suite 107 · 2101 Corporate Boulevard · Boca Raton, FL 33431-7343 · 561-998-7847

Marvin C. Gutter · a · Gutter Chaves Josepher · Boca Corporate Center, Suite 107 · 2101 Corporate Boulevard · Boca Raton, FL 33431-7343 · 561-998-7847

Richard E. Heath · 2% · Hodgson Russ · 1801 North Military Trail, Suite 200 · Boca Raton, FL 33431 · 561-394-0500

Richard A. Josepher · a · Gutter Chaves Josepher · Boca Corporate Center, Suite 107 · 2101 Corporate Boulevard · Boca Raton, FL 33431-7343 · 561-998-7847

Thomas O. Katz · Katz Baskies · http://www.katzbaskies.com · 2255 Glades Road, Suite 240 West · Boca Raton, FL 33431 · 561-910-5700

Marvin A. Kirsner · Greenberg Traurig · http://www.gtlaw.com · 5100 Town Center Circle, Suite 400 · Boca Raton, FL 33486 · 561-955-7600

Daniel D. Mielnicki · Berger Singerman · http://www.bergersingerman.com · 2650 North Military Trail, Suite 240 · Boca Raton, FL 33431 · 561-241-9500

David Pratt · Proskauer Rose · http://www.proskauer.com · 2255 Glades Road, Suite 340 West · Boca Raton, FL 33431-7383 · 561-241-7400

Donald R. Tescher · a · Tescher & Spallina · http://www.tescherlaw.com · Boca Corporate Center, Suite 107 · 2101 Corporate Boulevard · Boca Raton, FL 33431 · 561-998-7847

Bonita Springs

Hugh W. Nevin, Jr. · a · Cohen & Grigsby · 27200 Riverview Center Boulevard, Suite 309 · Bonita Springs, FL 34134-4317 · 239-390-1900

Clearwater

Bruce H. Bokor · 2) · Johnson, Pope, Bokor, Ruppel & Burns · http://www.jpfirm.com · 911 Chestnut Street · P.O. Box 1368 · Clearwater, FL 33756 · 727-461-1818

Coral Gables

Dennis Ginsburg · Packman, Neuwahl & Rosenberg · http://www.pnrlaw.com · 1500 San Remo Avenue, Suite 125 · Coral Gables, FL 33146 · 305-665-3311

Jose Nunez · Packman, Neuwahl & Rosenberg · http://www.pnrlaw.com · 1500 San Remo Avenue, Suite 125 · Coral Gables, FL 33146 · 305-665-3311

Michael Rosenberg · a · Packman, Neuwahl & Rosenberg · http://www.pnrlaw.com · 1500 San Remo Avenue, Suite 125 · Coral Gables, FL 33146 · 305-665-3311

Thomas O. Wells · Thomas O. Wells · 540 Biltmore Way · Coral Gables, FL 33134 · 305-444-0016

Fort Lauderdale

James B. Davis · 2) · Gunster, Yoakley & Stewart · Las Olas Centre, Suite 1400 · 450 East Las Olas Boulevard · Fort Lauderdale, FL 33301 · 954-462-2000

Gene K. Glasser · a · Greenspoon Marder · Trade Centre South, Suite 700 · 100 West Cypress Creek Road · Fort Lauderdale, FL 33309-2140 · 954-491-1120

Sheldon S. Polish · Berger Singerman · http://www.bergersingerman.com · 350 East Las Olas Boulevard, Suite 1000 · Fort Lauderdale, FL 33301 · 954-525-9900

Martin R. Press · Gunster, Yoakley & Stewart · Las Olas Centre, Suite 1400 · 450 East Las Olas Boulevard · Fort Lauderdale, FL 33301 · 954-462-2000

Jeffrey Rubinger · Holland & Knight · http://www.hklaw.com · One East Broward Boulevard, Suite 1300 · P.O. Box 14070 · Fort Lauderdale, FL 33302-4070 · 954-525-1000

William B. Sherman · Holland & Knight · http://www.hklaw.com · One East Broward Boulevard, Suite 1300 · P.O. Box 14070 · Fort Lauderdale, FL 33302-4070 · 954-525-1000

Fort Pierce

Michael D. Minton · Dean, Mead, Egerton, Bloodworth, Capouano & Bozarth · http://www.deanmead.com · 1903 South 25th Street, Suite 200 · Fort Pierce, FL 34947 · 772-464-7700

Jacksonville

Kenneth G. Anderson · 2% · Anderson & Stevens · 1301 Riverplace Boulevard, Suite 2640 · Jacksonville, FL 32207-9031 · 904-399-8000

Robert S. Bernstein · Foley & Lardner · One Independent Drive, Suite 1300 · P.O. Box 240 · Jacksonville, FL 32201 · 904-359-2000

Thomas M. Donahoo · Donahoo, Ball & McMenamy · 50 North Laura Street, Suite 2925 · Jacksonville, FL 32202 · 904-354-8080

Michael W. Fisher · a · Fisher, Tousey, Leas & Ball · 501 Riverside Avenue, Suite 600 · Jacksonville, FL 32202 · 904-356-2600

Peter O. Larsen · Akerman Senterfitt · http://www.akerman.com · 50 North Laura Street, Suite 2500 · Jacksonville, FL 32202-3646 · 904-798-3700

James L. Main · Holland & Knight · http://www.hklaw.com · 50 North Laura Street, Suite 3900 · P.O. Box 52687 · Jacksonville, FL 32202-2687 · 904-353-2000

Miami

James H. Barrett · Baker & McKenzie · Mellon Financial Center, Suite 1700 · 1111 Brickell Avenue · Miami, FL 33131 · 305-789-8900

Steven L. Cantor · Cantor & Webb · Brickell Bay Office Tower, Suite 3112 · 1001 Brickell Bay Drive · Miami, FL 33131 · 305-374-3886

Gary J. Cohen · Shutts & Bowen · http://www.shutts.com · Miami Center, Suite 1500 · 201 South Biscayne Boulevard · Miami, FL 33131 · 305-358-6300

L. Frank Cordero · Akerman Senterfitt · http://www.akerman.com · One Southeast Third Avenue, 25th Floor · Miami, FL 33131-1714 · 305-374-5600

Luis A. de Armas · Shutts & Bowen · http://www.shutts.com · Miami Center, Suite 1500 · 201 South Biscayne Boulevard · Miami, FL 33131 · 305-358-6300

Donald K. Duffy · Akerman Senterfitt · http://www.akerman.com · One Southeast Third Avenue, 25th Floor · Miami, FL 33131-1714 · 305-374-5600

Seth J. Entin · Greenberg Traurig · http://www.gtlaw.com · 1221 Brickell Avenue, 22nd Floor · Miami, FL 33131 · 305-579-0500

Guillermo J. Fernandez-Quincoces · Foley & Lardner · Bank of America Tower, Suite 1600 · 100 Southeast Second Street · Miami, FL 33131-2132 · 305-482-8400

Ivan A. Gomez · Gutierrez & Associates · 601 Brickell Key Drive, Suite 201 · Miami, FL 33131-0265 · 305-577-4500

K. Lawrence Gragg · a · White & Case · http://www.whitecase.com · Wachovia Financial Center, Suite 4900 · 200 South Biscayne Boulevard · Miami, FL 33131-2352 · 305-371-2700

Jerome M. Hesch · Greenberg Traurig · http://www.gtlaw.com · 1221 Brickell Avenue, 22nd Floor · Miami, FL 33131 · 305-579-0500

Robert F. Hudson, Jr. · 2) · Baker & McKenzie · Mellon Financial Center, Suite 1700 · 1111 Brickell Avenue · Miami, FL 33131 · 305-789-8900

Joel J. Karp · 2% · Cantor & Webb · Brickell Bay Office Tower, Suite 3112 · 1001 Brickell Bay Drive · Miami, FL 33131 · 305-374-3886

Stewart L. Kasner · Baker & McKenzie · Mellon Financial Center, Suite 1700 · 1111 Brickell Avenue · Miami, FL 33131 · 305-789-8900

Alan S. Lederman · Gunster, Yoakley & Stewart · One Biscayne Tower, Suite 3400 · Two South Biscayne Boulevard · Miami, FL 33131-1897 · 305-376-6000

Gregory M. Marks · Greenberg Traurig · http://www.gtlaw.com · 1221 Brickell Avenue, 22nd Floor · Miami, FL 33131 · 305-579-0500

Charles E. Muller II · a · Muller & Lebensburger · 7385 Galloway Road, Suite 200 · Miami, FL 33173 · 305-670-6770

Martin J. Nash · 2% · Adorno & Yoss · 2525 Ponce de Leon Boulevard, Suite 400 · Miami, FL 33134 · 305-460-1000

William H. Newton III · William H. Newton · 1000 Brickell Avenue, Suite 1025 · Miami, FL 33131-3015 305-373-0840

Louis Nostro · Shutts & Bowen · http://www.shutts.com · Miami Center, Suite 1500 · 201 South Biscayne Boulevard · Miami, FL 33131 · 305-358-6300

Robert E. Panoff · a · Robert E. Panoff · 9400 South Dadeland Boulevard, Suite 106 · Miami, FL 33156 305-670-6547

Henry H. Raattama, Jr. · 2) · Akerman Senterfitt · http://www.akerman.com · One Southeast Third Avenue, 25th Floor · Miami, FL 33131-1714 · 305-374-5600

Charles L. Ruffner · a · Charles L. Ruffner · 8830 Southwest 67th Court · Miami, FL 33156-1700 · 305-669-1904

Edward E. Sawyer · White & Case · http://www.whitecase.com · Wachovia Financial Center, Suite 4900 · 200 South Biscayne Boulevard · Miami, FL 33131-2352 · 305-371-2700

Ozzie A. Schindler · Greenberg Traurig · http://www.gtlaw.com · 1221 Brickell Avenue, 22nd Floor · Miami, FL 33131 · 305-579-0500

H. Allan Shore · a · Akerman Senterfitt · http://www.akerman.com · One Southeast Third Avenue, 25th Floor · Miami, FL 33131-1714 · 305-374-5600

Charles E. Stiver, Jr. · a · Greenberg Traurig · http://www.gtlaw.com · 1221 Brickell Avenue, 22nd Floor Miami, FL 33131 · 305-579-0500

Sydney S. Traum · a · Levey, Filler, Rodriguez, Kelso & De Bianchi · 555 North East 15 Street, Suite 104 · Miami, FL 33132 · 305-371-5250

Samuel C. Ullman · 2% · Bilzin Sumberg Baena Price & Axelrod · Wachovia Financial Center, Suite 2500 · 200 South Biscayne Boulevard · Miami, FL 33131 · 305-374-7580

Hal J. Webb · Cantor & Webb · Brickell Bay Office Tower, Suite 3112 · 1001 Brickell Bay Drive · Miami, FL 33131 · 305-374-3886

Andrew H. Weinstein · 2) · Holland & Knight · http://www.hklaw.com · 701 Brickell Avenue, Suite 3000 Miami, FL 33131 · 305-374-8500

Diana S. C. Zeydel · Greenberg Traurig · http://www.gtlaw.com · 1221 Brickell Avenue, 22nd Floor · Miami, FL 33131 · 305-579-0500

Naples

Jeffrey M. Folkman · Hahn Loeser & Parks · 800 Laurel Oak Drive, Suite 600 · Naples, FL 34108 · 239-254-2900

North Miami Beach

Barry A. Nelson · a · Nelson & Nelson · http://www.estatetaxlawyers.com · 2775 Sunny Isles Boulevard, Suite 118 · North Miami Beach, FL 33160 · 305-932-2000

Orlando

Jane Dunlap Callahan · Dean, Mead, Egerton, Bloodworth, Capouano & Bozarth · http://www.deanmead.com · 800 North Magnolia Avenue, Suite 1500 · P.O. Box 2346 · Orlando, FL 32802-2346 · 407-841-1200

Albert D. Capouano · Dean, Mead, Egerton, Bloodworth, Capouano & Bozarth · http://www.deanmead.com · 800 North Magnolia Avenue, Suite 1500 · P.O. Box 2346 · Orlando, FL 32802-2346 · 407-841-1200

Louis T. M. Conti · a · Holland & Knight · http://www.hklaw.com · 200 South Orange Avenue, Suite 2600 · P.O. Box 1526 · Orlando, FL 32802 · 407-425-8500

Charles H. Egerton · 2% · Dean, Mead, Egerton, Bloodworth, Capouano & Bozarth · http://www.deanmead.com · 800 North Magnolia Avenue, Suite 1500 · P.O. Box 2346 · Orlando, FL 32802-2346 · 407-841-1200

Russell B. Hale · Akerman Senterfitt · http://www.akerman.com · CNL Center II at City Commons, Suite 1200 · 420 South Orange Avenue · Orlando, FL 32801-3336 · 407-423-4000

Martha Anderson Hartley · Greenberg Traurig · http://www.gtlaw.com · 450 South Orange Avenue, Suite 650 · Orlando, FL 32801 · 407-420-1000

Russell P. Hintze · Greenberg Traurig · http://www.gtlaw.com · 450 South Orange Avenue, Suite 650 · Orlando, FL 32801 · 407-420-1000

Steven C. Lee · Dean, Mead, Egerton, Bloodworth, Capouano & Bozarth · http://www.deanmead.com · 800 North Magnolia Avenue, Suite 1500 · P.O. Box 2346 · Orlando, FL 32802-2346 · 407-841-1200

Stephen R. Looney · Dean, Mead, Egerton, Bloodworth, Capouano & Bozarth · http://www.deanmead.com · 800 North Magnolia Avenue, Suite 1500 · P.O. Box 2346 · Orlando, FL 32802-2346 · 407-841-1200

Joel D. Maser · Greenberg Traurig · http://www.gtlaw.com · 450 South Orange Avenue, Suite 650 · Orlando, FL 32801 · 407-420-1000

Richard M. Robinson · a · GrayRobinson · 301 East Pine Street, Suite 1400 · P.O. Box 3068 · Orlando, FL 32802-3068 · 407-843-8880

John A. Sanders · Foley & Lardner · 111 North Orange Avenue, Suite 1800 · P.O. Box 2193 · Orlando, FL 32802-2193 · 407-423-7656

Joel H. Sharp, Jr. · a · Baker Hostetler · http://www.bakerlaw.com · Sun Trust Center, Suite 2300 · 200 South Orange Avenue · Orlando, FL 32801-3432 · 407-649-4000

Palm Beach Gardens

Richard B. Comiter · a · Comiter, Singer & Baseman · 3801 PGA Boulevard, Suite 604 · Palm Beach Gardens, FL 33410 · 561-626-2101

Sarasota

William T. Harrison, Jr. · Williams Parker Harrison Dietz & Getzen · 200 South Orange Avenue · Sarasota, FL 34236 · 941-366-4800

St. Petersburg

Joel D. Bronstein · a · Bronstein, Carlson, Gleim & Smith · 150 Second Avenue North, Suite 1100 · St. Petersburg, FL 33701 · 727-898-6688

Susan W. Carlson · Bronstein, Carlson, Gleim & Smith · 150 Second Avenue North, Suite 1100 · St. Petersburg, FL 33701 · 727-898-6688

Tallahassee

Martha W. Barnett · a · Holland & Knight · http://www.hklaw.com · Bank of America Building, Suite 600 · 315 South Calhoun Street · Tallahassee, FL 32301 · 850-224-7000

James M. Ervin, Jr. · a · Holland & Knight · http://www.hklaw.com · Bank of America Building, Suite 600 · 315 South Calhoun Street · Tallahassee, FL 32301 · 850-224-7000

Robert S. Goldman · Madsen, Goldman & Holcomb · 1705 Metropolitan Boulevard, Suite 101 · Tallahassee, FL 32308-3765 · 850-523-0400

Kenneth R. Hart · Ausley & McMullen · Washington Square Building · 227 South Calhoun Street · P.O. Box 391 · Tallahassee, FL 32302 · 850-224-9115

Mark E. Holcomb · a · Madsen, Goldman & Holcomb · 1705 Metropolitan Boulevard, Suite 101 · Tallahassee, FL 32308-3765 · 850-523-0400

John T. Ledbeater · Ausley & McMullen · Washington Square Building · 227 South Calhoun Street · P.O. Box 391 · Tallahassee, FL 32302 · 850-224-9115

Robert A. Pierce · Ausley & McMullen · Washington Square Building · 227 South Calhoun Street · P.O. Box 391 · Tallahassee, FL 32302 · 850-224-9115

William D. Townsend · a · Fowler White Boggs Banker · 101 North Monroe Street, Suite 1090 · Tallahassee, FL 32301 · 850-681-0411

Rex D. Ware · Fowler White Boggs Banker · 101 North Monroe Street, Suite 1090 · Tallahassee, FL 32301 · 850-681-0411

Victoria L. Weber · Hopping Green & Sams · http://www.hgslaw.com · 123 South Calhoun Street · P.O. Box 6526 · Tallahassee, FL 32314 · 850-222-7598

Tampa

Michael D. Annis · 2) · Foley & Lardner · 100 North Tampa Street, Suite 2700 · P.O. Box 3391 · Tampa, FL 33602 · 813-229-2300

Leslie J. Barnett · 2% · Barnett, Bolt, Kirkwood, Long & McBride · http://www.barnettbolt.com · 601 Bayshore Boulevard, Suite 700 · P.O. Box 3287 · Tampa, FL 33606 · 813-253-2020

Bernard A. Barton, Jr. · a · Holland & Knight · http://www.hklaw.com · 100 North Tampa Street, Suite 4100 · P.O. Box 1288 · Tampa, FL 33601-1288 · 813-227-8500

E. Jackson Boggs · a · Fowler White Boggs Banker · 501 East Kennedy Boulevard, Suite 1700 · P.O. Box 1438 · Tampa, FL 33602-5239 · 813-228-7411

Hunter J. Brownlee · Fowler White Boggs Banker · 501 East Kennedy Boulevard, Suite 1700 · P.O. Box 1438 · Tampa, FL 33602-5239 · 813-228-7411

David P. Burke · Carlton Fields · Corporate Center Three at International Plaza, Suite 1000 · 4221 West Boy Scout Boulevard · Tampa, FL 33607 · 813-223-7000

Merritt A. Gardner · Gardner Law Firm · Watermark Five, Suite 200 · 5415 Mariner Street · Tampa, FL 33609 · 813-288-9600

Mitchell I. Horowitz · Fowler White Boggs Banker · 501 East Kennedy Boulevard, Suite 1700 · P.O. Box 1438 · Tampa, FL 33602-5239 · 813-228-7411

William Kalish · Akerman Senterfitt · http://www.akerman.com · SunTrust Financial Centre, Suite 1700 · 401 East Jackson Street · Tampa, FL 33602-5803 · 813-223-7333

Robert E. V. Kelley, Jr. · Hill, Ward & Henderson · http://www.hwhlaw.com · Bank of America Plaza, Suite 3700 · 101 East Kennedy Boulevard · Tampa, FL 33602 · 813-221-3900

Peter T. Kirkwood · Barnett, Bolt, Kirkwood, Long & McBride · http://www.barnettbolt.com · 601 Bayshore Boulevard, Suite 700 · P.O. Box 3287 · Tampa, FL 33606 · 813-253-2020

David L. Koche · Barnett, Bolt, Kirkwood, Long & McBride · http://www.barnettbolt.com · 601 Bayshore Boulevard, Suite 700 · P.O. Box 3287 · Tampa, FL 33606 · 813-253-2020

Jack A. Levine · Holland & Knight · http://www.hklaw.com · 100 North Tampa Street, Suite 4100 · P.O. Box 1288 · Tampa, FL 33601-1288 · 813-227-8500

Harold W. Mullis, Jr. · a · Trenam, Kemker, Scharf, Barkin, Frye, O'Neill & Mullis · http://www.trenam.com · 101 East Kennedy Boulevard, Suite 2700 · P.O. Box 1102 · Tampa, FL 33601-1102 · 813-223-7474

Albert C. O'Neill, Jr. · 2% · Trenam, Kemker, Scharf, Barkin, Frye, O'Neill & Mullis · http://www.trenam.com · 101 East Kennedy Boulevard, Suite 2700 · P.O. Box 1102 · Tampa, FL 33601-1102 · 813-223-7474

William M. Sharp · Sharp & Associates · 4890 West Kennedy Boulevard, Suite 900 · Tampa, FL 33609-1850 · 813-286-4199

Brian C. Sparks · Hill, Ward & Henderson · http://www.hwhlaw.com · Bank of America Plaza, Suite 3700 101 East Kennedy Boulevard · Tampa, FL 33602 · 813-221-3900

August M. Van Eepoel · Akerman Senterfitt · http://www.akerman.com · SunTrust Financial Centre, Suite 1700 · 401 East Jackson Street · Tampa, FL 33602-5803 · 813-223-7333

Douglas A. Wright · Holland & Knight · http://www.hklaw.com · 100 North Tampa Street, Suite 4100 · P.O. Box 1288 · Tampa, FL 33601-1288 · 813-227-8500

West Palm Beach

Jerald David August · a · Fox Rothschild · 222 Lakeview Avenue, Suite 700 · West Palm Beach, FL 33401 · 561-835-9600

David E. Bowers · a · Jones, Foster, Johnston & Stubbs · 505 South Flagler Drive, Suite 1100 · P.O. Box 3475 · West Palm Beach, FL 33402-3475 · 561-659-3000

Domenick R. Lioce · Nason, Yeager, Gerson, White & Lioce · Mellon United National Bank Tower, Suite 1200 · 1645 Palm Beach Lakes Boulevard · West Palm Beach, FL 33401 · 561-686-3307

Peter Matwiczyk · Matwiczyk & Brown · 625 North Flagler Drive, Suite 401 · West Palm Beach, FL 33401-4027 · 561-651-4004

Stephen G. Vogelsang · Gunster, Yoakley & Stewart · Phillips Point, Suite 500 East · 777 South Flagler Drive · West Palm Beach, FL 33401-6194 · 561-655-1980

TECHNOLOGY LAW

Boca Raton

Jon Gibbons · Fleit, Gibbons, Gutman, Bongini & Bianco · One Boca Commerce Center, Suite 111 · 551 NW 77th Street · Boca Raton, FL 33487 · 561-989-9811

Fort Lauderdale

Mark A. Albright · Perlman, Yevoli & Albright · 1500 North Federal Highway, Suite 250 · Fort Lauderdale, FL 33304 · 954-566-7117

Robert C. White, Jr. · Gunster, Yoakley & Stewart · Las Olas Centre, Suite 1400 · 450 East Las Olas Boulevard · Fort Lauderdale, FL 33301 · 954-462-2000

Lake Mary

Frank S. Ioppolo, Jr. · Precision Play Media, Inc. · 3300 W Lake Mary Boulevard, Suite 300 · Lake Mary, FL 32746 · 407-320-7229

Miami

Mark D. Grossman · Grossman Law Group · http://www.ecomputerlaw.com · 999 Ponce de Leon Boulevard, Suite 705 · Miami, FL 33134 · 305-443-8180

Kevin M. Levy · Gunster, Yoakley & Stewart · One Biscayne Tower, Suite 3400 · Two South Biscayne Boulevard · Miami, FL 33131-1897 · 305-376-6000

Samuel A. Lewis · Feldman Gale · http://www.feldmangale.com · One Biscayne Tower, 30th Floor · Two South Biscayne Boulevard · Miami, FL 33131 · 305-358-5001

José I. Rojas · Rojas Law Firm · Two Datran Center, Suite 1209 · 9130 South Dadeland Boulevard · Miami, FL 33156 · 305-446-4000

Manuel R. Valcarcel IV · Greenberg Traurig · http://www.gtlaw.com · 1221 Brickell Avenue, 22nd Floor · Miami, FL 33131 · 305-579-0500

West Palm Beach

David G. Bates · Gunster, Yoakley & Stewart · Phillips Point, Suite 500 East · 777 South Flagler Drive · West Palm Beach, FL 33401-6194 · 561-655-1980

TRANSPORTATION LAW

Coral Gables

Michael T. Moore · Moore & Company · http://www.moore-and-co.net · 355 Alhambra Circle, Suite 1100 Coral Gables, FL 33134 · 786-221-0600

Fort Lauderdale

Bruce David Green · Bruce David Green · 1313 South Andrews Avenue · Fort Lauderdale, FL 33316 · 954-522-8554

Jacksonville

Michael A. Abel · Holland & Knight · http://www.hklaw.com · 50 North Laura Street, Suite 3900 · P.O. Box 52687 · Jacksonville, FL 32202-2687 · 904-353-2000

Lawrence J. Hamilton II · Holland & Knight · http://www.hklaw.com · 50 North Laura Street, Suite 3900 P.O. Box 52687 · Jacksonville, FL 32202-2687 · 904-353-2000

Miami

James N. Hurley · Fowler White Burnett · Espirito Santo Plaza, 14th Floor · 1395 Brickell Avenue · Miami, FL 33131-3302 · 305-789-9200

George Mencio, Jr. · Holland & Knight · http://www.hklaw.com · 701 Brickell Avenue, Suite 3000 · Miami, FL 33131 · 305-374-8500

Timothy J. Norris · 2) · Duane Morris · 200 South Biscayne Boulevard, Suite 3400 · Miami, FL 33131-2397 · 305-960-2200

Tom Pennekamp, Jr. · Pennekamp Law · 2811 South West ThirdAve · Miami, FL 33129 · 305-860-4445

Jeffrey S. Tenen · Greenberg Traurig · http://www.gtlaw.com · 1221 Brickell Avenue, 22nd Floor · Miami, FL 33131 · 305-579-0500

Robert A. Zinn · Akerman Senterfitt · http://www.akerman.com · One Southeast Third Avenue, 25th Floor · Miami, FL 33131-1714 · 305-374-5600

Orlando

J. Gordon Arkin · Foley & Lardner · 111 North Orange Avenue, Suite 1800 · P.O. Box 2193 · Orlando, FL 32802-2193 · 407-423-7656

Tallahassee

John H. Beck · Beck Consulting Group · 2292-B Hampshire Way · Tallahassee, FL 32309 · 850-422-1011

A. J. James Spalla · Akerman Senterfitt · http://www.akerman.com · Highpoint Center, Suite 1200 · 106 East College Avenue · Tallahassee, FL 32301 · 850-224-9634

Jacob D. Varn · Fowler White Boggs Banker · 101 North Monroe Street, Suite 1090 · Tallahassee, FL 32301 · 850-681-0411

Tampa

Allen K. Von Spiegelfeld · Fowler White Boggs Banker · 501 East Kennedy Boulevard, Suite 1700 · P.O. Box 1438 · Tampa, FL 33602-5239 · 813-228-7411

TRUSTS AND ESTATES

Boca Raton

Jeffrey A. Baskies · Katz Baskies · http://www.katzbaskies.com · 2255 Glades Road, Suite 240 West · Boca Raton, FL 33431 · 561-910-5700

Peter J. Forman · Gutter Chaves Josepher · Boca Corporate Center, Suite 107 · 2101 Corporate Boulevard Boca Raton, FL 33431-7343 · 561-998-7847

Albert W. Gortz · Proskauer Rose · http://www.proskauer.com · 2255 Glades Road, Suite 340 West · Boca Raton, FL 33431-7383 · 561-241-7400

Ronald T. Martin · a · Greenspoon Marder · One Boca Place, Suite 414-E · 2255 Glades Road · Boca Raton, FL 33431 · 561-989-0400

David Pratt · Proskauer Rose · http://www.proskauer.com · 2255 Glades Road, Suite 340 West · Boca Raton, FL 33431-7383 · 561-241-7400

Donald R. Tescher · a · Tescher & Spallina · http://www.tescherlaw.com · Boca Corporate Center, Suite 107 · 2101 Corporate Boulevard · Boca Raton, FL 33431 · 561-998-7847

Jerome L. Wolf · Duane Morris · 2700 North Military Trail, Suite 300 · Boca Raton, FL 33431-1808 · 561-962-2100

Bonita Springs

William N. Horowitz · Cummings & Lockwood · http://www.cl-law.com · The Brooks Grand Plaza, Suite 300 · 8000 Health Center Boulevard · Bonita Springs, FL 34135 · 239-947-8811

Clearwater

Bruce H. Bokor · 2) · Johnson, Pope, Bokor, Ruppel & Burns · http://www.jpfirm.com · 911 Chestnut Street · P.O. Box 1368 · Clearwater, FL 33756 · 727-461-1818

Coral Gables

Neil R. Chrystal · Dunwody White & Landon · http://www.dwl-law.com · 550 Biltmore Way, Suite 810 · Coral Gables, FL 33134 · 305-529-1500

Jack A. Falk, Jr. · Dunwody White & Landon · http://www.dwl-law.com · 550 Biltmore Way, Suite 810 · Coral Gables, FL 33134 · 305-529-1500

Brian J. Felcoski · Goldman, Felcoski & Stone · 95 Merrick Way, Suite 440 · Coral Gables, FL 33134 · 305-446-2800

John J. Grundhauser · Dunwody White & Landon · http://www.dwl-law.com · 550 Biltmore Way, Suite 810 · Coral Gables, FL 33134 · 305-529-1500

William T. Muir · Dunwody White & Landon · http://www.dwl-law.com · 550 Biltmore Way, Suite 810 · Coral Gables, FL 33134 · 305-529-1500

Bruce M. Stone · 2) · Goldman, Felcoski & Stone · 95 Merrick Way, Suite 440 · Coral Gables, FL 33134 · 305-446-2800

Thomas O. Wells · Thomas O. Wells · 540 Biltmore Way · Coral Gables, FL 33134 · 305-444-0016

Robert A. White · 2% · Dunwody White & Landon · http://www.dwl-law.com · 550 Biltmore Way, Suite 810 · Coral Gables, FL 33134 · 305-529-1500

Davie

William A. Snyder · Snyder & Snyder · http://www.snyderlawpa.com · 7931 Southwest 45th Street · Davie, FL 33328 · 954-475-1139

Fort Lauderdale

Frank T. Adams · Katz Barron Squitero Faust · http://www.katzbarron.com · 100 Northeast Third Avenue, Suite 280 · Fort Lauderdale, FL 33301 · 954-522-3636

Francis B. Brogan, Jr. · Greenberg Traurig · http://www.gtlaw.com · 401 East Las Olas Boulevard, Suite 2000 · Fort Lauderdale, FL 33301 · 954-765-0500

James B. Davis · 2) · Gunster, Yoakley & Stewart · Las Olas Centre, Suite 1400 · 450 East Las Olas Boulevard · Fort Lauderdale, FL 33301 · 954-462-2000

Gene K. Glasser · a · Greenspoon Marder · Trade Centre South, Suite 700 · 100 West Cypress Creek Road · Fort Lauderdale, FL 33309-2140 · 954-491-1120

Robert B. Judd · Gunster, Yoakley & Stewart · Las Olas Centre, Suite 1400 · 450 East Las Olas Boulevard · Fort Lauderdale, FL 33301 · 954-462-2000

Rohan Kelley · 2) · The Kelley Law Firm · 5100 North Federal Highway, Suite 405 · Fort Lauderdale, FL 33308-3842 · 954-563-1400

Douglas B. Kniskern · a · Arnstein & Lehr · 200 East Las Olas Boulevard, Suite 1700 · Fort Lauderdale, FL 33301 · 954-713-7600

Paul McCawley · Greenberg Traurig · http://www.gtlaw.com · 401 East Las Olas Boulevard, Suite 2000 · Fort Lauderdale, FL 33301 · 954-765-0500

Carl Schuster · Ruden, McClosky, Smith, Schuster & Russell · 200 East Broward Boulevard · P.O. Box 1900 · Fort Lauderdale, FL 33302 · 954-764-6660

Michael L. Trop · a · Adorno & Yoss · 350 East Las Olas Boulevard, Suite 1700 · Fort Lauderdale, FL 33301 · 954-763-1200

Gainesville

Richard M. White, Jr. · White & Crouch PA · 5303 South West 91st Drive, Suite 200 · Gainesville, FL 32608 · 352-372-1011

Jacksonville

Thomas M. Donahoo · Donahoo, Ball & McMenamy · 50 North Laura Street, Suite 2925 · Jacksonville, FL 32202 · 904-354-8080

Timothy L. Flanagan · Purcell, Flanagan & Hay · 1548 Lancaster Terrace · P.O. Box 40749 · Jacksonville, FL 32203 · 904-355-0355

John G. Grimsley · 2% · Grimsley Marker & Iseley · 50 North Laura Street, Suite 2150 · Jacksonville, FL 32202-3607 · 904-354-9900

Thomas M. Reiter · Brant, Abraham, Reiter, McCormick & Greene · 50 North Laura Street, Suite 2750 · Jacksonville, FL 32202 · 904-358-2750

Richard L. Stockton · a · Holland & Knight · http://www.hklaw.com · 50 North Laura Street, Suite 3900 P.O. Box 52687 · Jacksonville, FL 32202-2687 · 904-353-2000

Clay B. Tousey, Jr. · Fisher, Tousey, Leas & Ball · 501 Riverside Avenue, Suite 600 · Jacksonville, FL 32202 · 904-356-2600

Lakeland

John K. Vreeland · GrayRobinson · One Lake Morton Drive · P.O. Box Three · Lakeland, FL 33802 · 863-284-2200

Maitland

Charles D. Wilder · Estate Planning and Legacy Law Center · 159 Lookout Place, Suite 101 · Maitland, FL 32751 · 407-647-7526

Melbourne

Charles Ian Nash · Nash, Moule & Kromash · 440 South Babcock Street · Melbourne, FL 32901 · 321-984-2440

Miami

Norman J. Benford · 2% · Greenberg Traurig · http://www.gtlaw.com · 1221 Brickell Avenue, 22nd Floor · Miami, FL 33131 · 305-579-0500

Christopher W. Boyett · Holland & Knight · http://www.hklaw.com · 701 Brickell Avenue, Suite 3000 · Miami, FL 33131 · 305-374-8500

David R. Carlisle · Duane Morris · 200 South Biscayne Boulevard, Suite 3400 · Miami, FL 33131-2397 · 305-960-2200

Nicholas E. Christin · Wicker, Smith, O'Hara, McCoy, Graham & Ford · Grove Plaza Building, Fifth Floor · 2900 Middle Street · Miami, FL 33133 · 305-448-3939

Michael A. Dribin · 10 · Broad and Cassel · One Biscayne Tower, Suite 2100 · Two South Biscayne Boulevard · Miami, FL 33131 · 305-373-9400

Dan P. Heller · Bilzin Sumberg Baena Price & Axelrod · Wachovia Financial Center, Suite 2500 · 200 South Biscayne Boulevard · Miami, FL 33131 · 305-374-7580

Charles H. Johnson · Richman Greer · http://www.richmangreer.com · Miami Center, 10th Floor · 201 South Biscayne Boulevard · Miami, FL 33131 · 305-373-4000

Michael E. Kavoukjian · White & Case · http://www.whitecase.com · Wachovia Financial Center, Suite 4900 · 200 South Biscayne Boulevard · Miami, FL 33131-2352 · 305-371-2700

Richard C. Milstein · Akerman Senterfitt · http://www.akerman.com · One Southeast Third Avenue, 25th Floor · Miami, FL 33131-1714 · 305-374-5600

Charles E. Muller II · 10 · Muller & Lebensburger · 7385 Galloway Road, Suite 200 · Miami, FL 33173 · 305-670-6770

Louis Nostro · Shutts & Bowen · http://www.shutts.com · Miami Center, Suite 1500 · 201 South Biscayne Boulevard · Miami, FL 33131 · 305-358-6300

Paul M. Stokes · 25 · Stokes McMillan & Maracini & Antúnez · One Southeast Third Avenue, Suite 1750 Miami, FL 33131 · 305-379-4008

Diana S. C. Zeydel · Greenberg Traurig · http://www.gtlaw.com · 1221 Brickell Avenue, 22nd Floor · Miami, FL 33131 · 305-579-0500

Naples

Todd L. Bradley · Cummings & Lockwood · 3001 Tamiami Trail North, Suite 400 · Naples, FL 34103 · 239-262-8311

Dorothy M. Breen · Goodman Breen & Gibbs · 3838 Tamiami Trail North, Suite 300 · Naples, FL 34103 · 239-403-3000

Jackson M. Bruce, Jr. · 20 · Dunwody White & Landon · http://www.dwl-law.com · 4001 Tamiami Trail North, Suite 200 · Naples, FL 34103 · 239-263-5885

Robert M. Buckel · Salvatori & Wood · Northern Trust Bank Building, Suite 330 · 4001 Tamiami Trail North · Naples, FL 34103-3060 · 239-263-1480

William M. Burke · Goodlette, Coleman & Johnson · 4001 Tamiami Trail North, Suite 300 · Naples, FL 34103 · 239-435-3535

Daniel K. Capes · Dunwody White & Landon · http://www.dwl-law.com · 4001 Tamiami Trail North, Suite 200 · Naples, FL 34103 · 239-263-5885

Joe B. Cox · Cox & Nici · 1185 Immokalee Road, Suite 110 · Naples, FL 34110 · 239-254-0706

Robert W. Goldman · 10 · Goldman, Felcoski & Stone · The 745 Building, Suite 101 · 745 Twelfth Avenue South · Naples, FL 34102 · 239-436-1988

Kenneth D. Goodman · Goodman Breen & Gibbs · 3838 Tamiami Trail North, Suite 300 · Naples, FL 34103 · 239-403-3000

F. Edward Johnson · Cheffy Passidomo Wilson & Johnson · 821 Fifth Avenue South, Suite 201 · Naples, FL 34102 · 239-261-9300

Kimberly L. Johnson · Quarles & Brady · http://www.quarles.com · 1395 Panther Lane, Suite 300 · Naples, FL 34109-7874 · 941-262-5959

Andrew J. Krause · Hahn Loeser & Parks · 800 Laurel Oak Drive, Suite 600 · Naples, FL 34108 · 239-254-2900

Robert D. W. Landon II · 2% · Dunwody White & Landon · http://www.dwl-law.com · 4001 Tamiami Trail North, Suite 200 · Naples, FL 34103 · 239-263-5885

Laird A. Lile · a · Laird A. Lile · http://www.lairdalile.com · 3033 Riviera Drive, Suite 104 · Naples, FL 34103 · 239-649-7778

G. Carson McEachern · Roetzel & Andress · http://www.ralaw.com · Trianon Centre, Third Floor · 850 Park Shore Drive · Naples, FL 34103 · 239-649-6200

William H. Myers · Porter, Wright, Morris & Arthur · http://www.porterwright.com · 5801 Pelican Bay Boulevard, Suite 300 · Naples, FL 34108-2709 · 239-593-2900

William M. Pearson · Grant, Fridkin, Pearson, Athan & Crown · Pelican Bay Corporate Centre, Suite 501 5551 Ridgewood Drive · Naples, FL 34108-2719 · 239-514-1000

Deborah L. Russell · Cummings & Lockwood · http://www.cl-law.com · 3001 Tamiami Trail North, Suite 400 · Naples, FL 34103 · 239-262-8311

Robert J. Stommel · Porter, Wright, Morris & Arthur · http://www.porterwright.com · 5801 Pelican Bay Boulevard, Suite 300 · Naples, FL 34108-2709 · 239-593-2900

Dennis R. White · a · Dennis R. White · 4501 Tamiami Trail North, Suite 210 · Naples, FL 34103-3018 239-261-4700

George A. Wilson II · Cheffy Passidomo Wilson & Johnson · 821 Fifth Avenue South, Suite 201 · Naples, FL 34102 · 239-261-9300

North Miami Beach

Barry A. Nelson · a · Nelson & Nelson · http://www.estatetaxlawyers.com · 2775 Sunny Isles Boulevard, Suite 118 · North Miami Beach, FL 33160 · 305-932-2000

Orlando

W. Michael Clifford · GrayRobinson · 301 East Pine Street, Suite 1400 · P.O. Box 3068 · Orlando, FL 32802-3068 · 407-843-8880

Lauren Y. Detzel · a · Dean, Mead, Egerton, Bloodworth, Capouano & Bozarth · http://www.deanmead.com · 800 North Magnolia Avenue, Suite 1500 · P.O. Box 2346 · Orlando, FL 32802-2346 · 407-841-1200

Stephen D. Dunegan · Dean, Mead, Egerton, Bloodworth, Capouano & Bozarth · http://www.deanmead.com · 800 North Magnolia Avenue, Suite 1500 · P.O. Box 2346 · Orlando, FL 32802-2346 · 407-841-1200

Julia L. Frey · Lowndes, Drosdick, Doster, Kantor & Reed · 215 North Eola Drive · Orlando, FL 32801 · 407-843-4600

Stewart Andrew Marshall III · Akerman Senterfitt · http://www.akerman.com · CNL Center II at City Commons, Suite 1200 · 420 South Orange Avenue · Orlando, FL 32801-3336 · 407-423-4000

John A. Sanders · Foley & Lardner · 111 North Orange Avenue, Suite 1800 · P.O. Box 2193 · Orlando, FL 32802-2193 · 407-423-7656

Norma Stanley · Lowndes, Drosdick, Doster, Kantor & Reed · 215 North Eola Drive · Orlando, FL 32801 · 407-843-4600

Palm Beach

Mark R. Parthemer · Bessemer Trust · 222 Royal Palm Way · Palm Beach, FL 33480-4394 · 561-655-4030

Palm Beach Gardens

Alan H. Baseman · Comiter, Singer & Baseman · 3801 PGA Boulevard, Suite 604 · Palm Beach Gardens, FL 33410 · 561-626-2101

Richard B. Comiter · a · Comiter, Singer & Baseman · 3801 PGA Boulevard, Suite 604 · Palm Beach Gardens, FL 33410 · 561-626-2101

Michael S. Singer · Comiter, Singer & Baseman · 3801 PGA Boulevard, Suite 604 · Palm Beach Gardens, FL 33410 · 561-626-2101

Punta Gorda

Guy S. Emerich · Farr, Farr, Emerich, Hackett and Carr · 99 Nesbit Street · Punta Gorda, FL 33950 · 941-639-1158

Sanibel

David M. Platt · Henderson, Franklin, Starnes & Holt · http://www.henlaw.com · Island Medical & Business Center, Suite B · 1648 Periwinkle Way · Sanibel, FL 33957 · 239-472-6700

Sarasota

John Berteau · Williams Parker Harrison Dietz & Getzen · 200 South Orange Avenue · Sarasota, FL 34236 · 941-366-4800

L. Howard Payne · The Payne Law Group · 240 South Pineapple Avenue, Suite 401 · Sarasota, FL 34236-3708 · 941-487-2800

Barry F. Spivey · Ruden, McClosky, Smith, Schuster & Russell · 1515 Ringling Boulevard, Suite 700 · Sarasota, FL 34236 · 941-316-7600

St. Petersburg

William Fletcher Belcher · a · William Fletcher Belcher · 540 Fourth Street North · St. Petersburg, FL 33701-2302 · 727-821-1249

Joel D. Bronstein · a · Bronstein, Carlson, Gleim & Smith · 150 Second Avenue North, Suite 1100 · St. Petersburg, FL 33701 · 727-898-6688

Bruce Marger · Trenam, Kemker, Scharf, Barkin, Frye, O'Neill & Mullis · http://www.trenam.com · 200 Central Avenue, Suite 1600 · P.O. Box 3542 · St. Petersburg, FL 33731-3542 · 727-896-7171

George F. Wilsey · a · Fisher & Wilsey · 1000 Sixteenth Street North · St. Petersburg, FL 33705 · 727-898-1181

Tallahassee

Frederick R. Dudley · Holland & Knight · http://www.hklaw.com · Bank of America Building, Suite 600 · 315 South Calhoun Street · Tallahassee, FL 32301 · 850-224-7000

Tampa

Thomas D. Aitken · Trenam, Kemker, Scharf, Barkin, Frye, O'Neill & Mullis · http://www.trenam.com · 101 East Kennedy Boulevard, Suite 2700 · P.O. Box 1102 · Tampa, FL 33601-1102 · 813-223-7474

Leslie J. Barnett · 2% · Barnett, Bolt, Kirkwood, Long & McBride · http://www.barnettbolt.com · 601 Bayshore Boulevard, Suite 700 · P.O. Box 3287 · Tampa, FL 33606 · 813-253-2020

E. Jackson Boggs · a · Fowler White Boggs Banker · 501 East Kennedy Boulevard, Suite 1700 · P.O. Box 1438 · Tampa, FL 33602-5239 · 813-228-7411

Amelia M. Campbell · Fowler White Boggs Banker · 501 East Kennedy Boulevard, Suite 1700 · P.O. Box 1438 · Tampa, FL 33602-5239 · 813-228-7411

Merritt A. Gardner · Gardner Law Firm · Watermark Five, Suite 200 · 5415 Mariner Street · Tampa, FL 33609 · 813-288-9600

Bruce H. Gordon · Shumaker, Loop & Kendrick · Bank of America Plaza, Suite 2800 · 101 East Kennedy Boulevard · Tampa, FL 33602-5150 · 813-229-7600

Linda C. Hanna · Linda C. Hanna Professional Association · 600 South Magnolia Avenue, Suite 125 · Tampa, FL 33606-2746 · 813-251-1666

Linda D. Hartley · Hill, Ward & Henderson · http://www.hwhlaw.com · Bank of America Plaza, Suite 3700 · 101 East Kennedy Boulevard · Tampa, FL 33602 · 813-221-3900

John Arthur Jones · 2) · Holland & Knight · http://www.hklaw.com · 100 North Tampa Street, Suite 4100 · P.O. Box 1288 · Tampa, FL 33601-1288 · 813-227-8500

Peter T. Kirkwood · Barnett, Bolt, Kirkwood, Long & McBride · http://www.barnettbolt.com · 601 Bayshore Boulevard, Suite 700 · P.O. Box 3287 · Tampa, FL 33606 · 813-253-2020

Edward F. Koren, Jr. · 2) · Holland & Knight · http://www.hklaw.com · 100 North Tampa Street, Suite 4100 · P.O. Box 1288 · Tampa, FL 33601-1288 · 813-227-8500

William R. Lane, Jr. · Holland & Knight · http://www.hklaw.com · 100 North Tampa Street, Suite 4100 · P.O. Box 1288 · Tampa, FL 33601-1288 · 813-227-8500

Michael J. Nolan II · GrayRobinson · 201 North Franklin Street, Suite 2200 · P.O. Box 3324 · Tampa, FL 33601 · 813-273-5000

Frank J. Rief · Akerman Senterfitt · http://www.akerman.com · SunTrust Financial Centre, Suite 1700 · 401 East Jackson Street · Tampa, FL 33602-5803 · 813-223-7333

Brian C. Sparks · Hill, Ward & Henderson · http://www.hwhlaw.com · Bank of America Plaza, Suite 3700 101 East Kennedy Boulevard · Tampa, FL 33602 · 813-221-3900

J. Eric Taylor · Trenam, Kemker, Scharf, Barkin, Frye, O'Neill & Mullis · http://www.trenam.com · 101 East Kennedy Boulevard, Suite 2700 · P.O. Box 1102 · Tampa, FL 33601-1102 · 813-223-7474

August M. Van Eepoel · Akerman Senterfitt · http://www.akerman.com · SunTrust Financial Centre, Suite 1700 · 401 East Jackson Street · Tampa, FL 33602-5803 · 813-223-7333

Robert H. Waltuch · Fowler White Boggs Banker · 501 East Kennedy Boulevard, Suite 1700 · P.O. Box 1438 · Tampa, FL 33602-5239 · 813-228-7411

Venice

Roger O. Isphording · 2) · Bechtold & Corbridge · 240 Nokomis Avenue South, Suite 200 · Venice, FL 34285 · 941-488-7751

West Palm Beach

Jerald David August · a · Fox Rothschild · 222 Lakeview Avenue, Suite 700 · West Palm Beach, FL 33401 · 561-835-9600

David E. Bowers · a · Jones, Foster, Johnston & Stubbs · 505 South Flagler Drive, Suite 1100 · P.O. Box 3475 · West Palm Beach, FL 33402-3475 · 561-659-3000

Daniel A. Hanley · Gunster, Yoakley & Stewart · Phillips Point, Suite 500 East · 777 South Flagler Drive · West Palm Beach, FL 33401-6194 · 561-655-1980

Peter Matwiczyk · Matwiczyk & Brown · 625 North Flagler Drive, Suite 401 · West Palm Beach, FL 33401-4027 · 561-651-4004

James G. Pressly, Jr. · 2% · Pressly & Pressly · Esperante Building, Suite 910 · 222 Lakeview Avenue · West Palm Beach, FL 33401-6112 · 561-659-4040

Peter A. Sachs · Jones, Foster, Johnston & Stubbs · 505 South Flagler Drive, Suite 1100 · P.O. Box 3475 · West Palm Beach, FL 33402-3475 · 561-659-3000

Lisa A. Schneider · Gunster, Yoakley & Stewart · Phillips Point, Suite 500 East · 777 South Flagler Drive West Palm Beach, FL 33401-6194 · 561-655-1980

Michael D. Simon · Gunster, Yoakley & Stewart · Phillips Point, Suite 500 East · 777 South Flagler Drive West Palm Beach, FL 33401-6194 · 561-655-1980

Stephen G. Vogelsang · Gunster, Yoakley & Stewart · Phillips Point, Suite 500 East · 777 South Flagler Drive · West Palm Beach, FL 33401-6194 · 561-655-1980

Winter Park

G. Charles Wohlust · G. Charles Wohlust Law Office · 341 North Maitland Avenue, Suite 346 · P.O. Box 1570 · Winter Park, FL 32790-1570 · 407-644-3206

VENTURE CAPITAL LAW

Miami

Ronald Albert, Jr. · Broad and Cassel · One Biscayne Tower, Suite 2100 · Two South Biscayne Boulevard · Miami, FL 33131 · 305-373-9400

Daniel H. Aronson · Bilzin Sumberg Baena Price & Axelrod · Wachovia Financial Center, Suite 2500 · 200 South Biscayne Boulevard · Miami, FL 33131 · 305-374-7580

Jonathan L. Awner · Akerman Senterfitt · http://www.akerman.com · One Southeast Third Avenue, 25th Floor · Miami, FL 33131-1714 · 305-374-5600

Martin G. Burkett · Akerman Senterfitt · http://www.akerman.com · One Southeast Third Avenue, 25th Floor · Miami, FL 33131-1714 · 305-374-5600

Bruce Jay Colan · Holland & Knight · http://www.hklaw.com · 701 Brickell Avenue, Suite 3000 · Miami, FL 33131 · 305-374-8500

Teddy D. Klinghoffer · Akerman Senterfitt · http://www.akerman.com · One Southeast Third Avenue, 25th Floor · Miami, FL 33131-1714 · 305-374-5600

Carl D. Roston · Akerman Senterfitt · http://www.akerman.com · One Southeast Third Avenue, 25th Floor · Miami, FL 33131-1714 · 305-374-5600

Tampa

David S. Felman · a · Hill, Ward & Henderson · http://www.hwhlaw.com · Bank of America Plaza, Suite 3700 · 101 East Kennedy Boulevard · Tampa, FL 33602 · 813-221-3900

WATER LAW

Jacksonville

Wayne E. Flowers · Lewis, Longman & Walker · http://www.llw-law.com · 245 Riverside Avenue, Suite 150 · Jacksonville, FL 32202 · 904-353-6410

Miami

Joseph Z. Fleming · 2% · Greenberg Traurig · http://www.gtlaw.com · 1221 Brickell Avenue, 22nd Floor · Miami, FL 33131 · 305-579-0500

Orlando

Roger W. Sims · a · Holland & Knight · http://www.hklaw.com · 200 South Orange Avenue, Suite 2600 · P.O. Box 1526 · Orlando, FL 32802 · 407-425-8500

Tallahassee

Eric T. Olsen · Hopping Green & Sams · http://www.hgslaw.com · 123 South Calhoun Street · P.O. Box 6526 · Tallahassee, FL 32314 · 850-222-7598

Philip S. Parsons · a · Young Van Assenderp · Gallie's Hall, Second Floor · 225 South Adams Street · P.O. Box 1833 · Tallahassee, FL 32302 · 850-222-7206

Lawrence E. Sellers · Holland & Knight · http://www.hklaw.com · Bank of America Building, Suite 600 · 315 South Calhoun Street · Tallahassee, FL 32301 · 850-224-7000

Jacob D. Varn · Fowler White Boggs Banker · 101 North Monroe Street, Suite 1090 · Tallahassee, FL 32301 · 850-681-0411

Tampa

Edward P. de la Parte, Jr. · de la Parte & Gilbert · Bank of America Plaza, Suite 3400 · 101 East Kennedy Boulevard · Tampa, FL 33602-5195 · 813-229-2775

Douglas P. Manson · Carey, O'Malley, Whitaker & Manson · 712 South Oregon Avenue · Tampa, FL 33606 · 813-250-0577

Roger D. Schwenke · 2) · Carlton Fields · Corporate Center Three at International Plaza, Suite 1000 · 4221 West Boy Scout Boulevard · Tampa, FL 33607 · 813-223-7000

WHITE-COLLAR CRIMINAL DEFENSE

Boca Raton

H. Dohn Williams, Jr. · a · H. Dohn Williams, Jr. · 990 Northwest Fifth Street · Boca Raton, FL 33486 · 561-929-5432

Clearwater

Denis M. de Vlaming · a · Denis M. de Vlaming · 1101 Turner Street · Clearwater, FL 33756 · 727-461-0525

George E. Tragos · Tragos & Sartres · Suntrust Bank Building, Suite 800 · 600 Cleveland Street · Clearwater, FL 33755 · 727-441-9030

Coral Gables

Joel Hirschhorn · 2% · Hirschhorn & Bieber · http://www.aquitall.com · 550 Biltmore Way, Penthouse 3-A Coral Gables, FL 33134 · 305-445-5320

Phillip A. Hubbart · Phillip Arthur Hubbart · 2655 South Le Jeune Road, Penthouse 1-G · Coral Gables, FL 33134 · 305-374-0650

Roberto Martinez · Colson, Hicks & Eidson · http://www.colsonhickseidson.com · 255 Aragon Avenue, Second Floor · Coral Gables, FL 33134 · 305-476-7400

Susan Johnson Tarbe · Colson, Hicks & Eidson · http://www.colsonhickseidson.com · 255 Aragon Avenue, Second Floor · Coral Gables, FL 33134 · 305-476-7400

Fort Lauderdale

J. David Bogenschutz · 2) · Bogenschutz, Dutko & Kroll · Third Fifth Bank Building, Suite 500 · 600 South Andrews Avenue · Fort Lauderdale, FL 33301 · 954-764-2500

Michael E. Dutko · Bogenschutz, Dutko & Kroll · Third Fifth Bank Building, Suite 500 · 600 South Andrews Avenue · Fort Lauderdale, FL 33301 · 954-764-2500

Fred Haddad · a · Fred Haddad · One Financial Plaza, Suite 2612 · Fort Lauderdale, FL 33394 · 954-467-6767

Bruce M. Lyons · 2) · Lyons and Sanders · 600 Northeast Third Avenue · Fort Lauderdale, FL 33304-2689 · 954-467-8700

Marc S. Nurik · Rothstein Rosenfeldt Adler · Bank of America Building, Suite 1650 · 401 East Las Olas Boulevard · Fort Lauderdale, FL 33301 · 954-522-3456

Bruce S. Rogow · 2) · Bruce S. Rogow · Broward Financial Centre, Suite 1930 · 500 East Broward Boulevard · Fort Lauderdale, FL 33394 · 954-767-8909

Bruce L. Udolf · Berger Singerman · http://www.bergersingerman.com · 350 East Las Olas Boulevard, Suite 1000 · Fort Lauderdale, FL 33301 · 954-525-9900

Theresa Van Vliet · Genovese Joblove & Battista · Fidelity Federal Center, Suite 1110 · 200 East Broward Boulevard · Fort Lauderdale, FL 33301 · 954-453-8000

Bruce A. Zimet · 2) · Bruce A. Zimet · One Financial Plaza, Suite 2612 · Fort Lauderdale, FL 33394 · 954-764-7081

Fort Myers

Peter D. Aiken · Peter D. Aiken · 2575 Cleveland Avenue · Fort Myers, FL 33901 · 239-334-8890

Gainesville

Robert S. Griscti · a · Law Firm of Robert S. Griscti · 204 West University Avenue, Suite Six · P.O. Box 508 · Gainesville, FL 32602 · 352-375-4460

Larry G. Turner · Turner & Jones · 204 West University Avenue, Suite Seven · Gainesville, FL 32601-5205 · 352-372-4263

Jacksonville

O. David Barksdale · Bedell, Dittmar, DeVault, Pillans & Coxe · http://www.bedellfirm.com · The Bedell Building · 101 East Adams Street · Jacksonville, FL 32202 · 904-353-0211

Thomas E. Bishop · Tanner Bishop · One Independent Drive, Suite 1700 · Jacksonville, FL 32202-5015 904-598-0034

Henry M. Coxe III · 2) · Bedell, Dittmar, DeVault, Pillans & Coxe · http://www.bedellfirm.com · The Bedell Building · 101 East Adams Street · Jacksonville, FL 32202 · 904-353-0211

Albert J. Datz · 2% · Datz & Datz · 4348 Southpoint Boulevard, Suite 330 · Jacksonville, FL 32216 · 904-296-7440

John A. DeVault III · 2) · Bedell, Dittmar, DeVault, Pillans & Coxe · http://www.bedellfirm.com · The Bedell Building · 101 East Adams Street · Jacksonville, FL 32202 · 904-353-0211

Samuel S. Jacobson · Bledsoe, Jacobson, Schmidt & Wright · 1301 Riverplace Boulevard, Suite 1818 · Jacksonville, FL 32207 · 904-398-1818

Charles B. Lembcke · Charles B. Lembcke · 1300 Riverplace Boulevard, Suite 605 · Jacksonville, FL 32207 · 904-355-5467

Charles P. Pillans III · a · Bedell, Dittmar, DeVault, Pillans & Coxe · http://www.bedellfirm.com · The Bedell Building · 101 East Adams Street · Jacksonville, FL 32202 · 904-353-0211

William J. Sheppard · a · Sheppard, White,Thomas & Kachergus · 215 North Washington Street · Jacksonville, FL 32202-2808 · 904-356-9661

D. Gray Thomas · Sheppard, White,Thomas & Kachergus · 215 North Washington Street · Jacksonville, FL 32202-2808 · 904-356-9661

Elizabeth L. White · a · Sheppard, White,Thomas & Kachergus · 215 North Washington Street · Jacksonville, FL 32202-2808 · 904-356-9661

Miami

William Aaron · Law Offices of William Aaron · Wachovia Financial Center, Suite 2770 · 200 South Biscayne Boulevard · Miami, FL 33131 · 305-371-5800

Gregory A. Baldwin · Holland & Knight · http://www.hklaw.com · 701 Brickell Avenue, Suite 3000 · Miami, FL 33131 · 305-374-8500

Joseph D. W. Beeler · Joseph Beeler, P.A. · 800 Brickell Avenue, Penthouse Two · Miami, FL 33131 · 305-372-5110

Donald I. Bierman · 2% · Bierman, Shohat, Loewy & Pizzi · 800 Brickell Avenue, Penthouse Two · Miami, FL 33131-2911 · 305-358-7000

Stephen J. Binhak · Greenberg Traurig · http://www.gtlaw.com · 1221 Brickell Avenue, 22nd Floor · Miami, FL 33131 · 305-579-0500

Melvin S. Black · a · Melvin S. Black · Grove Forest Plaza, Suite 202 · 2937 Southwest 27th Avenue · Miami, FL 33133 · 305-443-1600

Roy Black · 2) · Black, Srebnick Kornspan & Stumpf · http://www.royblack.com · Miami Center, Suite 1300 · 201 South Biscayne Boulevard · Miami, FL 33131 · 305-371-6421

Irwin J. Block · 2% · Adorno & Yoss · 2525 Ponce de Leon Boulevard, Suite 400 · Miami, FL 33134 · 305-460-1000

Stephen J. Bronis · a · Carlton Fields · 4000 International Place · 100 Southeast Second Street · P.O. Box 019101 · Miami, FL 33131-9101 · 305-530-0050

Edward A. Carhart · 2% · Edward A. Carhart · 5300 Southwest 76th Street · Miami, FL 33143-5852 · 305-567-1066

Joseph A. DeMaria · Tew Cardenas · http://www.tewlaw.com · Four Seasons Tower, 15th Floor · 1441 Brickell Avenue · Miami, FL 33131-3407 · 305-536-1112

Jack M. Denaro · 2% · Jack M. Denaro · 7700 North Kendall Drive, Suite 504 · Miami, FL 33156 · 305-274-9550

H. Scott Fingerhut · H. Scott Fingerhut · 2400 South Dixie Highway, Second Floor · Miami, FL 33133-3156 · 305-285-0500

Daniel S. Gelber · Akerman Senterfitt · http://www.akerman.com · One Southeast Third Avenue, 25th Floor · Miami, FL 33131-1714 · 305-374-5600

Martin B. Goldberg · Lash & Goldberg · http://www.lashgoldberg.com · Bank of America Tower, Suite 1200 · 100 Southeast Second Street · Miami, FL 33131-2158 · 305-347-4040

Jonathan Goodman · Akerman Senterfitt · http://www.akerman.com · One Southeast Third Avenue, 25th Floor · Miami, FL 33131-1714 · 305-374-5600

Douglas C. Hartman · Hartman & Cornely · 10680 Northwest 25th Street, Suite 200 · Miami, FL 33172-2108 · 305-477-1184

Steven E. M. Hartz · Akerman Senterfitt · http://www.akerman.com · One Southeast Third Avenue, 25th Floor · Miami, FL 33131-1714 · 305-374-5600

Milton Hirsch · a · Milton Hirsch · Two Datran Center, Suite 1200 · 9130 South Dadeland Boulevard · Miami, FL 33156 · 305-670-0077

James J. Hogan · a · Hogan, Greer & Shapiro · 2400 South Dixie Highway, Suite 200 · Miami, FL 33133-3153 · 305-854-8989

John M. Hogan · Holland & Knight · http://www.hklaw.com · 701 Brickell Avenue, Suite 3000 · Miami, FL 33131 · 305-374-8500

Robert C. Josefsberg · 2% · Podhurst Orseck · http://www.podhurst.com · City National Bank Building, Suite 800 · 25 West Flagler Street · Miami, FL 33130 · 305-358-2800

Albert J. Krieger · 2) · Albert J. Krieger, P.A. · 2701 South Bayshore Drive, Suite 315 · Miami, FL 33133-3307 · 786-573-4912

Ira N. Loewy · Bierman, Shohat, Loewy & Pizzi · 800 Brickell Avenue, Penthouse Two · Miami, FL 33131-2911 · 305-358-7000

David S. Mandel · Mandel & Mandel · Alfred I duPont Building, Suite 1200 · 169 East Flagler Street · Miami, FL 33131 · 305-374-7771

David Oscar Markus · David Oscar Markus · Alfred I. duPont Building, Suite 1200 · 169 East Flagler Street · Miami, FL 33131-1205 · 305-379-6667

Jane Wollner Moscowitz · a · Moscowitz & Moscowitz · Mellon Financial Center, Suite 2050 · 1111 Brickell Avenue · Miami, FL 33131 · 305-379-8300

Norman A. Moscowitz · a · Moscowitz & Moscowitz · Mellon Financial Center, Suite 2050 · 1111 Brickell Avenue · Miami, FL 33131 · 305-379-8300

Michael S. Pasano · Carlton Fields · 4000 International Place · 100 Southeast Second Street · P.O. Box 019101 · Miami, FL 33131-9101 · 305-530-0050

Rebekah J. Poston · Squire Sanders · http://www.ssd.com · 200 South Biscayne Boulevard, Suite 4000 · Miami, FL 33131-2398 · 305-577-7000

Peter Prieto · Holland & Knight · http://www.hklaw.com · 701 Brickell Avenue, Suite 3000 · Miami, FL 33131 · 305-374-8500

Jose M. Quiñon · a · Jose M. Quiñon · 2333 Brickell Avenue, Suite A-1 · Miami, FL 33129 · 305-858-5700

Jane S. Raskin · Raskin & Raskin · http://www.raskinlaw.com · 2601 South Bayshore Drive, Suite 725 · Miami, FL 33133 · 305-444-3400

Martin R. Raskin · Raskin & Raskin · http://www.raskinlaw.com · 2601 South Bayshore Drive, Suite 725 · Miami, FL 33133 · 305-444-3400

Robert Scott Reiff · Law Offices of Robert S. Reiff · 2400 South Dixie Highway, Suite 200 · Miami, FL 33133 · 305-854-5511

William L. Richey · a · William L. Richey · Miami Center, 34th Floor · 201 South Biscayne Boulevard · Miami, FL 33131-4325 · 305-372-8808

Andres Rivero · Rivero Palmer & Mestre · 2525 Ponce De Leon Boulevard, Suite 1000 · Miami, FL 33134-6046 · 305-445-2500

Michael J. Rosen · Michael J. Rosen · Grove Forest Plaza, Suite 101 · 2937 Southwest 27th Avenue · Miami, FL 33133 · 305-446-6116

Jon A. Sale · a · Sale & Weintraub · 200 Southeast Second Street, Suite 4300 · Miami, FL 33131-2112 · 305-374-1818

Elliot H. Scherker · Greenberg Traurig · http://www.gtlaw.com · 1221 Brickell Avenue, 22nd Floor · Miami, FL 33131 · 305-579-0500

Mark P. Schnapp · Greenberg Traurig · http://www.gtlaw.com · 1221 Brickell Avenue, 22nd Floor · Miami, FL 33131 · 305-579-0500

Thomas E. Scott · Cole, Scott & Kissane · http://www.csklegal.com · Pacific National Bank Building, Third Floor · 1390 Brickell Avenue · Miami, FL 33131 · 305-350-5300

Hy Shapiro · Hogan, Greer & Shapiro · 2400 South Dixie Highway, Suite 200 · Miami, FL 33133-3153 · 305-854-8989

Richard A. Sharpstein · a · Jorden Burt · 777 Brickell Avenue, Suite 500 · Miami, FL 33131-2803 · 305-371-2600

Edward R. Shohat · 2) · Bierman, Shohat, Loewy & Pizzi · 800 Brickell Avenue, Penthouse Two · Miami, FL 33131-2911 · 305-358-7000

Holly R. Skolnick · Greenberg Traurig · http://www.gtlaw.com · 1221 Brickell Avenue, 22nd Floor · Miami, FL 33131 · 305-579-0500

H. T. Smith, Jr. · a · H. T. Smith · 1017 Northwest Ninth Court · Miami, FL 33136-3012 · 305-324-1845

Neal R. Sonnett · 2% · Neal R. Sonnett · http://www.sonnettlaw.com · One Biscayne Tower, Twenty Sixth Floor · Two South Biscayne Boulevard · Miami, FL 33131-1802 · 305-358-2000

Howard M. Srebnick · Black, Srebnick Kornspan & Stumpf · http://www.royblack.com · Miami Center, Suite 1300 · 201 South Biscayne Boulevard · Miami, FL 33131 · 305-371-6421

Scott A. Srebnick · Law Offices of Scott Srebnick · 201 South Biscayne Boulevard, Suite 1380 · Miami, FL 33131 · 305-285-9019

Marty L. Steinberg · a · Hunton & Williams · Mellon Financial Center, Suite 2500 · 1111 Brickell Avenue · Miami, FL 33131 · 305-810-2500

G. Richard Strafer · a · G. Richard Strafer · 201 South Biscayne Boulevard, Suite 1380 · Miami, FL 33131 · 305-374-9091

Allan J. Sullivan · Baker & McKenzie · Mellon Financial Center, Suite 1700 · 1111 Brickell Avenue · Miami, FL 33131 · 305-789-8900

Naples

Yale T. Freeman · Yale T. Freeman · 2325 Stanford Court · Naples, FL 34112 · 239-530-2500

Orlando

Mark L. Horwitz · Law Offices of Mark L. Horwitz · http://www.mlhorwitzlaw.com · 17 East Pine Street · Orlando, FL 32801 · 407-401-7224

Robert A. Leventhal · Leventhal & Slaughter · 111 North Orange Avenue, Suite 700 · Orlando, FL 32801 · 407-849-6161

J. Cheney Mason · Law Offices of J. Cheney Mason · Bank of America Center, Suite 2100 · 390 North Orange Avenue · Orlando, FL 32801 · 407-843-5785

James M. Russ · 2% · Law Offices of James M. Russ · Tinker Building · 18 West Pine Street · Orlando, FL 32801-2697 · 407-849-6050

William J. Sheaffer · William J. Sheaffer · http://www.defenselaw.net · 609 East Central Boulevard · Orlando, FL 32801 · 407-423-1066

Harrison T. Slaughter, Jr. · Leventhal & Slaughter · 111 North Orange Avenue, Suite 700 · Orlando, FL 32801 · 407-849-6161

Pensacola

Barry W. Beroset · Beroset & Keene · 1622 North Ninth Avenue · Pensacola, FL 32503 · 850-438-3111

Leo A. Thomas · a · Levin, Papantonio, Thomas, Mitchell, Echsner & Proctor · 316 South Baylen Street, Suite 600 · P.O. Box 12308 · Pensacola, FL 32591 · 850-435-7000

Sarasota

Larry Byrd · a · The Byrd Law Firm · 2151 Main Street, Suite 201 · Sarasota, FL 34237 · 941-954-3400

Tallahassee

Stephen S. Dobson III · Dobson, Davis & Smith · 610 North Duval Street · Tallahassee, FL 32301 · 850-224-2683

W. Dexter Douglass · a · Douglass Law Firm · 211 East Call Street · P.O. Box 1674 · Tallahassee, FL 32302 · 850-224-6191

Stephen H. Grimes · Holland & Knight · http://www.hklaw.com · Bank of America Building, Suite 600 · 315 South Calhoun Street · Tallahassee, FL 32301 · 850-224-7000

Robert Augustus Harper · a · Harper & Harper · 325 West Park Avenue · P.O. Box 10132 · Tallahassee, FL 32302-2132 · 850-224-5900

Robert Augustus Harper III · Harper & Harper · 325 West Park Avenue · P.O. Box 10132 · Tallahassee, FL 32302-2132 · 850-224-5900

Melanie Ann Hines · Berger Singerman · http://www.bergersingerman.com · 125 South Gadsden Street, Suite 300 · Tallahassee, FL 32301 · 850-561-3010

James P. Judkins · a · Judkins, Simpson & High · 1102 North Gadsden Street · P.O. Box 10368 · Tallahassee, FL 32302 · 850-222-6040

E. C. Deeno Kitchen · 2) · Ervin Kitchen & Ervin · 223 South Gadsden Street · Tallahassee, FL 32302-1170 · 850-224-9135

Larry D. Simpson · a · Judkins, Simpson & High · 1102 North Gadsden Street · P.O. Box 10368 · Tallahassee, FL 32302 · 850-222-6040

Murray M. Wadsworth, Sr. · 2) · Gardner, Wadsworth, Duggar, Bist & Wiener · 1300 Thomaswood Drive · Tallahassee, FL 32308-7914 · 850-385-0070

Tampa

A. Brian Albritton · Holland & Knight · http://www.hklaw.com · 100 North Tampa Street, Suite 4100 · P.O. Box 1288 · Tampa, FL 33601-1288 · 813-227-8500

Ronald K. Cacciatore · 2% · Ronald K. Cacciatore · 100 North Tampa Street, Suite 2835 · Tampa, FL 33602 · 813-223-4831

Barry A. Cohen · 2% · Cohen, Jayson & Foster · 201 East Kennedy Boulevard, Suite 1000 · Tampa, FL 33602-5829 · 813-225-1655

Kevin J. Darken · Cohen, Jayson & Foster · 201 East Kennedy Boulevard, Suite 1000 · Tampa, FL 33602-5829 · 813-225-1655

James E. Felman · Kynes, Markman & Felman · 100 South Ashley Drive, Suite 1300 · P.O. Box 3396 · Tampa, FL 33601-3396 · 813-229-1118

Jack E. Fernandez, Jr. · Zuckerman Spaeder · http://www.zuckerman.com · 101 East Kennedy Boulevard, Suite 1200 · Tampa, FL 33602-5838 · 813-221-1010

John M. Fitzgibbons · a · John M. Fitzgibbons · 707 North Franklin Street, Suite 700 · Tampa, FL 33602 · 813-221-8800

D. Lee Fugate · Zuckerman Spaeder · http://www.zuckerman.com · 101 East Kennedy Boulevard, Suite 1200 · Tampa, FL 33602-5838 · 813-221-1010

Peter E. George · George & Titus · 100 South Ashley Drive, Suite 1290 · Tampa, FL 33602-5309 · 813-273-0355

Ronald P. Hanes · Trombley & Hanes · Tampa Theatre Building, 10th Floor · 707 North Franklin Street Tampa, FL 33602 · 813-229-7918

Marcelino J. Huerta III · Marcelino J. Huerta III · http://www.tampacase.com · 109 North Brush Street, Suite 200 · Tampa, FL 33602-4163 · 813-229-7623

William F. Jung · Jung & Sisco · http://www.jungandsisco.com · Wachovia Center, Suite 1240 · 100 South Ashley Drive · Tampa, FL 33602 · 813-225-1988

Stuart C. Markman · Kynes, Markman & Felman · 100 South Ashley Drive, Suite 1300 · P.O. Box 3396 · Tampa, FL 33601-3396 · 813-229-1118

Kevin J. Napper · Carlton Fields · Corporate Center Three at International Plaza, Suite 1000 · 4221 West Boy Scout Boulevard · Tampa, FL 33607 · 813-223-7000

Edward J. Page · Carlton Fields · Corporate Center Three at International Plaza, Suite 1000 · 4221 West Boy Scout Boulevard · Tampa, FL 33607 · 813-223-7000

Paul M. Sisco · Jung & Sisco · http://www.jungandsisco.com · Wachovia Center, Suite 1240 · 100 South Ashley Drive · Tampa, FL 33602 · 813-225-1988

Eduardo Suarez · Law Offices of Ed Suarez · Park Place · 1011 West Cleveland Street · Tampa, FL 33606 · 813-229-0040

Douglas J. Titus, Jr. · George & Titus · 100 South Ashley Drive, Suite 1290 · Tampa, FL 33602-5309 · 813-273-0355

Gary R. Trombley · 2) · Trombley & Hanes · Tampa Theatre Building, 10th Floor · 707 North Franklin Street · Tampa, FL 33602 · 813-229-7918

Morris Weinberg, Jr. · Zuckerman Spaeder · http://www.zuckerman.com · 101 East Kennedy Boulevard, Suite 1200 · Tampa, FL 33602-5838 · 813-221-1010

West Palm Beach

Joseph R. Atterbury · Atterbury, Goldberger, Richardson & Weiss · 250 Australian Avenue South, Suite 1400 · West Palm Beach, FL 33401-5012 · 561-659-8300

Jack A. Goldberger · Atterbury, Goldberger, Richardson & Weiss · 250 Australian Avenue South, Suite 1400 · West Palm Beach, FL 33401-5012 · 561-659-8300

Richard G. Lubin · a · Richard G. Lubin · 1217 South Flagler Drive, Second Floor · West Palm Beach, FL 33401-6706 · 561-655-2040

David Louis Roth · a · Roth & Duncan · 515 North Flagler Drive, Suite 325 · P.O. Box 770 · West Palm Beach, FL 33402 · 561-655-5529

Winter Park

Kirk N. Kirkconnell · Kirkconnell, Lindsey, Snure & Yates · 1150 Louisiana Avenue, Suite One · P.O. Box 2728 · Winter Park, FL 32790-2728 · 407-644-7600

Warren W. Lindsey · Kirkconnell, Lindsey, Snure & Yates · 1150 Louisiana Avenue, Suite One · P.O. Box 2728 · Winter Park, FL 32790-2728 · 407-644-7600

WORKERS' COMPENSATION LAW

Boca Raton

Charles Randal Morcroft · a · Charles Randal Morcroft · 1160 Southwest 19th Avenue · Boca Raton, FL 33486-8507 · 954-234-6681

Coral Gables

Robert J. Rodriguez · Miller, Kagan, Rodriguez & Silver · 201 Alhambra Circle, Suite 802 · Coral Gables, FL 33134 · 305-446-5228

Richard Anothony Sicking · a · Richard A. Sicking · 1313 Ponce de Leon Boulevard, Suite 300 · Coral Gables, FL 33134-3343 · 305-446-3700

Fort Myers

Matthew B. Wheeley · Fowler White Boggs Banker · 2235 First Street · Fort Myers, FL 33901 · 239-334-7892

Lake Worth

Randall T. Porcher · Gonzalez & Porcher · 2328 One Tenth Avenue North, Sixth Floor · Lake Worth, FL 33461 · 561-965-6550

Lithia

Rafael Gonzalez · a · Rafael Gonzalez · 6309 Wild Orchid Drive · Lithia, FL 33547-5043 · 813-967-7598

Miami

Lee Barry Keyfetz · a · L. Barry Keyfetz · 44 West Flagler Street, Suite 2400 · Miami, FL 33130 · 305-358-1740

Mark L. Zientz · Law Office of Mark L. Zientz · 9130 South Dadeland Boulevard, Suite 1619 · Miami, FL 33156 · 305-670-6275

Miami Lakes

Steven P. Kronenberg · a · Kelley Kronenberg · 15600 Northwest 67th Avenue, Suite 204 · Miami Lakes, FL 33014 · 305-826-7260

Orlando

Robert C. Barrett · a · Rissman, Weisberg, Barrett, Hurt, Donahue & McLain · Capital Plaza, 15th Floor 201 East Pine Street · P.O. Box 4940 · Orlando, FL 32801 · 407-839-0120

C. Thomas Ferrara · a · C. Thomas Ferrara · 1780 North Mills Avenue · P.O. Box 536636 · Orlando, FL 32853-6636 · 407-894-1112

Steve A. Rissman · a · Rissman, Weisberg, Barrett, Hurt, Donahue & McLain · Capital Plaza, 15th Floor 201 East Pine Street · P.O. Box 4940 · Orlando, FL 32801 · 407-839-0120

Dennis D. Smejkal · The Law Office of Dennis D. Smejkal · 214 East Lucerne Circle, Suite C · Orlando, FL 32801 · 407-649-7746

Glen D. Wieland · a · Wieland & Hilado · 790 North Orange Avenue · P.O. Box 944 · Orlando, FL 32802 · 407-841-7699

Plantation

Scott H. Silver · Miller, Kagan, Rodriguez & Silver · 1000 South Pine Island Road, Suite 520 · Plantation, FL 33324 · 954-776-9966

South Miami

Jeffrey Ira Jacobs · Malca & Jacobs · 5975 Sunset Drive, Suite 801 · South Miami, FL 33143 · 305-662-5500

Ramon Malca · a · Malca & Jacobs · 5975 Sunset Drive, Suite 801 · South Miami, FL 33143 · 305-662-5500

St. Petersburg

Gregory A. Brooks · Fowler White Boggs Banker · 501 First Avenue North, Suite 900 · St. Petersburg, FL 33701 · 727-896-0601

Tallahassee

James N. McConnaughhay · a · McConnaughhay, Duffy, Coonrad, Pope & Weaver · 1709 Hermitage Boulevard, Suite 200 · Tallahassee, FL 32308 · 850-222-8121

Tampa

Donald S. Bennett · Fowler White Boggs Banker · 501 East Kennedy Boulevard, Suite 1700 · P.O. Box 1438 · Tampa, FL 33602-5239 · 813-228-7411

David C. Lockwood · Fowler White Boggs Banker · 501 East Kennedy Boulevard, Suite 1700 · P.O. Box 1438 · Tampa, FL 33602-5239 · 813-228-7411

Stephen L. Rosen · a · Stephen L. Rosen · 3444 South Westshore Boulevard · Tampa, FL 33629-8221 · 813-902-1200

James H. Smith · a · Law Office of James H. Smith · 2918 Busch Lake Boulevard · Tampa, FL 33614 · 813-932-3304

Mary Ann Stiles · Stiles, Taylor, Grace & Smith · Old Hyde Park · 315 Plant Avenue · Tampa, FL 33606 813-251-2880

Timothy D. Wolf · Fowler White Boggs Banker · 501 East Kennedy Boulevard, Suite 1700 · P.O. Box 1438 · Tampa, FL 33602-5239 · 813-228-7411

West Palm Beach

H. George Kagan · a · Miller, Kagan, Rodriguez & Silver · 250 Australian Avenue South, Suite 1600 · West Palm Beach, FL 33401 · 561-833-1860

Gerald A. Rosenthal · a · Rosenthal & Levy · Mellon National Bank Building, Suite 350 · 1645 Palm Beach Lakes Boulevard · West Palm Beach, FL 33401-2289 · 561-478-2500

Winter Park

Geoffrey Bichler · Bichler & Kelley · 807 West Morse Boulevard, Suite 201 · Winter Park, FL 32789-3726 · 407-599-3777

J. David Parrish · a · Parrish & Smejkal · 807 West Morse Boulevard, Suite 203 · Winter Park, FL 32789-3726 · 407-843-1920

GEORGIA

ADMINISTRATIVE LAW

Atlanta

Anthony L. Cochran · ⑩ · Chilivis, Cochran, Larkins & Bever · 3127 Maple Drive, NE · Atlanta, GA 30305-2503 · 404-233-4171

Mark H. Cohen · Troutman Sanders · Bank of America Plaza, Suite 5200 · 600 Peachtree Street, NE · Atlanta, GA 30308-2216 · 404-885-3000

L. Craig Dowdy · ⑩ · McKenna Long & Aldridge · 303 Peachtree Street, NE, Suite 5300 · Atlanta, GA 30308 · 404-527-4000

Kevin C. Greene · ⑩ · Troutman Sanders · Bank of America Plaza, Suite 5200 · 600 Peachtree Street, NE Atlanta, GA 30308-2216 · 404-885-3000

Charles F. Palmer · Troutman Sanders · Bank of America Plaza, Suite 5200 · 600 Peachtree Street, NE · Atlanta, GA 30308-2216 · 404-885-3000

Robert B. Remar · Rogers & Hardin · 2700 International Tower · 229 Peachtree Street, NE · Atlanta, GA 30303 · 404-522-4700

ADVERTISING LAW

Atlanta

Jerre B. Swann · ⑩ · Kilpatrick Stockton · 1100 Peachtree Street, Suite 2800 · Atlanta, GA 30309-4530 · 404-815-6500

ALTERNATIVE DISPUTE RESOLUTION

Athens

J. Edward Allen, Jr. · Fortson, Bentley and Griffin · 2500 Daniell's Bridge Road, Building 200, Suite 3-A Athens, GA 30606 · 706-548-1151

Denny C. Galis · Denny Charles Galis · 735 South Milledge Avenue · P.O. Box 907 · Athens, GA 30603-0907 · 706-549-8242

Miles J. Alexander · ㉕ · Kilpatrick Stockton · 1100 Peachtree Street, Suite 2800 · Atlanta, GA 30309-4530 · 404-815-6500

John F. Allgood · Ford & Harrison · http://www.fordharrison.com · 1275 Peachtree Street, NE, Suite 600 Atlanta, GA 30309-3576 · 404-888-3800

Richard M. Asbill · ⑩ · Paul Hastings · 600 Peachtree Street, NE, 24th Floor · Atlanta, GA 30308 · 404-815-2400

R. Lawrence Ashe, Jr. · ⑩ · Ashe, Rafuse & Hill · South Tower, Suite 500 · 1355 Peachtree Street, NE · Atlanta, GA 30309-3232 · 404-253-6000

R. Neal Batson · ㉕ · Alston + Bird · http://www.alston.com · One Atlantic Center · 1201 West Peachtree Street · Atlanta, GA 30309-3424 · 404-881-7000

Joseph M. Beck · ⑩ · Kilpatrick Stockton · 1100 Peachtree Street, Suite 2800 · Atlanta, GA 30309-4530 · 404-815-6500

Jay D. Bennett · Alston + Bird · http://www.alston.com · One Atlantic Center · 1201 West Peachtree Street · Atlanta, GA 30309-3424 · 404-881-7000

Emmet J. Bondurant II · ㉕ · Bondurant, Mixson & Elmore · http://www.bmelaw.com · One Atlantic Center, Suite 3900 · 1201 West Peachtree Street, NW · Atlanta, GA 30309 · 404-881-4100

A. Stephens Clay IV · ⑩ · Kilpatrick Stockton · 1100 Peachtree Street, Suite 2800 · Atlanta, GA 30309-4530 · 404-815-6500

Terrence Lee Croft · King & Croft · The Candler Building, Suite 707 · 127 Peachtree Street, NE · Atlanta, GA 30303 · 404-577-8400

Taylor T. Daly · Nelson Mullins Riley & Scarborough · Atlantic Station, Suite 1700 · 201 Seventeenth Street, NW · Atlanta, GA 30363 · 404-817-6000

Arthur H. Glaser · Glaser, Currie & Bullman · 1455 Lincoln Parkway, Suite 300 · Atlanta, GA 30346 · 770-563-9300

William S. Goodman · Henning Mediation & Arbitration Services · Riverwood Building, Suite 75 · 3350 Riverwood Parkway · Atlanta, GA 30339 · 770-955-2252

Harry L. Griffin, Jr. · Sutherland · http://www.sutherland.com · 999 Peachtree Street, NE · Atlanta, GA 30309-3996 · 404-853-8000

James P. Groton · James P. Groton · 999 Peachtree Street, NE, Suite 2300 · Atlanta, GA 30309 · 404-853-8071

Shelby R. Grubbs · Miller & Martin · http://www.millermartin.com · 1170 Peachtree Street, NE, Suite 800 · Atlanta, GA 30309-3576 · 404-962-6100

John W. Hinchey · King & Spalding · 1180 Peachtree Street, NE · Atlanta, GA 30309-3521 · 404-572-4600

Allen I. Hirsch · Arnall Golden Gregory · 171 Seventeenth Street, NW, Suite 2100 · Atlanta, GA 30363-1031 · 404-873-8500

Hunter R. Hughes III · Rogers & Hardin · 2700 International Tower · 229 Peachtree Street, NE · Atlanta, GA 30303 · 404-522-4700

F. Carlton King, Jr. · King & Croft · The Candler Building, Suite 707 · 127 Peachtree Street, NE · Atlanta, GA 30303 · 404-577-8400

Linda A. Klein · Baker, Donelson, Bearman, Caldwell & Berkowitz · http://www.bakerdonelson.com · Six Concourse Parkway, Suite 3100 · Atlanta, GA 30328 · 678-406-8700

Clay C. Long · 20 · McKenna Long & Aldridge · 303 Peachtree Street, NE, Suite 5300 · Atlanta, GA 30308 · 404-527-4000

John T. Marshall · 25 · Powell Goldstein · http://www.pogolaw.com · One Atlantic Center, 14th Floor · 1201 West Peachtree Street, NE · Atlanta, GA 30309 · 404-572-6600

Albert M. Pearson III · 10 · Moraitakis, Kushel, Pearson & Gardner · 3445 Peachtree Road, NE, Suite 425 · Atlanta, GA 30326-3239 · 404-261-0016

Jonathan C. Peters, Jr. · Peters & Monyak · One Atlanta Plaza, Suite 2275 · 950 East Paces Ferry Road · Atlanta, GA 30326 · 404-607-0100

John A. Sherrill · Seyfarth Shaw · One Peachtree Pointe, Suite 700 · 1545 Peachtree Street, NE · Atlanta, GA 30309-2401 · 404-885-1500

Richard H. Sinkfield · 10 · Rogers & Hardin · 2700 International Tower · 229 Peachtree Street, NE · Atlanta, GA 30303 · 404-522-4700

Rex D. Smith · Mabry & McClelland · 2200 Century Parkway, NE, 10th Floor · Atlanta, GA 30345 · 404-325-4800

Sidney O. Smith, Jr. · Alston + Bird · http://www.alston.com · One Atlantic Center · 1201 West Peachtree Street · Atlanta, GA 30309-3424 · 404-881-7000

R. Wayne Thorpe · JAMS · 1100 Peachtree Street, NE, Suite 640 · Atlanta, GA 30309 · 404-588-0900

Thomas W. Tobin · Henning Mediation & Arbitration Services · Riverwood Building, Suite 75 · 3350 Riverwood Parkway · Atlanta, GA 30339 · 770-955-2252

William F. Welch · Merritt & Tenney · 200 Galleria Parkway, NW, Suite 500 · Atlanta, GA 30339-3183 · 770-952-6550

David M. Zacks · 10 · Kilpatrick Stockton · 1100 Peachtree Street, Suite 2800 · Atlanta, GA 30309-4530 · 404-815-6500

Augusta

Robert L. Allgood · Daniel, Allgood & Lowe · 2907 Professional Parkway · P.O. Box 211790 · Augusta, GA 30917 · 706-860-3747

Columbus

W. Nolan Murrah · Office of Dispute Resolution · 216 Tenth Street · Columbus, GA 31901 · 706-566-0586

Macon

Robert R. Gunn II · Martin Snow · http://www.martinsnow.com · 240 Third Street · P.O. Box 1606 · Macon, GA 31202-1606 · 478-749-1700

Daniel C. Cohen · Brannen, Searcy & Smith · 22 East Thirty-Fourth Street · P.O. Box 8002 · Savannah, GA 31412 · 912-234-8875

Robert E. Falligant, Jr. · Robert E. Falligant, Jr. · 317 West York Street · P.O. Box 8937 · Savannah, GA 31412 · 912-236-7007

Robert S. Glenn, Jr. · ⑩ · Hunter Maclean · http://www.huntermaclean.com · 200 East Saint Julian Street · P.O. Box 9848 · Savannah, GA 31412-0048 · 912-236-0261

Patrick T. O'Connor · ⑩ · Oliver Maner · http://www.olivermaner.com · 218 West State Street · P.O. Box 10186 · Savannah, GA 31412 · 912-236-3311

R. Clay Ratterree · ⑩ · Ellis, Painter, Ratterree & Adams · http://www.epra-law.com · Johnson Square Business Center, 10th Floor · Two East Bryan Street · P.O. Box 9946 · Savannah, GA 31412 · 912-233-9700

ANTITRUST LAW

Atlanta

Miles J. Alexander · ㉕ · Kilpatrick Stockton · 1100 Peachtree Street, Suite 2800 · Atlanta, GA 30309-4530 · 404-815-6500

Randall L. Allen · Alston + Bird · http://www.alston.com · One Atlantic Center · 1201 West Peachtree Street · Atlanta, GA 30309-3424 · 404-881-7000

Emmet J. Bondurant II · ㉕ · Bondurant, Mixson & Elmore · http://www.bmelaw.com · One Atlantic Center, Suite 3900 · 1201 West Peachtree Street, NW · Atlanta, GA 30309 · 404-881-4100

Jeffrey S. Cashdan · King & Spalding · 1180 Peachtree Street, NE · Atlanta, GA 30309-3521 · 404-572-4600

H. Stephen Harris, Jr. · Jones Day · 1420 Peachtree Street, NE, Suite 800 · Atlanta, GA 30309-3053 · 404-521-3939

Michael P. Kenny · Alston + Bird · http://www.alston.com · One Atlantic Center · 1201 West Peachtree Street · Atlanta, GA 30309-3424 · 404-881-7000

Peter Kontio · Alston + Bird · http://www.alston.com · One Atlantic Center · 1201 West Peachtree Street · Atlanta, GA 30309-3424 · 404-881-7000

Charles C. Murphy, Jr. · Vaughan & Murphy · 260 Peachtree Street, NW, Suite 1600 · Atlanta, GA 30303 · 404-577-6550

L. Trammel Newton, Jr. · Jones Day · 1420 Peachtree Street, NE, Suite 800 · Atlanta, GA 30309-3053 · 404-521-3939

Tony G. Powers · Rogers & Hardin · 2700 International Tower · 229 Peachtree Street, NE · Atlanta, GA 30303 · 404-522-4700

Thomas W. Rhodes · Smith, Gambrell & Russell · http://www.sgrlaw.com · Promenade II, Suite 3100 · 1230 Peachtree Street, NE · Atlanta, GA 30309-3592 · 404-815-3500

June Ann Sauntry · Troutman Sanders · Bank of America Plaza, Suite 5200 · 600 Peachtree Street, NE · Atlanta, GA 30308-2216 · 404-885-3000

C. David Vaughan · Vaughan & Murphy · 260 Peachtree Street, NW, Suite 1600 · Atlanta, GA 30303 · 404-577-6550

G. Patrick Watson · Powell Goldstein · http://www.pogolaw.com · One Atlantic Center, 14th Floor · 1201 West Peachtree Street, NE · Atlanta, GA 30309 · 404-572-6600

APPELLATE LAW

Atlanta

Emmet J. Bondurant II · 25 · Bondurant, Mixson & Elmore · http://www.bmelaw.com · One Atlantic Center, Suite 3900 · 1201 West Peachtree Street, NW · Atlanta, GA 30309 · 404-881-4100

Charles E. Campbell · 10 · McKenna Long & Aldridge · 303 Peachtree Street, NE, Suite 5300 · Atlanta, GA 30308 · 404-527-4000

Kenneth S. Canfield · Doffermyre, Shields, Canfield, Knowles & Devine · 1355 Peachtree Street, Suite 1600 · Atlanta, GA 30309 · 404-881-8900

Laurie Webb Daniel · Holland & Knight · http://www.hklaw.com · One Atlantic Center, Suite 2000 · 1201 West Peachtree Street, NE · Atlanta, GA 30309-3400 · 404-817-8500

John T. Marshall · 25 · Powell Goldstein · http://www.pogolaw.com · One Atlantic Center, 14th Floor · 1201 West Peachtree Street, NE · Atlanta, GA 30309 · 404-572-6600

Albert M. Pearson III · 10 · Moraitakis, Kushel, Pearson & Gardner · 3445 Peachtree Road, NE, Suite 425 · Atlanta, GA 30326-3239 · 404-261-0016

C. B. Rogers · 25 · Rogers & Hardin · 2700 International Tower · 229 Peachtree Street, NE · Atlanta, GA 30303 · 404-522-4700

Chilton D. Varner · 10 · King & Spalding · 1180 Peachtree Street, NE · Atlanta, GA 30309-3521 · 404-572-4600

Columbus

James E. Butler, Jr. · 20 · Butler, Wooten, Fryhofer, Daughtery & Sullivan · 105 Thirteenth Street · P.O. Box 2766 · Columbus, GA 31902 · 706-322-1990

Macon

Frank C. Jones · Jones, Cork & Miller · SunTrust Bank Building, Fifth Floor · 435 Second Street · P.O. Box 6437 · Macon, GA 31208-6437 · 478-745-2821

BANKING LAW

Atlanta

Bobbi Acord · Parker, Hudson, Rainer & Dobbs · 1500 Marquis Two Tower · 285 Peachtree Center Avenue, NE · Atlanta, GA 30303 · 404-523-5300

Carolyn Z. Alford · King & Spalding · 1180 Peachtree Street, NE · Atlanta, GA 30309-3521 · 404-572-4600

Gerald L. Blanchard · Powell Goldstein · http://www.pogolaw.com · One Atlantic Center, 14th Floor · 1201 West Peachtree Street, NE · Atlanta, GA 30309 · 404-572-6600

Rick D. Blumen · Alston + Bird · http://www.alston.com · One Atlantic Center · 1201 West Peachtree Street · Atlanta, GA 30309-3424 · 404-881-7000

T. Kennerly Carroll, Jr. · Miller & Martin · http://www.millermartin.com · 1170 Peachtree Street, NE, Suite 800 · Atlanta, GA 30309-3576 · 404-962-6100

Richard R. Cheatham · ⑩ · Kilpatrick Stockton · 1100 Peachtree Street, Suite 2800 · Atlanta, GA 30309-4530 · 404-815-6500

Kevin Conboy · Paul Hastings · 600 Peachtree Street, NE, 24th Floor · Atlanta, GA 30308 · 404-815-2400

Albert H. Conrad, Jr. · ⑩ · King & Spalding · 1180 Peachtree Street, NE · Atlanta, GA 30309-3521 · 404-572-4600

David W. Cranshaw · Morris, Manning & Martin · 1600 Atlanta Financial Center · 3343 Peachtree Road, NE · Atlanta, GA 30326 · 404-233-7000

Paul M. Cushing · Alston + Bird · http://www.alston.com · One Atlantic Center · 1201 West Peachtree Street · Atlanta, GA 30309-3424 · 404-881-7000

Hazen H. Dempster · Troutman Sanders · Bank of America Plaza, Suite 5200 · 600 Peachtree Street, NE · Atlanta, GA 30308-2216 · 404-885-3000

B. Knox Dobbins · ⑩ · Sutherland · http://www.sutherland.com · 999 Peachtree Street, NE · Atlanta, GA 30309-3996 · 404-853-8000

C. Edward Dobbs · ㉕ · Parker, Hudson, Rainer & Dobbs · 1500 Marquis Two Tower · 285 Peachtree Center Avenue, NE · Atlanta, GA 30303 · 404-523-5300

John L. Douglas · ⑩ · Paul Hastings · 600 Peachtree Street, NE, 24th Floor · Atlanta, GA 30308 · 404-815-2400

Steven S. Dunlevie · Womble Carlyle Sandridge & Rice · One Atlantic Center, Suite 3500 · 1201 West Peachtree Street · Atlanta, GA 30309 · 404-872-7000

Richard W. Grice · ⑩ · Alston + Bird · http://www.alston.com · One Atlantic Center · 1201 West Peachtree Street · Atlanta, GA 30309-3424 · 404-881-7000

Hilary P. Jordan · Kilpatrick Stockton · 1100 Peachtree Street, Suite 2800 · Atlanta, GA 30309-4530 · 404-815-6500

Kathryn L. Knudson · ⑩ · Powell Goldstein · http://www.pogolaw.com · One Atlantic Center, 14th Floor 1201 West Peachtree Street, NE · Atlanta, GA 30309 · 404-572-6600

Aldo L. LaFiandra · Jones Day · 1420 Peachtree Street, NE, Suite 800 · Atlanta, GA 30309-3053 · 404-521-3939

Hector E. Llorens, Jr. · King & Spalding · 1180 Peachtree Street, NE · Atlanta, GA 30309-3521 · 404-572-4600

Ralph F. MacDonald III · ⑩ · Jones Day · 1420 Peachtree Street, NE, Suite 800 · Atlanta, GA 30309-3053 · 404-521-3939

Walter G. Moeling IV · ⑩ · Powell Goldstein · http://www.pogolaw.com · One Atlantic Center, 14th Floor · 1201 West Peachtree Street, NE · Atlanta, GA 30309 · 404-572-6600

Chris D. Molen · Paul Hastings · 600 Peachtree Street, NE, 24th Floor · Atlanta, GA 30308 · 404-815-2400

Thomas O. Powell · Troutman Sanders · Bank of America Plaza, Suite 5200 · 600 Peachtree Street, NE · Atlanta, GA 30308-2216 · 404-885-3000

Michael E. Ray · Jones Walker · http://www.joneswalker.com · 100 Colony Square, Suite 1920 · 1175 Peachtree Street, NE · Atlanta, GA 30361 · 404-602-3700

Robert C. Schwartz · Smith, Gambrell & Russell · http://www.sgrlaw.com · Promenade II, Suite 3100 · 1230 Peachtree Street, NE · Atlanta, GA 30309-3592 · 404-815-3500

Edgar C. Snow, Jr. · Burr & Forman · http://www.burr.com · 171 Seventeenth Street, NW, Suite 1100 · Atlanta, GA 30363 · 404-815-3000

Rex R. Veal · Kilpatrick Stockton · 1100 Peachtree Street, Suite 2800 · Atlanta, GA 30309-4530 · 404-815-6500

Macon

Timothy K. Adams · ⑩ · Jones, Cork & Miller · SunTrust Bank Building, Fifth Floor · 435 Second Street P.O. Box 6437 · Macon, GA 31208-6437 · 478-745-2821

Edward J. Harrell · ⑳ · Martin Snow · http://www.martinsnow.com · 240 Third Street · P.O. Box 1606 · Macon, GA 31202-1606 · 478-749-1700

John T. McGoldrick, Jr. · Martin Snow · http://www.martinsnow.com · 240 Third Street · P.O. Box 1606 · Macon, GA 31202-1606 · 478-749-1700

Edward S. Sell III · ⑩ · Sell & Melton · Fickling & Company Building, 14th Floor · 577 Mulberry Street · P.O. Box 229 · Macon, GA 31202-0229 · 478-746-8521

BANKRUPTCY AND CREDITOR-DEBTOR RIGHTS LAW

Atlanta

Jesse H. Austin III · ⑩ · Paul Hastings · 600 Peachtree Street, NE, 24th Floor · Atlanta, GA 30308 · 404-815-2400

R. Neal Batson · ㉕ · Alston + Bird · http://www.alston.com · One Atlantic Center · 1201 West Peachtree Street · Atlanta, GA 30309-3424 · 404-881-7000

Sarah Robinson Borders · ⑩ · King & Spalding · 1180 Peachtree Street, NE · Atlanta, GA 30309-3521 · 404-572-4600

Charles E. Campbell · ⑩ · McKenna Long & Aldridge · 303 Peachtree Street, NE, Suite 5300 · Atlanta, GA 30308 · 404-527-4000

James C. Cifelli · Lamberth, Cifelli, Stokes, Ellis & Nason · Atlanta Financial Center, East Tower, Suite 550 · 3343 Peachtree Road, NE · Atlanta, GA 30326-1022 · 404-262-7373

Ezra H. Cohen · ㉕ · Troutman Sanders · Bank of America Plaza, Suite 5200 · 600 Peachtree Street, NE · Atlanta, GA 30308-2216 · 404-885-3000

Dennis J. Connolly · Alston + Bird · http://www.alston.com · One Atlantic Center · 1201 West Peachtree Street · Atlanta, GA 30309-3424 · 404-881-7000

C. Edward Dobbs · ㉕ · Parker, Hudson, Rainer & Dobbs · 1500 Marquis Two Tower · 285 Peachtree Center Avenue, NE · Atlanta, GA 30303 · 404-523-5300

Rufus T. Dorsey IV · Parker, Hudson, Rainer & Dobbs · 1500 Marquis Two Tower · 285 Peachtree Center Avenue, NE · Atlanta, GA 30303 · 404-523-5300

Paul K. Ferdinands · King & Spalding · 1180 Peachtree Street, NE · Atlanta, GA 30309-3521 · 404-572-4600

Mark S. Kaufman · McKenna Long & Aldridge · 303 Peachtree Street, NE, Suite 5300 · Atlanta, GA 30308 · 404-527-4000

Jeffrey W. Kelley · Troutman Sanders · Bank of America Plaza, Suite 5200 · 600 Peachtree Street, NE · Atlanta, GA 30308-2216 · 404-885-3000

Aldo L. LaFiandra · Jones Day · 1420 Peachtree Street, NE, Suite 800 · Atlanta, GA 30309-3053 · 404-521-3939

Alfred S. Lurey · ㉕ · Kilpatrick Stockton · 1100 Peachtree Street, Suite 2800 · Atlanta, GA 30309-4530 · 404-815-6500

Gary W. Marsh · McKenna Long & Aldridge · 303 Peachtree Street, NE, Suite 5300 · Atlanta, GA 30308 404-527-4000

Dennis S. Meir · ⑩ · Kilpatrick Stockton · 1100 Peachtree Street, Suite 2800 · Atlanta, GA 30309-4530 · 404-815-6500

E. Penn Nicholson · ⑩ · Powell Goldstein · http://www.pogolaw.com · One Atlantic Center, 14th Floor · 1201 West Peachtree Street, NE · Atlanta, GA 30309 · 404-572-6600

James A. Pardo, Jr. · ⑩ · King & Spalding · 1180 Peachtree Street, NE · Atlanta, GA 30309-3521 · 404-572-4600

Gus H. Small · ⑩ · Cohen Pollock Merlin & Small · 3350 Riverwood Parkway, Suite 1600 · Atlanta, GA 30339 · 770-858-1288

Grant T. Stein · ⑩ · Alston + Bird · http://www.alston.com · One Atlantic Center · 1201 West Peachtree Street · Atlanta, GA 30309-3424 · 404-881-7000

John C. Weitnauer · ⑩ · Alston + Bird · http://www.alston.com · One Atlantic Center · 1201 West Peachtree Street · Atlanta, GA 30309-3424 · 404-881-7000

Karen Fagin White · Cohen Pollock Merlin & Small · 3350 Riverwood Parkway, Suite 1600 · Atlanta, GA 30339 · 770-858-1288

J. Robert Williamson, Jr. · Scroggins & Williamson · 1500 The Candler Building · 127 Peachtree Street, NE · Atlanta, GA 30303 · 404-893-3880

Harris Winsberg · Troutman Sanders · Bank of America Plaza, Suite 5200 · 600 Peachtree Street, NE · Atlanta, GA 30308-2216 · 404-885-3000

Macon

Jerome L. Kaplan · ⑳ · Stone & Baxter · Fickling & Company Building, Suite 800 · 577 Mulberry Street · Macon, GA 31201 · 478-750-9898

John T. McGoldrick, Jr. · Martin Snow · http://www.martinsnow.com · 240 Third Street · P.O. Box 1606 · Macon, GA 31202-1606 · 478-749-1700

Edward S. Sell III · ⑩ · Sell & Melton · Fickling & Company Building, 14th Floor · 577 Mulberry Street · P.O. Box 229 · Macon, GA 31202-0229 · 478-746-8521

James P. Smith · Stone & Baxter · Fickling & Company Building, Suite 800 · 577 Mulberry Street · Macon, GA 31201 · 478-750-9898

Ward Stone, Jr. · ⑩ · Stone & Baxter · Fickling & Company Building, Suite 800 · 577 Mulberry Street · Macon, GA 31201 · 478-750-9898

Savannah

Mark Bulovic · McCallar Law Firm · 115 West Oglethorpe Avenue · P.O. Box 9026 · Savannah, GA 31412 · 912-234-1215

BET-THE-COMPANY LITIGATION

Atlanta

Emmet J. Bondurant II · ㉕ · Bondurant, Mixson & Elmore · http://www.bmelaw.com · One Atlantic Center, Suite 3900 · 1201 West Peachtree Street, NW · Atlanta, GA 30309 · 404-881-4100

Michael J. Bowers · Balch & Bingham · http://www.balch.com · 30 Ivan Allen, Jr. Boulevard, NW, Suite 700 · Atlanta, GA 30308 · 404-261-6020

Jeffrey O. Bramlett · Bondurant, Mixson & Elmore · http://www.bmelaw.com · One Atlantic Center, Suite 3900 · 1201 West Peachtree Street, NW · Atlanta, GA 30309 · 404-881-4100

John A. Chandler · ⑩ · Sutherland · http://www.sutherland.com · 999 Peachtree Street, NE · Atlanta, GA 30309-3996 · 404-853-8000

A. Stephens Clay IV · ⑩ · Kilpatrick Stockton · 1100 Peachtree Street, Suite 2800 · Atlanta, GA 30309-4530 · 404-815-6500

Harold T. Daniel · Holland & Knight · http://www.hklaw.com · One Atlantic Center, Suite 2000 · 1201 West Peachtree Street, NE · Atlanta, GA 30309-3400 · 404-817-8500

Laurie Webb Daniel · Holland & Knight · http://www.hklaw.com · One Atlantic Center, Suite 2000 · 1201 West Peachtree Street, NE · Atlanta, GA 30309-3400 · 404-817-8500

John H. Fleming · Sutherland · http://www.sutherland.com · 999 Peachtree Street, NE · Atlanta, GA 30309-3996 · 404-853-8000

Judson Graves · Alston + Bird · http://www.alston.com · One Atlantic Center · 1201 West Peachtree Street · Atlanta, GA 30309-3424 · 404-881-7000

Ralph B. Levy · King & Spalding · 1180 Peachtree Street, NE · Atlanta, GA 30309-3521 · 404-572-4600

L. Joseph Loveland, Jr. · King & Spalding · 1180 Peachtree Street, NE · Atlanta, GA 30309-3521 · 404-572-4600

John T. Marshall · ㉕ · Powell Goldstein · http://www.pogolaw.com · One Atlantic Center, 14th Floor · 1201 West Peachtree Street, NE · Atlanta, GA 30309 · 404-572-6600

Oscar N. Persons · Alston + Bird · http://www.alston.com · One Atlantic Center · 1201 West Peachtree Street · Atlanta, GA 30309-3424 · 404-881-7000

Robert B. Remar · Rogers & Hardin · 2700 International Tower · 229 Peachtree Street, NE · Atlanta, GA 30303 · 404-522-4700

C. B. Rogers · ㉕ · Rogers & Hardin · 2700 International Tower · 229 Peachtree Street, NE · Atlanta, GA 30303 · 404-522-4700

Michael C. Russ · ⑩ · King & Spalding · 1180 Peachtree Street, NE · Atlanta, GA 30309-3521 · 404-572-4600

Richard H. Sinkfield · ⑩ · Rogers & Hardin · 2700 International Tower · 229 Peachtree Street, NE · Atlanta, GA 30303 · 404-522-4700

Elizabeth V. Tanis · Sutherland · http://www.sutherland.com · 999 Peachtree Street, NE · Atlanta, GA 30309-3996 · 404-853-8000

Chilton D. Varner · ⑩ · King & Spalding · 1180 Peachtree Street, NE · Atlanta, GA 30309-3521 · 404-572-4600

Rome

Robert M. Brinson · ⑩ · Brinson, Askew, Berry, Seigler, Richardson & Davis · The Omberg House · 615 West First Street · P.O. Box 5513 · Rome, GA 30162-5513 · 706-291-8853

BIOTECHNOLOGY LAW

Atlanta

Jamie L. Greene · ⑩ · Kilpatrick Stockton · 1100 Peachtree Street, Suite 2800 · Atlanta, GA 30309-4530 · 404-815-6500

Robert A. Hodges · Arnall Golden Gregory · 171 Seventeenth Street, NW, Suite 2100 · Atlanta, GA 30363-1031 · 404-873-8500

David E. Huizenga · Arnall Golden Gregory · 171 Seventeenth Street, NW, Suite 2100 · Atlanta, GA 30363-1031 · 404-873-8500

William H. Kitchens · Arnall Golden Gregory · 171 Seventeenth Street, NW, Suite 2100 · Atlanta, GA 30363-1031 · 404-873-8500

COMMERCIAL LITIGATION

Athens

Gary B. Blasingame · ⑩ · Blasingame, Burch, Garrard & Ashley · http://www.bbgbalaw.com · 440 College Avenue North · P.O. Box 832 · Athens, GA 30603 · 706-354-4000

Atlanta

Alfred B. Adams III · Holland & Knight · http://www.hklaw.com · One Atlantic Center, Suite 2000 · 1201 West Peachtree Street, NE · Atlanta, GA 30309-3400 · 404-817-8500

Randall L. Allen · Alston + Bird · http://www.alston.com · One Atlantic Center · 1201 West Peachtree Street · Atlanta, GA 30309-3424 · 404-881-7000

John J. Almond · Rogers & Hardin · 2700 International Tower · 229 Peachtree Street, NE · Atlanta, GA 30303 · 404-522-4700

Peter J. Anderson · Sutherland · http://www.sutherland.com · 999 Peachtree Street, NE · Atlanta, GA 30309-3996 · 404-853-8000

David L. Balser · McKenna Long & Aldridge · 303 Peachtree Street, NE, Suite 5300 · Atlanta, GA 30308 404-527-4000

Peter Q. Bassett · Alston + Bird · http://www.alston.com · One Atlantic Center · 1201 West Peachtree Street · Atlanta, GA 30309-3424 · 404-881-7000

Jay D. Bennett · Alston + Bird · http://www.alston.com · One Atlantic Center · 1201 West Peachtree Street · Atlanta, GA 30309-3424 · 404-881-7000

Thomas D. Bever · Chilivis, Cochran, Larkins & Bever · 3127 Maple Drive, NE · Atlanta, GA 30305-2503 · 404-233-4171

James F. Bogan III · Kilpatrick Stockton · 1100 Peachtree Street, Suite 2800 · Atlanta, GA 30309-4530 · 404-815-6500

William H. Boice · Kilpatrick Stockton · 1100 Peachtree Street, Suite 2800 · Atlanta, GA 30309-4530 · 404-815-6500

Emmet J. Bondurant II · 25 · Bondurant, Mixson & Elmore · http://www.bmelaw.com · One Atlantic Center, Suite 3900 · 1201 West Peachtree Street, NW · Atlanta, GA 30309 · 404-881-4100

Michael J. Bowers · Balch & Bingham · http://www.balch.com · 30 Ivan Allen, Jr. Boulevard, NW, Suite 700 · Atlanta, GA 30308 · 404-261-6020

Jeffrey O. Bramlett · Bondurant, Mixson & Elmore · http://www.bmelaw.com · One Atlantic Center, Suite 3900 · 1201 West Peachtree Street, NW · Atlanta, GA 30309 · 404-881-4100

Thomas M. Byrne · Sutherland · http://www.sutherland.com · 999 Peachtree Street, NE · Atlanta, GA 30309-3996 · 404-853-8000

Susan A. Cahoon · 10 · Kilpatrick Stockton · 1100 Peachtree Street, Suite 2800 · Atlanta, GA 30309-4530 404-815-6500

Charles E. Campbell · 10 · McKenna Long & Aldridge · 303 Peachtree Street, NE, Suite 5300 · Atlanta, GA 30308 · 404-527-4000

Thomas S. Carlock · 10 · Carlock, Copeland, Semler & Stair · 2600 Marquis Two Tower · 285 Peachtree Center Avenue · Atlanta, GA 30303-1235 · 404-522-8220

Jeffrey S. Cashdan · King & Spalding · 1180 Peachtree Street, NE · Atlanta, GA 30309-3521 · 404-572-4600

John A. Chandler · 10 · Sutherland · http://www.sutherland.com · 999 Peachtree Street, NE · Atlanta, GA 30309-3996 · 404-853-8000

A. Stephens Clay IV · 10 · Kilpatrick Stockton · 1100 Peachtree Street, Suite 2800 · Atlanta, GA 30309-4530 · 404-815-6500

Steven M. Collins · Alston + Bird · http://www.alston.com · One Atlantic Center · 1201 West Peachtree Street · Atlanta, GA 30309-3424 · 404-881-7000

Stephen S. Cowen · King & Spalding · 1180 Peachtree Street, NE · Atlanta, GA 30309-3521 · 404-572-4600

Thomas A. Croft · King & Croft · The Candler Building, Suite 707 · 127 Peachtree Street, NE · Atlanta, GA 30303 · 404-577-8400

William V. Custer · Powell Goldstein · http://www.pogolaw.com · One Atlantic Center, 14th Floor · 1201 West Peachtree Street, NE · Atlanta, GA 30309 · 404-572-6600

John J. Dalton · ㉕ · Troutman Sanders · Bank of America Plaza, Suite 5200 · 600 Peachtree Street, NE · Atlanta, GA 30308-2216 · 404-885-3000

Harold T. Daniel · Holland & Knight · http://www.hklaw.com · One Atlantic Center, Suite 2000 · 1201 West Peachtree Street, NE · Atlanta, GA 30309-3400 · 404-817-8500

Laurie Webb Daniel · Holland & Knight · http://www.hklaw.com · One Atlantic Center, Suite 2000 · 1201 West Peachtree Street, NE · Atlanta, GA 30309-3400 · 404-817-8500

Todd R. David · Alston + Bird · http://www.alston.com · One Atlantic Center · 1201 West Peachtree Street · Atlanta, GA 30309-3424 · 404-881-7000

Dwight J. Davis · King & Spalding · 1180 Peachtree Street, NE · Atlanta, GA 30309-3521 · 404-572-4600

Cari K. Dawson · Alston + Bird · http://www.alston.com · One Atlantic Center · 1201 West Peachtree Street · Atlanta, GA 30309-3424 · 404-881-7000

Richard H. Deane, Jr. · Jones Day · 1420 Peachtree Street, NE, Suite 800 · Atlanta, GA 30309-3053 · 404-521-3939

Gregory J. Digel · Holland & Knight · http://www.hklaw.com · One Atlantic Center, Suite 2000 · 1201 West Peachtree Street, NE · Atlanta, GA 30309-3400 · 404-817-8500

Benjamin F. Easterlin IV · King & Spalding · 1180 Peachtree Street, NE · Atlanta, GA 30309-3521 · 404-572-4600

J. Randolph Evans · ⑩ · McKenna Long & Aldridge · 303 Peachtree Street, NE, Suite 5300 · Atlanta, GA 30308 · 404-527-4000

Scott A. Farrow · Troutman Sanders · Bank of America Plaza, Suite 5200 · 600 Peachtree Street, NE · Atlanta, GA 30308-2216 · 404-885-3000

R. Keegan Federal, Jr. · Keegan Federal & Associates · Two Ravinia Drive, Suite 1776 · Atlanta, GA 30346-2105 · 678-443-4044

J. D. Fleming, Jr. · ㉕ · Sutherland · http://www.sutherland.com · 999 Peachtree Street, NE · Atlanta, GA 30309-3996 · 404-853-8000

John H. Fleming · Sutherland · http://www.sutherland.com · 999 Peachtree Street, NE · Atlanta, GA 30309-3996 · 404-853-8000

John E. Floyd · Bondurant, Mixson & Elmore · http://www.bmelaw.com · One Atlantic Center, Suite 3900 · 1201 West Peachtree Street, NW · Atlanta, GA 30309 · 404-881-4100

Stephen M. Forte · Smith, Gambrell & Russell · http://www.sgrlaw.com · Promenade II, Suite 3100 · 1230 Peachtree Street, NE · Atlanta, GA 30309-3592 · 404-815-3500

Mary C. Gill · Alston + Bird · http://www.alston.com · One Atlantic Center · 1201 West Peachtree Street · Atlanta, GA 30309-3424 · 404-881-7000

Craig A. Gillen · Gillen Cromwell Withers & Brantley · One Securities Centre, Suite 1050 · 3490 Piedmont Road, NE · Atlanta, GA 30305 · 404-842-9700

James C. Grant · Alston + Bird · http://www.alston.com · One Atlantic Center · 1201 West Peachtree Street · Atlanta, GA 30309-3424 · 404-881-7000

Judson Graves · Alston + Bird · http://www.alston.com · One Atlantic Center · 1201 West Peachtree Street · Atlanta, GA 30309-3424 · 404-881-7000

H. Stephen Harris, Jr. · Jones Day · 1420 Peachtree Street, NE, Suite 800 · Atlanta, GA 30309-3053 · 404-521-3939

Joseph B. Haynes · King & Spalding · 1180 Peachtree Street, NE · Atlanta, GA 30309-3521 · 404-572-4600

Richard R. Hays · Alston + Bird · http://www.alston.com · One Atlantic Center · 1201 West Peachtree Street · Atlanta, GA 30309-3424 · 404-881-7000

William B. Hill, Jr. · Ashe, Rafuse & Hill · South Tower, Suite 500 · 1355 Peachtree Street, NE · Atlanta, GA 30309-3232 · 404-253-6000

Richard K. Hines V · ⑩ · Nelson Mullins Riley & Scarborough · Atlantic Station, Suite 1700 · 201 Seventeenth Street, NW · Atlanta, GA 30363 · 404-817-6000

Allen I. Hirsch · Arnall Golden Gregory · 171 Seventeenth Street, NW, Suite 2100 · Atlanta, GA 30363-1031 · 404-873-8500

Hunter R. Hughes III · Rogers & Hardin · 2700 International Tower · 229 Peachtree Street, NE · Atlanta, GA 30303 · 404-522-4700

Cary Ichter · Adorno & Yoss · Two Midtown Plaza, Suite 1500 · 1349 West Peachtree Street · Atlanta, GA 30309 · 404-347-8300

J. Scott Jacobson · Holt Ney Zatcoff & Wasserman · 100 Galleria Parkway, Suite 600 · Atlanta, GA 30339 · 770-956-9600

Michael P. Kenny · Alston + Bird · http://www.alston.com · One Atlantic Center · 1201 West Peachtree Street · Atlanta, GA 30309-3424 · 404-881-7000

Daniel J. King · King & Spalding · 1180 Peachtree Street, NE · Atlanta, GA 30309-3521 · 404-572-4600

F. Carlton King, Jr. · King & Croft · The Candler Building, Suite 707 · 127 Peachtree Street, NE · Atlanta, GA 30303 · 404-577-8400

Dan F. Laney · Rogers & Hardin · 2700 International Tower · 229 Peachtree Street, NE · Atlanta, GA 30303 · 404-522-4700

William C. Lanham · ⑳ · Johnson & Ward · The Equitable Building, Suite 2100 · 100 Peachtree Street, NW · Atlanta, GA 30303-1912 · 404-524-5626

John K. Larkins, Jr. · ⑩ · Chilivis, Cochran, Larkins & Bever · 3127 Maple Drive, NE · Atlanta, GA 30305-2503 · 404-233-4171

John L. Latham · Alston + Bird · http://www.alston.com · One Atlantic Center · 1201 West Peachtree Street · Atlanta, GA 30309-3424 · 404-881-7000

Ralph B. Levy · King & Spalding · 1180 Peachtree Street, NE · Atlanta, GA 30309-3521 · 404-572-4600

L. Joseph Loveland, Jr. · King & Spalding · 1180 Peachtree Street, NE · Atlanta, GA 30309-3521 · 404-572-4600

J. Allen Maines · Paul Hastings · 600 Peachtree Street, NE, 24th Floor · Atlanta, GA 30308 · 404-815-2400

John T. Marshall · 25 · Powell Goldstein · http://www.pogolaw.com · One Atlantic Center, 14th Floor · 1201 West Peachtree Street, NE · Atlanta, GA 30309 · 404-572-6600

H. Lamar Mixson · Bondurant, Mixson & Elmore · http://www.bmelaw.com · One Atlantic Center, Suite 3900 · 1201 West Peachtree Street, NW · Atlanta, GA 30309 · 404-881-4100

Paul J. Murphy · King & Spalding · 1180 Peachtree Street, NE · Atlanta, GA 30309-3521 · 404-572-4600

John G. Parker · Paul Hastings · 600 Peachtree Street, NE, 24th Floor · Atlanta, GA 30308 · 404-815-2400

Matthew H. Patton · Kilpatrick Stockton · 1100 Peachtree Street, Suite 2800 · Atlanta, GA 30309-4530 · 404-815-6500

Oscar N. Persons · Alston + Bird · http://www.alston.com · One Atlantic Center · 1201 West Peachtree Street · Atlanta, GA 30309-3424 · 404-881-7000

W. Ray Persons · King & Spalding · 1180 Peachtree Street, NE · Atlanta, GA 30309-3521 · 404-572-4600

Jill A. Pryor · Bondurant, Mixson & Elmore · http://www.bmelaw.com · One Atlantic Center, Suite 3900 · 1201 West Peachtree Street, NW · Atlanta, GA 30309 · 404-881-4100

William M. Ragland, Jr. · Womble Carlyle Sandridge & Rice · One Atlantic Center, Suite 3500 · 1201 West Peachtree Street · Atlanta, GA 30309 · 404-872-7000

J. Marbury Rainer · Parker, Hudson, Rainer & Dobbs · 1500 Marquis Two Tower · 285 Peachtree Center Avenue, NE · Atlanta, GA 30303 · 404-523-5300

Daniel S. Reinhardt · Troutman Sanders · Bank of America Plaza, Suite 5200 · 600 Peachtree Street, NE · Atlanta, GA 30308-2216 · 404-885-3000

Robert B. Remar · Rogers & Hardin · 2700 International Tower · 229 Peachtree Street, NE · Atlanta, GA 30303 · 404-522-4700

Thomas Richey · Powell Goldstein · http://www.pogolaw.com · One Atlantic Center, 14th Floor · 1201 West Peachtree Street, NE · Atlanta, GA 30309 · 404-572-6600

C. B. Rogers · 25 · Rogers & Hardin · 2700 International Tower · 229 Peachtree Street, NE · Atlanta, GA 30303 · 404-522-4700

Robert L. Rothman · Arnall Golden Gregory · 171 Seventeenth Street, NW, Suite 2100 · Atlanta, GA 30363-1031 · 404-873-8500

Michael C. Russ · 10 · King & Spalding · 1180 Peachtree Street, NE · Atlanta, GA 30309-3521 · 404-572-4600

David G. Russell · Parker, Hudson, Rainer & Dobbs · 1500 Marquis Two Tower · 285 Peachtree Center Avenue, NE · Atlanta, GA 30303 · 404-523-5300

Richard A. Schneider · King & Spalding · 1180 Peachtree Street, NE · Atlanta, GA 30309-3521 · 404-572-4600

Richard L. Shackelford · 10 · King & Spalding · 1180 Peachtree Street, NE · Atlanta, GA 30309-3521 · 404-572-4600

Robert E. Shields · Doffermyre, Shields, Canfield, Knowles & Devine · 1355 Peachtree Street, Suite 1600 · Atlanta, GA 30309 · 404-881-8900

Richard H. Sinkfield · ⑩ · Rogers & Hardin · 2700 International Tower · 229 Peachtree Street, NE · Atlanta, GA 30303 · 404-522-4700

Michael R. Smith · King & Spalding · 1180 Peachtree Street, NE · Atlanta, GA 30309-3521 · 404-572-4600

John E. Stephenson, Jr. · Alston + Bird · http://www.alston.com · One Atlantic Center · 1201 West Peachtree Street · Atlanta, GA 30309-3424 · 404-881-7000

Paul W. Stivers · ⑩ · Rogers & Hardin · 2700 International Tower · 229 Peachtree Street, NE · Atlanta, GA 30303 · 404-522-4700

Michael J. Sullivan · Womble Carlyle Sandridge & Rice · One Atlantic Center, Suite 3500 · 1201 West Peachtree Street · Atlanta, GA 30309 · 404-872-7000

Elizabeth V. Tanis · Sutherland · http://www.sutherland.com · 999 Peachtree Street, NE · Atlanta, GA 30309-3996 · 404-853-8000

Robert G. Tanner · ⑩ · Weinberg Wheeler Hudgins Gunn & Dial · 950 East Paces Ferry Road, Suite 3000 · Atlanta, GA 30326 · 404-876-2700

Michael B. Terry · Bondurant, Mixson & Elmore · http://www.bmelaw.com · One Atlantic Center, Suite 3900 · 1201 West Peachtree Street, NW · Atlanta, GA 30309 · 404-881-4100

M. Robert Thornton · King & Spalding · 1180 Peachtree Street, NE · Atlanta, GA 30309-3521 · 404-572-4600

Robert M. Travis · Powell Goldstein · http://www.pogolaw.com · One Atlantic Center, 14th Floor · 1201 West Peachtree Street, NE · Atlanta, GA 30309 · 404-572-6600

Chilton D. Varner · ⑩ · King & Spalding · 1180 Peachtree Street, NE · Atlanta, GA 30309-3521 · 404-572-4600

Woodrow W. Vaughan III · King & Spalding · 1180 Peachtree Street, NE · Atlanta, GA 30309-3521 · 404-572-4600

Allen S. C. Willingham · Troutman Sanders · Bank of America Plaza, Suite 5200 · 600 Peachtree Street, NE · Atlanta, GA 30308-2216 · 404-885-3000

William N. Withrow, Jr. · Troutman Sanders · Bank of America Plaza, Suite 5200 · 600 Peachtree Street, NE · Atlanta, GA 30308-2216 · 404-885-3000

Augusta

Raymond G. Chadwick, Jr. · Kilpatrick Stockton · Wachovia Bank Building, Suite 1400 · 699 Broad Street · Augusta, GA 30901-1453 · 706-724-2622

David E. Hudson · ⑩ · Hull, Towill, Norman, Barrett & Salley · SunTrust Bank Building, Suite 700 · 801 Broad Street · P.O. Box 1564 · Augusta, GA 30903-1564 · 706-722-4481

James W. Purcell · Fulcher Hagler · One 10th Street, Suite 700 · Augusta, GA 30901 · 706-724-0171

Patrick J. Rice · ⑩ · Hull, Towill, Norman, Barrett & Salley · SunTrust Bank Building, Suite 700 · 801 Broad Street · P.O. Box 1564 · Augusta, GA 30903-1564 · 706-722-4481

Thomas W. Tucker · ⑩ · Tucker, Everitt, Long, Brewton & Lanier · 453 Greene Street · P.O. Box 2426 · Augusta, GA 30903-2426 · 706-722-0771

James B. Wall · Burnside Wall · 454 Greene Street · P.O. Box 2125 · Augusta, GA 30903 · 706-993-3481

Carrollton

David H. Tisinger · ⑳ · Tisinger Vance · 100 Wagon Yard Plaza · P.O. Box 2069 · Carrollton, GA 30117-2069 · 770-834-4467

Columbus

William B. Hardegree · Hatcher, Stubbs, Land, Hollis & Rothschild · http://www.hatcherstubbs.com · The Corporate Center, Suite 500 · 233 Twelfth Street · P.O. Box 2707 · Columbus, GA 31902-2707 · 706-324-0201

W. G. Scrantom, Jr. · ⑳ · Page, Scrantom, Sprouse, Tucker & Ford · Synovus Centre, Third Floor · 1111 Bay Avenue · P.O. Box 1199 · Columbus, GA 31902 · 706-324-0251

Macon

F. Kennedy Hall · ⑩ · Hall, Bloch, Garland & Meyer · http://www.hbgm.com · Fickling & Company Building, Suite 1500 · 577 Mulberry Street · P.O. Box 5088 · Macon, GA 31208-5088 · 478-745-1625

John F. Kennedy · Hall, Bloch, Garland & Meyer · http://www.hbgm.com · Fickling & Company Building, Suite 1500 · 577 Mulberry Street · P.O. Box 5088 · Macon, GA 31208-5088 · 478-745-1625

Hubert C. Lovein, Jr. · ⑩ · Jones, Cork & Miller · SunTrust Bank Building, Fifth Floor · 435 Second Street · P.O. Box 6437 · Macon, GA 31208-6437 · 478-745-2821

John T. McGoldrick, Jr. · Martin Snow · http://www.martinsnow.com · 240 Third Street · P.O. Box 1606 · Macon, GA 31202-1606 · 478-749-1700

Edward S. Sell III · ⑩ · Sell & Melton · Fickling & Company Building, 14th Floor · 577 Mulberry Street · P.O. Box 229 · Macon, GA 31202-0229 · 478-746-8521

J. Steven Stewart · Hall, Bloch, Garland & Meyer · http://www.hbgm.com · Fickling & Company Building, Suite 1500 · 577 Mulberry Street · P.O. Box 5088 · Macon, GA 31208-5088 · 478-745-1625

H. Jerome Strickland · ⑩ · Jones, Cork & Miller · SunTrust Bank Building, Fifth Floor · 435 Second Street · P.O. Box 6437 · Macon, GA 31208-6437 · 478-745-2821

Marietta

Robert D. Ingram · Moore, Ingram, Johnson & Steele · 192 Anderson Street · P.O. Box 3305 · Marietta, GA 30061-3305 · 770-429-1499

Rome

Robert M. Brinson · ⑩ · Brinson, Askew, Berry, Seigler, Richardson & Davis · The Omberg House · 615 West First Street · P.O. Box 5513 · Rome, GA 30162-5513 · 706-291-8853

Savannah

Walter C. Hartridge · ⑩ · Bouhan, Williams & Levy · http://www.bouhan.com · The Armstrong House · 447 Bull Street · P.O. Box 2139 · Savannah, GA 31402-2139 · 912-236-2491

Patrick T. O'Connor · ⑩ · Oliver Maner · http://www.olivermaner.com · 218 West State Street · P.O. Box 10186 · Savannah, GA 31412 · 912-236-3311

Paul W. Painter, Jr. · ⑩ · Ellis, Painter, Ratterree & Adams · http://www.epra-law.com · Johnson Square Business Center, 10th Floor · Two East Bryan Street · P.O. Box 9946 · Savannah, GA 31412 · 912-233-9700

John M. Tatum · ⑩ · Hunter Maclean · http://www.huntermaclean.com · 200 East Saint Julian Street · P.O. Box 9848 · Savannah, GA 31412-0048 · 912-236-0261

Statesboro

Gerald M. Edenfield · Edenfield, Cox, Bruce & Classens · 115 Savannah Avenue · P.O. Box 1700 · Statesboro, GA 30459 · 912-764-8600

Tifton

George R. Reinhardt, Jr. · ⑩ · Reinhardt, Whitley, Wilmot, Summerlin & Pittman · 1001 North Central Avenue · P.O. Drawer 1287 · Tifton, GA 31793-1287 · 229-382-6135

COMMUNICATIONS LAW

Atlanta

Michael J. Egan III · King & Spalding · 1180 Peachtree Street, NE · Atlanta, GA 30309-3521 · 404-572-4600

CONSTRUCTION LAW

Atlanta

Thomas E. Abernathy IV · Smith, Currie & Hancock · 2700 Marquis One Tower · 245 Peachtree Center Avenue, NE · Atlanta, GA 30303-1227 · 404-521-3800

Thomas H. Asselin · Smith, Gambrell & Russell · http://www.sgrlaw.com · Promenade II, Suite 3100 · 1230 Peachtree Street, NE · Atlanta, GA 30309-3592 · 404-815-3500

Philip E. Beck · Smith, Currie & Hancock · 2700 Marquis One Tower · 245 Peachtree Center Avenue, NE · Atlanta, GA 30303-1227 · 404-521-3800

James K. Bidgood, Jr. · Smith, Currie & Hancock · 2700 Marquis One Tower · 245 Peachtree Center Avenue, NE · Atlanta, GA 30303-1227 · 404-521-3800

Arthur D. Brannan · DLA Piper · One Atlantic Center, Suite 2800 · 1201 West Peachtree Street · Atlanta, GA 30309-3450 · 404-736-7800

James F. Butler III · Smith, Currie & Hancock · 2700 Marquis One Tower · 245 Peachtree Center Avenue, NE · Atlanta, GA 30303-1227 · 404-521-3800

Bryan M. Cavan · Miller & Martin · http://www.millermartin.com · 1170 Peachtree Street, NE, Suite 800 · Atlanta, GA 30309-3576 · 404-962-6100

Robert C. Chambers · Smith, Currie & Hancock · 2700 Marquis One Tower · 245 Peachtree Center Avenue, NE · Atlanta, GA 30303-1227 · 404-521-3800

Aubrey L. Coleman, Jr. · Smith, Currie & Hancock · 2700 Marquis One Tower · 245 Peachtree Center Avenue, NE · Atlanta, GA 30303-1227 · 404-521-3800

Brian G. Corgan · Kilpatrick Stockton · 1100 Peachtree Street, Suite 2800 · Atlanta, GA 30309-4530 · 404-815-6500

Robert L. Crewdson · DLA Piper · One Atlantic Center, Suite 2800 · 1201 West Peachtree Street · Atlanta, GA 30309-3450 · 404-736-7800

Lee C. Davis · Sutherland · http://www.sutherland.com · 999 Peachtree Street, NE · Atlanta, GA 30309-3996 · 404-853-8000

David A. Dial · Weinberg Wheeler Hudgins Gunn & Dial · 950 East Paces Ferry Road, Suite 3000 · Atlanta, GA 30326 · 404-876-2700

William E. Dorris · Kilpatrick Stockton · 1100 Peachtree Street, Suite 2800 · Atlanta, GA 30309-4530 · 404-815-6500

R. Daniel Douglass · Stites & Harbison · http://www.stites.com · 2800 SunTrust Plaza · 303 Peachtree Street, NE · Atlanta, GA 30308 · 404-739-8800

Jennifer W. Fletcher · Sutherland · http://www.sutherland.com · 999 Peachtree Street, NE · Atlanta, GA 30309-3996 · 404-853-8000

John T. Flynn · Weinberg Wheeler Hudgins Gunn & Dial · 950 East Paces Ferry Road, Suite 3000 · Atlanta, GA 30326 · 404-876-2700

Ronald J. Garber · Shapiro Fussell Wedge & Martin · One Midtown Plaza, Suite 1200 · 1360 Peachtree Street · Atlanta, GA 30309-3214 · 404-870-2200

Ira Genberg · Troutman Sanders · Bank of America Plaza, Suite 5200 · 600 Peachtree Street, NE · Atlanta, GA 30308-2216 · 404-885-3000

Mark E. Grantham · DLA Piper · One Atlantic Center, Suite 2800 · 1201 West Peachtree Street · Atlanta, GA 30309-3450 · 404-736-7800

Randall F. Hafer · Kilpatrick Stockton · 1100 Peachtree Street, Suite 2800 · Atlanta, GA 30309-4530 · 404-815-6500

W. Hensell Harris, Jr. · Wasson, Sours & Harris · 300 Galleria Parkway, NW, Suite 1000 · Atlanta, GA 30339-5917 · 770-956-1700

David R. Hendrick · Hendrick, Phillips, Salzman & Flatt · 230 Peachtree Street, NW, Suite 2500 · Atlanta, GA 30303 · 404-522-1410

John W. Hinchey · King & Spalding · 1180 Peachtree Street, NE · Atlanta, GA 30309-3521 · 404-572-4600

William H. Hughes, Jr. · Alston + Bird · http://www.alston.com · One Atlantic Center · 1201 West Peachtree Street · Atlanta, GA 30309-3424 · 404-881-7000

J. D. Humphries III · Stites & Harbison · http://www.stites.com · 2800 SunTrust Plaza · 303 Peachtree Street, NE · Atlanta, GA 30308 · 404-739-8800

Thomas J. Kelleher, Jr. · Smith, Currie & Hancock · 2700 Marquis One Tower · 245 Peachtree Center Avenue, NE · Atlanta, GA 30303-1227 · 404-521-3800

David J. Larson · Weinberg Wheeler Hudgins Gunn & Dial · 950 East Paces Ferry Road, Suite 3000 · Atlanta, GA 30326 · 404-876-2700

H. Fielder Martin · Shapiro Fussell Wedge & Martin · One Midtown Plaza, Suite 1200 · 1360 Peachtree Street · Atlanta, GA 30309-3214 · 404-870-2200

Kamyar Molavi · Weissmann & Zucker · One Securities Center, Suite 650 · 3490 Piedmont Road · Atlanta, GA 30305 · 404-364-2300

W. Henry Parkman · Sutherland · http://www.sutherland.com · 999 Peachtree Street, NE · Atlanta, GA 30309-3996 · 404-853-8000

Stephen M. Phillips · Hendrick, Phillips, Salzman & Flatt · 230 Peachtree Street, NW, Suite 2500 · Atlanta, GA 30303 · 404-522-1410

William R. Poplin, Jr. · Kilpatrick Stockton · 1100 Peachtree Street, Suite 2800 · Atlanta, GA 30309-4530 404-815-6500

George C. Reid · George C. Reid · 4200 Northside Parkway, Suite 200 · Building One · Atlanta, GA 30327 · 404-365-6557

Frank E. Riggs, Jr. · Troutman Sanders · Bank of America Plaza, Suite 5200 · 600 Peachtree Street, NE · Atlanta, GA 30308-2216 · 404-885-3000

David A. Roberts · Roberts Construction Law · Three Piedmont Center, Suite 705 · 3565 Piedmont Road, NE · Atlanta, GA 30305 · 404-812-9424

Ronald G. Robey · Smith, Currie & Hancock · 2700 Marquis One Tower · 245 Peachtree Center Avenue, NE · Atlanta, GA 30303-1227 · 404-521-3800

Martin R. Salzman · Hendrick, Phillips, Salzman & Flatt · 230 Peachtree Street, NW, Suite 2500 · Atlanta, GA 30303 · 404-522-1410

J. Ben Shapiro · Shapiro Fussell Wedge & Martin · One Midtown Plaza, Suite 1200 · 1360 Peachtree Street · Atlanta, GA 30309-3214 · 404-870-2200

George Anthony Smith · Kilpatrick Stockton · 1100 Peachtree Street, Suite 2800 · Atlanta, GA 30309-4530 · 404-815-6500

Kent P. Smith · Smith, Currie & Hancock · 2700 Marquis One Tower · 245 Peachtree Center Avenue, NE · Atlanta, GA 30303-1227 · 404-521-3800

John I. Spangler III · Alston + Bird · http://www.alston.com · One Atlantic Center · 1201 West Peachtree Street · Atlanta, GA 30309-3424 · 404-881-7000

Kent T. Stair · Carlock, Copeland, Semler & Stair · 2600 Marquis Two Tower · 285 Peachtree Center Avenue · Atlanta, GA 30303-1235 · 404-522-8220

Neal J. Sweeney · Kilpatrick Stockton · 1100 Peachtree Street, Suite 2800 · Atlanta, GA 30309-4530 · 404-815-6500

William Wildman · Sutherland · http://www.sutherland.com · 999 Peachtree Street, NE · Atlanta, GA 30309-3996 · 404-853-8000

Savannah

Christopher W. Phillips · Hunter Maclean · http://www.huntermaclean.com · 200 East Saint Julian Street P.O. Box 9848 · Savannah, GA 31412-0048 · 912-236-0261

CORPORATE GOVERNANCE AND COMPLIANCE LAW

Atlanta

C. William Baxley · King & Spalding · 1180 Peachtree Street, NE · Atlanta, GA 30309-3521 · 404-572-4600

John D. Capers, Jr. · King & Spalding · 1180 Peachtree Street, NE · Atlanta, GA 30309-3521 · 404-572-4600

Todd R. David · Alston + Bird · http://www.alston.com · One Atlantic Center · 1201 West Peachtree Street · Atlanta, GA 30309-3424 · 404-881-7000

John D. Hopkins · Womble Carlyle Sandridge & Rice · One Atlantic Center, Suite 3500 · 1201 West Peachtree Street · Atlanta, GA 30309 · 404-872-7000

John J. Kelley III · King & Spalding · 1180 Peachtree Street, NE · Atlanta, GA 30309-3521 · 404-572-4600

John L. Latham · Alston + Bird · http://www.alston.com · One Atlantic Center · 1201 West Peachtree Street · Atlanta, GA 30309-3424 · 404-881-7000

Larry D. Ledbetter · Ledbetter Johnson Wanamaker · 100 Colony Square, Suite 1100 · 1175 Peachtree Street, NE · Atlanta, GA 30361 · 404-835-9500

Sidney J. Nurkin · ⑳ · Alston + Bird · http://www.alston.com · One Atlantic Center · 1201 West Peachtree Street · Atlanta, GA 30309-3424 · 404-881-7000

DeWitt R. Rogers · Troutman Sanders · Bank of America Plaza, Suite 5200 · 600 Peachtree Street, NE · Atlanta, GA 30308-2216 · 404-885-3000

Jeffrey M. Stein · King & Spalding · 1180 Peachtree Street, NE · Atlanta, GA 30309-3521 · 404-572-4600

David A. Stockton · ⑩ · Kilpatrick Stockton · 1100 Peachtree Street, Suite 2800 · Atlanta, GA 30309-4530 · 404-815-6500

CORPORATE LAW

Atlanta

Miles J. Alexander · ㉕ · Kilpatrick Stockton · 1100 Peachtree Street, Suite 2800 · Atlanta, GA 30309-4530 · 404-815-6500

Carolyn Z. Alford · King & Spalding · 1180 Peachtree Street, NE · Atlanta, GA 30309-3521 · 404-572-4600

Allen D. Altman · Greenberg Traurig · http://www.gtlaw.com · The Forum, Suite 400 · 3290 Northside Parkway, NE · Atlanta, GA 30327 · 678-553-2100

Raymond E. Baltz, Jr. · King & Spalding · 1180 Peachtree Street, NE · Atlanta, GA 30309-3521 · 404-572-4600

W. Benjamin Barkley · Kilpatrick Stockton · 1100 Peachtree Street, Suite 2800 · Atlanta, GA 30309-4530 404-815-6500

C. William Baxley · King & Spalding · 1180 Peachtree Street, NE · Atlanta, GA 30309-3521 · 404-572-4600

John C. Beane · McGuireWoods · http://www.mcguirewoods.com · The Proscenium, Suite 2100 · 1170 Peachtree Street, NE · Atlanta, GA 30309-7649 · 404-443-5500

W. Stanley Blackburn · Kilpatrick Stockton · 1100 Peachtree Street, Suite 2800 · Atlanta, GA 30309-4530 404-815-6500

Theodore I. Blum · Greenberg Traurig · http://www.gtlaw.com · The Forum, Suite 400 · 3290 Northside Parkway, NE · Atlanta, GA 30327 · 678-553-2100

Wayne N. Bradley · McKenna Long & Aldridge · 303 Peachtree Street, NE, Suite 5300 · Atlanta, GA 30308 · 404-527-4000

Terry C. Bridges · Troutman Sanders · Bank of America Plaza, Suite 5200 · 600 Peachtree Street, NE · Atlanta, GA 30308-2216 · 404-885-3000

Janine Brown · Alston + Bird · http://www.alston.com · One Atlantic Center · 1201 West Peachtree Street Atlanta, GA 30309-3424 · 404-881-7000

John D. Capers, Jr. · King & Spalding · 1180 Peachtree Street, NE · Atlanta, GA 30309-3521 · 404-572-4600

David M. Carter · Troutman Sanders · Bank of America Plaza, Suite 5200 · 600 Peachtree Street, NE · Atlanta, GA 30308-2216 · 404-885-3000

Richard R. Cheatham · ⑩ · Kilpatrick Stockton · 1100 Peachtree Street, Suite 2800 · Atlanta, GA 30309-4530 · 404-815-6500

Richard Cicchillo, Jr. · Kilpatrick Stockton · 1100 Peachtree Street, Suite 2800 · Atlanta, GA 30309-4530 404-815-6500

Gregory K. Cinnamon · Kilpatrick Stockton · 1100 Peachtree Street, Suite 2800 · Atlanta, GA 30309-4530 · 404-815-6500

George L. Cohen · ⑳ · Sutherland · http://www.sutherland.com · 999 Peachtree Street, NE · Atlanta, GA 30309-3996 · 404-853-8000

Albert H. Conrad, Jr. · ⑩ · King & Spalding · 1180 Peachtree Street, NE · Atlanta, GA 30309-3521 · 404-572-4600

J. Vaughan Curtis · ⑩ · Alston + Bird · http://www.alston.com · One Atlantic Center · 1201 West Peachtree Street · Atlanta, GA 30309-3424 · 404-881-7000

Paul M. Cushing · Alston + Bird · http://www.alston.com · One Atlantic Center · 1201 West Peachtree Street · Atlanta, GA 30309-3424 · 404-881-7000

Todd R. David · Alston + Bird · http://www.alston.com · One Atlantic Center · 1201 West Peachtree Street · Atlanta, GA 30309-3424 · 404-881-7000

Bryan E. Davis · Jones Day · 1420 Peachtree Street, NE, Suite 800 · Atlanta, GA 30309-3053 · 404-521-3939

Hazen H. Dempster · Troutman Sanders · Bank of America Plaza, Suite 5200 · 600 Peachtree Street, NE · Atlanta, GA 30308-2216 · 404-885-3000

W. Brinkley Dickerson · Troutman Sanders · Bank of America Plaza, Suite 5200 · 600 Peachtree Street, NE · Atlanta, GA 30308-2216 · 404-885-3000

C. Edward Dobbs · ㉕ · Parker, Hudson, Rainer & Dobbs · 1500 Marquis Two Tower · 285 Peachtree Center Avenue, NE · Atlanta, GA 30303 · 404-523-5300

Michael J. Egan III · King & Spalding · 1180 Peachtree Street, NE · Atlanta, GA 30309-3521 · 404-572-4600

Daniel T. Falstad · DLA Piper · One Atlantic Center, Suite 2800 · 1201 West Peachtree Street · Atlanta, GA 30309-3450 · 404-736-7800

Steven E. Fox · Rogers & Hardin · 2700 International Tower · 229 Peachtree Street, NE · Atlanta, GA 30303 · 404-522-4700

Charles D. Ganz · Sutherland · http://www.sutherland.com · 999 Peachtree Street, NE · Atlanta, GA 30309-3996 · 404-853-8000

Lawrence M. Gold · Carlton Fields · One Atlantic Center, Suite 300 · 1201 West Peachtree Street · Atlanta, GA 30309 · 404-815-3400

Jonathan Golden · ⑩ · Arnall Golden Gregory · 171 Seventeenth Street, NW, Suite 2100 · Atlanta, GA 30363-1031 · 404-873-8500

Douglas S. Gosden · Kilpatrick Stockton · 1100 Peachtree Street, Suite 2800 · Atlanta, GA 30309-4530 · 404-815-6500

Richard W. Grice · ⑩ · Alston + Bird · http://www.alston.com · One Atlantic Center · 1201 West Peachtree Street · Atlanta, GA 30309-3424 · 404-881-7000

Robert W. Grout · Troutman Sanders · Bank of America Plaza, Suite 5200 · 600 Peachtree Street, NE · Atlanta, GA 30308-2216 · 404-885-3000

Jeffrey K. Haidet · McKenna Long & Aldridge · 303 Peachtree Street, NE, Suite 5300 · Atlanta, GA 30308 · 404-527-4000

Edward J. Hardin · ⑳ · Rogers & Hardin · 2700 International Tower · 229 Peachtree Street, NE · Atlanta, GA 30303 · 404-522-4700

Jon R. Harris, Jr. · ⑩ · King & Spalding · 1180 Peachtree Street, NE · Atlanta, GA 30309-3521 · 404-572-4600

James L. Henderson III · Sutherland · http://www.sutherland.com · 999 Peachtree Street, NE · Atlanta, GA 30309-3996 · 404-853-8000

Thomas C. Herman · Sutherland · http://www.sutherland.com · 999 Peachtree Street, NE · Atlanta, GA 30309-3996 · 404-853-8000

Scott M. Hobby · Sutherland · http://www.sutherland.com · 999 Peachtree Street, NE · Atlanta, GA 30309-3996 · 404-853-8000

John D. Hopkins · Womble Carlyle Sandridge & Rice · One Atlantic Center, Suite 3500 · 1201 West Peachtree Street · Atlanta, GA 30309 · 404-872-7000

Paul L. Hudson, Jr. · ⑩ · Parker, Hudson, Rainer & Dobbs · 1500 Marquis Two Tower · 285 Peachtree Center Avenue, NE · Atlanta, GA 30303 · 404-523-5300

Hunter R. Hughes III · Rogers & Hardin · 2700 International Tower · 229 Peachtree Street, NE · Atlanta, GA 30303 · 404-522-4700

Thomas B. Hyman, Jr. · ⑩ · Sutherland · http://www.sutherland.com · 999 Peachtree Street, NE · Atlanta, GA 30309-3996 · 404-853-8000

David M. Ivey · McKenna Long & Aldridge · 303 Peachtree Street, NE, Suite 5300 · Atlanta, GA 30308 · 404-527-4000

M. Hill Jeffries · Alston + Bird · http://www.alston.com · One Atlantic Center · 1201 West Peachtree Street · Atlanta, GA 30309-3424 · 404-881-7000

Hilary P. Jordan · Kilpatrick Stockton · 1100 Peachtree Street, Suite 2800 · Atlanta, GA 30309-4530 · 404-815-6500

Walter E. Jospin · Paul Hastings · 600 Peachtree Street, NE, 24th Floor · Atlanta, GA 30308 · 404-815-2400

Mark D. Kaufman · Sutherland · http://www.sutherland.com · 999 Peachtree Street, NE · Atlanta, GA 30309-3996 · 404-853-8000

John J. Kelley III · King & Spalding · 1180 Peachtree Street, NE · Atlanta, GA 30309-3521 · 404-572-4600

Bennett Lexon Kight · ⑩ · Sutherland · http://www.sutherland.com · 999 Peachtree Street, NE · Atlanta, GA 30309-3996 · 404-853-8000

John L. Latham · Alston + Bird · http://www.alston.com · One Atlantic Center · 1201 West Peachtree Street · Atlanta, GA 30309-3424 · 404-881-7000

Frank Layson · Paul Hastings · 600 Peachtree Street, NE, 24th Floor · Atlanta, GA 30308 · 404-815-2400

Larry D. Ledbetter · Ledbetter Johnson Wanamaker · 100 Colony Square, Suite 1100 · 1175 Peachtree Street, NE · Atlanta, GA 30361 · 404-835-9500

Alan C. Leet · Rogers & Hardin · 2700 International Tower · 229 Peachtree Street, NE · Atlanta, GA 30303 · 404-522-4700

Colvin T. Leonard III · Kilpatrick Stockton · 1100 Peachtree Street, Suite 2800 · Atlanta, GA 30309-4530 404-815-6500

Clay C. Long · ⑳ · McKenna Long & Aldridge · 303 Peachtree Street, NE, Suite 5300 · Atlanta, GA 30308 · 404-527-4000

William B. Marianes · McGuireWoods · http://www.mcguirewoods.com · The Proscenium, Suite 2100 · 1170 Peachtree Street, NE · Atlanta, GA 30309-7649 · 404-443-5500

Teri Lynn McMahon · Alston + Bird · http://www.alston.com · One Atlantic Center · 1201 West Peachtree Street · Atlanta, GA 30309-3424 · 404-881-7000

Thomas R. McNeill · Powell Goldstein · http://www.pogolaw.com · One Atlantic Center, 14th Floor · 1201 West Peachtree Street, NE · Atlanta, GA 30309 · 404-572-6600

John B. Miller, Jr. · Sutherland · http://www.sutherland.com · 999 Peachtree Street, NE · Atlanta, GA 30309-3996 · 404-853-8000

Rick Miller · Powell Goldstein · http://www.pogolaw.com · One Atlantic Center, 14th Floor · 1201 West Peachtree Street, NE · Atlanta, GA 30309 · 404-572-6600

Walter G. Moeling IV · ⑩ · Powell Goldstein · http://www.pogolaw.com · One Atlantic Center, 14th Floor · 1201 West Peachtree Street, NE · Atlanta, GA 30309 · 404-572-6600

Chris D. Molen · Paul Hastings · 600 Peachtree Street, NE, 24th Floor · Atlanta, GA 30308 · 404-815-2400

F. Donald Nelms, Jr. · Powell Goldstein · http://www.pogolaw.com · One Atlantic Center, 14th Floor · 1201 West Peachtree Street, NE · Atlanta, GA 30309 · 404-572-6600

Sidney J. Nurkin · ⑳ · Alston + Bird · http://www.alston.com · One Atlantic Center · 1201 West Peachtree Street · Atlanta, GA 30309-3424 · 404-881-7000

Reinaldo Pascual · Paul Hastings · 600 Peachtree Street, NE, 24th Floor · Atlanta, GA 30308 · 404-815-2400

Steven L. Pottle · ⑩ · Alston + Bird · http://www.alston.com · One Atlantic Center · 1201 West Peachtree Street · Atlanta, GA 30309-3424 · 404-881-7000

Alan J. Prince · King & Spalding · 1180 Peachtree Street, NE · Atlanta, GA 30309-3521 · 404-572-4600

Robert C. Reynolds, Jr. · Alston + Bird · http://www.alston.com · One Atlantic Center · 1201 West Peachtree Street · Atlanta, GA 30309-3424 · 404-881-7000

Russell B. Richards · ⑩ · King & Spalding · 1180 Peachtree Street, NE · Atlanta, GA 30309-3521 · 404-572-4600

Lynn S. Scott · King & Spalding · 1180 Peachtree Street, NE · Atlanta, GA 30309-3521 · 404-572-4600

Jonathan R. Shils · Jonathan R. Shils · The Proscenium, Suite 2100 · 1170 Peachtree Street NE · Atlanta, GA 30309-7649 · 404-443-5500

Nathaniel G. Slaughter III · ⑳ · Slaughter & Virgin · http://www.slaughtervirgin.com · 400 Colony Square, Suite 1110 · 1201 Peachtree Street, NE · Atlanta, GA 30361 · 404-897-1110

James L. Smith III · ⑳ · Troutman Sanders · Bank of America Plaza, Suite 5200 · 600 Peachtree Street, NE · Atlanta, GA 30308-2216 · 404-885-3000

Jeffrey M. Stein · King & Spalding · 1180 Peachtree Street, NE · Atlanta, GA 30309-3521 · 404-572-4600

James D. Steinberg · Kilpatrick Stockton · 1100 Peachtree Street, Suite 2800 · Atlanta, GA 30309-4530 · 404-815-6500

David A. Stockton · ⑩ · Kilpatrick Stockton · 1100 Peachtree Street, Suite 2800 · Atlanta, GA 30309-4530 · 404-815-6500

Robert D. Strauss · Troutman Sanders · Bank of America Plaza, Suite 5200 · 600 Peachtree Street, NE · Atlanta, GA 30308-2216 · 404-885-3000

G. Kimbrough Taylor, Jr. · ⑩ · Kilpatrick Stockton · 1100 Peachtree Street, Suite 2800 · Atlanta, GA 30309-4530 · 404-815-6500

Lizanne Thomas · Jones Day · 1420 Peachtree Street, NE, Suite 800 · Atlanta, GA 30309-3053 · 404-521-3939

Bruce D. Wanamaker · Ledbetter Johnson Wanamaker · 100 Colony Square, Suite 1100 · 1175 Peachtree Street, NE · Atlanta, GA 30361 · 404-835-9500

Mark D. Wasserman · Sutherland · http://www.sutherland.com · 999 Peachtree Street, NE · Atlanta, GA 30309-3996 · 404-853-8000

Susan J. Wilson · Alston + Bird · http://www.alston.com · One Atlantic Center · 1201 West Peachtree Street · Atlanta, GA 30309-3424 · 404-881-7000

Gerald T. Woods · King & Spalding · 1180 Peachtree Street, NE · Atlanta, GA 30309-3521 · 404-572-4600

Dennis L. Zakas · McKenna Long & Aldridge · 303 Peachtree Street, NE, Suite 5300 · Atlanta, GA 30308 · 404-527-4000

John E. Zamer · Jones Day · 1420 Peachtree Street, NE, Suite 800 · Atlanta, GA 30309-3053 · 404-521-3939

Augusta

William Hale Barrett · ⑩ · Hull, Towill, Norman, Barrett & Salley · SunTrust Bank Building, Suite 700 · 801 Broad Street · P.O. Box 1564 · Augusta, GA 30903-1564 · 706-722-4481

Macon

Timothy K. Adams · ⑩ · Jones, Cork & Miller · SunTrust Bank Building, Fifth Floor · 435 Second Street P.O. Box 6437 · Macon, GA 31208-6437 · 478-745-2821

Edward J. Harrell · ⑳ · Martin Snow · http://www.martinsnow.com · 240 Third Street · P.O. Box 1606 · Macon, GA 31202-1606 · 478-749-1700

Hubert C. Lovein, Jr. · ⑩ · Jones, Cork & Miller · SunTrust Bank Building, Fifth Floor · 435 Second Street · P.O. Box 6437 · Macon, GA 31208-6437 · 478-745-2821

J. Patrick Meyer, Jr. · Hall, Bloch, Garland & Meyer · http://www.hbgm.com · Fickling & Company Building, Suite 1500 · 577 Mulberry Street · P.O. Box 5088 · Macon, GA 31208-5088 · 478-745-1625

Albert P. Reichert, Jr. · ⑳ · Anderson, Walker & Reichert · Fickling & Company Building, Suite 500 · 577 Mulberry Street · P.O. Box 6497 · Macon, GA 31208-6497 · 478-743-8651

G. Boone Smith III · ⑳ · Smith, Hawkins, Hollingsworth & Reeves · 688 Walnut Street, Suite 100 · P.O. Box 6495 · Macon, GA 31201 · 478-743-4436

Savannah

J. Wiley Ellis · ⑩ · Ellis, Painter, Ratterree & Adams · http://www.epra-law.com · Johnson Square Business Center, 10th Floor · Two East Bryan Street · P.O. Box 9946 · Savannah, GA 31412 · 912-233-9700

Thomas S. Gray, Jr. · ⑳ · Gray & Pannell · 218 West State Street, Third Floor · P.O. Box 8050 · Savannah, GA 31412-8050 · 912-443-4040

Walter C. Hartridge · ⑩ · Bouhan, Williams & Levy · http://www.bouhan.com · The Armstrong House · 447 Bull Street · P.O. Box 2139 · Savannah, GA 31402-2139 · 912-236-2491

John M. Hewson · Hunter Maclean · http://www.huntermaclean.com · 200 East Saint Julian Street · P.O. Box 9848 · Savannah, GA 31412-0048 · 912-236-0261

James L. Pannell · Gray & Pannell · 218 West State Street, Third Floor · P.O. Box 8050 · Savannah, GA 31412-8050 · 912-443-4040

DUI/DWI DEFENSE

Atlanta

Michael M. Hawkins · The Hawkins Law Firm · 1535 Mount Vernon Road, Suite 200 · Atlanta, GA 30338 · 404-272-8777

William C. Head · Head, Thomas, Webb & Willis · http://www.absolutely-not-guilty.com · Building Five, 750 Hammond Drive, NE · Atlanta, GA 30328-5532 · 404-250-1113

Michael S. Lascala · Arora & Lascala · 75 West Wieuca Road, NE · Atlanta, GA 30342 · 404-881-8866

Savannah

Douglas Andrews · Doug Andrews Law Office · 327 West York Street · Savannah, GA 31401 · 912-236-3020

EDUCATION LAW

Atlanta

Terrell W. Benton, Jr. · Hall Booth Smith & Slover · Atlantic Center Plaza, Suite 900 · 1180 West Peachtree, NW · Atlanta, GA 30309 · 404-954-5000

Rodney Gregory Moore · Greenberg Traurig · http://www.gtlaw.com · The Forum, Suite 400 · 3290 Northside Parkway, NE · Atlanta, GA 30327 · 678-553-2100

Rocco E. Testani · Sutherland · http://www.sutherland.com · 999 Peachtree Street, NE · Atlanta, GA 30309-3996 · 404-853-8000

EMINENT DOMAIN AND CONDEMNATION LAW

Atlanta

Richard N. Hubert · Chamberlain, Hrdlicka, White, Williams & Martin · 191 Peachtree Street, NE, 34th Floor · Atlanta, GA 30303-1747 · 404-659-1410

J. Scott Jacobson · Holt Ney Zatcoff & Wasserman · 100 Galleria Parkway, Suite 600 · Atlanta, GA 30339 · 770-956-9600

Donald W. Janney · Troutman Sanders · Bank of America Plaza, Suite 5200 · 600 Peachtree Street, NE · Atlanta, GA 30308-2216 · 404-885-3000

Scott W. Peters · Schreeder, Wheeler & Flint · 1100 Peachtree Street, Suite 800 · Atlanta, GA 30309 · 404-681-3450

Charles N. Pursley, Jr. · Pursley Lowery Meeks · 260 Peachtree Street, Suite 2000 · Atlanta, GA 30303 · 404-880-7180

Charles L. Ruffin · Baker, Donelson, Bearman, Caldwell & Berkowitz · http://www.bakerdonelson.com · Six Concourse Parkway, Suite 3100 · Atlanta, GA 30328 · 678-406-8700

Anne W. Sapp · Anne W. Sapp · 2100 Riveredge Parkway, Suite 700 · Atlanta, GA 30328 · 404-892-6668

Buford

Luther H. Beck, Jr. · Chandler, Britt, Jay & Beck · 4350 South Lee Street · Buford, GA 30518 · 770-271-2991

Richard B. Chandler, Jr. · Chandler, Britt, Jay & Beck · 4350 South Lee Street · Buford, GA 30518 · 770-271-2991

McDonough

Warren R. Power · Power & Cooper · 108 Atlanta Street · P.O. Box 70 · McDonough, GA 30253 · 770-957-1765

William A. White · Smith, Welch & Brittain · The Commerce Building, II · 2200 Keys Ferry Court · P.O. Box 10 · McDonough, GA 30253 · 770-957-3937

Atlanta

Eleanor Banister · King & Spalding · 1180 Peachtree Street, NE · Atlanta, GA 30309-3521 · 404-572-4600

Armin G. Brecher · Powell Goldstein · http://www.pogolaw.com · One Atlantic Center, 14th Floor · 1201 West Peachtree Street, NE · Atlanta, GA 30309 · 404-572-6600

Charles E. Elrod, Jr. · ⑳ · Parker, Hudson, Rainer & Dobbs · 1500 Marquis Two Tower · 285 Peachtree Center Avenue, NE · Atlanta, GA 30303 · 404-523-5300

William A. Gray · Ogletree Deakins · http://www.ogletreedeakins.com · Bank of America Plaza, Suite 2100 · 600 Peachtree Street, NE · Atlanta, GA 30308 · 404-881-1300

John R. Hickman · ⑩ · Alston + Bird · http://www.alston.com · One Atlantic Center · 1201 West Peachtree Street · Atlanta, GA 30309-3424 · 404-881-7000

H. Douglas Hinson · Alston + Bird · http://www.alston.com · One Atlantic Center · 1201 West Peachtree Street · Atlanta, GA 30309-3424 · 404-881-7000

Donald S. Kohla · ⑳ · King & Spalding · 1180 Peachtree Street, NE · Atlanta, GA 30309-3521 · 404-572-4600

James H. Landon · ⑳ · Jones Day · 1420 Peachtree Street, NE, Suite 800 · Atlanta, GA 30309-3053 · 404-521-3939

Craig R. Pett · Alston + Bird · http://www.alston.com · One Atlantic Center · 1201 West Peachtree Street · Atlanta, GA 30309-3424 · 404-881-7000

Susan Canter Reisner · King & Spalding · 1180 Peachtree Street, NE · Atlanta, GA 30309-3521 · 404-572-4600

Steven G. Schaffer · Powell Goldstein · http://www.pogolaw.com · One Atlantic Center, 14th Floor · 1201 West Peachtree Street, NE · Atlanta, GA 30309 · 404-572-6600

Jennifer Stobie Schumacher · Kilpatrick Stockton · 1100 Peachtree Street, Suite 2800 · Atlanta, GA 30309-4530 · 404-815-6500

Caroline Talley · Benefits Law Group · Resurgens Plaza, Suite 2515 · 945 East Paces Ferry Road · Atlanta, GA 30326 · 404-995-9505

Patricia E. Tate · McKenna Long & Aldridge · 303 Peachtree Street, NE, Suite 5300 · Atlanta, GA 30308 404-527-4000

Laura G. Thatcher · Alston + Bird · http://www.alston.com · One Atlantic Center · 1201 West Peachtree Street · Atlanta, GA 30309-3424 · 404-881-7000

William J. Vesely, Jr. · Kilpatrick Stockton · 1100 Peachtree Street, Suite 2800 · Atlanta, GA 30309-4530 404-815-6500

Columbus

Elizabeth R. Cook · Hatcher, Stubbs, Land, Hollis & Rothschild · http://www.hatcherstubbs.com · The Corporate Center, Suite 500 · 233 Twelfth Street · P.O. Box 2707 · Columbus, GA 31902-2707 · 706-324-0201

Morton A. Harris · (25) · Hatcher, Stubbs, Land, Hollis & Rothschild · http://www.hatcherstubbs.com · The Corporate Center, Suite 500 · 233 Twelfth Street · P.O. Box 2707 · Columbus, GA 31902-2707 · 706-324-0201

Macon

Albert P. Reichert, Jr. · (20) · Anderson, Walker & Reichert · Fickling & Company Building, Suite 500 · 577 Mulberry Street · P.O. Box 6497 · Macon, GA 31208-6497 · 478-743-8651

Savannah

Sally C. Nielsen · Hunter Maclean · http://www.huntermaclean.com · 200 East Saint Julian Street · P.O. Box 9848 · Savannah, GA 31412-0048 · 912-236-0261

ENERGY LAW

Atlanta

Peter M. Degnan · Alston + Bird · http://www.alston.com · One Atlantic Center · 1201 West Peachtree Street · Atlanta, GA 30309-3424 · 404-881-7000

L. Craig Dowdy · (10) · McKenna Long & Aldridge · 303 Peachtree Street, NE, Suite 5300 · Atlanta, GA 30308 · 404-527-4000

Robert P. Edwards, Jr. · Troutman Sanders · Bank of America Plaza, Suite 5200 · 600 Peachtree Street, NE · Atlanta, GA 30308-2216 · 404-885-3000

Robert H. Forry · Troutman Sanders · Bank of America Plaza, Suite 5200 · 600 Peachtree Street, NE · Atlanta, GA 30308-2216 · 404-885-3000

Cada T. Kilgore III · Cada T. Kilgore, III, Attorney at Law · 3280 Northside Parkway, Suite 613 · Atlanta, GA 30327 · 404-275-3948

Catherine D. Little · Hunton & Williams · Bank of America Plaza, Suite 4100 · 600 Peachtree Street, NE Atlanta, GA 30308-2216 · 404-888-4000

Thomas L. Penland, Jr. · Balch & Bingham · http://www.balch.com · 30 Ivan Allen, Jr. Boulevard, NW, Suite 700 · Atlanta, GA 30308 · 404-261-6020

DeWitt R. Rogers · Troutman Sanders · Bank of America Plaza, Suite 5200 · 600 Peachtree Street, NE · Atlanta, GA 30308-2216 · 404-885-3000

Della Wager Wells · Alston + Bird · http://www.alston.com · One Atlantic Center · 1201 West Peachtree Street · Atlanta, GA 30309-3424 · 404-881-7000

ENTERTAINMENT LAW

Atlanta

Joseph M. Beck · (10) · Kilpatrick Stockton · 1100 Peachtree Street, Suite 2800 · Atlanta, GA 30309-4530 · 404-815-6500

Martin J. Elgison · (10) · Alston + Bird · http://www.alston.com · One Atlantic Center · 1201 West Peachtree Street · Atlanta, GA 30309-3424 · 404-881-7000

Joel A. Katz · (20) · Greenberg Traurig · http://www.gtlaw.com · The Forum, Suite 400 · 3290 Northside Parkway, NE · Atlanta, GA 30327 · 678-553-2100

Jess L. Rosen · Greenberg Traurig · http://www.gtlaw.com · The Forum, Suite 400 · 3290 Northside Parkway, NE · Atlanta, GA 30327 · 678-553-2100

Bobby Rosenbloum · Greenberg Traurig · http://www.gtlaw.com · The Forum, Suite 400 · 3290 Northside Parkway, NE · Atlanta, GA 30327 · 678-553-2100

ENVIRONMENTAL LAW

Atlanta

Gordon R. Alphonso · McGuireWoods · http://www.mcguirewoods.com · The Proscenium, Suite 2100 · 1170 Peachtree Street, NE · Atlanta, GA 30309-7649 · 404-443-5500

Douglas S. Arnold · Alston + Bird · http://www.alston.com · One Atlantic Center · 1201 West Peachtree Street · Atlanta, GA 30309-3424 · 404-881-7000

Patricia T. Barmeyer · (10) · King & Spalding · 1180 Peachtree Street, NE · Atlanta, GA 30309-3521 · 404-572-4600

Gregory W. Blount · Troutman Sanders · Bank of America Plaza, Suite 5200 · 600 Peachtree Street, NE · Atlanta, GA 30308-2216 · 404-885-3000

Margaret C. Campbell · Troutman Sanders · Bank of America Plaza, Suite 5200 · 600 Peachtree Street, NE · Atlanta, GA 30308-2216 · 404-885-3000

J. Michael Childers · Balch & Bingham · http://www.balch.com · 30 Ivan Allen, Jr. Boulevard, NW, Suite 700 · Atlanta, GA 30308 · 404-261-6020

Douglas E. Cloud · Alston + Bird · http://www.alston.com · One Atlantic Center · 1201 West Peachtree Street · Atlanta, GA 30309-3424 · 404-881-7000

Peter M. Degnan · Alston + Bird · http://www.alston.com · One Atlantic Center · 1201 West Peachtree Street · Atlanta, GA 30309-3424 · 404-881-7000

Lee A. DeHihns III · (10) · Alston + Bird · http://www.alston.com · One Atlantic Center · 1201 West Peachtree Street · Atlanta, GA 30309-3424 · 404-881-7000

Barbara H. Gallo · Nelson Mullins Riley & Scarborough · Atlantic Station, Suite 1700 · 201 Seventeenth Street, NW · Atlanta, GA 30363 · 404-817-6000

Carol R. Geiger · McKenna Long & Aldridge · 303 Peachtree Street, NE, Suite 5300 · Atlanta, GA 30308 404-527-4000

Douglas A. Henderson · Troutman Sanders · Bank of America Plaza, Suite 5200 · 600 Peachtree Street, NE · Atlanta, GA 30308-2216 · 404-885-3000

Hollister A. Hill · Troutman Sanders · Bank of America Plaza, Suite 5200 · 600 Peachtree Street, NE · Atlanta, GA 30308-2216 · 404-885-3000

Robert E. Hogfoss · Hunton & Williams · Bank of America Plaza, Suite 4100 · 600 Peachtree Street, NE · Atlanta, GA 30308-2216 · 404-888-4000

Richard A. Horder · Kilpatrick Stockton · 1100 Peachtree Street, Suite 2800 · Atlanta, GA 30309-4530 · 404-815-6500

John H. Johnson, Jr. · Troutman Sanders · Bank of America Plaza, Suite 5200 · 600 Peachtree Street, NE · Atlanta, GA 30308-2216 · 404-885-3000

Edward A. Kazmarek · Kazmerek Geiger & Laseter · One Securities Center, Suite 201 · 3490 Piedmont Road, NE · Atlanta, GA 30305 · 404-812-0839

W. Scott Laseter · Kazmarek Geiger & Laseter · One Securities Center, Suite 201 · 3490 Piedmont Road, NE · Atlanta, GA 30305 · 404-812-0839

James D. Levine · McKenna Long & Aldridge · 303 Peachtree Street, NE, Suite 5300 · Atlanta, GA 30308 · 404-527-4000

Catherine D. Little · Hunton & Williams · Bank of America Plaza, Suite 4100 · 600 Peachtree Street, NE Atlanta, GA 30308-2216 · 404-888-4000

Robert D. Mowrey · Alston + Bird · http://www.alston.com · One Atlantic Center · 1201 West Peachtree Street · Atlanta, GA 30309-3424 · 404-881-7000

Stephen E. O'Day · Smith, Gambrell & Russell · http://www.sgrlaw.com · Promenade II, Suite 3100 · 1230 Peachtree Street, NE · Atlanta, GA 30309-3592 · 404-815-3500

Leslie A. Oakes · King & Spalding · 1180 Peachtree Street, NE · Atlanta, GA 30309-3521 · 404-572-4600

Gerald L. Pouncey, Jr. · Morris, Manning & Martin · 1600 Atlanta Financial Center · 3343 Peachtree Road, NE · Atlanta, GA 30326 · 404-233-7000

Randall D. Quintrell · Sutherland · http://www.sutherland.com · 999 Peachtree Street, NE · Atlanta, GA 30309-3996 · 404-853-8000

Susan H. Richardson · Kilpatrick Stockton · 1100 Peachtree Street, Suite 2800 · Atlanta, GA 30309-4530 404-815-6500

Andrea L. Rimer · Troutman Sanders · Bank of America Plaza, Suite 5200 · 600 Peachtree Street, NE · Atlanta, GA 30308-2216 · 404-885-3000

Harvey A. Rosenzweig · Troutman Sanders · Bank of America Plaza, Suite 5200 · 600 Peachtree Street, NE · Atlanta, GA 30308-2216 · 404-885-3000

Richard A. Schneider · King & Spalding · 1180 Peachtree Street, NE · Atlanta, GA 30309-3521 · 404-572-4600

John C. Spinrad · Arnall Golden Gregory · 171 Seventeenth Street, NW, Suite 2100 · Atlanta, GA 30363-1031 · 404-873-8500

Charles H. Tisdale, Jr. · ⑩ · King & Spalding · 1180 Peachtree Street, NE · Atlanta, GA 30309-3521 · 404-572-4600

Savannah

Andrew H. Ernst · ⑩ · Hunter Maclean · http://www.huntermaclean.com · 200 East Saint Julian Street · P.O. Box 9848 · Savannah, GA 31412-0048 · 912-236-0261

EQUIPMENT FINANCE LAW

Atlanta

Albert H. Conrad, Jr. · ⑩ · King & Spalding · 1180 Peachtree Street, NE · Atlanta, GA 30309-3521 · 404-572-4600

Paul M. Cushing · Alston + Bird · http://www.alston.com · One Atlantic Center · 1201 West Peachtree Street · Atlanta, GA 30309-3424 · 404-881-7000

C. Edward Dobbs · ㉕ · Parker, Hudson, Rainer & Dobbs · 1500 Marquis Two Tower · 285 Peachtree Center Avenue, NE · Atlanta, GA 30303 · 404-523-5300

Richard W. Grice · ⑩ · Alston + Bird · http://www.alston.com · One Atlantic Center · 1201 West Peachtree Street · Atlanta, GA 30309-3424 · 404-881-7000

Robert D. Strauss · Troutman Sanders · Bank of America Plaza, Suite 5200 · 600 Peachtree Street, NE · Atlanta, GA 30308-2216 · 404-885-3000

FAMILY LAW

Atlanta

Emily S. Bair · Emily S. Bair & Associates · 6100 Lake Forrest Drive, NW, Suite 480 · Atlanta, GA 30328 404-806-7330

Edward E. Bates, Jr. · ⑳ · Warner, Mayoue, Bates & Nolen · Riverwood 100 Building, Suite 2300 · 3350 Riverwood Parkway, SE · Atlanta, GA 30339-5948 · 770-951-2700

Robert D. Boyd · Boyd Collar Knight · http://www.lawbck.com · 400 Galleria Parkway, Suite 1920 · Atlanta, GA 30339 · 770-953-4300

J. Stephen Clifford · ⑩ · J. Stephen Clifford · One Securities Center, Suite 400 · 3490 Piedmont Road, NE · Atlanta, GA 30305-1743 · 404-233-2800

John L. Collar, Jr. · Boyd Collar Knight · http://www.lawbck.com · 400 Galleria Parkway, Suite 1920 · Atlanta, GA 30339 · 770-953-4300

Shiel G. Edlin · Stern & Edlin · 225 West Wieuca Road · Atlanta, GA 30342 · 404-256-0010

Kurt A. Kegel · Davis, Matthews & Quigley · Lenox Towers II, 14th Floor · 3400 Peachtree Road, NE · Atlanta, GA 30326 · 404-261-3900

Nancy F. Lawler · ⑩ · Lawler Green Givelber & Prinz · 3350 Riverwood Parkway, Suite 460 · Atlanta, GA 30339 · 770-563-8800

Elizabeth Green Lindsey · Davis, Matthews & Quigley · Lenox Towers II, 14th Floor · 3400 Peachtree Road, NE · Atlanta, GA 30326 · 404-261-3900

John C. Mayoue · ⑩ · Warner, Mayoue, Bates & Nolen · Riverwood 100 Building, Suite 2300 · 3350 Riverwood Parkway, SE · Atlanta, GA 30339-5948 · 770-951-2700

P. Joseph McGee · ⑩ · McGee & Oxford · Tower Place, Suite 2800 · 3340 Peachtree Road, NE · Atlanta, GA 30326-1000 · 404-231-1935

Barry B. McGough · ⑳ · Warner, Mayoue, Bates & Nolen · Riverwood 100 Building, Suite 2300 · 3350 Riverwood Parkway, SE · Atlanta, GA 30339-5948 · 770-951-2700

Christopher D. Olmstead · ⑩ · McLain & Merritt · 3445 Peachtree Road, NE, Suite 500 · Atlanta, GA 30326-1276 · 404-266-9171

Richard W. Schiffman, Jr. · ⑩ · Davis, Matthews & Quigley · Lenox Towers II, 14th Floor · 3400 Peachtree Road, NE · Atlanta, GA 30326 · 404-261-3900

George S. Stern · ⑩ · Stern & Edlin · 225 West Wieuca Road · Atlanta, GA 30342 · 404-256-0010

C. Wilbur Warner, Jr. · ㉕ · Warner, Mayoue, Bates & Nolen · Riverwood 100 Building, Suite 2300 · 3350 Riverwood Parkway, SE · Atlanta, GA 30339-5948 · 770-951-2700

Decatur

H. Martin Huddleston · ⑩ · H. Martin Huddleston, Attorney at Law · Wachovia Bank Building, Suite 850 · 315 West Ponce De Leon Avenue · Decatur, GA 30030 · 404-377-3441

M. T. Simmons, Jr. · ⑳ · Simmons & Szczecko · 315 West Ponce de Leon Avenue, Suite 850 · Decatur, GA 30030 · 404-378-1711

Joseph Szczecko · ⑩ · Simmons & Szczecko · 315 West Ponce de Leon Avenue, Suite 850 · Decatur, GA 30030 · 404-378-1711

Lawrenceville

Gerald Davidson, Jr. · ⑩ · Mahaffey Pickens Tucker · 1550 North Brown Road, Suite 125 · Lawrenceville, GA 30043 · 770-232-0000

Macon

Kice H. Stone, Jr. · ⑳ · The Stone Law Firm · http://www.stonechapmanlaw.com · 701 Nottingham Drive · P.O. Box 56701 · Macon, GA 31208-6701 · 478-741-0060

Marietta

Hylton B. Dupree, Jr. · Dupree & Kimbrough · 49 Green Street · P.O. Box 525 · Marietta, GA 30061 · 770-424-7171

Savannah

Carl S. Pedigo · Carl S. Pedigo, Jr · 105 North Marsh Road · Savannah, GA 31410 · 912-484-7481

FAMILY LAW MEDIATION

Atlanta

James E. Holmes · James E. Holmes · 434 Martietta Street, Suite 402 · Atlanta, GA 30313 · 404-523-6960

Susan A. Hurst · Bogart & Bogart · 6400 Powers Ferry Road, Suite 220 · Atlanta, GA 30339 · 770-988-9444

Decatur

M. T. Simmons, Jr. · ⑳ · Simmons & Szczecko · 315 West Ponce de Leon Avenue, Suite 850 · Decatur, GA 30030 · 404-378-1711

Marietta

Hylton B. Dupree, Jr. · Dupree & Kimbrough · 49 Green Street · P.O. Box 525 · Marietta, GA 30061 · 770-424-7171

Linda Wade Gettle · Linda Wade Gettle · 142 South Park Square, Suite F · Marietta, GA 30060 · 770-795-8000

F. Marian Weeks · F. Marian Weeks · 367 Atlanta Street, SE · Marietta, GA 30060 · 770-218-2600

J. Diane Woods · Huff, Woods and Hamby · Whitlock Park, Suite G-5 · 707 Whitlock Avenue, SW · Marietta, GA 30064-3033 · 770-429-1001

FIRST AMENDMENT LAW

Atlanta

David L. Balser · McKenna Long & Aldridge · 303 Peachtree Street, NE, Suite 5300 · Atlanta, GA 30308 404-527-4000

Emmet J. Bondurant II · ㉕ · Bondurant, Mixson & Elmore · http://www.bmelaw.com · One Atlantic Center, Suite 3900 · 1201 West Peachtree Street, NW · Atlanta, GA 30309 · 404-881-4100

Peter C. Canfield · ⑩ · Dow Lohnes · http://www.dowlohnes.com · Six Concourse Parkway, Suite 1800 · Atlanta, GA 30328-6117 · 770-901-8800

Thomas M. Clyde · Dow Lohnes · http://www.dowlohnes.com · Six Concourse Parkway, Suite 1800 · Atlanta, GA 30328-6117 · 770-901-8800

Judson Graves · Alston + Bird · http://www.alston.com · One Atlantic Center · 1201 West Peachtree Street · Atlanta, GA 30309-3424 · 404-881-7000

James C. Rawls · ⑩ · McKenna Long & Aldridge · 303 Peachtree Street, NE, Suite 5300 · Atlanta, GA 30308 · 404-527-4000

Daniel S. Reinhardt · Troutman Sanders · Bank of America Plaza, Suite 5200 · 600 Peachtree Street, NE · Atlanta, GA 30308-2216 · 404-885-3000

Robert B. Remar · Rogers & Hardin · 2700 International Tower · 229 Peachtree Street, NE · Atlanta, GA 30303 · 404-522-4700

Robert L. Rothman · Arnall Golden Gregory · 171 Seventeenth Street, NW, Suite 2100 · Atlanta, GA 30363-1031 · 404-873-8500

Augusta

James B. Ellington · Hull, Towill, Norman, Barrett & Salley · SunTrust Bank Building, Suite 700 · 801 Broad Street · P.O. Box 1564 · Augusta, GA 30903-1564 · 706-722-4481

David E. Hudson · ⑩ · Hull, Towill, Norman, Barrett & Salley · SunTrust Bank Building, Suite 700 · 801 Broad Street · P.O. Box 1564 · Augusta, GA 30903-1564 · 706-722-4481

Rome

Robert L. Berry · Brinson, Askew, Berry, Seigler, Richardson & Davis · The Omberg House · 615 West First Street · P.O. Box 5513 · Rome, GA 30162-5513 · 706-291-8853

FRANCHISE LAW

Atlanta

Morton H. Aronson · Kilpatrick Stockton · 1100 Peachtree Street, Suite 2800 · Atlanta, GA 30309-4530 · 404-815-6500

Richard M. Asbill · ⑩ · Paul Hastings · 600 Peachtree Street, NE, 24th Floor · Atlanta, GA 30308 · 404-815-2400

Rupert M. Barkoff · ⑩ · Kilpatrick Stockton · 1100 Peachtree Street, Suite 2800 · Atlanta, GA 30309-4530 · 404-815-6500

Christopher P. Bussert · Kilpatrick Stockton · 1100 Peachtree Street, Suite 2800 · Atlanta, GA 30309-4530 · 404-815-6500

Ronald T. Coleman, Jr. · Parker, Hudson, Rainer & Dobbs · 1500 Marquis Two Tower · 285 Peachtree Center Avenue, NE · Atlanta, GA 30303 · 404-523-5300

Dwight J. Davis · King & Spalding · 1180 Peachtree Street, NE · Atlanta, GA 30309-3521 · 404-572-4600

Richard G. Greenstein · DLA Piper · One Atlantic Center, Suite 2800 · 1201 West Peachtree Street · Atlanta, GA 30309-3450 · 404-736-7800

John G. Parker · Paul Hastings · 600 Peachtree Street, NE, 24th Floor · Atlanta, GA 30308 · 404-815-2400

W. Andrew Scott · Paul Hastings · 600 Peachtree Street, NE, 24th Floor · Atlanta, GA 30308 · 404-815-2400

Phillip Leslie Wharton · Epstein, Becker & Green · Resurgens Plaza, Suite 2700 · 945 East Paces Ferry Road · Atlanta, GA 30326 · 404-923-9000

GAMING LAW

Atlanta

William B. Marianes · McGuireWoods · http://www.mcguirewoods.com · The Proscenium, Suite 2100 · 1170 Peachtree Street, NE · Atlanta, GA 30309-7649 · 404-443-5500

Norman L. Underwood · Troutman Sanders · Bank of America Plaza, Suite 5200 · 600 Peachtree Street, NE · Atlanta, GA 30308-2216 · 404-885-3000

GOVERNMENT RELATIONS LAW

Atlanta

Mark H. Cohen · Troutman Sanders · Bank of America Plaza, Suite 5200 · 600 Peachtree Street, NE · Atlanta, GA 30308-2216 · 404-885-3000

Robert H. Forry · Troutman Sanders · Bank of America Plaza, Suite 5200 · 600 Peachtree Street, NE · Atlanta, GA 30308-2216 · 404-885-3000

Robert S. Highsmith, Jr. · Holland & Knight · http://www.hklaw.com · One Atlantic Center, Suite 2000 · 1201 West Peachtree Street, NE · Atlanta, GA 30309-3400 · 404-817-8500

Stanley S. Jones, Jr. · Nelson Mullins Riley & Scarborough · Atlantic Station, Suite 1700 · 201 Seventeenth Street, NW · Atlanta, GA 30363 · 404-817-6000

Pete Robinson · Troutman Sanders · Bank of America Plaza, Suite 5200 · 600 Peachtree Street, NE · Atlanta, GA 30308-2216 · 404-885-3000

Aubrey T. Villines · Magarahan, Villines & Honis · Park Ridge 85, Building One · 2900 Chamblee-Tucker Road · Atlanta, GA 30341 · 770-455-1350

Joe D. Whitley · Greenberg Traurig · http://www.gtlaw.com · The Forum, Suite 400 · 3290 Northside Parkway, NE · Atlanta, GA 30327 · 678-553-2100

Marietta

Charles B. Tanksley · The Barnes Law Group · 31 Atlanta Street · Marietta, GA 30060 · 770-227-6375

Newnan

Arthur B. Edge IV · Wood, Odom & Edge · 15 Jefferson Street · Newnan, GA 30263 · 770-253-9885

HEALTH CARE LAW

Atlanta

Armando L. Basarrate II · Parker, Hudson, Rainer & Dobbs · 1500 Marquis Two Tower · 285 Peachtree Center Avenue, NE · Atlanta, GA 30303 · 404-523-5300

J. Vaughan Curtis · ⑩ · Alston + Bird · http://www.alston.com · One Atlantic Center · 1201 West Peachtree Street · Atlanta, GA 30309-3424 · 404-881-7000

Glenn P. Hendrix · Arnall Golden Gregory · 171 Seventeenth Street, NW, Suite 2100 · Atlanta, GA 30363-1031 · 404-873-8500

Paul L. Hudson, Jr. · ⑩ · Parker, Hudson, Rainer & Dobbs · 1500 Marquis Two Tower · 285 Peachtree Center Avenue, NE · Atlanta, GA 30303 · 404-523-5300

Randall L. Hughes · Powell Goldstein · http://www.pogolaw.com · One Atlantic Center, 14th Floor · 1201 West Peachtree Street, NE · Atlanta, GA 30309 · 404-572-6600

Stanley S. Jones, Jr. · Nelson Mullins Riley & Scarborough · Atlantic Station, Suite 1700 · 201 Seventeenth Street, NW · Atlanta, GA 30363 · 404-817-6000

Robert M. Keenan III · King & Spalding · 1180 Peachtree Street, NE · Atlanta, GA 30309-3521 · 404-572-4600

James P. Kelly · Kelly Law Firm · http://www.kellylawfirm.com · 200 Galleria Parkway, Suite 1510 · Atlanta, GA 30339-5946 · 770-955-2770

Robert C. Lower · Alston + Bird · http://www.alston.com · One Atlantic Center · 1201 West Peachtree Street · Atlanta, GA 30309-3424 · 404-881-7000

Gary McClanahan · Baker, Donelson, Bearman, Caldwell & Berkowitz · http://www.bakerdonelson.com · Six Concourse Parkway, Suite 3100 · Atlanta, GA 30328 · 678-406-8700

John H. Parker, Jr. · ⑩ · Parker, Hudson, Rainer & Dobbs · 1500 Marquis Two Tower · 285 Peachtree Center Avenue, NE · Atlanta, GA 30303 · 404-523-5300

James C. Rawls · McKenna Long & Aldridge · 303 Peachtree Street, NE, Suite 5300 · Atlanta, GA 30308 404-527-4000

Glen A. Reed · ⑩ · King & Spalding · 1180 Peachtree Street, NE · Atlanta, GA 30309-3521 · 404-572-4600

Kim H. Roeder · ⑩ · King & Spalding · 1180 Peachtree Street, NE · Atlanta, GA 30309-3521 · 404-572-4600

Jonathan L. Rue · Parker, Hudson, Rainer & Dobbs · 1500 Marquis Two Tower · 285 Peachtree Center Avenue, NE · Atlanta, GA 30303 · 404-523-5300

Jack S. Schroder, Jr. · ⑩ · Alston + Bird · http://www.alston.com · One Atlantic Center · 1201 West Peachtree Street · Atlanta, GA 30309-3424 · 404-881-7000

Richard L. Shackelford · ⑩ · King & Spalding · 1180 Peachtree Street, NE · Atlanta, GA 30309-3521 · 404-572-4600

Phillip H. Street · Kilpatrick Stockton · 1100 Peachtree Street, Suite 2800 · Atlanta, GA 30309-4530 · 404-815-6500

Richard H. Vincent · Womble Carlyle Sandridge & Rice · One Atlantic Center, Suite 3500 · 1201 West Peachtree Street · Atlanta, GA 30309 · 404-872-7000

Sara Kay Wheeler · King & Spalding · 1180 Peachtree Street, NE · Atlanta, GA 30309-3521 · 404-572-4600

David M. Zacks · ⑩ · Kilpatrick Stockton · 1100 Peachtree Street, Suite 2800 · Atlanta, GA 30309-4530 · 404-815-6500

Augusta

Douglas D. Batchelor, Jr. · ⑩ · Hull, Towill, Norman, Barrett & Salley · SunTrust Bank Building, Suite 700 · 801 Broad Street · P.O. Box 1564 · Augusta, GA 30903-1564 · 706-722-4481

Savannah

T. Mills Fleming · Hunter Maclean · http://www.huntermaclean.com · 200 East Saint Julian Street · P.O. Box 9848 · Savannah, GA 31412-0048 · 912-236-0261

Stockbridge

Rod G. Meadows · ⑩ · Meadows & Lewis · 101 Eagle's Pointe Parkway · Stockbridge, GA 30281 · 770-957-1199

IMMIGRATION LAW

Atlanta

Robert E. Banta · ⑩ · Banta Immigration Law · 100 Colony Square, Suite 700 · 1175 Peachtree Street, NE · Atlanta, GA 30361 · 404-249-9300

Daryl R. Buffenstein · ⑩ · Paul Hastings · 600 Peachtree Street, NE, 24th Floor · Atlanta, GA 30308 · 404-815-2400

Carolina Colin- Antonini · Antonini Odom & Sullivan · One Georgia Center, Suite 2450 · 600 West Peachtree Street · Atlanta, GA 30308 · 404-523-8141

Joycelyn L. Fleming · Ford & Harrison · http://www.fordharrison.com · 1275 Peachtree Street, NE, Suite 600 · Atlanta, GA 30309-3576 · 404-888-3800

H. Glenn Fogle, Jr. · The Fogle Law Firm · The Grant Building, Suite 709 · 44 Broad Street, NW · Atlanta, GA 30303 · 404-522-1852

Romy Kapoor · Law Offices of Kapoor & Associates · 1447 Peachtree Street, Suite 600 · Atlanta, GA 30309 · 404-685-9940

Charles H. Kuck · Kuck Casablanca · http://www.immigration.net · 8010 Roswell Road, Suite 300 · Atlanta, GA 30350 · 404-816-8611

Deborah A. Marlowe · Paul Hastings · 600 Peachtree Street, NE, 24th Floor · Atlanta, GA 30308 · 404-815-2400

Mark J. Newman · ⑩ · Troutman Sanders · Bank of America Plaza, Suite 5200 · 600 Peachtree Street, NE Atlanta, GA 30308-2216 · 404-885-3000

Dale M. Schwartz · ⑩ · Dale M. Schwartz & Associates · River Edge One, Suite 450 · 5500 Interstate North Parkway · Atlanta, GA 30328-4662 · 770-951-1100

Eileen M. G. Scofield · Alston + Bird · http://www.alston.com · One Atlantic Center · 1201 West Peachtree Street · Atlanta, GA 30309-3424 · 404-881-7000

Kyle D. Sherman · Paul Hastings · 600 Peachtree Street, NE, 24th Floor · Atlanta, GA 30308 · 404-815-2400

Teri A. Simmons · Arnall Golden Gregory · 171 Seventeenth Street, NW, Suite 2100 · Atlanta, GA 30363-1031 · 404-873-8500

Jay I. Solomon · Jay I. Solomon · 900 Circle 75 Parkway, Suite 1350 · Atlanta, GA 30339-3035 · 770-955-1055

Karen B. Koenig Winarsky · Paul Hastings · 600 Peachtree Street, NE, 24th Floor · Atlanta, GA 30308 · 404-815-2400

Decatur

Myron N. Kramer · ⑩ · Kramer & Alfano · Two Decatur Town Center, Suite 330 · 125 Clairemont Avenue · Decatur, GA 30030 · 404-371-1835

Duluth

Socheat Chea · Law Offices of Socheat Chea · 3500 Duluth Park Lane, Building 300 · Duluth, GA 30096 770-623-8880

Marietta

Irene Steffas · Steffas & Associates · 4343 Shallowford Road, H-1 · Marietta, GA 30062-5024 · 770-642-6075

INFORMATION TECHNOLOGY LAW

Atlanta

Steven J. de Groot · King & Spalding · 1180 Peachtree Street, NE · Atlanta, GA 30309-3521 · 404-572-4600

James A. Harvey · Hunton & Williams · Bank of America Plaza, Suite 4100 · 600 Peachtree Street, NE · Atlanta, GA 30308-2216 · 404-888-4000

Scott M. Hobby · Sutherland · http://www.sutherland.com · 999 Peachtree Street, NE · Atlanta, GA 30309-3996 · 404-853-8000

John P. Hutchins · Troutman Sanders · Bank of America Plaza, Suite 5200 · 600 Peachtree Street, NE · Atlanta, GA 30308-2216 · 404-885-3000

James E. Meadows · FSB Legal Counsel · 191 Peachtree Street, Suite 3300 · Atlanta, GA 30303 · 678-318-3441

Robert C. Reynolds, Jr. · Alston + Bird · http://www.alston.com · One Atlantic Center · 1201 West Peachtree Street · Atlanta, GA 30309-3424 · 404-881-7000

William G. Roche · King & Spalding · 1180 Peachtree Street, NE · Atlanta, GA 30309-3521 · 404-572-4600

James D. Steinberg · Kilpatrick Stockton · 1100 Peachtree Street, Suite 2800 · Atlanta, GA 30309-4530 · 404-815-6500

INSURANCE LAW

Atlanta

J. Stephen Berry · McKenna Long & Aldridge · 303 Peachtree Street, NE, Suite 5300 · Atlanta, GA 30308 · 404-527-4000

Elizabeth J. Bondurant · Smith Moore Leatherwood · http://www.smithmoorelaw.com · One Atlantic Center, Suite 3700 · 1201 West Peachtree Street · Atlanta, GA 30309 · 404-962-1000

Dwight J. Davis · King & Spalding · 1180 Peachtree Street, NE · Atlanta, GA 30309-3521 · 404-572-4600

William D. Harrison · Mozley, Finlayson & Loggins · One Premier Plaza, Suite 900 · 5605 Glenridge Drive · Atlanta, GA 30342-1386 · 404-256-0700

Michael P. Kenny · Alston + Bird · http://www.alston.com · One Atlantic Center · 1201 West Peachtree Street · Atlanta, GA 30309-3424 · 404-881-7000

Hugh B. McNatt · Balch & Bingham · http://www.balch.com · 30 Ivan Allen, Jr. Boulevard, NW, Suite 700 Atlanta, GA 30308 · 404-261-6020

Philip W. Savrin · Freeman Mathis & Gary · 100 Galleria Parkway, Suite 1600 · Atlanta, GA 30339-5948 · 770-818-0000

Rex D. Smith · Mabry & McClelland · 2200 Century Parkway, NE, 10th Floor · Atlanta, GA 30345 · 404-325-4800

Caroline W. Spangenberg · Kilpatrick Stockton · 1100 Peachtree Street, Suite 2800 · Atlanta, GA 30309-4530 · 404-815-6500

Augusta

Robert C. Hagler · Fulcher Hagler · One 10th Street, Suite 700 · Augusta, GA 30901 · 706-724-0171

Rome

J. Clinton Sumner, Jr. · Magruder & Sumner · 701 Broad Street · P.O. Drawer 5187 · Rome, GA 30162-5187 · 706-291-7050

Savannah

Arnold C. Young · Hunter Maclean · http://www.huntermaclean.com · 200 East Saint Julian Street · P.O. Box 9848 · Savannah, GA 31412-0048 · 912-236-0261

Atlanta

Miles J. Alexander · ㉕ · Kilpatrick Stockton · 1100 Peachtree Street, Suite 2800 · Atlanta, GA 30309-4530 · 404-815-6500

Anthony B. Askew · ⑩ · King & Spalding · 1180 Peachtree Street, NE · Atlanta, GA 30309-3521 · 404-572-4600

Bruce W. Baber · ⑩ · King & Spalding · 1180 Peachtree Street, NE · Atlanta, GA 30309-3521 · 404-572-4600

Joseph M. Beck · ⑩ · Kilpatrick Stockton · 1100 Peachtree Street, Suite 2800 · Atlanta, GA 30309-4530 · 404-815-6500

William H. Boice · Kilpatrick Stockton · 1100 Peachtree Street, Suite 2800 · Atlanta, GA 30309-4530 · 404-815-6500

William H. Brewster · ⑩ · Kilpatrick Stockton · 1100 Peachtree Street, Suite 2800 · Atlanta, GA 30309-4530 · 404-815-6500

Christopher P. Bussert · Kilpatrick Stockton · 1100 Peachtree Street, Suite 2800 · Atlanta, GA 30309-4530 · 404-815-6500

Susan A. Cahoon · ⑩ · Kilpatrick Stockton · 1100 Peachtree Street, Suite 2800 · Atlanta, GA 30309-4530 404-815-6500

Theodore H. Davis, Jr. · Kilpatrick Stockton · 1100 Peachtree Street, Suite 2800 · Atlanta, GA 30309-4530 · 404-815-6500

Joan L. Dillon · ⑩ · Joan Dillon Law · 3522 Ashford Dunwoody Road, PMB 235 · Atlanta, GA 30319 · 404-257-1708

Martin J. Elgison · ⑩ · Alston + Bird · http://www.alston.com · One Atlantic Center · 1201 West Peachtree Street · Atlanta, GA 30309-3424 · 404-881-7000

James L. Ewing IV · ⑩ · Kilpatrick Stockton · 1100 Peachtree Street, Suite 2800 · Atlanta, GA 30309-4530 · 404-815-6500

J. D. Fleming, Jr. · ㉕ · Sutherland · http://www.sutherland.com · 999 Peachtree Street, NE · Atlanta, GA 30309-3996 · 404-853-8000

Patrick J. Flinn · Alston + Bird · http://www.alston.com · One Atlantic Center · 1201 West Peachtree Street · Atlanta, GA 30309-3424 · 404-881-7000

John P. Fry · Morris, Manning & Martin · 1600 Atlanta Financial Center · 3343 Peachtree Road, NE · Atlanta, GA 30326 · 404-233-7000

Jamie L. Greene · ⑩ · Kilpatrick Stockton · 1100 Peachtree Street, Suite 2800 · Atlanta, GA 30309-4530 · 404-815-6500

Holmes J. Hawkins III · King & Spalding · 1180 Peachtree Street, NE · Atlanta, GA 30309-3521 · 404-572-4600

Michael D. Hobbs, Jr. · Troutman Sanders · Bank of America Plaza, Suite 5200 · 600 Peachtree Street, NE · Atlanta, GA 30308-2216 · 404-885-3000

Ginabeth B. Hutchinson · Alston + Bird · http://www.alston.com · One Atlantic Center · 1201 West Peachtree Street · Atlanta, GA 30309-3424 · 404-881-7000

James D. Johnson · Swift, Currie, McGhee & Hiers · The Peachtree, Suite 300 · 1355 Peachtree Street, NE · Atlanta, GA 30309 · 404-874-8800

Gregory J. Kirsch · Ballard Spahr Andrews & Ingersoll · 999 Peachtree Street, Suite 1000 · Atlanta, GA 30309-3915 · 678-420-9300

Jeffrey R. Kuester · Thomas, Kayden, Horstemeyer & Risley · 600 Galleria Parkway, Suite 1500 · Atlanta, GA 30339-5948 · 770-933-9500

J. Rodgers Lunsford III · Smith, Gambrell & Russell · http://www.sgrlaw.com · Promenade II, Suite 3100 1230 Peachtree Street, NE · Atlanta, GA 30309-3592 · 404-815-3500

John K. McDonald · Kilpatrick Stockton · 1100 Peachtree Street, Suite 2800 · Atlanta, GA 30309-4530 · 404-815-6500

Robin L. McGrath · Alston + Bird · http://www.alston.com · One Atlantic Center · 1201 West Peachtree Street · Atlanta, GA 30309-3424 · 404-881-7000

Tina McKeon · Fish & Richardson · 1180 Peachtree Street, NE, 21st Floor · Atlanta, GA 30309 · 404-892-5005

William H. Needle · ⑩ · Ballard Spahr Andrews & Ingersoll · 999 Peachtree Street, Suite 1000 · Atlanta, GA 30309-3915 · 678-420-9300

Lawrence K. Nodine · ⑩ · Ballard Spahr Andrews & Ingersoll · 999 Peachtree Street, Suite 1000 · Atlanta, GA 30309-3915 · 678-420-9300

John L. North · Sutherland · http://www.sutherland.com · 999 Peachtree Street, NE · Atlanta, GA 30309-3996 · 404-853-8000

W. Scott Petty · King & Spalding · 1180 Peachtree Street, NE · Atlanta, GA 30309-3521 · 404-572-4600

Judith A. Powell · Kilpatrick Stockton · 1100 Peachtree Street, Suite 2800 · Atlanta, GA 30309-4530 · 404-815-6500

John S. Pratt · ⑩ · Kilpatrick Stockton · 1100 Peachtree Street, Suite 2800 · Atlanta, GA 30309-4530 · 404-815-6500

William M. Ragland, Jr. · Womble Carlyle Sandridge & Rice · One Atlantic Center, Suite 3500 · 1201 West Peachtree Street · Atlanta, GA 30309 · 404-872-7000

Courtland L. Reichman · King & Spalding · 1180 Peachtree Street, NE · Atlanta, GA 30309-3521 · 404-572-4600

Bobby Rosenbloum · Greenberg Traurig · http://www.gtlaw.com · The Forum, Suite 400 · 3290 Northside Parkway, NE · Atlanta, GA 30327 · 678-553-2100

Dean W. Russell · ⑩ · Kilpatrick Stockton · 1100 Peachtree Street, Suite 2800 · Atlanta, GA 30309-4530 · 404-815-6500

Douglas D. Salyers · Troutman Sanders · Bank of America Plaza, Suite 5200 · 600 Peachtree Street, NE · Atlanta, GA 30308-2216 · 404-885-3000

Stephen M. Schaetzel · King & Spalding · 1180 Peachtree Street, NE · Atlanta, GA 30309-3521 · 404-572-4600

Frank G. Smith III · Alston + Bird · http://www.alston.com · One Atlantic Center · 1201 West Peachtree Street · Atlanta, GA 30309-3424 · 404-881-7000

David J. Stewart · Alston + Bird · http://www.alston.com · One Atlantic Center · 1201 West Peachtree Street · Atlanta, GA 30309-3424 · 404-881-7000

Mitchell G. Stockwell · Kilpatrick Stockton · 1100 Peachtree Street, Suite 2800 · Atlanta, GA 30309-4530 404-815-6500

Jerre B. Swann · ⑩ · Kilpatrick Stockton · 1100 Peachtree Street, Suite 2800 · Atlanta, GA 30309-4530 · 404-815-6500

Roger D. Taylor · Finnegan, Henderson, Farabow, Garrett & Dunner · http://www.finnegan.com · 3500 SunTrust Plaza · 303 Peachtree Street, NE · Atlanta, GA 30308-3263 · 404-653-6400

Virginia S. Taylor · ⑩ · Kilpatrick Stockton · 1100 Peachtree Street, Suite 2800 · Atlanta, GA 30309-4530 404-815-6500

Daniel J. Warren · Sutherland · http://www.sutherland.com · 999 Peachtree Street, NE · Atlanta, GA 30309-3996 · 404-853-8000

Jeffrey E. Young · Alston + Bird · http://www.alston.com · One Atlantic Center · 1201 West Peachtree Street · Atlanta, GA 30309-3424 · 404-881-7000

INTERNATIONAL TRADE AND FINANCE LAW

Atlanta

Luis A. Aguilar · McKenna Long & Aldridge · 303 Peachtree Street, NE, Suite 5300 · Atlanta, GA 30308 404-527-4000

Timothy S. Perry · Miller & Martin · http://www.millermartin.com · 1170 Peachtree Street, NE, Suite 800 Atlanta, GA 30309-3576 · 404-962-6100

LABOR AND EMPLOYMENT LAW

Atlanta

John K. Anderson · Ogletree Deakins · http://www.ogletreedeakins.com · Bank of America Plaza, Suite 2100 · 600 Peachtree Street, NE · Atlanta, GA 30308 · 404-881-1300

R. Lawrence Ashe, Jr. · ⑩ · Ashe, Rafuse & Hill · South Tower, Suite 500 · 1355 Peachtree Street, NE · Atlanta, GA 30309-3232 · 404-253-6000

Jeffrey W. Bell · Ford & Harrison · http://www.fordharrison.com · 1275 Peachtree Street, NE, Suite 600 · Atlanta, GA 30309-3576 · 404-888-3800

William H. Boice · Kilpatrick Stockton · 1100 Peachtree Street, Suite 2800 · Atlanta, GA 30309-4530 · 404-815-6500

Richard R. Boisseau · ⑩ · Kilpatrick Stockton · 1100 Peachtree Street, Suite 2800 · Atlanta, GA 30309-4530 · 404-815-6500

Edward D. Buckley · Buckley & Klein · Atlantic Center Plaza, Suite 1100 · 1180 West Peachtree Street · Atlanta, GA 30309 · 404-781-1100

Daryl R. Buffenstein · ⑩ · Paul Hastings · 600 Peachtree Street, NE, 24th Floor · Atlanta, GA 30308 · 404-815-2400

Margaret Hutchins Campbell · Ogletree Deakins · http://www.ogletreedeakins.com · Bank of America Plaza, Suite 2100 · 600 Peachtree Street, NE · Atlanta, GA 30308 · 404-881-1300

Lisa H. Cassilly · Alston + Bird · http://www.alston.com · One Atlantic Center · 1201 West Peachtree Street · Atlanta, GA 30309-3424 · 404-881-7000

A. Craig Cleland · Ogletree Deakins · http://www.ogletreedeakins.com · Bank of America Plaza, Suite 2100 · 600 Peachtree Street, NE · Atlanta, GA 30308 · 404-881-1300

William A. Clineburg, Jr. · King & Spalding · 1180 Peachtree Street, NE · Atlanta, GA 30309-3521 · 404-572-4600

James H. Coil III · Kilpatrick Stockton · 1100 Peachtree Street, Suite 2800 · Atlanta, GA 30309-4530 · 404-815-6500

D. Gerald Coker · Ford & Harrison · http://www.fordharrison.com · 1275 Peachtree Street, NE, Suite 600 Atlanta, GA 30309-3576 · 404-888-3800

Homer L. Deakins, Jr. · ⑳ · Ogletree Deakins · http://www.ogletreedeakins.com · Bank of America Plaza, Suite 2100 · 600 Peachtree Street, NE · Atlanta, GA 30308 · 404-881-1300

Leslie A. Dent · Paul Hastings · 600 Peachtree Street, NE, 24th Floor · Atlanta, GA 30308 · 404-815-2400

L. Traywick Duffie · Hunton & Williams · Bank of America Plaza, Suite 4100 · 600 Peachtree Street, NE · Atlanta, GA 30308-2216 · 404-888-4000

James D. Fagan · ⑳ · Stanford Fagan · 1401 Peachtree Street, NE, Suite 238 · Atlanta, GA 30309 · 404-897-1000

Richard W. Gerakitis · Troutman Sanders · Bank of America Plaza, Suite 5200 · 600 Peachtree Street, NE · Atlanta, GA 30308-2216 · 404-885-3000

Patricia G. Griffith · ⑩ · Ford & Harrison · http://www.fordharrison.com · 1275 Peachtree Street, NE, Suite 600 · Atlanta, GA 30309-3576 · 404-888-3800

David C. Hagaman · ⑩ · Ford & Harrison · http://www.fordharrison.com · 1275 Peachtree Street, NE, Suite 600 · Atlanta, GA 30309-3576 · 404-888-3800

Donald B. Harden · Fisher & Phillips · http://www.laborlawyers.com · Resurgens Plaza, Suite 1500 · 945 East Paces Ferry Road · Atlanta, GA 30326 · 404-231-1400

C. Lash Harrison · ⑳ · Ford & Harrison · http://www.fordharrison.com · 1275 Peachtree Street, NE, Suite 600 · Atlanta, GA 30309-3576 · 404-888-3800

James C. Hoover · ⑩ · Ford & Harrison · http://www.fordharrison.com · 1275 Peachtree Street, NE, Suite 600 · Atlanta, GA 30309-3576 · 404-888-3800

Hunter R. Hughes III · Rogers & Hardin · 2700 International Tower · 229 Peachtree Street, NE · Atlanta, GA 30303 · 404-522-4700

Forrest W. Hunter · Alston + Bird · http://www.alston.com · One Atlantic Center · 1201 West Peachtree Street · Atlanta, GA 30309-3424 · 404-881-7000

Weyman T. Johnson, Jr. · ⑩ · Paul Hastings · 600 Peachtree Street, NE, 24th Floor · Atlanta, GA 30308 404-815-2400

Michael W. Johnston · King & Spalding · 1180 Peachtree Street, NE · Atlanta, GA 30309-3521 · 404-572-4600

Thomas J. Kassin · Ford & Harrison · http://www.fordharrison.com · 1275 Peachtree Street, NE, Suite 600 · Atlanta, GA 30309-3576 · 404-888-3800

J. Thomas Kilpatrick · Alston + Bird · http://www.alston.com · One Atlantic Center · 1201 West Peachtree Street · Atlanta, GA 30309-3424 · 404-881-7000

Ronald R. Kimzey · Ford & Harrison · http://www.fordharrison.com · 1275 Peachtree Street, NE, Suite 600 · Atlanta, GA 30309-3576 · 404-888-3800

Daniel M. Klein · Buckley & Klein · Atlantic Center Plaza, Suite 1100 · 1180 West Peachtree Street · Atlanta, GA 30309 · 404-781-1100

Michael L. Lowry · ⑩ · Ford & Harrison · http://www.fordharrison.com · 1275 Peachtree Street, NE, Suite 600 · Atlanta, GA 30309-3576 · 404-888-3800

Samuel M. Matchett · King & Spalding · 1180 Peachtree Street, NE · Atlanta, GA 30309-3521 · 404-572-4600

J. Timothy McDonald · Rogers & Hardin · 2700 International Tower · 229 Peachtree Street, NE · Atlanta, GA 30303 · 404-522-4700

C. L. McIver · Fisher & Phillips · http://www.laborlawyers.com · Resurgens Plaza, Suite 1500 · 945 East Paces Ferry Road · Atlanta, GA 30326 · 404-231-1400

John L. Monroe, Jr. · Ford & Harrison · http://www.fordharrison.com · 1275 Peachtree Street, NE, Suite 600 · Atlanta, GA 30309-3576 · 404-888-3800

A. Lee Parks · Parks, Chesin & Walbert · 75 Fourteenth Street, 26th Floor · Atlanta, GA 30309 · 404-873-8000

Penn Payne · Penn Payne · 3586 Tuxedo Park, NW · Atlanta, GA 30305 · 404-841-3295

Ann Margaret Pointer · Fisher & Phillips · http://www.laborlawyers.com · Resurgens Plaza, Suite 1500 · 945 East Paces Ferry Road · Atlanta, GA 30326 · 404-231-1400

Diane L. Prucino · Kilpatrick Stockton · 1100 Peachtree Street, Suite 2800 · Atlanta, GA 30309-4530 · 404-815-6500

Norman A. Quandt · Ford & Harrison · http://www.fordharrison.com · 1275 Peachtree Street, NE, Suite 600 · Atlanta, GA 30309-3576 · 404-888-3800

Roger K. Quillen · Fisher & Phillips · http://www.laborlawyers.com · Resurgens Plaza, Suite 1500 · 945 East Paces Ferry Road · Atlanta, GA 30326 · 404-231-1400

Nancy E. Rafuse · Ashe, Rafuse & Hill · South Tower, Suite 500 · 1355 Peachtree Street, NE · Atlanta, GA 30309-3232 · 404-253-6000

Stephen W. Riddell · Troutman Sanders · Bank of America Plaza, Suite 5200 · 600 Peachtree Street, NE · Atlanta, GA 30308-2216 · 404-885-3000

Michael E. Ross · Greenberg Traurig · http://www.gtlaw.com · The Forum, Suite 400 · 3290 Northside Parkway, NE · Atlanta, GA 30327 · 678-553-2100

Robert O. Sands · Ogletree Deakins · http://www.ogletreedeakins.com · Bank of America Plaza, Suite 2100 · 600 Peachtree Street, NE · Atlanta, GA 30308 · 404-881-1300

Lisa A. Schreter · Littler Mendelson · 3348 Peachtree Road, NE, Suite 1100 · Atlanta, GA 30326-1008 · 404-233-0330

Jeffrey A. Schwartz · Jackson Lewis · http://www.jacksonlewis.com · 1900 Marquis One Tower · 245 Peachtree Center Avenue, NE · Atlanta, GA 30303-1226 · 404-525-8200

Chad A. Shultz · Ford & Harrison · http://www.fordharrison.com · 1275 Peachtree Street, NE, Suite 600 · Atlanta, GA 30309-3576 · 404-888-3800

Frank Barry Shuster · ⓴ · Constangy, Brooks & Smith · http://www.constangy.com · 230 Peachtree Street, NW, Suite 2400 · Atlanta, GA 30303-1557 · 404-525-8622

Deborah A. Sudbury · Jones Day · 1420 Peachtree Street, NE, Suite 800 · Atlanta, GA 30309-3053 · 404-521-3939

Claude T. Sullivan · ❿ · Ford & Harrison · http://www.fordharrison.com · 1275 Peachtree Street, NE, Suite 600 · Atlanta, GA 30309-3576 · 404-888-3800

John E. Thompson · Fisher & Phillips · http://www.laborlawyers.com · Resurgens Plaza, Suite 1500 · 945 East Paces Ferry Road · Atlanta, GA 30326 · 404-231-1400

Patrick R. Tyson · Constangy, Brooks & Smith · http://www.constangy.com · 230 Peachtree Street, NW, Suite 2400 · Atlanta, GA 30303-1557 · 404-525-8622

James M. Walters · Fisher & Phillips · http://www.laborlawyers.com · Resurgens Plaza, Suite 1500 · 945 East Paces Ferry Road · Atlanta, GA 30326 · 404-231-1400

Frederick L. Warren · Ford & Harrison · http://www.fordharrison.com · 1275 Peachtree Street, NE, Suite 600 · Atlanta, GA 30309-3576 · 404-888-3800

C. Geoffrey Weirich · ❿ · Paul Hastings · 600 Peachtree Street, NE, 24th Floor · Atlanta, GA 30308 · 404-815-2400

Stanford G. Wilson · Elarbee, Thompson, Sapp & Wilson · 800 International Tower · 229 Peachtree Street, NE · Atlanta, GA 30303 · 404-659-6700

James W. Wimberly, Jr. · ⓴ · Wimberly, Lawson, Steckel, Nelson & Schneider · Lenox Towers, Suite 400 · 3400 Peachtree Road, NE · Atlanta, GA 30326 · 404-365-0900

John F. Wymer III · ❿ · Paul Hastings · 600 Peachtree Street, NE, 24th Floor · Atlanta, GA 30308 · 404-815-2400

Augusta

James B. Ellington · Hull, Towill, Norman, Barrett & Salley · SunTrust Bank Building, Suite 700 · 801 Broad Street · P.O. Box 1564 · Augusta, GA 30903-1564 · 706-722-4481

Decatur

John L. Quinn · ❿ · Nakamura, Quinn, Walls, Weaver & Davies · 3516 Covington Highway · Decatur, GA 30032 · 404-299-1211

Debra E. Schwartz · ❿ · Thompson Rollins Schwartz & Borowski · 160 Clairemont Avenue, Suite 595 · Decatur, GA 30030 · 404-377-7717

Macon

W. Melvin Haas III · Constangy, Brooks & Smith · http://www.constangy.com · 577 Mulberry Street, Suite 710 · Macon, GA 31201-1975 · 478-750-8600

Jeffrey L. Thompson · Constangy, Brooks & Smith · http://www.constangy.com · 577 Mulberry Street, Suite 710 · Macon, GA 31201-1975 · 478-750-8600

Savannah

Wade W. Herring II · Hunter Maclean · http://www.huntermaclean.com · 200 East Saint Julian Street · P.O. Box 9848 · Savannah, GA 31412-0048 · 912-236-0261

LAND USE & ZONING LAW

Atlanta

G. Douglas Dillard · Dillard & Galloway · 3500 Lenox Road, NE, Suite 760 · Atlanta, GA 30326 · 404-965-3680

Larry M. Dingle · Wilson Brock & Irby · Overlook I, Suite 700 · 2849 Paces Ferry Road · Atlanta, GA 30339 · 404-853-5050

David H. Flint · Schreeder, Wheeler & Flint · 1100 Peachtree Street, Suite 800 · Atlanta, GA 30309 · 404-681-3450

William Woodson Galloway · Dillard & Galloway · 3500 Lenox Road, NE, Suite 760 · Atlanta, GA 30326 · 404-965-3680

James M. Ney · ㉕ · Holt Ney Zatcoff & Wasserman · 100 Galleria Parkway, Suite 600 · Atlanta, GA 30339 · 770-956-9600

Charles F. Palmer · Troutman Sanders · Bank of America Plaza, Suite 5200 · 600 Peachtree Street, NE · Atlanta, GA 30308-2216 · 404-885-3000

T. Michael Tennant · Alston + Bird · http://www.alston.com · One Atlantic Center · 1201 West Peachtree Street · Atlanta, GA 30309-3424 · 404-881-7000

Carl E. Westmoreland, Jr. · Seyfarth Shaw · One Peachtree Pointe, Suite 700 · 1545 Peachtree Street, NE · Atlanta, GA 30309-2401 · 404-885-1500

Richard W. Wilson, Jr. · Wilson Brock & Irby · Overlook I, Suite 700 · 2849 Paces Ferry Road · Atlanta, GA 30339 · 404-853-5050

Kathryn M. Zickert · Smith, Gambrell & Russell · http://www.sgrlaw.com · Promenade II, Suite 3100 · 1230 Peachtree Street, NE · Atlanta, GA 30309-3592 · 404-815-3500

Conyers

Robert L. Zoeckler · Maddox, Nix, Bowman & Zoeckler · 945 Bank Street · P.O. Drawer 1017 · Conyers, GA 30012-1017 · 770-922-7700

Macon

Robert C. Norman, Jr. · Jones, Cork & Miller · SunTrust Bank Building, Fifth Floor · 435 Second Street P.O. Box 6437 · Macon, GA 31208-6437 · 478-745-2821

Marietta

John H. Moore · Moore, Ingram, Johnson & Steele · 192 Anderson Street · P.O. Box 3305 · Marietta, GA 30061-3305 · 770-429-1499

Garvis L. Sams, Jr. · Sams, Larkin & Huff · 376 Powder Springs Street, Suite 100 · Marietta, GA 30064 · 770-422-7016

Savannah

Harold B. Yellin · Hunter Maclean · http://www.huntermaclean.com · 200 East Saint Julian Street · P.O. Box 9848 · Savannah, GA 31412-0048 · 912-236-0261

LEGAL MALPRACTICE LAW

Atlanta

Frank J. Beltran · ⑩ · Beltran & Chandler · Atlantic Center Plaza, Suite 2450 · 1180 West Peachtree Street · Atlanta, GA 30309 · 404-892-3100

Steven M. Collins · Alston + Bird · http://www.alston.com · One Atlantic Center · 1201 West Peachtree Street · Atlanta, GA 30309-3424 · 404-881-7000

J. Randolph Evans · ⑩ · McKenna Long & Aldridge · 303 Peachtree Street, NE, Suite 5300 · Atlanta, GA 30308 · 404-527-4000

John H. Fleming · Sutherland · http://www.sutherland.com · 999 Peachtree Street, NE · Atlanta, GA 30309-3996 · 404-853-8000

James C. Grant · Alston + Bird · http://www.alston.com · One Atlantic Center · 1201 West Peachtree Street · Atlanta, GA 30309-3424 · 404-881-7000

Johannes S. Kingma · Carlock, Copeland, Semler & Stair · 2600 Marquis Two Tower · 285 Peachtree Center Avenue · Atlanta, GA 30303-1235 · 404-522-8220

Daryll Love · ⑩ · Troutman Sanders · Bank of America Plaza, Suite 5200 · 600 Peachtree Street, NE · Atlanta, GA 30308-2216 · 404-885-3000

John T. Marshall · ㉕ · Powell Goldstein · http://www.pogolaw.com · One Atlantic Center, 14th Floor · 1201 West Peachtree Street, NE · Atlanta, GA 30309 · 404-572-6600

Daniel S. Reinhardt · Troutman Sanders · Bank of America Plaza, Suite 5200 · 600 Peachtree Street, NE · Atlanta, GA 30308-2216 · 404-885-3000

Jeffrey M. Smith · ⑩ · Greenberg Traurig · http://www.gtlaw.com · The Forum, Suite 400 · 3290 Northside Parkway, NE · Atlanta, GA 30327 · 678-553-2100

H. Lane Young II · Hawkins & Parnell · 4000 SunTrust Plaza, 40th Floor · 303 Peachtree Street, NE · Atlanta, GA 30308-3243 · 404-614-7400

Augusta

George R. Hall · Hull, Towill, Norman, Barrett & Salley · SunTrust Bank Building, Suite 700 · 801 Broad Street · P.O. Box 1564 · Augusta, GA 30903-1564 · 706-722-4481

Savannah

Patrick T. O'Connor · ⑩ · Oliver Maner · http://www.olivermaner.com · 218 West State Street · P.O. Box 10186 · Savannah, GA 31412 · 912-236-3311

LEVERAGED BUYOUTS AND PRIVATE EQUITY LAW

Atlanta

Bert Adams · Sutherland · http://www.sutherland.com · 999 Peachtree Street, NE · Atlanta, GA 30309-3996 · 404-853-8000

John D. Capers, Jr. · King & Spalding · 1180 Peachtree Street, NE · Atlanta, GA 30309-3521 · 404-572-4600

B. Knox Dobbins · ⑩ · Sutherland · http://www.sutherland.com · 999 Peachtree Street, NE · Atlanta, GA 30309-3996 · 404-853-8000

Michael J. Egan III · King & Spalding · 1180 Peachtree Street, NE · Atlanta, GA 30309-3521 · 404-572-4600

Sidney J. Nurkin · ⑳ · Alston + Bird · http://www.alston.com · One Atlantic Center · 1201 West Peachtree Street · Atlanta, GA 30309-3424 · 404-881-7000

Russell B. Richards · ⑩ · King & Spalding · 1180 Peachtree Street, NE · Atlanta, GA 30309-3521 · 404-572-4600

Lynn S. Scott · King & Spalding · 1180 Peachtree Street, NE · Atlanta, GA 30309-3521 · 404-572-4600

Wade H. Stribling · Sutherland · http://www.sutherland.com · 999 Peachtree Street, NE · Atlanta, GA 30309-3996 · 404-853-8000

MARITIME LAW

Savannah

T. Langston Bass, Jr. · Brennan, Harris & Rominger · Two East Bryan Street, Suite 1300 · P.O. Box 2784 Savannah, GA 31402 · 912-233-3399

Robert S. Glenn, Jr. · ⑩ · Hunter Maclean · http://www.huntermaclean.com · 200 East Saint Julian Street · P.O. Box 9848 · Savannah, GA 31412-0048 · 912-236-0261

Walter C. Hartridge · ⑩ · Bouhan, Williams & Levy · http://www.bouhan.com · The Armstrong House · 447 Bull Street · P.O. Box 2139 · Savannah, GA 31402-2139 · 912-236-2491

Barnard M. Portman · Portman and Associates · P.O. Box 9087 · Savannah, GA 31401-9087 · 912-233-4175

Charles H. Raley · Raley & Raley · http://www.raleylawfirm.com · 9100 White Bluff Road, Suite 304 · P.O. Box 13488 · Savannah, GA 31416 · 912-925-9991

Edwin D. Robb, Jr. · ⑩ · Bouhan, Williams & Levy · http://www.bouhan.com · The Armstrong House · 447 Bull Street · P.O. Box 2139 · Savannah, GA 31402-2139 · 912-236-2491

David F. Sipple · ⑩ · Hunter Maclean · http://www.huntermaclean.com · 200 East Saint Julian Street · P.O. Box 9848 · Savannah, GA 31412-0048 · 912-236-0261

MASS TORT LITIGATION

Atlanta

Michael J. Bowers · Balch & Bingham · http://www.balch.com · 30 Ivan Allen, Jr. Boulevard, NW, Suite 700 · Atlanta, GA 30308 · 404-261-6020

Lori G. Cohen · Greenberg Traurig · http://www.gtlaw.com · The Forum, Suite 400 · 3290 Northside Parkway, NE · Atlanta, GA 30327 · 678-553-2100

Dwight J. Davis · King & Spalding · 1180 Peachtree Street, NE · Atlanta, GA 30309-3521 · 404-572-4600

N. Karen Deming · (10) · Troutman Sanders · Bank of America Plaza, Suite 5200 · 600 Peachtree Street, NE · Atlanta, GA 30308-2216 · 404-885-3000

C. Michael Evert, Jr. · Evert Weathersby Houff · http://www.ewhlaw.com · 3405 Piedmont Road, NE, Suite 200 · Atlanta, GA 30305 · 678-651-1200

William B. Hill, Jr. · Ashe, Rafuse & Hill · South Tower, Suite 500 · 1355 Peachtree Street, NE · Atlanta, GA 30309-3232 · 404-253-6000

Michael P. Kenny · Alston + Bird · http://www.alston.com · One Atlantic Center · 1201 West Peachtree Street · Atlanta, GA 30309-3424 · 404-881-7000

James A. Langlais · Alston + Bird · http://www.alston.com · One Atlantic Center · 1201 West Peachtree Street · Atlanta, GA 30309-3424 · 404-881-7000

Meghan Magruder · King & Spalding · 1180 Peachtree Street, NE · Atlanta, GA 30309-3521 · 404-572-4600

Laura Lewis Owens · Alston + Bird · http://www.alston.com · One Atlantic Center · 1201 West Peachtree Street · Atlanta, GA 30309-3424 · 404-881-7000

Stephanie E. Parker · Jones Day · 1420 Peachtree Street, NE, Suite 800 · Atlanta, GA 30309-3053 · 404-521-3939

Albert H. Parnell · (20) · Hawkins & Parnell · 4000 SunTrust Plaza, 40th Floor · 303 Peachtree Street, NE · Atlanta, GA 30308-3243 · 404-614-7400

W. Ray Persons · King & Spalding · 1180 Peachtree Street, NE · Atlanta, GA 30309-3521 · 404-572-4600

Richard A. Schneider · King & Spalding · 1180 Peachtree Street, NE · Atlanta, GA 30309-3521 · 404-572-4600

Bernard Taylor, Sr. · Alston + Bird · http://www.alston.com · One Atlantic Center · 1201 West Peachtree Street · Atlanta, GA 30309-3424 · 404-881-7000

Jane F. Thorpe · Alston + Bird · http://www.alston.com · One Atlantic Center · 1201 West Peachtree Street · Atlanta, GA 30309-3424 · 404-881-7000

Chilton D. Varner · (10) · King & Spalding · 1180 Peachtree Street, NE · Atlanta, GA 30309-3521 · 404-572-4600

H. Lane Young II · Hawkins & Parnell · 4000 SunTrust Plaza, 40th Floor · 303 Peachtree Street, NE · Atlanta, GA 30308-3243 · 404-614-7400

Marietta

Roy E. Barnes · The Barnes Law Group · 31 Atlanta Street · Marietta, GA 30060 · 770-227-6375

MEDICAL MALPRACTICE LAW

Athens

Gary B. Blasingame · ⑩ · Blasingame, Burch, Garrard & Ashley · http://www.bbgbalaw.com · 440 College Avenue North · P.O. Box 832 · Athens, GA 30603 · 706-354-4000

Henry G. Garrard III · ⑩ · Blasingame, Burch, Garrard & Ashley · http://www.bbgbalaw.com · 440 College Avenue North · P.O. Box 832 · Athens, GA 30603 · 706-354-4000

Atlanta

William L. Ballard · Scherffius, Ballard Still & Ayres · 400 Colony Square, Suite 1018 · 1201 Peachtree Street, NE · Atlanta, GA 30361 · 404-496-5628

William Q. Bird · ⑳ · Bird Law Group · 2170 DefoorHills Road · P.O. Box 19919 · Atlanta, GA 30325 · 404-873-4696

Alexander H. Booth · Hall Booth Smith & Slover · Atlantic Center Plaza, Suite 900 · 1180 West Peachtree, NW · Atlanta, GA 30309 · 404-954-5000

Lori G. Cohen · Greenberg Traurig · http://www.gtlaw.com · The Forum, Suite 400 · 3290 Northside Parkway, NE · Atlanta, GA 30327 · 678-553-2100

Philip C. Henry · ⑩ · Henry Spiegel Milling · 950 East Paces Ferry Road, Suite 2450 · Atlanta, GA 30326 404-832-8000

Thomas William Malone · ⑳ · Malone Law · http://www.malonepc.com · Two Ravinia Drive, Suite 300 · Atlanta, GA 30346 · 770-390-7550

James B. Matthews III · ⑩ · Matthews, Steel & Moss · 15 Piedmont Center, Suite 1560 · 3575 Piedmont Road, NE · Atlanta, GA 30305 · 404-264-1292

William Usher Norwood III · ⑩ · Pope, McGlamry, Kilpatrick, Morrison & Norwood · The Pinnacle, Suite 925 · 3455 Peachtree Road, NE · P.O. Box 191625 · Atlanta, GA 31119-1625 · 404-523-7706

Jonathan C. Peters, Jr. · Peters & Monyak · One Atlanta Plaza, Suite 2275 · 950 East Paces Ferry Road · Atlanta, GA 30326 · 404-607-0100

Jack G. Slover, Jr. · Hall Booth Smith & Slover · Atlantic Center Plaza, Suite 900 · 1180 West Peachtree, NW · Atlanta, GA 30309 · 404-954-5000

Bernard Taylor, Sr. · Alston + Bird · http://www.alston.com · One Atlantic Center · 1201 West Peachtree Street · Atlanta, GA 30309-3424 · 404-881-7000

Joseph W. Watkins · Watkins, Lourie, Roll & Chance · Tower Place 200, Suite 1050 · 3348 Peachtree Road, NE · Atlanta, GA 30326-1008 · 404-760-7400

Augusta

James V. Painter · Hull, Towill, Norman, Barrett & Salley · SunTrust Bank Building, Suite 700 · 801 Broad Street · P.O. Box 1564 · Augusta, GA 30903-1564 · 706-722-4481

Carrollton

David H. Tisinger · ⑳ · Tisinger Vance · 100 Wagon Yard Plaza · P.O. Box 2069 · Carrollton, GA 30117-2069 · 770-834-4467

Columbus

James E. Butler, Jr. · ⑳ · Butler, Wooten, Fryhofer, Daughtery & Sullivan · 105 Thirteenth Street · P.O. Box 2766 · Columbus, GA 31902 · 706-322-1990

Gainesville

Weymon H. Forrester · ⑩ · Forrester & Brim · 459 E.E. Butler Parkway, SE · P.O. Box 1688 · Gainesville, GA 30503-1688 · 770-531-0800

Macon

Thomas C. Alexander · Jones, Cork & Miller · SunTrust Bank Building, Fifth Floor · 435 Second Street · P.O. Box 6437 · Macon, GA 31208-6437 · 478-745-2821

Manley F. Brown · ⑩ · O'Neal, Brown & Clark · American Federal Building, Suite 1001 · 544 Mulberry Street · Macon, GA 31201 · 478-742-8981

R. William Buzzell · Buzzell, Graham & Welsh · 563 Walnut Street · Macon, GA 31201 · 478-742-8820

John C. Edwards · ⑩ · Martin Snow · http://www.martinsnow.com · 240 Third Street · P.O. Box 1606 · Macon, GA 31202-1606 · 478-749-1700

Savannah

Frederick S. Bergen · Bergen & Bergen · Marist Place Lafayette Square · 123 Charlton Street, East · Savannah, GA 31401-4603 · 912-233-6600

William P. Franklin, Jr. · ⑩ · Oliver Maner · http://www.olivermaner.com · 218 West State Street · P.O. Box 10186 · Savannah, GA 31412 · 912-236-3311

Kirby G. Mason · Hunter Maclean · http://www.huntermaclean.com · 200 East Saint Julian Street · P.O. Box 9848 · Savannah, GA 31412-0048 · 912-236-0261

Christopher L. Ray · Oliver Maner · http://www.olivermaner.com · 218 West State Street · P.O. Box 10186 · Savannah, GA 31412 · 912-236-3311

Frank W. Seiler · ㉕ · Bouhan, Williams & Levy · http://www.bouhan.com · The Armstrong House · 447 Bull Street · P.O. Box 2139 · Savannah, GA 31402-2139 · 912-236-2491

MERGERS & ACQUISITIONS LAW

Atlanta

Bert Adams · Sutherland · http://www.sutherland.com · 999 Peachtree Street, NE · Atlanta, GA 30309-3996 · 404-853-8000

Carolyn Z. Alford · King & Spalding · 1180 Peachtree Street, NE · Atlanta, GA 30309-3521 · 404-572-4600

Raymond E. Baltz, Jr. · King & Spalding · 1180 Peachtree Street, NE · Atlanta, GA 30309-3521 · 404-572-4600

W. Benjamin Barkley · Kilpatrick Stockton · 1100 Peachtree Street, Suite 2800 · Atlanta, GA 30309-4530 404-815-6500

C. William Baxley · King & Spalding · 1180 Peachtree Street, NE · Atlanta, GA 30309-3521 · 404-572-4600

W. Stanley Blackburn · Kilpatrick Stockton · 1100 Peachtree Street, Suite 2800 · Atlanta, GA 30309-4530 404-815-6500

Wayne N. Bradley · McKenna Long & Aldridge · 303 Peachtree Street, NE, Suite 5300 · Atlanta, GA 30308 · 404-527-4000

Janine Brown · Alston + Bird · http://www.alston.com · One Atlantic Center · 1201 West Peachtree Street Atlanta, GA 30309-3424 · 404-881-7000

John D. Capers, Jr. · King & Spalding · 1180 Peachtree Street, NE · Atlanta, GA 30309-3521 · 404-572-4600

Richard Cicchillo, Jr. · Kilpatrick Stockton · 1100 Peachtree Street, Suite 2800 · Atlanta, GA 30309-4530 404-815-6500

Paul J. Cox · ⑩ · Hartman, Simons, Spielman & Wood · 6400 Powers Ferry Road, NW, Suite 400 · Atlanta, GA 30339 · 770-955-3555

J. Vaughan Curtis · ⑩ · Alston + Bird · http://www.alston.com · One Atlantic Center · 1201 West Peachtree Street · Atlanta, GA 30309-3424 · 404-881-7000

Bryan E. Davis · Jones Day · 1420 Peachtree Street, NE, Suite 800 · Atlanta, GA 30309-3053 · 404-521-3939

Michael J. Egan III · King & Spalding · 1180 Peachtree Street, NE · Atlanta, GA 30309-3521 · 404-572-4600

Jonathan Golden · ⑩ · Arnall Golden Gregory · 171 Seventeenth Street, NW, Suite 2100 · Atlanta, GA 30363-1031 · 404-873-8500

Robert W. Grout · Troutman Sanders · Bank of America Plaza, Suite 5200 · 600 Peachtree Street, NE · Atlanta, GA 30308-2216 · 404-885-3000

Jon R. Harris, Jr. · ⑩ · King & Spalding · 1180 Peachtree Street, NE · Atlanta, GA 30309-3521 · 404-572-4600

Thomas C. Herman · Sutherland · http://www.sutherland.com · 999 Peachtree Street, NE · Atlanta, GA 30309-3996 · 404-853-8000

M. Hill Jeffries · Alston + Bird · http://www.alston.com · One Atlantic Center · 1201 West Peachtree Street · Atlanta, GA 30309-3424 · 404-881-7000

Mark D. Kaufman · Sutherland · http://www.sutherland.com · 999 Peachtree Street, NE · Atlanta, GA 30309-3996 · 404-853-8000

Frank Layson · Paul Hastings · 600 Peachtree Street, NE, 24th Floor · Atlanta, GA 30308 · 404-815-2400

Alan C. Leet · Rogers & Hardin · 2700 International Tower · 229 Peachtree Street, NE · Atlanta, GA 30303 · 404-522-4700

Teri Lynn McMahon · Alston + Bird · http://www.alston.com · One Atlantic Center · 1201 West Peachtree Street · Atlanta, GA 30309-3424 · 404-881-7000

Thomas R. McNeill · Powell Goldstein · http://www.pogolaw.com · One Atlantic Center, 14th Floor · 1201 West Peachtree Street, NE · Atlanta, GA 30309 · 404-572-6600

Rick Miller · Powell Goldstein · http://www.pogolaw.com · One Atlantic Center, 14th Floor · 1201 West Peachtree Street, NE · Atlanta, GA 30309 · 404-572-6600

Walter G. Moeling IV · ⑩ · Powell Goldstein · http://www.pogolaw.com · One Atlantic Center, 14th Floor · 1201 West Peachtree Street, NE · Atlanta, GA 30309 · 404-572-6600

F. Donald Nelms, Jr. · Powell Goldstein · http://www.pogolaw.com · One Atlantic Center, 14th Floor · 1201 West Peachtree Street, NE · Atlanta, GA 30309 · 404-572-6600

Sidney J. Nurkin · ⑳ · Alston + Bird · http://www.alston.com · One Atlantic Center · 1201 West Peachtree Street · Atlanta, GA 30309-3424 · 404-881-7000

Reinaldo Pascual · Paul Hastings · 600 Peachtree Street, NE, 24th Floor · Atlanta, GA 30308 · 404-815-2400

Robert J. Pile · Sutherland · http://www.sutherland.com · 999 Peachtree Street, NE · Atlanta, GA 30309-3996 · 404-853-8000

Steven L. Pottle · ⑩ · Alston + Bird · http://www.alston.com · One Atlantic Center · 1201 West Peachtree Street · Atlanta, GA 30309-3424 · 404-881-7000

Russell B. Richards · ⑩ · King & Spalding · 1180 Peachtree Street, NE · Atlanta, GA 30309-3521 · 404-572-4600

William B. Rowland · Jones Day · 1420 Peachtree Street, NE, Suite 800 · Atlanta, GA 30309-3053 · 404-521-3939

William B. Shearer, Jr. · Powell Goldstein · http://www.pogolaw.com · One Atlantic Center, 14th Floor · 1201 West Peachtree Street, NE · Atlanta, GA 30309 · 404-572-6600

William Calvin Smith · Troutman Sanders · Bank of America Plaza, Suite 5200 · 600 Peachtree Street, NE · Atlanta, GA 30308-2216 · 404-885-3000

MUNICIPAL LAW

Atlanta

Theodore Freeman · Freeman Mathis & Gary · 100 Galleria Parkway, Suite 1600 · Atlanta, GA 30339-5948 · 770-818-0000

Dana K. Maine · Freeman Mathis & Gary · 100 Galleria Parkway, Suite 1600 · Atlanta, GA 30339-5948 · 770-818-0000

Philip W. Savrin · Freeman Mathis & Gary · 100 Galleria Parkway, Suite 1600 · Atlanta, GA 30339-5948 · 770-818-0000

Matthew P. Stone · Freeman Mathis & Gary · 100 Galleria Parkway, Suite 1600 · Atlanta, GA 30339-5948 770-818-0000

Savannah

Patrick T. O'Connor · ⑩ · Oliver Maner · http://www.olivermaner.com · 218 West State Street · P.O. Box 10186 · Savannah, GA 31412 · 912-236-3311

R. Clay Ratterree · ⑩ · Ellis, Painter, Ratterree & Adams · http://www.epra-law.com · Johnson Square Business Center, 10th Floor · Two East Bryan Street · P.O. Box 9946 · Savannah, GA 31412 · 912-233-9700

NATURAL RESOURCES LAW

Atlanta

Lee A. DeHihns III · ⑩ · Alston + Bird · http://www.alston.com · One Atlantic Center · 1201 West Peachtree Street · Atlanta, GA 30309-3424 · 404-881-7000

Cada T. Kilgore III · Cada T. Kilgore, III, Attorney at Law · 3280 Northside Parkway, Suite 613 · Atlanta, GA 30327 · 404-275-3948

Della Wager Wells · Alston + Bird · http://www.alston.com · One Atlantic Center · 1201 West Peachtree Street · Atlanta, GA 30309-3424 · 404-881-7000

NON-PROFIT/CHARITIES LAW

Atlanta

Stephanie Casteel · King & Spalding · 1180 Peachtree Street, NE · Atlanta, GA 30309-3521 · 404-572-4600

James K. Hasson, Jr. · ⑳ · Sutherland · http://www.sutherland.com · 999 Peachtree Street, NE · Atlanta, GA 30309-3996 · 404-853-8000

Zoe M. Hicks · ⑩ · Hicks & Hicks · 1907 Mercedes Court · Atlanta, GA 30345-2739 · 404-788-1719

W. Marshall Sanders · Alston + Bird · http://www.alston.com · One Atlantic Center · 1201 West Peachtree Street · Atlanta, GA 30309-3424 · 404-881-7000

Wayne R. Vason · ⑳ · Troutman Sanders · Bank of America Plaza, Suite 5200 · 600 Peachtree Street, NE Atlanta, GA 30308-2216 · 404-885-3000

Benjamin T. White · ⑳ · Alston + Bird · http://www.alston.com · One Atlantic Center · 1201 West Peachtree Street · Atlanta, GA 30309-3424 · 404-881-7000

Columbus

Alan F. Rothschild, Jr. · Hatcher, Stubbs, Land, Hollis & Rothschild · http://www.hatcherstubbs.com · The Corporate Center, Suite 500 · 233 Twelfth Street · P.O. Box 2707 · Columbus, GA 31902-2707 · 706-324-0201

NON-WHITE-COLLAR CRIMINAL DEFENSE

Athens

Edward D. Tolley · ⑳ · Cook, Noell, Tolley, Bates & Michael · 304 East Washington Street · P.O. Box 1927 · Athens, GA 30603-1927 · 706-549-6111

Atlanta

Stephen B. Bright · ⑩ · Southern Center for Human Rights · 83 Poplar Street, NW · Atlanta, GA 30303-2122 · 404-688-1202

Jerome J. Froelich, Jr. · ⑳ · McKenney & Froelich · Two Midtown Plaza, Suite 1250 · 1349 West Peachtree Street, NW · Atlanta, GA 30309-2920 · 404-881-1111

Edward T. M. Garland · 25 · Garland, Samuel & Loeb · 3151 Maple Drive, NE · Atlanta, GA 30305 · 404-262-2225

Craig A. Gillen · Gillen Cromwell Withers & Brantley · One Securities Centre, Suite 1050 · 3490 Piedmont Road, NE · Atlanta, GA 30305 · 404-842-9700

John R. Martin · 20 · Martin Brothers · The Grant Building, Suite 500 · 44 Broad Street, NW · Atlanta, GA 30303-2327 · 404-522-0400

Wilmer Parker · Maloy Jenkins Parker · 75 Fourteenth Street, NW, 25th Floor · Atlanta, GA 30309 · 404-875-2700

Steven H. Sadow · 10 · Steven H. Sadow · 260 Peachtree St., N.W., Suite 2502 · Atlanta, GA 30303 · 404-577-1400

Donald F. Samuel · 10 · Garland, Samuel & Loeb · 3151 Maple Drive, NE · Atlanta, GA 30305 · 404-262-2225

Augusta

Michael C. Garrett · 10 · Garrett, Gilliard & Saul · 699 Broad Street, Suite 1010 · Augusta, GA 30901 · 706-724-1896

Columbus

Frank K. Martin · The Martin Firm · The Corporate Center, Suite 809 · 233 Twelfth Street · P.O. Box 1436 · Columbus, GA 31902 · 706-324-7371

Decatur

Douglas N. Peters · Peters, Roberts, Reynolds & Rubin · 2786 North Decatur Road, Suite 245 · Decatur, GA 30033 · 404-296-5300

Summerville

Bobby Lee Cook · 25 · Cook & Connelly · 128 South Commerce Street · P.O. Box 370 · Summerville, GA 30747-1339 · 706-857-3421

Valdosta

J. Converse Bright · 20 · J. Converse Bright · http://www.conversebright.com · The McKey Building, Fourth Floor · 101 East Central Avenue · P.O. Box 5889 · Valdosta, GA 31603 · 229-247-7846

PERSONAL INJURY LITIGATION

Athens

Gary B. Blasingame · 10 · Blasingame, Burch, Garrard & Ashley · http://www.bbgbalaw.com · 440 College Avenue North · P.O. Box 832 · Athens, GA 30603 · 706-354-4000

E. Davison Burch · 10 · Blasingame, Burch, Garrard & Ashley · http://www.bbgbalaw.com · 440 College Avenue North · P.O. Box 832 · Athens, GA 30603 · 706-354-4000

J. Vincent Cook · Cook, Noell, Tolley, Bates & Michael · 304 East Washington Street · P.O. Box 1927 · Athens, GA 30603-1927 · 706-549-6111

Henry G. Garrard III · ⑩ · Blasingame, Burch, Garrard & Ashley · http://www.bbgbalaw.com · 440 College Avenue North · P.O. Box 832 · Athens, GA 30603 · 706-354-4000

Andrew J. Hill III · Blasingame, Burch, Garrard & Ashley · http://www.bbgbalaw.com · 440 College Avenue North · P.O. Box 832 · Athens, GA 30603 · 706-354-4000

David R. Montgomery · Hudson, Montgomery & Kalivoda · 183 West Clayton Street · P.O. Box 8068 · Athens, GA 30603 · 706-549-9823

Atlanta

Alfred B. Adams III · Holland & Knight · http://www.hklaw.com · One Atlantic Center, Suite 2000 · 1201 West Peachtree Street, NE · Atlanta, GA 30309-3400 · 404-817-8500

William D. Barwick · Sutherland · http://www.sutherland.com · 999 Peachtree Street, NE · Atlanta, GA 30309-3996 · 404-853-8000

Andrew T. Bayman · King & Spalding · 1180 Peachtree Street, NE · Atlanta, GA 30309-3521 · 404-572-4600

William Q. Bird · ⑳ · Bird Law Group · 2170 DefoorHills Road · P.O. Box 19919 · Atlanta, GA 30325 · 404-873-4696

Thomas B. Branch III · Holland & Knight · http://www.hklaw.com · One Atlantic Center, Suite 2000 · 1201 West Peachtree Street, NE · Atlanta, GA 30309-3400 · 404-817-8500

Thomas S. Carlock · ⑩ · Carlock, Copeland, Semler & Stair · 2600 Marquis Two Tower · 285 Peachtree Center Avenue · Atlanta, GA 30303-1235 · 404-522-8220

W. Pitts Carr · ⑩ · Carr & Palmer · 10 North Parkway Square · 4200 Northside Parkway, NW · Atlanta, GA 30327 · 404-442-9000

Lori G. Cohen · Greenberg Traurig · http://www.gtlaw.com · The Forum, Suite 400 · 3290 Northside Parkway, NE · Atlanta, GA 30327 · 678-553-2100

N. Karen Deming · ⑩ · Troutman Sanders · Bank of America Plaza, Suite 5200 · 600 Peachtree Street, NE · Atlanta, GA 30308-2216 · 404-885-3000

Foy R. Devine · ⑳ · Doffermyre, Shields, Canfield, Knowles & Devine · 1355 Peachtree Street, Suite 1600 · Atlanta, GA 30309 · 404-881-8900

Michael G. Frick · Hall Booth Smith & Slover · Atlantic Center Plaza, Suite 900 · 1180 West Peachtree, NW · Atlanta, GA 30309 · 404-954-5000

Michael J. Goldman · Hawkins & Parnell · 4000 SunTrust Plaza, 40th Floor · 303 Peachtree Street, NE · Atlanta, GA 30308-3243 · 404-614-7400

Judson Graves · Alston + Bird · http://www.alston.com · One Atlantic Center · 1201 West Peachtree Street · Atlanta, GA 30309-3424 · 404-881-7000

John Hall · Hall Booth Smith & Slover · Atlantic Center Plaza, Suite 900 · 1180 West Peachtree, NW · Atlanta, GA 30309 · 404-954-5000

Robert D. Hays, Jr. · King & Spalding · 1180 Peachtree Street, NE · Atlanta, GA 30309-3521 · 404-572-4600

Philip C. Henry · ⑩ · Henry Spiegel Milling · 950 East Paces Ferry Road, Suite 2450 · Atlanta, GA 30326 404-832-8000

Alan F. Herman · Hawkins & Parnell · 4000 SunTrust Plaza, 40th Floor · 303 Peachtree Street, NE · Atlanta, GA 30308-3243 · 404-614-7400

Richard K. Hines V · ⑩ · Nelson Mullins Riley & Scarborough · Atlantic Station, Suite 1700 · 201 Seventeenth Street, NW · Atlanta, GA 30363 · 404-817-6000

A. Timothy Jones · ⑩ · Hawkins & Parnell · 4000 SunTrust Plaza, 40th Floor · 303 Peachtree Street, NE Atlanta, GA 30308-3243 · 404-614-7400

Glenn E. Kushel · Moraitakis, Kushel, Pearson & Gardner · 3445 Peachtree Road, NE, Suite 425 · Atlanta, GA 30326-3239 · 404-261-0016

William C. Lanham · ⑳ · Johnson & Ward · The Equitable Building, Suite 2100 · 100 Peachtree Street, NW · Atlanta, GA 30303-1912 · 404-524-5626

Peter A. Law · Peter A. Law · Tower Place 100, Suite 1530 · 3340 Peachtree Road, NE · Atlanta, GA 30326 · 404-814-3700

Daryll Love · ⑩ · Troutman Sanders · Bank of America Plaza, Suite 5200 · 600 Peachtree Street, NE · Atlanta, GA 30308-2216 · 404-885-3000

William H. Major III · Hawkins & Parnell · 4000 SunTrust Plaza, 40th Floor · 303 Peachtree Street, NE · Atlanta, GA 30308-3243 · 404-614-7400

Thomas William Malone · ⑳ · Malone Law · http://www.malonepc.com · Two Ravinia Drive, Suite 300 · Atlanta, GA 30346 · 770-390-7550

John T. Marshall · ㉕ · Powell Goldstein · http://www.pogolaw.com · One Atlantic Center, 14th Floor · 1201 West Peachtree Street, NE · Atlanta, GA 30309 · 404-572-6600

James B. Matthews III · ⑩ · Matthews, Steel & Moss · 15 Piedmont Center, Suite 1560 · 3575 Piedmont Road, NE · Atlanta, GA 30305 · 404-264-1292

James T. McDonald, Jr. · Swift, Currie, McGhee & Hiers · The Peachtree, Suite 300 · 1355 Peachtree Street, NE · Atlanta, GA 30309 · 404-874-8800

Wayne D. Mcgrew · Carlock, Copeland, Semler & Stair · 2600 Marquis Two Tower · 285 Peachtree Center Avenue · Atlanta, GA 30303-1235 · 404-522-8220

James Dartlin Meadows · Balch & Bingham · http://www.balch.com · 30 Ivan Allen, Jr. Boulevard, NW, Suite 700 · Atlanta, GA 30308 · 404-261-6020

Nicholas C. Moraitakis · Moraitakis, Kushel, Pearson & Gardner · 3445 Peachtree Road, NE, Suite 425 · Atlanta, GA 30326-3239 · 404-261-0016

William Usher Norwood III · ⑩ · Pope, McGlamry, Kilpatrick, Morrison & Norwood · The Pinnacle, Suite 925 · 3455 Peachtree Road, NE · P.O. Box 191625 · Atlanta, GA 31119-1625 · 404-523-7706

Albert H. Parnell · ⑳ · Hawkins & Parnell · 4000 SunTrust Plaza, 40th Floor · 303 Peachtree Street, NE · Atlanta, GA 30308-3243 · 404-614-7400

Albert M. Pearson III · ⑩ · Moraitakis, Kushel, Pearson & Gardner · 3445 Peachtree Road, NE, Suite 425 · Atlanta, GA 30326-3239 · 404-261-0016

Jonathan C. Peters, Jr. · Peters & Monyak · One Atlanta Plaza, Suite 2275 · 950 East Paces Ferry Road · Atlanta, GA 30326 · 404-607-0100

Elizabeth A. Price · Alston + Bird · http://www.alston.com · One Atlantic Center · 1201 West Peachtree Street · Atlanta, GA 30309-3424 · 404-881-7000

Thomas G. Sampson II · ⑩ · Thomas, Kennedy, Sampson & Patterson · 3355 Main Street · Atlanta, GA 30337 · 404-688-4503

Richard A. Schneider · King & Spalding · 1180 Peachtree Street, NE · Atlanta, GA 30309-3521 · 404-572-4600

Robert E. Shields · Doffermyre, Shields, Canfield, Knowles & Devine · 1355 Peachtree Street, Suite 1600 · Atlanta, GA 30309 · 404-881-8900

John D. Steel · Matthews, Steel & Moss · 15 Piedmont Center, Suite 1560 · 3575 Piedmont Road, NE · Atlanta, GA 30305 · 404-264-1292

Michael J. Sullivan · Womble Carlyle Sandridge & Rice · One Atlantic Center, Suite 3500 · 1201 West Peachtree Street · Atlanta, GA 30309 · 404-872-7000

Terrence C. Sullivan · Weinberg Wheeler Hudgins Gunn & Dial · 950 East Paces Ferry Road, Suite 3000 Atlanta, GA 30326 · 404-876-2700

Robert G. Tanner · ⑩ · Weinberg Wheeler Hudgins Gunn & Dial · 950 East Paces Ferry Road, Suite 3000 · Atlanta, GA 30326 · 404-876-2700

Bernard Taylor, Sr. · Alston + Bird · http://www.alston.com · One Atlantic Center · 1201 West Peachtree Street · Atlanta, GA 30309-3424 · 404-881-7000

Jane F. Thorpe · Alston + Bird · http://www.alston.com · One Atlantic Center · 1201 West Peachtree Street · Atlanta, GA 30309-3424 · 404-881-7000

Chilton D. Varner · ⑩ · King & Spalding · 1180 Peachtree Street, NE · Atlanta, GA 30309-3521 · 404-572-4600

H. Lane Young II · Hawkins & Parnell · 4000 SunTrust Plaza, 40th Floor · 303 Peachtree Street, NE · Atlanta, GA 30308-3243 · 404-614-7400

David M. Zacks · ⑩ · Kilpatrick Stockton · 1100 Peachtree Street, Suite 2800 · Atlanta, GA 30309-4530 · 404-815-6500

Augusta

John C. Bell, Jr. · Bell & Brigham · http://www.bellbrigham.com · 457 Greene Street · P.O. Box 1547 · Augusta, GA 30903-1547 · 706-722-2014

Raymond G. Chadwick, Jr. · Kilpatrick Stockton · Wachovia Bank Building, Suite 1400 · 699 Broad Street · Augusta, GA 30901-1453 · 706-724-2622

Raymond J. Doumar · Raymond J. Doumar · 431 Walker Street · Augusta, GA 30901 · 706-722-1700

George R. Hall · Hull, Towill, Norman, Barrett & Salley · SunTrust Bank Building, Suite 700 · 801 Broad Street · P.O. Box 1564 · Augusta, GA 30903-1564 · 706-722-4481

David E. Hudson · ⑩ · Hull, Towill, Norman, Barrett & Salley · SunTrust Bank Building, Suite 700 · 801 Broad Street · P.O. Box 1564 · Augusta, GA 30903-1564 · 706-722-4481

Pamela S. James · Pamela S. James · 431 Walker Street · Augusta, GA 30901 · 706-722-1700

John B. Long · ⑩ · Tucker, Everitt, Long, Brewton & Lanier · 453 Greene Street · P.O. Box 2426 · Augusta, GA 30903-2426 · 706-722-0771

James W. Purcell · Fulcher Hagler · One 10th Street, Suite 700 · Augusta, GA 30901 · 706-724-0171

Patrick J. Rice · ⑩ · Hull, Towill, Norman, Barrett & Salley · SunTrust Bank Building, Suite 700 · 801 Broad Street · P.O. Box 1564 · Augusta, GA 30903-1564 · 706-722-4481

Thomas W. Tucker · ⑩ · Tucker, Everitt, Long, Brewton & Lanier · 453 Greene Street · P.O. Box 2426 · Augusta, GA 30903-2426 · 706-722-0771

Blakely

William S. Stone · William S. Stone · 589 College Street · P.O. Drawer 70 · Blakely, GA 39823 · 229-723-3045

Brunswick

James B. Durham · Durham, McHugh & Duncan · 777 Gloucester Street, Suite 300 · P.O. Box 2177 · Brunswick, GA 31521-2177 · 912-264-1800

Wallace E. Harrell, Sr. · ⑳ · Gilbert, Harrell, Sumerford & Martin · Bank of America Plaza, Suite 200 · 777 Gloucester Street · P.O. Box 190 · Brunswick, GA 31521-0190 · 912-265-6700

Carrollton

David H. Tisinger · ⑳ · Tisinger Vance · 100 Wagon Yard Plaza · P.O. Box 2069 · Carrollton, GA 30117-2069 · 770-834-4467

Columbus

Ray L. Allison · Denney, Pease, Allison & Kirk · 945 Broadway, Suite 201 · P.O. Box 2648 · Columbus, GA 31902-2648 · 706-324-3711

Jerry A. Buchanan · Buchanan & Land · 1425 Wynnton Road · P.O. Box 2848 · Columbus, GA 31902 · 706-323-2848

James E. Butler, Jr. · ⑳ · Butler, Wooten, Fryhofer, Daughtery & Sullivan · 105 Thirteenth Street · P.O. Box 2766 · Columbus, GA 31902 · 706-322-1990

John W. Denney · ⑩ · Denney, Pease, Allison & Kirk · 945 Broadway, Suite 201 · P.O. Box 2648 · Columbus, GA 31902-2648 · 706-324-3711

William B. Hardegree · Hatcher, Stubbs, Land, Hollis & Rothschild · http://www.hatcherstubbs.com · The Corporate Center, Suite 500 · 233 Twelfth Street · P.O. Box 2707 · Columbus, GA 31902-2707 · 706-324-0201

C. Neal Pope · ⑳ · Pope, McGlamry, Kilpatrick, Morrison & Norwood · Synovus Building, Suite 450 · 1111 Bay Avenue · P.O. Box 2128 · Columbus, GA 31902-2128 · 706-324-0050

W. G. Scrantom, Jr. · ⑳ · Page, Scrantom, Sprouse, Tucker & Ford · Synovus Centre, Third Floor · 1111 Bay Avenue · P.O. Box 1199 · Columbus, GA 31902 · 706-324-0251

Cornelia

Dennis T. Cathey · Cathey & Strain · 649 Irvin Street · P.O. Box 689 · Cornelia, GA 30531-0689 · 706-778-2601

Edward E. Strain III · Cathey & Strain · 649 Irvin Street · P.O. Box 689 · Cornelia, GA 30531-0689 · 706-778-2601

Gainesville

Weymon H. Forrester · ⑩ · Forrester & Brim · 459 E.E. Butler Parkway, SE · P.O. Box 1688 · Gainesville, GA 30503-1688 · 770-531-0800

Charles W. Stephens · Stephens & Shuler · 210 Washington Street, NW, Suite 101 · Gainesville, GA 30501 · 770-536-7619

J. Douglas Stewart · ⑩ · Stewart, Melvin & Frost · Hunt Tower, Suite 600 · 200 Main Street · P.O. Box 3280 · Gainesville, GA 30503 · 770-536-0101

Hinesville

Billy Jones · Jones, Osteen & Jones · 206 East Court Street · P.O. Box 800 · Hinesville, GA 31310-0800 · 912-876-0888

Homerville

J. Jeffrey Helms, Jr. · The Helms Law Firm · http://www.helmslaw.com · 100 North College Street · P.O. Box 537 · Homerville, GA 31634-2104 · 912-487-5377

Macon

Thomas C. Alexander · Jones, Cork & Miller · SunTrust Bank Building, Fifth Floor · 435 Second Street · P.O. Box 6437 · Macon, GA 31208-6437 · 478-745-2821

Manley F. Brown · ⑩ · O'Neal, Brown & Clark · American Federal Building, Suite 1001 · 544 Mulberry Street · Macon, GA 31201 · 478-742-8981

R. William Buzzell · Buzzell, Graham & Welsh · 563 Walnut Street · Macon, GA 31201 · 478-742-8820

John C. Clark · O'Neal, Brown & Clark · American Federal Building, Suite 1001 · 544 Mulberry Street · Macon, GA 31201 · 478-742-8981

Carr G. Dodson · ⑩ · Jones, Cork & Miller · SunTrust Bank Building, Fifth Floor · 435 Second Street · P.O. Box 6437 · Macon, GA 31208-6437 · 478-745-2821

John C. Edwards · ⑩ · Martin Snow · http://www.martinsnow.com · 240 Third Street · P.O. Box 1606 · Macon, GA 31202-1606 · 478-749-1700

Robert R. Gunn II · Martin Snow · http://www.martinsnow.com · 240 Third Street · P.O. Box 1606 · Macon, GA 31202-1606 · 478-749-1700

John F. Kennedy · Hall, Bloch, Garland & Meyer · http://www.hbgm.com · Fickling & Company Building, Suite 1500 · 577 Mulberry Street · P.O. Box 5088 · Macon, GA 31208-5088 · 478-745-1625

William H. Larsen · Martin Snow · http://www.martinsnow.com · 240 Third Street · P.O. Box 1606 · Macon, GA 31202-1606 · 478-749-1700

Hubert C. Lovein, Jr. · ⑩ · Jones, Cork & Miller · SunTrust Bank Building, Fifth Floor · 435 Second Street · P.O. Box 6437 · Macon, GA 31208-6437 · 478-745-2821

W. Carl Reynolds · ⑩ · Reynolds, McArthur & Horne · 6320 Peake Road · P.O. Box 26610 · Macon, GA 31221-6610 · 478-405-0300

Cubbedge Snow III · Martin Snow · http://www.martinsnow.com · 240 Third Street · P.O. Box 1606 · Macon, GA 31202-1606 · 478-749-1700

J. Steven Stewart · Hall, Bloch, Garland & Meyer · http://www.hbgm.com · Fickling & Company Building, Suite 1500 · 577 Mulberry Street · P.O. Box 5088 · Macon, GA 31208-5088 · 478-745-1625

Marc T. Treadwell · ⑩ · Adams, Jordan & Treadwell · Fickling & Company Building, Suite 1250 · 577 Mulberry Street · P.O. Box 928 · Macon, GA 31202-0928 · 478-743-2159

Rome

Robert L. Berry · Brinson, Askew, Berry, Seigler, Richardson & Davis · The Omberg House · 615 West First Street · P.O. Box 5513 · Rome, GA 30162-5513 · 706-291-8853

Robert M. Brinson · ⑩ · Brinson, Askew, Berry, Seigler, Richardson & Davis · The Omberg House · 615 West First Street · P.O. Box 5513 · Rome, GA 30162-5513 · 706-291-8853

Savannah

Frederick S. Bergen · Bergen & Bergen · Marist Place Lafayette Square · 123 Charlton Street, East · Savannah, GA 31401-4603 · 912-233-6600

D. Michael Conner · Bouhan, Williams & Levy · http://www.bouhan.com · The Armstrong House · 447 Bull Street · P.O. Box 2139 · Savannah, GA 31402-2139 · 912-236-2491

William P. Franklin, Jr. · ⑩ · Oliver Maner · http://www.olivermaner.com · 218 West State Street · P.O. Box 10186 · Savannah, GA 31412 · 912-236-3311

I. Gregory Hodges · Oliver Maner · http://www.olivermaner.com · 218 West State Street · P.O. Box 10186 · Savannah, GA 31412 · 912-236-3311

Carlton E. Joyce · Bouhan, Williams & Levy · http://www.bouhan.com · The Armstrong House · 447 Bull Street · P.O. Box 2139 · Savannah, GA 31402-2139 · 912-236-2491

Paul W. Painter, Jr. · ⑩ · Ellis, Painter, Ratterree & Adams · http://www.epra-law.com · Johnson Square Business Center, 10th Floor · Two East Bryan Street · P.O. Box 9946 · Savannah, GA 31412 · 912-233-9700

William H. Pinson, Jr. · ⑩ · Savage, Turner, Pinson & Karsman · 304 East Bay Street · P.O. Box 10600 · Savannah, GA 31412 · 912-231-1140

R. Clay Ratterree · ⑩ · Ellis, Painter, Ratterree & Adams · http://www.epra-law.com · Johnson Square Business Center, 10th Floor · Two East Bryan Street · P.O. Box 9946 · Savannah, GA 31412 · 912-233-9700

Frank W. Seiler · ㉕ · Bouhan, Williams & Levy · http://www.bouhan.com · The Armstrong House · 447 Bull Street · P.O. Box 2139 · Savannah, GA 31402-2139 · 912-236-2491

John E. Suthers · Suthers Law Firm · 119 West Perry Street · Savannah, GA 31401 · 912-232-6767

Harvey Weitz · Weiner, Shearouse, Weitz, Greenberg & Shawe · 14 East State Street · P.O. Box 10105 · Savannah, GA 31412 · 912-233-2251

Arnold C. Young · Hunter Maclean · http://www.huntermaclean.com · 200 East Saint Julian Street · P.O. Box 9848 · Savannah, GA 31412-0048 · 912-236-0261

Statesboro

Gerald M. Edenfield · Edenfield, Cox, Bruce & Classens · 115 Savannah Avenue · P.O. Box 1700 · Statesboro, GA 30459 · 912-764-8600

Valdosta

Roger J. Dodd · ⑩ · Roger J. Dodd, Lawyers · 613 North Patterson Street · P.O. Box 1066 · Valdosta, GA 31601-1066 · 229-242-4470

PRODUCT LIABILITY LITIGATION

Athens

Gary B. Blasingame · ⑩ · Blasingame, Burch, Garrard & Ashley · http://www.bbgbalaw.com · 440 College Avenue North · P.O. Box 832 · Athens, GA 30603 · 706-354-4000

Henry G. Garrard III · ⑩ · Blasingame, Burch, Garrard & Ashley · http://www.bbgbalaw.com · 440 College Avenue North · P.O. Box 832 · Athens, GA 30603 · 706-354-4000

Atlanta

Andrew T. Bayman · King & Spalding · 1180 Peachtree Street, NE · Atlanta, GA 30309-3521 · 404-572-4600

Lori G. Cohen · Greenberg Traurig · http://www.gtlaw.com · The Forum, Suite 400 · 3290 Northside Parkway, NE · Atlanta, GA 30327 · 678-553-2100

N. Karen Deming · ⑩ · Troutman Sanders · Bank of America Plaza, Suite 5200 · 600 Peachtree Street, NE · Atlanta, GA 30308-2216 · 404-885-3000

Foy R. Devine · ⑳ · Doffermyre, Shields, Canfield, Knowles & Devine · 1355 Peachtree Street, Suite 1600 · Atlanta, GA 30309 · 404-881-8900

Thomas William Malone · ⑳ · Malone Law · http://www.malonepc.com · Two Ravinia Drive, Suite 300 · Atlanta, GA 30346 · 770-390-7550

John T. Marshall · ㉕ · Powell Goldstein · http://www.pogolaw.com · One Atlantic Center, 14th Floor · 1201 West Peachtree Street, NE · Atlanta, GA 30309 · 404-572-6600

James Dartlin Meadows · Balch & Bingham · http://www.balch.com · 30 Ivan Allen, Jr. Boulevard, NW, Suite 700 · Atlanta, GA 30308 · 404-261-6020

Robert P. Monyak · Peters & Monyak · One Atlanta Plaza, Suite 2275 · 950 East Paces Ferry Road · Atlanta, GA 30326 · 404-607-0100

Stephanie E. Parker · Jones Day · 1420 Peachtree Street, NE, Suite 800 · Atlanta, GA 30309-3053 · 404-521-3939

Albert M. Pearson III · ⑩ · Moraitakis, Kushel, Pearson & Gardner · 3445 Peachtree Road, NE, Suite 425 · Atlanta, GA 30326-3239 · 404-261-0016

Andrew M. Scherffius · Scherffius, Ballard Still & Ayres · 400 Colony Square, Suite 1018 · 1201 Peachtree Street, NE · Atlanta, GA 30361 · 404-496-5628

Richard A. Schneider · King & Spalding · 1180 Peachtree Street, NE · Atlanta, GA 30309-3521 · 404-572-4600

Bernard Taylor, Sr. · Alston + Bird · http://www.alston.com · One Atlantic Center · 1201 West Peachtree Street · Atlanta, GA 30309-3424 · 404-881-7000

Chilton D. Varner · ⑩ · King & Spalding · 1180 Peachtree Street, NE · Atlanta, GA 30309-3521 · 404-572-4600

Augusta

Raymond G. Chadwick, Jr. · Kilpatrick Stockton · Wachovia Bank Building, Suite 1400 · 699 Broad Street · Augusta, GA 30901-1453 · 706-724-2622

Columbus

James E. Butler, Jr. · ⑳ · Butler, Wooten, Fryhofer, Daughtery & Sullivan · 105 Thirteenth Street · P.O. Box 2766 · Columbus, GA 31902 · 706-322-1990

C. Neal Pope · ⑳ · Pope, McGlamry, Kilpatrick, Morrison & Norwood · Synovus Building, Suite 450 · 1111 Bay Avenue · P.O. Box 2128 · Columbus, GA 31902-2128 · 706-324-0050

Macon

Manley F. Brown · ⑩ · O'Neal, Brown & Clark · American Federal Building, Suite 1001 · 544 Mulberry Street · Macon, GA 31201 · 478-742-8981

Savannah

Paul W. Painter, Jr. · ⑩ · Ellis, Painter, Ratterree & Adams · http://www.epra-law.com · Johnson Square Business Center, 10th Floor · Two East Bryan Street · P.O. Box 9946 · Savannah, GA 31412 · 912-233-9700

Frank W. Seiler · ㉕ · Bouhan, Williams & Levy · http://www.bouhan.com · The Armstrong House · 447 Bull Street · P.O. Box 2139 · Savannah, GA 31402-2139 · 912-236-2491

Arnold C. Young · Hunter Maclean · http://www.huntermaclean.com · 200 East Saint Julian Street · P.O. Box 9848 · Savannah, GA 31412-0048 · 912-236-0261

PROFESSIONAL MALPRACTICE LAW

Atlanta

John T. Marshall · ㉕ · Powell Goldstein · http://www.pogolaw.com · One Atlantic Center, 14th Floor · 1201 West Peachtree Street, NE · Atlanta, GA 30309 · 404-572-6600

H. Lane Young II · Hawkins & Parnell · 4000 SunTrust Plaza, 40th Floor · 303 Peachtree Street, NE · Atlanta, GA 30308-3243 · 404-614-7400

PROJECT FINANCE LAW

Atlanta

Peter A. Fozzard · Sutherland · http://www.sutherland.com · 999 Peachtree Street, NE · Atlanta, GA 30309-3996 · 404-853-8000

John W. Hinchey · King & Spalding · 1180 Peachtree Street, NE · Atlanta, GA 30309-3521 · 404-572-4600

PUBLIC FINANCE LAW

Atlanta

William A. Holby · King & Spalding · 1180 Peachtree Street, NE · Atlanta, GA 30309-3521 · 404-572-4600

Leonard T. Marcinko · Bryant Miller & Olive · 430 Margate · Atlanta, GA 30328 · 770-399-7700

Karol V. Mason · Alston + Bird · http://www.alston.com · One Atlantic Center · 1201 West Peachtree Street · Atlanta, GA 30309-3424 · 404-881-7000

Floyd C. Newton III · King & Spalding · 1180 Peachtree Street, NE · Atlanta, GA 30309-3521 · 404-572-4600

Caryl Greenberg Smith · Hunton & Williams · Bank of America Plaza, Suite 4100 · 600 Peachtree Street, NE · Atlanta, GA 30308-2216 · 404-888-4000

Savannah

James L. Pannell · Gray & Pannell · 218 West State Street, Third Floor · P.O. Box 8050 · Savannah, GA 31412-8050 · 912-443-4040

RAILROAD LAW

Atlanta

Robert E. Casey, Jr. · Casey, Gilson & Leibel · Six Concourse Parkway, Suite 2200 · Atlanta, GA 30328 · 770-512-0300

REAL ESTATE LAW

Atlanta

Alfred G. Adams, Jr. · ⑩ · Sutherland · http://www.sutherland.com · 999 Peachtree Street, NE · Atlanta, GA 30309-3996 · 404-853-8000

James W. Addison · Troutman Sanders · Bank of America Plaza, Suite 5200 · 600 Peachtree Street, NE · Atlanta, GA 30308-2216 · 404-885-3000

Scott J. Arnold · King & Spalding · 1180 Peachtree Street, NE · Atlanta, GA 30309-3521 · 404-572-4600

Frank B. Bazzel · Morris, Manning & Martin · 1600 Atlanta Financial Center · 3343 Peachtree Road, NE · Atlanta, GA 30326 · 404-233-7000

Albert E. Bender, Jr. · Alston + Bird · http://www.alston.com · One Atlantic Center · 1201 West Peachtree Street · Atlanta, GA 30309-3424 · 404-881-7000

Brian P. Cain · Holt Ney Zatcoff & Wasserman · 100 Galleria Parkway, Suite 600 · Atlanta, GA 30339 · 770-956-9600

Maureen T. Callahan · Troutman Sanders · Bank of America Plaza, Suite 5200 · 600 Peachtree Street, NE Atlanta, GA 30308-2216 · 404-885-3000

Luther C. Curtis · Miller & Martin · http://www.millermartin.com · 1170 Peachtree Street, NE, Suite 800 Atlanta, GA 30309-3576 · 404-962-6100

Michael R. Davis · Alston + Bird · http://www.alston.com · One Atlantic Center · 1201 West Peachtree Street · Atlanta, GA 30309-3424 · 404-881-7000

Mark L. Elliott · Troutman Sanders · Bank of America Plaza, Suite 5200 · 600 Peachtree Street, NE · Atlanta, GA 30308-2216 · 404-885-3000

James G. Farris, Jr. · Alston + Bird · http://www.alston.com · One Atlantic Center · 1201 West Peachtree Street · Atlanta, GA 30309-3424 · 404-881-7000

Candace L. Fowler · Kilpatrick Stockton · 1100 Peachtree Street, Suite 2800 · Atlanta, GA 30309-4530 · 404-815-6500

William B. Fryer · ⑩ · King & Spalding · 1180 Peachtree Street, NE · Atlanta, GA 30309-3521 · 404-572-4600

W. Clay Gibson · King & Spalding · 1180 Peachtree Street, NE · Atlanta, GA 30309-3521 · 404-572-4600

Peter B. Glass · Ledbetter Johnson Wanamaker · 100 Colony Square, Suite 1100 · 1175 Peachtree Street, NE · Atlanta, GA 30361 · 404-835-9500

John W. Griffin · Troutman Sanders · Bank of America Plaza, Suite 5200 · 600 Peachtree Street, NE · Atlanta, GA 30308-2216 · 404-885-3000

H. Edward Hales, Jr. · Sutherland · http://www.sutherland.com · 999 Peachtree Street, NE · Atlanta, GA 30309-3996 · 404-853-8000

Victor P. Haley · Sutherland · http://www.sutherland.com · 999 Peachtree Street, NE · Atlanta, GA 30309-3996 · 404-853-8000

Dan L. Heller · King & Spalding · 1180 Peachtree Street, NE · Atlanta, GA 30309-3521 · 404-572-4600

Robert G. Holt · ㉕ · Holt Ney Zatcoff & Wasserman · 100 Galleria Parkway, Suite 600 · Atlanta, GA 30339 · 770-956-9600

Wayne S. Hyatt · Hyatt & Stubblefield · 1200 Peachtree Center, South Tower · 225 Peachtree Street, NE Atlanta, GA 30303 · 404-659-6600

James B. Jordan · ⑩ · Sutherland · http://www.sutherland.com · 999 Peachtree Street, NE · Atlanta, GA 30309-3996 · 404-853-8000

Joshua M. Kamin · King & Spalding · 1180 Peachtree Street, NE · Atlanta, GA 30309-3521 · 404-572-4600

M. Andrew Kauss · Kilpatrick Stockton · 1100 Peachtree Street, Suite 2800 · Atlanta, GA 30309-4530 · 404-815-6500

Michael G. Kerman · Sutherland · http://www.sutherland.com · 999 Peachtree Street, NE · Atlanta, GA 30309-3996 · 404-853-8000

Kenneth H. Kraft · Parker, Hudson, Rainer & Dobbs · 1500 Marquis Two Tower · 285 Peachtree Center Avenue, NE · Atlanta, GA 30303 · 404-523-5300

Jay J. Levin · Powell Goldstein · http://www.pogolaw.com · One Atlantic Center, 14th Floor · 1201 West Peachtree Street, NE · Atlanta, GA 30309 · 404-572-6600

David N. Minkin · Powell Goldstein · http://www.pogolaw.com · One Atlantic Center, 14th Floor · 1201 West Peachtree Street, NE · Atlanta, GA 30309 · 404-572-6600

James M. Ney · ㉕ · Holt Ney Zatcoff & Wasserman · 100 Galleria Parkway, Suite 600 · Atlanta, GA 30339 · 770-956-9600

A. Summey Orr III · Holland & Knight · http://www.hklaw.com · One Atlantic Center, Suite 2000 · 1201 West Peachtree Street, NE · Atlanta, GA 30309-3400 · 404-817-8500

Timothy J. Pakenham · Alston + Bird · http://www.alston.com · One Atlantic Center · 1201 West Peachtree Street · Atlanta, GA 30309-3424 · 404-881-7000

John R. Parks · Powell Goldstein · http://www.pogolaw.com · One Atlantic Center, 14th Floor · 1201 West Peachtree Street, NE · Atlanta, GA 30309 · 404-572-6600

Haynes R. Roberts · Sutherland · http://www.sutherland.com · 999 Peachtree Street, NE · Atlanta, GA 30309-3996 · 404-853-8000

Mark C. Rusche · Alston + Bird · http://www.alston.com · One Atlantic Center · 1201 West Peachtree Street · Atlanta, GA 30309-3424 · 404-881-7000

Christopher Glenn Sawyer · Alston + Bird · http://www.alston.com · One Atlantic Center · 1201 West Peachtree Street · Atlanta, GA 30309-3424 · 404-881-7000

Mason W. Stephenson · ⑩ · King & Spalding · 1180 Peachtree Street, NE · Atlanta, GA 30309-3521 · 404-572-4600

William F. Stevens · ⑳ · McKenna Long & Aldridge · 303 Peachtree Street, NE, Suite 5300 · Atlanta, GA 30308 · 404-527-4000

William J. Thompson · ㉕ · Powell Goldstein · http://www.pogolaw.com · One Atlantic Center, 14th Floor 1201 West Peachtree Street, NE · Atlanta, GA 30309 · 404-572-6600

Richard Vornholt · Holt Ney Zatcoff & Wasserman · 100 Galleria Parkway, Suite 600 · Atlanta, GA 30339 · 770-956-9600

Homer Lee Walker · Alston + Bird · http://www.alston.com · One Atlantic Center · 1201 West Peachtree Street · Atlanta, GA 30309-3424 · 404-881-7000

Stephen F. White · Nelson Mullins Riley & Scarborough · Atlantic Station, Suite 1700 · 201 Seventeenth Street, NW · Atlanta, GA 30363 · 404-817-6000

Andrew C. Williams · Morris, Manning & Martin · 1600 Atlanta Financial Center · 3343 Peachtree Road, NE · Atlanta, GA 30326 · 404-233-7000

Sanford H. Zatcoff · ⑩ · Holt Ney Zatcoff & Wasserman · 100 Galleria Parkway, Suite 600 · Atlanta, GA 30339 · 770-956-9600

Lawrenceville

Thomas J. Andersen · Andersen, Tate & Carr · http://www.atmlawfirm.com · 1505 Lakes Parkway, Suite 100 · P.O. Box 2000 · Lawrenceville, GA 30046 · 770-822-0900

Macon

V. J. Adams, Jr. · ⑩ · Adams & Adams · 155 College Street · Macon, GA 31201 · 478-745-4252

Wendell L. Bowden · ⑩ · Martin Snow · http://www.martinsnow.com · 240 Third Street · P.O. Box 1606 · Macon, GA 31202-1606 · 478-749-1700

J. Wayne Crowley · Bush, Crowley, Leverett & Leggett · 561 Cotton Avenue · P.O. Box 232 · Macon, GA 31202-0232 · 478-745-7461

John T. McGoldrick, Jr. · Martin Snow · http://www.martinsnow.com · 240 Third Street · P.O. Box 1606 · Macon, GA 31202-1606 · 478-749-1700

Steve L. Wilson · Jones, Cork & Miller · SunTrust Bank Building, Fifth Floor · 435 Second Street · P.O. Box 6437 · Macon, GA 31208-6437 · 478-745-2821

Marietta

Evelyn H. Coats · Coats Law Firm · 35 Johnson Ferry Road · Marietta, GA 30068 · 678-384-3070

John H. Moore · Moore, Ingram, Johnson & Steele · 192 Anderson Street · P.O. Box 3305 · Marietta, GA 30061-3305 · 770-429-1499

Savannah

LeeAnn W. Aldridge · Hunter Maclean · http://www.huntermaclean.com · 200 East Saint Julian Street · P.O. Box 9848 · Savannah, GA 31412-0048 · 912-236-0261

Marvin A. Fentress · Gray & Pannell · 218 West State Street, Third Floor · P.O. Box 8050 · Savannah, GA 31412-8050 · 912-443-4040

W. Brooks Stillwell III · ⑩ · Hunter Maclean · http://www.huntermaclean.com · 200 East Saint Julian Street · P.O. Box 9848 · Savannah, GA 31412-0048 · 912-236-0261

SECURITIES LAW

Atlanta

Peter J. Anderson · Sutherland · http://www.sutherland.com · 999 Peachtree Street, NE · Atlanta, GA 30309-3996 · 404-853-8000

W. Benjamin Barkley · Kilpatrick Stockton · 1100 Peachtree Street, Suite 2800 · Atlanta, GA 30309-4530 404-815-6500

Steven L. Berson · Nelson Mullins Riley & Scarborough · Atlantic Station, Suite 1700 · 201 Seventeenth Street, NW · Atlanta, GA 30363 · 404-817-6000

Terry C. Bridges · Troutman Sanders · Bank of America Plaza, Suite 5200 · 600 Peachtree Street, NE · Atlanta, GA 30308-2216 · 404-885-3000

J. Vaughan Curtis · ⑩ · Alston + Bird · http://www.alston.com · One Atlantic Center · 1201 West Peachtree Street · Atlanta, GA 30309-3424 · 404-881-7000

Bryan E. Davis · Jones Day · 1420 Peachtree Street, NE, Suite 800 · Atlanta, GA 30309-3053 · 404-521-3939

W. Brinkley Dickerson · Troutman Sanders · Bank of America Plaza, Suite 5200 · 600 Peachtree Street, NE · Atlanta, GA 30308-2216 · 404-885-3000

Daniel T. Falstad · DLA Piper · One Atlantic Center, Suite 2800 · 1201 West Peachtree Street · Atlanta, GA 30309-3450 · 404-736-7800

M. Hill Jeffries · Alston + Bird · http://www.alston.com · One Atlantic Center · 1201 West Peachtree Street · Atlanta, GA 30309-3424 · 404-881-7000

John J. Kelley III · King & Spalding · 1180 Peachtree Street, NE · Atlanta, GA 30309-3521 · 404-572-4600

John L. Latham · Alston + Bird · http://www.alston.com · One Atlantic Center · 1201 West Peachtree Street · Atlanta, GA 30309-3424 · 404-881-7000

Larry D. Ledbetter · Ledbetter Johnson Wanamaker · 100 Colony Square, Suite 1100 · 1175 Peachtree Street, NE · Atlanta, GA 30361 · 404-835-9500

Teri Lynn McMahon · Alston + Bird · http://www.alston.com · One Atlantic Center · 1201 West Peachtree Street · Atlanta, GA 30309-3424 · 404-881-7000

Thomas R. McNeill · Powell Goldstein · http://www.pogolaw.com · One Atlantic Center, 14th Floor · 1201 West Peachtree Street, NE · Atlanta, GA 30309 · 404-572-6600

Sidney J. Nurkin · ⑳ · Alston + Bird · http://www.alston.com · One Atlantic Center · 1201 West Peachtree Street · Atlanta, GA 30309-3424 · 404-881-7000

Steven L. Pottle · ⑩ · Alston + Bird · http://www.alston.com · One Atlantic Center · 1201 West Peachtree Street · Atlanta, GA 30309-3424 · 404-881-7000

Tony G. Powers · Rogers & Hardin · 2700 International Tower · 229 Peachtree Street, NE · Atlanta, GA 30303 · 404-522-4700

James L. Smith III · ⑳ · Troutman Sanders · Bank of America Plaza, Suite 5200 · 600 Peachtree Street, NE · Atlanta, GA 30308-2216 · 404-885-3000

Marlon F. Starr · Troutman Sanders · Bank of America Plaza, Suite 5200 · 600 Peachtree Street, NE · Atlanta, GA 30308-2216 · 404-885-3000

Jeffrey M. Stein · King & Spalding · 1180 Peachtree Street, NE · Atlanta, GA 30309-3521 · 404-572-4600

David A. Stockton · ⑩ · Kilpatrick Stockton · 1100 Peachtree Street, Suite 2800 · Atlanta, GA 30309-4530 · 404-815-6500

M. Robert Thornton · King & Spalding · 1180 Peachtree Street, NE · Atlanta, GA 30309-3521 · 404-572-4600

STRUCTURED FINANCE LAW

Atlanta

Thomas J. Biafore · Kilpatrick Stockton · 1100 Peachtree Street, Suite 2800 · Atlanta, GA 30309-4530 · 404-815-6500

Rick D. Blumen · Alston + Bird · http://www.alston.com · One Atlantic Center · 1201 West Peachtree Street · Atlanta, GA 30309-3424 · 404-881-7000

Sarah Robinson Borders · ⑩ · King & Spalding · 1180 Peachtree Street, NE · Atlanta, GA 30309-3521 · 404-572-4600

Gregory M. Chait · Alston + Bird · http://www.alston.com · One Atlantic Center · 1201 West Peachtree Street · Atlanta, GA 30309-3424 · 404-881-7000

Paul M. Cushing · Alston + Bird · http://www.alston.com · One Atlantic Center · 1201 West Peachtree Street · Atlanta, GA 30309-3424 · 404-881-7000

Hazen H. Dempster · Troutman Sanders · Bank of America Plaza, Suite 5200 · 600 Peachtree Street, NE · Atlanta, GA 30308-2216 · 404-885-3000

Carolyn B. Dobbins · Rogers & Hardin · 2700 International Tower · 229 Peachtree Street, NE · Atlanta, GA 30303 · 404-522-4700

C. Edward Dobbs · ㉕ · Parker, Hudson, Rainer & Dobbs · 1500 Marquis Two Tower · 285 Peachtree Center Avenue, NE · Atlanta, GA 30303 · 404-523-5300

Richard W. Grice · ⑩ · Alston + Bird · http://www.alston.com · One Atlantic Center · 1201 West Peachtree Street · Atlanta, GA 30309-3424 · 404-881-7000

Hilary P. Jordan · Kilpatrick Stockton · 1100 Peachtree Street, Suite 2800 · Atlanta, GA 30309-4530 · 404-815-6500

Mitchell M. Purvis · Parker, Hudson, Rainer & Dobbs · 1500 Marquis Two Tower · 285 Peachtree Center Avenue, NE · Atlanta, GA 30303 · 404-523-5300

Carolyn Peterson Richter · Troutman Sanders · Bank of America Plaza, Suite 5200 · 600 Peachtree Street, NE · Atlanta, GA 30308-2216 · 404-885-3000

William G. Rothschild · Sutherland · http://www.sutherland.com · 999 Peachtree Street, NE · Atlanta, GA 30309-3996 · 404-853-8000

Jonathan R. Shils · Jonathan R. Shils · The Proscenium, Suite 2100 · 1170 Peachtree Street NE · Atlanta, GA 30309-7649 · 404-443-5500

Robert D. Strauss · Troutman Sanders · Bank of America Plaza, Suite 5200 · 600 Peachtree Street, NE · Atlanta, GA 30308-2216 · 404-885-3000

Rex R. Veal · Kilpatrick Stockton · 1100 Peachtree Street, Suite 2800 · Atlanta, GA 30309-4530 · 404-815-6500

TAX LAW

Atlanta

Harold E. Abrams · ㉕ · Abrams, Davis, Mason & Long · 1100 Peachtree Street, Suite 2800 · Atlanta, GA 30309-4530 · 404-815-6060

Pinney L. Allen · ⑩ · Alston + Bird · http://www.alston.com · One Atlantic Center · 1201 West Peachtree Street · Atlanta, GA 30309-3424 · 404-881-7000

Saba Ashraf · Troutman Sanders · Bank of America Plaza, Suite 5200 · 600 Peachtree Street, NE · Atlanta, GA 30308-2216 · 404-885-3000

David D. Aughtry · Chamberlain, Hrdlicka, White, Williams & Martin · 191 Peachtree Street, NE, 34th Floor · Atlanta, GA 30303-1747 · 404-659-1410

Charles R. Beaudrot, Jr. · Morris, Manning & Martin · 1600 Atlanta Financial Center · 3343 Peachtree Road, NE · Atlanta, GA 30326 · 404-233-7000

Herschel M. Bloom · ⑳ · King & Spalding · 1180 Peachtree Street, NE · Atlanta, GA 30309-3521 · 404-572-4600

Raymond P. Carpenter · Holland & Knight · http://www.hklaw.com · One Atlantic Center, Suite 2000 · 1201 West Peachtree Street, NE · Atlanta, GA 30309-3400 · 404-817-8500

Reginald J. Clark · Sutherland · http://www.sutherland.com · 999 Peachtree Street, NE · Atlanta, GA 30309-3996 · 404-853-8000

John L. Coalson, Jr. · ⑩ · Alston + Bird · http://www.alston.com · One Atlantic Center · 1201 West Peachtree Street · Atlanta, GA 30309-3424 · 404-881-7000

N. Jerold Cohen · ⑳ · Sutherland · http://www.sutherland.com · 999 Peachtree Street, NE · Atlanta, GA 30309-3996 · 404-853-8000

Philip C. Cook · ⑳ · Alston + Bird · http://www.alston.com · One Atlantic Center · 1201 West Peachtree Street · Atlanta, GA 30309-3424 · 404-881-7000

Paul J. Cox · ⑩ · Hartman, Simons, Spielman & Wood · 6400 Powers Ferry Road, NW, Suite 400 · Atlanta, GA 30339 · 770-955-3555

Frank A. Crisafi · Powell Goldstein · http://www.pogolaw.com · One Atlantic Center, 14th Floor · 1201 West Peachtree Street, NE · Atlanta, GA 30309 · 404-572-6600

Scott M. Dayan · Kilpatrick Stockton · 1100 Peachtree Street, Suite 2800 · Atlanta, GA 30309-4530 · 404-815-6500

Charles E. Elrod, Jr. · ⑳ · Parker, Hudson, Rainer & Dobbs · 1500 Marquis Two Tower · 285 Peachtree Center Avenue, NE · Atlanta, GA 30303 · 404-523-5300

Peter J. Genz · King & Spalding · 1180 Peachtree Street, NE · Atlanta, GA 30309-3521 · 404-572-4600

Cleburne E. Gregory · Arnall Golden Gregory · 171 Seventeenth Street, NW, Suite 2100 · Atlanta, GA 30363-1031 · 404-873-8500

Stanley H. Hackett · Troutman Sanders · Bank of America Plaza, Suite 5200 · 600 Peachtree Street, NE · Atlanta, GA 30308-2216 · 404-885-3000

James K. Hasson, Jr. · ⑳ · Sutherland · http://www.sutherland.com · 999 Peachtree Street, NE · Atlanta, GA 30309-3996 · 404-853-8000

Michelle M. Henkel · Alston + Bird · http://www.alston.com · One Atlantic Center · 1201 West Peachtree Street · Atlanta, GA 30309-3424 · 404-881-7000

Robert H. Hishon · ⑳ · The Hishon Firm · 400 Colony Square, Suite 1000 · 1201 Peachtree Street, NE · Atlanta, GA 30361 · 404-817-7791

T. Jerry Jackson · Troutman Sanders · Bank of America Plaza, Suite 5200 · 600 Peachtree Street, NE · Atlanta, GA 30308-2216 · 404-885-3000

Sheldon Kay · Sutherland · http://www.sutherland.com · 999 Peachtree Street, NE · Atlanta, GA 30309-3996 · 404-853-8000

Sam K. Kaywood, Jr. · Alston + Bird · http://www.alston.com · One Atlantic Center · 1201 West Peachtree Street · Atlanta, GA 30309-3424 · 404-881-7000

James H. Lokey, Jr. · King & Spalding · 1180 Peachtree Street, NE · Atlanta, GA 30309-3521 · 404-572-4600

Philip J. Marzetti · Paul Hastings · 600 Peachtree Street, NE, 24th Floor · Atlanta, GA 30308 · 404-815-2400

Suzanne G. Mason · Abrams, Davis, Mason & Long · 1100 Peachtree Street, Suite 2800 · Atlanta, GA 30309-4530 · 404-815-6060

Timothy J. Peaden · Alston + Bird · http://www.alston.com · One Atlantic Center · 1201 West Peachtree Street · Atlanta, GA 30309-3424 · 404-881-7000

Michael T. Petrik · ⑩ · Alston + Bird · http://www.alston.com · One Atlantic Center · 1201 West Peachtree Street · Atlanta, GA 30309-3424 · 404-881-7000

M. Celeste Pickron · ⑩ · Sutherland · http://www.sutherland.com · 999 Peachtree Street, NE · Atlanta, GA 30309-3996 · 404-853-8000

E. Kendrick Smith · Jones Day · 1420 Peachtree Street, NE, Suite 800 · Atlanta, GA 30309-3053 · 404-521-3939

John A. Wallace · ㉕ · King & Spalding · 1180 Peachtree Street, NE · Atlanta, GA 30309-3521 · 404-572-4600

Michael G. Wasserman · ⑳ · Holt Ney Zatcoff & Wasserman · 100 Galleria Parkway, Suite 600 · Atlanta, GA 30339 · 770-956-9600

Robert G. Woodward · ⑳ · King & Spalding · 1180 Peachtree Street, NE · Atlanta, GA 30309-3521 · 404-572-4600

W. Scott Wright · Sutherland · http://www.sutherland.com · 999 Peachtree Street, NE · Atlanta, GA 30309-3996 · 404-853-8000

Augusta

Mark S. Burgreen · Hull, Towill, Norman, Barrett & Salley · SunTrust Bank Building, Suite 700 · 801 Broad Street · P.O. Box 1564 · Augusta, GA 30903-1564 · 706-722-4481

William F. Hammond · Hull, Towill, Norman, Barrett & Salley · SunTrust Bank Building, Suite 700 · 801 Broad Street · P.O. Box 1564 · Augusta, GA 30903-1564 · 706-722-4481

Russell V. Mobley · Fulcher Hagler · One 10th Street, Suite 700 · Augusta, GA 30901 · 706-724-0171

Columbus

Morton A. Harris · ㉕ · Hatcher, Stubbs, Land, Hollis & Rothschild · http://www.hatcherstubbs.com · The Corporate Center, Suite 500 · 233 Twelfth Street · P.O. Box 2707 · Columbus, GA 31902-2707 · 706-324-0201

S. Davis Laney · ⑩ · Page, Scrantom, Sprouse, Tucker & Ford · Synovus Centre, Third Floor · 1111 Bay Avenue · P.O. Box 1199 · Columbus, GA 31902 · 706-324-0251

Charles T. Staples · Hatcher, Stubbs, Land, Hollis & Rothschild · http://www.hatcherstubbs.com · The Corporate Center, Suite 500 · 233 Twelfth Street · P.O. Box 2707 · Columbus, GA 31902-2707 · 706-324-0201

Macon

W. Carter Bates III · Jemes, Bates, Pope & Spivey · 231 Riverside Drive, Suite 100 · Macon, GA 31201 · 478-742-4280

John B. Harris III · Harris & James · 3573 Vineville Avenue · P.O. Box 4866 · Macon, GA 31208-4866 · 478-745-9661

J. Patrick Meyer, Jr. · Hall, Bloch, Garland & Meyer · http://www.hbgm.com · Fickling & Company Building, Suite 1500 · 577 Mulberry Street · P.O. Box 5088 · Macon, GA 31208-5088 · 478-745-1625

Albert P. Reichert, Jr. · ⑳ · Anderson, Walker & Reichert · Fickling & Company Building, Suite 500 · 577 Mulberry Street · P.O. Box 6497 · Macon, GA 31208-6497 · 478-743-8651

G. Boone Smith III · 20 · Smith, Hawkins, Hollingsworth & Reeves · 688 Walnut Street, Suite 100 · P.O. Box 6495 · Macon, GA 31201 · 478-743-4436

Savannah

David H. Dickey · 20 · Oliver Maner · http://www.olivermaner.com · 218 West State Street · P.O. Box 10186 · Savannah, GA 31412 · 912-236-3311

H. Mitchell Dunn, Jr. · 25 · Hunter Maclean · http://www.huntermaclean.com · 200 East Saint Julian Street · P.O. Box 9848 · Savannah, GA 31412-0048 · 912-236-0261

Julian R. Friedman · 20 · Oliver Maner · http://www.olivermaner.com · 218 West State Street · P.O. Box 10186 · Savannah, GA 31412 · 912-236-3311

Paul D. Meyer · Bart, Meyer & Company · http://www.bart-law.com · Three Skidaway Village Square · P.O. Box 16089 · Savannah, GA 31416 · 912-598-5151

K. Russell Simpson · Simpson & Creasy · 7393 Hodgson Memorial Drive, Suite 102 · Savannah, GA 31406 · 912-925-7200

TIMBER LAW

Atlanta

Victor P. Haley · Sutherland · http://www.sutherland.com · 999 Peachtree Street, NE · Atlanta, GA 30309-3996 · 404-853-8000

Daniel R. McKeithen · Sutherland · http://www.sutherland.com · 999 Peachtree Street, NE · Atlanta, GA 30309-3996 · 404-853-8000

Mark G. Pottorff · Smith, Gambrell & Russell · http://www.sgrlaw.com · Promenade II, Suite 3100 · 1230 Peachtree Street, NE · Atlanta, GA 30309-3592 · 404-815-3500

Haynes R. Roberts · Sutherland · http://www.sutherland.com · 999 Peachtree Street, NE · Atlanta, GA 30309-3996 · 404-853-8000

TRUSTS AND ESTATES

Albany

Gregory L. Fullerton · 10 · Watson, Spence, Lowe & Chambless · 320 Residence Avenue · P.O. Box 2008 Albany, GA 31702-2008 · 229-436-1545

James E. Reynolds, Jr. · Perry & Walters · 212 North Westover Boulevard · P.O. Box 71209 · Albany, GA 31708-1209 · 229-439-4000

Atlanta

Harold E. Abrams · 25 · Abrams, Davis, Mason & Long · 1100 Peachtree Street, Suite 2800 · Atlanta, GA 30309-4530 · 404-815-6060

Henry L. Bowden, Jr. · 10 · The Bowden Law Firm · 191 Peachtree Street, NE, Suite 849 · Atlanta, GA 30303-1747 · 404-523-8337

Stephanie Casteel · King & Spalding · 1180 Peachtree Street, NE · Atlanta, GA 30309-3521 · 404-572-4600

Kimbrough A. Davis · Abrams, Davis, Mason & Long · 1100 Peachtree Street, Suite 2800 · Atlanta, GA 30309-4530 · 404-815-6060

Nikola R. Djuric · Sutherland · http://www.sutherland.com · 999 Peachtree Street, NE · Atlanta, GA 30309-3996 · 404-853-8000

Robert G. Edge · ㉕ · Alston + Bird · http://www.alston.com · One Atlantic Center · 1201 West Peachtree Street · Atlanta, GA 30309-3424 · 404-881-7000

Arnold L. Feinstein · Alston + Bird · http://www.alston.com · One Atlantic Center · 1201 West Peachtree Street · Atlanta, GA 30309-3424 · 404-881-7000

Adam R. Gaslowitz · Gaslowitz Frankel · 4500 SunTrust Plaza · 303 Peachtree Street, NE · Atlanta, GA 30308 · 404-892-9797

Milford B. Hatcher, Jr. · Jones Day · 1420 Peachtree Street, NE, Suite 800 · Atlanta, GA 30309-3053 · 404-521-3939

Zoe M. Hicks · ⑩ · Hicks & Hicks · 1907 Mercedes Court · Atlanta, GA 30345-2739 · 404-788-1719

Charles D. Hurt, Jr. · ⑩ · Sutherland · http://www.sutherland.com · 999 Peachtree Street, NE · Atlanta, GA 30309-3996 · 404-853-8000

Thomas E. Jones, Jr. · Chamberlain, Hrdlicka, White, Williams & Martin · 191 Peachtree Street, NE, 34th Floor · Atlanta, GA 30303-1747 · 404-659-1410

Bertram L. Levy · ⑩ · Arnall Golden Gregory · 171 Seventeenth Street, NW, Suite 2100 · Atlanta, GA 30363-1031 · 404-873-8500

William Joseph Linkous, Jr. · ㉕ · Powell Goldstein · http://www.pogolaw.com · One Atlantic Center, 14th Floor · 1201 West Peachtree Street, NE · Atlanta, GA 30309 · 404-572-6600

Edward M. Manigault · Jones Day · 1420 Peachtree Street, NE, Suite 800 · Atlanta, GA 30309-3053 · 404-521-3939

Frank S. McGaughey III · ⑩ · Powell Goldstein · http://www.pogolaw.com · One Atlantic Center, 14th Floor · 1201 West Peachtree Street, NE · Atlanta, GA 30309 · 404-572-6600

James H. Morgan, Jr. · Smith, Gambrell & Russell · http://www.sgrlaw.com · Promenade II, Suite 3100 · 1230 Peachtree Street, NE · Atlanta, GA 30309-3592 · 404-815-3500

Ralph R. Morrison · Jones Day · 1420 Peachtree Street, NE, Suite 800 · Atlanta, GA 30309-3053 · 404-521-3939

Ann Distler Salo · ⑩ · Salo & Walker · 3235 Roswell Road, Suite 400 · Atlanta, GA 30305 · 404-264-4555

John C. Sawyer · Alston + Bird · http://www.alston.com · One Atlantic Center · 1201 West Peachtree Street · Atlanta, GA 30309-3424 · 404-881-7000

James D. Spratt, Jr. · King & Spalding · 1180 Peachtree Street, NE · Atlanta, GA 30309-3521 · 404-572-4600

Douglas W. Stein · Smith, Gambrell & Russell · http://www.sgrlaw.com · Promenade II, Suite 3100 · 1230 Peachtree Street, NE · Atlanta, GA 30309-3592 · 404-815-3500

Wayne R. Vason · ⑳ · Troutman Sanders · Bank of America Plaza, Suite 5200 · 600 Peachtree Street, NE Atlanta, GA 30308-2216 · 404-885-3000

Melissa P. Walker · Salo & Walker · 3235 Roswell Road, Suite 400 · Atlanta, GA 30305 · 404-264-4555

John A. Wallace · ㉕ · King & Spalding · 1180 Peachtree Street, NE · Atlanta, GA 30309-3521 · 404-572-4600

Benjamin T. White · ⑳ · Alston + Bird · http://www.alston.com · One Atlantic Center · 1201 West Peachtree Street · Atlanta, GA 30309-3424 · 404-881-7000

Larry J. White · ⑳ · Sutherland · http://www.sutherland.com · 999 Peachtree Street, NE · Atlanta, GA 30309-3996 · 404-853-8000

R. Mark Williamson · Alston + Bird · http://www.alston.com · One Atlantic Center · 1201 West Peachtree Street · Atlanta, GA 30309-3424 · 404-881-7000

Augusta

Michael B. Hagler · Fulcher Hagler · One 10th Street, Suite 700 · Augusta, GA 30901 · 706-724-0171

Russell V. Mobley · Fulcher Hagler · One 10th Street, Suite 700 · Augusta, GA 30901 · 706-724-0171

Brunswick

Janet A. Shirley · Hunter Maclean · http://www.huntermaclean.com · Bank of America Plaza, Suite 305 · 777 Gloucester Street · Brunswick, GA 31520 · 912-262-5996

Rees M. Sumerford · ⑩ · Gilbert, Harrell, Sumerford & Martin · Bank of America Plaza, Suite 200 · 777 Gloucester Street · P.O. Box 190 · Brunswick, GA 31521-0190 · 912-265-6700

Columbus

Charles H. Ford, Jr. · ⑩ · Page, Scrantom, Sprouse, Tucker & Ford · Synovus Centre, Third Floor · 1111 Bay Avenue · P.O. Box 1199 · Columbus, GA 31902 · 706-324-0251

Morton A. Harris · ㉕ · Hatcher, Stubbs, Land, Hollis & Rothschild · http://www.hatcherstubbs.com · The Corporate Center, Suite 500 · 233 Twelfth Street · P.O. Box 2707 · Columbus, GA 31902-2707 · 706-324-0201

S. Davis Laney · ⑩ · Page, Scrantom, Sprouse, Tucker & Ford · Synovus Centre, Third Floor · 1111 Bay Avenue · P.O. Box 1199 · Columbus, GA 31902 · 706-324-0251

E. Lowery Reid, Jr. · Page, Scrantom, Sprouse, Tucker & Ford · Synovus Centre, Third Floor · 1111 Bay Avenue · P.O. Box 1199 · Columbus, GA 31902 · 706-324-0251

Alan F. Rothschild, Jr. · Hatcher, Stubbs, Land, Hollis & Rothschild · http://www.hatcherstubbs.com · The Corporate Center, Suite 500 · 233 Twelfth Street · P.O. Box 2707 · Columbus, GA 31902-2707 · 706-324-0201

John M. Sheftall · ⑩ · Hatcher, Stubbs, Land, Hollis & Rothschild · http://www.hatcherstubbs.com · The Corporate Center, Suite 500 · 233 Twelfth Street · P.O. Box 2707 · Columbus, GA 31902-2707 · 706-324-0201

Macon

Timothy K. Adams · ⑩ · Jones, Cork & Miller · SunTrust Bank Building, Fifth Floor · 435 Second Street P.O. Box 6437 · Macon, GA 31208-6437 · 478-745-2821

W. Carter Bates III · Jemes, Bates, Pope & Spivey · 231 Riverside Drive, Suite 100 · Macon, GA 31201 · 478-742-4280

John B. Harris III · Harris & James · 3573 Vineville Avenue · P.O. Box 4866 · Macon, GA 31208-4866 · 478-745-9661

J. Patrick Meyer, Jr. · Hall, Bloch, Garland & Meyer · http://www.hbgm.com · Fickling & Company Building, Suite 1500 · 577 Mulberry Street · P.O. Box 5088 · Macon, GA 31208-5088 · 478-745-1625

Albert P. Reichert, Jr. · ⑳ · Anderson, Walker & Reichert · Fickling & Company Building, Suite 500 · 577 Mulberry Street · P.O. Box 6497 · Macon, GA 31208-6497 · 478-743-8651

G. Boone Smith III · ⑳ · Smith, Hawkins, Hollingsworth & Reeves · 688 Walnut Street, Suite 100 · P.O. Box 6495 · Macon, GA 31201 · 478-743-4436

Rome

John M. Graham III · ⑩ · McRae, Stegall, Peek, Harmon, Smith and Manning · SunTrust Bank Building, Fourth Floor · 100 East Second Avenue · P.O. Box 29 · Rome, GA 30162-0029 · 706-291-6223

Savannah

Randall K. Bart · ⑩ · Bart, Meyer & Company · http://www.bart-law.com · Three Skidaway Village Square · P.O. Box 16089 · Savannah, GA 31416 · 912-598-5151

Neil A. Creasy · Simpson & Creasy · 7393 Hodgson Memorial Drive, Suite 102 · Savannah, GA 31406 · 912-925-7200

David H. Dickey · ⑳ · Oliver Maner · http://www.olivermaner.com · 218 West State Street · P.O. Box 10186 · Savannah, GA 31412 · 912-236-3311

H. Mitchell Dunn, Jr. · ㉕ · Hunter Maclean · http://www.huntermaclean.com · 200 East Saint Julian Street · P.O. Box 9848 · Savannah, GA 31412-0048 · 912-236-0261

Julian R. Friedman · ⑳ · Oliver Maner · http://www.olivermaner.com · 218 West State Street · P.O. Box 10186 · Savannah, GA 31412 · 912-236-3311

Frank S. Macgill · Hunter Maclean · http://www.huntermaclean.com · 200 East Saint Julian Street · P.O. Box 9848 · Savannah, GA 31412-0048 · 912-236-0261

Paul D. Meyer · Bart, Meyer & Company · http://www.bart-law.com · Three Skidaway Village Square · P.O. Box 16089 · Savannah, GA 31416 · 912-598-5151

M. Lane Morrison · Hunter Maclean · http://www.huntermaclean.com · 200 East Saint Julian Street · P.O. Box 9848 · Savannah, GA 31412-0048 · 912-236-0261

Robert W. Schivera · Oliver Maner · http://www.olivermaner.com · 218 West State Street · P.O. Box 10186 · Savannah, GA 31412 · 912-236-3311

K. Russell Simpson · Simpson & Creasy · 7393 Hodgson Memorial Drive, Suite 102 · Savannah, GA 31406 · 912-925-7200

Lee A. Summerford · Oliver Maner · http://www.olivermaner.com · 218 West State Street · P.O. Box 10186 · Savannah, GA 31412 · 912-236-3311

VENTURE CAPITAL LAW

Atlanta

Lynn S. Scott · King & Spalding · 1180 Peachtree Street, NE · Atlanta, GA 30309-3521 · 404-572-4600

Wade H. Stribling · Sutherland · http://www.sutherland.com · 999 Peachtree Street, NE · Atlanta, GA 30309-3996 · 404-853-8000

WHITE-COLLAR CRIMINAL DEFENSE

Athens

Edward D. Tolley · ⑳ · Cook, Noell, Tolley, Bates & Michael · 304 East Washington Street · P.O. Box 1927 · Athens, GA 30603-1927 · 706-549-6111

Atlanta

Thomas D. Bever · Chilivis, Cochran, Larkins & Bever · 3127 Maple Drive, NE · Atlanta, GA 30305-2503 · 404-233-4171

Anthony L. Cochran · ⑩ · Chilivis, Cochran, Larkins & Bever · 3127 Maple Drive, NE · Atlanta, GA 30305-2503 · 404-233-4171

Stephen S. Cowen · King & Spalding · 1180 Peachtree Street, NE · Atlanta, GA 30309-3521 · 404-572-4600

Jerome J. Froelich, Jr. · ⑳ · McKenney & Froelich · Two Midtown Plaza, Suite 1250 · 1349 West Peachtree Street, NW · Atlanta, GA 30309-2920 · 404-881-1111

Edward T. M. Garland · ㉕ · Garland, Samuel & Loeb · 3151 Maple Drive, NE · Atlanta, GA 30305 · 404-262-2225

Craig A. Gillen · Gillen Cromwell Withers & Brantley · One Securities Centre, Suite 1050 · 3490 Piedmont Road, NE · Atlanta, GA 30305 · 404-842-9700

Daniel P. Griffin · Miller & Martin · http://www.millermartin.com · 1170 Peachtree Street, NE, Suite 800 Atlanta, GA 30309-3576 · 404-962-6100

Bruce Maloy · Maloy Jenkins Parker · 75 Fourteenth Street, NW, 25th Floor · Atlanta, GA 30309 · 404-875-2700

John R. Martin · ⑳ · Martin Brothers · The Grant Building, Suite 500 · 44 Broad Street, NW · Atlanta, GA 30303-2327 · 404-522-0400

William R. Mitchelson, Jr. · Alston + Bird · http://www.alston.com · One Atlantic Center · 1201 West Peachtree Street · Atlanta, GA 30309-3424 · 404-881-7000

Bruce H. Morris · Finestone & Morris · Tower Place, Suite 2540 · 3340 Peachtree Road, NE · Atlanta, GA 30326 · 404-262-2500

Paul B. Murphy · King & Spalding · 1180 Peachtree Street, NE · Atlanta, GA 30309-3521 · 404-572-4600

Wilmer Parker · Maloy Jenkins Parker · 75 Fourteenth Street, NW, 25th Floor · Atlanta, GA 30309 · 404-875-2700

Steven H. Sadow · ⑩ · Steven H. Sadow · 260 Peachtree St., N.W., Suite 2502 · Atlanta, GA 30303 · 404-577-1400

Donald F. Samuel · ⑩ · Garland, Samuel & Loeb · 3151 Maple Drive, NE · Atlanta, GA 30305 · 404-262-2225

Augusta

Michael C. Garrett · ⑩ · Garrett, Gilliard & Saul · 699 Broad Street, Suite 1010 · Augusta, GA 30901 · 706-724-1896

Columbus

Frank K. Martin · The Martin Firm · The Corporate Center, Suite 809 · 233 Twelfth Street · P.O. Box 1436 · Columbus, GA 31902 · 706-324-7371

Kingsland

John J. Ossick, Jr. · John J. Ossick, Jr. · 230 South Lee Street · P.O. Box 1087 · Kingsland, GA 31548-1087 · 912-729-5864

Savannah

Alex L. Zipperer · ⑩ · Zipperer, Lorberbaum & Beauvais · 200 East Saint Julian Street · P.O. Box 9147 · Savannah, GA 31412 · 912-232-3770

Summerville

Bobby Lee Cook · ㉕ · Cook & Connelly · 128 South Commerce Street · P.O. Box 370 · Summerville, GA 30747-1339 · 706-857-3421

Valdosta

J. Converse Bright · ⑳ · J. Converse Bright · http://www.conversebright.com · The McKey Building, Fourth Floor · 101 East Central Avenue · P.O. Box 5889 · Valdosta, GA 31603 · 229-247-7846

WORKERS' COMPENSATION LAW

Athens

E. Davison Burch · ⑩ · Blasingame, Burch, Garrard & Ashley · http://www.bbgbalaw.com · 440 College Avenue North · P.O. Box 832 · Athens, GA 30603 · 706-354-4000

M. Steven Heath · Blasingame, Burch, Garrard & Ashley · http://www.bbgbalaw.com · 440 College Avenue North · P.O. Box 832 · Athens, GA 30603 · 706-354-4000

Atlanta

William N. Anderson · Hamilton, Westby, Antonowich & Anderson · One Georgia Center, 17th Floor · 600 West Peachtree Street, NW · Atlanta, GA 30308 · 404-872-3500

H. Michael Bagley · ⑩ · Drew Eckl & Farnham · 880 West Peachtree Street · P.O. Box 7600 · Atlanta, GA 30357-0600 · 404-885-1400

Douglas A. Bennett · ⑩ · Swift, Currie, McGhee & Hiers · The Peachtree, Suite 300 · 1355 Peachtree Street, NE · Atlanta, GA 30309 · 404-874-8800

John A. Ferguson, Jr. · Drew Eckl & Farnham · 880 West Peachtree Street · P.O. Box 7600 · Atlanta, GA 30357-0600 · 404-885-1400

Andrew J. Hamilton · ⑩ · Hamilton, Westby, Antonowich & Anderson · One Georgia Center, 17th Floor 600 West Peachtree Street, NW · Atlanta, GA 30308 · 404-872-3500

Robert R. Potter · ⑩ · Swift, Currie, McGhee & Hiers · The Peachtree, Suite 300 · 1355 Peachtree Street, NE · Atlanta, GA 30309 · 404-874-8800

Susan J. Sadow · Susan J. Sadow · http://www.sadowworkerscomplaw.com · 400 Galleria Parkway, SE, Suite 1500 · Atlanta, GA 30339 · 770-984-8900

E. Scott Slappey · Slappey & Sadd · 6100 Lake Forrest Drive, NW, Suite 570 · Atlanta, GA 30328 · 404-255-6677

John F. Sweet · Clements & Sweet · 175 Trinity Avenue, SW, Suite 300 · Atlanta, GA 30303-3618 · 404-688-6700

Steven A. Westby · Hamilton, Westby, Antonowich & Anderson · One Georgia Center, 17th Floor · 600 West Peachtree Street, NW · Atlanta, GA 30308 · 404-872-3500

Charles B. Zirkle, Jr. · ⑩ · Zirkle & Hoffman · http://www.zirklaw.com · Five Concourse Parkway, Suite 2900 · Atlanta, GA 30328 · 770-551-8700

Augusta

Larry N. Hollington · ⑩ · Larry N. Hollington · 1206 George C. Wilson Drive · Augusta, GA 30909 · 706-868-1090

Calhoun

Michael R. Eddings · Collins & Eddings · 417 Court Street · P.O. Box 1658 · Calhoun, GA 30703-1658 · 706-625-1513

Macon

James M. Elliott, Jr. · ⑩ · Wall & Elliott · 1902 Forsyth Street · P.O. Box 13870 · Macon, GA 31208-3870 478-745-1430

Neal Graham · Buzzell, Graham & Welsh · 563 Walnut Street · Macon, GA 31201 · 478-742-8820

David B. Higdon, Sr. · ⑩ · Chambless, Higdon, Richardson, Katz & Griggs · Ambrose Baber Building, Suite 200 · 577 Walnut Street · P.O. Box 246 · Macon, GA 31202-0246 · 478-745-1181

Stephen Welsh · Buzzell, Graham & Welsh · 563 Walnut Street · Macon, GA 31201 · 478-742-8820

Marietta

Robert D. Ingram · Moore, Ingram, Johnson & Steele · 192 Anderson Street · P.O. Box 3305 · Marietta, GA 30061-3305 · 770-429-1499

Valdosta

George T. Talley · Coleman, Talley, Newbern, Kurrie, Preston & Hollan · 910 North Patterson Street · Valdosta, GA 31601-4531 · 229-242-7562

HAWAII

ADMINISTRATIVE LAW

Honolulu

Richard J. Kowen · Alston Hunt Floyd & Ing · http://www.ahfi.com · American Savings Bank Tower, Suite 1800 · 1001 Bishop Street · Honolulu, HI 96813 · 808-524-1800

Dennis M. Lombardi · Case Lombardi & Pettit · http://www.caselombardi.com · Pacific Guardian Center, Mauka Tower, Suite 2600 · 737 Bishop Street · Honolulu, HI 96813-3283 · 808-547-5400

ALTERNATIVE DISPUTE RESOLUTION

Honolulu

Riki May Amano · Dispute Prevention & Resolution · Pauahi Tower, Suite 1155 · 1003 Bishop Street · Honolulu, HI 96813 · 808-523-1234

Daniel A. Bent · Dispute Prevention & Resolution · Pauahi Tower, Suite 1155 · 1003 Bishop Street · Honolulu, HI 96813 · 808-523-1234

Ellen Godbey Carson · Alston Hunt Floyd & Ing · http://www.ahfi.com · American Savings Bank Tower, Suite 1800 · 1001 Bishop Street · Honolulu, HI 96813 · 808-524-1800

Louis L. C. Chang · Louis L. C. Chang · 931 University Avenue, Room 202 · P.O. Box 61188 · Honolulu, HI 96839 · 808-384-2468

Gerald S. Clay · Clay Chapman Crumpton Iwamura & Pulice · 700 Bishop Street, Suite 2100 · Honolulu, HI 96813 · 808-535-8400

Charles W. Crumpton · Clay Chapman Crumpton Iwamura & Pulice · 700 Bishop Street, Suite 2100 · Honolulu, HI 96813 · 808-535-8400

David H. Franzel · David H. Franzel · 217 Prospect Street, Suite B-11 · Honolulu, HI 96813 · 808-371-0303

Michael L. Freed · Tom Petrus & Miller · http://www.tpm-hawaii.com · Finance Factors Center, Suite 650 · 1164 Bishop Street · Honolulu, HI 96813 · 808-792-5800

James K. Hoenig · Dispute Prevention & Resolution · Pauahi Tower, Suite 1155 · 1003 Bishop Street · Honolulu, HI 96813 · 808-523-1234

Michael R. Marsh · Case Lombardi & Pettit · http://www.caselombardi.com · Pacific Guardian Center, Mauka Tower, Suite 2600 · 737 Bishop Street · Honolulu, HI 96813-3283 · 808-547-5400

Marie N. Milks · Dispute Prevention & Resolution · Pauahi Tower, Suite 1155 · 1003 Bishop Street · Honolulu, HI 96813 · 808-523-1234

Michael F. Nauyokas · Michael F. Nauyokas · Pacific Guardian Center, Makai Tower, Suite 2300 · 733 Bishop Street · Honolulu, HI 96813 · 808-538-0553

Patricia Kim Park · Park Park & Remillard · 707 Richards Street, Suite 500 · Honolulu, HI 96813 · 808-536-3905

James T. Paul · ⑩ · Paul Johnson Park & Niles · http://www.pjpn.com · American Savings Bank Tower, Suite 1300 · 1001 Bishop Street · P.O. Box 4438 · Honolulu, HI 96812 · 808-524-1212

Patrick K. S. L. Yim · Dispute Prevention & Resolution · Pauahi Tower, Suite 1155 · 1003 Bishop Street Honolulu, HI 96813 · 808-523-1234

Kamuela

Jerry M. Hiatt · ⑩ · Law Offices of Jerry M. Hiatt · Parker Square, Suite 204 · 65-1279 Kawaihae Road · Kamuela, HI 96743 · 808-885-3400

ANTITRUST LAW

Honolulu

Paul D. Alston · ⑩ · Alston Hunt Floyd & Ing · http://www.ahfi.com · American Savings Bank Tower, Suite 1800 · 1001 Bishop Street · Honolulu, HI 96813 · 808-524-1800

Bert T. Kobayashi, Jr. · ⑩ · Kobayashi, Sugita & Goda · 999 Bishop Street, 26th Floor · Honolulu, HI 96813 · 808-539-8700

Lisa Woods Munger · ⑩ · Goodsill Anderson Quinn & Stifel · 1099 Alakea Street, Suite 1800 · Honolulu, HI 96813 · 808-547-5600

APPELLATE LAW

Honolulu

Paul D. Alston · ⑩ · Alston Hunt Floyd & Ing · http://www.ahfi.com · American Savings Bank Tower, Suite 1800 · 1001 Bishop Street · Honolulu, HI 96813 · 808-524-1800

BANKING LAW

Honolulu

John R. Aube · Watanabe Ing & Komeiji · 999 Bishop Street, 23rd Floor · Honolulu, HI 96813 · 808-544-8300

Deborah Macer Chun · ⑩ · Chun Rair & Yoshimoto · http://www.chunrair.com · 1000 Bishop Street, Suite 1000 · Honolulu, HI 96813 · 808-528-4200

Nicholas C. Dreher · ⑩ · Cades Schutte · 1000 Bishop Street, Suite 1200 · Honolulu, HI 96813 · 808-521-9200

Lani L. Ewart · ⑩ · Goodsill Anderson Quinn & Stifel · 1099 Alakea Street, Suite 1800 · Honolulu, HI 96813 · 808-547-5600

Gino L. Gabrio · ⑩ · Cades Schutte · 1000 Bishop Street, Suite 1200 · Honolulu, HI 96813 · 808-521-9200

Mark A. Hazlett · ⑩ · Cades Schutte · 1000 Bishop Street, Suite 1200 · Honolulu, HI 96813 · 808-521-9200

Lawrence S. Okinaga · Carlsmith Ball · ASB Tower, Suite 2200 · 1001 Bishop Street · P.O. Box 656 · Honolulu, HI 96813 · 808-523-2500

David K. Rair · Chun Rair & Yoshimoto · http://www.chunrair.com · 1000 Bishop Street, Suite 1000 · Honolulu, HI 96813 · 808-528-4200

Larry T. Takumi · ⑩ · Cades Schutte · 1000 Bishop Street, Suite 1200 · Honolulu, HI 96813 · 808-521-9200

Janel M. Yoshimoto · Chun Rair & Yoshimoto · http://www.chunrair.com · 1000 Bishop Street, Suite 1000 · Honolulu, HI 96813 · 808-528-4200

BANKRUPTCY AND CREDITOR-DEBTOR RIGHTS LAW

Honolulu

Chuck C. Choi · Wagner, Choi & Evers · Topa Financial Center, Fort Street Tower, Suite 1900 · 745 Fort Street · Honolulu, HI 96813 · 808-533-1877

Nicholas C. Dreher · ⑩ · Cades Schutte · 1000 Bishop Street, Suite 1200 · Honolulu, HI 96813 · 808-521-9200

James N. Duca · ⑳ · Kessner, Duca, Umebayashi, Bain & Matsunaga · Central Pacific Plaza, 19th Floor · 220 South King Street · Honolulu, HI 96813 · 808-536-1900

Don Jeffrey Gelber · 20 · Gelber Gelber & Ingersoll · Topa Financial Center, Fort Street Tower, Suite 1400 · 745 Fort Street · Honolulu, HI 96813-3823 · 808-524-0155

Stephen M. Gelber · 20 · Gelber Gelber & Ingersoll · Topa Financial Center, Fort Street Tower, Suite 1400 · 745 Fort Street · Honolulu, HI 96813-3823 · 808-524-0155

Jerrold K. Guben · 10 · Reinwald O'Connor & Playdon · Pacific Guardian Center, Makai Tower, 24th Floor · 733 Bishop Street · P.O. Box 3199 · Honolulu, HI 96813 · 808-524-8350

Simon Klevansky · 10 · Klevansky Piper Van Etten · Bishop Square, Pauahi Tower, Suite 770 · 1003 Bishop Street · Honolulu, HI 96813 · 808-536-0200

Ted N. Pettit · Case Lombardi & Pettit · http://www.caselombardi.com · Pacific Guardian Center, Mauka Tower, Suite 2600 · 737 Bishop Street · Honolulu, HI 96813-3283 · 808-547-5400

Cuyler E. Shaw · 10 · Ashford & Wriston · Ali'i Place, Suite 1400 · 1099 Alakea Street · Honolulu, HI 96813 · 808-539-0400

Susan Tius · Rush Moore · 737 Bishop Street, Suite 2400 · Honolulu, HI 96813 · 808-521-0400

James A. Wagner · 20 · Wagner, Choi & Evers · Topa Financial Center, Fort Street Tower, Suite 1900 · 745 Fort Street · Honolulu, HI 96813 · 808-533-1877

BET-THE-COMPANY LITIGATION

Honolulu

Paul D. Alston · 10 · Alston Hunt Floyd & Ing · http://www.ahfi.com · American Savings Bank Tower, Suite 1800 · 1001 Bishop Street · Honolulu, HI 96813 · 808-524-1800

Edmund Burke · 25 · Burke, McPheeters, Bordner & Estes · 3100 Mauka Tower, Pacific Guardian Center 737 Bishop Street · Honolulu, HI 96813 · 808-523-9833

William C. McCorriston · 10 · McCorriston Miller Mukai MacKinnon · Five Waterfront Plaza, Fourth Floor · 500 Ala Moana Boulevard · P.O. Box 2800 · Honolulu, HI 96803-2800 · 808-529-7300

Kamuela

Jerry M. Hiatt · 10 · Law Offices of Jerry M. Hiatt · Parker Square, Suite 204 · 65-1279 Kawaihae Road · Kamuela, HI 96743 · 808-885-3400

COMMERCIAL LITIGATION

Honolulu

Paul D. Alston · 10 · Alston Hunt Floyd & Ing · http://www.ahfi.com · American Savings Bank Tower, Suite 1800 · 1001 Bishop Street · Honolulu, HI 96813 · 808-524-1800

Nadine Y. Ando · Bickerton Saunders Dang & Sullivan · Topa Financial Center, Fort Street Tower, Suite 801 · 745 Fort Street · Honolulu, HI 96813 · 808-599-3811

A. Bernard Bays · Bays, Deaver, Lung, Rose & Holma · Ali'i Place, Suite 1600 · 1099 Alakea Street · P.O. Box 1760 · Honolulu, HI 96813 · 808-523-9000

Edmund Burke · (25) · Burke, McPheeters, Bordner & Estes · 3100 Mauka Tower, Pacific Guardian Center 737 Bishop Street · Honolulu, HI 96813 · 808-523-9833

Phillip L. Deaver · Bays, Deaver, Lung, Rose & Holma · Ali'i Place, Suite 1600 · 1099 Alakea Street · P.O. Box 1760 · Honolulu, HI 96813 · 808-523-9000

Mark B. Desmarais · Tom Petrus & Miller · http://www.tpm-hawaii.com · Finance Factors Center, Suite 650 · 1164 Bishop Street · Honolulu, HI 96813 · 808-792-5800

Jacqueline Earle · Goodsill Anderson Quinn & Stifel · 1099 Alakea Street, Suite 1800 · Honolulu, HI 96813 · 808-547-5600

John S. Edmunds · (25) · Edmunds & Verga · Davies Pacific Center, Suite 2104 · 841 Bishop Street · Honolulu, HI 96813 · 808-524-2000

Shelby Anne Floyd · Alston Hunt Floyd & Ing · http://www.ahfi.com · American Savings Bank Tower, Suite 1800 · 1001 Bishop Street · Honolulu, HI 96813 · 808-524-1800

Diane D. Hastert · Damon Key Leong Kupchak Hastert · Pauahi Tower, Suite 1600 · 1003 Bishop Street · Honolulu, HI 96813 · 808-531-8031

C. Michael Heihre · (10) · Cades Schutte · 1000 Bishop Street, Suite 1200 · Honolulu, HI 96813 · 808-521-9200

Susan M. Ichinose · (10) · Susan M. Ichinose · Dillingham Transportation Building, Street Level · 701 Bishop Street · Honolulu, HI 96813-4814 · 808-585-0333

Louise K. Y. Ing · Alston Hunt Floyd & Ing · http://www.ahfi.com · American Savings Bank Tower, Suite 1800 · 1001 Bishop Street · Honolulu, HI 96813 · 808-524-1800

James A. Kawachika · Reinwald O'Connor & Playdon · Pacific Guardian Center, Makai Tower, 24th Floor · 733 Bishop Street · P.O. Box 3199 · Honolulu, HI 96813 · 808-524-8350

Bert T. Kobayashi, Jr. · (10) · Kobayashi, Sugita & Goda · 999 Bishop Street, 26th Floor · Honolulu, HI 96813 · 808-539-8700

John T. Komeiji · (10) · Watanabe Ing & Komeiji · 999 Bishop Street, 23rd Floor · Honolulu, HI 96813 · 808-544-8300

Kenneth R. Kupchak · Damon Key Leong Kupchak Hastert · Pauahi Tower, Suite 1600 · 1003 Bishop Street · Honolulu, HI 96813 · 808-531-8031

Bruce L. Lamon · Goodsill Anderson Quinn & Stifel · 1099 Alakea Street, Suite 1800 · Honolulu, HI 96813 · 808-547-5600

Harvey J. Lung · Bays, Deaver, Lung, Rose & Holma · Ali'i Place, Suite 1600 · 1099 Alakea Street · P.O. Box 1760 · Honolulu, HI 96813 · 808-523-9000

William C. McCorriston · (10) · McCorriston Miller Mukai MacKinnon · Five Waterfront Plaza, Fourth Floor · 500 Ala Moana Boulevard · P.O. Box 2800 · Honolulu, HI 96803-2800 · 808-529-7300

James C. McWhinnie · Damon Key Leong Kupchak Hastert · Pauahi Tower, Suite 1600 · 1003 Bishop Street · Honolulu, HI 96813 · 808-531-8031

William K. Meheula · Winer Meheula & Devens · 707 Richards Street, Penthouse One · Honolulu, HI 96813-4623 · 808-254-5855

Sheryl L. Nicholson · Paul Johnson Park & Niles · http://www.pjpn.com · American Savings Bank Tower, Suite 1300 · 1001 Bishop Street · P.O. Box 4438 · Honolulu, HI 96812 · 808-524-1212

Ke-Ching Ning · Ning, Lilly & Jones · 707 Richards Street, Suite 700 · Honolulu, HI 96813 · 808-528-1100

Dennis E. W. O'Connor, Sr. · ㉕ · Reinwald O'Connor & Playdon · Pacific Guardian Center, Makai Tower, 24th Floor · 733 Bishop Street · P.O. Box 3199 · Honolulu, HI 96813 · 808-524-8350

Terence James O'Toole · Starn O'Toole Marcus & Fisher · Pacific Guardian Center, Makai Tower, Suite 1900 · 733 Bishop Street · Honolulu, HI 96813 · 808-537-6100

Corey Park · Paul Johnson Park & Niles · http://www.pjpn.com · American Savings Bank Tower, Suite 1300 · 1001 Bishop Street · P.O. Box 4438 · Honolulu, HI 96812 · 808-524-1212

James T. Paul · ⑩ · Paul Johnson Park & Niles · http://www.pjpn.com · American Savings Bank Tower, Suite 1300 · 1001 Bishop Street · P.O. Box 4438 · Honolulu, HI 96812 · 808-524-1212

George W. Playdon, Jr. · ⑩ · Reinwald O'Connor & Playdon · Pacific Guardian Center, Makai Tower, 24th Floor · 733 Bishop Street · P.O. Box 3199 · Honolulu, HI 96813 · 808-524-8350

Jeffrey S. Portnoy · ⑩ · Cades Schutte · 1000 Bishop Street, Suite 1200 · Honolulu, HI 96813 · 808-521-9200

Crystal K. Rose · Bays, Deaver, Lung, Rose & Holma · Ali'i Place, Suite 1600 · 1099 Alakea Street · P.O. Box 1760 · Honolulu, HI 96813 · 808-523-9000

David Schulmeister · Cades Schutte · 1000 Bishop Street, Suite 1200 · Honolulu, HI 96813 · 808-521-9200

Lex R. Smith · Kobayashi, Sugita & Goda · 999 Bishop Street, 26th Floor · Honolulu, HI 96813 · 808-539-8700

Roy A. Vitousek III · Cades Schutte · 1000 Bishop Street, Suite 1200 · Honolulu, HI 96813 · 808-521-9200

Kamuela

Jerry M. Hiatt · ⑩ · Law Offices of Jerry M. Hiatt · Parker Square, Suite 204 · 65-1279 Kawaihae Road · Kamuela, HI 96743 · 808-885-3400

CONSTRUCTION LAW

Honolulu

Gerald S. Clay · Clay Chapman Crumpton Iwamura & Pulice · 700 Bishop Street, Suite 2100 · Honolulu, HI 96813 · 808-535-8400

Phillip L. Deaver · Bays, Deaver, Lung, Rose & Holma · Ali'i Place, Suite 1600 · 1099 Alakea Street · P.O. Box 1760 · Honolulu, HI 96813 · 808-523-9000

C. Michael Heihre · ⑩ · Cades Schutte · 1000 Bishop Street, Suite 1200 · Honolulu, HI 96813 · 808-521-9200

Karin L. Holma · Bays, Deaver, Lung, Rose & Holma · Ali'i Place, Suite 1600 · 1099 Alakea Street · P.O. Box 1760 · Honolulu, HI 96813 · 808-523-9000

Bert T. Kobayashi, Jr. · ⑩ · Kobayashi, Sugita & Goda · 999 Bishop Street, 26th Floor · Honolulu, HI 96813 · 808-539-8700

Kenneth R. Kupchak · Damon Key Leong Kupchak Hastert · Pauahi Tower, Suite 1600 · 1003 Bishop Street · Honolulu, HI 96813 · 808-531-8031

James H. Lawhn · Oliver, Lau, Lawhn, Ogawa & Nakamura · 707 Richards Street, Suite 600 · P.O. Box 2690 · Honolulu, HI 96803-2690 · 808-533-3999

Harvey J. Lung · Bays, Deaver, Lung, Rose & Holma · Ali'i Place, Suite 1600 · 1099 Alakea Street · P.O. Box 1760 · Honolulu, HI 96813 · 808-523-9000

Terence James O'Toole · Starn O'Toole Marcus & Fisher · Pacific Guardian Center, Makai Tower, Suite 1900 · 733 Bishop Street · Honolulu, HI 96813 · 808-537-6100

Brad S. Petrus · Tom Petrus & Miller · http://www.tpm-hawaii.com · Finance Factors Center, Suite 650 · 1164 Bishop Street · Honolulu, HI 96813 · 808-792-5800

David Schulmeister · Cades Schutte · 1000 Bishop Street, Suite 1200 · Honolulu, HI 96813 · 808-521-9200

Michael D. Tom · Tom Petrus & Miller · http://www.tpm-hawaii.com · Finance Factors Center, Suite 650 1164 Bishop Street · Honolulu, HI 96813 · 808-792-5800

CORPORATE LAW

Honolulu

Daniel H. Case · ㉕ · Case Lombardi & Pettit · http://www.caselombardi.com · Pacific Guardian Center, Mauka Tower, Suite 2600 · 737 Bishop Street · Honolulu, HI 96813-3283 · 808-547-5400

James H. Case · ⑳ · Carlsmith Ball · ASB Tower, Suite 2200 · 1001 Bishop Street · P.O. Box 656 · Honolulu, HI 96813 · 808-523-2500

Wesley Y. S. Chang · ⑩ · Law Offices of Wesley Y. S. Chang · Harbor Court, Suite 2800 · 55 Merchant Street · Honolulu, HI 96813 · 808-534-4807

James M. Cribley · ⑩ · Case Lombardi & Pettit · http://www.caselombardi.com · Pacific Guardian Center, Mauka Tower, Suite 2600 · 737 Bishop Street · Honolulu, HI 96813-3283 · 808-547-5400

Richard K. Ingersoll · ⑩ · Gelber Gelber & Ingersoll · Topa Financial Center, Fort Street Tower, Suite 1400 · 745 Fort Street · Honolulu, HI 96813-3823 · 808-524-0155

Gregory R. Kim · Vantage Counsel · Pacific Guardian Center, Makai Tower, Suite 2500 · 733 Bishop Street · Honolulu, HI 96813 · 808-538-9200

Kenneth R. Kupchak · Damon Key Leong Kupchak Hastert · Pauahi Tower, Suite 1600 · 1003 Bishop Street · Honolulu, HI 96813 · 808-531-8031

Stewart Pressman · McCorriston Miller Mukai MacKinnon · Five Waterfront Plaza, Fourth Floor · 500 Ala Moana Boulevard · P.O. Box 2800 · Honolulu, HI 96803-2800 · 808-529-7300

David J. Reber · ⑩ · Goodsill Anderson Quinn & Stifel · 1099 Alakea Street, Suite 1800 · Honolulu, HI 96813 · 808-547-5600

E. Gunner Schull · ⑳ · Cades Schutte · 1000 Bishop Street, Suite 1200 · Honolulu, HI 96813 · 808-521-9200

Tod Z. Tanaka · Schneider Tanaka Radovich Andrew & Tanaka · Alakea Corporate Tower, Suite 2100 · 1100 Alakea Street · Honolulu, HI 96813 · 808-792-4200

Kahului

Paul R. Mancini · Mancini, Welch & Geiger · The Kahului Building, Suite 470 · 33 Lono Avenue · Kahului, HI 96732-1681 · 808-871-8351

EDUCATION LAW

Honolulu

Shelby Anne Floyd · Alston Hunt Floyd & Ing · http://www.ahfi.com · American Savings Bank Tower, Suite 1800 · 1001 Bishop Street · Honolulu, HI 96813 · 808-524-1800

EMINENT DOMAIN AND CONDEMNATION LAW

Honolulu

Rosemary T. Fazio · ⑩ · Ashford & Wriston · Ali'i Place, Suite 1400 · 1099 Alakea Street · Honolulu, HI 96813 · 808-539-0400

C. Michael Heihre · ⑩ · Cades Schutte · 1000 Bishop Street, Suite 1200 · Honolulu, HI 96813 · 808-521-9200

Philip J. Leas · Cades Schutte · 1000 Bishop Street, Suite 1200 · Honolulu, HI 96813 · 808-521-9200

James K. Mee · Ashford & Wriston · Ali'i Place, Suite 1400 · 1099 Alakea Street · Honolulu, HI 96813 · 808-539-0400

Wayne P. Nasser · Ashford & Wriston · Ali'i Place, Suite 1400 · 1099 Alakea Street · Honolulu, HI 96813 · 808-539-0400

EMPLOYEE BENEFITS LAW

Honolulu

John J. D'Amato · D'Amato & Associates · http://www.benefitslawyers.com · Davies Pacific Center, Suite 1881 · 841 Bishop Street · Honolulu, HI 96813 · 808-546-5200

Roger W. Fonseca · ⑳ · Cades Schutte · 1000 Bishop Street, Suite 1200 · Honolulu, HI 96813 · 808-521-9200

Gregory M. Hansen · Case Lombardi & Pettit · http://www.caselombardi.com · Pacific Guardian Center, Mauka Tower, Suite 2600 · 737 Bishop Street · Honolulu, HI 96813-3283 · 808-547-5400

Lant A. Johnson · Goodsill Anderson Quinn & Stifel · 1099 Alakea Street, Suite 1800 · Honolulu, HI 96813 · 808-547-5600

John C. Khil · ⑩ · Carlsmith Ball · ASB Tower, Suite 2200 · 1001 Bishop Street · P.O. Box 656 · Honolulu, HI 96813 · 808-523-2500

J. Thomas Maloney, Jr. · Carlsmith Ball · ASB Tower, Suite 2200 · 1001 Bishop Street · P.O. Box 656 · Honolulu, HI 96813 · 808-523-2500

James L. Starshak · ㉕ · Carlsmith Ball · ASB Tower, Suite 2200 · 1001 Bishop Street · P.O. Box 656 · Honolulu, HI 96813 · 808-523-2500

ENERGY LAW

Honolulu

Michael H. Q. L. Lau · Morihara Lau & Fong · Davies Pacific Center, Suite 400 · 841 Bishop Street · Honolulu, HI 96813 · 808-526-2888

Kent D. Morihara · Morihara Lau & Fong · Davies Pacific Center, Suite 400 · 841 Bishop Street · Honolulu, HI 96813 · 808-526-2888

Craig I. Nakanishi · Rush Moore · 737 Bishop Street, Suite 2400 · Honolulu, HI 96813 · 808-521-0400

Thomas W. Williams, Jr. · ⑩ · Goodsill Anderson Quinn & Stifel · 1099 Alakea Street, Suite 1800 · Honolulu, HI 96813 · 808-547-5600

ENVIRONMENTAL LAW

Honolulu

Grace Nihei Kido · Cades Schutte · 1000 Bishop Street, Suite 1200 · Honolulu, HI 96813 · 808-521-9200

Lisa Woods Munger · ⑩ · Goodsill Anderson Quinn & Stifel · 1099 Alakea Street, Suite 1800 · Honolulu, HI 96813 · 808-547-5600

Ian L. Sandison · Carlsmith Ball · ASB Tower, Suite 2200 · 1001 Bishop Street · P.O. Box 656 · Honolulu, HI 96813 · 808-523-2500

EQUIPMENT FINANCE LAW

Honolulu

Mark B. Desmarais · Tom Petrus & Miller · http://www.tpm-hawaii.com · Finance Factors Center, Suite 650 · 1164 Bishop Street · Honolulu, HI 96813 · 808-792-5800

Larry T. Takumi · ⑩ · Cades Schutte · 1000 Bishop Street, Suite 1200 · Honolulu, HI 96813 · 808-521-9200

FAMILY LAW

Honolulu

William C. Darrah · ⑳ · Law Office of William C. Darrah · http://www.wcdlawhawaii.com · Pacific Guardian Center, Mauka Tower, Suite 2820 · 737 Bishop Street · Honolulu, HI 96813 · 808-533-2930

Geoffrey Hamilton · ㉕ · Char Hamilton Campbell & Yoshida · Pacific Guardian Center, Mauka Tower, Suite 2100 · 737 Bishop Street · Honolulu, HI 96813 · 808-524-3800

Charles T. Kleintop · ⑳ · Stirling & Kleintop · Alakea Corporate Tower, 20th Floor · 1100 Alakea Street · Honolulu, HI 96813 · 808-524-5183

Edward R. Lebb · Law Offices of Edward R. Lebb · Pacific Guardian Center, Makai Tower, Suite 1478 · 733 Bishop Street · Honolulu, HI 96813 · 808-542-9000

Timothy F. Luria · Stirling & Kleintop · Alakea Corporate Tower, 20th Floor · 1100 Alakea Street · Honolulu, HI 96813 · 808-524-5183

Dyan M. Medeiros · Stirling & Kleintop · Alakea Corporate Tower, 20th Floor · 1100 Alakea Street · Honolulu, HI 96813 · 808-524-5183

Stephanie A. Rezents · ⑩ · Rezents & Crowley · Dillingham Transportation Building, Suite 205 · 735 Bishop Street · Honolulu, HI 96813 · 808-532-9020

Thomas L. Stirling, Jr. · ㉕ · Stirling & Kleintop · Alakea Corporate Tower, 20th Floor · 1100 Alakea Street · Honolulu, HI 96813 · 808-524-5183

FAMILY LAW MEDIATION

Honolulu

James K. Hoenig · Dispute Prevention & Resolution · Pauahi Tower, Suite 1155 · 1003 Bishop Street · Honolulu, HI 96813 · 808-523-1234

FIRST AMENDMENT LAW

Honolulu

Paul D. Alston · ⑩ · Alston Hunt Floyd & Ing · http://www.ahfi.com · American Savings Bank Tower, Suite 1800 · 1001 Bishop Street · Honolulu, HI 96813 · 808-524-1800

James J. Bickerton · ⑩ · Bickerton Saunders Dang & Sullivan · Topa Financial Center, Fort Street Tower, Suite 801 · 745 Fort Street · Honolulu, HI 96813 · 808-599-3811

Jeffrey S. Portnoy · ⑩ · Cades Schutte · 1000 Bishop Street, Suite 1200 · Honolulu, HI 96813 · 808-521-9200

GOVERNMENT RELATIONS LAW

Honolulu

Robert K. Ichikawa · ⑩ · Kobayashi, Sugita & Goda · 999 Bishop Street, 26th Floor · Honolulu, HI 96813 · 808-539-8700

William M. Kaneko · Alston Hunt Floyd & Ing · http://www.ahfi.com · American Savings Bank Tower, Suite 1800 · 1001 Bishop Street · Honolulu, HI 96813 · 808-524-1800

Gary M. Slovin · Goodsill Anderson Quinn & Stifel · 1099 Alakea Street, Suite 1800 · Honolulu, HI 96813 · 808-547-5600

HEALTH CARE LAW

Honolulu

Ellen Godbey Carson · Alston Hunt Floyd & Ing · http://www.ahfi.com · American Savings Bank Tower, Suite 1800 · 1001 Bishop Street · Honolulu, HI 96813 · 808-524-1800

Wesley Y. S. Chang · ⑩ · Law Offices of Wesley Y. S. Chang · Harbor Court, Suite 2800 · 55 Merchant Street · Honolulu, HI 96813 · 808-534-4807

J. George Hetherington · Torkildson Katz Moore Hetherington & Harris · http://www.torkildson.com · Topa Financial Center Building, 15th Floor · 700 Bishop Street · Honolulu, HI 96813-4187 · 808-523-6000

Robert S. Katz · (25) · Torkildson Katz Moore Hetherington & Harris · http://www.torkildson.com · Topa Financial Center Building, 15th Floor · 700 Bishop Street · Honolulu, HI 96813-4187 · 808-523-6000

IMMIGRATION LAW

Honolulu

KahBo Dye-Chiew · Law Office of KahBo Dye-Chiew · 201 Merchant Street, Suite 2302 · Honolulu, HI 96813 · 808-542-5572

Maile M. Hirota · Lynch Ichida Thompson Kim & Hirota · 1132 Bishop Street, Suite 1405 · Honolulu, HI 96813 · 808-528-0100

Robert K. Ichikawa · (10) · Kobayashi, Sugita & Goda · 999 Bishop Street, 26th Floor · Honolulu, HI 96813 · 808-539-8700

Peter T. Kashiwa · (10) · Goodsill Anderson Quinn & Stifel · 1099 Alakea Street, Suite 1800 · Honolulu, HI 96813 · 808-547-5600

Alan W. C. Ma · (10) · Law Offices of Alan W. C. Ma · Pan Am Building, Suite 1018 · 1600 Kapiolani Boulevard · P.O. Box 23014 · Honolulu, HI 96823-3014 · 808-944-1188

Ruth K. Oh · Kobayashi, Sugita & Goda · 999 Bishop Street, 26th Floor · Honolulu, HI 96813 · 808-539-8700

INSURANCE LAW

Honolulu

James Kawashima · (10) · Kawashima Lorusso & Harada · Topa Financial Center, Fort Street Tower, Suite 500 · 745 Fort Street · Honolulu, HI 96813 · 808-275-0300

Richard B. Miller · Tom Petrus & Miller · http://www.tpm-hawaii.com · Finance Factors Center, Suite 650 · 1164 Bishop Street · Honolulu, HI 96813 · 808-792-5800

Peter W. Olson · Cades Schutte · 1000 Bishop Street, Suite 1200 · Honolulu, HI 96813 · 808-521-9200

Jeffrey S. Portnoy · (10) · Cades Schutte · 1000 Bishop Street, Suite 1200 · Honolulu, HI 96813 · 808-521-9200

George W. Van Buren · Van Buren Campbell & Shimizu · Topa Financial Center, Fort Street Tower, Suite 1950 · 745 Fort Street Mall · Honolulu, HI 96813 · 808-522-0420

Bruce H. Wakuzawa · Law Office Of Bruce H. Wakuzawa · Topa Financial Center, Fort Street Tower, Suite 1950 · 745 Fort Street · Honolulu, HI 96813 · 808-523-1007

INTELLECTUAL PROPERTY LAW

Honolulu

Edward R. Bendet · ⑩ · Bendet Fidell Sakai & Lee · The Davies Pacific Center, Suite 1500 · 841 Bishop Street · Honolulu, HI 96813 · 808-524-0544

Mark D. Bernstein · ⑩ · Mark D. Bernstein · 63 Merchant Street · Honolulu, HI 96813 · 808-537-3327

Robert Carson Godbey · ⑩ · Godbey Griffiths & Reiss · http://www.lawhi.com · Pauahi Tower, Suite 2300 · 1003 Bishop Street · Honolulu, HI 96813 · 808-523-8894

Martin E. Hsia · ⑩ · Cades Schutte · 1000 Bishop Street, Suite 1200 · Honolulu, HI 96813 · 808-521-9200

Paul Maki · Paul Maki · Alakea Corporate Tower, 23rd Floor · 1100 Alakea Street · Honolulu, HI 96813 · 808-545-1122

Robert J. Smolenski · ⑩ · Smolenski & Wooddell · Davies Pacific Center, Suite 1717 · 841 Bishop Street Honolulu, HI 96813-3970 · 808-524-5750

Elise O. Thorn · Clay Chapman Crumpton Iwamura & Pulice · 700 Bishop Street, Suite 2100 · Honolulu, HI 96813 · 808-535-8400

LABOR AND EMPLOYMENT LAW

Honolulu

David F. E. Banks · Cades Schutte · 1000 Bishop Street, Suite 1200 · Honolulu, HI 96813 · 808-521-9200

Dean D. Choy · ⑩ · Dean D. Choy · The Merchant House, Suite 209 · 222 Merchant Street · Honolulu, HI 96813 · 808-538-7087

Lowell K. Y. Chun-Hoon · ⑩ · King, Nakamura & Chun-Hoon · Central Pacific Plaza, Suite 980 · 220 South King Street · Honolulu, HI 96813-4539 · 808-521-8041

Perry W. Confalone · Carlsmith Ball · ASB Tower, Suite 2200 · 1001 Bishop Street · P.O. Box 656 · Honolulu, HI 96813 · 808-523-2500

Anna Elento-Sneed · Alston Hunt Floyd & Ing · http://www.ahfi.com · American Savings Bank Tower, Suite 1800 · 1001 Bishop Street · Honolulu, HI 96813 · 808-524-1800

Colleen Hanabusa · ⑩ · Colleen Hanabusa · Alakea Corporate Tower, Suite 1200 · 1100 Alakea Street · Honolulu, HI 96813 · 808-523-5777

Jeffrey S. Harris · Torkildson Katz Moore Hetherington & Harris · http://www.torkildson.com · Topa Financial Center Building, 15th Floor · 700 Bishop Street · Honolulu, HI 96813-4187 · 808-523-6000

Susan M. Ichinose · ⑩ · Susan M. Ichinose · Dillingham Transportation Building, Street Level · 701 Bishop Street · Honolulu, HI 96813-4814 · 808-585-0333

Patrick H. Jones · Marr Jones & Wang · Pauahi Tower, Suite 1550 · 1003 Bishop Street · Honolulu, HI 96813 · 808-536-4900

Robert S. Katz · ㉕ · Torkildson Katz Moore Hetherington & Harris · http://www.torkildson.com · Topa Financial Center Building, 15th Floor · 700 Bishop Street · Honolulu, HI 96813-4187 · 808-523-6000

John L. Knorek · Torkildson Katz Moore Hetherington & Harris · http://www.torkildson.com · Topa Financial Center Building, 15th Floor · 700 Bishop Street · Honolulu, HI 96813-4187 · 808-523-6000

Ronald Y. K. Leong · Watanabe Ing & Komeiji · 999 Bishop Street, 23rd Floor · Honolulu, HI 96813 · 808-544-8300

Barry W. Marr · ⑩ · Marr Jones & Wang · Pauahi Tower, Suite 1550 · 1003 Bishop Street · Honolulu, HI 96813 · 808-536-4900

Ernest C. Moore III · ⑩ · Torkildson Katz Moore Hetherington & Harris · http://www.torkildson.com · Topa Financial Center Building, 15th Floor · 700 Bishop Street · Honolulu, HI 96813-4187 · 808-523-6000

Steven M. Nakashima · Marr Jones & Wang · Pauahi Tower, Suite 1550 · 1003 Bishop Street · Honolulu, HI 96813 · 808-536-4900

Michael F. Nauyokas · Michael F. Nauyokas · Pacific Guardian Center, Makai Tower, Suite 2300 · 733 Bishop Street · Honolulu, HI 96813 · 808-538-0553

Ke-Ching Ning · Ning, Lilly & Jones · 707 Richards Street, Suite 700 · Honolulu, HI 96813 · 808-528-1100

Barbara A. Petrus · Goodsill Anderson Quinn & Stifel · 1099 Alakea Street, Suite 1800 · Honolulu, HI 96813 · 808-547-5600

Richard M. Rand · Marr Jones & Wang · Pauahi Tower, Suite 1550 · 1003 Bishop Street · Honolulu, HI 96813 · 808-536-4900

Gregory M. Sato · Kobayashi, Sugita & Goda · 999 Bishop Street, 26th Floor · Honolulu, HI 96813 · 808-539-8700

David F. Simons · The Law Offices of David F. Simons · Ocean View Center, Penthouse One · 707 Richards Street · Honolulu, HI 96813 · 808-536-3255

Herbert R. Takahashi · ⑳ · Takahashi, Vasconcellos & Covert · 345 Queen Street, Suite 506 · Honolulu, HI 96813 · 808-526-3003

Lynne T. Toyofuku · Marr Jones & Wang · Pauahi Tower, Suite 1550 · 1003 Bishop Street · Honolulu, HI 96813 · 808-536-4900

Sarah O. Wang · Marr Jones & Wang · Pauahi Tower, Suite 1550 · 1003 Bishop Street · Honolulu, HI 96813 · 808-536-4900

Christopher S. Yeh · Marr Jones & Wang · Pauahi Tower, Suite 1550 · 1003 Bishop Street · Honolulu, HI 96813 · 808-536-4900

Kamuela

Jerry M. Hiatt · ⑩ · Law Offices of Jerry M. Hiatt · Parker Square, Suite 204 · 65-1279 Kawaihae Road · Kamuela, HI 96743 · 808-885-3400

LAND USE & ZONING LAW

Honolulu

Michael W. Gibson · Ashford & Wriston · Ali'i Place, Suite 1400 · 1099 Alakea Street · Honolulu, HI 96813 · 808-539-0400

Benjamin A. Kudo · Imanaka Kudo & Fujimoto · Topa Financial Center, Fort Street Tower, 17th floor · 745 Fort Street · Honolulu, HI 96813 · 808-521-9500

Roy A. Vitousek III · Cades Schutte · 1000 Bishop Street, Suite 1200 · Honolulu, HI 96813 · 808-521-9200

Lihue

Michael J. Belles · Belles, Graham, Proudfoot & Wilson · Watumull Plaza, Suite 202 · 4334 Rice Street · Lihue, HI 96766-1388 · 808-245-4705

Wailuku

B. Martin Luna · Carlsmith Ball · One Main Plaza, Suite 400 · 2200 Main Street · Wailuku, HI 96793-1086 · 808-242-4535

LEGAL MALPRACTICE LAW

Honolulu

A. Bernard Bays · Bays, Deaver, Lung, Rose & Holma · Ali'i Place, Suite 1600 · 1099 Alakea Street · P.O. Box 1760 · Honolulu, HI 96813 · 808-523-9000

James J. Bickerton · ⑩ · Bickerton Saunders Dang & Sullivan · Topa Financial Center, Fort Street Tower, Suite 801 · 745 Fort Street · Honolulu, HI 96813 · 808-599-3811

William A. Bordner · Burke, McPheeters, Bordner & Estes · 3100 Mauka Tower, Pacific Guardian Center · 737 Bishop Street · Honolulu, HI 96813 · 808-523-9833

James Kawashima · ⑩ · Kawashima Lorusso & Harada · Topa Financial Center, Fort Street Tower, Suite 500 · 745 Fort Street · Honolulu, HI 96813 · 808-275-0300

William C. McCorriston · ⑩ · McCorriston Miller Mukai MacKinnon · Five Waterfront Plaza, Fourth Floor · 500 Ala Moana Boulevard · P.O. Box 2800 · Honolulu, HI 96803-2800 · 808-529-7300

William K. Meheula · Winer Meheula & Devens · 707 Richards Street, Penthouse One · Honolulu, HI 96813-4623 · 808-254-5855

William S. Miller · ⑩ · Goodsill Anderson Quinn & Stifel · 1099 Alakea Street, Suite 1800 · Honolulu, HI 96813 · 808-547-5600

John Francis Perkin · Perkin & Faria · Davies Pacific Center, Suite 2000 · 841 Bishop Street · Honolulu, HI 96813 · 808-523-2300

George W. Playdon, Jr. · ⑩ · Reinwald O'Connor & Playdon · Pacific Guardian Center, Makai Tower, 24th Floor · 733 Bishop Street · P.O. Box 3199 · Honolulu, HI 96813 · 808-524-8350

Jeffrey S. Portnoy · ⑩ · Cades Schutte · 1000 Bishop Street, Suite 1200 · Honolulu, HI 96813 · 808-521-9200

MARITIME LAW

Honolulu

Mark B. Desmarais · Tom Petrus & Miller · http://www.tpm-hawaii.com · Finance Factors Center, Suite 650 · 1164 Bishop Street · Honolulu, HI 96813 · 808-792-5800

Robert G. Frame · Frame & Nakano · Four Waterfront Plaza, Suite 575 · 500 Ala Moana Boulevard · Honolulu, HI 96813 · 808-545-3043

John R. Lacy · ⑩ · Goodsill Anderson Quinn & Stifel · 1099 Alakea Street, Suite 1800 · Honolulu, HI 96813 · 808-547-5600

Dean H. Robb · Carlsmith Ball · ASB Tower, Suite 2200 · 1001 Bishop Street · P.O. Box 656 · Honolulu, HI 96813 · 808-523-2500

Lihue

David W. Proudfoot · ⑩ · Belles, Graham, Proudfoot & Wilson · Watumull Plaza, Suite 202 · 4334 Rice Street · Lihue, HI 96766-1388 · 808-245-4705

MASS TORT LITIGATION

Honolulu

Gary O. Galiher · Galiher DeRobertis Ono · 610 Ward Avenue, Second Floor · Honolulu, HI 96814 · 808-597-1400

Bruce H. Wakuzawa · Law Office Of Bruce H. Wakuzawa · Topa Financial Center, Fort Street Tower, Suite 1950 · 745 Fort Street · Honolulu, HI 96813 · 808-523-1007

MEDICAL MALPRACTICE LAW

Honolulu

James J. Bickerton · ⑩ · Bickerton Saunders Dang & Sullivan · Topa Financial Center, Fort Street Tower, Suite 801 · 745 Fort Street · Honolulu, HI 96813 · 808-599-3811

Edmund Burke · ㉕ · Burke, McPheeters, Bordner & Estes · 3100 Mauka Tower, Pacific Guardian Center 737 Bishop Street · Honolulu, HI 96813 · 808-523-9833

Thomas E. Cook · Lyons Brandt Cook & Hiramatsu · Davies Pacific Center, Suite 1800 · 841 Bishop Street · Honolulu, HI 96813 · 808-524-7030

Mark S. Davis · ⑩ · Davis Levin Livingston · http://www.davislevin.com · Davis Levin Livingston Place, Suite 400 · 851 Fort Street · Honolulu, HI 96813 · 808-524-7500

L. Richard Fried, Jr. · ㉕ · Cronin, Fried, Sekiya, Kekina & Fairbanks · Davies Pacific Center, Suite 600 · 841 Bishop Street · Honolulu, HI 96813-3962 · 808-524-1433

William S. Hunt · Alston Hunt Floyd & Ing · http://www.ahfi.com · American Savings Bank Tower, Suite 1800 · 1001 Bishop Street · Honolulu, HI 96813 · 808-524-1800

Michael K. Livingston · Davis Levin Livingston · http://www.davislevin.com · Davis Levin Livingston Place, Suite 400 · 851 Fort Street · Honolulu, HI 96813 · 808-524-7500

John S. Nishimoto · Ayabe, Chong, Nishimoto, Sia & Nakamura · Pauahi Tower, Suite 2500 · 1003 Bishop Street · Honolulu, HI 96813 · 808-537-6119

Arthur F. Roeca · Roeca, Louie & Hiraoka · Davies Pacific Center, Suite 900 · 841 Bishop Street · Honolulu, HI 96813-3917 · 808-538-7500

Kamuela

Jerry M. Hiatt · ⑩ · Law Offices of Jerry M. Hiatt · Parker Square, Suite 204 · 65-1279 Kawaihae Road · Kamuela, HI 96743 · 808-885-3400

MERGERS & ACQUISITIONS LAW

Honolulu

Stewart Pressman · McCorriston Miller Mukai MacKinnon · Five Waterfront Plaza, Fourth Floor · 500 Ala Moana Boulevard · P.O. Box 2800 · Honolulu, HI 96803-2800 · 808-529-7300

E. Gunner Schull · ⑳ · Cades Schutte · 1000 Bishop Street, Suite 1200 · Honolulu, HI 96813 · 808-521-9200

J. Thomas Van Winkle · Carlsmith Ball · ASB Tower, Suite 2200 · 1001 Bishop Street · P.O. Box 656 · Honolulu, HI 96813 · 808-523-2500

NATURAL RESOURCES LAW

Honolulu

Gino L. Gabrio · ⑩ · Cades Schutte · 1000 Bishop Street, Suite 1200 · Honolulu, HI 96813 · 808-521-9200

NON-PROFIT/CHARITIES LAW

Honolulu

James L. Starshak · ㉕ · Carlsmith Ball · ASB Tower, Suite 2200 · 1001 Bishop Street · P.O. Box 656 · Honolulu, HI 96813 · 808-523-2500

NON-WHITE-COLLAR CRIMINAL DEFENSE

Honolulu

John S. Edmunds · ㉕ · Edmunds & Verga · Davies Pacific Center, Suite 2104 · 841 Bishop Street · Honolulu, HI 96813 · 808-524-2000

David W. Hall · ⑩ · David W. Hall · Dillingham Transportation Building, Suite 236 · 735 Bishop Street · Honolulu, HI 96813-4816 · 808-526-0402

William A. Harrison · Harrison & Matsuoka · http://www.hamlaw.net · Davies Pacific Center, Suite 800 · 841 Bishop Street · Honolulu, HI 96813 · 808-523-7041

Brook Hart · ㉕ · Brook Hart, Attorney at Law · http://www.hart-law.net · Melim Building, Suite 610 · 333 Queen Street · Honolulu, HI 96813 · 808-526-0811

Howard K. K. Luke · Law Office of Howard K. K. Luke · Davies Pacific Center, Suite 2022 · 841 Bishop Street · Honolulu, HI 96813 · 808-545-5000

Wailuku

Philip H. Lowenthal · ㉕ · Philip H. Lowenthal · 33 North Market Street, Suite 101 · Wailuku, HI 96793 808-242-5000

PERSONAL INJURY LITIGATION

Honolulu

Paul D. Alston · ⑩ · Alston Hunt Floyd & Ing · http://www.ahfi.com · American Savings Bank Tower, Suite 1800 · 1001 Bishop Street · Honolulu, HI 96813 · 808-524-1800

Sidney A. Ayabe · Ayabe, Chong, Nishimoto, Sia & Nakamura · Pauahi Tower, Suite 2500 · 1003 Bishop Street · Honolulu, HI 96813 · 808-537-6119

James J. Bickerton · ⑩ · Bickerton Saunders Dang & Sullivan · Topa Financial Center, Fort Street Tower, Suite 801 · 745 Fort Street · Honolulu, HI 96813 · 808-599-3811

William A. Bordner · Burke, McPheeters, Bordner & Estes · 3100 Mauka Tower, Pacific Guardian Center · 737 Bishop Street · Honolulu, HI 96813 · 808-523-9833

Sherry P. Broder · ⑩ · Law Offices of Sherry P. Broder · Davies Pacific Center, Suite 800 · 841 Bishop Street · Honolulu, HI 96813 · 808-531-1411

Edmund Burke · ㉕ · Burke, McPheeters, Bordner & Estes · 3100 Mauka Tower, Pacific Guardian Center 737 Bishop Street · Honolulu, HI 96813 · 808-523-9833

Thomas E. Cook · Lyons Brandt Cook & Hiramatsu · Davies Pacific Center, Suite 1800 · 841 Bishop Street · Honolulu, HI 96813 · 808-524-7030

Jeffrey P. Crabtree · Law Offices of Jeff Crabtree · http://www.consumerlaw.com · 820 Mililani Street, Suite 701 · Honolulu, HI 96813 · 808-536-6260

Paul F. Cronin · ⑩ · Cronin, Fried, Sekiya, Kekina & Fairbanks · Davies Pacific Center, Suite 600 · 841 Bishop Street · Honolulu, HI 96813-3962 · 808-524-1433

Mark S. Davis · ⑩ · Davis Levin Livingston · http://www.davislevin.com · Davis Levin Livingston Place, Suite 400 · 851 Fort Street · Honolulu, HI 96813 · 808-524-7500

John S. Edmunds · ㉕ · Edmunds & Verga · Davies Pacific Center, Suite 2104 · 841 Bishop Street · Honolulu, HI 96813 · 808-524-2000

David L. Fairbanks · ⑳ · Cronin, Fried, Sekiya, Kekina & Fairbanks · Davies Pacific Center, Suite 600 · 841 Bishop Street · Honolulu, HI 96813-3962 · 808-524-1433

L. Richard Fried, Jr. · ㉕ · Cronin, Fried, Sekiya, Kekina & Fairbanks · Davies Pacific Center, Suite 600 · 841 Bishop Street · Honolulu, HI 96813-3962 · 808-524-1433

William S. Hunt · Alston Hunt Floyd & Ing · http://www.ahfi.com · American Savings Bank Tower, Suite 1800 · 1001 Bishop Street · Honolulu, HI 96813 · 808-524-1800

James Kawashima · ⑩ · Kawashima Lorusso & Harada · Topa Financial Center, Fort Street Tower, Suite 500 · 745 Fort Street · Honolulu, HI 96813 · 808-275-0300

Bert T. Kobayashi, Jr. · ⑩ · Kobayashi, Sugita & Goda · 999 Bishop Street, 26th Floor · Honolulu, HI 96813 · 808-539-8700

John T. Komeiji · 10 · Watanabe Ing & Komeiji · 999 Bishop Street, 23rd Floor · Honolulu, HI 96813 · 808-544-8300

John R. Lacy · 10 · Goodsill Anderson Quinn & Stifel · 1099 Alakea Street, Suite 1800 · Honolulu, HI 96813 · 808-547-5600

Michael K. Livingston · Davis Levin Livingston · http://www.davislevin.com · Davis Levin Livingston Place, Suite 400 · 851 Fort Street · Honolulu, HI 96813 · 808-524-7500

William C. McCorriston · 10 · McCorriston Miller Mukai MacKinnon · Five Waterfront Plaza, Fourth Floor · 500 Ala Moana Boulevard · P.O. Box 2800 · Honolulu, HI 96803-2800 · 808-529-7300

John S. Nishimoto · Ayabe, Chong, Nishimoto, Sia & Nakamura · Pauahi Tower, Suite 2500 · 1003 Bishop Street · Honolulu, HI 96813 · 808-537-6119

Dennis E. W. O'Connor, Sr. · 25 · Reinwald O'Connor & Playdon · Pacific Guardian Center, Makai Tower, 24th Floor · 733 Bishop Street · P.O. Box 3199 · Honolulu, HI 96813 · 808-524-8350

George W. Playdon, Jr. · 10 · Reinwald O'Connor & Playdon · Pacific Guardian Center, Makai Tower, 24th Floor · 733 Bishop Street · P.O. Box 3199 · Honolulu, HI 96813 · 808-524-8350

Jeffrey S. Portnoy · 10 · Cades Schutte · 1000 Bishop Street, Suite 1200 · Honolulu, HI 96813 · 808-521-9200

Kenneth S. Robbins · 10 · Robbins & Associates · Davies Pacific Center, Suite 2200 · 841 Bishop Street · Honolulu, HI 96813 · 808-524-2355

Arthur F. Roeca · Roeca, Louie & Hiraoka · Davies Pacific Center, Suite 900 · 841 Bishop Street · Honolulu, HI 96813-3917 · 808-538-7500

Gerald Y. Sekiya · 20 · Cronin, Fried, Sekiya, Kekina & Fairbanks · Davies Pacific Center, Suite 600 · 841 Bishop Street · Honolulu, HI 96813-3962 · 808-524-1433

Raymond J. Tam · 25 · Tam & Stanford · American Savings Bank Tower, Suite 1100 · 1001 Bishop Street Honolulu, HI 96813 · 808-522-9111

Alan Van Etten · Klevansky Piper Van Etten · Bishop Square, Pauahi Tower, Suite 770 · 1003 Bishop Street · Honolulu, HI 96813 · 808-536-0200

Jan M. Weinberg · 10 · Jan M. Weinberg · http://www.janweinberg.com · 1164 Bishop Street, Suite 1200 · Honolulu, HI 96813 · 808-523-9477

Wailuku

James Krueger · 25 · Krueger Wong · Wailuku Business Plaza, Suite 102 · 2065 Main Street · P.O. Box 1460 · Wailuku, HI 96793-1693 · 808-244-7444

PRODUCT LIABILITY LITIGATION

Honolulu

Sherry P. Broder · 10 · Law Offices of Sherry P. Broder · Davies Pacific Center, Suite 800 · 841 Bishop Street · Honolulu, HI 96813 · 808-531-1411

Edmund Burke · 25 · Burke, McPheeters, Bordner & Estes · 3100 Mauka Tower, Pacific Guardian Center 737 Bishop Street · Honolulu, HI 96813 · 808-523-9833

PUBLIC FINANCE LAW

Honolulu

Wesley Y. S. Chang · ⑩ · Law Offices of Wesley Y. S. Chang · Harbor Court, Suite 2800 · 55 Merchant Street · Honolulu, HI 96813 · 808-534-4807

Brian T. Hirai · McCorriston Miller Mukai MacKinnon · Five Waterfront Plaza, Fourth Floor · 500 Ala Moana Boulevard · P.O. Box 2800 · Honolulu, HI 96803-2800 · 808-529-7300

David J. Reber · ⑩ · Goodsill Anderson Quinn & Stifel · 1099 Alakea Street, Suite 1800 · Honolulu, HI 96813 · 808-547-5600

REAL ESTATE LAW

Hilo

Steven S. C. Lim · Carlsmith Ball · 121 Waianuenue Avenue · P.O. Box 686 · Hilo, HI 96721-0686 · 808-935-6644

Honolulu

David F. Andrew · Schneider Tanaka Radovich Andrew & Tanaka · Alakea Corporate Tower, Suite 2100 1100 Alakea Street · Honolulu, HI 96813 · 808-792-4200

Walter Beh II · Rush Moore · 737 Bishop Street, Suite 2400 · Honolulu, HI 96813 · 808-521-0400

Edward R. Brooks · Brooks Tom Porter & Quitiquit · 841 Bishop Street, Suite 2125 · Honolulu, HI 96813 · 808-526-3011

Gilbert D. Butson · ⑩ · Reinwald O'Connor & Playdon · Pacific Guardian Center, Makai Tower, 24th Floor · 733 Bishop Street · P.O. Box 3199 · Honolulu, HI 96813 · 808-524-8350

Daniel H. Case · ㉕ · Case Lombardi & Pettit · http://www.caselombardi.com · Pacific Guardian Center, Mauka Tower, Suite 2600 · 737 Bishop Street · Honolulu, HI 96813-3283 · 808-547-5400

Wesley Y. S. Chang · ⑩ · Law Offices of Wesley Y. S. Chang · Harbor Court, Suite 2800 · 55 Merchant Street · Honolulu, HI 96813 · 808-534-4807

Deborah Macer Chun · ⑩ · Chun Rair & Yoshimoto · http://www.chunrair.com · 1000 Bishop Street, Suite 1000 · Honolulu, HI 96813 · 808-528-4200

Edward Y. C. Chun · ㉕ · Chun, Kerr, Dodd, Beaman & Wong · Fort Street Tower, Topa Financial Center, Ninth Floor · 745 Fort Street · Honolulu, HI 96813-3815 · 808-528-8200

Rosemary T. Fazio · ⑩ · Ashford & Wriston · Ali'i Place, Suite 1400 · 1099 Alakea Street · Honolulu, HI 96813 · 808-539-0400

Stacey W. E. Foy · Case Lombardi & Pettit · http://www.caselombardi.com · Pacific Guardian Center, Mauka Tower, Suite 2600 · 737 Bishop Street · Honolulu, HI 96813-3283 · 808-547-5400

Gino L. Gabrio · ⑩ · Cades Schutte · 1000 Bishop Street, Suite 1200 · Honolulu, HI 96813 · 808-521-9200

Stephen M. Gelber · ⑳ · Gelber Gelber & Ingersoll · Topa Financial Center, Fort Street Tower, Suite 1400 · 745 Fort Street · Honolulu, HI 96813-3823 · 808-524-0155

Michael W. Gibson · Ashford & Wriston · Ali'i Place, Suite 1400 · 1099 Alakea Street · Honolulu, HI 96813 · 808-539-0400

Robert Bruce Graham, Jr. · ⑩ · Ashford & Wriston · Ali'i Place, Suite 1400 · 1099 Alakea Street · Honolulu, HI 96813 · 808-539-0400

Nancy N. Grekin · ⑩ · McCorriston Miller Mukai MacKinnon · Five Waterfront Plaza, Fourth Floor · 500 Ala Moana Boulevard · P.O. Box 2800 · Honolulu, HI 96803-2800 · 808-529-7300

C. Michael Heihre · ⑩ · Cades Schutte · 1000 Bishop Street, Suite 1200 · Honolulu, HI 96813 · 808-521-9200

Neil F. Hulbert · Alston Hunt Floyd & Ing · http://www.ahfi.com · American Savings Bank Tower, Suite 1800 · 1001 Bishop Street · Honolulu, HI 96813 · 808-524-1800

Raymond S. Iwamoto · Schlack Ito Lockwood Piper & Elkind · Topa Financial Center, Suite 1500 · 745 Fort Street · Honolulu, HI 96813 · 808-523-6040

Eric A. James · Carlsmith Ball · ASB Tower, Suite 2200 · 1001 Bishop Street · P.O. Box 656 · Honolulu, HI 96813 · 808-523-2500

John Jubinsky · ⑳ · John Jubinsky · Title Guaranty Building, Seventh Floor · 235 Queen Street · P.O. Box 3595 · Honolulu, HI 96811 · 808-533-5808

Charles W. Key · ⑩ · Damon Key Leong Kupchak Hastert · Pauahi Tower, Suite 1600 · 1003 Bishop Street · Honolulu, HI 96813 · 808-531-8031

Grace Nihei Kido · Cades Schutte · 1000 Bishop Street, Suite 1200 · Honolulu, HI 96813 · 808-521-9200

Galen C. K. Leong · Ashford & Wriston · Ali'i Place, Suite 1400 · 1099 Alakea Street · Honolulu, HI 96813 · 808-539-0400

Bernice Littman · ⑩ · Cades Schutte · 1000 Bishop Street, Suite 1200 · Honolulu, HI 96813 · 808-521-9200

Dennis M. Lombardi · Case Lombardi & Pettit · http://www.caselombardi.com · Pacific Guardian Center, Mauka Tower, Suite 2600 · 737 Bishop Street · Honolulu, HI 96813-3283 · 808-547-5400

D. Scott MacKinnon · ⑩ · McCorriston Miller Mukai MacKinnon · Five Waterfront Plaza, Fourth Floor · 500 Ala Moana Boulevard · P.O. Box 2800 · Honolulu, HI 96803-2800 · 808-529-7300

Kenneth B. Marcus · Starn O'Toole Marcus & Fisher · Pacific Guardian Center, Makai Tower, Suite 1900 · 733 Bishop Street · Honolulu, HI 96813 · 808-537-6100

James K. Mee · Ashford & Wriston · Ali'i Place, Suite 1400 · 1099 Alakea Street · Honolulu, HI 96813 · 808-539-0400

Clifford J. Miller · ㉕ · McCorriston Miller Mukai MacKinnon · Five Waterfront Plaza, Fourth Floor · 500 Ala Moana Boulevard · P.O. Box 2800 · Honolulu, HI 96803-2800 · 808-529-7300

Joyce Y. Neeley · Neeley & Anderson · Pacific Guardian Center, Makai Tower, Suite 2301 · 737 Bishop Street · Honolulu, HI 96813 · 808-536-8177

Charles E. Pear, Jr. · McCorriston Miller Mukai MacKinnon · Five Waterfront Plaza, Fourth Floor · 500 Ala Moana Boulevard · P.O. Box 2800 · Honolulu, HI 96803-2800 · 808-529-7300

Vincent A. Piekarski · Goodsill Anderson Quinn & Stifel · 1099 Alakea Street, Suite 1800 · Honolulu, HI 96813 · 808-547-5600

Scott D. Radovich · Schneider Tanaka Radovich Andrew & Tanaka · Alakea Corporate Tower, Suite 2100 · 1100 Alakea Street · Honolulu, HI 96813 · 808-792-4200

Carl J. Schlack, Jr. · Schlack Ito Lockwood Piper & Elkind · Topa Financial Center, Suite 1500 · 745 Fort Street · Honolulu, HI 96813 · 808-523-6040

Robert F. Schneider · ⑩ · Schneider Tanaka Radovich Andrew & Tanaka · Alakea Corporate Tower, Suite 2100 · 1100 Alakea Street · Honolulu, HI 96813 · 808-792-4200

David S. Shibata · Rush Moore · 737 Bishop Street, Suite 2400 · Honolulu, HI 96813 · 808-521-0400

Peter Starn · Starn O'Toole Marcus & Fisher · Pacific Guardian Center, Makai Tower, Suite 1900 · 733 Bishop Street · Honolulu, HI 96813 · 808-537-6100

Randall K. Steverson · Goodsill Anderson Quinn & Stifel · 1099 Alakea Street, Suite 1800 · Honolulu, HI 96813 · 808-547-5600

Robert E. Strand · Carlsmith Ball · ASB Tower, Suite 2200 · 1001 Bishop Street · P.O. Box 656 · Honolulu, HI 96813 · 808-523-2500

Larry T. Takumi · ⑩ · Cades Schutte · 1000 Bishop Street, Suite 1200 · Honolulu, HI 96813 · 808-521-9200

Gail M. Tamashiro · ⑩ · Cades Schutte · 1000 Bishop Street, Suite 1200 · Honolulu, HI 96813 · 808-521-9200

Danton S. Wong · ⑩ · Chun, Kerr, Dodd, Beaman & Wong · Fort Street Tower, Topa Financial Center, Ninth Floor · 745 Fort Street · Honolulu, HI 96813-3815 · 808-528-8200

A. James Wriston, Jr. · ⑩ · Ashford & Wriston · Ali'i Place, Suite 1400 · 1099 Alakea Street · Honolulu, HI 96813 · 808-539-0400

Janel M. Yoshimoto · Chun Rair & Yoshimoto · http://www.chunrair.com · 1000 Bishop Street, Suite 1000 · Honolulu, HI 96813 · 808-528-4200

Leighton J. H. S. Yuen · Goodsill Anderson Quinn & Stifel · 1099 Alakea Street, Suite 1800 · Honolulu, HI 96813 · 808-547-5600

Kahului

Richard J. Kiefer · Kiefer Merchant & Garneau · 444 Hana Highway, Suite 204 · Kahului, HI 96732-2315 808-871-9700

Paul R. Mancini · Mancini, Welch & Geiger · The Kahului Building, Suite 470 · 33 Lono Avenue · Kahului, HI 96732-1681 · 808-871-8351

Thomas D. Welch, Jr. · Mancini, Welch & Geiger · The Kahului Building, Suite 470 · 33 Lono Avenue · Kahului, HI 96732-1681 · 808-871-8351

Kailua-Kona

Sylvester V. Quitiquit · Brooks Tom Porter & Quitiquit · 75-1000 Henry Street, Suite 208 · Kailua-Kona, HI 96740 · 808-326-7300

Robert D. Triantos · Carlsmith Ball · 75-1000 Henry Street, Suite 209 · P.O. Box 1720 · Kailua-Kona, HI 96745-1720 · 808-329-6464

Lihue

Michael J. Belles · Belles, Graham, Proudfoot & Wilson · Watumull Plaza, Suite 202 · 4334 Rice Street · Lihue, HI 96766-1388 · 808-245-4705

Wailuku

B. Martin Luna · Carlsmith Ball · One Main Plaza, Suite 400 · 2200 Main Street · Wailuku, HI 96793-1086 · 808-242-4535

STRUCTURED FINANCE LAW

Honolulu

Mark A. Hazlett · ⑩ · Cades Schutte · 1000 Bishop Street, Suite 1200 · Honolulu, HI 96813 · 808-521-9200

Larry T. Takumi · ⑩ · Cades Schutte · 1000 Bishop Street, Suite 1200 · Honolulu, HI 96813 · 808-521-9200

TAX LAW

Honolulu

Wesley Y. S. Chang · ⑩ · Law Offices of Wesley Y. S. Chang · Harbor Court, Suite 2800 · 55 Merchant Street · Honolulu, HI 96813 · 808-534-4807

Roger H. Epstein · ⑳ · Cades Schutte · 1000 Bishop Street, Suite 1200 · Honolulu, HI 96813 · 808-521-9200

Vito Galati · Cades Schutte · 1000 Bishop Street, Suite 1200 · Honolulu, HI 96813 · 808-521-9200

Stephen M. Gelber · ⑳ · Gelber Gelber & Ingersoll · Topa Financial Center, Fort Street Tower, Suite 1400 · 745 Fort Street · Honolulu, HI 96813-3823 · 808-524-0155

Ronald I. Heller · ⑩ · Torkildson Katz Moore Hetherington & Harris · http://www.torkildson.com · Topa Financial Center Building, 15th Floor · 700 Bishop Street · Honolulu, HI 96813-4187 · 808-523-6000

Richard K. Ingersoll · ⑩ · Gelber Gelber & Ingersoll · Topa Financial Center, Fort Street Tower, Suite 1400 · 745 Fort Street · Honolulu, HI 96813-3823 · 808-524-0155

Ray K. Kamikawa · Chun, Kerr, Dodd, Beaman & Wong · Fort Street Tower, Topa Financial Center, Ninth Floor · 745 Fort Street · Honolulu, HI 96813-3815 · 808-528-8200

Chris S. Mashiba · Cades Schutte · 1000 Bishop Street, Suite 1200 · Honolulu, HI 96813 · 808-521-9200

Miki Okumura · Goodsill Anderson Quinn & Stifel · 1099 Alakea Street, Suite 1800 · Honolulu, HI 96813 · 808-547-5600

Arthur B. Reinwald · ㉕ · Reinwald O'Connor & Playdon · Pacific Guardian Center, Makai Tower, 24th Floor · 733 Bishop Street · P.O. Box 3199 · Honolulu, HI 96813 · 808-524-8350

Steven L. Rinesmith · Rinesmith & Sekiguchi · Pacific Guardian Center, Mauka Tower, Suite 2775 · 737 Bishop Street · Honolulu, HI 96813 · 808-534-4951

TRUSTS AND ESTATES

Honolulu

Daniel H. Case · ㉕ · Case Lombardi & Pettit · http://www.caselombardi.com · Pacific Guardian Center, Mauka Tower, Suite 2600 · 737 Bishop Street · Honolulu, HI 96813-3283 · 808-547-5400

Heather K. L. Conahan · Loden & Conahan · 737 Bishop Street, Suite 2990 · Honolulu, HI 96813 · 808-524-8099

Mary Jane Connell · ⑩ · Carlsmith Ball · ASB Tower, Suite 2200 · 1001 Bishop Street · P.O. Box 656 · Honolulu, HI 96813 · 808-523-2500

Rhonda L. Griswold · Cades Schutte · 1000 Bishop Street, Suite 1200 · Honolulu, HI 96813 · 808-521-9200

Ronda K. Kent · Ashford & Wriston · Ali'i Place, Suite 1400 · 1099 Alakea Street · Honolulu, HI 96813 · 808-539-0400

David C. Larsen · ⑳ · Cades Schutte · 1000 Bishop Street, Suite 1200 · Honolulu, HI 96813 · 808-521-9200

Judy Yuriko Lee · Goodsill Anderson Quinn & Stifel · 1099 Alakea Street, Suite 1800 · Honolulu, HI 96813 · 808-547-5600

Patricia Y. Lee · ⑩ · Goodsill Anderson Quinn & Stifel · 1099 Alakea Street, Suite 1800 · Honolulu, HI 96813 · 808-547-5600

John A. Lockwood · Ashford & Wriston · Ali'i Place, Suite 1400 · 1099 Alakea Street · Honolulu, HI 96813 · 808-539-0400

Elliot H. Loden · ㉕ · Loden & Conahan · 737 Bishop Street, Suite 2990 · Honolulu, HI 96813 · 808-524-8099

Joy M. Miyasaki · Law Offices of Shuichi Miyasaki · American Savings Bank Tower, Suite 1030 · 1001 Bishop Street · Honolulu, HI 96813 · 808-521-3255

Raymond K. Okada · ⑩ · Goodsill Anderson Quinn & Stifel · 1099 Alakea Street, Suite 1800 · Honolulu, HI 96813 · 808-547-5600

Russell A. Ota · ⑩ · Law Office of Russell A. Ota · Pioneer Plaza, Suite 1602 · 900 Fort Street Mall · Honolulu, HI 96813 · 808-532-3100

Arthur B. Reinwald · ㉕ · Reinwald O'Connor & Playdon · Pacific Guardian Center, Makai Tower, 24th Floor · 733 Bishop Street · P.O. Box 3199 · Honolulu, HI 96813 · 808-524-8350

Douglas C. Smith · Damon Key Leong Kupchak Hastert · Pauahi Tower, Suite 1600 · 1003 Bishop Street Honolulu, HI 96813 · 808-531-8031

James L. Starshak · ㉕ · Carlsmith Ball · ASB Tower, Suite 2200 · 1001 Bishop Street · P.O. Box 656 · Honolulu, HI 96813 · 808-523-2500

Carroll S. Taylor · ⑩ · Taylor, Leong & Chee · Pacific Guardian Center, Suite 2060 · 737 Bishop Street · Honolulu, HI 96813 · 808-528-2222

Randall M. L. Yee · Law Office of Randall M. L. Yee · Cades Schutte Building, Suite 908 · 1000 Bishop Street · Honolulu, HI 96813 · 808-524-4501

Curtis B. K. Yuen · Law Offices of Curtis B. K. Yuen · Pioneer Plaza, Suite 1505 · 900 Fort Street Mall · Honolulu, HI 96813-3713 · 808-532-3103

Kamuela

Robert Williams Hastings II · ⑳ · Robert W. Hastings II · Carter Professional Center, Suite B-20 · 65-1230 Mamalaho Highway · Kamuela, HI 96743 · 808-885-4554

WATER LAW

Honolulu

Gino L. Gabrio · ⑩ · Cades Schutte · 1000 Bishop Street, Suite 1200 · Honolulu, HI 96813 · 808-521-9200

Yvonne Y. Izu · Morihara Lau & Fong · Davies Pacific Center, Suite 400 · 841 Bishop Street · Honolulu, HI 96813 · 808-526-2888

William M. Tam · Alston Hunt Floyd & Ing · http://www.ahfi.com · American Savings Bank Tower, Suite 1800 · 1001 Bishop Street · Honolulu, HI 96813 · 808-524-1800

WHITE-COLLAR CRIMINAL DEFENSE

Honolulu

John S. Edmunds · ㉕ · Edmunds & Verga · Davies Pacific Center, Suite 2104 · 841 Bishop Street · Honolulu, HI 96813 · 808-524-2000

David W. Hall · ⑩ · David W. Hall · Dillingham Transportation Building, Suite 236 · 735 Bishop Street · Honolulu, HI 96813-4816 · 808-526-0402

William A. Harrison · Harrison & Matsuoka · http://www.hamlaw.net · Davies Pacific Center, Suite 800 · 841 Bishop Street · Honolulu, HI 96813 · 808-523-7041

Brook Hart · ㉕ · Brook Hart, Attorney at Law · http://www.hart-law.net · Melim Building, Suite 610 · 333 Queen Street · Honolulu, HI 96813 · 808-526-0811

Howard K. K. Luke · Law Office of Howard K. K. Luke · Davies Pacific Center, Suite 2022 · 841 Bishop Street · Honolulu, HI 96813 · 808-545-5000

William C. McCorriston · ⑩ · McCorriston Miller Mukai MacKinnon · Five Waterfront Plaza, Fourth Floor · 500 Ala Moana Boulevard · P.O. Box 2800 · Honolulu, HI 96803-2800 · 808-529-7300

Wailuku

Philip H. Lowenthal · ㉕ · Philip H. Lowenthal · 33 North Market Street, Suite 101 · Wailuku, HI 96793 808-242-5000

WORKERS' COMPENSATION LAW

Honolulu

Lowell K. Y. Chun-Hoon · ⑩ · King, Nakamura & Chun-Hoon · Central Pacific Plaza, Suite 980 · 220 South King Street · Honolulu, HI 96813-4539 · 808-521-8041

IDAHO

ALTERNATIVE DISPUTE RESOLUTION

Boise

Robert E. Bakes · Moffatt, Thomas, Barrett, Rock & Fields · 101 South Capitol Boulevard, 10th Floor · P.O. Box 829 · Boise, ID 83701-0829 · 208-345-2000

Merlyn W. Clark · ⑩ · Hawley Troxell Ennis & Hawley · 877 Main Street, Suite 1000 · P.O. Box 1617 · Boise, ID 83701 · 208-344-6000

James R. Gillespie · James R. Gillespie · 300 West Myrtle, Suite 100 · P.O. Box 2337 · Boise, ID 83701 · 208-344-8400

David D. Goss · ⑩ · Risch Goss Insinger Gustavel · 407 West Jefferson Street · Boise, ID 83702 · 208-345-9974

John Magel · Elam & Burke · 251 East Front Street, Suite 300 · P.O. Box 1539 · Boise, ID 83701 · 208-343-5454

Twin Falls

J. Robert Alexander · ⑩ · Benoit, Alexander, Harwood, High & Butler · 126 Second Avenue North · P.O. Box 366 · Twin Falls, ID 83301 · 208-733-5463

APPELLATE LAW

Boise

John W. Barrett · ⑩ · Moffatt, Thomas, Barrett, Rock & Fields · 101 South Capitol Boulevard, 10th Floor P.O. Box 829 · Boise, ID 83701-0829 · 208-345-2000

Bobbi K. Dominick · Gjording & Fouser · 509 West Hays Street · P.O. Box 2837 · Boise, ID 83701 · 208-336-9777

Idaho Falls

C. Timothy Hopkins · Hopkins Roden Crockett Hansen & Hoopes · Salisbury Building · 428 Park Avenue · P.O. Box 51219 · Idaho Falls, ID 83405-1219 · 208-523-4445

Twin Falls

Lloyd J. Webb · Webb, Webb & Guerry · 155 Second Avenue North · P.O. Box 1768 · Twin Falls, ID 83303-1768 · 208-734-1616

BANKING LAW

Boise

Conrad J. Aiken · Racine, Olson, Nye, Budge & Bailey · U.S. Bank Plaza, Suite 208 · 101 South Capital Boulevard · Boise, ID 83704 · 208-395-0011

BANKRUPTCY AND CREDITOR-DEBTOR RIGHTS LAW

Boise

Joseph M. Meier · Cosho Humphrey · 800 Park Boulevard, Suite 790 · P.O. Box 9518 · Boise, ID 83707-9518 · 208-344-7811

Randall A. Peterman · ⑩ · Moffatt, Thomas, Barrett, Rock & Fields · 101 South Capitol Boulevard, 10th Floor · P.O. Box 829 · Boise, ID 83701-0829 · 208-345-2000

Larry E. Prince · ⑩ · Holland & Hart · U.S. Bank Plaza, Suite 1400 · 101 South Capitol Boulevard · Boise, ID 83702 · 208-342-5000

Pocatello

Daniel C. Green · Racine, Olson, Nye, Budge & Bailey · 201 East Center Street · P.O. Box 1391 · Pocatello, ID 83204 · 208-232-6101

Sandpoint

Ford Elsaesser · ⑩ · Elsaesser Jarzabek Anderson Marks & Elliott · Lake Plaza Building · 123 South Third · P.O. Box 1049 · Sandpoint, ID 83864 · 208-263-8517

COMMERCIAL LITIGATION

Boise

Walter H. Bithell · ⑩ · Holland & Hart · U.S. Bank Plaza, Suite 1400 · 101 South Capitol Boulevard · Boise, ID 83702 · 208-342-5000

Richard C. Boardman · Perkins Coie · http://www.perkinscoie.com · 251 East Front Street, Suite 400 · Boise, ID 83702-7310 · 208-343-3434

Christopher C. Burke · Greener Burke Shoemaker · 950 West Bannock Street, Suite 900 · Boise, ID 83702 · 208-319-2600

Merlyn W. Clark · ⑩ · Hawley Troxell Ennis & Hawley · 877 Main Street, Suite 1000 · P.O. Box 1617 · Boise, ID 83701 · 208-344-6000

David E. Comstock · ⑩ · Comstock & Bush · 199 North Capitol Boulevard, Suite 500 · P.O. Box 2774 · Boise, ID 83701-2774 · 208-344-7700

M. Allyn Dingel, Jr. · ⑩ · M. Allyn Dingel · 950 West Bannock Street, Suite 520 · Boise, ID 83702 · 208-333-8540

William G. Dryden · Elam & Burke · 251 East Front Street, Suite 300 · P.O. Box 1539 · Boise, ID 83701 · 208-343-5454

Richard C. Fields · ⑩ · Moffatt, Thomas, Barrett, Rock & Fields · 101 South Capitol Boulevard, 10th Floor · P.O. Box 829 · Boise, ID 83701-0829 · 208-345-2000

Mark S. Geston · Stoel Rives · http://www.stoel.com · 101 South Capitol Boulevard, Suite 1900 · Boise, ID 83702-7705 · 208-389-9000

Richard H. Greener · ⑩ · Greener Burke Shoemaker · 950 West Bannock Street, Suite 900 · Boise, ID 83702 · 208-319-2600

Richard E. Hall · ⑩ · Hall, Farley, Oberrecht & Blanton · http://www.hallfarley.com · Key Financial Center, Suite 700 · 702 West Idaho Street · P.O. Box 1271 · Boise, ID 83701 · 208-395-8500

Larry C. Hunter · Moffatt, Thomas, Barrett, Rock & Fields · 101 South Capitol Boulevard, 10th Floor · P.O. Box 829 · Boise, ID 83701-0829 · 208-345-2000

James D. LaRue · Elam & Burke · 251 East Front Street, Suite 300 · P.O. Box 1539 · Boise, ID 83701 · 208-343-5454

John Magel · Elam & Burke · 251 East Front Street, Suite 300 · P.O. Box 1539 · Boise, ID 83701 · 208-343-5454

Craig L. Meadows · ⑩ · Hawley Troxell Ennis & Hawley · 877 Main Street, Suite 1000 · P.O. Box 1617 · Boise, ID 83701 · 208-344-6000

Phillip S. Oberrecht · Hall, Farley, Oberrecht & Blanton · http://www.hallfarley.com · Key Financial Center, Suite 700 · 702 West Idaho Street · P.O. Box 1271 · Boise, ID 83701 · 208-395-8500

J. Walter Sinclair · Stoel Rives · http://www.stoel.com · 101 South Capitol Boulevard, Suite 1900 · Boise, ID 83702-7705 · 208-389-9000

B. Newal Squyres · Holland & Hart · U.S. Bank Plaza, Suite 1400 · 101 South Capitol Boulevard · Boise, ID 83702 · 208-342-5000

Burley

William A. Parsons · Parsons, Smith & Stone · 137 West 13th Street · P.O. Box 910 · Burley, ID 83318 · 208-878-8382

Coeur d'Alene

Micheal E. Ramsden · Ramsden & Lyons · 618 North Fourth Street · P.O. Box 1336 · Coeur d'Alene, ID 83816-1336 · 208-664-5818

Idaho Falls

C. Timothy Hopkins · Hopkins Roden Crockett Hansen & Hoopes · Salisbury Building · 428 Park Avenue · P.O. Box 51219 · Idaho Falls, ID 83405-1219 · 208-523-4445

Lewiston

Robert P. Brown · ⑩ · Clements, Brown & McNichols · 321 Thirteenth Street · P.O. Box 1510 · Lewiston, ID 83501 · 208-743-6538

Michael E. McNichols · ⑩ · Clements, Brown & McNichols · 321 Thirteenth Street · P.O. Box 1510 · Lewiston, ID 83501 · 208-743-6538

Pocatello

W. Marcus W. Nye · ⑩ · Racine, Olson, Nye, Budge & Bailey · 201 East Center Street · P.O. Box 1391 · Pocatello, ID 83204 · 208-232-6101

Post Falls

Charles B. Lempesis · Charles B. Lempesis · West 201 Seventh Avenue · Post Falls, ID 83854 · 208-777-8815

Twin Falls

Thomas B. High · Benoit, Alexander, Harwood, High & Butler · 126 Second Avenue North · P.O. Box 366 · Twin Falls, ID 83301 · 208-733-5463

Steven K. Tolman · Tolman & Brizee · 132 Third Avenue East · Twin Falls, ID 83303 · 208-733-5566

CONSTRUCTION LAW

Boise

Robert A. Anderson · Anderson, Julian & Hull · C.W. Moore Plaza, Suite 700 · 250 South Fifth Street · P.O. Box 7426 · Boise, ID 83707-7426 · 208-344-5800

Richard C. Boardman · Perkins Coie · http://www.perkinscoie.com · 251 East Front Street, Suite 400 · Boise, ID 83702-7310 · 208-343-3434

Geoffrey J. McConnell · Meuleman Mollerup · 755 West Front Street, Suite 200 · Boise, ID 83702-5802 · 208-342-6066

Wayne V. Meuleman · Meuleman Mollerup · 755 West Front Street, Suite 200 · Boise, ID 83702-5802 · 208-342-6066

Phillip S. Oberrecht · Hall, Farley, Oberrecht & Blanton · http://www.hallfarley.com · Key Financial Center, Suite 700 · 702 West Idaho Street · P.O. Box 1271 · Boise, ID 83701 · 208-395-8500

CORPORATE LAW

Boise

Conrad J. Aiken · Racine, Olson, Nye, Budge & Bailey · U.S. Bank Plaza, Suite 208 · 101 South Capital Boulevard · Boise, ID 83704 · 208-395-0011

Paul M. Boyd · Stoel Rives · http://www.stoel.com · 101 South Capitol Boulevard, Suite 1900 · Boise, ID 83702-7705 · 208-389-9000

Loren Ipsen · Elam & Burke · 251 East Front Street, Suite 300 · P.O. Box 1539 · Boise, ID 83701 · 208-343-5454

J. Frederick Mack · Holland & Hart · U.S. Bank Plaza, Suite 1400 · 101 South Capitol Boulevard · Boise, ID 83702 · 208-342-5000

William J. McKlveen · Eberle, Berlin, Kading, Turnbow McKlveen & Jones · 1111 West Jefferson Street, Suite 530 · Boise, ID 83701 · 208-344-8535

Nicholas G. Miller · ⑩ · Hawley Troxell Ennis & Hawley · 877 Main Street, Suite 1000 · P.O. Box 1617 · Boise, ID 83701 · 208-344-6000

Kris J. Ormseth · Stoel Rives · http://www.stoel.com · 101 South Capitol Boulevard, Suite 1900 · Boise, ID 83702-7705 · 208-389-9000

Richard A. Riley · Hawley Troxell Ennis & Hawley · 877 Main Street, Suite 1000 · P.O. Box 1617 · Boise, ID 83701 · 208-344-6000

John S. Simko · Moffatt, Thomas, Barrett, Rock & Fields · 101 South Capitol Boulevard, 10th Floor · P.O. Box 829 · Boise, ID 83701-0829 · 208-345-2000

Robert M. Turnbow · ⑩ · Eberle, Berlin, Kading, Turnbow McKlveen & Jones · 1111 West Jefferson Street, Suite 530 · Boise, ID 83701 · 208-344-8535

John C. Ward · Moffatt, Thomas, Barrett, Rock & Fields · 101 South Capitol Boulevard, 10th Floor · P.O. Box 829 · Boise, ID 83701-0829 · 208-345-2000

Idaho Falls

Gary L. Meikle · Holden, Kidwell, Hahn & Crapo · 1000 Riverwalk Drive, Suite 200 · P.O. Box 50130 · Idaho Falls, ID 83405 · 208-523-0620

Lewiston

Eric K. Peterson · Clements, Brown & McNichols · 321 Thirteenth Street · P.O. Box 1510 · Lewiston, ID 83501 · 208-743-6538

DUI/DWI DEFENSE

Boise

Michael Bartlett · Nevin, Benjamin, McKay & Bartlett · 303 West Bannock Street · P.O. Box 2772 · Boise, ID 83701 · 208-343-1000

EDUCATION LAW

Boise

Amy G. White · Anderson, Julian & Hull · C.W. Moore Plaza, Suite 700 · 250 South Fifth Street · P.O. Box 7426 · Boise, ID 83707-7426 · 208-344-5800

ELDER LAW

Pocatello

Kirk B. Hadley · Racine, Olson, Nye, Budge & Bailey · 201 East Center Street · P.O. Box 1391 · Pocatello, ID 83204 · 208-232-6101

EMINENT DOMAIN AND CONDEMNATION LAW

Boise

E. Don Copple · Davison, Copple, Copple & Cox · 199 North Capitol Boulevard, Suite 600 · P.O. Box 1583 · Boise, ID 83701 · 208-342-3658

Heather A. Cunningham · Davison, Copple, Copple & Cox · 199 North Capitol Boulevard, Suite 600 · P.O. Box 1583 · Boise, ID 83701 · 208-342-3658

Kimbell D. Gourley · Trout Jones Gledhill Fuhrman · Ninth & Idaho Center, Suite 820 · 225 North Ninth Street · Boise, ID 83701 · 208-331-1170

EMPLOYEE BENEFITS LAW

Boise

Steven E. Alkire · Eberle, Berlin, Kading, Turnbow McKlveen & Jones · 1111 West Jefferson Street, Suite 530 · Boise, ID 83701 · 208-344-8535

Andrew M. Chasan · Chasan & Walton · 1459 Tyrell Lane · Boise, ID 83706 · 208-345-3760

James C. Dale · Stoel Rives · http://www.stoel.com · 101 South Capitol Boulevard, Suite 1900 · Boise, ID 83702-7705 · 208-389-9000

Alan K. Hull · Anderson, Julian & Hull · C.W. Moore Plaza, Suite 700 · 250 South Fifth Street · P.O. Box 7426 · Boise, ID 83707-7426 · 208-344-5800

Gerald T. Husch · Moffatt, Thomas, Barrett, Rock & Fields · 101 South Capitol Boulevard, 10th Floor · P.O. Box 829 · Boise, ID 83701-0829 · 208-345-2000

Jeffery Mandell · ⑩ · The ERISA Law Group · 205 North 10th Street, Suite 300 · P.O. Box 853 · Boise, ID 83701 · 208-342-5522

William Breck Seiniger, Jr. · Seiniger Law Offices · 942 West Myrtle Street · Boise, ID 83702 · 208-345-1000

Joseph H. Uberuaga II · ⑩ · Eberle, Berlin, Kading, Turnbow McKlveen & Jones · 1111 West Jefferson Street, Suite 530 · Boise, ID 83701 · 208-344-8535

Priest River

Nicholas M. Lamanna · ⑩ · Lamanna Law Firm · Priest River Professional Center · 102 Ninth Street · P.O. Box 789 · Priest River, ID 83856-0789 · 208-448-1221

ENERGY LAW

Boise

Scott L. Campbell · Moffatt, Thomas, Barrett, Rock & Fields · 101 South Capitol Boulevard, 10th Floor · P.O. Box 829 · Boise, ID 83701-0829 · 208-345-2000

John M. Eustermann · Stoel Rives · http://www.stoel.com · 101 South Capitol Boulevard, Suite 1900 · Boise, ID 83702-7705 · 208-389-9000

Jeffrey C. Fereday · ⑩ · Givens Pursley · http://www.givenspursley.com · 601 West Bannock Street · P.O. Box 2720 · Boise, ID 83701 · 208-388-1200

Robert Maynard · Perkins Coie · http://www.perkinscoie.com · 251 East Front Street, Suite 400 · Boise, ID 83702-7310 · 208-343-3434

Conley E. Ward, Jr. · ⑩ · Givens Pursley · http://www.givenspursley.com · 601 West Bannock Street · P.O. Box 2720 · Boise, ID 83701 · 208-388-1200

Pocatello

Randall C. Budge · Racine, Olson, Nye, Budge & Bailey · 201 East Center Street · P.O. Box 1391 · Pocatello, ID 83204 · 208-232-6101

Rexburg

Jerry Rigby · Rigby, Andrus & Moeller · 25 North Second East · P.O. Box 250 · Rexburg, ID 83440 · 208-356-3633

Rupert

Roger D. Ling · ⑩ · Ling, Robinson & Walker · 615 H Street · P.O. Box 396 · Rupert, ID 83350 · 208-436-4717

ENVIRONMENTAL LAW

Boise

Kevin J. Beaton · Stoel Rives · http://www.stoel.com · 101 South Capitol Boulevard, Suite 1900 · Boise, ID 83702-7705 · 208-389-9000

Michael C. Creamer · Givens Pursley · http://www.givenspursley.com · 601 West Bannock Street · P.O. Box 2720 · Boise, ID 83701 · 208-388-1200

Roy Lewis Eiguren · ⑩ · Eiguren Public Law & Policy · http://www.royeiguren.com · 702 West Idaho Street, Suite 1000 · Boise, ID 83702 · 208-947-7252

Murray D. Feldman · Holland & Hart · U.S. Bank Plaza, Suite 1400 · 101 South Capitol Boulevard · Boise, ID 83702 · 208-342-5000

Jeffrey C. Fereday · ⑩ · Givens Pursley · http://www.givenspursley.com · 601 West Bannock Street · P.O. Box 2720 · Boise, ID 83701 · 208-388-1200

Larry C. Hunter · Moffatt, Thomas, Barrett, Rock & Fields · 101 South Capitol Boulevard, 10th Floor · P.O. Box 829 · Boise, ID 83701-0829 · 208-345-2000

Robert Maynard · Perkins Coie · http://www.perkinscoie.com · 251 East Front Street, Suite 400 · Boise, ID 83702-7310 · 208-343-3434

Krista K. McIntyre · ⑩ · Stoel Rives · http://www.stoel.com · 101 South Capitol Boulevard, Suite 1900 · Boise, ID 83702-7705 · 208-389-9000

Christopher H. Meyer · Givens Pursley · http://www.givenspursley.com · 601 West Bannock Street · P.O. Box 2720 · Boise, ID 83701 · 208-388-1200

William G. Myers III · Holland & Hart · U.S. Bank Plaza, Suite 1400 · 101 South Capitol Boulevard · Boise, ID 83702 · 208-342-5000

FAMILY LAW

Boise

James A. Bevis · ⑩ · Bevis, Johnson & Thiry · http://www.bevislaw.com · 960 Broadway Avenue, Suite 220 · P.O. Box 827 · Boise, ID 83706-3667 · 208-345-1040

Debrha J. Carnahan · Carnahan Law Offices · 101 South Capitol Boulevard, Suite 400 · P.O. Box 2125 · Boise, ID 83701 · 208-338-1420

Glenna M. Christensen · Moffatt, Thomas, Barrett, Rock & Fields · 101 South Capitol Boulevard, 10th Floor · P.O. Box 829 · Boise, ID 83701-0829 · 208-345-2000

David D. Goss · ⑩ · Risch Goss Insinger Gustavel · 407 West Jefferson Street · Boise, ID 83702 · 208-345-9974

Jean R. Uranga · Uranga & Uranga · 714 North Fifth Street · P.O. Box 1678 · Boise, ID 83701 · 208-342-8931

Stanley W. Welsh · ㉕ · Cosho Humphrey · 800 Park Boulevard, Suite 790 · P.O. Box 9518 · Boise, ID 83707-9518 · 208-344-7811

FAMILY LAW MEDIATION

Boise

Stephen L. Beer · Beer & Cain · 302 West Idaho · Boise, ID 83702-6039 · 208-336-2323

David D. Goss · ⑩ · Risch Goss Insinger Gustavel · 407 West Jefferson Street · Boise, ID 83702 · 208-345-9974

Jean R. Uranga · Uranga & Uranga · 714 North Fifth Street · P.O. Box 1678 · Boise, ID 83701 · 208-342-8931

HEALTH CARE LAW

Boise

Richard C. Fields · ⑩ · Moffatt, Thomas, Barrett, Rock & Fields · 101 South Capitol Boulevard, 10th Floor · P.O. Box 829 · Boise, ID 83701-0829 · 208-345-2000

L. Edward Miller · ⑩ · Givens Pursley · http://www.givenspursley.com · 601 West Bannock Street · P.O. Box 2720 · Boise, ID 83701 · 208-388-1200

Patrick J. Miller · Givens Pursley · http://www.givenspursley.com · 601 West Bannock Street · P.O. Box 2720 · Boise, ID 83701 · 208-388-1200

J. Kevin West · Hall, Farley, Oberrecht & Blanton · http://www.hallfarley.com · Key Financial Center, Suite 700 · 702 West Idaho Street · P.O. Box 1271 · Boise, ID 83701 · 208-395-8500

Coeur d'Alene

Peter C. Erbland · Paine, Hamblen · 701 Front Avenue, Suite 101 · P.O. Box E · Coeur d'Alene, ID 83816 · 208-664-8115

Patrick E. Miller · Paine, Hamblen · 701 Front Avenue, Suite 101 · P.O. Box E · Coeur d'Alene, ID 83816 · 208-664-8115

IMMIGRATION LAW

Boise

Ernest A. Hoidal · Hoidal Law Office · 960 Broadway Avenue, Suite 220 · Boise, ID 83706 · 208-342-4647

INSURANCE LAW

Boise

Richard E. Hall · ⑩ · Hall, Farley, Oberrecht & Blanton · http://www.hallfarley.com · Key Financial Center, Suite 700 · 702 West Idaho Street · P.O. Box 1271 · Boise, ID 83701 · 208-395-8500

Gerald T. Husch · Moffatt, Thomas, Barrett, Rock & Fields · 101 South Capitol Boulevard, 10th Floor · P.O. Box 829 · Boise, ID 83701-0829 · 208-345-2000

Brian K. Julian · Anderson, Julian & Hull · C.W. Moore Plaza, Suite 700 · 250 South Fifth Street · P.O. Box 7426 · Boise, ID 83707-7426 · 208-344-5800

James D. LaRue · Elam & Burke · 251 East Front Street, Suite 300 · P.O. Box 1539 · Boise, ID 83701 · 208-343-5454

James L. Martin · Moffatt, Thomas, Barrett, Rock & Fields · 101 South Capitol Boulevard, 10th Floor · P.O. Box 829 · Boise, ID 83701-0829 · 208-345-2000

Mark Prusynski · Moffatt, Thomas, Barrett, Rock & Fields · 101 South Capitol Boulevard, 10th Floor · P.O. Box 829 · Boise, ID 83701-0829 · 208-345-2000

J. Kevin West · Hall, Farley, Oberrecht & Blanton · http://www.hallfarley.com · Key Financial Center, Suite 700 · 702 West Idaho Street · P.O. Box 1271 · Boise, ID 83701 · 208-395-8500

Pocatello

John A. Bailey, Jr. · Racine, Olson, Nye, Budge & Bailey · 201 East Center Street · P.O. Box 1391 · Pocatello, ID 83204 · 208-232-6101

William D. Olson · Racine, Olson, Nye, Budge & Bailey · 201 East Center Street · P.O. Box 1391 · Pocatello, ID 83204 · 208-232-6101

LABOR AND EMPLOYMENT LAW

Boise

Steven W. Berenter · Hawley Troxell Ennis & Hawley · 877 Main Street, Suite 1000 · P.O. Box 1617 · Boise, ID 83701 · 208-344-6000

James C. Dale · Stoel Rives · http://www.stoel.com · 101 South Capitol Boulevard, Suite 1900 · Boise, ID 83702-7705 · 208-389-9000

Richard C. Fields · ⑩ · Moffatt, Thomas, Barrett, Rock & Fields · 101 South Capitol Boulevard, 10th Floor · P.O. Box 829 · Boise, ID 83701-0829 · 208-345-2000

Alan Herzfeld · Herzfeld & Piotrowski · 713 West Franklin Street · P.O. Box 2864 · Boise, ID 83701 · 208-331-9200

Brian K. Julian · Anderson, Julian & Hull · C.W. Moore Plaza, Suite 700 · 250 South Fifth Street · P.O. Box 7426 · Boise, ID 83707-7426 · 208-344-5800

Patricia M. Olsson · ⑩ · Moffatt, Thomas, Barrett, Rock & Fields · 101 South Capitol Boulevard, 10th Floor · P.O. Box 829 · Boise, ID 83701-0829 · 208-345-2000

Robert B. White · Givens Pursley · http://www.givenspursley.com · 601 West Bannock Street · P.O. Box 2720 · Boise, ID 83701 · 208-388-1200

LAND USE & ZONING LAW

Boise

Gary G. Allen · Givens Pursley · http://www.givenspursley.com · 601 West Bannock Street · P.O. Box 2720 · Boise, ID 83701 · 208-388-1200

Steve Bradbury · Williams Bradbury · 1015 West Hays Street · Boise, ID 83702 · 208-344-6633

JoAnn C. Butler · Spink Butler · 251 East Front Street, Suite 200 · P.O. Box 639 · Boise, ID 83701 · 208-388-1000

Christopher H. Meyer · Givens Pursley · http://www.givenspursley.com · 601 West Bannock Street · P.O. Box 2720 · Boise, ID 83701 · 208-388-1200

Timothy W. Tyree · Hawley Troxell Ennis & Hawley · 877 Main Street, Suite 1000 · P.O. Box 1617 · Boise, ID 83701 · 208-344-6000

Geoffrey M. Wardle · Hawley Troxell Ennis & Hawley · 877 Main Street, Suite 1000 · P.O. Box 1617 · Boise, ID 83701 · 208-344-6000

MEDICAL MALPRACTICE LAW

Boise

Keely E. Duke · Hall, Farley, Oberrecht & Blanton · http://www.hallfarley.com · Key Financial Center, Suite 700 · 702 West Idaho Street · P.O. Box 1271 · Boise, ID 83701 · 208-395-8500

Richard E. Hall · ⑩ · Hall, Farley, Oberrecht & Blanton · http://www.hallfarley.com · Key Financial Center, Suite 700 · 702 West Idaho Street · P.O. Box 1271 · Boise, ID 83701 · 208-395-8500

David R. Lombardi · ⑩ · Givens Pursley · http://www.givenspursley.com · 601 West Bannock Street · P.O. Box 2720 · Boise, ID 83701 · 208-388-1200

Raymond D. Powers · Powers Thomson · 345 Bobwhite Court, Suite 150 · P.O. Box 9756 · Boise, ID 83707 · 208-577-5100

Pocatello

Gary T. Dance · Moffatt, Thomas, Barrett, Rock & Fields · 412 West Center, Suite 2000 · P.O. Box 817 · Pocatello, ID 83204-0817 · 208-233-2001

MERGERS & ACQUISITIONS LAW

Boise

Paul M. Boyd · Stoel Rives · http://www.stoel.com · 101 South Capitol Boulevard, Suite 1900 · Boise, ID 83702-7705 · 208-389-9000

J. Frederick Mack · Holland & Hart · U.S. Bank Plaza, Suite 1400 · 101 South Capitol Boulevard · Boise, ID 83702 · 208-342-5000

Kris J. Ormseth · Stoel Rives · http://www.stoel.com · 101 South Capitol Boulevard, Suite 1900 · Boise, ID 83702-7705 · 208-389-9000

Richard A. Riley · Hawley Troxell Ennis & Hawley · 877 Main Street, Suite 1000 · P.O. Box 1617 · Boise, ID 83701 · 208-344-6000

MINING LAW

Boise

John S. Simko · Moffatt, Thomas, Barrett, Rock & Fields · 101 South Capitol Boulevard, 10th Floor · P.O. Box 829 · Boise, ID 83701-0829 · 208-345-2000

NATURAL RESOURCES LAW

Boise

Michael C. Creamer · Givens Pursley · http://www.givenspursley.com · 601 West Bannock Street · P.O. Box 2720 · Boise, ID 83701 · 208-388-1200

Jeffrey C. Fereday · ⑩ · Givens Pursley · http://www.givenspursley.com · 601 West Bannock Street · P.O. Box 2720 · Boise, ID 83701 · 208-388-1200

Robert Maynard · Perkins Coie · http://www.perkinscoie.com · 251 East Front Street, Suite 400 · Boise, ID 83702-7310 · 208-343-3434

Christopher H. Meyer · Givens Pursley · http://www.givenspursley.com · 601 West Bannock Street · P.O. Box 2720 · Boise, ID 83701 · 208-388-1200

Daniel V. Steenson · Ringert Clark · 455 South Third Street · Boise, ID 83701 · 208-342-4591

Pocatello

Randall C. Budge · Racine, Olson, Nye, Budge & Bailey · 201 East Center Street · P.O. Box 1391 · Pocatello, ID 83204 · 208-232-6101

Rexburg

Jerry Rigby · Rigby, Andrus & Moeller · 25 North Second East · P.O. Box 250 · Rexburg, ID 83440 · 208-356-3633

Ray W. Rigby · ⑩ · Rigby, Andrus & Moeller · 25 North Second East · P.O. Box 250 · Rexburg, ID 83440 208-356-3633

Twin Falls

John A. Rosholt · ⑩ · Barker Rosholt & Simpson · 113 Main Avenue West, Suite 303 · P.O. Box 485 · Twin Falls, ID 83303-0485 · 208-733-0700

NON-WHITE-COLLAR CRIMINAL DEFENSE

Boise

Dennis Benjamin · Nevin, Benjamin, McKay & Bartlett · 303 West Bannock Street · P.O. Box 2772 · Boise, ID 83701 · 208-343-1000

Mark H. Manweiler · Manweiler, Breen, Ball & Hancock · 290 Bobwhite Court, Suite 300 · P.O. Box 937 Boise, ID 83701-0937 · 208-424-9100

Scott McKay · Nevin, Benjamin, McKay & Bartlett · 303 West Bannock Street · P.O. Box 2772 · Boise, ID 83701 · 208-343-1000

David Z. Nevin · ⑩ · Nevin, Benjamin, McKay & Bartlett · 303 West Bannock Street · P.O. Box 2772 · Boise, ID 83701 · 208-343-1000

Charles F. Peterson, Jr. · Law Office of Charles F. Peterson · 913 West River Street, Suite 420 · Boise, ID 83702 · 208-342-4633

Paul L. Westberg · ⑩ · Westberg, McCabe & Collins · The Tullis Building, Lower Level · 516 West Franklin Street · P.O. Box 2836 · Boise, ID 83702 · 208-336-5200

Ketchum

Brian E. Elkins · Brian E. Elkins · Bitterroot Square Professional Building · 208 Spruce Avenue North · P.O. Box 766 · Ketchum, ID 83340 · 208-726-4338

Andrew H. Parnes · ⑩ · Law Office of Andrew Parnes · 671 First Avenue North · P.O. Box 5988 · Ketchum, ID 83340 · 208-726-1010

Moscow

James E. Siebe · ⑩ · Siebe Law Office · 202 East Second Street · P.O. Box 9045 · Moscow, ID 83843 · 208-883-0622

PERSONAL INJURY LITIGATION

Boise

Steven B. Andersen · Holland & Hart · U.S. Bank Plaza, Suite 1400 · 101 South Capitol Boulevard · Boise, ID 83702 · 208-342-5000

Robert A. Anderson · Anderson, Julian & Hull · C.W. Moore Plaza, Suite 700 · 250 South Fifth Street · P.O. Box 7426 · Boise, ID 83707-7426 · 208-344-5800

Walter H. Bithell · ⑩ · Holland & Hart · U.S. Bank Plaza, Suite 1400 · 101 South Capitol Boulevard · Boise, ID 83702 · 208-342-5000

David E. Comstock · ⑩ · Comstock & Bush · 199 North Capitol Boulevard, Suite 500 · P.O. Box 2774 · Boise, ID 83701-2774 · 208-344-7700

William G. Dryden · Elam & Burke · 251 East Front Street, Suite 300 · P.O. Box 1539 · Boise, ID 83701 · 208-343-5454

Keely E. Duke · Hall, Farley, Oberrecht & Blanton · http://www.hallfarley.com · Key Financial Center, Suite 700 · 702 West Idaho Street · P.O. Box 1271 · Boise, ID 83701 · 208-395-8500

Donald J. Farley · Hall, Farley, Oberrecht & Blanton · http://www.hallfarley.com · Key Financial Center, Suite 700 · 702 West Idaho Street · P.O. Box 1271 · Boise, ID 83701 · 208-395-8500

Jack S. Gjording · ⑩ · Gjording & Fouser · 509 West Hays Street · P.O. Box 2837 · Boise, ID 83701 · 208-336-9777

Richard E. Hall · ⑩ · Hall, Farley, Oberrecht & Blanton · http://www.hallfarley.com · Key Financial Center, Suite 700 · 702 West Idaho Street · P.O. Box 1271 · Boise, ID 83701 · 208-395-8500

Chris H. Hansen · Anderson, Julian & Hull · C.W. Moore Plaza, Suite 700 · 250 South Fifth Street · P.O. Box 7426 · Boise, ID 83707-7426 · 208-344-5800

J. Charles Hepworth, Jr. · Hepworth, Lezamiz & Janis · 537 West Bannock · P.O. Box 2582 · Boise, ID 83701-2582 · 208-343-7510

Larry C. Hunter · Moffatt, Thomas, Barrett, Rock & Fields · 101 South Capitol Boulevard, 10th Floor · P.O. Box 829 · Boise, ID 83701-0829 · 208-345-2000

Gerald T. Husch · Moffatt, Thomas, Barrett, Rock & Fields · 101 South Capitol Boulevard, 10th Floor · P.O. Box 829 · Boise, ID 83701-0829 · 208-345-2000

John J. Janis · Hepworth, Lezamiz & Janis · 537 West Bannock · P.O. Box 2582 · Boise, ID 83701-2582 · 208-343-7510

Brian K. Julian · Anderson, Julian & Hull · C.W. Moore Plaza, Suite 700 · 250 South Fifth Street · P.O. Box 7426 · Boise, ID 83707-7426 · 208-344-5800

James D. LaRue · Elam & Burke · 251 East Front Street, Suite 300 · P.O. Box 1539 · Boise, ID 83701 · 208-343-5454

David R. Lombardi · ⑩ · Givens Pursley · http://www.givenspursley.com · 601 West Bannock Street · P.O. Box 2720 · Boise, ID 83701 · 208-388-1200

Raymond D. Powers · Powers Thomson · 345 Bobwhite Court, Suite 150 · P.O. Box 9756 · Boise, ID 83707 · 208-577-5100

Mark Prusynski · Moffatt, Thomas, Barrett, Rock & Fields · 101 South Capitol Boulevard, 10th Floor · P.O. Box 829 · Boise, ID 83701-0829 · 208-345-2000

B. Newal Squyres · Holland & Hart · U.S. Bank Plaza, Suite 1400 · 101 South Capitol Boulevard · Boise, ID 83702 · 208-342-5000

Burley

William A. Parsons · Parsons, Smith & Stone · 137 West 13th Street · P.O. Box 910 · Burley, ID 83318 · 208-878-8382

Coeur d'Alene

Peter C. Erbland · Paine, Hamblen · 701 Front Avenue, Suite 101 · P.O. Box E · Coeur d'Alene, ID 83816 · 208-664-8115

Kenneth B. Howard, Jr. · ⑩ · Kenneth B. Howard · 250 Northwest Boulevard, Suite 107-A · P.O. Box 2528 · Coeur d'Alene, ID 83816-2528 · 208-676-8890

R. Bruce Owens · ⑩ · Owens & Crandall · 1859 North Lakewood Drive, Suite 104 · Coeur d'Alene, ID 83814 · 208-667-8989

Idaho Falls

D. Fredrick Hoopes · Hopkins Roden Crockett Hansen & Hoopes · Salisbury Building · 428 Park Avenue · P.O. Box 51219 · Idaho Falls, ID 83405-1219 · 208-523-4445

Lewiston

Darrell Aherin · Aherin, Rice & Anegon · 1212 Idaho Street · P.O. Drawer 698 · Lewiston, ID 83501 · 208-746-3646

Robert P. Brown · ⑩ · Clements, Brown & McNichols · 321 Thirteenth Street · P.O. Box 1510 · Lewiston, ID 83501 · 208-743-6538

Michael E. McNichols · ⑩ · Clements, Brown & McNichols · 321 Thirteenth Street · P.O. Box 1510 · Lewiston, ID 83501 · 208-743-6538

Pocatello

Gary T. Dance · Moffatt, Thomas, Barrett, Rock & Fields · 412 West Center, Suite 2000 · P.O. Box 817 · Pocatello, ID 83204-0817 · 208-233-2001

W. Marcus W. Nye · ⑩ · Racine, Olson, Nye, Budge & Bailey · 201 East Center Street · P.O. Box 1391 · Pocatello, ID 83204 · 208-232-6101

Priest River

Nicholas M. Lamanna · ⑩ · Lamanna Law Firm · Priest River Professional Center · 102 Ninth Street · P.O. Box 789 · Priest River, ID 83856-0789 · 208-448-1221

Twin Falls

J. Robert Alexander · ⑩ · Benoit, Alexander, Harwood, High & Butler · 126 Second Avenue North · P.O. Box 366 · Twin Falls, ID 83301 · 208-733-5463

John T. Lezamiz · ⑩ · Hepworth, Lezamiz & Janis · 133 Shoshone Street North · P.O. Box 389 · Twin Falls, ID 83303-0389 · 208-734-7510

Kenneth L. Pedersen · ⑩ · Pedersen and Whitehead · 161 Fifth Avenue South, Suite 301 · P.O. Box 2349 Twin Falls, ID 83303-2349 · 208-734-2552

PRODUCT LIABILITY LITIGATION

Boise

Donald J. Farley · Hall, Farley, Oberrecht & Blanton · http://www.hallfarley.com · Key Financial Center, Suite 700 · 702 West Idaho Street · P.O. Box 1271 · Boise, ID 83701 · 208-395-8500

James D. LaRue · Elam & Burke · 251 East Front Street, Suite 300 · P.O. Box 1539 · Boise, ID 83701 · 208-343-5454

Raymond D. Powers · Powers Thomson · 345 Bobwhite Court, Suite 150 · P.O. Box 9756 · Boise, ID 83707 · 208-577-5100

Coeur d'Alene

Kenneth B. Howard, Jr. · ⑩ · Kenneth B. Howard · 250 Northwest Boulevard, Suite 107-A · P.O. Box 2528 · Coeur d'Alene, ID 83816-2528 · 208-676-8890

Lewiston

Darrell Aherin · Aherin, Rice & Anegon · 1212 Idaho Street · P.O. Drawer 698 · Lewiston, ID 83501 · 208-746-3646

Michael E. McNichols · ⑩ · Clements, Brown & McNichols · 321 Thirteenth Street · P.O. Box 1510 · Lewiston, ID 83501 · 208-743-6538

Pocatello

W. Marcus W. Nye · ⑩ · Racine, Olson, Nye, Budge & Bailey · 201 East Center Street · P.O. Box 1391 · Pocatello, ID 83204 · 208-232-6101

PROFESSIONAL MALPRACTICE LAW

Boise

Mark Prusynski · Moffatt, Thomas, Barrett, Rock & Fields · 101 South Capitol Boulevard, 10th Floor · P.O. Box 829 · Boise, ID 83701-0829 · 208-345-2000

PUBLIC FINANCE LAW

Boise

Nicholas G. Miller · ⑩ · Hawley Troxell Ennis & Hawley · 877 Main Street, Suite 1000 · P.O. Box 1617 · Boise, ID 83701 · 208-344-6000

REAL ESTATE LAW

Boise

Brian L. Ballard · Hawley Troxell Ennis & Hawley · 877 Main Street, Suite 1000 · P.O. Box 1617 · Boise, ID 83701 · 208-344-6000

Christopher J. Beeson · Givens Pursley · http://www.givenspursley.com · 601 West Bannock Street · P.O. Box 2720 · Boise, ID 83701 · 208-388-1200

Robert B. Burns · Moffatt, Thomas, Barrett, Rock & Fields · 101 South Capitol Boulevard, 10th Floor · P.O. Box 829 · Boise, ID 83701-0829 · 208-345-2000

JoAnn C. Butler · Spink Butler · 251 East Front Street, Suite 200 · P.O. Box 639 · Boise, ID 83701 · 208-388-1000

William J. McKlveen · Eberle, Berlin, Kading, Turnbow McKlveen & Jones · 1111 West Jefferson Street, Suite 530 · Boise, ID 83701 · 208-344-8535

L. Edward Miller · ⑩ · Givens Pursley · http://www.givenspursley.com · 601 West Bannock Street · P.O. Box 2720 · Boise, ID 83701 · 208-388-1200

Michael T. Spink · Spink Butler · 251 East Front Street, Suite 200 · P.O. Box 639 · Boise, ID 83701 · 208-388-1000

Idaho Falls

Charles A. Homer · Holden, Kidwell, Hahn & Crapo · 1000 Riverwalk Drive, Suite 200 · P.O. Box 50130 Idaho Falls, ID 83405 · 208-523-0620

Lewiston

Eric K. Peterson · Clements, Brown & McNichols · 321 Thirteenth Street · P.O. Box 1510 · Lewiston, ID 83501 · 208-743-6538

Meridian

Kenneth L. Mallea · Mallea Law Offices · 78 Southwest Fifth Avenue, Suite One · P.O. Box 857 · Meridian, ID 83680 · 208-888-2790

SECURITIES LAW

Boise

Loren Ipsen · Elam & Burke · 251 East Front Street, Suite 300 · P.O. Box 1539 · Boise, ID 83701 · 208-343-5454

TAX LAW

Boise

Steven E. Alkire · Eberle, Berlin, Kading, Turnbow McKlveen & Jones · 1111 West Jefferson Street, Suite 530 · Boise, ID 83701 · 208-344-8535

John McGown, Jr. · Hawley Troxell Ennis & Hawley · 877 Main Street, Suite 1000 · P.O. Box 1617 · Boise, ID 83701 · 208-344-6000

Joseph H. Uberuaga II · ⑩ · Eberle, Berlin, Kading, Turnbow McKlveen & Jones · 1111 West Jefferson Street, Suite 530 · Boise, ID 83701 · 208-344-8535

Idaho Falls

Stephen E. Martin · ⑳ · Martin & Eskelson · 425 South Holmes Avenue · P.O. Box 3189 · Idaho Falls, ID 83403 · 208-523-6644

Pocatello

Thomas J. Holmes · Jones Chartered · 203 South Garfield · P.O. Box 967 · Pocatello, ID 83204-0967 · 208-232-5911

D. James Manning · Moffatt, Thomas, Barrett, Rock & Fields · 412 West Center, Suite 2000 · P.O. Box 817 · Pocatello, ID 83204-0817 · 208-233-2001

Eric L. Olsen · Racine, Olson, Nye, Budge & Bailey · 201 East Center Street · P.O. Box 1391 · Pocatello, ID 83204 · 208-232-6101

TIMBER LAW

Boise

Robert Maynard · Perkins Coie · http://www.perkinscoie.com · 251 East Front Street, Suite 400 · Boise, ID 83702-7310 · 208-343-3434

Bruce M. Smith · Moore, Smith, Buxton & Turcke · 950 West Bannock Street, Suite 520 · Boise, ID 83702 · 208-331-1800

TRUSTS AND ESTATES

Boise

Edward D. Ahrens · Ahrens & DeAngeli · 101 South Capitol Boulevard, Suite 300 · P.O. Box 6561 · Boise, ID 83707-6561 · 208-395-0001

Darin DeAngeli · Ahrens & DeAngeli · 101 South Capitol Boulevard, Suite 300 · P.O. Box 6561 · Boise, ID 83707-6561 · 208-395-0001

Loren Ipsen · Elam & Burke · 251 East Front Street, Suite 300 · P.O. Box 1539 · Boise, ID 83701 · 208-343-5454

John McGown, Jr. · Hawley Troxell Ennis & Hawley · 877 Main Street, Suite 1000 · P.O. Box 1617 · Boise, ID 83701 · 208-344-6000

Michael W. McGreaham · Moffatt, Thomas, Barrett, Rock & Fields · 101 South Capitol Boulevard, 10th Floor · P.O. Box 829 · Boise, ID 83701-0829 · 208-345-2000

Joseph H. Uberuaga II · ⑩ · Eberle, Berlin, Kading, Turnbow McKlveen & Jones · 1111 West Jefferson Street, Suite 530 · Boise, ID 83701 · 208-344-8535

Coeur d'Alene

Marc E. Wallace · Wallace & Cusack · 2370 North Merritt Creek Loop, Suite One · Coeur d'Alene, ID 83814 · 208-667-2264

Eagle

Sandra L. Clapp · Sanda L. Clapp & Associates · http://www.clapp-legal.com · 1025 South Bridgeway Place, Suite 180 · P.O. Box 2660 · Eagle, ID 83616 · 208-938-2660

Idaho Falls

Stephen E. Martin · ⑳ · Martin & Eskelson · 425 South Holmes Avenue · P.O. Box 3189 · Idaho Falls, ID 83403 · 208-523-6644

Gary L. Meikle · Holden, Kidwell, Hahn & Crapo · 1000 Riverwalk Drive, Suite 200 · P.O. Box 50130 · Idaho Falls, ID 83405 · 208-523-0620

Pocatello

Thomas J. Holmes · Jones Chartered · 203 South Garfield · P.O. Box 967 · Pocatello, ID 83204-0967 · 208-232-5911

D. James Manning · Moffatt, Thomas, Barrett, Rock & Fields · 412 West Center, Suite 2000 · P.O. Box 817 · Pocatello, ID 83204-0817 · 208-233-2001

Eric L. Olsen · Racine, Olson, Nye, Budge & Bailey · 201 East Center Street · P.O. Box 1391 · Pocatello, ID 83204 · 208-232-6101

WATER LAW

Boise

Kevin J. Beaton · Stoel Rives · http://www.stoel.com · 101 South Capitol Boulevard, Suite 1900 · Boise, ID 83702-7705 · 208-389-9000

Michael C. Creamer · Givens Pursley · http://www.givenspursley.com · 601 West Bannock Street · P.O. Box 2720 · Boise, ID 83701 · 208-388-1200

Jeffrey C. Fereday · ⑩ · Givens Pursley · http://www.givenspursley.com · 601 West Bannock Street · P.O. Box 2720 · Boise, ID 83701 · 208-388-1200

Christopher H. Meyer · Givens Pursley · http://www.givenspursley.com · 601 West Bannock Street · P.O. Box 2720 · Boise, ID 83701 · 208-388-1200

Pocatello

Randall C. Budge · Racine, Olson, Nye, Budge & Bailey · 201 East Center Street · P.O. Box 1391 · Pocatello, ID 83204 · 208-232-6101

Rexburg

Jerry Rigby · Rigby, Andrus & Moeller · 25 North Second East · P.O. Box 250 · Rexburg, ID 83440 · 208-356-3633

Ray W. Rigby · ⑩ · Rigby, Andrus & Moeller · 25 North Second East · P.O. Box 250 · Rexburg, ID 83440 208-356-3633

Twin Falls

John A. Rosholt · ⑩ · Barker Rosholt & Simpson · 113 Main Avenue West, Suite 303 · P.O. Box 485 · Twin Falls, ID 83303-0485 · 208-733-0700

WHITE-COLLAR CRIMINAL DEFENSE

Boise

Scott McKay · Nevin, Benjamin, McKay & Bartlett · 303 West Bannock Street · P.O. Box 2772 · Boise, ID 83701 · 208-343-1000

David Z. Nevin · ⑩ · Nevin, Benjamin, McKay & Bartlett · 303 West Bannock Street · P.O. Box 2772 · Boise, ID 83701 · 208-343-1000

Charles F. Peterson, Jr. · Law Office of Charles F. Peterson · 913 West River Street, Suite 420 · Boise, ID 83702 · 208-342-4633

Paul L. Westberg · ⑩ · Westberg, McCabe & Collins · The Tullis Building, Lower Level · 516 West Franklin Street · P.O. Box 2836 · Boise, ID 83702 · 208-336-5200

Ketchum

Andrew H. Parnes · ⑩ · Law Office of Andrew Parnes · 671 First Avenue North · P.O. Box 5988 · Ketchum, ID 83340 · 208-726-1010

Moscow

James E. Siebe · ⑩ · Siebe Law Office · 202 East Second Street · P.O. Box 9045 · Moscow, ID 83843 · 208-883-0622

WORKERS' COMPENSATION LAW

Boise

John W. Barrett · ⑩ · Moffatt, Thomas, Barrett, Rock & Fields · 101 South Capitol Boulevard, 10th Floor P.O. Box 829 · Boise, ID 83701-0829 · 208-345-2000

Glenna M. Christensen · Moffatt, Thomas, Barrett, Rock & Fields · 101 South Capitol Boulevard, 10th Floor · P.O. Box 829 · Boise, ID 83701-0829 · 208-345-2000

James A. Ford · Elam & Burke · 251 East Front Street, Suite 300 · P.O. Box 1539 · Boise, ID 83701 · 208-343-5454

Alan K. Hull · Anderson, Julian & Hull · C.W. Moore Plaza, Suite 700 · 250 South Fifth Street · P.O. Box 7426 · Boise, ID 83707-7426 · 208-344-5800

Lynn Michael Luker · Lynn M. Luker · 1010 North Orchard, Suite Four · P.O. Box 190929 · Boise, ID 83719 · 208-343-0022

Hugh V. Mossman · Mossman Law Office · 611 West Hays Street · Boise, ID 83702 · 208-342-6900

William Breck Seiniger, Jr. · Seiniger Law Offices · 942 West Myrtle Street · Boise, ID 83702 · 208-345-1000

Lewiston

Darrell Aherin · Aherin, Rice & Anegon · 1212 Idaho Street · P.O. Drawer 698 · Lewiston, ID 83501 · 208-746-3646

Nicholas M. Lamanna · ⑩ · Lamanna Law Firm · Priest River Professional Center · 102 Ninth Street · P.O. Box 789 · Priest River, ID 83856-0789 · 208-448-1221

ILLINOIS

ADMINISTRATIVE LAW

Chicago

Christian F. Binnig · Mayer Brown · 71 South Wacker Drive · Chicago, IL 60606 · 312-782-0600

David W. Carpenter · Sidley Austin · One South Dearborn Street · Chicago, IL 60603 · 312-853-7000

J. Tyson Covey · Mayer Brown · 71 South Wacker Drive · Chicago, IL 60606 · 312-782-0600

Theodore A. Livingston, Jr. · Mayer Brown · 71 South Wacker Drive · Chicago, IL 60606 · 312-782-0600

John E. Muench · Mayer Brown · 71 South Wacker Drive · Chicago, IL 60606 · 312-782-0600

E. Glenn Rippie · Foley & Lardner · 321 North Clark Street, Suite 2800 · Chicago, IL 60654 · 312-832-4500

Dale E. Thomas · Sidley Austin · One South Dearborn Street · Chicago, IL 60603 · 312-853-7000

ADVERTISING LAW

Chicago

Jeffrey H. Brown · Michael Best & Friedrich · Two Prudential Plaza, Suite 2000 · 180 North Stetson Avenue · Chicago, IL 60601 · 312-222-0800

Darren S. Cahr · Drinker Biddle & Reath · 191 North Wacker Drive, Suite 3700 · Chicago, IL 60606-1698 · 312-569-1000

Stephen P. Durchslag · Winston & Strawn · 35 West Wacker Drive · Chicago, IL 60601-9703 · 312-558-5600

Brian L. Heidelberger · Winston & Strawn · 35 West Wacker Drive · Chicago, IL 60601-9703 · 312-558-5600

Mary Hutchings Reed · Winston & Strawn · 35 West Wacker Drive · Chicago, IL 60601-9703 · 312-558-5600

Larry L. Saret · Michael Best & Friedrich · Two Prudential Plaza, Suite 2000 · 180 North Stetson Avenue Chicago, IL 60601 · 312-222-0800

Eugene F. Zelek, Jr. · Freeborn & Peters · 311 South Wacker Drive, Suite 3000 · Chicago, IL 60606-6677 · 312-360-6000

ALTERNATIVE DISPUTE RESOLUTION

Chicago

Lee N. Abrams · Mayer Brown · 71 South Wacker Drive · Chicago, IL 60606 · 312-782-0600

Peter V. Baugher · Schopf & Weiss · One South Wacker Drive, 28th Floor · Chicago, IL 60606-4617 · 312-701-9300

John C. Berghoff, Jr. · Mayer Brown · 71 South Wacker Drive · Chicago, IL 60606 · 312-782-0600

Vincent J. Connelly · ⑩ · Mayer Brown · 71 South Wacker Drive · Chicago, IL 60606 · 312-782-0600

Brian L. Crowe · Shefsky & Froelich · 111 East Wacker Drive, Suite 2800 · Chicago, IL 60601 · 312-527-4000

Richard M. Franklin · Baker & McKenzie · One Prudential Plaza · 130 East Randolph Drive · Chicago, IL 60601 · 312-861-8000

William R. Jentes · ㉕ · William R. Jentes · 1500 North Lake Shore Drive, Suite 4-C · Chicago, IL 60610 312-643-0024

Kent Lawrence · Lawrence, Kamin, Saunders & Uhlenhop · 300 South Wacker Drive, Suite 500 · Chicago, IL 60606 · 312-372-1947

Warren Lupel · Lupel & Weininger · 30 North La Salle Street, Suite 3520 · Chicago, IL 60602 · 312-260-7700

George P. McAndrews · McAndrews, Held & Malloy · 500 West Madison Street, 34th Floor · Chicago, IL 60661 · 312-775-8000

Jonathan C. Medow · Mayer Brown · 71 South Wacker Drive · Chicago, IL 60606 · 312-782-0600

Scott A. Meyers · Levenfeld Pearlstein · http://www.lplegal.com · Two North LaSalle Street, Suite 1300 · Chicago, IL 60602 · 312-346-8380

Michael A. Olsen · Mayer Brown · 71 South Wacker Drive · Chicago, IL 60606 · 312-782-0600

Jeffrey S. Piell · Quarles & Brady · http://www.quarles.com · Citigroup Center, Suite 3700 · 500 West Madison Street · Chicago, IL 60661-2511 · 312-715-5000

Kenneth M. Roberts · Schiff Hardin · Sears Tower, Suite 6600 · 233 South Wacker Drive · Chicago, IL 60606-6473 · 312-258-5500

Gerald G. Saltarelli · Butler Rubin Saltarelli & Boyd · 70 West Madison Street, Suite 1800 · Chicago, IL 60602 · 312-444-9660

Zaldwaynaka Scott · Mayer Brown · 71 South Wacker Drive · Chicago, IL 60606 · 312-782-0600

John M. Touhy · Mayer Brown · 71 South Wacker Drive · Chicago, IL 60606 · 312-782-0600

Thomas R. Woodrow · Holland & Knight · http://www.hklaw.com · 131 South Dearborn Street, 30th Floor · Chicago, IL 60603 · 312-263-3600

Evanston

John H. Morrison · John H. Morrison · 2550 Princeton Avenue · Evanston, IL 60201-4941 · 847-869-5950

ANTITRUST LAW

Chicago

Lee N. Abrams · Mayer Brown · 71 South Wacker Drive · Chicago, IL 60606 · 312-782-0600

Roxane C. Busey · Baker & McKenzie · One Prudential Plaza · 130 East Randolph Drive · Chicago, IL 60601 · 312-861-8000

Joel G. Chefitz · McDermott Will & Emery · 227 West Monroe Street · Chicago, IL 60606-5096 · 312-372-2000

Charles W. Douglas · Sidley Austin · One South Dearborn Street · Chicago, IL 60603 · 312-853-7000

Nathan P. Eimer · Eimer Stahl Klevorn & Solberg · 224 South Michigan Avenue, Suite 1100 · Chicago, IL 60604 · 312-660-7600

Robert F. Finke · Mayer Brown · 71 South Wacker Drive · Chicago, IL 60606 · 312-782-0600

James K. Gardner · Neal, Gerber & Eisenberg · http://www.ngelaw.com · Two North LaSalle Street, Suite 2200 · Chicago, IL 60602-3801 · 312-269-8000

Robert T. Joseph · Sonnenschein Nath & Rosenthal · Sears Tower, Suite 7800 · 233 South Wacker Drive Chicago, IL 60606-6404 · 312-876-8000

Andrew G. Klevorn · Eimer Stahl Klevorn & Solberg · 224 South Michigan Avenue, Suite 1100 · Chicago, IL 60604 · 312-660-7600

Steven M. Kowal · Bell, Boyd & Lloyd · Three First National Plaza, Suite 3100 · 70 West Madison Street Chicago, IL 60602 · 312-372-1121

J. Andrew Langan · Kirkland & Ellis · 200 East Randolph Drive · Chicago, IL 60601-6636 · 312-861-2000

Andrew S. Marovitz · Mayer Brown · 71 South Wacker Drive · Chicago, IL 60606 · 312-782-0600

R. Mark McCareins · Winston & Strawn · 35 West Wacker Drive · Chicago, IL 60601-9703 · 312-558-5600

T. Mark McLaughlin · Mayer Brown · 71 South Wacker Drive · Chicago, IL 60606 · 312-782-0600

James H. Mutchnik · Kirkland & Ellis · 200 East Randolph Drive · Chicago, IL 60601-6636 · 312-861-2000

Phil C. Neal · Neal, Gerber & Eisenberg · http://www.ngelaw.com · Two North LaSalle Street, Suite 2200 Chicago, IL 60602-3801 · 312-269-8000

Thomas F. Ryan · Sidley Austin · One South Dearborn Street · Chicago, IL 60603 · 312-853-7000

Michael Sennett · Jones Day · 77 West Wacker Drive · Chicago, IL 60601-1692 · 312-782-3939

Alan H. Silberman · Sonnenschein Nath & Rosenthal · Sears Tower, Suite 7800 · 233 South Wacker Drive · Chicago, IL 60606-6404 · 312-876-8000

Paul E. Slater · Sperling & Slater · 55 West Monroe Street, Suite 3200 · Chicago, IL 60603 · 312-641-3200

John W. Treece · Sidley Austin · One South Dearborn Street · Chicago, IL 60603 · 312-853-7000

APPELLATE LAW

Carbondale

Edward J. Kionka · Southern Illinois University · Lesar Law Building · 1150 Douglas Drive, MS 6804 · Carbondale, IL 62901 · 618-521-5555

Chicago

Joel Bertocchi · Hinshaw & Culbertson · http://www.hinshawlaw.com · 222 North LaSalle Street, Suite 300 · Chicago, IL 60601-1081 · 312-704-3000

Timothy S. Bishop · Mayer Brown · 71 South Wacker Drive · Chicago, IL 60606 · 312-782-0600

J. Timothy Eaton · Shefsky & Froelich · 111 East Wacker Drive, Suite 2800 · Chicago, IL 60601 · 312-527-4000

James T. Ferrini · Clausen Miller · 10 South LaSalle Street, Suite 1600 · Chicago, IL 60603-1098 · 312-855-1010

Kevin M. Forde · ⑳ · Kevin M. Forde · 111 West Washington Street, Suite 1100 · Chicago, IL 60602-2768 · 312-641-1441

Celia G. Gamrath · Schiller DuCanto and Fleck · http://www.sdflaw.com · 200 North LaSalle Street, 30th Floor · Chicago, IL 60601-1089 · 312-641-5560

Hugh C. Griffin · Hall Prangle & Schoonveld · 200 South Wacker Drive, Suite 3300 · Chicago, IL 60606 · 312-345-9600

William J. Harte · ㉕ · William J. Harte · 111 West Washington Street, Suite 1100 · Chicago, IL 60602 · 312-726-5015

Edward M. Kay · Clausen Miller · 10 South LaSalle Street, Suite 1600 · Chicago, IL 60603-1098 · 312-855-1010

Howard A. London · Beermann Swerdlove · 161 North Clark Street, Suite 2600 · Chicago, IL 60601-3297 · 312-621-9700

Michele L. Odorizzi · Mayer Brown · 71 South Wacker Drive · Chicago, IL 60606 · 312-782-0600

Michael A. Pollard · Baker & McKenzie · One Prudential Plaza · 130 East Randolph Drive · Chicago, IL 60601 · 312-861-8000

Richard J. Prendergast · ⑩ · Richard J. Prendergast · 111 West Washington Street, Suite 1100 · Chicago, IL 60602 · 312-641-0881

William R. Quinlan · Quinlan & Carroll · 30 North LaSalle Street, Suite 2900 · Chicago, IL 60602 · 312-263-0900

Michael W. Rathsack · Law Office of Michael W. Rathsack · 111 West Washington Street, Suite 962 · Chicago, IL 60602-2711 · 312-726-5433

Michael L. Resis · O'Hagan, Smith & Amundsen · 150 North Michigan Avenue, Suite 3300 · Chicago, IL 60601 · 312-894-3200

Jeffrey W. Sarles · Mayer Brown · 71 South Wacker Drive · Chicago, IL 60606 · 312-782-0600

James C. Schroeder · Mayer Brown · 71 South Wacker Drive · Chicago, IL 60606 · 312-782-0600

Stephen M. Shapiro · Mayer Brown · 71 South Wacker Drive · Chicago, IL 60606 · 312-782-0600

Sarane C. Siewerth · Schiller DuCanto and Fleck · http://www.sdflaw.com · 200 North LaSalle Street, 30th Floor · Chicago, IL 60601-1089 · 312-641-5560

Robert M. Stephenson · ⑳ · Locke Lord Bissell & Liddell · 111 South Wacker Drive · Chicago, IL 60606-4410 · 312-443-0700

Stephen R. Swofford · Hinshaw & Culbertson · http://www.hinshawlaw.com · 222 North LaSalle Street, Suite 300 · Chicago, IL 60601-1081 · 312-704-3000

Mattoon

Richard F. Record, Jr. · Craig & Craig · 1807 Broadway · P.O. Box 689 · Mattoon, IL 61938-0689 · 217-234-6481

Peoria

Karen L. Kendall · Heyl, Royster, Voelker & Allen · Chase Building, Suite 600 · 124 Southwest Adams Street · Peoria, IL 61602 · 309-676-0400

BANKING LAW

Chicago

Thomas W. Albrecht · Sidley Austin · One South Dearborn Street · Chicago, IL 60603 · 312-853-7000

Robert C. Baptista, Jr. · Mayer Brown · 71 South Wacker Drive · Chicago, IL 60606 · 312-782-0600

Peter H. Barrow · Neal, Gerber & Eisenberg · http://www.ngelaw.com · Two North LaSalle Street, Suite 2200 · Chicago, IL 60602-3801 · 312-269-8000

H. Bruce Bernstein · ㉕ · Sidley Austin · One South Dearborn Street · Chicago, IL 60603 · 312-853-7000

Willis R. Buck, Jr. · Sidley Austin · One South Dearborn Street · Chicago, IL 60603 · 312-853-7000

James E. Clark · Sidley Austin · One South Dearborn Street · Chicago, IL 60603 · 312-853-7000

Jill A. Coleman · Neal, Gerber & Eisenberg · http://www.ngelaw.com · Two North LaSalle Street, Suite 2200 · Chicago, IL 60602-3801 · 312-269-8000

David G. Crumbaugh · Latham & Watkins · Sears Tower, Suite 5800 · 233 South Wacker Drive · Chicago, IL 60606-6401 · 312-876-7700

Debora de Hoyos · Mayer Brown · 71 South Wacker Drive · Chicago, IL 60606 · 312-782-0600

Edwin S. del Hierro · Barack Ferrazzano Kirschbaum Perlman & Nagelberg · 200 West Madison Street, Suite 3900 · Chicago, IL 60606 · 312-984-3100

Douglas A. Doetsch · Mayer Brown · 71 South Wacker Drive · Chicago, IL 60606 · 312-782-0600

James W. Doran · Latham & Watkins · Sears Tower, Suite 5800 · 233 South Wacker Drive · Chicago, IL 60606-6401 · 312-876-7700

David L. Dranoff · Goldberg, Kohn, Bell, Black, Rosenbloom & Moritz · 55 East Monroe Street, Suite 3300 · Chicago, IL 60603-5792 · 312-201-4000

J. Paul Forrester · Mayer Brown · 71 South Wacker Drive · Chicago, IL 60606 · 312-782-0600

Marc P. Franson · Chapman and Cutler · 111 West Monroe Street · Chicago, IL 60603-4080 · 312-845-3000

John E. Freechack · Barack Ferrazzano Kirschbaum Perlman & Nagelberg · 200 West Madison Street, Suite 3900 · Chicago, IL 60606 · 312-984-3100

Michael L. Gold · Sidley Austin · One South Dearborn Street · Chicago, IL 60603 · 312-853-7000

Kevin J. Hochberg · Sidley Austin · One South Dearborn Street · Chicago, IL 60603 · 312-853-7000

Robert F. Hugi · Mayer Brown · 71 South Wacker Drive · Chicago, IL 60606 · 312-782-0600

Ronald H. Jacobson · Winston & Strawn · 35 West Wacker Drive · Chicago, IL 60601-9703 · 312-558-5600

Seth E. Jacobson · Skadden, Arps, Slate, Meagher & Flom · 333 West Wacker Drive · Chicago, IL 60606 312-407-0700

Donald L. Johnson · 20 · Law Offices of Donald L. Johnson · 33 North Dearborn Street, Suite 1401 · Chicago, IL 60602 · 312-263-7000

Andrew M. Kaufman · Kirkland & Ellis · 200 East Randolph Drive · Chicago, IL 60601-6636 · 312-861-2000

Carter H. Klein · Jenner & Block · http://www.jenner.com · 330 North Wabash Avenue · Chicago, IL 60611-7603 · 312-222-9350

Richard M. Kohn · Goldberg, Kohn, Bell, Black, Rosenbloom & Moritz · 55 East Monroe Street, Suite 3300 · Chicago, IL 60603-5792 · 312-201-4000

Kenneth A. Latimer · Duane Morris · 190 South LaSalle Street, Suite 3700 · Chicago, IL 60603-3433 · 312-499-6700

James R. Looman · Sidley Austin · One South Dearborn Street · Chicago, IL 60603 · 312-853-7000

David M. Mason · Goldberg, Kohn, Bell, Black, Rosenbloom & Moritz · 55 East Monroe Street, Suite 3300 · Chicago, IL 60603-5792 · 312-201-4000

John T. McEnroe · Vedder Price · 222 North LaSalle Street · Chicago, IL 60601-1003 · 312-609-7500

Lynn M. McGovern · Skadden, Arps, Slate, Meagher & Flom · 333 West Wacker Drive · Chicago, IL 60606 · 312-407-0700

J. Robert McMenamin · McDermott Will & Emery · 227 West Monroe Street · Chicago, IL 60606-5096 · 312-372-2000

Scott J. Moore · Jones Day · 77 West Wacker Drive · Chicago, IL 60601-1692 · 312-782-3939

Kenneth P. Morrison · Kirkland & Ellis · 200 East Randolph Drive · Chicago, IL 60601-6636 · 312-861-2000

Gary L. Mowder · ⑩ · Schiff Hardin · Sears Tower, Suite 6600 · 233 South Wacker Drive · Chicago, IL 60606-6473 · 312-258-5500

Arthur B. Muir · McGuireWoods · http://www.mcguirewoods.com · 77 West Wacker Drive, Suite 4100 · Chicago, IL 60601-1818 · 312-849-8100

Gregory S. Murray · Winston & Strawn · 35 West Wacker Drive · Chicago, IL 60601-9703 · 312-558-5600

John R. Mussman · Holland & Knight · http://www.hklaw.com · 131 South Dearborn Street, 30th Floor · Chicago, IL 60603 · 312-263-3600

Daniel O'Rourke · Vedder Price · 222 North LaSalle Street · Chicago, IL 60601-1003 · 312-609-7500

Michael L. Owen · Bell, Boyd & Lloyd · Three First National Plaza, Suite 3100 · 70 West Madison Street Chicago, IL 60602 · 312-372-1121

George A. Pecoulas · Mayer Brown · 71 South Wacker Drive · Chicago, IL 60606 · 312-782-0600

Philip J. Perzek · Latham & Watkins · Sears Tower, Suite 5800 · 233 South Wacker Drive · Chicago, IL 60606-6401 · 312-876-7700

Scott E. Pickens · Schiff Hardin · Sears Tower, Suite 6600 · 233 South Wacker Drive · Chicago, IL 60606-6473 · 312-258-5500

Vik Puri · Latham & Watkins · Sears Tower, Suite 5800 · 233 South Wacker Drive · Chicago, IL 60606-6401 · 312-876-7700

Ronald E. Rokosz · Chapman and Cutler · 111 West Monroe Street · Chicago, IL 60603-4080 · 312-845-3000

Peter L. Rossiter · Schiff Hardin · Sears Tower, Suite 6600 · 233 South Wacker Drive · Chicago, IL 60606-6473 · 312-258-5500

Donald L. Schwartz · Latham & Watkins · Sears Tower, Suite 5800 · 233 South Wacker Drive · Chicago, IL 60606-6401 · 312-876-7700

Ami G. Scott · Mayer Brown · 71 South Wacker Drive · Chicago, IL 60606 · 312-782-0600

Stuart P. Shulruff · Katten Muchin Rosenman · 525 West Monroe Street · Chicago, IL 60661-3693 · 312-902-5200

Gary B. Stern · Sidley Austin · One South Dearborn Street · Chicago, IL 60603 · 312-853-7000

Angela M. Ulum · Mayer Brown · 71 South Wacker Drive · Chicago, IL 60606 · 312-782-0600

Gary T. Zussman · Goldberg, Kohn, Bell, Black, Rosenbloom & Moritz · 55 East Monroe Street, Suite 3300 · Chicago, IL 60603-5792 · 312-201-4000

BANKRUPTCY AND CREDITOR-DEBTOR RIGHTS LAW

Chicago

Howard L. Adelman · ⑩ · Adelman, Gettleman, Merens, Berish & Carter · 53 West Jackson Boulevard, Suite 1050 · Chicago, IL 60604 · 312-435-1050

Ronald Barliant · Goldberg, Kohn, Bell, Black, Rosenbloom & Moritz · 55 East Monroe Street, Suite 3300 · Chicago, IL 60603-5792 · 312-201-4000

Mark A. Berkoff · DLA Piper · 203 North LaSalle Street, Suite 1900 · Chicago, IL 60601-1293 · 312-368-4000

H. Bruce Bernstein · ㉕ · Sidley Austin · One South Dearborn Street · Chicago, IL 60603 · 312-853-7000

Matthew J. Botica · Winston & Strawn · 35 West Wacker Drive · Chicago, IL 60601-9703 · 312-558-5600

John William Butler, Jr. · Skadden, Arps, Slate, Meagher & Flom · 333 West Wacker Drive · Chicago, IL 60606 · 312-407-0700

James F. Conlan · Sidley Austin · One South Dearborn Street · Chicago, IL 60603 · 312-853-7000

David S. Curry · Mayer Brown · 71 South Wacker Drive · Chicago, IL 60606 · 312-782-0600

Robert M. Fishman · ⑩ · Shaw Gussis Fishman Glantz Wolfson & Towbin · 321 North Clark Street, Suite 800 · Chicago, IL 60654 · 312-541-0151

Michael L. Gesas · Arnstein & Lehr · 120 South Riverside Plaza, Suite 1200 · Chicago, IL 60606 · 312-876-7100

Paul E. Harner · Paul Hastings · 191 North Wacker Drive, 30th Floor · Chicago, IL 60606 · 312-499-6060

David S. Heller · Latham & Watkins · Sears Tower, Suite 5800 · 233 South Wacker Drive · Chicago, IL 60606-6401 · 312-876-7700

Janet E. Henderson · Sidley Austin · One South Dearborn Street · Chicago, IL 60603 · 312-853-7000

J. Eric Ivester · Skadden, Arps, Slate, Meagher & Flom · 333 West Wacker Drive · Chicago, IL 60606 · 312-407-0700

Fruman Jacobson · Sonnenschein Nath & Rosenthal · Sears Tower, Suite 7800 · 233 South Wacker Drive · Chicago, IL 60606-6404 · 312-876-8000

Harold L. Kaplan · Foley & Lardner · 321 North Clark Street, Suite 2800 · Chicago, IL 60654 · 312-832-4500

Marc Kieselstein · Kirkland & Ellis · 200 East Randolph Drive · Chicago, IL 60601-6636 · 312-861-2000

Thomas S. Kiriakos · Mayer Brown · 71 South Wacker Drive · Chicago, IL 60606 · 312-782-0600

David N. Missner · ⑳ · DLA Piper · 203 North LaSalle Street, Suite 1900 · Chicago, IL 60601-1293 · 312-368-4000

Michael L. Molinaro · Loeb & Loeb · 321 North Clark, Suite 2300 · Chicago, IL 60654 · 312-464-3100

Daniel R. Murray · ⑩ · Jenner & Block · http://www.jenner.com · 330 North Wabash Avenue · Chicago, IL 60611-7603 · 312-222-9350

Larry J. Nyhan · Sidley Austin · One South Dearborn Street · Chicago, IL 60603 · 312-853-7000

George N. Panagakis · Skadden, Arps, Slate, Meagher & Flom · 333 West Wacker Drive · Chicago, IL 60606 · 312-407-0700

Felicia Gerber Perlman · Skadden, Arps, Slate, Meagher & Flom · 333 West Wacker Drive · Chicago, IL 60606 · 312-407-0700

Nancy A. Peterman · Greenberg Traurig · http://www.gtlaw.com · 77 West Wacker Drive, Suite 2500 · Chicago, IL 60601 · 312-456-8400

Ronald R. Peterson · ⑩ · Jenner & Block · http://www.jenner.com · 330 North Wabash Avenue · Chicago, IL 60611-7603 · 312-222-9350

Timothy R. Pohl · Skadden, Arps, Slate, Meagher & Flom · 333 West Wacker Drive · Chicago, IL 60606 312-407-0700

Lewis S. Rosenbloom · ⑩ · Dewey & LeBoeuf · Two Prudential Plaza, Suite 3700 · 180 North Stetson Avenue · Chicago, IL 60601 · 312-794-8000

Stuart M. Rozen · Mayer Brown · 71 South Wacker Drive · Chicago, IL 60606 · 312-782-0600

Jeffrey M. Schwartz · Drinker Biddle & Reath · 191 North Wacker Drive, Suite 3700 · Chicago, IL 60606-1698 · 312-569-1000

Keith J. Shapiro · Greenberg Traurig · http://www.gtlaw.com · 77 West Wacker Drive, Suite 2500 · Chicago, IL 60601 · 312-456-8400

Alan P. Solow · Goldberg, Kohn, Bell, Black, Rosenbloom & Moritz · 55 East Monroe Street, Suite 3300 · Chicago, IL 60603-5792 · 312-201-4000

Michael B. Solow · Kaye Scholer · Three First National Plaza, Suite 4100 · 70 West Madison Street · Chicago, IL 60602-4231 · 312-583-2300

Catherine L. Steege · Jenner & Block · http://www.jenner.com · 330 North Wabash Avenue · Chicago, IL 60611-7603 · 312-222-9350

James A. Stempel · Kirkland & Ellis · 200 East Randolph Drive · Chicago, IL 60601-6636 · 312-861-2000

J. Robert Stoll · Mayer Brown · 71 South Wacker Drive · Chicago, IL 60606 · 312-782-0600

Steven B. Towbin · Shaw Gussis Fishman Glantz Wolfson & Towbin · 321 North Clark Street, Suite 800 Chicago, IL 60654 · 312-541-0151

Neal L. Wolf · Katten Muchin Rosenman · 525 West Monroe Street · Chicago, IL 60661-3693 · 312-902-5200

Daniel A. Zazove · Perkins Coie · http://www.perkinscoie.com · 131 South Dearborn Street, Suite 1700 · Chicago, IL 60603-5559 · 312-324-8400

BET-THE-COMPANY LITIGATION

Chicago

Fred H. Bartlit, Jr. · ⑳ · Bartlit, Beck, Herman, Palenchar & Scott · Courthouse Place, Suite 300 · 54 West Hubbard Street · Chicago, IL 60610 · 312-494-4400

Philip S. Beck · ⑩ · Bartlit, Beck, Herman, Palenchar & Scott · Courthouse Place, Suite 300 · 54 West Hubbard Street · Chicago, IL 60610 · 312-494-4400

Vincent J. Connelly · ⑩ · Mayer Brown · 71 South Wacker Drive · Chicago, IL 60606 · 312-782-0600

Brian L. Crowe · Shefsky & Froelich · 111 East Wacker Drive, Suite 2800 · Chicago, IL 60601 · 312-527-4000

Tyrone C. Fahner · ⑩ · Mayer Brown · 71 South Wacker Drive · Chicago, IL 60606 · 312-782-0600

James R. Ferguson · Mayer Brown · 71 South Wacker Drive · Chicago, IL 60606 · 312-782-0600

James R. Figliulo · ⑩ · Figliulo & Silverman · 10 South LaSalle Street, Suite 3600 · Chicago, IL 60603 · 312-251-4600

Kevin M. Forde · ⑳ · Kevin M. Forde · 111 West Washington Street, Suite 1100 · Chicago, IL 60602-2768 · 312-641-1441

Lee A. Freeman, Jr. · ⑩ · Jenner & Block · http://www.jenner.com · 330 North Wabash Avenue · Chicago, IL 60611-7603 · 312-222-9350

William J. Harte · ㉕ · William J. Harte · 111 West Washington Street, Suite 1100 · Chicago, IL 60602 · 312-726-5015

Scott R. Lassar · Sidley Austin · One South Dearborn Street · Chicago, IL 60603 · 312-853-7000

Richard J. Prendergast · ⑩ · Richard J. Prendergast · 111 West Washington Street, Suite 1100 · Chicago, IL 60602 · 312-641-0881

Daniel E. Reidy · ⑩ · Jones Day · 77 West Wacker Drive · Chicago, IL 60601-1692 · 312-782-3939

Lowell E. Sachnoff · ㉕ · Reed Smith · 10 South Wacker Drive, 40th Floor · Chicago, IL 60606-7507 · 312-207-1000

Alan N. Salpeter · ⑩ · Dewey & LeBoeuf · Two Prudential Plaza, Suite 3700 · 180 North Stetson Avenue Chicago, IL 60601 · 312-794-8000

Jerold S. Solovy · ⑩ · Jenner & Block · http://www.jenner.com · 330 North Wabash Avenue · Chicago, IL 60611-7603 · 312-222-9350

Thomas P. Sullivan · ㉕ · Jenner & Block · http://www.jenner.com · 330 North Wabash Avenue · Chicago, IL 60611-7603 · 312-222-9350

Anton R. Valukas · ㉕ · Jenner & Block · http://www.jenner.com · 330 North Wabash Avenue · Chicago, IL 60611-7603 · 312-222-9350

Dan K. Webb · ⑳ · Winston & Strawn · 35 West Wacker Drive · Chicago, IL 60601-9703 · 312-558-5600

BIOTECHNOLOGY LAW

Chicago

Timothy S. Bishop · Mayer Brown · 71 South Wacker Drive · Chicago, IL 60606 · 312-782-0600

Misty S. Gruber · Dykema · http://www.dykema.com · 10 South Wacker Drive, Suite 2300 · Chicago, IL 60606 · 312-876-1700

Alice O. Martin · Barnes & Thornburg · http://www.btlaw.com · One North Wacker Drive, Suite 4400 · Chicago, IL 60606-2833 · 312-357-1313

Kevin E. Noonan · McDonnell Boehnen Hulbert & Berghoff · 300 South Wacker Drive, Suite 31 · Chicago, IL 60606-6709 · 312-913-0001

Matthew A. Rooney · Mayer Brown · 71 South Wacker Drive · Chicago, IL 60606 · 312-782-0600

Deborah Schavey Ruff · Mayer Brown · 71 South Wacker Drive · Chicago, IL 60606 · 312-782-0600

Donald W. Rupert · Marshall, Gerstein & Borun · 6300 Sears Tower · 233 South Wacker Drive · Chicago, IL 60606-6357 · 312-474-6300

COLLABORATIVE LAW: FAMILY LAW

Chicago

Brigitte Bell · Brigitte Bell Mediation · 53 West Jackson Boulevard, Suite 1230 · Chicago, IL 60604 · 847-733-0933

James H. Feldman · ㉕ · Jenner & Block · http://www.jenner.com · 330 North Wabash Avenue · Chicago, IL 60611-7603 · 312-222-9350

James R. Galvin · Schiller DuCanto and Fleck · http://www.sdflaw.com · 200 North LaSalle Street, 30th Floor · Chicago, IL 60601-1089 · 312-641-5560

Lake Forest

Carlton R. Marcyan · Schiller DuCanto and Fleck · http://www.sdflaw.com · 225 East Deerpath Road, Suite 270 · Lake Forest, IL 60045-1937 · 847-615-8300

COMMERCIAL LITIGATION

Chicago

Fred H. Bartlit, Jr. · ⑳ · Bartlit, Beck, Herman, Palenchar & Scott · Courthouse Place, Suite 300 · 54 West Hubbard Street · Chicago, IL 60610 · 312-494-4400

Philip S. Beck · ⑩ · Bartlit, Beck, Herman, Palenchar & Scott · Courthouse Place, Suite 300 · 54 West Hubbard Street · Chicago, IL 60610 · 312-494-4400

Alvin R. Becker · ⑩ · Beermann Swerdlove · 161 North Clark Street, Suite 2600 · Chicago, IL 60601-3297 · 312-621-9700

H. Nicholas Berberian · Neal, Gerber & Eisenberg · http://www.ngelaw.com · Two North LaSalle Street, Suite 2200 · Chicago, IL 60602-3801 · 312-269-8000

David M. Bernick · Kirkland & Ellis · 200 East Randolph Drive · Chicago, IL 60601-6636 · 312-861-2000

William T. Cahill · Perkins Coie · http://www.perkinscoie.com · 131 South Dearborn Street, Suite 1700 · Chicago, IL 60603-5559 · 312-324-8400

Walter C. Carlson · Sidley Austin · One South Dearborn Street · Chicago, IL 60603 · 312-853-7000

Joel G. Chefitz · McDermott Will & Emery · 227 West Monroe Street · Chicago, IL 60606-5096 · 312-372-2000

Frank Cicero, Jr. · ㉕ · Kirkland & Ellis · 200 East Randolph Drive · Chicago, IL 60601-6636 · 312-861-2000

Francis A. Citera · Greenberg Traurig · http://www.gtlaw.com · 77 West Wacker Drive, Suite 2500 · Chicago, IL 60601 · 312-456-8400

Fay Clayton · ⑩ · Robinson, Curley & Clayton · 300 South Wacker Drive, Suite 1700 · Chicago, IL 60606 312-663-3100

Robert A. Clifford · ⑩ · Clifford Law Offices · http://www.cliffordlaw.com · 120 North LaSalle Street, Suite 3100 · Chicago, IL 60602 · 312-899-9090

Jeffrey D. Colman · Jenner & Block · http://www.jenner.com · 330 North Wabash Avenue · Chicago, IL 60611-7603 · 312-222-9350

William F. Conlon · Sidley Austin · One South Dearborn Street · Chicago, IL 60603 · 312-853-7000

Vincent J. Connelly · 10 · Mayer Brown · 71 South Wacker Drive · Chicago, IL 60606 · 312-782-0600

Michael M. Conway · 10 · Foley & Lardner · 321 North Clark Street, Suite 2800 · Chicago, IL 60654 · 312-832-4500

Sean B. Crotty · Robert F. Coleman & Associates · 77 West Wacker Drive · Chicago, IL 60601 · 312-444-1000

Brian L. Crowe · Shefsky & Froelich · 111 East Wacker Drive, Suite 2800 · Chicago, IL 60601 · 312-527-4000

Julian C. D'Esposito, Jr. · Mayer Brown · 71 South Wacker Drive · Chicago, IL 60606 · 312-782-0600

Charles W. Douglas · Sidley Austin · One South Dearborn Street · Chicago, IL 60603 · 312-853-7000

Thomas M. Durkin · Mayer Brown · 71 South Wacker Drive · Chicago, IL 60606 · 312-782-0600

Gary M. Elden · Grippo & Elden · 111 South Wacker Drive · Chicago, IL 60606 · 312-704-7700

Tyrone C. Fahner · 10 · Mayer Brown · 71 South Wacker Drive · Chicago, IL 60606 · 312-782-0600

Michael R. Feagley · Mayer Brown · 71 South Wacker Drive · Chicago, IL 60606 · 312-782-0600

James R. Ferguson · Mayer Brown · 71 South Wacker Drive · Chicago, IL 60606 · 312-782-0600

James R. Figliulo · 10 · Figliulo & Silverman · 10 South LaSalle Street, Suite 3600 · Chicago, IL 60603 · 312-251-4600

Sheila M. Finnegan · Mayer Brown · 71 South Wacker Drive · Chicago, IL 60606 · 312-782-0600

Kevin M. Flynn · Kevin M. Flynn & Associates · 77 West Wacker Drive, Suite 4800 · Chicago, IL 60601 · 312-456-0240

Michael P. Foradas · Kirkland & Ellis · 200 East Randolph Drive · Chicago, IL 60601-6636 · 312-861-2000

Kevin M. Forde · 20 · Kevin M. Forde · 111 West Washington Street, Suite 1100 · Chicago, IL 60602-2768 · 312-641-1441

Michael K. Forde · Mayer Brown · 71 South Wacker Drive · Chicago, IL 60606 · 312-782-0600

Lee A. Freeman, Jr. · 10 · Jenner & Block · http://www.jenner.com · 330 North Wabash Avenue · Chicago, IL 60611-7603 · 312-222-9350

John N. Gallo · Sidley Austin · One South Dearborn Street · Chicago, IL 60603 · 312-853-7000

James K. Gardner · Neal, Gerber & Eisenberg · http://www.ngelaw.com · Two North LaSalle Street, Suite 2200 · Chicago, IL 60602-3801 · 312-269-8000

Terry M. Grimm · Winston & Strawn · 35 West Wacker Drive · Chicago, IL 60601-9703 · 312-558-5600

Michael T. Hannafan · 10 · Hannafan & Hannafan · One East Wacker Drive, Suite 2800 · Chicago, IL 60601 · 312-527-0055

Steven J. Harper · Kirkland & Ellis · 200 East Randolph Drive · Chicago, IL 60601-6636 · 312-861-2000

William J. Harte · ㉕ · William J. Harte · 111 West Washington Street, Suite 1100 · Chicago, IL 60602 · 312-726-5015

John F. Hartmann · Kirkland & Ellis · 200 East Randolph Drive · Chicago, IL 60601-6636 · 312-861-2000

Reuben L. Hedlund · ㉕ · Hedlund & Hanley · 77 West Wacker Drive, Suite 4800 · Chicago, IL 60601 · 312-606-8686

J. Patrick Herald · Baker & McKenzie · One Prudential Plaza · 130 East Randolph Drive · Chicago, IL 60601 · 312-861-8000

John T. Hickey, Jr. · Kirkland & Ellis · 200 East Randolph Drive · Chicago, IL 60601-6636 · 312-861-2000

Peter C. John · ⑩ · Williams, Montgomery & John · 20 North Wacker Drive, Suite 2100 · Chicago, IL 60606-3094 · 312-443-3200

Garrett B. Johnson · Kirkland & Ellis · 200 East Randolph Drive · Chicago, IL 60601-6636 · 312-861-2000

Jack Joseph · Hedlund & Hanley · 77 West Wacker Drive, Suite 4800 · Chicago, IL 60601 · 312-606-8686

Chester T. Kamin · Jenner & Block · http://www.jenner.com · 330 North Wabash Avenue · Chicago, IL 60611-7603 · 312-222-9350

James A. Klenk · ⑩ · Sonnenschein Nath & Rosenthal · Sears Tower, Suite 7800 · 233 South Wacker Drive · Chicago, IL 60606-6404 · 312-876-8000

Andrew R. Laidlaw · ⑳ · Seyfarth Shaw · 131 South Dearborn Street, Suite 2400 · Chicago, IL 60603-5577 · 312-460-5000

Scott R. Lassar · Sidley Austin · One South Dearborn Street · Chicago, IL 60603 · 312-853-7000

Warren Lupel · Lupel & Weininger · 30 North La Salle Street, Suite 3520 · Chicago, IL 60602 · 312-260-7700

Hugh R. McCombs, Jr. · Mayer Brown · 71 South Wacker Drive · Chicago, IL 60606 · 312-782-0600

Steven D. McCormick · Kirkland & Ellis · 200 East Randolph Drive · Chicago, IL 60601-6636 · 312-861-2000

William J. McKenna · Foley & Lardner · 321 North Clark Street, Suite 2800 · Chicago, IL 60654 · 312-832-4500

Jerry S. Menge · Robert F. Coleman & Associates · 77 West Wacker Drive · Chicago, IL 60601 · 312-444-1000

C. Barry Montgomery · ⑩ · Williams, Montgomery & John · 20 North Wacker Drive, Suite 2100 · Chicago, IL 60606-3094 · 312-443-3200

Thomas Mulroy III · Hinshaw & Culbertson · http://www.hinshawlaw.com · 222 North LaSalle Street, Suite 300 · Chicago, IL 60601-1081 · 312-704-3000

Christopher J. Murdoch · Holland & Knight · http://www.hklaw.com · 131 South Dearborn Street, 30th Floor · Chicago, IL 60603 · 312-263-3600

Gordon B. Nash, Jr. · Drinker Biddle & Reath · 191 North Wacker Drive, Suite 3700 · Chicago, IL 60606-1698 · 312-569-1000

Phil C. Neal · Neal, Gerber & Eisenberg · http://www.ngelaw.com · Two North LaSalle Street, Suite 2200 Chicago, IL 60602-3801 · 312-269-8000

Emily Nicklin · ⑩ · Kirkland & Ellis · 200 East Randolph Drive · Chicago, IL 60601-6636 · 312-861-2000

Michele L. Odorizzi · Mayer Brown · 71 South Wacker Drive · Chicago, IL 60606 · 312-782-0600

Stephen R. Patton · Kirkland & Ellis · 200 East Randolph Drive · Chicago, IL 60601-6636 · 312-861-2000

Eugene I. Pavalon · ⑩ · Pavalon, Gifford & Laatsch · http://www.pglmlaw.com · Two North LaSalle Street, Suite 1600 · Chicago, IL 60602-4036 · 312-419-7400

Michael A. Pope · McDermott Will & Emery · 227 West Monroe Street · Chicago, IL 60606-5096 · 312-372-2000

Richard J. Prendergast · ⑩ · Richard J. Prendergast · 111 West Washington Street, Suite 1100 · Chicago, IL 60602 · 312-641-0881

Daniel E. Reidy · ⑩ · Jones Day · 77 West Wacker Drive · Chicago, IL 60601-1692 · 312-782-3939

Kenneth P. Ross · Robert F. Coleman & Associates · 77 West Wacker Drive · Chicago, IL 60601 · 312-444-1000

Lowell E. Sachnoff · ㉕ · Reed Smith · 10 South Wacker Drive, 40th Floor · Chicago, IL 60606-7507 · 312-207-1000

Alan N. Salpeter · ⑩ · Dewey & LeBoeuf · Two Prudential Plaza, Suite 3700 · 180 North Stetson Avenue Chicago, IL 60601 · 312-794-8000

William L. Schaller · Baker & McKenzie · One Prudential Plaza · 130 East Randolph Drive · Chicago, IL 60601 · 312-861-8000

Eugene J. Schiltz · Robert F. Coleman & Associates · 77 West Wacker Drive · Chicago, IL 60601 · 312-444-1000

Stephen M. Shapiro · Mayer Brown · 71 South Wacker Drive · Chicago, IL 60606 · 312-782-0600

John B. Simon · Jenner & Block · http://www.jenner.com · 330 North Wabash Avenue · Chicago, IL 60611-7603 · 312-222-9350

Charles B. Sklarsky · Jenner & Block · http://www.jenner.com · 330 North Wabash Avenue · Chicago, IL 60611-7603 · 312-222-9350

Jerold S. Solovy · ⑩ · Jenner & Block · http://www.jenner.com · 330 North Wabash Avenue · Chicago, IL 60611-7603 · 312-222-9350

Jeffrey E. Stone · McDermott Will & Emery · 227 West Monroe Street · Chicago, IL 60606-5096 · 312-372-2000

Thomas P. Sullivan · ㉕ · Jenner & Block · http://www.jenner.com · 330 North Wabash Avenue · Chicago, IL 60611-7603 · 312-222-9350

Christina M. Tchen · Skadden, Arps, Slate, Meagher & Flom · 333 West Wacker Drive · Chicago, IL 60606 · 312-407-0700

René A. Torrado, Jr. · ⑩ · Corboy & Demetrio · http://www.corboydemetrio.com · 33 North Dearborn Street, Suite 2100 · Chicago, IL 60602 · 312-346-3191

Howard J. Trienens · ㉕ · Sidley Austin · One South Dearborn Street · Chicago, IL 60603 · 312-853-7000

Anton R. Valukas · ㉕ · Jenner & Block · http://www.jenner.com · 330 North Wabash Avenue · Chicago, IL 60611-7603 · 312-222-9350

William N. Weaver, Jr. · Reed Smith · 10 South Wacker Drive, 40th Floor · Chicago, IL 60606-7507 · 312-207-1000

Dan K. Webb · ⑳ · Winston & Strawn · 35 West Wacker Drive · Chicago, IL 60601-9703 · 312-558-5600

Sarah R. Wolff · Reed Smith · 10 South Wacker Drive, 40th Floor · Chicago, IL 60606-7507 · 312-207-1000

Herbert L. Zarov · Mayer Brown · 71 South Wacker Drive · Chicago, IL 60606 · 312-782-0600

Edward J. Zulkey · ⑩ · Baker & McKenzie · One Prudential Plaza · 130 East Randolph Drive · Chicago, IL 60601 · 312-861-8000

Moline

Martin H. Katz · ⑩ · Katz, Huntoon & Fieweger · 1000 Thirty-Sixth Avenue · Moline, IL 61265 · 309-797-3000

Sterling

Ole Bly Pace III · Ward, Murray, Pace & Johnson · 202 East Fifth Street · P.O. Box 400 · Sterling, IL 61081 · 815-625-8200

COMMUNICATIONS LAW

Champaign

Joseph D. Murphy · Meyer Capel · Athenaeum Building · 306 West Church Street · P.O. Box 6750 · Champaign, IL 61826-6750 · 217-352-1800

Chicago

Christian F. Binnig · Mayer Brown · 71 South Wacker Drive · Chicago, IL 60606 · 312-782-0600

David W. Carpenter · Sidley Austin · One South Dearborn Street · Chicago, IL 60603 · 312-853-7000

J. Tyson Covey · Mayer Brown · 71 South Wacker Drive · Chicago, IL 60606 · 312-782-0600

Dennis G. Friedman · Mayer Brown · 71 South Wacker Drive · Chicago, IL 60606 · 312-782-0600

John J. Hamill · Jenner & Block · http://www.jenner.com · 330 North Wabash Avenue · Chicago, IL 60611-7603 · 312-222-9350

John R. Harrington · Jenner & Block · http://www.jenner.com · 330 North Wabash Avenue · Chicago, IL 60611-7603 · 312-222-9350

Theodore A. Livingston, Jr. · Mayer Brown · 71 South Wacker Drive · Chicago, IL 60606 · 312-782-0600

Terri L. Mascherin · Jenner & Block · http://www.jenner.com · 330 North Wabash Avenue · Chicago, IL 60611-7603 · 312-222-9350

John E. Muench · Mayer Brown · 71 South Wacker Drive · Chicago, IL 60606 · 312-782-0600

CONSTRUCTION LAW

Chicago

Ross J. Altman · DLA Piper · 203 North LaSalle Street, Suite 1900 · Chicago, IL 60601-1293 · 312-368-4000

Joseph G. Bisceglia · Jenner & Block · http://www.jenner.com · 330 North Wabash Avenue · Chicago, IL 60611-7603 · 312-222-9350

Daniel S. Brennan · DLA Piper · 203 North LaSalle Street, Suite 1900 · Chicago, IL 60601-1293 · 312-368-4000

Philip L. Bruner · JAMS · 71 South Wacker Drive, Suite 3090 · Chicago, IL 60606 · 312-655-0555

Timothy P. Callahan · Paul Hastings · 191 North Wacker Drive, 30th Floor · Chicago, IL 60606 · 312-499-6060

Alexandra R. Cole · Perkins Coie · http://www.perkinscoie.com · 131 South Dearborn Street, Suite 1700 · Chicago, IL 60603-5559 · 312-324-8400

Timothy R. Conway · Conway & Mrowiec · http://www.cmcontractors.com · 20 South Clark Street, Suite 1000 · Chicago, IL 60603 · 312-658-1100

Mark C. Friedlander · Schiff Hardin · Sears Tower, Suite 6600 · 233 South Wacker Drive · Chicago, IL 60606-6473 · 312-258-5500

Robert J. Harris · Stein, Ray & Harris · http://www.steinrayharris.com · 222 West Adams Street, Suite 1800 · Chicago, IL 60606 · 312-641-3700

Stephen P. Kikoler · Much Shelist Freed Denenberg Ament & Rubenstein · 191 North Wacker Drive, Suite 1800 · Chicago, IL 60606-1615 · 312-521-2000

Ty D. Laurie · DLA Piper · 203 North LaSalle Street, Suite 1900 · Chicago, IL 60601-1293 · 312-368-4000

Josh M. Leavitt · Bell, Boyd & Lloyd · Three First National Plaza, Suite 3100 · 70 West Madison Street · Chicago, IL 60602 · 312-372-1121

Charles B. Lewis · Duane Morris · 190 South LaSalle Street, Suite 3700 · Chicago, IL 60603-3433 · 312-499-6700

Paul M. Lurie · Schiff Hardin · Sears Tower, Suite 6600 · 233 South Wacker Drive · Chicago, IL 60606-6473 · 312-258-5500

John S. Mrowiec · Conway & Mrowiec · http://www.cmcontractors.com · 20 South Clark Street, Suite 1000 · Chicago, IL 60603 · 312-658-1100

James N. Nowacki · Kirkland & Ellis · 200 East Randolph Drive · Chicago, IL 60601-6636 · 312-861-2000

Dennis J. Powers · DLA Piper · 203 North LaSalle Street, Suite 1900 · Chicago, IL 60601-1293 · 312-368-4000

Stephen E. Ray · Stein, Ray & Harris · http://www.steinrayharris.com · 222 West Adams Street, Suite 1800 · Chicago, IL 60606 · 312-641-3700

Cornelius F. Riordan · Riordan, Donnelly, Lipinski & McKee · 10 North Dearborn Street, Fourth Floor · Chicago, IL 60602 · 312-663-9400

Kenneth M. Roberts · Schiff Hardin · Sears Tower, Suite 6600 · 233 South Wacker Drive · Chicago, IL 60606-6473 · 312-258-5500

Randolph E. Ruff · Ogletree Deakins · http://www.ogletreedeakins.com · Two First National Plaza, 25th Floor · 20 South Clark Street · Chicago, IL 60603-1891 · 312-558-1220

Werner A. Sabo · Sabo & Zahn · 401 North Michigan Avenue, Suite 2050 · Chicago, IL 60611 · 312-655-8620

Bruce H. Schoumacher · Querrey & Harrow · 175 West Jackson Boulevard, Suite 1600 · Chicago, IL 60604-2827 · 312-540-7000

Clifford J. Shapiro · Barnes & Thornburg · http://www.btlaw.com · One North Wacker Drive, Suite 4400 Chicago, IL 60606-2833 · 312-357-1313

Stanley P. Sklar · Bell, Boyd & Lloyd · Three First National Plaza, Suite 3100 · 70 West Madison Street · Chicago, IL 60602 · 312-372-1121

Lorence H. Slutzky · Robbins, Schwartz, Nicholas, Lifton & Taylor · 20 North Clark Street, Suite 900 · Chicago, IL 60602 · 312-332-7760

Steven G. M. Stein · Stein, Ray & Harris · http://www.steinrayharris.com · 222 West Adams Street, Suite 1800 · Chicago, IL 60606 · 312-641-3700

Jeffrey H. Winick · Stein, Ray & Harris · http://www.steinrayharris.com · 222 West Adams Street, Suite 1800 · Chicago, IL 60606 · 312-641-3700

Lisle

Eric L. Singer · Ice Miller · 2300 Cabot Drive, Suite 455 · Lisle, IL 60532 · 630-955-0555

Oak Brook

William D. Lyman · Lyman & Nielsen · 1301 West 22nd Street, Suite 914 · Oak Brook, IL 60523-2018 · 630-575-0020

Jennifer A. Nielsen · Lyman & Nielsen · 1301 West 22nd Street, Suite 914 · Oak Brook, IL 60523-2018 · 630-575-0020

CORPORATE GOVERNANCE AND COMPLIANCE LAW

Chicago

Edward S. Best · Mayer Brown · 71 South Wacker Drive · Chicago, IL 60606 · 312-782-0600

Thomas A. Cole · ⑳ · Sidley Austin · One South Dearborn Street · Chicago, IL 60603 · 312-853-7000

Carter W. Emerson · ⑩ · Kirkland & Ellis · 200 East Randolph Drive · Chicago, IL 60601-6636 · 312-861-2000

R. Scott Falk · Kirkland & Ellis · 200 East Randolph Drive · Chicago, IL 60601-6636 · 312-861-2000

William R. Kunkel · Skadden, Arps, Slate, Meagher & Flom · 333 West Wacker Drive · Chicago, IL 60606 · 312-407-0700

Jack S. Levin · ㉕ · Kirkland & Ellis · 200 East Randolph Drive · Chicago, IL 60601-6636 · 312-861-2000

Peter H. Lieberman · Greenberg Traurig · http://www.gtlaw.com · 77 West Wacker Drive, Suite 2500 · Chicago, IL 60601 · 312-456-8400

Charles W. Mulaney, Jr. · ⑳ · Skadden, Arps, Slate, Meagher & Flom · 333 West Wacker Drive · Chicago, IL 60606 · 312-407-0700

Edward J. Schneidman · Mayer Brown · 71 South Wacker Drive · Chicago, IL 60606 · 312-782-0600

Paul B. Uhlenhop · ⑩ · Lawrence, Kamin, Saunders & Uhlenhop · 300 South Wacker Drive, Suite 500 · Chicago, IL 60606 · 312-372-1947

H. Kurt von Moltke · Kirkland & Ellis · 200 East Randolph Drive · Chicago, IL 60601-6636 · 312-861-2000

Herbert S. Wander · ㉕ · Katten Muchin Rosenman · 525 West Monroe Street · Chicago, IL 60661-3693 · 312-902-5200

CORPORATE LAW

Chicago

J. Trent Anderson · Mayer Brown · 71 South Wacker Drive · Chicago, IL 60606 · 312-782-0600

Richard W. Astle · Sidley Austin · One South Dearborn Street · Chicago, IL 60603 · 312-853-7000

Cameron S. Avery · ⑳ · Bell, Boyd & Lloyd · Three First National Plaza, Suite 3100 · 70 West Madison Street · Chicago, IL 60602 · 312-372-1121

Larry A. Barden · Sidley Austin · One South Dearborn Street · Chicago, IL 60603 · 312-853-7000

Robert L. Berner, Jr. · ㉕ · Baker & McKenzie · One Prudential Plaza · 130 East Randolph Drive · Chicago, IL 60601 · 312-861-8000

Edward S. Best · Mayer Brown · 71 South Wacker Drive · Chicago, IL 60606 · 312-782-0600

Jack R. Bierig · ⑩ · Sidley Austin · One South Dearborn Street · Chicago, IL 60603 · 312-853-7000

John H. Bitner · ㉕ · Bell, Boyd & Lloyd · Three First National Plaza, Suite 3100 · 70 West Madison Street · Chicago, IL 60602 · 312-372-1121

John C. Blew · ⑳ · Bell, Boyd & Lloyd · Three First National Plaza, Suite 3100 · 70 West Madison Street Chicago, IL 60602 · 312-372-1121

Addison D. Braendel · Baker & McKenzie · One Prudential Plaza · 130 East Randolph Drive · Chicago, IL 60601 · 312-861-8000

Dennis J. Carlin · Drinker Biddle & Reath · 191 North Wacker Drive, Suite 3700 · Chicago, IL 60606-1698 · 312-569-1000

Paul L. Choi · Sidley Austin · One South Dearborn Street · Chicago, IL 60603 · 312-853-7000

Peter D. Clarke · Jones Day · 77 West Wacker Drive · Chicago, IL 60601-1692 · 312-782-3939

Thomas A. Cole · ⑳ · Sidley Austin · One South Dearborn Street · Chicago, IL 60603 · 312-853-7000

Dewey B. Crawford · ⑳ · Foley & Lardner · 321 North Clark Street, Suite 2800 · Chicago, IL 60654 · 312-832-4500

James R. Cruger · Perkins Coie · http://www.perkinscoie.com · 131 South Dearborn Street, Suite 1700 · Chicago, IL 60603-5559 · 312-324-8400

Gary P. Cullen · Skadden, Arps, Slate, Meagher & Flom · 333 West Wacker Drive · Chicago, IL 60606 · 312-407-0700

Robert E. Curley · Mayer Brown · 71 South Wacker Drive · Chicago, IL 60606 · 312-782-0600

Scott J. Davis · Mayer Brown · 71 South Wacker Drive · Chicago, IL 60606 · 312-782-0600

Edwin R. Dunn · ㉕ · Baker & McKenzie · One Prudential Plaza · 130 East Randolph Drive · Chicago, IL 60601 · 312-861-8000

Paul H. Dykstra · ㉕ · Bell, Boyd & Lloyd · Three First National Plaza, Suite 3100 · 70 West Madison Street · Chicago, IL 60602 · 312-372-1121

Marshall E. Eisenberg · ⑩ · Neal, Gerber & Eisenberg · http://www.ngelaw.com · Two North LaSalle Street, Suite 2200 · Chicago, IL 60602-3801 · 312-269-8000

Carter W. Emerson · ⑩ · Kirkland & Ellis · 200 East Randolph Drive · Chicago, IL 60601-6636 · 312-861-2000

Ross D. Emmerman · Neal, Gerber & Eisenberg · http://www.ngelaw.com · Two North LaSalle Street, Suite 2200 · Chicago, IL 60602-3801 · 312-269-8000

Jay A. Erens · ⑳ · Foley & Lardner · 321 North Clark Street, Suite 2800 · Chicago, IL 60654 · 312-832-4500

Bruce I. Ettelson · Kirkland & Ellis · 200 East Randolph Drive · Chicago, IL 60601-6636 · 312-861-2000

Jill Sugar Factor · Perkins Coie · http://www.perkinscoie.com · 131 South Dearborn Street, Suite 1700 · Chicago, IL 60603-5559 · 312-324-8400

Peter V. Fazio, Jr. · ⑩ · Schiff Hardin · Sears Tower, Suite 6600 · 233 South Wacker Drive · Chicago, IL 60606-6473 · 312-258-5500

Michael M. Froy · Sonnenschein Nath & Rosenthal · Sears Tower, Suite 7800 · 233 South Wacker Drive · Chicago, IL 60606-6404 · 312-876-8000

Norman M. Gold · ⑳ · Perkins Coie · http://www.perkinscoie.com · 131 South Dearborn Street, Suite 1700 · Chicago, IL 60603-5559 · 312-324-8400

Stanford J. Goldblatt · ⑳ · Winston & Strawn · 35 West Wacker Drive · Chicago, IL 60601-9703 · 312-558-5600

Stuart L. Goodman · ⑳ · Schiff Hardin · Sears Tower, Suite 6600 · 233 South Wacker Drive · Chicago, IL 60606-6473 · 312-258-5500

Phillip Gordon · Perkins Coie · http://www.perkinscoie.com · 131 South Dearborn Street, Suite 1700 · Chicago, IL 60603-5559 · 312-324-8400

Victor E. Grimm · ㉕ · Bell, Boyd & Lloyd · Three First National Plaza, Suite 3100 · 70 West Madison Street · Chicago, IL 60602 · 312-372-1121

Arthur W. Hahn · ⑩ · Katten Muchin Rosenman · 525 West Monroe Street · Chicago, IL 60661-3693 · 312-902-5200

Lawrence R. Hamilton · Mayer Brown · 71 South Wacker Drive · Chicago, IL 60606 · 312-782-0600

Frederick L. Hartmann · ⑳ · Schiff Hardin · Sears Tower, Suite 6600 · 233 South Wacker Drive · Chicago, IL 60606-6473 · 312-258-5500

Thomas Z. Hayward, Jr. · ⑩ · Bell, Boyd & Lloyd · Three First National Plaza, Suite 3100 · 70 West Madison Street · Chicago, IL 60602 · 312-372-1121

Robert A. Helman · ㉕ · Mayer Brown · 71 South Wacker Drive · Chicago, IL 60606 · 312-782-0600

Lawrence H. Hunt, Jr. · Sidley Austin · One South Dearborn Street · Chicago, IL 60603 · 312-853-7000

Donald L. Johnson · ⑳ · Law Offices of Donald L. Johnson · 33 North Dearborn Street, Suite 1401 · Chicago, IL 60602 · 312-263-7000

Harold L. Kaplan · Foley & Lardner · 321 North Clark Street, Suite 2800 · Chicago, IL 60654 · 312-832-4500

David N. Kay · Drinker Biddle & Reath · 191 North Wacker Drive, Suite 3700 · Chicago, IL 60606-1698 · 312-569-1000

Peter C. Krupp · Skadden, Arps, Slate, Meagher & Flom · 333 West Wacker Drive · Chicago, IL 60606 · 312-407-0700

William R. Kucera · Mayer Brown · 71 South Wacker Drive · Chicago, IL 60606 · 312-782-0600

William R. Kunkel · Skadden, Arps, Slate, Meagher & Flom · 333 West Wacker Drive · Chicago, IL 60606 · 312-407-0700

Jack S. Levin · ㉕ · Kirkland & Ellis · 200 East Randolph Drive · Chicago, IL 60601-6636 · 312-861-2000

Frederick C. Lowinger · ⑩ · Sidley Austin · One South Dearborn Street · Chicago, IL 60603 · 312-853-7000

Donald G. Lubin · ⑳ · Sonnenschein Nath & Rosenthal · Sears Tower, Suite 7800 · 233 South Wacker Drive · Chicago, IL 60606-6404 · 312-876-8000

Cary J. Malkin · Mayer Brown · 71 South Wacker Drive · Chicago, IL 60606 · 312-782-0600

Elias N. Matsakis · Holland & Knight · http://www.hklaw.com · 131 South Dearborn Street, 30th Floor · Chicago, IL 60603 · 312-263-3600

David M. Matteson · Drinker Biddle & Reath · 191 North Wacker Drive, Suite 3700 · Chicago, IL 60606-1698 · 312-569-1000

John T. McCarthy · ⑳ · Bell, Boyd & Lloyd · Three First National Plaza, Suite 3100 · 70 West Madison Street · Chicago, IL 60602 · 312-372-1121

Paul T. Metzger · Bell, Boyd & Lloyd · Three First National Plaza, Suite 3100 · 70 West Madison Street · Chicago, IL 60602 · 312-372-1121

Michael L. Meyer · ㉕ · Schiff Hardin · Sears Tower, Suite 6600 · 233 South Wacker Drive · Chicago, IL 60606-6473 · 312-258-5500

Robert J. Moran · Vedder Price · 222 North LaSalle Street · Chicago, IL 60601-1003 · 312-609-7500

Gary L. Mowder · ⑩ · Schiff Hardin · Sears Tower, Suite 6600 · 233 South Wacker Drive · Chicago, IL 60606-6473 · 312-258-5500

Allan B. Muchin · ⑳ · Katten Muchin Rosenman · 525 West Monroe Street · Chicago, IL 60661-3693 · 312-902-5200

Charles W. Mulaney, Jr. · ⑳ · Skadden, Arps, Slate, Meagher & Flom · 333 West Wacker Drive · Chicago, IL 60606 · 312-407-0700

John W. Noell, Jr. · Mayer Brown · 71 South Wacker Drive · Chicago, IL 60606 · 312-782-0600

James P. O'Brien · Baker & McKenzie · One Prudential Plaza · 130 East Randolph Drive · Chicago, IL 60601 · 312-861-8000

Dennis V. Osimitz · Sidley Austin · One South Dearborn Street · Chicago, IL 60603 · 312-853-7000

Gerald M. Penner · ⑳ · Katten Muchin Rosenman · 525 West Monroe Street · Chicago, IL 60661-3693 · 312-902-5200

Imad I. Qasim · Sidley Austin · One South Dearborn Street · Chicago, IL 60603 · 312-853-7000

Stephen L. Ritchie · Kirkland & Ellis · 200 East Randolph Drive · Chicago, IL 60601-6636 · 312-861-2000

Lowell E. Sachnoff · ㉕ · Reed Smith · 10 South Wacker Drive, 40th Floor · Chicago, IL 60606-7507 · 312-207-1000

John R. Schmidt · Mayer Brown · 71 South Wacker Drive · Chicago, IL 60606 · 312-782-0600

David S. Stone · Neal, Gerber & Eisenberg · http://www.ngelaw.com · Two North LaSalle Street, Suite 2200 · Chicago, IL 60602-3801 · 312-269-8000

Philip F. Suse · ⑩ · Baker & McKenzie · One Prudential Plaza · 130 East Randolph Drive · Chicago, IL 60601 · 312-861-8000

Steven Sutherland · Sidley Austin · One South Dearborn Street · Chicago, IL 60603 · 312-853-7000

Edward T. Swan · Kirkland & Ellis · 200 East Randolph Drive · Chicago, IL 60601-6636 · 312-861-2000

Christina M. Tchen · Skadden, Arps, Slate, Meagher & Flom · 333 West Wacker Drive · Chicago, IL 60606 · 312-407-0700

Theodore R. Tetzlaff · Ungaretti & Harris · Three First National Plaza, Suite 3500 · 70 West Madison Street · Chicago, IL 60602-4283 · 312-977-4400

Paul B. Uhlenhop · ⑩ · Lawrence, Kamin, Saunders & Uhlenhop · 300 South Wacker Drive, Suite 500 · Chicago, IL 60606 · 312-372-1947

L. Byron Vance III · Skadden, Arps, Slate, Meagher & Flom · 333 West Wacker Drive · Chicago, IL 60606 · 312-407-0700

Kenneth J. Vaughan · ⑳ · Chapman and Cutler · 111 West Monroe Street · Chicago, IL 60603-4080 · 312-845-3000

Robert F. Wall · ⑩ · Winston & Strawn · 35 West Wacker Drive · Chicago, IL 60601-9703 · 312-558-5600

Joseph A. Walsh, Jr. · Winston & Strawn · 35 West Wacker Drive · Chicago, IL 60601-9703 · 312-558-5600

Priscilla A. Walter · ⑳ · Drinker Biddle & Reath · 191 North Wacker Drive, Suite 3700 · Chicago, IL 60606-1698 · 312-569-1000

Herbert S. Wander · ㉕ · Katten Muchin Rosenman · 525 West Monroe Street · Chicago, IL 60661-3693 · 312-902-5200

Jonathan D. Wasserman · Neal, Gerber & Eisenberg · http://www.ngelaw.com · Two North LaSalle Street, Suite 2200 · Chicago, IL 60602-3801 · 312-269-8000

William N. Weaver, Jr. · Reed Smith · 10 South Wacker Drive, 40th Floor · Chicago, IL 60606-7507 · 312-207-1000

Walter S. Weinberg · Katten Muchin Rosenman · 525 West Monroe Street · Chicago, IL 60661-3693 · 312-902-5200

Wayne W. Whalen · ⑳ · Skadden, Arps, Slate, Meagher & Flom · 333 West Wacker Drive · Chicago, IL 60606 · 312-407-0700

Robert J. Wilczek · ⑩ · Drinker Biddle & Reath · 191 North Wacker Drive, Suite 3700 · Chicago, IL 60606-1698 · 312-569-1000

David J. Zampa · Sidley Austin · One South Dearborn Street · Chicago, IL 60603 · 312-853-7000

DERIVATIVES LAW

Chicago

Scott E. Early · Foley & Lardner · 321 North Clark Street, Suite 2800 · Chicago, IL 60654 · 312-832-4500

Kevin M. Foley · Katten Muchin Rosenman · 525 West Monroe Street · Chicago, IL 60661-3693 · 312-902-5200

Arthur W. Hahn · ⑩ · Katten Muchin Rosenman · 525 West Monroe Street · Chicago, IL 60661-3693 · 312-902-5200

Joseph H. Harrison, Jr. · Sidley Austin · One South Dearborn Street · Chicago, IL 60603 · 312-853-7000

Lawrence H. Hunt, Jr. · Sidley Austin · One South Dearborn Street · Chicago, IL 60603 · 312-853-7000

William J. Nissen · Sidley Austin · One South Dearborn Street · Chicago, IL 60603 · 312-853-7000

Michael M. Philipp · Winston & Strawn · 35 West Wacker Drive · Chicago, IL 60601-9703 · 312-558-5600

Kenneth M. Rosenzweig · Katten Muchin Rosenman · 525 West Monroe Street · Chicago, IL 60661-3693 · 312-902-5200

Carl A. Royal · Schiff Hardin · Sears Tower, Suite 6600 · 233 South Wacker Drive · Chicago, IL 60606-6473 · 312-258-5500

Jerrold E. Salzman · Skadden, Arps, Slate, Meagher & Flom · 333 West Wacker Drive · Chicago, IL 60606 · 312-407-0700

John H. Stassen · Kirkland & Ellis · 200 East Randolph Drive · Chicago, IL 60601-6636 · 312-861-2000

Kathryn M. Trkla · Foley & Lardner · 321 North Clark Street, Suite 2800 · Chicago, IL 60654 · 312-832-4500

Paul B. Uhlenhop · ⑩ · Lawrence, Kamin, Saunders & Uhlenhop · 300 South Wacker Drive, Suite 500 · Chicago, IL 60606 · 312-372-1947

James D. Van De Graaf · Katten Muchin Rosenman · 525 West Monroe Street · Chicago, IL 60661-3693 312-902-5200

EDUCATION LAW

Chicago

Lisa Scruggs · Jenner & Block · http://www.jenner.com · 330 North Wabash Avenue · Chicago, IL 60611-7603 · 312-222-9350

Elaine Waterhouse Wilson · Quarles & Brady · http://www.quarles.com · Citigroup Center, Suite 3700 · 500 West Madison Street · Chicago, IL 60661-2511 · 312-715-5000

EMINENT DOMAIN AND CONDEMNATION LAW

Chicago

Celeste P. Cinquino · Righeimer Martin & Cinquino · 20 North Clark, Suite 1900 · Chicago, IL 60602 · 312-726-5646

Leo N. Cinquino · Righeimer Martin & Cinquino · 20 North Clark, Suite 1900 · Chicago, IL 60602 · 312-726-5646

John J. Foran · Foran, O'Toole & Burke · 321 North Clark Street, Suite 2450 · Chicago, IL 60610 · 312-644-1414

Michael D. Leroy · Neal & Leroy · 203 North LaSalle Street, Suite 2300 · Chicago, IL 60601-1213 · 312-641-7144

Langdon D. Neal · Neal & Leroy · 203 North LaSalle Street, Suite 2300 · Chicago, IL 60601-1213 · 312-641-7144

William E. Ryan · Ryan and Ryan · 33 North Dearborn Street, Suite 1530 · Chicago, IL 60602 · 312-236-1386

Fairview Heights

Harry J. Sterling · Harry J. Sterling · Six Canty Lane · Fairview Heights, IL 62208 · 618-397-9403

EMPLOYEE BENEFITS LAW

Chicago

David Ackerman · Morgan Lewis & Bockius · 77 West Wacker Drive · Chicago, IL 60601 · 312-324-1000

Joni L. Andrioff · Jones Day · 77 West Wacker Drive · Chicago, IL 60601-1692 · 312-782-3939

Pamela Baker · ⑩ · Sonnenschein Nath & Rosenthal · Sears Tower, Suite 7800 · 233 South Wacker Drive Chicago, IL 60606-6404 · 312-876-8000

Wilber H. Boies · McDermott Will & Emery · 227 West Monroe Street · Chicago, IL 60606-5096 · 312-372-2000

Gregory K. Brown · (10) · Katten Muchin Rosenman · 525 West Monroe Street · Chicago, IL 60661-3693 · 312-902-5200

Patricia S. Cain · Neal, Gerber & Eisenberg · http://www.ngelaw.com · Two North LaSalle Street, Suite 2200 · Chicago, IL 60602-3801 · 312-269-8000

Susan J. Daley · (10) · Perkins Coie · http://www.perkinscoie.com · 131 South Dearborn Street, Suite 1700 · Chicago, IL 60603-5559 · 312-324-8400

Beth J. Dickstein · Sidley Austin · One South Dearborn Street · Chicago, IL 60603 · 312-853-7000

David W. Ellis · Baker & McKenzie · One Prudential Plaza · 130 East Randolph Drive · Chicago, IL 60601 · 312-861-8000

Karen F. R. Grotberg · Mayer Brown · 71 South Wacker Drive · Chicago, IL 60606 · 312-782-0600

Vicki Vallen Hood · Kirkland & Ellis · 200 East Randolph Drive · Chicago, IL 60601-6636 · 312-861-2000

Gary W. Howell · Katten Muchin Rosenman · 525 West Monroe Street · Chicago, IL 60661-3693 · 312-902-5200

Sally Doubet King · McGuireWoods · http://www.mcguirewoods.com · 77 West Wacker Drive, Suite 4100 Chicago, IL 60601-1818 · 312-849-8100

Leslie A. Klein · Greenberg Traurig · http://www.gtlaw.com · 77 West Wacker Drive, Suite 2500 · Chicago, IL 60601 · 312-456-8400

Ian S. Kopelman · DLA Piper · 203 North LaSalle Street, Suite 1900 · Chicago, IL 60601-1293 · 312-368-4000

Herbert W. Krueger · (20) · Mayer Brown · 71 South Wacker Drive · Chicago, IL 60606 · 312-782-0600

Henry deVos Lawrie, Jr. · (10) · McGuireWoods · http://www.mcguirewoods.com · 77 West Wacker Drive, Suite 4100 · Chicago, IL 60601-1818 · 312-849-8100

Wayne R. Luepker · Mayer Brown · 71 South Wacker Drive · Chicago, IL 60606 · 312-782-0600

Maura Ann McBreen · Baker & McKenzie · One Prudential Plaza · 130 East Randolph Drive · Chicago, IL 60601 · 312-861-8000

Michael S. Melbinger · Winston & Strawn · 35 West Wacker Drive · Chicago, IL 60601-9703 · 312-558-5600

Richard L. Menson · (20) · McGuireWoods · http://www.mcguirewoods.com · 77 West Wacker Drive, Suite 4100 · Chicago, IL 60601-1818 · 312-849-8100

Alan D. Nesburg · (20) · McDermott Will & Emery · 227 West Monroe Street · Chicago, IL 60606-5096 · 312-372-2000

Lee T. Polk · Barnes & Thornburg · http://www.btlaw.com · One North Wacker Drive, Suite 4400 · Chicago, IL 60606-2833 · 312-357-1313

Michael D. Rosenbaum · Drinker Biddle & Reath · 191 North Wacker Drive, Suite 3700 · Chicago, IL 60606-1698 · 312-569-1000

Priscilla E. Ryan · Sidley Austin · One South Dearborn Street · Chicago, IL 60603 · 312-853-7000

Stewart R. Shepherd · Sidley Austin · One South Dearborn Street · Chicago, IL 60603 · 312-853-7000

Robert J. Stucker · Vedder Price · 222 North LaSalle Street · Chicago, IL 60601-1003 · 312-609-7500

Mark S. Weisberg · Winston & Strawn · 35 West Wacker Drive · Chicago, IL 60601-9703 · 312-558-5600

David L. Wolfe · ⑩ · Drinker Biddle & Reath · 191 North Wacker Drive, Suite 3700 · Chicago, IL 60606-1698 · 312-569-1000

ENERGY LAW

Chicago

Richard W. Astle · Sidley Austin · One South Dearborn Street · Chicago, IL 60603 · 312-853-7000

Peter V. Fazio, Jr. · ⑩ · Schiff Hardin · Sears Tower, Suite 6600 · 233 South Wacker Drive · Chicago, IL 60606-6473 · 312-258-5500

Christopher Flynn · Jones Day · 77 West Wacker Drive · Chicago, IL 60601-1692 · 312-782-3939

Paul F. Hanzlik · Foley & Lardner · 321 North Clark Street, Suite 2800 · Chicago, IL 60654 · 312-832-4500

Robert A. Helman · ㉕ · Mayer Brown · 71 South Wacker Drive · Chicago, IL 60606 · 312-782-0600

Owen E. MacBride · Schiff Hardin · Sears Tower, Suite 6600 · 233 South Wacker Drive · Chicago, IL 60606-6473 · 312-258-5500

E. Glenn Rippie · Foley & Lardner · 321 North Clark Street, Suite 2800 · Chicago, IL 60654 · 312-832-4500

John E. Rooney · Sonnenschein Nath & Rosenthal · Sears Tower, Suite 7800 · 233 South Wacker Drive · Chicago, IL 60606-6404 · 312-876-8000

Paul T. Ruxin · ⑩ · Jones Day · 77 West Wacker Drive · Chicago, IL 60601-1692 · 312-782-3939

Dale E. Thomas · Sidley Austin · One South Dearborn Street · Chicago, IL 60603 · 312-853-7000

Christopher J. Townsend · DLA Piper · 203 North LaSalle Street, Suite 1900 · Chicago, IL 60601-1293 · 312-368-4000

Granite City

R. Eric Robertson · Lueders, Robertson & Konzen · 1939 Delmar Avenue · P.O. Box 735 · Granite City, IL 62040 · 618-876-8500

ENTERTAINMENT LAW

Chicago

Jeffrey H. Brown · Michael Best & Friedrich · Two Prudential Plaza, Suite 2000 · 180 North Stetson Avenue · Chicago, IL 60601 · 312-222-0800

Luke W. Demarte · Michael Best & Friedrich · Two Prudential Plaza, Suite 2000 · 180 North Stetson Avenue · Chicago, IL 60601 · 312-222-0800

Stephen P. Durchslag · Winston & Strawn · 35 West Wacker Drive · Chicago, IL 60601-9703 · 312-558-5600

Andrew L. Goldstein · Freeborn & Peters · 311 South Wacker Drive, Suite 3000 · Chicago, IL 60606-6677 · 312-360-6000

Robert J. Labate · Holland & Knight · http://www.hklaw.com · 131 South Dearborn Street, 30th Floor · Chicago, IL 60603 · 312-263-3600

Linda S. Mensch · Linda S. Mensch · 200 South Michigan Avenue, Suite 1240 · Chicago, IL 60604 · 312-922-2910

Mary Hutchings Reed · Winston & Strawn · 35 West Wacker Drive · Chicago, IL 60601-9703 · 312-558-5600

David M. Saltiel · Bell, Boyd & Lloyd · Three First National Plaza, Suite 3100 · 70 West Madison Street · Chicago, IL 60602 · 312-372-1121

Peter Jeffrey Strand · Holland & Knight · http://www.hklaw.com · 131 South Dearborn Street, 30th Floor Chicago, IL 60603 · 312-263-3600

Eugene F. Zelek, Jr. · Freeborn & Peters · 311 South Wacker Drive, Suite 3000 · Chicago, IL 60606-6677 · 312-360-6000

ENVIRONMENTAL LAW

Chicago

John C. Berghoff, Jr. · Mayer Brown · 71 South Wacker Drive · Chicago, IL 60606 · 312-782-0600

Timothy S. Bishop · Mayer Brown · 71 South Wacker Drive · Chicago, IL 60606 · 312-782-0600

Eric E. Boyd · Seyfarth Shaw · 131 South Dearborn Street, Suite 2400 · Chicago, IL 60603-5577 · 312-460-5000

James N. Cahan · Sidley Austin · One South Dearborn Street · Chicago, IL 60603 · 312-853-7000

Russell R. Eggert · Reed Smith · 10 South Wacker Drive, 40th Floor · Chicago, IL 60606-7507 · 312-207-1000

Bill S. Forcade · Jenner & Block · http://www.jenner.com · 330 North Wabash Avenue · Chicago, IL 60611-7603 · 312-222-9350

Jeffrey C. Fort · Sonnenschein Nath & Rosenthal · Sears Tower, Suite 7800 · 233 South Wacker Drive · Chicago, IL 60606-6404 · 312-876-8000

Susan M. Franzetti · Franzetti Law Firm · 10 South LaSalle Street, Suite 3600 · Chicago, IL 60603 · 312-251-5590

E. Lynn Grayson · Jenner & Block · http://www.jenner.com · 330 North Wabash Avenue · Chicago, IL 60611-7603 · 312-222-9350

Eleni Kouimelis · Winston & Strawn · 35 West Wacker Drive · Chicago, IL 60601-9703 · 312-558-5600

Janine M. Landow-Esser · Quarles & Brady · http://www.quarles.com · Citigroup Center, Suite 3700 · 500 West Madison Street · Chicago, IL 60661-2511 · 312-715-5000

Jerome I. Maynard · Dykema · http://www.dykema.com · 10 South Wacker Drive, Suite 2300 · Chicago, IL 60606 · 312-876-1700

Jennifer T. Nijman · Nijman Franzetti · 10 South LaSalle Street, Suite 3600 · Chicago, IL 60603 · 312-251-5250

Robert M. Olian · Sidley Austin · One South Dearborn Street · Chicago, IL 60603 · 312-853-7000

Gabriel M. Rodriguez · Schiff Hardin · Sears Tower, Suite 6600 · 233 South Wacker Drive · Chicago, IL 60606-6473 · 312-258-5500

J. Andrew Schlickman · Sidley Austin · One South Dearborn Street · Chicago, IL 60603 · 312-853-7000

A. Bruce White · Karaganis, White & Magel · 414 North Orleans Street, Suite 810 · Chicago, IL 60610-4421 · 312-836-1177

Sheldon A. Zabel · ⑳ · Schiff Hardin · Sears Tower, Suite 6600 · 233 South Wacker Drive · Chicago, IL 60606-6473 · 312-258-5500

Springfield

Fred C. Prillaman · Mohan, Alewet, Prillaman & Adami · One North Old Capitol Plaza, Suite 325 · Springfield, IL 62701-1323 · 217-528-2517

Wilmette

Mark C. Furse · Furse Law · 1025 Ashland Avenue · Wilmette, IL 60091 · 847-251-1614

EQUIPMENT FINANCE LAW

Chicago

H. Bruce Bernstein · ㉕ · Sidley Austin · One South Dearborn Street · Chicago, IL 60603 · 312-853-7000

James E. Clark · Sidley Austin · One South Dearborn Street · Chicago, IL 60603 · 312-853-7000

J. Mark Fisher · Schiff Hardin · Sears Tower, Suite 6600 · 233 South Wacker Drive · Chicago, IL 60606-6473 · 312-258-5500

Dean N. Gerber · Vedder Price · 222 North LaSalle Street · Chicago, IL 60601-1003 · 312-609-7500

Seth E. Jacobson · Skadden, Arps, Slate, Meagher & Flom · 333 West Wacker Drive · Chicago, IL 60606 312-407-0700

Robert A. Kelman · Mayer Brown · 71 South Wacker Drive · Chicago, IL 60606 · 312-782-0600

Richard M. Kohn · Goldberg, Kohn, Bell, Black, Rosenbloom & Moritz · 55 East Monroe Street, Suite 3300 · Chicago, IL 60603-5792 · 312-201-4000

Kenneth A. Latimer · Duane Morris · 190 South LaSalle Street, Suite 3700 · Chicago, IL 60603-3433 · 312-499-6700

Andre LeDuc · Skadden, Arps, Slate, Meagher & Flom · 333 West Wacker Drive · Chicago, IL 60606 · 312-407-0700

James R. Looman · Sidley Austin · One South Dearborn Street · Chicago, IL 60603 · 312-853-7000

Daniel R. Murray · ⑩ · Jenner & Block · http://www.jenner.com · 330 North Wabash Avenue · Chicago, IL 60611-7603 · 312-222-9350

ETHICS AND PROFESSIONAL RESPONSIBILITY LAW

Chicago

Deane B. Brown · Beermann Swerdlove · 161 North Clark Street, Suite 2600 · Chicago, IL 60601-3297 · 312-621-9700

FAMILY LAW

Bannockburn

Stephen H. Katz · 25 · Katz, Goldstein & Warren · 2345 Waukeegan Road, Suite 150 · Bannockburn, IL 60015 · 847-317-9500

Chicago

Miles N. Beermann · 25 · Beermann Swerdlove · 161 North Clark Street, Suite 2600 · Chicago, IL 60601-3297 · 312-621-9700

Michael J. Berger · Berger Schatz · 111 West Washington Street, Suite 937 · Chicago, IL 60602 · 312-782-3456

Arthur M. Berman · 25 · Kirsh & Berman · 10 South LaSalle Street, Suite 2424 · Chicago, IL 60603 · 312-782-3020

Muller Davis · 20 · Davis Friedman · 135 South LaSalle Street, 36th Floor · Chicago, IL 60603 · 312-782-2220

James H. Feldman · 25 · Jenner & Block · http://www.jenner.com · 330 North Wabash Avenue · Chicago, IL 60611-7603 · 312-222-9350

Meighan A. Harmon · Schiller DuCanto and Fleck · http://www.sdflaw.com · 200 North LaSalle Street, 30th Floor · Chicago, IL 60601-1089 · 312-641-5560

Burton S. Hochberg · Schiller DuCanto and Fleck · http://www.sdflaw.com · 200 North LaSalle Street, 30th Floor · Chicago, IL 60601-1089 · 312-641-5560

Pamela J. Hutul · Beermann Swerdlove · 161 North Clark Street, Suite 2600 · Chicago, IL 60601-3297 · 312-621-9700

Larry R. Kane · 10 · Davis Friedman · 135 South LaSalle Street, 36th Floor · Chicago, IL 60603 · 312-782-2220

Frances H. Krasnow · Holland & Knight · http://www.hklaw.com · 131 South Dearborn Street, 30th Floor · Chicago, IL 60603 · 312-263-3600

Howard A. London · Beermann Swerdlove · 161 North Clark Street, Suite 2600 · Chicago, IL 60601-3297 · 312-621-9700

Dorene Marcus · Davis Friedman · 135 South LaSalle Street, 36th Floor · Chicago, IL 60603 · 312-782-2220

Sandra R. Murphy · 10 · McDermott Will & Emery · 227 West Monroe Street · Chicago, IL 60606-5096 · 312-372-2000

Bernard B. Rinella · 25 · Rinella and Rinella · One North LaSalle Street, Suite 3400 · Chicago, IL 60602-4004 · 312-236-5454

Howard H. Rosenfeld · ⑩ · Rosenfeld, Hafron, Shapiro & Farmer · http://www.shapiro-lawyers.com · 221 North LaSalle Street, Suite 1763 · Chicago, IL 60601 · 312-372-6058

Donald C. Schiller · ㉕ · Schiller DuCanto and Fleck · http://www.sdflaw.com · 200 North LaSalle Street, 30th Floor · Chicago, IL 60601-1089 · 312-641-5560

Sarane C. Siewerth · Schiller DuCanto and Fleck · http://www.sdflaw.com · 200 North LaSalle Street, 30th Floor · Chicago, IL 60601-1089 · 312-641-5560

Arnold B. Stein · ⑩ · Schiller DuCanto and Fleck · http://www.sdflaw.com · 200 North LaSalle Street, 30th Floor · Chicago, IL 60601-1089 · 312-641-5560

Errol Zavett · ⑳ · Davis Friedman · 135 South LaSalle Street, 36th Floor · Chicago, IL 60603 · 312-782-2220

Lake Forest

Charles J. Fleck · ⑳ · Schiller DuCanto and Fleck · http://www.sdflaw.com · 225 East Deerpath Road, Suite 270 · Lake Forest, IL 60045-1937 · 847-615-8300

Carlton R. Marcyan · Schiller DuCanto and Fleck · http://www.sdflaw.com · 225 East Deerpath Road, Suite 270 · Lake Forest, IL 60045-1937 · 847-615-8300

Eric L. Schulman · Schiller DuCanto and Fleck · http://www.sdflaw.com · 225 East Deerpath Road, Suite 270 · Lake Forest, IL 60045-1937 · 847-615-8300

Wheaton

Timothy Daw · Schiller DuCanto and Fleck · http://www.sdflaw.com · 311 South County Farm Road, Suite G · Wheaton, IL 60187-2477 · 630-665-5800

Woodstock

Gunnar J. Gitlin · The Gitlin Law Firm · http://www.gitlinlawfirm.com · 663 East Calhoun Street · Woodstock, IL 60098-4262 · 815-338-9401

H. Joseph Gitlin · ㉕ · Gitlin, Haaff & Kasper · http://www.gitlin.com · 111 Dean Street · Woodstock, IL 60098-3220 · 815-338-0021

FIRST AMENDMENT LAW

Chicago

Michael M. Conway · ⑩ · Foley & Lardner · 321 North Clark Street, Suite 2800 · Chicago, IL 60654 · 312-832-4500

Samuel Fifer · ⑩ · Sonnenschein Nath & Rosenthal · Sears Tower, Suite 7800 · 233 South Wacker Drive · Chicago, IL 60606-6404 · 312-876-8000

James A. Klenk · ⑩ · Sonnenschein Nath & Rosenthal · Sears Tower, Suite 7800 · 233 South Wacker Drive · Chicago, IL 60606-6404 · 312-876-8000

Kenneth E. Kraus · Schopf & Weiss · One South Wacker Drive, 28th Floor · Chicago, IL 60606-4617 · 312-701-9300

Richard J. O'Brien · Sidley Austin · One South Dearborn Street · Chicago, IL 60603 · 312-853-7000

David P. Sanders · ⑩ · Jenner & Block · http://www.jenner.com · 330 North Wabash Avenue · Chicago, IL 60611-7603 · 312-222-9350

Natalie Spears · Sonnenschein Nath & Rosenthal · Sears Tower, Suite 7800 · 233 South Wacker Drive · Chicago, IL 60606-6404 · 312-876-8000

FRANCHISE LAW

Chicago

Lee N. Abrams · Mayer Brown · 71 South Wacker Drive · Chicago, IL 60606 · 312-782-0600

John R. F. Baer · Sonnenschein Nath & Rosenthal · Sears Tower, Suite 7800 · 233 South Wacker Drive · Chicago, IL 60606-6404 · 312-876-8000

Michael G. Brennan · DLA Piper · 203 North LaSalle Street, Suite 1900 · Chicago, IL 60601-1293 · 312-368-4000

Amy Cheng · Cheng Cohen · 1101 West Fulton Market, Suite 2000 · Chicago, IL 60607 · 312-243-1701

Fredric A. Cohen · Cheng Cohen · 1101 West Fulton Market, Suite 2000 · Chicago, IL 60607 · 312-243-1701

Stuart Hershman · DLA Piper · 203 North LaSalle Street, Suite 1900 · Chicago, IL 60601-1293 · 312-368-4000

Robert T. Joseph · Sonnenschein Nath & Rosenthal · Sears Tower, Suite 7800 · 233 South Wacker Drive Chicago, IL 60606-6404 · 312-876-8000

Norman M. Leon · DLA Piper · 203 North LaSalle Street, Suite 1900 · Chicago, IL 60601-1293 · 312-368-4000

William M. McErlean · Barnes & Thornburg · http://www.btlaw.com · One North Wacker Drive, Suite 4400 · Chicago, IL 60606-2833 · 312-357-1313

Paula J. Morency · Schiff Hardin · Sears Tower, Suite 6600 · 233 South Wacker Drive · Chicago, IL 60606-6473 · 312-258-5500

Marc P. Seidler · DLA Piper · 203 North LaSalle Street, Suite 1900 · Chicago, IL 60601-1293 · 312-368-4000

Joseph W. Sheyka · DLA Piper · 203 North LaSalle Street, Suite 1900 · Chicago, IL 60601-1293 · 312-368-4000

Alan H. Silberman · Sonnenschein Nath & Rosenthal · Sears Tower, Suite 7800 · 233 South Wacker Drive · Chicago, IL 60606-6404 · 312-876-8000

John F. Verhey · DLA Piper · 203 North LaSalle Street, Suite 1900 · Chicago, IL 60601-1293 · 312-368-4000

Dennis E. Wieczorek · DLA Piper · 203 North LaSalle Street, Suite 1900 · Chicago, IL 60601-1293 · 312-368-4000

GAMING LAW

Chicago

Michael A. Ficaro · Ungaretti & Harris · Three First National Plaza, Suite 3500 · 70 West Madison Street Chicago, IL 60602-4283 · 312-977-4400

Cezar Froelich · Shefsky & Froelich · 111 East Wacker Drive, Suite 2800 · Chicago, IL 60601 · 312-527-4000

James S. Montana, Jr. · Vedder Price · 222 North LaSalle Street · Chicago, IL 60601-1003 · 312-609-7500

Springfield

J. William Roberts · Hinshaw & Culbertson · http://www.hinshawlaw.com · 400 South Ninth Street, Suite 200 · Springfield, IL 62701 · 217-528-7375

GOVERNMENT RELATIONS LAW

Chicago

Barbara A. Adams · Holland & Knight · http://www.hklaw.com · 131 South Dearborn Street, 30th Floor · Chicago, IL 60603 · 312-263-3600

Roger H. Bickel · Freeborn & Peters · 311 South Wacker Drive, Suite 3000 · Chicago, IL 60606-6677 · 312-360-6000

Demetrius E. Carney · Perkins Coie · http://www.perkinscoie.com · 131 South Dearborn Street, Suite 1700 · Chicago, IL 60603-5559 · 312-324-8400

Julian C. D'Esposito, Jr. · Mayer Brown · 71 South Wacker Drive · Chicago, IL 60606 · 312-782-0600

Steven Elrod · Holland & Knight · http://www.hklaw.com · 131 South Dearborn Street, 30th Floor · Chicago, IL 60603 · 312-263-3600

John A. Janicik · Mayer Brown · 71 South Wacker Drive · Chicago, IL 60606 · 312-782-0600

Roger J. Kiley, Jr. · Mayer Brown · 71 South Wacker Drive · Chicago, IL 60606 · 312-782-0600

David Narefsky · Mayer Brown · 71 South Wacker Drive · Chicago, IL 60606 · 312-782-0600

George A. Ranney, Jr. · Mayer Brown · 71 South Wacker Drive · Chicago, IL 60606 · 312-782-0600

Mary B. Richardson-Lowry · Mayer Brown · 71 South Wacker Drive · Chicago, IL 60606 · 312-782-0600

Sanford M. Stein · Drinker Biddle & Reath · 191 North Wacker Drive, Suite 3700 · Chicago, IL 60606-1698 · 312-569-1000

John E. Stevens · Freeborn & Peters · 311 South Wacker Drive, Suite 3000 · Chicago, IL 60606-6677 · 312-360-6000

Richard Stock · Drinker Biddle & Reath · 191 North Wacker Drive, Suite 3700 · Chicago, IL 60606-1698 312-569-1000

HEALTH CARE LAW

Chicago

Michael F. Anthony · ⑩ · McDermott Will & Emery · 227 West Monroe Street · Chicago, IL 60606-5096 312-372-2000

Scott Becker · McGuireWoods · http://www.mcguirewoods.com · 77 West Wacker Drive, Suite 4100 · Chicago, IL 60601-1818 · 312-849-8100

Jack R. Bierig · ⑩ · Sidley Austin · One South Dearborn Street · Chicago, IL 60603 · 312-853-7000

Bernadette M. Broccolo · ⑩ · McDermott Will & Emery · 227 West Monroe Street · Chicago, IL 60606-5096 · 312-372-2000

L. Edward Bryant, Jr. · ⑩ · Drinker Biddle & Reath · 191 North Wacker Drive, Suite 3700 · Chicago, IL 60606-1698 · 312-569-1000

Michael R. Callahan · ⑩ · Katten Muchin Rosenman · 525 West Monroe Street · Chicago, IL 60661-3693 312-902-5200

Thomas Campbell · Baker & McKenzie · One Prudential Plaza · 130 East Randolph Drive · Chicago, IL 60601 · 312-861-8000

Douglas R. Carlson · Wildman, Harrold, Allen & Dixon · 225 West Wacker Drive, Suite 3000 · Chicago, IL 60606 · 312-201-2000

Julian C. D'Esposito, Jr. · Mayer Brown · 71 South Wacker Drive · Chicago, IL 60606 · 312-782-0600

James C. Dechene · ⑩ · Sidley Austin · One South Dearborn Street · Chicago, IL 60603 · 312-853-7000

Monte I. Dube · McDermott Will & Emery · 227 West Monroe Street · Chicago, IL 60606-5096 · 312-372-2000

Thomas M. Fahey · ⑩ · Ungaretti & Harris · Three First National Plaza, Suite 3500 · 70 West Madison Street · Chicago, IL 60602-4283 · 312-977-4400

Stephen M. Fatum · Barnes & Thornburg · http://www.btlaw.com · One North Wacker Drive, Suite 4400 Chicago, IL 60606-2833 · 312-357-1313

D. Louis Glaser II · Sonnenschein Nath & Rosenthal · Sears Tower, Suite 7800 · 233 South Wacker Drive · Chicago, IL 60606-6404 · 312-876-8000

Gerald M. Griffith · ⑩ · Jones Day · 77 West Wacker Drive · Chicago, IL 60601-1692 · 312-782-3939

Robert G. Hoban · McDermott Will & Emery · 227 West Monroe Street · Chicago, IL 60606-5096 · 312-372-2000

Steven B. Kite · Sonnenschein Nath & Rosenthal · Sears Tower, Suite 7800 · 233 South Wacker Drive · Chicago, IL 60606-6404 · 312-876-8000

Jeffrey G. Kraft · Neal, Gerber & Eisenberg · http://www.ngelaw.com · Two North LaSalle Street, Suite 2200 · Chicago, IL 60602-3801 · 312-269-8000

John P. Marren · Hogan Marren · 180 North Wacker Drive, Suite 600 · Chicago, IL 60606 · 312-946-1800

David Marx, Jr. · McDermott Will & Emery · 227 West Monroe Street · Chicago, IL 60606-5096 · 312-372-2000

Jane K. McCahill · Bell, Boyd & Lloyd · Three First National Plaza, Suite 3100 · 70 West Madison Street Chicago, IL 60602 · 312-372-1121

Michael W. Peregrine · ⑩ · McDermott Will & Emery · 227 West Monroe Street · Chicago, IL 60606-5096 · 312-372-2000

Richard D. Raskin · Sidley Austin · One South Dearborn Street · Chicago, IL 60603 · 312-853-7000

Michael E. Reed · Vedder Price · 222 North LaSalle Street · Chicago, IL 60601-1003 · 312-609-7500

William H. Roach, Jr. · ⑩ · McDermott Will & Emery · 227 West Monroe Street · Chicago, IL 60606-5096 · 312-372-2000

Jack A. Rovner · Neal, Gerber & Eisenberg · http://www.ngelaw.com · Two North LaSalle Street, Suite 2200 · Chicago, IL 60602-3801 · 312-269-8000

Mark E. Rust · Barnes & Thornburg · http://www.btlaw.com · One North Wacker Drive, Suite 4400 · Chicago, IL 60606-2833 · 312-357-1313

Thomas C. Shields · ⑩ · Bell, Boyd & Lloyd · Three First National Plaza, Suite 3100 · 70 West Madison Street · Chicago, IL 60602 · 312-372-1121

Roger D. Strode, Jr. · McDermott Will & Emery · 227 West Monroe Street · Chicago, IL 60606-5096 · 312-372-2000

Mary G. Wilson · Sonnenschein Nath & Rosenthal · Sears Tower, Suite 7800 · 233 South Wacker Drive · Chicago, IL 60606-6404 · 312-876-8000

Robert J. Zimmerman · ⑩ · Foley & Lardner · 321 North Clark Street, Suite 2800 · Chicago, IL 60654 · 312-832-4500

Rock Island

Peter J. Benson · ⑩ · Lane & Waterman · 224 Eighteenth Street, Suite 500 · Rock Island, IL 61201 · 309-786-1600

IMMIGRATION LAW

Chicago

Robert D. Ahlgren · ⑩ · Robert D. Ahlgren · 105 West Madison Street, Suite 508 · Chicago, IL 60602-4604 · 312-782-1804

Douglas Bristol · ⑩ · Douglas Bristol · 321 South Plymouth Court, Suite 1525 · Chicago, IL 60604 · 312-663-4466

Susan Compernolle · Rubman & Compernolle · 53 West Jackson Boulevard, Suite 750 · Chicago, IL 60604 · 312-341-1907

James Hallagan · Minsky, McCormick & Hallagan · The Clark Adams Building, Suite 2025 · 210 South Clark Street · Chicago, IL 60604 · 312-427-6163

Donald B. Kempster · ⑩ · Kempster, Keller & Lenz-Calvo · 332 South Michigan Avenue, Suite 1428 · Chicago, IL 60604 · 312-341-9730

Susan M. MacLean · Zulkie Partners · 222 South Riverside Plaza, Suite 2300 · Chicago, IL 60606-6101 · 312-648-2244

Margaret H. McCormick · ⑩ · Minsky, McCormick & Hallagan · The Clark Adams Building, Suite 2025 210 South Clark Street · Chicago, IL 60604 · 312-427-6163

Timothy G. Payne · Sidley Austin · One South Dearborn Street · Chicago, IL 60603 · 312-853-7000

Carlina Tapia-Ruano · Tapia-Ruano & Gunn · 53 West Jackson Boulevard, Suite 852 · Chicago, IL 60604 · 312-281-4867

Paul L. Zulkie · ⑩ · Zulkie Partners · 222 South Riverside Plaza, Suite 2300 · Chicago, IL 60606-6101 · 312-648-2244

INFORMATION TECHNOLOGY LAW

Barrington

Karen J. O' Connor · Gallitano & O'Connor · 257 East Main Street, Suite 300 · Barrington, IL 60010 · 224-633-5000

Chicago

Ruth Hill Bro · Baker & McKenzie · One Prudential Plaza · 130 East Randolph Drive · Chicago, IL 60601 · 312-861-8000

Rebecca S. Eisner · Mayer Brown · 71 South Wacker Drive · Chicago, IL 60606 · 312-782-0600

Gregg Kirchhoefer · Kirkland & Ellis · 200 East Randolph Drive · Chicago, IL 60601-6636 · 312-861-2000

Diana J. P. McKenzie · Neal, Gerber & Eisenberg · http://www.ngelaw.com · Two North LaSalle Street, Suite 2200 · Chicago, IL 60602-3801 · 312-269-8000

Michael S. Mensik · Baker & McKenzie · One Prudential Plaza · 130 East Randolph Drive · Chicago, IL 60601 · 312-861-8000

Paul J. N. Roy · Mayer Brown · 71 South Wacker Drive · Chicago, IL 60606 · 312-782-0600

Vincent A. Sanchez · DLA Piper · 203 North LaSalle Street, Suite 1900 · Chicago, IL 60601-1293 · 312-368-4000

Thomas J. Smedinghoff · Wildman, Harrold, Allen & Dixon · 225 West Wacker Drive, Suite 3000 · Chicago, IL 60606 · 312-201-2000

Robert M. Weiss · Neal, Gerber & Eisenberg · http://www.ngelaw.com · Two North LaSalle Street, Suite 2200 · Chicago, IL 60602-3801 · 312-269-8000

Larry M. Zanger · Holland & Knight · http://www.hklaw.com · 131 South Dearborn Street, 30th Floor · Chicago, IL 60603 · 312-263-3600

INSURANCE LAW

Chicago

Robert J. Bates, Jr. · Bates & Carey · 191 North Wacker Drive, Suite 2400 · Chicago, IL 60606 · 312-762-3100

Jill B. Berkeley · Howrey · 321 North Clark Street, Suite 3400 · Chicago, IL 60654 · 312-595-1239

Jon Biasetti · Locke Lord Bissell & Liddell · 111 South Wacker Drive · Chicago, IL 60606-4410 · 312-443-0700

Scott L. Carey · Bates & Carey · 191 North Wacker Drive, Suite 2400 · Chicago, IL 60606 · 312-762-3100

Robert Marc Chemers · Pretzel & Stouffer · One South Wacker Drive, Suite 2500 · Chicago, IL 60606-8242 · 312-346-1973

George W. Craven · Mayer Brown · 71 South Wacker Drive · Chicago, IL 60606 · 312-782-0600

Nick J. DiGiovanni · Locke Lord Bissell & Liddell · 111 South Wacker Drive · Chicago, IL 60606-4410 · 312-443-0700

James R. Dwyer · Dewey & LeBoeuf · Two Prudential Plaza, Suite 3700 · 180 North Stetson Avenue · Chicago, IL 60601 · 312-794-8000

John N. Gavin · Foley & Lardner · 321 North Clark Street, Suite 2800 · Chicago, IL 60654 · 312-832-4500

Steven R. Gilford · Proskauer Rose · http://www.proskauer.com · 222 South Riverside Plaza, 29th Floor · Chicago, IL 60606-5808 · 312-962-3550

Michael P. Goldman · Sidley Austin · One South Dearborn Street · Chicago, IL 60603 · 312-853-7000

Mark R. Goodman · Dewey & LeBoeuf · Two Prudential Plaza, Suite 3700 · 180 North Stetson Avenue · Chicago, IL 60601 · 312-794-8000

John B. Haarlow · Locke Lord Bissell & Liddell · 111 South Wacker Drive · Chicago, IL 60606-4410 · 312-443-0700

Peter C. John · ⑩ · Williams, Montgomery & John · 20 North Wacker Drive, Suite 2100 · Chicago, IL 60606-3094 · 312-443-3200

Robert A. Knuti · Locke Lord Bissell & Liddell · 111 South Wacker Drive · Chicago, IL 60606-4410 · 312-443-0700

Paul L. Langer · Proskauer Rose · http://www.proskauer.com · 222 South Riverside Plaza, 29th Floor · Chicago, IL 60606-5808 · 312-962-3550

Michael M. Marick · Meckler Bulger Tilson Marick & Pearson · 123 North Wacker Drive, Suite 1800 · Chicago, IL 60606 · 312-474-7900

Thomas A. Marrinson · Reed Smith · 10 South Wacker Drive, 40th Floor · Chicago, IL 60606-7507 · 312-207-1000

Alan J. Martin · Barnes & Thornburg · http://www.btlaw.com · One North Wacker Drive, Suite 4400 · Chicago, IL 60606-2833 · 312-357-1313

John H. Mathias, Jr. · Jenner & Block · http://www.jenner.com · 330 North Wabash Avenue · Chicago, IL 60611-7603 · 312-222-9350

David E. Mendelsohn · DLA Piper · 203 North LaSalle Street, Suite 1900 · Chicago, IL 60601-1293 · 312-368-4000

Stephen M. Murray · Locke Lord Bissell & Liddell · 111 South Wacker Drive · Chicago, IL 60606-4410 312-443-0700

Stanley C. Nardoni · Mayer Brown · 71 South Wacker Drive · Chicago, IL 60606 · 312-782-0600

Marc E. Rosenthal · Proskauer Rose · http://www.proskauer.com · 222 South Riverside Plaza, 29th Floor · Chicago, IL 60606-5808 · 312-962-3550

James I. Rubin · Butler Rubin Saltarelli & Boyd · 70 West Madison Street, Suite 1800 · Chicago, IL 60602 · 312-444-9660

Stephen W. Schwab · DLA Piper · 203 North LaSalle Street, Suite 1900 · Chicago, IL 60601-1293 · 312-368-4000

John D. Shugrue · Reed Smith · 10 South Wacker Drive, 40th Floor · Chicago, IL 60606-7507 · 312-207-1000

William M. Sneed · Sidley Austin · One South Dearborn Street · Chicago, IL 60603 · 312-853-7000

David M. Spector · Schiff Hardin · Sears Tower, Suite 6600 · 233 South Wacker Drive · Chicago, IL 60606-6473 · 312-258-5500

Philip C. Stahl · Grippo & Elden · 111 South Wacker Drive · Chicago, IL 60606 · 312-704-7700

James R. Stinson · Sidley Austin · One South Dearborn Street · Chicago, IL 60603 · 312-853-7000

Susan A. Stone · Sidley Austin · One South Dearborn Street · Chicago, IL 60603 · 312-853-7000

John S. Vishneski III · Reed Smith · 10 South Wacker Drive, 40th Floor · Chicago, IL 60606-7507 · 312-207-1000

Edward J. Zulkey · ⑩ · Baker & McKenzie · One Prudential Plaza · 130 East Randolph Drive · Chicago, IL 60601 · 312-861-8000

INTELLECTUAL PROPERTY LAW

Chicago

Meredith Martin Addy · Brinks Hofer Gilson & Lione · NBC Tower, Suite 3600 · 455 North Cityfront Plaza Drive · Chicago, IL 60611-5599 · 312-321-4200

James M. Amend · Kirkland & Ellis · 200 East Randolph Drive · Chicago, IL 60601-6636 · 312-861-2000

Thomas P. Arden · Holland & Knight · http://www.hklaw.com · 131 South Dearborn Street, 30th Floor · Chicago, IL 60603 · 312-263-3600

Jack C. Berenzweig · Brinks Hofer Gilson & Lione · NBC Tower, Suite 3600 · 455 North Cityfront Plaza Drive · Chicago, IL 60611-5599 · 312-321-4200

Leslie A. Bertagnolli · Baker & McKenzie · One Prudential Plaza · 130 East Randolph Drive · Chicago, IL 60601 · 312-861-8000

Daniel A. Boehnen · McDonnell Boehnen Hulbert & Berghoff · 300 South Wacker Drive, Suite 31 · Chicago, IL 60606-6709 · 312-913-0001

David C. Brezina · Barnes & Thornburg · http://www.btlaw.com · One North Wacker Drive, Suite 4400 · Chicago, IL 60606-2833 · 312-357-1313

Henry L. Brinks · Brinks Hofer Gilson & Lione · NBC Tower, Suite 3600 · 455 North Cityfront Plaza Drive · Chicago, IL 60611-5599 · 312-321-4200

Robert E. Browne · Neal, Gerber & Eisenberg · http://www.ngelaw.com · Two North LaSalle Street, Suite 2200 · Chicago, IL 60602-3801 · 312-269-8000

Richard A. Cederoth · Sidley Austin · One South Dearborn Street · Chicago, IL 60603 · 312-853-7000

Granger Cook, Jr. · ⑩ · Cook Alex · 200 West Adams Street, Suite 2850 · Chicago, IL 60606 · 312-236-8500

Timothy Q. Delaney · Brinks Hofer Gilson & Lione · NBC Tower, Suite 3600 · 455 North Cityfront Plaza Drive · Chicago, IL 60611-5599 · 312-321-4200

Robert J. Depke · Rockey, Depke, Lyons & Kitzinger · Sears Tower, Suite 5450 · 233 South Wacker Drive · Chicago, IL 60606 · 312-277-2006

Stephen P. Durchslag · Winston & Strawn · 35 West Wacker Drive · Chicago, IL 60601-9703 · 312-558-5600

Mark I. Feldman · DLA Piper · 203 North LaSalle Street, Suite 1900 · Chicago, IL 60601-1293 · 312-368-4000

Ralph J. Gabric · Brinks Hofer Gilson & Lione · NBC Tower, Suite 3600 · 455 North Cityfront Plaza Drive · Chicago, IL 60611-5599 · 312-321-4200

Raymond I. Geraldson, Jr. · ⑩ · Pattishall, McAuliffe, Newbury, Hilliard & Geraldson · 311 South Wacker Drive, Suite 5000 · Chicago, IL 60606 · 312-554-8000

Allen H. Gerstein · ⑩ · Marshall, Gerstein & Borun · 6300 Sears Tower · 233 South Wacker Drive · Chicago, IL 60606-6357 · 312-474-6300

Jerome Gilson · ⑩ · Brinks Hofer Gilson & Lione · NBC Tower, Suite 3600 · 455 North Cityfront Plaza Drive · Chicago, IL 60611-5599 · 312-321-4200

H. Michael Hartmann · Leydig, Voit & Mayer · http://www.leydig.com · Two Prudential Plaza, Suite 4900 · 180 North Stetson Avenue · Chicago, IL 60601-6731 · 312-616-5600

John J. Held · McAndrews, Held & Malloy · 500 West Madison Street, 34th Floor · Chicago, IL 60661 · 312-775-8000

David Craig Hilliard · ⑩ · Pattishall, McAuliffe, Newbury, Hilliard & Geraldson · 311 South Wacker Drive, Suite 5000 · Chicago, IL 60606 · 312-554-8000

Roy E. Hofer · ⑩ · Brinks Hofer Gilson & Lione · NBC Tower, Suite 3600 · 455 North Cityfront Plaza Drive · Chicago, IL 60611-5599 · 312-321-4200

Jerold A. Jacover · Brinks Hofer Gilson & Lione · NBC Tower, Suite 3600 · 455 North Cityfront Plaza Drive · Chicago, IL 60611-5599 · 312-321-4200

John W. Kozak · Leydig, Voit & Mayer · http://www.leydig.com · Two Prudential Plaza, Suite 4900 · 180 North Stetson Avenue · Chicago, IL 60601-6731 · 312-616-5600

Charles A. Laff · Michael Best & Friedrich · Two Prudential Plaza, Suite 2000 · 180 North Stetson Avenue · Chicago, IL 60601 · 312-222-0800

Russell E. Levine · Kirkland & Ellis · 200 East Randolph Drive · Chicago, IL 60601-6636 · 312-861-2000

Richard G. Lione · Brinks Hofer Gilson & Lione · NBC Tower, Suite 3600 · 455 North Cityfront Plaza Drive · Chicago, IL 60611-5599 · 312-321-4200

Joseph A. Mahoney · Mayer Brown · 71 South Wacker Drive · Chicago, IL 60606 · 312-782-0600

Timothy J. Malloy · ⑩ · McAndrews, Held & Malloy · 500 West Madison Street, 34th Floor · Chicago, IL 60661 · 312-775-8000

John J. McDonnell · McDonnell Boehnen Hulbert & Berghoff · 300 South Wacker Drive, Suite 31 · Chicago, IL 60606-6709 · 312-913-0001

Dennis M. McWilliams · Barnes & Thornburg · http://www.btlaw.com · One North Wacker Drive, Suite 4400 · Chicago, IL 60606-2833 · 312-357-1313

Robert M. Newbury · ⑩ · Pattishall, McAuliffe, Newbury, Hilliard & Geraldson · 311 South Wacker Drive, Suite 5000 · Chicago, IL 60606 · 312-554-8000

Raymond P. Niro · Niro, Scavone, Haller & Niro · 181 West Madison Street, Suite 4600 · Chicago, IL 60602-4515 · 312-236-0733

Scott W. Petersen · Holland & Knight · http://www.hklaw.com · 131 South Dearborn Street, 30th Floor · Chicago, IL 60603 · 312-263-3600

Harry J. Roper · ⑩ · Jenner & Block · http://www.jenner.com · 330 North Wabash Avenue · Chicago, IL 60611-7603 · 312-222-9350

Gary M. Ropski · Brinks Hofer Gilson & Lione · NBC Tower, Suite 3600 · 455 North Cityfront Plaza Drive · Chicago, IL 60611-5599 · 312-321-4200

Larry L. Saret · Michael Best & Friedrich · Two Prudential Plaza, Suite 2000 · 180 North Stetson Avenue Chicago, IL 60601 · 312-222-0800

Thomas G. Scavone · Niro, Scavone, Haller & Niro · 181 West Madison Street, Suite 4600 · Chicago, IL 60602-4515 · 312-236-0733

Keith P. Schoeneberger · Dewey & LeBoeuf · Two Prudential Plaza, Suite 3700 · 180 North Stetson Avenue · Chicago, IL 60601 · 312-794-8000

James R. Sobieraj · Brinks Hofer Gilson & Lione · NBC Tower, Suite 3600 · 455 North Cityfront Plaza Drive · Chicago, IL 60611-5599 · 312-321-4200

Mary M. Squyres · Brinks Hofer Gilson & Lione · NBC Tower, Suite 3600 · 455 North Cityfront Plaza Drive · Chicago, IL 60611-5599 · 312-321-4200

Lewis T. Steadman, Jr. · Wildman, Harrold, Allen & Dixon · 225 West Wacker Drive, Suite 3000 · Chicago, IL 60606 · 312-201-2000

Lewis T. Steadman, Sr. · Rockey, Depke, Lyons & Kitzinger · Sears Tower, Suite 5450 · 233 South Wacker Drive · Chicago, IL 60606 · 312-277-2006

William A. Streff, Jr. · Kirkland & Ellis · 200 East Randolph Drive · Chicago, IL 60601-6636 · 312-861-2000

Barry Sufrin · Drinker Biddle & Reath · 191 North Wacker Drive, Suite 3700 · Chicago, IL 60606-1698 · 312-569-1000

Michael O. Warnecke · Perkins Coie · http://www.perkinscoie.com · 131 South Dearborn Street, Suite 1700 · Chicago, IL 60603-5559 · 312-324-8400

David L. Witcoff · Jones Day · 77 West Wacker Drive · Chicago, IL 60601-1692 · 312-782-3939

Richard W. Young · Drinker Biddle & Reath · 191 North Wacker Drive, Suite 3700 · Chicago, IL 60606-1698 · 312-569-1000

Larry M. Zanger · Holland & Knight · http://www.hklaw.com · 131 South Dearborn Street, 30th Floor · Chicago, IL 60603 · 312-263-3600

INTERNATIONAL ARBITRATION

Chicago

Ethan A. Berghoff · Baker & McKenzie · One Prudential Plaza · 130 East Randolph Drive · Chicago, IL 60601 · 312-861-8000

Richard M. Franklin · Baker & McKenzie · One Prudential Plaza · 130 East Randolph Drive · Chicago, IL 60601 · 312-861-8000

William R. Jentes · ㉕ · William R. Jentes · 1500 North Lake Shore Drive, Suite 4-C · Chicago, IL 60610 312-643-0024

David N. Kay · Drinker Biddle & Reath · 191 North Wacker Drive, Suite 3700 · Chicago, IL 60606-1698 · 312-569-1000

Michael L. Morkin · Baker & McKenzie · One Prudential Plaza · 130 East Randolph Drive · Chicago, IL 60601 · 312-861-8000

James H. Schink · Kirkland & Ellis · 200 East Randolph Drive · Chicago, IL 60601-6636 · 312-861-2000

Evanston

John H. Morrison · John H. Morrison · 2550 Princeton Avenue · Evanston, IL 60201-4941 · 847-869-5950

INTERNATIONAL TRADE AND FINANCE LAW

Chicago

Robert L. Berner, Jr. · ㉕ · Baker & McKenzie · One Prudential Plaza · 130 East Randolph Drive · Chicago, IL 60601 · 312-861-8000

John J. Conroy, Jr. · Baker & McKenzie · One Prudential Plaza · 130 East Randolph Drive · Chicago, IL 60601 · 312-861-8000

Richard T. Greenberg · McGuireWoods · http://www.mcguirewoods.com · 77 West Wacker Drive, Suite 4100 · Chicago, IL 60601-1818 · 312-849-8100

LABOR AND EMPLOYMENT LAW

Chicago

Vicki L. Abrahamson · Abrahamson Vorachek & Levinson · 120 North LaSalle Street, Suite 1050 · Chicago, IL 60602 · 312-263-2698

Harvey M. Adelstein · Neal, Gerber & Eisenberg · http://www.ngelaw.com · Two North LaSalle Street, Suite 2200 · Chicago, IL 60602-3801 · 312-269-8000

Margaret Angelucci · Asher, Gittler, Greenfield & D'Alba · 200 West Jackson Boulevard, Suite 1900 · Chicago, IL 60606 · 312-263-1500

Howard L. Bernstein · Neal, Gerber & Eisenberg · http://www.ngelaw.com · Two North LaSalle Street, Suite 2200 · Chicago, IL 60602-3801 · 312-269-8000

Roger T. Brice · Sonnenschein Nath & Rosenthal · Sears Tower, Suite 7800 · 233 South Wacker Drive · Chicago, IL 60606-6404 · 312-876-8000

Max G. Brittain, Jr. · Schiff Hardin · Sears Tower, Suite 6600 · 233 South Wacker Drive · Chicago, IL 60606-6473 · 312-258-5500

Brian W. Bulger · Meckler Bulger Tilson Marick & Pearson · 123 North Wacker Drive, Suite 1800 · Chicago, IL 60606 · 312-474-7900

Joseph M. Burns · Jacobs, Burns, Orlove, Stanton & Hernandez · 122 South Michigan Avenue, Suite 1720 · Chicago, IL 60603-6145 · 312-372-1646

Lawrence J. Casazza · Vedder Price · 222 North LaSalle Street · Chicago, IL 60601-1003 · 312-609-7500

Robert P. Casey · Ogletree Deakins · http://www.ogletreedeakins.com · Two First National Plaza, 25th Floor · 20 South Clark Street · Chicago, IL 60603-1891 · 312-558-1220

R. Theodore Clark, Jr. · ⑳ · Seyfarth Shaw · 131 South Dearborn Street, Suite 2400 · Chicago, IL 60603-5577 · 312-460-5000

Fay Clayton · ⑩ · Robinson, Curley & Clayton · 300 South Wacker Drive, Suite 1700 · Chicago, IL 60606 312-663-3100

Gilbert A. Cornfield · ㉕ · Cornfield & Feldman · 25 East Washington Street, Suite 1400 · Chicago, IL 60602 · 312-236-7800

Jules I. Crystal · Bryan Cave · 161 North Clark Street, Suite 4300 · Chicago, IL 60601-3315 · 312-602-5000

Joel A. D'Alba · ⑩ · Asher, Gittler, Greenfield & D'Alba · 200 West Jackson Boulevard, Suite 1900 · Chicago, IL 60606 · 312-263-1500

Thomas E. Deer · Ogletree Deakins · http://www.ogletreedeakins.com · Two First National Plaza, 25th Floor · 20 South Clark Street · Chicago, IL 60603-1891 · 312-558-1220

Lawrence C. DiNardo · Jones Day · 77 West Wacker Drive · Chicago, IL 60601-1692 · 312-782-3939

Kenneth R. Dolin · Seyfarth Shaw · 131 South Dearborn Street, Suite 2400 · Chicago, IL 60603-5577 · 312-460-5000

Michael W. Duffee · Ford & Harrison · http://www.fordharrison.com · 55 East Monroe Street, Suite 2900 · Chicago, IL 60603 · 312-332-0777

Lori D. Ecker · Law Office of Lori D. Ecker · http://www.loriecker.com · 120 North La Salle Street, Suite 1050 · Chicago, IL 60602 · 312-855-1880

Gilbert Feldman · ⑳ · Cornfield & Feldman · 25 East Washington Street, Suite 1400 · Chicago, IL 60602 312-236-7800

Elaine S. Fox · Seyfarth Shaw · 131 South Dearborn Street, Suite 2400 · Chicago, IL 60603-5577 · 312-460-5000

James C. Franczek, Jr. · ⑳ · Franczek Sullivan · 300 South Wacker Drive, Suite 3400 · Chicago, IL 60606-6785 · 312-986-0300

Joseph M. Gagliardo · Laner, Muchin, Dombrow, Becker, Levin and Tominberg · http://www.lanermuchin.com · 515 North State Street, Suite 2800 · Chicago, IL 60654 · 312-467-9800

Columbus R. Gangemi, Jr. · Winston & Strawn · 35 West Wacker Drive · Chicago, IL 60601-9703 · 312-558-5600

Marvin Gittler · ⑳ · Asher, Gittler, Greenfield & D'Alba · 200 West Jackson Boulevard, Suite 1900 · Chicago, IL 60606 · 312-263-1500

Brian J. Gold · Sidley Austin · One South Dearborn Street · Chicago, IL 60603 · 312-853-7000

Gerald A. Golden · Neal, Gerber & Eisenberg · http://www.ngelaw.com · Two North LaSalle Street, Suite 2200 · Chicago, IL 60602-3801 · 312-269-8000

Barry A. Hartstein · Morgan Lewis & Bockius · 77 West Wacker Drive · Chicago, IL 60601 · 312-324-1000

Ronald J. Hein, Jr. · Franczek Sullivan · 300 South Wacker Drive, Suite 3400 · Chicago, IL 60606-6785 · 312-986-0300

James D. Holzhauer · Mayer Brown · 71 South Wacker Drive · Chicago, IL 60606 · 312-782-0600

Charles C. Jackson · Morgan Lewis & Bockius · 77 West Wacker Drive · Chicago, IL 60601 · 312-324-1000

Edward C. Jepson, Jr. · Vedder Price · 222 North LaSalle Street · Chicago, IL 60601-1003 · 312-609-7500

Penny Nathan Kahan · Penny Nathan Kahan & Associates · 150 North Wacker Drive, Suite 2236 · Chicago, IL 60606 · 312-855-1660

Joel H. Kaplan · ⑩ · Seyfarth Shaw · 131 South Dearborn Street, Suite 2400 · Chicago, IL 60603-5577 · 312-460-5000

Michael D. Karpeles · Goldberg, Kohn, Bell, Black, Rosenbloom & Moritz · 55 East Monroe Street, Suite 3300 · Chicago, IL 60603-5792 · 312-201-4000

Harold A. Katz · ㉕ · Katz, Friedman, Eagle, Eisenstein & Johnson · 77 West Washington Street, 20th Floor · Chicago, IL 60602 · 312-263-6330

Richard E. Lieberman · McGuireWoods · http://www.mcguirewoods.com · 77 West Wacker Drive, Suite 4100 · Chicago, IL 60601-1818 · 312-849-8100

Richard L. Marcus · ㉕ · Sonnenschein Nath & Rosenthal · Sears Tower, Suite 7800 · 233 South Wacker Drive · Chicago, IL 60606-6404 · 312-876-8000

George J. Matkov, Jr. · Ford & Harrison · http://www.fordharrison.com · 55 East Monroe Street, Suite 2900 · Chicago, IL 60603 · 312-332-0777

Jane M. McFetridge · Jackson Lewis · http://www.jacksonlewis.com · 320 West Ohio Street, Suite 500 · Chicago, IL 60654 · 312-787-4949

Donald J. McNeil · Barnes & Thornburg · http://www.btlaw.com · One North Wacker Drive, Suite 4400 · Chicago, IL 60606-2833 · 312-357-1313

Philip A. Miscimarra · Morgan Lewis & Bockius · 77 West Wacker Drive · Chicago, IL 60601 · 312-324-1000

Ralph A. Morris · Schiff Hardin · Sears Tower, Suite 6600 · 233 South Wacker Drive · Chicago, IL 60606-6473 · 312-258-5500

Thomas J. Piskorski · Seyfarth Shaw · 131 South Dearborn Street, Suite 2400 · Chicago, IL 60603-5577 · 312-460-5000

John W. Powers · Seyfarth Shaw · 131 South Dearborn Street, Suite 2400 · Chicago, IL 60603-5577 · 312-460-5000

David P. Radelet · Franczek Sullivan · 300 South Wacker Drive, Suite 3400 · Chicago, IL 60606-6785 · 312-986-0300

David B. Ritter · Neal, Gerber & Eisenberg · http://www.ngelaw.com · Two North LaSalle Street, Suite 2200 · Chicago, IL 60602-3801 · 312-269-8000

Richard H. Schnadig · Vedder Price · 222 North LaSalle Street · Chicago, IL 60601-1003 · 312-609-7500

Rex L. Sessions · Winston & Strawn · 35 West Wacker Drive · Chicago, IL 60601-9703 · 312-558-5600

Patricia Costello Slovak · Schiff Hardin · Sears Tower, Suite 6600 · 233 South Wacker Drive · Chicago, IL 60606-6473 · 312-258-5500

Michael H. Slutsky · Allison, Slutsky & Kennedy · 230 West Monroe Street, Suite 2600 · Chicago, IL 60606 · 312-364-9400

Arthur B. Smith, Jr. · Ogletree Deakins · http://www.ogletreedeakins.com · Two First National Plaza, 25th Floor · 20 South Clark Street · Chicago, IL 60603-1891 · 312-558-1220

Nina G. Stillman · ⑩ · Morgan Lewis & Bockius · 77 West Wacker Drive · Chicago, IL 60601 · 312-324-1000

William R. Sullivan, Jr. · ⑩ · Franczek Sullivan · 300 South Wacker Drive, Suite 3400 · Chicago, IL 60606-6785 · 312-986-0300

Joseph E. Tilson · Meckler Bulger Tilson Marick & Pearson · 123 North Wacker Drive, Suite 1800 · Chicago, IL 60606 · 312-474-7900

Carl S. Tominberg · Laner, Muchin, Dombrow, Becker, Levin and Tominberg · http://www.lanermuchin.com · 515 North State Street, Suite 2800 · Chicago, IL 60654 · 312-467-9800

Joseph J. Torres · Winston & Strawn · 35 West Wacker Drive · Chicago, IL 60601-9703 · 312-558-5600

William Widmer · Carmell, Charone, Widmer, Mathews & Moss · 230 West Monroe, Suite 1900 · Chicago, IL 60606 · 312-236-8033

Joseph H. Yastrow · Laner, Muchin, Dombrow, Becker, Levin and Tominberg · http://www.lanermuchin.com · 515 North State Street, Suite 2800 · Chicago, IL 60654 · 312-467-9800

Peoria

Patricia C. Benassi · Benassi & Benassi · 300 Northeast Perry Avenue · Peoria, IL 61603 · 309-674-3556

Springfield

Mary Lee C. Leahy · Leahy Law Office · 308 East Canedy · Springfield, IL 62703 · 217-522-4411

Swansea

William K. Cavanagh, Jr. · Cavanagh & O'Hara · 1609 North Illinois Street · Swansea, IL 62226 · 618-222-5945

LAND USE & ZONING LAW

Chicago

Steven Elrod · Holland & Knight · http://www.hklaw.com · 131 South Dearborn Street, 30th Floor · Chicago, IL 60603 · 312-263-3600

Victor P. Filippini, Jr. · Holland & Knight · http://www.hklaw.com · 131 South Dearborn Street, 30th Floor · Chicago, IL 60603 · 312-263-3600

Harold W. Francke · DLA Piper · 203 North LaSalle Street, Suite 1900 · Chicago, IL 60601-1293 · 312-368-4000

Graham C. Grady · Bell, Boyd & Lloyd · Three First National Plaza, Suite 3100 · 70 West Madison Street · Chicago, IL 60602 · 312-372-1121

Jack Guthman · Shefsky & Froelich · 111 East Wacker Drive, Suite 2800 · Chicago, IL 60601 · 312-527-4000

Joseph Karaganis · Karaganis, White & Magel · 414 North Orleans Street, Suite 810 · Chicago, IL 60610-4421 · 312-836-1177

Richard F. Klawiter · DLA Piper · 203 North LaSalle Street, Suite 1900 · Chicago, IL 60601-1293 · 312-368-4000

Danielle B. Meltzer Cassel · Vedder Price · 222 North LaSalle Street · Chicago, IL 60601-1003 · 312-609-7500

Theodore J. Novak · DLA Piper · 203 North LaSalle Street, Suite 1900 · Chicago, IL 60601-1293 · 312-368-4000

David L. Reifman · DLA Piper · 203 North LaSalle Street, Suite 1900 · Chicago, IL 60601-1293 · 312-368-4000

Paul Shadle · DLA Piper · 203 North LaSalle Street, Suite 1900 · Chicago, IL 60601-1293 · 312-368-4000

LEGAL MALPRACTICE LAW

Chicago

Donald J. Brown, Jr. · Donohue Brown Mathewson & Smyth · 140 South Dearborn Street, Suite 800 · Chicago, IL 60603 · 312-422-0900

Robert F. Coleman · ⑩ · Robert F. Coleman & Associates · 77 West Wacker Drive · Chicago, IL 60601 · 312-444-1000

James R. Figliulo · ⑩ · Figliulo & Silverman · 10 South LaSalle Street, Suite 3600 · Chicago, IL 60603 · 312-251-4600

Robert A. Merrick, Jr. · Robert A. Merrick, Jr. · 53 West Jackson Boulevard, Suite 1235 · Chicago, IL 60604 · 312-922-0772

Eugene A. Schoon · Sidley Austin · One South Dearborn Street · Chicago, IL 60603 · 312-853-7000

George W. Spellmire, Jr. · ⑩ · Spellmire & Sommer · 77 West Wacker Drive, Suite 4800 · Chicago, IL 60601 · 312-606-8721

Edward J. Zulkey · ⑩ · Baker & McKenzie · One Prudential Plaza · 130 East Randolph Drive · Chicago, IL 60601 · 312-861-8000

LEVERAGED BUYOUTS AND PRIVATE EQUITY LAW

Chicago

Jon A. Ballis · Kirkland & Ellis · 200 East Randolph Drive · Chicago, IL 60601-6636 · 312-861-2000

Kevin R. Evanich · Kirkland & Ellis · 200 East Randolph Drive · Chicago, IL 60601-6636 · 312-861-2000

Jeffrey C. Hammes · Kirkland & Ellis · 200 East Randolph Drive · Chicago, IL 60601-6636 · 312-861-2000

Peter C. Krupp · Skadden, Arps, Slate, Meagher & Flom · 333 West Wacker Drive · Chicago, IL 60606 · 312-407-0700

Jack S. Levin · ㉕ · Kirkland & Ellis · 200 East Randolph Drive · Chicago, IL 60601-6636 · 312-861-2000

Kenneth W. Miller · Katten Muchin Rosenman · 525 West Monroe Street · Chicago, IL 60661-3693 · 312-902-5200

Steven V. Napolitano · DLA Piper · 203 North LaSalle Street, Suite 1900 · Chicago, IL 60601-1293 · 312-368-4000

S. Michael Peck · Sidley Austin · One South Dearborn Street · Chicago, IL 60603 · 312-853-7000

Sanford E. Perl · Kirkland & Ellis · 200 East Randolph Drive · Chicago, IL 60601-6636 · 312-861-2000

Stephen L. Ritchie · Kirkland & Ellis · 200 East Randolph Drive · Chicago, IL 60601-6636 · 312-861-2000

John A. Schoenfeld · Kirkland & Ellis · 200 East Randolph Drive · Chicago, IL 60601-6636 · 312-861-2000

Matthew E. Steinmetz · Kirkland & Ellis · 200 East Randolph Drive · Chicago, IL 60601-6636 · 312-861-2000

Walter S. Weinberg · Katten Muchin Rosenman · 525 West Monroe Street · Chicago, IL 60661-3693 · 312-902-5200

MARITIME LAW

Chicago

Steven B. Belgrade · Belgrade & O'Donnell · 20 North Wacker Drive, Suite 1900 · Chicago, IL 60606 · 312-422-1700

Sandor Korein · ⑩ · Korein Tillery · 205 North Michigan, Suite 1950 · Chicago, IL 60601 · 312-641-9750

Warren J. Marwedel · ⑳ · Marwedel, Minichello & Reeb · 10 South Riverside Plaza, Suite 720 · Chicago, IL 60606 · 312-902-1600

Dennis Minichello · ⑩ · Marwedel, Minichello & Reeb · 10 South Riverside Plaza, Suite 720 · Chicago, IL 60606 · 312-902-1600

John A. O'Donnell · Belgrade & O'Donnell · 20 North Wacker Drive, Suite 1900 · Chicago, IL 60606 · 312-422-1700

Robert Reeb · Marwedel, Minichello & Reeb · 10 South Riverside Plaza, Suite 720 · Chicago, IL 60606 · 312-902-1600

Palos Heights

Michael A. Snyder · ⑳ · Snyder McGovern · 12750 South Harlem Avenue, Suite 2-A · Palos Heights, IL 60463 · 708-448-9700

MASS TORT LITIGATION

Chicago

David M. Bernick · Kirkland & Ellis · 200 East Randolph Drive · Chicago, IL 60601-6636 · 312-861-2000

James T. Conlon · Sedgwick, Detert, Moran & Arnold · One North Wacker Drive, Suite 4200 · Chicago, IL 60606-2841 · 312-641-9050

John D. Cooney · Cooney and Conway · 120 North LaSalle Street, Suite 3000 · Chicago, IL 60602 · 312-236-6166

Edward M. Crane · Skadden, Arps, Slate, Meagher & Flom · 333 West Wacker Drive · Chicago, IL 60606 · 312-407-0700

Michael W. Davis · Sidley Austin · One South Dearborn Street · Chicago, IL 60603 · 312-853-7000

Richard L. Fenton · Sonnenschein Nath & Rosenthal · Sears Tower, Suite 7800 · 233 South Wacker Drive · Chicago, IL 60606-6404 · 312-876-8000

William J. Harte · ㉕ · William J. Harte · 111 West Washington Street, Suite 1100 · Chicago, IL 60602 · 312-726-5015

Joseph J. O'Hara, Jr. · Schiff Hardin · Sears Tower, Suite 6600 · 233 South Wacker Drive · Chicago, IL 60606-6473 · 312-258-5500

Michael A. Pope · McDermott Will & Emery · 227 West Monroe Street · Chicago, IL 60606-5096 · 312-372-2000

Robert H. Riley, Jr. · Schiff Hardin · Sears Tower, Suite 6600 · 233 South Wacker Drive · Chicago, IL 60606-6473 · 312-258-5500

Todd A. Smith · ⑩ · Power Rogers & Smith · Three First National Plaza, 55th Floor · 70 West Madison Street · Chicago, IL 60602 · 312-236-9381

R. Ryan Stoll · Skadden, Arps, Slate, Meagher & Flom · 333 West Wacker Drive · Chicago, IL 60606 · 312-407-0700

Dan K. Webb · ⑳ · Winston & Strawn · 35 West Wacker Drive · Chicago, IL 60601-9703 · 312-558-5600

Edwardsville

Gordon R. Broom · Hepler, Broom, MacDonald, Hebrank, True & Noce · Two Mark Twain Plaza, Suite 300 · 103 West Vandalia Street · P.O. Box 510 · Edwardsville, IL 62025-0510 · 618-656-0184

Jeffrey S. Hebrank · Hepler, Broom, MacDonald, Hebrank, True & Noce · Two Mark Twain Plaza, Suite 300 · 103 West Vandalia Street · P.O. Box 510 · Edwardsville, IL 62025-0510 · 618-656-0184

Larry E. Hepler · Hepler, Broom, MacDonald, Hebrank, True & Noce · Two Mark Twain Plaza, Suite 300 · 103 West Vandalia Street · P.O. Box 510 · Edwardsville, IL 62025-0510 · 618-656-0184

Robert H. Shultz, Jr. · Heyl, Royster, Voelker & Allen · Mark Twain Plaza II, Suite 100 · 103 West Vandalia Street · P.O. Box 467 · Edwardsville, IL 62025 · 618-656-4646

Peoria

Christopher Larson · Heyl, Royster, Voelker & Allen · Chase Building, Suite 600 · 124 Southwest Adams Street · Peoria, IL 61602 · 309-676-0400

MEDICAL MALPRACTICE LAW

Chicago

Robert A. Clifford · ⑩ · Clifford Law Offices · http://www.cliffordlaw.com · 120 North LaSalle Street, Suite 3100 · Chicago, IL 60602 · 312-899-9090

Thomas A. Demetrio · ⑳ · Corboy & Demetrio · http://www.corboydemetrio.com · 33 North Dearborn Street, Suite 2100 · Chicago, IL 60602 · 312-346-3191

Richard H. Donohue · Donohue Brown Mathewson & Smyth · 140 South Dearborn Street, Suite 800 · Chicago, IL 60603 · 312-422-0900

William V. Johnson · ⑳ · Johnson & Bell · 33 West Monroe Street, Suite 2700 · Chicago, IL 60603-5404 · 312-372-0770

C. Barry Montgomery · ⑩ · Williams, Montgomery & John · 20 North Wacker Drive, Suite 2100 · Chicago, IL 60606-3094 · 312-443-3200

Bruce R. Pfaff · Pfaff & Gill · http://www.pfaffgill.com · One East Wacker Drive, Suite 3310 · Chicago, IL 60601 · 312-828-9666

Joseph A. Power, Jr. · ⑳ · Power Rogers & Smith · Three First National Plaza, 55th Floor · 70 West Madison Street · Chicago, IL 60602 · 312-236-9381

Neil K. Quinn · ㉕ · Pretzel & Stouffer · One South Wacker Drive, Suite 2500 · Chicago, IL 60606-8242 · 312-346-1973

Rudolph G. Schade, Jr. · Cassiday Schade · 20 North Wacker Drive, Suite 1040 · Chicago, IL 60606-2903 · 312-641-3100

East St. Louis

Rex Carr · ㉕ · Rex Carr Law Firm · 412 Missouri Avenue · East St. Louis, IL 62201-3050 · 618-274-0434

Rock Island

Michael J. Warner · Michael J. Warner & Associates · 1600 Fourth Avenue, Suite 410 · P.O. Box 3544 · Rock Island, IL 61204-3544 · 309-794-1660

Springfield

Thomas F. Londrigan · ⑳ · Londrigan, Potter & Randle · 1227 South Seventh Street · P.O. Box 399 · Springfield, IL 62705 · 217-544-9823

Waukegan

Patrick A. Salvi · Salvi, Schostok & Pritchard · 218 North Martin Luther King Jr. Avenue · Waukegan, IL 60085 · 847-249-1227

Michael P. Schostok · Salvi, Schostok & Pritchard · 218 North Martin Luther King Jr. Avenue · Waukegan, IL 60085 · 847-249-1227

MERGERS & ACQUISITIONS LAW

Chicago

Neal Aizenstein · Sonnenschein Nath & Rosenthal · Sears Tower, Suite 7800 · 233 South Wacker Drive · Chicago, IL 60606-6404 · 312-876-8000

Frank D. Ballantine · Reed Smith · 10 South Wacker Drive, 40th Floor · Chicago, IL 60606-7507 · 312-207-1000

Jon A. Ballis · Kirkland & Ellis · 200 East Randolph Drive · Chicago, IL 60601-6636 · 312-861-2000

Larry A. Barden · Sidley Austin · One South Dearborn Street · Chicago, IL 60603 · 312-853-7000

Robert L. Berner, Jr. · ㉕ · Baker & McKenzie · One Prudential Plaza · 130 East Randolph Drive · Chicago, IL 60601 · 312-861-8000

Edward S. Best · Mayer Brown · 71 South Wacker Drive · Chicago, IL 60606 · 312-782-0600

Timothy R. M. Bryant · McDermott Will & Emery · 227 West Monroe Street · Chicago, IL 60606-5096 · 312-372-2000

Paul L. Choi · Sidley Austin · One South Dearborn Street · Chicago, IL 60603 · 312-853-7000

Keith S. Crow · Kirkland & Ellis · 200 East Randolph Drive · Chicago, IL 60601-6636 · 312-861-2000

Gary P. Cullen · Skadden, Arps, Slate, Meagher & Flom · 333 West Wacker Drive · Chicago, IL 60606 · 312-407-0700

Scott J. Davis · Mayer Brown · 71 South Wacker Drive · Chicago, IL 60606 · 312-782-0600

Brian W. Duwe · Skadden, Arps, Slate, Meagher & Flom · 333 West Wacker Drive · Chicago, IL 60606 · 312-407-0700

Carter W. Emerson · ❿ · Kirkland & Ellis · 200 East Randolph Drive · Chicago, IL 60601-6636 · 312-861-2000

Kevin R. Evanich · Kirkland & Ellis · 200 East Randolph Drive · Chicago, IL 60601-6636 · 312-861-2000

R. Scott Falk · Kirkland & Ellis · 200 East Randolph Drive · Chicago, IL 60601-6636 · 312-861-2000

Willard G. Fraumann · Kirkland & Ellis · 200 East Randolph Drive · Chicago, IL 60601-6636 · 312-861-2000

Helen R. Friedli · McDermott Will & Emery · 227 West Monroe Street · Chicago, IL 60606-5096 · 312-372-2000

Michael M. Froy · Sonnenschein Nath & Rosenthal · Sears Tower, Suite 7800 · 233 South Wacker Drive · Chicago, IL 60606-6404 · 312-876-8000

Steven J. Gavin · Winston & Strawn · 35 West Wacker Drive · Chicago, IL 60601-9703 · 312-558-5600

Mark D. Gerstein · Latham & Watkins · Sears Tower, Suite 5800 · 233 South Wacker Drive · Chicago, IL 60606-6401 · 312-876-7700

Joseph P. Gromacki · Jenner & Block · http://www.jenner.com · 330 North Wabash Avenue · Chicago, IL 60611-7603 · 312-222-9350

Jeffrey C. Hammes · Kirkland & Ellis · 200 East Randolph Drive · Chicago, IL 60601-6636 · 312-861-2000

Michael H. Kerr · Kirkland & Ellis · 200 East Randolph Drive · Chicago, IL 60601-6636 · 312-861-2000

Elizabeth Clough Kitslaar · Jones Day · 77 West Wacker Drive · Chicago, IL 60601-1692 · 312-782-3939

Peter C. Krupp · Skadden, Arps, Slate, Meagher & Flom · 333 West Wacker Drive · Chicago, IL 60606 · 312-407-0700

William R. Kunkel · Skadden, Arps, Slate, Meagher & Flom · 333 West Wacker Drive · Chicago, IL 60606 · 312-407-0700

James T. Lidbury · Ropes & Gray · http://www.ropesgray.com · One South Dearborn Street, Suite 2100 · Chicago, IL 60603-2302 · 312-212-4410

Peter H. Lieberman · Greenberg Traurig · http://www.gtlaw.com · 77 West Wacker Drive, Suite 2500 · Chicago, IL 60601 · 312-456-8400

Stanley H. Meadows · McDermott Will & Emery · 227 West Monroe Street · Chicago, IL 60606-5096 · 312-372-2000

Kenneth W. Miller · Katten Muchin Rosenman · 525 West Monroe Street · Chicago, IL 60661-3693 · 312-902-5200

Robert J. Minkus · Schiff Hardin · Sears Tower, Suite 6600 · 233 South Wacker Drive · Chicago, IL 60606-6473 · 312-258-5500

Charles W. Mulaney, Jr. · ⑳ · Skadden, Arps, Slate, Meagher & Flom · 333 West Wacker Drive · Chicago, IL 60606 · 312-407-0700

Steven V. Napolitano · DLA Piper · 203 North LaSalle Street, Suite 1900 · Chicago, IL 60601-1293 · 312-368-4000

S. Michael Peck · Sidley Austin · One South Dearborn Street · Chicago, IL 60603 · 312-853-7000

Sanford E. Perl · Kirkland & Ellis · 200 East Randolph Drive · Chicago, IL 60601-6636 · 312-861-2000

Imad I. Qasim · Sidley Austin · One South Dearborn Street · Chicago, IL 60603 · 312-853-7000

E. Paul Quinn · Greenberg Traurig · http://www.gtlaw.com · 77 West Wacker Drive, Suite 2500 · Chicago, IL 60601 · 312-456-8400

Stephen L. Ritchie · Kirkland & Ellis · 200 East Randolph Drive · Chicago, IL 60601-6636 · 312-861-2000

Edward J. Schneidman · Mayer Brown · 71 South Wacker Drive · Chicago, IL 60606 · 312-782-0600

Richard W. Shepro · Mayer Brown · 71 South Wacker Drive · Chicago, IL 60606 · 312-782-0600

Marc F. Sperber · Mayer Brown · 71 South Wacker Drive · Chicago, IL 60606 · 312-782-0600

Matthew E. Steinmetz · Kirkland & Ellis · 200 East Randolph Drive · Chicago, IL 60601-6636 · 312-861-2000

Paul W. Theiss · Mayer Brown · 71 South Wacker Drive · Chicago, IL 60606 · 312-782-0600

Frederick B. Thomas · Mayer Brown · 71 South Wacker Drive · Chicago, IL 60606 · 312-782-0600

Michael G. Timmers · Kirkland & Ellis · 200 East Randolph Drive · Chicago, IL 60601-6636 · 312-861-2000

Bruce A. Toth · Winston & Strawn · 35 West Wacker Drive · Chicago, IL 60601-9703 · 312-558-5600

Robert F. Wall · ⑩ · Winston & Strawn · 35 West Wacker Drive · Chicago, IL 60601-9703 · 312-558-5600

Herbert S. Wander · ㉕ · Katten Muchin Rosenman · 525 West Monroe Street · Chicago, IL 60661-3693 · 312-902-5200

MUNICIPAL LAW

Chicago

Ronald S. Cope · Ungaretti & Harris · Three First National Plaza, Suite 3500 · 70 West Madison Street · Chicago, IL 60602-4283 · 312-977-4400

Lewis Greenbaum · Katten Muchin Rosenman · 525 West Monroe Street · Chicago, IL 60661-3693 · 312-902-5200

Roger J. Kiley, Jr. · Mayer Brown · 71 South Wacker Drive · Chicago, IL 60606 · 312-782-0600

John B. Murphey · Rosenthal, Murphey & Coblentz · 30 North LaSalle Street, Suite 1624 · Chicago, IL 60602 · 312-541-1070

MUTUAL FUNDS LAW

Chicago

Cameron S. Avery · ⑳ · Bell, Boyd & Lloyd · Three First National Plaza, Suite 3100 · 70 West Madison Street · Chicago, IL 60602 · 312-372-1121

Paul H. Dykstra · ㉕ · Bell, Boyd & Lloyd · Three First National Plaza, Suite 3100 · 70 West Madison Street · Chicago, IL 60602 · 312-372-1121

Michael L. Meyer · ㉕ · Schiff Hardin · Sears Tower, Suite 6600 · 233 South Wacker Drive · Chicago, IL 60606-6473 · 312-258-5500

Paulita A. Pike · Bell, Boyd & Lloyd · Three First National Plaza, Suite 3100 · 70 West Madison Street · Chicago, IL 60602 · 312-372-1121

Charles B. Taylor · Skadden, Arps, Slate, Meagher & Flom · 333 West Wacker Drive · Chicago, IL 60606 312-407-0700

Paul B. Uhlenhop · ⑩ · Lawrence, Kamin, Saunders & Uhlenhop · 300 South Wacker Drive, Suite 500 · Chicago, IL 60606 · 312-372-1947

Wayne W. Whalen · ⑳ · Skadden, Arps, Slate, Meagher & Flom · 333 West Wacker Drive · Chicago, IL 60606 · 312-407-0700

NON-PROFIT/CHARITIES LAW

Chicago

Larry D. Berning · ㉕ · Sidley Austin · One South Dearborn Street · Chicago, IL 60603 · 312-853-7000

Jack R. Bierig · ⑩ · Sidley Austin · One South Dearborn Street · Chicago, IL 60603 · 312-853-7000

Thomas E. Chomicz · Quarles & Brady · http://www.quarles.com · Citigroup Center, Suite 3700 · 500 West Madison Street · Chicago, IL 60661-2511 · 312-715-5000

Michael A. Clark · Sidley Austin · One South Dearborn Street · Chicago, IL 60603 · 312-853-7000

Quin R. Frazer · Drinker Biddle & Reath · 191 North Wacker Drive, Suite 3700 · Chicago, IL 60606-1698 · 312-569-1000

Paula Cozzi Goedert · Barnes & Thornburg · http://www.btlaw.com · One North Wacker Drive, Suite 4400 · Chicago, IL 60606-2833 · 312-357-1313

Gerald M. Griffith · ⑩ · Jones Day · 77 West Wacker Drive · Chicago, IL 60601-1692 · 312-782-3939

James R. Hellige · Foley & Lardner · 321 North Clark Street, Suite 2800 · Chicago, IL 60654 · 312-832-4500

Jed R. Mandel · Neal, Gerber & Eisenberg · http://www.ngelaw.com · Two North LaSalle Street, Suite 2200 · Chicago, IL 60602-3801 · 312-269-8000

Howard M. McCue III · ㉕ · Mayer Brown · 71 South Wacker Drive · Chicago, IL 60606 · 312-782-0600

Janice E. Rodgers · Quarles & Brady · http://www.quarles.com · Citigroup Center, Suite 3700 · 500 West Madison Street · Chicago, IL 60661-2511 · 312-715-5000

Richard L. Sevcik · Bell, Boyd & Lloyd · Three First National Plaza, Suite 3100 · 70 West Madison Street · Chicago, IL 60602 · 312-372-1121

NON-WHITE-COLLAR CRIMINAL DEFENSE

Chicago

Edward M. Genson · ⑳ · Genson & Gillespie · 53 West Jackson Boulevard, Suite 1420 · Chicago, IL 60604 · 312-726-9015

Cynthia Giacchetti · Law Offices of Cynthia Giacchetti · 53 West Jackson Boulevard, Suite 1460 · Chicago, IL 60604 · 312-939-6440

Terrence P. Gillespie · ⑩ · Genson & Gillespie · 53 West Jackson Boulevard, Suite 1420 · Chicago, IL 60604 · 312-726-9015

Marc W. Martin · Marc W. Martin · 53 West Jackson Boulevard, Suite 1420 · Chicago, IL 60604 · 312-408-1111

William J. Martin · ㉕ · William J. Martin · 6832 West North Avenue, Suite 4-B · Chicago, IL 60707 · 773-622-5350

Michael D. Monico · ⑩ · Monico, Pavich & Spevack · 20 South Clark Street, Suite 700 · Chicago, IL 60603 · 312-782-8500

Craig D. Tobin · ⑩ · Tobin Petkus & Muñoz · http://www.barristers.com · Three First National Plaza, Suite 1950 · Chicago, IL 60602-4298 · 312-641-1321

Springfield

Michael B. Metnick · Metnick, Cherry, Frazier, Sabin & Perrin · Myers Building, Suite 200 · One West Old State Capitol Plaza · P.O. Box 12140 · Springfield, IL 62791 · 217-753-4242

PERSONAL INJURY LITIGATION

Chicago

John W. Bell · ⑩ · Johnson & Bell · 33 West Monroe Street, Suite 2700 · Chicago, IL 60603-5404 · 312-372-0770

Kevin G. Burke · Burke, Mahoney, Wise · 161 North Clark Street, Suite 2240 · Chicago, IL 60601 · 312-580-2040

William J. Burke · Costello, McMahon & Burke · 150 North Wacker Drive, Suite 3050 · Chicago, IL 60606 · 312-541-9700

Robert A. Clifford · ⑩ · Clifford Law Offices · http://www.cliffordlaw.com · 120 North LaSalle Street, Suite 3100 · Chicago, IL 60602 · 312-899-9090

Philip H. Corboy · ㉕ · Corboy & Demetrio · http://www.corboydemetrio.com · 33 North Dearborn Street, Suite 2100 · Chicago, IL 60602 · 312-346-3191

Philip Harnett Corboy, Jr. · Corboy & Demetrio · http://www.corboydemetrio.com · 33 North Dearborn Street, Suite 2100 · Chicago, IL 60602 · 312-346-3191

Thomas M. Crisham · Crisham & Kubes · 30 North LaSalle Street, Suite 2800 · Chicago, IL 60602 · 312-327-2500

Michael K. Demetrio · Corboy & Demetrio · http://www.corboydemetrio.com · 33 North Dearborn Street, Suite 2100 · Chicago, IL 60602 · 312-346-3191

Thomas A. Demetrio · ⑳ · Corboy & Demetrio · http://www.corboydemetrio.com · 33 North Dearborn Street, Suite 2100 · Chicago, IL 60602 · 312-346-3191

Thomas M. Durkin · Mayer Brown · 71 South Wacker Drive · Chicago, IL 60606 · 312-782-0600

Brian C. Fetzer · Johnson & Bell · 33 West Monroe Street, Suite 2700 · Chicago, IL 60603-5404 · 312-372-0770

Geoffrey L. Gifford · ⑩ · Pavalon, Gifford & Laatsch · http://www.pglmlaw.com · Two North LaSalle Street, Suite 1600 · Chicago, IL 60602-4036 · 312-419-7400

Albert F. Hofeld · ㉕ · Hofeld and Schaffner · 30 North LaSalle Street, Suite 3120 · Chicago, IL 60602-2506 · 312-372-4250

William V. Johnson · ⑳ · Johnson & Bell · 33 West Monroe Street, Suite 2700 · Chicago, IL 60603-5404 · 312-372-0770

Bruce M. Kohen · ⑩ · Anesi, Ozmon, Rodin, Novak & Kohen · http://www.anesilaw.com · 161 North Clark Street, 21st Floor · Chicago, IL 60601 · 312-372-3822

Sandor Korein · ⑩ · Korein Tillery · 205 North Michigan, Suite 1950 · Chicago, IL 60601 · 312-641-9750

Warren Lupel · Lupel & Weininger · 30 North La Salle Street, Suite 3520 · Chicago, IL 60602 · 312-260-7700

Kevin T. Martin · Swanson, Martin & Bell · 330 North Wabash, Suite 3300 · Chicago, IL 60611 · 312-321-9100

C. Barry Montgomery · ⑩ · Williams, Montgomery & John · 20 North Wacker Drive, Suite 2100 · Chicago, IL 60606-3094 · 312-443-3200

Eugene I. Pavalon · ⑩ · Pavalon, Gifford & Laatsch · http://www.pglmlaw.com · Two North LaSalle Street, Suite 1600 · Chicago, IL 60602-4036 · 312-419-7400

Bruce R. Pfaff · Pfaff & Gill · http://www.pfaffgill.com · One East Wacker Drive, Suite 3310 · Chicago, IL 60601 · 312-828-9666

Joseph A. Power, Jr. · ⑳ · Power Rogers & Smith · Three First National Plaza, 55th Floor · 70 West Madison Street · Chicago, IL 60602 · 312-236-9381

Lorna E. Propes · ⑩ · Propes & Kaveny · 833 West Jackson, Suite 200 · Chicago, IL 60607 · 312-334-3100

Neil K. Quinn · ㉕ · Pretzel & Stouffer · One South Wacker Drive, Suite 2500 · Chicago, IL 60606-8242 · 312-346-1973

Curt N. Rodin · ⑩ · Anesi, Ozmon, Rodin, Novak & Kohen · http://www.anesilaw.com · 161 North Clark Street, 21st Floor · Chicago, IL 60601 · 312-372-3822

Larry R. Rogers, Sr. · ⑩ · Power Rogers & Smith · Three First National Plaza, 55th Floor · 70 West Madison Street · Chicago, IL 60602 · 312-236-9381

Howard Schaffner · ⑩ · Hofeld and Schaffner · 30 North LaSalle Street, Suite 3120 · Chicago, IL 60602-2506 · 312-372-4250

Colin P. Smith · Holland & Knight · http://www.hklaw.com · 131 South Dearborn Street, 30th Floor · Chicago, IL 60603 · 312-263-3600

Todd A. Smith · ⑩ · Power Rogers & Smith · Three First National Plaza, 55th Floor · 70 West Madison Street · Chicago, IL 60602 · 312-236-9381

East St. Louis

Rex Carr · ㉕ · Rex Carr Law Firm · 412 Missouri Avenue · East St. Louis, IL 62201-3050 · 618-274-0434

Rock Island

Michael J. Warner · Michael J. Warner & Associates · 1600 Fourth Avenue, Suite 410 · P.O. Box 3544 · Rock Island, IL 61204-3544 · 309-794-1660

Springfield

Thomas F. Londrigan · ⑳ · Londrigan, Potter & Randle · 1227 South Seventh Street · P.O. Box 399 · Springfield, IL 62705 · 217-544-9823

Waukegan

Patrick A. Salvi · Salvi, Schostok & Pritchard · 218 North Martin Luther King Jr. Avenue · Waukegan, IL 60085 · 847-249-1227

Michael P. Schostok · Salvi, Schostok & Pritchard · 218 North Martin Luther King Jr. Avenue · Waukegan, IL 60085 · 847-249-1227

PRIVATE FUNDS LAW

Chicago

James B. Biery · Sidley Austin · One South Dearborn Street · Chicago, IL 60603 · 312-853-7000

Bruce I. Ettelson · Kirkland & Ellis · 200 East Randolph Drive · Chicago, IL 60601-6636 · 312-861-2000

Joseph H. Harrison, Jr. · Sidley Austin · One South Dearborn Street · Chicago, IL 60603 · 312-853-7000

William D. Kerr · Sidley Austin · One South Dearborn Street · Chicago, IL 60603 · 312-853-7000

David M. Matteson · Drinker Biddle & Reath · 191 North Wacker Drive, Suite 3700 · Chicago, IL 60606-1698 · 312-569-1000

Deborah A. Monson · Ropes & Gray · http://www.ropesgray.com · One South Dearborn Street, Suite 2100 · Chicago, IL 60603-2302 · 312-212-4410

Wesley G. Nissen · Winston & Strawn · 35 West Wacker Drive · Chicago, IL 60601-9703 · 312-558-5600

John W. Noell, Jr. · Mayer Brown · 71 South Wacker Drive · Chicago, IL 60606 · 312-782-0600

Michele Ilene Ruiz · Sidley Austin · One South Dearborn Street · Chicago, IL 60603 · 312-853-7000

David R. Sawyier · Sidley Austin · One South Dearborn Street · Chicago, IL 60603 · 312-853-7000

James D. Van De Graaf · Katten Muchin Rosenman · 525 West Monroe Street · Chicago, IL 60661-3693 312-902-5200

PRODUCT LIABILITY LITIGATION

Chicago

Michael Borders · Dykema · http://www.dykema.com · 10 South Wacker Drive, Suite 2300 · Chicago, IL 60606 · 312-876-1700

Robert A. Clifford · ⑩ · Clifford Law Offices · http://www.cliffordlaw.com · 120 North LaSalle Street, Suite 3100 · Chicago, IL 60602 · 312-899-9090

Thomas M. Crisham · Crisham & Kubes · 30 North LaSalle Street, Suite 2800 · Chicago, IL 60602 · 312-327-2500

James P. Dorr · Wildman, Harrold, Allen & Dixon · 225 West Wacker Drive, Suite 3000 · Chicago, IL 60606 · 312-201-2000

Thomas M. Durkin · Mayer Brown · 71 South Wacker Drive · Chicago, IL 60606 · 312-782-0600

Mark Herrmann · Jones Day · 77 West Wacker Drive · Chicago, IL 60601-1692 · 312-782-3939

Neil K. Quinn · ㉕ · Pretzel & Stouffer · One South Wacker Drive, Suite 2500 · Chicago, IL 60606-8242 · 312-346-1973

Dale G. Wills · Swanson, Martin & Bell · 330 North Wabash, Suite 3300 · Chicago, IL 60611 · 312-321-9100

Springfield

Thomas F. Londrigan · ⑳ · Londrigan, Potter & Randle · 1227 South Seventh Street · P.O. Box 399 · Springfield, IL 62705 · 217-544-9823

PROFESSIONAL MALPRACTICE LAW

Chicago

Thomas R. Hill · Dykema · http://www.dykema.com · 10 South Wacker Drive, Suite 2300 · Chicago, IL 60606 · 312-876-1700

Carrie K. Huff · Mayer Brown · 71 South Wacker Drive · Chicago, IL 60606 · 312-782-0600

Kevin O'Hagan · O'Hagan Spencer · http://www.ohaganspencer.com · One East Wacker Drive, 34th Floor Chicago, IL 60601 · 312-422-6100

Neil K. Quinn · ㉕ · Pretzel & Stouffer · One South Wacker Drive, Suite 2500 · Chicago, IL 60606-8242 · 312-346-1973

PROJECT FINANCE LAW

Chicago

Cynthia A. Baker · Chapman and Cutler · 111 West Monroe Street · Chicago, IL 60603-4080 · 312-845-3000

J. Paul Forrester · Mayer Brown · 71 South Wacker Drive · Chicago, IL 60606 · 312-782-0600

Barry N. Machlin · Mayer Brown · 71 South Wacker Drive · Chicago, IL 60606 · 312-782-0600

James P. O'Brien · Baker & McKenzie · One Prudential Plaza · 130 East Randolph Drive · Chicago, IL 60601 · 312-861-8000

PUBLIC FINANCE LAW

Chicago

William E. Corbin · Perkins Coie · http://www.perkinscoie.com · 131 South Dearborn Street, Suite 1700 · Chicago, IL 60603-5559 · 312-324-8400

Darryl R. Davidson · Miller Canfield Paddock and Stone · http://www.millercanfield.com · 225 West Washington Street, Suite 2600 · Chicago, IL 60606 · 312-460-4200

Thomas M. Fahey · ⑩ · Ungaretti & Harris · Three First National Plaza, Suite 3500 · 70 West Madison Street · Chicago, IL 60602-4283 · 312-977-4400

Janet Goelz Hoffman · Katten Muchin Rosenman · 525 West Monroe Street · Chicago, IL 60661-3693 · 312-902-5200

Steven B. Kite · Sonnenschein Nath & Rosenthal · Sears Tower, Suite 7800 · 233 South Wacker Drive · Chicago, IL 60606-6404 · 312-876-8000

Paul C. Marengo · Schiff Hardin · Sears Tower, Suite 6600 · 233 South Wacker Drive · Chicago, IL 60606-6473 · 312-258-5500

Michael J. Mitchell · Jones Day · 77 West Wacker Drive · Chicago, IL 60601-1692 · 312-782-3939

David Narefsky · Mayer Brown · 71 South Wacker Drive · Chicago, IL 60606 · 312-782-0600

Mary G. Wilson · Sonnenschein Nath & Rosenthal · Sears Tower, Suite 7800 · 233 South Wacker Drive · Chicago, IL 60606-6404 · 312-876-8000

Lisle

James M. Snyder · Ice Miller · 2300 Cabot Drive, Suite 455 · Lisle, IL 60532 · 630-955-0555

RAILROAD LAW

Belleville

Richard E. Boyle · Gundlach, Lee, Eggmann, Boyle & Roessler · 5000 West Main Street · P.O. Box 23560 · Belleville, IL 62223-0560 · 618-277-9000

Thomas E. Jones · Thompson Coburn · 525 West Main Street · Belleville, IL 62220-1534 · 618-277-4700

REAL ESTATE LAW

Chicago

Anthony J. Aiello · Sidley Austin · One South Dearborn Street · Chicago, IL 60603 · 312-853-7000

Virginia L. Aronson · Sidley Austin · One South Dearborn Street · Chicago, IL 60603 · 312-853-7000

Jana Cohen Barbe · Sonnenschein Nath & Rosenthal · Sears Tower, Suite 7800 · 233 South Wacker Drive · Chicago, IL 60606-6404 · 312-876-8000

James L. Beard · DLA Piper · 203 North LaSalle Street, Suite 1900 · Chicago, IL 60601-1293 · 312-368-4000

Stephen B. Bell · Goldberg, Kohn, Bell, Black, Rosenbloom & Moritz · 55 East Monroe Street, Suite 3300 Chicago, IL 60603-5792 · 312-201-4000

Robert M. Berger · ⑩ · Krasnow Saunders Cornblath · The Boyce Building, Second Floor · 500 North Dearborn Street · Chicago, IL 60654 · 312-755-5700

Stephen L. Berger · Neal, Gerber & Eisenberg · http://www.ngelaw.com · Two North LaSalle Street, Suite 2200 · Chicago, IL 60602-3801 · 312-269-8000

Adam T. Berkoff · DLA Piper · 203 North LaSalle Street, Suite 1900 · Chicago, IL 60601-1293 · 312-368-4000

Roy L. Bernstein · Arnstein & Lehr · 120 South Riverside Plaza, Suite 1200 · Chicago, IL 60606 · 312-876-7100

Suzanne Bessette-Smith · Barack Ferrazzano Kirschbaum Perlman & Nagelberg · 200 West Madison Street, Suite 3900 · Chicago, IL 60606 · 312-984-3100

David J. Bryant · Katten Muchin Rosenman · 525 West Monroe Street · Chicago, IL 60661-3693 · 312-902-5200

Terrence E. Budny · Bell, Boyd & Lloyd · Three First National Plaza, Suite 3100 · 70 West Madison Street · Chicago, IL 60602 · 312-372-1121

Louis S. Cohen · DLA Piper · 203 North LaSalle Street, Suite 1900 · Chicago, IL 60601-1293 · 312-368-4000

Michael F. Csar · Drinker Biddle & Reath · 191 North Wacker Drive, Suite 3700 · Chicago, IL 60606-1698 · 312-569-1000

D. Albert Daspin · Daspin & Aument · 227 West Monroe Street, Suite 3500 · Chicago, IL 60606 · 312-258-1600

Steven R. Davidson · Sonnenschein Nath & Rosenthal · Sears Tower, Suite 7800 · 233 South Wacker Drive · Chicago, IL 60606-6404 · 312-876-8000

Charles L. Edwards · ⓴ · DLA Piper · 203 North LaSalle Street, Suite 1900 · Chicago, IL 60601-1293 · 312-368-4000

Steven Elrod · Holland & Knight · http://www.hklaw.com · 131 South Dearborn Street, 30th Floor · Chicago, IL 60603 · 312-263-3600

Fred I. Feinstein · ㉕ · McDermott Will & Emery · 227 West Monroe Street · Chicago, IL 60606-5096 · 312-372-2000

Dennis Ferrazzano · Barack Ferrazzano Kirschbaum Perlman & Nagelberg · 200 West Madison Street, Suite 3900 · Chicago, IL 60606 · 312-984-3100

Victor P. Filippini, Jr. · Holland & Knight · http://www.hklaw.com · 131 South Dearborn Street, 30th Floor · Chicago, IL 60603 · 312-263-3600

Paul E. Fisher · McGuireWoods · http://www.mcguirewoods.com · 77 West Wacker Drive, Suite 4100 · Chicago, IL 60601-1818 · 312-849-8100

H. James Fox · Quarles & Brady · http://www.quarles.com · Citigroup Center, Suite 3700 · 500 West Madison Street · Chicago, IL 60661-2511 · 312-715-5000

John J. Gearen · ❿ · Mayer Brown · 71 South Wacker Drive · Chicago, IL 60606 · 312-782-0600

David Glickstein · ㉕ · DLA Piper · 203 North LaSalle Street, Suite 1900 · Chicago, IL 60601-1293 · 312-368-4000

Joy S. Goldman · Meltzer, Purtill & Stelle · 300 South Wacker Drive, Suite 3500 · Chicago, IL 60606-6704 · 312-987-9900

Robert H. Goldman · DLA Piper · 203 North LaSalle Street, Suite 1900 · Chicago, IL 60601-1293 · 312-368-4000

Jack Guthman · Shefsky & Froelich · 111 East Wacker Drive, Suite 2800 · Chicago, IL 60601 · 312-527-4000

Wayne R. Hannah, Jr. · ㉕ · Sonnenschein Nath & Rosenthal · Sears Tower, Suite 7800 · 233 South Wacker Drive · Chicago, IL 60606-6404 · 312-876-8000

Mark Henning · Winston & Strawn · 35 West Wacker Drive · Chicago, IL 60601-9703 · 312-558-5600

Thomas C. Homburger · ㉕ · Bell, Boyd & Lloyd · Three First National Plaza, Suite 3100 · 70 West Madison Street · Chicago, IL 60602 · 312-372-1121

Paul Homer · ⓴ · DLA Piper · 203 North LaSalle Street, Suite 1900 · Chicago, IL 60601-1293 · 312-368-4000

Kenneth M. Jacobson · Katten Muchin Rosenman · 525 West Monroe Street · Chicago, IL 60661-3693 · 312-902-5200

Marc S. Joseph · Levenfeld Pearlstein · http://www.lplegal.com · Two North LaSalle Street, Suite 1300 · Chicago, IL 60602 · 312-346-8380

Howard E. Kane · ㉕ · DLA Piper · 203 North LaSalle Street, Suite 1900 · Chicago, IL 60601-1293 · 312-368-4000

Ivan P. Kane · Mayer Brown · 71 South Wacker Drive · Chicago, IL 60606 · 312-782-0600

Alvin C. Katz · Mayer Brown · 71 South Wacker Drive · Chicago, IL 60606 · 312-782-0600

Sandra Y. Kellman · DLA Piper · 203 North LaSalle Street, Suite 1900 · Chicago, IL 60601-1293 · 312-368-4000

Howard J. Kirschbaum · Barack Ferrazzano Kirschbaum Perlman & Nagelberg · 200 West Madison Street, Suite 3900 · Chicago, IL 60606 · 312-984-3100

Henry C. Krasnow · Krasnow Saunders Cornblath · The Boyce Building, Second Floor · 500 North Dearborn Street · Chicago, IL 60654 · 312-755-5700

Michael S. Kurtzon · ㉕ · Dykema · http://www.dykema.com · 10 South Wacker Drive, Suite 2300 · Chicago, IL 60606 · 312-876-1700

Robert C. Lee · Jones Day · 77 West Wacker Drive · Chicago, IL 60601-1692 · 312-782-3939

Eugene J. M. Leone · Pircher, Nichols & Meeks · 900 North Michigan Avenue, Suite 1050 · Chicago, IL 60611 · 312-915-3112

Anthony R. Licata · ❿ · Shefsky & Froelich · 111 East Wacker Drive, Suite 2800 · Chicago, IL 60601 · 312-527-4000

Bruce D. Loring · Holland & Knight · http://www.hklaw.com · 131 South Dearborn Street, 30th Floor · Chicago, IL 60603 · 312-263-3600

Nina B. Matis · ❿ · Katten Muchin Rosenman · 525 West Monroe Street · Chicago, IL 60661-3693 · 312-902-5200

Mark F. Mehlman · Sonnenschein Nath & Rosenthal · Sears Tower, Suite 7800 · 233 South Wacker Drive · Chicago, IL 60606-6404 · 312-876-8000

Paul E. Meyer · Mayer Brown · 71 South Wacker Drive · Chicago, IL 60606 · 312-782-0600

Lee I. Miller · DLA Piper · 203 North LaSalle Street, Suite 1900 · Chicago, IL 60601-1293 · 312-368-4000

Michael D. Miselman · Seyfarth Shaw · 131 South Dearborn Street, Suite 2400 · Chicago, IL 60603-5577 312-460-5000

Patrick G. Moran · ❿ · Sonnenschein Nath & Rosenthal · Sears Tower, Suite 7800 · 233 South Wacker Drive · Chicago, IL 60606-6404 · 312-876-8000

Portia Owen Morrison · DLA Piper · 203 North LaSalle Street, Suite 1900 · Chicago, IL 60601-1293 · 312-368-4000

Christopher D. Murtaugh · ❿ · Winston & Strawn · 35 West Wacker Drive · Chicago, IL 60601-9703 · 312-558-5600

Howard A. Nagelberg · Barack Ferrazzano Kirschbaum Perlman & Nagelberg · 200 West Madison Street, Suite 3900 · Chicago, IL 60606 · 312-984-3100

Theodore J. Novak · DLA Piper · 203 North LaSalle Street, Suite 1900 · Chicago, IL 60601-1293 · 312-368-4000

Keith D. Pascus · Katten Muchin Rosenman · 525 West Monroe Street · Chicago, IL 60661-3693 · 312-902-5200

Mark D. Pearlstein · Levenfeld Pearlstein · http://www.lplegal.com · Two North LaSalle Street, Suite 1300 · Chicago, IL 60602 · 312-346-8380

Daniel J. Perlman · Paul Hastings · 191 North Wacker Drive, 30th Floor · Chicago, IL 60606 · 312-499-6060

Gregory P. L. Pierce · Katten Muchin Rosenman · 525 West Monroe Street · Chicago, IL 60661-3693 · 312-902-5200

Harold B. Pomerantz · DLA Piper · 203 North LaSalle Street, Suite 1900 · Chicago, IL 60601-1293 · 312-368-4000

Benjamin J. Randall · ⑩ · Randall & Kenig · NBC Tower, Suite 2510 · 455 North Cityfront Plaza · Chicago, IL 60611 · 312-822-0800

David L. Reifman · DLA Piper · 203 North LaSalle Street, Suite 1900 · Chicago, IL 60601-1293 · 312-368-4000

Donald I. Resnick · Jenner & Block · http://www.jenner.com · 330 North Wabash Avenue · Chicago, IL 60611-7603 · 312-222-9350

Howard M. Richard · ⑩ · Katten Muchin Rosenman · 525 West Monroe Street · Chicago, IL 60661-3693 312-902-5200

James B. Rosenbloom · Goldberg, Kohn, Bell, Black, Rosenbloom & Moritz · 55 East Monroe Street, Suite 3300 · Chicago, IL 60603-5792 · 312-201-4000

Joel D. Rubin · ⑩ · Seyfarth Shaw · 131 South Dearborn Street, Suite 2400 · Chicago, IL 60603-5577 · 312-460-5000

Paul D. Rudnick · ㉕ · DLA Piper · 203 North LaSalle Street, Suite 1900 · Chicago, IL 60601-1293 · 312-368-4000

Peter A. Sarasek · Quarles & Brady · http://www.quarles.com · Citigroup Center, Suite 3700 · 500 West Madison Street · Chicago, IL 60661-2511 · 312-715-5000

Eric M. Schiller · Sonnenschein Nath & Rosenthal · Sears Tower, Suite 7800 · 233 South Wacker Drive · Chicago, IL 60606-6404 · 312-876-8000

Charles E. Schrank · Sidley Austin · One South Dearborn Street · Chicago, IL 60603 · 312-853-7000

Michael F. Sexton · Dykema · http://www.dykema.com · 10 South Wacker Drive, Suite 2300 · Chicago, IL 60606 · 312-876-1700

Gerald J. Sherman · Sonnenschein Nath & Rosenthal · Sears Tower, Suite 7800 · 233 South Wacker Drive · Chicago, IL 60606-6404 · 312-876-8000

David B. Sickle · DLA Piper · 203 North LaSalle Street, Suite 1900 · Chicago, IL 60601-1293 · 312-368-4000

Mark C. Simon · Katten Muchin Rosenman · 525 West Monroe Street · Chicago, IL 60661-3693 · 312-902-5200

Andrew D. Small · Katten Muchin Rosenman · 525 West Monroe Street · Chicago, IL 60661-3693 · 312-902-5200

Lee M. Smolen · Sidley Austin · One South Dearborn Street · Chicago, IL 60603 · 312-853-7000

Marcia W. Sullivan · Katten Muchin Rosenman · 525 West Monroe Street · Chicago, IL 60661-3693 · 312-902-5200

Stephen G. Tomlinson · Kirkland & Ellis · 200 East Randolph Drive · Chicago, IL 60601-6636 · 312-861-2000

Michael J. Tuchman · Levenfeld Pearlstein · http://www.lplegal.com · Two North LaSalle Street, Suite 1300 · Chicago, IL 60602 · 312-346-8380

Jeffrey A. Usow · Mayer Brown · 71 South Wacker Drive · Chicago, IL 60606 · 312-782-0600

Raymond J. Werner · Arnstein & Lehr · 120 South Riverside Plaza, Suite 1200 · Chicago, IL 60606 · 312-876-7100

Edward E. Wicks · Perkins Coie · http://www.perkinscoie.com · 131 South Dearborn Street, Suite 1700 · Chicago, IL 60603-5559 · 312-324-8400

Theodore I. Yi · DLA Piper · 203 North LaSalle Street, Suite 1900 · Chicago, IL 60601-1293 · 312-368-4000

Mark D. Yurà · DLA Piper · 203 North LaSalle Street, Suite 1900 · Chicago, IL 60601-1293 · 312-368-4000

Schaumburg

Brian Meltzer · ⑳ · Meltzer, Purtill & Stelle · 1515 East Woodfield Road, Second Floor · Schaumburg, IL 60173 · 847-330-2400

Wheaton

Arthur E. Pape · ⑩ · The Pape Law Firm · Building 3A, Suite 102 · 100 West Roosevelt Road · Wheaton, IL 60187 · 630-933-9300

SECURITIES LAW

Chicago

Edward S. Best · Mayer Brown · 71 South Wacker Drive · Chicago, IL 60606 · 312-782-0600

Dewey B. Crawford · ⑳ · Foley & Lardner · 321 North Clark Street, Suite 2800 · Chicago, IL 60654 · 312-832-4500

Robert E. Curley · Mayer Brown · 71 South Wacker Drive · Chicago, IL 60606 · 312-782-0600

Carter W. Emerson · ⑩ · Kirkland & Ellis · 200 East Randolph Drive · Chicago, IL 60601-6636 · 312-861-2000

Steven J. Gavin · Winston & Strawn · 35 West Wacker Drive · Chicago, IL 60601-9703 · 312-558-5600

Mark D. Gerstein · Latham & Watkins · Sears Tower, Suite 5800 · 233 South Wacker Drive · Chicago, IL 60606-6401 · 312-876-7700

Stuart L. Goodman · 20 · Schiff Hardin · Sears Tower, Suite 6600 · 233 South Wacker Drive · Chicago, IL 60606-6473 · 312-258-5500

Joseph P. Gromacki · Jenner & Block · http://www.jenner.com · 330 North Wabash Avenue · Chicago, IL 60611-7603 · 312-222-9350

Alton B. Harris · Ungaretti & Harris · Three First National Plaza, Suite 3500 · 70 West Madison Street · Chicago, IL 60602-4283 · 312-977-4400

Robert M. Hayward · Kirkland & Ellis · 200 East Randolph Drive · Chicago, IL 60601-6636 · 312-861-2000

Michael L. Hermsen · Mayer Brown · 71 South Wacker Drive · Chicago, IL 60606 · 312-782-0600

James J. Junewicz · Winston & Strawn · 35 West Wacker Drive · Chicago, IL 60601-9703 · 312-558-5600

Jonathan A. Koff · Chapman and Cutler · 111 West Monroe Street · Chicago, IL 60603-4080 · 312-845-3000

Cary J. Malkin · Mayer Brown · 71 South Wacker Drive · Chicago, IL 60606 · 312-782-0600

Robert J. Minkus · Schiff Hardin · Sears Tower, Suite 6600 · 233 South Wacker Drive · Chicago, IL 60606-6473 · 312-258-5500

Thomas J. Murphy · McDermott Will & Emery · 227 West Monroe Street · Chicago, IL 60606-5096 · 312-372-2000

Dennis M. Myers · Kirkland & Ellis · 200 East Randolph Drive · Chicago, IL 60601-6636 · 312-861-2000

Philip J. Niehoff · Mayer Brown · 71 South Wacker Drive · Chicago, IL 60606 · 312-782-0600

John J. Sabl · Sidley Austin · One South Dearborn Street · Chicago, IL 60603 · 312-853-7000

Lowell E. Sachnoff · 25 · Reed Smith · 10 South Wacker Drive, 40th Floor · Chicago, IL 60606-7507 · 312-207-1000

John R. Sagan · Mayer Brown · 71 South Wacker Drive · Chicago, IL 60606 · 312-782-0600

John R. Schmidt · Mayer Brown · 71 South Wacker Drive · Chicago, IL 60606 · 312-782-0600

Edward J. Schneidman · Mayer Brown · 71 South Wacker Drive · Chicago, IL 60606 · 312-782-0600

David A. Schuette · Mayer Brown · 71 South Wacker Drive · Chicago, IL 60606 · 312-782-0600

Paul W. Theiss · Mayer Brown · 71 South Wacker Drive · Chicago, IL 60606 · 312-782-0600

Bruce A. Toth · Winston & Strawn · 35 West Wacker Drive · Chicago, IL 60601-9703 · 312-558-5600

Paul B. Uhlenhop · 10 · Lawrence, Kamin, Saunders & Uhlenhop · 300 South Wacker Drive, Suite 500 · Chicago, IL 60606 · 312-372-1947

H. Kurt von Moltke · Kirkland & Ellis · 200 East Randolph Drive · Chicago, IL 60601-6636 · 312-861-2000

Robert F. Wall · 10 · Winston & Strawn · 35 West Wacker Drive · Chicago, IL 60601-9703 · 312-558-5600

Herbert S. Wander · ㉕ · Katten Muchin Rosenman · 525 West Monroe Street · Chicago, IL 60661-3693 · 312-902-5200

Michael Wise · Lawrence, Kamin, Saunders & Uhlenhop · 300 South Wacker Drive, Suite 500 · Chicago, IL 60606 · 312-372-1947

SPORTS LAW

Chicago

Lee N. Abrams · Mayer Brown · 71 South Wacker Drive · Chicago, IL 60606 · 312-782-0600

Julian C. D'Esposito, Jr. · Mayer Brown · 71 South Wacker Drive · Chicago, IL 60606 · 312-782-0600

Daniel W. Luther · Mayer Brown · 71 South Wacker Drive · Chicago, IL 60606 · 312-782-0600

John R. McCambridge · Grippo & Elden · 111 South Wacker Drive · Chicago, IL 60606 · 312-704-7700

STRUCTURED FINANCE LAW

Chicago

Thomas W. Albrecht · Sidley Austin · One South Dearborn Street · Chicago, IL 60603 · 312-853-7000

Thomas P. Brown · Sidley Austin · One South Dearborn Street · Chicago, IL 60603 · 312-853-7000

Willis R. Buck, Jr. · Sidley Austin · One South Dearborn Street · Chicago, IL 60603 · 312-853-7000

Mary C. Fontaine · Mayer Brown · 71 South Wacker Drive · Chicago, IL 60606 · 312-782-0600

Dean N. Gerber · Vedder Price · 222 North LaSalle Street · Chicago, IL 60601-1003 · 312-609-7500

Carol A. Hitselberger · Mayer Brown · 71 South Wacker Drive · Chicago, IL 60606 · 312-782-0600

Kevin J. Hochberg · Sidley Austin · One South Dearborn Street · Chicago, IL 60603 · 312-853-7000

Robert F. Hugi · Mayer Brown · 71 South Wacker Drive · Chicago, IL 60606 · 312-782-0600

Stuart M. Litwin · Mayer Brown · 71 South Wacker Drive · Chicago, IL 60606 · 312-782-0600

Reid A. Mandel · Katten Muchin Rosenman · 525 West Monroe Street · Chicago, IL 60661-3693 · 312-902-5200

Kenneth P. Morrison · Kirkland & Ellis · 200 East Randolph Drive · Chicago, IL 60601-6636 · 312-861-2000

George A. Pecoulas · Mayer Brown · 71 South Wacker Drive · Chicago, IL 60606 · 312-782-0600

Randall J. Rademaker · Skadden, Arps, Slate, Meagher & Flom · 333 West Wacker Drive · Chicago, IL 60606 · 312-407-0700

Gary B. Stern · Sidley Austin · One South Dearborn Street · Chicago, IL 60603 · 312-853-7000

TAX LAW

Chicago

Suresh T. Advani · Sidley Austin · One South Dearborn Street · Chicago, IL 60603 · 312-853-7000

Sheldon I. Banoff · ⑳ · Katten Muchin Rosenman · 525 West Monroe Street · Chicago, IL 60661-3693 · 312-902-5200

James R. Barry · Mayer Brown · 71 South Wacker Drive · Chicago, IL 60606 · 312-782-0600

John A. Biek · Neal, Gerber & Eisenberg · http://www.ngelaw.com · Two North LaSalle Street, Suite 2200 · Chicago, IL 60602-3801 · 312-269-8000

Thomas C. Borders · McDermott Will & Emery · 227 West Monroe Street · Chicago, IL 60606-5096 · 312-372-2000

Thomas W. Bottomlee · Mayer Brown · 71 South Wacker Drive · Chicago, IL 60606 · 312-782-0600

Stephen S. Bowen · ⑳ · Latham & Watkins · Sears Tower, Suite 5800 · 233 South Wacker Drive · Chicago, IL 60606-6401 · 312-876-7700

Gary S. Colton, Jr. · Mayer Brown · 71 South Wacker Drive · Chicago, IL 60606 · 312-782-0600

George W. Craven · Mayer Brown · 71 South Wacker Drive · Chicago, IL 60606 · 312-782-0600

Robert J. Cunningham · Baker & McKenzie · One Prudential Plaza · 130 East Randolph Drive · Chicago, IL 60601 · 312-861-8000

Stuart Duhl · Harrison & Held · 333 West Wacker Drive, Suite 1700 · Chicago, IL 60606-1247 · 312-332-1111

Thomas C. Durham · Mayer Brown · 71 South Wacker Drive · Chicago, IL 60606 · 312-782-0600

Marshall E. Eisenberg · ⑩ · Neal, Gerber & Eisenberg · http://www.ngelaw.com · Two North LaSalle Street, Suite 2200 · Chicago, IL 60602-3801 · 312-269-8000

Glenn E. Ferencz · ⑩ · Drinker Biddle & Reath · 191 North Wacker Drive, Suite 3700 · Chicago, IL 60606-1698 · 312-569-1000

Louis S. Freeman · ㉕ · Skadden, Arps, Slate, Meagher & Flom · 333 West Wacker Drive · Chicago, IL 60606 · 312-407-0700

Steven G. Frost · Chapman and Cutler · 111 West Monroe Street · Chicago, IL 60603-4080 · 312-845-3000

Bruce L. Gelman · Kirkland & Ellis · 200 East Randolph Drive · Chicago, IL 60601-6636 · 312-861-2000

Thomas A. Geraghty · Kirkland & Ellis · 200 East Randolph Drive · Chicago, IL 60601-6636 · 312-861-2000

Frederic L. Hahn · ⑩ · Mayer Brown · 71 South Wacker Drive · Chicago, IL 60606 · 312-782-0600

Kenneth L. Harris · Neal, Gerber & Eisenberg · http://www.ngelaw.com · Two North LaSalle Street, Suite 2200 · Chicago, IL 60602-3801 · 312-269-8000

Roger J. Jones · Latham & Watkins · Sears Tower, Suite 5800 · 233 South Wacker Drive · Chicago, IL 60606-6401 · 312-876-7700

Jared Kaplan · ㉕ · McDermott Will & Emery · 227 West Monroe Street · Chicago, IL 60606-5096 · 312-372-2000

Anne Marie Konopack · Mayer Brown · 71 South Wacker Drive · Chicago, IL 60606 · 312-782-0600

Andrea S. Kramer · McDermott Will & Emery · 227 West Monroe Street · Chicago, IL 60606-5096 · 312-372-2000

Andre LeDuc · Skadden, Arps, Slate, Meagher & Flom · 333 West Wacker Drive · Chicago, IL 60606 · 312-407-0700

Gregg D. Lemein · Baker & McKenzie · One Prudential Plaza · 130 East Randolph Drive · Chicago, IL 60601 · 312-861-8000

Jack S. Levin · ㉕ · Kirkland & Ellis · 200 East Randolph Drive · Chicago, IL 60601-6636 · 312-861-2000

William A. Levy · Mayer Brown · 71 South Wacker Drive · Chicago, IL 60606 · 312-782-0600

Richard M. Lipton · ⑩ · Baker & McKenzie · One Prudential Plaza · 130 East Randolph Drive · Chicago, IL 60601 · 312-861-8000

George A. Luscombe II · ⑩ · Mayer Brown · 71 South Wacker Drive · Chicago, IL 60606 · 312-782-0600

James M. Lynch · ⑩ · Winston & Strawn · 35 West Wacker Drive · Chicago, IL 60601-9703 · 312-558-5600

Todd F. Maynes · Kirkland & Ellis · 200 East Randolph Drive · Chicago, IL 60601-6636 · 312-861-2000

John B. Palmer · Foley & Lardner · 321 North Clark Street, Suite 2800 · Chicago, IL 60654 · 312-832-4500

John D. Rayis · Skadden, Arps, Slate, Meagher & Flom · 333 West Wacker Drive · Chicago, IL 60606 · 312-407-0700

Donald E. Rocap · ⑩ · Kirkland & Ellis · 200 East Randolph Drive · Chicago, IL 60601-6636 · 312-861-2000

William A. Schmalzl · Mayer Brown · 71 South Wacker Drive · Chicago, IL 60606 · 312-782-0600

Jeffrey T. Sheffield · ⑩ · Kirkland & Ellis · 200 East Randolph Drive · Chicago, IL 60601-6636 · 312-861-2000

Timothy C. Sherck · ⑩ · Mayer Brown · 71 South Wacker Drive · Chicago, IL 60606 · 312-782-0600

Sharp Sorensen · Sidley Austin · One South Dearborn Street · Chicago, IL 60603 · 312-853-7000

Thomas M. Stephens · Sonnenschein Nath & Rosenthal · Sears Tower, Suite 7800 · 233 South Wacker Drive · Chicago, IL 60606-6404 · 312-876-8000

B. Alan Van Dyke · Mayer Brown · 71 South Wacker Drive · Chicago, IL 60606 · 312-782-0600

Keith E. Villmow · Kirkland & Ellis · 200 East Randolph Drive · Chicago, IL 60601-6636 · 312-861-2000

Louis J. Weber III · Winston & Strawn · 35 West Wacker Drive · Chicago, IL 60601-9703 · 312-558-5600

William R. Welke · ⑩ · Kirkland & Ellis · 200 East Randolph Drive · Chicago, IL 60601-6636 · 312-861-2000

Raymond P. Wexler · ⑩ · Kirkland & Ellis · 200 East Randolph Drive · Chicago, IL 60601-6636 · 312-861-2000

Joel V. Williamson · ⑩ · Mayer Brown · 71 South Wacker Drive · Chicago, IL 60606 · 312-782-0600

Lowell D. Yoder · McDermott Will & Emery · 227 West Monroe Street · Chicago, IL 60606-5096 · 312-372-2000

Jay H. Zimbler · Sidley Austin · One South Dearborn Street · Chicago, IL 60603 · 312-853-7000

Farmer City

William A. Peithmann · ⑩ · The Peithmann Law Office · 111 South Main Street · P.O. Box 228 · Farmer City, IL 61842 · 309-928-3390

TECHNOLOGY LAW

Chicago

J. Ross Docksey · Sonnenschein Nath & Rosenthal · Sears Tower, Suite 7800 · 233 South Wacker Drive · Chicago, IL 60606-6404 · 312-876-8000

Rebecca S. Eisner · Mayer Brown · 71 South Wacker Drive · Chicago, IL 60606 · 312-782-0600

Todd H. Flaming · Schopf & Weiss · One South Wacker Drive, 28th Floor · Chicago, IL 60606-4617 · 312-701-9300

Rosemary Gullikson · Sonnenschein Nath & Rosenthal · Sears Tower, Suite 7800 · 233 South Wacker Drive · Chicago, IL 60606-6404 · 312-876-8000

Marcelo Halpern · Latham & Watkins · Sears Tower, Suite 5800 · 233 South Wacker Drive · Chicago, IL 60606-6401 · 312-876-7700

Neil S. Hirshman · Kirkland & Ellis · 200 East Randolph Drive · Chicago, IL 60601-6636 · 312-861-2000

Gregg Kirchhoefer · Kirkland & Ellis · 200 East Randolph Drive · Chicago, IL 60601-6636 · 312-861-2000

Michael S. Mensik · Baker & McKenzie · One Prudential Plaza · 130 East Randolph Drive · Chicago, IL 60601 · 312-861-8000

Brad L. Peterson · Mayer Brown · 71 South Wacker Drive · Chicago, IL 60606 · 312-782-0600

Paul J. N. Roy · Mayer Brown · 71 South Wacker Drive · Chicago, IL 60606 · 312-782-0600

TRUSTS AND ESTATES

Chicago

Thomas W. Abendroth · Schiff Hardin · Sears Tower, Suite 6600 · 233 South Wacker Drive · Chicago, IL 60606-6473 · 312-258-5500

Christine A. Albright · Winston & Strawn · 35 West Wacker Drive · Chicago, IL 60601-9703 · 312-558-5600

David A. Baker · McDermott Will & Emery · 227 West Monroe Street · Chicago, IL 60606-5096 · 312-372-2000

Susan T. Bart · Sidley Austin · One South Dearborn Street · Chicago, IL 60603 · 312-853-7000

Larry D. Berning · ㉕ · Sidley Austin · One South Dearborn Street · Chicago, IL 60603 · 312-853-7000

Scott Bieber · Schiff Hardin · Sears Tower, Suite 6600 · 233 South Wacker Drive · Chicago, IL 60606-6473 · 312-258-5500

John T. Brooks · Foley & Lardner · 321 North Clark Street, Suite 2800 · Chicago, IL 60654 · 312-832-4500

Richard A. Campbell · Mayer Brown · 71 South Wacker Drive · Chicago, IL 60606 · 312-782-0600

James A. Casey · Mayer Brown · 71 South Wacker Drive · Chicago, IL 60606 · 312-782-0600

Richard L. Dees · ⑩ · McDermott Will & Emery · 227 West Monroe Street · Chicago, IL 60606-5096 · 312-372-2000

John D. English · Ungaretti & Harris · Three First National Plaza, Suite 3500 · 70 West Madison Street · Chicago, IL 60602-4283 · 312-977-4400

Quin R. Frazer · Drinker Biddle & Reath · 191 North Wacker Drive, Suite 3700 · Chicago, IL 60606-1698 · 312-569-1000

Andrew R. Gelman · Holland & Knight · http://www.hklaw.com · 131 South Dearborn Street, 30th Floor Chicago, IL 60603 · 312-263-3600

Donald A. Gillies · ㉕ · Holland & Knight · http://www.hklaw.com · 131 South Dearborn Street, 30th Floor · Chicago, IL 60603 · 312-263-3600

David A. Handler · Kirkland & Ellis · 200 East Randolph Drive · Chicago, IL 60601-6636 · 312-861-2000

Carol A. Harrington · ⑩ · McDermott Will & Emery · 227 West Monroe Street · Chicago, IL 60606-5096 · 312-372-2000

Louis S. Harrison · ⑩ · Harrison & Held · 333 West Wacker Drive, Suite 1700 · Chicago, IL 60606-1247 312-332-1111

Michael O. Hartz · Katten Muchin Rosenman · 525 West Monroe Street · Chicago, IL 60661-3693 · 312-902-5200

Quentin G. Heisler, Jr. · ⑩ · McDermott Will & Emery · 227 West Monroe Street · Chicago, IL 60606-5096 · 312-372-2000

James R. Hellige · Foley & Lardner · 321 North Clark Street, Suite 2800 · Chicago, IL 60654 · 312-832-4500

David A. Herpe · ⑩ · McDermott Will & Emery · 227 West Monroe Street · Chicago, IL 60606-5096 · 312-372-2000

David R. Hodgman · Schiff Hardin · Sears Tower, Suite 6600 · 233 South Wacker Drive · Chicago, IL 60606-6473 · 312-258-5500

Kirk A. Hoopingarner · Wildman, Harrold, Allen & Dixon · 225 West Wacker Drive, Suite 3000 · Chicago, IL 60606 · 312-201-2000

Richard M. Horwood · Horwood, Marcus & Berk · 180 North LaSalle Street, Suite 3700 · Chicago, IL 60601 · 312-606-3200

Neil T. Kawashima · McDermott Will & Emery · 227 West Monroe Street · Chicago, IL 60606-5096 · 312-372-2000

Richard A. Lang · ⑩ · McDermott Will & Emery · 227 West Monroe Street · Chicago, IL 60606-5096 · 312-372-2000

Daniel W. Luther · Mayer Brown · 71 South Wacker Drive · Chicago, IL 60606 · 312-782-0600

Karen K. MacKay · ⑩ · Burke, Warren, MacKay & Serritella · 330 North Wabash Avenue, 22nd Floor · Chicago, IL 60611-3607 · 312-840-7000

Howard M. McCue III · ㉕ · Mayer Brown · 71 South Wacker Drive · Chicago, IL 60606 · 312-782-0600

Judith W. McCue · ⑩ · McDermott Will & Emery · 227 West Monroe Street · Chicago, IL 60606-5096 · 312-372-2000

Donna E. Morgan · Mayer Brown · 71 South Wacker Drive · Chicago, IL 60606 · 312-782-0600

Michael K. Moyers · Levin & Schreder · 120 North LaSalle Street, 38th Floor · Chicago, IL 60602 · 312-332-6300

Franklin W. Nitikman · ⑳ · McDermott Will & Emery · 227 West Monroe Street · Chicago, IL 60606-5096 · 312-372-2000

Lawrence I. Richman · Neal, Gerber & Eisenberg · http://www.ngelaw.com · Two North LaSalle Street, Suite 2200 · Chicago, IL 60602-3801 · 312-269-8000

Robert A. Romanoff · Levenfeld Pearlstein · http://www.lplegal.com · Two North LaSalle Street, Suite 1300 · Chicago, IL 60602 · 312-346-8380

Joseph O. Rubinelli, Jr. · ⑩ · McDermott Will & Emery · 227 West Monroe Street · Chicago, IL 60606-5096 · 312-372-2000

Bernard T. Wall · ⑩ · Harrison & Held · 333 West Wacker Drive, Suite 1700 · Chicago, IL 60606-1247 · 312-332-1111

William C. Weinsheimer · ⑳ · Foley & Lardner · 321 North Clark Street, Suite 2800 · Chicago, IL 60654 312-832-4500

Lyman W. Welch · ⑩ · Sidley Austin · One South Dearborn Street · Chicago, IL 60603 · 312-853-7000

Farmer City

William A. Peithmann · ⑩ · The Peithmann Law Office · 111 South Main Street · P.O. Box 228 · Farmer City, IL 61842 · 309-928-3390

Peoria

Jerold I. Horn · ㉕ · Jerold I. Horn · 124 Southwest Adams Street, Suite 515 · Peoria, IL 61602-1320 · 309-676-2778

Springfield

James M. Lestikow · Hinshaw & Culbertson · http://www.hinshawlaw.com · 400 South Ninth Street, Suite 200 · Springfield, IL 62701 · 217-528-7375

Sterling

Philip H. Ward · Ward, Murray, Pace & Johnson · 202 East Fifth Street · P.O. Box 400 · Sterling, IL 61081 · 815-625-8200

VENTURE CAPITAL LAW

Chicago

Laurence R. Bronska · DLA Piper · 203 North LaSalle Street, Suite 1900 · Chicago, IL 60601-1293 · 312-368-4000

Kenneth M. Crane · Perkins Coie · http://www.perkinscoie.com · 131 South Dearborn Street, Suite 1700 · Chicago, IL 60603-5559 · 312-324-8400

Jack S. Levin · [25] · Kirkland & Ellis · 200 East Randolph Drive · Chicago, IL 60601-6636 · 312-861-2000

Andrew McCune · DLA Piper · 203 North LaSalle Street, Suite 1900 · Chicago, IL 60601-1293 · 312-368-4000

Jonathan D. Wasserman · Neal, Gerber & Eisenberg · http://www.ngelaw.com · Two North LaSalle Street, Suite 2200 · Chicago, IL 60602-3801 · 312-269-8000

WHITE-COLLAR CRIMINAL DEFENSE

Chicago

Jonathan Bunge · Kirkland & Ellis · 200 East Randolph Drive · Chicago, IL 60601-6636 · 312-861-2000

Jeffrey D. Colman · Jenner & Block · http://www.jenner.com · 330 North Wabash Avenue · Chicago, IL 60611-7603 · 312-222-9350

Vincent J. Connelly · [10] · Mayer Brown · 71 South Wacker Drive · Chicago, IL 60606 · 312-782-0600

Brian L. Crowe · Shefsky & Froelich · 111 East Wacker Drive, Suite 2800 · Chicago, IL 60601 · 312-527-4000

Thomas D. Decker · [25] · Thomas D. Decker and Associates · 321 South Plymouth Court, Suite 1500 · Chicago, IL 60604 · 312-922-4180

Joseph J. Duffy · [10] · Stetler & Duffy · 11 South LaSalle Street, Suite 1200 · Chicago, IL 60603 · 312-338-0200

Tyrone C. Fahner · [10] · Mayer Brown · 71 South Wacker Drive · Chicago, IL 60606 · 312-782-0600

James R. Ferguson · Mayer Brown · 71 South Wacker Drive · Chicago, IL 60606 · 312-782-0600

Chris C. Gair · Jenner & Block · http://www.jenner.com · 330 North Wabash Avenue · Chicago, IL 60611-7603 · 312-222-9350

Edward M. Genson · [20] · Genson & Gillespie · 53 West Jackson Boulevard, Suite 1420 · Chicago, IL 60604 · 312-726-9015

Cynthia Giacchetti · Law Offices of Cynthia Giacchetti · 53 West Jackson Boulevard, Suite 1460 · Chicago, IL 60604 · 312-939-6440

Terrence P. Gillespie · ⑩ · Genson & Gillespie · 53 West Jackson Boulevard, Suite 1420 · Chicago, IL 60604 · 312-726-9015

Ted S. Helwig · Katten Muchin Rosenman · 525 West Monroe Street · Chicago, IL 60661-3693 · 312-902-5200

Steven M. Kowal · Bell, Boyd & Lloyd · Three First National Plaza, Suite 3100 · 70 West Madison Street Chicago, IL 60602 · 312-372-1121

Scott R. Lassar · Sidley Austin · One South Dearborn Street · Chicago, IL 60603 · 312-853-7000

Bradley E. Lerman · Winston & Strawn · 35 West Wacker Drive · Chicago, IL 60601-9703 · 312-558-5600

William Joseph Linklater · ⑩ · Baker & McKenzie · One Prudential Plaza · 130 East Randolph Drive · Chicago, IL 60601 · 312-861-8000

Marc W. Martin · Marc W. Martin · 53 West Jackson Boulevard, Suite 1420 · Chicago, IL 60604 · 312-408-1111

Royal B. Martin · ⑳ · Martin, Brown & Sullivan · 321 South Plymouth Court, 10th Floor · Chicago, IL 60604 · 312-360-5000

William J. Martin · ㉕ · William J. Martin · 6832 West North Avenue, Suite 4-B · Chicago, IL 60707 · 773-622-5350

Michael D. Monico · ⑩ · Monico, Pavich & Spevack · 20 South Clark Street, Suite 700 · Chicago, IL 60603 · 312-782-8500

James S. Montana, Jr. · Vedder Price · 222 North LaSalle Street · Chicago, IL 60601-1003 · 312-609-7500

Gordon B. Nash, Jr. · Drinker Biddle & Reath · 191 North Wacker Drive, Suite 3700 · Chicago, IL 60606-1698 · 312-569-1000

Michael B. Nash · ㉕ · Michael B. Nash · 53 West Jackson Boulevard, Suite 620 · Chicago, IL 60604 · 312-236-8788

Daniel E. Reidy · ⑩ · Jones Day · 77 West Wacker Drive · Chicago, IL 60601-1692 · 312-782-3939

James G. Richmond · Greenberg Traurig · http://www.gtlaw.com · 77 West Wacker Drive, Suite 2500 · Chicago, IL 60601 · 312-456-8400

Leigh D. Roadman · Martin, Brown & Sullivan · 321 South Plymouth Court, 10th Floor · Chicago, IL 60604 · 312-360-5000

David S. Rosenbloom · McDermott Will & Emery · 227 West Monroe Street · Chicago, IL 60606-5096 · 312-372-2000

Ronald S. Safer · Schiff Hardin · Sears Tower, Suite 6600 · 233 South Wacker Drive · Chicago, IL 60606-6473 · 312-258-5500

Charles B. Sklarsky · Jenner & Block · http://www.jenner.com · 330 North Wabash Avenue · Chicago, IL 60611-7603 · 312-222-9350

Julian Solotorovsky · Kelley Drye & Warren · 333 West Wacker Drive, 26th Floor · Chicago, IL 60606 · 312-857-7070

Robert M. Stephenson · ⑳ · Locke Lord Bissell & Liddell · 111 South Wacker Drive · Chicago, IL 60606-4410 · 312-443-0700

David J. Stetler · Stetler & Duffy · 11 South LaSalle Street, Suite 1200 · Chicago, IL 60603 · 312-338-0200

James R. Streicker · ⑳ · Cotsirilos, Tighe & Streicker · 33 North Dearborn Street, Suite 600 · Chicago, IL 60602-3104 · 312-263-0345

Thomas P. Sullivan · ㉕ · Jenner & Block · http://www.jenner.com · 330 North Wabash Avenue · Chicago, IL 60611-7603 · 312-222-9350

Anton R. Valukas · ㉕ · Jenner & Block · http://www.jenner.com · 330 North Wabash Avenue · Chicago, IL 60611-7603 · 312-222-9350

Dan K. Webb · ⑳ · Winston & Strawn · 35 West Wacker Drive · Chicago, IL 60601-9703 · 312-558-5600

Sheldon T. Zenner · ⑩ · Katten Muchin Rosenman · 525 West Monroe Street · Chicago, IL 60661-3693 · 312-902-5200

Edwardsville

J. William Lucco · Lucco Brown Threlkeld Dawson · 224 St. Louis Street · Edwardsville, IL 62025-1906 618-656-2321

Springfield

Michael B. Metnick · Metnick, Cherry, Frazier, Sabin & Perrin · Myers Building, Suite 200 · One West Old State Capitol Plaza · P.O. Box 12140 · Springfield, IL 62791 · 217-753-4242

J. William Roberts · Hinshaw & Culbertson · http://www.hinshawlaw.com · 400 South Ninth Street, Suite 200 · Springfield, IL 62701 · 217-528-7375

WORKERS' COMPENSATION LAW

Aurora

Kim Edward Presbrey · Presbrey & Associates · http://www.presbrey.com · 821 West Galena Boulevard · Aurora, IL 60506-3749 · 630-264-7300

Chicago

Gregory E. Ahern · Kane Doy & Harrington · One North LaSalle Street, Suite 1825 · Chicago, IL 60602 312-236-7788

Richard Aleksy · Corti, Aleksy & Castaneda · http://www.workcompguys.com · 180 North LaSalle Street, Suite 2910 · Chicago, IL 60601-2501 · 312-782-8372

Philip A. Bareck · Katz, Friedman, Eagle, Eisenstein & Johnson · 77 West Washington Street, 20th Floor Chicago, IL 60602 · 312-263-6330

John T. Bowman · Bowman & Corday · 20 North Clark Street, Suite 500 · Chicago, IL 60602 · 312-606-9675

Michael J. Brennan · Kane Doy & Harrington · One North LaSalle Street, Suite 1825 · Chicago, IL 60602 · 312-236-7788

Douglas A. Colby · Anesi, Ozmon, Rodin, Novak & Kohen · http://www.anesilaw.com · 161 North Clark Street, 21st Floor · Chicago, IL 60601 · 312-372-3822

Peter D. Corti · ⑩ · Corti, Aleksy & Castaneda · http://www.workcompguys.com · 180 North LaSalle Street, Suite 2910 · Chicago, IL 60601-2501 · 312-782-8372

George J. Cullen · ⑩ · Cullen, Haskins, Nicholson & Menchetti · 35 East Wacker Drive · Chicago, IL 60601-2201 · 312-332-2545

Frank I. Gaughan · Steven B Salk & Associates · 150 North Wacker Drive, Suite 2570 · Chicago, IL 60606 · 312-782-3529

Charles G. Haskins, Jr. · ⑩ · Cullen, Haskins, Nicholson & Menchetti · 35 East Wacker Drive · Chicago, IL 60601-2201 · 312-332-2545

Richard K. Johnson · Katz, Friedman, Eagle, Eisenstein & Johnson · 77 West Washington Street, 20th Floor · Chicago, IL 60602 · 312-263-6330

William A. Lowry · Nyhan, Pfister, Bambrick, Kinzie & Lowry · 20 North Clark Street, Suite 1000 · Chicago, IL 60602 · 312-629-9800

Robert E. Maciorowski · Maciorowski, Sackmann & Ulrich · 10 South Riverside Plaza, Suite 2290 · Chicago, IL 60606 · 312-627-0600

David B. Menchetti · Cullen, Haskins, Nicholson & Menchetti · 35 East Wacker Drive · Chicago, IL 60601-2201 · 312-332-2545

Patrick B. Nicholson · Cullen, Haskins, Nicholson & Menchetti · 35 East Wacker Drive · Chicago, IL 60601-2201 · 312-332-2545

Kenneth D. Peters · ⑩ · Cronin, Peters & Cook · 221 North LaSalle Street, Suite 1454 · Chicago, IL 60601 · 312-372-1872

Arnold G. Rubin · ⑩ · Arnold G. Rubin · 100 West Monroe Street, Suite 1100 · Chicago, IL 60603 · 312-899-8333

Scott Schreiber · Garofalo, Schreiber, Hart & Storm · 55 West Wacker Drive, Tenth Floor · Chicago, IL 60601 · 312-670-2000

Ross Tyrrell · ⑩ · Ross Tyrrell · 111 West Washington Street, Suite 1120 · Chicago, IL 60602 · 312-726-5322

Frank J. Wiedner · ⑩ · Wiedner & McAuliffe · One North Franklin Street, Suite 1900 · Chicago, IL 60606 · 312-855-1105

Mark C. Wiedner · Wiedner & McAuliffe · One North Franklin Street, Suite 1900 · Chicago, IL 60606 · 312-855-1105

Paul W. Wiedner · ⑩ · Wiedner & McAuliffe · One North Franklin Street, Suite 1900 · Chicago, IL 60606 · 312-855-1105

Mark D. Wilkening · Wiedner & McAuliffe · One North Franklin Street, Suite 1900 · Chicago, IL 60606 312-855-1105

East St. Louis

Michael H. Korein · Glass & Korein · 412 Missouri Avenue · East St. Louis, IL 62201 · 618-274-0434

John L. Shepherd · Williams & McCarthy · 120 West State Street, Fourth Floor · P.O. Box 219 · Rockford, IL 61105-0219 · 815-987-8900

INDIANA

ADMINISTRATIVE LAW

Indianapolis

Charles B. Baldwin · Ogletree Deakins · http://www.ogletreedeakins.com · 111 Monument Circle, Suite 4600 · Indianapolis, IN 46204 · 317-916-1300

J. Murray Clark · Baker & Daniels · http://www.bakerdaniels.com · 300 North Meridian Street, Suite 2700 · Indianapolis, IN 46204 · 317-237-0300

Richard T. Freije, Jr. · Baker & Daniels · http://www.bakerdaniels.com · 300 North Meridian Street, Suite 2700 · Indianapolis, IN 46204 · 317-237-0300

Kathleen G. Lucas · Bose McKinney & Evans · http://www.boselaw.com · First Indiana Plaza, Suite 2700 135 North Pennsylvania Street · Indianapolis, IN 46204 · 317-684-5000

Terre Haute

Stephen L. Williams · ⑩ · Mann Law Firm · 646 Walnut Street · P.O. Box 1643 · Terre Haute, IN 47808-1643 · 812-232-0107

ALTERNATIVE DISPUTE RESOLUTION

Bloomington

Samuel R. Ardery · Bunger & Robertson · 226 South College Square · P.O. Box 910 · Bloomington, IN 47402-0910 · 812-332-9295

Joseph D. O'Connor · Bunger & Robertson · 226 South College Square · P.O. Box 910 · Bloomington, IN 47402-0910 · 812-332-9295

Columbia City

John W. Whiteleather, Jr. · Bloom, Gates, Sigler & Whiteleather · 119 South Main Street · Columbia City, IN 46725 · 260-248-8900

Columbus

John A. Stroh · Sharpnack, Bigley, Stroh & Washburn · 321 Washington Street · P.O. Box 310 · Columbus, IN 47202-0310 · 812-372-1553

Evansville

Ross E. Rudolph · Rudolph, Fine, Porter & Johnson · 221 Northwest Fifth Street · P.O. Box 1507 · Evansville, IN 47708 · 812-422-9444

Fort Wayne

Sherrill William Colvin · ⑳ · Haller & Colvin · 444 East Main Street · Fort Wayne, IN 46802 · 260-426-0444

John F. Lyons · Barrett & McNagny · 215 East Berry Street · P.O. Box 2263 · Fort Wayne, IN 46802 · 260-423-9551

Greenwood

Brian C. Hewitt · Williams, Hewitt, Barrett & Wilkowski · 600 North Emerson Avenue · P.O. Box 405 · Greenwood, IN 46142 · 317-888-1121

Indianapolis

T. Neil Bemenderfer · The Mediation Group · 8888 Keystone Crossing, Suite 1500 · Indianapolis, IN 46240 · 317-569-3000

Michael P. Bishop · Cohen, Garelick & Glazier · 8888 Keystone Crossing Boulevard, Suite 800 · Indianapolis, IN 46240 · 317-573-8888

Lee C. Christie · Cline, Farrell, Christie, Lee & Caress · 951 North Delaware Street · Indianapolis, IN 46202-3377 · 317-488-5500

Robert Clemens · Bose McKinney & Evans · http://www.boselaw.com · First Indiana Plaza, Suite 2700 · 135 North Pennsylvania Street · Indianapolis, IN 46204 · 317-684-5000

James A. Fels · The Mediation Group · 8888 Keystone Crossing, Suite 1500 · Indianapolis, IN 46240 · 317-569-3000

Robert W. Geddes · Hume Smith Geddes Green & Simmons · 54 Monument Circle, Fourth Floor · Indianapolis, IN 46204-2996 · 317-632-4402

Douglas J. Hill · Hill, Fulwider, McDowell, Funk & Matthews · One Indiana Square, Suite 2000 · 211 North Pennsylvania Street · Indianapolis, IN 46204-2031 · 317-488-2000

John T. Hume III · Hume Smith Geddes Green & Simmons · 54 Monument Circle, Fourth Floor · Indianapolis, IN 46204-2996 · 317-632-4402

Dick Kraege · The Mediation Group · 8888 Keystone Crossing, Suite 1500 · Indianapolis, IN 46240 · 317-569-3000

Denise Page · The Mediation Group · 8888 Keystone Crossing, Suite 1500 · Indianapolis, IN 46240 · 317-569-3000

Robert W. Strohmeyer, Jr. · Law Offices of Robert W. Strohmeyer · 3815 River Crossing Parkway, Suite 100 · Indianapolis, IN 46240-0000 · 317-652-4360

John R. Van Winkle · Van Winkle, Baten, Rimstidt, Dispute Resolution · 111 Monument Circle, Suite 302 · Indianapolis, IN 46204 · 317-231-6320

Lafayette

Joseph T. Bumbleburg · Ball Eggleston · 201 Main Street · P.O. Box 1535 · Lafayette, IN 47902-1535 · 765-742-9046

Madison

George A. Leininger, Jr. · Kemper, Collins & Hensley · 307 Jefferson Street · Madison, IN 47250 · 812-265-3311

Merrillville

Ronald P. Kuker · Hoeppner, Wagner & Evans · South Tower, Suite 606 · 1000 East 80th Place · P.O. Box 10627 · Merrillville, IN 46411-0627 · 219-769-6552

New Albany

Barry N. Bitzegaio · Lorch & Naville · 506 State Street · New Albany, IN 47150 · 866-852-5710

South Bend

Robert M. Edwards, Jr. · Jones Obenchain · Key Bank Building, Suite 600 · 202 South Michigan Street · P.O. Box 4577 · South Bend, IN 46634-4577 · 574-233-1194

Robert J. Konopa · ⑳ · Tuesley Hall Konopa · RiverPlace Professional Center, Suite 100 · 212 East LaSalle Avenue · South Bend, IN 46617 · 574-232-3538

Terre Haute

Gus Sacopulos · ⑩ · Sacopulos, Johnson & Sacopulos · 676 Ohio Street · Terre Haute, IN 47807-3604 · 812-238-2565

Warsaw

Thomas R. Lemon · Miner Lemon & Walston · 523 South Buffalo Street · P.O. Box 720 · Warsaw, IN 46581-0720 · 574-268-9911

ANTITRUST LAW

Indianapolis

Kendall C. Crook · Bose McKinney & Evans · http://www.boselaw.com · First Indiana Plaza, Suite 2700 · 135 North Pennsylvania Street · Indianapolis, IN 46204 · 317-684-5000

Jerry R. Jenkins · Baker & Daniels · http://www.bakerdaniels.com · 600 East 96th Street, Suite 600 · Indianapolis, IN 46240 · 317-569-9600

Donald E. Knebel · ⑩ · Barnes & Thornburg · http://www.btlaw.com · 11 South Meridian Street · Indianapolis, IN 46204-3535 · 317-236-1313

Philip Whistler · Ice Miller · One American Square, Suite 3100 · Indianapolis, IN 46282-0200 · 317-236-2100

APPELLATE LAW

Indianapolis

Arend J. Abel · Cohen & Malad · One Indiana Square, Suite 1400 · Indianapolis, IN 46204 · 317-636-6481

Nelson D. Alexander · Locke Reynolds · http://www.locke.com · 201 North Illinois Street, Suite 1000 · P.O. Box 44961 · Indianapolis, IN 46244-0961 · 317-237-3800

Bryan H. Babb · Bose McKinney & Evans · http://www.boselaw.com · First Indiana Plaza, Suite 2700 · 135 North Pennsylvania Street · Indianapolis, IN 46204 · 317-684-5000

A. Scott Chinn · Baker & Daniels · http://www.bakerdaniels.com · 300 North Meridian Street, Suite 2700 Indianapolis, IN 46204 · 317-237-0300

Stanley C. Fickle · Barnes & Thornburg · http://www.btlaw.com · 11 South Meridian Street · Indianapolis, IN 46204-3535 · 317-236-1313

Julia B. Gelinas · Locke Reynolds · http://www.locke.com · 201 North Illinois Street, Suite 1000 · P.O. Box 44961 · Indianapolis, IN 46244-0961 · 317-237-3800

Jon B. Laramore · Baker & Daniels · http://www.bakerdaniels.com · 300 North Meridian Street, Suite 2700 · Indianapolis, IN 46204 · 317-237-0300

John R. Maley · Barnes & Thornburg · http://www.btlaw.com · 11 South Meridian Street · Indianapolis, IN 46204-3535 · 317-236-1313

Lee B. McTurnan · ⑳ · Bingham McHale · Market Tower Building, Suite 2700 · 10 West Market Street · Indianapolis, IN 46204 · 317-635-8900

Lloyd H. Milliken, Jr. · ⑳ · Locke Reynolds · http://www.locke.com · 201 North Illinois Street, Suite 1000 · P.O. Box 44961 · Indianapolis, IN 46244-0961 · 317-237-3800

Karl L. Mulvaney · Bingham McHale · Market Tower Building, Suite 2700 · 10 West Market Street · Indianapolis, IN 46204 · 317-635-8900

Nana Quay-Smith · Bingham McHale · Market Tower Building, Suite 2700 · 10 West Market Street · Indianapolis, IN 46204 · 317-635-8900

Maggie L. Smith · Locke Reynolds · http://www.locke.com · 201 North Illinois Street, Suite 1000 · P.O. Box 44961 · Indianapolis, IN 46244-0961 · 317-237-3800

Wayne C. Turner · Bingham McHale · Market Tower Building, Suite 2700 · 10 West Market Street · Indianapolis, IN 46204 · 317-635-8900

BANKING LAW

Indianapolis

Mark B. Barnes · Ice Miller · One American Square, Suite 3100 · Indianapolis, IN 46282-0200 · 317-236-2100

Alan W. Becker · Bose McKinney & Evans · http://www.boselaw.com · First Indiana Plaza, Suite 2700 · 135 North Pennsylvania Street · Indianapolis, IN 46204 · 317-684-5000

David Butcher · ⑩ · Bose McKinney & Evans · http://www.boselaw.com · First Indiana Plaza, Suite 2700 135 North Pennsylvania Street · Indianapolis, IN 46204 · 317-684-5000

James E. Carlberg · ㉕ · Bose McKinney & Evans · http://www.boselaw.com · First Indiana Plaza, Suite 2700 · 135 North Pennsylvania Street · Indianapolis, IN 46204 · 317-684-5000

Stephen A. Claffey · ⑩ · Baker & Daniels · http://www.bakerdaniels.com · 300 North Meridian Street, Suite 2700 · Indianapolis, IN 46204 · 317-237-0300

David A. Foster · Baker & Daniels · http://www.bakerdaniels.com · 600 East 96th Street, Suite 600 · Indianapolis, IN 46240 · 317-569-9600

Jay P. Kennedy · Kroger, Gardis & Regas · http://www.kgrlaw.com · 111 Monument Circle, Suite 900 · Indianapolis, IN 46204-5125 · 317-692-9000

Theodore J. Nowacki · Bose McKinney & Evans · http://www.boselaw.com · First Indiana Plaza, Suite 2700 · 135 North Pennsylvania Street · Indianapolis, IN 46204 · 317-684-5000

David R. Prechtel · Bingham McHale · Market Tower Building, Suite 2700 · 10 West Market Street · Indianapolis, IN 46204 · 317-635-8900

Rebecca A. Richardson · Baker & Daniels · http://www.bakerdaniels.com · 300 North Meridian Street, Suite 2700 · Indianapolis, IN 46204 · 317-237-0300

Claudia V. Swhier · (10) · Barnes & Thornburg · http://www.btlaw.com · 11 South Meridian Street · Indianapolis, IN 46204-3535 · 317-236-1313

John W. Tanselle · Krieg DeVault · One Indiana Square, Suite 2800 · Indianapolis, IN 46204-2079 · 317-636-4341

David C. Worrell · (10) · Baker & Daniels · http://www.bakerdaniels.com · 600 East 96th Street, Suite 600 · Indianapolis, IN 46240 · 317-569-9600

South Bend

Richard L. Mintz · (10) · Barnes & Thornburg · http://www.btlaw.com · First Source Bank Center, Suite 600 · 100 North Michigan Street · South Bend, IN 46601 · 574-233-1171

BANKRUPTCY AND CREDITOR-DEBTOR RIGHTS LAW

Elkhart

James R. Byron · Thorne Grodnik · 228 West High Street · Elkhart, IN 46516-3176 · 574-294-7473

Fort Wayne

John Burns · Baker & Daniels · http://www.bakerdaniels.com · 111 East Wayne Street, Suite 800 · Fort Wayne, IN 46802 · 260-424-8000

Howard B. Sandler · (20) · Beckman Lawson · Standard Federal Plaza, Suite 800 · 200 East Main Street · Fort Wayne, IN 46801-0800 · 260-422-0800

Mark Warsco · Rothberg, Logan & Warsco · National City Center, Suite 2100 · 110 West Berry Street · Fort Wayne, IN 46802 · 260-422-9454

Thomas P. Yoder · (10) · Barrett & McNagny · 215 East Berry Street · P.O. Box 2263 · Fort Wayne, IN 46802 · 260-423-9551

Indianapolis

Jon B. Abels · Dann, Pecar, Newman & Kleiman · http://www.dannpecar.com · One American Square, Suite 2300 · Indianapolis, IN 46282 · 317-632-3232

Jerald I. Ancel · (20) · Taft Stettinius & Hollister · http://www.taftlaw.com · One Indiana Square, Suite 3500 · Indianapolis, IN 46204 · 317-713-3500

Steven H. Ancel · ㉕ · Taft Stettinius & Hollister · http://www.taftlaw.com · One Indiana Square, Suite 3500 · Indianapolis, IN 46204 · 317-713-3500

James E. Carlberg · ㉕ · Bose McKinney & Evans · http://www.boselaw.com · First Indiana Plaza, Suite 2700 · 135 North Pennsylvania Street · Indianapolis, IN 46204 · 317-684-5000

James M. Carr · ⑳ · Baker & Daniels · http://www.bakerdaniels.com · 300 North Meridian Street, Suite 2700 · Indianapolis, IN 46204 · 317-237-0300

Ben T. Caughey · Ice Miller · One American Square, Suite 3100 · Indianapolis, IN 46282-0200 · 317-236-2100

Stephen A. Claffey · ⑩ · Baker & Daniels · http://www.bakerdaniels.com · 300 North Meridian Street, Suite 2700 · Indianapolis, IN 46204 · 317-237-0300

Paul T. Deignan · Taft Stettinius & Hollister · http://www.taftlaw.com · One Indiana Square, Suite 3500 · Indianapolis, IN 46204 · 317-713-3500

Henry Efroymson · ⑩ · Ice Miller · One American Square, Suite 3100 · Indianapolis, IN 46282-0200 · 317-236-2100

Jeffrey A. Hokanson · Hostetler & Kowalik · 101 West Ohio Street, Suite 2100 · Indianapolis, IN 46204 · 317-262-1001

Gary Lynn Hostetler · Hostetler & Kowalik · 101 West Ohio Street, Suite 2100 · Indianapolis, IN 46204 · 317-262-1001

Jay Jaffe · ⑩ · Baker & Daniels · http://www.bakerdaniels.com · 600 East 96th Street, Suite 600 · Indianapolis, IN 46240 · 317-569-9600

David H. Kleiman · ㉕ · Dann, Pecar, Newman & Kleiman · http://www.dannpecar.com · One American Square, Suite 2300 · Indianapolis, IN 46282 · 317-632-3232

James A. Knauer · ⑳ · Kroger, Gardis & Regas · http://www.kgrlaw.com · 111 Monument Circle, Suite 900 · Indianapolis, IN 46204-5125 · 317-692-9000

Elliott D. Levin · ⑳ · Rubin & Levin · 500 Marott Center · 342 Massachusetts Avenue · Indianapolis, IN 46204-2161 · 317-634-0300

Michael K. McCrory · Barnes & Thornburg · http://www.btlaw.com · 11 South Meridian Street · Indianapolis, IN 46204-3535 · 317-236-1313

James P. Moloy · Dann, Pecar, Newman & Kleiman · http://www.dannpecar.com · One American Square, Suite 2300 · Indianapolis, IN 46282 · 317-632-3232

Michael P. O'Neil · Taft Stettinius & Hollister · http://www.taftlaw.com · One Indiana Square, Suite 3500 Indianapolis, IN 46204 · 317-713-3500

Marlene Reich · Taft Stettinius & Hollister · http://www.taftlaw.com · One Indiana Square, Suite 3500 · Indianapolis, IN 46204 · 317-713-3500

Thomas C. Scherer · ⑩ · Bingham McHale · Market Tower Building, Suite 2700 · 10 West Market Street Indianapolis, IN 46204 · 317-635-8900

Mishawaka

Steven L. Hostetler · ⑩ · Thorne Grodnik · 420 Lincoln Way West · P.O. Box 1210 · Mishawaka, IN 46545-5689 · 574-256-5660

South Bend

Michael B. Watkins · ⑩ · Barnes & Thornburg · http://www.btlaw.com · First Source Bank Center, Suite 600 · 100 North Michigan Street · South Bend, IN 46601 · 574-233-1171

BET-THE-COMPANY LITIGATION

Fort Wayne

Leonard E. Eilbacher · ⑳ · Eilbacher Fletcher · 803 South Calhoun Street, Suite 400 · Fort Wayne, IN 46802 · 260-425-9777

Hammond

David C. Jensen · ㉕ · Eichhorn & Eichhorn · 200 Russell Street, Sixth Floor · P.O. Box 6328 · Hammond, IN 46325 · 219-931-0560

Indianapolis

David K. Herzog · Baker & Daniels · http://www.bakerdaniels.com · 300 North Meridian Street, Suite 2700 · Indianapolis, IN 46204 · 317-237-0300

Donald E. Knebel · ⑩ · Barnes & Thornburg · http://www.btlaw.com · 11 South Meridian Street · Indianapolis, IN 46204-3535 · 317-236-1313

John R. Maley · Barnes & Thornburg · http://www.btlaw.com · 11 South Meridian Street · Indianapolis, IN 46204-3535 · 317-236-1313

Lee B. McTurnan · ⑳ · Bingham McHale · Market Tower Building, Suite 2700 · 10 West Market Street · Indianapolis, IN 46204 · 317-635-8900

Lloyd H. Milliken, Jr. · ⑳ · Locke Reynolds · http://www.locke.com · 201 North Illinois Street, Suite 1000 · P.O. Box 44961 · Indianapolis, IN 46244-0961 · 317-237-3800

Hugh E. Reynolds, Jr. · ⑩ · Locke Reynolds · http://www.locke.com · 201 North Illinois Street, Suite 1000 · P.O. Box 44961 · Indianapolis, IN 46244-0961 · 317-237-3800

Christopher G. Scanlon · ⑳ · Baker & Daniels · http://www.bakerdaniels.com · 300 North Meridian Street, Suite 2700 · Indianapolis, IN 46204 · 317-237-0300

Robert K. Stanley · Baker & Daniels · http://www.bakerdaniels.com · 300 North Meridian Street, Suite 2700 · Indianapolis, IN 46204 · 317-237-0300

South Bend

Robert J. Konopa · ⑳ · Tuesley Hall Konopa · RiverPlace Professional Center, Suite 100 · 212 East LaSalle Avenue · South Bend, IN 46617 · 574-232-3538

Thomas H. Singer · ⑳ · Nickle & Piasecki · 205 West Jefferson Boulevard, Suite 600 · South Bend, IN 46601 · 574-232-4747

BIOTECHNOLOGY LAW

Indianapolis

Daniel L. Boeglin · Baker & Daniels · http://www.bakerdaniels.com · 600 East 96th Street, Suite 600 · Indianapolis, IN 46240 · 317-569-9600

John A. Millspaugh · Bose McKinney & Evans · http://www.boselaw.com · First Indiana Plaza, Suite 2700 · 135 North Pennsylvania Street · Indianapolis, IN 46204 · 317-684-5000

Craig E. Pinkus · ⑩ · Bose McKinney & Evans · http://www.boselaw.com · First Indiana Plaza, Suite 2700 · 135 North Pennsylvania Street · Indianapolis, IN 46204 · 317-684-5000

COMMERCIAL LITIGATION

Fort Wayne

Kathleen M. Anderson · Barnes & Thornburg · http://www.btlaw.com · One Summit Square, Suite 600 · Fort Wayne, IN 46802-3119 · 260-423-9440

Leonard E. Eilbacher · ⑳ · Eilbacher Fletcher · 803 South Calhoun Street, Suite 400 · Fort Wayne, IN 46802 · 260-425-9777

James P. Fenton · ⑩ · Eilbacher Fletcher · 803 South Calhoun Street, Suite 400 · Fort Wayne, IN 46802 260-425-9777

Martin T. Fletcher, Sr. · Eilbacher Fletcher · 803 South Calhoun Street, Suite 400 · Fort Wayne, IN 46802 · 260-425-9777

Frank J. Gray · Gray and Friend · Harrison Professional Center, Second Floor · 927 South Harrison Street Fort Wayne, IN 46802 · 260-407-7130

Thomas A. Herr · Barrett & McNagny · 215 East Berry Street · P.O. Box 2263 · Fort Wayne, IN 46802 · 260-423-9551

Steven L. Jackson · Baker & Daniels · http://www.bakerdaniels.com · 111 East Wayne Street, Suite 800 · Fort Wayne, IN 46802 · 260-424-8000

Robert T. Keen, Jr. · Carson Boxberger · 1400 One Summit Square · Fort Wayne, IN 46802-3173 · 260-423-9411

Milford M. Miller, Jr. · ⑩ · Miller Murphy · http://www.millermurphylaw.com · 110 West Berry Street, Suite 1500 · Fort Wayne, IN 46802 · 260-423-1500

Alan VerPlanck · ⑩ · Eilbacher Fletcher · 803 South Calhoun Street, Suite 400 · Fort Wayne, IN 46802 · 260-425-9777

Goshen

John D. Ulmer · ⑩ · Yoder, Ainlay, Ulmer & Buckingham · 130 North Main Street · P.O. Box 575 · Goshen, IN 46527-0575 · 574-533-1171

Hammond

David C. Jensen · ㉕ · Eichhorn & Eichhorn · 200 Russell Street, Sixth Floor · P.O. Box 6328 · Hammond, IN 46325 · 219-931-0560

Highland

Terrance L. Smith · Smith & DeBonis · Professional Building · 9696 Gordon Drive · Highland, IN 46322 219-922-1000

Indianapolis

Steven M. Badger · Bose McKinney & Evans · http://www.boselaw.com · First Indiana Plaza, Suite 2700 · 135 North Pennsylvania Street · Indianapolis, IN 46204 · 317-684-5000

Thomas A. Barnard · Taft Stettinius & Hollister · http://www.taftlaw.com · One Indiana Square, Suite 3500 · Indianapolis, IN 46204 · 317-713-3500

Jackie M. Bennett, Jr. · Taft Stettinius & Hollister · http://www.taftlaw.com · One Indiana Square, Suite 3500 · Indianapolis, IN 46204 · 317-713-3500

Terrence L. Brookie · Locke Reynolds · http://www.locke.com · 201 North Illinois Street, Suite 1000 · P.O. Box 44961 · Indianapolis, IN 46244-0961 · 317-237-3800

Alan S. Brown · ⑩ · Locke Reynolds · http://www.locke.com · 201 North Illinois Street, Suite 1000 · P.O. Box 44961 · Indianapolis, IN 46244-0961 · 317-237-3800

Brian K. Burke · Baker & Daniels · http://www.bakerdaniels.com · 300 North Meridian Street, Suite 2700 Indianapolis, IN 46204 · 317-237-0300

David C. Campbell · Bingham McHale · Market Tower Building, Suite 2700 · 10 West Market Street · Indianapolis, IN 46204 · 317-635-8900

Joseph C. Chapelle · Barnes & Thornburg · http://www.btlaw.com · 11 South Meridian Street · Indianapolis, IN 46204-3535 · 317-236-1313

Robert Clemens · Bose McKinney & Evans · http://www.boselaw.com · First Indiana Plaza, Suite 2700 · 135 North Pennsylvania Street · Indianapolis, IN 46204 · 317-684-5000

Ralph A. Cohen · ⑩ · Ice Miller · One American Square, Suite 3100 · Indianapolis, IN 46282-0200 · 317-236-2100

Michael R. Conner · ⑩ · Barnes & Thornburg · http://www.btlaw.com · 11 South Meridian Street · Indianapolis, IN 46204-3535 · 317-236-1313

Edward O. DeLaney · ⑩ · DeLaney & DeLaney · 3640 North Washington Boulevard · Indianapolis, IN 46205 · 317-920-0400

Kathleen A. Delaney · DeLaney & DeLaney · 3640 North Washington Boulevard · Indianapolis, IN 46205 · 317-920-0400

Anne N. DePrez · ⑩ · Barnes & Thornburg · http://www.btlaw.com · 11 South Meridian Street · Indianapolis, IN 46204-3535 · 317-236-1313

Andrew J. Detherage · Barnes & Thornburg · http://www.btlaw.com · 11 South Meridian Street · Indianapolis, IN 46204-3535 · 317-236-1313

Richard J. Dick · Mitchell Hurst Jacobs & Dick · 152 East Washington Street · Indianapolis, IN 46204 · 317-636-0808

James Dimos · Locke Reynolds · http://www.locke.com · 201 North Illinois Street, Suite 1000 · P.O. Box 44961 · Indianapolis, IN 46244-0961 · 317-237-3800

Ronald E. Elberger · ⑩ · Bose McKinney & Evans · http://www.boselaw.com · First Indiana Plaza, Suite 2700 · 135 North Pennsylvania Street · Indianapolis, IN 46204 · 317-684-5000

Michael R. Fruehwald · Barnes & Thornburg · http://www.btlaw.com · 11 South Meridian Street · Indianapolis, IN 46204-3535 · 317-236-1313

Jeffrey R. Gaither · Bose McKinney & Evans · http://www.boselaw.com · First Indiana Plaza, Suite 2700 · 135 North Pennsylvania Street · Indianapolis, IN 46204 · 317-684-5000

Robert W. Geddes · Hume Smith Geddes Green & Simmons · 54 Monument Circle, Fourth Floor · Indianapolis, IN 46204-2996 · 317-632-4402

James H. Ham · Baker & Daniels · http://www.bakerdaniels.com · 300 North Meridian Street, Suite 2700 Indianapolis, IN 46204 · 317-237-0300

Robert L. Hartley · Locke Reynolds · http://www.locke.com · 201 North Illinois Street, Suite 1000 · P.O. Box 44961 · Indianapolis, IN 46244-0961 · 317-237-3800

David K. Herzog · Baker & Daniels · http://www.bakerdaniels.com · 300 North Meridian Street, Suite 2700 · Indianapolis, IN 46204 · 317-237-0300

Jeffrey A. Hokanson · Hostetler & Kowalik · 101 West Ohio Street, Suite 2100 · Indianapolis, IN 46204 · 317-262-1001

John T. Hume III · Hume Smith Geddes Green & Simmons · 54 Monument Circle, Fourth Floor · Indianapolis, IN 46204-2996 · 317-632-4402

Kenneth H. Inskeep · Barnes & Thornburg · http://www.btlaw.com · 11 South Meridian Street · Indianapolis, IN 46204-3535 · 317-236-1313

J. Richard Kiefer · ⑳ · Bingham McHale · Market Tower Building, Suite 2700 · 10 West Market Street · Indianapolis, IN 46204 · 317-635-8900

Donald E. Knebel · ⑩ · Barnes & Thornburg · http://www.btlaw.com · 11 South Meridian Street · Indianapolis, IN 46204-3535 · 317-236-1313

Wayne C. Kreuscher · Barnes & Thornburg · http://www.btlaw.com · 11 South Meridian Street · Indianapolis, IN 46204-3535 · 317-236-1313

V. Samuel Laurin · Bose McKinney & Evans · http://www.boselaw.com · First Indiana Plaza, Suite 2700 · 135 North Pennsylvania Street · Indianapolis, IN 46204 · 317-684-5000

Michael J. Lewinski · Ice Miller · One American Square, Suite 3100 · Indianapolis, IN 46282-0200 · 317-236-2100

Robert D. MacGill · Barnes & Thornburg · http://www.btlaw.com · 11 South Meridian Street · Indianapolis, IN 46204-3535 · 317-236-1313

John R. Maley · Barnes & Thornburg · http://www.btlaw.com · 11 South Meridian Street · Indianapolis, IN 46204-3535 · 317-236-1313

David M. Mattingly · Ice Miller · One American Square, Suite 3100 · Indianapolis, IN 46282-0200 · 317-236-2100

Lee B. McTurnan · ⑳ · Bingham McHale · Market Tower Building, Suite 2700 · 10 West Market Street · Indianapolis, IN 46204 · 317-635-8900

Lloyd H. Milliken, Jr. · ⑳ · Locke Reynolds · http://www.locke.com · 201 North Illinois Street, Suite 1000 · P.O. Box 44961 · Indianapolis, IN 46244-0961 · 317-237-3800

Marvin H. Mitchell · ⑳ · Mitchell Hurst Jacobs & Dick · 152 East Washington Street · Indianapolis, IN 46204 · 317-636-0808

Theodore J. Nowacki · Bose McKinney & Evans · http://www.boselaw.com · First Indiana Plaza, Suite 2700 · 135 North Pennsylvania Street · Indianapolis, IN 46204 · 317-684-5000

Linda L. Pence · Taft Stettinius & Hollister · http://www.taftlaw.com · One Indiana Square, Suite 3500 · Indianapolis, IN 46204 · 317-713-3500

James L. Petersen · Ice Miller · One American Square, Suite 3100 · Indianapolis, IN 46282-0200 · 317-236-2100

Henry J. Price · ㉕ · Price, Waicukauski & Riley · The Hammond Block Building · 301 Massachusetts Avenue · Indianapolis, IN 46204 · 317-633-8787

Hugh E. Reynolds, Jr. · ⑩ · Locke Reynolds · http://www.locke.com · 201 North Illinois Street, Suite 1000 · P.O. Box 44961 · Indianapolis, IN 46244-0961 · 317-237-3800

Michael Rosiello · ⑩ · Barnes & Thornburg · http://www.btlaw.com · 11 South Meridian Street · Indianapolis, IN 46204-3535 · 317-236-1313

Christopher G. Scanlon · ⑳ · Baker & Daniels · http://www.bakerdaniels.com · 300 North Meridian Street, Suite 2700 · Indianapolis, IN 46204 · 317-237-0300

John R. Schaibley · Baker & Daniels · http://www.bakerdaniels.com · 300 North Meridian Street, Suite 2700 · Indianapolis, IN 46204 · 317-237-0300

Steven C. Shockley · Taft Stettinius & Hollister · http://www.taftlaw.com · One Indiana Square, Suite 3500 · Indianapolis, IN 46204 · 317-713-3500

Donald M. Snemis · Ice Miller · One American Square, Suite 3100 · Indianapolis, IN 46282-0200 · 317-236-2100

Robert K. Stanley · Baker & Daniels · http://www.bakerdaniels.com · 300 North Meridian Street, Suite 2700 · Indianapolis, IN 46204 · 317-237-0300

Thomas G. Stayton · Baker & Daniels · http://www.bakerdaniels.com · 300 North Meridian Street, Suite 2700 · Indianapolis, IN 46204 · 317-237-0300

Michael C. Terrell · Taft Stettinius & Hollister · http://www.taftlaw.com · One Indiana Square, Suite 3500 · Indianapolis, IN 46204 · 317-713-3500

David O. Tittle · Bingham McHale · Market Tower Building, Suite 2700 · 10 West Market Street · Indianapolis, IN 46204 · 317-635-8900

Wayne C. Turner · Bingham McHale · Market Tower Building, Suite 2700 · 10 West Market Street · Indianapolis, IN 46204 · 317-635-8900

Lynn C. Tyler · Barnes & Thornburg · http://www.btlaw.com · 11 South Meridian Street · Indianapolis, IN 46204-3535 · 317-236-1313

Mark A. Voigtmann · Baker & Daniels · http://www.bakerdaniels.com · 300 North Meridian Street, Suite 2700 · Indianapolis, IN 46204 · 317-237-0300

Ronald J. Waicukauski · Price, Waicukauski & Riley · The Hammond Block Building · 301 Massachusetts Avenue · Indianapolis, IN 46204 · 317-633-8787

Brian W. Welch · Bingham McHale · Market Tower Building, Suite 2700 · 10 West Market Street · Indianapolis, IN 46204 · 317-635-8900

Philip Whistler · Ice Miller · One American Square, Suite 3100 · Indianapolis, IN 46282-0200 · 317-236-2100

Michael A. Wilkins · Ice Miller · One American Square, Suite 3100 · Indianapolis, IN 46282-0200 · 317-236-2100

Judy L. Woods · Bose McKinney & Evans · http://www.boselaw.com · First Indiana Plaza, Suite 2700 · 135 North Pennsylvania Street · Indianapolis, IN 46204 · 317-684-5000

Joseph H. Yeager, Jr. · Baker & Daniels · http://www.bakerdaniels.com · 300 North Meridian Street, Suite 2700 · Indianapolis, IN 46204 · 317-237-0300

La Porte

David P. Jones · Newby, Lewis, Kaminski & Jones · 916 Lincoln Way · La Porte, IN 46350 · 219-362-1577

Martin W. Kus · Newby, Lewis, Kaminski & Jones · 916 Lincoln Way · La Porte, IN 46350 · 219-362-1577

Marion

H. Joseph Certain · Kiley, Harker & Certain · 300 West Third Street · Marion, IN 46952 · 765-664-9041

South Bend

Timothy J. Abeska · Barnes & Thornburg · http://www.btlaw.com · First Source Bank Center, Suite 600 · 100 North Michigan Street · South Bend, IN 46601 · 574-233-1171

Thomas J. Brunner · Baker & Daniels · http://www.bakerdaniels.com · 205 West Jefferson Boulevard, Suite 250 · South Bend, IN 46601 · 574-234-4149

Robert J. Konopa · ⑳ · Tuesley Hall Konopa · RiverPlace Professional Center, Suite 100 · 212 East LaSalle Avenue · South Bend, IN 46617 · 574-232-3538

Richard W. Morgan · ⑳ · Pfeifer Morgan & Stesiak · 53600 North Ironwood Drive · South Bend, IN 46635 · 574-272-2870

Patrick D. Murphy · Boveri Murphy Rice · http://www.bmrl-law.com · 400 Plaza Building · 210 South Michigan Street · South Bend, IN 46601 · 574-232-0300

Thomas H. Singer · ⑳ · Nickle & Piasecki · 205 West Jefferson Boulevard, Suite 600 · South Bend, IN 46601 · 574-232-4747

Valparaiso

Larry G. Evans · Hoeppner, Wagner & Evans · Chase Building · 103 East Lincolnway · P.O. Box 2357 · Valparaiso, IN 46384-2357 · 219-464-4961

COMMUNICATIONS LAW

Indianapolis

Michael B. Cracraft · Hackman Hulett & Cracraft · http://www.hhclaw.com · 111 Monument Circle, Suite 3500 · Indianapolis, IN 46204-2030 · 317-636-5401

Teresa E. Morton · Barnes & Thornburg · http://www.btlaw.com · 11 South Meridian Street · Indianapolis, IN 46204-3535 · 317-236-1313

Nikki Gray Shoultz · Bose McKinney & Evans · http://www.boselaw.com · First Indiana Plaza, Suite 2700 · 135 North Pennsylvania Street · Indianapolis, IN 46204 · 317-684-5000

David L. Wills · Bose McKinney & Evans · http://www.boselaw.com · First Indiana Plaza, Suite 2700 · 135 North Pennsylvania Street · Indianapolis, IN 46204 · 317-684-5000

CONSTRUCTION LAW

Evansville

Dirck H. Stahl · Ziemer, Stayman, Weitzel & Shoulders · One Riverfront Place, Ninth Floor · 20 Northwest First Street · P.O. Box 916 · Evansville, IN 47706-0916 · 812-424-7575

Fort Wayne

G. William Fishering · Beers Mallers Backs & Salin · National City Bank Building, Suite 1100 · 110 West Berry Street · Fort Wayne, IN 46802 · 260-426-9706

Michael L. James · Baker & Daniels · http://www.bakerdaniels.com · 111 East Wayne Street, Suite 800 · Fort Wayne, IN 46802 · 260-424-8000

Indianapolis

Terrill Albright · Baker & Daniels · http://www.bakerdaniels.com · 300 North Meridian Street, Suite 2700 Indianapolis, IN 46204 · 317-237-0300

Terrence L. Brookie · Locke Reynolds · http://www.locke.com · 201 North Illinois Street, Suite 1000 · P.O. Box 44961 · Indianapolis, IN 46244-0961 · 317-237-3800

Michael F. Drewry · Drewry Simmons Vornehm · http://www.drewrysimmons.com · 8888 Keystone Crossing, Suite 1200 · Indianapolis, IN 46240 · 317-580-4848

Julia B. Gelinas · Locke Reynolds · http://www.locke.com · 201 North Illinois Street, Suite 1000 · P.O. Box 44961 · Indianapolis, IN 46244-0961 · 317-237-3800

Alan H. Goldstein · Ice Miller · One American Square, Suite 3100 · Indianapolis, IN 46282-0200 · 317-236-2100

William J. Hancock · Harrison & Moberly · http://www.harrisonmoberly.net · Market Tower, Suite 700 · 10 West Market · Indianapolis, IN 46204 · 317-639-4511

V. Samuel Laurin · Bose McKinney & Evans · http://www.boselaw.com · First Indiana Plaza, Suite 2700 · 135 North Pennsylvania Street · Indianapolis, IN 46204 · 317-684-5000

Hugh E. Reynolds, Jr. · ⑩ · Locke Reynolds · http://www.locke.com · 201 North Illinois Street, Suite 1000 · P.O. Box 44961 · Indianapolis, IN 46244-0961 · 317-237-3800

Steven Strawbridge · Locke Reynolds · http://www.locke.com · 201 North Illinois Street, Suite 1000 · P.O. Box 44961 · Indianapolis, IN 46244-0961 · 317-237-3800

CORPORATE GOVERNANCE AND COMPLIANCE LAW

Elkhart

Glenn E. Killoren · Barnes & Thornburg · http://www.btlaw.com · 121 West Franklin, Suite 200 · Elkhart, IN 46516 · 219-293-0681

Indianapolis

Alan W. Becker · Bose McKinney & Evans · http://www.boselaw.com · First Indiana Plaza, Suite 2700 · 135 North Pennsylvania Street · Indianapolis, IN 46204 · 317-684-5000

David Butcher · ⑩ · Bose McKinney & Evans · http://www.boselaw.com · First Indiana Plaza, Suite 2700 135 North Pennsylvania Street · Indianapolis, IN 46204 · 317-684-5000

Stephen J. Dutton · Barnes & Thornburg · http://www.btlaw.com · 11 South Meridian Street · Indianapolis, IN 46204-3535 · 317-236-1313

Eric R. Moy · Barnes & Thornburg · http://www.btlaw.com · 11 South Meridian Street · Indianapolis, IN 46204-3535 · 317-236-1313

James A. Strain · ㉕ · Taft Stettinius & Hollister · http://www.taftlaw.com · One Indiana Square, Suite 3500 · Indianapolis, IN 46204 · 317-713-3500

CORPORATE LAW

Fort Wayne

Philip L. Carson · ⑳ · Carson Boxberger · 1400 One Summit Square · Fort Wayne, IN 46802-3173 · 260-423-9411

Steven H. Hazelrigg · Baker & Daniels · http://www.bakerdaniels.com · 111 East Wayne Street, Suite 800 Fort Wayne, IN 46802 · 260-424-8000

Vincent J. Heiny · Haller & Colvin · 444 East Main Street · Fort Wayne, IN 46802 · 260-426-0444

John P. Martin · ⑩ · Barrett & McNagny · 215 East Berry Street · P.O. Box 2263 · Fort Wayne, IN 46802 260-423-9551

Richard D. Robinson · Barrett & McNagny · 215 East Berry Street · P.O. Box 2263 · Fort Wayne, IN 46802 · 260-423-9551

Thomas M. Shoaff · ⑳ · Baker & Daniels · http://www.bakerdaniels.com · 111 East Wayne Street, Suite 800 · Fort Wayne, IN 46802 · 260-424-8000

N. Reed Silliman · ⑩ · Baker & Daniels · http://www.bakerdaniels.com · 111 East Wayne Street, Suite 800 · Fort Wayne, IN 46802 · 260-424-8000

Dennis D. Sutton · Burt, Blee, Dixon & Sutton · 1000 Standard Federal Plaza · 200 East Main Street · P.O. Box 10810 · Fort Wayne, IN 46854-0810 · 219-426-1300

Robert S. Walters · Barrett & McNagny · 215 East Berry Street · P.O. Box 2263 · Fort Wayne, IN 46802 · 260-423-9551

James A. Aschleman · 20 · Baker & Daniels · http://www.bakerdaniels.com · 300 North Meridian Street, Suite 2700 · Indianapolis, IN 46204 · 317-237-0300

Mark B. Barnes · Ice Miller · One American Square, Suite 3100 · Indianapolis, IN 46282-0200 · 317-236-2100

Daniel L. Boeglin · Baker & Daniels · http://www.bakerdaniels.com · 600 East 96th Street, Suite 600 · Indianapolis, IN 46240 · 317-569-9600

Catherine L. Bridge · Barnes & Thornburg · http://www.btlaw.com · 11 South Meridian Street · Indianapolis, IN 46204-3535 · 317-236-1313

J. Jeffrey Brown · Baker & Daniels · http://www.bakerdaniels.com · 600 East 96th Street, Suite 600 · Indianapolis, IN 46240 · 317-569-9600

David Butcher · 10 · Bose McKinney & Evans · http://www.boselaw.com · First Indiana Plaza, Suite 2700 135 North Pennsylvania Street · Indianapolis, IN 46204 · 317-684-5000

Patrick Callahan · Baker & Daniels · http://www.bakerdaniels.com · 300 North Meridian Street, Suite 2700 · Indianapolis, IN 46204 · 317-237-0300

Kendall C. Crook · Bose McKinney & Evans · http://www.boselaw.com · First Indiana Plaza, Suite 2700 · 135 North Pennsylvania Street · Indianapolis, IN 46204 · 317-684-5000

Patrick Cross · Baker & Daniels · http://www.bakerdaniels.com · 600 East 96th Street, Suite 600 · Indianapolis, IN 46240 · 317-569-9600

Joseph E. DeGroff · Ice Miller · One American Square, Suite 3100 · Indianapolis, IN 46282-0200 · 317-236-2100

Donald K. Densborn · Taft Stettinius & Hollister · http://www.taftlaw.com · 8888 Keystone Crossing, Suite 1400 · Indianapolis, IN 46240-5609 · 317-844-4744

Stephen J. Dutton · Barnes & Thornburg · http://www.btlaw.com · 11 South Meridian Street · Indianapolis, IN 46204-3535 · 317-236-1313

Brian S. Fennerty · Baker & Daniels · http://www.bakerdaniels.com · 600 East 96th Street, Suite 600 · Indianapolis, IN 46240 · 317-569-9600

Thomas Froehle · Baker & Daniels · http://www.bakerdaniels.com · 300 North Meridian Street, Suite 2700 · Indianapolis, IN 46204 · 317-237-0300

G. Frederick Glass · Baker & Daniels · http://www.bakerdaniels.com · 300 North Meridian Street, Suite 2700 · Indianapolis, IN 46204 · 317-237-0300

Robert A. Greising · Krieg DeVault · One Indiana Square, Suite 2800 · Indianapolis, IN 46204-2079 · 317-636-4341

Stephen J. Hackman · Ice Miller · One American Square, Suite 3100 · Indianapolis, IN 46282-0200 · 317-236-2100

Robert J. Hicks · Taft Stettinius & Hollister · http://www.taftlaw.com · One Indiana Square, Suite 3500 · Indianapolis, IN 46204 · 317-713-3500

Steven K. Humke · Ice Miller · One American Square, Suite 3100 · Indianapolis, IN 46282-0200 · 317-236-2100

Roberts E. Inveiss · Bose McKinney & Evans · http://www.boselaw.com · First Indiana Plaza, Suite 2700 135 North Pennsylvania Street · Indianapolis, IN 46204 · 317-684-5000

David L. Johnson · Baker & Daniels · http://www.bakerdaniels.com · 300 North Meridian Street, Suite 2700 · Indianapolis, IN 46204 · 317-237-0300

Robert P. Kassing · ⑩ · Bose McKinney & Evans · http://www.boselaw.com · First Indiana Plaza, Suite 2700 · 135 North Pennsylvania Street · Indianapolis, IN 46204 · 317-684-5000

Tibor D. Klopfer · Baker & Daniels · http://www.bakerdaniels.com · 300 North Meridian Street, Suite 2700 · Indianapolis, IN 46204 · 317-237-0300

Scott M. Kosnoff · Baker & Daniels · http://www.bakerdaniels.com · 300 North Meridian Street, Suite 2700 · Indianapolis, IN 46204 · 317-237-0300

David B. Millard · ⑩ · Barnes & Thornburg · http://www.btlaw.com · 11 South Meridian Street · Indianapolis, IN 46204-3535 · 317-236-1313

Eric R. Moy · Barnes & Thornburg · http://www.btlaw.com · 11 South Meridian Street · Indianapolis, IN 46204-3535 · 317-236-1313

Erick D. Ponader · Taft Stettinius & Hollister · http://www.taftlaw.com · One Indiana Square, Suite 3500 Indianapolis, IN 46204 · 317-713-3500

Michael J. Schneider · Bose McKinney & Evans · http://www.boselaw.com · First Indiana Plaza, Suite 2700 · 135 North Pennsylvania Street · Indianapolis, IN 46204 · 317-684-5000

Regina M. Sharrow · Baker & Daniels · http://www.bakerdaniels.com · 600 East 96th Street, Suite 600 · Indianapolis, IN 46240 · 317-569-9600

James A. Strain · ㉕ · Taft Stettinius & Hollister · http://www.taftlaw.com · One Indiana Square, Suite 3500 · Indianapolis, IN 46204 · 317-713-3500

John R. Thornburgh · ⑩ · Ice Miller · One American Square, Suite 3100 · Indianapolis, IN 46282-0200 · 317-236-2100

Steven W. Thornton · Barnes & Thornburg · http://www.btlaw.com · 11 South Meridian Street · Indianapolis, IN 46204-3535 · 317-236-1313

Richard J. Thrapp · Ice Miller · One American Square, Suite 3100 · Indianapolis, IN 46282-0200 · 317-236-2100

Robert T. Wildman · Bose McKinney & Evans · http://www.boselaw.com · First Indiana Plaza, Suite 2700 · 135 North Pennsylvania Street · Indianapolis, IN 46204 · 317-684-5000

David L. Wills · Bose McKinney & Evans · http://www.boselaw.com · First Indiana Plaza, Suite 2700 · 135 North Pennsylvania Street · Indianapolis, IN 46204 · 317-684-5000

David C. Worrell · ⑩ · Baker & Daniels · http://www.bakerdaniels.com · 600 East 96th Street, Suite 600 · Indianapolis, IN 46240 · 317-569-9600

Robert S. Wynne · Baker & Daniels · http://www.bakerdaniels.com · 600 East 96th Street, Suite 600 · Indianapolis, IN 46240 · 317-569-9600

South Bend

Richard L. Hill · Baker & Daniels · http://www.bakerdaniels.com · 205 West Jefferson Boulevard, Suite 250 · South Bend, IN 46601 · 574-234-4149

Richard L. Mintz · ⑩ · Barnes & Thornburg · http://www.btlaw.com · First Source Bank Center, Suite 600 · 100 North Michigan Street · South Bend, IN 46601 · 574-233-1171

Nelson J. Vogel, Jr. · ㉕ · Barnes & Thornburg · http://www.btlaw.com · First Source Bank Center, Suite 600 · 100 North Michigan Street · South Bend, IN 46601 · 574-233-1171

Terre Haute

Michael J. Sacopulos · Sacopulos, Johnson & Sacopulos · 676 Ohio Street · Terre Haute, IN 47807-3604 812-238-2565

DUI/DWI DEFENSE

Evansville

Dennis L. Brinkmeyer · Dennis L. Brinkmeyer · 525 Sycamore Street · P.O. Box 1005 · Evansville, IN 47706-1005 · 812-423-3125

Mark A. Foster · Foster Montgomery & O'Daniel · 3820 Oak Hill Road · Evansville, IN 47711 · 812-424-8101

EDUCATION LAW

Indianapolis

Jeffrey O. Lewis · Ice Miller · One American Square, Suite 3100 · Indianapolis, IN 46282-0200 · 317-236-2100

Joseph E. Miller · Baker & Daniels · http://www.bakerdaniels.com · 300 North Meridian Street, Suite 2700 · Indianapolis, IN 46204 · 317-237-0300

D. William Moreau, Jr. · Barnes & Thornburg · http://www.btlaw.com · 11 South Meridian Street · Indianapolis, IN 46204-3535 · 317-236-1313

Charles R. Rubright · Bose McKinney & Evans · http://www.boselaw.com · First Indiana Plaza, Suite 2700 · 135 North Pennsylvania Street · Indianapolis, IN 46204 · 317-684-5000

Susan Traynor Chastain · Bose McKinney & Evans · http://www.boselaw.com · First Indiana Plaza, Suite 2700 · 135 North Pennsylvania Street · Indianapolis, IN 46204 · 317-684-5000

D. Michael Wallman · Rund Wallman & Robbins · Market Square Center, Suite 520 · 151 North Delaware Street · Indianapolis, IN 46204-2535 · 317-639-2224

Thomas E. Wheeler II · Locke Reynolds · http://www.locke.com · 201 North Illinois Street, Suite 1000 · P.O. Box 44961 · Indianapolis, IN 46244-0961 · 317-237-3800

Lafayette

Anthony S. Benton · Stuart & Branigin · 300 Main Street, Suite 900 · P.O. Box 1010 · Lafayette, IN 47902-1010 · 765-423-1561

Noblesville

David R. Day · Church, Church, Hittle & Antrim · 938 Conner Street · P.O. Box 10 · Noblesville, IN 46061-0010 · 317-773-2190

South Bend

Edward A. Sullivan · Baker & Daniels · http://www.bakerdaniels.com · 205 West Jefferson Boulevard, Suite 250 · South Bend, IN 46601 · 574-234-4149

ELDER LAW

Beech Grove

William J. Holwager · Holwager, Byer & Caughey · 1818 Main Street, Suite A · Beech Grove, IN 46107-1418 · 317-787-8395

Bluffton

Keith Huffman · Dale & Huffman · 1127 North Main Street · P.O. Box 277 · Bluffton, IN 46714 · 260-824-5566

Carmel

George G. Slater II · Slater & Associates · 301 East Carmel Drive, Building G · Carmel, IN 46032 · 317-571-9600

Elkhart

Timothy A. Weaver · Barnes & Thornburg · http://www.btlaw.com · 121 West Franklin, Suite 200 · Elkhart, IN 46516 · 219-293-0681

Indianapolis

Robert W. Fechtman · Fechtman Law Office · 8555 River Road, Suite 420 · Indianapolis, IN 46240 · 317-655-5140

Claire E. Lewis · Claire E. Lewis · 115 North Girls School Road · Indianapolis, IN 46214 · 317-484-8115

Scott R. Severns · Severns & Associates · 10293 North Meridian Street, Suite 150 · Indianapolis, IN 46290 · 317-817-0300

Marion

Warren Haas · Warren Haas · 514 South Washington Street · Marion, IN 46953 · 765-662-7777

Warsaw

W. Wayne Walston · Miner Lemon & Walston · 523 South Buffalo Street · P.O. Box 720 · Warsaw, IN 46581-0720 · 574-268-9911

EMINENT DOMAIN AND CONDEMNATION LAW

Indianapolis

David A. Given · Baker & Daniels · http://www.bakerdaniels.com · 300 North Meridian Street, Suite 2700 Indianapolis, IN 46204 · 317-237-0300

Alan S. Townsend · Bose McKinney & Evans · http://www.boselaw.com · First Indiana Plaza, Suite 2700 135 North Pennsylvania Street · Indianapolis, IN 46204 · 317-684-5000

Zeff A. Weiss · ⑩ · Ice Miller · One American Square, Suite 3100 · Indianapolis, IN 46282-0200 · 317-236-2100

EMPLOYEE BENEFITS LAW

Fort Wayne

N. Thomas Horton II · ⑳ · Barrett & McNagny · 215 East Berry Street · P.O. Box 2263 · Fort Wayne, IN 46802 · 260-423-9551

Thomas J. Markle · Barrett & McNagny · 215 East Berry Street · P.O. Box 2263 · Fort Wayne, IN 46802 · 260-423-9551

Michael J. Nader · Baker & Daniels · http://www.bakerdaniels.com · 111 East Wayne Street, Suite 800 · Fort Wayne, IN 46802 · 260-424-8000

Indianapolis

Mary Beth Braitman · ⑳ · Ice Miller · One American Square, Suite 3100 · Indianapolis, IN 46282-0200 · 317-236-2100

Craig C. Burke · Ice Miller · One American Square, Suite 3100 · Indianapolis, IN 46282-0200 · 317-236-2100

John L. Egloff · ⑩ · Riley Bennett & Egloff · 141 East Washington Street, Fourth Floor · Indianapolis, IN 46204 · 317-636-8000

James D. Kemper · ⑳ · Ice Miller · One American Square, Suite 3100 · Indianapolis, IN 46282-0200 · 317-236-2100

Alan A. Levin · ⑩ · Barnes & Thornburg · http://www.btlaw.com · 11 South Meridian Street · Indianapolis, IN 46204-3535 · 317-236-1313

John W. Purcell · ⑩ · Baker & Daniels · http://www.bakerdaniels.com · 300 North Meridian Street, Suite 2700 · Indianapolis, IN 46204 · 317-237-0300

Melissa Proffitt Reese · Ice Miller · One American Square, Suite 3100 · Indianapolis, IN 46282-0200 · 317-236-2100

Charles F. Rolph III · Dann, Pecar, Newman & Kleiman · http://www.dannpecar.com · One American Square, Suite 2300 · Indianapolis, IN 46282 · 317-632-3232

Marc W. Seiscoe · ⑳ · Ice Miller · One American Square, Suite 3100 · Indianapolis, IN 46282-0200 · 317-236-2100

Christopher S. Sears · Ice Miller · One American Square, Suite 3100 · Indianapolis, IN 46282-0200 · 317-236-2100

Gayle L. Skolnik · Baker & Daniels · http://www.bakerdaniels.com · 300 North Meridian Street, Suite 2700 · Indianapolis, IN 46204 · 317-237-0300

Stephen D. Smith · Krieg DeVault · One Indiana Square, Suite 2800 · Indianapolis, IN 46204-2079 · 317-636-4341

South Bend

Brian J. Lake · ⑳ · Barnes & Thornburg · http://www.btlaw.com · First Source Bank Center, Suite 600 · 100 North Michigan Street · South Bend, IN 46601 · 574-233-1171

Richard B. Urda, Jr. · ⑳ · Urda Professional Corporation · 112 West Jefferson Boulevard, Suite 503 · South Bend, IN 46601 · 574-234-2161

ENERGY LAW

Evansville

George A. Porch · ⑩ · Bowers Harrison · 25 Northwest Riverside Drive, Second Floor · P.O. Box 1287 · Evansville, IN 47708 · 812-426-1231

Indianapolis

Michael B. Cracraft · Hackman Hulett & Cracraft · http://www.hhclaw.com · 111 Monument Circle, Suite 3500 · Indianapolis, IN 46204-2030 · 317-636-5401

Stanley C. Fickle · Barnes & Thornburg · http://www.btlaw.com · 11 South Meridian Street · Indianapolis, IN 46204-3535 · 317-236-1313

Nicholas K. Kile · Barnes & Thornburg · http://www.btlaw.com · 11 South Meridian Street · Indianapolis, IN 46204-3535 · 317-236-1313

Daniel W. McGill · ⑩ · Barnes & Thornburg · http://www.btlaw.com · 11 South Meridian Street · Indianapolis, IN 46204-3535 · 317-236-1313

Teresa E. Morton · Barnes & Thornburg · http://www.btlaw.com · 11 South Meridian Street · Indianapolis, IN 46204-3535 · 317-236-1313

Fred E. Schlegel · ⑩ · Baker & Daniels · http://www.bakerdaniels.com · 300 North Meridian Street, Suite 2700 · Indianapolis, IN 46204 · 317-237-0300

P. Jason Stephenson · Barnes & Thornburg · http://www.btlaw.com · 11 South Meridian Street · Indianapolis, IN 46204-3535 · 317-236-1313

Larry J. Wallace · ⑩ · Parr Richey Obremskey & Morton · http://www.parrlaw.com · Capital Center South, Suite 300 · 201 North Illinois Street · Indianapolis, IN 46204 · 317-269-2500

ENTERTAINMENT LAW

Indianapolis

Ronald E. Elberger · ⑩ · Bose McKinney & Evans · http://www.boselaw.com · First Indiana Plaza, Suite 2700 · 135 North Pennsylvania Street · Indianapolis, IN 46204 · 317-684-5000

Craig E. Pinkus · ⑩ · Bose McKinney & Evans · http://www.boselaw.com · First Indiana Plaza, Suite 2700 · 135 North Pennsylvania Street · Indianapolis, IN 46204 · 317-684-5000

ENVIRONMENTAL LAW

Evansville

G. Michael Schopmeyer · Kahn, Dees, Donovan & Kahn · 501 Main Street, Suite 305 · Evansville, IN 47708 · 812-423-3183

Indianapolis

Christopher J. Braun · Plews Shadley Racher Braun · 1346 North Delaware Street · Indianapolis, IN 46202-2415 · 317-637-0700

Robert R. Clark · Taft Stettinius & Hollister · http://www.taftlaw.com · One Indiana Square, Suite 3500 · Indianapolis, IN 46204 · 317-713-3500

Frank J. Deveau · ⑩ · Taft Stettinius & Hollister · http://www.taftlaw.com · One Indiana Square, Suite 3500 · Indianapolis, IN 46204 · 317-713-3500

S. Curtis DeVoe · Plews Shadley Racher Braun · 1346 North Delaware Street · Indianapolis, IN 46202-2415 · 317-637-0700

E. Sean Griggs · Barnes & Thornburg · http://www.btlaw.com · 11 South Meridian Street · Indianapolis, IN 46204-3535 · 317-236-1313

John M. Kyle III · Barnes & Thornburg · http://www.btlaw.com · 11 South Meridian Street · Indianapolis, IN 46204-3535 · 317-236-1313

Kathleen G. Lucas · Bose McKinney & Evans · http://www.boselaw.com · First Indiana Plaza, Suite 2700 135 North Pennsylvania Street · Indianapolis, IN 46204 · 317-684-5000

Donna C. Marron · Plews Shadley Racher Braun · 1346 North Delaware Street · Indianapolis, IN 46202-2415 · 317-637-0700

Daniel P. McInerny · Bose McKinney & Evans · http://www.boselaw.com · First Indiana Plaza, Suite 2700 · 135 North Pennsylvania Street · Indianapolis, IN 46204 · 317-684-5000

George M. Plews · Plews Shadley Racher Braun · 1346 North Delaware Street · Indianapolis, IN 46202-2415 · 317-637-0700

Peter M. Racher · Plews Shadley Racher Braun · 1346 North Delaware Street · Indianapolis, IN 46202-2415 · 317-637-0700

Michael T. Scanlon · Barnes & Thornburg · http://www.btlaw.com · 11 South Meridian Street · Indianapolis, IN 46204-3535 · 317-236-1313

Sue A. Shadley · ⑩ · Plews Shadley Racher Braun · 1346 North Delaware Street · Indianapolis, IN 46202-2415 · 317-637-0700

Jacqueline A. Simmons · Baker & Daniels · http://www.bakerdaniels.com · 300 North Meridian Street, Suite 2700 · Indianapolis, IN 46204 · 317-237-0300

Rosemary G. Spalding · Spalding & Hilmes · 330 South Downey Avenue · Indianapolis, IN 46219 · 317-375-0448

Stephen A. Studer · Plews Shadley Racher Braun · 1346 North Delaware Street · Indianapolis, IN 46202-2415 · 317-637-0700

Anthony C. Sullivan · Barnes & Thornburg · http://www.btlaw.com · 11 South Meridian Street · Indianapolis, IN 46204-3535 · 317-236-1313

Richard S. VanRheenen · Bose McKinney & Evans · http://www.boselaw.com · First Indiana Plaza, Suite 2700 · 135 North Pennsylvania Street · Indianapolis, IN 46204 · 317-684-5000

Terre Haute

Peter J. Sacopulos · Sacopulos, Johnson & Sacopulos · 676 Ohio Street · Terre Haute, IN 47807-3604 · 812-238-2565

ETHICS AND PROFESSIONAL RESPONSIBILITY LAW

Indianapolis

Kevin P. McGoff · Bingham McHale · Market Tower Building, Suite 2700 · 10 West Market Street · Indianapolis, IN 46204 · 317-635-8900

William H. Thompson · ⑩ · Hall, Render, Killian, Heath & Lyman · One American Square, Suite 2000 · P.O. Box 82064 · Indianapolis, IN 46282 · 317-633-4884

FAMILY LAW

Bloomington

Andrew C. Mallor · ⑳ · Mallor Clendening Grodner & Bohrer · http://www.mcgb.com · 511 Woodscrest Drive · P.O. Box 5787 · Bloomington, IN 47407 · 812-336-0200

Carmel

Deborah L. Farmer · ⑩ · Campbell Kyle Proffitt · 11595 North Meridian Street, Suite 701 · Carmel, IN 46032 · 317-846-6514

John D. Proffitt · ㉕ · Campbell Kyle Proffitt · 11595 North Meridian Street, Suite 701 · Carmel, IN 46032 · 317-846-6514

Fort Wayne

John H. Brandt · Beckman Lawson · Standard Federal Plaza, Suite 800 · 200 East Main Street · Fort Wayne, IN 46801-0800 · 260-422-0800

Sherie L. Hampshire · ⑩ · Hampshire & Associates · Courtside Building, Suite 201 · 803 South Calhoun Street · Fort Wayne, IN 46802-2305 · 260-423-3637

Cornelius B. Hayes · ⑩ · Hayes and Hayes · http://www.hayesandhayeslaw.com · Eight Ten Building, Third Floor · 810 South Calhoun Street · Fort Wayne, IN 46802 · 260-420-1800

Hammond

Thomas E. Rucinski · Sachs & Hess · http://www.sachsandhess.com · 5832 Hohman Avenue · Hammond, IN 46320 · 219-932-6070

Highland

Debra L. Dubovich · Levy & Dubovich · 2850 Forty-Fifth Street, Suite A · Highland, IN 46322-2905 · 219-922-1200

Samuel J. Goodman · ⑩ · Goodman, Katz, Scheele & Bauswell · 9013 Indianapolis Boulevard · Highland, IN 46322 · 219-838-9200

Indianapolis

Nancy L. Cross · ⑩ · Cross, Woolsey & Glazier · 500 East 96th Street, Suite 100 · Indianapolis, IN 46240-3733 · 317-582-1040

Jill E. Goldenberg · Cohen, Garelick & Glazier · 8888 Keystone Crossing Boulevard, Suite 800 · Indianapolis, IN 46240 · 317-573-8888

Kevin P. McGoff · Bingham McHale · Market Tower Building, Suite 2700 · 10 West Market Street · Indianapolis, IN 46204 · 317-635-8900

Franklin I. Miroff · ㉕ · Cross, Woolsey & Glazier · 500 East 96th Street, Suite 100 · Indianapolis, IN 46240-3733 · 317-582-1040

Marvin H. Mitchell · ⑳ · Mitchell Hurst Jacobs & Dick · 152 East Washington Street · Indianapolis, IN 46204 · 317-636-0808

Timothy J. O'Hara · Bose McKinney & Evans · http://www.boselaw.com · First Indiana Plaza, Suite 2700 135 North Pennsylvania Street · Indianapolis, IN 46204 · 317-684-5000

Bruce M. Pennamped · ⑩ · Pennamped & Associates · 3925 River Crossing Parkway, Suite 280 · Indianapolis, IN 46240 · 317-815-9736

James A. Reed · ⑩ · Bingham McHale · Market Tower Building, Suite 2700 · 10 West Market Street · Indianapolis, IN 46204 · 317-635-8900

Mark J. Roberts · Locke Reynolds · http://www.locke.com · 201 North Illinois Street, Suite 1000 · P.O. Box 44961 · Indianapolis, IN 46244-0961 · 317-237-3800

Andrew Z. Soshnick · ⑩ · Baker & Daniels · http://www.bakerdaniels.com · 300 North Meridian Street, Suite 2700 · Indianapolis, IN 46204 · 317-237-0300

Merrillville

Paul A. Leonard, Jr. · Burke Costanza and Cuppy · 9191 Broadway · Merrillville, IN 46410 · 219-769-1313

Munster

J. Douglas Angel · Law Offices of J. Douglas Angel & Associates · 9245 Calumet Avenue, Suite 203 · Munster, IN 46321 · 219-836-3133

Vincennes

J. David Roellgen · Emison, Doolittle, Kolb & Roellgen · 801 Busseron Street · P.O. Box 215 · Vincennes, IN 47591 · 812-882-2280

FAMILY LAW MEDIATION

Fort Wayne

Edward Beck · Shambaugh, Kast, Beck & Williams · http://www.skbw.com · 229 West Berry Street, Suite 400 · P.O. Box 11648 · Fort Wayne, IN 46859-1648 · 260-423-1430

Dan J. Borgmann · Helmke Beams · 202 West Berry Street · Fort Wayne, IN 46802 · 260-422-7422

Douglas E. Johnston · Tourkow, Crell, Rosenblatt & Johnston · http://www.tcrjlaw.com · 203 East Berry Street, Suite 814 · Fort Wayne, IN 46802 · 260-426-0545

Vincennes

J. David Roellgen · Emison, Doolittle, Kolb & Roellgen · 801 Busseron Street · P.O. Box 215 · Vincennes, IN 47591 · 812-882-2280

FIRST AMENDMENT LAW

Indianapolis

Steven M. Badger · Bose McKinney & Evans · http://www.boselaw.com · First Indiana Plaza, Suite 2700 · 135 North Pennsylvania Street · Indianapolis, IN 46204 · 317-684-5000

Daniel P. Byron · Bingham McHale · Market Tower Building, Suite 2700 · 10 West Market Street · Indianapolis, IN 46204 · 317-635-8900

Jan M. Carroll · ⑩ · Barnes & Thornburg · http://www.btlaw.com · 11 South Meridian Street · Indianapolis, IN 46204-3535 · 317-236-1313

South Bend

Gerald F. Lutkus · Barnes & Thornburg · http://www.btlaw.com · First Source Bank Center, Suite 600 · 100 North Michigan Street · South Bend, IN 46601 · 574-233-1171

GAMING LAW

Indianapolis

Mary Kay Fleming · Ice Miller · One American Square, Suite 3100 · Indianapolis, IN 46282-0200 · 317-236-2100

Thomas Froehle · Baker & Daniels · http://www.bakerdaniels.com · 300 North Meridian Street, Suite 2700 · Indianapolis, IN 46204 · 317-237-0300

Lacy Johnson · Ice Miller · One American Square, Suite 3100 · Indianapolis, IN 46282-0200 · 317-236-2100

Joseph E. Loftus · Barnes & Thornburg · http://www.btlaw.com · 11 South Meridian Street · Indianapolis, IN 46204-3535 · 317-236-1313

Peter J. Rusthoven · Barnes & Thornburg · http://www.btlaw.com · 11 South Meridian Street · Indianapolis, IN 46204-3535 · 317-236-1313

John J. Thar · Ice Miller · One American Square, Suite 3100 · Indianapolis, IN 46282-0200 · 317-236-2100

GOVERNMENT RELATIONS LAW

Indianapolis

John V. Barnett, Jr. · Bose McKinney & Evans · http://www.boselaw.com · First Indiana Plaza, Suite 2700 · 135 North Pennsylvania Street · Indianapolis, IN 46204 · 317-684-5000

Brian L. Burdick · Barnes & Thornburg · http://www.btlaw.com · 11 South Meridian Street · Indianapolis, IN 46204-3535 · 317-236-1313

J. Murray Clark · Baker & Daniels · http://www.bakerdaniels.com · 300 North Meridian Street, Suite 2700 · Indianapolis, IN 46204 · 317-237-0300

Miriam S. Dant · Dant Advocacy · http://www.dantadvocacy.com · 54 Monument Circle, Suite 300 · Indianapolis, IN 46204 · 317-450-6182

John R. Hammond III · Ice Miller · One American Square, Suite 3100 · Indianapolis, IN 46282-0200 · 317-236-2100

John S. Keeler · Baker & Daniels · http://www.bakerdaniels.com · 300 North Meridian Street, Suite 2700 Indianapolis, IN 46204 · 317-237-0300

Robert Kuzman · Ice Miller · One American Square, Suite 3100 · Indianapolis, IN 46282-0200 · 317-236-2100

Joseph E. Loftus · Barnes & Thornburg · http://www.btlaw.com · 11 South Meridian Street · Indianapolis, IN 46204-3535 · 317-236-1313

Paul S. Mannweiler · Bose McKinney & Evans · http://www.boselaw.com · First Indiana Plaza, Suite 2700 · 135 North Pennsylvania Street · Indianapolis, IN 46204 · 317-684-5000

Daniel B. Seitz · Bose McKinney & Evans · http://www.boselaw.com · First Indiana Plaza, Suite 2700 · 135 North Pennsylvania Street · Indianapolis, IN 46204 · 317-684-5000

Joseph L. Smith, Jr. · Baker & Daniels · http://www.bakerdaniels.com · 300 North Meridian Street, Suite 2700 · Indianapolis, IN 46204 · 317-237-0300

South Bend

Phillip J. Faccenda, Jr. · Barnes & Thornburg · http://www.btlaw.com · First Source Bank Center, Suite 600 · 100 North Michigan Street · South Bend, IN 46601 · 574-233-1171

Anthony M. Zappia · Zappia, Zappia & Stipp · 52582 U.S. 33 · South Bend, IN 46637 · 219-277-8720

HEALTH CARE LAW

Carmel

Thomas R. Neal · ⑩ · Krieg DeVault · 12800 North Meridian Street, Suite 300 · Carmel, IN 46032-9422 · 317-566-1110

Fort Wayne

Steven L. Jackson · Baker & Daniels · http://www.bakerdaniels.com · 111 East Wayne Street, Suite 800 · Fort Wayne, IN 46802 · 260-424-8000

Richard D. Robinson · Barrett & McNagny · 215 East Berry Street · P.O. Box 2263 · Fort Wayne, IN 46802 · 260-423-9551

Franklin

Brian J. Deppe · ⑩ · Deppe, Fredbeck & Boll · Nine East Court · Franklin, IN 46131-2303 · 317-736-5138

Indianapolis

Dave C. Bromund · Taft Stettinius & Hollister · http://www.taftlaw.com · One Indiana Square, Suite 3500 · Indianapolis, IN 46204 · 317-713-3500

Mary Beth Claus · Baker & Daniels · http://www.bakerdaniels.com · 300 North Meridian Street, Suite 2700 · Indianapolis, IN 46204 · 317-237-0300

Patrick Cross · Baker & Daniels · http://www.bakerdaniels.com · 600 East 96th Street, Suite 600 · Indianapolis, IN 46240 · 317-569-9600

Sherry A. Fabina-Abney · Ice Miller · One American Square, Suite 3100 · Indianapolis, IN 46282-0200 · 317-236-2100

Terry R. Heath · Hall, Render, Killian, Heath & Lyman · One American Square, Suite 2000 · P.O. Box 82064 · Indianapolis, IN 46282 · 317-633-4884

Brenda Horn · ⑩ · Ice Miller · One American Square, Suite 3100 · Indianapolis, IN 46282-0200 · 317-236-2100

David E. Jose · ⑩ · Krieg DeVault · One Indiana Square, Suite 2800 · Indianapolis, IN 46204-2079 · 317-636-4341

Leah S. Mannweiler · Krieg DeVault · One Indiana Square, Suite 2800 · Indianapolis, IN 46204-2079 · 317-636-4341

Gregory L. Pemberton · ⑩ · Ice Miller · One American Square, Suite 3100 · Indianapolis, IN 46282-0200 317-236-2100

David R. Prechtel · Bingham McHale · Market Tower Building, Suite 2700 · 10 West Market Street · Indianapolis, IN 46204 · 317-635-8900

John C. Render · ⑩ · Hall, Render, Killian, Heath & Lyman · One American Square, Suite 2000 · P.O. Box 82064 · Indianapolis, IN 46282 · 317-633-4884

Myra C. Selby · Ice Miller · One American Square, Suite 3100 · Indianapolis, IN 46282-0200 · 317-236-2100

William H. Thompson · ⑩ · Hall, Render, Killian, Heath & Lyman · One American Square, Suite 2000 · P.O. Box 82064 · Indianapolis, IN 46282 · 317-633-4884

Kevin C. Woodhouse · Ice Miller · One American Square, Suite 3100 · Indianapolis, IN 46282-0200 · 317-236-2100

Noblesville

Glenn T. Troyer · ⑩ · Krieg DeVault · 949 East Conner Street, Suite 200 · Noblesville, IN 46060 · 317-773-7818

South Bend

Robert A. Wade · Baker & Daniels · http://www.bakerdaniels.com · 205 West Jefferson Boulevard, Suite 250 · South Bend, IN 46601 · 574-234-4149

IMMIGRATION LAW

Indianapolis

Jenifer M. Brown · Ice Miller · One American Square, Suite 3100 · Indianapolis, IN 46282-0200 · 317-236-2100

Mariana Richmond · Barnes & Thornburg · http://www.btlaw.com · 11 South Meridian Street · Indianapolis, IN 46204-3535 · 317-236-1313

Robert W. Rund · Rund Wallman & Robbins · Market Square Center, Suite 520 · 151 North Delaware Street · Indianapolis, IN 46204-2535 · 317-639-2224

Steven L. Tuchman · Lewis & Kappes · One American Square, Suite 2500 · Indianapolis, IN 46282-0003 317-639-1210

INFORMATION TECHNOLOGY LAW

Indianapolis

Stephen J. Dutton · Barnes & Thornburg · http://www.btlaw.com · 11 South Meridian Street · Indianapolis, IN 46204-3535 · 317-236-1313

Thomas A. Walsh · Ice Miller · One American Square, Suite 3100 · Indianapolis, IN 46282-0200 · 317-236-2100

INSURANCE LAW

Indianapolis

Scott M. Kosnoff · Baker & Daniels · http://www.bakerdaniels.com · 300 North Meridian Street, Suite 2700 · Indianapolis, IN 46204 · 317-237-0300

George M. Plews · Plews Shadley Racher Braun · 1346 North Delaware Street · Indianapolis, IN 46202-2415 · 317-637-0700

La Porte

Mark A. Lienhoop · Newby, Lewis, Kaminski & Jones · 916 Lincoln Way · La Porte, IN 46350 · 219-362-1577

South Bend

Robert G. Devetski · Barnes & Thornburg · http://www.btlaw.com · First Source Bank Center, Suite 600 100 North Michigan Street · South Bend, IN 46601 · 574-233-1171

INTELLECTUAL PROPERTY LAW

Fort Wayne

D. Randall Brown · Barnes & Thornburg · http://www.btlaw.com · One Summit Square, Suite 600 · Fort Wayne, IN 46802-3119 · 260-423-9440

Bobby B. Gillenwater · ⑩ · Barnes & Thornburg · http://www.btlaw.com · One Summit Square, Suite 600 · Fort Wayne, IN 46802-3119 · 260-423-9440

John F. Hoffman · ⑩ · Baker & Daniels · http://www.bakerdaniels.com · 111 East Wayne Street, Suite 800 · Fort Wayne, IN 46802 · 260-424-8000

David P. Irmscher · Baker & Daniels · http://www.bakerdaniels.com · 111 East Wayne Street, Suite 800 · Fort Wayne, IN 46802 · 260-424-8000

Indianapolis

Bradford G. Addison · Barnes & Thornburg · http://www.btlaw.com · 11 South Meridian Street · Indianapolis, IN 46204-3535 · 317-236-1313

James A. Coles · ⑩ · Bose McKinney & Evans · http://www.boselaw.com · First Indiana Plaza, Suite 2700 135 North Pennsylvania Street · Indianapolis, IN 46204 · 317-684-5000

Richard D. Conard · ⑩ · Barnes & Thornburg · http://www.btlaw.com · 11 South Meridian Street · Indianapolis, IN 46204-3535 · 317-236-1313

Kevin Erdman · Baker & Daniels · http://www.bakerdaniels.com · 300 North Meridian Street, Suite 2700 Indianapolis, IN 46204 · 317-237-0300

Eric J. Groen · Baker & Daniels · http://www.bakerdaniels.com · 300 North Meridian Street, Suite 2700 · Indianapolis, IN 46204 · 317-237-0300

Thomas Q. Henry · ⑩ · Woodard, Emhardt, Moriarty, McNett & Henry · 111 Monument Circle, Suite 3700 · Indianapolis, IN 46204-5137 · 317-634-3456

Donald E. Knebel · ⑩ · Barnes & Thornburg · http://www.btlaw.com · 11 South Meridian Street · Indianapolis, IN 46204-3535 · 317-236-1313

Dwight D. Lueck · Barnes & Thornburg · http://www.btlaw.com · 11 South Meridian Street · Indianapolis, IN 46204-3535 · 317-236-1313

Jeffrey A. Michael · Barnes & Thornburg · http://www.btlaw.com · 11 South Meridian Street · Indianapolis, IN 46204-3535 · 317-236-1313

Timothy E. Niednagel · Baker & Daniels · http://www.bakerdaniels.com · 300 North Meridian Street, Suite 2700 · Indianapolis, IN 46204 · 317-237-0300

James R. Sweeney II · Barnes & Thornburg · http://www.btlaw.com · 11 South Meridian Street · Indianapolis, IN 46204-3535 · 317-236-1313

INTERNATIONAL TRADE AND FINANCE LAW

Indianapolis

M. Angella Castille · Baker & Daniels · http://www.bakerdaniels.com · 600 East 96th Street, Suite 600 · Indianapolis, IN 46240 · 317-569-9600

LABOR AND EMPLOYMENT LAW

Evansville

Dirck H. Stahl · Ziemer, Stayman, Weitzel & Shoulders · One Riverfront Place, Ninth Floor · 20 Northwest First Street · P.O. Box 916 · Evansville, IN 47706-0916 · 812-424-7575

Fort Wayne

Kathleen M. Anderson · Barnes & Thornburg · http://www.btlaw.com · One Summit Square, Suite 600 · Fort Wayne, IN 46802-3119 · 260-423-9440

Kathryn A. Brogan · Eilbacher Fletcher · 803 South Calhoun Street, Suite 400 · Fort Wayne, IN 46802 · 260-425-9777

William T. Hopkins, Jr. · ⑩ · Barnes & Thornburg · http://www.btlaw.com · One Summit Square, Suite 600 · Fort Wayne, IN 46802-3119 · 260-423-9440

David W. Miller · ⑳ · Baker & Daniels · http://www.bakerdaniels.com · 111 East Wayne Street, Suite 800 Fort Wayne, IN 46802 · 260-424-8000

Indianapolis

Michael H. Boldt · ⑩ · Ice Miller · One American Square, Suite 3100 · Indianapolis, IN 46282-0200 · 317-236-2100

Gregory N. Dale · Baker & Daniels · http://www.bakerdaniels.com · 300 North Meridian Street, Suite 2700 · Indianapolis, IN 46204 · 317-237-0300

Kathleen A. Delaney · DeLaney & DeLaney · 3640 North Washington Boulevard · Indianapolis, IN 46205 · 317-920-0400

Frederick W. Dennerline III · ㉕ · Fillenwarth, Dennerline, Groth & Towe · 1213 North Arlington Avenue, Suite 204 · Indianapolis, IN 46219 · 317-353-9363

Kim F. Ebert · ⑩ · Ogletree Deakins · http://www.ogletreedeakins.com · 111 Monument Circle, Suite 4600 · Indianapolis, IN 46204 · 317-916-1300

Daniel C. Emerson · Bose McKinney & Evans · http://www.boselaw.com · First Indiana Plaza, Suite 2700 135 North Pennsylvania Street · Indianapolis, IN 46204 · 317-684-5000

Edward J. Fillenwarth, Jr. · ⑳ · Fillenwarth, Dennerline, Groth & Towe · 1213 North Arlington Avenue, Suite 204 · Indianapolis, IN 46219 · 317-353-9363

William R. Groth · ㉕ · Fillenwarth, Dennerline, Groth & Towe · 1213 North Arlington Avenue, Suite 204 · Indianapolis, IN 46219 · 317-353-9363

Barry A. Macey · ⑳ · Macey Swanson & Allman · 445 North Pennsylvania Street, Suite 401 · Indianapolis, IN 46204 · 317-637-2345

Nora L. Macey · ⑩ · Macey Swanson & Allman · 445 North Pennsylvania Street, Suite 401 · Indianapolis, IN 46204 · 317-637-2345

John R. Maley · Barnes & Thornburg · http://www.btlaw.com · 11 South Meridian Street · Indianapolis, IN 46204-3535 · 317-236-1313

Brian L. McDermott · Ogletree Deakins · http://www.ogletreedeakins.com · 111 Monument Circle, Suite 4600 · Indianapolis, IN 46204 · 317-916-1300

Peter A. Morse, Jr. · Barnes & Thornburg · http://www.btlaw.com · 11 South Meridian Street · Indianapolis, IN 46204-3535 · 317-236-1313

Byron L. Myers · Ice Miller · One American Square, Suite 3100 · Indianapolis, IN 46282-0200 · 317-236-2100

John T. Neighbours · ⑩ · Baker & Daniels · http://www.bakerdaniels.com · 300 North Meridian Street, Suite 2700 · Indianapolis, IN 46204 · 317-237-0300

Todd M. Nierman · Littler Mendelson · 111 Monument Circle, Suite 702 · Indianapolis, IN 46204 · 317-287-3600

Hudnall A. Pfeiffer · Baker & Daniels · http://www.bakerdaniels.com · 300 North Meridian Street, Suite 2700 · Indianapolis, IN 46204 · 317-237-0300

Paul H. Sinclair · Ice Miller · One American Square, Suite 3100 · Indianapolis, IN 46282-0200 · 317-236-2100

David Swider · Bose McKinney & Evans · http://www.boselaw.com · First Indiana Plaza, Suite 2700 · 135 North Pennsylvania Street · Indianapolis, IN 46204 · 317-684-5000

Michael C. Terrell · Taft Stettinius & Hollister · http://www.taftlaw.com · One Indiana Square, Suite 3500 · Indianapolis, IN 46204 · 317-713-3500

Michael L. Tooley · Ice Miller · One American Square, Suite 3100 · Indianapolis, IN 46282-0200 · 317-236-2100

Gregory J. Utken · Baker & Daniels · http://www.bakerdaniels.com · 300 North Meridian Street, Suite 2700 · Indianapolis, IN 46204 · 317-237-0300

Kenneth J. Yerkes · ⑩ · Barnes & Thornburg · http://www.btlaw.com · 11 South Meridian Street · Indianapolis, IN 46204-3535 · 317-236-1313

South Bend

Kathleen K. Brickley · Barnes & Thornburg · http://www.btlaw.com · First Source Bank Center, Suite 600 · 100 North Michigan Street · South Bend, IN 46601 · 574-233-1171

John D. LaDue · LaDue Curran & Kuehn · 200 First Bank Building · 205 West Jefferson Boulevard · South Bend, IN 46601 · 574-968-0760

Patrick D. Murphy · Boveri Murphy Rice · http://www.bmrl-law.com · 400 Plaza Building · 210 South Michigan Street · South Bend, IN 46601 · 574-232-0300

LAND USE & ZONING LAW

Indianapolis

Philip A. Nicely · ⑳ · Bose McKinney & Evans · http://www.boselaw.com · Meridian Corporate Plaza Two, Suite 300 · 301 Pennsylvania Parkway · Indianapolis, IN 46280 · 317-684-5300

Joseph M. Scimia · Baker & Daniels · http://www.bakerdaniels.com · 600 East 96th Street, Suite 600 · Indianapolis, IN 46240 · 317-569-9600

Mary E. Solada · Bingham McHale · Market Tower Building, Suite 2700 · 10 West Market Street · Indianapolis, IN 46204 · 317-635-8900

Zeff A. Weiss · ⑩ · Ice Miller · One American Square, Suite 3100 · Indianapolis, IN 46282-0200 · 317-236-2100

LEGAL MALPRACTICE LAW

Indianapolis

Michael E. Brown · Kightlinger & Gray · Market Square Center, Suite 600 · 151 North Delaware Street · Indianapolis, IN 46204 · 317-638-4521

Ronald E. Elberger · ⑩ · Bose McKinney & Evans · http://www.boselaw.com · First Indiana Plaza, Suite 2700 · 135 North Pennsylvania Street · Indianapolis, IN 46204 · 317-684-5000

David T. Kasper · Locke Reynolds · http://www.locke.com · 201 North Illinois Street, Suite 1000 · P.O. Box 44961 · Indianapolis, IN 46244-0961 · 317-237-3800

Kevin P. McGoff · Bingham McHale · Market Tower Building, Suite 2700 · 10 West Market Street · Indianapolis, IN 46204 · 317-635-8900

Karl L. Mulvaney · Bingham McHale · Market Tower Building, Suite 2700 · 10 West Market Street · Indianapolis, IN 46204 · 317-635-8900

LEVERAGED BUYOUTS AND PRIVATE EQUITY LAW

Indianapolis

J. Jeffrey Brown · Baker & Daniels · http://www.bakerdaniels.com · 600 East 96th Street, Suite 600 · Indianapolis, IN 46240 · 317-569-9600

David L. Johnson · Baker & Daniels · http://www.bakerdaniels.com · 300 North Meridian Street, Suite 2700 · Indianapolis, IN 46204 · 317-237-0300

Michael E. Millikan · Ice Miller · One American Square, Suite 3100 · Indianapolis, IN 46282-0200 · 317-236-2100

John R. Thornburgh · ⑩ · Ice Miller · One American Square, Suite 3100 · Indianapolis, IN 46282-0200 · 317-236-2100

MASS TORT LITIGATION

Fort Wayne

Albert J. Dahm · Locke Reynolds · http://www.locke.com · 9604 Coldwater Road, Suite 201 · Fort Wayne, IN 46825 · 260-497-6000

Indianapolis

Michael A. Bergin · Locke Reynolds · http://www.locke.com · 201 North Illinois Street, Suite 1000 · P.O. Box 44961 · Indianapolis, IN 46244-0961 · 317-237-3800

Patricia Polis McCrory · Locke Reynolds · http://www.locke.com · 201 North Illinois Street, Suite 1000 · P.O. Box 44961 · Indianapolis, IN 46244-0961 · 317-237-3800

MEDIA LAW

Indianapolis

Michael A. Wilkins · Ice Miller · One American Square, Suite 3100 · Indianapolis, IN 46282-0200 · 317-236-2100

MEDICAL MALPRACTICE LAW

Bloomington

Edward J. Liptak · Carson Boxberger · 3100 John Hinkle Place, Suite 106 · Bloomington, IN 47408-2611 812-333-1225

Fort Wayne

Mark W. Baeverstad · Rothberg, Logan & Warsco · National City Center, Suite 2100 · 110 West Berry Street · Fort Wayne, IN 46802 · 260-422-9454

Sherrill William Colvin · ⑳ · Haller & Colvin · 444 East Main Street · Fort Wayne, IN 46802 · 260-426-0444

David L. Farnbauch · Sweeney Law Firm · 8109-B Lima Road · Fort Wayne, IN 46818 · 260-420-3137

Milford M. Miller, Jr. · ⑩ · Miller Murphy · http://www.millermurphylaw.com · 110 West Berry Street, Suite 1500 · Fort Wayne, IN 46802 · 260-423-1500

Edward L. Murphy, Jr. · Miller Murphy · http://www.millermurphylaw.com · 110 West Berry Street, Suite 1500 · Fort Wayne, IN 46802 · 260-423-1500

Daniel A. Roby · ⑩ · Roby & Manges · 200 East Main Street, Suite 520 · Fort Wayne, IN 46802 · 260-423-3366

Stanley L. Rosenblatt · Tourkow, Crell, Rosenblatt & Johnston · http://www.tcrjlaw.com · 203 East Berry Street, Suite 814 · Fort Wayne, IN 46802 · 260-426-0545

Indianapolis

Stephen B. Caplin · Caplin & Park · 135 North Pennyslvania Street, Suite 1150 · Indianapolis, IN 46204 317-231-1100

Lance D. Cline · ⑩ · Cline, Farrell, Christie, Lee & Caress · 951 North Delaware Street · Indianapolis, IN 46202-3377 · 317-488-5500

Mary Arlien Findling · Findling Garau Germano & Pennington · 151 North Delaware Street, Suite 1515 · Indianapolis, IN 46204 · 317-822-9530

F. Boyd Hovde · ⑳ · Hovde Dassow & Deets · http://www.hovdelaw.com · Meridian Tower, Suite 500 · 201 West 103rd Street · Indianapolis, IN 46290 · 317-818-3100

George E. Purdy · Bose McKinney & Evans · http://www.boselaw.com · First Indiana Plaza, Suite 2700 · 135 North Pennsylvania Street · Indianapolis, IN 46204 · 317-684-5000

La Porte

Mark A. Lienhoop · Newby, Lewis, Kaminski & Jones · 916 Lincoln Way · La Porte, IN 46350 · 219-362-1577

Merrillville

Barry D. Rooth · Theodoros & Rooth · http://www.theodorosrooth.com · 8750 Broadway, Suite A · Merrillville, IN 46410 · 219-769-6393

South Bend

R. Kent Rowe · ⑩ · Rowe & Rowe · 1003 North Hickory · South Bend, IN 46615 · 574-233-8200

R. Kent Rowe III · ⑩ · Rowe & Rowe · 1003 North Hickory · South Bend, IN 46615 · 574-233-8200

MERGERS & ACQUISITIONS LAW

Indianapolis

Mark B. Barnes · Ice Miller · One American Square, Suite 3100 · Indianapolis, IN 46282-0200 · 317-236-2100

Alan W. Becker · Bose McKinney & Evans · http://www.boselaw.com · First Indiana Plaza, Suite 2700 · 135 North Pennsylvania Street · Indianapolis, IN 46204 · 317-684-5000

J. Jeffrey Brown · Baker & Daniels · http://www.bakerdaniels.com · 600 East 96th Street, Suite 600 · Indianapolis, IN 46240 · 317-569-9600

David Butcher · ⑩ · Bose McKinney & Evans · http://www.boselaw.com · First Indiana Plaza, Suite 2700 135 North Pennsylvania Street · Indianapolis, IN 46204 · 317-684-5000

Kendall C. Crook · Bose McKinney & Evans · http://www.boselaw.com · First Indiana Plaza, Suite 2700 · 135 North Pennsylvania Street · Indianapolis, IN 46204 · 317-684-5000

Joseph E. DeGroff · Ice Miller · One American Square, Suite 3100 · Indianapolis, IN 46282-0200 · 317-236-2100

Donald K. Densborn · Taft Stettinius & Hollister · http://www.taftlaw.com · 8888 Keystone Crossing, Suite 1400 · Indianapolis, IN 46240-5609 · 317-844-4744

Robert A. Greising · Krieg DeVault · One Indiana Square, Suite 2800 · Indianapolis, IN 46204-2079 · 317-636-4341

Stephen J. Hackman · Ice Miller · One American Square, Suite 3100 · Indianapolis, IN 46282-0200 · 317-236-2100

Eugene L. Henderson · Bose McKinney & Evans · http://www.boselaw.com · First Indiana Plaza, Suite 2700 · 135 North Pennsylvania Street · Indianapolis, IN 46204 · 317-684-5000

Robert J. Hicks · Taft Stettinius & Hollister · http://www.taftlaw.com · One Indiana Square, Suite 3500 · Indianapolis, IN 46204 · 317-713-3500

Steven K. Humke · Ice Miller · One American Square, Suite 3100 · Indianapolis, IN 46282-0200 · 317-236-2100

Roberts E. Inveiss · Bose McKinney & Evans · http://www.boselaw.com · First Indiana Plaza, Suite 2700 135 North Pennsylvania Street · Indianapolis, IN 46204 · 317-684-5000

Robert P. Kassing · ⑩ · Bose McKinney & Evans · http://www.boselaw.com · First Indiana Plaza, Suite 2700 · 135 North Pennsylvania Street · Indianapolis, IN 46204 · 317-684-5000

Tibor D. Klopfer · Baker & Daniels · http://www.bakerdaniels.com · 300 North Meridian Street, Suite 2700 · Indianapolis, IN 46204 · 317-237-0300

Erick D. Ponader · Taft Stettinius & Hollister · http://www.taftlaw.com · One Indiana Square, Suite 3500 Indianapolis, IN 46204 · 317-713-3500

Michael J. Schneider · Bose McKinney & Evans · http://www.boselaw.com · First Indiana Plaza, Suite 2700 · 135 North Pennsylvania Street · Indianapolis, IN 46204 · 317-684-5000

Regina M. Sharrow · Baker & Daniels · http://www.bakerdaniels.com · 600 East 96th Street, Suite 600 · Indianapolis, IN 46240 · 317-569-9600

John R. Thornburgh · ⑩ · Ice Miller · One American Square, Suite 3100 · Indianapolis, IN 46282-0200 · 317-236-2100

Steven W. Thornton · Barnes & Thornburg · http://www.btlaw.com · 11 South Meridian Street · Indianapolis, IN 46204-3535 · 317-236-1313

Richard J. Thrapp · Ice Miller · One American Square, Suite 3100 · Indianapolis, IN 46282-0200 · 317-236-2100

Robert T. Wildman · Bose McKinney & Evans · http://www.boselaw.com · First Indiana Plaza, Suite 2700 · 135 North Pennsylvania Street · Indianapolis, IN 46204 · 317-684-5000

David L. Wills · Bose McKinney & Evans · http://www.boselaw.com · First Indiana Plaza, Suite 2700 · 135 North Pennsylvania Street · Indianapolis, IN 46204 · 317-684-5000

Robert S. Wynne · Baker & Daniels · http://www.bakerdaniels.com · 600 East 96th Street, Suite 600 · Indianapolis, IN 46240 · 317-569-9600

MUNICIPAL LAW

Indianapolis

Brian L. Burdick · Barnes & Thornburg · http://www.btlaw.com · 11 South Meridian Street · Indianapolis, IN 46204-3535 · 317-236-1313

Amy M. Corsaro · Ice Miller · One American Square, Suite 3100 · Indianapolis, IN 46282-0200 · 317-236-2100

Robert T. Grand · Barnes & Thornburg · http://www.btlaw.com · 11 South Meridian Street · Indianapolis, IN 46204-3535 · 317-236-1313

Paul S. Mannweiler · Bose McKinney & Evans · http://www.boselaw.com · First Indiana Plaza, Suite 2700 · 135 North Pennsylvania Street · Indianapolis, IN 46204 · 317-684-5000

NON-PROFIT/CHARITIES LAW

Indianapolis

Ben W. Blanton · Baker & Daniels · http://www.bakerdaniels.com · 300 North Meridian Street, Suite 2700 · Indianapolis, IN 46204 · 317-237-0300

Gina M. Giacone · Ice Miller · One American Square, Suite 3100 · Indianapolis, IN 46282-0200 · 317-236-2100

Paul Lowell Haines · Baker & Daniels · http://www.bakerdaniels.com · 300 North Meridian Street, Suite 2700 · Indianapolis, IN 46204 · 317-237-0300

Jennett M. Hill · Baker & Daniels · http://www.bakerdaniels.com · 300 North Meridian Street, Suite 2700 Indianapolis, IN 46204 · 317-237-0300

Joseph E. Miller · Baker & Daniels · http://www.bakerdaniels.com · 300 North Meridian Street, Suite 2700 · Indianapolis, IN 46204 · 317-237-0300

Marilee J. Springer · Ice Miller · One American Square, Suite 3100 · Indianapolis, IN 46282-0200 · 317-236-2100

Lisa A. Stone · 10 · Ice Miller · One American Square, Suite 3100 · Indianapolis, IN 46282-0200 · 317-236-2100

Gordon D. Wishard · 20 · Ice Miller · One American Square, Suite 3100 · Indianapolis, IN 46282-0200 · 317-236-2100

C. Daniel Yates · Bose McKinney & Evans · http://www.boselaw.com · First Indiana Plaza, Suite 2700 · 135 North Pennsylvania Street · Indianapolis, IN 46204 · 317-684-5000

NON-WHITE-COLLAR CRIMINAL DEFENSE

Anderson

Jeffrey A. Lockwood · 20 · Jeffrey A. Lockwood · 403 West Eigth Street, Suite Three · Anderson, IN 46016 · 765-649-1144

Evansville

Dennis L. Brinkmeyer · Dennis L. Brinkmeyer · 525 Sycamore Street · P.O. Box 1005 · Evansville, IN 47706-1005 · 812-423-3125

Jeffery L. Lantz · Jeffery Lantz Law Office · 525 Sycamore Street · Evansville, IN 47706 · 812-464-0044

Fort Wayne

Charles F. Leonard · 10 · Leonard, Hammond, Thoma & Terrill · 800 South Calhoun Street · Fort Wayne, IN 46802-2302 · 260-420-6000

Indianapolis

Robert W. Hammerle · 20 · Hammerle & Allen · 1455 North Pennsylvania Street · Indianapolis, IN 46202-2420 · 317-630-0137

Richard Kammen · 25 · Gilroy & Kammen · One Indiana Square, Suite 150 · Indianapolis, IN 46204 · 317-236-0400

J. Richard Kiefer · 20 · Bingham McHale · Market Tower Building, Suite 2700 · 10 West Market Street · Indianapolis, IN 46204 · 317-635-8900

Kevin P. McGoff · Bingham McHale · Market Tower Building, Suite 2700 · 10 West Market Street · Indianapolis, IN 46204 · 317-635-8900

James H. Voyles, Jr. · ㉕ · Voyles, Zahn, Paul, Hogan & Merriman · 141 East Washington Street, Suite 300 · Indianapolis, IN 46204 · 317-632-4463

Dennis E. Zahn · ⑩ · Voyles, Zahn, Paul, Hogan & Merriman · 141 East Washington Street, Suite 300 · Indianapolis, IN 46204 · 317-632-4463

La Porte

Martin W. Kus · Newby, Lewis, Kaminski & Jones · 916 Lincoln Way · La Porte, IN 46350 · 219-362-1577

Merrillville

Nick J. Thiros · ㉕ · Cohen & Thiros · 200 East 90th Drive · Merrillville, IN 46410-8102 · 219-769-1600

Terre Haute

William G. Smock · Smock & Etling · 77 Cherry Street · Terre Haute, IN 47807 · 812-238-1751

PERSONAL INJURY LITIGATION

Anderson

Theodore F. Smith, Jr. · Theodore F. Smith, Jr. · http://www.smithlaw.bz · 215 Historical West Eighth Street · Anderson, IN 46016-1374 · 765-644-8410

Evansville

Charles L. Berger · ⑳ · Berger & Berger · 313 Main Street · Evansville, IN 47708 · 812-425-8101

Fort Wayne

Mark W. Baeverstad · Rothberg, Logan & Warsco · National City Center, Suite 2100 · 110 West Berry Street · Fort Wayne, IN 46802 · 260-422-9454

Edward Beck · Shambaugh, Kast, Beck & Williams · http://www.skbw.com · 229 West Berry Street, Suite 400 · P.O. Box 11648 · Fort Wayne, IN 46859-1648 · 260-423-1430

Sherrill William Colvin · ⑳ · Haller & Colvin · 444 East Main Street · Fort Wayne, IN 46802 · 260-426-0444

Leonard E. Eilbacher · ⑳ · Eilbacher Fletcher · 803 South Calhoun Street, Suite 400 · Fort Wayne, IN 46802 · 260-425-9777

John O. Feighner · Haller & Colvin · 444 East Main Street · Fort Wayne, IN 46802 · 260-426-0444

Robert T. Keen, Jr. · Carson Boxberger · 1400 One Summit Square · Fort Wayne, IN 46802-3173 · 260-423-9411

Branch R. Lew · Hunt Suedhoff Kalamaros · 803 South Calhoun Street, Ninth Floor · P.O. Box 11489 · Fort Wayne, IN 46858-1489 · 260-423-1311

Edward L. Murphy, Jr. · Miller Murphy · http://www.millermurphylaw.com · 110 West Berry Street, Suite 1500 · Fort Wayne, IN 46802 · 260-423-1500

Daniel A. Roby · ⑩ · Roby & Manges · 200 East Main Street, Suite 520 · Fort Wayne, IN 46802 · 260-423-3366

Stanley L. Rosenblatt · Tourkow, Crell, Rosenblatt & Johnston · http://www.tcrjlaw.com · 203 East Berry Street, Suite 814 · Fort Wayne, IN 46802 · 260-426-0545

Richard P. Samek · Carson Boxberger · 1400 One Summit Square · Fort Wayne, IN 46802-3173 · 260-423-9411

James J. Shea · Hunt Suedhoff Kalamaros · 803 South Calhoun Street, Ninth Floor · P.O. Box 11489 · Fort Wayne, IN 46858-1489 · 260-423-1311

Arthur Surguine · Hunt Suedhoff Kalamaros · 803 South Calhoun Street, Ninth Floor · P.O. Box 11489 · Fort Wayne, IN 46858-1489 · 260-423-1311

Robert L. Thompson · ⑩ · Thompson & Rogers · 444 East Main Street, Suite 202 · Fort Wayne, IN 46802 · 260-426-0674

Franklin

George Hoffman III · Hoffman Admire & Newcomb · 250 East Jefferson Street · Franklin, IN 46131 · 317-736-1982

Goshen

John D. Ulmer · ⑩ · Yoder, Ainlay, Ulmer & Buckingham · 130 North Main Street · P.O. Box 575 · Goshen, IN 46527-0575 · 574-533-1171

Hammond

Harold Abrahamson · ⑩ · Abrahamson & Reed · 200 Russell Street · Hammond, IN 46320-1818 · 219-937-1500

Highland

Anthony DeBonis, Jr. · Smith & DeBonis · Professional Building · 9696 Gordon Drive · Highland, IN 46322 · 219-922-1000

Indianapolis

Theodore J. Blanford · Hume Smith Geddes Green & Simmons · 54 Monument Circle, Fourth Floor · Indianapolis, IN 46204-2996 · 317-632-4402

Robert Clemens · Bose McKinney & Evans · http://www.boselaw.com · First Indiana Plaza, Suite 2700 · 135 North Pennsylvania Street · Indianapolis, IN 46204 · 317-684-5000

Lance D. Cline · ⑩ · Cline, Farrell, Christie, Lee & Caress · 951 North Delaware Street · Indianapolis, IN 46202-3377 · 317-488-5500

Ralph A. Cohen · ⑩ · Ice Miller · One American Square, Suite 3100 · Indianapolis, IN 46282-0200 · 317-236-2100

Michael R. Conner · ⑩ · Barnes & Thornburg · http://www.btlaw.com · 11 South Meridian Street · Indianapolis, IN 46204-3535 · 317-236-1313

William F. Conour · Conour Law Firm · http://www.conour.com · Four Parkwood Crossing, Suite 150 · 500 East 96th Street · Indianapolis, IN 46240-3765 · 317-846-5550

Thomas L. Davis · Locke Reynolds · http://www.locke.com · 201 North Illinois Street, Suite 1000 · P.O. Box 44961 · Indianapolis, IN 46244-0961 · 317-237-3800

Andrew J. Detherage · Barnes & Thornburg · http://www.btlaw.com · 11 South Meridian Street · Indianapolis, IN 46204-3535 · 317-236-1313

Kevin P. Farrell · Cline, Farrell, Christie, Lee & Caress · 951 North Delaware Street · Indianapolis, IN 46202-3377 · 317-488-5500

Robert W. Geddes · Hume Smith Geddes Green & Simmons · 54 Monument Circle, Fourth Floor · Indianapolis, IN 46204-2996 · 317-632-4402

George C. Gray · Gray, Robinson, Ryan & Fox · 8122 South Meridian Street · Indianapolis, IN 46217-4939 · 317-881-2501

Richard Douglas Hailey · ⑩ · Ramey & Hailey · 3891 Eagle Creek Parkway, Suite C · Indianapolis, IN 46254-2600 · 317-634-9978

F. Boyd Hovde · ⑳ · Hovde Dassow & Deets · http://www.hovdelaw.com · Meridian Tower, Suite 500 · 201 West 103rd Street · Indianapolis, IN 46290 · 317-818-3100

Frederick R. Hovde · Hovde Dassow & Deets · http://www.hovdelaw.com · Meridian Tower, Suite 500 · 201 West 103rd Street · Indianapolis, IN 46290 · 317-818-3100

John T. Hume III · Hume Smith Geddes Green & Simmons · 54 Monument Circle, Fourth Floor · Indianapolis, IN 46204-2996 · 317-632-4402

William W. Hurst · ⑳ · Mitchell Hurst Jacobs & Dick · 152 East Washington Street · Indianapolis, IN 46204 · 317-636-0808

Samuel L. Jacobs · ⑩ · Mitchell Hurst Jacobs & Dick · 152 East Washington Street · Indianapolis, IN 46204 · 317-636-0808

D. Bruce Kehoe · ⑩ · Wilson, Kehoe & Winingham · 2859 North Meridian Street · P.O. Box 1317 · Indianapolis, IN 46206-1317 · 317-920-6400

Mark C. Ladendorf · Ladendorf & Ladendorf · 7310 North Shadeland Avenue · Indianapolis, IN 46250 · 317-842-5800

Lloyd H. Milliken, Jr. · ⑳ · Locke Reynolds · http://www.locke.com · 201 North Illinois Street, Suite 1000 · P.O. Box 44961 · Indianapolis, IN 46244-0961 · 317-237-3800

Marvin H. Mitchell · ⑳ · Mitchell Hurst Jacobs & Dick · 152 East Washington Street · Indianapolis, IN 46204 · 317-636-0808

W. Scott Montross · ⑳ · Townsend & Montross · 230 East Ohio Street · Indianapolis, IN 46204-2149 · 317-264-4444

Eric A. Riegner · Locke Reynolds · http://www.locke.com · 201 North Illinois Street, Suite 1000 · P.O. Box 44961 · Indianapolis, IN 46244-0961 · 317-237-3800

Randall R. Riggs · Locke Reynolds · http://www.locke.com · 201 North Illinois Street, Suite 1000 · P.O. Box 44961 · Indianapolis, IN 46244-0961 · 317-237-3800

Kevin C. Schiferl · Locke Reynolds · http://www.locke.com · 201 North Illinois Street, Suite 1000 · P.O. Box 44961 · Indianapolis, IN 46244-0961 · 317-237-3800

W. Brent Threlkeld · Threlkeld Reynolds · Century Building, Suite 720 · 36 South Pennsylvania Street · Indianapolis, IN 46204 · 317-655-5200

John F. Townsend, Jr. · ⑩ · Townsend & Montross · 230 East Ohio Street · Indianapolis, IN 46204-2149 · 317-264-4444

Robert F. Wagner · Lewis Wagner, LLP · 501 Indiana Avenue, Suite 200 · Indianapolis, IN 46202-6150 · 317-237-0500

William E. Winingham, Jr. · Wilson, Kehoe & Winingham · 2859 North Meridian Street · P.O. Box 1317 Indianapolis, IN 46206-1317 · 317-920-6400

Louis Buddy Yosha · ㉕ · The Law Offices of Buddy Yosha · http://www.yoshalaw.com · Pyramid I, Fourth Floor · 3500 DePauw Boulevard · Indianapolis, IN 46268-1137 · 317-334-9200

Kokomo

Daniel J. Harrigan · ⑩ · Bayliff, Harrigan, Cord & Maugans · 123 North Buckeye Street · P.O. Box 2249 · Kokomo, IN 46904-2249 · 765-459-3941

James R. Martin · Martin and Humphrey · 1517 Rockford Court · P.O. Box 2797 · Kokomo, IN 46902 · 765-453-2777

La Porte

Gene M. Jones · ⑩ · Newby, Lewis, Kaminski & Jones · 916 Lincoln Way · La Porte, IN 46350 · 219-362-1577

Martin W. Kus · Newby, Lewis, Kaminski & Jones · 916 Lincoln Way · La Porte, IN 46350 · 219-362-1577

Lafayette

Stephen R. Pennell · Stuart & Branigin · 300 Main Street, Suite 900 · P.O. Box 1010 · Lafayette, IN 47902-1010 · 765-423-1561

Michael J. Stapleton · Ball Eggleston · 201 Main Street · P.O. Box 1535 · Lafayette, IN 47902-1535 · 765-742-9046

Charles R. Vaughan, Sr. · ⑩ · Vaughan and Vaughan · Chase Building, Suite 909 · 201 Main Street · P.O. Box 498 · Lafayette, IN 47901 · 765-742-0056

Charles V. Vaughan · Vaughan and Vaughan · Chase Building, Suite 909 · 201 Main Street · P.O. Box 498 Lafayette, IN 47901 · 765-742-0056

Lebanon

Peter L. Obremskey · ⑩ · Parr Richey Obremskey & Morton · http://www.parrlaw.com · 225 West Main Street · P.O. Box 668 · Lebanon, IN 46052 · 765-482-0110

Anthony W. Patterson · Parr Richey Obremskey & Morton · http://www.parrlaw.com · 225 West Main Street · P.O. Box 668 · Lebanon, IN 46052 · 765-482-0110

Merrillville

Thomas A. Clements · Clements & Vann · http://www.clementsvann.com · 500 East 86th Avenue · Merrillville, IN 46410 · 219-793-2990

John E. Hughes · Hoeppner, Wagner & Evans · South Tower, Suite 606 · 1000 East 80th Place · P.O. Box 10627 · Merrillville, IN 46411-0627 · 219-769-6552

Mooresville

John A. Young · ⑳ · John A. Young · 36 South Pennsylvania Street, Suite 630 · Mooresville, IN 46158 · 317-633-4200

Muncie

P. Gregory Cross · ⑩ · The Cross Law Firm · Historic Riley-Jones House · 315 East Charles Street · Muncie, IN 47305 · 765-747-1953

New Albany

Donald R. Forrest · Forrest & Bourne · 117 East Spring Street, Suite 216 · P.O. Box 785 · New Albany, IN 47150 · 812-945-9151

David V. Scott · ⑩ · Dave Scott · 157 East Main Street · P.O. Box 785 · New Albany, IN 47150 · 812-945-4555

Seymour

Roger L. Pardieck · ⑳ · The Pardieck Law Firm · 100 North Chestnut Street · P.O. Box 608 · Seymour, IN 47274 · 812-523-8686

South Bend

Douglas K. Dieterly · Barnes & Thornburg · http://www.btlaw.com · First Source Bank Center, Suite 600 100 North Michigan Street · South Bend, IN 46601 · 574-233-1171

Robert F. Gonderman, Jr. · Gonderman Legal Corporation · 54391 Thirtieth Street · P.O. Box 6456 · South Bend, IN 46601 · 574-272-9931

Robert J. Konopa · ⑳ · Tuesley Hall Konopa · RiverPlace Professional Center, Suite 100 · 212 East LaSalle Avenue · South Bend, IN 46617 · 574-232-3538

Carmen M. Piasecki · Nickle & Piasecki · 205 West Jefferson Boulevard, Suite 600 · South Bend, IN 46601 · 574-232-4747

R. Kent Rowe · ⑩ · Rowe & Rowe · 1003 North Hickory · South Bend, IN 46615 · 574-233-8200

R. Kent Rowe III · ⑩ · Rowe & Rowe · 1003 North Hickory · South Bend, IN 46615 · 574-233-8200

Thomas H. Singer · ⑳ · Nickle & Piasecki · 205 West Jefferson Boulevard, Suite 600 · South Bend, IN 46601 · 574-232-4747

Terre Haute

Bruce D. Aukerman · Mann Law Firm · 646 Walnut Street · P.O. Box 1643 · Terre Haute, IN 47808-1643 · 812-232-0107

G. Steven Fleschner · ⑩ · Fleschner, Stark, Tanoos & Newlin · 201 Ohio Street · Terre Haute, IN 47807 812-232-2000

James O. McDonald · Everett, Everett & McDonald · 648 Walnut Street · P.O. Box 8328 · Terre Haute, IN 47808-8328 · 812-238-2456

Thomas C. Newlin · Fleschner, Stark, Tanoos & Newlin · 201 Ohio Street · Terre Haute, IN 47807 · 812-232-2000

Gus Sacopulos · ⑩ · Sacopulos, Johnson & Sacopulos · 676 Ohio Street · Terre Haute, IN 47807-3604 · 812-238-2565

Stephen L. Williams · ⑩ · Mann Law Firm · 646 Walnut Street · P.O. Box 1643 · Terre Haute, IN 47808-1643 · 812-232-0107

Robert L. Wright · Wright Shagley & Lowery · 500 Ohio Street · P.O. Box 8448 · Terre Haute, IN 47808-8448 · 812-232-3388

PRIVATE FUNDS LAW

Indianapolis

Alan W. Becker · Bose McKinney & Evans · http://www.boselaw.com · First Indiana Plaza, Suite 2700 · 135 North Pennsylvania Street · Indianapolis, IN 46204 · 317-684-5000

Karen Woods · Krieg DeVault · One Indiana Square, Suite 2800 · Indianapolis, IN 46204-2079 · 317-636-4341

PRODUCT LIABILITY LITIGATION

Fort Wayne

Sherrill William Colvin · ⑳ · Haller & Colvin · 444 East Main Street · Fort Wayne, IN 46802 · 260-426-0444

Albert J. Dahm · Locke Reynolds · http://www.locke.com · 9604 Coldwater Road, Suite 201 · Fort Wayne, IN 46825 · 260-497-6000

Indianapolis

Michael R. Conner · ⑩ · Barnes & Thornburg · http://www.btlaw.com · 11 South Meridian Street · Indianapolis, IN 46204-3535 · 317-236-1313

Joseph G. Eaton · Barnes & Thornburg · http://www.btlaw.com · 11 South Meridian Street · Indianapolis, IN 46204-3535 · 317-236-1313

Bonnie L. Gallivan · Ice Miller · One American Square, Suite 3100 · Indianapolis, IN 46282-0200 · 317-236-2100

F. Boyd Hovde · ⑳ · Hovde Dassow & Deets · http://www.hovdelaw.com · Meridian Tower, Suite 500 · 201 West 103rd Street · Indianapolis, IN 46290 · 317-818-3100

Wayne C. Kreuscher · Barnes & Thornburg · http://www.btlaw.com · 11 South Meridian Street · Indianapolis, IN 46204-3535 · 317-236-1313

Mary Nold Larimore · Ice Miller · One American Square, Suite 3100 · Indianapolis, IN 46282-0200 · 317-236-2100

Lloyd H. Milliken, Jr. · ⑳ · Locke Reynolds · http://www.locke.com · 201 North Illinois Street, Suite 1000 · P.O. Box 44961 · Indianapolis, IN 46244-0961 · 317-237-3800

Judy S. Okenfuss · Ice Miller · One American Square, Suite 3100 · Indianapolis, IN 46282-0200 · 317-236-2100

George E. Purdy · Bose McKinney & Evans · http://www.boselaw.com · First Indiana Plaza, Suite 2700 · 135 North Pennsylvania Street · Indianapolis, IN 46204 · 317-684-5000

Randall R. Riggs · Locke Reynolds · http://www.locke.com · 201 North Illinois Street, Suite 1000 · P.O. Box 44961 · Indianapolis, IN 46244-0961 · 317-237-3800

Kevin C. Schiferl · Locke Reynolds · http://www.locke.com · 201 North Illinois Street, Suite 1000 · P.O. Box 44961 · Indianapolis, IN 46244-0961 · 317-237-3800

Thomas G. Stayton · Baker & Daniels · http://www.bakerdaniels.com · 300 North Meridian Street, Suite 2700 · Indianapolis, IN 46204 · 317-237-0300

John Joseph Tanner · Baker & Daniels · http://www.bakerdaniels.com · 300 North Meridian Street, Suite 2700 · Indianapolis, IN 46204 · 317-237-0300

William E. Winingham, Jr. · Wilson, Kehoe & Winingham · 2859 North Meridian Street · P.O. Box 1317 Indianapolis, IN 46206-1317 · 317-920-6400

South Bend

Douglas K. Dieterly · Barnes & Thornburg · http://www.btlaw.com · First Source Bank Center, Suite 600 100 North Michigan Street · South Bend, IN 46601 · 574-233-1171

Joseph R. Fullenkamp · Barnes & Thornburg · http://www.btlaw.com · First Source Bank Center, Suite 600 · 100 North Michigan Street · South Bend, IN 46601 · 574-233-1171

Robert J. Konopa · 20 · Tuesley Hall Konopa · RiverPlace Professional Center, Suite 100 · 212 East LaSalle Avenue · South Bend, IN 46617 · 574-232-3538

PROFESSIONAL MALPRACTICE LAW

Indianapolis

Ronald E. Elberger · 10 · Bose McKinney & Evans · http://www.boselaw.com · First Indiana Plaza, Suite 2700 · 135 North Pennsylvania Street · Indianapolis, IN 46204 · 317-684-5000

South Bend

R. Kent Rowe · 10 · Rowe & Rowe · 1003 North Hickory · South Bend, IN 46615 · 574-233-8200

PUBLIC FINANCE LAW

Indianapolis

Bruce D. Donaldson · Barnes & Thornburg · http://www.btlaw.com · 11 South Meridian Street · Indianapolis, IN 46204-3535 · 317-236-1313

Thomas Froehle · Baker & Daniels · http://www.bakerdaniels.com · 300 North Meridian Street, Suite 2700 · Indianapolis, IN 46204 · 317-237-0300

Philip C. Genetos · Ice Miller · One American Square, Suite 3100 · Indianapolis, IN 46282-0200 · 317-236-2100

Michael P. Lucas · Barnes & Thornburg · http://www.btlaw.com · 11 South Meridian Street · Indianapolis, IN 46204-3535 · 317-236-1313

Richard C. Starkey · Barnes & Thornburg · http://www.btlaw.com · 11 South Meridian Street · Indianapolis, IN 46204-3535 · 317-236-1313

Neal W. Steinbart · Barnes & Thornburg · http://www.btlaw.com · 11 South Meridian Street · Indianapolis, IN 46204-3535 · 317-236-1313

South Bend

Alan B. Feldbaum · Barnes & Thornburg · http://www.btlaw.com · First Source Bank Center, Suite 600 · 100 North Michigan Street · South Bend, IN 46601 · 574-233-1171

RAILROAD LAW

Hammond

Harold Abrahamson · ⑩ · Abrahamson & Reed · 200 Russell Street · Hammond, IN 46320-1818 · 219-937-1500

Indianapolis

Bruce Hugon · Stuart & Branigin · 8888 Keystone Crossing, Suite 640 · Indianapolis, IN 46240 · 317-574-7245

Lafayette

John C. Duffey · Stuart & Branigin · 300 Main Street, Suite 900 · P.O. Box 1010 · Lafayette, IN 47902-1010 · 765-423-1561

REAL ESTATE LAW

Fort Wayne

Jon A. Bomberger · Baker & Daniels · http://www.bakerdaniels.com · 111 East Wayne Street, Suite 800 · Fort Wayne, IN 46802 · 260-424-8000

Jack W. Lawson · ⑩ · Beckman Lawson · Standard Federal Plaza, Suite 800 · 200 East Main Street · Fort Wayne, IN 46801-0800 · 260-422-0800

Indianapolis

Jeffrey A. Abrams · Dann, Pecar, Newman & Kleiman · http://www.dannpecar.com · One American Square, Suite 2300 · Indianapolis, IN 46282 · 317-632-3232

John B. Baxter · Barnes & Thornburg · http://www.btlaw.com · 11 South Meridian Street · Indianapolis, IN 46204-3535 · 317-236-1313

Phillip L. Bayt · Ice Miller · One American Square, Suite 3100 · Indianapolis, IN 46282-0200 · 317-236-2100

James C. Carlino · Bose McKinney & Evans · http://www.boselaw.com · Meridian Corporate Plaza Two, Suite 300 · 301 Pennsylvania Parkway · Indianapolis, IN 46280 · 317-684-5300

Thomas W. Dinwiddie · Wooden & McLaughlin · One Indiana Square, Suite 1800 · Indianapolis, IN 46204 · 317-639-6151

Karl P. Haas · Wallack Somers & Haas · http://www.wshlaw.com · One Indiana Square, Suite 1500 · Indianapolis, IN 46204 · 317-231-9000

John W. Hamilton · Wooden & McLaughlin · One Indiana Square, Suite 1800 · Indianapolis, IN 46204 · 317-639-6151

Thomas Hanahan · Wooden & McLaughlin · One Indiana Square, Suite 1800 · Indianapolis, IN 46204 · 317-639-6151

Dennis A. Johnson · Barnes & Thornburg · http://www.btlaw.com · 11 South Meridian Street · Indianapolis, IN 46204-3535 · 317-236-1313

Stephen W. Lee · Barnes & Thornburg · http://www.btlaw.com · 11 South Meridian Street · Indianapolis, IN 46204-3535 · 317-236-1313

Mary Katherine Lisher · Baker & Daniels · http://www.bakerdaniels.com · 300 North Meridian Street, Suite 2700 · Indianapolis, IN 46204 · 317-237-0300

Marvin H. Mitchell · ⑳ · Mitchell Hurst Jacobs & Dick · 152 East Washington Street · Indianapolis, IN 46204 · 317-636-0808

Norman R. Newman · ㉕ · Dann, Pecar, Newman & Kleiman · http://www.dannpecar.com · One American Square, Suite 2300 · Indianapolis, IN 46282 · 317-632-3232

Philip A. Nicely · ⑳ · Bose McKinney & Evans · http://www.boselaw.com · Meridian Corporate Plaza Two, Suite 300 · 301 Pennsylvania Parkway · Indianapolis, IN 46280 · 317-684-5300

Rory O'Bryan · ⑩ · Harrison & Moberly · http://www.harrisonmoberly.net · Market Tower, Suite 700 · 10 West Market · Indianapolis, IN 46204 · 317-639-4511

Timothy E. Ochs · Ice Miller · One American Square, Suite 3100 · Indianapolis, IN 46282-0200 · 317-236-2100

Stephen H. Paul · ⑩ · Baker & Daniels · http://www.bakerdaniels.com · 300 North Meridian Street, Suite 2700 · Indianapolis, IN 46204 · 317-237-0300

Benjamin Pecar · Barnes & Thornburg · http://www.btlaw.com · 11 South Meridian Street · Indianapolis, IN 46204-3535 · 317-236-1313

James H. Schwarz · Dann, Pecar, Newman & Kleiman · http://www.dannpecar.com · One American Square, Suite 2300 · Indianapolis, IN 46282 · 317-632-3232

Joseph M. Scimia · Baker & Daniels · http://www.bakerdaniels.com · 600 East 96th Street, Suite 600 · Indianapolis, IN 46240 · 317-569-9600

George W. Somers · ⑩ · Wallack Somers & Haas · http://www.wshlaw.com · One Indiana Square, Suite 1500 · Indianapolis, IN 46204 · 317-231-9000

Barry Z. Wallack · ⑩ · Wallack Somers & Haas · http://www.wshlaw.com · One Indiana Square, Suite 1500 · Indianapolis, IN 46204 · 317-231-9000

David R. Warshauer · Barnes & Thornburg · http://www.btlaw.com · 11 South Meridian Street · Indianapolis, IN 46204-3535 · 317-236-1313

Zeff A. Weiss · ⑩ · Ice Miller · One American Square, Suite 3100 · Indianapolis, IN 46282-0200 · 317-236-2100

Brantly H. Wright · Bose McKinney & Evans · http://www.boselaw.com · First Indiana Plaza, Suite 2700 · 135 North Pennsylvania Street · Indianapolis, IN 46204 · 317-684-5000

Lafayette

Thomas R. McCully · ⑳ · Stuart & Branigin · 300 Main Street, Suite 900 · P.O. Box 1010 · Lafayette, IN 47902-1010 · 765-423-1561

South Bend

Richard L. Mintz · ⑩ · Barnes & Thornburg · http://www.btlaw.com · First Source Bank Center, Suite 600 · 100 North Michigan Street · South Bend, IN 46601 · 574-233-1171

SECURITIES LAW

Fort Wayne

Robert S. Walters · Barrett & McNagny · 215 East Berry Street · P.O. Box 2263 · Fort Wayne, IN 46802 · 260-423-9551

Indianapolis

James A. Aschleman · ⑳ · Baker & Daniels · http://www.bakerdaniels.com · 300 North Meridian Street, Suite 2700 · Indianapolis, IN 46204 · 317-237-0300

David Butcher · ⑩ · Bose McKinney & Evans · http://www.boselaw.com · First Indiana Plaza, Suite 2700 135 North Pennsylvania Street · Indianapolis, IN 46204 · 317-684-5000

Anne N. DePrez · ⑩ · Barnes & Thornburg · http://www.btlaw.com · 11 South Meridian Street · Indianapolis, IN 46204-3535 · 317-236-1313

James H. Ham · Baker & Daniels · http://www.bakerdaniels.com · 300 North Meridian Street, Suite 2700 Indianapolis, IN 46204 · 317-237-0300

Eric R. Moy · Barnes & Thornburg · http://www.btlaw.com · 11 South Meridian Street · Indianapolis, IN 46204-3535 · 317-236-1313

SPORTS LAW

Indianapolis

Stephen E. DeVoe · Bose McKinney & Evans · http://www.boselaw.com · First Indiana Plaza, Suite 2700 135 North Pennsylvania Street · Indianapolis, IN 46204 · 317-684-5000

Ronald E. Elberger · ⑩ · Bose McKinney & Evans · http://www.boselaw.com · First Indiana Plaza, Suite 2700 · 135 North Pennsylvania Street · Indianapolis, IN 46204 · 317-684-5000

Daniel C. Emerson · Bose McKinney & Evans · http://www.boselaw.com · First Indiana Plaza, Suite 2700 135 North Pennsylvania Street · Indianapolis, IN 46204 · 317-684-5000

Robert J. Salyers · ⑩ · Salyers Eiteljorg & Pulice · 1712 East 66th Street · Indianapolis, IN 46221-1202 · 317-634-2070

John R. Thornburgh · ⑩ · Ice Miller · One American Square, Suite 3100 · Indianapolis, IN 46282-0200 · 317-236-2100

Roanoke

Eugene Parker · ⑩ · Maximum Sports Management · 196 North Main Street · P.O. Box 637 · Roanoke, IN 46783 · 260-672-9480

STRUCTURED FINANCE LAW

Indianapolis

Alan W. Becker · Bose McKinney & Evans · http://www.boselaw.com · First Indiana Plaza, Suite 2700 · 135 North Pennsylvania Street · Indianapolis, IN 46204 · 317-684-5000

Eric R. Moy · Barnes & Thornburg · http://www.btlaw.com · 11 South Meridian Street · Indianapolis, IN 46204-3535 · 317-236-1313

Bryan B. Woodruff · Bose McKinney & Evans · http://www.boselaw.com · First Indiana Plaza, Suite 2700 135 North Pennsylvania Street · Indianapolis, IN 46204 · 317-684-5000

Karen Woods · Krieg DeVault · One Indiana Square, Suite 2800 · Indianapolis, IN 46204-2079 · 317-636-4341

TAX LAW

Carmel

Michael J. Rusnak · Harrison & Moberly · http://www.harrisonmoberly.net · 11611 North Meridian Street, Suite 150 · Carmel, IN 46032 · 317-639-4511

Fort Wayne

Dennis C. Becker · Barnes & Thornburg · http://www.btlaw.com · One Summit Square, Suite 600 · Fort Wayne, IN 46802-3119 · 260-423-9440

James Koday · ⑩ · Bewley & Koday · http://www.bewleykoday.com · 110 West Berry Street, Suite 2006 · Fort Wayne, IN 46802 · 260-424-0566

John P. Martin · ⑩ · Barrett & McNagny · 215 East Berry Street · P.O. Box 2263 · Fort Wayne, IN 46802 260-423-9551

Stephen J. Williams · ⑳ · Shambaugh, Kast, Beck & Williams · http://www.skbw.com · 229 West Berry Street, Suite 400 · P.O. Box 11648 · Fort Wayne, IN 46859-1648 · 260-423-1430

Indianapolis

Donald P. Bennett · ⑳ · Baker & Daniels · http://www.bakerdaniels.com · 600 East 96th Street, Suite 600 Indianapolis, IN 46240 · 317-569-9600

John W. Boyd · ⑩ · Barnes & Thornburg · http://www.btlaw.com · 11 South Meridian Street · Indianapolis, IN 46204-3535 · 317-236-1313

Francina A. Dlouhy · ⑳ · Baker & Daniels · http://www.bakerdaniels.com · 300 North Meridian Street, Suite 2700 · Indianapolis, IN 46204 · 317-237-0300

Daniel H. FitzGibbon · ⑳ · Barnes & Thornburg · http://www.btlaw.com · 11 South Meridian Street · Indianapolis, IN 46204-3535 · 317-236-1313

Mark J. Richards · Ice Miller · One American Square, Suite 3100 · Indianapolis, IN 46282-0200 · 317-236-2100

Timothy J. Riffle · ⑩ · Barnes & Thornburg · http://www.btlaw.com · 11 South Meridian Street · Indianapolis, IN 46204-3535 · 317-236-1313

Thomas F. Schnellenberger, Jr. · Ice Miller · One American Square, Suite 3100 · Indianapolis, IN 46282-0200 · 317-236-2100

Barton T. Sprunger · ⑳ · Ice Miller · One American Square, Suite 3100 · Indianapolis, IN 46282-0200 · 317-236-2100

Larry J. Stroble · Barnes & Thornburg · http://www.btlaw.com · 11 South Meridian Street · Indianapolis, IN 46204-3535 · 317-236-1313

South Bend

Timothy D. Hernly · ⑩ · Barnes & Thornburg · http://www.btlaw.com · First Source Bank Center, Suite 600 · 100 North Michigan Street · South Bend, IN 46601 · 574-233-1171

Nelson J. Vogel, Jr. · ㉕ · Barnes & Thornburg · http://www.btlaw.com · First Source Bank Center, Suite 600 · 100 North Michigan Street · South Bend, IN 46601 · 574-233-1171

TECHNOLOGY LAW

Indianapolis

James A. Coles · ⑩ · Bose McKinney & Evans · http://www.boselaw.com · First Indiana Plaza, Suite 2700 135 North Pennsylvania Street · Indianapolis, IN 46204 · 317-684-5000

TRUSTS AND ESTATES

Bluffton

Daniel R. Gordon · Gordon & Associates · 119 East Oak Forest Drive · Bluffton, IN 46714 · 260-824-9377

Columbia City

Benton E. Gates, Jr. · ⑩ · Benton E. Gates, Jr. · 407 Pinecrest Drive · P.O. Box 251 · Columbia City, IN 46725 · 260-244-5175

Columbus

Thomas C. Bigley, Jr. · ⑩ · Sharpnack, Bigley, Stroh & Washburn · 321 Washington Street · P.O. Box 310 Columbus, IN 47202-0310 · 812-372-1553

Elkhart

Samuel S. Thompson · Barnes & Thornburg · http://www.btlaw.com · 121 West Franklin, Suite 200 · Elkhart, IN 46516 · 219-293-0681

Evansville

Diane L. Bender · Diane L. Bender · 111 Southeast Third Street, Suite 402 · P.O. Box 1536 · Evansville, IN 47706-1536 · 812-423-8558

Brian K. Carroll · Johnson Carroll Norton Kent & Straus · 2230 West Franklin Street · Evansville, IN 47712 · 812-425-4466

Sheila M. Corcoran · Berger & Berger · 313 Main Street · Evansville, IN 47708 · 812-425-8101

Randall K. Craig · Law Offices of Randall K. Craig · http://www.rkcraiglaw.com · 5000 East Virginia Street, Suite One · Evansville, IN 47715-2672 · 812-477-3337

Fort Wayne

George N. Bewley, Jr. · ⑩ · Bewley & Koday · http://www.bewleykoday.com · 110 West Berry Street, Suite 2006 · Fort Wayne, IN 46802 · 260-424-0566

James Koday · ⑩ · Bewley & Koday · http://www.bewleykoday.com · 110 West Berry Street, Suite 2006 · Fort Wayne, IN 46802 · 260-424-0566

Jeannie E. Longsworth · Longsworth Law Offices · 7030 Pointe Inverness Way, Suite 330 · Fort Wayne, IN 46804 · 260-625-6316

Stephen J. Williams · ⑳ · Shambaugh, Kast, Beck & Williams · http://www.skbw.com · 229 West Berry Street, Suite 400 · P.O. Box 11648 · Fort Wayne, IN 46859-1648 · 260-423-1430

Greenwood

Brian C. Hewitt · Williams, Hewitt, Barrett & Wilkowski · 600 North Emerson Avenue · P.O. Box 405 · Greenwood, IN 46142 · 317-888-1121

Indianapolis

Aline F. Anderson · ⑩ · Aline F. Anderson · 7104 U.S. Highway 31 South · Indianapolis, IN 46227-8537 · 317-888-8868

Vicki Anderson · Hackman Hulett & Cracraft · http://www.hhclaw.com · 111 Monument Circle, Suite 3500 · Indianapolis, IN 46204-2030 · 317-636-5401

MaryEllen K. Bishop · Bose McKinney & Evans · http://www.boselaw.com · Meridian Corporate Plaza Two, Suite 300 · 301 Pennsylvania Parkway · Indianapolis, IN 46280 · 317-684-5300

Gerald L. Cowan · ⑩ · Law Offices of Gerald L. Cowan · http://www.geraldlcowan.com · 3815 River Crossing Parkway, Suite 100 · Indianapolis, IN 46240-7766 · 800-345-5505

Robert W. Elzer · ⑩ · Baker & Daniels · http://www.bakerdaniels.com · 600 East 96th Street, Suite 600 · Indianapolis, IN 46240 · 317-569-9600

Thomas P. Ewbank · Krieg DeVault · One Indiana Square, Suite 2800 · Indianapolis, IN 46204-2079 · 317-636-4341

Kristin G. Fruehwald · ⑳ · Barnes & Thornburg · http://www.btlaw.com · 11 South Meridian Street · Indianapolis, IN 46204-3535 · 317-236-1313

John A. Gardner · ⑩ · Baker & Daniels · http://www.bakerdaniels.com · 600 East 96th Street, Suite 600 · Indianapolis, IN 46240 · 317-569-9600

Gina M. Giacone · Ice Miller · One American Square, Suite 3100 · Indianapolis, IN 46282-0200 · 317-236-2100

Marc A. Hetzner · ⑩ · Krieg DeVault · One Indiana Square, Suite 2800 · Indianapolis, IN 46204-2079 · 317-636-4341

Kent A. Rollison · Baker & Daniels · http://www.bakerdaniels.com · 600 East 96th Street, Suite 600 · Indianapolis, IN 46240 · 317-569-9600

G. Pearson Smith, Jr. · Bose McKinney & Evans · http://www.boselaw.com · First Indiana Plaza, Suite 2700 · 135 North Pennsylvania Street · Indianapolis, IN 46204 · 317-684-5000

Lisa A. Stone · ⑩ · Ice Miller · One American Square, Suite 3100 · Indianapolis, IN 46282-0200 · 317-236-2100

Gordon D. Wishard · ⑳ · Ice Miller · One American Square, Suite 3100 · Indianapolis, IN 46282-0200 · 317-236-2100

C. Daniel Yates · Bose McKinney & Evans · http://www.boselaw.com · First Indiana Plaza, Suite 2700 · 135 North Pennsylvania Street · Indianapolis, IN 46204 · 317-684-5000

Noblesville

Eric A. Manterfield · ⑩ · Krieg DeVault · 949 East Conner Street, Suite 200 · Noblesville, IN 46060 · 317-773-7818

South Bend

Nancy L. Ickler · ⑩ · Barnes & Thornburg · http://www.btlaw.com · First Source Bank Center, Suite 600 · 100 North Michigan Street · South Bend, IN 46601 · 574-233-1171

Greta Roemer Lewis · Barnes & Thornburg · http://www.btlaw.com · First Source Bank Center, Suite 600 · 100 North Michigan Street · South Bend, IN 46601 · 574-233-1171

Vincennes

Jeffrey B. Kolb · Emison, Doolittle, Kolb & Roellgen · 801 Busseron Street · P.O. Box 215 · Vincennes, IN 47591 · 812-882-2280

VENTURE CAPITAL LAW

Indianapolis

J. Jeffrey Brown · Baker & Daniels · http://www.bakerdaniels.com · 600 East 96th Street, Suite 600 · Indianapolis, IN 46240 · 317-569-9600

David Butcher · ⑩ · Bose McKinney & Evans · http://www.boselaw.com · First Indiana Plaza, Suite 2700 135 North Pennsylvania Street · Indianapolis, IN 46204 · 317-684-5000

Brian S. Fennerty · Baker & Daniels · http://www.bakerdaniels.com · 600 East 96th Street, Suite 600 · Indianapolis, IN 46240 · 317-569-9600

John A. Millspaugh · Bose McKinney & Evans · http://www.boselaw.com · First Indiana Plaza, Suite 2700 · 135 North Pennsylvania Street · Indianapolis, IN 46204 · 317-684-5000

John R. Thornburgh · ⑩ · Ice Miller · One American Square, Suite 3100 · Indianapolis, IN 46282-0200 · 317-236-2100

WATER LAW

Indianapolis

J. Christopher Janak · Bose McKinney & Evans · http://www.boselaw.com · First Indiana Plaza, Suite 2700 · 135 North Pennsylvania Street · Indianapolis, IN 46204 · 317-684-5000

Nicholas K. Kile · Barnes & Thornburg · http://www.btlaw.com · 11 South Meridian Street · Indianapolis, IN 46204-3535 · 317-236-1313

L. Parvin Price · Bose McKinney & Evans · http://www.boselaw.com · First Indiana Plaza, Suite 2700 · 135 North Pennsylvania Street · Indianapolis, IN 46204 · 317-684-5000

WHITE-COLLAR CRIMINAL DEFENSE

Anderson

Jeffrey A. Lockwood · (20) · Jeffrey A. Lockwood · 403 West Eigth Street, Suite Three · Anderson, IN 46016 · 765-649-1144

Evansville

Dennis L. Brinkmeyer · Dennis L. Brinkmeyer · 525 Sycamore Street · P.O. Box 1005 · Evansville, IN 47706-1005 · 812-423-3125

Jeffery L. Lantz · Jeffery Lantz Law Office · 525 Sycamore Street · Evansville, IN 47706 · 812-464-0044

Fort Wayne

Frank J. Gray · Gray and Friend · Harrison Professional Center, Second Floor · 927 South Harrison Street Fort Wayne, IN 46802 · 260-407-7130

Charles F. Leonard · (10) · Leonard, Hammond, Thoma & Terrill · 800 South Calhoun Street · Fort Wayne, IN 46802-2302 · 260-420-6000

Indianapolis

Jackie M. Bennett, Jr. · Taft Stettinius & Hollister · http://www.taftlaw.com · One Indiana Square, Suite 3500 · Indianapolis, IN 46204 · 317-713-3500

Robert W. Hammerle · (20) · Hammerle & Allen · 1455 North Pennsylvania Street · Indianapolis, IN 46202-2420 · 317-630-0137

Richard Kammen · (25) · Gilroy & Kammen · One Indiana Square, Suite 150 · Indianapolis, IN 46204 · 317-236-0400

J. Richard Kiefer · (20) · Bingham McHale · Market Tower Building, Suite 2700 · 10 West Market Street · Indianapolis, IN 46204 · 317-635-8900

Larry A. Mackey · Barnes & Thornburg · http://www.btlaw.com · 11 South Meridian Street · Indianapolis, IN 46204-3535 · 317-236-1313

Kevin P. McGoff · Bingham McHale · Market Tower Building, Suite 2700 · 10 West Market Street · Indianapolis, IN 46204 · 317-635-8900

Linda L. Pence · Taft Stettinius & Hollister · http://www.taftlaw.com · One Indiana Square, Suite 3500 · Indianapolis, IN 46204 · 317-713-3500

C. Joseph Russell · Bose McKinney & Evans · http://www.boselaw.com · First Indiana Plaza, Suite 2700 · 135 North Pennsylvania Street · Indianapolis, IN 46204 · 317-684-5000

James H. Voyles, Jr. · (25) · Voyles, Zahn, Paul, Hogan & Merriman · 141 East Washington Street, Suite 300 · Indianapolis, IN 46204 · 317-632-4463

Bradley L. Williams · Ice Miller · One American Square, Suite 3100 · Indianapolis, IN 46282-0200 · 317-236-2100

La Porte

Martin W. Kus · Newby, Lewis, Kaminski & Jones · 916 Lincoln Way · La Porte, IN 46350 · 219-362-1577

Merrillville

Nick J. Thiros · (25) · Cohen & Thiros · 200 East 90th Drive · Merrillville, IN 46410-8102 · 219-769-1600

South Bend

George E. Horn, Jr. · Barnes & Thornburg · http://www.btlaw.com · First Source Bank Center, Suite 600 100 North Michigan Street · South Bend, IN 46601 · 574-233-1171

Terre Haute

William G. Smock · Smock & Etling · 77 Cherry Street · Terre Haute, IN 47807 · 812-238-1751

WORKERS' COMPENSATION LAW

Crown Point

George C. Patrick · George C. Patrick & Associates · 706 Merrillville Road · Crown Point, IN 46307 · 219-662-7959

Evansville

Stephen S. Lavallo · McCray Lavallo Frank & Klingler · 5000 East Virginia Street, Suite Four · Evansville, IN 47715 · 812-477-6510

Diana L. Wann · McCray Lavallo Frank & Klingler · 5000 East Virginia Street, Suite Four · Evansville, IN 47715 · 812-477-6510

Indianapolis

Robert A. Fanning · (10) · Due Doyle Fanning & Metzger · Circle Tower Building, Suite 900 · 55 Monument Circle · Indianapolis, IN 46204 · 317-635-7700

Patricia L. Odgen · Barnes & Thornburg · http://www.btlaw.com · 11 South Meridian Street · Indianapolis, IN 46204-3535 · 317-236-1313

Richard J. Swanson · (10) · Macey Swanson & Allman · 445 North Pennsylvania Street, Suite 401 · Indianapolis, IN 46204 · 317-637-2345

David Swider · Bose McKinney & Evans · http://www.boselaw.com · First Indiana Plaza, Suite 2700 · 135 North Pennsylvania Street · Indianapolis, IN 46204 · 317-684-5000

Sally A. Voland · Dugan, Voland & Meagher · 3388 Founders Road, Suite A · Indianapolis, IN 46268 · 317-872-3836

South Bend

Thomas F. Cohen · ⑩ · Hunt Suedhoff Kalamaros · 120 West LaSalle Avenue, 12th Floor · P.O. Box 4156 South Bend, IN 46601 · 574-232-4801

Robert D. Woods · ⑩ · Hunt Suedhoff Kalamaros · 120 West LaSalle Avenue, 12th Floor · P.O. Box 4156 South Bend, IN 46601 · 574-232-4801

Terre Haute

Anthony A. Tanoos · Fleschner, Stark, Tanoos & Newlin · 201 Ohio Street · Terre Haute, IN 47807 · 812-232-2000

Valparaiso

David L. Hollenbeck · ⑩ · Blachly, Tabor, Bozik & Hartman · 56 South Washington Street, Suite 401 · Valparaiso, IN 46383 · 219-464-1041

Jeffrey S. Sturm · Sturm & Phillips · 175 Lincolnway, Suite D · Valparaiso, IN 46383-5559 · 219-476-7557

IOWA

ADMINISTRATIVE LAW

Cedar Rapids

John M. Bickel · ⑩ · Shuttleworth & Ingersoll · 115 Third Street, SE, Suite 500 · Cedar Rapids, IA 52401
319-365-9461

Douglas R. Oelschlaeger · Shuttleworth & Ingersoll · 115 Third Street, SE, Suite 500 · Cedar Rapids, IA 52401 · 319-365-9461

ALTERNATIVE DISPUTE RESOLUTION

Waterloo

Peter J. Gartelos · Gartelos, Wagner & Ament · 2115 La Porte Road · Waterloo, IA 50702 · 319-234-3500

West Des Moines

Richard M. Calkins · Richard M. Calkins · 2700 West Town Parkway, Suite 220 · West Des Moines, IA 50266 · 515-283-0331

ANTITRUST LAW

Des Moines

John C. Cortesio, Jr. · ⑩ · Bradshaw, Fowler, Proctor & Fairgrave · 801 Grand Avenue, Suite 3700 · Des Moines, IA 50309-8004 · 515-243-4191

Edward W. Remsburg · Ahlers & Cooney · 100 Court Avenue, Suite 600 · Des Moines, IA 50309-2231 · 515-243-7611

Stanley J. Thompson · Davis, Brown, Koehn, Shors & Roberts · The Davis Brown Tower, Suite 1300 · 215 Tenth Street · Des Moines, IA 50309-3993 · 515-288-2500

James C. Wine · Nyemaster, Goode, West, Hansell & O'Brien · 700 Walnut Street, Suite 1600 · Des Moines, IA 50309-3899 · 515-283-3100

APPELLATE LAW

Cedar Rapids

Sarah J. Gayer · Shuttleworth & Ingersoll · 115 Third Street, SE, Suite 500 · Cedar Rapids, IA 52401 · 319-365-9461

Robert M. Hogg · Elderkin & Pirnie · 115 First Avenue, SE · Cedar Rapids, IA 52401 · 319-362-2137

Diane H. Kutzko · ⑩ · Shuttleworth & Ingersoll · 115 Third Street, SE, Suite 500 · Cedar Rapids, IA 52401 · 319-365-9461

Nancy J. Penner · Shuttleworth & Ingersoll · 115 Third Street, SE, Suite 500 · Cedar Rapids, IA 52401 · 319-365-9461

Des Moines

Robert G. Allbee · Ahlers & Cooney · 100 Court Avenue, Suite 600 · Des Moines, IA 50309-2231 · 515-243-7611

David L. Brown · ⑩ · Hansen, McClintock & Riley · Fleming Building, Eighth Floor · 218 Sixth Avenue Des Moines, IA 50309-4092 · 515-244-2141

Brent B. Green · ⑩ · Duncan, Green, Brown & Langeness · 400 Locust Street, Suite 380 · Des Moines, IA 50309 · 515-288-6440

Mark McCormick · ⑩ · Belin Lamson McCormick Zumbach Flynn · http://www.belinlaw.com · 666 Walnut Street, Suite 2000 · Des Moines, IA 50309-3989 · 515-243-7100

BANKING LAW

Cedar Rapids

Carroll J. Reasoner · ⑩ · Shuttleworth & Ingersoll · 115 Third Street, SE, Suite 500 · Cedar Rapids, IA 52401 · 319-365-9461

Des Moines

Thomas L. Flynn · ㉕ · Belin Lamson McCormick Zumbach Flynn · http://www.belinlaw.com · 666 Walnut Street, Suite 2000 · Des Moines, IA 50309-3989 · 515-243-7100

Robert A. Gamble · Davis, Brown, Koehn, Shors & Roberts · The Davis Brown Tower, Suite 1300 · 215 Tenth Street · Des Moines, IA 50309-3993 · 515-288-2500

Howard O. Hagen · ⑩ · Dickinson, Mackaman, Tyler & Hagen · http://www.dickinsonlaw.com · 699 Walnut Street, Suite 1600 · Des Moines, IA 50309-3929 · 515-244-2600

Robert A. Mullen · Belin Lamson McCormick Zumbach Flynn · http://www.belinlaw.com · 666 Walnut Street, Suite 2000 · Des Moines, IA 50309-3989 · 515-243-7100

Gregory P. Page · ⑩ · Nyemaster, Goode, West, Hansell & O'Brien · 700 Walnut Street, Suite 1600 · Des Moines, IA 50309-3899 · 515-283-3100

John T. Seitz · Belin Lamson McCormick Zumbach Flynn · http://www.belinlaw.com · 666 Walnut Street, Suite 2000 · Des Moines, IA 50309-3989 · 515-243-7100

J. Marc Ward · Dickinson, Mackaman, Tyler & Hagen · http://www.dickinsonlaw.com · 699 Walnut Street, Suite 1600 · Des Moines, IA 50309-3929 · 515-244-2600

BANKRUPTCY AND CREDITOR-DEBTOR RIGHTS LAW

Cedar Rapids

Dan Childers · ⑩ · Elderkin & Pirnie · 115 First Avenue, SE · Cedar Rapids, IA 52401 · 319-362-2137

Larry G. Gutz · ⑳ · Moyer & Bergman · http://www.moyerbergman.com · 2720 First Avenue, NE · P.O. Box 1943 · Cedar Rapids, IA 52402 · 319-366-7331

Eric W. Lam · ⑩ · Moyer & Bergman · http://www.moyerbergman.com · 2720 First Avenue, NE · P.O. Box 1943 · Cedar Rapids, IA 52402 · 319-366-7331

Council Bluffs

Charles R. Hannan · ⑳ · Hannan & Dreismeier · http://rphlaw.bluffsonline.net · 215 South Main Street · P.O. Box 1016 · Council Bluffs, IA 51502-1016 · 712-328-1575

Charles L. Smith · ⑩ · Telpner, Peterson, Smith, Ruesch & Thomas · 25 Main Place, Suite 200 · P.O. Box 248 · Council Bluffs, IA 51502 · 712-325-9000

Des Moines

Thomas L. Flynn · ㉕ · Belin Lamson McCormick Zumbach Flynn · http://www.belinlaw.com · 666 Walnut Street, Suite 2000 · Des Moines, IA 50309-3989 · 515-243-7100

Donald F. Neiman · ⑳ · Bradshaw, Fowler, Proctor & Fairgrave · 801 Grand Avenue, Suite 3700 · Des Moines, IA 50309-8004 · 515-243-4191

Gary A. Norton · Whitfield & Eddy · 317 Sixth Avenue, Suite 1200 · Des Moines, IA 50309-4195 · 515-288-6041

Jon P. Sullivan · Dickinson, Mackaman, Tyler & Hagen · http://www.dickinsonlaw.com · 699 Walnut Street, Suite 1600 · Des Moines, IA 50309-3929 · 515-244-2600

Mark D. Walz · Davis, Brown, Koehn, Shors & Roberts · The Davis Brown Tower, Suite 1300 · 215 Tenth Street · Des Moines, IA 50309-3993 · 515-288-2500

Mason City

Larry S. Eide · ⑩ · Pappajohn, Shriver, Eide & Nicholas · 103 East State Street, Suite 800 · P.O. Box 1588 Mason City, IA 50402-1588 · 641-423-4264

Sioux City

A. Frank Baron · ⑳ · Baron, Sar, Goodwin, Gill & Lohr · 750 Pierce Street · P.O. Box 717 · Sioux City, IA 51101 · 712-277-1015

BET-THE-COMPANY LITIGATION

Cedar Rapids

Patrick M. Roby · ⑳ · Elderkin & Pirnie · 115 First Avenue, SE · Cedar Rapids, IA 52401 · 319-362-2137

Davenport

Robert V. P. Waterman, Jr. · Lane & Waterman · 220 North Main Street, Suite 600 · Davenport, IA 52801 · 563-324-3246

Des Moines

Mark McCormick · ⑩ · Belin Lamson McCormick Zumbach Flynn · http://www.belinlaw.com · 666 Walnut Street, Suite 2000 · Des Moines, IA 50309-3989 · 515-243-7100

David L. Phipps · Whitfield & Eddy · 317 Sixth Avenue, Suite 1200 · Des Moines, IA 50309-4195 · 515-288-6041

Waterloo

David J. Dutton · ⑩ · Dutton, Braun, Staack & Hellman · 3151 Brockway Road · P.O. Box 810 · Waterloo, IA 50704 · 319-234-4471

COMMERCIAL LITIGATION

Cedar Rapids

Stephen J. Holtman · ⑩ · Simmons, Perrine, Albright & Ellwood · 115 Third Street, SE, Suite 1200 · Cedar Rapids, IA 52401-1266 · 319-366-7641

Robert D. Houghton · Shuttleworth & Ingersoll · 115 Third Street, SE, Suite 500 · Cedar Rapids, IA 52401 · 319-365-9461

Glenn L. Johnson · Shuttleworth & Ingersoll · 115 Third Street, SE, Suite 500 · Cedar Rapids, IA 52401 319-365-9461

Gregory M. Lederer · Lederer, Weston, Craig · 118 Third Avenue SE, Suite 700 · P.O. Box 1927 · Cedar Rapids, IA 52406 · 319-365-1184

Patrick M. Roby · ⑳ · Elderkin & Pirnie · 115 First Avenue, SE · Cedar Rapids, IA 52401 · 319-362-2137

Davenport

Robert V. P. Waterman, Jr. · Lane & Waterman · 220 North Main Street, Suite 600 · Davenport, IA 52801 · 563-324-3246

Thomas D. Waterman · Lane & Waterman · 220 North Main Street, Suite 600 · Davenport, IA 52801 · 563-324-3246

Des Moines

Nicholas Critelli · ⑩ · Law Chambers of Nicholas Critelli · 317 Sixth Avenue, Suite 950 · Des Moines, IA 50309 · 515-243-3122

Robert L. Fanter · Whitfield & Eddy · 317 Sixth Avenue, Suite 1200 · Des Moines, IA 50309-4195 · 515-288-6041

R. Todd Gaffney · Finley, Alt, Smith, Scharnberg, Craig, Hilmes & Gaffney · 699 Walnut Street, Suite 1900 · Des Moines, IA 50309 · 515-288-0145

Brent B. Green · ⑩ · Duncan, Green, Brown & Langeness · 400 Locust Street, Suite 380 · Des Moines, IA 50309 · 515-288-6440

Joseph R. Gunderson · Gunderson, Sharp & Walke · 317 Sixth Avenue, Suite 600 · Des Moines, IA 50309-4115 · 515-288-0219

Thomas D. Hanson · ⑩ · Hanson, Bjork & Russell · 405 Sixth Avenue, Suite 1300 · Des Moines, IA 50309 · 515-244-0177

Wade R. Hauser III · Ahlers & Cooney · 100 Court Avenue, Suite 600 · Des Moines, IA 50309-2231 · 515-243-7611

John D. Hilmes · ⑩ · Finley, Alt, Smith, Scharnberg, Craig, Hilmes & Gaffney · 699 Walnut Street, Suite 1900 · Des Moines, IA 50309 · 515-288-0145

Dwight W. James · ⑩ · The James Law Firm · 604 Locust Street, Suite 630 · Des Moines, IA 50309 · 866-566-8291

Dennis W. Johnson · Dorsey & Whitney · 801 Grand Avenue, Suite 3900 · Des Moines, IA 50309-2790 · 515-283-1000

F. Richard Lyford · Dickinson, Mackaman, Tyler & Hagen · http://www.dickinsonlaw.com · 699 Walnut Street, Suite 1600 · Des Moines, IA 50309-3929 · 515-244-2600

Edward M. Mansfield · Belin Lamson McCormick Zumbach Flynn · http://www.belinlaw.com · 666 Walnut Street, Suite 2000 · Des Moines, IA 50309-3989 · 515-243-7100

Mark McCormick · ⑩ · Belin Lamson McCormick Zumbach Flynn · http://www.belinlaw.com · 666 Walnut Street, Suite 2000 · Des Moines, IA 50309-3989 · 515-243-7100

David L. Phipps · Whitfield & Eddy · 317 Sixth Avenue, Suite 1200 · Des Moines, IA 50309-4195 · 515-288-6041

Edward W. Remsburg · Ahlers & Cooney · 100 Court Avenue, Suite 600 · Des Moines, IA 50309-2231 · 515-243-7611

Richard G. Santi · ⑩ · Ahlers & Cooney · 100 Court Avenue, Suite 600 · Des Moines, IA 50309-2231 · 515-243-7611

Randall H. Stefani · Ahlers & Cooney · 100 Court Avenue, Suite 600 · Des Moines, IA 50309-2231 · 515-243-7611

David M. Swinton · Belin Lamson McCormick Zumbach Flynn · http://www.belinlaw.com · 666 Walnut Street, Suite 2000 · Des Moines, IA 50309-3989 · 515-243-7100

Deborah M. Tharnish · Davis, Brown, Koehn, Shors & Roberts · The Davis Brown Tower, Suite 1300 · 215 Tenth Street · Des Moines, IA 50309-3993 · 515-288-2500

Michael W. Thrall · Nyemaster, Goode, West, Hansell & O'Brien · 700 Walnut Street, Suite 1600 · Des Moines, IA 50309-3899 · 515-283-3100

Mark L. Tripp · Bradshaw, Fowler, Proctor & Fairgrave · 801 Grand Avenue, Suite 3700 · Des Moines, IA 50309-8004 · 515-243-4191

Steven P. Wandro · Wandro, Lyons & Baer · 2501 Grand Avenue, Suite B · Des Moines, IA 50312 · 515-281-1475

Mark E. Weinhardt · Belin Lamson McCormick Zumbach Flynn · http://www.belinlaw.com · 666 Walnut Street, Suite 2000 · Des Moines, IA 50309-3989 · 515-243-7100

Iowa City

John W. Hayek · ⑩ · Hayek, Hayek, Brown, Moreland & Hayek · 120 East Washington Street · Iowa City, IA 52240-3924 · 319-337-9606

Thomas D. Hobart · ⑩ · Meardon, Sueppel & Downer · 122 South Linn Street · Iowa City, IA 52240 · 319-338-9222

Muscatine

David J. Meloy · Stanley, Lande & Hunter · 301 Iowa Avenue, Suite 400 · Muscatine, IA 52761 · 563-264-5000

Sioux City

Maurice B. Nieland · ⑩ · Rawlings, Nieland, Killinger, Ellwanger, Jacobs, Mohrhauser, Nelson & Early · 522 Fourth Street, Suite 300 · Sioux City, IA 51101 · 712-277-2373

Waterloo

David J. Dutton · ⑩ · Dutton, Braun, Staack & Hellman · 3151 Brockway Road · P.O. Box 810 · Waterloo, IA 50704 · 319-234-4471

Edward J. Gallagher, Jr. · ㉕ · Gallagher, Langlas & Gallagher · Law Building · 405 East Fifth Street · P.O. Box 2615 · Waterloo, IA 50704 · 319-233-6163

James R. Hellman · Dutton, Braun, Staack & Hellman · 3151 Brockway Road · P.O. Box 810 · Waterloo, IA 50704 · 319-234-4471

COMMUNICATIONS LAW

Cedar Rapids

Dean R. Einck · ⑩ · Shuttleworth & Ingersoll · 115 Third Street, SE, Suite 500 · Cedar Rapids, IA 52401 319-365-9461

Des Moines

Bret A. Dublinske · Dickinson, Mackaman, Tyler & Hagen · http://www.dickinsonlaw.com · 699 Walnut Street, Suite 1600 · Des Moines, IA 50309-3929 · 515-244-2600

Robert F. Holz, Jr. · ⑩ · Davis, Brown, Koehn, Shors & Roberts · The Davis Brown Tower, Suite 1300 · 215 Tenth Street · Des Moines, IA 50309-3993 · 515-288-2500

Richard W. Lozier, Jr. · Belin Lamson McCormick Zumbach Flynn · http://www.belinlaw.com · 666 Walnut Street, Suite 2000 · Des Moines, IA 50309-3989 · 515-243-7100

Philip E. Stoffregen · ⑩ · Brown, Winick, Graves, Gross, Baskerville & Schoenebaum · Ruan Center, Suite 2000 · 666 Grand Avenue · Des Moines, IA 50309-2510 · 515-242-2400

Sheila K. Tipton · ⑩ · Belin Lamson McCormick Zumbach Flynn · http://www.belinlaw.com · 666 Walnut Street, Suite 2000 · Des Moines, IA 50309-3989 · 515-243-7100

CONSTRUCTION LAW

Cedar Rapids

Kevin H. Collins · Shuttleworth & Ingersoll · 115 Third Street, SE, Suite 500 · Cedar Rapids, IA 52401 · 319-365-9461

Donald G. Thompson · Bradley & Riley · http://www.bradleyriley.com · 2007 First Avenue, SE · P.O. Box 2804 · Cedar Rapids, IA 52406-2804 · 319-363-0101

Des Moines

Kevin J. Driscoll · Finley, Alt, Smith, Scharnberg, Craig, Hilmes & Gaffney · 699 Walnut Street, Suite 1900 · Des Moines, IA 50309 · 515-288-0145

Brian P. Rickert · Brown, Winick, Graves, Gross, Baskerville & Schoenebaum · Ruan Center, Suite 2000 666 Grand Avenue · Des Moines, IA 50309-2510 · 515-242-2400

Muscatine

Steven J. Havercamp · Stanley, Lande & Hunter · 301 Iowa Avenue, Suite 400 · Muscatine, IA 52761 · 563-264-5000

West Des Moines

John A. Templer, Jr. · Whitfield & Eddy · 3737 Woodland Avenue, Suite 400 · West Des Moines, IA 50266 · 515-558-0111

CORPORATE LAW

Cedar Falls

David R. Mason · ⑩ · Redfern, Mason, Larsen & Moore · 415 Clay Street · P.O. Box 627 · Cedar Falls, IA 50613 · 319-277-6830

Cedar Rapids

Brian D. Bergstrom · Shuttleworth & Ingersoll · 115 Third Street, SE, Suite 500 · Cedar Rapids, IA 52401 · 319-365-9461

Dennis J. McMenimen · Shuttleworth & Ingersoll · 115 Third Street, SE, Suite 500 · Cedar Rapids, IA 52401 · 319-365-9461

Carroll J. Reasoner · ⑩ · Shuttleworth & Ingersoll · 115 Third Street, SE, Suite 500 · Cedar Rapids, IA 52401 · 319-365-9461

Byron G. Riley · ⑩ · Bradley & Riley · http://www.bradleyriley.com · 2007 First Avenue, SE · P.O. Box 2804 · Cedar Rapids, IA 52406-2804 · 319-363-0101

Davenport

C. Dana Waterman III · ⑩ · Lane & Waterman · 220 North Main Street, Suite 600 · Davenport, IA 52801 · 563-324-3246

Des Moines

Garth D. Adams · Belin Lamson McCormick Zumbach Flynn · http://www.belinlaw.com · 666 Walnut Street, Suite 2000 · Des Moines, IA 50309-3989 · 515-243-7100

Bradford L. Austin · Nyemaster, Goode, West, Hansell & O'Brien · 700 Walnut Street, Suite 1600 · Des Moines, IA 50309-3899 · 515-283-3100

Willard L. Boyd III · Nyemaster, Goode, West, Hansell & O'Brien · 700 Walnut Street, Suite 1600 · Des Moines, IA 50309-3899 · 515-283-3100

Quentin R. Boyken · Belin Lamson McCormick Zumbach Flynn · http://www.belinlaw.com · 666 Walnut Street, Suite 2000 · Des Moines, IA 50309-3989 · 515-243-7100

Donald J. Brown · ㉕ · Davis, Brown, Koehn, Shors & Roberts · The Davis Brown Tower, Suite 1300 · 215 Tenth Street · Des Moines, IA 50309-3993 · 515-288-2500

Frank J. Carroll · ㉕ · Davis, Brown, Koehn, Shors & Roberts · The Davis Brown Tower, Suite 1300 · 215 Tenth Street · Des Moines, IA 50309-3993 · 515-288-2500

John C. Cortesio, Jr. · ⑩ · Bradshaw, Fowler, Proctor & Fairgrave · 801 Grand Avenue, Suite 3700 · Des Moines, IA 50309-8004 · 515-243-4191

Mark C. Dickinson · Nyemaster, Goode, West, Hansell & O'Brien · 700 Walnut Street, Suite 1600 · Des Moines, IA 50309-3899 · 515-283-3100

Kent M. Forney · ⑩ · Bradshaw, Fowler, Proctor & Fairgrave · 801 Grand Avenue, Suite 3700 · Des Moines, IA 50309-8004 · 515-243-4191

Edgar F. Hansell · ㉕ · Nyemaster, Goode, West, Hansell & O'Brien · 700 Walnut Street, Suite 1600 · Des Moines, IA 50309-3899 · 515-283-3100

John D. Hintze · Ahlers & Cooney · 100 Court Avenue, Suite 600 · Des Moines, IA 50309-2231 · 515-243-7611

Rod Kubat · Nyemaster, Goode, West, Hansell & O'Brien · 700 Walnut Street, Suite 1600 · Des Moines, IA 50309-3899 · 515-283-3100

Gordon R. Neumann, Jr. · ⑩ · Nyemaster, Goode, West, Hansell & O'Brien · 700 Walnut Street, Suite 1600 · Des Moines, IA 50309-3899 · 515-283-3100

Gregory P. Page · ⑩ · Nyemaster, Goode, West, Hansell & O'Brien · 700 Walnut Street, Suite 1600 · Des Moines, IA 50309-3899 · 515-283-3100

Stephen W. Roberts · Davis, Brown, Koehn, Shors & Roberts · The Davis Brown Tower, Suite 1300 · 215 Tenth Street · Des Moines, IA 50309-3993 · 515-288-2500

Fred R. Schneider · Smith, Schneider, Stiles & Serangeli · The Equitable Building, Suite 1000 · 604 Locust Street · Des Moines, IA 50309 · 515-245-6789

Wade Schut · Nyemaster, Goode, West, Hansell & O'Brien · 700 Walnut Street, Suite 1600 · Des Moines, IA 50309-3899 · 515-283-3100

John D. Shors · ⑩ · Davis, Brown, Koehn, Shors & Roberts · The Davis Brown Tower, Suite 1300 · 215 Tenth Street · Des Moines, IA 50309-3993 · 515-288-2500

J. Marc Ward · Dickinson, Mackaman, Tyler & Hagen · http://www.dickinsonlaw.com · 699 Walnut Street, Suite 1600 · Des Moines, IA 50309-3929 · 515-244-2600

Gregory B. Wilcox · Nyemaster, Goode, West, Hansell & O'Brien · 700 Walnut Street, Suite 1600 · Des Moines, IA 50309-3899 · 515-283-3100

Steven E. Zumbach · ⑩ · Belin Lamson McCormick Zumbach Flynn · http://www.belinlaw.com · 666 Walnut Street, Suite 2000 · Des Moines, IA 50309-3989 · 515-243-7100

Iowa City

Robert N. Downer · ⑩ · Meardon, Sueppel & Downer · 122 South Linn Street · Iowa City, IA 52240 · 319-338-9222

Thomas H. Gelman · Phelan, Tucker, Mullen, Walker, Tucker & Gelman · 321 East Market Street · P.O. Box 2150 · Iowa City, IA 52244-2150 · 319-354-1104

Mason City

Gerald M. Stambaugh · ⑩ · Heiny, McManigal, Duffy, Stambaugh & Anderson · 11 Fourth Street, NE · P.O. Box 1567 · Mason City, IA 50402-1567 · 641-423-5154

Muscatine

Roger L. Lande · ⑩ · Stanley, Lande & Hunter · 301 Iowa Avenue, Suite 400 · Muscatine, IA 52761 · 563-264-5000

Sioux City

Marvin S. Berenstein · ⑳ · Berenstein, Moore, Berenstein, Heffernan & Moeller · 501 Pierce Street, Suite 300 · P.O. Box 3207 · Sioux City, IA 51101 · 712-252-0020

Dale C. Tigges · Vriezelaar, Tigges, Edgington, Bottaro, Boden & Ross · 421 Nebraska Street · P.O. Box 1557 · Sioux City, IA 51102 · 712-252-3226

Waterloo

W. Louis Beecher · ⑳ · Beecher, Field, Walker, Morris, Hoffman & Johnson · Court Square Building, Suite 300 · 620 Lafayette Street · P.O. Box 178 · Waterloo, IA 50704-0178 · 319-234-1766

Steven A. Weidner · ⑳ · Swisher & Cohrt · 528 West Fourth Street · P.O. Box 1200 · Waterloo, IA 50704 319-232-6555

DUI/DWI DEFENSE

Des Moines

Dean A. Stowers · Rosenberg, Stowers & Morse · http://www.rosenbergstowersmorse.com · 505 Fifth Avenue, Suite 1010 · Des Moines, IA 50309 · 515-243-7600

EDUCATION LAW

Cedar Rapids

Douglas R. Oelschlaeger · Shuttleworth & Ingersoll · 115 Third Street, SE, Suite 500 · Cedar Rapids, IA 52401 · 319-365-9461

ELDER LAW

Des Moines

Gregory L. Kenyon · Bradshaw, Fowler, Proctor & Fairgrave · 801 Grand Avenue, Suite 3700 · Des Moines, IA 50309-8004 · 515-243-4191

Thomas T. Tarbox · Thomas T. Tarbox Law Office · 309 Court Avenue, Suite 240 · Des Moines, IA 50309 · 515-875-4884

West Des Moines

J. Michael Deege · ⑩ · Wilson, Deege, Dollar & Despotovich · West Bank Building, Suite 300 · 1601 Twenty-Second Street · West Des Moines, IA 50266 · 515-327-1000

Phyllis Pearson · Phyllis Pearson · 6600 West Town Parkway, Suite 160 · West Des Moines, IA 50266 · 515-727-0986

Donald B. Young · Young & Rogers · 4800 Mills Civic Parkway, Suite 205 · West Des Moines, IA 50265 · 515-440-2175

EMINENT DOMAIN AND CONDEMNATION LAW

Altoona

Edwin Skinner · Skinner Law Offices · 204 Eighth Street, SE · P.O. Box 367 · Altoona, IA 50009-0367 · 515-967-4264

Des Moines

Antonio Colacino · Nyemaster, Goode, West, Hansell & O'Brien · 700 Walnut Street, Suite 1600 · Des Moines, IA 50309-3899 · 515-283-3100

William J. Lillis · Connolly, O'Malley, Lillis, Hansen & Olson · 317 Sixth Avenue, Suite 300 · Des Moines, IA 50309-4127 · 515-243-8157

Daniel L. Manning · Connolly, O'Malley, Lillis, Hansen & Olson · 317 Sixth Avenue, Suite 300 · Des Moines, IA 50309-4127 · 515-243-8157

Frank Murray Smith · Frank Murray Smith · 4215 Hubbell Avenue · Des Moines, IA 50317 · 515-265-6210

West Des Moines

Douglas A. Fulton · Brick, Gentry, Bowers, Swartz & Levis · 6701 Westown Parkway, Suite 100 · West Des Moines, IA 50266 · 515-274-1450

EMPLOYEE BENEFITS LAW

Cedar Rapids

J. Scott Bogguss · 20 · Moyer & Bergman · http://www.moyerbergman.com · 2720 First Avenue, NE · P.O. Box 1943 · Cedar Rapids, IA 52402 · 319-366-7331

Gilda L. Boyer · Shuttleworth & Ingersoll · 115 Third Street, SE, Suite 500 · Cedar Rapids, IA 52401 · 319-365-9461

Gary J. Streit · 20 · Shuttleworth & Ingersoll · 115 Third Street, SE, Suite 500 · Cedar Rapids, IA 52401 · 319-365-9461

Davenport

David A. Dettmann · 10 · Lane & Waterman · 220 North Main Street, Suite 600 · Davenport, IA 52801 · 563-324-3246

Gene H. Snapp, Jr. · 20 · Gene H. Snapp, Jr. · 4500 North Brady Street, Suite 205 · Davenport, IA 52806 563-445-1710

Des Moines

Ronni F. Begleiter · 10 · Brown, Winick, Graves, Gross, Baskerville & Schoenebaum · Ruan Center, Suite 2000 · 666 Grand Avenue · Des Moines, IA 50309-2510 · 515-242-2400

David C. Craig · 10 · Finley, Alt, Smith, Scharnberg, Craig, Hilmes & Gaffney · 699 Walnut Street, Suite 1900 · Des Moines, IA 50309 · 515-288-0145

Terry C. Hancock · Nyemaster, Goode, West, Hansell & O'Brien · 700 Walnut Street, Suite 1600 · Des Moines, IA 50309-3899 · 515-283-3100

Alice E. Helle · 10 · Brown, Winick, Graves, Gross, Baskerville & Schoenebaum · Ruan Center, Suite 2000 · 666 Grand Avenue · Des Moines, IA 50309-2510 · 515-242-2400

R. Craig Shives · 20 · Nyemaster, Goode, West, Hansell & O'Brien · 700 Walnut Street, Suite 1600 · Des Moines, IA 50309-3899 · 515-283-3100

Margaret D. Van Houten · 10 · Davis, Brown, Koehn, Shors & Roberts · The Davis Brown Tower, Suite 1300 · 215 Tenth Street · Des Moines, IA 50309-3993 · 515-288-2500

Sioux City

Kenton B. Vriezelaar · ⑩ · Vriezelaar, Tigges, Edgington, Bottaro, Boden & Ross · 421 Nebraska Street · P.O. Box 1557 · Sioux City, IA 51102 · 712-252-3226

ENERGY LAW

Cedar Rapids

Steven J. Pace · Shuttleworth & Ingersoll · 115 Third Street, SE, Suite 500 · Cedar Rapids, IA 52401 · 319-365-9461

Des Moines

Bret A. Dublinske · Dickinson, Mackaman, Tyler & Hagen · http://www.dickinsonlaw.com · 699 Walnut Street, Suite 1600 · Des Moines, IA 50309-3929 · 515-244-2600

Robert F. Holz, Jr. · ⑩ · Davis, Brown, Koehn, Shors & Roberts · The Davis Brown Tower, Suite 1300 · 215 Tenth Street · Des Moines, IA 50309-3993 · 515-288-2500

Philip E. Stoffregen · ⑩ · Brown, Winick, Graves, Gross, Baskerville & Schoenebaum · Ruan Center, Suite 2000 · 666 Grand Avenue · Des Moines, IA 50309-2510 · 515-242-2400

Sheila K. Tipton · ⑩ · Belin Lamson McCormick Zumbach Flynn · http://www.belinlaw.com · 666 Walnut Street, Suite 2000 · Des Moines, IA 50309-3989 · 515-243-7100

ENVIRONMENTAL LAW

Cedar Rapids

Steven J. Pace · Shuttleworth & Ingersoll · 115 Third Street, SE, Suite 500 · Cedar Rapids, IA 52401 · 319-365-9461

Des Moines

Charles F. Becker · Belin Lamson McCormick Zumbach Flynn · http://www.belinlaw.com · 666 Walnut Street, Suite 2000 · Des Moines, IA 50309-3989 · 515-243-7100

Jane B. McCallister · Ahlers & Cooney · 100 Court Avenue, Suite 600 · Des Moines, IA 50309-2231 · 515-243-7611

James L. Pray · Brown, Winick, Graves, Gross, Baskerville & Schoenebaum · Ruan Center, Suite 2000 · 666 Grand Avenue · Des Moines, IA 50309-2510 · 515-242-2400

West Des Moines

Mark Landa · Sullivan & Ward · 6601 Westown Parkway, Suite 200 · West Des Moines, IA 50266-7733 · 515-244-3500

Lawrence P. McLellan · Sullivan & Ward · 6601 Westown Parkway, Suite 200 · West Des Moines, IA 50266-7733 · 515-244-3500

Decorah

Marion L. Beatty · Miller, Pearson, Gloe, Burns, Beatty & Cowie · 301 West Broadway · P.O. Box 28 · Decorah, IA 52101 · 563-382-4226

Des Moines

Harvey L. Harrison · Harrison & Dietz-Kilen · 423 East Court Avenue, Suite 200 · Des Moines, IA 50309 · 515-284-1433

Robert Laden · Laden & Pearson · 3231 East Euclid Avenue, Suite 300 · Des Moines, IA 50317 · 515-266-6000

Steven H. Lytle · ⑩ · Nyemaster, Goode, West, Hansell & O'Brien · 700 Walnut Street, Suite 1600 · Des Moines, IA 50309-3899 · 515-283-3100

Timothy G. Pearson · Laden & Pearson · 3231 East Euclid Avenue, Suite 300 · Des Moines, IA 50317 · 515-266-6000

Patricia A. Shoff · ⑩ · Belin Lamson McCormick Zumbach Flynn · http://www.belinlaw.com · 666 Walnut Street, Suite 2000 · Des Moines, IA 50309-3989 · 515-243-7100

John K. Vernon · Dickinson, Mackaman, Tyler & Hagen · http://www.dickinsonlaw.com · 699 Walnut Street, Suite 1600 · Des Moines, IA 50309-3929 · 515-244-2600

Harlan

J. C. Salvo · Salvo, Deren, Schenck & Lauterbach · 711 Court Street · P.O. Box 509 · Harlan, IA 51537-0509 · 712-755-3141

Iowa City

Daniel L. Bray · ⑩ · Bray & Klockau · 402 South Linn Street · Iowa City, IA 52240 · 319-338-7968

John W. Hayek · ⑩ · Hayek, Hayek, Brown, Moreland & Hayek · 120 East Washington Street · Iowa City, IA 52240-3924 · 319-337-9606

Chad A. Kepros · Bray & Klockau · 402 South Linn Street · Iowa City, IA 52240 · 319-338-7968

Sharon A. Mellon · ⑳ · Mellon & Spies · 312 East College Street, Suite 216 · Iowa City, IA 52240 · 319-337-4193

Randall B. Willman · Leff Law Firm · 222 South Linn Street · P.O. Box 2447 · Iowa City, IA 52244-2447 319-338-7551

Waterloo

Thomas W. Langlas · ⑩ · Gallagher, Langlas & Gallagher · Law Building · 405 East Fifth Street · P.O. Box 2615 · Waterloo, IA 50704 · 319-233-6163

West Des Moines

Thomas J. Levis · Brick, Gentry, Bowers, Swartz & Levis · 6701 Westown Parkway, Suite 100 · West Des Moines, IA 50266 · 515-274-1450

James M. Meade · ⑩ · James M. Meade · 2700 Westown Parkway, Suite 310 · West Des Moines, IA 50266-1411 · 515-225-1100

FIRST AMENDMENT LAW

Des Moines

Michael A. Giudicessi · ⑩ · Faegre & Benson · 801 Grand Avenue, Suite 3100 · Des Moines, IA 50309-8002 · 515-248-9000

Kim J. Walker · ⑩ · Faegre & Benson · 801 Grand Avenue, Suite 3100 · Des Moines, IA 50309-8002 · 515-248-9000

FRANCHISE LAW

Des Moines

Mark C. Dickinson · Nyemaster, Goode, West, Hansell & O'Brien · 700 Walnut Street, Suite 1600 · Des Moines, IA 50309-3899 · 515-283-3100

Iowa City

Mark T. Hamer · ⑩ · Meardon, Sueppel & Downer · 122 South Linn Street · Iowa City, IA 52240 · 319-338-9222

GAMING LAW

Des Moines

Thomas L. Flynn · ㉕ · Belin Lamson McCormick Zumbach Flynn · http://www.belinlaw.com · 666 Walnut Street, Suite 2000 · Des Moines, IA 50309-3989 · 515-243-7100

GOVERNMENT RELATIONS LAW

Des Moines

James W. Carney · Carney Appleby Law Firm · 303 Locust Street · 400 Homestead Building · Des Moines, IA 50309-1740 · 515-282-6803

Stephen W. Roberts · Davis, Brown, Koehn, Shors & Roberts · The Davis Brown Tower, Suite 1300 · 215 Tenth Street · Des Moines, IA 50309-3993 · 515-288-2500

Steven C. Schoenebaum · Brown, Winick, Graves, Gross, Baskerville & Schoenebaum · Ruan Center, Suite 2000 · 666 Grand Avenue · Des Moines, IA 50309-2510 · 515-242-2400

James B. West · Nyemaster, Goode, West, Hansell & O'Brien · 700 Walnut Street, Suite 1600 · Des Moines, IA 50309-3899 · 515-283-3100

West Des Moines

William J. Wimmer · Wasker, Dorr, Wimmer & Marcouiller · Three Fountains Office Park, Suite 250 · 4201 Westown Parkway · West Des Moines, IA 50266-6720 · 515-283-1801

HEALTH CARE LAW

Cedar Rapids

Diane H. Kutzko · ⑩ · Shuttleworth & Ingersoll · 115 Third Street, SE, Suite 500 · Cedar Rapids, IA 52401 · 319-365-9461

Carroll J. Reasoner · ⑩ · Shuttleworth & Ingersoll · 115 Third Street, SE, Suite 500 · Cedar Rapids, IA 52401 · 319-365-9461

Des Moines

Willard L. Boyd III · Nyemaster, Goode, West, Hansell & O'Brien · 700 Walnut Street, Suite 1600 · Des Moines, IA 50309-3899 · 515-283-3100

Edgar F. Hansell · ㉕ · Nyemaster, Goode, West, Hansell & O'Brien · 700 Walnut Street, Suite 1600 · Des Moines, IA 50309-3899 · 515-283-3100

Norene D. Jacobs · ⑩ · Kutak Rock · Highland Building, Suite 124 · 4201 Westown Parkway · Des Moines, IA 50266-6720 · 515-224-1266

Edwin N. McIntosh · Dorsey & Whitney · 801 Grand Avenue, Suite 3900 · Des Moines, IA 50309-2790 · 515-283-1000

Sally A. Reavely · Whitfield & Eddy · 317 Sixth Avenue, Suite 1200 · Des Moines, IA 50309-4195 · 515-288-6041

John D. Shors · ⑩ · Davis, Brown, Koehn, Shors & Roberts · The Davis Brown Tower, Suite 1300 · 215 Tenth Street · Des Moines, IA 50309-3993 · 515-288-2500

Kendall Watkins · Davis, Brown, Koehn, Shors & Roberts · The Davis Brown Tower, Suite 1300 · 215 Tenth Street · Des Moines, IA 50309-3993 · 515-288-2500

Sioux City

Cynthia C. Moser · ⑩ · Heidman, Redmond, Fredregill, Patterson, Plaza, Dykstra & Prahl · 1128 Historic Fourth Street · P.O. Box 3086 · Sioux City, IA 51101 · 712-255-8838

IMMIGRATION LAW

Des Moines

Lori T. Chesser · Davis, Brown, Koehn, Shors & Roberts · The Davis Brown Tower, Suite 1300 · 215 Tenth Street · Des Moines, IA 50309-3993 · 515-288-2500

Fairfield

James D. Pearson · James D. Pearson · 506 North Fourth Street · Fairfield, IA 52556 · 641-472-6095

INSURANCE LAW

Cedar Rapids

Philip D. Brooks · Moyer & Bergman · http://www.moyerbergman.com · 2720 First Avenue, NE · P.O. Box 1943 · Cedar Rapids, IA 52402 · 319-366-7331

Douglas R. Oelschlaeger · Shuttleworth & Ingersoll · 115 Third Street, SE, Suite 500 · Cedar Rapids, IA 52401 · 319-365-9461

Des Moines

Kent M. Forney · ⑩ · Bradshaw, Fowler, Proctor & Fairgrave · 801 Grand Avenue, Suite 3700 · Des Moines, IA 50309-8004 · 515-243-4191

Michael D. Treinen · Brown, Winick, Graves, Gross, Baskerville & Schoenebaum · Ruan Center, Suite 2000 · 666 Grand Avenue · Des Moines, IA 50309-2510 · 515-242-2400

Mark L. Tripp · Bradshaw, Fowler, Proctor & Fairgrave · 801 Grand Avenue, Suite 3700 · Des Moines, IA 50309-8004 · 515-243-4191

James B. West · Nyemaster, Goode, West, Hansell & O'Brien · 700 Walnut Street, Suite 1600 · Des Moines, IA 50309-3899 · 515-283-3100

West Des Moines

William J. Wimmer · Wasker, Dorr, Wimmer & Marcouiller · Three Fountains Office Park, Suite 250 · 4201 Westown Parkway · West Des Moines, IA 50266-6720 · 515-283-1801

INTELLECTUAL PROPERTY LAW

Cedar Rapids

James C. Nemmers · ⑩ · Shuttleworth & Ingersoll · 115 Third Street, SE, Suite 500 · Cedar Rapids, IA 52401 · 319-365-9461

Des Moines

Kent A. Herink · ⑩ · Davis, Brown, Koehn, Shors & Roberts · The Davis Brown Tower, Suite 1300 · 215 Tenth Street · Des Moines, IA 50309-3993 · 515-288-2500

Brian J. Laurenzo · Dorsey & Whitney · 801 Grand Avenue, Suite 3900 · Des Moines, IA 50309-2790 · 515-283-1000

Bruce W. McKee · ⑩ · McKee, Voorhees & Sease · 801 Grand Avenue, Suite 3200 · Des Moines, IA 50309-2721 · 515-288-3667

Edmund J. Sease · McKee, Voorhees & Sease · 801 Grand Avenue, Suite 3200 · Des Moines, IA 50309-2721 · 515-288-3667

Michael O. Sturm · ⑩ · Sturm & Fix · 206 Sixth Avenue, Suite 1213 · Des Moines, IA 50309-4076 · 515-288-9589

Michael G. Voorhees · ⑩ · McKee, Voorhees & Sease · 801 Grand Avenue, Suite 3200 · Des Moines, IA 50309-2721 · 515-288-3667

West Des Moines

G. Brian Pingel · ⑩ · Brown, Winick, Graves, Gross, Baskerville & Schoenebaum · Regency West Five, Suite 277 · 4500 Westown Parkway · West Des Moines, IA 50266-6717 · 515-242-2400

Cedar Rapids

Kelly R. Baier · ⑩ · Bradley & Riley · http://www.bradleyriley.com · 2007 First Avenue, SE · P.O. Box 2804 · Cedar Rapids, IA 52406-2804 · 319-363-0101

Iris E. Muchmore · ⑩ · Simmons, Perrine, Albright & Ellwood · 115 Third Street, SE, Suite 1200 · Cedar Rapids, IA 52401-1266 · 319-366-7641

Mark L. Zaiger · ⑩ · Shuttleworth & Ingersoll · 115 Third Street, SE, Suite 500 · Cedar Rapids, IA 52401 319-365-9461

Des Moines

Helen C. Adams · Dickinson, Mackaman, Tyler & Hagen · http://www.dickinsonlaw.com · 699 Walnut Street, Suite 1600 · Des Moines, IA 50309-3929 · 515-244-2600

Roxanne B. Conlin · ⑩ · Roxanne B. Conlin & Associates · 319 Seventh Street, Suite 600 · Des Moines, IA 50309-3826 · 515-283-1111

Thomas W. Foley · Nyemaster, Goode, West, Hansell & O'Brien · 700 Walnut Street, Suite 1600 · Des Moines, IA 50309-3899 · 515-283-3100

Frank B. Harty · Nyemaster, Goode, West, Hansell & O'Brien · 700 Walnut Street, Suite 1600 · Des Moines, IA 50309-3899 · 515-283-3100

Elizabeth Gregg Kennedy · ⑩ · Ahlers & Cooney · 100 Court Avenue, Suite 600 · Des Moines, IA 50309-2231 · 515-243-7611

Jeffrey A. Krausman · Dickinson, Mackaman, Tyler & Hagen · http://www.dickinsonlaw.com · 699 Walnut Street, Suite 1600 · Des Moines, IA 50309-3929 · 515-244-2600

Gene R. La Suer · ⑩ · Davis, Brown, Koehn, Shors & Roberts · The Davis Brown Tower, Suite 1300 · 215 Tenth Street · Des Moines, IA 50309-3993 · 515-288-2500

Edward W. Remsburg · Ahlers & Cooney · 100 Court Avenue, Suite 600 · Des Moines, IA 50309-2231 · 515-243-7611

Russell L. Samson · Dickinson, Mackaman, Tyler & Hagen · http://www.dickinsonlaw.com · 699 Walnut Street, Suite 1600 · Des Moines, IA 50309-3929 · 515-244-2600

Jaki K. Samuelson · Whitfield & Eddy · 317 Sixth Avenue, Suite 1200 · Des Moines, IA 50309-4195 · 515-288-6041

Patricia A. Shoff · ⑩ · Belin Lamson McCormick Zumbach Flynn · http://www.belinlaw.com · 666 Walnut Street, Suite 2000 · Des Moines, IA 50309-3989 · 515-243-7100

James R. Swanger · ⑩ · Belin Lamson McCormick Zumbach Flynn · http://www.belinlaw.com · 666 Walnut Street, Suite 2000 · Des Moines, IA 50309-3989 · 515-243-7100

Sioux City

MacDonald Smith · ⑳ · Smith & McElwain · 505 Fifth Street, Suite 530 · P.O. Box 1194 · Sioux City, IA 51102 · 712-255-8094

Urbandale

Paige E. Fiedler · Fiedler & Newkirk · 2900 One Hundredth Street, Suite 209 · Urbandale, IA 50322 · 515-254-1999

LAND USE & ZONING LAW

Cedar Rapids

William P. Prowell · Shuttleworth & Ingersoll · 115 Third Street, SE, Suite 500 · Cedar Rapids, IA 52401 319-365-9461

Des Moines

Streetar Cameron · Connolly, O'Malley, Lillis, Hansen & Olson · 317 Sixth Avenue, Suite 300 · Des Moines, IA 50309-4127 · 515-243-8157

William J. Lillis · Connolly, O'Malley, Lillis, Hansen & Olson · 317 Sixth Avenue, Suite 300 · Des Moines, IA 50309-4127 · 515-243-8157

Daniel L. Manning · Connolly, O'Malley, Lillis, Hansen & Olson · 317 Sixth Avenue, Suite 300 · Des Moines, IA 50309-4127 · 515-243-8157

Christopher R. Pose · Connolly, O'Malley, Lillis, Hansen & Olson · 317 Sixth Avenue, Suite 300 · Des Moines, IA 50309-4127 · 515-243-8157

West Des Moines

Michael J. Green · Brown, Winick, Graves, Gross, Baskerville & Schoenebaum · Regency West Five, Suite 277 · 4500 Westown Parkway · West Des Moines, IA 50266-6717 · 515-242-2400

LEGAL MALPRACTICE LAW

Cedar Rapids

Patrick M. Roby · ⑳ · Elderkin & Pirnie · 115 First Avenue, SE · Cedar Rapids, IA 52401 · 319-362-2137

Davenport

Robert V. P. Waterman, Jr. · Lane & Waterman · 220 North Main Street, Suite 600 · Davenport, IA 52801 · 563-324-3246

Waterloo

David J. Dutton · ⑩ · Dutton, Braun, Staack & Hellman · 3151 Brockway Road · P.O. Box 810 · Waterloo, IA 50704 · 319-234-4471

LEVERAGED BUYOUTS AND PRIVATE EQUITY LAW

Cedar Rapids

Brian D. Bergstrom · Shuttleworth & Ingersoll · 115 Third Street, SE, Suite 500 · Cedar Rapids, IA 52401 · 319-365-9461

Cedar Rapids

Constance M. Alt · Shuttleworth & Ingersoll · 115 Third Street, SE, Suite 500 · Cedar Rapids, IA 52401 · 319-365-9461

Robert D. Houghton · Shuttleworth & Ingersoll · 115 Third Street, SE, Suite 500 · Cedar Rapids, IA 52401 · 319-365-9461

John L. Riccolo · ⑩ · Riccolo & Semelroth · 425 Second Street, SE, Suite 1140 · Cedar Rapids, IA 52401 319-365-9200

Jennifer Rinden · Shuttleworth & Ingersoll · 115 Third Street, SE, Suite 500 · Cedar Rapids, IA 52401 · 319-365-9461

Council Bluffs

John M. French · Peters Law Firm · 233 Pearl Street · P.O. Box 1078 · Council Bluffs, IA 51502 · 712-328-3157

Davenport

Michael K. Bush · ⑩ · Bush, Motto, Creen, Koury & Halligan · 5505 Victoria Avenue, Suite 100 · Davenport, IA 52807 · 563-344-4900

Greg A. Egbers · Betty, Neuman & McMahon · 111 East Third Street, Suite 600 · Davenport, IA 52801 · 563-326-4491

Craig A. Levien · Betty, Neuman & McMahon · 111 East Third Street, Suite 600 · Davenport, IA 52801 · 563-326-4491

Charles E. Miller · Lane & Waterman · 220 North Main Street, Suite 600 · Davenport, IA 52801 · 563-324-3246

Robert V. P. Waterman, Jr. · Lane & Waterman · 220 North Main Street, Suite 600 · Davenport, IA 52801 · 563-324-3246

Des Moines

Nicholas Critelli · ⑩ · Law Chambers of Nicholas Critelli · 317 Sixth Avenue, Suite 950 · Des Moines, IA 50309 · 515-243-3122

Michael H. Figenshaw · ⑩ · Bradshaw, Fowler, Proctor & Fairgrave · 801 Grand Avenue, Suite 3700 · Des Moines, IA 50309-8004 · 515-243-4191

Thomas A. Finley · ⑩ · Finley, Alt, Smith, Scharnberg, Craig, Hilmes & Gaffney · 699 Walnut Street, Suite 1900 · Des Moines, IA 50309 · 515-288-0145

John D. Hilmes · ⑩ · Finley, Alt, Smith, Scharnberg, Craig, Hilmes & Gaffney · 699 Walnut Street, Suite 1900 · Des Moines, IA 50309 · 515-288-0145

Dwight W. James · ⑩ · The James Law Firm · 604 Locust Street, Suite 630 · Des Moines, IA 50309 · 866-566-8291

Gregory W. Landry · LaMarca & Landry · 1820 Northwest 118th Street, Suite 200 · Des Moines, IA 50325 · 515-225-2600

Iowa City

James P. Hayes · ⑳ · Hayes Lorenzen Lawyers · Plaza Centre One, Suite 580 · 125 South Dubuque Street · Iowa City, IA 52240 · 319-887-3688

Karen A. Lorenzen · Hayes Lorenzen Lawyers · Plaza Centre One, Suite 580 · 125 South Dubuque Street · Iowa City, IA 52240 · 319-887-3688

Richard M. Tucker · Phelan, Tucker, Mullen, Walker, Tucker & Gelman · 321 East Market Street · P.O. Box 2150 · Iowa City, IA 52244-2150 · 319-354-1104

Sioux City

Maurice B. Nieland · ⑩ · Rawlings, Nieland, Killinger, Ellwanger, Jacobs, Mohrhauser, Nelson & Early · 522 Fourth Street, Suite 300 · Sioux City, IA 51101 · 712-277-2373

MERGERS & ACQUISITIONS LAW

Cedar Rapids

Brian D. Bergstrom · Shuttleworth & Ingersoll · 115 Third Street, SE, Suite 500 · Cedar Rapids, IA 52401 · 319-365-9461

Dean R. Einck · ⑩ · Shuttleworth & Ingersoll · 115 Third Street, SE, Suite 500 · Cedar Rapids, IA 52401 319-365-9461

Davenport

Scott Van Vooren · Lane & Waterman · 220 North Main Street, Suite 600 · Davenport, IA 52801 · 563-324-3246

C. Dana Waterman III · ⑩ · Lane & Waterman · 220 North Main Street, Suite 600 · Davenport, IA 52801 · 563-324-3246

Des Moines

Garth D. Adams · Belin Lamson McCormick Zumbach Flynn · http://www.belinlaw.com · 666 Walnut Street, Suite 2000 · Des Moines, IA 50309-3989 · 515-243-7100

Frank J. Carroll · ㉕ · Davis, Brown, Koehn, Shors & Roberts · The Davis Brown Tower, Suite 1300 · 215 Tenth Street · Des Moines, IA 50309-3993 · 515-288-2500

John D. Hintze · Ahlers & Cooney · 100 Court Avenue, Suite 600 · Des Moines, IA 50309-2231 · 515-243-7611

Steven E. Zumbach · ⑩ · Belin Lamson McCormick Zumbach Flynn · http://www.belinlaw.com · 666 Walnut Street, Suite 2000 · Des Moines, IA 50309-3989 · 515-243-7100

MUNICIPAL LAW

Iowa City

William F. Sueppel, Sr. · Meardon, Sueppel & Downer · 122 South Linn Street · Iowa City, IA 52240 · 319-338-9222

NON-PROFIT/CHARITIES LAW

Cedar Rapids

Gilda L. Boyer · Shuttleworth & Ingersoll · 115 Third Street, SE, Suite 500 · Cedar Rapids, IA 52401 · 319-365-9461

Des Moines

William A. Boatwright · Davis, Brown, Koehn, Shors & Roberts · The Davis Brown Tower, Suite 1300 · 215 Tenth Street · Des Moines, IA 50309-3993 · 515-288-2500

Willard L. Boyd III · Nyemaster, Goode, West, Hansell & O'Brien · 700 Walnut Street, Suite 1600 · Des Moines, IA 50309-3899 · 515-283-3100

Bruce I. Campbell · ㉕ · Davis, Brown, Koehn, Shors & Roberts · The Davis Brown Tower, Suite 1300 · 215 Tenth Street · Des Moines, IA 50309-3993 · 515-288-2500

Steven E. Zumbach · ⑩ · Belin Lamson McCormick Zumbach Flynn · http://www.belinlaw.com · 666 Walnut Street, Suite 2000 · Des Moines, IA 50309-3989 · 515-243-7100

NON-WHITE-COLLAR CRIMINAL DEFENSE

Des Moines

Alfredo G. Parrish · ⑩ · Parrish, Kruidenier, Moss, Dunn, Boles, Gribble, Cook, Parish & Gentry · 2910 Grand Avenue · Des Moines, IA 50312 · 515-284-5737

Paul H. Rosenberg · Paul Rosenberg & Associates · 666 Grand Avenue, Suite 1837 · Des Moines, IA 50309 · 515-245-3828

Dean A. Stowers · Rosenberg, Stowers & Morse · http://www.rosenbergstowersmorse.com · 505 Fifth Avenue, Suite 1010 · Des Moines, IA 50309 · 515-243-7600

Iowa City

Leon F. Spies · ㉕ · Mellon & Spies · 312 East College Street, Suite 216 · Iowa City, IA 52240 · 319-337-4193

PERSONAL INJURY LITIGATION

Cedar Falls

Mark W. Fransdal · Redfern, Mason, Larsen & Moore · 415 Clay Street · P.O. Box 627 · Cedar Falls, IA 50613 · 319-277-6830

Cedar Rapids

Richard S. Fry · Shuttleworth & Ingersoll · 115 Third Street, SE, Suite 500 · Cedar Rapids, IA 52401 · 319-365-9461

Richard C. Garberson · Shuttleworth & Ingersoll · 115 Third Street, SE, Suite 500 · Cedar Rapids, IA 52401 · 319-365-9461

Tom Riley · ⑩ · Tom Riley Law Firm · 4040 First Avenue, NE · P.O. Box 998 · Cedar Rapids, IA 52406 · 319-363-4040

Patrick M. Roby · ⑳ · Elderkin & Pirnie · 115 First Avenue, SE · Cedar Rapids, IA 52401 · 319-362-2137

Council Bluffs

John M. French · Peters Law Firm · 233 Pearl Street · P.O. Box 1078 · Council Bluffs, IA 51502 · 712-328-3157

Dennis M. Gray · ⑩ · Peters Law Firm · 233 Pearl Street · P.O. Box 1078 · Council Bluffs, IA 51502 · 712-328-3157

Kristopher K. Madsen · Stuart, Tinley, Peters, Thorn & Hughes · Northwestern Bell Building, Second Floor · 310 West Kanesville Boulevard · P.O. Box 398 · Council Bluffs, IA 51502-0398 · 712-322-4033

Philip J. Willson · ⑩ · Willson & Pechacek · 421 West Broadway, Suite 200 · P.O. Box 2029 · Council Bluffs, IA 51503 · 712-322-6000

Davenport

Michael K. Bush · ⑩ · Bush, Motto, Creen, Koury & Halligan · 5505 Victoria Avenue, Suite 100 · Davenport, IA 52807 · 563-344-4900

Greg A. Egbers · Betty, Neuman & McMahon · 111 East Third Street, Suite 600 · Davenport, IA 52801 · 563-326-4491

Craig A. Levien · Betty, Neuman & McMahon · 111 East Third Street, Suite 600 · Davenport, IA 52801 · 563-326-4491

Michael C. Walker · Hopkins & Huebner · Northwest Bank Tower, Suite 704 · 100 East Kimberly Road · Davenport, IA 52806-5944 · 563-445-2264

Decorah

Marion L. Beatty · Miller, Pearson, Gloe, Burns, Beatty & Cowie · 301 West Broadway · P.O. Box 28 · Decorah, IA 52101 · 563-382-4226

Des Moines

David L. Brown · ⑩ · Hansen, McClintock & Riley · Fleming Building, Eighth Floor · 218 Sixth Avenue Des Moines, IA 50309-4092 · 515-244-2141

Roxanne B. Conlin · ⑩ · Roxanne B. Conlin & Associates · 319 Seventh Street, Suite 600 · Des Moines, IA 50309-3826 · 515-283-1111

Nicholas Critelli · ⑩ · Law Chambers of Nicholas Critelli · 317 Sixth Avenue, Suite 950 · Des Moines, IA 50309 · 515-243-3122

William L. Dawe · ⑩ · Hopkins & Huebner · Terrace Center, Suite 111 · 2700 Grand Avenue · Des Moines, IA 50312-5213 · 515-244-0111

Michael H. Figenshaw · ⑩ · Bradshaw, Fowler, Proctor & Fairgrave · 801 Grand Avenue, Suite 3700 · Des Moines, IA 50309-8004 · 515-243-4191

Thomas A. Finley · ⑩ · Finley, Alt, Smith, Scharnberg, Craig, Hilmes & Gaffney · 699 Walnut Street, Suite 1900 · Des Moines, IA 50309 · 515-288-0145

John D. Hilmes · ⑩ · Finley, Alt, Smith, Scharnberg, Craig, Hilmes & Gaffney · 699 Walnut Street, Suite 1900 · Des Moines, IA 50309 · 515-288-0145

Dwight W. James · ⑩ · The James Law Firm · 604 Locust Street, Suite 630 · Des Moines, IA 50309 · 866-566-8291

Jeff H. Jeffries · Hopkins & Huebner · Terrace Center, Suite 111 · 2700 Grand Avenue · Des Moines, IA 50312-5213 · 515-244-0111

George LaMarca · LaMarca & Landry · 1820 Northwest 118th Street, Suite 200 · Des Moines, IA 50325 · 515-225-2600

John A. McClintock · ⑩ · Hansen, McClintock & Riley · Fleming Building, Eighth Floor · 218 Sixth Avenue · Des Moines, IA 50309-4092 · 515-244-2141

Mark McCormick · ⑩ · Belin Lamson McCormick Zumbach Flynn · http://www.belinlaw.com · 666 Walnut Street, Suite 2000 · Des Moines, IA 50309-3989 · 515-243-7100

Richard J. Sapp · ⑩ · Nyemaster, Goode, West, Hansell & O'Brien · 700 Walnut Street, Suite 1600 · Des Moines, IA 50309-3899 · 515-283-3100

Steven K. Scharnberg · Finley, Alt, Smith, Scharnberg, Craig, Hilmes & Gaffney · 699 Walnut Street, Suite 1900 · Des Moines, IA 50309 · 515-288-0145

Estherville

Joseph L. Fitzgibbons · ⑩ · Fitzgibbons Law Firm · 108 North Seventh Street · P.O. Box 496 · Estherville, IA 51334 · 712-362-7215

Harlan

J. C. Salvo · Salvo, Deren, Schenck & Lauterbach · 711 Court Street · P.O. Box 509 · Harlan, IA 51537-0509 · 712-755-3141

Iowa City

David E. Brown · Hayek, Hayek, Brown, Moreland & Hayek · 120 East Washington Street · Iowa City, IA 52240-3924 · 319-337-9606

James P. Hayes · ⑳ · Hayes Lorenzen Lawyers · Plaza Centre One, Suite 580 · 125 South Dubuque Street · Iowa City, IA 52240 · 319-887-3688

Thomas D. Hobart · ⑩ · Meardon, Sueppel & Downer · 122 South Linn Street · Iowa City, IA 52240 · 319-338-9222

Richard M. Tucker · Phelan, Tucker, Mullen, Walker, Tucker & Gelman · 321 East Market Street · P.O. Box 2150 · Iowa City, IA 52244-2150 · 319-354-1104

Bruce L. Walker · Phelan, Tucker, Mullen, Walker, Tucker & Gelman · 321 East Market Street · P.O. Box 2150 · Iowa City, IA 52244-2150 · 319-354-1104

Mason City

David E. Funkhouser · ⑩ · Brown, Kinsey, Funkhouser & Lander · 214 North Adams Avenue · P.O. Box 679 · Mason City, IA 50402-0679 · 641-423-6223

Sioux City

Michael W. Ellwanger · Rawlings, Nieland, Killinger, Ellwanger, Jacobs, Mohrhauser, Nelson & Early · 522 Fourth Street, Suite 300 · Sioux City, IA 51101 · 712-277-2373

Maurice B. Nieland · ⑩ · Rawlings, Nieland, Killinger, Ellwanger, Jacobs, Mohrhauser, Nelson & Early · 522 Fourth Street, Suite 300 · Sioux City, IA 51101 · 712-277-2373

N. Richard Willia, Jr. · ⑩ · Willia, Stahle & Andreasen · U.S. Bank Building, Suite 400 · 501 Pierce Street P.O. Box 1768 · Sioux City, IA 51102 · 712-277-0686

Spencer

Richard J. Barry · ⑩ · Montgomery, Barry & Bovee · Southwest Plaza · 316 Eleventh Street · P.O. Box 500 · Spencer, IA 51301-0500 · 712-262-1150

Urbandale

Marc Humphrey · Humphrey Law Firm · 2755 One-Hundred-Sixth Street · Urbandale, IA 50322 · 515-274-8340

Waterloo

David J. Dutton · ⑩ · Dutton, Braun, Staack & Hellman · 3151 Brockway Road · P.O. Box 810 · Waterloo, IA 50704 · 319-234-4471

Edward J. Gallagher, Jr. · ㉕ · Gallagher, Langlas & Gallagher · Law Building · 405 East Fifth Street · P.O. Box 2615 · Waterloo, IA 50704 · 319-233-6163

James R. Hellman · Dutton, Braun, Staack & Hellman · 3151 Brockway Road · P.O. Box 810 · Waterloo, IA 50704 · 319-234-4471

PRODUCT LIABILITY LITIGATION

Cedar Rapids

Robert D. Houghton · Shuttleworth & Ingersoll · 115 Third Street, SE, Suite 500 · Cedar Rapids, IA 52401 · 319-365-9461

Des Moines

Robert L. Fanter · Whitfield & Eddy · 317 Sixth Avenue, Suite 1200 · Des Moines, IA 50309-4195 · 515-288-6041

Richard J. Sapp · ⑩ · Nyemaster, Goode, West, Hansell & O'Brien · 700 Walnut Street, Suite 1600 · Des Moines, IA 50309-3899 · 515-283-3100

David A. Tank · Davis, Brown, Koehn, Shors & Roberts · The Davis Brown Tower, Suite 1300 · 215 Tenth Street · Des Moines, IA 50309-3993 · 515-288-2500

Sioux City

Maurice B. Nieland · ⑩ · Rawlings, Nieland, Killinger, Ellwanger, Jacobs, Mohrhauser, Nelson & Early · 522 Fourth Street, Suite 300 · Sioux City, IA 51101 · 712-277-2373

Waterloo

David J. Dutton · ⑩ · Dutton, Braun, Staack & Hellman · 3151 Brockway Road · P.O. Box 810 · Waterloo, IA 50704 · 319-234-4471

Edward J. Gallagher, Jr. · ㉕ · Gallagher, Langlas & Gallagher · Law Building · 405 East Fifth Street · P.O. Box 2615 · Waterloo, IA 50704 · 319-233-6163

PROFESSIONAL MALPRACTICE LAW

Cedar Rapids

Richard S. Fry · Shuttleworth & Ingersoll · 115 Third Street, SE, Suite 500 · Cedar Rapids, IA 52401 · 319-365-9461

Waterloo

David J. Dutton · ⑩ · Dutton, Braun, Staack & Hellman · 3151 Brockway Road · P.O. Box 810 · Waterloo, IA 50704 · 319-234-4471

PUBLIC FINANCE LAW

Des Moines

David L. Claypool · Dorsey & Whitney · 801 Grand Avenue, Suite 3900 · Des Moines, IA 50309-2790 · 515-283-1000

David D. Grossklaus · Dorsey & Whitney · 801 Grand Avenue, Suite 3900 · Des Moines, IA 50309-2790 515-283-1000

Robert E. Josten · Dorsey & Whitney · 801 Grand Avenue, Suite 3900 · Des Moines, IA 50309-2790 · 515-283-1000

Linda L. Kniep · Ahlers & Cooney · 100 Court Avenue, Suite 600 · Des Moines, IA 50309-2231 · 515-243-7611

David B. Van Sickel · Davis, Brown, Koehn, Shors & Roberts · The Davis Brown Tower, Suite 1300 · 215 Tenth Street · Des Moines, IA 50309-3993 · 515-288-2500

REAL ESTATE LAW

Cedar Rapids

Linda M. Kirsch · Shuttleworth & Ingersoll · 115 Third Street, SE, Suite 500 · Cedar Rapids, IA 52401 · 319-365-9461

David W. Kubicek · ⑳ · Simmons, Perrine, Albright & Ellwood · 115 Third Street, SE, Suite 1200 · Cedar Rapids, IA 52401-1266 · 319-366-7641

Dennis J. McMenimen · Shuttleworth & Ingersoll · 115 Third Street, SE, Suite 500 · Cedar Rapids, IA 52401 · 319-365-9461

William P. Prowell · Shuttleworth & Ingersoll · 115 Third Street, SE, Suite 500 · Cedar Rapids, IA 52401 319-365-9461

Greg J. Seyfer · ⑩ · Bradley & Riley · http://www.bradleyriley.com · 2007 First Avenue, SE · P.O. Box 2804 · Cedar Rapids, IA 52406-2804 · 319-363-0101

William R. Shuttleworth · ⑩ · Shuttleworth & Ingersoll · 115 Third Street, SE, Suite 500 · Cedar Rapids, IA 52401 · 319-365-9461

Council Bluffs

Steven H. Krohn · Smith Peterson · 35 Main Place, Suite 300 · P.O. Box 249 · Council Bluffs, IA 51502 · 712-328-1833

Davenport

David A. Dettmann · ⑩ · Lane & Waterman · 220 North Main Street, Suite 600 · Davenport, IA 52801 · 563-324-3246

Catherine E. E. Hult · Lane & Waterman · 220 North Main Street, Suite 600 · Davenport, IA 52801 · 563-324-3246

Des Moines

Robert D. Andeweg · Nyemaster, Goode, West, Hansell & O'Brien · 700 Walnut Street, Suite 1600 · Des Moines, IA 50309-3899 · 515-283-3100

Bradford L. Austin · Nyemaster, Goode, West, Hansell & O'Brien · 700 Walnut Street, Suite 1600 · Des Moines, IA 50309-3899 · 515-283-3100

William D. Bartine · ⑩ · Belin Lamson McCormick Zumbach Flynn · http://www.belinlaw.com · 666 Walnut Street, Suite 2000 · Des Moines, IA 50309-3989 · 515-243-7100

Streetar Cameron · Connolly, O'Malley, Lillis, Hansen & Olson · 317 Sixth Avenue, Suite 300 · Des Moines, IA 50309-4127 · 515-243-8157

Antonio Colacino · Nyemaster, Goode, West, Hansell & O'Brien · 700 Walnut Street, Suite 1600 · Des Moines, IA 50309-3899 · 515-283-3100

Robert J. Douglas · Davis, Brown, Koehn, Shors & Roberts · The Davis Brown Tower, Suite 1300 · 215 Tenth Street · Des Moines, IA 50309-3993 · 515-288-2500

David M. Erickson · ⑩ · Davis, Brown, Koehn, Shors & Roberts · The Davis Brown Tower, Suite 1300 · 215 Tenth Street · Des Moines, IA 50309-3993 · 515-288-2500

James M. Holcomb · ⑩ · Bradshaw, Fowler, Proctor & Fairgrave · 801 Grand Avenue, Suite 3700 · Des Moines, IA 50309-8004 · 515-243-4191

William J. Lillis · Connolly, O'Malley, Lillis, Hansen & Olson · 317 Sixth Avenue, Suite 300 · Des Moines, IA 50309-4127 · 515-243-8157

Anthony A. Longnecker · Nyemaster, Goode, West, Hansell & O'Brien · 700 Walnut Street, Suite 1600 · Des Moines, IA 50309-3899 · 515-283-3100

Richard W. Lozier, Jr. · Belin Lamson McCormick Zumbach Flynn · http://www.belinlaw.com · 666 Walnut Street, Suite 2000 · Des Moines, IA 50309-3989 · 515-243-7100

Daniel L. Manning · Connolly, O'Malley, Lillis, Hansen & Olson · 317 Sixth Avenue, Suite 300 · Des Moines, IA 50309-4127 · 515-243-8157

Eugene E. Olson · Connolly, O'Malley, Lillis, Hansen & Olson · 317 Sixth Avenue, Suite 300 · Des Moines, IA 50309-4127 · 515-243-8157

Christopher R. Pose · Connolly, O'Malley, Lillis, Hansen & Olson · 317 Sixth Avenue, Suite 300 · Des Moines, IA 50309-4127 · 515-243-8157

James V. Sarcone, Jr. · Belin Lamson McCormick Zumbach Flynn · http://www.belinlaw.com · 666 Walnut Street, Suite 2000 · Des Moines, IA 50309-3989 · 515-243-7100

Jeremy C. Sharpe · Belin Lamson McCormick Zumbach Flynn · http://www.belinlaw.com · 666 Walnut Street, Suite 2000 · Des Moines, IA 50309-3989 · 515-243-7100

Jon P. Sullivan · Dickinson, Mackaman, Tyler & Hagen · http://www.dickinsonlaw.com · 699 Walnut Street, Suite 1600 · Des Moines, IA 50309-3929 · 515-244-2600

Paul R. Tyler · Dickinson, Mackaman, Tyler & Hagen · http://www.dickinsonlaw.com · 699 Walnut Street, Suite 1600 · Des Moines, IA 50309-3929 · 515-244-2600

Ivan T. Webber · Ahlers & Cooney · 100 Court Avenue, Suite 600 · Des Moines, IA 50309-2231 · 515-243-7611

Jonathan C. Wilson · Davis, Brown, Koehn, Shors & Roberts · The Davis Brown Tower, Suite 1300 · 215 Tenth Street · Des Moines, IA 50309-3993 · 515-288-2500

James C. Wine · Nyemaster, Goode, West, Hansell & O'Brien · 700 Walnut Street, Suite 1600 · Des Moines, IA 50309-3899 · 515-283-3100

Iowa City

John W. Hayek · ⑩ · Hayek, Hayek, Brown, Moreland & Hayek · 120 East Washington Street · Iowa City, IA 52240-3924 · 319-337-9606

C. Joseph Holland · C. Joseph Holland · 123 North Linn Street, Suite 300 · Iowa City, IA 52245-2143 · 319-354-0331

Douglas D. Ruppert · Meardon, Sueppel & Downer · 122 South Linn Street · Iowa City, IA 52240 · 319-338-9222

Mason City

Scott D. Brown · Brown, Kinsey, Funkhouser & Lander · 214 North Adams Avenue · P.O. Box 679 · Mason City, IA 50402-0679 · 641-423-6223

Gerald M. Stambaugh · ⑩ · Heiny, McManigal, Duffy, Stambaugh & Anderson · 11 Fourth Street, NE · P.O. Box 1567 · Mason City, IA 50402-1567 · 641-423-5154

Muscatine

Robert L. Lande · Stanley, Lande & Hunter · 301 Iowa Avenue, Suite 400 · Muscatine, IA 52761 · 563-264-5000

Sioux City

John B. Anderson · ㉕ · Corbett, Anderson, Corbett & Vellinga · 423 Sixth Street, Suite 400 · P.O. Box 3527 · Sioux City, IA 51102-3527 · 712-277-1261

Dan A. Moore · ⑩ · Berenstein, Moore, Berenstein, Heffernan & Moeller · 501 Pierce Street, Suite 300 · P.O. Box 3207 · Sioux City, IA 51101 · 712-252-0020

SECURITIES LAW

Cedar Rapids

Brian D. Bergstrom · Shuttleworth & Ingersoll · 115 Third Street, SE, Suite 500 · Cedar Rapids, IA 52401 · 319-365-9461

Davenport

C. Dana Waterman III · ⑩ · Lane & Waterman · 220 North Main Street, Suite 600 · Davenport, IA 52801 · 563-324-3246

TAX LAW

Algona

A. David Bibler · ⑩ · Buchanan, Bibler, Buchanan & Gabor · 111 North Dodge Street · P.O. Box 617 · Algona, IA 50511 · 515-295-3565

Atlantic

David W. Chase · ⑩ · Cambridge, Feilmeyer, Landsness & Chase · 707 Poplar Street · P.O. Box 496 · Atlantic, IA 50022 · 712-243-1663

Cedar Falls

Steven D. Moore · ⑩ · Redfern, Mason, Larsen & Moore · 415 Clay Street · P.O. Box 627 · Cedar Falls, IA 50613 · 319-277-6830

Cedar Rapids

J. Scott Bogguss · ⑳ · Moyer & Bergman · http://www.moyerbergman.com · 2720 First Avenue, NE · P.O. Box 1943 · Cedar Rapids, IA 52402 · 319-366-7331

Patrick M. Courtney · ⑩ · Bradley & Riley · http://www.bradleyriley.com · 2007 First Avenue, SE · P.O. Box 2804 · Cedar Rapids, IA 52406-2804 · 319-363-0101

Dean R. Einck · ⑩ · Shuttleworth & Ingersoll · 115 Third Street, SE, Suite 500 · Cedar Rapids, IA 52401 319-365-9461

Gary J. Streit · ⑳ · Shuttleworth & Ingersoll · 115 Third Street, SE, Suite 500 · Cedar Rapids, IA 52401 · 319-365-9461

Denison

James D. Lohman · ⑩ · Reimer, Lohman & Reitz · 25 South Main Street · Denison, IA 51442 · 712-263-4627

Des Moines

Bruce W. Baker · Nyemaster, Goode, West, Hansell & O'Brien · 700 Walnut Street, Suite 1600 · Des Moines, IA 50309-3899 · 515-283-3100

Donald J. Brown · ㉕ · Davis, Brown, Koehn, Shors & Roberts · The Davis Brown Tower, Suite 1300 · 215 Tenth Street · Des Moines, IA 50309-3993 · 515-288-2500

William C. Brown · ⑩ · Brown, Winick, Graves, Gross, Baskerville & Schoenebaum · Ruan Center, Suite 2000 · 666 Grand Avenue · Des Moines, IA 50309-2510 · 515-242-2400

Bruce I. Campbell · ㉕ · Davis, Brown, Koehn, Shors & Roberts · The Davis Brown Tower, Suite 1300 · 215 Tenth Street · Des Moines, IA 50309-3993 · 515-288-2500

Paul E. Carey · Brown, Winick, Graves, Gross, Baskerville & Schoenebaum · Ruan Center, Suite 2000 · 666 Grand Avenue · Des Moines, IA 50309-2510 · 515-242-2400

Frank J. Carroll · ㉕ · Davis, Brown, Koehn, Shors & Roberts · The Davis Brown Tower, Suite 1300 · 215 Tenth Street · Des Moines, IA 50309-3993 · 515-288-2500

David M. Repp · Dickinson, Mackaman, Tyler & Hagen · http://www.dickinsonlaw.com · 699 Walnut Street, Suite 1600 · Des Moines, IA 50309-3929 · 515-244-2600

Steven J. Roy · Nyemaster, Goode, West, Hansell & O'Brien · 700 Walnut Street, Suite 1600 · Des Moines, IA 50309-3899 · 515-283-3100

John D. Shors · ⑩ · Davis, Brown, Koehn, Shors & Roberts · The Davis Brown Tower, Suite 1300 · 215 Tenth Street · Des Moines, IA 50309-3993 · 515-288-2500

Jon L. Staudt · ⑳ · Belin Lamson McCormick Zumbach Flynn · http://www.belinlaw.com · 666 Walnut Street, Suite 2000 · Des Moines, IA 50309-3989 · 515-243-7100

Margaret D. Van Houten · ⑩ · Davis, Brown, Koehn, Shors & Roberts · The Davis Brown Tower, Suite 1300 · 215 Tenth Street · Des Moines, IA 50309-3993 · 515-288-2500

Dubuque

James E. Goodman, Jr. · O'Connor & Thomas · Dubuque Building, Suite 200 · 700 Locust Street · P.O. Box 599 · Dubuque, IA 52004-0599 · 563-557-8400

John C. O'Connor · ⑩ · O'Connor & Thomas · Dubuque Building, Suite 200 · 700 Locust Street · P.O. Box 599 · Dubuque, IA 52004-0599 · 563-557-8400

Muscatine

James A. Nepple · ⑩ · Nepple Law · Hershey Professional Center, Suite 500 · 216 Sycamore Street · Muscatine, IA 52761-3809 · 563-264-6840

Sioux City

Marvin S. Berenstein · ⑳ · Berenstein, Moore, Berenstein, Heffernan & Moeller · 501 Pierce Street, Suite 300 · P.O. Box 3207 · Sioux City, IA 51101 · 712-252-0020

Victor

Orville W. Bloethe · ㉕ · Bloethe, Elwood & Buchanan · 702 Third Street · Victor, IA 52347 · 319-647-3121

Waterloo

C. Kevin McCrindle · Kevin McCrindle · 607 Sycamore Street, Suite 500 · P.O. Box 928 · Waterloo, IA 50703 · 319-234-0535

West Des Moines

John V. Donnelly · 25 · Sullivan & Ward · 6601 Westown Parkway, Suite 200 · West Des Moines, IA 50266-7733 · 515-244-3500

TRUSTS AND ESTATES

Atlantic

David W. Chase · 10 · Cambridge, Feilmeyer, Landsness & Chase · 707 Poplar Street · P.O. Box 496 · Atlantic, IA 50022 · 712-243-1663

Cedar Falls

John C. Larsen · 10 · Redfern, Mason, Larsen & Moore · 415 Clay Street · P.O. Box 627 · Cedar Falls, IA 50613 · 319-277-6830

Cedar Rapids

J. Scott Bogguss · 20 · Moyer & Bergman · http://www.moyerbergman.com · 2720 First Avenue, NE · P.O. Box 1943 · Cedar Rapids, IA 52402 · 319-366-7331

Patrick M. Courtney · 10 · Bradley & Riley · http://www.bradleyriley.com · 2007 First Avenue, SE · P.O. Box 2804 · Cedar Rapids, IA 52406-2804 · 319-363-0101

Dean R. Einck · 10 · Shuttleworth & Ingersoll · 115 Third Street, SE, Suite 500 · Cedar Rapids, IA 52401 319-365-9461

William S. Hochstetler · Shuttleworth & Ingersoll · 115 Third Street, SE, Suite 500 · Cedar Rapids, IA 52401 · 319-365-9461

Janice J. Kerkove · Bradley & Riley · http://www.bradleyriley.com · 2007 First Avenue, SE · P.O. Box 2804 · Cedar Rapids, IA 52406-2804 · 319-363-0101

Michael O. McDermott · 10 · Shuttleworth & Ingersoll · 115 Third Street, SE, Suite 500 · Cedar Rapids, IA 52401 · 319-365-9461

Darrel A. Morf · 20 · Simmons, Perrine, Albright & Ellwood · 115 Third Street, SE, Suite 1200 · Cedar Rapids, IA 52401-1266 · 319-366-7641

Paul P. Morf · Simmons, Perrine, Albright & Ellwood · 115 Third Street, SE, Suite 1200 · Cedar Rapids, IA 52401-1266 · 319-366-7641

Lorie Reins-Schweer · Simmons, Perrine, Albright & Ellwood · 115 Third Street, SE, Suite 1200 · Cedar Rapids, IA 52401-1266 · 319-366-7641

Gary J. Streit · 20 · Shuttleworth & Ingersoll · 115 Third Street, SE, Suite 500 · Cedar Rapids, IA 52401 · 319-365-9461

Davenport

David A. Dettmann · 10 · Lane & Waterman · 220 North Main Street, Suite 600 · Davenport, IA 52801 · 563-324-3246

Des Moines

Mark W. Beerman · Ahlers & Cooney · 100 Court Avenue, Suite 600 · Des Moines, IA 50309-2231 · 515-243-7611

Ronni F. Begleiter · ⑩ · Brown, Winick, Graves, Gross, Baskerville & Schoenebaum · Ruan Center, Suite 2000 · 666 Grand Avenue · Des Moines, IA 50309-2510 · 515-242-2400

William A. Boatwright · Davis, Brown, Koehn, Shors & Roberts · The Davis Brown Tower, Suite 1300 · 215 Tenth Street · Des Moines, IA 50309-3993 · 515-288-2500

Donald J. Brown · ㉕ · Davis, Brown, Koehn, Shors & Roberts · The Davis Brown Tower, Suite 1300 · 215 Tenth Street · Des Moines, IA 50309-3993 · 515-288-2500

Bruce I. Campbell · ㉕ · Davis, Brown, Koehn, Shors & Roberts · The Davis Brown Tower, Suite 1300 · 215 Tenth Street · Des Moines, IA 50309-3993 · 515-288-2500

Edward E. Johnson · ⑩ · Bradshaw, Fowler, Proctor & Fairgrave · 801 Grand Avenue, Suite 3700 · Des Moines, IA 50309-8004 · 515-243-4191

Carlton T. King · Nyemaster, Goode, West, Hansell & O'Brien · 700 Walnut Street, Suite 1600 · Des Moines, IA 50309-3899 · 515-283-3100

James B. Langeness · ⑩ · Duncan, Green, Brown & Langeness · 400 Locust Street, Suite 380 · Des Moines, IA 50309 · 515-288-6440

Christine B. Long · Duncan, Green, Brown & Langeness · 400 Locust Street, Suite 380 · Des Moines, IA 50309 · 515-288-6440

David M. Repp · Dickinson, Mackaman, Tyler & Hagen · http://www.dickinsonlaw.com · 699 Walnut Street, Suite 1600 · Des Moines, IA 50309-3929 · 515-244-2600

Steven J. Roy · Nyemaster, Goode, West, Hansell & O'Brien · 700 Walnut Street, Suite 1600 · Des Moines, IA 50309-3899 · 515-283-3100

Margaret D. Van Houten · ⑩ · Davis, Brown, Koehn, Shors & Roberts · The Davis Brown Tower, Suite 1300 · 215 Tenth Street · Des Moines, IA 50309-3993 · 515-288-2500

Robert A. VanOrsdel · ⑩ · Nyemaster, Goode, West, Hansell & O'Brien · 700 Walnut Street, Suite 1600 · Des Moines, IA 50309-3899 · 515-283-3100

Steven E. Zumbach · ⑩ · Belin Lamson McCormick Zumbach Flynn · http://www.belinlaw.com · 666 Walnut Street, Suite 2000 · Des Moines, IA 50309-3989 · 515-243-7100

Iowa City

Robert N. Downer · ⑩ · Meardon, Sueppel & Downer · 122 South Linn Street · Iowa City, IA 52240 · 319-338-9222

Mason City

Scott D. Brown · Brown, Kinsey, Funkhouser & Lander · 214 North Adams Avenue · P.O. Box 679 · Mason City, IA 50402-0679 · 641-423-6223

Socrates G. Pappajohn · ⑩ · Pappajohn, Shriver, Eide & Nicholas · 103 East State Street, Suite 800 · P.O. Box 1588 · Mason City, IA 50402-1588 · 641-423-4264

Gerald M. Stambaugh · 10 · Heiny, McManigal, Duffy, Stambaugh & Anderson · 11 Fourth Street, NE · P.O. Box 1567 · Mason City, IA 50402-1567 · 641-423-5154

Harold R. Winston · 20 · Winston & Byrne · 119 Second Street, NW · Mason City, IA 50401 · 641-423-1913

Sioux City

John B. Anderson · 25 · Corbett, Anderson, Corbett & Vellinga · 423 Sixth Street, Suite 400 · P.O. Box 3527 · Sioux City, IA 51102-3527 · 712-277-1261

Marvin S. Berenstein · 20 · Berenstein, Moore, Berenstein, Heffernan & Moeller · 501 Pierce Street, Suite 300 · P.O. Box 3207 · Sioux City, IA 51101 · 712-252-0020

Ray H. Edgington · Vriezelaar, Tigges, Edgington, Bottaro, Boden & Ross · 421 Nebraska Street · P.O. Box 1557 · Sioux City, IA 51102 · 712-252-3226

Victor

Orville W. Bloethe · 25 · Bloethe, Elwood & Buchanan · 702 Third Street · Victor, IA 52347 · 319-647-3121

Waterloo

Theresa E. Hoffman · Beecher, Field, Walker, Morris, Hoffman & Johnson · Court Square Building, Suite 300 · 620 Lafayette Street · P.O. Box 178 · Waterloo, IA 50704-0178 · 319-234-1766

C. Kevin McCrindle · Kevin McCrindle · 607 Sycamore Street, Suite 500 · P.O. Box 928 · Waterloo, IA 50703 · 319-234-0535

West Des Moines

J. Michael Deege · 10 · Wilson, Deege, Dollar & Despotovich · West Bank Building, Suite 300 · 1601 Twenty-Second Street · West Des Moines, IA 50266 · 515-327-1000

Thomas J. Houser · Davis, Brown, Koehn, Shors & Roberts · The Highland Building, Suite 300 · 4201 Westown Parkway · West Des Moines, IA 50266 · 515-288-2500

Donald B. Young · Young & Rogers · 4800 Mills Civic Parkway, Suite 205 · West Des Moines, IA 50265 · 515-440-2175

VENTURE CAPITAL LAW

Cedar Rapids

Brian D. Bergstrom · Shuttleworth & Ingersoll · 115 Third Street, SE, Suite 500 · Cedar Rapids, IA 52401 · 319-365-9461

WHITE-COLLAR CRIMINAL DEFENSE

Des Moines

Guy R. Cook · Grefe & Sidney · 2222 Grand Avenue · P.O. Box 10434 · Des Moines, IA 50306 · 515-245-4300

Thomas D. Hanson · ⑩ · Hanson, Bjork & Russell · 405 Sixth Avenue, Suite 1300 · Des Moines, IA 50309 · 515-244-0177

Alfredo G. Parrish · ⑩ · Parrish, Kruidenier, Moss, Dunn, Boles, Gribble, Cook, Parish & Gentry · 2910 Grand Avenue · Des Moines, IA 50312 · 515-284-5737

Dean A. Stowers · Rosenberg, Stowers & Morse · http://www.rosenbergstowersmorse.com · 505 Fifth Avenue, Suite 1010 · Des Moines, IA 50309 · 515-243-7600

Mark E. Weinhardt · Belin Lamson McCormick Zumbach Flynn · http://www.belinlaw.com · 666 Walnut Street, Suite 2000 · Des Moines, IA 50309-3989 · 515-243-7100

Iowa City

Leon F. Spies · ㉕ · Mellon & Spies · 312 East College Street, Suite 216 · Iowa City, IA 52240 · 319-337-4193

WORKERS' COMPENSATION LAW

Cedar Rapids

John M. Bickel · ⑩ · Shuttleworth & Ingersoll · 115 Third Street, SE, Suite 500 · Cedar Rapids, IA 52401 319-365-9461

Theresa C. Davis · Shuttleworth & Ingersoll · 115 Third Street, SE, Suite 500 · Cedar Rapids, IA 52401 · 319-365-9461

Richard C. Garberson · Shuttleworth & Ingersoll · 115 Third Street, SE, Suite 500 · Cedar Rapids, IA 52401 · 319-365-9461

Pete Leehey · Pete Leehey Law Firm · http://www.leeheylaw.com · 425 Second Street, SE, Suite 1250 · P.O. Box 547 · Cedar Rapids, IA 52406-0547 · 319-294-4424

Robert R. Rush · Rush & Nicholson · 100 First Street, SW · Cedar Rapids, IA 52404 · 319-363-5209

Thomas M. Wertz · Wertz Law Firm · 1500 Center Street, NE · P.O. Box 849 · Cedar Rapids, IA 52406 · 319-861-3001

Coralville

Paul J. McAndrew, Jr. · ⑩ · Paul McAndrew Law Firm · 2771 Oakdale Boulevard, Suite Six · Coralville, IA 52241 · 319-887-1690

Council Bluffs

Jacob J. Peters · Peters Law Firm · 233 Pearl Street · P.O. Box 1078 · Council Bluffs, IA 51502 · 712-328-3157

James E. Thorn · ⑩ · Stuart, Tinley, Peters, Thorn & Hughes · Northwestern Bell Building, Second Floor · 310 West Kanesville Boulevard · P.O. Box 398 · Council Bluffs, IA 51502-0398 · 712-322-4033

Davenport

Greg A. Egbers · Betty, Neuman & McMahon · 111 East Third Street, Suite 600 · Davenport, IA 52801 · 563-326-4491

Craig A. Levien · Betty, Neuman & McMahon · 111 East Third Street, Suite 600 · Davenport, IA 52801 · 563-326-4491

Des Moines

Tom L. Drew · Drew Law Firm · 554 Twenty-Eighth Street · P.O. Box 12129 · Des Moines, IA 50312-9403 · 515-323-5640

E. J. Giovannetti · ⑩ · Hopkins & Huebner · Terrace Center, Suite 111 · 2700 Grand Avenue · Des Moines, IA 50312-5213 · 515-244-0111

Dennis L. Hanssen · Hopkins & Huebner · Terrace Center, Suite 111 · 2700 Grand Avenue · Des Moines, IA 50312-5213 · 515-244-0111

Frank T. Harrison · Hopkins & Huebner · Terrace Center, Suite 111 · 2700 Grand Avenue · Des Moines, IA 50312-5213 · 515-244-0111

David L. Jenkins · Bradshaw, Fowler, Proctor & Fairgrave · 801 Grand Avenue, Suite 3700 · Des Moines, IA 50309-8004 · 515-243-4191

Jason D. Neifert · Max Schott & Associates · 6611 University Avenue, Suite 200 · Des Moines, IA 50311-1655 · 866-388-2068

Martin Ozga · Max Schott & Associates · 6611 University Avenue, Suite 200 · Des Moines, IA 50311-1655 · 866-388-2068

Gregory T. Racette · Hopkins & Huebner · Terrace Center, Suite 111 · 2700 Grand Avenue · Des Moines, IA 50312-5213 · 515-244-0111

Max Schott · Max Schott & Associates · 6611 University Avenue, Suite 200 · Des Moines, IA 50311-1655 866-388-2068

Fort Dodge

Janece M. Valentine · Valentine Law Office · 809 Central Avenue · 415 Boston Center · P.O. Box 1414 · Fort Dodge, IA 50501-1414 · 515-955-5544

Mason City

Robert S. Kinsey III · ⑩ · Brown, Kinsey, Funkhouser & Lander · 214 North Adams Avenue · P.O. Box 679 · Mason City, IA 50402-0679 · 641-423-6223

Mindi M. Vervaecke · Fitzsimmons & Vervaecke, Law Firm · Five North Federal Avenue, Suite 200 · P.O. Box 1661 · Mason City, IA 50402-1661 · 641-422-0066

Richard R. Winga · ⑩ · Heiny, McManigal, Duffy, Stambaugh & Anderson · 11 Fourth Street, NE · P.O. Box 1567 · Mason City, IA 50402-1567 · 641-423-5154

Waterloo

Robert C. Andres · Fulton, Martin & Andres · First National Building, Suite 600 · 607 Sycamore Street · Waterloo, IA 50703 · 319-234-7741

David W. Stamp · Ball, Kirk & Holm · 3324 Kimball Avenue · P.O. Box 2696 · Waterloo, IA 50704 · 319-234-2638

Mark S. Soldat · ⑩ · Mark S. Soldat · 3737 Woodland Avenue, Suite 130 · West Des Moines, IA 50266 · 515-222-3133

KANSAS

ALTERNATIVE DISPUTE RESOLUTION

Great Bend

Thomas J. Berscheidt · Thomas J. Berscheidt · 2107 Forest Avenue · P.O. Box 550 · Great Bend, KS 67530-0550 · 620-792-7777

Lake Quivira

M. Warren McCamish · a · McCamish Law · 480 Terrace Trail East · Lake Quivira, KS 66217 · 913-268-5771

Overland Park

J. Nick Badgerow · Spencer Fane Britt & Browne · http://www.spencerfane.com · 40 Corporate Woods, Suite 700 · 9401 Indian Creek Parkway · Overland Park, KS 66210-2005 · 913-345-8100

Topeka

Jerry R. Palmer · 2) · Palmer, Leatherman & White · 627 Southwest Topeka Boulevard, Suite A · Topeka, KS 66603 · 785-233-1836

Wichita

Dennis L. Gillen · Depew Gillen Rathbun & McInteer · 8301 East 21st Street, N, Suite 450 · Wichita, KS 67206-2936 · 316-262-4000

Bryson E. Mills · Bryson E. Mills · 1359 South Broadway Street · Wichita, KS 67211 · 316-263-8251

ANTITRUST LAW

Mission Hills

Thomas J. H. Brill · Thomas H. Brill · 6552 Sagamore Road · Mission Hills, KS 66208-1945 · 913-677-2004

APPELLATE LAW

Kansas City

Douglas M. Greenwald · McAnany, Van Cleave & Phillips · 707 Minnesota Avenue, Fourth Floor · P.O. Box 171300 · Kansas City, KS 66101 · 913-371-3838

Terry Karnaze · Terry Karnaze · 1707 North 77th Terrace · Kansas City, KS 66112 · 913-299-0626

Overland Park

James D. Oliver · a · Foulston Siefkin · http://www.foulston.com · Nine Corporate Woods, Suite 450 · 9200 Indian Creek Parkway · Overland Park, KS 66210 · 913-498-2100

Wichita

Stephen M. Kerwick · Foulston Siefkin · http://www.foulston.com · 1551 North Waterfront Parkway, Suite 100 · Wichita, KS 67206-4466 · 316-267-6371

Roger M. Theis · Hinkle Elkouri Law Firm · http://www.hinklaw.com · Epic Center, Suite 2000 · 301 North Main Street · Wichita, KS 67202 · 316-267-2000

Lyndon W. Vix · Fleeson, Gooing, Coulson & Kitch · http://www.fleeson.com · Epic Center, Suite 1900 · 301 North Main Street · Wichita, KS 67202 · 316-267-7361

BANKING LAW

Cimarron

Philip D. Ridenour · 2% · Ridenour and Ridenour · 109 South Main Street · P.O. Box 1028 · Cimarron, KS 67835 · 620-855-7051

Wichita

William R. Wood II · ⑩ · Foulston Siefkin · http://www.foulston.com · 1551 North Waterfront Parkway, Suite 100 · Wichita, KS 67206-4466 · 316-267-6371

BANKRUPTCY AND CREDITOR-DEBTOR RIGHTS LAW

Lenexa

Cynthia F. Grimes · Grimes & Rebein · 15301 West 87th Street, Suite 200 · Lenexa, KS 66219 · 913-888-4800

Overland Park

Michael H. Berman · ⑳ · Berman & Rabin · 10660 Barkley Street · Overland Park, KS 66212 · 913-649-1555

Carl R. Clark · Lentz & Clark · 9260 Glenwood Street · P.O. Box 12167 · Overland Park, KS 66282-2167 · 913-648-0600

Chris W. Henry · ⑳ · Payne & Jones · 11000 King Street · P.O. Box 25625 · Overland Park, KS 66225-5625 · 913-469-4100

Shawnee

Thomas M. Mullinix III · ㉕ · Evans & Mullinix · 7225 Renner Road, Suite 200 · Shawnee, KS 66217-3043 · 913-962-8700

Topeka

Robert L. Baer · ⑳ · Cosgrove, Webb & Oman · 534 South Kansas Avenue, Suite 1100 · Topeka, KS 66603 · 785-235-9511

Patricia Hamilton · Henson, Hutton, Mudrick & Gragson · Commerce Bank Building, Second Floor · 100 Southeast Ninth Street · P.O. 3555 · Topeka, KS 66601-3555 · 785-232-2200

Justice B. King · ⑩ · Fisher, Patterson, Sayler & Smith · 3550 Southwest Fifth Street · P.O. Box 949 · Topeka, KS 66601 · 785-232-7761

Wesley F. Smith · Stumbo, Hanson & Hendricks · 2887 Southwest MacVicar Avenue · Topeka, KS 66611 · 785-267-3410

Wichita

Terry C. Cupps · ⑩ · Foulston Siefkin · http://www.foulston.com · 1551 North Waterfront Parkway, Suite 100 · Wichita, KS 67206-4466 · 316-267-6371

Jack C. Marvin · Stinson Morrison Hecker · http://www.stinson.com · 1625 North Waterfront Parkway, Suite 300 · Wichita, KS 67206-6602 · 316-265-8800

J. Michael Morris · Klenda, Mitchell, Austerman & Zuercher · Epic Center, Suite 1600 · 301 North Main Wichita, KS 67202-4888 · 316-267-0331

Edward J. Nazar · ⑩ · Redmond & Nazar · 245 North Waco, Suite 402 · Wichita, KS 67202 · 316-262-8361

Linda S. Parks · Hite, Fanning & Honeyman · 100 North Broadway, Suite 950 · Wichita, KS 67202-2209 316-265-7741

William B. Sorensen, Jr. · a · Morris, Laing, Evans, Brock & Kennedy · Old Town Square, Suite 200 · 300 North Meade · Wichita, KS 67202-2745 · 316-262-2671

BET-THE-COMPANY LITIGATION

Overland Park

Mark D. Hinderks · Stinson Morrison Hecker · http://www.stinson.com · 12 Corporate Woods, Suite 550 · 10975 Benson · Overland Park, KS 66210 · 913-451-8600

Greg L. Musil · Shughart Thomson & Kilroy · http://www.stklaw.com · 32 Corporate Woods, Suite 1100 · 9225 Indian Creek Parkway · Overland Park, KS 66210 · 913-451-3355

James D. Oliver · a · Foulston Siefkin · http://www.foulston.com · Nine Corporate Woods, Suite 450 · 9200 Indian Creek Parkway · Overland Park, KS 66210 · 913-498-2100

Roger D. Stanton · a · Law Offices of Roger D. Stanton · Building 51, 500 Corporate Woods · 9393 West 110th Street · Overland Park, KS 66210 · 913-451-6958

Topeka

Arthur E. Palmer · 2) · Goodell, Stratton, Edmonds & Palmer · 515 South Kansas Avenue · Topeka, KS 66603-3999 · 785-233-0593

Wichita

James M. Armstrong · a · Foulston Siefkin · http://www.foulston.com · 1551 North Waterfront Parkway, Suite 100 · Wichita, KS 67206-4466 · 316-267-6371

Jack Focht · 2% · Foulston Siefkin · http://www.foulston.com · 1551 North Waterfront Parkway, Suite 100 · Wichita, KS 67206-4466 · 316-267-6371

Jay F. Fowler · a · Foulston Siefkin · http://www.foulston.com · 1551 North Waterfront Parkway, Suite 100 · Wichita, KS 67206-4466 · 316-267-6371

Richard C. Hite · 2% · Hite, Fanning & Honeyman · 100 North Broadway, Suite 950 · Wichita, KS 67202-2209 · 316-265-7741

Mikel L. Stout · 2) · Foulston Siefkin · http://www.foulston.com · 1551 North Waterfront Parkway, Suite 100 · Wichita, KS 67206-4466 · 316-267-6371

Darrell L. Warta · a · Foulston Siefkin · http://www.foulston.com · 1551 North Waterfront Parkway, Suite 100 · Wichita, KS 67206-4466 · 316-267-6371

Lee H. Woodard · a · Woodard, Hernandez, Roth & Day · Emprise Bank Center, Suite 300 · 257 North Broadway · Wichita, KS 67202 · 316-263-4958

BIOTECHNOLOGY LAW

Topeka

Steve A. Schwarm · Polsinelli Shalton Flanigan Suelthaus · http://www.polsinelli.com · One AmVestors Place, Suite 101 · 555 Kansas Avenue · Topeka, KS 66603 · 785-233-1446

COMMERCIAL LITIGATION

Dodge City

David J. Rebein · a · Rebein Bangerter · http://www.rebeinbangerter.com · 810 West Frontview · P.O. Box 1147 · Dodge City, KS 67801 · 620-227-8126

Leawood

Diane A. Nygaard · a · The Nygaard Law Firm · http://www.nygaardlaw.com · 4501 College Boulevard, Suite 260 · Leawood, KS 66211 · 913-469-5544

Olathe

George A. Lowe · 2) · Lowe, Farmer, Bacon & Roe · 105 South Kansas Avenue · P.O. Box 580 · Olathe, KS 66061-0580 · 913-782-0422

Overland Park

Thomas A. Hamill · Thomas A. Hamill · 6900 College Boulevard, Suite 700 · Overland Park, KS 66211 · 913-491-5500

Mark D. Hinderks · Stinson Morrison Hecker · http://www.stinson.com · 12 Corporate Woods, Suite 550 · 10975 Benson · Overland Park, KS 66210 · 913-451-8600

Greg L. Musil · Shughart Thomson & Kilroy · http://www.stklaw.com · 32 Corporate Woods, Suite 1100 · 9225 Indian Creek Parkway · Overland Park, KS 66210 · 913-451-3355

Michael G. Norris · Norris & Keplinger · Financial Plaza II, Suite 630 · 6800 College Boulevard · Overland Park, KS 66211 · 913-663-2000

James D. Oliver · a · Foulston Siefkin · http://www.foulston.com · Nine Corporate Woods, Suite 450 · 9200 Indian Creek Parkway · Overland Park, KS 66210 · 913-498-2100

Anthony F. Rupp · Shughart Thomson & Kilroy · http://www.stklaw.com · 32 Corporate Woods, Suite 1100 · 9225 Indian Creek Parkway · Overland Park, KS 66210 · 913-451-3355

Roger D. Stanton · a · Law Offices of Roger D. Stanton · Building 51, 500 Corporate Woods · 9393 West 110th Street · Overland Park, KS 66210 · 913-451-6958

Topeka

Edward L. Bailey · Cosgrove, Webb & Oman · 534 South Kansas Avenue, Suite 1100 · Topeka, KS 66603 · 785-235-9511

Randall J. Forbes · Frieden & Forbes · 555 South Kansas Avenue, Suite 303 · P.O. Box 639 · Topeka, KS 66601-0639 · 785-232-7266

John C. Frieden · a · Frieden & Forbes · 555 South Kansas Avenue, Suite 303 · P.O. Box 639 · Topeka, KS 66601-0639 · 785-232-7266

Richard F. Hayse · Morris, Laing, Evans, Brock & Kennedy · U.S. Bank Building, Thirteenth Floor · 800 Southwest Jackson · Topeka, KS 66612-1216 · 785-232-2662

Arthur E. Palmer · 2) · Goodell, Stratton, Edmonds & Palmer · 515 South Kansas Avenue · Topeka, KS 66603-3999 · 785-233-0593

Wichita

James M. Armstrong · a · Foulston Siefkin · http://www.foulston.com · 1551 North Waterfront Parkway, Suite 100 · Wichita, KS 67206-4466 · 316-267-6371

Gary L. Ayers · Foulston Siefkin · http://www.foulston.com · 1551 North Waterfront Parkway, Suite 100 · Wichita, KS 67206-4466 · 316-267-6371

David E. Bengtson · Stinson Morrison Hecker · http://www.stinson.com · 1625 North Waterfront Parkway, Suite 300 · Wichita, KS 67206-6602 · 316-265-8800

Mark A. Biberstein · Foulston Siefkin · http://www.foulston.com · 1551 North Waterfront Parkway, Suite 100 · Wichita, KS 67206-4466 · 316-267-6371

Ronald L. Campbell · Fleeson, Gooing, Coulson & Kitch · http://www.fleeson.com · Epic Center, Suite 1900 · 301 North Main Street · Wichita, KS 67202 · 316-267-7361

Richard D. Ewy · a · Foulston Siefkin · http://www.foulston.com · 1551 North Waterfront Parkway, Suite 100 · Wichita, KS 67206-4466 · 316-267-6371

Jack Focht · 2% · Foulston Siefkin · http://www.foulston.com · 1551 North Waterfront Parkway, Suite 100 · Wichita, KS 67206-4466 · 316-267-6371

Jay F. Fowler · a · Foulston Siefkin · http://www.foulston.com · 1551 North Waterfront Parkway, Suite 100 · Wichita, KS 67206-4466 · 316-267-6371

John H. Gibson · a · Gilliland & Hayes · 301 North Main Street, Suite 1300 · Wichita, KS 67202-4813 · 316-264-7321

Kurt A. Harper · Sherwood, Harper, Dakan, Unruh & Pratt · 833 North Waco · P.O. Box 830 · Wichita, KS 67201 · 316-267-1281

Richard C. Hite · 2% · Hite, Fanning & Honeyman · 100 North Broadway, Suite 950 · Wichita, KS 67202-2209 · 316-265-7741

Jeffery A. Jordan · Foulston Siefkin · http://www.foulston.com · 1551 North Waterfront Parkway, Suite 100 · Wichita, KS 67206-4466 · 316-267-6371

Stephen M. Kerwick · Foulston Siefkin · http://www.foulston.com · 1551 North Waterfront Parkway, Suite 100 · Wichita, KS 67206-4466 · 316-267-6371

Thomas J. Lasater · Fleeson, Gooing, Coulson & Kitch · http://www.fleeson.com · Epic Center, Suite 1900 · 301 North Main Street · Wichita, KS 67202 · 316-267-7361

Robert Martin · 2% · Martin, Pringle, Oliver, Wallace & Bauer · 100 North Broadway, Suite 500 · Wichita, KS 67202 · 316-265-9311

Charles E. Millsap · a · Fleeson, Gooing, Coulson & Kitch · http://www.fleeson.com · Epic Center, Suite 1900 · 301 North Main Street · Wichita, KS 67202 · 316-267-7361

Linda S. Parks · Hite, Fanning & Honeyman · 100 North Broadway, Suite 950 · Wichita, KS 67202-2209 316-265-7741

Ken M. Peterson · a · Morris, Laing, Evans, Brock & Kennedy · Old Town Square, Suite 200 · 300 North Meade · Wichita, KS 67202-2745 · 316-262-2671

F. James Robinson, Jr. · Hite, Fanning & Honeyman · 100 North Broadway, Suite 950 · Wichita, KS 67202-2209 · 316-265-7741

Roger Sherwood · Sherwood, Harper, Dakan, Unruh & Pratt · 833 North Waco · P.O. Box 830 · Wichita, KS 67201 · 316-267-1281

Mikel L. Stout · 2) · Foulston Siefkin · http://www.foulston.com · 1551 North Waterfront Parkway, Suite 100 · Wichita, KS 67206-4466 · 316-267-6371

James A. Walker · Triplett, Woolf & Garretson · http://www.twgfirm.com · 2959 North Rock Road, Suite 300 · Wichita, KS 67226 · 316-630-8100

Darrell L. Warta · a · Foulston Siefkin · http://www.foulston.com · 1551 North Waterfront Parkway, Suite 100 · Wichita, KS 67206-4466 · 316-267-6371

Lee H. Woodard · a · Woodard, Hernandez, Roth & Day · Emprise Bank Center, Suite 300 · 257 North Broadway · Wichita, KS 67202 · 316-263-4958

John P. Woolf · Triplett, Woolf & Garretson · http://www.twgfirm.com · 2959 North Rock Road, Suite 300 · Wichita, KS 67226 · 316-630-8100

COMMUNICATIONS LAW

Topeka

Robert A. Fox · a · Foulston Siefkin · http://www.foulston.com · Bank of America Tower, Suite 1400 · 534 South Kansas Avenue · Topeka, KS 66603-3436 · 785-233-3600

CONSTRUCTION LAW

Overland Park

Michael G. Norris · Norris & Keplinger · Financial Plaza II, Suite 630 · 6800 College Boulevard · Overland Park, KS 66211 · 913-663-2000

Wichita

Ronald L. Campbell · Fleeson, Gooing, Coulson & Kitch · http://www.fleeson.com · Epic Center, Suite 1900 · 301 North Main Street · Wichita, KS 67202 · 316-267-7361

J. Phillip Davidson · Hinkle Elkouri Law Firm · http://www.hinklaw.com · Epic Center, Suite 2000 · 301 North Main Street · Wichita, KS 67202 · 316-267-2000

Wyatt A. Hoch · Foulston Siefkin · http://www.foulston.com · 1551 North Waterfront Parkway, Suite 100 · Wichita, KS 67206-4466 · 316-267-6371

Jeffrey D. Leonard · Triplett, Woolf & Garretson · http://www.twgfirm.com · 2959 North Rock Road, Suite 300 · Wichita, KS 67226 · 316-630-8100

Charles E. Millsap · a · Fleeson, Gooing, Coulson & Kitch · http://www.fleeson.com · Epic Center, Suite 1900 · 301 North Main Street · Wichita, KS 67202 · 316-267-7361

Roger Sherwood · Sherwood, Harper, Dakan, Unruh & Pratt · 833 North Waco · P.O. Box 830 · Wichita, KS 67201 · 316-267-1281

CORPORATE GOVERNANCE AND COMPLIANCE LAW

Wichita

William R. Wood II · a · Foulston Siefkin · http://www.foulston.com · 1551 North Waterfront Parkway, Suite 100 · Wichita, KS 67206-4466 · 316-267-6371

CORPORATE LAW

Cimarron

Philip D. Ridenour · 2% · Ridenour and Ridenour · 109 South Main Street · P.O. Box 1028 · Cimarron, KS 67835 · 620-855-7051

Lawrence

Webster L. Golden · 2% · Stevens & Brand · 900 Massachusetts Street, Suite 500 · P.O. Box 189 · Lawrence, KS 66044-0189 · 785-843-0811

Manhattan

Charles S. Arthur III · 2% · Arthur Green Law Firm · 801 Poyntz Avenue · Manhattan, KS 66502 · 785-537-1345

Overland Park

Alson R. Martin · 2% · Lathrop & Gage · Building 82, Suite 1000 · 10851 Mastin Boulevard · Overland Park, KS 66210-1669 · 913-451-5100

James D. Oliver · a · Foulston Siefkin · http://www.foulston.com · Nine Corporate Woods, Suite 450 · 9200 Indian Creek Parkway · Overland Park, KS 66210 · 913-498-2100

R. Douglas Reagan · Foulston Siefkin · http://www.foulston.com · Nine Corporate Woods, Suite 450 · 9200 Indian Creek Parkway · Overland Park, KS 66210 · 913-498-2100

William P. Trenkle, Jr. · 2% · Foulston Siefkin · http://www.foulston.com · Nine Corporate Woods, Suite 450 · 9200 Indian Creek Parkway · Overland Park, KS 66210 · 913-498-2100

Topeka

H. Philip Elwood · 2% · Goodell, Stratton, Edmonds & Palmer · 515 South Kansas Avenue · Topeka, KS 66603-3999 · 785-233-0593

Richard F. Hayse · Morris, Laing, Evans, Brock & Kennedy · U.S. Bank Building, Thirteenth Floor · 800 Southwest Jackson · Topeka, KS 66612-1216 · 785-232-2662

Wichita

Stanley G. Andeel · 2% · Foulston Siefkin · http://www.foulston.com · 1551 North Waterfront Parkway, Suite 100 · Wichita, KS 67206-4466 · 316-267-6371

J. Eric Engstrom · 2% · Fleeson, Gooing, Coulson & Kitch · http://www.fleeson.com · Epic Center, Suite 1900 · 301 North Main Street · Wichita, KS 67202 · 316-267-7361

Thomas P. Garretson · Triplett, Woolf & Garretson · http://www.twgfirm.com · 2959 North Rock Road, Suite 300 · Wichita, KS 67226 · 316-630-8100

Thomas J. Lasater · Fleeson, Gooing, Coulson & Kitch · http://www.fleeson.com · Epic Center, Suite 1900 · 301 North Main Street · Wichita, KS 67202 · 316-267-7361

Jack C. Marvin · Stinson Morrison Hecker · http://www.stinson.com · 1625 North Waterfront Parkway, Suite 300 · Wichita, KS 67206-6602 · 316-265-8800

Harvey R. Sorensen · a · Foulston Siefkin · http://www.foulston.com · 1551 North Waterfront Parkway, Suite 100 · Wichita, KS 67206-4466 · 316-267-6371

Willard B. Thompson · 2% · Fleeson, Gooing, Coulson & Kitch · http://www.fleeson.com · Epic Center, Suite 1900 · 301 North Main Street · Wichita, KS 67202 · 316-267-7361

Thomas C. Triplett · 2% · Triplett, Woolf & Garretson · http://www.twgfirm.com · 2959 North Rock Road, Suite 300 · Wichita, KS 67226 · 316-630-8100

DUI/DWI DEFENSE

Wichita

Roger L. Falk · Roger L. Falk & Associates · 301 West Central Avenue · Wichita, KS 67202-1077 · 316-265-5115

Leslie F. Hulnick · Hulnick, Stang & Rapp · 310 West Central at Waco, Suite 111 · Wichita, KS 67202 · 316-263-7596

ELDER LAW

Lawrence

Molly M. Wood · Stevens & Brand · 900 Massachusetts Street, Suite 500 · P.O. Box 189 · Lawrence, KS 66044-0189 · 785-843-0811

Wichita

Robert M. Collins · Collins & Collins · 100 North Main Street, Suite 608 · Wichita, KS 67202 · 316-267-0235

Timothy P. O'Sullivan · a · Foulston Siefkin · http://www.foulston.com · 1551 North Waterfront Parkway, Suite 100 · Wichita, KS 67206-4466 · 316-267-6371

Ronald B. Rose · Martin, Pringle, Oliver, Wallace & Bauer · 100 North Broadway, Suite 500 · Wichita, KS 67202 · 316-265-9311

EMINENT DOMAIN AND CONDEMNATION LAW

Overland Park

Timothy P. Orrick · Foth & Orrick · 11900 College Boulevard, Suite 210 · Overland Park, KS 66210 · 913-888-1777

Eldon J. Shields · Gates, Biles, Shields & Ryan · 10990 Quivira Road, Suite 200 · Overland Park, KS 66210 · 913-661-0222

Topeka

John R. Hamilton · Hamilton, Laughlin, Barker, Johnson & Watson · 3649 Southwest Burlingame Road · Topeka, KS 66611 · 785-267-2410

David E. Watson · Hamilton, Laughlin, Barker, Johnson & Watson · 3649 Southwest Burlingame Road · Topeka, KS 66611 · 785-267-2410

Wichita

Robert W. Kaplan · Kaplan, McMillan & Harris · 430 North Market Street · Wichita, KS 67202 · 316-262-5175

David M. Rapp · Hinkle Elkouri Law Firm · http://www.hinklaw.com · Epic Center, Suite 2000 · 301 North Main Street · Wichita, KS 67202 · 316-267-2000

Roger Sherwood · Sherwood, Harper, Dakan, Unruh & Pratt · 833 North Waco · P.O. Box 830 · Wichita, KS 67201 · 316-267-1281

Bradley A. Stout · Adams Jones Law Firm · 1635 North Waterfront Parkway, Suite 200 · Wichita, KS 67206-6623 · 316-265-8591

EMPLOYEE BENEFITS LAW

Overland Park

Gregory L. Ash · Spencer Fane Britt & Browne · http://www.spencerfane.com · 40 Corporate Woods, Suite 700 · 9401 Indian Creek Parkway · Overland Park, KS 66210-2005 · 913-345-8100

Alson R. Martin · 2% · Lathrop & Gage · Building 82, Suite 1000 · 10851 Mastin Boulevard · Overland Park, KS 66210-1669 · 913-451-5100

Kenneth A. Mason · Spencer Fane Britt & Browne · http://www.spencerfane.com · 40 Corporate Woods, Suite 700 · 9401 Indian Creek Parkway · Overland Park, KS 66210-2005 · 913-345-8100

John L. Utz · a · Utz Miller & Kuhn · 7285 West 132nd Street, Suite 320 · Overland Park, KS 66213-1164 · 913-685-0970

Salina

Peter L. Peterson · 2% · Clark, Mize & Linville · 129 South Eighth Street · P.O. Box 380 · Salina, KS 67402-0380 · 785-823-6325

Topeka

James P. Rankin · 2) · Foulston Siefkin · http://www.foulston.com · Bank of America Tower, Suite 1400 · 534 South Kansas Avenue · Topeka, KS 66603-3436 · 785-233-3600

Wichita

Douglas Hanisch · a · Foulston Siefkin · http://www.foulston.com · 1551 North Waterfront Parkway, Suite 100 · Wichita, KS 67206-4466 · 316-267-6371

R. Chris Robe · a · Bever Dye · http://www.beverdye.com · Epic Center, Suite 600 · 301 North Main Street · Wichita, KS 67202-4806 · 316-263-8294

ENERGY LAW

Ottawa

James G. Flaherty · Anderson, Byrd, Richeson, Flaherty & Henrichs · 216 South Hickory · P.O. Box 17 · Ottawa, KS 66067 · 785-242-1234

Overland Park

Frank A. Caro, Jr. · Polsinelli Shalton Flanigan Suelthaus · http://www.polsinelli.com · 6201 College Boulevard, Suite 500 · Overland Park, KS 66211-2423 · 913-451-8788

James P. Zakoura · a · Smithyman & Zakoura · Commerce Plaza, Building II, Suite 750 · 7400 West 110th Street · Overland Park, KS 66210-2362 · 913-661-9800

Topeka

Robert A. Fox · a · Foulston Siefkin · http://www.foulston.com · Bank of America Tower, Suite 1400 · 534 South Kansas Avenue · Topeka, KS 66603-3436 · 785-233-3600

Wichita

Ralph R. Brock · 2) · Morris, Laing, Evans, Brock & Kennedy · Old Town Square, Suite 200 · 300 North Meade · Wichita, KS 67202-2745 · 316-262-2671

Jim H. Goering · Foulston Siefkin · http://www.foulston.com · 1551 North Waterfront Parkway, Suite 100 Wichita, KS 67206-4466 · 316-267-6371

Charles J. Woodin · a · Foulston Siefkin · http://www.foulston.com · 1551 North Waterfront Parkway, Suite 100 · Wichita, KS 67206-4466 · 316-267-6371

ENVIRONMENTAL LAW

Wichita

Charles P. Efflandt · a · Foulston Siefkin · http://www.foulston.com · 1551 North Waterfront Parkway, Suite 100 · Wichita, KS 67206-4466 · 316-267-6371

Jeff Kennedy · Martin, Pringle, Oliver, Wallace & Bauer · 100 North Broadway, Suite 500 · Wichita, KS 67202 · 316-265-9311

Randall K. Rathbun · a · Depew Gillen Rathbun & McInteer · 8301 East 21st Street, N, Suite 450 · Wichita, KS 67206-2936 · 316-262-4000

Charles C. Steincamp · Depew Gillen Rathbun & McInteer · 8301 East 21st Street, N, Suite 450 · Wichita, KS 67206-2936 · 316-262-4000

David M. Traster · Foulston Siefkin · http://www.foulston.com · 1551 North Waterfront Parkway, Suite 100 · Wichita, KS 67206-4466 · 316-267-6371

EQUIPMENT FINANCE LAW

Wichita

Larry G. Rapp · Foulston Siefkin · http://www.foulston.com · 1551 North Waterfront Parkway, Suite 100 · Wichita, KS 67206-4466 · 316-267-6371

FAMILY LAW

Lawrence

Sherri E. Loveland · Stevens & Brand · 900 Massachusetts Street, Suite 500 · P.O. Box 189 · Lawrence, KS 66044-0189 · 785-843-0811

Leawood

Regina Keelan Bass · a · Bass Family Law Firm · State Line Executive Office Park, Suite 100 · 8014 State Line Road · Leawood, KS 66208 · 913-385-0555

Olathe

Dana L. Parks · Norton, Hubbard, Ruzicka, Kreamer & Kincaid · 130 North Cherry Street · P.O. Box 550 Olathe, KS 66061 · 913-782-2350

Overland Park

Ray L. Borth · 2) · Short, Borth & Thilges · 55 Corporate Woods, Suite 500 · 9300 West 110th Street · Overland Park, KS 66210 · 913-491-4400

Anne E. Burke · a · Manson & Karbank · http://www.mansonkarbanklaw.com · 84 Corporate Woods, Suite 430 · 10801 Mastin Street · Overland Park, KS 66210 · 913-498-8080

T. Bradley Manson · 2) · Manson & Karbank · http://www.mansonkarbanklaw.com · 84 Corporate Woods, Suite 430 · 10801 Mastin Street · Overland Park, KS 66210 · 913-498-8080

J. Bradley Short · 2) · Short, Borth & Thilges · 55 Corporate Woods, Suite 500 · 9300 West 110th Street · Overland Park, KS 66210 · 913-491-4400

Amanda A. Thilges · Short, Borth & Thilges · 55 Corporate Woods, Suite 500 · 9300 West 110th Street · Overland Park, KS 66210 · 913-491-4400

Topeka

James R. McEntire · Sloan Eisenbarth Glassman McEntire & Jarboe · Bank of America Tower, Suite 1000 · 534 South Kansas Avenue · Topeka, KS 66603-3456 · 785-357-6311

Wichita

Stephen J. Blaylock · 2) · Blaylock & Cleous · Emprise Bank Center, Suite 300 · 257 North Broadway · Wichita, KS 67202 · 316-263-4958

Cindy L. Cleous · Justice Suites · 444 North Market Street · Wichita, KS 67202 · 316-262-4550

Sheila J. Floodman · a · Floodman, Wagle & West · 323 North Market Street · Wichita, KS 67202 · 316-269-1950

Ann Soderberg Gottberg · Lambdin, Soderberg & Lambdin · 830 North Main Street · P.O. Box 797 · Wichita, KS 67201-0454 · 316-265-3285

Donald E. Lambdin · 2% · Lambdin, Soderberg & Lambdin · 830 North Main Street · P.O. Box 797 · Wichita, KS 67201-0454 · 316-265-3285

FIRST AMENDMENT LAW

Overland Park

Samuel L. Colville · a · Holman Hansen & Colville · 10740 Nall Avenue, Suite 200 · Overland Park, KS 66211 · 913-648-7272

Topeka

Michael W. Merriam · a · Michael W. Merriam · 700 Southwest Jackson Street, Roof Garden Suite · Topeka, KS 66603 · 785-233-3700

Wichita

William P. Tretbar · Fleeson, Gooing, Coulson & Kitch · http://www.fleeson.com · Epic Center, Suite 1900 · 301 North Main Street · Wichita, KS 67202 · 316-267-7361

Lyndon W. Vix · Fleeson, Gooing, Coulson & Kitch · http://www.fleeson.com · Epic Center, Suite 1900 · 301 North Main Street · Wichita, KS 67202 · 316-267-7361

GOVERNMENT RELATIONS LAW

Topeka

James P. Rankin · 2) · Foulston Siefkin · http://www.foulston.com · Bank of America Tower, Suite 1400 · 534 South Kansas Avenue · Topeka, KS 66603-3436 · 785-233-3600

William W. Sneed · Polsinelli Shalton Flanigan Suelthaus · http://www.polsinelli.com · One AmVestors Place, Suite 101 · 555 Kansas Avenue · Topeka, KS 66603 · 785-233-1446

HEALTH CARE LAW

Lawrence

Peter K. Curran · Stevens & Brand · 900 Massachusetts Street, Suite 500 · P.O. Box 189 · Lawrence, KS 66044-0189 · 785-843-0811

Overland Park

Jeffrey O. Ellis · a · Lathrop & Gage · Building 82, Suite 1000 · 10851 Mastin Boulevard · Overland Park, KS 66210-1669 · 913-451-5100

Andrew R. Ramirez · Lathrop & Gage · Building 82, Suite 1000 · 10851 Mastin Boulevard · Overland Park, KS 66210-1669 · 913-451-5100

Salina

John W. Mize · a · Clark, Mize & Linville · 129 South Eighth Street · P.O. Box 380 · Salina, KS 67402-0380 · 785-823-6325

Topeka

H. Philip Elwood · 2% · Goodell, Stratton, Edmonds & Palmer · 515 South Kansas Avenue · Topeka, KS 66603-3999 · 785-233-0593

Charles R. Hay · a · Foulston Siefkin · http://www.foulston.com · Bank of America Tower, Suite 1400 · 534 South Kansas Avenue · Topeka, KS 66603-3436 · 785-233-3600

Wayne T. Stratton · 2) · Goodell, Stratton, Edmonds & Palmer · 515 South Kansas Avenue · Topeka, KS 66603-3999 · 785-233-0593

Thomas L. Theis · Foulston Siefkin · http://www.foulston.com · Bank of America Tower, Suite 1400 · 534 South Kansas Avenue · Topeka, KS 66603-3436 · 785-233-3600

Wichita

Stanley G. Andeel · 2% · Foulston Siefkin · http://www.foulston.com · 1551 North Waterfront Parkway, Suite 100 · Wichita, KS 67206-4466 · 316-267-6371

Gary L. Ayers · Foulston Siefkin · http://www.foulston.com · 1551 North Waterfront Parkway, Suite 100 · Wichita, KS 67206-4466 · 316-267-6371

John H. Gibson · a · Gilliland & Hayes · 301 North Main Street, Suite 1300 · Wichita, KS 67202-4813 · 316-264-7321

Amy Liebau · Hinkle Elkouri Law Firm · http://www.hinklaw.com · Epic Center, Suite 2000 · 301 North Main Street · Wichita, KS 67202 · 316-267-2000

Dixie F. Madden · Adams Jones Law Firm · 1635 North Waterfront Parkway, Suite 200 · Wichita, KS 67206-6623 · 316-265-8591

Scott C. Palecki · Foulston Siefkin · http://www.foulston.com · 1551 North Waterfront Parkway, Suite 100 · Wichita, KS 67206-4466 · 316-267-6371

INFORMATION TECHNOLOGY LAW

Overland Park

James J. Kernell · Chase Law Firm · 4400 College Boulevard, Suite 130 · Overland Park, KS 66211 · 913-339-9666

INSURANCE LAW

Wichita

William L. Townsley III · Fleeson, Gooing, Coulson & Kitch · http://www.fleeson.com · Epic Center, Suite 1900 · 301 North Main Street · Wichita, KS 67202 · 316-267-7361

Lyndon W. Vix · Fleeson, Gooing, Coulson & Kitch · http://www.fleeson.com · Epic Center, Suite 1900 · 301 North Main Street · Wichita, KS 67202 · 316-267-7361

INTELLECTUAL PROPERTY LAW

Overland Park

D. A. N. Chase · (10) · Chase Law Firm · 4400 College Boulevard, Suite 130 · Overland Park, KS 66211 · 913-339-9666

John M. Collins · (10) · Hovey Williams · 84 Corporate Woods, Suite 1000 · 10801 Mastin Boulevard · Overland Park, KS 66210 · 816-474-9050

Gerald M. Kraai · Lathrop & Gage · Building 82, Suite 1000 · 10851 Mastin Boulevard · Overland Park, KS 66210-1669 · 913-451-5100

Lawrence A. Swain · Shughart Thomson & Kilroy · http://www.stklaw.com · 32 Corporate Woods, Suite 1100 · 9225 Indian Creek Parkway · Overland Park, KS 66210 · 913-451-3355

Stephen D. Timmons · Hovey Williams · 84 Corporate Woods, Suite 1000 · 10801 Mastin Boulevard · Overland Park, KS 66210 · 816-474-9050

Michael Yakimo, Jr. · (10) · Chase Law Firm · 4400 College Boulevard, Suite 130 · Overland Park, KS 66211 · 913-339-9666

Topeka

Bruce J. Clark · Henson, Hutton, Mudrick & Gragson · Commerce Bank Building, Second Floor · 100 Southeast Ninth Street · P.O. 3555 · Topeka, KS 66601-3555 · 785-232-2200

Wichita

Jim H. Goering · Foulston Siefkin · http://www.foulston.com · 1551 North Waterfront Parkway, Suite 100 Wichita, KS 67206-4466 · 316-267-6371

William P. Matthews · Foulston Siefkin · http://www.foulston.com · 1551 North Waterfront Parkway, Suite 100 · Wichita, KS 67206-4466 · 316-267-6371

Kent A. Meyerhoff · Fleeson, Gooing, Coulson & Kitch · http://www.fleeson.com · Epic Center, Suite 1900 · 301 North Main Street · Wichita, KS 67202 · 316-267-7361

Jerald W. Rogers · Triplett, Woolf & Garretson · http://www.twgfirm.com · 2959 North Rock Road, Suite 300 · Wichita, KS 67226 · 316-630-8100

LABOR AND EMPLOYMENT LAW

Kansas City

Joseph W. Moreland · (20) · Blake & Uhlig · 475 New Brotherhood Building · 753 State Avenue · Kansas City, KS 66101 · 913-321-8884

James R. Waers · (10) · Blake & Uhlig · 475 New Brotherhood Building · 753 State Avenue · Kansas City, KS 66101 · 913-321-8884

Overland Park

Richard L. Connors · Stinson Morrison Hecker · http://www.stinson.com · 12 Corporate Woods, Suite 550 · 10975 Benson · Overland Park, KS 66210 · 913-451-8600

Wyatt M. Wright · Foulston Siefkin · http://www.foulston.com · Nine Corporate Woods, Suite 450 · 9200 Indian Creek Parkway · Overland Park, KS 66210 · 913-498-2100

Topeka

Deanne W. Hay · Parker & Hay · 400 South Kansas Avenue, Suite 200 · Topeka, KS 66603 · 785-228-5736

David P. Mudrick · Henson, Hutton, Mudrick & Gragson · Commerce Bank Building, Second Floor · 100 Southeast Ninth Street · P.O. 3555 · Topeka, KS 66601-3555 · 785-232-2200

Arthur E. Palmer · ⑳ · Goodell, Stratton, Edmonds & Palmer · 515 South Kansas Avenue · Topeka, KS 66603-3999 · 785-233-0593

J. Steven Pigg · ⑩ · Fisher, Patterson, Sayler & Smith · 3550 Southwest Fifth Street · P.O. Box 949 · Topeka, KS 66601 · 785-232-7761

Patricia E. Riley · Weathers, Riley & Sheppeard · 4848 Southwest 21st Street, Suite 202 · P.O. Box 67209 Topeka, KS 66667-0209 · 785-273-2020

Wichita

Boyd A. Byers · Foulston Siefkin · http://www.foulston.com · 1551 North Waterfront Parkway, Suite 100 · Wichita, KS 67206-4466 · 316-267-6371

W. Stanley Churchill · ㉕ · Martin & Churchill · 8415 East 21st North, Suite 210 · Wichita, KS 67206 · 316-263-3200

Donald E. Hill · Martin & Churchill · 8415 East 21st North, Suite 210 · Wichita, KS 67206 · 316-263-3200

Ross A. Hollander · Joseph & Hollander · 500 North Market Street · Wichita, KS 67214-3514 · 316-262-9393

Terry L. Mann · Martin, Pringle, Oliver, Wallace & Bauer · 100 North Broadway, Suite 500 · Wichita, KS 67202 · 316-265-9311

Eric B. Metz · Triplett, Woolf & Garretson · http://www.twgfirm.com · 2959 North Rock Road, Suite 300 · Wichita, KS 67226 · 316-630-8100

Robert D. Overman · ⑩ · Morris, Laing, Evans, Brock & Kennedy · Old Town Square, Suite 200 · 300 North Meade · Wichita, KS 67202-2745 · 316-262-2671

Jay M. Rector · Foulston Siefkin · http://www.foulston.com · 1551 North Waterfront Parkway, Suite 100 · Wichita, KS 67206-4466 · 316-267-6371

Alan L. Rupe · Kutak Rock · Capitol Federal Building, Suite 370 · 8301 East 21st Street North · Wichita, KS 67206-2935 · 316-609-7900

David G. Seely · Fleeson, Gooing, Coulson & Kitch · http://www.fleeson.com · Epic Center, Suite 1900 · 301 North Main Street · Wichita, KS 67202 · 316-267-7361

Douglas L. Stanley · Foulston Siefkin · http://www.foulston.com · 1551 North Waterfront Parkway, Suite 100 · Wichita, KS 67206-4466 · 316-267-6371

Todd N. Tedesco · Foulston Siefkin · http://www.foulston.com · 1551 North Waterfront Parkway, Suite 100 · Wichita, KS 67206-4466 · 316-267-6371

Trisha A. Thelen · Foulston Siefkin · http://www.foulston.com · 1551 North Waterfront Parkway, Suite 100 · Wichita, KS 67206-4466 · 316-267-6371

Diane S. Worth · Morris, Laing, Evans, Brock & Kennedy · Old Town Square, Suite 200 · 300 North Meade · Wichita, KS 67202-2745 · 316-262-2671

LAND USE & ZONING LAW

Overland Park

Lewis A. Heaven, Jr. · a · Lathrop & Gage · Building 82, Suite 1000 · 10851 Mastin Boulevard · Overland Park, KS 66210-1669 · 913-451-5100

Greg L. Musil · Shughart Thomson & Kilroy · http://www.stklaw.com · 32 Corporate Woods, Suite 1100 · 9225 Indian Creek Parkway · Overland Park, KS 66210 · 913-451-3355

Timothy J. Sear · Polsinelli Shalton Flanigan Suelthaus · http://www.polsinelli.com · 6201 College Boulevard, Suite 500 · Overland Park, KS 66211-2423 · 913-451-8788

LEGAL MALPRACTICE LAW

Overland Park

Roger W. Warren · Sanders Conkright & Warren · http://www.sanconwar.com · 40 Corporate Woods, Suite 1250 · 9401 Indian Creek Parkway · Overland Park, KS 66210 · 913-234-6103

Roeland Park

Daniel F. Church · McAnany, Van Cleave & Phillips · 5125 Roe Boulevard, Suite 200 · Roeland Park, KS 66205 · 913-371-3838

Wichita

James M. Armstrong · a · Foulston Siefkin · http://www.foulston.com · 1551 North Waterfront Parkway, Suite 100 · Wichita, KS 67206-4466 · 316-267-6371

Jack Focht · 2% · Foulston Siefkin · http://www.foulston.com · 1551 North Waterfront Parkway, Suite 100 · Wichita, KS 67206-4466 · 316-267-6371

Steven D. Gough · Withers, Gough, Pike, Pfaff & Peterson · http://www.withersgough.com · O.W. Garvey Building, Suite 1010 · 200 West Douglas · Wichita, KS 67202 · 316-267-1562

John Terry Moore · a · Moore Martin · 622 East Douglas · Wichita, KS 67202 · 316-267-6000

MASS TORT LITIGATION

Wichita

Mark Hutton · a · Hutton & Hutton · 8100 East 22nd Street North, Building 1200 · P.O. Box 638 · Wichita, KS 67201-0638 · 316-688-1166

Fairway

David A. Hoffman · Vasos Law Offices · 4400 Shawnee Mission Parkway, Suite 100 · Fairway, KS 66205-2518 · 913-362-4400

Donald W. Vasos · 2% · Vasos Law Offices · 4400 Shawnee Mission Parkway, Suite 100 · Fairway, KS 66205-2518 · 913-362-4400

Leawood

James Bartimus · a · Bartimus, Frickleton, Robertson & Gorny · 11150 Overbrook Road, Suite 200 · Leawood, KS 66211 · 913-266-2300

Kirk J. Goza · Goza & Honnold · 11150 Overbrook Road, Suite 250 · Leawood, KS 66211 · 816-512-2171

Overland Park

Reid F. Holbrook · Holbrook & Osborn · Commerce Plaza II, Suite 600 · 7400 West 110 Street · Overland Park, KS 66210-2362 · 913-342-2500

Mark A. Lynch · Holbrook & Osborn · Commerce Plaza II, Suite 600 · 7400 West 110 Street · Overland Park, KS 66210-2362 · 913-342-2500

Anthony F. Rupp · Shughart Thomson & Kilroy · http://www.stklaw.com · 32 Corporate Woods, Suite 1100 · 9225 Indian Creek Parkway · Overland Park, KS 66210 · 913-451-3355

Topeka

Jerry R. Palmer · 2) · Palmer, Leatherman & White · 627 Southwest Topeka Boulevard, Suite A · Topeka, KS 66603 · 785-233-1836

Gene E. Schroer · 2% · Gene E. Schroer · 115 Southeast Seventh Street · Topeka, KS 66603 · 785-357-7300

Bryan Smith · Cavanaugh & Lemon · 2942A Southwest Wanamaker Drive, Suite 100 · Topeka, KS 66614-4135 · 785-440-4000

Kyle J. Steadman · Foulston Siefkin · http://www.foulston.com · Bank of America Tower, Suite 1400 · 534 South Kansas Avenue · Topeka, KS 66603-3436 · 785-233-3600

Wayne T. Stratton · 2) · Goodell, Stratton, Edmonds & Palmer · 515 South Kansas Avenue · Topeka, KS 66603-3999 · 785-233-0593

Thomas L. Theis · Foulston Siefkin · http://www.foulston.com · Bank of America Tower, Suite 1400 · 534 South Kansas Avenue · Topeka, KS 66603-3436 · 785-233-3600

Wichita

Gary M. Austerman · Klenda, Mitchell, Austerman & Zuercher · Epic Center, Suite 1600 · 301 North Main · Wichita, KS 67202-4888 · 316-267-0331

Arden J. Bradshaw · 2) · Arden J. Bradshaw Attorney at Law · 245 North Waco, Suite 405 · Wichita, KS 67202 · 316-687-2400

Steven C. Day · Woodard, Hernandez, Roth & Day · Emprise Bank Center, Suite 300 · 257 North Broadway · Wichita, KS 67202 · 316-263-4958

Don D. Gribble · Hite, Fanning & Honeyman · 100 North Broadway, Suite 950 · Wichita, KS 67202-2209 316-265-7741

James Z. Hernandez · Woodard, Hernandez, Roth & Day · Emprise Bank Center, Suite 300 · 257 North Broadway · Wichita, KS 67202 · 316-263-4958

Mark Hutton · a · Hutton & Hutton · 8100 East 22nd Street North, Building 1200 · P.O. Box 638 · Wichita, KS 67201-0638 · 316-688-1166

Amy S. Lemley · a · Foulston Siefkin · http://www.foulston.com · 1551 North Waterfront Parkway, Suite 100 · Wichita, KS 67206-4466 · 316-267-6371

Brad Prochaska · Prochaska, Giroux & Howell · 7701 East Kellogg, Suite 415 · Wichita, KS 67207-1709 · 316-683-9080

Randy J. Troutt · Hite, Fanning & Honeyman · 100 North Broadway, Suite 950 · Wichita, KS 67202-2209 · 316-265-7741

MERGERS & ACQUISITIONS LAW

Wichita

David S. Elkouri · Hinkle Elkouri Law Firm · http://www.hinklaw.com · Epic Center, Suite 2000 · 301 North Main Street · Wichita, KS 67202 · 316-267-2000

J. Eric Engstrom · 2% · Fleeson, Gooing, Coulson & Kitch · http://www.fleeson.com · Epic Center, Suite 1900 · 301 North Main Street · Wichita, KS 67202 · 316-267-7361

Ronald H. Harnden · Triplett, Woolf & Garretson · http://www.twgfirm.com · 2959 North Rock Road, Suite 300 · Wichita, KS 67226 · 316-630-8100

Jack C. Marvin · Stinson Morrison Hecker · http://www.stinson.com · 1625 North Waterfront Parkway, Suite 300 · Wichita, KS 67206-6602 · 316-265-8800

Harvey R. Sorensen · a · Foulston Siefkin · http://www.foulston.com · 1551 North Waterfront Parkway, Suite 100 · Wichita, KS 67206-4466 · 316-267-6371

Connie D. Tatum · Hinkle Elkouri Law Firm · http://www.hinklaw.com · Epic Center, Suite 2000 · 301 North Main Street · Wichita, KS 67202 · 316-267-2000

William R. Wood II · a · Foulston Siefkin · http://www.foulston.com · 1551 North Waterfront Parkway, Suite 100 · Wichita, KS 67206-4466 · 316-267-6371

MINING LAW

Wichita

Jim H. Goering · Foulston Siefkin · http://www.foulston.com · 1551 North Waterfront Parkway, Suite 100 Wichita, KS 67206-4466 · 316-267-6371

Steven D. Gough · Withers, Gough, Pike, Pfaff & Peterson · http://www.withersgough.com · O.W. Garvey Building, Suite 1010 · 200 West Douglas · Wichita, KS 67202 · 316-267-1562

Jeff Kennedy · Martin, Pringle, Oliver, Wallace & Bauer · 100 North Broadway, Suite 500 · Wichita, KS 67202 · 316-265-9311

Charles J. Woodin · a · Foulston Siefkin · http://www.foulston.com · 1551 North Waterfront Parkway, Suite 100 · Wichita, KS 67206-4466 · 316-267-6371

MUNICIPAL LAW

Olathe

Thomas A. Glinstra · Thomas A. Glinstra · 100 East Santa Fe, Third Floor · P.O. Box 768 · Olathe, KS 66051 · 913-971-8726

Overland Park

Anthony F. Rupp · Shughart Thomson & Kilroy · http://www.stklaw.com · 32 Corporate Woods, Suite 1100 · 9225 Indian Creek Parkway · Overland Park, KS 66210 · 913-451-3355

Michael K. Seck · Fisher, Patterson, Sayler & Smith · 51 Corporate Woods, Suite 300 · 9393 West 110th Street · Overland Park, KS 66210-1406 · 913-339-6757

Neil R. Shortlidge · Stinson Morrison Hecker · http://www.stinson.com · 12 Corporate Woods, Suite 550 · 10975 Benson · Overland Park, KS 66210 · 913-451-8600

Topeka

J. Steven Pigg · a · Fisher, Patterson, Sayler & Smith · 3550 Southwest Fifth Street · P.O. Box 949 · Topeka, KS 66601 · 785-232-7761

Wichita

Alan L. Rupe · Kutak Rock · Capitol Federal Building, Suite 370 · 8301 East 21st Street North · Wichita, KS 67206-2935 · 316-609-7900

NATURAL RESOURCES LAW

Garden City

Michael K. Ramsey · Hope, Mills, Bolin, Collins & Ramsey · 607 North Seventh Street · Garden City, KS 67846 · 620-276-3203

Wichita

Ralph R. Brock · 2) · Morris, Laing, Evans, Brock & Kennedy · Old Town Square, Suite 200 · 300 North Meade · Wichita, KS 67202-2745 · 316-262-2671

Jim H. Goering · Foulston Siefkin · http://www.foulston.com · 1551 North Waterfront Parkway, Suite 100 Wichita, KS 67206-4466 · 316-267-6371

Thomas D. Kitch · Fleeson, Gooing, Coulson & Kitch · http://www.fleeson.com · Epic Center, Suite 1900 301 North Main Street · Wichita, KS 67202 · 316-267-7361

Timothy E. McKee · Triplett, Woolf & Garretson · http://www.twgfirm.com · 2959 North Rock Road, Suite 300 · Wichita, KS 67226 · 316-630-8100

Gregory J. Stucky · Fleeson, Gooing, Coulson & Kitch · http://www.fleeson.com · Epic Center, Suite 1900 · 301 North Main Street · Wichita, KS 67202 · 316-267-7361

Charles J. Woodin · a · Foulston Siefkin · http://www.foulston.com · 1551 North Waterfront Parkway, Suite 100 · Wichita, KS 67206-4466 · 316-267-6371

NON-PROFIT/CHARITIES LAW

Overland Park

William K. Waugh III · a · Lathrop & Gage · Building 82, Suite 1000 · 10851 Mastin Boulevard · Overland Park, KS 66210-1669 · 913-451-5100

Salina

Peter L. Peterson · 2% · Clark, Mize & Linville · 129 South Eighth Street · P.O. Box 380 · Salina, KS 67402-0380 · 785-823-6325

Topeka

Donald J. Horttor · 2% · Cosgrove, Webb & Oman · 534 South Kansas Avenue, Suite 1100 · Topeka, KS 66603 · 785-235-9511

Wichita

Jack D. Flesher · a · Bever Dye · http://www.beverdye.com · Epic Center, Suite 600 · 301 North Main Street · Wichita, KS 67202-4806 · 316-263-8294

Eric J. Larson · a · Bever Dye · http://www.beverdye.com · Epic Center, Suite 600 · 301 North Main Street · Wichita, KS 67202-4806 · 316-263-8294

NON-WHITE-COLLAR CRIMINAL DEFENSE

Holton

J. Richard Lake · Lake Law Firm · 110 West Fifth Street · Holton, KS 66436 · 785-364-4161

Kansas City

John M. Duma · Duma Law Firm · 831 Armstrong Avenue · Kansas City, KS 66101-2604 · 913-342-7070

Olathe

Carl E. Cornwell · Cornwell Erickson Travis Breer & Scherff · 201 East Loula, Suite 101 · Olathe, KS 66061 · 913-254-7600

Thomas J. Erker · Erker Norton & Hare · 130 North Cherry, Suite 203 · Olathe, KS 66061 · 913-829-2500

Overland Park

Thomas J. Bath, Jr. · Bath & Edmonds · Historic Voigts Building · 7944 Santa Fe Drive · Overland Park, KS 66204 · 913-652-9800

Topeka

John J. Ambrosio · a · John J. Ambrosio · 5897 Southwest 29th Street · Topeka, KS 66614-2486 · 785-233-0524

Mark L. Bennett, Jr. · 2) · Bennett & Hendrix · 5605 Southwest Barrington Court South, Suite 201 · Topeka, KS 66614 · 785-271-0800

Peter Luis Irigonegaray · a · Peter Luis Irigonegaray · 1535 Southwest 29th Street · Topeka, KS 66611 · 785-267-6115

M. Kristine Savage · Joseph & Hollander · 1508 Southwest Topeka Boulevard · Topeka, KS 66612-1887 785-234-3272

Wichita

Leslie F. Hulnick · Hulnick, Stang & Rapp · 310 West Central at Waco, Suite 111 · Wichita, KS 67202 · 316-263-7596

Stephen M. Joseph · 2) · Joseph & Hollander · 500 North Market Street · Wichita, KS 67214-3514 · 316-262-9393

Daniel E. Monnat · 2) · Monnat & Spurrier · http://www.monnat.com · Olive West Garvey Building, Suite 830 · 200 West Douglas · Wichita, KS 67202 · 316-264-2800

Richard A. Ney · a · Ney, Adams & Sylvester · Orpheum Center, Suite 300 · 200 North Broadway · Wichita, KS 67202 · 316-264-0100

OIL & GAS LAW

Wichita

Ralph R. Brock · 2) · Morris, Laing, Evans, Brock & Kennedy · Old Town Square, Suite 200 · 300 North Meade · Wichita, KS 67202-2745 · 316-262-2671

Jim H. Goering · Foulston Siefkin · http://www.foulston.com · 1551 North Waterfront Parkway, Suite 100 Wichita, KS 67206-4466 · 316-267-6371

Thomas D. Kitch · Fleeson, Gooing, Coulson & Kitch · http://www.fleeson.com · Epic Center, Suite 1900 301 North Main Street · Wichita, KS 67202 · 316-267-7361

David G. Seely · Fleeson, Gooing, Coulson & Kitch · http://www.fleeson.com · Epic Center, Suite 1900 · 301 North Main Street · Wichita, KS 67202 · 316-267-7361

Gregory J. Stucky · Fleeson, Gooing, Coulson & Kitch · http://www.fleeson.com · Epic Center, Suite 1900 · 301 North Main Street · Wichita, KS 67202 · 316-267-7361

PERSONAL INJURY LITIGATION

Dodge City

David J. Rebein · a · Rebein Bangerter · http://www.rebeinbangerter.com · 810 West Frontview · P.O. Box 1147 · Dodge City, KS 67801 · 620-227-8126

Fairway

Donald W. Vasos · 2% · Vasos Law Offices · 4400 Shawnee Mission Parkway, Suite 100 · Fairway, KS 66205-2518 · 913-362-4400

Fort Scott

Leigh C. Hudson · a · Hudson & Mullies · 710 West Eighth Street, Suite 203 · P.O. Box 866 · Fort Scott, KS 66701 · 620-223-2900

Lake Quivira

M. Warren McCamish · a · McCamish Law · 480 Terrace Trail East · Lake Quivira, KS 66217 · 913-268-5771

Leavenworth

Michael P. Crow · Crow, Clothier & Associates · 302 Shawnee Street · P.O. Box 707 · Leavenworth, KS 66048-0707 · 913-682-0166

Leawood

James Bartimus · a · Bartimus, Frickleton, Robertson & Gorny · 11150 Overbrook Road, Suite 200 · Leawood, KS 66211 · 913-266-2300

Bryson R. Cloon · Cloon Law Firm · One Hallbrook Place, Suite 350 · 11150 Overbrook Road · Leawood, KS 66211 · 913-661-9600

James P. Frickleton · Bartimus, Frickleton, Robertson & Gorny · 11150 Overbrook Road, Suite 200 · Leawood, KS 66211 · 913-266-2300

Steve Gorny · Bartimus, Frickleton, Robertson & Gorny · 11150 Overbrook Road, Suite 200 · Leawood, KS 66211 · 913-266-2300

Kirk J. Goza · Goza & Honnold · 11150 Overbrook Road, Suite 250 · Leawood, KS 66211 · 816-512-2171

Brad Honnold · Goza & Honnold · 11150 Overbrook Road, Suite 250 · Leawood, KS 66211 · 816-512-2171

Liberal

Kerry E. McQueen · a · Sharp, McQueen, McKinley, McQueen & Dodge · 419 North Kansas Avenue · P.O. Box 2619 · Liberal, KS 67905-2619 · 620-624-2548

Gene H. Sharp · 2) · Sharp, McQueen, McKinley, McQueen & Dodge · 419 North Kansas Avenue · P.O. Box 2619 · Liberal, KS 67905-2619 · 620-624-2548

Overland Park

Bruce Keplinger · a · Norris & Keplinger · Financial Plaza II, Suite 630 · 6800 College Boulevard · Overland Park, KS 66211 · 913-663-2000

Anthony F. Rupp · Shughart Thomson & Kilroy · http://www.stklaw.com · 32 Corporate Woods, Suite 1100 · 9225 Indian Creek Parkway · Overland Park, KS 66210 · 913-451-3355

Steven D. Ruse · Shughart Thomson & Kilroy · http://www.stklaw.com · 32 Corporate Woods, Suite 1100 9225 Indian Creek Parkway · Overland Park, KS 66210 · 913-451-3355

Edwin Dudley Smith · a · Fisher, Patterson, Sayler & Smith · 51 Corporate Woods, Suite 300 · 9393 West 110th Street · Overland Park, KS 66210-1406 · 913-339-6757

Pittsburg

Fred Spigarelli · a · The Spigarelli Law Firm · 100 South Broadway, Suite 200 · P.O. Box 1449 · Pittsburg, KS 66762 · 620-231-1290

Roeland Park

Daniel F. Church · McAnany, Van Cleave & Phillips · 5125 Roe Boulevard, Suite 200 · Roeland Park, KS 66205 · 913-371-3838

Salina

Debra E. James · a · Hampton & Royce · United Building, Ninth and Tenth Floors · 119 West Iron Street · P.O. Box 1247 · Salina, KS 67402-1247 · 785-827-7251

Shawnee Mission

Michael L. Sexton · a · Sexton, Shelor, Latimer & Pryor · 6700 Antioch Street, Suite 120 · Shawnee Mission, KS 66204 · 913-789-7477

Topeka

N. Larry Bork · Goodell, Stratton, Edmonds & Palmer · 515 South Kansas Avenue · Topeka, KS 66603-3999 · 785-233-0593

Peter Luis Irigonegaray · a · Peter Luis Irigonegaray · 1535 Southwest 29th Street · Topeka, KS 66611 · 785-267-6115

James P. Nordstrom · Fisher, Patterson, Sayler & Smith · 3550 Southwest Fifth Street · P.O. Box 949 · Topeka, KS 66601 · 785-232-7761

Jerry R. Palmer · 2) · Palmer, Leatherman & White · 627 Southwest Topeka Boulevard, Suite A · Topeka, KS 66603 · 785-233-1836

Donald Patterson · 2% · Fisher, Patterson, Sayler & Smith · 3550 Southwest Fifth Street · P.O. Box 949 · Topeka, KS 66601 · 785-232-7761

Ronald R. Pope · Ralston, Pope & Diehl · 2913 Southwest Maupin Lane · Topeka, KS 66614 · 785-273-8002

Gene E. Schroer · 2% · Gene E. Schroer · 115 Southeast Seventh Street · Topeka, KS 66603 · 785-357-7300

Bryan Smith · Cavanaugh & Lemon · 2942A Southwest Wanamaker Drive, Suite 100 · Topeka, KS 66614-4135 · 785-440-4000

Wayne T. Stratton · 2) · Goodell, Stratton, Edmonds & Palmer · 515 South Kansas Avenue · Topeka, KS 66603-3999 · 785-233-0593

Thomas L. Theis · Foulston Siefkin · http://www.foulston.com · Bank of America Tower, Suite 1400 · 534 South Kansas Avenue · Topeka, KS 66603-3436 · 785-233-3600

Wesley A. Weathers · 2) · Weathers, Riley & Sheppeard · 4848 Southwest 21st Street, Suite 202 · P.O. Box 67209 · Topeka, KS 66667-0209 · 785-273-2020

Gary D. White, Jr. · Palmer, Leatherman & White · 627 Southwest Topeka Boulevard, Suite A · Topeka, KS 66603 · 785-233-1836

Arden J. Bradshaw · 2) · Arden J. Bradshaw Attorney at Law · 245 North Waco, Suite 405 · Wichita, KS 67202 · 316-687-2400

Jeffery L. Carmichael · Morris, Laing, Evans, Brock & Kennedy · Old Town Square, Suite 200 · 300 North Meade · Wichita, KS 67202-2745 · 316-262-2671

Steven C. Day · Woodard, Hernandez, Roth & Day · Emprise Bank Center, Suite 300 · 257 North Broadway · Wichita, KS 67202 · 316-263-4958

Jack Focht · 2% · Foulston Siefkin · http://www.foulston.com · 1551 North Waterfront Parkway, Suite 100 · Wichita, KS 67206-4466 · 316-267-6371

James Z. Hernandez · Woodard, Hernandez, Roth & Day · Emprise Bank Center, Suite 300 · 257 North Broadway · Wichita, KS 67202 · 316-263-4958

Richard C. Hite · 2% · Hite, Fanning & Honeyman · 100 North Broadway, Suite 950 · Wichita, KS 67202-2209 · 316-265-7741

Richard Honeyman · Hite, Fanning & Honeyman · 100 North Broadway, Suite 950 · Wichita, KS 67202-2209 · 316-265-7741

Edward J. Hund · a · Edward J. Hund · 622 East Douglas · Wichita, KS 67202 · 316-685-1747

Andrew Hutton · a · Hutton & Hutton · 8100 East 22nd Street North, Building 1200 · P.O. Box 638 · Wichita, KS 67201-0638 · 316-688-1166

Mark Hutton · a · Hutton & Hutton · 8100 East 22nd Street North, Building 1200 · P.O. Box 638 · Wichita, KS 67201-0638 · 316-688-1166

John W. Johnson · a · Morris, Laing, Evans, Brock & Kennedy · Old Town Square, Suite 200 · 300 North Meade · Wichita, KS 67202-2745 · 316-262-2671

Amy S. Lemley · a · Foulston Siefkin · http://www.foulston.com · 1551 North Waterfront Parkway, Suite 100 · Wichita, KS 67206-4466 · 316-267-6371

Ken M. Peterson · a · Morris, Laing, Evans, Brock & Kennedy · Old Town Square, Suite 200 · 300 North Meade · Wichita, KS 67202-2745 · 316-262-2671

Bradley Post · a · Bradley Post · 322 North Main Street · Wichita, KS 67202-2078 · 316-267-6391

David E. Rogers · Foulston Siefkin · http://www.foulston.com · 1551 North Waterfront Parkway, Suite 100 · Wichita, KS 67206-4466 · 316-267-6371

Craig Shultz · Craig Shultz · 205 East Central Avenue · Wichita, KS 67202 · 316-269-2284

Mikel L. Stout · 2) · Foulston Siefkin · http://www.foulston.com · 1551 North Waterfront Parkway, Suite 100 · Wichita, KS 67206-4466 · 316-267-6371

Darrell L. Warta · a · Foulston Siefkin · http://www.foulston.com · 1551 North Waterfront Parkway, Suite 100 · Wichita, KS 67206-4466 · 316-267-6371

Craig W. West · Foulston Siefkin · http://www.foulston.com · 1551 North Waterfront Parkway, Suite 100 · Wichita, KS 67206-4466 · 316-267-6371

Ronald P. Williams · Stinson Morrison Hecker · http://www.stinson.com · 1625 North Waterfront Parkway, Suite 300 · Wichita, KS 67206-6602 · 316-265-8800

PRODUCT LIABILITY LITIGATION

Fairway

Donald W. Vasos · 2% · Vasos Law Offices · 4400 Shawnee Mission Parkway, Suite 100 · Fairway, KS 66205-2518 · 913-362-4400

Leawood

James P. Frickleton · Bartimus, Frickleton, Robertson & Gorny · 11150 Overbrook Road, Suite 200 · Leawood, KS 66211 · 913-266-2300

Steve Gorny · Bartimus, Frickleton, Robertson & Gorny · 11150 Overbrook Road, Suite 200 · Leawood, KS 66211 · 913-266-2300

Kirk J. Goza · Goza & Honnold · 11150 Overbrook Road, Suite 250 · Leawood, KS 66211 · 816-512-2171

Roeland Park

Daniel F. Church · McAnany, Van Cleave & Phillips · 5125 Roe Boulevard, Suite 200 · Roeland Park, KS 66205 · 913-371-3838

Topeka

Wesley A. Weathers · 2) · Weathers, Riley & Sheppeard · 4848 Southwest 21st Street, Suite 202 · P.O. Box 67209 · Topeka, KS 66667-0209 · 785-273-2020

Wichita

Mark A. Biberstein · Foulston Siefkin · http://www.foulston.com · 1551 North Waterfront Parkway, Suite 100 · Wichita, KS 67206-4466 · 316-267-6371

Arden J. Bradshaw · 2) · Arden J. Bradshaw Attorney at Law · 245 North Waco, Suite 405 · Wichita, KS 67202 · 316-687-2400

Mark Hutton · a · Hutton & Hutton · 8100 East 22nd Street North, Building 1200 · P.O. Box 638 · Wichita, KS 67201-0638 · 316-688-1166

David E. Rogers · Foulston Siefkin · http://www.foulston.com · 1551 North Waterfront Parkway, Suite 100 · Wichita, KS 67206-4466 · 316-267-6371

Darrell L. Warta · a · Foulston Siefkin · http://www.foulston.com · 1551 North Waterfront Parkway, Suite 100 · Wichita, KS 67206-4466 · 316-267-6371

Ronald P. Williams · Stinson Morrison Hecker · http://www.stinson.com · 1625 North Waterfront Parkway, Suite 300 · Wichita, KS 67206-6602 · 316-265-8800

PROFESSIONAL MALPRACTICE LAW

Topeka

Jerry R. Palmer · 2) · Palmer, Leatherman & White · 627 Southwest Topeka Boulevard, Suite A · Topeka, KS 66603 · 785-233-1836

Wayne T. Stratton · 2) · Goodell, Stratton, Edmonds & Palmer · 515 South Kansas Avenue · Topeka, KS 66603-3999 · 785-233-0593

RAILROAD LAW

Roeland Park

Daniel F. Church · McAnany, Van Cleave & Phillips · 5125 Roe Boulevard, Suite 200 · Roeland Park, KS 66205 · 913-371-3838

REAL ESTATE LAW

Lawrence

Mark A. Andersen · Barber Emerson · 1211 Massachusetts Street · P.O. Box 667 · Lawrence, KS 66044-3351 · 785-843-6600

Peter K. Curran · Stevens & Brand · 900 Massachusetts Street, Suite 500 · P.O. Box 189 · Lawrence, KS 66044-0189 · 785-843-0811

Richard L. Zinn · a · Barber Emerson · 1211 Massachusetts Street · P.O. Box 667 · Lawrence, KS 66044-3351 · 785-843-6600

Overland Park

Lewis A. Heaven, Jr. · a · Lathrop & Gage · Building 82, Suite 1000 · 10851 Mastin Boulevard · Overland Park, KS 66210-1669 · 913-451-5100

Richard H. Hertel · Spencer Fane Britt & Browne · http://www.spencerfane.com · 40 Corporate Woods, Suite 700 · 9401 Indian Creek Parkway · Overland Park, KS 66210-2005 · 913-345-8100

John D. Petersen · Polsinelli Shalton Flanigan Suelthaus · http://www.polsinelli.com · 6201 College Boulevard, Suite 500 · Overland Park, KS 66211-2423 · 913-451-8788

Neil R. Shortlidge · Stinson Morrison Hecker · http://www.stinson.com · 12 Corporate Woods, Suite 550 · 10975 Benson · Overland Park, KS 66210 · 913-451-8600

Larry W. Winn III · Polsinelli Shalton Flanigan Suelthaus · http://www.polsinelli.com · 6201 College Boulevard, Suite 500 · Overland Park, KS 66211-2423 · 913-451-8788

Stanley N. Woodworth · Polsinelli Shalton Flanigan Suelthaus · http://www.polsinelli.com · 6201 College Boulevard, Suite 500 · Overland Park, KS 66211-2423 · 913-451-8788

Topeka

Gerald L. Goodell · a · Goodell, Stratton, Edmonds & Palmer · 515 South Kansas Avenue · Topeka, KS 66603-3999 · 785-233-0593

Richard F. Hayse · Morris, Laing, Evans, Brock & Kennedy · U.S. Bank Building, Thirteenth Floor · 800 Southwest Jackson · Topeka, KS 66612-1216 · 785-232-2662

Vernon L. Jarboe · Sloan Eisenbarth Glassman McEntire & Jarboe · Bank of America Tower, Suite 1000 534 South Kansas Avenue · Topeka, KS 66603-3456 · 785-357-6311

Wichita

Philip L. Bowman · 2) · Adams Jones Law Firm · 1635 North Waterfront Parkway, Suite 200 · Wichita, KS 67206-6623 · 316-265-8591

Mert F. Buckley · Adams Jones Law Firm · 1635 North Waterfront Parkway, Suite 200 · Wichita, KS 67206-6623 · 316-265-8591

Kenneth G. Gale · Adams Jones Law Firm · 1635 North Waterfront Parkway, Suite 200 · Wichita, KS 67206-6623 · 316-265-8591

Ronald H. Harnden · Triplett, Woolf & Garretson · http://www.twgfirm.com · 2959 North Rock Road, Suite 300 · Wichita, KS 67226 · 316-630-8100

Roger D. Hughey · Adams Jones Law Firm · 1635 North Waterfront Parkway, Suite 200 · Wichita, KS 67206-6623 · 316-265-8591

Scott D. Jensen · Bever Dye · http://www.beverdye.com · Epic Center, Suite 600 · 301 North Main Street Wichita, KS 67202-4806 · 316-263-8294

Ted E. Knopp · Ted E. Knopp · The Quarters, Suite 203 · 310 West Central Avenue · Wichita, KS 67202-1004 · 316-265-5882

Jack C. Marvin · Stinson Morrison Hecker · http://www.stinson.com · 1625 North Waterfront Parkway, Suite 300 · Wichita, KS 67206-6602 · 316-265-8800

Donald E. Schrag · Morris, Laing, Evans, Brock & Kennedy · Old Town Square, Suite 200 · 300 North Meade · Wichita, KS 67202-2745 · 316-262-2671

John R. Stallings · Hinkle Elkouri Law Firm · http://www.hinklaw.com · 8621 East 21st Street North, Suite 200 · Wichita, KS 67206 · 316-267-2000

Stephen M. Stark · Fleeson, Gooing, Coulson & Kitch · http://www.fleeson.com · Epic Center, Suite 1900 · 301 North Main Street · Wichita, KS 67202 · 316-267-7361

Monte Vines · Adams Jones Law Firm · 1635 North Waterfront Parkway, Suite 200 · Wichita, KS 67206-6623 · 316-265-8591

William R. Wood II · a · Foulston Siefkin · http://www.foulston.com · 1551 North Waterfront Parkway, Suite 100 · Wichita, KS 67206-4466 · 316-267-6371

SPORTS LAW

Overland Park

Richard J. Evrard · Bond, Schoeneck & King · 7500 College Boulevard, Suite 910 · Overland Park, KS 66210-4035 · 913-234-4400

Michael S. Glazier · Bond, Schoeneck & King · 7500 College Boulevard, Suite 910 · Overland Park, KS 66210-4035 · 913-234-4400

Stephen R. Morgan · Bond, Schoeneck & King · 7500 College Boulevard, Suite 910 · Overland Park, KS 66210-4035 · 913-234-4400

TAX LAW

Cimarron

Philip D. Ridenour · 2% · Ridenour and Ridenour · 109 South Main Street · P.O. Box 1028 · Cimarron, KS 67835 · 620-855-7051

Lawrence

Martin B. Dickinson, Jr. · 2% · Martin B. Dickinson, Jr. · University of Kansas School of Law · 1535 West 15th Street · Lawrence, KS 66045 · 785-864-4550

Manhattan

Charles S. Arthur III · 2% · Arthur Green Law Firm · 801 Poyntz Avenue · Manhattan, KS 66502 · 785-537-1345

Overland Park

Eric L. Hansen · Holman Hansen & Colville · 10740 Nall Avenue, Suite 200 · Overland Park, KS 66211 · 913-648-7272

Thomas K. Jones · a · Payne & Jones · 11000 King Street · P.O. Box 25625 · Overland Park, KS 66225-5625 · 913-469-4100

James K. Logan · Foulston Siefkin · http://www.foulston.com · Nine Corporate Woods, Suite 450 · 9200 Indian Creek Parkway · Overland Park, KS 66210 · 913-498-2100

Alson R. Martin · 2% · Lathrop & Gage · Building 82, Suite 1000 · 10851 Mastin Boulevard · Overland Park, KS 66210-1669 · 913-451-5100

Lyle D. Pishny · a · Lathrop & Gage · Building 82, Suite 1000 · 10851 Mastin Boulevard · Overland Park, KS 66210-1669 · 913-451-5100

William P. Trenkle, Jr. · 2% · Foulston Siefkin · http://www.foulston.com · Nine Corporate Woods, Suite 450 · 9200 Indian Creek Parkway · Overland Park, KS 66210 · 913-498-2100

William K. Waugh III · a · Lathrop & Gage · Building 82, Suite 1000 · 10851 Mastin Boulevard · Overland Park, KS 66210-1669 · 913-451-5100

David N. Zimmerman · Shughart Thomson & Kilroy · http://www.stklaw.com · 32 Corporate Woods, Suite 1100 · 9225 Indian Creek Parkway · Overland Park, KS 66210 · 913-451-3355

Salina

Peter L. Peterson · 2% · Clark, Mize & Linville · 129 South Eighth Street · P.O. Box 380 · Salina, KS 67402-0380 · 785-823-6325

Topeka

S. Lucky DeFries · a · Coffman, DeFries & Nothern · 534 South Kansas Avenue, Suite 925 · Topeka, KS 66603-3407 · 785-234-3461

Donald J. Horttor · 2% · Cosgrove, Webb & Oman · 534 South Kansas Avenue, Suite 1100 · Topeka, KS 66603 · 785-235-9511

Gerald J. Letourneau · a · Goodell, Stratton, Edmonds & Palmer · 515 South Kansas Avenue · Topeka, KS 66603-3999 · 785-233-0593

R. Austin Nothern · 2% · Coffman, DeFries & Nothern · 534 South Kansas Avenue, Suite 925 · Topeka, KS 66603-3407 · 785-234-3461

Wichita

Stanley G. Andeel · 2% · Foulston Siefkin · http://www.foulston.com · 1551 North Waterfront Parkway, Suite 100 · Wichita, KS 67206-4466 · 316-267-6371

William M. Cobb · 2% · Bever Dye · http://www.beverdye.com · Epic Center, Suite 600 · 301 North Main Street · Wichita, KS 67202-4806 · 316-263-8294

Jack D. Flesher · a · Bever Dye · http://www.beverdye.com · Epic Center, Suite 600 · 301 North Main Street · Wichita, KS 67202-4806 · 316-263-8294

Gregory L. Franken · Bever Dye · http://www.beverdye.com · Epic Center, Suite 600 · 301 North Main Street · Wichita, KS 67202-4806 · 316-263-8294

Christopher M. Hurst · Foulston Siefkin · http://www.foulston.com · 1551 North Waterfront Parkway, Suite 100 · Wichita, KS 67206-4466 · 316-267-6371

Eric J. Larson · a · Bever Dye · http://www.beverdye.com · Epic Center, Suite 600 · 301 North Main Street · Wichita, KS 67202-4806 · 316-263-8294

Harvey R. Sorensen · a · Foulston Siefkin · http://www.foulston.com · 1551 North Waterfront Parkway, Suite 100 · Wichita, KS 67206-4466 · 316-267-6371

Thomas C. Triplett · 2% · Triplett, Woolf & Garretson · http://www.twgfirm.com · 2959 North Rock Road, Suite 300 · Wichita, KS 67226 · 316-630-8100

TRUSTS AND ESTATES

Cimarron

Philip D. Ridenour · 2% · Ridenour and Ridenour · 109 South Main Street · P.O. Box 1028 · Cimarron, KS 67835 · 620-855-7051

Lawrence

Martin B. Dickinson, Jr. · 2% · Martin B. Dickinson, Jr. · University of Kansas School of Law · 1535 West 15th Street · Lawrence, KS 66045 · 785-864-4550

Webster L. Golden · 2% · Stevens & Brand · 900 Massachusetts Street, Suite 500 · P.O. Box 189 · Lawrence, KS 66044-0189 · 785-843-0811

Evan H. Ice · Stevens & Brand · 900 Massachusetts Street, Suite 500 · P.O. Box 189 · Lawrence, KS 66044-0189 · 785-843-0811

Calvin J. Karlin · Barber Emerson · 1211 Massachusetts Street · P.O. Box 667 · Lawrence, KS 66044-3351 · 785-843-6600

Richard L. Zinn · a · Barber Emerson · 1211 Massachusetts Street · P.O. Box 667 · Lawrence, KS 66044-3351 · 785-843-6600

Manhattan

Charles S. Arthur III · 2% · Arthur Green Law Firm · 801 Poyntz Avenue · Manhattan, KS 66502 · 785-537-1345

Overland Park

Jodde Olsen Lanning · Payne & Jones · 11000 King Street · P.O. Box 25625 · Overland Park, KS 66225-5625 · 913-469-4100

James K. Logan · Foulston Siefkin · http://www.foulston.com · Nine Corporate Woods, Suite 450 · 9200 Indian Creek Parkway · Overland Park, KS 66210 · 913-498-2100

John S. Schmidt · Shughart Thomson & Kilroy · http://www.stklaw.com · 32 Corporate Woods, Suite 1100 · 9225 Indian Creek Parkway · Overland Park, KS 66210 · 913-451-3355

William P. Trenkle, Jr. · 2% · Foulston Siefkin · http://www.foulston.com · Nine Corporate Woods, Suite 450 · 9200 Indian Creek Parkway · Overland Park, KS 66210 · 913-498-2100

William K. Waugh III · a · Lathrop & Gage · Building 82, Suite 1000 · 10851 Mastin Boulevard · Overland Park, KS 66210-1669 · 913-451-5100

Richard D. Woods · 2) · Kirkland & Woods · 6201 College Boulevard, Suite 250 · Overland Park, KS 66211 · 913-469-0900

Salina

Peter L. Peterson · 2% · Clark, Mize & Linville · 129 South Eighth Street · P.O. Box 380 · Salina, KS 67402-0380 · 785-823-6325

Topeka

Michael L. Clutter · Clutter & Aadalen · 2201 Southwest 29th Street · Topeka, KS 66611 · 785-266-5121

H. Hurst Coffman · a · Coffman, DeFries & Nothern · 534 South Kansas Avenue, Suite 925 · Topeka, KS 66603-3407 · 785-234-3461

Donald J. Horttor · 2% · Cosgrove, Webb & Oman · 534 South Kansas Avenue, Suite 1100 · Topeka, KS 66603 · 785-235-9511

Craig R. McKinney · McKinney & McKinney · 700 South Kansas Avenue, Suite 508 · Topeka, KS 66603-3823 · 785-233-1321

R. Austin Nothern · 2% · Coffman, DeFries & Nothern · 534 South Kansas Avenue, Suite 925 · Topeka, KS 66603-3407 · 785-234-3461

Wichita

Stanley G. Andeel · 2% · Foulston Siefkin · http://www.foulston.com · 1551 North Waterfront Parkway, Suite 100 · Wichita, KS 67206-4466 · 316-267-6371

Robert K. Anderson · Morris, Laing, Evans, Brock & Kennedy · Old Town Square, Suite 200 · 300 North Meade · Wichita, KS 67202-2745 · 316-262-2671

William M. Cobb · 2% · Bever Dye · http://www.beverdye.com · Epic Center, Suite 600 · 301 North Main Street · Wichita, KS 67202-4806 · 316-263-8294

Charles E. Cole, Jr. · Fleeson, Gooing, Coulson & Kitch · http://www.fleeson.com · Epic Center, Suite 1900 · 301 North Main Street · Wichita, KS 67202 · 316-267-7361

Linda K. Constable · 2) · Fleeson, Gooing, Coulson & Kitch · http://www.fleeson.com · Epic Center, Suite 1900 · 301 North Main Street · Wichita, KS 67202 · 316-267-7361

Jack D. Flesher · a · Bever Dye · http://www.beverdye.com · Epic Center, Suite 600 · 301 North Main Street · Wichita, KS 67202-4806 · 316-263-8294

Gregory L. Franken · Bever Dye · http://www.beverdye.com · Epic Center, Suite 600 · 301 North Main Street · Wichita, KS 67202-4806 · 316-263-8294

Theron E. Fry · Triplett, Woolf & Garretson · http://www.twgfirm.com · 2959 North Rock Road, Suite 300 · Wichita, KS 67226 · 316-630-8100

Hugh W. Gill · Hinkle Elkouri Law Firm · http://www.hinklaw.com · Epic Center, Suite 2000 · 301 North Main Street · Wichita, KS 67202 · 316-267-2000

Robert I. Guenthner · a · Morris, Laing, Evans, Brock & Kennedy · Old Town Square, Suite 200 · 300 North Meade · Wichita, KS 67202-2745 · 316-262-2671

Hellen Haag · Bever Dye · http://www.beverdye.com · Epic Center, Suite 600 · 301 North Main Street · Wichita, KS 67202-4806 · 316-263-8294

Robert M. Hughes · Bever Dye · http://www.beverdye.com · Epic Center, Suite 600 · 301 North Main Street · Wichita, KS 67202-4806 · 316-263-8294

Eric J. Larson · a · Bever Dye · http://www.beverdye.com · Epic Center, Suite 600 · 301 North Main Street · Wichita, KS 67202-4806 · 316-263-8294

Kent A. Meyerhoff · Fleeson, Gooing, Coulson & Kitch · http://www.fleeson.com · Epic Center, Suite 1900 · 301 North Main Street · Wichita, KS 67202 · 316-267-7361

Timothy P. O'Sullivan · a · Foulston Siefkin · http://www.foulston.com · 1551 North Waterfront Parkway, Suite 100 · Wichita, KS 67206-4466 · 316-267-6371

Dan C. Peare · Hinkle Elkouri Law Firm · http://www.hinklaw.com · Epic Center, Suite 2000 · 301 North Main Street · Wichita, KS 67202 · 316-267-2000

Don B. Stahr · a · Bever Dye · http://www.beverdye.com · Epic Center, Suite 600 · 301 North Main Street · Wichita, KS 67202-4806 · 316-263-8294

Willard B. Thompson · 2% · Fleeson, Gooing, Coulson & Kitch · http://www.fleeson.com · Epic Center, Suite 1900 · 301 North Main Street · Wichita, KS 67202 · 316-267-7361

Thomas C. Triplett · 2% · Triplett, Woolf & Garretson · http://www.twgfirm.com · 2959 North Rock Road, Suite 300 · Wichita, KS 67226 · 316-630-8100

John A. Vetter · Stinson Morrison Hecker · http://www.stinson.com · 1625 North Waterfront Parkway, Suite 300 · Wichita, KS 67206-6602 · 316-265-8800

Stewart T. Weaver · Foulston Siefkin · http://www.foulston.com · 1551 North Waterfront Parkway, Suite 100 · Wichita, KS 67206-4466 · 316-267-6371

WATER LAW

Garden City

Michael K. Ramsey · Hope, Mills, Bolin, Collins & Ramsey · 607 North Seventh Street · Garden City, KS 67846 · 620-276-3203

Overland Park

John C. Peck · Foulston Siefkin · http://www.foulston.com · Nine Corporate Woods, Suite 450 · 9200 Indian Creek Parkway · Overland Park, KS 66210 · 913-498-2100

Wichita

David M. Traster · Foulston Siefkin · http://www.foulston.com · 1551 North Waterfront Parkway, Suite 100 · Wichita, KS 67206-4466 · 316-267-6371

WHITE-COLLAR CRIMINAL DEFENSE

Overland Park

Thomas J. Bath, Jr. · Bath & Edmonds · Historic Voigts Building · 7944 Santa Fe Drive · Overland Park, KS 66204 · 913-652-9800

Robin D. Fowler · Bath & Edmonds · Historic Voigts Building · 7944 Santa Fe Drive · Overland Park, KS 66204 · 913-652-9800

Prairie Village

James L. Eisenbrandt · ⑳ · Berkowitz Oliver Williams Shaw & Eisenbrandt · 4200 Somerset, Suite 150 · Prairie Village, KS 66208 · 913-649-7007

Topeka

John J. Ambrosio · ⑩ · John J. Ambrosio · 5897 Southwest 29th Street · Topeka, KS 66614-2486 · 785-233-0524

Mark L. Bennett, Jr. · ⑳ · Bennett & Hendrix · 5605 Southwest Barrington Court South, Suite 201 · Topeka, KS 66614 · 785-271-0800

Thomas D. Haney · ⑩ · Henson, Hutton, Mudrick & Gragson · Commerce Bank Building, Second Floor · 100 Southeast Ninth Street · P.O. 3555 · Topeka, KS 66601-3555 · 785-232-2200

Peter Luis Irigonegaray · ⑩ · Peter Luis Irigonegaray · 1535 Southwest 29th Street · Topeka, KS 66611 · 785-267-6115

Wichita

Jack Focht · ㉕ · Foulston Siefkin · http://www.foulston.com · 1551 North Waterfront Parkway, Suite 100 · Wichita, KS 67206-4466 · 316-267-6371

Stephen M. Joseph · ⑳ · Joseph & Hollander · 500 North Market Street · Wichita, KS 67214-3514 · 316-262-9393

Daniel E. Monnat · ⑳ · Monnat & Spurrier · http://www.monnat.com · Olive West Garvey Building, Suite 830 · 200 West Douglas · Wichita, KS 67202 · 316-264-2800

Stephen E. Robison · ⑳ · Fleeson, Gooing, Coulson & Kitch · http://www.fleeson.com · Epic Center, Suite 1900 · 301 North Main Street · Wichita, KS 67202 · 316-267-7361

Dodge City

D. Shane Bangerter · Rebein Bangerter · http://www.rebeinbangerter.com · 810 West Frontview · P.O. Box 1147 · Dodge City, KS 67801 · 620-227-8126

David J. Rebein · a · Rebein Bangerter · http://www.rebeinbangerter.com · 810 West Frontview · P.O. Box 1147 · Dodge City, KS 67801 · 620-227-8126

Emporia

Stanley R. Ausemus · Stanley R. Ausemus · 413 Commercial Street · Emporia, KS 66801 · 620-342-8717

Kansas City

Frederick J. Greenbaum · McAnany, Van Cleave & Phillips · 707 Minnesota Avenue, Fourth Floor · P.O. Box 171300 · Kansas City, KS 66101 · 913-371-3838

Denise E. Tomasic · Tomasic & Rehorn · Historic Strawberry Hill · 419 North Sixth Street · P.O. Box 171855 · Kansas City, KS 66117-0855 · 913-371-5750

Lawrence

Patrick Nichols · a · Associates in Dispute Resolution · 5200 Bob Billings Parkway, Suite 302 · Lawrence, KS 66049 · 785-865-3700

Lenexa

Wade A. Dorothy · a · The Dorothy Law Firm · 8675 West 96th Street, Suite 203 · Lenexa, KS 66212 · 913-888-7888

Mark E. Kolich · a · Mark E. Kolich · 13420 Santa Fe Trail Drive · Lenexa, KS 66215 · 913-888-7100

Ottawa

Derek R. Chappell · Jordan & Chappell · 313 South Hickory Street · P.O. Box 927 · Ottawa, KS 66067 · 785-242-5566

Gary L. Jordan · a · Jordan & Chappell · 313 South Hickory Street · P.O. Box 927 · Ottawa, KS 66067 · 785-242-5566

Overland Park

Vaughn Burkholder · a · Foulston Siefkin · http://www.foulston.com · Nine Corporate Woods, Suite 450 9200 Indian Creek Parkway · Overland Park, KS 66210 · 913-498-2100

Rex W. Henoch · Dorothy & Henoch · 8675 West 96th Street, Suite 203 · Overland Park, KS 66212 · 913-888-7888

Timothy G. Lutz · Wallace, Saunders, Austin, Brown & Enochs · 10111 West 87th Street · P.O. Box 12290 Overland Park, KS 66282-2290 · 913-888-1000

James E. Martin · Law Offices of James E. Martin · 8826 Sante Fe Drive, Suite 218 · Overland Park, KS 66212 · 913-385-0500

Gary R. Terrill · a · Wallace, Saunders, Austin, Brown & Enochs · 10111 West 87th Street · P.O. Box 12290 · Overland Park, KS 66282-2290 · 913-888-1000

Roeland Park

John David Jurcyk · McAnany, Van Cleave & Phillips · 5125 Roe Boulevard, Suite 200 · Roeland Park, KS 66205 · 913-371-3838

Salina

Jeffrey E. King · a · Hampton & Royce · United Building, Ninth and Tenth Floors · 119 West Iron Street · P.O. Box 1247 · Salina, KS 67402-1247 · 785-827-7251

Shawnee Mission

Michael R. Wallace · a · Law Office of Michael R. Wallace · 4400 Shawnee Mission Parkway, Suite 100 · Shawnee Mission, KS 66205 · 913-362-5400

Topeka

John Bryan · Bryan, Lykin, Hejtmanek & Fincher · 222 Southwest Seventh Street · P.O. Box 797 · Topeka, KS 66601-0797 · 785-235-5678

Jeff Cooper · Cooper & Lee · 100 Southeast Ninth Street, Third Floor · Topeka, KS 66601 · 785-233-9988

Jan Fisher · McCullough, Wareheim & LaBunker · 1501 Southwest Topeka Boulevard · P.O. Box 1453 · Topeka, KS 66601 · 785-233-2323

John M. Ostrowski · a · John M. Ostrowski · 1507 Southwest Topeka Boulevard · P.O. Box 1453 · Topeka, KS 66601-1453 · 785-233-2323

Patrick M. Salsbury · a · Goodell, Stratton, Edmonds & Palmer · 515 South Kansas Avenue · Topeka, KS 66603-3999 · 785-233-0593

Michael J. Unrein · a · Davis, Unrein, McCallister, Biggs & Head · Commerce Bank Building, Third Floor · 100 Southeast Ninth Street · P.O. Box 3575 · Topeka, KS 66601-3575 · 785-354-1100

James C. Wright · a · Wright Law Office · 700 Southwest Jackson Street, Roof Garden Suite · Topeka, KS 66603 · 785-234-0059

Mitchell D. Wulfekoetter · McCullough, Wareheim & LaBunker · 1501 Southwest Topeka Boulevard · P.O. Box 1453 · Topeka, KS 66601 · 785-233-2323

Wichita

P. Kelly Donley · McDonald, Tinker, Skaer, Quinn & Herrington · 300 West Douglas Street, Suite 500 · P.O. Box 207 · Wichita, KS 67202-2909 · 316-263-5851

Larry Gurney · a · Wilson, Lee, Gurney & Hess · 1861 North Rock Road, Suite 320 · Wichita, KS 67206 316-685-2245

Thomas E. Hammond · a · Hammond, Zongker & Farris · 727 North Waco Street, Suite 200 · P.O. Box 47370 · Wichita, KS 67201 · 316-262-6800

Charles W. Hess · Wilson, Lee, Gurney & Hess · 1861 North Rock Road, Suite 320 · Wichita, KS 67206 · 316-685-2245

Kelly W. Johnston · a · Johnston Law Offices · 800 North Market Street · P.O. Box 3089 · Wichita, KS 67201-3089 · 316-263-2173

Eric K. Kuhn · Foulston Siefkin · http://www.foulston.com · 1551 North Waterfront Parkway, Suite 100 · Wichita, KS 67206-4466 · 316-267-6371

Robert R. Lee · Wilson, Lee, Gurney & Hess · 1861 North Rock Road, Suite 320 · Wichita, KS 67206 · 316-685-2245

Kim R. Martens · Hite, Fanning & Honeyman · 100 North Broadway, Suite 950 · Wichita, KS 67202-2209 · 316-265-7741

William L. Townsley III · Fleeson, Gooing, Coulson & Kitch · http://www.fleeson.com · Epic Center, Suite 1900 · 301 North Main Street · Wichita, KS 67202 · 316-267-7361

Steve Wilson · Wilson, Lee, Gurney & Hess · 1861 North Rock Road, Suite 320 · Wichita, KS 67206 · 316-685-2245

James B. Zongker · a · Hammond, Zongker & Farris · 727 North Waco Street, Suite 200 · P.O. Box 47370 · Wichita, KS 67201 · 316-262-6800

KENTUCKY

ADMINISTRATIVE LAW

Frankfort

Bruce F. Clark · ⑩ · Stites & Harbison · http://www.stites.com · 421 West Main Street · P.O. Box 634 · Frankfort, KY 40602-0634 · 502-223-3477

William D. Kirkland · ⑩ · McBrayer, McGinnis, Leslie & Kirkland · Whitaker Bank Building, Suite 300 · P.O. Box 1100 · Frankfort, KY 40602-1100 · 502-223-1200

Mark Overstreet · ⑩ · Stites & Harbison · http://www.stites.com · 421 West Main Street · P.O. Box 634 · Frankfort, KY 40602-0634 · 502-223-3477

Michele M. Whittington · Stites & Harbison · http://www.stites.com · 421 West Main Street · P.O. Box 634 · Frankfort, KY 40602-0634 · 502-223-3477

Louisville

Carole D. Christian · ⑩ · Wyatt, Tarrant & Combs · http://www.wyattfirm.com · PNC Plaza, Suite 2800 · 500 West Jefferson Street · Louisville, KY 40202-2898 · 502-589-5235

Kenneth S. Handmaker · Middleton Reutlinger · Brown & Williamson Tower, Suite 2500 · 401 South Fourth Street · Louisville, KY 40202-3410 · 502-584-1135

C. Kent Hatfield · ⑩ · Stoll Keenon Ogden · http://www.skofirm.com · PNC Plaza, Suite 2000 · 500 West Jefferson Street · Louisville, KY 40202-2828 · 502-333-6000

Holland N. McTyeire V · Greenebaum Doll & McDonald · http://www.gdm.com · National City Tower, Suite 3500 · 101 South Fifth Street · Louisville, KY 40202-3140 · 502-589-4200

Kendrick R. Riggs · ⑩ · Stoll Keenon Ogden · http://www.skofirm.com · PNC Plaza, Suite 2000 · 500 West Jefferson Street · Louisville, KY 40202-2828 · 502-333-6000

John E. Selent · Dinsmore & Shohl · http://www.dinslaw.com · 1400 PNC Plaza · 500 West Jefferson Street · Louisville, KY 40202 · 502-540-2300

ALTERNATIVE DISPUTE RESOLUTION

Edgewood

Harry D. Rankin · Sutton Rankin Law · 130 Dudley Road, Suite 250 · Edgewood, KY 41017 · 859-331-8883

Lexington

Pierce W. Hamblin · Landrum & Shouse · 106 West Vine Street, Suite 800 · P.O. Box 951 · Lexington, KY 40588-0951 · 859-255-2424

J. Clarke Keller · Stites & Harbison · http://www.stites.com · 250 West Main Street, Suite 2300 · Lexington, KY 40507-1758 · 859-226-2300

Louisville

John T. Ballantine · ⑳ · Stoll Keenon Ogden · http://www.skofirm.com · PNC Plaza, Suite 2000 · 500 West Jefferson Street · Louisville, KY 40202-2828 · 502-333-6000

William D. Grubbs · ⑳ · Woodward, Hobson & Fulton · http://www.whf-law.com · 2500 National City Tower · 101 South Fifth Street · Louisville, KY 40202-3175 · 502-581-8000

Thomas J. Knopf · Retired Judges and Associates Mediation Service · P.O. Box 70318 · Louisville, KY 40270 · 502-721-9900

Gary M. Weiss · ⑩ · Weiss & Cobb · PNC Building, 16th Floor · 500 West Jefferson Street · Louisville, KY 40220 · 502-493-1394

Union

Henry L. Stephens, Jr. · Henry L. Stephens, Jr. · 710 Gallant Fox Lane · Union, KY 41091 · 859-630-1204

ANTITRUST LAW

Louisville

Robert L. Brown · Greenebaum Doll & McDonald · http://www.gdm.com · National City Tower, Suite 3500 · 101 South Fifth Street · Louisville, KY 40202-3140 · 502-589-4200

John K. Bush · Greenebaum Doll & McDonald · http://www.gdm.com · National City Tower, Suite 3500 101 South Fifth Street · Louisville, KY 40202-3140 · 502-589-4200

Holland N. McTyeire V · Greenebaum Doll & McDonald · http://www.gdm.com · National City Tower, Suite 3500 · 101 South Fifth Street · Louisville, KY 40202-3140 · 502-589-4200

Kenneth J. Tuggle · ㉕ · Frost Brown Todd · http://www.frostbrowntodd.com · 400 West Market Street, 32nd Floor · Louisville, KY 40202-3363 · 502-589-5400

Jeffrey Kent Wicker · Reed Wicker · http://www.reedwicker.com · 2100 Waterfront Plaza · 321 West Main Street · Louisville, KY 40202 · 502-572-2500

APPELLATE LAW

Bowling Green

Charles E. English, Sr. · English, Lucas, Priest & Owsley · 1101 College Street · P.O. Box 770 · Bowling Green, KY 42102-0770 · 270-781-6500

Covington

Mark G. Arnzen · ⑳ · Arnzen, Wentz, Molloy, Laber & Storm · 600 Greenup Street · P.O. Box 472 · Covington, KY 41012-0472 · 859-431-6100

Lexington

Anne A. Chesnut · Greenebaum Doll & McDonald · http://www.gdm.com · 300 West Vine Street, Suite 1100 · Lexington, KY 40507-1622 · 859-231-8500

Barbara B. Edelman · ⑩ · Dinsmore & Shohl · http://www.dinslaw.com · Lexington Financial Center, Suite 1400 · 250 West Main Street · Lexington, KY 40507 · 859-425-1000

David A. Owen · Greenebaum Doll & McDonald · http://www.gdm.com · 300 West Vine Street, Suite 1100 · Lexington, KY 40507-1622 · 859-231-8500

W. Keith Ransdell · Ransdell and Roach · 176 Pasadena Drive, Building One · Lexington, KY 40503 · 859-276-6262

Joe C. Savage · ㉕ · Savage, Elliott, Houlihan, Moore, Mullins & Erdmann · PNC Bank Plaza, Suite 810 · 200 West Vine Street · Lexington, KY 40507 · 859-233-2700

Ashley W. Ward · Stites & Harbison · http://www.stites.com · 250 West Main Street, Suite 2300 · Lexington, KY 40507-1758 · 859-226-2300

Louisville

Brent R. Baughman · Greenebaum Doll & McDonald · http://www.gdm.com · National City Tower, Suite 3500 · 101 South Fifth Street · Louisville, KY 40202-3140 · 502-589-4200

Bethany A. Breetz · Stites & Harbison · http://www.stites.com · 400 West Market Street, Suite 1800 · Louisville, KY 40202-3352 · 502-587-3400

John K. Bush · Greenebaum Doll & McDonald · http://www.gdm.com · National City Tower, Suite 3500 101 South Fifth Street · Louisville, KY 40202-3140 · 502-589-4200

David A. Friedman · Fernandez Friedman Grossman & Kohn · 1807 One Riverfront Plaza · 401 West Main Street · Louisville, KY 40202 · 502-589-1001

Virginia Hamilton Snell · Wyatt, Tarrant & Combs · http://www.wyattfirm.com · PNC Plaza, Suite 2800 · 500 West Jefferson Street · Louisville, KY 40202-2898 · 502-589-5235

Sheryl G. Snyder · Frost Brown Todd · http://www.frostbrowntodd.com · 400 West Market Street, 32nd Floor · Louisville, KY 40202-3363 · 502-589-5400

BANKING LAW

Lexington

Walter R. Byrne, Jr. · Stites & Harbison · http://www.stites.com · 250 West Main Street, Suite 2300 · Lexington, KY 40507-1758 · 859-226-2300

J. David Smith, Jr. · Stoll Keenon Ogden · http://www.skofirm.com · 300 West Vine Street, Suite 2100 · Lexington, KY 40507-1801 · 859-231-3000

Louisville

Scott W. Brinkman · ⑩ · Stoll Keenon Ogden · http://www.skofirm.com · PNC Plaza, Suite 2000 · 500 West Jefferson Street · Louisville, KY 40202-2828 · 502-333-6000

Stewart E. Conner · ㉕ · Wyatt, Tarrant & Combs · http://www.wyattfirm.com · PNC Plaza, Suite 2800 · 500 West Jefferson Street · Louisville, KY 40202-2898 · 502-589-5235

Ivan M. Diamond · ⑩ · Greenebaum Doll & McDonald · http://www.gdm.com · National City Tower, Suite 3500 · 101 South Fifth Street · Louisville, KY 40202-3140 · 502-589-4200

James A. Giesel · Frost Brown Todd · http://www.frostbrowntodd.com · 400 West Market Street, 32nd Floor · Louisville, KY 40202-3363 · 502-589-5400

W. Thomas Halbleib, Jr. · Stites & Harbison · http://www.stites.com · 400 West Market Street, Suite 1800 · Louisville, KY 40202-3352 · 502-587-3400

David W. Harper · ⑩ · David W. Harper · 313 Pepperbush Road · Louisville, KY 40207 · 502-551-1746

John T. McGarvery · Morgan & Pottinger · 601 West Main Street · Louisville, KY 40202 · 502-589-2780

Caryn F. Price · Wyatt, Tarrant & Combs · http://www.wyattfirm.com · PNC Plaza, Suite 2800 · 500 West Jefferson Street · Louisville, KY 40202-2898 · 502-589-5235

David E. Saffer · Stites & Harbison · http://www.stites.com · 400 West Market Street, Suite 1800 · Louisville, KY 40202-3352 · 502-587-3400

R. James Straus · ⑩ · Frost Brown Todd · http://www.frostbrowntodd.com · 400 West Market Street, 32nd Floor · Louisville, KY 40202-3363 · 502-589-5400

Cynthia W. Young · Wyatt, Tarrant & Combs · http://www.wyattfirm.com · PNC Plaza, Suite 2800 · 500 West Jefferson Street · Louisville, KY 40202-2898 · 502-589-5235

BANKRUPTCY AND CREDITOR-DEBTOR RIGHTS LAW

Bowling Green

Scott A. Bachert · Harned, Bachert & Denton · 324 East 10th Avenue · P.O. Box 1270 · Bowling Green, KY 42102-1270 · 270-782-3938

Glasgow

Charles A. Goodman · ⑩ · Garmon & Goodman · 139 North Public Square · P.O. Box 663 · Glasgow, KY 42142 · 270-651-8812

Henderson

Merritt S. Deitz, Jr. · ⑩ · Deitz & Freeburger · 101 First Street · P.O. Box 21 · Henderson, KY 42420 · 270-830-0830

Sandra D. Freeburger · ⑩ · Deitz & Freeburger · 101 First Street · P.O. Box 21 · Henderson, KY 42420 · 270-830-0830

Lexington

Robert J. Brown · Wyatt, Tarrant & Combs · http://www.wyattfirm.com · Lexington Financial Center, Suite 1600 · 250 West Main Street · Lexington, KY 40507 · 859-233-2012

Laura Day DelCotto · Wise DelCotto · 200 North Upper Street · Lexington, KY 40507 · 859-231-5800

Mary L. Fullington · Wyatt, Tarrant & Combs · http://www.wyattfirm.com · Lexington Financial Center, Suite 1600 · 250 West Main Street · Lexington, KY 40507 · 859-233-2012

Taft A. McKinstry · ⑩ · Fowler, Measle & Bell · http://www.fmblaw.com · 300 West Vine Street, Suite 600 · Lexington, KY 40507-1660 · 859-252-6700

Robert S. Ryan · ⑩ · Fowler, Measle & Bell · http://www.fmblaw.com · 300 West Vine Street, Suite 600 · Lexington, KY 40507-1660 · 859-252-6700

Robert V. Sartin · Frost Brown Todd · http://www.frostbrowntodd.com · Lexington Financial Center, Suite 2800 · 250 West Main Street · Lexington, KY 40507-1749 · 859-231-0000

John S. Sawyer · ⑩ · Frost Brown Todd · http://www.frostbrowntodd.com · Lexington Financial Center, Suite 2800 · 250 West Main Street · Lexington, KY 40507-1749 · 859-231-0000

Gregory R. Schaaf · Greenebaum Doll & McDonald · http://www.gdm.com · 300 West Vine Street, Suite 1100 · Lexington, KY 40507-1622 · 859-231-8500

Elizabeth L. Thompson · Stites & Harbison · http://www.stites.com · 250 West Main Street, Suite 2300 · Lexington, KY 40507-1758 · 859-226-2300

Tracey Wise · ⑩ · Wise DelCotto · 200 North Upper Street · Lexington, KY 40507 · 859-231-5800

Louisville

John W. Ames · ⑳ · Greenebaum Doll & McDonald · http://www.gdm.com · National City Tower, Suite 3500 · 101 South Fifth Street · Louisville, KY 40202-3140 · 502-589-4200

C. R. Bowles · Greenebaum Doll & McDonald · http://www.gdm.com · National City Tower, Suite 3500 · 101 South Fifth Street · Louisville, KY 40202-3140 · 502-589-4200

David M. Cantor · ⑩ · Seiller & Waterman · Meidinger Tower, Suite 2200 · 462 South Fourth Street · Louisville, KY 40202 · 502-584-7400

John S. Egan · Frost Brown Todd · http://www.frostbrowntodd.com · 400 West Market Street, 32nd Floor Louisville, KY 40202-3363 · 502-589-5400

James S. Goldberg · Stoll Keenon Ogden · http://www.skofirm.com · PNC Plaza, Suite 2000 · 500 West Jefferson Street · Louisville, KY 40202-2828 · 502-333-6000

Charles R. Keeton · Frost Brown Todd · http://www.frostbrowntodd.com · 400 West Market Street, 32nd Floor · Louisville, KY 40202-3363 · 502-589-5400

Edward M. King · Frost Brown Todd · http://www.frostbrowntodd.com · 400 West Market Street, 32nd Floor · Louisville, KY 40202-3363 · 502-589-5400

John P. Reisz · ⑳ · Wyatt, Tarrant & Combs · http://www.wyattfirm.com · PNC Plaza, Suite 2800 · 500 West Jefferson Street · Louisville, KY 40202-2898 · 502-589-5235

Owensboro

Ronald J. Bamberger · ⑩ · Bamberger, Abshier & Brancato · P.O. 1598 · Owensboro, KY 42302 · 270-926-4545

Michael A. Fiorella · Sullivan, Mountjoy, Stainback & Miller · 100 St. Ann Street · P.O. Box 727 · Owensboro, KY 42302 · 270-926-4000

Seebree

Tommy Joe Fridy · ⑩ · Fridy Law Offices · 7106 Main Street · P.O. Box 468 · Seebree, KY 42455-0468 · 270-835-7571

BET-THE-COMPANY LITIGATION

Lexington

Robert F. Houlihan, Jr. · ⑩ · Savage, Elliott, Houlihan, Moore, Mullins & Erdmann · PNC Bank Plaza, Suite 810 · 200 West Vine Street · Lexington, KY 40507 · 859-233-2700

Louisville

Charles J. Cronan IV · ⑩ · Stites & Harbison · http://www.stites.com · 400 West Market Street, Suite 1800 · Louisville, KY 40202-3352 · 502-587-3400

K. Gregory Haynes · ⑳ · Wyatt, Tarrant & Combs · http://www.wyattfirm.com · PNC Plaza, Suite 2800 · 500 West Jefferson Street · Louisville, KY 40202-2898 · 502-589-5235

John S. Reed · ⑩ · Reed Weitkamp Schell & Vice · http://www.rwsvlaw.com · 500 West Jefferson Street, Suite 2400 · Louisville, KY 40202 · 502-589-1000

Sheryl G. Snyder · Frost Brown Todd · http://www.frostbrowntodd.com · 400 West Market Street, 32nd Floor · Louisville, KY 40202-3363 · 502-589-5400

BIOTECHNOLOGY LAW

Louisville

Stephen C. Hall · Stoll Keenon Ogden · http://www.skofirm.com · PNC Plaza, Suite 2000 · 500 West Jefferson Street · Louisville, KY 40202-2828 · 502-333-6000

COMMERCIAL LITIGATION

Bowling Green

Joe B. Campbell · ⑩ · Joe B. Campbell · 1011 Lehman Avenue, Suite 105 · Bowling Green, KY 42103 · 270-782-8228

John David Cole, Sr. · ⑳ · Cole & Moore · Phoenix Place · 921 College Street · P.O. Box 10240 · Bowling Green, KY 42102-7240 · 270-782-6666

Charles E. English, Sr. · English, Lucas, Priest & Owsley · 1101 College Street · P.O. Box 770 · Bowling Green, KY 42102-0770 · 270-781-6500

Covington

Gerald F. Dusing · ⑩ · Adams, Stepner, Woltermann & Dusing · 40 West Pike Street · P.O. Box 861 · Covington, KY 41012-0861 · 859-394-6200

Beverly R. Storm · Arnzen, Wentz, Molloy, Laber & Storm · 600 Greenup Street · P.O. Box 472 · Covington, KY 41012-0472 · 859-431-6100

Frankfort

Donald Duff · ⑩ · Donald Duff · 212 Washington Street · P.O. Box 1160 · Frankfort, KY 40602 · 502-223-7656

William E. Johnson · ㉕ · Johnson, True & Guarnieri · http://www.jtgattorneys.com · 326 West Main Street · Frankfort, KY 40601-1887 · 502-875-6000

William D. Kirkland · ⑩ · McBrayer, McGinnis, Leslie & Kirkland · Whitaker Bank Building, Suite 300 · P.O. Box 1100 · Frankfort, KY 40602-1100 · 502-223-1200

J. Guthrie True · ⑩ · Johnson, True & Guarnieri · http://www.jtgattorneys.com · 326 West Main Street · Frankfort, KY 40601-1887 · 502-875-6000

Lexington

P. Douglas Barr · Stoll Keenon Ogden · http://www.skofirm.com · 300 West Vine Street, Suite 2100 · Lexington, KY 40507-1801 · 859-231-3000

Robert F. Duncan · Jackson Kelly · 175 East Main Street · Lexington, KY 40507 · 859-255-9500

Barbara B. Edelman · ⑩ · Dinsmore & Shohl · http://www.dinslaw.com · Lexington Financial Center, Suite 1400 · 250 West Main Street · Lexington, KY 40507 · 859-425-1000

Buckner Hinkle, Jr. · Stites & Harbison · http://www.stites.com · 250 West Main Street, Suite 2300 · Lexington, KY 40507-1758 · 859-226-2300

Robert F. Houlihan, Jr. · ⑩ · Savage, Elliott, Houlihan, Moore, Mullins & Erdmann · PNC Bank Plaza, Suite 810 · 200 West Vine Street · Lexington, KY 40507 · 859-233-2700

Thomas W. Miller · Miller, Griffin & Marks · Security Trust Building, Suite 600 · 271 West Short Street · Lexington, KY 40507 · 859-255-6676

David A. Owen · Greenebaum Doll & McDonald · http://www.gdm.com · 300 West Vine Street, Suite 1100 · Lexington, KY 40507-1622 · 859-231-8500

Phillip D. Scott · Greenebaum Doll & McDonald · http://www.gdm.com · 300 West Vine Street, Suite 1100 · Lexington, KY 40507-1622 · 859-231-8500

Paul E. Sullivan · ⑩ · Frost Brown Todd · http://www.frostbrowntodd.com · Lexington Financial Center, Suite 2800 · 250 West Main Street · Lexington, KY 40507-1749 · 859-231-0000

Richard C. Ward · ⑩ · Wyatt, Tarrant & Combs · http://www.wyattfirm.com · Lexington Financial Center, Suite 1600 · 250 West Main Street · Lexington, KY 40507 · 859-233-2012

Louisville

Douglas C. Ballantine · Stoll Keenon Ogden · http://www.skofirm.com · PNC Plaza, Suite 2000 · 500 West Jefferson Street · Louisville, KY 40202-2828 · 502-333-6000

John W. Bilby · Stoll Keenon Ogden · http://www.skofirm.com · PNC Plaza, Suite 2000 · 500 West Jefferson Street · Louisville, KY 40202-2828 · 502-333-6000

Frank F. Chuppe · Wyatt, Tarrant & Combs · http://www.wyattfirm.com · PNC Plaza, Suite 2800 · 500 West Jefferson Street · Louisville, KY 40202-2898 · 502-589-5235

Richard H. C. Clay · Woodward, Hobson & Fulton · http://www.whf-law.com · 2500 National City Tower 101 South Fifth Street · Louisville, KY 40202-3175 · 502-581-8000

Philip W. Collier · Stites & Harbison · http://www.stites.com · 400 West Market Street, Suite 1800 · Louisville, KY 40202-3352 · 502-587-3400

Robert M. Connolly · Stites & Harbison · http://www.stites.com · 400 West Market Street, Suite 1800 · Louisville, KY 40202-3352 · 502-587-3400

Cornelius E. Coryell II · Wyatt, Tarrant & Combs · http://www.wyattfirm.com · PNC Plaza, Suite 2800 · 500 West Jefferson Street · Louisville, KY 40202-2898 · 502-589-5235

Donald L. Cox · Lynch, Cox, Gilman & Mahan · 500 West Jefferson Street, Suite 2100 · Louisville, KY 40202 · 502-589-4215

John R. Crockett III · Frost Brown Todd · http://www.frostbrowntodd.com · 400 West Market Street, 32nd Floor · Louisville, KY 40202-3363 · 502-589-5400

Charles J. Cronan IV · ⑩ · Stites & Harbison · http://www.stites.com · 400 West Market Street, Suite 1800 · Louisville, KY 40202-3352 · 502-587-3400

Scott T. Dickens · Fultz Maddox Hovious & Dickens · 2700 National City Tower · 101 South Fifth Street · Louisville, KY 40202 · 502-588-2000

Frank P. Doheny, Jr. · ⑳ · Dinsmore & Shohl · http://www.dinslaw.com · 1400 PNC Plaza · 500 West Jefferson Street · Louisville, KY 40202 · 502-540-2300

Hiram Ely III · Greenebaum Doll & McDonald · http://www.gdm.com · National City Tower, Suite 3500 101 South Fifth Street · Louisville, KY 40202-3140 · 502-589-4200

Robert W. Griffith · Stites & Harbison · http://www.stites.com · 400 West Market Street, Suite 1800 · Louisville, KY 40202-3352 · 502-587-3400

Joseph L. Hamilton · Stites & Harbison · http://www.stites.com · 400 West Market Street, Suite 1800 · Louisville, KY 40202-3352 · 502-587-3400

K. Gregory Haynes · ⑳ · Wyatt, Tarrant & Combs · http://www.wyattfirm.com · PNC Plaza, Suite 2800 · 500 West Jefferson Street · Louisville, KY 40202-2898 · 502-589-5235

Samuel D. Hinkle IV · Stoll Keenon Ogden · http://www.skofirm.com · PNC Plaza, Suite 2000 · 500 West Jefferson Street · Louisville, KY 40202-2828 · 502-333-6000

Marvin J. Hirn · ⑳ · Dinsmore & Shohl · http://www.dinslaw.com · 1400 PNC Plaza · 500 West Jefferson Street · Louisville, KY 40202 · 502-540-2300

Eric L. Ison · Greenebaum Doll & McDonald · http://www.gdm.com · National City Tower, Suite 3500 · 101 South Fifth Street · Louisville, KY 40202-3140 · 502-589-4200

Janet P. Jakubowicz · Greenebaum Doll & McDonald · http://www.gdm.com · National City Tower, Suite 3500 · 101 South Fifth Street · Louisville, KY 40202-3140 · 502-589-4200

Margaret E. Keane · ⑩ · Greenebaum Doll & McDonald · http://www.gdm.com · National City Tower, Suite 3500 · 101 South Fifth Street · Louisville, KY 40202-3140 · 502-589-4200

W. Gregory King · Stoll Keenon Ogden · http://www.skofirm.com · PNC Plaza, Suite 2000 · 500 West Jefferson Street · Louisville, KY 40202-2828 · 502-333-6000

Byron E. Leet · Wyatt, Tarrant & Combs · http://www.wyattfirm.com · PNC Plaza, Suite 2800 · 500 West Jefferson Street · Louisville, KY 40202-2898 · 502-589-5235

Winston E. Miller · Frost Brown Todd · http://www.frostbrowntodd.com · 400 West Market Street, 32nd Floor · Louisville, KY 40202-3363 · 502-589-5400

James E. Milliman · Middleton Reutlinger · Brown & Williamson Tower, Suite 2500 · 401 South Fourth Street · Louisville, KY 40202-3410 · 502-584-1135

David R. Monohan · Woodward, Hobson & Fulton · http://www.whf-law.com · 2500 National City Tower 101 South Fifth Street · Louisville, KY 40202-3175 · 502-581-8000

Marc S. Murphy · Stites & Harbison · http://www.stites.com · 400 West Market Street, Suite 1800 · Louisville, KY 40202-3352 · 502-587-3400

M. Stephen Pitt · Wyatt, Tarrant & Combs · http://www.wyattfirm.com · PNC Plaza, Suite 2800 · 500 West Jefferson Street · Louisville, KY 40202-2898 · 502-589-5235

John S. Reed · ⑩ · Reed Weitkamp Schell & Vice · http://www.rwsvlaw.com · 500 West Jefferson Street, Suite 2400 · Louisville, KY 40202 · 502-589-1000

Mark S. Riddle · Greenebaum Doll & McDonald · http://www.gdm.com · National City Tower, Suite 3500 · 101 South Fifth Street · Louisville, KY 40202-3140 · 502-589-4200

Virginia Hamilton Snell · Wyatt, Tarrant & Combs · http://www.wyattfirm.com · PNC Plaza, Suite 2800 · 500 West Jefferson Street · Louisville, KY 40202-2898 · 502-589-5235

Sheryl G. Snyder · Frost Brown Todd · http://www.frostbrowntodd.com · 400 West Market Street, 32nd Floor · Louisville, KY 40202-3363 · 502-589-5400

David B. Tachau · Tachau Meek · 2400 National City Tower · 101 South Fifth Street · Louisville, KY 40202-3115 · 502-238-9900

John L. Tate · ⑩ · Stites & Harbison · http://www.stites.com · 400 West Market Street, Suite 1800 · Louisville, KY 40202-3352 · 502-587-3400

Kenneth J. Tuggle · ㉕ · Frost Brown Todd · http://www.frostbrowntodd.com · 400 West Market Street, 32nd Floor · Louisville, KY 40202-3363 · 502-589-5400

COMMUNICATIONS LAW

Frankfort

Mark Overstreet · ⑩ · Stites & Harbison · http://www.stites.com · 421 West Main Street · P.O. Box 634 · Frankfort, KY 40602-0634 · 502-223-3477

Louisville

C. Kent Hatfield · ⑩ · Stoll Keenon Ogden · http://www.skofirm.com · PNC Plaza, Suite 2000 · 500 West Jefferson Street · Louisville, KY 40202-2828 · 502-333-6000

Holland N. McTyeire V · Greenebaum Doll & McDonald · http://www.gdm.com · National City Tower, Suite 3500 · 101 South Fifth Street · Louisville, KY 40202-3140 · 502-589-4200

Kendrick R. Riggs · ⑩ · Stoll Keenon Ogden · http://www.skofirm.com · PNC Plaza, Suite 2000 · 500 West Jefferson Street · Louisville, KY 40202-2828 · 502-333-6000

John E. Selent · Dinsmore & Shohl · http://www.dinslaw.com · 1400 PNC Plaza · 500 West Jefferson Street · Louisville, KY 40202 · 502-540-2300

CONSTRUCTION LAW

Fort Mitchell

William G. Geisen · Graydon, Head & Ritchey · 2400 Chamber Center Drive, Suite 300 · Fort Mitchell, KY 41017 · 859-282-8800

Lexington

Anne E. Gorham · Stites & Harbison · http://www.stites.com · 250 West Main Street, Suite 2300 · Lexington, KY 40507-1758 · 859-226-2300

Buckner Hinkle, Jr. · Stites & Harbison · http://www.stites.com · 250 West Main Street, Suite 2300 · Lexington, KY 40507-1758 · 859-226-2300

Gregory P. Parsons · Stites & Harbison · http://www.stites.com · 250 West Main Street, Suite 2300 · Lexington, KY 40507-1758 · 859-226-2300

Louisville

David B. Blandford · Ackerson & Yann · One Riverfront Plaza, Suite 1200 · 401 West Main Street · Louisville, KY 40202 · 502-583-7400

Robert M. Brooks · Boehl Stopher & Graves · AEGON Center, Suite 2300 · 400 West Market Street · Louisville, KY 40202 · 502-589-5980

Matthew Gillies · Stites & Harbison · http://www.stites.com · 400 West Market Street, Suite 1800 · Louisville, KY 40202-3352 · 502-587-3400

Joseph Hardesty · Stites & Harbison · http://www.stites.com · 400 West Market Street, Suite 1800 · Louisville, KY 40202-3352 · 502-587-3400

George P. Parker · Parker & O'Connell · The Starks Building, Suite 930 · 455 South Fourth Avenue · Louisville, KY 40202 · 502-584-7196

David B. Ratterman · Stites & Harbison · http://www.stites.com · 400 West Market Street, Suite 1800 · Louisville, KY 40202-3352 · 502-587-3400

Gerald L. Stovall · Hall, Render, Killian, Heath & Lyman · 614 West Main Street, Suite 4000 · Louisville, KY 40202 · 502-568-1890

CORPORATE GOVERNANCE AND COMPLIANCE LAW

Lexington

R. David Lester · ⑩ · Stoll Keenon Ogden · http://www.skofirm.com · 300 West Vine Street, Suite 2100 · Lexington, KY 40507-1801 · 859-231-3000

Louisville

June N. King · Greenebaum Doll & McDonald · http://www.gdm.com · National City Tower, Suite 3500 · 101 South Fifth Street · Louisville, KY 40202-3140 · 502-589-4200

Thomas E. Rutledge · Stoll Keenon Ogden · http://www.skofirm.com · PNC Plaza, Suite 2000 · 500 West Jefferson Street · Louisville, KY 40202-2828 · 502-333-6000

William G. Strench · Frost Brown Todd · http://www.frostbrowntodd.com · 400 West Market Street, 32nd Floor · Louisville, KY 40202-3363 · 502-589-5400

CORPORATE LAW

Bowling Green

Charles E. English, Sr. · English, Lucas, Priest & Owsley · 1101 College Street · P.O. Box 770 · Bowling Green, KY 42102-0770 · 270-781-6500

Frankfort

Bruce F. Clark · ⑩ · Stites & Harbison · http://www.stites.com · 421 West Main Street · P.O. Box 634 · Frankfort, KY 40602-0634 · 502-223-3477

William E. Johnson · ㉕ · Johnson, True & Guarnieri · http://www.jtgattorneys.com · 326 West Main Street · Frankfort, KY 40601-1887 · 502-875-6000

Lexington

P. Douglas Barr · Stoll Keenon Ogden · http://www.skofirm.com · 300 West Vine Street, Suite 2100 · Lexington, KY 40507-1801 · 859-231-3000

Robert M. Beck, Jr. · Stites & Harbison · http://www.stites.com · 250 West Main Street, Suite 2300 · Lexington, KY 40507-1758 · 859-226-2300

Jeffrey L. Hallos · Frost Brown Todd · http://www.frostbrowntodd.com · Lexington Financial Center, Suite 2800 · 250 West Main Street · Lexington, KY 40507-1749 · 859-231-0000

Warren J. Hoffmann · Frost Brown Todd · http://www.frostbrowntodd.com · Lexington Financial Center, Suite 2800 · 250 West Main Street · Lexington, KY 40507-1749 · 859-231-0000

R. David Lester · 10 · Stoll Keenon Ogden · http://www.skofirm.com · 300 West Vine Street, Suite 2100 · Lexington, KY 40507-1801 · 859-231-3000

Dan M. Rose · Stoll Keenon Ogden · http://www.skofirm.com · 300 West Vine Street, Suite 2100 · Lexington, KY 40507-1801 · 859-231-3000

Kenneth R. Sagan · Stites & Harbison · http://www.stites.com · 250 West Main Street, Suite 2300 · Lexington, KY 40507-1758 · 859-226-2300

Phillip D. Scott · Greenebaum Doll & McDonald · http://www.gdm.com · 300 West Vine Street, Suite 1100 · Lexington, KY 40507-1622 · 859-231-8500

J. David Smith, Jr. · Stoll Keenon Ogden · http://www.skofirm.com · 300 West Vine Street, Suite 2100 · Lexington, KY 40507-1801 · 859-231-3000

Paul E. Sullivan · 10 · Frost Brown Todd · http://www.frostbrowntodd.com · Lexington Financial Center, Suite 2800 · 250 West Main Street · Lexington, KY 40507-1749 · 859-231-0000

Joseph H. Terry · Dinsmore & Shohl · http://www.dinslaw.com · Lexington Financial Center, Suite 1400 250 West Main Street · Lexington, KY 40507 · 859-425-1000

Job D. Turner III · Greenebaum Doll & McDonald · http://www.gdm.com · 300 West Vine Street, Suite 1100 · Lexington, KY 40507-1622 · 859-231-8500

Louisville

P. Richard Anderson, Jr. · Greenebaum Doll & McDonald · http://www.gdm.com · National City Tower, Suite 3500 · 101 South Fifth Street · Louisville, KY 40202-3140 · 502-589-4200

Craig C. Bradley, Jr. · Stites & Harbison · http://www.stites.com · 400 West Market Street, Suite 1800 · Louisville, KY 40202-3352 · 502-587-3400

Scott W. Brinkman · 10 · Stoll Keenon Ogden · http://www.skofirm.com · PNC Plaza, Suite 2000 · 500 West Jefferson Street · Louisville, KY 40202-2828 · 502-333-6000

H. Alexander Campbell · Wyatt, Tarrant & Combs · http://www.wyattfirm.com · PNC Plaza, Suite 2800 · 500 West Jefferson Street · Louisville, KY 40202-2898 · 502-589-5235

Stewart E. Conner · 25 · Wyatt, Tarrant & Combs · http://www.wyattfirm.com · PNC Plaza, Suite 2800 · 500 West Jefferson Street · Louisville, KY 40202-2898 · 502-589-5235

Brian A. Cromer · Stites & Harbison · http://www.stites.com · 400 West Market Street, Suite 1800 · Louisville, KY 40202-3352 · 502-587-3400

Ivan M. Diamond · 10 · Greenebaum Doll & McDonald · http://www.gdm.com · National City Tower, Suite 3500 · 101 South Fifth Street · Louisville, KY 40202-3140 · 502-589-4200

A. Robert Doll · ㉕ · Greenebaum Doll & McDonald · http://www.gdm.com · National City Tower, Suite 3500 · 101 South Fifth Street · Louisville, KY 40202-3140 · 502-589-4200

Scott W. Dolson · Frost Brown Todd · http://www.frostbrowntodd.com · 400 West Market Street, 32nd Floor · Louisville, KY 40202-3363 · 502-589-5400

Michael M. Fleishman · ㉕ · Greenebaum Doll & McDonald · http://www.gdm.com · National City Tower, Suite 3500 · 101 South Fifth Street · Louisville, KY 40202-3140 · 502-589-4200

C. Edward Glasscock · ⑩ · Frost Brown Todd · http://www.frostbrowntodd.com · 400 West Market Street, 32nd Floor · Louisville, KY 40202-3363 · 502-589-5400

Kevin J. Hable · ⑩ · Wyatt, Tarrant & Combs · http://www.wyattfirm.com · PNC Plaza, Suite 2800 · 500 West Jefferson Street · Louisville, KY 40202-2898 · 502-589-5235

W. Thomas Halbleib, Jr. · Stites & Harbison · http://www.stites.com · 400 West Market Street, Suite 1800 · Louisville, KY 40202-3352 · 502-587-3400

David W. Harper · ⑩ · David W. Harper · 313 Pepperbush Road · Louisville, KY 40207 · 502-551-1746

Michael de León Hawthorne · Greenebaum Doll & McDonald · http://www.gdm.com · National City Tower, Suite 3500 · 101 South Fifth Street · Louisville, KY 40202-3140 · 502-589-4200

Robert A. Heath · Wyatt, Tarrant & Combs · http://www.wyattfirm.com · PNC Plaza, Suite 2800 · 500 West Jefferson Street · Louisville, KY 40202-2898 · 502-589-5235

T. Kennedy Helm III · ⑩ · Stites & Harbison · http://www.stites.com · 400 West Market Street, Suite 1800 · Louisville, KY 40202-3352 · 502-587-3400

Franklin K. Jelsma · Wyatt, Tarrant & Combs · http://www.wyattfirm.com · PNC Plaza, Suite 2800 · 500 West Jefferson Street · Louisville, KY 40202-2898 · 502-589-5235

June N. King · Greenebaum Doll & McDonald · http://www.gdm.com · National City Tower, Suite 3500 · 101 South Fifth Street · Louisville, KY 40202-3140 · 502-589-4200

Peggy B. Lyndrup · ⑩ · Greenebaum Doll & McDonald · http://www.gdm.com · National City Tower, Suite 3500 · 101 South Fifth Street · Louisville, KY 40202-3140 · 502-589-4200

Alan K. MacDonald · Frost Brown Todd · http://www.frostbrowntodd.com · 400 West Market Street, 32nd Floor · Louisville, KY 40202-3363 · 502-589-5400

Patrick Mattingly · Wyatt, Tarrant & Combs · http://www.wyattfirm.com · PNC Plaza, Suite 2800 · 500 West Jefferson Street · Louisville, KY 40202-2898 · 502-589-5235

Jeffrey A. McKenzie · Greenebaum Doll & McDonald · http://www.gdm.com · National City Tower, Suite 3500 · 101 South Fifth Street · Louisville, KY 40202-3140 · 502-589-4200

Francis J. Mellen · Wyatt, Tarrant & Combs · http://www.wyattfirm.com · PNC Plaza, Suite 2800 · 500 West Jefferson Street · Louisville, KY 40202-2898 · 502-589-5235

Patrick R. Northam · Greenebaum Doll & McDonald · http://www.gdm.com · National City Tower, Suite 3500 · 101 South Fifth Street · Louisville, KY 40202-3140 · 502-589-4200

Richard Northern · Wyatt, Tarrant & Combs · http://www.wyattfirm.com · PNC Plaza, Suite 2800 · 500 West Jefferson Street · Louisville, KY 40202-2898 · 502-589-5235

Edwin H. Perry · ⑳ · Greenebaum Doll & McDonald · http://www.gdm.com · National City Tower, Suite 3500 · 101 South Fifth Street · Louisville, KY 40202-3140 · 502-589-4200

Thomas E. Rutledge · Stoll Keenon Ogden · http://www.skofirm.com · PNC Plaza, Suite 2000 · 500 West Jefferson Street · Louisville, KY 40202-2828 · 502-333-6000

James C. Seiffert · Stites & Harbison · http://www.stites.com · 400 West Market Street, Suite 1800 · Louisville, KY 40202-3352 · 502-587-3400

R. James Straus · ⑩ · Frost Brown Todd · http://www.frostbrowntodd.com · 400 West Market Street, 32nd Floor · Louisville, KY 40202-3363 · 502-589-5400

William G. Strench · Frost Brown Todd · http://www.frostbrowntodd.com · 400 West Market Street, 32nd Floor · Louisville, KY 40202-3363 · 502-589-5400

Patrick J. Welsh · Greenebaum Doll & McDonald · http://www.gdm.com · National City Tower, Suite 3500 · 101 South Fifth Street · Louisville, KY 40202-3140 · 502-589-4200

Ernest W. Williams · ⑩ · Stoll Keenon Ogden · http://www.skofirm.com · PNC Plaza, Suite 2000 · 500 West Jefferson Street · Louisville, KY 40202-2828 · 502-333-6000

Cynthia W. Young · Wyatt, Tarrant & Combs · http://www.wyattfirm.com · PNC Plaza, Suite 2800 · 500 West Jefferson Street · Louisville, KY 40202-2898 · 502-589-5235

DUI/DWI DEFENSE

Florence

Wilbur M. Zevely · Busald Funk Zevely · 226 Main Street · P.O. Box 6910 · Florence, KY 41022-6910 · 859-371-3600

Lexington

Fred E. Peters · Fred E. Peters · 226 East High Street · Lexington, KY 40588-2043 · 606-255-7857

Randolph T. Richardson III · Baldani, Rowland & Richardson · 300 West Short Street · Lexington, KY 40507-1204 · 859-259-0727

Jerry L. Wright · Herren & Adams · 148 North Broadway · Lexington, KY 40507 · 859-254-0024

Louisville

Keith E. Kamenish · Kamenish Law Firm · 1916 Kentucky Home Life Building · 239 South Fifth Street · Louisville, KY 40202 · 502-584-1402

Mount Vernon

Jerry J. Cox · Jerry J. Cox · 115 Richmond Street · P.O. Box 1350 · Mount Vernon, KY 40456-1350 · 606-256-5111

EDUCATION LAW

Lexington

Arthur L. Brooks · ⑩ · Brooks, McComb & Fields · 1204 Winchester Road, Suite 100 · Lexington, KY 40505 · 859-233-3366

ELDER LAW

Louisville

Brian Borellis · Brian Borellis · http://www.brianborellislaw.com · 802 Stone Creek Parkway, Suite Eight · Louisville, KY 40223 · 502-425-5297

Mary Zeller Wing Ceridan · ⑩ · Sturm, Paletti & Wilson · 713 East Market Street, Suite 100 · Louisville, KY 40202 · 502-589-9254

Maria A. Fernandez · Fernandez Friedman Grossman & Kohn · 1807 One Riverfront Plaza · 401 West Main Street · Louisville, KY 40202 · 502-589-1001

Jefferey M. Yussman · ⑩ · Wyatt, Tarrant & Combs · http://www.wyattfirm.com · PNC Plaza, Suite 2800 500 West Jefferson Street · Louisville, KY 40202-2898 · 502-589-5235

EMPLOYEE BENEFITS LAW

Covington

Nicholas W. Ferrigno, Jr. · Greenebaum Doll & McDonald · http://www.gdm.com · 1800 RiverCenter I · 50 East RiverCenter Boulevard · Covington, KY 41011-1660 · 859-655-4200

Lexington

C. Joseph Beavin · Stoll Keenon Ogden · http://www.skofirm.com · 300 West Vine Street, Suite 2100 · Lexington, KY 40507-1801 · 859-231-3000

Gayle B. McGrath · Wyatt, Tarrant & Combs · http://www.wyattfirm.com · Lexington Financial Center, Suite 1600 · 250 West Main Street · Lexington, KY 40507 · 859-233-2012

Bruce M. Reynolds · ⑩ · Stites & Harbison · http://www.stites.com · 250 West Main Street, Suite 2300 · Lexington, KY 40507-1758 · 859-226-2300

Deborah H. Tudor · ⑩ · Frost Brown Todd · http://www.frostbrowntodd.com · Lexington Financial Center, Suite 2800 · 250 West Main Street · Lexington, KY 40507-1749 · 859-231-0000

Louisville

John A. Bartlett · Stites & Harbison · http://www.stites.com · 400 West Market Street, Suite 1800 · Louisville, KY 40202-3352 · 502-587-3400

Mark C. Blackwell · ⑩ · Wyatt, Tarrant & Combs · http://www.wyattfirm.com · PNC Plaza, Suite 2800 · 500 West Jefferson Street · Louisville, KY 40202-2898 · 502-589-5235

Mary G. Eaves · ⑩ · Greenebaum Doll & McDonald · http://www.gdm.com · National City Tower, Suite 3500 · 101 South Fifth Street · Louisville, KY 40202-3140 · 502-589-4200

Sheldon G. Gilman · Lynch, Cox, Gilman & Mahan · 500 West Jefferson Street, Suite 2100 · Louisville, KY 40202 · 502-589-4215

G. Alexander Hamilton · ⑳ · Wyatt, Tarrant & Combs · http://www.wyattfirm.com · PNC Plaza, Suite 2800 · 500 West Jefferson Street · Louisville, KY 40202-2898 · 502-589-5235

Sharon A. Mattingly · ⑩ · Stoll Keenon Ogden · http://www.skofirm.com · PNC Plaza, Suite 2000 · 500 West Jefferson Street · Louisville, KY 40202-2828 · 502-333-6000

Alan D. Pauw · Reed Weitkamp Schell & Vice · http://www.rwsvlaw.com · 500 West Jefferson Street, Suite 2400 · Louisville, KY 40202 · 502-589-1000

Debbie Reiss Hardesty · ⑩ · Frost Brown Todd · http://www.frostbrowntodd.com · 400 West Market Street, 32nd Floor · Louisville, KY 40202-3363 · 502-589-5400

George B. Sanders, Jr. · ⑩ · Stites & Harbison · http://www.stites.com · 400 West Market Street, Suite 1800 · Louisville, KY 40202-3352 · 502-587-3400

Ivan J. Schell · ⑳ · Reed Weitkamp Schell & Vice · http://www.rwsvlaw.com · 500 West Jefferson Street, Suite 2400 · Louisville, KY 40202 · 502-589-1000

Alison M. Stemler · Frost Brown Todd · http://www.frostbrowntodd.com · 400 West Market Street, 32nd Floor · Louisville, KY 40202-3363 · 502-589-5400

Gordon B. Wright · Wyatt, Tarrant & Combs · http://www.wyattfirm.com · PNC Plaza, Suite 2800 · 500 West Jefferson Street · Louisville, KY 40202-2898 · 502-589-5235

ENERGY LAW

Frankfort

Bruce F. Clark · ⑩ · Stites & Harbison · http://www.stites.com · 421 West Main Street · P.O. Box 634 · Frankfort, KY 40602-0634 · 502-223-3477

Mark Overstreet · ⑩ · Stites & Harbison · http://www.stites.com · 421 West Main Street · P.O. Box 634 · Frankfort, KY 40602-0634 · 502-223-3477

Lexington

Stephen G. Allen · Stites & Harbison · http://www.stites.com · 250 West Main Street, Suite 2300 · Lexington, KY 40507-1758 · 859-226-2300

Bruce E. Cryder · ⑩ · Greenebaum Doll & McDonald · http://www.gdm.com · 300 West Vine Street, Suite 1100 · Lexington, KY 40507-1622 · 859-231-8500

Chauncey S. R. Curtz · ⑩ · Dinsmore & Shohl · http://www.dinslaw.com · Lexington Financial Center, Suite 1400 · 250 West Main Street · Lexington, KY 40507 · 859-425-1000

William T. Gorton III · Stites & Harbison · http://www.stites.com · 250 West Main Street, Suite 2300 · Lexington, KY 40507-1758 · 859-226-2300

Warren J. Hoffmann · Frost Brown Todd · http://www.frostbrowntodd.com · Lexington Financial Center, Suite 2800 · 250 West Main Street · Lexington, KY 40507-1749 · 859-231-0000

Lindsey W. Ingram, Jr. · Stoll Keenon Ogden · http://www.skofirm.com · 300 West Vine Street, Suite 2100 · Lexington, KY 40507-1801 · 859-231-3000

Thomas E. Meng · Stites & Harbison · http://www.stites.com · 250 West Main Street, Suite 2300 · Lexington, KY 40507-1758 · 859-226-2300

Marco M. Rajkovich, Jr. · Rajkovich, Williams, Kilpatrick and True · 2333 Alumni Park Plaza, Suite 310 · Lexington, KY 40517 · 859-245-1059

John R. Rhorer, Jr. · ⑩ · Dinsmore & Shohl · http://www.dinslaw.com · Lexington Financial Center, Suite 1400 · 250 West Main Street · Lexington, KY 40507 · 859-425-1000

Gregory R. Schaaf · Greenebaum Doll & McDonald · http://www.gdm.com · 300 West Vine Street, Suite 1100 · Lexington, KY 40507-1622 · 859-231-8500

Richard C. Ward · ⑩ · Wyatt, Tarrant & Combs · http://www.wyattfirm.com · Lexington Financial Center, Suite 1600 · 250 West Main Street · Lexington, KY 40507 · 859-233-2012

Robert M. Watt III · Stoll Keenon Ogden · http://www.skofirm.com · 300 West Vine Street, Suite 2100 · Lexington, KY 40507-1801 · 859-231-3000

Joseph J. Zaluski · ⑳ · Wyatt, Tarrant & Combs · http://www.wyattfirm.com · Lexington Financial Center, Suite 1600 · 250 West Main Street · Lexington, KY 40507 · 859-233-2012

Louisville

C. Kent Hatfield · ⑩ · Stoll Keenon Ogden · http://www.skofirm.com · PNC Plaza, Suite 2000 · 500 West Jefferson Street · Louisville, KY 40202-2828 · 502-333-6000

Kendrick R. Riggs · ⑩ · Stoll Keenon Ogden · http://www.skofirm.com · PNC Plaza, Suite 2000 · 500 West Jefferson Street · Louisville, KY 40202-2828 · 502-333-6000

Pikeville

Charles J. Baird · Baird & Baird · 162 Second Street · P.O. Box 351 · Pikeville, KY 41502 · 606-437-6276

ENVIRONMENTAL LAW

Bowling Green

LaJuana S. Wilcher · English, Lucas, Priest & Owsley · 1101 College Street · P.O. Box 770 · Bowling Green, KY 42102-0770 · 270-781-6500

Frankfort

Carl W. Breeding · ⑩ · Greenebaum Doll & McDonald · http://www.gdm.com · 229 West Main Street, Suite 101 · Frankfort, KY 40601-1847 · 502-875-0050

Lloyd R. Cress, Jr. · Greenebaum Doll & McDonald · http://www.gdm.com · 229 West Main Street, Suite 101 · Frankfort, KY 40601-1847 · 502-875-0050

Lexington

Stephen G. Allen · Stites & Harbison · http://www.stites.com · 250 West Main Street, Suite 2300 · Lexington, KY 40507-1758 · 859-226-2300

John C. Bender · ⑩ · Greenebaum Doll & McDonald · http://www.gdm.com · 300 West Vine Street, Suite 1100 · Lexington, KY 40507-1622 · 859-231-8500

Carolyn M. Brown · ⑩ · Greenebaum Doll & McDonald · http://www.gdm.com · 300 West Vine Street, Suite 1100 · Lexington, KY 40507-1622 · 859-231-8500

Martin J. Cunningham · Greenebaum Doll & McDonald · http://www.gdm.com · 300 West Vine Street, Suite 1100 · Lexington, KY 40507-1622 · 859-231-8500

W. Blaine Early III · Stites & Harbison · http://www.stites.com · 250 West Main Street, Suite 2300 · Lexington, KY 40507-1758 · 859-226-2300

Laura D. Keller · Stites & Harbison · http://www.stites.com · 250 West Main Street, Suite 2300 · Lexington, KY 40507-1758 · 859-226-2300

Thomas E. Meng · Stites & Harbison · http://www.stites.com · 250 West Main Street, Suite 2300 · Lexington, KY 40507-1758 · 859-226-2300

Marco M. Rajkovich, Jr. · Rajkovich, Williams, Kilpatrick and True · 2333 Alumni Park Plaza, Suite 310 · Lexington, KY 40517 · 859-245-1059

Joseph J. Zaluski · ⑳ · Wyatt, Tarrant & Combs · http://www.wyattfirm.com · Lexington Financial Center, Suite 1600 · 250 West Main Street · Lexington, KY 40507 · 859-233-2012

Louisville

Dennis J. Conniff · Frost Brown Todd · http://www.frostbrowntodd.com · 400 West Market Street, 32nd Floor · Louisville, KY 40202-3363 · 502-589-5400

Bradley E. Dillon · Greenebaum Doll & McDonald · http://www.gdm.com · National City Tower, Suite 3500 · 101 South Fifth Street · Louisville, KY 40202-3140 · 502-589-4200

Timothy J. Hagerty · Frost Brown Todd · http://www.frostbrowntodd.com · 400 West Market Street, 32nd Floor · Louisville, KY 40202-3363 · 502-589-5400

H. Carl Horneman · Wyatt, Tarrant & Combs · http://www.wyattfirm.com · PNC Plaza, Suite 2800 · 500 West Jefferson Street · Louisville, KY 40202-2898 · 502-589-5235

W. Patrick Stallard · Stites & Harbison · http://www.stites.com · 400 West Market Street, Suite 1800 · Louisville, KY 40202-3352 · 502-587-3400

FAMILY LAW

Frankfort

Steven G. Bolton · ⑩ · Bolton Law Office · 413 Shelby Street · P.O. Box 502 · Frankfort, KY 40602 · 502-227-2001

Lexington

Glen S. Bagby · ⑩ · Woodward, Hobson & Fulton · http://www.whf-law.com · 200 West Vine Street, Fifth Floor · P.O. Box 1720 · Lexington, KY 40588-1720 · 859-244-7100

Anita M. Britton · Stoll Keenon Ogden · http://www.skofirm.com · 300 West Vine Street, Suite 2100 · Lexington, KY 40507-1801 · 859-231-3000

W. Stokes Harris, Jr. · ⑩ · Harris & Johnson · 177 North Limestone · Lexington, KY 40507 · 859-255-2039

Crystal L. Osborne · Stoll Keenon Ogden · http://www.skofirm.com · 300 West Vine Street, Suite 2100 · Lexington, KY 40507-1801 · 859-231-3000

Martha A. Rosenberg · Rosenberg Law Office · 183 North Upper Street · Lexington, KY 40507 · 859-233-7972

Natalie S. Wilson · ⑳ · Gess Mattingly & Atchison · 201 West Short Street · Lexington, KY 40507-1269 · 859-252-9000

Catesby Woodford · ⑩ · Miller, Griffin & Marks · Security Trust Building, Suite 600 · 271 West Short Street · Lexington, KY 40507 · 859-255-6676

Louisville

Mitchell A. Charney · ⑩ · Goldberg & Simpson · 9301 Dayflower Street · Louisville, KY 40059 · 502-589-4440

Laurel S. Doheny · Greenebaum Doll & McDonald · http://www.gdm.com · National City Tower, Suite 3500 · 101 South Fifth Street · Louisville, KY 40202-3140 · 502-589-4200

Margaret E. Keane · ⑩ · Greenebaum Doll & McDonald · http://www.gdm.com · National City Tower, Suite 3500 · 101 South Fifth Street · Louisville, KY 40202-3140 · 502-589-4200

Mark Mulloy · Mulloy and Mulloy · First Trust Centre, Suite 400 North · 200 South Fifth Street · Louisville, KY 40202 · 502-583-1895

Ann B. Oldfather · ⑩ · Oldfather Law Firm · http://www.oldfather.com · 1330 South Third Street · Louisville, KY 40208 · 502-637-7200

Diana L. Skaggs · Diana L. Skaggs + Associates · http://www.louisvilledivorce.com · 623 West Main Street · Louisville, KY 40202 · 502-562-0050

FAMILY LAW MEDIATION

Lexington

Suzanne Baumgardner · Dawahare & Kershaw · 333 West Vine Street, Suite 1201 · Lexington, KY 40507 · 859-381-1145

Valerie S. Kershaw · Dawahare & Kershaw · 333 West Vine Street, Suite 1201 · Lexington, KY 40507 · 859-381-1145

Martha A. Rosenberg · Rosenberg Law Office · 183 North Upper Street · Lexington, KY 40507 · 859-233-7972

Catesby Woodford · ⑩ · Miller, Griffin & Marks · Security Trust Building, Suite 600 · 271 West Short Street · Lexington, KY 40507 · 859-255-6676

FIRST AMENDMENT LAW

Lexington

Robert F. Houlihan, Jr. · ⑩ · Savage, Elliott, Houlihan, Moore, Mullins & Erdmann · PNC Bank Plaza, Suite 810 · 200 West Vine Street · Lexington, KY 40507 · 859-233-2700

Louisville

Jon L. Fleischaker · ⑩ · Dinsmore & Shohl · http://www.dinslaw.com · 1400 PNC Plaza · 500 West Jefferson Street · Louisville, KY 40202 · 502-540-2300

GOVERNMENT RELATIONS LAW

Covington

Thomas R. Nienaber · Berger, Cox & Nienaber · 401 Madison Avenue · Covington, KY 41011 · 859-491-9088

Frankfort

Carl W. Breeding · ⑩ · Greenebaum Doll & McDonald · http://www.gdm.com · 229 West Main Street, Suite 101 · Frankfort, KY 40601-1847 · 502-875-0050

HEALTH CARE LAW

Crestview Hills

Gerald E. Benzinger · ⑩ · Deters, Benzinger & LaVelle · 207 Thomas More Parkway · Crestview Hills, KY 41017-2596 · 859-341-1881

James A. Dietz · Deters, Benzinger & LaVelle · 207 Thomas More Parkway · Crestview Hills, KY 41017-2596 · 859-341-1881

Mathew R. Klein, Jr. · Deters, Benzinger & LaVelle · 207 Thomas More Parkway · Crestview Hills, KY 41017-2596 · 859-341-1881

Robert G. Stevens · ⑩ · Deters, Benzinger & LaVelle · 207 Thomas More Parkway · Crestview Hills, KY 41017-2596 · 859-341-1881

Flemingsburg

Frank H. McCartney · ⑩ · Suit, McCartney, Price, Price & Ruark · 207 Court Square · Flemingsburg, KY 41041 · 606-849-2338

Frankfort

Marie Alagia Cull · ⑩ · Cull, Hayden & Vance · 210 Washington Street · P.O. Box 1515 · Frankfort, KY 40602-1515 · 502-226-4157

Marian J. Hayden · Cull, Hayden & Vance · 210 Washington Street · P.O. Box 1515 · Frankfort, KY 40602-1515 · 502-226-4157

David H. Vance · Cull, Hayden & Vance · 210 Washington Street · P.O. Box 1515 · Frankfort, KY 40602-1515 · 502-226-4157

Lexington

Mike D. Baker · ⑩ · Wyatt, Tarrant & Combs · http://www.wyattfirm.com · Lexington Financial Center, Suite 1600 · 250 West Main Street · Lexington, KY 40507 · 859-233-2012

Janet A. Craig · ⑩ · Stites & Harbison · http://www.stites.com · 250 West Main Street, Suite 2300 · Lexington, KY 40507-1758 · 859-226-2300

David T. Enlow · ⑩ · Enlow & Enlow · 1850 Lexington Financial Center · 250 West Main Street · Lexington, KY 40507 · 859-252-0851

William A. Hoskins III · Jackson Kelly · 175 East Main Street · Lexington, KY 40507 · 859-255-9500

Phillip D. Scott · Greenebaum Doll & McDonald · http://www.gdm.com · 300 West Vine Street, Suite 1100 · Lexington, KY 40507-1622 · 859-231-8500

Dean T. Wellman · Piper, Wellman & Bowers · 147 East Third Street, Suite 150 · Lexington, KY 40508 · 859-231-1012

Louisville

Vickie Yates Brown · Greenebaum Doll & McDonald · http://www.gdm.com · National City Tower, Suite 3500 · 101 South Fifth Street · Louisville, KY 40202-3140 · 502-589-4200

J. Larry Cashen · ⑩ · Wyatt, Tarrant & Combs · http://www.wyattfirm.com · PNC Plaza, Suite 2800 · 500 West Jefferson Street · Louisville, KY 40202-2898 · 502-589-5235

Mary Zeller Wing Ceridan · ⑩ · Sturm, Paletti & Wilson · 713 East Market Street, Suite 100 · Louisville, KY 40202 · 502-589-9254

Carole D. Christian · ⑩ · Wyatt, Tarrant & Combs · http://www.wyattfirm.com · PNC Plaza, Suite 2800 · 500 West Jefferson Street · Louisville, KY 40202-2898 · 502-589-5235

Charles J. Cronan IV · ⑩ · Stites & Harbison · http://www.stites.com · 400 West Market Street, Suite 1800 · Louisville, KY 40202-3352 · 502-587-3400

John R. Cummins · ⑳ · Greenebaum Doll & McDonald · http://www.gdm.com · National City Tower, Suite 3500 · 101 South Fifth Street · Louisville, KY 40202-3140 · 502-589-4200

Barbara Reid Hartung · Greenebaum Doll & McDonald · http://www.gdm.com · National City Tower, Suite 3500 · 101 South Fifth Street · Louisville, KY 40202-3140 · 502-589-4200

Thomas A. Hoy · ⑩ · Woodward, Hobson & Fulton · http://www.whf-law.com · 2500 National City Tower · 101 South Fifth Street · Louisville, KY 40202-3175 · 502-581-8000

Kathie McDonald-McClure · Wyatt, Tarrant & Combs · http://www.wyattfirm.com · PNC Plaza, Suite 2800 · 500 West Jefferson Street · Louisville, KY 40202-2898 · 502-589-5235

Theodore T. Myre · Wyatt, Tarrant & Combs · http://www.wyattfirm.com · PNC Plaza, Suite 2800 · 500 West Jefferson Street · Louisville, KY 40202-2898 · 502-589-5235

Stephen R. Price, Sr. · Wyatt, Tarrant & Combs · http://www.wyattfirm.com · PNC Plaza, Suite 2800 · 500 West Jefferson Street · Louisville, KY 40202-2898 · 502-589-5235

Rene Remek Savarise · Hall, Render, Killian, Heath & Lyman · 614 West Main Street, Suite 4000 · Louisville, KY 40202 · 502-568-1890

IMMIGRATION LAW

Lexington

Glen M. Krebs · ⑩ · Wyatt, Tarrant & Combs · http://www.wyattfirm.com · Lexington Financial Center, Suite 1600 · 250 West Main Street · Lexington, KY 40507 · 859-233-2012

Louisville

J. Gregory Clare · ⑩ · Wetterer and Clare · 2933 Bowman Avenue · Louisville, KY 40205 · 502-451-3030

Rusty O'Brien · Clare & O'Brien · 745 West Main Street, Suite 500 · Louisville, KY 40202 · 502-587-7400

Danny L. Owens · ⑩ · Frost Brown Todd · http://www.frostbrowntodd.com · 400 West Market Street, 32nd Floor · Louisville, KY 40202-3363 · 502-589-5400

Ron Russell · Russell Immigration Law Firm · 1012 South Fourth Street · Louisville, KY 40203 · 502-587-7791

INFORMATION TECHNOLOGY LAW

Louisville

Joel T. Beres · Stites & Harbison · http://www.stites.com · 400 West Market Street, Suite 1800 · Louisville, KY 40202-3352 · 502-587-3400

Charles R. Keeton · Frost Brown Todd · http://www.frostbrowntodd.com · 400 West Market Street, 32nd Floor · Louisville, KY 40202-3363 · 502-589-5400

Cynthia L. Stewart · Frost Brown Todd · http://www.frostbrowntodd.com · 400 West Market Street, 32nd Floor · Louisville, KY 40202-3363 · 502-589-5400

Kenneth J. Tuggle · ㉕ · Frost Brown Todd · http://www.frostbrowntodd.com · 400 West Market Street, 32nd Floor · Louisville, KY 40202-3363 · 502-589-5400

INSURANCE LAW

Bowling Green

Joe B. Campbell · ⑩ · Joe B. Campbell · 1011 Lehman Avenue, Suite 105 · Bowling Green, KY 42103 · 270-782-8228

Lexington

Guy R. Colson · Fowler, Measle & Bell · http://www.fmblaw.com · 300 West Vine Street, Suite 600 · Lexington, KY 40507-1660 · 859-252-6700

D. Craig Dance · Greenebaum Doll & McDonald · http://www.gdm.com · 300 West Vine Street, Suite 1100 · Lexington, KY 40507-1622 · 859-231-8500

Greg E. Mitchell · Frost Brown Todd · http://www.frostbrowntodd.com · Lexington Financial Center, Suite 2800 · 250 West Main Street · Lexington, KY 40507-1749 · 859-231-0000

Louisville

Barbara Reid Hartung · Greenebaum Doll & McDonald · http://www.gdm.com · National City Tower, Suite 3500 · 101 South Fifth Street · Louisville, KY 40202-3140 · 502-589-4200

David B. Tachau · Tachau Meek · 2400 National City Tower · 101 South Fifth Street · Louisville, KY 40202-3115 · 502-238-9900

INTELLECTUAL PROPERTY LAW

Lexington

J. Ralph King · ⑩ · King and Schickli · 247 North Broadway · Lexington, KY 40507 · 859-252-0889

Louisville

Joel T. Beres · Stites & Harbison · http://www.stites.com · 400 West Market Street, Suite 1800 · Louisville, KY 40202-3352 · 502-587-3400

Amy B. Berge · Greenebaum Doll & McDonald · http://www.gdm.com · National City Tower, Suite 3500 101 South Fifth Street · Louisville, KY 40202-3140 · 502-589-4200

James C. Eaves, Jr. · Greenebaum Doll & McDonald · http://www.gdm.com · National City Tower, Suite 3500 · 101 South Fifth Street · Louisville, KY 40202-3140 · 502-589-4200

James R. Higgins, Jr. · ⑩ · Middleton Reutlinger · Brown & Williamson Tower, Suite 2500 · 401 South Fourth Street · Louisville, KY 40202-3410 · 502-584-1135

William H. Hollander · Wyatt, Tarrant & Combs · http://www.wyattfirm.com · PNC Plaza, Suite 2800 · 500 West Jefferson Street · Louisville, KY 40202-2898 · 502-589-5235

Charles G. Lamb, Jr. · ⑩ · Middleton Reutlinger · Brown & Williamson Tower, Suite 2500 · 401 South Fourth Street · Louisville, KY 40202-3410 · 502-584-1135

John F. Salazar · Middleton Reutlinger · Brown & Williamson Tower, Suite 2500 · 401 South Fourth Street · Louisville, KY 40202-3410 · 502-584-1135

Cynthia L. Stewart · Frost Brown Todd · http://www.frostbrowntodd.com · 400 West Market Street, 32nd Floor · Louisville, KY 40202-3363 · 502-589-5400

Jack A. Wheat · Stites & Harbison · http://www.stites.com · 400 West Market Street, Suite 1800 · Louisville, KY 40202-3352 · 502-587-3400

LABOR AND EMPLOYMENT LAW

Covington

Robert D. Hudson · Greenebaum Doll & McDonald · http://www.gdm.com · 1800 RiverCenter I · 50 East RiverCenter Boulevard · Covington, KY 41011-1660 · 859-655-4200

Lexington

Stephen L. Barker · Sturgill, Turner, Barker & Moloney · 333 West Vine Street, Suite 1400 · Lexington, KY 40507 · 859-255-8581

Wendy Bryant Becker · Greenebaum Doll & McDonald · http://www.gdm.com · 300 West Vine Street, Suite 1100 · Lexington, KY 40507-1622 · 859-231-8500

Arthur L. Brooks · ⑩ · Brooks, McComb & Fields · 1204 Winchester Road, Suite 100 · Lexington, KY 40505 · 859-233-3366

Debra H. Dawahare · Wyatt, Tarrant & Combs · http://www.wyattfirm.com · Lexington Financial Center, Suite 1600 · 250 West Main Street · Lexington, KY 40507 · 859-233-2012

Richard G. Griffith · Stoll Keenon Ogden · http://www.skofirm.com · 300 West Vine Street, Suite 2100 · Lexington, KY 40507-1801 · 859-231-3000

Douglas L. McSwain · Sturgill, Turner, Barker & Moloney · 333 West Vine Street, Suite 1400 · Lexington, KY 40507 · 859-255-8581

Christopher D. Miller · Rambicure & Miller · 219 East High Street · P.O. Box 34188 · Lexington, KY 40588-4188 · 859-253-6713

George J. Miller · Wyatt, Tarrant & Combs · http://www.wyattfirm.com · Lexington Financial Center, Suite 1600 · 250 West Main Street · Lexington, KY 40507 · 859-233-2012

W. Keith Ransdell · Ransdell and Roach · 176 Pasadena Drive, Building One · Lexington, KY 40503 · 859-276-6262

John Roach · Ransdell and Roach · 176 Pasadena Drive, Building One · Lexington, KY 40503 · 859-276-6262

Susan C. Sears · Dinsmore & Shohl · http://www.dinslaw.com · Lexington Financial Center, Suite 1400 · 250 West Main Street · Lexington, KY 40507 · 859-425-1000

Richard C. Stephenson · Stoll Keenon Ogden · http://www.skofirm.com · 300 West Vine Street, Suite 2100 · Lexington, KY 40507-1801 · 859-231-3000

Donald P. Wagner · Stoll Keenon Ogden · http://www.skofirm.com · 300 West Vine Street, Suite 2100 · Lexington, KY 40507-1801 · 859-231-3000

Louisville

Oliver H. Barber, Jr. · Barber Banaszynski & Glidewell · 100 North Sixth Street, Fifth Floor · Louisville, KY 40202 · 502-585-2100

Thomas J. Birchfield · Greenebaum Doll & McDonald · http://www.gdm.com · National City Tower, Suite 3500 · 101 South Fifth Street · Louisville, KY 40202-3140 · 502-589-4200

Richard S. Cleary · Greenebaum Doll & McDonald · http://www.gdm.com · National City Tower, Suite 3500 · 101 South Fifth Street · Louisville, KY 40202-3140 · 502-589-4200

James D. Cockrum · Frost Brown Todd · http://www.frostbrowntodd.com · 400 West Market Street, 32nd Floor · Louisville, KY 40202-3363 · 502-589-5400

Tony C. Coleman · Frost Brown Todd · http://www.frostbrowntodd.com · 400 West Market Street, 32nd Floor · Louisville, KY 40202-3363 · 502-589-5400

Irwin H. Cutler, Jr. · ⑩ · Priddy, Cutler, Miller & Meade · 800 Republic Building · 429 West Muhammad Ali Boulevard · Louisville, KY 40202 · 502-569-2741

Raymond C. Haley · Woodward, Hobson & Fulton · http://www.whf-law.com · 2500 National City Tower 101 South Fifth Street · Louisville, KY 40202-3175 · 502-581-8000

Edwin S. Hopson · Wyatt, Tarrant & Combs · http://www.wyattfirm.com · PNC Plaza, Suite 2800 · 500 West Jefferson Street · Louisville, KY 40202-2898 · 502-589-5235

Michael K. Kirk · Wyatt, Tarrant & Combs · http://www.wyattfirm.com · PNC Plaza, Suite 2800 · 500 West Jefferson Street · Louisville, KY 40202-2898 · 502-589-5235

John T. Lovett · ⑩ · Frost Brown Todd · http://www.frostbrowntodd.com · 400 West Market Street, 32nd Floor · Louisville, KY 40202-3363 · 502-589-5400

Don C. Meade · Priddy, Cutler, Miller & Meade · 800 Republic Building · 429 West Muhammad Ali Boulevard · Louisville, KY 40202 · 502-569-2741

D. Patton Pelfrey · ㉕ · Frost Brown Todd · http://www.frostbrowntodd.com · 400 West Market Street, 32nd Floor · Louisville, KY 40202-3363 · 502-589-5400

Donna King Perry · Woodward, Hobson & Fulton · http://www.whf-law.com · 2500 National City Tower 101 South Fifth Street · Louisville, KY 40202-3175 · 502-581-8000

Alton D. Priddy · 20 · Priddy, Cutler, Miller & Meade · 800 Republic Building · 429 West Muhammad Ali Boulevard · Louisville, KY 40202 · 502-569-2741

Kathryn A. Quesenberry · Woodward, Hobson & Fulton · http://www.whf-law.com · 2500 National City Tower · 101 South Fifth Street · Louisville, KY 40202-3175 · 502-581-8000

Walter L. Sales · 10 · Stoll Keenon Ogden · http://www.skofirm.com · PNC Plaza, Suite 2000 · 500 West Jefferson Street · Louisville, KY 40202-2828 · 502-333-6000

Jeffrey A. Savarise · Greenebaum Doll & McDonald · http://www.gdm.com · National City Tower, Suite 3500 · 101 South Fifth Street · Louisville, KY 40202-3140 · 502-589-4200

Herbert L. Segal · 25 · Segal, Lindsay & Janes · 515 Park Avenue · Louisville, KY 40208 · 502-568-5600

James U. Smith III · 20 · Smith and Smith · 300 South First Trust Centre · 200 South Fifth Street · Louisville, KY 40202 · 502-587-0761

W. Kevin Smith · Smith and Smith · 300 South First Trust Centre · 200 South Fifth Street · Louisville, KY 40202 · 502-587-0761

Thomas M. Williams · Stoll Keenon Ogden · http://www.skofirm.com · PNC Plaza, Suite 2000 · 500 West Jefferson Street · Louisville, KY 40202-2828 · 502-333-6000

C. Laurence Woods III · 10 · Frost Brown Todd · http://www.frostbrowntodd.com · 400 West Market Street, 32nd Floor · Louisville, KY 40202-3363 · 502-589-5400

LAND USE & ZONING LAW

Lexington

William M. Lear, Jr. · 20 · Stoll Keenon Ogden · http://www.skofirm.com · 300 West Vine Street, Suite 2100 · Lexington, KY 40507-1801 · 859-231-3000

Stephen M. Ruschell · Stites & Harbison · http://www.stites.com · 250 West Main Street, Suite 2300 · Lexington, KY 40507-1758 · 859-226-2300

Job D. Turner III · Greenebaum Doll & McDonald · http://www.gdm.com · 300 West Vine Street, Suite 1100 · Lexington, KY 40507-1622 · 859-231-8500

Rena G. Wiseman · 10 · Stoll Keenon Ogden · http://www.skofirm.com · 300 West Vine Street, Suite 2100 Lexington, KY 40507-1801 · 859-231-3000

Louisville

William B. Bardenwerper · Bardenwerper Talbott & Roberts · http://www.bardlaw.net · 8311 Shelbyville Road · Louisville, KY 40222 · 502-426-6688

Deborah A. Bilitski · Wyatt, Tarrant & Combs · http://www.wyattfirm.com · PNC Plaza, Suite 2800 · 500 West Jefferson Street · Louisville, KY 40202-2898 · 502-589-5235

Alfred S. Joseph III · 25 · Stites & Harbison · http://www.stites.com · 400 West Market Street, Suite 1800 Louisville, KY 40202-3352 · 502-587-3400

Glenn A. Price, Jr. · 10 · Frost Brown Todd · http://www.frostbrowntodd.com · 400 West Market Street, 32nd Floor · Louisville, KY 40202-3363 · 502-589-5400

Paul B. Whitty · ⑩ · Greenebaum Doll & McDonald · http://www.gdm.com · National City Tower, Suite 3500 · 101 South Fifth Street · Louisville, KY 40202-3140 · 502-589-4200

LEGAL MALPRACTICE LAW

Louisville

Elizabeth U. Mendel · Woodward, Hobson & Fulton · http://www.whf-law.com · 2500 National City Tower · 101 South Fifth Street · Louisville, KY 40202-3175 · 502-581-8000

Ann B. Oldfather · ⑩ · Oldfather Law Firm · http://www.oldfather.com · 1330 South Third Street · Louisville, KY 40208 · 502-637-7200

Raymond G. Smith · Boehl Stopher & Graves · AEGON Center, Suite 2300 · 400 West Market Street · Louisville, KY 40202 · 502-589-5980

Edward H. Stopher · ㉕ · Boehl Stopher & Graves · AEGON Center, Suite 2300 · 400 West Market Street · Louisville, KY 40202 · 502-589-5980

Gary M. Weiss · ⑩ · Weiss & Cobb · PNC Building, 16th Floor · 500 West Jefferson Street · Louisville, KY 40220 · 502-493-1394

Prospect

Douglas H. Morris II · ⑩ · Morris & Player · http://www.morrisplayer.com · 5924 Timber Ridge Drive, Suite 202 · Prospect, KY 40052 · 502-228-0664

MASS TORT LITIGATION

Louisville

Carol Dan Browning · Stites & Harbison · http://www.stites.com · 400 West Market Street, Suite 1800 · Louisville, KY 40202-3352 · 502-587-3400

Gregory J. Bubalo · Bubalo, Hiestand & Rotman · http://www.bhtriallaw.com · 401 South Fourth Street, Suite 800 · Louisville, KY 40202 · 502-753-1626

Ann B. Oldfather · ⑩ · Oldfather Law Firm · http://www.oldfather.com · 1330 South Third Street · Louisville, KY 40208 · 502-637-7200

Charles M. Pritchett, Jr. · Frost Brown Todd · http://www.frostbrowntodd.com · 400 West Market Street, 32nd Floor · Louisville, KY 40202-3363 · 502-589-5400

Edward H. Stopher · ㉕ · Boehl Stopher & Graves · AEGON Center, Suite 2300 · 400 West Market Street · Louisville, KY 40202 · 502-589-5980

MEDICAL MALPRACTICE LAW

Bowling Green

John David Cole, Sr. · ⑳ · Cole & Moore · Phoenix Place · 921 College Street · P.O. Box 10240 · Bowling Green, KY 42102-7240 · 270-782-6666

Thomas N. Kerrick · Kerrick, Stivers, Coyle & Van Zant · 1025 State Street · P.O. Box 9547 · Bowling Green, KY 42102-9547 · 270-782-8160

Frank Hampton Moore, Jr. · Cole & Moore · Phoenix Place · 921 College Street · P.O. Box 10240 · Bowling Green, KY 42102-7240 · 270-782-6666

Covington

Mark G. Arnzen · 20 · Arnzen, Wentz, Molloy, Laber & Storm · 600 Greenup Street · P.O. Box 472 · Covington, KY 41012-0472 · 859-431-6100

Richard D. Lawrence · 10 · The Lawrence Firm · 606 Philadelphia Street · Covington, KY 41011 · 859-578-9130

Robert E. Sanders · 10 · The Sanders Law Firm · The Charles H. Fisk House · 1017 Russell Street · Covington, KY 41011 · 859-491-3000

Lexington

Gregory K. Jenkins · Jenkins, Robinson, Epling & Smith · Court Square Building, Suite 100 · 269 West Main Street · Lexington, KY 40507 · 859-225-9625

Mark E. Nichols · Fulkerson, Nichols & Kinkel · 239 North Broadway · Lexington, KY 40507 · 859-253-0523

Margaret M. Pisacano · Jenkins, Robinson, Epling & Smith · Court Square Building, Suite 100 · 269 West Main Street · Lexington, KY 40507 · 859-225-9625

Larry S. Roberts · Larry S. Roberts · 110 West Vine Street · Lexington, KY 40507 · 859-254-4941

Joe C. Savage · 25 · Savage, Elliott, Houlihan, Moore, Mullins & Erdmann · PNC Bank Plaza, Suite 810 · 200 West Vine Street · Lexington, KY 40507 · 859-233-2700

Kenneth W. Smith · Jenkins, Robinson, Epling & Smith · Court Square Building, Suite 100 · 269 West Main Street · Lexington, KY 40507 · 859-225-9625

Louisville

Martin A. Arnett · Phillips Parker Orberson & Moore · 716 West Main Street, Suite 300 · Louisville, KY 40202 · 502-583-9900

John T. Ballantine · 20 · Stoll Keenon Ogden · http://www.skofirm.com · PNC Plaza, Suite 2000 · 500 West Jefferson Street · Louisville, KY 40202-2828 · 502-333-6000

Donald K. Brown, Jr. · O'Bryan, Brown & Toner · http://www.obtlaw.com · Starks Building, Suite 1500 · 455 South Fourth Street · Louisville, KY 40202 · 502-585-4700

Carol Dan Browning · Stites & Harbison · http://www.stites.com · 400 West Market Street, Suite 1800 · Louisville, KY 40202-3352 · 502-587-3400

Donald W. Darby · Darby & Gazak · 3220 Office Point Place, Suite 200 · Louisville, KY 40220 · 502-412-5020

Frank P. Doheny, Jr. · 20 · Dinsmore & Shohl · http://www.dinslaw.com · 1400 PNC Plaza · 500 West Jefferson Street · Louisville, KY 40202 · 502-540-2300

Douglass C. E. Farnsley · Stites & Harbison · http://www.stites.com · 400 West Market Street, Suite 1800 Louisville, KY 40202-3352 · 502-587-3400

Larry B. Franklin · ⑳ · Franklin and Hance · The Speed House · 505 West Ormsby Avenue · Louisville, KY 40203 · 502-637-6000

David B. Gazak · Darby & Gazak · 3220 Office Point Place, Suite 200 · Louisville, KY 40220 · 502-412-5020

James P. Grohmann · O'Bryan, Brown & Toner · http://www.obtlaw.com · Starks Building, Suite 1500 · 455 South Fourth Street · Louisville, KY 40202 · 502-585-4700

Michael R. Hance · Franklin and Hance · The Speed House · 505 West Ormsby Avenue · Louisville, KY 40203 · 502-637-6000

Ron Hillerich · Gary R. Hillerich · Kentucky Home Life Building, Suite 1800 · 239 South Fifth Street · Louisville, KY 40202 · 502-736-8100

Craig Louis Johnson · Whonsetler & Johnson · 6011 Brownsboro Park Boulevard, Suite E · Louisville, KY 40207 · 502-895-2297

W. Gregory King · Stoll Keenon Ogden · http://www.skofirm.com · PNC Plaza, Suite 2000 · 500 West Jefferson Street · Louisville, KY 40202-2828 · 502-333-6000

Christopher P. O'Bryan · O'Bryan, Brown & Toner · http://www.obtlaw.com · Starks Building, Suite 1500 · 455 South Fourth Street · Louisville, KY 40202 · 502-585-4700

Ann B. Oldfather · ⑩ · Oldfather Law Firm · http://www.oldfather.com · 1330 South Third Street · Louisville, KY 40208 · 502-637-7200

John W. Phillips · ⑩ · Phillips Parker Orberson & Moore · 716 West Main Street, Suite 300 · Louisville, KY 40202 · 502-583-9900

Susan D. Phillips · Phillips Parker Orberson & Moore · 716 West Main Street, Suite 300 · Louisville, KY 40202 · 502-583-9900

Gerald R. Toner · O'Bryan, Brown & Toner · http://www.obtlaw.com · Starks Building, Suite 1500 · 455 South Fourth Street · Louisville, KY 40202 · 502-585-4700

Ronald M. Wilt · Dolt, Thompson, Shepherd, Kinney & Wilt · 13800 Lake Point Circle · Louisville, KY 40223 · 502-410-3809

Paducah

Jonathan Freed · Bradley & Freed · 1634 Broadway · Paducah, KY 42001 · 270-443-0040

E. Frederick Straub, Jr. · Whitlow, Roberts, Houston & Straub · Old National Bank Building · 300 Broadway · P.O. Box 995 · Paducah, KY 42002-0995 · 270-443-4516

Prospect

Douglas H. Morris II · ⑩ · Morris & Player · http://www.morrisplayer.com · 5924 Timber Ridge Drive, Suite 202 · Prospect, KY 40052 · 502-228-0664

Somerset

John G. Prather, Jr. · John G. Prather · 48 Public Square · P.O. Box 616 · Somerset, KY 42502 · 606-679-1626

Lexington

Robert M. Beck, Jr. · Stites & Harbison · http://www.stites.com · 250 West Main Street, Suite 2300 · Lexington, KY 40507-1758 · 859-226-2300

Jeffrey L. Hallos · Frost Brown Todd · http://www.frostbrowntodd.com · Lexington Financial Center, Suite 2800 · 250 West Main Street · Lexington, KY 40507-1749 · 859-231-0000

R. David Lester · ⑩ · Stoll Keenon Ogden · http://www.skofirm.com · 300 West Vine Street, Suite 2100 · Lexington, KY 40507-1801 · 859-231-3000

Dan M. Rose · Stoll Keenon Ogden · http://www.skofirm.com · 300 West Vine Street, Suite 2100 · Lexington, KY 40507-1801 · 859-231-3000

Joseph H. Terry · Dinsmore & Shohl · http://www.dinslaw.com · Lexington Financial Center, Suite 1400 250 West Main Street · Lexington, KY 40507 · 859-425-1000

Louisville

P. Richard Anderson, Jr. · Greenebaum Doll & McDonald · http://www.gdm.com · National City Tower, Suite 3500 · 101 South Fifth Street · Louisville, KY 40202-3140 · 502-589-4200

Craig C. Bradley, Jr. · Stites & Harbison · http://www.stites.com · 400 West Market Street, Suite 1800 · Louisville, KY 40202-3352 · 502-587-3400

Brian A. Cromer · Stites & Harbison · http://www.stites.com · 400 West Market Street, Suite 1800 · Louisville, KY 40202-3352 · 502-587-3400

Scott W. Dolson · Frost Brown Todd · http://www.frostbrowntodd.com · 400 West Market Street, 32nd Floor · Louisville, KY 40202-3363 · 502-589-5400

Daniel E. Fisher · Greenebaum Doll & McDonald · http://www.gdm.com · National City Tower, Suite 3500 · 101 South Fifth Street · Louisville, KY 40202-3140 · 502-589-4200

C. Edward Glasscock · ⑩ · Frost Brown Todd · http://www.frostbrowntodd.com · 400 West Market Street, 32nd Floor · Louisville, KY 40202-3363 · 502-589-5400

Michael de León Hawthorne · Greenebaum Doll & McDonald · http://www.gdm.com · National City Tower, Suite 3500 · 101 South Fifth Street · Louisville, KY 40202-3140 · 502-589-4200

Robert A. Heath · Wyatt, Tarrant & Combs · http://www.wyattfirm.com · PNC Plaza, Suite 2800 · 500 West Jefferson Street · Louisville, KY 40202-2898 · 502-589-5235

T. Kennedy Helm III · ⑩ · Stites & Harbison · http://www.stites.com · 400 West Market Street, Suite 1800 · Louisville, KY 40202-3352 · 502-587-3400

Franklin K. Jelsma · Wyatt, Tarrant & Combs · http://www.wyattfirm.com · PNC Plaza, Suite 2800 · 500 West Jefferson Street · Louisville, KY 40202-2898 · 502-589-5235

June N. King · Greenebaum Doll & McDonald · http://www.gdm.com · National City Tower, Suite 3500 · 101 South Fifth Street · Louisville, KY 40202-3140 · 502-589-4200

Peggy B. Lyndrup · ⑩ · Greenebaum Doll & McDonald · http://www.gdm.com · National City Tower, Suite 3500 · 101 South Fifth Street · Louisville, KY 40202-3140 · 502-589-4200

Alan K. MacDonald · Frost Brown Todd · http://www.frostbrowntodd.com · 400 West Market Street, 32nd Floor · Louisville, KY 40202-3363 · 502-589-5400

Patrick Mattingly · Wyatt, Tarrant & Combs · http://www.wyattfirm.com · PNC Plaza, Suite 2800 · 500 West Jefferson Street · Louisville, KY 40202-2898 · 502-589-5235

Patrick R. Northam · Greenebaum Doll & McDonald · http://www.gdm.com · National City Tower, Suite 3500 · 101 South Fifth Street · Louisville, KY 40202-3140 · 502-589-4200

Thomas E. Rutledge · Stoll Keenon Ogden · http://www.skofirm.com · PNC Plaza, Suite 2000 · 500 West Jefferson Street · Louisville, KY 40202-2828 · 502-333-6000

James C. Seiffert · Stites & Harbison · http://www.stites.com · 400 West Market Street, Suite 1800 · Louisville, KY 40202-3352 · 502-587-3400

R. James Straus · ⓾ · Frost Brown Todd · http://www.frostbrowntodd.com · 400 West Market Street, 32nd Floor · Louisville, KY 40202-3363 · 502-589-5400

Patrick J. Welsh · Greenebaum Doll & McDonald · http://www.gdm.com · National City Tower, Suite 3500 · 101 South Fifth Street · Louisville, KY 40202-3140 · 502-589-4200

Cynthia W. Young · Wyatt, Tarrant & Combs · http://www.wyattfirm.com · PNC Plaza, Suite 2800 · 500 West Jefferson Street · Louisville, KY 40202-2898 · 502-589-5235

MINING LAW

Lexington

Stephen G. Allen · Stites & Harbison · http://www.stites.com · 250 West Main Street, Suite 2300 · Lexington, KY 40507-1758 · 859-226-2300

Bruce E. Cryder · ⓾ · Greenebaum Doll & McDonald · http://www.gdm.com · 300 West Vine Street, Suite 1100 · Lexington, KY 40507-1622 · 859-231-8500

Martin J. Cunningham · Greenebaum Doll & McDonald · http://www.gdm.com · 300 West Vine Street, Suite 1100 · Lexington, KY 40507-1622 · 859-231-8500

Chauncey S. R. Curtz · ⓾ · Dinsmore & Shohl · http://www.dinslaw.com · Lexington Financial Center, Suite 1400 · 250 West Main Street · Lexington, KY 40507 · 859-425-1000

William T. Gorton III · Stites & Harbison · http://www.stites.com · 250 West Main Street, Suite 2300 · Lexington, KY 40507-1758 · 859-226-2300

Karen J. Greenwell · Wyatt, Tarrant & Combs · http://www.wyattfirm.com · Lexington Financial Center, Suite 1600 · 250 West Main Street · Lexington, KY 40507 · 859-233-2012

Warren J. Hoffmann · Frost Brown Todd · http://www.frostbrowntodd.com · Lexington Financial Center, Suite 2800 · 250 West Main Street · Lexington, KY 40507-1749 · 859-231-0000

Thomas E. Meng · Stites & Harbison · http://www.stites.com · 250 West Main Street, Suite 2300 · Lexington, KY 40507-1758 · 859-226-2300

John R. Rhorer, Jr. · ⓾ · Dinsmore & Shohl · http://www.dinslaw.com · Lexington Financial Center, Suite 1400 · 250 West Main Street · Lexington, KY 40507 · 859-425-1000

Jeff A. Woods · Wyatt, Tarrant & Combs · http://www.wyattfirm.com · Lexington Financial Center, Suite 1600 · 250 West Main Street · Lexington, KY 40507 · 859-233-2012

Louisville

Timothy J. Hagerty · Frost Brown Todd · http://www.frostbrowntodd.com · 400 West Market Street, 32nd Floor · Louisville, KY 40202-3363 · 502-589-5400

Pikeville

Charles J. Baird · Baird & Baird · 162 Second Street · P.O. Box 351 · Pikeville, KY 41502 · 606-437-6276

NATURAL RESOURCES LAW

Henderson

David H. Thomason · Stoll Keenon Ogden · http://www.skofirm.com · 201C North Main Street · Henderson, KY 42420 · 270-831-1900

Lexington

Stephen G. Allen · Stites & Harbison · http://www.stites.com · 250 West Main Street, Suite 2300 · Lexington, KY 40507-1758 · 859-226-2300

Bruce E. Cryder · ⑩ · Greenebaum Doll & McDonald · http://www.gdm.com · 300 West Vine Street, Suite 1100 · Lexington, KY 40507-1622 · 859-231-8500

Chauncey S. R. Curtz · ⑩ · Dinsmore & Shohl · http://www.dinslaw.com · Lexington Financial Center, Suite 1400 · 250 West Main Street · Lexington, KY 40507 · 859-425-1000

William T. Gorton III · Stites & Harbison · http://www.stites.com · 250 West Main Street, Suite 2300 · Lexington, KY 40507-1758 · 859-226-2300

Karen J. Greenwell · Wyatt, Tarrant & Combs · http://www.wyattfirm.com · Lexington Financial Center, Suite 1600 · 250 West Main Street · Lexington, KY 40507 · 859-233-2012

Warren J. Hoffmann · Frost Brown Todd · http://www.frostbrowntodd.com · Lexington Financial Center, Suite 2800 · 250 West Main Street · Lexington, KY 40507-1749 · 859-231-0000

Thomas E. Meng · Stites & Harbison · http://www.stites.com · 250 West Main Street, Suite 2300 · Lexington, KY 40507-1758 · 859-226-2300

Marco M. Rajkovich, Jr. · Rajkovich, Williams, Kilpatrick and True · 2333 Alumni Park Plaza, Suite 310 · Lexington, KY 40517 · 859-245-1059

John R. Rhorer, Jr. · ⑩ · Dinsmore & Shohl · http://www.dinslaw.com · Lexington Financial Center, Suite 1400 · 250 West Main Street · Lexington, KY 40507 · 859-425-1000

Richard C. Ward · ⑩ · Wyatt, Tarrant & Combs · http://www.wyattfirm.com · Lexington Financial Center, Suite 1600 · 250 West Main Street · Lexington, KY 40507 · 859-233-2012

NON-WHITE-COLLAR CRIMINAL DEFENSE

Covington

Robert W. Carran · ⑩ · Taliaferro, Mehling, Shirooni, Carran & Keys · 1005 Madison Avenue · Covington, KY 41011-3113 · 859-291-9900

Florence

Wilbur M. Zevely · Busald Funk Zevely · 226 Main Street · P.O. Box 6910 · Florence, KY 41022-6910 · 859-371-3600

Frankfort

William E. Johnson · ㉕ · Johnson, True & Guarnieri · http://www.jtgattorneys.com · 326 West Main Street · Frankfort, KY 40601-1887 · 502-875-6000

J. Guthrie True · ⑩ · Johnson, True & Guarnieri · http://www.jtgattorneys.com · 326 West Main Street · Frankfort, KY 40601-1887 · 502-875-6000

Glasgow

Bobby H. Richardson · Richardson, Gardner, Barrickman & Alexander · 117 East Washington Street · P.O. Box 368 · Glasgow, KY 42142-0368 · 270-651-2116

Lexington

James I. Lowry IV · James I. Lowry IV · Security Trust Building, Suite 812 · 271 West Short Street · Lexington, KY 40507 · 859-233-4441

R. Burl McCoy · ⑩ · Stoll Keenon Ogden · http://www.skofirm.com · 300 West Vine Street, Suite 2100 · Lexington, KY 40507-1801 · 859-231-3000

Larry S. Roberts · Larry S. Roberts · 110 West Vine Street · Lexington, KY 40507 · 859-254-4941

James A. Shuffett · ㉕ · James A. Shuffett · 400 Security Trust Building · 271 West Short Street · Lexington, KY 40507-1292 · 859-252-5794

Kenneth W. Smith · Jenkins, Robinson, Epling & Smith · Court Square Building, Suite 100 · 269 West Main Street · Lexington, KY 40507 · 859-225-9625

Louisville

James Barton Adams, Jr. · James Barton Adams & Associates · 500 Kentucky Home Life Building · 239 South Fifth Street · Louisville, KY 40202 · 502-583-4881

Scott C. Cox · Cox & Mazzoli · 600 West Main Street, Suite 300 · Louisville, KY 40202 · 502-589-6190

David A. Lambertus · ⑩ · Interchange Law Office · 600 West Main Street, Suite 300 · Louisville, KY 40202 · 502-589-6190

John Tim McCall · ⑩ · Interchange Law Office · 600 West Main Street, Suite 300 · Louisville, KY 40202 502-589-6190

Steve Romines · Romines Weis & Young · 600 West Main Street, Suite 100 · Louisville, KY 40202 · 502-587-8822

OIL & GAS LAW

Lexington

Robert M. Watt III · Stoll Keenon Ogden · http://www.skofirm.com · 300 West Vine Street, Suite 2100 · Lexington, KY 40507-1801 · 859-231-3000

Owensboro

Bryan R. Reynolds · Sullivan, Mountjoy, Stainback & Miller · 100 St. Ann Street · P.O. Box 727 · Owensboro, KY 42302 · 270-926-4000

PERSONAL INJURY LITIGATION

Ashland

David O. Welch · David O. Welch · 340 Seventeenth Street · P.O. Box 1653 · Ashland, KY 41105-1653 · 606-325-8446

Barbourville

Samuel E. Davies · ⑩ · Samuel E. Davies · 230 Knox Street · Barbourville, KY 40906 · 606-546-5196

Bowling Green

John David Cole, Sr. · ⑳ · Cole & Moore · Phoenix Place · 921 College Street · P.O. Box 10240 · Bowling Green, KY 42102-7240 · 270-782-6666

Steven D. Downey · Law Offices of Steven D. Downey · 537 East 10th Avenue, Suite 300 · P.O. Box 3250 · Bowling Green, KY 42102 · 270-782-3580

Thomas N. Kerrick · Kerrick, Stivers, Coyle & Van Zant · 1025 State Street · P.O. Box 9547 · Bowling Green, KY 42102-9547 · 270-782-8160

Covington

Mark G. Arnzen · ⑳ · Arnzen, Wentz, Molloy, Laber & Storm · 600 Greenup Street · P.O. Box 472 · Covington, KY 41012-0472 · 859-431-6100

Gerald F. Dusing · ⑩ · Adams, Stepner, Woltermann & Dusing · 40 West Pike Street · P.O. Box 861 · Covington, KY 41012-0861 · 859-394-6200

Richard D. Lawrence · ⑩ · The Lawrence Firm · 606 Philadelphia Street · Covington, KY 41011 · 859-578-9130

Jeffrey C. Mando · ⑩ · Adams, Stepner, Woltermann & Dusing · 40 West Pike Street · P.O. Box 861 · Covington, KY 41012-0861 · 859-394-6200

Mary K. Molloy · Arnzen, Wentz, Molloy, Laber & Storm · 600 Greenup Street · P.O. Box 472 · Covington, KY 41012-0472 · 859-431-6100

Robert E. Sanders · ⑩ · The Sanders Law Firm · The Charles H. Fisk House · 1017 Russell Street · Covington, KY 41011 · 859-491-3000

Donald L. Stepner · ⑩ · Adams, Stepner, Woltermann & Dusing · 40 West Pike Street · P.O. Box 861 · Covington, KY 41012-0861 · 859-394-6200

Jeffrey A. Stepner · Adams, Stepner, Woltermann & Dusing · 40 West Pike Street · P.O. Box 861 · Covington, KY 41012-0861 · 859-394-6200

Beverly R. Storm · Arnzen, Wentz, Molloy, Laber & Storm · 600 Greenup Street · P.O. Box 472 · Covington, KY 41012-0472 · 859-431-6100

Philip Taliaferro III · ⓴ · Taliaferro, Mehling, Shirooni, Carran & Keys · 1005 Madison Avenue · Covington, KY 41011-3113 · 859-291-9900

Edgewood

Harry D. Rankin · Sutton Rankin Law · 130 Dudley Road, Suite 250 · Edgewood, KY 41017 · 859-331-8883

Florence

E. Andre' Busald · ⓴ · Busald Funk Zevely · 226 Main Street · P.O. Box 6910 · Florence, KY 41022-6910 859-371-3600

William J. Kathman, Jr. · ⓾ · Busald Funk Zevely · 226 Main Street · P.O. Box 6910 · Florence, KY 41022-6910 · 859-371-3600

Frankfort

Michael L. Hawkins · Michael L. Hawkins & Associates · 420 Ann Street · Frankfort, KY 40601 · 502-223-3459

Lexington

Charles C. Adams, Jr. · Herren & Adams · 148 North Broadway · Lexington, KY 40507 · 859-254-0024

Perry M. Bentley · Stoll Keenon Ogden · http://www.skofirm.com · 300 West Vine Street, Suite 2100 · Lexington, KY 40507-1801 · 859-231-3000

Larry C. Deener · Landrum & Shouse · 106 West Vine Street, Suite 800 · P.O. Box 951 · Lexington, KY 40588-0951 · 859-255-2424

Robert L. Elliott · ⓾ · Savage, Elliott, Houlihan, Moore, Mullins & Erdmann · PNC Bank Plaza, Suite 810 · 200 West Vine Street · Lexington, KY 40507 · 859-233-2700

John M. Famularo · ⓾ · Stites & Harbison · http://www.stites.com · 250 West Main Street, Suite 2300 · Lexington, KY 40507-1758 · 859-226-2300

William R. Garmer · ⓴ · Garmer & O'Brien · http://www.garmerobrienlaw.com · Opera House Building · 141 North Broadway · Lexington, KY 40507 · 859-254-9352

John G. McNeill · Landrum & Shouse · 106 West Vine Street, Suite 800 · P.O. Box 951 · Lexington, KY 40588-0951 · 859-255-2424

Donald P. Moloney II · ⓾ · Sturgill, Turner, Barker & Moloney · 333 West Vine Street, Suite 1400 · Lexington, KY 40507 · 859-255-8581

Peter Perlman · ⓾ · Peter Perlman Law Offices · 388 South Broadway · Lexington, KY 40508-0251 · 859-253-3919

George C. Piper · ⓾ · Piper, Wellman & Bowers · 147 East Third Street, Suite 150 · Lexington, KY 40508 · 859-231-1012

Larry S. Roberts · Larry S. Roberts · 110 West Vine Street · Lexington, KY 40507 · 859-254-4941

Joe C. Savage · ㉕ · Savage, Elliott, Houlihan, Moore, Mullins & Erdmann · PNC Bank Plaza, Suite 810 · 200 West Vine Street · Lexington, KY 40507 · 859-233-2700

Kenneth W. Smith · Jenkins, Robinson, Epling & Smith · Court Square Building, Suite 100 · 269 West Main Street · Lexington, KY 40507 · 859-225-9625

Linsey W. West · Woodward, Hobson & Fulton · http://www.whf-law.com · 200 West Vine Street, Fifth Floor · P.O. Box 1720 · Lexington, KY 40588-1720 · 859-244-7100

Louisville

John T. Ballantine · ⑳ · Stoll Keenon Ogden · http://www.skofirm.com · PNC Plaza, Suite 2000 · 500 West Jefferson Street · Louisville, KY 40202-2828 · 502-333-6000

Donald K. Brown, Jr. · O'Bryan, Brown & Toner · http://www.obtlaw.com · Starks Building, Suite 1500 · 455 South Fourth Street · Louisville, KY 40202 · 502-585-4700

Carol Dan Browning · Stites & Harbison · http://www.stites.com · 400 West Market Street, Suite 1800 · Louisville, KY 40202-3352 · 502-587-3400

Richard H. C. Clay · Woodward, Hobson & Fulton · http://www.whf-law.com · 2500 National City Tower 101 South Fifth Street · Louisville, KY 40202-3175 · 502-581-8000

F. Thomas Conway · ⑩ · F. Thomas Conway · Kentucky Home Life Building, Suite 1800 · 239 South Fifth Street · Louisville, KY 40202 · 502-736-8100

Charles J. Cronan IV · ⑩ · Stites & Harbison · http://www.stites.com · 400 West Market Street, Suite 1800 · Louisville, KY 40202-3352 · 502-587-3400

Donald W. Darby · Darby & Gazak · 3220 Office Point Place, Suite 200 · Louisville, KY 40220 · 502-412-5020

Frank P. Doheny, Jr. · ⑳ · Dinsmore & Shohl · http://www.dinslaw.com · 1400 PNC Plaza · 500 West Jefferson Street · Louisville, KY 40202 · 502-540-2300

Richard Edwards · Boehl Stopher & Graves · AEGON Center, Suite 2300 · 400 West Market Street · Louisville, KY 40202 · 502-589-5980

Douglass C. E. Farnsley · Stites & Harbison · http://www.stites.com · 400 West Market Street, Suite 1800 Louisville, KY 40202-3352 · 502-587-3400

Larry B. Franklin · ⑳ · Franklin and Hance · The Speed House · 505 West Ormsby Avenue · Louisville, KY 40203 · 502-637-6000

James P. Grohmann · O'Bryan, Brown & Toner · http://www.obtlaw.com · Starks Building, Suite 1500 · 455 South Fourth Street · Louisville, KY 40202 · 502-585-4700

Gary R. Hillerich · ⑩ · Gary R. Hillerich · Kentucky Home Life Building, Suite 1800 · 239 South Fifth Street · Louisville, KY 40202 · 502-736-8100

W. Gregory King · Stoll Keenon Ogden · http://www.skofirm.com · PNC Plaza, Suite 2000 · 500 West Jefferson Street · Louisville, KY 40202-2828 · 502-333-6000

David T. Klapheke · Boehl Stopher & Graves · AEGON Center, Suite 2300 · 400 West Market Street · Louisville, KY 40202 · 502-589-5980

John R. Martin, Jr. · ⑩ · Landrum & Shouse · The LG&E Building, Suite 1900 · 220 West Main Street · Louisville, KY 40202-3349 · 502-589-7616

Winston E. Miller · Frost Brown Todd · http://www.frostbrowntodd.com · 400 West Market Street, 32nd Floor · Louisville, KY 40202-3363 · 502-589-5400

David R. Monohan · Woodward, Hobson & Fulton · http://www.whf-law.com · 2500 National City Tower 101 South Fifth Street · Louisville, KY 40202-3175 · 502-581-8000

Christopher P. O'Bryan · O'Bryan, Brown & Toner · http://www.obtlaw.com · Starks Building, Suite 1500 · 455 South Fourth Street · Louisville, KY 40202 · 502-585-4700

Ann B. Oldfather · ⑩ · Oldfather Law Firm · http://www.oldfather.com · 1330 South Third Street · Louisville, KY 40208 · 502-637-7200

John F. Parker, Jr. · Phillips Parker Orberson & Moore · 716 West Main Street, Suite 300 · Louisville, KY 40202 · 502-583-9900

John W. Phillips · ⑩ · Phillips Parker Orberson & Moore · 716 West Main Street, Suite 300 · Louisville, KY 40202 · 502-583-9900

Susan D. Phillips · Phillips Parker Orberson & Moore · 716 West Main Street, Suite 300 · Louisville, KY 40202 · 502-583-9900

Edward H. Stopher · ㉕ · Boehl Stopher & Graves · AEGON Center, Suite 2300 · 400 West Market Street · Louisville, KY 40202 · 502-589-5980

Robert E. Stopher · Boehl Stopher & Graves · AEGON Center, Suite 2300 · 400 West Market Street · Louisville, KY 40202 · 502-589-5980

John L. Tate · ⑩ · Stites & Harbison · http://www.stites.com · 400 West Market Street, Suite 1800 · Louisville, KY 40202-3352 · 502-587-3400

Tyler S. Thompson · Dolt, Thompson, Shepherd, Kinney & Wilt · 13800 Lake Point Circle · Louisville, KY 40223 · 502-410-3809

Gerald R. Toner · O'Bryan, Brown & Toner · http://www.obtlaw.com · Starks Building, Suite 1500 · 455 South Fourth Street · Louisville, KY 40202 · 502-585-4700

Gary M. Weiss · ⑩ · Weiss & Cobb · PNC Building, 16th Floor · 500 West Jefferson Street · Louisville, KY 40220 · 502-493-1394

R. Kent Westberry · Landrum & Shouse · The LG&E Building, Suite 1900 · 220 West Main Street · Louisville, KY 40202-3349 · 502-589-7616

Owensboro

Charles E. Moore · Moore, Malone & Safreed · 104 East Fourth Street · P.O. Box 549 · Owensboro, KY 42302-0549 · 270-683-4513

Marvin P. Nunley · McCarroll, Nunley & Hartz · 111 East Third Street · P.O. Box 925 · Owensboro, KY 42302-0925 · 270-683-3535

R. Frank Stainback · Sullivan, Mountjoy, Stainback & Miller · 100 St. Ann Street · P.O. Box 727 · Owensboro, KY 42302 · 270-926-4000

Ronald M. Sullivan · Sullivan, Mountjoy, Stainback & Miller · 100 St. Ann Street · P.O. Box 727 · Owensboro, KY 42302 · 270-926-4000

Paducah

J. David Boswell · Boswell, Sims & Vasseur · 425 South Sixth Street · P.O. Box 1265 · Paducah, KY 42002-1265 · 270-442-9237

Richard C. Roberts · Whitlow, Roberts, Houston & Straub · Old National Bank Building · 300 Broadway P.O. Box 995 · Paducah, KY 42002-0995 · 270-443-4516

Richard L. Walter · Boehl Stopher & Graves · 410 Broadway · Paducah, KY 42001 · 270-442-4369

Prospect

Douglas H. Morris II · ⑩ · Morris & Player · http://www.morrisplayer.com · 5924 Timber Ridge Drive, Suite 202 · Prospect, KY 40052 · 502-228-0664

Somerset

Richard W. Hay · ⑩ · Law Office of Richard W. Hay · 203 West Columbia Street · P.O. Box 1124 · Somerset, KY 42502 · 606-679-2214

PRODUCT LIABILITY LITIGATION

Covington

Robert E. Sanders · ⑩ · The Sanders Law Firm · The Charles H. Fisk House · 1017 Russell Street · Covington, KY 41011 · 859-491-3000

Lexington

Perry M. Bentley · Stoll Keenon Ogden · http://www.skofirm.com · 300 West Vine Street, Suite 2100 · Lexington, KY 40507-1801 · 859-231-3000

Robert F. Duncan · Jackson Kelly · 175 East Main Street · Lexington, KY 40507 · 859-255-9500

Peter Perlman · ⑩ · Peter Perlman Law Offices · 388 South Broadway · Lexington, KY 40508-0251 · 859-253-3919

Linsey W. West · Woodward, Hobson & Fulton · http://www.whf-law.com · 200 West Vine Street, Fifth Floor · P.O. Box 1720 · Lexington, KY 40588-1720 · 859-244-7100

Louisville

Carol Dan Browning · Stites & Harbison · http://www.stites.com · 400 West Market Street, Suite 1800 · Louisville, KY 40202-3352 · 502-587-3400

Charles J. Cronan IV · ⑩ · Stites & Harbison · http://www.stites.com · 400 West Market Street, Suite 1800 · Louisville, KY 40202-3352 · 502-587-3400

Frank P. Doheny, Jr. · ⑳ · Dinsmore & Shohl · http://www.dinslaw.com · 1400 PNC Plaza · 500 West Jefferson Street · Louisville, KY 40202 · 502-540-2300

Richard Edwards · Boehl Stopher & Graves · AEGON Center, Suite 2300 · 400 West Market Street · Louisville, KY 40202 · 502-589-5980

Douglass C. E. Farnsley · Stites & Harbison · http://www.stites.com · 400 West Market Street, Suite 1800 Louisville, KY 40202-3352 · 502-587-3400

W. Gregory King · Stoll Keenon Ogden · http://www.skofirm.com · PNC Plaza, Suite 2000 · 500 West Jefferson Street · Louisville, KY 40202-2828 · 502-333-6000

Edward H. Stopher · ㉕ · Boehl Stopher & Graves · AEGON Center, Suite 2300 · 400 West Market Street · Louisville, KY 40202 · 502-589-5980

John L. Tate · ⑩ · Stites & Harbison · http://www.stites.com · 400 West Market Street, Suite 1800 · Louisville, KY 40202-3352 · 502-587-3400

Prospect

Douglas H. Morris II · ⑩ · Morris & Player · http://www.morrisplayer.com · 5924 Timber Ridge Drive, Suite 202 · Prospect, KY 40052 · 502-228-0664

PROFESSIONAL MALPRACTICE LAW

Louisville

John T. Ballantine · ⑳ · Stoll Keenon Ogden · http://www.skofirm.com · PNC Plaza, Suite 2000 · 500 West Jefferson Street · Louisville, KY 40202-2828 · 502-333-6000

W. Gregory King · Stoll Keenon Ogden · http://www.skofirm.com · PNC Plaza, Suite 2000 · 500 West Jefferson Street · Louisville, KY 40202-2828 · 502-333-6000

Ann B. Oldfather · ⑩ · Oldfather Law Firm · http://www.oldfather.com · 1330 South Third Street · Louisville, KY 40208 · 502-637-7200

Edward H. Stopher · ㉕ · Boehl Stopher & Graves · AEGON Center, Suite 2300 · 400 West Market Street · Louisville, KY 40202 · 502-589-5980

Gerald R. Toner · O'Bryan, Brown & Toner · http://www.obtlaw.com · Starks Building, Suite 1500 · 455 South Fourth Street · Louisville, KY 40202 · 502-585-4700

Prospect

Douglas H. Morris II · ⑩ · Morris & Player · http://www.morrisplayer.com · 5924 Timber Ridge Drive, Suite 202 · Prospect, KY 40052 · 502-228-0664

PUBLIC FINANCE LAW

Covington

Roger L. Peterman · Peck, Shaffer · 118 West Fifth Street · Covington, KY 41011 · 859-431-7000

Louisville

Stephen D. Berger · Wyatt, Tarrant & Combs · http://www.wyattfirm.com · PNC Plaza, Suite 2800 · 500 West Jefferson Street · Louisville, KY 40202-2898 · 502-589-5235

William W. Davis · Stoll Keenon Ogden · http://www.skofirm.com · PNC Plaza, Suite 2000 · 500 West Jefferson Street · Louisville, KY 40202-2828 · 502-333-6000

Spencer E. Harper, Jr. · Stoll Keenon Ogden · http://www.skofirm.com · PNC Plaza, Suite 2000 · 500 West Jefferson Street · Louisville, KY 40202-2828 · 502-333-6000

T. Kennedy Helm III · ⑩ · Stites & Harbison · http://www.stites.com · 400 West Market Street, Suite 1800 · Louisville, KY 40202-3352 · 502-587-3400

Alex P. Herrington, Jr. · Stites & Harbison · http://www.stites.com · 400 West Market Street, Suite 1800 Louisville, KY 40202-3352 · 502-587-3400

Charles S. Musson · Rubin & Hays · Kentucky Home Trust Building · 450 South Third Street · Louisville, KY 40202-1410 · 502-569-7525

William L. Skees, Jr. · Frost Brown Todd · http://www.frostbrowntodd.com · 400 West Market Street, 32nd Floor · Louisville, KY 40202-3363 · 502-589-5400

RAILROAD LAW

Ashland

James E. Cleveland III · Huddleston Bolen · 1422 Winchester Avenue · P.O. Box 770 · Ashland, KY 41105 · 606-329-8771

Lexington

Larry C. Deener · Landrum & Shouse · 106 West Vine Street, Suite 800 · P.O. Box 951 · Lexington, KY 40588-0951 · 859-255-2424

Linsey W. West · Woodward, Hobson & Fulton · http://www.whf-law.com · 200 West Vine Street, Fifth Floor · P.O. Box 1720 · Lexington, KY 40588-1720 · 859-244-7100

Louisville

David R. Monohan · Woodward, Hobson & Fulton · http://www.whf-law.com · 2500 National City Tower 101 South Fifth Street · Louisville, KY 40202-3175 · 502-581-8000

REAL ESTATE LAW

Lexington

Michael L. Ades · ⑳ · Greenebaum Doll & McDonald · http://www.gdm.com · 300 West Vine Street, Suite 1100 · Lexington, KY 40507-1622 · 859-231-8500

Gary W. Barr · ⑳ · Stoll Keenon Ogden · http://www.skofirm.com · 300 West Vine Street, Suite 2100 · Lexington, KY 40507-1801 · 859-231-3000

J. Mark Burton · Wyatt, Tarrant & Combs · http://www.wyattfirm.com · Lexington Financial Center, Suite 1600 · 250 West Main Street · Lexington, KY 40507 · 859-233-2012

Kermin E. Fleming · Woodward, Hobson & Fulton · http://www.whf-law.com · 200 West Vine Street, Fifth Floor · P.O. Box 1720 · Lexington, KY 40588-1720 · 859-244-7100

James T. Hodge · ⑳ · Wyatt, Tarrant & Combs · http://www.wyattfirm.com · Lexington Financial Center, Suite 1600 · 250 West Main Street · Lexington, KY 40507 · 859-233-2012

Richard M. Hopgood · ⑩ · Wyatt, Tarrant & Combs · http://www.wyattfirm.com · Lexington Financial Center, Suite 1600 · 250 West Main Street · Lexington, KY 40507 · 859-233-2012

William M. Lear, Jr. · ⑳ · Stoll Keenon Ogden · http://www.skofirm.com · 300 West Vine Street, Suite 2100 · Lexington, KY 40507-1801 · 859-231-3000

Thomas E. Meng · Stites & Harbison · http://www.stites.com · 250 West Main Street, Suite 2300 · Lexington, KY 40507-1758 · 859-226-2300

Richard V. Murphy · ⑩ · Murphy and Martin · Lexington Financial Center, Suite 2950 · 250 West Main Street · Lexington, KY 40507 · 859-233-9811

Richard A. Nunnelly · Stoll Keenon Ogden · http://www.skofirm.com · 300 West Vine Street, Suite 2100 · Lexington, KY 40507-1801 · 859-231-3000

Foster Ockerman, Sr. · ⑳ · Ockerman, Brabant & Baugh · 200 North Upper Street · Lexington, KY 40507 · 859-254-4401

Edward A. Receski · Frost Brown Todd · http://www.frostbrowntodd.com · Lexington Financial Center, Suite 2800 · 250 West Main Street · Lexington, KY 40507-1749 · 859-231-0000

John R. Rhorer, Jr. · ⑩ · Dinsmore & Shohl · http://www.dinslaw.com · Lexington Financial Center, Suite 1400 · 250 West Main Street · Lexington, KY 40507 · 859-425-1000

Dan M. Rose · Stoll Keenon Ogden · http://www.skofirm.com · 300 West Vine Street, Suite 2100 · Lexington, KY 40507-1801 · 859-231-3000

Stephen M. Ruschell · Stites & Harbison · http://www.stites.com · 250 West Main Street, Suite 2300 · Lexington, KY 40507-1758 · 859-226-2300

Thomas Bruce Simpson, Jr. · McBrayer, McGinnis, Leslie & Kirkland · 201 East Main Street, Suite 1000 · Lexington, KY 40507 · 859-231-8780

Job D. Turner III · Greenebaum Doll & McDonald · http://www.gdm.com · 300 West Vine Street, Suite 1100 · Lexington, KY 40507-1622 · 859-231-8500

Frank L. Wilford · Stoll Keenon Ogden · http://www.skofirm.com · 300 West Vine Street, Suite 2100 · Lexington, KY 40507-1801 · 859-231-3000

Rena G. Wiseman · ⑩ · Stoll Keenon Ogden · http://www.skofirm.com · 300 West Vine Street, Suite 2100 Lexington, KY 40507-1801 · 859-231-3000

Louisville

Dale E. Ahearn · ⑩ · Frost Brown Todd · http://www.frostbrowntodd.com · 400 West Market Street, 32nd Floor · Louisville, KY 40202-3363 · 502-589-5400

L. Jude Clark, Jr. · Frost Brown Todd · http://www.frostbrowntodd.com · 400 West Market Street, 32nd Floor · Louisville, KY 40202-3363 · 502-589-5400

Marshall P. Eldred, Jr. · Frost Brown Todd · http://www.frostbrowntodd.com · 400 West Market Street, 32nd Floor · Louisville, KY 40202-3363 · 502-589-5400

Michael M. Fleishman · ㉕ · Greenebaum Doll & McDonald · http://www.gdm.com · National City Tower, Suite 3500 · 101 South Fifth Street · Louisville, KY 40202-3140 · 502-589-4200

William H. Haden · Stites & Harbison · http://www.stites.com · 400 West Market Street, Suite 1800 · Louisville, KY 40202-3352 · 502-587-3400

Barry A. Hines · Stites & Harbison · http://www.stites.com · 400 West Market Street, Suite 1800 · Louisville, KY 40202-3352 · 502-587-3400

Alfred S. Joseph III · ㉕ · Stites & Harbison · http://www.stites.com · 400 West Market Street, Suite 1800 Louisville, KY 40202-3352 · 502-587-3400

Timothy W. Martin · ⑩ · Frost Brown Todd · http://www.frostbrowntodd.com · 400 West Market Street, 32nd Floor · Louisville, KY 40202-3363 · 502-589-5400

Tandy C. Patrick · Greenebaum Doll & McDonald · http://www.gdm.com · National City Tower, Suite 3500 · 101 South Fifth Street · Louisville, KY 40202-3140 · 502-589-4200

Grover C. Potts, Jr. · Wyatt, Tarrant & Combs · http://www.wyattfirm.com · PNC Plaza, Suite 2800 · 500 West Jefferson Street · Louisville, KY 40202-2898 · 502-589-5235

Arthur A. Rouse · Wyatt, Tarrant & Combs · http://www.wyattfirm.com · PNC Plaza, Suite 2800 · 500 West Jefferson Street · Louisville, KY 40202-2898 · 502-589-5235

David E. Saffer · Stites & Harbison · http://www.stites.com · 400 West Market Street, Suite 1800 · Louisville, KY 40202-3352 · 502-587-3400

Michael G. Shaikun · 25 · Greenebaum Doll & McDonald · http://www.gdm.com · National City Tower, Suite 3500 · 101 South Fifth Street · Louisville, KY 40202-3140 · 502-589-4200

Michael B. Vincenti · 10 · Wyatt, Tarrant & Combs · http://www.wyattfirm.com · PNC Plaza, Suite 2800 · 500 West Jefferson Street · Louisville, KY 40202-2898 · 502-589-5235

Richard L. Wood · Frost Brown Todd · http://www.frostbrowntodd.com · 400 West Market Street, 32nd Floor · Louisville, KY 40202-3363 · 502-589-5400

Scottsville

James S. Secrest, Jr. · Secrest & Secrest · 210 West Main Street · Scottsville, KY 42164 · 270-237-3616

SECURITIES LAW

Louisville

Craig C. Bradley, Jr. · Stites & Harbison · http://www.stites.com · 400 West Market Street, Suite 1800 · Louisville, KY 40202-3352 · 502-587-3400

Ivan M. Diamond · 10 · Greenebaum Doll & McDonald · http://www.gdm.com · National City Tower, Suite 3500 · 101 South Fifth Street · Louisville, KY 40202-3140 · 502-589-4200

James A. Giesel · Frost Brown Todd · http://www.frostbrowntodd.com · 400 West Market Street, 32nd Floor · Louisville, KY 40202-3363 · 502-589-5400

Michael de León Hawthorne · Greenebaum Doll & McDonald · http://www.gdm.com · National City Tower, Suite 3500 · 101 South Fifth Street · Louisville, KY 40202-3140 · 502-589-4200

Robert A. Heath · Wyatt, Tarrant & Combs · http://www.wyattfirm.com · PNC Plaza, Suite 2800 · 500 West Jefferson Street · Louisville, KY 40202-2898 · 502-589-5235

Franklin K. Jelsma · Wyatt, Tarrant & Combs · http://www.wyattfirm.com · PNC Plaza, Suite 2800 · 500 West Jefferson Street · Louisville, KY 40202-2898 · 502-589-5235

June N. King · Greenebaum Doll & McDonald · http://www.gdm.com · National City Tower, Suite 3500 · 101 South Fifth Street · Louisville, KY 40202-3140 · 502-589-4200

Alan K. MacDonald · Frost Brown Todd · http://www.frostbrowntodd.com · 400 West Market Street, 32nd Floor · Louisville, KY 40202-3363 · 502-589-5400

William G. Strench · Frost Brown Todd · http://www.frostbrowntodd.com · 400 West Market Street, 32nd Floor · Louisville, KY 40202-3363 · 502-589-5400

Cynthia W. Young · Wyatt, Tarrant & Combs · http://www.wyattfirm.com · PNC Plaza, Suite 2800 · 500 West Jefferson Street · Louisville, KY 40202-2898 · 502-589-5235

Crescent Springs

Martin J. Horwitz · The Horwitz Law Firm · 541 Buttermilk Pike, Suite 305 · Crescent Springs, KY 41017 · 859-578-1000

Frankfort

Bruce F. Clark · ⑩ · Stites & Harbison · http://www.stites.com · 421 West Main Street · P.O. Box 634 · Frankfort, KY 40602-0634 · 502-223-3477

Lexington

Bruce M. Reynolds · ⑩ · Stites & Harbison · http://www.stites.com · 250 West Main Street, Suite 2300 · Lexington, KY 40507-1758 · 859-226-2300

Douglas P. Romaine · Stoll Keenon Ogden · http://www.skofirm.com · 300 West Vine Street, Suite 2100 · Lexington, KY 40507-1801 · 859-231-3000

Jennifer S. Smart · Greenebaum Doll & McDonald · http://www.gdm.com · 300 West Vine Street, Suite 1100 · Lexington, KY 40507-1622 · 859-231-8500

Jeffrey J. Yost · Jackson Kelly · 175 East Main Street · Lexington, KY 40507 · 859-255-9500

Louisville

Thomas A. Brown · ⑩ · Greenebaum Doll & McDonald · http://www.gdm.com · National City Tower, Suite 3500 · 101 South Fifth Street · Louisville, KY 40202-3140 · 502-589-4200

Timothy J. Eifler · Stoll Keenon Ogden · http://www.skofirm.com · PNC Plaza, Suite 2000 · 500 West Jefferson Street · Louisville, KY 40202-2828 · 502-333-6000

Charles Fassler · ⑳ · Greenebaum Doll & McDonald · http://www.gdm.com · National City Tower, Suite 3500 · 101 South Fifth Street · Louisville, KY 40202-3140 · 502-589-4200

Charles J. Lavelle · ⑩ · Greenebaum Doll & McDonald · http://www.gdm.com · National City Tower, Suite 3500 · 101 South Fifth Street · Louisville, KY 40202-3140 · 502-589-4200

Thomas J. Luber · ⑳ · Wyatt, Tarrant & Combs · http://www.wyattfirm.com · PNC Plaza, Suite 2800 · 500 West Jefferson Street · Louisville, KY 40202-2898 · 502-589-5235

James B. Martin, Jr. · Stoll Keenon Ogden · http://www.skofirm.com · PNC Plaza, Suite 2000 · 500 West Jefferson Street · Louisville, KY 40202-2828 · 502-333-6000

Theodore T. Myre · Wyatt, Tarrant & Combs · http://www.wyattfirm.com · PNC Plaza, Suite 2800 · 500 West Jefferson Street · Louisville, KY 40202-2898 · 502-589-5235

James C. Seiffert · Stites & Harbison · http://www.stites.com · 400 West Market Street, Suite 1800 · Louisville, KY 40202-3352 · 502-587-3400

Mark F. Sommer · ⑩ · Greenebaum Doll & McDonald · http://www.gdm.com · National City Tower, Suite 3500 · 101 South Fifth Street · Louisville, KY 40202-3140 · 502-589-4200

Robert C. Webb · Frost Brown Todd · http://www.frostbrowntodd.com · 400 West Market Street, 32nd Floor · Louisville, KY 40202-3363 · 502-589-5400

Gary R. Weitkamp · 10 · Reed Weitkamp Schell & Vice · http://www.rwsvlaw.com · 500 West Jefferson Street, Suite 2400 · Louisville, KY 40202 · 502-589-1000

TRANSPORTATION LAW

Convington

Wilbert L. Ziegler · Ziegler & Schneider · 541 Buttermilk Pike · P.O. Box 175710 · Convington, KY 41017-5710 · 859-426-1300

TRUSTS AND ESTATES

Crescent Springs

Martin J. Horwitz · The Horwitz Law Firm · 541 Buttermilk Pike, Suite 305 · Crescent Springs, KY 41017 · 859-578-1000

Lexington

Glen S. Bagby · 10 · Woodward, Hobson & Fulton · http://www.whf-law.com · 200 West Vine Street, Fifth Floor · P.O. Box 1720 · Lexington, KY 40588-1720 · 859-244-7100

Jack R. Cunningham · Frost Brown Todd · http://www.frostbrowntodd.com · Lexington Financial Center, Suite 2800 · 250 West Main Street · Lexington, KY 40507-1749 · 859-231-0000

Robert W. Fleming · Woodward, Hobson & Fulton · http://www.whf-law.com · 200 West Vine Street, Fifth Floor · P.O. Box 1720 · Lexington, KY 40588-1720 · 859-244-7100

James E. Hargrove · Stoll Keenon Ogden · http://www.skofirm.com · 300 West Vine Street, Suite 2100 · Lexington, KY 40507-1801 · 859-231-3000

J. David Porter · Stites & Harbison · http://www.stites.com · 250 West Main Street, Suite 2300 · Lexington, KY 40507-1758 · 859-226-2300

Henry C.T. Richmond III · Greenebaum Doll & McDonald · http://www.gdm.com · 300 West Vine Street, Suite 1100 · Lexington, KY 40507-1622 · 859-231-8500

Louisville

Turney P. Berry · 10 · Wyatt, Tarrant & Combs · http://www.wyattfirm.com · PNC Plaza, Suite 2800 · 500 West Jefferson Street · Louisville, KY 40202-2898 · 502-589-5235

John T. Bondurant · 20 · Frost Brown Todd · http://www.frostbrowntodd.com · 400 West Market Street, 32nd Floor · Louisville, KY 40202-3363 · 502-589-5400

James L. Coorssen · 20 · Wyatt, Tarrant & Combs · http://www.wyattfirm.com · PNC Plaza, Suite 2800 · 500 West Jefferson Street · Louisville, KY 40202-2898 · 502-589-5235

John R. Cummins · 20 · Greenebaum Doll & McDonald · http://www.gdm.com · National City Tower, Suite 3500 · 101 South Fifth Street · Louisville, KY 40202-3140 · 502-589-4200

Bruce K. Dudley · Wyatt, Tarrant & Combs · http://www.wyattfirm.com · PNC Plaza, Suite 2800 · 500 West Jefferson Street · Louisville, KY 40202-2898 · 502-589-5235

Sheldon G. Gilman · Lynch, Cox, Gilman & Mahan · 500 West Jefferson Street, Suite 2100 · Louisville, KY 40202 · 502-589-4215

F. Gerald Greenwell · ⑳ · Frost Brown Todd · http://www.frostbrowntodd.com · 400 West Market Street, 32nd Floor · Louisville, KY 40202-3363 · 502-589-5400

Robert L. Hallenberg · Woodward, Hobson & Fulton · http://www.whf-law.com · 2500 National City Tower · 101 South Fifth Street · Louisville, KY 40202-3175 · 502-581-8000

Kelly S. Henry · Wyatt, Tarrant & Combs · http://www.wyattfirm.com · PNC Plaza, Suite 2800 · 500 West Jefferson Street · Louisville, KY 40202-2898 · 502-589-5235

John S. Lueken · Greenebaum Doll & McDonald · http://www.gdm.com · National City Tower, Suite 3500 · 101 South Fifth Street · Louisville, KY 40202-3140 · 502-589-4200

Homer Parrent III · ⑩ · Parrent & Oyler · First Trust Center, Suite 610 North · 200 South Fifth Street · Louisville, KY 40202 · 502-584-7500

Gordon B. Wright · Wyatt, Tarrant & Combs · http://www.wyattfirm.com · PNC Plaza, Suite 2800 · 500 West Jefferson Street · Louisville, KY 40202-2898 · 502-589-5235

Jefferey M. Yussman · ⑩ · Wyatt, Tarrant & Combs · http://www.wyattfirm.com · PNC Plaza, Suite 2800 500 West Jefferson Street · Louisville, KY 40202-2898 · 502-589-5235

Owensboro

George Thacker II · ⑩ · Thacker, Bickel, Hodskins & Thacker · 209 West Fourth Street · P.O. Box 39 · Owensboro, KY 42302 · 270-926-4500

Paducah

Gary B. Houston · ⑩ · Whitlow, Roberts, Houston & Straub · Old National Bank Building · 300 Broadway · P.O. Box 995 · Paducah, KY 42002-0995 · 270-443-4516

VENTURE CAPITAL LAW

Louisville

William G. Strench · Frost Brown Todd · http://www.frostbrowntodd.com · 400 West Market Street, 32nd Floor · Louisville, KY 40202-3363 · 502-589-5400

WATER LAW

Frankfort

Lloyd R. Cress, Jr. · Greenebaum Doll & McDonald · http://www.gdm.com · 229 West Main Street, Suite 101 · Frankfort, KY 40601-1847 · 502-875-0050

Lexington

John C. Bender · ⑩ · Greenebaum Doll & McDonald · http://www.gdm.com · 300 West Vine Street, Suite 1100 · Lexington, KY 40507-1622 · 859-231-8500

W. Blaine Early III · Stites & Harbison · http://www.stites.com · 250 West Main Street, Suite 2300 · Lexington, KY 40507-1758 · 859-226-2300

WHITE-COLLAR CRIMINAL DEFENSE

Frankfort

William E. Johnson · ㉕ · Johnson, True & Guarnieri · http://www.jtgattorneys.com · 326 West Main Street · Frankfort, KY 40601-1887 · 502-875-6000

J. Guthrie True · ⑩ · Johnson, True & Guarnieri · http://www.jtgattorneys.com · 326 West Main Street · Frankfort, KY 40601-1887 · 502-875-6000

Glasgow

Bobby H. Richardson · Richardson, Gardner, Barrickman & Alexander · 117 East Washington Street · P.O. Box 368 · Glasgow, KY 42142-0368 · 270-651-2116

Lexington

James I. Lowry IV · James I. Lowry IV · Security Trust Building, Suite 812 · 271 West Short Street · Lexington, KY 40507 · 859-233-4441

R. Burl McCoy · ⑩ · Stoll Keenon Ogden · http://www.skofirm.com · 300 West Vine Street, Suite 2100 · Lexington, KY 40507-1801 · 859-231-3000

Larry S. Roberts · Larry S. Roberts · 110 West Vine Street · Lexington, KY 40507 · 859-254-4941

James A. Shuffett · ㉕ · James A. Shuffett · 400 Security Trust Building · 271 West Short Street · Lexington, KY 40507-1292 · 859-252-5794

Kenneth W. Smith · Jenkins, Robinson, Epling & Smith · Court Square Building, Suite 100 · 269 West Main Street · Lexington, KY 40507 · 859-225-9625

Louisville

James Barton Adams, Jr. · James Barton Adams & Associates · 500 Kentucky Home Life Building · 239 South Fifth Street · Louisville, KY 40202 · 502-583-4881

Scott C. Cox · Cox & Mazzoli · 600 West Main Street, Suite 300 · Louisville, KY 40202 · 502-589-6190

David A. Lambertus · ⑩ · Interchange Law Office · 600 West Main Street, Suite 300 · Louisville, KY 40202 · 502-589-6190

Michael R. Mazzoli · Cox & Mazzoli · 600 West Main Street, Suite 300 · Louisville, KY 40202 · 502-589-6190

John Tim McCall · ⑩ · Interchange Law Office · 600 West Main Street, Suite 300 · Louisville, KY 40202 502-589-6190

Steve Romines · Romines Weis & Young · 600 West Main Street, Suite 100 · Louisville, KY 40202 · 502-587-8822

R. Kent Westberry · Landrum & Shouse · The LG&E Building, Suite 1900 · 220 West Main Street · Louisville, KY 40202-3349 · 502-589-7616

Barbourville

John E. Anderson · Cole, Cole, Anderson & Nagle · 108 Knox Street · P.O. Box 250 · Barbourville, KY 40906-0250 · 606-546-3117

Bowling Green

Norman E. Harned · ⑩ · Harned, Bachert & Denton · 324 East 10th Avenue · P.O. Box 1270 · Bowling Green, KY 42102-1270 · 270-782-3938

Covington

Gregory N. Schabell · ⑩ · Berger, Cox & Nienaber · 401 Madison Avenue · Covington, KY 41011 · 859-491-9088

Florence

Kenneth J. Dietz · Jones, Dietz & Schrand · 51 Cavalier Boulevard, Suite 260 · P.O. Box 0095 · Florence, KY 41022-0095 · 859-594-4200

H. Douglas Jones · Jones, Dietz & Schrand · 51 Cavalier Boulevard, Suite 260 · P.O. Box 0095 · Florence, KY 41022-0095 · 859-594-4200

Frankfort

Richard M. Guarnieri · Johnson, True & Guarnieri · http://www.jtgattorneys.com · 326 West Main Street Frankfort, KY 40601-1887 · 502-875-6000

Lexington

L. Davis Bussey · ⑩ · Bussey & Fouts · 501 Darby Creek Road, Suite 13 · Lexington, KY 40509 · 859-263-1140

Guillermo Carlos · ⑩ · Boehl Stopher & Graves · 444 West Second Street · Lexington, KY 40507 · 859-252-6721

Lloyd R. Edens · Wilson, Polites & McQueen · 444 East Main Street, Suite 201 · Lexington, KY 40507-2373 · 859-253-2373

C. David Emerson · ⑩ · Emerson Law Office · 501 Darby Creek Road, Unit 41 · Lexington, KY 40509 · 859-264-1664

Mark J. Hinkel · ⑩ · Landrum & Shouse · 106 West Vine Street, Suite 800 · P.O. Box 951 · Lexington, KY 40588-0951 · 859-255-2424

Charles E. Lowther · Boehl Stopher & Graves · 444 West Second Street · Lexington, KY 40507 · 859-252-6721

Walter A. Ward · ⑩ · Clark & Ward · The World Trade Center, Suite 1100 · 333 West Vine Street · Lexington, KY 40507 · 859-422-6000

Timothy J. Wilson · Wilson, Polites & McQueen · 444 East Main Street, Suite 201 · Lexington, KY 40507-2373 · 859-253-2373

Robert L. Catlett, Jr. · ⑩ · Sales Tillman Wallbaum Catlett & Satterley · 1900 Waterfront Plaza · 325 West Main Street · Louisville, KY 40202 · 502-589-5600

Tamara Todd Cotton · ⑩ · Cotton & Evensen · Republic Building, Suite 1102 · 429 West Muhammad Ali Boulevard · Louisville, KY 40202 · 502-569-2711

Wayne C. Daub · ⑩ · Interchange Law Office · 600 West Main Street, Suite 300 · Louisville, KY 40202 · 502-589-6190

Judson F. Devlin · Fulton & Devlin · 2000 Warrington Way, Suite 165 · Louisville, KY 40222-6409 · 502-327-0099

Christopher P. Evensen · Evensen Law Office · 325 West Main Street · 2000 Waterfront Plaza · Louisville, KY 40202 · 502-719-3145

Thomas L. Ferreri · Ferreri & Fogle · Speed Building, Suite 203 · 333 Guthrie Green · Louisville, KY 40202 · 502-582-1381

James G. Fogle · Ferreri & Fogle · Speed Building, Suite 203 · 333 Guthrie Green · Louisville, KY 40202 502-582-1381

Wesley G. Gatlin, Jr. · ⑩ · Boehl Stopher & Graves · AEGON Center, Suite 2300 · 400 West Market Street · Louisville, KY 40202 · 502-589-5980

Peter J. Glauber · ⑩ · Boehl Stopher & Graves · AEGON Center, Suite 2300 · 400 West Market Street · Louisville, KY 40202 · 502-589-5980

Walter E. Harding · Boehl Stopher & Graves · AEGON Center, Suite 2300 · 400 West Market Street · Louisville, KY 40202 · 502-589-5980

Larry L. Johnson · ⑩ · Boehl Stopher & Graves · AEGON Center, Suite 2300 · 400 West Market Street · Louisville, KY 40202 · 502-589-5980

Denis S. Kline · Ferreri & Fogle · Speed Building, Suite 203 · 333 Guthrie Green · Louisville, KY 40202 · 502-582-1381

W. David Klingman · ⑩ · W. David Klingman · 429 West Muhammad Ali Boulevard, Suite 504 · Louisville, KY 40202 · 502-587-7004

Robert M. Lindsay · ⑩ · Segal, Lindsay & Janes · 515 Park Avenue · Louisville, KY 40208 · 502-568-5600

Scott M. Miller · Priddy, Cutler, Miller & Meade · 800 Republic Building · 429 West Muhammad Ali Boulevard · Louisville, KY 40202 · 502-569-2741

Timothy P. O'Mara · ⑩ · Middleton Reutlinger · Brown & Williamson Tower, Suite 2500 · 401 South Fourth Street · Louisville, KY 40202-3410 · 502-584-1135

Philip J. Reverman · ⑩ · Boehl Stopher & Graves · AEGON Center, Suite 2300 · 400 West Market Street Louisville, KY 40202 · 502-589-5980

Douglas A. U'Sellis · ⑩ · U'Sellis & Kitchen · 600 East Main Street, Suite 100 · Louisville, KY 40202 · 502-736-3600

James R. Wagoner · Ferreri & Fogle · Speed Building, Suite 203 · 333 Guthrie Green · Louisville, KY 40202 · 502-582-1381

Madisonville

Ronald K. Bruce · Bruce Law Firm · 238 Union Street · Madisonville, KY 42431-2532 · 270-821-0920

Jerry P. Rhoads · ⑩ · Rhoads & Rhoads · Nine East Center Street · P.O. Box 1705 · Madisonville, KY 42431 · 270-825-1490

Tom M. Rhoads · ⑩ · Rhoads & Rhoads · Nine East Center Street · P.O. Box 1705 · Madisonville, KY 42431 · 270-825-1490

Pikeville

R. Roland Case · ⑩ · R. Roland Case Law Offices · 149 Main Street · P.O. Box 1410 · Pikeville, KY 41502 · 606-432-8175

Versailles

John W. Hardin · ⑩ · Stuart & Hardin · 102 North Main Street · Versailles, KY 40383 · 859-879-9393

LOUISIANA

ADMINISTRATIVE LAW

New Orleans

O. Ray Cornelius · Adams and Reese · http://www.adamsandreese.com · One Shell Square, Suite 4500 · 701 Poydras Street · New Orleans, LA 70139 · 504-581-3234

ALTERNATIVE DISPUTE RESOLUTION

Baton Rouge

Vincent P. Fornias · MAPS · United Plaza Two, Suite 904 · 8550 United Plaza Boulevard · Baton Rouge, LA 70809 · 225-769-4553

John W. Perry, Jr. · Perry, Atkinson, Balhoff, Mengis & Burns · 2141 Quail Run Drive · P.O. Box 83260 · Baton Rouge, LA 70884-3260 · 225-767-7730

Mandeville

Danny G. Shaw · Baker, Donelson, Bearman, Caldwell & Berkowitz · http://www.bakerdonelson.com · Three Sanctuary Boulevard, Suite 201 · Mandeville, LA 70471 · 985-819-8400

Metairie

Thomas K. Foutz · ADR Incorporated · 3838 North Causeway Boulevard, Suite 2880 · Metairie, LA 70002 · 504-838-6100

C. Joseph Murray · ADR Incorporated · 3838 North Causeway Boulevard, Suite 2880 · Metairie, LA 70002 · 504-838-6100

William R. Pitts · William R. Pitts · 300 Bella Drive · Metairie, LA 70005 · 504-831-5050

David R. M. Williams · ADR Incorporated · 3838 North Causeway Boulevard, Suite 2880 · Metairie, LA 70002 · 504-838-6100

Monroe

Ben R. Hanchey · Hanchey Mediation Services · 2304 Point Drive · P.O. Box 14547 · Monroe, LA 71207-4547 · 318-388-0841

New Orleans

M. Nan Alessandra · Phelps Dunbar · http://www.phelpsdunbar.com · Canal Place, Suite 2000 · 365 Canal Street · New Orleans, LA 70130-6534 · 504-566-1311

Nancy Scott Degan · Baker, Donelson, Bearman, Caldwell & Berkowitz · http://www.bakerdonelson.com 201 St. Charles Avenue, Suite 3600 · New Orleans, LA 70170-1000 · 504-566-5200

E. Phelps Gay · Christovich & Kearney · 601 Poydras Street, Suite 2300 · New Orleans, LA 70130 · 504-561-5700

Joseph I. Giarrusso, Jr. · Law Office of Joe Giarrusso, Jr. · 3557 Inwood Avenue · New Orleans, LA 70131 · 504-554-2678

Harvey C. Koch · Montgomery, Barnett, Brown, Read, Hammond & Mintz · http://www.monbar.com · 1100 Poydras Street, Suite 3200 · New Orleans, LA 70163-3200 · 504-585-3200

John M. McCollam · 2) · Gordon, Arata, McCollam, Duplantis & Eagan · http://www.gordonarata.com · Place St. Charles, Suite 4000 · 201 St. Charles Avenue · New Orleans, LA 70170-4000 · 504-582-1111

Leopold Z. Sher · Sher Garner Cahill Richter Klein & Hilbert · http://www.shergarner.com · 909 Poydras Street, Suite 2800 · New Orleans, LA 70112 · 504-299-2100

Ronald J. Sholes · Adams and Reese · http://www.adamsandreese.com · One Shell Square, Suite 4500 · 701 Poydras Street · New Orleans, LA 70139 · 504-581-3234

H. Bruce Shreves · Simon, Peragine, Smith & Redfearn · Energy Centre, 30th Floor · 1100 Poydras Street · New Orleans, LA 70163-3000 · 504-569-2030

ANTITRUST LAW

New Orleans

Mark R. Beebe · Adams and Reese · http://www.adamsandreese.com · One Shell Square, Suite 4500 · 701 Poydras Street · New Orleans, LA 70139 · 504-581-3234

Amelia Williams Koch · Baker, Donelson, Bearman, Caldwell & Berkowitz · http://www.bakerdonelson.com · 201 St. Charles Avenue, Suite 3600 · New Orleans, LA 70170-1000 · 504-566-5200

Gene W. Lafitte · 2% · Liskow & Lewis · http://www.liskow.com · One Shell Square, Suite 5000 · 701 Poydras Street · New Orleans, LA 70139-5099 · 504-581-7979

John M. Landis · Stone Pigman Walther Wittmann · http://www.stonepigman.com · 546 Carondelet Street · New Orleans, LA 70130-3588 · 504-581-3200

Charles W. Lane III · a · Jones Walker · http://www.joneswalker.com · 201 St. Charles Avenue · New Orleans, LA 70170-5100 · 504-582-8000

David G. Radlauer · Jones Walker · http://www.joneswalker.com · 201 St. Charles Avenue · New Orleans, LA 70170-5100 · 504-582-8000

Bruce V. Schewe · Phelps Dunbar · http://www.phelpsdunbar.com · Canal Place, Suite 2000 · 365 Canal Street · New Orleans, LA 70130-6534 · 504-566-1311

APPELLATE LAW

Baton Rouge

H. Alston Johnson III · Phelps Dunbar · http://www.phelpsdunbar.com · City Plaza, Suite 701 · 445 North Boulevard · Baton Rouge, LA 70802 · 225-346-0285

Michael H. Rubin · a · McGlinchey Stafford · http://www.mcglinchey.com · One American Place, 14th Floor · 301 Main Street · Baton Rouge, LA 70825-0001 · 225-383-9000

New Orleans

Roy C. Cheatwood · a · Baker, Donelson, Bearman, Caldwell & Berkowitz · http://www.bakerdonelson.com · 201 St. Charles Avenue, Suite 3600 · New Orleans, LA 70170-1000 · 504-566-5200

Thomas M. Flanagan · Stanley, Flanagan & Reuter · http://www.sfrlawfirm.com · 909 Poydras Street, Suite 2500 · New Orleans, LA 70112 · 504-523-1580

Michael R. Fontham · a · Stone Pigman Walther Wittmann · http://www.stonepigman.com · 546 Carondelet Street · New Orleans, LA 70130-3588 · 504-581-3200

James M. Garner · Sher Garner Cahill Richter Klein & Hilbert · http://www.shergarner.com · 909 Poydras Street, Suite 2800 · New Orleans, LA 70112 · 504-299-2100

Harry Simms Hardin III · Jones Walker · http://www.joneswalker.com · 201 St. Charles Avenue · New Orleans, LA 70170-5100 · 504-582-8000

Russ M. Herman · 2% · Herman, Herman, Katz & Cotlar · http://www.hhkc.com · 820 O'Keefe Avenue · New Orleans, LA 70113 · 504-581-4892

Gene W. Lafitte · 2% · Liskow & Lewis · http://www.liskow.com · One Shell Square, Suite 5000 · 701 Poydras Street · New Orleans, LA 70139-5099 · 504-581-7979

Joseph L. McReynolds · Deutsch, Kerrigan & Stiles · http://www.dkslaw.com · 755 Magazine Street · New Orleans, LA 70130-3672 · 504-581-5141

Martin A. Stern · Adams and Reese · http://www.adamsandreese.com · One Shell Square, Suite 4500 · 701 Poydras Street · New Orleans, LA 70139 · 504-581-3234

Shreveport

F. Drake Lee · Cook, Yancey, King & Galloway · 333 Texas Street, Suite 1700 · P.O. Box 22260 · Shreveport, LA 71120-2260 · 318-221-6277

BANKING LAW

Baton Rouge

J. Michael Cutshaw · J. Michael Cutshaw · 2203 Sassy Lane · Baton Rouge, LA 70808 · 225-343-6117

Mary Terrel Joseph · McGlinchey Stafford · http://www.mcglinchey.com · One American Place, 14th Floor · 301 Main Street · Baton Rouge, LA 70825-0001 · 225-383-9000

Lee C. Kantrow · a · Kantrow, Spaht, Weaver & Blitzer · City Plaza Building, Suite 300 · 445 North Boulevard · P.O. Box 2997 · Baton Rouge, LA 70821-2997 · 225-383-4703

Randy P. Roussel · Phelps Dunbar · http://www.phelpsdunbar.com · City Plaza, Suite 701 · 445 North Boulevard · Baton Rouge, LA 70802 · 225-346-0285

Michael H. Rubin · a · McGlinchey Stafford · http://www.mcglinchey.com · One American Place, 14th Floor · 301 Main Street · Baton Rouge, LA 70825-0001 · 225-383-9000

Natchitoches

Ronald E. Corken, Jr. · Watson, Murchison, Crews, Arthur & Corken · 616 Front Street · P.O. Box 1036 · Natchitoches, LA 71457 · 318-352-2302

Henry Cole Gahagan, Jr. · a · Henry C. Gahagan, Jr. · 1950 Williams Avenue · P.O. Box 1188 · Natchitoches, LA 71458 · 318-352-7397

New Orleans

Wm. Blake Bennett · Liskow & Lewis · http://www.liskow.com · One Shell Square, Suite 5000 · 701 Poydras Street · New Orleans, LA 70139-5099 · 504-581-7979

Philip deV. Claverie, Sr. · a · Phelps Dunbar · http://www.phelpsdunbar.com · Canal Place, Suite 2000 · 365 Canal Street · New Orleans, LA 70130-6534 · 504-566-1311

Anthony J. Correro III · 2% · Adams and Reese · http://www.adamsandreese.com · One Shell Square, Suite 4500 · 701 Poydras Street · New Orleans, LA 70139 · 504-581-3234

Louis Y. Fishman · 2% · Fishman Haygood Phelps Walmsley Willis & Swanson · http://www.cfhlaw.com · 201 St. Charles Avenue, 46th Floor · New Orleans, LA 70170-4600 · 504-586-5252

F. Frank Fontenot · Milling Benson Woodward · 909 Poydras Street, Suite 2300 · New Orleans, LA 70112-1010 · 504-569-7000

William H. Hines · a · Jones Walker · http://www.joneswalker.com · 201 St. Charles Avenue · New Orleans, LA 70170-5100 · 504-582-8000

Bennet Scott Koren · a · McGlinchey Stafford · http://www.mcglinchey.com · 643 Magazine Street · New Orleans, LA 70130 · 504-586-1200

J. Marshall Page III · Jones Walker · http://www.joneswalker.com · 201 St. Charles Avenue · New Orleans, LA 70170-5100 · 504-582-8000

Leon J. Reymond, Jr. · Liskow & Lewis · http://www.liskow.com · One Shell Square, Suite 5000 · 701 Poydras Street · New Orleans, LA 70139-5099 · 504-581-7979

James A. Stuckey · a · Phelps Dunbar · http://www.phelpsdunbar.com · Canal Place, Suite 2000 · 365 Canal Street · New Orleans, LA 70130-6534 · 504-566-1311

Susan Gayle Talley · a · Stone Pigman Walther Wittmann · http://www.stonepigman.com · 546 Carondelet Street · New Orleans, LA 70130-3588 · 504-581-3200

Frank A. Tessier · Carver, Darden, Koretzky, Tessier, Finn, Blossman & Areaux · Energy Centre, Suite 3100 · 1100 Poydras Street · New Orleans, LA 70163 · 504-585-3800

Harvey D. Wagar III · Phelps Dunbar · http://www.phelpsdunbar.com · Canal Place, Suite 2000 · 365 Canal Street · New Orleans, LA 70130-6534 · 504-566-1311

David S. Willenzik · a · McGlinchey Stafford · http://www.mcglinchey.com · 643 Magazine Street · New Orleans, LA 70130 · 504-586-1200

Sterling Scott Willis · Fishman Haygood Phelps Walmsley Willis & Swanson · http://www.cfhlaw.com · 201 St. Charles Avenue, 46th Floor · New Orleans, LA 70170-4600 · 504-586-5252

John D. Wogan · a · Liskow & Lewis · http://www.liskow.com · One Shell Square, Suite 5000 · 701 Poydras Street · New Orleans, LA 70139-5099 · 504-581-7979

Shreveport

L. David Cromwell · a · Pettiette, Armand, Dunkelman, Woodley, Byrd & Cromwell · 400 Texas Street, Suite 400 · P.O. Box 1786 · Shreveport, LA 71166-1786 · 318-221-1800

BANKRUPTCY AND CREDITOR-DEBTOR RIGHTS LAW

Baton Rouge

Patricia B. McMurray · Adams and Reese · http://www.adamsandreese.com · 450 Laurel Street, Suite 1900 · Baton Rouge, LA 70801 · 225-336-5200

Louis M. Phillips · Gordon, Arata, McCollam, Duplantis & Eagan · http://www.gordonarata.com · One American Place, Suite 1600 · 301 Main Street · Baton Rouge, LA 70801-1916 · 225-381-9643

David S. Rubin · 2) · Kantrow, Spaht, Weaver & Blitzer · City Plaza Building, Suite 300 · 445 North Boulevard · P.O. Box 2997 · Baton Rouge, LA 70821-2997 · 225-383-4703

William E. Steffes · 2) · Steffes, Vingiello & McKenzie · 13702 Coursey Boulevard, Building Three · Baton Rouge, LA 70817 · 225-751-1751

Stephen P. Strohschein · McGlinchey Stafford · http://www.mcglinchey.com · One American Place, 14th Floor · 301 Main Street · Baton Rouge, LA 70825-0001 · 225-383-9000

Lafayette

Gerald H. Schiff · Gordon, Arata, McCollam, Duplantis & Eagan · http://www.gordonarata.com · 400 East Kaliste Saloom Road, Suite 4200 · Lafayette, LA 70508-8517 · 337-237-0132

New Orleans

Brent B. Barriere · Phelps Dunbar · http://www.phelpsdunbar.com · Canal Place, Suite 2000 · 365 Canal Street · New Orleans, LA 70130-6534 · 504-566-1311

Rudy J. Cerone · McGlinchey Stafford · http://www.mcglinchey.com · 643 Magazine Street · New Orleans, LA 70130 · 504-586-1200

Douglas S. Draper · 2) · Heller, Draper, Hayden, Patrick & Horn · 650 Poydras Street, Suite 2500 · New Orleans, LA 70130 · 504-299-3300

John M. Duck · Adams and Reese · http://www.adamsandreese.com · One Shell Square, Suite 4500 · 701 Poydras Street · New Orleans, LA 70139 · 504-581-3234

J. David Forsyth · a · Sessions, Fishman, Nathan & Israel · http://www.sessions-law.com · Place St. Charles, Suite 3500 · 201 St. Charles Avenue · New Orleans, LA 70170-3500 · 504-582-1500

Elizabeth J. Futrell · a · Jones Walker · http://www.joneswalker.com · 201 St. Charles Avenue · New Orleans, LA 70170-5100 · 504-582-8000

Jan M. Hayden · a · Heller, Draper, Hayden, Patrick & Horn · 650 Poydras Street, Suite 2500 · New Orleans, LA 70130 · 504-299-3300

Edward M. Heller · 2% · Heller, Draper, Hayden, Patrick & Horn · 650 Poydras Street, Suite 2500 · New Orleans, LA 70130 · 504-299-3300

Sessions Ault Hootsell III · Phelps Dunbar · http://www.phelpsdunbar.com · Canal Place, Suite 2000 · 365 Canal Street · New Orleans, LA 70130-6534 · 504-566-1311

Patrick Johnson, Jr. · Lemle & Kelleher · http://www.lemle.com · Pan American Life Center, Suite 2100 601 Poydras Street · New Orleans, LA 70130-6097 · 504-586-1241

Phillip K. Jones, Jr. · Liskow & Lewis · http://www.liskow.com · One Shell Square, Suite 5000 · 701 Poydras Street · New Orleans, LA 70139-5099 · 504-581-7979

Omer F. Kuebel III · Locke Lord Bissell & Liddell · 601 Poydras Street, Suite 2660 · New Orleans, LA 70130-6036 · 504-558-5100

John M. Landis · Stone Pigman Walther Wittmann · http://www.stonepigman.com · 546 Carondelet Street · New Orleans, LA 70130-3588 · 504-581-3200

R. Lewis McHenry · a · Jones Walker · http://www.joneswalker.com · 201 St. Charles Avenue · New Orleans, LA 70170-5100 · 504-582-8000

William H. Patrick III · a · Heller, Draper, Hayden, Patrick & Horn · 650 Poydras Street, Suite 2500 · New Orleans, LA 70130 · 504-299-3300

R. Patrick Vance · a · Jones Walker · http://www.joneswalker.com · 201 St. Charles Avenue · New Orleans, LA 70170-5100 · 504-582-8000

BET-THE-COMPANY LITIGATION

Baton Rouge

G. William Jarman · Kean, Miller, Hawthorne, D'Armond, McCowan & Jarman · One American Place, 22nd Floor · P.O. Box 3513 · Baton Rouge, LA 70821 · 225-387-0999

Michael H. Rubin · a · McGlinchey Stafford · http://www.mcglinchey.com · One American Place, 14th Floor · 301 Main Street · Baton Rouge, LA 70825-0001 · 225-383-9000

New Orleans

Judy Y. Barrasso · Barrasso Usdin Kupperman Freeman & Sarver · http://www.barrassousdin.com · 909 Poydras Street, 24th Floor · New Orleans, LA 70112 · 504-589-9700

Roy C. Cheatwood · a · Baker, Donelson, Bearman, Caldwell & Berkowitz · http://www.bakerdonelson.com · 201 St. Charles Avenue, Suite 3600 · New Orleans, LA 70170-1000 · 504-566-5200

Ewell E. Eagan, Jr. · Gordon, Arata, McCollam, Duplantis & Eagan · http://www.gordonarata.com · Place St. Charles, Suite 4000 · 201 St. Charles Avenue · New Orleans, LA 70170-4000 · 504-582-1111

Gene W. Lafitte · 2% · Liskow & Lewis · http://www.liskow.com · One Shell Square, Suite 5000 · 701 Poydras Street · New Orleans, LA 70139-5099 · 504-581-7979

Daniel Lund · a · Montgomery, Barnett, Brown, Read, Hammond & Mintz · http://www.monbar.com · 1100 Poydras Street, Suite 3200 · New Orleans, LA 70163-3200 · 504-585-3200

Steven W. Usdin · Barrasso Usdin Kupperman Freeman & Sarver · http://www.barrassousdin.com · 909 Poydras Street, 24th Floor · New Orleans, LA 70112 · 504-589-9700

R. Patrick Vance · a · Jones Walker · http://www.joneswalker.com · 201 St. Charles Avenue · New Orleans, LA 70170-5100 · 504-582-8000

Phillip A. Wittmann · 2% · Stone Pigman Walther Wittmann · http://www.stonepigman.com · 546 Carondelet Street · New Orleans, LA 70130-3588 · 504-581-3200

COMMERCIAL LITIGATION

Baton Rouge

Gary A. Bezet · Kean, Miller, Hawthorne, D'Armond, McCowan & Jarman · One American Place, 22nd Floor · P.O. Box 3513 · Baton Rouge, LA 70821 · 225-387-0999

G. Blane Clark, Jr. · Kean, Miller, Hawthorne, D'Armond, McCowan & Jarman · One American Place, 22nd Floor · P.O. Box 3513 · Baton Rouge, LA 70821 · 225-387-0999

Michael D. Ferachi · McGlinchey Stafford · http://www.mcglinchey.com · One American Place, 14th Floor · 301 Main Street · Baton Rouge, LA 70825-0001 · 225-383-9000

Leon Gary, Jr. · Jones Walker · http://www.joneswalker.com · Four United Plaza, Suite 500 · 8555 United Plaza Boulevard · Baton Rouge, LA 70809-7000 · 225-248-2000

Eugene R. Groves · Taylor, Porter, Brooks & Phillips · Chase Tower South, Eighth Floor · 451 Florida Street · P.O. Box 2471 · Baton Rouge, LA 70821-2471 · 225-387-3221

Michael D. Hunt · Phelps Dunbar · http://www.phelpsdunbar.com · City Plaza, Suite 701 · 445 North Boulevard · Baton Rouge, LA 70802 · 225-346-0285

G. William Jarman · Kean, Miller, Hawthorne, D'Armond, McCowan & Jarman · One American Place, 22nd Floor · P.O. Box 3513 · Baton Rouge, LA 70821 · 225-387-0999

F. Scott Kaiser · Phelps Dunbar · http://www.phelpsdunbar.com · City Plaza, Suite 701 · 445 North Boulevard · Baton Rouge, LA 70802 · 225-346-0285

William C. Kaufman III · Seale Smith Zuber & Barnette · Two United Plaza, Suite 200 · 8550 United Plaza Boulevard · Baton Rouge, LA 70809 · 225-924-1600

Charles S. McCowan III · Kean, Miller, Hawthorne, D'Armond, McCowan & Jarman · One American Place, 22nd Floor · P.O. Box 3513 · Baton Rouge, LA 70821 · 225-387-0999

James C. Percy · Jones Walker · http://www.joneswalker.com · Four United Plaza, Suite 500 · 8555 United Plaza Boulevard · Baton Rouge, LA 70809-7000 · 225-248-2000

Claude F. Reynaud, Jr. · Breazeale, Sachse and Wilson · One American Place, Suite 2300 · P.O. Box 3197 Baton Rouge, LA 70821-3197 · 225-387-4000

Larry M. Roedel · Roedel, Parsons, Koch, Blache, Balhoff & McCollister · 8440 Jefferson Highway, Suite 301 · Baton Rouge, LA 70809 · 225-929-7033

Michael H. Rubin · a · McGlinchey Stafford · http://www.mcglinchey.com · One American Place, 14th Floor · 301 Main Street · Baton Rouge, LA 70825-0001 · 225-383-9000

Charles A. Schutte, Jr. · Guglielmo, Marks, Schutte, Terhoeve & Love · http://www.gmstl.com · 320 Somerulos Street · Baton Rouge, LA 70802-6129 · 225-387-6966

Paul H. Spaht · Kantrow, Spaht, Weaver & Blitzer · City Plaza Building, Suite 300 · 445 North Boulevard P.O. Box 2997 · Baton Rouge, LA 70821-2997 · 225-383-4703

Fredrick R. Tulley · Taylor, Porter, Brooks & Phillips · Chase Tower South, Eighth Floor · 451 Florida Street · P.O. Box 2471 · Baton Rouge, LA 70821-2471 · 225-387-3221

Dan E. West · McGlinchey Stafford · http://www.mcglinchey.com · One American Place, 14th Floor · 301 Main Street · Baton Rouge, LA 70825-0001 · 225-383-9000

Richard F. Zimmerman, Jr. · Kantrow, Spaht, Weaver & Blitzer · City Plaza Building, Suite 300 · 445 North Boulevard · P.O. Box 2997 · Baton Rouge, LA 70821-2997 · 225-383-4703

Lake Charles

William B. Monk · Stockwell, Sievert, Viccellio, Clements & Shaddock · One Lakeside Plaza, Fourth Floor · P.O. Box 2900 · Lake Charles, LA 70602 · 337-436-9491

John B. Scofield · 2) · Scofield, Gerard, Singletary & Pohorelsky · 901 Lakeshore Drive, Suite 900 · Lake Charles, LA 70601 · 337-433-9436

J. Michael Veron · Bice, Palermo & Veron · 721 Kirby Street · P.O. Box 2125 · Lake Charles, LA 70602 · 337-310-1600

Mandeville

Danny G. Shaw · Baker, Donelson, Bearman, Caldwell & Berkowitz · http://www.bakerdonelson.com · Three Sanctuary Boulevard, Suite 201 · Mandeville, LA 70471 · 985-819-8400

Monroe

Robert P. McLeod · a · McLeod Verlander · 1900 North 18th Street, Suite 610 · P.O. Box 2270 · Monroe, LA 71207-2270 · 318-325-7000

New Orleans

Jack M. Alltmont · Sessions, Fishman, Nathan & Israel · http://www.sessions-law.com · Place St. Charles, Suite 3500 · 201 St. Charles Avenue · New Orleans, LA 70170-3500 · 504-582-1500

Barry W. Ashe · Stone Pigman Walther Wittmann · http://www.stonepigman.com · 546 Carondelet Street New Orleans, LA 70130-3588 · 504-581-3200

Robert E. Barkley, Jr. · 2) · Barkley & Thompson · 1515 Poydras Street, Suite 2350 · New Orleans, LA 70112 · 504-595-3350

Judy Y. Barrasso · Barrasso Usdin Kupperman Freeman & Sarver · http://www.barrassousdin.com · 909 Poydras Street, 24th Floor · New Orleans, LA 70112 · 504-589-9700

Brent B. Barriere · Phelps Dunbar · http://www.phelpsdunbar.com · Canal Place, Suite 2000 · 365 Canal Street · New Orleans, LA 70130-6534 · 504-566-1311

Edward H. Bergin · Jones Walker · http://www.joneswalker.com · 201 St. Charles Avenue · New Orleans, LA 70170-5100 · 504-582-8000

Robert B. Bieck, Jr. · Jones Walker · http://www.joneswalker.com · 201 St. Charles Avenue · New Orleans, LA 70170-5100 · 504-582-8000

James A. Brown · Liskow & Lewis · http://www.liskow.com · One Shell Square, Suite 5000 · 701 Poydras Street · New Orleans, LA 70139-5099 · 504-581-7979

Thomas A. Casey, Jr. · Jones Walker · http://www.joneswalker.com · 201 St. Charles Avenue · New Orleans, LA 70170-5100 · 504-582-8000

Roy C. Cheatwood · a · Baker, Donelson, Bearman, Caldwell & Berkowitz · http://www.bakerdonelson.com · 201 St. Charles Avenue, Suite 3600 · New Orleans, LA 70170-1000 · 504-566-5200

Mark Cunningham · Jones Walker · http://www.joneswalker.com · 201 St. Charles Avenue · New Orleans, LA 70170-5100 · 504-582-8000

Nancy Scott Degan · Baker, Donelson, Bearman, Caldwell & Berkowitz · http://www.bakerdonelson.com 201 St. Charles Avenue, Suite 3600 · New Orleans, LA 70170-1000 · 504-566-5200

George Denegre, Jr. · Liskow & Lewis · http://www.liskow.com · One Shell Square, Suite 5000 · 701 Poydras Street · New Orleans, LA 70139-5099 · 504-581-7979

Ewell E. Eagan, Jr. · Gordon, Arata, McCollam, Duplantis & Eagan · http://www.gordonarata.com · Place St. Charles, Suite 4000 · 201 St. Charles Avenue · New Orleans, LA 70170-4000 · 504-582-1111

Matt J. Farley · Krebs, Farley & Pelleteri · http://www.kfplaw.com · 400 Poydras Street, Suite 2500 · New Orleans, LA 70130 · 504-299-3570

Larry Feldman, Jr. · McGlinchey Stafford · http://www.mcglinchey.com · 643 Magazine Street · New Orleans, LA 70130 · 504-586-1200

William R. Forrester, Jr. · Lemle & Kelleher · http://www.lemle.com · Pan American Life Center, Suite 2100 · 601 Poydras Street · New Orleans, LA 70130-6097 · 504-586-1241

George C. Freeman III · Barrasso Usdin Kupperman Freeman & Sarver · http://www.barrassousdin.com · 909 Poydras Street, 24th Floor · New Orleans, LA 70112 · 504-589-9700

James M. Garner · Sher Garner Cahill Richter Klein & Hilbert · http://www.shergarner.com · 909 Poydras Street, Suite 2800 · New Orleans, LA 70112 · 504-299-2100

Covert J. Geary · Jones Walker · http://www.joneswalker.com · 201 St. Charles Avenue · New Orleans, LA 70170-5100 · 504-582-8000

A. Gregory Grimsal · Gordon, Arata, McCollam, Duplantis & Eagan · http://www.gordonarata.com · Place St. Charles, Suite 4000 · 201 St. Charles Avenue · New Orleans, LA 70170-4000 · 504-582-1111

James C. Gulotta, Jr. · Stone Pigman Walther Wittmann · http://www.stonepigman.com · 546 Carondelet Street · New Orleans, LA 70130-3588 · 504-581-3200

Harry Simms Hardin III · Jones Walker · http://www.joneswalker.com · 201 St. Charles Avenue · New Orleans, LA 70170-5100 · 504-582-8000

Pauline F. Hardin · Jones Walker · http://www.joneswalker.com · 201 St. Charles Avenue · New Orleans, LA 70170-5100 · 504-582-8000

L. Eades Hogue · Lemle & Kelleher · http://www.lemle.com · Pan American Life Center, Suite 2100 · 601 Poydras Street · New Orleans, LA 70130-6097 · 504-586-1241

Grady S. Hurley · Jones Walker · http://www.joneswalker.com · 201 St. Charles Avenue · New Orleans, LA 70170-5100 · 504-582-8000

James K. Irvin · Milling Benson Woodward · 909 Poydras Street, Suite 2300 · New Orleans, LA 70112-1010 · 504-569-7000

Robert E. Kerrigan, Jr. · a · Deutsch, Kerrigan & Stiles · http://www.dkslaw.com · 755 Magazine Street · New Orleans, LA 70130-3672 · 504-581-5141

Amelia Williams Koch · Baker, Donelson, Bearman, Caldwell & Berkowitz · http://www.bakerdonelson.com · 201 St. Charles Avenue, Suite 3600 · New Orleans, LA 70170-1000 · 504-566-5200

Harvey C. Koch · Montgomery, Barnett, Brown, Read, Hammond & Mintz · http://www.monbar.com · 1100 Poydras Street, Suite 3200 · New Orleans, LA 70163-3200 · 504-585-3200

David J. Krebs · Krebs, Farley & Pelleteri · http://www.kfplaw.com · 400 Poydras Street, Suite 2500 · New Orleans, LA 70130 · 504-299-3570

Stephen Kupperman · Barrasso Usdin Kupperman Freeman & Sarver · http://www.barrassousdin.com · 909 Poydras Street, 24th Floor · New Orleans, LA 70112 · 504-589-9700

Gene W. Lafitte · 2% · Liskow & Lewis · http://www.liskow.com · One Shell Square, Suite 5000 · 701 Poydras Street · New Orleans, LA 70139-5099 · 504-581-7979

Charles W. Lane III · a · Jones Walker · http://www.joneswalker.com · 201 St. Charles Avenue · New Orleans, LA 70170-5100 · 504-582-8000

Andrew R. Lee · Jones Walker · http://www.joneswalker.com · 201 St. Charles Avenue · New Orleans, LA 70170-5100 · 504-582-8000

Wayne J. Lee · Stone Pigman Walther Wittmann · http://www.stonepigman.com · 546 Carondelet Street · New Orleans, LA 70130-3588 · 504-581-3200

Daniel Lund · a · Montgomery, Barnett, Brown, Read, Hammond & Mintz · http://www.monbar.com · 1100 Poydras Street, Suite 3200 · New Orleans, LA 70163-3200 · 504-585-3200

Joseph Maselli, Jr. · Plauché, Maselli, Landry & Parkerson · One Shell Square, Suite 3800 · 701 Poydras Street · New Orleans, LA 70139 · 504-582-1142

Joe B. Norman · Liskow & Lewis · http://www.liskow.com · One Shell Square, Suite 5000 · 701 Poydras Street · New Orleans, LA 70139-5099 · 504-581-7979

C. Lawrence Orlansky · Stone Pigman Walther Wittmann · http://www.stonepigman.com · 546 Carondelet Street · New Orleans, LA 70130-3588 · 504-581-3200

G. Bruce Parkerson · Plauché, Maselli, Landry & Parkerson · One Shell Square, Suite 3800 · 701 Poydras Street · New Orleans, LA 70139 · 504-582-1142

Maura Z. Pelleteri · Krebs, Farley & Pelleteri · http://www.kfplaw.com · 400 Poydras Street, Suite 2500 · New Orleans, LA 70130 · 504-299-3570

Thomas A. Roberts · Barrasso Usdin Kupperman Freeman & Sarver · http://www.barrassousdin.com · 909 Poydras Street, 24th Floor · New Orleans, LA 70112 · 504-589-9700

Robert S. Rooth · Chaffe McCall · 2300 Energy Centre · 1100 Poydras Street · New Orleans, LA 70163-2300 · 504-585-7000

Harry Rosenberg · Phelps Dunbar · http://www.phelpsdunbar.com · Canal Place, Suite 2000 · 365 Canal Street · New Orleans, LA 70130-6534 · 504-566-1311

James H. Roussel · Baker, Donelson, Bearman, Caldwell & Berkowitz · http://www.bakerdonelson.com · 201 St. Charles Avenue, Suite 3600 · New Orleans, LA 70170-1000 · 504-566-5200

Richard E. Sarver · Barrasso Usdin Kupperman Freeman & Sarver · http://www.barrassousdin.com · 909 Poydras Street, 24th Floor · New Orleans, LA 70112 · 504-589-9700

Howard E. Sinor, Jr. · Gordon, Arata, McCollam, Duplantis & Eagan · http://www.gordonarata.com · Place St. Charles, Suite 4000 · 201 St. Charles Avenue · New Orleans, LA 70170-4000 · 504-582-1111

Benjamin R. Slater III · Lemle & Kelleher · http://www.lemle.com · Pan American Life Center, Suite 2100 · 601 Poydras Street · New Orleans, LA 70130-6097 · 504-586-1241

Richard C. Stanley · Stanley, Flanagan & Reuter · http://www.sfrlawfirm.com · 909 Poydras Street, Suite 2500 · New Orleans, LA 70112 · 504-523-1580

James R. Swanson · Fishman Haygood Phelps Walmsley Willis & Swanson · http://www.cfhlaw.com · 201 St. Charles Avenue, 46th Floor · New Orleans, LA 70170-4600 · 504-586-5252

Walter C. Thompson, Jr. · 2) · Barkley & Thompson · 1515 Poydras Street, Suite 2350 · New Orleans, LA 70112 · 504-595-3350

Steven W. Usdin · Barrasso Usdin Kupperman Freeman & Sarver · http://www.barrassousdin.com · 909 Poydras Street, 24th Floor · New Orleans, LA 70112 · 504-589-9700

R. Patrick Vance · a · Jones Walker · http://www.joneswalker.com · 201 St. Charles Avenue · New Orleans, LA 70170-5100 · 504-582-8000

Robert A. Vosbein · Adams and Reese · http://www.adamsandreese.com · One Shell Square, Suite 4500 · 701 Poydras Street · New Orleans, LA 70139 · 504-581-3234

Edward Dirk Wegmann · Jones Walker · http://www.joneswalker.com · 201 St. Charles Avenue · New Orleans, LA 70170-5100 · 504-582-8000

John M. Wilson · Liskow & Lewis · http://www.liskow.com · One Shell Square, Suite 5000 · 701 Poydras Street · New Orleans, LA 70139-5099 · 504-581-7979

Rachel W. Wisdom · Stone Pigman Walther Wittmann · http://www.stonepigman.com · 546 Carondelet Street · New Orleans, LA 70130-3588 · 504-581-3200

Anne Derbes Wittman · Baker, Donelson, Bearman, Caldwell & Berkowitz · http://www.bakerdonelson.com · 201 St. Charles Avenue, Suite 3600 · New Orleans, LA 70170-1000 · 504-566-5200

Phillip A. Wittmann · 2% · Stone Pigman Walther Wittmann · http://www.stonepigman.com · 546 Carondelet Street · New Orleans, LA 70130-3588 · 504-581-3200

William E. Wright, Jr. · Deutsch, Kerrigan & Stiles · http://www.dkslaw.com · 755 Magazine Street · New Orleans, LA 70130-3672 · 504-581-5141

Shreveport

F. Drake Lee · Cook, Yancey, King & Galloway · 333 Texas Street, Suite 1700 · P.O. Box 22260 · Shreveport, LA 71120-2260 · 318-221-6277

Kay Cowden Medlin · Lemle & Kelleher · http://www.lemle.com · Louisiana Tower, 10th Floor · 401 Edwards Street · Shreveport, LA 71101-3289 · 318-227-1131

Billy R. Pesnell · 2) · The Pesnell Law Firm · H.C. Beck Building, Suite 1100 · 400 Travis Street · P.O. Box 1794 · Shreveport, LA 71166-1794 · 318-226-5577

Herschel E. Richard, Jr. · a · Cook, Yancey, King & Galloway · 333 Texas Street, Suite 1700 · P.O. Box 22260 · Shreveport, LA 71120-2260 · 318-221-6277

Joseph L. Shea, Jr. · Lemle & Kelleher · http://www.lemle.com · Louisiana Tower, 10th Floor · 401 Edwards Street · Shreveport, LA 71101-3289 · 318-227-1131

COMMUNICATIONS LAW

Baton Rouge

Janet S. Boles · The Boles Law Firm · 7914 Wrenwood Boulevard, Suite A · Baton Rouge, LA 70809 · 225-924-2686

Katherine W. King · Kean, Miller, Hawthorne, D'Armond, McCowan & Jarman · One American Place, 22nd Floor · P.O. Box 3513 · Baton Rouge, LA 70821 · 225-387-0999

New Orleans

James R. Swanson · Fishman Haygood Phelps Walmsley Willis & Swanson · http://www.cfhlaw.com · 201 St. Charles Avenue, 46th Floor · New Orleans, LA 70170-4600 · 504-586-5252

Constance Charles Willems · McGlinchey Stafford · http://www.mcglinchey.com · 643 Magazine Street · New Orleans, LA 70130 · 504-586-1200

CONSTRUCTION LAW

Baton Rouge

Michael D. Hunt · Phelps Dunbar · http://www.phelpsdunbar.com · City Plaza, Suite 701 · 445 North Boulevard · Baton Rouge, LA 70802 · 225-346-0285

Paul H. Spaht · Kantrow, Spaht, Weaver & Blitzer · City Plaza Building, Suite 300 · 445 North Boulevard P.O. Box 2997 · Baton Rouge, LA 70821-2997 · 225-383-4703

Lake Charles

Emmett C. Sole · Stockwell, Sievert, Viccellio, Clements & Shaddock · One Lakeside Plaza, Fourth Floor · P.O. Box 2900 · Lake Charles, LA 70602 · 337-436-9491

Mandeville

Mark W. Mercante · Baker, Donelson, Bearman, Caldwell & Berkowitz · http://www.bakerdonelson.com Three Sanctuary Boulevard, Suite 201 · Mandeville, LA 70471 · 985-819-8400

Danny G. Shaw · Baker, Donelson, Bearman, Caldwell & Berkowitz · http://www.bakerdonelson.com · Three Sanctuary Boulevard, Suite 201 · Mandeville, LA 70471 · 985-819-8400

New Orleans

Gerardo R. Barrios · Baker, Donelson, Bearman, Caldwell & Berkowitz · http://www.bakerdonelson.com 201 St. Charles Avenue, Suite 3600 · New Orleans, LA 70170-1000 · 504-566-5200

Terrence L. Brennan · Deutsch, Kerrigan & Stiles · http://www.dkslaw.com · 755 Magazine Street · New Orleans, LA 70130-3672 · 504-581-5141

Jay H. Kern · Simon, Peragine, Smith & Redfearn · Energy Centre, 30th Floor · 1100 Poydras Street · New Orleans, LA 70163-3000 · 504-569-2030

David J. Krebs · Krebs, Farley & Pelleteri · http://www.kfplaw.com · 400 Poydras Street, Suite 2500 · New Orleans, LA 70130 · 504-299-3570

Denise C. Puente · Simon, Peragine, Smith & Redfearn · Energy Centre, 30th Floor · 1100 Poydras Street New Orleans, LA 70163-3000 · 504-569-2030

Gary J. Rouse · Couhig Partners · 1100 Poydras Street, Suite 1150 · New Orleans, LA 70163 · 504-588-1288

Michael R. Schneider · Stone Pigman Walther Wittmann · http://www.stonepigman.com · 546 Carondelet Street · New Orleans, LA 70130-3588 · 504-581-3200

Charles F. Seemann, Jr. · Deutsch, Kerrigan & Stiles · http://www.dkslaw.com · 755 Magazine Street · New Orleans, LA 70130-3672 · 504-581-5141

Lloyd N. Shields · Shields Mott Lund · http://www.shieldsmottlund.com · 650 Poydras Street, Suite 2600 New Orleans, LA 70130 · 504-581-4445

H. Bruce Shreves · Simon, Peragine, Smith & Redfearn · Energy Centre, 30th Floor · 1100 Poydras Street · New Orleans, LA 70163-3000 · 504-569-2030

Howard E. Sinor, Jr. · Gordon, Arata, McCollam, Duplantis & Eagan · http://www.gordonarata.com · Place St. Charles, Suite 4000 · 201 St. Charles Avenue · New Orleans, LA 70170-4000 · 504-582-1111

Richard J. Tyler · Jones Walker · http://www.joneswalker.com · 201 St. Charles Avenue · New Orleans, LA 70170-5100 · 504-582-8000

CORPORATE GOVERNANCE AND COMPLIANCE LAW

Shreveport

Herschel E. Richard, Jr. · a · Cook, Yancey, King & Galloway · 333 Texas Street, Suite 1700 · P.O. Box 22260 · Shreveport, LA 71120-2260 · 318-221-6277

CORPORATE LAW

Alexandria

Charles S. Weems III · Gold, Weems, Bruser, Sues & Rundell · 2001 MacArthur Drive · P.O. Box 6118 · Alexandria, LA 71307-6118 · 318-445-6471

Baton Rouge

Rodolfo J. Aguilar, Jr. · McGlinchey Stafford · http://www.mcglinchey.com · One American Place, 14th Floor · 301 Main Street · Baton Rouge, LA 70825-0001 · 225-383-9000

John S. Campbell, Jr. · Taylor, Porter, Brooks & Phillips · Chase Tower South, Eighth Floor · 451 Florida Street · P.O. Box 2471 · Baton Rouge, LA 70821-2471 · 225-387-3221

G. Blane Clark, Jr. · Kean, Miller, Hawthorne, D'Armond, McCowan & Jarman · One American Place, 22nd Floor · P.O. Box 3513 · Baton Rouge, LA 70821 · 225-387-0999

Lee C. Kantrow · a · Kantrow, Spaht, Weaver & Blitzer · City Plaza Building, Suite 300 · 445 North Boulevard · P.O. Box 2997 · Baton Rouge, LA 70821-2997 · 225-383-4703

B. Michael Mauldin · Jones Walker · http://www.joneswalker.com · Four United Plaza, Suite 500 · 8555 United Plaza Boulevard · Baton Rouge, LA 70809-7000 · 225-248-2000

Ben R. Miller, Jr. · 2) · Kean, Miller, Hawthorne, D'Armond, McCowan & Jarman · One American Place, 22nd Floor · P.O. Box 3513 · Baton Rouge, LA 70821 · 225-387-0999

B. Troy Villa · Breazeale, Sachse and Wilson · One American Place, Suite 2300 · P.O. Box 3197 · Baton Rouge, LA 70821-3197 · 225-387-4000

Paul S. West · a · McGlinchey Stafford · http://www.mcglinchey.com · One American Place, 14th Floor · 301 Main Street · Baton Rouge, LA 70825-0001 · 225-383-9000

New Orleans

Joseph L. Caverly · Stone Pigman Walther Wittmann · http://www.stonepigman.com · 546 Carondelet Street · New Orleans, LA 70130-3588 · 504-581-3200

David J. Conroy · a · Milling Benson Woodward · 909 Poydras Street, Suite 2300 · New Orleans, LA 70112-1010 · 504-569-7000

O. Ray Cornelius · Adams and Reese · http://www.adamsandreese.com · One Shell Square, Suite 4500 · 701 Poydras Street · New Orleans, LA 70139 · 504-581-3234

Anthony J. Correro III · 2% · Adams and Reese · http://www.adamsandreese.com · One Shell Square, Suite 4500 · 701 Poydras Street · New Orleans, LA 70139 · 504-581-3234

Louis Y. Fishman · 2% · Fishman Haygood Phelps Walmsley Willis & Swanson · http://www.cfhlaw.com · 201 St. Charles Avenue, 46th Floor · New Orleans, LA 70170-4600 · 504-586-5252

Mark A. Fullmer · Phelps Dunbar · http://www.phelpsdunbar.com · Canal Place, Suite 2000 · 365 Canal Street · New Orleans, LA 70130-6534 · 504-566-1311

Edward N. George · Chaffe McCall · 2300 Energy Centre · 1100 Poydras Street · New Orleans, LA 70163-2300 · 504-585-7000

Paul M. Haygood · 2% · Fishman Haygood Phelps Walmsley Willis & Swanson · http://www.cfhlaw.com · 201 St. Charles Avenue, 46th Floor · New Orleans, LA 70170-4600 · 504-586-5252

Curtis R. Hearn · a · Jones Walker · http://www.joneswalker.com · 201 St. Charles Avenue · New Orleans, LA 70170-5100 · 504-582-8000

William H. Hines · a · Jones Walker · http://www.joneswalker.com · 201 St. Charles Avenue · New Orleans, LA 70170-5100 · 504-582-8000

F. Rivers Lelong, Jr. · Jones Walker · http://www.joneswalker.com · 201 St. Charles Avenue · New Orleans, LA 70170-5100 · 504-582-8000

Kenneth J. Najder · Jones Walker · http://www.joneswalker.com · 201 St. Charles Avenue · New Orleans, LA 70170-5100 · 504-582-8000

William N. Norton · Baker, Donelson, Bearman, Caldwell & Berkowitz · http://www.bakerdonelson.com · 201 St. Charles Avenue, Suite 3600 · New Orleans, LA 70170-1000 · 504-566-5200

J. Marshall Page III · Jones Walker · http://www.joneswalker.com · 201 St. Charles Avenue · New Orleans, LA 70170-5100 · 504-582-8000

Leon J. Reymond III · Stone Pigman Walther Wittmann · http://www.stonepigman.com · 546 Carondelet Street · New Orleans, LA 70130-3588 · 504-581-3200

Leon J. Reymond, Jr. · Liskow & Lewis · http://www.liskow.com · One Shell Square, Suite 5000 · 701 Poydras Street · New Orleans, LA 70139-5099 · 504-581-7979

Dionne M. Rousseau · a · Jones Walker · http://www.joneswalker.com · 201 St. Charles Avenue · New Orleans, LA 70170-5100 · 504-582-8000

Charles A. Snyder · 2) · Milling Benson Woodward · 909 Poydras Street, Suite 2300 · New Orleans, LA 70112-1010 · 504-569-7000

Harvey D. Wagar III · Phelps Dunbar · http://www.phelpsdunbar.com · Canal Place, Suite 2000 · 365 Canal Street · New Orleans, LA 70130-6534 · 504-566-1311

Robert M. Walmsley, Jr. · a · Fishman Haygood Phelps Walmsley Willis & Swanson · http://www.cfhlaw.com · 201 St. Charles Avenue, 46th Floor · New Orleans, LA 70170-4600 · 504-586-5252

Scott T. Whittaker · Stone Pigman Walther Wittmann · http://www.stonepigman.com · 546 Carondelet Street · New Orleans, LA 70130-3588 · 504-581-3200

John D. Wogan · a · Liskow & Lewis · http://www.liskow.com · One Shell Square, Suite 5000 · 701 Poydras Street · New Orleans, LA 70139-5099 · 504-581-7979

Richard P. Wolfe · a · Jones Walker · http://www.joneswalker.com · 201 St. Charles Avenue · New Orleans, LA 70170-5100 · 504-582-8000

DERIVATIVES LAW

New Orleans

O. Ray Cornelius · Adams and Reese · http://www.adamsandreese.com · One Shell Square, Suite 4500 · 701 Poydras Street · New Orleans, LA 70139 · 504-581-3234

DUI/DWI DEFENSE

Shreveport

Kenneth Craig Smith, Jr. · Smith & John · http://www.smith-john.com · 3646 Youree Drive · Shreveport, LA 71105 · 318-219-1001

Jason W. Waltman · Jason W. Waltman · 3646 Youree Drive · Shreveport, LA 71105 · 318-861-4394

ELDER LAW

New Orleans

Roselyn B. Koretzky · Milling Benson Woodward · 909 Poydras Street, Suite 2300 · New Orleans, LA 70112-1010 · 504-569-7000

John A. Rouchell · a · Baldwin Haspel Burke & Mayer · Energy Centre, Suite 2200 · 1100 Poydras Street · New Orleans, LA 70163-2200 · 504-585-7711

Kenneth A. Weiss · a · McGlinchey Stafford · http://www.mcglinchey.com · 643 Magazine Street · New Orleans, LA 70130 · 504-586-1200

EMINENT DOMAIN AND CONDEMNATION LAW

New Orleans

O. Ray Cornelius · Adams and Reese · http://www.adamsandreese.com · One Shell Square, Suite 4500 · 701 Poydras Street · New Orleans, LA 70139 · 504-581-3234

EMPLOYEE BENEFITS LAW

Baton Rouge

John C. Blackman IV · 2) · Jones Walker · http://www.joneswalker.com · Four United Plaza, Suite 500 · 8555 United Plaza Boulevard · Baton Rouge, LA 70809-7000 · 225-248-2000

Robert C. Schmidt · 2) · Adams and Reese · http://www.adamsandreese.com · 450 Laurel Street, Suite 1900 · Baton Rouge, LA 70801 · 225-336-5200

New Orleans

Jane E. Armstrong · 2) · Phelps Dunbar · http://www.phelpsdunbar.com · Canal Place, Suite 2000 · 365 Canal Street · New Orleans, LA 70130-6534 · 504-566-1311

Hilton S. Bell · 2) · Milling Benson Woodward · 909 Poydras Street, Suite 2300 · New Orleans, LA 70112-1010 · 504-569-7000

Susan K. Chambers · Jones Walker · http://www.joneswalker.com · 201 St. Charles Avenue · New Orleans, LA 70170-5100 · 504-582-8000

Katherine Conklin · McGlinchey Stafford · http://www.mcglinchey.com · 643 Magazine Street · New Orleans, LA 70130 · 504-586-1200

Sandra M. Feingerts · a · Fisher & Phillips · http://www.laborlawyers.com · 201 St. Charles Avenue, Suite 3710 · New Orleans, LA 70170 · 504-529-3303

Michael E. Guarisco · 2) · Guarisco & Cordes · 301 St. Charles Avenue, Suite 250 · New Orleans, LA 70130 · 504-587-7007

Edward F. Martin · 2) · Jones Walker · http://www.joneswalker.com · 201 St. Charles Avenue · New Orleans, LA 70170-5100 · 504-582-8000

Rudolph R. Ramelli · 2) · Jones Walker · http://www.joneswalker.com · 201 St. Charles Avenue · New Orleans, LA 70170-5100 · 504-582-8000

Howard Shapiro · a · Proskauer Rose · http://www.proskauer.com · 909 Poydras Street, Suite 1100 · New Orleans, LA 70112-4017 · 504-310-4088

Randye C. Snyder · Liskow & Lewis · http://www.liskow.com · One Shell Square, Suite 5000 · 701 Poydras Street · New Orleans, LA 70139-5099 · 504-581-7979

ENERGY LAW

Baton Rouge

James L. Ellis · a · Taylor, Porter, Brooks & Phillips · Chase Tower South, Eighth Floor · 451 Florida Street · P.O. Box 2471 · Baton Rouge, LA 70821-2471 · 225-387-3221

G. William Jarman · Kean, Miller, Hawthorne, D'Armond, McCowan & Jarman · One American Place, 22nd Floor · P.O. Box 3513 · Baton Rouge, LA 70821 · 225-387-0999

Katherine W. King · Kean, Miller, Hawthorne, D'Armond, McCowan & Jarman · One American Place, 22nd Floor · P.O. Box 3513 · Baton Rouge, LA 70821 · 225-387-0999

Robert W. Scheffy, Jr. · Jones Walker · http://www.joneswalker.com · Four United Plaza, Suite 500 · 8555 United Plaza Boulevard · Baton Rouge, LA 70809-7000 · 225-248-2000

J. Randy Young · Kean, Miller, Hawthorne, D'Armond, McCowan & Jarman · One American Place, 22nd Floor · P.O. Box 3513 · Baton Rouge, LA 70821 · 225-387-0999

Lafayette

Robert L. Cabes · Milling Benson Woodward · 101 La Rue France, Suite 200 · Lafayette, LA 70508 · 337-232-3929

Bob J. Duplantis · Gordon, Arata, McCollam, Duplantis & Eagan · http://www.gordonarata.com · 400 East Kaliste Saloom Road, Suite 4200 · Lafayette, LA 70508-8517 · 337-237-0132

James N. Mansfield III · Liskow & Lewis · http://www.liskow.com · 822 Harding Street · P.O. Box 52008 Lafayette, LA 70505-2008 · 337-232-7424

Richard W. Revels, Jr. · Liskow & Lewis · http://www.liskow.com · 822 Harding Street · P.O. Box 52008 Lafayette, LA 70505-2008 · 337-232-7424

George H. Robinson, Jr. · Liskow & Lewis · http://www.liskow.com · 822 Harding Street · P.O. Box 52008 · Lafayette, LA 70505-2008 · 337-232-7424

Monroe

Daniel Ryan Sartor, Jr. · 2) · Snellings, Breard, Sartor, Inabnett & Trascher · 1503 North 19th Street · P.O. Box 2055 · Monroe, LA 71207-2055 · 318-387-8000

New Orleans

Thomas Beron · Liskow & Lewis · http://www.liskow.com · One Shell Square, Suite 5000 · 701 Poydras Street · New Orleans, LA 70139-5099 · 504-581-7979

Ewell E. Eagan, Jr. · Gordon, Arata, McCollam, Duplantis & Eagan · http://www.gordonarata.com · Place St. Charles, Suite 4000 · 201 St. Charles Avenue · New Orleans, LA 70170-4000 · 504-582-1111

Ernest L. Edwards, Jr. · Lemle & Kelleher · http://www.lemle.com · Pan American Life Center, Suite 2100 · 601 Poydras Street · New Orleans, LA 70130-6097 · 504-586-1241

Michael R. Fontham · a · Stone Pigman Walther Wittmann · http://www.stonepigman.com · 546 Carondelet Street · New Orleans, LA 70130-3588 · 504-581-3200

C. Peck Hayne, Jr. · Gordon, Arata, McCollam, Duplantis & Eagan · http://www.gordonarata.com · Place St. Charles, Suite 4000 · 201 St. Charles Avenue · New Orleans, LA 70170-4000 · 504-582-1111

Jonathan A. Hunter · Liskow & Lewis · http://www.liskow.com · One Shell Square, Suite 5000 · 701 Poydras Street · New Orleans, LA 70139-5099 · 504-581-7979

Gene W. Lafitte · 2% · Liskow & Lewis · http://www.liskow.com · One Shell Square, Suite 5000 · 701 Poydras Street · New Orleans, LA 70139-5099 · 504-581-7979

John M. McCollam · 2) · Gordon, Arata, McCollam, Duplantis & Eagan · http://www.gordonarata.com · Place St. Charles, Suite 4000 · 201 St. Charles Avenue · New Orleans, LA 70170-4000 · 504-582-1111

Edward B. Poitevent II · Baker, Donelson, Bearman, Caldwell & Berkowitz · http://www.bakerdonelson.com · 201 St. Charles Avenue, Suite 3600 · New Orleans, LA 70170-1000 · 504-566-5200

Alan C. Wolf · Phelps Dunbar · http://www.phelpsdunbar.com · Canal Place, Suite 2000 · 365 Canal Street · New Orleans, LA 70130-6534 · 504-566-1311

Paul L. Zimmering · a · Stone Pigman Walther Wittmann · http://www.stonepigman.com · 546 Carondelet Street · New Orleans, LA 70130-3588 · 504-581-3200

Shreveport

Arthur R. Carmody, Jr. · a · Wilkinson, Carmody & Gilliam · 400 Travis Street, Suite 1700 · Shreveport, LA 71101 · 318-221-4196

J. William Fleming · Cook, Yancey, King & Galloway · 333 Texas Street, Suite 1700 · P.O. Box 22260 · Shreveport, LA 71120-2260 · 318-221-6277

Bobby S. Gilliam · Wilkinson, Carmody & Gilliam · 400 Travis Street, Suite 1700 · Shreveport, LA 71101 · 318-221-4196

Joseph L. Hargrove, Jr. · Hargrove, Smelley, Strickland & Langley · American Towers, Suite 600 · 401 Market Street · P.O. Box 59 · Shreveport, LA 71161-0059 · 318-429-7200

David L. Smelley · Hargrove, Smelley, Strickland & Langley · American Towers, Suite 600 · 401 Market Street · P.O. Box 59 · Shreveport, LA 71161-0059 · 318-429-7200

ENVIRONMENTAL LAW

Baton Rouge

Robert L. Coco · Taylor, Porter, Brooks & Phillips · Chase Tower South, Eighth Floor · 451 Florida Street · P.O. Box 2471 · Baton Rouge, LA 70821-2471 · 225-387-3221

Paul O. Dicharry · Taylor, Porter, Brooks & Phillips · Chase Tower South, Eighth Floor · 451 Florida Street · P.O. Box 2471 · Baton Rouge, LA 70821-2471 · 225-387-3221

Maureen N. Harbourt · Kean, Miller, Hawthorne, D'Armond, McCowan & Jarman · One American Place, 22nd Floor · P.O. Box 3513 · Baton Rouge, LA 70821 · 225-387-0999

Leonard L. Kilgore III · Kean, Miller, Hawthorne, D'Armond, McCowan & Jarman · One American Place, 22nd Floor · P.O. Box 3513 · Baton Rouge, LA 70821 · 225-387-0999

Gerald L. Walter, Jr. · a · Taylor, Porter, Brooks & Phillips · Chase Tower South, Eighth Floor · 451 Florida Street · P.O. Box 2471 · Baton Rouge, LA 70821-2471 · 225-387-3221

Lafayette

Thomas M. McNamara · a · Johnson Gray McNamara · 200 West Congress Street, Suite 900 · P.O. Box 51165 · Lafayette, LA 70505 · 337-412-6003

Mandeville

Mary Johnson · Johnson Gray McNamara · 21357 Marion Lane, Suite 300 · Mandeville, LA 70471 · 985-246-6544

New Orleans

Michael A. Chernekoff · Jones Walker · http://www.joneswalker.com · 201 St. Charles Avenue · New Orleans, LA 70170-5100 · 504-582-8000

George A. Frilot III · a · Frilot · 1100 Poydras Street, Suite 3600 · New Orleans, LA 70163 · 504-599-8000

Thomas M. Nosewicz · Jones Walker · http://www.joneswalker.com · 201 St. Charles Avenue · New Orleans, LA 70170-5100 · 504-582-8000

Glen M. Pilie · Adams and Reese · http://www.adamsandreese.com · One Shell Square, Suite 4500 · 701 Poydras Street · New Orleans, LA 70139 · 504-581-3234

Andrew L. Plauché, Jr. · Plauché, Maselli, Landry & Parkerson · One Shell Square, Suite 3800 · 701 Poydras Street · New Orleans, LA 70139 · 504-582-1142

EQUIPMENT FINANCE LAW

Baton Rouge

R. Marshall Grodner · McGlinchey Stafford · http://www.mcglinchey.com · One American Place, 14th Floor · 301 Main Street · Baton Rouge, LA 70825-0001 · 225-383-9000

New Orleans

Edward H. Arnold III · Baker, Donelson, Bearman, Caldwell & Berkowitz · http://www.bakerdonelson.com · 201 St. Charles Avenue, Suite 3600 · New Orleans, LA 70170-1000 · 504-566-5200

O. Ray Cornelius · Adams and Reese · http://www.adamsandreese.com · One Shell Square, Suite 4500 · 701 Poydras Street · New Orleans, LA 70139 · 504-581-3234

James A. Stuckey · a · Phelps Dunbar · http://www.phelpsdunbar.com · Canal Place, Suite 2000 · 365 Canal Street · New Orleans, LA 70130-6534 · 504-566-1311

David S. Willenzik · a · McGlinchey Stafford · http://www.mcglinchey.com · 643 Magazine Street · New Orleans, LA 70130 · 504-586-1200

Sterling Scott Willis · Fishman Haygood Phelps Walmsley Willis & Swanson · http://www.cfhlaw.com · 201 St. Charles Avenue, 46th Floor · New Orleans, LA 70170-4600 · 504-586-5252

FAMILY LAW

Baton Rouge

Paul M. Hebert, Jr. · Breazeale, Sachse and Wilson · One American Place, Suite 2300 · P.O. Box 3197 · Baton Rouge, LA 70821-3197 · 225-387-4000

Donna Wright Lee · Lee & Walsh · 628 North Boulevard · Baton Rouge, LA 70802 · 225-344-0474

Lake Charles

Randy J. Fuerst · Fuerst & Godley · 130 West Kirby Street · Lake Charles, LA 70601 · 337-436-3332

John Green, Jr. · John Green, Jr. · 1135 Hodges Street · Lake Charles, LA 70601 · 337-990-0060

Walter M. Sanchez · The Sanchez Law Firm · 901 Lakeshore Drive, Suite 1050 · Lake Charles, LA 70601 · 337-433-4405

Metairie

Philip R. Riegel, Jr. · 2% · Riegel Law Firm · 3017 Twenty-First Street, Suite 150 · Metairie, LA 70002 · 504-834-5345

Frank P. Tranchina, Jr. · a · Dutel & Tranchina · Two Lakeway Center, Suite 1130 · 3850 North Causeway Boulevard · Metairie, LA 70002 · 504-831-0055

New Orleans

Steven J. Lane · Herman, Herman, Katz & Cotlar · http://www.hhkc.com · 820 O'Keefe Avenue · New Orleans, LA 70113 · 504-581-4892

Robert C. Lowe · 2% · Lowe, Stein, Hoffman, Allweiss & Hauver · One Shell Square, Suite 3600 · 701 Poydras Street · New Orleans, LA 70139-7735 · 504-581-2450

Shreveport

Hani E. Dehan · 2) · Love, Rigby, Dehan & McDaniel · 330 Marshall Street, Suite 1030 · P.O. Box 1835 · Shreveport, LA 71166-1835 · 318-226-1880

Kenneth Rigby · 2% · Love, Rigby, Dehan & McDaniel · 330 Marshall Street, Suite 1030 · P.O. Box 1835 · Shreveport, LA 71166-1835 · 318-226-1880

H. F. Sockrider, Jr. · 2) · Sockrider, Bolin, Anglin & Batte · 327 Crockett Street · Shreveport, LA 71101 · 318-221-5503

FIRST AMENDMENT LAW

New Orleans

Mary Ellen Roy · a · Phelps Dunbar · http://www.phelpsdunbar.com · Canal Place, Suite 2000 · 365 Canal Street · New Orleans, LA 70130-6534 · 504-566-1311

FRANCHISE LAW

Baton Rouge

Patrick Ragan Richard · Phelps Dunbar · http://www.phelpsdunbar.com · City Plaza, Suite 701 · 445 North Boulevard · Baton Rouge, LA 70802 · 225-346-0285

GAMING LAW

Baton Rouge

John S. Campbell, Jr. · Taylor, Porter, Brooks & Phillips · Chase Tower South, Eighth Floor · 451 Florida Street · P.O. Box 2471 · Baton Rouge, LA 70821-2471 · 225-387-3221

Paul S. West · a · McGlinchey Stafford · http://www.mcglinchey.com · One American Place, 14th Floor · 301 Main Street · Baton Rouge, LA 70825-0001 · 225-383-9000

New Orleans

Wm. Blake Bennett · Liskow & Lewis · http://www.liskow.com · One Shell Square, Suite 5000 · 701 Poydras Street · New Orleans, LA 70139-5099 · 504-581-7979

J. Kelly Duncan · Jones Walker · http://www.joneswalker.com · 201 St. Charles Avenue · New Orleans, LA 70170-5100 · 504-582-8000

C. Lawrence Orlansky · Stone Pigman Walther Wittmann · http://www.stonepigman.com · 546 Carondelet Street · New Orleans, LA 70130-3588 · 504-581-3200

Brian D. Wallace · Phelps Dunbar · http://www.phelpsdunbar.com · Canal Place, Suite 2000 · 365 Canal Street · New Orleans, LA 70130-6534 · 504-566-1311

GOVERNMENT RELATIONS LAW

Baton Rouge

Deborah Duplechin Harkins · McGlinchey Stafford · http://www.mcglinchey.com · One American Place, 14th Floor · 301 Main Street · Baton Rouge, LA 70825-0001 · 225-383-9000

Dickie Patterson · Baker, Donelson, Bearman, Caldwell & Berkowitz · http://www.bakerdonelson.com · One American Place, Suite 810 · 301 North Main Street · Baton Rouge, LA 70825 · 225-381-7000

New Orleans

O. Ray Cornelius · Adams and Reese · http://www.adamsandreese.com · One Shell Square, Suite 4500 · 701 Poydras Street · New Orleans, LA 70139 · 504-581-3234

Donna D. Fraiche · a · Baker, Donelson, Bearman, Caldwell & Berkowitz · http://www.bakerdonelson.com · 201 St. Charles Avenue, Suite 3600 · New Orleans, LA 70170-1000 · 504-566-5200

HEALTH CARE LAW

Baton Rouge

Errol J. King · a · McGlinchey Stafford · http://www.mcglinchey.com · One American Place, 14th Floor · 301 Main Street · Baton Rouge, LA 70825-0001 · 225-383-9000

Linda G. Rodrigue · Kean, Miller, Hawthorne, D'Armond, McCowan & Jarman · One American Place, 22nd Floor · P.O. Box 3513 · Baton Rouge, LA 70821 · 225-387-0999

Patrick D. Seiter · Taylor, Porter, Brooks & Phillips · Chase Tower South, Eighth Floor · 451 Florida Street · P.O. Box 2471 · Baton Rouge, LA 70821-2471 · 225-387-3221

Lake Charles

Richard B. Cappel · a · Raggio, Cappel, Chozen & Berniard · 1011 Lakeshore Drive, Suite 500 · Lake Charles, LA 70601 · 337-436-9481

New Orleans

Donna D. Fraiche · a · Baker, Donelson, Bearman, Caldwell & Berkowitz · http://www.bakerdonelson.com · 201 St. Charles Avenue, Suite 3600 · New Orleans, LA 70170-1000 · 504-566-5200

Joseph I. Giarrusso, Jr. · Law Office of Joe Giarrusso, Jr. · 3557 Inwood Avenue · New Orleans, LA 70131 · 504-554-2678

Donna G. Klein · a · McGlinchey Stafford · http://www.mcglinchey.com · 643 Magazine Street · New Orleans, LA 70130 · 504-586-1200

Roselyn B. Koretzky · Milling Benson Woodward · 909 Poydras Street, Suite 2300 · New Orleans, LA 70112-1010 · 504-569-7000

Peter E. Sperling · Frilot · 1100 Poydras Street, Suite 3600 · New Orleans, LA 70163 · 504-599-8000

Danielle L. Trostorff · a · Baker, Donelson, Bearman, Caldwell & Berkowitz · http://www.bakerdonelson.com · 201 St. Charles Avenue, Suite 3600 · New Orleans, LA 70170-1000 · 504-566-5200

IMMIGRATION LAW

Metairie

David A. M. Ware · a · David Ware & Associates · Two Lakeway Center, Suite 555 · 3850 North Causeway Boulevard · Metairie, LA 70002-1752 · 504-830-5900

New Orleans

Thomas P. Adams · a · Thomas P. Adams · 631 St. Charles Avenue · New Orleans, LA 70130 · 504-523-3815

Malvern C. Burnett · Law Offices of Malvern C. Burnett · 1523 Polymnia Street · New Orleans, LA 70130 · 504-586-1922

Lawrence B. Fabacher · a · Lawrence B. Fabacher · One Canal Place, Suite 2340 · 365 Canal Street · New Orleans, LA 70130 · 504-522-2800

INSURANCE LAW

Baton Rouge

John F. Jakuback · Kean, Miller, Hawthorne, D'Armond, McCowan & Jarman · One American Place, 22nd Floor · P.O. Box 3513 · Baton Rouge, LA 70821 · 225-387-0999

W. Shelby McKenzie · Taylor, Porter, Brooks & Phillips · Chase Tower South, Eighth Floor · 451 Florida Street · P.O. Box 2471 · Baton Rouge, LA 70821-2471 · 225-387-3221

Marshall M. Redmon · Phelps Dunbar · http://www.phelpsdunbar.com · City Plaza, Suite 701 · 445 North Boulevard · Baton Rouge, LA 70802 · 225-346-0285

Lafayette

John A. Jeansonne, Jr. · Jeansonne & Remondet · 200 West Congress Street, Suite 1100 · P.O. Box 91530 · Lafayette, LA 70509 · 337-237-4370

New Orleans

Sidney W. Degan III · Degan, Blanchard & Nash · Texaco Center, Suite 2600 · 400 Poydras Street · New Orleans, LA 70130 · 504-529-3333

Richard N. Dicharry · Phelps Dunbar · http://www.phelpsdunbar.com · Canal Place, Suite 2000 · 365 Canal Street · New Orleans, LA 70130-6534 · 504-566-1311

George D. Fagan · a · Leake & Andersson · Energy Centre, Suite 1700 · 1100 Poydras Street · New Orleans, LA 70163-1701 · 504-585-7500

George B. Hall, Jr. · Phelps Dunbar · http://www.phelpsdunbar.com · Canal Place, Suite 2000 · 365 Canal Street · New Orleans, LA 70130-6534 · 504-566-1311

Stephen P. Hall · Phelps Dunbar · http://www.phelpsdunbar.com · Canal Place, Suite 2000 · 365 Canal Street · New Orleans, LA 70130-6534 · 504-566-1311

William H. Hines · a · Jones Walker · http://www.joneswalker.com · 201 St. Charles Avenue · New Orleans, LA 70170-5100 · 504-582-8000

James K. Irvin · Milling Benson Woodward · 909 Poydras Street, Suite 2300 · New Orleans, LA 70112-1010 · 504-569-7000

Harvey C. Koch · Montgomery, Barnett, Brown, Read, Hammond & Mintz · http://www.monbar.com · 1100 Poydras Street, Suite 3200 · New Orleans, LA 70163-3200 · 504-585-3200

Wayne J. Lee · Stone Pigman Walther Wittmann · http://www.stonepigman.com · 546 Carondelet Street · New Orleans, LA 70130-3588 · 504-581-3200

Andrew L. Plauché, Jr. · Plauché, Maselli, Landry & Parkerson · One Shell Square, Suite 3800 · 701 Poydras Street · New Orleans, LA 70139 · 504-582-1142

William D. Treeby · Stone Pigman Walther Wittmann · http://www.stonepigman.com · 546 Carondelet Street · New Orleans, LA 70130-3588 · 504-581-3200

Hal C. Welch · Lemle & Kelleher · http://www.lemle.com · Pan American Life Center, Suite 2100 · 601 Poydras Street · New Orleans, LA 70130-6097 · 504-586-1241

INTELLECTUAL PROPERTY LAW

Baton Rouge

Allen D. Darden · Phelps Dunbar · http://www.phelpsdunbar.com · City Plaza, Suite 701 · 445 North Boulevard · Baton Rouge, LA 70802 · 225-346-0285

Bonnie J. Davis · Taylor, Porter, Brooks & Phillips · Chase Tower South, Eighth Floor · 451 Florida Street · P.O. Box 2471 · Baton Rouge, LA 70821-2471 · 225-387-3221

Warner Delaune · Baker, Donelson, Bearman, Caldwell & Berkowitz · http://www.bakerdonelson.com · One American Place, Suite 810 · 301 North Main Street · Baton Rouge, LA 70825 · 225-381-7000

R. Andrew Patty · McGlinchey Stafford · http://www.mcglinchey.com · One American Place, 14th Floor · 301 Main Street · Baton Rouge, LA 70825-0001 · 225-383-9000

Russel O. Primeaux · Kean, Miller, Hawthorne, D'Armond, McCowan & Jarman · One American Place, 22nd Floor · P.O. Box 3513 · Baton Rouge, LA 70821 · 225-387-0999

Robert C. Tucker · Jones Walker · http://www.joneswalker.com · Four United Plaza, Suite 500 · 8555 United Plaza Boulevard · Baton Rouge, LA 70809-7000 · 225-248-2000

Metairie

Charles C. Garvey, Jr. · Garvey, Smith, Nehrbass & North · Three Lakeway Center, Suite 3290 · 3838 North Causeway Boulevard · Metairie, LA 70002 · 504-835-2000

Seth M. Nehrbass · Garvey, Smith, Nehrbass & North · Three Lakeway Center, Suite 3290 · 3838 North Causeway Boulevard · Metairie, LA 70002 · 504-835-2000

New Orleans

Joseph W. Looney · Adams and Reese · http://www.adamsandreese.com · One Shell Square, Suite 4500 · 701 Poydras Street · New Orleans, LA 70139 · 504-581-3234

Mary Ellen Roy · a · Phelps Dunbar · http://www.phelpsdunbar.com · Canal Place, Suite 2000 · 365 Canal Street · New Orleans, LA 70130-6534 · 504-566-1311

INTERNATIONAL ARBITRATION

Metairie

Thomas K. Foutz · ADR Incorporated · 3838 North Causeway Boulevard, Suite 2880 · Metairie, LA 70002 · 504-838-6100

INTERNATIONAL TRADE AND FINANCE LAW

New Orleans

William H. Hines · a · Jones Walker · http://www.joneswalker.com · 201 St. Charles Avenue · New Orleans, LA 70170-5100 · 504-582-8000

J. Marshall Page III · Jones Walker · http://www.joneswalker.com · 201 St. Charles Avenue · New Orleans, LA 70170-5100 · 504-582-8000

Richard P. Wolfe · a · Jones Walker · http://www.joneswalker.com · 201 St. Charles Avenue · New Orleans, LA 70170-5100 · 504-582-8000

LABOR AND EMPLOYMENT LAW

Baton Rouge

Vicki M. Crochet · Taylor, Porter, Brooks & Phillips · Chase Tower South, Eighth Floor · 451 Florida Street · P.O. Box 2471 · Baton Rouge, LA 70821-2471 · 225-387-3221

Thomas H. Kiggans · Phelps Dunbar · http://www.phelpsdunbar.com · City Plaza, Suite 701 · 445 North Boulevard · Baton Rouge, LA 70802 · 225-346-0285

William M. McGoey · a · Casteel & Associates · 138 McGehee Drive · Baton Rouge, LA 70815 · 225-273-4442

Covington

Michael T. Tusa · The Tusa Law Firm · 512 South Tyler Street, Suite B · Covington, LA 70433 · 985-809-1405

Lafayette

Greg Guidry · Onebane Law Firm · http://www.onebane.com · 1200 Camellia Boulevard, Suite 300 · P.O. Drawer 3507 · Lafayette, LA 70502-3507 · 337-237-2660

Lake Charles

John S. Bradford · Stockwell, Sievert, Viccellio, Clements & Shaddock · One Lakeside Plaza, Fourth Floor · P.O. Box 2900 · Lake Charles, LA 70602 · 337-436-9491

Metairie

William H. Reinhardt, Jr. · a · Blue Williams · 3421 North Causeway Boulevard, Suite 900 · Metairie, LA 70002 · 504-831-4091

Louis L. Robein, Jr. · 2) · Robein, Urann, Spencer, Picard & Cangemi · 2540 Severn Avenue, Suite 400 · P.O. Box 6768 · Metairie, LA 70009-6768 · 504-885-9994

New Orleans

H. Mark Adams · Jones Walker · http://www.joneswalker.com · 201 St. Charles Avenue · New Orleans, LA 70170-5100 · 504-582-8000

M. Nan Alessandra · Phelps Dunbar · http://www.phelpsdunbar.com · Canal Place, Suite 2000 · 365 Canal Street · New Orleans, LA 70130-6534 · 504-566-1311

William F. Banta · a · The Kullman Firm · 1600 Energy Centre · 1100 Poydras Street · P.O. Box 60118 · New Orleans, LA 70160 · 504-524-4162

Stephen P. Beiser · McGlinchey Stafford · http://www.mcglinchey.com · 643 Magazine Street · New Orleans, LA 70130 · 504-586-1200

Brooke Duncan III · Adams and Reese · http://www.adamsandreese.com · One Shell Square, Suite 4500 · 701 Poydras Street · New Orleans, LA 70139 · 504-581-3234

Cornelius R. Heusel · Jones Walker · http://www.joneswalker.com · 201 St. Charles Avenue · New Orleans, LA 70170-5100 · 504-582-8000

Clyde H. Jacob III · Coats, Rose, Yale, Ryman & Lee · 400 Poydras Street, Suite 1440 · New Orleans, LA 70130 · 504-299-3070

S. Mark Klyza · The Kullman Firm · 1600 Energy Centre · 1100 Poydras Street · P.O. Box 60118 · New Orleans, LA 70160 · 504-524-4162

Sidney F. Lewis V · Jones Walker · http://www.joneswalker.com · 201 St. Charles Avenue · New Orleans, LA 70170-5100 · 504-582-8000

Julie D. Livaudais · Chaffe McCall · 2300 Energy Centre · 1100 Poydras Street · New Orleans, LA 70163-2300 · 504-585-7000

Mark N. Mallery · Kiesewetter Wise Kaplan Prather · 639 Loyola Avenue, Suite 2550 · New Orleans, LA 70113 · 504-648-3840

Ernest R. Malone, Jr. · The Kullman Firm · 1600 Energy Centre · 1100 Poydras Street · P.O. Box 60118 · New Orleans, LA 70160 · 504-524-4162

Robert K. McCalla · 2) · Fisher & Phillips · http://www.laborlawyers.com · 201 St. Charles Avenue, Suite 3710 · New Orleans, LA 70170 · 504-529-3303

Thomas J. McGoey II · Liskow & Lewis · http://www.liskow.com · One Shell Square, Suite 5000 · 701 Poydras Street · New Orleans, LA 70139-5099 · 504-581-7979

Michael S. Mitchell · Fisher & Phillips · http://www.laborlawyers.com · 201 St. Charles Avenue, Suite 3710 · New Orleans, LA 70170 · 504-529-3303

Christopher E. Moore · Coats, Rose, Yale, Ryman & Lee · 400 Poydras Street, Suite 1440 · New Orleans, LA 70130 · 504-299-3070

Ellis B. Murov · Deutsch, Kerrigan & Stiles · http://www.dkslaw.com · 755 Magazine Street · New Orleans, LA 70130-3672 · 504-581-5141

Keith M. Pyburn, Jr. · a · Fisher & Phillips · http://www.laborlawyers.com · 201 St. Charles Avenue, Suite 3710 · New Orleans, LA 70170 · 504-529-3303

Charles F. Seemann III · Proskauer Rose · http://www.proskauer.com · 909 Poydras Street, Suite 1100 · New Orleans, LA 70112-4017 · 504-310-4088

Howard Shapiro · a · Proskauer Rose · http://www.proskauer.com · 909 Poydras Street, Suite 1100 · New Orleans, LA 70112-4017 · 504-310-4088

Robert F. Spencer, Jr. · The Kullman Firm · 1600 Energy Centre · 1100 Poydras Street · P.O. Box 60118 New Orleans, LA 70160 · 504-524-4162

Robert B. Worley, Jr. · Jones Walker · http://www.joneswalker.com · 201 St. Charles Avenue · New Orleans, LA 70170-5100 · 504-582-8000

LAND USE & ZONING LAW

New Orleans

Richard P. Richter · Sher Garner Cahill Richter Klein & Hilbert · http://www.shergarner.com · 909 Poydras Street, Suite 2800 · New Orleans, LA 70112 · 504-299-2100

Leopold Z. Sher · Sher Garner Cahill Richter Klein & Hilbert · http://www.shergarner.com · 909 Poydras Street, Suite 2800 · New Orleans, LA 70112 · 504-299-2100

LEGAL MALPRACTICE LAW

Lafayette

Patrick A. Juneau, Jr. · a · Juneau Law Firm · The Harding Center, Suite 202 · 1018 Harding Street · P.O. Drawer 51268 · Lafayette, LA 70505-1268 · 337-269-0052

Lake Charles

Allen L. Smith, Jr. · a · Plauché, Smith & Nieset · 1123 Pithon Street · P.O. Drawer 1705 · Lake Charles, LA 70602 · 337-436-0522

New Orleans

Robert B. Acomb, Jr. · 2% · Jones Walker · http://www.joneswalker.com · 201 St. Charles Avenue · New Orleans, LA 70170-5100 · 504-582-8000

W. Paul Andersson · a · Leake & Andersson · Energy Centre, Suite 1700 · 1100 Poydras Street · New Orleans, LA 70163-1701 · 504-585-7500

James A. Brown · Liskow & Lewis · http://www.liskow.com · One Shell Square, Suite 5000 · 701 Poydras Street · New Orleans, LA 70139-5099 · 504-581-7979

Roy C. Cheatwood · a · Baker, Donelson, Bearman, Caldwell & Berkowitz · http://www.bakerdonelson.com · 201 St. Charles Avenue, Suite 3600 · New Orleans, LA 70170-1000 · 504-566-5200

William K. Christovich · 2% · Christovich & Kearney · 601 Poydras Street, Suite 2300 · New Orleans, LA 70130 · 504-561-5700

Gus A. Fritchie III · Irwin Fritchie Urquhart & Moore · 400 Poydras Street, Suite 2700 · New Orleans, LA 70130 · 504-310-2100

Harvey C. Koch · Montgomery, Barnett, Brown, Read, Hammond & Mintz · http://www.monbar.com · 1100 Poydras Street, Suite 3200 · New Orleans, LA 70163-3200 · 504-585-3200

Harvey J. Lewis · 2% · Lewis, Kullman, Sterbcow & Abramson · Pan American Life Center, Suite 2615 · 601 Poydras Street · New Orleans, LA 70130 · 504-588-1500

Daniel Lund · a · Montgomery, Barnett, Brown, Read, Hammond & Mintz · http://www.monbar.com · 1100 Poydras Street, Suite 3200 · New Orleans, LA 70163-3200 · 504-585-3200

Ernest L. O'Bannon · a · Bienvenu, Foster, Ryan & O'Bannon · 1010 Common Street, Suite 2200 · New Orleans, LA 70112 · 504-310-1500

Richard C. Stanley · Stanley, Flanagan & Reuter · http://www.sfrlawfirm.com · 909 Poydras Street, Suite 2500 · New Orleans, LA 70112 · 504-523-1580

Shreveport

Herschel E. Richard, Jr. · a · Cook, Yancey, King & Galloway · 333 Texas Street, Suite 1700 · P.O. Box 22260 · Shreveport, LA 71120-2260 · 318-221-6277

LEVERAGED BUYOUTS AND PRIVATE EQUITY LAW

New Orleans

Anthony J. Correro III · 2% · Adams and Reese · http://www.adamsandreese.com · One Shell Square, Suite 4500 · 701 Poydras Street · New Orleans, LA 70139 · 504-581-3234

MARITIME LAW

Alexandria

Richard J. Arsenault · a · Neblett, Beard & Arsenault · 2220 Bonaventure Court · P.O. Box 1190 · Alexandria, LA 71309-1190 · 318-487-9874

Baton Rouge

James A. George · a · George & George · 346 Shady Lake Parkway · Baton Rouge, LA 70810 · 225-769-3064

Lafayette

Lawrence K. Burleigh, Sr. · 2) · Lawrence K. Burleigh · Gordon Square, Suite 160 · 100 East Vermilion Street · Lafayette, LA 70501 · 337-234-6222

Lawrence N. Curtis · Lawrence N. Curtis · http://www.larrycurtis.com · 300 Rue Beauregard, Building C · Lafayette, LA 70508 · 337-235-1825

Patrick A. Juneau, Jr. · a · Juneau Law Firm · The Harding Center, Suite 202 · 1018 Harding Street · P.O. Drawer 51268 · Lafayette, LA 70505-1268 · 337-269-0052

Cliffe E. Laborde III · Laborde & Neuner · One Petroleum Center, Suite 200 · 1001 West Pinhook Road P.O. Drawer 52828 · Lafayette, LA 70505-2828 · 337-237-7000

Edwin G. Preis, Jr. · Preis & Roy · http://www.preisroy.com · Versailles Centre, Suite 400 · 102 Versailles Boulevard · P.O. Drawer 94-C · Lafayette, LA 70509 · 337-237-6062

George H. Robinson, Jr. · Liskow & Lewis · http://www.liskow.com · 822 Harding Street · P.O. Box 52008 · Lafayette, LA 70505-2008 · 337-232-7424

James Parkerson Roy · a · Domengeaux Wright Roy & Edwards · 556 Jefferson Street, Suite 500 · P.O. Box 3668 · Lafayette, LA 70501 · 337-233-3033

Randall K. Theunissen · Allen & Gooch · 1015 St. John Street · P.O. Box 3768 · Lafayette, LA 70502-3768 · 337-291-1000

Bob F. Wright · a · Domengeaux Wright Roy & Edwards · 556 Jefferson Street, Suite 500 · P.O. Box 3668 · Lafayette, LA 70501 · 337-233-3033

Lake Charles

Allen L. Smith, Jr. · a · Plauché, Smith & Nieset · 1123 Pithon Street · P.O. Drawer 1705 · Lake Charles, LA 70602 · 337-436-0522

New Orleans

Donald R. Abaunza · 2) · Liskow & Lewis · http://www.liskow.com · One Shell Square, Suite 5000 · 701 Poydras Street · New Orleans, LA 70139-5099 · 504-581-7979

Robert B. Acomb III · McAlpine & Cozad · 365 Canal Street, Suite 3180 · New Orleans, LA 70130-0323 504-561-1671

Robert B. Acomb, Jr. · 2% · Jones Walker · http://www.joneswalker.com · 201 St. Charles Avenue · New Orleans, LA 70170-5100 · 504-582-8000

Robert J. Barbier · Phelps Dunbar · http://www.phelpsdunbar.com · Canal Place, Suite 2000 · 365 Canal Street · New Orleans, LA 70130-6534 · 504-566-1311

Francis J. Barry, Jr. · Deutsch, Kerrigan & Stiles · http://www.dkslaw.com · 755 Magazine Street · New Orleans, LA 70130-3672 · 504-581-5141

John A. Bolles · a · Phelps Dunbar · http://www.phelpsdunbar.com · Canal Place, Suite 2000 · 365 Canal Street · New Orleans, LA 70130-6534 · 504-566-1311

John J. Broders · Jones Walker · http://www.joneswalker.com · 201 St. Charles Avenue · New Orleans, LA 70170-5100 · 504-582-8000

Kathleen K. Charvet · McGlinchey Stafford · http://www.mcglinchey.com · 643 Magazine Street · New Orleans, LA 70130 · 504-586-1200

William K. Christovich · 2% · Christovich & Kearney · 601 Poydras Street, Suite 2300 · New Orleans, LA 70130 · 504-561-5700

Christopher O. Davis · Baker, Donelson, Bearman, Caldwell & Berkowitz · http://www.bakerdonelson.com · 201 St. Charles Avenue, Suite 3600 · New Orleans, LA 70170-1000 · 504-566-5200

J. Kelly Duncan · Jones Walker · http://www.joneswalker.com · 201 St. Charles Avenue · New Orleans, LA 70170-5100 · 504-582-8000

S. Gene Fendler · Liskow & Lewis · http://www.liskow.com · One Shell Square, Suite 5000 · 701 Poydras Street · New Orleans, LA 70139-5099 · 504-581-7979

Joshua S. Force · Sher Garner Cahill Richter Klein & Hilbert · http://www.shergarner.com · 909 Poydras Street, Suite 2800 · New Orleans, LA 70112 · 504-299-2100

George J. Fowler III · Fowler Rodriguez · http://www.frc-law.com · 400 Poydras Street, 30th Floor · New Orleans, LA 70130 · 504-523-2600

George A. Frilot III · a · Frilot · 1100 Poydras Street, Suite 3600 · New Orleans, LA 70163 · 504-599-8000

John B. Gooch, Jr. · 2) · Montgomery, Barnett, Brown, Read, Hammond & Mintz · http://www.monbar.com · 1100 Poydras Street, Suite 3200 · New Orleans, LA 70163-3200 · 504-585-3200

Glenn G. Goodier · Jones Walker · http://www.joneswalker.com · 201 St. Charles Avenue · New Orleans, LA 70170-5100 · 504-582-8000

A. Gordon Grant, Jr. · a · Montgomery, Barnett, Brown, Read, Hammond & Mintz · http://www.monbar.com · 1100 Poydras Street, Suite 3200 · New Orleans, LA 70163-3200 · 504-585-3200

Don K. Haycraft · Liskow & Lewis · http://www.liskow.com · One Shell Square, Suite 5000 · 701 Poydras Street · New Orleans, LA 70139-5099 · 504-581-7979

Peter L. Hilbert, Jr. · Sher Garner Cahill Richter Klein & Hilbert · http://www.shergarner.com · 909 Poydras Street, Suite 2800 · New Orleans, LA 70112 · 504-299-2100

Grady S. Hurley · Jones Walker · http://www.joneswalker.com · 201 St. Charles Avenue · New Orleans, LA 70170-5100 · 504-582-8000

Ronald A. Johnson · Johnson, Johnson, Barrios & Yacoubian · http://www.jjbylaw.com · One Shell Square, Suite 4700 · 701 Poydras Street · New Orleans, LA 70139-7701 · 504-528-3001

Edward J. Koehl, Jr. · Jones Walker · http://www.joneswalker.com · 201 St. Charles Avenue · New Orleans, LA 70170-5100 · 504-582-8000

David B. Lawton · Phelps Dunbar · http://www.phelpsdunbar.com · Canal Place, Suite 2000 · 365 Canal Street · New Orleans, LA 70130-6534 · 504-566-1311

J. Dwight LeBlanc III · Frilot · 1100 Poydras Street, Suite 3600 · New Orleans, LA 70163 · 504-599-8000

J. Dwight LeBlanc, Jr. · a · Chaffe McCall · 2300 Energy Centre · 1100 Poydras Street · New Orleans, LA 70163-2300 · 504-585-7000

David W. Leefe · Liskow & Lewis · http://www.liskow.com · One Shell Square, Suite 5000 · 701 Poydras Street · New Orleans, LA 70139-5099 · 504-581-7979

Robert T. Lemon II · Jones Walker · http://www.joneswalker.com · 201 St. Charles Avenue · New Orleans, LA 70170-5100 · 504-582-8000

Harvey J. Lewis · 2% · Lewis, Kullman, Sterbcow & Abramson · Pan American Life Center, Suite 2615 · 601 Poydras Street · New Orleans, LA 70130 · 504-588-1500

Stewart F. Peck · Lugenbuhl, Wheaton, Peck, Rankin & Hubbard · Pan-American Life Center, 27th Floor · 601 Poydras Street · New Orleans, LA 70130 · 504-568-1990

Antonio J. Rodriguez · Fowler Rodriguez · http://www.frc-law.com · 400 Poydras Street, 30th Floor · New Orleans, LA 70130 · 504-523-2600

James H. Roussel · Baker, Donelson, Bearman, Caldwell & Berkowitz · http://www.bakerdonelson.com · 201 St. Charles Avenue, Suite 3600 · New Orleans, LA 70170-1000 · 504-566-5200

Mark J. Spansel · Adams and Reese · http://www.adamsandreese.com · One Shell Square, Suite 4500 · 701 Poydras Street · New Orleans, LA 70139 · 504-581-3234

Hugh R. Straub · Phelps Dunbar · http://www.phelpsdunbar.com · Canal Place, Suite 2000 · 365 Canal Street · New Orleans, LA 70130-6534 · 504-566-1311

MASS TORT LITIGATION

Abita Springs

Edward F. Kohnke IV · Hamlin, Griffin & Kohnke · 71648 Maple Street · Abita Springs, LA 70420 · 985-246-6001

Baton Rouge

David M. Bienvenu, Jr. · Taylor, Porter, Brooks & Phillips · Chase Tower South, Eighth Floor · 451 Florida Street · P.O. Box 2471 · Baton Rouge, LA 70821-2471 · 225-387-3221

Charles S. McCowan, Jr. · a · Kean, Miller, Hawthorne, D'Armond, McCowan & Jarman · One American Place, 22nd Floor · P.O. Box 3513 · Baton Rouge, LA 70821 · 225-387-0999

John Michael Parker · Taylor, Porter, Brooks & Phillips · Chase Tower South, Eighth Floor · 451 Florida Street · P.O. Box 2471 · Baton Rouge, LA 70821-2471 · 225-387-3221

Lewis O. Unglesby · 2) · Unglesby & Marionneaux · http://www.unglesbyandmarionneaux.com · 246 Napoleon Street · Baton Rouge, LA 70802 · 225-387-0120

Denham Springs

Calvin C. Fayard, Jr. · Fayard & Honeycutt · 519 Florida Avenue, SW · Denham Springs, LA 70726 · 225-664-0304

Lake Charles

William B. Monk · Stockwell, Sievert, Viccellio, Clements & Shaddock · One Lakeside Plaza, Fourth Floor · P.O. Box 2900 · Lake Charles, LA 70602 · 337-436-9491

New Orleans

Robert E. Barkley, Jr. · 2) · Barkley & Thompson · 1515 Poydras Street, Suite 2350 · New Orleans, LA 70112 · 504-595-3350

Mark C. Dodart · Phelps Dunbar · http://www.phelpsdunbar.com · Canal Place, Suite 2000 · 365 Canal Street · New Orleans, LA 70130-6534 · 504-566-1311

Robert S. Emmett · Baker, Donelson, Bearman, Caldwell & Berkowitz · http://www.bakerdonelson.com · 201 St. Charles Avenue, Suite 3600 · New Orleans, LA 70170-1000 · 504-566-5200

James M. Garner · Sher Garner Cahill Richter Klein & Hilbert · http://www.shergarner.com · 909 Poydras Street, Suite 2800 · New Orleans, LA 70112 · 504-299-2100

Russ M. Herman · 25 · Herman, Herman, Katz & Cotlar · http://www.hhkc.com · 820 O'Keefe Avenue · New Orleans, LA 70113 · 504-581-4892

William H. Howard III · Baker, Donelson, Bearman, Caldwell & Berkowitz · http://www.bakerdonelson.com · 201 St. Charles Avenue, Suite 3600 · New Orleans, LA 70170-1000 · 504-566-5200

Keith Alex Kornman · Degan, Blanchard & Nash · Texaco Center, Suite 2600 · 400 Poydras Street · New Orleans, LA 70130 · 504-529-3333

John P. Manard, Jr. · Phelps Dunbar · http://www.phelpsdunbar.com · Canal Place, Suite 2000 · 365 Canal Street · New Orleans, LA 70130-6534 · 504-566-1311

Gerald E. Meunier · 10 · Gainsburgh, Benjamin, David, Meunier & Warshauer · http://www.gainsburghbenjamin.com · 2800 Energy Centre · 1100 Poydras Street · New Orleans, LA 70163-2800 · 504-522-2304

James H. Roussel · Baker, Donelson, Bearman, Caldwell & Berkowitz · http://www.bakerdonelson.com · 201 St. Charles Avenue, Suite 3600 · New Orleans, LA 70170-1000 · 504-566-5200

Benjamin R. Slater III · Lemle & Kelleher · http://www.lemle.com · Pan American Life Center, Suite 2100 · 601 Poydras Street · New Orleans, LA 70130-6097 · 504-586-1241

A. Wendel Stout III · Deutsch, Kerrigan & Stiles · http://www.dkslaw.com · 755 Magazine Street · New Orleans, LA 70130-3672 · 504-581-5141

MEDICAL MALPRACTICE LAW

Baton Rouge

Vance A. Gibbs · Kean, Miller, Hawthorne, D'Armond, McCowan & Jarman · One American Place, 22nd Floor · P.O. Box 3513 · Baton Rouge, LA 70821 · 225-387-0999

Lake Charles

Richard B. Cappel · 10 · Raggio, Cappel, Chozen & Berniard · 1011 Lakeshore Drive, Suite 500 · Lake Charles, LA 70601 · 337-436-9481

Metairie

Kurt S. Blankenship · Blue Williams · 3421 North Causeway Boulevard, Suite 900 · Metairie, LA 70002 · 504-831-4091

New Orleans

Henry B. Alsobrook, Jr. · 25 · Adams and Reese · http://www.adamsandreese.com · One Shell Square, Suite 4500 · 701 Poydras Street · New Orleans, LA 70139 · 504-581-3234

C. William Bradley, Jr. · Lemle & Kelleher · http://www.lemle.com · Pan American Life Center, Suite 2100 · 601 Poydras Street · New Orleans, LA 70130-6097 · 504-586-1241

Robert J. David · a · Gainsburgh, Benjamin, David, Meunier & Warshauer · http://www.gainsburghbenjamin.com · 2800 Energy Centre · 1100 Poydras Street · New Orleans, LA 70163-2800 · 504-522-2304

Monica A. Frois · McGlinchey Stafford · http://www.mcglinchey.com · 643 Magazine Street · New Orleans, LA 70130 · 504-586-1200

Charles F. Gay, Jr. · Adams and Reese · http://www.adamsandreese.com · One Shell Square, Suite 4500 · 701 Poydras Street · New Orleans, LA 70139 · 504-581-3234

Lawrence S. Kullman · Lewis, Kullman, Sterbcow & Abramson · Pan American Life Center, Suite 2615 · 601 Poydras Street · New Orleans, LA 70130 · 504-588-1500

Peter E. Sperling · Frilot · 1100 Poydras Street, Suite 3600 · New Orleans, LA 70163 · 504-599-8000

Shreveport

Troy E. Bain · 2) · Troy E. Bain · 1700 Irving Place · Shreveport, LA 71101 · 318-221-8644

Robert G. Pugh, Jr. · a · Pugh, Pugh & Pugh · 333 Texas Street, Suite 2100 · Shreveport, LA 71101-3680 · 318-227-2270

Herschel E. Richard, Jr. · a · Cook, Yancey, King & Galloway · 333 Texas Street, Suite 1700 · P.O. Box 22260 · Shreveport, LA 71120-2260 · 318-221-6277

MERGERS & ACQUISITIONS LAW

Baton Rouge

John S. Campbell, Jr. · Taylor, Porter, Brooks & Phillips · Chase Tower South, Eighth Floor · 451 Florida Street · P.O. Box 2471 · Baton Rouge, LA 70821-2471 · 225-387-3221

Dean P. Cazenave · Kean, Miller, Hawthorne, D'Armond, McCowan & Jarman · One American Place, 22nd Floor · P.O. Box 3513 · Baton Rouge, LA 70821 · 225-387-0999

G. Blane Clark, Jr. · Kean, Miller, Hawthorne, D'Armond, McCowan & Jarman · One American Place, 22nd Floor · P.O. Box 3513 · Baton Rouge, LA 70821 · 225-387-0999

Ben R. Miller, Jr. · 2) · Kean, Miller, Hawthorne, D'Armond, McCowan & Jarman · One American Place, 22nd Floor · P.O. Box 3513 · Baton Rouge, LA 70821 · 225-387-0999

B. Troy Villa · Breazeale, Sachse and Wilson · One American Place, Suite 2300 · P.O. Box 3197 · Baton Rouge, LA 70821-3197 · 225-387-4000

New Orleans

Virginia Boulet · Adams and Reese · http://www.adamsandreese.com · One Shell Square, Suite 4500 · 701 Poydras Street · New Orleans, LA 70139 · 504-581-3234

Patrick J. Butler, Jr. · Phelps Dunbar · http://www.phelpsdunbar.com · Canal Place, Suite 2000 · 365 Canal Street · New Orleans, LA 70130-6534 · 504-566-1311

Joseph L. Caverly · Stone Pigman Walther Wittmann · http://www.stonepigman.com · 546 Carondelet Street · New Orleans, LA 70130-3588 · 504-581-3200

Louis Y. Fishman · 2% · Fishman Haygood Phelps Walmsley Willis & Swanson · http://www.cfhlaw.com · 201 St. Charles Avenue, 46th Floor · New Orleans, LA 70170-4600 · 504-586-5252

Mark A. Fullmer · Phelps Dunbar · http://www.phelpsdunbar.com · Canal Place, Suite 2000 · 365 Canal Street · New Orleans, LA 70130-6534 · 504-566-1311

Paul M. Haygood · 2% · Fishman Haygood Phelps Walmsley Willis & Swanson · http://www.cfhlaw.com · 201 St. Charles Avenue, 46th Floor · New Orleans, LA 70170-4600 · 504-586-5252

Curtis R. Hearn · a · Jones Walker · http://www.joneswalker.com · 201 St. Charles Avenue · New Orleans, LA 70170-5100 · 504-582-8000

William N. Norton · Baker, Donelson, Bearman, Caldwell & Berkowitz · http://www.bakerdonelson.com · 201 St. Charles Avenue, Suite 3600 · New Orleans, LA 70170-1000 · 504-566-5200

Leon J. Reymond III · Stone Pigman Walther Wittmann · http://www.stonepigman.com · 546 Carondelet Street · New Orleans, LA 70130-3588 · 504-581-3200

Scott T. Whittaker · Stone Pigman Walther Wittmann · http://www.stonepigman.com · 546 Carondelet Street · New Orleans, LA 70130-3588 · 504-581-3200

MINING LAW

New Orleans

John Y. Pearce · Montgomery, Barnett, Brown, Read, Hammond & Mintz · http://www.monbar.com · 1100 Poydras Street, Suite 3200 · New Orleans, LA 70163-3200 · 504-585-3200

MUNICIPAL LAW

New Orleans

William D. Aaron, Jr. · Goins Aaron · 201 St. Charles Avenue, Suite 3800 · New Orleans, LA 70170 · 504-569-1800

NATURAL RESOURCES LAW

Lafayette

Robert L. Cabes · Milling Benson Woodward · 101 La Rue France, Suite 200 · Lafayette, LA 70508 · 337-232-3929

Patrick Gray · Johnson Gray McNamara · 200 West Congress Street, Suite 900 · P.O. Box 51165 · Lafayette, LA 70505 · 337-412-6003

Richard W. Revels, Jr. · Liskow & Lewis · http://www.liskow.com · 822 Harding Street · P.O. Box 52008 Lafayette, LA 70505-2008 · 337-232-7424

Lawrence P. Simon, Jr. · Liskow & Lewis · http://www.liskow.com · 822 Harding Street · P.O. Box 52008 · Lafayette, LA 70505-2008 · 337-232-7424

Monroe

Daniel Ryan Sartor, Jr. · 2) · Snellings, Breard, Sartor, Inabnett & Trascher · 1503 North 19th Street · P.O. Box 2055 · Monroe, LA 71207-2055 · 318-387-8000

New Orleans

Gene W. Lafitte · 2% · Liskow & Lewis · http://www.liskow.com · One Shell Square, Suite 5000 · 701 Poydras Street · New Orleans, LA 70139-5099 · 504-581-7979

Charles D. Marshall, Jr. · Milling Benson Woodward · 909 Poydras Street, Suite 2300 · New Orleans, LA 70112-1010 · 504-569-7000

John M. McCollam · 2) · Gordon, Arata, McCollam, Duplantis & Eagan · http://www.gordonarata.com · Place St. Charles, Suite 4000 · 201 St. Charles Avenue · New Orleans, LA 70170-4000 · 504-582-1111

John Y. Pearce · Montgomery, Barnett, Brown, Read, Hammond & Mintz · http://www.monbar.com · 1100 Poydras Street, Suite 3200 · New Orleans, LA 70163-3200 · 504-585-3200

NON-PROFIT/CHARITIES LAW

New Orleans

Thomas B. Lemann · 2% · Liskow & Lewis · http://www.liskow.com · One Shell Square, Suite 5000 · 701 Poydras Street · New Orleans, LA 70139-5099 · 504-581-7979

Max Nathan, Jr. · 2% · Sessions, Fishman, Nathan & Israel · http://www.sessions-law.com · Place St. Charles, Suite 3500 · 201 St. Charles Avenue · New Orleans, LA 70170-3500 · 504-582-1500

Carole Cukell Neff · a · Sessions, Fishman, Nathan & Israel · http://www.sessions-law.com · Place St. Charles, Suite 3500 · 201 St. Charles Avenue · New Orleans, LA 70170-3500 · 504-582-1500

Jerome J. Reso, Jr. · 2% · Baldwin Haspel Burke & Mayer · Energy Centre, Suite 2200 · 1100 Poydras Street · New Orleans, LA 70163-2200 · 504-585-7711

Leon H. Rittenberg III · Baldwin Haspel Burke & Mayer · Energy Centre, Suite 2200 · 1100 Poydras Street · New Orleans, LA 70163-2200 · 504-585-7711

Kenneth A. Weiss · a · McGlinchey Stafford · http://www.mcglinchey.com · 643 Magazine Street · New Orleans, LA 70130 · 504-586-1200

NON-WHITE-COLLAR CRIMINAL DEFENSE

Alexandria

J. Michael Small · 2) · Law Offices of J. Michael Small · 1412 Centre Court, Suite 406 · P.O. Box 1470 · Alexandria, LA 71309 · 318-487-8963

Baton Rouge

James E. Boren · a · The Law Office of James E. Boren · http://www.jameseboren.com · 830 Main Street Baton Rouge, LA 70802-5528 · 225-387-5786

C. Frank Holthaus · a · deGravelles, Palmintier, Holthaus & Fruge · 618 Main Street · Baton Rouge, LA 70801-1910 · 225-344-3735

Karl J. Koch · Karl J. Koch · 214 Third Street, Suite 2-C · Baton Rouge, LA 70801 · 225-223-6215

Lewis O. Unglesby · 2) · Unglesby & Marionneaux · http://www.unglesbyandmarionneaux.com · 246 Napoleon Street · Baton Rouge, LA 70802 · 225-387-0120

Lake Charles

Thomas L. Lorenzi · Lorenzi & Barnett · 518 Pujo Street · P.O. Box 3305 · Lake Charles, LA 70602-3305 337-436-8401

Metairie

Julian R. Murray, Jr. · 2% · Chehardy, Sherman, Ellis, Breslin & Murray · One Galleria Boulevard, Suite 1100 · P.O. Box 931 · Metairie, LA 70004-9312 · 504-833-5600

Monroe

Thomas W. Davenport, Jr. · a · Davenport, Files & Kelly · 1509 Lamy Lane · P.O. Box 4787 · Monroe, LA 71211-4787 · 318-387-6453

Napoleonville

Risley C. Triche · 2) · Law Office of Risley C. Triche · 4759 Highway One · P.O. Drawer 339 · Napoleonville, LA 70390-8517 · 985-369-6168

New Orleans

Robert Glass · 2% · Glass & Reed · 530 Natchez Street · New Orleans, LA 70130 · 504-581-9083

John Wilson Reed · 2% · Glass & Reed · 530 Natchez Street · New Orleans, LA 70130 · 504-581-9083

Shreveport

Kenneth Craig Smith, Jr. · Smith & John · http://www.smith-john.com · 3646 Youree Drive · Shreveport, LA 71105 · 318-219-1001

A. M. Stroud III · Tutt, Stroud & McKay · 920 Pierremont Road, Suite 308 · Shreveport, LA 71106 · 318-868-6633

OIL & GAS LAW

Baton Rouge

G. William Jarman · Kean, Miller, Hawthorne, D'Armond, McCowan & Jarman · One American Place, 22nd Floor · P.O. Box 3513 · Baton Rouge, LA 70821 · 225-387-0999

Charles S. McCowan III · Kean, Miller, Hawthorne, D'Armond, McCowan & Jarman · One American Place, 22nd Floor · P.O. Box 3513 · Baton Rouge, LA 70821 · 225-387-0999

Robert W. Scheffy, Jr. · Jones Walker · http://www.joneswalker.com · Four United Plaza, Suite 500 · 8555 United Plaza Boulevard · Baton Rouge, LA 70809-7000 · 225-248-2000

Lafayette

George Arceneaux III · Liskow & Lewis · http://www.liskow.com · 822 Harding Street · P.O. Box 52008 · Lafayette, LA 70505-2008 · 337-232-7424

William F. Bailey · Gordon, Arata, McCollam, Duplantis & Eagan · http://www.gordonarata.com · 400 East Kaliste Saloom Road, Suite 4200 · Lafayette, LA 70508-8517 · 337-237-0132

Robert L. Cabes · Milling Benson Woodward · 101 La Rue France, Suite 200 · Lafayette, LA 70508 · 337-232-3929

Bob J. Duplantis · Gordon, Arata, McCollam, Duplantis & Eagan · http://www.gordonarata.com · 400 East Kaliste Saloom Road, Suite 4200 · Lafayette, LA 70508-8517 · 337-237-0132

Patrick Gray · Johnson Gray McNamara · 200 West Congress Street, Suite 900 · P.O. Box 51165 · Lafayette, LA 70505 · 337-412-6003

James N. Mansfield III · Liskow & Lewis · http://www.liskow.com · 822 Harding Street · P.O. Box 52008 Lafayette, LA 70505-2008 · 337-232-7424

Richard W. Revels, Jr. · Liskow & Lewis · http://www.liskow.com · 822 Harding Street · P.O. Box 52008 Lafayette, LA 70505-2008 · 337-232-7424

Lawrence P. Simon, Jr. · Liskow & Lewis · http://www.liskow.com · 822 Harding Street · P.O. Box 52008 · Lafayette, LA 70505-2008 · 337-232-7424

Randall C. Songy · Onebane Law Firm · http://www.onebane.com · 1200 Camellia Boulevard, Suite 300 · P.O. Drawer 3507 · Lafayette, LA 70502-3507 · 337-237-2660

Lake Charles

Patrick D. Gallaugher, Jr. · Scofield, Gerard, Singletary & Pohorelsky · 901 Lakeshore Drive, Suite 900 · Lake Charles, LA 70601 · 337-433-9436

New Orleans

Thomas Beron · Liskow & Lewis · http://www.liskow.com · One Shell Square, Suite 5000 · 701 Poydras Street · New Orleans, LA 70139-5099 · 504-581-7979

M. Hampton Carver · Carver, Darden, Koretzky, Tessier, Finn, Blossman & Areaux · Energy Centre, Suite 3100 · 1100 Poydras Street · New Orleans, LA 70163 · 504-585-3800

M. Taylor Darden · Carver, Darden, Koretzky, Tessier, Finn, Blossman & Areaux · Energy Centre, Suite 3100 · 1100 Poydras Street · New Orleans, LA 70163 · 504-585-3800

C. Peck Hayne, Jr. · Gordon, Arata, McCollam, Duplantis & Eagan · http://www.gordonarata.com · Place St. Charles, Suite 4000 · 201 St. Charles Avenue · New Orleans, LA 70170-4000 · 504-582-1111

Jonathan A. Hunter · Liskow & Lewis · http://www.liskow.com · One Shell Square, Suite 5000 · 701 Poydras Street · New Orleans, LA 70139-5099 · 504-581-7979

Gene W. Lafitte · 2% · Liskow & Lewis · http://www.liskow.com · One Shell Square, Suite 5000 · 701 Poydras Street · New Orleans, LA 70139-5099 · 504-581-7979

Charles D. Marshall, Jr. · Milling Benson Woodward · 909 Poydras Street, Suite 2300 · New Orleans, LA 70112-1010 · 504-569-7000

John M. McCollam · 2) · Gordon, Arata, McCollam, Duplantis & Eagan · http://www.gordonarata.com · Place St. Charles, Suite 4000 · 201 St. Charles Avenue · New Orleans, LA 70170-4000 · 504-582-1111

Robert B. McNeal · Liskow & Lewis · http://www.liskow.com · One Shell Square, Suite 5000 · 701 Poydras Street · New Orleans, LA 70139-5099 · 504-581-7979

Joe B. Norman · Liskow & Lewis · http://www.liskow.com · One Shell Square, Suite 5000 · 701 Poydras Street · New Orleans, LA 70139-5099 · 504-581-7979

Scott A. O'Connor · Gordon, Arata, McCollam, Duplantis & Eagan · http://www.gordonarata.com · Place St. Charles, Suite 4000 · 201 St. Charles Avenue · New Orleans, LA 70170-4000 · 504-582-1111

John Y. Pearce · Montgomery, Barnett, Brown, Read, Hammond & Mintz · http://www.monbar.com · 1100 Poydras Street, Suite 3200 · New Orleans, LA 70163-3200 · 504-585-3200

Edward B. Poitevent II · Baker, Donelson, Bearman, Caldwell & Berkowitz · http://www.bakerdonelson.com · 201 St. Charles Avenue, Suite 3600 · New Orleans, LA 70170-1000 · 504-566-5200

Carl D. Rosenblum · Jones Walker · http://www.joneswalker.com · 201 St. Charles Avenue · New Orleans, LA 70170-5100 · 504-582-8000

Gerald F. Slattery, Jr. · Schully, Roberts, Slattery, Jaubert & Marino · 1100 Poydras Street, Suite 1800 · New Orleans, LA 70163-1800 · 504-585-7800

Shreveport

David R. Taggart · Lemle & Kelleher · http://www.lemle.com · Louisiana Tower, 10th Floor · 401 Edwards Street · Shreveport, LA 71101-3289 · 318-227-1131

PERSONAL INJURY LITIGATION

Alexandria

Henry B. Bruser III · Gold, Weems, Bruser, Sues & Rundell · 2001 MacArthur Drive · P.O. Box 6118 · Alexandria, LA 71307-6118 · 318-445-6471

Baton Rouge

Paul H. Dué · a · Dué, Price, Guidry, Piedrahita & Andrews · 8201 Jefferson Highway · Baton Rouge, LA 70809 · 225-929-7481

Charles S. McCowan, Jr. · a · Kean, Miller, Hawthorne, D'Armond, McCowan & Jarman · One American Place, 22nd Floor · P.O. Box 3513 · Baton Rouge, LA 70821 · 225-387-0999

Lewis O. Unglesby · 2) · Unglesby & Marionneaux · http://www.unglesbyandmarionneaux.com · 246 Napoleon Street · Baton Rouge, LA 70802 · 225-387-0120

Cameron

Glenn W. Alexander · Jones & Alexander, LLC · 128 Smith Circle · P.O. Box 1550 · Cameron, LA 70631 337-775-5714

Jennifer A. Jones · Jones Law Firm · 128 Smith Circle · Cameron, LA 70631 · 337-775-5714

Convington

Frank E. Lamothe III · 2% · Lamothe Law Firm · 100 Innwood Drive, Suite B · Convington, LA 70433 · 985-249-6800

Covington

Janet L. MacDonell · a · Janet L. MacDonell · 21452 Lowe Davis Road · Covington, LA 70435 · 985-867-9971

Denham Springs

Calvin C. Fayard, Jr. · Fayard & Honeycutt · 519 Florida Avenue, SW · Denham Springs, LA 70726 · 225-664-0304

Gonzales

Victor L. Marcello · Talbot, Carmouche & Marcello · 214 West Cornerview · P.O. Box 759 · Gonzales, LA 70707 · 225-644-7777

Lafayette

Lawrence K. Burleigh, Sr. · 2) · Lawrence K. Burleigh · Gordon Square, Suite 160 · 100 East Vermilion Street · Lafayette, LA 70501 · 337-234-6222

Lawrence N. Curtis · Lawrence N. Curtis · http://www.larrycurtis.com · 300 Rue Beauregard, Building C · Lafayette, LA 70508 · 337-235-1825

Patrick A. Juneau, Jr. · a · Juneau Law Firm · The Harding Center, Suite 202 · 1018 Harding Street · P.O. Drawer 51268 · Lafayette, LA 70505-1268 · 337-269-0052

Cliffe E. Laborde III · Laborde & Neuner · One Petroleum Center, Suite 200 · 1001 West Pinhook Road P.O. Drawer 52828 · Lafayette, LA 70505-2828 · 337-237-7000

Edwin G. Preis, Jr. · Preis & Roy · http://www.preisroy.com · Versailles Centre, Suite 400 · 102 Versailles Boulevard · P.O. Drawer 94-C · Lafayette, LA 70509 · 337-237-6062

James Parkerson Roy · a · Domengeaux Wright Roy & Edwards · 556 Jefferson Street, Suite 500 · P.O. Box 3668 · Lafayette, LA 70501 · 337-233-3033

Randall K. Theunissen · Allen & Gooch · 1015 St. John Street · P.O. Box 3768 · Lafayette, LA 70502-3768 · 337-291-1000

Bob F. Wright · a · Domengeaux Wright Roy & Edwards · 556 Jefferson Street, Suite 500 · P.O. Box 3668 · Lafayette, LA 70501 · 337-233-3033

Lake Charles

William B. Baggett, Sr. · 2% · Baggett, McCall, Burgess & Watson · 3006 Country Club Road · P.O. Drawer 7820 · Lake Charles, LA 70606-7820 · 337-478-8888

Jere Jay Bice · Bice, Palermo & Veron · 721 Kirby Street · P.O. Box 2125 · Lake Charles, LA 70602 · 337-310-1600

Steven Broussard · Broussard & Hart · 1301 Common Street · Lake Charles, LA 70601 · 337-439-2450

Roger G. Burgess · Baggett, McCall, Burgess & Watson · 3006 Country Club Road · P.O. Drawer 7820 · Lake Charles, LA 70606-7820 · 337-478-8888

Richard B. Cappel · a · Raggio, Cappel, Chozen & Berniard · 1011 Lakeshore Drive, Suite 500 · Lake Charles, LA 70601 · 337-436-9481

Hunter W. Lundy · Lundy & Davis · 501 Broad Street · P.O. Box 3010 · Lake Charles, LA 70602 · 337-439-0707

Michael J. McNulty III · Plauché, Smith & Nieset · 1123 Pithon Street · P.O. Drawer 1705 · Lake Charles, LA 70602 · 337-436-0522

James R. Nieset · a · Plauché, Smith & Nieset · 1123 Pithon Street · P.O. Drawer 1705 · Lake Charles, LA 70602 · 337-436-0522

J. Rock Palermo · Bice, Palermo & Veron · 721 Kirby Street · P.O. Box 2125 · Lake Charles, LA 70602 · 337-310-1600

Thomas W. Sanders · a · Thomas W. Sanders · 411 Clarence Street · P.O. Box 3032, Zip 70602 · Lake Charles, LA 70601 · 337-433-1691

John B. Scofield · 2) · Scofield, Gerard, Singletary & Pohorelsky · 901 Lakeshore Drive, Suite 900 · Lake Charles, LA 70601 · 337-433-9436

Allen L. Smith, Jr. · a · Plauché, Smith & Nieset · 1123 Pithon Street · P.O. Drawer 1705 · Lake Charles, LA 70602 · 337-436-0522

Russell T. Tritico, Sr. · Tritico Law Office · 921 Ryan Street, Suite C · Lake Charles, LA 70601 · 337-436-6648

J. Michael Veron · Bice, Palermo & Veron · 721 Kirby Street · P.O. Box 2125 · Lake Charles, LA 70602 · 337-310-1600

Frank M. Walker, Jr. · Plauché, Smith & Nieset · 1123 Pithon Street · P.O. Drawer 1705 · Lake Charles, LA 70602 · 337-436-0522

Mandeville

Mary Johnson · Johnson Gray McNamara · 21357 Marion Lane, Suite 300 · Mandeville, LA 70471 · 985-246-6544

Metairie

Thomas A. Gennusa II · a · Gennusa, Piacun & Ruli · 4405 North I-10 Service Road, West, Suite 200 · Metairie, LA 70006 · 504-455-0442

Monroe

Robert P. McLeod · a · McLeod Verlander · 1900 North 18th Street, Suite 610 · P.O. Box 2270 · Monroe, LA 71207-2270 · 318-325-7000

Natchitoches

Ronald E. Corken, Jr. · Watson, Murchison, Crews, Arthur & Corken · 616 Front Street · P.O. Box 1036 · Natchitoches, LA 71457 · 318-352-2302

Edwin Dunahoe · Dunahoe Law Firm · 402 Second Street · P.O. Box 607 · Natchitoches, LA 71458 · 318-352-1999

Henry Cole Gahagan, Jr. · a · Henry C. Gahagan, Jr. · 1950 Williams Avenue · P.O. Box 1188 · Natchitoches, LA 71458 · 318-352-7397

New Orleans

Robert B. Acomb, Jr. · 2% · Jones Walker · http://www.joneswalker.com · 201 St. Charles Avenue · New Orleans, LA 70170-5100 · 504-582-8000

William Ryan Acomb · a · Porteous, Hainkel and Johnson · 704 Carondelet Street · New Orleans, LA 70130-3774 · 504-581-3838

Michael Allweiss · Lowe, Stein, Hoffman, Allweiss & Hauver · One Shell Square, Suite 3600 · 701 Poydras Street · New Orleans, LA 70139-7735 · 504-581-2450

Henry B. Alsobrook, Jr. · 2% · Adams and Reese · http://www.adamsandreese.com · One Shell Square, Suite 4500 · 701 Poydras Street · New Orleans, LA 70139 · 504-581-3234

W. Paul Andersson · a · Leake & Andersson · Energy Centre, Suite 1700 · 1100 Poydras Street · New Orleans, LA 70163-1701 · 504-585-7500

Frederick R. Bott · Deutsch, Kerrigan & Stiles · http://www.dkslaw.com · 755 Magazine Street · New Orleans, LA 70130-3672 · 504-581-5141

C. William Bradley, Jr. · Lemle & Kelleher · http://www.lemle.com · Pan American Life Center, Suite 2100 · 601 Poydras Street · New Orleans, LA 70130-6097 · 504-586-1241

Bertrand M. Cass, Jr. · Deutsch, Kerrigan & Stiles · http://www.dkslaw.com · 755 Magazine Street · New Orleans, LA 70130-3672 · 504-581-5141

Alvin R. Christovich, Jr. · 2% · Christovich & Kearney · 601 Poydras Street, Suite 2300 · New Orleans, LA 70130 · 504-561-5700

William K. Christovich · 2% · Christovich & Kearney · 601 Poydras Street, Suite 2300 · New Orleans, LA 70130 · 504-561-5700

Robert J. David · a · Gainsburgh, Benjamin, David, Meunier & Warshauer · http://www.gainsburghbenjamin.com · 2800 Energy Centre · 1100 Poydras Street · New Orleans, LA 70163-2800 · 504-522-2304

Ewell E. Eagan, Jr. · Gordon, Arata, McCollam, Duplantis & Eagan · http://www.gordonarata.com · Place St. Charles, Suite 4000 · 201 St. Charles Avenue · New Orleans, LA 70170-4000 · 504-582-1111

S. Gene Fendler · Liskow & Lewis · http://www.liskow.com · One Shell Square, Suite 5000 · 701 Poydras Street · New Orleans, LA 70139-5099 · 504-581-7979

James M. Garner · Sher Garner Cahill Richter Klein & Hilbert · http://www.shergarner.com · 909 Poydras Street, Suite 2800 · New Orleans, LA 70112 · 504-299-2100

Charles F. Gay, Jr. · Adams and Reese · http://www.adamsandreese.com · One Shell Square, Suite 4500 · 701 Poydras Street · New Orleans, LA 70139 · 504-581-3234

Terry Christovich Gay · Christovich & Kearney · 601 Poydras Street, Suite 2300 · New Orleans, LA 70130 · 504-561-5700

Russ M. Herman · 2% · Herman, Herman, Katz & Cotlar · http://www.hhkc.com · 820 O'Keefe Avenue · New Orleans, LA 70113 · 504-581-4892

Grady S. Hurley · Jones Walker · http://www.joneswalker.com · 201 St. Charles Avenue · New Orleans, LA 70170-5100 · 504-582-8000

James B. Irwin · Irwin Fritchie Urquhart & Moore · 400 Poydras Street, Suite 2700 · New Orleans, LA 70130 · 504-310-2100

C. Gordon Johnson, Jr. · Porteous, Hainkel and Johnson · 704 Carondelet Street · New Orleans, LA 70130-3774 · 504-581-3838

Robert E. Kerrigan, Jr. · a · Deutsch, Kerrigan & Stiles · http://www.dkslaw.com · 755 Magazine Street · New Orleans, LA 70130-3672 · 504-581-5141

Lawrence S. Kullman · Lewis, Kullman, Sterbcow & Abramson · Pan American Life Center, Suite 2615 · 601 Poydras Street · New Orleans, LA 70130 · 504-588-1500

Charles E. Leche · Deutsch, Kerrigan & Stiles · http://www.dkslaw.com · 755 Magazine Street · New Orleans, LA 70130-3672 · 504-581-5141

Wayne J. Lee · Stone Pigman Walther Wittmann · http://www.stonepigman.com · 546 Carondelet Street · New Orleans, LA 70130-3588 · 504-581-3200

David W. Leefe · Liskow & Lewis · http://www.liskow.com · One Shell Square, Suite 5000 · 701 Poydras Street · New Orleans, LA 70139-5099 · 504-581-7979

Harvey J. Lewis · 2% · Lewis, Kullman, Sterbcow & Abramson · Pan American Life Center, Suite 2615 · 601 Poydras Street · New Orleans, LA 70130 · 504-588-1500

Daniel Lund · a · Montgomery, Barnett, Brown, Read, Hammond & Mintz · http://www.monbar.com · 1100 Poydras Street, Suite 3200 · New Orleans, LA 70163-3200 · 504-585-3200

Kathleen A. Manning · McGlinchey Stafford · http://www.mcglinchey.com · 643 Magazine Street · New Orleans, LA 70130 · 504-586-1200

Nancy J. Marshall · a · Deutsch, Kerrigan & Stiles · http://www.dkslaw.com · 755 Magazine Street · New Orleans, LA 70130-3672 · 504-581-5141

Joseph Maselli, Jr. · Plauché, Maselli, Landry & Parkerson · One Shell Square, Suite 3800 · 701 Poydras Street · New Orleans, LA 70139 · 504-582-1142

Gerald E. Meunier · a · Gainsburgh, Benjamin, David, Meunier & Warshauer · http://www.gainsburghbenjamin.com · 2800 Energy Centre · 1100 Poydras Street · New Orleans, LA 70163-2800 · 504-522-2304

Stephen B. Murray · 2% · Murray Law Firm · 650 Poydras Street, Suite 1100 · New Orleans, LA 70130 · 504-525-8100

Robert B. Nolan · Adams and Reese · http://www.adamsandreese.com · One Shell Square, Suite 4500 · 701 Poydras Street · New Orleans, LA 70139 · 504-581-3234

Michael M. Noonan · McGlinchey Stafford · http://www.mcglinchey.com · 643 Magazine Street · New Orleans, LA 70130 · 504-586-1200

Colvin G. Norwood, Jr. · a · McGlinchey Stafford · http://www.mcglinchey.com · 643 Magazine Street · New Orleans, LA 70130 · 504-586-1200

Ernest L. O'Bannon · a · Bienvenu, Foster, Ryan & O'Bannon · 1010 Common Street, Suite 2200 · New Orleans, LA 70112 · 504-310-1500

Edward J. Rice, Jr. · Adams and Reese · http://www.adamsandreese.com · One Shell Square, Suite 4500 · 701 Poydras Street · New Orleans, LA 70139 · 504-581-3234

Ronald J. Sholes · Adams and Reese · http://www.adamsandreese.com · One Shell Square, Suite 4500 · 701 Poydras Street · New Orleans, LA 70139 · 504-581-3234

Mark C. Surprenant · Adams and Reese · http://www.adamsandreese.com · One Shell Square, Suite 4500 701 Poydras Street · New Orleans, LA 70139 · 504-581-3234

Irving J. Warshauer · Gainsburgh, Benjamin, David, Meunier & Warshauer · http://www.gainsburghbenjamin.com · 2800 Energy Centre · 1100 Poydras Street · New Orleans, LA 70163-2800 · 504-522-2304

Lawrence D. Wiedemann · 2) · Wiedemann & Wiedemann · 821 Baronne Street · P.O. Box 30648 · New Orleans, LA 70113 · 504-581-6180

Phillip A. Wittmann · 2% · Stone Pigman Walther Wittmann · http://www.stonepigman.com · 546 Carondelet Street · New Orleans, LA 70130-3588 · 504-581-3200

Henri Wolbrette III · McGlinchey Stafford · http://www.mcglinchey.com · 643 Magazine Street · New Orleans, LA 70130 · 504-586-1200

Thomas J. Wyllie · 2) · Adams and Reese · http://www.adamsandreese.com · One Shell Square, Suite 4500 · 701 Poydras Street · New Orleans, LA 70139 · 504-581-3234

Opelousas

Leslie J. Schiff · 2) · Schiff Law Corporation · 117 West Landry Street · P.O. Box 10 · Opelousas, LA 70571-0910 · 337-942-9771

Ruston

A. Kennon Goff III · 2% · Goff and Goff · 612 North Vienna Street · P.O. Box 2050 · Ruston, LA 71273-2050 · 318-255-1760

Shreveport

Leland H. Ayres · Ayres, Warren, Shelton & Williams · Regions Tower, Suite 1400 · 333 Texas Street · P.O. Box 1764 · Shreveport, LA 71166 · 318-227-3500

Troy E. Bain · 2) · Troy E. Bain · 1700 Irving Place · Shreveport, LA 71101 · 318-221-8644

Samuel W. Caverlee · Cook, Yancey, King & Galloway · 333 Texas Street, Suite 1700 · P.O. Box 22260 · Shreveport, LA 71120-2260 · 318-221-6277

Kenneth Mascagni · Cook, Yancey, King & Galloway · 333 Texas Street, Suite 1700 · P.O. Box 22260 · Shreveport, LA 71120-2260 · 318-221-6277

Lawrence W. Pettiette, Jr. · Pettiette, Armand, Dunkelman, Woodley, Byrd & Cromwell · 400 Texas Street, Suite 400 · P.O. Box 1786 · Shreveport, LA 71166-1786 · 318-221-1800

Robert G. Pugh, Jr. · a · Pugh, Pugh & Pugh · 333 Texas Street, Suite 2100 · Shreveport, LA 71101-3680 · 318-227-2270

Herschel E. Richard, Jr. · a · Cook, Yancey, King & Galloway · 333 Texas Street, Suite 1700 · P.O. Box 22260 · Shreveport, LA 71120-2260 · 318-221-6277

Gordon E. Rountree · a · Rountree, Cox & Guin · Beck Building, Suite 1200 · 400 Travis Street · Shreveport, LA 71101 · 318-226-0993

Charles W. Salley · 2) · Lunn, Irion, Salley, Carlisle & Gardner · 330 Marshall Street, Suite 500 · P.O. Box 1534 · Shreveport, LA 71101 · 318-222-0665

PRODUCT LIABILITY LITIGATION

Baton Rouge

Paul H. Dué · a · Dué, Price, Guidry, Piedrahita & Andrews · 8201 Jefferson Highway · Baton Rouge, LA 70809 · 225-929-7481

Lewis O. Unglesby · 2) · Unglesby & Marionneaux · http://www.unglesbyandmarionneaux.com · 246 Napoleon Street · Baton Rouge, LA 70802 · 225-387-0120

Lafayette

Patrick A. Juneau, Jr. · a · Juneau Law Firm · The Harding Center, Suite 202 · 1018 Harding Street · P.O. Drawer 51268 · Lafayette, LA 70505-1268 · 337-269-0052

New Orleans

Robert E. Barkley, Jr. · 2) · Barkley & Thompson · 1515 Poydras Street, Suite 2350 · New Orleans, LA 70112 · 504-595-3350

Carmelite M. Bertaut · Stone Pigman Walther Wittmann · http://www.stonepigman.com · 546 Carondelet Street · New Orleans, LA 70130-3588 · 504-581-3200

William K. Christovich · 2% · Christovich & Kearney · 601 Poydras Street, Suite 2300 · New Orleans, LA 70130 · 504-561-5700

James M. Garner · Sher Garner Cahill Richter Klein & Hilbert · http://www.shergarner.com · 909 Poydras Street, Suite 2800 · New Orleans, LA 70112 · 504-299-2100

Charles F. Gay, Jr. · Adams and Reese · http://www.adamsandreese.com · One Shell Square, Suite 4500 · 701 Poydras Street · New Orleans, LA 70139 · 504-581-3234

Terry Christovich Gay · Christovich & Kearney · 601 Poydras Street, Suite 2300 · New Orleans, LA 70130 · 504-561-5700

Alan H. Goodman · Lemle & Kelleher · http://www.lemle.com · Pan American Life Center, Suite 2100 · 601 Poydras Street · New Orleans, LA 70130-6097 · 504-586-1241

Arthur Landry · Arthur W. Landry & Jeanne Andry Landry · 710 Carondelet Street · New Orleans, LA 70130 · 504-581-4334

Nancy J. Marshall · a · Deutsch, Kerrigan & Stiles · http://www.dkslaw.com · 755 Magazine Street · New Orleans, LA 70130-3672 · 504-581-5141

Joseph Maselli, Jr. · Plauché, Maselli, Landry & Parkerson · One Shell Square, Suite 3800 · 701 Poydras Street · New Orleans, LA 70139 · 504-582-1142

Mary L. Meyer · Adams and Reese · http://www.adamsandreese.com · One Shell Square, Suite 4500 · 701 Poydras Street · New Orleans, LA 70139 · 504-581-3234

Colvin G. Norwood, Jr. · a · McGlinchey Stafford · http://www.mcglinchey.com · 643 Magazine Street · New Orleans, LA 70130 · 504-586-1200

G. Bruce Parkerson · Plauché, Maselli, Landry & Parkerson · One Shell Square, Suite 3800 · 701 Poydras Street · New Orleans, LA 70139 · 504-582-1142

Edward J. Rice, Jr. · Adams and Reese · http://www.adamsandreese.com · One Shell Square, Suite 4500 · 701 Poydras Street · New Orleans, LA 70139 · 504-581-3234

Mark C. Surprenant · Adams and Reese · http://www.adamsandreese.com · One Shell Square, Suite 4500 701 Poydras Street · New Orleans, LA 70139 · 504-581-3234

Henri Wolbrette III · McGlinchey Stafford · http://www.mcglinchey.com · 643 Magazine Street · New Orleans, LA 70130 · 504-586-1200

Shreveport

Troy E. Bain · 2) · Troy E. Bain · 1700 Irving Place · Shreveport, LA 71101 · 318-221-8644

Herschel E. Richard, Jr. · a · Cook, Yancey, King & Galloway · 333 Texas Street, Suite 1700 · P.O. Box 22260 · Shreveport, LA 71120-2260 · 318-221-6277

PROFESSIONAL MALPRACTICE LAW

Baton Rouge

Marshall M. Redmon · Phelps Dunbar · http://www.phelpsdunbar.com · City Plaza, Suite 701 · 445 North Boulevard · Baton Rouge, LA 70802 · 225-346-0285

Lake Charles

Emmett C. Sole · Stockwell, Sievert, Viccellio, Clements & Shaddock · One Lakeside Plaza, Fourth Floor · P.O. Box 2900 · Lake Charles, LA 70602 · 337-436-9491

Mandeville

Danny G. Shaw · Baker, Donelson, Bearman, Caldwell & Berkowitz · http://www.bakerdonelson.com · Three Sanctuary Boulevard, Suite 201 · Mandeville, LA 70471 · 985-819-8400

New Orleans

Terrence L. Brennan · Deutsch, Kerrigan & Stiles · http://www.dkslaw.com · 755 Magazine Street · New Orleans, LA 70130-3672 · 504-581-5141

Roy C. Cheatwood · a · Baker, Donelson, Bearman, Caldwell & Berkowitz · http://www.bakerdonelson.com · 201 St. Charles Avenue, Suite 3600 · New Orleans, LA 70170-1000 · 504-566-5200

William K. Christovich · 2% · Christovich & Kearney · 601 Poydras Street, Suite 2300 · New Orleans, LA 70130 · 504-561-5700

William R. Forrester, Jr. · Lemle & Kelleher · http://www.lemle.com · Pan American Life Center, Suite 2100 · 601 Poydras Street · New Orleans, LA 70130-6097 · 504-586-1241

Amelia Williams Koch · Baker, Donelson, Bearman, Caldwell & Berkowitz · http://www.bakerdonelson.com · 201 St. Charles Avenue, Suite 3600 · New Orleans, LA 70170-1000 · 504-566-5200

Nancy J. Marshall · a · Deutsch, Kerrigan & Stiles · http://www.dkslaw.com · 755 Magazine Street · New Orleans, LA 70130-3672 · 504-581-5141

William E. Wright, Jr. · Deutsch, Kerrigan & Stiles · http://www.dkslaw.com · 755 Magazine Street · New Orleans, LA 70130-3672 · 504-581-5141

Shreveport

Herschel E. Richard, Jr. · a · Cook, Yancey, King & Galloway · 333 Texas Street, Suite 1700 · P.O. Box 22260 · Shreveport, LA 71120-2260 · 318-221-6277

PROJECT FINANCE LAW

New Orleans

O. Ray Cornelius · Adams and Reese · http://www.adamsandreese.com · One Shell Square, Suite 4500 · 701 Poydras Street · New Orleans, LA 70139 · 504-581-3234

William H. Hines · a · Jones Walker · http://www.joneswalker.com · 201 St. Charles Avenue · New Orleans, LA 70170-5100 · 504-582-8000

PUBLIC FINANCE LAW

Baton Rouge

Fred L. Chevalier · Jones Walker · http://www.joneswalker.com · Four United Plaza, Suite 500 · 8555 United Plaza Boulevard · Baton Rouge, LA 70809-7000 · 225-248-2000

New Orleans

O. Ray Cornelius · Adams and Reese · http://www.adamsandreese.com · One Shell Square, Suite 4500 · 701 Poydras Street · New Orleans, LA 70139 · 504-581-3234

Lisa E. Maurer · McGlinchey Stafford · http://www.mcglinchey.com · 643 Magazine Street · New Orleans, LA 70130 · 504-586-1200

Susan Weeks · Foley & Judell · One Canal Place, Suite 2600 · 365 Canal Street · New Orleans, LA 70130 504-568-1249

RAILROAD LAW

Baton Rouge

Steven J. Levine · Phelps Dunbar · http://www.phelpsdunbar.com · City Plaza, Suite 701 · 445 North Boulevard · Baton Rouge, LA 70802 · 225-346-0285

Lafayette

John E. McElligott, Jr. · Davidson, Meaux, Sonnier & McElligott · 810 South Buchanan Street · P.O. Drawer 2908 · Lafayette, LA 70502 · 337-237-1660

Mandeville

Benjamin B. Saunders · a · Davis and Saunders · 500 Mariners Village Plaza, Suite 504 · Mandeville, LA 70448 · 985-612-3070

New Orleans

Alissa J. Allison · Baker, Donelson, Bearman, Caldwell & Berkowitz · http://www.bakerdonelson.com · 201 St. Charles Avenue, Suite 3600 · New Orleans, LA 70170-1000 · 504-566-5200

F. Frank Fontenot · Milling Benson Woodward · 909 Poydras Street, Suite 2300 · New Orleans, LA 70112-1010 · 504-569-7000

William H. Howard III · Baker, Donelson, Bearman, Caldwell & Berkowitz · http://www.bakerdonelson.com · 201 St. Charles Avenue, Suite 3600 · New Orleans, LA 70170-1000 · 504-566-5200

David S. Kelly · Lemle & Kelleher · http://www.lemle.com · Pan American Life Center, Suite 2100 · 601 Poydras Street · New Orleans, LA 70130-6097 · 504-586-1241

Benjamin R. Slater III · Lemle & Kelleher · http://www.lemle.com · Pan American Life Center, Suite 2100 · 601 Poydras Street · New Orleans, LA 70130-6097 · 504-586-1241

Brent Talbot · Chaffe McCall · 2300 Energy Centre · 1100 Poydras Street · New Orleans, LA 70163-2300 504-585-7000

Patrick A. Talley, Jr. · Frilot · 1100 Poydras Street, Suite 3600 · New Orleans, LA 70163 · 504-599-8000

Shreveport

Arthur R. Carmody, Jr. · a · Wilkinson, Carmody & Gilliam · 400 Travis Street, Suite 1700 · Shreveport, LA 71101 · 318-221-4196

Samuel W. Caverlee · Cook, Yancey, King & Galloway · 333 Texas Street, Suite 1700 · P.O. Box 22260 · Shreveport, LA 71120-2260 · 318-221-6277

REAL ESTATE LAW

Baton Rouge

Samuel A. Bacot · McGlinchey Stafford · http://www.mcglinchey.com · One American Place, 14th Floor · 301 Main Street · Baton Rouge, LA 70825-0001 · 225-383-9000

Donald E. Bradford · 2) · Donald E. Bradford · 7809 Jefferson Highway, Suite D-2 · Baton Rouge, LA 70809-1200 · 225-932-0030

Isaac M. Gregorie, Jr. · Kean, Miller, Hawthorne, D'Armond, McCowan & Jarman · One American Place, 22nd Floor · P.O. Box 3513 · Baton Rouge, LA 70821 · 225-387-0999

Ralph E. Hood · a · Kizer, Hood & Morgan · 2111 Quail Run Drive · Baton Rouge, LA 70808-4127 · 225-761-0001

Charles A. Landry · a · Jones Walker · http://www.joneswalker.com · Four United Plaza, Suite 500 · 8555 United Plaza Boulevard · Baton Rouge, LA 70809-7000 · 225-248-2000

Louis S. Quinn, Jr. · Jones Walker · http://www.joneswalker.com · Four United Plaza, Suite 500 · 8555 United Plaza Boulevard · Baton Rouge, LA 70809-7000 · 225-248-2000

Randy P. Roussel · Phelps Dunbar · http://www.phelpsdunbar.com · City Plaza, Suite 701 · 445 North Boulevard · Baton Rouge, LA 70802 · 225-346-0285

Lake Charles

John R. Pohorelsky · Scofield, Gerard, Singletary & Pohorelsky · 901 Lakeshore Drive, Suite 900 · Lake Charles, LA 70601 · 337-433-9436

New Orleans

Marguerite L. Adams · Liskow & Lewis · http://www.liskow.com · One Shell Square, Suite 5000 · 701 Poydras Street · New Orleans, LA 70139-5099 · 504-581-7979

Philip deV. Claverie, Sr. · a · Phelps Dunbar · http://www.phelpsdunbar.com · Canal Place, Suite 2000 · 365 Canal Street · New Orleans, LA 70130-6534 · 504-566-1311

R. Keith Colvin · a · McGlinchey Stafford · http://www.mcglinchey.com · 643 Magazine Street · New Orleans, LA 70130 · 504-586-1200

James R. Conway III · Lemle & Kelleher · http://www.lemle.com · Pan American Life Center, Suite 2100 · 601 Poydras Street · New Orleans, LA 70130-6097 · 504-586-1241

E. Howell Crosby · Chaffe McCall · 2300 Energy Centre · 1100 Poydras Street · New Orleans, LA 70163-2300 · 504-585-7000

Victoria M. DeLisle · Locke Lord Bissell & Liddell · 601 Poydras Street, Suite 2660 · New Orleans, LA 70130-6036 · 504-558-5100

Gary J. Elkins · Elkins · 201 St. Charles Avenue, Suite 4400 · New Orleans, LA 70170 · 504-529-3600

Lillian E. Eyrich · The Steeg Law Firm · http://www.steeglaw.com · 201 St. Charles Avenue, Suite 3201 · New Orleans, LA 70170-3201 · 504-582-1199

William H. Hines · a · Jones Walker · http://www.joneswalker.com · 201 St. Charles Avenue · New Orleans, LA 70170-5100 · 504-582-8000

Rose M. Le Breton · The Steeg Law Firm · http://www.steeglaw.com · 201 St. Charles Avenue, Suite 3201 · New Orleans, LA 70170-3201 · 504-582-1199

Jon F. Leyens, Jr. · The Steeg Law Firm · http://www.steeglaw.com · 201 St. Charles Avenue, Suite 3201 New Orleans, LA 70170-3201 · 504-582-1199

A. Kelton Longwell · Coats, Rose, Yale, Ryman & Lee · 400 Poydras Street, Suite 1440 · New Orleans, LA 70130 · 504-299-3070

R. Lewis McHenry · a · Jones Walker · http://www.joneswalker.com · 201 St. Charles Avenue · New Orleans, LA 70170-5100 · 504-582-8000

Malcolm A. Meyer · Adams and Reese · http://www.adamsandreese.com · One Shell Square, Suite 4500 · 701 Poydras Street · New Orleans, LA 70139 · 504-581-3234

Deborah J. Moench · Sher Garner Cahill Richter Klein & Hilbert · http://www.shergarner.com · 909 Poydras Street, Suite 2800 · New Orleans, LA 70112 · 504-299-2100

Henry F. O'Connor, Jr. · 2) · O'Connor & O'Connor · 228 St. Charles Avenue, Suite 1030 · New Orleans, LA 70130 · 504-592-8230

Leon J. Reymond, Jr. · Liskow & Lewis · http://www.liskow.com · One Shell Square, Suite 5000 · 701 Poydras Street · New Orleans, LA 70139-5099 · 504-581-7979

Richard P. Richter · Sher Garner Cahill Richter Klein & Hilbert · http://www.shergarner.com · 909 Poydras Street, Suite 2800 · New Orleans, LA 70112 · 504-299-2100

Michael R. Schneider · Stone Pigman Walther Wittmann · http://www.stonepigman.com · 546 Carondelet Street · New Orleans, LA 70130-3588 · 504-581-3200

Leopold Z. Sher · Sher Garner Cahill Richter Klein & Hilbert · http://www.shergarner.com · 909 Poydras Street, Suite 2800 · New Orleans, LA 70112 · 504-299-2100

Moise S. Steeg, Jr. · 2% · The Steeg Law Firm · http://www.steeglaw.com · 201 St. Charles Avenue, Suite 3201 · New Orleans, LA 70170-3201 · 504-582-1199

Robert M. Steeg · a · The Steeg Law Firm · http://www.steeglaw.com · 201 St. Charles Avenue, Suite 3201 · New Orleans, LA 70170-3201 · 504-582-1199

James A. Stuckey · a · Phelps Dunbar · http://www.phelpsdunbar.com · Canal Place, Suite 2000 · 365 Canal Street · New Orleans, LA 70130-6534 · 504-566-1311

Susan Gayle Talley · a · Stone Pigman Walther Wittmann · http://www.stonepigman.com · 546 Carondelet Street · New Orleans, LA 70130-3588 · 504-581-3200

Peter S. Title · a · Sessions, Fishman, Nathan & Israel · http://www.sessions-law.com · Place St. Charles, Suite 3500 · 201 St. Charles Avenue · New Orleans, LA 70170-3500 · 504-582-1500

Susan M. Tyler · McGlinchey Stafford · http://www.mcglinchey.com · 643 Magazine Street · New Orleans, LA 70130 · 504-586-1200

Harvey D. Wagar III · Phelps Dunbar · http://www.phelpsdunbar.com · Canal Place, Suite 2000 · 365 Canal Street · New Orleans, LA 70130-6534 · 504-566-1311

Emile A. Wagner III · Milling Benson Woodward · 909 Poydras Street, Suite 2300 · New Orleans, LA 70112-1010 · 504-569-7000

Scott T. Whittaker · Stone Pigman Walther Wittmann · http://www.stonepigman.com · 546 Carondelet Street · New Orleans, LA 70130-3588 · 504-581-3200

SECURITIES LAW

New Orleans

O. Ray Cornelius · Adams and Reese · http://www.adamsandreese.com · One Shell Square, Suite 4500 · 701 Poydras Street · New Orleans, LA 70139 · 504-581-3234

Anthony J. Correro III · 2% · Adams and Reese · http://www.adamsandreese.com · One Shell Square, Suite 4500 · 701 Poydras Street · New Orleans, LA 70139 · 504-581-3234

Louis Y. Fishman · 2% · Fishman Haygood Phelps Walmsley Willis & Swanson · http://www.cfhlaw.com · 201 St. Charles Avenue, 46th Floor · New Orleans, LA 70170-4600 · 504-586-5252

Mark A. Fullmer · Phelps Dunbar · http://www.phelpsdunbar.com · Canal Place, Suite 2000 · 365 Canal Street · New Orleans, LA 70130-6534 · 504-566-1311

Curtis R. Hearn · a · Jones Walker · http://www.joneswalker.com · 201 St. Charles Avenue · New Orleans, LA 70170-5100 · 504-582-8000

Kenneth J. Najder · Jones Walker · http://www.joneswalker.com · 201 St. Charles Avenue · New Orleans, LA 70170-5100 · 504-582-8000

Dionne M. Rousseau · a · Jones Walker · http://www.joneswalker.com · 201 St. Charles Avenue · New Orleans, LA 70170-5100 · 504-582-8000

Richard P. Wolfe · a · Jones Walker · http://www.joneswalker.com · 201 St. Charles Avenue · New Orleans, LA 70170-5100 · 504-582-8000

STRUCTURED FINANCE LAW

New Orleans

O. Ray Cornelius · Adams and Reese · http://www.adamsandreese.com · One Shell Square, Suite 4500 · 701 Poydras Street · New Orleans, LA 70139 · 504-581-3234

TAX LAW

Baton Rouge

John C. Blackman IV · 2) · Jones Walker · http://www.joneswalker.com · Four United Plaza, Suite 500 · 8555 United Plaza Boulevard · Baton Rouge, LA 70809-7000 · 225-248-2000

Robert R. Casey · 2% · Jones Walker · http://www.joneswalker.com · Four United Plaza, Suite 500 · 8555 United Plaza Boulevard · Baton Rouge, LA 70809-7000 · 225-248-2000

Christopher J. Dicharry · Kean, Miller, Hawthorne, D'Armond, McCowan & Jarman · One American Place, 22nd Floor · P.O. Box 3513 · Baton Rouge, LA 70821 · 225-387-0999

Jeffrey W. Koonce · Phelps Dunbar · http://www.phelpsdunbar.com · City Plaza, Suite 701 · 445 North Boulevard · Baton Rouge, LA 70802 · 225-346-0285

Carey J. Messina · a · Kean, Miller, Hawthorne, D'Armond, McCowan & Jarman · One American Place, 22nd Floor · P.O. Box 3513 · Baton Rouge, LA 70821 · 225-387-0999

Lake Charles

David L. Sigler · David Sigler & Associates · 630 Kirby Street · P.O. Box 1550 · Lake Charles, LA 70602 · 337-439-2033

Russell J. Stutes, Jr. · Stutes Lavergne · http://www.stuteslaw.com · 713 Kirby Street · P.O. Box 1644 · Lake Charles, LA 70601 · 337-433-0022

James A. Watson · Roddy, Watson & Everett · 400 East College Street · Lake Charles, LA 70602 · 337-474-4886

Metairie

Paul H. Waldman · Waldman Law Corporation · 113 Rosa Avenue, Suite A · Metairie, LA 70005 · 504-834-7077

New Orleans

Robert S. Angelico · Liskow & Lewis · http://www.liskow.com · One Shell Square, Suite 5000 · 701 Poydras Street · New Orleans, LA 70139-5099 · 504-581-7979

William M. Backstrom, Jr. · a · Jones Walker · http://www.joneswalker.com · 201 St. Charles Avenue · New Orleans, LA 70170-5100 · 504-582-8000

Hilton S. Bell · 2) · Milling Benson Woodward · 909 Poydras Street, Suite 2300 · New Orleans, LA 70112-1010 · 504-569-7000

Edward B. Benjamin, Jr. · 2% · Jones Walker · http://www.joneswalker.com · 201 St. Charles Avenue · New Orleans, LA 70170-5100 · 504-582-8000

Jaye A. Calhoun · McGlinchey Stafford · http://www.mcglinchey.com · 643 Magazine Street · New Orleans, LA 70130 · 504-586-1200

John W. Colbert · a · Stone Pigman Walther Wittmann · http://www.stonepigman.com · 546 Carondelet Street · New Orleans, LA 70130-3588 · 504-581-3200

Paul Cordes · Guarisco & Cordes · 301 St. Charles Avenue, Suite 250 · New Orleans, LA 70130 · 504-587-7007

Gary J. Elkins · Elkins · 201 St. Charles Avenue, Suite 4400 · New Orleans, LA 70170 · 504-529-3600

James C. Exnicios · Liskow & Lewis · http://www.liskow.com · One Shell Square, Suite 5000 · 701 Poydras Street · New Orleans, LA 70139-5099 · 504-581-7979

William C. Gambel · 2% · Milling Benson Woodward · 909 Poydras Street, Suite 2300 · New Orleans, LA 70112-1010 · 504-569-7000

Michael E. Guarisco · 2) · Guarisco & Cordes · 301 St. Charles Avenue, Suite 250 · New Orleans, LA 70130 · 504-587-7007

Maunsel W. Hickey · a · Hickey & Riess · 1139 Arabella Street · New Orleans, LA 70115 · 504-525-1120

Steven I. Klein · Sher Garner Cahill Richter Klein & Hilbert · http://www.shergarner.com · 909 Poydras Street, Suite 2800 · New Orleans, LA 70112 · 504-299-2100

Thomas B. Lemann · 2% · Liskow & Lewis · http://www.liskow.com · One Shell Square, Suite 5000 · 701 Poydras Street · New Orleans, LA 70139-5099 · 504-581-7979

Donald H. McDaniel · a · Perez, McDaniel & Faust · One Shell Square, Suite 3640 · 701 Poydras Street · New Orleans, LA 70139-7700 · 504-717-4639

Max Nathan, Jr. · 2% · Sessions, Fishman, Nathan & Israel · http://www.sessions-law.com · Place St. Charles, Suite 3500 · 201 St. Charles Avenue · New Orleans, LA 70170-3500 · 504-582-1500

Robert W. Nuzum · Baker, Donelson, Bearman, Caldwell & Berkowitz · http://www.bakerdonelson.com · 201 St. Charles Avenue, Suite 3600 · New Orleans, LA 70170-1000 · 504-566-5200

Robert Perez · Perez, McDaniel & Faust · One Shell Square, Suite 3640 · 701 Poydras Street · New Orleans, LA 70139-7700 · 504-717-4639

Rudolph R. Ramelli · 2) · Jones Walker · http://www.joneswalker.com · 201 St. Charles Avenue · New Orleans, LA 70170-5100 · 504-582-8000

Jerome J. Reso, Jr. · 2% · Baldwin Haspel Burke & Mayer · Energy Centre, Suite 2200 · 1100 Poydras Street · New Orleans, LA 70163-2200 · 504-585-7711

F. Kelleher Riess · a · Hickey & Riess · 1139 Arabella Street · New Orleans, LA 70115 · 504-525-1120

John A. Rouchell · a · Baldwin Haspel Burke & Mayer · Energy Centre, Suite 2200 · 1100 Poydras Street · New Orleans, LA 70163-2200 · 504-585-7711

Mark S. Stein · Lowe, Stein, Hoffman, Allweiss & Hauver · One Shell Square, Suite 3600 · 701 Poydras Street · New Orleans, LA 70139-7735 · 504-581-2450

Alex P. Trostorff · a · Jones Walker · http://www.joneswalker.com · 201 St. Charles Avenue · New Orleans, LA 70170-5100 · 504-582-8000

John J. Weiler · 2% · Weiler & Rees · 650 Poydras Street, Suite 2210 · New Orleans, LA 70130 · 504-524-2944

Kenneth A. Weiss · a · McGlinchey Stafford · http://www.mcglinchey.com · 643 Magazine Street · New Orleans, LA 70130 · 504-586-1200

Shreveport

Allen P. Jones · Wiener, Weiss & Madison · AM South Bank Tower, Suite 2350 · 333 Texas Street · P.O. Box 21990 · Shreveport, LA 71120-1990 · 318-226-9100

J. Benjamin Warren, Jr. · Ayres, Warren, Shelton & Williams · Regions Tower, Suite 1400 · 333 Texas Street · P.O. Box 1764 · Shreveport, LA 71166 · 318-227-3500

TIMBER LAW

Lake Charles

James P. Doré · Kean Miller Hawthorne D'Armond McCowan & Jarman · One Lakeshore Drive, Suite 1150 · Lake Charles, LA 70629 · 337-430-0350

Terrence D. Mccay · Kean Miller Hawthorne D'Armond McCowan & Jarman · One Lakeshore Drive, Suite 1150 · Lake Charles, LA 70629 · 337-430-0350

TRANSPORTATION LAW

New Orleans

William H. Howard III · Baker, Donelson, Bearman, Caldwell & Berkowitz · http://www.bakerdonelson.com · 201 St. Charles Avenue, Suite 3600 · New Orleans, LA 70170-1000 · 504-566-5200

TRUSTS AND ESTATES

Baton Rouge

Alton E. Bayard III · a · Baker, Donelson, Bearman, Caldwell & Berkowitz · http://www.bakerdonelson.com · One American Place, Suite 810 · 301 North Main Street · Baton Rouge, LA 70825 · 225-381-7000

John C. Blackman IV · 2) · Jones Walker · http://www.joneswalker.com · Four United Plaza, Suite 500 · 8555 United Plaza Boulevard · Baton Rouge, LA 70809-7000 · 225-248-2000

Sidney M. Blitzer, Jr. · 2) · Kantrow, Spaht, Weaver & Blitzer · City Plaza Building, Suite 300 · 445 North Boulevard · P.O. Box 2997 · Baton Rouge, LA 70821-2997 · 225-383-4703

Robert R. Casey · 2% · Jones Walker · http://www.joneswalker.com · Four United Plaza, Suite 500 · 8555 United Plaza Boulevard · Baton Rouge, LA 70809-7000 · 225-248-2000

Mary C. Hester · Taylor, Porter, Brooks & Phillips · Chase Tower South, Eighth Floor · 451 Florida Street · P.O. Box 2471 · Baton Rouge, LA 70821-2471 · 225-387-3221

Jeffrey W. Koonce · Phelps Dunbar · http://www.phelpsdunbar.com · City Plaza, Suite 701 · 445 North Boulevard · Baton Rouge, LA 70802 · 225-346-0285

B. Michael Mauldin · Jones Walker · http://www.joneswalker.com · Four United Plaza, Suite 500 · 8555 United Plaza Boulevard · Baton Rouge, LA 70809-7000 · 225-248-2000

Carey J. Messina · a · Kean, Miller, Hawthorne, D'Armond, McCowan & Jarman · One American Place, 22nd Floor · P.O. Box 3513 · Baton Rouge, LA 70821 · 225-387-0999

Ben R. Miller, Jr. · 2) · Kean, Miller, Hawthorne, D'Armond, McCowan & Jarman · One American Place, 22nd Floor · P.O. Box 3513 · Baton Rouge, LA 70821 · 225-387-0999

Lake Charles

William E. Shaddock · 2) · Stockwell, Sievert, Viccellio, Clements & Shaddock · One Lakeside Plaza, Fourth Floor · P.O. Box 2900 · Lake Charles, LA 70602 · 337-436-9491

David L. Sigler · David Sigler & Associates · 630 Kirby Street · P.O. Box 1550 · Lake Charles, LA 70602 · 337-439-2033

Monroe

Daniel Ryan Sartor, Jr. · 2) · Snellings, Breard, Sartor, Inabnett & Trascher · 1503 North 19th Street · P.O. Box 2055 · Monroe, LA 71207-2055 · 318-387-8000

New Orleans

Hirschel T. Abbott, Jr. · Stone Pigman Walther Wittmann · http://www.stonepigman.com · 546 Carondelet Street · New Orleans, LA 70130-3588 · 504-581-3200

Marguerite L. Adams · Liskow & Lewis · http://www.liskow.com · One Shell Square, Suite 5000 · 701 Poydras Street · New Orleans, LA 70139-5099 · 504-581-7979

Edward B. Benjamin, Jr. · 2% · Jones Walker · http://www.joneswalker.com · 201 St. Charles Avenue · New Orleans, LA 70170-5100 · 504-582-8000

David F. Edwards · a · Jones Walker · http://www.joneswalker.com · 201 St. Charles Avenue · New Orleans, LA 70170-5100 · 504-582-8000

Miriam W. Henry · Jones Walker · http://www.joneswalker.com · 201 St. Charles Avenue · New Orleans, LA 70170-5100 · 504-582-8000

Maunsel W. Hickey · a · Hickey & Riess · 1139 Arabella Street · New Orleans, LA 70115 · 504-525-1120

Thomas B. Lemann · 2% · Liskow & Lewis · http://www.liskow.com · One Shell Square, Suite 5000 · 701 Poydras Street · New Orleans, LA 70139-5099 · 504-581-7979

Edward F. Martin · 2) · Jones Walker · http://www.joneswalker.com · 201 St. Charles Avenue · New Orleans, LA 70170-5100 · 504-582-8000

Max Nathan, Jr. · 2% · Sessions, Fishman, Nathan & Israel · http://www.sessions-law.com · Place St. Charles, Suite 3500 · 201 St. Charles Avenue · New Orleans, LA 70170-3500 · 504-582-1500

Carole Cukell Neff · a · Sessions, Fishman, Nathan & Israel · http://www.sessions-law.com · Place St. Charles, Suite 3500 · 201 St. Charles Avenue · New Orleans, LA 70170-3500 · 504-582-1500

Robert Perez · Perez, McDaniel & Faust · One Shell Square, Suite 3640 · 701 Poydras Street · New Orleans, LA 70139-7700 · 504-717-4639

Jerome J. Reso, Jr. · 2% · Baldwin Haspel Burke & Mayer · Energy Centre, Suite 2200 · 1100 Poydras Street · New Orleans, LA 70163-2200 · 504-585-7711

F. Kelleher Riess · a · Hickey & Riess · 1139 Arabella Street · New Orleans, LA 70115 · 504-525-1120

Leon H. Rittenberg III · Baldwin Haspel Burke & Mayer · Energy Centre, Suite 2200 · 1100 Poydras Street · New Orleans, LA 70163-2200 · 504-585-7711

Kenneth A. Weiss · a · McGlinchey Stafford · http://www.mcglinchey.com · 643 Magazine Street · New Orleans, LA 70130 · 504-586-1200

Shreveport

Allen P. Jones · Wiener, Weiss & Madison · AM South Bank Tower, Suite 2350 · 333 Texas Street · P.O. Box 21990 · Shreveport, LA 71120-1990 · 318-226-9100

William C. Kalmbach III · Cook, Yancey, King & Galloway · 333 Texas Street, Suite 1700 · P.O. Box 22260 · Shreveport, LA 71120-2260 · 318-221-6277

VENTURE CAPITAL LAW

New Orleans

Joseph L. Caverly · Stone Pigman Walther Wittmann · http://www.stonepigman.com · 546 Carondelet Street · New Orleans, LA 70130-3588 · 504-581-3200

Anthony J. Correro III · 2% · Adams and Reese · http://www.adamsandreese.com · One Shell Square, Suite 4500 · 701 Poydras Street · New Orleans, LA 70139 · 504-581-3234

Mark A. Fullmer · Phelps Dunbar · http://www.phelpsdunbar.com · Canal Place, Suite 2000 · 365 Canal Street · New Orleans, LA 70130-6534 · 504-566-1311

Curtis R. Hearn · a · Jones Walker · http://www.joneswalker.com · 201 St. Charles Avenue · New Orleans, LA 70170-5100 · 504-582-8000

William N. Norton · Baker, Donelson, Bearman, Caldwell & Berkowitz · http://www.bakerdonelson.com · 201 St. Charles Avenue, Suite 3600 · New Orleans, LA 70170-1000 · 504-566-5200

J. Marshall Page III · Jones Walker · http://www.joneswalker.com · 201 St. Charles Avenue · New Orleans, LA 70170-5100 · 504-582-8000

Scott T. Whittaker · Stone Pigman Walther Wittmann · http://www.stonepigman.com · 546 Carondelet Street · New Orleans, LA 70130-3588 · 504-581-3200

WATER LAW

Baton Rouge

Kyle B. Beall · Kean, Miller, Hawthorne, D'Armond, McCowan & Jarman · One American Place, 22nd Floor · P.O. Box 3513 · Baton Rouge, LA 70821 · 225-387-0999

WHITE-COLLAR CRIMINAL DEFENSE

Alexandria

J. Michael Small · 2) · Law Offices of J. Michael Small · 1412 Centre Court, Suite 406 · P.O. Box 1470 · Alexandria, LA 71309 · 318-487-8963

Baton Rouge

James E. Boren · a · The Law Office of James E. Boren · http://www.jameseboren.com · 830 Main Street Baton Rouge, LA 70802-5528 · 225-387-5786

C. Frank Holthaus · a · deGravelles, Palmintier, Holthaus & Fruge · 618 Main Street · Baton Rouge, LA 70801-1910 · 225-344-3735

Karl J. Koch · Karl J. Koch · 214 Third Street, Suite 2-C · Baton Rouge, LA 70801 · 225-223-6215

Lewis O. Unglesby · 2) · Unglesby & Marionneaux · http://www.unglesbyandmarionneaux.com · 246 Napoleon Street · Baton Rouge, LA 70802 · 225-387-0120

Lake Charles

Thomas L. Lorenzi · Lorenzi & Barnett · 518 Pujo Street · P.O. Box 3305 · Lake Charles, LA 70602-3305 337-436-8401

Metairie

Julian R. Murray, Jr. · 2% · Chehardy, Sherman, Ellis, Breslin & Murray · One Galleria Boulevard, Suite 1100 · P.O. Box 931 · Metairie, LA 70004-9312 · 504-833-5600

Monroe

Thomas W. Davenport, Jr. · a · Davenport, Files & Kelly · 1509 Lamy Lane · P.O. Box 4787 · Monroe, LA 71211-4787 · 318-387-6453

Napoleonville

Risley C. Triche · 2) · Law Office of Risley C. Triche · 4759 Highway One · P.O. Drawer 339 · Napoleonville, LA 70390-8517 · 985-369-6168

New Orleans

Robert Glass · 2% · Glass & Reed · 530 Natchez Street · New Orleans, LA 70130 · 504-581-9083

John Wilson Reed · 2% · Glass & Reed · 530 Natchez Street · New Orleans, LA 70130 · 504-581-9083

Shreveport

Kenneth Craig Smith, Jr. · Smith & John · http://www.smith-john.com · 3646 Youree Drive · Shreveport, LA 71105 · 318-219-1001

A. M. Stroud III · Tutt, Stroud & McKay · 920 Pierremont Road, Suite 308 · Shreveport, LA 71106 · 318-868-6633

WORKERS' COMPENSATION LAW

Baton Rouge

H. Alston Johnson III · Phelps Dunbar · http://www.phelpsdunbar.com · City Plaza, Suite 701 · 445 North Boulevard · Baton Rouge, LA 70802 · 225-346-0285

MAINE

ADMINISTRATIVE LAW

Augusta

Severin M. Beliveau · Preti, Flaherty, Beliveau & Pachios · http://www.preti.com · 45 Memorial Circle · P.O. Box 1058 · Augusta, ME 04332-1058 · 207-623-5300

Peter B. Bickerman · Verrill Dana · http://www.verrilldana.com · 45 Memorial Circle · Augusta, ME 04332-5307 · 207-623-3889

Charles F. Dingman · Preti, Flaherty, Beliveau & Pachios · http://www.preti.com · 45 Memorial Circle · P.O. Box 1058 · Augusta, ME 04332-1058 · 207-623-5300

Bruce C. Gerrity · Preti, Flaherty, Beliveau & Pachios · http://www.preti.com · 45 Memorial Circle · P.O. Box 1058 · Augusta, ME 04332-1058 · 207-623-5300

Ann R. Robinson · Preti, Flaherty, Beliveau & Pachios · http://www.preti.com · 45 Memorial Circle · P.O. Box 1058 · Augusta, ME 04332-1058 · 207-623-5300

Michael Seitzinger · Kozak & Gayer · 160 Capitol Street, Suite Four · Augusta, ME 04330 · 207-621-4390

Charles C. Soltan · Charles C. Soltan · 45 Memorial Circle, Suite 301 · P.O. Box 188 · Augusta, ME 04332-0188 · 207-621-6300

Portland

Kenneth M. Cole III · Jensen Baird Gardner & Henry · Ten Free Street · P.O. Box 4510 · Portland, ME 04112-4510 · 207-775-7271

William H. Dale · Jensen Baird Gardner & Henry · Ten Free Street · P.O. Box 4510 · Portland, ME 04112-4510 · 207-775-7271

John D. Delahanty · Pierce Atwood · One Monument Square, Seventh Floor · Portland, ME 04101 · 207-791-1100

Beth Dobson · a · Verrill Dana · http://www.verrilldana.com · One Portland Square · P.O. Box 586 · Portland, ME 04112-0586 · 207-774-4000

D. Michael Frink · Curtis Thaxter · One Canal Plaza, Suite 1000 · P.O. Box 7320 · Portland, ME 04112-7320 · 207-774-9000

William S. Harwood · a · Verrill Dana · http://www.verrilldana.com · One Portland Square · P.O. Box 586 · Portland, ME 04112-0586 · 207-774-4000

Geoffrey H. Hole · Bernstein Shur · West Tower · 100 Middle Street · P.O. Box 9729 · Portland, ME 04104-5029 · 207-774-1200

Kimball L. Kenway · a · Curtis Thaxter · One Canal Plaza, Suite 1000 · P.O. Box 7320 · Portland, ME 04112-7320 · 207-774-9000

Kenneth W. Lehman · Bernstein Shur · West Tower · 100 Middle Street · P.O. Box 9729 · Portland, ME 04104-5029 · 207-774-1200

Patrick J. Scully · Bernstein Shur · West Tower · 100 Middle Street · P.O. Box 9729 · Portland, ME 04104-5029 · 207-774-1200

Christopher L. Vaniotis · Bernstein Shur · West Tower · 100 Middle Street · P.O. Box 9729 · Portland, ME 04104-5029 · 207-774-1200

ALTERNATIVE DISPUTE RESOLUTION

Portland

George F. Burns · Bernstein Shur · West Tower · 100 Middle Street · P.O. Box 9729 · Portland, ME 04104-5029 · 207-774-1200

Jerrol A. Crouter · Drummond Woodsum & MacMahon · http://www.dwmlaw.com · 245 Commercial Street · P.O. Box 9781 · Portland, ME 04104-5081 · 207-772-1941

Christopher C. Dinan · Monaghan Leahy · 95 Exchange Street · P.O. Box 7046 · Portland, ME 04112-7046 · 207-774-3906

Charles Harvey · Harvey and Frank · Two City Center, Suite Four · P.O. Box 126 · Portland, ME 04101-0126 · 207-775-1300

Vincent L. McKusick · Pierce Atwood · One Monument Square, Seventh Floor · Portland, ME 04101 · 207-791-1100

Richard O'Meara · Murray, Plumb & Murray · 75 Pearl Street · P.O. Box 9785 · Portland, ME 04104 · 207-773-5651

Gerald F. Petruccelli · 2) · Petruccelli, Martin & Haddow · http://www.pmhlegal.com · 50 Monument Square · P.O. Box 17555 · Portland, ME 04112-8555 · 207-775-0200

Jotham D. Pierce, Jr. · a · Pierce Atwood · One Monument Square, Seventh Floor · Portland, ME 04101 · 207-791-1100

Daniel Rapaport · Preti, Flaherty, Beliveau & Pachios · http://www.preti.com · One City Center · P.O. Box 9546 · Portland, ME 04112-9546 · 207-791-3000

David P. Ray · Bernstein Shur · West Tower · 100 Middle Street · P.O. Box 9729 · Portland, ME 04104-5029 · 207-774-1200

Daniel E. Wathen · Pierce Atwood · One Monument Square, Seventh Floor · Portland, ME 04101 · 207-791-1100

Raymond

Patrick Campbell Coughlan · Conflict Solutions · 112 Plains Road · Raymond, ME 04071 · 207-655-6677

Saco

Peter W. Schroeter · Smith Elliott Smith & Garmey · 199 Main Street · P.O. Box 1079 · Saco, ME 04072 207-282-1527

ANTITRUST LAW

Portland

Robert S. Frank · Harvey and Frank · Two City Center, Suite Four · P.O. Box 126 · Portland, ME 04101-0126 · 207-775-1300

John M. R. Paterson · a · Bernstein Shur · West Tower · 100 Middle Street · P.O. Box 9729 · Portland, ME 04104-5029 · 207-774-1200

Jeffrey M. White · a · Pierce Atwood · One Monument Square, Seventh Floor · Portland, ME 04101 · 207-791-1100

APPELLATE LAW

Augusta

Peter B. Bickerman · Verrill Dana · http://www.verrilldana.com · 45 Memorial Circle · Augusta, ME 04332-5307 · 207-623-3889

Lewiston

Paul F. Macri · Berman & Simmons · 129 Lisbon Street · P.O. Box 961 · Lewiston, ME 04243-0961 · 207-784-3576

Portland

Catherine R. Connors · Pierce Atwood · One Monument Square, Seventh Floor · Portland, ME 04101 · 207-791-1100

John M. R. Paterson · a · Bernstein Shur · West Tower · 100 Middle Street · P.O. Box 9729 · Portland, ME 04104-5029 · 207-774-1200

Gerald F. Petruccelli · 2) · Petruccelli, Martin & Haddow · http://www.pmhlegal.com · 50 Monument Square · P.O. Box 17555 · Portland, ME 04112-8555 · 207-775-0200

James D. Poliquin · Norman, Hanson & DeTroy · 415 Congress Street · P.O. Box 4600 · Portland, ME 04112-4600 · 207-774-7000

Peter J. Rubin · 2% · Bernstein Shur · West Tower · 100 Middle Street · P.O. Box 9729 · Portland, ME 04104-5029 · 207-774-1200

Jeffrey A. Thaler · 2) · Bernstein Shur · West Tower · 100 Middle Street · P.O. Box 9729 · Portland, ME 04104-5029 · 207-774-1200

BANKING LAW

Portland

Beth Dobson · a · Verrill Dana · http://www.verrilldana.com · One Portland Square · P.O. Box 586 · Portland, ME 04112-0586 · 207-774-4000

Mark K. Googins · Verrill Dana · http://www.verrilldana.com · One Portland Square · P.O. Box 586 · Portland, ME 04112-0586 · 207-774-4000

Richard P. Hackett · a · Pierce Atwood · One Monument Square, Seventh Floor · Portland, ME 04101 · 207-791-1100

Michael E. High · a · Drummond Woodsum & MacMahon · http://www.dwmlaw.com · 245 Commercial Street · P.O. Box 9781 · Portland, ME 04104-5081 · 207-772-1941

William E. Saufley · William E. Saufley · PMB 1251 · 89 Auburn Street · Portland, ME 04103-2103 · 207-650-2190

Mark P. Snow · Perkins Thompson · http://www.perkinsthompson.com · One Canal Plaza · P.O. Box 426 Portland, ME 04112-0426 · 207-774-2635

James B. Zimpritch · a · Pierce Atwood · One Monument Square, Seventh Floor · Portland, ME 04101 · 207-791-1100

BANKRUPTCY AND CREDITOR-DEBTOR RIGHTS LAW

Portland

Daniel Amory · 2) · Drummond Woodsum & MacMahon · http://www.dwmlaw.com · 245 Commercial Street · P.O. Box 9781 · Portland, ME 04104-5081 · 207-772-1941

Fred W. Bopp III · Perkins Thompson · http://www.perkinsthompson.com · One Canal Plaza · P.O. Box 426 · Portland, ME 04112-0426 · 207-774-2635

Roger A. Clement, Jr. · Verrill Dana · http://www.verrilldana.com · One Portland Square · P.O. Box 586 · Portland, ME 04112-0586 · 207-774-4000

Randy J. Creswell · Perkins Thompson · http://www.perkinsthompson.com · One Canal Plaza · P.O. Box 426 · Portland, ME 04112-0426 · 207-774-2635

Keith J. Cunningham · Pierce Atwood · One Monument Square, Seventh Floor · Portland, ME 04101 · 207-791-1100

Jonathan R. Doolittle · Verrill Dana · http://www.verrilldana.com · One Portland Square · P.O. Box 586 · Portland, ME 04112-0586 · 207-774-4000

Joshua R. Dow · Pearce & Dow · Two Monument Square, Suite 901 · P.O. Box 108 · Portland, ME 04101 · 207-822-9900

Michael A. Fagone · Bernstein Shur · West Tower · 100 Middle Street · P.O. Box 9729 · Portland, ME 04104-5029 · 207-774-1200

Jay S. Geller · Law Office of Jay S. Geller · One Monument Way, Suite 200 · Portland, ME 04101-4078 · 207-772-6668

Leonard M. Gulino · Bernstein Shur · West Tower · 100 Middle Street · P.O. Box 9729 · Portland, ME 04104-5029 · 207-774-1200

David C. Hillman · a · Verrill Dana · http://www.verrilldana.com · One Portland Square · P.O. Box 586 · Portland, ME 04112-0586 · 207-774-4000

Robert J. Keach · a · Bernstein Shur · West Tower · 100 Middle Street · P.O. Box 9729 · Portland, ME 04104-5029 · 207-774-1200

Jacob A. Manheimer · a · Pierce Atwood · One Monument Square, Seventh Floor · Portland, ME 04101 207-791-1100

Benjamin E. Marcus · Drummond Woodsum & MacMahon · http://www.dwmlaw.com · 245 Commercial Street · P.O. Box 9781 · Portland, ME 04104-5081 · 207-772-1941

George J. Marcus · 2) · Marcus, Clegg & Mistretta · East Tower · 100 Middle Street · Portland, ME 04101 · 207-828-8000

Michael J. Pearce · Pearce & Dow · Two Monument Square, Suite 901 · P.O. Box 108 · Portland, ME 04101 · 207-822-9900

Gregory A. Tselikis · 2% · Bernstein Shur · West Tower · 100 Middle Street · P.O. Box 9729 · Portland, ME 04104-5029 · 207-774-1200

BET-THE-COMPANY LITIGATION

Lewiston

William D. Robitzek · a · Berman & Simmons · 129 Lisbon Street · P.O. Box 961 · Lewiston, ME 04243-0961 · 207-784-3576

Jack H. Simmons · 2% · Berman & Simmons · 129 Lisbon Street · P.O. Box 961 · Lewiston, ME 04243-0961 · 207-784-3576

Portland

Peter J. DeTroy III · 2) · Norman, Hanson & DeTroy · 415 Congress Street · P.O. Box 4600 · Portland, ME 04112-4600 · 207-774-7000

Robert S. Frank · Harvey and Frank · Two City Center, Suite Four · P.O. Box 126 · Portland, ME 04101-0126 · 207-775-1300

William J. Kayatta, Jr. · a · Pierce Atwood · One Monument Square, Seventh Floor · Portland, ME 04101 · 207-791-1100

Ralph I. Lancaster, Jr. · 2% · Pierce Atwood · One Monument Square, Seventh Floor · Portland, ME 04101 · 207-791-1100

Peter J. Rubin · 2% · Bernstein Shur · West Tower · 100 Middle Street · P.O. Box 9729 · Portland, ME 04104-5029 · 207-774-1200

COMMERCIAL LITIGATION

Lewiston

George S. Isaacson · Brann & Isaacson · http://www.brannlaw.com · 184 Main Street · P.O. Box 3070 · Lewiston, ME 04243-3070 · 207-786-3566

William D. Robitzek · a · Berman & Simmons · 129 Lisbon Street · P.O. Box 961 · Lewiston, ME 04243-0961 · 207-784-3576

Jack H. Simmons · 2% · Berman & Simmons · 129 Lisbon Street · P.O. Box 961 · Lewiston, ME 04243-0961 · 207-784-3576

Portland

John J. Aromando · Pierce Atwood · One Monument Square, Seventh Floor · Portland, ME 04101 · 207-791-1100

David E. Barry · Pierce Atwood · One Monument Square, Seventh Floor · Portland, ME 04101 · 207-791-1100

George F. Burns · Bernstein Shur · West Tower · 100 Middle Street · P.O. Box 9729 · Portland, ME 04104-5029 · 207-774-1200

Jerrol A. Crouter · Drummond Woodsum & MacMahon · http://www.dwmlaw.com · 245 Commercial Street · P.O. Box 9781 · Portland, ME 04104-5081 · 207-772-1941

Peter W. Culley · a · Pierce Atwood · One Monument Square, Seventh Floor · Portland, ME 04101 · 207-791-1100

Peter J. DeTroy III · 2) · Norman, Hanson & DeTroy · 415 Congress Street · P.O. Box 4600 · Portland, ME 04112-4600 · 207-774-7000

Robert S. Frank · Harvey and Frank · Two City Center, Suite Four · P.O. Box 126 · Portland, ME 04101-0126 · 207-775-1300

Joseph H. Groff III · Jensen Baird Gardner & Henry · Ten Free Street · P.O. Box 4510 · Portland, ME 04112-4510 · 207-775-7271

Gregory P. Hansel · Preti, Flaherty, Beliveau & Pachios · http://www.preti.com · One City Center · P.O. Box 9546 · Portland, ME 04112-9546 · 207-791-3000

Charles Harvey · Harvey and Frank · Two City Center, Suite Four · P.O. Box 126 · Portland, ME 04101-0126 · 207-775-1300

Melissa A. Hewey · Drummond Woodsum & MacMahon · http://www.dwmlaw.com · 245 Commercial Street · P.O. Box 9781 · Portland, ME 04104-5081 · 207-772-1941

William J. Kayatta, Jr. · a · Pierce Atwood · One Monument Square, Seventh Floor · Portland, ME 04101 · 207-791-1100

James T. Kilbreth · a · Verrill Dana · http://www.verrilldana.com · One Portland Square · P.O. Box 586 · Portland, ME 04112-0586 · 207-774-4000

Ralph I. Lancaster, Jr. · 2% · Pierce Atwood · One Monument Square, Seventh Floor · Portland, ME 04101 · 207-791-1100

Michael A. Nelson · Jensen Baird Gardner & Henry · Ten Free Street · P.O. Box 4510 · Portland, ME 04112-4510 · 207-775-7271

Thomas Newman · Murray, Plumb & Murray · 75 Pearl Street · P.O. Box 9785 · Portland, ME 04104 · 207-773-5651

Robert O. Newton · Preti, Flaherty, Beliveau & Pachios · http://www.preti.com · One City Center · P.O. Box 9546 · Portland, ME 04112-9546 · 207-791-3000

Gerald F. Petruccelli · 2) · Petruccelli, Martin & Haddow · http://www.pmhlegal.com · 50 Monument Square · P.O. Box 17555 · Portland, ME 04112-8555 · 207-775-0200

Jotham D. Pierce, Jr. · a · Pierce Atwood · One Monument Square, Seventh Floor · Portland, ME 04101 · 207-791-1100

Jonathan S. Piper · a · Preti, Flaherty, Beliveau & Pachios · http://www.preti.com · One City Center · P.O. Box 9546 · Portland, ME 04112-9546 · 207-791-3000

James D. Poliquin · Norman, Hanson & DeTroy · 415 Congress Street · P.O. Box 4600 · Portland, ME 04112-4600 · 207-774-7000

Peter J. Rubin · 2% · Bernstein Shur · West Tower · 100 Middle Street · P.O. Box 9729 · Portland, ME 04104-5029 · 207-774-1200

Jeffrey A. Thaler · 2) · Bernstein Shur · West Tower · 100 Middle Street · P.O. Box 9729 · Portland, ME 04104-5029 · 207-774-1200

Jeffrey M. White · a · Pierce Atwood · One Monument Square, Seventh Floor · Portland, ME 04101 · 207-791-1100

COMMUNICATIONS LAW

Augusta

Joseph G. Donahue · Preti, Flaherty, Beliveau & Pachios · http://www.preti.com · 45 Memorial Circle · P.O. Box 1058 · Augusta, ME 04332-1058 · 207-623-5300

CONSTRUCTION LAW

Brunswick

David C. Pierson · Eaton Peabody · 167 Park Row · P.O. Box Nine · Brunswick, ME 04011-0009 · 207-729-1144

Cape Elizabeth

Mary DeLano · Mary DeLano · 15 Linwood Street · Cape Elizabeth, ME 04107 · 207-767-3009

Portland

Michael R. Bosse · Bernstein Shur · West Tower · 100 Middle Street · P.O. Box 9729 · Portland, ME 04104-5029 · 207-774-1200

Debra L. Brown · Law Offices of Debra L. Brown · 22 Free Street, Suite 302 · P.O. Box 373 · Portland, ME 04112 · 207-774-7887

George F. Burns · Bernstein Shur · West Tower · 100 Middle Street · P.O. Box 9729 · Portland, ME 04104-5029 · 207-774-1200

Rebecca H. Farnum · Thompson & Bowie · Three Canal Plaza · P.O. Box 4630 · Portland, ME 04112-4630 · 207-774-2500

John P. Giffune · Verrill Dana · http://www.verrilldana.com · One Portland Square · P.O. Box 586 · Portland, ME 04112-0586 · 207-774-4000

Gordon F. Grimes · 2% · Bernstein Shur · West Tower · 100 Middle Street · P.O. Box 9729 · Portland, ME 04104-5029 · 207-774-1200

John A. Hobson · Perkins Thompson · http://www.perkinsthompson.com · One Canal Plaza · P.O. Box 426 · Portland, ME 04112-0426 · 207-774-2635

Arnold C. Macdonald · Bernstein Shur · West Tower · 100 Middle Street · P.O. Box 9729 · Portland, ME 04104-5029 · 207-774-1200

Deborah M. Mann · Jensen Baird Gardner & Henry · Ten Free Street · P.O. Box 4510 · Portland, ME 04112-4510 · 207-775-7271

John H. Montgomery III · Bernstein Shur · West Tower · 100 Middle Street · P.O. Box 9729 · Portland, ME 04104-5029 · 207-774-1200

Gerald F. Petruccelli · 2) · Petruccelli, Martin & Haddow · http://www.pmhlegal.com · 50 Monument Square · P.O. Box 17555 · Portland, ME 04112-8555 · 207-775-0200

Jotham D. Pierce, Jr. · a · Pierce Atwood · One Monument Square, Seventh Floor · Portland, ME 04101 · 207-791-1100

David P. Ray · Bernstein Shur · West Tower · 100 Middle Street · P.O. Box 9729 · Portland, ME 04104-5029 · 207-774-1200

Peter J. Rubin · 2% · Bernstein Shur · West Tower · 100 Middle Street · P.O. Box 9729 · Portland, ME 04104-5029 · 207-774-1200

A. Robert Ruesch · Verrill Dana · http://www.verrilldana.com · One Portland Square · P.O. Box 586 · Portland, ME 04112-0586 · 207-774-4000

CORPORATE GOVERNANCE AND COMPLIANCE LAW

Portland

John L. Carpenter · Bernstein Shur · West Tower · 100 Middle Street · P.O. Box 9729 · Portland, ME 04104-5029 · 207-774-1200

James B. Zimpritch · a · Pierce Atwood · One Monument Square, Seventh Floor · Portland, ME 04101 · 207-791-1100

CORPORATE LAW

Bangor

David M. Austin · Eaton Peabody · 80 Exchange Street · P.O. Box 1210 · Bangor, ME 04402-1210 · 207-947-0111

George F. Eaton II · Rudman & Winchell · The Graham Building · 84 Harlow Street · P.O. Box 1401 · Bangor, ME 04402-1401 · 207-947-4501

Daniel G. McKay · a · Eaton Peabody · 80 Exchange Street · P.O. Box 1210 · Bangor, ME 04402-1210 · 207-947-0111

Portland

Norman R. Belanger · a · Van Meer & Belanger · 20 York Street · Portland, ME 04101-4556 · 207-871-7500

George F. Burns · Bernstein Shur · West Tower · 100 Middle Street · P.O. Box 9729 · Portland, ME 04104-5029 · 207-774-1200

John L. Carpenter · Bernstein Shur · West Tower · 100 Middle Street · P.O. Box 9729 · Portland, ME 04104-5029 · 207-774-1200

David J. Champoux · Pierce Atwood · One Monument Square, Seventh Floor · Portland, ME 04101 · 207-791-1100

Bruce A. Coggeshall · a · Pierce Atwood · One Monument Square, Seventh Floor · Portland, ME 04101 207-791-1100

Frank H. Frye · Jensen Baird Gardner & Henry · Ten Free Street · P.O. Box 4510 · Portland, ME 04112-4510 · 207-775-7271

Gregory S. Fryer · Verrill Dana · http://www.verrilldana.com · One Portland Square · P.O. Box 586 · Portland, ME 04112-0586 · 207-774-4000

Philip H. Gleason · Bernstein Shur · West Tower · 100 Middle Street · P.O. Box 9729 · Portland, ME 04104-5029 · 207-774-1200

Mark K. Googins · Verrill Dana · http://www.verrilldana.com · One Portland Square · P.O. Box 586 · Portland, ME 04112-0586 · 207-774-4000

Gordon F. Grimes · 2% · Bernstein Shur · West Tower · 100 Middle Street · P.O. Box 9729 · Portland, ME 04104-5029 · 207-774-1200

Michael E. High · a · Drummond Woodsum & MacMahon · http://www.dwmlaw.com · 245 Commercial Street · P.O. Box 9781 · Portland, ME 04104-5081 · 207-772-1941

Keith C. Jones · Verrill Dana · http://www.verrilldana.com · One Portland Square · P.O. Box 586 · Portland, ME 04112-0586 · 207-774-4000

Susan E. LoGiudice · Preti, Flaherty, Beliveau & Pachios · http://www.preti.com · One City Center · P.O. Box 9546 · Portland, ME 04112-9546 · 207-791-3000

Arnold C. Macdonald · Bernstein Shur · West Tower · 100 Middle Street · P.O. Box 9729 · Portland, ME 04104-5029 · 207-774-1200

Alan D. MacEwan · Verrill Dana · http://www.verrilldana.com · One Portland Square · P.O. Box 586 · Portland, ME 04112-0586 · 207-774-4000

Christopher S. McLoon · Verrill Dana · http://www.verrilldana.com · One Portland Square · P.O. Box 586 Portland, ME 04112-0586 · 207-774-4000

Leonard M. Nelson · 2% · Bernstein Shur · West Tower · 100 Middle Street · P.O. Box 9729 · Portland, ME 04104-5029 · 207-774-1200

Harold C. Pachios · a · Preti, Flaherty, Beliveau & Pachios · http://www.preti.com · One City Center · P.O. Box 9546 · Portland, ME 04112-9546 · 207-791-3000

Michael Peisner · Curtis Thaxter · One Canal Plaza, Suite 1000 · P.O. Box 7320 · Portland, ME 04112-7320 · 207-774-9000

Roderick R. Rovzar · Norman, Hanson & DeTroy · 415 Congress Street · P.O. Box 4600 · Portland, ME 04112-4600 · 207-774-7000

Eric F. Saunders · a · Bernstein Shur · West Tower · 100 Middle Street · P.O. Box 9729 · Portland, ME 04104-5029 · 207-774-1200

Michael L. Sheehan · Preti, Flaherty, Beliveau & Pachios · http://www.preti.com · One City Center · P.O. Box 9546 · Portland, ME 04112-9546 · 207-791-3000

Christopher R. Smith · Verrill Dana · http://www.verrilldana.com · One Portland Square · P.O. Box 586 · Portland, ME 04112-0586 · 207-774-4000

Eric P. Stauffer · a · Preti, Flaherty, Beliveau & Pachios · http://www.preti.com · One City Center · P.O. Box 9546 · Portland, ME 04112-9546 · 207-791-3000

John S. Upton · Perkins Thompson · http://www.perkinsthompson.com · One Canal Plaza · P.O. Box 426 Portland, ME 04112-0426 · 207-774-2635

David E. Warren · Verrill Dana · http://www.verrilldana.com · One Portland Square · P.O. Box 586 · Portland, ME 04112-0586 · 207-774-4000

Peter B. Webster · 2% · Verrill Dana · http://www.verrilldana.com · One Portland Square · P.O. Box 586 · Portland, ME 04112-0586 · 207-774-4000

James B. Zimpritch · a · Pierce Atwood · One Monument Square, Seventh Floor · Portland, ME 04101 · 207-791-1100

DUI/DWI DEFENSE

Auburn

Leonard I. Sharon · Sharon, Leary & Detroy · 90 Main Street · Auburn, ME 04210 · 207-782-3275

EDUCATION LAW

Portland

Eric Herlan · Drummond Woodsum & MacMahon · http://www.dwmlaw.com · 245 Commercial Street · P.O. Box 9781 · Portland, ME 04104-5081 · 207-772-1941

Melissa A. Hewey · Drummond Woodsum & MacMahon · http://www.dwmlaw.com · 245 Commercial Street · P.O. Box 9781 · Portland, ME 04104-5081 · 207-772-1941

Hugh G. E. MacMahon · a · Drummond Woodsum & MacMahon · http://www.dwmlaw.com · 245 Commercial Street · P.O. Box 9781 · Portland, ME 04104-5081 · 207-772-1941

Richard O'Meara · Murray, Plumb & Murray · 75 Pearl Street · P.O. Box 9785 · Portland, ME 04104 · 207-773-5651

Harry R. Pringle · a · Drummond Woodsum & MacMahon · http://www.dwmlaw.com · 245 Commercial Street · P.O. Box 9781 · Portland, ME 04104-5081 · 207-772-1941

Bruce W. Smith · Drummond Woodsum & MacMahon · http://www.dwmlaw.com · 245 Commercial Street · P.O. Box 9781 · Portland, ME 04104-5081 · 207-772-1941

Richard A. Spencer · Drummond Woodsum & MacMahon · http://www.dwmlaw.com · 245 Commercial Street · P.O. Box 9781 · Portland, ME 04104-5081 · 207-772-1941

E. William Stockmeyer · Drummond Woodsum & MacMahon · http://www.dwmlaw.com · 245 Commercial Street · P.O. Box 9781 · Portland, ME 04104-5081 · 207-772-1941

Amy K. Tchao · Drummond Woodsum & MacMahon · http://www.dwmlaw.com · 245 Commercial Street P.O. Box 9781 · Portland, ME 04104-5081 · 207-772-1941

ELDER LAW

Portland

Patricia A. Nelson-Reade · Patricia A. Nelson-Reade · 813 Washington Avenue · Portland, ME 04103 · 207-828-1597

EMINENT DOMAIN AND CONDEMNATION LAW

Portland

Christopher L. Vaniotis · Bernstein Shur · West Tower · 100 Middle Street · P.O. Box 9729 · Portland, ME 04104-5029 · 207-774-1200

EMPLOYEE BENEFITS LAW

Portland

Eric D. Altholz · Verrill Dana · http://www.verrilldana.com · One Portland Square · P.O. Box 586 · Portland, ME 04112-0586 · 207-774-4000

Lisa S. Boehm · Verrill Dana · http://www.verrilldana.com · One Portland Square · P.O. Box 586 · Portland, ME 04112-0586 · 207-774-4000

Kimberly S. Couch · Verrill Dana · http://www.verrilldana.com · One Portland Square · P.O. Box 586 · Portland, ME 04112-0586 · 207-774-4000

Gregg H. Ginn · Verrill Dana · http://www.verrilldana.com · One Portland Square · P.O. Box 586 · Portland, ME 04112-0586 · 207-774-4000

Leslie C. Hallock · Wakelin, Hallock & O'Donovan · 57 Exchange Street, Suite 100 · Portland, ME 04101-5000 · 207-774-3595

James A. Houle · Bernstein Shur · West Tower · 100 Middle Street · P.O. Box 9729 · Portland, ME 04104-5029 · 207-774-1200

Suzanne E. Meeker · Verrill Dana · http://www.verrilldana.com · One Portland Square · P.O. Box 586 · Portland, ME 04112-0586 · 207-774-4000

Anne E. O'Donovan · Wakelin, Hallock & O'Donovan · 57 Exchange Street, Suite 100 · Portland, ME 04101-5000 · 207-774-3595

David S. Wakelin · Wakelin, Hallock & O'Donovan · 57 Exchange Street, Suite 100 · Portland, ME 04101-5000 · 207-774-3595

ENERGY LAW

Auburn

Alan G. Stone · a · Skelton, Taintor & Abbott · 95 Main Street · P.O. Box 3200 · Auburn, ME 04212-3200 · 207-784-3200

Augusta

Anthony W. Buxton · a · Preti, Flaherty, Beliveau & Pachios · http://www.preti.com · 45 Memorial Circle · P.O. Box 1058 · Augusta, ME 04332-1058 · 207-623-5300

Joseph G. Donahue · Preti, Flaherty, Beliveau & Pachios · http://www.preti.com · 45 Memorial Circle · P.O. Box 1058 · Augusta, ME 04332-1058 · 207-623-5300

Donald J. Sipe · Preti, Flaherty, Beliveau & Pachios · http://www.preti.com · 45 Memorial Circle · P.O. Box 1058 · Augusta, ME 04332-1058 · 207-623-5300

Portland

Gordon F. Grimes · 2% · Bernstein Shur · West Tower · 100 Middle Street · P.O. Box 9729 · Portland, ME 04104-5029 · 207-774-1200

John W. Gulliver · a · Pierce Atwood · One Monument Square, Seventh Floor · Portland, ME 04101 · 207-791-1100

William S. Harwood · a · Verrill Dana · http://www.verrilldana.com · One Portland Square · P.O. Box 586 · Portland, ME 04112-0586 · 207-774-4000

Kimball L. Kenway · a · Curtis Thaxter · One Canal Plaza, Suite 1000 · P.O. Box 7320 · Portland, ME 04112-7320 · 207-774-9000

Charles Micoleau · Curtis Thaxter · One Canal Plaza, Suite 1000 · P.O. Box 7320 · Portland, ME 04112-7320 · 207-774-9000

Patrick J. Scully · Bernstein Shur · West Tower · 100 Middle Street · P.O. Box 9729 · Portland, ME 04104-5029 · 207-774-1200

Louise K. Thomas · Pierce Atwood · One Monument Square, Seventh Floor · Portland, ME 04101 · 207-791-1100

ENVIRONMENTAL LAW

Augusta

Clifford H. Goodall · 2) · Dyer Goodall and Denison · 61 Winthrop Street · Augusta, ME 04330 · 207-622-3693

Portland

Philip F. W. Ahrens III · a · Pierce Atwood · One Monument Square, Seventh Floor · Portland, ME 04101 · 207-791-1100

Juliet T. Browne · Verrill Dana · http://www.verrilldana.com · One Portland Square · P.O. Box 586 · Portland, ME 04112-0586 · 207-774-4000

Thomas R. Doyle · a · Pierce Atwood · One Monument Square, Seventh Floor · Portland, ME 04101 · 207-791-1100

Kenneth Fairbanks Gray · a · Pierce Atwood · One Monument Square, Seventh Floor · Portland, ME 04101 · 207-791-1100

James T. Kilbreth · a · Verrill Dana · http://www.verrilldana.com · One Portland Square · P.O. Box 586 · Portland, ME 04112-0586 · 207-774-4000

Matthew D. Manahan · Pierce Atwood · One Monument Square, Seventh Floor · Portland, ME 04101 · 207-791-1100

Dixon P. Pike · Pierce Atwood · One Monument Square, Seventh Floor · Portland, ME 04101 · 207-791-1100

William E. Taylor · Pierce Atwood · One Monument Square, Seventh Floor · Portland, ME 04101 · 207-791-1100

Jeffrey A. Thaler · 2) · Bernstein Shur · West Tower · 100 Middle Street · P.O. Box 9729 · Portland, ME 04104-5029 · 207-774-1200

David B. Van Slyke · Preti, Flaherty, Beliveau & Pachios · http://www.preti.com · One City Center · P.O. Box 9546 · Portland, ME 04112-9546 · 207-791-3000

FAMILY LAW

Auburn

Ronald P. Lebel · Skelton, Taintor & Abbott · 95 Main Street · P.O. Box 3200 · Auburn, ME 04212-3200 207-784-3200

Augusta

Kristin A. Gustafson · Dyer & Gustafson · One Weston Court · P. O. Box 2147 · Augusta, ME 04338-2147 · 207-623-5088

Roger J. Katz · 2) · Lipman, Katz & McKee · 227 Water Street · P.O. Box 1051 · Augusta, ME 04332-1051 · 207-622-3711

Bangor

Susan R. Kominsky · 2) · Vafiades, Brountas and Kominsky · Key Plaza · 23 Water Street · P.O. Box 919 · Bangor, ME 04402-0919 · 207-947-6915

Kennebunk

Gene R. Libby · Libby O'Brien Kingsley · http://www.lokllc.com · 62 Portland Road, Unit 17 · Kennebunk, ME 04043-0147 · 207-985-1815

Portland

David S. Abramson · Verrill Dana · http://www.verrilldana.com · One Portland Square · P.O. Box 586 · Portland, ME 04112-0586 · 207-774-4000

Michael P. Asen · a · Mittel Asen · http://www.mittelasen.com · 85 Exchange Street · P.O. Box 427 · Portland, ME 04112-0427 · 207-775-3101

Diane Dusini · Mittel Asen · http://www.mittelasen.com · 85 Exchange Street · P.O. Box 427 · Portland, ME 04112-0427 · 207-775-3101

Margaret C. Lavoie · Givertz, Hambley, Scheffee & Lavoie · 215 Commercial Street · P.O. Box 4801 · Portland, ME 04112-4801 · 207-772-8373

Patricia A. Nelson-Reade · Patricia A. Nelson-Reade · 813 Washington Avenue · Portland, ME 04103 · 207-828-1597

Barry Zimmerman · 2) · Kelly, Remmel & Zimmerman · 53 Exchange Street, Third Floor · P.O. Box 597 Portland, ME 04112-0597 · 207-775-1020

FIRST AMENDMENT LAW

Bangor

Bernard J. Kubetz · a · Eaton Peabody · 80 Exchange Street · P.O. Box 1210 · Bangor, ME 04402-1210 · 207-947-0111

Portland

John M. R. Paterson · a · Bernstein Shur · West Tower · 100 Middle Street · P.O. Box 9729 · Portland, ME 04104-5029 · 207-774-1200

Jonathan S. Piper · a · Preti, Flaherty, Beliveau & Pachios · http://www.preti.com · One City Center · P.O. Box 9546 · Portland, ME 04112-9546 · 207-791-3000

Sigmund D. Schutz · Preti, Flaherty, Beliveau & Pachios · http://www.preti.com · One City Center · P.O. Box 9546 · Portland, ME 04112-9546 · 207-791-3000

FRANCHISE LAW

Augusta

Bruce C. Gerrity · Preti, Flaherty, Beliveau & Pachios · http://www.preti.com · 45 Memorial Circle · P.O. Box 1058 · Augusta, ME 04332-1058 · 207-623-5300

Portland

Timothy J. Bryant · Preti, Flaherty, Beliveau & Pachios · http://www.preti.com · One City Center · P.O. Box 9546 · Portland, ME 04112-9546 · 207-791-3000

John L. Carpenter · Bernstein Shur · West Tower · 100 Middle Street · P.O. Box 9729 · Portland, ME 04104-5029 · 207-774-1200

Robert F. Macdonald, Jr. · Bernstein Shur · West Tower · 100 Middle Street · P.O. Box 9729 · Portland, ME 04104-5029 · 207-774-1200

GOVERNMENT RELATIONS LAW

Augusta

Severin M. Beliveau · Preti, Flaherty, Beliveau & Pachios · http://www.preti.com · 45 Memorial Circle · P.O. Box 1058 · Augusta, ME 04332-1058 · 207-623-5300

Daniel P. Riley, Jr. · Bernstein Shur · 146 Capitol Street · P.O. Box 5057 · Augusta, ME 04332-5057 · 207-623-1596

Michael V. Saxl · Verrill Dana · http://www.verrilldana.com · 45 Memorial Circle · Augusta, ME 04332-5307 · 207-623-3889

Portland

James I. Cohen · Verrill Dana · http://www.verrilldana.com · One Portland Square · P.O. Box 586 · Portland, ME 04112-0586 · 207-774-4000

John D. Delahanty · Pierce Atwood · One Monument Square, Seventh Floor · Portland, ME 04101 · 207-791-1100

HEALTH CARE LAW

Augusta

Julius Ciembroniewicz · Kozak & Gayer · 160 Capitol Street, Suite Four · Augusta, ME 04330 · 207-621-4390

Joseph M. Kozak · a · Kozak & Gayer · 160 Capitol Street, Suite Four · Augusta, ME 04330 · 207-621-4390

Michael Seitzinger · Kozak & Gayer · 160 Capitol Street, Suite Four · Augusta, ME 04330 · 207-621-4390

Benjamin P. Townsend · Kozak & Gayer · 160 Capitol Street, Suite Four · Augusta, ME 04330 · 207-621-4390

Portland

Eric D. Altholz · Verrill Dana · http://www.verrilldana.com · One Portland Square · P.O. Box 586 · Portland, ME 04112-0586 · 207-774-4000

Norman R. Belanger · a · Van Meer & Belanger · 20 York Street · Portland, ME 04101-4556 · 207-871-7500

Beth Dobson · a · Verrill Dana · http://www.verrilldana.com · One Portland Square · P.O. Box 586 · Portland, ME 04112-0586 · 207-774-4000

John P. Doyle, Jr. · a · Preti, Flaherty, Beliveau & Pachios · http://www.preti.com · One City Center · P.O. Box 9546 · Portland, ME 04112-9546 · 207-791-3000

John D. Gleason · Curtis Thaxter · One Canal Plaza, Suite 1000 · P.O. Box 7320 · Portland, ME 04112-7320 · 207-774-9000

Kenneth W. Lehman · Bernstein Shur · West Tower · 100 Middle Street · P.O. Box 9729 · Portland, ME 04104-5029 · 207-774-1200

William H. Stiles · Verrill Dana · http://www.verrilldana.com · One Portland Square · P.O. Box 586 · Portland, ME 04112-0586 · 207-774-4000

IMMIGRATION LAW

Portland

Anthony R. Derosby · Pierce Atwood · One Monument Square, Seventh Floor · Portland, ME 04101 · 207-791-1100

Peter J. Landis · Landis & Arn · 115 Middle Street, Suite 300 · Portland, ME 04101 · 207-775-6371

James J. O'Keefe · Immigration Law Group · http://www.immigration-group.com · 57 Exchange Street, Suite 401 · Portland, ME 04101 · 207-871-0099

INSURANCE LAW

Portland

Mark E. Dunlap · Norman, Hanson & DeTroy · 415 Congress Street · P.O. Box 4600 · Portland, ME 04112-4600 · 207-774-7000

Michael K. Martin · Petruccelli, Martin & Haddow · http://www.pmhlegal.com · 50 Monument Square · P.O. Box 17555 · Portland, ME 04112-8555 · 207-775-0200

John H. Montgomery III · Bernstein Shur · West Tower · 100 Middle Street · P.O. Box 9729 · Portland, ME 04104-5029 · 207-774-1200

James D. Poliquin · Norman, Hanson & DeTroy · 415 Congress Street · P.O. Box 4600 · Portland, ME 04112-4600 · 207-774-7000

Louise K. Thomas · Pierce Atwood · One Monument Square, Seventh Floor · Portland, ME 04101 · 207-791-1100

INTELLECTUAL PROPERTY LAW

Portland

Alfred C. Frawley III · Preti, Flaherty, Beliveau & Pachios · http://www.preti.com · One City Center · P.O. Box 9546 · Portland, ME 04112-9546 · 207-791-3000

James G. Goggin · Verrill Dana · http://www.verrilldana.com · One Portland Square · P.O. Box 586 · Portland, ME 04112-0586 · 207-774-4000

Robert E. Mittel · Mittel Asen · http://www.mittelasen.com · 85 Exchange Street · P.O. Box 427 · Portland, ME 04112-0427 · 207-775-3101

Thomas Newman · Murray, Plumb & Murray · 75 Pearl Street · P.O. Box 9785 · Portland, ME 04104 · 207-773-5651

Gloria A. Pinza · Pierce Atwood · One Monument Square, Seventh Floor · Portland, ME 04101 · 207-791-1100

Robert H. Stier, Jr. · a · Pierce Atwood · One Monument Square, Seventh Floor · Portland, ME 04101 · 207-791-1100

LABOR AND EMPLOYMENT LAW

Augusta

David G. Webbert · Johnson & Webbert · http://www.johnsonwebbert.com · 160 Capitol Street, Suite Three · P.O. Box 79 · Augusta, ME 04332-0079 · 207-623-5110

Bangor

Thomas C. Johnston · a · Eaton Peabody · 80 Exchange Street · P.O. Box 1210 · Bangor, ME 04402-1210 · 207-947-0111

Frank T. McGuire · Rudman & Winchell · The Graham Building · 84 Harlow Street · P.O. Box 1401 · Bangor, ME 04402-1401 · 207-947-4501

Clare Hudson Payne · Eaton Peabody · 80 Exchange Street · P.O. Box 1210 · Bangor, ME 04402-1210 · 207-947-0111

Gorham

Edward F. Feibel · Edward F. Feibel · 88 Files Road · Gorham, ME 04038 · 207-839-8368

Portland

Peter Bennett · The Bennett Law Firm · 121 Middle Street, Suite 300 · P.O. Box 7799 · Portland, ME 04112-7799 · 207-773-4775

Douglas P. Currier · Verrill Dana · http://www.verrilldana.com · One Portland Square · P.O. Box 586 · Portland, ME 04112-0586 · 207-774-4000

Charles S. Einsiedler, Jr. · a · Pierce Atwood · One Monument Square, Seventh Floor · Portland, ME 04101 · 207-791-1100

James R. Erwin · Pierce Atwood · One Monument Square, Seventh Floor · Portland, ME 04101 · 207-791-1100

F. Paul Frinsko · Bernstein Shur · West Tower · 100 Middle Street · P.O. Box 9729 · Portland, ME 04104-5029 · 207-774-1200

Melissa A. Hewey · Drummond Woodsum & MacMahon · http://www.dwmlaw.com · 245 Commercial Street · P.O. Box 9781 · Portland, ME 04104-5081 · 207-772-1941

Peter H. Jacobs · 2) · Pierce Atwood · One Monument Square, Seventh Floor · Portland, ME 04101 · 207-791-1100

Margaret Coughlin LePage · Pierce Atwood · One Monument Square, Seventh Floor · Portland, ME 04101 · 207-791-1100

Hugh G. E. MacMahon · a · Drummond Woodsum & MacMahon · http://www.dwmlaw.com · 245 Commercial Street · P.O. Box 9781 · Portland, ME 04104-5081 · 207-772-1941

Linda D. McGill · a · Bernstein Shur · West Tower · 100 Middle Street · P.O. Box 9729 · Portland, ME 04104-5029 · 207-774-1200

Michael G. Messerschmidt · Preti, Flaherty, Beliveau & Pachios · http://www.preti.com · One City Center · P.O. Box 9546 · Portland, ME 04112-9546 · 207-791-3000

Richard G. Moon · a · Verrill Dana · http://www.verrilldana.com · One Portland Square · P.O. Box 586 · Portland, ME 04112-0586 · 207-774-4000

Philip J. Moss · Moss Shapiro · 400 Congress Street, Fourth Floor · Portland, ME 04101 · 207-774-6001

Richard O'Meara · Murray, Plumb & Murray · 75 Pearl Street · P.O. Box 9785 · Portland, ME 04104 · 207-773-5651

Patricia A. Peard · Bernstein Shur · West Tower · 100 Middle Street · P.O. Box 9729 · Portland, ME 04104-5029 · 207-774-1200

S. Mason Pratt, Jr. · 2) · Pierce Atwood · One Monument Square, Seventh Floor · Portland, ME 04101 · 207-791-1100

Harry R. Pringle · a · Drummond Woodsum & MacMahon · http://www.dwmlaw.com · 245 Commercial Street · P.O. Box 9781 · Portland, ME 04104-5081 · 207-772-1941

Howard T. Reben · 2) · Reben, Benjamin and March · 97 India Street · P.O. Box 7060 · Portland, ME 04112-7060 · 207-874-4771

Daniel J. Rose · Drummond Woodsum & MacMahon · http://www.dwmlaw.com · 245 Commercial Street P.O. Box 9781 · Portland, ME 04104-5081 · 207-772-1941

Jonathan Shapiro · Moss Shapiro · 400 Congress Street, Fourth Floor · Portland, ME 04101 · 207-774-6001

Eric J. Uhl · Moss Shapiro · 400 Congress Street, Fourth Floor · Portland, ME 04101 · 207-774-6001

Topsham

Jeffrey N. Young · McTeague, Higbee, Case, Cohen, Whitney & Toker · Four Union Park · P.O. Box 5000 · Topsham, ME 04086-5000 · 207-725-5581

LAND USE & ZONING LAW

Augusta

Lee K. Bragg · Bernstein Shur · 146 Capitol Street · P.O. Box 5057 · Augusta, ME 04332-5057 · 207-623-1596

Virginia E. Davis · Preti, Flaherty, Beliveau & Pachios · http://www.preti.com · 45 Memorial Circle · P.O. Box 1058 · Augusta, ME 04332-1058 · 207-623-5300

Clifford H. Goodall · 2) · Dyer Goodall and Denison · 61 Winthrop Street · Augusta, ME 04330 · 207-622-3693

Bangor

Edmund J. Bearor · Rudman & Winchell · The Graham Building · 84 Harlow Street · P.O. Box 1401 · Bangor, ME 04402-1401 · 207-947-4501

P. Andrew Hamilton · Eaton Peabody · 80 Exchange Street · P.O. Box 1210 · Bangor, ME 04402-1210 · 207-947-0111

Roger L. Huber · Farrell, Rosenblatt & Russell · 61 Main Street, Suite One · Bangor, ME 04401 · 207-990-3314

Thomas A. Russell · Farrell, Rosenblatt & Russell · 61 Main Street, Suite One · Bangor, ME 04401 · 207-990-3314

Portland

John Bannon · Murray, Plumb & Murray · 75 Pearl Street · P.O. Box 9785 · Portland, ME 04104 · 207-773-5651

William H. Dale · Jensen Baird Gardner & Henry · Ten Free Street · P.O. Box 4510 · Portland, ME 04112-4510 · 207-775-7271

William L. Plouffe · Drummond Woodsum & MacMahon · http://www.dwmlaw.com · 245 Commercial Street · P.O. Box 9781 · Portland, ME 04104-5081 · 207-772-1941

Christopher L. Vaniotis · Bernstein Shur · West Tower · 100 Middle Street · P.O. Box 9729 · Portland, ME 04104-5029 · 207-774-1200

LEGAL MALPRACTICE LAW

Augusta

Phillip E. Johnson · Johnson & Webbert · http://www.johnsonwebbert.com · 160 Capitol Street, Suite Three · P.O. Box 79 · Augusta, ME 04332-0079 · 207-623-5110

Portland

James M. Bowie · Thompson & Bowie · Three Canal Plaza · P.O. Box 4630 · Portland, ME 04112-4630 · 207-774-2500

Michael A. Nelson · Jensen Baird Gardner & Henry · Ten Free Street · P.O. Box 4510 · Portland, ME 04112-4510 · 207-775-7271

Peter J. Rubin · 2% · Bernstein Shur · West Tower · 100 Middle Street · P.O. Box 9729 · Portland, ME 04104-5029 · 207-774-1200

MARITIME LAW

Camden

William H. Welte · Welte and Welte · 13 Wood Street · Camden, ME 04843 · 207-236-7786

Portland

John R. Bass II · Thompson, Bull, Furey, Bass & MacColl · 120 Exchange Street, Sixth Floor · P.O. Box 447 · Portland, ME 04112-0447 · 207-774-7600

R. Terrance Duddy · Kelly, Remmel & Zimmerman · 53 Exchange Street, Third Floor · P.O. Box 597 · Portland, ME 04112-0597 · 207-775-1020

Michael Kaplan · Preti, Flaherty, Beliveau & Pachios · http://www.preti.com · One City Center · P.O. Box 9546 · Portland, ME 04112-9546 · 207-791-3000

Leonard W. Langer · Tompkins, Clough, Hirshon & Langer · Three Canal Plaza, Sixth Floor · P.O. Box 15060 · Portland, ME 04112-5060 · 207-874-6700

MASS TORT LITIGATION

Portland

Peter W. Culley · a · Pierce Atwood · One Monument Square, Seventh Floor · Portland, ME 04101 · 207-791-1100

Thomas Newman · Murray, Plumb & Murray · 75 Pearl Street · P.O. Box 9785 · Portland, ME 04104 · 207-773-5651

Peter J. Rubin · 2% · Bernstein Shur · West Tower · 100 Middle Street · P.O. Box 9729 · Portland, ME 04104-5029 · 207-774-1200

MEDICAL MALPRACTICE LAW

Augusta

Sumner H. Lipman · Lipman, Katz & McKee · 227 Water Street · P.O. Box 1051 · Augusta, ME 04332-1051 · 207-622-3711

Malcolm L. Lyons · a · Pierce Atwood · 77 Winthrop Street · Augusta, ME 04330 · 207-622-6311

Robert J. Stolt · Lipman, Katz & McKee · 227 Water Street · P.O. Box 1051 · Augusta, ME 04332-1051 · 207-622-3711

Bangor

David C. King · Rudman & Winchell · The Graham Building · 84 Harlow Street · P.O. Box 1401 · Bangor, ME 04402-1401 · 207-947-4501

Lewiston

Jodi L. Nofsinger · Berman & Simmons · 129 Lisbon Street · P.O. Box 961 · Lewiston, ME 04243-0961 · 207-784-3576

Steven D. Silin · a · Berman & Simmons · 129 Lisbon Street · P.O. Box 961 · Lewiston, ME 04243-0961 207-784-3576

Jack H. Simmons · 2% · Berman & Simmons · 129 Lisbon Street · P.O. Box 961 · Lewiston, ME 04243-0961 · 207-784-3576

Julian L. Sweet · a · Berman & Simmons · 129 Lisbon Street · P.O. Box 961 · Lewiston, ME 04243-0961 207-784-3576

Portland

Philip M. Coffin III · Lamber Coffin · 477 Congress Street · P.O. Box 15215 · Portland, ME 04112-5215 · 207-874-4000

Terrence D. Garmey · a · Smith Elliott Smith & Garmey · Seven Custom House Street, Fifth Floor · Portland, ME 04101 · 207-774-3199

John N. Kelly · a · Kelly, Remmel & Zimmerman · 53 Exchange Street, Third Floor · P.O. Box 597 · Portland, ME 04112-0597 · 207-775-1020

Mark G. Lavoie · Norman, Hanson & DeTroy · 415 Congress Street · P.O. Box 4600 · Portland, ME 04112-4600 · 207-774-7000

Christopher D. Nyhan · a · Preti, Flaherty, Beliveau & Pachios · http://www.preti.com · One City Center · P.O. Box 9546 · Portland, ME 04112-9546 · 207-791-3000

Daniel Rapaport · Preti, Flaherty, Beliveau & Pachios · http://www.preti.com · One City Center · P.O. Box 9546 · Portland, ME 04112-9546 · 207-791-3000

Peter J. Rubin · 2% · Bernstein Shur · West Tower · 100 Middle Street · P.O. Box 9729 · Portland, ME 04104-5029 · 207-774-1200

MERGERS & ACQUISITIONS LAW

Bangor

Daniel G. McKay · a · Eaton Peabody · 80 Exchange Street · P.O. Box 1210 · Bangor, ME 04402-1210 · 207-947-0111

Portland

John L. Carpenter · Bernstein Shur · West Tower · 100 Middle Street · P.O. Box 9729 · Portland, ME 04104-5029 · 207-774-1200

David J. Champoux · Pierce Atwood · One Monument Square, Seventh Floor · Portland, ME 04101 · 207-791-1100

Gregory S. Fryer · Verrill Dana · http://www.verrilldana.com · One Portland Square · P.O. Box 586 · Portland, ME 04112-0586 · 207-774-4000

Mark K. Googins · Verrill Dana · http://www.verrilldana.com · One Portland Square · P.O. Box 586 · Portland, ME 04112-0586 · 207-774-4000

Michael E. High · a · Drummond Woodsum & MacMahon · http://www.dwmlaw.com · 245 Commercial Street · P.O. Box 9781 · Portland, ME 04104-5081 · 207-772-1941

Christopher E. Howard · Pierce Atwood · One Monument Square, Seventh Floor · Portland, ME 04101 · 207-791-1100

Keith C. Jones · Verrill Dana · http://www.verrilldana.com · One Portland Square · P.O. Box 586 · Portland, ME 04112-0586 · 207-774-4000

James B. Zimpritch · a · Pierce Atwood · One Monument Square, Seventh Floor · Portland, ME 04101 · 207-791-1100

MUNICIPAL LAW

Augusta

Clifford H. Goodall · 2) · Dyer Goodall and Denison · 61 Winthrop Street · Augusta, ME 04330 · 207-622-3693

Bangor

Edmund J. Bearor · Rudman & Winchell · The Graham Building · 84 Harlow Street · P.O. Box 1401 · Bangor, ME 04402-1401 · 207-947-4501

Kennebunk

Durward W. Parkinson · Bergen and Parkinson · 62 Portland Road, Suite 25 · Kennebunk, ME 04043 · 207-985-7000

Portland

Robert J. Crawford · Bernstein Shur · West Tower · 100 Middle Street · P.O. Box 9729 · Portland, ME 04104-5029 · 207-774-1200

Joan M. Fortin · Bernstein Shur · West Tower · 100 Middle Street · P.O. Box 9729 · Portland, ME 04104-5029 · 207-774-1200

William L. Plouffe · Drummond Woodsum & MacMahon · http://www.dwmlaw.com · 245 Commercial Street · P.O. Box 9781 · Portland, ME 04104-5081 · 207-772-1941

Christopher L. Vaniotis · Bernstein Shur · West Tower · 100 Middle Street · P.O. Box 9729 · Portland, ME 04104-5029 · 207-774-1200

NATIVE AMERICAN LAW

Portland

Robert L. Gips · Drummond Woodsum & MacMahon · http://www.dwmlaw.com · 245 Commercial Street · P.O. Box 9781 · Portland, ME 04104-5081 · 207-772-1941

Gregory W. Sample · Drummond Woodsum & MacMahon · http://www.dwmlaw.com · 245 Commercial Street · P.O. Box 9781 · Portland, ME 04104-5081 · 207-772-1941

Kaighn Smith, Jr. · Drummond Woodsum & MacMahon · http://www.dwmlaw.com · 245 Commercial Street · P.O. Box 9781 · Portland, ME 04104-5081 · 207-772-1941

NATURAL RESOURCES LAW

Portland

Philip F. W. Ahrens III · a · Pierce Atwood · One Monument Square, Seventh Floor · Portland, ME 04101 · 207-791-1100

James T. Kilbreth · a · Verrill Dana · http://www.verrilldana.com · One Portland Square · P.O. Box 586 · Portland, ME 04112-0586 · 207-774-4000

Jeffrey A. Thaler · 2) · Bernstein Shur · West Tower · 100 Middle Street · P.O. Box 9729 · Portland, ME 04104-5029 · 207-774-1200

NON-WHITE-COLLAR CRIMINAL DEFENSE

Lewiston

Jack H. Simmons · 2% · Berman & Simmons · 129 Lisbon Street · P.O. Box 961 · Lewiston, ME 04243-0961 · 207-784-3576

Portland

Peter J. DeTroy III · 2) · Norman, Hanson & DeTroy · 415 Congress Street · P.O. Box 4600 · Portland, ME 04112-4600 · 207-774-7000

Ralph I. Lancaster, Jr. · 2% · Pierce Atwood · One Monument Square, Seventh Floor · Portland, ME 04101 · 207-791-1100

Daniel G. Lilley · 2% · Daniel G. Lilley Law Offices · 39 Portland Pier · P.O. Box 4803 · Portland, ME 04112 · 207-774-6206

Peter J. Rubin · 2% · Bernstein Shur · West Tower · 100 Middle Street · P.O. Box 9729 · Portland, ME 04104-5029 · 207-774-1200

PERSONAL INJURY LITIGATION

Auburn

Stephen B. Wade · Skelton, Taintor & Abbott · 95 Main Street · P.O. Box 3200 · Auburn, ME 04212-3200 · 207-784-3200

Augusta

Malcolm L. Lyons · a · Pierce Atwood · 77 Winthrop Street · Augusta, ME 04330 · 207-622-6311

Elsworth

Barry K. Mills · Hale & Hamlin · Four State Street · P.O. Box 729 · Elsworth, ME 04605-0729 · 207-667-2561

Lewiston

William D. Robitzek · a · Berman & Simmons · 129 Lisbon Street · P.O. Box 961 · Lewiston, ME 04243-0961 · 207-784-3576

Steven D. Silin · a · Berman & Simmons · 129 Lisbon Street · P.O. Box 961 · Lewiston, ME 04243-0961 207-784-3576

Jack H. Simmons · 2% · Berman & Simmons · 129 Lisbon Street · P.O. Box 961 · Lewiston, ME 04243-0961 · 207-784-3576

Julian L. Sweet · a · Berman & Simmons · 129 Lisbon Street · P.O. Box 961 · Lewiston, ME 04243-0961 207-784-3576

Portland

Jonathan W. Brogan · Norman, Hanson & DeTroy · 415 Congress Street · P.O. Box 4600 · Portland, ME 04112-4600 · 207-774-7000

Philip M. Coffin III · Lamber Coffin · 477 Congress Street · P.O. Box 15215 · Portland, ME 04112-5215 · 207-874-4000

Peter J. DeTroy III · 2) · Norman, Hanson & DeTroy · 415 Congress Street · P.O. Box 4600 · Portland, ME 04112-4600 · 207-774-7000

R. Terrance Duddy · Kelly, Remmel & Zimmerman · 53 Exchange Street, Third Floor · P.O. Box 597 · Portland, ME 04112-0597 · 207-775-1020

Terrence D. Garmey · a · Smith Elliott Smith & Garmey · Seven Custom House Street, Fifth Floor · Portland, ME 04101 · 207-774-3199

Charles Harvey · Harvey and Frank · Two City Center, Suite Four · P.O. Box 126 · Portland, ME 04101-0126 · 207-775-1300

John N. Kelly · a · Kelly, Remmel & Zimmerman · 53 Exchange Street, Third Floor · P.O. Box 597 · Portland, ME 04112-0597 · 207-775-1020

Ralph I. Lancaster, Jr. · 2% · Pierce Atwood · One Monument Square, Seventh Floor · Portland, ME 04101 · 207-791-1100

Wendell G. Large · Richardson, Whitman, Large & Badger · 465 Congress Street · P.O. Box 9545 · Portland, ME 04112-9545 · 207-774-7474

Mark G. Lavoie · Norman, Hanson & DeTroy · 415 Congress Street · P.O. Box 4600 · Portland, ME 04112-4600 · 207-774-7000

Thomas S. Marjerison · Norman, Hanson & DeTroy · 415 Congress Street · P.O. Box 4600 · Portland, ME 04112-4600 · 207-774-7000

Robert O. Newton · Preti, Flaherty, Beliveau & Pachios · http://www.preti.com · One City Center · P.O. Box 9546 · Portland, ME 04112-9546 · 207-791-3000

Christopher D. Nyhan · a · Preti, Flaherty, Beliveau & Pachios · http://www.preti.com · One City Center · P.O. Box 9546 · Portland, ME 04112-9546 · 207-791-3000

Gerald F. Petruccelli · 2) · Petruccelli, Martin & Haddow · http://www.pmhlegal.com · 50 Monument Square · P.O. Box 17555 · Portland, ME 04112-8555 · 207-775-0200

Daniel Rapaport · Preti, Flaherty, Beliveau & Pachios · http://www.preti.com · One City Center · P.O. Box 9546 · Portland, ME 04112-9546 · 207-791-3000

Harrison L. Richardson · a · Richardson, Whitman, Large & Badger · 465 Congress Street · P.O. Box 9545 · Portland, ME 04112-9545 · 207-774-7474

Peter J. Rubin · 2% · Bernstein Shur · West Tower · 100 Middle Street · P.O. Box 9729 · Portland, ME 04104-5029 · 207-774-1200

PRODUCT LIABILITY LITIGATION

Auburn

Stephen B. Wade · Skelton, Taintor & Abbott · 95 Main Street · P.O. Box 3200 · Auburn, ME 04212-3200 · 207-784-3200

Lewiston

John E. Sedgewick · Berman & Simmons · 129 Lisbon Street · P.O. Box 961 · Lewiston, ME 04243-0961 207-784-3576

Jack H. Simmons · 2% · Berman & Simmons · 129 Lisbon Street · P.O. Box 961 · Lewiston, ME 04243-0961 · 207-784-3576

Portland

Peter W. Culley · a · Pierce Atwood · One Monument Square, Seventh Floor · Portland, ME 04101 · 207-791-1100

Harold J. Friedman · Friedman Gaythwaite Wolfe & Leavitt · Six City Center, Suite 400 · P.O. Box 4726 Portland, ME 04112-4726 · 207-761-0900

Peter J. Rubin · 2% · Bernstein Shur · West Tower · 100 Middle Street · P.O. Box 9729 · Portland, ME 04104-5029 · 207-774-1200

PROFESSIONAL MALPRACTICE LAW

Portland

Peter J. Rubin · 2% · Bernstein Shur · West Tower · 100 Middle Street · P.O. Box 9729 · Portland, ME 04104-5029 · 207-774-1200

PUBLIC FINANCE LAW

Augusta

James C. Pitney, Jr. · Preti, Flaherty, Beliveau & Pachios · http://www.preti.com · 45 Memorial Circle · P.O. Box 1058 · Augusta, ME 04332-1058 · 207-623-5300

Portland

Bruce A. Coggeshall · a · Pierce Atwood · One Monument Square, Seventh Floor · Portland, ME 04101 207-791-1100

Ronald A. Epstein · Jensen Baird Gardner & Henry · Ten Free Street · P.O. Box 4510 · Portland, ME 04112-4510 · 207-775-7271

F. Paul Frinsko · Bernstein Shur · West Tower · 100 Middle Street · P.O. Box 9729 · Portland, ME 04104-5029 · 207-774-1200

James M. Saffian · Pierce Atwood · One Monument Square, Seventh Floor · Portland, ME 04101 · 207-791-1100

Richard A. Spencer · Drummond Woodsum & MacMahon · http://www.dwmlaw.com · 245 Commercial Street · P.O. Box 9781 · Portland, ME 04104-5081 · 207-772-1941

E. William Stockmeyer · Drummond Woodsum & MacMahon · http://www.dwmlaw.com · 245 Commercial Street · P.O. Box 9781 · Portland, ME 04104-5081 · 207-772-1941

REAL ESTATE LAW

Augusta

Michael J. Gentile · Preti, Flaherty, Beliveau & Pachios · http://www.preti.com · 45 Memorial Circle · P.O. Box 1058 · Augusta, ME 04332-1058 · 207-623-5300

Lester F. Wilkinson, Jr. · Bernstein Shur · 146 Capitol Street · P.O. Box 5057 · Augusta, ME 04332-5057 207-623-1596

Brunswick

John A. Cunningham · a · Eaton Peabody · 167 Park Row · P.O. Box Nine · Brunswick, ME 04011-0009 207-729-1144

Falmouth

James B. Barns · James B. Barns · 361 U.S. Route One · Falmouth, ME 04105-1345 · 207-781-7677

Kingfield

Donald A. Fowler, Jr. · a · Donald A. Fowler, Jr. · 243 Main Street · P.O. Box 576 · Kingfield, ME 04947 · 207-265-2002

Portland

Drew Anderson · Murray, Plumb & Murray · 75 Pearl Street · P.O. Box 9785 · Portland, ME 04104 · 207-773-5651

Anthony M. Calcagni · Verrill Dana · http://www.verrilldana.com · One Portland Square · P.O. Box 586 · Portland, ME 04112-0586 · 207-774-4000

Lawrence R. Clough · a · Tompkins, Clough, Hirshon & Langer · Three Canal Plaza, Sixth Floor · P.O. Box 15060 · Portland, ME 04112-5060 · 207-874-6700

Christopher J. W. Coggeshall · Verrill Dana · http://www.verrilldana.com · One Portland Square · P.O. Box 586 · Portland, ME 04112-0586 · 207-774-4000

Kenneth M. Cole III · Jensen Baird Gardner & Henry · Ten Free Street · P.O. Box 4510 · Portland, ME 04112-4510 · 207-775-7271

Paul F. Driscoll · Norman, Hanson & DeTroy · 415 Congress Street · P.O. Box 4600 · Portland, ME 04112-4600 · 207-774-7000

Ronald A. Epstein · Jensen Baird Gardner & Henry · Ten Free Street · P.O. Box 4510 · Portland, ME 04112-4510 · 207-775-7271

William M. Fletcher · Verrill Dana · http://www.verrilldana.com · One Portland Square · P.O. Box 586 · Portland, ME 04112-0586 · 207-774-4000

David S. Galgay, Jr. · Verrill Dana · http://www.verrilldana.com · One Portland Square · P.O. Box 586 · Portland, ME 04112-0586 · 207-774-4000

Tom S. Hanson · Bernstein Shur · West Tower · 100 Middle Street · P.O. Box 9729 · Portland, ME 04104-5029 · 207-774-1200

David J. Jones · Jensen Baird Gardner & Henry · Ten Free Street · P.O. Box 4510 · Portland, ME 04112-4510 · 207-775-7271

Dennis C. Keeler · Pierce Atwood · One Monument Square, Seventh Floor · Portland, ME 04101 · 207-791-1100

Leslie E. Lowry III · Jensen Baird Gardner & Henry · Ten Free Street · P.O. Box 4510 · Portland, ME 04112-4510 · 207-775-7271

Charles E. Miller · a · Bernstein Shur · West Tower · 100 Middle Street · P.O. Box 9729 · Portland, ME 04104-5029 · 207-774-1200

Timothy H. Norton · Kelly, Remmel & Zimmerman · 53 Exchange Street, Third Floor · P.O. Box 597 · Portland, ME 04112-0597 · 207-775-1020

Charles R. Oestreicher · Verrill Dana · http://www.verrilldana.com · One Portland Square · P.O. Box 586 · Portland, ME 04112-0586 · 207-774-4000

James C. Palmer · Verrill Dana · http://www.verrilldana.com · One Portland Square · P.O. Box 586 · Portland, ME 04112-0586 · 207-774-4000

Paul D. Pietropaoli · Perkins Thompson · http://www.perkinsthompson.com · One Canal Plaza · P.O. Box 426 · Portland, ME 04112-0426 · 207-774-2635

Richard D. Prentice · Pierce Atwood · One Monument Square, Seventh Floor · Portland, ME 04101 · 207-791-1100

Roderick R. Rovzar · Norman, Hanson & DeTroy · 415 Congress Street · P.O. Box 4600 · Portland, ME 04112-4600 · 207-774-7000

Dennis C. Sbrega · Preti, Flaherty, Beliveau & Pachios · http://www.preti.com · One City Center · P.O. Box 9546 · Portland, ME 04112-9546 · 207-791-3000

Jaimie P. Schwartz · Bernstein Shur · West Tower · 100 Middle Street · P.O. Box 9729 · Portland, ME 04104-5029 · 207-774-1200

Maurice A. Selinger III · Curtis Thaxter · One Canal Plaza, Suite 1000 · P.O. Box 7320 · Portland, ME 04112-7320 · 207-774-9000

Richard A. Shinay · Drummond Woodsum & MacMahon · http://www.dwmlaw.com · 245 Commercial Street · P.O. Box 9781 · Portland, ME 04104-5081 · 207-772-1941

Nathan H. Smith · a · Bernstein Shur · West Tower · 100 Middle Street · P.O. Box 9729 · Portland, ME 04104-5029 · 207-774-1200

Richard W. Smith · Bernstein Shur · West Tower · 100 Middle Street · P.O. Box 9729 · Portland, ME 04104-5029 · 207-774-1200

Richard H. Spencer, Jr. · Jensen Baird Gardner & Henry · Ten Free Street · P.O. Box 4510 · Portland, ME 04112-4510 · 207-775-7271

Robert E. Stevens · Curtis Thaxter · One Canal Plaza, Suite 1000 · P.O. Box 7320 · Portland, ME 04112-7320 · 207-774-9000

Christopher L. Vaniotis · Bernstein Shur · West Tower · 100 Middle Street · P.O. Box 9729 · Portland, ME 04104-5029 · 207-774-1200

Ronald N. Ward · Drummond Woodsum & MacMahon · http://www.dwmlaw.com · 245 Commercial Street · P.O. Box 9781 · Portland, ME 04104-5081 · 207-772-1941

William M. Welch · Bernstein Shur · West Tower · 100 Middle Street · P.O. Box 9729 · Portland, ME 04104-5029 · 207-774-1200

Judith Fletcher Woodbury · Pierce Atwood · One Monument Square, Seventh Floor · Portland, ME 04101 · 207-791-1100

SECURITIES LAW

Bangor

Daniel G. McKay · a · Eaton Peabody · 80 Exchange Street · P.O. Box 1210 · Bangor, ME 04402-1210 · 207-947-0111

Camden

Susan E. Bryant · Bryant Law · http://www.bryantlawgroup.com · 39 ½ Main Street · P.O. Box 596 · Camden, ME 04843 · 207-230-0066

Portland

David J. Champoux · Pierce Atwood · One Monument Square, Seventh Floor · Portland, ME 04101 · 207-791-1100

Gregory S. Fryer · Verrill Dana · http://www.verrilldana.com · One Portland Square · P.O. Box 586 · Portland, ME 04112-0586 · 207-774-4000

Michael E. High · a · Drummond Woodsum & MacMahon · http://www.dwmlaw.com · 245 Commercial Street · P.O. Box 9781 · Portland, ME 04104-5081 · 207-772-1941

Herbert F. Janick III · Bingham McCutchen · http://www.bingham.com · 85 Exchange Street, Suite 300 · Portland, ME 04101-5045 · 207-780-8274

Keith C. Jones · Verrill Dana · http://www.verrilldana.com · One Portland Square · P.O. Box 586 · Portland, ME 04112-0586 · 207-774-4000

SPORTS LAW

Cumberland

Janet P. Judge · Sports Law Associates · 97 Range Road · Cumberland, ME 04021 · 207-776-4551

Kennebunk

Timothy J. O'Brien · Libby O'Brien Kingsley · http://www.lokllc.com · 62 Portland Road, Unit 17 · Kennebunk, ME 04043-0147 · 207-985-1815

Portland

David S. Abramson · Verrill Dana · http://www.verrilldana.com · One Portland Square · P.O. Box 586 · Portland, ME 04112-0586 · 207-774-4000

Peter S. Carlisle · Preti, Flaherty, Beliveau & Pachios · http://www.preti.com · One City Center · P.O. Box 9546 · Portland, ME 04112-9546 · 207-791-3000

TAX LAW

Auburn

Bryan M. Dench · a · Skelton, Taintor & Abbott · 95 Main Street · P.O. Box 3200 · Auburn, ME 04212-3200 · 207-784-3200

Lewiston

Martin I. Eisenstein · Brann & Isaacson · http://www.brannlaw.com · 184 Main Street · P.O. Box 3070 · Lewiston, ME 04243-3070 · 207-786-3566

Portland

Sarah H. Beard · Pierce Atwood · One Monument Square, Seventh Floor · Portland, ME 04101 · 207-791-1100

Norman R. Belanger · a · Van Meer & Belanger · 20 York Street · Portland, ME 04101-4556 · 207-871-7500

Timothy P. Benoit · Perkins Thompson · http://www.perkinsthompson.com · One Canal Plaza · P.O. Box 426 · Portland, ME 04112-0426 · 207-774-2635

Jonathan A. Block · Pierce Atwood · One Monument Square, Seventh Floor · Portland, ME 04101 · 207-791-1100

John W. Geismar · Norman, Hanson & DeTroy · 415 Congress Street · P.O. Box 4600 · Portland, ME 04112-4600 · 207-774-7000

James G. Good · Pierce Atwood · One Monument Square, Seventh Floor · Portland, ME 04101 · 207-791-1100

John S. Kaminski · Drummond Woodsum & MacMahon · http://www.dwmlaw.com · 245 Commercial Street · P.O. Box 9781 · Portland, ME 04104-5081 · 207-772-1941

Karen B. Lovell · Bernstein Shur · West Tower · 100 Middle Street · P.O. Box 9729 · Portland, ME 04104-5029 · 207-774-1200

Christopher S. McLoon · Verrill Dana · http://www.verrilldana.com · One Portland Square · P.O. Box 586 Portland, ME 04112-0586 · 207-774-4000

Robert B. Ravenelle · Pierce Atwood · One Monument Square, Seventh Floor · Portland, ME 04101 · 207-791-1100

Michael L. Sheehan · Preti, Flaherty, Beliveau & Pachios · http://www.preti.com · One City Center · P.O. Box 9546 · Portland, ME 04112-9546 · 207-791-3000

Nelson A. Toner · Bernstein Shur · West Tower · 100 Middle Street · P.O. Box 9729 · Portland, ME 04104-5029 · 207-774-1200

Thomas J. Van Meer · 2) · Van Meer & Belanger · 20 York Street · Portland, ME 04101-4556 · 207-871-7500

TIMBER LAW

Portland

George F. Burns · Bernstein Shur · West Tower · 100 Middle Street · P.O. Box 9729 · Portland, ME 04104-5029 · 207-774-1200

TRUSTS AND ESTATES

Auburn

Jill A. Checkoway · Skelton, Taintor & Abbott · 95 Main Street · P.O. Box 3200 · Auburn, ME 04212-3200 · 207-784-3200

Ellsworth

Jeffrey W. Jones · a · Jeffrey W. Jones · 104 Main Street · P.O. Box 622 · Ellsworth, ME 04605-0622 · 207-664-0002

Portland

David J. Backer · Drummond Woodsum & MacMahon · http://www.dwmlaw.com · 245 Commercial Street · P.O. Box 9781 · Portland, ME 04104-5081 · 207-772-1941

Judith M. Coburn · a · Verrill Dana · http://www.verrilldana.com · One Portland Square · P.O. Box 586 · Portland, ME 04112-0586 · 207-774-4000

Abigail K. Diggins · LeBlanc & Young · Two Canal Plaza, Suite 400 · P.O. Box 7950 · Portland, ME 04112-7950 · 207-772-2800

Eileen M. L. Epstein · a · Epstein & O'Donovan · Two Monument Square · Portland, ME 04101-4036 · 207-772-4100

Elizabeth T. High · LeBlanc & Young · Two Canal Plaza, Suite 400 · P.O. Box 7950 · Portland, ME 04112-7950 · 207-772-2800

James A. Houle · Bernstein Shur · West Tower · 100 Middle Street · P.O. Box 9729 · Portland, ME 04104-5029 · 207-774-1200

David E. Hunt · a · Law Office of David E. Hunt · 511 Congress Street · Portland, ME 04101-3464 · 207-773-5100

Philip C. Hunt · a · Perkins Thompson · http://www.perkinsthompson.com · One Canal Plaza · P.O. Box 426 · Portland, ME 04112-0426 · 207-774-2635

Susan E. Hunter · Law Offices of Susan E. Hunter · 75 Pearl Street, Suite 420 · P.O. Box 455 · Portland, ME 04112 · 207-775-6341

Everett P. Ingalls III · Pierce Atwood · One Monument Square, Seventh Floor · Portland, ME 04101 · 207-791-1100

Kurt E. Klebe · Verrill Dana · http://www.verrilldana.com · One Portland Square · P.O. Box 586 · Portland, ME 04112-0586 · 207-774-4000

Richard P. LeBlanc · 2) · LeBlanc & Young · Two Canal Plaza, Suite 400 · P.O. Box 7950 · Portland, ME 04112-7950 · 207-772-2800

Karen B. Lovell · Bernstein Shur · West Tower · 100 Middle Street · P.O. Box 9729 · Portland, ME 04104-5029 · 207-774-1200

Elizabeth T. McCandless · McCandless · 14 York Street · Portland, ME 04101 · 207-523-3434

Mary McQuillen · Verrill Dana · http://www.verrilldana.com · One Portland Square · P.O. Box 586 · Portland, ME 04112-0586 · 207-774-4000

Thomas J. Van Meer · 2) · Van Meer & Belanger · 20 York Street · Portland, ME 04101-4556 · 207-871-7500

Barbara K. Wheaton · a · Pierce Atwood · One Monument Square, Seventh Floor · Portland, ME 04101 207-791-1100

James H. Young II · a · LeBlanc & Young · Two Canal Plaza, Suite 400 · P.O. Box 7950 · Portland, ME 04112-7950 · 207-772-2800

WHITE-COLLAR CRIMINAL DEFENSE

Lewiston

Jack H. Simmons · 2% · Berman & Simmons · 129 Lisbon Street · P.O. Box 961 · Lewiston, ME 04243-0961 · 207-784-3576

Portland

David E. Barry · Pierce Atwood · One Monument Square, Seventh Floor · Portland, ME 04101 · 207-791-1100

Peter J. DeTroy III · 2) · Norman, Hanson & DeTroy · 415 Congress Street · P.O. Box 4600 · Portland, ME 04112-4600 · 207-774-7000

Joseph H. Groff III · Jensen Baird Gardner & Henry · Ten Free Street · P.O. Box 4510 · Portland, ME 04112-4510 · 207-775-7271

Ralph I. Lancaster, Jr. · 2% · Pierce Atwood · One Monument Square, Seventh Floor · Portland, ME 04101 · 207-791-1100

Daniel G. Lilley · 2% · Daniel G. Lilley Law Offices · 39 Portland Pier · P.O. Box 4803 · Portland, ME 04112 · 207-774-6206

Alexia Pappas · Verrill Dana · http://www.verrilldana.com · One Portland Square · P.O. Box 586 · Portland, ME 04112-0586 · 207-774-4000

Peter J. Rubin · 2% · Bernstein Shur · West Tower · 100 Middle Street · P.O. Box 9729 · Portland, ME 04104-5029 · 207-774-1200

Portland

Robert W. Bower, Jr. · Norman, Hanson & DeTroy · 415 Congress Street · P.O. Box 4600 · Portland, ME 04112-4600 · 207-774-7000

Robert C. Brooks · Verrill Dana · http://www.verrilldana.com · One Portland Square · P.O. Box 586 · Portland, ME 04112-0586 · 207-774-4000

Kevin M. Gillis · Troubh Heisler · 511 Congress Street · P.O. Box 9711 · Portland, ME 04104-5011 · 207-780-6789

Evan M. Hansen · Preti, Flaherty, Beliveau & Pachios · http://www.preti.com · One City Center · P.O. Box 9546 · Portland, ME 04112-9546 · 207-791-3000

Stephen Hessert · a · Norman, Hanson & DeTroy · 415 Congress Street · P.O. Box 4600 · Portland, ME 04112-4600 · 207-774-7000

John M. McCallum · a · Robinson, Kriger & McCallum · 12 Portland Pier · P.O. Box 568 · Portland, ME 04112-0568 · 207-772-6565

Stephen W. Moriarty · Norman, Hanson & DeTroy · 415 Congress Street · P.O. Box 4600 · Portland, ME 04112-4600 · 207-774-7000

Allan M. Muir · a · Pierce Atwood · One Monument Square, Seventh Floor · Portland, ME 04101 · 207-791-1100

Richard F. van Antwerp · Robinson, Kriger & McCallum · 12 Portland Pier · P.O. Box 568 · Portland, ME 04112-0568 · 207-772-6565

Topsham

G. William Higbee · McTeague, Higbee, Case, Cohen, Whitney & Toker · Four Union Park · P.O. Box 5000 · Topsham, ME 04086-5000 · 207-725-5581

Yarmouth

Robert J. Piampiano · a · Piampiano Law Offices · 45 Forest Falls Drive, Suite B4 · Yarmouth, ME 04096 · 207-846-4500

MARYLAND

ADMINISTRATIVE LAW

Baltimore

Carville B. Collins · DLA Piper · 6225 Smith Avenue · Baltimore, MD 21209-3600 · 410-580-3000

Michael C. Powell · ⑩ · Gordon, Feinblatt, Rothman, Hoffberger & Hollander · http://www.gfrlaw.com · The Garrett Building · 233 East Redwood Street · Baltimore, MD 21202 · 410-576-4000

Paul A. Tiburzi · DLA Piper · 6225 Smith Avenue · Baltimore, MD 21209-3600 · 410-580-3000

ADVERTISING LAW

Baltimore

James B. Astrachan · Astrachan, Gunst & Thomas · http://www.agtlawyers.com · 217 East Redwood Street, Suite 2100 · Baltimore, MD 21202 · 410-783-3550

ALTERNATIVE DISPUTE RESOLUTION

Annapolis

Rignal W. Baldwin, Jr. · Brassel Baldwin Kagan & May · 112 West Street · Annapolis, MD 21401 · 410-974-9200

Tarrant H. Lomax · Tarrant H. Lomax · 940 Bay Ridge Avenue · Annapolis, MD 21403-3033 · 410-267-6151

Baltimore

George Beall · ⑳ · Hogan & Hartson · 111 South Calvert Street, Suite 1600 · Baltimore, MD 21202 · 410-659-2700

Paul D. Bekman · ⑳ · Salsbury, Clements, Bekman, Marder & Adkins · 300 West Pratt Street, Suite 450 · Baltimore, MD 21201 · 410-539-6633

Herbert J. Belgrad · Tydings & Rosenberg · http://www.tydingslaw.com · 100 East Pratt Street, 26th Floor · Baltimore, MD 21202 · 410-752-9700

Herbert Better · Zuckerman Spaeder · http://www.zuckerman.com · 100 East Pratt Street, Suite 2440 · Baltimore, MD 21202-1031 · 410-332-0444

Paul A. Dorf · Adelberg, Rudow, Dorf & Hendler · http://www.adelbergrudow.com · Wachovia Building, Suite 600 · Seven St. Paul Street · Baltimore, MD 21202 · 410-539-5195

Howard G. Goldberg · Goldberg, Pike & Besche · Tower II, Suite 1001 · 100 South Charles Street · Baltimore, MD 21201-2728 · 410-539-1004

Andrew Jay Graham · ⑩ · Kramon & Graham · http://www.kramonandgraham.com · One South Street, Suite 2600 · Baltimore, MD 21202 · 410-752-6030

Lawrence S. Greenwald · Gordon, Feinblatt, Rothman, Hoffberger & Hollander · http://www.gfrlaw.com The Garrett Building · 233 East Redwood Street · Baltimore, MD 21202 · 410-576-4000

Edward J. Gutman · Edward J. Gutman · 25 South Charles Street, 14th Floor · Baltimore, MD 21201 · 410-576-4809

M. Natalie McSherry · Kramon & Graham · http://www.kramonandgraham.com · One South Street, Suite 2600 · Baltimore, MD 21202 · 410-752-6030

J. Michael McWilliams · McWilliams Dispute Resolution · 1106 North Charles Street, Suite 300 · Baltimore, MD 21201-5557 · 410-244-8124

Benjamin Rosenberg · Rosenberg | Martin | Greenberg · 25 South Charles Street, Suite 2115 · Baltimore, MD 21201 · 410-547-7163

Sheila K. Sachs · ⑩ · Gordon, Feinblatt, Rothman, Hoffberger & Hollander · http://www.gfrlaw.com · The Garrett Building · 233 East Redwood Street · Baltimore, MD 21202 · 410-576-4000

David W. Skeen · ⑳ · Wright, Constable & Skeen · One Charles Center, 16th Floor · 100 North Charles Street · Baltimore, MD 21201 · 410-539-5541

William B. Whiteford · ⑳ · Whiteford, Taylor & Preston · http://www.wtplaw.com · Seven Saint Paul Street · Baltimore, MD 21202-1636 · 410-347-8700

M. Hamilton Whitman, Jr. · ⑳ · Ober, Kaler, Grimes & Shriver · http://www.ober.com · 120 East Baltimore Street, Suite 800 · Baltimore, MD 21202-1643 · 410-685-1120

John Anthony Wolf · ⑩ · Ober, Kaler, Grimes & Shriver · http://www.ober.com · 120 East Baltimore Street, Suite 800 · Baltimore, MD 21202-1643 · 410-685-1120

Robert M. Wright · Whiteford, Taylor & Preston · http://www.wtplaw.com · Seven Saint Paul Street · Baltimore, MD 21202-1636 · 410-347-8700

Catonsville

John E. Sandbower III · ㉕ · Sandbower & Gabler · 505 Patleigh Road · Catonsville, MD 21228-5634 · 410-494-6380

Greenbelt

Howard S. Chasanow · Howard S. Chasanow · 7849 Belle Point Drive · Greenbelt, MD 20770 · 301-441-3366

Pasedena

Charles E. Iliff, Jr. · Iliff & Meredith · 8055 Ritchie Highway, Suites 201-203 · Pasedena, MD 21122-1067 · 410-685-1166

Rockville

Allan Goodman · Allan Goodman · 401 Green Pasture Drive · Rockville, MD 20852-4232 · 301-770-4463

Sherwood Forrest

Timothy J. Bloomfield · ㉕ · Law Offices of Timothy J. Bloomfield · 534 Little John Hill · Sherwood Forrest, MD 21405-2024 · 410-849-2105

ANTITRUST LAW

Baltimore

Charles O. Monk II · Saul Ewing · 500 East Pratt Street, Suite 900 · Baltimore, MD 21202 · 410-332-8600

Thomas M. Wilson III · Tydings & Rosenberg · http://www.tydingslaw.com · 100 East Pratt Street, 26th Floor · Baltimore, MD 21202 · 410-752-9700

Sherwood Forrest

Timothy J. Bloomfield · ㉕ · Law Offices of Timothy J. Bloomfield · 534 Little John Hill · Sherwood Forrest, MD 21405-2024 · 410-849-2105

APPELLATE LAW

Baltimore

Andrew H. Baida · Rosenberg | Martin | Greenberg · 25 South Charles Street, Suite 2115 · Baltimore, MD 21201 · 410-547-7163

Benjamin Rosenberg · Rosenberg | Martin | Greenberg · 25 South Charles Street, Suite 2115 · Baltimore, MD 21201 · 410-547-7163

Melvin J. Sykes · Melvin J. Sykes · 120 East Baltimore Street, Suite 1701 · Baltimore, MD 21202-6701 · 410-727-3078

BANKING LAW

Baltimore

Frank C. Bonaventure, Jr. · Ober, Kaler, Grimes & Shriver · http://www.ober.com · 120 East Baltimore Street, Suite 800 · Baltimore, MD 21202-1643 · 410-685-1120

Marjorie A. Corwin · Gordon, Feinblatt, Rothman, Hoffberger & Hollander · http://www.gfrlaw.com · The Garrett Building · 233 East Redwood Street · Baltimore, MD 21202 · 410-576-4000

Cleaveland D. Miller · ⑩ · Semmes Bowen & Semmes · http://www.semmes.com · 25 South Charles Street, Suite 1400 · Baltimore, MD 21201 · 410-539-5040

Frederick W. Runge, Jr. · Miles & Stockbridge · http://www.milesstockbridge.com · 10 Light Street · Baltimore, MD 21202-1487 · 410-727-6464

Carla Stone Witzel · Gordon, Feinblatt, Rothman, Hoffberger & Hollander · http://www.gfrlaw.com · The Garrett Building · 233 East Redwood Street · Baltimore, MD 21202 · 410-576-4000

Hanover

Thomas B. Hudson · Hudson Cook · 7250 Parkway Drive, Fifth Floor · Hanover, MD 21076 · 410-712-6990

BANKRUPTCY AND CREDITOR-DEBTOR RIGHTS LAW

Ashton

Roger M. Whelan · ⑳ · Roger M. Whelan · 17908 Ednor View Terrace · Ashton, MD 20861 · 301-260-7707

Baltimore

Lawrence D. Coppel · ⑩ · Gordon, Feinblatt, Rothman, Hoffberger & Hollander · http://www.gfrlaw.com · The Garrett Building · 233 East Redwood Street · Baltimore, MD 21202 · 410-576-4000

Deborah Hunt Devan · ⑩ · Neuberger, Quinn, Gielen, Rubin & Gibber · http://www.nqgrg.com · One South Street, 27th Floor · Baltimore, MD 21202 · 410-332-8550

Linda V. Donhauser · Miles & Stockbridge · http://www.milesstockbridge.com · 10 Light Street · Baltimore, MD 21202-1487 · 410-727-6464

Martin T. Fletcher · ⑩ · Whiteford, Taylor & Preston · http://www.wtplaw.com · Seven Saint Paul Street Baltimore, MD 21202-1636 · 410-347-8700

Mark J. Friedman · ⑩ · DLA Piper · 6225 Smith Avenue · Baltimore, MD 21209-3600 · 410-580-3000

Alan M. Grochal · Tydings & Rosenberg · http://www.tydingslaw.com · 100 East Pratt Street, 26th Floor · Baltimore, MD 21202 · 410-752-9700

Richard M. Kremen · ⑳ · DLA Piper · 6225 Smith Avenue · Baltimore, MD 21209-3600 · 410-580-3000

Joyce A. Kuhns · Saul Ewing · 500 East Pratt Street, Suite 900 · Baltimore, MD 21202 · 410-332-8600

Paul M. Nussbaum · Whiteford, Taylor & Preston · http://www.wtplaw.com · Seven Saint Paul Street · Baltimore, MD 21202-1636 · 410-347-8700

David E. Rice · Venable · http://www.venable.com · 750 East Pratt Street, Suite 900 · Baltimore, MD 21202 · 410-244-7400

Joel I. Sher · Shapiro Sher Guinot & Sandler · 36 South Charles Street, Suite 2000 · Baltimore, MD 21201-3147 · 410-385-0202

Jay A. Shulman · ⑩ · Saul Ewing · 500 East Pratt Street, Suite 900 · Baltimore, MD 21202 · 410-332-8600

Irving E. Walker · ⑩ · Cole, Schotz, Meisel, Forman & Leonard · http://www.coleschotz.com · 111 South Calvert Street, Suite 2350 · Baltimore, MD 21202 · 410-230-0660

Richard L. Wasserman · ⑩ · Venable · http://www.venable.com · 750 East Pratt Street, Suite 900 · Baltimore, MD 21202 · 410-244-7400

Bethesda

Nelson Deckelbaum · ⑳ · Deckelbaum Ogens & Raftery · Three Bethesda Metro Center, Suite 200 · Bethesda, MD 20814 · 301-961-9200

Paul J. Sweeney · Linowes & Blocher · http://www.linowes-law.com · 7200 Wisconsin Avenue, Suite 800 · Bethesda, MD 20814-4842 · 301-654-0504

Rockville

Morton A. Faller · Shulman, Rogers, Gandal, Pordy & Ecker · 11921 Rockville Pike · Rockville, MD 20852-2743 · 301-230-5200

Alan S. Kerxton · ⑩ · Stein, Sperling, Bennett, De Jong, Driscoll & Greenfeig · 25 West Middle Lane · Rockville, MD 20850-2204 · 301-340-2020

BET-THE-COMPANY LITIGATION

Baltimore

Francis B. Burch, Jr. · (20) · DLA Piper · 6225 Smith Avenue · Baltimore, MD 21209-3600 · 410-580-3000

Andrew Jay Graham · (10) · Kramon & Graham · http://www.kramonandgraham.com · One South Street, Suite 2600 · Baltimore, MD 21202 · 410-752-6030

James P. Ulwick · (10) · Kramon & Graham · http://www.kramonandgraham.com · One South Street, Suite 2600 · Baltimore, MD 21202 · 410-752-6030

COLLABORATIVE LAW: FAMILY LAW

Annapolis

Nancy Leibowitz Weller · Nancy Leibowitz Weller · 22- 1/2 West Street · Annapolis, MD 21401 · 410-263-3660

Bethesda

Deborah E. Reiser · Lerch, Early & Brewer · Three Bethesda Metro Center, Suite 460 · Bethesda, MD 20814-5367 · 301-986-1300

Rockville

Cynthia Callahan · Dragga, Callahan, Hannon & Hessler · 110 North Washington Street, Suite 300 · Rockville, MD 20850-2223 · 301-340-9090

Stuart S. Greenfeig · Stein, Sperling, Bennett, De Jong, Driscoll & Greenfeig · 25 West Middle Lane · Rockville, MD 20850-2204 · 301-340-2020

Darcy A. Shoop · Stein, Sperling, Bennett, De Jong, Driscoll & Greenfeig · 25 West Middle Lane · Rockville, MD 20850-2204 · 301-340-2020

COMMERCIAL LITIGATION

Baltimore

Philip M. Andrews · Kramon & Graham · http://www.kramonandgraham.com · One South Street, Suite 2600 · Baltimore, MD 21202 · 410-752-6030

Kevin F. Arthur · Kramon & Graham · http://www.kramonandgraham.com · One South Street, Suite 2600 Baltimore, MD 21202 · 410-752-6030

George Beall · (20) · Hogan & Hartson · 111 South Calvert Street, Suite 1600 · Baltimore, MD 21202 · 410-659-2700

Herbert J. Belgrad · Tydings & Rosenberg · http://www.tydingslaw.com · 100 East Pratt Street, 26th Floor · Baltimore, MD 21202 · 410-752-9700

Herbert Better · Zuckerman Spaeder · http://www.zuckerman.com · 100 East Pratt Street, Suite 2440 · Baltimore, MD 21202-1031 · 410-332-0444

Robert S. Brennen · Miles & Stockbridge · http://www.milesstockbridge.com · 10 Light Street · Baltimore, MD 21202-1487 · 410-727-6464

Francis B. Burch, Jr. · ⑳ · DLA Piper · 6225 Smith Avenue · Baltimore, MD 21209-3600 · 410-580-3000

Benjamin R. Civiletti · ⑳ · Venable · http://www.venable.com · 750 East Pratt Street, Suite 900 · Baltimore, MD 21202 · 410-244-7400

Ward B. Coe III · ⑩ · Gallagher, Evelius & Jones · 218 North Charles Street, Suite 400 · Baltimore, MD 21201 · 410-727-7702

Joel A. Dewey · DLA Piper · 6225 Smith Avenue · Baltimore, MD 21209-3600 · 410-580-3000

Neil J. Dilloff · DLA Piper · 6225 Smith Avenue · Baltimore, MD 21209-3600 · 410-580-3000

Joseph G. Finnerty, Jr. · ⑩ · DLA Piper · 6225 Smith Avenue · Baltimore, MD 21209-3600 · 410-580-3000

Lawrence Fletcher-Hill · Gordon, Feinblatt, Rothman, Hoffberger & Hollander · http://www.gfrlaw.com The Garrett Building · 233 East Redwood Street · Baltimore, MD 21202 · 410-576-4000

Mark D. Gately · Hogan & Hartson · 111 South Calvert Street, Suite 1600 · Baltimore, MD 21202 · 410-659-2700

Price O. Gielen · ⑩ · Neuberger, Quinn, Gielen, Rubin & Gibber · http://www.nqgrg.com · One South Street, 27th Floor · Baltimore, MD 21202 · 410-332-8550

Andrew Jay Graham · ⑩ · Kramon & Graham · http://www.kramonandgraham.com · One South Street, Suite 2600 · Baltimore, MD 21202 · 410-752-6030

James E. Gray · Venable · http://www.venable.com · 750 East Pratt Street, Suite 900 · Baltimore, MD 21202 · 410-244-7400

Lawrence S. Greenwald · Gordon, Feinblatt, Rothman, Hoffberger & Hollander · http://www.gfrlaw.com The Garrett Building · 233 East Redwood Street · Baltimore, MD 21202 · 410-576-4000

Martin S. Himeles, Jr. · Zuckerman Spaeder · http://www.zuckerman.com · 100 East Pratt Street, Suite 2440 · Baltimore, MD 21202-1031 · 410-332-0444

Stephen J. Immelt · ⑩ · Hogan & Hartson · 111 South Calvert Street, Suite 1600 · Baltimore, MD 21202 410-659-2700

Sidney G. Leech · Goodell, DeVries, Leech & Dann · http://www.gdlglaw.com · One South Street, 20th Floor · Baltimore, MD 21202 · 410-783-4000

Andrew D. Levy · ⑩ · Brown, Goldstein & Levy · 120 East Baltimore Street, Suite 1700 · Baltimore, MD 21202 · 410-962-1030

Ava E. Lias-Booker · ⑩ · McGuireWoods · http://www.mcguirewoods.com · Seven Saint Paul Street, Suite 1000 · Baltimore, MD 21202-1671 · 410-659-4400

Richard J. Magid · Whiteford, Taylor & Preston · http://www.wtplaw.com · Seven Saint Paul Street · Baltimore, MD 21202-1636 · 410-347-8700

Gerard P. Martin · Rosenberg | Martin | Greenberg · 25 South Charles Street, Suite 2115 · Baltimore, MD 21201 · 410-547-7163

James D. Mathias · DLA Piper · 6225 Smith Avenue · Baltimore, MD 21209-3600 · 410-580-3000

Robert J. Mathias · ⑩ · DLA Piper · 6225 Smith Avenue · Baltimore, MD 21209-3600 · 410-580-3000

M. Natalie McSherry · Kramon & Graham · http://www.kramonandgraham.com · One South Street, Suite 2600 · Baltimore, MD 21202 · 410-752-6030

Albert Mezzanotte, Jr. · Whiteford, Taylor & Preston · http://www.wtplaw.com · Seven Saint Paul Street Baltimore, MD 21202-1636 · 410-347-8700

Charles O. Monk II · Saul Ewing · 500 East Pratt Street, Suite 900 · Baltimore, MD 21202 · 410-332-8600

William J. Murphy · ⑩ · Murphy & Shaffer · http://www.murphyshaffer.com · 36 South Charles Street, Suite 1400 · Baltimore, MD 21201 · 410-783-7000

Lee H. Ogburn · Kramon & Graham · http://www.kramonandgraham.com · One South Street, Suite 2600 · Baltimore, MD 21202 · 410-752-6030

Benjamin Rosenberg · Rosenberg | Martin | Greenberg · 25 South Charles Street, Suite 2115 · Baltimore, MD 21201 · 410-547-7163

William Ryan, Jr. · Whiteford, Taylor & Preston · http://www.wtplaw.com · Seven Saint Paul Street · Baltimore, MD 21202-1636 · 410-347-8700

Michael Schatzow · Venable · http://www.venable.com · 750 East Pratt Street, Suite 900 · Baltimore, MD 21202 · 410-244-7400

Charles P. Scheeler · DLA Piper · 6225 Smith Avenue · Baltimore, MD 21209-3600 · 410-580-3000

Robert T. Shaffer III · Murphy & Shaffer · http://www.murphyshaffer.com · 36 South Charles Street, Suite 1400 · Baltimore, MD 21201 · 410-783-7000

James L. Shea · ⑩ · Venable · http://www.venable.com · 750 East Pratt Street, Suite 900 · Baltimore, MD 21202 · 410-244-7400

Shale D. Stiller · ㉕ · DLA Piper · 6225 Smith Avenue · Baltimore, MD 21209-3600 · 410-580-3000

Paul F. Strain · Venable · http://www.venable.com · 750 East Pratt Street, Suite 900 · Baltimore, MD 21202 · 410-244-7400

Kenneth L. Thompson · DLA Piper · 6225 Smith Avenue · Baltimore, MD 21209-3600 · 410-580-3000

Jerrold A. Thrope · Gordon, Feinblatt, Rothman, Hoffberger & Hollander · http://www.gfrlaw.com · The Garrett Building · 233 East Redwood Street · Baltimore, MD 21202 · 410-576-4000

James P. Ulwick · ⑩ · Kramon & Graham · http://www.kramonandgraham.com · One South Street, Suite 2600 · Baltimore, MD 21202 · 410-752-6030

John Anthony Wolf · ⑩ · Ober, Kaler, Grimes & Shriver · http://www.ober.com · 120 East Baltimore Street, Suite 800 · Baltimore, MD 21202-1643 · 410-685-1120

Thomas M. Wood IV · Neuberger, Quinn, Gielen, Rubin & Gibber · http://www.nqgrg.com · One South Street, 27th Floor · Baltimore, MD 21202 · 410-332-8550

Linda S. Woolf · Goodell, DeVries, Leech & Dann · http://www.gdlglaw.com · One South Street, 20th Floor · Baltimore, MD 21202 · 410-783-4000

Jefferson V. Wright · Miles & Stockbridge · http://www.milesstockbridge.com · 10 Light Street · Baltimore, MD 21202-1487 · 410-727-6464

Bethesda

Gerald W. Heller · Linowes & Blocher · http://www.linowes-law.com · 7200 Wisconsin Avenue, Suite 800 Bethesda, MD 20814-4842 · 301-654-0504

Easton

David R. Thompson · Cowdrey, Thompson & Karsten · 130 North Washington Street · P.O. Box 1747 · Easton, MD 21601-1747 · 410-822-6800

Rockville

Thomas D. Murphy · Murphy & Mood · Adams Law Center, Suite Two · 31 Wood Lane · Rockville, MD 20850 · 301-424-0400

Sherwood Forrest

Timothy J. Bloomfield · (25) · Law Offices of Timothy J. Bloomfield · 534 Little John Hill · Sherwood Forrest, MD 21405-2024 · 410-849-2105

Towson

Kieron F. Quinn · (20) · Quinn, Gordon & Wolf · 102 West Pennsylvania Avenue, Suite 402 · Towson, MD 21204 · 410-825-2300

CONSTRUCTION LAW

Baltimore

Thomas A. Baker · Thomas A. Baker · Charles Center South, Suite 2402 · 36 South Charles Street · Baltimore, MD 21201 · 410-332-1507

Neil J. Dilloff · DLA Piper · 6225 Smith Avenue · Baltimore, MD 21209-3600 · 410-580-3000

Howard G. Goldberg · Goldberg, Pike & Besche · Tower II, Suite 1001 · 100 South Charles Street · Baltimore, MD 21201-2728 · 410-539-1004

Christopher J. Heffernan · Niles, Barton & Wilmer · http://www.niles-law.com · 111 South Calvert Street, Suite 1400 · Baltimore, MD 21202-6185 · 410-783-6300

Joseph C. Kovars · Ober, Kaler, Grimes & Shriver · http://www.ober.com · 120 East Baltimore Street, Suite 800 · Baltimore, MD 21202-1643 · 410-685-1120

Anthony L. Meagher · DLA Piper · 6225 Smith Avenue · Baltimore, MD 21209-3600 · 410-580-3000

Patrick M. Pike · Goldberg, Pike & Besche · Tower II, Suite 1001 · 100 South Charles Street · Baltimore, MD 21201-2728 · 410-539-1004

J. Snowden Stanley, Jr. · Semmes Bowen & Semmes · http://www.semmes.com · 25 South Charles Street, Suite 1400 · Baltimore, MD 21201 · 410-539-5040

John Anthony Wolf · (10) · Ober, Kaler, Grimes & Shriver · http://www.ober.com · 120 East Baltimore Street, Suite 800 · Baltimore, MD 21202-1643 · 410-685-1120

Robert M. Wright · Whiteford, Taylor & Preston · http://www.wtplaw.com · Seven Saint Paul Street · Baltimore, MD 21202-1636 · 410-347-8700

Sherwood Forrest

Timothy J. Bloomfield · ㉕ · Law Offices of Timothy J. Bloomfield · 534 Little John Hill · Sherwood Forrest, MD 21405-2024 · 410-849-2105

CORPORATE GOVERNANCE AND COMPLIANCE LAW

Baltimore

Benjamin R. Civiletti · ⑳ · Venable · http://www.venable.com · 750 East Pratt Street, Suite 900 · Baltimore, MD 21202 · 410-244-7400

James J. Hanks, Jr. · Venable · http://www.venable.com · 750 East Pratt Street, Suite 900 · Baltimore, MD 21202 · 410-244-7400

Cleaveland D. Miller · ⑩ · Semmes Bowen & Semmes · http://www.semmes.com · 25 South Charles Street, Suite 1400 · Baltimore, MD 21201 · 410-539-5040

Charles R. Moran · Ballard Spahr Andrews & Ingersoll · 300 East Lombard Street, 18th Floor · Baltimore, MD 21202 · 410-528-5600

Wilbert H. Sirota · Duane Morris · 111 South Calvert Street, Suite 2000 · Baltimore, MD 21202 · 410-949-2913

R. W. Smith, Jr. · ⑩ · DLA Piper · 6225 Smith Avenue · Baltimore, MD 21209-3600 · 410-580-3000

Shale D. Stiller · ㉕ · DLA Piper · 6225 Smith Avenue · Baltimore, MD 21209-3600 · 410-580-3000

Towson

Lowell R. Bowen · ㉕ · Miles & Stockbridge · http://www.milesstockbridge.com · One West Pennsylvania Avenue, Suite 900 · Towson, MD 21204-3965 · 410-821-6565

CORPORATE LAW

Baltimore

Kenneth B. Abel · Ober, Kaler, Grimes & Shriver · http://www.ober.com · 120 East Baltimore Street, Suite 800 · Baltimore, MD 21202-1643 · 410-685-1120

Michael J. Baader · Venable · http://www.venable.com · 750 East Pratt Street, Suite 900 · Baltimore, MD 21202 · 410-244-7400

Bryson L. Cook · ⑩ · Venable · http://www.venable.com · 750 East Pratt Street, Suite 900 · Baltimore, MD 21202 · 410-244-7400

Robert B. Curran · Whiteford, Taylor & Preston · http://www.wtplaw.com · Seven Saint Paul Street · Baltimore, MD 21202-1636 · 410-347-8700

William M. Davidow, Jr. · Whiteford, Taylor & Preston · http://www.wtplaw.com · Seven Saint Paul Street · Baltimore, MD 21202-1636 · 410-347-8700

John B. Frisch · Miles & Stockbridge · http://www.milesstockbridge.com · 10 Light Street · Baltimore, MD 21202-1487 · 410-727-6464

James J. Hanks, Jr. · Venable · http://www.venable.com · 750 East Pratt Street, Suite 900 · Baltimore, MD 21202 · 410-244-7400

Frank S. Jones, Jr. · Whiteford, Taylor & Preston · http://www.wtplaw.com · Seven Saint Paul Street · Baltimore, MD 21202-1636 · 410-347-8700

Walter G. Lohr, Jr. · Hogan & Hartson · 111 South Calvert Street, Suite 1600 · Baltimore, MD 21202 · 410-659-2700

Charles R. Moran · Ballard Spahr Andrews & Ingersoll · 300 East Lombard Street, 18th Floor · Baltimore, MD 21202 · 410-528-5600

Stephen L. Owen · ⑩ · DLA Piper · 6225 Smith Avenue · Baltimore, MD 21209-3600 · 410-580-3000

Marshall B. Paul · Saul Ewing · 500 East Pratt Street, Suite 900 · Baltimore, MD 21202 · 410-332-8600

Abba David Poliakoff · Gordon, Feinblatt, Rothman, Hoffberger & Hollander · http://www.gfrlaw.com · The Garrett Building · 233 East Redwood Street · Baltimore, MD 21202 · 410-576-4000

David B. Rudow · Adelberg, Rudow, Dorf & Hendler · http://www.adelbergrudow.com · Wachovia Building, Suite 600 · Seven St. Paul Street · Baltimore, MD 21202 · 410-539-5195

Frederick W. Runge, Jr. · Miles & Stockbridge · http://www.milesstockbridge.com · 10 Light Street · Baltimore, MD 21202-1487 · 410-727-6464

Michael J. Silver · Hogan & Hartson · 111 South Calvert Street, Suite 1600 · Baltimore, MD 21202 · 410-659-2700

Wilbert H. Sirota · Duane Morris · 111 South Calvert Street, Suite 2000 · Baltimore, MD 21202 · 410-949-2913

R. W. Smith, Jr. · ⑩ · DLA Piper · 6225 Smith Avenue · Baltimore, MD 21209-3600 · 410-580-3000

Shale D. Stiller · ㉕ · DLA Piper · 6225 Smith Avenue · Baltimore, MD 21209-3600 · 410-580-3000

Thomas D. Washburne, Jr. · Venable · http://www.venable.com · 750 East Pratt Street, Suite 900 · Baltimore, MD 21202 · 410-244-7400

J. W. Thompson Webb · Miles & Stockbridge · http://www.milesstockbridge.com · 10 Light Street · Baltimore, MD 21202-1487 · 410-727-6464

Earl S. Wellschlager · DLA Piper · 6225 Smith Avenue · Baltimore, MD 21209-3600 · 410-580-3000

Towson

Lowell R. Bowen · ㉕ · Miles & Stockbridge · http://www.milesstockbridge.com · One West Pennsylvania Avenue, Suite 900 · Towson, MD 21204-3965 · 410-821-6565

DUI/DWI DEFENSE

College Park

James E. McCollum, Jr. · McCollum & Associates · 7309 Baltimore Avenue, Suite 117 · P.O. Box 1717 · College Park, MD 20741-1717 · 301-864-6070

Columbia

Jason A. Shapiro · Shapiro & Mack · http://www.shapiroandmack.com · 7226 Lee Deforest Drive, Suite 207 · Columbia, MD 21046 · 410-884-6100

Frederick

Richard P. Bricken · Richard P. Bricken · 317 West Patrick Street · Frederick, MD 21701 · 301-694-5850

Greenbelt

Leonard R. Stamm · Goldstein & Stamm · Capital Office Park, Suite 504 · 6301 Ivy Lane · Greenbelt, MD 20770 · 301-345-0122

Owings Mills

Leonard H. Shapiro · Leonard H. Shapiro · The Owings Centre, Suite 203 · 10220 South Dolfield Road · Owings Mills, MD 21117-3660 · 410-363-3311

Rockville

Philip H. Armstrong · Armstrong & Page · 204 Monroe Street, Suite 109 · Rockville, MD 20850 · 301-762-0505

John P. Kudel · Law Office of John P. Kudel · One Metro Square, Suite 600 · 51 Monroe Street · Rockville, MD 20850 · 301-762-3770

Michael J. McAuliffe · Ethridge, Quinn, McAuliffe, Rowan & Hartinger · 33 Wood Lane · Rockville, MD 20850 · 301-762-1696

Towson

Gary S. Bernstein · Gary S. Bernstein · 29 West Susquehanna Avenue, Suite 700 · Towson, MD 21204 · 410-337-7770

David B. Irwin · Irwin Green & Dexter · 301 West Pennsylvania Avenue · Towson, MD 21204 · 410-832-0111

EMINENT DOMAIN AND CONDEMNATION LAW

Baltimore

Kurt J. Fischer · DLA Piper · 6225 Smith Avenue · Baltimore, MD 21209-3600 · 410-580-3000

John C. Murphy · John C. Murphy · 516 North Charles Street, Suite 206 · Baltimore, MD 21201 · 410-625-4828

Rockville

James L. Thompson · Miller, Miller & Canby · http://www.millermillercanby.com · 200-B Monroe Street Rockville, MD 20850 · 301-762-5212

EMPLOYEE BENEFITS LAW

Baltimore

Edward J. Adkins · Miles & Stockbridge · http://www.milesstockbridge.com · 10 Light Street · Baltimore, MD 21202-1487 · 410-727-6464

Barry D. Berman · Thomas & Libowitz · 100 Light Street, 11th Floor · Baltimore, MD 21202-1053 · 410-752-2468

Mary Claire Chesshire · Whiteford, Taylor & Preston · http://www.wtplaw.com · Seven Saint Paul Street Baltimore, MD 21202-1636 · 410-347-8700

Kenneth R. Hoffman · Venable · http://www.venable.com · 750 East Pratt Street, Suite 900 · Baltimore, MD 21202 · 410-244-7400

John E. Kratz · DLA Piper · 6225 Smith Avenue · Baltimore, MD 21209-3600 · 410-580-3000

Matthew P. Mellin · Gordon, Feinblatt, Rothman, Hoffberger & Hollander · http://www.gfrlaw.com · The Garrett Building · 233 East Redwood Street · Baltimore, MD 21202 · 410-576-4000

Mark Muedeking · DLA Piper · 6225 Smith Avenue · Baltimore, MD 21209-3600 · 410-580-3000

Marika McVey Ostendorf · Baldwin Law Group · http://www.blglaw.org · 600 Washington Avenue, Suite 302 · Baltimore, MD 21204-3916 · 410-828-5510

Barbara E. Schlaff · Venable · http://www.venable.com · 750 East Pratt Street, Suite 900 · Baltimore, MD 21202 · 410-244-7400

Henry A. Smith III · Smith & Downey · One West Pennsylvania Avenue, Suite 950 · Baltimore, MD 21204 · 410-321-9000

Thomas J. St. Ville · Miles & Stockbridge · http://www.milesstockbridge.com · 10 Light Street · Baltimore, MD 21202-1487 · 410-727-6464

Linda Marotta Thomas · DLA Piper · 6225 Smith Avenue · Baltimore, MD 21209-3600 · 410-580-3000

Robert L. Waldman · Venable · http://www.venable.com · 750 East Pratt Street, Suite 900 · Baltimore, MD 21202 · 410-244-7400

Towson

Katrina Kamantauskas-Holder · Holder Law Group · 406 Allegheny Avenue · P.O. Box 10509 · Towson, MD 21285-0509 · 410-296-9550

ENERGY LAW

Baltimore

Carville B. Collins · DLA Piper · 6225 Smith Avenue · Baltimore, MD 21209-3600 · 410-580-3000

Marta D. Harting · DLA Piper · 6225 Smith Avenue · Baltimore, MD 21209-3600 · 410-580-3000

ENTERTAINMENT LAW

Baltimore

Francis J. Gorman · Gorman & Williams · Two North Charles Street · Baltimore, MD 21201-3754 · 410-528-0600

E. Scott Johnson · Ober, Kaler, Grimes & Shriver · http://www.ober.com · 120 East Baltimore Street, Suite 800 · Baltimore, MD 21202-1643 · 410-685-1120

Charles F. Morgan · Astrachan, Gunst & Thomas · http://www.agtlawyers.com · 217 East Redwood Street, Suite 2100 · Baltimore, MD 21202 · 410-783-3550

Joel A. Smith · (20) · Kahn, Smith & Collins · 201 North Charles Street, 10th Floor · Baltimore, MD 21201 410-244-1010

Towson

David N. Pessin · Hodes, Pessin & Katz · http://www.hpklegal.com · 901 Dulaney Valley Road, Suite 400 Towson, MD 21204 · 410-938-8800

ENVIRONMENTAL LAW

Baltimore

Marian C. Hwang · Miles & Stockbridge · http://www.milesstockbridge.com · 10 Light Street · Baltimore, MD 21202-1487 · 410-727-6464

Deborah E. Jennings · (10) · DLA Piper · 111 South Calvert Street, Suite 1950 · Baltimore, MD 21202-6174 · 410-580-3000

Randall M. Lutz · (10) · Saul Ewing · 500 East Pratt Street, Suite 900 · Baltimore, MD 21202 · 410-332-8600

Michael C. Powell · (10) · Gordon, Feinblatt, Rothman, Hoffberger & Hollander · http://www.gfrlaw.com · The Garrett Building · 233 East Redwood Street · Baltimore, MD 21202 · 410-576-4000

Robert G. Smith · (20) · Venable · http://www.venable.com · 750 East Pratt Street, Suite 900 · Baltimore, MD 21202 · 410-244-7400

EQUIPMENT FINANCE LAW

Baltimore

Alan J. Mogol · Ober, Kaler, Grimes & Shriver · http://www.ober.com · 120 East Baltimore Street, Suite 800 · Baltimore, MD 21202-1643 · 410-685-1120

FAMILY LAW

Annapolis

Leslie G. Billman · Trainor, Billman, Bennett, Milko & McCabe · 113 Cathedral Street, Suite E · Annapolis, MD 21401 · 410-280-1700

Stephen P. Krohn · Krohn & Krissoff · 133 Defense Highway, Suite 203 · Annapolis, MD 21401 · 410-266-1136

Roger A. Perkins · Roger A. Perkins · The Courtyards, Suite 202 · 133 Defense Highway · Annapolis, MD 21401-8907 · 410-266-3558

Baltimore

Michael G. Hendler · ⑩ · Adelberg, Rudow, Dorf & Hendler · http://www.adelbergrudow.com · Wachovia Building, Suite 600 · Seven St. Paul Street · Baltimore, MD 21202 · 410-539-5195

Sheila K. Sachs · ⑩ · Gordon, Feinblatt, Rothman, Hoffberger & Hollander · http://www.gfrlaw.com · The Garrett Building · 233 East Redwood Street · Baltimore, MD 21202 · 410-576-4000

Jerrold A. Thrope · Gordon, Feinblatt, Rothman, Hoffberger & Hollander · http://www.gfrlaw.com · The Garrett Building · 233 East Redwood Street · Baltimore, MD 21202 · 410-576-4000

Bethesda

Glenn M. Cooper · Paley, Rothman, Goldstein, Rosenberg, Eig & Cooper · 4800 Hampden Lane, Seventh Floor · Bethesda, MD 20814-2930 · 301-656-7603

Linda A. Delaney · Delaney McKinney · Three Bethesda Metro Center, Suite 500 · Bethesda, MD 20814 · 301-913-5236

Kathleen Dumais · Paley, Rothman, Goldstein, Rosenberg, Eig & Cooper · 4800 Hampden Lane, Seventh Floor · Bethesda, MD 20814-2930 · 301-656-7603

Hadrian N. Hatfield · Strickler, Sachitano & Hatfield · 4550 Montgomery Avenue, Suite 900 North · Bethesda, MD 20814 · 301-657-8805

Heather Hostetter · Strickler, Sachitano & Hatfield · 4550 Montgomery Avenue, Suite 900 North · Bethesda, MD 20814 · 301-657-8805

Ronald Ogens · Deckelbaum Ogens & Raftery · Three Bethesda Metro Center, Suite 200 · Bethesda, MD 20814 · 301-961-9200

Joseph C. Paradiso · Paradiso, Dack, Taub & Sinay · Three Bethesda Metro Center, Suite 640 · Bethesda, MD 20814 · 301-986-7900

Linda J. Ravdin · Pasternak & Fidis · Fairmont Building, Suite 1100 · 7735 Old Georgetown Road · Bethesda, MD 20814-6183 · 301-656-8850

Deborah E. Reiser · Lerch, Early & Brewer · Three Bethesda Metro Center, Suite 460 · Bethesda, MD 20814-5367 · 301-986-1300

Scott Strickler · Strickler, Sachitano & Hatfield · 4550 Montgomery Avenue, Suite 900 North · Bethesda, MD 20814 · 301-657-8805

Robin B. Taub · Paradiso, Dack, Taub & Sinay · Three Bethesda Metro Center, Suite 640 · Bethesda, MD 20814 · 301-986-7900

Anne White · Pasternak & Fidis · Fairmont Building, Suite 1100 · 7735 Old Georgetown Road · Bethesda, MD 20814-6183 · 301-656-8850

Greenbelt

David Bulitt · Joseph, Greenwald & Laake · Capital Office Park, Suite 400 · 6404 Ivy Lane · Greenbelt, MD 20770 · 301-220-2200

Rockville

Cynthia Callahan · Dragga, Callahan, Hannon & Hessler · 110 North Washington Street, Suite 300 · Rockville, MD 20850-2223 · 301-340-9090

Patrick Dragga · Dragga, Callahan, Hannon & Hessler · 110 North Washington Street, Suite 300 · Rockville, MD 20850-2223 · 301-340-9090

Stuart S. Greenfeig · Stein, Sperling, Bennett, De Jong, Driscoll & Greenfeig · 25 West Middle Lane · Rockville, MD 20850-2204 · 301-340-2020

Jeffrey Hannon · Dragga, Callahan, Hannon & Hessler · 110 North Washington Street, Suite 300 · Rockville, MD 20850-2223 · 301-340-9090

Cheryl Lynn Hepfer · ⑩ · Cheryl Lynn Hepfer · 220 North Adams Street · Rockville, MD 20850 · 301-762-5500

Joseph M. Quirk · Law Office of Joseph M. Quirk · The Adams Law Center · 27 Wood Lane · Rockville, MD 20850 · 301-762-4050

Donna Van Scoy · The Law Office of Donna E. Van Scoy · 50 West Montgomery Avenue, Suite 105 · Rockville, MD 20850-4250 · 301-610-0110

Silver Spring

Walter W. Johnson, Jr. · Walter W. Johnson · 8701 Georgia Avenue · Silver Spring, MD 20910-3713 · 301-587-2090

Towson

Richard B. Jacobs · Hooper & Jacobs · 40 West Chesapeake Avenue, Suite 400 · Towson, MD 21204-4856 · 410-821-8718

Thomas C. Ries · ⑩ · Kaufman, Ries & Elgin · The Exchange, Suite 113 · 1122 Kenilworth Drive · Towson, MD 21204-2139 · 410-828-6100

Ann McKenrick Turnbull · Turnbull & Sanders · 29 West Susquehanna Avenue, Suite 202 · Towson, MD 21204 · 410-339-4100

Upper Marlboro

Paul J. Reinstein · Sasscer, Clagett & Bucher · 5407 Water Street, Suite 101 · Upper Marlboro, MD 20772 · 301-627-5500

FAMILY LAW MEDIATION

Baltimore

Herbert J. Belgrad · Tydings & Rosenberg · http://www.tydingslaw.com · 100 East Pratt Street, 26th Floor · Baltimore, MD 21202 · 410-752-9700

Sheila K. Sachs · ⑩ · Gordon, Feinblatt, Rothman, Hoffberger & Hollander · http://www.gfrlaw.com · The Garrett Building · 233 East Redwood Street · Baltimore, MD 21202 · 410-576-4000

Towson

Richard B. Jacobs · Hooper & Jacobs · 40 West Chesapeake Avenue, Suite 400 · Towson, MD 21204-4856 · 410-821-8718

Thomas C. Ries · (10) · Kaufman, Ries & Elgin · The Exchange, Suite 113 · 1122 Kenilworth Drive · Towson, MD 21204-2139 · 410-828-6100

FIRST AMENDMENT LAW

Baltimore

Henry R. Abrams · Saul Ewing · 500 East Pratt Street, Suite 900 · Baltimore, MD 21202 · 410-332-8600

C. Christopher Brown · (10) · Brown, Goldstein & Levy · 120 East Baltimore Street, Suite 1700 · Baltimore, MD 21202 · 410-962-1030

GOVERNMENT RELATIONS LAW

Baltimore

Robert Enten · Gordon, Feinblatt, Rothman, Hoffberger & Hollander · http://www.gfrlaw.com · The Garrett Building · 233 East Redwood Street · Baltimore, MD 21202 · 410-576-4000

Joseph A. Schwartz III · Schwartz & Metz · 10 West Madison Street · Baltimore, MD 21201 · 410-244-7000

Paul A. Tiburzi · DLA Piper · 6225 Smith Avenue · Baltimore, MD 21209-3600 · 410-580-3000

HEALTH CARE LAW

Annapolis

S. Allan Adelman · Adelman, Sheff & Smith · 180 Admiral Cochrane Drive, Suite 370 · Annapolis, MD 21401 · 410-224-3000

Baltimore

Constance H. Baker · (10) · Venable · http://www.venable.com · 750 East Pratt Street, Suite 900 · Baltimore, MD 21202 · 410-244-7400

S. Craig Holden · Ober, Kaler, Grimes & Shriver · http://www.ober.com · 120 East Baltimore Street, Suite 800 · Baltimore, MD 21202-1643 · 410-685-1120

Leonard C. Homer · (10) · Ober, Kaler, Grimes & Shriver · http://www.ober.com · 120 East Baltimore Street, Suite 800 · Baltimore, MD 21202-1643 · 410-685-1120

Rose M. Matricciani · Whiteford, Taylor & Preston · http://www.wtplaw.com · Seven Saint Paul Street · Baltimore, MD 21202-1636 · 410-347-8700

M. Natalie McSherry · Kramon & Graham · http://www.kramonandgraham.com · One South Street, Suite 2600 · Baltimore, MD 21202 · 410-752-6030

Peter P. Parvis · (10) · Venable · http://www.venable.com · 750 East Pratt Street, Suite 900 · Baltimore, MD 21202 · 410-244-7400

Barry F. Rosen · (10) · Gordon, Feinblatt, Rothman, Hoffberger & Hollander · http://www.gfrlaw.com · The Garrett Building · 233 East Redwood Street · Baltimore, MD 21202 · 410-576-4000

Howard L. Sollins · ⑩ · Ober, Kaler, Grimes & Shriver · http://www.ober.com · 120 East Baltimore Street, Suite 800 · Baltimore, MD 21202-1643 · 410-685-1120

Sanford V. Teplitzky · ⑩ · Ober, Kaler, Grimes & Shriver · http://www.ober.com · 120 East Baltimore Street, Suite 800 · Baltimore, MD 21202-1643 · 410-685-1120

Jack C. Tranter · ⑩ · Gallagher, Evelius & Jones · 218 North Charles Street, Suite 400 · Baltimore, MD 21201 · 410-727-7702

Bethesda

Robert G. Brewer, Jr. · ⑩ · Lerch, Early & Brewer · Three Bethesda Metro Center, Suite 460 · Bethesda, MD 20814-5367 · 301-986-1300

IMMIGRATION LAW

Baltimore

Mary Ryan · Taylor & Ryan · http://www.taylor-ryan.com · Commercentre East, Suite 280 · 1777 Reisterstown Road · Baltimore, MD 21208 · 410-486-5800

Henry J. Suelau · Miles & Stockbridge · http://www.milesstockbridge.com · 10 Light Street · Baltimore, MD 21202-1487 · 410-727-6464

Frances O'Connell Taylor · Taylor & Ryan · http://www.taylor-ryan.com · Commercentre East, Suite 280 1777 Reisterstown Road · Baltimore, MD 21208 · 410-486-5800

Geoffrey S. Tobias · Ober, Kaler, Grimes & Shriver · http://www.ober.com · 120 East Baltimore Street, Suite 800 · Baltimore, MD 21202-1643 · 410-685-1120

Ana Claudia Zigel · Law Office of Ana Claudia Zigel · Commerce Center East, Suite 280 · 1777 Reisterstown Road · Baltimore, MD 21208 · 410-602-2155

Rockville

Denise C. Hammond · Hammond Claxton · http://www.hammondclaxton.com · Rockville Metro Plaza I, Suite 400 · 111 Rockville Pike · Rockville, MD 20850 · 301-917-6900

Severna Park

Ann L. Lamdin · Corbin, Schaffer & Aviles · Four Evergreen Road · Severna Park, MD 21146 · 410-544-0314

INFORMATION TECHNOLOGY LAW

Baltimore

Ned T. Himmelrich · Gordon, Feinblatt, Rothman, Hoffberger & Hollander · http://www.gfrlaw.com · The Garrett Building · 233 East Redwood Street · Baltimore, MD 21202 · 410-576-4000

Martha Lessman Katz · Miles & Stockbridge · http://www.milesstockbridge.com · 10 Light Street · Baltimore, MD 21202-1487 · 410-727-6464

William A. McComas · Shapiro Sher Guinot & Sandler · 36 South Charles Street, Suite 2000 · Baltimore, MD 21201-3147 · 410-385-0202

Donald A. Rea · McGuireWoods · http://www.mcguirewoods.com · Seven Saint Paul Street, Suite 1000 · Baltimore, MD 21202-1671 · 410-659-4400

Roszel C. Thomsen II · Thomsen & Burke · http://www.t-b.com · One North Charles Street, Suite 400 · Baltimore, MD 21201 · 410-539-2595

Towson

Michael D. Oliver · Bowie & Jensen · 29 West Susquehanna Avenue, Suite 600 · Towson, MD 21204 · 410-583-2400

INSURANCE LAW

Baltimore

George J. Bachrach · Whiteford, Taylor & Preston · http://www.wtplaw.com · Seven Saint Paul Street · Baltimore, MD 21202-1636 · 410-347-8700

Bryan D. Bolton · Funk & Bolton · 36 South Charles Street, 12th Floor · Baltimore, MD 21201-3111 · 410-659-7700

David M. Funk · Funk & Bolton · 36 South Charles Street, 12th Floor · Baltimore, MD 21201-3111 · 410-659-7700

Alan N. Gamse · Semmes Bowen & Semmes · http://www.semmes.com · 25 South Charles Street, Suite 1400 · Baltimore, MD 21201 · 410-539-5040

Joseph A. Schwartz III · Schwartz & Metz · 10 West Madison Street · Baltimore, MD 21201 · 410-244-7000

Grantsville

Gary C. Harriger · Funk & Bolton · 148 Main Street · P.O. Box 656 · Grantsville, MD 21536 · 301-895-3331

Towson

Patricia McHugh Lambert · Hodes, Pessin & Katz · http://www.hpklegal.com · 901 Dulaney Valley Road, Suite 400 · Towson, MD 21204 · 410-938-8800

INTELLECTUAL PROPERTY LAW

Baltimore

James B. Astrachan · Astrachan, Gunst & Thomas · http://www.agtlawyers.com · 217 East Redwood Street, Suite 2100 · Baltimore, MD 21202 · 410-783-3550

Francis J. Gorman · Gorman & Williams · Two North Charles Street · Baltimore, MD 21201-3754 · 410-528-0600

Ned T. Himmelrich · Gordon, Feinblatt, Rothman, Hoffberger & Hollander · http://www.gfrlaw.com · The Garrett Building · 233 East Redwood Street · Baltimore, MD 21202 · 410-576-4000

E. Scott Johnson · Ober, Kaler, Grimes & Shriver · http://www.ober.com · 120 East Baltimore Street, Suite 800 · Baltimore, MD 21202-1643 · 410-685-1120

Gregory M. Stone · Whiteford, Taylor & Preston · http://www.wtplaw.com · Seven Saint Paul Street · Baltimore, MD 21202-1636 · 410-347-8700

Steven E. Tiller · Whiteford, Taylor & Preston · http://www.wtplaw.com · Seven Saint Paul Street · Baltimore, MD 21202-1636 · 410-347-8700

Bethesda

Gregory L. Hillyer · Feldman Gale · http://www.feldmangale.com · 4720 Montgomery Lane, Suite 400 · Bethesda, MD 20814 · 800-489-9814

Towson

Michael D. Oliver · Bowie & Jensen · 29 West Susquehanna Avenue, Suite 600 · Towson, MD 21204 · 410-583-2400

INTERNATIONAL ARBITRATION

Baltimore

M. Hamilton Whitman, Jr. · ⑳ · Ober, Kaler, Grimes & Shriver · http://www.ober.com · 120 East Baltimore Street, Suite 800 · Baltimore, MD 21202-1643 · 410-685-1120

John Anthony Wolf · ⑩ · Ober, Kaler, Grimes & Shriver · http://www.ober.com · 120 East Baltimore Street, Suite 800 · Baltimore, MD 21202-1643 · 410-685-1120

INTERNATIONAL TRADE AND FINANCE LAW

Baltimore

Bryson L. Cook · ⑩ · Venable · http://www.venable.com · 750 East Pratt Street, Suite 900 · Baltimore, MD 21202 · 410-244-7400

LABOR AND EMPLOYMENT LAW

Baltimore

Gil A. Abramson · Hogan & Hartson · 111 South Calvert Street, Suite 1600 · Baltimore, MD 21202 · 410-659-2700

Arthur M. Brewer · Shawe Rosenthal · 20 South Charles Street, 11th Floor · Baltimore, MD 21201 · 410-752-1040

Kathleen Cahill · The Law Offices of Kathleen Cahill · 15 East Chesapeake Avenue · Baltimore, MD 21286 · 410-321-6171

Harriet E. Cooperman · ⑩ · Saul Ewing · 500 East Pratt Street, Suite 900 · Baltimore, MD 21202 · 410-332-8600

Steven D. Frenkil · Miles & Stockbridge · http://www.milesstockbridge.com · 10 Light Street · Baltimore, MD 21202-1487 · 410-727-6464

Russell H. Gardner · DLA Piper · 6225 Smith Avenue · Baltimore, MD 21209-3600 · 410-580-3000

Stephen W. Godoff · ⑳ · Abato, Rubenstein & Abato · 809 Gleneagles Court, Suite 320 · Baltimore, MD 21286 · 410-321-0990

Richard J. Hafets · DLA Piper · 6225 Smith Avenue · Baltimore, MD 21209-3600 · 410-580-3000

Bruce S. Harrison · ⑩ · Shawe Rosenthal · 20 South Charles Street, 11th Floor · Baltimore, MD 21201 · 410-752-1040

H. Victoria Hedian · Abato, Rubenstein & Abato · 809 Gleneagles Court, Suite 320 · Baltimore, MD 21286 · 410-321-0990

Eric Hemmendinger · Shawe Rosenthal · 20 South Charles Street, 11th Floor · Baltimore, MD 21201 · 410-752-1040

Todd J. Horn · Venable · http://www.venable.com · 750 East Pratt Street, Suite 900 · Baltimore, MD 21202 · 410-244-7400

George W. Johnston · ⑩ · Venable · http://www.venable.com · 750 East Pratt Street, Suite 900 · Baltimore, MD 21202 · 410-244-7400

Robert C. Kellner · Gordon, Feinblatt, Rothman, Hoffberger & Hollander · http://www.gfrlaw.com · The Garrett Building · 233 East Redwood Street · Baltimore, MD 21202 · 410-576-4000

Stefan Jan Marculewicz · Miles & Stockbridge · http://www.milesstockbridge.com · 10 Light Street · Baltimore, MD 21202-1487 · 410-727-6464

Emmett F. McGee · DLA Piper · 6225 Smith Avenue · Baltimore, MD 21209-3600 · 410-580-3000

J. Michael McGuire · Shawe Rosenthal · 20 South Charles Street, 11th Floor · Baltimore, MD 21201 · 410-752-1040

Jeanne M. Phelan · ⑩ · Whiteford, Taylor & Preston · http://www.wtplaw.com · Seven Saint Paul Street · Baltimore, MD 21202-1636 · 410-347-8700

Kathleen Pontone · Miles & Stockbridge · http://www.milesstockbridge.com · 10 Light Street · Baltimore, MD 21202-1487 · 410-727-6464

Larry R. Seegull · DLA Piper · 6225 Smith Avenue · Baltimore, MD 21209-3600 · 410-580-3000

Stephen D. Shawe · ㉕ · Shawe Rosenthal · 20 South Charles Street, 11th Floor · Baltimore, MD 21201 · 410-752-1040

Stephen M. Silvestri · Miles & Stockbridge · http://www.milesstockbridge.com · 10 Light Street · Baltimore, MD 21202-1487 · 410-727-6464

Gary L. Simpler · Shawe Rosenthal · 20 South Charles Street, 11th Floor · Baltimore, MD 21201 · 410-752-1040

Joel A. Smith · ⑳ · Kahn, Smith & Collins · 201 North Charles Street, 10th Floor · Baltimore, MD 21201 410-244-1010

Ronald W. Taylor · Venable · http://www.venable.com · 750 East Pratt Street, Suite 900 · Baltimore, MD 21202 · 410-244-7400

Douglas M. Topolski · McGuireWoods · http://www.mcguirewoods.com · Seven Saint Paul Street, Suite 1000 · Baltimore, MD 21202-1671 · 410-659-4400

Larry M. Wolf · ⑳ · Whiteford, Taylor & Preston · http://www.wtplaw.com · Seven Saint Paul Street · Baltimore, MD 21202-1636 · 410-347-8700

Bethesda

Hope B. Eastman · Paley, Rothman, Goldstein, Rosenberg, Eig & Cooper · 4800 Hampden Lane, Seventh Floor · Bethesda, MD 20814-2930 · 301-656-7603

Owings Mills

John M. Singleton · Singleton Gendler · 400 Redland Court, Suite 107 · Owings Mills, MD 21117 · 410-902-0073

Timonium

J. Eric Paltell · Kollman & Saucier · The Business Law Building · 1823 York Road · Timonium, MD 21093 · 410-727-4300

Darrell R. VanDeusen · Kollman & Saucier · The Business Law Building · 1823 York Road · Timonium, MD 21093 · 410-727-4300

Towson

Jeffrey P. Ayres · Venable · http://www.venable.com · 210 Allegheny Avenue · Towson, MD 21204 · 410-494-6200

Stephen B. Lebau · Lebau & Neuworth · 606 Baltimore Avenue, Suite 201 · Towson, MD 21204 · 410-296-3030

LAND USE & ZONING LAW

Baltimore

G. Scott Barhight · Whiteford, Taylor & Preston · http://www.wtplaw.com · Seven Saint Paul Street · Baltimore, MD 21202-1636 · 410-347-8700

Stanley S. Fine · Rosenberg | Martin | Greenberg · 25 South Charles Street, Suite 2115 · Baltimore, MD 21201 · 410-547-7163

Jon M. Laria · Ballard Spahr Andrews & Ingersoll · 300 East Lombard Street, 18th Floor · Baltimore, MD 21202 · 410-528-5600

Bethesda

Stanley D. Abrams · Abrams & West · 4550 Montgomery Avenue, Suite 760 North · Bethesda, MD 20814-3379 · 301-951-1540

Robert G. Brewer, Jr. · ⑩ · Lerch, Early & Brewer · Three Bethesda Metro Center, Suite 460 · Bethesda, MD 20814-5367 · 301-986-1300

C. Robert Dalrymple · Linowes & Blocher · http://www.linowes-law.com · 7200 Wisconsin Avenue, Suite 800 · Bethesda, MD 20814-4842 · 301-654-0504

John J. Delaney · Linowes & Blocher · http://www.linowes-law.com · 7200 Wisconsin Avenue, Suite 800 · Bethesda, MD 20814-4842 · 301-654-0504

Stephen P. Elmendorf · Linowes & Blocher · http://www.linowes-law.com · 7200 Wisconsin Avenue, Suite 800 · Bethesda, MD 20814-4842 · 301-654-0504

Robert Roland Harris · Holland & Knight · http://www.hklaw.com · Three Bethesda Metro Center, Suite 800 · Bethesda, MD 20814 · 301-654-7800

Stephen Z. Kaufman · Linowes & Blocher · http://www.linowes-law.com · 7200 Wisconsin Avenue, Suite 800 · Bethesda, MD 20814-4842 · 301-654-0504

William Kominers · Holland & Knight · http://www.hklaw.com · Three Bethesda Metro Center, Suite 800 · Bethesda, MD 20814 · 301-654-7800

Harry W. Lerch · Lerch, Early & Brewer · Three Bethesda Metro Center, Suite 460 · Bethesda, MD 20814-5367 · 301-986-1300

Steven A. Robins · Lerch, Early & Brewer · Three Bethesda Metro Center, Suite 460 · Bethesda, MD 20814-5367 · 301-986-1300

Barbara A. Sears · Linowes & Blocher · http://www.linowes-law.com · 7200 Wisconsin Avenue, Suite 800 Bethesda, MD 20814-4842 · 301-654-0504

Rockville

Joel S. Kline · Miller, Miller & Canby · http://www.millermillercanby.com · 200-B Monroe Street · Rockville, MD 20850 · 301-762-5212

LEGAL MALPRACTICE LAW

Baltimore

Neil J. Dilloff · DLA Piper · 6225 Smith Avenue · Baltimore, MD 21209-3600 · 410-580-3000

Alvin I. Frederick · ⑩ · Eccleston & Wolf · Baltimore-Washington Law Center, Fourth Floor · 7240 Parkway Drive · Baltimore, MD 21076 · 410-752-7474

Jeffrey J. Hines · Goodell, DeVries, Leech & Dann · http://www.gdlglaw.com · One South Street, 20th Floor · Baltimore, MD 21202 · 410-783-4000

Edward J. Hutchins, Jr. · Eccleston & Wolf · Baltimore-Washington Law Center, Fourth Floor · 7240 Parkway Drive · Baltimore, MD 21076 · 410-752-7474

Pasedena

Charles E. Iliff, Jr. · Iliff & Meredith · 8055 Ritchie Highway, Suites 201-203 · Pasedena, MD 21122-1067 · 410-685-1166

LEVERAGED BUYOUTS AND PRIVATE EQUITY LAW

Baltimore

Wilbert H. Sirota · Duane Morris · 111 South Calvert Street, Suite 2000 · Baltimore, MD 21202 · 410-949-2913

Towson

George S. Lawler · Whiteford, Taylor & Preston · http://www.wtplaw.com · Towson Commons, Suite 300 One West Pennsylvania Avenue · Towson, MD 21204-5025 · 410-832-2000

MARITIME LAW

Baltimore

James W. Bartlett III · ⑩ · Semmes Bowen & Semmes · http://www.semmes.com · 25 South Charles Street, Suite 1400 · Baltimore, MD 21201 · 410-539-5040

Paul D. Bekman · ⑳ · Salsbury, Clements, Bekman, Marder & Adkins · 300 West Pratt Street, Suite 450 · Baltimore, MD 21201 · 410-539-6633

Donald C. Greenman · ⑳ · Ober, Kaler, Grimes & Shriver · http://www.ober.com · 120 East Baltimore Street, Suite 800 · Baltimore, MD 21202-1643 · 410-685-1120

Robert B. Hopkins · Duane Morris · 111 South Calvert Street, Suite 2000 · Baltimore, MD 21202 · 410-949-2913

David W. Skeen · ⑳ · Wright, Constable & Skeen · One Charles Center, 16th Floor · 100 North Charles Street · Baltimore, MD 21201 · 410-539-5541

Geoffrey S. Tobias · Ober, Kaler, Grimes & Shriver · http://www.ober.com · 120 East Baltimore Street, Suite 800 · Baltimore, MD 21202-1643 · 410-685-1120

Stephen F. White · Wright, Constable & Skeen · One Charles Center, 16th Floor · 100 North Charles Street · Baltimore, MD 21201 · 410-539-5541

M. Hamilton Whitman, Jr. · ⑳ · Ober, Kaler, Grimes & Shriver · http://www.ober.com · 120 East Baltimore Street, Suite 800 · Baltimore, MD 21202-1643 · 410-685-1120

JoAnne Zawitoski · Semmes Bowen & Semmes · http://www.semmes.com · 25 South Charles Street, Suite 1400 · Baltimore, MD 21201 · 410-539-5040

Towson

Kieron F. Quinn · ⑳ · Quinn, Gordon & Wolf · 102 West Pennsylvania Avenue, Suite 402 · Towson, MD 21204 · 410-825-2300

MASS TORT LITIGATION

Baltimore

Joel A. Dewey · DLA Piper · 6225 Smith Avenue · Baltimore, MD 21209-3600 · 410-580-3000

Charles P. Goodell, Jr. · Goodell, DeVries, Leech & Dann · http://www.gdlglaw.com · One South Street, 20th Floor · Baltimore, MD 21202 · 410-783-4000

Joseph Hovermill · Miles & Stockbridge · http://www.milesstockbridge.com · 10 Light Street · Baltimore, MD 21202-1487 · 410-727-6464

Robert K. Jenner · Janet, Jenner & Suggs · Woodholme Center, Suite 320 · 1829 Reisterstown Road · Baltimore, MD 21208 · 410-653-3200

Harry S. Johnson · Whiteford, Taylor & Preston · http://www.wtplaw.com · Seven Saint Paul Street · Baltimore, MD 21202-1636 · 410-347-8700

Kenneth L. Thompson · DLA Piper · 6225 Smith Avenue · Baltimore, MD 21209-3600 · 410-580-3000

Towson

Martin E. Wolf · Quinn, Gordon & Wolf · 102 West Pennsylvania Avenue, Suite 402 · Towson, MD 21204 · 410-825-2300

MEDICAL MALPRACTICE LAW

Annapolis

David A. Levin · ⑩ · Wharton, Levin, Ehrmantraut & Klein · 104 West Street · P.O. Box 551 · Annapolis, MD 21401-0551 · 410-263-5900

Baltimore

E. Dale Adkins III · ⑩ · Salsbury, Clements, Bekman, Marder & Adkins · 300 West Pratt Street, Suite 450 · Baltimore, MD 21201 · 410-539-6633

Michael J. Baxter · Baxter Baker Sidle Conn & Jones · http://www.bbsclaw.com · 120 East Baltimore Street · Baltimore, MD 21202 · 410-230-3800

Paul D. Bekman · ⑳ · Salsbury, Clements, Bekman, Marder & Adkins · 300 West Pratt Street, Suite 450 · Baltimore, MD 21201 · 410-539-6633

Daniel M. Clements · Salsbury, Clements, Bekman, Marder & Adkins · 300 West Pratt Street, Suite 450 · Baltimore, MD 21201 · 410-539-6633

Donald L. DeVries, Jr. · ⑩ · Goodell, DeVries, Leech & Dann · http://www.gdlglaw.com · One South Street, 20th Floor · Baltimore, MD 21202 · 410-783-4000

Philip C. Federico · Schochor, Federico and Staton · 1211 Saint Paul Street · Baltimore, MD 21202 · 410-234-1000

Joseph G. Finnerty, Jr. · ⑩ · DLA Piper · 6225 Smith Avenue · Baltimore, MD 21209-3600 · 410-580-3000

E. Philip Franke III · Anderson, Coe & King · http://www.acklaw.com · 201 North Charles Street, Suite 2000 · Baltimore, MD 21201 · 410-752-1630

Amy B. Heinrich · Goodell, DeVries, Leech & Dann · http://www.gdlglaw.com · One South Street, 20th Floor · Baltimore, MD 21202 · 410-783-4000

Howard A. Janet · Janet, Jenner & Suggs · Woodholme Center, Suite 320 · 1829 Reisterstown Road · Baltimore, MD 21208 · 410-653-3200

M. Natalie McSherry · Kramon & Graham · http://www.kramonandgraham.com · One South Street, Suite 2600 · Baltimore, MD 21202 · 410-752-6030

Craig B. Merkle · Goodell, DeVries, Leech & Dann · http://www.gdlglaw.com · One South Street, 20th Floor · Baltimore, MD 21202 · 410-783-4000

Susan T. Preston · Goodell, DeVries, Leech & Dann · http://www.gdlglaw.com · One South Street, 20th Floor · Baltimore, MD 21202 · 410-783-4000

Stuart M. Salsbury · ⑩ · Salsbury, Clements, Bekman, Marder & Adkins · 300 West Pratt Street, Suite 450 · Baltimore, MD 21201 · 410-539-6633

Jonathan Schochor · Schochor, Federico and Staton · 1211 Saint Paul Street · Baltimore, MD 21202 · 410-234-1000

Marcus Z. Shar · Shar, Rosen & Warshaw · 26 South Street · Baltimore, MD 21202-3399 · 410-244-1155

Kerry D. Staton · Schochor, Federico and Staton · 1211 Saint Paul Street · Baltimore, MD 21202 · 410-234-1000

Catherine W. Steiner · Whiteford, Taylor & Preston · http://www.wtplaw.com · Seven Saint Paul Street · Baltimore, MD 21202-1636 · 410-347-8700

Robert J. Weltchek · Snyder, Weltchek & Snyder · 1829 Reisterstown Road, Suite 100 · Baltimore, MD 21208 · 410-653-3700

Bethesda

Steven A. Hamilton · ⑩ · Hamilton Altman Canale & Dillon · 4600 East-West Highway, Suite 201 · Bethesda, MD 20814 · 301-652-7332

Greenbelt

Andrew E. Greenwald · Joseph, Greenwald & Laake · Capital Office Park, Suite 400 · 6404 Ivy Lane · Greenbelt, MD 20770 · 301-220-2200

W. Scott Sonntag · Law Office of W. Scott Sonntag · 7841 Belle Point Drive · Greenbelt, MD 20770-3338 · 301-982-1255

Hunt Valley

Mary Alane Downs · Morgan Carlo Downs & Everton · Executive Plaza Four, Suite 100 · 11350 McCormick Road · Hunt Valley, MD 21031 · 410-584-2800

Pasedena

Kathleen Meredith · Iliff & Meredith · 8055 Ritchie Highway, Suites 201-203 · Pasedena, MD 21122-1067 · 410-685-1166

Rockville

H. Kenneth Armstrong · ⑩ · Armstrong, Donohue, Ceppos & Vaughn · 204 Monroe Street, Suite 101 · Rockville, MD 20850 · 301-251-0440

Albert D. Brault · ⑳ · Brault, Graham, Scott & Brault · 101 South Washington Street · Rockville, MD 20850 · 301-424-1060

Michael F. Flynn, Jr. · Gleason, Flynn, Emig & Fogleman · 11 North Washington Street, Suite 400 · Rockville, MD 20850 · 301-294-2110

James P. Gleason · Gleason, Flynn, Emig & Fogleman · 11 North Washington Street, Suite 400 · Rockville, MD 20850 · 301-294-2110

Robert R. Michael · ⑩ · Shadoan, Michael & Wells · http://www.smwlawfirm.com · 108 Park Avenue · Rockville, MD 20850 · 301-762-5150

George W. Shadoan · ⑳ · Shadoan, Michael & Wells · http://www.smwlawfirm.com · 108 Park Avenue · Rockville, MD 20850 · 301-762-5150

Gregory Wells · Shadoan, Michael & Wells · http://www.smwlawfirm.com · 108 Park Avenue · Rockville, MD 20850 · 301-762-5150

Townsend

James R. Chason · Chason, Rosner, Leary & Marshall · 401 Washington Avenue, Fifth Floor · Townsend, MD 21204 · 410-494-3700

James F. Rosner · Chason, Rosner, Leary & Marshall · 401 Washington Avenue, Fifth Floor · Townsend, MD 21204 · 410-494-3700

Towson

Natalie C. Magdeburger · Whiteford, Taylor & Preston · http://www.wtplaw.com · Towson Commons, Suite 300 · One West Pennsylvania Avenue · Towson, MD 21204-5025 · 410-832-2000

Paul M. Vettori · Kenny & Vettori · 502 Washington Avenue, Suite 720 · Towson, MD 21204 · 410-825-1050

MERGERS & ACQUISITIONS LAW

Baltimore

Kenneth B. Abel · Ober, Kaler, Grimes & Shriver · http://www.ober.com · 120 East Baltimore Street, Suite 800 · Baltimore, MD 21202-1643 · 410-685-1120

Michael J. Baader · Venable · http://www.venable.com · 750 East Pratt Street, Suite 900 · Baltimore, MD 21202 · 410-244-7400

Bryson L. Cook · ⑩ · Venable · http://www.venable.com · 750 East Pratt Street, Suite 900 · Baltimore, MD 21202 · 410-244-7400

William M. Davidow, Jr. · Whiteford, Taylor & Preston · http://www.wtplaw.com · Seven Saint Paul Street · Baltimore, MD 21202-1636 · 410-347-8700

John B. Frisch · Miles & Stockbridge · http://www.milesstockbridge.com · 10 Light Street · Baltimore, MD 21202-1487 · 410-727-6464

James J. Hanks, Jr. · Venable · http://www.venable.com · 750 East Pratt Street, Suite 900 · Baltimore, MD 21202 · 410-244-7400

Frank S. Jones, Jr. · Whiteford, Taylor & Preston · http://www.wtplaw.com · Seven Saint Paul Street · Baltimore, MD 21202-1636 · 410-347-8700

Henry D. Kahn · Hogan & Hartson · 111 South Calvert Street, Suite 1600 · Baltimore, MD 21202 · 410-659-2700

Walter G. Lohr, Jr. · Hogan & Hartson · 111 South Calvert Street, Suite 1600 · Baltimore, MD 21202 · 410-659-2700

R. W. Smith, Jr. · ⑩ · DLA Piper · 6225 Smith Avenue · Baltimore, MD 21209-3600 · 410-580-3000

Thomas D. Washburne, Jr. · Venable · http://www.venable.com · 750 East Pratt Street, Suite 900 · Baltimore, MD 21202 · 410-244-7400

J. W. Thompson Webb · Miles & Stockbridge · http://www.milesstockbridge.com · 10 Light Street · Baltimore, MD 21202-1487 · 410-727-6464

NON-PROFIT/CHARITIES LAW

Baltimore

Jeffrey K. Gonya · Venable · http://www.venable.com · 750 East Pratt Street, Suite 900 · Baltimore, MD 21202 · 410-244-7400

Stephen M. Sharkey · DLA Piper · 6225 Smith Avenue · Baltimore, MD 21209-3600 · 410-580-3000

Lee A. Sheller · DLA Piper · 6225 Smith Avenue · Baltimore, MD 21209-3600 · 410-580-3000

Robert L. Waldman · Venable · http://www.venable.com · 750 East Pratt Street, Suite 900 · Baltimore, MD 21202 · 410-244-7400

Columbia

Jonathan Z. May · Whiteford, Taylor & Preston · http://www.wtplaw.com · 50 Corporate Center, Suite 750 · 10500 Little Patuxent Parkway · Columbia, MD 21044-3585 · 410-884-0700

NON-WHITE-COLLAR CRIMINAL DEFENSE

Baltimore

Larry Allen Nathans · Nathans & Biddle · http://www.nathanslaw.com · 120 East Baltimore Street, Suite 1800 · Baltimore, MD 21202 · 410-783-0272

Bethesda

Stanley J. Reed · Lerch, Early & Brewer · Three Bethesda Metro Center, Suite 460 · Bethesda, MD 20814-5367 · 301-986-1300

Greenbelt

Robert C. Bonsib · Marcus & Bonsib · http://www.robertbonsib.com · 6411 Ivy Lane, Suite 116 · Greenbelt, MD 20770 · 301-441-3000

Rockville

Philip H. Armstrong · Armstrong & Page · 204 Monroe Street, Suite 109 · Rockville, MD 20850 · 301-762-0505

Towson

Steven A. Allen · Hodes, Pessin & Katz · http://www.hpklegal.com · 901 Dulaney Valley Road, Suite 400 Towson, MD 21204 · 410-938-8800

David B. Irwin · Irwin Green & Dexter · 301 West Pennsylvania Avenue · Towson, MD 21204 · 410-832-0111

PERSONAL INJURY LITIGATION

Annapolis

Rignal W. Baldwin, Jr. · Brassel Baldwin Kagan & May · 112 West Street · Annapolis, MD 21401 · 410-974-9200

Jon W. Brassel · Brassel Baldwin Kagan & May · 112 West Street · Annapolis, MD 21401 · 410-974-9200

David A. Levin · ⑩ · Wharton, Levin, Ehrmantraut & Klein · 104 West Street · P.O. Box 551 · Annapolis, MD 21401-0551 · 410-263-5900

Baltimore

E. Dale Adkins III · ⑩ · Salsbury, Clements, Bekman, Marder & Adkins · 300 West Pratt Street, Suite 450 · Baltimore, MD 21201 · 410-539-6633

Michael J. Baxter · Baxter Baker Sidle Conn & Jones · http://www.bbsclaw.com · 120 East Baltimore Street · Baltimore, MD 21202 · 410-230-3800

Paul D. Bekman · ⑳ · Salsbury, Clements, Bekman, Marder & Adkins · 300 West Pratt Street, Suite 450 · Baltimore, MD 21201 · 410-539-6633

Daniel M. Clements · Salsbury, Clements, Bekman, Marder & Adkins · 300 West Pratt Street, Suite 450 · Baltimore, MD 21201 · 410-539-6633

Donald L. DeVries, Jr. · ⑩ · Goodell, DeVries, Leech & Dann · http://www.gdlglaw.com · One South Street, 20th Floor · Baltimore, MD 21202 · 410-783-4000

Neil J. Dilloff · DLA Piper · 6225 Smith Avenue · Baltimore, MD 21209-3600 · 410-580-3000

Joseph G. Finnerty, Jr. · ⑩ · DLA Piper · 6225 Smith Avenue · Baltimore, MD 21209-3600 · 410-580-3000

James E. Gray · Venable · http://www.venable.com · 750 East Pratt Street, Suite 900 · Baltimore, MD 21202 · 410-244-7400

Howard A. Janet · Janet, Jenner & Suggs · Woodholme Center, Suite 320 · 1829 Reisterstown Road · Baltimore, MD 21208 · 410-653-3200

Robert K. Jenner · Janet, Jenner & Suggs · Woodholme Center, Suite 320 · 1829 Reisterstown Road · Baltimore, MD 21208 · 410-653-3200

Harry S. Johnson · Whiteford, Taylor & Preston · http://www.wtplaw.com · Seven Saint Paul Street · Baltimore, MD 21202-1636 · 410-347-8700

Sidney G. Leech · Goodell, DeVries, Leech & Dann · http://www.gdlglaw.com · One South Street, 20th Floor · Baltimore, MD 21202 · 410-783-4000

Leonard Orman · Shar, Rosen & Warshaw · 26 South Street · Baltimore, MD 21202-3399 · 410-244-1155

Marc S. Rosen · Shar, Rosen & Warshaw · 26 South Street · Baltimore, MD 21202-3399 · 410-244-1155

Stuart M. Salsbury · ⑩ · Salsbury, Clements, Bekman, Marder & Adkins · 300 West Pratt Street, Suite 450 · Baltimore, MD 21201 · 410-539-6633

Paul Mark Sandler · ⑩ · Shapiro Sher Guinot & Sandler · 36 South Charles Street, Suite 2000 · Baltimore, MD 21201-3147 · 410-385-0202

Robert E. Scott, Jr. · ⑩ · Semmes Bowen & Semmes · http://www.semmes.com · 25 South Charles Street, Suite 1400 · Baltimore, MD 21201 · 410-539-5040

Marcus Z. Shar · Shar, Rosen & Warshaw · 26 South Street · Baltimore, MD 21202-3399 · 410-244-1155

Donald E. Sharpe · ㉕ · DLA Piper · 6225 Smith Avenue · Baltimore, MD 21209-3600 · 410-580-3000

H. Russell Smouse · ⑩ · Law Offices of Peter G. Angelos · One Charles Center, 20th Floor · 100 North Charles Street · Baltimore, MD 21201 · 410-649-2000

Robert C. Verderaime · ⑩ · Verderaime & DuBois · 1231 North Calvert Street · Baltimore, MD 21202 · 410-752-8888

William B. Whiteford · ⑳ · Whiteford, Taylor & Preston · http://www.wtplaw.com · Seven Saint Paul Street · Baltimore, MD 21202-1636 · 410-347-8700

Bel Air

Augustus F. Brown · Brown, Brown & Young · 200 South Main Street · Bel Air, MD 21014 · 410-838-5500

Bethesda

Francis J. Ford · ⑩ · Francis J. Ford · 7700 Old Georgetown Road, Suite 520 · Bethesda, MD 20814 · 301-279-2000

Bowie

Kevin J. McCarthy · ⑩ · McCarthy & Winkelman · http://www.mccarthywinkelman.com · One Town Center, Suite 410 · 4201 Northview Drive · Bowie, MD 20716-2668 · 301-262-7422

Catonsville

John E. Sandbower III · ㉕ · Sandbower & Gabler · 505 Patleigh Road · Catonsville, MD 21228-5634 · 410-494-6380

Easton

Roy B. Cowdrey, Jr. · Cowdrey, Thompson & Karsten · 130 North Washington Street · P.O. Box 1747 · Easton, MD 21601-1747 · 410-822-6800

Greenbelt

Dov Apfel · Joseph, Greenwald & Laake · Capital Office Park, Suite 400 · 6404 Ivy Lane · Greenbelt, MD 20770 · 301-220-2200

Andrew E. Greenwald · Joseph, Greenwald & Laake · Capital Office Park, Suite 400 · 6404 Ivy Lane · Greenbelt, MD 20770 · 301-220-2200

Hunt Valley

Mary Alane Downs · Morgan Carlo Downs & Everton · Executive Plaza Four, Suite 100 · 11350 McCormick Road · Hunt Valley, MD 21031 · 410-584-2800

Pasedena

Kathleen Meredith · Iliff & Meredith · 8055 Ritchie Highway, Suites 201-203 · Pasedena, MD 21122-1067 · 410-685-1166

Rockville

H. Kenneth Armstrong · ⑩ · Armstrong, Donohue, Ceppos & Vaughn · 204 Monroe Street, Suite 101 · Rockville, MD 20850 · 301-251-0440

Albert D. Brault · 20 · Brault, Graham, Scott & Brault · 101 South Washington Street · Rockville, MD 20850 · 301-424-1060

Larry A. Ceppos · Armstrong, Donohue, Ceppos & Vaughn · 204 Monroe Street, Suite 101 · Rockville, MD 20850 · 301-251-0440

Gerard J. Emig · Gleason, Flynn, Emig & Fogleman · 11 North Washington Street, Suite 400 · Rockville, MD 20850 · 301-294-2110

Michael F. Flynn, Jr. · Gleason, Flynn, Emig & Fogleman · 11 North Washington Street, Suite 400 · Rockville, MD 20850 · 301-294-2110

James P. Gleason · Gleason, Flynn, Emig & Fogleman · 11 North Washington Street, Suite 400 · Rockville, MD 20850 · 301-294-2110

Gerald I. Holtz · Gerald I. Holtz · 50 West Montgomery Avenue, Suite 200 · Rockville, MD 20850 · 301-610-0777

Ronald A. Karp · Karp, Frosh, Lapidus, Wigodsky & Norwind · 2273 Research Boulevard, Suite 200 · Rockville, MD 20850 · 301-948-3800

Robert R. Michael · 10 · Shadoan, Michael & Wells · http://www.smwlawfirm.com · 108 Park Avenue · Rockville, MD 20850 · 301-762-5150

John M. Quinn · 10 · Ethridge, Quinn, McAuliffe, Rowan & Hartinger · 33 Wood Lane · Rockville, MD 20850 · 301-762-1696

Leo A. Roth · Brault, Graham, Scott & Brault · 101 South Washington Street · Rockville, MD 20850 · 301-424-1060

George W. Shadoan · 20 · Shadoan, Michael & Wells · http://www.smwlawfirm.com · 108 Park Avenue · Rockville, MD 20850 · 301-762-5150

Daniel L. Shea · Brault, Graham, Scott & Brault · 101 South Washington Street · Rockville, MD 20850 · 301-424-1060

Benjamin S. Vaughan · Armstrong, Donohue, Ceppos & Vaughn · 204 Monroe Street, Suite 101 · Rockville, MD 20850 · 301-251-0440

Gregory Wells · Shadoan, Michael & Wells · http://www.smwlawfirm.com · 108 Park Avenue · Rockville, MD 20850 · 301-762-5150

James S. Wilson · Brault, Graham, Scott & Brault · 101 South Washington Street · Rockville, MD 20850 · 301-424-1060

Towson

Ronald M. Cherry · Cherry & Jenifer · 7825 York Road · Towson, MD 21204-7445 · 410-494-4954

Paul M. Vettori · Kenny & Vettori · 502 Washington Avenue, Suite 720 · Towson, MD 21204 · 410-825-1050

PRIVATE FUNDS LAW

Baltimore

Wilbert H. Sirota · Duane Morris · 111 South Calvert Street, Suite 2000 · Baltimore, MD 21202 · 410-949-2913

PRODUCT LIABILITY LITIGATION

Baltimore

Paul D. Bekman · ⑳ · Salsbury, Clements, Bekman, Marder & Adkins · 300 West Pratt Street, Suite 450 · Baltimore, MD 21201 · 410-539-6633

Joel A. Dewey · DLA Piper · 6225 Smith Avenue · Baltimore, MD 21209-3600 · 410-580-3000

Joseph G. Finnerty, Jr. · ⑩ · DLA Piper · 6225 Smith Avenue · Baltimore, MD 21209-3600 · 410-580-3000

John B. Isbister · Tydings & Rosenberg · http://www.tydingslaw.com · 100 East Pratt Street, 26th Floor · Baltimore, MD 21202 · 410-752-9700

Harry S. Johnson · Whiteford, Taylor & Preston · http://www.wtplaw.com · Seven Saint Paul Street · Baltimore, MD 21202-1636 · 410-347-8700

Timothy L. Mullin, Jr. · Miles & Stockbridge · http://www.milesstockbridge.com · 10 Light Street · Baltimore, MD 21202-1487 · 410-727-6464

Deborah L. Robinson · Robinson Woolson · Redwood Tower, Suite 1500 · 217 East Redwood Street · Baltimore, MD 21202 · 410-625-0000

Marc S. Rosen · Shar, Rosen & Warshaw · 26 South Street · Baltimore, MD 21202-3399 · 410-244-1155

Donald E. Sharpe · ㉕ · DLA Piper · 6225 Smith Avenue · Baltimore, MD 21209-3600 · 410-580-3000

John Parker Sweeney · Womble Carlyle Sandridge & Rice · 250 West Pratt Street, Suite 1300 · Baltimore, MD 21201 · 410-545-5800

Warren N. Weaver · Whiteford, Taylor & Preston · http://www.wtplaw.com · Seven Saint Paul Street · Baltimore, MD 21202-1636 · 410-347-8700

T. Sky Woodward · Womble Carlyle Sandridge & Rice · 250 West Pratt Street, Suite 1300 · Baltimore, MD 21201 · 410-545-5800

Thurman W. Zollicoffer, Jr. · Whiteford, Taylor & Preston · http://www.wtplaw.com · Seven Saint Paul Street · Baltimore, MD 21202-1636 · 410-347-8700

Rockville

Robert R. Michael · ⑩ · Shadoan, Michael & Wells · http://www.smwlawfirm.com · 108 Park Avenue · Rockville, MD 20850 · 301-762-5150

George W. Shadoan · ⑳ · Shadoan, Michael & Wells · http://www.smwlawfirm.com · 108 Park Avenue · Rockville, MD 20850 · 301-762-5150

Gregory Wells · Shadoan, Michael & Wells · http://www.smwlawfirm.com · 108 Park Avenue · Rockville, MD 20850 · 301-762-5150

PROFESSIONAL MALPRACTICE LAW

Annapolis

Paul J. Weber · Hyatt & Weber · http://www.hwlaw.com · 200 Westgate Circle, Suite 500 · Annapolis, MD 21401 · 410-266-0626

Baltimore

Thomas Althauser · Eccleston & Wolf · Baltimore-Washington Law Center, Fourth Floor · 7240 Parkway Drive · Baltimore, MD 21076 · 410-752-7474

Kevin F. Arthur · Kramon & Graham · http://www.kramonandgraham.com · One South Street, Suite 2600 Baltimore, MD 21202 · 410-752-6030

Charles Martinez · Eccleston & Wolf · Baltimore-Washington Law Center, Fourth Floor · 7240 Parkway Drive · Baltimore, MD 21076 · 410-752-7474

Catherine W. Steiner · Whiteford, Taylor & Preston · http://www.wtplaw.com · Seven Saint Paul Street · Baltimore, MD 21202-1636 · 410-347-8700

Lanham

Alan R. Siciliano · DeCaro, Doran, Siciliano, Gallagher & DeBlasis · 4601 Forbes Boulevard, Suite 200 · Lanham, MD 20706 · 301-306-4300

Rockville

Albert D. Brault · 20 · Brault, Graham, Scott & Brault · 101 South Washington Street · Rockville, MD 20850 · 301-424-1060

George W. Shadoan · 20 · Shadoan, Michael & Wells · http://www.smwlawfirm.com · 108 Park Avenue · Rockville, MD 20850 · 301-762-5150

Gregory Wells · Shadoan, Michael & Wells · http://www.smwlawfirm.com · 108 Park Avenue · Rockville, MD 20850 · 301-762-5150

Townsend

James R. Chason · Chason, Rosner, Leary & Marshall · 401 Washington Avenue, Fifth Floor · Townsend, MD 21204 · 410-494-3700

PROJECT FINANCE LAW

Baltimore

Edward C. Sledge · 10 · Hogan & Hartson · 111 South Calvert Street, Suite 1600 · Baltimore, MD 21202 · 410-659-2700

PUBLIC FINANCE LAW

Baltimore

Harold Altscher · Miles & Stockbridge · http://www.milesstockbridge.com · 10 Light Street · Baltimore, MD 21202-1487 · 410-727-6464

Alan C. Cason · McGuireWoods · http://www.mcguirewoods.com · Seven Saint Paul Street, Suite 1000 · Baltimore, MD 21202-1671 · 410-659-4400

James E. Cumbie · Venable · http://www.venable.com · 750 East Pratt Street, Suite 900 · Baltimore, MD 21202 · 410-244-7400

Deborah H. Diehl · Whiteford, Taylor & Preston · http://www.wtplaw.com · Seven Saint Paul Street · Baltimore, MD 21202-1636 · 410-347-8700

Robert L. Doory, Jr. · Miles & Stockbridge · http://www.milesstockbridge.com · 10 Light Street · Baltimore, MD 21202-1487 · 410-727-6464

David M. Funk · Funk & Bolton · 36 South Charles Street, 12th Floor · Baltimore, MD 21201-3111 · 410-659-7700

Elizabeth A. McKennon · McKennon Shelton & Henn · 401 East Pratt Street, Suite 2315 · Baltimore, MD 21202 · 410-843-3500

Emery B. McRill · McGuireWoods · http://www.mcguirewoods.com · Seven Saint Paul Street, Suite 1000 Baltimore, MD 21202-1671 · 410-659-4400

John A. Stalfort · Miles & Stockbridge · http://www.milesstockbridge.com · 10 Light Street · Baltimore, MD 21202-1487 · 410-727-6464

Ernest G. Wilson · McGuireWoods · http://www.mcguirewoods.com · Seven Saint Paul Street, Suite 1000 Baltimore, MD 21202-1671 · 410-659-4400

RAILROAD LAW

Baltimore

Stephen B. Caplis · Whiteford, Taylor & Preston · http://www.wtplaw.com · Seven Saint Paul Street · Baltimore, MD 21202-1636 · 410-347-8700

Bethesda

Lawrence M. Mann · ⑩ · Alper & Mann · 9205 Redwood Avenue · Bethesda, MD 20817 · 301-469-8985

REAL ESTATE LAW

Baltimore

Thomas C. Barbuti · Whiteford, Taylor & Preston · http://www.wtplaw.com · Seven Saint Paul Street · Baltimore, MD 21202-1636 · 410-347-8700

Timothy D. A. Chriss · ⑩ · Gordon, Feinblatt, Rothman, Hoffberger & Hollander · http://www.gfrlaw.com · The Garrett Building · 233 East Redwood Street · Baltimore, MD 21202 · 410-576-4000

Morton P. Fisher, Jr. · ⑳ · Ballard Spahr Andrews & Ingersoll · 300 East Lombard Street, 18th Floor · Baltimore, MD 21202 · 410-528-5600

David H. Fishman · ⑳ · Gordon, Feinblatt, Rothman, Hoffberger & Hollander · http://www.gfrlaw.com · The Garrett Building · 233 East Redwood Street · Baltimore, MD 21202 · 410-576-4000

Christopher J. Fritz · Ballard Spahr Andrews & Ingersoll · 300 East Lombard Street, 18th Floor · Baltimore, MD 21202 · 410-528-5600

Marci I. Gordon · Ballard Spahr Andrews & Ingersoll · 300 East Lombard Street, 18th Floor · Baltimore, MD 21202 · 410-528-5600

Barry C. Greenberg · Rosenberg | Martin | Greenberg · 25 South Charles Street, Suite 2115 · Baltimore, MD 21201 · 410-547-7163

Jan K. Guben · Venable · http://www.venable.com · 750 East Pratt Street, Suite 900 · Baltimore, MD 21202 · 410-244-7400

Nancy Haas · Abramoff, Neuberger & Linder · 250 West Pratt Street, Suite 800 · Baltimore, MD 21201-2500 · 410-539-8300

Jon M. Laria · Ballard Spahr Andrews & Ingersoll · 300 East Lombard Street, 18th Floor · Baltimore, MD 21202 · 410-528-5600

Edward J. Levin · ⑳ · DLA Piper · 6225 Smith Avenue · Baltimore, MD 21209-3600 · 410-580-3000

Richard E. Levine · ⑩ · DLA Piper · 6225 Smith Avenue · Baltimore, MD 21209-3600 · 410-580-3000

John P. Machen · DLA Piper · 6225 Smith Avenue · Baltimore, MD 21209-3600 · 410-580-3000

Searle E. Mitnick · Gordon, Feinblatt, Rothman, Hoffberger & Hollander · http://www.gfrlaw.com · The Garrett Building · 233 East Redwood Street · Baltimore, MD 21202 · 410-576-4000

James C. Oliver · ⑩ · Lenrow, Kohn & Oliver · Wachovia Tower, Suite 940 · Seven St. Paul Street · Baltimore, MD 21202-1628 · 410-962-0550

Mark Pollak · ⑩ · Ballard Spahr Andrews & Ingersoll · 300 East Lombard Street, 18th Floor · Baltimore, MD 21202 · 410-528-5600

Russell Ronald Reno, Jr. · ⑳ · Venable · http://www.venable.com · 750 East Pratt Street, Suite 900 · Baltimore, MD 21202 · 410-244-7400

Richard Rubin · Neuberger, Quinn, Gielen, Rubin & Gibber · http://www.nqgrg.com · One South Street, 27th Floor · Baltimore, MD 21202 · 410-332-8550

Jeffrey H. Scherr · Kramon & Graham · http://www.kramonandgraham.com · One South Street, Suite 2600 · Baltimore, MD 21202 · 410-752-6030

Kevin Shepherd · Venable · http://www.venable.com · 750 East Pratt Street, Suite 900 · Baltimore, MD 21202 · 410-244-7400

Raymond G. Truitt · ⑩ · Ballard Spahr Andrews & Ingersoll · 300 East Lombard Street, 18th Floor · Baltimore, MD 21202 · 410-528-5600

Jane A. Wilson · DLA Piper · 6225 Smith Avenue · Baltimore, MD 21209-3600 · 410-580-3000

Fred Wolf III · Ballard Spahr Andrews & Ingersoll · 300 East Lombard Street, 18th Floor · Baltimore, MD 21202 · 410-528-5600

James W. D. Wright · ⑩ · Venable · http://www.venable.com · 750 East Pratt Street, Suite 900 · Baltimore, MD 21202 · 410-244-7400

Bethesda

Douglas M. Bregman · Bregman, Berbert, Schwartz & Gilday · 7315 Wisconsin Avenue, Suite 800 West · Bethesda, MD 20814 · 301-656-2707

David M. Cohen · Linowes & Blocher · http://www.linowes-law.com · 7200 Wisconsin Avenue, Suite 800 Bethesda, MD 20814-4842 · 301-654-0504

Andrew M. Goldstein · Linowes & Blocher · http://www.linowes-law.com · 7200 Wisconsin Avenue, Suite 800 · Bethesda, MD 20814-4842 · 301-654-0504

Robert Roland Harris · Holland & Knight · http://www.hklaw.com · Three Bethesda Metro Center, Suite 800 · Bethesda, MD 20814 · 301-654-7800

Daniel P. Hodin · Paley, Rothman, Goldstein, Rosenberg, Eig & Cooper · 4800 Hampden Lane, Seventh Floor · Bethesda, MD 20814-2930 · 301-656-7603

Andrew L. Isaacson · Linowes & Blocher · http://www.linowes-law.com · 7200 Wisconsin Avenue, Suite 800 · Bethesda, MD 20814-4842 · 301-654-0504

Stephen Z. Kaufman · Linowes & Blocher · http://www.linowes-law.com · 7200 Wisconsin Avenue, Suite 800 · Bethesda, MD 20814-4842 · 301-654-0504

William Kominers · Holland & Knight · http://www.hklaw.com · Three Bethesda Metro Center, Suite 800 · Bethesda, MD 20814 · 301-654-7800

Harry W. Lerch · Lerch, Early & Brewer · Three Bethesda Metro Center, Suite 460 · Bethesda, MD 20814-5367 · 301-986-1300

Linda D. Schwartz · Paley, Rothman, Goldstein, Rosenberg, Eig & Cooper · 4800 Hampden Lane, Seventh Floor · Bethesda, MD 20814-2930 · 301-656-7603

Barbara A. Sears · Linowes & Blocher · http://www.linowes-law.com · 7200 Wisconsin Avenue, Suite 800 Bethesda, MD 20814-4842 · 301-654-0504

Roger D. Winston · Ballard Spahr Andrews & Ingersoll · 4800 Montgomery Lane, Seventh Floor · Bethesda, MD 20814-3458 · 301-664-6200

Richard Zeidman · Linowes & Blocher · http://www.linowes-law.com · 7200 Wisconsin Avenue, Suite 800 Bethesda, MD 20814-4842 · 301-654-0504

Chevy Chase

Robert L. Brownell · Furey, Doolan & Abell · 8401 Connecticut Avenue, Suite 1100 · Chevy Chase, MD 20815 · 301-652-6880

Rockville

Brian E. Frosh · Karp, Frosh, Lapidus, Wigodsky & Norwind · 2273 Research Boulevard, Suite 200 · Rockville, MD 20850 · 301-948-3800

David M. Kochanski · Shulman, Rogers, Gandal, Pordy & Ecker · 11921 Rockville Pike · Rockville, MD 20852-2743 · 301-230-5200

Lawrence A. Shulman · Shulman, Rogers, Gandal, Pordy & Ecker · 11921 Rockville Pike · Rockville, MD 20852-2743 · 301-230-5200

Samuel M. Spiritos · Shulman, Rogers, Gandal, Pordy & Ecker · 11921 Rockville Pike · Rockville, MD 20852-2743 · 301-230-5200

Towson

Sandra L. Howard · Miles & Stockbridge · http://www.milesstockbridge.com · One West Pennsylvania Avenue, Suite 900 · Towson, MD 21204-3965 · 410-821-6565

SECURITIES LAW

Baltimore

Francis B. Burch, Jr. · ⑳ · DLA Piper · 6225 Smith Avenue · Baltimore, MD 21209-3600 · 410-580-3000

Henry D. Kahn · Hogan & Hartson · 111 South Calvert Street, Suite 1600 · Baltimore, MD 21202 · 410-659-2700

James D. Mathias · DLA Piper · 6225 Smith Avenue · Baltimore, MD 21209-3600 · 410-580-3000

Abba David Poliakoff · Gordon, Feinblatt, Rothman, Hoffberger & Hollander · http://www.gfrlaw.com · The Garrett Building · 233 East Redwood Street · Baltimore, MD 21202 · 410-576-4000

Michael J. Silver · Hogan & Hartson · 111 South Calvert Street, Suite 1600 · Baltimore, MD 21202 · 410-659-2700

R. W. Smith, Jr. · ⑩ · DLA Piper · 6225 Smith Avenue · Baltimore, MD 21209-3600 · 410-580-3000

J. W. Thompson Webb · Miles & Stockbridge · http://www.milesstockbridge.com · 10 Light Street · Baltimore, MD 21202-1487 · 410-727-6464

Towson

Alan R. Sachs · Alan R. Sachs · West Road Corporate Center, Suite 227 · 110 West Road · Towson, MD 21204 · 410-847-9100

SPORTS LAW

Baltimore

Charles F. Morgan · Astrachan, Gunst & Thomas · http://www.agtlawyers.com · 217 East Redwood Street, Suite 2100 · Baltimore, MD 21202 · 410-783-3550

Ronald M. Shapiro · ⑩ · Shapiro Sher Guinot & Sandler · 36 South Charles Street, Suite 2000 · Baltimore, MD 21201-3147 · 410-385-0202

Joel A. Smith · ⑳ · Kahn, Smith & Collins · 201 North Charles Street, 10th Floor · Baltimore, MD 21201 410-244-1010

Hunt Valley

Michael D. Maas · Shapiro, Robinson & Associates · Four North Park Drive, Suite 110 · Hunt Valley, MD 21030 · 410-329-1999

Towson

David N. Pessin · Hodes, Pessin & Katz · http://www.hpklegal.com · 901 Dulaney Valley Road, Suite 400 Towson, MD 21204 · 410-938-8800

TAX LAW

Baltimore

Walter R. Calvert · Venable · http://www.venable.com · 750 East Pratt Street, Suite 900 · Baltimore, MD 21202 · 410-244-7400

Bryson L. Cook · ⑩ · Venable · http://www.venable.com · 750 East Pratt Street, Suite 900 · Baltimore, MD 21202 · 410-244-7400

Robert B. Curran · Whiteford, Taylor & Preston · http://www.wtplaw.com · Seven Saint Paul Street · Baltimore, MD 21202-1636 · 410-347-8700

Robert M. Ercole · Neuberger, Quinn, Gielen, Rubin & Gibber · http://www.nqgrg.com · One South Street, 27th Floor · Baltimore, MD 21202 · 410-332-8550

Theodore W. Hirsh · ⑩ · Theodore W. Hirsh · http://theodorehirshlaw.com · 100 North Charles Street, Suite 602 · Baltimore, MD 21201 · 410-244-5900

Richard E. Levine · ⑩ · DLA Piper · 6225 Smith Avenue · Baltimore, MD 21209-3600 · 410-580-3000

Jeffrey A. Markowitz · Miles & Stockbridge · http://www.milesstockbridge.com · 10 Light Street · Baltimore, MD 21202-1487 · 410-727-6464

Brian J. O'Connor · Venable · http://www.venable.com · 750 East Pratt Street, Suite 900 · Baltimore, MD 21202 · 410-244-7400

Stephen L. Owen · ⑩ · DLA Piper · 6225 Smith Avenue · Baltimore, MD 21209-3600 · 410-580-3000

Herman B. Rosenthal · Whiteford, Taylor & Preston · http://www.wtplaw.com · Seven Saint Paul Street · Baltimore, MD 21202-1636 · 410-347-8700

David B. Rudow · Adelberg, Rudow, Dorf & Hendler · http://www.adelbergrudow.com · Wachovia Building, Suite 600 · Seven St. Paul Street · Baltimore, MD 21202 · 410-539-5195

Stephen M. Sharkey · DLA Piper · 6225 Smith Avenue · Baltimore, MD 21209-3600 · 410-580-3000

Daryl J. Sidle · Baxter Baker Sidle Conn & Jones · http://www.bbsclaw.com · 120 East Baltimore Street · Baltimore, MD 21202 · 410-230-3800

Robert A. Snyder, Jr. · Thomas & Libowitz · 100 Light Street, 11th Floor · Baltimore, MD 21202-1053 · 410-752-2468

Shale D. Stiller · ㉕ · DLA Piper · 6225 Smith Avenue · Baltimore, MD 21209-3600 · 410-580-3000

Robert L. Waldman · Venable · http://www.venable.com · 750 East Pratt Street, Suite 900 · Baltimore, MD 21202 · 410-244-7400

TECHNOLOGY LAW

Baltimore

Ned T. Himmelrich · Gordon, Feinblatt, Rothman, Hoffberger & Hollander · http://www.gfrlaw.com · The Garrett Building · 233 East Redwood Street · Baltimore, MD 21202 · 410-576-4000

Gregory M. Stone · Whiteford, Taylor & Preston · http://www.wtplaw.com · Seven Saint Paul Street · Baltimore, MD 21202-1636 · 410-347-8700

Baltimore

Albert S. Barr III · ㉕ · Albert S. Barr III · 111 South Calvert Street, Suite 2700 · Baltimore, MD 21202 · 410-385-5212

Max E. Blumenthal · ⑳ · Stewart, Plant & Blumenthal · Seven St. Paul Street, Suite 910 · Baltimore, MD 21202 · 410-347-0506

Jonathan David Eisner · DLA Piper · 6225 Smith Avenue · Baltimore, MD 21209-3600 · 410-580-3000

Allan J. Gibber · ⑩ · Neuberger, Quinn, Gielen, Rubin & Gibber · http://www.nqgrg.com · One South Street, 27th Floor · Baltimore, MD 21202 · 410-332-8550

Sandra P. Gohn · ⑩ · DLA Piper · 6225 Smith Avenue · Baltimore, MD 21209-3600 · 410-580-3000

Jeffrey K. Gonya · Venable · http://www.venable.com · 750 East Pratt Street, Suite 900 · Baltimore, MD 21202 · 410-244-7400

Marianne Schmitt Hellauer · ⑩ · DLA Piper · 6225 Smith Avenue · Baltimore, MD 21209-3600 · 410-580-3000

Donald R. Mering · ⑩ · Ober, Kaler, Grimes & Shriver · http://www.ober.com · 120 East Baltimore Street, Suite 800 · Baltimore, MD 21202-1643 · 410-685-1120

Hugh A. Mitchell, Jr. · Stewart, Plant & Blumenthal · Seven St. Paul Street, Suite 910 · Baltimore, MD 21202 · 410-347-0506

A. MacDonough Plant · ㉕ · Stewart, Plant & Blumenthal · Seven St. Paul Street, Suite 910 · Baltimore, MD 21202 · 410-347-0506

Jeffrey J. Radowich · ⑩ · Venable · http://www.venable.com · 750 East Pratt Street, Suite 900 · Baltimore, MD 21202 · 410-244-7400

George K. Reynolds III · Miles & Stockbridge · http://www.milesstockbridge.com · 10 Light Street · Baltimore, MD 21202-1487 · 410-727-6464

David B. Rudow · Adelberg, Rudow, Dorf & Hendler · http://www.adelbergrudow.com · Wachovia Building, Suite 600 · Seven St. Paul Street · Baltimore, MD 21202 · 410-539-5195

Lynn B. Sassin · DLA Piper · 6225 Smith Avenue · Baltimore, MD 21209-3600 · 410-580-3000

William E. Scholtes · Saul Ewing · 500 East Pratt Street, Suite 900 · Baltimore, MD 21202 · 410-332-8600

Shale D. Stiller · ㉕ · DLA Piper · 6225 Smith Avenue · Baltimore, MD 21209-3600 · 410-580-3000

Melvin J. Sykes · Melvin J. Sykes · 120 East Baltimore Street, Suite 1701 · Baltimore, MD 21202-6701 · 410-727-3078

Earl S. Wellschlager · DLA Piper · 6225 Smith Avenue · Baltimore, MD 21209-3600 · 410-580-3000

Charles Winner · Fisher & Winner · 2002 Clipper Park Road, Suite 108 · Baltimore, MD 21211 · 410-385-2000

Robert C. Young · Stewart, Plant & Blumenthal · Seven St. Paul Street, Suite 910 · Baltimore, MD 21202 · 410-347-0506

Bethesda

Eric M. Core · Lerch, Early & Brewer · Three Bethesda Metro Center, Suite 460 · Bethesda, MD 20814-5367 · 301-986-1300

Nicholas P. Damico · Law Offices of Nicholas D'Amico · 7272 Wisconsin Avenue, Suite 300 · Bethesda, MD 20814 · 301-941-1957

Nancy G. Fax · Pasternak & Fidis · Fairmont Building, Suite 1100 · 7735 Old Georgetown Road · Bethesda, MD 20814-6183 · 301-656-8850

Marc R. Feinberg · West & Feinberg · 4550 Montgomery Avenue, Suite 775 North · Bethesda, MD 20814 · 301-951-1500

Marcia C. Fidis · Pasternak & Fidis · Fairmont Building, Suite 1100 · 7735 Old Georgetown Road · Bethesda, MD 20814-6183 · 301-656-8850

Richard L. Lyon · Law Offices of Richard L. Lyon · 8120 Woodmont Avenue, Suite 650 · Bethesda, MD 20814 · 301-770-2200

Steven A. Widdes · Paley, Rothman, Goldstein, Rosenberg, Eig & Cooper · 4800 Hampden Lane, Seventh Floor · Bethesda, MD 20814-2930 · 301-656-7603

Chevy Chase

W. Shepherdson Abell · ⑩ · Furey, Doolan & Abell · 8401 Connecticut Avenue, Suite 1100 · Chevy Chase, MD 20815 · 301-652-6880

Shelton M. Binstock · Binstock, Torchinsky and Associates · The Barlow Building, Suite 1340 · 5454 Wisconsin Avenue · Chevy Chase, MD 20815 · 301-657-5555

Julia L. O'Brien · Furey, Doolan & Abell · 8401 Connecticut Avenue, Suite 1100 · Chevy Chase, MD 20815 · 301-652-6880

Philip L. O'Donoghue · ⑩ · Furey, Doolan & Abell · 8401 Connecticut Avenue, Suite 1100 · Chevy Chase, MD 20815 · 301-652-6880

Rockville

Mark B. Weinberg · Weinberg & Jacobs · One Central Plaza, Suite 1200 · 11300 Rockville Pike · Rockville, MD 20852 · 301-468-5500

Silver Spring

Dena C. Feeney · Feeney & Kuwamura · 1010 Wayne Avenue, Suite 220 · Silver Spring, MD 20910-5660 301-587-2240

Towson

Edwin G. Fee, Jr. · Whiteford, Taylor & Preston · http://www.wtplaw.com · Towson Commons, Suite 300 · One West Pennsylvania Avenue · Towson, MD 21204-5025 · 410-832-2000

VENTURE CAPITAL LAW

Baltimore

Frank S. Jones, Jr. · Whiteford, Taylor & Preston · http://www.wtplaw.com · Seven Saint Paul Street · Baltimore, MD 21202-1636 · 410-347-8700

Wilbert H. Sirota · Duane Morris · 111 South Calvert Street, Suite 2000 · Baltimore, MD 21202 · 410-949-2913

WHITE-COLLAR CRIMINAL DEFENSE

Annapolis

Harry J. Trainor, Jr. · Trainor, Billman, Bennett, Milko & McCabe · 113 Cathedral Street, Suite E · Annapolis, MD 21401 · 410-280-1700

Baltimore

Gregg L. Bernstein · Zuckerman Spaeder · http://www.zuckerman.com · 100 East Pratt Street, Suite 2440 Baltimore, MD 21202-1031 · 410-332-0444

Herbert Better · Zuckerman Spaeder · http://www.zuckerman.com · 100 East Pratt Street, Suite 2440 · Baltimore, MD 21202-1031 · 410-332-0444

Benjamin R. Civiletti · ⑳ · Venable · http://www.venable.com · 750 East Pratt Street, Suite 900 · Baltimore, MD 21202 · 410-244-7400

Price O. Gielen · ⑩ · Neuberger, Quinn, Gielen, Rubin & Gibber · http://www.nqgrg.com · One South Street, 27th Floor · Baltimore, MD 21202 · 410-332-8550

Andrew Jay Graham · ⑩ · Kramon & Graham · http://www.kramonandgraham.com · One South Street, Suite 2600 · Baltimore, MD 21202 · 410-752-6030

Martin S. Himeles, Jr. · Zuckerman Spaeder · http://www.zuckerman.com · 100 East Pratt Street, Suite 2440 · Baltimore, MD 21202-1031 · 410-332-0444

Stephen J. Immelt · ⑩ · Hogan & Hartson · 111 South Calvert Street, Suite 1600 · Baltimore, MD 21202 410-659-2700

Andrew D. Levy · ⑩ · Brown, Goldstein & Levy · 120 East Baltimore Street, Suite 1700 · Baltimore, MD 21202 · 410-962-1030

Gerard P. Martin · Rosenberg | Martin | Greenberg · 25 South Charles Street, Suite 2115 · Baltimore, MD 21201 · 410-547-7163

Robert J. Mathias · ⑩ · DLA Piper · 6225 Smith Avenue · Baltimore, MD 21209-3600 · 410-580-3000

William J. Murphy · ⑩ · Murphy & Shaffer · http://www.murphyshaffer.com · 36 South Charles Street, Suite 1400 · Baltimore, MD 21201 · 410-783-7000

Larry Allen Nathans · Nathans & Biddle · http://www.nathanslaw.com · 120 East Baltimore Street, Suite 1800 · Baltimore, MD 21202 · 410-783-0272

Michael Schatzow · Venable · http://www.venable.com · 750 East Pratt Street, Suite 900 · Baltimore, MD 21202 · 410-244-7400

Charles P. Scheeler · DLA Piper · 6225 Smith Avenue · Baltimore, MD 21209-3600 · 410-580-3000

Joshua R. Treem · Schulman, Treem, Kaminkow, Gilden & Ravenell · http://www.stkgrlaw.com · The World Trade Center, Suite 1800 · 401 East Pratt Street · Baltimore, MD 21202-3004 · 410-332-0850

James P. Ulwick · ⑩ · Kramon & Graham · http://www.kramonandgraham.com · One South Street, Suite 2600 · Baltimore, MD 21202 · 410-752-6030

Arnold M. Weiner · ㉕ · The Law Offices of Arnold M. Weiner · 2002 Clipper Park Road, Suite 108 · Baltimore, MD 21211 · 410-769-8080

Bethesda

Stanley J. Reed · Lerch, Early & Brewer · Three Bethesda Metro Center, Suite 460 · Bethesda, MD 20814-5367 · 301-986-1300

Greenbelt

Robert C. Bonsib · Marcus & Bonsib · http://www.robertbonsib.com · 6411 Ivy Lane, Suite 116 · Greenbelt, MD 20770 · 301-441-3000

William C. Brennan, Jr. · Brennan, Sullivan & McKenna · 6305 Ivy Lane, Suite 700 · Greenbelt, MD 20770 · 301-474-0044

Rockville

Paul F. Kemp · Venable · http://www.venable.com · One Church Street, Fifth Floor · Rockville, MD 20850 · 301-217-5600

Towson

Steven A. Allen · Hodes, Pessin & Katz · http://www.hpklegal.com · 901 Dulaney Valley Road, Suite 400 Towson, MD 21204 · 410-938-8800

David B. Irwin · Irwin Green & Dexter · 301 West Pennsylvania Avenue · Towson, MD 21204 · 410-832-0111

WORKERS' COMPENSATION LAW

Baltimore

Rudolph L. Rose · Semmes Bowen & Semmes · http://www.semmes.com · 25 South Charles Street, Suite 1400 · Baltimore, MD 21201 · 410-539-5040

Rockville

Martin Gerel · Ashcraft & Gerel · 1300 Rockville Pike · Rockville, MD 20852 · 301-770-3737

MASSACHUSETTS

ADMINISTRATIVE LAW

Boston

Jeffrey F. Jones · a · Edwards Angell Palmer & Dodge · Prudential Center · 111 Huntington Avenue · Boston, MA 02199-7613 · 617-239-0100

David S. Rosenzweig · Keegan Werlin · 265 Franklin Street · Boston, MA 02110-3113 · 617-951-1400

Robert A. Sherman · Greenberg Traurig · http://www.gtlaw.com · One International Place · Boston, MA 02110 · 617-310-6000

Michael D. Vhay · DLA Piper · 33 Arch Street, 26th Floor · Boston, MA 02110-1447 · 617-406-6000

Cambridge

Scott P. Lewis · Anderson & Kreiger · One Canal Park, Suite 200 · Cambridge, MA 02141 · 617-621-6500

ALTERNATIVE DISPUTE RESOLUTION

Boston

Samuel Adams · 2) · K&L Gates · State Street Financial Center · One Lincoln Street · Boston, MA 02111-2950 · 617-261-3100

John W. Fieldsteel · Urbelis & Fieldsteel · 155 Federal Street · Boston, MA 02110-1727 · 617-338-2200

John P. Fitzgerald · Cogavin and Waystack · One Center Plaza, Suite 310 · Boston, MA 02108 · 617-742-3340

David H. Gibbs · Bowditch & Dewey · One International Place, 44th Floor · Boston, MA 02110-2602 · 617-757-6500

Dwight Golann · Suffolk University Law School · 120 Tremont Street · Boston, MA 02108-4977 · 617-573-8000

Eric D. Green · Resolutions · 222 Berkeley Street, Suite 1060 · Boston, MA 02116 · 617-556-0800

David A. Hoffman · Boston Law Collaborative · 99 Summer Street, Suite 1600 · Boston, MA 02110 · 617-439-4700

Joseph L. Kociubes · a · Bingham McCutchen · http://www.bingham.com · One Federal Street · Boston, MA 02110-1726 · 617-951-8000

James E. McGuire · JAMS · One Beacon Street, Suite 2300 · Boston, MA 02108-3106 · 617-228-0200

Carmin C. Reiss · Resolutions · 222 Berkeley Street, Suite 1060 · Boston, MA 02116 · 617-556-0800

James V. Ryan · JAMS · One Beacon Street, Suite 2300 · Boston, MA 02108-3106 · 617-228-0200

Eileen M. Shaevel · Dispute Resolution Alternatives · Two Center Plaza, Suite 530 · Boston, MA 02108-1906 · 617-367-3998

Jeffrey S. Stern · Sugarman, Rogers, Barshak & Cohen · http://www.srbc.com · 101 Merrimac Street, Ninth Floor · Boston, MA 02114-4737 · 617-227-3030

Eric E. Van Loon · JAMS · One Beacon Street, Suite 2300 · Boston, MA 02108-3106 · 617-228-0200

Maria C. Walsh · JAMS · One Beacon Street, Suite 2300 · Boston, MA 02108-3106 · 617-228-0200

Brookline

Brad Honoroff · The Mediation Group · http://www.themediationgroup.org · Three Harvard Avenue, Suite Three · Brookline, MA 02446 · 617-277-9232

Mark L. Irvings · Mark L. Irvings · 24 Elba Street · Brookline, MA 02446 · 617-734-3278

Framingham

Lauren Stiller Rikleen · a · Bowditch & Dewey · 175 Crossing Boulevard, Suite 500 · Framingham, MA 01702 · 508-879-5700

Newton

Diane Zaar Cochran · Diane Zaar Cochran · 22 Cabot Street · Newton, MA 02458 · 617-964-1461

Northampton

Peter Contuzzi · Peter Contuzzi · 70 Massasoit Street · Northampton, MA 01060 · 413-586-8030

Pittsfield

David Burbank · Burbank Mediation · 440 South Street · Pittsfield, MA 01201-8243 · 413-445-5141

ANTITRUST LAW

Boston

Cary Armistead · Ropes & Gray · http://www.ropesgray.com · One International Place · Boston, MA 02110-2624 · 617-951-7000

Robert M. Buchanan, Jr. · Choate, Hall & Stewart · http://www.choate.com · Two International Place · Boston, MA 02110 · 617-248-5000

James C. Burling · WilmerHale · http://www.wilmerhale.com · 60 State Street · Boston, MA 02109 · 617-526-6000

Daniel L. Goldberg · Bingham McCutchen · http://www.bingham.com · One Federal Street · Boston, MA 02110-1726 · 617-951-8000

David A. Martland · Nixon Peabody · 100 Summer Street · Boston, MA 02110-1832 · 617-345-1000

Michelle D. Miller · WilmerHale · http://www.wilmerhale.com · 60 State Street · Boston, MA 02109 · 617-526-6000

Neil P. Motenko · Nutter McClennen & Fish · http://www.nutter.com · World Trade Center West · 155 Seaport Boulevard · Boston, MA 02210 · 617-439-2000

William L. Patton · a · Ropes & Gray · http://www.ropesgray.com · One International Place · Boston, MA 02110-2624 · 617-951-7000

Daniel S. Savrin · Bingham McCutchen · http://www.bingham.com · One Federal Street · Boston, MA 02110-1726 · 617-951-8000

Thane D. Scott · Bingham McCutchen · http://www.bingham.com · One Federal Street · Boston, MA 02110-1726 · 617-951-8000

Jane E. Willis · Ropes & Gray · http://www.ropesgray.com · One International Place · Boston, MA 02110-2624 · 617-951-7000

Lisa C. Wood · Foley Hoag · http://www.foleyhoag.com · Seaport World Trade Center West · 155 Seaport Boulevard · Boston, MA 02210-2600 · 617-832-1000

Richard J. Yurko · Yurko, Salvesen & Remz · One Washington Mall, 11th Floor · Boston, MA 02108-2603 · 617-723-6900

APPELLATE LAW

Boston

David E. Cherny · a · Atwood & Cherny · http://www.atwoodcherny.com · 101 Huntington Avenue, 25th Floor · Boston, MA 02199 · 617-262-6400

Richard M. Egbert · a · Richard M. Egbert · 99 Summer Street, Suite 1800 · Boston, MA 02110 · 617-737-8222

William F. Lee · a · WilmerHale · http://www.wilmerhale.com · 60 State Street · Boston, MA 02109 · 617-526-6000

Richard L. Neumeier · Morrison Mahoney · 250 Summer Street · Boston, MA 02210 · 617-439-7500

Charles W. Rankin, Jr. · a · Rankin & Sultan · 151 Merrimac Street, Second Floor · Boston, MA 02114 · 617-720-0011

John R. Salsberg · a · Salsberg & Schneider · 95 Commercial Wharf · Boston, MA 02110 · 617-227-7788

James L. Sultan · a · Rankin & Sultan · 151 Merrimac Street, Second Floor · Boston, MA 02114 · 617-720-0011

Michael Traft · Carney & Bassil · 20 Park Plaza, Suite 1405 · Boston, MA 02116 · 617-338-5566

Cambridge

Roberta F. Benjamin · a · Benjamin & Benson · Bulfinch Square · 43 Thorndike Street · Cambridge, MA 02141 · 617-577-1515

Alan M. Dershowitz · a · Harvard Law School · 1563 Massachusetts Avenue · Cambridge, MA 02138 · 617-495-3100

Laurence H. Tribe · a · Harvard Law School · 1563 Massachusetts Avenue · Cambridge, MA 02138 · 617-495-3100

BANKING LAW

Boston

Lynne B. Barr · Goodwin Procter · Exchange Place · 53 State Street · Boston, MA 02109-2881 · 617-570-1000

Lyman G. Bullard, Jr. · Choate, Hall & Stewart · http://www.choate.com · Two International Place · Boston, MA 02110 · 617-248-5000

Peter W. Coogan · a · Foley Hoag · http://www.foleyhoag.com · Seaport World Trade Center West · 155 Seaport Boulevard · Boston, MA 02210-2600 · 617-832-1000

Stephen J. Coukos · a · Chu, Ring & Hazel · 241 A Street, Suite 300 · Boston, MA 02210 · 617-443-9800

Neal J. Curtin · a · Bingham McCutchen · http://www.bingham.com · One Federal Street · Boston, MA 02110-1726 · 617-951-8000

Thomas B. Draper · Ropes & Gray · http://www.ropesgray.com · One International Place · Boston, MA 02110-2624 · 617-951-7000

Kenneth F. Ehrlich · Nutter McClennen & Fish · http://www.nutter.com · World Trade Center West · 155 Seaport Boulevard · Boston, MA 02210 · 617-439-2000

Kevin J. Handly · Pierce Atwood · 225 Franklin Street, 17th Floor, Suite 1740 · Boston, MA 02110 · 857-277-6900

David F. Hannon · a · Craig and Macauley · http://www.craigmacauley.com · Federal Reserve Plaza · 600 Atlantic Avenue · Boston, MA 02210 · 617-367-9500

Jonathon R. Harris · Edwards Angell Palmer & Dodge · Prudential Center · 111 Huntington Avenue · Boston, MA 02199-7613 · 617-239-0100

Amy L. Kyle · Bingham McCutchen · http://www.bingham.com · One Federal Street · Boston, MA 02110-1726 · 617-951-8000

Gregory Lyons · Goodwin Procter · Exchange Place · 53 State Street · Boston, MA 02109-2881 · 617-570-1000

William P. Mayer · a · Goodwin Procter · Exchange Place · 53 State Street · Boston, MA 02109-2881 · 617-570-1000

James A. McDaniel · Choate, Hall & Stewart · http://www.choate.com · Two International Place · Boston, MA 02110 · 617-248-5000

David A. McKay · Ropes & Gray · http://www.ropesgray.com · One International Place · Boston, MA 02110-2624 · 617-951-7000

Regina M. Pisa · a · Goodwin Procter · Exchange Place · 53 State Street · Boston, MA 02109-2881 · 617-570-1000

Carol Hempfling Pratt · Foley Hoag · http://www.foleyhoag.com · Seaport World Trade Center West · 155 Seaport Boulevard · Boston, MA 02210-2600 · 617-832-1000

Stanley Ragalevsky · K&L Gates · State Street Financial Center · One Lincoln Street · Boston, MA 02111-2950 · 617-261-3100

Alfred O. Rose · a · Ropes & Gray · http://www.ropesgray.com · One International Place · Boston, MA 02110-2624 · 617-951-7000

Michael J. Ruberto · Ruberto, Israel & Weiner · 100 North Washington Street · Boston, MA 02114-2128 · 617-742-4200

David Ruediger · Edwards Angell Palmer & Dodge · Prudential Center · 111 Huntington Avenue · Boston, MA 02199-7613 · 617-239-0100

Susan E. Siebert · Edwards Angell Palmer & Dodge · Prudential Center · 111 Huntington Avenue · Boston, MA 02199-7613 · 617-239-0100

Edwin E. Smith · a · Bingham McCutchen · http://www.bingham.com · One Federal Street · Boston, MA 02110-1726 · 617-951-8000

Philip J. Smith · Ropes & Gray · http://www.ropesgray.com · One International Place · Boston, MA 02110-2624 · 617-951-7000

George Ticknor · Edwards Angell Palmer & Dodge · Prudential Center · 111 Huntington Avenue · Boston, MA 02199-7613 · 617-239-0100

Springfield

Stephen A. Shatz · a · Shatz, Schwartz and Fentin · 1441 Main Street, Suite 1100 · Springfield, MA 01103 · 413-737-1131

BANKRUPTCY AND CREDITOR-DEBTOR RIGHTS LAW

Boston

Mitchel Appelbaum · WilmerHale · http://www.wilmerhale.com · 60 State Street · Boston, MA 02109 · 617-526-6000

William R. Baldiga · Brown Rudnick · http://www.brbilaw.com · One Financial Center · Boston, MA 02111 · 617-856-8200

Charles R. Bennett, Jr. · Hanify & King · One Beacon Street, 21st Floor · Boston, MA 02108-3107 · 617-423-0400

Mark N. Berman · 2) · Nixon Peabody · 100 Summer Street · Boston, MA 02110-1832 · 617-345-1000

Janet E. Bostwick · Janet E. Bostwick · 295 Devonshire Street · Boston, MA 02110 · 617-956-2670

Daniel C. Cohn · a · Cohn, Whitesell & Goldberg · 101 Arch Street, Suite 1600 · Boston, MA 02110 · 617-951-2505

Howard M. Cooper · Todd & Weld · http://www.toddweld.com · 28 State Street, 31st Floor · Boston, MA 02109 · 617-720-2626

Charles A. Dale III · K&L Gates · State Street Financial Center · One Lincoln Street · Boston, MA 02111-2950 · 617-261-3100

Paul P. Daley · 2) · WilmerHale · http://www.wilmerhale.com · 60 State Street · Boston, MA 02109 · 617-526-6000

Don S. De Amicis · Ropes & Gray · http://www.ropesgray.com · One International Place · Boston, MA 02110-2624 · 617-951-7000

Mark G. DeGiacomo · Murtha Cullina · 99 High Street, 20th Floor · Boston, MA 02110 · 617-457-4000

Charles R. Dougherty · a · Foley & Lardner · 111 Huntington Avenue · Boston, MA 02199 · 617-342-4000

Charles L. Glerum · a · Choate, Hall & Stewart · http://www.choate.com · Two International Place · Boston, MA 02110 · 617-248-5000

Daniel M. Glosband · 2) · Goodwin Procter · Exchange Place · 53 State Street · Boston, MA 02109-2881 · 617-570-1000

Michael J. Goldberg · Cohn, Whitesell & Goldberg · 101 Arch Street, Suite 1600 · Boston, MA 02110 · 617-951-2505

Douglas R. Gooding · Choate, Hall & Stewart · http://www.choate.com · Two International Place · Boston, MA 02110 · 617-248-5000

Richard Hiersteiner · Edwards Angell Palmer & Dodge · Prudential Center · 111 Huntington Avenue · Boston, MA 02199-7613 · 617-239-0100

Steven T. Hoort · a · Ropes & Gray · http://www.ropesgray.com · One International Place · Boston, MA 02110-2624 · 617-951-7000

Jeffrey L. Jonas · Brown Rudnick · http://www.brbilaw.com · One Financial Center · Boston, MA 02111 · 617-856-8200

William W. Kannel · Mintz, Levin, Cohn, Ferris, Glovsky and Popeo · One Financial Center, 40th Floor · Boston, MA 02111 · 617-542-6000

Richard L. Levine · 2) · Nelson, Kinder, Mosseau & Saturley · http://www.nkms.com · 45 Milk Street, Seventh Floor · Boston, MA 02109 · 617-778-7500

Steven B. Levine · Brown Rudnick · http://www.brbilaw.com · One Financial Center · Boston, MA 02111 617-856-8200

Christine D. Lynch · Goulston & Storrs · 400 Atlantic Avenue · Boston, MA 02110-3333 · 617-482-1776

William F. Macauley · a · Craig and Macauley · http://www.craigmacauley.com · Federal Reserve Plaza · 600 Atlantic Avenue · Boston, MA 02210 · 617-367-9500

D. Ross Martin · Ropes & Gray · http://www.ropesgray.com · One International Place · Boston, MA 02110-2624 · 617-951-7000

Gina Lynn Martin · Goodwin Procter · Exchange Place · 53 State Street · Boston, MA 02109-2881 · 617-570-1000

Richard E. Mikels · 2% · Mintz, Levin, Cohn, Ferris, Glovsky and Popeo · One Financial Center, 40th Floor · Boston, MA 02111 · 617-542-6000

John J. Monaghan · Holland & Knight · http://www.hklaw.com · 10 Saint James Avenue, 11th Floor · Boston, MA 02116 · 617-523-2700

Paul D. Moore · a · Duane Morris · 470 Atlantic Avenue, Suite 500 · Boston, MA 02210-2600 · 857-488-4200

William R. Moorman · Craig and Macauley · http://www.craigmacauley.com · Federal Reserve Plaza · 600 Atlantic Avenue · Boston, MA 02210 · 617-367-9500

John T. Morrier · Mintz, Levin, Cohn, Ferris, Glovsky and Popeo · One Financial Center, 40th Floor · Boston, MA 02111 · 617-542-6000

Guy B. Moss · a · Riemer & Braunstein · Three Center Plaza, Sixth Floor · Boston, MA 02108 · 617-523-9000

Harold B. Murphy · a · Hanify & King · One Beacon Street, 21st Floor · Boston, MA 02108-3107 · 617-423-0400

Christopher J. Panos · a · Craig and Macauley · http://www.craigmacauley.com · Federal Reserve Plaza · 600 Atlantic Avenue · Boston, MA 02210 · 617-367-9500

Michael J. Pappone · 2) · Goodwin Procter · Exchange Place · 53 State Street · Boston, MA 02109-2881 · 617-570-1000

Paul J. Ricotta · Mintz, Levin, Cohn, Ferris, Glovsky and Popeo · One Financial Center, 40th Floor · Boston, MA 02111 · 617-542-6000

Douglas B. Rosner · Goulston & Storrs · 400 Atlantic Avenue · Boston, MA 02110-3333 · 617-482-1776

Joseph F. Ryan · a · Brown Rudnick · http://www.brbilaw.com · One Financial Center · Boston, MA 02111 · 617-856-8200

Jon D. Schneider · 2) · Goodwin Procter · Exchange Place · 53 State Street · Boston, MA 02109-2881 · 617-570-1000

Andrew Z. Schwartz · Foley Hoag · http://www.foleyhoag.com · Seaport World Trade Center West · 155 Seaport Boulevard · Boston, MA 02210-2600 · 617-832-1000

John D. Sigel · a · WilmerHale · http://www.wilmerhale.com · 60 State Street · Boston, MA 02109 · 617-526-6000

Edwin E. Smith · a · Bingham McCutchen · http://www.bingham.com · One Federal Street · Boston, MA 02110-1726 · 617-951-8000

John V. Snellings · Nixon Peabody · 100 Summer Street · Boston, MA 02110-1832 · 617-345-1000

C. Hall Swaim · 2) · WilmerHale · http://www.wilmerhale.com · 60 State Street · Boston, MA 02109 · 617-526-6000

John F. Ventola · Choate, Hall & Stewart · http://www.choate.com · Two International Place · Boston, MA 02110 · 617-248-5000

James F. Wallack · Goulston & Storrs · 400 Atlantic Avenue · Boston, MA 02110-3333 · 617-482-1776

A. Davis Whitesell · Cohn, Whitesell & Goldberg · 101 Arch Street, Suite 1600 · Boston, MA 02110 · 617-951-2505

John L. Whitlock · 2) · Edwards Angell Palmer & Dodge · Prudential Center · 111 Huntington Avenue · Boston, MA 02199-7613 · 617-239-0100

P. Sabin Willett · Bingham McCutchen · http://www.bingham.com · One Federal Street · Boston, MA 02110-1726 · 617-951-8000

James M. Wilton · Ropes & Gray · http://www.ropesgray.com · One International Place · Boston, MA 02110-2624 · 617-951-7000

Springfield

Joseph B. Collins · 2) · Hendel & Collins · 101 State Street · Springfield, MA 01103 · 413-734-6411

Mark D. Cress · Bulkley, Richardson and Gelinas · 1500 Main Street, Suite 2700 · P.O. Box 15507 · Springfield, MA 01115-5507 · 413-781-2820

Henry E. Geberth, Jr. · Hendel & Collins · 101 State Street · Springfield, MA 01103 · 413-734-6411

Philip J. Hendel · 2) · Hendel & Collins · 101 State Street · Springfield, MA 01103 · 413-734-6411

George I. Roumeliotis · Hendel & Collins · 101 State Street · Springfield, MA 01103 · 413-734-6411

Paul R. Salvage · a · Bacon & Wilson · 33 State Street · Springfield, MA 01103 · 413-781-0560

Gary M. Weiner · Weiner & Lange · 95 State Street, Suite 918 · Springfield, MA 01103 · 413-732-6840

Steven Weiss · Shatz, Schwartz and Fentin · 1441 Main Street, Suite 1100 · Springfield, MA 01103 · 413-737-1131

Westborough

Joseph H. Baldiga · Mirick O'Connell DeMallie & Lougee · 1700 West Park Drive · Westborough, MA 01581-3941 · 508-898-1501

Worcester

Kevin C. McGee · Seder & Chandler · Burnside Building · 339 Main Street · Worcester, MA 01608-1585 · 508-757-7721

J. Robert Seder · 2) · Seder & Chandler · Burnside Building · 339 Main Street · Worcester, MA 01608-1585 · 508-757-7721

Richard A. Sheils, Jr. · a · Bowditch & Dewey · 311 Main Street · P.O. Box 15156 · Worcester, MA 01615-0156 · 508-791-3511

George W. Tetler III · 2) · Bowditch & Dewey · 311 Main Street · P.O. Box 15156 · Worcester, MA 01615-0156 · 508-791-3511

BET-THE-COMPANY LITIGATION

Boston

R. Jack Cinquegrana · Choate, Hall & Stewart · http://www.choate.com · Two International Place · Boston, MA 02110 · 617-248-5000

Michael B. Keating · 2) · Foley Hoag · http://www.foleyhoag.com · Seaport World Trade Center West · 155 Seaport Boulevard · Boston, MA 02210-2600 · 617-832-1000

Joseph L. Kociubes · a · Bingham McCutchen · http://www.bingham.com · One Federal Street · Boston, MA 02110-1726 · 617-951-8000

William F. Lee · a · WilmerHale · http://www.wilmerhale.com · 60 State Street · Boston, MA 02109 · 617-526-6000

Edward P. Leibensperger · a · McDermott Will & Emery · 28 State Street, 34th Floor · Boston, MA 02109-1775 · 617-535-4000

Joan A. Lukey · a · Ropes & Gray · http://www.ropesgray.com · One International Place · Boston, MA 02110-2624 · 617-951-7000

John T. Montgomery · Ropes & Gray · http://www.ropesgray.com · One International Place · Boston, MA 02110-2624 · 617-951-7000

Robert J. Muldoon, Jr. · 2) · Sherin and Lodgen · 101 Federal Street · Boston, MA 02110 · 617-646-2000

R. Robert Popeo · 2) · Mintz, Levin, Cohn, Ferris, Glovsky and Popeo · One Financial Center, 40th Floor · Boston, MA 02111 · 617-542-6000

Richard W. Renehan · 2% · Goulston & Storrs · 400 Atlantic Avenue · Boston, MA 02110-3333 · 617-482-1776

Paul F. Ware, Jr. · a · Goodwin Procter · Exchange Place · 53 State Street · Boston, MA 02109-2881 · 617-570-1000

Worcester

Michael P. Angelini · 2) · Bowditch & Dewey · 311 Main Street · P.O. Box 15156 · Worcester, MA 01615-0156 · 508-791-3511

BIOTECHNOLOGY LAW

Boston

Mitchell S. Bloom · Goodwin Procter · Exchange Place · 53 State Street · Boston, MA 02109-2881 · 617-570-1000

Christopher J. Denn · Goodwin Procter · Exchange Place · 53 State Street · Boston, MA 02109-2881 · 617-570-1000

Jonathan L. Kravetz · Mintz, Levin, Cohn, Ferris, Glovsky and Popeo · One Financial Center, 40th Floor · Boston, MA 02111 · 617-542-6000

David E. Redlick · a · WilmerHale · http://www.wilmerhale.com · 60 State Street · Boston, MA 02109 · 617-526-6000

Steven D. Singer · WilmerHale · http://www.wilmerhale.com · 60 State Street · Boston, MA 02109 · 617-526-6000

Kingsley L. Taft · Goodwin Procter · Exchange Place · 53 State Street · Boston, MA 02109-2881 · 617-570-1000

Thomas A. Turano · K&L Gates · State Street Financial Center · One Lincoln Street · Boston, MA 02111-2950 · 617-261-3100

Julio Vega · Bingham McCutchen · http://www.bingham.com · One Federal Street · Boston, MA 02110-1726 · 617-951-8000

Jeffrey M. Wiesen · Mintz, Levin, Cohn, Ferris, Glovsky and Popeo · One Financial Center, 40th Floor · Boston, MA 02111 · 617-542-6000

Steven A. Wilcox · Ropes & Gray · http://www.ropesgray.com · One International Place · Boston, MA 02110-2624 · 617-951-7000

Lawrence S. Wittenberg · Goodwin Procter · Exchange Place · 53 State Street · Boston, MA 02109-2881 · 617-570-1000

CIVIL RIGHTS LAW

Boston

Juliane Balliro · a · WolfBlock · http://wolfblock.com · One Boston Place, 40th Floor · Boston, MA 02108 · 617-226-4000

Howard Friedman · Law Offices of Howard Friedman · 90 Canal Street, Fifth Floor · Boston, MA 02114 617-742-4100

Patricia Garin · Stern Shapiro Weissberg & Garin · 90 Canal Street, Fifth Floor · Boston, MA 02114-2022 617-742-5800

Michael S. Greco · K&L Gates · State Street Financial Center · One Lincoln Street · Boston, MA 02111-2950 · 617-261-3100

Paul V. Holtzman · Krokidas & Bluestein · 600 Atlantic Avenue · Boston, MA 02210 · 617-482-7211

Jonathan Shapiro · a · Stern Shapiro Weissberg & Garin · 90 Canal Street, Fifth Floor · Boston, MA 02114-2022 · 617-742-5800

Max D. Stern · 2) · Stern Shapiro Weissberg & Garin · 90 Canal Street, Fifth Floor · Boston, MA 02114-2022 · 617-742-5800

Lynn Weissberg · Stern Shapiro Weissberg & Garin · 90 Canal Street, Fifth Floor · Boston, MA 02114-2022 · 617-742-5800

COLLABORATIVE LAW: FAMILY LAW

Boston

Valerie Browne-Matherly · Valerie Browne-Matherly · 85 Devonshire Street, Suite 1000 · Boston, MA 02109 · 617-227-7493

David A. Hoffman · Boston Law Collaborative · 99 Summer Street, Suite 1600 · Boston, MA 02110 · 617-439-4700

Brookline

Rita S. Pollak · Rita S. Pollak · Three Harvard Avenue, Suite Three · Brookline, MA 02446 · 617-232-2009

Cambridge

John A. Moos · Bowman, Moos, Elder & Noe · http://www.bmenlaw.com · 222 Third Street, Suite 3220 · Cambridge, MA 02142 · 617-494-8808

Douglas C. Reynolds · The New Law Center · 545 Concord Avenue, Suite 15 · Cambridge, MA 02138 · 617-492-4400

Chelmsford

Lynda J. Robbins · Lynda J. Robbins · 11 Summer Street · Chelmsford, MA 01824 · 978-256-8178

Chicopee

Eileen Z. Sorentino · Law Office of Eileen Sorrentino · 279 Front Street · P.O. Box 119 · Chicopee, MA 01014-0119 · 413-594-7500

Lowell

Karen J. Levitt · Levitt Law Group · Old Central Firehouse · 134 Middle Street, Suite 220 · Lowell, MA 01852 · 978-458-5550

Newton

Howard I. Goldstein · Rosenberg, Freedman & Goldstein · 246 Walnut Street · Newton, MA 02460-6734 · 617-964-7000

Doris Tennant · Tennant Lubell · http://www.tllawgroup.com · 288 Walnut Street, Suite 500 · Newton, MA 02460 · 617-969-9610

Wellesley

Daniel J. Finn · Daniel J. Finn · 60 Walnut Street · Wellesley, MA 02481 · 781-997-1600

COMMERCIAL LITIGATION

Boston

Edward J. Barshak · 25 · Sugarman, Rogers, Barshak & Cohen · http://www.srbc.com · 101 Merrimac Street, Ninth Floor · Boston, MA 02114-4737 · 617-227-3030

R. Jack Cinquegrana · Choate, Hall & Stewart · http://www.choate.com · Two International Place · Boston, MA 02110 · 617-248-5000

Michael A. Collora · 10 · Dwyer & Collora · 600 Atlantic Avenue, 12th Floor · Boston, MA 02210-2211 · 617-371-1000

John J. Curtin, Jr. · 25 · Bingham McCutchen · http://www.bingham.com · One Federal Street · Boston, MA 02110-1726 · 617-951-8000

James R. DeGiacomo · 10 · Murtha Cullina · 99 High Street, 20th Floor · Boston, MA 02110 · 617-457-4000

Stephen R. Delinsky · Eckert Seamans Cherin & Mellott · One International Place, 18th Floor · Boston, MA 02110-2602 · 617-342-6800

Michael DeMarco · K&L Gates · State Street Financial Center · One Lincoln Street · Boston, MA 02111-2950 · 617-261-3100

James S. Dittmar · Goodwin Procter · Exchange Place · 53 State Street · Boston, MA 02109-2881 · 617-570-1000

Anthony M. Doniger · Sugarman, Rogers, Barshak & Cohen · http://www.srbc.com · 101 Merrimac Street, Ninth Floor · Boston, MA 02114-4737 · 617-227-3030

John D. Donovan, Jr. · 10 · Ropes & Gray · http://www.ropesgray.com · One International Place · Boston, MA 02110-2624 · 617-951-7000

Bruce E. Falby · DLA Piper · 33 Arch Street, 26th Floor · Boston, MA 02110-1447 · 617-406-6000

John Kenneth Felter · Goodwin Procter · Exchange Place · 53 State Street · Boston, MA 02109-2881 · 617-570-1000

George P. Field · Verrill Dana · http://www.verrilldana.com · One Boston Place, Suite 2330 · Boston, MA 02108-4427 · 617-309-2600

Francis H. Fox · 2% · Bingham McCutchen · http://www.bingham.com · One Federal Street · Boston, MA 02110-1726 · 617-951-8000

Robert S. Frank, Jr. · a · Choate, Hall & Stewart · http://www.choate.com · Two International Place · Boston, MA 02110 · 617-248-5000

John A.D. Gilmore · DLA Piper · 33 Arch Street, 26th Floor · Boston, MA 02110-1447 · 617-406-6000

Daniel J. Gleason · a · Nutter McClennen & Fish · http://www.nutter.com · World Trade Center West · 155 Seaport Boulevard · Boston, MA 02210 · 617-439-2000

Daniel L. Goldberg · Bingham McCutchen · http://www.bingham.com · One Federal Street · Boston, MA 02110-1726 · 617-951-8000

Michael S. Greco · K&L Gates · State Street Financial Center · One Lincoln Street · Boston, MA 02111-2950 · 617-261-3100

John D. Hanify · a · Hanify & King · One Beacon Street, 21st Floor · Boston, MA 02108-3107 · 617-423-0400

Michell H. Kaplan · Choate, Hall & Stewart · http://www.choate.com · Two International Place · Boston, MA 02110 · 617-248-5000

Michael B. Keating · 2) · Foley Hoag · http://www.foleyhoag.com · Seaport World Trade Center West · 155 Seaport Boulevard · Boston, MA 02210-2600 · 617-832-1000

Dennis J. Kelly · Burns & Levinson · http://www.burnslev.com · 125 Summer Street · Boston, MA 02110-1624 · 617-345-3000

Michael D. Kendall · McDermott Will & Emery · 28 State Street, 34th Floor · Boston, MA 02109-1775 · 617-535-4000

Joseph L. Kociubes · a · Bingham McCutchen · http://www.bingham.com · One Federal Street · Boston, MA 02110-1726 · 617-951-8000

Joel A. Kozol · 2) · Friedman & Atherton · 53 State Street, Second Floor · Boston, MA 02109 · 617-227-5540

William F. Lee · a · WilmerHale · http://www.wilmerhale.com · 60 State Street · Boston, MA 02109 · 617-526-6000

Edward P. Leibensperger · a · McDermott Will & Emery · 28 State Street, 34th Floor · Boston, MA 02109-1775 · 617-535-4000

Natasha C. Lisman · Sugarman, Rogers, Barshak & Cohen · http://www.srbc.com · 101 Merrimac Street, Ninth Floor · Boston, MA 02114-4737 · 617-227-3030

William F. Looney, Jr. · a · Looney & Grossman · 101 Arch Street, Ninth Floor · Boston, MA 02110 · 617-951-2800

Joan A. Lukey · a · Ropes & Gray · http://www.ropesgray.com · One International Place · Boston, MA 02110-2624 · 617-951-7000

Gael Mahony · ㉕ · Holland & Knight · http://www.hklaw.com · 10 Saint James Avenue, 11th Floor · Boston, MA 02116 · 617-523-2700

Ieuan G. Mahony · Holland & Knight · http://www.hklaw.com · 10 Saint James Avenue, 11th Floor · Boston, MA 02116 · 617-523-2700

William A. McCormack · ⑩ · Sally & Fitch · One Beacon Street · Boston, MA 02108 · 617-542-5542

John T. Montgomery · Ropes & Gray · http://www.ropesgray.com · One International Place · Boston, MA 02110-2624 · 617-951-7000

George Marshall Moriarty · ⑩ · Ropes & Gray · http://www.ropesgray.com · One International Place · Boston, MA 02110-2624 · 617-951-7000

Robert J. Muldoon, Jr. · ⑳ · Sherin and Lodgen · 101 Federal Street · Boston, MA 02110 · 617-646-2000

John A. Nadas · Choate, Hall & Stewart · http://www.choate.com · Two International Place · Boston, MA 02110 · 617-248-5000

Brien T. O'Connor · Ropes & Gray · http://www.ropesgray.com · One International Place · Boston, MA 02110-2624 · 617-951-7000

A. John Pappalardo · Greenberg Traurig · http://www.gtlaw.com · One International Place · Boston, MA 02110 · 617-310-6000

Kenneth J. Parsigian · Goodwin Procter · Exchange Place · 53 State Street · Boston, MA 02109-2881 · 617-570-1000

Mark W. Pearlstein · McDermott Will & Emery · 28 State Street, 34th Floor · Boston, MA 02109-1775 · 617-535-4000

R. Robert Popeo · ⑳ · Mintz, Levin, Cohn, Ferris, Glovsky and Popeo · One Financial Center, 40th Floor · Boston, MA 02111 · 617-542-6000

Alan K. Posner · Rubin and Rudman · 50 Rowes Wharf · Boston, MA 02110-3319 · 617-330-7000

M. Frederick Pritzker · ⑩ · Brown Rudnick · http://www.brbilaw.com · One Financial Center · Boston, MA 02111 · 617-856-8200

Richard W. Renehan · ㉕ · Goulston & Storrs · 400 Atlantic Avenue · Boston, MA 02110-3333 · 617-482-1776

Alan D. Rose, Sr. · ⑩ · Rose, Chinitz & Rose · http://www.rose-law.net · One Beacon Street, Fourth Floor · Boston, MA 02108 · 617-536-0040

Jeffrey B. Rudman · ⑳ · WilmerHale · http://www.wilmerhale.com · 60 State Street · Boston, MA 02109 · 617-526-6000

Thomas J. Sartory · ⑳ · Goulston & Storrs · 400 Atlantic Avenue · Boston, MA 02110-3333 · 617-482-1776

Joseph F. Savage, Jr. · Goodwin Procter · Exchange Place · 53 State Street · Boston, MA 02109-2881 · 617-570-1000

A. Hugh Scott · Choate, Hall & Stewart · http://www.choate.com · Two International Place · Boston, MA 02110 · 617-248-5000

Bruce Singal · Donoghue, Barrett & Singal · http://www.dbslawfirm.com · One Beacon Street · Boston, MA 02108-3113 · 617-720-5090

James D. Smeallie · Holland & Knight · http://www.hklaw.com · 10 Saint James Avenue, 11th Floor · Boston, MA 02116 · 617-523-2700

Joseph D. Steinfield · 2) · Prince, Lobel, Glovsky & Tye · http://www.princelobel.com · 100 Cambridge Street, Suite 2200 · Boston, MA 02114 · 617-456-8000

Donald K. Stern · Cooley Godward Kronish · The Prudential Tower, 46th Floor · 800 Boylston Street · Boston, MA 02199 · 617-937-2300

Robert E. Sullivan · a · Sullivan, Weinstein & McQuay · Two Park Plaza, Suite 610 · Boston, MA 02116-3902 · 617-348-4300

Jeffrey Swope · Edwards Angell Palmer & Dodge · Prudential Center · 111 Huntington Avenue · Boston, MA 02199-7613 · 617-239-0100

J. Owen Todd · 2% · Todd & Weld · http://www.toddweld.com · 28 State Street, 31st Floor · Boston, MA 02109 · 617-720-2626

Roscoe Trimmier, Jr. · Ropes & Gray · http://www.ropesgray.com · One International Place · Boston, MA 02110-2624 · 617-951-7000

Michael J. Tuteur · Foley & Lardner · 111 Huntington Avenue · Boston, MA 02199 · 617-342-4000

Paul F. Ware, Jr. · a · Goodwin Procter · Exchange Place · 53 State Street · Boston, MA 02109-2881 · 617-570-1000

Harvey J. Wolkoff · Ropes & Gray · http://www.ropesgray.com · One International Place · Boston, MA 02110-2624 · 617-951-7000

Richard M. Zielinski · Goulston & Storrs · 400 Atlantic Avenue · Boston, MA 02110-3333 · 617-482-1776

Cambridge

Scott P. Lewis · Anderson & Kreiger · One Canal Park, Suite 200 · Cambridge, MA 02141 · 617-621-6500

Springfield

Charles K. Bergin, Jr. · a · Charles K. Bergin, Jr. · 73 Chestnut Street · Springfield, MA 01103 · 413-739-0333

Francis D. Dibble, Jr. · a · Bulkley, Richardson and Gelinas · 1500 Main Street, Suite 2700 · P.O. Box 15507 · Springfield, MA 01115-5507 · 413-781-2820

Kevin C. Maynard · Bulkley, Richardson and Gelinas · 1500 Main Street, Suite 2700 · P.O. Box 15507 · Springfield, MA 01115-5507 · 413-781-2820

Paul Peter Nicolai · Nicolai Law Group · http://www.niclawgrp.com · Tarbell-Watters Building · 146 Chestnut Street · Springfield, MA 01103-1539 · 413-272-2000

Worcester

Michael P. Angelini · 2) · Bowditch & Dewey · 311 Main Street · P.O. Box 15156 · Worcester, MA 01615-0156 · 508-791-3511

Roy A. Bourgeois · Bourgeois, Dresser, White & Beard · Four Dix Street · Worcester, MA 01609 · 508-798-8801

Burton Chandler · a · Seder & Chandler · Burnside Building · 339 Main Street · Worcester, MA 01608-1585 · 508-757-7721

John O. Mirick · a · Mirick O'Connell DeMallie & Lougee · 100 Front Street, Suite 1700 · Worcester, MA 01608-1477 · 508-791-8500

Vincent F. O'Rourke, Jr. · a · Bowditch & Dewey · 311 Main Street · P.O. Box 15156 · Worcester, MA 01615-0156 · 508-791-3511

Seymour Weinstein · 2) · Weinstein & Weinstein · 10 Mechanic Street, Suite 300 · Worcester, MA 01608 508-757-7000

COMMUNICATIONS LAW

Boston

Robert A. Bertsche · Prince, Lobel, Glovsky & Tye · http://www.princelobel.com · 100 Cambridge Street, Suite 2200 · Boston, MA 02114 · 617-456-8000

CONSTRUCTION LAW

Boston

Loring A. Cook III · Murtha Cullina · 99 High Street, 20th Floor · Boston, MA 02110 · 617-457-4000

David J. Hatem · Donovan Hatem · World Trade Center East · Two Seaport Lane · Boston, MA 02210 · 617-406-4500

Robert J. Kaler · McCarter & English · 265 Franklin Street · Boston, MA 02110 · 617-449-6500

Joel Lewin · Hinckley, Allen & Snyder · http://www.haslaw.com · 28 State Street, 29th Floor · Boston, MA 02109-1775 · 617-345-9000

Stanley A. Martin · Holland & Knight · http://www.hklaw.com · 10 Saint James Avenue, 11th Floor · Boston, MA 02116 · 617-523-2700

James J. Myers · McCarter & English · 265 Franklin Street · Boston, MA 02110 · 617-449-6500

M. Frederick Pritzker · a · Brown Rudnick · http://www.brbilaw.com · One Financial Center · Boston, MA 02111 · 617-856-8200

Charles E. Schaub, Jr. · Hinckley, Allen & Snyder · http://www.haslaw.com · 28 State Street, 29th Floor · Boston, MA 02109-1775 · 617-345-9000

William G. Southard · Bingham McCutchen · http://www.bingham.com · One Federal Street · Boston, MA 02110-1726 · 617-951-8000

Springfield

Daniel J. Finnegan · Bulkley, Richardson and Gelinas · 1500 Main Street, Suite 2700 · P.O. Box 15507 · Springfield, MA 01115-5507 · 413-781-2820

Worcester

Burton Chandler · a · Seder & Chandler · Burnside Building · 339 Main Street · Worcester, MA 01608-1585 · 508-757-7721

CORPORATE GOVERNANCE AND COMPLIANCE LAW

Boston

William B. Asher, Jr. · a · Choate, Hall & Stewart · http://www.choate.com · Two International Place · Boston, MA 02110 · 617-248-5000

Harvey E. Bines · Sullivan & Worcester · One Post Office Square · Boston, MA 02109 · 617-338-2800

Mark G. Borden · a · WilmerHale · http://www.wilmerhale.com · 60 State Street · Boston, MA 02109 · 617-526-6000

R. Jack Cinquegrana · Choate, Hall & Stewart · http://www.choate.com · Two International Place · Boston, MA 02110 · 617-248-5000

Matthew J. Gardella · Edwards Angell Palmer & Dodge · Prudential Center · 111 Huntington Avenue · Boston, MA 02199-7613 · 617-239-0100

Stanley Keller · 2) · Edwards Angell Palmer & Dodge · Prudential Center · 111 Huntington Avenue · Boston, MA 02199-7613 · 617-239-0100

Alexander A. Notopoulos · Sullivan & Worcester · One Post Office Square · Boston, MA 02109 · 617-338-2800

Robert L. Nutt · 2) · Ropes & Gray · http://www.ropesgray.com · One International Place · Boston, MA 02110-2624 · 617-951-7000

Brian E. Pastuszenski · Goodwin Procter · Exchange Place · 53 State Street · Boston, MA 02109-2881 · 617-570-1000

Jonathan Wolfman · WilmerHale · http://www.wilmerhale.com · 60 State Street · Boston, MA 02109 · 617-526-6000

CORPORATE LAW

Boston

Constantine Alexander · 2) · Nutter McClennen & Fish · http://www.nutter.com · World Trade Center West · 155 Seaport Boulevard · Boston, MA 02210 · 617-439-2000

William B. Asher, Jr. · a · Choate, Hall & Stewart · http://www.choate.com · Two International Place · Boston, MA 02110 · 617-248-5000

Mitchell S. Bloom · Goodwin Procter · Exchange Place · 53 State Street · Boston, MA 02109-2881 · 617-570-1000

Mark G. Borden · a · WilmerHale · http://www.wilmerhale.com · 60 State Street · Boston, MA 02109 · 617-526-6000

Johan V. Brigham · Bingham McCutchen · http://www.bingham.com · One Federal Street · Boston, MA 02110-1726 · 617-951-8000

James R. Burke · WilmerHale · http://www.wilmerhale.com · 60 State Street · Boston, MA 02109 · 617-526-6000

Mark H. Burnett · Goodwin Procter · Exchange Place · 53 State Street · Boston, MA 02109-2881 · 617-570-1000

Stuart M. Cable · Goodwin Procter · Exchange Place · 53 State Street · Boston, MA 02109-2881 · 617-570-1000

David C. Chapin · Ropes & Gray · http://www.ropesgray.com · One International Place · Boston, MA 02110-2624 · 617-951-7000

Peter W. Coogan · a · Foley Hoag · http://www.foleyhoag.com · Seaport World Trade Center West · 155 Seaport Boulevard · Boston, MA 02210-2600 · 617-832-1000

William J. Curry · Sullivan & Worcester · One Post Office Square · Boston, MA 02109 · 617-338-2800

Roslyn G. Daum · a · Choate, Hall & Stewart · http://www.choate.com · Two International Place · Boston, MA 02110 · 617-248-5000

James E. Dawson · Nutter McClennen & Fish · http://www.nutter.com · World Trade Center West · 155 Seaport Boulevard · Boston, MA 02210 · 617-439-2000

John J. Egan III · Goodwin Procter · Exchange Place · 53 State Street · Boston, MA 02109-2881 · 617-570-1000

Roger D. Feldman · Fish & Richardson · 225 Franklin Street · Boston, MA 02110-2804 · 617-542-5070

Matthew J. Gardella · Edwards Angell Palmer & Dodge · Prudential Center · 111 Huntington Avenue · Boston, MA 02199-7613 · 617-239-0100

Louis A. Goodman · Skadden, Arps, Slate, Meagher & Flom · One Beacon Street · Boston, MA 02108-3194 · 617-573-4800

Kenneth J. Gordon · Goodwin Procter · Exchange Place · 53 State Street · Boston, MA 02109-2881 · 617-570-1000

Keith F. Higgins · a · Ropes & Gray · http://www.ropesgray.com · One International Place · Boston, MA 02110-2624 · 617-951-7000

Laura Hodges Taylor · a · Goodwin Procter · Exchange Place · 53 State Street · Boston, MA 02109-2881 617-570-1000

Robert V. Jahrling III · Choate, Hall & Stewart · http://www.choate.com · Two International Place · Boston, MA 02110 · 617-248-5000

Virginia Kapner · Virginia Kapner · 711 Bolyston Street · Boston, MA 02116 · 617-233-8839

Stanley Keller · 2) · Edwards Angell Palmer & Dodge · Prudential Center · 111 Huntington Avenue · Boston, MA 02199-7613 · 617-239-0100

Michael J. Kendall · Goodwin Procter · Exchange Place · 53 State Street · Boston, MA 02109-2881 · 617-570-1000

William R. Kolb · Foley Hoag · http://www.foleyhoag.com · Seaport World Trade Center West · 155 Seaport Boulevard · Boston, MA 02210-2600 · 617-832-1000

John R. LeClaire · Goodwin Procter · Exchange Place · 53 State Street · Boston, MA 02109-2881 · 617-570-1000

Brian P. Lenihan · Choate, Hall & Stewart · http://www.choate.com · Two International Place · Boston, MA 02110 · 617-248-5000

Mark J. Macenka · Goodwin Procter · Exchange Place · 53 State Street · Boston, MA 02109-2881 · 617-570-1000

R. Bradford Malt · a · Ropes & Gray · http://www.ropesgray.com · One International Place · Boston, MA 02110-2624 · 617-951-7000

Anthony J. Medaglia, Jr. · 2% · Goodwin Procter · Exchange Place · 53 State Street · Boston, MA 02109-2881 · 617-570-1000

Gilbert G. Menna · a · Goodwin Procter · Exchange Place · 53 State Street · Boston, MA 02109-2881 · 617-570-1000

Stephen O. Meredith · Edwards Angell Palmer & Dodge · Prudential Center · 111 Huntington Avenue · Boston, MA 02199-7613 · 617-239-0100

John M. Mutkoski · Goodwin Procter · Exchange Place · 53 State Street · Boston, MA 02109-2881 · 617-570-1000

Alexander A. Notopoulos · Sullivan & Worcester · One Post Office Square · Boston, MA 02109 · 617-338-2800

Robert L. Nutt · 2) · Ropes & Gray · http://www.ropesgray.com · One International Place · Boston, MA 02110-2624 · 617-951-7000

Robin A. Painter · Proskauer Rose · http://www.proskauer.com · One International Place · Boston, MA 02110-2600 · 617-526-9600

Regina M. Pisa · a · Goodwin Procter · Exchange Place · 53 State Street · Boston, MA 02109-2881 · 617-570-1000

James Pollock · Holland & Knight · http://www.hklaw.com · 10 Saint James Avenue, 11th Floor · Boston, MA 02116 · 617-523-2700

David E. Redlick · a · WilmerHale · http://www.wilmerhale.com · 60 State Street · Boston, MA 02109 · 617-526-6000

Patrick J. Rondeau · WilmerHale · http://www.wilmerhale.com · 60 State Street · Boston, MA 02109 · 617-526-6000

Peter M. Rosenblum · a · Foley Hoag · http://www.foleyhoag.com · Seaport World Trade Center West · 155 Seaport Boulevard · Boston, MA 02210-2600 · 617-832-1000

Ettore A. Santucci · Goodwin Procter · Exchange Place · 53 State Street · Boston, MA 02109-2881 · 617-570-1000

William J. Schnoor, Jr. · Goodwin Procter · Exchange Place · 53 State Street · Boston, MA 02109-2881 · 617-570-1000

Steven D. Singer · WilmerHale · http://www.wilmerhale.com · 60 State Street · Boston, MA 02109 · 617-526-6000

Edwin E. Smith · a · Bingham McCutchen · http://www.bingham.com · One Federal Street · Boston, MA 02110-1726 · 617-951-8000

R. Newcomb Stillwell · Ropes & Gray · http://www.ropesgray.com · One International Place · Boston, MA 02110-2624 · 617-951-7000

H. Lawrence Tafe III · Day Pitney · One International Place, 17th Floor · Boston, MA 02110-3179 · 617-345-4600

George W. Thibeault · 2) · Law Office of George W. Thibeault · 125 High Street · Boston, MA 02100 · 617-248-7520

George Ticknor · Edwards Angell Palmer & Dodge · Prudential Center · 111 Huntington Avenue · Boston, MA 02199-7613 · 617-239-0100

John R. Utzschneider · Bingham McCutchen · http://www.bingham.com · One Federal Street · Boston, MA 02110-1726 · 617-951-8000

David W. Watson · Goodwin Procter · Exchange Place · 53 State Street · Boston, MA 02109-2881 · 617-570-1000

Mary E. Weber · Ropes & Gray · http://www.ropesgray.com · One International Place · Boston, MA 02110-2624 · 617-951-7000

David A. Westenberg · WilmerHale · http://www.wilmerhale.com · 60 State Street · Boston, MA 02109 · 617-526-6000

James R. Westra · Weil Gotshal & Manges · 100 Federal Street, 34th Floor · Boston, MA 02110 · 617-772-8300

Jeffrey M. Wiesen · Mintz, Levin, Cohn, Ferris, Glovsky and Popeo · One Financial Center, 40th Floor · Boston, MA 02111 · 617-542-6000

Springfield

Mark D. Cress · Bulkley, Richardson and Gelinas · 1500 Main Street, Suite 2700 · P.O. Box 15507 · Springfield, MA 01115-5507 · 413-781-2820

Paul S. Doherty · 2) · Doherty, Wallace, Pillsbury and Murphy · One Monarch Place, Suite 1900 · 1414 Main Street · Springfield, MA 01144-1900 · 413-733-3111

Richard M. Gaberman · a · Robinson Donovan · http://www.robinson-donovan.com · 1500 Main Street, Suite 1600 · P.O. Box 15609 · Springfield, MA 01115 · 413-732-2301

Timothy P. Mulhern · Shatz, Schwartz and Fentin · 1441 Main Street, Suite 1100 · Springfield, MA 01103 · 413-737-1131

David A. Parke · Bulkley, Richardson and Gelinas · 1500 Main Street, Suite 2700 · P.O. Box 15507 · Springfield, MA 01115-5507 · 413-781-2820

Jeffrey W. Roberts · a · Robinson Donovan · http://www.robinson-donovan.com · 1500 Main Street, Suite 1600 · P.O. Box 15609 · Springfield, MA 01115 · 413-732-2301

Stephen A. Shatz · a · Shatz, Schwartz and Fentin · 1441 Main Street, Suite 1100 · Springfield, MA 01103 · 413-737-1131

Ronald P. Weiss · a · Bulkley, Richardson and Gelinas · 1500 Main Street, Suite 2700 · P.O. Box 15507 · Springfield, MA 01115-5507 · 413-781-2820

Waltham

John H. Chory · WilmerHale · http://www.wilmerhale.com · Bay Colony Corporate Center · 1100 Winter Street · Waltham, MA 02451 · 781-966-2000

Worcester

Michael P. Angelini · 2) · Bowditch & Dewey · 311 Main Street · P.O. Box 15156 · Worcester, MA 01615-0156 · 508-791-3511

Henry W. Beth · Mountain, Dearborn & Whiting · 370 Main Street, Eighth Floor · Worcester, MA 01608-1778 · 508-756-2423

Burton Chandler · ⑩ · Seder & Chandler · Burnside Building · 339 Main Street · Worcester, MA 01608-1585 · 508-757-7721

Phillips S. Davis · ⑳ · Fletcher, Tilton & Whipple · http://www.ftwlaw.com · 370 Main Street, 12th Floor Worcester, MA 01608-1779 · 508-459-8000

Robert P. Lombardi · ⑩ · Mirick O'Connell DeMallie & Lougee · 100 Front Street, Suite 1700 · Worcester, MA 01608-1477 · 508-791-8500

David L. Lougee · ⑳ · Mirick O'Connell DeMallie & Lougee · 100 Front Street, Suite 1700 · Worcester, MA 01608-1477 · 508-791-8500

Robert J. Martin · ⑩ · Mirick O'Connell DeMallie & Lougee · 100 Front Street, Suite 1700 · Worcester, MA 01608-1477 · 508-791-8500

Dennis Pojani · Pojani Hurley Ritter & Salvidio · 446 Main Street, 21st Floor · Worcester, MA 01608 · 508-798-2480

J. Robert Seder · ⑳ · Seder & Chandler · Burnside Building · 339 Main Street · Worcester, MA 01608-1585 · 508-757-7721

David E. Surprenant · ⑩ · Mirick O'Connell DeMallie & Lougee · 100 Front Street, Suite 1700 · Worcester, MA 01608-1477 · 508-791-8500

EDUCATION LAW

Boston

Paul G. Lannon, Jr. · Holland & Knight · http://www.hklaw.com · 10 Saint James Avenue, 11th Floor · Boston, MA 02116 · 617-523-2700

Daryl J. Lapp · Edwards Angell Palmer & Dodge · Prudential Center · 111 Huntington Avenue · Boston, MA 02199-7613 · 617-239-0100

Miriam J. McKendall · Holland & Knight · http://www.hklaw.com · 10 Saint James Avenue, 11th Floor · Boston, MA 02116 · 617-523-2700

Harold W. Potter, Jr. · Holland & Knight · http://www.hklaw.com · 10 Saint James Avenue, 11th Floor · Boston, MA 02116 · 617-523-2700

Alan D. Rose, Sr. · ⑩ · Rose, Chinitz & Rose · http://www.rose-law.net · One Beacon Street, Fourth Floor · Boston, MA 02108 · 617-536-0040

James D. Smeallie · Holland & Knight · http://www.hklaw.com · 10 Saint James Avenue, 11th Floor · Boston, MA 02116 · 617-523-2700

Jeffrey Swope · Edwards Angell Palmer & Dodge · Prudential Center · 111 Huntington Avenue · Boston, MA 02199-7613 · 617-239-0100

Richard J. Yurko · Yurko, Salvesen & Remz · One Washington Mall, 11th Floor · Boston, MA 02108-2603 · 617-723-6900

Framingham

Mary T. Feeney · Bowditch & Dewey · 175 Crossing Boulevard, Suite 500 · Framingham, MA 01702 · 508-879-5700

Worcester

Vincent F. O'Rourke, Jr. · a · Bowditch & Dewey · 311 Main Street · P.O. Box 15156 · Worcester, MA 01615-0156 · 508-791-3511

ELDER LAW

Fitchburg

Emily S. Starr · Ciota, Starr & Vander Linden · 625 Main Street · Fitchburg, MA 01420 · 978-345-6791

Newton

Donald N. Freedman · Rosenberg, Freedman & Goldstein · 246 Walnut Street · Newton, MA 02460-6734 · 617-964-7000

Susan H. Levin · Rosenberg, Freedman & Goldstein · 246 Walnut Street · Newton, MA 02460-6734 · 617-964-7000

Springfield

Carol C. Klyman · Shatz, Schwartz and Fentin · 1441 Main Street, Suite 1100 · Springfield, MA 01103 · 413-737-1131

Ronda G. Parish · Robinson Donovan · http://www.robinson-donovan.com · 1500 Main Street, Suite 1600 P.O. Box 15609 · Springfield, MA 01115 · 413-732-2301

Ann I. Weber · Shatz, Schwartz and Fentin · 1441 Main Street, Suite 1100 · Springfield, MA 01103 · 413-737-1131

EMINENT DOMAIN AND CONDEMNATION LAW

Boston

Mark S. Bourbeau · Bourbeau & Associates · 266 Beacon Street · Boston, MA 02116 · 617-536-9695

Ernest P. DeSimone · Lynch DeSimone & Nylen · 12 Post Office Square, Sixth Floor · Boston, MA 02109 · 617-348-4500

John S. Leonard · Menard, Murphy & Walsh · 60 State Street, 34th Floor · Boston, MA 02109 · 617-832-2500

James D. Masterman · Greenberg Traurig · http://www.gtlaw.com · One International Place · Boston, MA 02110 · 617-310-6000

George A. McLaughlin III · a · The McLaughlin Brothers · One Beacon Street, 17th Floor · Boston, MA 02108 · 617-523-7165

Stephen H. Oleskey · WilmerHale · http://www.wilmerhale.com · 60 State Street · Boston, MA 02109 · 617-526-6000

J. Owen Todd · 2% · Todd & Weld · http://www.toddweld.com · 28 State Street, 31st Floor · Boston, MA 02109 · 617-720-2626

Neal C. Tully · Masterman, Culbert & Tully · One Lewis Wharf · Boston, MA 02110 · 617-227-8010

Eric L. Wodlinger · Rackemann, Sawyer & Brewster · http://www.rackemann.com · 160 Federal Street, 13th-15th Floor · Boston, MA 02110-1700 · 617-542-2300

Saugus

Peter E. Flynn · The Law Offices of Peter E. Flynn · 78 Essex Street · Saugus, MA 01906-4312 · 781-233-2284

EMPLOYEE BENEFITS LAW

Boston

Alden J. Bianchi · a · Mintz, Levin, Cohn, Ferris, Glovsky and Popeo · One Financial Center, 40th Floor Boston, MA 02111 · 617-542-6000

Carol C. Brown · Parker Brown & Macaulay · Four Faneuil Hall Marketplace · Boston, MA 02109 · 617-350-7701

John J. Cleary · 2) · Goodwin Procter · Exchange Place · 53 State Street · Boston, MA 02109-2881 · 617-570-1000

Daniel P. Condon · a · Goodwin Procter · Exchange Place · 53 State Street · Boston, MA 02109-2881 · 617-570-1000

Russell A. Gaudreau, Jr. · 2) · Ropes & Gray · http://www.ropesgray.com · One International Place · Boston, MA 02110-2624 · 617-951-7000

Natascha S. George · Bingham McCutchen · http://www.bingham.com · One Federal Street · Boston, MA 02110-1726 · 617-951-8000

Richard M. Harter · 2) · Bingham McCutchen · http://www.bingham.com · One Federal Street · Boston, MA 02110-1726 · 617-951-8000

Joseph A. Hugg · DLA Piper · 33 Arch Street, 26th Floor · Boston, MA 02110-1447 · 617-406-6000

Russell E. Isaia · Bingham McCutchen · http://www.bingham.com · One Federal Street · Boston, MA 02110-1726 · 617-951-8000

Robert Macaulay, Jr. · Parker Brown & Macaulay · Four Faneuil Hall Marketplace · Boston, MA 02109 · 617-350-7701

Peter J. Marathas · Proskauer Rose · http://www.proskauer.com · One International Place · Boston, MA 02110-2600 · 617-526-9600

R. Hardin Matthews · a · Ropes & Gray · http://www.ropesgray.com · One International Place · Boston, MA 02110-2624 · 617-951-7000

Arthur S. Meyers · Seyfarth Shaw · World Trade Center East, Suite 300 · Two Seaport Lane · Boston, MA 02210-2028 · 617-946-4800

Wayne H. Miller · a · Goulston & Storrs · 400 Atlantic Avenue · Boston, MA 02110-3333 · 617-482-1776

C. Stephen Parker, Jr. · a · Parker Brown & Macaulay · Four Faneuil Hall Marketplace · Boston, MA 02109 · 617-350-7701

David L. Raish · 2) · Ropes & Gray · http://www.ropesgray.com · One International Place · Boston, MA 02110-2624 · 617-951-7000

Loretta R. Richard · Ropes & Gray · http://www.ropesgray.com · One International Place · Boston, MA 02110-2624 · 617-951-7000

Peter N. Rosenberg · Ropes & Gray · http://www.ropesgray.com · One International Place · Boston, MA 02110-2624 · 617-951-7000

M. James Shumaker · a · Choate, Hall & Stewart · http://www.choate.com · Two International Place · Boston, MA 02110 · 617-248-5000

Leslie Crane Slavin · Lourie & Cutler · 60 State Street, Ninth Floor · Boston, MA 02109 · 617-742-6720

Marian A. Tse · a · Goodwin Procter · Exchange Place · 53 State Street · Boston, MA 02109-2881 · 617-570-1000

Marcia S. Wagner · a · The Wagner Law Group · 99 Summer Street, 13th Floor · Boston, MA 02110 · 617-357-5200

Springfield

Ronda G. Parish · Robinson Donovan · http://www.robinson-donovan.com · 1500 Main Street, Suite 1600 P.O. Box 15609 · Springfield, MA 01115 · 413-732-2301

Melissa M. Shea · Sullivan, Hayes & Quinn · One Monarch Place, Suite 1200 · Springfield, MA 01144 · 413-736-4538

ENERGY LAW

Boston

John A. DeTore · a · Rubin and Rudman · 50 Rowes Wharf · Boston, MA 02110-3319 · 617-330-7000

Mary Beth Gentleman · a · Foley Hoag · http://www.foleyhoag.com · Seaport World Trade Center West 155 Seaport Boulevard · Boston, MA 02210-2600 · 617-832-1000

Jeffrey F. Jones · a · Edwards Angell Palmer & Dodge · Prudential Center · 111 Huntington Avenue · Boston, MA 02199-7613 · 617-239-0100

Robert J. Keegan · a · Keegan Werlin · 265 Franklin Street · Boston, MA 02110-3113 · 617-951-1400

E. Randolph Tucker · DLA Piper · 33 Arch Street, 26th Floor · Boston, MA 02110-1447 · 617-406-6000

ENTERTAINMENT LAW

Boston

Mark A. Fischer · a · Fish & Richardson · 225 Franklin Street · Boston, MA 02110-2804 · 617-542-5070

John Taylor Williams · a · Fish & Richardson · 225 Franklin Street · Boston, MA 02110-2804 · 617-542-5070

Boston

Ned Abelson · Goulston & Storrs · 400 Atlantic Avenue · Boston, MA 02110-3333 · 617-482-1776

Jeffrey C. Bates · McDermott Will & Emery · 28 State Street, 34th Floor · Boston, MA 02109-1775 · 617-535-4000

Gregory A. Bibler · Goodwin Procter · Exchange Place · 53 State Street · Boston, MA 02109-2881 · 617-570-1000

Susan M. Cooke · 2) · McDermott Will & Emery · 28 State Street, 34th Floor · Boston, MA 02109-1775 · 617-535-4000

Donald D. Cooper · Nixon Peabody · 100 Summer Street · Boston, MA 02110-1832 · 617-345-1000

Christopher P. Davis · a · Goodwin Procter · Exchange Place · 53 State Street · Boston, MA 02109-2881 617-570-1000

Jonathan M. Ettinger · Foley Hoag · http://www.foleyhoag.com · Seaport World Trade Center West · 155 Seaport Boulevard · Boston, MA 02210-2600 · 617-832-1000

Lisa C. Goodheart · Sugarman, Rogers, Barshak & Cohen · http://www.srbc.com · 101 Merrimac Street, Ninth Floor · Boston, MA 02114-4737 · 617-227-3030

H. Hamilton Hackney III · Greenberg Traurig · http://www.gtlaw.com · One International Place · Boston, MA 02110 · 617-310-6000

Martin R. Healy · a · Goodwin Procter · Exchange Place · 53 State Street · Boston, MA 02109-2881 · 617-570-1000

Seth D. Jaffe · Foley Hoag · http://www.foleyhoag.com · Seaport World Trade Center West · 155 Seaport Boulevard · Boston, MA 02210-2600 · 617-832-1000

Adam P. Kahn · Foley Hoag · http://www.foleyhoag.com · Seaport World Trade Center West · 155 Seaport Boulevard · Boston, MA 02210-2600 · 617-832-1000

Robert C. Kirsch · WilmerHale · http://www.wilmerhale.com · 60 State Street · Boston, MA 02109 · 617-526-6000

Michael P. Last · 2) · Rackemann, Sawyer & Brewster · http://www.rackemann.com · 160 Federal Street, 13th-15th Floor · Boston, MA 02110-1700 · 617-542-2300

Michael A. Leon · Nutter McClennen & Fish · http://www.nutter.com · World Trade Center West · 155 Seaport Boulevard · Boston, MA 02210 · 617-439-2000

Stephen M. Leonard · Brown Rudnick · http://www.brbilaw.com · One Financial Center · Boston, MA 02111 · 617-856-8200

Thomas A. Mackie · Mackie Shea O'Brien · 137 Newbury Street, Sixth Floor · Boston, MA 02116 · 617-266-5700

Michelle N. O'Brien · Mackie Shea O'Brien · 137 Newbury Street, Sixth Floor · Boston, MA 02116 · 617-266-5700

Jonathan Z. Pearlson · Goulston & Storrs · 400 Atlantic Avenue · Boston, MA 02110-3333 · 617-482-1776

Martin C. Pentz · a · Foley Hoag · http://www.foleyhoag.com · Seaport World Trade Center West · 155 Seaport Boulevard · Boston, MA 02210-2600 · 617-832-1000

Jeffrey R. Porter · Mintz, Levin, Cohn, Ferris, Glovsky and Popeo · One Financial Center, 40th Floor · Boston, MA 02111 · 617-542-6000

David P. Rosenblatt · a · Burns & Levinson · http://www.burnslev.com · 125 Summer Street · Boston, MA 02110-1624 · 617-345-3000

Mary K. Ryan · 2) · Nutter McClennen & Fish · http://www.nutter.com · World Trade Center West · 155 Seaport Boulevard · Boston, MA 02210 · 617-439-2000

Robert S. Sanoff · Foley Hoag · http://www.foleyhoag.com · Seaport World Trade Center West · 155 Seaport Boulevard · Boston, MA 02210-2600 · 617-832-1000

John F. Shea · Mackie Shea O'Brien · 137 Newbury Street, Sixth Floor · Boston, MA 02116 · 617-266-5700

Cambridge

Stephen D. Anderson · Anderson & Kreiger · One Canal Park, Suite 200 · Cambridge, MA 02141 · 617-621-6500

Donald L. Anglehart · Law Offices of Donald L. Anglehart · One Broadway, 14th Floor · Cambridge, MA 02142 · 617-401-3350

Wendy B. Jacobs · Harvard Law School · 1563 Massachusetts Avenue · Cambridge, MA 02138 · 617-495-3100

Arthur P. Kreiger · Anderson & Kreiger · One Canal Park, Suite 200 · Cambridge, MA 02141 · 617-621-6500

Framingham

Norman E. Bartlett II · Bowditch & Dewey · 175 Crossing Boulevard, Suite 500 · Framingham, MA 01702 · 508-879-5700

Lauren Stiller Rikleen · a · Bowditch & Dewey · 175 Crossing Boulevard, Suite 500 · Framingham, MA 01702 · 508-879-5700

Springfield

Christopher B. Myhrum · a · Bulkley, Richardson and Gelinas · 1500 Main Street, Suite 2700 · P.O. Box 15507 · Springfield, MA 01115-5507 · 413-781-2820

Worcester

Robert D. Cox, Jr. · Bowditch & Dewey · 311 Main Street · P.O. Box 15156 · Worcester, MA 01615-0156 508-791-3511

EQUIPMENT FINANCE LAW

Boston

Jonathan K. Bernstein · Bingham McCutchen · http://www.bingham.com · One Federal Street · Boston, MA 02110-1726 · 617-951-8000

Amy L. Kyle · Bingham McCutchen · http://www.bingham.com · One Federal Street · Boston, MA 02110-1726 · 617-951-8000

Robert L. Nutt · 2) · Ropes & Gray · http://www.ropesgray.com · One International Place · Boston, MA 02110-2624 · 617-951-7000

Philip R. Rosenblatt · Nutter McClennen & Fish · http://www.nutter.com · World Trade Center West · 155 Seaport Boulevard · Boston, MA 02210 · 617-439-2000

Richard S. Rosenstein · Nutter McClennen & Fish · http://www.nutter.com · World Trade Center West · 155 Seaport Boulevard · Boston, MA 02210 · 617-439-2000

Edwin E. Smith · a · Bingham McCutchen · http://www.bingham.com · One Federal Street · Boston, MA 02110-1726 · 617-951-8000

Philip J. Smith · Ropes & Gray · http://www.ropesgray.com · One International Place · Boston, MA 02110-2624 · 617-951-7000

FAMILY LAW

Amherst

Stephen B. Monsein · Bacon & Wilson · Six South East Street · P.O. Box 2060 · Amherst, MA 01004-2060 · 413-256-6701

Boston

Joan P. Armstrong · Murtha Cullina · 99 High Street, 20th Floor · Boston, MA 02110 · 617-457-4000

Jacob M. Atwood · a · Atwood & Cherny · http://www.atwoodcherny.com · 101 Huntington Avenue, 25th Floor · Boston, MA 02199 · 617-262-6400

Peter M. Barlow · Foley & Lardner · 111 Huntington Avenue · Boston, MA 02199 · 617-342-4000

Edward J. Barshak · 2% · Sugarman, Rogers, Barshak & Cohen · http://www.srbc.com · 101 Merrimac Street, Ninth Floor · Boston, MA 02114-4737 · 617-227-3030

Janice Bassil · Carney & Bassil · 20 Park Plaza, Suite 1405 · Boston, MA 02116 · 617-338-5566

Amy Lyn Blake · Casner & Edwards · http://www.casneredwards.com · 303 Congress Street · Boston, MA 02210 · 617-426-5900

David E. Cherny · a · Atwood & Cherny · http://www.atwoodcherny.com · 101 Huntington Avenue, 25th Floor · Boston, MA 02199 · 617-262-6400

Gene D. Dahmen · Verrill Dana · http://www.verrilldana.com · One Boston Place, Suite 2330 · Boston, MA 02108-4427 · 617-309-2600

James R. DeGiacomo · a · Murtha Cullina · 99 High Street, 20th Floor · Boston, MA 02110 · 617-457-4000

Anthony M. Doniger · Sugarman, Rogers, Barshak & Cohen · http://www.srbc.com · 101 Merrimac Street, Ninth Floor · Boston, MA 02114-4737 · 617-227-3030

Elaine M. Epstein · Todd & Weld · http://www.toddweld.com · 28 State Street, 31st Floor · Boston, MA 02109 · 617-720-2626

Phyllis E. Federico · Packenham, Schmidt & Federico · 10 Saint James Avenue, 16th Floor · Boston, MA 02116 · 617-695-0021

George M. Ford · 2% · Conn, Kavanaugh, Rosenthal, Peisch & Ford · 10 Post Office Square, Fourth Floor Boston, MA 02109 · 617-482-8200

Melanie J. Gargas · Gargas & Associates · 75 Federal Street, Second Floor · Boston, MA 02110 · 617-542-4200

Norman I. Jacobs · 2% · Esdaile, Barrett & Esdaile · 75 Federal Street, 16th Floor · Boston, MA 02110 · 617-482-0333

Paul M. Kane · 2) · McGrath & Kane · One Longfellow Place, Suite 3610 · Boston, MA 02114 · 617-523-5600

Haskell A. Kassler · 2% · Casner & Edwards · http://www.casneredwards.com · 303 Congress Street · Boston, MA 02210 · 617-426-5900

Robert J. Kates · 2) · Foley & Lardner · 111 Huntington Avenue · Boston, MA 02199 · 617-342-4000

David H. Lee · 2% · Lee & Levine · 222 Berkeley Street, Suite 1400 · Boston, MA 02116 · 617-266-6262

William M. Levine · a · Lee & Levine · 222 Berkeley Street, Suite 1400 · Boston, MA 02116 · 617-266-6262

Edward Malik · a · Malik & Cyr · 68 Commercial Wharf · Boston, MA 02110 · 617-367-0662

Robert F. McGrath · a · McGrath & Kane · One Longfellow Place, Suite 3610 · Boston, MA 02114 · 617-523-5600

Paul P. Perocchi · 2% · Brown Rudnick · http://www.brbilaw.com · One Financial Center · Boston, MA 02111 · 617-856-8200

Robert J. Rivers, Jr. · Lee & Levine · 222 Berkeley Street, Suite 1400 · Boston, MA 02116 · 617-266-6262

Steven J. Ryan · Witmer, Karp, Warner & Ryan · http://www.wkwrlaw.com · 22 Batterymarch Street · Boston, MA 02109 · 617-423-7250

Mark Smith · Atwood & Cherny · http://www.atwoodcherny.com · 101 Huntington Avenue, 25th Floor · Boston, MA 02199 · 617-262-6400

James Takacs · Casner & Edwards · http://www.casneredwards.com · 303 Congress Street · Boston, MA 02210 · 617-426-5900

Karen Tosh · a · Karen Tosh · 77 Franklin Street, Fourth Floor · Boston, MA 02110-1510 · 617-723-2525

Mark J. Warner · Witmer, Karp, Warner & Ryan · http://www.wkwrlaw.com · 22 Batterymarch Street · Boston, MA 02109 · 617-423-7250

Ronald A. Witmer · 2) · Witmer, Karp, Warner & Ryan · http://www.wkwrlaw.com · 22 Batterymarch Street · Boston, MA 02109 · 617-423-7250

Cambridge

Roberta F. Benjamin · a · Benjamin & Benson · Bulfinch Square · 43 Thorndike Street · Cambridge, MA 02141 · 617-577-1515

Danvers

Rudolf A. Jaworski · R. A. Jaworski · 317 Liberty Square · 10 Liberty Street · Danvers, MA 01923-2577 · 978-777-1010

Franklin

Paul A. Cataldo · ⓴ · Cataldo Law Offices · 1000 Franklin Village Drive · Franklin, MA 02038-4001 · 508-570-2062

Greenfield

Mark I. Berson · ❿ · Mark I. Berson · http://www.markiberson.com · One Federal Street, Second Floor · P.O. Box 1538 · Greenfield, MA 01302-1538 · 413-774-3741

Newton

Joanne E. Romanow · Schlesinger and Buchbinder · 1200 Walnut Street · Newton, MA 02461-1267 · 617-965-3500

North Andover

Patricia Fernandez · Patricia S. Fernandez · 510 Turnpike Street, Suite 203 · North Andover, MA 01845 978-681-5454

Joyce G. Perocchi · Perocchi Family Law Group · http://www.nalegal.com · 859 Turnpike Street, Suite 232 · North Andover, MA 01845 · 978-681-5665

Northampton

Merry L. Nasser · Lesser, Newman & Nasser · 39 Main Street, Suite Eight · Northampton, MA 01060 · 413-584-7331

Pittsfield

Diane M. DeGiacomo · Cain Hibbard Myers & Cook · 66 West Street · Pittsfield, MA 01201-5764 · 413-443-4771

Salem

John S. Legasey · ❿ · Legasey & Associates · http://www.legaseylaw.com · 100 Museum Place · Salem, MA 01970 · 978-745-6600

Springfield

Efrem A. Gordon · ⓴ · Efrem A. Gordon · 101 State Street, Suite 410 · Springfield, MA 01103 · 413-737-4316

Wellesley

Fern Frolin · Grindle, Robinson, Goodhue & Frolin · 40 Grove Street, Suite 190 · Wellesley, MA 02482-7708 · 781-235-3300

Steve Grindle · Grindle, Robinson, Goodhue & Frolin · 40 Grove Street, Suite 190 · Wellesley, MA 02482-7708 · 781-235-3300

Michael L. Leshin · Ginsburg & Leshin · http://www.glmediation.com · One Hollis Street, Suite 423 · Wellesley, MA 02482 · 781-235-3332

Williamstown

Bruce D. Grinnell · ⑩ · Grinnell & Smith · One Bank Street · P.O. Box 576 · Williamstown, MA 01267-0576 · 413-458-9601

FAMILY LAW MEDIATION

Amherst

Oran E. Kaufman · Amherst Mediation Services · 190 University Avenue · Amherst, MA 01002 · 413-253-3900

Boston

Charles J. Bowser, Jr. · ㉕ · Charles J. Bowser, Jr. · 95 Commercial Wharf · Boston, MA 02110 · 617-227-0146

David A. Hoffman · Boston Law Collaborative · 99 Summer Street, Suite 1600 · Boston, MA 02110 · 617-439-4700

Eileen M. Shaevel · Dispute Resolution Alternatives · Two Center Plaza, Suite 530 · Boston, MA 02108-1906 · 617-367-3998

Cambridge

John A. Fiske · Healy, Fiske, Richmond & Matthew · 189 Cambridge Street · Cambridge, MA 02141 · 617-354-7133

John A. Moos · Bowman, Moos, Elder & Noe · http://www.bmenlaw.com · 222 Third Street, Suite 3220 · Cambridge, MA 02142 · 617-494-8808

Philip D. Woodbury · Healy, Fiske, Richmond & Matthew · 189 Cambridge Street · Cambridge, MA 02141 · 617-354-7133

Centerville

Peter R. Hickey · Forman, Terry, Hickey & Garrahan · 1185 Falmouth Road · Centerville, MA 02632 · 508-771-3363

Chelmsford

Lynda J. Robbins · Lynda J. Robbins · 11 Summer Street · Chelmsford, MA 01824 · 978-256-8178

Springfield

Bruce D. Clarkin · Divorce Mediation Group · 1441 Main Street, Suite 806 · Springfield, MA 01103 · 413-733-4444

Kathleen A. Townsend · Divorce Mediation Group · 1441 Main Street, Suite 806 · Springfield, MA 01103 · 413-733-4444

Wellesley

Julie E. Ginsburg · Ginsburg & Leshin · http://www.glmediation.com · One Hollis Street, Suite 423 · Wellesley, MA 02482 · 781-235-3332

Michael L. Leshin · Ginsburg & Leshin · http://www.glmediation.com · One Hollis Street, Suite 423 · Wellesley, MA 02482 · 781-235-3332

FIRST AMENDMENT LAW

Boston

Jonathan M. Albano · a · Bingham McCutchen · http://www.bingham.com · One Federal Street · Boston, MA 02110-1726 · 617-951-8000

Robert A. Bertsche · Prince, Lobel, Glovsky & Tye · http://www.princelobel.com · 100 Cambridge Street, Suite 2200 · Boston, MA 02114 · 617-456-8000

Howard M. Cooper · Todd & Weld · http://www.toddweld.com · 28 State Street, 31st Floor · Boston, MA 02109 · 617-720-2626

Joseph L. Kociubes · a · Bingham McCutchen · http://www.bingham.com · One Federal Street · Boston, MA 02110-1726 · 617-951-8000

Evan T. Lawson · a · Lawson & Weitzen · http://www.lawson-weitzen.com · 88 Black Falcon Avenue · Boston, MA 02210 · 617-439-4990

Joan A. Lukey · a · Ropes & Gray · http://www.ropesgray.com · One International Place · Boston, MA 02110-2624 · 617-951-7000

Elizabeth A. Ritvo · Brown Rudnick · http://www.brbilaw.com · One Financial Center · Boston, MA 02111 · 617-856-8200

Joseph D. Steinfield · 2) · Prince, Lobel, Glovsky & Tye · http://www.princelobel.com · 100 Cambridge Street, Suite 2200 · Boston, MA 02114 · 617-456-8000

John Taylor Williams · a · Fish & Richardson · 225 Franklin Street · Boston, MA 02110-2804 · 617-542-5070

Cambridge

Laurence H. Tribe · a · Harvard Law School · 1563 Massachusetts Avenue · Cambridge, MA 02138 · 617-495-3100

FRANCHISE LAW

Boston

Eric H. Karp · Witmer, Karp, Warner & Ryan · http://www.wkwrlaw.com · 22 Batterymarch Street · Boston, MA 02109 · 617-423-7250

Arthur L. Pressman · Nixon Peabody · 100 Summer Street · Boston, MA 02110-1832 · 617-345-1000

L. Seth Stadfeld · Weston, Patrick, Willard & Redding · 84 State Street, 11th Floor · Boston, MA 02109 · 617-742-9310

GOVERNMENT RELATIONS LAW

Boston

Robert P. Rodophele · Ferriter, Scobbo & Rodophele · 125 High Street, 26th Floor · Boston, MA 02110 · 617-737-1800

Boston

Kenneth A. Behar · a · Behar & Kalman · Six Beacon Street, Suite 312 · Boston, MA 02108 · 617-227-7660

Stephen W. Bernstein · McDermott Will & Emery · 28 State Street, 34th Floor · Boston, MA 02109-1775 · 617-535-4000

Michael L. Blau · Foley & Lardner · 111 Huntington Avenue · Boston, MA 02199 · 617-342-4000

Charles R. Buck · McDermott Will & Emery · 28 State Street, 34th Floor · Boston, MA 02109-1775 · 617-535-4000

Nancy E. Forbes · Ropes & Gray · http://www.ropesgray.com · One International Place · Boston, MA 02110-2624 · 617-951-7000

Jennifer Gallop · Krokidas & Bluestein · 600 Atlantic Avenue · Boston, MA 02210 · 617-482-7211

Michele M. Garvin · Ropes & Gray · http://www.ropesgray.com · One International Place · Boston, MA 02110-2624 · 617-951-7000

Robert J. Griffin · Krokidas & Bluestein · 600 Atlantic Avenue · Boston, MA 02210 · 617-482-7211

Jeffrey L. Heidt · a · Ropes & Gray · http://www.ropesgray.com · One International Place · Boston, MA 02110-2624 · 617-951-7000

Ellen L. Janos · Mintz, Levin, Cohn, Ferris, Glovsky and Popeo · One Financial Center, 40th Floor · Boston, MA 02111 · 617-542-6000

Christopher M. Jedrey · McDermott Will & Emery · 28 State Street, 34th Floor · Boston, MA 02109-1775 · 617-535-4000

Edward D. Kalman · a · Behar & Kalman · Six Beacon Street, Suite 312 · Boston, MA 02108 · 617-227-7660

William A. Knowlton · a · Ropes & Gray · http://www.ropesgray.com · One International Place · Boston, MA 02110-2624 · 617-951-7000

Timothy M. McCrystal · Ropes & Gray · http://www.ropesgray.com · One International Place · Boston, MA 02110-2624 · 617-951-7000

Anne Phillips Ogilby · Ropes & Gray · http://www.ropesgray.com · One International Place · Boston, MA 02110-2624 · 617-951-7000

Daniel T. Roble · a · Ropes & Gray · http://www.ropesgray.com · One International Place · Boston, MA 02110-2624 · 617-951-7000

Regina S. Rockefeller · a · Nixon Peabody · 100 Summer Street · Boston, MA 02110-1832 · 617-345-1000

David W. Rosenberg · a · Rosenberg & Schapiro · 44 School Street, Suite 800 · Boston, MA 02108 · 617-723-7440

Gary A. Rosenberg · Behar & Kalman · Six Beacon Street, Suite 312 · Boston, MA 02108 · 617-227-7660

Michael F. Sexton · Ropes & Gray · http://www.ropesgray.com · One International Place · Boston, MA 02110-2624 · 617-951-7000

Christine G. Solt · Choate, Hall & Stewart · http://www.choate.com · Two International Place · Boston, MA 02110 · 617-248-5000

Susan T. Valente · a · Nixon Peabody · 100 Summer Street · Boston, MA 02110-1832 · 617-345-1000

Lawrence W. Vernaglia · Foley & Lardner · 111 Huntington Avenue · Boston, MA 02199 · 617-342-4000

Stephen M. Weiner · a · Mintz, Levin, Cohn, Ferris, Glovsky and Popeo · One Financial Center, 40th Floor · Boston, MA 02111 · 617-542-6000

Springfield

Theodore C. Brown · Egan, Flanagan and Cohen · 67 Market Street · P.O. Box 9035 · Springfield, MA 01102 · 413-737-0260

IMMIGRATION LAW

Boston

Lawrence D. Bastone · a · Sullivan & Worcester · One Post Office Square · Boston, MA 02109 · 617-338-2800

Francis E. Chin · a · Chin & Curtis · 75 Federal Street, Suite 210 · Boston, MA 02110 · 617-482-1775

Susan J. Cohen · Mintz, Levin, Cohn, Ferris, Glovsky and Popeo · One Financial Center, 40th Floor · Boston, MA 02111 · 617-542-6000

Phillip C. Curtis · Chin & Curtis · 75 Federal Street, Suite 210 · Boston, MA 02110 · 617-482-1775

Kerry E. Doyle · Graves & Doyle · 77 Franklin Street, Third Floor · Boston, MA 02110 · 617-542-6400

Scott J. FitzGerald · Fragomen, Del Rey, Bernsen & Loewy · http://www.fragomen.com · Two Liberty Square, 11th Floor · Boston, MA 02109-4892 · 617-574-0400

Jeremiah Friedman · Kaplan, O'Sullivan & Friedman · 10 Winthrop Square, Third Floor · Boston, MA 02110-1264 · 617-482-4500

William E. Graves, Jr. · Graves & Doyle · 77 Franklin Street, Third Floor · Boston, MA 02110 · 617-542-6400

Ilana Greenstein · Kaplan, O'Sullivan & Friedman · 10 Winthrop Square, Third Floor · Boston, MA 02110-1264 · 617-482-4500

Richard L. Iandoli · a · Richard L. Iandoli & Associates · One Appleton Street, Suite 200 · Boston, MA 02116 · 617-482-1010

Harvey Kaplan · a · Kaplan, O'Sullivan & Friedman · 10 Winthrop Square, Third Floor · Boston, MA 02110-1264 · 617-482-4500

Maureen O'Sullivan · a · Kaplan, O'Sullivan & Friedman · 10 Winthrop Square, Third Floor · Boston, MA 02110-1264 · 617-482-4500

Sharryn E. Ross · a · Ross, Silverman & Levy · http://www.rsl-law.net · 59 Temple Place, Suite 605 · Boston, MA 02111 · 617-542-5111

Bennett R. Savitz · Savitz Law Offices · http://www.immigrationoptions.com · Six Beacon Street, Suite 900 · Boston, MA 02108 · 617-723-7111

Howard A. Silverman · Ross, Silverman & Levy · http://www.rsl-law.net · 59 Temple Place, Suite 605 · Boston, MA 02111 · 617-542-5111

Cambridge

Steven A. Clark · a · Flynn & Clark · One Main Street, Eighth Floor · Cambridge, MA 02142-1531 · 617-299-4200

Alan M. Pampanin · a · Pampanin Law Offices · 2343 Massachusetts Avenue · Cambridge, MA 02140-1294 · 617-498-0900

INFORMATION TECHNOLOGY LAW

Boston

David J. Goldstone · Goodwin Procter · Exchange Place · 53 State Street · Boston, MA 02109-2881 · 617-570-1000

Kathleen M. Porter · Robinson & Cole · http://www.rc.com · One Boston Place, 25th Floor · 201 Washington Street · Boston, MA 02108-4404 · 617-557-5900

David A. Westenberg · WilmerHale · http://www.wilmerhale.com · 60 State Street · Boston, MA 02109 · 617-526-6000

INSURANCE LAW

Boston

George A. Berman · Peabody & Arnold · http://www.peabodyarnold.com · Federal Reserve Plaza · 600 Atlantic Avenue · Boston, MA 02210-2261 · 617-951-2100

Mark D. Cahill · Choate, Hall & Stewart · http://www.choate.com · Two International Place · Boston, MA 02110 · 617-248-5000

Michael P. Duffy · Peabody & Arnold · http://www.peabodyarnold.com · Federal Reserve Plaza · 600 Atlantic Avenue · Boston, MA 02210-2261 · 617-951-2100

Kenneth W. Erickson · Ropes & Gray · http://www.ropesgray.com · One International Place · Boston, MA 02110-2624 · 617-951-7000

Samuel M. Furgang · Sugarman, Rogers, Barshak & Cohen · http://www.srbc.com · 101 Merrimac Street, Ninth Floor · Boston, MA 02114-4737 · 617-227-3030

Susan A. Hartnett · Sugarman, Rogers, Barshak & Cohen · http://www.srbc.com · 101 Merrimac Street, Ninth Floor · Boston, MA 02114-4737 · 617-227-3030

J. David Leslie · Rackemann, Sawyer & Brewster · http://www.rackemann.com · 160 Federal Street, 13th-15th Floor · Boston, MA 02110-1700 · 617-542-2300

Natasha C. Lisman · Sugarman, Rogers, Barshak & Cohen · http://www.srbc.com · 101 Merrimac Street, Ninth Floor · Boston, MA 02114-4737 · 617-227-3030

Kim V. Marrkand · Mintz, Levin, Cohn, Ferris, Glovsky and Popeo · One Financial Center, 40th Floor · Boston, MA 02111 · 617-542-6000

Michael B. Meyer · a · Meyer, Connolly, Simons & Keuthen · 12 Post Office Square, Fifth Floor · Boston, MA 02109 · 617-423-2254

George Marshall Moriarty · a · Ropes & Gray · http://www.ropesgray.com · One International Place · Boston, MA 02110-2624 · 617-951-7000

John A. Nadas · Choate, Hall & Stewart · http://www.choate.com · Two International Place · Boston, MA 02110 · 617-248-5000

Regina E. Roman · Sugarman, Rogers, Barshak & Cohen · http://www.srbc.com · 101 Merrimac Street, Ninth Floor · Boston, MA 02114-4737 · 617-227-3030

Rosanna Sattler · Posternak, Blankstein & Lund · The Prudential Tower · 800 Boylston Street · Boston, MA 02199-8004 · 617-973-6100

Steven L. Schreckinger · Lynch, Brewer, Hoffman & Fink · 101 Federal Street, 22nd Floor · Boston, MA 02110 · 617-951-0800

Harvey Weiner · Peabody & Arnold · http://www.peabodyarnold.com · Federal Reserve Plaza · 600 Atlantic Avenue · Boston, MA 02210-2261 · 617-951-2100

Tamara S. Wolfson · Lynch, Brewer, Hoffman & Fink · 101 Federal Street, 22nd Floor · Boston, MA 02110 · 617-951-0800

Framingham

Christopher A. Kenney · Kenney & Sams · Framingham Corporate Center · 492 Old Connecticut Path · Framingham, MA 01701 · 508-665-4299

INTELLECTUAL PROPERTY LAW

Attleboro

Thomas R. Noel · Noel & Gyorgy · Eight North Main Street, Suite 403 · Attleboro, MA 02703 · 508-223-5800

Boston

D. Dennis Allegretti · a · Duane Morris · 470 Atlantic Avenue, Suite 500 · Boston, MA 02210-2600 · 857-488-4200

Beth E. Arnold · Foley Hoag · http://www.foleyhoag.com · Seaport World Trade Center West · 155 Seaport Boulevard · Boston, MA 02210-2600 · 617-832-1000

Steven M. Bauer · Proskauer Rose · http://www.proskauer.com · One International Place · Boston, MA 02110-2600 · 617-526-9600

Lee Carl Bromberg · Bromberg & Sunstein · 125 Summer Street · Boston, MA 02110-1618 · 617-443-9292

Paul T. Clark · Clark & Elbing · 101 Federal Street, 15th Floor · Boston, MA 02110-1800 · 617-428-0200

Jerry Cohen · Burns & Levinson · http://www.burnslev.com · 125 Summer Street · Boston, MA 02110-1624 · 617-345-3000

Sarah Chapin Columbia · McDermott Will & Emery · 28 State Street, 34th Floor · Boston, MA 02109-1775 · 617-535-4000

David G. Conlin · a · Edwards Angell Palmer & Dodge · Prudential Center · 111 Huntington Avenue · Boston, MA 02199-7613 · 617-239-0100

J. Anthony Downs · Goodwin Procter · Exchange Place · 53 State Street · Boston, MA 02109-2881 · 617-570-1000

John C. Englander · Goodwin Procter · Exchange Place · 53 State Street · Boston, MA 02109-2881 · 617-570-1000

David L. Feigenbaum · Fish & Richardson · 225 Franklin Street · Boston, MA 02110-2804 · 617-542-5070

Robert S. Frank, Jr. · a · Choate, Hall & Stewart · http://www.choate.com · Two International Place · Boston, MA 02110 · 617-248-5000

Timothy A. French · Fish & Richardson · 225 Franklin Street · Boston, MA 02110-2804 · 617-542-5070

Edward R. Gates · Wolf, Greenfield & Sacks · 600 Atlantic Avenue · Boston, MA 02210-2206 · 617-646-8000

Lawrence M. Green · Wolf, Greenfield & Sacks · 600 Atlantic Avenue · Boston, MA 02210-2206 · 617-646-8000

George L. Greenfield · a · Wolf, Greenfield & Sacks · 600 Atlantic Avenue · Boston, MA 02210-2206 · 617-646-8000

Gilbert H. Hennessey · Fish & Richardson · 225 Franklin Street · Boston, MA 02110-2804 · 617-542-5070

Steven J. Henry · Wolf, Greenfield & Sacks · 600 Atlantic Avenue · Boston, MA 02210-2206 · 617-646-8000

Charles Hieken · Fish & Richardson · 225 Franklin Street · Boston, MA 02110-2804 · 617-542-5070

Robert E. Hillman · a · Fish & Richardson · 225 Franklin Street · Boston, MA 02110-2804 · 617-542-5070

James B. Lampert · a · WilmerHale · http://www.wilmerhale.com · 60 State Street · Boston, MA 02109 · 617-526-6000

William F. Lee · a · WilmerHale · http://www.wilmerhale.com · 60 State Street · Boston, MA 02109 · 617-526-6000

P. Louis Myers · Fish & Richardson · 225 Franklin Street · Boston, MA 02110-2804 · 617-542-5070

Martin J. O'Donnell · Cesari and McKenna · 88 Black Falcon Avenue · Boston, MA 02210-2414 · 617-951-2500

Sam Pasternack · Choate, Hall & Stewart · http://www.choate.com · Two International Place · Boston, MA 02110 · 617-248-5000

Edward F. Perlman · Wolf, Greenfield & Sacks · 600 Atlantic Avenue · Boston, MA 02210-2206 · 617-646-8000

Victor H. Polk, Jr. · Greenberg Traurig · http://www.gtlaw.com · One International Place · Boston, MA 02110 · 617-310-6000

Frank P. Porcelli · Fish & Richardson · 225 Franklin Street · Boston, MA 02110-2804 · 617-542-5070

Shepard M. Remis · Goodwin Procter · Exchange Place · 53 State Street · Boston, MA 02109-2881 · 617-570-1000

Frank E. Scherkenbach · Fish & Richardson · 225 Franklin Street · Boston, MA 02110-2804 · 617-542-5070

Gary A. Walpert · a · K&L Gates · State Street Financial Center · One Lincoln Street · Boston, MA 02111-2950 · 617-261-3100

Donald R. Ware · Foley Hoag · http://www.foleyhoag.com · Seaport World Trade Center West · 155 Seaport Boulevard · Boston, MA 02210-2600 · 617-832-1000

David Wolf · a · Wolf, Greenfield & Sacks · 600 Atlantic Avenue · Boston, MA 02210-2206 · 617-646-8000

Cambridge

Ronald E. Myrick · Finnegan, Henderson, Farabow, Garrett & Dunner · http://www.finnegan.com · 55 Cambridge Parkway · Cambridge, MA 02142-1215 · 617-452-1600

Worcester

Louis M. Ciavarra · Bowditch & Dewey · 311 Main Street · P.O. Box 15156 · Worcester, MA 01615-0156 508-791-3511

INTERNATIONAL ARBITRATION

Boston

Kenneth W. Erickson · Ropes & Gray · http://www.ropesgray.com · One International Place · Boston, MA 02110-2624 · 617-951-7000

Adolfo R. Garcia · Ropes & Gray · http://www.ropesgray.com · One International Place · Boston, MA 02110-2624 · 617-951-7000

Richard A. Johnston · WilmerHale · http://www.wilmerhale.com · 60 State Street · Boston, MA 02109 · 617-526-6000

Natasha C. Lisman · Sugarman, Rogers, Barshak & Cohen · http://www.srbc.com · 101 Merrimac Street, Ninth Floor · Boston, MA 02114-4737 · 617-227-3030

George Marshall Moriarty · a · Ropes & Gray · http://www.ropesgray.com · One International Place · Boston, MA 02110-2624 · 617-951-7000

Philip D. O'Neill, Jr. · Edwards Angell Palmer & Dodge · Prudential Center · 111 Huntington Avenue · Boston, MA 02199-7613 · 617-239-0100

William W. Park · Boston University · 765 Commonwealth Avenue · Boston, MA 02215 · 617-353-3149

INTERNATIONAL TRADE AND FINANCE LAW

Boston

Cary Armistead · Ropes & Gray · http://www.ropesgray.com · One International Place · Boston, MA 02110-2624 · 617-951-7000

William C. Benjamin · WilmerHale · http://www.wilmerhale.com · 60 State Street · Boston, MA 02109 · 617-526-6000

John A. Burgess · WilmerHale · http://www.wilmerhale.com · 60 State Street · Boston, MA 02109 · 617-526-6000

Howard A. Cubell · 2) · Goodwin Procter · Exchange Place · 53 State Street · Boston, MA 02109-2881 · 617-570-1000

Adolfo R. Garcia · Ropes & Gray · http://www.ropesgray.com · One International Place · Boston, MA 02110-2624 · 617-951-7000

Marc A. Rubenstein · Ropes & Gray · http://www.ropesgray.com · One International Place · Boston, MA 02110-2624 · 617-951-7000

Stephen E. Shay · a · Ropes & Gray · http://www.ropesgray.com · One International Place · Boston, MA 02110-2624 · 617-951-7000

Rom P. Watson · Ropes & Gray · http://www.ropesgray.com · One International Place · Boston, MA 02110-2624 · 617-951-7000

LABOR AND EMPLOYMENT LAW

Boston

Joan Ackerstein · Jackson Lewis · http://www.jacksonlewis.com · 75 Park Plaza, Fourth Floor · Boston, MA 02116 · 617-367-0025

John F. Adkins · Bingham McCutchen · http://www.bingham.com · One Federal Street · Boston, MA 02110-1726 · 617-951-8000

Richard L. Alfred · Seyfarth Shaw · World Trade Center East, Suite 300 · Two Seaport Lane · Boston, MA 02210-2028 · 617-946-4800

Joseph W. Ambash · Greenberg Traurig · http://www.gtlaw.com · One International Place · Boston, MA 02110 · 617-310-6000

Mark Batten · Proskauer Rose · http://www.proskauer.com · One International Place · Boston, MA 02110-2600 · 617-526-9600

Wilfred J. Benoit, Jr. · Goodwin Procter · Exchange Place · 53 State Street · Boston, MA 02109-2881 · 617-570-1000

Inga S. Bernstein · Zalkind Rodriguez Lunt & Duncan · http://www.zrld.com · 65A Atlantic Avenue · Boston, MA 02110 · 617-742-6020

Michael R. Brown · 2) · Cooley Manion Jones · 21 Custom House Street, Sixth Floor · Boston, MA 02110 617-737-3100

James W. Bucking · Foley Hoag · http://www.foleyhoag.com · Seaport World Trade Center West · 155 Seaport Boulevard · Boston, MA 02210-2600 · 617-832-1000

David C. Casey · Littler Mendelson · One International Place, Suite 2700 · Boston, MA 02110 · 617-378-6000

Lisa J. Damon · Seyfarth Shaw · World Trade Center East, Suite 300 · Two Seaport Lane · Boston, MA 02210-2028 · 617-946-4800

Joshua M. Davis · Goulston & Storrs · 400 Atlantic Avenue · Boston, MA 02110-3333 · 617-482-1776

Laurence J. Donoghue · Morgan, Brown & Joy · 200 State Street, 11th Floor · Boston, MA 02109 · 617-523-6666

Peter L. Ebb · Ropes & Gray · http://www.ropesgray.com · One International Place · Boston, MA 02110-2624 · 617-951-7000

Andrew L. Eisenberg · Seyfarth Shaw · World Trade Center East, Suite 300 · Two Seaport Lane · Boston, MA 02210-2028 · 617-946-4800

Michael A. Feinberg · 2) · Feinberg, Campbell & Zack · 177 Milk Street, Suite 300 · Boston, MA 02109 · 617-338-1976

Robert M. Hale · Goodwin Procter · Exchange Place · 53 State Street · Boston, MA 02109-2881 · 617-570-1000

Jeffrey L. Hirsch · Hirsch, Roberts & Weinstein · Two Park Plaza · Boston, MA 02116 · 617-348-4300

Kay H. Hodge · Stoneman, Chandler & Miller · 99 High Street, Suite 1601 · Boston, MA 02110 · 617-542-6789

Paul V. Holtzman · Krokidas & Bluestein · 600 Atlantic Avenue · Boston, MA 02210 · 617-482-7211

Neil Jacobs · WilmerHale · http://www.wilmerhale.com · 60 State Street · Boston, MA 02109 · 617-526-6000

Robert P. Joy · Morgan, Brown & Joy · 200 State Street, 11th Floor · Boston, MA 02109 · 617-523-6666

William F. Joy, Jr. · Morgan, Brown & Joy · 200 State Street, 11th Floor · Boston, MA 02109 · 617-523-6666

Mark G. Kaplan · a · Krakow & Souris · 225 Friend Street, Fifth Floor · Boston, MA 02114 · 617-723-8440

Ellen C. Kearns · Foley & Lardner · 111 Huntington Avenue · Boston, MA 02199 · 617-342-4000

Gregory Keating · Littler Mendelson · One International Place, Suite 2700 · Boston, MA 02110 · 617-378-6000

Paul F. Kelly · Segal Roitman · 111 Devonshire Street, Fifth Floor · Boston, MA 02109 · 617-742-0208

William B. Koffel · Foley Hoag · http://www.foleyhoag.com · Seaport World Trade Center West · 155 Seaport Boulevard · Boston, MA 02210-2600 · 617-832-1000

Shelley B. Kroll · Segal Roitman · 111 Devonshire Street, Fifth Floor · Boston, MA 02109 · 617-742-0208

Harold L. Lichten · Pyle, Rome, Lichten, Ehrenberg & Liss-Riordan · 18 Tremont Street, Suite 500 · Boston, MA 02108 · 617-367-7200

Shannon Liss- Riordan · Pyle, Rome, Lichten, Ehrenberg & Liss-Riordan · 18 Tremont Street, Suite 500 · Boston, MA 02108 · 617-367-7200

Sharen Litwin · Kotin, Crabtree & Strong · http://www.kcslegal.com · One Bowdoin Square · Boston, MA 02114-2925 · 617-227-7031

Joan A. Lukey · a · Ropes & Gray · http://www.ropesgray.com · One International Place · Boston, MA 02110-2624 · 617-951-7000

David M. Mandel · Ropes & Gray · http://www.ropesgray.com · One International Place · Boston, MA 02110-2624 · 617-951-7000

John M. McKelway, Jr. · McCarter & English · 265 Franklin Street · Boston, MA 02110 · 617-449-6500

Alan S. Miller · 2% · Stoneman, Chandler & Miller · 99 High Street, Suite 1601 · Boston, MA 02110 · 617-542-6789

Scott C. Moriearty · Bingham McCutchen · http://www.bingham.com · One Federal Street · Boston, MA 02110-1726 · 617-951-8000

Jean A. Musiker · Sugarman, Rogers, Barshak & Cohen · http://www.srbc.com · 101 Merrimac Street, Ninth Floor · Boston, MA 02114-4737 · 617-227-3030

James W. Nagle · Goodwin Procter · Exchange Place · 53 State Street · Boston, MA 02109-2881 · 617-570-1000

Jody L. Newman · Dwyer & Collora · 600 Atlantic Avenue, 12th Floor · Boston, MA 02210-2211 · 617-371-1000

Stephen B. Perlman · 2) · Ropes & Gray · http://www.ropesgray.com · One International Place · Boston, MA 02110-2624 · 617-951-7000

Andrew C. Pickett · Jackson Lewis · http://www.jacksonlewis.com · 75 Park Plaza, Fourth Floor · Boston, MA 02116 · 617-367-0025

Warren H. Pyle · 2% · Pyle, Rome, Lichten, Ehrenberg & Liss-Riordan · 18 Tremont Street, Suite 500 · Boston, MA 02108 · 617-367-7200

David Rapaport · Davis, Malm & D'Agostine · One Boston Place · 201 Washington Street · Boston, MA 02108 · 617-367-2500

Anthony D. Rizzotti · Littler Mendelson · One International Place, Suite 2700 · Boston, MA 02110 · 617-378-6000

Louis A. Rodriques · Bingham McCutchen · http://www.bingham.com · One Federal Street · Boston, MA 02110-1726 · 617-951-8000

Mark E. Schreiber · 2) · Edwards Angell Palmer & Dodge · Prudential Center · 111 Huntington Avenue · Boston, MA 02199-7613 · 617-239-0100

Thomas E. Shirley · Choate, Hall & Stewart · http://www.choate.com · Two International Place · Boston, MA 02110 · 617-248-5000

Donald J. Siegel · 2) · Segal Roitman · 111 Devonshire Street, Fifth Floor · Boston, MA 02109 · 617-742-0208

Ira Sills · 2) · Segal Roitman · 111 Devonshire Street, Fifth Floor · Boston, MA 02109 · 617-742-0208

Diane M. Soubly · Seyfarth Shaw · World Trade Center East, Suite 300 · Two Seaport Lane · Boston, MA 02210-2028 · 617-946-4800

Laura R. Studen · Burns & Levinson · http://www.burnslev.com · 125 Summer Street · Boston, MA 02110-1624 · 617-345-3000

Mary T. Sullivan · a · Segal Roitman · 111 Devonshire Street, Fifth Floor · Boston, MA 02109 · 617-742-0208

Ilene Robinson Sunshine · Sullivan & Worcester · One Post Office Square · Boston, MA 02109 · 617-338-2800

Arthur G. Telegen · Foley Hoag · http://www.foleyhoag.com · Seaport World Trade Center West · 155 Seaport Boulevard · Boston, MA 02210-2600 · 617-832-1000

Danielle Y. Vanderzanden · Day Pitney · One International Place, 17th Floor · Boston, MA 02110-3179 · 617-345-4600

E. David Wanger · 2) · Angoff, Goldman, Manning, Wanger & Hynes · 45 Bromfield Street, Eighth Floor Boston, MA 02108 · 617-723-5500

Jerome N. Weinstein · a · Hirsch, Roberts & Weinstein · Two Park Plaza · Boston, MA 02116 · 617-348-4300

John F. Welsh · Bello Black & Welsh · One Exeter Plaza, Tenth Floor · 699 Boyleston Street · Boston, MA 02116 · 617-247-4100

Framingham

John D. O'Reilly III · 2% · O'Reilly, Grosso & Gross · 1671 Worcester Road, Suite 205 · Framingham, MA 01701 · 508-620-0055

Southborough

James F. Lamond · McDonald, Lamond & Canzoneri · Cordaville Office Center, Suite 320 · 153 Cordaville Road · Southborough, MA 01772-1834 · 508-485-6600

Alan J. McDonald · 2) · McDonald, Lamond & Canzoneri · Cordaville Office Center, Suite 320 · 153 Cordaville Road · Southborough, MA 01772-1834 · 508-485-6600

Springfield

Ralph F. Abbott, Jr. · 2) · Skoler, Abbott & Presser · One Monarch Place, Suite 2000 · Springfield, MA 01144 · 413-737-4753

John H. Glenn · a · Skoler, Abbott & Presser · One Monarch Place, Suite 2000 · Springfield, MA 01144 · 413-737-4753

Richard D. Hayes · a · Sullivan, Hayes & Quinn · One Monarch Place, Suite 1200 · Springfield, MA 01144 · 413-736-4538

Jay M. Presser · a · Skoler, Abbott & Presser · One Monarch Place, Suite 2000 · Springfield, MA 01144 · 413-737-4753

Gordon D. Quinn · Sullivan, Hayes & Quinn · One Monarch Place, Suite 1200 · Springfield, MA 01144 · 413-736-4538

John C. Sikorski · a · Robinson Donovan · http://www.robinson-donovan.com · 1500 Main Street, Suite 1600 · P.O. Box 15609 · Springfield, MA 01115 · 413-732-2301

Frederick L. Sullivan · 2) · Sullivan, Hayes & Quinn · One Monarch Place, Suite 1200 · Springfield, MA 01144 · 413-736-4538

Meghan B. Sullivan · Sullivan, Hayes & Quinn · One Monarch Place, Suite 1200 · Springfield, MA 01144 413-736-4538

Worcester

Michael P. Angelini · 2) · Bowditch & Dewey · 311 Main Street · P.O. Box 15156 · Worcester, MA 01615-0156 · 508-791-3511

James E. Wallace, Jr. · 2) · Bowditch & Dewey · 311 Main Street · P.O. Box 15156 · Worcester, MA 01615-0156 · 508-791-3511

LAND USE & ZONING LAW

Boston

Katharine E. Bachman · a · WilmerHale · http://www.wilmerhale.com · 60 State Street · Boston, MA 02109 · 617-526-6000

Robert C. Davis · 2) · Goulston & Storrs · 400 Atlantic Avenue · Boston, MA 02110-3333 · 617-482-1776

Robert A. Fishman · Nutter McClennen & Fish · http://www.nutter.com · World Trade Center West · 155 Seaport Boulevard · Boston, MA 02210 · 617-439-2000

Martin R. Healy · a · Goodwin Procter · Exchange Place · 53 State Street · Boston, MA 02109-2881 · 617-570-1000

Douglas M. Husid · Goulston & Storrs · 400 Atlantic Avenue · Boston, MA 02110-3333 · 617-482-1776

Matthew J. Kiefer · Goulston & Storrs · 400 Atlantic Avenue · Boston, MA 02110-3333 · 617-482-1776

James D. Masterman · Greenberg Traurig · http://www.gtlaw.com · One International Place · Boston, MA 02110 · 617-310-6000

William R. O'Reilly, Jr. · WilmerHale · http://www.wilmerhale.com · 60 State Street · Boston, MA 02109 617-526-6000

Myrna Putziger · a · Rubin and Rudman · 50 Rowes Wharf · Boston, MA 02110-3319 · 617-330-7000

Melvin R. Shuman · WilmerHale · http://www.wilmerhale.com · 60 State Street · Boston, MA 02109 · 617-526-6000

Robert Tuchmann · 2) · WilmerHale · http://www.wilmerhale.com · 60 State Street · Boston, MA 02109 · 617-526-6000

West Harwich

Michael D. Ford · The Law Office of Michael D. Ford · 72 Main Street · P.O. Box 485 · West Harwich, MA 02671 · 508-430-1900

LEGAL MALPRACTICE LAW

Boston

Clyde D. Bergstresser · Campbell Campbell Edwards & Conroy · One Constitution Plaza, Third Floor · Boston, MA 02129 · 617-241-3000

George A. Berman · Peabody & Arnold · http://www.peabodyarnold.com · Federal Reserve Plaza · 600 Atlantic Avenue · Boston, MA 02210-2261 · 617-951-2100

William J. Dailey, Jr. · a · Sloane & Walsh · Three Center Plaza, Eighth Floor · Boston, MA 02108 · 617-523-6010

James R. DeGiacomo · a · Murtha Cullina · 99 High Street, 20th Floor · Boston, MA 02110 · 617-457-4000

Erik Lund · a · Posternak, Blankstein & Lund · The Prudential Tower · 800 Boylston Street · Boston, MA 02199-8004 · 617-973-6100

Robert J. Muldoon, Jr. · 2) · Sherin and Lodgen · 101 Federal Street · Boston, MA 02110 · 617-646-2000

Richard W. Renehan · 2% · Goulston & Storrs · 400 Atlantic Avenue · Boston, MA 02110-3333 · 617-482-1776

Regina E. Roman · Sugarman, Rogers, Barshak & Cohen · http://www.srbc.com · 101 Merrimac Street, Ninth Floor · Boston, MA 02114-4737 · 617-227-3030

John P. Ryan · a · Sloane & Walsh · Three Center Plaza, Eighth Floor · Boston, MA 02108 · 617-523-6010

Thomas J. Sartory · 2) · Goulston & Storrs · 400 Atlantic Avenue · Boston, MA 02110-3333 · 617-482-1776

Harvey Weiner · Peabody & Arnold · http://www.peabodyarnold.com · Federal Reserve Plaza · 600 Atlantic Avenue · Boston, MA 02210-2261 · 617-951-2100

Richard M. Zielinski · Goulston & Storrs · 400 Atlantic Avenue · Boston, MA 02110-3333 · 617-482-1776

LEVERAGED BUYOUTS AND PRIVATE EQUITY LAW

Boston

C. Todd Boes · Ropes & Gray · http://www.ropesgray.com · One International Place · Boston, MA 02110-2624 · 617-951-7000

David C. Chapin · Ropes & Gray · http://www.ropesgray.com · One International Place · Boston, MA 02110-2624 · 617-951-7000

Byung W. Choi · Ropes & Gray · http://www.ropesgray.com · One International Place · Boston, MA 02110-2624 · 617-951-7000

Patrick Diaz · Ropes & Gray · http://www.ropesgray.com · One International Place · Boston, MA 02110-2624 · 617-951-7000

John J. Egan III · Goodwin Procter · Exchange Place · 53 State Street · Boston, MA 02109-2881 · 617-570-1000

Daniel S. Evans · Ropes & Gray · http://www.ropesgray.com · One International Place · Boston, MA 02110-2624 · 617-951-7000

Laura Hodges Taylor · a · Goodwin Procter · Exchange Place · 53 State Street · Boston, MA 02109-2881 617-570-1000

R. Bradford Malt · a · Ropes & Gray · http://www.ropesgray.com · One International Place · Boston, MA 02110-2624 · 617-951-7000

Robert L. Nutt · 2) · Ropes & Gray · http://www.ropesgray.com · One International Place · Boston, MA 02110-2624 · 617-951-7000

Steven M. Peck · Weil Gotshal & Manges · 100 Federal Street, 34th Floor · Boston, MA 02110 · 617-772-8300

Charles W. Robins · Weil Gotshal & Manges · 100 Federal Street, 34th Floor · Boston, MA 02110 · 617-772-8300

Alfred O. Rose · a · Ropes & Gray · http://www.ropesgray.com · One International Place · Boston, MA 02110-2624 · 617-951-7000

William J. Schnoor, Jr. · Goodwin Procter · Exchange Place · 53 State Street · Boston, MA 02109-2881 · 617-570-1000

R. Newcomb Stillwell · Ropes & Gray · http://www.ropesgray.com · One International Place · Boston, MA 02110-2624 · 617-951-7000

Paul F. Van Houten · Ropes & Gray · http://www.ropesgray.com · One International Place · Boston, MA 02110-2624 · 617-951-7000

James R. Westra · Weil Gotshal & Manges · 100 Federal Street, 34th Floor · Boston, MA 02110 · 617-772-8300

Robert M. Wolf · Bingham McCutchen · http://www.bingham.com · One Federal Street · Boston, MA 02110-1726 · 617-951-8000

MASS TORT LITIGATION

Boston

Kevin G. Kenneally · LeClair Ryan · One International Place, 11th Floor · Boston, MA 02110 · 617-502-8200

Neil T. Leifer · Thornton & Naumes · 100 Summer Street, 30th Floor · Boston, MA 02110 · 617-720-1333

Alex H. MacDonald · MacDonald Rothweiler Eisenberg · One Bowdoin Square, Eighth Floor · Boston, MA 02114 · 617-747-7550

John J. McGivney · Rubin and Rudman · 50 Rowes Wharf · Boston, MA 02110-3319 · 617-330-7000

Kenneth J. Parsigian · Goodwin Procter · Exchange Place · 53 State Street · Boston, MA 02109-2881 · 617-570-1000

Michael P. Thornton · Thornton & Naumes · 100 Summer Street, 30th Floor · Boston, MA 02110 · 617-720-1333

Malden

Richard M. Sandman · Rodman, Rodman & Sandman · 442 Main Street, Suite 300 · Malden, MA 02148-5122 · 781-322-3720

MEDIA LAW

Boston

Jonathan M. Albano · a · Bingham McCutchen · http://www.bingham.com · One Federal Street · Boston, MA 02110-1726 · 617-951-8000

Robert A. Bertsche · Prince, Lobel, Glovsky & Tye · http://www.princelobel.com · 100 Cambridge Street, Suite 2200 · Boston, MA 02114 · 617-456-8000

John Taylor Williams · a · Fish & Richardson · 225 Franklin Street · Boston, MA 02110-2804 · 617-542-5070

MEDICAL MALPRACTICE LAW

Boston

Lisa G. Arrowood · Todd & Weld · http://www.toddweld.com · 28 State Street, 31st Floor · Boston, MA 02109 · 617-720-2626

David A. Barry · Sugarman, Rogers, Barshak & Cohen · http://www.srbc.com · 101 Merrimac Street, Ninth Floor · Boston, MA 02114-4737 · 617-227-3030

Clyde D. Bergstresser · Campbell Campbell Edwards & Conroy · One Constitution Plaza, Third Floor · Boston, MA 02129 · 617-241-3000

Leo V. Boyle · 2) · Meehan, Boyle, Black & Bogdanow · Two Center Plaza, Suite 600 · Boston, MA 02108-1922 · 617-523-8300

Thomas W. Braun · Moquin & Daley · 388 Commonwealth Avenue · Boston, MA 02215 · 617-536-0606

Robert W. Casby · a · Sugarman and Sugarman · One Beacon Street, 13th Floor · Boston, MA 02108 · 617-542-1000

John D. Cassidy · Ficksman & Conley · 98 North Washington Street, Suite 500 · Boston, MA 02114 · 617-720-1515

Ellen Epstein Cohen · Adler, Cohen, Harvey, Wakeman & Guekguezian · 75 Federal Street · Boston, MA 02110 · 617-423-6674

William J. Dailey, Jr. · a · Sloane & Walsh · Three Center Plaza, Eighth Floor · Boston, MA 02108 · 617-523-6010

Edmund P. Daley · a · Moquin & Daley · 388 Commonwealth Avenue · Boston, MA 02215 · 617-536-0606

Joseph L. Doherty · Doherty & Quill · 225 Franklin Street, 26th Floor · Boston, MA 02110 · 617-217-2837

David M. Gould · Ficksman & Conley · 98 North Washington Street, Suite 500 · Boston, MA 02114 · 617-720-1515

Daniel J. Griffin, Jr. · Martin, Magnuson, McCarthy & Kenney · http://www.mmmk.com · 101 Merrimac Street, Suite 700 · Boston, MA 02114 · 617-227-3240

A. Bernard Guekguezian · Adler, Cohen, Harvey, Wakeman & Guekguezian · 75 Federal Street · Boston, MA 02110 · 617-423-6674

Robert M. Higgins · Lubin & Meyer · 100 City Hall Plaza, Fourth Floor · Boston, MA 02108 · 617-720-4447

Edward T. Hinchey · Sloane & Walsh · Three Center Plaza, Eighth Floor · Boston, MA 02108 · 617-523-6010

Patrick T. Jones · Cooley Manion Jones · 21 Custom House Street, Sixth Floor · Boston, MA 02110 · 617-737-3100

Paul R. Keane · Martin, Magnuson, McCarthy & Kenney · http://www.mmmk.com · 101 Merrimac Street, Suite 700 · Boston, MA 02114 · 617-227-3240

Peter C. Knight · Morrison Mahoney · 250 Summer Street · Boston, MA 02210 · 617-439-7500

Edward F. Mahoney · Martin, Magnuson, McCarthy & Kenney · http://www.mmmk.com · 101 Merrimac Street, Suite 700 · Boston, MA 02114 · 617-227-3240

Paul M. McTague · Martin, Magnuson, McCarthy & Kenney · http://www.mmmk.com · 101 Merrimac Street, Suite 700 · Boston, MA 02114 · 617-227-3240

Andrew C. Meyer, Jr. · a · Lubin & Meyer · 100 City Hall Plaza, Fourth Floor · Boston, MA 02108 · 617-720-4447

Michael E. Mone, Sr. · 2% · Esdaile, Barrett & Esdaile · 75 Federal Street, 16th Floor · Boston, MA 02110 617-482-0333

Elizabeth Mulvey · a · Crowe and Mulvey · 141 Tremont Street, Eighth Floor · Boston, MA 02111 · 617-426-4488

Charles P. Reidy III · 2) · Martin, Magnuson, McCarthy & Kenney · http://www.mmmk.com · 101 Merrimac Street, Suite 700 · Boston, MA 02114 · 617-227-3240

John P. Ryan · a · Sloane & Walsh · Three Center Plaza, Eighth Floor · Boston, MA 02108 · 617-523-6010

Camille Francis Sarrouf, Sr. · 2) · Sarrouf Corso · 95 Commercial Wharf · Boston, MA 02110-3816 · 617-227-5800

Steven H. Schafer · Steven H. Schafer & Associates · 141 Tremont Street, Sixth Floor · Boston, MA 02111-1209 · 617-423-2447

Neil Sugarman · 2) · Sugarman and Sugarman · One Beacon Street, 13th Floor · Boston, MA 02108 · 617-542-1000

Anthony Tarricone · a · Kreindler & Kreindler · 277 Dartmouth Street · Boston, MA 02116 · 617-424-9100

George E. Wakeman, Jr. · Adler, Cohen, Harvey, Wakeman & Guekguezian · 75 Federal Street · Boston, MA 02110 · 617-423-6674

Nancy L. Watson · Ficksman & Conley · 98 North Washington Street, Suite 500 · Boston, MA 02114 · 617-720-1515

Cambridge

Robert L. Bouley · McCarthy Bouley & Barry · The Bulfinch Building · 47 Thorndike Street · Cambridge, MA 02141 · 617-225-2211

Edward D. McCarthy · McCarthy Bouley & Barry · The Bulfinch Building · 47 Thorndike Street · Cambridge, MA 02141 · 617-225-2211

Springfield

Michael H. Burke · a · Bulkley, Richardson and Gelinas · 1500 Main Street, Suite 2700 · P.O. Box 15507 Springfield, MA 01115-5507 · 413-781-2820

Ronald C. Kidd · a · Robinson Donovan · http://www.robinson-donovan.com · 1500 Main Street, Suite 1600 · P.O. Box 15609 · Springfield, MA 01115 · 413-732-2301

Matthew J. King · Robinson Donovan · http://www.robinson-donovan.com · 1500 Main Street, Suite 1600 P.O. Box 15609 · Springfield, MA 01115 · 413-732-2301

Melinda Phelps · Bulkley, Richardson and Gelinas · 1500 Main Street, Suite 2700 · P.O. Box 15507 · Springfield, MA 01115-5507 · 413-781-2820

Woburn

Philip E. Murray, Jr. · Murray, Kelly & Bertrand · 600 Unicorn Park Drive · Woburn, MA 01801 · 781-569-0020

MERGERS & ACQUISITIONS LAW

Boston

Mark G. Borden · a · WilmerHale · http://www.wilmerhale.com · 60 State Street · Boston, MA 02109 · 617-526-6000

Jay E. Bothwick · WilmerHale · http://www.wilmerhale.com · 60 State Street · Boston, MA 02109 · 617-526-6000

Johan V. Brigham · Bingham McCutchen · http://www.bingham.com · One Federal Street · Boston, MA 02110-1726 · 617-951-8000

Margaret A. Brown · Skadden, Arps, Slate, Meagher & Flom · One Beacon Street · Boston, MA 02108-3194 · 617-573-4800

John A. Burgess · WilmerHale · http://www.wilmerhale.com · 60 State Street · Boston, MA 02109 · 617-526-6000

Mark H. Burnett · Goodwin Procter · Exchange Place · 53 State Street · Boston, MA 02109-2881 · 617-570-1000

David C. Chapin · Ropes & Gray · http://www.ropesgray.com · One International Place · Boston, MA 02110-2624 · 617-951-7000

Stephen M. L. Cohen · Choate, Hall & Stewart · http://www.choate.com · Two International Place · Boston, MA 02110 · 617-248-5000

Roslyn G. Daum · a · Choate, Hall & Stewart · http://www.choate.com · Two International Place · Boston, MA 02110 · 617-248-5000

Roger D. Feldman · Fish & Richardson · 225 Franklin Street · Boston, MA 02110-2804 · 617-542-5070

Kathy A. Fields · Goodwin Procter · Exchange Place · 53 State Street · Boston, MA 02109-2881 · 617-570-1000

Gabor Garai · Foley & Lardner · 111 Huntington Avenue · Boston, MA 02199 · 617-342-4000

William P. Gelnaw, Jr. · Choate, Hall & Stewart · http://www.choate.com · Two International Place · Boston, MA 02110 · 617-248-5000

Louis A. Goodman · Skadden, Arps, Slate, Meagher & Flom · One Beacon Street · Boston, MA 02108-3194 · 617-573-4800

Joseph L. Johnson III · Goodwin Procter · Exchange Place · 53 State Street · Boston, MA 02109-2881 · 617-570-1000

William R. Kolb · Foley Hoag · http://www.foleyhoag.com · Seaport World Trade Center West · 155 Seaport Boulevard · Boston, MA 02210-2600 · 617-832-1000

Edouard C. Lefevre · Foley & Lardner · 111 Huntington Avenue · Boston, MA 02199 · 617-342-4000

R. Bradford Malt · a · Ropes & Gray · http://www.ropesgray.com · One International Place · Boston, MA 02110-2624 · 617-951-7000

Susan E. Pravda · Foley & Lardner · 111 Huntington Avenue · Boston, MA 02199 · 617-342-4000

Patrick J. Rondeau · WilmerHale · http://www.wilmerhale.com · 60 State Street · Boston, MA 02109 · 617-526-6000

Steven D. Singer · WilmerHale · http://www.wilmerhale.com · 60 State Street · Boston, MA 02109 · 617-526-6000

John R. Utzschneider · Bingham McCutchen · http://www.bingham.com · One Federal Street · Boston, MA 02110-1726 · 617-951-8000

Mary E. Weber · Ropes & Gray · http://www.ropesgray.com · One International Place · Boston, MA 02110-2624 · 617-951-7000

David A. Westenberg · WilmerHale · http://www.wilmerhale.com · 60 State Street · Boston, MA 02109 · 617-526-6000

James R. Westra · Weil Gotshal & Manges · 100 Federal Street, 34th Floor · Boston, MA 02110 · 617-772-8300

Jeffrey M. Wiesen · Mintz, Levin, Cohn, Ferris, Glovsky and Popeo · One Financial Center, 40th Floor · Boston, MA 02111 · 617-542-6000

Springfield

Ronald P. Weiss · a · Bulkley, Richardson and Gelinas · 1500 Main Street, Suite 2700 · P.O. Box 15507 · Springfield, MA 01115-5507 · 413-781-2820

Worcester

David L. Lougee · 2) · Mirick O'Connell DeMallie & Lougee · 100 Front Street, Suite 1700 · Worcester, MA 01608-1477 · 508-791-8500

David E. Surprenant · a · Mirick O'Connell DeMallie & Lougee · 100 Front Street, Suite 1700 · Worcester, MA 01608-1477 · 508-791-8500

MUTUAL FUNDS LAW

Boston

Joseph R. Fleming · Dechert · 200 Clarendon Street, 27th Floor · Boston, MA 02116-5021 · 617-728-7100

John W. Gerstmayr · Ropes & Gray · http://www.ropesgray.com · One International Place · Boston, MA 02110-2624 · 617-951-7000

Christopher P. Harvey · WilmerHale · http://www.wilmerhale.com · 60 State Street · Boston, MA 02109 · 617-526-6000

Roger P. Joseph · Bingham McCutchen · http://www.bingham.com · One Federal Street · Boston, MA 02110-1726 · 617-951-8000

Geoffrey R. T. Kenyon · Dechert · 200 Clarendon Street, 27th Floor · Boston, MA 02116-5021 · 617-728-7100

John M. Loder · Ropes & Gray · http://www.ropesgray.com · One International Place · Boston, MA 02110-2624 · 617-951-7000

Philip H. Newman · Goodwin Procter · Exchange Place · 53 State Street · Boston, MA 02109-2881 · 617-570-1000

John V. O'Hanlon · Dechert · 200 Clarendon Street, 27th Floor · Boston, MA 02116-5021 · 617-728-7100

Gregory D. Sheehan · Ropes & Gray · http://www.ropesgray.com · One International Place · Boston, MA 02110-2624 · 617-951-7000

NON-PROFIT/CHARITIES LAW

Boston

Richard C. Allen · Casner & Edwards · http://www.casneredwards.com · 303 Congress Street · Boston, MA 02210 · 617-426-5900

Robert E. Cowden III · Casner & Edwards · http://www.casneredwards.com · 303 Congress Street · Boston, MA 02210 · 617-426-5900

Peter C. Erichsen · Ropes & Gray · http://www.ropesgray.com · One International Place · Boston, MA 02110-2624 · 617-951-7000

Christopher M. Jedrey · McDermott Will & Emery · 28 State Street, 34th Floor · Boston, MA 02109-1775 · 617-535-4000

Frederic J. Marx · Hemenway & Barnes · 60 State Street, Eighth Floor · Boston, MA 02109-1899 · 617-227-7940

Carolyn M. Osteen · a · Ropes & Gray · http://www.ropesgray.com · One International Place · Boston, MA 02110-2624 · 617-951-7000

Kendi E. Ozmon · Ropes & Gray · http://www.ropesgray.com · One International Place · Boston, MA 02110-2624 · 617-951-7000

Amy R. Segal · WilmerHale · http://www.wilmerhale.com · 60 State Street · Boston, MA 02109 · 617-526-6000

Adelbert L. Spitzer · Ropes & Gray · http://www.ropesgray.com · One International Place · Boston, MA 02110-2624 · 617-951-7000

NON-WHITE-COLLAR CRIMINAL DEFENSE

Amherst

David P. Hoose · Sasson Hoose & Turnbull · 190 University Drive · Amherst, MA 01002 · 413-732-1939

Boston

Michael Avery · a · Suffolk University Law School · 120 Tremont Street · Boston, MA 02108-4977 · 617-573-8000

Joseph J. Balliro, Sr. · 2% · Balliro & Mondano · 99 Summer Street, Suite 1800 · Boston, MA 02110 · 617-737-8442

Juliane Balliro · a · WolfBlock · http://wolfblock.com · One Boston Place, 40th Floor · Boston, MA 02108 · 617-226-4000

Janice Bassil · Carney & Bassil · 20 Park Plaza, Suite 1405 · Boston, MA 02116 · 617-338-5566

Anthony M. Cardinale · a · Law Office of Anthony M. Cardinale · 655 Summer Street · Boston, MA 02210 · 617-345-5400

J. W. Carney, Jr. · a · Carney & Bassil · 20 Park Plaza, Suite 1405 · Boston, MA 02116 · 617-338-5566

R. Jack Cinquegrana · Choate, Hall & Stewart · http://www.choate.com · Two International Place · Boston, MA 02110 · 617-248-5000

Michael A. Collora · a · Dwyer & Collora · 600 Atlantic Avenue, 12th Floor · Boston, MA 02210-2211 · 617-371-1000

James S. Dilday · a · Grayer & Dilday · 27 School Street, Suite 400 · Boston, MA 02108 · 617-227-3470

Francis J. DiMento · 2% · DiMento & Sullivan · Seven Faneuil Hall Market Place, Third Floor · Boston, MA 02109 · 617-523-5253

James M. Doyle · Carney & Bassil · 20 Park Plaza, Suite 1405 · Boston, MA 02116 · 617-338-5566

Thomas Drechsler · Byrne & Drechsler · Eastern Harbor Office Park, Suite 201 · 50 Redfield Street · Boston, MA 02122 · 617-265-3900

David Duncan · Zalkind Rodriguez Lunt & Duncan · http://www.zrld.com · 65A Atlantic Avenue · Boston, MA 02110 · 617-742-6020

Maria R. Durant · Dwyer & Collora · 600 Atlantic Avenue, 12th Floor · Boston, MA 02210-2211 · 617-371-1000

Richard M. Egbert · a · Richard M. Egbert · 99 Summer Street, Suite 1800 · Boston, MA 02110 · 617-737-8222

Richard A. Gargiulo · Gargiulo Rudnick · 66 Long Wharf · Boston, MA 02110 · 617-742-3833

Randy Gioia · Law Office of Randy Gioia · 151 Merrimac Street, Second Floor · Boston, MA 02114 · 617-367-2480

Andrew H. Good · 2) · Good & Cormier · 83 Atlantic Avenue · Boston, MA 02110-3711 · 617-523-5933

Thomas M. Hoopes · a · Libby Hoopes · 175 Federal Street, Eighth Floor · Boston, MA 02110 · 617-338-9300

William H. Kettlewell · Dwyer & Collora · 600 Atlantic Avenue, 12th Floor · Boston, MA 02210-2211 · 617-371-1000

James W. Lawson · a · Prince, Lobel, Glovsky & Tye · http://www.princelobel.com · 100 Cambridge Street, Suite 2200 · Boston, MA 02114 · 617-456-8000

Elizabeth Lunt · Zalkind Rodriguez Lunt & Duncan · http://www.zrld.com · 65A Atlantic Avenue · Boston, MA 02110 · 617-742-6020

Martin F. Murphy · Foley Hoag · http://www.foleyhoag.com · Seaport World Trade Center West · 155 Seaport Boulevard · Boston, MA 02210-2600 · 617-832-1000

Wayne Murphy · Murphy & Associates · 600 Atlantic Avenue, 12th Floor · Boston, MA 02210 · 617-227-7777

Joseph S. Oteri · 2% · Oteri, Weinberg & Lawson · 20 Park Plaza, Suite 905 · Boston, MA 02116 · 617-227-3700

Walter B. Prince · Prince, Lobel, Glovsky & Tye · http://www.princelobel.com · 100 Cambridge Street, Suite 2200 · Boston, MA 02114 · 617-456-8000

Charles W. Rankin, Jr. · a · Rankin & Sultan · 151 Merrimac Street, Second Floor · Boston, MA 02114 · 617-720-0011

Arnold R. Rosenfeld · K&L Gates · State Street Financial Center · One Lincoln Street · Boston, MA 02111-2950 · 617-261-3100

Martin R. Rosenthal · a · Martin R. Rosenthal · 65-A Atlantic Avenue · Boston, MA 02110 · 617-742-0606

Michael R. Schneider · Salsberg & Schneider · 95 Commercial Wharf · Boston, MA 02110 · 617-227-7788

Jonathan Shapiro · a · Stern Shapiro Weissberg & Garin · 90 Canal Street, Fifth Floor · Boston, MA 02114-2022 · 617-742-5800

Robert L. Sheketoff · a · Sheketoff & Homan · One McKinley Square, Third Floor · Boston, MA 02109 617-367-3449

Max D. Stern · 2) · Stern Shapiro Weissberg & Garin · 90 Canal Street, Fifth Floor · Boston, MA 02114-2022 · 617-742-5800

James L. Sultan · a · Rankin & Sultan · 151 Merrimac Street, Second Floor · Boston, MA 02114 · 617-720-0011

John G. Swomley · Swomley & Associates · 227 Lewis Wharf · Boston, MA 02110 · 617-227-9443

Kathy B. Weinman · Dwyer & Collora · 600 Atlantic Avenue, 12th Floor · Boston, MA 02210-2211 · 617-371-1000

Elliot M. Weinstein · a · Elliot M. Weinstein · 83 Atlantic Avenue · Boston, MA 02110 · 617-367-9334

Norman S. Zalkind · a · Zalkind Rodriguez Lunt & Duncan · http://www.zrld.com · 65A Atlantic Avenue · Boston, MA 02110 · 617-742-6020

Brockton

Martin Kenneth Leppo · 2% · Leppo & Leppo · Seven Christy's Drive, Suite One · Brockton, MA 02301 · 508-580-3733

Kevin J. Reddington · a · Kevin J. Reddington · Williamsburg Square, Suite 203 · 1342 Belmont Street · Brockton, MA 02301 · 508-583-4280

Cambridge

Judith L. Lindahl · a · Judith L. Lindahl · Two Worthington Street · Cambridge, MA 02138 · 617-864-1089

Charlestown

Charles A. Clifford · a · Clifford Law Office · 305 Main Street · Charlestown, MA 02129 · 617-241-7440

Northampton

John Pucci · Fierst, Pucci & Kinder · 64 Gothic Street · Northampton, MA 01060 · 413-584-8067

Pittsfield

Leonard H. Cohen · Cain Hibbard Myers & Cook · 66 West Street · Pittsfield, MA 01201-5764 · 413-443-4771

Quincy

Martin S. Cosgrove · Cosgrove, Eisenberg and Kiley · 803 Hancock Street · P.O. Box 189 · Quincy, MA 02170 · 617-479-7770

Shrewsbury

Michael M. Monopoli · 2) · Michael M. Monopoli · 415 Boston Turnpike Road, Suite 212 · Shrewsbury, MA 01545 · 508-754-2229

Springfield

Vincent A. Bongiorni · a · Bongiorni & Mastroianni · 95 State Street, Suite 309 · Springfield, MA 01103 413-732-0222

Efrem A. Gordon · 2) · Efrem A. Gordon · 101 State Street, Suite 410 · Springfield, MA 01103 · 413-737-4316

Michael O. Jennings · a · Michael O. Jennings · 73 Chestnut Street · Springfield, MA 01103 · 413-737-7349

Jack F. St. Clair · 2% · Jack F. St. Clair · 73 Chestnut Street · Springfield, MA 01103 · 413-737-5000

Worcester

Peter L. Ettenberg · 2) · Gould & Ettenberg · 370 Main Street, Suite 1050 · Worcester, MA 01608 · 508-752-6733

James J. Gribouski · a · Glickman, Sugarman, Kneeland & Gribouski · 11 Harvard Street · P.O. Box 2917 · Worcester, MA 01613-2917 · 508-756-6206

Boston

Lisa G. Arrowood · Todd & Weld · http://www.toddweld.com · 28 State Street, 31st Floor · Boston, MA 02109 · 617-720-2626

Charles W. Barrett, Jr. · 2) · Esdaile, Barrett & Esdaile · 75 Federal Street, 16th Floor · Boston, MA 02110 · 617-482-0333

Edward J. Barshak · 2% · Sugarman, Rogers, Barshak & Cohen · http://www.srbc.com · 101 Merrimac Street, Ninth Floor · Boston, MA 02114-4737 · 617-227-3030

Leo V. Boyle · 2) · Meehan, Boyle, Black & Bogdanow · Two Center Plaza, Suite 600 · Boston, MA 02108-1922 · 617-523-8300

Thomas W. Braun · Moquin & Daley · 388 Commonwealth Avenue · Boston, MA 02215 · 617-536-0606

Thomas D. Burns · 2) · Burns & Levinson · http://www.burnslev.com · 125 Summer Street · Boston, MA 02110-1624 · 617-345-3000

Richard P. Campbell · Campbell Campbell Edwards & Conroy · One Constitution Plaza, Third Floor · Boston, MA 02129 · 617-241-3000

Robert W. Casby · a · Sugarman and Sugarman · One Beacon Street, 13th Floor · Boston, MA 02108 · 617-542-1000

John D. Cassidy · Ficksman & Conley · 98 North Washington Street, Suite 500 · Boston, MA 02114 · 617-720-1515

Lawrence Cetrulo · Cetrulo & Capone · Two Seaport Lane, 10th Floor · Boston, MA 02210 · 617-217-5500

Ellen Epstein Cohen · Adler, Cohen, Harvey, Wakeman & Guekguezian · 75 Federal Street · Boston, MA 02110 · 617-423-6674

William J. Dailey, Jr. · a · Sloane & Walsh · Three Center Plaza, Eighth Floor · Boston, MA 02108 · 617-523-6010

Edmund P. Daley · a · Moquin & Daley · 388 Commonwealth Avenue · Boston, MA 02215 · 617-536-0606

Michael DeMarco · K&L Gates · State Street Financial Center · One Lincoln Street · Boston, MA 02111-2950 · 617-261-3100

Joseph L. Doherty · Doherty & Quill · 225 Franklin Street, 26th Floor · Boston, MA 02110 · 617-217-2837

William J. Doyle, Jr. · a · Leavis & Rest · 83 Central Street, Third Floor · Boston, MA 02109-3413 · 617-742-1700

Leo J. Dunn III · Crowe & Dunn · 141 Tremont Street · Boston, MA 02111 · 617-367-6767

James N. Esdaile, Jr. · 2% · Esdaile, Barrett & Esdaile · 75 Federal Street, 16th Floor · Boston, MA 02110 617-482-0333

John B. Flemming · Law Office of John Flemming · 35 India Street · Boston, MA 02110-3816 · 617-523-0911

David M. Gould · Ficksman & Conley · 98 North Washington Street, Suite 500 · Boston, MA 02114 · 617-720-1515

A. Bernard Guekguezian · Adler, Cohen, Harvey, Wakeman & Guekguezian · 75 Federal Street · Boston, MA 02110 · 617-423-6674

David G. Hanrahan · Gilman, McLaughlin & Hanrahan · 101 Merrimac Street · P.O. Box 9601 · Boston, MA 02114-9601 · 617-227-9999

David J. Hatem · Donovan Hatem · World Trade Center East · Two Seaport Lane · Boston, MA 02210 · 617-406-4500

Edward T. Hinchey · Sloane & Walsh · Three Center Plaza, Eighth Floor · Boston, MA 02108 · 617-523-6010

Patrick T. Jones · Cooley Manion Jones · 21 Custom House Street, Sixth Floor · Boston, MA 02110 · 617-737-3100

Patricia L. Kelly · Esdaile, Barrett & Esdaile · 75 Federal Street, 16th Floor · Boston, MA 02110 · 617-482-0333

Lawrence J. Kenney, Jr. · Sloane & Walsh · Three Center Plaza, Eighth Floor · Boston, MA 02108 · 617-523-6010

Peter C. Knight · Morrison Mahoney · 250 Summer Street · Boston, MA 02210 · 617-439-7500

John F. X. Lawler · Adler Pollock & Sheehan · 175 Federal Street, 10th Floor · Boston, MA 02110-2210 · 617-482-0600

Paul F. Leavis · a · Leavis & Rest · 83 Central Street, Third Floor · Boston, MA 02109-3413 · 617-742-1700

Marianne C. LeBlanc · Sugarman and Sugarman · One Beacon Street, 13th Floor · Boston, MA 02108 · 617-542-1000

Joan A. Lukey · a · Ropes & Gray · http://www.ropesgray.com · One International Place · Boston, MA 02110-2624 · 617-951-7000

David McMorris · Thornton & Naumes · 100 Summer Street, 30th Floor · Boston, MA 02110 · 617-720-1333

Andrew C. Meyer, Jr. · a · Lubin & Meyer · 100 City Hall Plaza, Fourth Floor · Boston, MA 02108 · 617-720-4447

Michael E. Mone, Sr. · 2% · Esdaile, Barrett & Esdaile · 75 Federal Street, 16th Floor · Boston, MA 02110 617-482-0333

Elizabeth Mulvey · a · Crowe and Mulvey · 141 Tremont Street, Eighth Floor · Boston, MA 02111 · 617-426-4488

Jodi M. Petrucelli · Sugarman and Sugarman · One Beacon Street, 13th Floor · Boston, MA 02108 · 617-542-1000

Charles P. Reidy III · 2) · Martin, Magnuson, McCarthy & Kenney · http://www.mmmk.com · 101 Merrimac Street, Suite 700 · Boston, MA 02114 · 617-227-3240

Peter Resnik · McDermott Will & Emery · 28 State Street, 34th Floor · Boston, MA 02109-1775 · 617-535-4000

Neil Rossman · Rossman & Rossman · Market Place Center, Three North · 200 State Street · Boston, MA 02109 · 617-439-9559

John P. Ryan · a · Sloane & Walsh · Three Center Plaza, Eighth Floor · Boston, MA 02108 · 617-523-6010

Francis J. Sally · Sally & Fitch · One Beacon Street · Boston, MA 02108 · 617-542-5542

Camille Francis Sarrouf, Sr. · 2) · Sarrouf Corso · 95 Commercial Wharf · Boston, MA 02110-3816 · 617-227-5800

Steven H. Schafer · Steven H. Schafer & Associates · 141 Tremont Street, Sixth Floor · Boston, MA 02111-1209 · 617-423-2447

W. Thomas Smith · a · Sugarman and Sugarman · One Beacon Street, 13th Floor · Boston, MA 02108 · 617-542-1000

Neil Sugarman · 2) · Sugarman and Sugarman · One Beacon Street, 13th Floor · Boston, MA 02108 · 617-542-1000

Paul R. Sugarman · a · Sugarman and Sugarman · One Beacon Street, 13th Floor · Boston, MA 02108 · 617-542-1000

Edward M. Swartz · Swartz & Swartz · 10 Marshall Street · Boston, MA 02108 · 617-742-1900

Anthony Tarricone · a · Kreindler & Kreindler · 277 Dartmouth Street · Boston, MA 02116 · 617-424-9100

J. Owen Todd · 2% · Todd & Weld · http://www.toddweld.com · 28 State Street, 31st Floor · Boston, MA 02109 · 617-720-2626

Edwin L. Wallace · Thornton & Naumes · 100 Summer Street, 30th Floor · Boston, MA 02110 · 617-720-1333

Michael D. Weisman · Weisman & McIntyre · 99 Summer Street, Suite 2010 · Boston, MA 02110 · 617-720-2727

Valerie A. Yarashus · Yarashus Wagner Cook Freiberger & Washienko · One Beacon Street, 33rd Floor · Boston, MA 02108 · 617-723-0008

Richard M. Zielinski · Goulston & Storrs · 400 Atlantic Avenue · Boston, MA 02110-3333 · 617-482-1776

Cambridge

Robert V. Costello · a · Ferriter and Costello · 171 Third Street · Cambridge, MA 02141 · 617-547-5600

Northampton

Harry L. Miles · a · Green, Miles, Lipton & Fitz-Gibbon · 77 Pleasant Street · P.O. Box 210 · Northampton, MA 01061-0210 · 413-586-8218

Pittsfield

Leonard H. Cohen · Cain Hibbard Myers & Cook · 66 West Street · Pittsfield, MA 01201-5764 · 413-443-4771

Quincy

Martin S. Cosgrove · Cosgrove, Eisenberg and Kiley · 803 Hancock Street · P.O. Box 189 · Quincy, MA 02170 · 617-479-7770

Lewis C. Eisenberg · Cosgrove, Eisenberg and Kiley · 803 Hancock Street · P.O. Box 189 · Quincy, MA 02170 · 617-479-7770

Salem

Walter A. Costello, Jr. · a · Costello & Associates · 314 Essex Street · Salem, MA 01970 · 978-740-0700

South Easton

Francis J. Lynch III · Lynch & Lynch · 45 Bristol Drive · South Easton, MA 02375 · 508-230-2500

Springfield

Charles K. Bergin, Jr. · a · Charles K. Bergin, Jr. · 73 Chestnut Street · Springfield, MA 01103 · 413-739-0333

Donald W. Blakesley · a · Pellegrini, Seeley, Ryan & Blakesley · 1145 Main Street, Suite 308 · P.O. Box 30009 · Springfield, MA 01103-0009 · 413-785-5300

Michael H. Burke · a · Bulkley, Richardson and Gelinas · 1500 Main Street, Suite 2700 · P.O. Box 15507 Springfield, MA 01115-5507 · 413-781-2820

Philip J. Callan, Jr. · a · Doherty, Wallace, Pillsbury and Murphy · One Monarch Place, Suite 1900 · 1414 Main Street · Springfield, MA 01144-1900 · 413-733-3111

John J. Egan · Egan, Flanagan and Cohen · 67 Market Street · P.O. Box 9035 · Springfield, MA 01102 · 413-737-0260

Robert A. Gelinas · a · Bulkley, Richardson and Gelinas · 1500 Main Street, Suite 2700 · P.O. Box 15507 Springfield, MA 01115-5507 · 413-781-2820

Ronald C. Kidd · a · Robinson Donovan · http://www.robinson-donovan.com · 1500 Main Street, Suite 1600 · P.O. Box 15609 · Springfield, MA 01115 · 413-732-2301

Matthew J. King · Robinson Donovan · http://www.robinson-donovan.com · 1500 Main Street, Suite 1600 P.O. Box 15609 · Springfield, MA 01115 · 413-732-2301

Jeffrey L. McCormick · Robinson Donovan · http://www.robinson-donovan.com · 1500 Main Street, Suite 1600 · P.O. Box 15609 · Springfield, MA 01115 · 413-732-2301

Edward J. McDonough, Jr. · Egan, Flanagan and Cohen · 67 Market Street · P.O. Box 9035 · Springfield, MA 01102 · 413-737-0260

L. Jeffrey Meehan · Doherty, Wallace, Pillsbury and Murphy · One Monarch Place, Suite 1900 · 1414 Main Street · Springfield, MA 01144-1900 · 413-733-3111

Nancy Frankel Pelletier · Robinson Donovan · http://www.robinson-donovan.com · 1500 Main Street, Suite 1600 · P.O. Box 15609 · Springfield, MA 01115 · 413-732-2301

Melinda Phelps · Bulkley, Richardson and Gelinas · 1500 Main Street, Suite 2700 · P.O. Box 15507 · Springfield, MA 01115-5507 · 413-781-2820

Waltham

Leonard A. Simon · a · Leonard A. Simon · 1000 Winter Street, Suite 1100 · Waltham, MA 02451 · 781-290-5788

Woburn

Philip E. Murray, Jr. · Murray, Kelly & Bertrand · 600 Unicorn Park Drive · Woburn, MA 01801 · 781-569-0020

Worcester

William E. Bernstein · 2) · Bernstein, Burwick & Tucker · 10 Mechanic Street, Suite 150 · Worcester, MA 01608 · 508-755-5555

Thomas B. Farrey III · Burns & Farrey · 446 Main Street, 22nd Floor · Worcester, MA 01608-2302 · 508-756-6288

John F. Hurley, Jr. · Pojani Hurley Ritter & Salvidio · 446 Main Street, 21st Floor · Worcester, MA 01608 · 508-798-2480

John F. Keenan · 2) · Wolfson, Keenan, Cotton & Meagher · 390 Main Street, Suite 1000 · Worcester, MA 01608-2575 · 508-791-8181

Gerard R. Laurence · 2) · Milton, Laurence & Dixon · 100 Front Street, Suite 1510 · Worcester, MA 01608-1430 · 508-791-6386

Elizabeth W. Morse · Tashjian, Simsarian & Wickstrom · 370 Main Street · Worcester, MA 01608-1763 · 508-756-1578

Paul P. O'Connor · Milton, Laurence & Dixon · 100 Front Street, Suite 1510 · Worcester, MA 01608-1430 · 508-791-6386

Richard T. Tucker · Bernstein, Burwick & Tucker · 10 Mechanic Street, Suite 150 · Worcester, MA 01608 · 508-755-5555

Seymour Weinstein · 2) · Weinstein & Weinstein · 10 Mechanic Street, Suite 300 · Worcester, MA 01608 508-757-7000

John A. Wickstrom · 2) · Tashjian, Simsarian & Wickstrom · 370 Main Street · Worcester, MA 01608-1763 · 508-756-1578

Timothy P. Wickstrom · Tashjian, Simsarian & Wickstrom · 370 Main Street · Worcester, MA 01608-1763 · 508-756-1578

David A. Wojcik · Christopher, Hays, Wojcik & Mavricos · 370 Main Street, Suite 700 · Worcester, MA 01608 · 508-792-2800

Daniel M. Wrenn · Milton, Laurence & Dixon · 100 Front Street, Suite 1510 · Worcester, MA 01608-1430 · 508-791-6386

PRIVATE FUNDS LAW

Boston

Thomas A. Beaudoin · WilmerHale · http://www.wilmerhale.com · 60 State Street · Boston, MA 02109 · 617-526-6000

Daniel P. Finkelman · Proskauer Rose · http://www.proskauer.com · One International Place · Boston, MA 02110-2600 · 617-526-9600

Elizabeth Shea Fries · Goodwin Procter · Exchange Place · 53 State Street · Boston, MA 02109-2881 · 617-570-1000

David P. Kreisler · Weil Gotshal & Manges · 100 Federal Street, 34th Floor · Boston, MA 02110 · 617-772-8300

Mary B. Kuusiato · Proskauer Rose · http://www.proskauer.com · One International Place · Boston, MA 02110-2600 · 617-526-9600

R. Bradford Malt · a · Ropes & Gray · http://www.ropesgray.com · One International Place · Boston, MA 02110-2624 · 617-951-7000

Raj Marphatia · Ropes & Gray · http://www.ropesgray.com · One International Place · Boston, MA 02110-2624 · 617-951-7000

Arnold P. May · Proskauer Rose · http://www.proskauer.com · One International Place · Boston, MA 02110-2600 · 617-526-9600

Ann L. Milner · Ropes & Gray · http://www.ropesgray.com · One International Place · Boston, MA 02110-2624 · 617-951-7000

Malcolm B. Nicholls III · Proskauer Rose · http://www.proskauer.com · One International Place · Boston, MA 02110-2600 · 617-526-9600

Robin A. Painter · Proskauer Rose · http://www.proskauer.com · One International Place · Boston, MA 02110-2600 · 617-526-9600

Charles W. Robins · Weil Gotshal & Manges · 100 Federal Street, 34th Floor · Boston, MA 02110 · 617-772-8300

Alfred O. Rose · a · Ropes & Gray · http://www.ropesgray.com · One International Place · Boston, MA 02110-2624 · 617-951-7000

Sarah Rothermel · WilmerHale · http://www.wilmerhale.com · 60 State Street · Boston, MA 02109 · 617-526-6000

Larry Jordan Rowe · Ropes & Gray · http://www.ropesgray.com · One International Place · Boston, MA 02110-2624 · 617-951-7000

Gregory D. Sheehan · Ropes & Gray · http://www.ropesgray.com · One International Place · Boston, MA 02110-2624 · 617-951-7000

R. Newcomb Stillwell · Ropes & Gray · http://www.ropesgray.com · One International Place · Boston, MA 02110-2624 · 617-951-7000

Andrew E. Taylor, Jr. · Choate, Hall & Stewart · http://www.choate.com · Two International Place · Boston, MA 02110 · 617-248-5000

David W. Tegeler · Proskauer Rose · http://www.proskauer.com · One International Place · Boston, MA 02110-2600 · 617-526-9600

James R. Westra · Weil Gotshal & Manges · 100 Federal Street, 34th Floor · Boston, MA 02110 · 617-772-8300

PRODUCT LIABILITY LITIGATION

Boston

David A. Barry · Sugarman, Rogers, Barshak & Cohen · http://www.srbc.com · 101 Merrimac Street, Ninth Floor · Boston, MA 02114-4737 · 617-227-3030

Richard P. Campbell · Campbell Campbell Edwards & Conroy · One Constitution Plaza, Third Floor · Boston, MA 02129 · 617-241-3000

Lawrence Cetrulo · Cetrulo & Capone · Two Seaport Lane, 10th Floor · Boston, MA 02210 · 617-217-5500

James J. Dillon · Foley Hoag · http://www.foleyhoag.com · Seaport World Trade Center West · 155 Seaport Boulevard · Boston, MA 02210-2600 · 617-832-1000

David R. Geiger · Foley Hoag · http://www.foleyhoag.com · Seaport World Trade Center West · 155 Seaport Boulevard · Boston, MA 02210-2600 · 617-832-1000

Thomas J. Griffin · Goodwin Procter · Exchange Place · 53 State Street · Boston, MA 02109-2881 · 617-570-1000

Joseph J. Leghorn · Nixon Peabody · 100 Summer Street · Boston, MA 02110-1832 · 617-345-1000

Neil T. Leifer · Thornton & Naumes · 100 Summer Street, 30th Floor · Boston, MA 02110 · 617-720-1333

Andrew J. McElaney, Jr. · Nutter McClennen & Fish · http://www.nutter.com · World Trade Center West · 155 Seaport Boulevard · Boston, MA 02210 · 617-439-2000

Kenneth J. Parsigian · Goodwin Procter · Exchange Place · 53 State Street · Boston, MA 02109-2881 · 617-570-1000

Charles P. Reidy III · 2) · Martin, Magnuson, McCarthy & Kenney · http://www.mmmk.com · 101 Merrimac Street, Suite 700 · Boston, MA 02114 · 617-227-3240

Camille Francis Sarrouf, Sr. · 2) · Sarrouf Corso · 95 Commercial Wharf · Boston, MA 02110-3816 · 617-227-5800

Neil Sugarman · 2) · Sugarman and Sugarman · One Beacon Street, 13th Floor · Boston, MA 02108 · 617-542-1000

Anthony Tarricone · a · Kreindler & Kreindler · 277 Dartmouth Street · Boston, MA 02116 · 617-424-9100

Quincy

Lewis C. Eisenberg · Cosgrove, Eisenberg and Kiley · 803 Hancock Street · P.O. Box 189 · Quincy, MA 02170 · 617-479-7770

PROFESSIONAL MALPRACTICE LAW

Boston

David J. Hatem · Donovan Hatem · World Trade Center East · Two Seaport Lane · Boston, MA 02210 · 617-406-4500

Charles P. Reidy III · 2) · Martin, Magnuson, McCarthy & Kenney · http://www.mmmk.com · 101 Merrimac Street, Suite 700 · Boston, MA 02114 · 617-227-3240

Wilson D. Rogers, Jr. · The Rogers Law Firm · 100 Cambridge Street, 20th Floor, Suite 2000 · Boston, MA 02114 · 617-723-1100

PROJECT FINANCE LAW

Boston

William P. Gelnaw, Jr. · Choate, Hall & Stewart · http://www.choate.com · Two International Place · Boston, MA 02110 · 617-248-5000

James A. McDaniel · Choate, Hall & Stewart · http://www.choate.com · Two International Place · Boston, MA 02110 · 617-248-5000

Peter M. Palladino · Choate, Hall & Stewart · http://www.choate.com · Two International Place · Boston, MA 02110 · 617-248-5000

Marc A. Reardon · Bingham McCutchen · http://www.bingham.com · One Federal Street · Boston, MA 02110-1726 · 617-951-8000

PUBLIC FINANCE LAW

Boston

Neil P. Arkuss · a · Edwards Angell Palmer & Dodge · Prudential Center · 111 Huntington Avenue · Boston, MA 02199-7613 · 617-239-0100

Lawrence D. Bragg III · Ropes & Gray · http://www.ropesgray.com · One International Place · Boston, MA 02110-2624 · 617-951-7000

Meghan B. Burke · Mintz, Levin, Cohn, Ferris, Glovsky and Popeo · One Financial Center, 40th Floor · Boston, MA 02111 · 617-542-6000

Robert H. Hale · Edwards Angell Palmer & Dodge · Prudential Center · 111 Huntington Avenue · Boston, MA 02199-7613 · 617-239-0100

Richard A. Manley, Jr. · Edwards Angell Palmer & Dodge · Prudential Center · 111 Huntington Avenue Boston, MA 02199-7613 · 617-239-0100

Thomas W. Merrill · Edwards Angell Palmer & Dodge · Prudential Center · 111 Huntington Avenue · Boston, MA 02199-7613 · 617-239-0100

John R. Regier · Mintz, Levin, Cohn, Ferris, Glovsky and Popeo · One Financial Center, 40th Floor · Boston, MA 02111 · 617-542-6000

Loretta R. Richard · Ropes & Gray · http://www.ropesgray.com · One International Place · Boston, MA 02110-2624 · 617-951-7000

Gregory A. Sandomirsky · Mintz, Levin, Cohn, Ferris, Glovsky and Popeo · One Financial Center, 40th Floor · Boston, MA 02111 · 617-542-6000

Maxwell D. Solet · Mintz, Levin, Cohn, Ferris, Glovsky and Popeo · One Financial Center, 40th Floor · Boston, MA 02111 · 617-542-6000

Walter J. St. Onge III · Edwards Angell Palmer & Dodge · Prudential Center · 111 Huntington Avenue · Boston, MA 02199-7613 · 617-239-0100

Roger P. Vacco · Edwards Angell Palmer & Dodge · Prudential Center · 111 Huntington Avenue · Boston, MA 02199-7613 · 617-239-0100

REAL ESTATE LAW

Boston

Marianne Ajemian · Nutter McClennen & Fish · http://www.nutter.com · World Trade Center West · 155 Seaport Boulevard · Boston, MA 02210 · 617-439-2000

Stephen Carr Anderson · 2% · Law Office of Stephen Carr Anderson · 160 Federal Street · Boston, MA 02110 · 617-426-1450

Katharine E. Bachman · a · WilmerHale · http://www.wilmerhale.com · 60 State Street · Boston, MA 02109 · 617-526-6000

Christopher B. Barker · Goodwin Procter · Exchange Place · 53 State Street · Boston, MA 02109-2881 · 617-570-1000

Keith R. Barnett · WilmerHale · http://www.wilmerhale.com · 60 State Street · Boston, MA 02109 · 617-526-6000

Sean T. Boulger · WilmerHale · http://www.wilmerhale.com · 60 State Street · Boston, MA 02109 · 617-526-6000

James M. Broderick · Goodwin Procter · Exchange Place · 53 State Street · Boston, MA 02109-2881 · 617-570-1000

Stephen I. Burr · Foley & Lardner · 111 Huntington Avenue · Boston, MA 02199 · 617-342-4000

Joseph J. Christian · DLA Piper · 33 Arch Street, 26th Floor · Boston, MA 02110-1447 · 617-406-6000

Andrew H. Cohn · a · WilmerHale · http://www.wilmerhale.com · 60 State Street · Boston, MA 02109 · 617-526-6000

Scott E. Cooper · Holland & Knight · http://www.hklaw.com · 10 Saint James Avenue, 11th Floor · Boston, MA 02116 · 617-523-2700

Robert C. Davis · 2) · Goulston & Storrs · 400 Atlantic Avenue · Boston, MA 02110-3333 · 617-482-1776

Robert A. Fishman · Nutter McClennen & Fish · http://www.nutter.com · World Trade Center West · 155 Seaport Boulevard · Boston, MA 02210 · 617-439-2000

William B. Forbush III · DLA Piper · 33 Arch Street, 26th Floor · Boston, MA 02110-1447 · 617-406-6000

Michael H. Glazer · Goodwin Procter · Exchange Place · 53 State Street · Boston, MA 02109-2881 · 617-570-1000

Alan P. Gottlieb · Hinckley, Allen & Snyder · http://www.haslaw.com · 28 State Street, 29th Floor · Boston, MA 02109-1775 · 617-345-9000

John J. Griffin, Jr. · 2% · Edwards Angell Palmer & Dodge · Prudential Center · 111 Huntington Avenue · Boston, MA 02199-7613 · 617-239-0100

Francis X. Hanlon · a · Ropes & Gray · http://www.ropesgray.com · One International Place · Boston, MA 02110-2624 · 617-951-7000

Michael J. Haroz · Goulston & Storrs · 400 Atlantic Avenue · Boston, MA 02110-3333 · 617-482-1776

Martin R. Healy · a · Goodwin Procter · Exchange Place · 53 State Street · Boston, MA 02109-2881 · 617-570-1000

Edward S. Hershfeld · Brown Rudnick · http://www.brbilaw.com · One Financial Center · Boston, MA 02111 · 617-856-8200

Kenneth B. Hoffman · Holland & Knight · http://www.hklaw.com · 10 Saint James Avenue, 11th Floor · Boston, MA 02116 · 617-523-2700

Geoffrey A. Howell · DLA Piper · 33 Arch Street, 26th Floor · Boston, MA 02110-1447 · 617-406-6000

Paul Jakubowski · WilmerHale · http://www.wilmerhale.com · 60 State Street · Boston, MA 02109 · 617-526-6000

Minta E. Kay · Goodwin Procter · Exchange Place · 53 State Street · Boston, MA 02109-2881 · 617-570-1000

Cynthia B. Keliher · McCarter & English · 265 Franklin Street · Boston, MA 02110 · 617-449-6500

Jordan P. Krasnow · 2% · Goulston & Storrs · 400 Atlantic Avenue · Boston, MA 02110-3333 · 617-482-1776

Raymond M. Kwasnick · Goulston & Storrs · 400 Atlantic Avenue · Boston, MA 02110-3333 · 617-482-1776

Philip S. Lapatin · Holland & Knight · http://www.hklaw.com · 10 Saint James Avenue, 11th Floor · Boston, MA 02116 · 617-523-2700

Stephen P. Lindsay · 2% · Ropes & Gray · http://www.ropesgray.com · One International Place · Boston, MA 02110-2624 · 617-951-7000

Walter R. McCabe III · Ropes & Gray · http://www.ropesgray.com · One International Place · Boston, MA 02110-2624 · 617-951-7000

Diane M. McDermott · McCarter & English · 265 Franklin Street · Boston, MA 02110 · 617-449-6500

Beth H. Mitchell · Nutter McClennen & Fish · http://www.nutter.com · World Trade Center West · 155 Seaport Boulevard · Boston, MA 02210 · 617-439-2000

William R. O'Reilly, Jr. · WilmerHale · http://www.wilmerhale.com · 60 State Street · Boston, MA 02109 617-526-6000

Daniel J. Ossoff · Rackemann, Sawyer & Brewster · http://www.rackemann.com · 160 Federal Street, 13th-15th Floor · Boston, MA 02110-1700 · 617-542-2300

Gregory D. Peterson · DLA Piper · 33 Arch Street, 26th Floor · Boston, MA 02110-1447 · 617-406-6000

Frederick J. Pittaro · a · Mintz, Levin, Cohn, Ferris, Glovsky and Popeo · One Financial Center, 40th Floor · Boston, MA 02111 · 617-542-6000

Myrna Putziger · a · Rubin and Rudman · 50 Rowes Wharf · Boston, MA 02110-3319 · 617-330-7000

John E. Rattigan, Jr. · DLA Piper · 33 Arch Street, 26th Floor · Boston, MA 02110-1447 · 617-406-6000

Joel Reck · Brown Rudnick · http://www.brbilaw.com · One Financial Center · Boston, MA 02111 · 617-856-8200

Alan W. Rottenberg · 2% · Goulston & Storrs · 400 Atlantic Avenue · Boston, MA 02110-3333 · 617-482-1776

Eli Rubenstein · a · Goulston & Storrs · 400 Atlantic Avenue · Boston, MA 02110-3333 · 617-482-1776

Richard D. Rudman · DLA Piper · 33 Arch Street, 26th Floor · Boston, MA 02110-1447 · 617-406-6000

Edward A. Saxe · Bingham McCutchen · http://www.bingham.com · One Federal Street · Boston, MA 02110-1726 · 617-951-8000

Paul D. Schwartz · Goodwin Procter · Exchange Place · 53 State Street · Boston, MA 02109-2881 · 617-570-1000

Joel H. Sirkin · WilmerHale · http://www.wilmerhale.com · 60 State Street · Boston, MA 02109 · 617-526-6000

Timothy M. Smith · Nutter McClennen & Fish · http://www.nutter.com · World Trade Center West · 155 Seaport Boulevard · Boston, MA 02210 · 617-439-2000

Michael S. Sophocles · Choate, Hall & Stewart · http://www.choate.com · Two International Place · Boston, MA 02110 · 617-248-5000

John L. Sullivan · DLA Piper · 33 Arch Street, 26th Floor · Boston, MA 02110-1447 · 617-406-6000

Elliot M. Surkin · 2% · DLA Piper · 33 Arch Street, 26th Floor · Boston, MA 02110-1447 · 617-406-6000

Daniel A. Taylor · a · DLA Piper · 33 Arch Street, 26th Floor · Boston, MA 02110-1447 · 617-406-6000

Henry H. Thayer · 2% · Rackemann, Sawyer & Brewster · http://www.rackemann.com · 160 Federal Street, 13th-15th Floor · Boston, MA 02110-1700 · 617-542-2300

Richard A. Toelke · Bingham McCutchen · http://www.bingham.com · One Federal Street · Boston, MA 02110-1726 · 617-951-8000

Robert Tuchmann · 2) · WilmerHale · http://www.wilmerhale.com · 60 State Street · Boston, MA 02109 · 617-526-6000

Lawrence E. Uchill · a · DLA Piper · 33 Arch Street, 26th Floor · Boston, MA 02110-1447 · 617-406-6000

Springfield

A. Craig Brown · a · Doherty, Wallace, Pillsbury and Murphy · One Monarch Place, Suite 1900 · 1414 Main Street · Springfield, MA 01144-1900 · 413-733-3111

Richard M. Gaberman · a · Robinson Donovan · http://www.robinson-donovan.com · 1500 Main Street, Suite 1600 · P.O. Box 15609 · Springfield, MA 01115 · 413-732-2301

Michael S. Ratner · 2) · Bacon & Wilson · 33 State Street · Springfield, MA 01103 · 413-781-0560

Stephen A. Shatz · a · Shatz, Schwartz and Fentin · 1441 Main Street, Suite 1100 · Springfield, MA 01103 · 413-737-1131

Worcester

Joseph W. Allen III · a · Dunn, McGee & Allen · 446 Main Street, Suite 1900 · Worcester, MA 01608 · 508-754-8100

SECURITIES LAW

Boston

William B. Asher, Jr. · a · Choate, Hall & Stewart · http://www.choate.com · Two International Place · Boston, MA 02110 · 617-248-5000

Randall W. Bodner · Ropes & Gray · http://www.ropesgray.com · One International Place · Boston, MA 02110-2624 · 617-951-7000

Mark G. Borden · a · WilmerHale · http://www.wilmerhale.com · 60 State Street · Boston, MA 02109 · 617-526-6000

Steven C. Browne · Bingham McCutchen · http://www.bingham.com · One Federal Street · Boston, MA 02110-1726 · 617-951-8000

John A. Burgess · WilmerHale · http://www.wilmerhale.com · 60 State Street · Boston, MA 02109 · 617-526-6000

James R. Carroll · Skadden, Arps, Slate, Meagher & Flom · One Beacon Street · Boston, MA 02108-3194 617-573-4800

Roslyn G. Daum · a · Choate, Hall & Stewart · http://www.choate.com · Two International Place · Boston, MA 02110 · 617-248-5000

John D. Donovan, Jr. · a · Ropes & Gray · http://www.ropesgray.com · One International Place · Boston, MA 02110-2624 · 617-951-7000

Thomas J. Dougherty · Skadden, Arps, Slate, Meagher & Flom · One Beacon Street · Boston, MA 02108-3194 · 617-573-4800

Michael L. Fantozzi · Mintz, Levin, Cohn, Ferris, Glovsky and Popeo · One Financial Center, 40th Floor Boston, MA 02111 · 617-542-6000

Jason D. Frank · Bingham McCutchen · http://www.bingham.com · One Federal Street · Boston, MA 02110-1726 · 617-951-8000

Richard M. Gelb · Gelb & Gelb · 84 State Street · Boston, MA 02109 · 617-345-0010

Jordan D. Hershman · Bingham McCutchen · http://www.bingham.com · One Federal Street · Boston, MA 02110-1726 · 617-951-8000

Keith F. Higgins · a · Ropes & Gray · http://www.ropesgray.com · One International Place · Boston, MA 02110-2624 · 617-951-7000

Julie H. Jones · Ropes & Gray · http://www.ropesgray.com · One International Place · Boston, MA 02110-2624 · 617-951-7000

Paul M. Kinsella · Ropes & Gray · http://www.ropesgray.com · One International Place · Boston, MA 02110-2624 · 617-951-7000

Jonathan L. Kravetz · Mintz, Levin, Cohn, Ferris, Glovsky and Popeo · One Financial Center, 40th Floor · Boston, MA 02111 · 617-542-6000

Edwin L. Miller, Jr. · Sullivan & Worcester · One Post Office Square · Boston, MA 02109 · 617-338-2800

Robert L. Nutt · 2) · Ropes & Gray · http://www.ropesgray.com · One International Place · Boston, MA 02110-2624 · 617-951-7000

Patrick O'Brien · Ropes & Gray · http://www.ropesgray.com · One International Place · Boston, MA 02110-2624 · 617-951-7000

William H. Paine · WilmerHale · http://www.wilmerhale.com · 60 State Street · Boston, MA 02109 · 617-526-6000

Brian E. Pastuszenski · Goodwin Procter · Exchange Place · 53 State Street · Boston, MA 02109-2881 · 617-570-1000

Stephen D. Poss · a · Goodwin Procter · Exchange Place · 53 State Street · Boston, MA 02109-2881 · 617-570-1000

Gerald Rath · Bingham McCutchen · http://www.bingham.com · One Federal Street · Boston, MA 02110-1726 · 617-951-8000

Patrick J. Rondeau · WilmerHale · http://www.wilmerhale.com · 60 State Street · Boston, MA 02109 · 617-526-6000

Jeffrey B. Rudman · 2) · WilmerHale · http://www.wilmerhale.com · 60 State Street · Boston, MA 02109 · 617-526-6000

Ettore A. Santucci · Goodwin Procter · Exchange Place · 53 State Street · Boston, MA 02109-2881 · 617-570-1000

John R. Utzschneider · Bingham McCutchen · http://www.bingham.com · One Federal Street · Boston, MA 02110-1726 · 617-951-8000

Harvey J. Wolkoff · Ropes & Gray · http://www.ropesgray.com · One International Place · Boston, MA 02110-2624 · 617-951-7000

STRUCTURED FINANCE LAW

Boston

Alyson Allen · Ropes & Gray · http://www.ropesgray.com · One International Place · Boston, MA 02110-2624 · 617-951-7000

Robert A.J. Barry · Bingham McCutchen · http://www.bingham.com · One Federal Street · Boston, MA 02110-1726 · 617-951-8000

Jonathan K. Bernstein · Bingham McCutchen · http://www.bingham.com · One Federal Street · Boston, MA 02110-1726 · 617-951-8000

Ronald S. Borod · Brown Rudnick · http://www.brbilaw.com · One Financial Center · Boston, MA 02111 617-856-8200

Thomas B. Draper · Ropes & Gray · http://www.ropesgray.com · One International Place · Boston, MA 02110-2624 · 617-951-7000

Matthew F. Furlong · Bingham McCutchen · http://www.bingham.com · One Federal Street · Boston, MA 02110-1726 · 617-951-8000

Dennis L. Jenkins · WilmerHale · http://www.wilmerhale.com · 60 State Street · Boston, MA 02109 · 617-526-6000

Robert L. Nutt · 2) · Ropes & Gray · http://www.ropesgray.com · One International Place · Boston, MA 02110-2624 · 617-951-7000

Peter M. Palladino · Choate, Hall & Stewart · http://www.choate.com · Two International Place · Boston, MA 02110 · 617-248-5000

Alfred O. Rose · a · Ropes & Gray · http://www.ropesgray.com · One International Place · Boston, MA 02110-2624 · 617-951-7000

Philip J. Smith · Ropes & Gray · http://www.ropesgray.com · One International Place · Boston, MA 02110-2624 · 617-951-7000

TAX LAW

Boston

Donald-Bruce Abrams · Bingham McCutchen · http://www.bingham.com · One Federal Street · Boston, MA 02110-1726 · 617-951-8000

Martin Allen · K&L Gates · State Street Financial Center · One Lincoln Street · Boston, MA 02111-2950 617-261-3100

David R. Andelman · 2% · Lourie & Cutler · 60 State Street, Ninth Floor · Boston, MA 02109 · 617-742-6720

Neil P. Arkuss · a · Edwards Angell Palmer & Dodge · Prudential Center · 111 Huntington Avenue · Boston, MA 02199-7613 · 617-239-0100

William C. Benjamin · WilmerHale · http://www.wilmerhale.com · 60 State Street · Boston, MA 02109 · 617-526-6000

John S. Brown · a · Bingham McCutchen · http://www.bingham.com · One Federal Street · Boston, MA 02110-1726 · 617-951-8000

Joel R. Carpenter · Sullivan & Worcester · One Post Office Square · Boston, MA 02109 · 617-338-2800

Howard A. Cubell · 2) · Goodwin Procter · Exchange Place · 53 State Street · Boston, MA 02109-2881 · 617-570-1000

Michael M. Davis · 2) · Sullivan & Worcester · One Post Office Square · Boston, MA 02109 · 617-338-2800

M. Gordon Ehrlich · 2% · Bingham McCutchen · http://www.bingham.com · One Federal Street · Boston, MA 02110-1726 · 617-951-8000

Steven P. Eichel · Choate, Hall & Stewart · http://www.choate.com · Two International Place · Boston, MA 02110 · 617-248-5000

Eric M. Elfman · Ropes & Gray · http://www.ropesgray.com · One International Place · Boston, MA 02110-2624 · 617-951-7000

Karl P. Fryzel · Edwards Angell Palmer & Dodge · Prudential Center · 111 Huntington Avenue · Boston, MA 02199-7613 · 617-239-0100

Richard W. Giuliani · 2) · WilmerHale · http://www.wilmerhale.com · 60 State Street · Boston, MA 02109 · 617-526-6000

Edward L. Glazer · 2) · Goodwin Procter · Exchange Place · 53 State Street · Boston, MA 02109-2881 · 617-570-1000

Kenneth A. Glusman · Choate, Hall & Stewart · http://www.choate.com · Two International Place · Boston, MA 02110 · 617-248-5000

John R. Grumbacher · Goulston & Storrs · 400 Atlantic Avenue · Boston, MA 02110-3333 · 617-482-1776

Susan A. Johnston · Ropes & Gray · http://www.ropesgray.com · One International Place · Boston, MA 02110-2624 · 617-951-7000

Christopher M. Leich · Ropes & Gray · http://www.ropesgray.com · One International Place · Boston, MA 02110-2624 · 617-951-7000

Louis J. Marett · Choate, Hall & Stewart · http://www.choate.com · Two International Place · Boston, MA 02110 · 617-248-5000

Michael E. Mooney · 2) · Nutter McClennen & Fish · http://www.nutter.com · World Trade Center West 155 Seaport Boulevard · Boston, MA 02210 · 617-439-2000

Michael F. O'Connell · Rackemann, Sawyer & Brewster · http://www.rackemann.com · 160 Federal Street, 13th-15th Floor · Boston, MA 02110-1700 · 617-542-2300

Carolyn M. Osteen · a · Ropes & Gray · http://www.ropesgray.com · One International Place · Boston, MA 02110-2624 · 617-951-7000

Steven L. Paul · Edwards Angell Palmer & Dodge · Prudential Center · 111 Huntington Avenue · Boston, MA 02199-7613 · 617-239-0100

Ameek Ashok Ponda · Sullivan & Worcester · One Post Office Square · Boston, MA 02109 · 617-338-2800

James P. Redding · Greenberg Traurig · http://www.gtlaw.com · One International Place · Boston, MA 02110 · 617-310-6000

Loretta R. Richard · Ropes & Gray · http://www.ropesgray.com · One International Place · Boston, MA 02110-2624 · 617-951-7000

Roger M. Ritt · a · WilmerHale · http://www.wilmerhale.com · 60 State Street · Boston, MA 02109 · 617-526-6000

H. Neal Sandford · Goodwin Procter · Exchange Place · 53 State Street · Boston, MA 02109-2881 · 617-570-1000

Matthew D. Schnall · Bingham McCutchen · http://www.bingham.com · One Federal Street · Boston, MA 02110-1726 · 617-951-8000

Leonard Schneidman · 2) · Pepper Hamilton · http://www.pepperlaw.com · Oliver Street Tower, 15th Floor · 125 High Street · Boston, MA 02110-2736 · 617-204-5100

Stephen E. Shay · a · Ropes & Gray · http://www.ropesgray.com · One International Place · Boston, MA 02110-2624 · 617-951-7000

David Scott Sloan · Holland & Knight · http://www.hklaw.com · 10 Saint James Avenue, 11th Floor · Boston, MA 02116 · 617-523-2700

Maxwell D. Solet · Mintz, Levin, Cohn, Ferris, Glovsky and Popeo · One Financial Center, 40th Floor · Boston, MA 02111 · 617-542-6000

Walter G. Van Dorn · 2% · K&L Gates · State Street Financial Center · One Lincoln Street · Boston, MA 02111-2950 · 617-261-3100

Rom P. Watson · Ropes & Gray · http://www.ropesgray.com · One International Place · Boston, MA 02110-2624 · 617-951-7000

William H. Whitledge · Goodwin Procter · Exchange Place · 53 State Street · Boston, MA 02109-2881 · 617-570-1000

Jonathan M. Zorn · Ropes & Gray · http://www.ropesgray.com · One International Place · Boston, MA 02110-2624 · 617-951-7000

Newton

Kenneth J. Vacovec · Vacovec, Mayotte & Singer · Two Newton Place, Suite 340 · 255 Washington Street · Newton, MA 02458-1634 · 617-964-0500

Springfield

Richard M. Gaberman · a · Robinson Donovan · http://www.robinson-donovan.com · 1500 Main Street, Suite 1600 · P.O. Box 15609 · Springfield, MA 01115 · 413-732-2301

Timothy P. Mulhern · Shatz, Schwartz and Fentin · 1441 Main Street, Suite 1100 · Springfield, MA 01103 · 413-737-1131

Ronda G. Parish · Robinson Donovan · http://www.robinson-donovan.com · 1500 Main Street, Suite 1600 P.O. Box 15609 · Springfield, MA 01115 · 413-732-2301

Ronald P. Weiss · a · Bulkley, Richardson and Gelinas · 1500 Main Street, Suite 2700 · P.O. Box 15507 · Springfield, MA 01115-5507 · 413-781-2820

Worcester

Stuart A. Hammer · a · Mountain, Dearborn & Whiting · 370 Main Street, Eighth Floor · Worcester, MA 01608-1778 · 508-756-2423

Andrew B. O'Donnell · 2) · Mirick O'Connell DeMallie & Lougee · 100 Front Street, Suite 1700 · Worcester, MA 01608-1477 · 508-791-8500

TECHNOLOGY LAW

Boston

Mark T. Bettencourt · Goodwin Procter · Exchange Place · 53 State Street · Boston, MA 02109-2881 · 617-570-1000

David L. Feigenbaum · Fish & Richardson · 225 Franklin Street · Boston, MA 02110-2804 · 617-542-5070

Jonathan L. Kravetz · Mintz, Levin, Cohn, Ferris, Glovsky and Popeo · One Financial Center, 40th Floor · Boston, MA 02111 · 617-542-6000

Richard S. Sanders · Cooley Godward Kronish · The Prudential Tower, 46th Floor · 800 Boylston Street · Boston, MA 02199 · 617-937-2300

David B. Walek · Ropes & Gray · http://www.ropesgray.com · One International Place · Boston, MA 02110-2624 · 617-951-7000

David A. Westenberg · WilmerHale · http://www.wilmerhale.com · 60 State Street · Boston, MA 02109 · 617-526-6000

TRUSTS AND ESTATES

Boston

David R. Andelman · 2% · Lourie & Cutler · 60 State Street, Ninth Floor · Boston, MA 02109 · 617-742-6720

Patricia M. Annino · Prince, Lobel, Glovsky & Tye · http://www.princelobel.com · 100 Cambridge Street, Suite 2200 · Boston, MA 02114 · 617-456-8000

Katherine L. Babson, Jr. · a · Nixon Peabody · 100 Summer Street · Boston, MA 02110-1832 · 617-345-1000

Mark D. Balk · Goulston & Storrs · 400 Atlantic Avenue · Boston, MA 02110-3333 · 617-482-1776

Thomas Bator · Nichols & Pratt · 50 Congress Street · Boston, MA 02109 · 617-523-6800

Thomas H. Belknap · 2) · Ropes & Gray · http://www.ropesgray.com · One International Place · Boston, MA 02110-2624 · 617-951-7000

George W. Butterworth · Goodwin Procter · Exchange Place · 53 State Street · Boston, MA 02109-2881 · 617-570-1000

Stefanie D. Cantor · Foley Hoag · http://www.foleyhoag.com · Seaport World Trade Center West · 155 Seaport Boulevard · Boston, MA 02210-2600 · 617-832-1000

Natalie B. Choate · a · Nutter McClennen & Fish · http://www.nutter.com · World Trade Center West · 155 Seaport Boulevard · Boston, MA 02210 · 617-439-2000

Mark M. Christopher · Edwards Angell Palmer & Dodge · Prudential Center · 111 Huntington Avenue · Boston, MA 02199-7613 · 617-239-0100

John H. Clymer · a · Nixon Peabody · 100 Summer Street · Boston, MA 02110-1832 · 617-345-1000

Lawrence B. Cohen · Edwards Angell Palmer & Dodge · Prudential Center · 111 Huntington Avenue · Boston, MA 02199-7613 · 617-239-0100

Virginia F. Coleman · a · Ropes & Gray · http://www.ropesgray.com · One International Place · Boston, MA 02110-2624 · 617-951-7000

George L. Cushing · a · K&L Gates · State Street Financial Center · One Lincoln Street · Boston, MA 02111-2950 · 617-261-3100

F. Davis Dassori · a · Choate, Hall & Stewart · http://www.choate.com · Two International Place · Boston, MA 02110 · 617-248-5000

James R. DeGiacomo · a · Murtha Cullina · 99 High Street, 20th Floor · Boston, MA 02110 · 617-457-4000

Nancy E. Dempze · Hemenway & Barnes · 60 State Street, Eighth Floor · Boston, MA 02109-1899 · 617-227-7940

M. Gordon Ehrlich · 2% · Bingham McCutchen · http://www.bingham.com · One Federal Street · Boston, MA 02110-1726 · 617-951-8000

John C. Emery · a · Sullivan & Worcester · One Post Office Square · Boston, MA 02109 · 617-338-2800

Michael L. Fay · a · WilmerHale · http://www.wilmerhale.com · 60 State Street · Boston, MA 02109 · 617-526-6000

Magda L. Fleckner · Ropes & Gray · http://www.ropesgray.com · One International Place · Boston, MA 02110-2624 · 617-951-7000

Albert M. Fortier, Jr. · a · Rackemann, Sawyer & Brewster · http://www.rackemann.com · 160 Federal Street, 13th-15th Floor · Boston, MA 02110-1700 · 617-542-2300

A. Silvana Giner · WilmerHale · http://www.wilmerhale.com · 60 State Street · Boston, MA 02109 · 617-526-6000

Robert P. Goldman · Goulston & Storrs · 400 Atlantic Avenue · Boston, MA 02110-3333 · 617-482-1776

Kenneth L. Grinnell · a · Foley Hoag · http://www.foleyhoag.com · Seaport World Trade Center West · 155 Seaport Boulevard · Boston, MA 02210-2600 · 617-832-1000

Laurie J. Hall · Edwards Angell Palmer & Dodge · Prudential Center · 111 Huntington Avenue · Boston, MA 02199-7613 · 617-239-0100

Martin Hall · Ropes & Gray · http://www.ropesgray.com · One International Place · Boston, MA 02110-2624 · 617-951-7000

Charles M. Hamann · Casner & Edwards · http://www.casneredwards.com · 303 Congress Street · Boston, MA 02210 · 617-426-5900

Thomas P. Jalkut · a · Nutter McClennen & Fish · http://www.nutter.com · World Trade Center West · 155 Seaport Boulevard · Boston, MA 02210 · 617-439-2000

William D. Kirchick · Bingham McCutchen · http://www.bingham.com · One Federal Street · Boston, MA 02110-1726 · 617-951-8000

Shari Levitan · Holland & Knight · http://www.hklaw.com · 10 Saint James Avenue, 11th Floor · Boston, MA 02116 · 617-523-2700

Winifred I. Li · a · Ropes & Gray · http://www.ropesgray.com · One International Place · Boston, MA 02110-2624 · 617-951-7000

William Amory Lowell · a · Choate, Hall & Stewart · http://www.choate.com · Two International Place · Boston, MA 02110 · 617-248-5000

George P. Mair · a · Bingham McCutchen · http://www.bingham.com · One Federal Street · Boston, MA 02110-1726 · 617-951-8000

Eric F. Menoyo · a · Edwards Angell Palmer & Dodge · Prudential Center · 111 Huntington Avenue · Boston, MA 02199-7613 · 617-239-0100

Peter M. Miller · Mintz, Levin, Cohn, Ferris, Glovsky and Popeo · One Financial Center, 40th Floor · Boston, MA 02111 · 617-542-6000

Mary-Kathleen O'Connell · Goodwin Procter · Exchange Place · 53 State Street · Boston, MA 02109-2881 · 617-570-1000

Thomas E. Peckham · Bingham McCutchen · http://www.bingham.com · One Federal Street · Boston, MA 02110-1726 · 617-951-8000

Lawrence T. Perera · 2% · Hemenway & Barnes · 60 State Street, Eighth Floor · Boston, MA 02109-1899 · 617-227-7940

Robert C. Pomeroy · 2) · Goodwin Procter · Exchange Place · 53 State Street · Boston, MA 02109-2881 · 617-570-1000

Hanson S. Reynolds · 2) · Rackemann, Sawyer & Brewster · http://www.rackemann.com · 160 Federal Street, 13th-15th Floor · Boston, MA 02110-1700 · 617-542-2300

Jay D. Rosenbaum · Edwards Angell Palmer & Dodge · Prudential Center · 111 Huntington Avenue · Boston, MA 02199-7613 · 617-239-0100

Nancy B. Samiljan · Goulston & Storrs · 400 Atlantic Avenue · Boston, MA 02110-3333 · 617-482-1776

Thomas G. Sitzmann · a · Goulston & Storrs · 400 Atlantic Avenue · Boston, MA 02110-3333 · 617-482-1776

David Scott Sloan · Holland & Knight · http://www.hklaw.com · 10 Saint James Avenue, 11th Floor · Boston, MA 02116 · 617-523-2700

Janet M. Smith · a · Rackemann, Sawyer & Brewster · http://www.rackemann.com · 160 Federal Street, 13th-15th Floor · Boston, MA 02110-1700 · 617-542-2300

Jennifer C. Snyder · WilmerHale · http://www.wilmerhale.com · 60 State Street · Boston, MA 02109 · 617-526-6000

Kurt F. Somerville · Hemenway & Barnes · 60 State Street, Eighth Floor · Boston, MA 02109-1899 · 617-227-7940

Jon E. Steffensen · a · Steffensen, Herman & Doggett · 45 School Street · Boston, MA 02108-3204 · 617-523-7935

Robert A. Vigoda · Edwards Angell Palmer & Dodge · Prudential Center · 111 Huntington Avenue · Boston, MA 02199-7613 · 617-239-0100

Barbara Freedman Wand · Bingham McCutchen · http://www.bingham.com · One Federal Street · Boston, MA 02110-1726 · 617-951-8000

R. Robert Woodburn, Jr. · a · Edwards Angell Palmer & Dodge · Prudential Center · 111 Huntington Avenue · Boston, MA 02199-7613 · 617-239-0100

Raymond H. Young · 2% · Young & Bayle · 150 Federal Street · Boston, MA 02110 · 617-737-0404

Stephen Ziobrowski · Day Pitney · One International Place, 17th Floor · Boston, MA 02110-3179 · 617-345-4600

Gloucester

Robert G. Stewart · Robert G. Stewart · Three Heritage Way · Gloucester, MA 01930 · 978-281-6020

Needham

Kenneth P. Brier · a · Brier & Associates · http://www.brierlaw.com · 160 Gould Street, Suite 320 · Needham, MA 02494-2300 · 781-453-0030

Orleans

Lawrence O. Spaulding, Jr. · La Tanzi, Spaulding & Landreth · Eight Cardinal Lane · P.O. Box 2300 · Orleans, MA 02653 · 508-255-2133

Springfield

Richard M. Gaberman · a · Robinson Donovan · http://www.robinson-donovan.com · 1500 Main Street, Suite 1600 · P.O. Box 15609 · Springfield, MA 01115 · 413-732-2301

Ronda G. Parish · Robinson Donovan · http://www.robinson-donovan.com · 1500 Main Street, Suite 1600 P.O. Box 15609 · Springfield, MA 01115 · 413-732-2301

Jeffrey W. Roberts · a · Robinson Donovan · http://www.robinson-donovan.com · 1500 Main Street, Suite 1600 · P.O. Box 15609 · Springfield, MA 01115 · 413-732-2301

Wellesley

Bruce J. Bettigole · a · Gilmore, Rees & Carlson · 20 Walnut Street, Suite 200 · Wellesley, MA 02481 · 781-431-9788

Paul D. Bishop · a · Gilmore, Rees & Carlson · 20 Walnut Street, Suite 200 · Wellesley, MA 02481 · 781-431-9788

Christopher T. Carlson · a · Gilmore, Rees & Carlson · 20 Walnut Street, Suite 200 · Wellesley, MA 02481 · 781-431-9788

Michael H. Riley · King & Navins · 20 William Street, Suite G-75 · Wellesley, MA 02481-4102 · 781-237-0150

Sidney A. Slobodkin · Gilmore, Rees & Carlson · 20 Walnut Street, Suite 200 · Wellesley, MA 02481 · 781-431-9788

Worcester

Richard C. Barry, Jr. · Fletcher, Tilton & Whipple · http://www.ftwlaw.com · 370 Main Street, 12th Floor · Worcester, MA 01608-1779 · 508-459-8000

Michael D. Brockelman · a · Bowditch & Dewey · 311 Main Street · P.O. Box 15156 · Worcester, MA 01615-0156 · 508-791-3511

Janet Wilson Moore · a · Mirick O'Connell DeMallie & Lougee · 100 Front Street, Suite 1700 · Worcester, MA 01608-1477 · 508-791-8500

Marvin S. Silver · Seder & Chandler · Burnside Building · 339 Main Street · Worcester, MA 01608-1585 · 508-757-7721

VENTURE CAPITAL LAW

Boston

Kevin M. Barry · Bingham McCutchen · http://www.bingham.com · One Federal Street · Boston, MA 02110-1726 · 617-951-8000

Robert L. Birnbaum · Foley Hoag · http://www.foleyhoag.com · Seaport World Trade Center West · 155 Seaport Boulevard · Boston, MA 02210-2600 · 617-832-1000

Mark G. Borden · a · WilmerHale · http://www.wilmerhale.com · 60 State Street · Boston, MA 02109 · 617-526-6000

Steven C. Browne · Bingham McCutchen · http://www.bingham.com · One Federal Street · Boston, MA 02110-1726 · 617-951-8000

John J. Concannon III · Bingham McCutchen · http://www.bingham.com · One Federal Street · Boston, MA 02110-1726 · 617-951-8000

John J. Egan III · Goodwin Procter · Exchange Place · 53 State Street · Boston, MA 02109-2881 · 617-570-1000

Lester J. Fagen · Cooley Godward Kronish · The Prudential Tower, 46th Floor · 800 Boylston Street · Boston, MA 02199 · 617-937-2300

John Hession · Cooley Godward Kronish · The Prudential Tower, 46th Floor · 800 Boylston Street · Boston, MA 02199 · 617-937-2300

Mark J. Macenka · Goodwin Procter · Exchange Place · 53 State Street · Boston, MA 02109-2881 · 617-570-1000

Gregory E. Moore · Ropes & Gray · http://www.ropesgray.com · One International Place · Boston, MA 02110-2624 · 617-951-7000

John M. Mutkoski · Goodwin Procter · Exchange Place · 53 State Street · Boston, MA 02109-2881 · 617-570-1000

Jeffrey L. Quillen · Foley Hoag · http://www.foleyhoag.com · Seaport World Trade Center West · 155 Seaport Boulevard · Boston, MA 02210-2600 · 617-832-1000

Patrick J. Rondeau · WilmerHale · http://www.wilmerhale.com · 60 State Street · Boston, MA 02109 · 617-526-6000

William J. Schnoor, Jr. · Goodwin Procter · Exchange Place · 53 State Street · Boston, MA 02109-2881 · 617-570-1000

Julio Vega · Bingham McCutchen · http://www.bingham.com · One Federal Street · Boston, MA 02110-1726 · 617-951-8000

David A. Westenberg · WilmerHale · http://www.wilmerhale.com · 60 State Street · Boston, MA 02109 · 617-526-6000

Waltham

Michael D. Bain · WilmerHale · http://www.wilmerhale.com · Bay Colony Corporate Center · 1100 Winter Street · Waltham, MA 02451 · 781-966-2000

John H. Chory · WilmerHale · http://www.wilmerhale.com · Bay Colony Corporate Center · 1100 Winter Street · Waltham, MA 02451 · 781-966-2000

Marc F. Dupré · Gunderson Dettmer Stough Villeneuve Franklin & Hachigian · 610 Lincoln Street · Waltham, MA 02451 · 781-890-8800

Jay K. Hachigian · Gunderson Dettmer Stough Villeneuve Franklin & Hachigian · 610 Lincoln Street · Waltham, MA 02451 · 781-890-8800

Susan L. Mazur · WilmerHale · http://www.wilmerhale.com · Bay Colony Corporate Center · 1100 Winter Street · Waltham, MA 02451 · 781-966-2000

Amherst

David P. Hoose · Sasson Hoose & Turnbull · 190 University Drive · Amherst, MA 01002 · 413-732-1939

Boston

Michael Avery · a · Suffolk University Law School · 120 Tremont Street · Boston, MA 02108-4977 · 617-573-8000

Joseph J. Balliro, Sr. · 2% · Balliro & Mondano · 99 Summer Street, Suite 1800 · Boston, MA 02110 · 617-737-8442

Juliane Balliro · a · WolfBlock · http://wolfblock.com · One Boston Place, 40th Floor · Boston, MA 02108 · 617-226-4000

Anthony M. Cardinale · a · Law Office of Anthony M. Cardinale · 655 Summer Street · Boston, MA 02210 · 617-345-5400

J. W. Carney, Jr. · a · Carney & Bassil · 20 Park Plaza, Suite 1405 · Boston, MA 02116 · 617-338-5566

R. Jack Cinquegrana · Choate, Hall & Stewart · http://www.choate.com · Two International Place · Boston, MA 02110 · 617-248-5000

Daniel J. Cloherty · Dwyer & Collora · 600 Atlantic Avenue, 12th Floor · Boston, MA 02210-2211 · 617-371-1000

Michael A. Collora · a · Dwyer & Collora · 600 Atlantic Avenue, 12th Floor · Boston, MA 02210-2211 · 617-371-1000

Albert F. Cullen, Jr. · 2% · Albert F. Cullen, Jr. · 60 K Street · Boston, MA 02127 · 617-268-2240

John H. Cunha · a · Cunha & Holcomb · One State Street, Suite 500 · Boston, MA 02109-3507 · 617-523-4300

Stephen R. Delinsky · Eckert Seamans Cherin & Mellott · One International Place, 18th Floor · Boston, MA 02110-2602 · 617-342-6800

Francis J. DiMento · 2% · DiMento & Sullivan · Seven Faneuil Hall Market Place, Third Floor · Boston, MA 02109 · 617-523-5253

James M. Doyle · Carney & Bassil · 20 Park Plaza, Suite 1405 · Boston, MA 02116 · 617-338-5566

Thomas Drechsler · Byrne & Drechsler · Eastern Harbor Office Park, Suite 201 · 50 Redfield Street · Boston, MA 02122 · 617-265-3900

David Duncan · Zalkind Rodriguez Lunt & Duncan · http://www.zrld.com · 65A Atlantic Avenue · Boston, MA 02110 · 617-742-6020

Maria R. Durant · Dwyer & Collora · 600 Atlantic Avenue, 12th Floor · Boston, MA 02210-2211 · 617-371-1000

Thomas E. Dwyer, Jr. · 2) · Dwyer & Collora · 600 Atlantic Avenue, 12th Floor · Boston, MA 02210-2211 617-371-1000

Richard M. Egbert · a · Richard M. Egbert · 99 Summer Street, Suite 1800 · Boston, MA 02110 · 617-737-8222

Thomas C. Frongillo · Weil Gotshal & Manges · 100 Federal Street, 34th Floor · Boston, MA 02110 · 617-772-8300

Richard A. Gargiulo · Gargiulo Rudnick · 66 Long Wharf · Boston, MA 02110 · 617-742-3833

Andrew H. Good · 2) · Good & Cormier · 83 Atlantic Avenue · Boston, MA 02110-3711 · 617-523-5933

Karen F. Green · WilmerHale · http://www.wilmerhale.com · 60 State Street · Boston, MA 02109 · 617-526-6000

Thomas M. Hoopes · a · Libby Hoopes · 175 Federal Street, Eighth Floor · Boston, MA 02110 · 617-338-9300

Robert D. Keefe · WilmerHale · http://www.wilmerhale.com · 60 State Street · Boston, MA 02109 · 617-526-6000

Michael D. Kendall · McDermott Will & Emery · 28 State Street, 34th Floor · Boston, MA 02109-1775 · 617-535-4000

William H. Kettlewell · Dwyer & Collora · 600 Atlantic Avenue, 12th Floor · Boston, MA 02210-2211 · 617-371-1000

Jonathan Kotlier · Nutter McClennen & Fish · http://www.nutter.com · World Trade Center West · 155 Seaport Boulevard · Boston, MA 02210 · 617-439-2000

James W. Lawson · a · Prince, Lobel, Glovsky & Tye · http://www.princelobel.com · 100 Cambridge Street, Suite 2200 · Boston, MA 02114 · 617-456-8000

Frank A. Libby, Jr. · Libby Hoopes · 175 Federal Street, Eighth Floor · Boston, MA 02110 · 617-338-9300

Martin F. Murphy · Foley Hoag · http://www.foleyhoag.com · Seaport World Trade Center West · 155 Seaport Boulevard · Boston, MA 02210-2600 · 617-832-1000

Brien T. O'Connor · Ropes & Gray · http://www.ropesgray.com · One International Place · Boston, MA 02110-2624 · 617-951-7000

Joseph S. Oteri · 2% · Oteri, Weinberg & Lawson · 20 Park Plaza, Suite 905 · Boston, MA 02116 · 617-227-3700

A. John Pappalardo · Greenberg Traurig · http://www.gtlaw.com · One International Place · Boston, MA 02110 · 617-310-6000

Mark W. Pearlstein · McDermott Will & Emery · 28 State Street, 34th Floor · Boston, MA 02109-1775 · 617-535-4000

R. Robert Popeo · 2) · Mintz, Levin, Cohn, Ferris, Glovsky and Popeo · One Financial Center, 40th Floor · Boston, MA 02111 · 617-542-6000

Walter B. Prince · Prince, Lobel, Glovsky & Tye · http://www.princelobel.com · 100 Cambridge Street, Suite 2200 · Boston, MA 02114 · 617-456-8000

Charles W. Rankin, Jr. · a · Rankin & Sultan · 151 Merrimac Street, Second Floor · Boston, MA 02114 · 617-720-0011

Mark E. Robinson · Bingham McCutchen · http://www.bingham.com · One Federal Street · Boston, MA 02110-1726 · 617-951-8000

Alan D. Rose, Sr. · ⑩ · Rose, Chinitz & Rose · http://www.rose-law.net · One Beacon Street, Fourth Floor · Boston, MA 02108 · 617-536-0040

Arnold R. Rosenfeld · K&L Gates · State Street Financial Center · One Lincoln Street · Boston, MA 02111-2950 · 617-261-3100

Martin R. Rosenthal · ⑩ · Martin R. Rosenthal · 65-A Atlantic Avenue · Boston, MA 02110 · 617-742-0606

John R. Salsberg · ⑩ · Salsberg & Schneider · 95 Commercial Wharf · Boston, MA 02110 · 617-227-7788

Joseph F. Savage, Jr. · Goodwin Procter · Exchange Place · 53 State Street · Boston, MA 02109-2881 · 617-570-1000

Michael R. Schneider · Salsberg & Schneider · 95 Commercial Wharf · Boston, MA 02110 · 617-227-7788

A. Hugh Scott · Choate, Hall & Stewart · http://www.choate.com · Two International Place · Boston, MA 02110 · 617-248-5000

Jonathan Shapiro · ⑩ · Stern Shapiro Weissberg & Garin · 90 Canal Street, Fifth Floor · Boston, MA 02114-2022 · 617-742-5800

Robert L. Sheketoff · ⑩ · Sheketoff & Homan · One McKinley Square, Third Floor · Boston, MA 02109 617-367-3449

Harvey A. Silverglate · ㉕ · Good & Cormier · 83 Atlantic Avenue · Boston, MA 02110-3711 · 617-523-5933

Bruce Singal · Donoghue, Barrett & Singal · http://www.dbslawfirm.com · One Beacon Street · Boston, MA 02108-3113 · 617-720-5090

Max D. Stern · ⑳ · Stern Shapiro Weissberg & Garin · 90 Canal Street, Fifth Floor · Boston, MA 02114-2022 · 617-742-5800

James L. Sultan · ⑩ · Rankin & Sultan · 151 Merrimac Street, Second Floor · Boston, MA 02114 · 617-720-0011

Nicholas C. Theodorou · Foley Hoag · http://www.foleyhoag.com · Seaport World Trade Center West · 155 Seaport Boulevard · Boston, MA 02210-2600 · 617-832-1000

Michael J. Tuteur · Foley & Lardner · 111 Huntington Avenue · Boston, MA 02199 · 617-342-4000

Robert L. Ullmann · Nutter McClennen & Fish · http://www.nutter.com · World Trade Center West · 155 Seaport Boulevard · Boston, MA 02210 · 617-439-2000

Martin G. Weinberg · ⑳ · Oteri, Weinberg & Lawson · 20 Park Plaza, Suite 905 · Boston, MA 02116 · 617-227-3700

Kathy B. Weinman · Dwyer & Collora · 600 Atlantic Avenue, 12th Floor · Boston, MA 02210-2211 · 617-371-1000

Elliot M. Weinstein · ⑩ · Elliot M. Weinstein · 83 Atlantic Avenue · Boston, MA 02110 · 617-367-9334

Norman S. Zalkind · ⑩ · Zalkind Rodriguez Lunt & Duncan · http://www.zrld.com · 65A Atlantic Avenue · Boston, MA 02110 · 617-742-6020

Brockton

Martin Kenneth Leppo · 2% · Leppo & Leppo · Seven Christy's Drive, Suite One · Brockton, MA 02301 · 508-580-3733

Kevin J. Reddington · a · Kevin J. Reddington · Williamsburg Square, Suite 203 · 1342 Belmont Street · Brockton, MA 02301 · 508-583-4280

Cambridge

Alan M. Dershowitz · a · Harvard Law School · 1563 Massachusetts Avenue · Cambridge, MA 02138 · 617-495-3100

Judith L. Lindahl · a · Judith L. Lindahl · Two Worthington Street · Cambridge, MA 02138 · 617-864-1089

Charlestown

Charles A. Clifford · a · Clifford Law Office · 305 Main Street · Charlestown, MA 02129 · 617-241-7440

Northampton

John Pucci · Fierst, Pucci & Kinder · 64 Gothic Street · Northampton, MA 01060 · 413-584-8067

Pittsfield

Leonard H. Cohen · Cain Hibbard Myers & Cook · 66 West Street · Pittsfield, MA 01201-5764 · 413-443-4771

Quincy

Martin S. Cosgrove · Cosgrove, Eisenberg and Kiley · 803 Hancock Street · P.O. Box 189 · Quincy, MA 02170 · 617-479-7770

Springfield

Vincent A. Bongiorni · a · Bongiorni & Mastroianni · 95 State Street, Suite 309 · Springfield, MA 01103 413-732-0222

Efrem A. Gordon · 2) · Efrem A. Gordon · 101 State Street, Suite 410 · Springfield, MA 01103 · 413-737-4316

Michael O. Jennings · a · Michael O. Jennings · 73 Chestnut Street · Springfield, MA 01103 · 413-737-7349

Jack F. St. Clair · 2% · Jack F. St. Clair · 73 Chestnut Street · Springfield, MA 01103 · 413-737-5000

Worcester

Peter L. Ettenberg · 2) · Gould & Ettenberg · 370 Main Street, Suite 1050 · Worcester, MA 01608 · 508-752-6733

James J. Gribouski · a · Glickman, Sugarman, Kneeland & Gribouski · 11 Harvard Street · P.O. Box 2917 · Worcester, MA 01613-2917 · 508-756-6206

Boston

Gerard B. Carney · a · Carney and Troupe · 10 High Street, Fifth Floor · Boston, MA 02110 · 617-426-9797

William H. Murphy · a · Curtin, Murphy & O'Reilly · 31 Saint James Avenue · Boston, MA 02110 · 617-574-1700

Thomas P. O'Reilly · Curtin, Murphy & O'Reilly · 31 Saint James Avenue · Boston, MA 02110 · 617-574-1700

William H. Troupe · a · Carney and Troupe · 10 High Street, Fifth Floor · Boston, MA 02110 · 617-426-9797

Braintree

Paul S. Danahy · Law Office of Paul S. Danahy · 420 Washington Street, Suite 400 · Braintree, MA 02184-4745 · 781-848-8807

Brockton

Bernard Mulholland · a · Ford, Mulholland & Moran · 288 North Main Street · P.O. Box 4499 · Brockton, MA 02303-4499 · 508-586-5353

Fall River

Deborah G. Kohl · Law Offices of Deborah G. Kohl · 191 Bedford Street · Fall River, MA 02720 · 508-677-4900

Lynnfield

Salvatore J. Perra · a · Salvatore J. Perra · 220 Broadway · P.O. Box 938 · Lynnfield, MA 01940 · 781-596-9600

North Adams

J. Norman O'Connor, Jr. · a · Donovan & O'Connor · 1330 Mass MoCa Way · North Adams, MA 01247 413-663-3200

Salem

Alan S. Pierce · Alan S. Pierce & Associates · http://www.alanspierce.com · Shetland Office Park, Suite 301 · 27 Congress Street · Salem, MA 01970 · 978-745-0914

Springfield

Donald W. Blakesley · a · Pellegrini, Seeley, Ryan & Blakesley · 1145 Main Street, Suite 308 · P.O. Box 30009 · Springfield, MA 01103-0009 · 413-785-5300

Charles R. Casartello · Pellegrini, Seeley, Ryan & Blakesley · 1145 Main Street, Suite 308 · P.O. Box 30009 · Springfield, MA 01103-0009 · 413-785-5300

Ronald C. Kidd · a · Robinson Donovan · http://www.robinson-donovan.com · 1500 Main Street, Suite 1600 · P.O. Box 15609 · Springfield, MA 01115 · 413-732-2301

Earlon L. Seeley, Jr. · a · Pellegrini, Seeley, Ryan & Blakesley · 1145 Main Street, Suite 308 · P.O. Box 30009 · Springfield, MA 01103-0009 · 413-785-5300

Stoughton

James F. Fitzgerald, Jr. · a · James F. Fitzgerald, Jr. · One Cabot Place · Stoughton, MA 02072 · 781-297-9959

Wareham

Michael Ready · Ready, Kiernan & McNally · 267 Main Street · Wareham, MA 02571 · 508-295-0286

Wellesley

John D. Hislop III · a · Law Office of John D. Hislop III · 15 Walnut Street, Suite 400 · Wellesley, MA 02481 · 781-237-7871

Worcester

Paul L. Durkee · McGuire & McGuire · 14 Harvard Street · Worcester, MA 01609 · 508-754-3291

John K. McGuire, Jr. · McGuire & McGuire · 14 Harvard Street · Worcester, MA 01609 · 508-754-3291

Joseph E. McGuire · a · McGuire & McGuire · 14 Harvard Street · Worcester, MA 01609 · 508-754-3291

Christine Griggs Narcisse · McGuire & McGuire · 14 Harvard Street · Worcester, MA 01609 · 508-754-3291

MICHIGAN

ADMINISTRATIVE LAW

Lansing

Michael E. Cavanaugh · (20) · Fraser Trebilcock Davis & Dunlap · 124 West Allegan Street, Suite 1000 · Lansing, MI 48933 · 517-482-5800

Peter H. Ellsworth · Dickinson Wright · http://www.dickinsonwright.com · 215 South Washington Square, Suite 200 · Lansing, MI 48933-1816 · 517-371-1730

Karl L. Gotting · Loomis, Ewert, Parsley, Davis & Gotting · 124 West Allegan Street, Suite 700 · Lansing, MI 48933-1707 · 517-482-2400

Michael J. Hodge · Miller Canfield Paddock and Stone · http://www.millercanfield.com · One Michigan Avenue, Suite 900 · Lansing, MI 48933 · 517-487-2070

Max R. Hoffman, Jr. · Butzel Long · http://www.butzel.com · 110 West Michigan, Suite 1100 · Lansing, MI 48933 · 517-372-6622

David E. S. Marvin · (10) · Fraser Trebilcock Davis & Dunlap · 124 West Allegan Street, Suite 1000 · Lansing, MI 48933 · 517-482-5800

Richard D. McLellan · Dykema · http://www.dykema.com · 201 Townsend Street, Suite 900 · Lansing, MI 48933 · 517-374-9100

Harvey J. Messing · (10) · Miller Canfield Paddock and Stone · http://www.millercanfield.com · One Michigan Avenue, Suite 900 · Lansing, MI 48933 · 517-487-2070

Thomas L. Sparks · Butzel Long · http://www.butzel.com · 110 West Michigan, Suite 1100 · Lansing, MI 48933 · 517-372-6622

Robert W. Stocker II · Dickinson Wright · http://www.dickinsonwright.com · 215 South Washington Square, Suite 200 · Lansing, MI 48933-1816 · 517-371-1730

Okemos

William K. Fahey · Fahey Schultz Burzych Rhodes · http://www.fsblawyers.com · 4151 Okemos Road · Okemos, MI 48864 · 517-381-0100

ALTERNATIVE DISPUTE RESOLUTION

Ann Arbor

Allyn D. Kantor · (10) · Miller Canfield Paddock and Stone · http://www.millercanfield.com · 101 North Main Street, Seventh Floor · Ann Arbor, MI 48104-1400 · 734-663-2445

Richard A. Soble · Soble Rowe Krichbaum · 221 North Main Street, Suite 200 · Ann Arbor, MI 48104 · 734-996-5600

Bingham Farms

Sheldon G. Larky · Sheldon G. Larky · 30600 Telegraph Road, Suite 3350 · Bingham Farms, MI 48025-4533 · 248-642-4660

Birmingham

Martin I. Reisig · Martin Reisig · 401 South Old Woodward Avenue, Suite 456 · Birmingham, MI 48009 · 248-258-6222

Bloomfield Hills

James P. Feeney · Dykema · http://www.dykema.com · 39577 Woodward Avenue, Suite 300 · Bloomfield Hills, MI 48304-2820 · 248-203-0700

Alan M. Kanter · Vestevich, Mallender, DuBois & Dritsas · 6905 Telegraph Road, Suite 300 · Bloomfield Hills, MI 48301-3160 · 248-642-1920

Detroit

Tracy L. Allen · Bodman · http://www.bodmanllp.com · Sixth Floor at Ford Field · 1901 Saint Antoine Street · Detroit, MI 48226 · 313-259-7777

Samuel C. Damren · Dykema · http://www.dykema.com · 400 Renaissance Center · Detroit, MI 48243 · 313-568-6800

Kevin S. Hendrick · Clark Hill · http://www.clarkhill.com · 500 Woodward Avenue, Suite 3500 · Detroit, MI 48226-3435 · 313-965-8300

Peter M. Kellett · Dykema · http://www.dykema.com · 400 Renaissance Center · Detroit, MI 48243 · 313-568-6800

Michael G. Nowakowski · Federal Mediation & Conciliation Service · McNamara Federal Building, Suite 1155 · 477 Michigan Avenue · Detroit, MI 48226-2559 · 313-226-7769

East Lansing

Mary A. Bedikian · MSU Detroit College of Law · 405B Law College Building · East Lansing, MI 48824 517-432-6889

Ted W. Stroud · Oade, Stroud & Kleiman · http://www.osklaw.com · 200 Woodland Pass · P.O. Box 1296 · East Lansing, MI 48826 · 517-351-6501

Grand Rapids

Frederick D. Dilley · ⑩ · DilleyHaney · 330 East Fulton · Grand Rapids, MI 49503 · 616-235-2300

William W. Jack, Jr. · ⑩ · Smith, Haughey, Rice & Roegge · Calder Plaza Building, Suite 200 · 250 Monroe Avenue, NW · Grand Rapids, MI 49503-2251 · 616-774-8000

Jon G. March · ⑩ · Miller Johnson · http://www.millerjohnson.com · Calder Plaza Building, Suite 800 · 250 Monroe Avenue, NW · P.O. Box 306 · Grand Rapids, MI 49503-2250 · 616-831-1700

Jon R. Muth · Miller Johnson · http://www.millerjohnson.com · Calder Plaza Building, Suite 800 · 250 Monroe Avenue, NW · P.O. Box 306 · Grand Rapids, MI 49503-2250 · 616-831-1700

Bruce W. Neckers · ⑩ · Rhoades McKee · 161 Ottawa Avenue, NW, Suite 600 · Grand Rapids, MI 49503 616-235-3500

H. Rhett Pinsky · ⑳ · Pinsky, Smith, Fayette & Kennedy · 146 Monroe Center, NW, Suite 805 · Grand Rapids, MI 49503 · 616-451-8496

Robert E. Lee Wright · Miller Canfield Paddock and Stone · http://www.millercanfield.com · 99 Monroe Avenue, NW, Suite 1200 · Grand Rapids, MI 49503 · 616-454-8656

Kalamazoo

Pamela C. Enslen · Miller Canfield Paddock and Stone · http://www.millercanfield.com · 277 South Rose Street, Suite 5000 · Kalamazoo, MI 49007-3751 · 269-381-7030

Amy Glass · Michigan Mediation & Arbitration Services · P.O. Box 51662 · Kalamazoo, MI 49005-1662 · 269-342-9046

Lansing

Patrick A. Aseltyne · Johnson, Rosati, LaBarge, Aseltyne & Field · 303 S Waverly Road · Lansing, MI 48917 · 517-886-3800

Peter L. Dunlap · ⑩ · Fraser Trebilcock Davis & Dunlap · 124 West Allegan Street, Suite 1000 · Lansing, MI 48933 · 517-482-5800

Michael G. Harrison · Foster, Swift, Collins & Smith · http://www.fosterswift.com · 313 South Washington Square · Lansing, MI 48933-2193 · 517-371-8100

Paula K. Manis · Worman, Dixon & Manis · 2400 Lake Lansing Road, Suite E · Lansing, MI 48912 · 517-485-0400

Rochester Hills

Barbara A. Johannessen · Mediation Specialists · 757 Redwood Court · Rochester Hills, MI 48309-2446 248-375-9411

Royal Oak

Stuart M. Israel · Martens, Ice, Klass, Legghio & Israel · 306 South Washington Avenue, Suite 600 · Royal Oak, MI 48067-3837 · 248-398-5900

Southfield

Richard J. Maddin · Maddin, Hauser, Wartell, Roth & Heller · http://www.maddinhauser.com · Essex Centre, Third Floor · 28400 Northwestern Highway · Southfield, MI 48034-1839 · 248-354-4030

Troy

Paul F. Monicatti · Paul F. Monicatti · 1111 West Long Lake Road, Suite 201 · Troy, MI 48098-6349 · 248-641-0060

ANTITRUST LAW

Ann Arbor

Gregory L. Curtner · Miller Canfield Paddock and Stone · http://www.millercanfield.com · 101 North Main Street, Seventh Floor · Ann Arbor, MI 48104-1400 · 734-663-2445

Bloomfield Hills

Howard B. Iwrey · Dykema · http://www.dykema.com · 39577 Woodward Avenue, Suite 300 · Bloomfield Hills, MI 48304-2820 · 248-203-0700

Detroit

David A. Ettinger · Honigman Miller Schwartz and Cohn · First National Building, Suite 2290 · 660 Woodward Avenue · Detroit, MI 48226-3506 · 313-465-7000

Monte D. Jahnke · ⑩ · Kerr, Russell and Weber · Detroit Center, Suite 2500 · 500 Woodward Avenue · Detroit, MI 48226-3427 · 313-961-0200

Philip J. Kessler · ⑩ · Butzel Long · http://www.butzel.com · 150 West Jefferson Avenue, Suite 100 · Detroit, MI 48226 · 313-225-7000

William A. Sankbeil · ㉕ · Kerr, Russell and Weber · Detroit Center, Suite 2500 · 500 Woodward Avenue · Detroit, MI 48226-3427 · 313-961-0200

Larry J. Saylor · Miller Canfield Paddock and Stone · http://www.millercanfield.com · 150 West Jefferson Avenue, Suite 2500 · Detroit, MI 48226 · 313-963-6420

Grand Rapids

Daniel R. Gravelyn · Barnes & Thornburg · http://www.btlaw.com · 300 Ottawa Avenue, NW, Suite 500 · Grand Rapids, MI 49503 · 616-742-3930

Troy

Irwin M. Alterman · ⑳ · Kemp, Klein, Umphrey, Endelman & May · 201 West Big Beaver Road, Suite 600 · Troy, MI 48084 · 248-528-1111

APPELLATE LAW

Birmingham

Neil H. Fink · ㉕ · Law Offices of Neil H. Fink · 185 Oakland Avenue, Suite 250 · Birmingham, MI 48009 · 248-258-3181

Bloomfield Hills

Robert G. Kamenec · Plunkett Cooney · 38505 Woodward Avenue, Suite 2000 · Bloomfield Hills, MI 48304 · 248-901-4000

Mary Massaron Ross · Plunkett Cooney · 38505 Woodward Avenue, Suite 2000 · Bloomfield Hills, MI 48304 · 248-901-4000

Detroit

Mark R. Bendure · Bendure & Thomas · 30700 Telegraph Road, Suite 3475 · Detroit, MI 48025-4527 · 248-646-5255

James E. Brenner · Clark Hill · http://www.clarkhill.com · 500 Woodward Avenue, Suite 3500 · Detroit, MI 48226-3435 · 313-965-8300

James G. Gross · Gross, Nemeth & Silverman · 615 Griswold, Suite 1305 · Detroit, MI 48226 · 313-963-8200

Elizabeth L. Jacobs · Law Office of Elizabeth Jacobs · 615 Griswold Street, Suite 1125 · Detroit, MI 48226 · 313-962-4090

John P. Jacobs · John P. Jacobs · http://www.jpjpc.com · The Guardian Building, Suite 2825 · 500 Griswold Street · Detroit, MI 48226 · 313-965-1900

Christine D. Oldani · Plunkett Cooney · Buhl Building, Suite 2400 · 535 Griswold Street · Detroit, MI 48226 · 313-965-3900

Rosalind Rochkind · Garan Lucow & Miller · Woodbridge Place · 1000 Woodbridge Street · Detroit, MI 48207-3192 · 313-446-1530

Daniel S. Saylor · Garan Lucow & Miller · Woodbridge Place · 1000 Woodbridge Street · Detroit, MI 48207-3192 · 313-446-1530

Okemos

William K. Fahey · Fahey Schultz Burzych Rhodes · http://www.fsblawyers.com · 4151 Okemos Road · Okemos, MI 48864 · 517-381-0100

Royal Oak

Mark R. Granzotto · Mark Granzotto · 225 South Troy Street, Suite 120 · Royal Oak, MI 48067 · 248-546-4649

Southfield

Raymond W. Morganti · Siemion, Huckabay, Bodary, Padilla, Morganti & Bowerman · One Towne Square, Suite 1400 · P.O. Box 5068 · Southfield, MI 48086-5068 · 248-357-1400

Brian G. Shannon · Jaffe Raitt Heuer & Weiss · 27777 Franklin Road, Suite 2500 · Southfield, MI 48034-8214 · 248-351-3000

Noreen L. Slank · Collins, Einhorn, Farrell & Ulanoff · http://www.ceflawyers.com · 4000 Town Center, Suite 909 · Southfield, MI 48075-1473 · 248-355-4141

BANKING LAW

Bloomfield Hills

Craig W. Hammond · Dickinson Wright · http://www.dickinsonwright.com · 38525 Woodward Avenue, Suite 2000 · Bloomfield Hills, MI 48304-2970 · 248-433-7200

Patrick J. Ledwidge · ⑩ · Dickinson Wright · http://www.dickinsonwright.com · 38525 Woodward Avenue, Suite 2000 · Bloomfield Hills, MI 48304-2970 · 248-433-7200

Detroit

Robert J. Diehl, Jr. · ⑩ · Bodman · http://www.bodmanllp.com · Sixth Floor at Ford Field · 1901 Saint Antoine Street · Detroit, MI 48226 · 313-259-7777

John J. Hern, Jr. · Clark Hill · http://www.clarkhill.com · 500 Woodward Avenue, Suite 3500 · Detroit, MI 48226-3435 · 313-965-8300

Kathleen O'Callaghan Hickey · Bodman · http://www.bodmanllp.com · Sixth Floor at Ford Field · 1901 Saint Antoine Street · Detroit, MI 48226 · 313-259-7777

Douglas M. Kilbourne · Miller Canfield Paddock and Stone · http://www.millercanfield.com · 150 West Jefferson Avenue, Suite 2500 · Detroit, MI 48226 · 313-963-6420

Joseph J. Kochanek · Bodman · http://www.bodmanllp.com · Sixth Floor at Ford Field · 1901 Saint Antoine Street · Detroit, MI 48226 · 313-259-7777

John K. Lawrence · Dickinson Wright · http://www.dickinsonwright.com · 500 Woodward Avenue, Suite 4000 · Detroit, MI 48226-3425 · 313-223-3500

Thomas W. Linn · Miller Canfield Paddock and Stone · http://www.millercanfield.com · 150 West Jefferson Avenue, Suite 2500 · Detroit, MI 48226 · 313-963-6420

David K. McLeod · Miller Canfield Paddock and Stone · http://www.millercanfield.com · 150 West Jefferson Avenue, Suite 2500 · Detroit, MI 48226 · 313-963-6420

Cyril Moscow · 25 · Honigman Miller Schwartz and Cohn · First National Building, Suite 2290 · 660 Woodward Avenue · Detroit, MI 48226-3506 · 313-465-7000

David K. Page · 25 · Honigman Miller Schwartz and Cohn · First National Building, Suite 2290 · 660 Woodward Avenue · Detroit, MI 48226-3506 · 313-465-7000

Steven A. Roach · Miller Canfield Paddock and Stone · http://www.millercanfield.com · 150 West Jefferson Avenue, Suite 2500 · Detroit, MI 48226 · 313-963-6420

Nicholas P. Scavone, Jr. · Bodman · http://www.bodmanllp.com · Sixth Floor at Ford Field · 1901 Saint Antoine Street · Detroit, MI 48226 · 313-259-7777

William P. Shield, Jr. · Dickinson Wright · http://www.dickinsonwright.com · 500 Woodward Avenue, Suite 4000 · Detroit, MI 48226-3425 · 313-223-3500

Larry R. Shulman · Bodman · http://www.bodmanllp.com · Sixth Floor at Ford Field · 1901 Saint Antoine Street · Detroit, MI 48226 · 313-259-7777

Amanda Van Dusen · Miller Canfield Paddock and Stone · http://www.millercanfield.com · 150 West Jefferson Avenue, Suite 2500 · Detroit, MI 48226 · 313-963-6420

Carl H. von Ende · 10 · Miller Canfield Paddock and Stone · http://www.millercanfield.com · 150 West Jefferson Avenue, Suite 2500 · Detroit, MI 48226 · 313-963-6420

Grand Rapids

Jeffrey S. Ammon · Miller Johnson · http://www.millerjohnson.com · Calder Plaza Building, Suite 800 · 250 Monroe Avenue, NW · P.O. Box 306 · Grand Rapids, MI 49503-2250 · 616-831-1700

James H. Breay · 10 · Warner Norcross & Judd · http://www.wnj.com · 900 Fifth Third Center · 111 Lyon Street, NW · Grand Rapids, MI 49503-2487 · 616-752-2000

Harvey Koning · Varnum, Riddering, Schmidt & Howlett · Bridgewater Place · 333 Bridge Street, NW · P.O. Box 352 · Grand Rapids, MI 49501-0352 · 616-336-6000

Daniel R. Kubiak · Mika Meyers Beckett & Jones · 900 Monroe Avenue, NW · Grand Rapids, MI 49503 616-632-8000

Gordon R. Lewis · 10 · Warner Norcross & Judd · http://www.wnj.com · 900 Fifth Third Center · 111 Lyon Street, NW · Grand Rapids, MI 49503-2487 · 616-752-2000

Rodney D. Martin · 10 · Warner Norcross & Judd · http://www.wnj.com · 900 Fifth Third Center · 111 Lyon Street, NW · Grand Rapids, MI 49503-2487 · 616-752-2000

Ronald E. Roden · Miller Johnson · http://www.millerjohnson.com · Calder Plaza Building, Suite 800 · 250 Monroe Avenue, NW · P.O. Box 306 · Grand Rapids, MI 49503-2250 · 616-831-1700

Alan C. Schwartz · Miller Johnson · http://www.millerjohnson.com · Calder Plaza Building, Suite 800 · 250 Monroe Avenue, NW · P.O. Box 306 · Grand Rapids, MI 49503-2250 · 616-831-1700

Lansing

William J. Danhof · Miller Canfield Paddock and Stone · http://www.millercanfield.com · One Michigan Avenue, Suite 900 · Lansing, MI 48933 · 517-487-2070

Matt G. Hrebec · Foster, Swift, Collins & Smith · http://www.fosterswift.com · 313 South Washington Square · Lansing, MI 48933-2193 · 517-371-8100

Lori McAllister · Dykema · http://www.dykema.com · 201 Townsend Street, Suite 900 · Lansing, MI 48933 · 517-374-9100

Southfield

Robert S. Bolton · (25) · Jaffe Raitt Heuer & Weiss · 27777 Franklin Road, Suite 2500 · Southfield, MI 48034-8214 · 248-351-3000

Troy

James L. Allen · Miller Canfield Paddock and Stone · http://www.millercanfield.com · 840 West Long Lake Road, Suite 200 · Troy, MI 48098-6358 · 248-879-2000

David D. Joswick · (10) · Miller Canfield Paddock and Stone · http://www.millercanfield.com · 840 West Long Lake Road, Suite 200 · Troy, MI 48098-6358 · 248-879-2000

James A. Simpson · Miller Canfield Paddock and Stone · http://www.millercanfield.com · 840 West Long Lake Road, Suite 200 · Troy, MI 48098-6358 · 248-879-2000

BANKRUPTCY AND CREDITOR-DEBTOR RIGHTS LAW

Ann Arbor

Douglas S. Ellmann · (10) · Ellmann & Ellmann · 308 West Huron Street · Ann Arbor, MI 48103 · 734-668-4800

Auburn Hills

Richardo I. Kilpatrick · Kilpatrick and Associates · 903 North Opdyke Road, Suite C · Auburn Hills, MI 48326 · 248-377-0700

Bay City

Susan M. Cook · Lambert, Leser, Isackson, Cook & Giunta · http://www.lambertleser.com · Davidson Building, Suite 309 · 916 Washington Avenue · Bay City, MI 48707 · 989-893-3518

Rozanne M. Giunta · Lambert, Leser, Isackson, Cook & Giunta · http://www.lambertleser.com · Davidson Building, Suite 309 · 916 Washington Avenue · Bay City, MI 48707 · 989-893-3518

Bloomfield Hills

Joseph M. Fischer · (10) · Carson Fischer · 4111 Andover Road West, Second Floor · Bloomfield Hills, MI 48302-1924 · 248-644-4840

Marc M. Bakst · Bodman · http://www.bodmanllp.com · Sixth Floor at Ford Field · 1901 Saint Antoine Street · Detroit, MI 48226 · 313-259-7777

Donald F. Baty, Jr. · Honigman Miller Schwartz and Cohn · First National Building, Suite 2290 · 660 Woodward Avenue · Detroit, MI 48226-3506 · 313-465-7000

William T. Burgess · Dickinson Wright · http://www.dickinsonwright.com · 500 Woodward Avenue, Suite 4000 · Detroit, MI 48226-3425 · 313-223-3500

I. William Cohen · 25 · Pepper Hamilton · http://www.pepperlaw.com · 100 Renaissance Center, Suite 3600 · Detroit, MI 48243-1157 · 313-259-7110

Robert J. Diehl, Jr. · 10 · Bodman · http://www.bodmanllp.com · Sixth Floor at Ford Field · 1901 Saint Antoine Street · Detroit, MI 48226 · 313-259-7777

Jonathan S. Green · 20 · Miller Canfield Paddock and Stone · http://www.millercanfield.com · 150 West Jefferson Avenue, Suite 2500 · Detroit, MI 48226 · 313-963-6420

Robert S. Hertzberg · 10 · Pepper Hamilton · http://www.pepperlaw.com · 100 Renaissance Center, Suite 3600 · Detroit, MI 48243-1157 · 313-259-7110

Edgar C. Howbert · 10 · Dickinson Wright · http://www.dickinsonwright.com · 500 Woodward Avenue, Suite 4000 · Detroit, MI 48226-3425 · 313-223-3500

Steven G. Howell · Dickinson Wright · http://www.dickinsonwright.com · 500 Woodward Avenue, Suite 4000 · Detroit, MI 48226-3425 · 313-223-3500

Dennis S. Kayes · 10 · Pepper Hamilton · http://www.pepperlaw.com · 100 Renaissance Center, Suite 3600 · Detroit, MI 48243-1157 · 313-259-7110

Kay Standridge Kress · Pepper Hamilton · http://www.pepperlaw.com · 100 Renaissance Center, Suite 3600 · Detroit, MI 48243-1157 · 313-259-7110

Stephen S. LaPlante · Miller Canfield Paddock and Stone · http://www.millercanfield.com · 150 West Jefferson Avenue, Suite 2500 · Detroit, MI 48226 · 313-963-6420

Ralph E. McDowell · Bodman · http://www.bodmanllp.com · Sixth Floor at Ford Field · 1901 Saint Antoine Street · Detroit, MI 48226 · 313-259-7777

Judy A. O'Neill · 10 · Foley & Lardner · One Detroit Center, Suite 2700 · 500 Woodward Avenue · Detroit, MI 48226-3489 · 313-234-7100

James A. Plemmons · Dickinson Wright · http://www.dickinsonwright.com · 500 Woodward Avenue, Suite 4000 · Detroit, MI 48226-3425 · 313-223-3500

Barbara Rom · 20 · Pepper Hamilton · http://www.pepperlaw.com · 100 Renaissance Center, Suite 3600 · Detroit, MI 48243-1157 · 313-259-7110

Ronald L. Rose · 20 · Dykema · http://www.dykema.com · 400 Renaissance Center · Detroit, MI 48243 · 313-568-6800

E. Todd Sable · Honigman Miller Schwartz and Cohn · First National Building, Suite 2290 · 660 Woodward Avenue · Detroit, MI 48226-3506 · 313-465-7000

Sheryl L. Toby · Dykema · http://www.dykema.com · 400 Renaissance Center · Detroit, MI 48243 · 313-568-6800

Michael H. Traison · Miller Canfield Paddock and Stone · http://www.millercanfield.com · 150 West Jefferson Avenue, Suite 2500 · Detroit, MI 48226 · 313-963-6420

Robert B. Weiss · ⑩ · Honigman Miller Schwartz and Cohn · First National Building, Suite 2290 · 660 Woodward Avenue · Detroit, MI 48226-3506 · 313-465-7000

Scott A. Wolfson · Honigman Miller Schwartz and Cohn · First National Building, Suite 2290 · 660 Woodward Avenue · Detroit, MI 48226-3506 · 313-465-7000

Grand Blanc

Dennis M. Haley · Winegarden, Haley, Lindholm & Robertson · G-9460 South Saginaw Street, Suite A · Grand Blanc, MI 48439 · 810-579-3600

Grand Rapids

James B. Frakie · ⑳ · James B. Frakie · 2812 East Beltline Lane, NE · Grand Rapids, MI 49525 · 616-363-3330

Stephen B. Grow · Warner Norcross & Judd · http://www.wnj.com · 900 Fifth Third Center · 111 Lyon Street, NW · Grand Rapids, MI 49503-2487 · 616-752-2000

Timothy Hillegonds · Warner Norcross & Judd · http://www.wnj.com · 900 Fifth Third Center · 111 Lyon Street, NW · Grand Rapids, MI 49503-2487 · 616-752-2000

Scott H. Hogan · Foster, Swift, Collins & Smith · http://www.fosterswift.com · 1700 East Beltline, NE, Suite 200 · Grand Rapids, MI 49525-2076 · 616-726-2200

Patrick E. Mears · ⑩ · Barnes & Thornburg · http://www.btlaw.com · 300 Ottawa Avenue, NW, Suite 500 Grand Rapids, MI 49503 · 616-742-3930

Thomas P. Sarb · ⑩ · Miller Johnson · http://www.millerjohnson.com · Calder Plaza Building, Suite 800 · 250 Monroe Avenue, NW · P.O. Box 306 · Grand Rapids, MI 49503-2250 · 616-831-1700

Robert H. Skilton III · Warner Norcross & Judd · http://www.wnj.com · 900 Fifth Third Center · 111 Lyon Street, NW · Grand Rapids, MI 49503-2487 · 616-752-2000

Gordon J. Toering · Warner Norcross & Judd · http://www.wnj.com · 900 Fifth Third Center · 111 Lyon Street, NW · Grand Rapids, MI 49503-2487 · 616-752-2000

Robert F. Wardrop II · Wardrop & Wardrop · Frey Building, Suite 150 · 300 Ottawa Avenue, NW · Grand Rapids, MI 49503 · 616-459-1225

Southfield

Earle I. Erman · ⑩ · Erman, Teicher, Miller, Zucker & Freedman · 400 Galleria Officentre, Suite 444 · Southfield, MI 48034 · 248-827-4100

Wallace M. Handler · ㉕ · Sullivan, Ward, Asher & Patton · 1000 Maccabees Center · 25800 Northwestern Highway · Southfield, MI 48075-1000 · 248-746-0700

Louis P. Rochkind · ㉕ · Jaffe Raitt Heuer & Weiss · 27777 Franklin Road, Suite 2500 · Southfield, MI 48034-8214 · 248-351-3000

Sheldon S. Toll · ⑳ · Law Office of Sheldon S. Toll · http://www.tolllaw.com · 2000 Town Center, Suite 2100 · Southfield, MI 48075-1130 · 248-358-2460

Jay L. Welford · Jaffe Raitt Heuer & Weiss · 27777 Franklin Road, Suite 2500 · Southfield, MI 48034-8214 · 248-351-3000

Wyoming

Perry G. Pastula · Dunn, Schouten & Snoap · 2745 DeHoop Avenue, SW · Wyoming, MI 49509 · 616-538-6380

Thomas W. Schouten · ⑩ · Dunn, Schouten & Snoap · 2745 DeHoop Avenue, SW · Wyoming, MI 49509 · 616-538-6380

BET-THE-COMPANY LITIGATION

Bloomfield Hills

Keefe A. Brooks · Butzel Long · http://www.butzel.com · Stoneridge West · 41000 Woodward Avenue · Bloomfield Hills, MI 48304 · 248-258-1616

James P. Feeney · Dykema · http://www.dykema.com · 39577 Woodward Avenue, Suite 300 · Bloomfield Hills, MI 48304-2820 · 248-203-0700

Edward H. Pappas · Dickinson Wright · http://www.dickinsonwright.com · 38525 Woodward Avenue, Suite 2000 · Bloomfield Hills, MI 48304-2970 · 248-433-7200

Detroit

Norman C. Ankers · Honigman Miller Schwartz and Cohn · First National Building, Suite 2290 · 660 Woodward Avenue · Detroit, MI 48226-3506 · 313-465-7000

Lawrence G. Campbell · ⑳ · Dickinson Wright · http://www.dickinsonwright.com · 500 Woodward Avenue, Suite 4000 · Detroit, MI 48226-3425 · 313-223-3500

Eugene Driker · ⑳ · Barris, Sott, Denn & Driker · http://www.bsdd.com · 211 West Fort Street, 15th Floor · Detroit, MI 48226-3202 · 313-965-9725

Philip J. Kessler · ⑩ · Butzel Long · http://www.butzel.com · 150 West Jefferson Avenue, Suite 100 · Detroit, MI 48226 · 313-225-7000

Richard E. Rassel · ⑳ · Butzel Long · http://www.butzel.com · 150 West Jefferson Avenue, Suite 100 · Detroit, MI 48226 · 313-225-7000

William A. Sankbeil · ㉕ · Kerr, Russell and Weber · Detroit Center, Suite 2500 · 500 Woodward Avenue · Detroit, MI 48226-3427 · 313-961-0200

Carl H. von Ende · ⑩ · Miller Canfield Paddock and Stone · http://www.millercanfield.com · 150 West Jefferson Avenue, Suite 2500 · Detroit, MI 48226 · 313-963-6420

Sharon M. Woods · ⑩ · Barris, Sott, Denn & Driker · http://www.bsdd.com · 211 West Fort Street, 15th Floor · Detroit, MI 48226-3202 · 313-965-9725

Grand Rapids

Douglas A. Dozeman · Warner Norcross & Judd · http://www.wnj.com · 900 Fifth Third Center · 111 Lyon Street, NW · Grand Rapids, MI 49503-2487 · 616-752-2000

David J. Gass · Miller Johnson · http://www.millerjohnson.com · Calder Plaza Building, Suite 800 · 250 Monroe Avenue, NW · P.O. Box 306 · Grand Rapids, MI 49503-2250 · 616-831-1700

William K. Holmes · ⑩ · Warner Norcross & Judd · http://www.wnj.com · 900 Fifth Third Center · 111 Lyon Street, NW · Grand Rapids, MI 49503-2487 · 616-752-2000

Richard A. Kay · Varnum, Riddering, Schmidt & Howlett · Bridgewater Place · 333 Bridge Street, NW · P.O. Box 352 · Grand Rapids, MI 49501-0352 · 616-336-6000

Jon G. March · ⑩ · Miller Johnson · http://www.millerjohnson.com · Calder Plaza Building, Suite 800 · 250 Monroe Avenue, NW · P.O. Box 306 · Grand Rapids, MI 49503-2250 · 616-831-1700

Jon R. Muth · Miller Johnson · http://www.millerjohnson.com · Calder Plaza Building, Suite 800 · 250 Monroe Avenue, NW · P.O. Box 306 · Grand Rapids, MI 49503-2250 · 616-831-1700

Bruce W. Neckers · ⑩ · Rhoades McKee · 161 Ottawa Avenue, NW, Suite 600 · Grand Rapids, MI 49503 616-235-3500

Lansing

Peter H. Ellsworth · Dickinson Wright · http://www.dickinsonwright.com · 215 South Washington Square, Suite 200 · Lansing, MI 48933-1816 · 517-371-1730

Troy

Thomas W. Cranmer · ⑩ · Miller Canfield Paddock and Stone · http://www.millercanfield.com · 840 West Long Lake Road, Suite 200 · Troy, MI 48098-6358 · 248-879-2000

CIVIL RIGHTS LAW

Bloomfield Hills

Patricia A. Stamler · Hertz Schram · 1760 South Telegraph Road, Suite 300 · Bloomfield Hills, MI 48302-0183 · 248-335-5000

COMMERCIAL LITIGATION

Ann Arbor

Mark T. Boonstra · Miller Canfield Paddock and Stone · http://www.millercanfield.com · 101 North Main Street, Seventh Floor · Ann Arbor, MI 48104-1400 · 734-663-2445

Charles W. Borgsdorf · ⑩ · Hooper, Hathaway, Price, Beuche & Wallace · 126 South Main Street · Ann Arbor, MI 48104-1945 · 734-662-4426

James M. Cameron, Jr. · Dykema · http://www.dykema.com · 2723 South State Street, Suite 400 · Ann Arbor, MI 48104 · 734-214-7600

Pat D. Conner · ⑩ · Ellis, Eby, Conner, Smillie & Bourque · 320 North Main Street, Suite 300 · Ann Arbor, MI 48104 · 734-769-2691

E. Edward Hood · ⑩ · Dykema · http://www.dykema.com · 2723 South State Street, Suite 400 · Ann Arbor, MI 48104 · 734-214-7600

Allyn D. Kantor · ⑩ · Miller Canfield Paddock and Stone · http://www.millercanfield.com · 101 North Main Street, Seventh Floor · Ann Arbor, MI 48104-1400 · 734-663-2445

Richard J. Landau · RJ Landau Partners · 5340 Plymouth Road, Suite 200 · Ann Arbor, MI 48105 · 734-865-1585

Marta A. Manildi · Miller Canfield Paddock and Stone · http://www.millercanfield.com · 101 North Main Street, Seventh Floor · Ann Arbor, MI 48104-1400 · 734-663-2445

Sonal Hope Mithani · Miller Canfield Paddock and Stone · http://www.millercanfield.com · 101 North Main Street, Seventh Floor · Ann Arbor, MI 48104-1400 · 734-663-2445

Allen J. Philbrick · ⑩ · Conlin, McKenney & Philbrick · 350 South Main Street, Suite 400 · Ann Arbor, MI 48104-2131 · 734-761-9000

John A. Shea · John A. Shea · 120 North Fourth Avenue · Ann Arbor, MI 48104 · 734-995-4646

Bruce T. Wallace · Hooper, Hathaway, Price, Beuche & Wallace · 126 South Main Street · Ann Arbor, MI 48104-1945 · 734-662-4426

Birmingham

David S. Mendelson · Law Offices of David Mendelson · 322 North Old Woodward Avenue · Birmingham, MI 48009 · 248-646-8277

Thomas G. Plunkett · Williams, Williams, Rattner & Plunkett · 380 North Old Woodward Avenue, Suite 300 · Birmingham, MI 48009 · 248-642-0333

Bloomfield Hills

Joseph Aviv · Honigman Miller Schwartz and Cohn · 38500 Woodward Avenue, Suite 100 · Bloomfield Hills, MI 48304-5048 · 248-566-8301

Keefe A. Brooks · Butzel Long · http://www.butzel.com · Stoneridge West · 41000 Woodward Avenue · Bloomfield Hills, MI 48304 · 248-258-1616

Robert M. Carson · Carson Fischer · 4111 Andover Road West, Second Floor · Bloomfield Hills, MI 48302-1924 · 248-644-4840

James P. Feeney · Dykema · http://www.dykema.com · 39577 Woodward Avenue, Suite 300 · Bloomfield Hills, MI 48304-2820 · 248-203-0700

Dennis M. Haffey · ⑩ · Dykema · http://www.dykema.com · 39577 Woodward Avenue, Suite 300 · Bloomfield Hills, MI 48304-2820 · 248-203-0700

Norman Hyman · ⑩ · Honigman Miller Schwartz and Cohn · 38500 Woodward Avenue, Suite 100 · Bloomfield Hills, MI 48304-5048 · 248-566-8301

Edward H. Pappas · Dickinson Wright · http://www.dickinsonwright.com · 38525 Woodward Avenue, Suite 2000 · Bloomfield Hills, MI 48304-2970 · 248-433-7200

Marilyn A. Peters · Dykema · http://www.dykema.com · 39577 Woodward Avenue, Suite 300 · Bloomfield Hills, MI 48304-2820 · 248-203-0700

Peter M. Alter · Honigman Miller Schwartz and Cohn · First National Building, Suite 2290 · 660 Woodward Avenue · Detroit, MI 48226-3506 · 313-465-7000

Norman C. Ankers · Honigman Miller Schwartz and Cohn · First National Building, Suite 2290 · 660 Woodward Avenue · Detroit, MI 48226-3506 · 313-465-7000

Susan Artinian · Dykema · http://www.dykema.com · 400 Renaissance Center · Detroit, MI 48243 · 313-568-6800

Lawrence G. Campbell · 20 · Dickinson Wright · http://www.dickinsonwright.com · 500 Woodward Avenue, Suite 4000 · Detroit, MI 48226-3425 · 313-223-3500

Samuel C. Damren · Dykema · http://www.dykema.com · 400 Renaissance Center · Detroit, MI 48243 · 313-568-6800

Eugene Driker · 20 · Barris, Sott, Denn & Driker · http://www.bsdd.com · 211 West Fort Street, 15th Floor · Detroit, MI 48226-3202 · 313-965-9725

W. Mack Faison · Miller Canfield Paddock and Stone · http://www.millercanfield.com · 150 West Jefferson Avenue, Suite 2500 · Detroit, MI 48226 · 313-963-6420

Robert J. Franzinger · 10 · Dykema · http://www.dykema.com · 400 Renaissance Center · Detroit, MI 48243 · 313-568-6800

Michael W. Hartmann · 10 · Miller Canfield Paddock and Stone · http://www.millercanfield.com · 150 West Jefferson Avenue, Suite 2500 · Detroit, MI 48226 · 313-963-6420

Raymond W. Henney · Honigman Miller Schwartz and Cohn · First National Building, Suite 2290 · 660 Woodward Avenue · Detroit, MI 48226-3506 · 313-465-7000

Robert M. Jackson · Honigman Miller Schwartz and Cohn · First National Building, Suite 2290 · 660 Woodward Avenue · Detroit, MI 48226-3506 · 313-465-7000

John P. Jacobs · John P. Jacobs · http://www.jpjpc.com · The Guardian Building, Suite 2825 · 500 Griswold Street · Detroit, MI 48226 · 313-965-1900

Peter M. Kellett · Dykema · http://www.dykema.com · 400 Renaissance Center · Detroit, MI 48243 · 313-568-6800

Philip J. Kessler · 10 · Butzel Long · http://www.butzel.com · 150 West Jefferson Avenue, Suite 100 · Detroit, MI 48226 · 313-225-7000

Kathleen A. Lang · Dickinson Wright · http://www.dickinsonwright.com · 500 Woodward Avenue, Suite 4000 · Detroit, MI 48226-3425 · 313-223-3500

Daniel P. Malone · Butzel Long · http://www.butzel.com · 150 West Jefferson Avenue, Suite 100 · Detroit, MI 48226 · 313-225-7000

Thomas G. McNeill · Dickinson Wright · http://www.dickinsonwright.com · 500 Woodward Avenue, Suite 4000 · Detroit, MI 48226-3425 · 313-223-3500

Thomas G. Parachini · Miller Canfield Paddock and Stone · http://www.millercanfield.com · 150 West Jefferson Avenue, Suite 2500 · Detroit, MI 48226 · 313-963-6420

Clarence L. Pozza, Jr. · Miller Canfield Paddock and Stone · http://www.millercanfield.com · 150 West Jefferson Avenue, Suite 2500 · Detroit, MI 48226 · 313-963-6420

Richard E. Rassel · ⑳ · Butzel Long · http://www.butzel.com · 150 West Jefferson Avenue, Suite 100 · Detroit, MI 48226 · 313-225-7000

William A. Sankbeil · ㉕ · Kerr, Russell and Weber · Detroit Center, Suite 2500 · 500 Woodward Avenue · Detroit, MI 48226-3427 · 313-961-0200

Bruce L. Sendek · Butzel Long · http://www.butzel.com · 150 West Jefferson Avenue, Suite 100 · Detroit, MI 48226 · 313-225-7000

Mark A. Stern · Honigman Miller Schwartz and Cohn · First National Building, Suite 2290 · 660 Woodward Avenue · Detroit, MI 48226-3506 · 313-465-7000

Carl H. von Ende · ⑩ · Miller Canfield Paddock and Stone · http://www.millercanfield.com · 150 West Jefferson Avenue, Suite 2500 · Detroit, MI 48226 · 313-963-6420

I. W. Winsten · Honigman Miller Schwartz and Cohn · First National Building, Suite 2290 · 660 Woodward Avenue · Detroit, MI 48226-3506 · 313-465-7000

Timothy D. Wittlinger · Clark Hill · http://www.clarkhill.com · 500 Woodward Avenue, Suite 3500 · Detroit, MI 48226-3435 · 313-965-8300

Sharon M. Woods · ⑩ · Barris, Sott, Denn & Driker · http://www.bsdd.com · 211 West Fort Street, 15th Floor · Detroit, MI 48226-3202 · 313-965-9725

Richard E. Zuckerman · Honigman Miller Schwartz and Cohn · First National Building, Suite 2290 · 660 Woodward Avenue · Detroit, MI 48226-3506 · 313-465-7000

Farmington Hills

William P. Hampton · ⑩ · Secrest, Wardle, Lynch, Hampton, Truex and Morley · 30903 Northwestern Highway · P.O. Box 3040 · Farmington Hills, MI 48333-3040 · 248-851-9500

Grand Rapids

Stephen P. Afendoulis · Varnum, Riddering, Schmidt & Howlett · Bridgewater Place · 333 Bridge Street, NW · P.O. Box 352 · Grand Rapids, MI 49501-0352 · 616-336-6000

Charles F. Behler · Smith, Haughey, Rice & Roegge · Calder Plaza Building, Suite 200 · 250 Monroe Avenue, NW · Grand Rapids, MI 49503-2251 · 616-774-8000

James S. Brady · Miller Johnson · http://www.millerjohnson.com · Calder Plaza Building, Suite 800 · 250 Monroe Avenue, NW · P.O. Box 306 · Grand Rapids, MI 49503-2250 · 616-831-1700

Scott S. Brinkmeyer · Mika Meyers Beckett & Jones · 900 Monroe Avenue, NW · Grand Rapids, MI 49503 · 616-632-8000

Robert J. Buchanan · Buchanan & Buchanan · http://www.buchananfirm.com · 171 Monroe Avenue, NW, Suite 750 · Grand Rapids, MI 49503 · 616-458-2464

John J. Bursch · Warner Norcross & Judd · http://www.wnj.com · 900 Fifth Third Center · 111 Lyon Street, NW · Grand Rapids, MI 49503-2487 · 616-752-2000

Robert L. DeJong · Miller Canfield Paddock and Stone · http://www.millercanfield.com · 99 Monroe Avenue, NW, Suite 1200 · Grand Rapids, MI 49503 · 616-454-8656

Douglas A. Dozeman · Warner Norcross & Judd · http://www.wnj.com · 900 Fifth Third Center · 111 Lyon Street, NW · Grand Rapids, MI 49503-2487 · 616-752-2000

David J. Gass · Miller Johnson · http://www.millerjohnson.com · Calder Plaza Building, Suite 800 · 250 Monroe Avenue, NW · P.O. Box 306 · Grand Rapids, MI 49503-2250 · 616-831-1700

William K. Holmes · 10 · Warner Norcross & Judd · http://www.wnj.com · 900 Fifth Third Center · 111 Lyon Street, NW · Grand Rapids, MI 49503-2487 · 616-752-2000

Richard A. Kay · Varnum, Riddering, Schmidt & Howlett · Bridgewater Place · 333 Bridge Street, NW · P.O. Box 352 · Grand Rapids, MI 49501-0352 · 616-336-6000

Jon G. March · 10 · Miller Johnson · http://www.millerjohnson.com · Calder Plaza Building, Suite 800 · 250 Monroe Avenue, NW · P.O. Box 306 · Grand Rapids, MI 49503-2250 · 616-831-1700

Molly E. McManus · Warner Norcross & Judd · http://www.wnj.com · 900 Fifth Third Center · 111 Lyon Street, NW · Grand Rapids, MI 49503-2487 · 616-752-2000

Jon R. Muth · Miller Johnson · http://www.millerjohnson.com · Calder Plaza Building, Suite 800 · 250 Monroe Avenue, NW · P.O. Box 306 · Grand Rapids, MI 49503-2250 · 616-831-1700

Bruce W. Neckers · 10 · Rhoades McKee · 161 Ottawa Avenue, NW, Suite 600 · Grand Rapids, MI 49503 616-235-3500

L. Roland Roegge · 20 · Smith, Haughey, Rice & Roegge · Calder Plaza Building, Suite 200 · 250 Monroe Avenue, NW · Grand Rapids, MI 49503-2251 · 616-774-8000

Paul T. Sorensen · Warner Norcross & Judd · http://www.wnj.com · 900 Fifth Third Center · 111 Lyon Street, NW · Grand Rapids, MI 49503-2487 · 616-752-2000

Stanley J. Stek · Miller Canfield Paddock and Stone · http://www.millercanfield.com · 99 Monroe Avenue, NW, Suite 1200 · Grand Rapids, MI 49503 · 616-454-8656

Robert D. VanderLaan · VanderLaan & Associates · 80 Ottawa Avenue, NW, Suite 300 · Grand Rapids, MI 49503 · 616-454-0900

Douglas E. Wagner · 10 · Warner Norcross & Judd · http://www.wnj.com · 900 Fifth Third Center · 111 Lyon Street, NW · Grand Rapids, MI 49503-2487 · 616-752-2000

Michael C. Walton · Rhoades McKee · 161 Ottawa Avenue, NW, Suite 600 · Grand Rapids, MI 49503 · 616-235-3500

James L. Wernstrom · Clark Hill · http://www.clarkhill.com · 200 Ottawa Avenue, NW, Suite 500 · Grand Rapids, MI 49503 · 616-608-1100

Kalamazoo

John W. Allen · Varnum, Riddering, Schmidt & Howlett · 251 North Rose Street, Fourth Floor · Kalamazoo, MI 49007-3823 · 269-382-2300

Stephen M. Denenfeld · Lewis Reed & Allen · 136 East Michigan Avenue · Kalamazoo, MI 49007-3945 · 269-388-7600

Pamela C. Enslen · Miller Canfield Paddock and Stone · http://www.millercanfield.com · 277 South Rose Street, Suite 5000 · Kalamazoo, MI 49007-3751 · 269-381-7030

Craig H. Lubben · Miller Johnson · http://www.millerjohnson.com · Rose Street Market Building, Suite 600 · 303 North Rose Street · Kalamazoo, MI 49007-3850 · 269-226-2950

Lawrence J. Murphy · Varnum, Riddering, Schmidt & Howlett · 251 North Rose Street, Fourth Floor · Kalamazoo, MI 49007-3823 · 269-382-2300

B. Jay Yelton III · Miller Canfield Paddock and Stone · http://www.millercanfield.com · 277 South Rose Street, Suite 5000 · Kalamazoo, MI 49007-3751 · 269-381-7030

Lansing

Jeffrey Bracken · Warner Norcross & Judd · http://www.wnj.com · 201 North Washington Square, Suite 920 · Lansing, MI 48933-1323 · 517-679-7400

Kenneth T. Brooks · Honigman Miller Schwartz and Cohn · 222 North Washington Square, Suite 400 · Lansing, MI 48933-1800 · 517-484-8282

Michael E. Cavanaugh · ⑳ · Fraser Trebilcock Davis & Dunlap · 124 West Allegan Street, Suite 1000 · Lansing, MI 48933 · 517-482-5800

Eric J. Eggan · Honigman Miller Schwartz and Cohn · 222 North Washington Square, Suite 400 · Lansing, MI 48933-1800 · 517-484-8282

Peter H. Ellsworth · Dickinson Wright · http://www.dickinsonwright.com · 215 South Washington Square, Suite 200 · Lansing, MI 48933-1816 · 517-371-1730

Joseph A. Fink · ⑩ · Dickinson Wright · http://www.dickinsonwright.com · 215 South Washington Square, Suite 200 · Lansing, MI 48933-1816 · 517-371-1730

David M. Lick · Foster, Swift, Collins & Smith · http://www.fosterswift.com · 313 South Washington Square · Lansing, MI 48933-2193 · 517-371-8100

Scott L. Mandel · Foster, Swift, Collins & Smith · http://www.fosterswift.com · 313 South Washington Square · Lansing, MI 48933-2193 · 517-371-8100

Lori McAllister · Dykema · http://www.dykema.com · 201 Townsend Street, Suite 900 · Lansing, MI 48933 · 517-374-9100

John D. Pirich · ⑩ · Honigman Miller Schwartz and Cohn · 222 North Washington Square, Suite 400 · Lansing, MI 48933-1800 · 517-484-8282

Webb A. Smith · ⑩ · Foster, Swift, Collins & Smith · http://www.fosterswift.com · 313 South Washington Square · Lansing, MI 48933-2193 · 517-371-8100

Robert W. Stocker II · Dickinson Wright · http://www.dickinsonwright.com · 215 South Washington Square, Suite 200 · Lansing, MI 48933-1816 · 517-371-1730

Scott A. Storey · Foster, Swift, Collins & Smith · http://www.fosterswift.com · 313 South Washington Square · Lansing, MI 48933-2193 · 517-371-8100

Deanna Swisher · Foster, Swift, Collins & Smith · http://www.fosterswift.com · 313 South Washington Square · Lansing, MI 48933-2193 · 517-371-8100

Rochester

E. Powell Miller · The Miller Law Firm · 950 West University Drive, Suite 300 · Rochester, MI 48307 · 248-841-2200

Royal Oak

Stephen F. Wasinger · Stephen Wasinger · 32121 Woodward Avenue, Suite 300 · Royal Oak, MI 48073 · 248-554-6306

Southfield

Jeffrey G. Heuer · Jaffe Raitt Heuer & Weiss · 27777 Franklin Road, Suite 2500 · Southfield, MI 48034-8214 · 248-351-3000

William R. Jansen · Warner Norcross & Judd · http://www.wnj.com · 2000 Town Center, Suite 2700 · Southfield, MI 48075-1318 · 248-784-5000

Joel H. Serlin · Seyburn, Kahn, Ginn, Bess & Serlin · 2000 Town Center, Suite 1500 · Southfield, MI 48075 · 248-353-7620

Rodger D. Young · Young & Susser · Westview Office Center, Suite 305 · 26200 American Drive · Southfield, MI 48034 · 248-353-8620

Traverse City

Mark P. Bickel · Smith, Haughey, Rice & Roegge · 202 East State Street, Suite 100 · Traverse City, MI 49685-0848 · 231-929-4878

Troy

Irwin M. Alterman · ⓴ · Kemp, Klein, Umphrey, Endelman & May · 201 West Big Beaver Road, Suite 600 · Troy, MI 48084 · 248-528-1111

Thomas W. Cranmer · ❿ · Miller Canfield Paddock and Stone · http://www.millercanfield.com · 840 West Long Lake Road, Suite 200 · Troy, MI 48098-6358 · 248-879-2000

Michael B. Lewiston · Bodman · http://www.bodmanllp.com · 201 West Big Beaver Road, Suite 500 · Troy, MI 48084 · 248-743-6000

Thomas J. Tallerico · Bodman · http://www.bodmanllp.com · 201 West Big Beaver Road, Suite 500 · Troy, MI 48084 · 248-743-6000

Thomas Van Dusen · Bodman · http://www.bodmanllp.com · 201 West Big Beaver Road, Suite 500 · Troy, MI 48084 · 248-743-6000

COMMUNICATIONS LAW

Lansing

Roderick S. Coy · ❿ · Clark Hill · http://www.clarkhill.com · 212 East Grand River Avenue · Lansing, MI 48906-4328 · 517-318-3100

Eric J. Schneidewind · Varnum, Riddering, Schmidt & Howlett · The Victor Center, Suite 810 · 201 North Washington Square · Lansing, MI 48933 · 517-482-6237

CONSTRUCTION LAW

Ann Arbor

Harvey W. Berman · Bodman · http://www.bodmanllp.com · 201 South Division Street, Suite 400 · Ann Arbor, MI 48104 · 734-761-3780

Auburn Hills

Mark L. McAlpine · McAlpine & Associates · http://www.mcalpinelawfirm.com · 3201 University Drive, Suite 100 · Auburn Hills, MI 48326-2361 · 248-373-3700

Bloomfield Hills

Ronald P. Strote · May, Simpson & Strote · 100 West Long Lake Road, Suite 200 · P.O. Box 1134 · Bloomfield Hills, MI 48303-1134 · 248-646-9500

Detroit

James R. Case · Kerr, Russell and Weber · Detroit Center, Suite 2500 · 500 Woodward Avenue · Detroit, MI 48226-3427 · 313-961-0200

Lawrence M. Dudek · Miller Canfield Paddock and Stone · http://www.millercanfield.com · 150 West Jefferson Avenue, Suite 2500 · Detroit, MI 48226 · 313-963-6420

Margaret E. Greene · Honigman Miller Schwartz and Cohn · First National Building, Suite 2290 · 660 Woodward Avenue · Detroit, MI 48226-3506 · 313-465-7000

David M. Hayes · Clark Hill · http://www.clarkhill.com · 500 Woodward Avenue, Suite 3500 · Detroit, MI 48226-3435 · 313-965-8300

Kevin S. Hendrick · Clark Hill · http://www.clarkhill.com · 500 Woodward Avenue, Suite 3500 · Detroit, MI 48226-3435 · 313-965-8300

James A. Samborn · Dickinson Wright · http://www.dickinsonwright.com · 500 Woodward Avenue, Suite 4000 · Detroit, MI 48226-3425 · 313-223-3500

Stuart H. Teger · Honigman Miller Schwartz and Cohn · First National Building, Suite 2290 · 660 Woodward Avenue · Detroit, MI 48226-3506 · 313-465-7000

East Lansing

Ted W. Stroud · Oade, Stroud & Kleiman · http://www.osklaw.com · 200 Woodland Pass · P.O. Box 1296 · East Lansing, MI 48826 · 517-351-6501

Grand Rapids

Jeffrey S. Ammon · Miller Johnson · http://www.millerjohnson.com · Calder Plaza Building, Suite 800 · 250 Monroe Avenue, NW · P.O. Box 306 · Grand Rapids, MI 49503-2250 · 616-831-1700

Charles F. Behler · Smith, Haughey, Rice & Roegge · Calder Plaza Building, Suite 200 · 250 Monroe Avenue, NW · Grand Rapids, MI 49503-2251 · 616-774-8000

John G. Cameron, Jr. · ⑩ · Dickinson Wright · http://www.dickinsonwright.com · 200 Ottawa Avenue, NW, Suite 900 · Grand Rapids, MI 49503-2427 · 616-458-1300

Stephen A. Hilger · Rhoades McKee · 161 Ottawa Avenue, NW, Suite 600 · Grand Rapids, MI 49503 · 616-235-3500

Grosse Pointe Farms

John K. Grylls · John K. Grylls · 18430 Mack Avenue · Grosse Pointe Farms, MI 48236 · 248-548-0100

Kalamazoo

James E. Spurr · Miller Canfield Paddock and Stone · http://www.millercanfield.com · 277 South Rose Street, Suite 5000 · Kalamazoo, MI 49007-3751 · 269-381-7030

Lansing

David M. Lick · Foster, Swift, Collins & Smith · http://www.fosterswift.com · 313 South Washington Square · Lansing, MI 48933-2193 · 517-371-8100

Gregory L. McClelland · ⑩ · McClelland & Anderson · 1305 South Washington Avenue, Suite 102 · Lansing, MI 48910 · 517-482-4890

James J. Urban · Butzel Long · http://www.butzel.com · 110 West Michigan, Suite 1100 · Lansing, MI 48933 · 517-372-6622

Mt. Clemens

John M. Sier · Kitch Drutchas Wagner Valitutti & Sherbrook · Towne Square Development, Suite 200 · 10 South Main Street · Mt. Clemens, MI 48043-7908 · 586-463-9770

Southfield

Kevin J. Gleeson · Sullivan, Ward, Asher & Patton · 1000 Maccabees Center · 25800 Northwestern Highway · Southfield, MI 48075-1000 · 248-746-0700

Jeffrey G. Heuer · Jaffe Raitt Heuer & Weiss · 27777 Franklin Road, Suite 2500 · Southfield, MI 48034-8214 · 248-351-3000

Troy

Ronald E. Hodess · Miller Canfield Paddock and Stone · http://www.millercanfield.com · 840 West Long Lake Road, Suite 200 · Troy, MI 48098-6358 · 248-879-2000

CORPORATE GOVERNANCE AND COMPLIANCE LAW

Detroit

Patrick D. Daugherty · Foley & Lardner · One Detroit Center, Suite 2700 · 500 Woodward Avenue · Detroit, MI 48226-3489 · 313-234-7100

David Foltyn · ⑩ · Honigman Miller Schwartz and Cohn · First National Building, Suite 2290 · 660 Woodward Avenue · Detroit, MI 48226-3506 · 313-465-7000

Justin G. Klimko · ⑩ · Butzel Long · http://www.butzel.com · 150 West Jefferson Avenue, Suite 100 · Detroit, MI 48226 · 313-225-7000

Donald J. Kunz · Honigman Miller Schwartz and Cohn · First National Building, Suite 2290 · 660 Woodward Avenue · Detroit, MI 48226-3506 · 313-465-7000

Mark A. Metz · Dykema · http://www.dykema.com · 400 Renaissance Center · Detroit, MI 48243 · 313-568-6800

Aleksandra A. Miziolek · Dykema · http://www.dykema.com · 400 Renaissance Center · Detroit, MI 48243 · 313-568-6800

Cyril Moscow · ㉕ · Honigman Miller Schwartz and Cohn · First National Building, Suite 2290 · 660 Woodward Avenue · Detroit, MI 48226-3506 · 313-465-7000

Grand Rapids

Craig N. Meurlin · Warner Norcross & Judd · http://www.wnj.com · 900 Fifth Third Center · 111 Lyon Street, NW · Grand Rapids, MI 49503-2487 · 616-752-2000

Ann Arbor

James R. Beuche · Hooper, Hathaway, Price, Beuche & Wallace · 126 South Main Street · Ann Arbor, MI 48104-1945 · 734-662-4426

Charles W. Borgsdorf · ⑩ · Hooper, Hathaway, Price, Beuche & Wallace · 126 South Main Street · Ann Arbor, MI 48104-1945 · 734-662-4426

Timothy R. Damschroder · Bodman · http://www.bodmanllp.com · 201 South Division Street, Suite 400 · Ann Arbor, MI 48104 · 734-761-3780

James L. Hughes · Butzel Long · http://www.butzel.com · 350 South Main Street, Suite 300 · Ann Arbor, MI 48104 · 734-995-3110

Barbara A. Kaye · Honigman Miller Schwartz and Cohn · 130 South First Street, Fourth Floor · Ann Arbor, MI 48104-1386 · 734-418-4200

Joseph W. Kimmell · Butzel Long · http://www.butzel.com · 350 South Main Street, Suite 300 · Ann Arbor, MI 48104 · 734-995-3110

George E. Kuehn · Butzel Long · http://www.butzel.com · 350 South Main Street, Suite 300 · Ann Arbor, MI 48104 · 734-995-3110

Chris L. McKenney · ⑳ · Conlin, McKenney & Philbrick · 350 South Main Street, Suite 400 · Ann Arbor, MI 48104-2131 · 734-761-9000

David N. Parsigian · Honigman Miller Schwartz and Cohn · 130 South First Street, Fourth Floor · Ann Arbor, MI 48104-1386 · 734-418-4200

Randolph S. Perry · Randolph S. Perry · 2475 Whitmore Lake Road · Ann Arbor, MI 48105 · 734-677-7738

Ian J. Reach · Reach Law Firm · 121 West Washington Street, Suite 400 · Ann Arbor, MI 48104 · 734-994-1400

Raynold A. Schmick · ⑩ · Schmick Law Offices · 325 East Eisenhower Parkway, Suite Two · Ann Arbor, MI 48108-3307 · 734-332-0033

James A. Schriemer · Conlin, McKenney & Philbrick · 350 South Main Street, Suite 400 · Ann Arbor, MI 48104-2131 · 734-761-9000

Erik H. Serr · Miller Canfield Paddock and Stone · http://www.millercanfield.com · 101 North Main Street, Seventh Floor · Ann Arbor, MI 48104-1400 · 734-663-2445

Birmingham

Daniel H. Minkus · Clark Hill · http://www.clarkhill.com · 255 South Old Woodward Avenue, Third Floor Birmingham, MI 48009-6179 · 248-642-9692

Bloomfield Hills

Patrick J. Ledwidge · ⑩ · Dickinson Wright · http://www.dickinsonwright.com · 38525 Woodward Avenue, Suite 2000 · Bloomfield Hills, MI 48304-2970 · 248-433-7200

Jeffrey H. Miro · ⑩ · Honigman Miller Schwartz and Cohn · 38500 Woodward Avenue, Suite 100 · Bloomfield Hills, MI 48304-5048 · 248-566-8301

Bruce D. Birgbauer · ㉕ · Miller Canfield Paddock and Stone · http://www.millercanfield.com · 150 West Jefferson Avenue, Suite 2500 · Detroit, MI 48226 · 313-963-6420

Richard M. Bolton · Dickinson Wright · http://www.dickinsonwright.com · 500 Woodward Avenue, Suite 4000 · Detroit, MI 48226-3425 · 313-223-3500

James C. Bruno · ⑩ · Butzel Long · http://www.butzel.com · 150 West Jefferson Avenue, Suite 100 · Detroit, MI 48226 · 313-225-7000

James R. Cambridge · Kerr, Russell and Weber · Detroit Center, Suite 2500 · 500 Woodward Avenue · Detroit, MI 48226-3427 · 313-961-0200

Herold Deason · Bodman · http://www.bodmanllp.com · Sixth Floor at Ford Field · 1901 Saint Antoine Street · Detroit, MI 48226 · 313-259-7777

Laurence B. Deitch · Bodman · http://www.bodmanllp.com · Sixth Floor at Ford Field · 1901 Saint Antoine Street · Detroit, MI 48226 · 313-259-7777

Bernadette M. Dennehy · Dickinson Wright · http://www.dickinsonwright.com · 500 Woodward Avenue, Suite 4000 · Detroit, MI 48226-3425 · 313-223-3500

Arthur Dudley II · Butzel Long · http://www.butzel.com · 150 West Jefferson Avenue, Suite 100 · Detroit, MI 48226 · 313-225-7000

Patrick T. Duerr · ⑩ · Honigman Miller Schwartz and Cohn · First National Building, Suite 2290 · 660 Woodward Avenue · Detroit, MI 48226-3506 · 313-465-7000

David Foltyn · ⑩ · Honigman Miller Schwartz and Cohn · First National Building, Suite 2290 · 660 Woodward Avenue · Detroit, MI 48226-3506 · 313-465-7000

Verne C. Hampton II · Dickinson Wright · http://www.dickinsonwright.com · 500 Woodward Avenue, Suite 4000 · Detroit, MI 48226-3425 · 313-223-3500

John J. Hern, Jr. · Clark Hill · http://www.clarkhill.com · 500 Woodward Avenue, Suite 3500 · Detroit, MI 48226-3435 · 313-965-8300

Mark R. High · Dickinson Wright · http://www.dickinsonwright.com · 500 Woodward Avenue, Suite 4000 Detroit, MI 48226-3425 · 313-223-3500

Robert A. Hudson · ⑩ · Butzel Long · http://www.butzel.com · 150 West Jefferson Avenue, Suite 100 · Detroit, MI 48226 · 313-225-7000

Justin G. Klimko · ⑩ · Butzel Long · http://www.butzel.com · 150 West Jefferson Avenue, Suite 100 · Detroit, MI 48226 · 313-225-7000

Jin-Kyu Koh · Dykema · http://www.dykema.com · 400 Renaissance Center · Detroit, MI 48243 · 313-568-6800

Donald J. Kunz · Honigman Miller Schwartz and Cohn · First National Building, Suite 2290 · 660 Woodward Avenue · Detroit, MI 48226-3506 · 313-465-7000

F. Thomas Lewand · Bodman · http://www.bodmanllp.com · Sixth Floor at Ford Field · 1901 Saint Antoine Street · Detroit, MI 48226 · 313-259-7777

Mark A. Metz · Dykema · http://www.dykema.com · 400 Renaissance Center · Detroit, MI 48243 · 313-568-6800

Aleksandra A. Miziolek · Dykema · http://www.dykema.com · 400 Renaissance Center · Detroit, MI 48243 · 313-568-6800

Cyril Moscow · ㉕ · Honigman Miller Schwartz and Cohn · First National Building, Suite 2290 · 660 Woodward Avenue · Detroit, MI 48226-3506 · 313-465-7000

David K. Page · ㉕ · Honigman Miller Schwartz and Cohn · First National Building, Suite 2290 · 660 Woodward Avenue · Detroit, MI 48226-3506 · 313-465-7000

Alex L. Parrish · Honigman Miller Schwartz and Cohn · First National Building, Suite 2290 · 660 Woodward Avenue · Detroit, MI 48226-3506 · 313-465-7000

Paul R. Rentenbach · ⑩ · Dykema · http://www.dykema.com · 400 Renaissance Center · Detroit, MI 48243 · 313-568-6800

Rex E. Schlaybaugh, Jr. · Dykema · http://www.dykema.com · 400 Renaissance Center · Detroit, MI 48243 · 313-568-6800

Alan E. Schwartz · ㉕ · Honigman Miller Schwartz and Cohn · First National Building, Suite 2290 · 660 Woodward Avenue · Detroit, MI 48226-3506 · 313-465-7000

Alan S. Schwartz · ⑳ · Honigman Miller Schwartz and Cohn · First National Building, Suite 2290 · 660 Woodward Avenue · Detroit, MI 48226-3506 · 313-465-7000

Jerome M. Schwartz · Dickinson Wright · http://www.dickinsonwright.com · 500 Woodward Avenue, Suite 4000 · Detroit, MI 48226-3425 · 313-223-3500

Samuel T. Stahl · ⑩ · Honigman Miller Schwartz and Cohn · First National Building, Suite 2290 · 660 Woodward Avenue · Detroit, MI 48226-3506 · 313-465-7000

Nicholas J. Stasevich · Butzel Long · http://www.butzel.com · 150 West Jefferson Avenue, Suite 100 · Detroit, MI 48226 · 313-225-7000

Duane L. Tarnacki · Clark Hill · http://www.clarkhill.com · 500 Woodward Avenue, Suite 3500 · Detroit, MI 48226-3435 · 313-965-8300

Thomas S. Vaughn · Dykema · http://www.dykema.com · 400 Renaissance Center · Detroit, MI 48243 · 313-568-6800

Farmington Hills

Mark Shaevsky · ⑩ · Mark Shaevsky & Associates · 30833 Northwestern Highway, Suite 200 · Farmington Hills, MI 48334 · 248-737-0808

Grand Rapids

Jeffrey S. Ammon · Miller Johnson · http://www.millerjohnson.com · Calder Plaza Building, Suite 800 · 250 Monroe Avenue, NW · P.O. Box 306 · Grand Rapids, MI 49503-2250 · 616-831-1700

Jeffrey S. Battershall · Warner Norcross & Judd · http://www.wnj.com · 900 Fifth Third Center · 111 Lyon Street, NW · Grand Rapids, MI 49503-2487 · 616-752-2000

James H. Breay · ⑩ · Warner Norcross & Judd · http://www.wnj.com · 900 Fifth Third Center · 111 Lyon Street, NW · Grand Rapids, MI 49503-2487 · 616-752-2000

Michael G. Campbell · Barnes & Thornburg · http://www.btlaw.com · 300 Ottawa Avenue, NW, Suite 500 · Grand Rapids, MI 49503 · 616-742-3930

Cameron S. DeLong · ⑩ · Warner Norcross & Judd · http://www.wnj.com · 900 Fifth Third Center · 111 Lyon Street, NW · Grand Rapids, MI 49503-2487 · 616-752-2000

Frank G. Dunten · ⑩ · Dickinson Wright · http://www.dickinsonwright.com · 200 Ottawa Avenue, NW, Suite 900 · Grand Rapids, MI 49503-2427 · 616-458-1300

R. Paul Guerre · Barnes & Thornburg · http://www.btlaw.com · 300 Ottawa Avenue, NW, Suite 500 · Grand Rapids, MI 49503 · 616-742-3930

Shane B. Hansen · Warner Norcross & Judd · http://www.wnj.com · 900 Fifth Third Center · 111 Lyon Street, NW · Grand Rapids, MI 49503-2487 · 616-752-2000

Thomas P. Hogan · Rhoades McKee · 161 Ottawa Avenue, NW, Suite 600 · Grand Rapids, MI 49503 · 616-235-3500

Scott A. Huizenga · Varnum, Riddering, Schmidt & Howlett · Bridgewater Place · 333 Bridge Street, NW P.O. Box 352 · Grand Rapids, MI 49501-0352 · 616-336-6000

Richard C. Lague · Varnum, Riddering, Schmidt & Howlett · Bridgewater Place · 333 Bridge Street, NW P.O. Box 352 · Grand Rapids, MI 49501-0352 · 616-336-6000

Tracy T. Larsen · ⑩ · Barnes & Thornburg · http://www.btlaw.com · 300 Ottawa Avenue, NW, Suite 500 · Grand Rapids, MI 49503 · 616-742-3930

Gordon R. Lewis · ⑩ · Warner Norcross & Judd · http://www.wnj.com · 900 Fifth Third Center · 111 Lyon Street, NW · Grand Rapids, MI 49503-2487 · 616-752-2000

Hugh H. Makens · ㉕ · Warner Norcross & Judd · http://www.wnj.com · 900 Fifth Third Center · 111 Lyon Street, NW · Grand Rapids, MI 49503-2487 · 616-752-2000

Charles E. McCallum · ㉕ · Warner Norcross & Judd · http://www.wnj.com · 900 Fifth Third Center · 111 Lyon Street, NW · Grand Rapids, MI 49503-2487 · 616-752-2000

Daniel C. Molhoek · ⑩ · Varnum, Riddering, Schmidt & Howlett · Bridgewater Place · 333 Bridge Street, NW · P.O. Box 352 · Grand Rapids, MI 49501-0352 · 616-336-6000

Robert L. Nelson · ㉕ · Myers Nelson Dillon & Shierk · 125 Ottawa Avenue, NW, Suite 270 · Grand Rapids, MI 49503 · 616-233-9640

Brian J. Page · Dykema · http://www.dykema.com · 300 Ottawa Avenue, NW, Suite 700 · Grand Rapids, MI 49503-2304 · 616-776-7500

Robert R. Stead · Barnes & Thornburg · http://www.btlaw.com · 300 Ottawa Avenue, NW, Suite 500 · Grand Rapids, MI 49503 · 616-742-3930

Stephen C. Waterbury · ⑩ · Warner Norcross & Judd · http://www.wnj.com · 900 Fifth Third Center · 111 Lyon Street, NW · Grand Rapids, MI 49503-2487 · 616-752-2000

Michael G. Wooldridge · Varnum, Riddering, Schmidt & Howlett · Bridgewater Place · 333 Bridge Street, NW · P.O. Box 352 · Grand Rapids, MI 49501-0352 · 616-336-6000

Kalamazoo

Eric V. Brown, Jr. · ⑩ · Miller Canfield Paddock and Stone · http://www.millercanfield.com · 277 South Rose Street, Suite 5000 · Kalamazoo, MI 49007-3751 · 269-381-7030

John R. Cook · Miller Canfield Paddock and Stone · http://www.millercanfield.com · 277 South Rose Street, Suite 5000 · Kalamazoo, MI 49007-3751 · 269-381-7030

Robert R. Lennon · Miller Canfield Paddock and Stone · http://www.millercanfield.com · 277 South Rose Street, Suite 5000 · Kalamazoo, MI 49007-3751 · 269-381-7030

Lansing

Stephen L. Burlingame · ⑩ · Fraser Trebilcock Davis & Dunlap · 124 West Allegan Street, Suite 1000 · Lansing, MI 48933 · 517-482-5800

James B. Jensen, Jr. · Foster, Swift, Collins & Smith · http://www.fosterswift.com · 313 South Washington Square · Lansing, MI 48933-2193 · 517-371-8100

Iris K. Linder · Fraser Trebilcock Davis & Dunlap · 124 West Allegan Street, Suite 1000 · Lansing, MI 48933 · 517-482-5800

David E. S. Marvin · ⑩ · Fraser Trebilcock Davis & Dunlap · 124 West Allegan Street, Suite 1000 · Lansing, MI 48933 · 517-482-5800

John D. Pirich · ⑩ · Honigman Miller Schwartz and Cohn · 222 North Washington Square, Suite 400 · Lansing, MI 48933-1800 · 517-484-8282

Peter S. Sheldon · ㉕ · Dickinson Wright · http://www.dickinsonwright.com · 215 South Washington Square, Suite 200 · Lansing, MI 48933-1816 · 517-371-1730

Southfield

Ira J. Jaffe · ㉕ · Jaffe Raitt Heuer & Weiss · 27777 Franklin Road, Suite 2500 · Southfield, MI 48034-8214 · 248-351-3000

Peter Sugar · Jaffe Raitt Heuer & Weiss · 27777 Franklin Road, Suite 2500 · Southfield, MI 48034-8214 · 248-351-3000

Troy

Thomas G. Appleman · Miller Canfield Paddock and Stone · http://www.millercanfield.com · 840 West Long Lake Road, Suite 200 · Troy, MI 48098-6358 · 248-879-2000

Brad B. Arbuckle · Miller Canfield Paddock and Stone · http://www.millercanfield.com · 840 West Long Lake Road, Suite 200 · Troy, MI 48098-6358 · 248-879-2000

David D. Joswick · ⑩ · Miller Canfield Paddock and Stone · http://www.millercanfield.com · 840 West Long Lake Road, Suite 200 · Troy, MI 48098-6358 · 248-879-2000

DUI/DWI DEFENSE

Birmingham

Patrick T. Barone · Barone Defense Firm · 280 North Old Woodward Avenue, Suite 200 · Birmingham, MI 48009 · 248-594-4554

Kimberly W. Stout · Kimberly W. Stout · 185 Oakland Avenue, Suite 250 · Birmingham, MI 48009-3478 248-258-3181

Bloomfield Hills

Robert W. Larin · Larin & Leonard · 36400 Woodward Avenue, Suite 111 · Bloomfield Hills, MI 48304 · 248-647-3151

Okemos

George Zulakis · Baird & Zulakis · 4127 Okemos Road, Suite Four · Okemos, MI 48864-2821 · 517-349-5011

EDUCATION LAW

Grand Rapids

Craig A. Mutch · Miller Johnson · http://www.millerjohnson.com · Calder Plaza Building, Suite 800 · 250 Monroe Avenue, NW · P.O. Box 306 · Grand Rapids, MI 49503-2250 · 616-831-1700

ELDER LAW

East Lansing

Douglas G. Chalgian · Chalgian & Tripp Law Offices · 139 West Lake Lansing Road, Suite 200 · East Lansing, MI 48823 · 517-332-3800

Grand Rapids

Lauretta K. Murphy · Miller Johnson · http://www.millerjohnson.com · Calder Plaza Building, Suite 800 · 250 Monroe Avenue, NW · P.O. Box 306 · Grand Rapids, MI 49503-2250 · 616-831-1700

Lansing

Douglas A. Mielock · Foster, Swift, Collins & Smith · http://www.fosterswift.com · 313 South Washington Square · Lansing, MI 48933-2193 · 517-371-8100

Okemos

Michelyn E. Pasteur · Foster Zack Little Pasteur & Manning · http://www.fosterzack.com · 2125 University Park Drive, Suite 250 · Okemos, MI 48864 · 517-706-0000

EMINENT DOMAIN AND CONDEMNATION LAW

Birmingham

H. Adam Cohen · Steinhardt Pesick & Cohen · 380 North Old Woodward Avenue, Suite 120 · Birmingham, MI 48009 · 248-356-5888

Jerome P. Pesick · Steinhardt Pesick & Cohen · 380 North Old Woodward Avenue, Suite 120 · Birmingham, MI 48009 · 248-356-5888

Bloomfield Hills

Alan T. Ackerman · Ackerman Ackerman & Dynowski · http://www.ackerman-ackerman.com · 100 West Long Lake Road · Bloomfield Hills, MI 48304 · 248-537-1155

Darius W. Dynkowski · Ackerman Ackerman & Dynowski · http://www.ackerman-ackerman.com · 100 West Long Lake Road · Bloomfield Hills, MI 48304 · 248-537-1155

Detroit

Norman C. Ankers · Honigman Miller Schwartz and Cohn · First National Building, Suite 2290 · 660 Woodward Avenue · Detroit, MI 48226-3506 · 313-465-7000

Farmington Hills

Mark J. Zausmer · Zausmer, Kaufman, August & Caldwell · 31700 Middlebelt Road, Suite 150 · Farmington Hills, MI 48334-2374 · 248-851-4111

EMPLOYEE BENEFITS LAW

Ann Arbor

Larry J. Ferguson · ⑩ · Ferguson & Widmayer · http://www.fw-pc.com · 538 North Division Street · Ann Arbor, MI 48104 · 734-662-0222

Nancy Keppelman · ⑩ · Stevenson Keppelman Associates · http://www.skalaw.com · 444 South Main Street · Ann Arbor, MI 48104 · 734-747-7050

Jordan S. Schreier · Butzel Long · http://www.butzel.com · 350 South Main Street, Suite 300 · Ann Arbor, MI 48104 · 734-995-3110

Robert B. Stevenson · ⑳ · Stevenson Keppelman Associates · http://www.skalaw.com · 444 South Main Street · Ann Arbor, MI 48104 · 734-747-7050

Warren J. Widmayer · ⑩ · Ferguson & Widmayer · http://www.fw-pc.com · 538 North Division Street · Ann Arbor, MI 48104 · 734-662-0222

Bloomfield Hills

Alexander B. Bragdon · Butzel Long · http://www.butzel.com · Stoneridge West · 41000 Woodward Avenue · Bloomfield Hills, MI 48304 · 248-258-1616

Roberta Granadier · Butzel Long · http://www.butzel.com · Stoneridge West · 41000 Woodward Avenue · Bloomfield Hills, MI 48304 · 248-258-1616

Theresa C. Joswick · ⑩ · Law Office of Theresa C. Joswick · 41000 Woodward Avenue, Suite 345 · Bloomfield Hills, MI 48304-5130 · 248-540-6760

David M. Rosenberger · ⑳ · Rosenberger Law Group · 4111 Andover Road, Suite 100 W · Bloomfield Hills, MI 48302 · 248-723-7001

Detroit

Orin D. Brustad · ⑩ · Miller Canfield Paddock and Stone · http://www.millercanfield.com · 150 West Jefferson Avenue, Suite 2500 · Detroit, MI 48226 · 313-963-6420

Robert G. Buydens · ⑳ · Butzel Long · http://www.butzel.com · 150 West Jefferson Avenue, Suite 100 · Detroit, MI 48226 · 313-225-7000

Margaret A. Hunter · Dykema · http://www.dykema.com · 400 Renaissance Center · Detroit, MI 48243 · 313-568-6800

Christopher A. McMican · Miller Canfield Paddock and Stone · http://www.millercanfield.com · 150 West Jefferson Avenue, Suite 2500 · Detroit, MI 48226 · 313-963-6420

Andrew Nickelhoff · Sachs Waldman · 1000 Farmer Street · Detroit, MI 48226-2899 · 313-965-3464

Deborah W. Thompson · ⑩ · Miller Canfield Paddock and Stone · http://www.millercanfield.com · 150 West Jefferson Avenue, Suite 2500 · Detroit, MI 48226 · 313-963-6420

Grand Rapids

Mary V. Bauman · Miller Johnson · http://www.millerjohnson.com · Calder Plaza Building, Suite 800 · 250 Monroe Avenue, NW · P.O. Box 306 · Grand Rapids, MI 49503-2250 · 616-831-1700

Frank E. Berrodin · Miller Johnson · http://www.millerjohnson.com · Calder Plaza Building, Suite 800 · 250 Monroe Avenue, NW · P.O. Box 306 · Grand Rapids, MI 49503-2250 · 616-831-1700

James C. Bruinsma · ⑳ · Miller Johnson · http://www.millerjohnson.com · Calder Plaza Building, Suite 800 · 250 Monroe Avenue, NW · P.O. Box 306 · Grand Rapids, MI 49503-2250 · 616-831-1700

Sue O. Conway · Warner Norcross & Judd · http://www.wnj.com · 900 Fifth Third Center · 111 Lyon Street, NW · Grand Rapids, MI 49503-2487 · 616-752-2000

Jeffrey A. DeVree · Clark Hill · http://www.clarkhill.com · 200 Ottawa Avenue, NW, Suite 500 · Grand Rapids, MI 49503 · 616-608-1100

William R. Hineline · ⑩ · Law, Weathers & Richardson · Bridgewater Place, Suite 800 · 333 Bridge Street, NW · Grand Rapids, MI 49504-5320 · 616-459-1171

Anthony J. Kolenic, Jr. · ⑩ · Warner Norcross & Judd · http://www.wnj.com · 900 Fifth Third Center · 111 Lyon Street, NW · Grand Rapids, MI 49503-2487 · 616-752-2000

Vernon P. Saper · ⑳ · Warner Norcross & Judd · http://www.wnj.com · 900 Fifth Third Center · 111 Lyon Street, NW · Grand Rapids, MI 49503-2487 · 616-752-2000

Larry J. Titley · ⑩ · Varnum, Riddering, Schmidt & Howlett · Bridgewater Place · 333 Bridge Street, NW P.O. Box 352 · Grand Rapids, MI 49501-0352 · 616-336-6000

Timothy J. Tornga · Varnum, Riddering, Schmidt & Howlett · Bridgewater Place · 333 Bridge Street, NW · P.O. Box 352 · Grand Rapids, MI 49501-0352 · 616-336-6000

George L. Whitfield · ⑳ · Warner Norcross & Judd · http://www.wnj.com · 900 Fifth Third Center · 111 Lyon Street, NW · Grand Rapids, MI 49503-2487 · 616-752-2000

Lansing

Stephen I. Jurmu · ⑳ · Foster, Swift, Collins & Smith · http://www.fosterswift.com · 313 South Washington Square · Lansing, MI 48933-2193 · 517-371-8100

Darrell A. Lindman · ⑩ · Fraser Trebilcock Davis & Dunlap · 124 West Allegan Street, Suite 1000 · Lansing, MI 48933 · 517-482-5800

Stephen J. Lowney · Foster, Swift, Collins & Smith · http://www.fosterswift.com · 313 South Washington Square · Lansing, MI 48933-2193 · 517-371-8100

Sherry A. Stein · Foster, Swift, Collins & Smith · http://www.fosterswift.com · 313 South Washington Square · Lansing, MI 48933-2193 · 517-371-8100

Muskegon

John H. McKendry, Jr. · ⑩ · Warner Norcross & Judd · http://www.wnj.com · 400 Terrace Plaza · P.O. Box 900 · Muskegon, MI 49443-0900 · 231-727-2600

Pittsfield Twp.

John H. Eggertsen · ⑳ · John H. Eggertsen · 6270 Munger Road · Pittsfield Twp., MI 48197 · 734-794-7100

Southfield

Mary Jo Larson · Warner Norcross & Judd · http://www.wnj.com · 2000 Town Center, Suite 2700 · Southfield, MI 48075-1318 · 248-784-5000

Charles M. Lax · Maddin, Hauser, Wartell, Roth & Heller · http://www.maddinhauser.com · Essex Centre, Third Floor · 28400 Northwestern Highway · Southfield, MI 48034-1839 · 248-354-4030

Troy

Kalman G. Goren · Miller Canfield Paddock and Stone · http://www.millercanfield.com · 840 West Long Lake Road, Suite 200 · Troy, MI 48098-6358 · 248-879-2000

David B. Walters · Bodman · http://www.bodmanllp.com · 201 West Big Beaver Road, Suite 500 · Troy, MI 48084 · 248-743-6000

ENERGY LAW

Detroit

Joseph M. Polito · ⑳ · Honigman Miller Schwartz and Cohn · First National Building, Suite 2290 · 660 Woodward Avenue · Detroit, MI 48226-3506 · 313-465-7000

Peter W. Waldmeir · Miller Canfield Paddock and Stone · http://www.millercanfield.com · 150 West Jefferson Avenue, Suite 2500 · Detroit, MI 48226 · 313-963-6420

Lansing

Ronald W. Bloomberg · Miller Canfield Paddock and Stone · http://www.millercanfield.com · One Michigan Avenue, Suite 900 · Lansing, MI 48933 · 517-487-2070

Roderick S. Coy · ⑩ · Clark Hill · http://www.clarkhill.com · 212 East Grand River Avenue · Lansing, MI 48906-4328 · 517-318-3100

Albert Ernst · ⑩ · Dykema · http://www.dykema.com · 201 Townsend Street, Suite 900 · Lansing, MI 48933 · 517-374-9100

Harvey J. Messing · ⑩ · Miller Canfield Paddock and Stone · http://www.millercanfield.com · One Michigan Avenue, Suite 900 · Lansing, MI 48933 · 517-487-2070

James R. Neal · ⑩ · Loomis, Ewert, Parsley, Davis & Gotting · 124 West Allegan Street, Suite 700 · Lansing, MI 48933-1707 · 517-482-2400

Eric J. Schneidewind · Varnum, Riddering, Schmidt & Howlett · The Victor Center, Suite 810 · 201 North Washington Square · Lansing, MI 48933 · 517-482-6237

Webb A. Smith · ⑩ · Foster, Swift, Collins & Smith · http://www.fosterswift.com · 313 South Washington Square · Lansing, MI 48933-2193 · 517-371-8100

Sherri A. Wellman · Miller Canfield Paddock and Stone · http://www.millercanfield.com · One Michigan Avenue, Suite 900 · Lansing, MI 48933 · 517-487-2070

Okemos

Richard J. Aaron · Fahey Schultz Burzych Rhodes · http://www.fsblawyers.com · 4151 Okemos Road · Okemos, MI 48864 · 517-381-0100

William K. Fahey · Fahey Schultz Burzych Rhodes · http://www.fsblawyers.com · 4151 Okemos Road · Okemos, MI 48864 · 517-381-0100

ENTERTAINMENT LAW

Bloomfield Hills

Howard Hertz · Hertz Schram · 1760 South Telegraph Road, Suite 300 · Bloomfield Hills, MI 48302-0183 · 248-335-5000

Troy

Michael A. Novak · Giarmarco, Mullins & Horton · Columbia Center, 10th Floor · 101 West Big Beaver Road · Troy, MI 48084-5280 · 248-457-7000

ENVIRONMENTAL LAW

Bloomfield Hills

Philip A. Grashoff, Jr. · 10 · Strobl & Sharp · http://www.stroblpc.com · 300 East Long Lake Road, Suite 200 · Bloomfield Hills, MI 48304 · 248-540-2300

Jeffrey K. Haynes · 20 · Beier Howlett · 200 East Long Lake Road, Suite 110 · Bloomfield Hills, MI 48304-2328 · 248-645-9400

Jack D. Shumate · Butzel Long · http://www.butzel.com · Stoneridge West · 41000 Woodward Avenue · Bloomfield Hills, MI 48304 · 248-258-1616

Detroit

Margaret A. Coughlin · Dickinson Wright · http://www.dickinsonwright.com · 500 Woodward Avenue, Suite 4000 · Detroit, MI 48226-3425 · 313-223-3500

Fredrick J. Dindoffer · Bodman · http://www.bodmanllp.com · Sixth Floor at Ford Field · 1901 Saint Antoine Street · Detroit, MI 48226 · 313-259-7777

Kenneth C. Gold · Honigman Miller Schwartz and Cohn · First National Building, Suite 2290 · 660 Woodward Avenue · Detroit, MI 48226-3506 · 313-465-7000

Steven C. Nadeau · 10 · Honigman Miller Schwartz and Cohn · First National Building, Suite 2290 · 660 Woodward Avenue · Detroit, MI 48226-3506 · 313-465-7000

Joseph M. Polito · 20 · Honigman Miller Schwartz and Cohn · First National Building, Suite 2290 · 660 Woodward Avenue · Detroit, MI 48226-3506 · 313-465-7000

Thomas P. Wilczak · Pepper Hamilton · http://www.pepperlaw.com · 100 Renaissance Center, Suite 3600 Detroit, MI 48243-1157 · 313-259-7110

Grand Rapids

John V. Byl · Warner Norcross & Judd · http://www.wnj.com · 900 Fifth Third Center · 111 Lyon Street, NW · Grand Rapids, MI 49503-2487 · 616-752-2000

Charles M. Denton II · ⑩ · Barnes & Thornburg · http://www.btlaw.com · 300 Ottawa Avenue, NW, Suite 500 · Grand Rapids, MI 49503 · 616-742-3930

John D. Dunn · ⑩ · Warner Norcross & Judd · http://www.wnj.com · 900 Fifth Third Center · 111 Lyon Street, NW · Grand Rapids, MI 49503-2487 · 616-752-2000

Dustin Ordway · Miller Johnson · http://www.millerjohnson.com · Calder Plaza Building, Suite 800 · 250 Monroe Avenue, NW · P.O. Box 306 · Grand Rapids, MI 49503-2250 · 616-831-1700

Mary Jane Rhoades · Rhoades McKee · 161 Ottawa Avenue, NW, Suite 600 · Grand Rapids, MI 49503 · 616-235-3500

Michael L. Robinson · ⑳ · Warner Norcross & Judd · http://www.wnj.com · 900 Fifth Third Center · 111 Lyon Street, NW · Grand Rapids, MI 49503-2487 · 616-752-2000

Alan C. Schwartz · Miller Johnson · http://www.millerjohnson.com · Calder Plaza Building, Suite 800 · 250 Monroe Avenue, NW · P.O. Box 306 · Grand Rapids, MI 49503-2250 · 616-831-1700

Eugene E. Smary · ⑩ · Warner Norcross & Judd · http://www.wnj.com · 900 Fifth Third Center · 111 Lyon Street, NW · Grand Rapids, MI 49503-2487 · 616-752-2000

J. Michael Smith · Miller Johnson · http://www.millerjohnson.com · Calder Plaza Building, Suite 800 · 250 Monroe Avenue, NW · P.O. Box 306 · Grand Rapids, MI 49503-2250 · 616-831-1700

Peter W. Steketee · ⑳ · Peter W. Steketee · 2060 Robinson Road, SE · Grand Rapids, MI 49506 · 616-949-6551

Kalamazoo

Ronald E. Baylor · Miller Canfield Paddock and Stone · http://www.millercanfield.com · 277 South Rose Street, Suite 5000 · Kalamazoo, MI 49007-3751 · 269-381-7030

Michael B. Ortega · Lewis Reed & Allen · 136 East Michigan Avenue · Kalamazoo, MI 49007-3945 · 269-388-7600

Lansing

Charles E. Barbieri · ⑩ · Foster, Swift, Collins & Smith · http://www.fosterswift.com · 313 South Washington Square · Lansing, MI 48933-2193 · 517-371-8100

Douglas W. Crim · Miller Canfield Paddock and Stone · http://www.millercanfield.com · One Michigan Avenue, Suite 900 · Lansing, MI 48933 · 517-487-2070

James R. Lancaster · Miller Canfield Paddock and Stone · http://www.millercanfield.com · One Michigan Avenue, Suite 900 · Lansing, MI 48933 · 517-487-2070

Thomas C. Phillips · Miller Canfield Paddock and Stone · http://www.millercanfield.com · One Michigan Avenue, Suite 900 · Lansing, MI 48933 · 517-487-2070

Steven D. Weyhing · Kelley Cawthorne · 208 North Capitol Avenue, Third Floor · Lansing, MI 48933 · 517-371-1400

Troy

Anna M. Maiuri · Miller Canfield Paddock and Stone · http://www.millercanfield.com · 840 West Long Lake Road, Suite 200 · Troy, MI 48098-6358 · 248-879-2000

James K. O'Brien · Dean & Fulkerson · 801 West Big Beaver Road, Suite 500 · Troy, MI 48084-4767 · 248-362-1300

FAMILY LAW

Ann Arbor

Diana Raimi · Moran, Raimi & Goethal · 320 North Main Street, Suite 101 · Ann Arbor, MI 48104 · 734-769-6838

Birmingham

Mark A. Bank · The Law Firm of John F. Schaefer · 380 North Old Woodward Avenue, Suite 320 · Birmingham, MI 48009 · 248-642-6655

John F. Mills · Williams, Williams, Rattner & Plunkett · 380 North Old Woodward Avenue, Suite 300 · Birmingham, MI 48009 · 248-642-0333

John F. Schaefer · ㉕ · The Law Firm of John F. Schaefer · 380 North Old Woodward Avenue, Suite 320 Birmingham, MI 48009 · 248-642-6655

Kurt E. Schnelz · Schnelz Wells · 280 North Old Woodward Road, Suite 250 · Birmingham, MI 48009 · 248-258-7074

Bloomfield Hills

Joseph Aviv · Honigman Miller Schwartz and Cohn · 38500 Woodward Avenue, Suite 100 · Bloomfield Hills, MI 48304-5048 · 248-566-8301

Frederick G. Buesser III · ㉕ · Butzel Long · http://www.butzel.com · Stoneridge West · 41000 Woodward Avenue · Bloomfield Hills, MI 48304 · 248-258-1616

Timothy T. Fryhoff · ⑩ · Fryhoff & Lynch · 40701 Woodward Avenue, Suite 50 · Bloomfield Hills, MI 48304 · 248-644-1366

Edward D. Gold · ⑩ · Butzel Long · http://www.butzel.com · Stoneridge West · 41000 Woodward Avenue Bloomfield Hills, MI 48304 · 248-258-1616

Hanley M. Gurwin · ㉕ · Dickinson Wright · http://www.dickinsonwright.com · 38525 Woodward Avenue, Suite 2000 · Bloomfield Hills, MI 48304-2970 · 248-433-7200

William O. Lynch · Meyer, Kirk, Snyder & Lynch · 100 West Long Lake Road, Suite 100 · Bloomfield Hills, MI 48304 · 248-647-5111

Richard S. Victor · Law Offices of Victor and Victor · http://www.richardsvictor.com · 100 West Long Lake Road, Suite 250 · Bloomfield Hills, MI 48304 · 248-646-7177

Detroit

Carole L. Chiamp · ⑳ · Chiamp & Associates · 333 West Fort Street, Suite 1800 · Detroit, MI 48226-3186 · 313-962-4600

East Lansing

Nan Elizabeth Casey · Oade, Stroud & Kleiman · http://www.osklaw.com · 200 Woodland Pass · P.O. Box 1296 · East Lansing, MI 48826 · 517-351-6501

Maurice E. Schoenberger · Maurice E. Schoenberger · 1675 Watertower Place, Suite 500 · East Lansing, MI 48823 · 517-337-0600

Farmington Hills

William P. Hampton · ⑩ · Secrest, Wardle, Lynch, Hampton, Truex and Morley · 30903 Northwestern Highway · P.O. Box 3040 · Farmington Hills, MI 48333-3040 · 248-851-9500

Franklin

Harriet B. Rotter · ⑩ · Harriet B. Rotter · 32710 Franklin Road · Franklin, MI 48025-1136 · 248-855-5200

Grand Rapids

Michael B. Quinn · Miller Johnson · http://www.millerjohnson.com · Calder Plaza Building, Suite 800 · 250 Monroe Avenue, NW · P.O. Box 306 · Grand Rapids, MI 49503-2250 · 616-831-1700

Richard A. Roane · Warner Norcross & Judd · http://www.wnj.com · 900 Fifth Third Center · 111 Lyon Street, NW · Grand Rapids, MI 49503-2487 · 616-752-2000

David C. Sarnacki · The Sarnacki Law Firm · 800 McKay Tower · 146 Monroe Center, NW · Grand Rapids, MI 49503-2833 · 616-988-9500

Connie R. Thacker · Rhoades McKee · 161 Ottawa Avenue, NW, Suite 600 · Grand Rapids, MI 49503 · 616-235-3500

James W. Zerrenner · ⑩ · James W. Zerrenner · Grand Plaza Place, Suite 450 · 220 Lyon Square, NW · Grand Rapids, MI 49503 · 616-774-4414

Grosse Pointe

Kenneth E. Prather · ㉕ · Kenneth E. Prather, Sr. · Five Sratford Place · Grosse Pointe, MI 48230 · 313-884-5622

Lansing

Bernard F. Finn · Sinas, Dramis, Brake, Boughton & McIntyre · 3380 Pine Tree Road · Lansing, MI 48911-4207 · 517-394-7500

Frank H. Reynolds · The Reynolds Law Firm · Oakhill Professional Park, Suite A · 2400 Lake Lansing Road · Lansing, MI 48912-3674 · 517-372-0676

Southfield

William M. Brukoff · Sommers Schwartz · http://www.sommerspc.com · 2000 Town Center, Suite 900 · Southfield, MI 48075-1100 · 248-355-0300

Troy

Robert Z. Feldstein · ⑩ · Kemp, Klein, Umphrey, Endelman & May · 201 West Big Beaver Road, Suite 600 · Troy, MI 48084 · 248-528-1111

Donald E. McGinnis, Jr. · Donald E. McGinnis, Jr · 1721 Crooks Road, Suite 101 · Troy, MI 48084 · 248-643-6002

FIRST AMENDMENT LAW

Ann Arbor

Leonard M. Niehoff · Butzel Long · http://www.butzel.com · 350 South Main Street, Suite 300 · Ann Arbor, MI 48104 · 734-995-3110

James E. Stewart · (10) · Butzel Long · http://www.butzel.com · 350 South Main Street, Suite 300 · Ann Arbor, MI 48104 · 734-995-3110

Detroit

Herschel P. Fink · (10) · Honigman Miller Schwartz and Cohn · First National Building, Suite 2290 · 660 Woodward Avenue · Detroit, MI 48226-3506 · 313-465-7000

Laurie J. Michelson · Butzel Long · http://www.butzel.com · 150 West Jefferson Avenue, Suite 100 · Detroit, MI 48226 · 313-225-7000

Richard E. Rassel · (20) · Butzel Long · http://www.butzel.com · 150 West Jefferson Avenue, Suite 100 · Detroit, MI 48226 · 313-225-7000

Grand Rapids

James S. Brady · Miller Johnson · http://www.millerjohnson.com · Calder Plaza Building, Suite 800 · 250 Monroe Avenue, NW · P.O. Box 306 · Grand Rapids, MI 49503-2250 · 616-831-1700

J. A. Cragwall, Jr. · (10) · Warner Norcross & Judd · http://www.wnj.com · 900 Fifth Third Center · 111 Lyon Street, NW · Grand Rapids, MI 49503-2487 · 616-752-2000

Lansing

Charles E. Barbieri · (10) · Foster, Swift, Collins & Smith · http://www.fosterswift.com · 313 South Washington Square · Lansing, MI 48933-2193 · 517-371-8100

Webb A. Smith · (10) · Foster, Swift, Collins & Smith · http://www.fosterswift.com · 313 South Washington Square · Lansing, MI 48933-2193 · 517-371-8100

Plymouth

John J. Ronayne III · (10) · Bernardi, Ronayne & Glusac · 1058 Maple Street, Suite 100 · Plymouth, MI 48170 · 734-416-1780

FRANCHISE LAW

Detroit

David A. Ettinger · Honigman Miller Schwartz and Cohn · First National Building, Suite 2290 · 660 Woodward Avenue · Detroit, MI 48226-3506 · 313-465-7000

Okemos

Mark J. Burzych · Fahey Schultz Burzych Rhodes · http://www.fsblawyers.com · 4151 Okemos Road · Okemos, MI 48864 · 517-381-0100

GAMING LAW

East Lansing

David D. Waddell · Regulatory Management Counselors · University Place Center, Suite 450 · 333 Albert Avenue · East Lansing, MI 48823 · 517-507-3860

Lansing

R. Lance Boldrey · Dykema · http://www.dykema.com · 201 Townsend Street, Suite 900 · Lansing, MI 48933 · 517-374-9100

Eric J. Eggan · Honigman Miller Schwartz and Cohn · 222 North Washington Square, Suite 400 · Lansing, MI 48933-1800 · 517-484-8282

Peter H. Ellsworth · Dickinson Wright · http://www.dickinsonwright.com · 215 South Washington Square, Suite 200 · Lansing, MI 48933-1816 · 517-371-1730

Kevin J. Moody · Miller Canfield Paddock and Stone · http://www.millercanfield.com · One Michigan Avenue, Suite 900 · Lansing, MI 48933 · 517-487-2070

Robert W. Stocker II · Dickinson Wright · http://www.dickinsonwright.com · 215 South Washington Square, Suite 200 · Lansing, MI 48933-1816 · 517-371-1730

Leonard C. Wolfe · Dykema · http://www.dykema.com · 201 Townsend Street, Suite 900 · Lansing, MI 48933 · 517-374-9100

GOVERNMENT RELATIONS LAW

Detroit

George W. Ash · Foley & Lardner · One Detroit Center, Suite 2700 · 500 Woodward Avenue · Detroit, MI 48226-3489 · 313-234-7100

G. Scott Romney · Honigman Miller Schwartz and Cohn · First National Building, Suite 2290 · 660 Woodward Avenue · Detroit, MI 48226-3506 · 313-465-7000

Lansing

Peter H. Ellsworth · Dickinson Wright · http://www.dickinsonwright.com · 215 South Washington Square, Suite 200 · Lansing, MI 48933-1816 · 517-371-1730

James R. Lancaster · Miller Canfield Paddock and Stone · http://www.millercanfield.com · One Michigan Avenue, Suite 900 · Lansing, MI 48933 · 517-487-2070

William J. Perrone · Dykema · http://www.dykema.com · 201 Townsend Street, Suite 900 · Lansing, MI 48933 · 517-374-9100

John D. Pirich · ⑩ · Honigman Miller Schwartz and Cohn · 222 North Washington Square, Suite 400 · Lansing, MI 48933-1800 · 517-484-8282

Robert W. Stocker II · Dickinson Wright · http://www.dickinsonwright.com · 215 South Washington Square, Suite 200 · Lansing, MI 48933-1816 · 517-371-1730

Leonard C. Wolfe · Dykema · http://www.dykema.com · 201 Townsend Street, Suite 900 · Lansing, MI 48933 · 517-374-9100

Okemos

Mark J. Burzych · Fahey Schultz Burzych Rhodes · http://www.fsblawyers.com · 4151 Okemos Road · Okemos, MI 48864 · 517-381-0100

HEALTH CARE LAW

Ann Arbor

Bettye S. Elkins · ⑩ · Miller Canfield Paddock and Stone · http://www.millercanfield.com · 101 North Main Street, Seventh Floor · Ann Arbor, MI 48104-1400 · 734-663-2445

James L. Hughes · Butzel Long · http://www.butzel.com · 350 South Main Street, Suite 300 · Ann Arbor, MI 48104 · 734-995-3110

Joseph G. Nuyen, Jr. · ⑩ · Nuyen, Tomtishen and Aoun · 2001 Commonwealth Boulevard, Suite 300 · Ann Arbor, MI 48105 · 734-372-4100

Roselyn R. Parmenter · Miller Canfield Paddock and Stone · http://www.millercanfield.com · 101 North Main Street, Seventh Floor · Ann Arbor, MI 48104-1400 · 734-663-2445

Timothy D. Sochocki · ⑩ · Miller Canfield Paddock and Stone · http://www.millercanfield.com · 101 North Main Street, Seventh Floor · Ann Arbor, MI 48104-1400 · 734-663-2445

Birmingham

Keith J. Soltis · Kotz, Sangster, Wysocki & Berg · 300 Park Street, Suite 265 · Birmingham, MI 48009-3429 · 248-646-1050

Bloomfield Hills

Maria B. Abrahamsen · ⑩ · Dykema · http://www.dykema.com · 39577 Woodward Avenue, Suite 300 · Bloomfield Hills, MI 48304-2820 · 248-203-0700

Detroit

William M. Cassetta · Honigman Miller Schwartz and Cohn · First National Building, Suite 2290 · 660 Woodward Avenue · Detroit, MI 48226-3506 · 313-465-7000

William O. Hochkammer · ⑩ · Honigman Miller Schwartz and Cohn · First National Building, Suite 2290 · 660 Woodward Avenue · Detroit, MI 48226-3506 · 313-465-7000

Monte D. Jahnke · ⑩ · Kerr, Russell and Weber · Detroit Center, Suite 2500 · 500 Woodward Avenue · Detroit, MI 48226-3427 · 313-961-0200

Kathrin E. Kudner · ⑩ · Dykema · http://www.dykema.com · 400 Renaissance Center · Detroit, MI 48243 · 313-568-6800

Seth M. Lloyd · ⑩ · Dykema · http://www.dykema.com · 400 Renaissance Center · Detroit, MI 48243 · 313-568-6800

Stuart M. Lockman · ⑩ · Honigman Miller Schwartz and Cohn · First National Building, Suite 2290 · 660 Woodward Avenue · Detroit, MI 48226-3506 · 313-465-7000

Kenneth Marcus · Honigman Miller Schwartz and Cohn · First National Building, Suite 2290 · 660 Woodward Avenue · Detroit, MI 48226-3506 · 313-465-7000

Thomas J. McGraw · Dykema · http://www.dykema.com · 400 Renaissance Center · Detroit, MI 48243 · 313-568-6800

Julie E. Robertson · Honigman Miller Schwartz and Cohn · First National Building, Suite 2290 · 660 Woodward Avenue · Detroit, MI 48226-3506 · 313-465-7000

Linda S. Ross · Honigman Miller Schwartz and Cohn · First National Building, Suite 2290 · 660 Woodward Avenue · Detroit, MI 48226-3506 · 313-465-7000

Chris E. Rossman · ⑩ · Foley & Lardner · One Detroit Center, Suite 2700 · 500 Woodward Avenue · Detroit, MI 48226-3489 · 313-234-7100

Farmington Hills

Gilbert M. Frimet · Foster, Swift, Collins & Smith · http://www.fosterswift.com · 32300 Northwestern Highway, Suite 230 · Farmington Hills, MI 48334 · 248-539-9900

Alan Gilchrist · Foster, Swift, Collins & Smith · http://www.fosterswift.com · 32300 Northwestern Highway, Suite 230 · Farmington Hills, MI 48334 · 248-539-9900

Alan T. Rogalski · Foster, Swift, Collins & Smith · http://www.fosterswift.com · 32300 Northwestern Highway, Suite 230 · Farmington Hills, MI 48334 · 248-539-9900

Grand Haven

Thomas R. Reinsma · ⑩ · Scholten & Fant · 100 North Third Street · P.O. Box 454 · Grand Haven, MI 49417-0454 · 616-842-3030

Grand Rapids

Richard L. Bouma · Warner Norcross & Judd · http://www.wnj.com · 900 Fifth Third Center · 111 Lyon Street, NW · Grand Rapids, MI 49503-2487 · 616-752-2000

Lawrence P. Burns · ⑩ · Varnum, Riddering, Schmidt & Howlett · Bridgewater Place · 333 Bridge Street, NW · P.O. Box 352 · Grand Rapids, MI 49501-0352 · 616-336-6000

Richard E. Cassard · ⑩ · Warner Norcross & Judd · http://www.wnj.com · 900 Fifth Third Center · 111 Lyon Street, NW · Grand Rapids, MI 49503-2487 · 616-752-2000

Kenneth G. Hofman · Miller Johnson · http://www.millerjohnson.com · Calder Plaza Building, Suite 800 · 250 Monroe Avenue, NW · P.O. Box 306 · Grand Rapids, MI 49503-2250 · 616-831-1700

Richard C. Lague · Varnum, Riddering, Schmidt & Howlett · Bridgewater Place · 333 Bridge Street, NW P.O. Box 352 · Grand Rapids, MI 49501-0352 · 616-336-6000

Devin S. Schindler · Warner Norcross & Judd · http://www.wnj.com · 900 Fifth Third Center · 111 Lyon Street, NW · Grand Rapids, MI 49503-2487 · 616-752-2000

Lansing

Gary J. McRay · ⑩ · Foster, Swift, Collins & Smith · http://www.fosterswift.com · 313 South Washington Square · Lansing, MI 48933-2193 · 517-371-8100

Royal Oak

Andrew B. Wachler · Wachler & Associates · 210 East Third Street, Suite 204 · Royal Oak, MI 48067 · 248-544-0888

IMMIGRATION LAW

Bingham Farms

Dorothy H. Basmaji · Vercruysse Murray & Calzone · http://www.vmclaw.com · 31780 Telegraph Road, Suite 200 · Bingham Farms, MI 48025-3469 · 248-540-8019

Debra Auerbach Clephane · Vercruysse Murray & Calzone · http://www.vmclaw.com · 31780 Telegraph Road, Suite 200 · Bingham Farms, MI 48025-3469 · 248-540-8019

Bloomfield Hills

Elise S. Levasseur · Dickinson Wright · http://www.dickinsonwright.com · 38525 Woodward Avenue, Suite 2000 · Bloomfield Hills, MI 48304-2970 · 248-433-7200

Larry J. Stringer · ⑩ · Dickinson Wright · http://www.dickinsonwright.com · 38525 Woodward Avenue, Suite 2000 · Bloomfield Hills, MI 48304-2970 · 248-433-7200

Detroit

William H. Dance · ⑩ · Abbott, Nicholson, Quilter, Esshaki & Youngblood · 300 River Place, Suite 3000 · Detroit, MI 48207 · 313-566-2500

Carol A. Friend · Honigman Miller Schwartz and Cohn · First National Building, Suite 2290 · 660 Woodward Avenue · Detroit, MI 48226-3506 · 313-465-7000

Clara DeMatteis Mager · Butzel Long · http://www.butzel.com · 150 West Jefferson Avenue, Suite 100 · Detroit, MI 48226 · 313-225-7000

Derek I. Meier · Dykema · http://www.dykema.com · 400 Renaissance Center · Detroit, MI 48243 · 313-568-6800

Reginald A. Pacis · Butzel Long · http://www.butzel.com · 150 West Jefferson Avenue, Suite 100 · Detroit, MI 48226 · 313-225-7000

Grand Rapids

Kathleen M. Hanenburg · Warner Norcross & Judd · http://www.wnj.com · 900 Fifth Third Center · 111 Lyon Street, NW · Grand Rapids, MI 49503-2487 · 616-752-2000

Grosse Pointe Park

Ingrid K. Brey · ⑩ · Ingrid K. Brey · 15124 Kercheval Avenue · Grosse Pointe Park, MI 48230 · 313-822-8888

Southfield

Thomas A. Bassett · Thomas Bassett and Associates · 28444 Franklin Road · Southfield, MI 48034 · 248-827-4110

Charles Steven Owen · ⑩ · Owen & Associates · 25899 West Twelve Mile Road, Suite 120 · Southfield, MI 48034 · 248-353-7000

Troy

Christian S. Allen · Ellis Porter · 2701 Troy Center Drive, Suite 100 · Troy, MI 48084 · 248-519-9900

Scott F. Cooper · Fragomen, Del Rey, Bernsen & Loewy · http://www.fragomen.com · 2301 West Big Beaver Road, Suite 225 · Troy, MI 48084-3325 · 248-649-5404

Leila Freijy · Fragomen, Del Rey, Bernsen & Loewy · http://www.fragomen.com · 2301 West Big Beaver Road, Suite 225 · Troy, MI 48084-3325 · 248-649-5404

David H. Paruch · ⑩ · Law Offices of David H. Paruch · 525 East Big Beaver Road, Suite 250 · Troy, MI 48083 · 248-743-0470

INFORMATION TECHNOLOGY LAW

Ann Arbor

Bettye S. Elkins · ⑩ · Miller Canfield Paddock and Stone · http://www.millercanfield.com · 101 North Main Street, Seventh Floor · Ann Arbor, MI 48104-1400 · 734-663-2445

Marta A. Manildi · Miller Canfield Paddock and Stone · http://www.millercanfield.com · 101 North Main Street, Seventh Floor · Ann Arbor, MI 48104-1400 · 734-663-2445

Detroit

Kathryn L. Ossian · Miller Canfield Paddock and Stone · http://www.millercanfield.com · 150 West Jefferson Avenue, Suite 2500 · Detroit, MI 48226 · 313-963-6420

Linda S. Ross · Honigman Miller Schwartz and Cohn · First National Building, Suite 2290 · 660 Woodward Avenue · Detroit, MI 48226-3506 · 313-465-7000

Stephen L. Tupper · Dykema · http://www.dykema.com · 400 Renaissance Center · Detroit, MI 48243 · 313-568-6800

Southfield

Holli Hart Targan · Jaffe Raitt Heuer & Weiss · 27777 Franklin Road, Suite 2500 · Southfield, MI 48034-8214 · 248-351-3000

INSURANCE LAW

Detroit

William M. Cassetta · Honigman Miller Schwartz and Cohn · First National Building, Suite 2290 · 660 Woodward Avenue · Detroit, MI 48226-3506 · 313-465-7000

William O. Hochkammer · ⑩ · Honigman Miller Schwartz and Cohn · First National Building, Suite 2290 · 660 Woodward Avenue · Detroit, MI 48226-3506 · 313-465-7000

Monte D. Jahnke · ⑩ · Kerr, Russell and Weber · Detroit Center, Suite 2500 · 500 Woodward Avenue · Detroit, MI 48226-3427 · 313-961-0200

Julie E. Robertson · Honigman Miller Schwartz and Cohn · First National Building, Suite 2290 · 660 Woodward Avenue · Detroit, MI 48226-3506 · 313-465-7000

Rosalind Rochkind · Garan Lucow & Miller · Woodbridge Place · 1000 Woodbridge Street · Detroit, MI 48207-3192 · 313-446-1530

Daniel S. Saylor · Garan Lucow & Miller · Woodbridge Place · 1000 Woodbridge Street · Detroit, MI 48207-3192 · 313-446-1530

Grand Rapids

Gary A. Maximiuk · Wheeler Upham · http://www.wheelerupham.com · Trust Building, Second Floor · 40 Pearl Street, NW · Grand Rapids, MI 49503-3001 · 616-459-7100

Lansing

Timothy S. Knowlton · Honigman Miller Schwartz and Cohn · 222 North Washington Square, Suite 400 · Lansing, MI 48933-1800 · 517-484-8282

James E. Lozier · Dickinson Wright · http://www.dickinsonwright.com · 215 South Washington Square, Suite 200 · Lansing, MI 48933-1816 · 517-371-1730

Scott L. Mandel · Foster, Swift, Collins & Smith · http://www.fosterswift.com · 313 South Washington Square · Lansing, MI 48933-2193 · 517-371-8100

Lori McAllister · Dykema · http://www.dykema.com · 201 Townsend Street, Suite 900 · Lansing, MI 48933 · 517-374-9100

John D. Pirich · 10 · Honigman Miller Schwartz and Cohn · 222 North Washington Square, Suite 400 · Lansing, MI 48933-1800 · 517-484-8282

Royal Oak

John R. Monnich · John R. Monnich · 306 South Washington Avenue, Suite 207 · Royal Oak, MI 48067 · 248-548-4747

Traverse City

Todd W. Millar · Smith, Haughey, Rice & Roegge · 202 East State Street, Suite 100 · Traverse City, MI 49685-0848 · 231-929-4878

INTELLECTUAL PROPERTY LAW

Ann Arbor

James M. Cameron, Jr. · Dykema · http://www.dykema.com · 2723 South State Street, Suite 400 · Ann Arbor, MI 48104 · 734-214-7600

Alan N. Harris · Bodman · http://www.bodmanllp.com · 201 South Division Street, Suite 400 · Ann Arbor, MI 48104 · 734-761-3780

J. Michael Huget · Butzel Long · http://www.butzel.com · 350 South Main Street, Suite 300 · Ann Arbor, MI 48104 · 734-995-3110

Lawrence R. Jordan · Jaffe Raitt Heuer & Weiss · 201 South Main, Suite 300 · Ann Arbor, MI 48104 · 734-222-4776

Susan M. Kornfield · Bodman · http://www.bodmanllp.com · 201 South Division Street, Suite 400 · Ann Arbor, MI 48104 · 734-761-3780

Marta A. Manildi · Miller Canfield Paddock and Stone · http://www.millercanfield.com · 101 North Main Street, Seventh Floor · Ann Arbor, MI 48104-1400 · 734-663-2445

Steven L. Oberholtzer · Brinks Hofer Gilson & Lione · 524 South Main, Suite 200 · Ann Arbor, MI 48104-2921 · 734-302-6000

Bloomfield Hills

Bernard J. Cantor · ⑩ · Bernard J. Cantor · 5685 Forman Drive · Bloomfield Hills, MI 48301 · 248-626-5259

Richard D. Grauer · ⑩ · Rader, Fishman and Grauer · 39533 Woodward Avenue, Suite 140 · Bloomfield Hills, MI 48304 · 248-594-0600

William H. Honaker · Dickinson Wright · http://www.dickinsonwright.com · 38525 Woodward Avenue, Suite 2000 · Bloomfield Hills, MI 48304-2970 · 248-433-7200

Michael A. Lisi · Honigman Miller Schwartz and Cohn · 38500 Woodward Avenue, Suite 100 · Bloomfield Hills, MI 48304-5048 · 248-566-8301

R. Terrance Rader · Rader, Fishman and Grauer · 39533 Woodward Avenue, Suite 140 · Bloomfield Hills, MI 48304 · 248-594-0600

Michael B. Stewart · Rader, Fishman and Grauer · 39533 Woodward Avenue, Suite 140 · Bloomfield Hills, MI 48304 · 248-594-0600

Detroit

Marjory G. Basile · Miller Canfield Paddock and Stone · http://www.millercanfield.com · 150 West Jefferson Avenue, Suite 2500 · Detroit, MI 48226 · 313-963-6420

Grand Rapids

Charles E. Burpee · ⑩ · Warner Norcross & Judd · http://www.wnj.com · 900 Fifth Third Center · 111 Lyon Street, NW · Grand Rapids, MI 49503-2487 · 616-752-2000

Catherine S. Collins · Van Dyke, Gardner, Linn & Burkhart · 2851 Charlevoix Drive, SE, Suite 207 · P.O. Box 888695 · Grand Rapids, MI 49588-8695 · 616-975-5500

Timothy A. Flory · Van Dyke, Gardner, Linn & Burkhart · 2851 Charlevoix Drive, SE, Suite 207 · P.O. Box 888695 · Grand Rapids, MI 49588-8695 · 616-975-5500

Richard A. Gaffin · Miller Canfield Paddock and Stone · http://www.millercanfield.com · 99 Monroe Avenue, NW, Suite 1200 · Grand Rapids, MI 49503 · 616-454-8656

Donald S. Gardner · ⑩ · Van Dyke, Gardner, Linn & Burkhart · 2851 Charlevoix Drive, SE, Suite 207 · P.O. Box 888695 · Grand Rapids, MI 49588-8695 · 616-975-5500

Terence J. Linn · Van Dyke, Gardner, Linn & Burkhart · 2851 Charlevoix Drive, SE, Suite 207 · P.O. Box 888695 · Grand Rapids, MI 49588-8695 · 616-975-5500

James A. Mitchell · ⑩ · Varnum, Riddering, Schmidt & Howlett · Bridgewater Place · 333 Bridge Street, NW · P.O. Box 352 · Grand Rapids, MI 49501-0352 · 616-336-6000

Harold W. Reick · Price, Heneveld, Cooper, DeWitt & Litton · 695 Kenmoor Avenue, SE · P.O. Box 2567 · Grand Rapids, MI 49501 · 616-949-9610

Lansing

Mark R. Fox · Fraser Trebilcock Davis & Dunlap · 124 West Allegan Street, Suite 1000 · Lansing, MI 48933 · 517-482-5800

Pontiac

Eric M. Dobrusin · Dobrusin & Thennisch · http://www.patentco.com · 29 West Lawrence Street, Suite 210 · Pontiac, MI 48342-2813 · 248-292-2920

Southfield

Frank A. Angileri · Brooks Kushman · http://www.brookskushman.com · 1000 Town Center, 22nd Floor · Southfield, MI 48075 · 248-358-4400

Mark Cantor · Brooks Kushman · http://www.brookskushman.com · 1000 Town Center, 22nd Floor · Southfield, MI 48075 · 248-358-4400

Troy

Thomas N. Young · Young Basile · 3001 West Big Beaver Road, Suite 624 · Troy, MI 48084-3107 · 248-649-3333

INTERNATIONAL TRADE AND FINANCE LAW

Detroit

Bruce D. Birgbauer · ㉕ · Miller Canfield Paddock and Stone · http://www.millercanfield.com · 150 West Jefferson Avenue, Suite 2500 · Detroit, MI 48226 · 313-963-6420

James C. Bruno · ⑩ · Butzel Long · http://www.butzel.com · 150 West Jefferson Avenue, Suite 100 · Detroit, MI 48226 · 313-225-7000

D. Kerry Crenshaw · Clark Hill · http://www.clarkhill.com · 500 Woodward Avenue, Suite 3500 · Detroit, MI 48226-3435 · 313-965-8300

Robert A. Hudson · ⑩ · Butzel Long · http://www.butzel.com · 150 West Jefferson Avenue, Suite 100 · Detroit, MI 48226 · 313-225-7000

Grand Rapids

Cameron S. DeLong · ⑩ · Warner Norcross & Judd · http://www.wnj.com · 900 Fifth Third Center · 111 Lyon Street, NW · Grand Rapids, MI 49503-2487 · 616-752-2000

Charles E. McCallum · ㉕ · Warner Norcross & Judd · http://www.wnj.com · 900 Fifth Third Center · 111 Lyon Street, NW · Grand Rapids, MI 49503-2487 · 616-752-2000

Daniel C. Molhoek · ⑩ · Varnum, Riddering, Schmidt & Howlett · Bridgewater Place · 333 Bridge Street, NW · P.O. Box 352 · Grand Rapids, MI 49501-0352 · 616-336-6000

LABOR AND EMPLOYMENT LAW

Ann Arbor

Linda O. Goldberg · Miller Canfield Paddock and Stone · http://www.millercanfield.com · 101 North Main Street, Seventh Floor · Ann Arbor, MI 48104-1400 · 734-663-2445

Christine A. Green · Green, Green, Adams & Kent · Atrium One Office Center, Suite 370 · 900 Victor's Way · Ann Arbor, MI 48108 · 734-665-4036

Philip Green · ⑩ · Green, Green, Adams & Kent · Atrium One Office Center, Suite 370 · 900 Victor's Way · Ann Arbor, MI 48108 · 734-665-4036

Melvin J. Muskovitz · Dykema · http://www.dykema.com · 2723 South State Street, Suite 400 · Ann Arbor, MI 48104 · 734-214-7600

Ronald J. Santo · ⑳ · Dykema · http://www.dykema.com · 2723 South State Street, Suite 400 · Ann Arbor, MI 48104 · 734-214-7600

Bingham Farms

Kathleen L. Bogas · ⑳ · Law Offices of Kathleen Bogas · 31700 Telegraph Road, Suite 160 · Bingham Farms, MI 48025 · 248-502-5000

David B. Calzone · Vercruysse Murray & Calzone · http://www.vmclaw.com · 31780 Telegraph Road, Suite 200 · Bingham Farms, MI 48025-3469 · 248-540-8019

Gregory V. Murray · ⑩ · Vercruysse Murray & Calzone · http://www.vmclaw.com · 31780 Telegraph Road, Suite 200 · Bingham Farms, MI 48025-3469 · 248-540-8019

Robert M. Vercruysse · ⑳ · Vercruysse Murray & Calzone · http://www.vmclaw.com · 31780 Telegraph Road, Suite 200 · Bingham Farms, MI 48025-3469 · 248-540-8019

Birmingham

Dennis P. Brescoll · Brescoll & Brescoll · 222 Merrill Street · Birmingham, MI 48009 · 248-540-4300

James A. Brescoll · ⑩ · Brescoll & Brescoll · 222 Merrill Street · Birmingham, MI 48009 · 248-540-4300

John L. Gierak · Clark Hill · http://www.clarkhill.com · 255 South Old Woodward Avenue, Third Floor · Birmingham, MI 48009-6179 · 248-642-9692

Elizabeth P. Hardy · Kienbaum Opperwall Hardy & Pelton · http://www.kohp.com · 280 North Old Woodward Avenue, Suite 400 · Birmingham, MI 48009 · 248-645-0000

Thomas G. Kienbaum · ㉕ · Kienbaum Opperwall Hardy & Pelton · http://www.kohp.com · 280 North Old Woodward Avenue, Suite 400 · Birmingham, MI 48009 · 248-645-0000

Theodore R. Opperwall · ⑩ · Kienbaum Opperwall Hardy & Pelton · http://www.kohp.com · 280 North Old Woodward Avenue, Suite 400 · Birmingham, MI 48009 · 248-645-0000

Eric J. Pelton · Kienbaum Opperwall Hardy & Pelton · http://www.kohp.com · 280 North Old Woodward Avenue, Suite 400 · Birmingham, MI 48009 · 248-645-0000

Bloomfield Hills

Dennis M. Devaney · Strobl & Sharp · http://www.stroblpc.com · 300 East Long Lake Road, Suite 200 · Bloomfield Hills, MI 48304 · 248-540-2300

Sue Ellen Eisenberg · Sue Ellen Eisenberg & Associates · 33 Bloomfield Hills Parkway, Suite 145 · Bloomfield Hills, MI 48304-2945 · 248-258-6080

Deborah L. Gordon · ⑳ · Deborah L. Gordon · 33 Bloomfield Hills Parkway, Suite 275 · Bloomfield Hills, MI 48304 · 248-258-2500

Stanley C. Moore III · Plunkett Cooney · 38505 Woodward Avenue, Suite 2000 · Bloomfield Hills, MI 48304 · 248-901-4000

Patricia A. Stamler · Hertz Schram · 1760 South Telegraph Road, Suite 300 · Bloomfield Hills, MI 48302-0183 · 248-335-5000

Cedar Springs

Jack R. Clary · ⑳ · Jack R. Clary · 2600 Indian Lakes Road · P.O. Box 400 · Cedar Springs, MI 49319 · 616-696-8636

Detroit

William B. Balke · Littler Mendelson · 200 Renaissance Center, Suite 3110 · Detroit, MI 48243-1301 · 313-446-6400

Fred W. Batten · Clark Hill · http://www.clarkhill.com · 500 Woodward Avenue, Suite 3500 · Detroit, MI 48226-3435 · 313-965-8300

Thomas P. Brady · ⑩ · Clark Hill · http://www.clarkhill.com · 500 Woodward Avenue, Suite 3500 · Detroit, MI 48226-3435 · 313-965-8300

Daniel J. Bretz · ⑩ · Clark Hill · http://www.clarkhill.com · 500 Woodward Avenue, Suite 3500 · Detroit, MI 48226-3435 · 313-965-8300

Beverly H. Burns · Miller Canfield Paddock and Stone · http://www.millercanfield.com · 150 West Jefferson Avenue, Suite 2500 · Detroit, MI 48226 · 313-963-6420

Connie M. Cessante · Clark Hill · http://www.clarkhill.com · 500 Woodward Avenue, Suite 3500 · Detroit, MI 48226-3435 · 313-965-8300

Paul W. Coughenour · Clark Hill · http://www.clarkhill.com · 500 Woodward Avenue, Suite 3500 · Detroit, MI 48226-3435 · 313-965-8300

Lynne E. Deitch · Butzel Long · http://www.butzel.com · 150 West Jefferson Avenue, Suite 100 · Detroit, MI 48226 · 313-225-7000

David R. Deromedi · Dickinson Wright · http://www.dickinsonwright.com · 500 Woodward Avenue, Suite 4000 · Detroit, MI 48226-3425 · 313-223-3500

Carey A. Dewitt · Butzel Long · http://www.butzel.com · 150 West Jefferson Avenue, Suite 100 · Detroit, MI 48226 · 313-225-7000

Charles C. DeWitt, Jr. · ⑩ · Littler Mendelson · 200 Renaissance Center, Suite 3110 · Detroit, MI 48243-1301 · 313-446-6400

Donna J. Donati · Miller Canfield Paddock and Stone · http://www.millercanfield.com · 150 West Jefferson Avenue, Suite 2500 · Detroit, MI 48226 · 313-963-6420

John A. Entenman · Dykema · http://www.dykema.com · 400 Renaissance Center · Detroit, MI 48243 · 313-568-6800

Martin Jay Galvin · Dykema · http://www.dykema.com · 400 Renaissance Center · Detroit, MI 48243 · 313-568-6800

Leonard D. Givens · Miller Canfield Paddock and Stone · http://www.millercanfield.com · 150 West Jefferson Avenue, Suite 2500 · Detroit, MI 48226 · 313-963-6420

Gordon A. Gregory · ㉕ · Gregory, Moore, Jeakle, Heinen & Brooks · 65 Cadillac Square, Suite 3727 · Detroit, MI 48226-2844 · 313-964-5600

John P. Hancock, Jr. · ⑩ · Butzel Long · http://www.butzel.com · 150 West Jefferson Avenue, Suite 100 · Detroit, MI 48226 · 313-225-7000

Thomas M. J. Hathaway · Clark Hill · http://www.clarkhill.com · 500 Woodward Avenue, Suite 3500 · Detroit, MI 48226-3435 · 313-965-8300

Ronald R. Helveston · ⑳ · Helveston & Helveston · 3327 Cadillac Tower · Detroit, MI 48226 · 313-963-7220

Timothy H. Howlett · Dickinson Wright · http://www.dickinsonwright.com · 500 Woodward Avenue, Suite 4000 · Detroit, MI 48226-3425 · 313-223-3500

Linn A. Hynds · Honigman Miller Schwartz and Cohn · First National Building, Suite 2290 · 660 Woodward Avenue · Detroit, MI 48226-3506 · 313-465-7000

Seth M. Lloyd · ⑩ · Dykema · http://www.dykema.com · 400 Renaissance Center · Detroit, MI 48243 · 313-568-6800

James M. Moore · ⑩ · Gregory, Moore, Jeakle, Heinen & Brooks · 65 Cadillac Square, Suite 3727 · Detroit, MI 48226-2844 · 313-964-5600

Andrew Nickelhoff · Sachs Waldman · 1000 Farmer Street · Detroit, MI 48226-2899 · 313-965-3464

Megan P. Norris · Miller Canfield Paddock and Stone · http://www.millercanfield.com · 150 West Jefferson Avenue, Suite 2500 · Detroit, MI 48226 · 313-963-6420

Joseph A. Ritok, Jr. · ⑩ · Dykema · http://www.dykema.com · 400 Renaissance Center · Detroit, MI 48243 · 313-568-6800

John R. Runyan, Jr. · ⑳ · Sachs Waldman · 1000 Farmer Street · Detroit, MI 48226-2899 · 313-965-3464

William D. Sargent · Honigman Miller Schwartz and Cohn · First National Building, Suite 2290 · 660 Woodward Avenue · Detroit, MI 48226-3506 · 313-465-7000

Richard J. Seryak · Miller Canfield Paddock and Stone · http://www.millercanfield.com · 150 West Jefferson Avenue, Suite 2500 · Detroit, MI 48226 · 313-963-6420

Louis Theros · Dickinson Wright · http://www.dickinsonwright.com · 500 Woodward Avenue, Suite 4000 · Detroit, MI 48226-3425 · 313-223-3500

Daniel B. Tukel · Butzel Long · http://www.butzel.com · 150 West Jefferson Avenue, Suite 100 · Detroit, MI 48226 · 313-225-7000

Reginald M. Turner, Jr. · Clark Hill · http://www.clarkhill.com · 500 Woodward Avenue, Suite 3500 · Detroit, MI 48226-3435 · 313-965-8300

Jerome R. Watson · Miller Canfield Paddock and Stone · http://www.millercanfield.com · 150 West Jefferson Avenue, Suite 2500 · Detroit, MI 48226 · 313-963-6420

Farmington Hills

Donald J. Gasiorek · ⑩ · Gasiorek, Morgan & Greco · http://www.gmgpc.com · 30500 Northwestern Highway, Suite 425 · Farmington Hills, MI 48334 · 248-865-0001

J. Douglas Korney · ⑳ · Law Offices of J. Douglas Korney · 32300 Northwestern Highway, Suite 200 · Farmington Hills, MI 48334 · 248-865-9214

David A. Kotzian · ⑩ · David A. Kotzian · http://www.davidkotzian.com · 31700 Middlebelt Road, Suite 150 · Farmington Hills, MI 48334 · 248-737-9991

Sam G. Morgan · Gasiorek, Morgan & Greco · http://www.gmgpc.com · 30500 Northwestern Highway, Suite 425 · Farmington Hills, MI 48334 · 248-865-0001

Flint

Glen N. Lenhoff · ⑩ · Glen N. Lenhoff · North Building, Eighth Floor · 328 South Saginaw Street · Flint, MI 48502 · 810-235-5660

Grand Rapids

Thomas J. Barnes · Varnum, Riddering, Schmidt & Howlett · Bridgewater Place · 333 Bridge Street, NW P.O. Box 352 · Grand Rapids, MI 49501-0352 · 616-336-6000

Gary A. Chamberlin · Miller Johnson · http://www.millerjohnson.com · Calder Plaza Building, Suite 800 · 250 Monroe Avenue, NW · P.O. Box 306 · Grand Rapids, MI 49503-2250 · 616-831-1700

Robert J. Chovanec · Warner Norcross & Judd · http://www.wnj.com · 900 Fifth Third Center · 111 Lyon Street, NW · Grand Rapids, MI 49503-2487 · 616-752-2000

Ann M. Cooper · Drew Cooper & Anding · 300 Ledyard Building · 125 Ottawa Avenue, NW · Grand Rapids, MI 49503 · 616-454-8300

Steven R. Drew · Drew Cooper & Anding · 300 Ledyard Building · 125 Ottawa Avenue, NW · Grand Rapids, MI 49503 · 616-454-8300

Scott E. Dwyer · Mika Meyers Beckett & Jones · 900 Monroe Avenue, NW · Grand Rapids, MI 49503 · 616-632-8000

William H. Fallon · Miller Johnson · http://www.millerjohnson.com · Calder Plaza Building, Suite 800 · 250 Monroe Avenue, NW · P.O. Box 306 · Grand Rapids, MI 49503-2250 · 616-831-1700

Michael L. Fayette · ⑳ · Pinsky, Smith, Fayette & Kennedy · 146 Monroe Center, NW, Suite 805 · Grand Rapids, MI 49503 · 616-451-8496

David R. Fernstrum · Mika Meyers Beckett & Jones · 900 Monroe Avenue, NW · Grand Rapids, MI 49503 · 616-632-8000

Jeffrey J. Fraser · Varnum, Riddering, Schmidt & Howlett · Bridgewater Place · 333 Bridge Street, NW · P.O. Box 352 · Grand Rapids, MI 49501-0352 · 616-336-6000

Bradley K. Glazier · Bos & Glazier · 990 Monroe Avenue, NW · Grand Rapids, MI 49503 · 616-458-6814

Henry L. Guikema · Guikema & Hulbert · Ledyard Building, Suite 333 · 125 Ottawa, NW · Grand Rapids, MI 49503 · 616-235-2601

Theodore M. Iorio · ⑳ · Kalniz, Iorio & Feldstein · 4981 Cascade Road, SE · Grand Rapids, MI 49546 · 616-940-1911

David E. Khorey · Varnum, Riddering, Schmidt & Howlett · Bridgewater Place · 333 Bridge Street, NW · P.O. Box 352 · Grand Rapids, MI 49501-0352 · 616-336-6000

Peter J. Kok · ⑩ · Miller Johnson · http://www.millerjohnson.com · Calder Plaza Building, Suite 800 · 250 Monroe Avenue, NW · P.O. Box 306 · Grand Rapids, MI 49503-2250 · 616-831-1700

Donald P. Lawless · Varnum, Riddering, Schmidt & Howlett · Bridgewater Place · 333 Bridge Street, NW · P.O. Box 352 · Grand Rapids, MI 49501-0352 · 616-336-6000

Jon G. March · ⑩ · Miller Johnson · http://www.millerjohnson.com · Calder Plaza Building, Suite 800 · 250 Monroe Avenue, NW · P.O. Box 306 · Grand Rapids, MI 49503-2250 · 616-831-1700

Craig A. Mutch · Miller Johnson · http://www.millerjohnson.com · Calder Plaza Building, Suite 800 · 250 Monroe Avenue, NW · P.O. Box 306 · Grand Rapids, MI 49503-2250 · 616-831-1700

H. Rhett Pinsky · ⑳ · Pinsky, Smith, Fayette & Kennedy · 146 Monroe Center, NW, Suite 805 · Grand Rapids, MI 49503 · 616-451-8496

Louis C. Rabaut · Warner Norcross & Judd · http://www.wnj.com · 900 Fifth Third Center · 111 Lyon Street, NW · Grand Rapids, MI 49503-2487 · 616-752-2000

Brent R. Rector · Miller Johnson · http://www.millerjohnson.com · Calder Plaza Building, Suite 800 · 250 Monroe Avenue, NW · P.O. Box 306 · Grand Rapids, MI 49503-2250 · 616-831-1700

David A. Rhem · Varnum, Riddering, Schmidt & Howlett · Bridgewater Place · 333 Bridge Street, NW · P.O. Box 352 · Grand Rapids, MI 49501-0352 · 616-336-6000

Timothy J. Ryan · Ryan Im Knecht · 44 Grandville Avenue, SW, Suite 270 · Grand Rapids, MI 49503 · 616-242-0540

Robert W. Sikkel · ⑩ · Barnes & Thornburg · http://www.btlaw.com · 300 Ottawa Avenue, NW, Suite 500 · Grand Rapids, MI 49503 · 616-742-3930

Edward M. Smith · ⑩ · Pinsky, Smith, Fayette & Kennedy · 146 Monroe Center, NW, Suite 805 · Grand Rapids, MI 49503 · 616-451-8496

Michael A. Snapper · ⑩ · Barnes & Thornburg · http://www.btlaw.com · 300 Ottawa Avenue, NW, Suite 500 · Grand Rapids, MI 49503 · 616-742-3930

Kent J. Vana · ⑳ · Varnum, Riddering, Schmidt & Howlett · Bridgewater Place · 333 Bridge Street, NW · P.O. Box 352 · Grand Rapids, MI 49501-0352 · 616-336-6000

Joseph J. Vogan · Varnum, Riddering, Schmidt & Howlett · Bridgewater Place · 333 Bridge Street, NW · P.O. Box 352 · Grand Rapids, MI 49501-0352 · 616-336-6000

John Patrick White · Varnum, Riddering, Schmidt & Howlett · Bridgewater Place · 333 Bridge Street, NW · P.O. Box 352 · Grand Rapids, MI 49501-0352 · 616-336-6000

Thomas R. Wurst · Miller Johnson · http://www.millerjohnson.com · Calder Plaza Building, Suite 800 · 250 Monroe Avenue, NW · P.O. Box 306 · Grand Rapids, MI 49503-2250 · 616-831-1700

Kalamazoo

Lawrence J. Murphy · Varnum, Riddering, Schmidt & Howlett · 251 North Rose Street, Fourth Floor · Kalamazoo, MI 49007-3823 · 269-382-2300

Lansing

David J. Houston · Dickinson Wright · http://www.dickinsonwright.com · 215 South Washington Square, Suite 200 · Lansing, MI 48933-1816 · 517-371-1730

Muskegon

Donald J. Veldman · ⑳ · Warner Norcross & Judd · http://www.wnj.com · 400 Terrace Plaza · P.O. Box 900 · Muskegon, MI 49443-0900 · 231-727-2600

Novi

Richard A. Hooker · Varnum, Riddering, Schmidt & Howlett · 39500 High Pointe Boulevard, Suite 350 · Novi, MI 48375 · 248-567-7400

Okemos

Jeffrey S. Donahue · White, Schneider Young & Chiodini · 2300 Jolly Oak Road · Okemos, MI 48864 · 517-349-7744

Stephen O. Schultz · Fahey Schultz Burzych Rhodes · http://www.fsblawyers.com · 4151 Okemos Road · Okemos, MI 48864 · 517-381-0100

Pleasant Ridge

Ronald J. Reosti · ⑳ · Reosti, James & Sirlin · 23880 Woodward Avenue · Pleasant Ridge, MI 48069-1133 · 248-691-4200

Royal Oak

Darcie R. Brault · Dib, Fagan and Brault · http://www.dibandfagan.com · 25892 Woodward Avenue · Royal Oak, MI 48067-0910 · 248-542-6300

Joseph A. Golden · ⑩ · Pitt, McGehee, Palmer, Rivers & Golden · 117 West Fourth Street, Suite 200 · Royal Oak, MI 48067 · 248-398-9800

Stuart M. Israel · Martens, Ice, Klass, Legghio & Israel · 306 South Washington Avenue, Suite 600 · Royal Oak, MI 48067-3837 · 248-398-5900

Cary S. McGehee · Pitt, McGehee, Palmer, Rivers & Golden · 117 West Fourth Street, Suite 200 · Royal Oak, MI 48067 · 248-398-9800

Robert W. Palmer · Pitt, McGehee, Palmer, Rivers & Golden · 117 West Fourth Street, Suite 200 · Royal Oak, MI 48067 · 248-398-9800

Michael L. Pitt · ⑳ · Pitt, McGehee, Palmer, Rivers & Golden · 117 West Fourth Street, Suite 200 · Royal Oak, MI 48067 · 248-398-9800

Southfield

Brian S. Ahearn · ⑳ · Sullivan, Ward, Asher & Patton · 1000 Maccabees Center · 25800 Northwestern Highway · Southfield, MI 48075-1000 · 248-746-0700

Samuel C. McKnight · ⑳ · Klimist, McKnight, Sale, McClow & Canzano · 400 Galleria Officentre, Suite 117 · Southfield, MI 48034 · 248-354-9650

Daniel D. Swanson · ⑩ · Sommers Schwartz · http://www.sommerspc.com · 2000 Town Center, Suite 900 Southfield, MI 48075-1100 · 248-355-0300

Troy

John C. Cashen · Bodman · http://www.bodmanllp.com · 201 West Big Beaver Road, Suite 500 · Troy, MI 48084 · 248-743-6000

Thomas E. Marshall · ⑩ · Thomas E. Marshall · 2041 East Square Lake Road, Suite 500 · Troy, MI 48085 · 248-828-4440

LAND USE & ZONING LAW

Ann Arbor

Karl R. Frankena · Conlin, McKenney & Philbrick · 350 South Main Street, Suite 400 · Ann Arbor, MI 48104-2131 · 734-761-9000

Birmingham

Richard D. Rattner · Williams, Williams, Rattner & Plunkett · 380 North Old Woodward Avenue, Suite 300 · Birmingham, MI 48009 · 248-642-0333

Bloomfield Hills

Susan K. Friedlaender · Honigman Miller Schwartz and Cohn · 38500 Woodward Avenue, Suite 100 · Bloomfield Hills, MI 48304-5048 · 248-566-8301

Alan M. Greene · Dykema · http://www.dykema.com · 39577 Woodward Avenue, Suite 300 · Bloomfield Hills, MI 48304-2820 · 248-203-0700

Norman Hyman · ⑩ · Honigman Miller Schwartz and Cohn · 38500 Woodward Avenue, Suite 100 · Bloomfield Hills, MI 48304-5048 · 248-566-8301

Lawrence R. Ternan · Beier Howlett · 200 East Long Lake Road, Suite 110 · Bloomfield Hills, MI 48304-2328 · 248-645-9400

Detroit

Joseph F. Galvin · Miller Canfield Paddock and Stone · http://www.millercanfield.com · 150 West Jefferson Avenue, Suite 2500 · Detroit, MI 48226 · 313-963-6420

Farmington Hills

David W. Berry · Berry, Reynolds & Rogowski · 33493 West 14 Mile Road, Suite 100 · Farmington Hills, MI 48331-1587 · 248-851-3434

Grand Rapids

Jeffrey S. Ammon · Miller Johnson · http://www.millerjohnson.com · Calder Plaza Building, Suite 800 · 250 Monroe Avenue, NW · P.O. Box 306 · Grand Rapids, MI 49503-2250 · 616-831-1700

Lansing

David E. Pierson · McClelland & Anderson · 1305 South Washington Avenue, Suite 102 · Lansing, MI 48910 · 517-482-4890

Okemos

William K. Fahey · Fahey Schultz Burzych Rhodes · http://www.fsblawyers.com · 4151 Okemos Road · Okemos, MI 48864 · 517-381-0100

Royal Oak

Edward F. Kickham · Kickham Hanley · http://www.kickhamhanley.com · 300 Balmoral Centre · 32121 Woodward Avenue · Royal Oak, MI 48073-0943 · 248-554-6300

LEGAL MALPRACTICE LAW

Ann Arbor

Thomas H. Blaske · ⑩ · Blaske & Blaske · 500 South Main Street · Ann Arbor, MI 48104 · 734-747-7055

Barry J. Gates · ⑩ · Barry J. Gates · 2017 Marra Drive · Ann Arbor, MI 48103 · 734-769-5855

Bloomfield Hills

Lawrence J. Acker · ⑩ · Lawrence J. Acker · 44 East Long Lake Road · Bloomfield Hills, MI 48304 · 248-594-7277

Michael P. Ashcraft, Jr. · Plunkett Cooney · 38505 Woodward Avenue, Suite 2000 · Bloomfield Hills, MI 48304 · 248-901-4000

Detroit

David W. Christensen · ⑩ · Charfoos & Christensen · Smiley Mansion · 5510 Woodward Avenue · Detroit, MI 48202 · 313-875-8080

Michael W. Hartmann · ⑩ · Miller Canfield Paddock and Stone · http://www.millercanfield.com · 150 West Jefferson Avenue, Suite 2500 · Detroit, MI 48226 · 313-963-6420

Grand Rapids

William S. Farr · ⑩ · Farr Oosterhouse & Krissoff · Ledyard Building, Suite 333 · 125 Ottawa Avenue, NW · Grand Rapids, MI 49503 · 616-459-3355

William W. Jack, Jr. · ⑩ · Smith, Haughey, Rice & Roegge · Calder Plaza Building, Suite 200 · 250 Monroe Avenue, NW · Grand Rapids, MI 49503-2251 · 616-774-8000

Joel E. Krissoff · Farr Oosterhouse & Krissoff · Ledyard Building, Suite 333 · 125 Ottawa Avenue, NW · Grand Rapids, MI 49503 · 616-459-3355

Paul A. McCarthy · Rhoades McKee · 161 Ottawa Avenue, NW, Suite 600 · Grand Rapids, MI 49503 · 616-235-3500

Jon R. Muth · Miller Johnson · http://www.millerjohnson.com · Calder Plaza Building, Suite 800 · 250 Monroe Avenue, NW · P.O. Box 306 · Grand Rapids, MI 49503-2250 · 616-831-1700

John R. Oostema · Smith, Haughey, Rice & Roegge · Calder Plaza Building, Suite 200 · 250 Monroe Avenue, NW · Grand Rapids, MI 49503-2251 · 616-774-8000

L. Roland Roegge · ⑳ · Smith, Haughey, Rice & Roegge · Calder Plaza Building, Suite 200 · 250 Monroe Avenue, NW · Grand Rapids, MI 49503-2251 · 616-774-8000

Kalamazoo

John W. Allen · Varnum, Riddering, Schmidt & Howlett · 251 North Rose Street, Fourth Floor · Kalamazoo, MI 49007-3823 · 269-382-2300

Southfield

David M. Black · Sommers Schwartz · http://www.sommerspc.com · 2000 Town Center, Suite 900 · Southfield, MI 48075-1100 · 248-355-0300

Harvey R. Heller · Maddin, Hauser, Wartell, Roth & Heller · http://www.maddinhauser.com · Essex Centre, Third Floor · 28400 Northwestern Highway · Southfield, MI 48034-1839 · 248-354-4030

Steven M. Wolock · Maddin, Hauser, Wartell, Roth & Heller · http://www.maddinhauser.com · Essex Centre, Third Floor · 28400 Northwestern Highway · Southfield, MI 48034-1839 · 248-354-4030

LEVERAGED BUYOUTS AND PRIVATE EQUITY LAW

Ann Arbor

David N. Parsigian · Honigman Miller Schwartz and Cohn · 130 South First Street, Fourth Floor · Ann Arbor, MI 48104-1386 · 734-418-4200

Detroit

David Foltyn · ⑩ · Honigman Miller Schwartz and Cohn · First National Building, Suite 2290 · 660 Woodward Avenue · Detroit, MI 48226-3506 · 313-465-7000

Donald J. Kunz · Honigman Miller Schwartz and Cohn · First National Building, Suite 2290 · 660 Woodward Avenue · Detroit, MI 48226-3506 · 313-465-7000

MASS TORT LITIGATION

Troy

Robert J. Haddad · Miller Canfield Paddock and Stone · http://www.millercanfield.com · 840 West Long Lake Road, Suite 200 · Troy, MI 48098-6358 · 248-879-2000

Stephen J. Ott · Miller Canfield Paddock and Stone · http://www.millercanfield.com · 840 West Long Lake Road, Suite 200 · Troy, MI 48098-6358 · 248-879-2000

Brian S. Westenberg · Miller Canfield Paddock and Stone · http://www.millercanfield.com · 840 West Long Lake Road, Suite 200 · Troy, MI 48098-6358 · 248-879-2000

MEDICAL MALPRACTICE LAW

Ann Arbor

Peter A. Davis · ⑩ · Davis & Kuhnke · 405 North Main Street · Ann Arbor, MI 48104 · 734-663-2233

Heidi L. Salter-Ferris · Ferris & Salter · 4158 Washtenaw Avenue · Ann Arbor, MI 48108 · 734-677-2020

Edward R. Stein · ⑩ · Smith, Haughey, Rice & Roegge · 213 South Ashley, Suite 400 · Ann Arbor, MI 48104 · 734-213-8000

Bloomfield Hills

William C. Gage · Gage & Little · 300 East Long Lake Road, Suite 280 · Bloomfield Hills, MI 48304 · 248-593-8900

Russell Gregory · Gregory & Reiter · http://www.abclawcenters.com · 122 Concord Road · Bloomfield Hills, MI 48304 · 248-593-5100

Jesse M. Reiter · Gregory & Reiter · http://www.abclawcenters.com · 122 Concord Road · Bloomfield Hills, MI 48304 · 248-593-5100

Robert P. Roth · Portnoy & Roth · 3883 Telegraph, Suite 103 · Bloomfield Hills, MI 48302 · 248-647-4242

D. J. Watters · ⑩ · Plunkett Cooney · 38505 Woodward Avenue, Suite 2000 · Bloomfield Hills, MI 48304 248-901-4000

Detroit

David W. Christensen · ⑩ · Charfoos & Christensen · Smiley Mansion · 5510 Woodward Avenue · Detroit, MI 48202 · 313-875-8080

Richard M. Goodman · ㉕ · Goodman Kalahar · 1394 East Jefferson Avenue · Detroit, MI 48207 · 313-567-6165

Stephen D. McGraw · Kerr, Russell and Weber · Detroit Center, Suite 2500 · 500 Woodward Avenue · Detroit, MI 48226-3427 · 313-961-0200

Thomas L. Misuraca · Garan Lucow & Miller · Woodbridge Place · 1000 Woodbridge Street · Detroit, MI 48207-3192 · 313-446-1530

John Patrick O'Leary · ⑩ · O'Leary & O'Leary · 535 Griswold Street, Suite 1400 · Detroit, MI 48226 · 313-234-4786

Barry P. Waldman · ⑩ · Sachs Waldman · 1000 Farmer Street · Detroit, MI 48226-2899 · 313-965-3464

East Lansing

Brett J. Bean · Hackney Grover Hoover & Bean · 1715 Abbey Road, Suite A · East Lansing, MI 48823 · 517-333-0306

Farmington Hills

Bruce A. Vande Vusse · Foster, Swift, Collins & Smith · http://www.fosterswift.com · 32300 Northwestern Highway, Suite 230 · Farmington Hills, MI 48334 · 248-539-9900

Grand Rapids

Bruce M. Bieneman · Bruce Bieneman · 660 Cascade West Parkway, SE, Suite 220 · Grand Rapids, MI 49546 · 616-464-3497

Albert J. Engel III · Smith, Haughey, Rice & Roegge · Calder Plaza Building, Suite 200 · 250 Monroe Avenue, NW · Grand Rapids, MI 49503-2251 · 616-774-8000

Mark E. Fatum · Rhoades McKee · 161 Ottawa Avenue, NW, Suite 600 · Grand Rapids, MI 49503 · 616-235-3500

Troy W. Haney · DilleyHaney · 330 East Fulton · Grand Rapids, MI 49503 · 616-235-2300

William W. Jack, Jr. · ⑩ · Smith, Haughey, Rice & Roegge · Calder Plaza Building, Suite 200 · 250 Monroe Avenue, NW · Grand Rapids, MI 49503-2251 · 616-774-8000

John M. Kruis · Smith, Haughey, Rice & Roegge · Calder Plaza Building, Suite 200 · 250 Monroe Avenue, NW · Grand Rapids, MI 49503-2251 · 616-774-8000

Richard G. Leonard · Rhoades McKee · 161 Ottawa Avenue, NW, Suite 600 · Grand Rapids, MI 49503 · 616-235-3500

Bruce W. Neckers · ⑩ · Rhoades McKee · 161 Ottawa Avenue, NW, Suite 600 · Grand Rapids, MI 49503 616-235-3500

John C. O'Loughlin · Smith, Haughey, Rice & Roegge · Calder Plaza Building, Suite 200 · 250 Monroe Avenue, NW · Grand Rapids, MI 49503-2251 · 616-774-8000

Norman H. Pylman · Gruel, Mills, Nims and Pylman · 50 Monroe Avenue, Suite 700-W · Grand Rapids, MI 49503 · 616-235-5500

L. Roland Roegge · ⑳ · Smith, Haughey, Rice & Roegge · Calder Plaza Building, Suite 200 · 250 Monroe Avenue, NW · Grand Rapids, MI 49503-2251 · 616-774-8000

William J. Waddell · ⑳ · Law Offices of William J. Waddell · http://www.wjwlaw.com · 1025 Spaulding Avenue, SE, Suite D · Grand Rapids, MI 49546 · 616-957-5800

Grandville

Richard K. Grover, Jr. · Hackney Grover Hoover & Bean · 3514 Rivertown Point Court, SW, Suite 102 · Grandville, MI 49418 · 616-257-3900

Mount Clemens

James N. Martin · ⑩ · Martin, Bacon & Martin · 44 First Street · Mount Clemens, MI 48043 · 586-979-6500

Southfield

Norman H. Rosen · Erlich, Rosen and Bartnick · 29201 Telegraph, Suite 330 · Southfield, MI 48034 · 248-356-0999

Robert P. Siemion · Siemion, Huckabay, Bodary, Padilla, Morganti & Bowerman · One Towne Square, Suite 1400 · P.O. Box 5068 · Southfield, MI 48086-5068 · 248-357-1400

Judith Susskind · The Thurswell Law Group · 1000 Town Center, Suite 500 · Southfield, MI 48075 · 248-354-2222

Gerald Thurswell · The Thurswell Law Group · 1000 Town Center, Suite 500 · Southfield, MI 48075 · 248-354-2222

J. Lee Tilson · Lee Tilson · 28145 Greenfield Road · Southfield, MI 48076 · 313-550-7500

Norman D. Tucker · ⑩ · Sommers Schwartz · http://www.sommerspc.com · 2000 Town Center, Suite 900 Southfield, MI 48075-1100 · 248-355-0300

MERGERS & ACQUISITIONS LAW

Ann Arbor

Timothy R. Damschroder · Bodman · http://www.bodmanllp.com · 201 South Division Street, Suite 400 · Ann Arbor, MI 48104 · 734-761-3780

Bloomfield Hills

Gerald T. Lievois · Dykema · http://www.dykema.com · 39577 Woodward Avenue, Suite 300 · Bloomfield Hills, MI 48304-2820 · 248-203-0700

Jeffrey H. Miro · ⑩ · Honigman Miller Schwartz and Cohn · 38500 Woodward Avenue, Suite 100 · Bloomfield Hills, MI 48304-5048 · 248-566-8301

Detroit

J. Michael Bernard · Dykema · http://www.dykema.com · 400 Renaissance Center · Detroit, MI 48243 · 313-568-6800

David Foltyn · ⑩ · Honigman Miller Schwartz and Cohn · First National Building, Suite 2290 · 660 Woodward Avenue · Detroit, MI 48226-3506 · 313-465-7000

Justin G. Klimko · ⑩ · Butzel Long · http://www.butzel.com · 150 West Jefferson Avenue, Suite 100 · Detroit, MI 48226 · 313-225-7000

Donald J. Kunz · Honigman Miller Schwartz and Cohn · First National Building, Suite 2290 · 660 Woodward Avenue · Detroit, MI 48226-3506 · 313-465-7000

Cyril Moscow · ㉕ · Honigman Miller Schwartz and Cohn · First National Building, Suite 2290 · 660 Woodward Avenue · Detroit, MI 48226-3506 · 313-465-7000

Alan S. Schwartz · ⑳ · Honigman Miller Schwartz and Cohn · First National Building, Suite 2290 · 660 Woodward Avenue · Detroit, MI 48226-3506 · 313-465-7000

Samuel T. Stahl · ⑩ · Honigman Miller Schwartz and Cohn · First National Building, Suite 2290 · 660 Woodward Avenue · Detroit, MI 48226-3506 · 313-465-7000

Grand Rapids

Jeffrey S. Ammon · Miller Johnson · http://www.millerjohnson.com · Calder Plaza Building, Suite 800 · 250 Monroe Avenue, NW · P.O. Box 306 · Grand Rapids, MI 49503-2250 · 616-831-1700

Tracy T. Larsen · ⑩ · Barnes & Thornburg · http://www.btlaw.com · 300 Ottawa Avenue, NW, Suite 500 · Grand Rapids, MI 49503 · 616-742-3930

John W. McNeil · ㉕ · Miller Johnson · http://www.millerjohnson.com · Calder Plaza Building, Suite 800 · 250 Monroe Avenue, NW · P.O. Box 306 · Grand Rapids, MI 49503-2250 · 616-831-1700

Mark E. Rizik · Miller Johnson · http://www.millerjohnson.com · Calder Plaza Building, Suite 800 · 250 Monroe Avenue, NW · P.O. Box 306 · Grand Rapids, MI 49503-2250 · 616-831-1700

Ronald E. Roden · Miller Johnson · http://www.millerjohnson.com · Calder Plaza Building, Suite 800 · 250 Monroe Avenue, NW · P.O. Box 306 · Grand Rapids, MI 49503-2250 · 616-831-1700

John M. Sommerdyke · Miller Canfield Paddock and Stone · http://www.millercanfield.com · 99 Monroe Avenue, NW, Suite 1200 · Grand Rapids, MI 49503 · 616-454-8656

Robert R. Stead · Barnes & Thornburg · http://www.btlaw.com · 300 Ottawa Avenue, NW, Suite 500 · Grand Rapids, MI 49503 · 616-742-3930

Troy

David D. Joswick · ⑩ · Miller Canfield Paddock and Stone · http://www.millercanfield.com · 840 West Long Lake Road, Suite 200 · Troy, MI 48098-6358 · 248-879-2000

MUNICIPAL LAW

Bloomfield Hills

Terence M. Donnelly · Dickinson Wright · http://www.dickinsonwright.com · 38525 Woodward Avenue, Suite 2000 · Bloomfield Hills, MI 48304-2970 · 248-433-7200

Detroit

Joseph F. Galvin · Miller Canfield Paddock and Stone · http://www.millercanfield.com · 150 West Jefferson Avenue, Suite 2500 · Detroit, MI 48226 · 313-963-6420

Farmington Hills

William P. Hampton · 10 · Secrest, Wardle, Lynch, Hampton, Truex and Morley · 30903 Northwestern Highway · P.O. Box 3040 · Farmington Hills, MI 48333-3040 · 248-851-9500

Grand Rapids

Randall W. Kraker · Varnum, Riddering, Schmidt & Howlett · Bridgewater Place · 333 Bridge Street, NW · P.O. Box 352 · Grand Rapids, MI 49501-0352 · 616-336-6000

Richard A. Wendt · Dickinson Wright · http://www.dickinsonwright.com · 200 Ottawa Avenue, NW, Suite 900 · Grand Rapids, MI 49503-2427 · 616-458-1300

Kalamazoo

Michael S. Bogren · Plunkett Cooney · Skyrise Business Center, Suite 256 · 535 South Burdick Street · Kalamazoo, MI 49007 · 269-382-5935

Don M. Schmidt · Miller Canfield Paddock and Stone · http://www.millercanfield.com · 277 South Rose Street, Suite 5000 · Kalamazoo, MI 49007-3751 · 269-381-7030

NATIVE AMERICAN LAW

Ann Arbor

Riyaz Kanji · Kanji & Katzen · 101 North Main Street, Suite 555 · Ann Arbor, MI 48104 · 734-769-5400

Lansing

Kevin J. Moody · Miller Canfield Paddock and Stone · http://www.millercanfield.com · One Michigan Avenue, Suite 900 · Lansing, MI 48933 · 517-487-2070

NATURAL RESOURCES LAW

Detroit

Joseph M. Polito · 20 · Honigman Miller Schwartz and Cohn · First National Building, Suite 2290 · 660 Woodward Avenue · Detroit, MI 48226-3506 · 313-465-7000

Grand Rapids

Eugene E. Smary · 10 · Warner Norcross & Judd · http://www.wnj.com · 900 Fifth Third Center · 111 Lyon Street, NW · Grand Rapids, MI 49503-2487 · 616-752-2000

Lansing

Charles E. Barbieri · ⑩ · Foster, Swift, Collins & Smith · http://www.fosterswift.com · 313 South Washington Square · Lansing, MI 48933-2193 · 517-371-8100

Harvey J. Messing · ⑩ · Miller Canfield Paddock and Stone · http://www.millercanfield.com · One Michigan Avenue, Suite 900 · Lansing, MI 48933 · 517-487-2070

James R. Neal · ⑩ · Loomis, Ewert, Parsley, Davis & Gotting · 124 West Allegan Street, Suite 700 · Lansing, MI 48933-1707 · 517-482-2400

Webb A. Smith · ⑩ · Foster, Swift, Collins & Smith · http://www.fosterswift.com · 313 South Washington Square · Lansing, MI 48933-2193 · 517-371-8100

NON-PROFIT/CHARITIES LAW

Ann Arbor

Christopher A. Ballard · Bodman · http://www.bodmanllp.com · 201 South Division Street, Suite 400 · Ann Arbor, MI 48104 · 734-761-3780

James L. Hughes · Butzel Long · http://www.butzel.com · 350 South Main Street, Suite 300 · Ann Arbor, MI 48104 · 734-995-3110

Randolph S. Perry · Randolph S. Perry · 2475 Whitmore Lake Road · Ann Arbor, MI 48105 · 734-677-7738

Detroit

Christopher J. Dine · Bodman · http://www.bodmanllp.com · Sixth Floor at Ford Field · 1901 Saint Antoine Street · Detroit, MI 48226 · 313-259-7777

Jane Forbes · Dykema · http://www.dykema.com · 400 Renaissance Center · Detroit, MI 48243 · 313-568-6800

Charles Nida · ⑩ · Honigman Miller Schwartz and Cohn · First National Building, Suite 2290 · 660 Woodward Avenue · Detroit, MI 48226-3506 · 313-465-7000

Duane L. Tarnacki · Clark Hill · http://www.clarkhill.com · 500 Woodward Avenue, Suite 3500 · Detroit, MI 48226-3435 · 313-965-8300

Harvey B. Wallace II · ⑩ · Berry Moorman · Buhl Building, Suite 1900 · 535 Griswold Street · Detroit, MI 48226-3679 · 313-496-1200

Grand Rapids

Jeffrey B. Power · ⑩ · Warner Norcross & Judd · http://www.wnj.com · 900 Fifth Third Center · 111 Lyon Street, NW · Grand Rapids, MI 49503-2487 · 616-752-2000

W. Michael Van Haren · ⑳ · Warner Norcross & Judd · http://www.wnj.com · 900 Fifth Third Center · 111 Lyon Street, NW · Grand Rapids, MI 49503-2487 · 616-752-2000

NON-WHITE-COLLAR CRIMINAL DEFENSE

Ann Arbor

Don Ferris · ⑩ · Ferris & Salter · 4158 Washtenaw Avenue · Ann Arbor, MI 48108 · 734-677-2020

Douglas R. Mullkoff · Kessler, Mulkoff & Hooberman · 402 West Liberty Street · Ann Arbor, MI 48103 · 734-761-8585

John A. Shea · John A. Shea · 120 North Fourth Avenue · Ann Arbor, MI 48104 · 734-995-4646

Joseph A. Simon · Simon & Geherin · 1310 South Main Street, Suite 11 · Ann Arbor, MI 48104 · 734-997-0870

Birmingham

Neil H. Fink · ㉕ · Law Offices of Neil H. Fink · 185 Oakland Avenue, Suite 250 · Birmingham, MI 48009 · 248-258-3181

Bloomfield Hills

Steven J. Fishman · Fishman Group · 40950 Woodward Avenue, Suite 350 · Bloomfield Hills, MI 48304 · 248-258-8700

Robert S. Harrison · ㉕ · Robert Harrison & Associates · 200 East Long Lake Road, Suite 110 · Bloomfield Hills, MI 48304 · 248-283-1600

Detroit

Anthony T. Chambers · Anthony T. Chambers · 220 West Congress Street, Fifth Floor · Detroit, MI 48226 · 313-964-5557

Elizabeth L. Jacobs · Law Office of Elizabeth Jacobs · 615 Griswold Street, Suite 1125 · Detroit, MI 48226 · 313-962-4090

Robert M. Morgan · ⑩ · Robert M. Morgan · Ford Building, Suite 1125 · 615 Griswold Street · Detroit, MI 48226-4211 · 313-961-7070

James C. Thomas · Plunkett Cooney · Buhl Building, Suite 2400 · 535 Griswold Street · Detroit, MI 48226 · 313-965-3900

Grand Rapids

James S. Brady · Miller Johnson · http://www.millerjohnson.com · Calder Plaza Building, Suite 800 · 250 Monroe Avenue, NW · P.O. Box 306 · Grand Rapids, MI 49503-2250 · 616-831-1700

Charles E. Chamberlain, Jr. · Willey & Chamberlain · 940 Trust Building · 40 Pearl Street, NW · Grand Rapids, MI 49503 · 616-458-2212

Paul L. Mitchell · Mitchell & Zambon · 161 Ottawa Avenue, NW, Suite 507 · Grand Rapids, MI 49503 · 616-456-7831

Larry C. Willey · ⑩ · Willey & Chamberlain · 940 Trust Building · 40 Pearl Street, NW · Grand Rapids, MI 49503 · 616-458-2212

Kalamazoo

Randall S. Levine · Levine & Levine · http://www.levine-levine.com · 427 South Burdick Street · Kalamazoo, MI 49007 · 269-382-0444

Lansing

Donald E. Martin · Foster, Swift, Collins & Smith · http://www.fosterswift.com · 313 South Washington Square · Lansing, MI 48933-2193 · 517-371-8100

Frank H. Reynolds · The Reynolds Law Firm · Oakhill Professional Park, Suite A · 2400 Lake Lansing Road · Lansing, MI 48912-3674 · 517-372-0676

Troy

Thomas W. Cranmer · ⑩ · Miller Canfield Paddock and Stone · http://www.millercanfield.com · 840 West Long Lake Road, Suite 200 · Troy, MI 48098-6358 · 248-879-2000

Matthew F. Leitman · Miller Canfield Paddock and Stone · http://www.millercanfield.com · 840 West Long Lake Road, Suite 200 · Troy, MI 48098-6358 · 248-879-2000

OIL & GAS LAW

Bloomfield Hills

John H. Norris · Dickinson Wright · http://www.dickinsonwright.com · 38525 Woodward Avenue, Suite 2000 · Bloomfield Hills, MI 48304-2970 · 248-433-7200

Concord

J. Donel Moore · J. Donel Moore · 14444 Behling Road · P.O. Box 426 · Concord, MI 49237 · 517-524-8774

Grand Rapids

John M. DeVries · Mika Meyers Beckett & Jones · 900 Monroe Avenue, NW · Grand Rapids, MI 49503 · 616-632-8000

Michael C. Haines · Mika Meyers Beckett & Jones · 900 Monroe Avenue, NW · Grand Rapids, MI 49503 616-632-8000

William A. Horn · Mika Meyers Beckett & Jones · 900 Monroe Avenue, NW · Grand Rapids, MI 49503 · 616-632-8000

Lansing

Paula K. Manis · Worman, Dixon & Manis · 2400 Lake Lansing Road, Suite E · Lansing, MI 48912 · 517-485-0400

Harvey J. Messing · ⑩ · Miller Canfield Paddock and Stone · http://www.millercanfield.com · One Michigan Avenue, Suite 900 · Lansing, MI 48933 · 517-487-2070

James R. Neal · ⑩ · Loomis, Ewert, Parsley, Davis & Gotting · 124 West Allegan Street, Suite 700 · Lansing, MI 48933-1707 · 517-482-2400

Michael H. Rhodes · Loomis, Ewert, Parsley, Davis & Gotting · 124 West Allegan Street, Suite 700 · Lansing, MI 48933-1707 · 517-482-2400

Webb A. Smith · ⑩ · Foster, Swift, Collins & Smith · http://www.fosterswift.com · 313 South Washington Square · Lansing, MI 48933-2193 · 517-371-8100

Gary L. Worman · Worman, Dixon & Manis · 2400 Lake Lansing Road, Suite E · Lansing, MI 48912 · 517-485-0400

Mount Pleasant

John J. Lynch · Lynch, Gallagher, Lynch & Martineau · 555 North Main Street · P.O. Box 446 · Mount Pleasant, MI 48858 · 989-773-9961

PERSONAL INJURY LITIGATION

Ann Arbor

Mark R. Daane · Hooper, Hathaway, Price, Beuche & Wallace · 126 South Main Street · Ann Arbor, MI 48104-1945 · 734-662-4426

Peter A. Davis · ⑩ · Davis & Kuhnke · 405 North Main Street · Ann Arbor, MI 48104 · 734-663-2233

Don Ferris · ⑩ · Ferris & Salter · 4158 Washtenaw Avenue · Ann Arbor, MI 48108 · 734-677-2020

Robert E. Logeman · Logeman, Iafrate & Pollard · 2950 South State Street, Suite 400 · Ann Arbor, MI 48104 · 734-994-0200

Thomas C. O'Brien · Miller Canfield Paddock and Stone · http://www.millercanfield.com · 101 North Main Street, Seventh Floor · Ann Arbor, MI 48104-1400 · 734-663-2445

Allen J. Philbrick · ⑩ · Conlin, McKenney & Philbrick · 350 South Main Street, Suite 400 · Ann Arbor, MI 48104-2131 · 734-761-9000

Heidi L. Salter-Ferris · Ferris & Salter · 4158 Washtenaw Avenue · Ann Arbor, MI 48108 · 734-677-2020

Edward R. Stein · ⑩ · Smith, Haughey, Rice & Roegge · 213 South Ashley, Suite 400 · Ann Arbor, MI 48104 · 734-213-8000

Berkley

Jules B. Olsman · Olsman, Mueller & James · 2684 West 11 Mile Road · Berkley, MI 48072 · 248-591-2300

Birmingham

William R. Buesser · ⑩ · Buesser & Buesser · 401 South Old Woodward Avenue, Suite 315 · Birmingham, MI 48009 · 248-642-7880

Bloomfield Hills

William D. Booth · ⑳ · Plunkett Cooney · 38505 Woodward Avenue, Suite 2000 · Bloomfield Hills, MI 48304 · 248-901-4000

Jerome A. Galante · Plunkett Cooney · 38505 Woodward Avenue, Suite 2000 · Bloomfield Hills, MI 48304 · 248-901-4000

George A. Googasian · ⑩ · The Googasian Firm · 6895 Telegraph Road · Bloomfield Hills, MI 48301-3138 · 248-540-3333

Arthur Y. Liss · Liss Seder & Andrews · The Pinehurst Building, Suite 200 · 39400 Woodward Avenue · Bloomfield Hills, MI 48304 · 248-647-9700

D. J. Watters · ⑩ · Plunkett Cooney · 38505 Woodward Avenue, Suite 2000 · Bloomfield Hills, MI 48304 248-901-4000

Detroit

Lawrence S. Charfoos · Charfoos & Christensen · Smiley Mansion · 5510 Woodward Avenue · Detroit, MI 48202 · 313-875-8080

David W. Christensen · ⑩ · Charfoos & Christensen · Smiley Mansion · 5510 Woodward Avenue · Detroit, MI 48202 · 313-875-8080

Wilson A. Copeland II · ⑩ · Grier, Copeland & Williams · 615 Griswold Street, Suite 400 · Detroit, MI 48226-3978 · 313-961-2600

Richard M. Goodman · ㉕ · Goodman Kalahar · 1394 East Jefferson Avenue · Detroit, MI 48207 · 313-567-6165

John P. Jacobs · John P. Jacobs · http://www.jpjpc.com · The Guardian Building, Suite 2825 · 500 Griswold Street · Detroit, MI 48226 · 313-965-1900

Edward M. Kronk · ⑩ · Butzel Long · http://www.butzel.com · 150 West Jefferson Avenue, Suite 100 · Detroit, MI 48226 · 313-225-7000

Kathleen A. Lang · Dickinson Wright · http://www.dickinsonwright.com · 500 Woodward Avenue, Suite 4000 · Detroit, MI 48226-3425 · 313-223-3500

Daniel P. Malone · Butzel Long · http://www.butzel.com · 150 West Jefferson Avenue, Suite 100 · Detroit, MI 48226 · 313-225-7000

Stephen D. McGraw · Kerr, Russell and Weber · Detroit Center, Suite 2500 · 500 Woodward Avenue · Detroit, MI 48226-3427 · 313-961-0200

John Patrick O'Leary · ⑩ · O'Leary & O'Leary · 535 Griswold Street, Suite 1400 · Detroit, MI 48226 · 313-234-4786

Daniel J. Scully, Jr. · Clark Hill · http://www.clarkhill.com · 500 Woodward Avenue, Suite 3500 · Detroit, MI 48226-3435 · 313-965-8300

Barry P. Waldman · ⑩ · Sachs Waldman · 1000 Farmer Street · Detroit, MI 48226-2899 · 313-965-3464

James E. Wynne · Butzel Long · http://www.butzel.com · 150 West Jefferson Avenue, Suite 100 · Detroit, MI 48226 · 313-225-7000

East Lansing

Brett J. Bean · Hackney Grover Hoover & Bean · 1715 Abbey Road, Suite A · East Lansing, MI 48823 · 517-333-0306

C. Mark Hoover · Hackney Grover Hoover & Bean · 1715 Abbey Road, Suite A · East Lansing, MI 48823 · 517-333-0306

Grand Rapids

Bruce M. Bieneman · Bruce Bieneman · 660 Cascade West Parkway, SE, Suite 220 · Grand Rapids, MI 49546 · 616-464-3497

James S. Brady · Miller Johnson · http://www.millerjohnson.com · Calder Plaza Building, Suite 800 · 250 Monroe Avenue, NW · P.O. Box 306 · Grand Rapids, MI 49503-2250 · 616-831-1700

John C. Buchanan · ⑩ · Buchanan & Buchanan · http://www.buchananfirm.com · 171 Monroe Avenue, NW, Suite 750 · Grand Rapids, MI 49503 · 616-458-2464

Robert J. Buchanan · Buchanan & Buchanan · http://www.buchananfirm.com · 171 Monroe Avenue, NW, Suite 750 · Grand Rapids, MI 49503 · 616-458-2464

Frederick D. Dilley · ⑩ · DilleyHaney · 330 East Fulton · Grand Rapids, MI 49503 · 616-235-2300

Troy W. Haney · DilleyHaney · 330 East Fulton · Grand Rapids, MI 49503 · 616-235-2300

William W. Jack, Jr. · ⑩ · Smith, Haughey, Rice & Roegge · Calder Plaza Building, Suite 200 · 250 Monroe Avenue, NW · Grand Rapids, MI 49503-2251 · 616-774-8000

Jon G. March · ⑩ · Miller Johnson · http://www.millerjohnson.com · Calder Plaza Building, Suite 800 · 250 Monroe Avenue, NW · P.O. Box 306 · Grand Rapids, MI 49503-2250 · 616-831-1700

E. Thomas McCarthy, Jr. · Halpert, Weston, Wuori & Sawusch · 200 Ottawa Avenue, NW · Grand Rapids, MI 49503 · 616-458-4400

William F. Mills · ⑩ · Gruel, Mills, Nims and Pylman · 50 Monroe Avenue, Suite 700-W · Grand Rapids, MI 49503 · 616-235-5500

Bruce W. Neckers · ⑩ · Rhoades McKee · 161 Ottawa Avenue, NW, Suite 600 · Grand Rapids, MI 49503 616-235-3500

Norman H. Pylman · Gruel, Mills, Nims and Pylman · 50 Monroe Avenue, Suite 700-W · Grand Rapids, MI 49503 · 616-235-5500

L. Roland Roegge · ⑳ · Smith, Haughey, Rice & Roegge · Calder Plaza Building, Suite 200 · 250 Monroe Avenue, NW · Grand Rapids, MI 49503-2251 · 616-774-8000

William J. Waddell · ⑳ · Law Offices of William J. Waddell · http://www.wjwlaw.com · 1025 Spaulding Avenue, SE, Suite D · Grand Rapids, MI 49546 · 616-957-5800

Michael D. Wade · Garan Lucow & Miller · 300 Ottawa Avenue, NW, Eighth Floor · Grand Rapids, MI 49503 · 616-742-5500

Kalamazoo

Richard L. Halpert · Halpert, Weston, Wuori & Sawusch · The Fifth Third Bank Building, Suite 1050 · 136 East Michigan Avenue · Kalamazoo, MI 49007 · 269-388-4800

Craig H. Lubben · Miller Johnson · http://www.millerjohnson.com · Rose Street Market Building, Suite 600 · 303 North Rose Street · Kalamazoo, MI 49007-3850 · 269-226-2950

Lake Orion

Marietta S. Robinson · ⑩ · Law Offices of Marietta S. Robinson · 436 South Broadway Street, Suite C · Lake Orion, MI 48362 · 248-693-6245

Lansing

Timothy J. Donovan · Sinas, Dramis, Brake, Boughton & McIntyre · 3380 Pine Tree Road · Lansing, MI 48911-4207 · 517-394-7500

Peter L. Dunlap · ⑩ · Fraser Trebilcock Davis & Dunlap · 124 West Allegan Street, Suite 1000 · Lansing, MI 48933 · 517-482-5800

James Graves · Sinas, Dramis, Brake, Boughton & McIntyre · 3380 Pine Tree Road · Lansing, MI 48911-4207 · 517-394-7500

William N. Kritselis · ⑳ · Church, Kritselis & Wyble · 2827 East Saginaw Street · Lansing, MI 48912 · 517-372-1011

James E. Lozier · Dickinson Wright · http://www.dickinsonwright.com · 215 South Washington Square, Suite 200 · Lansing, MI 48933-1816 · 517-371-1730

David S. Mittleman · Church, Kritselis & Wyble · 2827 East Saginaw Street · Lansing, MI 48912 · 517-372-1011

George T. Sinas · ⑳ · Sinas, Dramis, Brake, Boughton & McIntyre · 3380 Pine Tree Road · Lansing, MI 48911-4207 · 517-394-7500

Bryan J. Waldman · Sinas, Dramis, Brake, Boughton & McIntyre · 3380 Pine Tree Road · Lansing, MI 48911-4207 · 517-394-7500

Mount Clemens

James N. Martin · ⑩ · Martin, Bacon & Martin · 44 First Street · Mount Clemens, MI 48043 · 586-979-6500

Saginaw

Harvey E. van Benschoten · van Benschoten Law Offices · 905 North Michigan Avenue · Saginaw, MI 48602 · 989-753-2444

Southfield

Richard D. Fox · Sommers Schwartz · http://www.sommerspc.com · 2000 Town Center, Suite 900 · Southfield, MI 48075-1100 · 248-355-0300

David R. Getto · ⑩ · Sommers Schwartz · http://www.sommerspc.com · 2000 Town Center, Suite 900 · Southfield, MI 48075-1100 · 248-355-0300

Richard L. Groffsky · Sommers Schwartz · http://www.sommerspc.com · 2000 Town Center, Suite 900 · Southfield, MI 48075-1100 · 248-355-0300

Lawrence E. Gursten · Gursten, Koltonow, Gursten, Christensen & Rait · http://www.michiganautolaw.com · 26555 Evergreen Road, Suite 1530 · Southfield, MI 48076 · 248-353-7575

Steven M. Gursten · Gursten, Koltonow, Gursten, Christensen & Rait · http://www.michiganautolaw.com 26555 Evergreen Road, Suite 1530 · Southfield, MI 48076 · 248-353-7575

Paul W. Hines · Sommers Schwartz · http://www.sommerspc.com · 2000 Town Center, Suite 900 · Southfield, MI 48075-1100 · 248-355-0300

Charles A. Huckabay · Siemion, Huckabay, Bodary, Padilla, Morganti & Bowerman · One Towne Square, Suite 1400 · P.O. Box 5068 · Southfield, MI 48086-5068 · 248-357-1400

Frank Mafrice · Frank Mafrice · 17000 West Ten Mile Road, Suite 100 · Southfield, MI 48075 · 248-552-0600

Wayne Miller · Miller & Tischler · 26711 Northwestern Highway, Suite 200 · Southfield, MI 48033-2159
248-945-1040

Paul A. Rosen · Rosen and Lovell · 25505 West 12 Mile Road, Suite 1000 · Southfield, MI 48034 · 313-961-7510

Joseph C. Smith · Smith & Gibson · One Northwestern Plaza, Suite 1275 · 28411 Northwestern Highway
Southfield, MI 48034 · 248-353-0600

Judith Susskind · The Thurswell Law Group · 1000 Town Center, Suite 500 · Southfield, MI 48075 · 248-354-2222

Gerald Thurswell · The Thurswell Law Group · 1000 Town Center, Suite 500 · Southfield, MI 48075 · 248-354-2222

Norman D. Tucker · ⑩ · Sommers Schwartz · http://www.sommerspc.com · 2000 Town Center, Suite 900
Southfield, MI 48075-1100 · 248-355-0300

St. Claire Shores

Robert F. Garvey · Robert F. Garvey · 24825 Little Mack Avenue · St. Claire Shores, MI 48080 · 586-779-7810

St. Joseph

Barry R. Conybeare · Conybeare Law Office · 519 Main Street · St. Joseph, MI 49085 · 269-983-0561

Stevensville

Michael D. Marrs · ⑩ · Michael D. Marrs · 5709 Red Arrow Highway · P.O. Box 618 · Stevensville, MI 49085 · 269-982-4000

Suttons Bay

Dean A. Robb · ㉕ · The Dean Robb Law Firm · 416 Saint Joseph Street · P.O. Box 879 · Suttons Bay, MI 49682 · 231-271-6350

Troy

James L. Borin · Garan Lucow & Miller · 1111 West Long Lake Road, Suite 300 · Troy, MI 48098-6333 · 248-641-7600

Dennis M. Goebel · Harvey Kruse · 1050 Wilshire Drive, Suite 320 · Troy, MI 48084-1526 · 248-649-7800

Stephen J. Ott · Miller Canfield Paddock and Stone · http://www.millercanfield.com · 840 West Long Lake Road, Suite 200 · Troy, MI 48098-6358 · 248-879-2000

William C. Schaefer · Driggers, Schutz & Herbst · Bank Of America Financial Center, Suite 550 · 2600 West Big Beaver Road · Troy, MI 48084-3323 · 248-643-8491

Roger A. Smith · Garan Lucow & Miller · 1111 West Long Lake Road, Suite 300 · Troy, MI 48098-6333
248-641-7600

Ypsilanti

Andrew S. Muth · ⑩ · Muth and Shapiro · 301 West Michigan Avenue, Suite 302 · Ypsilanti, MI 48197 · 734-481-8800

PRIVATE FUNDS LAW

Grand Rapids

Ronald E. Roden · Miller Johnson · http://www.millerjohnson.com · Calder Plaza Building, Suite 800 · 250 Monroe Avenue, NW · P.O. Box 306 · Grand Rapids, MI 49503-2250 · 616-831-1700

John M. Sommerdyke · Miller Canfield Paddock and Stone · http://www.millercanfield.com · 99 Monroe Avenue, NW, Suite 1200 · Grand Rapids, MI 49503 · 616-454-8656

Robert R. Stead · Barnes & Thornburg · http://www.btlaw.com · 300 Ottawa Avenue, NW, Suite 500 · Grand Rapids, MI 49503 · 616-742-3930

PRODUCT LIABILITY LITIGATION

Ann Arbor

James M. Cameron, Jr. · Dykema · http://www.dykema.com · 2723 South State Street, Suite 400 · Ann Arbor, MI 48104 · 734-214-7600

Peter A. Davis · ⑩ · Davis & Kuhnke · 405 North Main Street · Ann Arbor, MI 48104 · 734-663-2233

Bloomfield Hills

James P. Feeney · Dykema · http://www.dykema.com · 39577 Woodward Avenue, Suite 300 · Bloomfield Hills, MI 48304-2820 · 248-203-0700

Detroit

David W. Christensen · ⑩ · Charfoos & Christensen · Smiley Mansion · 5510 Woodward Avenue · Detroit, MI 48202 · 313-875-8080

Richard M. Goodman · ㉕ · Goodman Kalahar · 1394 East Jefferson Avenue · Detroit, MI 48207 · 313-567-6165

Peter M. Kellett · Dykema · http://www.dykema.com · 400 Renaissance Center · Detroit, MI 48243 · 313-568-6800

Edward M. Kronk · ⑩ · Butzel Long · http://www.butzel.com · 150 West Jefferson Avenue, Suite 100 · Detroit, MI 48226 · 313-225-7000

Daniel J. Scully, Jr. · Clark Hill · http://www.clarkhill.com · 500 Woodward Avenue, Suite 3500 · Detroit, MI 48226-3435 · 313-965-8300

Barry P. Waldman · ⑩ · Sachs Waldman · 1000 Farmer Street · Detroit, MI 48226-2899 · 313-965-3464

Lansing

William N. Kritselis · ⑳ · Church, Kritselis & Wyble · 2827 East Saginaw Street · Lansing, MI 48912 · 517-372-1011

Scott A. Storey · Foster, Swift, Collins & Smith · http://www.fosterswift.com · 313 South Washington Square · Lansing, MI 48933-2193 · 517-371-8100

Mount Clemens

James N. Martin · ⑩ · Martin, Bacon & Martin · 44 First Street · Mount Clemens, MI 48043 · 586-979-6500

Troy

Stephen J. Ott · Miller Canfield Paddock and Stone · http://www.millercanfield.com · 840 West Long Lake Road, Suite 200 · Troy, MI 48098-6358 · 248-879-2000

PROFESSIONAL MALPRACTICE LAW

Birmingham

William R. Buesser · ⑩ · Buesser & Buesser · 401 South Old Woodward Avenue, Suite 315 · Birmingham, MI 48009 · 248-642-7880

Bloomfield Hills

George A. Googasian · ⑩ · The Googasian Firm · 6895 Telegraph Road · Bloomfield Hills, MI 48301-3138 · 248-540-3333

Detroit

David W. Christensen · ⑩ · Charfoos & Christensen · Smiley Mansion · 5510 Woodward Avenue · Detroit, MI 48202 · 313-875-8080

Michael W. Hartmann · ⑩ · Miller Canfield Paddock and Stone · http://www.millercanfield.com · 150 West Jefferson Avenue, Suite 2500 · Detroit, MI 48226 · 313-963-6420

Sharon M. Woods · ⑩ · Barris, Sott, Denn & Driker · http://www.bsdd.com · 211 West Fort Street, 15th Floor · Detroit, MI 48226-3202 · 313-965-9725

Grand Rapids

Mark E. Fatum · Rhoades McKee · 161 Ottawa Avenue, NW, Suite 600 · Grand Rapids, MI 49503 · 616-235-3500

Jon G. March · ⑩ · Miller Johnson · http://www.millerjohnson.com · Calder Plaza Building, Suite 800 · 250 Monroe Avenue, NW · P.O. Box 306 · Grand Rapids, MI 49503-2250 · 616-831-1700

Jon R. Muth · Miller Johnson · http://www.millerjohnson.com · Calder Plaza Building, Suite 800 · 250 Monroe Avenue, NW · P.O. Box 306 · Grand Rapids, MI 49503-2250 · 616-831-1700

Southfield

Steven M. Wolock · Maddin, Hauser, Wartell, Roth & Heller · http://www.maddinhauser.com · Essex Centre, Third Floor · 28400 Northwestern Highway · Southfield, MI 48034-1839 · 248-354-4030

PUBLIC FINANCE LAW

Bloomfield Hills

Terence M. Donnelly · Dickinson Wright · http://www.dickinsonwright.com · 38525 Woodward Avenue, Suite 2000 · Bloomfield Hills, MI 48304-2970 · 248-433-7200

Robert L. Schwartz · Butzel Long · http://www.butzel.com · Stoneridge West · 41000 Woodward Avenue Bloomfield Hills, MI 48304 · 248-258-1616

Detroit

Harold W. Bulger, Jr. · Miller Canfield Paddock and Stone · http://www.millercanfield.com · 150 West Jefferson Avenue, Suite 2500 · Detroit, MI 48226 · 313-963-6420

Brant A. Freer · Miller Canfield Paddock and Stone · http://www.millercanfield.com · 150 West Jefferson Avenue, Suite 2500 · Detroit, MI 48226 · 313-963-6420

Donald W. Keim · Miller Canfield Paddock and Stone · http://www.millercanfield.com · 150 West Jefferson Avenue, Suite 2500 · Detroit, MI 48226 · 313-963-6420

Jeffrey M. McHugh · Miller Canfield Paddock and Stone · http://www.millercanfield.com · 150 West Jefferson Avenue, Suite 2500 · Detroit, MI 48226 · 313-963-6420

Joel L. Piell · Miller Canfield Paddock and Stone · http://www.millercanfield.com · 150 West Jefferson Avenue, Suite 2500 · Detroit, MI 48226 · 313-963-6420

Jerry T. Rupley · Miller Canfield Paddock and Stone · http://www.millercanfield.com · 150 West Jefferson Avenue, Suite 2500 · Detroit, MI 48226 · 313-963-6420

Amanda Van Dusen · Miller Canfield Paddock and Stone · http://www.millercanfield.com · 150 West Jefferson Avenue, Suite 2500 · Detroit, MI 48226 · 313-963-6420

Grand Rapids

Richard A. Wendt · Dickinson Wright · http://www.dickinsonwright.com · 200 Ottawa Avenue, NW, Suite 900 · Grand Rapids, MI 49503-2427 · 616-458-1300

James K. White · Mika Meyers Beckett & Jones · 900 Monroe Avenue, NW · Grand Rapids, MI 49503 · 616-632-8000

Susan M. Wyngaarden · Varnum, Riddering, Schmidt & Howlett · Bridgewater Place · 333 Bridge Street, NW · P.O. Box 352 · Grand Rapids, MI 49501-0352 · 616-336-6000

Lansing

James W. Bliss · Dickinson Wright · http://www.dickinsonwright.com · 215 South Washington Square, Suite 200 · Lansing, MI 48933-1816 · 517-371-1730

William J. Danhof · Miller Canfield Paddock and Stone · http://www.millercanfield.com · One Michigan Avenue, Suite 900 · Lansing, MI 48933 · 517-487-2070

Christopher J. Dembowski · Miller Canfield Paddock and Stone · http://www.millercanfield.com · One Michigan Avenue, Suite 900 · Lansing, MI 48933 · 517-487-2070

Ann D. Fillingham · Dykema · http://www.dykema.com · 201 Townsend Street, Suite 900 · Lansing, MI 48933 · 517-374-9100

Southfield

Stephen G. Schafer · Jaffe Raitt Heuer & Weiss · 27777 Franklin Road, Suite 2500 · Southfield, MI 48034-8214 · 248-351-3000

REAL ESTATE LAW

Ann Arbor

Paul R. Dimond · Miller Canfield Paddock and Stone · http://www.millercanfield.com · 101 North Main Street, Seventh Floor · Ann Arbor, MI 48104-1400 · 734-663-2445

Joseph M. Fazio · Miller Canfield Paddock and Stone · http://www.millercanfield.com · 101 North Main Street, Seventh Floor · Ann Arbor, MI 48104-1400 · 734-663-2445

Karl R. Frankena · Conlin, McKenney & Philbrick · 350 South Main Street, Suite 400 · Ann Arbor, MI 48104-2131 · 734-761-9000

Robert E. Gilbert · 25 · Miller Canfield Paddock and Stone · http://www.millercanfield.com · 101 North Main Street, Seventh Floor · Ann Arbor, MI 48104-1400 · 734-663-2445

Joseph Lloyd · 10 · Chard & Lloyd · 201 East Washington Street · Ann Arbor, MI 48104-2007 · 734-668-1522

Ian J. Reach · Reach Law Firm · 121 West Washington Street, Suite 400 · Ann Arbor, MI 48104 · 734-994-1400

Brad M. Tomtishen · Nuyen, Tomtishen and Aoun · 2001 Commonwealth Boulevard, Suite 300 · Ann Arbor, MI 48105 · 734-372-4100

Bloomfield Hills

James C. Adams · Butzel Long · http://www.butzel.com · Stoneridge West · 41000 Woodward Avenue · Bloomfield Hills, MI 48304 · 248-258-1616

C. Leslie Banas · Honigman Miller Schwartz and Cohn · 38500 Woodward Avenue, Suite 100 · Bloomfield Hills, MI 48304-5048 · 248-566-8301

Jorge I. Beltran · Butzel Long · http://www.butzel.com · Stoneridge West · 41000 Woodward Avenue · Bloomfield Hills, MI 48304 · 248-258-1616

Stephen A. Bromberg · 20 · Butzel Long · http://www.butzel.com · Stoneridge West · 41000 Woodward Avenue · Bloomfield Hills, MI 48304 · 248-258-1616

Richard J. Burstein · 10 · Honigman Miller Schwartz and Cohn · 38500 Woodward Avenue, Suite 100 · Bloomfield Hills, MI 48304-5048 · 248-566-8301

Edward C. Dawda · Dawda, Mann, Mulcahy & Sadler · http://www.dmms.com · 39533 Woodward Avenue, Suite 200 · Bloomfield Hills, MI 48304-5103 · 248-642-3700

Stephen E. Dawson · 25 · Dickinson Wright · http://www.dickinsonwright.com · 38525 Woodward Avenue, Suite 2000 · Bloomfield Hills, MI 48304-2970 · 248-433-7200

Gordon N. Didier · Butzel Long · http://www.butzel.com · Stoneridge West · 41000 Woodward Avenue · Bloomfield Hills, MI 48304 · 248-258-1616

Fred J. Fechheimer · Dykema · http://www.dykema.com · 39577 Woodward Avenue, Suite 300 · Bloomfield Hills, MI 48304-2820 · 248-203-0700

Susan K. Friedlaender · Honigman Miller Schwartz and Cohn · 38500 Woodward Avenue, Suite 100 · Bloomfield Hills, MI 48304-5048 · 248-566-8301

Howard B. Goldman · Butzel Long · http://www.butzel.com · Stoneridge West · 41000 Woodward Avenue · Bloomfield Hills, MI 48304 · 248-258-1616

Alan M. Greene · Dykema · http://www.dykema.com · 39577 Woodward Avenue, Suite 300 · Bloomfield Hills, MI 48304-2820 · 248-203-0700

Alan M. Hurvitz · 10 · Honigman Miller Schwartz and Cohn · 38500 Woodward Avenue, Suite 100 · Bloomfield Hills, MI 48304-5048 · 248-566-8301

Norman Hyman · 10 · Honigman Miller Schwartz and Cohn · 38500 Woodward Avenue, Suite 100 · Bloomfield Hills, MI 48304-5048 · 248-566-8301

Martin L. Katz · Honigman Miller Schwartz and Cohn · 38500 Woodward Avenue, Suite 100 · Bloomfield Hills, MI 48304-5048 · 248-566-8301

Joel D. Kellman · Dykema · http://www.dykema.com · 39577 Woodward Avenue, Suite 300 · Bloomfield Hills, MI 48304-2820 · 248-203-0700

Howard N. Luckoff · Honigman Miller Schwartz and Cohn · 38500 Woodward Avenue, Suite 100 · Bloomfield Hills, MI 48304-5048 · 248-566-8301

Michael D. Mulcahy · Dawda, Mann, Mulcahy & Sadler · http://www.dmms.com · 39533 Woodward Avenue, Suite 200 · Bloomfield Hills, MI 48304-5103 · 248-642-3700

William T. Myers · 25 · Myers Nelson Dillon & Shierk · 40701 Woodward Avenue, Suite 235 · Bloomfield Hills, MI 48034 · 248-203-2040

Allan Nachman · Butzel Long · http://www.butzel.com · Stoneridge West · 41000 Woodward Avenue · Bloomfield Hills, MI 48304 · 248-258-1616

Robert V. Peterson · Dickinson Wright · http://www.dickinsonwright.com · 38525 Woodward Avenue, Suite 2000 · Bloomfield Hills, MI 48304-2970 · 248-433-7200

J. Adam Rothstein · Honigman Miller Schwartz and Cohn · 38500 Woodward Avenue, Suite 100 · Bloomfield Hills, MI 48304-5048 · 248-566-8301

Anthony J. Saulino, Jr. · Butzel Long · http://www.butzel.com · Stoneridge West · 41000 Woodward Avenue · Bloomfield Hills, MI 48304 · 248-258-1616

C. Kim Shierk · Myers Nelson Dillon & Shierk · 40701 Woodward Avenue, Suite 235 · Bloomfield Hills, MI 48034 · 248-203-2040

Laurence E. Winokur · Dickinson Wright · http://www.dickinsonwright.com · 38525 Woodward Avenue, Suite 2000 · Bloomfield Hills, MI 48304-2970 · 248-433-7200

Detroit

Joel S. Adelman · 10 · Honigman Miller Schwartz and Cohn · First National Building, Suite 2290 · 660 Woodward Avenue · Detroit, MI 48226-3506 · 313-465-7000

William G. Barris · 20 · Barris, Sott, Denn & Driker · http://www.bsdd.com · 211 West Fort Street, 15th Floor · Detroit, MI 48226-3202 · 313-965-9725

Maurice S. Binkow · 25 · Honigman Miller Schwartz and Cohn · First National Building, Suite 2290 · 660 Woodward Avenue · Detroit, MI 48226-3506 · 313-465-7000

James N. Candler, Jr. · 10 · Dickinson Wright · http://www.dickinsonwright.com · 500 Woodward Avenue, Suite 4000 · Detroit, MI 48226-3425 · 313-223-3500

Lawrence M. Dudek · Miller Canfield Paddock and Stone · http://www.millercanfield.com · 150 West Jefferson Avenue, Suite 2500 · Detroit, MI 48226 · 313-963-6420

William B. Dunn · 20 · Clark Hill · http://www.clarkhill.com · 500 Woodward Avenue, Suite 3500 · Detroit, MI 48226-3435 · 313-965-8300

James S. Fontichiaro · Barris, Sott, Denn & Driker · http://www.bsdd.com · 211 West Fort Street, 15th Floor · Detroit, MI 48226-3202 · 313-965-9725

Joseph F. Galvin · Miller Canfield Paddock and Stone · http://www.millercanfield.com · 150 West Jefferson Avenue, Suite 2500 · Detroit, MI 48226 · 313-963-6420

Vicki R. Harding · Pepper Hamilton · http://www.pepperlaw.com · 100 Renaissance Center, Suite 3600 · Detroit, MI 48243-1157 · 313-259-7110

Carl W. Herstein · Honigman Miller Schwartz and Cohn · First National Building, Suite 2290 · 660 Woodward Avenue · Detroit, MI 48226-3506 · 313-465-7000

Timothy M. Koltun · Clark Hill · http://www.clarkhill.com · 500 Woodward Avenue, Suite 3500 · Detroit, MI 48226-3435 · 313-965-8300

Lawrence D. McLaughlin · 10 · Honigman Miller Schwartz and Cohn · First National Building, Suite 2290 · 660 Woodward Avenue · Detroit, MI 48226-3506 · 313-465-7000

Robert R. Nix II · 10 · Kerr, Russell and Weber · Detroit Center, Suite 2500 · 500 Woodward Avenue · Detroit, MI 48226-3427 · 313-961-0200

Cameron H. Piggott · Dykema · http://www.dykema.com · 400 Renaissance Center · Detroit, MI 48243 · 313-568-6800

Michael B. Shapiro · 10 · Honigman Miller Schwartz and Cohn · First National Building, Suite 2290 · 660 Woodward Avenue · Detroit, MI 48226-3506 · 313-465-7000

Daniel M. Share · Barris, Sott, Denn & Driker · http://www.bsdd.com · 211 West Fort Street, 15th Floor · Detroit, MI 48226-3202 · 313-965-9725

Wilfred A. Steiner, Jr. · Dykema · http://www.dykema.com · 400 Renaissance Center · Detroit, MI 48243 · 313-568-6800

Sheldon P. Winkelman · 25 · Honigman Miller Schwartz and Cohn · First National Building, Suite 2290 · 660 Woodward Avenue · Detroit, MI 48226-3506 · 313-465-7000

William J. Zousmer · 25 · Honigman Miller Schwartz and Cohn · First National Building, Suite 2290 · 660 Woodward Avenue · Detroit, MI 48226-3506 · 313-465-7000

Farmington Hills

Robert A. Berlow · Taubman, Nadis & Neuman · 32255 Northwestern Highway, Suite 200 · Farmington Hills, MI 48334 · 248-865-3700

William P. Hampton · 10 · Secrest, Wardle, Lynch, Hampton, Truex and Morley · 30903 Northwestern Highway · P.O. Box 3040 · Farmington Hills, MI 48333-3040 · 248-851-9500

Grand Rapids

Jeffrey S. Ammon · Miller Johnson · http://www.millerjohnson.com · Calder Plaza Building, Suite 800 · 250 Monroe Avenue, NW · P.O. Box 306 · Grand Rapids, MI 49503-2250 · 616-831-1700

Jonathan W. Anderson · Varnum, Riddering, Schmidt & Howlett · Bridgewater Place · 333 Bridge Street, NW · P.O. Box 352 · Grand Rapids, MI 49501-0352 · 616-336-6000

James R. Brown · ⑳ · Mika Meyers Beckett & Jones · 900 Monroe Avenue, NW · Grand Rapids, MI 49503 · 616-632-8000

John G. Cameron, Jr. · ⑩ · Dickinson Wright · http://www.dickinsonwright.com · 200 Ottawa Avenue, NW, Suite 900 · Grand Rapids, MI 49503-2427 · 616-458-1300

Nyal D. Deems · ⑩ · Varnum, Riddering, Schmidt & Howlett · Bridgewater Place · 333 Bridge Street, NW · P.O. Box 352 · Grand Rapids, MI 49501-0352 · 616-336-6000

William W. Hall · ⑩ · Warner Norcross & Judd · http://www.wnj.com · 900 Fifth Third Center · 111 Lyon Street, NW · Grand Rapids, MI 49503-2487 · 616-752-2000

Todd A. Hendricks · Rhoades McKee · 161 Ottawa Avenue, NW, Suite 600 · Grand Rapids, MI 49503 · 616-235-3500

Randall W. Kraker · Varnum, Riddering, Schmidt & Howlett · Bridgewater Place · 333 Bridge Street, NW · P.O. Box 352 · Grand Rapids, MI 49501-0352 · 616-336-6000

Robert L. Nelson · ㉕ · Myers Nelson Dillon & Shierk · 125 Ottawa Avenue, NW, Suite 270 · Grand Rapids, MI 49503 · 616-233-9640

James J. Rabaut · Warner Norcross & Judd · http://www.wnj.com · 900 Fifth Third Center · 111 Lyon Street, NW · Grand Rapids, MI 49503-2487 · 616-752-2000

David L. Smith · ⑩ · McShane & Bowie · Campau Square Plaza, Suite 1100 · 99 Monroe Avenue, NW · P.O. Box 360 · Grand Rapids, MI 49501-0360 · 616-732-5000

William K. Van't Hof · ⑩ · Charron & Hanisch · 4949 Plainfield Avenue, NE · Grand Rapids, MI 49525 · 616-363-0300

Michael C. Walton · Rhoades McKee · 161 Ottawa Avenue, NW, Suite 600 · Grand Rapids, MI 49503 · 616-235-3500

Kalamazoo

Robert R. Lennon · Miller Canfield Paddock and Stone · http://www.millercanfield.com · 277 South Rose Street, Suite 5000 · Kalamazoo, MI 49007-3751 · 269-381-7030

Lansing

Gail A. Anderson · McClelland & Anderson · 1305 South Washington Avenue, Suite 102 · Lansing, MI 48910 · 517-482-4890

Douglas J. Austin · ⑳ · Fraser Trebilcock Davis & Dunlap · 124 West Allegan Street, Suite 1000 · Lansing, MI 48933 · 517-482-5800

Kenneth W. Beall · Loomis, Ewert, Parsley, Davis & Gotting · 124 West Allegan Street, Suite 700 · Lansing, MI 48933-1707 · 517-482-2400

Jack C. Davis · Loomis, Ewert, Parsley, Davis & Gotting · 124 West Allegan Street, Suite 700 · Lansing, MI 48933-1707 · 517-482-2400

Karl L. Gotting · Loomis, Ewert, Parsley, Davis & Gotting · 124 West Allegan Street, Suite 700 · Lansing, MI 48933-1707 · 517-482-2400

Jeffrey L. Green · Loomis, Ewert, Parsley, Davis & Gotting · 124 West Allegan Street, Suite 700 · Lansing, MI 48933-1707 · 517-482-2400

Gregory L. McClelland · 10 · McClelland & Anderson · 1305 South Washington Avenue, Suite 102 · Lansing, MI 48910 · 517-482-4890

Steven L. Owen · Foster, Swift, Collins & Smith · http://www.fosterswift.com · 313 South Washington Square · Lansing, MI 48933-2193 · 517-371-8100

David E. Pierson · McClelland & Anderson · 1305 South Washington Avenue, Suite 102 · Lansing, MI 48910 · 517-482-4890

Brent A. Titus · Foster, Swift, Collins & Smith · http://www.fosterswift.com · 313 South Washington Square · Lansing, MI 48933-2193 · 517-371-8100

Okemos

William K. Fahey · Fahey Schultz Burzych Rhodes · http://www.fsblawyers.com · 4151 Okemos Road · Okemos, MI 48864 · 517-381-0100

Royal Oak

Edward F. Kickham · Kickham Hanley · http://www.kickhamhanley.com · 300 Balmoral Centre · 32121 Woodward Avenue · Royal Oak, MI 48073-0943 · 248-554-6300

Southfield

Robert S. Bolton · 25 · Jaffe Raitt Heuer & Weiss · 27777 Franklin Road, Suite 2500 · Southfield, MI 48034-8214 · 248-351-3000

Mark R. Hauser · 10 · Maddin, Hauser, Wartell, Roth & Heller · http://www.maddinhauser.com · Essex Centre, Third Floor · 28400 Northwestern Highway · Southfield, MI 48034-1839 · 248-354-4030

John E. Jacobs · Maddin, Hauser, Wartell, Roth & Heller · http://www.maddinhauser.com · Essex Centre, Third Floor · 28400 Northwestern Highway · Southfield, MI 48034-1839 · 248-354-4030

Michael W. Maddin · Maddin, Hauser, Wartell, Roth & Heller · http://www.maddinhauser.com · Essex Centre, Third Floor · 28400 Northwestern Highway · Southfield, MI 48034-1839 · 248-354-4030

Richard J. Maddin · Maddin, Hauser, Wartell, Roth & Heller · http://www.maddinhauser.com · Essex Centre, Third Floor · 28400 Northwestern Highway · Southfield, MI 48034-1839 · 248-354-4030

Lowell D. Salesin · Maddin, Hauser, Wartell, Roth & Heller · http://www.maddinhauser.com · Essex Centre, Third Floor · 28400 Northwestern Highway · Southfield, MI 48034-1839 · 248-354-4030

Gary A. Taback · 20 · Sommers Schwartz · http://www.sommerspc.com · 2000 Town Center, Suite 900 · Southfield, MI 48075-1100 · 248-355-0300

Arthur A. Weiss · Jaffe Raitt Heuer & Weiss · 27777 Franklin Road, Suite 2500 · Southfield, MI 48034-8214 · 248-351-3000

Richard A. Zussman · Jaffe Raitt Heuer & Weiss · 27777 Franklin Road, Suite 2500 · Southfield, MI 48034-8214 · 248-351-3000

Troy

David W. Hipp · Bodman · http://www.bodmanllp.com · 201 West Big Beaver Road, Suite 500 · Troy, MI 48084 · 248-743-6000

Ronald E. Hodess · Miller Canfield Paddock and Stone · http://www.millercanfield.com · 840 West Long Lake Road, Suite 200 · Troy, MI 48098-6358 · 248-879-2000

Stephen G. Palms · ㉕ · Miller Canfield Paddock and Stone · http://www.millercanfield.com · 840 West Long Lake Road, Suite 200 · Troy, MI 48098-6358 · 248-879-2000

Leon M. Schurgin · Bodman · http://www.bodmanllp.com · 201 West Big Beaver Road, Suite 500 · Troy, MI 48084 · 248-743-6000

Andrew Z. Spilkin · Bodman · http://www.bodmanllp.com · 201 West Big Beaver Road, Suite 500 · Troy, MI 48084 · 248-743-6000

J. Kevin Trimmer · Miller Canfield Paddock and Stone · http://www.millercanfield.com · 840 West Long Lake Road, Suite 200 · Troy, MI 48098-6358 · 248-879-2000

SECURITIES LAW

Ann Arbor

Barbara A. Kaye · Honigman Miller Schwartz and Cohn · 130 South First Street, Fourth Floor · Ann Arbor, MI 48104-1386 · 734-418-4200

David N. Parsigian · Honigman Miller Schwartz and Cohn · 130 South First Street, Fourth Floor · Ann Arbor, MI 48104-1386 · 734-418-4200

Bloomfield Hills

D. Richard McDonald · Dykema · http://www.dykema.com · 39577 Woodward Avenue, Suite 300 · Bloomfield Hills, MI 48304-2820 · 248-203-0700

Detroit

Patrick D. Daugherty · Foley & Lardner · One Detroit Center, Suite 2700 · 500 Woodward Avenue · Detroit, MI 48226-3489 · 313-234-7100

David Foltyn · ⑩ · Honigman Miller Schwartz and Cohn · First National Building, Suite 2290 · 660 Woodward Avenue · Detroit, MI 48226-3506 · 313-465-7000

Justin G. Klimko · ⑩ · Butzel Long · http://www.butzel.com · 150 West Jefferson Avenue, Suite 100 · Detroit, MI 48226 · 313-225-7000

Jin-Kyu Koh · Dykema · http://www.dykema.com · 400 Renaissance Center · Detroit, MI 48243 · 313-568-6800

Donald J. Kunz · Honigman Miller Schwartz and Cohn · First National Building, Suite 2290 · 660 Woodward Avenue · Detroit, MI 48226-3506 · 313-465-7000

Mark A. Metz · Dykema · http://www.dykema.com · 400 Renaissance Center · Detroit, MI 48243 · 313-568-6800

Cyril Moscow · ㉕ · Honigman Miller Schwartz and Cohn · First National Building, Suite 2290 · 660 Woodward Avenue · Detroit, MI 48226-3506 · 313-465-7000

Rex E. Schlaybaugh, Jr. · Dykema · http://www.dykema.com · 400 Renaissance Center · Detroit, MI 48243 · 313-568-6800

Alan E. Schwartz · ㉕ · Honigman Miller Schwartz and Cohn · First National Building, Suite 2290 · 660 Woodward Avenue · Detroit, MI 48226-3506 · 313-465-7000

Alan S. Schwartz · (20) · Honigman Miller Schwartz and Cohn · First National Building, Suite 2290 · 660 Woodward Avenue · Detroit, MI 48226-3506 · 313-465-7000

Thomas S. Vaughn · Dykema · http://www.dykema.com · 400 Renaissance Center · Detroit, MI 48243 · 313-568-6800

Grand Rapids

Shane B. Hansen · Warner Norcross & Judd · http://www.wnj.com · 900 Fifth Third Center · 111 Lyon Street, NW · Grand Rapids, MI 49503-2487 · 616-752-2000

Timothy L. Horner · Warner Norcross & Judd · http://www.wnj.com · 900 Fifth Third Center · 111 Lyon Street, NW · Grand Rapids, MI 49503-2487 · 616-752-2000

Gordon R. Lewis · (10) · Warner Norcross & Judd · http://www.wnj.com · 900 Fifth Third Center · 111 Lyon Street, NW · Grand Rapids, MI 49503-2487 · 616-752-2000

Hugh H. Makens · (25) · Warner Norcross & Judd · http://www.wnj.com · 900 Fifth Third Center · 111 Lyon Street, NW · Grand Rapids, MI 49503-2487 · 616-752-2000

Lansing

Iris K. Linder · Fraser Trebilcock Davis & Dunlap · 124 West Allegan Street, Suite 1000 · Lansing, MI 48933 · 517-482-5800

Southfield

Peter Sugar · Jaffe Raitt Heuer & Weiss · 27777 Franklin Road, Suite 2500 · Southfield, MI 48034-8214 · 248-351-3000

Troy

Thomas G. Appleman · Miller Canfield Paddock and Stone · http://www.millercanfield.com · 840 West Long Lake Road, Suite 200 · Troy, MI 48098-6358 · 248-879-2000

Brad B. Arbuckle · Miller Canfield Paddock and Stone · http://www.millercanfield.com · 840 West Long Lake Road, Suite 200 · Troy, MI 48098-6358 · 248-879-2000

SPORTS LAW

Ann Arbor

Gregory L. Curtner · Miller Canfield Paddock and Stone · http://www.millercanfield.com · 101 North Main Street, Seventh Floor · Ann Arbor, MI 48104-1400 · 734-663-2445

TAX LAW

Ann Arbor

Randolph S. Perry · Randolph S. Perry · 2475 Whitmore Lake Road · Ann Arbor, MI 48105 · 734-677-7738

Warren J. Widmayer · (10) · Ferguson & Widmayer · http://www.fw-pc.com · 538 North Division Street · Ann Arbor, MI 48104 · 734-662-0222

Bloomfield Hills

Lynn M. Brimer · Strobl & Sharp · http://www.stroblpc.com · 300 East Long Lake Road, Suite 200 · Bloomfield Hills, MI 48304 · 248-540-2300

Jeffrey H. Miro · 10 · Honigman Miller Schwartz and Cohn · 38500 Woodward Avenue, Suite 100 · Bloomfield Hills, MI 48304-5048 · 248-566-8301

Linda A. Wasserman · Honigman Miller Schwartz and Cohn · 38500 Woodward Avenue, Suite 100 · Bloomfield Hills, MI 48304-5048 · 248-566-8301

Detroit

Roger Cook · 10 · Honigman Miller Schwartz and Cohn · First National Building, Suite 2290 · 660 Woodward Avenue · Detroit, MI 48226-3506 · 313-465-7000

Brant A. Freer · Miller Canfield Paddock and Stone · http://www.millercanfield.com · 150 West Jefferson Avenue, Suite 2500 · Detroit, MI 48226 · 313-963-6420

Steven E. Grob · 10 · Dykema · http://www.dykema.com · 400 Renaissance Center · Detroit, MI 48243 · 313-568-6800

Michael A. Indenbaum · 10 · Honigman Miller Schwartz and Cohn · First National Building, Suite 2290 · 660 Woodward Avenue · Detroit, MI 48226-3506 · 313-465-7000

Stewart L. Mandell · Honigman Miller Schwartz and Cohn · First National Building, Suite 2290 · 660 Woodward Avenue · Detroit, MI 48226-3506 · 313-465-7000

Samuel J. McKim III · 25 · Miller Canfield Paddock and Stone · http://www.millercanfield.com · 150 West Jefferson Avenue, Suite 2500 · Detroit, MI 48226 · 313-963-6420

Charles Nida · 10 · Honigman Miller Schwartz and Cohn · First National Building, Suite 2290 · 660 Woodward Avenue · Detroit, MI 48226-3506 · 313-465-7000

Richard S. Soble · Honigman Miller Schwartz and Cohn · First National Building, Suite 2290 · 660 Woodward Avenue · Detroit, MI 48226-3506 · 313-465-7000

Stevan Uzelac · 25 · Honigman Miller Schwartz and Cohn · First National Building, Suite 2290 · 660 Woodward Avenue · Detroit, MI 48226-3506 · 313-465-7000

Grand Rapids

Robert D. Brower · 20 · Miller Johnson · http://www.millerjohnson.com · Calder Plaza Building, Suite 800 250 Monroe Avenue, NW · P.O. Box 306 · Grand Rapids, MI 49503-2250 · 616-831-1700

Edward B. Goodrich · 25 · Rhoades McKee · 161 Ottawa Avenue, NW, Suite 600 · Grand Rapids, MI 49503 · 616-235-3500

Carol J. Karr · 10 · Miller Johnson · http://www.millerjohnson.com · Calder Plaza Building, Suite 800 · 250 Monroe Avenue, NW · P.O. Box 306 · Grand Rapids, MI 49503-2250 · 616-831-1700

Stephen R. Kretschman · 20 · Warner Norcross & Judd · http://www.wnj.com · 900 Fifth Third Center · 111 Lyon Street, NW · Grand Rapids, MI 49503-2487 · 616-752-2000

John W. McNeil · 25 · Miller Johnson · http://www.millerjohnson.com · Calder Plaza Building, Suite 800 · 250 Monroe Avenue, NW · P.O. Box 306 · Grand Rapids, MI 49503-2250 · 616-831-1700

J. Lee Murphy · ⑳ · Miller Johnson · http://www.millerjohnson.com · Calder Plaza Building, Suite 800 · 250 Monroe Avenue, NW · P.O. Box 306 · Grand Rapids, MI 49503-2250 · 616-831-1700

Mark E. Rizik · Miller Johnson · http://www.millerjohnson.com · Calder Plaza Building, Suite 800 · 250 Monroe Avenue, NW · P.O. Box 306 · Grand Rapids, MI 49503-2250 · 616-831-1700

Holland

John R. Marquis · ⑩ · Warner Norcross & Judd · http://www.wnj.com · 85 East Eighth Street, Suite 310 · Holland, MI 49423-2920 · 616-396-9800

Lansing

Allan J. Claypool · ㉕ · Foster, Swift, Collins & Smith · http://www.fosterswift.com · 313 South Washington Square · Lansing, MI 48933-2193 · 517-371-8100

James B. Jensen, Jr. · Foster, Swift, Collins & Smith · http://www.fosterswift.com · 313 South Washington Square · Lansing, MI 48933-2193 · 517-371-8100

Patricia M. Ouellette · Bernick Omer Radner & Ouellette · 2400 Lake Lansing Road, Suite F · Lansing, MI 48912 · 517-371-5361

Peter S. Sheldon · ㉕ · Dickinson Wright · http://www.dickinsonwright.com · 215 South Washington Square, Suite 200 · Lansing, MI 48933-1816 · 517-371-1730

Patrick R. Van Tiflin · Honigman Miller Schwartz and Cohn · 222 North Washington Square, Suite 400 · Lansing, MI 48933-1800 · 517-484-8282

Okemos

Joe C. Foster, Jr. · ㉕ · Foster Zack Little Pasteur & Manning · http://www.fosterzack.com · 2125 University Park Drive, Suite 250 · Okemos, MI 48864 · 517-706-0000

Richard C. Lowe · ⑩ · Lowe Law Firm · 2375 Woodlake Drive, Suite 380 · Okemos, MI 48864 · 517-908-0909

Southfield

Steven J. Schwartz · Sommers Schwartz · http://www.sommerspc.com · 2000 Town Center, Suite 900 · Southfield, MI 48075-1100 · 248-355-0300

St. Clair Shores

Robert B. Joslyn · ㉕ · Robert B. Joslyn · http://www.rbjoslynpc.com · 200 Maple Park Boulevard, Suite 201 · St. Clair Shores, MI 48081-2211 · 586-773-3323

TECHNOLOGY LAW

Ann Arbor

Susan M. Kornfield · Bodman · http://www.bodmanllp.com · 201 South Division Street, Suite 400 · Ann Arbor, MI 48104 · 734-761-3780

TRUSTS AND ESTATES

Ann Arbor

Marie R. Deveney · Dykema · http://www.dykema.com · 2723 South State Street, Suite 400 · Ann Arbor, MI 48104 · 734-214-7600

Dennis M. Mitzel · Berry Moorman · 900 Victors Way, Suite 300 · Ann Arbor, MI 48108 · 734-668-4100

Susan S. Westerman · ⑳ · Westerman & Associates · 345 South Division Street · Ann Arbor, MI 48104 · 734-995-9731

Bingham Farms

Lauren M. Underwood · Lauren M. Underwood · 32100 Telegraph Road, Suite 200 · Bingham Farms, MI 48025 · 248-594-1919

Birmingham

George W. Gregory · ⑩ · George W. Gregory · 401 South Old Woodward Avenue, Suite 456 · Birmingham, MI 48009 · 248-647-5700

J. Thomas MacFarlane · Clark Hill · http://www.clarkhill.com · 255 South Old Woodward Avenue, Third Floor · Birmingham, MI 48009-6179 · 248-642-9692

Thomas F. Sweeney · Clark Hill · http://www.clarkhill.com · 255 South Old Woodward Avenue, Third Floor · Birmingham, MI 48009-6179 · 248-642-9692

Bloomfield Hills

Michael G. Cumming · Dykema · http://www.dykema.com · 39577 Woodward Avenue, Suite 300 · Bloomfield Hills, MI 48304-2820 · 248-203-0700

Henry M. Grix · Dickinson Wright · http://www.dickinsonwright.com · 38525 Woodward Avenue, Suite 2000 · Bloomfield Hills, MI 48304-2970 · 248-433-7200

Stephen W. Jones · ⑩ · Beier Howlett · 200 East Long Lake Road, Suite 110 · Bloomfield Hills, MI 48304-2328 · 248-645-9400

Judith F. Layne · Dickinson Wright · http://www.dickinsonwright.com · 38525 Woodward Avenue, Suite 2000 · Bloomfield Hills, MI 48304-2970 · 248-433-7200

Marguerite Munson Lentz · Honigman Miller Schwartz and Cohn · 38500 Woodward Avenue, Suite 100 · Bloomfield Hills, MI 48304-5048 · 248-566-8301

James H. LoPrete · LoPrete & Lyneis · 40950 Woodward Avenue, Suite 306 · Bloomfield Hills, MI 48304-5128 · 248-594-5770

David W. Sommerfeld · ⑩ · Butzel Long · http://www.butzel.com · Stoneridge West · 41000 Woodward Avenue · Bloomfield Hills, MI 48304 · 248-258-1616

Linda A. Wasserman · Honigman Miller Schwartz and Cohn · 38500 Woodward Avenue, Suite 100 · Bloomfield Hills, MI 48304-5048 · 248-566-8301

Detroit

Joseph A. Bonventre · Clark Hill · http://www.clarkhill.com · 500 Woodward Avenue, Suite 3500 · Detroit, MI 48226-3435 · 313-965-8300

Andrew H. Curoe · Bodman · http://www.bodmanllp.com · Sixth Floor at Ford Field · 1901 Saint Antoine Street · Detroit, MI 48226 · 313-259-7777

James M. Elsworth · ⑩ · Dykema · http://www.dykema.com · 400 Renaissance Center · Detroit, MI 48243 · 313-568-6800

William E. Fisher · ⑩ · Dykema · http://www.dykema.com · 400 Renaissance Center · Detroit, MI 48243 313-568-6800

David M. Hempstead · ⑩ · Bodman · http://www.bodmanllp.com · Sixth Floor at Ford Field · 1901 Saint Antoine Street · Detroit, MI 48226 · 313-259-7777

Frederick H. Hoops III · Clark Hill · http://www.clarkhill.com · 500 Woodward Avenue, Suite 3500 · Detroit, MI 48226-3435 · 313-965-8300

Robert E. Kass · Barris, Sott, Denn & Driker · http://www.bsdd.com · 211 West Fort Street, 15th Floor · Detroit, MI 48226-3202 · 313-965-9725

David P. Larsen · Bodman · http://www.bodmanllp.com · Sixth Floor at Ford Field · 1901 Saint Antoine Street · Detroit, MI 48226 · 313-259-7777

Charles Nida · ⑩ · Honigman Miller Schwartz and Cohn · First National Building, Suite 2290 · 660 Woodward Avenue · Detroit, MI 48226-3506 · 313-465-7000

Douglas J. Rasmussen · ㉕ · Clark Hill · http://www.clarkhill.com · 500 Woodward Avenue, Suite 3500 · Detroit, MI 48226-3435 · 313-965-8300

Harvey B. Wallace II · ⑩ · Berry Moorman · Buhl Building, Suite 1900 · 535 Griswold Street · Detroit, MI 48226-3679 · 313-496-1200

East Lansing

John E. Bos · Chalgian & Tripp Law Offices · 139 West Lake Lansing Road, Suite 200 · East Lansing, MI 48823 · 517-332-3800

Farmington Hills

John D. Mabley · ⑩ · Smith & Mabley · 31313 Northwestern Highway, Suite 215 · Farmington Hills, MI 48334-2577 · 248-851-0700

Patricia Gormely Prince · The Prince Law Firm · 31300 Northwestern Highway · Farmington Hills, MI 48334 · 248-865-8810

Grand Rapids

Robert D. Brower · ⑳ · Miller Johnson · http://www.millerjohnson.com · Calder Plaza Building, Suite 800 250 Monroe Avenue, NW · P.O. Box 306 · Grand Rapids, MI 49503-2250 · 616-831-1700

Carl W. Dufendach · Warner Norcross & Judd · http://www.wnj.com · 900 Fifth Third Center · 111 Lyon Street, NW · Grand Rapids, MI 49503-2487 · 616-752-2000

Christopher L. Edgar · Miller Johnson · http://www.millerjohnson.com · Calder Plaza Building, Suite 800 250 Monroe Avenue, NW · P.O. Box 306 · Grand Rapids, MI 49503-2250 · 616-831-1700

Dirk C. Hoffius · ⑳ · Varnum, Riddering, Schmidt & Howlett · Bridgewater Place · 333 Bridge Street, NW · P.O. Box 352 · Grand Rapids, MI 49501-0352 · 616-336-6000

John M. Huff · Law, Weathers & Richardson · Bridgewater Place, Suite 800 · 333 Bridge Street, NW · Grand Rapids, MI 49504-5320 · 616-459-1171

Carol J. Karr · 10 · Miller Johnson · http://www.millerjohnson.com · Calder Plaza Building, Suite 800 · 250 Monroe Avenue, NW · P.O. Box 306 · Grand Rapids, MI 49503-2250 · 616-831-1700

Thomas G. Kyros · Varnum, Riddering, Schmidt & Howlett · Bridgewater Place · 333 Bridge Street, NW P.O. Box 352 · Grand Rapids, MI 49501-0352 · 616-336-6000

Marilyn A. Lankfer · 10 · Varnum, Riddering, Schmidt & Howlett · Bridgewater Place · 333 Bridge Street, NW · P.O. Box 352 · Grand Rapids, MI 49501-0352 · 616-336-6000

Susan Gell Meyers · Warner Norcross & Judd · http://www.wnj.com · 900 Fifth Third Center · 111 Lyon Street, NW · Grand Rapids, MI 49503-2487 · 616-752-2000

Lauretta K. Murphy · Miller Johnson · http://www.millerjohnson.com · Calder Plaza Building, Suite 800 · 250 Monroe Avenue, NW · P.O. Box 306 · Grand Rapids, MI 49503-2250 · 616-831-1700

Jeffrey B. Power · 10 · Warner Norcross & Judd · http://www.wnj.com · 900 Fifth Third Center · 111 Lyon Street, NW · Grand Rapids, MI 49503-2487 · 616-752-2000

Jerome M. Smith · 10 · Warner Norcross & Judd · http://www.wnj.com · 900 Fifth Third Center · 111 Lyon Street, NW · Grand Rapids, MI 49503-2487 · 616-752-2000

Fredric A. Sytsma · 20 · Varnum, Riddering, Schmidt & Howlett · Bridgewater Place · 333 Bridge Street, NW · P.O. Box 352 · Grand Rapids, MI 49501-0352 · 616-336-6000

Michael J. Taylor · Miller Johnson · http://www.millerjohnson.com · Calder Plaza Building, Suite 800 · 250 Monroe Avenue, NW · P.O. Box 306 · Grand Rapids, MI 49503-2250 · 616-831-1700

Pamela J. Tyler · 10 · Varnum, Riddering, Schmidt & Howlett · Bridgewater Place · 333 Bridge Street, NW · P.O. Box 352 · Grand Rapids, MI 49501-0352 · 616-336-6000

W. Michael Van Haren · 20 · Warner Norcross & Judd · http://www.wnj.com · 900 Fifth Third Center · 111 Lyon Street, NW · Grand Rapids, MI 49503-2487 · 616-752-2000

Holland

Mark K. Harder · Warner Norcross & Judd · http://www.wnj.com · 85 East Eighth Street, Suite 310 · Holland, MI 49423-2920 · 616-396-9800

Lansing

Allan J. Claypool · 25 · Foster, Swift, Collins & Smith · http://www.fosterswift.com · 313 South Washington Square · Lansing, MI 48933-2193 · 517-371-8100

Charles A. Janssen · 10 · Foster, Swift, Collins & Smith · http://www.fosterswift.com · 313 South Washington Square · Lansing, MI 48933-2193 · 517-371-8100

Douglas A. Mielock · Foster, Swift, Collins & Smith · http://www.fosterswift.com · 313 South Washington Square · Lansing, MI 48933-2193 · 517-371-8100

Patricia M. Ouellette · Bernick Omer Radner & Ouellette · 2400 Lake Lansing Road, Suite F · Lansing, MI 48912 · 517-371-5361

Marquette

Kenneth J. Seavoy · Kendricks, Bordeau, Adamini, Chilman & Greenlee · 128 West Spring Street · Marquette, MI 49855 · 906-226-2543

Okemos

Joe C. Foster, Jr. · ㉕ · Foster Zack Little Pasteur & Manning · http://www.fosterzack.com · 2125 University Park Drive, Suite 250 · Okemos, MI 48864 · 517-706-0000

Nancy L. Little · ⑩ · Foster Zack Little Pasteur & Manning · http://www.fosterzack.com · 2125 University Park Drive, Suite 250 · Okemos, MI 48864 · 517-706-0000

Richard C. Lowe · ⑩ · Lowe Law Firm · 2375 Woodlake Drive, Suite 380 · Okemos, MI 48864 · 517-908-0909

Paw Paw

Harold Schuitmaker · Schuitmaker, Cooper, Schuitmaker & Cypher · 181 West Michigan Avenue, Suite One · P.O. Box 520 · Paw Paw, MI 49079-0520 · 269-657-3177

Southfield

Joel S. Golden · Jaffe Raitt Heuer & Weiss · 27777 Franklin Road, Suite 2500 · Southfield, MI 48034-8214 · 248-351-3000

Shirley A. Kaigler · Jaffe Raitt Heuer & Weiss · 27777 Franklin Road, Suite 2500 · Southfield, MI 48034-8214 · 248-351-3000

James P. Spica · Warner Norcross & Judd · http://www.wnj.com · 2000 Town Center, Suite 2700 · Southfield, MI 48075-1318 · 248-784-5000

St. Clair Shores

Robert B. Joslyn · ㉕ · Robert B. Joslyn · http://www.rbjoslynpc.com · 200 Maple Park Boulevard, Suite 201 · St. Clair Shores, MI 48081-2211 · 586-773-3323

Traverse City

George F. Bearup · ⑩ · Smith, Haughey, Rice & Roegge · 202 East State Street, Suite 100 · Traverse City, MI 49685-0848 · 231-929-4878

John A. Scott · John A. Scott · 1000 South Garfield Avenue, Suite Three · Traverse City, MI 49686 · 231-933-5322

Troy

James E. Beall · ㉕ · Stark Reagan · 1111 West Long Lake Road, Suite 202 · Troy, MI 48098-6310 · 248-641-9955

Joseph P. Buttiglieri · Kemp, Klein, Umphrey, Endelman & May · 201 West Big Beaver Road, Suite 600 Troy, MI 48084 · 248-528-1111

Gregory V. DiCenso · Miller Canfield Paddock and Stone · http://www.millercanfield.com · 840 West Long Lake Road, Suite 200 · Troy, MI 48098-6358 · 248-879-2000

Sebastian V. Grassi, Jr. · Grassi & Toering · 888 West Big Beaver Road, Suite 750 · Troy, MI 48084-4745 · 248-269-2020

Kenneth E. Konop · ⑩ · Miller Canfield Paddock and Stone · http://www.millercanfield.com · 840 West Long Lake Road, Suite 200 · Troy, MI 48098-6358 · 248-879-2000

Leonard J. Prekel · ⑩ · Morris, Rowland, Prekel & Lewinski · 3221 West Big Beaver Road, Suite 102 · Troy, MI 48084-3332 · 248-649-2910

David M. Thoms · Miller Canfield Paddock and Stone · http://www.millercanfield.com · 840 West Long Lake Road, Suite 200 · Troy, MI 48098-6358 · 248-879-2000

James W. Williams · Miller Canfield Paddock and Stone · http://www.millercanfield.com · 840 West Long Lake Road, Suite 200 · Troy, MI 48098-6358 · 248-879-2000

West Bloomfield

Nancy H. Welber · ⑩ · Nancy H. Welber · 6960 Orchard Lake Road, Suite 204 · West Bloomfield, MI 48322 · 248-932-1230

VENTURE CAPITAL LAW

Detroit

Donald J. Kunz · Honigman Miller Schwartz and Cohn · First National Building, Suite 2290 · 660 Woodward Avenue · Detroit, MI 48226-3506 · 313-465-7000

Cyril Moscow · ㉕ · Honigman Miller Schwartz and Cohn · First National Building, Suite 2290 · 660 Woodward Avenue · Detroit, MI 48226-3506 · 313-465-7000

Michael B. Staebler · Pepper Hamilton · http://www.pepperlaw.com · 100 Renaissance Center, Suite 3600 · Detroit, MI 48243-1157 · 313-259-7110

WHITE-COLLAR CRIMINAL DEFENSE

Ann Arbor

Don Ferris · ⑩ · Ferris & Salter · 4158 Washtenaw Avenue · Ann Arbor, MI 48108 · 734-677-2020

Douglas R. Mullkoff · Kessler, Mulkoff & Hooberman · 402 West Liberty Street · Ann Arbor, MI 48103 · 734-761-8585

Thomas C. O'Brien · Miller Canfield Paddock and Stone · http://www.millercanfield.com · 101 North Main Street, Seventh Floor · Ann Arbor, MI 48104-1400 · 734-663-2445

John A. Shea · John A. Shea · 120 North Fourth Avenue · Ann Arbor, MI 48104 · 734-995-4646

Joseph A. Simon · Simon & Geherin · 1310 South Main Street, Suite 11 · Ann Arbor, MI 48104 · 734-997-0870

Birmingham

Neil H. Fink · ㉕ · Law Offices of Neil H. Fink · 185 Oakland Avenue, Suite 250 · Birmingham, MI 48009 · 248-258-3181

Bloomfield Hills

Steven J. Fishman · Fishman Group · 40950 Woodward Avenue, Suite 350 · Bloomfield Hills, MI 48304 · 248-258-8700

Robert S. Harrison · ㉕ · Robert Harrison & Associates · 200 East Long Lake Road, Suite 110 · Bloomfield Hills, MI 48304 · 248-283-1600

Walter J. Piszczatowski · Hertz Schram · 1760 South Telegraph Road, Suite 300 · Bloomfield Hills, MI 48302-0183 · 248-335-5000

Detroit

Anthony T. Chambers · Anthony T. Chambers · 220 West Congress Street, Fifth Floor · Detroit, MI 48226 · 313-964-5557

David F. DuMouchel · ㉕ · Butzel Long · http://www.butzel.com · 150 West Jefferson Avenue, Suite 100 · Detroit, MI 48226 · 313-225-7000

Robert M. Morgan · ⑩ · Robert M. Morgan · Ford Building, Suite 1125 · 615 Griswold Street · Detroit, MI 48226-4211 · 313-961-7070

James C. Thomas · Plunkett Cooney · Buhl Building, Suite 2400 · 535 Griswold Street · Detroit, MI 48226 · 313-965-3900

Richard E. Zuckerman · Honigman Miller Schwartz and Cohn · First National Building, Suite 2290 · 660 Woodward Avenue · Detroit, MI 48226-3506 · 313-465-7000

Grand Rapids

James S. Brady · Miller Johnson · http://www.millerjohnson.com · Calder Plaza Building, Suite 800 · 250 Monroe Avenue, NW · P.O. Box 306 · Grand Rapids, MI 49503-2250 · 616-831-1700

Charles E. Chamberlain, Jr. · Willey & Chamberlain · 940 Trust Building · 40 Pearl Street, NW · Grand Rapids, MI 49503 · 616-458-2212

Paul L. Mitchell · Mitchell & Zambon · 161 Ottawa Avenue, NW, Suite 507 · Grand Rapids, MI 49503 · 616-456-7831

Larry C. Willey · ⑩ · Willey & Chamberlain · 940 Trust Building · 40 Pearl Street, NW · Grand Rapids, MI 49503 · 616-458-2212

Kalamazoo

Randall S. Levine · Levine & Levine · http://www.levine-levine.com · 427 South Burdick Street · Kalamazoo, MI 49007 · 269-382-0444

Lansing

Donald E. Martin · Foster, Swift, Collins & Smith · http://www.fosterswift.com · 313 South Washington Square · Lansing, MI 48933-2193 · 517-371-8100

Frank H. Reynolds · The Reynolds Law Firm · Oakhill Professional Park, Suite A · 2400 Lake Lansing Road · Lansing, MI 48912-3674 · 517-372-0676

Southfield

Christopher A. Andreoff · Jaffe Raitt Heuer & Weiss · 27777 Franklin Road, Suite 2500 · Southfield, MI 48034-8214 · 248-351-3000

Troy

Thomas W. Cranmer · ⑩ · Miller Canfield Paddock and Stone · http://www.millercanfield.com · 840 West Long Lake Road, Suite 200 · Troy, MI 48098-6358 · 248-879-2000

Matthew F. Leitman · Miller Canfield Paddock and Stone · http://www.millercanfield.com · 840 West Long Lake Road, Suite 200 · Troy, MI 48098-6358 · 248-879-2000

WORKERS' COMPENSATION LAW

Bingham Farms

Donald G. Ducey · ⑩ · Conklin Benham · Bingham Center, Suite 2580 · 30700 Telegraph Road · Bingham Farms, MI 48025 · 248-593-2450

T. F. Felker, Jr. · Conklin Benham · Bingham Center, Suite 2580 · 30700 Telegraph Road · Bingham Farms, MI 48025 · 248-593-2450

Walter Noeske · Conklin Benham · Bingham Center, Suite 2580 · 30700 Telegraph Road · Bingham Farms, MI 48025 · 248-593-2450

Birmingham

Gerald M. Marcinkoski · Lacey & Jones · 600 South Adams Road, Suite 300 · Birmingham, MI 48009-6827 · 248-433-1414

Detroit

Norton J. Cohen · ⑩ · Miller Cohen · http://www.millercohen.com · 600 West Lafayette Boulevard, Fourth Floor · Detroit, MI 48226-0840 · 313-964-4454

East Lansing

Michael S. Brenton · Murphy, Brenton & Spagnuolo · 4572 South Hagadorn, Suite 1-A · East Lansing, MI 48823 · 517-351-2020

Farmington Hills

Myron B. Charfoos · Charfoos, Reiter, Peterson, Jones, Dorland & Hébert · 30500 Northwestern Highway, Suite 200 · Farmington Hills, MI 46334-3179 · 248-826-7300

James Reiter · Charfoos, Reiter, Peterson, Jones, Dorland & Hébert · 30500 Northwestern Highway, Suite 200 · Farmington Hills, MI 46334-3179 · 248-826-7300

Grand Rapids

Leonard M. Hickey · Hickey Combs · 3358 Eagle Run Drive, Suite 100 · Grand Rapids, MI 49525 · 616-364-2550

Kenneth R. Oosterhouse · ⑩ · Farr Oosterhouse & Krissoff · Ledyard Building, Suite 333 · 125 Ottawa Avenue, NW · Grand Rapids, MI 49503 · 616-459-3355

Richard R. Symons · Varnum, Riddering, Schmidt & Howlett · Bridgewater Place · 333 Bridge Street, NW · P.O. Box 352 · Grand Rapids, MI 49501-0352 · 616-336-6000

Lansing

Brian G. Goodenough · Foster, Swift, Collins & Smith · http://www.fosterswift.com · 313 South Washington Square · Lansing, MI 48933-2193 · 517-371-8100

Michael D. Sanders · Foster, Swift, Collins & Smith · http://www.fosterswift.com · 313 South Washington Square · Lansing, MI 48933-2193 · 517-371-8100

Mount Clemens

James R. Geroux · Plunkett Cooney · 10 South Main, Suite 400 · Mount Clemens, MI 48043 · 586-465-7000

Southfield

Richard L. Warsh · Richard L. Warsh · 29566 Northwestern Highway, Suite 120 · Southfield, MI 48037 · 248-357-7013

Troy

John P. Charters · ⑩ · Charters, Heck, O'Donnell & Petrulis · 888 West Big Beaver Road, Suite 1490 · Troy, MI 48084-4738 · 248-362-4700

Donald L. Petrulis · Charters, Heck, O'Donnell & Petrulis · 888 West Big Beaver Road, Suite 1490 · Troy, MI 48084-4738 · 248-362-4700

MINNESOTA

ALTERNATIVE DISPUTE RESOLUTION

Eden Prairie

Robert G. Schiefelbein · Robert G. Schiefelbein · 10125 Juniper Lane · Eden Prairie, MN 55347 · 952-944-1618

Fairmont

Michael T. O'Rourke · Erickson Zierke Kuderer Madsen · 114 West Second Street · Fairmont, MN 56031 · 507-238-4711

Fergus Falls

Richard L. Pemberton, Sr. · a · Pemberton, Sorlie, Rufer & Kershner · Law Office Building · 110 North Mill Street · P.O. Box 866 · Fergus Falls, MN 56538-0866 · 218-736-5493

Minneapolis

Gregory M. Bistram · Briggs and Morgan · IDS Center, Suite 2200 · 80 South Eighth Street · Minneapolis, MN 55402 · 612-977-8400

R. Scott Davies · a · Briggs and Morgan · IDS Center, Suite 2200 · 80 South Eighth Street · Minneapolis, MN 55402 · 612-977-8400

Thomas S. Fraser · Fredrikson & Byron · 200 South Sixth Street, Suite 4000 · Minneapolis, MN 55402-1425 · 612-492-7000

John M. Harens · Moore, Costello & Hart · International Centre I, Suite 1500 · 900 Second Avenue South Minneapolis, MN 55402-5079 · 612-673-0148

Lowell J. Noteboom · a · Leonard, Street and Deinard · http://www.leonard.com · 150 South Fifth Street, Suite 2300 · Minneapolis, MN 55402 · 612-335-1500

Michael R. O'Brien · Leonard, O'Brien, Spencer Gayle & Sayre · 100 South Fifth Street, Suite 2500 · Minneapolis, MN 55402 · 612-332-1030

Lewis A. Remele, Jr. · a · Bassford Remele · http://www.bassford.com · 33 South Sixth Street, Suite 3800 Minneapolis, MN 55402-3707 · 612-333-3000

Leo G. Stern · Fredrikson & Byron · 200 South Sixth Street, Suite 4000 · Minneapolis, MN 55402-1425 · 612-492-7000

ANTITRUST LAW

Minneapolis

Peter W. Carter · Dorsey & Whitney · 50 South Sixth Street, Suite 1500 · Minneapolis, MN 55402-1498 · 612-340-2600

Robert L. DeMay · Leonard, Street and Deinard · http://www.leonard.com · 150 South Fifth Street, Suite 2300 · Minneapolis, MN 55402 · 612-335-1500

Richard A. Duncan · a · Faegre & Benson · Wells Fargo Center, Suite 2200 · 90 South Seventh Street · Minneapolis, MN 55402-3901 · 612-766-7000

William L. Greene · Leonard, Street and Deinard · http://www.leonard.com · 150 South Fifth Street, Suite 2300 · Minneapolis, MN 55402 · 612-335-1500

Michael A. Lindsay · Dorsey & Whitney · 50 South Sixth Street, Suite 1500 · Minneapolis, MN 55402-1498 · 612-340-2600

Brian B. O'Neill · a · Faegre & Benson · Wells Fargo Center, Suite 2200 · 90 South Seventh Street · Minneapolis, MN 55402-3901 · 612-766-7000

Daniel R. Shulman · a · Gray, Plant, Mooty, Mooty & Bennett · IDS Center, Suite 500 · 80 South Eighth Street · Minneapolis, MN 55402-3796 · 612-632-3000

APPELLATE LAW

Minneapolis

Thomas H. Boyd · Winthrop & Weinstine · http://www.winthrop.com · 225 South Sixth Street, Suite 3500 Minneapolis, MN 55402-4629 · 612-604-6400

Samuel L. Hanson · Briggs and Morgan · IDS Center, Suite 2200 · 80 South Eighth Street · Minneapolis, MN 55402 · 612-977-8400

David F. Herr · a · Maslon Edelman Borman & Brand · 3300 Wells Fargo Center · 90 South Seventh Street · Minneapolis, MN 55402-4140 · 612-672-8200

Kay Nord Hunt · Lommen, Abdo, Cole, King & Stageberg · 2000 IDS Center · 80 South Eighth Street · Minneapolis, MN 55402 · 612-339-8131

Charles E. Lundberg · Bassford Remele · http://www.bassford.com · 33 South Sixth Street, Suite 3800 · Minneapolis, MN 55402-3707 · 612-333-3000

Marianne D. Short · Dorsey & Whitney · 50 South Sixth Street, Suite 1500 · Minneapolis, MN 55402-1498 · 612-340-2600

Michael J. Wahoske · Dorsey & Whitney · 50 South Sixth Street, Suite 1500 · Minneapolis, MN 55402-1498 · 612-340-2600

BANKING LAW

Minneapolis

Kevin M. Busch · Moss & Barnett · http://www.moss-barnett.com · Wells Fargo Center, Suite 4800 · 90 South Seventh Street · Minneapolis, MN 55402-4129 · 612-877-5000

J. Kevin Costley · a · Lindquist & Vennum · http://www.lindquist.com · IDS Center, Suite 4200 · 80 South Eighth Street · Minneapolis, MN 55402-2205 · 612-371-3211

Edward J. Drenttel · a · Winthrop & Weinstine · http://www.winthrop.com · 225 South Sixth Street, Suite 3500 · Minneapolis, MN 55402-4629 · 612-604-6400

Lynn M. Gardin · Fredrikson & Byron · 200 South Sixth Street, Suite 4000 · Minneapolis, MN 55402-1425 · 612-492-7000

L. Joseph Genereux · Dorsey & Whitney · 50 South Sixth Street, Suite 1500 · Minneapolis, MN 55402-1498 · 612-340-2600

Karen L. Grandstrand · Fredrikson & Byron · 200 South Sixth Street, Suite 4000 · Minneapolis, MN 55402-1425 · 612-492-7000

Charles R. Haynor · a · Briggs and Morgan · IDS Center, Suite 2200 · 80 South Eighth Street · Minneapolis, MN 55402 · 612-977-8400

Richard A. Hoel · a · Winthrop & Weinstine · http://www.winthrop.com · 225 South Sixth Street, Suite 3500 · Minneapolis, MN 55402-4629 · 612-604-6400

Jon J. Hoganson · Winthrop & Weinstine · http://www.winthrop.com · 225 South Sixth Street, Suite 3500 Minneapolis, MN 55402-4629 · 612-604-6400

Steven J. Johnson · a · Lindquist & Vennum · http://www.lindquist.com · IDS Center, Suite 4200 · 80 South Eighth Street · Minneapolis, MN 55402-2205 · 612-371-3211

David Kantor · Leonard, Street and Deinard · http://www.leonard.com · 150 South Fifth Street, Suite 2300 · Minneapolis, MN 55402 · 612-335-1500

Jay L. Kim · Dorsey & Whitney · 50 South Sixth Street, Suite 1500 · Minneapolis, MN 55402-1498 · 612-340-2600

James M. Pfau · Faegre & Benson · Wells Fargo Center, Suite 2200 · 90 South Seventh Street · Minneapolis, MN 55402-3901 · 612-766-7000

Donald C. Shepard · Faegre & Benson · Wells Fargo Center, Suite 2200 · 90 South Seventh Street · Minneapolis, MN 55402-3901 · 612-766-7000

James P. Stephenson · a · Faegre & Benson · Wells Fargo Center, Suite 2200 · 90 South Seventh Street Minneapolis, MN 55402-3901 · 612-766-7000

Patrick W. Weber · Winthrop & Weinstine · http://www.winthrop.com · 225 South Sixth Street, Suite 3500 · Minneapolis, MN 55402-4629 · 612-604-6400

Mark W. Westra · a · Fabyanske, Westra, Hart & Thomson · http://www.fwhlaw.com · 800 LaSalle Avenue, Suite 1900 · Minneapolis, MN 55402 · 612-338-0115

Robert B. Whitlock · a · Fredrikson & Byron · 200 South Sixth Street, Suite 4000 · Minneapolis, MN 55402-1425 · 612-492-7000

BANKRUPTCY AND CREDITOR-DEBTOR RIGHTS LAW

Minneapolis

James L. Baillie · 2) · Fredrikson & Byron · 200 South Sixth Street, Suite 4000 · Minneapolis, MN 55402-1425 · 612-492-7000

Hart Kuller · Winthrop & Weinstine · http://www.winthrop.com · 225 South Sixth Street, Suite 3500 · Minneapolis, MN 55402-4629 · 612-604-6400

Michael L. Meyer · a · Ravich, Meyer, Kirkman, McGrath & Nauman · 4545 IDS Center · 80 South Eighth Street · Minneapolis, MN 55402 · 612-332-8511

James A. Rubenstein · Moss & Barnett · http://www.moss-barnett.com · Wells Fargo Center, Suite 4800 · 90 South Seventh Street · Minneapolis, MN 55402-4129 · 612-877-5000

Michael R. Stewart · a · Faegre & Benson · Wells Fargo Center, Suite 2200 · 90 South Seventh Street · Minneapolis, MN 55402-3901 · 612-766-7000

St. Cloud

Philip L. Kunkel · a · Gray, Plant, Mooty, Mooty & Bennett · 1010 West St. German Street, Suite 600 · St. Cloud, MN 56301-3406 · 320-252-4414

BET-THE-COMPANY LITIGATION

Minneapolis

Joseph W. Anthony · Anthony Ostlund & Baer · 3600 Wells Fargo Building · 90 South Seventh Street · Minneapolis, MN 55402 · 612-349-6969

Michael V. Ciresi · a · Robins, Kaplan, Miller & Ciresi · 2800 LaSalle Plaza · 800 LaSalle Avenue · Minneapolis, MN 55402 · 612-349-8500

Thomas S. Fraser · Fredrikson & Byron · 200 South Sixth Street, Suite 4000 · Minneapolis, MN 55402-1425 · 612-492-7000

Peter S. Hendrixson · a · Dorsey & Whitney · 50 South Sixth Street, Suite 1500 · Minneapolis, MN 55402-1498 · 612-340-2600

David F. Herr · a · Maslon Edelman Borman & Brand · 3300 Wells Fargo Center · 90 South Seventh Street · Minneapolis, MN 55402-4140 · 612-672-8200

Timothy D. Kelly · 2) · Kelly & Berens · IDS Center, Suite 3720 · 80 South Eighth Street · Minneapolis, MN 55402 · 612-349-6171

Andrew M. Luger · Greene Espel · 200 South Sixth Street, Suite 1200 · Minneapolis, MN 55402-1415 · 612-373-0830

Brian B. O'Neill · a · Faegre & Benson · Wells Fargo Center, Suite 2200 · 90 South Seventh Street · Minneapolis, MN 55402-3901 · 612-766-7000

Lewis A. Remele, Jr. · a · Bassford Remele · http://www.bassford.com · 33 South Sixth Street, Suite 3800 Minneapolis, MN 55402-3707 · 612-333-3000

COMMERCIAL LITIGATION

Duluth

Steven C. Overom · Maki & Overom · 31 West Superior Street, Suite 402 · Duluth, MN 55802 · 218-726-0805

Minneapolis

David A. Allgeyer · Lindquist & Vennum · http://www.lindquist.com · IDS Center, Suite 4200 · 80 South Eighth Street · Minneapolis, MN 55402-2205 · 612-371-3211

Joseph W. Anthony · Anthony Ostlund & Baer · 3600 Wells Fargo Building · 90 South Seventh Street · Minneapolis, MN 55402 · 612-349-6969

Thomas H. Boyd · Winthrop & Weinstine · http://www.winthrop.com · 225 South Sixth Street, Suite 3500 Minneapolis, MN 55402-4629 · 612-604-6400

Mark Briol · Briol & Associates · 3700 IDS Center · 80 South Eighth Street · Minneapolis, MN 55402 · 612-337-8410

James G. Bullard · Leonard, Street and Deinard · http://www.leonard.com · 150 South Fifth Street, Suite 2300 · Minneapolis, MN 55402 · 612-335-1500

Peter W. Carter · Dorsey & Whitney · 50 South Sixth Street, Suite 1500 · Minneapolis, MN 55402-1498 · 612-340-2600

Michael V. Ciresi · a · Robins, Kaplan, Miller & Ciresi · 2800 LaSalle Plaza · 800 LaSalle Avenue · Minneapolis, MN 55402 · 612-349-8500

Michael R. Cunningham · Gray, Plant, Mooty, Mooty & Bennett · IDS Center, Suite 500 · 80 South Eighth Street · Minneapolis, MN 55402-3796 · 612-632-3000

R. Scott Davies · a · Briggs and Morgan · IDS Center, Suite 2200 · 80 South Eighth Street · Minneapolis, MN 55402 · 612-977-8400

Robert L. DeMay · Leonard, Street and Deinard · http://www.leonard.com · 150 South Fifth Street, Suite 2300 · Minneapolis, MN 55402 · 612-335-1500

Craig D. Diviney · a · Dorsey & Whitney · 50 South Sixth Street, Suite 1500 · Minneapolis, MN 55402-1498 · 612-340-2600

Joseph T. Dixon, Jr. · Henson & Efron · 220 South Sixth Street, Suite 1800 · Minneapolis, MN 55402-4503 · 612-339-2500

Lawrence J. Field · a · Leonard, Street and Deinard · http://www.leonard.com · 150 South Fifth Street, Suite 2300 · Minneapolis, MN 55402 · 612-335-1500

Terrence J. Fleming · Lindquist & Vennum · http://www.lindquist.com · IDS Center, Suite 4200 · 80 South Eighth Street · Minneapolis, MN 55402-2205 · 612-371-3211

David C. Forsberg · 2% · Briggs and Morgan · IDS Center, Suite 2200 · 80 South Eighth Street · Minneapolis, MN 55402 · 612-977-8400

Thomas S. Fraser · Fredrikson & Byron · 200 South Sixth Street, Suite 4000 · Minneapolis, MN 55402-1425 · 612-492-7000

Terence M. Fruth · 2) · Fruth, Jamison & Elsass · 3902 IDS Center · 80 South Eighth Street · Minneapolis, MN 55402 · 612-344-9700

John B. Gordon · Faegre & Benson · Wells Fargo Center, Suite 2200 · 90 South Seventh Street · Minneapolis, MN 55402-3901 · 612-766-7000

Clifford M. Greene · Greene Espel · 200 South Sixth Street, Suite 1200 · Minneapolis, MN 55402-1415 · 612-373-0830

William L. Greene · Leonard, Street and Deinard · http://www.leonard.com · 150 South Fifth Street, Suite 2300 · Minneapolis, MN 55402 · 612-335-1500

Samuel L. Hanson · Briggs and Morgan · IDS Center, Suite 2200 · 80 South Eighth Street · Minneapolis, MN 55402 · 612-977-8400

Peter S. Hendrixson · a · Dorsey & Whitney · 50 South Sixth Street, Suite 1500 · Minneapolis, MN 55402-1498 · 612-340-2600

Robert J. Hennessey · a · Lindquist & Vennum · http://www.lindquist.com · IDS Center, Suite 4200 · 80 South Eighth Street · Minneapolis, MN 55402-2205 · 612-371-3211

David F. Herr · a · Maslon Edelman Borman & Brand · 3300 Wells Fargo Center · 90 South Seventh Street · Minneapolis, MN 55402-4140 · 612-672-8200

Richard Ihrig · Lindquist & Vennum · http://www.lindquist.com · IDS Center, Suite 4200 · 80 South Eighth Street · Minneapolis, MN 55402-2205 · 612-371-3211

Geoffrey P. Jarpe · Winthrop & Weinstine · http://www.winthrop.com · 225 South Sixth Street, Suite 3500 · Minneapolis, MN 55402-4629 · 612-604-6400

Randall E. Kahnke · Faegre & Benson · Wells Fargo Center, Suite 2200 · 90 South Seventh Street · Minneapolis, MN 55402-3901 · 612-766-7000

Elliot S. Kaplan · 2) · Robins, Kaplan, Miller & Ciresi · 2800 LaSalle Plaza · 800 LaSalle Avenue · Minneapolis, MN 55402 · 612-349-8500

Timothy D. Kelly · 2) · Kelly & Berens · IDS Center, Suite 3720 · 80 South Eighth Street · Minneapolis, MN 55402 · 612-349-6171

Martin R. Lueck · Robins, Kaplan, Miller & Ciresi · 2800 LaSalle Plaza · 800 LaSalle Avenue · Minneapolis, MN 55402 · 612-349-8500

Andrew M. Luger · Greene Espel · 200 South Sixth Street, Suite 1200 · Minneapolis, MN 55402-1415 · 612-373-0830

Alan H. Maclin · Briggs and Morgan · IDS Center, Suite 2200 · 80 South Eighth Street · Minneapolis, MN 55402 · 612-977-8400

Roger J. Magnuson · Dorsey & Whitney · 50 South Sixth Street, Suite 1500 · Minneapolis, MN 55402-1498 · 612-340-2600

John J. McDonald, Jr. · Meagher & Geer · http://www.meagher.com · 33 South Sixth Street, Suite 4400 · Minneapolis, MN 55402 · 612-338-0661

Frederick W. Morris · Leonard, Street and Deinard · http://www.leonard.com · 150 South Fifth Street, Suite 2300 · Minneapolis, MN 55402 · 612-335-1500

Thomas F. Nelson · Leonard, Street and Deinard · http://www.leonard.com · 150 South Fifth Street, Suite 2300 · Minneapolis, MN 55402 · 612-335-1500

Lowell J. Noteboom · a · Leonard, Street and Deinard · http://www.leonard.com · 150 South Fifth Street, Suite 2300 · Minneapolis, MN 55402 · 612-335-1500

Todd A. Noteboom · Leonard, Street and Deinard · http://www.leonard.com · 150 South Fifth Street, Suite 2300 · Minneapolis, MN 55402 · 612-335-1500

Brian B. O'Neill · a · Faegre & Benson · Wells Fargo Center, Suite 2200 · 90 South Seventh Street · Minneapolis, MN 55402-3901 · 612-766-7000

Richard T. Ostlund · Anthony Ostlund & Baer · 3600 Wells Fargo Building · 90 South Seventh Street · Minneapolis, MN 55402 · 612-349-6969

David P. Pearson · Winthrop & Weinstine · http://www.winthrop.com · 225 South Sixth Street, Suite 3500 · Minneapolis, MN 55402-4629 · 612-604-6400

William Z. Pentelovitch · a · Maslon Edelman Borman & Brand · 3300 Wells Fargo Center · 90 South Seventh Street · Minneapolis, MN 55402-4140 · 612-672-8200

Lewis A. Remele, Jr. · a · Bassford Remele · http://www.bassford.com · 33 South Sixth Street, Suite 3800 Minneapolis, MN 55402-3707 · 612-333-3000

James F. Roegge · Meagher & Geer · http://www.meagher.com · 33 South Sixth Street, Suite 4400 · Minneapolis, MN 55402 · 612-338-0661

Charles B. Rogers · Briggs and Morgan · IDS Center, Suite 2200 · 80 South Eighth Street · Minneapolis, MN 55402 · 612-977-8400

Allen I. Saeks · Leonard, Street and Deinard · http://www.leonard.com · 150 South Fifth Street, Suite 2300 · Minneapolis, MN 55402 · 612-335-1500

Robert L. Schnell, Jr. · Faegre & Benson · Wells Fargo Center, Suite 2200 · 90 South Seventh Street · Minneapolis, MN 55402-3901 · 612-766-7000

Marianne D. Short · Dorsey & Whitney · 50 South Sixth Street, Suite 1500 · Minneapolis, MN 55402-1498 · 612-340-2600

Daniel R. Shulman · a · Gray, Plant, Mooty, Mooty & Bennett · IDS Center, Suite 500 · 80 South Eighth Street · Minneapolis, MN 55402-3796 · 612-632-3000

Alan I. Silver · Bassford Remele · http://www.bassford.com · 33 South Sixth Street, Suite 3800 · Minneapolis, MN 55402-3707 · 612-333-3000

James S. Simonson · 2% · Gray, Plant, Mooty, Mooty & Bennett · IDS Center, Suite 500 · 80 South Eighth Street · Minneapolis, MN 55402-3796 · 612-632-3000

Peter W. Sipkins · a · Dorsey & Whitney · 50 South Sixth Street, Suite 1500 · Minneapolis, MN 55402-1498 · 612-340-2600

Jerry W. Snider · Faegre & Benson · Wells Fargo Center, Suite 2200 · 90 South Seventh Street · Minneapolis, MN 55402-3901 · 612-766-7000

Stephen J. Snyder · a · Snyder & Snyder · 100 South Fifth Street, Suite 410 · Minneapolis, MN 55402 · 612-787-3100

Byron E. Starns · a · Leonard, Street and Deinard · http://www.leonard.com · 150 South Fifth Street, Suite 2300 · Minneapolis, MN 55402 · 612-335-1500

Jan D. Stuurmans · a · Jan Stuurmans · 12 South Sixth Street, Suite 1008 · Minneapolis, MN 55402 · 612-336-4455

Madge S. Thorsen · Thorsen Kaplan · 310 Groveland Avenue · Minneapolis, MN 55403 · 612-767-3040

Thomas W. Tinkham · 2) · Dorsey & Whitney · 50 South Sixth Street, Suite 1500 · Minneapolis, MN 55402-1498 · 612-340-2600

James Volling · Faegre & Benson · Wells Fargo Center, Suite 2200 · 90 South Seventh Street · Minneapolis, MN 55402-3901 · 612-766-7000

Charles F. Webber · Faegre & Benson · Wells Fargo Center, Suite 2200 · 90 South Seventh Street · Minneapolis, MN 55402-3901 · 612-766-7000

Robert R. Weinstine · a · Winthrop & Weinstine · http://www.winthrop.com · 225 South Sixth Street, Suite 3500 · Minneapolis, MN 55402-4629 · 612-604-6400

Gregory M. Weyandt · Dorsey & Whitney · 50 South Sixth Street, Suite 1500 · Minneapolis, MN 55402-1498 · 612-340-2600

Wendy J. Wildung · Faegre & Benson · Wells Fargo Center, Suite 2200 · 90 South Seventh Street · Minneapolis, MN 55402-3901 · 612-766-7000

Rochester

Ronald L. Seeger · 2) · Dunlap & Seeger · 206 South Broadway, Suite 505 · P.O. Box 549 · Rochester, MN 55903-0549 · 507-288-9111

CONSTRUCTION LAW

Minneapolis

Marvin T. Fabyanske · Fabyanske, Westra, Hart & Thomson · http://www.fwhlaw.com · 800 LaSalle Avenue, Suite 1900 · Minneapolis, MN 55402 · 612-338-0115

Peter C. Halls · Faegre & Benson · Wells Fargo Center, Suite 2200 · 90 South Seventh Street · Minneapolis, MN 55402-3901 · 612-766-7000

Thomas M. Hart · Winthrop & Weinstine · http://www.winthrop.com · 225 South Sixth Street, Suite 3500 Minneapolis, MN 55402-4629 · 612-604-6400

John H. Hinderaker · Faegre & Benson · Wells Fargo Center, Suite 2200 · 90 South Seventh Street · Minneapolis, MN 55402-3901 · 612-766-7000

David L. Lillehaug · Fredrikson & Byron · 200 South Sixth Street, Suite 4000 · Minneapolis, MN 55402-1425 · 612-492-7000

Steven R. Lindemann · Leonard, Street and Deinard · http://www.leonard.com · 150 South Fifth Street, Suite 2300 · Minneapolis, MN 55402 · 612-335-1500

Lowell J. Noteboom · a · Leonard, Street and Deinard · http://www.leonard.com · 150 South Fifth Street, Suite 2300 · Minneapolis, MN 55402 · 612-335-1500

Timothy M. O'Brien · Faegre & Benson · Wells Fargo Center, Suite 2200 · 90 South Seventh Street · Minneapolis, MN 55402-3901 · 612-766-7000

Patrick John O'Connor, Jr. · Faegre & Benson · Wells Fargo Center, Suite 2200 · 90 South Seventh Street · Minneapolis, MN 55402-3901 · 612-766-7000

Michael G. Taylor · Leonard, Street and Deinard · http://www.leonard.com · 150 South Fifth Street, Suite 2300 · Minneapolis, MN 55402 · 612-335-1500

CORPORATE GOVERNANCE AND COMPLIANCE LAW

Minneapolis

Philip S. Garon · a · Faegre & Benson · Wells Fargo Center, Suite 2200 · 90 South Seventh Street · Minneapolis, MN 55402-3901 · 612-766-7000

Timothy S. Hearn · Dorsey & Whitney · 50 South Sixth Street, Suite 1500 · Minneapolis, MN 55402-1498 · 612-340-2600

Charles P. Moorse · a · Lindquist & Vennum · http://www.lindquist.com · IDS Center, Suite 4200 · 80 South Eighth Street · Minneapolis, MN 55402-2205 · 612-371-3211

Robert A. Rosenbaum · Dorsey & Whitney · 50 South Sixth Street, Suite 1500 · Minneapolis, MN 55402-1498 · 612-340-2600

Jay L. Swanson · Dorsey & Whitney · 50 South Sixth Street, Suite 1500 · Minneapolis, MN 55402-1498 · 612-340-2600

Gary L. Tygesson · Dorsey & Whitney · 50 South Sixth Street, Suite 1500 · Minneapolis, MN 55402-1498 · 612-340-2600

David M. Vander Haar · Faegre & Benson · Wells Fargo Center, Suite 2200 · 90 South Seventh Street · Minneapolis, MN 55402-3901 · 612-766-7000

CORPORATE LAW

Minneapolis

Andris A. Baltins · a · Kaplan, Strangis and Kaplan · 5500 Wells Fargo Center · 90 South Seventh Street · Minneapolis, MN 55402 · 612-375-1138

William R. Busch · a · Faegre & Benson · Wells Fargo Center, Suite 2200 · 90 South Seventh Street · Minneapolis, MN 55402-3901 · 612-766-7000

Kenneth L. Cutler · Dorsey & Whitney · 50 South Sixth Street, Suite 1500 · Minneapolis, MN 55402-1498 · 612-340-2600

Stanley Efron · 2) · Henson & Efron · 220 South Sixth Street, Suite 1800 · Minneapolis, MN 55402-4503 612-339-2500

Bruce M. Engler · Faegre & Benson · Wells Fargo Center, Suite 2200 · 90 South Seventh Street · Minneapolis, MN 55402-3901 · 612-766-7000

Lynn M. Gardin · Fredrikson & Byron · 200 South Sixth Street, Suite 4000 · Minneapolis, MN 55402-1425 · 612-492-7000

Philip S. Garon · a · Faegre & Benson · Wells Fargo Center, Suite 2200 · 90 South Seventh Street · Minneapolis, MN 55402-3901 · 612-766-7000

David C. Grorud · Fredrikson & Byron · 200 South Sixth Street, Suite 4000 · Minneapolis, MN 55402-1425 · 612-492-7000

Andrew G. Humphrey · Faegre & Benson · Wells Fargo Center, Suite 2200 · 90 South Seventh Street · Minneapolis, MN 55402-3901 · 612-766-7000

Susan L. Jacobson · Faegre & Benson · Wells Fargo Center, Suite 2200 · 90 South Seventh Street · Minneapolis, MN 55402-3901 · 612-766-7000

Samuel L. Kaplan · 2) · Kaplan, Strangis and Kaplan · 5500 Wells Fargo Center · 90 South Seventh Street Minneapolis, MN 55402 · 612-375-1138

D. William Kaufman · Oppenheimer Wolff & Donnelly · Plaza VII, Suite 3300 · 45 South Seventh Street Minneapolis, MN 55402 · 612-607-7000

Richard J. Kelber · Moss & Barnett · http://www.moss-barnett.com · Wells Fargo Center, Suite 4800 · 90 South Seventh Street · Minneapolis, MN 55402-4129 · 612-877-5000

Steven C. Kennedy · Faegre & Benson · Wells Fargo Center, Suite 2200 · 90 South Seventh Street · Minneapolis, MN 55402-3901 · 612-766-7000

Thomas R. King · Fredrikson & Byron · 200 South Sixth Street, Suite 4000 · Minneapolis, MN 55402-1425 · 612-492-7000

Richard G. Lareau · 2% · Oppenheimer Wolff & Donnelly · Plaza VII, Suite 3300 · 45 South Seventh Street · Minneapolis, MN 55402 · 612-607-7000

Thomas A. Letscher · Oppenheimer Wolff & Donnelly · Plaza VII, Suite 3300 · 45 South Seventh Street · Minneapolis, MN 55402 · 612-607-7000

Keith A. Libbey · a · Fredrikson & Byron · 200 South Sixth Street, Suite 4000 · Minneapolis, MN 55402-1425 · 612-492-7000

Bruce A. Machmeier · Oppenheimer Wolff & Donnelly · Plaza VII, Suite 3300 · 45 South Seventh Street Minneapolis, MN 55402 · 612-607-7000

Gale R. Mellum · a · Mellum & Welsh · 3833 Thomas Avenue South · Minneapolis, MN 55410 · 612-819-4213

David B. Miller · Faegre & Benson · Wells Fargo Center, Suite 2200 · 90 South Seventh Street · Minneapolis, MN 55402-3901 · 612-766-7000

Charles P. Moorse · a · Lindquist & Vennum · http://www.lindquist.com · IDS Center, Suite 4200 · 80 South Eighth Street · Minneapolis, MN 55402-2205 · 612-371-3211

Thomas G. Morgan · a · Faegre & Benson · Wells Fargo Center, Suite 2200 · 90 South Seventh Street · Minneapolis, MN 55402-3901 · 612-766-7000

William B. Payne · Dorsey & Whitney · 50 South Sixth Street, Suite 1500 · Minneapolis, MN 55402-1498 612-340-2600

Richard G. Pepin, Jr. · Leonard, Street and Deinard · http://www.leonard.com · 150 South Fifth Street, Suite 2300 · Minneapolis, MN 55402 · 612-335-1500

Robert K. Ranum · Fredrikson & Byron · 200 South Sixth Street, Suite 4000 · Minneapolis, MN 55402-1425 · 612-492-7000

Robert A. Rosenbaum · Dorsey & Whitney · 50 South Sixth Street, Suite 1500 · Minneapolis, MN 55402-1498 · 612-340-2600

Thomas P. Sanders · Leonard, Street and Deinard · http://www.leonard.com · 150 South Fifth Street, Suite 2300 · Minneapolis, MN 55402 · 612-335-1500

Timothy J. Scallen · Oppenheimer Wolff & Donnelly · Plaza VII, Suite 3300 · 45 South Seventh Street · Minneapolis, MN 55402 · 612-607-7000

Kris Sharpe · a · Faegre & Benson · Wells Fargo Center, Suite 2200 · 90 South Seventh Street · Minneapolis, MN 55402-3901 · 612-766-7000

Morris M. Sherman · 2) · Leonard, Street and Deinard · http://www.leonard.com · 150 South Fifth Street, Suite 2300 · Minneapolis, MN 55402 · 612-335-1500

Roger V. Stageberg · a · Lommen, Abdo, Cole, King & Stageberg · 2000 IDS Center · 80 South Eighth Street · Minneapolis, MN 55402 · 612-339-8131

James P. Stephenson · a · Faegre & Benson · Wells Fargo Center, Suite 2200 · 90 South Seventh Street Minneapolis, MN 55402-3901 · 612-766-7000

Ralph Strangis · 2) · Kaplan, Strangis and Kaplan · 5500 Wells Fargo Center · 90 South Seventh Street · Minneapolis, MN 55402 · 612-375-1138

Jay L. Swanson · Dorsey & Whitney · 50 South Sixth Street, Suite 1500 · Minneapolis, MN 55402-1498 · 612-340-2600

David M. Vander Haar · Faegre & Benson · Wells Fargo Center, Suite 2200 · 90 South Seventh Street · Minneapolis, MN 55402-3901 · 612-766-7000

Albert A. Woodward · Leonard, Street and Deinard · http://www.leonard.com · 150 South Fifth Street, Suite 2300 · Minneapolis, MN 55402 · 612-335-1500

John F. Wurm · Fredrikson & Byron · 200 South Sixth Street, Suite 4000 · Minneapolis, MN 55402-1425 612-492-7000

DUI/DWI DEFENSE

Barrett

Kent D. Marshall · Kent D. Marshall · 15086 Two-Hundred-Twentieth Street · Barrett, MN 56311-0097 320-528-2564

Bloomington

Douglas V. Hazelton · Halberg Criminal Defense · http://www.halbergdefense.com · Northland Plaza Building, Suite 1590 · 3800 American Boulevard · Bloomington, MN 55431 · 952-224-4848

Eagan

Jeffrey S. Sheridan · Strandemo, Sheridan & Dulas · 1380 Corporate Center Curve, Suite 320 · Eagan, MN 55121 · 651-686-8800

Mendota Heights

David L. Ayers · Ayers & Riehm · Riverwood Place, Suite 100 · 880 Sibley Memorial Highway · Mendota Heights, MN 55118-1736 · 651-552-8400

Minneapolis

John C. Brink · Brink & Gerdts · 331Second Avenue South, Suite 110 · Minneapolis, MN 55401 · 612-371-0722

Charles L. Hawkins · a · Charles L. Hawkins · 150 South Fifth Street, Suite 3260 · Minneapolis, MN 55402 · 612-339-6921

Faison T. Sessoms · F. T. Sessoms · http://sessoms.com · Tritech Office Center, Suite 840 · 331 Second Avenue South · Minneapolis, MN 55401 · 612-344-1505

David L. Valentini · Valentini & Associates · 247 Third Avenue South · Minneapolis, MN 55415 · 612-341-0900

Shakopee

Samuel A. McCloud · Samuel A. McCloud · P.O. Box 216 · Shakopee, MN 55379 · 952-445-6595

ELDER LAW

St. Paul

Jeffrey W. Schmidt · a · Schmitz & Schmidt · 400 North Robert Street, Suite 1840 · St. Paul, MN 55101 651-291-2405

Stuart E. Schmitz · Schmitz & Schmidt · 400 North Robert Street, Suite 1840 · St. Paul, MN 55101 · 651-291-2405

EMINENT DOMAIN AND CONDEMNATION LAW

Minneapolis

Steven K. Champlin · Dorsey & Whitney · 50 South Sixth Street, Suite 1500 · Minneapolis, MN 55402-1498 · 612-340-2600

John E. Drawz · Fredrikson & Byron · 200 South Sixth Street, Suite 4000 · Minneapolis, MN 55402-1425 612-492-7000

Bruce D. Malkerson · Malkerson Gilliland Martin · U.S. Bank Plaza South, Suite 1900 · 220 South Sixth Street · Minneapolis, MN 55402-4502 · 612-344-1111

Daniel N. Rosen · Parker Rosen · 133 First Avenue North · Minneapolis, MN 55401 · 612-767-3000

Howard A. Roston · Malkerson Gilliland Martin · U.S. Bank Plaza South, Suite 1900 · 220 South Sixth Street · Minneapolis, MN 55402-4502 · 612-344-1111

Mark D. Savin · Faegre & Benson · Wells Fargo Center, Suite 2200 · 90 South Seventh Street · Minneapolis, MN 55402-3901 · 612-766-7000

EMPLOYEE BENEFITS LAW

Minneapolis

Leslie Anderson · Dorsey & Whitney · 50 South Sixth Street, Suite 1500 · Minneapolis, MN 55402-1498 612-340-2600

Mark E. Baumann · Maslon Edelman Borman & Brand · 3300 Wells Fargo Center · 90 South Seventh Street · Minneapolis, MN 55402-4140 · 612-672-8200

Brian G. Belisle · a · Oppenheimer Wolff & Donnelly · Plaza VII, Suite 3300 · 45 South Seventh Street · Minneapolis, MN 55402 · 612-607-7000

Angela M. Bohmann · a · Leonard, Street and Deinard · http://www.leonard.com · 150 South Fifth Street, Suite 2300 · Minneapolis, MN 55402 · 612-335-1500

Jeffrey P. Cairns · Leonard, Street and Deinard · http://www.leonard.com · 150 South Fifth Street, Suite 2300 · Minneapolis, MN 55402 · 612-335-1500

Don D. Carlson · 2) · Dorsey & Whitney · 50 South Sixth Street, Suite 1500 · Minneapolis, MN 55402-1498 · 612-340-2600

Jude Anne Carluccio · Parsinen Kaplan Rosberg & Gotlieb · 100 South Fifth Street, Suite 1100 · Minneapolis, MN 55402-1298 · 612-333-2111

Glenn R. Drury · a · Mackall, Crounse & Moore · 1400 AT&T Tower · 901 Marquette Avenue · Minneapolis, MN 55402 · 612-305-1400

Hubert V. Forcier · 2) · Faegre & Benson · Wells Fargo Center, Suite 2200 · 90 South Seventh Street · Minneapolis, MN 55402-3901 · 612-766-7000

Richard A. Hackett · a · Gray, Plant, Mooty, Mooty & Bennett · IDS Center, Suite 500 · 80 South Eighth Street · Minneapolis, MN 55402-3796 · 612-632-3000

Robert J. Hartman · a · Lindquist & Vennum · http://www.lindquist.com · IDS Center, Suite 4200 · 80 South Eighth Street · Minneapolis, MN 55402-2205 · 612-371-3211

Douglas J. Heffernan · a · Faegre & Benson · Wells Fargo Center, Suite 2200 · 90 South Seventh Street · Minneapolis, MN 55402-3901 · 612-766-7000

Bradley S. Keil · a · Oppenheimer Wolff & Donnelly · Plaza VII, Suite 3300 · 45 South Seventh Street · Minneapolis, MN 55402 · 612-607-7000

Bruce J. McNeil · Leonard, Street and Deinard · http://www.leonard.com · 150 South Fifth Street, Suite 2300 · Minneapolis, MN 55402 · 612-335-1500

John H. Merkle · a · Fredrikson & Byron · 200 South Sixth Street, Suite 4000 · Minneapolis, MN 55402-1425 · 612-492-7000

Richard A. Nelson · a · Faegre & Benson · Wells Fargo Center, Suite 2200 · 90 South Seventh Street · Minneapolis, MN 55402-3901 · 612-766-7000

John M. Nichols · 2) · Gray, Plant, Mooty, Mooty & Bennett · IDS Center, Suite 500 · 80 South Eighth Street · Minneapolis, MN 55402-3796 · 612-632-3000

Timothy R. Quinn · Oppenheimer Wolff & Donnelly · Plaza VII, Suite 3300 · 45 South Seventh Street · Minneapolis, MN 55402 · 612-607-7000

Pam Thein · Oppenheimer Wolff & Donnelly · Plaza VII, Suite 3300 · 45 South Seventh Street · Minneapolis, MN 55402 · 612-607-7000

Thomas A. Walker · Winthrop & Weinstine · http://www.winthrop.com · 225 South Sixth Street, Suite 3500 · Minneapolis, MN 55402-4629 · 612-604-6400

Edward J. Wegerson · Lindquist & Vennum · http://www.lindquist.com · IDS Center, Suite 4200 · 80 South Eighth Street · Minneapolis, MN 55402-2205 · 612-371-3211

ENERGY LAW

Minneapolis

James J. Bertrand · Leonard, Street and Deinard · http://www.leonard.com · 150 South Fifth Street, Suite 2300 · Minneapolis, MN 55402 · 612-335-1500

Michael J. Bradley · Moss & Barnett · http://www.moss-barnett.com · Wells Fargo Center, Suite 4800 · 90 South Seventh Street · Minneapolis, MN 55402-4129 · 612-877-5000

Richard J. Johnson · a · Moss & Barnett · http://www.moss-barnett.com · Wells Fargo Center, Suite 4800 · 90 South Seventh Street · Minneapolis, MN 55402-4129 · 612-877-5000

Michael C. Krikava · Briggs and Morgan · IDS Center, Suite 2200 · 80 South Eighth Street · Minneapolis, MN 55402 · 612-977-8400

Robert S. Lee · a · Mackall, Crounse & Moore · 1400 AT&T Tower · 901 Marquette Avenue · Minneapolis, MN 55402 · 612-305-1400

Byron E. Starns · a · Leonard, Street and Deinard · http://www.leonard.com · 150 South Fifth Street, Suite 2300 · Minneapolis, MN 55402 · 612-335-1500

Eric F. Swanson · Winthrop & Weinstine · http://www.winthrop.com · 225 South Sixth Street, Suite 3500 Minneapolis, MN 55402-4629 · 612-604-6400

Minneapolis

John M. Anderson · Bassford Remele · http://www.bassford.com · 33 South Sixth Street, Suite 3800 · Minneapolis, MN 55402-3707 · 612-333-3000

B. Andrew Brown · Dorsey & Whitney · 50 South Sixth Street, Suite 1500 · Minneapolis, MN 55402-1498 · 612-340-2600

Bob Cattanach · Dorsey & Whitney · 50 South Sixth Street, Suite 1500 · Minneapolis, MN 55402-1498 · 612-340-2600

Dennis M. Coyne · a · Dennis M. Coyne · 821 Marquette Avenue South, Suite 1000 · Minneapolis, MN 55402 · 612-375-0155

Richard A. Duncan · a · Faegre & Benson · Wells Fargo Center, Suite 2200 · 90 South Seventh Street · Minneapolis, MN 55402-3901 · 612-766-7000

Delmar R. Ehrich · Faegre & Benson · Wells Fargo Center, Suite 2200 · 90 South Seventh Street · Minneapolis, MN 55402-3901 · 612-766-7000

Lloyd W. Grooms · Winthrop & Weinstine · http://www.winthrop.com · 225 South Sixth Street, Suite 3500 · Minneapolis, MN 55402-4629 · 612-604-6400

John H. Herman · 2) · Faegre & Benson · Wells Fargo Center, Suite 2200 · 90 South Seventh Street · Minneapolis, MN 55402-3901 · 612-766-7000

Thaddeus R. Lightfoot · Environmental Law Group · 133 First Avenue, North · Minneapolis, MN 55401 612-378-3700

Charles N. Nauen · a · Lockridge Grindal Nauen · 100 Washington Avenue South, Suite 2200 · Minneapolis, MN 55401 · 612-339-6900

Brian B. O'Neill · a · Faegre & Benson · Wells Fargo Center, Suite 2200 · 90 South Seventh Street · Minneapolis, MN 55402-3901 · 612-766-7000

James A. Payne · a · Environmental Law Group · 133 First Avenue, North · Minneapolis, MN 55401 · 612-378-3700

Dennis P. Reis · a · Briggs and Morgan · IDS Center, Suite 2200 · 80 South Eighth Street · Minneapolis, MN 55402 · 612-977-8400

Elizabeth Hendricks Schmiesing · Faegre & Benson · Wells Fargo Center, Suite 2200 · 90 South Seventh Street · Minneapolis, MN 55402-3901 · 612-766-7000

Byron E. Starns · a · Leonard, Street and Deinard · http://www.leonard.com · 150 South Fifth Street, Suite 2300 · Minneapolis, MN 55402 · 612-335-1500

Carolyn V. Wolski · Leonard, Street and Deinard · http://www.leonard.com · 150 South Fifth Street, Suite 2300 · Minneapolis, MN 55402 · 612-335-1500

Edina

Lorraine S. Clugg · Clugg, Linder, Dittberner & Bryant · http://www.cldblaw.com · 3205 West 76th Street, Suite Two · Edina, MN 55435-5244 · 952-896-1099

Michael Dittberner · Clugg, Linder, Dittberner & Bryant · http://www.cldblaw.com · 3205 West 76th Street, Suite Two · Edina, MN 55435-5244 · 952-896-1099

Martin L. Swaden · a · Swaden Law Offices · http://www.swaden.com · 7301 Ohms Lane, Suite 550 · Edina, MN 55439 · 952-832-5990

Faribault

Gary L. Voegele · Voegele Law Firm · 102 Fourth Street, NW · Faribault, MN 55021 · 507-334-2045

Mankato

Joseph P. Bluth · a · Manahan, Bluth & Kohlmeyer Law Office · 110 South Broad Street · P.O. Box 287 · Mankato, MN 56002-0287 · 507-387-5661

Maplewood

Thomas W. Tuft · Tuft & Arnold · 2109 County Road D East · Maplewood, MN 55109-2643 · 651-771-0050

Minneapolis

Nancy Zalusky Berg · a · Walling, Berg & Debele · http://www.wbdlaw.com · 121 South Eighth Street, Suite 1100 · Minneapolis, MN 55402 · 612-340-1150

Gary A. Debele · Walling, Berg & Debele · http://www.wbdlaw.com · 121 South Eighth Street, Suite 1100 · Minneapolis, MN 55402 · 612-340-1150

Alan C. Eidsness · a · Henson & Efron · 220 South Sixth Street, Suite 1800 · Minneapolis, MN 55402-4503 · 612-339-2500

Karim El-Ghazzawy · El-Ghazzawy Law Office · 309 Clifton Avenue · Minneapolis, MN 55403 · 612-659-0199

William F. Forsyth · a · Henson & Efron · 220 South Sixth Street, Suite 1800 · Minneapolis, MN 55402-4503 · 612-339-2500

Richard D. Goff · a · Richard D. Goff & Associates · 3908 IDS Center · 80 South Eighth Street · Minneapolis, MN 55402 · 612-630-0010

Ben M. Henschel · Moss & Barnett · http://www.moss-barnett.com · Wells Fargo Center, Suite 4800 · 90 South Seventh Street · Minneapolis, MN 55402-4129 · 612-877-5000

A. Larry Katz · 2% · Katz, Manka, Teplinsky, Due & Sobol · 225 South Sixth Street, Suite 4150 · Minneapolis, MN 55402 · 612-333-1671

Susan M. Lach · a · Messerli & Kramer · Fifth Street Towers, Suite 1800 · 150 South Fifth Street · Minneapolis, MN 55402-4218 · 612-672-3600

Raymond M. Lazar · a · Fredrikson & Byron · 200 South Sixth Street, Suite 4000 · Minneapolis, MN 55402-1425 · 612-492-7000

Kathleen M. Picotte Newman · a · Kathleen M. Newman & Associates · 225 South Sixth Street, Suite 1775 · Minneapolis, MN 55402 · 612-746-5525

Nathalie S. Rabause · Walling, Berg & Debele · http://www.wbdlaw.com · 121 South Eighth Street, Suite 1100 · Minneapolis, MN 55402 · 612-340-1150

Susan C. Rhode · a · Moss & Barnett · http://www.moss-barnett.com · Wells Fargo Center, Suite 4800 · 90 South Seventh Street · Minneapolis, MN 55402-4129 · 612-877-5000

Douglas G. Sauter · Barna, Guzy & Steffen · 400 Northtown Financial Center · 200 Coon Rapids Boulevard · Minneapolis, MN 55433-5894 · 763-780-8500

Wright S. Walling · Walling, Berg & Debele · http://www.wbdlaw.com · 121 South Eighth Street, Suite 1100 · Minneapolis, MN 55402 · 612-340-1150

Edward L. Winer · 2% · Moss & Barnett · http://www.moss-barnett.com · Wells Fargo Center, Suite 4800 · 90 South Seventh Street · Minneapolis, MN 55402-4129 · 612-877-5000

Debra E. Yerigan · Messerli & Kramer · Fifth Street Towers, Suite 1800 · 150 South Fifth Street · Minneapolis, MN 55402-4218 · 612-672-3600

Rochester

Lawrence D. Downing · 2) · Downing, Dittrich & Lawrence · 330 Wells Fargo Center · 21 First Street, SW · Rochester, MN 55902 · 507-288-8432

St. Paul

Joan Lucas · Lucas Family Law · 889 Grand Avenue · St. Paul, MN 55105 · 651-294-0894

D. Patrick McCullough · a · McCullough, Bowden & Cyr · http://www.mcculloughlawyers.com · Maple Hills Center · 905 Parkway Drive · St. Paul, MN 55117-3198 · 651-772-3446

Dan O'Connell · Collins, Buckley, Sauntry and Haugh · First National Bank Building, Suite West 1100 · 332 Minnesota Street · St. Paul, MN 55101-1379 · 651-227-0611

J. Peter Wolf · a · Wolf, Rohr & McKenzie · 400 North Robert Street, Suite 1860 · St. Paul, MN 55101 · 651-222-6341

FAMILY LAW MEDIATION

Edina

Christine M. Leick · Christine M. Leick · 3300 Edinborough Way, Suite 550 · Edina, MN 55435 · 952-921-7272

Martin L. Swaden · a · Swaden Law Offices · http://www.swaden.com · 7301 Ohms Lane, Suite 550 · Edina, MN 55439 · 952-832-5990

Minneapolis

Alan C. Eidsness · a · Henson & Efron · 220 South Sixth Street, Suite 1800 · Minneapolis, MN 55402-4503 · 612-339-2500

William E. Mullin · a · Maslon Edelman Borman & Brand · 3300 Wells Fargo Center · 90 South Seventh Street · Minneapolis, MN 55402-4140 · 612-672-8200

Andrea Niemi · Niemi, Barr & Jerabek · 510 Marquette Avenue, Suite 200 · Minneapolis, MN 55402-1110 · 612-333-2400

Susan C. Rhode · a · Moss & Barnett · http://www.moss-barnett.com · Wells Fargo Center, Suite 4800 · 90 South Seventh Street · Minneapolis, MN 55402-4129 · 612-877-5000

Gary A. Weissman · Gary A. Weissman · 701 Fourth Avenue South, Suite 300 · Minneapolis, MN 55415 · 612-370-1110

Rochester

Kathryn M. Snyder · a · Conflict Management & Resolution · 3510 Eighth Street, NW, Suite 300 · Rochester, MN 55901 · 507-288-6653

FIRST AMENDMENT LAW

Minneapolis

Mark R. Anfinson · a · Mark R. Anfinson · 3109 Hennepin Avenue South · Minneapolis, MN 55408 · 612-827-5611

John P. Borger · a · Faegre & Benson · Wells Fargo Center, Suite 2200 · 90 South Seventh Street · Minneapolis, MN 55402-3901 · 612-766-7000

Paul R. Hannah · a · Kelly & Berens · IDS Center, Suite 3720 · 80 South Eighth Street · Minneapolis, MN 55402 · 612-349-6171

Eric E. Jorstad · Faegre & Benson · Wells Fargo Center, Suite 2200 · 90 South Seventh Street · Minneapolis, MN 55402-3901 · 612-766-7000

FRANCHISE LAW

Minneapolis

Kerry L. Bundy · Faegre & Benson · Wells Fargo Center, Suite 2200 · 90 South Seventh Street · Minneapolis, MN 55402-3901 · 612-766-7000

Lawrence R. Commers · a · Mackall, Crounse & Moore · 1400 AT&T Tower · 901 Marquette Avenue · Minneapolis, MN 55402 · 612-305-1400

J. Michael Dady · a · Dady & Garner · http://www.dadygarner.com · 5100 IDS Center · 80 South Eighth Street · Minneapolis, MN 55402 · 612-359-9000

Joseph J. Fittante · Larkin, Hoffman, Daly & Lindgren · Wells Fargo Plaza, Suite 1500 · 7900 Xerxes Avenue South · Minneapolis, MN 55431-1194 · 952-835-3800

Ronald K. Gardner, Jr. · Dady & Garner · http://www.dadygarner.com · 5100 IDS Center · 80 South Eighth Street · Minneapolis, MN 55402 · 612-359-9000

W. Michael Garner · Dady & Garner · http://www.dadygarner.com · 5100 IDS Center · 80 South Eighth Street · Minneapolis, MN 55402 · 612-359-9000

William L. Killion · Faegre & Benson · Wells Fargo Center, Suite 2200 · 90 South Seventh Street · Minneapolis, MN 55402-3901 · 612-766-7000

Scott E. Korzenowski · Dady & Garner · http://www.dadygarner.com · 5100 IDS Center · 80 South Eighth Street · Minneapolis, MN 55402 · 612-359-9000

G. Thomas MacIntosh II · a · Krass Monroe · 8000 Norman Center Drive, Suite 1000 · Minneapolis, MN 55437 · 952-885-5999

Charles S. Modell · Larkin, Hoffman, Daly & Lindgren · Wells Fargo Plaza, Suite 1500 · 7900 Xerxes Avenue South · Minneapolis, MN 55431-1194 · 952-835-3800

Dennis L. Monroe · Krass Monroe · 8000 Norman Center Drive, Suite 1000 · Minneapolis, MN 55437 · 952-885-5999

Brian B. Schnell · Faegre & Benson · Wells Fargo Center, Suite 2200 · 90 South Seventh Street · Minneapolis, MN 55402-3901 · 612-766-7000

Andrew C. Selden · a · Briggs and Morgan · IDS Center, Suite 2200 · 80 South Eighth Street · Minneapolis, MN 55402 · 612-977-8400

GAMING LAW

Minneapolis

Mark A. Jarboe · Dorsey & Whitney · 50 South Sixth Street, Suite 1500 · Minneapolis, MN 55402-1498 · 612-340-2600

Kent E. Richey · Faegre & Benson · Wells Fargo Center, Suite 2200 · 90 South Seventh Street · Minneapolis, MN 55402-3901 · 612-766-7000

St. Paul

Thomas J. Foley · Foley Law Group · 332 Minnesota Street, Suite W-1450 · St. Paul, MN 55101 · 651-602-6262

Kevin C. Quigley · Hamilton, Quigley & Twait · http://www.hqt-law.com · First National Bank Building, Suite W 1450 · 332 Minnesota Street · St. Paul, MN 55101-1314 · 651-602-6262

GOVERNMENT RELATIONS LAW

Minneapolis

John A. Knapp · Winthrop & Weinstine · http://www.winthrop.com · 225 South Sixth Street, Suite 3500 · Minneapolis, MN 55402-4629 · 612-604-6400

HEALTH CARE LAW

Minneapolis

Jay D. Christiansen · a · Faegre & Benson · Wells Fargo Center, Suite 2200 · 90 South Seventh Street · Minneapolis, MN 55402-3901 · 612-766-7000

Konrad J. Friedemann · a · Fredrikson & Byron · 200 South Sixth Street, Suite 4000 · Minneapolis, MN 55402-1425 · 612-492-7000

Daniel J. McInerney, Jr. · Leonard, Street and Deinard · http://www.leonard.com · 150 South Fifth Street, Suite 2300 · Minneapolis, MN 55402 · 612-335-1500

Thomas S. Schroeder · Faegre & Benson · Wells Fargo Center, Suite 2200 · 90 South Seventh Street · Minneapolis, MN 55402-3901 · 612-766-7000

Margo S. Struthers · a · Oppenheimer Wolff & Donnelly · Plaza VII, Suite 3300 · 45 South Seventh Street · Minneapolis, MN 55402 · 612-607-7000

IMMIGRATION LAW

Minneapolis

Scott M. Borene · Borene Law Firm · IDS Center, Suite 3950 · 80 South Eighth Street · Minneapolis, MN 55402 · 612-321-0082

Howard S. Myers III · a · Myers Thompson · 10 South Fifth Street, Suite 200 · Minneapolis, MN 55402 612-349-3030

Elizabeth A. Thompson · a · Myers Thompson · 10 South Fifth Street, Suite 200 · Minneapolis, MN 55402 · 612-349-3030

Scott W. Wright · Faegre & Benson · Wells Fargo Center, Suite 2200 · 90 South Seventh Street · Minneapolis, MN 55402-3901 · 612-766-7000

INFORMATION TECHNOLOGY LAW

Minneapolis

Stephen J. Davidson · Leonard, Street and Deinard · http://www.leonard.com · 150 South Fifth Street, Suite 2300 · Minneapolis, MN 55402 · 612-335-1500

INSURANCE LAW

Minneapolis

John M. Anderson · Bassford Remele · http://www.bassford.com · 33 South Sixth Street, Suite 3800 · Minneapolis, MN 55402-3707 · 612-333-3000

Bradley M. Jones · Meagher & Geer · http://www.meagher.com · 33 South Sixth Street, Suite 4400 · Minneapolis, MN 55402 · 612-338-0661

John A. Knapp · Winthrop & Weinstine · http://www.winthrop.com · 225 South Sixth Street, Suite 3500 · Minneapolis, MN 55402-4629 · 612-604-6400

Charles E. Spevacek · Meagher & Geer · http://www.meagher.com · 33 South Sixth Street, Suite 4400 · Minneapolis, MN 55402 · 612-338-0661

Peter H. Thrane · Leonard, Street and Deinard · http://www.leonard.com · 150 South Fifth Street, Suite 2300 · Minneapolis, MN 55402 · 612-335-1500

Timothy P. Tobin · Gislason & Hunter · 701 Xenia Avenue South, Suite 500 · Minneapolis, MN 55416 · 763-225-6000

Jeanne H. Unger · Bassford Remele · http://www.bassford.com · 33 South Sixth Street, Suite 3800 · Minneapolis, MN 55402-3707 · 612-333-3000

Minneapolis

David A. Allgeyer · Lindquist & Vennum · http://www.lindquist.com · IDS Center, Suite 4200 · 80 South Eighth Street · Minneapolis, MN 55402-2205 · 612-371-3211

Felicia J. Boyd · Faegre & Benson · Wells Fargo Center, Suite 2200 · 90 South Seventh Street · Minneapolis, MN 55402-3901 · 612-766-7000

Alan G. Carlson · a · Carlson, Caspers, Vandenburgh & Lindquist · 225 South Sixth Street, Suite 3200 · Minneapolis, MN 55402 · 612-436-9600

Philip P. Caspers · Carlson, Caspers, Vandenburgh & Lindquist · 225 South Sixth Street, Suite 3200 · Minneapolis, MN 55402 · 612-436-9600

Jan M. Conlin · Robins, Kaplan, Miller & Ciresi · 2800 LaSalle Plaza · 800 LaSalle Avenue · Minneapolis, MN 55402 · 612-349-8500

Kevin D. Conneely · Leonard, Street and Deinard · http://www.leonard.com · 150 South Fifth Street, Suite 2300 · Minneapolis, MN 55402 · 612-335-1500

Craig D. Diviney · a · Dorsey & Whitney · 50 South Sixth Street, Suite 1500 · Minneapolis, MN 55402-1498 · 612-340-2600

Mark S. Ellinger · Fish & Richardson · 3300 RBC Plaza · 60 South Sixth Street · Minneapolis, MN 55402 612-335-5070

David J. F. Gross · Faegre & Benson · Wells Fargo Center, Suite 2200 · 90 South Seventh Street · Minneapolis, MN 55402-3901 · 612-766-7000

Denise M. Kettelberger · Merchant & Gould · IDS Center, Suite 3200 · 80 South Eighth Street · Minneapolis, MN 55402 · 612-332-5300

Kenneth A. Liebman · Faegre & Benson · Wells Fargo Center, Suite 2200 · 90 South Seventh Street · Minneapolis, MN 55402-3901 · 612-766-7000

Timothy A. Lindquist · Carlson, Caspers, Vandenburgh & Lindquist · 225 South Sixth Street, Suite 3200 Minneapolis, MN 55402 · 612-436-9600

Calvin L. Litsey · Faegre & Benson · Wells Fargo Center, Suite 2200 · 90 South Seventh Street · Minneapolis, MN 55402-3901 · 612-766-7000

Martin R. Lueck · Robins, Kaplan, Miller & Ciresi · 2800 LaSalle Plaza · 800 LaSalle Avenue · Minneapolis, MN 55402 · 612-349-8500

Malcolm L. Moore · a · Moore, Hansen & Sumner · 225 South Sixth Street, Suite 4850 · Minneapolis, MN 55402 · 612-332-8200

Ronald J. Schutz · Robins, Kaplan, Miller & Ciresi · 2800 LaSalle Plaza · 800 LaSalle Avenue · Minneapolis, MN 55402 · 612-349-8500

J. Derek Vandenburgh · Carlson, Caspers, Vandenburgh & Lindquist · 225 South Sixth Street, Suite 3200 · Minneapolis, MN 55402 · 612-436-9600

Dorothy P. Whelan · Fish & Richardson · 3300 RBC Plaza · 60 South Sixth Street · Minneapolis, MN 55402 · 612-335-5070

Douglas J. Williams · a · Fulbright & Jaworski · http://www.fulbright.com · 2100 IDS Center · 80 South Eighth Street · Minneapolis, MN 55402-2112 · 612-321-2800

Anthony R. Zeuli · Merchant & Gould · IDS Center, Suite 3200 · 80 South Eighth Street · Minneapolis, MN 55402 · 612-332-5300

LABOR AND EMPLOYMENT LAW

Fergus Falls

Richard L. Pemberton, Sr. · a · Pemberton, Sorlie, Rufer & Kershner · Law Office Building · 110 North Mill Street · P.O. Box 866 · Fergus Falls, MN 56538-0866 · 218-736-5493

Minneapolis

Dominic J. Cecere · Leonard, Street and Deinard · http://www.leonard.com · 150 South Fifth Street, Suite 2300 · Minneapolis, MN 55402 · 612-335-1500

Barbara Jean D'Aquila · a · Fulbright & Jaworski · http://www.fulbright.com · 2100 IDS Center · 80 South Eighth Street · Minneapolis, MN 55402-2112 · 612-321-2800

R. Scott Davies · a · Briggs and Morgan · IDS Center, Suite 2200 · 80 South Eighth Street · Minneapolis, MN 55402 · 612-977-8400

James M. Dawson · Felhaber Larson Fenlon & Vogt · U.S. Bank Plaza, Suite 2200 · 220 South Sixth Street · Minneapolis, MN 55402-4504 · 612-339-6321

Jan D. Halverson · Felhaber Larson Fenlon & Vogt · U.S. Bank Plaza, Suite 2200 · 220 South Sixth Street · Minneapolis, MN 55402-4504 · 612-339-6321

Robert L. Hobbins · a · Dorsey & Whitney · 50 South Sixth Street, Suite 1500 · Minneapolis, MN 55402-1498 · 612-340-2600

R. Ann Huntrods · a · Briggs and Morgan · IDS Center, Suite 2200 · 80 South Eighth Street · Minneapolis, MN 55402 · 612-977-8400

James H. Kaster · a · Nichols, Kaster & Anderson · 4600 IDS Center · 80 South Eighth Street · Minneapolis, MN 55402-2242 · 612-338-1919

Judith Bevis Langevin · a · Gray, Plant, Mooty, Mooty & Bennett · IDS Center, Suite 500 · 80 South Eighth Street · Minneapolis, MN 55402-3796 · 612-632-3000

Dennis J. Merley · Felhaber Larson Fenlon & Vogt · U.S. Bank Plaza, Suite 2200 · 220 South Sixth Street Minneapolis, MN 55402-4504 · 612-339-6321

Richard A. Miller · 2) · Miller O'Brien · One Financial Plaza, Suite 2400 · 120 South Sixth Street · Minneapolis, MN 55402 · 612-333-5831

Donald H. Nichols · Nichols, Kaster & Anderson · 4600 IDS Center · 80 South Eighth Street · Minneapolis, MN 55402-2242 · 612-338-1919

Maurice W. O'Brien · Miller O'Brien · One Financial Plaza, Suite 2400 · 120 South Sixth Street · Minneapolis, MN 55402 · 612-333-5831

Anne M. Radolinski · Fredrikson & Byron · 200 South Sixth Street, Suite 4000 · Minneapolis, MN 55402-1425 · 612-492-7000

Melissa Raphan · Dorsey & Whitney · 50 South Sixth Street, Suite 1500 · Minneapolis, MN 55402-1498 · 612-340-2600

Robert R. Reinhart · a · Dorsey & Whitney · 50 South Sixth Street, Suite 1500 · Minneapolis, MN 55402-1498 · 612-340-2600

Richard A. Ross · Fredrikson & Byron · 200 South Sixth Street, Suite 4000 · Minneapolis, MN 55402-1425 · 612-492-7000

Ellen G. Sampson · Leonard, Street and Deinard · http://www.leonard.com · 150 South Fifth Street, Suite 2300 · Minneapolis, MN 55402 · 612-335-1500

Karen G. Schanfield · Fredrikson & Byron · 200 South Sixth Street, Suite 4000 · Minneapolis, MN 55402-1425 · 612-492-7000

Mark W. Schneider · Littler Mendelson · 1300 IDS Center · 80 South Eighth Street · Minneapolis, MN 55402-2136 · 612-630-1000

Stephen J. Snyder · a · Snyder & Snyder · 100 South Fifth Street, Suite 410 · Minneapolis, MN 55402 · 612-787-3100

Gregory J. Stenmoe · a · Briggs and Morgan · IDS Center, Suite 2200 · 80 South Eighth Street · Minneapolis, MN 55402 · 612-977-8400

Mary E. Stumo · a · Faegre & Benson · Wells Fargo Center, Suite 2200 · 90 South Seventh Street · Minneapolis, MN 55402-3901 · 612-766-7000

John D. Thompson · a · Oberman Thompson & Segal · One Financial Plaza, Suite 850 · 120 South Sixth Street · Minneapolis, MN 55402 · 612-217-6440

Nancy B. Vollertsen · Lindquist & Vennum · http://www.lindquist.com · IDS Center, Suite 4200 · 80 South Eighth Street · Minneapolis, MN 55402-2205 · 612-371-3211

Daniel R. Wachtler · a · Briggs and Morgan · IDS Center, Suite 2200 · 80 South Eighth Street · Minneapolis, MN 55402 · 612-977-8400

Daniel G. Wilczek · a · Faegre & Benson · Wells Fargo Center, Suite 2200 · 90 South Seventh Street · Minneapolis, MN 55402-3901 · 612-766-7000

Paul J. Zech · Felhaber Larson Fenlon & Vogt · U.S. Bank Plaza, Suite 2200 · 220 South Sixth Street · Minneapolis, MN 55402-4504 · 612-339-6321

Robert Zeglovitch · Law Offices of Robert Zeglovitch · One Financial Plaza, Suite 2400 · 120 South Sixth Street · Minneapolis, MN 55402 · 612-334-9025

Rochester

Ronald L. Seeger · 2) · Dunlap & Seeger · 206 South Broadway, Suite 505 · P.O. Box 549 · Rochester, MN 55903-0549 · 507-288-9111

St. Louis Park

Gregg M. Corwin · 2) · Gregg M. Corwin & Associates · 508 East Parkdale Plaza Building, Suite 508-E · 1660 South Highway 100 · St. Louis Park, MN 55416-1534 · 952-544-7774

Michael J. Galvin, Jr. · a · Briggs and Morgan · First National Bank Building, Suite W2200 · 332 Minnesota Street · St. Paul, MN 55101-1396 · 651-808-6600

Roger A. Jensen · 2) · Jensen, Bell, Converse & Erickson · 1500 Wells Fargo Place · 30 East Seventh Street · St. Paul, MN 55101 · 651-223-4999

LAND USE & ZONING LAW

Minneapolis

Peter J. Coyle · Larkin, Hoffman, Daly & Lindgren · Wells Fargo Plaza, Suite 1500 · 7900 Xerxes Avenue South · Minneapolis, MN 55431-1194 · 952-835-3800

Joseph M. Finley · a · Leonard, Street and Deinard · http://www.leonard.com · 150 South Fifth Street, Suite 2300 · Minneapolis, MN 55402 · 612-335-1500

Eric H. Galatz · Leonard, Street and Deinard · http://www.leonard.com · 150 South Fifth Street, Suite 2300 · Minneapolis, MN 55402 · 612-335-1500

Gary L. Gandrud · Faegre & Benson · Wells Fargo Center, Suite 2200 · 90 South Seventh Street · Minneapolis, MN 55402-3901 · 612-766-7000

Bradley J. Gunn · Malkerson Gilliland Martin · U.S. Bank Plaza South, Suite 1900 · 220 South Sixth Street · Minneapolis, MN 55402-4502 · 612-344-1111

John H. Herman · 2) · Faegre & Benson · Wells Fargo Center, Suite 2200 · 90 South Seventh Street · Minneapolis, MN 55402-3901 · 612-766-7000

Robert L. Hoffman · a · Larkin, Hoffman, Daly & Lindgren · Wells Fargo Plaza, Suite 1500 · 7900 Xerxes Avenue South · Minneapolis, MN 55431-1194 · 952-835-3800

Jay R. Lindgren · Dorsey & Whitney · 50 South Sixth Street, Suite 1500 · Minneapolis, MN 55402-1498 · 612-340-2600

Bruce D. Malkerson · Malkerson Gilliland Martin · U.S. Bank Plaza South, Suite 1900 · 220 South Sixth Street · Minneapolis, MN 55402-4502 · 612-344-1111

Michael T. Norton · Kennedy & Graven · 470 U.S. Bank Plaza · 200 South Sixth Street · Minneapolis, MN 55402 · 612-337-9300

Walt H. Rockenstein II · Faegre & Benson · Wells Fargo Center, Suite 2200 · 90 South Seventh Street · Minneapolis, MN 55402-3901 · 612-766-7000

Rebecca L. Rom · Faegre & Benson · Wells Fargo Center, Suite 2200 · 90 South Seventh Street · Minneapolis, MN 55402-3901 · 612-766-7000

David C. Sellergren · a · Fredrikson & Byron · 200 South Sixth Street, Suite 4000 · Minneapolis, MN 55402-1425 · 612-492-7000

LEGAL MALPRACTICE LAW

Duluth

John D. Kelly · a · Hanft Fride · 1000 U.S. Bank Place · 130 West Superior Street · Duluth, MN 55802-2094 · 218-722-4766

Minneapolis

John W. Carey · a · Sieben, Grose, Von Holtum & Carey · 800 Marquette Avenue, Suite 900 · Minneapolis, MN 55402 · 612-333-4500

Phillip A. Cole · a · Lommen, Abdo, Cole, King & Stageberg · 2000 IDS Center · 80 South Eighth Street Minneapolis, MN 55402 · 612-339-8131

Charles E. Lundberg · Bassford Remele · http://www.bassford.com · 33 South Sixth Street, Suite 3800 · Minneapolis, MN 55402-3707 · 612-333-3000

Lewis A. Remele, Jr. · a · Bassford Remele · http://www.bassford.com · 33 South Sixth Street, Suite 3800 Minneapolis, MN 55402-3707 · 612-333-3000

Allen I. Saeks · Leonard, Street and Deinard · http://www.leonard.com · 150 South Fifth Street, Suite 2300 · Minneapolis, MN 55402 · 612-335-1500

LEVERAGED BUYOUTS AND PRIVATE EQUITY LAW

Minneapolis

Bruce M. Engler · Faegre & Benson · Wells Fargo Center, Suite 2200 · 90 South Seventh Street · Minneapolis, MN 55402-3901 · 612-766-7000

Dennis M. O'Malley · Lindquist & Vennum · http://www.lindquist.com · IDS Center, Suite 4200 · 80 South Eighth Street · Minneapolis, MN 55402-2205 · 612-371-3211

MASS TORT LITIGATION

Minneapolis

Michael V. Ciresi · a · Robins, Kaplan, Miller & Ciresi · 2800 LaSalle Plaza · 800 LaSalle Avenue · Minneapolis, MN 55402 · 612-349-8500

Jack M. Fribley · Faegre & Benson · Wells Fargo Center, Suite 2200 · 90 South Seventh Street · Minneapolis, MN 55402-3901 · 612-766-7000

James A. O'Neal · Faegre & Benson · Wells Fargo Center, Suite 2200 · 90 South Seventh Street · Minneapolis, MN 55402-3901 · 612-766-7000

Charles E. Spevacek · Meagher & Geer · http://www.meagher.com · 33 South Sixth Street, Suite 4400 · Minneapolis, MN 55402 · 612-338-0661

Roberta B. Walburn · Robins, Kaplan, Miller & Ciresi · 2800 LaSalle Plaza · 800 LaSalle Avenue · Minneapolis, MN 55402 · 612-349-8500

Charles S. Zimmerman · Zimmerman Reed · 651 Nicollet Mall, Suite 501 · Minneapolis, MN 55402 · 612-341-0400

MEDICAL MALPRACTICE LAW

Duluth

Paul F. Schweiger · Sieben, Grose, Von Holtum & Carey · Duluth Technology Village, Suite 320 · 11 East Superior Street · Duluth, MN 55802 · 218-722-6848

Fergus Falls

Richard L. Pemberton, Sr. · a · Pemberton, Sorlie, Rufer & Kershner · Law Office Building · 110 North Mill Street · P.O. Box 866 · Fergus Falls, MN 56538-0866 · 218-736-5493

Minneapolis

John F. Eisberg · 2) · Robins, Kaplan, Miller & Ciresi · 2800 LaSalle Plaza · 800 LaSalle Avenue · Minneapolis, MN 55402 · 612-349-8500

Rodger A. Hagen · Meagher & Geer · http://www.meagher.com · 33 South Sixth Street, Suite 4400 · Minneapolis, MN 55402 · 612-338-0661

Richard G. Hunegs · 2% · Hunegs, Stone, LeNeave, Kvas & Thornton · 1650 International Centre Building · 900 Second Avenue South · Minneapolis, MN 55402 · 612-339-4511

Kathleen Flynn Peterson · a · Robins, Kaplan, Miller & Ciresi · 2800 LaSalle Plaza · 800 LaSalle Avenue · Minneapolis, MN 55402 · 612-349-8500

John P. Sheehy · Meshbesher & Spence · 1616 Park Avenue · Minneapolis, MN 55404 · 612-339-9121

Jan D. Stuurmans · a · Jan Stuurmans · 12 South Sixth Street, Suite 1008 · Minneapolis, MN 55402 · 612-336-4455

Barbara A. Zurek · Meagher & Geer · http://www.meagher.com · 33 South Sixth Street, Suite 4400 · Minneapolis, MN 55402 · 612-338-0661

St. Paul

Robert M. Mahoney · Geraghty, O'Loughlin & Kenney · Alliance Bank Center, Suite 1100 · 55 East Fifth Street · St. Paul, MN 55101-1812 · 651-291-1177

MERGERS & ACQUISITIONS LAW

Minneapolis

J. Kevin Costley · a · Lindquist & Vennum · http://www.lindquist.com · IDS Center, Suite 4200 · 80 South Eighth Street · Minneapolis, MN 55402-2205 · 612-371-3211

Kenneth L. Cutler · Dorsey & Whitney · 50 South Sixth Street, Suite 1500 · Minneapolis, MN 55402-1498 · 612-340-2600

Bruce M. Engler · Faegre & Benson · Wells Fargo Center, Suite 2200 · 90 South Seventh Street · Minneapolis, MN 55402-3901 · 612-766-7000

Philip S. Garon · a · Faegre & Benson · Wells Fargo Center, Suite 2200 · 90 South Seventh Street · Minneapolis, MN 55402-3901 · 612-766-7000

Andrew G. Humphrey · Faegre & Benson · Wells Fargo Center, Suite 2200 · 90 South Seventh Street · Minneapolis, MN 55402-3901 · 612-766-7000

Richard J. Kelber · Moss & Barnett · http://www.moss-barnett.com · Wells Fargo Center, Suite 4800 · 90 South Seventh Street · Minneapolis, MN 55402-4129 · 612-877-5000

Keith A. Libbey · a · Fredrikson & Byron · 200 South Sixth Street, Suite 4000 · Minneapolis, MN 55402-1425 · 612-492-7000

Bruce A. Machmeier · Oppenheimer Wolff & Donnelly · Plaza VII, Suite 3300 · 45 South Seventh Street Minneapolis, MN 55402 · 612-607-7000

Charles P. Moorse · a · Lindquist & Vennum · http://www.lindquist.com · IDS Center, Suite 4200 · 80 South Eighth Street · Minneapolis, MN 55402-2205 · 612-371-3211

William B. Payne · Dorsey & Whitney · 50 South Sixth Street, Suite 1500 · Minneapolis, MN 55402-1498 612-340-2600

Robert K. Ranum · Fredrikson & Byron · 200 South Sixth Street, Suite 4000 · Minneapolis, MN 55402-1425 · 612-492-7000

Robert A. Rosenbaum · Dorsey & Whitney · 50 South Sixth Street, Suite 1500 · Minneapolis, MN 55402-1498 · 612-340-2600

Timothy J. Scallen · Oppenheimer Wolff & Donnelly · Plaza VII, Suite 3300 · 45 South Seventh Street · Minneapolis, MN 55402 · 612-607-7000

Michael A. Stanchfield · Faegre & Benson · Wells Fargo Center, Suite 2200 · 90 South Seventh Street · Minneapolis, MN 55402-3901 · 612-766-7000

Jay L. Swanson · Dorsey & Whitney · 50 South Sixth Street, Suite 1500 · Minneapolis, MN 55402-1498 · 612-340-2600

David M. Vander Haar · Faegre & Benson · Wells Fargo Center, Suite 2200 · 90 South Seventh Street · Minneapolis, MN 55402-3901 · 612-766-7000

MUNICIPAL LAW

Eden Prairie

George C. Hoff · Hoff, Barry & Kozar · 775 Prairie Center Drive, Suite 160 · Eden Prairie, MN 55344 · 952-941-9220

MUTUAL FUNDS LAW

Minneapolis

Michael J. Radmer · Dorsey & Whitney · 50 South Sixth Street, Suite 1500 · Minneapolis, MN 55402-1498 · 612-340-2600

NATIVE AMERICAN LAW

Minneapolis

Kurt V. BlueDog · BlueDog, Paulson & Small · Southgate Office Plaza, Suite 500 · 5001 American Boulevard West · Minneapolis, MN 55437 · 952-893-1813

Thomas B. Heffelfinger · Best & Flanagan · 225 South Sixth Street, Suite 4000 · Minneapolis, MN 55402-4690 · 612-339-7121

Kent E. Richey · Faegre & Benson · Wells Fargo Center, Suite 2200 · 90 South Seventh Street · Minneapolis, MN 55402-3901 · 612-766-7000

St Paul

Henry M. Buffalo, Jr. · Jacobson Buffalo Magnuson Anderson & Hogen · Energy Park Financial Center, Suite 210 · 1360 Energy Park Drive · St Paul, MN 55108 · 651-644-4710

Vanya S. Hogen · Jacobson Buffalo Magnuson Anderson & Hogen · Energy Park Financial Center, Suite 210 · 1360 Energy Park Drive · St Paul, MN 55108 · 651-644-4710

John E. Jacobson · Jacobson Buffalo Magnuson Anderson & Hogen · Energy Park Financial Center, Suite 210 · 1360 Energy Park Drive · St Paul, MN 55108 · 651-644-4710

NON-PROFIT/CHARITIES LAW

Minneapolis

William J. Brody · a · Fredrikson & Byron · 200 South Sixth Street, Suite 4000 · Minneapolis, MN 55402-1425 · 612-492-7000

William S. Forsberg · Leonard, Street and Deinard · http://www.leonard.com · 150 South Fifth Street, Suite 2300 · Minneapolis, MN 55402 · 612-335-1500

J. Hazen Graves · Faegre & Benson · Wells Fargo Center, Suite 2200 · 90 South Seventh Street · Minneapolis, MN 55402-3901 · 612-766-7000

Sidney Kaplan · 2% · Parsinen Kaplan Rosberg & Gotlieb · 100 South Fifth Street, Suite 1100 · Minneapolis, MN 55402-1298 · 612-333-2111

Clinton A. Schroeder · 2% · Gray, Plant, Mooty, Mooty & Bennett · IDS Center, Suite 500 · 80 South Eighth Street · Minneapolis, MN 55402-3796 · 612-632-3000

NON-WHITE-COLLAR CRIMINAL DEFENSE

Burnsville

Howard Bass · Bass Law Firm · 14101 Southcross Drive West, Suite 100 · Burnsville, MN 55337 · 952-224-0182

Minneapolis

Joseph S. Friedberg · 2% · Joseph S. Friedberg · Fifth Street Towers, Suite 320 · 150 South Fifth Street · Minneapolis, MN 55402 · 612-339-8626

Charles L. Hawkins · a · Charles L. Hawkins · 150 South Fifth Street, Suite 3260 · Minneapolis, MN 55402 · 612-339-6921

William J. Mauzy · 2% · Mauzy Law Firm · 510 First Avenue North, Suite 610 · Minneapolis, MN 55403 · 612-340-9108

Ronald I. Meshbesher · 2% · Meshbesher & Spence · 1616 Park Avenue · Minneapolis, MN 55404 · 612-339-9121

St. Paul

Earl P. Gray · a · Gray & Malacko · 332 Minnesota Street, Suite W1610 · St. Paul, MN 55101 · 651-223-5175

OIL & GAS LAW

Minneapolis

Brian B. O'Neill · a · Faegre & Benson · Wells Fargo Center, Suite 2200 · 90 South Seventh Street · Minneapolis, MN 55402-3901 · 612-766-7000

Timothy R. Thornton · Briggs and Morgan · IDS Center, Suite 2200 · 80 South Eighth Street · Minneapolis, MN 55402 · 612-977-8400

PERSONAL INJURY LITIGATION

Duluth

James W. Balmer · Falsani, Balmer, Peterson, Quinn & Beyer · http://www.duluthtriallawyers.com · 1200 Alworth Building · 306 West Superior Street · Duluth, MN 55802-1800 · 218-723-1990

Paul F. Schweiger · Sieben, Grose, Von Holtum & Carey · Duluth Technology Village, Suite 320 · 11 East Superior Street · Duluth, MN 55802 · 218-722-6848

Thomas R. Thibodeau · Thibodeau, Johnson & Feriancek · http://www.trialgroupnorth.com · 800 Lonsdale Building · 302 West Superior Street · Duluth, MN 55802 · 218-722-0073

Fergus Falls

Richard L. Pemberton, Sr. · a · Pemberton, Sorlie, Rufer & Kershner · Law Office Building · 110 North Mill Street · P.O. Box 866 · Fergus Falls, MN 56538-0866 · 218-736-5493

Hastings

Richard A. LaVerdiere · Sieben, Polk, LaVerdiere & Dusich · 1640 South Frontage Road, Suite 200 · Hastings, MN 55003 · 651-437-3148

Michael S. Polk · Sieben, Polk, LaVerdiere & Dusich · 1640 South Frontage Road, Suite 200 · Hastings, MN 55003 · 651-437-3148

Michael R. Sieben · Sieben, Polk, LaVerdiere & Dusich · 1640 South Frontage Road, Suite 200 · Hastings, MN 55003 · 651-437-3148

Hibbing

Edward J. Matonich · a · Matonich & Persson · 2031 Second Avenue East · P.O. Box 127 · Hibbing, MN 55746 · 218-263-8881

Mankato

Gerald L. Maschka · a · Maschka, Riedy & Ries · Union Square Business Center, Suite 200 · 201 North Broad Street · P.O. Box Seven · Mankato, MN 56002-0007 · 507-625-6600

Minneapolis

David D. Alsop · Gislason & Hunter · 701 Xenia Avenue South, Suite 500 · Minneapolis, MN 55416 · 763-225-6000

John M. Anderson · Bassford Remele · http://www.bassford.com · 33 South Sixth Street, Suite 3800 · Minneapolis, MN 55402-3707 · 612-333-3000

William M. Beadie · a · Moore, Costello & Hart · International Centre I, Suite 1500 · 900 Second Avenue South · Minneapolis, MN 55402-5079 · 612-673-0148

J. Richard Bland · a · Meagher & Geer · http://www.meagher.com · 33 South Sixth Street, Suite 4400 · Minneapolis, MN 55402 · 612-338-0661

Richard A. Bowman · 2) · Bowman and Brooke · 150 South Fifth Street, Suite 3000 · Minneapolis, MN 55402 · 612-339-8682

James P. Carey · Sieben, Grose, Von Holtum & Carey · 800 Marquette Avenue, Suite 900 · Minneapolis, MN 55402 · 612-333-4500

John W. Carey · a · Sieben, Grose, Von Holtum & Carey · 800 Marquette Avenue, Suite 900 · Minneapolis, MN 55402 · 612-333-4500

Michael V. Ciresi · a · Robins, Kaplan, Miller & Ciresi · 2800 LaSalle Plaza · 800 LaSalle Avenue · Minneapolis, MN 55402 · 612-349-8500

Phillip A. Cole · a · Lommen, Abdo, Cole, King & Stageberg · 2000 IDS Center · 80 South Eighth Street Minneapolis, MN 55402 · 612-339-8131

J. Michael Dady · a · Dady & Garner · http://www.dadygarner.com · 5100 IDS Center · 80 South Eighth Street · Minneapolis, MN 55402 · 612-359-9000

John M. Dornik · Mackenzie & Dornik · 150 South Fifth Street, Suite 2500 · Minneapolis, MN 55402 · 612-335-3500

John F. Eisberg · 2) · Robins, Kaplan, Miller & Ciresi · 2800 LaSalle Plaza · 800 LaSalle Avenue · Minneapolis, MN 55402 · 612-349-8500

Leo F. Feeney · a · Robins, Kaplan, Miller & Ciresi · 2800 LaSalle Plaza · 800 LaSalle Avenue · Minneapolis, MN 55402 · 612-349-8500

James L. Fetterly · 2) · Robins, Kaplan, Miller & Ciresi · 2800 LaSalle Plaza · 800 LaSalle Avenue · Minneapolis, MN 55402 · 612-349-8500

Wilbur W. Fluegel · Fluegel Law Office · 150 South Fifth Street, Suite 3475 · Minneapolis, MN 55402 · 612-238-3540

George W. Flynn · a · Flynn, Gaskins & Bennett · 333 South Seventh Street, Suite 2900 · Minneapolis, MN 55402-2440 · 612-333-9500

Edward F. Fox · Bassford Remele · http://www.bassford.com · 33 South Sixth Street, Suite 3800 · Minneapolis, MN 55402-3707 · 612-333-3000

Jack M. Fribley · Faegre & Benson · Wells Fargo Center, Suite 2200 · 90 South Seventh Street · Minneapolis, MN 55402-3901 · 612-766-7000

Paul E. Godlewski · Schwebel Goetz & Sieben · http://www.schwebel.com · IDS Center, Suite 5120 · 80 South Eighth Street · Minneapolis, MN 55402-2246 · 612-377-7777

John C. Goetz · a · Schwebel Goetz & Sieben · http://www.schwebel.com · IDS Center, Suite 5120 · 80 South Eighth Street · Minneapolis, MN 55402-2246 · 612-377-7777

Jan M. Gunderson · Bassford Remele · http://www.bassford.com · 33 South Sixth Street, Suite 3800 · Minneapolis, MN 55402-3707 · 612-333-3000

Rodger A. Hagen · Meagher & Geer · http://www.meagher.com · 33 South Sixth Street, Suite 4400 · Minneapolis, MN 55402 · 612-338-0661

Susan M. Holden · Sieben, Grose, Von Holtum & Carey · 800 Marquette Avenue, Suite 900 · Minneapolis, MN 55402 · 612-333-4500

John C. Hughes · Meagher & Geer · http://www.meagher.com · 33 South Sixth Street, Suite 4400 · Minneapolis, MN 55402 · 612-338-0661

Richard G. Hunegs · 2% · Hunegs, Stone, LeNeave, Kvas & Thornton · 1650 International Centre Building · 900 Second Avenue South · Minneapolis, MN 55402 · 612-339-4511

Michael D. Hutchens · Meagher & Geer · http://www.meagher.com · 33 South Sixth Street, Suite 4400 · Minneapolis, MN 55402 · 612-338-0661

Charles T. Hvass, Jr. · 2% · Hvass, Weisman & King · 825 Nicollet Mall, Suite 1025 · Minneapolis, MN 55402 · 612-333-0201

David W. H. Jorstad · McCoy Peterson & Jorstad · Butler Square Building, Suite 550-A · 100 North Sixth Street · Minneapolis, MN 55403 · 612-333-3999

Robert J. King, Jr. · Lommen, Abdo, Cole, King & Stageberg · 2000 IDS Center · 80 South Eighth Street Minneapolis, MN 55402 · 612-339-8131

Reed K. Mackenzie · a · Mackenzie & Dornik · 150 South Fifth Street, Suite 2500 · Minneapolis, MN 55402 · 612-335-3500

Julie A. Matonich · Matonich & Persson · 220 South Sixth Street, Suite 215 · Minneapolis, MN 55402 · 612-677-1708

Rebecca Egge Moos · Bassford Remele · http://www.bassford.com · 33 South Sixth Street, Suite 3800 · Minneapolis, MN 55402-3707 · 612-333-3000

Frederick W. Morris · Leonard, Street and Deinard · http://www.leonard.com · 150 South Fifth Street, Suite 2300 · Minneapolis, MN 55402 · 612-335-1500

Richard J. Nygaard · a · Schwebel Goetz & Sieben · http://www.schwebel.com · IDS Center, Suite 5120 80 South Eighth Street · Minneapolis, MN 55402-2246 · 612-377-7777

Kathleen Flynn Peterson · a · Robins, Kaplan, Miller & Ciresi · 2800 LaSalle Plaza · 800 LaSalle Avenue · Minneapolis, MN 55402 · 612-349-8500

Joseph M. Price · Faegre & Benson · Wells Fargo Center, Suite 2200 · 90 South Seventh Street · Minneapolis, MN 55402-3901 · 612-766-7000

Fred H. Pritzker · Pritzker Ruohonen & Associates · Plaza VII, Suite 2950 · 45 South Seventh Street · Minneapolis, MN 55402-1652 · 612-338-0202

Lewis A. Remele, Jr. · a · Bassford Remele · http://www.bassford.com · 33 South Sixth Street, Suite 3800 Minneapolis, MN 55402-3707 · 612-333-3000

Peter W. Riley · Schwebel Goetz & Sieben · http://www.schwebel.com · IDS Center, Suite 5120 · 80 South Eighth Street · Minneapolis, MN 55402-2246 · 612-377-7777

Roger R. Roe · a · Bassford Remele · http://www.bassford.com · 33 South Sixth Street, Suite 3800 · Minneapolis, MN 55402-3707 · 612-333-3000

Timothy R. Schupp · Flynn, Gaskins & Bennett · 333 South Seventh Street, Suite 2900 · Minneapolis, MN 55402-2440 · 612-333-9500

James R. Schwebel · 2) · Schwebel Goetz & Sieben · http://www.schwebel.com · IDS Center, Suite 5120 80 South Eighth Street · Minneapolis, MN 55402-2246 · 612-377-7777

John P. Sheehy · Meshbesher & Spence · 1616 Park Avenue · Minneapolis, MN 55404 · 612-339-9121

Harry A. Sieben, Jr. · Sieben, Grose, Von Holtum & Carey · 800 Marquette Avenue, Suite 900 · Minneapolis, MN 55402 · 612-333-4500

William R. Sieben · a · Schwebel Goetz & Sieben · http://www.schwebel.com · IDS Center, Suite 5120 · 80 South Eighth Street · Minneapolis, MN 55402-2246 · 612-377-7777

Louis J. Speltz · Bassford Remele · http://www.bassford.com · 33 South Sixth Street, Suite 3800 · Minneapolis, MN 55402-3707 · 612-333-3000

Byron E. Starns · a · Leonard, Street and Deinard · http://www.leonard.com · 150 South Fifth Street, Suite 2300 · Minneapolis, MN 55402 · 612-335-1500

Jan D. Stuurmans · a · Jan Stuurmans · 12 South Sixth Street, Suite 1008 · Minneapolis, MN 55402 · 612-336-4455

Michael D. Tewksbury · Tewksbury & Kerfeld · http://www.tkz.com · 88 South Tenth Street, Suite 300 · Minneapolis, MN 55403 · 612-334-3399

Richard L. Tousignant · Schwebel Goetz & Sieben · http://www.schwebel.com · IDS Center, Suite 5120 80 South Eighth Street · Minneapolis, MN 55402-2246 · 612-377-7777

Peter G. Van Bergen · Cousineau McGuire · 1550 Utica Avenue South, Suite 600 · Minneapolis, MN 55416 · 952-546-8400

Barry G. Vermeer · Gislason & Hunter · 701 Xenia Avenue South, Suite 500 · Minneapolis, MN 55416 · 763-225-6000

James G. Weinmeyer · Schwebel Goetz & Sieben · http://www.schwebel.com · IDS Center, Suite 5120 · 80 South Eighth Street · Minneapolis, MN 55402-2246 · 612-377-7777

Gregory M. Weyandt · Dorsey & Whitney · 50 South Sixth Street, Suite 1500 · Minneapolis, MN 55402-1498 · 612-340-2600

Minnetonka

Mark N. Stageberg · 2) · Mark N. Stageberg · 5101 Thimsen Avenue, Suite 201 · Minnetonka, MN 55345 · 952-470-5242

Plymouth

Mark Kosieradzki · Kosieradzki Smith Law Firm · 3675 Plymouth Boulevard, Suite 105 · Plymouth, MN 55446 · 763-746-7800

Rochester

Stephen S. Fuller · Fuller Law Firm · Riverside Building · 206 Fourth Street, SE · Rochester, MN 55904-3753 · 507-288-4800

Charles J. Suk · Suk Law Firm · Five East Center Street, Suite 200 · Rochester, MN 55904 · 507-281-0000

St. Paul

William M. Bradt · a · Hansen, Dordell, Bradt, Odlaug & Bradt · 3900 Northwoods Drive, Suite 250 · St. Paul, MN 55112 · 651-482-8900

J. Mark Catron · Hansen, Dordell, Bradt, Odlaug & Bradt · 3900 Northwoods Drive, Suite 250 · St. Paul, MN 55112 · 651-482-8900

Mark A. Hallberg · a · Hallberg & McClain · 380 St. Peter Street, Suite 715 · St. Paul, MN 55102 · 651-255-6810

David C. Hutchinson · a · Geraghty, O'Loughlin & Kenney · Alliance Bank Center, Suite 1100 · 55 East Fifth Street · St. Paul, MN 55101-1812 · 651-291-1177

Lawrence R. King · a · Larson King · 2800 Wells Fargo Place · 30 East Seventh Street · St. Paul, MN 55101 · 651-312-6500

Steven J. Kirsch · Murnane Brandt · 30 East Seventh Street, Suite 3200 · St. Paul, MN 55101-4919 · 651-227-9411

Terence J. O'Loughlin · a · Geraghty, O'Loughlin & Kenney · Alliance Bank Center, Suite 1100 · 55 East Fifth Street · St. Paul, MN 55101-1812 · 651-291-1177

Mark A. Solheim · Larson King · 2800 Wells Fargo Place · 30 East Seventh Street · St. Paul, MN 55101 · 651-312-6500

Wadena

Charles R. Kennedy · a · Kennedy & Nervig · 503 Jefferson Street South · P.O. Box 647 · Wadena, MN 56482-0647 · 218-631-2505

Willmar

Joe E. Thompson · a · Johnson, Moody, Schmidt, & Kleinhuzen · 320 First Street, South · P.O. Box 913 Willmar, MN 56201-0913 · 320-235-2000

PRODUCT LIABILITY LITIGATION

Fergus Falls

Richard L. Pemberton, Sr. · a · Pemberton, Sorlie, Rufer & Kershner · Law Office Building · 110 North Mill Street · P.O. Box 866 · Fergus Falls, MN 56538-0866 · 218-736-5493

Minneapolis

Michael V. Ciresi · a · Robins, Kaplan, Miller & Ciresi · 2800 LaSalle Plaza · 800 LaSalle Avenue · Minneapolis, MN 55402 · 612-349-8500

John M. Dornik · Mackenzie & Dornik · 150 South Fifth Street, Suite 2500 · Minneapolis, MN 55402 · 612-335-3500

James L. Fetterly · 2) · Robins, Kaplan, Miller & Ciresi · 2800 LaSalle Plaza · 800 LaSalle Avenue · Minneapolis, MN 55402 · 612-349-8500

Richard G. Hunegs · 2% · Hunegs, Stone, LeNeave, Kvas & Thornton · 1650 International Centre Building · 900 Second Avenue South · Minneapolis, MN 55402 · 612-339-4511

Frederick W. Morris · Leonard, Street and Deinard · http://www.leonard.com · 150 South Fifth Street, Suite 2300 · Minneapolis, MN 55402 · 612-335-1500

James A. O'Neal · Faegre & Benson · Wells Fargo Center, Suite 2200 · 90 South Seventh Street · Minneapolis, MN 55402-3901 · 612-766-7000

Joseph M. Price · Faegre & Benson · Wells Fargo Center, Suite 2200 · 90 South Seventh Street · Minneapolis, MN 55402-3901 · 612-766-7000

Winthrop A. Rockwell · Faegre & Benson · Wells Fargo Center, Suite 2200 · 90 South Seventh Street · Minneapolis, MN 55402-3901 · 612-766-7000

John M. Sheran · Leonard, Street and Deinard · http://www.leonard.com · 150 South Fifth Street, Suite 2300 · Minneapolis, MN 55402 · 612-335-1500

Peter G. Van Bergen · Cousineau McGuire · 1550 Utica Avenue South, Suite 600 · Minneapolis, MN 55416 · 952-546-8400

PROFESSIONAL MALPRACTICE LAW

Fergus Falls

Richard L. Pemberton, Sr. · a · Pemberton, Sorlie, Rufer & Kershner · Law Office Building · 110 North Mill Street · P.O. Box 866 · Fergus Falls, MN 56538-0866 · 218-736-5493

Minneapolis

David D. Alsop · Gislason & Hunter · 701 Xenia Avenue South, Suite 500 · Minneapolis, MN 55416 · 763-225-6000

James L. Fetterly · 2) · Robins, Kaplan, Miller & Ciresi · 2800 LaSalle Plaza · 800 LaSalle Avenue · Minneapolis, MN 55402 · 612-349-8500

Thomas J. Shroyer · Moss & Barnett · http://www.moss-barnett.com · Wells Fargo Center, Suite 4800 · 90 South Seventh Street · Minneapolis, MN 55402-4129 · 612-877-5000

PUBLIC FINANCE LAW

Minneapolis

Jerome P. Gilligan · Dorsey & Whitney · 50 South Sixth Street, Suite 1500 · Minneapolis, MN 55402-1498 · 612-340-2600

Stephen C. Rosholt · Faegre & Benson · Wells Fargo Center, Suite 2200 · 90 South Seventh Street · Minneapolis, MN 55402-3901 · 612-766-7000

Thomas D. Vander Molen · Dorsey & Whitney · 50 South Sixth Street, Suite 1500 · Minneapolis, MN 55402-1498 · 612-340-2600

RAILROAD LAW

Eagan

David A. Donna · a · Donna & Hurley · 1460 Buffet Way, Suite 150 · Eagan, MN 55121 · 651-406-4242

Minneapolis

Ronald J. Barczak · a · Yaeger, Jungbauer & Barczak · http://www.yjblaw.com · 745 Kasota Avenue · Minneapolis, MN 55414 · 612-333-6371

Robert T. Dolan · Yaeger, Jungbauer & Barczak · http://www.yjblaw.com · 745 Kasota Avenue · Minneapolis, MN 55414 · 612-333-6371

Louis E. Jungbauer · Yaeger, Jungbauer & Barczak · http://www.yjblaw.com · 745 Kasota Avenue · Minneapolis, MN 55414 · 612-333-6371

William G. Jungbauer · a · Yaeger, Jungbauer & Barczak · http://www.yjblaw.com · 745 Kasota Avenue · Minneapolis, MN 55414 · 612-333-6371

David B. Potter · Oppenheimer Wolff & Donnelly · Plaza VII, Suite 3300 · 45 South Seventh Street · Minneapolis, MN 55402 · 612-607-7000

Michael L. Weiner · Yaeger, Jungbauer & Barczak · http://www.yjblaw.com · 745 Kasota Avenue · Minneapolis, MN 55414 · 612-333-6371

Gregory T. Yaeger · Yaeger, Jungbauer & Barczak · http://www.yjblaw.com · 745 Kasota Avenue · Minneapolis, MN 55414 · 612-333-6371

St. Paul

Julius W. Gernes · Spence, Ricke, Sweeney & Gernes · Degree of Honor Building, Suite 600 · 325 Cedar Street · St. Paul, MN 55101 · 651-223-8000

Megan K. Ricke · Spence, Ricke, Sweeney & Gernes · Degree of Honor Building, Suite 600 · 325 Cedar Street · St. Paul, MN 55101 · 651-223-8000

Patrick J. Sweeney · Spence, Ricke, Sweeney & Gernes · Degree of Honor Building, Suite 600 · 325 Cedar Street · St. Paul, MN 55101 · 651-223-8000

REAL ESTATE LAW

Duluth

William M. Burns · 2) · Hanft Fride · 1000 U.S. Bank Place · 130 West Superior Street · Duluth, MN 55802-2094 · 218-722-4766

Minneapolis

Scott A. Anderegg · Faegre & Benson · Wells Fargo Center, Suite 2200 · 90 South Seventh Street · Minneapolis, MN 55402-3901 · 612-766-7000

Angela M. Christy · Faegre & Benson · Wells Fargo Center, Suite 2200 · 90 South Seventh Street · Minneapolis, MN 55402-3901 · 612-766-7000

Stephen J. Davis · 2% · Stephen J. Davis · 4601 Excelsior Boulevard, Suite 500 · Minneapolis, MN 55416-4960 · 952-285-9200

David B. Eide · Felhaber Larson Fenlon & Vogt · U.S. Bank Plaza, Suite 2200 · 220 South Sixth Street · Minneapolis, MN 55402-4504 · 612-339-6321

Gary C. Eidson · Fabyanske, Westra, Hart & Thomson · http://www.fwhlaw.com · 800 LaSalle Avenue, Suite 1900 · Minneapolis, MN 55402 · 612-338-0115

Charles S. Ferrell · 2) · Faegre & Benson · Wells Fargo Center, Suite 2200 · 90 South Seventh Street · Minneapolis, MN 55402-3901 · 612-766-7000

Joseph M. Finley · a · Leonard, Street and Deinard · http://www.leonard.com · 150 South Fifth Street, Suite 2300 · Minneapolis, MN 55402 · 612-335-1500

Larry B. Guthrie · Lindquist & Vennum · http://www.lindquist.com · IDS Center, Suite 4200 · 80 South Eighth Street · Minneapolis, MN 55402-2205 · 612-371-3211

Mark E. Hamel · a · Dorsey & Whitney · 50 South Sixth Street, Suite 1500 · Minneapolis, MN 55402-1498 · 612-340-2600

Robyn Hansen · Leonard, Street and Deinard · http://www.leonard.com · 150 South Fifth Street, Suite 2300 · Minneapolis, MN 55402 · 612-335-1500

Thomas M. Hart · Winthrop & Weinstine · http://www.winthrop.com · 225 South Sixth Street, Suite 3500 Minneapolis, MN 55402-4629 · 612-604-6400

William A. Haug · Moss & Barnett · http://www.moss-barnett.com · Wells Fargo Center, Suite 4800 · 90 South Seventh Street · Minneapolis, MN 55402-4129 · 612-877-5000

Charles R. Haynor · a · Briggs and Morgan · IDS Center, Suite 2200 · 80 South Eighth Street · Minneapolis, MN 55402 · 612-977-8400

Robert L. Hoffman · a · Larkin, Hoffman, Daly & Lindgren · Wells Fargo Plaza, Suite 1500 · 7900 Xerxes Avenue South · Minneapolis, MN 55431-1194 · 952-835-3800

Jon J. Hoganson · Winthrop & Weinstine · http://www.winthrop.com · 225 South Sixth Street, Suite 3500 Minneapolis, MN 55402-4629 · 612-604-6400

David W. Kelley · a · Leonard, Street and Deinard · http://www.leonard.com · 150 South Fifth Street, Suite 2300 · Minneapolis, MN 55402 · 612-335-1500

Lloyd G. Kepple · Oppenheimer Wolff & Donnelly · Plaza VII, Suite 3300 · 45 South Seventh Street · Minneapolis, MN 55402 · 612-607-7000

David E. Kirkman · Ravich, Meyer, Kirkman, McGrath & Nauman · 4545 IDS Center · 80 South Eighth Street · Minneapolis, MN 55402 · 612-332-8511

John M. Koneck · a · Fredrikson & Byron · 200 South Sixth Street, Suite 4000 · Minneapolis, MN 55402-1425 · 612-492-7000

Richard H. Massopust, Jr. · 2) · Oppenheimer Wolff & Donnelly · Plaza VII, Suite 3300 · 45 South Seventh Street · Minneapolis, MN 55402 · 612-607-7000

Thomas M. Mayerle · 2% · Faegre & Benson · Wells Fargo Center, Suite 2200 · 90 South Seventh Street · Minneapolis, MN 55402-3901 · 612-766-7000

Paul S. Moe · Faegre & Benson · Wells Fargo Center, Suite 2200 · 90 South Seventh Street · Minneapolis, MN 55402-3901 · 612-766-7000

Donald P. Norwich · a · Oppenheimer Wolff & Donnelly · Plaza VII, Suite 3300 · 45 South Seventh Street · Minneapolis, MN 55402 · 612-607-7000

Bruce G. Odlaug · a · Lindquist & Vennum · http://www.lindquist.com · IDS Center, Suite 4200 · 80 South Eighth Street · Minneapolis, MN 55402-2205 · 612-371-3211

Charles A. Parsons, Jr. · Moss & Barnett · http://www.moss-barnett.com · Wells Fargo Center, Suite 4800 · 90 South Seventh Street · Minneapolis, MN 55402-4129 · 612-877-5000

Mary S. Ranum · Fredrikson & Byron · 200 South Sixth Street, Suite 4000 · Minneapolis, MN 55402-1425 · 612-492-7000

Paul H. Ravich · 2% · Ravich, Meyer, Kirkman, McGrath & Nauman · 4545 IDS Center · 80 South Eighth Street · Minneapolis, MN 55402 · 612-332-8511

Rebecca L. Rom · Faegre & Benson · Wells Fargo Center, Suite 2200 · 90 South Seventh Street · Minneapolis, MN 55402-3901 · 612-766-7000

David C. Sellergren · a · Fredrikson & Byron · 200 South Sixth Street, Suite 4000 · Minneapolis, MN 55402-1425 · 612-492-7000

John W. Thiel · 2% · Gray, Plant, Mooty, Mooty & Bennett · IDS Center, Suite 500 · 80 South Eighth Street · Minneapolis, MN 55402-3796 · 612-632-3000

Mark W. Westra · a · Fabyanske, Westra, Hart & Thomson · http://www.fwhlaw.com · 800 LaSalle Avenue, Suite 1900 · Minneapolis, MN 55402 · 612-338-0115

John R. Wheaton · a · Faegre & Benson · Wells Fargo Center, Suite 2200 · 90 South Seventh Street · Minneapolis, MN 55402-3901 · 612-766-7000

SECURITIES LAW

Minneapolis

Jonathan B. Abram · Dorsey & Whitney · 50 South Sixth Street, Suite 1500 · Minneapolis, MN 55402-1498 · 612-340-2600

Philip S. Garon · a · Faegre & Benson · Wells Fargo Center, Suite 2200 · 90 South Seventh Street · Minneapolis, MN 55402-3901 · 612-766-7000

Steven C. Kennedy · Faegre & Benson · Wells Fargo Center, Suite 2200 · 90 South Seventh Street · Minneapolis, MN 55402-3901 · 612-766-7000

Thomas R. King · Fredrikson & Byron · 200 South Sixth Street, Suite 4000 · Minneapolis, MN 55402-1425 · 612-492-7000

David B. Miller · Faegre & Benson · Wells Fargo Center, Suite 2200 · 90 South Seventh Street · Minneapolis, MN 55402-3901 · 612-766-7000

Michael J. Radmer · Dorsey & Whitney · 50 South Sixth Street, Suite 1500 · Minneapolis, MN 55402-1498 · 612-340-2600

Melodie R. Rose · Fredrikson & Byron · 200 South Sixth Street, Suite 4000 · Minneapolis, MN 55402-1425 · 612-492-7000

Kris Sharpe · a · Faegre & Benson · Wells Fargo Center, Suite 2200 · 90 South Seventh Street · Minneapolis, MN 55402-3901 · 612-766-7000

Mark S. Weitz · Leonard, Street and Deinard · http://www.leonard.com · 150 South Fifth Street, Suite 2300 · Minneapolis, MN 55402 · 612-335-1500

SPORTS LAW

Minneapolis

Richard G. Pepin, Jr. · Leonard, Street and Deinard · http://www.leonard.com · 150 South Fifth Street, Suite 2300 · Minneapolis, MN 55402 · 612-335-1500

STRUCTURED FINANCE LAW

Minneapolis

Kevin M. Busch · Moss & Barnett · http://www.moss-barnett.com · Wells Fargo Center, Suite 4800 · 90 South Seventh Street · Minneapolis, MN 55402-4129 · 612-877-5000

James M. Pfau · Faegre & Benson · Wells Fargo Center, Suite 2200 · 90 South Seventh Street · Minneapolis, MN 55402-3901 · 612-766-7000

TAX LAW

Duluth

James H. Stewart · 2) · Fryberger, Buchanan, Smith & Frederick · 302 West Superior Street, Suite 700 · Duluth, MN 55802 · 218-722-0861

Edina

Jack W. Carlson · 2% · Thomsen & Nybeck · 3300 Edinborough Way, Suite 600 · Edina, MN 55435 · 952-835-7000

Minneapolis

Bruce A. Ackerman · Faegre & Benson · Wells Fargo Center, Suite 2200 · 90 South Seventh Street · Minneapolis, MN 55402-3901 · 612-766-7000

David C. Bahls · Gray, Plant, Mooty, Mooty & Bennett · IDS Center, Suite 500 · 80 South Eighth Street · Minneapolis, MN 55402-3796 · 612-632-3000

Douglas J. Brown · Brown & Carlson · 5411 Circle Down Avenue, Suite 100 · Minneapolis, MN 55416-1311 · 763-591-9950

Martin A. Culhane III · a · Oppenheimer Wolff & Donnelly · Plaza VII, Suite 3300 · 45 South Seventh Street · Minneapolis, MN 55402 · 612-607-7000

Kimball J. Devoy · 2% · Lindquist & Vennum · http://www.lindquist.com · IDS Center, Suite 4200 · 80 South Eighth Street · Minneapolis, MN 55402-2205 · 612-371-3211

John J. Erhart · a · Fredrikson & Byron · 200 South Sixth Street, Suite 4000 · Minneapolis, MN 55402-1425 · 612-492-7000

Myron L. Frans · a · Faegre & Benson · Wells Fargo Center, Suite 2200 · 90 South Seventh Street · Minneapolis, MN 55402-3901 · 612-766-7000

William R. Goetz · Dorsey & Whitney · 50 South Sixth Street, Suite 1500 · Minneapolis, MN 55402-1498 612-340-2600

David N. Haynes · Leonard, Street and Deinard · http://www.leonard.com · 150 South Fifth Street, Suite 2300 · Minneapolis, MN 55402 · 612-335-1500

William D. Klein · Gray, Plant, Mooty, Mooty & Bennett · IDS Center, Suite 500 · 80 South Eighth Street · Minneapolis, MN 55402-3796 · 612-632-3000

Paul J. Linstroth · Malkerson Gilliland Martin · U.S. Bank Plaza South, Suite 1900 · 220 South Sixth Street · Minneapolis, MN 55402-4502 · 612-344-1111

Phillip H. Martin · 2) · Dorsey & Whitney · 50 South Sixth Street, Suite 1500 · Minneapolis, MN 55402-1498 · 612-340-2600

Thomas R. Muck · a · Fredrikson & Byron · 200 South Sixth Street, Suite 4000 · Minneapolis, MN 55402-1425 · 612-492-7000

Sue Ann Nelson · Fredrikson & Byron · 200 South Sixth Street, Suite 4000 · Minneapolis, MN 55402-1425 · 612-492-7000

Walter A. Pickhardt · a · Faegre & Benson · Wells Fargo Center, Suite 2200 · 90 South Seventh Street · Minneapolis, MN 55402-3901 · 612-766-7000

Clinton A. Schroeder · 2% · Gray, Plant, Mooty, Mooty & Bennett · IDS Center, Suite 500 · 80 South Eighth Street · Minneapolis, MN 55402-3796 · 612-632-3000

Bruce J. Shnider · 2) · Dorsey & Whitney · 50 South Sixth Street, Suite 1500 · Minneapolis, MN 55402-1498 · 612-340-2600

John K. Steffen · 2) · Faegre & Benson · Wells Fargo Center, Suite 2200 · 90 South Seventh Street · Minneapolis, MN 55402-3901 · 612-766-7000

John W. Windhorst, Jr. · 2% · Dorsey & Whitney · 50 South Sixth Street, Suite 1500 · Minneapolis, MN 55402-1498 · 612-340-2600

Peter J. Withoff · Faegre & Benson · Wells Fargo Center, Suite 2200 · 90 South Seventh Street · Minneapolis, MN 55402-3901 · 612-766-7000

St. Paul

Terrance A. Costello · Terrance A. Costello · The Lakes & Plains Office Building · 842 Raymond Avenue · St. Paul, MN 55114 · 251-246-5459

Jerome A. Geis · 2% · Briggs and Morgan · First National Bank Building, Suite W2200 · 332 Minnesota Street · St. Paul, MN 55101-1396 · 651-808-6600

TIMBER LAW

Duluth

David R. Oberstar · Fryberger, Buchanan, Smith & Frederick · 302 West Superior Street, Suite 700 · Duluth, MN 55802 · 218-722-0861

Minneapolis

Richard A. Duncan · a · Faegre & Benson · Wells Fargo Center, Suite 2200 · 90 South Seventh Street · Minneapolis, MN 55402-3901 · 612-766-7000

TRUSTS AND ESTATES

Duluth

Richard R. Burns · 2) · Hanft Fride · 1000 U.S. Bank Place · 130 West Superior Street · Duluth, MN 55802-2094 · 218-722-4766

Mark T. Signorelli · 2) · Mark T. Signorelli · Alworth Building, Suite 300 · 306 West Superior Street · Duluth, MN 55802 · 218-722-5380

James H. Stewart · 2) · Fryberger, Buchanan, Smith & Frederick · 302 West Superior Street, Suite 700 · Duluth, MN 55802 · 218-722-0861

Edina

Bonnie M. Fleming · Bonnie M. Fleming · 5200 Willson Road, Suite 150 · Edina, MN 55424

Hopkins

Nancy S. Bender-Kelner · a · Bender-Kelner Wills, Trusts & Estates · Wells Fargo Bank Building, Suite 444 · 1011 First Street South · Hopkins, MN 55343 · 952-930-3700

Minneapolis

Edward M. Arundel · 2) · Gray, Plant, Mooty, Mooty & Bennett · IDS Center, Suite 500 · 80 South Eighth Street · Minneapolis, MN 55402-3796 · 612-632-3000

William J. Berens · a · Dorsey & Whitney · 50 South Sixth Street, Suite 1500 · Minneapolis, MN 55402-1498 · 612-340-2600

Bruce W. Blackburn · Oppenheimer Wolff & Donnelly · Plaza VII, Suite 3300 · 45 South Seventh Street Minneapolis, MN 55402 · 612-607-7000

Steve A. Brand · 2) · Robins, Kaplan, Miller & Ciresi · 2800 LaSalle Plaza · 800 LaSalle Avenue · Minneapolis, MN 55402 · 612-349-8500

Andrea S. Breckner · Olson & Breckner · 150 South Fifth Street, Suite 3275 · Minneapolis, MN 55402 · 612-455-1000

William J. Brody · a · Fredrikson & Byron · 200 South Sixth Street, Suite 4000 · Minneapolis, MN 55402-1425 · 612-492-7000

Ann Barry Burns · a · Gray, Plant, Mooty, Mooty & Bennett · IDS Center, Suite 500 · 80 South Eighth Street · Minneapolis, MN 55402-3796 · 612-632-3000

John A. Burton, Jr. · a · Best & Flanagan · 225 South Sixth Street, Suite 4000 · Minneapolis, MN 55402-4690 · 612-339-7121

Thomas D. Carlson · Lindquist & Vennum · http://www.lindquist.com · IDS Center, Suite 4200 · 80 South Eighth Street · Minneapolis, MN 55402-2205 · 612-371-3211

Bronwen L. Cound · Fredrikson & Byron · 200 South Sixth Street, Suite 4000 · Minneapolis, MN 55402-1425 · 612-492-7000

Robert L. Crosby · 2) · Best & Flanagan · 225 South Sixth Street, Suite 4000 · Minneapolis, MN 55402-4690 · 612-339-7121

William S. Forsberg · Leonard, Street and Deinard · http://www.leonard.com · 150 South Fifth Street, Suite 2300 · Minneapolis, MN 55402 · 612-335-1500

Jane F. Godfrey · Leonard, Street and Deinard · http://www.leonard.com · 150 South Fifth Street, Suite 2300 · Minneapolis, MN 55402 · 612-335-1500

Mark W. Greiner · Fredrikson & Byron · 200 South Sixth Street, Suite 4000 · Minneapolis, MN 55402-1425 · 612-492-7000

Larry R. Henneman · 2% · Gray, Plant, Mooty, Mooty & Bennett · IDS Center, Suite 500 · 80 South Eighth Street · Minneapolis, MN 55402-3796 · 612-632-3000

E. Burke Hinds · Inrelex Law Group · 4626 Wentworth Avenue South · P.O. Box 19649 · Minneapolis, MN 55419 · 612-309-5340

Christopher B. Hunt · a · Fredrikson & Byron · 200 South Sixth Street, Suite 4000 · Minneapolis, MN 55402-1425 · 612-492-7000

Gary M. Johnson · a · Dorsey & Whitney · 50 South Sixth Street, Suite 1500 · Minneapolis, MN 55402-1498 · 612-340-2600

Sidney Kaplan · 2% · Parsinen Kaplan Rosberg & Gotlieb · 100 South Fifth Street, Suite 1100 · Minneapolis, MN 55402-1298 · 612-333-2111

E. Joseph LaFave · Best & Flanagan · 225 South Sixth Street, Suite 4000 · Minneapolis, MN 55402-4690 612-339-7121

Stephen R. Litman · Leonard, Street and Deinard · http://www.leonard.com · 150 South Fifth Street, Suite 2300 · Minneapolis, MN 55402 · 612-335-1500

Bridget A. Logstrom Koci · Dorsey & Whitney · 50 South Sixth Street, Suite 1500 · Minneapolis, MN 55402-1498 · 612-340-2600

Thomas E. Lund · a · Oppenheimer Wolff & Donnelly · Plaza VII, Suite 3300 · 45 South Seventh Street Minneapolis, MN 55402 · 612-607-7000

Gary D. McDowell · a · Lindquist & Vennum · http://www.lindquist.com · IDS Center, Suite 4200 · 80 South Eighth Street · Minneapolis, MN 55402-2205 · 612-371-3211

Gene C. Olson · a · Olson & Breckner · 150 South Fifth Street, Suite 3275 · Minneapolis, MN 55402 · 612-455-1000

Charles T. Parks, Jr. · a · Faegre & Benson · Wells Fargo Center, Suite 2200 · 90 South Seventh Street · Minneapolis, MN 55402-3901 · 612-766-7000

Stanley M. Rein · a · Dorsey & Whitney · 50 South Sixth Street, Suite 1500 · Minneapolis, MN 55402-1498 · 612-340-2600

Dale J. Schoonover · Fredrikson & Byron · 200 South Sixth Street, Suite 4000 · Minneapolis, MN 55402-1425 · 612-492-7000

Clinton A. Schroeder · 2% · Gray, Plant, Mooty, Mooty & Bennett · IDS Center, Suite 500 · 80 South Eighth Street · Minneapolis, MN 55402-3796 · 612-632-3000

David J. Shannon · a · Faegre & Benson · Wells Fargo Center, Suite 2200 · 90 South Seventh Street · Minneapolis, MN 55402-3901 · 612-766-7000

Alan I. Silver · Bassford Remele · http://www.bassford.com · 33 South Sixth Street, Suite 3800 · Minneapolis, MN 55402-3707 · 612-333-3000

Lowell V. Stortz · Leonard, Street and Deinard · http://www.leonard.com · 150 South Fifth Street, Suite 2300 · Minneapolis, MN 55402 · 612-335-1500

Mavis J. Van Sambeek · Lindquist & Vennum · http://www.lindquist.com · IDS Center, Suite 4200 · 80 South Eighth Street · Minneapolis, MN 55402-2205 · 612-371-3211

Rochester

Alan J. Yanowitz · a · Alan J. Yanowitz · 18 Third Street, SW, Suite 300 · Rochester, MN 55902 · 507-252-8997

St. Cloud

Gerald L. Thoreen · Quinlivan & Hughes · 400 South First Street, Suite 600 · St. Cloud, MN 56302 · 320-251-1414

St. Louis Park

Ross A. Sussman · Ross A. Sussman · 5353 Wayzata Boulevard, Suite 205 · St. Louis Park, MN 55416 · 952-541-1122

St. Paul

Terence N. Doyle · 2) · Briggs and Morgan · First National Bank Building, Suite W2200 · 332 Minnesota Street · St. Paul, MN 55101-1396 · 651-808-6600

Martin H. Fisk · Briggs and Morgan · First National Bank Building, Suite W2200 · 332 Minnesota Street · St. Paul, MN 55101-1396 · 651-808-6600

Gregory A. Kvam · a · Briggs and Morgan · First National Bank Building, Suite W2200 · 332 Minnesota Street · St. Paul, MN 55101-1396 · 651-808-6600

John J. McNeely · 2% · Briggs and Morgan · First National Bank Building, Suite W2200 · 332 Minnesota Street · St. Paul, MN 55101-1396 · 651-808-6600

McNeil V. Seymour · 2% · Briggs and Morgan · First National Bank Building, Suite W2200 · 332 Minnesota Street · St. Paul, MN 55101-1396 · 651-808-6600

Terry L. Slye · a · Briggs and Morgan · First National Bank Building, Suite W2200 · 332 Minnesota Street · St. Paul, MN 55101-1396 · 651-808-6600

Richard A. Wilhoit · 2% · Briggs and Morgan · First National Bank Building, Suite W2200 · 332 Minnesota Street · St. Paul, MN 55101-1396 · 651-808-6600

Wayzata

Edward G. Heilman · a · Heilman & Schlotthauer · 1000 Twelve Oaks Center Drive, Suite 101 · Wayzata, MN 55391 · 952-767-0409

WATER LAW

Minneapolis

Byron E. Starns · a · Leonard, Street and Deinard · http://www.leonard.com · 150 South Fifth Street, Suite 2300 · Minneapolis, MN 55402 · 612-335-1500

WHITE-COLLAR CRIMINAL DEFENSE

Minneapolis

Joseph S. Friedberg · 2% · Joseph S. Friedberg · Fifth Street Towers, Suite 320 · 150 South Fifth Street · Minneapolis, MN 55402 · 612-339-8626

Charles L. Hawkins · a · Charles L. Hawkins · 150 South Fifth Street, Suite 3260 · Minneapolis, MN 55402 · 612-339-6921

John W. Lundquist · Fredrikson & Byron · 200 South Sixth Street, Suite 4000 · Minneapolis, MN 55402-1425 · 612-492-7000

William J. Mauzy · 2% · Mauzy Law Firm · 510 First Avenue North, Suite 610 · Minneapolis, MN 55403 · 612-340-9108

Ronald I. Meshbesher · 2% · Meshbesher & Spence · 1616 Park Avenue · Minneapolis, MN 55404 · 612-339-9121

St. Paul

Earl P. Gray · a · Gray & Malacko · 332 Minnesota Street, Suite W1610 · St. Paul, MN 55101 · 651-223-5175

WORKERS' COMPENSATION LAW

Bloomington

Christopher Middlebrook · Christopher Middlebrook · 8030 Old Cedar Avenue South, Suite 215 · Bloomington, MN 55425 · 952-883-0880

Coon Rapids

David B. Kempston · Law Office of Thomas D. Mottaz · 3340 Northdale Boulevard, NW, Suite 140 · Coon Rapids, MN 55448 · 763-421-8226

Thomas D. Mottaz · a · Law Office of Thomas D. Mottaz · 3340 Northdale Boulevard, NW, Suite 140 · Coon Rapids, MN 55448 · 763-421-8226

Duluth

Robert C. Falsani · a · Falsani, Balmer, Peterson, Quinn & Beyer · http://www.duluthtriallawyers.com · 1200 Alworth Building · 306 West Superior Street · Duluth, MN 55802-1800 · 218-723-1990

Lake Elmo

Eugene J. Flick · a · Jardine, Logan & O'Brien · 8519 Eagle Point Boulevard, Suite 100 · Lake Elmo, MN 55042 · 651-290-6500

Minneapolis

Michael D. Aafedt · a · Aafedt, Forde, Gray, Monson & Hager · 150 South Fifth Street, Suite 2600 · Minneapolis, MN 55402-4226 · 612-339-8965

Kathryn Hipp Carlson · Miller & Carlson · 150 South Fifth Street, Suite 1490 · Minneapolis, MN 55402 · 612-333-8600

Thomas F. Coleman · Cousineau McGuire · 1550 Utica Avenue South, Suite 600 · Minneapolis, MN 55416 · 952-546-8400

Michael Forde · a · Aafedt, Forde, Gray, Monson & Hager · 150 South Fifth Street, Suite 2600 · Minneapolis, MN 55402-4226 · 612-339-8965

Thomas P. Kieselbach · a · Cousineau McGuire · 1550 Utica Avenue South, Suite 600 · Minneapolis, MN 55416 · 952-546-8400

Mark A. Kleinschmidt · Cousineau McGuire · 1550 Utica Avenue South, Suite 600 · Minneapolis, MN 55416 · 952-546-8400

Timothy J. McCoy · a · McCoy Peterson & Jorstad · Butler Square Building, Suite 550-A · 100 North Sixth Street · Minneapolis, MN 55403 · 612-333-3999

Janet Monson · Aafedt, Forde, Gray, Monson & Hager · 150 South Fifth Street, Suite 2600 · Minneapolis, MN 55402-4226 · 612-339-8965

Mark G. Olive · Sieben, Grose, Von Holtum & Carey · 800 Marquette Avenue, Suite 900 · Minneapolis, MN 55402 · 612-333-4500

Raymond R. Peterson · a · McCoy Peterson & Jorstad · Butler Square Building, Suite 550-A · 100 North Sixth Street · Minneapolis, MN 55403 · 612-333-3999

Peter J. Pustorino · a · Pustorino, Tilton, Parrington & Lindquist · 4005 West 65th Street, Suite 200 · Minneapolis, MN 55435 · 952-925-3001

James R. Waldhauser · a · Cousineau McGuire · 1550 Utica Avenue South, Suite 600 · Minneapolis, MN 55416 · 952-546-8400

St. Paul

William M. Bradt · a · Hansen, Dordell, Bradt, Odlaug & Bradt · 3900 Northwoods Drive, Suite 250 · St. Paul, MN 55112 · 651-482-8900

Jay T. Hartman · a · Heacox, Hartman, Mattaini, Koshmrl, Cosgriff & Johnson · 550 Hamm Building · 408 St. Peter Street · St. Paul, MN 55102 · 651-222-2922

Steven D. Hawn · a · Steven D. Hawn · 366 Jackson Street, Suite 200 · St. Paul, MN 55101 · 651-222-4146

Gregory G. Heacox · a · Heacox, Hartman, Mattaini, Koshmrl, Cosgriff & Johnson · 550 Hamm Building 408 St. Peter Street · St. Paul, MN 55102 · 651-222-2922

Gregg A. Johnson · Heacox, Hartman, Mattaini, Koshmrl, Cosgriff & Johnson · 550 Hamm Building · 408 St. Peter Street · St. Paul, MN 55102 · 651-222-2922

Michael J. Koshmrl · Heacox, Hartman, Mattaini, Koshmrl, Cosgriff & Johnson · 550 Hamm Building · 408 St. Peter Street · St. Paul, MN 55102 · 651-222-2922

David J. Odlaug · a · Hansen, Dordell, Bradt, Odlaug & Bradt · 3900 Northwoods Drive, Suite 250 · St. Paul, MN 55112 · 651-482-8900

MISSISSIPPI

ADMINISTRATIVE LAW

Jackson

David B. Grishman · a · Watkins Ludlam Winter & Stennis · http://www.watkinsludlam.com · 633 North State Street · P.O. Box 427 · Jackson, MS 39205-0427 · 601-949-4900

David L. Martin · Watkins Ludlam Winter & Stennis · http://www.watkinsludlam.com · 633 North State Street · P.O. Box 427 · Jackson, MS 39205-0427 · 601-949-4900

Edward A. Wilmesherr · a · Butler, Snow, O'Mara, Stevens and Cannada · http://www.butlersnow.com · AmSouth Plaza, Suite 1700 · 210 East Capitol Street · P.O. Box 22567 · Jackson, MS 39225-2567 · 601-948-5711

ALTERNATIVE DISPUTE RESOLUTION

Biloxi

Donald C. Dornan, Jr. · Spyridon, Palermo & Dornan · 154 Porter Avenue · Biloxi, MS 39533 · 228-374-2013

Britt R. Singletary · Singletary & Thrash · 177 Lameuse Street · P.O. Box 1229 · Biloxi, MS 39533-1229 · 228-432-8900

Columbia

Thomas D. McNeese · McNeese & Hahn · 338 Church Street · P.O. Drawer 948 · Columbia, MS 39429-0948 · 601-731-5020

Greenwood

Charles J. Swayze, Jr. · Whittington, Brock & Swayze · 308 Fulton Street · P.O. Box 941 · Greenwood, MS 38935-0941 · 662-453-7325

Jackson

Reuben V. Anderson · Phelps Dunbar · http://www.phelpsdunbar.com · 111 East Capitol Street, Suite 600 · P.O. Box 23066 · Jackson, MS 39225-3066 · 601-352-2300

Fred L. Banks, Jr. · Phelps Dunbar · http://www.phelpsdunbar.com · 111 East Capitol Street, Suite 600 · P.O. Box 23066 · Jackson, MS 39225-3066 · 601-352-2300

Richard T. Bennett · 2% · Bennett, Lotterhos, Sulser & Wilson · http://www.blswlaw.com · One Jackson Place, Suite 1400 · 188 East Capitol Street · P.O. Box 98 · Jackson, MS 39205-0098 · 601-944-0466

Thomas W. Crockett · a · Watkins Ludlam Winter & Stennis · http://www.watkinsludlam.com · 633 North State Street · P.O. Box 427 · Jackson, MS 39205-0427 · 601-949-4900

Kenneth E. Milam · 2) · Watkins & Eager · http://www.watkinseager.com · The Emporium Building · 400 East Capitol Street · P.O. Box 650 · Jackson, MS 39205 · 601-965-1900

Harold D. Miller, Jr. · a · Butler, Snow, O'Mara, Stevens and Cannada · http://www.butlersnow.com · AmSouth Plaza, Suite 1700 · 210 East Capitol Street · P.O. Box 22567 · Jackson, MS 39225-2567 · 601-948-5711

Patrick H. Scanlon · 2% · Pat H. Scanlon · The Quarter, Suite L-15 · 1855 Lakeland Drive · Jackson, MS 39232 · 601-936-8924

Robert W. Sneed · Robert W. Sneed · Five Old River Place, Suite 205 · P.O. Box 2251 · Jackson, MS 39225-2251 · 601-354-0044

Oxford

Jack F. Dunbar · 2% · Holcomb Dunbar · Courthouse Square · 1217 Jackson Avenue · P.O. Drawer 707 · Oxford, MS 38655 · 662-234-8775

Ridgeland

William Larry Latham · Latham & Burwell · 618 Crescent Boulevard, Suite 200 · Ridgeland, MS 39157 · 601-427-4470

ANTITRUST LAW

Jackson

Robert E. Hauberg, Jr. · a · Baker, Donelson, Bearman, Caldwell & Berkowitz · http://www.bakerdonelson.com · Meadowbrook Office Park · 4268 I-55 North · P.O. Box 14167 · Jackson, MS 39236 · 601-351-2400

APPELLATE LAW

Jackson

Fred L. Banks, Jr. · Phelps Dunbar · http://www.phelpsdunbar.com · 111 East Capitol Street, Suite 600 · P.O. Box 23066 · Jackson, MS 39225-3066 · 601-352-2300

James Craig · Phelps Dunbar · http://www.phelpsdunbar.com · 111 East Capitol Street, Suite 600 · P.O. Box 23066 · Jackson, MS 39225-3066 · 601-352-2300

Margaret Oertling Cupples · Bradley Arant Rose & White · http://www.bradleyarant.com · One Jackson Place, Suite 450 · 188 East Capitol Street · Jackson, MS 39201 · 601-948-8000

W. Wayne Drinkwater, Jr. · a · Bradley Arant Rose & White · http://www.bradleyarant.com · One Jackson Place, Suite 450 · 188 East Capitol Street · Jackson, MS 39201 · 601-948-8000

William F. Goodman, Jr. · 2% · Watkins & Eager · http://www.watkinseager.com · The Emporium Building · 400 East Capitol Street · P.O. Box 650 · Jackson, MS 39205 · 601-965-1900

John C. Henegan · a · Butler, Snow, O'Mara, Stevens and Cannada · http://www.butlersnow.com · AmSouth Plaza, Suite 1700 · 210 East Capitol Street · P.O. Box 22567 · Jackson, MS 39225-2567 · 601-948-5711

Donna Brown Jacobs · Butler, Snow, O'Mara, Stevens and Cannada · http://www.butlersnow.com · AmSouth Plaza, Suite 1700 · 210 East Capitol Street · P.O. Box 22567 · Jackson, MS 39225-2567 · 601-948-5711

John L. Maxey II · 2% · Maxey Wann · AmSouth Plaza, Suite 2100 · 210 East Capitol Street · P.O. Box 3977 · Jackson, MS 39207-3977 · 601-355-8855

Robert B. McDuff · Robert Bruce McDuff · 767 North Congress Street · Jackson, MS 39202 · 601-969-0802

Luther T. Munford · a · Phelps Dunbar · http://www.phelpsdunbar.com · 111 East Capitol Street, Suite 600 · P.O. Box 23066 · Jackson, MS 39225-3066 · 601-352-2300

Michael B. Wallace · Wise Carter Child & Caraway · Heritage Building, Suite 600 · 401 East Capitol Street · Jackson, MS 39205 · 601-968-5500

J. Collins Wohner, Jr. · Watkins & Eager · http://www.watkinseager.com · The Emporium Building · 400 East Capitol Street · P.O. Box 650 · Jackson, MS 39205 · 601-965-1900

BANKING LAW

Gulfport

John M. Harral · Butler, Snow, O'Mara, Stevens and Cannada · http://www.butlersnow.com · Whitney National Bank Building, Suite 204 · 1300 Twenty-Fifth Avenue · P.O. Drawer 4248 · Gulfport, MS 39502 228-864-1170

Jackson

Paul A. Carrubba · Adams and Reese · http://www.adamsandreese.com · 111 East Capitol Street, Suite 350 · P.O. Box 24297 · Jackson, MS 39201 · 601-353-3234

George R. Fair · 2) · Watkins & Eager · http://www.watkinseager.com · The Emporium Building · 400 East Capitol Street · P.O. Box 650 · Jackson, MS 39205 · 601-965-1900

William F. Goodman, Jr. · 2% · Watkins & Eager · http://www.watkinseager.com · The Emporium Building · 400 East Capitol Street · P.O. Box 650 · Jackson, MS 39205 · 601-965-1900

J. Clifford Harrison · a · Butler, Snow, O'Mara, Stevens and Cannada · http://www.butlersnow.com · AmSouth Plaza, Suite 1700 · 210 East Capitol Street · P.O. Box 22567 · Jackson, MS 39225-2567 · 601-948-5711

E. Clifton Hodge, Jr. · a · Mockbee Hall Drake & Hodge · Capital Towers, Suite 1820 · 125 South Congress Street · Jackson, MS 39201 · 601-353-0035

Craig N. Landrum · a · Watkins Ludlam Winter & Stennis · http://www.watkinsludlam.com · 633 North State Street · P.O. Box 427 · Jackson, MS 39205-0427 · 601-949-4900

David L. Martin · Watkins Ludlam Winter & Stennis · http://www.watkinsludlam.com · 633 North State Street · P.O. Box 427 · Jackson, MS 39205-0427 · 601-949-4900

Charles N. Parrott · Adams and Reese · http://www.adamsandreese.com · 111 East Capitol Street, Suite 350 · P.O. Box 24297 · Jackson, MS 39201 · 601-353-3234

Keith R. Raulston · a · Watkins Ludlam Winter & Stennis · http://www.watkinsludlam.com · 633 North State Street · P.O. Box 427 · Jackson, MS 39205-0427 · 601-949-4900

Granville Tate, Jr. · Brunini, Grantham, Grower & Hewes · http://www.brunini.com · 1400 Trustmark Building · 248 East Capitol Street · P.O. Drawer 119 · Jackson, MS 39205 · 601-948-3101

Edward A. Wilmesherr · a · Butler, Snow, O'Mara, Stevens and Cannada · http://www.butlersnow.com · AmSouth Plaza, Suite 1700 · 210 East Capitol Street · P.O. Box 22567 · Jackson, MS 39225-2567 · 601-948-5711

Biloxi

Robert Alan Byrd · a · Byrd & Wiser · 145 Main Street · P.O. Box 1939 · Biloxi, MS 39533 · 228-432-8123

Hattiesburg

J. C. Bell · 2% · Office of Chapter 13 Trustee · 1210 West Pine Street · P.O. Box 566 · Hattiesburg, MS 39403 · 601-582-5011

Jackson

J.Thomas Ash · J. Thomas Ash · 4915 I-55 North, Suite 203-B · P.O. Box 13219 · Jackson, MS 39236-3219 · 601-981-5600

Jeffrey R. Barber · Watkins Ludlam Winter & Stennis · http://www.watkinsludlam.com · 633 North State Street · P.O. Box 427 · Jackson, MS 39205-0427 · 601-949-4900

Richard T. Bennett · 2% · Bennett, Lotterhos, Sulser & Wilson · http://www.blswlaw.com · One Jackson Place, Suite 1400 · 188 East Capitol Street · P.O. Box 98 · Jackson, MS 39205-0098 · 601-944-0466

Derek A. Henderson · a · Derek A. Henderson · 111 East Capitol Street, Suite 455 · Jackson, MS 39201-2403 · 601-948-3167

Kristina M. Johnson · Watkins Ludlam Winter & Stennis · http://www.watkinsludlam.com · 633 North State Street · P.O. Box 427 · Jackson, MS 39205-0427 · 601-949-4900

Robert W. King · 2% · King & Spencer · 235 East Capitol Street · P.O. Box 123 · Jackson, MS 39205-0123 601-948-1547

Douglas C. Noble · Phelps Dunbar · http://www.phelpsdunbar.com · 111 East Capitol Street, Suite 600 · P.O. Box 23066 · Jackson, MS 39225-3066 · 601-352-2300

James W. O'Mara · 2% · Phelps Dunbar · http://www.phelpsdunbar.com · 111 East Capitol Street, Suite 600 · P.O. Box 23066 · Jackson, MS 39225-3066 · 601-352-2300

Stephen W. Rosenblatt · a · Butler, Snow, O'Mara, Stevens and Cannada · http://www.butlersnow.com · AmSouth Plaza, Suite 1700 · 210 East Capitol Street · P.O. Box 22567 · Jackson, MS 39225-2567 · 601-948-5711

Patrick H. Scanlon · 2% · Pat H. Scanlon · The Quarter, Suite L-15 · 1855 Lakeland Drive · Jackson, MS 39232 · 601-936-8924

Eileen N. Shaffer · Law Office of Eileen N. Shaffer · 401 East Capitol Street, Suite 316 · P.O. Box 1177 · Jackson, MS 39201 · 601-969-3006

Jim F. Spencer, Jr. · Watkins & Eager · http://www.watkinseager.com · The Emporium Building · 400 East Capitol Street · P.O. Box 650 · Jackson, MS 39205 · 601-965-1900

Larry Spencer · King & Spencer · 235 East Capitol Street · P.O. Box 123 · Jackson, MS 39205-0123 · 601-948-1547

Marcus M. Wilson · a · Bennett, Lotterhos, Sulser & Wilson · http://www.blswlaw.com · One Jackson Place, Suite 1400 · 188 East Capitol Street · P.O. Box 98 · Jackson, MS 39205-0098 · 601-944-0466

Meridian

Thomas L. Webb · a · Thomas L. Webb · 613 Twenty-Second Avenue · P.O. Box 308 · Meridian, MS 39302-0308 · 601-483-1200

Oxford

D. Andrew Phillips · Mitchell, McNutt & Sams · http://www.mitchellmcnutt.com · 1216 Van Buren · P.O. Box 947 · Oxford, MS 38655 · 662-234-4845

Nina Stubblefield Tollison · a · Law Offices of Nina S. Tollison · P.O. Box 1192 · Oxford, MS 38655-1192 · 662-816-7755

Ridgeland

Craig M. Geno · a · Harris Jernigan & Geno · 587 Highland Colony Parkway · P.O. Box 3380 · Ridgeland, MS 39158-3380 · 601-427-0048

William H. Leech, Sr. · Copeland Cook Taylor & Bush · http://www.cctb.com · Concourse 600, Suite 100 1076 Highland Colony Parkway · P.O. Box 6020 · Ridgeland, MS 39158 · 601-856-7200

BET-THE-COMPANY LITIGATION

Jackson

John G. Corlew · Watkins & Eager · http://www.watkinseager.com · The Emporium Building · 400 East Capitol Street · P.O. Box 650 · Jackson, MS 39205 · 601-965-1900

W. Wayne Drinkwater, Jr. · a · Bradley Arant Rose & White · http://www.bradleyarant.com · One Jackson Place, Suite 450 · 188 East Capitol Street · Jackson, MS 39201 · 601-948-8000

William F. Goodman, Jr. · 2% · Watkins & Eager · http://www.watkinseager.com · The Emporium Building · 400 East Capitol Street · P.O. Box 650 · Jackson, MS 39205 · 601-965-1900

David W. Mockbee · Mockbee Hall Drake & Hodge · Capital Towers, Suite 1820 · 125 South Congress Street · Jackson, MS 39201 · 601-353-0035

Alan W. Perry · 2% · Forman Perry Watkins Krutz & Tardy · http://www.fpwk.com · City Center, Suite 100 · 200 South Lamar Street · P.O. Box 22608 · Jackson, MS 39225-2608 · 601-960-8600

Christopher A. Shapley · a · Brunini, Grantham, Grower & Hewes · http://www.brunini.com · 1400 Trustmark Building · 248 East Capitol Street · P.O. Drawer 119 · Jackson, MS 39205 · 601-948-3101

Lee Davis Thames · 2% · Butler, Snow, O'Mara, Stevens and Cannada · http://www.butlersnow.com · AmSouth Plaza, Suite 1700 · 210 East Capitol Street · P.O. Box 22567 · Jackson, MS 39225-2567 · 601-948-5711

COMMERCIAL LITIGATION

Biloxi

Nicholas Van Wiser · Byrd & Wiser · 145 Main Street · P.O. Box 1939 · Biloxi, MS 39533 · 228-432-8123

Gulfport

Henry F. Laird, Jr. · Watkins Ludlam Winter & Stennis · http://www.watkinsludlam.com · One Hancock Plaza, Suite 1125 · 2510 Fourteenth Street · P.O. Box 160 · Gulfport, MS 39502-0160 · 228-864-3094

Hattiesburg

Frank D. Montague, Jr. · 2% · Montague, Pittman & Varnado · 525 Main Street · P.O. Drawer 1975 · Hattiesburg, MS 39403-1975 · 601-544-1234

Carey R. Varnado · Montague, Pittman & Varnado · 525 Main Street · P.O. Drawer 1975 · Hattiesburg, MS 39403-1975 · 601-544-1234

Jackson

Phil B. Abernethy · Butler, Snow, O'Mara, Stevens and Cannada · http://www.butlersnow.com · AmSouth Plaza, Suite 1700 · 210 East Capitol Street · P.O. Box 22567 · Jackson, MS 39225-2567 · 601-948-5711

Lawrence E. Allison, Jr. · Brunini, Grantham, Grower & Hewes · http://www.brunini.com · 1400 Trustmark Building · 248 East Capitol Street · P.O. Drawer 119 · Jackson, MS 39205 · 601-948-3101

Reuben V. Anderson · Phelps Dunbar · http://www.phelpsdunbar.com · 111 East Capitol Street, Suite 600 · P.O. Box 23066 · Jackson, MS 39225-3066 · 601-352-2300

Fred L. Banks, Jr. · Phelps Dunbar · http://www.phelpsdunbar.com · 111 East Capitol Street, Suite 600 · P.O. Box 23066 · Jackson, MS 39225-3066 · 601-352-2300

Ross F. Bass, Jr. · Phelps Dunbar · http://www.phelpsdunbar.com · 111 East Capitol Street, Suite 600 · P.O. Box 23066 · Jackson, MS 39225-3066 · 601-352-2300

David W. Clark · Bradley Arant Rose & White · http://www.bradleyarant.com · One Jackson Place, Suite 450 · 188 East Capitol Street · Jackson, MS 39201 · 601-948-8000

John G. Corlew · Watkins & Eager · http://www.watkinseager.com · The Emporium Building · 400 East Capitol Street · P.O. Box 650 · Jackson, MS 39205 · 601-965-1900

Luther M. Dove · Dove & Chill · 200 East Capitol Street, Suite 1010 · Jackson, MS 39211 · 601-352-0999

W. Wayne Drinkwater, Jr. · a · Bradley Arant Rose & White · http://www.bradleyarant.com · One Jackson Place, Suite 450 · 188 East Capitol Street · Jackson, MS 39201 · 601-948-8000

C. Michael Ellingburg · a · Daniel, Coker, Horton and Bell · http://www.danielcoker.com · 4400 Old Canton Road, Suite 400 · P.O. Box 1084 · Jackson, MS 39215-1084 · 601-969-7607

William F. Goodman, Jr. · 2% · Watkins & Eager · http://www.watkinseager.com · The Emporium Building · 400 East Capitol Street · P.O. Box 650 · Jackson, MS 39205 · 601-965-1900

John C. Henegan · a · Butler, Snow, O'Mara, Stevens and Cannada · http://www.butlersnow.com · AmSouth Plaza, Suite 1700 · 210 East Capitol Street · P.O. Box 22567 · Jackson, MS 39225-2567 · 601-948-5711

E. Clifton Hodge, Jr. · a · Mockbee Hall Drake & Hodge · Capital Towers, Suite 1820 · 125 South Congress Street · Jackson, MS 39201 · 601-353-0035

Walker W. Jones III · Baker, Donelson, Bearman, Caldwell & Berkowitz · http://www.bakerdonelson.com · Meadowbrook Office Park · 4268 I-55 North · P.O. Box 14167 · Jackson, MS 39236 · 601-351-2400

William Trey Jones III · Brunini, Grantham, Grower & Hewes · http://www.brunini.com · 1400 Trustmark Building · 248 East Capitol Street · P.O. Drawer 119 · Jackson, MS 39205 · 601-948-3101

R. David Kaufman · Brunini, Grantham, Grower & Hewes · http://www.brunini.com · 1400 Trustmark Building · 248 East Capitol Street · P.O. Drawer 119 · Jackson, MS 39205 · 601-948-3101

David W. Mockbee · Mockbee Hall Drake & Hodge · Capital Towers, Suite 1820 · 125 South Congress Street · Jackson, MS 39201 · 601-353-0035

Luther T. Munford · a · Phelps Dunbar · http://www.phelpsdunbar.com · 111 East Capitol Street, Suite 600 · P.O. Box 23066 · Jackson, MS 39225-3066 · 601-352-2300

Charles T. Ozier · Wise Carter Child & Caraway · Heritage Building, Suite 600 · 401 East Capitol Street · Jackson, MS 39205 · 601-968-5500

Alan W. Perry · 2% · Forman Perry Watkins Krutz & Tardy · http://www.fpwk.com · City Center, Suite 100 · 200 South Lamar Street · P.O. Box 22608 · Jackson, MS 39225-2608 · 601-960-8600

Keith R. Raulston · a · Watkins Ludlam Winter & Stennis · http://www.watkinsludlam.com · 633 North State Street · P.O. Box 427 · Jackson, MS 39205-0427 · 601-949-4900

William F. Ray · Watkins & Eager · http://www.watkinseager.com · The Emporium Building · 400 East Capitol Street · P.O. Box 650 · Jackson, MS 39205 · 601-965-1900

William N. Reed · Baker, Donelson, Bearman, Caldwell & Berkowitz · http://www.bakerdonelson.com · Meadowbrook Office Park · 4268 I-55 North · P.O. Box 14167 · Jackson, MS 39236 · 601-351-2400

James L. Robertson · Wise Carter Child & Caraway · Heritage Building, Suite 600 · 401 East Capitol Street · Jackson, MS 39205 · 601-968-5500

Patrick H. Scanlon · 2% · Pat H. Scanlon · The Quarter, Suite L-15 · 1855 Lakeland Drive · Jackson, MS 39232 · 601-936-8924

Christopher A. Shapley · a · Brunini, Grantham, Grower & Hewes · http://www.brunini.com · 1400 Trustmark Building · 248 East Capitol Street · P.O. Drawer 119 · Jackson, MS 39205 · 601-948-3101

Paul H. Stephenson III · Watkins & Eager · http://www.watkinseager.com · The Emporium Building · 400 East Capitol Street · P.O. Box 650 · Jackson, MS 39205 · 601-965-1900

Lee Davis Thames · 2% · Butler, Snow, O'Mara, Stevens and Cannada · http://www.butlersnow.com · AmSouth Plaza, Suite 1700 · 210 East Capitol Street · P.O. Box 22567 · Jackson, MS 39225-2567 · 601-948-5711

Stephen L. Thomas · a · Bradley Arant Rose & White · http://www.bradleyarant.com · One Jackson Place, Suite 450 · 188 East Capitol Street · Jackson, MS 39201 · 601-948-8000

John E. Wade · Brunini, Grantham, Grower & Hewes · http://www.brunini.com · 1400 Trustmark Building · 248 East Capitol Street · P.O. Drawer 119 · Jackson, MS 39205 · 601-948-3101

Michael B. Wallace · Wise Carter Child & Caraway · Heritage Building, Suite 600 · 401 East Capitol Street · Jackson, MS 39205 · 601-968-5500

W. Scott Welch III · a · Baker, Donelson, Bearman, Caldwell & Berkowitz · http://www.bakerdonelson.com · Meadowbrook Office Park · 4268 I-55 North · P.O. Box 14167 · Jackson, MS 39236 · 601-351-2400

Joshua J. Wiener · Butler, Snow, O'Mara, Stevens and Cannada · http://www.butlersnow.com · AmSouth Plaza, Suite 1700 · 210 East Capitol Street · P.O. Box 22567 · Jackson, MS 39225-2567 · 601-948-5711

Oxford

J. Cal Mayo, Jr. · ⑩ · Mayo Mallette · http://www.mayomallette.com · Five University Office Park, Suite 200 · 2094 Old Taylor Road · Oxford, MS 38655 · 662-236-0055

Ridgeland

William Larry Latham · Latham & Burwell · 618 Crescent Boulevard, Suite 200 · Ridgeland, MS 39157 · 601-427-4470

Tupelo

L. F. Sams, Jr. · ㉕ · Mitchell, McNutt & Sams · http://www.mitchellmcnutt.com · 105 South Front Street P.O. Box 7120 · Tupelo, MS 38802-7120 · 662-842-3871

COMMUNICATIONS LAW

Jackson

James L. Halford · Brunini, Grantham, Grower & Hewes · http://www.brunini.com · 1400 Trustmark Building · 248 East Capitol Street · P.O. Drawer 119 · Jackson, MS 39205 · 601-948-3101

Charles L. McBride, Jr. · Brunini, Grantham, Grower & Hewes · http://www.brunini.com · 1400 Trustmark Building · 248 East Capitol Street · P.O. Drawer 119 · Jackson, MS 39205 · 601-948-3101

Stanley Q. Smith · Watkins Ludlam Winter & Stennis · http://www.watkinsludlam.com · 633 North State Street · P.O. Box 427 · Jackson, MS 39205-0427 · 601-949-4900

CONSTRUCTION LAW

Jackson

Phil B. Abernethy · Butler, Snow, O'Mara, Stevens and Cannada · http://www.butlersnow.com · AmSouth Plaza, Suite 1700 · 210 East Capitol Street · P.O. Box 22567 · Jackson, MS 39225-2567 · 601-948-5711

Samuel C. Kelly · Brunini, Grantham, Grower & Hewes · http://www.brunini.com · 1400 Trustmark Building · 248 East Capitol Street · P.O. Drawer 119 · Jackson, MS 39205 · 601-948-3101

David W. Mockbee · Mockbee Hall Drake & Hodge · Capital Towers, Suite 1820 · 125 South Congress Street · Jackson, MS 39201 · 601-353-0035

William R. Purdy · Bradley Arant Rose & White · http://www.bradleyarant.com · One Jackson Place, Suite 450 · Jackson, MS 39201 · 601-948-8000

Patrick H. Scanlon · ㉕ · Pat H. Scanlon · The Quarter, Suite L-15 · 1855 Lakeland Drive · Jackson, MS 39232 · 601-936-8924

Ron A. Yarbrough · Brunini, Grantham, Grower & Hewes · http://www.brunini.com · 1400 Trustmark Building · 248 East Capitol Street · P.O. Drawer 119 · Jackson, MS 39205 · 601-948-3101

Madison

Thomas W. Prewitt · Thomas W. Prewitt · P.O. Box 2327 · Madison, MS 39130-2330 · 601-427-2327

CORPORATE GOVERNANCE AND COMPLIANCE LAW

Jackson

Robert E. Hauberg, Jr. · a · Baker, Donelson, Bearman, Caldwell & Berkowitz · http://www.bakerdonelson.com · Meadowbrook Office Park · 4268 I-55 North · P.O. Box 14167 · Jackson, MS 39236 · 601-351-2400

Craig N. Landrum · a · Watkins Ludlam Winter & Stennis · http://www.watkinsludlam.com · 633 North State Street · P.O. Box 427 · Jackson, MS 39205-0427 · 601-949-4900

L. Keith Parsons · Watkins Ludlam Winter & Stennis · http://www.watkinsludlam.com · 633 North State Street · P.O. Box 427 · Jackson, MS 39205-0427 · 601-949-4900

James B. Tucker · Butler, Snow, O'Mara, Stevens and Cannada · http://www.butlersnow.com · AmSouth Plaza, Suite 1700 · 210 East Capitol Street · P.O. Box 22567 · Jackson, MS 39225-2567 · 601-948-5711

CORPORATE LAW

Jackson

Charles P. Adams, Jr. · Adams and Reese · http://www.adamsandreese.com · 111 East Capitol Street, Suite 350 · P.O. Box 24297 · Jackson, MS 39201 · 601-353-3234

R. Barry Cannada · Butler, Snow, O'Mara, Stevens and Cannada · http://www.butlersnow.com · AmSouth Plaza, Suite 1700 · 210 East Capitol Street · P.O. Box 22567 · Jackson, MS 39225-2567 · 601-948-5711

Henry E. Chatham, Jr. · a · Wise Carter Child & Caraway · Heritage Building, Suite 600 · 401 East Capitol Street · Jackson, MS 39205 · 601-968-5500

Robert D. Drinkwater · a · Brunini, Grantham, Grower & Hewes · http://www.brunini.com · 1400 Trustmark Building · 248 East Capitol Street · P.O. Drawer 119 · Jackson, MS 39205 · 601-948-3101

George R. Fair · 2) · Watkins & Eager · http://www.watkinseager.com · The Emporium Building · 400 East Capitol Street · P.O. Box 650 · Jackson, MS 39205 · 601-965-1900

Jerome C. Hafter · a · Phelps Dunbar · http://www.phelpsdunbar.com · 111 East Capitol Street, Suite 600 · P.O. Box 23066 · Jackson, MS 39225-3066 · 601-352-2300

Daniel G. Hise · a · Butler, Snow, O'Mara, Stevens and Cannada · http://www.butlersnow.com · AmSouth Plaza, Suite 1700 · 210 East Capitol Street · P.O. Box 22567 · Jackson, MS 39225-2567 · 601-948-5711

E. Clifton Hodge, Jr. · a · Mockbee Hall Drake & Hodge · Capital Towers, Suite 1820 · 125 South Congress Street · Jackson, MS 39201 · 601-353-0035

Jamie G. Houston III · a · Watkins & Eager · http://www.watkinseager.com · The Emporium Building · 400 East Capitol Street · P.O. Box 650 · Jackson, MS 39205 · 601-965-1900

Gina M. Jacobs · Watkins Ludlam Winter & Stennis · http://www.watkinsludlam.com · 633 North State Street · P.O. Box 427 · Jackson, MS 39205-0427 · 601-949-4900

Robert S. Lazarus · Watkins Ludlam Winter & Stennis · http://www.watkinsludlam.com · 633 North State Street · P.O. Box 427 · Jackson, MS 39205-0427 · 601-949-4900

William S. Mendenhall · a · Baker, Donelson, Bearman, Caldwell & Berkowitz · http://www.bakerdonelson.com · Meadowbrook Office Park · 4268 I-55 North · P.O. Box 14167 · Jackson, MS 39236 · 601-351-2400

William S. Painter · a · Baker, Donelson, Bearman, Caldwell & Berkowitz · http://www.bakerdonelson.com · Meadowbrook Office Park · 4268 I-55 North · P.O. Box 14167 · Jackson, MS 39236 · 601-351-2400

L. Keith Parsons · Watkins Ludlam Winter & Stennis · http://www.watkinsludlam.com · 633 North State Street · P.O. Box 427 · Jackson, MS 39205-0427 · 601-949-4900

Alan W. Perry · 2% · Forman Perry Watkins Krutz & Tardy · http://www.fpwk.com · City Center, Suite 100 · 200 South Lamar Street · P.O. Box 22608 · Jackson, MS 39225-2608 · 601-960-8600

Thomas B. Shepherd III · Watkins Ludlam Winter & Stennis · http://www.watkinsludlam.com · 633 North State Street · P.O. Box 427 · Jackson, MS 39205-0427 · 601-949-4900

Zachary Taylor III · Watkins Ludlam Winter & Stennis · http://www.watkinsludlam.com · 633 North State Street · P.O. Box 427 · Jackson, MS 39205-0427 · 601-949-4900

Randall B. Wall · Watkins Ludlam Winter & Stennis · http://www.watkinsludlam.com · 633 North State Street · P.O. Box 427 · Jackson, MS 39205-0427 · 601-949-4900

Walter S. Weems · a · Brunini, Grantham, Grower & Hewes · http://www.brunini.com · 1400 Trustmark Building · 248 East Capitol Street · P.O. Drawer 119 · Jackson, MS 39205 · 601-948-3101

M. Binford Williams, Jr. · Watkins & Eager · http://www.watkinseager.com · The Emporium Building · 400 East Capitol Street · P.O. Box 650 · Jackson, MS 39205 · 601-965-1900

Margaret H. Williams · Wise Carter Child & Caraway · Heritage Building, Suite 600 · 401 East Capitol Street · Jackson, MS 39205 · 601-968-5500

Stephen M. Wilson · Phelps Dunbar · http://www.phelpsdunbar.com · 111 East Capitol Street, Suite 600 · P.O. Box 23066 · Jackson, MS 39225-3066 · 601-352-2300

Ridgeland

Thomas A. Cook · a · Copeland Cook Taylor & Bush · http://www.cctb.com · Concourse 600, Suite 100 · 1076 Highland Colony Parkway · P.O. Box 6020 · Ridgeland, MS 39158 · 601-856-7200

Tupelo

F. M. Bush III · 2% · Phelps Dunbar · http://www.phelpsdunbar.com · One Mississippi Plaza, Seventh Floor · 201 South Spring Street · Tupelo, MS 38804 · 662-842-7907

ELDER LAW

Jackson

Barry K. Jones · Wise Carter Child & Caraway · Heritage Building, Suite 600 · 401 East Capitol Street · Jackson, MS 39205 · 601-968-5500

Oxford

Catherine V. Kilgore · North Mississippi Rural Legal Services · 2134 West Jackson Avenue · P.O. Box 767 · Oxford, MS 38655-0767 · 662-234-8731

EMINENT DOMAIN AND CONDEMNATION LAW

Hernando

Paul R. Scott · Smith, Phillips, Mitchell, Scott & Nowak · http://www.smithphillips.com · P.O. Box 346 · Hernando, MS 38632 · 662-429-5041

EMPLOYEE BENEFITS LAW

Jackson

Deborah S. Dees · Phelps Dunbar · http://www.phelpsdunbar.com · 111 East Capitol Street, Suite 600 · P.O. Box 23066 · Jackson, MS 39225-3066 · 601-352-2300

Linda Bounds Keng · Watkins Ludlam Winter & Stennis · http://www.watkinsludlam.com · 633 North State Street · P.O. Box 427 · Jackson, MS 39205-0427 · 601-949-4900

William Eugene Magee · Butler, Snow, O'Mara, Stevens and Cannada · http://www.butlersnow.com · AmSouth Plaza, Suite 1700 · 210 East Capitol Street · P.O. Box 22567 · Jackson, MS 39225-2567 · 601-948-5711

Gilbert C. Van Loon · a · Butler, Snow, O'Mara, Stevens and Cannada · http://www.butlersnow.com · AmSouth Plaza, Suite 1700 · 210 East Capitol Street · P.O. Box 22567 · Jackson, MS 39225-2567 · 601-948-5711

ENERGY LAW

Gulfport

Ricky J. Cox · Balch & Bingham · http://www.balch.com · 1310 Twenty-Fifth Avenue · P.O. Box 130 · Gulfport, MS 39502 · 228-864-9900

Ben H. Stone · a · Balch & Bingham · http://www.balch.com · 1310 Twenty-Fifth Avenue · P.O. Box 130 Gulfport, MS 39502 · 228-864-9900

H. Rodger Wilder · a · Balch & Bingham · http://www.balch.com · 1310 Twenty-Fifth Avenue · P.O. Box 130 · Gulfport, MS 39502 · 228-864-9900

Jackson

James K. Child, Jr. · a · Wise Carter Child & Caraway · Heritage Building, Suite 600 · 401 East Capitol Street · Jackson, MS 39205 · 601-968-5500

Thomas R. Crews · 2) · Watkins & Eager · http://www.watkinseager.com · The Emporium Building · 400 East Capitol Street · P.O. Box 650 · Jackson, MS 39205 · 601-965-1900

William F. Goodman, Jr. · 2% · Watkins & Eager · http://www.watkinseager.com · The Emporium Building · 400 East Capitol Street · P.O. Box 650 · Jackson, MS 39205 · 601-965-1900

James L. Halford · Brunini, Grantham, Grower & Hewes · http://www.brunini.com · 1400 Trustmark Building · 248 East Capitol Street · P.O. Drawer 119 · Jackson, MS 39205 · 601-948-3101

Henderson S. Hall, Jr. · Wise Carter Child & Caraway · Heritage Building, Suite 600 · 401 East Capitol Street · Jackson, MS 39205 · 601-968-5500

Otis Johnson, Jr. · 2) · Robinson Biggs Ingram Solop & Farris · 111 East Capitol Street, Suite 101 · Jackson, MS 39201 · 601-713-1192

Douglas E. Levanway · Wise Carter Child & Caraway · Heritage Building, Suite 600 · 401 East Capitol Street · Jackson, MS 39205 · 601-968-5500

Dennis W. Miller · Watkins Ludlam Winter & Stennis · http://www.watkinsludlam.com · 633 North State Street · P.O. Box 427 · Jackson, MS 39205-0427 · 601-949-4900

Powell G. Ogletree, Jr. · Adams and Reese · http://www.adamsandreese.com · 111 East Capitol Street, Suite 350 · P.O. Box 24297 · Jackson, MS 39201 · 601-353-3234

A. Jerry Sheldon · Adams and Reese · http://www.adamsandreese.com · 111 East Capitol Street, Suite 350 · P.O. Box 24297 · Jackson, MS 39201 · 601-353-3234

Stanley Q. Smith · Watkins Ludlam Winter & Stennis · http://www.watkinsludlam.com · 633 North State Street · P.O. Box 427 · Jackson, MS 39205-0427 · 601-949-4900

Jefferson D. Stewart · 2) · Adams and Reese · http://www.adamsandreese.com · 111 East Capitol Street, Suite 350 · P.O. Box 24297 · Jackson, MS 39201 · 601-353-3234

Robert P. Wise · Sharpe & Wise · 120 North Congress Street, Suite 902 · Jackson, MS 39201 · 601-968-5561

Natchez

W. Marion Smith · 2) · Truly, Smith & Latham · 100 South Pearl Street · P.O. Box 1307 · Natchez, MS 39121-1307 · 601-442-6495

Ridgeland

Glenn Gates Taylor · 2) · Copeland Cook Taylor & Bush · http://www.cctb.com · Concourse 600, Suite 100 · 1076 Highland Colony Parkway · P.O. Box 6020 · Ridgeland, MS 39158 · 601-856-7200

ENVIRONMENTAL LAW

Gulfport

Terese T. Wyly · a · Balch & Bingham · http://www.balch.com · 1310 Twenty-Fifth Avenue · P.O. Box 130 · Gulfport, MS 39502 · 228-864-9900

Jackson

Trudy B. Allen · Watkins Ludlam Winter & Stennis · http://www.watkinsludlam.com · 633 North State Street · P.O. Box 427 · Jackson, MS 39205-0427 · 601-949-4900

John G. Corlew · Watkins & Eager · http://www.watkinseager.com · The Emporium Building · 400 East Capitol Street · P.O. Box 650 · Jackson, MS 39205 · 601-965-1900

John A. Crawford · a · Butler, Snow, O'Mara, Stevens and Cannada · http://www.butlersnow.com · AmSouth Plaza, Suite 1700 · 210 East Capitol Street · P.O. Box 22567 · Jackson, MS 39225-2567 · 601-948-5711

Michael T. Dawkins · Baker, Donelson, Bearman, Caldwell & Berkowitz · http://www.bakerdonelson.com · Meadowbrook Office Park · 4268 I-55 North · P.O. Box 14167 · Jackson, MS 39236 · 601-351-2400

James T. Mccafferty III · James T. McCafferty Attorney At Law · P.O. Box 5092 · Jackson, MS 39296 · 601-366-3506

John E. Milner · a · Brunini, Grantham, Grower & Hewes · http://www.brunini.com · 1400 Trustmark Building · 248 East Capitol Street · P.O. Drawer 119 · Jackson, MS 39205 · 601-948-3101

Virginia T. Munford · Watkins & Eager · http://www.watkinseager.com · The Emporium Building · 400 East Capitol Street · P.O. Box 650 · Jackson, MS 39205 · 601-965-1900

Daniel L. Singletary · a · Baker, Donelson, Bearman, Caldwell & Berkowitz · http://www.bakerdonelson.com · Meadowbrook Office Park · 4268 I-55 North · P.O. Box 14167 · Jackson, MS 39236 · 601-351-2400

Jefferson D. Stewart · 2) · Adams and Reese · http://www.adamsandreese.com · 111 East Capitol Street, Suite 350 · P.O. Box 24297 · Jackson, MS 39201 · 601-353-3234

Ridgeland

Glenn Gates Taylor · 2) · Copeland Cook Taylor & Bush · http://www.cctb.com · Concourse 600, Suite 100 · 1076 Highland Colony Parkway · P.O. Box 6020 · Ridgeland, MS 39158 · 601-856-7200

FAMILY LAW

Ashland

John S. Farese · Farese, Farese & Farese · http://www.fareselaw.com · 122 Church Street · P.O. Box 98 · Ashland, MS 38603 · 662-224-6211

Gulfport

Joseph R. Meadows · 2) · Meadows Law Firm · 1902 Twenty-First Avenue · P.O. Box 1076 · Gulfport, MS 39502-1076 · 228-868-7717

Jackson

Thomas W. Crockett · a · Watkins Ludlam Winter & Stennis · http://www.watkinsludlam.com · 633 North State Street · P.O. Box 427 · Jackson, MS 39205-0427 · 601-949-4900

N. Shelton Hand, Jr. · a · Mississippi College School of Law · 151 East Griffith Street · Jackson, MS 39201 · 601-925-7145

Robert W. King · 2% · King & Spencer · 235 East Capitol Street · P.O. Box 123 · Jackson, MS 39205-0123 601-948-1547

William R. Wright · Wright Law Firm · 400 River Hill Tower · 1675 Lakeland Drive · Jackson, MS 39216-4852 · 601-366-8090

Laurel

Billie J. Graham · a · Billie J. Graham · 315 Sawmill Road, Suite 216 · P.O. Box 683 · Laurel, MS 39441-0683 · 601-426-9900

Ridgeland

L. C. James · 2% · James & O'Brien Family Law Group · 682 Towne Center Boulevard, Suite 101 · P.O. Box 2623 · Ridgeland, MS 39158-2623 · 601-952-0050

William Larry Latham · Latham & Burwell · 618 Crescent Boulevard, Suite 200 · Ridgeland, MS 39157 · 601-427-4470

Richard C. Roberts III · a · Richard C. Roberts III · 599 Highland Colony Parkway, Suite 110 · Ridgeland, MS 39157 · 601-607-4144

University

Deborah H. Bell · University Of Mississippi School of Law · Lamar Law Center · P.O. Box 1848 · University, MS 38667 · 662-915-7361

FAMILY LAW MEDIATION

Jackson

Thomas W. Crockett · a · Watkins Ludlam Winter & Stennis · http://www.watkinsludlam.com · 633 North State Street · P.O. Box 427 · Jackson, MS 39205-0427 · 601-949-4900

Ridgeland

William Larry Latham · Latham & Burwell · 618 Crescent Boulevard, Suite 200 · Ridgeland, MS 39157 · 601-427-4470

FIRST AMENDMENT LAW

Gulfport

George F. Bloss III · Watkins Ludlam Winter & Stennis · http://www.watkinsludlam.com · One Hancock Plaza, Suite 1125 · 2510 Fourteenth Street · P.O. Box 160 · Gulfport, MS 39502-0160 · 228-864-3094

Henry F. Laird, Jr. · Watkins Ludlam Winter & Stennis · http://www.watkinsludlam.com · One Hancock Plaza, Suite 1125 · 2510 Fourteenth Street · P.O. Box 160 · Gulfport, MS 39502-0160 · 228-864-3094

Jackson

John C. Henegan · a · Butler, Snow, O'Mara, Stevens and Cannada · http://www.butlersnow.com · AmSouth Plaza, Suite 1700 · 210 East Capitol Street · P.O. Box 22567 · Jackson, MS 39225-2567 · 601-948-5711

Luther T. Munford · a · Phelps Dunbar · http://www.phelpsdunbar.com · 111 East Capitol Street, Suite 600 · P.O. Box 23066 · Jackson, MS 39225-3066 · 601-352-2300

Leonard D. Van Slyke, Jr. · a · Watkins Ludlam Winter & Stennis · http://www.watkinsludlam.com · 633 North State Street · P.O. Box 427 · Jackson, MS 39205-0427 · 601-949-4900

Tupelo

Thomas A. Wicker · a · Holland, Ray, Upchurch & Hillen · 322 Jefferson Street · P.O. Drawer 409 · Tupelo, MS 38802 · 662-842-1721

FRANCHISE LAW

Jackson

David B. Grishman · a · Watkins Ludlam Winter & Stennis · http://www.watkinsludlam.com · 633 North State Street · P.O. Box 427 · Jackson, MS 39205-0427 · 601-949-4900

Bridgforth R. Rutledge · Phelps Dunbar · http://www.phelpsdunbar.com · 111 East Capitol Street, Suite 600 · P.O. Box 23066 · Jackson, MS 39225-3066 · 601-352-2300

GAMING LAW

Gulfport

Leonard A. Blackwell II · Blackwell's Lawyers & Counselors · 1613 Twenty-Third Avenue · Gulfport, MS 39501 · 228-864-1484

Ben H. Stone · a · Balch & Bingham · http://www.balch.com · 1310 Twenty-Fifth Avenue · P.O. Box 130 Gulfport, MS 39502 · 228-864-9900

Jackson

Scott E. Andress · Balch & Bingham · http://www.balch.com · 401 East Capitol Street, Suite 200 · Jackson, MS 39201-2608 · 601-961-9900

Heather J. Camp · Phelps Dunbar · http://www.phelpsdunbar.com · 111 East Capitol Street, Suite 600 · P.O. Box 23066 · Jackson, MS 39225-3066 · 601-352-2300

Daniel G. Hise · a · Butler, Snow, O'Mara, Stevens and Cannada · http://www.butlersnow.com · AmSouth Plaza, Suite 1700 · 210 East Capitol Street · P.O. Box 22567 · Jackson, MS 39225-2567 · 601-948-5711

Dan M. McDaniel, Jr. · Phelps Dunbar · http://www.phelpsdunbar.com · 111 East Capitol Street, Suite 600 · P.O. Box 23066 · Jackson, MS 39225-3066 · 601-352-2300

Thomas B. Shepherd III · Watkins Ludlam Winter & Stennis · http://www.watkinsludlam.com · 633 North State Street · P.O. Box 427 · Jackson, MS 39205-0427 · 601-949-4900

GOVERNMENT RELATIONS LAW

Jackson

Michael D. Caples · Butler, Snow, O'Mara, Stevens and Cannada · http://www.butlersnow.com · AmSouth Plaza, Suite 1700 · 210 East Capitol Street · P.O. Box 22567 · Jackson, MS 39225-2567 · 601-948-5711

Tommie S. Cardin · Butler, Snow, O'Mara, Stevens and Cannada · http://www.butlersnow.com · AmSouth Plaza, Suite 1700 · 210 East Capitol Street · P.O. Box 22567 · Jackson, MS 39225-2567 · 601-948-5711

Tim Ford · Balch & Bingham · http://www.balch.com · 401 East Capitol Street, Suite 200 · Jackson, MS 39201-2608 · 601-961-9900

Mark W. Garriga · Butler, Snow, O'Mara, Stevens and Cannada · http://www.butlersnow.com · AmSouth Plaza, Suite 1700 · 210 East Capitol Street · P.O. Box 22567 · Jackson, MS 39225-2567 · 601-948-5711

Samuel W. Keyes, Jr. · Butler, Snow, O'Mara, Stevens and Cannada · http://www.butlersnow.com · AmSouth Plaza, Suite 1700 · 210 East Capitol Street · P.O. Box 22567 · Jackson, MS 39225-2567 · 601-948-5711

Dennis W. Miller · Watkins Ludlam Winter & Stennis · http://www.watkinsludlam.com · 633 North State Street · P.O. Box 427 · Jackson, MS 39205-0427 · 601-949-4900

HEALTH CARE LAW

Hattiesburg

R. Webster Heidelberg III · Heidelberg Law Firm · 301 West Pine Street · P.O. Box 1070 · Hattiesburg, MS 39403-1070 · 601-545-8180

J. Robert Ramsay · Ramsay & Hammond · 106 Madison Plaza, Suite B · P.O. Box 16567 · Hattiesburg, MS 39404-6567 · 601-264-4499

Jackson

John B. Beard · Baker, Donelson, Bearman, Caldwell & Berkowitz · http://www.bakerdonelson.com · Meadowbrook Office Park · 4268 I-55 North · P.O. Box 14167 · Jackson, MS 39236 · 601-351-2400

Edmund L. Brunini, Jr. · a · Brunini, Grantham, Grower & Hewes · http://www.brunini.com · 1400 Trustmark Building · 248 East Capitol Street · P.O. Drawer 119 · Jackson, MS 39205 · 601-948-3101

Barry K. Cockrell · a · Baker, Donelson, Bearman, Caldwell & Berkowitz · http://www.bakerdonelson.com · Meadowbrook Office Park · 4268 I-55 North · P.O. Box 14167 · Jackson, MS 39236 · 601-351-2400

Charles W. Ferguson · Baker, Donelson, Bearman, Caldwell & Berkowitz · http://www.bakerdonelson.com · Meadowbrook Office Park · 4268 I-55 North · P.O. Box 14167 · Jackson, MS 39236 · 601-351-2400

Kathryn R. Gilchrist · Adams and Reese · http://www.adamsandreese.com · 111 East Capitol Street, Suite 350 · P.O. Box 24297 · Jackson, MS 39201 · 601-353-3234

D. Colllier Graham, Jr. · Wise Carter Child & Caraway · Heritage Building, Suite 600 · 401 East Capitol Street · Jackson, MS 39205 · 601-968-5500

L. Carl Hagwood · a · Wilkins, Stephens & Tipton · One LeFleur's Square, Suite 108 · 4735 Old Canton Road · P.O. Box 13429 · Jackson, MS 39236-3429 · 601-366-4343

R. Mark Hodges · Wise Carter Child & Caraway · Heritage Building, Suite 600 · 401 East Capitol Street · Jackson, MS 39205 · 601-968-5500

Eugene R. Naylor · Wise Carter Child & Caraway · Heritage Building, Suite 600 · 401 East Capitol Street Jackson, MS 39205 · 601-968-5500

William S. Painter · a · Baker, Donelson, Bearman, Caldwell & Berkowitz · http://www.bakerdonelson.com · Meadowbrook Office Park · 4268 I-55 North · P.O. Box 14167 · Jackson, MS 39236 · 601-351-2400

George H. Ritter · Wise Carter Child & Caraway · Heritage Building, Suite 600 · 401 East Capitol Street · Jackson, MS 39205 · 601-968-5500

Margaret H. Williams · Wise Carter Child & Caraway · Heritage Building, Suite 600 · 401 East Capitol Street · Jackson, MS 39205 · 601-968-5500

Jonell B. Williamson · Baker, Donelson, Bearman, Caldwell & Berkowitz · http://www.bakerdonelson.com · Meadowbrook Office Park · 4268 I-55 North · P.O. Box 14167 · Jackson, MS 39236 · 601-351-2400

Ridgeland

Thomas L. Kirkland, Jr. · Copeland Cook Taylor & Bush · http://www.cctb.com · Concourse 600, Suite 100 · 1076 Highland Colony Parkway · P.O. Box 6020 · Ridgeland, MS 39158 · 601-856-7200

Tupelo

F. M. Bush III · 2% · Phelps Dunbar · http://www.phelpsdunbar.com · One Mississippi Plaza, Seventh Floor · 201 South Spring Street · Tupelo, MS 38804 · 662-842-7907

Jeffrey S. Moore · Phelps Dunbar · http://www.phelpsdunbar.com · One Mississippi Plaza, Seventh Floor 201 South Spring Street · Tupelo, MS 38804 · 662-842-7907

INFORMATION TECHNOLOGY LAW

Jackson

W. Whitaker Rayner · Watkins Ludlam Winter & Stennis · http://www.watkinsludlam.com · 633 North State Street · P.O. Box 427 · Jackson, MS 39205-0427 · 601-949-4900

INSURANCE LAW

Jackson

William C. Griffin · Currie Johnson Griffin Gaines & Myers · http://www.curriejohnson.com · 1044 River Oaks Drive · P.O. Box 750 · Jackson, MS 39205-0750 · 601-969-1010

Michael O. Gwin · Watkins & Eager · http://www.watkinseager.com · The Emporium Building · 400 East Capitol Street · P.O. Box 650 · Jackson, MS 39205 · 601-965-1900

Walter T. Johnson · Watkins & Eager · http://www.watkinseager.com · The Emporium Building · 400 East Capitol Street · P.O. Box 650 · Jackson, MS 39205 · 601-965-1900

Richard T. Lawrence · Watkins & Eager · http://www.watkinseager.com · The Emporium Building · 400 East Capitol Street · P.O. Box 650 · Jackson, MS 39205 · 601-965-1900

David L. Martin · Watkins Ludlam Winter & Stennis · http://www.watkinsludlam.com · 633 North State Street · P.O. Box 427 · Jackson, MS 39205-0427 · 601-949-4900

Keith R. Raulston · a · Watkins Ludlam Winter & Stennis · http://www.watkinsludlam.com · 633 North State Street · P.O. Box 427 · Jackson, MS 39205-0427 · 601-949-4900

Ridgeland

Charles G. Copeland · Copeland Cook Taylor & Bush · http://www.cctb.com · Concourse 600, Suite 100 · 1076 Highland Colony Parkway · P.O. Box 6020 · Ridgeland, MS 39158 · 601-856-7200

J. Tucker Mitchell · Copeland Cook Taylor & Bush · http://www.cctb.com · Concourse 600, Suite 100 · 1076 Highland Colony Parkway · P.O. Box 6020 · Ridgeland, MS 39158 · 601-856-7200

James R. Moore · Copeland Cook Taylor & Bush · http://www.cctb.com · Concourse 600, Suite 100 · 1076 Highland Colony Parkway · P.O. Box 6020 · Ridgeland, MS 39158 · 601-856-7200

INTELLECTUAL PROPERTY LAW

Jackson

Stephen J. Carmody · Brunini, Grantham, Grower & Hewes · http://www.brunini.com · 1400 Trustmark Building · 248 East Capitol Street · P.O. Drawer 119 · Jackson, MS 39205 · 601-948-3101

R. Pepper Crutcher, Jr. · Balch & Bingham · http://www.balch.com · 401 East Capitol Street, Suite 200 · Jackson, MS 39201-2608 · 601-961-9900

John J. Healy III · Butler, Snow, O'Mara, Stevens and Cannada · http://www.butlersnow.com · AmSouth Plaza, Suite 1700 · 210 East Capitol Street · P.O. Box 22567 · Jackson, MS 39225-2567 · 601-948-5711

W. Whitaker Rayner · Watkins Ludlam Winter & Stennis · http://www.watkinsludlam.com · 633 North State Street · P.O. Box 427 · Jackson, MS 39205-0427 · 601-949-4900

Oxford

Stephan L. McDavid · Harris Shelton Hanover Walsh · 1109 Van Buren Avenue · Oxford, MS 38655 · 662-281-8300

LABOR AND EMPLOYMENT LAW

Columbus

Taylor B. Smith · The Kullman Firm · Court Square Towers, Suite 505 · 200 Sixth Street North · P.O. Box 827 · Columbus, MS 39703 · 662-244-8824

Gulfport

Susan Fahey Desmond · Watkins Ludlam Winter & Stennis · http://www.watkinsludlam.com · One Hancock Plaza, Suite 1125 · 2510 Fourteenth Street · P.O. Box 160 · Gulfport, MS 39502-0160 · 228-864-3094

Jackson

Walter J. Brand · Watkins & Eager · http://www.watkinseager.com · The Emporium Building · 400 East Capitol Street · P.O. Box 650 · Jackson, MS 39205 · 601-965-1900

R. Pepper Crutcher, Jr. · Balch & Bingham · http://www.balch.com · 401 East Capitol Street, Suite 200 · Jackson, MS 39201-2608 · 601-961-9900

Gary E. Friedman · Phelps Dunbar · http://www.phelpsdunbar.com · 111 East Capitol Street, Suite 600 · P.O. Box 23066 · Jackson, MS 39225-3066 · 601-352-2300

Peyton S. Irby, Jr. · a · Watkins Ludlam Winter & Stennis · http://www.watkinsludlam.com · 633 North State Street · P.O. Box 427 · Jackson, MS 39205-0427 · 601-949-4900

John L. Maxey II · 2% · Maxey Wann · AmSouth Plaza, Suite 2100 · 210 East Capitol Street · P.O. Box 3977 · Jackson, MS 39207-3977 · 601-355-8855

Kenneth E. Milam · 2) · Watkins & Eager · http://www.watkinseager.com · The Emporium Building · 400 East Capitol Street · P.O. Box 650 · Jackson, MS 39205 · 601-965-1900

Armin J. Moeller, Jr. · 2) · Balch & Bingham · http://www.balch.com · 401 East Capitol Street, Suite 200 Jackson, MS 39201-2608 · 601-961-9900

W. Thomas Siler, Jr. · Phelps Dunbar · http://www.phelpsdunbar.com · 111 East Capitol Street, Suite 600 · P.O. Box 23066 · Jackson, MS 39225-3066 · 601-352-2300

Jeffrey A. Walker · a · Butler, Snow, O'Mara, Stevens and Cannada · http://www.butlersnow.com · AmSouth Plaza, Suite 1700 · 210 East Capitol Street · P.O. Box 22567 · Jackson, MS 39225-2567 · 601-948-5711

Barbara C. Wallace · a · Wise Carter Child & Caraway · Heritage Building, Suite 600 · 401 East Capitol Street · Jackson, MS 39205 · 601-968-5500

S. Mark Wann · Maxey Wann · AmSouth Plaza, Suite 2100 · 210 East Capitol Street · P.O. Box 3977 · Jackson, MS 39207-3977 · 601-355-8855

Madison

Dennis L. Horn · a · Horn & Payne · 137 Executive Drive, Suite C · P.O. Box 2754 · Madison, MS 39130-2754 · 601-853-6090

Ridgeland

Herbert C. Ehrhardt · a · Ogletree Deakins · http://www.ogletreedeakins.com · 100 Concourse, Suite 204 · 1052 Highland Colony Parkway · Ridgeland, MS 39157 · 601-360-8444

Timothy W. Lindsay · Ogletree Deakins · http://www.ogletreedeakins.com · 100 Concourse, Suite 204 · 1052 Highland Colony Parkway · Ridgeland, MS 39157 · 601-360-8444

M. Curtiss McKee · 2) · Ogletree Deakins · http://www.ogletreedeakins.com · 100 Concourse, Suite 204 · 1052 Highland Colony Parkway · Ridgeland, MS 39157 · 601-360-8444

Emile C. Ott · 2) · Ogletree Deakins · http://www.ogletreedeakins.com · 100 Concourse, Suite 204 · 1052 Highland Colony Parkway · Ridgeland, MS 39157 · 601-360-8444

Jerrald L. Shivers · Ogletree Deakins · http://www.ogletreedeakins.com · 100 Concourse, Suite 204 · 1052 Highland Colony Parkway · Ridgeland, MS 39157 · 601-360-8444

Tupelo

Mark N. Halbert · Phelps Dunbar · http://www.phelpsdunbar.com · One Mississippi Plaza, Seventh Floor 201 South Spring Street · Tupelo, MS 38804 · 662-842-7907

James D. Waide III · Waide & Associates · 332 North Spring Street · P.O. Box 1357 · Tupelo, MS 38802-1357 · 662-842-7324

LAND USE & ZONING LAW

Jackson

W. Rodney Clement, Jr. · a · Brunini, Grantham, Grower & Hewes · http://www.brunini.com · 1400 Trustmark Building · 248 East Capitol Street · P.O. Drawer 119 · Jackson, MS 39205 · 601-948-3101

Kathryn H. Hester · Watkins Ludlam Winter & Stennis · http://www.watkinsludlam.com · 633 North State Street · P.O. Box 427 · Jackson, MS 39205-0427 · 601-949-4900

Crane D. Kipp · Wise Carter Child & Caraway · Heritage Building, Suite 600 · 401 East Capitol Street · Jackson, MS 39205 · 601-968-5500

James A. Peden, Jr. · Stennett, Wilkinson & Peden · 401 Legacy Park, Suite A · P.O. Box 13308 · Jackson, MS 39236-3308 · 601-206-1816

William C. Smith III · Watkins & Eager · http://www.watkinseager.com · The Emporium Building · 400 East Capitol Street · P.O. Box 650 · Jackson, MS 39205 · 601-965-1900

LEGAL MALPRACTICE LAW

Jackson

Reuben V. Anderson · Phelps Dunbar · http://www.phelpsdunbar.com · 111 East Capitol Street, Suite 600 · P.O. Box 23066 · Jackson, MS 39225-3066 · 601-352-2300

Ross F. Bass, Jr. · Phelps Dunbar · http://www.phelpsdunbar.com · 111 East Capitol Street, Suite 600 · P.O. Box 23066 · Jackson, MS 39225-3066 · 601-352-2300

Thomas W. Crockett · a · Watkins Ludlam Winter & Stennis · http://www.watkinsludlam.com · 633 North State Street · P.O. Box 427 · Jackson, MS 39205-0427 · 601-949-4900

Keith R. Raulston · a · Watkins Ludlam Winter & Stennis · http://www.watkinsludlam.com · 633 North State Street · P.O. Box 427 · Jackson, MS 39205-0427 · 601-949-4900

MARITIME LAW

Greenville

Franklin S. Thackston, Jr. · Lake Tindall · 127 South Poplar · P.O. Box 918 · Greenville, MS 38702-0918 · 662-378-2121

Jackson

James L. Robertson · Wise Carter Child & Caraway · Heritage Building, Suite 600 · 401 East Capitol Street · Jackson, MS 39205 · 601-968-5500

MASS TORT LITIGATION

Jackson

John G. Corlew · Watkins & Eager · http://www.watkinseager.com · The Emporium Building · 400 East Capitol Street · P.O. Box 650 · Jackson, MS 39205 · 601-965-1900

W. Wayne Drinkwater, Jr. · a · Bradley Arant Rose & White · http://www.bradleyarant.com · One Jackson Place, Suite 450 · 188 East Capitol Street · Jackson, MS 39201 · 601-948-8000

Richard L. Forman · Forman Perry Watkins Krutz & Tardy · http://www.fpwk.com · City Center, Suite 100 · 200 South Lamar Street · P.O. Box 22608 · Jackson, MS 39225-2608 · 601-960-8600

William M. Gage · Butler, Snow, O'Mara, Stevens and Cannada · http://www.butlersnow.com · AmSouth Plaza, Suite 1700 · 210 East Capitol Street · P.O. Box 22567 · Jackson, MS 39225-2567 · 601-948-5711

William F. Goodman III · Watkins & Eager · http://www.watkinseager.com · The Emporium Building · 400 East Capitol Street · P.O. Box 650 · Jackson, MS 39205 · 601-965-1900

Walker W. Jones III · Baker, Donelson, Bearman, Caldwell & Berkowitz · http://www.bakerdonelson.com · Meadowbrook Office Park · 4268 I-55 North · P.O. Box 14167 · Jackson, MS 39236 · 601-351-2400

Fred Krutz · Forman Perry Watkins Krutz & Tardy · http://www.fpwk.com · City Center, Suite 100 · 200 South Lamar Street · P.O. Box 22608 · Jackson, MS 39225-2608 · 601-960-8600

J. William Manuel · Bradley Arant Rose & White · http://www.bradleyarant.com · One Jackson Place, Suite 450 · 188 East Capitol Street · Jackson, MS 39201 · 601-948-8000

Steven D. Orlansky · Watkins & Eager · http://www.watkinseager.com · The Emporium Building · 400 East Capitol Street · P.O. Box 650 · Jackson, MS 39205 · 601-965-1900

Christopher A. Shapley · a · Brunini, Grantham, Grower & Hewes · http://www.brunini.com · 1400 Trustmark Building · 248 East Capitol Street · P.O. Drawer 119 · Jackson, MS 39205 · 601-948-3101

John P. Sneed · Wise Carter Child & Caraway · Heritage Building, Suite 600 · 401 East Capitol Street · Jackson, MS 39205 · 601-968-5500

Thomas W. Tardy III · Forman Perry Watkins Krutz & Tardy · http://www.fpwk.com · City Center, Suite 100 · 200 South Lamar Street · P.O. Box 22608 · Jackson, MS 39225-2608 · 601-960-8600

Michael W. Ulmer · a · Watkins & Eager · http://www.watkinseager.com · The Emporium Building · 400 East Capitol Street · P.O. Box 650 · Jackson, MS 39205 · 601-965-1900

Walter G. Watkins, Jr. · Forman Perry Watkins Krutz & Tardy · http://www.fpwk.com · City Center, Suite 100 · 200 South Lamar Street · P.O. Box 22608 · Jackson, MS 39225-2608 · 601-960-8600

MEDICAL MALPRACTICE LAW

Clarksdale

Ralph E. Chapman · a · Chapman, Lewis & Swan · 501 First Street · P.O. Box 428 · Clarksdale, MS 38614 · 662-627-4105

John H. Cocke · Merkel & Cocke · http://www.merkel-cocke.com · 30 Delta Avenue · P.O. Box 1388 · Clarksdale, MS 38614-1388 · 662-627-9641

Charles M. Merkel, Jr. · 2) · Merkel & Cocke · http://www.merkel-cocke.com · 30 Delta Avenue · P.O. Box 1388 · Clarksdale, MS 38614-1388 · 662-627-9641

Greenwood

Tommie G. Williams · Upshaw, Williams, Biggers, Beckham & Riddick · 309 Fulton Street · P.O. Drawer 8230 · Greenwood, MS 38935-8230 · 662-455-1613

Gulfport

Harry R. Allen · 2) · Allen, Cobb, Hood & Atkinson · 2512 Twenty-Fifth Avenue, Suite Three · Gulfport, MS 39501 · 228-864-4011

George F. Bloss III · Watkins Ludlam Winter & Stennis · http://www.watkinsludlam.com · One Hancock Plaza, Suite 1125 · 2510 Fourteenth Street · P.O. Box 160 · Gulfport, MS 39502-0160 · 228-864-3094

Ben F. Galloway III · Owen & Galloway · Owen Building · 1414 Twenty-Fifth Avenue · P.O. Drawer 420 Gulfport, MS 39502-0420 · 228-868-2821

Hattiesburg

J. Robert Ramsay · Ramsay & Hammond · 106 Madison Plaza, Suite B · P.O. Box 16567 · Hattiesburg, MS 39404-6567 · 601-264-4499

Jackson

Mark P. Caraway · Wise Carter Child & Caraway · Heritage Building, Suite 600 · 401 East Capitol Street Jackson, MS 39205 · 601-968-5500

William C. Griffin · Currie Johnson Griffin Gaines & Myers · http://www.curriejohnson.com · 1044 River Oaks Drive · P.O. Box 750 · Jackson, MS 39205-0750 · 601-969-1010

L. Carl Hagwood · a · Wilkins, Stephens & Tipton · One LeFleur's Square, Suite 108 · 4735 Old Canton Road · P.O. Box 13429 · Jackson, MS 39236-3429 · 601-366-4343

Walter T. Johnson · Watkins & Eager · http://www.watkinseager.com · The Emporium Building · 400 East Capitol Street · P.O. Box 650 · Jackson, MS 39205 · 601-965-1900

Whitman B. Johnson III · Currie Johnson Griffin Gaines & Myers · http://www.curriejohnson.com · 1044 River Oaks Drive · P.O. Box 750 · Jackson, MS 39205-0750 · 601-969-1010

Mildred M. Morris · Watkins & Eager · http://www.watkinseager.com · The Emporium Building · 400 East Capitol Street · P.O. Box 650 · Jackson, MS 39205 · 601-965-1900

Eugene R. Naylor · Wise Carter Child & Caraway · Heritage Building, Suite 600 · 401 East Capitol Street Jackson, MS 39205 · 601-968-5500

Michael W. Ulmer · a · Watkins & Eager · http://www.watkinseager.com · The Emporium Building · 400 East Capitol Street · P.O. Box 650 · Jackson, MS 39205 · 601-965-1900

Christopher J. Walker · Markow Walker · 599 Highland Colony Parkway, Suite 100 · P.O. Box 13669 · Jackson, MS 39236-3669 · 601-853-1911

Pascagoula

James H. Heidelberg · a · Heidelberg, Steinberger, Colmer & Burrow · 711 Delmas Avenue · P.O. Box 1407 · Pascagoula, MS 39568-1407 · 228-762-8021

Ridgeland

Bobby L. Dallas · Sessums, Dallas & Morrison · 240 Trace Colony Park Drive, Suite 100 · Ridgeland, MS 39157 · 601-933-2040

J. Leray McNamara · Copeland Cook Taylor & Bush · http://www.cctb.com · Concourse 600, Suite 100 · 1076 Highland Colony Parkway · P.O. Box 6020 · Ridgeland, MS 39158 · 601-856-7200

Walter C. Morrison IV · Sessums, Dallas & Morrison · 240 Trace Colony Park Drive, Suite 100 · Ridgeland, MS 39157 · 601-933-2040

Robert B. Sessums · a · Sessums, Dallas & Morrison · 240 Trace Colony Park Drive, Suite 100 · Ridgeland, MS 39157 · 601-933-2040

Tupelo

L. F. Sams, Jr. · 2% · Mitchell, McNutt & Sams · http://www.mitchellmcnutt.com · 105 South Front Street P.O. Box 7120 · Tupelo, MS 38802-7120 · 662-842-3871

David W. Upchurch · Holland, Ray, Upchurch & Hillen · 322 Jefferson Street · P.O. Drawer 409 · Tupelo, MS 38802 · 662-842-1721

Robert K. Upchurch · Holland, Ray, Upchurch & Hillen · 322 Jefferson Street · P.O. Drawer 409 · Tupelo, MS 38802 · 662-842-1721

John G. Wheeler · Mitchell, McNutt & Sams · http://www.mitchellmcnutt.com · 105 South Front Street · P.O. Box 7120 · Tupelo, MS 38802-7120 · 662-842-3871

Vicksburg

R. Eugene Parker, Jr. · Varner, Parker & Sessums · http://www.vpslaw.com · Court House Square · 1110 Jackson Street · P.O. Box 1237 · Vicksburg, MS 39181 · 601-638-8741

MERGERS & ACQUISITIONS LAW

Jackson

R. Barry Cannada · Butler, Snow, O'Mara, Stevens and Cannada · http://www.butlersnow.com · AmSouth Plaza, Suite 1700 · 210 East Capitol Street · P.O. Box 22567 · Jackson, MS 39225-2567 · 601-948-5711

E. Clifton Hodge, Jr. · a · Mockbee Hall Drake & Hodge · Capital Towers, Suite 1820 · 125 South Congress Street · Jackson, MS 39201 · 601-353-0035

Walter S. Weems · a · Brunini, Grantham, Grower & Hewes · http://www.brunini.com · 1400 Trustmark Building · 248 East Capitol Street · P.O. Drawer 119 · Jackson, MS 39205 · 601-948-3101

Tupelo

F. M. Bush III · 2% · Phelps Dunbar · http://www.phelpsdunbar.com · One Mississippi Plaza, Seventh Floor · 201 South Spring Street · Tupelo, MS 38804 · 662-842-7907

MUNICIPAL LAW

Batesville

Richard T. Phillips · Smith, Phillips, Mitchell, Scott & Nowak · http://www.smithphillips.com · 695 Shamrock Drive · P.O. Box 1586 · Batesville, MS 38606-1586 · 662-563-4613

Clarksdale

Thomas T. Ross, Jr. · Hunt Ross & Allen A Professional Assoc · 123 Court Street · P.O. Box 1196 · Clarksdale, MS 38614 · 662-627-5251

Cleveland

Benjamin E. Griffith · Griffith & Griffith · http://www.griffithlaw.net · 123 South Court Street · P.O. Drawer 1680 · Cleveland, MS 38732 · 662-843-6100

Jackson

Alan L. Moore · Baker, Donelson, Bearman, Caldwell & Berkowitz · http://www.bakerdonelson.com · Meadowbrook Office Park · 4268 I-55 North · P.O. Box 14167 · Jackson, MS 39236 · 601-351-2400

Zachary Taylor III · Watkins Ludlam Winter & Stennis · http://www.watkinsludlam.com · 633 North State Street · P.O. Box 427 · Jackson, MS 39205-0427 · 601-949-4900

H. Hunter Twiford III · McGlinchey Stafford · http://www.mcglinchey.com · City Centre, Suite 1100 · 200 South Lamar Street · P.O. Box 22949 · Jackson, MS 39225-2949 · 601-960-8400

Randall B. Wall · Watkins Ludlam Winter & Stennis · http://www.watkinsludlam.com · 633 North State Street · P.O. Box 427 · Jackson, MS 39205-0427 · 601-949-4900

Oxford

Jack F. Dunbar · 2% · Holcomb Dunbar · Courthouse Square · 1217 Jackson Avenue · P.O. Drawer 707 · Oxford, MS 38655 · 662-234-8775

David D. O'Donnell · Clayton O'Donnell · http://www.northmslaw.com · 1005 Jackson Avenue · P. O. Drawer 676 · Oxford, MS 38655 · 662-234-0900

NATURAL RESOURCES LAW

Brandon

William F. Blair · Blair & Bondurant · 1368 Old Fannin Road, Suite 300 · P.O. Box 321423 · Brandon, MS 39232-1423 · 601-992-4477

Si Morgan Bondurant · Blair & Bondurant · 1368 Old Fannin Road, Suite 300 · P.O. Box 321423 · Brandon, MS 39232-1423 · 601-992-4477

Jackson

Trudy B. Allen · Watkins Ludlam Winter & Stennis · http://www.watkinsludlam.com · 633 North State Street · P.O. Box 427 · Jackson, MS 39205-0427 · 601-949-4900

Thomas R. Crews · 2) · Watkins & Eager · http://www.watkinseager.com · The Emporium Building · 400 East Capitol Street · P.O. Box 650 · Jackson, MS 39205 · 601-965-1900

William F. Goodman, Jr. · 2% · Watkins & Eager · http://www.watkinseager.com · The Emporium Building · 400 East Capitol Street · P.O. Box 650 · Jackson, MS 39205 · 601-965-1900

Kathryn H. Hester · Watkins Ludlam Winter & Stennis · http://www.watkinsludlam.com · 633 North State Street · P.O. Box 427 · Jackson, MS 39205-0427 · 601-949-4900

Otis Johnson, Jr. · 2) · Robinson Biggs Ingram Solop & Farris · 111 East Capitol Street, Suite 101 · Jackson, MS 39201 · 601-713-1192

Powell G. Ogletree, Jr. · Adams and Reese · http://www.adamsandreese.com · 111 East Capitol Street, Suite 350 · P.O. Box 24297 · Jackson, MS 39201 · 601-353-3234

A. Jerry Sheldon · Adams and Reese · http://www.adamsandreese.com · 111 East Capitol Street, Suite 350 · P.O. Box 24297 · Jackson, MS 39201 · 601-353-3234

Daniel L. Singletary · a · Baker, Donelson, Bearman, Caldwell & Berkowitz · http://www.bakerdonelson.com · Meadowbrook Office Park · 4268 I-55 North · P.O. Box 14167 · Jackson, MS 39236 · 601-351-2400

Jefferson D. Stewart · 2) · Adams and Reese · http://www.adamsandreese.com · 111 East Capitol Street, Suite 350 · P.O. Box 24297 · Jackson, MS 39201 · 601-353-3234

Natchez

W. Marion Smith · 2) · Truly, Smith & Latham · 100 South Pearl Street · P.O. Box 1307 · Natchez, MS 39121-1307 · 601-442-6495

Ridgeland

Glenn Gates Taylor · 2) · Copeland Cook Taylor & Bush · http://www.cctb.com · Concourse 600, Suite 100 · 1076 Highland Colony Parkway · P.O. Box 6020 · Ridgeland, MS 39158 · 601-856-7200

NON-PROFIT/CHARITIES LAW

Jackson

James K. Dossett, Jr. · a · Baker, Donelson, Bearman, Caldwell & Berkowitz · http://www.bakerdonelson.com · Meadowbrook Office Park · 4268 I-55 North · P.O. Box 14167 · Jackson, MS 39236 · 601-351-2400

NON-WHITE-COLLAR CRIMINAL DEFENSE

Ashland

Anthony L. Farese · Farese, Farese & Farese · http://www.fareselaw.com · 122 Church Street · P.O. Box 98 · Ashland, MS 38603 · 662-224-6211

Steven E. Farese, Sr. · a · Farese, Farese & Farese · http://www.fareselaw.com · 122 Church Street · P.O. Box 98 · Ashland, MS 38603 · 662-224-6211

Canton

Julie Ann Epps · a · Julie A. Epps · 504 East Peace Street · Canton, MS 39046 · 601-407-1410

Gulfport

Joe Sam Owen · a · Owen & Galloway · Owen Building · 1414 Twenty-Fifth Avenue · P.O. Drawer 420 · Gulfport, MS 39502-0420 · 228-868-2821

Hernando

Gerald W. Chatham, Sr. · Chatham Damaré Pittman · 291 Losher Street · Hernando, MS 38632-2235 · 662-429-9871

Jackson

Merrida P. Coxwell, Jr. · a · Coxwell & Associates · 500 North State Street · P.O. Drawer 1337 · Jackson, MS 39215-1337 · 601-948-1600

Weaver E. Gore, Jr. · 2) · Weaver E. Gore, Jr. · 419 South State Street · P.O. Box 186 · Jackson, MS 39205 · 601-355-8775

William B. Kirksey · a · Kirksey & Associates · 401 East Capitol Street, Suite 100-M · P.O. Box 33 · Jackson, MS 39205-0033 · 601-354-4662

James W. Kitchens · a · Kitchens & Ellis · 610 North Street · Jackson, MS 39202 · 601-355-7444

Thomas E. Royals · 2) · Royals & Mayfield · The Plaza Building, Suite 500 · 120 North Congress Street · P.O. Box 22909 · Jackson, MS 39225-2909 · 601-948-7777

Frank W. Trapp · Phelps Dunbar · http://www.phelpsdunbar.com · 111 East Capitol Street, Suite 600 · P.O. Box 23066 · Jackson, MS 39225-3066 · 601-352-2300

Samuel H. Wilkins · Samuel H. Wilkins · 555 Tombigbee Street, Suite 101 · P.O. Box 504 · Jackson, MS 39205-0504 · 601-354-0770

Madison

Cynthia H. Speetjens · Cynthia H. Speetjens · 2088 Main Street, Suite A · P.O. Box 2629 · Madison, MS 39130 · 601-856-0515

Cynthia A. Stewart · a · Cynthia Stewart · 2088 Main Street, Suite A · P.O. Box 2629 · Madison, MS 39130 · 601-856-0515

Meridian

Daniel P. Self, Jr. · a · Self, Jacob & Kieronski · 509 Constitution Avenue · P.O. Box 949 · Meridian, MS 39302-0949 · 601-693-6994

OIL & GAS LAW

Brandon

William F. Blair · Blair & Bondurant · 1368 Old Fannin Road, Suite 300 · P.O. Box 321423 · Brandon, MS 39232-1423 · 601-992-4477

Si Morgan Bondurant · Blair & Bondurant · 1368 Old Fannin Road, Suite 300 · P.O. Box 321423 · Brandon, MS 39232-1423 · 601-992-4477

Jackson

Edmund L. Brunini, Jr. · a · Brunini, Grantham, Grower & Hewes · http://www.brunini.com · 1400 Trustmark Building · 248 East Capitol Street · P.O. Drawer 119 · Jackson, MS 39205 · 601-948-3101

Thomas R. Crews · 2) · Watkins & Eager · http://www.watkinseager.com · The Emporium Building · 400 East Capitol Street · P.O. Box 650 · Jackson, MS 39205 · 601-965-1900

Paul N. Davis · Butler, Snow, O'Mara, Stevens and Cannada · http://www.butlersnow.com · AmSouth Plaza, Suite 1700 · 210 East Capitol Street · P.O. Box 22567 · Jackson, MS 39225-2567 · 601-948-5711

William F. Goodman, Jr. · 2% · Watkins & Eager · http://www.watkinseager.com · The Emporium Building · 400 East Capitol Street · P.O. Box 650 · Jackson, MS 39205 · 601-965-1900

Otis Johnson, Jr. · 2) · Robinson Biggs Ingram Solop & Farris · 111 East Capitol Street, Suite 101 · Jackson, MS 39201 · 601-713-1192

Daniel L. Singletary · a · Baker, Donelson, Bearman, Caldwell & Berkowitz · http://www.bakerdonelson.com · Meadowbrook Office Park · 4268 I-55 North · P.O. Box 14167 · Jackson, MS 39236 · 601-351-2400

Paul H. Stephenson III · Watkins & Eager · http://www.watkinseager.com · The Emporium Building · 400 East Capitol Street · P.O. Box 650 · Jackson, MS 39205 · 601-965-1900

Jefferson D. Stewart · 2) · Adams and Reese · http://www.adamsandreese.com · 111 East Capitol Street, Suite 350 · P.O. Box 24297 · Jackson, MS 39201 · 601-353-3234

Natchez

W. Marion Smith · 2) · Truly, Smith & Latham · 100 South Pearl Street · P.O. Box 1307 · Natchez, MS 39121-1307 · 601-442-6495

Ridgeland

C. Glen Bush · Copeland Cook Taylor & Bush · http://www.cctb.com · Concourse 600, Suite 100 · 1076 Highland Colony Parkway · P.O. Box 6020 · Ridgeland, MS 39158 · 601-856-7200

Glenn Gates Taylor · 2) · Copeland Cook Taylor & Bush · http://www.cctb.com · Concourse 600, Suite 100 · 1076 Highland Colony Parkway · P.O. Box 6020 · Ridgeland, MS 39158 · 601-856-7200

PERSONAL INJURY LITIGATION

Ashland

John Booth Farese · a · Farese, Farese & Farese · http://www.fareselaw.com · 122 Church Street · P.O. Box 98 · Ashland, MS 38603 · 662-224-6211

Biloxi

William E. Whitfield III · Copeland Cook Taylor & Bush · http://www.cctb.com · Gulf Coast Professional Towers, Suite 200 · 2781 C.T. Switzer Senior Drive · Biloxi, MS 39531 · 228-863-6101

Clarksdale

Ralph E. Chapman · a · Chapman, Lewis & Swan · 501 First Street · P.O. Box 428 · Clarksdale, MS 38614 · 662-627-4105

Charles M. Merkel, Jr. · 2) · Merkel & Cocke · http://www.merkel-cocke.com · 30 Delta Avenue · P.O. Box 1388 · Clarksdale, MS 38614-1388 · 662-627-9641

Columbus

J. Gordon Flowers · Brunini, Grantham, Grower & Hewes · http://www.brunini.com · 3499 Bluecutt Road · P.O. Box 752O · Columbus, MS 39705-0024 · 662-240-9744

Greenwood

James E. Upshaw · Upshaw, Williams, Biggers, Beckham & Riddick · 309 Fulton Street · P.O. Drawer 8230 · Greenwood, MS 38935-8230 · 662-455-1613

Gulfport

Harry R. Allen · 2) · Allen, Cobb, Hood & Atkinson · 2512 Twenty-Fifth Avenue, Suite Three · Gulfport, MS 39501 · 228-864-4011

Paul J. Delcambre, Jr. · Balch & Bingham · http://www.balch.com · 1310 Twenty-Fifth Avenue · P.O. Box 130 · Gulfport, MS 39502 · 228-864-9900

Ben F. Galloway III · Owen & Galloway · Owen Building · 1414 Twenty-Fifth Avenue · P.O. Drawer 420 Gulfport, MS 39502-0420 · 228-868-2821

Robert C. Galloway · a · Butler, Snow, O'Mara, Stevens and Cannada · http://www.butlersnow.com · Whitney National Bank Building, Suite 204 · 1300 Twenty-Fifth Avenue · P.O. Drawer 4248 · Gulfport, MS 39502 · 228-864-1170

Timothy C. Holleman · Boyce Holleman & Associates · 11240 Highway 49, Suite 400 · Gulfport, MS 39503 · 228-539-9600

Alben N. Hopkins · Hopkins, Barvié & Hopkins · 2701 Twenty-Fourth Avenue · P.O. Box 1510 · Gulfport, MS 39501-4941 · 228-864-2200

Joe Sam Owen · a · Owen & Galloway · Owen Building · 1414 Twenty-Fifth Avenue · P.O. Drawer 420 · Gulfport, MS 39502-0420 · 228-868-2821

Edward C. Taylor · Daniel, Coker, Horton and Bell · http://www.danielcoker.com · 1712 Fifteenth Street P.O. Box 416 · Gulfport, MS 39502-0416 · 228-864-8117

Thomas E. Vaughn · Vaughn, Bowden & Wooten · 2304 Nineteenth Street, Suite 102 · P.O. Drawer 240 · Gulfport, MS 39502 · 228-863-5656

James G. Wyly III · Phelps Dunbar · http://www.phelpsdunbar.com · NorthCourt One, Suite 300 · 2304 Nineteenth Street · Gulfport, MS 39501 · 228-679-1130

Hattiesburg

J. Robert Ramsay · Ramsay & Hammond · 106 Madison Plaza, Suite B · P.O. Box 16567 · Hattiesburg, MS 39404-6567 · 601-264-4499

Tom W. Tyner · Aultman, Tyner & Ruffin · 315 Hemphill Street · P.O. Drawer 750 · Hattiesburg, MS 39403-0750 · 601-583-2671

Carey R. Varnado · Montague, Pittman & Varnado · 525 Main Street · P.O. Drawer 1975 · Hattiesburg, MS 39403-1975 · 601-544-1234

Hernando

Gerald W. Chatham, Sr. · Chatham Damaré Pittman · 291 Losher Street · Hernando, MS 38632-2235 · 662-429-9871

Jackson

David L. Ayers · Watkins & Eager · http://www.watkinseager.com · The Emporium Building · 400 East Capitol Street · P.O. Box 650 · Jackson, MS 39205 · 601-965-1900

F. Hall Bailey · Watkins Ludlam Winter & Stennis · http://www.watkinsludlam.com · 633 North State Street · P.O. Box 427 · Jackson, MS 39205-0427 · 601-949-4900

Roy D. Campbell III · Bradley Arant Rose & White · http://www.bradleyarant.com · One Jackson Place, Suite 450 · 188 East Capitol Street · Jackson, MS 39201 · 601-948-8000

John B. Clark · Daniel, Coker, Horton and Bell · http://www.danielcoker.com · 4400 Old Canton Road, Suite 400 · P.O. Box 1084 · Jackson, MS 39215-1084 · 601-969-7607

James P. Cothren · 2% · Cothren Law Firm · 820 North State Street · P.O. Box 1329 · Jackson, MS 39215-1329 · 601-354-1115

Edward J. Currie, Jr. · Currie Johnson Griffin Gaines & Myers · http://www.curriejohnson.com · 1044 River Oaks Drive · P.O. Box 750 · Jackson, MS 39205-0750 · 601-969-1010

Barry W. Ford · Baker, Donelson, Bearman, Caldwell & Berkowitz · http://www.bakerdonelson.com · Meadowbrook Office Park · 4268 I-55 North · P.O. Box 14167 · Jackson, MS 39236 · 601-351-2400

James B. Galloway · Butler, Snow, O'Mara, Stevens and Cannada · http://www.butlersnow.com · AmSouth Plaza, Suite 1700 · 210 East Capitol Street · P.O. Box 22567 · Jackson, MS 39225-2567 · 601-948-5711

Robert L. Gibbs · Brunini, Grantham, Grower & Hewes · http://www.brunini.com · 1400 Trustmark Building · 248 East Capitol Street · P.O. Drawer 119 · Jackson, MS 39205 · 601-948-3101

William F. Goodman, Jr. · 2% · Watkins & Eager · http://www.watkinseager.com · The Emporium Building · 400 East Capitol Street · P.O. Box 650 · Jackson, MS 39205 · 601-965-1900

Christy D. Jones · a · Butler, Snow, O'Mara, Stevens and Cannada · http://www.butlersnow.com · AmSouth Plaza, Suite 1700 · 210 East Capitol Street · P.O. Box 22567 · Jackson, MS 39225-2567 · 601-948-5711

John Griffin Jones · a · Jones, Funderburg, Sessums, Peterson & Lee · 901 North State Street · P.O. Box 13960 · Jackson, MS 39236-3960 · 601-355-5200

Walker W. Jones III · Baker, Donelson, Bearman, Caldwell & Berkowitz · http://www.bakerdonelson.com · Meadowbrook Office Park · 4268 I-55 North · P.O. Box 14167 · Jackson, MS 39236 · 601-351-2400

R. David Kaufman · Brunini, Grantham, Grower & Hewes · http://www.brunini.com · 1400 Trustmark Building · 248 East Capitol Street · P.O. Drawer 119 · Jackson, MS 39205 · 601-948-3101

William H. Liston · 2) · Liston/Lancaster · http://www.listonlancaster.com · 304 North Congress Street · P.O. Box 22983 · Jackson, MS 39225 · 601-944-0820

James W. Nobles, Jr. · a · James W. Nobles, Jr. · 431 Tombigbee Street · P.O. Box 1733 · Jackson, MS 39215-1733 · 601-948-1757

John D. Price · Wise Carter Child & Caraway · Heritage Building, Suite 600 · 401 East Capitol Street · Jackson, MS 39205 · 601-968-5500

Keith R. Raulston · a · Watkins Ludlam Winter & Stennis · http://www.watkinsludlam.com · 633 North State Street · P.O. Box 427 · Jackson, MS 39205-0427 · 601-949-4900

George H. Ritter · Wise Carter Child & Caraway · Heritage Building, Suite 600 · 401 East Capitol Street · Jackson, MS 39205 · 601-968-5500

Christopher A. Shapley · a · Brunini, Grantham, Grower & Hewes · http://www.brunini.com · 1400 Trustmark Building · 248 East Capitol Street · P.O. Drawer 119 · Jackson, MS 39205 · 601-948-3101

Forrest Stringfellow · Daniel, Coker, Horton and Bell · http://www.danielcoker.com · 4400 Old Canton Road, Suite 400 · P.O. Box 1084 · Jackson, MS 39215-1084 · 601-969-7607

Lee Davis Thames · 2% · Butler, Snow, O'Mara, Stevens and Cannada · http://www.butlersnow.com · AmSouth Plaza, Suite 1700 · 210 East Capitol Street · P.O. Box 22567 · Jackson, MS 39225-2567 · 601-948-5711

Stephen L. Thomas · a · Bradley Arant Rose & White · http://www.bradleyarant.com · One Jackson Place, Suite 450 · 188 East Capitol Street · Jackson, MS 39201 · 601-948-8000

Michael W. Ulmer · a · Watkins & Eager · http://www.watkinseager.com · The Emporium Building · 400 East Capitol Street · P.O. Box 650 · Jackson, MS 39205 · 601-965-1900

John E. Wade · Brunini, Grantham, Grower & Hewes · http://www.brunini.com · 1400 Trustmark Building · 248 East Capitol Street · P.O. Drawer 119 · Jackson, MS 39205 · 601-948-3101

W. Scott Welch III · a · Baker, Donelson, Bearman, Caldwell & Berkowitz · http://www.bakerdonelson.com · Meadowbrook Office Park · 4268 I-55 North · P.O. Box 14167 · Jackson, MS 39236 · 601-351-2400

Laurel

Leonard B. Melvin, Jr. · 2% · Melvin & Melvin · 424 Sawmill Road · P.O. Box 142 · Laurel, MS 39441 · 601-426-6306

Oxford

Jack F. Dunbar · 2% · Holcomb Dunbar · Courthouse Square · 1217 Jackson Avenue · P.O. Drawer 707 · Oxford, MS 38655 · 662-234-8775

John H. Dunbar · Dunbar Davis · 324 Jackson Avenue East, Suite A · Oxford, MS 38655 · 662-281-0001

J. Rhea Tannehill, Jr. · Tannehill & Carmean · http://www.tannehillcarmean.com · 829 North Lamar, Suite One · Oxford, MS 38655 · 662-236-9996

Grady F. Tollison, Jr. · a · Tollison Law Firm · 100 Courthouse Square · P.O. Box 1216 · Oxford, MS 38655 · 662-234-7070

Pascagoula

James H. Heidelberg · a · Heidelberg, Steinberger, Colmer & Burrow · 711 Delmas Avenue · P.O. Box 1407 · Pascagoula, MS 39568-1407 · 228-762-8021

Roy C. Williams · a · Heidelberg, Steinberger, Colmer & Burrow · 711 Delmas Avenue · P.O. Box 1407 · Pascagoula, MS 39568-1407 · 228-762-8021

Ridgeland

Bobby L. Dallas · Sessums, Dallas & Morrison · 240 Trace Colony Park Drive, Suite 100 · Ridgeland, MS 39157 · 601-933-2040

Robert B. Sessums · a · Sessums, Dallas & Morrison · 240 Trace Colony Park Drive, Suite 100 · Ridgeland, MS 39157 · 601-933-2040

Robert P. Thompson · Copeland Cook Taylor & Bush · http://www.cctb.com · Concourse 600, Suite 100 1076 Highland Colony Parkway · P.O. Box 6020 · Ridgeland, MS 39158 · 601-856-7200

Tupelo

L. F. Sams, Jr. · 2% · Mitchell, McNutt & Sams · http://www.mitchellmcnutt.com · 105 South Front Street P.O. Box 7120 · Tupelo, MS 38802-7120 · 662-842-3871

PRODUCT LIABILITY LITIGATION

Clarksdale

Ralph E. Chapman · a · Chapman, Lewis & Swan · 501 First Street · P.O. Box 428 · Clarksdale, MS 38614 · 662-627-4105

Columbus

J. Gordon Flowers · Brunini, Grantham, Grower & Hewes · http://www.brunini.com · 3499 Bluecutt Road · P.O. Box 752O · Columbus, MS 39705-0024 · 662-240-9744

Gulfport

Harry R. Allen · 2) · Allen, Cobb, Hood & Atkinson · 2512 Twenty-Fifth Avenue, Suite Three · Gulfport, MS 39501 · 228-864-4011

Jackson

David L. Ayers · Watkins & Eager · http://www.watkinseager.com · The Emporium Building · 400 East Capitol Street · P.O. Box 650 · Jackson, MS 39205 · 601-965-1900

William F. Goodman III · Watkins & Eager · http://www.watkinseager.com · The Emporium Building · 400 East Capitol Street · P.O. Box 650 · Jackson, MS 39205 · 601-965-1900

Christy D. Jones · a · Butler, Snow, O'Mara, Stevens and Cannada · http://www.butlersnow.com · AmSouth Plaza, Suite 1700 · 210 East Capitol Street · P.O. Box 22567 · Jackson, MS 39225-2567 · 601-948-5711

Walker W. Jones III · Baker, Donelson, Bearman, Caldwell & Berkowitz · http://www.bakerdonelson.com · Meadowbrook Office Park · 4268 I-55 North · P.O. Box 14167 · Jackson, MS 39236 · 601-351-2400

Shane F. Langston · Langston & Langston · 201 North President Street · Jackson, MS 39201 · 601-969-1356

Robert A. Miller · Butler, Snow, O'Mara, Stevens and Cannada · http://www.butlersnow.com · AmSouth Plaza, Suite 1700 · 210 East Capitol Street · P.O. Box 22567 · Jackson, MS 39225-2567 · 601-948-5711

William N. Reed · Baker, Donelson, Bearman, Caldwell & Berkowitz · http://www.bakerdonelson.com · Meadowbrook Office Park · 4268 I-55 North · P.O. Box 14167 · Jackson, MS 39236 · 601-351-2400

Lee Davis Thames · 2% · Butler, Snow, O'Mara, Stevens and Cannada · http://www.butlersnow.com · AmSouth Plaza, Suite 1700 · 210 East Capitol Street · P.O. Box 22567 · Jackson, MS 39225-2567 · 601-948-5711

Stephen L. Thomas · a · Bradley Arant Rose & White · http://www.bradleyarant.com · One Jackson Place, Suite 450 · 188 East Capitol Street · Jackson, MS 39201 · 601-948-8000

J. Carter Thompson, Jr. · Baker, Donelson, Bearman, Caldwell & Berkowitz · http://www.bakerdonelson.com · Meadowbrook Office Park · 4268 I-55 North · P.O. Box 14167 · Jackson, MS 39236 · 601-351-2400

W. Scott Welch III · a · Baker, Donelson, Bearman, Caldwell & Berkowitz · http://www.bakerdonelson.com · Meadowbrook Office Park · 4268 I-55 North · P.O. Box 14167 · Jackson, MS 39236 · 601-351-2400

Thomas E. Williams · Butler, Snow, O'Mara, Stevens and Cannada · http://www.butlersnow.com · AmSouth Plaza, Suite 1700 · 210 East Capitol Street · P.O. Box 22567 · Jackson, MS 39225-2567 · 601-948-5711

Tupelo

Claude F. Clayton, Jr. · Clayton O'Donnell · http://www.northmslaw.com · 115 North Broadway Street · P.O. Box 755 · Tupelo, MS 38802 · 662-620-7938

William C. Murphree · Mitchell, McNutt & Sams · http://www.mitchellmcnutt.com · 105 South Front Street · P.O. Box 7120 · Tupelo, MS 38802-7120 · 662-842-3871

L. F. Sams, Jr. · 2% · Mitchell, McNutt & Sams · http://www.mitchellmcnutt.com · 105 South Front Street P.O. Box 7120 · Tupelo, MS 38802-7120 · 662-842-3871

William C. Spencer, Sr. · Mitchell, McNutt & Sams · http://www.mitchellmcnutt.com · 105 South Front Street · P.O. Box 7120 · Tupelo, MS 38802-7120 · 662-842-3871

PROFESSIONAL MALPRACTICE LAW

Jackson

John B. Clark · Daniel, Coker, Horton and Bell · http://www.danielcoker.com · 4400 Old Canton Road, Suite 400 · P.O. Box 1084 · Jackson, MS 39215-1084 · 601-969-7607

John D. Price · Wise Carter Child & Caraway · Heritage Building, Suite 600 · 401 East Capitol Street · Jackson, MS 39205 · 601-968-5500

Phillip S. Sykes · Forman Perry Watkins Krutz & Tardy · http://www.fpwk.com · City Center, Suite 100 · 200 South Lamar Street · P.O. Box 22608 · Jackson, MS 39225-2608 · 601-960-8600

Thomas E. Williams · Butler, Snow, O'Mara, Stevens and Cannada · http://www.butlersnow.com · AmSouth Plaza, Suite 1700 · 210 East Capitol Street · P.O. Box 22567 · Jackson, MS 39225-2567 · 601-948-5711

Tupelo

L. F. Sams, Jr. · 2% · Mitchell, McNutt & Sams · http://www.mitchellmcnutt.com · 105 South Front Street P.O. Box 7120 · Tupelo, MS 38802-7120 · 662-842-3871

Robert K. Upchurch · Holland, Ray, Upchurch & Hillen · 322 Jefferson Street · P.O. Drawer 409 · Tupelo, MS 38802 · 662-842-1721

John G. Wheeler · Mitchell, McNutt & Sams · http://www.mitchellmcnutt.com · 105 South Front Street · P.O. Box 7120 · Tupelo, MS 38802-7120 · 662-842-3871

PROJECT FINANCE LAW

Jackson

Robert S. Lazarus · Watkins Ludlam Winter & Stennis · http://www.watkinsludlam.com · 633 North State Street · P.O. Box 427 · Jackson, MS 39205-0427 · 601-949-4900

Zachary Taylor III · Watkins Ludlam Winter & Stennis · http://www.watkinsludlam.com · 633 North State Street · P.O. Box 427 · Jackson, MS 39205-0427 · 601-949-4900

Randall B. Wall · Watkins Ludlam Winter & Stennis · http://www.watkinsludlam.com · 633 North State Street · P.O. Box 427 · Jackson, MS 39205-0427 · 601-949-4900

M. Binford Williams, Jr. · Watkins & Eager · http://www.watkinseager.com · The Emporium Building · 400 East Capitol Street · P.O. Box 650 · Jackson, MS 39205 · 601-965-1900

PUBLIC FINANCE LAW

Jackson

Stephen C. Edds · Baker, Donelson, Bearman, Caldwell & Berkowitz · http://www.bakerdonelson.com · Meadowbrook Office Park · 4268 I-55 North · P.O. Box 14167 · Jackson, MS 39236 · 601-351-2400

John F. England · Butler, Snow, O'Mara, Stevens and Cannada · http://www.butlersnow.com · AmSouth Plaza, Suite 1700 · 210 East Capitol Street · P.O. Box 22567 · Jackson, MS 39225-2567 · 601-948-5711

Wilton J. Johnson III · Baker, Donelson, Bearman, Caldwell & Berkowitz · http://www.bakerdonelson.com · Meadowbrook Office Park · 4268 I-55 North · P.O. Box 14167 · Jackson, MS 39236 · 601-351-2400

Samuel W. Keyes, Jr. · Butler, Snow, O'Mara, Stevens and Cannada · http://www.butlersnow.com · AmSouth Plaza, Suite 1700 · 210 East Capitol Street · P.O. Box 22567 · Jackson, MS 39225-2567 · 601-948-5711

Robert S. Lazarus · Watkins Ludlam Winter & Stennis · http://www.watkinsludlam.com · 633 North State Street · P.O. Box 427 · Jackson, MS 39205-0427 · 601-949-4900

Zachary Taylor III · Watkins Ludlam Winter & Stennis · http://www.watkinsludlam.com · 633 North State Street · P.O. Box 427 · Jackson, MS 39205-0427 · 601-949-4900

Thad W. Varner · Butler, Snow, O'Mara, Stevens and Cannada · http://www.butlersnow.com · AmSouth Plaza, Suite 1700 · 210 East Capitol Street · P.O. Box 22567 · Jackson, MS 39225-2567 · 601-948-5711

Randall B. Wall · Watkins Ludlam Winter & Stennis · http://www.watkinsludlam.com · 633 North State Street · P.O. Box 427 · Jackson, MS 39205-0427 · 601-949-4900

RAILROAD LAW

Greenwood

Glenn F. Beckham · Upshaw, Williams, Biggers, Beckham & Riddick · 309 Fulton Street · P.O. Drawer 8230 · Greenwood, MS 38935-8230 · 662-455-1613

Hattiesburg

Vicki R. Leggett · Zachary and Leggett · 211 South 29th Avenue, Suite 100 · Hattiesburg, MS 39402 · 601-264-0300

Patrick H. Zachary · Zachary and Leggett · 211 South 29th Avenue, Suite 100 · Hattiesburg, MS 39402 · 601-264-0300

Jackson

Stuart G. Kruger · Kruger Law Firm · 2329 East Manor Drive · P.O. Box 16665 · Jackson, MS 39236 · 601-362-3268

Charles T. Ozier · Wise Carter Child & Caraway · Heritage Building, Suite 600 · 401 East Capitol Street · Jackson, MS 39205 · 601-968-5500

George H. Ritter · Wise Carter Child & Caraway · Heritage Building, Suite 600 · 401 East Capitol Street · Jackson, MS 39205 · 601-968-5500

Charles E. Ross · Wise Carter Child & Caraway · Heritage Building, Suite 600 · 401 East Capitol Street · Jackson, MS 39205 · 601-968-5500

Biloxi

Lawrence C. Corban, Jr. · a · Corban Gunn & Van Cleave · 146 Porter Avenue · P.O. Drawer 1916 · Biloxi, MS 39533-1916 · 228-432-7826

Gulfport

John L. Galloway · Butler, Snow, O'Mara, Stevens and Cannada · http://www.butlersnow.com · Whitney National Bank Building, Suite 204 · 1300 Twenty-Fifth Avenue · P.O. Drawer 4248 · Gulfport, MS 39502 228-864-1170

Walter Rayford Jones · 2% · Jones, Jones & Jones · 1605 Twenty-Third Avenue · P.O. Box 4227 · Gulfport, MS 39502-4227 · 228-864-8965

Hattiesburg

J. Kearney Travis, Jr. · a · Travis & Travis · 614 Main Street · P.O. Box 590 · Hattiesburg, MS 39403-0590 · 601-582-5591

Jackson

Don B. Cannada · a · Butler, Snow, O'Mara, Stevens and Cannada · http://www.butlersnow.com · AmSouth Plaza, Suite 1700 · 210 East Capitol Street · P.O. Box 22567 · Jackson, MS 39225-2567 · 601-948-5711

W. Rodney Clement, Jr. · a · Brunini, Grantham, Grower & Hewes · http://www.brunini.com · 1400 Trustmark Building · 248 East Capitol Street · P.O. Drawer 119 · Jackson, MS 39205 · 601-948-3101

Mark T. Davis · Watkins Ludlam Winter & Stennis · http://www.watkinsludlam.com · 633 North State Street · P.O. Box 427 · Jackson, MS 39205-0427 · 601-949-4900

Paul L. Gunn · Watkins & Eager · http://www.watkinseager.com · The Emporium Building · 400 East Capitol Street · P.O. Box 650 · Jackson, MS 39205 · 601-965-1900

Steven M. Hendrix · Forman Perry Watkins Krutz & Tardy · http://www.fpwk.com · City Center, Suite 100 · 200 South Lamar Street · P.O. Box 22608 · Jackson, MS 39225-2608 · 601-960-8600

John Sanford McDavid · YoungWilliams · 210 East Capitol Street, Suite 2000 · P.O. Box 23059 · Jackson, MS 39225-3059 · 601-948-6100

Powell G. Ogletree, Jr. · Adams and Reese · http://www.adamsandreese.com · 111 East Capitol Street, Suite 350 · P.O. Box 24297 · Jackson, MS 39201 · 601-353-3234

Daniel L. Singletary · a · Baker, Donelson, Bearman, Caldwell & Berkowitz · http://www.bakerdonelson.com · Meadowbrook Office Park · 4268 I-55 North · P.O. Box 14167 · Jackson, MS 39236 · 601-351-2400

William C. Smith, Jr. · 2) · Watkins & Eager · http://www.watkinseager.com · The Emporium Building · 400 East Capitol Street · P.O. Box 650 · Jackson, MS 39205 · 601-965-1900

Jim B. Tohill · 2) · Watkins Ludlam Winter & Stennis · http://www.watkinsludlam.com · 633 North State Street · P.O. Box 427 · Jackson, MS 39205-0427 · 601-949-4900

M. Binford Williams, Jr. · Watkins & Eager · http://www.watkinseager.com · The Emporium Building · 400 East Capitol Street · P.O. Box 650 · Jackson, MS 39205 · 601-965-1900

Roger W. Williams · Watkins & Eager · http://www.watkinseager.com · The Emporium Building · 400 East Capitol Street · P.O. Box 650 · Jackson, MS 39205 · 601-965-1900

Macon

Charles G. Perkins · Charles G. Perkins · 417 South Jefferson Street · P.O. Drawer 570 · Macon, MS 39341-0570 · 662-726-4276

Olive Branch

Gary P. Snyder · Watkins Ludlam Winter & Stennis · http://www.watkinsludlam.com · 6897 Crumpler Boulevard, Suite 100 · P.O. Box 1456 · Olive Branch, MS 38564 · 662-895-2996

James E. Woods · Watkins Ludlam Winter & Stennis · http://www.watkinsludlam.com · 6897 Crumpler Boulevard, Suite 100 · P.O. Box 1456 · Olive Branch, MS 38564 · 662-895-2996

SECURITIES LAW

Jackson

Charles P. Adams, Jr. · Adams and Reese · http://www.adamsandreese.com · 111 East Capitol Street, Suite 350 · P.O. Box 24297 · Jackson, MS 39201 · 601-353-3234

E. Clifton Hodge, Jr. · a · Mockbee Hall Drake & Hodge · Capital Towers, Suite 1820 · 125 South Congress Street · Jackson, MS 39201 · 601-353-0035

L. Keith Parsons · Watkins Ludlam Winter & Stennis · http://www.watkinsludlam.com · 633 North State Street · P.O. Box 427 · Jackson, MS 39205-0427 · 601-949-4900

STRUCTURED FINANCE LAW

Jackson

Zachary Taylor III · Watkins Ludlam Winter & Stennis · http://www.watkinsludlam.com · 633 North State Street · P.O. Box 427 · Jackson, MS 39205-0427 · 601-949-4900

TAX LAW

Gulfport

Frederick T. Hoff, Jr. · a · Newton & Hoff · 2019 Twenty-Third Avenue · P.O. Box 910 · Gulfport, MS 39502-0910 · 228-863-8827

Paul M. Newton, Jr. · 2) · Newton & Hoff · 2019 Twenty-Third Avenue · P.O. Box 910 · Gulfport, MS 39502-0910 · 228-863-8827

Jackson

Alveno N. Castilla · a · Watkins Ludlam Winter & Stennis · http://www.watkinsludlam.com · 633 North State Street · P.O. Box 427 · Jackson, MS 39205-0427 · 601-949-4900

James K. Dossett, Jr. · a · Baker, Donelson, Bearman, Caldwell & Berkowitz · http://www.bakerdonelson.com · Meadowbrook Office Park · 4268 I-55 North · P.O. Box 14167 · Jackson, MS 39236 · 601-351-2400

William E. Dossett · a · Watkins Ludlam Winter & Stennis · http://www.watkinsludlam.com · 633 North State Street · P.O. Box 427 · Jackson, MS 39205-0427 · 601-949-4900

Louis G. Fuller · Brunini, Grantham, Grower & Hewes · http://www.brunini.com · 1400 Trustmark Building · 248 East Capitol Street · P.O. Drawer 119 · Jackson, MS 39205 · 601-948-3101

David B. Grishman · a · Watkins Ludlam Winter & Stennis · http://www.watkinsludlam.com · 633 North State Street · P.O. Box 427 · Jackson, MS 39205-0427 · 601-949-4900

Jamie G. Houston III · a · Watkins & Eager · http://www.watkinseager.com · The Emporium Building · 400 East Capitol Street · P.O. Box 650 · Jackson, MS 39205 · 601-965-1900

James Stanford Nippes · Nippes & Healy · 6360 I-55 North, Suite 250 · P. O. Box 13492 · Jackson, MS 39236 · 601-952-2592

William S. Painter · a · Baker, Donelson, Bearman, Caldwell & Berkowitz · http://www.bakerdonelson.com · Meadowbrook Office Park · 4268 I-55 North · P.O. Box 14167 · Jackson, MS 39236 · 601-351-2400

James L. Pettis · Wyatt, Tarrant & Combs · http://www.wyattfirm.com · 4450 Old Canton Road, Suite 210 Jackson, MS 39211 · 601-987-5300

Stacy E. Thomas · Baker, Donelson, Bearman, Caldwell & Berkowitz · http://www.bakerdonelson.com · Meadowbrook Office Park · 4268 I-55 North · P.O. Box 14167 · Jackson, MS 39236 · 601-351-2400

Leonard D. Van Slyke, Jr. · a · Watkins Ludlam Winter & Stennis · http://www.watkinsludlam.com · 633 North State Street · P.O. Box 427 · Jackson, MS 39205-0427 · 601-949-4900

J. Paul Varner · a · Butler, Snow, O'Mara, Stevens and Cannada · http://www.butlersnow.com · AmSouth Plaza, Suite 1700 · 210 East Capitol Street · P.O. Box 22567 · Jackson, MS 39225-2567 · 601-948-5711

David P. Webb · Baker, Donelson, Bearman, Caldwell & Berkowitz · http://www.bakerdonelson.com · Meadowbrook Office Park · 4268 I-55 North · P.O. Box 14167 · Jackson, MS 39236 · 601-351-2400

Walter S. Weems · a · Brunini, Grantham, Grower & Hewes · http://www.brunini.com · 1400 Trustmark Building · 248 East Capitol Street · P.O. Drawer 119 · Jackson, MS 39205 · 601-948-3101

Tupelo

Gregory D. Pirkle · Phelps Dunbar · http://www.phelpsdunbar.com · One Mississippi Plaza, Seventh Floor · 201 South Spring Street · Tupelo, MS 38804 · 662-842-7907

TIMBER LAW

Jackson

Powell G. Ogletree, Jr. · Adams and Reese · http://www.adamsandreese.com · 111 East Capitol Street, Suite 350 · P.O. Box 24297 · Jackson, MS 39201 · 601-353-3234

TRUSTS AND ESTATES

Clarksdale

Edward P. Connell, Sr. · 2% · Edward P. Connell, Sr. · 152 Delta Avenue · P.O. Box 368 · Clarksdale, MS 38614-0368 · 662-627-2241

Columbus

Hunter M. Gholson · a · Hunter M. Gholson · 710 Main Street, Second Floor · P.O. Box 1111 · Columbus, MS 39703 · 662-243-7302

Gulfport

Paul M. Newton, Jr. · 2) · Newton & Hoff · 2019 Twenty-Third Avenue · P.O. Box 910 · Gulfport, MS 39502-0910 · 228-863-8827

Jackson

Holmes S. Adams · a · Adams and Reese · http://www.adamsandreese.com · 111 East Capitol Street, Suite 350 · P.O. Box 24297 · Jackson, MS 39201 · 601-353-3234

James K. Dossett, Jr. · a · Baker, Donelson, Bearman, Caldwell & Berkowitz · http://www.bakerdonelson.com · Meadowbrook Office Park · 4268 I-55 North · P.O. Box 14167 · Jackson, MS 39236 · 601-351-2400

William E. Dossett · a · Watkins Ludlam Winter & Stennis · http://www.watkinsludlam.com · 633 North State Street · P.O. Box 427 · Jackson, MS 39205-0427 · 601-949-4900

Lynne K. Green · Brunini, Grantham, Grower & Hewes · http://www.brunini.com · 1400 Trustmark Building · 248 East Capitol Street · P.O. Drawer 119 · Jackson, MS 39205 · 601-948-3101

David B. Grishman · a · Watkins Ludlam Winter & Stennis · http://www.watkinsludlam.com · 633 North State Street · P.O. Box 427 · Jackson, MS 39205-0427 · 601-949-4900

Jamie G. Houston III · a · Watkins & Eager · http://www.watkinseager.com · The Emporium Building · 400 East Capitol Street · P.O. Box 650 · Jackson, MS 39205 · 601-965-1900

Linda Bounds Keng · Watkins Ludlam Winter & Stennis · http://www.watkinsludlam.com · 633 North State Street · P.O. Box 427 · Jackson, MS 39205-0427 · 601-949-4900

Ronald I. Loeb · Butler, Snow, O'Mara, Stevens and Cannada · http://www.butlersnow.com · AmSouth Plaza, Suite 1700 · 210 East Capitol Street · P.O. Box 22567 · Jackson, MS 39225-2567 · 601-948-5711

Leonard C. Martin · Baker, Donelson, Bearman, Caldwell & Berkowitz · http://www.bakerdonelson.com Meadowbrook Office Park · 4268 I-55 North · P.O. Box 14167 · Jackson, MS 39236 · 601-351-2400

W. McDonald Nichols · a · Wise Carter Child & Caraway · Heritage Building, Suite 600 · 401 East Capitol Street · Jackson, MS 39205 · 601-968-5500

Jay A. Travis III · 2) · Butler, Snow, O'Mara, Stevens and Cannada · http://www.butlersnow.com · AmSouth Plaza, Suite 1700 · 210 East Capitol Street · P.O. Box 22567 · Jackson, MS 39225-2567 · 601-948-5711

Leonard D. Van Slyke, Jr. · a · Watkins Ludlam Winter & Stennis · http://www.watkinsludlam.com · 633 North State Street · P.O. Box 427 · Jackson, MS 39205-0427 · 601-949-4900

J. Paul Varner · a · Butler, Snow, O'Mara, Stevens and Cannada · http://www.butlersnow.com · AmSouth Plaza, Suite 1700 · 210 East Capitol Street · P.O. Box 22567 · Jackson, MS 39225-2567 · 601-948-5711

Ridgeland

Robert E. Williford · Williford McAllister Jacobus · 303 Highland Park Cove, Suite A · Ridgeland, MS 39157 · 601-991-2000

R. James Young · a · Wells Marble & Hurst · http://www.wellsmar.com · 300 Concourse Boulevard, Suite 200 · Ridgeland, MS 39157 · 601-605-6900

Tupelo

F. M. Bush III · 2% · Phelps Dunbar · http://www.phelpsdunbar.com · One Mississippi Plaza, Seventh Floor · 201 South Spring Street · Tupelo, MS 38804 · 662-842-7907

VENTURE CAPITAL LAW

Jackson

James A. Lowe III · Watkins & Eager · http://www.watkinseager.com · The Emporium Building · 400 East Capitol Street · P.O. Box 650 · Jackson, MS 39205 · 601-965-1900

James Stanford Nippes · Nippes & Healy · 6360 I-55 North, Suite 250 · P. O. Box 13492 · Jackson, MS 39236 · 601-952-2592

WATER LAW

Brandon

William F. Blair · Blair & Bondurant · 1368 Old Fannin Road, Suite 300 · P.O. Box 321423 · Brandon, MS 39232-1423 · 601-992-4477

Jackson

John A. Crawford · a · Butler, Snow, O'Mara, Stevens and Cannada · http://www.butlersnow.com · AmSouth Plaza, Suite 1700 · 210 East Capitol Street · P.O. Box 22567 · Jackson, MS 39225-2567 · 601-948-5711

Jefferson D. Stewart · 2) · Adams and Reese · http://www.adamsandreese.com · 111 East Capitol Street, Suite 350 · P.O. Box 24297 · Jackson, MS 39201 · 601-353-3234

Ridgeland

Glenn Gates Taylor · 2) · Copeland Cook Taylor & Bush · http://www.cctb.com · Concourse 600, Suite 100 · 1076 Highland Colony Parkway · P.O. Box 6020 · Ridgeland, MS 39158 · 601-856-7200

WHITE-COLLAR CRIMINAL DEFENSE

Ashland

Anthony L. Farese · Farese, Farese & Farese · http://www.fareselaw.com · 122 Church Street · P.O. Box 98 · Ashland, MS 38603 · 662-224-6211

Steven E. Farese, Sr. · a · Farese, Farese & Farese · http://www.fareselaw.com · 122 Church Street · P.O. Box 98 · Ashland, MS 38603 · 662-224-6211

Canton

Julie Ann Epps · a · Julie A. Epps · 504 East Peace Street · Canton, MS 39046 · 601-407-1410

Gulfport

Joe Sam Owen · a · Owen & Galloway · Owen Building · 1414 Twenty-Fifth Avenue · P.O. Drawer 420 · Gulfport, MS 39502-0420 · 228-868-2821

Hernando

Gerald W. Chatham, Sr. · Chatham Damaré Pittman · 291 Losher Street · Hernando, MS 38632-2235 · 662-429-9871

Jackson

Merrida P. Coxwell, Jr. · a · Coxwell & Associates · 500 North State Street · P.O. Drawer 1337 · Jackson, MS 39215-1337 · 601-948-1600

Robert E. Hauberg, Jr. · a · Baker, Donelson, Bearman, Caldwell & Berkowitz · http://www.bakerdonelson.com · Meadowbrook Office Park · 4268 I-55 North · P.O. Box 14167 · Jackson, MS 39236 · 601-351-2400

William B. Kirksey · a · Kirksey & Associates · 401 East Capitol Street, Suite 100-M · P.O. Box 33 · Jackson, MS 39205-0033 · 601-354-4662

James W. Kitchens · a · Kitchens & Ellis · 610 North Street · Jackson, MS 39202 · 601-355-7444

Thomas E. Royals · 2) · Royals & Mayfield · The Plaza Building, Suite 500 · 120 North Congress Street · P.O. Box 22909 · Jackson, MS 39225-2909 · 601-948-7777

Frank W. Trapp · Phelps Dunbar · http://www.phelpsdunbar.com · 111 East Capitol Street, Suite 600 · P.O. Box 23066 · Jackson, MS 39225-3066 · 601-352-2300

Samuel H. Wilkins · Samuel H. Wilkins · 555 Tombigbee Street, Suite 101 · P.O. Box 504 · Jackson, MS 39205-0504 · 601-354-0770

Madison

Cynthia H. Speetjens · Cynthia H. Speetjens · 2088 Main Street, Suite A · P.O. Box 2629 · Madison, MS 39130 · 601-856-0515

Cynthia A. Stewart · a · Cynthia Stewart · 2088 Main Street, Suite A · P.O. Box 2629 · Madison, MS 39130 · 601-856-0515

Meridian

Daniel P. Self, Jr. · a · Self, Jacob & Kieronski · 509 Constitution Avenue · P.O. Box 949 · Meridian, MS 39302-0949 · 601-693-6994

Oxford

Grady F. Tollison, Jr. · a · Tollison Law Firm · 100 Courthouse Square · P.O. Box 1216 · Oxford, MS 38655 · 662-234-7070

WORKERS' COMPENSATION LAW

Biloxi

Ronald T. Russell · a · Copeland Cook Taylor & Bush · http://www.cctb.com · Gulf Coast Professional Towers, Suite 200 · 2781 C.T. Switzer Senior Drive · Biloxi, MS 39531 · 228-863-6101

Greenwood

Roger C. Riddick · Upshaw, Williams, Biggers, Beckham & Riddick · 309 Fulton Street · P.O. Drawer 8230 · Greenwood, MS 38935-8230 · 662-455-1613

Hattiesburg

Louie F. Ruffin · a · Aultman, Tyner & Ruffin · 315 Hemphill Street · P.O. Drawer 750 · Hattiesburg, MS 39403-0750 · 601-583-2671

Jackson

Clifford B. Ammons · a · Watkins & Eager · http://www.watkinseager.com · The Emporium Building · 400 East Capitol Street · P.O. Box 650 · Jackson, MS 39205 · 601-965-1900

Donald V. Burch · a · Daniel, Coker, Horton and Bell · http://www.danielcoker.com · 4400 Old Canton Road, Suite 400 · P.O. Box 1084 · Jackson, MS 39215-1084 · 601-969-7607

Roger K. Doolittle · Doolittle and Doolittle · Briarwood One Building, Suite 500 · 460 Briarwood Drive · Jackson, MS 39206-3060 · 601-957-9777

Steven H. Funderburg · Jones, Funderburg, Sessums, Peterson & Lee · 901 North State Street · P.O. Box 13960 · Jackson, MS 39236-3960 · 601-355-5200

James E. Higginbotham · Watkins & Eager · http://www.watkinseager.com · The Emporium Building · 400 East Capitol Street · P.O. Box 650 · Jackson, MS 39205 · 601-965-1900

Gary K. Jones · Daniel, Coker, Horton and Bell · http://www.danielcoker.com · 4400 Old Canton Road, Suite 400 · P.O. Box 1084 · Jackson, MS 39215-1084 · 601-969-7607

John Griffin Jones · a · Jones, Funderburg, Sessums, Peterson & Lee · 901 North State Street · P.O. Box 13960 · Jackson, MS 39236-3960 · 601-355-5200

G. Davis Peterson · Jones, Funderburg, Sessums, Peterson & Lee · 901 North State Street · P.O. Box 13960 · Jackson, MS 39236-3960 · 601-355-5200

Andrew D. Sweat · Wise Carter Child & Caraway · Heritage Building, Suite 600 · 401 East Capitol Street Jackson, MS 39205 · 601-968-5500

Ridgeland

James M. Anderson · a · Anderson Crawley & Burke · http://www.acblaw.com · 805 South Wheatley, Suite 400 · P.O. Box 2540 · Ridgeland, MS 39158-2540 · 601-977-8977

Robert P. Thompson · Copeland Cook Taylor & Bush · http://www.cctb.com · Concourse 600, Suite 100 1076 Highland Colony Parkway · P.O. Box 6020 · Ridgeland, MS 39158 · 601-856-7200

Tupelo

Dennis W. Voge · Mitchell, McNutt & Sams · http://www.mitchellmcnutt.com · 105 South Front Street · P.O. Box 7120 · Tupelo, MS 38802-7120 · 662-842-3871

MISSOURI

ADMINISTRATIVE LAW

Columbia

Sarah J. Read · Law Offices of Sarah J. Read · 1905 Cherry Hill Drive, Suite 200 · Columbia, MO 65203 · 573-447-2349

St. Louis

Norman W. Pressman · Goldstein & Pressman · 121 Hunter Avenue, Suite 101 · St. Louis, MO 63124 · 314-727-1717

ALTERNATIVE DISPUTE RESOLUTION

Cape Girardeau

Stanley A. Grimm · Stanley A. Grimm · 2208 Crown Point Drive · Cape Girardeau, MO 63701 · 573-335-3253

Clayton

Leonard J. Frankel · Frankel, Rubin, Bond, Dubin, Siegel & Klein · Bemiston Tower, Suite 1111 · 231 South Bemiston · Clayton, MO 63105 · 314-725-8000

Kansas City

John R. Phillips · ⑩ · Husch Blackwell Sanders · http://www.huschblackwell.com · 4801 Main Street, Suite 1000 · Kansas City, MO 64112 · 816-983-8000

Richard H. Ralston · Armstrong Teasdale · http://www.armstrongteasdale.com · 2345 Grand Boulevard, Suite 2000 · Kansas City, MO 64108-2617 · 816-221-3420

Walter R. Simpson · ⑩ · Sanders & Simpson · 1125 Grand Boulevard, 15th Floor · Kansas City, MO 64106 · 816-471-6444

Kent Sullivan · Stinson Morrison Hecker · http://www.stinson.com · 1201 Walnut Street, Suite 2900 · Kansas City, MO 64106-2150 · 816-842-8600

Springfield

Gary R. Cunningham · Lathrop & Gage · 1845 South National · P.O. Box 4288 · Springfield, MO 65804 · 417-886-2000

James S. Newberry · The Law Office of Jim Newberry · 4730 South National, Suite A-2 · Springfield, MO 65810-2773 · 417-447-1212

Michael J. Patton · Turner, Reid, Duncan, Loomer & Patton · 1355 East Bradford Parkway, Suite A · P.O. Box 4043 · Springfield, MO 65808 · 417-883-2102

St. Louis

Thomas M. Blumenthal · Paule, Camazine & Blumenthal · 165 North Meramec Avenue, Sixth Floor · St. Louis, MO 63105 · 314-727-2266

Thomas Cummings · Armstrong Teasdale · http://www.armstrongteasdale.com · One Metropolitan Square, Suite 2600 · 211 North Broadway · St. Louis, MO 63102-2740 · 314-621-5070

Jerome A. Diekemper · ㉕ · Jerome A. Diekemper · 7730 Carondelet Avenue, Suite 200 · St. Louis, MO 63105 · 314-727-1015

George L. Fitzsimmons · ⑩ · Holloran, Stewart & Schwartz · 2000 South Eighth Street · St. Louis, MO 63104 · 314-621-2121

Alan E. Freed · Paule, Camazine & Blumenthal · 165 North Meramec Avenue, Sixth Floor · St. Louis, MO 63105 · 314-727-2266

Michael S. Geigerman · Michael S. Geigerman · 720 Olive Street, Suite 2300 · St. Louis, MO 63101 · 314-231-4642

Brendan Ryan · Thompson Coburn · One U.S. Bank Plaza · St. Louis, MO 63101-1611 · 314-552-6000

Richard P. Sher · Devereux Murphy · The Plaza at Clayton, Suite 1100 · 190 Carondelet · St. Louis, MO 63105 · 314-721-1516

ANTITRUST LAW

Clayton

Alan E. Popkin · ⑩ · Husch Blackwell Sanders · http://www.huschblackwell.com · The Plaza in Clayton Office Tower, Suite 600 · 190 Carondelet Plaza · Clayton, MO 63105-3441 · 314-480-1500

Kansas City

Thomas Bradshaw · ⑩ · Bradshaw Herrington · 2345 Grand Boulevard, Suite 600 · Kansas City, MO 64108-2655 · 816-285-1030

James R. Eiszner, Jr. · Shook, Hardy & Bacon · 2555 Grand Boulevard · Kansas City, MO 64108 · 816-474-6550

David E. Everson · Stinson Morrison Hecker · http://www.stinson.com · 1201 Walnut Street, Suite 2900 · Kansas City, MO 64106-2150 · 816-842-8600

Floyd R. Finch, Jr. · Husch Blackwell Sanders · http://www.huschblackwell.com · 4801 Main Street, Suite 1000 · Kansas City, MO 64112 · 816-983-8000

George E. Leonard · Shughart Thomson & Kilroy · http://www.stklaw.com · 12 Wyandotte Plaza, Suite 1800 · 120 West 12th Street · Kansas City, MO 64105 · 816-421-3355

David A. Rameden · Shook, Hardy & Bacon · 2555 Grand Boulevard · Kansas City, MO 64108 · 816-474-6550

R. Lawrence Ward · ⑩ · Shughart Thomson & Kilroy · http://www.stklaw.com · 12 Wyandotte Plaza, Suite 1800 · 120 West 12th Street · Kansas City, MO 64105 · 816-421-3355

Curtis E. Woods · Sonnenschein Nath & Rosenthal · 4520 Main Street, Suite 1100 · Kansas City, MO 64111-7700 · 816-460-2400

St. Louis

John Michael Clear · ㉕ · Bryan Cave · One Metropolitan Square, Suite 3600 · 211 North Broadway · St. Louis, MO 63102-2750 · 314-259-2000

Glenn E. Davis · Armstrong Teasdale · http://www.armstrongteasdale.com · One Metropolitan Square, Suite 2600 · 211 North Broadway · St. Louis, MO 63102-2740 · 314-621-5070

Don M. Downing · Gray, Ritter & Graham · http://www.grayrittergraham.com · Gateway One on The Mall, Suite 800 · 701 Market Street · St. Louis, MO 63101-1826 · 314-241-5620

Dale R. Joerling · Thompson Coburn · One U.S. Bank Plaza · St. Louis, MO 63101-1611 · 314-552-6000

E. Perry Johnson · Bryan Cave · One Metropolitan Square, Suite 3600 · 211 North Broadway · St. Louis, MO 63102-2750 · 314-259-2000

W. Stanley Walch · ㉕ · Thompson Coburn · One U.S. Bank Plaza · St. Louis, MO 63101-1611 · 314-552-6000

APPELLATE LAW

Clayton

Mark G. Arnold · Husch Blackwell Sanders · http://www.huschblackwell.com · The Plaza in Clayton Office Tower, Suite 600 · 190 Carondelet Plaza · Clayton, MO 63105-3441 · 314-480-1500

Jefferson City

Ann K. Covington · Bryan Cave · Riverview Office Center · 221 Bolivar Street · Jefferson City, MO 65101-1574 · 573-556-6620

Kansas City

William E. Quirk · Shughart Thomson & Kilroy · http://www.stklaw.com · 12 Wyandotte Plaza, Suite 1800 · 120 West 12th Street · Kansas City, MO 64105 · 816-421-3355

R. Kent Sellers · Lathrop & Gage · 2345 Grand Boulevard, Suite 2800 · Kansas City, MO 64108 · 816-292-2000

Springfield

John C. Holstein · Shughart Thomson & Kilroy · http://www.stklaw.com · The Hammons Tower, Suite 1200 · 901 St. Louis Street · Springfield, MO 65806 · 417-869-3353

St. Louis

Ann E. Buckley · Buckley & Buckley · 1139 Olive Street, Suite 800 · St. Louis, MO 63101-1928 · 314-621-3434

Jordan B. Cherrick · Greensfelder, Hemker & Gale · Equitable Building, Suite 2000 · 10 South Broadway · St. Louis, MO 63102 · 314-241-9090

James W. Erwin · Thompson Coburn · One U.S. Bank Plaza · St. Louis, MO 63101-1611 · 314-552-6000

Gretchen Garrison · Gray, Ritter & Graham · http://www.grayrittergraham.com · Gateway One on The Mall, Suite 800 · 701 Market Street · St. Louis, MO 63101-1826 · 314-241-5620

Bruce D. Ryder · Thompson Coburn · One U.S. Bank Plaza · St. Louis, MO 63101-1611 · 314-552-6000

Erwin O. Switzer III · Greensfelder, Hemker & Gale · Equitable Building, Suite 2000 · 10 South Broadway · St. Louis, MO 63102 · 314-241-9090

Thomas E. Wack · ⑩ · Bryan Cave · One Metropolitan Square, Suite 3600 · 211 North Broadway · St. Louis, MO 63102-2750 · 314-259-2000

Thomas C. Walsh · ⑩ · Bryan Cave · One Metropolitan Square, Suite 3600 · 211 North Broadway · St. Louis, MO 63102-2750 · 314-259-2000

Thomas B. Weaver · Armstrong Teasdale · http://www.armstrongteasdale.com · One Metropolitan Square, Suite 2600 · 211 North Broadway · St. Louis, MO 63102-2740 · 314-621-5070

BANKING LAW

Clayton

Maury B. Poscover · ⑩ · Husch Blackwell Sanders · http://www.huschblackwell.com · The Plaza in Clayton Office Tower, Suite 600 · 190 Carondelet Plaza · Clayton, MO 63105-3441 · 314-480-1500

Kansas City

Richard N. Bien · Lathrop & Gage · 2345 Grand Boulevard, Suite 2800 · Kansas City, MO 64108 · 816-292-2000

Brent C. Erwood · Stinson Morrison Hecker · http://www.stinson.com · 1201 Walnut Street, Suite 2900 · Kansas City, MO 64106-2150 · 816-842-8600

Daniel J. Flanigan · Polsinelli Shalton Flanigan Suelthaus · http://www.polsinelli.com · 700 West 47th Street, Suite 1000 · Kansas City, MO 64112 · 816-753-1000

Norman E. Fretwell · Spencer Fane Britt & Browne · http://www.spencerfane.com · 1000 Walnut Street, Suite 1400 · Kansas City, MO 64106-2140 · 816-474-8100

Karen L. Garrett · Bryan Cave · One Kansas City Place, Suite 3500 · 1200 Main Street · Kansas City, MO 64105-2100 · 816-374-3200

H. Steven Graham · Lathrop & Gage · 2345 Grand Boulevard, Suite 2800 · Kansas City, MO 64108 · 816-292-2000

Mark Hargrave · Stinson Morrison Hecker · http://www.stinson.com · 1201 Walnut Street, Suite 2900 · Kansas City, MO 64106-2150 · 816-842-8600

Mike W. Lochmann · Stinson Morrison Hecker · http://www.stinson.com · 1201 Walnut Street, Suite 2900 · Kansas City, MO 64106-2150 · 816-842-8600

Howard H. Mick · ⑩ · Stinson Morrison Hecker · http://www.stinson.com · 1201 Walnut Street, Suite 2900 · Kansas City, MO 64106-2150 · 816-842-8600

C. Robert Monroe · Stinson Morrison Hecker · http://www.stinson.com · 1201 Walnut Street, Suite 2900 · Kansas City, MO 64106-2150 · 816-842-8600

Richard N. Nixon · ⑩ · Stinson Morrison Hecker · http://www.stinson.com · 1201 Walnut Street, Suite 2900 · Kansas City, MO 64106-2150 · 816-842-8600

Christopher J. Rockers · Husch Blackwell Sanders · http://www.huschblackwell.com · 1200 Main Street, Suite 2300 · Kansas City, MO 64105 · 816-421-4800

Thomas H. Stahl · Lathrop & Gage · 2345 Grand Boulevard, Suite 2800 · Kansas City, MO 64108 · 816-292-2000

Springfield

Thomas J. O'Neal · Shughart Thomson & Kilroy · http://www.stklaw.com · The Hammons Tower, Suite 1200 · 901 St. Louis Street · Springfield, MO 65806 · 417-869-3353

Randell D. Wallace · Lathrop & Gage · 1845 South National · P.O. Box 4288 · Springfield, MO 65804 · 417-886-2000

St. Louis

John G. Boyle · Bryan Cave · One Metropolitan Square, Suite 3600 · 211 North Broadway · St. Louis, MO 63102-2750 · 314-259-2000

Steven C. Drapekin · Lewis, Rice & Fingersh · 500 North Broadway, Suite 2000 · St. Louis, MO 63102-2147 · 314-444-7600

Thomas C. Erb · Lewis, Rice & Fingersh · 500 North Broadway, Suite 2000 · St. Louis, MO 63102-2147 · 314-444-7600

Peter A. Fanchi · ⑩ · Thompson Coburn · One U.S. Bank Plaza · St. Louis, MO 63101-1611 · 314-552-6000

John J. Inkley · Armstrong Teasdale · http://www.armstrongteasdale.com · One Metropolitan Square, Suite 2600 · 211 North Broadway · St. Louis, MO 63102-2740 · 314-621-5070

Thomas B. Kinsock · Thompson Coburn · One U.S. Bank Plaza · St. Louis, MO 63101-1611 · 314-552-6000

Thomas E. Lowther · ⑩ · The Stolar Partnership · http://www.stolarlaw.com · The Lammert Building · 911 Washington Avenue · St. Louis, MO 63101-1290 · 314-231-2800

Linda M. Martinez · Bryan Cave · One Metropolitan Square, Suite 3600 · 211 North Broadway · St. Louis, MO 63102-2750 · 314-259-2000

Gregory D. Omer · Thompson Coburn · One U.S. Bank Plaza · St. Louis, MO 63101-1611 · 314-552-6000

Joseph T. Porter, Jr. · Polsinelli Shalton Flanigan Suelthaus · http://www.polsinelli.com · 100 South Fourth Street, Suite 1100 · St. Louis, MO 63102 · 314-231-1950

Kenneth H. Suelthaus · ⑩ · Polsinelli Shalton Flanigan Suelthaus · http://www.polsinelli.com · 7733 Forsyth Boulevard, Suite 1200 · St. Louis, MO 63105 · 314-889-8000

John L. Sullivan · Armstrong Teasdale · http://www.armstrongteasdale.com · One Metropolitan Square, Suite 2600 · 211 North Broadway · St. Louis, MO 63102-2740 · 314-621-5070

Michael R. Turley · Lewis, Rice & Fingersh · 500 North Broadway, Suite 2000 · St. Louis, MO 63102-2147 · 314-444-7600

BANKRUPTCY AND CREDITOR-DEBTOR RIGHTS LAW

Cape Girardeau

Paul H. Berens · Bradshaw, Steele, Cochrane & Berens · 3113 Independence Street · P.O. Box 1300 · Cape Girardeau, MO 63702-1300 · 573-334-0555

Carthage

J. Kevin Checkett · Checkett & Pauly · 517 South Main Street · P.O. Box 409 · Carthage, MO 64836 · 417-358-4049

Kansas City

Brett D. Anders · Polsinelli Shalton Flanigan Suelthaus · http://www.polsinelli.com · 700 West 47th Street, Suite 1000 · Kansas City, MO 64112 · 816-753-1000

Gary D. Barnes · ⑩ · Husch Blackwell Sanders · http://www.huschblackwell.com · 1200 Main Street, Suite 2300 · Kansas City, MO 64105 · 816-421-4800

Mark T. Benedict · Husch Blackwell Sanders · http://www.huschblackwell.com · 1200 Main Street, Suite 2300 · Kansas City, MO 64105 · 816-421-4800

James E. Bird · Polsinelli Shalton Flanigan Suelthaus · http://www.polsinelli.com · 700 West 47th Street, Suite 1000 · Kansas City, MO 64112 · 816-753-1000

John J. Cruciani · Husch Blackwell Sanders · http://www.huschblackwell.com · 4801 Main Street, Suite 1000 · Kansas City, MO 64112 · 816-983-8000

Brian T. Fenimore · Lathrop & Gage · 2345 Grand Boulevard, Suite 2800 · Kansas City, MO 64108 · 816-292-2000

Daniel J. Flanigan · Polsinelli Shalton Flanigan Suelthaus · http://www.polsinelli.com · 700 West 47th Street, Suite 1000 · Kansas City, MO 64112 · 816-753-1000

Laurence M. Frazen · ⑩ · Bryan Cave · One Kansas City Place, Suite 3500 · 1200 Main Street · Kansas City, MO 64105-2100 · 816-374-3200

Scott J. Goldstein · ⑩ · Spencer Fane Britt & Browne · http://www.spencerfane.com · 1000 Walnut Street, Suite 1400 · Kansas City, MO 64106-2140 · 816-474-8100

Paul M. Hoffmann · Stinson Morrison Hecker · http://www.stinson.com · 1201 Walnut Street, Suite 2900 · Kansas City, MO 64106-2150 · 816-842-8600

Benjamin F. Mann · ⑩ · Husch Blackwell Sanders · http://www.huschblackwell.com · 4801 Main Street, Suite 1000 · Kansas City, MO 64112 · 816-983-8000

Christopher J. Redmond · ⑳ · Husch Blackwell Sanders · http://www.huschblackwell.com · 1200 Main Street, Suite 2300 · Kansas City, MO 64105 · 816-421-4800

Mark A. Shaiken · ⑩ · Stinson Morrison Hecker · http://www.stinson.com · 1201 Walnut Street, Suite 2900 · Kansas City, MO 64106-2150 · 816-842-8600

Paul D. Sinclair · Shughart Thomson & Kilroy · http://www.stklaw.com · 12 Wyandotte Plaza, Suite 1800 120 West 12th Street · Kansas City, MO 64105 · 816-421-3355

R. Pete Smith · ⑳ · McDowell, Rice, Smith & Buchanan · Skelly Building, Suite 350 · 605 West 47th Street · Kansas City, MO 64112 · 816-753-5400

Mark G. Stingley · Bryan Cave · One Kansas City Place, Suite 3500 · 1200 Main Street · Kansas City, MO 64105-2100 · 816-374-3200

Springfield

Dan R. Nelson · Lathrop & Gage · 1845 South National · P.O. Box 4288 · Springfield, MO 65804 · 417-886-2000

Thomas J. O'Neal · Shughart Thomson & Kilroy · http://www.stklaw.com · The Hammons Tower, Suite 1200 · 901 St. Louis Street · Springfield, MO 65806 · 417-869-3353

St. Louis

Mark V. Bossi · Thompson Coburn · One U.S. Bank Plaza · St. Louis, MO 63101-1611 · 314-552-6000

Robert H. Brownlee · ⑩ · Thompson Coburn · One U.S. Bank Plaza · St. Louis, MO 63101-1611 · 314-552-6000

Francis X. Buckley, Jr. · Thompson Coburn · One U.S. Bank Plaza · St. Louis, MO 63101-1611 · 314-552-6000

Steven N. Cousins · ⑩ · Armstrong Teasdale · http://www.armstrongteasdale.com · One Metropolitan Square, Suite 2600 · 211 North Broadway · St. Louis, MO 63102-2740 · 314-621-5070

David L. Going · Armstrong Teasdale · http://www.armstrongteasdale.com · One Metropolitan Square, Suite 2600 · 211 North Broadway · St. Louis, MO 63102-2740 · 314-621-5070

Steven Goldstein · ⑳ · Goldstein & Pressman · 121 Hunter Avenue, Suite 101 · St. Louis, MO 63124 · 314-727-1717

David A. Lander · ⑳ · Thompson Coburn · One U.S. Bank Plaza · St. Louis, MO 63101-1611 · 314-552-6000

Lloyd A. Palans · ⑳ · Bryan Cave · One Metropolitan Square, Suite 3600 · 211 North Broadway · St. Louis, MO 63102-2750 · 314-259-2000

David A. Sosne · Summers, Compton, Wells and Hamburg · 8909 Ladue Road · St. Louis, MO 63124 · 314-991-4999

David A. Warfield · ⑩ · Husch Blackwell Sanders · http://www.huschblackwell.com · 720 Olive Street, Suite 2400 · St. Louis, MO 63101 · 314-345-6000

Gregory D. Willard · ⑳ · Bryan Cave · One Metropolitan Square, Suite 3600 · 211 North Broadway · St. Louis, MO 63102-2750 · 314-259-2000

BET-THE-COMPANY LITIGATION

Caruthersville

James E. Reeves · ⑩ · Ward & Reeves · 711 Ward Avenue · P.O. Box 169 · Caruthersville, MO 63830 · 573-333-2396

Clayton

Alan E. Popkin · ⑩ · Husch Blackwell Sanders · http://www.huschblackwell.com · The Plaza in Clayton Office Tower, Suite 600 · 190 Carondelet Plaza · Clayton, MO 63105-3441 · 314-480-1500

Kansas City

John C. Aisenbrey · ⑩ · Stinson Morrison Hecker · http://www.stinson.com · 1201 Walnut Street, Suite 2900 · Kansas City, MO 64106-2150 · 816-842-8600

J. Eugene Balloun · ㉕ · Shook, Hardy & Bacon · 2555 Grand Boulevard · Kansas City, MO 64108 · 816-474-6550

W. Perry Brandt · ⑩ · Bryan Cave · One Kansas City Place, Suite 3500 · 1200 Main Street · Kansas City, MO 64105-2100 · 816-374-3200

Spencer J. Brown · ⑳ · Deacy and Deacy · http://www.deacylawfirm.com · Ten Main Center, Suite 1900 920 Main Street · Kansas City, MO 64105 · 816-421-4000

Charles W. German · Rouse Hendricks German May · One Petticoat Lane Building, Suite 400 · 1010 Walnut Street · Kansas City, MO 64106 · 816-471-7700

James D. Griffin · ⑩ · Husch Blackwell Sanders · http://www.huschblackwell.com · 4801 Main Street, Suite 1000 · Kansas City, MO 64112 · 816-983-8000

R. Lawrence Ward · ⑩ · Shughart Thomson & Kilroy · http://www.stklaw.com · 12 Wyandotte Plaza, Suite 1800 · 120 West 12th Street · Kansas City, MO 64105 · 816-421-3355

Curtis E. Woods · Sonnenschein Nath & Rosenthal · 4520 Main Street, Suite 1100 · Kansas City, MO 64111-7700 · 816-460-2400

St. Louis

Gerard T. Carmody · ⑩ · Carmody MacDonald · 120 South Central, Suite 1800 · St. Louis, MO 63105-1705 · 314-854-8600

John Gianoulakis · Kohn, Shands, Elbert, Gianoulakis & Giljum · One U.S. Bank Plaza, Suite 2410 · 505 North Seventh Street · St. Louis, MO 63101 · 314-241-3963

Maurice B. Graham · Gray, Ritter & Graham · http://www.grayrittergraham.com · Gateway One on The Mall, Suite 800 · 701 Market Street · St. Louis, MO 63101-1826 · 314-241-5620

Alan C. Kohn · ⑩ · Kohn, Shands, Elbert, Gianoulakis & Giljum · One U.S. Bank Plaza, Suite 2410 · 505 North Seventh Street · St. Louis, MO 63101 · 314-241-3963

Robert F. Ritter · ⑩ · Gray, Ritter & Graham · http://www.grayrittergraham.com · Gateway One on The Mall, Suite 800 · 701 Market Street · St. Louis, MO 63101-1826 · 314-241-5620

Thomas E. Wack · ⑩ · Bryan Cave · One Metropolitan Square, Suite 3600 · 211 North Broadway · St. Louis, MO 63102-2750 · 314-259-2000

Thomas C. Walsh · ⑩ · Bryan Cave · One Metropolitan Square, Suite 3600 · 211 North Broadway · St. Louis, MO 63102-2750 · 314-259-2000

BIOTECHNOLOGY LAW

Kansas City

G. Melissa Ince · Bryan Cave · One Kansas City Place, Suite 3500 · 1200 Main Street · Kansas City, MO 64105-2100 · 816-374-3200

Harvey L. Kaplan · Shook, Hardy & Bacon · 2555 Grand Boulevard · Kansas City, MO 64108 · 816-474-6550

Anne S. O'Brien · Polsinelli Shalton Flanigan Suelthaus · http://www.polsinelli.com · 700 West 47th Street, Suite 1000 · Kansas City, MO 64112 · 816-753-1000

Kevin R. Sweeney · Polsinelli Shalton Flanigan Suelthaus · http://www.polsinelli.com · 700 West 47th Street, Suite 1000 · Kansas City, MO 64112 · 816-753-1000

St. Louis

G. Harley Blosser · Sonnenschein Nath & Rosenthal · One Metropolitan Square, Suite 3000 · 211 North Broadway · St. Louis, MO 63102-2741 · 314-241-1800

Andrew Hoyne · Armstrong Teasdale · http://www.armstrongteasdale.com · One Metropolitan Square, Suite 2600 · 211 North Broadway · St. Louis, MO 63102-2740 · 314-621-5070

David B. Jennings · Armstrong Teasdale · http://www.armstrongteasdale.com · One Metropolitan Square, Suite 2600 · 211 North Broadway · St. Louis, MO 63102-2740 · 314-621-5070

CIVIL RIGHTS LAW

Kansas City

Arthur A. Benson II · ⑩ · Benson & Associates · http://www.bensonlaw.com · 4006 Central Street · P.O. Box 119007 · Kansas City, MO 64171-9007 · 816-531-6565

COLLABORATIVE LAW: FAMILY LAW

St. Charles

Rebecca T. Magruder · Rebecca T. Magruder · 118 North Second Street, Suite 300 · St. Charles, MO 63301 · 636-947-9273

St. Louis

Susan L. Amato · Susan L. Amato · http://www.susanamato.com · 230 South Bemiston, Suite 510 · St. Louis, MO 63105 · 314-862-0330

Gregory B. Brough · Gregory Brough · 8000 Maryland Avenue, Suite 1000 · St. Louis, MO 63105 · 314-725-0001

Alan E. Freed · Paule, Camazine & Blumenthal · 165 North Meramec Avenue, Sixth Floor · St. Louis, MO 63105 · 314-727-2266

COMMERCIAL LITIGATION

Caruthersville

James E. Reeves · ⑩ · Ward & Reeves · 711 Ward Avenue · P.O. Box 169 · Caruthersville, MO 63830 · 573-333-2396

Clayton

Mark G. Arnold · Husch Blackwell Sanders · http://www.huschblackwell.com · The Plaza in Clayton Office Tower, Suite 600 · 190 Carondelet Plaza · Clayton, MO 63105-3441 · 314-480-1500

Joseph P. Conran · Husch Blackwell Sanders · http://www.huschblackwell.com · The Plaza in Clayton Office Tower, Suite 600 · 190 Carondelet Plaza · Clayton, MO 63105-3441 · 314-480-1500

Kenneth R. Heineman · Husch Blackwell Sanders · http://www.huschblackwell.com · The Plaza in Clayton Office Tower, Suite 600 · 190 Carondelet Plaza · Clayton, MO 63105-3441 · 314-480-1500

Alan E. Popkin · ⑩ · Husch Blackwell Sanders · http://www.huschblackwell.com · The Plaza in Clayton Office Tower, Suite 600 · 190 Carondelet Plaza · Clayton, MO 63105-3441 · 314-480-1500

Jefferson City

Ann K. Covington · Bryan Cave · Riverview Office Center · 221 Bolivar Street · Jefferson City, MO 65101-1574 · 573-556-6620

Kansas City

John C. Aisenbrey · ⑩ · Stinson Morrison Hecker · http://www.stinson.com · 1201 Walnut Street, Suite 2900 · Kansas City, MO 64106-2150 · 816-842-8600

Jennifer Gille Bacon · Shughart Thomson & Kilroy · http://www.stklaw.com · 12 Wyandotte Plaza, Suite 1800 · 120 West 12th Street · Kansas City, MO 64105 · 816-421-3355

J. Eugene Balloun · ㉕ · Shook, Hardy & Bacon · 2555 Grand Boulevard · Kansas City, MO 64108 · 816-474-6550

Irvin V. Belzer · Bryan Cave · One Kansas City Place, Suite 3500 · 1200 Main Street · Kansas City, MO 64105-2100 · 816-374-3200

Lawrence M. Berkowitz · ⑩ · Berkowitz Oliver Williams Shaw & Eisenbrandt · 2600 Grand Boulevard, Suite 1200 · Kansas City, MO 64108 · 816-561-7007

W. Perry Brandt · ⑩ · Bryan Cave · One Kansas City Place, Suite 3500 · 1200 Main Street · Kansas City, MO 64105-2100 · 816-374-3200

Spencer J. Brown · ⑳ · Deacy and Deacy · http://www.deacylawfirm.com · Ten Main Center, Suite 1900 920 Main Street · Kansas City, MO 64105 · 816-421-4000

Douglas R. Dalgleish · Lathrop & Gage · 2345 Grand Boulevard, Suite 2800 · Kansas City, MO 64108 · 816-292-2000

Robert L. Driscoll · ⑳ · Stinson Morrison Hecker · http://www.stinson.com · 1201 Walnut Street, Suite 2900 · Kansas City, MO 64106-2150 · 816-842-8600

David E. Everson · Stinson Morrison Hecker · http://www.stinson.com · 1201 Walnut Street, Suite 2900 · Kansas City, MO 64106-2150 · 816-842-8600

Floyd R. Finch, Jr. · Husch Blackwell Sanders · http://www.huschblackwell.com · 4801 Main Street, Suite 1000 · Kansas City, MO 64112 · 816-983-8000

Mark S. Foster · Stinson Morrison Hecker · http://www.stinson.com · 1201 Walnut Street, Suite 2900 · Kansas City, MO 64106-2150 · 816-842-8600

Charles W. German · Rouse Hendricks German May · One Petticoat Lane Building, Suite 400 · 1010 Walnut Street · Kansas City, MO 64106 · 816-471-7700

J. Michael Grier · Warden Triplett Grier · 420 Nichols Road, Suite 200 · Kansas City, MO 64112 · 816-877-8100

James D. Griffin · ⑩ · Husch Blackwell Sanders · http://www.huschblackwell.com · 4801 Main Street, Suite 1000 · Kansas City, MO 64112 · 816-983-8000

Alan V. Hallquist · Husch Blackwell Sanders · http://www.huschblackwell.com · 4801 Main Street, Suite 1000 · Kansas City, MO 64112 · 816-983-8000

Robert A. Henderson · Shughart Thomson & Kilroy · http://www.stklaw.com · 12 Wyandotte Plaza, Suite 1800 · 120 West 12th Street · Kansas City, MO 64105 · 816-421-3355

Randall E. Hendricks · Rouse Hendricks German May · One Petticoat Lane Building, Suite 400 · 1010 Walnut Street · Kansas City, MO 64106 · 816-471-7700

James R. Hobbs · ⑩ · Wyrsch Hobbs & Mirakian · 1000 Walnut Street, Suite 1600 · Kansas City, MO 64106 · 816-221-0080

Russell S. Jones, Jr. · Shughart Thomson & Kilroy · http://www.stklaw.com · 12 Wyandotte Plaza, Suite 1800 · 120 West 12th Street · Kansas City, MO 64105 · 816-421-3355

John M. Kilroy, Jr. · Shughart Thomson & Kilroy · http://www.stklaw.com · 12 Wyandotte Plaza, Suite 1800 · 120 West 12th Street · Kansas City, MO 64105 · 816-421-3355

Larry L. McMullen · ㉕ · Husch Blackwell Sanders · http://www.huschblackwell.com · 4801 Main Street, Suite 1000 · Kansas City, MO 64112 · 816-983-8000

Timothy K. McNamara · Lathrop & Gage · 2345 Grand Boulevard, Suite 2800 · Kansas City, MO 64108 · 816-292-2000

David F. Oliver · Berkowitz Oliver Williams Shaw & Eisenbrandt · 2600 Grand Boulevard, Suite 1200 · Kansas City, MO 64108 · 816-561-7007

David A. Rameden · Shook, Hardy & Bacon · 2555 Grand Boulevard · Kansas City, MO 64108 · 816-474-6550

Joseph M. Rebein · Shook, Hardy & Bacon · 2555 Grand Boulevard · Kansas City, MO 64108 · 816-474-6550

William R. Sampson · ⑩ · Shook, Hardy & Bacon · 2555 Grand Boulevard · Kansas City, MO 64108 · 816-474-6550

Thomas P. Schult · Berkowitz Oliver Williams Shaw & Eisenbrandt · 2600 Grand Boulevard, Suite 1200 · Kansas City, MO 64108 · 816-561-7007

J. Stanley Sexton · ⑩ · Shook, Hardy & Bacon · 2555 Grand Boulevard · Kansas City, MO 64108 · 816-474-6550

John W. Shaw · Berkowitz Oliver Williams Shaw & Eisenbrandt · 2600 Grand Boulevard, Suite 1200 · Kansas City, MO 64108 · 816-561-7007

Kent Sullivan · Stinson Morrison Hecker · http://www.stinson.com · 1201 Walnut Street, Suite 2900 · Kansas City, MO 64106-2150 · 816-842-8600

Robert M. Thompson · Bryan Cave · One Kansas City Place, Suite 3500 · 1200 Main Street · Kansas City, MO 64105-2100 · 816-374-3200

Laurence R. Tucker · ⑩ · Armstrong Teasdale · http://www.armstrongteasdale.com · 2345 Grand Boulevard, Suite 2000 · Kansas City, MO 64108-2617 · 816-221-3420

Matthew J. Verschelden · Stinson Morrison Hecker · http://www.stinson.com · 1201 Walnut Street, Suite 2900 · Kansas City, MO 64106-2150 · 816-842-8600

Gene E. Voigts · Shook, Hardy & Bacon · 2555 Grand Boulevard · Kansas City, MO 64108 · 816-474-6550

R. Lawrence Ward · ⑩ · Shughart Thomson & Kilroy · http://www.stklaw.com · 12 Wyandotte Plaza, Suite 1800 · 120 West 12th Street · Kansas City, MO 64105 · 816-421-3355

W. Russell Welsh · Polsinelli Shalton Flanigan Suelthaus · http://www.polsinelli.com · 700 West 47th Street, Suite 1000 · Kansas City, MO 64112 · 816-753-1000

Curtis E. Woods · Sonnenschein Nath & Rosenthal · 4520 Main Street, Suite 1100 · Kansas City, MO 64111-7700 · 816-460-2400

Karl Zobrist · Sonnenschein Nath & Rosenthal · 4520 Main Street, Suite 1100 · Kansas City, MO 64111-7700 · 816-460-2400

Springfield

Gary R. Cunningham · Lathrop & Gage · 1845 South National · P.O. Box 4288 · Springfield, MO 65804 · 417-886-2000

Frank M. Evans III · Lathrop & Gage · 1845 South National · P.O. Box 4288 · Springfield, MO 65804 · 417-886-2000

Virginia L. Fry · Husch Blackwell Sanders · http://www.huschblackwell.com · The Hammons Tower, Suite 1900 · 901 St. Louis Street · Springfield, MO 65806 · 417-268-4000

John C. Holstein · Shughart Thomson & Kilroy · http://www.stklaw.com · The Hammons Tower, Suite 1200 · 901 St. Louis Street · Springfield, MO 65806 · 417-869-3353

Randy P. Scheer · Husch Blackwell Sanders · http://www.huschblackwell.com · The Hammons Tower, Suite 1900 · 901 St. Louis Street · Springfield, MO 65806 · 417-268-4000

St. Joseph

R. Dan Boulware · Shughart Thomson & Kilroy · http://www.stklaw.com · 3101 Frederick Avenue · St. Joseph, MO 64506 · 816-364-2117

St. Louis

Gordon L. Ankney · Thompson Coburn · One U.S. Bank Plaza · St. Louis, MO 63101-1611 · 314-552-6000

James F. Bennett · Dowd Bennett · http://www.dowdbennett.com · 7733 Forsyth Boulevard, Suite 1410 · St. Louis, MO 63105 · 314-889-7300

Gerard T. Carmody · ⑩ · Carmody MacDonald · 120 South Central, Suite 1800 · St. Louis, MO 63105-1705 · 314-854-8600

John Michael Clear · ㉕ · Bryan Cave · One Metropolitan Square, Suite 3600 · 211 North Broadway · St. Louis, MO 63102-2750 · 314-259-2000

Glenn E. Davis · Armstrong Teasdale · http://www.armstrongteasdale.com · One Metropolitan Square, Suite 2600 · 211 North Broadway · St. Louis, MO 63102-2740 · 314-621-5070

Don M. Downing · Gray, Ritter & Graham · http://www.grayrittergraham.com · Gateway One on The Mall, Suite 800 · 701 Market Street · St. Louis, MO 63101-1826 · 314-241-5620

John Gianoulakis · Kohn, Shands, Elbert, Gianoulakis & Giljum · One U.S. Bank Plaza, Suite 2410 · 505 North Seventh Street · St. Louis, MO 63101 · 314-241-3963

Maurice B. Graham · Gray, Ritter & Graham · http://www.grayrittergraham.com · Gateway One on The Mall, Suite 800 · 701 Market Street · St. Louis, MO 63101-1826 · 314-241-5620

Frank N. Gundlach · ⑩ · Armstrong Teasdale · http://www.armstrongteasdale.com · One Metropolitan Square, Suite 2600 · 211 North Broadway · St. Louis, MO 63102-2740 · 314-621-5070

John M. Hessel · Lewis, Rice & Fingersh · 500 North Broadway, Suite 2000 · St. Louis, MO 63102-2147 · 314-444-7600

Jeffery J. Kalinowski · Husch Blackwell Sanders · http://www.huschblackwell.com · 720 Olive Street, Suite 2400 · St. Louis, MO 63101 · 314-345-6000

Alan C. Kohn · ⑩ · Kohn, Shands, Elbert, Gianoulakis & Giljum · One U.S. Bank Plaza, Suite 2410 · 505 North Seventh Street · St. Louis, MO 63101 · 314-241-3963

Paul E. Kovacs · ⑩ · Armstrong Teasdale · http://www.armstrongteasdale.com · One Metropolitan Square, Suite 2600 · 211 North Broadway · St. Louis, MO 63102-2740 · 314-621-5070

Theodore J. MacDonald, Jr. · Hepler, Broom, MacDonald, Hebrank, True & Noce · 800 Market Street, Suite 2300 · St. Louis, MO 63101 · 314-241-6160

W. Dudley McCarter · Behr, McCarter & Potter · 7777 Bonhomme Avenue, Suite 1400 · St. Louis, MO 63105 · 314-862-3800

John R. Musgrave · Thompson Coburn · One U.S. Bank Plaza · St. Louis, MO 63101-1611 · 314-552-6000

J. William Newbold · Thompson Coburn · One U.S. Bank Plaza · St. Louis, MO 63101-1611 · 314-552-6000

Michael D. O'Keefe · ⑩ · Thompson Coburn · One U.S. Bank Plaza · St. Louis, MO 63101-1611 · 314-552-6000

G. Keith Phoenix · ⑩ · Sandberg, Phoenix & von Gontard · http://www.spvg.com · One City Centre, 15th Floor · 515 North Sixth Street · St. Louis, MO 63101-1880 · 314-231-3332

Robert F. Ritter · ⑩ · Gray, Ritter & Graham · http://www.grayrittergraham.com · Gateway One on The Mall, Suite 800 · 701 Market Street · St. Louis, MO 63101-1826 · 314-241-5620

Andrew Rothschild · Lewis, Rice & Fingersh · 500 North Broadway, Suite 2000 · St. Louis, MO 63102-2147 · 314-444-7600

Stephen H. Rovak · ⑩ · Sonnenschein Nath & Rosenthal · One Metropolitan Square, Suite 3000 · 211 North Broadway · St. Louis, MO 63102-2741 · 314-241-1800

Steven P. Sanders · ㉕ · Williams Venker & Sanders · http://www.wvslaw.com · Bank of America Tower, 21st Floor · 100 North Broadway · St. Louis, MO 63102 · 314-345-5000

Richard B. Scherrer · ⑩ · Armstrong Teasdale · http://www.armstrongteasdale.com · One Metropolitan Square, Suite 2600 · 211 North Broadway · St. Louis, MO 63102-2740 · 314-621-5070

Charles Alan Seigel · ⑩ · The Stolar Partnership · http://www.stolarlaw.com · The Lammert Building · 911 Washington Avenue · St. Louis, MO 63101-1290 · 314-231-2800

Barry A. Short · Lewis, Rice & Fingersh · 500 North Broadway, Suite 2000 · St. Louis, MO 63102-2147 · 314-444-7600

James J. Virtel · ⑩ · Armstrong Teasdale · http://www.armstrongteasdale.com · One Metropolitan Square, Suite 2600 · 211 North Broadway · St. Louis, MO 63102-2740 · 314-621-5070

Thomas E. Wack · ⑩ · Bryan Cave · One Metropolitan Square, Suite 3600 · 211 North Broadway · St. Louis, MO 63102-2750 · 314-259-2000

W. Stanley Walch · ㉕ · Thompson Coburn · One U.S. Bank Plaza · St. Louis, MO 63101-1611 · 314-552-6000

Richard B. Walsh, Jr. · Lewis, Rice & Fingersh · 500 North Broadway, Suite 2000 · St. Louis, MO 63102-2147 · 314-444-7600

Thomas C. Walsh · ⑩ · Bryan Cave · One Metropolitan Square, Suite 3600 · 211 North Broadway · St. Louis, MO 63102-2750 · 314-259-2000

Charles A. Weiss · ⑩ · Bryan Cave · One Metropolitan Square, Suite 3600 · 211 North Broadway · St. Louis, MO 63102-2750 · 314-259-2000

W. David Wells · Thompson Coburn · One U.S. Bank Plaza · St. Louis, MO 63101-1611 · 314-552-6000

COMMUNICATIONS LAW

Jefferson City

Mark W. Comley · Newman, Comley & Ruth · 601 Monroe Street, Suite 301 · P.O. Box 537 · Jefferson City, MO 65102-0537 · 573-634-2266

William R. England III · ⑩ · Brydon, Swearengen & England · http://www.brydonlaw.com · 312 East Capitol Avenue · P.O. Box 456 · Jefferson City, MO 65102-0456 · 573-635-7166

St. Louis

Leland B. Curtis · ⑩ · Curtis, Heinz, Garrett & O'Keefe · 130 South Bemiston Avenue, Suite 200 · St. Louis, MO 63105-1913 · 314-725-8788

Carl J. Lumley · Curtis, Heinz, Garrett & O'Keefe · 130 South Bemiston Avenue, Suite 200 · St. Louis, MO 63105-1913 · 314-725-8788

Chesterfield

Matthew D. Menghini · McCarthy, Leonard, Kaemmerer, Owen, McGovern, Striler & Menghini · 400 South Woods Mill, Suite 250 · Chesterfield, MO 63017 · 314-392-5200

Kansas City

Jerome V. Bales · Lathrop & Gage · 2345 Grand Boulevard, Suite 2800 · Kansas City, MO 64108 · 816-292-2000

Roy Bash · Shughart Thomson & Kilroy · http://www.stklaw.com · 12 Wyandotte Plaza, Suite 1800 · 120 West 12th Street · Kansas City, MO 64105 · 816-421-3355

J. Michael Grier · Warden Triplett Grier · 420 Nichols Road, Suite 200 · Kansas City, MO 64112 · 816-877-8100

Susan Linden McGreevy · Stinson Morrison Hecker · http://www.stinson.com · 1201 Walnut Street, Suite 2900 · Kansas City, MO 64106-2150 · 816-842-8600

David R. Raymond · Husch Blackwell Sanders · http://www.huschblackwell.com · 4801 Main Street, Suite 1000 · Kansas City, MO 64112 · 816-983-8000

Jeffrey B. Rosen · Polsinelli Shalton Flanigan Suelthaus · http://www.polsinelli.com · 700 West 47th Street, Suite 1000 · Kansas City, MO 64112 · 816-753-1000

G. Steven Ruprecht · Brown & Dunn · 911 Main Street, Suite 2300 · Kansas City, MO 64105-5319 · 816-471-7000

St. Louis

Steven M. Cockriel · Cockriel & Christofferson · 3660 South Geyer, Suite 320 · St. Louis, MO 63127-1223 · 314-821-4200

Joseph A. Colagiovanni, Jr. · Sonnenschein Nath & Rosenthal · One Metropolitan Square, Suite 3000 · 211 North Broadway · St. Louis, MO 63102-2741 · 314-241-1800

Byron E. Francis · Armstrong Teasdale · http://www.armstrongteasdale.com · One Metropolitan Square, Suite 2600 · 211 North Broadway · St. Louis, MO 63102-2740 · 314-621-5070

Richard R. Hardcastle III · Greensfelder, Hemker & Gale · Equitable Building, Suite 2000 · 10 South Broadway · St. Louis, MO 63102 · 314-241-9090

John R. Haug · Sonnenschein Nath & Rosenthal · One Metropolitan Square, Suite 3000 · 211 North Broadway · St. Louis, MO 63102-2741 · 314-241-1800

David G. Loseman · Armstrong Teasdale · http://www.armstrongteasdale.com · One Metropolitan Square, Suite 2600 · 211 North Broadway · St. Louis, MO 63102-2740 · 314-621-5070

Paul M. Macon · Thompson Coburn · One U.S. Bank Plaza · St. Louis, MO 63101-1611 · 314-552-6000

Andrew W. Manuel · Greensfelder, Hemker & Gale · Equitable Building, Suite 2000 · 10 South Broadway · St. Louis, MO 63102 · 314-241-9090

Kenneth A. Slavens · Husch Blackwell Sanders · http://www.huschblackwell.com · 720 Olive Street, Suite 2400 · St. Louis, MO 63101 · 314-345-6000

Timothy R. Thornton · Greensfelder, Hemker & Gale · Equitable Building, Suite 2000 · 10 South Broadway · St. Louis, MO 63102 · 314-241-9090

Michael E. Wilson · Greensfelder, Hemker & Gale · Equitable Building, Suite 2000 · 10 South Broadway St. Louis, MO 63102 · 314-241-9090

CORPORATE GOVERNANCE AND COMPLIANCE LAW

Kansas City

John A. Granda · ⑩ · Stinson Morrison Hecker · http://www.stinson.com · 1201 Walnut Street, Suite 2900 Kansas City, MO 64106-2150 · 816-842-8600

Kip A. Wiggins · Stinson Morrison Hecker · http://www.stinson.com · 1201 Walnut Street, Suite 2900 · Kansas City, MO 64106-2150 · 816-842-8600

St. Louis

Karl R. Barnickol · Husch Blackwell Sanders · http://www.huschblackwell.com · 720 Olive Street, Suite 2400 · St. Louis, MO 63101 · 314-345-6000

Edward L. Dowd, Jr. · Dowd Bennett · http://www.dowdbennett.com · 7733 Forsyth Boulevard, Suite 1410 · St. Louis, MO 63105 · 314-889-7300

Don G. Lents · ⑩ · Bryan Cave · One Metropolitan Square, Suite 3600 · 211 North Broadway · St. Louis, MO 63102-2750 · 314-259-2000

Thomas A. Litz · Thompson Coburn · One U.S. Bank Plaza · St. Louis, MO 63101-1611 · 314-552-6000

James G. Martin · Armstrong Teasdale · http://www.armstrongteasdale.com · One Metropolitan Square, Suite 2600 · 211 North Broadway · St. Louis, MO 63102-2740 · 314-621-5070

James L. Nouss, Jr. · ⑩ · Bryan Cave · One Metropolitan Square, Suite 3600 · 211 North Broadway · St. Louis, MO 63102-2750 · 314-259-2000

William F. Seabaugh · Bryan Cave · One Metropolitan Square, Suite 3600 · 211 North Broadway · St. Louis, MO 63102-2750 · 314-259-2000

Joseph S. von Kaenel · Armstrong Teasdale · http://www.armstrongteasdale.com · One Metropolitan Square, Suite 2600 · 211 North Broadway · St. Louis, MO 63102-2740 · 314-621-5070

CORPORATE LAW

Clayton

Mary Anne O'Connell · Husch Blackwell Sanders · http://www.huschblackwell.com · The Plaza in Clayton Office Tower, Suite 600 · 190 Carondelet Plaza · Clayton, MO 63105-3441 · 314-480-1500

Maury B. Poscover · ⑩ · Husch Blackwell Sanders · http://www.huschblackwell.com · The Plaza in Clayton Office Tower, Suite 600 · 190 Carondelet Plaza · Clayton, MO 63105-3441 · 314-480-1500

James V. Stepleton · Husch Blackwell Sanders · http://www.huschblackwell.com · The Plaza in Clayton Office Tower, Suite 600 · 190 Carondelet Plaza · Clayton, MO 63105-3441 · 314-480-1500

James W. Allen · Stinson Morrison Hecker · http://www.stinson.com · 1201 Walnut Street, Suite 2900 · Kansas City, MO 64106-2150 · 816-842-8600

James M. Ash · ⑩ · Husch Blackwell Sanders · http://www.huschblackwell.com · 4801 Main Street, Suite 1000 · Kansas City, MO 64112 · 816-983-8000

Robert M. Barnes · Bryan Cave · One Kansas City Place, Suite 3500 · 1200 Main Street · Kansas City, MO 64105-2100 · 816-374-3200

Jacob W. Bayer, Jr. · Shughart Thomson & Kilroy · http://www.stklaw.com · 12 Wyandotte Plaza, Suite 1800 · 120 West 12th Street · Kansas City, MO 64105 · 816-421-3355

Steven F. Carman · Husch Blackwell Sanders · http://www.huschblackwell.com · 4801 Main Street, Suite 1000 · Kansas City, MO 64112 · 816-983-8000

Craig L. Evans · Stinson Morrison Hecker · http://www.stinson.com · 1201 Walnut Street, Suite 2900 · Kansas City, MO 64106-2150 · 816-842-8600

G. Robert Fisher · ⑩ · Sonnenschein Nath & Rosenthal · 4520 Main Street, Suite 1100 · Kansas City, MO 64111-7700 · 816-460-2400

John A. Granda · ⑩ · Stinson Morrison Hecker · http://www.stinson.com · 1201 Walnut Street, Suite 2900 Kansas City, MO 64106-2150 · 816-842-8600

William A. Hirsch · ⑳ · Stinson Morrison Hecker · http://www.stinson.com · 1201 Walnut Street, Suite 2900 · Kansas City, MO 64106-2150 · 816-842-8600

Mike W. Lochmann · Stinson Morrison Hecker · http://www.stinson.com · 1201 Walnut Street, Suite 2900 · Kansas City, MO 64106-2150 · 816-842-8600

William W. Mahood III · Polsinelli Shalton Flanigan Suelthaus · http://www.polsinelli.com · 700 West 47th Street, Suite 1000 · Kansas City, MO 64112 · 816-753-1000

John F. Marvin · ㉕ · Sonnenschein Nath & Rosenthal · 4520 Main Street, Suite 1100 · Kansas City, MO 64111-7700 · 816-460-2400

Joseph W. Medved · Lathrop & Gage · 2345 Grand Boulevard, Suite 2800 · Kansas City, MO 64108 · 816-292-2000

Howard H. Mick · ⑩ · Stinson Morrison Hecker · http://www.stinson.com · 1201 Walnut Street, Suite 2900 · Kansas City, MO 64106-2150 · 816-842-8600

C. Robert Monroe · Stinson Morrison Hecker · http://www.stinson.com · 1201 Walnut Street, Suite 2900 · Kansas City, MO 64106-2150 · 816-842-8600

Richard N. Nixon · ⑩ · Stinson Morrison Hecker · http://www.stinson.com · 1201 Walnut Street, Suite 2900 · Kansas City, MO 64106-2150 · 816-842-8600

James A. Polsinelli · ⑩ · Polsinelli Shalton Flanigan Suelthaus · http://www.polsinelli.com · 700 West 47th Street, Suite 1000 · Kansas City, MO 64112 · 816-753-1000

James P. Pryde · Bryan Cave · One Kansas City Place, Suite 3500 · 1200 Main Street · Kansas City, MO 64105-2100 · 816-374-3200

Patrick J. Respeliers · Stinson Morrison Hecker · http://www.stinson.com · 1201 Walnut Street, Suite 2900 · Kansas City, MO 64106-2150 · 816-842-8600

Kevin R. Sweeney · Polsinelli Shalton Flanigan Suelthaus · http://www.polsinelli.com · 700 West 47th Street, Suite 1000 · Kansas City, MO 64112 · 816-753-1000

Thomas W. Van Dyke · ⓴ · Bryan Cave · One Kansas City Place, Suite 3500 · 1200 Main Street · Kansas City, MO 64105-2100 · 816-374-3200

Kip A. Wiggins · Stinson Morrison Hecker · http://www.stinson.com · 1201 Walnut Street, Suite 2900 · Kansas City, MO 64106-2150 · 816-842-8600

Springfield

David C. Agee · Husch Blackwell Sanders · http://www.huschblackwell.com · The Hammons Tower, Suite 1900 · 901 St. Louis Street · Springfield, MO 65806 · 417-268-4000

St. Charles

Wm. Randolph Weber · Hazelwood & Weber · 200 North Third Street · St. Charles, MO 63301 · 636-947-4700

St. Louis

Craig A. Adoor · Husch Blackwell Sanders · http://www.huschblackwell.com · 720 Olive Street, Suite 2400 · St. Louis, MO 63101 · 314-345-6000

John Fox Arnold · Lashly & Baer · 714 Locust Street · St. Louis, MO 63101 · 314-621-2939

John W. Dillane · Greensfelder, Hemker & Gale · Equitable Building, Suite 2000 · 10 South Broadway · St. Louis, MO 63102 · 314-241-9090

Thomas C. Erb · Lewis, Rice & Fingersh · 500 North Broadway, Suite 2000 · St. Louis, MO 63102-2147 · 314-444-7600

John W. Finger · Stinson Morrison Hecker · http://www.stinson.com · 100 South Fourth Street, Suite 700 St. Louis, MO 63102 · 314-259-4500

John L. Gillis, Jr. · Armstrong Teasdale · http://www.armstrongteasdale.com · One Metropolitan Square, Suite 2600 · 211 North Broadway · St. Louis, MO 63102-2740 · 314-621-5070

William G. Guerri · ㉕ · Thompson Coburn · One U.S. Bank Plaza · St. Louis, MO 63101-1611 · 314-552-6000

Stephen C. Jones · Armstrong Teasdale · http://www.armstrongteasdale.com · One Metropolitan Square, Suite 2600 · 211 North Broadway · St. Louis, MO 63102-2740 · 314-621-5070

Michael F. Lause · ❿ · Thompson Coburn · One U.S. Bank Plaza · St. Louis, MO 63101-1611 · 314-552-6000

Don G. Lents · ❿ · Bryan Cave · One Metropolitan Square, Suite 3600 · 211 North Broadway · St. Louis, MO 63102-2750 · 314-259-2000

Thomas G. Lewin · Gallop, Johnson & Neuman · 101 South Hanley Road, Suite 1700 · St. Louis, MO 63105 · 314-615-6000

Thomas E. Lowther · ❿ · The Stolar Partnership · http://www.stolarlaw.com · The Lammert Building · 911 Washington Avenue · St. Louis, MO 63101-1290 · 314-231-2800

Denis P. McCusker · ❿ · Bryan Cave · One Metropolitan Square, Suite 3600 · 211 North Broadway · St. Louis, MO 63102-2750 · 314-259-2000

Walter L. Metcalfe, Jr. · 20 · Bryan Cave · One Metropolitan Square, Suite 3600 · 211 North Broadway · St. Louis, MO 63102-2750 · 314-259-2000

Thomas J. Minogue · Thompson Coburn · One U.S. Bank Plaza · St. Louis, MO 63101-1611 · 314-552-6000

Jay A. Nathanson · Greensfelder, Hemker & Gale · Equitable Building, Suite 2000 · 10 South Broadway · St. Louis, MO 63102 · 314-241-9090

James L. Nouss, Jr. · 10 · Bryan Cave · One Metropolitan Square, Suite 3600 · 211 North Broadway · St. Louis, MO 63102-2750 · 314-259-2000

Jeffrey H. Pass · The Stolar Partnership · http://www.stolarlaw.com · The Lammert Building · 911 Washington Avenue · St. Louis, MO 63101-1290 · 314-231-2800

Donald W. Paule · Paule, Camazine & Blumenthal · 165 North Meramec Avenue, Sixth Floor · St. Louis, MO 63105 · 314-727-2266

Joseph T. Porter, Jr. · Polsinelli Shalton Flanigan Suelthaus · http://www.polsinelli.com · 100 South Fourth Street, Suite 1100 · St. Louis, MO 63102 · 314-231-1950

John K. Pruellage · Lewis, Rice & Fingersh · 500 North Broadway, Suite 2000 · St. Louis, MO 63102-2147 · 314-444-7600

John J. Riffle · Lewis, Rice & Fingersh · 500 North Broadway, Suite 2000 · St. Louis, MO 63102-2147 · 314-444-7600

William F. Seabaugh · Bryan Cave · One Metropolitan Square, Suite 3600 · 211 North Broadway · St. Louis, MO 63102-2750 · 314-259-2000

John R. Short · 10 · Husch Blackwell Sanders · http://www.huschblackwell.com · 720 Olive Street, Suite 2400 · St. Louis, MO 63101 · 314-345-6000

Kenneth H. Suelthaus · 10 · Polsinelli Shalton Flanigan Suelthaus · http://www.polsinelli.com · 7733 Forsyth Boulevard, Suite 1200 · St. Louis, MO 63105 · 314-889-8000

Peter D. Van Cleve · Bryan Cave · One Metropolitan Square, Suite 3600 · 211 North Broadway · St. Louis, MO 63102-2750 · 314-259-2000

W. Stanley Walch · 25 · Thompson Coburn · One U.S. Bank Plaza · St. Louis, MO 63101-1611 · 314-552-6000

R. Randall Wang · Bryan Cave · One Metropolitan Square, Suite 3600 · 211 North Broadway · St. Louis, MO 63102-2750 · 314-259-2000

Joseph H. Weyhrich · Lewis, Rice & Fingersh · 500 North Broadway, Suite 2000 · St. Louis, MO 63102-2147 · 314-444-7600

Tom W. Zook · Lewis, Rice & Fingersh · 500 North Broadway, Suite 2000 · St. Louis, MO 63102-2147 · 314-444-7600

DUI/DWI DEFENSE

Clayton

Donald L. Wolff · 25 · Wolff and D'Agrosa · 8019 Forsyth Boulevard · Clayton, MO 63105 · 314-725-8019

Independence

Michael C. McIntosh · ⑩ · Schaffer, McIntosh & Effertz · 14701 East 42nd Street · Independence, MO 64055 · 816-373-5590

St. Louis

Travis L. Noble, Jr. · Sindel, Sindel & Noble · 8008 Carondelet, Suite 301 · St. Louis, MO 63105 · 314-721-6040

Washington

Carl M. Ward · Law Office of Carl M. Ward · 216 West Main Street · Washington, MO 63090-2123 · 636-390-0070

EDUCATION LAW

Chesterfield

Thomas A. Mickes · Doster Mickes James Ullom Benson & Guest · 17107 Chesterfield Airport Road, Suite 300 · Chesterfield, MO 63005 · 636-532-0042

Kansas City

Stanley D. Davis · Shook, Hardy & Bacon · 2555 Grand Boulevard · Kansas City, MO 64108 · 816-474-6550

St. Louis

John R. Munich · Stinson Morrison Hecker · http://www.stinson.com · 100 South Fourth Street, Suite 700 St. Louis, MO 63102 · 314-259-4500

ELDER LAW

Kansas City

Craig C. Reaves · Reaves Law Firm · 4400 Madison Avenue · Kansas City, MO 64111 · 816-756-2100

EMINENT DOMAIN AND CONDEMNATION LAW

Clayton

Gary H. Feder · Husch Blackwell Sanders · http://www.huschblackwell.com · The Plaza in Clayton Office Tower, Suite 600 · 190 Carondelet Plaza · Clayton, MO 63105-3441 · 314-480-1500

Paul J. Puricelli · Stone, Leyton & Gershman · 7733 Forsyth Boulevard, Suite 500 · Clayton, MO 63105-1817 · 314-721-7011

Gregory R. Smith · Husch Blackwell Sanders · http://www.huschblackwell.com · The Plaza in Clayton Office Tower, Suite 600 · 190 Carondelet Plaza · Clayton, MO 63105-3441 · 314-480-1500

Kansas City

Steven E. Mauer · Bryan Cave · One Kansas City Place, Suite 3500 · 1200 Main Street · Kansas City, MO 64105-2100 · 816-374-3200

Spencer R. Thomson · Husch Blackwell Sanders · http://www.huschblackwell.com · 4801 Main Street, Suite 1000 · Kansas City, MO 64112 · 816-983-8000

St. Louis

Donald U. Beimdiek · ㉕ · Armstrong Teasdale · http://www.armstrongteasdale.com · One Metropolitan Square, Suite 2600 · 211 North Broadway · St. Louis, MO 63102-2740 · 314-621-5070

Mary M. Bonacorsi · Thompson Coburn · One U.S. Bank Plaza · St. Louis, MO 63101-1611 · 314-552-6000

Gerard T. Carmody · ⑩ · Carmody MacDonald · 120 South Central, Suite 1800 · St. Louis, MO 63105-1705 · 314-854-8600

Robert Denlow · Denlow & Henry · http://www.denlow.com · 7777 Bonhomme, Suite 1910 · St. Louis, MO 63105 · 314-725-5151

Paul G. Henry · Denlow & Henry · http://www.denlow.com · 7777 Bonhomme, Suite 1910 · St. Louis, MO 63105 · 314-725-5151

Jay L. Levitch · The Stolar Partnership · http://www.stolarlaw.com · The Lammert Building · 911 Washington Avenue · St. Louis, MO 63101-1290 · 314-231-2800

Jerome Wallach · The Wallach Law Firm · http://www.wallachlawfirm.com · Three City Place Drive, Suite 1070 · St. Louis, MO 63141 · 314-997-4050

Stanley J. Wallach · The Wallach Law Firm · http://www.wallachlawfirm.com · Three City Place Drive, Suite 1070 · St. Louis, MO 63141 · 314-997-4050

Thomas B. Weaver · Armstrong Teasdale · http://www.armstrongteasdale.com · One Metropolitan Square, Suite 2600 · 211 North Broadway · St. Louis, MO 63102-2740 · 314-621-5070

EMPLOYEE BENEFITS LAW

Clayton

Ruth Hays · ⑩ · Husch Blackwell Sanders · http://www.huschblackwell.com · The Plaza in Clayton Office Tower, Suite 600 · 190 Carondelet Plaza · Clayton, MO 63105-3441 · 314-480-1500

Kansas City

Thomas R. Brous · ⑩ · Stinson Morrison Hecker · http://www.stinson.com · 1201 Walnut Street, Suite 2900 · Kansas City, MO 64106-2150 · 816-842-8600

Michael V. Conger · Polsinelli Shalton Flanigan Suelthaus · http://www.polsinelli.com · 700 West 47th Street, Suite 1000 · Kansas City, MO 64112 · 816-753-1000

Robert D. Grossman · Lathrop & Gage · 2345 Grand Boulevard, Suite 2800 · Kansas City, MO 64108 · 816-292-2000

Christopher R. Hoyt · University of Missouri - Kansas City School of Law · 5100 Rockhill Road · Kansas City, MO 64110-2449 · 816-235-1644

James R. Hudek · ⑩ · Spencer Fane Britt & Browne · http://www.spencerfane.com · 1000 Walnut Street, Suite 1400 · Kansas City, MO 64106-2140 · 816-474-8100

Craig A. Kovarik · Husch Blackwell Sanders · http://www.huschblackwell.com · 4801 Main Street, Suite 1000 · Kansas City, MO 64112 · 816-983-8000

Patricia L. Martin · Husch Blackwell Sanders · http://www.huschblackwell.com · 4801 Main Street, Suite 1000 · Kansas City, MO 64112 · 816-983-8000

Philip C. McKnight · Stinson Morrison Hecker · http://www.stinson.com · 1201 Walnut Street, Suite 2900 Kansas City, MO 64106-2150 · 816-842-8600

Martin J. Moderson · Sonnenschein Nath & Rosenthal · 4520 Main Street, Suite 1100 · Kansas City, MO 64111-7700 · 816-460-2400

Maurice J. O'Sullivan, Jr. · ⑩ · Lathrop & Gage · 2345 Grand Boulevard, Suite 2800 · Kansas City, MO 64108 · 816-292-2000

Myron E. Sildon · ㉕ · Sildon Law Group · 500 Plaza Center Building, Suite 500 · 800 West 47th Street · Kansas City, MO 64112-1240 · 816-531-8877

Margo C. Soulé · Sonnenschein Nath & Rosenthal · 4520 Main Street, Suite 1100 · Kansas City, MO 64111-7700 · 816-460-2400

Michel A. Thompson · ⑩ · Lathrop & Gage · 2345 Grand Boulevard, Suite 2800 · Kansas City, MO 64108 · 816-292-2000

Perry M. Toll · ⑳ · Shughart Thomson & Kilroy · http://www.stklaw.com · 12 Wyandotte Plaza, Suite 1800 · 120 West 12th Street · Kansas City, MO 64105 · 816-421-3355

Mark D. Welker · ⑩ · Husch Blackwell Sanders · http://www.huschblackwell.com · 4801 Main Street, Suite 1000 · Kansas City, MO 64112 · 816-983-8000

Lees Summit

Thomas C. Graves · ⑳ · Haynes Benefits · 1650 Northeast Grand Avenue, Suite 201 · Lees Summit, MO 64086 · 816-875-1919

St. Louis

Brian W. Berglund · ⑩ · Bryan Cave · One Metropolitan Square, Suite 3600 · 211 North Broadway · St. Louis, MO 63102-2750 · 314-259-2000

Paul G. Griesemer · ⑳ · Thompson Coburn · One U.S. Bank Plaza · St. Louis, MO 63101-1611 · 314-552-6000

Lori W. Jones · Thompson Coburn · One U.S. Bank Plaza · St. Louis, MO 63101-1611 · 314-552-6000

Jamie Zveitel Kwiatek · Polsinelli Shalton Flanigan Suelthaus · http://www.polsinelli.com · 7733 Forsyth Boulevard, Suite 1200 · St. Louis, MO 63105 · 314-889-8000

Richard J. Pautler · Thompson Coburn · One U.S. Bank Plaza · St. Louis, MO 63101-1611 · 314-552-6000

Pamela D. Perdue · ⑩ · Summers, Compton, Wells and Hamburg · 8909 Ladue Road · St. Louis, MO 63124 · 314-991-4999

Douglas D. Ritterskamp · ⑳ · Bryan Cave · One Metropolitan Square, Suite 3600 · 211 North Broadway · St. Louis, MO 63102-2750 · 314-259-2000

Daniel J. Schwartz · Greensfelder, Hemker & Gale · Equitable Building, Suite 2000 · 10 South Broadway St. Louis, MO 63102 · 314-241-9090

Larry M. Sewell · ⑩ · Armstrong Teasdale · http://www.armstrongteasdale.com · One Metropolitan Square, Suite 2600 · 211 North Broadway · St. Louis, MO 63102-2740 · 314-621-5070

James I. Singer · Schuchat, Cook & Werner · The Shell Building, Second Floor · 1221 Locust Street · St. Louis, MO 63103-2364 · 314-621-2626

Sarah Roe Sise · Bryan Cave · One Metropolitan Square, Suite 3600 · 211 North Broadway · St. Louis, MO 63102-2750 · 314-259-2000

Ruth A. Streit · Thompson Coburn · One U.S. Bank Plaza · St. Louis, MO 63101-1611 · 314-552-6000

Lisa A. Van Fleet · ⑩ · Bryan Cave · One Metropolitan Square, Suite 3600 · 211 North Broadway · St. Louis, MO 63102-2750 · 314-259-2000

ENERGY LAW

Columbia

Sarah J. Read · Law Offices of Sarah J. Read · 1905 Cherry Hill Drive, Suite 200 · Columbia, MO 65203 · 573-447-2349

Jefferson City

Paul Boudreau · Brydon, Swearengen & England · http://www.brydonlaw.com · 312 East Capitol Avenue P.O. Box 456 · Jefferson City, MO 65102-0456 · 573-635-7166

Dean L. Cooper · Brydon, Swearengen & England · http://www.brydonlaw.com · 312 East Capitol Avenue · P.O. Box 456 · Jefferson City, MO 65102-0456 · 573-635-7166

Gary W. Duffy · ⑩ · Brydon, Swearengen & England · http://www.brydonlaw.com · 312 East Capitol Avenue · P.O. Box 456 · Jefferson City, MO 65102-0456 · 573-635-7166

William R. England III · ⑩ · Brydon, Swearengen & England · http://www.brydonlaw.com · 312 East Capitol Avenue · P.O. Box 456 · Jefferson City, MO 65102-0456 · 573-635-7166

James C. Swearengen · ⑩ · Brydon, Swearengen & England · http://www.brydonlaw.com · 312 East Capitol Avenue · P.O. Box 456 · Jefferson City, MO 65102-0456 · 573-635-7166

Kansas City

Spencer J. Brown · ⑳ · Deacy and Deacy · http://www.deacylawfirm.com · Ten Main Center, Suite 1900 920 Main Street · Kansas City, MO 64105 · 816-421-4000

Martin M. Loring · Husch Blackwell Sanders · http://www.huschblackwell.com · 4801 Main Street, Suite 1000 · Kansas City, MO 64112 · 816-983-8000

Karl Zobrist · Sonnenschein Nath & Rosenthal · 4520 Main Street, Suite 1100 · Kansas City, MO 64111-7700 · 816-460-2400

St. Louis

Ann E. Buckley · Buckley & Buckley · 1139 Olive Street, Suite 800 · St. Louis, MO 63101-1928 · 314-621-3434

Leland B. Curtis · ⑩ · Curtis, Heinz, Garrett & O'Keefe · 130 South Bemiston Avenue, Suite 200 · St. Louis, MO 63105-1913 · 314-725-8788

Daniel J. Godar · Armstrong Teasdale · http://www.armstrongteasdale.com · One Metropolitan Square, Suite 2600 · 211 North Broadway · St. Louis, MO 63102-2740 · 314-621-5070

James J. Virtel · ⑩ · Armstrong Teasdale · http://www.armstrongteasdale.com · One Metropolitan Square, Suite 2600 · 211 North Broadway · St. Louis, MO 63102-2740 · 314-621-5070

ENTERTAINMENT LAW

Chesterfield

Daniel R. Friedman · Daniel R. Friedman · 377 Dinsdoor Drive · Chesterfield, MO 63017 · 314-469-7113

St. Louis

Michael A. Kahn · Bryan Cave · One Metropolitan Square, Suite 3600 · 211 North Broadway · St. Louis, MO 63102-2750 · 314-259-2000

Eric F. Kayira · Kayira Law · 1001 Craig Road, Suite 357 · St. Louis, MO 63146 · 314-872-2141

Danica L. Mathes · Kayira Law · 1001 Craig Road, Suite 357 · St. Louis, MO 63146 · 314-872-2141

Peter Salsich III · Husch Blackwell Sanders · http://www.huschblackwell.com · 720 Olive Street, Suite 2400 · St. Louis, MO 63101 · 314-345-6000

ENVIRONMENTAL LAW

Clayton

Joseph G. Nassif · Husch Blackwell Sanders · http://www.huschblackwell.com · The Plaza in Clayton Office Tower, Suite 600 · 190 Carondelet Plaza · Clayton, MO 63105-3441 · 314-480-1500

Jefferson City

David A. Shorr · Lathrop & Gage · 314 East High Street · Jefferson City, MO 65101 · 573-893-4336

Kansas City

William G. Beck · Lathrop & Gage · 2345 Grand Boulevard, Suite 2800 · Kansas City, MO 64108 · 816-292-2000

Robert L. Driscoll · ⑳ · Stinson Morrison Hecker · http://www.stinson.com · 1201 Walnut Street, Suite 2900 · Kansas City, MO 64106-2150 · 816-842-8600

David R. Erickson · Shook, Hardy & Bacon · 2555 Grand Boulevard · Kansas City, MO 64108 · 816-474-6550

Parthenia B. Evans · Stinson Morrison Hecker · http://www.stinson.com · 1201 Walnut Street, Suite 2900 Kansas City, MO 64106-2150 · 816-842-8600

William F. Ford · Lathrop & Gage · 2345 Grand Boulevard, Suite 2800 · Kansas City, MO 64108 · 816-292-2000

Carl H. Helmstetter · (10) · Spencer Fane Britt & Browne · http://www.spencerfane.com · 1000 Walnut Street, Suite 1400 · Kansas City, MO 64106-2140 · 816-474-8100

Michael D. Hockley · Spencer Fane Britt & Browne · http://www.spencerfane.com · 1000 Walnut Street, Suite 1400 · Kansas City, MO 64106-2140 · 816-474-8100

James L. Moeller · Sonnenschein Nath & Rosenthal · 4520 Main Street, Suite 1100 · Kansas City, MO 64111-7700 · 816-460-2400

James T. Price · (20) · Spencer Fane Britt & Browne · http://www.spencerfane.com · 1000 Walnut Street, Suite 1400 · Kansas City, MO 64106-2140 · 816-474-8100

Stanley A. Reigel · (10) · Stinson Morrison Hecker · http://www.stinson.com · 1201 Walnut Street, Suite 2900 · Kansas City, MO 64106-2150 · 816-842-8600

Terry J. Satterlee · Shook, Hardy & Bacon · 2555 Grand Boulevard · Kansas City, MO 64108 · 816-474-6550

David R. Tripp · (10) · Stinson Morrison Hecker · http://www.stinson.com · 1201 Walnut Street, Suite 2900 Kansas City, MO 64106-2150 · 816-842-8600

Jerome T. Wolf · (10) · Sonnenschein Nath & Rosenthal · 4520 Main Street, Suite 1100 · Kansas City, MO 64111-7700 · 816-460-2400

Teresa A. Woody · Woody Law Firm · 1044 Main Street, Suite 500 · Kansas City, MO 64105 · 816-421-4246

St. Louis

Dale A. Guariglia · Bryan Cave · One Metropolitan Square, Suite 3600 · 211 North Broadway · St. Louis, MO 63102-2750 · 314-259-2000

Frank H. Hackmann · (10) · Sonnenschein Nath & Rosenthal · One Metropolitan Square, Suite 3000 · 211 North Broadway · St. Louis, MO 63102-2741 · 314-241-1800

Bradley S. Hiles · (10) · Husch Blackwell Sanders · http://www.huschblackwell.com · 720 Olive Street, Suite 2400 · St. Louis, MO 63101 · 314-345-6000

Stephen G. Jeffery · Thompson Coburn · One U.S. Bank Plaza · St. Louis, MO 63101-1611 · 314-552-6000

Maxine I. Lipeles · (10) · Interdisciplinary Environmental Clinic · Washington University School of Law · One Brookings Drive · P.O. Box 1120 · St. Louis, MO 63130 · 314-935-5837

Frank L. Pellegrini · Armstrong Teasdale · http://www.armstrongteasdale.com · One Metropolitan Square, Suite 2600 · 211 North Broadway · St. Louis, MO 63102-2740 · 314-621-5070

Steven J. Poplawski · Bryan Cave · One Metropolitan Square, Suite 3600 · 211 North Broadway · St. Louis, MO 63102-2750 · 314-259-2000

Peter S. Strassner · Thompson Coburn · One U.S. Bank Plaza · St. Louis, MO 63101-1611 · 314-552-6000

George M. von Stamwitz · (10) · Armstrong Teasdale · http://www.armstrongteasdale.com · One Metropolitan Square, Suite 2600 · 211 North Broadway · St. Louis, MO 63102-2740 · 314-621-5070

EQUIPMENT FINANCE LAW

Clayton

Maury B. Poscover · ⑩ · Husch Blackwell Sanders · http://www.huschblackwell.com · The Plaza in Clayton Office Tower, Suite 600 · 190 Carondelet Plaza · Clayton, MO 63105-3441 · 314-480-1500

Kansas City

Christopher J. Rockers · Husch Blackwell Sanders · http://www.huschblackwell.com · 1200 Main Street, Suite 2300 · Kansas City, MO 64105 · 816-421-4800

St. Louis

Ruthanne Hammett · Thompson Coburn · One U.S. Bank Plaza · St. Louis, MO 63101-1611 · 314-552-6000

David A. Lander · ⑳ · Thompson Coburn · One U.S. Bank Plaza · St. Louis, MO 63101-1611 · 314-552-6000

James J. Murphy · Thompson Coburn · One U.S. Bank Plaza · St. Louis, MO 63101-1611 · 314-552-6000

FAMILY LAW

Blue Springs

Jack A. Cochran · ㉕ · Cochran, Oswald & Roam · 601 Northwest Jefferson · P.O. Box 550 · Blue Springs, MO 64013-0550 · 816-229-8121

Susan Green · Cochran, Oswald & Roam · 601 Northwest Jefferson · P.O. Box 550 · Blue Springs, MO 64013-0550 · 816-229-8121

Clayton

David B. Lacks · ㉕ · David B. Lacks · 231 South Beniston, Suite 910 · Clayton, MO 63105 · 314-863-4100

Cary J. Mogerman · ⑩ · Zerman & Mogerman · http://www.zermanmogerman.com · Park Place, Suite 325 · 100 South Brentwood Boulevard · Clayton, MO 63105 · 314-862-4444

Allan H. Zerman · ⑩ · Zerman & Mogerman · http://www.zermanmogerman.com · Park Place, Suite 325 · 100 South Brentwood Boulevard · Clayton, MO 63105 · 314-862-4444

Independence

Michael S. J. Albano · ㉕ · Welch, Martin & Albano · 311 West Kansas Avenue · Independence, MO 64050 · 816-836-8000

John W. Dennis, Jr. · ⑳ · Welch, Martin & Albano · 311 West Kansas Avenue · Independence, MO 64050 · 816-836-8000

David Kimminau · ⑩ · McElligott, Ewan, Hall & Kimminau · 233 West Walnut · Independence, MO 64050-3825 · 816-833-1222

Michael C. McIntosh · ⑩ · Schaffer, McIntosh & Effertz · 14701 East 42nd Street · Independence, MO 64055 · 816-373-5590

Jefferson City

Lori J. Levine · ⑳ · Carson & Coil · 515 East High Street · P.O. Box 28 · Jefferson City, MO 65102 · 573-636-2177

Kansas City

Jill C. Allison · Law Offices of Blond & Allison · One Ward Parkway, Suite 118 · Kansas City, MO 64112 816-756-0080

Sheldon Bernstein · ⑩ · Bernstein, Rodarte & Hatheway · 9237 Ward Parkway, Suite 106 · Kansas City, MO 64114 · 816-444-8030

James T. Cook · ⑩ · Berkowitz, Cook & Gondring · 4420 Madison Avenue, Suite 100 · Kansas City, MO 64111 · 816-753-5000

Tamara S. Hatheway · Bernstein, Rodarte & Hatheway · 9237 Ward Parkway, Suite 106 · Kansas City, MO 64114 · 816-444-8030

Karen A. Plax · ⑩ · Law Office of Karen A. Plax · http://www.plaxlaw.com · United Missouri Bank Building, Suite 300 · 1310 Carondelet Drive · Kansas City, MO 64114 · 816-942-1900

Anita I. Rodarte · Bernstein, Rodarte & Hatheway · 9237 Ward Parkway, Suite 106 · Kansas City, MO 64114 · 816-444-8030

Lee's Summit

Rebecca Leonard · Leonard and Finley · 3300 Northeast Ralph Powell Road · Lee's Summit, MO 64064 816-836-9950

Lees Summit

James H. Young · James H. Young & Associates · http://www.jameshyoung.com · 3300 Northeast Ralph Powell Road · Lees Summit, MO 64064 · 816-246-9981

Rolla

J. Kent Robinson · Williams, Robinson, Rigler & Buschjost · 901 North Pine Street, Fourth Floor · P.O. Box 47 · Rolla, MO 65401 · 573-341-2266

Springfield

C. Ronald Baird · Baird, Lightner, Millsap & Harpool · Two Corporate Centre, Suite 2-102 · 1949 East Sunshine Street · Springfield, MO 65804-1605 · 417-887-0133

Lisa Ghan Blumenstock · Lowther Johnson · 901 St. Louis Street, 20th Floor · Springfield, MO 65806 · 417-866-7777

John S. Pratt · ⑩ · Pratt, Fossard, Jensen & Masters · 3432 South Culpepper Court, Suite A · Springfield, MO 65804-3755 · 417-883-8200

F. Richard Van Pelt · Van Pelt and Van Pelt · http://www.vanpeltlaw.com · 1524 East Primrose Street, Suite A · Springfield, MO 65804 · 417-886-9080

St. Charles

Michael A. Turken · ⑩ · Turken & Associates · 320 North Fifth Street, Lower Level · St. Charles, MO 63301-1899 · 636-940-7500

St. Joseph

Grace S. Day · Shughart Thomson & Kilroy · http://www.stklaw.com · 3101 Frederick Avenue · St. Joseph, MO 64506 · 816-364-2117

St. Louis

Alisse C. Camazine · ⑩ · Paule, Camazine & Blumenthal · 165 North Meramec Avenue, Sixth Floor · St. Louis, MO 63105 · 314-727-2266

James P. Carmondy · Carmody MacDonald · 120 South Central, Suite 1800 · St. Louis, MO 63105-1705 · 314-854-8600

Justin C. Cordonnier · ⑩ · Green Cordonnier & House · http://www.greencordonnierhouse.com · 8000 Maryland Avenue, Suite 400 · St. Louis, MO 63105 · 314-726-0455

Bruce E. Friedman · Paule, Camazine & Blumenthal · 165 North Meramec Avenue, Sixth Floor · St. Louis, MO 63105 · 314-727-2266

Merle L. Silverstein · ⑳ · Rosenblum, Goldenhersh, Silverstein & Zafft · 7733 Forsyth Boulevard, Fourth Floor · St. Louis, MO 63105 · 314-726-6868

Daniel R. Sokol · ⑩ · Capes, Sokol, Goodman & Sarachan · Pierre Laclede Center, 12th Floor · 7701 Forsyth Boulevard · St. Louis, MO 63105-1818 · 314-721-7701

Allan F. Stewart · ⑩ · Stewart, Mittleman, Heggie & Henry · 222 South Central Avenue, Suite 501 · St. Louis, MO 63105-3509 · 314-863-8484

Robert F. Summers · Summers, Compton, Wells and Hamburg · 8909 Ladue Road · St. Louis, MO 63124 · 314-991-4999

FAMILY LAW MEDIATION

Clayton

Leonard J. Frankel · Frankel, Rubin, Bond, Dubin, Siegel & Klein · Bemiston Tower, Suite 1111 · 231 South Bemiston · Clayton, MO 63105 · 314-725-8000

Springfield

Lisa Ghan Blumenstock · Lowther Johnson · 901 St. Louis Street, 20th Floor · Springfield, MO 65806 · 417-866-7777

St. Charles

Rebecca T. Magruder · Rebecca T. Magruder · 118 North Second Street, Suite 300 · St. Charles, MO 63301 · 636-947-9273

St. Louis

Susan L. Amato · Susan L. Amato · http://www.susanamato.com · 230 South Bemiston, Suite 510 · St. Louis, MO 63105 · 314-862-0330

Alan E. Freed · Paule, Camazine & Blumenthal · 165 North Meramec Avenue, Sixth Floor · St. Louis, MO 63105 · 314-727-2266

FIRST AMENDMENT LAW

Kansas City

M. Errol Copilevitz · ⑩ · Copilevitz & Canter · 310 West 20th Street, Suite 300 · Kansas City, MO 64108 816-472-9000

Mark P. Johnson · ⑩ · Sonnenschein Nath & Rosenthal · 4520 Main Street, Suite 1100 · Kansas City, MO 64111-7700 · 816-460-2400

Jean A. Maneke · Jean A. Maneke · 910 One Main Plaza · 4435 Main Street · Kansas City, MO 64111 · 816-753-9000

Bernard J. Rhodes · Lathrop & Gage · 2345 Grand Boulevard, Suite 2800 · Kansas City, MO 64108 · 816-292-2000

St. Louis

Michael A. Kahn · Bryan Cave · One Metropolitan Square, Suite 3600 · 211 North Broadway · St. Louis, MO 63102-2750 · 314-259-2000

Joseph E. Martineau · Lewis, Rice & Fingersh · 500 North Broadway, Suite 2000 · St. Louis, MO 63102-2147 · 314-444-7600

Gerald R. Ortbals · Bryan Cave · One Metropolitan Square, Suite 3600 · 211 North Broadway · St. Louis, MO 63102-2750 · 314-259-2000

Mark Sableman · ⑩ · Thompson Coburn · One U.S. Bank Plaza · St. Louis, MO 63101-1611 · 314-552-6000

FRANCHISE LAW

Kansas City

Donald A. Culp · ⑩ · Husch Blackwell Sanders · http://www.huschblackwell.com · 4801 Main Street, Suite 1000 · Kansas City, MO 64112 · 816-983-8000

Edward M. Dolson · ⑩ · Swanson Midgley · 2420 Pershing Road, Suite 400 · Kansas City, MO 64108-2505 · 816-842-6100

Joseph L. Hiersteiner · Seigfreid, Bingham, Levy, Selzer & Gee · http://www.sblsg.com · 2800 Commerce Tower · 911 Main Street · Kansas City, MO 64105-2009 · 816-421-4460

Dennis D. Palmer · ⑩ · Shughart Thomson & Kilroy · http://www.stklaw.com · 12 Wyandotte Plaza, Suite 1800 · 120 West 12th Street · Kansas City, MO 64105 · 816-421-3355

Edward R. Spalty · ⑩ · Armstrong Teasdale · http://www.armstrongteasdale.com · 2345 Grand Boulevard, Suite 2000 · Kansas City, MO 64108-2617 · 816-221-3420

St. Louis

Jane E. Cohen · ⑩ · Jane Cohen · 230 South Bemiston Avenue, Suite 1200 · St. Louis, MO 63105 · 314-862-3333

Glenn E. Davis · Armstrong Teasdale · http://www.armstrongteasdale.com · One Metropolitan Square, Suite 2600 · 211 North Broadway · St. Louis, MO 63102-2740 · 314-621-5070

Stephen H. Rovak · ⑩ · Sonnenschein Nath & Rosenthal · One Metropolitan Square, Suite 3000 · 211 North Broadway · St. Louis, MO 63102-2741 · 314-241-1800

Leonard D. Vines · ⑩ · Greensfelder, Hemker & Gale · Equitable Building, Suite 2000 · 10 South Broadway · St. Louis, MO 63102 · 314-241-9090

GAMING LAW

Jefferson City

James B. Deutsch · Blitz, Bardgett & Deutsch · 308 East High Street, Suite 301 · Jefferson City, MO 65101-3237 · 573-634-2500

Kansas City

Harold L. Fridkin · Lathrop & Gage · 2345 Grand Boulevard, Suite 2800 · Kansas City, MO 64108 · 816-292-2000

Jerome D. Riffel · Lathrop & Gage · 2345 Grand Boulevard, Suite 2800 · Kansas City, MO 64108 · 816-292-2000

GOVERNMENT RELATIONS LAW

Jefferson City

Sherry L. Doctorian · Armstrong Teasdale · http://www.armstrongteasdale.com · 3405 West Truman Boulevard, Suite 210 · Jefferson City, MO 65109-5713 · 573-636-8394

Charles W. Hatfield · Stinson Morrison Hecker · http://www.stinson.com · 230 West McCarty Street · Jefferson City, MO 65101 · 573-636-6263

Kansas City

John C. Craft · Lathrop & Gage · 2345 Grand Boulevard, Suite 2800 · Kansas City, MO 64108 · 816-292-2000

St. Louis

Jonathan F. Dalton · Lewis, Rice & Fingersh · 500 North Broadway, Suite 2000 · St. Louis, MO 63102-2147 · 314-444-7600

Erwin O. Switzer III · Greensfelder, Hemker & Gale · Equitable Building, Suite 2000 · 10 South Broadway · St. Louis, MO 63102 · 314-241-9090

HEALTH CARE LAW

Jefferson City

Harvey M. Tettlebaum · ⑩ · Husch Blackwell Sanders · http://www.huschblackwell.com · 235 East High Street · P.O. Box 1251 · Jefferson City, MO 65101-1251 · 573-635-9118

Kansas City

Stephen T. Adams · ⑩ · Husch Blackwell Sanders · http://www.huschblackwell.com · 4801 Main Street, Suite 1000 · Kansas City, MO 64112 · 816-983-8000

Larry J. Bingham · ⑩ · Seigfreid, Bingham, Levy, Selzer & Gee · http://www.sblsg.com · 2800 Commerce Tower · 911 Main Street · Kansas City, MO 64105-2009 · 816-421-4460

Mary Beth Blake · ⑩ · Polsinelli Shalton Flanigan Suelthaus · http://www.polsinelli.com · 700 West 47th Street, Suite 1000 · Kansas City, MO 64112 · 816-753-1000

Curt J. Chase · Husch Blackwell Sanders · http://www.huschblackwell.com · 4801 Main Street, Suite 1000 · Kansas City, MO 64112 · 816-983-8000

Joseph L. Hiersteiner · Seigfreid, Bingham, Levy, Selzer & Gee · http://www.sblsg.com · 2800 Commerce Tower · 911 Main Street · Kansas City, MO 64105-2009 · 816-421-4460

Michelle Stark Kaufman · Sonnenschein Nath & Rosenthal · 4520 Main Street, Suite 1100 · Kansas City, MO 64111-7700 · 816-460-2400

Thomas G. Kokoruda · ⑩ · Shughart Thomson & Kilroy · http://www.stklaw.com · 12 Wyandotte Plaza, Suite 1800 · 120 West 12th Street · Kansas City, MO 64105 · 816-421-3355

George E. Leonard · Shughart Thomson & Kilroy · http://www.stklaw.com · 12 Wyandotte Plaza, Suite 1800 · 120 West 12th Street · Kansas City, MO 64105 · 816-421-3355

Charles F. Myers · ⑩ · Lathrop & Gage · 2345 Grand Boulevard, Suite 2800 · Kansas City, MO 64108 · 816-292-2000

Martha A. Ross · Lathrop & Gage · 2345 Grand Boulevard, Suite 2800 · Kansas City, MO 64108 · 816-292-2000

G. Mark Sappington · ⑩ · Kutak Rock · 1010 Grand Boulevard, Suite 500 · Kansas City, MO 64106-2220 816-960-0090

Mark R. Thompson · Seigfreid, Bingham, Levy, Selzer & Gee · http://www.sblsg.com · 2800 Commerce Tower · 911 Main Street · Kansas City, MO 64105-2009 · 816-421-4460

St. Louis

Kenneth W. Bean · Sandberg, Phoenix & von Gontard · http://www.spvg.com · One City Centre, 15th Floor · 515 North Sixth Street · St. Louis, MO 63101-1880 · 314-231-3332

John W. Dillane · Greensfelder, Hemker & Gale · Equitable Building, Suite 2000 · 10 South Broadway · St. Louis, MO 63102 · 314-241-9090

Diane E. Felix · ⑩ · Armstrong Teasdale · http://www.armstrongteasdale.com · One Metropolitan Square, Suite 2600 · 211 North Broadway · St. Louis, MO 63102-2740 · 314-621-5070

James L. Fogle · Thompson Coburn · One U.S. Bank Plaza · St. Louis, MO 63101-1611 · 314-552-6000

Randy S. Gerber · Polsinelli Shalton Flanigan Suelthaus · http://www.polsinelli.com · 100 South Fourth Street, Suite 1100 · St. Louis, MO 63102 · 314-231-1950

Mark H. Goran · Bryan Cave · One Metropolitan Square, Suite 3600 · 211 North Broadway · St. Louis, MO 63102-2750 · 314-259-2000

James F. Gunn · Thompson Coburn · One U.S. Bank Plaza · St. Louis, MO 63101-1611 · 314-552-6000

David M. Harris · ⑩ · Greensfelder, Hemker & Gale · Equitable Building, Suite 2000 · 10 South Broadway · St. Louis, MO 63102 · 314-241-9090

Linda M. Martinez · Bryan Cave · One Metropolitan Square, Suite 3600 · 211 North Broadway · St. Louis, MO 63102-2750 · 314-259-2000

Tracy L. Mathis · ⑩ · Lewis, Rice & Fingersh · 500 North Broadway, Suite 2000 · St. Louis, MO 63102-2147 · 314-444-7600

Stacey L. Murphy · Fulbright & Jaworski · http://www.fulbright.com · 8000 Maryland Avenue, Suite 1190 St. Louis, MO 63105 · 314-505-8800

John J. Riffle · Lewis, Rice & Fingersh · 500 North Broadway, Suite 2000 · St. Louis, MO 63102-2147 · 314-444-7600

Richard D. Watters · ⑩ · Lashly & Baer · 714 Locust Street · St. Louis, MO 63101 · 314-621-2939

James George Wiehl · ⑩ · Fulbright & Jaworski · http://www.fulbright.com · 8000 Maryland Avenue, Suite 1190 · St. Louis, MO 63105 · 314-505-8800

IMMIGRATION LAW

Clayton

Larry Carp · ⑩ · Carp and Sexauer · The Parkway Tower Building, Suite 325 · 225 South Meramec Avenue · Clayton, MO 63105 · 314-863-4300

Kansas City

Adele A. McGrath · The McGrath Law Firm · 2300 Main Street, Ninth Floor · Kansas City, MO 64108 · 816-448-3400

St. Louis

Arthur G. Carr III · ⑩ · Arthur G. Carr III · 5701 Columbia Avenue · St. Louis, MO 63139 · 314-862-0900

Melanie Gurley Keeney · ⑩ · Tueth Keeney Cooper Mohan & Jackstadt · 34 North Meramec Avenue, Suite 600 · St. Louis, MO 63105 · 314-880-3600

George S. Newman · ⑩ · Stinson Morrison Hecker · http://www.stinson.com · 168 North Meramec Avenue, Suite 400 · St. Louis, MO 63105 · 314-863-0800

Linda L. Shapiro · Thompson Coburn · One U.S. Bank Plaza · St. Louis, MO 63101-1611 · 314-552-6000

INFORMATION TECHNOLOGY LAW

Clayton

Arthur L. Smith · Husch Blackwell Sanders · http://www.huschblackwell.com · The Plaza in Clayton Office Tower, Suite 600 · 190 Carondelet Plaza · Clayton, MO 63105-3441 · 314-480-1500

Charles H. Fendell · Thompson Coburn · One U.S. Bank Plaza · St. Louis, MO 63101-1611 · 314-552-6000

Andrew Hoyne · Armstrong Teasdale · http://www.armstrongteasdale.com · One Metropolitan Square, Suite 2600 · 211 North Broadway · St. Louis, MO 63102-2740 · 314-621-5070

Benjamin Hulsey · Thompson Coburn · One U.S. Bank Plaza · St. Louis, MO 63101-1611 · 314-552-6000

INSURANCE LAW

Kansas City

Bruce E. Baty · Sonnenschein Nath & Rosenthal · 4520 Main Street, Suite 1100 · Kansas City, MO 64111-7700 · 816-460-2400

William G. Beck · Lathrop & Gage · 2345 Grand Boulevard, Suite 2800 · Kansas City, MO 64108 · 816-292-2000

Richard N. Bien · Lathrop & Gage · 2345 Grand Boulevard, Suite 2800 · Kansas City, MO 64108 · 816-292-2000

Steven G. Emerson · Stinson Morrison Hecker · http://www.stinson.com · 1201 Walnut Street, Suite 2900 Kansas City, MO 64106-2150 · 816-842-8600

Scott C. Hecht · Stinson Morrison Hecker · http://www.stinson.com · 1201 Walnut Street, Suite 2900 · Kansas City, MO 64106-2150 · 816-842-8600

Gerald A. King · Armstrong Teasdale · http://www.armstrongteasdale.com · 2345 Grand Boulevard, Suite 2000 · Kansas City, MO 64108-2617 · 816-221-3420

Laurence R. Tucker · ⑩ · Armstrong Teasdale · http://www.armstrongteasdale.com · 2345 Grand Boulevard, Suite 2000 · Kansas City, MO 64108-2617 · 816-221-3420

Lisa A. Weixelman · Polsinelli Shalton Flanigan Suelthaus · http://www.polsinelli.com · 700 West 47th Street, Suite 1000 · Kansas City, MO 64112 · 816-753-1000

Springfield

Michael J. Patton · Turner, Reid, Duncan, Loomer & Patton · 1355 East Bradford Parkway, Suite A · P.O. Box 4043 · Springfield, MO 65808 · 417-883-2102

St. Louis

Ann E. Buckley · Buckley & Buckley · 1139 Olive Street, Suite 800 · St. Louis, MO 63101-1928 · 314-621-3434

Thomas A. Buckley · Buckley & Buckley · 1139 Olive Street, Suite 800 · St. Louis, MO 63101-1928 · 314-621-3434

Clark H. Cole · Armstrong Teasdale · http://www.armstrongteasdale.com · One Metropolitan Square, Suite 2600 · 211 North Broadway · St. Louis, MO 63102-2740 · 314-621-5070

Patrick J. Kenny · Armstrong Teasdale · http://www.armstrongteasdale.com · One Metropolitan Square, Suite 2600 · 211 North Broadway · St. Louis, MO 63102-2740 · 314-621-5070

Kansas City

Russell S. Jones, Jr. · Shughart Thomson & Kilroy · http://www.stklaw.com · 12 Wyandotte Plaza, Suite 1800 · 120 West 12th Street · Kansas City, MO 64105 · 816-421-3355

William B. Kircher · ⑩ · Husch Blackwell Sanders · http://www.huschblackwell.com · 4801 Main Street, Suite 1000 · Kansas City, MO 64112 · 816-983-8000

Malcolm A. Litman · ⑩ · Shughart Thomson & Kilroy · http://www.stklaw.com · 12 Wyandotte Plaza, Suite 1800 · 120 West 12th Street · Kansas City, MO 64105 · 816-421-3355

I. Edward Marquette · ⑩ · Sonnenschein Nath & Rosenthal · 4520 Main Street, Suite 1100 · Kansas City, MO 64111-7700 · 816-460-2400

Penny R. Slicer · Stinson Morrison Hecker · http://www.stinson.com · 1201 Walnut Street, Suite 2900 · Kansas City, MO 64106-2150 · 816-842-8600

J. David Wharton · Stinson Morrison Hecker · http://www.stinson.com · 1201 Walnut Street, Suite 2900 · Kansas City, MO 64106-2150 · 816-842-8600

St. Louis

John S. Beulick · Armstrong Teasdale · http://www.armstrongteasdale.com · One Metropolitan Square, Suite 2600 · 211 North Broadway · St. Louis, MO 63102-2740 · 314-621-5070

G. Harley Blosser · Sonnenschein Nath & Rosenthal · One Metropolitan Square, Suite 3000 · 211 North Broadway · St. Louis, MO 63102-2741 · 314-241-1800

J. Bennett Clark · Bryan Cave · One Metropolitan Square, Suite 3600 · 211 North Broadway · St. Louis, MO 63102-2750 · 314-259-2000

William B. Cunningham · ⑩ · Polster, Lieder, Woodruff & Lucchesi · 12412 Powerscourt Drive, Suite 200 · St. Louis, MO 63131-3615 · 314-238-2400

Paul M. Denk · ⑩ · Patent Law Office · 763 South New Ballas Road, Suite 170 · St. Louis, MO 63141 · 314-872-8136

Samuel Digirolamo · Husch Blackwell Sanders · http://www.huschblackwell.com · 720 Olive Street, Suite 2400 · St. Louis, MO 63101 · 314-345-6000

Michael E. Godar · ⑩ · Senniger, Powers, Leavitt & Roedel · One Metropolitan Square, Suite 1600 · 211 North Broadway · St. Louis, MO 63102 · 314-231-5400

John M. Howell · ⑩ · Thompson Coburn · One U.S. Bank Plaza · St. Louis, MO 63101-1611 · 314-552-6000

Frank B. Janoski · Lewis, Rice & Fingersh · 500 North Broadway, Suite 2000 · St. Louis, MO 63102-2147 · 314-444-7600

Michael A. Kahn · Bryan Cave · One Metropolitan Square, Suite 3600 · 211 North Broadway · St. Louis, MO 63102-2750 · 314-259-2000

McPherson D. Moore · ⑩ · Polster, Lieder, Woodruff & Lucchesi · 12412 Powerscourt Drive, Suite 200 · St. Louis, MO 63131-3615 · 314-238-2400

Alan S. Nemes · Husch Blackwell Sanders · http://www.huschblackwell.com · 720 Olive Street, Suite 2400 · St. Louis, MO 63101 · 314-345-6000

Thomas A. Polcyn · Thompson Coburn · One U.S. Bank Plaza · St. Louis, MO 63101-1611 · 314-552-6000

J. Philip Polster · Polster, Lieder, Woodruff & Lucchesi · 12412 Powerscourt Drive, Suite 200 · St. Louis, MO 63131-3615 · 314-238-2400

Philip B. Polster · ⑩ · Polster, Lieder, Woodruff & Lucchesi · 12412 Powerscourt Drive, Suite 200 · St. Louis, MO 63131-3615 · 314-238-2400

John H. Quinn III · Armstrong Teasdale · http://www.armstrongteasdale.com · One Metropolitan Square, Suite 2600 · 211 North Broadway · St. Louis, MO 63102-2740 · 314-621-5070

John K. Roedel, Jr. · ⑩ · Senniger, Powers, Leavitt & Roedel · One Metropolitan Square, Suite 1600 · 211 North Broadway · St. Louis, MO 63102 · 314-231-5400

David A. Roodman · Bryan Cave · One Metropolitan Square, Suite 3600 · 211 North Broadway · St. Louis, MO 63102-2750 · 314-259-2000

INTERNATIONAL TRADE AND FINANCE LAW

St. Louis

Frederick W. Bartelsmeyer · Bryan Cave · One Metropolitan Square, Suite 3600 · 211 North Broadway · St. Louis, MO 63102-2750 · 314-259-2000

Thomas H. Bottini · Armstrong Teasdale · http://www.armstrongteasdale.com · One Metropolitan Square, Suite 2600 · 211 North Broadway · St. Louis, MO 63102-2740 · 314-621-5070

A.J. Chivetta · Armstrong Teasdale · http://www.armstrongteasdale.com · One Metropolitan Square, Suite 2600 · 211 North Broadway · St. Louis, MO 63102-2740 · 314-621-5070

Don G. Lents · ⑩ · Bryan Cave · One Metropolitan Square, Suite 3600 · 211 North Broadway · St. Louis, MO 63102-2750 · 314-259-2000

Denis P. McCusker · ⑩ · Bryan Cave · One Metropolitan Square, Suite 3600 · 211 North Broadway · St. Louis, MO 63102-2750 · 314-259-2000

LABOR AND EMPLOYMENT LAW

Chesterfield

Ronald K. Fisher · ⑳ · Harris, Dowell, Fisher & Harris · 15400 South Outer Forty, Suite 202 · Chesterfield, MO 63017 · 636-532-0300

Michael E. Kaemmerer · ⑩ · McCarthy, Leonard, Kaemmerer, Owen, McGovern, Striler & Menghini · 400 South Woods Mill, Suite 250 · Chesterfield, MO 63017 · 314-392-5200

Clayton

Cary W. Hammond · ⑩ · Hammond, Shinners, Turcotte and Larrew & Young · 7730 Carondelet Avenue, Suite 200 · Clayton, MO 63105 · 314-727-1015

D. Michael Linihan · ⑩ · The Lowenbaum Partnership · 222 South Central Avenue, Suite 901 · Clayton, MO 63105 · 314-863-0092

Independence

Gene P. Graham, Jr. · White, Allinder, Graham & Buckley · 19049 East Valley View Parkway, Suite C · Independence, MO 64055 · 816-373-9080

Kansas City

Arthur A. Benson II · ⑩ · Benson & Associates · http://www.bensonlaw.com · 4006 Central Street · P.O. Box 119007 · Kansas City, MO 64171-9007 · 816-531-6565

Michael L. Blumenthal · Seyferth Blumenthal & Harris · 300 Wyandotte Street, Suite 430 · Kansas City, MO 64105 · 816-756-0700

Stanley E. Craven · Spencer Fane Britt & Browne · http://www.spencerfane.com · 1000 Walnut Street, Suite 1400 · Kansas City, MO 64106-2140 · 816-474-8100

Paul E. Donnelly · Stinson Morrison Hecker · http://www.stinson.com · 1201 Walnut Street, Suite 2900 · Kansas City, MO 64106-2150 · 816-842-8600

Denise K. Drake · Spencer Fane Britt & Browne · http://www.spencerfane.com · 1000 Walnut Street, Suite 1400 · Kansas City, MO 64106-2140 · 816-474-8100

Dennis E. Egan · ⑩ · The Popham Law Firm · 712 Broadway, Suite 100 · Kansas City, MO 64105 · 816-221-2288

Brian J. Finucane · Fisher & Phillips · http://www.laborlawyers.com · The Stilwell Building, Suite 400 · 104 West Ninth Street · Kansas City, MO 63105 · 816-842-8770

Karen Glickstein · Shughart Thomson & Kilroy · http://www.stklaw.com · 12 Wyandotte Plaza, Suite 1800 · 120 West 12th Street · Kansas City, MO 64105 · 816-421-3355

Robert J. Janowitz · Constangy, Brooks & Smith · http://www.constangy.com · 2600 Grand Boulevard, Suite 300 · Kansas City, MO 64108-4600 · 816-472-6400

William A. Jolley · ㉕ · Jolley, Walsh, Hurley & Raisher · 204 West Linwood Boulevard · Kansas City, MO 64111 · 816-561-3755

Larry W. Joye · Stinson Morrison Hecker · http://www.stinson.com · 1201 Walnut Street, Suite 2900 · Kansas City, MO 64106-2150 · 816-842-8600

Michael S. Ketchmark · Davis, Ketchmark & McCreight · 2345 Grand Boulevard, Suite 2110 · Kansas City, MO 64108-2617 · 816-842-1515

W. Terrence Kilroy · Shughart Thomson & Kilroy · http://www.stklaw.com · 12 Wyandotte Plaza, Suite 1800 · 120 West 12th Street · Kansas City, MO 64105 · 816-421-3355

William C. Martucci · ⑩ · Shook, Hardy & Bacon · 2555 Grand Boulevard · Kansas City, MO 64108 · 816-474-6550

Rosalee M. McNamara · Lathrop & Gage · 2345 Grand Boulevard, Suite 2800 · Kansas City, MO 64108 · 816-292-2000

Martin M. Meyers · The Meyers Law Firm · 222 West Gregory, Suite 340 · Kansas City, MO 64113 · 816-444-8500

John R. Phillips · ⑩ · Husch Blackwell Sanders · http://www.huschblackwell.com · 4801 Main Street, Suite 1000 · Kansas City, MO 64112 · 816-983-8000

Jack D. Rowe · ⑩ · Lathrop & Gage · 2345 Grand Boulevard, Suite 2800 · Kansas City, MO 64108 · 816-292-2000

Larry M. Schumaker · Schumaker Center for Employment Law · 10401 Holmes Road, Suite 480 · Kansas City, MO 64131 · 816-941-9994

Paul D. Seyferth · Seyferth Blumenthal & Harris · 300 Wyandotte Street, Suite 430 · Kansas City, MO 64105 · 816-756-0700

John A. Vering III · Armstrong Teasdale · http://www.armstrongteasdale.com · 2345 Grand Boulevard, Suite 2000 · Kansas City, MO 64108-2617 · 816-221-3420

Sue K. Willman · Spencer Fane Britt & Browne · http://www.spencerfane.com · 1000 Walnut Street, Suite 1400 · Kansas City, MO 64106-2140 · 816-474-8100

David L. Wing · Spencer Fane Britt & Browne · http://www.spencerfane.com · 1000 Walnut Street, Suite 1400 · Kansas City, MO 64106-2140 · 816-474-8100

Springfield

Virginia L. Fry · Husch Blackwell Sanders · http://www.huschblackwell.com · The Hammons Tower, Suite 1900 · 901 St. Louis Street · Springfield, MO 65806 · 417-268-4000

Paul W. King · Paul W. King · The Hammons Tower, Suite 1501 · 901 St. Louis Street · Springfield, MO 65806-2505 · 417-862-6100

St. Louis

Michael J. Bobroff · Bobroff, Hesse, Lindmark & Martone · 1650 Des Peres Road, Suite 200 · St. Louis, MO 63131 · 314-862-0300

Michael P. Burke · Bryan Cave · One Metropolitan Square, Suite 3600 · 211 North Broadway · St. Louis, MO 63102-2750 · 314-259-2000

James K. Cook · ㉕ · Schuchat, Cook & Werner · The Shell Building, Second Floor · 1221 Locust Street · St. Louis, MO 63103-2364 · 314-621-2626

Jerome A. Diekemper · ㉕ · Jerome A. Diekemper · 7730 Carondelet Avenue, Suite 200 · St. Louis, MO 63105 · 314-727-1015

Jerome J. Dobson · Dobson, Goldberg, Moreland & Berns · 906 Olive Street, Suite 900 · St. Louis, MO 63101 · 314-621-8363

Dennis C. Donnelly · ⑳ · Bryan Cave · One Metropolitan Square, Suite 3600 · 211 North Broadway · St. Louis, MO 63102-2750 · 314-259-2000

Charles S. Elbert · Kohn, Shands, Elbert, Gianoulakis & Giljum · One U.S. Bank Plaza, Suite 2410 · 505 North Seventh Street · St. Louis, MO 63101 · 314-241-3963

Clifford A. Godiner · Thompson Coburn · One U.S. Bank Plaza · St. Louis, MO 63101-1611 · 314-552-6000

Christopher T. Hexter · Schuchat, Cook & Werner · The Shell Building, Second Floor · 1221 Locust Street · St. Louis, MO 63103-2364 · 314-621-2626

Jerry M. Hunter · Bryan Cave · One Metropolitan Square, Suite 3600 · 211 North Broadway · St. Louis, MO 63102-2750 · 314-259-2000

Richard E. Jaudes · Thompson Coburn · One U.S. Bank Plaza · St. Louis, MO 63101-1611 · 314-552-6000

Robert A. Kaiser · Armstrong Teasdale · http://www.armstrongteasdale.com · One Metropolitan Square, Suite 2600 · 211 North Broadway · St. Louis, MO 63102-2740 · 314-621-5070

Fred Leicht, Jr. · ⑳ · Armstrong Teasdale · http://www.armstrongteasdale.com · One Metropolitan Square, Suite 2600 · 211 North Broadway · St. Louis, MO 63102-2740 · 314-621-5070

Ned O. Lemkemeier · ⑳ · Bryan Cave · One Metropolitan Square, Suite 3600 · 211 North Broadway · St. Louis, MO 63102-2750 · 314-259-2000

Arthur J. Martin · Schuchat, Cook & Werner · The Shell Building, Second Floor · 1221 Locust Street · St. Louis, MO 63103-2364 · 314-621-2626

Thomas O. McCarthy · ⑩ · McMahon Berger · 2730 North Ballas Road, Suite 200 · P.O. Box 31901 · St. Louis, MO 63131-3039 · 314-567-7350

Vance D. Miller · Armstrong Teasdale · http://www.armstrongteasdale.com · One Metropolitan Square, Suite 2600 · 211 North Broadway · St. Louis, MO 63102-2740 · 314-621-5070

Howard Kent Munson · The Stolar Partnership · http://www.stolarlaw.com · The Lammert Building · 911 Washington Avenue · St. Louis, MO 63101-1290 · 314-231-2800

Daniel K. O'Toole · Armstrong Teasdale · http://www.armstrongteasdale.com · One Metropolitan Square, Suite 2600 · 211 North Broadway · St. Louis, MO 63102-2740 · 314-621-5070

Mary Beth Ortbals · Greensfelder, Hemker & Gale · Equitable Building, Suite 2000 · 10 South Broadway St. Louis, MO 63102 · 314-241-9090

Susan Nell Rowe · The Stolar Partnership · http://www.stolarlaw.com · The Lammert Building · 911 Washington Avenue · St. Louis, MO 63101-1290 · 314-231-2800

Mary Anne Sedey · ⑩ · Sedey & Harper · 2711 Clifton Avenue · St. Louis, MO 63139 · 314-773-3566

George O. Suggs · Schuchat, Cook & Werner · The Shell Building, Second Floor · 1221 Locust Street · St. Louis, MO 63103-2364 · 314-621-2626

Marilyn S. Teitelbaum · Schuchat, Cook & Werner · The Shell Building, Second Floor · 1221 Locust Street · St. Louis, MO 63103-2364 · 314-621-2626

Robert J. Tomaso · Husch Blackwell Sanders · http://www.huschblackwell.com · 720 Olive Street, Suite 2400 · St. Louis, MO 63101 · 314-345-6000

Paul N. Venker · Williams Venker & Sanders · http://www.wvslaw.com · Bank of America Tower, 21st Floor · 100 North Broadway · St. Louis, MO 63102 · 314-345-5000

David W. Welch · ⑩ · Armstrong Teasdale · http://www.armstrongteasdale.com · One Metropolitan Square, Suite 2600 · 211 North Broadway · St. Louis, MO 63102-2740 · 314-621-5070

Harry W. Wellford, Jr. · Littler Mendelson · Two CityPlace Drive, Suite 200 · St. Louis, MO 63141 · 314-432-4797

Charles A. Werner · ㉕ · Schuchat, Cook & Werner · The Shell Building, Second Floor · 1221 Locust Street · St. Louis, MO 63103-2364 · 314-621-2626

David F. Yates · ⑩ · Polsinelli Shalton Flanigan Suelthaus · http://www.polsinelli.com · 7733 Forsyth Boulevard, Suite 1200 · St. Louis, MO 63105 · 314-889-8000

LAND USE & ZONING LAW

Clayton

Gary H. Feder · Husch Blackwell Sanders · http://www.huschblackwell.com · The Plaza in Clayton Office Tower, Suite 600 · 190 Carondelet Plaza · Clayton, MO 63105-3441 · 314-480-1500

John P. King · Lathrop & Gage · Pierre Laclede Center, Suite 400 · 7701 Forsyth Boulevard · Clayton, MO 63105 · 314-613-2800

David G. Richardson · Husch Blackwell Sanders · http://www.huschblackwell.com · The Plaza in Clayton Office Tower, Suite 600 · 190 Carondelet Plaza · Clayton, MO 63105-3441 · 314-480-1500

Gregory R. Smith · Husch Blackwell Sanders · http://www.huschblackwell.com · The Plaza in Clayton Office Tower, Suite 600 · 190 Carondelet Plaza · Clayton, MO 63105-3441 · 314-480-1500

Kansas City

James C. Bowers, Jr. · White Goss Bowers March Schulte & Weisenfels · 4510 Belleview Avenue, Suite 300 · Kansas City, MO 64111 · 816-753-9200

Stephen P. Chinn · Stinson Morrison Hecker · http://www.stinson.com · 1201 Walnut Street, Suite 2900 · Kansas City, MO 64106-2150 · 816-842-8600

Daniel R. Cofran · Spencer Fane Britt & Browne · http://www.spencerfane.com · 1000 Walnut Street, Suite 1400 · Kansas City, MO 64106-2140 · 816-474-8100

David A. Fenley · ⑩ · Husch Blackwell Sanders · http://www.huschblackwell.com · 4801 Main Street, Suite 1000 · Kansas City, MO 64112 · 816-983-8000

Aaron G. March · White Goss Bowers March Schulte & Weisenfels · 4510 Belleview Avenue, Suite 300 · Kansas City, MO 64111 · 816-753-9200

Charles F. Miller · ⑩ · Lewis, Rice & Fingersh · One Petticoat Lane, Suite 500 · 1010 Walnut Street · Kansas City, MO 64106 · 816-421-2500

Jerome D. Riffel · Lathrop & Gage · 2345 Grand Boulevard, Suite 2800 · Kansas City, MO 64108 · 816-292-2000

Spencer R. Thomson · Husch Blackwell Sanders · http://www.huschblackwell.com · 4801 Main Street, Suite 1000 · Kansas City, MO 64112 · 816-983-8000

Michael T. White · ⑩ · White Goss Bowers March Schulte & Weisenfels · 4510 Belleview Avenue, Suite 300 · Kansas City, MO 64111 · 816-753-9200

St. Louis

Donald U. Beimdiek · ㉕ · Armstrong Teasdale · http://www.armstrongteasdale.com · One Metropolitan Square, Suite 2600 · 211 North Broadway · St. Louis, MO 63102-2740 · 314-621-5070

Craig S. Biesterfeld · ⑩ · Husch Blackwell Sanders · http://www.huschblackwell.com · 720 Olive Street, Suite 2400 · St. Louis, MO 63101 · 314-345-6000

Edward J. Griesedieck III · Herzog Crebs · 100 North Broadway, 14th Floor · St. Louis, MO 63102-2728 314-231-6700

Stephen L. Kling, Jr. · Jenkins & Kling · http://www.jenkinskling.com · 10 South Brentwood, Suite 200 · St. Louis, MO 63105 · 314-721-2525

S. Jerome Pratter · The Stolar Partnership · http://www.stolarlaw.com · The Lammert Building · 911 Washington Avenue · St. Louis, MO 63101-1290 · 314-231-2800

Timothy J. Tryniecki · Armstrong Teasdale · http://www.armstrongteasdale.com · One Metropolitan Square, Suite 2600 · 211 North Broadway · St. Louis, MO 63102-2740 · 314-621-5070

LEGAL MALPRACTICE LAW

Clayton

Alan E. Popkin · ⑩ · Husch Blackwell Sanders · http://www.huschblackwell.com · The Plaza in Clayton Office Tower, Suite 600 · 190 Carondelet Plaza · Clayton, MO 63105-3441 · 314-480-1500

Kansas City

Arthur A. Benson II · ⑩ · Benson & Associates · http://www.bensonlaw.com · 4006 Central Street · P.O. Box 119007 · Kansas City, MO 64171-9007 · 816-531-6565

Spencer J. Brown · ⑳ · Deacy and Deacy · http://www.deacylawfirm.com · Ten Main Center, Suite 1900 920 Main Street · Kansas City, MO 64105 · 816-421-4000

Daniel E. Hamann · Deacy and Deacy · http://www.deacylawfirm.com · Ten Main Center, Suite 1900 · 920 Main Street · Kansas City, MO 64105 · 816-421-4000

Springfield

Kent O. Hyde · Hyde, Love & Overby · 1121 South Glenstone · Springfield, MO 65807 · 417-831-4046

St. Louis

Brent W. Baldwin · ⑩ · Lathrop & Gage · The Equitable Building, Suite 1300 · 10 South Broadway · St. Louis, MO 63102-1708 · 314-613-2500

John Gianoulakis · Kohn, Shands, Elbert, Gianoulakis & Giljum · One U.S. Bank Plaza, Suite 2410 · 505 North Seventh Street · St. Louis, MO 63101 · 314-241-3963

Alan C. Kohn · ⑩ · Kohn, Shands, Elbert, Gianoulakis & Giljum · One U.S. Bank Plaza, Suite 2410 · 505 North Seventh Street · St. Louis, MO 63101 · 314-241-3963

Paul E. Kovacs · ⑩ · Armstrong Teasdale · http://www.armstrongteasdale.com · One Metropolitan Square, Suite 2600 · 211 North Broadway · St. Louis, MO 63102-2740 · 314-621-5070

Robert F. Ritter · ⑩ · Gray, Ritter & Graham · http://www.grayrittergraham.com · Gateway One on The Mall, Suite 800 · 701 Market Street · St. Louis, MO 63101-1826 · 314-241-5620

Robert S. Rosenthal · ⑩ · Brown & James · http://www.bjpc.com · 1010 Market Street, 20th Floor · St. Louis, MO 63101-2000 · 314-421-3400

Richard C. Wuestling · Wuestling & James · http://www.wuestlingandjames.com · The Laclede Gas Building, Suite 2020 · 720 Olive Street · St. Louis, MO 63101 · 314-421-6500

LEVERAGED BUYOUTS AND PRIVATE EQUITY LAW

Kansas City

Steven F. Carman · Husch Blackwell Sanders · http://www.huschblackwell.com · 4801 Main Street, Suite 1000 · Kansas City, MO 64112 · 816-983-8000

Michael J. Van Dyke · Sonnenschein Nath & Rosenthal · 4520 Main Street, Suite 1100 · Kansas City, MO 64111-7700 · 816-460-2400

Kip A. Wiggins · Stinson Morrison Hecker · http://www.stinson.com · 1201 Walnut Street, Suite 2900 · Kansas City, MO 64106-2150 · 816-842-8600

MARITIME LAW

St. Louis

Alan K. Goldstein · ⑩ · Goldstein and Price · One Memorial Drive, Suite 1000 · St. Louis, MO 63102 · 314-421-0710

John R. Halpern · ⑩ · Goldstein and Price · One Memorial Drive, Suite 1000 · St. Louis, MO 63102 · 314-421-0710

Raymond L. Massey · ⑩ · Thompson Coburn · One U.S. Bank Plaza · St. Louis, MO 63101-1611 · 314-552-6000

Michael D. O'Keefe · ⑩ · Thompson Coburn · One U.S. Bank Plaza · St. Louis, MO 63101-1611 · 314-552-6000

Gary T. Sacks · ⑩ · Goldstein and Price · One Memorial Drive, Suite 1000 · St. Louis, MO 63102 · 314-421-0710

Daryl F. Sohn · ⑩ · Goldstein and Price · One Memorial Drive, Suite 1000 · St. Louis, MO 63102 · 314-421-0710

MASS TORT LITIGATION

Clayton

Kenneth R. Heineman · Husch Blackwell Sanders · http://www.huschblackwell.com · The Plaza in Clayton Office Tower, Suite 600 · 190 Carondelet Plaza · Clayton, MO 63105-3441 · 314-480-1500

Kansas City

Douglas R. Dalgleish · Lathrop & Gage · 2345 Grand Boulevard, Suite 2800 · Kansas City, MO 64108 · 816-292-2000

Dennis J. Dobbels · Polsinelli Shalton Flanigan Suelthaus · http://www.polsinelli.com · 700 West 47th Street, Suite 1000 · Kansas City, MO 64112 · 816-753-1000

David R. Erickson · Shook, Hardy & Bacon · 2555 Grand Boulevard · Kansas City, MO 64108 · 816-474-6550

Thomas P. Schult · Berkowitz Oliver Williams Shaw & Eisenbrandt · 2600 Grand Boulevard, Suite 1200 · Kansas City, MO 64108 · 816-561-7007

Springfield

Gary R. Cunningham · Lathrop & Gage · 1845 South National · P.O. Box 4288 · Springfield, MO 65804 · 417-886-2000

St. Louis

Raymond R. Fournie · Armstrong Teasdale · http://www.armstrongteasdale.com · One Metropolitan Square, Suite 2600 · 211 North Broadway · St. Louis, MO 63102-2740 · 314-621-5070

Michael B. Minton · Thompson Coburn · One U.S. Bank Plaza · St. Louis, MO 63101-1611 · 314-552-6000

MEDIA LAW

St. Louis

Michael A. Kahn · Bryan Cave · One Metropolitan Square, Suite 3600 · 211 North Broadway · St. Louis, MO 63102-2750 · 314-259-2000

Joseph E. Martineau · Lewis, Rice & Fingersh · 500 North Broadway, Suite 2000 · St. Louis, MO 63102-2147 · 314-444-7600

Mark Sableman · ⑩ · Thompson Coburn · One U.S. Bank Plaza · St. Louis, MO 63101-1611 · 314-552-6000

MEDICAL MALPRACTICE LAW

Kansas City

P. John Brady · Shughart Thomson & Kilroy · http://www.stklaw.com · 12 Wyandotte Plaza, Suite 1800 · 120 West 12th Street · Kansas City, MO 64105 · 816-421-3355

Thomas P. Cartmell · Wagstaff & Cartmell · 4740 Grand Avenue, Suite 300 · Kansas City, MO 64112 · 816-701-1100

James D. Griffin · ⑩ · Husch Blackwell Sanders · http://www.huschblackwell.com · 4801 Main Street, Suite 1000 · Kansas City, MO 64112 · 816-983-8000

Robert A. Henderson · Shughart Thomson & Kilroy · http://www.stklaw.com · 12 Wyandotte Plaza, Suite 1800 · 120 West 12th Street · Kansas City, MO 64105 · 816-421-3355

Lynn R. Johnson · ⑳ · Shamberg, Johnson & Bergman · http://www.sjblaw.com · 2600 Grand Boulevard, Suite 550 · Kansas City, MO 64108 · 816-474-0004

Thomas G. Kokoruda · ⑩ · Shughart Thomson & Kilroy · http://www.stklaw.com · 12 Wyandotte Plaza, Suite 1800 · 120 West 12th Street · Kansas City, MO 64105 · 816-421-3355

William A. Lynch · Husch Blackwell Sanders · http://www.huschblackwell.com · 1200 Main Street, Suite 2300 · Kansas City, MO 64105 · 816-421-4800

Larry L. McMullen · ㉕ · Husch Blackwell Sanders · http://www.huschblackwell.com · 4801 Main Street, Suite 1000 · Kansas City, MO 64112 · 816-983-8000

Timothy W. Monsees · Monsees Miller Mayer Presley & Amick · 4717 Grand Avenue, Suite 820 · Kansas City, MO 64112-2258 · 816-361-5550

William Dirk Vandever · ⑩ · The Popham Law Firm · 712 Broadway, Suite 100 · Kansas City, MO 64105 · 816-221-2288

Lantz Welch · ㉕ · Lantz Welch · 10000 Northwest 75th Street · Kansas City, MO 64152 · 816-587-3773

Springfield

Monte P. Clithero · Taylor, Stafford, Clithero, Fitzgerald & Harris · 3315 East Ridgeview, Suite 1000 · Springfield, MO 65804 · 417-887-2020

Kent O. Hyde · Hyde, Love & Overby · 1121 South Glenstone · Springfield, MO 65807 · 417-831-4046

St. Charles

James J. Hennelly · Hazelwood & Weber · 200 North Third Street · St. Charles, MO 63301 · 636-947-4700

St. Louis

Brent W. Baldwin · ⑩ · Lathrop & Gage · The Equitable Building, Suite 1300 · 10 South Broadway · St. Louis, MO 63102-1708 · 314-613-2500

Kenneth W. Bean · Sandberg, Phoenix & von Gontard · http://www.spvg.com · One City Centre, 15th Floor · 515 North Sixth Street · St. Louis, MO 63101-1880 · 314-231-3332

Anthony R. Behr · Behr, McCarter & Potter · 7777 Bonhomme Avenue, Suite 1400 · St. Louis, MO 63105 · 314-862-3800

Kenneth C. Brostron · ⑩ · Lashly & Baer · 714 Locust Street · St. Louis, MO 63101 · 314-621-2939

David P. Ellington · Brown & James · http://www.bjpc.com · 1010 Market Street, 20th Floor · St. Louis, MO 63101-2000 · 314-421-3400

Timothy J. Gearin · Armstrong Teasdale · http://www.armstrongteasdale.com · One Metropolitan Square, Suite 2600 · 211 North Broadway · St. Louis, MO 63102-2740 · 314-621-5070

Maurice B. Graham · Gray, Ritter & Graham · http://www.grayrittergraham.com · Gateway One on The Mall, Suite 800 · 701 Market Street · St. Louis, MO 63101-1826 · 314-241-5620

Kevin F. O'Malley · Greensfelder, Hemker & Gale · Equitable Building, Suite 2000 · 10 South Broadway St. Louis, MO 63102 · 314-241-9090

G. Keith Phoenix · ⑩ · Sandberg, Phoenix & von Gontard · http://www.spvg.com · One City Centre, 15th Floor · 515 North Sixth Street · St. Louis, MO 63101-1880 · 314-231-3332

Jonathan Ries · Sandberg, Phoenix & von Gontard · http://www.spvg.com · One City Centre, 15th Floor · 515 North Sixth Street · St. Louis, MO 63101-1880 · 314-231-3332

Robert F. Ritter · ⑩ · Gray, Ritter & Graham · http://www.grayrittergraham.com · Gateway One on The Mall, Suite 800 · 701 Market Street · St. Louis, MO 63101-1826 · 314-241-5620

Robert S. Rosenthal · ⑩ · Brown & James · http://www.bjpc.com · 1010 Market Street, 20th Floor · St. Louis, MO 63101-2000 · 314-421-3400

Donald L. Schlapprizzi · ⑩ · Donald L. Schlapprizzi · Gateway One on The Mall, Suite 1550 · 701 Market Street · St. Louis, MO 63101 · 314-241-0763

Peter F. Spataro · Moser and Marsalek · St. Louis Place, Suite 700 · 200 North Broadway · St. Louis, MO 63102-2753 · 314-421-5364

Paul N. Venker · Williams Venker & Sanders · http://www.wvslaw.com · Bank of America Tower, 21st Floor · 100 North Broadway · St. Louis, MO 63102 · 314-345-5000

Peter von Gontard · Sandberg, Phoenix & von Gontard · http://www.spvg.com · One City Centre, 15th Floor · 515 North Sixth Street · St. Louis, MO 63101-1880 · 314-231-3332

John S. Wallach · Wallach & Wolff · 100 South Brentwood Boulevard, Suite 300 · St. Louis, MO 63105 · 314-241-2500

Philip L. Willman · Moser and Marsalek · St. Louis Place, Suite 700 · 200 North Broadway · St. Louis, MO 63102-2753 · 314-421-5364

Alvin A. Wolff, Jr. · Wallach & Wolff · 100 South Brentwood Boulevard, Suite 300 · St. Louis, MO 63105 314-241-2500

West Plains

H. Lynn Henry · Henry & Henry · http://www.henrylawfirm.com · 1207 Porter Wagoner Boulevard · P.O. Box 617 · West Plains, MO 65775-1826 · 417-256-8133

MERGERS & ACQUISITIONS LAW

Clayton

Mary Anne O'Connell · Husch Blackwell Sanders · http://www.huschblackwell.com · The Plaza in Clayton Office Tower, Suite 600 · 190 Carondelet Plaza · Clayton, MO 63105-3441 · 314-480-1500

Kansas City

James W. Allen · Stinson Morrison Hecker · http://www.stinson.com · 1201 Walnut Street, Suite 2900 · Kansas City, MO 64106-2150 · 816-842-8600

James M. Ash · ⑩ · Husch Blackwell Sanders · http://www.huschblackwell.com · 4801 Main Street, Suite 1000 · Kansas City, MO 64112 · 816-983-8000

Robert M. Barnes · Bryan Cave · One Kansas City Place, Suite 3500 · 1200 Main Street · Kansas City, MO 64105-2100 · 816-374-3200

Craig L. Evans · Stinson Morrison Hecker · http://www.stinson.com · 1201 Walnut Street, Suite 2900 · Kansas City, MO 64106-2150 · 816-842-8600

G. Robert Fisher · ⑩ · Sonnenschein Nath & Rosenthal · 4520 Main Street, Suite 1100 · Kansas City, MO 64111-7700 · 816-460-2400

James G. Goettsch · Husch Blackwell Sanders · http://www.huschblackwell.com · 4801 Main Street, Suite 1000 · Kansas City, MO 64112 · 816-983-8000

John A. Granda · ⑩ · Stinson Morrison Hecker · http://www.stinson.com · 1201 Walnut Street, Suite 2900 Kansas City, MO 64106-2150 · 816-842-8600

Gregory G. Johnson · Bryan Cave · One Kansas City Place, Suite 3500 · 1200 Main Street · Kansas City, MO 64105-2100 · 816-374-3200

Mike W. Lochmann · Stinson Morrison Hecker · http://www.stinson.com · 1201 Walnut Street, Suite 2900 · Kansas City, MO 64106-2150 · 816-842-8600

C. Robert Monroe · Stinson Morrison Hecker · http://www.stinson.com · 1201 Walnut Street, Suite 2900 · Kansas City, MO 64106-2150 · 816-842-8600

James A. Polsinelli · ⑩ · Polsinelli Shalton Flanigan Suelthaus · http://www.polsinelli.com · 700 West 47th Street, Suite 1000 · Kansas City, MO 64112 · 816-753-1000

James P. Pryde · Bryan Cave · One Kansas City Place, Suite 3500 · 1200 Main Street · Kansas City, MO 64105-2100 · 816-374-3200

St. Louis

Brian Bouquet · Lewis, Rice & Fingersh · 500 North Broadway, Suite 2000 · St. Louis, MO 63102-2147 · 314-444-7600

Donald B. Dorwart · Thompson Coburn · One U.S. Bank Plaza · St. Louis, MO 63101-1611 · 314-552-6000

Thomas C. Erb · Lewis, Rice & Fingersh · 500 North Broadway, Suite 2000 · St. Louis, MO 63102-2147 · 314-444-7600

John W. Finger · Stinson Morrison Hecker · http://www.stinson.com · 100 South Fourth Street, Suite 700 St. Louis, MO 63102 · 314-259-4500

Robert M. LaRose · Thompson Coburn · One U.S. Bank Plaza · St. Louis, MO 63101-1611 · 314-552-6000

Don G. Lents · ⑩ · Bryan Cave · One Metropolitan Square, Suite 3600 · 211 North Broadway · St. Louis, MO 63102-2750 · 314-259-2000

Thomas A. Litz · Thompson Coburn · One U.S. Bank Plaza · St. Louis, MO 63101-1611 · 314-552-6000

Thomas A. Prince · Husch Blackwell Sanders · http://www.huschblackwell.com · 720 Olive Street, Suite 2400 · St. Louis, MO 63101 · 314-345-6000

John K. Pruellage · Lewis, Rice & Fingersh · 500 North Broadway, Suite 2000 · St. Louis, MO 63102-2147 · 314-444-7600

Joseph S. von Kaenel · Armstrong Teasdale · http://www.armstrongteasdale.com · One Metropolitan Square, Suite 2600 · 211 North Broadway · St. Louis, MO 63102-2740 · 314-621-5070

R. Randall Wang · Bryan Cave · One Metropolitan Square, Suite 3600 · 211 North Broadway · St. Louis, MO 63102-2750 · 314-259-2000

MUNICIPAL LAW

Kansas City

Gary A. Anderson · Gilmore & Bell · 2405 Grand Boulevard, Suite 1100 · Kansas City, MO 64108 · 816-221-1000

Stephen P. Chinn · Stinson Morrison Hecker · http://www.stinson.com · 1201 Walnut Street, Suite 2900 · Kansas City, MO 64106-2150 · 816-842-8600

St. Charles

Wm. Randolph Weber · Hazelwood & Weber · 200 North Third Street · St. Charles, MO 63301 · 636-947-4700

St. Louis

D. Keith Henson · Paule, Camazine & Blumenthal · 165 North Meramec Avenue, Sixth Floor · St. Louis, MO 63105 · 314-727-2266

John M. Hessel · Lewis, Rice & Fingersh · 500 North Broadway, Suite 2000 · St. Louis, MO 63102-2147 · 314-444-7600

Kevin M. O'Keefe · Curtis, Heinz, Garrett & O'Keefe · 130 South Bemiston Avenue, Suite 200 · St. Louis, MO 63105-1913 · 314-725-8788

Stephen M. Ryals · Ryals & Breed · 3120 Locust Street · St. Louis, MO 63103 · 314-862-6262

Helmut Starr · Polsinelli Shalton Flanigan Suelthaus · http://www.polsinelli.com · 7733 Forsyth Boulevard, Suite 1200 · St. Louis, MO 63105 · 314-889-8000

MUTUAL FUNDS LAW

St. Louis

Dee Anne Sjogren · Thompson Coburn · One U.S. Bank Plaza · St. Louis, MO 63101-1611 · 314-552-6000

NON-PROFIT/CHARITIES LAW

Jefferson City

Charles W. Hatfield · Stinson Morrison Hecker · http://www.stinson.com · 230 West McCarty Street · Jefferson City, MO 65101 · 573-636-6263

Kansas City

Douglas Anning · Polsinelli Shalton Flanigan Suelthaus · http://www.polsinelli.com · 700 West 47th Street, Suite 1000 · Kansas City, MO 64112 · 816-753-1000

Bruce C. Davison · Sonnenschein Nath & Rosenthal · 4520 Main Street, Suite 1100 · Kansas City, MO 64111-7700 · 816-460-2400

Virginia C. Gross · Polsinelli Shalton Flanigan Suelthaus · http://www.polsinelli.com · 700 West 47th Street, Suite 1000 · Kansas City, MO 64112 · 816-753-1000

Bruce R. Hopkins · Polsinelli Shalton Flanigan Suelthaus · http://www.polsinelli.com · 700 West 47th Street, Suite 1000 · Kansas City, MO 64112 · 816-753-1000

Russell D. Jones · Lathrop & Gage · 2345 Grand Boulevard, Suite 2800 · Kansas City, MO 64108 · 816-292-2000

Patrick E. McGrath · Wallace, Saunders, Austin, Brown & Enochs · 2300 Main Street, Ninth Floor · Kansas City, MO 64108 · 816-942-8080

St. Louis

Lawrence P. Katzenstein · ⑳ · Thompson Coburn · One U.S. Bank Plaza · St. Louis, MO 63101-1611 · 314-552-6000

David J. Krauss · ⑩ · The Stolar Partnership · http://www.stolarlaw.com · The Lammert Building · 911 Washington Avenue · St. Louis, MO 63101-1290 · 314-231-2800

Richard L. Lawton · ⑩ · Thompson Coburn · One U.S. Bank Plaza · St. Louis, MO 63101-1611 · 314-552-6000

Leonard J. Pranschke · The Stolar Partnership · http://www.stolarlaw.com · The Lammert Building · 911 Washington Avenue · St. Louis, MO 63101-1290 · 314-231-2800

NON-WHITE-COLLAR CRIMINAL DEFENSE

Clayton

Paul J. D'Agrosa · Wolff and D'Agrosa · 8019 Forsyth Boulevard · Clayton, MO 63105 · 314-725-8019

Arthur S. Margulis · Margulis Grant & Margulis · 11 South Meramec Avenue, Suite 1330 · Clayton, MO 63105-1716 · 314-721-6677

Donald L. Wolff · ㉕ · Wolff and D'Agrosa · 8019 Forsyth Boulevard · Clayton, MO 63105 · 314-725-8019

Columbia

Patrick J. Eng · Eng & Woods · 903 East Ash Street · Columbia, MO 65201 · 573-874-4190

Dan Viets · Dan Viets · 15 North 10th Street · Columbia, MO 65201 · 573-443-6866

Independence

Robert C. Welch · ㉕ · Welch, Martin & Albano · 311 West Kansas Avenue · Independence, MO 64050 · 816-836-8000

Jefferson City

Joseph Bednar · Armstrong Teasdale · http://www.armstrongteasdale.com · 3405 West Truman Boulevard, Suite 210 · Jefferson City, MO 65109-5713 · 573-636-8394

Kansas City

W. Brian Gaddy · Gaddy Geiger & Brown · 2345 Grand Boulevard, Suite 675 · Kansas City, MO 64108 · 816-221-8989

Gerald M. Handley · ㉕ · Gerald M. Handley · 1100 Main Street, Suite 2800 · Kansas City, MO 64105 · 816-471-7145

James R. Hobbs · ⑩ · Wyrsch Hobbs & Mirakian · 1000 Walnut Street, Suite 1600 · Kansas City, MO 64106 · 816-221-0080

Bruce C. Houdek · ⑩ · Bruce C. Houdek · 818 Grand Avenue · Kansas City, MO 64106 · 816-842-2575

Patrick A. McInerney · Husch Blackwell Sanders · http://www.huschblackwell.com · 4801 Main Street, Suite 1000 · Kansas City, MO 64112 · 816-983-8000

John P. O'Connor · Wagstaff & Cartmell · 4740 Grand Avenue, Suite 300 · Kansas City, MO 64112 · 816-701-1100

Kevin E. J. Regan · The Regan Law Firm · http://www.reganlawfirm.com · 1821 Wyandotte Street, Suite 200 · Kansas City, MO 64108 · 816-221-5357

Charles M. Rogers · Wyrsch Hobbs & Mirakian · 1000 Walnut Street, Suite 1600 · Kansas City, MO 64106 · 816-221-0080

Bruce W. Simon · ⑩ · Simon and Simon · 105 East Fifth Street, Suite 201 · Kansas City, MO 64106-1179 816-471-3430

James R. Wyrsch · ㉕ · Wyrsch Hobbs & Mirakian · 1000 Walnut Street, Suite 1600 · Kansas City, MO 64106 · 816-221-0080

Springfield

Thomas D. Carver · Thomas D. Carver · 2103 East Sunshine · Springfield, MO 65806 · 417-886-3330

Joseph S. Passanise · The Law Offices of Dee Wampler and Joseph Passanise · 2974 East Battlefield · Springfield, MO 65804 · 417-882-9300

Dee Wampler · The Law Offices of Dee Wampler and Joseph Passanise · 2974 East Battlefield · Springfield, MO 65804 · 417-882-9300

St. Louis

Irl B. Baris · ㉕ · Baris Law Firm · The Shell Building, 10th Floor · 1221 Locust Street · St. Louis, MO 63103 · 314-421-6644

N. Scott Rosenblum · Rosenblum, Schwartz, Rogers & Glass · 120 South Central Avenue, Suite 130 · St. Louis, MO 63105 · 314-862-4332

Burton H. Shostak · Shostak & Shostak · The Berkley Building · 8015 Forsyth Boulevard · St. Louis, MO 63105 · 314-725-3200

Richard H. Sindel · Sindel, Sindel & Noble · 8008 Carondelet, Suite 301 · St. Louis, MO 63105 · 314-721-6040

OIL & GAS LAW

Jefferson City

James C. Swearengen · ⑩ · Brydon, Swearengen & England · http://www.brydonlaw.com · 312 East Capitol Avenue · P.O. Box 456 · Jefferson City, MO 65102-0456 · 573-635-7166

PERSONAL INJURY LITIGATION

Clayton

James E. Hullverson, Jr. · ㉕ · Hullverson & Hullverson · The Sevens Building, Suite 1616 · 7777 Bonhomme Avenue · Clayton, MO 63105 · 314-725-1616

Independence

Kenneth B. McClain · Humphrey Farrington & McClain · 221 West Lexington Avenue, Suite 400 · P.O. Box 900 · Independence, MO 64051 · 816-836-5050

Jefferson City

Dale C. Doerhoff · ⑩ · Cook, Vetter, Doerhoff and Landwehr · 231 Madison Street · Jefferson City, MO 65101 · 573-635-7977

J. Kent Lowry · Armstrong Teasdale · http://www.armstrongteasdale.com · 3405 West Truman Boulevard, Suite 210 · Jefferson City, MO 65109-5713 · 573-636-8394

Joplin

Edward James Hershewe · The Hershewe Law Firm · 431 South Virginia Avenue · Joplin, MO 64801-2399 · 417-782-3790

Kansas City

Robert T. Adams · Shook, Hardy & Bacon · 2555 Grand Boulevard · Kansas City, MO 64108 · 816-474-6550

Dale L. Beckerman · Deacy and Deacy · http://www.deacylawfirm.com · Ten Main Center, Suite 1900 · 920 Main Street · Kansas City, MO 64105 · 816-421-4000

Victor A. Bergman · ⑳ · Shamberg, Johnson & Bergman · http://www.sjblaw.com · 2600 Grand Boulevard, Suite 550 · Kansas City, MO 64108 · 816-474-0004

Scott S. Bethune · Davis, Bethune & Jones · 1100 Main Street, Suite 2930 · Kansas City, MO 64105 · 816-421-1600

James R. Borthwick · Husch Blackwell Sanders · http://www.huschblackwell.com · 4801 Main Street, Suite 1000 · Kansas City, MO 64112 · 816-983-8000

P. John Brady · Shughart Thomson & Kilroy · http://www.stklaw.com · 12 Wyandotte Plaza, Suite 1800 · 120 West 12th Street · Kansas City, MO 64105 · 816-421-3355

Spencer J. Brown · ⑳ · Deacy and Deacy · http://www.deacylawfirm.com · Ten Main Center, Suite 1900 920 Main Street · Kansas City, MO 64105 · 816-421-4000

Thomas P. Cartmell · Wagstaff & Cartmell · 4740 Grand Avenue, Suite 300 · Kansas City, MO 64112 · 816-701-1100

Douglas R. Dalgleish · Lathrop & Gage · 2345 Grand Boulevard, Suite 2800 · Kansas City, MO 64108 · 816-292-2000

Grant L. Davis · Davis, Bethune & Jones · 1100 Main Street, Suite 2930 · Kansas City, MO 64105 · 816-421-1600

Tim E. Dollar · The Law Offices of Dollar, Burns & Becker · 1100 Main Street, Suite 2600 · Kansas City, MO 64105 · 816-221-3443

W. James Foland · ⑩ · Foland, Wickens, Eisfelder, Roper & Hofer · Commerce Tower Building, Suite 3000 · 911 Main Street · Kansas City, MO 64105 · 816-472-7474

James D. Griffin · ⑩ · Husch Blackwell Sanders · http://www.huschblackwell.com · 4801 Main Street, Suite 1000 · Kansas City, MO 64112 · 816-983-8000

Robert A. Henderson · Shughart Thomson & Kilroy · http://www.stklaw.com · 12 Wyandotte Plaza, Suite 1800 · 120 West 12th Street · Kansas City, MO 64105 · 816-421-3355

Sylvester James, Jr. · Sly James Firm · 802 Broadway, Seventh Floor · Kansas City, MO 64105 · 816-472-6800

Lynn R. Johnson · ⑳ · Shamberg, Johnson & Bergman · http://www.sjblaw.com · 2600 Grand Boulevard, Suite 550 · Kansas City, MO 64108 · 816-474-0004

John S. Johnston · 10 · Shook, Hardy & Bacon · 2555 Grand Boulevard · Kansas City, MO 64108 · 816-474-6550

John M. Klamann · Klamann & Hubbard · 929 Walnut Street, Suite 800 · Kansas City, MO 64106 · 816-421-2626

Thomas G. Kokoruda · 10 · Shughart Thomson & Kilroy · http://www.stklaw.com · 12 Wyandotte Plaza, Suite 1800 · 120 West 12th Street · Kansas City, MO 64105 · 816-421-3355

John W. Kurtz · Hubbard & Kurtz · 1718 Walnut Street · Kansas City, MO 64108 · 816-472-4673

C. Patrick McLarney · 20 · Shook, Hardy & Bacon · 2555 Grand Boulevard · Kansas City, MO 64108 · 816-474-6550

Richard E. McLeod · 10 · McLeod and Heinricks · http://www.mcleodlaw.com · City Center Square, Suite 2900 · 1100 Main Street · Kansas City, MO 64105 · 816-421-5656

Larry L. McMullen · 25 · Husch Blackwell Sanders · http://www.huschblackwell.com · 4801 Main Street, Suite 1000 · Kansas City, MO 64112 · 816-983-8000

Stephen B. Millin, Jr. · 10 · Law Firm of Stephen B. Millin, Jr. · City Center Square, Suite 2800 · 1100 Main Street · Kansas City, MO 64105 · 816-842-1130

Kirk R. Presley · Monsees Miller Mayer Presley & Amick · 4717 Grand Avenue, Suite 820 · Kansas City, MO 64112-2258 · 816-361-5550

Gary C. Robb · Robb & Robb · http://www.robbrobb.com · One Kansas City Place, Suite 3900 · 1200 Main Street · Kansas City, MO 64105 · 816-474-8080

Joseph J. Roper · Foland, Wickens, Eisfelder, Roper & Hofer · Commerce Tower Building, Suite 3000 · 911 Main Street · Kansas City, MO 64105 · 816-472-7474

Scott W. Sayler · Shook, Hardy & Bacon · 2555 Grand Boulevard · Kansas City, MO 64108 · 816-474-6550

Todd A. Scharnhorst · Scharnhorst Ast & Kennard · http://www.sakfirm.com · 1000 Walnut, Suite 1550 · Kansas City, MO 64106 · 816-268-8300

Thomas P. Schult · Berkowitz Oliver Williams Shaw & Eisenbrandt · 2600 Grand Boulevard, Suite 1200 · Kansas City, MO 64108 · 816-561-7007

Andrew See · 10 · Shook, Hardy & Bacon · 2555 Grand Boulevard · Kansas City, MO 64108 · 816-474-6550

J. Stanley Sexton · 10 · Shook, Hardy & Bacon · 2555 Grand Boulevard · Kansas City, MO 64108 · 816-474-6550

Walter R. Simpson · 10 · Sanders & Simpson · 1125 Grand Boulevard, 15th Floor · Kansas City, MO 64106 · 816-471-6444

John E. Turner · 10 · Turner & Sweeny · 10401 Holmes Road, Suite 450 · Kansas City, MO 64131 · 816-942-5100

William Dirk Vandever · 10 · The Popham Law Firm · 712 Broadway, Suite 100 · Kansas City, MO 64105 · 816-221-2288

Thomas W. Wagstaff · Wagstaff & Cartmell · 4740 Grand Avenue, Suite 300 · Kansas City, MO 64112 · 816-701-1100

R. Lawrence Ward · ⑩ · Shughart Thomson & Kilroy · http://www.stklaw.com · 12 Wyandotte Plaza, Suite 1800 · 120 West 12th Street · Kansas City, MO 64105 · 816-421-3355

James M. Warden · ⑩ · Warden Triplett Grier · 420 Nichols Road, Suite 200 · Kansas City, MO 64112 · 816-877-8100

Lantz Welch · ㉕ · Lantz Welch · 10000 Northwest 75th Street · Kansas City, MO 64152 · 816-587-3773

W. Russell Welsh · Polsinelli Shalton Flanigan Suelthaus · http://www.polsinelli.com · 700 West 47th Street, Suite 1000 · Kansas City, MO 64112 · 816-753-1000

Paul L. Wickens · Foland, Wickens, Eisfelder, Roper & Hofer · Commerce Tower Building, Suite 3000 · 911 Main Street · Kansas City, MO 64105 · 816-472-7474

Lee's Summit

Cynthia Reams- Martin · Cynthia L. Reams-Martin · 408 Southeast Douglas · Lee's Summit, MO 64063 816-554-6444

Springfield

Monte P. Clithero · Taylor, Stafford, Clithero, Fitzgerald & Harris · 3315 East Ridgeview, Suite 1000 · Springfield, MO 65804 · 417-887-2020

Gary R. Cunningham · Lathrop & Gage · 1845 South National · P.O. Box 4288 · Springfield, MO 65804 · 417-886-2000

Steven B. Garner · Strong, Garner & Bauer · 415 East Chestnut Expressway · Springfield, MO 65802 · 417-887-4300

Steven D. Harrell · Bartimus, Frickleton, Robertson & Gorny · 1442 East Bradford Parkway · Springfield, MO 65804 · 417-882-2112

Rodney E. Loomer · ⑩ · Turner, Reid, Duncan, Loomer & Patton · 1355 East Bradford Parkway, Suite A P.O. Box 4043 · Springfield, MO 65808 · 417-883-2102

Robert M. N. Palmer · Law Offices of Palmer Oliver · The Holland Building, Suite 511 · 205 Park Central East · P.O. Box 5720 · Springfield, MO 65801-5720 · 417-865-3234

Thomas G. Strong · ㉕ · Strong, Garner & Bauer · 415 East Chestnut Expressway · Springfield, MO 65802 · 417-887-4300

St. Charles

James J. Hennelly · Hazelwood & Weber · 200 North Third Street · St. Charles, MO 63301 · 636-947-4700

St. Joseph

R. Dan Boulware · Shughart Thomson & Kilroy · http://www.stklaw.com · 3101 Frederick Avenue · St. Joseph, MO 64506 · 816-364-2117

St. Louis

Brent W. Baldwin · ⑩ · Lathrop & Gage · The Equitable Building, Suite 1300 · 10 South Broadway · St. Louis, MO 63102-1708 · 314-613-2500

Dan H. Ball · Bryan Cave · One Metropolitan Square, Suite 3600 · 211 North Broadway · St. Louis, MO 63102-2750 · 314-259-2000

Kenneth W. Bean · Sandberg, Phoenix & von Gontard · http://www.spvg.com · One City Centre, 15th Floor · 515 North Sixth Street · St. Louis, MO 63101-1880 · 314-231-3332

Anthony R. Behr · Behr, McCarter & Potter · 7777 Bonhomme Avenue, Suite 1400 · St. Louis, MO 63105 · 314-862-3800

Kenneth C. Brostron · ⑩ · Lashly & Baer · 714 Locust Street · St. Louis, MO 63101 · 314-621-2939

Clark H. Cole · Armstrong Teasdale · http://www.armstrongteasdale.com · One Metropolitan Square, Suite 2600 · 211 North Broadway · St. Louis, MO 63102-2740 · 314-621-5070

Morry S. Cole · Gray, Ritter & Graham · http://www.grayrittergraham.com · Gateway One on The Mall, Suite 800 · 701 Market Street · St. Louis, MO 63101-1826 · 314-241-5620

William M. Corrigan, Jr. · Armstrong Teasdale · http://www.armstrongteasdale.com · One Metropolitan Square, Suite 2600 · 211 North Broadway · St. Louis, MO 63102-2740 · 314-621-5070

David P. Ellington · Brown & James · http://www.bjpc.com · 1010 Market Street, 20th Floor · St. Louis, MO 63101-2000 · 314-421-3400

Maurice B. Graham · Gray, Ritter & Graham · http://www.grayrittergraham.com · Gateway One on The Mall, Suite 800 · 701 Market Street · St. Louis, MO 63101-1826 · 314-241-5620

Lawrence B. Grebel · ⑩ · Brown & James · http://www.bjpc.com · 1010 Market Street, 20th Floor · St. Louis, MO 63101-2000 · 314-421-3400

Frank N. Gundlach · ⑩ · Armstrong Teasdale · http://www.armstrongteasdale.com · One Metropolitan Square, Suite 2600 · 211 North Broadway · St. Louis, MO 63102-2740 · 314-621-5070

Amy Collignon Gunn · Simon Passanante · 701 Market Street, Suite 1450 · St. Louis, MO 63101 · 314-241-2929

Patrick J. Hagerty · Gray, Ritter & Graham · http://www.grayrittergraham.com · Gateway One on The Mall, Suite 800 · 701 Market Street · St. Louis, MO 63101-1826 · 314-241-5620

Theodore H. Hoffman · ⑩ · Hoffman & Gelfman · 133 South 11th Street, Suite 310 · St. Louis, MO 63102 · 314-241-1020

James P. Holloran · ⑩ · Holloran, Stewart & Schwartz · 2000 South Eighth Street · St. Louis, MO 63104 314-621-2121

Paul E. Kovacs · ⑩ · Armstrong Teasdale · http://www.armstrongteasdale.com · One Metropolitan Square, Suite 2600 · 211 North Broadway · St. Louis, MO 63102-2740 · 314-621-5070

Nicholas J. Lamb · Thompson Coburn · One U.S. Bank Plaza · St. Louis, MO 63101-1611 · 314-552-6000

Theodore J. MacDonald, Jr. · Hepler, Broom, MacDonald, Hebrank, True & Noce · 800 Market Street, Suite 2300 · St. Louis, MO 63101 · 314-241-6160

Thomas J. Magee · Moser and Marsalek · St. Louis Place, Suite 700 · 200 North Broadway · St. Louis, MO 63102-2753 · 314-421-5364

John R. Musgrave · Thompson Coburn · One U.S. Bank Plaza · St. Louis, MO 63101-1611 · 314-552-6000

Gerard T. Noce · ⑩ · Hepler, Broom, MacDonald, Hebrank, True & Noce · 800 Market Street, Suite 2300 · St. Louis, MO 63101 · 314-241-6160

Kevin F. O'Malley · Greensfelder, Hemker & Gale · Equitable Building, Suite 2000 · 10 South Broadway St. Louis, MO 63102 · 314-241-9090

David G. Ott · Armstrong Teasdale · http://www.armstrongteasdale.com · One Metropolitan Square, Suite 2600 · 211 North Broadway · St. Louis, MO 63102-2740 · 314-621-5070

G. Keith Phoenix · ⑩ · Sandberg, Phoenix & von Gontard · http://www.spvg.com · One City Centre, 15th Floor · 515 North Sixth Street · St. Louis, MO 63101-1880 · 314-231-3332

Daniel T. Rabbitt · ⑳ · Rabbitt, Pitzer & Snodgrass · 100 South Fourth Street, Suite 400 · St. Louis, MO 63102-1821 · 314-421-5545

Stephen H. Ringkamp · Hullverson Law Firm · 1010 Market Street, Suite 1480 · St. Louis, MO 63101-2091 · 314-421-2313

Robert F. Ritter · ⑩ · Gray, Ritter & Graham · http://www.grayrittergraham.com · Gateway One on The Mall, Suite 800 · 701 Market Street · St. Louis, MO 63101-1826 · 314-241-5620

Sam P. Rynearson · ⑩ · Rynearson, Suess, Schnurbusch & Champion · One South Memorial Drive, Suite 1800 · St. Louis, MO 63102 · 314-421-4430

John S. Sandberg · Sandberg, Phoenix & von Gontard · http://www.spvg.com · One City Centre, 15th Floor · 515 North Sixth Street · St. Louis, MO 63101-1880 · 314-231-3332

Steven P. Sanders · ㉕ · Williams Venker & Sanders · http://www.wvslaw.com · Bank of America Tower, 21st Floor · 100 North Broadway · St. Louis, MO 63102 · 314-345-5000

Donald L. Schlapprizzi · ⑩ · Donald L. Schlapprizzi · Gateway One on The Mall, Suite 1550 · 701 Market Street · St. Louis, MO 63101 · 314-241-0763

Jerome J. Schlichter · Schlichter, Bogard & Denton · 100 South Fourth Street, Suite 900 · St. Louis, MO 63102 · 314-621-6115

John G. Simon · Simon Passanante · 701 Market Street, Suite 1450 · St. Louis, MO 63101 · 314-241-2929

Gary E. Snodgrass · Rabbitt, Pitzer & Snodgrass · 100 South Fourth Street, Suite 400 · St. Louis, MO 63102-1821 · 314-421-5545

Paul N. Venker · Williams Venker & Sanders · http://www.wvslaw.com · Bank of America Tower, 21st Floor · 100 North Broadway · St. Louis, MO 63102 · 314-345-5000

James J. Virtel · ⑩ · Armstrong Teasdale · http://www.armstrongteasdale.com · One Metropolitan Square, Suite 2600 · 211 North Broadway · St. Louis, MO 63102-2740 · 314-621-5070

Peter von Gontard · Sandberg, Phoenix & von Gontard · http://www.spvg.com · One City Centre, 15th Floor · 515 North Sixth Street · St. Louis, MO 63101-1880 · 314-231-3332

John S. Wallach · Wallach & Wolff · 100 South Brentwood Boulevard, Suite 300 · St. Louis, MO 63105 · 314-241-2500

Thomas C. Walsh · ⑩ · Bryan Cave · One Metropolitan Square, Suite 3600 · 211 North Broadway · St. Louis, MO 63102-2750 · 314-259-2000

Theodore J. Williams, Jr. · ⑩ · Williams Venker & Sanders · http://www.wvslaw.com · Bank of America Tower, 21st Floor · 100 North Broadway · St. Louis, MO 63102 · 314-345-5000

Stephen R. Woodley · Gray, Ritter & Graham · http://www.grayrittergraham.com · Gateway One on The Mall, Suite 800 · 701 Market Street · St. Louis, MO 63101-1826 · 314-241-5620

Richard C. Wuestling · Wuestling & James · http://www.wuestlingandjames.com · The Laclede Gas Building, Suite 2020 · 720 Olive Street · St. Louis, MO 63101 · 314-421-6500

West Plains

H. Lynn Henry · Henry & Henry · http://www.henrylawfirm.com · 1207 Porter Wagoner Boulevard · P.O. Box 617 · West Plains, MO 65775-1826 · 417-256-8133

PRODUCT LIABILITY LITIGATION

Columbia

W. Hamp Ford, Jr. · Ford, Parshall & Baker · 3210 Bluff Creek Drive · Columbia, MO 65201-3525 · 573-449-2613

Kansas City

Louis C. Accurso · Accurso Law Firm · 4646 Roanoke Parkway · Kansas City, MO 64112-1227 · 816-561-3900

Robert T. Adams · Shook, Hardy & Bacon · 2555 Grand Boulevard · Kansas City, MO 64108 · 816-474-6550

Victor A. Bergman · 20 · Shamberg, Johnson & Bergman · http://www.sjblaw.com · 2600 Grand Boulevard, Suite 550 · Kansas City, MO 64108 · 816-474-0004

Walter L. Cofer · Shook, Hardy & Bacon · 2555 Grand Boulevard · Kansas City, MO 64108 · 816-474-6550

W. James Foland · 10 · Foland, Wickens, Eisfelder, Roper & Hofer · Commerce Tower Building, Suite 3000 · 911 Main Street · Kansas City, MO 64105 · 816-472-7474

Robert A. Henderson · Shughart Thomson & Kilroy · http://www.stklaw.com · 12 Wyandotte Plaza, Suite 1800 · 120 West 12th Street · Kansas City, MO 64105 · 816-421-3355

Leonard J. Johnson · Stinson Morrison Hecker · http://www.stinson.com · 1201 Walnut Street, Suite 2900 · Kansas City, MO 64106-2150 · 816-842-8600

Lynn R. Johnson · 20 · Shamberg, Johnson & Bergman · http://www.sjblaw.com · 2600 Grand Boulevard, Suite 550 · Kansas City, MO 64108 · 816-474-0004

Harvey L. Kaplan · Shook, Hardy & Bacon · 2555 Grand Boulevard · Kansas City, MO 64108 · 816-474-6550

Gary R. Long · Shook, Hardy & Bacon · 2555 Grand Boulevard · Kansas City, MO 64108 · 816-474-6550

Craig S. O'Dear · Bryan Cave · One Kansas City Place, Suite 3500 · 1200 Main Street · Kansas City, MO 64105-2100 · 816-374-3200

David F. Oliver · Berkowitz Oliver Williams Shaw & Eisenbrandt · 2600 Grand Boulevard, Suite 1200 · Kansas City, MO 64108 · 816-561-7007

Gary C. Robb · Robb & Robb · http://www.robbrobb.com · One Kansas City Place, Suite 3900 · 1200 Main Street · Kansas City, MO 64105 · 816-474-8080

Thomas P. Schult · Berkowitz Oliver Williams Shaw & Eisenbrandt · 2600 Grand Boulevard, Suite 1200 · Kansas City, MO 64108 · 816-561-7007

John W. Shaw · Berkowitz Oliver Williams Shaw & Eisenbrandt · 2600 Grand Boulevard, Suite 1200 · Kansas City, MO 64108 · 816-561-7007

John E. Turner · ⑩ · Turner & Sweeny · 10401 Holmes Road, Suite 450 · Kansas City, MO 64131 · 816-942-5100

Lantz Welch · ㉕ · Lantz Welch · 10000 Northwest 75th Street · Kansas City, MO 64152 · 816-587-3773

W. Russell Welsh · Polsinelli Shalton Flanigan Suelthaus · http://www.polsinelli.com · 700 West 47th Street, Suite 1000 · Kansas City, MO 64112 · 816-753-1000

Marie S. Woodbury · Shook, Hardy & Bacon · 2555 Grand Boulevard · Kansas City, MO 64108 · 816-474-6550

Rolla

Daniel L. Birdsong · Thomas, Birdsong & Mills · 1100 North Elm Street · P.O. Box 248 · Rolla, MO 65402-0248 · 573-364-4097

Springfield

Gary R. Cunningham · Lathrop & Gage · 1845 South National · P.O. Box 4288 · Springfield, MO 65804 · 417-886-2000

Steven D. Harrell · Bartimus, Frickleton, Robertson & Gorny · 1442 East Bradford Parkway · Springfield, MO 65804 · 417-882-2112

Kent O. Hyde · Hyde, Love & Overby · 1121 South Glenstone · Springfield, MO 65807 · 417-831-4046

Rodney E. Loomer · ⑩ · Turner, Reid, Duncan, Loomer & Patton · 1355 East Bradford Parkway, Suite A P.O. Box 4043 · Springfield, MO 65808 · 417-883-2102

Robert M. N. Palmer · Law Offices of Palmer Oliver · The Holland Building, Suite 511 · 205 Park Central East · P.O. Box 5720 · Springfield, MO 65801-5720 · 417-865-3234

Michael J. Patton · Turner, Reid, Duncan, Loomer & Patton · 1355 East Bradford Parkway, Suite A · P.O. Box 4043 · Springfield, MO 65808 · 417-883-2102

Randy P. Scheer · Husch Blackwell Sanders · http://www.huschblackwell.com · The Hammons Tower, Suite 1900 · 901 St. Louis Street · Springfield, MO 65806 · 417-268-4000

St. Louis

Dan H. Ball · Bryan Cave · One Metropolitan Square, Suite 3600 · 211 North Broadway · St. Louis, MO 63102-2750 · 314-259-2000

Anthony R. Behr · Behr, McCarter & Potter · 7777 Bonhomme Avenue, Suite 1400 · St. Louis, MO 63105 · 314-862-3800

Lawrence B. Grebel · ⑩ · Brown & James · http://www.bjpc.com · 1010 Market Street, 20th Floor · St. Louis, MO 63101-2000 · 314-421-3400

Richard A. Mueller · Thompson Coburn · One U.S. Bank Plaza · St. Louis, MO 63101-1611 · 314-552-6000

G. Keith Phoenix · ⑩ · Sandberg, Phoenix & von Gontard · http://www.spvg.com · One City Centre, 15th Floor · 515 North Sixth Street · St. Louis, MO 63101-1880 · 314-231-3332

Jonathan Ries · Sandberg, Phoenix & von Gontard · http://www.spvg.com · One City Centre, 15th Floor · 515 North Sixth Street · St. Louis, MO 63101-1880 · 314-231-3332

Robert F. Ritter · ⑩ · Gray, Ritter & Graham · http://www.grayrittergraham.com · Gateway One on The Mall, Suite 800 · 701 Market Street · St. Louis, MO 63101-1826 · 314-241-5620

John S. Sandberg · Sandberg, Phoenix & von Gontard · http://www.spvg.com · One City Centre, 15th Floor · 515 North Sixth Street · St. Louis, MO 63101-1880 · 314-231-3332

Steven P. Sanders · ㉕ · Williams Venker & Sanders · http://www.wvslaw.com · Bank of America Tower, 21st Floor · 100 North Broadway · St. Louis, MO 63102 · 314-345-5000

John G. Simon · Simon Passanante · 701 Market Street, Suite 1450 · St. Louis, MO 63101 · 314-241-2929

Peter von Gontard · Sandberg, Phoenix & von Gontard · http://www.spvg.com · One City Centre, 15th Floor · 515 North Sixth Street · St. Louis, MO 63101-1880 · 314-231-3332

PROFESSIONAL MALPRACTICE LAW

Columbia

W. Hamp Ford, Jr. · Ford, Parshall & Baker · 3210 Bluff Creek Drive · Columbia, MO 65201-3525 · 573-449-2613

Kansas City

Lynn R. Johnson · ⑳ · Shamberg, Johnson & Bergman · http://www.sjblaw.com · 2600 Grand Boulevard, Suite 550 · Kansas City, MO 64108 · 816-474-0004

Rolla

Daniel L. Birdsong · Thomas, Birdsong & Mills · 1100 North Elm Street · P.O. Box 248 · Rolla, MO 65402-0248 · 573-364-4097

PROJECT FINANCE LAW

Kansas City

David W. Frantze · ⑩ · Stinson Morrison Hecker · http://www.stinson.com · 1201 Walnut Street, Suite 2900 · Kansas City, MO 64106-2150 · 816-842-8600

Webb R. Gilmore · Gilmore & Bell · 2405 Grand Boulevard, Suite 1100 · Kansas City, MO 64108 · 816-221-1000

Charles D. Horner · Husch Blackwell Sanders · http://www.huschblackwell.com · 4801 Main Street, Suite 1000 · Kansas City, MO 64112 · 816-983-8000

James W. Winn · Gilmore & Bell · 2405 Grand Boulevard, Suite 1100 · Kansas City, MO 64108 · 816-221-1000

St. Louis

O. Kirby Colson III · Armstrong Teasdale · http://www.armstrongteasdale.com · One Metropolitan Square, Suite 2600 · 211 North Broadway · St. Louis, MO 63102-2740 · 314-621-5070

Michael F. Lause · ⑩ · Thompson Coburn · One U.S. Bank Plaza · St. Louis, MO 63101-1611 · 314-552-6000

PUBLIC FINANCE LAW

Kansas City

Christopher D. Ahrens · Gilmore & Bell · 2405 Grand Boulevard, Suite 1100 · Kansas City, MO 64108 · 816-221-1000

Gary A. Anderson · Gilmore & Bell · 2405 Grand Boulevard, Suite 1100 · Kansas City, MO 64108 · 816-221-1000

E. Sid Douglas III · Gilmore & Bell · 2405 Grand Boulevard, Suite 1100 · Kansas City, MO 64108 · 816-221-1000

Webb R. Gilmore · Gilmore & Bell · 2405 Grand Boulevard, Suite 1100 · Kansas City, MO 64108 · 816-221-1000

Nancy N.C. Lear · Gilmore & Bell · 2405 Grand Boulevard, Suite 1100 · Kansas City, MO 64108 · 816-221-1000

Lynd K. Mische · Gilmore & Bell · 2405 Grand Boulevard, Suite 1100 · Kansas City, MO 64108 · 816-221-1000

David W. Queen · Gilmore & Bell · 2405 Grand Boulevard, Suite 1100 · Kansas City, MO 64108 · 816-221-1000

James W. Winn · Gilmore & Bell · 2405 Grand Boulevard, Suite 1100 · Kansas City, MO 64108 · 816-221-1000

Richard M. Wright, Jr. · Gilmore & Bell · 2405 Grand Boulevard, Suite 1100 · Kansas City, MO 64108 · 816-221-1000

St. Louis

Robert P. Ballsrud · Gilmore & Bell · One Metropolitan Square, Suite 2350 · 211 North Broadway · St. Louis, MO 63102 · 314-436-1000

Mark A. Boatman · Armstrong Teasdale · http://www.armstrongteasdale.com · One Metropolitan Square, Suite 2600 · 211 North Broadway · St. Louis, MO 63102-2740 · 314-621-5070

O. Kirby Colson III · Armstrong Teasdale · http://www.armstrongteasdale.com · One Metropolitan Square, Suite 2600 · 211 North Broadway · St. Louis, MO 63102-2740 · 314-621-5070

Mark D. Grimm · Gilmore & Bell · One Metropolitan Square, Suite 2350 · 211 North Broadway · St. Louis, MO 63102 · 314-436-1000

Claire Halpern · Gilmore & Bell · One Metropolitan Square, Suite 2350 · 211 North Broadway · St. Louis, MO 63102 · 314-436-1000

Michael F. Lause · ⑩ · Thompson Coburn · One U.S. Bank Plaza · St. Louis, MO 63101-1611 · 314-552-6000

Thomas E. Lowther · ⑩ · The Stolar Partnership · http://www.stolarlaw.com · The Lammert Building · 911 Washington Avenue · St. Louis, MO 63101-1290 · 314-231-2800

Linda M. Martinez · Bryan Cave · One Metropolitan Square, Suite 3600 · 211 North Broadway · St. Louis, MO 63102-2750 · 314-259-2000

James E. Mello · Armstrong Teasdale · http://www.armstrongteasdale.com · One Metropolitan Square, Suite 2600 · 211 North Broadway · St. Louis, MO 63102-2740 · 314-621-5070

RAILROAD LAW

Kansas City

Douglas R. Dalgleish · Lathrop & Gage · 2345 Grand Boulevard, Suite 2800 · Kansas City, MO 64108 · 816-292-2000

St. Louis

William A. Brasher · ⑩ · Brasher Law Firm · One Metropolitan Square, Suite 2300 · 211 North Broadway St. Louis, MO 63102 · 314-621-7700

C. Marshall Friedman · ⑩ · C. Marshall Friedman · 1010 Market Street, 13th Floor · St. Louis, MO 63101 · 314-621-8400

Nicholas J. Lamb · Thompson Coburn · One U.S. Bank Plaza · St. Louis, MO 63101-1611 · 314-552-6000

Jerome J. Schlichter · Schlichter, Bogard & Denton · 100 South Fourth Street, Suite 900 · St. Louis, MO 63102 · 314-621-6115

Theodore J. Williams, Jr. · ⑩ · Williams Venker & Sanders · http://www.wvslaw.com · Bank of America Tower, 21st Floor · 100 North Broadway · St. Louis, MO 63102 · 314-345-5000

REAL ESTATE LAW

Clayton

Gary H. Feder · Husch Blackwell Sanders · http://www.huschblackwell.com · The Plaza in Clayton Office Tower, Suite 600 · 190 Carondelet Plaza · Clayton, MO 63105-3441 · 314-480-1500

Gregory R. Smith · Husch Blackwell Sanders · http://www.huschblackwell.com · The Plaza in Clayton Office Tower, Suite 600 · 190 Carondelet Plaza · Clayton, MO 63105-3441 · 314-480-1500

Kansas City

Stephen T. Adams · ⑩ · Husch Blackwell Sanders · http://www.huschblackwell.com · 4801 Main Street, Suite 1000 · Kansas City, MO 64112 · 816-983-8000

Ralph E. Bellar, Jr. · Lewis, Rice & Fingersh · One Petticoat Lane, Suite 500 · 1010 Walnut Street · Kansas City, MO 64106 · 816-421-2500

William E. Carr · ⑩ · Lewis, Rice & Fingersh · One Petticoat Lane, Suite 500 · 1010 Walnut Street · Kansas City, MO 64106 · 816-421-2500

Carl J. Circo · ⑩ · Stinson Morrison Hecker · http://www.stinson.com · 1201 Walnut Street, Suite 2900 · Kansas City, MO 64106-2150 · 816-842-8600

Don F. Dagenais · Lathrop & Gage · 2345 Grand Boulevard, Suite 2800 · Kansas City, MO 64108 · 816-292-2000

Peter M. DiGiovanni · ⑩ · Lewis, Rice & Fingersh · One Petticoat Lane, Suite 500 · 1010 Walnut Street · Kansas City, MO 64106 · 816-421-2500

David A. Fenley · ⑩ · Husch Blackwell Sanders · http://www.huschblackwell.com · 4801 Main Street, Suite 1000 · Kansas City, MO 64112 · 816-983-8000

Jack N. Fingersh · ㉕ · Lewis, Rice & Fingersh · One Petticoat Lane, Suite 500 · 1010 Walnut Street · Kansas City, MO 64106 · 816-421-2500

David W. Frantze · ⑩ · Stinson Morrison Hecker · http://www.stinson.com · 1201 Walnut Street, Suite 2900 · Kansas City, MO 64106-2150 · 816-842-8600

John C. Hickey · ⑩ · Lewis, Rice & Fingersh · One Petticoat Lane, Suite 500 · 1010 Walnut Street · Kansas City, MO 64106 · 816-421-2500

Michele McCue · Lewis, Rice & Fingersh · One Petticoat Lane, Suite 500 · 1010 Walnut Street · Kansas City, MO 64106 · 816-421-2500

Charles F. Miller · ⑩ · Lewis, Rice & Fingersh · One Petticoat Lane, Suite 500 · 1010 Walnut Street · Kansas City, MO 64106 · 816-421-2500

Ford R. Nelson, Jr. · Armstrong Teasdale · http://www.armstrongteasdale.com · 2345 Grand Boulevard, Suite 2000 · Kansas City, MO 64108-2617 · 816-221-3420

Richard W. Scarritt · ㉕ · Spencer Fane Britt & Browne · http://www.spencerfane.com · 1000 Walnut Street, Suite 1400 · Kansas City, MO 64106-2140 · 816-474-8100

Lonnie J. Shalton · Polsinelli Shalton Flanigan Suelthaus · http://www.polsinelli.com · 700 West 47th Street, Suite 1000 · Kansas City, MO 64112 · 816-753-1000

John L. Snyder · Sonnenschein Nath & Rosenthal · 4520 Main Street, Suite 1100 · Kansas City, MO 64111-7700 · 816-460-2400

Springfield

Randell D. Wallace · Lathrop & Gage · 1845 South National · P.O. Box 4288 · Springfield, MO 65804 · 417-886-2000

St. Charles

Keith W. Hazelwood · Hazelwood & Weber · 200 North Third Street · St. Charles, MO 63301 · 636-947-4700

St. Louis

Fred E. Arnold · ㉕ · Thompson Coburn · One U.S. Bank Plaza · St. Louis, MO 63101-1611 · 314-552-6000

Donald U. Beimdiek · ㉕ · Armstrong Teasdale · http://www.armstrongteasdale.com · One Metropolitan Square, Suite 2600 · 211 North Broadway · St. Louis, MO 63102-2740 · 314-621-5070

Craig S. Biesterfeld · ⑩ · Husch Blackwell Sanders · http://www.huschblackwell.com · 720 Olive Street, Suite 2400 · St. Louis, MO 63101 · 314-345-6000

Christopher M. Blanton · ⑩ · The Stolar Partnership · http://www.stolarlaw.com · The Lammert Building · 911 Washington Avenue · St. Louis, MO 63101-1290 · 314-231-2800

John A. Blumenfeld · ㉕ · Stinson Morrison Hecker · http://www.stinson.com · 168 North Meramec Avenue, Suite 400 · St. Louis, MO 63105 · 314-863-0800

Alan B. Bornstein · Sonnenschein Nath & Rosenthal · One Metropolitan Square, Suite 3000 · 211 North Broadway · St. Louis, MO 63102-2741 · 314-241-1800

Harold R. Burroughs · Bryan Cave · One Metropolitan Square, Suite 3600 · 211 North Broadway · St. Louis, MO 63102-2750 · 314-259-2000

Michael A. Chivell · Armstrong Teasdale · http://www.armstrongteasdale.com · One Metropolitan Square, Suite 2600 · 211 North Broadway · St. Louis, MO 63102-2740 · 314-621-5070

Joseph A. Colagiovanni, Jr. · Sonnenschein Nath & Rosenthal · One Metropolitan Square, Suite 3000 · 211 North Broadway · St. Louis, MO 63102-2741 · 314-241-1800

Kathryn J. Giddings · The Stolar Partnership · http://www.stolarlaw.com · The Lammert Building · 911 Washington Avenue · St. Louis, MO 63101-1290 · 314-231-2800

Victoria G. Goldson · Bryan Cave · One Metropolitan Square, Suite 3600 · 211 North Broadway · St. Louis, MO 63102-2750 · 314-259-2000

Harvey A. Harris · ㉕ · The Stolar Partnership · http://www.stolarlaw.com · The Lammert Building · 911 Washington Avenue · St. Louis, MO 63101-1290 · 314-231-2800

Mark B. Hillis · ⑩ · Carmody MacDonald · 120 South Central, Suite 1800 · St. Louis, MO 63105-1705 · 314-854-8600

John W. Hoffman · Bryan Cave · One Metropolitan Square, Suite 3600 · 211 North Broadway · St. Louis, MO 63102-2750 · 314-259-2000

Lisa Greenman Kraner · Paster West & Kraner · http://www.pwklaw.com · 138 North Meramec Avenue · St. Louis, MO 63105 · 314-721-7080

Carl C. Lang · Rosenblum, Goldenhersh, Silverstein & Zafft · 7733 Forsyth Boulevard, Fourth Floor · St. Louis, MO 63105 · 314-726-6868

Paul M. Macon · Thompson Coburn · One U.S. Bank Plaza · St. Louis, MO 63101-1611 · 314-552-6000

Linda M. Martinez · Bryan Cave · One Metropolitan Square, Suite 3600 · 211 North Broadway · St. Louis, MO 63102-2750 · 314-259-2000

John P. McNearney · Husch Blackwell Sanders · http://www.huschblackwell.com · 720 Olive Street, Suite 2400 · St. Louis, MO 63101 · 314-345-6000

George V. Meisel · ㉕ · Bryan Cave · One Metropolitan Square, Suite 3600 · 211 North Broadway · St. Louis, MO 63102-2750 · 314-259-2000

Charles G. Misko · Stinson Morrison Hecker · http://www.stinson.com · 100 South Fourth Street, Suite 700 · St. Louis, MO 63102 · 314-259-4500

Kathleen T. Mueller · Husch Blackwell Sanders · http://www.huschblackwell.com · 720 Olive Street, Suite 2400 · St. Louis, MO 63101 · 314-345-6000

George E. Murray III · ⑩ · Bryan Cave · One Metropolitan Square, Suite 3600 · 211 North Broadway · St. Louis, MO 63102-2750 · 314-259-2000

Craig A. Olschansky · Thompson Coburn · One U.S. Bank Plaza · St. Louis, MO 63101-1611 · 314-552-6000

S. Jerome Pratter · The Stolar Partnership · http://www.stolarlaw.com · The Lammert Building · 911 Washington Avenue · St. Louis, MO 63101-1290 · 314-231-2800

Laura K. Rebbe · Husch Blackwell Sanders · http://www.huschblackwell.com · 720 Olive Street, Suite 2400 · St. Louis, MO 63101 · 314-345-6000

Jacob W. Reby · Lewis, Rice & Fingersh · 500 North Broadway, Suite 2000 · St. Louis, MO 63102-2147 · 314-444-7600

Thomas L. Story · Greensfelder, Hemker & Gale · Equitable Building, Suite 2000 · 10 South Broadway · St. Louis, MO 63102 · 314-241-9090

Timothy J. Tryniecki · Armstrong Teasdale · http://www.armstrongteasdale.com · One Metropolitan Square, Suite 2600 · 211 North Broadway · St. Louis, MO 63102-2740 · 314-621-5070

Harold A. Tzinberg · ⑩ · Stinson Morrison Hecker · http://www.stinson.com · 168 North Meramec Avenue, Suite 400 · St. Louis, MO 63105 · 314-863-0800

Bryan C. West · Paster West & Kraner · http://www.pwklaw.com · 138 North Meramec Avenue · St. Louis, MO 63105 · 314-721-7080

Daniel R. Wofsey · Armstrong Teasdale · http://www.armstrongteasdale.com · One Metropolitan Square, Suite 2600 · 211 North Broadway · St. Louis, MO 63102-2740 · 314-621-5070

Stuart H. Zimbalist · Polsinelli Shalton Flanigan Suelthaus · http://www.polsinelli.com · 7733 Forsyth Boulevard, Suite 1200 · St. Louis, MO 63105 · 314-889-8000

SECURITIES LAW

Kansas City

John A. Granda · ⑩ · Stinson Morrison Hecker · http://www.stinson.com · 1201 Walnut Street, Suite 2900 Kansas City, MO 64106-2150 · 816-842-8600

Jeffrey T. Haughey · Husch Blackwell Sanders · http://www.huschblackwell.com · 4801 Main Street, Suite 1000 · Kansas City, MO 64112 · 816-983-8000

George E. Rider · Stinson Morrison Hecker · http://www.stinson.com · 1201 Walnut Street, Suite 2900 · Kansas City, MO 64106-2150 · 816-842-8600

Carl W. Struby · Lathrop & Gage · 2345 Grand Boulevard, Suite 2800 · Kansas City, MO 64108 · 816-292-2000

St. Louis

John Michael Clear · ㉕ · Bryan Cave · One Metropolitan Square, Suite 3600 · 211 North Broadway · St. Louis, MO 63102-2750 · 314-259-2000

John L. Gillis, Jr. · Armstrong Teasdale · http://www.armstrongteasdale.com · One Metropolitan Square, Suite 2600 · 211 North Broadway · St. Louis, MO 63102-2740 · 314-621-5070

J. Mark Klamer · Bryan Cave · One Metropolitan Square, Suite 3600 · 211 North Broadway · St. Louis, MO 63102-2750 · 314-259-2000

Don G. Lents · ⑩ · Bryan Cave · One Metropolitan Square, Suite 3600 · 211 North Broadway · St. Louis, MO 63102-2750 · 314-259-2000

Thomas G. Lewin · Gallop, Johnson & Neuman · 101 South Hanley Road, Suite 1700 · St. Louis, MO 63105 · 314-615-6000

Thomas A. Litz · Thompson Coburn · One U.S. Bank Plaza · St. Louis, MO 63101-1611 · 314-552-6000

James L. Nouss, Jr. · ⑩ · Bryan Cave · One Metropolitan Square, Suite 3600 · 211 North Broadway · St. Louis, MO 63102-2750 · 314-259-2000

William F. Seabaugh · Bryan Cave · One Metropolitan Square, Suite 3600 · 211 North Broadway · St. Louis, MO 63102-2750 · 314-259-2000

John R. Short · ⑩ · Husch Blackwell Sanders · http://www.huschblackwell.com · 720 Olive Street, Suite 2400 · St. Louis, MO 63101 · 314-345-6000

W. Stanley Walch · ㉕ · Thompson Coburn · One U.S. Bank Plaza · St. Louis, MO 63101-1611 · 314-552-6000

Thomas C. Walsh · ⑩ · Bryan Cave · One Metropolitan Square, Suite 3600 · 211 North Broadway · St. Louis, MO 63102-2750 · 314-259-2000

Tom W. Zook · Lewis, Rice & Fingersh · 500 North Broadway, Suite 2000 · St. Louis, MO 63102-2147 · 314-444-7600

SPORTS LAW

Kansas City

John S. Black · Shughart Thomson & Kilroy · http://www.stklaw.com · 12 Wyandotte Plaza, Suite 1800 · 120 West 12th Street · Kansas City, MO 64105 · 816-421-3355

Judith S. Heeter · Shughart Thomson & Kilroy · http://www.stklaw.com · 12 Wyandotte Plaza, Suite 1800 120 West 12th Street · Kansas City, MO 64105 · 816-421-3355

St. Louis

Robert H. Lattinville · Stinson Morrison Hecker · http://www.stinson.com · 100 South Fourth Street, Suite 700 · St. Louis, MO 63102 · 314-259-4500

STRUCTURED FINANCE LAW

Kansas City

Russell A. Brien · Stinson Morrison Hecker · http://www.stinson.com · 1201 Walnut Street, Suite 2900 · Kansas City, MO 64106-2150 · 816-842-8600

Kraig M. Kohring · Polsinelli Shalton Flanigan Suelthaus · http://www.polsinelli.com · 700 West 47th Street, Suite 1000 · Kansas City, MO 64112 · 816-753-1000

Maribeth S. McMahon · Polsinelli Shalton Flanigan Suelthaus · http://www.polsinelli.com · 700 West 47th Street, Suite 1000 · Kansas City, MO 64112 · 816-753-1000

Patrick J. Respeliers · Stinson Morrison Hecker · http://www.stinson.com · 1201 Walnut Street, Suite 2900 · Kansas City, MO 64106-2150 · 816-842-8600

Kenda K. Tomes · Stinson Morrison Hecker · http://www.stinson.com · 1201 Walnut Street, Suite 2900 · Kansas City, MO 64106-2150 · 816-842-8600

TAX LAW

Clayton

Dave L. Cornfeld · (25) · Husch Blackwell Sanders · http://www.huschblackwell.com · The Plaza in Clayton Office Tower, Suite 600 · 190 Carondelet Plaza · Clayton, MO 63105-3441 · 314-480-1500

Bennett S. Keller · Lathrop & Gage · Pierre Laclede Center, Suite 400 · 7701 Forsyth Boulevard · Clayton, MO 63105 · 314-613-2800

Kansas City

Bruce C. Davison · Sonnenschein Nath & Rosenthal · 4520 Main Street, Suite 1100 · Kansas City, MO 64111-7700 · 816-460-2400

Ernest M. Fleischer · (10) · Husch Blackwell Sanders · http://www.huschblackwell.com · 4801 Main Street, Suite 1000 · Kansas City, MO 64112 · 816-983-8000

Ben W. Hobert · Stinson Morrison Hecker · http://www.stinson.com · 1201 Walnut Street, Suite 2900 · Kansas City, MO 64106-2150 · 816-842-8600

Russell D. Jones · Lathrop & Gage · 2345 Grand Boulevard, Suite 2800 · Kansas City, MO 64108 · 816-292-2000

H. Elvin Knight, Jr. · (10) · Husch Blackwell Sanders · http://www.huschblackwell.com · 4801 Main Street, Suite 1000 · Kansas City, MO 64112 · 816-983-8000

Ronald L. Langstaff · (20) · Spencer Fane Britt & Browne · http://www.spencerfane.com · 1000 Walnut Street, Suite 1400 · Kansas City, MO 64106-2140 · 816-474-8100

Paul E. McLaughlin · Stinson Morrison Hecker · http://www.stinson.com · 1201 Walnut Street, Suite 2900 · Kansas City, MO 64106-2150 · 816-842-8600

Thomas J. McMahon · (10) · Lathrop & Gage · 2345 Grand Boulevard, Suite 2800 · Kansas City, MO 64108 · 816-292-2000

William B. Prugh · Shughart Thomson & Kilroy · http://www.stklaw.com · 12 Wyandotte Plaza, Suite 1800 · 120 West 12th Street · Kansas City, MO 64105 · 816-421-3355

Jason A. Reschly · Husch Blackwell Sanders · http://www.huschblackwell.com · 4801 Main Street, Suite 1000 · Kansas City, MO 64112 · 816-983-8000

Sylvan Siegler · (25) · Shook, Hardy & Bacon · 2555 Grand Boulevard · Kansas City, MO 64108 · 816-474-6550

Myron E. Sildon · (25) · Sildon Law Group · 500 Plaza Center Building, Suite 500 · 800 West 47th Street · Kansas City, MO 64112-1240 · 816-531-8877

John W. Simpson · Shook, Hardy & Bacon · 2555 Grand Boulevard · Kansas City, MO 64108 · 816-474-6550

J. Harlan Stamper · Shughart Thomson & Kilroy · http://www.stklaw.com · 12 Wyandotte Plaza, Suite 1800 · 120 West 12th Street · Kansas City, MO 64105 · 816-421-3355

Stanley P. Weiner · ㉕ · Shook, Hardy & Bacon · 2555 Grand Boulevard · Kansas City, MO 64108 · 816-474-6550

St. Louis

Lawrence Brody · ㉕ · Bryan Cave · One Metropolitan Square, Suite 3600 · 211 North Broadway · St. Louis, MO 63102-2750 · 314-259-2000

Edward J. Buchholz · ⑩ · Thompson Coburn · One U.S. Bank Plaza · St. Louis, MO 63101-1611 · 314-552-6000

David V. Capes · Capes, Sokol, Goodman & Sarachan · Pierre Laclede Center, 12th Floor · 7701 Forsyth Boulevard · St. Louis, MO 63105-1818 · 314-721-7701

William J. Falk · ⑩ · Lewis, Rice & Fingersh · 500 North Broadway, Suite 2000 · St. Louis, MO 63102-2147 · 314-444-7600

Joseph P. Giljum · ⑩ · Kohn, Shands, Elbert, Gianoulakis & Giljum · One U.S. Bank Plaza, Suite 2410 · 505 North Seventh Street · St. Louis, MO 63101 · 314-241-3963

Robert Lewis Jackson · ⑩ · Armstrong Teasdale · http://www.armstrongteasdale.com · One Metropolitan Square, Suite 2600 · 211 North Broadway · St. Louis, MO 63102-2740 · 314-621-5070

David J. Krauss · ⑩ · The Stolar Partnership · http://www.stolarlaw.com · The Lammert Building · 911 Washington Avenue · St. Louis, MO 63101-1290 · 314-231-2800

Raymond S. Kreienkamp · Husch Blackwell Sanders · http://www.huschblackwell.com · 720 Olive Street, Suite 2400 · St. Louis, MO 63101 · 314-345-6000

Richard L. Lawton · ⑩ · Thompson Coburn · One U.S. Bank Plaza · St. Louis, MO 63101-1611 · 314-552-6000

Janette M. Lohman · Thompson Coburn · One U.S. Bank Plaza · St. Louis, MO 63101-1611 · 314-552-6000

Michael A. Markenson · Rosenblum, Goldenhersh, Silverstein & Zafft · 7733 Forsyth Boulevard, Fourth Floor · St. Louis, MO 63105 · 314-726-6868

Thomas Mug · Gallop, Johnson & Neuman · 101 South Hanley Road, Suite 1700 · St. Louis, MO 63105 · 314-615-6000

Jay A. Nathanson · Greensfelder, Hemker & Gale · Equitable Building, Suite 2000 · 10 South Broadway · St. Louis, MO 63102 · 314-241-9090

Sanford S. Neuman · ⑩ · Gallop, Johnson & Neuman · 101 South Hanley Road, Suite 1700 · St. Louis, MO 63105 · 314-615-6000

Michael N. Newmark · ㉕ · Bryan Cave · One Metropolitan Square, Suite 3600 · 211 North Broadway · St. Louis, MO 63102-2750 · 314-259-2000

Albert S. Rose · Lewis, Rice & Fingersh · 500 North Broadway, Suite 2000 · St. Louis, MO 63102-2147 · 314-444-7600

Thomas E. Venker, Jr. · ⑩ · The Stolar Partnership · http://www.stolarlaw.com · The Lammert Building 911 Washington Avenue · St. Louis, MO 63101-1290 · 314-231-2800

Lawrence H. Weltman · ⑩ · Lewis, Rice & Fingersh · 500 North Broadway, Suite 2000 · St. Louis, MO 63102-2147 · 314-444-7600

Philip B. Wright · Bryan Cave · One Metropolitan Square, Suite 3600 · 211 North Broadway · St. Louis, MO 63102-2750 · 314-259-2000

TECHNOLOGY LAW

Kansas City

Timothy J. Feathers · Stinson Morrison Hecker · http://www.stinson.com · 1201 Walnut Street, Suite 2900 · Kansas City, MO 64106-2150 · 816-842-8600

Herbert M. Kohn · Bryan Cave · One Kansas City Place, Suite 3500 · 1200 Main Street · Kansas City, MO 64105-2100 · 816-374-3200

I. Edward Marquette · ⑩ · Sonnenschein Nath & Rosenthal · 4520 Main Street, Suite 1100 · Kansas City, MO 64111-7700 · 816-460-2400

William A. Rudy · Lathrop & Gage · 2345 Grand Boulevard, Suite 2800 · Kansas City, MO 64108 · 816-292-2000

St. Louis

Frank P. Wolff, Jr. · Bryan Cave · One Metropolitan Square, Suite 3600 · 211 North Broadway · St. Louis, MO 63102-2750 · 314-259-2000

TRUSTS AND ESTATES

Clayton

Dave L. Cornfeld · ㉕ · Husch Blackwell Sanders · http://www.huschblackwell.com · The Plaza in Clayton Office Tower, Suite 600 · 190 Carondelet Plaza · Clayton, MO 63105-3441 · 314-480-1500

Robert P. Edler · ⑩ · Husch Blackwell Sanders · http://www.huschblackwell.com · The Plaza in Clayton Office Tower, Suite 600 · 190 Carondelet Plaza · Clayton, MO 63105-3441 · 314-480-1500

Christopher E. Erblich · Husch Blackwell Sanders · http://www.huschblackwell.com · The Plaza in Clayton Office Tower, Suite 600 · 190 Carondelet Plaza · Clayton, MO 63105-3441 · 314-480-1500

Patricia D. Gray · Gray & Hoffman · 7733 Forsyth Boulevard, Suite 2050 · Clayton, MO 63105-1882 · 314-726-6970

Kenneth W. Kingma · Husch Blackwell Sanders · http://www.huschblackwell.com · The Plaza in Clayton Office Tower, Suite 600 · 190 Carondelet Plaza · Clayton, MO 63105-3441 · 314-480-1500

James Robert Penninger, Jr. · Husch Blackwell Sanders · http://www.huschblackwell.com · The Plaza in Clayton Office Tower, Suite 600 · 190 Carondelet Plaza · Clayton, MO 63105-3441 · 314-480-1500

Edward F. Reilly · Muhm & Reilly · 8000 Maryland, Suite 320 · Clayton, MO 63205-3752 · 314-721-7778

James R. Strong · Husch Blackwell Sanders · http://www.huschblackwell.com · The Plaza in Clayton Office Tower, Suite 600 · 190 Carondelet Plaza · Clayton, MO 63105-3441 · 314-480-1500

Hillsboro

John W. Howald · ⑩ · Thurman, Howald, Weber, Senkel & Norrick · One Thurman Court · 301 Second Street · P.O. Box 800 · Hillsboro, MO 63050 · 636-797-2601

Independence

Buford L. Farrington · ⑩ · Humphrey Farrington & McClain · 221 West Lexington Avenue, Suite 400 · P.O. Box 900 · Independence, MO 64051 · 816-836-5050

Byron A. Stewart, Jr. · ㉕ · Stewart, Cook, Constance, Minton & Wight · 501 West Lexington Avenue · Independence, MO 64050 · 816-833-1800

Kansas City

Christopher J. Anderson · Armstrong Teasdale · http://www.armstrongteasdale.com · 2345 Grand Boulevard, Suite 2000 · Kansas City, MO 64108-2617 · 816-221-3420

James Betterman · Lathrop & Gage · 2345 Grand Boulevard, Suite 2800 · Kansas City, MO 64108 · 816-292-2000

Larry J. Bingham · ⑩ · Seigfreid, Bingham, Levy, Selzer & Gee · http://www.sblsg.com · 2800 Commerce Tower · 911 Main Street · Kansas City, MO 64105-2009 · 816-421-4460

Scott E. Blakesley · ⑩ · Husch Blackwell Sanders · http://www.huschblackwell.com · 4801 Main Street, Suite 1000 · Kansas City, MO 64112 · 816-983-8000

Peter W. Brown · ⑳ · Lathrop & Gage · 2345 Grand Boulevard, Suite 2800 · Kansas City, MO 64108 · 816-292-2000

Heywood H. Davis · ⑩ · Dicus, Davis, Sands & Collins · 1930 City Center Square · 1100 Main Street · Kansas City, MO 64105 · 816-221-8188

John C. Davis · ⑳ · Stinson Morrison Hecker · http://www.stinson.com · 1201 Walnut Street, Suite 2900 · Kansas City, MO 64106-2150 · 816-842-8600

Richard L. English · Stinson Morrison Hecker · http://www.stinson.com · 1201 Walnut Street, Suite 2900 Kansas City, MO 64106-2150 · 816-842-8600

George R. Haydon, Jr. · ⑳ · Husch Blackwell Sanders · http://www.huschblackwell.com · 4801 Main Street, Suite 1000 · Kansas City, MO 64112 · 816-983-8000

Christopher R. Hoyt · University of Missouri - Kansas City School of Law · 5100 Rockhill Road · Kansas City, MO 64110-2449 · 816-235-1644

Roger T. Hurwitz · ㉕ · Slagle, Bernard & Gorman · 600 Plaza West Building · 4600 Madison Avenue · Kansas City, MO 64112-3031 · 816-410-4600

H. Elvin Knight, Jr. · ⑩ · Husch Blackwell Sanders · http://www.huschblackwell.com · 4801 Main Street, Suite 1000 · Kansas City, MO 64112 · 816-983-8000

Scott K. Martinsen · Husch Blackwell Sanders · http://www.huschblackwell.com · 4801 Main Street, Suite 1000 · Kansas City, MO 64112 · 816-983-8000

Wendy Byers Marvin · Sonnenschein Nath & Rosenthal · 4520 Main Street, Suite 1100 · Kansas City, MO 64111-7700 · 816-460-2400

Maurice J. O'Sullivan, Jr. · ⑩ · Lathrop & Gage · 2345 Grand Boulevard, Suite 2800 · Kansas City, MO 64108 · 816-292-2000

H. Joseph Price, Jr. · Spencer Fane Britt & Browne · http://www.spencerfane.com · 1000 Walnut Street, Suite 1400 · Kansas City, MO 64106-2140 · 816-474-8100

Nancy Schmidt Roush · ⑳ · Lathrop & Gage · 2345 Grand Boulevard, Suite 2800 · Kansas City, MO 64108 · 816-292-2000

Edward A. Setzler · ㉕ · Lathrop & Gage · 2345 Grand Boulevard, Suite 2800 · Kansas City, MO 64108 · 816-292-2000

Sylvan Siegler · ㉕ · Shook, Hardy & Bacon · 2555 Grand Boulevard · Kansas City, MO 64108 · 816-474-6550

Kent V. Stallard · Stinson Morrison Hecker · http://www.stinson.com · 1201 Walnut Street, Suite 2900 · Kansas City, MO 64106-2150 · 816-842-8600

Joel B. Voran · Lathrop & Gage · 2345 Grand Boulevard, Suite 2800 · Kansas City, MO 64108 · 816-292-2000

Stanley P. Weiner · Shook, Hardy & Bacon · 2555 Grand Boulevard · Kansas City, MO 64108 · 816-474-6550

David L. West · ⑳ · Husch Blackwell Sanders · http://www.huschblackwell.com · 4801 Main Street, Suite 1000 · Kansas City, MO 64112 · 816-983-8000

Liberty

Robert Kirkland · ⑩ · Kirkland & Woods · 132 Westwoods Drive · Liberty, MO 64068 · 816-792-8300

Springfield

Clifford S. Brown · ⑩ · Carnahan, Evans, Cantwell & Brown · 2805 South Ingram Mill Road · Springfield, MO 65804 · 417-447-4400

J. Richard Owensby · Neale & Newman · 1949 East Sunshine Street, Suite 1-130 · P.O. Box 10327 · Springfield, MO 65808 · 417-841-4600

St. Louis

Lawrence Brody · ㉕ · Bryan Cave · One Metropolitan Square, Suite 3600 · 211 North Broadway · St. Louis, MO 63102-2750 · 314-259-2000

T. Jack Challis · Polsinelli Shalton Flanigan Suelthaus · http://www.polsinelli.com · 7733 Forsyth Boulevard, Suite 1200 · St. Louis, MO 63105 · 314-889-8000

Thomas R. Corbett · ⑩ · Thompson Coburn · One U.S. Bank Plaza · St. Louis, MO 63101-1611 · 314-552-6000

Stephen E. Cupples · ⑩ · Thompson Coburn · One U.S. Bank Plaza · St. Louis, MO 63101-1611 · 314-552-6000

John E. Dooling, Jr. · Armstrong Teasdale · http://www.armstrongteasdale.com · One Metropolitan Square, Suite 2600 · 211 North Broadway · St. Louis, MO 63102-2740 · 314-621-5070

Steven B. Gorin · Thompson Coburn · One U.S. Bank Plaza · St. Louis, MO 63101-1611 · 314-552-6000

Kenneth E. Hand · ⑩ · Polsinelli Shalton Flanigan Suelthaus · http://www.polsinelli.com · 7733 Forsyth Boulevard, Suite 1200 · St. Louis, MO 63105 · 314-889-8000

William H. Hobson · The Stolar Partnership · http://www.stolarlaw.com · The Lammert Building · 911 Washington Avenue · St. Louis, MO 63101-1290 · 314-231-2800

Jonathan W. Igoe · Armstrong Teasdale · http://www.armstrongteasdale.com · One Metropolitan Square, Suite 2600 · 211 North Broadway · St. Louis, MO 63102-2740 · 314-621-5070

Lawrence P. Katzenstein · ⑳ · Thompson Coburn · One U.S. Bank Plaza · St. Louis, MO 63101-1611 · 314-552-6000

Mark R. Leuchtmann · Husch Blackwell Sanders · http://www.huschblackwell.com · 720 Olive Street, Suite 2400 · St. Louis, MO 63101 · 314-345-6000

Matthew J. Madsen · Lewis, Rice & Fingersh · 500 North Broadway, Suite 2000 · St. Louis, MO 63102-2147 · 314-444-7600

Lisa D. McLaughlin · ⑩ · Polsinelli Shalton Flanigan Suelthaus · http://www.polsinelli.com · 7733 Forsyth Boulevard, Suite 1200 · St. Louis, MO 63105 · 314-889-8000

Marian V. Mehan · ⑩ · Lewis, Rice & Fingersh · 500 North Broadway, Suite 2000 · St. Louis, MO 63102-2147 · 314-444-7600

Jaime R. Mendez · Lewis, Rice & Fingersh · 500 North Broadway, Suite 2000 · St. Louis, MO 63102-2147 · 314-444-7600

Michael D. Mulligan · ⑳ · Lewis, Rice & Fingersh · 500 North Broadway, Suite 2000 · St. Louis, MO 63102-2147 · 314-444-7600

Sanford S. Neuman · ⑩ · Gallop, Johnson & Neuman · 101 South Hanley Road, Suite 1700 · St. Louis, MO 63105 · 314-615-6000

Matthew G. Perlow · Husch Blackwell Sanders · http://www.huschblackwell.com · 720 Olive Street, Suite 2400 · St. Louis, MO 63101 · 314-345-6000

Charles A. Redd · ⑩ · Sonnenschein Nath & Rosenthal · One Metropolitan Square, Suite 3000 · 211 North Broadway · St. Louis, MO 63102-2741 · 314-241-1800

Albert S. Rose · Lewis, Rice & Fingersh · 500 North Broadway, Suite 2000 · St. Louis, MO 63102-2147 · 314-444-7600

Robert J. Selsor · Polsinelli Shalton Flanigan Suelthaus · http://www.polsinelli.com · 7733 Forsyth Boulevard, Suite 1200 · St. Louis, MO 63105 · 314-889-8000

Kathleen R. Sherby · ⑳ · Bryan Cave · One Metropolitan Square, Suite 3600 · 211 North Broadway · St. Louis, MO 63102-2750 · 314-259-2000

Kimberly N. Springer · Kimberly N. Springer · 8777 Big Bend Boulevard · St. Louis, MO 63119 · 314-962-6500

Jason P. Thein · Thompson Coburn · One U.S. Bank Plaza · St. Louis, MO 63101-1611 · 314-552-6000

Thomas E. Venker, Jr. · ⑩ · The Stolar Partnership · http://www.stolarlaw.com · The Lammert Building 911 Washington Avenue · St. Louis, MO 63101-1290 · 314-231-2800

Franklin F. Wallis · ⑳ · Bryan Cave · One Metropolitan Square, Suite 3600 · 211 North Broadway · St. Louis, MO 63102-2750 · 314-259-2000

VENTURE CAPITAL LAW

Kansas City

Robert C. Hunter · Stinson Morrison Hecker · http://www.stinson.com · 1201 Walnut Street, Suite 2900 · Kansas City, MO 64106-2150 · 816-842-8600

WATER LAW

Kansas City

Parthenia B. Evans · Stinson Morrison Hecker · http://www.stinson.com · 1201 Walnut Street, Suite 2900 Kansas City, MO 64106-2150 · 816-842-8600

James T. Price · (20) · Spencer Fane Britt & Browne · http://www.spencerfane.com · 1000 Walnut Street, Suite 1400 · Kansas City, MO 64106-2140 · 816-474-8100

St. Louis

George M. von Stamwitz · (10) · Armstrong Teasdale · http://www.armstrongteasdale.com · One Metropolitan Square, Suite 2600 · 211 North Broadway · St. Louis, MO 63102-2740 · 314-621-5070

WHITE-COLLAR CRIMINAL DEFENSE

Clayton

Paul J. D'Agrosa · Wolff and D'Agrosa · 8019 Forsyth Boulevard · Clayton, MO 63105 · 314-725-8019

Arthur S. Margulis · Margulis Grant & Margulis · 11 South Meramec Avenue, Suite 1330 · Clayton, MO 63105-1716 · 314-721-6677

Donald L. Wolff · (25) · Wolff and D'Agrosa · 8019 Forsyth Boulevard · Clayton, MO 63105 · 314-725-8019

Columbia

Patrick J. Eng · Eng & Woods · 903 East Ash Street · Columbia, MO 65201 · 573-874-4190

Jefferson City

Joseph Bednar · Armstrong Teasdale · http://www.armstrongteasdale.com · 3405 West Truman Boulevard, Suite 210 · Jefferson City, MO 65109-5713 · 573-636-8394

Kansas City

John C. Aisenbrey · (10) · Stinson Morrison Hecker · http://www.stinson.com · 1201 Walnut Street, Suite 2900 · Kansas City, MO 64106-2150 · 816-842-8600

Jean Paul Bradshaw II · Lathrop & Gage · 2345 Grand Boulevard, Suite 2800 · Kansas City, MO 64108 · 816-292-2000

Thomas Bradshaw · (10) · Bradshaw Herrington · 2345 Grand Boulevard, Suite 600 · Kansas City, MO 64108-2655 · 816-285-1030

W. Brian Gaddy · Gaddy Geiger & Brown · 2345 Grand Boulevard, Suite 675 · Kansas City, MO 64108 · 816-221-8989

Charles W. German · Rouse Hendricks German May · One Petticoat Lane Building, Suite 400 · 1010 Walnut Street · Kansas City, MO 64106 · 816-471-7700

Gerald M. Handley · ㉕ · Gerald M. Handley · 1100 Main Street, Suite 2800 · Kansas City, MO 64105 · 816-471-7145

James R. Hobbs · ⑩ · Wyrsch Hobbs & Mirakian · 1000 Walnut Street, Suite 1600 · Kansas City, MO 64106 · 816-221-0080

Bruce C. Houdek · ⑩ · Bruce C. Houdek · 818 Grand Avenue · Kansas City, MO 64106 · 816-842-2575

Patrick A. McInerney · Husch Blackwell Sanders · http://www.huschblackwell.com · 4801 Main Street, Suite 1000 · Kansas City, MO 64112 · 816-983-8000

Jeffrey D. Morris · Berkowitz Oliver Williams Shaw & Eisenbrandt · 2600 Grand Boulevard, Suite 1200 · Kansas City, MO 64108 · 816-561-7007

John P. O'Connor · Wagstaff & Cartmell · 4740 Grand Avenue, Suite 300 · Kansas City, MO 64112 · 816-701-1100

Bruce W. Simon · ⑩ · Simon and Simon · 105 East Fifth Street, Suite 201 · Kansas City, MO 64106-1179 816-471-3430

Mark A. Thornhill · Spencer Fane Britt & Browne · http://www.spencerfane.com · 1000 Walnut Street, Suite 1400 · Kansas City, MO 64106-2140 · 816-474-8100

James R. Wyrsch · ㉕ · Wyrsch Hobbs & Mirakian · 1000 Walnut Street, Suite 1600 · Kansas City, MO 64106 · 816-221-0080

Springfield

Thomas D. Carver · Thomas D. Carver · 2103 East Sunshine · Springfield, MO 65806 · 417-886-3330

Joseph S. Passanise · The Law Offices of Dee Wampler and Joseph Passanise · 2974 East Battlefield · Springfield, MO 65804 · 417-882-9300

Dee Wampler · The Law Offices of Dee Wampler and Joseph Passanise · 2974 East Battlefield · Springfield, MO 65804 · 417-882-9300

St. Louis

Gordon L. Ankney · Thompson Coburn · One U.S. Bank Plaza · St. Louis, MO 63101-1611 · 314-552-6000

Irl B. Baris · ㉕ · Baris Law Firm · The Shell Building, 10th Floor · 1221 Locust Street · St. Louis, MO 63103 · 314-421-6644

David V. Capes · Capes, Sokol, Goodman & Sarachan · Pierre Laclede Center, 12th Floor · 7701 Forsyth Boulevard · St. Louis, MO 63105-1818 · 314-721-7701

Jeffrey T. Demerath · Armstrong Teasdale · http://www.armstrongteasdale.com · One Metropolitan Square, Suite 2600 · 211 North Broadway · St. Louis, MO 63102-2740 · 314-621-5070

Edward L. Dowd, Jr. · Dowd Bennett · http://www.dowdbennett.com · 7733 Forsyth Boulevard, Suite 1410 · St. Louis, MO 63105 · 314-889-7300

David B. B. Helfrey · Helfrey, Neiers & Jones · 120 South Central Avenue, Suite 1500 · St. Louis, MO 63105 · 314-725-9100

James G. Martin · Armstrong Teasdale · http://www.armstrongteasdale.com · One Metropolitan Square, Suite 2600 · 211 North Broadway · St. Louis, MO 63102-2740 · 314-621-5070

Kevin F. O'Malley · Greensfelder, Hemker & Gale · Equitable Building, Suite 2000 · 10 South Broadway St. Louis, MO 63102 · 314-241-9090

N. Scott Rosenblum · Rosenblum, Schwartz, Rogers & Glass · 120 South Central Avenue, Suite 130 · St. Louis, MO 63105 · 314-862-4332

Barry A. Short · Lewis, Rice & Fingersh · 500 North Broadway, Suite 2000 · St. Louis, MO 63102-2147 · 314-444-7600

Burton H. Shostak · Shostak & Shostak · The Berkley Building · 8015 Forsyth Boulevard · St. Louis, MO 63105 · 314-725-3200

Richard H. Sindel · Sindel, Sindel & Noble · 8008 Carondelet, Suite 301 · St. Louis, MO 63105 · 314-721-6040

WORKERS' COMPENSATION LAW

Kansas City

Kip A. Kubin · ⑩ · Bottaro, Morefield & Kubin · 1001 East 101st Terrace, Suite 120 · Kansas City, MO 64131 · 816-256-4660

St. Louis

Wilbur L. Tomlinson · Armstrong Teasdale · http://www.armstrongteasdale.com · One Metropolitan Square, Suite 2600 · 211 North Broadway · St. Louis, MO 63102-2740 · 314-621-5070

MONTANA

ALTERNATIVE DISPUTE RESOLUTION

Billings

Charles R. Cashmore · Cashmore & Grant · 2722 Third Avenue North, Suite 321 · Billings, MT 59101 · 406-245-2194

Ronald R. Lodders · Ronald R. Lodders · 5315 Cheyenne Trail · Billings, MT 59106 · 406-651-5738

Butte

R. D. Corette · a · Corette Pohlman & Kebe · Mayer Building · 129 West Park Street · Butte, MT 59701 406-782-5800

Helena

Thomas M. Keegan · Thomas M. Keegan · 212 North Rodney Street · Helena, MT 59601 · 406-442-8711

Stuart L. Kellner · 2) · Hughes, Kellner, Sullivan & Alke · 40 West Lawrence Street, Suite A · P.O. Box 1166 · Helena, MT 59624 · 406-442-3690

Kalispell

Tracy Axelberg · Christensen, Moore, Cockrell, Cummings & Axelberg · Two Medicine Building, Suite 104 · 160 Heritage Way · P.O. Box 7370 · Kalispell, MT 59904-0370 · 406-751-6000

APPELLATE LAW

Billings

Steven R. Milch · Crowley, Haughey, Hanson, Toole & Dietrich · http://www.crowleylaw.com · 490 North 31st Street, Suite 500 · P.O. Box 2529 · Billings, MT 59103-2529 · 406-252-3441

Bozeman

James H. Goetz · a · Goetz, Gallik & Baldwin · 35 North Grand Avenue · P.O. Box 6580 · Bozeman, MT 59771-6580 · 406-587-0618

Helena

Ronald F. Waterman · a · Gough, Shanahan, Johnson & Waterman · 33 South Last Chance Gulch · P.O. Box 1715 · Helena, MT 59624-1715 · 406-442-8560

BANKING LAW

Billings

Charles W. Hingle · a · Holland & Hart · 401 North 31st Street, Suite 1500 · Billings, MT 59101-1200 · 406-252-2166

Doug James · Moulton, Bellingham · http://www.moultonlawfirm.com · Crowne Plaza, Suite 1900 · P.O. Box 2559 · Billings, MT 59103-2559 · 406-248-7731

William D. Lamdin III · a · Crowley, Haughey, Hanson, Toole & Dietrich · http://www.crowleylaw.com 490 North 31st Street, Suite 500 · P.O. Box 2529 · Billings, MT 59103-2529 · 406-252-3441

Gerald B. Murphy · a · Moulton, Bellingham · http://www.moultonlawfirm.com · Crowne Plaza, Suite 1900 · P.O. Box 2559 · Billings, MT 59103-2559 · 406-248-7731

Laurence W. Petersen · a · Holland & Hart · 401 North 31st Street, Suite 1500 · Billings, MT 59101-1200 · 406-252-2166

Missoula

Ronald A. Bender · Worden Thane · http://www.wthlaw.net · 111 North Higgins Avenue, Suite 600 · P.O. Box 4747 · Missoula, MT 59806 · 406-721-3400

David R. Chisholm · a · Christian, Samson, Jones & Chisholm · 310 West Spruce Street · Missoula, MT 59802 · 406-721-7772

David B. Cotner · Datsopoulos, MacDonald & Lind · 201 West Main Street, Suite 201 · Missoula, MT 59801 · 406-728-0810

Martin S. King · Worden Thane · http://www.wthlaw.net · 111 North Higgins Avenue, Suite 600 · P.O. Box 4747 · Missoula, MT 59806 · 406-721-3400

BANKRUPTCY AND CREDITOR-DEBTOR RIGHTS LAW

Billings

Malcolm H. Goodrich · Goodrich Law Firm · 2619 Saint Johns Avenue, Suite F · P.O. Box 1899 · Billings, MT 59103 · 406-256-3663

Joel E. Guthals · a · Guthals, Hunnes, Reuss & Thompson · Windsor Court · 10 North 27th Street · P.O. Box 1977 · Billings, MT 59103-1977 · 406-245-3071

Charles W. Hingle · a · Holland & Hart · 401 North 31st Street, Suite 1500 · Billings, MT 59101-1200 · 406-252-2166

Doug James · Moulton, Bellingham · http://www.moultonlawfirm.com · Crowne Plaza, Suite 1900 · P.O. Box 2559 · Billings, MT 59103-2559 · 406-248-7731

Missoula

Harold V. Dye · 2) · Dye & Moe · Studebaker Building, Suite 200 · 216 West Main Street · P.O. Box 9198 Missoula, MT 59807-9198 · 406-542-5205

Martin S. King · Worden Thane · http://www.wthlaw.net · 111 North Higgins Avenue, Suite 600 · P.O. Box 4747 · Missoula, MT 59806 · 406-721-3400

BET-THE-COMPANY LITIGATION

Bozeman

James H. Goetz · a · Goetz, Gallik & Baldwin · 35 North Grand Avenue · P.O. Box 6580 · Bozeman, MT 59771-6580 · 406-587-0618

Great Falls

Alexander Blewett III · a · Hoyt & Blewett · 501 Second Avenue North · P.O. Box 2807 · Great Falls, MT 59403-2807 · 406-761-1960

Tom L. Lewis · a · Lewis, Slovak & Kovacich · 725 Third Avenue North · P.O. Box 2325 · Great Falls, MT 59403 · 406-761-5595

Missoula

Gary L. Graham · a · Garlington, Lohn & Robinson · http://www.garlington.com · 199 West Pine Street · P.O. Box 7909 · Missoula, MT 59807-7909 · 406-523-2500

William Evan Jones · a · Garlington, Lohn & Robinson · http://www.garlington.com · 199 West Pine Street · P.O. Box 7909 · Missoula, MT 59807-7909 · 406-523-2500

CIVIL RIGHTS LAW

Billings

Steven R. Milch · Crowley, Haughey, Hanson, Toole & Dietrich · http://www.crowleylaw.com · 490 North 31st Street, Suite 500 · P.O. Box 2529 · Billings, MT 59103-2529 · 406-252-3441

COMMERCIAL LITIGATION

Billings

David L. Charles · Crowley, Haughey, Hanson, Toole & Dietrich · http://www.crowleylaw.com · 490 North 31st Street, Suite 500 · P.O. Box 2529 · Billings, MT 59103-2529 · 406-252-3441

Lawrence B. Cozzens · Harman, Warren & Harris · 550 North 31st Street, Suite 250 · Billings, MT 59101 406-294-2000

John G. Crist · Crist Law Firm · Securities Building, Suite 300 · 2708 First Avenue North · Billings, MT 59101 · 406-255-0400

Michael S. Dockery · Crowley, Haughey, Hanson, Toole & Dietrich · http://www.crowleylaw.com · 490 North 31st Street, Suite 500 · P.O. Box 2529 · Billings, MT 59103-2529 · 406-252-3441

A. Clifford Edwards · ⑳ · Edwards Frickle & Culver · http://www.edwardslawfirm.org · 1601 Lewis Avenue, Suite 206 · P.O. Box 20039 · Billings, MT 59104-0039 · 406-256-8155

William A. Forsythe · ⑩ · Moulton, Bellingham · http://www.moultonlawfirm.com · Crowne Plaza, Suite 1900 · P.O. Box 2559 · Billings, MT 59103-2559 · 406-248-7731

Joel E. Guthals · ⑩ · Guthals, Hunnes, Reuss & Thompson · Windsor Court · 10 North 27th Street · P.O. Box 1977 · Billings, MT 59103-1977 · 406-245-3071

Harlan B. Krogh · Crist, Krogh & Nord · 2708 First Avenue North, Suite 300 · Billings, MT 59101 · 406-255-0400

Carey E. Matovich · Matovich & Keller · 2812 First Avenue North, Suite 225 · P.O. Box 1098 · Billings, MT 59103 · 406-252-5500

Gregory G. Murphy · Moulton, Bellingham · http://www.moultonlawfirm.com · Crowne Plaza, Suite 1900 P.O. Box 2559 · Billings, MT 59103-2559 · 406-248-7731

Mark D. Parker · Parker, Heitz & Cosgrove · 401 North 31st Street, Suite 805 · P.O. Box 7212 · Billings, MT 59103-7212 · 406-245-9991

Robert L. Sterup · Holland & Hart · 401 North 31st Street, Suite 1500 · Billings, MT 59101-1200 · 406-252-2166

Bozeman

James H. Goetz · ⑩ · Goetz, Gallik & Baldwin · 35 North Grand Avenue · P.O. Box 6580 · Bozeman, MT 59771-6580 · 406-587-0618

Butte

Donald C. Robinson · ⑳ · Poore, Roth & Robinson · 1341 Harrison Avenue · P.O. Box 2000 · Butte, MT 59702 · 406-497-1200

Great Falls

Alexander Blewett III · ⑩ · Hoyt & Blewett · 501 Second Avenue North · P.O. Box 2807 · Great Falls, MT 59403-2807 · 406-761-1960

Tom L. Lewis · ⑩ · Lewis, Slovak & Kovacich · 725 Third Avenue North · P.O. Box 2325 · Great Falls, MT 59403 · 406-761-5595

John D. Stephenson · 2) · Jardine, Stephenson, Blewett and Weaver · U.S. Bank Building, Seventh Floor 300 Central Avenue · P.O. Box 2269 · Great Falls, MT 59403 · 406-727-5000

Gary M. Zadick · Ugrin, Alexander, Zadick & Higgins · Two Railroad Square, Suite B · Great Falls, MT 59401 · 406-771-0007

Helena

Gary L. Davis · Luxan & Murfitt · Montana Club Building · 24 West Sixth Avenue · P.O. Box 1144 · Helena, MT 59624-1144 · 406-442-7450

Stanley T. Kaleczyc · Browning, Kaleczyc, Berry and Hoven · 139 North Last Chance Gulch · P.O. Box 1697 · Helena, MT 59624 · 406-443-6820

Ronald F. Waterman · a · Gough, Shanahan, Johnson & Waterman · 33 South Last Chance Gulch · P.O. Box 1715 · Helena, MT 59624-1715 · 406-442-8560

Kalispell

Tracy Axelberg · Christensen, Moore, Cockrell, Cummings & Axelberg · Two Medicine Building, Suite 104 · 160 Heritage Way · P.O. Box 7370 · Kalispell, MT 59904-0370 · 406-751-6000

Allan M. McGarvey · McGarvey, Heberling, Sullivan & McGarvey · 745 South Main · Kalispell, MT 59901-5399 · 406-752-5566

Michael L. Moore · Christensen, Moore, Cockrell, Cummings & Axelberg · Two Medicine Building, Suite 104 · 160 Heritage Way · P.O. Box 7370 · Kalispell, MT 59904-0370 · 406-751-6000

Livingston

Joseph T. Swindlehurst · Huppert & Swindlehurst · 420 South Second Street · P.O. Box 523 · Livingston, MT 59047 · 406-222-2023

Missoula

Ronald A. Bender · Worden Thane · http://www.wthlaw.net · 111 North Higgins Avenue, Suite 600 · P.O. Box 4747 · Missoula, MT 59806 · 406-721-3400

David B. Cotner · Datsopoulos, MacDonald & Lind · 201 West Main Street, Suite 201 · Missoula, MT 59801 · 406-728-0810

Lawrence F. Daly · Garlington, Lohn & Robinson · http://www.garlington.com · 199 West Pine Street · P.O. Box 7909 · Missoula, MT 59807-7909 · 406-523-2500

Patrick G. Frank · Worden Thane · http://www.wthlaw.net · 111 North Higgins Avenue, Suite 600 · P.O. Box 4747 · Missoula, MT 59806 · 406-721-3400

Gary L. Graham · a · Garlington, Lohn & Robinson · http://www.garlington.com · 199 West Pine Street · P.O. Box 7909 · Missoula, MT 59807-7909 · 406-523-2500

William Evan Jones · a · Garlington, Lohn & Robinson · http://www.garlington.com · 199 West Pine Street · P.O. Box 7909 · Missoula, MT 59807-7909 · 406-523-2500

Martin S. King · Worden Thane · http://www.wthlaw.net · 111 North Higgins Avenue, Suite 600 · P.O. Box 4747 · Missoula, MT 59806 · 406-721-3400

W. Carl Mendenhall · Worden Thane · http://www.wthlaw.net · 111 North Higgins Avenue, Suite 600 · P.O. Box 4747 · Missoula, MT 59806 · 406-721-3400

Robert J. Sullivan · Boone Karlberg · Central Square, Suite 300 · 201 West Main Street · P.O. Box 9199 · Missoula, MT 59807-9199 · 406-543-6646

CONSTRUCTION LAW

Missoula

Patrick G. Frank · Worden Thane · http://www.wthlaw.net · 111 North Higgins Avenue, Suite 600 · P.O. Box 4747 · Missoula, MT 59806 · 406-721-3400

CORPORATE LAW

Billings

Lance R. Hoskins · a · Brekke & Hoskins · 1280 First Interstate Center · 401 North 31st Street · P.O. Box 7197 · Billings, MT 59103 · 406-869-1100

Laurence W. Petersen · a · Holland & Hart · 401 North 31st Street, Suite 1500 · Billings, MT 59101-1200 · 406-252-2166

Thomas F. Topel · Brekke & Hoskins · 1280 First Interstate Center · 401 North 31st Street · P.O. Box 7197 · Billings, MT 59103 · 406-869-1100

Great Falls

Gary W. Bjelland · a · Jardine, Stephenson, Blewett and Weaver · U.S. Bank Building, Seventh Floor · 300 Central Avenue · P.O. Box 2269 · Great Falls, MT 59403 · 406-727-5000

Helena

Ward A. Shanahan · a · Gough, Shanahan, Johnson & Waterman · 33 South Last Chance Gulch · P.O. Box 1715 · Helena, MT 59624-1715 · 406-442-8560

Missoula

Thomas H. Boone · 2) · Boone Karlberg · Central Square, Suite 300 · 201 West Main Street · P.O. Box 9199 · Missoula, MT 59807-9199 · 406-543-6646

Gary B. Chumrau · Garlington, Lohn & Robinson · http://www.garlington.com · 199 West Pine Street · P.O. Box 7909 · Missoula, MT 59807-7909 · 406-523-2500

Patrick D. Dougherty · Worden Thane · http://www.wthlaw.net · 111 North Higgins Avenue, Suite 600 · P.O. Box 4747 · Missoula, MT 59806 · 406-721-3400

John W. Manning · a · Dorsey & Whitney · 125 Bank Street, Suite 600 · Missoula, MT 59802-4407 · 406-721-6025

EDUCATION LAW

Missoula

W. Carl Mendenhall · Worden Thane · http://www.wthlaw.net · 111 North Higgins Avenue, Suite 600 · P.O. Box 4747 · Missoula, MT 59806 · 406-721-3400

EMINENT DOMAIN AND CONDEMNATION LAW

Missoula

William Evan Jones · a · Garlington, Lohn & Robinson · http://www.garlington.com · 199 West Pine Street · P.O. Box 7909 · Missoula, MT 59807-7909 · 406-523-2500

EMPLOYEE BENEFITS LAW

Billings

Elizabeth A. Nedrow · Holland & Hart · 401 North 31st Street, Suite 1500 · Billings, MT 59101-1200 · 406-252-2166

ENERGY LAW

Billings

Gary G. Broeder · a · Crowley, Haughey, Hanson, Toole & Dietrich · http://www.crowleylaw.com · 490 North 31st Street, Suite 500 · P.O. Box 2529 · Billings, MT 59103-2529 · 406-252-3441

John R. Lee · Crowley, Haughey, Hanson, Toole & Dietrich · http://www.crowleylaw.com · 490 North 31st Street, Suite 500 · P.O. Box 2529 · Billings, MT 59103-2529 · 406-252-3441

Christopher Mangen, Jr. · a · Crowley, Haughey, Hanson, Toole & Dietrich · http://www.crowleylaw.com · 490 North 31st Street, Suite 500 · P.O. Box 2529 · Billings, MT 59103-2529 · 406-252-3441

Laurence W. Petersen · a · Holland & Hart · 401 North 31st Street, Suite 1500 · Billings, MT 59101-1200 · 406-252-2166

Donald W. Quander · Holland & Hart · 401 North 31st Street, Suite 1500 · Billings, MT 59101-1200 · 406-252-2166

Steven P. Ruffatto · a · Crowley, Haughey, Hanson, Toole & Dietrich · http://www.crowleylaw.com · 490 North 31st Street, Suite 500 · P.O. Box 2529 · Billings, MT 59103-2529 · 406-252-3441

Helena

John L. Alke · a · Hughes, Kellner, Sullivan & Alke · 40 West Lawrence Street, Suite A · P.O. Box 1166 · Helena, MT 59624 · 406-442-3690

ENVIRONMENTAL LAW

Billings

Donald W. Quander · Holland & Hart · 401 North 31st Street, Suite 1500 · Billings, MT 59101-1200 · 406-252-2166

John Walker Ross · Brown Law Firm · 315 North 24th Street · P.O. Drawer 849 · Billings, MT 59103-0849 · 406-248-2611

David A. Veeder · Veeder Law Firm · 2795 Enterprise Avenue · P.O. Box 80946 · Billings, MT 59108-0946 · 406-248-9156

Bozeman

James H. Goetz · a · Goetz, Gallik & Baldwin · 35 North Grand Avenue · P.O. Box 6580 · Bozeman, MT 59771-6580 · 406-587-0618

Helena

Frank C. Crowley · a · Doney, Crowley, Bloomquist, Payne & Uda · Diamond Block Building, Suite 200 44 West Sixth Avenue · P.O. Box 1185 · Helena, MT 59624-1185 · 406-443-2211

Alan L. Joscelyn · a · Gough, Shanahan, Johnson & Waterman · 33 South Last Chance Gulch · P.O. Box 1715 · Helena, MT 59624-1715 · 406-442-8560

Missoula

Stephen R. Brown · a · Garlington, Lohn & Robinson · http://www.garlington.com · 199 West Pine Street · P.O. Box 7909 · Missoula, MT 59807-7909 · 406-523-2500

FAMILY LAW

Bozeman

Kent M. Kasting · a · Kasting, Kauffman & Mersen · 716 South 20th Avenue, Suite 101 · Bozeman, MT 59718 · 406-586-4383

Hamilton

Gail H. Goheen · a · Gail H. Goheen · 345 West Main Street · P.O. Box 997 · Hamilton, MT 59840-0997 406-363-2722

Missoula

Cynthia K. Thiel · Boone Karlberg · Central Square, Suite 300 · 201 West Main Street · P.O. Box 9199 · Missoula, MT 59807-9199 · 406-543-6646

FIRST AMENDMENT LAW

Bozeman

James H. Goetz · a · Goetz, Gallik & Baldwin · 35 North Grand Avenue · P.O. Box 6580 · Bozeman, MT 59771-6580 · 406-587-0618

Helena

Peter M. Meloy · Meloy Trieweiler · Bluestone Building · 80 South Warren · P.O. Box 1241 · Helena, MT 59624 · 406-442-8670

HEALTH CARE LAW

Billings

John T. Jones · a · Moulton, Bellingham · http://www.moultonlawfirm.com · Crowne Plaza, Suite 1900 · P.O. Box 2559 · Billings, MT 59103-2559 · 406-248-7731

Missoula

Gary B. Chumrau · Garlington, Lohn & Robinson · http://www.garlington.com · 199 West Pine Street · P.O. Box 7909 · Missoula, MT 59807-7909 · 406-523-2500

Candace C. Fetscher · a · Garlington, Lohn & Robinson · http://www.garlington.com · 199 West Pine Street · P.O. Box 7909 · Missoula, MT 59807-7909 · 406-523-2500

W. Carl Mendenhall · Worden Thane · http://www.wthlaw.net · 111 North Higgins Avenue, Suite 600 · P.O. Box 4747 · Missoula, MT 59806 · 406-721-3400

Jeremy G. Thane · a · Worden Thane · http://www.wthlaw.net · 111 North Higgins Avenue, Suite 600 · P.O. Box 4747 · Missoula, MT 59806 · 406-721-3400

INSURANCE LAW

Billings

Randall G. Nelson · Nelson & Dahle · http://www.nelson-dahle.com · 316 North 25th Street · Billings, MT 59101 · 406-867-7000

Guy W. Rogers · Brown Law Firm · 315 North 24th Street · P.O. Drawer 849 · Billings, MT 59103-0849 · 406-248-2611

Great Falls

Robert F. James · Ugrin, Alexander, Zadick & Higgins · Two Railroad Square, Suite B · Great Falls, MT 59401 · 406-771-0007

Missoula

Ronald A. Bender · Worden Thane · http://www.wthlaw.net · 111 North Higgins Avenue, Suite 600 · P.O. Box 4747 · Missoula, MT 59806 · 406-721-3400

Gary L. Graham · a · Garlington, Lohn & Robinson · http://www.garlington.com · 199 West Pine Street · P.O. Box 7909 · Missoula, MT 59807-7909 · 406-523-2500

Bradley J. Luck · a · Garlington, Lohn & Robinson · http://www.garlington.com · 199 West Pine Street · P.O. Box 7909 · Missoula, MT 59807-7909 · 406-523-2500

W. Carl Mendenhall · Worden Thane · http://www.wthlaw.net · 111 North Higgins Avenue, Suite 600 · P.O. Box 4747 · Missoula, MT 59806 · 406-721-3400

INTELLECTUAL PROPERTY LAW

Billings

Shane P. Coleman · Holland & Hart · 401 North 31st Street, Suite 1500 · Billings, MT 59101-1200 · 406-252-2166

Missoula

Robert C. Lukes · Garlington, Lohn & Robinson · http://www.garlington.com · 199 West Pine Street · P.O. Box 7909 · Missoula, MT 59807-7909 · 406-523-2500

Shane A. Vannatta · Worden Thane · http://www.wthlaw.net · 111 North Higgins Avenue, Suite 600 · P.O. Box 4747 · Missoula, MT 59806 · 406-721-3400

LABOR AND EMPLOYMENT LAW

Billings

Jeanne Matthews Bender · Holland & Hart · 401 North 31st Street, Suite 1500 · Billings, MT 59101-1200 · 406-252-2166

John G. Crist · Crist Law Firm · Securities Building, Suite 300 · 2708 First Avenue North · Billings, MT 59101 · 406-255-0400

Steven J. Lehman · Crowley, Haughey, Hanson, Toole & Dietrich · http://www.crowleylaw.com · 490 North 31st Street, Suite 500 · P.O. Box 2529 · Billings, MT 59103-2529 · 406-252-3441

Butte

Donald C. Robinson · 2) · Poore, Roth & Robinson · 1341 Harrison Avenue · P.O. Box 2000 · Butte, MT 59702 · 406-497-1200

Great Falls

Jean Faure · Church, Harris, Johnson & Williams · Wells Fargo Bank Building, Third Floor · 21 Third Street North · P.O. Box 1645 · Great Falls, MT 59403 · 406-761-3000

D. Patrick McKittrick · 2) · McKittrick Law Firm · Strain Building, Suite 622 · 410 Central Avenue · P.O. Box 1184 · Great Falls, MT 59403 · 406-727-4041

Gary M. Zadick · Ugrin, Alexander, Zadick & Higgins · Two Railroad Square, Suite B · Great Falls, MT 59401 · 406-771-0007

Helena

Thomas E. Hattersley III · a · Gough, Shanahan, Johnson & Waterman · 33 South Last Chance Gulch · P.O. Box 1715 · Helena, MT 59624-1715 · 406-442-8560

Peter M. Meloy · Meloy Trieweiler · Bluestone Building · 80 South Warren · P.O. Box 1241 · Helena, MT 59624 · 406-442-8670

John F. Sullivan · Hughes, Kellner, Sullivan & Alke · 40 West Lawrence Street, Suite A · P.O. Box 1166 · Helena, MT 59624 · 406-442-3690

Missoula

Ronald A. Bender · Worden Thane · http://www.wthlaw.net · 111 North Higgins Avenue, Suite 600 · P.O. Box 4747 · Missoula, MT 59806 · 406-721-3400

Candace C. Fetscher · a · Garlington, Lohn & Robinson · http://www.garlington.com · 199 West Pine Street · P.O. Box 7909 · Missoula, MT 59807-7909 · 406-523-2500

Lucy T. France · Garlington, Lohn & Robinson · http://www.garlington.com · 199 West Pine Street · P.O. Box 7909 · Missoula, MT 59807-7909 · 406-523-2500

Jeremy G. Thane · a · Worden Thane · http://www.wthlaw.net · 111 North Higgins Avenue, Suite 600 · P.O. Box 4747 · Missoula, MT 59806 · 406-721-3400

LAND USE & ZONING LAW

Bozeman

Andrew C. Dana · Conservation Law Associates · 115 West Kagy Boulevard, Suite P · Bozeman, MT 59715 · 406-586-9270

LEGAL MALPRACTICE LAW

Helena

Michael F. McMahon · Hughes, Kellner, Sullivan & Alke · 40 West Lawrence Street, Suite A · P.O. Box 1166 · Helena, MT 59624 · 406-442-3690

Missoula

Gary L. Graham · a · Garlington, Lohn & Robinson · http://www.garlington.com · 199 West Pine Street · P.O. Box 7909 · Missoula, MT 59807-7909 · 406-523-2500

William Evan Jones · a · Garlington, Lohn & Robinson · http://www.garlington.com · 199 West Pine Street · P.O. Box 7909 · Missoula, MT 59807-7909 · 406-523-2500

Bradley J. Luck · a · Garlington, Lohn & Robinson · http://www.garlington.com · 199 West Pine Street · P.O. Box 7909 · Missoula, MT 59807-7909 · 406-523-2500

MEDICAL MALPRACTICE LAW

Billings

John J. Russel · Brown Law Firm · 315 North 24th Street · P.O. Drawer 849 · Billings, MT 59103-0849 · 406-248-2611

Bozeman

John L. Amsden · Beck, Amsden & Ruggiero · 1946 Stadium Drive, Suite One · Bozeman, MT 59715 · 406-586-8700

Great Falls

John D. Alexander · Ugrin, Alexander, Zadick & Higgins · Two Railroad Square, Suite B · Great Falls, MT 59401 · 406-771-0007

Alexander Blewett III · a · Hoyt & Blewett · 501 Second Avenue North · P.O. Box 2807 · Great Falls, MT 59403-2807 · 406-761-1960

Kalispell

Dana L. Christensen · a · Christensen, Moore, Cockrell, Cummings & Axelberg · Two Medicine Building, Suite 104 · 160 Heritage Way · P.O. Box 7370 · Kalispell, MT 59904-0370 · 406-751-6000

Missoula

Douglas A. Buxbaum · Buxbaum, Daue & Fitzpatrick · 228 West Main Street, Suite A · P.O. Box 8209 · Missoula, MT 59807 · 406-327-8677

E. Craig Daue · Buxbaum, Daue & Fitzpatrick · 228 West Main Street, Suite A · P.O. Box 8209 · Missoula, MT 59807 · 406-327-8677

W. Carl Mendenhall · Worden Thane · http://www.wthlaw.net · 111 North Higgins Avenue, Suite 600 · P.O. Box 4747 · Missoula, MT 59806 · 406-721-3400

Larry E. Riley · ⑳ · Garlington, Lohn & Robinson · http://www.garlington.com · 199 West Pine Street · P.O. Box 7909 · Missoula, MT 59807-7909 · 406-523-2500

William A. Rossbach · ⑩ · Rossbach Hart Bechtold · 401 North Washington Street · P.O. Box 8988 · Missoula, MT 59807 · 406-543-5156

Jeremy G. Thane · ⑩ · Worden Thane · http://www.wthlaw.net · 111 North Higgins Avenue, Suite 600 · P.O. Box 4747 · Missoula, MT 59806 · 406-721-3400

MERGERS & ACQUISITIONS LAW

Missoula

Gary B. Chumrau · Garlington, Lohn & Robinson · http://www.garlington.com · 199 West Pine Street · P.O. Box 7909 · Missoula, MT 59807-7909 · 406-523-2500

MINING LAW

Helena

Alan L. Joscelyn · ⑩ · Gough, Shanahan, Johnson & Waterman · 33 South Last Chance Gulch · P.O. Box 1715 · Helena, MT 59624-1715 · 406-442-8560

Ward A. Shanahan · ⑩ · Gough, Shanahan, Johnson & Waterman · 33 South Last Chance Gulch · P.O. Box 1715 · Helena, MT 59624-1715 · 406-442-8560

MUNICIPAL LAW

Billings

Harlan B. Krogh · Crist, Krogh & Nord · 2708 First Avenue North, Suite 300 · Billings, MT 59101 · 406-255-0400

Butte

Brendon J. Rohan · Poore, Roth & Robinson · 1341 Harrison Avenue · P.O. Box 2000 · Butte, MT 59702 406-497-1200

Great Falls

Kevin C. Meek · Ugrin, Alexander, Zadick & Higgins · Two Railroad Square, Suite B · Great Falls, MT 59401 · 406-771-0007

Helena

Allen B. Chronister · Harlen, Chronister, Parish & Larson · 36 West Sixth Avenue · P.O. Box 1152 · Helena, MT 59624 · 406-443-0360

Stanley T. Kaleczyc · Browning, Kaleczyc, Berry and Hoven · 139 North Last Chance Gulch · P.O. Box 1697 · Helena, MT 59624 · 406-443-6820

Missoula

William L. Crowley · Boone Karlberg · Central Square, Suite 300 · 201 West Main Street · P.O. Box 9199 · Missoula, MT 59807-9199 · 406-543-6646

NATIVE AMERICAN LAW

Billings

Colby L. Branch · Crowley, Haughey, Hanson, Toole & Dietrich · http://www.crowleylaw.com · 490 North 31st Street, Suite 500 · P.O. Box 2529 · Billings, MT 59103-2529 · 406-252-3441

Bozeman

Neil G. Westesen · Crowley, Haughey, Hanson, Toole & Dietrich · http://www.crowleylaw.com · 45 Discovery Drive · P.O. Box 10969 · Bozeman, MT 59719-0969 · 406-556-1430

NATURAL RESOURCES LAW

Billings

Gary G. Broeder · a · Crowley, Haughey, Hanson, Toole & Dietrich · http://www.crowleylaw.com · 490 North 31st Street, Suite 500 · P.O. Box 2529 · Billings, MT 59103-2529 · 406-252-3441

John R. Lee · Crowley, Haughey, Hanson, Toole & Dietrich · http://www.crowleylaw.com · 490 North 31st Street, Suite 500 · P.O. Box 2529 · Billings, MT 59103-2529 · 406-252-3441

Christopher Mangen, Jr. · a · Crowley, Haughey, Hanson, Toole & Dietrich · http://www.crowleylaw.com · 490 North 31st Street, Suite 500 · P.O. Box 2529 · Billings, MT 59103-2529 · 406-252-3441

Laurence W. Petersen · a · Holland & Hart · 401 North 31st Street, Suite 1500 · Billings, MT 59101-1200 · 406-252-2166

Steven P. Ruffatto · a · Crowley, Haughey, Hanson, Toole & Dietrich · http://www.crowleylaw.com · 490 North 31st Street, Suite 500 · P.O. Box 2529 · Billings, MT 59103-2529 · 406-252-3441

Helena

Jon Metropolous · Gough, Shanahan, Johnson & Waterman · 33 South Last Chance Gulch · P.O. Box 1715 · Helena, MT 59624-1715 · 406-442-8560

NON-WHITE-COLLAR CRIMINAL DEFENSE

Helena

Gregory A. Jackson · 2) · Jackson Law Firm · 320 Eleventh Avenue · Helena, MT 59601 · 406-443-2140

Missoula

Milton Datsopoulos · Datsopoulos, MacDonald & Lind · 201 West Main Street, Suite 201 · Missoula, MT 59801 · 406-728-0810

OIL & GAS LAW

Billings

Colby L. Branch · Crowley, Haughey, Hanson, Toole & Dietrich · http://www.crowleylaw.com · 490 North 31st Street, Suite 500 · P.O. Box 2529 · Billings, MT 59103-2529 · 406-252-3441

Gary G. Broeder · a · Crowley, Haughey, Hanson, Toole & Dietrich · http://www.crowleylaw.com · 490 North 31st Street, Suite 500 · P.O. Box 2529 · Billings, MT 59103-2529 · 406-252-3441

Christopher Mangen, Jr. · a · Crowley, Haughey, Hanson, Toole & Dietrich · http://www.crowleylaw.com · 490 North 31st Street, Suite 500 · P.O. Box 2529 · Billings, MT 59103-2529 · 406-252-3441

PERSONAL INJURY LITIGATION

Anaconda

Bernard J. Everett · a · Knight, Dahood, Everett & Sievers · 113 East Third Street · P.O. Box 727 · Anaconda, MT 59711 · 406-563-3424

Billings

Roberta Anner-Hughes · Anner-Hughes Law Firm · 175 North 27th Street, Suite 1206 · Billings, MT 59103-1156 · 406-256-8155

L. Randall Bishop · a · Jarussi & Bishop · 303 North Broadway, Suite 705 · P.O. Box 3353 · Billings, MT 59103 · 406-245-7555

David L. Charles · Crowley, Haughey, Hanson, Toole & Dietrich · http://www.crowleylaw.com · 490 North 31st Street, Suite 500 · P.O. Box 2529 · Billings, MT 59103-2529 · 406-252-3441

John G. Crist · Crist Law Firm · Securities Building, Suite 300 · 2708 First Avenue North · Billings, MT 59101 · 406-255-0400

Brent R. Cromley · Moulton, Bellingham · http://www.moultonlawfirm.com · Crowne Plaza, Suite 1900 · P.O. Box 2559 · Billings, MT 59103-2559 · 406-248-7731

A. Clifford Edwards · 2) · Edwards Frickle & Culver · http://www.edwardslawfirm.org · 1601 Lewis Avenue, Suite 206 · P.O. Box 20039 · Billings, MT 59104-0039 · 406-256-8155

Steven J. Harman · a · Harman, Warren & Harris · 550 North 31st Street, Suite 250 · Billings, MT 59101 406-294-2000

Donald Harris · Harman, Warren & Harris · 550 North 31st Street, Suite 250 · Billings, MT 59101 · 406-294-2000

Gene R. Jarussi · a · Jarussi & Bishop · 303 North Broadway, Suite 705 · P.O. Box 3353 · Billings, MT 59103 · 406-245-7555

Mark D. Parker · Parker, Heitz & Cosgrove · 401 North 31st Street, Suite 805 · P.O. Box 7212 · Billings, MT 59103-7212 · 406-245-9991

James J. Ragain · Ragain Christensen Fulton & Filz · 2825 Third Avenue North, Suite 100 · P.O. Box 339 · Billings, MT 59103 · 406-248-3100

Guy W. Rogers · Brown Law Firm · 315 North 24th Street · P.O. Drawer 849 · Billings, MT 59103-0849 · 406-248-2611

Calvin J. Stacey · Stacey and Funyak · The Grand Building, Suite 700 · 100 North 27th Street · P.O. Box 1139 · Billings, MT 59101 · 406-259-4545

Bozeman

Monte D. Beck · Beck, Amsden & Ruggiero · 1946 Stadium Drive, Suite One · Bozeman, MT 59715 · 406-586-8700

Michael D. Cok · Cok, Wheat & Kinzler · 35 North Bozeman Avenue · P.O. Box 1105 · Bozeman, MT 59771-1105 · 406-587-4445

Butte

R. D. Corette · a · Corette Pohlman & Kebe · Mayer Building · 129 West Park Street · Butte, MT 59701 406-782-5800

Michael J. McKeon · a · McKeon & Anderson · 2825 Lexington Avenue · P.O. Box 3329 · Butte, MT 59702-3329 · 406-494-8890

Marshal L. Mickelson · Corette Pohlman & Kebe · Mayer Building · 129 West Park Street · Butte, MT 59701 · 406-782-5800

Donald C. Robinson · 2) · Poore, Roth & Robinson · 1341 Harrison Avenue · P.O. Box 2000 · Butte, MT 59702 · 406-497-1200

Thomas M. Welsch · Poore, Roth & Robinson · 1341 Harrison Avenue · P.O. Box 2000 · Butte, MT 59702 · 406-497-1200

Great Falls

Alexander Blewett III · a · Hoyt & Blewett · 501 Second Avenue North · P.O. Box 2807 · Great Falls, MT 59403-2807 · 406-761-1960

Dennis P. Conner · a · Conner Shannon & Pinski · 520 Third Avenue North · P.O. Box 3028 · Great Falls, MT 59403-3028 · 406-727-3550

Joseph P. Cosgrove · Hoyt & Blewett · 501 Second Avenue North · P.O. Box 2807 · Great Falls, MT 59403-2807 · 406-761-1960

Maxon R. Davis · a · Davis, Hatley, Haffeman & Tighe · The Milwaukee Station, Third Floor · 101 River Drive North · P.O. Box 2103 · Great Falls, MT 59403 · 406-761-5243

Kurt M. Jackson · a · Hoyt & Blewett · 501 Second Avenue North · P.O. Box 2807 · Great Falls, MT 59403-2807 · 406-761-1960

Tom L. Lewis · a · Lewis, Slovak & Kovacich · 725 Third Avenue North · P.O. Box 2325 · Great Falls, MT 59403 · 406-761-5595

J. David Slovak · Lewis, Slovak & Kovacich · 725 Third Avenue North · P.O. Box 2325 · Great Falls, MT 59403 · 406-761-5595

Gary M. Zadick · Ugrin, Alexander, Zadick & Higgins · Two Railroad Square, Suite B · Great Falls, MT 59401 · 406-771-0007

Helena

Thomas M. Keegan · Thomas M. Keegan · 212 North Rodney Street · Helena, MT 59601 · 406-442-8711

Stuart L. Kellner · 2) · Hughes, Kellner, Sullivan & Alke · 40 West Lawrence Street, Suite A · P.O. Box 1166 · Helena, MT 59624 · 406-442-3690

Michael F. Lamb · Lamb & Carey · 2601 Broadway · Helena, MT 59601 · 406-457-1100

David M. McLean · a · Browning, Kaleczyc, Berry and Hoven · 139 North Last Chance Gulch · P.O. Box 1697 · Helena, MT 59624 · 406-443-6820

James P. Molloy · Molloy Law Firm · 30 West 14th Street, Suite 204 · P.O. Box 1182 · Helena, MT 59624-1182 · 406-442-2440

Erik B. Thueson · a · Thueson Law Office · 213 Fifth Avenue · P.O. Box 280 · Helena, MT 59624-0280 406-449-8200

Kalispell

Joe R. Bottomly · Bottomly & Ellingson · 1230 Whitefish Stage Road · Kalispell, MT 59901 · 406-752-3303

Dana L. Christensen · a · Christensen, Moore, Cockrell, Cummings & Axelberg · Two Medicine Building, Suite 104 · 160 Heritage Way · P.O. Box 7370 · Kalispell, MT 59904-0370 · 406-751-6000

Michael L. Moore · Christensen, Moore, Cockrell, Cummings & Axelberg · Two Medicine Building, Suite 104 · 160 Heritage Way · P.O. Box 7370 · Kalispell, MT 59904-0370 · 406-751-6000

Roger M. Sullivan, Jr. · McGarvey, Heberling, Sullivan & McGarvey · 745 South Main · Kalispell, MT 59901-5399 · 406-752-5566

Missoula

Douglas A. Buxbaum · Buxbaum, Daue & Fitzpatrick · 228 West Main Street, Suite A · P.O. Box 8209 · Missoula, MT 59807 · 406-327-8677

Randy J. Cox · Boone Karlberg · Central Square, Suite 300 · 201 West Main Street · P.O. Box 9199 · Missoula, MT 59807-9199 · 406-543-6646

Lawrence F. Daly · Garlington, Lohn & Robinson · http://www.garlington.com · 199 West Pine Street · P.O. Box 7909 · Missoula, MT 59807-7909 · 406-523-2500

E. Craig Daue · Buxbaum, Daue & Fitzpatrick · 228 West Main Street, Suite A · P.O. Box 8209 · Missoula, MT 59807 · 406-327-8677

Gary L. Graham · a · Garlington, Lohn & Robinson · http://www.garlington.com · 199 West Pine Street · P.O. Box 7909 · Missoula, MT 59807-7909 · 406-523-2500

William Evan Jones · a · Garlington, Lohn & Robinson · http://www.garlington.com · 199 West Pine Street · P.O. Box 7909 · Missoula, MT 59807-7909 · 406-523-2500

Bradley J. Luck · a · Garlington, Lohn & Robinson · http://www.garlington.com · 199 West Pine Street · P.O. Box 7909 · Missoula, MT 59807-7909 · 406-523-2500

Larry E. Riley · 2) · Garlington, Lohn & Robinson · http://www.garlington.com · 199 West Pine Street · P.O. Box 7909 · Missoula, MT 59807-7909 · 406-523-2500

William A. Rossbach · a · Rossbach Hart Bechtold · 401 North Washington Street · P.O. Box 8988 · Missoula, MT 59807 · 406-543-5156

Jeremy G. Thane · a · Worden Thane · http://www.wthlaw.net · 111 North Higgins Avenue, Suite 600 · P.O. Box 4747 · Missoula, MT 59806 · 406-721-3400

White Fish

Terry N. Trieweiler · Trieweiler Law Firm · P.O. Box 5509 · White Fish, MT 59937 · 406-862-4597

PRODUCT LIABILITY LITIGATION

Anaconda

Bernard J. Everett · a · Knight, Dahood, Everett & Sievers · 113 East Third Street · P.O. Box 727 · Anaconda, MT 59711 · 406-563-3424

Billings

Scott G. Gratton · Brown Law Firm · 315 North 24th Street · P.O. Drawer 849 · Billings, MT 59103-0849 406-248-2611

Brooke B. Murphy · Matovich & Keller · 2812 First Avenue North, Suite 225 · P.O. Box 1098 · Billings, MT 59103 · 406-252-5500

T. Thomas Singer · Axilon Law Group · Electric Building, Suite 310 · 115 North Broadway · Billings, MT 59101 · 406-294-9466

Bozeman

John L. Amsden · Beck, Amsden & Ruggiero · 1946 Stadium Drive, Suite One · Bozeman, MT 59715 · 406-586-8700

Monte D. Beck · Beck, Amsden & Ruggiero · 1946 Stadium Drive, Suite One · Bozeman, MT 59715 · 406-586-8700

Michael D. Cok · Cok, Wheat & Kinzler · 35 North Bozeman Avenue · P.O. Box 1105 · Bozeman, MT 59771-1105 · 406-587-4445

Helena

Michael F. Lamb · Lamb & Carey · 2601 Broadway · Helena, MT 59601 · 406-457-1100

Missoula

Ronald A. Bender · Worden Thane · http://www.wthlaw.net · 111 North Higgins Avenue, Suite 600 · P.O. Box 4747 · Missoula, MT 59806 · 406-721-3400

Paul C. Meismer · Meismer & Associates · 335 West Spruce Street, Suite 201 · P.O. Box 8989 · Missoula, MT 59807-8989 · 406-829-1766

David R. Paoli · Paoli, Latino, Kutzman & Jasper · 257 West Front Street, Suite A · P.O. Box 8131 · Missoula, MT 59802 · 406-542-3330

William A. Rossbach · a · Rossbach Hart Bechtold · 401 North Washington Street · P.O. Box 8988 · Missoula, MT 59807 · 406-543-5156

Jeremy G. Thane · a · Worden Thane · http://www.wthlaw.net · 111 North Higgins Avenue, Suite 600 · P.O. Box 4747 · Missoula, MT 59806 · 406-721-3400

PROJECT FINANCE LAW

Billings

Laurence W. Petersen · a · Holland & Hart · 401 North 31st Street, Suite 1500 · Billings, MT 59101-1200 · 406-252-2166

PUBLIC FINANCE LAW

Missoula

Mae Nan Ellingson · Dorsey & Whitney · 125 Bank Street, Suite 600 · Missoula, MT 59802-4407 · 406-721-6025

RAILROAD LAW

Billings

Jon M. Moyers · Hedgers Moyers · 2800 Central Avenue · Billings, MT 59102 · 406-896-4100

Russell Yerger · a · The Yerger Law Firm · 2722 Third Avenue North, Suite 400 · Billings, MT 59101 · 406-256-1500

Great Falls

Alexander Blewett III · a · Hoyt & Blewett · 501 Second Avenue North · P.O. Box 2807 · Great Falls, MT 59403-2807 · 406-761-1960

Joseph P. Cosgrove · Hoyt & Blewett · 501 Second Avenue North · P.O. Box 2807 · Great Falls, MT 59403-2807 · 406-761-1960

Kurt M. Jackson · a · Hoyt & Blewett · 501 Second Avenue North · P.O. Box 2807 · Great Falls, MT 59403-2807 · 406-761-1960

Missoula

Randy J. Cox · Boone Karlberg · Central Square, Suite 300 · 201 West Main Street · P.O. Box 9199 · Missoula, MT 59807-9199 · 406-543-6646

Robert E. Sheridan · Garlington, Lohn & Robinson · http://www.garlington.com · 199 West Pine Street · P.O. Box 7909 · Missoula, MT 59807-7909 · 406-523-2500

Big Timber

Richard W. Josephson · 2) · Josephson Law Firm · 115 West Second Avenue · P.O. Box 1047 · Big Timber, MT 59011 · 406-932-5900

Billings

Michael S. Dockery · Crowley, Haughey, Hanson, Toole & Dietrich · http://www.crowleylaw.com · 490 North 31st Street, Suite 500 · P.O. Box 2529 · Billings, MT 59103-2529 · 406-252-3441

Lance R. Hoskins · a · Brekke & Hoskins · 1280 First Interstate Center · 401 North 31st Street · P.O. Box 7197 · Billings, MT 59103 · 406-869-1100

Allan L. Karell · Karell Dyre Haney · Wells Fargo Center, Suite 1303 · 175 North 27th Street · Billings, MT 59101 · 406-294-8484

Laurence W. Petersen · a · Holland & Hart · 401 North 31st Street, Suite 1500 · Billings, MT 59101-1200 · 406-252-2166

Thomas E. Smith · Moulton, Bellingham · http://www.moultonlawfirm.com · Crowne Plaza, Suite 1900 · P.O. Box 2559 · Billings, MT 59103-2559 · 406-248-7731

Bozeman

Andrew C. Dana · Conservation Law Associates · 115 West Kagy Boulevard, Suite P · Bozeman, MT 59715 · 406-586-9270

Columbus

Richard W. Heard · a · Heard & Howard · 219 North Fourth Street · P.O. Box 926 · Columbus, MT 59019 · 406-322-4429

Kalispell

Stephen E. Cummings · Christensen, Moore, Cockrell, Cummings & Axelberg · Two Medicine Building, Suite 104 · 160 Heritage Way · P.O. Box 7370 · Kalispell, MT 59904-0370 · 406-751-6000

Missoula

Ronald A. Bender · Worden Thane · http://www.wthlaw.net · 111 North Higgins Avenue, Suite 600 · P.O. Box 4747 · Missoula, MT 59806 · 406-721-3400

James A. Bowditch · Boone Karlberg · Central Square, Suite 300 · 201 West Main Street · P.O. Box 9199 · Missoula, MT 59807-9199 · 406-543-6646

Kirby S. Christian · Christian, Samson, Jones & Chisholm · 310 West Spruce Street · Missoula, MT 59802 · 406-721-7772

Peter S. Dayton · Worden Thane · http://www.wthlaw.net · 111 North Higgins Avenue, Suite 600 · P.O. Box 4747 · Missoula, MT 59806 · 406-721-3400

Patrick D. Dougherty · Worden Thane · http://www.wthlaw.net · 111 North Higgins Avenue, Suite 600 · P.O. Box 4747 · Missoula, MT 59806 · 406-721-3400

Martin S. King · Worden Thane · http://www.wthlaw.net · 111 North Higgins Avenue, Suite 600 · P.O. Box 4747 · Missoula, MT 59806 · 406-721-3400

Robert M. Knight · 2) · Robert M. Knight · 526 East Front Street · P.O. Box 8899 · Missoula, MT 59807-8899 · 406-721-5440

Helena S. Maclay · a · Maclay Law Firm · 828 Ronald Avenue · P.O. Box 9197 · Missoula, MT 59807-9197 · 406-721-4210

Dean A. Stensland · Boone Karlberg · Central Square, Suite 300 · 201 West Main Street · P.O. Box 9199 · Missoula, MT 59807-9199 · 406-543-6646

William T. Wagner · Garlington, Lohn & Robinson · http://www.garlington.com · 199 West Pine Street · P.O. Box 7909 · Missoula, MT 59807-7909 · 406-523-2500

SECURITIES LAW

Missoula

John W. Manning · a · Dorsey & Whitney · 125 Bank Street, Suite 600 · Missoula, MT 59802-4407 · 406-721-6025

TAX LAW

Billings

Eric K. Anderson · Anderson & Heard · 3116 McBride Street · Billings, MT 59102 · 406-869-8869

Richard A. Brekke · a · Brekke & Hoskins · 1280 First Interstate Center · 401 North 31st Street · P.O. Box 7197 · Billings, MT 59103 · 406-869-1100

Scott Heard · Anderson & Heard · 3116 McBride Street · Billings, MT 59102 · 406-869-8869

Lance R. Hoskins · a · Brekke & Hoskins · 1280 First Interstate Center · 401 North 31st Street · P.O. Box 7197 · Billings, MT 59103 · 406-869-1100

John T. Jones · a · Moulton, Bellingham · http://www.moultonlawfirm.com · Crowne Plaza, Suite 1900 · P.O. Box 2559 · Billings, MT 59103-2559 · 406-248-7731

Laurence W. Petersen · a · Holland & Hart · 401 North 31st Street, Suite 1500 · Billings, MT 59101-1200 · 406-252-2166

Thomas F. Topel · Brekke & Hoskins · 1280 First Interstate Center · 401 North 31st Street · P.O. Box 7197 · Billings, MT 59103 · 406-869-1100

Bozeman

Larry A. Holle · a · Crowley, Haughey, Hanson, Toole & Dietrich · http://www.crowleylaw.com · 45 Discovery Drive · P.O. Box 10969 · Bozeman, MT 59719-0969 · 406-556-1430

Missoula

Patrick D. Dougherty · Worden Thane · http://www.wthlaw.net · 111 North Higgins Avenue, Suite 600 · P.O. Box 4747 · Missoula, MT 59806 · 406-721-3400

Gregory L. Hanson · a · Garlington, Lohn & Robinson · http://www.garlington.com · 199 West Pine Street · P.O. Box 7909 · Missoula, MT 59807-7909 · 406-523-2500

Shane N. Reely · Reely Law Firm · 3819 Stephens Avenue, Suite 201 · Missoula, MT 59801 · 406-541-9700

Gerald W. Steinbrenner · Milodragovich, Dale, Steinbrenner & Nygren · 620 High Park Way · P.O. Box 4947 · Missoula, MT 59806-4947 · 406-728-1455

TRUSTS AND ESTATES

Billings

Eric K. Anderson · Anderson & Heard · 3116 McBride Street · Billings, MT 59102 · 406-869-8869

Richard A. Brekke · a · Brekke & Hoskins · 1280 First Interstate Center · 401 North 31st Street · P.O. Box 7197 · Billings, MT 59103 · 406-869-1100

Angus B. Fulton · a · Ragain Christensen Fulton & Filz · 2825 Third Avenue North, Suite 100 · P.O. Box 339 · Billings, MT 59103 · 406-248-3100

Lance R. Hoskins · a · Brekke & Hoskins · 1280 First Interstate Center · 401 North 31st Street · P.O. Box 7197 · Billings, MT 59103 · 406-869-1100

John T. Jones · a · Moulton, Bellingham · http://www.moultonlawfirm.com · Crowne Plaza, Suite 1900 · P.O. Box 2559 · Billings, MT 59103-2559 · 406-248-7731

Laurence W. Petersen · a · Holland & Hart · 401 North 31st Street, Suite 1500 · Billings, MT 59101-1200 · 406-252-2166

Great Falls

Gary W. Bjelland · a · Jardine, Stephenson, Blewett and Weaver · U.S. Bank Building, Seventh Floor · 300 Central Avenue · P.O. Box 2269 · Great Falls, MT 59403 · 406-727-5000

W. Bjarne Johnson · a · Church, Harris, Johnson & Williams · Wells Fargo Bank Building, Third Floor · 21 Third Street North · P.O. Box 1645 · Great Falls, MT 59403 · 406-761-3000

Helena

Daniel N. McLean · Crowley, Haughey, Hanson, Toole & Dietrich · http://www.crowleylaw.com · 100 North Park Avenue, Suite 300 · P.O. Box 797 · Helena, MT 59625-0797 · 406-449-4165

Missoula

Patrick D. Dougherty · Worden Thane · http://www.wthlaw.net · 111 North Higgins Avenue, Suite 600 · P.O. Box 4747 · Missoula, MT 59806 · 406-721-3400

Gregory L. Hanson · a · Garlington, Lohn & Robinson · http://www.garlington.com · 199 West Pine Street · P.O. Box 7909 · Missoula, MT 59807-7909 · 406-523-2500

Shane N. Reely · Reely Law Firm · 3819 Stephens Avenue, Suite 201 · Missoula, MT 59801 · 406-541-9700

WATER LAW

Helena

John E. Bloomquist · Doney, Crowley, Bloomquist, Payne & Uda · Diamond Block Building, Suite 200 · 44 West Sixth Avenue · P.O. Box 1185 · Helena, MT 59624-1185 · 406-443-2211

Holly J. Franz · Franz & Driscoll · 21 North Last Chance Gulch Street, Suite 210 · Helena, MT 59601 · 406-442-0005

Alan L. Joscelyn · a · Gough, Shanahan, Johnson & Waterman · 33 South Last Chance Gulch · P.O. Box 1715 · Helena, MT 59624-1715 · 406-442-8560

WHITE-COLLAR CRIMINAL DEFENSE

Helena

Gregory A. Jackson · 2) · Jackson Law Firm · 320 Eleventh Avenue · Helena, MT 59601 · 406-443-2140

Missoula

Milton Datsopoulos · Datsopoulos, MacDonald & Lind · 201 West Main Street, Suite 201 · Missoula, MT 59801 · 406-728-0810

WORKERS' COMPENSATION LAW

Anaconda

Bernard J. Everett · a · Knight, Dahood, Everett & Sievers · 113 East Third Street · P.O. Box 727 · Anaconda, MT 59711 · 406-563-3424

Billings

Michael P. Heringer · Brown Law Firm · 315 North 24th Street · P.O. Drawer 849 · Billings, MT 59103-0849 · 406-248-2611

Thomas J. Lynaugh · a · Lynaugh, Fitzgerald, Eiselein & Grubbs · 225 North 23rd Street · P.O. Box 1729 · Billings, MT 59103-1729 · 406-252-3461

Joe C. Maynard, Jr. · a · Crowley, Haughey, Hanson, Toole & Dietrich · http://www.crowleylaw.com · 490 North 31st Street, Suite 500 · P.O. Box 2529 · Billings, MT 59103-2529 · 406-252-3441

Patrick R. Sheehy · a · Halverson, Sheehy & Plath · 550 North 31st Street, Suite 111 · P.O. Box 1817 · Billings, MT 59101 · 406-256-2000

Great Falls

Tom L. Lewis · a · Lewis, Slovak & Kovacich · 725 Third Avenue North · P.O. Box 2325 · Great Falls, MT 59403 · 406-761-5595

Helena

Norman H. Grosfield · a · Norman H. Grosfield · 314 North Last Chance Gulch Street · Helena, MT 59601 · 406-443-7250

Andrew J. Utick · a · Andrew J. Utick · 1424 National Avenue · Helena, MT 59601 · 406-443-7250

Missoula

Bradley J. Luck · a · Garlington, Lohn & Robinson · http://www.garlington.com · 199 West Pine Street · P.O. Box 7909 · Missoula, MT 59807-7909 · 406-523-2500

W. Carl Mendenhall · Worden Thane · http://www.wthlaw.net · 111 North Higgins Avenue, Suite 600 · P.O. Box 4747 · Missoula, MT 59806 · 406-721-3400

NEBRASKA

ALTERNATIVE DISPUTE RESOLUTION

Lincoln

James M. Bausch · a · Cline, Williams, Wright, Johnson & Oldfather · 1900 U.S. Bank Building · 233 South 13th Street · Lincoln, NE 68508-2095 · 402-474-6900

Mark A. Christensen · Cline, Williams, Wright, Johnson & Oldfather · 1900 U.S. Bank Building · 233 South 13th Street · Lincoln, NE 68508-2095 · 402-474-6900

Fredric H. Kauffman · 2) · Cline, Williams, Wright, Johnson & Oldfather · 1900 U.S. Bank Building · 233 South 13th Street · Lincoln, NE 68508-2095 · 402-474-6900

Con M. Keating · 2) · Keating, O'Gara, Davis & Nedved · 530 South 13th Street, Suite 100 · Lincoln, NE 68508 · 402-475-8230

Omaha

John C. Brownrigg · Erickson & Sederstrom · Regency Westpointe, Suite 100 · 10330 Regency Parkway Drive · Omaha, NE 68114-3761 · 402-397-2200

D. Nick Caporale · Baird Holm · http://www.bairdholm.com · Woodmen Tower, Suite 1500 · 1700 Farnam Street · Omaha, NE 68102-2068 · 402-344-0500

J. Terry Macnamara · McGrath North · http://www.mcgrathnorth.com · First National Tower, Suite 3700 1601 Dodge Street · Omaha, NE 68102 · 402-341-3070

Matthew G. Miller · Matthew G. Miller · http://www.mgmillerlaw.com · 6910 Pacific Street, Suite 200 · Omaha, NE 68106 · 402-558-4900

Michael G. Mullin · Kutak Rock · The Omaha Building · 1650 Farnam Street · Omaha, NE 68102-2186 · 402-346-6000

BANKING LAW

Lincoln

Victor E. Covalt III · Ballew, Colvalt · 1045 Lincoln Mall, Suite 200 · Lincoln, NE 68508 · 402-436-3030

John M. Guthery · Perry, Guthery, Haase & Gessford · 233 South 13th Street, Suite 1400 · Lincoln, NE 68508 · 402-476-9200

Robert J. Routh · 2) · Cline, Williams, Wright, Johnson & Oldfather · 1900 U.S. Bank Building · 233 South 13th Street · Lincoln, NE 68508-2095 · 402-474-6900

Norfolk

Thomas H. DeLay · Jewell, Collins & DeLay · 105 South Second Street · P.O. Box 1367 · Norfolk, NE 68701 · 402-371-4844

Omaha

Joyce A. Dixon · Husch Blackwell Sanders · http://www.huschblackwell.com · 1620 Dodge Street, Suite 2100 · Omaha, NE 68102 · 402-964-5000

Steven C. Turner · 2) · Baird Holm · http://www.bairdholm.com · Woodmen Tower, Suite 1500 · 1700 Farnam Street · Omaha, NE 68102-2068 · 402-344-0500

John S. Zeilinger · a · Baird Holm · http://www.bairdholm.com · Woodmen Tower, Suite 1500 · 1700 Farnam Street · Omaha, NE 68102-2068 · 402-344-0500

BANKRUPTCY AND CREDITOR-DEBTOR RIGHTS LAW

Lincoln

Joseph H. Badami · 2) · Woods & Aitken · 301 South 13th Street, Suite 500 · Lincoln, NE 68508 · 402-437-8500

Victor E. Covalt III · Ballew, Colvalt · 1045 Lincoln Mall, Suite 200 · Lincoln, NE 68508 · 402-436-3030

Richard P. Garden, Jr. · Cline, Williams, Wright, Johnson & Oldfather · 1900 U.S. Bank Building · 233 South 13th Street · Lincoln, NE 68508-2095 · 402-474-6900

John M. Guthery · Perry, Guthery, Haase & Gessford · 233 South 13th Street, Suite 1400 · Lincoln, NE 68508 · 402-476-9200

Rick D. Lange · Rembolt Ludtke · 1201 Lincoln Mall, Suite 102 · Lincoln, NE 68508 · 402-475-5100

Stephen H. Nelsen · Cline, Williams, Wright, Johnson & Oldfather · 1900 U.S. Bank Building · 233 South 13th Street · Lincoln, NE 68508-2095 · 402-474-6900

Omaha

Robert J. Bothe · McGrath North · http://www.mcgrathnorth.com · First National Tower, Suite 3700 · 1601 Dodge Street · Omaha, NE 68102 · 402-341-3070

James B. Cavanagh · Lieben, Whitted, Houghton, Slowiaczek & Cavanagh · 100 Scoular Building · 2027 Dodge Street · Omaha, NE 68102 · 402-344-4000

Robert V. Ginn · Husch Blackwell Sanders · http://www.huschblackwell.com · 1620 Dodge Street, Suite 2100 · Omaha, NE 68102 · 402-964-5000

Richard D. Myers · McGill, Gotsdiner, Workman & Lepp · http://www.mgwl.com · First National Plaza, Suite 500 · 11404 West Dodge Road · Omaha, NE 68154 · 402-492-9200

Jerrold L. Strasheim · 2% · Baird Holm · http://www.bairdholm.com · Woodmen Tower, Suite 1500 · 1700 Farnam Street · Omaha, NE 68102-2068 · 402-344-0500

Donald L. Swanson · Koley Jessen · One Pacific Place, Suite 800 · 1125 South 103rd Street · Omaha, NE 68124 · 402-390-9500

Mary L. Swick · Baird Holm · http://www.bairdholm.com · Woodmen Tower, Suite 1500 · 1700 Farnam Street · Omaha, NE 68102-2068 · 402-344-0500

Steven C. Turner · 2) · Baird Holm · http://www.bairdholm.com · Woodmen Tower, Suite 1500 · 1700 Farnam Street · Omaha, NE 68102-2068 · 402-344-0500

T. Randall Wright · Baird Holm · http://www.bairdholm.com · Woodmen Tower, Suite 1500 · 1700 Farnam Street · Omaha, NE 68102-2068 · 402-344-0500

BET-THE-COMPANY LITIGATION

Lincoln

Fredric H. Kauffman · 2) · Cline, Williams, Wright, Johnson & Oldfather · 1900 U.S. Bank Building · 233 South 13th Street · Lincoln, NE 68508-2095 · 402-474-6900

Omaha

John R. Douglas · a · Cassem, Tierney, Adams, Gotch & Douglas · 8805 Indian Hills Drive, Suite 300 · Omaha, NE 68114 · 402-390-0300

Charles F. Gotch · 2% · Cassem, Tierney, Adams, Gotch & Douglas · 8805 Indian Hills Drive, Suite 300 · Omaha, NE 68114 · 402-390-0300

William M. Lamson, Jr. · a · Lamson, Dugan and Murray · 10306 Regency Parkway Drive · Omaha, NE 68114 · 402-397-7300

Joseph K. Meusey · 2% · Fraser Stryker · http://www.fraserstryker.com · 500 Energy Plaza · 409 South 17th Street · Omaha, NE 68102-2663 · 402-341-6000

COMMERCIAL LITIGATION

Lincoln

James M. Bausch · a · Cline, Williams, Wright, Johnson & Oldfather · 1900 U.S. Bank Building · 233 South 13th Street · Lincoln, NE 68508-2095 · 402-474-6900

Timothy R. Engler · Harding & Shultz · 800 Lincoln Square · 121 South 13th Street · P.O. Box 82028 · Lincoln, NE 68501-2028 · 402-434-3000

Fredric H. Kauffman · 2) · Cline, Williams, Wright, Johnson & Oldfather · 1900 U.S. Bank Building · 233 South 13th Street · Lincoln, NE 68508-2095 · 402-474-6900

Allen L. Overcash · a · Woods & Aitken · 301 South 13th Street, Suite 500 · Lincoln, NE 68508 · 402-437-8500

Omaha

Steven E. Achelpohl · Steven E. Achelpohl · 1010 Historic Library Plaza · 1823 Harney Street · Omaha, NE 68102 · 402-346-1900

Kirk S. Blecha · Baird Holm · http://www.bairdholm.com · Woodmen Tower, Suite 1500 · 1700 Farnam Street · Omaha, NE 68102-2068 · 402-344-0500

James B. Cavanagh · Lieben, Whitted, Houghton, Slowiaczek & Cavanagh · 100 Scoular Building · 2027 Dodge Street · Omaha, NE 68102 · 402-344-4000

Thomas J. Culhane · Erickson & Sederstrom · Regency Westpointe, Suite 100 · 10330 Regency Parkway Drive · Omaha, NE 68114-3761 · 402-397-2200

Kelly R. Dahl · Baird Holm · http://www.bairdholm.com · Woodmen Tower, Suite 1500 · 1700 Farnam Street · Omaha, NE 68102-2068 · 402-344-0500

Thomas H. Dahlk · Husch Blackwell Sanders · http://www.huschblackwell.com · 1620 Dodge Street, Suite 2100 · Omaha, NE 68102 · 402-964-5000

Steven D. Davidson · Baird Holm · http://www.bairdholm.com · Woodmen Tower, Suite 1500 · 1700 Farnam Street · Omaha, NE 68102-2068 · 402-344-0500

William G. Dittrick · Baird Holm · http://www.bairdholm.com · Woodmen Tower, Suite 1500 · 1700 Farnam Street · Omaha, NE 68102-2068 · 402-344-0500

John R. Douglas · a · Cassem, Tierney, Adams, Gotch & Douglas · 8805 Indian Hills Drive, Suite 300 · Omaha, NE 68114 · 402-390-0300

Daniel J. Duffy · a · Cassem, Tierney, Adams, Gotch & Douglas · 8805 Indian Hills Drive, Suite 300 · Omaha, NE 68114 · 402-390-0300

Mark F. Enenbach · McGrath North · http://www.mcgrathnorth.com · First National Tower, Suite 3700 · 1601 Dodge Street · Omaha, NE 68102 · 402-341-3070

James P. Fitzgerald · McGrath North · http://www.mcgrathnorth.com · First National Tower, Suite 3700 · 1601 Dodge Street · Omaha, NE 68102 · 402-341-3070

Gerald L. Friedrichsen · Fitzgerald, Schorr, Barmettler & Brennan · 13220 California Street, Suite 400 · Omaha, NE 68154 · 402-342-1000

Charles F. Gotch · 2% · Cassem, Tierney, Adams, Gotch & Douglas · 8805 Indian Hills Drive, Suite 300 · Omaha, NE 68114 · 402-390-0300

William F. Hargens · McGrath North · http://www.mcgrathnorth.com · First National Tower, Suite 3700 · 1601 Dodge Street · Omaha, NE 68102 · 402-341-3070

David S. Houghton · Lieben, Whitted, Houghton, Slowiaczek & Cavanagh · 100 Scoular Building · 2027 Dodge Street · Omaha, NE 68102 · 402-344-4000

Thomas E. Johnson · a · Baird Holm · http://www.bairdholm.com · Woodmen Tower, Suite 1500 · 1700 Farnam Street · Omaha, NE 68102-2068 · 402-344-0500

Joseph E. Jones · Fraser Stryker · http://www.fraserstryker.com · 500 Energy Plaza · 409 South 17th Street · Omaha, NE 68102-2663 · 402-341-6000

Michael F. Kinney · Cassem, Tierney, Adams, Gotch & Douglas · 8805 Indian Hills Drive, Suite 300 · Omaha, NE 68114 · 402-390-0300

William M. Lamson, Jr. · a · Lamson, Dugan and Murray · 10306 Regency Parkway Drive · Omaha, NE 68114 · 402-397-7300

Gerald P. Laughlin · a · Baird Holm · http://www.bairdholm.com · Woodmen Tower, Suite 1500 · 1700 Farnam Street · Omaha, NE 68102-2068 · 402-344-0500

Wayne J. Mark · Fraser Stryker · http://www.fraserstryker.com · 500 Energy Plaza · 409 South 17th Street Omaha, NE 68102-2663 · 402-341-6000

Bartholomew L. McLeay · Kutak Rock · The Omaha Building · 1650 Farnam Street · Omaha, NE 68102-2186 · 402-346-6000

Joseph K. Meusey · 2% · Fraser Stryker · http://www.fraserstryker.com · 500 Energy Plaza · 409 South 17th Street · Omaha, NE 68102-2663 · 402-341-6000

John P. Passarelli · Kutak Rock · The Omaha Building · 1650 Farnam Street · Omaha, NE 68102-2186 · 402-346-6000

Patrick G. Vipond · Lamson, Dugan and Murray · 10306 Regency Parkway Drive · Omaha, NE 68114 · 402-397-7300

Edward G. Warin · a · McGrath North · http://www.mcgrathnorth.com · First National Tower, Suite 3700 · 1601 Dodge Street · Omaha, NE 68102 · 402-341-3070

CONSTRUCTION LAW

Lincoln

Timothy R. Engler · Harding & Shultz · 800 Lincoln Square · 121 South 13th Street · P.O. Box 82028 · Lincoln, NE 68501-2028 · 402-434-3000

Allen L. Overcash · a · Woods & Aitken · 301 South 13th Street, Suite 500 · Lincoln, NE 68508 · 402-437-8500

Omaha

Paul Scott Dye · Baird Holm · http://www.bairdholm.com · Woodmen Tower, Suite 1500 · 1700 Farnam Street · Omaha, NE 68102-2068 · 402-344-0500

Lawrence E. Kritenbrink · Baird Holm · http://www.bairdholm.com · Woodmen Tower, Suite 1500 · 1700 Farnam Street · Omaha, NE 68102-2068 · 402-344-0500

Wayne J. Mark · Fraser Stryker · http://www.fraserstryker.com · 500 Energy Plaza · 409 South 17th Street Omaha, NE 68102-2663 · 402-341-6000

CORPORATE GOVERNANCE AND COMPLIANCE LAW

Omaha

Dennis J. Fogland · Baird Holm · http://www.bairdholm.com · Woodmen Tower, Suite 1500 · 1700 Farnam Street · Omaha, NE 68102-2068 · 402-344-0500

Paul C. Jessen · a · Koley Jessen · One Pacific Place, Suite 800 · 1125 South 103rd Street · Omaha, NE 68124 · 402-390-9500

CORPORATE LAW

Lincoln

Donald F. Burt · a · Cline, Williams, Wright, Johnson & Oldfather · 1900 U.S. Bank Building · 233 South 13th Street · Lincoln, NE 68508-2095 · 402-474-6900

Robert L. Nefsky · a · Rembolt Ludtke · 1201 Lincoln Mall, Suite 102 · Lincoln, NE 68508 · 402-475-5100

Robert J. Routh · 2) · Cline, Williams, Wright, Johnson & Oldfather · 1900 U.S. Bank Building · 233 South 13th Street · Lincoln, NE 68508-2095 · 402-474-6900

Mark A. Scudder · Scudder Law Firm · 411 South Thirteenth Street, Suite 200 · Lincoln, NE 68508 · 402-435-3223

Omaha

Joe E. Armstrong · a · Kutak Rock · The Omaha Building · 1650 Farnam Street · Omaha, NE 68102-2186 · 402-346-6000

Joseph J. Barmettler · a · Fitzgerald, Schorr, Barmettler & Brennan · 13220 California Street, Suite 400 · Omaha, NE 68154 · 402-342-1000

Thomas R. Burke · 2% · Lamson, Dugan and Murray · 10306 Regency Parkway Drive · Omaha, NE 68114 402-397-7300

Joyce A. Dixon · Husch Blackwell Sanders · http://www.huschblackwell.com · 1620 Dodge Street, Suite 2100 · Omaha, NE 68102 · 402-964-5000

Donald L. Erftmier, Jr. · Lamson, Dugan and Murray · 10306 Regency Parkway Drive · Omaha, NE 68114 · 402-397-7300

Dennis J. Fogland · Baird Holm · http://www.bairdholm.com · Woodmen Tower, Suite 1500 · 1700 Farnam Street · Omaha, NE 68102-2068 · 402-344-0500

Robert L. Freeman · Fraser Stryker · http://www.fraserstryker.com · 500 Energy Plaza · 409 South 17th Street · Omaha, NE 68102-2663 · 402-341-6000

David E. Gardels · Husch Blackwell Sanders · http://www.huschblackwell.com · 1620 Dodge Street, Suite 2100 · Omaha, NE 68102 · 402-964-5000

Stephen E. Gehring · a · Cline, Williams, Wright, Johnson & Oldfather · One Pacific Place, Suite 320 · 1125 South 103rd Street · Omaha, NE 68124 · 402-397-1700

Gary M. Gotsdiner · McGill, Gotsdiner, Workman & Lepp · http://www.mgwl.com · First National Plaza, Suite 500 · 11404 West Dodge Road · Omaha, NE 68154 · 402-492-9200

Deryl F. Hamann · 2% · Baird Holm · http://www.bairdholm.com · Woodmen Tower, Suite 1500 · 1700 Farnam Street · Omaha, NE 68102-2068 · 402-344-0500

David L. Hefflinger · 2% · McGrath North · http://www.mcgrathnorth.com · First National Tower, Suite 3700 · 1601 Dodge Street · Omaha, NE 68102 · 402-341-3070

John W. Herdzina · Abrahams Kaslow & Cassman · http://www.akclaw.com · 8712 West Dodge Road, Suite 300 · Omaha, NE 68114-3419 · 402-392-1250

Michael M. Hupp · Koley Jessen · One Pacific Place, Suite 800 · 1125 South 103rd Street · Omaha, NE 68124 · 402-390-9500

Thomas E. Johnson · a · Baird Holm · http://www.bairdholm.com · Woodmen Tower, Suite 1500 · 1700 Farnam Street · Omaha, NE 68102-2068 · 402-344-0500

Howard J. Kaslow · 2) · Abrahams Kaslow & Cassman · http://www.akclaw.com · 8712 West Dodge Road, Suite 300 · Omaha, NE 68114-3419 · 402-392-1250

John S. Katelman · Husch Blackwell Sanders · http://www.huschblackwell.com · 1620 Dodge Street, Suite 2100 · Omaha, NE 68102 · 402-964-5000

Douglas D. Murray · Baird Holm · http://www.bairdholm.com · Woodmen Tower, Suite 1500 · 1700 Farnam Street · Omaha, NE 68102-2068 · 402-344-0500

Robert J. Murray · Lamson, Dugan and Murray · 10306 Regency Parkway Drive · Omaha, NE 68114 · 402-397-7300

Richard E. Putnam · Baird Holm · http://www.bairdholm.com · Woodmen Tower, Suite 1500 · 1700 Farnam Street · Omaha, NE 68102-2068 · 402-344-0500

Todd A. Richardson · Husch Blackwell Sanders · http://www.huschblackwell.com · 1620 Dodge Street, Suite 2100 · Omaha, NE 68102 · 402-964-5000

T. Parker Schenken · Baird Holm · http://www.bairdholm.com · Woodmen Tower, Suite 1500 · 1700 Farnam Street · Omaha, NE 68102-2068 · 402-344-0500

Bruce D. Vosburg · Fitzgerald, Schorr, Barmettler & Brennan · 13220 California Street, Suite 400 · Omaha, NE 68154 · 402-342-1000

Roger W. Wells · McGrath North · http://www.mcgrathnorth.com · First National Tower, Suite 3700 · 1601 Dodge Street · Omaha, NE 68102 · 402-341-3070

R. Thomas Workman · McGill, Gotsdiner, Workman & Lepp · http://www.mgwl.com · First National Plaza, Suite 500 · 11404 West Dodge Road · Omaha, NE 68154 · 402-492-9200

John S. Zeilinger · a · Baird Holm · http://www.bairdholm.com · Woodmen Tower, Suite 1500 · 1700 Farnam Street · Omaha, NE 68102-2068 · 402-344-0500

EDUCATION LAW

Lincoln

Kelley Baker · Harding & Shultz · 800 Lincoln Square · 121 South 13th Street · P.O. Box 82028 · Lincoln, NE 68501-2028 · 402-434-3000

James B. Gessford · Perry, Guthery, Haase & Gessford · 233 South 13th Street, Suite 1400 · Lincoln, NE 68508 · 402-476-9200

Karen A. Haase · Harding & Shultz · 800 Lincoln Square · 121 South 13th Street · P.O. Box 82028 · Lincoln, NE 68501-2028 · 402-434-3000

Scott J. Norby · McGuire & Norby · 605 South 14th Street, Suite 100 · Lincoln, NE 68508 · 402-434-2390

Gregory H. Perry · Perry, Guthery, Haase & Gessford · 233 South 13th Street, Suite 1400 · Lincoln, NE 68508 · 402-476-9200

Rex R. Schultze · a · Perry, Guthery, Haase & Gessford · 233 South 13th Street, Suite 1400 · Lincoln, NE 68508 · 402-476-9200

Omaha

Elizabeth Eynon-Kokrda · Baird Holm · http://www.bairdholm.com · Woodmen Tower, Suite 1500 · 1700 Farnam Street · Omaha, NE 68102-2068 · 402-344-0500

David M. Pedersen · Baird Holm · http://www.bairdholm.com · Woodmen Tower, Suite 1500 · 1700 Farnam Street · Omaha, NE 68102-2068 · 402-344-0500

EMPLOYEE BENEFITS LAW

Lincoln

Michael C. Mueller · a · Cline, Williams, Wright, Johnson & Oldfather · 1900 U.S. Bank Building · 233 South 13th Street · Lincoln, NE 68508-2095 · 402-474-6900

L. Bruce Wright · 2) · Cline, Williams, Wright, Johnson & Oldfather · 1900 U.S. Bank Building · 233 South 13th Street · Lincoln, NE 68508-2095 · 402-474-6900

Omaha

Gary N. Clatterbuck · a · Baird Holm · http://www.bairdholm.com · Woodmen Tower, Suite 1500 · 1700 Farnam Street · Omaha, NE 68102-2068 · 402-344-0500

Peter C. Langdon · Kutak Rock · The Omaha Building · 1650 Farnam Street · Omaha, NE 68102-2186 · 402-346-6000

T. Geoffrey Lieben · 2% · Lieben, Whitted, Houghton, Slowiaczek & Cavanagh · 100 Scoular Building · 2027 Dodge Street · Omaha, NE 68102 · 402-344-4000

Randal M. Limbeck · a · McGrath North · http://www.mcgrathnorth.com · First National Tower, Suite 3700 · 1601 Dodge Street · Omaha, NE 68102 · 402-341-3070

Gary W. Radil · a · Baird Holm · http://www.bairdholm.com · Woodmen Tower, Suite 1500 · 1700 Farnam Street · Omaha, NE 68102-2068 · 402-344-0500

John E. Schembari · Kutak Rock · The Omaha Building · 1650 Farnam Street · Omaha, NE 68102-2186 402-346-6000

Daniel J. Wintz · Fraser Stryker · http://www.fraserstryker.com · 500 Energy Plaza · 409 South 17th Street Omaha, NE 68102-2663 · 402-341-6000

ENVIRONMENTAL LAW

Lincoln

Donald G. Blankenau · Husch Blackwell Sanders · http://www.huschblackwell.com · 206 South 13th Street, Suite 1400 · Lincoln, NE 68508 · 402-458-1500

Thomas R. Wilmoth · Husch Blackwell Sanders · http://www.huschblackwell.com · 206 South 13th Street, Suite 1400 · Lincoln, NE 68508 · 402-458-1500

Omaha

John A. Andreasen · McGrath North · http://www.mcgrathnorth.com · First National Tower, Suite 3700 · 1601 Dodge Street · Omaha, NE 68102 · 402-341-3070

Stephen M. Bruckner · a · Fraser Stryker · http://www.fraserstryker.com · 500 Energy Plaza · 409 South 17th Street · Omaha, NE 68102-2663 · 402-341-6000

Steven P. Case · McGrath North · http://www.mcgrathnorth.com · First National Tower, Suite 3700 · 1601 Dodge Street · Omaha, NE 68102 · 402-341-3070

Kelly R. Dahl · Baird Holm · http://www.bairdholm.com · Woodmen Tower, Suite 1500 · 1700 Farnam Street · Omaha, NE 68102-2068 · 402-344-0500

John P. Heil · a · Baird Holm · http://www.bairdholm.com · Woodmen Tower, Suite 1500 · 1700 Farnam Street · Omaha, NE 68102-2068 · 402-344-0500

Thomas C. McGowan · McGrath North · http://www.mcgrathnorth.com · First National Tower, Suite 3700 · 1601 Dodge Street · Omaha, NE 68102 · 402-341-3070

Michael S. Mostek · Koley Jessen · One Pacific Place, Suite 800 · 1125 South 103rd Street · Omaha, NE 68124 · 402-390-9500

FAMILY LAW

Kearney

Kent A. Schroeder · a · Ross, Schroeder & Ramatzke · 220 West 15th Street · P.O. Box 1685 · Kearney, NE 68845 · 308-237-5187

Lincoln

John W. Ballew, Jr. · Ballew, Colvalt · 1045 Lincoln Mall, Suite 200 · Lincoln, NE 68508 · 402-436-3030

Steven J. Flodman · a · Johnson, Flodman, Guenzel & Widger · 1227 Lincoln Mall · P.O. Box 81686 · Lincoln, NE 68501-1686 · 402-475-4240

Paul E. Galter · 2% · Butler, Galter, O'Brien & Boehm · 811 South 13th Street · Lincoln, NE 68508 · 402-475-0811

Con M. Keating · 2) · Keating, O'Gara, Davis & Nedved · 530 South 13th Street, Suite 100 · Lincoln, NE 68508 · 402-475-8230

Rex R. Schultze · a · Perry, Guthery, Haase & Gessford · 233 South 13th Street, Suite 1400 · Lincoln, NE 68508 · 402-476-9200

Omaha

Michael B. Lustgarten · Lustgarten and Roberts · 1625 Farnam Street, Suite 900 · Omaha, NE 68102 · 402-346-1920

Steven J. Lustgarten · 2% · Lustgarten and Roberts · 1625 Farnam Street, Suite 900 · Omaha, NE 68102 · 402-346-1920

Donald A. Roberts · Lustgarten and Roberts · 1625 Farnam Street, Suite 900 · Omaha, NE 68102 · 402-346-1920

John S. Slowiaczek · a · Lieben, Whitted, Houghton, Slowiaczek & Cavanagh · 100 Scoular Building · 2027 Dodge Street · Omaha, NE 68102 · 402-344-4000

FAMILY LAW MEDIATION

Lincoln

Paul E. Galter · 2% · Butler, Galter, O'Brien & Boehm · 811 South 13th Street · Lincoln, NE 68508 · 402-475-0811

Con M. Keating · 2) · Keating, O'Gara, Davis & Nedved · 530 South 13th Street, Suite 100 · Lincoln, NE 68508 · 402-475-8230

FIRST AMENDMENT LAW

Lincoln

Alan E. Peterson · a · Cline, Williams, Wright, Johnson & Oldfather · 1900 U.S. Bank Building · 233 South 13th Street · Lincoln, NE 68508-2095 · 402-474-6900

Shawn D. Renner · Cline, Williams, Wright, Johnson & Oldfather · 1900 U.S. Bank Building · 233 South 13th Street · Lincoln, NE 68508-2095 · 402-474-6900

Omaha

Michael C. Cox · Koley Jessen · One Pacific Place, Suite 800 · 1125 South 103rd Street · Omaha, NE 68124 · 402-390-9500

FRANCHISE LAW

Omaha

Gary R. Batenhorst · Stinson Morrison Hecker · http://www.stinson.com · Landmark Building, Suite 1501 · 1299 Farnam Street · Omaha, NE 68102 · 402-342-1700

John W. Herdzina · Abrahams Kaslow & Cassman · http://www.akclaw.com · 8712 West Dodge Road, Suite 300 · Omaha, NE 68114-3419 · 402-392-1250

John P. Passarelli · Kutak Rock · The Omaha Building · 1650 Farnam Street · Omaha, NE 68102-2186 · 402-346-6000

Michael L. Sullivan · Baird Holm · http://www.bairdholm.com · Woodmen Tower, Suite 1500 · 1700 Farnam Street · Omaha, NE 68102-2068 · 402-344-0500

GOVERNMENT RELATIONS LAW

Lincoln

William J. Mueller · Ruth Mueller Robak · 530 South Thirteenth Street, Suite 110 · Lincoln, NE 68508 · 402-434-3399

Kim Robak · Ruth Mueller Robak · 530 South Thirteenth Street, Suite 110 · Lincoln, NE 68508 · 402-434-3399

Omaha

David J. Kramer · Baird Holm · http://www.bairdholm.com · Woodmen Tower, Suite 1500 · 1700 Farnam Street · Omaha, NE 68102-2068 · 402-344-0500

HEALTH CARE LAW

Lincoln

Jill Gossin Jensen · Cline, Williams, Wright, Johnson & Oldfather · 1900 U.S. Bank Building · 233 South 13th Street · Lincoln, NE 68508-2095 · 402-474-6900

William H. Lewis · a · William H. Lewis · 44 Corporate Place, Suite 207 · 300 North 44th Street · Lincoln, NE 68503 · 402-467-3617

Charles M. Pallesen, Jr. · a · Cline, Williams, Wright, Johnson & Oldfather · 1900 U.S. Bank Building · 233 South 13th Street · Lincoln, NE 68508-2095 · 402-474-6900

Omaha

Vickie J. Brady · Baird Holm · http://www.bairdholm.com · Woodmen Tower, Suite 1500 · 1700 Farnam Street · Omaha, NE 68102-2068 · 402-344-0500

Alex M. Clarke · a · Baird Holm · http://www.bairdholm.com · Woodmen Tower, Suite 1500 · 1700 Farnam Street · Omaha, NE 68102-2068 · 402-344-0500

Andrew E. Grimm · a · Andrew E. Grimm · 4242 Farnam Street, Suite 267 · Omaha, NE 68131 · 402-552-3483

Wayne B. Henry · Stinson Morrison Hecker · http://www.stinson.com · Landmark Building, Suite 1501 · 1299 Farnam Street · Omaha, NE 68102 · 402-342-1700

John R. Holdenried · a · Baird Holm · http://www.bairdholm.com · Woodmen Tower, Suite 1500 · 1700 Farnam Street · Omaha, NE 68102-2068 · 402-344-0500

Jennifer Wolfe Jerram · Stinson Morrison Hecker · http://www.stinson.com · Landmark Building, Suite 1501 · 1299 Farnam Street · Omaha, NE 68102 · 402-342-1700

Julie A. Knutson · Baird Holm · http://www.bairdholm.com · Woodmen Tower, Suite 1500 · 1700 Farnam Street · Omaha, NE 68102-2068 · 402-344-0500

Amy L. Longo · Ellick, Jones, Buelt, Blazek & Longo · 8805 Indian Hills Drive, Suite 280 · Omaha, NE 68114 · 402-390-0390

Thomas R. Pansing, Jr. · Pansing Hogan Ernst & Bachman · Regency Center, Suite 300 · 10250 Regency Circle · Omaha, NE 68114 · 402-397-5500

Barbara E. Person · Baird Holm · http://www.bairdholm.com · Woodmen Tower, Suite 1500 · 1700 Farnam Street · Omaha, NE 68102-2068 · 402-344-0500

Charles V. Sederstrom · a · Erickson & Sederstrom · Regency Westpointe, Suite 100 · 10330 Regency Parkway Drive · Omaha, NE 68114-3761 · 402-397-2200

Karen M. Shuler · Koley Jessen · One Pacific Place, Suite 800 · 1125 South 103rd Street · Omaha, NE 68124 · 402-390-9500

Patricia A. Zieg · a · Stinson Morrison Hecker · http://www.stinson.com · Landmark Building, Suite 1501 1299 Farnam Street · Omaha, NE 68102 · 402-342-1700

IMMIGRATION LAW

Omaha

A. Stevenson Bogue · a · McGrath North · http://www.mcgrathnorth.com · First National Tower, Suite 3700 · 1601 Dodge Street · Omaha, NE 68102 · 402-341-3070

Amy L. Erlbacher-Anderson · Baird Holm · http://www.bairdholm.com · Woodmen Tower, Suite 1500 · 1700 Farnam Street · Omaha, NE 68102-2068 · 402-344-0500

M. Angela Krieger · Krieger & Krieger · 9290 West Dodge Road, Suite 302 · Omaha, NE 68114 · 402-392-1280

Stanley A. Krieger · a · Krieger & Krieger · 9290 West Dodge Road, Suite 302 · Omaha, NE 68114 · 402-392-1280

Gregory B. Minter · Fitzgerald, Schorr, Barmettler & Brennan · 13220 California Street, Suite 400 · Omaha, NE 68154 · 402-342-1000

Scott S. Moore · Baird Holm · http://www.bairdholm.com · Woodmen Tower, Suite 1500 · 1700 Farnam Street · Omaha, NE 68102-2068 · 402-344-0500

INFORMATION TECHNOLOGY LAW

Omaha

Terrence P. Maher · Baird Holm · http://www.bairdholm.com · Woodmen Tower, Suite 1500 · 1700 Farnam Street · Omaha, NE 68102-2068 · 402-344-0500

James E. O'Connor · Baird Holm · http://www.bairdholm.com · Woodmen Tower, Suite 1500 · 1700 Farnam Street · Omaha, NE 68102-2068 · 402-344-0500

INSURANCE LAW

Omaha

Edward Hotz · Hotz, Weaver, Flood, Breitkreutz & Grant · 444 Regency Parkway Drive, Suite 310 · Omaha, NE 68114 · 402-397-1140

Michael G. Mullin · Kutak Rock · The Omaha Building · 1650 Farnam Street · Omaha, NE 68102-2186 · 402-346-6000

Robert D. Mullin, Jr. · McGrath North · http://www.mcgrathnorth.com · First National Tower, Suite 3700 · 1601 Dodge Street · Omaha, NE 68102 · 402-341-3070

Terrence D. O'Hare · McGrath North · http://www.mcgrathnorth.com · First National Tower, Suite 3700 1601 Dodge Street · Omaha, NE 68102 · 402-341-3070

INTELLECTUAL PROPERTY LAW

Omaha

Jill Robb Ackerman · Baird Holm · http://www.bairdholm.com · Woodmen Tower, Suite 1500 · 1700 Farnam Street · Omaha, NE 68102-2068 · 402-344-0500

Denise C. Mazour · McGrath North · First National Tower, Suite 3700 · 1601 Dodge Street · Omaha, NE 68102 · 402-341-3070

James E. O'Connor · Baird Holm · http://www.bairdholm.com · Woodmen Tower, Suite 1500 · 1700 Farnam Street · Omaha, NE 68102-2068 · 402-344-0500

John P. Passarelli · Kutak Rock · The Omaha Building · 1650 Farnam Street · Omaha, NE 68102-2186 · 402-346-6000

Dennis L. Thomte · ⑩ · Thomte Mazour & Niebergall · 2120 South 72nd Street, Suite 1111 · Omaha, NE 68124 · 402-392-2280

Bruce D. Vosburg · Fitzgerald, Schorr, Barmettler & Brennan · 13220 California Street, Suite 400 · Omaha, NE 68154 · 402-342-1000

INTERNATIONAL TRADE AND FINANCE LAW

Omaha

David E. Gardels · Husch Blackwell Sanders · http://www.huschblackwell.com · 1620 Dodge Street, Suite 2100 · Omaha, NE 68102 · 402-964-5000

LABOR AND EMPLOYMENT LAW

Lincoln

David R. Buntain · ⑩ · Cline, Williams, Wright, Johnson & Oldfather · 1900 U.S. Bank Building · 233 South 13th Street · Lincoln, NE 68508-2095 · 402-474-6900

Mark A. Fahleson · Rembolt Ludtke · 1201 Lincoln Mall, Suite 102 · Lincoln, NE 68508 · 402-475-5100

William A. Harding · ㉕ · Harding & Shultz · 800 Lincoln Square · 121 South 13th Street · P.O. Box 82028 · Lincoln, NE 68501-2028 · 402-434-3000

Mark D. McGuire · ⑩ · McGuire & Norby · 605 South 14th Street, Suite 100 · Lincoln, NE 68508 · 402-434-2390

Jack L. Shultz · ⑩ · Harding & Shultz · 800 Lincoln Square · 121 South 13th Street · P.O. Box 82028 · Lincoln, NE 68501-2028 · 402-434-3000

Omaha

Patrick J. Barrett · a · Fraser Stryker · http://www.fraserstryker.com · 500 Energy Plaza · 409 South 17th Street · Omaha, NE 68102-2663 · 402-341-6000

A. Stevenson Bogue · a · McGrath North · http://www.mcgrathnorth.com · First National Tower, Suite 3700 · 1601 Dodge Street · Omaha, NE 68102 · 402-341-3070

Robert V. Broom · a · Broom, Johnson, Clarkson & Lanphier · 310 Flatiron Building · 1722 St. Mary's Avenue · Omaha, NE 68102 · 402-346-8323

Robert T. Cannella · Fitzgerald, Schorr, Barmettler & Brennan · 13220 California Street, Suite 400 · Omaha, NE 68154 · 402-342-1000

Christopher R. Hedican · Baird Holm · http://www.bairdholm.com · Woodmen Tower, Suite 1500 · 1700 Farnam Street · Omaha, NE 68102-2068 · 402-344-0500

Thomas F. Hoarty, Jr. · Byam & Hoarty · 317 American National Building · 8990 West Dodge Road · Omaha, NE 68114 · 402-397-0303

Timothy D. Loudon · Berens & Tate · 10050 Regency Circle, Suite 400 · Omaha, NE 68114 · 402-391-1991

Roger J. Miller · 2) · McGrath North · http://www.mcgrathnorth.com · First National Tower, Suite 3700 · 1601 Dodge Street · Omaha, NE 68102 · 402-341-3070

Robert F. Rossiter, Jr. · a · Fraser Stryker · http://www.fraserstryker.com · 500 Energy Plaza · 409 South 17th Street · Omaha, NE 68102-2663 · 402-341-6000

R. J. Stevenson · Baird Holm · http://www.bairdholm.com · Woodmen Tower, Suite 1500 · 1700 Farnam Street · Omaha, NE 68102-2068 · 402-344-0500

LAND USE & ZONING LAW

Omaha

Steven D. Johnson · Steven D. Johnson · 1864 South 155th Circle · Omaha, NE 68144 · 402-334-7729

LEGAL MALPRACTICE LAW

Lincoln

Fredric H. Kauffman · 2) · Cline, Williams, Wright, Johnson & Oldfather · 1900 U.S. Bank Building · 233 South 13th Street · Lincoln, NE 68508-2095 · 402-474-6900

Omaha

John R. Douglas · a · Cassem, Tierney, Adams, Gotch & Douglas · 8805 Indian Hills Drive, Suite 300 · Omaha, NE 68114 · 402-390-0300

Joseph K. Meusey · 2% · Fraser Stryker · http://www.fraserstryker.com · 500 Energy Plaza · 409 South 17th Street · Omaha, NE 68102-2663 · 402-341-6000

MEDICAL MALPRACTICE LAW

Omaha

John R. Douglas · a · Cassem, Tierney, Adams, Gotch & Douglas · 8805 Indian Hills Drive, Suite 300 · Omaha, NE 68114 · 402-390-0300

Charles F. Gotch · 2% · Cassem, Tierney, Adams, Gotch & Douglas · 8805 Indian Hills Drive, Suite 300 · Omaha, NE 68114 · 402-390-0300

Michael F. Kinney · Cassem, Tierney, Adams, Gotch & Douglas · 8805 Indian Hills Drive, Suite 300 · Omaha, NE 68114 · 402-390-0300

William M. Lamson, Jr. · a · Lamson, Dugan and Murray · 10306 Regency Parkway Drive · Omaha, NE 68114 · 402-397-7300

Scottsbluff

Robert P. Chaloupka · 2) · Chaloupka, Holyoke, Hofmeister, Snyder & Chaloupka · 1714 Second Avenue · Scottsbluff, NE 69363 · 308-635-5000

MERGERS & ACQUISITIONS LAW

Lincoln

Robert J. Routh · 2) · Cline, Williams, Wright, Johnson & Oldfather · 1900 U.S. Bank Building · 233 South 13th Street · Lincoln, NE 68508-2095 · 402-474-6900

L. Bruce Wright · 2) · Cline, Williams, Wright, Johnson & Oldfather · 1900 U.S. Bank Building · 233 South 13th Street · Lincoln, NE 68508-2095 · 402-474-6900

Omaha

Dennis J. Fogland · Baird Holm · http://www.bairdholm.com · Woodmen Tower, Suite 1500 · 1700 Farnam Street · Omaha, NE 68102-2068 · 402-344-0500

Robert L. Freeman · Fraser Stryker · http://www.fraserstryker.com · 500 Energy Plaza · 409 South 17th Street · Omaha, NE 68102-2663 · 402-341-6000

Keith A. Green · McGill, Gotsdiner, Workman & Lepp · http://www.mgwl.com · First National Plaza, Suite 500 · 11404 West Dodge Road · Omaha, NE 68154 · 402-492-9200

David L. Hefflinger · 2% · McGrath North · http://www.mcgrathnorth.com · First National Tower, Suite 3700 · 1601 Dodge Street · Omaha, NE 68102 · 402-341-3070

Robert J. Kmiecik · Heartland Automotive Services, Inc · 11308 Davenport Street · Omaha, NE 68154 · 402-333-0990

Todd A. Richardson · Husch Blackwell Sanders · http://www.huschblackwell.com · 1620 Dodge Street, Suite 2100 · Omaha, NE 68102 · 402-964-5000

Roger W. Wells · McGrath North · http://www.mcgrathnorth.com · First National Tower, Suite 3700 · 1601 Dodge Street · Omaha, NE 68102 · 402-341-3070

John S. Zeilinger · a · Baird Holm · http://www.bairdholm.com · Woodmen Tower, Suite 1500 · 1700 Farnam Street · Omaha, NE 68102-2068 · 402-344-0500

MUNICIPAL LAW

Omaha

Timothy M. Kenny · Abrahams Kaslow & Cassman · http://www.akclaw.com · 8712 West Dodge Road, Suite 300 · Omaha, NE 68114-3419 · 402-392-1250

NATURAL RESOURCES LAW

Lincoln

Donald G. Blankenau · Husch Blackwell Sanders · http://www.huschblackwell.com · 206 South 13th Street, Suite 1400 · Lincoln, NE 68508 · 402-458-1500

NON-PROFIT/CHARITIES LAW

Omaha

Howard Fredrick Hahn · a · Husch Blackwell Sanders · http://www.huschblackwell.com · 1620 Dodge Street, Suite 2100 · Omaha, NE 68102 · 402-964-5000

NON-WHITE-COLLAR CRIMINAL DEFENSE

Lincoln

Kirk E. Naylor, Jr. · 2% · Naylor Law Office · 1111 Lincoln Mall, Suite 300 · Lincoln, NE 68508 · 402-474-5529

Omaha

Steven E. Achelpohl · Steven E. Achelpohl · 1010 Historic Library Plaza · 1823 Harney Street · Omaha, NE 68102 · 402-346-1900

J. William Gallup · 2% · Gallup & Schaefer · 1001 Farnam Street, Third Floor · Omaha, NE 68102-1827 · 402-341-0700

Alan G. Stoler · Alan G. Stoler · 1823 Harney Street, Suite 1004 · Omaha, NE 68102 · 402-346-1733

PERSONAL INJURY LITIGATION

Omaha

Michael F. Coyle · Fraser Stryker · http://www.fraserstryker.com · 500 Energy Plaza · 409 South 17th Street · Omaha, NE 68102-2663 · 402-341-6000

Charles F. Gotch · 2% · Cassem, Tierney, Adams, Gotch & Douglas · 8805 Indian Hills Drive, Suite 300 · Omaha, NE 68114 · 402-390-0300

Thomas A. Grennan · Gross & Welch · 1500 Omaha Tower · 2120 South 72nd Street · Omaha, NE 68124-2342 · 402-392-1500

Michael F. Kinney · Cassem, Tierney, Adams, Gotch & Douglas · 8805 Indian Hills Drive, Suite 300 · Omaha, NE 68114 · 402-390-0300

William M. Lamson, Jr. · a · Lamson, Dugan and Murray · 10306 Regency Parkway Drive · Omaha, NE 68114 · 402-397-7300

Joseph K. Meusey · 2% · Fraser Stryker · http://www.fraserstryker.com · 500 Energy Plaza · 409 South 17th Street · Omaha, NE 68102-2663 · 402-341-6000

Michael J. Mooney · Gross & Welch · 1500 Omaha Tower · 2120 South 72nd Street · Omaha, NE 68124-2342 · 402-392-1500

Michael G. Mullin · Kutak Rock · The Omaha Building · 1650 Farnam Street · Omaha, NE 68102-2186 · 402-346-6000

Robert D. Mullin, Jr. · McGrath North · http://www.mcgrathnorth.com · First National Tower, Suite 3700 · 1601 Dodge Street · Omaha, NE 68102 · 402-341-3070

Robert E. O'Connor, Jr. · O'Connor Law Firm · http://www.dlcoconnor.com · 2433 South 130th Circle · Omaha, NE 68144 · 402-330-5906

E. Terry Sibbernsen · Sibbernsen & Strigenz · 1111 North 102nd Court, Suite 330 · Omaha, NE 68114 · 402-493-7221

Scottsbluff

Robert P. Chaloupka · 2) · Chaloupka, Holyoke, Hofmeister, Snyder & Chaloupka · 1714 Second Avenue · Scottsbluff, NE 69363 · 308-635-5000

PRODUCT LIABILITY LITIGATION

Omaha

Charles F. Gotch · 2% · Cassem, Tierney, Adams, Gotch & Douglas · 8805 Indian Hills Drive, Suite 300 · Omaha, NE 68114 · 402-390-0300

Michael F. Kinney · Cassem, Tierney, Adams, Gotch & Douglas · 8805 Indian Hills Drive, Suite 300 · Omaha, NE 68114 · 402-390-0300

Scottsbluff

Robert P. Chaloupka · 2) · Chaloupka, Holyoke, Hofmeister, Snyder & Chaloupka · 1714 Second Avenue · Scottsbluff, NE 69363 · 308-635-5000

PROFESSIONAL MALPRACTICE LAW

Omaha

Patrick G. Vipond · Lamson, Dugan and Murray · 10306 Regency Parkway Drive · Omaha, NE 68114 · 402-397-7300

PUBLIC FINANCE LAW

Omaha

Charles J. Addy · Baird Holm · http://www.bairdholm.com · Woodmen Tower, Suite 1500 · 1700 Farnam Street · Omaha, NE 68102-2068 · 402-344-0500

Richard J. Pedersen · Baird Holm · http://www.bairdholm.com · Woodmen Tower, Suite 1500 · 1700 Farnam Street · Omaha, NE 68102-2068 · 402-344-0500

Patricia S. Peterson · Kutak Rock · The Omaha Building · 1650 Farnam Street · Omaha, NE 68102-2186 402-346-6000

REAL ESTATE LAW

Lincoln

Thomas J. Fitchett · 2) · Thomas J. Fitchett · 6717 Flint Ridge Road · Lincoln, NE 68506 · 402-489-9009

Thomas C. Huston · Cline, Williams, Wright, Johnson & Oldfather · 1900 U.S. Bank Building · 233 South 13th Street · Lincoln, NE 68508-2095 · 402-474-6900

Jennifer J. Strand · Woods & Aitken · 301 South 13th Street, Suite 500 · Lincoln, NE 68508 · 402-437-8500

Omaha

John Q. Bachman · Pansing Hogan Ernst & Bachman · Regency Center, Suite 300 · 10250 Regency Circle · Omaha, NE 68114 · 402-397-5500

James D. Buser · Pansing Hogan Ernst & Bachman · Regency Center, Suite 300 · 10250 Regency Circle · Omaha, NE 68114 · 402-397-5500

Paul Scott Dye · Baird Holm · http://www.bairdholm.com · Woodmen Tower, Suite 1500 · 1700 Farnam Street · Omaha, NE 68102-2068 · 402-344-0500

John H. Fullenkamp · 2) · Fullenkamp, Doyle & Jobeun · 11440 West Center Road, Suite C · Omaha, NE 68144 · 402-334-0700

Lee H. Hamann · McGrath North · http://www.mcgrathnorth.com · First National Tower, Suite 3700 · 1601 Dodge Street · Omaha, NE 68102 · 402-341-3070

Dennis P. Hogan III · a · Pansing Hogan Ernst & Bachman · Regency Center, Suite 300 · 10250 Regency Circle · Omaha, NE 68114 · 402-397-5500

Larry A. Jobeun · Fullenkamp, Doyle & Jobeun · 11440 West Center Road, Suite C · Omaha, NE 68144 402-334-0700

Steven D. Johnson · Steven D. Johnson · 1864 South 155th Circle · Omaha, NE 68144 · 402-334-7729

John S. Katelman · Husch Blackwell Sanders · http://www.huschblackwell.com · 1620 Dodge Street, Suite 2100 · Omaha, NE 68102 · 402-964-5000

Michael F. Kivett · Walentine O'Toole McQuillan & Gordon · 11240 Davenport Street · Omaha, NE 68154-0125 · 402-330-6300

Lawrence E. Kritenbrink · Baird Holm · http://www.bairdholm.com · Woodmen Tower, Suite 1500 · 1700 Farnam Street · Omaha, NE 68102-2068 · 402-344-0500

Michael D. Matejka · Woods & Aitken · 10250 Regency Circle, Suite 525 · Omaha, NE 68114 · 402-898-7400

Frank J. Mihulka · Fitzgerald, Schorr, Barmettler & Brennan · 13220 California Street, Suite 400 · Omaha, NE 68154 · 402-342-1000

Scott P. Moore · Baird Holm · http://www.bairdholm.com · Woodmen Tower, Suite 1500 · 1700 Farnam Street · Omaha, NE 68102-2068 · 402-344-0500

Robert W. Rieke · Fraser Stryker · http://www.fraserstryker.com · 500 Energy Plaza · 409 South 17th Street · Omaha, NE 68102-2663 · 402-341-6000

SECURITIES LAW

Lincoln

David J. Routh · Cline, Williams, Wright, Johnson & Oldfather · 1900 U.S. Bank Building · 233 South 13th Street · Lincoln, NE 68508-2095 · 402-474-6900

Robert J. Routh · ⑳ · Cline, Williams, Wright, Johnson & Oldfather · 1900 U.S. Bank Building · 233 South 13th Street · Lincoln, NE 68508-2095 · 402-474-6900

Omaha

Dennis J. Fogland · Baird Holm · http://www.bairdholm.com · Woodmen Tower, Suite 1500 · 1700 Farnam Street · Omaha, NE 68102-2068 · 402-344-0500

David L. Hefflinger · ㉕ · McGrath North · http://www.mcgrathnorth.com · First National Tower, Suite 3700 · 1601 Dodge Street · Omaha, NE 68102 · 402-341-3070

TAX LAW

Lincoln

M. Douglas Deitchler · ⑳ · Baylor, Evnen, Curtiss, Grimit & Witt · 1248 O Street, Suite 600 · Lincoln, NE 68508 · 402-475-1075

Don R. Janssen · ⑩ · Cline, Williams, Wright, Johnson & Oldfather · 1900 U.S. Bank Building · 233 South 13th Street · Lincoln, NE 68508-2095 · 402-474-6900

David A. Ludtke · ㉕ · Rembolt Ludtke · 1201 Lincoln Mall, Suite 102 · Lincoln, NE 68508 · 402-475-5100

Omaha

Howard Fredrick Hahn · ⑩ · Husch Blackwell Sanders · http://www.huschblackwell.com · 1620 Dodge Street, Suite 2100 · Omaha, NE 68102 · 402-964-5000

Deryl F. Hamann · ㉕ · Baird Holm · http://www.bairdholm.com · Woodmen Tower, Suite 1500 · 1700 Farnam Street · Omaha, NE 68102-2068 · 402-344-0500

David L. Hefflinger · ㉕ · McGrath North · http://www.mcgrathnorth.com · First National Tower, Suite 3700 · 1601 Dodge Street · Omaha, NE 68102 · 402-341-3070

Paul C. Jessen · ⑩ · Koley Jessen · One Pacific Place, Suite 800 · 1125 South 103rd Street · Omaha, NE 68124 · 402-390-9500

Howard N. Kaplan · ⑩ · Law Office of Howard N. Kaplan · 9290 West Dodge Road, Suite 205 · Omaha, NE 68114 · 402-397-8988

T. Geoffrey Lieben · 2% · Lieben, Whitted, Houghton, Slowiaczek & Cavanagh · 100 Scoular Building · 2027 Dodge Street · Omaha, NE 68102 · 402-344-4000

Thomas R. Pansing, Jr. · Pansing Hogan Ernst & Bachman · Regency Center, Suite 300 · 10250 Regency Circle · Omaha, NE 68114 · 402-397-5500

Jeffrey J. Pirruccello · a · McGrath North · http://www.mcgrathnorth.com · First National Tower, Suite 3700 · 1601 Dodge Street · Omaha, NE 68102 · 402-341-3070

Gary W. Radil · a · Baird Holm · http://www.bairdholm.com · Woodmen Tower, Suite 1500 · 1700 Farnam Street · Omaha, NE 68102-2068 · 402-344-0500

TRUSTS AND ESTATES

Lincoln

Rick A. Damkroger · Harding & Shultz · 800 Lincoln Square · 121 South 13th Street · P.O. Box 82028 · Lincoln, NE 68501-2028 · 402-434-3000

M. Douglas Deitchler · 2) · Baylor, Evnen, Curtiss, Grimit & Witt · 1248 O Street, Suite 600 · Lincoln, NE 68508 · 402-475-1075

Thomas J. Fitchett · 2) · Thomas J. Fitchett · 6717 Flint Ridge Road · Lincoln, NE 68506 · 402-489-9009

Thomas M. Haase · a · Perry, Guthery, Haase & Gessford · 233 South 13th Street, Suite 1400 · Lincoln, NE 68508 · 402-476-9200

John C. Hurd · a · Wolfe, Snowden, Hurd, Luers & Ahl · Wells Fargo Center, Suite 800 · 1248 O Street · Lincoln, NE 68508-1424 · 402-474-1507

Don R. Janssen · a · Cline, Williams, Wright, Johnson & Oldfather · 1900 U.S. Bank Building · 233 South 13th Street · Lincoln, NE 68508-2095 · 402-474-6900

David A. Ludtke · 2% · Rembolt Ludtke · 1201 Lincoln Mall, Suite 102 · Lincoln, NE 68508 · 402-475-5100

William E. Olson, Jr. · Demars, Gordon, Olson & Zalewski · Federal Trust Building, Suite 800 · 134 South 13th Street · P.O. Box 81607 · Lincoln, NE 68501-1607 · 402-438-2500

James E. Rembolt · a · Rembolt Ludtke · 1201 Lincoln Mall, Suite 102 · Lincoln, NE 68508 · 402-475-5100

Gary B. Schneider · Pinnacle Bank · 3939 South Street · Lincoln, NE 68506 · 402-434-3128

Daniel R. Stogsdill · Cline, Williams, Wright, Johnson & Oldfather · 1900 U.S. Bank Building · 233 South 13th Street · Lincoln, NE 68508-2095 · 402-474-6900

Norfolk

Dennis W. Collins · a · Jewell, Collins & DeLay · 105 South Second Street · P.O. Box 1367 · Norfolk, NE 68701 · 402-371-4844

Omaha

Thomas R. Burke · 2% · Lamson, Dugan and Murray · 10306 Regency Parkway Drive · Omaha, NE 68114 402-397-7300

Deryl F. Hamann · 2% · Baird Holm · http://www.bairdholm.com · Woodmen Tower, Suite 1500 · 1700 Farnam Street · Omaha, NE 68102-2068 · 402-344-0500

David L. Hefflinger · 2% · McGrath North · http://www.mcgrathnorth.com · First National Tower, Suite 3700 · 1601 Dodge Street · Omaha, NE 68102 · 402-341-3070

Ronald C. Jensen · Baird Holm · http://www.bairdholm.com · Woodmen Tower, Suite 1500 · 1700 Farnam Street · Omaha, NE 68102-2068 · 402-344-0500

Paul C. Jessen · a · Koley Jessen · One Pacific Place, Suite 800 · 1125 South 103rd Street · Omaha, NE 68124 · 402-390-9500

Michael D. Jones · 2) · Ellick, Jones, Buelt, Blazek & Longo · 8805 Indian Hills Drive, Suite 280 · Omaha, NE 68114 · 402-390-0390

Sharon R. Kresha · a · Baird Holm · http://www.bairdholm.com · Woodmen Tower, Suite 1500 · 1700 Farnam Street · Omaha, NE 68102-2068 · 402-344-0500

T. Geoffrey Lieben · 2% · Lieben, Whitted, Houghton, Slowiaczek & Cavanagh · 100 Scoular Building · 2027 Dodge Street · Omaha, NE 68102 · 402-344-4000

Thomas J. Malicki · Abrahams Kaslow & Cassman · http://www.akclaw.com · 8712 West Dodge Road, Suite 300 · Omaha, NE 68114-3419 · 402-392-1250

Gary W. Radil · a · Baird Holm · http://www.bairdholm.com · Woodmen Tower, Suite 1500 · 1700 Farnam Street · Omaha, NE 68102-2068 · 402-344-0500

Susan J. Spahn · Fitzgerald, Schorr, Barmettler & Brennan · 13220 California Street, Suite 400 · Omaha, NE 68154 · 402-342-1000

Michael L. Sullivan · Baird Holm · http://www.bairdholm.com · Woodmen Tower, Suite 1500 · 1700 Farnam Street · Omaha, NE 68102-2068 · 402-344-0500

Nick R. Taylor · a · Fitzgerald, Schorr, Barmettler & Brennan · 13220 California Street, Suite 400 · Omaha, NE 68154 · 402-342-1000

Kurt F. Tjaden · Koley Jessen · One Pacific Place, Suite 800 · 1125 South 103rd Street · Omaha, NE 68124 · 402-390-9500

Jeffrey D. Toberer · a · Stinson Morrison Hecker · http://www.stinson.com · Landmark Building, Suite 1501 · 1299 Farnam Street · Omaha, NE 68102 · 402-342-1700

WATER LAW

Lincoln

Donald G. Blankenau · Husch Blackwell Sanders · http://www.huschblackwell.com · 206 South 13th Street, Suite 1400 · Lincoln, NE 68508 · 402-458-1500

Thomas R. Wilmoth · Husch Blackwell Sanders · http://www.huschblackwell.com · 206 South 13th Street, Suite 1400 · Lincoln, NE 68508 · 402-458-1500

Lincoln

Kirk E. Naylor, Jr. · 2% · Naylor Law Office · 1111 Lincoln Mall, Suite 300 · Lincoln, NE 68508 · 402-474-5529

Omaha

Steven E. Achelpohl · Steven E. Achelpohl · 1010 Historic Library Plaza · 1823 Harney Street · Omaha, NE 68102 · 402-346-1900

J. William Gallup · 2% · Gallup & Schaefer · 1001 Farnam Street, Third Floor · Omaha, NE 68102-1827 · 402-341-0700

Edward G. Warin · a · McGrath North · http://www.mcgrathnorth.com · First National Tower, Suite 3700 · 1601 Dodge Street · Omaha, NE 68102 · 402-341-3070